T0391303

THE EUROPA INTERNATIONAL FOUNDATION DIRECTORY 2025

THE EUROPA INTERNATIONAL FOUNDATION DIRECTORY 2025

Routledge
Taylor & Francis Group

LONDON AND NEW YORK

Thirty-fourth edition published 2025
by Routledge
4 Park Square, Milton Park, Abingdon, Oxon OX14 4RN
and by Routledge
605 Third Avenue, New York, NY 10158
Routledge is an imprint of the Taylor & Francis Group, an informa business

© 2025 Routledge

All rights reserved. No part of this book may be reprinted or reproduced or utilised in any form or by any electronic, mechanical, or other means, now known or hereafter invented, including photocopying and recording, or in any information storage or retrieval system, without permission in writing from the publishers.

Trademark notice: Product or corporate names may be trademarks or registered trademarks, and are used only for identification and explanation without intent to infringe.

First published 1974

ISBN: 978-1-041-05305-7 (hbk)
ISBN: 978-1-003-63257-3 (ebk)
ISSN: 1366-8048
DOI: 10.4324/9781003632573
Typeset in Century Schoolbook
by AMA DataSet Limited, Preston

Senior Editor: Cathy Hartley
Editorial Assistant: Avi Sharma
Contributing Editor: Anna Thomas

The publishers make no representation, express or implied, with regard to the accuracy of the information contained in this book and cannot accept any legal responsibility for any errors or omissions that may take place.

Foreword

Since it was first published in 1974 as *The International Foundation Directory* (Consultant Editor H. V. Hodson), this book has undergone many revisions. Now in its 34th edition, *The Europa International Foundation Directory* includes some 2,660 directory entries, a bibliography and comprehensive indexes, and aims to provide a thorough and up-to-date overview of grantmaking civil society worldwide.

The Directory includes not only foundations and trusts (private, operating, grantmaking and corporate), but also charities and other NGOs, some of which make grants to organizations and individuals, while others carry out their own programmes and projects.

To gain entry to the publication, an organization must be international, or, where operating on a purely national basis, must be important enough to have a widespread impact; it must have charitable or public benefit status; and must have significant funds available, or make significant charitable donations, or run its own projects of importance (however, the Editors have no predetermined figure to establish inclusion, as the importance of an organization's funds is relative, depending on the wealth of the country in which it is located). The Editors have excluded foundations established purely for the benefit of a particular named hospital or school; moreover, governmental bodies may only be included if they are independent of political control. Community foundations are included where they are a major source of funding, or offer support to organizations working internationally.

The book contains a directory section and three indexes. The directory section is organized by country or territory, with entries arranged alphabetically under the appropriate heading: Co-ordinating Bodies; or Foundations and Non-Profits. A bibliography is followed by three indexes: a full index of organizations; an index by main activity (where organizations are listed under headings including conservation and the environment, education, medicine and health, and social welfare); and an index by geographical area of activity, allowing the reader to find organizations active in, for example, South America, Central America and the Caribbean, Central and South-Eastern Europe, or South Asia.

The Editors and publishers of *The Europa International Foundation Directory* are greatly indebted to the many people who advised and helped with its compilation, and offer their sincere thanks. They gratefully acknowledge the assistance of those foundations, trusts, NGOs and other non-profit organizations that updated their entries to ensure accuracy, and would like to thank the governmental bodies and other national and international institutions, foundation centres and co-ordinating bodies that have helped provide information on foundations and NGOs in all parts of the world.

June 2025

Contents

Abbreviations	ix	Germany	118
International Telephone Codes	xi	Ghana	143
		Gibraltar	144
Directory		Greece	144
		Guatemala	147
Afghanistan	3	Guinea	149
Albania	4	Haiti	149
Angola	5	Honduras	150
Anguilla	5	Hong Kong	150
Argentina	6	Hungary	152
Armenia	9	Iceland	154
Australia	10	India	154
Austria	20	Indonesia	161
Azerbaijan	23	Iran	163
Bahamas	24	Iraq	164
Bangladesh	24	Ireland	165
Barbados	25	Israel	168
Belarus	25	Italy	171
Belgium	26	Jamaica	184
Benin	35	Japan	185
Bermuda	35	Jordan	195
Bolivia	36	Kazakhstan	197
Bosnia and Herzegovina	37	Kenya	197
Botswana	37	The Republic of Korea	200
Brazil	38	Kosovo	202
Bulgaria	42	Kuwait	203
Burkina Faso	44	Latvia	204
Burundi	45	Lebanon	205
Cabo Verde	45	Lesotho	207
Cambodia	46	Libya	207
Cameroon	47	Liechtenstein	207
Canada	47	Lithuania	208
Central African Republic	63	Luxembourg	209
Chad	64	Madagascar	210
Channel Islands	64	Malawi	210
Chile	64	Malaysia	211
The People's Republic of China	66	Maldives	212
Colombia	70	Mali	213
Democratic Republic of the Congo	72	Malta	213
Republic of the Congo	73	Mauritania	214
Costa Rica	73	Mauritius	214
Côte d'Ivoire	75	Mexico	214
Croatia	76	Moldova	216
Curaçao	77	Monaco	217
Cyprus	77	Mongolia	218
Czech Republic (Czechia)	78	Montenegro	219
Denmark	82	Morocco	219
Dominican Republic	87	Mozambique	221
Ecuador	87	Myanmar	221
Egypt	89	Namibia	222
El Salvador	91	Nepal	223
Estonia	92	Netherlands	223
Eswatini	93	New Zealand	232
Ethiopia	93	Niger	236
Fiji	94	Nigeria	236
Finland	95	North Macedonia	239
France	99	Norway	240
The Gambia	117	Oman	244
Georgia	117	Pakistan	244

CONTENTS

Palestinian Territories	246	Switzerland	305
Panama	247	Taiwan	321
Papua New Guinea	247	Tanzania	322
Paraguay	248	Thailand	323
Peru	248	Timor-Leste	325
Philippines	250	Trinidad and Tobago	326
Poland	253	Tunisia	326
Portugal	258	Türkiye (Turkey)	327
Puerto Rico	261	Uganda	331
Qatar	262	Ukraine	332
Réunion	262	United Arab Emirates	334
Romania	263	United Kingdom	335
Russian Federation	264	United States of America	393
Rwanda	268	Uruguay	485
Saint Lucia	268	Uzbekistan	485
Saudi Arabia	268	Vatican City	486
Senegal	270	Venezuela	487
Serbia	271	Viet Nam	488
Seychelles	272	Yemen	489
Singapore	272	Zambia	490
Slovakia	273	Zimbabwe	490
Slovenia	276		
Somalia	277	Select Bibliography	493
South Africa	278		
South Sudan	285	**Indexes**	
Spain	285		
Sri Lanka	297	Index of Foundations	499
Sudan	297	Index of Main Activities	520
Sweden	298	Index by Area of Activity	596

Abbreviations

AB	Alberta	Dr.	Drive
AC	Companion of the Order of Australia	DRC	Democratic Republic of the Congo
ACT	Australian Capital Territory	Drs	Doctorandus
Admin	Administration	ECOSOC	Economic and Social Council (United Nations)
Admin.	Administrative, Administrator	Ed.	Editor
AG	Aktiengesellschaft (Joint Stock Company)	Edif.	Edificio (building)
a.i.	ad interim	Eds	Editors
AIDS	acquired immune deficiency syndrome	E.h.	ehrenhalber (Honorary)
al.	aleja (alley, avenue)	Emer.	Emeritus
Amb.	Ambassador	Eng.	Engineer
Apdo	Apartado (Post Box)	etc.	et cetera
approx.	approximately	EU	European Union
Apt	Apartment	eV	eingetragener Verein
AR	Arkansas	Exec.	Executive
ASEAN	Association of Southeast Asian Nations	f.	founded
Assoc.	associate	FL	Florida
Asst	assistant	fmr (ly)	former (ly)
Aug.	August	Fr	Father
Av.	Avenida (avenue)	G20	Group of Twenty
Avda	Avenida (avenue)	GA	Georgia
Ave	Avenue	Gdns	Gardens
AZ	Arizona	Gen.	General
BC	British Columbia	gGmbH	gemeinnützige Gesellschaft mit beschränkter Haftung
Bldg	Building		
Blvd	Boulevard	GmbH	Gesellschaft mit beschränkter Haftung
BP	Boîte Postale	ha	hectares
Bte	Boîte (Post Box)	h.c.	honoris causa (honorary)
bul.	bulvar (boulevard)	HE	His (Her) Excellency
c.	circa (about); cuadra(s) (block(s))	HH	His (Her) Highness
CA	California	HI	Hawaii
Cad.	Caddesi (street)	HIH	His Imperial Highness
CEO	Chief Executive Officer	HIV	human immunodeficiency virus
CFO	Chief Financial Officer	HM	His (Her) Majesty
Chair.	Chairman/woman, Chairmen/women	Hon.	Honourable; honorary
CIS	Commonwealth of Independent States	HRH	His (Her) Royal Highness
Cl.	Close	HSH	His (Her) Serene Highness
cnr	corner	IA	Iowa
CO	Colorado	ICT	information and communications technology
Co	Company, County	i.e.	id est (that is to say)
Col	Colonel	IL	Illinois
Col.	Colonia	IN	Indiana
COO	Chief Operating Officer	Inc	Incorporated
Corpn	Corporation	incl.	including
CP	Case (Casa) Postale	Ing.	Engineer (German, Spanish)
Cres.	Crescent	Int.	International
CSO	civil society organization	Ir	Engineer (Dutch)
CT	Connecticut	IT	information technology
Ct	Court	Izq.	Izquierda (left)
Cttee	Committee	Jan.	January
DC	District of Columbia	Jl.	Jalan (Street)
DE	Delaware	Jr	Junior
Dec.	December	km	kilometre
Dem.	Democratic	Latinx	Latino/Latina
Dept	Department	LGBT	lesbian, gay, bisexual, transgender
DF	Distrito Federal	LGBTQI+	lesbian, gay, bisexual, transgender, queer and intersex
Dir(s)	Director(s)		
DNA	deoxyribonucleic acid	Lic.	Licenciado (Spanish)
Dott.	Dottore	Lt	Lieutenant
Dr	Doctor	Ltd	Limited

ABBREVIATIONS

m.	million
MA	Massachusetts
Ma.	María
Maj.	Major
Man.	Manager, Managing
MB	Manitoba
MBA	Master of Business Administration
MD	Maryland, Doctor of Medicine
Mgr	Monseigneur, Monsignor
MI	Michigan
MN	Minnesota
MO	Missouri
Mons.	Monsignor
MP	Member of Parliament
MS	Mississippi
MSc	Master of Science
n.a.	not available
Nat.	National
NATO	North Atlantic Treaty Organization
NC	North Carolina
NGO	non-governmental organization
NH	New Hampshire
NJ	New Jersey
No(.)	Numéro, Número, Number
Nov.	November
nr	near
NRs	Nepalese rupees
NSW	New South Wales
NV	Naamloze Vennootschap
NW	North West
NY	New York
Oct.	October
OECD	Organisation for Economic Co-operation and Development
Of.	Oficina (Office)
OH	Ohio
ON	Ontario
On.	Honourable (Italian)
PA	Pennsylvania
per.	pereulok (lane, alley)
PhD	Doctor of Philosophy
Pl.	Place
PLC	Public Limited Company
POB	Post Office Box
PR	Public Relations
Preb.	Prebendal, Prebendary
Pres(.)	President, Presidents
Prof.	Professor
Pty	Proprietary
QC	Québec
Qld	Queensland
qq.v.	quae vide (see, plural)
q.v.	quod vide (see)
Rd	Road
Rep.	Representative
Repub.	Republic
Retd	Retired
Rev.	Reverend
RI	Rhode Island
Rm	Room
Rs	rupees
Rt Hon.	Right Honourable
Rt Rev.	Right Reverend
s/n	sin número (no number)
SA	South Australia
SAR	Special Administrative Region
Sec.	Secretary
Sec.-Gen.	Secretary-General
Sept.	September
Sok.	Sokak (street)
SpA	Società per Azioni (Joint-Stock Company)
Sq.	Square
Sr	Senior
St	Saint, Street
Str.	Strasse (street)
Treas.	Treasurer
TX	Texas
u./út	utca (street)
UAE	United Arab Emirates
UK	United Kingdom
ul.	ulitsa (street)
UN	United Nations
UNESCO	United Nations Educational, Scientific and Cultural Organization
UNHCR	United Nations High Commissioner for Refugees
UNICEF	United Nations Children's Fund
US (A)	United States (of America)
USSR	Union of Soviet Socialist Republics
UT	Utah
VA	Virginia
Vic	Victoria
vol.(s)	volume(s)
vul.	vulitsa (street)
WA	Washington (state), Western Australia
WHO	World Health Organization
WI	Wisconsin
YMCA	Young Men's Christian Association

International Telephone Codes

The following codes should be added to the relevant contact numbers listed in the Directory. The code and number must be preceded by the International Dialling Code of the country from which you are calling.

Country	Code
Afghanistan	93
Albania	355
Angola	244
Anguilla	1 264
Argentina	54
Armenia	374
Australia	61
Austria	43
Azerbaijan	994
Bahamas	1 242
Bangladesh	880
Barbados	1 246
Belarus	375
Belgium	32
Benin	229
Bermuda	1 441
Bolivia	591
Bosnia and Herzegovina	387
Botswana	267
Brazil	55
Bulgaria	359
Burkina Faso	226
Burundi	257
Cabo Verde	238
Cambodia	855
Cameroon	237
Canada	1
Central African Republic	236
Chad	235
Channel Islands	44
Chile	56
China (People's Republic)	86
Colombia	57
Congo (Democratic Republic)	243
Congo (Republic)	242
Costa Rica	506
Côte d'Ivoire	225
Croatia	385
Curaçao	599
Cyprus	357
Czech Republic (Czechia)	420
Denmark	45
Dominican Republic	1 809
Ecuador	593
Egypt	20
El Salvador	503
Estonia	372
Eswatini	268
Ethiopia	251
Fiji	679
Finland	358
France	33
Gambia	220
Georgia	995
Germany	49
Ghana	233
Gibraltar	350
Greece	30
Guatemala	502
Guinea	224
Haiti	509
Honduras	504
Hong Kong	852
Hungary	36
Iceland	354
India	91
Indonesia	62
Iran	98
Iraq	964
Ireland	353
Israel	972
Italy	39
Jamaica	1 876
Japan	81
Jordan	962
Kazakhstan	7
Kenya	254
Korea (Republic)	82
Kosovo	383
Kuwait	965
Latvia	371
Lebanon	961
Lesotho	266
Libya	218
Liechtenstein	423
Lithuania	370
Luxembourg	352
Madagascar	261
Malawi	265
Malaysia	60
Maldives	960
Mali	223
Malta	356
Mauritania	222
Mauritius	230
Mexico	52
Moldova	373
Monaco	377
Mongolia	976
Montenegro	382
Morocco	212
Mozambique	258
Myanmar	95
Namibia	264
Nepal	977
Netherlands	31
New Zealand	64
Niger	227
Nigeria	234
North Macedonia	389
Norway	47
Oman	968
Pakistan	92
Palestinian Territories	970/972
Panama	507
Papua New Guinea	675
Paraguay	595
Peru	51
Philippines	63
Poland	48
Portugal	351
Puerto Rico	1 787
Qatar	974
Réunion	262
Romania	40
Russian Federation	7
Rwanda	250
Saint Lucia	1 758
Saudi Arabia	966
Senegal	221
Serbia	381
Seychelles	248
Singapore	65
Slovakia	421
Slovenia	386
Somalia	252
South Africa	27
South Sudan	211
Spain	34
Sri Lanka	94
Sudan	249
Sweden	46
Switzerland	41
Taiwan	886
Tanzania	255
Thailand	66
Timor-Leste	670
Trinidad and Tobago	1 868
Tunisia	216
Türkiye (Turkey)	90
Uganda	256
Ukraine	380
United Arab Emirates	971
United Kingdom	44
United States of America	1
Uruguay	598
Uzbekistan	998
Vatican City	39
Venezuela	58
Viet Nam	84
Yemen	967
Zambia	260
Zimbabwe	263

Directory

AFGHANISTAN

CO-ORDINATING BODIES

Afghanistan Institute for Civil Society—AICS

Established in 2014 with support from the Aga Khan Foundation and Counterpart International.

Activities: Encourages the growth of civil society and promotes pluralism and participatory development through capacity building and certification of local NGOs. The Institute carries out policy research and advocates reforms; and organizes National Civil Society Week and provincial roundtables, bringing together representatives from civil society, the media, academia and government. It hosts the secretariat of the South Asia Hub of the Innovation for Change (I4C) global network, an initiative of CIVICUS (q.v.), co-ordinating regional activities and events. AICS is also actively engaged in various sectors, including education, health, nutrition, WASH & hygiene, economic empowerment, climate change, capacity building, and others.

Geographical Area of Activity: South Asia.

Publications: Annual Report; newsletter; policy briefs; policy reference manuals; CSO Directory; SEECA Research; audit reports.

Finance: Annual Budget $1.5m. (2025).

Board of Directors: Dr Najmuddin Najm (Chair.).

Principal Staff: CEO Mohammad Hashim Amiri.

Contact Details: House #3, St 12, District #10, Qalah-e-Fatullah, Golahi Paikob, opp. Sehat Afghan Clinic, Kabul; tel. 0798650999; e-mail info@aicsafg.org; internet aicsafg.org.

Civil Society and Human Rights Organization—CSHRO

Established in 2004 by 24 human rights organizations as the Civil Society and Human Rights Network; present name adopted in 2011.

Activities: Promotes human rights, democracy and respect for the rule of law; strengthens the role of NGOs; acts as a co-ordination centre for CSOs; and carries out educational programmes. Current programme areas include: promoting the role of women in peace, security and stability; conflict transformation; reduction of domestic violence; access to information; and minority rights. Organized as a national network of 162 CSOs. It has offices in Jalalabad, Mazar-i-Sharif and Herat.

Geographical Area of Activity: Afghanistan.

Publications: Annual Report; thematic and research reports; manuals.

Principal Staff: Exec. Dir Sayed Hussain Anosh.

Contact Details: House 30, 12 St, Kart-e-3, Kabul; tel. 799796945; e-mail info@cshrn.org; internet www.cshrn.org.

FOUNDATIONS AND NON-PROFITS

Afghan Women's Network

Established in 1995 by Mary Akrami, founder of the Afghan Women Skills Development Center, following the UN Fourth World Conference on Women; an umbrella organization.

Activities: Operates in three main fields: networking and co-ordinating with national and international organizations and individuals, sharing expertise and experience; advocacy and lobbying, representing and promoting Afghan women; and capacity building, to help women to participate in rehabilitating the country and reviving state institutions. The Network has regional offices in Balkh, Bamyan, Herat, Jalalabad, Kandahar, Kunduz and Paktia, and works with partner organizations in other provinces. It comprises more than 3,500 individual members and 125 female-led organizations.

Geographical Area of Activity: Afghanistan (and Afghan diaspora).

Publications: Annual Report; newsletter; policy briefs; discussion papers; position papers.

Board: Mahbouba Seraj (Dir).

Principal Staff: Exec. Dir Faizia Sadat.

Contact Details: Kolola Poshta, Kabul; tel. 788383505; e-mail admin@awn-af.net; internet www.awn-af.net.

Afghanistan Research and Evaluation Unit

Established in 2002 as an independent research institute, with the assistance of the international community in Afghanistan.

Activities: Carries out quantitative and qualitative public policy research on all aspects of Afghan society. Thematic areas cover: Afghanistan studies; culture; gender; humanitarian assistance; governance and political economy; natural resource management; regional co-operation and migration studies; and social protection. The Visiting Scholars Programme is open to academics, postgraduate students and researchers for visits of up to three months. The Unit maintains a library of over 20,000 books and periodicals on Afghanistan, in print and digitally, in Dari, Pashto and English.

Geographical Area of Activity: Afghanistan.

Publications: Newsletter (quarterly); *The Intersection* (blog); briefing papers; case studies; discussion papers; issues papers; policy notes; synthesis papers; *A to Z Guide to Afghanistan Assistance* (annual).

Board: Sayed Jawad Jawed (Chair.).

Contact Details: House 27, Heratiyan Mosque St, District 4, Shahr-e Naw, Kabul 1003; tel. 799608548; e-mail areu@areu.org.af; internet www.areu.org.af.

Armanshahr Foundation—OPEN ASIA

Established in 2006; a member of the International Federation for Human Rights—FIDH (q.v.).

Activities: Promotes human rights, democratic values, women's empowerment and justice. The Foundation's activities include awareness raising, promoting dialogue and public discussion, education programmes, organizing conferences and events, issuing publications, and research. It holds an International Women's Film Festival annually. The International Simorgh Peace Prize is awarded for works of literature and music. Has sister organizations in Tajikistan (f. 1995), Iran and France (f. 2000).

Geographical Area of Activity: Afghanistan, France, Iran, Tajikistan.

Publications: Newsletter; journals; briefing notes; reports; handbooks; guides; poetry anthologies; e-books.

Principal Staff: Exec. Dir Guissou Jahangiri.

Contact Details: House 195, 5th street on the left, Rashid St, Qassabi St, Baharestan Cinema, Karte Parwarn, Kabul; tel. 662153297; e-mail contact@openasia.org; internet openasia.org.

Foundation for Culture and Civil Society—FCCS

Established in 2003 to promote Afghan culture and to strengthen civil society.

Activities: Assists CSOs through providing technical advice on sociocultural activities. The Foundation helps Afghan artists to travel abroad and hosts events by those living abroad. In 2019, with funding from the British Council (q.v.), it began the restoration of paintings from the Afghan National Gallery collection, which was destroyed by the Taliban. Has cultural centres in Baghlan, Frayab, Herat, Jalalabad, Kandahar, Khost and Mazar-i-Sharif.

Geographical Area of Activity: Afghanistan.

Finance: Receives funding from international donors.

Principal Staff: Chair. Mir Ahammad Joyenda; Exec. Dir Timor Hakimyar.

Ghazanfar Foundation

Ghazanfar Foundation

Established in 2008 by Ghazanfar Group, a business conglomerate, inspired by Islamic, moral and humanitarian values.

Activities: Works to improve living conditions and provide opportunities to disadvantaged people through promoting rural and economic development. Main programme areas are: community development and rehabilitation; education; healthcare; employment; and housing. The Foundation offers scholarships and skills training, and carries out general charitable activities.

Geographical Area of Activity: Afghanistan.

Publications: *Ghazanfar Foundation Magazine*; reports.

Finance: Funded by the Ghazanfar Group.

Principal Staff: Chair. Al-Hajj Mohammad Ibrahim Ghazanfar.

Contact Details: Burj Ghazanfar, Baihaqi St, Mazar-i-Sharif; tel. 793101700; e-mail info@ghazanfargroup.com; internet www.ghazanfargroup.com/ghazanfar-foundation.php?lang=en.

MTN Afghanistan Foundation

Established in 2009 by MTN Afghanistan, a telecommunications company; part of the MTN Foundations network.

Activities: Administers MTN Afghanistan's social investment programmes in three main areas: community and health; education; and national development. Initiatives include: assisting internally displaced people and returnees; helping with orphanages; providing emergency medical relief and humanitarian assistance following natural disasters; restoring and renovating classrooms, schools and mosques; creating libraries and computer laboratories; providing books and academic materials to schoolchildren; offering educational opportunities and scholarships to young people; and organizing capacity-building seminars. The Foundation also encourages employee volunteering.

Geographical Area of Activity: Afghanistan.

Principal Staff: MTN Afghanistan Gen. Man., Corporate Affairs Hidayatullah Zahid.

Contact Details: POB 700, MTN Park Plaza, opp. Shar-e-Naw Park, Kabul; tel. 772222779; e-mail customerservices.af@mtn.com; internet mtn.com.af/foundation.

Transparent Election Foundation of Afghanistan—TEFA (Benaad Enetkhabat Shafaf Afghanistan)

Established in 2009 by Mohammad Naeem Ayubzada as an election-monitoring organization; an umbrella organization.

Activities: Promotes transparency and justice in political and social processes and mutual trust between the public and government, based on democratic values and principles. The Foundation supports women's rights, promoting their increased participation in elections; and strengthens the effectiveness of CSOs in the fields of social affairs, electoral reforms, advocacy and professional and impartial monitoring at all stages of elections. Internationally, it has monitored elections in seven countries and participated in international conferences. Comprises 48 CSOs.

Geographical Area of Activity: Afghanistan.

Publications: Surveys; training manuals; election guidelines.

Principal Staff: Dir Mohammad Naeem Ayubzada.

Contact Details: Second St, Taimani Sabeqa, Kabul; tel. 795868730; e-mail tefa.afghan@gmail.com.

ALBANIA

FOUNDATIONS AND NON-PROFITS

Albanian Institute for International Studies—AIIS

Established in 1998 as a research institute by a group of academics and analysts.

Activities: Carries out applied public policy research and analysis in the fields of foreign policy and national security; studies political, economic, security, ethnic, cultural, and religious developments in the Balkans region; and promotes conflict resolution, dialogue and reconciliation. Programme areas include: security studies; democracy; the market economy; Euro-Atlantic integration; NATO membership; regional co-operation; and EU integration. The Institute organizes the Foreign Policy Forum and maintains a library on international relations.

Geographical Area of Activity: Balkans region.

Publications: Newsletter; *Europa* (magazine); *Tirana Observatory* (quarterly magazine); policy papers; working papers; reports; essays; books.

Board of Directors: Artan Hajdari (Chair.).

Principal Staff: Chair. Dr Albert Rakipi; Exec. Dir Alba Çela.

Contact Details: Anton Zako Çajupi No. 20/5, Tirana; tel. (4) 4400084; e-mail aiis@aiis-albania.org; internet www.aiis-albania.org.

Fondacioni Shqiptar për të Drejtat e Personave me Aftësi të Kufizuar—FSHDPAK (Albanian Disability Rights Foundation)

Established in 1994 as an Oxfam (q.v.) disability programme in Albania; became an independent local NGO in 1996.

Activities: Empowers disabled people by improving their capacity to support their integration into society. The Foundation helps people with disabilities, their families, disability NGOs, and professionals who work directly with the disabled. It works in the areas of information and documentation services, hosting the National Center of Information and Documentation on Disability; runs a training and technical assistance centre; provides counselling and free legal aid; and carries out advocacy and awareness-raising activities.

Geographical Area of Activity: Albania.

Publications: Annual Report; *Bulletin Informativ* (2 a year); information sheets; studies and research; books; manuals; guides.

Principal Staff: Exec. Dir Blerta Çani Drenofci.

Contact Details: Rr. Bogdani (ish-A. Z. Çajupi), pall. 15, kati III (3), Tirana; tel. (4) 2269426; e-mail info@adrf.al; internet adrf.al.

Institute for Policy and Legal Studies—IPLS

Established in 1999 with the assistance of the US-based East West Management Institute; a think tank, registered as a foundation.

Activities: Provides legal assistance and training to government, non-government and international organizations working in Albania; and policy analysis and recommendations on the implementation of laws and their public impact. Main programme areas include: capacity building of public institutions; decentralization and governance; empowering civil society; EU integration; judicial reform; legislative advocacy; media policies and regulatory reform; and public administration reform.

Geographical Area of Activity: Albania.

Publications: Newsletter; action plans.

Principal Staff: Exec. Dir Lidra Elezi.

Contact Details: Sheshi 'Skenderbej', Pallati Kultures (QTZHK), kati II, No. 9, Tirana; tel. (4) 2267009; e-mail info@ipls.org; internet ipls.org.

Open Society Foundation—Western Balkans

Established in 1992 as Open Society Foundation for Albania—OSFA; part of the Open Society Foundations (q.v.) network.

Activities: Works in the fields of good governance and EU integration, justice and human rights, and social inclusion. Programme areas include: EU integration and regional co-operation; green energy transition and democratization; and digital transformation. The Foundation co-operates with other foundations in the Open Society Foundations network on international programmes, and aims to assist with the integration of the Western Balkans into the EU. Has offices in Bosnia and Herzegovina, Kosovo, North Macedonia and Serbia.

Geographical Area of Activity: Albania, Bosnia and Herzegovina, Kosovo, North Macedonia, Serbia.

Publications: Annual Report; books; brochures; policy briefs.

Principal Staff: Dir Andi Dobrushi; Deputy Dir Miodrag Milosavljevic.

Contact Details: ABA Business Center, 12th Floor, Papa Gjon Pali II St, 1010 Tirana; tel. (4) 4501700; e-mail info@osfwb.org; internet osfwb.org.

Vodafone Albania Foundation

Established in 2007 by Vodafone Albania, a telecommunications company; part of the Vodafone Foundation (q.v.) network.

Activities: Makes grants to projects in the fields of education, healthcare, support for vulnerable groups and emergency response. The Foundation promotes employee volunteering and provides technology to unsupported communities and people affected by natural disasters. Under the Vodafone Distinction Bursary Fund it offers scholarships to study Master's degrees at international universities in subjects that require digital skills.

Geographical Area of Activity: Albania.

Restrictions: Scholarships are open to Albanian graduates aged up to 35 years who are residing in Albania.

Publications: Annual Report.

Finance: Annual disbursements 52m. lek.

Board of Directors: Christina Samoulada (Chair.); Artur Tomini (Treas.).

Principal Staff: Exec. Dir Viola Puci.

Contact Details: Autostrada Tirane-Durrës, Rr. Pavarësia 61, Kashar, Tirana 1050; tel. (4) 2283072; e-mail foundation.al@vodafone.com; internet www.vodafone.al/fondacioni.

ANGOLA

FOUNDATIONS AND NON-PROFITS

Fundação Sindika Dokolo (Sindika Dokolo Foundation)

Established in 2007 by Sindika Dokolo, a Congolese business person and art collector, and Fernando Alvim, an artist, to support the development of contemporary African art, the first edition of the Trienal de Luanda and the creation of the first African pavilion at the 52nd Venice Biennale.

Activities: Manages and exhibits a collection of around 5,000 contemporary African works of art. The Foundation works in partnership with African cities and nations, and international institutions to promote African culture. It hosts exhibitions, loans works of art and maintains a database of artists.

Geographical Area of Activity: International.

Publications: Newsletter.

Principal Staff: Pres. Sindika Dokolo; Vice-Pres. Fernando Alvim.

Contact Details: Palacio de Ferro, Rua Major Kanhangulo, Ingombota, Luanda; e-mail contact@fondation-sindikadokolo.com; internet www.fondation-sindikadokolo.com.

Nesr Art Foundation

Founded in 2021 by philanthropists Hiba and Wissam Nesr.

Activities: Supports Angolan artists and other African artists through a programme of dialogue and exchange both across the continent and internationally. Offers a residency programme for six emerging artists per year who attend the 10-week residency in Luanda.

Geographical Area of Activity: Angola, Cape Verde, Guinea-Bissau, Mozambique, São Tomé e Príncipe.

Principal Staff: Project Manager Edna Bettencourt.

Contact Details: Boavista, Luanda; e-mail info@nesrartfoundation.com; internet www.nesrartfoundation.com.

ANGUILLA

FOUNDATIONS AND NON-PROFITS

Anguilla Community Fund

Established in 1999 with the support of the Social Security Development Fund.

Activities: Promotes local philanthropy. The organization manages eight funds: the General Endowment, a long-term fund which supports NGOs, projects and other initiatives; the Mouton Scholarship Fund, providing scholarships for general tertiary-level education abroad; the Anguilla College Scholarship Fund, providing scholarships for tertiary-level education abroad in the fields of information technology and medicine; the David Berglund Scholarship Fund, providing scholarships to study veterinary medicine and services; the David and Pauline Farmer Fund, providing services for senior citizens and lesbian and gay young people; the Teacher Noonie Fund, focusing on early childhood development; the Lydia and Jeremiah Gumbs Fund, providing care for the mentally ill; and the Anguilla Cares Fund, which awards grants every 12–18 months based on community needs.

Geographical Area of Activity: Anguilla.

Restrictions: Grants to individuals are limited to scholarship assistance.

Board: Bonnie Richardson Lake (Chair.); Seymour Hodge (Treas.); Lavelle Niles (Sec.).

Principal Staff: Dir Carrolle Devonish.

Anguilla National Trust

Contact Details: POB 1097, The Valley 2640; Devonish Art Gallery Bldg, West End; tel. 4765162; e-mail brichardsonlake@yahoo.com; internet www.acf.org.ai.

Anguilla National Trust—ANT
Founded in 1989.
Activities: The ANT's mandate is to sustain Anguilla's natural and cultural heritage through active management and educational programmes. Has been instrumental in the creation and maintenance of national parks, conservation areas, and heritage sites. Conducts essential research and conservation work, including habitat and species monitoring, and works to raise public awareness of the complexity and fragility of natural and cultural resources.
Geographical Area of Activity: Anguilla.
Principal Staff: Exec. Dir Farah Mukhida.
Contact Details: Museum Bldg, Albert Lake Dr, POB 1234, AI-2640 The Valley; tel. 2355297; e-mail antadmin@axanationaltrust.com; internet www.axanationaltrust.org.

ARGENTINA

CO-ORDINATING BODY

Grupo de Fundaciones y Empresas (Group of Foundations and Businesses)
Established in 1995 to promote the development of foundations in Argentina.
Activities: Promotes the development of philanthropy and provides information to foundations about philanthropy, social investment and volunteering. The Group maintains online databases on foundations and projects operated by not-for-profit organizations; offers a diploma in education policy aimed at business people and leaders of companies and foundations; and established the Observatorio de Salud on public health policy. Has 80 member organizations.
Geographical Area of Activity: Argentina.
Publications: Annual Report; newsletter (monthly); *Proyectos Aprobados* (quarterly publication on projects funded by foundations).
Board of Directors: Gustavo Castagnino (Pres.); Mariana Corti (Vice-Pres.); Javier di Biase (Treas.); Lucia de la Vega (Sec.).
Principal Staff: Exec. Dir Javier García Moritan.
Contact Details: Av. Pres. Roque Sáenz Peña 615, piso 9, Of. 911, C1035AAB Buenos Aires; tel. (11) 5272-0513; e-mail gdfe@gdfe.org.ar; internet www.gdfe.org.ar.

FOUNDATIONS AND NON-PROFITS

Consejo Argentino para las Relaciones Internacionales—CARI (Argentine Council for International Relations)
Established in 1978 by former Foreign Minister Dr Carlos Manuel Muñiz and a group of international affairs professionals as an independent non-profit organization; a think tank.
Activities: Studies and analyses the political, economic, cultural and social aspects of Argentina's international relations. Thematic areas of study include: Argentina's foreign policy; defence and security; democracy and human rights; economy; energy and environment; global and regional governance; science and technology; and society and culture. The Council carries out work through permanent study committees and working groups; and established the Institute of International Law (f. 1993) and the Institute for International Security and Strategic Affairs (f. 1994). It organizes bilateral dialogue forums, conferences, lectures, meetings and seminars; and comprises the Documentation Center for African Studies. The Young Group contributes to the training and development of young professionals aged 25–40 years.
Geographical Area of Activity: International.
Publications: Academic Report (annual); *Artículos y Testimonios* (series); *Crónicas del Foro* (series); *Los Diplomáticos* (series); newsletters; bulletins; working papers; books.
Executive Committee: Francisco de Santibañes (Pres.); Dr Carola Ramón (Vice-Pres.); Lila Roldán Vázquez (Gen. Sec.); Victoria Costoya (Treas.).
Contact Details: Uruguay 1037, piso 1, C1016ACA Buenos Aires; tel. (11) 4811-0072; e-mail cari@cari.org.ar; internet cari.org.ar.

Consejo Latinoamericano de Ciencias Sociales—CLACSO (Latin American Council of Social Sciences)
Established in 1967 as an international NGO; a think tank.
Activities: Promotes social research on issues of importance to Latin America and the Caribbean through academic research, and South–South and North–South co-operation and dialogue. Areas of interest include: combating poverty and inequality; strengthening human rights and democratic participation; economically, socially and environmentally sustainable development; and the democratization of access to knowledge and evidence-based research. The Council supports the formation of networks and institutions working in the fields of the social sciences and humanities, offering scholarships and research grants, organizing international seminars and working groups, and publishing research findings. It comprises 937 research and postgraduate centres from 56 countries; and has associative status with ECOSOC.
Geographical Area of Activity: International.
Publications: Annual Report; newsletter; *Cuadernos del Pensamiento Crítico Latinoamericano* (series); policy briefs; working group newsletters; working groups collections; South–South collection; books; magazines; encyclopaedias.
Principal Staff: Exec. Sec. Dr Karina Batthyány.
Contact Details: Estados Unidos 1168, C1101AAX Buenos Aires; tel. (11) 4304-9145; e-mail clacsoinst@clacso.edu.ar; internet www.clacso.org.

Fundación Acindar (Acíndar Foundation)
Founded in 1962 by Acindar (Industria Argentina de Aceros SA), a steel manufacturer, now Acindar Grupo ArcelorMittal.
Activities: Works mainly in the areas of education and social welfare. The Foundation collaborates with the Government, educational institutions and CSOs; supports initiatives that promote science, technology, engineering and mathematics (STEM); and offers scholarships to the children of employees for secondary and higher education. It operates in five cities in Argentina where the company has a presence, principally in Villa Constitución, Santa Fe province.
Geographical Area of Activity: Argentina.
Publications: Annual Report; reports.
Board of Directors: Arturo T. Acevedo (Pres.); Federico Amos (Vice-Pres.).
Contact Details: Estanislas Zeballos 2739, 1643 Beccar, Buenos Aires; tel. (11) 5077-5000; e-mail fundacion.acindar@arcelormittal.com.ar; internet www.fundacionacindar.org.ar.

ARGENTINA

Fundación Ambiente y Recursos Naturales—FARN (Environment and Natural Resources Foundation)

Founded in 1985 by Dr Guillermo J. Cano, a lawyer and diplomat.

Activities: Promotes democratic and participatory citizenship and sustainable development through environmental advocacy. Programme areas include: agriculture; biodiversity; climate change; economics and environmental policy; energy and infrastructure; environmental justice and rights; mining and glaciers; and pollution. The Foundation awards the annual Adriana Schiffrin Prize for innovation for the environment. It has consultative status with ECOSOC.

Geographical Area of Activity: International.

Publications: Annual Report; Annual Environmental Report; *Pulso Ambiental* (digital magazine, 2 a year); *Environmental Law Supplement* (quarterly, in Spanish); articles, reports, papers and other publications.

Finance: Annual income 376.2m. pesos, expenditure 375.9m. pesos (30 June 2023).

Board of Directors: Daniel Ryan (Pres.); Jorge Schiffrin (Vice-Pres.); Margarita Carlés (Treas.); Marta Inés Andelman (Sec.).

Principal Staff: Exec. Dir Andrés Nápoli; Deputy Exec. Dirs Ana Di Pangracio, Pia Marchegiani.

Contact Details: Sánchez de Bustamante 27, piso 1, C1173AAA Buenos Aires; tel. (11) 4865-1707; e-mail info@farn.org.ar; internet www.farn.org.ar.

Fundación Bariloche (Bariloche Foundation)

Founded in 1963 by a group of business people and scientists from the National Atomic Energy Commission.

Activities: Focuses on four main fields of interest: energy economics and planning, with an emphasis on developing countries; environmental policy and sustainable development; quality of life; and philosophy. Main programmes are: Environment and Development; Complex Systems Analysis; Energy; and Integrated Policy and Development. The Foundation issues publications and takes part in regional conferences and symposia. It maintains a library containing approx. 10,000 books and monographs; maintains an office in Buenos Aires.

Geographical Area of Activity: Argentina.

Publications: *Boletín Bibliográfico* (2 a year); *Revista Desarrollo y Energía* (2 a year); *Revista Patagónica de Filosofía* (journal); books; periodicals; journals; working papers.

Finance: Annual budget of the Foundation and its associated groups approx. US $1.1m.

Principal Staff: Chief Exec. Nicolás di Sbroiavacca; Exec. Vice-Pres. Gustavo Nadal.

Contact Details: Bustillo Ave 9500, R8402AGP, San Carlos de Bariloche, Río Negro; tel. (11) 4331-1816; e-mail fb@fundacionbariloche.org.ar; internet www.fundacionbariloche.org.ar.

Fundación Bunge y Born (Bunge y Born Foundation)

Founded in 1963 by the Bunge Group of agribusiness companies.

Activities: Operates in the fields of education, scientific research, health and culture; and provides emergency aid and medical equipment during natural or humanitarian disasters. The Foundation offers grants for research into infectious diseases and social vulnerability. It also awards scholarships for young Argentinians to carry out doctoral research in scientific disciplines at universities and research centres in Germany and the USA; for university and professional training in nursing; and training in cultural management for administrators and civil servants.

Geographical Area of Activity: Argentina, Germany, USA.

Publications: Annual Report; newsletter; books.

Board of Directors: Jorge Born (Pres.); Jenefer Féraud (Vice-Pres.).

Principal Staff: Exec. Dir Gerardo della Paolera.

Contact Details: 25 de Mayo 501, piso 6, C1002ABK, 1002 Buenos Aires; tel. (11) 4318-6096; e-mail info@fundacionbyb.org; internet www.fundacionbyb.org.

Fundación para Estudio e Investigación de la Mujer—FEIM (Foundation for Women's Research and Studies)

Established in 1989 by a group of women gender experts; has consultative status at the UN.

Activities: Works in the area of girls' and women's rights, providing services such as healthcare and health education (especially regarding AIDS and reproductive health); promotes the development of small enterprises; conducts research; and maintains a library. The Foundation also operates in the area of the environment, promoting recycling, solar energy and the development of environmental organizations in Argentina.

Geographical Area of Activity: Argentina.

Publications: Newsletter; books; information on health matters.

Finance: Annual budget approx. US $100,000.

Board of Directors: Dr Mabel Bianco (Pres.); Lidia Heller (Treas.); Dr Laura Pagani (Sec.).

Contact Details: Paraná 135, piso 3, Of. 13, C1017AAC Buenos Aires; tel. (11) 4372-2763; e-mail feim@feim.org.ar; internet www.feim.org.ar.

Fundación de Investigaciones Económicas Latinoamericanas—FIEL (Foundation for Latin American Economic Research)

Founded in 1964 by the Chamber of Commerce of Argentina, the Stock Exchange of Buenos Aires, the Argentine Industrial Union and the Cattle Breeders' Association.

Activities: Operates in the field of economic affairs, through conducting public policy analysis and research on business trends and structural problems of the Argentinian and Central and South American economies. Areas of interest include: analysis and design of social policies in health, education, and social and employment programmes; the energy economy; environmental economics; fiscal growth, monetary policy, the financial sector, banking and insurance; foreign trade and international negotiations; income distribution and poverty; industry, agriculture, commerce and services; law and economics; municipal and provincial socioeconomic development, business and public policy; national and regional macroeconomics; price indexes and monitoring; and small and medium-sized businesses. The Foundation co-operates with similar Central and South American organizations. It maintains a library and database.

Geographical Area of Activity: Central and South America (mainly Argentina).

Publications: Annual Report; *FIEL News* (monthly); *Partes de Prensa* (monthly); *Indicadores de Coyuntura* (monthly); *Documentos de Trabajo* (quarterly); *Indicadores de Actividad y Precios* (monthly); books; studies; surveys; working papers.

Finance: Annual income 558.2m. pesos, expenditure 574.5m. pesos (31 Dec. 2023).

Board of Directors: Dr Daniel Herrero (Pres.); Dr Carlos Ormachea (First Vice-Pres.); Dr María Carmen Tettamanti (Second Vice-Pres.); Martin Zarich (Third Vice-Pres.); Gustavo Canzani, Dr Patricia Galli (Treas); Franco Livini (Sec.).

Contact Details: Córdoba 637, piso 4, C1054AAF Buenos Aires; tel. (11) 4314-1990; e-mail info@fiel.org.ar; internet www.fiel.org.

Fundación Mediterránea—IERAL (Mediterranean Foundation)

Founded in 1977 by 34 companies from Córdoba province.

Activities: Promotes national and regional economic research and analysis. The Foundation carries out research and issues publications, and organizes conferences. It

Fundación Mujeres en Igualdad ARGENTINA

established the Institute for Studies on the Argentine and Latin American Reality, a think tank which carries out regional socioeconomic research and analysis in the national interest.

Geographical Area of Activity: Central and South America.

Publications: *Revista Novedades* (magazine); *Monitor/Foco Fiscal*; discussion papers; agroindustry reports; situation reports; studies.

Board: María Pía Astori (Pres.); Marcos Brito (First Vice-Pres.); José Enrique Martín (Second Vice-Pres.); Sergio Oscar Roggio (Sec.).

Principal Staff: Exec. Dir Myrian R. Martínez.

Contact Details: Ituzaingó 1368, 5000 Córdoba; tel. (351) 463-0000; e-mail info@fundmediterranea.org.ar; internet ieral.org.

Fundación Mujeres en Igualdad—MEI (Women in Equality Foundation)

Established in 1990 by Zita Montes de Oca, a women's rights advocate.

Activities: Challenges gender violence and discrimination; and promotes women's social, economic, cultural and political development. The Foundation supports women's empowerment, with a focus on gender violence, trafficking and pimping, the digital world, gender and corruption, and gender and sports. MEI also established Femplea, a digital platform to create job opportunities for and provide training to women. It organizes international women's forums against corruption; it has consultative status at ECOSOC.

Geographical Area of Activity: Mainly Argentina.

Publications: *Mujeres en Política* (magazine); bulletins; brochures; handbooks.

Board of Trustees: Silvia Carmen Ferraro (Pres.); Sonia Santoro (Vice-Pres.); María Inés Rodríguez Aguilar (Treas.); Myrtha Schalom (Sec.).

Principal Staff: Exec. Dir Monique Thiteux Altschul.

Contact Details: Urquiza 1835, 1602 Florida, Buenos Aires; tel. (11) 4791-0821; e-mail it@mujeresenigualdad.org; internet mujeresenigualdad.org.

Fundación SES—Sustentabilidad, Educación, Solidaridad (SES Foundation—Sustainability, Education, Solidarity)

Established in 1999.

Activities: Promotes sustainability, education and social inclusion. The Foundation carries out activities in the areas of: inclusive, quality education; institutional capacity building of CSOs; job opportunities for young people; and youth participation. It develops training initiatives for the social and political inclusion of young people; funds projects in schools and higher education institutions; and provides technical and financial assistance to CSOs and NGOs.

Geographical Area of Activity: Central and South America, Europe.

Restrictions: No grants to individuals; grants only to partner organizations.

Publications: Annual Report; *Boletín* (electronic newsletter); reports; surveys; toolkits.

Principal Staff: Exec. Dir Alejandra Solla.

Contact Details: Bulnes 1455, 4th Floor, D – Buenos Aires; tel. (11) 5368-8370; e-mail info@fundses.org.ar; internet www.fundses.org.ar.

Fundación Telefónica Movistar Argentina (Telefónica Movistar Argentina Foundation)

Established in 1999 by Telefónica-Movistar, a telecommunications company; part of the Fundación Telefónica (q.v.) network.

Activities: Carries out activities in the areas of digital culture, education, employability and volunteering. The Foundation offers free online training and digital tools via the Conecta Empleo platform. It works with partners in the private, public and third sectors, carrying out research and organizing conferences, exhibitions and workshops.

Geographical Area of Activity: Argentina.

Publications: Newsletter.

Board of Trustees: Marcelo Ricardo Tarakdjian (Pres.); Sebastián Minoyetti (Treas.); Alejandro Pinedo (Sec.).

Principal Staff: Man. Gustavo Blanco García Ordás.

Contact Details: Arenales 1540, C1061AAR Buenos Aires; tel. (11) 4333-1301; e-mail educacion.ar@telefonica.com; internet www.fundaciontelefonica.com.ar.

Fundación Torcuato Di Tella—FTDT (Torcuato Di Tella Foundation)

Established in 1958 by Torcuato Di Tella, an industrialist.

Activities: Carries out research projects and provides technical assistance in relation to environmental issues, climate change and energy. Areas of interest include: adaptation; carbon pricing; climate financing; deep decarbonization; the economics of climate change; knowledge platforms; and wetlands. In 2002, in conjunction with the Instituto di Tella, the Foundation established the Centro de Estudios en Cambio Climático Global (CECcG), which works with the Universidad de Torcuato di Tella to investigate the impacts of climate change, influence public policy and contribute to the debate about environmental issues and governance. It co-ordinates the activities of the Argentinian delegation of Delta Alliance; and has observer status at meetings of the UN Framework Convention on Climate Change.

Geographical Area of Activity: Argentina.

Publications: Newsletter; working papers; books; blog.

Board of Directors: Daniel Perczyk (Chair.).

Contact Details: Esmeralda 1376, Buenos Aires; tel. (11) 5697-5394; internet ftdt.cc.

Instituto para la Integración de América Latina y el Caribe—BID-INTAL (Institute for Latin American and Caribbean Integration)

Founded in 1965 by an agreement between the Inter-American Development Bank and the Government of Argentina to promote regional integration; a unit of the Inter-American Development Bank.

Activities: Promotes the economic, digital and political integration of Latin American and the Caribbean, through providing technical, financial and operational support. Main activities include: producing and publishing information on integration processes, foreign direct investment and trade in services developing technologies and platforms to foster the exchange of ideas and trade regionally; capacity building in the public and private sectors; and promoting strategic dialogue.

Geographical Area of Activity: Latin America and the Caribbean.

Publications: *Conexión INTAL* (monthly newsletter); *Revista Integración & Comercio* (2 a year, magazine in English and Spanish); *Eco integración de América Latina* (magazine); *Latinobarómetro*; *Informe MERCOSUR*; *Monitor de Comercio*; databases; monographs; newsletters; periodicals; reports; technical notes.

Principal Staff: Dir Ana Ines Basco.

Contact Details: Esmeralda 130, Piso 16, Buenos Aires; tel. (11) 4323-2363; e-mail intal@iadb.org; internet www.iadb.org/es/quienes-somos/tematicas/comercio/intal.

ARMENIA

CO-ORDINATING BODY

NGO Center—NGOC
Founded in 1994 as the Armenian Assembly of America, to provide training and technical assistance on advocacy and public policy advocacy; registered as a local NGO in 2005.

Activities: Offers a database of knowledge, information and experience for civil society organizations, and contributes to the empowerment of civil society organizations through training, consultancy, research, awareness raising and capacity-building programmes and services. Its mission is to promote citizen participation in development processes of the state through continuous and systematic capacity enhancement.

Geographical Area of Activity: Armenia.

Publications: *Armenian NGO News in Brief* (annual); *NGOC Gazette* (annual); studies; newsletters; reports.

Finance: Annual budget €261,000 (2023).

Principal Staff: Dir Arpine Hakobyan.

Contact Details: Vanadzor, Khorenatsi St 6/1; tel. (91) 743315; e-mail info@ngoc.am; internet www.ngoc.am.

FOUNDATIONS AND NON-PROFITS

Caucasus Research Resource Center Armenia Foundation—CRRC
Established in 2003 with support from the Carnegie Corporation, the Eurasia Partnership Foundation and Yerevan University; became an independent body in 2013.

Activities: Carries out social science and public policy research, analysis and data collection on regional socioeconomic and political issues. Research areas include: CSOs, human rights and civic education; the economy and the labour market; education, skills and research capacity building; gender; health and the environment; media; and migration. Provides the Caucusus Barometer online data analysis tool covering the South Causasus. Offers grants and training, and organizes conferences and summer schools. It maintains a social science library of more than 2,000 publications.

Geographical Area of Activity: Armenia, Azerbaijan, Georgia.

Publications: Annual Report; *Caucasus Barometer*; surveys; datasets; guides; blogs.

Finance: Total assets US $857,423 (31 Dec. 2023).

Board of Trustees: Mary Sheehan (Pres.); Michael Johnson (Treas.).

Principal Staff: CEO Sona Balasanyan.

Contact Details: Yerevan 0018, 47/1 Tigran Mets Ave; tel. (98) 948548; e-mail crrc@crrc.am; internet www.crrc.am.

Eurasia Partnership Foundation-Armenia—EPF-Armenia
Established in 1995 as an office of the Eurasia Foundation (q.v.); became part of the Eurasia Partnership Foundation network in 2007.

Activities: Carries out policy research and analysis in the promotion of social justice and economic prosperity. Programme areas include: human rights and justice reform; peace building and conflict transformation; civil society capacity building and youth empowerment; good governance; and policy advocacy. Organizes discussions and conferences; and offers training, professional exchange tours of Armenia and internships. It has a branch office in Ijevan (EPF North) and works with regional NGO partners. Has special consultative status with ECOSOC.

Geographical Area of Activity: South Caucasus.

Restrictions: Grants only for specific projects.

Publications: Annual Report; newsletter; policy briefs; reports; country reports; conference reports; guidebooks.

Finance: Total assets US $2m. (31 Dec. 2023).

Board of Trustees: Mary Sheehan (Pres.).

Principal Staff: CEO Gevorg Ter-Gabrielyan.

Contact Details: Yerevan 0037, Suite 23, Azatutyan Ave 1/21; tel. (10) 251575; e-mail info-epf@epfound.am; internet epfarmenia.am.

Future in Our Hands Youth NGO—FIOH
Established in 2011 by Tigranuhi Aleksanyan.

Activities: Promotes youth education, participation in civil society and democracy through providing opportunities for young Armenians to travel abroad, organizing volunteering placements and training, and exchanges for young people from other countries to travel to Armenia. Participates in the EU's Erasmus+ and European Voluntary Service programmes, offers English-language tuition and holds seminars on social entrepreneurship.

Geographical Area of Activity: Armenia, People's Repub. of China, EU, Georgia, Türkiye (Turkey).

Publications: Newsletter.

Principal Staff: Dir Tigranuhi Aleksanyan.

Contact Details: Yerevan 0014, Ghapantsian 8A; tel. (95) 337873; e-mail info@fioh-ngo.com; internet fioh-ngo.com.

Open Society Foundations—Armenia
Established in 1996; an independent organization, part of the Open Society Foundations (q.v.) network. Formerly known as the Open Society Institute Assistance Foundation, Armenia—OSIAFA.

Activities: Supports local NGOs to promote accountability, human rights, justice, the rule of law and transparency. Programme areas include: civil society; education; information and the media; law and criminal justice; strategic litigation; public health; and women. Awards scholarships for annual summer university courses and postgraduate study abroad at the Central European University; and also offers the Policy Fellowships for independent policy-orientated research and Academic Fellowships to encourage young scholars to return to Armenia to take up positions in universities. It hosts the Partnership for Open Society, a coalition of more than 60 CSOs.

Geographical Area of Activity: Armenia.

Publications: Annual Report; newsletter; reports; briefings.

Finance: Annual budget US $3.6m. (2019).

Principal Staff: Exec. Dir Larisa Minasyan; Deputy Dir (Programmes) David Amiryan.

Contact Details: Yerevan 375002, 7/1 cul-de-sac #2 off Tumanian St; tel. (77) 533862; e-mail info@osi.am; internet www.osf.am.

Ucom Foundation
Established in 2011 as Orange Foundation Armenia by telecommunications provider Orange; present name adopted in 2016 after Ucom's acquisition of Orange Armenia.

Activities: Carries out activities in the fields of healthcare, education and culture. The Foundation helps vulnerable people, through creating economic and social stability and development opportunities.

Geographical Area of Activity: Armenia.

Publications: Annual Report.

Principal Staff: CEO Ara Khachatryan.

Contact Details: Yerevan 0069, 'Ucom' CJSC, 8/4 Davit Anhaght St; tel. (11) 444444; e-mail info@ucom.am; internet www.ucom.am/en/footer/foundation.

AUSTRALIA

CO-ORDINATING BODIES

Good2Give
Established in 2000 as Charities Aid Foundation (CAF) Australia; present name adopted in 2016. A member of the Global Alliance of the Charities Aid Foundation.

Activities: Provides financial services and advice to companies, their employees and customers on workplace giving and volunteering; and administrative, regulatory and finance management services for corporate foundations. The organization maintains an online directory of 2,000 charities linked with its workplace giving platform.

Geographical Area of Activity: Australia, New Zealand.

Publications: Annual Review; *World Giving Index*; Charity Directory (online); guides; case studies; research reports; toolkits; blog.

Board of Directors: Michael Graf, Nerida Caesar (Co-Chair.); Thomas Bodger (Sec.).

Principal Staff: CEO David Mann.

Contact Details: 12 Holtermann St, Crows Nest, Sydney, NSW 2065; tel. (2) 9929 9633; e-mail info@good2give.ngo; internet good2give.ngo.

Philanthropy Australia
Established in 1975; formerly known as the Australian Association of Philanthropy.

Activities: Represents the philanthropic sector through carrying out policy advocacy. The organization promotes philanthropy by the community, business and government sectors; inspires and supports new philanthropists; increases the effectiveness of philanthropy through providing information, resources and networking opportunities; and promotes strong and transparent governance standards in the philanthropic sector. It organizes the Australian Philanthropy Awards; and has around 700 institutional and individual members.

Geographical Area of Activity: Australia.

Restrictions: Supports grantmakers, but does not make grants itself.

Publications: Annual Report; *Philanthropy Weekly* (weekly); Directory of Funders (online); Foundation Maps: Australia (online); Advocacy Toolkit (online); papers; reports.

Finance: Annual income A$5.8m., expenditure A$5.7m. (2023).

Board: Lisa George, Amanda Miller (Co-Chair.).

Principal Staff: CEO Maree Sidey.

Contact Details: Level 14, 90 Collins St, Melbourne, VIC 3000; tel. (3) 9662 9299; e-mail info@philanthropy.org.au; internet www.philanthropy.org.au.

FOUNDATIONS AND NON-PROFITS

Action on Poverty
Established in 1968, originally to co-ordinate philanthropic programmes in the Pacific region; formerly known as the Australian Foundation for the Peoples of Asia and the Pacific—AFAP.

Activities: Supports sustainable development in poor and vulnerable communities, with a focus on women, people with disabilities and ethnic minorities. Main programme areas include: food and water security and climate resilience; governance and social accountability; health; livelihoods and economic empowerment. The organization works in 16 countries and has a representative office in Hanoi, Viet Nam.

Geographical Area of Activity: Asia-Pacific, Australia, South and South-East Asia, sub-Saharan Africa.

Publications: Annual Report; *Action on Poverty NOW* (newsletter); reports.

Finance: Annual revenue A$8.9m., expenditure A$9.0m. (30 June 2024).

Board of Directors: Tim Lovitt (Chair.).

Principal Staff: CEO Brayden Howie.

Contact Details: 383 George St, Sydney, NSW 2000; tel. (2) 9906 3792; e-mail info@actiononpoverty.org; internet actiononpoverty.org.

AMP Foundation
Established in 1992 by the AMP Group, a financial services company; merged with the AXA Charitable Trust in 2011.

Activities: Invests in two main areas: capacity building, focusing on young people's education and employment and the sustainability of the non-profit sector; and community involvement, supporting the work of AMP employees and financial planners in the community, including an employee volunteering programme. The Foundation comprises the AMP Foundation Trust, which also funds grants made through the Tomorrow Fund; the AMP Foundation Charitable Trust; and the AMP Community Trust (formerly AXA Charitable Trust).

Geographical Area of Activity: Australia, New Zealand.

Restrictions: Does not accept unsolicited applications.

Publications: Annual Report; Community Report (annual).

Finance: Annual revenue A$3.0m., expenditure $2.6m. (31 Dec. 2023).

Board of Directors: Alexis George (Chair.).

Principal Staff: Gen. Man. Nicola Stokes.

Contact Details: 50 Bridge St, Sydney NSW 2000; POB 4134, Sydney 2001; tel. (2) 9257 5334; e-mail amp_foundation@amp.com.au; internet ampfoundation.com.au.

Apex Foundation
Founded in 1976 by the Association of Apex Clubs, an association of community service clubs.

Activities: Works to improve the quality of life for young Australians with special needs. The Foundation manages five trusts: the Apex Foundation Charitable Trust, which funds research on autism, children's cancer and leukaemia, craniofacial, diabetes mellitus and melanoma; the Underprivileged Children's Trust, which funds the construction, maintenance and operation of short-term respite accommodation and care facilities for disadvantaged, chronically ill and disabled children and young adults and their families; the Fine Arts Trust, which offers scholarships for young artists to compete in the Hans Gabor Belvedere Competition; the Civilian Widows NSW Trust, which supports disadvantaged individuals and families in need; and the Apex Foundation Community Fund, which supports Apex Clubs to provide programmes for children and families at risk with grants worth up to A$3,000.

Geographical Area of Activity: Australia.

Restrictions: Researchers may be of any nationality, but must undertake their research in Australia.

Publications: Annual Report; *The Apex Newsletter* (quarterly); *Apex in Action*.

Board of Directors: Jamie Vincent (Chair.); Lindsay Carthew (Vice-Chair.); Mike Fitze (Sec.).

Contact Details: POB 331, Wollongong, NSW 2520; tel. (4) 9317 1870; e-mail info@apexfoundation.org.au; internet www.apexfoundation.org.au.

Arthritis Australia
Established in 1999 as the Arthritis Foundation of Australia.

Activities: Provides advocacy, information and support to people with arthritis and related conditions; and promotes medical and scientific research in the field. The organization acts as the national secretariat for affiliated foundations

throughout Australia. It assists medical, scientific and allied health professions through providing investigator or allied health grants (A$10,000–A$15,000), project grants and grants in aid (A$15,000–A$50,000), scholarships (A$20,000–A$25,000) and fellowships (A$50,000).
Geographical Area of Activity: Australia, UK, USA.
Publications: Annual Report; *Arthritis Insights* (newsletter); information sheets; reports; books.
Finance: Annual income A$3.6m., expenditure A$3.3m. (30 June 2024).
Board of Directors: Kaylene Hubbard (Chair.); Paul Ritchie (Deputy Chair. and Treas.); John Butt (Sec.).
Principal Staff: CEO Jonathan Smithers.
Contact Details: Level 2, 255 Broadway, Glebe, NSW 2037; POB 550, Broadway, NSW 2007; tel. (2) 9518 4441; e-mail info@arthritisaustralia.com.au; internet arthritisaustralia.com.au.

Australian Academy of the Humanities

Established in 1969 by the Australian Humanities Research Council.
Activities: Aims to advance knowledge in the field of the humanities, in particular: archaeology; the arts; Asian studies; classical studies; cultural and communication studies; English; European languages and cultures; history; linguistics; philosophy and the history of ideas; and religion. The Academy offers the John Mulvaney Fellowship, worth A$4,000, for Aboriginal and Torres Strait Islander researchers and doctoral students working in the humanities; Humanities Travelling Fellowships of up to A$4,000 for early career researchers; publication subsidies of up to A$3,000; every two years, the Max Crawford Medal for achievement in the humanities and the Medal for Excellence in Translation; and every 3–4 years, the McCredie Musicological Award. Through the Ernst & Rosemarie Keller Fund it offers travelling fellowships of up to A$5,000 for scholars in Australia researching German history, literature, language, politics or culture, or German contributions in Australia or the Asia-Pacific region. Has more than 730 Fellows.
Geographical Area of Activity: Australia.
Publications: Annual Report; *Humanities Australia* (annual journal); symposium papers; monographs; occasional papers; edited collections.
Finance: Annual income A$1.5m., expenditure A$1.4m. (30 June 2024).
Council: Prof. Stephen Garton (Pres.); Prof. Elizabeth Minchin (Hon. Sec. and Vice-Pres.); Prof. Chris Hilliard (Treas.).
Principal Staff: Exec. Dir Inga Davis.
Contact Details: WOTSO, 490 Northbourne Ave, Dickson, ACT, 2602; tel. (2) 6189 6982; e-mail enquiries@humanities.org.au; internet www.humanities.org.au.

Australian Academy of Science

Founded in 1954 by Australian Fellows of the Royal Society of London; an independent body of Australia's research scientists.
Activities: Champions, celebrates and supports excellence in Australian science. The Academy promotes international scientific engagement; builds public awareness and understanding of science; and provides independent, authoritative and influential scientific advice. Each year, up to 20 new Fellows are elected. It maintains the Basser Library (f. 1960), which contains books and journals; and the Fenner Archives (f. 1962), which contain manuscript and archival collections.
Geographical Area of Activity: Mainly Australia.
Publications: Annual Report; newsletters.
Finance: Total revenue A$15.0m., expenditure A$15.4m. (30 June 2024).
Exec. Committee: Prof. Chennupati Jagadish (Pres.); Prof. Marilyn Anderson (Treas.); Prof. Ivan Marusic (Sec. for Physical Sciences); Prof. Bob Graham (Sec. for Biological Sciences); Prof. Ian Chubb (Sec. for Science Policy); Prof. Lyn Beazley (Sec. for Education and Public Awareness); Prof. Frances Separovic (Foreign Sec.).
Principal Staff: Chief Exec. Anna-Maria Arabia.
Contact Details: Ian Potter House, 9 Gordon St, Acton, ACT 2601; GPO Box 783, Canberra, ACT 2601; tel. (2) 6201 9400; e-mail aas@science.org.au; internet www.science.org.au.

Australian Academy of Technological Sciences and Engineering

Established in 1976 as the Australian Academy of Technological Sciences; renamed in 1987 to incorporate Engineering.
Activities: Works in the fields of science, technology and engineering. Programme areas include: agriculture and food; digital futures; education; energy; health and medical technology; industry and innovation; infrastructure; mineral resources; and water. The Academy facilitates a network of forums, working groups and advisory groups on a range of key issues. It disseminates information nationally through its STELR (Science and Technology Education Leveraging Relevance) Project; and offers awards for the application of science and technology to benefit Australia economically, socially or environmentally. Fellowships are awarded in the areas of applied physical science and technology, applied biological science and technology, engineering and management, and development and leadership. Comprises almost 900 Fellows.
Geographical Area of Activity: International.
Publications: Annual Report; Annual Review; *#TechKnow* (newsletter); *Focus* (magazine, 6 a year); discussion papers; policy papers; position statements; reports.
Finance: Annual income A$6.5m., expenditure A$8.7m. (30 June 2023).
Board of Directors: Dr Katherine Woodthorpe (Pres.); Prof. Mark Hoffman, Sue MacLeman, Prof. Anne Green (Vice-Pres).
Principal Staff: CEO Kylie Walker.
Contact Details: Level 2, 28 National Circuit, Forrest, ACT 2603; POB 4776, Kingston, ACT 2604; tel. (2) 6185 3240; e-mail info@atse.org.au; internet www.atse.org.au.

Australian-American Fulbright Commission

Founded in 1949 by the Governments of Australia and the USA to further mutual understanding between the people of the two nations through educational and cultural exchanges.
Activities: Works in the field of education, running the Fulbright Scholarship programme for Americans and Australians to undertake research, study or lecturing assignments in Australia or the USA, respectively. Awards cover all academic disciplines and professions, at various academic and career stages including graduate, postgraduate, postdoctoral, and professorial and associate professorial levels.
Geographical Area of Activity: Australia, USA.
Restrictions: Scholarships are open to Australian and US citizens only.
Publications: Annual Report; *Minds & Hearts* (newsletter).
Finance: Annual revenue A$10.1m., expenditure A$7.9m. (30 Sept. 2023).
Board of Directors: Prof. Brian P. Schmidt (Chair.); Jeff Anderson (Treas.).
Principal Staff: Exec. Dir Dr Varuni Kulasekera.
Contact Details: POB 9541, Deakin, ACT 2600; tel. (2) 6260 4460; e-mail fulbright@fulbright.org.au; internet www.fulbright.org.au.

Australian Cancer Research Foundation—ACRF

Established in 1984 by Sir Peter Abeles and Lady Sonia McMahon.
Activities: Operates nationally in the field of cancer research through providing technology, equipment and infrastructure. The Foundation supports cancer research at Australian

institutes, hospitals and universities. It offers grants for capital projects and equipment, research and seed funding. Grant amounts range from A$1.5m. to A$5m.

Geographical Area of Activity: Australia.

Publications: Annual Report; newsletter (annual).

Finance: Annual income A$14.6m., expenditure A$9.2m. (31 Dec. 2023).

Board of Trustees: Tom S. Dery (Chair.).

Principal Staff: CEO Kerry Strydom.

Contact Details: Suite 903, 50 Margaret St, Sydney, NSW 2000; POB 9989, Sydney, NSW 2001; tel. (2) 9223 7833; e-mail info@acrf.com.au; internet www.acrf.com.au.

Australian Communities Foundation

Established in 1997 as the Melbourne Community Foundation; present name adopted in 2011.

Activities: Generates and distributes philanthropic resources in partnership with donors and others in response to social issues and community needs. The Foundation provides services for donors to establish sub-funds without incurring the administrative and legal costs of starting up independent foundations; and grantmaking expertise and in-depth knowledge of community issues to help donors to make effective grants. The Impact Fund provides large grants and agile/seed grants for advocacy, campaigning research and scaling up in the areas of inequality, democracy, indigenous self-determination and the environment. Grants range from A$500 to A$300,000. Comprises more than 630 foundations and funds.

Geographical Area of Activity: Australia.

Publications: Annual Review; factsheets.

Finance: Annual revenue A$56.5m., expenditure A$46.0m. (15 months to 30 Sept. 2024).

Board of Directors: Fiona McLeay (Chair.).

Principal Staff: CEO Andrew Binns.

Contact Details: Level 6, 126 Wellington Parade, East Melbourne, VIC 3002; tel. (3) 9412 0412; e-mail info @communityfoundation.org.au; internet www.community foundation.org.au.

Australian Conservation Foundation—ACF

Founded in 1965 to oppose plans to mine the Great Barrier Reef.

Activities: Works to prevent climate damage and habitat destruction. Main campaigns focus on: solving the climate crisis; protecting nature; redesigning the economy; and strengthening democracy. The Foundation has more than 700,000 members.

Geographical Area of Activity: Asia-Pacific, Australia.

Restrictions: Not a grantmaking organization.

Publications: Annual Report; *Habitat* (magazine, 6 a year); newsletter; background briefs; reports; toolkits.

Finance: Annual revenue A$17.1m., expenditure A$10.4m. (30 June 2024).

Board: Ros Harvey (Pres.); Stephen Lightfoot, Shar Molloy (Vice-Pres); Leon Cermak (Sec.); Joshua Gilbert (Treas.).

Principal Staff: CEO Kelly O'Shanassy.

Contact Details: Level 1, 60 Leicester St, Carlton, VIC 3053; tel. (3) 9345 1111; e-mail acf@acf.org.au; internet www.acf.org.au.

Australian Council for International Development—ACFID

Founded in 1965; formerly known as the Australian Council for Overseas Aid—ACFOA.

Activities: Co-ordinates the activities of member organizations during international disasters or emergencies through the International Disaster Emergencies Committee; and has sub-committees co-ordinating activities in areas such as North–South relations, the Pacific, Indo-China and regional human rights. A development education programme coordinates the educational activities of member agencies; and informs and educates particular groups in the community that have a special opportunity to promote international development and cooperation, such as teachers, students and those engaged in voluntary aid administration. The Council holds specialized conferences and consultations; and promotes more stringent self-regulation by the aid sector, particularly through developing a Code of Conduct for NGOs. Has more than 130 members working in 93 developing countries.

Geographical Area of Activity: International.

Publications: Annual Report; newsletter; *ACFID Research in Development Series*; *ACFID-IHS Working Paper Series*; position papers and analysis; practice notes; research papers; blog.

Finance: Annual income A$4.0m., expenditure A$4.6m. (30 June 2023).

Board: Susan Pascoe (Pres.); Lyn Morgain, Surika Goringe, Michelle Higelin (Vice-Pres).

Principal Staff: Interim CEO Matthew Maury.

Contact Details: 14 Napier Close, Deakin, ACT 2600; Private Bag 3, Deakin, ACT 2600; tel. (2) 6285 1816; e-mail main@acfid.asn.au; internet www.acfid.asn.au.

Australian Institute of International Affairs—AIIA

Founded in 1924; established as a federal body in 1933.

Activities: Work covers international relations, economics, trade, strategic and defence studies, and international law. The Institute carries out research; issues publications; and organizes lectures, seminars and national and international conferences. Its Fellows programme recognizes contributions to Australia's international affairs.

Geographical Area of Activity: Australia.

Publications: Annual Review; newsletter; *Australian Outlook* (weekly newsletter); *Australian Journal of International Affairs*—*AJIA* (journal, five a year); *Australia in World Affairs* (series); occasional papers; conference proceedings.

Finance: Annual income A$1,246.6m., expenditure A$1,560.5m. (30 June 2024).

National Executive: Dr Heather Smith (Nat. Pres.); Zara Kimpton (Nat. Vice-Pres.); Sophie England (Treas.).

Principal Staff: Nat. Exec. Dr Bryce Wakefield.

Contact Details: Stephen House, 32 Thesiger Ct, Deakin, ACT 2600; tel. (2) 6282 2133; e-mail info@internationalaffairs.org.au; internet www.internationalaffairs.org.au.

Australian Multicultural Foundation—AMF

Established in 1988 as an initiative of the Australian Bicentennial Authority and the Federation of Ethnic Communities' Councils of Australia National Conference.

Activities: Develops intercultural activities in consultation with community organizations, foundations, government departments, and employer and employee bodies. Programme areas include: citizen participation in CSOs and institutions; raising awareness of the contribution of diversity to development, including English language and literacy and foreign language skills; increasing tolerance, including through improving community relations, social justice and mutual benefit; and youth leadership.

Geographical Area of Activity: Australia, People's Repub. of China, Europe.

Restrictions: Not a grantmaking organization.

Publications: Annual Report; newsletter; project reports; research and projects archive.

Finance: Annual income A$1.9m., expenditure A$1.9m. (30 June 2024).

Board of Directors: Dr Bulent Hass Dellal (Chair.).

Principal Staff: Exec. Dir Hakan Akyol; Sec. Lynn Cain.

Contact Details: Level 1, 185 Faraday St, Carlton, VIC 3053; POB 538, Carlton South, Vic 3053; tel. (3) 9347 6622; e-mail info@amf.net.au; internet www.amf.net.au.

AUSTRALIA

Australian Volunteers International—AVI

Founded in 1961 as the Overseas Service Bureau; an initiative of the Australian Government.

Activities: Recruits, prepares and sends volunteers to work in less-developed countries, in partnership with local communities, for placements of 3–18 months' duration; and manages the government-funded Australian Volunteers Program. Programme areas include: law and justice; disability; vocational education and training; health; engineering, architecture and skilled trades; finance, economics and governance; media, communication and arts; human resources, management, IT and business; agriculture, environment and natural resources; education and libraries; community and social development; and fundraising and resource mobilization. Former volunteers can join the Returned Australian Volunteer Network, an alumni network that raises awareness of volunteering and promotes Australian aid.

Geographical Area of Activity: East Asia and South-East Asia, Oceania, South Asia, sub-Saharan Africa.

Restrictions: Open to Australian citizens or permanent residents or New Zealand citizens permanently residing in Australia; applicants must hold a degree or have demonstrable and relevant professional experience.

Publications: Annual Report; newsletter; practice notes.

Finance: Annual revenue A$26.8m., expenditure A$26.8m. (30 June 2024).

Board of Directors: Julie Hamblin (Chair.).

Principal Staff: CEO Melanie Gow.

Contact Details: 160 Johnston St, POB 350, Fitzroy, VIC 3065; e-mail enquiries@avi.org.au; internet www.avi.org.au.

Baker Heart & Diabetes Institute

Founded in 1926 with a donation from Thomas Baker, his wife Alice and sister Eleanor Shaw.

Activities: Works to diagnose, prevent and treat diabetes, cardiovascular disease and obesity. The Institute carries out laboratory research, clinical research trials and large-scale community studies. A national programme addresses health disadvantages in Aboriginal communities and collaborates on international projects. The Bright Sparks programme offers travel awards, research and career development grants, scholarships and fellowships, ranging from A$500 to A$120,000.

Geographical Area of Activity: International.

Publications: Annual Report; Impact Report; newsletter research articles; books; factsheets.

Finance: Annual revenue A$59.6m., expenditure A$62.8m. (31 Dec. 2023).

Board: Peter Scott (Chair.).

Principal Staff: Dir and Chief Exec. Prof. John Greenwood.

Contact Details: 75 Commercial Rd, Melbourne, VIC 3004; POB 6492, Melbourne, VIC 3004; tel. (3) 8532 1111; e-mail reception@baker.edu.au; internet www.baker.edu.au.

Cancer Council Australia

Established in 1961 as the Australian Cancer Society.

Activities: Operates in the field of health and welfare. The Council and its eight member organizations, operating in each state and territory of Australia, undertake and fund cancer research, cancer prevention and control; conduct policy analysis and advocacy; and provide information and support services. It awards fellowships and research grants; and runs a telephone helpline.

Geographical Area of Activity: Australia.

Publications: Annual Report; *National Cancer Prevention Policy*; *Research Highlights*; *Cancer Forum*.

Finance: Annual revenue A$27.3m., expenditure A$31.1m. (30 June 2024).

Board of Directors: Prof. Maxine Morand (Chair.); Anne Pleash (Deputy Chair.).

Principal Staff: CEO Mark Nevin.

Contact Details: 320 Pitt St, Sydney, NSW 2000; POB 4708, Sydney, NSW 2001; tel. (2) 8256 4100; e-mail info@cancer.org.au; internet www.cancer.org.au.

Children's Medical Research Institute—CMRI

Established in 1958 to undertake and carry out paediatric research; affiliated to the Children's Hospital Westmead and the University of Sydney. The Institute's flagship fundraising campaign is Jeans for Genes.

Activities: Operates in the fields of medical and biological research. The Institute grants funds to students carrying out research, in particular research into childhood diseases, especially cancer, genetic disorders, leukaemia and neurosciences, and to those using recombinant DNA technology. It also offers grants for postdoctoral research to Australian residents, and fellowships to postgraduates from outside Australia.

Geographical Area of Activity: Australia.

Restrictions: Grants to students who are Australian residents and internationally to postgraduate students.

Publications: Annual Report; newsletter.

Finance: Annual revenue A$44.1m., expenditure A$50.0m. (31 Dec. 2023).

Board of Directors: Prof. Frank J. Martin (Pres.); Carolyn Forster (Vice-Pres.); Jeremy Waine (Treas.).

Principal Staff: Deputy Dir Prof. Patrick Tam.

Contact Details: 214 Hawkesbury Rd, Westmead, NSW 2145; Locked Bag 2023, Wentworthville, NSW 2145; tel. (2) 8865 2800; e-mail info@cmri.org.au; internet www.cmrijeansforgenes.org.au.

Clean Up Australia

Founded in 1990 by Ian Kiernan AO.

Activities: Clean Up Australia inspires and mobilizes communities to improve and conserve the environment, eliminate litter and end waste.

Geographical Area of Activity: National.

Publications: Annual Report; Litter *Report*; factsheets; educational materials; blog.

Finance: Annual income A$10.0m., expenditure A$9.5m. (30 June 2023).

Board of Directors: Pip Kiernan (Chair.); Brett Hearnden (Sec.).

Principal Staff: CEO Jenny Geddes.

Contact Details: Level 4, 233 Castlereagh St, Sydney, NSW 2000; tel. (2) 8197 3400; e-mail cleanup@cleanup.com.au; internet www.cleanup.org.au.

Collier Charitable Fund

Established in 1954 by the wills of Alice, Annette and Edith Collier, who inherited the fortune of their father Jenkin Collier, a grazier and railway builder.

Activities: Operates in the fields of education, public health and welfare. In Victoria, the Fund makes grants to benevolent institutions and hospitals; and across Australia, for educational and religious purposes, poverty relief, to support the children of civilian service and military personnel, and to support the Australian Red Cross.

Geographical Area of Activity: Australia.

Restrictions: Grants only for activities in Australia.

Publications: Annual Review.

Finance: Annual income A$7.9m., expenditure A$815,508 (30 June 2024).

Trustees: Michael Kingston (Chair.).

Principal Staff: Exec. Officer and Sec. Wendy Lewis.

Contact Details: 570 Bourke St, Level 31, Melbourne, VIC 3000; tel. (3) 9670 1647; e-mail wlewis@colliercharitable.org; internet www.colliercharitable.org.

Foundation for National Parks & Wildlife

Established in 1970 by Tom Lewis, a former Lands Minister and Premier of New South Wales.

Activities: Works in the fields of conservation of the environment and of heritage through self-conducted programmes, funding and education. The Foundation makes grants to government agencies, private landowners, community groups and scientists to support nature conservation projects, environmental education programmes and cultural heritage conservation.

Geographical Area of Activity: Australia.

Publications: Annual Report; *PAWS Newsletter*; *PAW Prints Update*.

Finance: Annual income A$8.5m., expenditure A$8.7m. (31 Dec. 2023).

Board of Directors: David Knowles (Chair.); Helen Schuler (Treas.).

Principal Staff: CEO Ian Darbyshire.

Contact Details: L8, 50 Clarence St, Sydney, NSW 2000; GPO Box 2666, Sydney, NSW 2001; tel. (2) 9221 1949; e-mail fnpw@fnpw.org.au; internet www.fnpw.org.au.

Foundation for Rural & Regional Renewal—FRRR

Established in 2000 following a proposal made at the 1999 National Regional Summit.

Activities: Serves all remote, rural and regional Australians by carrying out self-conducted activities in three main areas: people, place, and disaster resilience and climate solutions. Grantmaking ranges from broad programmes that are open all year round to non-profit organizations; to place-based programmes where the Foundation helps communities to identify and develop opportunities.

Geographical Area of Activity: Remote, rural and regional Australia.

Publications: Annual Review; newsletter.

Finance: Total income A$7.1m., expenditure A$7.1m. (30 June 2024).

Board of Directors: Tim Fairfax (Chair.); Sue Middleton (Deputy Chair.).

Principal Staff: CEO Natalie Egleton.

Contact Details: 101a/141 Mollison St, Bendigo, VIC 3550; POB 41, Bendigo, VIC 3552; tel. (3) 5430 2399; e-mail info@frrr.org.au; internet www.frrr.org.au.

The Foundation for Young Australians—FYA

Established in 2000 following the merger of the Queen's Trust for Young Australians and the Australian Youth Foundation.

Activities: Supports young people aged 14–25 years by carrying out self-conducted programmes, advocacy, policy analysis and research. The Foundation supports youth-led social change organizations and youth empowerment initiatives that help young people to overcome structural disadvantages or injustice through coaching, leadership development and training, and grantmaking. In 2016 YLab was established as a consulting, learning and co-design agency, recruiting associates aged 18–30 years to work on projects in the areas of employment, the environment, First Nations representation and self-determination, health and wellbeing, learning, and power and decisionmaking. Affiliated to the International Youth Foundation (USA, q.v.); a member of the International Youth Foundation Global Network of Partners.

Geographical Area of Activity: Australia.

Restrictions: Funding is provided only to benefit young Australians.

Publications: Annual Report; newsletters (weekly, fortnightly); New Work Order (series); reports; evaluations.

Finance: Annual income A$2.9m., expenditure A$8.9m. (31 Dec. 2023).

Board of Directors: Jason Glanville (Chair.); Maya Marcus (Deputy Chair.); Zoe Myers (Treas.).

Principal Staff: CEO Molly Whelan.

Contact Details: Level 1, 136 Exhibition St, Melbourne, VIC 3000; POB 24091, Melbourne, VIC 3000; tel. (3) 7046 3837; e-mail info@fya.org.au; internet www.fya.org.au.

The Fred Hollows Foundation

Established in 1992 by Gabi Hollows to continue the work of her husband, eye doctor Prof. Fred Hollows.

Activities: Operates worldwide in the field of medicine and health. Main initiatives are: Ending Avoidable Blindness and the Indigenous Australia Program. The Foundation provides funding, training and expertise to assist with the treatment of the cataract blind in developing countries; and works with local agencies to develop programmes to provide modern cataract surgery and support eye health infrastructure. It has links with various international blindness-prevention programmes, including Vision 2020: The Right to Sight; and works in more than 25 countries, with local programme offices in Australia, Cambodia, the People's Republic of China, New Zealand, Pakistan, South Africa and Viet Nam, and offices in Hong Kong, the United Kingdom and the USA. The Fred Hollows Humanity Award recognizes Year 6 students' care and compassion for others.

Geographical Area of Activity: Asia, Australasia, Middle East, sub-Saharan Africa.

Restrictions: Not a grantmaking organization.

Publications: Annual Report; *Sharing the Vision* (quarterly newsletter); *Strategic Framework: Seeing is Believing* (monthly e-newsletter).

Finance: Total income A$116.7m., expenditure A$117.0m. (31 Dec. 2023).

Board of Directors: Jane Madden (Chair.); Michael Johnson, Tina Wyer (Co-Deputy Chair.).

Principal Staff: CEO Ross Piper.

Contact Details: Level 9, 320 Pitt St, Sydney, NSW 2000; Locked Bag 5021, Alexandria, NSW 2015; tel. (2) 8741 1900; e-mail fhf@hollows.org; internet www.hollows.org.

Ian Potter Foundation

Established in 1964 by Sir Ian Potter, a business person and financier.

Activities: Supports initiatives in the fields of arts and culture, community wellbeing, early childhood development, the environment, medical research equipment and public health research. In 1993 it established the Ian Potter Cultural Trust to support emerging Australian artists. The Trust offers grants for early career artists to undertake professional development, usually overseas.

Geographical Area of Activity: Australia.

Restrictions: No grants to individuals (except through the Ian Potter Cultural Trust); major grants by invitation only.

Publications: Annual Grants Report; *The Seahorse* (quarterly newsletter).

Finance: Annual revenue (investments) A$41.2m., expenditure A$33.3m. (30 June 2023).

Board of Governors: Craig Drummond (Chair.).

Principal Staff: CEO Paul Conroy.

Contact Details: Level 3, 111 Collins St, Melbourne, VIC 3000; tel. (3) 9650 3188; e-mail admin@ianpotter.org.au; internet www.ianpotter.org.au.

Lord Mayor's Charitable Foundation

Established in 1923.

Activities: Launched after the First World War to help Melbourne recover and prosper. Areas of focus are: homelessness and affordable housing; inclusive and sustainable economy and employment; health and climate resilience; the environment and sustainability. Initiatives to encourage generous charitable giving within the Melbourne community.

Geographical Area of Activity: Australia.

Publications: Annual reports; newsletters; videos.

Finance: Annual income A$28.1m., expenditure A$5.3m. (30 June 2024).
Board: Janina Gawler (Chair.); Bernadette Murdoch (Deputy Chair.).
Principal Staff: CEO Peter Walton.
Contact Details: Level 4, 454 Queen St, Melbourne, VIC 3000; GPOB 1851, Melbourne, VIC 3001; tel. (3) 9633 0033; e-mail info@lmcf.org.au; internet www.lmcf.org.au.

Lowy Institute for International Policy

Established in 2003 by Frank Lowy, Chair. and former CEO of Westfield Corpn, a retail shopping group; a think tank.
Activities: Conducts research on international affairs; hosts speeches by leading figures and holds conferences; collaborates with think tanks and foundations worldwide to promote an Asia-Pacific perspective on world issues. Main programmes include: China and East Asia; Southeast Asia; Indo-Pacific development; Pacific Islands; International Security; International Economy; Transnational Challenges; and Public Opinion and Foreign Policy. The Institute offers the Distinguished International Fellowship and Michael and Deborah Thawley Scholarship in International Security; and awards the annual Lowy Institute Media Award to Australian journalists writing on international policy issues.
Geographical Area of Activity: Worldwide.
Restrictions: Does not accept private commissions; publishes all research.
Publications: *The Interpreter* (daily); Lowy Institute Papers (Penguin Specials); Global Diplomacy Index; Asia Power Index; Lowy Institute Pacific Aid Map; Lowy Institute Poll (annual); analyses; policy briefs; reports; research notes.
Finance: Annual income A$13.7m., expenditure A$10.2m. (30 June 2024).
Board of Directors: Sir Frank Lowy (Chair.); Steven M. Lowy (Deputy Chair.).
Principal Staff: Exec. Dir Dr Michael Fullilove.
Contact Details: 31 Bligh St, Sydney, NSW 2000; tel. (2) 8238 9000; e-mail reception@lowyinstitute.org; internet www.lowyinstitute.org.

Macquarie Group Foundation

Established in 1985 by the Macquarie Group, a banking and financial services provider.
Activities: The Macquarie Group Foundation drives social impact work for the Macquarie Group. The Foundation provides support to community organizations globally each year through financial support, volunteering and skills sharing, predominantly in the locations in which Macquarie operates. The work of the Foundation focuses on capacity building within the community sector and increasing social and economic mobility.
Geographical Area of Activity: International.
Restrictions: Does not accept unsolicited applications.
Publications: Annual Review.
Finance: Total disbursements A$641m. (since 1985).
Committee: Alexander Harvey (Chair.).
Principal Staff: Global Head Lisa George.
Contact Details: POB 4294, Sydney, NSW, 1164; tel. (2) 8232 3333; e-mail foundation@macquarie.com; internet www.macquarie.com/community.

Menzies Foundation

Founded in 1979 in memory of former Prime Minister Sir Robert Menzies; formerly known as the Sir Robert Menzies Memorial Foundation.
Activities: Menzies Foundation aspires to raise the profile and importance of 'outstanding' leadership by encouraging Australians to reflect on leadership, build their leadership capability and act for the greater good. Supports leadership platforms which facilitate the exploration, deepen understanding, and codification of approaches to leadership. Examines various dimensions of leadership from diverse perspectives to reinforce the Foundation's commitment to identifying the essential leadership qualities and attributes required for effective leadership in both the Australian and global contexts. Shares these insights with the Australian and Global community; contributing to the leadership discourse.
Geographical Area of Activity: Australia.
Publications: Annual Report; newsletter.
Finance: Total assets A$29.3m. (31 Dec. 2023).
Board of Directors: Peter Jopling AM KC (Chair.).
Principal Staff: CEO Liz Gillies.
Contact Details: Central House, L3, 489 Toorak Road, VIC 3142; tel. (3) 9070 3489; e-mail menzies@menziesfoundation.org.au; internet www.menziesfoundation.org.au.

Minderoo Foundation

Established in 2001 as the Australian Children's Trust by Andrew Forrest, founder of Fortescue Metals Group and Minderoo Group, and his wife Nicola; present name adopted in 2013.
Activities: A philanthropic organization working to forge a fair future and a society that value all people and natural eco-systems through four key functions: advocacy and engagement; effective philanthropy; finance, technology and operations; and people and culture. In 2024 the Foundation went through a transformation as part of its 2030 strategy, establishing three core Focus Areas: gender equality, including Walk Free, a human rights organization targeting modern slavery; natural eco-systems; and communities.
Geographical Area of Activity: Australia, Asia-Pacific.
Publications: Annual Report; Global Fishing Index; Global Slavery Index; flyers.
Finance: Annual revenue A$5,062.9m., expenditure A$268.8m. (30 June 2023).
Board: Allen Myers (Chair.); Dr Andrew Forrest, Nicola Forrest (Co-Chair.).
Principal Staff: CEO John Hartman.
Contact Details: POB 3155, Broadway Nedlands, WA 6009; tel. (8) 6460 4949; e-mail hello@minderoo.com.au; internet www.minderoo.com.au.

Murdoch Children's Research Institute—MCRI

Established in 1960 as the Royal Children's Hospital Research Foundation; merged with the Murdoch Institute (f. 1986) in 2000.
Activities: Works in the field of medicine and particularly the health of children and adolescents. The Institute conducts, supports and promotes research in five areas: infection and immunity; cell biology; clinical sciences; genetics; and population health. It offers scholarships for students and postgraduate researchers; and travel awards to support presentations at conferences.
Geographical Area of Activity: International.
Publications: Annual Report; newsletter.
Finance: Total assets A$276.2m. (31 Dec. 2023).
Board of Directors: Patrick Houlihan (Chair.); Sarah Murdoch (Co-Chair.).
Principal Staff: Dir Prof. Kathryn North; Deputy Dir Prof. Andrew Sinclair.
Contact Details: Royal Children's Hospital, Flemington Rd, Parkville, VIC 3052; tel. (3) 8341 6200; e-mail mcri@mcri.edu.au; internet www.mcri.edu.au.

National Heart Foundation of Australia

Established in 1959 by a group of doctors, lawyers and business people; a federation, comprising a national body and eight state and territory divisions.

Oxfam Australia   AUSTRALIA

Activities: Promotes public awareness about the treatment and prevention of cardiac diseases. The Foundation supports individuals and organizations in researching the causes, diagnosis, cure and prevention of cardiac diseases. It offers a range of awards, grants, scholarships and fellowships.
Geographical Area of Activity: Australia.
Publications: Annual Report; Annual Review; e-newsletter.
Finance: Total revenue A$55.9m., expenditure A$54.4m. (31 Dec. 2023).
Board of Directors: Mario D'Orazio (Chair.).
Principal Staff: CEO David Lloyd.
Contact Details: Suite 9.02, Level 9, 565 Bourke St, Melbourne, VIC 3000; e-mail contactus@heartfoundation.org.au; internet www.heartfoundation.org.au.

Oxfam Australia

Established in 1992 by the merger of Community Aid Abroad (f. 1953 as Food for Peace Campaign) and the Australian Freedom from Hunger Campaign (f. 1962); became part of the Oxfam confederation of organizations (qq.v.) in 1995, changing its name to Oxfam Community Aid Abroad in 2001. Present name adopted in 2005.
Activities: Works to reduce extreme poverty and inequality through aid and development. Programmes include: emergency response; ethical trading; food security and climate change; health and nutrition; Indigenous Australia; infrastructure and environment; mining; water and sanitation; and women's rights. The organization works in 86 countries as part of the global Oxfam confederation.
Geographical Area of Activity: Australasia, East and South-East Asia, Middle East, South Asia, sub-Saharan Africa.
Restrictions: Does not make loans or grants to individuals.
Publications: Annual Report; newsletter; policy papers; reports; books.
Finance: Annual income A$65.3m., expenditure A$66.6m. (31 March 2024).
Board of Directors: Dr Judith Slocombe (Chair.).
Principal Staff: Acting Chief Exec. Dr Chrisanta Muli.
Contact Details: 355 William St, West Melbourne, VIC 3003; Locked Bag 20004, Melbourne, VIC 3001; tel. (3) 9289 9444; e-mail enquire@oxfam.org.au; internet www.oxfam.org.au.

OzChild—Children Australia Inc

Established in 1993, through the merger of Family Action (f. 1851), Family Focus (f. 1893) and the National Children's Bureau of Australia (f. 1971).
Activities: Supports children, young people and their families. The organization provides services in areas including: assessing, accrediting and placing children with foster carers; supporting and training kinship carers; early intervention and prevention programmes; family support; family law; matching volunteers with disadvantaged children and families; connecting Aboriginal children and young people with their communities and cultures; education; and disability.
Geographical Area of Activity: Australia (Victoria, New South Wales, Queensland, Australian Capital Territory).
Publications: Annual Report; newsletter; *OzChild Matters* (magazine).
Finance: Annual revenue A$66.7m., expenditure A$67.3m. (30 June 2024).
Board of Directors: Helen Maxwell-Wright (Pres.); Stephen Fontana, Cathrerine Dunlop (Vice-Pres); Michael Wooten (Treas.).
Principal Staff: CEO Dr Lisa J. Griffiths.
Contact Details: POB 1312 South Melbourne, VIC 3205; tel. (3) 9695 2200; e-mail hello@ozchild.org.au; internet www.ozchild.org.au.

Pancare Foundation

Founded in 2011 by Dr Mehrdad Nikfarjam.
Activities: Raises awareness of pancreatic and upper gastrointestinal cancers. Provides care and support for patients. Funds research into early diagnosis and better treatment options to improve survival rates.
Geographical Area of Activity: Australia.
Publications: Annual Report.
Finance: Revenue A$2.3m., expenditure A$2.7m. (30 June 2021).
Board: Clive Appleton (Chair.).
PanSupport Advisory Committee: Prof. Meinir Krishnasamy (Chair.).
Principal Staff: CEO Doug Hawkins.
Contact Details: 70 Yarra St, Heidelberg, VIC 3084; e-mail info@pancare.org.au; internet www.pancare.org.au.

Partners for Equity

Established in 2015.
Activities: Supports disadvantaged and poor communities through working in partnership with non-governmental, community-based and local organizations. Main programmes focus on health, education, livelihoods, human rights and street children/disabled children.
Geographical Area of Activity: Australia, South and South-East Asia, Africa.
Finance: Annual income A$25.7m., expenditure A$24.1m. (30 June 2024).
Principal Staff: CEO Linda Fox.
Contact Details: Level 6, 126 Wellington Parade, East Melbourne, VIC 3006; e-mail info@partnersforequity.org; internet partnersforequity.org.

The Paul Ramsay Foundation

Established in 2006 by Paul Ramsay, a healthcare entrepreneur.
Activities: Works to identify the root causes of disadvantage. The Foundation carries out activities in the areas of children, disaster response and resilience, education, first nation populations, housing, justice and safety, mental health, and communities. Has an office in Melbourne.
Geographical Area of Activity: Australia.
Publications: Newsletter.
Finance: Total assets A$2,703.2m. (30 June 2024).
Board of Directors: Michael Traill (Chair.).
Principal Staff: CEO Kristy Muir.
Contact Details: 262 Liverpool St, Darlinghurst, NSW 2010; tel. (2) 8582 4000; e-mail hello@paulramsayfoundation.org.au; internet www.paulramsayfoundation.org.au.

Perpetual Foundation

Established in 1998 by Perpetual Trustees Australia, a trustee company operating throughout Australia.
Activities: Administers more than 1,000 charitable trusts and endowments operating in Australia. The Foundation distributes the income to charitable organizations, in accordance with the wishes of the founders of the managed trusts, supporting initiatives in the areas of social and community welfare, education, medical and scientific research, arts and culture, and conservation and the environment.
Geographical Area of Activity: Australia.
Restrictions: Does not make grants to individuals.
Finance: Annual income A$58.3m., expenditure A$18.0m. (30 June 2024).
Principal Staff: Man. Partner Caitriona Fay; Nat. Man. Jane Magor.

Contact Details: Level 12, 123 Pitt St, Sydney, NSW 2000; POB 4172, Sydney, NSW 2001; tel. (2) 9229 9633; e-mail philanthropy@perpetual.com.au; internet www.perpetual.com.au/philanthropy.

Pratt Foundation

Established in 1978 by Richard Pratt, Chair. of packaging, paper and recycling company Visy, and his wife Jeanne; part of the Pratt Philanthropies, in addition to The Pratt Family Foundation and Visy Cares.

Activities: Supports initiatives in the areas of mental health, the arts, education, cancer care, Jewish life, Aboriginal advancement and the environment; and promotes Australia-Israel relations. Richard Pratt Fellowships in Prostate Cancer worth A$100,000 are awarded annually for translational research. A sister organization operates in Israel (f. 1998).

Geographical Area of Activity: Australia, Israel, USA.

Restrictions: Does not accept unsolicited applications.

Finance: Annual income A$722,481, expenditure A$759,016 (30 June 2024).

Principal Staff: Sec. Robert Kay.

Contact Details: Level 11, 2 Southbank Blvd, South Melbourne, VIC 3006; POB 5182, South Melbourne, VIC 3205; tel. (3) 9247 4798; internet www.theprattfoundation.org.

Ramaciotti Foundations

Established in 1970 by Vera Ramaciotti with the proceeds from the sale of the Theatre Royal and other properties in Sydney, in memory of her brother Clive; formerly known as The Clive and Vera Ramaciotti Foundations.

Activities: Operate in the field of biomedical research, in particular molecular biology, immunology and genetics. The Foundations offer health investment grants of up to A$150,000 to individuals in universities, public hospitals or institutes for health or medical research. They also offer the Ramaciotti Medal for Excellence in Biomedical Research, worth A$50,000; and, every two years, the Ramaciotti Biomedical Research Award, worth A$1m., to a group or individual for biomedical research in universities, public hospitals, medical research institutes or similar organizations.

Geographical Area of Activity: Australia.

Finance: Ramaciotti Australia Foundation: annual income A$3.0m., expenditure A$1.8m.; Ramaciotti NSW Foundation: annual income A$3.6m., expenditure A$1.1m. (30 June 2024).

Principal Staff: Dir Mark Smith.

Contact Details: c/o Perpetual Trustee Co Ltd, GPO Box 4172, Sydney, NSW 2001; tel. (2) 9229 9633; e-mail philanthropy@perpetual.com.au; internet www.perpetual.com.au/ramaciotti.

The Ross Trust

Founded in 1970 by the will of Roy Everard Ross, the founder of Hillview Quarries.

Activities: Makes grants in two programme areas: providing equitable access to secondary education; and conserving and protecting biodiversity. The Trust offers a range of three-year grants, annually worth up to A$40,000 for Smart Grants; up to A$50,000 for Advocacy Grants; and between A$40,000 and A$100,000 for Challenge and Change Grants.

Geographical Area of Activity: Australia (Victoria).

Restrictions: Grants only to charities in Victoria state; Challenge and Change Grants are by invitation only.

Publications: Annual Report; *The Ross Trust Update* (newsletter).

Finance: Annual income A$4.0m., expenditure A$1.7m. (30 June 2024).

Board of Trustees: Jon Webster (Chair.).

Principal Staff: CEO Sarah Hardy.

Contact Details: Ground Level, Suite 2, 43 Agnes St, East Melbourne, VIC 3002; tel. (3) 9690 6255; e-mail information@rosstrust.org.au; internet www.rosstrust.org.au.

The Royal Australasian College of Physicians—RACP

Founded in 1938; established the Research and Education Foundation in 1991 to increase funding to its medical research awards programme.

Activities: Promotes the study of the science and art of medicine, and research in clinical science and the institutes of medicine; brings together physicians for their common benefit, and for scientific discussions and clinical demonstrations; and disseminates knowledge of the principles and practice of medicine. The College presents the views of physicians and paediatricians on questions of medical importance to the Government and other bodies; encourages continuing education for qualified physicians; conducts a training and examination programme for admission of trainees to Fellowship; provides lecturers for medical teaching in the Asia-Pacific region; and publishes the results of research and study. It has more than 70 Honorary Fellows and over 28,000 Fellows and trainees; and maintains a library of 40,000 vols, including the Ford Collection. The RACP Foundation offers: research awards and career grants for Fellows and trainees; college and congress prizes; regional awards and prizes; indigenous scholarships and prizes for Fellows, trainees, medical students and junior medical officers; exam prizes; medical student scholarships and prizes; and international grants worth up to A$10,000 to medical graduates or specialists from outside Australia and New Zealand.

Geographical Area of Activity: Asia-Pacific, Australia, New Zealand.

Publications: Annual Report; *Internal Medicine Journal*; *The Journal of Paediatrics and Child Health*; research reports; magazine.

Finance: Annual income A$2.0m., expenditure A$2.5m. (31 Dec. 2024).

Board: Prof Jennifer Martin (Pres.); Sharmila Ramessur Chandran (Viice-Pres.); Kim Davis (Sec.).

Principal Staff: CEO Lee Whitney.

Contact Details: 145 Macquarie St, Sydney, NSW 2000; tel. (2) 9256 5444; e-mail racp@racp.edu.au; internet www.racp.edu.au/about/foundation.

Royal Flying Doctor Service of Australia—RFDS

Established in 1928 by the Rev. John Flynn; comprises seven federated entities.

Activities: Delivers primary healthcare and 24-hour emergency service to people living, working and travelling throughout Australia. The Service provides emergency health services; primary healthcare clinics at remote sites; telehealth radio and telephone consultations; medical chests to be stored in isolated areas; inter-hospital transfers; and mental and dental health. It operates from 23 air bases and 292 healthcare road vehicles throughout Australia.

Geographical Area of Activity: Australia.

Restrictions: Not a grantmaking organization.

Publications: Annual Report.

Finance: Total assets A$45.3m. (30 June 2024).

Federation Board: Tracey Hayes (Chair.); Dr John O'Donnell (Deputy Chair.).

Principal Staff: Exec. Dir Frank Quinlan.

Contact Details: Level 2, 10–12 Brisbane Ave, Barton, ACT 2600; POB 4350, Kingston, ACT 2604; tel. (2) 6269 5500; e-mail enquiries@rfds.org.au; internet www.flyingdoctor.org.au.

Seeds of Affinity

Founded in 2006 by women with lived experience of the prison system.

Activities: Works to challenge the stigma and discrimination of women leaving the prison system, including advocacy and court support, and to provide programmes in the community

Sidney Myer Fund & The Myer Foundation

for women to develop a sense of belonging and self worth. Runs activities and promotional events as well as a community vegetable garden.

Geographical Area of Activity: Southern Australia.

Board: Michele Jarldorn (Chair.); Bec Neill (Treas.); Quynh Nguyen (Sec.).

Principal Staff: Patron Heather Stokes.

Contact Details: 146–150 Semaphore Rd, Exeter, SA 5019; tel. (8) 8242 7210; e-mail soasemaphore@gmail.com; internet seedsofaffinity.org.

Sidney Myer Fund & The Myer Foundation

The Sidney Myer Fund was established in 1934 by the will of Sidney Myer; and The Myer Foundation in 1959 by his sons Kenneth B. Myer and S. Baillieu Myer.

Activities: Operate separately, offering grants in the fields of the arts and humanities, poverty and disadvantage, mental health, and sustainability and the environment. The Foundation offers annual Sydney Myer Performing Arts Awards, collectively worth A$175,000; and Sidney Myer Creative Fellowships, worth A$160,000 over two years, to artists, arts managers and thought leaders in the humanities; and also offers grants in the field of human, civil and legal rights. The Fund established the Kenneth Myer Innovation Fellowships, each worth A$120,000, to support the development of solutions to social and environmental challenges; and through the Small Grants Program offers grants worth up to A$10,000 to organizations and communities working to address poverty and disadvantage. The Merlyn Myer Fund focuses on the wellbeing of women in Australia, addressing their disadvantages and providing opportunities.

Geographical Area of Activity: Asia-Pacific, Australia.

Restrictions: Does not support medical research, scholarships, travel, film or video; no grants to individuals.

Publications: Annual Report; *Aged Care: 2020 A Vision for Aged Care in Australia*; *Sidney Myer Centenary Celebration*.

Finance: Fund: annual income A$3.3m., expenditure A$1.8m.; Foundation: annual income A$5.4m., expenditure A$2.0m. (30 June 2024).

Fund Board of Trustees: Andrew Myer (Chair.).

Foundation Board of Directors: Rupert Myer (Pres.); Hang Truong (Sec.).

Principal Staff: CEO Leonard Vary.

Contact Details: 171 Collins St, Melbourne, VIC 3000; POB 29, Flinders Lane, VIC 8009; tel. (3) 8609 3150; e-mail admin@myerfoundation.org.au; internet www.myerfoundation.org.au.

The Snow Foundation

Established in 1991 by Terry and George Snow.

Activities: Initially focused on providing grants for disadvantaged youth, people with disabilities, food programmes, and schools in need in the Canberra area. Expanded outside of Canberra over time to offer support to social entrepreneurs and projects looking to implement social change. Has an office in Sydney.

Geographical Area of Activity: Australia.

Finance: Annual revenue A$7.9m., expenditure $15.5m. (30 June 2024).

Principal Staff: CEO Georgina Byron; Exec. Dir Scarlett Gaffey.

Contact Details: Level 4, 21 Terminal Ave, Plaza Offices—West, Canberra Airport, ACT 2609; tel. (2) 6175 3333; e-mail enquiries@snowfoundation.org.au; internet www.snowfoundation.org.au.

SpinalCure Australia

Established in 1994 by Joanna Knott, Prof. Perry Bartlett and Stewart Yesner; formerly known as the Australasian Spinal Research Trust. Incorporated the Spinal Research Foundation in 2004.

Activities: Funds and promotes research into curing spinal cord injury. The organization fosters co-operation between all disciplines involved in central nervous system research; disseminates information about research progress; and co-operates with international efforts in the same field. It offers career development fellowships; and funds equipment grants and travel grants (A$3,000 for international travel and A$1,000 for domestic travel) for researchers and clinicians.

Geographical Area of Activity: Australia.

Restrictions: Travel and equipment grants only for applicants working or studying in Australia.

Publications: Annual Report; newsletters; e-newsletters; impact reports.

Finance: Annual income A$2.0m., expenditure A$1.4m. (30 June 2024).

Board of Directors: Joanna Knott (Chair.); Duncan Adams (Sec.); Prof. Perry Bartlett (Scientific Chair.); Gabriel McDowell (Exec. Chair.).

Principal Staff: CEO Kathryn Borkovic; Exec. Dir Duncan Wallace.

Contact Details: Suite 3.04, 80 Clarence St, Sydney, NSW 2000; POB 908, Mona Vale NSW 1660 Australia; tel. (2) 9356 8321; e-mail research@spinalcure.org.au; internet www.spinalcure.org.au.

Sylvia and Charles Viertel Charitable Foundation

Established in 1999 by the will of Charles Viertel, an accountant and business person.

Activities: Supports medical research, and disadvantaged, homeless and elderly people. The Foundation has longstanding partnerships with several organizations based in Queensland. Its flagship programme is the Senior Medical Research Fellowship, worth A$275,000 a year for five years, helping researchers to establish research careers in Australia. It makes five annual Clinical Investigator awards of A$90,000 each.

Geographical Area of Activity: Australia.

Restrictions: Fellowship applicants must be medical or clinical graduates who have completed training, normally to doctoral level.

Finance: Annual income A$29.0m., expenditure A$673,365 (30 June 2024).

Trustees: Justice Debra Mullins (Chair.).

Principal Staff: Co-Chair. of Medical Advisory Board Prof. Christina Mitchell, Associate Prof. Paul Ekert.

Contact Details: GPOB 2307, Melbourne, VIC 3016; tel. (3) 8623 5008; e-mail charities@eqt.com.au; internet viertel.org.au.

Talk Out Loud

Founded in 2016 by Mary Galouzis.

Activities: Provides youth mental health services across Southern Australia, including school programmes, youth empowerment camps and mental health first aid training.

Geographical Area of Activity: Southern Australia.

Finance: Annual income A$364,336, expenditure A$348,401 (30 June 2024).

Board: Brett Knowles (Chair.); Gary McCourt (Vice-Chair.); Ming Lyn Hii (Sec.); Linda Jury (Treas.).

Principal Staff: CEO Mary Galouzis.

Contact Details: 3/1267 North East Rd, Ridgehaven, SA 5097; tel. (4) 6748 5880; e-mail info@talkoutloud.com.au; internet talkoutloud.com.au.

Tearfund Australia

Established in 1971, as The Evangelical Alliance Relief (TEAR) Fund, an arm of the Australian Evangelical Alliance; a Christian organization.

Activities: Works in the field of relief and development. Programme areas include: community building; education; emergency response; empowering Australians; food and livelihoods; health; impact investing; indigenous Australia; and water and sanitation. The organization supports 14 local partners in 11 countries.

Geographical Area of Activity: International.

Publications: Annual Report; *Tearfund Update* (monthly newsletter); *Target Magazine* (2 a year).

Finance: Annual income A$15.9m., expenditure A$15.9m. (30 June 2024).

Board of Trustees: Joanna Lee (Chair.); Peter Lochore (Deputy Chair.); Stephen Gunaratnam (Sec.).

Principal Staff: CEO Bec Oates.

Contact Details: Unit 1, 4 Solwood Lane, Blackburn, VIC 3130; POB 110, Forest Hill, VIC 3131; tel. (3) 9264 7000; e-mail info@tearfund.org.au; internet www.tearfund.org.au.

TPG Telecom Foundation

Established in 2002 by Vodafone Australia, a telecommunications company; part of the Vodafone Foundation (q.v.) network; present name adopted in 2022 following the merger of Vodafone Australia and TPG Telecom.

Activities: Promotes better health, wellbeing and education through technology. Partners with the Garvan Institute of Medical Research and Infoxchange. Works with communities in remote and disaster-prone areas to co-design locally-led solutions using social connectivity and digital tools to improve disaster preparedness and community resilience.

Geographical Area of Activity: Australia.

Publications: Annual Report.

Finance: Annual income A$2.2m., expenditure A$2.3m. (31 March 2024).

Board of Trustees: Dan Lloyd (Chair.); Lisa Maddock (Sec.).

Contact Details: Level 27, Tower Two, International Towers, Sydney, Barangaroo NSW 2000; tel. (4) 3632 3188; internet www.tpgtelecom.com.au/foundation.

The Trawalla Foundation

Established in 2004.

Activities: The Trawalla Foundation works with individuals and organizations, focused on strengthening gender equality, creativity, sustainability and social justice. Works to support female leaders, especially in business, media and politics. Works in a variety of ways, including offering grants and investments, skills initiatives, networks and advocacy.

Geographical Area of Activity: Australia.

Finance: Annual revenue A$3.2m., expenditure $4.7m. (30 June 2024).

Principal Staff: Chair. Carol Schwartz; CEO Sarah Buckley.

Contact Details: Level 4, 167 Flinders Lane, Melbourne, VIC 3000; internet www.trawallafoundation.com.au.

Union Aid Abroad—APHEDA

Established in 1984 as Australian People For Health Education & Development Abroad, the overseas humanitarian aid agency of the Australian Council of Trade Unions (ACTU).

Activities: Works with local communities and trade unions to promote skills development, better employment opportunities, education, sustainable agriculture, healthcare and workers' rights. The organization has more than 39 training projects in 14 locations, working with 42 local trade unions and community organizations. In South-East Asia, it supports trade unionists and campaigners to ban asbestos and eliminate asbestos-related diseases.

Geographical Area of Activity: Middle East, Pacific, South-East Asia, Southern Africa.

Publications: Annual Report; *Solidarity Partnerships* (quarterly newsletter); monthly e-bulletin; reports and submissions.

Finance: Annual income A$6.6m., expenditure A$6.1m. (30 June 2024).

Board: Lori-Anne Sharp (Chair.); Michele O'Neil (Vice-Chair.).

Principal Staff: Exec. Officer Kate Lee.

Contact Details: Level 1, 365–375 Sussex St, Sydney, NSW 2000; tel. (2) 9264 9343; e-mail office@apheda.org.au; internet apheda.org.au.

Vincent Fairfax Family Foundation—VFFF

Established in 1962 by Sir Vincent Fairfax, a business person and farmer.

Activities: Operates in the areas of education, agriculture, Christianity and community wellbeing. The Foundation awards grants under two programmes: Thriving People and Places and Christianity. Grants for more than A$50,000 are available to organizations in New South Wales (NSW); and between A$20,000 to A$50,000 for organizations in NSW and Queensland. Fellowships are offered to senior executive leaders through the Cranlana Centre for Ethical Leadership, Monash University, and last for 12 months.

Geographical Area of Activity: Australia (mainly NSW and Queensland).

Restrictions: Grants only to charities registered in Australia; grants support core operations, organizational capacity building and programme costs.

Publications: Newsletter.

Finance: Annual income A$7.2m., expenditure A$26.5m. (30 June 2020).

Board of Directors: Rosemary Vilgan (Chair.); Ruth Armytage (Deputy Chair.).

Principal Staff: CEO Jenny Wheatley; Foundation Man. Claire Mannion.

Contact Details: Level 14, 131 Macquarie St, Sydney, NSW 2000; GPO Box 1551, Sydney, NSW 2001; tel. (2) 9291 2727; e-mail foundation@vfff.org.au; internet www.vfff.org.au.

William Buckland Foundation

Established in 1964 by the will of William Buckland, a business person and pastoralist, to benefit Victoria and Victorians.

Activities: Aims to improve the lives of disadvantaged people through grant programmes in areas including: agriculture; education; employment and housing; and health. Also funds initiatives that build resilience in rural and regional communities. Since its establishment, the Foundation has distributed over A$135m.

Geographical Area of Activity: Australia.

Restrictions: All programmes work exclusively in Victoria and for the benefit of Victorians.

Publications: Annual Report.

Finance: Annual revenue A$15.3m., expenditure $1.3m. (30 June 2024).

Board of Trustees: Jennifer McGregor (Chair.).

Contact Details: c/o Equity Trustees, Philanthropy Services, Level 2, 575 Bourke St, Melbourne, VIC 3000; GPO Box 2307, Melbourne, VIC 3001; tel. (3) 8623 5000; e-mail info@williambucklandfoundation.org.au; internet www.williambucklandfoundation.org.au.

Winston Churchill Memorial Trust

Founded in 1965 in memory of former British Prime Minister Sir Winston Churchill.

Activities: Awards approximately 100 Churchill Fellowships each year to Australian citizens to undertake overseas investigative projects of a kind not available in Australia. There are no prescribed qualifications, academic or otherwise: merit is the primary test, whether based on past achievements or on demonstrated ability for future achievement in any field. The value of applicants' work to the community and the extent to which it will be enhanced by overseas study are also important criteria. Fellowships are worth more than A$28,000 on average.

Geographical Area of Activity: Fellowships can be completed anywhere in the world, but cannot contribute to tertiary education or gaining work experience; applicants must be over 18 years old.
Restrictions: Australian citizens only.
Publications: Annual Report; *Churchill Chatter* (newsletter).
Finance: Total assets A$129.7m. (31 Jan. 2024).
Board of Directors: A/Prof. Richard Roylance (Nat. Chair.).
Principal Staff: CEO Christine Dacey.
Contact Details: Churchill House, 30 Balmain Cresc., Acton, ACT 2601; GPO Box 1536, Canberra, ACT 2601; tel. (2) 6247 8333; e-mail info@churchilltrust.com.au; internet www.churchilltrust.com.au.

AUSTRIA

CO-ORDINATING BODIES

Verband für Gemeinnütziges Stiften (Association for Public Benefit Foundations)
Established in 2014.
Activities: Provides members with opportunities for networking, development and training; and information and knowledge exchange. The Association offers consultancy and administrative services, and lobbies government on behalf of members. It has over 90 member organizations working in areas including: education and social affairs, art and culture, science and research, and the environment; and is a member of Philea (q.v.).
Geographical Area of Activity: Austria.
Restrictions: Only funds member organizations.
Publications: Annual Report; Foundation Report, newsletter; factsheets.
Finance: Annual revenue €300,000, expenditure €290,000 (2024).
Board of Directors: Katharina Turnauer (Pres.); Franz Karl Prüller (Vice-Pres.).
Principal Staff: Man. Günther Lutschinger.
Contact Details: Schottenring 16/3 OG, 1010 Vienna; tel. (1) 6645441090; e-mail office@gemeinnuetzig-stiften.at; internet gemeinnuetzig-stiften.at.

The World of NGOs
Founded in 1997 by Christiana Weidel and Christian Pichler-Stainern.
Activities: Operates nationally and throughout Europe in the fields of education, human rights, co-operation of civil society and civil dialogue. The organization provides information; carries out self-conducted programmes and research; organizes conferences and training courses; and issues publications. Recent projects have focused on social inclusion of migrants, elderly people, women and young people; preventing human trafficking; developing rural areas; and innovations in education and participation. Comprises around 60 member organizations, including umbrella organizations, citizens' initiatives and research institutes.
Geographical Area of Activity: Europe.
Restrictions: Does not make grants.
Publications: Activity Report; brochures; other publications.
Finance: Funded through membership fees, public funds and project finance.
Board of Directors: Christiana Pordes (Weidel) (Chair.); Prof. Dr Jürgen Nautz (Vice-Chair.).
Contact Details: Himmelpfortgasse 17/14, 1010 Vienna; tel. (676) 3359715; e-mail office@ngo.at; internet www.ngo.at.

FOUNDATIONS AND NON-PROFITS

AMINA—aktiv für Menschen in Not Austria (Active for People in Need Austria)
Founded in 2003 as AMURT (Austria) and was a member of the AMURT (q.v.) network from 2005 until 2011; has carried out its own projects since 2009.
Activities: Works in the fields of emergency relief, sustainable development and co-operation. The organization helps communities in need to develop survival strategies. It focuses on disadvantaged groups, including children, women, the elderly, and sick and disabled people.
Geographical Area of Activity: Ethiopia, Georgia, Kenya, Moldova, Mozambique, Niger, Senegal.
Restrictions: Exclusively charitable.
Finance: Annual income €277,691, expenditure €277,691 (2024).
Board of Directors: Dr Ines Kohl (Chair.); Katharina Zlattinger (Treas.); Laura Oberhuber (Sec.).
Principal Staff: Project Officer (South and East) Gertraud Hödl; Office Man. Joachim Frank.
Contact Details: Hütteldorferstr. 253A, 1140 Vienna; tel. (1) 92916701; e-mail info@aktivfuermenschen.at; internet www.aktivfuermenschen.at.

Bruno Kreisky Forum für internationalen Dialog (Bruno Kreisky Forum for International Dialogue)
Established in 1991 by Franz Vranitzky, in memory of Bruno Kreisky, former Foreign Minister and Chancellor of Austria; a think tank.
Activities: Operates as a centre for dialogue and exchange of ideas between politicians, scientists and intellectuals to analyse complex questions and to propose solutions to global problems. Main programme areas include: democracy and identity; economy and social change; Europe; international politics; and an annual theme, which in 2024 was politics and religion. The Forum conducts research projects and organizes conferences, discussions, fellowship programmes, lectures, roundtables, seminars and symposia. It maintains the Bruno Kreisky Archives; and established the Bruno Kreisky Foundation for Outstanding Achievements in Human Rights.
Geographical Area of Activity: Austria.
Publications: Annual Report; newsletter; Dialogue Series; reports.
Board of Directors: Rudolf Scholten (Pres.); Eva Nowotny (Vice-Pres.); Georg Lennkh (Treas.); Helfried Carl (Sec.).
Principal Staff: Sec.-Gen. Sabine Kroissenbrunner.
Contact Details: Armbrustergasse 15, 1190 Vienna; tel. (1) 3188260; e-mail kreiskyforum@kreisky-forum.org; internet www.kreisky-forum.org.

Entwicklungshilfe-Klub (Aid for Development Club)
Established in 1973 by Gerhard Dorffner and Helmut Novy.
Activities: Supports community development initiatives in the developing world. The Club provides disaster relief and long-term grants to micro, small micro and macro projects, working with local partner organizations.
Geographical Area of Activity: Africa, Asia, Central and South America, Eastern Europe, North Africa.
Publications: Annual Report; newsletter; project reports.
Finance: Annual income €3.5m., expenditure €3.5m. (2024).
Board: Manfred Formanek (Chair.); Hilbert Heikenwälder (Deputy Chair.).

Principal Staff: Dir Brita Wilfling.
Contact Details: Böcklinstr. 44, 1020 Vienna; tel. (1) 7205150; e-mail office@eh-klub.at; internet www.eh-klub.at.

ERSTE Stiftung—Die ERSTE Österreichische Spar-Casse Privatstiftung (ERSTE Foundation)

Established in 2006 by Erste Group, a financial services provider.
Activities: Funds initiatives in the fields of social innovation, financial literacy, European cohesion and democracy, and contemporary culture. The Foundation established the Igor Zabel Association for Culture and Theory (f. 2007) and offers the Igor Zabel Award for Culture and Theory, worth a total of €85,000, which is awarded to international curators, art historians and theorists, writers or critics who are from or live and/or work in the region. It has a research library on Central, Eastern and South-Eastern European countries containing approximately 12,000 items (mainly in English and German).
Geographical Area of Activity: Central and South-Eastern Europe.
Publications: Annual Reports; newsletter; catalogues; books; series; studies; other publications.
Finance: Total assets €727.1m. (31 Dec. 2023).
Supervisory Board: Andreas Treichl (Chair.); Manfred Wimmer (Deputy Chair.).
Principal Staff: CEO Boris Marte; Deputy CEO Wolfgang Schopf.
Contact Details: Am Belvedere 1, 1100 Vienna; tel. (501) 0015100; e-mail office@erstestiftung.org; internet www.erstestiftung.org.

European Centre for Social Welfare Policy and Research

Established in 1974 in Vienna as the European Centre for Social Welfare Training and Research; an autonomous, UN-affiliated intergovernmental organization; present name adopted in 1989.
Activities: Carries out research through two main units: the Work and Welfare Unit; and the Health and Care Unit. The Centre's expertise includes demographic development; work and employment; income, poverty and social exclusion; social security; migration and social integration; human security; care; and health and wellbeing. It offers training; and organizes conferences, seminars and workshops.
Geographical Area of Activity: Canada, Europe, Israel, USA.
Publications: Annual Report; newsletters; policy briefs; books; reports; working papers.
Board of Directors: Ghada Fathi Waly (Chair.); Angela Me (Acting Chair.).
Principal Staff: Exec. Dir Dr Kai Leichsenring; Deputy Dir Anette Scoppetta.
Contact Details: Berggasse 17, 1090 Vienna; tel. (1) 31945050; e-mail ec@euro.centre.org; internet www.euro.centre.org.

FWF—Österreichischer Wissenschaftsfonds (Austrian Science Fund)

Founded in 1967.
Activities: Provides finance for basic research in all fields of science, including the humanities. The Fund assists in the formulation and implementation of national science policy; public relations work relating to science; and the promotion of the internationalization (in particular Europeanization) of the scientific sector in Austria. It supports non-Austrian scientists working at Austrian science institutes; and Austrian postgraduate students wishing to carry out scientific research abroad. The alpha+ Stiftung was established in 2019 to assist philanthropic funders in supporting scientific research.
Geographical Area of Activity: Austria.
Publications: Annual Report; *scilog* (online magazine in German and English); statistical publications.
Finance: Grants awarded €407.8m. (2024).
Executive Board: Prof. Christof Gattringer (Pres.); Ursula Jakubek (Exec. Vice-Pres.).
Contact Details: Georg-Coch-Platz 2 (Eingang Wiesingerstraße 4), 1010 Vienna; tel. (1) 5056740; e-mail office@fwf.ac.at; internet www.fwf.ac.at.

International Institute for Applied Systems Analysis—IIASA

Founded in 1972 by representatives of the Union of Soviet Socialist Republics (USSR), the USA and 10 other countries from the Eastern and Western blocs as a non-governmental interdisciplinary research institute.
Activities: Conducts policy-orientated research into complex problems, such as climate change, energy security and sustainable development. The Institute provides decisionmaking tools to policymakers; and services to researchers, including hosting key databases on climate and population. It runs capacity-building activities for PhD and postdoctoral students and policymakers and offers fellowships. The flagship Young Scientists Summer Program (YSSP) strengthens the skills of emerging researchers and the Postdoctoral Program gives early career scientists experience of solving real-world problems, with financial support from the YSSP Fund. Has members in 19 countries.
Geographical Area of Activity: International.
Publications: Annual Report; *Options* (biannual magazine); research reports; working papers (approx. 75 a year); brochures; information sheets; blog.
Council: Dr Kazu Takemoto (Chair.); Prof. Debra Knopman (Vice-Chair.).
Principal Staff: Dir-Gen. Prof. Dr Hans Joachim Schellnhuber; Deputy Dir-Gen. Karen R. Lips.
Contact Details: Schlossplatz 1, 2361 Laxenburg; tel. (2) 2368070; e-mail info@iiasa.ac.at; internet www.iiasa.ac.at.

International Press Institute—IPI

Founded in 1950 in New York, USA; a network of editors, media executives and journalists.
Activities: Defends freedom of expression; and supports the protection and strengthening of the freedom to collect and disseminate news and carry out journalism. The Institute raises awareness about the challenges journalists face; conducts advocacy and dialogue with authorities, working with local journalists; and informs journalists about their role in the democratic process. It leads a consortium that manages the IJ4EU—Investigative Journalism for Europe fund (f. 2018). It offers grants under its Investigation Support Scheme for new projects carried out by teams or organizations based in at least two EU countries or one EU country and one EU candidate country—grants are worth up to €50,000; and the Freelancer Support Scheme, worth up to €20,000.
Geographical Area of Activity: Worldwide.
Publications: Newsletter; research and investigation reports; training manuals; mission reports.
Finance: Annual income €2.5m., expenditure €2.4m. (2022).
Executive Board: Márton Gergely (Chair.).
Principal Staff: Exec. Dir Scott Griffen.
Contact Details: Spiegelgasse 2, 1010 Vienna; tel. (1) 5129011; e-mail info@ipi.media; internet ipi.media.

Ludwig Boltzmann Gesellschaft

Established in 1960; a non-profit association.
Activities: Comprises 20 institutes, which carry out research in thematic clusters: history; cardiovascular research; oncology; translational oncology; rare diseases; archaeological prospection; traumatology; biography; mental health, etc. Most institutes are located in Vienna, Graz and Innsbruck (Austria). Also a part of Ludwig Boltzmann Gesellschaft: LBG Open Innovation in Science Center and LBG Career Center.
Geographical Area of Activity: Europe.

Publications: Annual Report; monographs; policy papers.
Finance: Annual income €38.4m. (2024).
Executive Committee: Prof. Dr Freyja-Maria Smolle-Jüttner (Pres.); Christoph Neumayer (Treas.); Dr Michael Stampfer (Sec.).
Principal Staff: Man. Dirs Dr Elvira Welzig, Marisa Radatz.
Contact Details: Nußdorferstr. 64, 6th Floor, 1090 Vienna; tel. (1) 5132750; e-mail office@lbg.ac.at; internet www.lbg.ac.at.

OeAD

Established in 1961 as an association of the Austrian Rectors' Conference; in 2020 it took over the activities of KulturKontakt Austria (f. 1989).
Activities: Operates international mobility and co-operation programmes in the fields of education, science, research and culture, overseeing international exchanges of students, apprentices, lecturers and researchers, and carrying out international educational projects. In Austria, the Agency co-ordinates education programmes including Erasmus+, the Central European Exchange Programme for University Studies (CEEPUS), Citizen Science and Sparkling Science; runs national co-ordination, service and contact centres for the Bologna Process, the European Credit System for Vocational Training and Education (ECVET), Euroguidance, Europass, eTwinning, the Electronic Platform for Adult Learning in Europe (EPALE) and the National Qualification Framework; provides information on grants, scholarships and research funding; and supports higher education for refugees living in Austria. It has seven regional offices in Austria and co-operation offices in Azerbaijan, the People's Republic of China and Ukraine.
Geographical Area of Activity: Europe, Central and East Asia.
Publications: Annual Report; *oead.news* (newsletter); brochure; e-books.
Finance: Annual budget €137m. (2023).
Supervisory Board: Elmar Pichl (Chair.); Doris Wagner (Deputy Chair.).
Principal Staff: Man. Dir Dr Jakob Calice.
Contact Details: Ebendorferstr. 7, 1010 Vienna; tel. (1) 534080; e-mail info@oead.at; internet www.oead.at.

ORF Nachbar in Not (Neighbour in Need)

Established in 1992 to offer aid those affected by armed conflict and natural disasters; became a foundation in 2003.
Activities: Supports people in need as a result of war, natural disaster, armed conflict or politicala and economic crises. Plans, organizes and implements fundraising campaigns in co-operation with partner organizations. Comprises Austrian humanitarian assistance organizations, incl. CARE Österreich, Caritas Österreich, Hilfswerk International, Österreichisches Rotes Kreuz, Volkshilfe Österreich.
Geographical Area of Activity: International.
Finance: Annual budget €44.3m. (2023).
Board: Andreas Knapp, Michael Opriesnig, Reinhard Trink.
Contact Details: Wiedner Hauptstr. 32, 1040 Vienna; tel. (1) 58900517; e-mail spenden@nachbarinnot.at; internet nachbarinnot.orf.at.

Österreichische Forschungsstiftung für Internationale Entwicklung—ÖFSE (Austrian Foundation for Development Research)

Founded in 1967 by the Afro-Asiatisches Institut in Wien (q.v.) and the Österreichischer Auslandsstudentendienst.
Activities: Carries out research in the fields of Austrian and international development policy. Main programmes include: development policy and co-operation; education and development; stakeholder participation, process support and moderation; and the world economy and development. The Foundation organizes conferences and workshops; and maintains databases on Austrian development co-operation projects and organizations. Jointly with BAOBAB and Frauen*solidarität, it operates the C3-Library for International Development, which specializes in international development, global learning, and women's and gender issues.
Geographical Area of Activity: International.
Publications: Annual Report; *Österreichische Entwicklungspolitik*; *ÖFSE-Forum*; *ÖFSE-Edition*; *ÖFSE-Newsletter* (monthly e-newsletter); briefing papers; policy notes; research reports; working papers.
Supervisory Board: Prof. Dr Ulrich Brand (Chair.); Johanna Mang (Deputy Chair.).
Principal Staff: Dir Werner Raza; Deputy Dir Irene Vogel.
Contact Details: C3 Centrum für Internationale Entwicklung, Sensengasse 3, 1090 Vienna; tel. (1) 3174010; e-mail office@oefse.at; internet oefse.at.

Österreichische Gesellschaft für Aussenpolitik und Internationale Beziehungen—ÖGAVN (Foreign Policy and United Nations Association of Austria—UNA-AUSTRIA)

Formed in 2008 by the merger of the Austrian League for the UN (f. 1945) and the Austrian Society for Foreign Policy and International Relations (f. 1958).
Activities: Operates in the fields of foreign affairs and international relations. The Association informs the public about the goals and achievements of foreign policy and the UN, raising awareness about international relations and deepening understanding of current affairs in foreign, economic, development and cultural policy fields. It organizes international conferences, lectures and panel discussions, including foreign policy talks at Hernstein Castle.
Geographical Area of Activity: Austria.
Publications: *Global View* (quarterly magazine); *Society* (magazine, 2 a year); *GAP-Journal* (annual); newsletter; monographs.
Board of Directors: Dr Wolfgang Schüssel (Pres.).
Principal Staff: Sec.-Gen. Bernd Hermann.
Contact Details: Hofburg/Stallburg, Reitschulgasse 2/2. OG, 1010 Vienna; tel. (1) 5354627; e-mail office@oegavn.org; internet www.oegavn.org.

Salzburg Global Seminar

Established in 1947, as the Salzburg Seminar in American Studies, by Clemens Heller, a graduate of Harvard University; comprises the Salzburg Seminar American Studies Association, the Salzburg Academy on Media and Global Change (f. 2007) and the Salzburg Global Forum for Young Cultural Innovators (f. 2014).
Activities: Promotes international collaboration and networking through convening meetings between leaders on issues of global importance. Main programme areas are: finance and governance, including philanthropy and social investment, and law and technology; justice and security, comprising human rights and the rule of law; culture, arts and society; planet and health, including urban conservation and pandemic preparedness; global media and voice; and education and work, with a focus on interdisciplinary research on meeting the UN Sustainable Development Goals. The organization hosts workshops and a lecture series; offers grants and scholarships to Fellows; and provides seed funding for new projects and partnerships through the Fund for Program Excellence. Fellows from more than 170 countries. Has an office in Washington, DC, USA.
Geographical Area of Activity: International.
Restrictions: Grants and scholarships only available to Fellows.
Publications: President's Report; newsletter; reports.
Finance: Annual revenue US $17.7m., expenditure $13.0m. (31 Dec. 2023).
Board of Directors: Grant Cambridge (Chair.); Christopher F. Lee (Vice-Chair.); Adena Testa (Sec.).

AZERBAIJAN

Principal Staff: Pres. and CEO Martin Weiss.
Contact Details: Schloss Leopoldskron, Leopoldskron Str. 56–58, 5020 Salzburg; tel. (662) 839830; e-mail info@salzburgglobal.org; internet www.salzburgglobal.org.

South East Europe Media Organisation—SEEMO
(Südosteuropäische Medienorganisation)

Established in 2000 in Zagreb, Croatia, by 23 media organizations from nine countries.

Activities: Promotes freedom of the media and freedom of expression. Activities include fostering understanding between journalists and other media professionals; improving standards and practices; ensuring the safety of journalists; and promoting co-operation. Programmes include a Media Aid Programme, a Media Law Programme and a Media in Transition Programme. Through the SEEMO South-East Europe Media Foundation for Emergency Help, the Organisation offers support for projects in the region. It awards the annual Busek Award for Better Understanding, worth €2,500, to a journalist, editor or media executive in South-Eastern Europe who has promoted better understanding among peoples and worked to end ethnic divisions, racism and xenophobia. Additional awards include the CEI SEEMO Award for investigative journalism, worth €5,000, the SEEMO Human Rights Award and the SEEMO Photo Human Rights Award. The SEEMO Emergency Fund supports journalists in need in South-Eastern Europe.

Geographical Area of Activity: Central and South-Eastern Europe, Eastern Europe, Russian Federation, Central Asia, Italy, San Marino, Türkiye (Turkey), Vatican City.

Publications: *SEEMO Media Handbook* (annually, in English); *SEEMO Review*; *DeScripto* (quarterly journal); *SEEMO Investigative Journalism Handbook*; newsletter; publications in local languages.

Principal Staff: Sec.-Gen. Oliver Vujović.
Contact Details: Spiegelgasse 2/29 (SEEMO IPI office), 1010 Vienna; tel. (1) 5133940; e-mail info@seemo.org; internet www.seemo.org.

VIDC—Vienna Institute for International Dialogue and Co-operation

Founded in 1987 as successor to the Vienna Institute for Development (f. 1962 by Minister of Foreign Affairs Bruno Kreisky); a think tank.

Activities: Works in the fields of democracy and human rights, gender, migration and the economy. Main activities include promoting critical public discourse; initiating cultural co-operation; and supporting diversity and opposing discrimination in sport. The Institute conducts research programmes; holds conferences, seminars and workshops on development policy and developing countries; and issues publications on international development. It runs a cultural exchange programme with the countries of the global South; and is the lead agency of Fairplay (f. 1997), a Europe-wide network of sports organizations addressing racism and discrimination both within and outside sport. Members come from 20 countries. Has consultative status with ECOSOC.

Geographical Area of Activity: Asia, Europe, Latin America, Middle East and North Africa, sub-Saharan Africa.

Publications: Annual Report; newsletter; *Spotlight* (online magazine); thematic studies.

Board of Trustees: Gabriele Heinisch-Hosek (Pres.).
Principal Staff: Man. Dir Sybille Straubinger; Deputy Man. Dir Franz Schmidjell.
Contact Details: Möllwaldplatz 5/9, 1040 Vienna; tel. (1) 7133594; e-mail office@vidc.org; internet www.vidc.org.

AZERBAIJAN

FOUNDATIONS AND NON-PROFITS

Center for Economic & Social Development—CESD

Established in 2005 by Dr Vugar Bayramov; a think tank.

Activities: Supports socioeconomic development through increasing transparency and reducing corruption. Projects include the School of European Studies, promoting European integration and increasing awareness about the EU in Azerbaijan; and the School of Public Policy, carrying out research and education on public policy reform in Azerbaijan and the wider region, in co-operation with the Government and CSOs. The Center carries out research and analysis; organizes seminars, workshops and presentations; offers training for CSOs and small businesses; and publishes research findings. It runs an internship and traineeship programme for national and international economics graduates.

Geographical Area of Activity: Azerbaijan, Cyprus, Georgia, Kazakhstan, Türkiye (Turkey).

Publications: Annual Presentation; policy briefs; reports.
Principal Staff: Dir Karamat Ismayilov.
Contact Details: 1065 Baku, Caspian Pl., 3rd Block, 14th Floor, J. Jabbarli Str. 44; tel. (12) 594-36-65; e-mail info@cesd.az; internet www.cesd.az.

Heydar Aliyev Fondu (Heydar Aliyev Foundation)

Established in 2004 in memory of former President Heydar Aliyev.

Activities: Supports socioeconomic development with projects in the areas of education, public health, the environment, science and technology, culture and sport. Promotes the study and implementation of policies that support the goals of the organization, and works with other national and international organizations with similar objectives.

Geographical Area of Activity: Azerbaijan, International.
Publications: Publications about Azerbaijani culture and history; biographies; music.
Trustees: Mehriban Arif gyzy Aliyeva (Pres.); Leyla Ilham gyzy Aliyeva (Vice-Pres.).
Principal Staff: Exec. Dir Anar Alakbarov.
Contact Details: 1000 Baku, Niyazi Str. 5; tel. (12) 525-13-31; e-mail public@heydar-aliyev-foundation.org; internet heydar-aliyev-foundation.org.

Uluchay Social-Economic Innovation Center

Established in 1995.

Activities: Carries out policy research and implements programmes to support the socioeconomic development of Azerbaijan's regions. The Center focuses on young people, women, farmers, small and medium-sized enterprises, internally displaced people and refugees. It funds community projects and supports businesses; provides training and capacity building; carries out public education and awareness-raising campaigns; and publishes research findings.

Geographical Area of Activity: Azerbaijan.
Publications: Policy briefs; reports.
Board of Directors: Dr Mayis Safarov (Chair.); Arzu Huseynova (Sec.).
Principal Staff: Exec. Dir Ilyas Safarli.
Contact Details: 5500 Sheki, Galgali Bulag Str. 31A; tel. (2424) 45447; e-mail office@uluchay.org; internet uluchay.org.

BAHAMAS

FOUNDATIONS AND NON-PROFITS

Lyford Cay Foundations
Established in 1969 as the American Friends of The Bahamas by Robert Blum and William Robbins; present name adopted in 1979.

Activities: Primarily interested in education: the FOCUS and Cutillas Scholars programmes support access to higher education in the Bahamas for high school leavers. The Foundation offers community grants worth between US $5,000 and $10,000 to national organizations; partial scholarships, worth up to $25,000, for Bahamians to pursue graduate or undergraduate technical and vocational qualifications abroad; and grants towards studying at the University of the Bahamas. Has an office in New York, USA. The Canadian Lyford Cay Foundation (f. 1977) operates in Canada.

Geographical Area of Activity: International.

Publications: Annual Report; *Caystone* (newsletter).

Finance: Annual revenue US $2.9m., expenditure $1.5m. (31 Dec. 2023).

Board of Directors: Basil P. Goulandris (Chair.); Sarah A. Farrington (Vice-Chair.); Judith Whitehead (Pres.); Jon T. Crone, IV (Treas.); E. Parker Neave (Sec.); Mary Filippelli Hall (Chair., Canada).

Principal Staff: Exec. Dir Nicola Virgill-Rolle.

Contact Details: POB N 7776, Templeton Global Advisors Bldg, West Bay St, Lyford Cay, Nassau; tel. 362-4910; e-mail info@lyfordcayfoundation.org; internet lyfordcayfoundations.org.

Templeton Religion Trust
Established in 1984 by Sir John Templeton, an investor and fund manager; part of the Templeton Philanthropies, with the John Templeton Foundation (q.v.) in the USA and the Templeton World Charity Foundation. Active since 2012.

Activities: Supports projects that advance the understanding of religion and its benefits, and provide opportunities for spiritual growth. The Foundation funds research in areas including: art and culture, philosophy, science, society and theology. With the Templeton World Charity Foundation, it co-funds the Templeton Prize (f. 1972) for scientific insights about religion, worth £1m., which is administered by the Templeton Foundation.

Geographical Area of Activity: International.

Publications: Newsletter; grantee articles.

Principal Staff: Man., Grant Operations Melinda Cartwright.

Contact Details: c/o First Trust Bank Ltd, Templeton Bldg, Lyford Cay, Nassau; e-mail communications@templetonreligiontrust.org; internet templetonreligion@brk;trust.org.

TK Foundation
Established in 2002 to continue the work of J. Torben Karlshoej, founder of the Teekay Shipping Group.

Activities: Aims to advance knowledge of oceanography, marine biology, marine engineering, naval architecture, seamanship and other maritime sciences. The Foundation also aims to relieve poverty and promote the welfare of impoverished, sick or injured seafarers. Current priorities are youth development for disadvantaged young people aged 15–25 years; and maritime education, awarding scholarship grants worth up to US $10,000 per year for up to 3 years for maritime majors at US universities.

Geographical Area of Activity: International.

Restrictions: Grants only to registered non-profit organizations; youth development projects must be in the Foundation's geographical areas of interest: North America, Latin America and the Caribbean, South Africa or Europe.

Publications: Impact Report.

Finance: Total grants awarded since 2002 c. US $46m.

Board of Directors: Bruce Chan (Chair.).

Principal Staff: Man. Dir Susan Karlshoej.

Contact Details: c/o Teekay Corpn, 1st Floor, Bayside House, Bayside Executive Park, West Bay St and Blake Rd, POB AP 59214, Nassau; tel. 502-8827; internet thetkfoundation.org.

BANGLADESH

FOUNDATIONS AND NON-PROFITS

AID Foundation
Founded in 1992 by Tarikul Islam Palash; formerly known as Action in Development—AID.

Activities: Works to improve the socioeconomic conditions of disadvantaged people, including women, children, people with disabilities, labourers and farmers. The organization carries out self-conducted programmes in the areas of disability, human development and income generation. It collaborates internationally with similar organizations; and organizes conferences and seminars. Has an office in Dhaka.

Geographical Area of Activity: Bangladesh.

Publications: Annual Report.

Principal Staff: Gen Sec. Afrina Yesmen.

Contact Details: AID Complex, Shatbaria, POB 03, Jhenaidah 7300; 3/13 Humayan Rd, Block B, 3rd Floor, Mohammadpur, Dhaka 1207; tel. 967221221; e-mail info@aid-bd.org; internet aid-bd.org.

Bangladesh Freedom Foundation—BFF
Established in 1997 to take over the work of the Ford Foundation (q.v.), when the latter ceased operating in Bangladesh.

Activities: Supports programmes that work to free people from poverty, ignorance and oppression. The Foundation focuses on promoting secondary-level science education, through student-led extracurricular activities such as science clubs, science fairs, leadership development, etc. Other activities include capacity building of teachers; establishing mini-science labs; organizing national events, such as the Bangladesh Junior Science Olympiad, the National School Science Debate and the Junior Science Congress; and advocacy. It annually awards grants to NGOs worth around 10m. taka; grants typically range from 400,000 to 800,000 taka per year for three years or more. Research fellowships are also offered.

Geographical Area of Activity: Bangladesh.

Restrictions: Does not accept unsolicited applications; grants only to organizations registered with the Department of Social Welfare or the NGO Affairs Bureau.

Publications: Annual Report; *Science Newsletters*; research findings; reports.

Board of Trustees: Mahfuz Anam (Chair.); Dr Rezaur Rahman (Treas.).

Principal Staff: Exec. Dir Sazzadur Rahman Chowdhury.

Contact Details: Level 5, 6/5A Sir Syed Rd, Mohammadpur, Dhaka 1207; tel. (2) 41022916; e-mail info@freedomfound.org; internet www.freedomfound.org.

BRAC

Established in 1972 by Sir Fazle Hasan Abed as the Bangladesh Rehabilitation Assistance Committee, originally as a relief organization; later renamed the Bangladesh Rural Advancement Committee, and subsequently known as Building Resources Across Communities (BRAC).

Activities: Works in the field of social development through carrying out research and advocacy. Main programme areas include: climate change and emergencies; eliminating extreme poverty; expanding financial choices; gender equality; humanitarian crisis management; universal healthcare; pro-poor urban development; and investing in the next generation. The organization runs the BRAC University (comprising the BRAC Institute of Governance and Development—BIGD), BRAC Bank, and social enterprises, including craft shops and food projects. It has affiliate offices in the Netherlands, the United Kingdom and the USA.

Geographical Area of Activity: Afghanistan, Bangladesh, Liberia, Myanmar, Nepal, Netherlands, Philippines, Rwanda, Sierra Leone, South Sudan, Tanzania, Uganda, UK, USA.

Publications: Annual Report; newsletter; factsheets; guidelines; reports; blog.

Finance: Annual income 140,616.3m. taka, expenditure 111,893.2m. taka (30 June 2024).

BRAC Global Board: Dr Martha Chen (Chair.).

Governing Body: Dr Hossain Zillur Rahman (Chair.).

Principal Staff: Exec. Dir (BRAC Bangladesh) Asif Saleh; Exec. Dir (BRAC International) Shameran Abed.

Contact Details: BRAC Centre, 75 Mohakhali, Dhaka 1212; tel. (2) 222281265; e-mail info@brac.net; internet www.brac.net.

Dutch-Bangla Bank Foundation

Established in 1995 by M. Sahabuddin Ahmed, Founder Chair. of Dutch-Bangla Bank Ltd.

Activities: Supports socioeconomic development in Bangladesh. The Foundation carries out philanthropic activities in the areas of education, health, conservation and social care. It offers scholarships for secondary- and tertiary-level education to students in financial need; scholarships are worth 2,500 taka per month for 3–5 years, with a reading materials grant of 5,000 taka.

Geographical Area of Activity: Bangladesh.

Publications: Social causes report.

Board of Directors: Sahabuddin Ahmed (Chair.).

Contact Details: Level 8, 47 Motijheel Commercial Area, Dhaka 1000; tel. (2) 47110465; internet www.dutchbanglabank.com/social/social-cause.html.

BARBADOS

CO-ORDINATING BODY

Caribbean Policy Development Centre—CPDC

Established in 1991 as an umbrella body representing the major national and regional NGO networks in the Caribbean.

Activities: Represents Caribbean NGOs in regional and international forums. The Centre's main areas of interest are: capacity building; governance and participation; sustainable development; and trade liberalization and economic development. Current projects include disaster risk management and mobilizing resources for NGOs. In partnership with Munich Climate Insurance Initiative it established the Risk Resilience Hub, which comprises a library of climate and disaster risk finance and insurance materials. Has 33 individual and institutional members.

Geographical Area of Activity: Caribbean.

Publications: Newsletter; Regional CPDC NGO Directory (online); *Caribbean NGO Trends*; conference proceedings; discussion papers; factsheets; manuals; reports; research findings; toolkits.

Principal Staff: Officer in Charge Richard Jones.

Contact Details: POB 57, Halsworth, Welches Rd, St Michael 11000; tel. 437-6055; e-mail cpdc@caribsurf.com; internet www.cpdcngo.org.

FOUNDATIONS AND NON-PROFITS

Barbados Entrepreneurship Foundation Inc

Established in 2010 to support business and promote Barbados as an entrepreneurial hub.

Activities: Aims to achieve a model of 'Growing Sustainable Entrepreneurship' supported by five pillars: Access to Finance; Business Facilitation; Business Mentorship & Networking; Government Policy; and Education and Talent Development. The Foundation conducts research into best practices for each pillar. Projects include the $20 Challenge and related Agricultural Business Challenge, microfinance initiatives which are aimed at schoolchildren; WiFi Barbados, to provide free Wi-Fi nationally; and an online Mentorship Forum.

Geographical Area of Activity: Barbados.

Publications: Annual Report; newsletter; blog; webinars.

Board of Directors: Celeste Foster (Exec. Chair.).

Contact Details: Lex Caribbean, Worthing Corporate Centre, Worthing, Christ Church; tel. 435-3308; e-mail info@barbadosentrepreneurshipfoundation.org; internet www.barbadosentrepreneurshipfoundation.org.

BELARUS

CO-ORDINATING BODY

Abjadnany Šliach (United Way—Belarus/NGO Development Centre)

Established in 1995.

Activities: Operates as an information portal, disseminating information on the Belarusian third sector. The Centre promotes capacity building through collaboration, consultation and organizing training programmes. It maintains databases of Belarusian NGOs; offers legislative and NGO management services; monitors the Belarusian press; provides an online platform for searching for partners, volunteers and scholarships, and a computer-aided system that automatically generates documents required for NGO activities. Has a library containing 4,000 reference books and periodicals on NGO management, strategic planning, organizational development, marketing, etc.

Geographical Area of Activity: Belarus.

Publications: *GURT* (newsletter); NGO directories; handbooks; monographs; research papers.

Principal Staff: Exec. Dir Alicia Shybitskaya.

Contact Details: 9 Masherov Ave, 220000 Minsk; tel. (29) 630-32-76; e-mail uwb@ngo.by; internet www.ngo.by.

BELGIUM

CO-ORDINATING BODIES

CONCORD—European NGO Confederation for Relief and Development

Established in 2003.

Activities: Comprises 57 member organizations, representing more than 2,600 European NGOs. The Confederation represents its members in dealing with EU institutions. Priority areas include: tackling rising inequality and building a sustainable economy; EU policy coherence, with a focus on migration and trade; and monitoring international donors' commitments to funding and financing. Cross-cutting themes are civil society, gender equality, global citizenship, the private sector and regional alliances. It maintains an online research library.

Geographical Area of Activity: Europe.

Publications: Annual Report; newsletter; guides; policy briefs; reaction papers; reports.

Finance: Annual income €2.2m., expenditure €2.2m. (31 Dec. 2023).

Board: Rilli Lappalainen (Pres.); Javier García de la Oliva (Vice-Pres.); Ida Ragnarsson (Sec.).

Principal Staff: Dir Tanya Cox.

Contact Details: 10 rue de l'Industrie, 1000 Brussels; tel. (2) 743-87-60; e-mail secretariat@concordeurope.org; internet concordeurope.org.

European Food Banks Federation—EFBF (Fédération Européenne des Banques Alimentaires—FEBA)

Established in 1986 in France by Bernard Dandrel and André Hubert; relocated to Brussels in 2018.

Activities: Prevents food waste and contributes to reducing food insecurity through supporting and developing food banks in countries where they are most needed in Europe. The Federation represents over 351 food banks from 25 full members and five associate members in 30 European countries. Members are either national organizations or individual food banks.

Geographical Area of Activity: Europe.

Publications: Annual Report; leaflet; reports.

Finance: Total assets €3.1m. (31 Dec. 2023).

Board of Directors: Bernard Valluis (Pres.); Lindsay Boswell (Vice-Pres.); Tom Hillemans (Treas.); Pedro Castaños (Sec.).

Principal Staff: CEO Esteban Arriaga Miranda.

Contact Details: 775 chaussée de Louvain, 1140 Brussels; tel. (2) 538-94-50; e-mail info@eurofoodbank.org; internet www.eurofoodbank.org.

European Think Tanks Group—ETTG

Established in 2010.

Activities: Supports and promotes the role of the EU in relation to developing countries and more broadly. The Group comprises six research institutes concerned with international development and humanitarian policy: the German Institute of Development and Sustainability—IDOS (q.v.); the European Centre for Development Policy Management; the Real Instituto Elcano (Elcano Royal Institute, see Fundación Real Instituto Elcano); the Istituto Affari Internazionali (Institute of International Affairs, q.v.); the Institut du Développement Durable et des Relations Internationales (Institute for Sustainable Development and International Relations) and ODI (formerly known as the Overseas Development Institute, q.v.). It issues publications; and organizes conferences, workshops and webinars.

Geographical Area of Activity: International.

Publications: Newsletter; reports; blog.

Principal Staff: Dir Iliana Olivié.

Contact Details: 44 ave des Arts, 1000 Brussels; tel. (2) 237-43-82; e-mail ettginfo@ettg.eu; internet ettg.eu.

Fédération Belge des Fondations Philanthropiques (Belgian Federation of Philanthropic Foundations)

Established in 2004 by the Centre Européen pour Enfants Disparus et Sexuellement Exploits, Cera Holding (q.v.), Fondation Belge de la Vocation, Fondation Bernheim, Fondation Charcot, Fondation Evens (q.v.), Fondation Francqui (q.v.), Fondation pour les Générations Futures, Fondation Roi Baudouin and Fortis Foundation Belgium, and administered by the Köning Boudewijnstichting/Fondation Roi Baudouin (q.v.); formerly known as the Réseau Belge de Fondations.

Activities: Works to make the Belgian foundations sector more transparent. The Federation has six main working groups: education; family foundations; law, taxation and accounting; medical research; societal impact of foundations; and wealth management. It represents the interests of its members; organizes workshops and training; provides information to the public; and promotes transparency. It has 130 member foundations. Is a member of Philea (q.v.).

Geographical Area of Activity: Belgium.

Publications: *Les Fondations en Belgique*; brochures; surveys; studies.

Board of Directors: Cecile Coune (Pres.); Frédéric Lecok (Vice-Pres.); Ludwig Forrest (Sec.).

Principal Staff: Sec.-Gen. Pascale Van Durme.

Contact Details: 21 rue Brederode, 1000 Brussels; tel. (474) 88-19-85; e-mail info@lesfondations.be; internet www.lesfondations.be.

Fédération Européenne des Associations Nationales Travaillant avec les Sans-Abri—FEANTSA (European Federation of National Organisations Working with the Homeless)

Established in 1989; an umbrella body for not-for-profit organizations.

Activities: Prevents and alleviates the poverty and social exclusion of people threatened by or living with homelessness. Main programme areas include: employment; energy poverty; health; housing; housing as a human right; migration; participation; trends and statistics; women's homelessness; and young people. The Federation engages with European institutions, and national and regional governments, to develop and implement measures to fight homelessness; conducts research and data collection; organizes conferences, seminars and workshops; and raises public awareness. In 2016 it co-founded the Housing First Europe Hub with the Y-Foundation and more than 15 other European partner organizations. The Ending

Homelessness Awards recognize projects that have changed the lives of homeless people. Has more than 130 member organizations from 29 countries.

Geographical Area of Activity: Europe.

Publications: Annual Report; *Homeless in Europe* (magazine, 3 a year); *Flash* (monthly newsletter); *Health and Homelessness Newsletter* (quarterly newsletter); *Housing Rights Watch* (newsletter); *Migration & Homelessness Newsletter*; *Cities Bulletin*; *European Observatory on Homelessness*; *European Journal on Homelessness* (2 a year); *Comparative Studies* (1 a year); briefings; handbooks; glossaries; policy statements; research reports.

Executive Committee: Jules Van Dam (Pres.); Boroka Feher, Marthe Yonh (Vice-Pres); Alexander Machatschke (Treas.).

Principal Staff: Dir Freek Spinnewijn; Deputy Dir Ruth Owen.

Contact Details: 194 chaussée de Louvain, 1210 Brussels; tel. (2) 538-66-69; e-mail information@feantsa.org; internet www.feantsa.org.

Impact Europe

Established in 2004, as EVPA—European Venture Philanthropy Association, by Doug Miller; registered in the United Kingdom; name changed in 2025.

Activities: Promotes venture philanthropy and uses social investment tools to target social impact. The Association's members include venture philanthropy funds, social investors, grantmaking foundations, impact investing funds, private equity firms and professional service firms, philanthropy advisers, banks and business schools. It has 350 members from over 30 countries.

Geographical Area of Activity: Asia, Europe, Middle East, USA.

Publications: Newsletter; guides; cases studies; good practices; surveys.

Finance: Total income €3.1m., expenditure €3.0m. (2021).

Board of Directors: Leslie Johnston (Chair.).

Principal Staff: CEO Roberta Bosurgi.

Contact Details: Impact Europe Philanthropy House, 94 rue Royale, 1000 Brussels; tel. (2) 513-21-31; internet www.impacteurope.net.

Network of European Foundations—NEF

Established in 1976 as the European Fund for Cooperation; renamed as the International Association for European Co-operation in 1996. Present name adopted in 2002.

Activities: Carries out activities in the fields of social inclusion, democracy and international development. Projects that the Network supports include: the European Programme on Integration and Migration; Transnational Forum on Integrated Community Care; European Foundations' Initiative on Dementia; European Practice Exchange on Deradicalisation; Fund for Democracy and Solidarity in Europe; Fikra-Tunisia Joint Fund; European Fund for the Balkans; FutureLab Europe; Philanthropy in a Disruptive Era: Discovering Philanthropy, Discovering America; Children and Violence Evaluation Challenge Fund; Joint Action for Farmers' Organisations in West Africa; The Global Fund for Community Foundations; the Ariadne peer-to-peer network; and the *Alliance* magazine. It comprises 13 member foundations; and hosts the Civitates initiative (f. 2019), a network of 12 foundations.

Geographical Area of Activity: International.

Publications: Triennial Report; newsletter (quarterly).

Finance: Total assets €21.3m. (31 Dec. 2024).

Board of Directors: Alexandre Giraud (Chair.); Shannon Lawder (Vice-Chair.); Stefan Schaefers (Treas.); Markus Lux (Sec.).

Principal Staff: Exec. Dir Peggy Saïller.

Contact Details: Philanthropy House, 94 rue Royale, 1000 Brussels; tel. (2) 235-24-13; e-mail info@nef-europe.org; internet nef-europe.org.

Philanthropy Europe Association—Philea

Established in 2021 by the merger of Donors and Foundations Networks in Europe—DAFNE (f. 2006) and the European Foundation Centre—EFC (1989).

Activities: Works to strengthen the philanthropic sector in Europe and to enhance the professionalism and effectiveness of national associations. The organization carries out activities in the areas of advocacy, capability building, promotion of philanthropy and research. Comprising over 30 member associations, it has a collective membership of more than 7,500 foundations and grantmakers. The organization is a member of WINGS (q.v.), an associate partner of the Network of Foundations Working for Development (netFWD) (q.v.) and runs the Philanthropy Advocacy project.

Geographical Area of Activity: Europe.

Publications: Annual Report; *APhileated*, *Climate and Philanthropy*, and *PEXnews* (monthly newsletters); reports; consultations.

Board: Angel Font Vidal (Pres.); Carola Carazzone (Vice-Pres.); Christina Lambropoulou (Treas.).

Principal Staff: CEO Delphine Moralis.

Contact Details: Philanthropy House, 94 rue Royale, 1000 Brussels; tel. (2) 512-89-38; e-mail info@philea.eu; internet philea.eu.

Transnational Giving Europe—TGE

Established in 1999 by a group of European foundations; a network of philanthropic organizations.

Activities: Fosters charitable giving in Europe through facilitating tax-effective, cross-border cash donations. The network provides legal and administrative support to member organizations; and organizes the Conference for Practical Philanthropy across Europe. It comprises members from 19 European countries.

Geographical Area of Activity: Europe.

Publications: Newsletters, brochures, reports.

Finance: Financed by a 5% charge on donations of up to €100,000 with a degressive fee structure on the donated amount above this mark.

Principal Staff: Network Man. Anne-Laure Paquot.

Contact Details: c/o King Baudouin Foundation, 21 rue Bréderode, 1000 Brussels; tel. (2) 549-02-31; e-mail info@transnationalgiving.eu; internet transnationalgiving.eu.

Union des Associations Internationales—UAI (Union of International Associations—UIA/Unie van de Internationale Verenigingen—UIV)

Founded 1907 as the Central Office of International Associations by Henri La Fontaine, Nobel Peace Prize winner in 1913, and Paul Otlet, Sec.-Gen. of the then International Institute of Bibliography; present name adopted in 1910 at the First World Congress of International Organizations.

Activities: Facilitates the development of the worldwide network of non-profit organizations. The Union collects and disseminates information on non-profit organizations; promotes understanding of their role in global society; and carries out research on the legal and administrative problems they face. It organizes an annual roundtable; and maintains a database of c. 73,000 international associations, including international NGOs and intergovernmental organizations, and around 505,000 of their meetings. Has special consultative status with ECOSOC, associate status with UNESCO and Special List status with the International Labour Organization (ILO).

Geographical Area of Activity: International.

Publications: *International Congress Calendar Online*; *Yearbook of International Organizations Online*; *Encyclopaedia of World Problems and Human Potential* (online); *Open Yearbook and Open Calendar* (online); UIA's *World of Associations* (e-newsletter); *International Meetings Statistics Report*; *Survey on International Meeting Habits Issues*.

Council and Bureau: Cyril Ritchie (Pres.); Dragana Avramov, Esperanza Duran, Marilyn Mehlmann (Vice-Pres); Brigitte Motte (Treas.); Jacques de Mévius (Sec.-Gen.).

Contact Details: 40 rue Washington, 1050 Brussels; tel. (2) 640-18-08; e-mail uia@uia.org; internet www.uia.org.

FOUNDATIONS AND NON-PROFITS

Action Damien/Damiaanactie

Founded in 1964 as Les amis du père Damien (Friends of Fr Damian); a medical development organization.

Activities: Operates in developing countries to provide specialist medical assistance, aiming to eradicate leprosy, tuberculosis and leishmaniasis, through long-term projects, research and international co-operation; and also in Belgium, in partnership with BELTA (Belgian Lung and Tuberculosis Association), to eliminate tuberculosis among homeless people. The organization provides screening services and medical treatment; socioeconomic assistance to patients; information, awareness raising and training; and technical support to national authorities. It also carries out scientific research. In 2020, the Dr Hemerijckx Award was established, offering an Impact Award, worth €25,000, for efforts to address leprosy in developing countries; and a Research Award, worth €10,000, to encourage student research on the disease. Active in 14 countries.

Geographical Area of Activity: Bangladesh, Belgium, Bolivia, Burundi, Comoros, Dem. Repub. of the Congo, Guatemala, Guinea, India, Nepal, Nicaragua, Niger, Nigeria, Senegal.

Publications: Annual Report; newsletter (monthly); *Perspectives* (quarterly, in Dutch and French); teaching materials; blog.

Finance: Annual income €16.6m. (2023).

Board of Directors: Steven Osaer (Chair.).

Principal Staff: Gen. Man. Pascale Barnich.

Contact Details: 263 blvd Léopold II, 1081 Brussels; tel. (2) 422-59-11; e-mail info@actiondamien.be; internet www.actiondamien.be.

Association Internationale des Charités—AIC (International Association of Charities)

Founded in 1617 by Saint Vincent de Paul as the Confraternity of Ladies of Charity; re-established under Belgian law in 1986.

Activities: Operates internationally in the field of welfare. The Association works with member organizations to eliminate poverty and sustain the promotion and development of the underprivileged; and encourages voluntary work for and with the poor. Activities include social work, mainly to fight poverty of women; supporting drug addicts and alcoholics; caring for the elderly and the sick; helping single mothers; assisting the lonely; defending human rights; and working towards a culture of solidarity, respect and peace. It runs literacy and other educational workshops; provides technical training; and offers loans to individuals in need. In 2019 the Claire and Delva Prize was launched for initiatives to prevent violence against women. Has more than 150,000 local volunteers, mainly women, in 57 countries.

Geographical Area of Activity: International.

Restrictions: Not a grantmaking organization.

Publications: Activity Report; newsletter; *Initiation to Associative Life*; *AIC Volunteers Today*; training booklets.

Executive Board: Tayde de Callataÿ (Int. Pres.); Milagros Galisteo Moya, Guillermina Vergara Macip (Vice-Pres); Gloria Amparo Benitez (Treas.); Lisette Maillet (Sec.).

Principal Staff: Gen. Man. Bénédicte de Bellefroid.

Contact Details: 23 rampe des Ardennais, 1348 Louvain la Neuve; tel. (10) 45-63-53; e-mail info@aic-international.org; internet www.aic-international.org.

Bruegel—Brussels European and Global Economic Laboratory

An independent think tank, established in 2005, developed by French economists Jean Pisani-Ferry and Nicolas Véron and endorsed by French President Jacques Chirac and German Chancellor Gerhard Schröder. At the time, it had 10 founding member states.

Activities: Carries out evidence-based economic policy research and analysis, and organizes workshops and conferences, in the areas of: banking and capital markets; digital economy, labour markets, skills and health; global economy and trade policy; energy and climate policy; and macroeconomic policy and governance. The organization undertakes EU-funded projects, multinational research projects with academic institutions and private research partnerships. The Visiting Fellowship Programme is open to researchers and practitioners from academia, think tanks, and policy and business institutions, for visits of up to one year on a full- or part-time basis. Members include governments of EU member states, international corporations and institutions.

Geographical Area of Activity: International.

Publications: Annual Report; newsletter (weekly); working papers; policy contributions; data sets; essays; blogs; podcasts.

Finance: Annual revenue €7.8m., expenditure €7.2m. (2024).

Board: Erkki Liikanen (Chair.).

Scientific Council: Elena Carletti (Chair.).

Principal Staff: Dir Jeromin Zettelmeyer.

Contact Details: 33 rue de la Charité, 1210 Saint-Josse-ten-Noode, Brussels; tel. (2) 227-42-10; e-mail operations@bruegel.org; internet www.bruegel.org.

Cera

Established in 1998 as the Cera Foundation, a division of Cera Holding, a co-operative financial group, following the merger of CERA Bank with Kreditbank and ABB Insurance; present name adopted in 2004.

Activities: Supports projects that promote co-operative principles for the development of society. The Foundation makes investments at regional, supraregional (in Wallonia and Brussels), national and international level in the areas of: social inclusion and poverty alleviation; art and culture; services and community care; agriculture, horticulture and sustainable development; education and young people; co-operative entrepreneurship; and microfinance and microinsurance in the global South. The affiliated Belgische Raiffeisenstichting carries out international operations; and Cera Coopburo provides co-operatives with advice, coaching and training, and carries out research and development. Has around 400,000 partners.

Geographical Area of Activity: International.

Restrictions: Does not fund projects that receive substantial financial support from other financial institutions; no direct support for individuals, with the exception of art and culture grants.

Publications: Annual Report; newsletter; *Cera Scoop* (magazine); *Cera Select* (magazine, 2 a year); brochure.

Finance: Total assets €2,879.2m. (2022).

Board: Mathilde Remy (Chair.); Liesbet Okkerse, Luc Vandecatseye (Vice-Chair.).

Principal Staff: Man. Dirs Franky Depickere, Frederik Vandepitte, Marc De Ceuster.

Contact Details: Muntstraat 1, 3000 Leuven; tel. (800) 62340; e-mail info@cera.coop; internet www.cera.coop.

Churches' Commission for Migrants in Europe (Commission des Eglises auprès des Migrants en Europe/Kommission der Kirchen für Migranten in Europa)

Established in 1964; a network of churches and ecumenical groups.

Activities: Operates in Europe in the area of human rights. The Commission raises awareness of migration problems in Europe and develops the role of religious organizations in solving these. It aims to defend the rights of migrants and asylum seekers in Europe, and lobbies various European institutions. It also conducts studies on problems relating to European migration policies and racial discrimination and anti-trafficking; and organizes seminars and conferences on migration and related legal issues. The Commission participates in a network of NGOs throughout Europe. It comprises 39 Anglican, Orthodox and Protestant churches and church-related agencies from 19 European countries.

Geographical Area of Activity: Europe.

Publications: Annual Report; reports; guidelines; guides; conference reports; leaflets.

Executive Committee: Fiona Kendall (Moderator); Despoina Georgiadou (Vice-Moderator); Dr Goos Minderman (Treas.).

Principal Staff: Gen. Sec. Dr Torsten Moritz.

Contact Details: 174 rue Joseph II, 1000 Brussels; tel. (2) 234-68-00; e-mail info@ccme.eu; internet www.ccme.eu.

CIDSE—Together for Global Justice

Established in 1967; a network of Catholic social justice organizations; formerly known as Coopération Internationale pour le Développement et la Solidarité.

Activities: Operates in the field of aid to less-developed countries through advocating and campaigning for the reform of current policymaking. Programme areas include: systemic change; gender equality; climate justice; corporate regulation; land rights; Israel and the Palestinian Territories; energy systems; food systems; and sustainable lifestyles.

Geographical Area of Activity: International.

Restrictions: Not a grantmaking organization.

Publications: Annual Report; *CIDSE Highlights* (newsletter, 5 a year); policy papers.

Finance: Annual income €2.0m., expenditure €1.9m. (31 Dec. 2023).

Executive Committee: Caoimhe de Barra (Pres.); Thomas Vercruysse (Treas.).

Principal Staff: Sec.-Gen. Josianne Gauthier.

Contact Details: 16 rue Stévin, 1000 Brussels; tel. (2) 230-77-22; e-mail postmaster@cidse.org; internet www.cidse.org.

Concawe—Oil Companies' European Association for Environment, Health and Safety in Refining and Distribution

Founded in 1963 as the Oil Companies' International Study Group for Conservation of Clean Air and Water in Europe; a division of the European Petroleum Refiners Association. In 2013 it merged with EUROPIA, which represented the European oil-refining and marketing industry.

Activities: Carries out research and disseminates scientific, technical and economic information on environmental and health protection related to the petroleum-refining industry. Main programme areas include: air quality; fuel quality and emissions; health; oil pipelines; petroleum products; refinery technology; regulation; safety; water, soil and waste. The Association collates environmental and health data; assesses proposed environmental legislation; promotes co-operation between petroleum companies, industry and governments; and publishes reports and other information. It has observer status at the UN Economic Council for Europe (UNECE), the OSPAR Commission for the protection of the North-East Atlantic and the WHO. Has 40 members in 19 OECD European countries and one associate member in Eastern Europe.

Geographical Area of Activity: Europe.

Publications: *Concawe Review* (2 a year); *Concawe Reports*; briefing notes; factsheets.

Board of Directors: Luis Cabra (Pres.).

Principal Staff: Dir-Gen. Liana Gouta; Concawe Dir Jean-Marc Sohier.

Contact Details: 165 blvd du Souverain, 1160 Brussels; tel. (2) 566-91-60; e-mail info@concawe.eu; internet www.concawe.eu.

EGMONT—Institut Royal des Relations Internationales (Royal Institute of International Relations—Egmont Institute)

Established in 1947 to further studies into foreign politics, international law and economics, in particular in relation to the foreign policies of Belgium, Luxembourg and the Netherlands.

Activities: Operates internationally through self-conducted programmes, including research projects, carried out on an international basis. Main research programmes are: Africa; European Affairs; Europe in the World; and Training Programmes. The Institute also organizes national and international conferences and lectures, hosts working groups and issues publications.

Geographical Area of Activity: International.

Publications: Newsletter; *Egmont Papers*; *Studia Diplomatica*; Africa Policy Briefs; European Policy Briefs; Security Policy Briefs; books; commentaries.

Finance: Total assets €1.1m.; net annual income €14,158 (31 Dec. 2020).

Board of Directors: François-Xavier de Donnea (Chair.); Peter Moors (Vice-Chair.).

Principal Staff: Dir-Gen. Pol de Witte.

Contact Details: 24A rue des Petits Carmes, 1000 Brussels; 15 rue des Petits Carmes, 1000 Brussels; tel. (2) 213-40-20; e-mail info@egmontinstitute.be; internet www.egmontinstitute.be.

EURODAD—European Network on Debt and Development

Established in 1990, growing out of FONDAD—Forum on Debt and Development (q.v.), a network based in the Netherlands.

Activities: Focuses on debt justice, development finance and tax justice, targeting European governments, the World Bank, the International Monetary Fund and OECD. The Network offers a platform for exploring issues, collecting intelligence and ideas, and undertaking collective advocacy. It promotes responsible financial principles and practices, and redesigning financial architecture. Comprises 60 European NGOs in 28 countries.

Geographical Area of Activity: International.

Publications: Annual Report; newsletter; reports; blog.

Finance: Annual income €3.4m., expenditure €3.4m. (2023).

Board of Directors: Dominik Gross (Chair.); Kristina Rehbein (Treas.).

Principal Staff: Dir Jean Saldanha.

Contact Details: 18–26 rue d'Edimbourg, Mundo B Bldg, 3rd Floor, 1050 Ixelles, Brussels; tel. (2) 894-46-40; e-mail comms@eurodad.org; internet www.eurodad.org.

European Anti-Poverty Network—EAPN (Réseau Européen des Associations de Lutte contre la Pauvreté et l'Exclusion Sociale)

Established in 1990; an independent coalition of national and international NGOs.

Activities: Works to eliminate poverty and social exclusion and ensure co-operation at EU level. Main programme areas include: access to public services; employment; EU funds; Europe 2020 Strategy; participation of people experiencing poverty; poverty and fundamental rights; the future of Europe; and wealth and inequality. The Network raises public awareness; advocates for people and groups affected by poverty; and carries out training. It has consultative status with the Council of Europe and is a founding member of the Social Platform (Platform of European Social NGOs). Comprises more than 31 national networks and 13 European organizations.

European Environmental Bureau   BELGIUM

Geographical Area of Activity: EU, Iceland, North Macedonia, Norway, Serbia.

Publications: Annual Report; *EAPN Flash* (newsletter, 2 month); *Anti-Poverty Magazine*; *European Manual on the Management of the Structural Funds*; books; booklets; briefings; position papers; reports; toolkits.

Bureau: Carlos Susias (Pres.).

Principal Staff: Dir Juliana Wahlgren.

Contact Details: 11 blvd Bischofsheim, 1000 Brussels; tel. (2) 226-58-50; e-mail team@eapn.eu; internet www.eapn.eu.

European Environmental Bureau—EEB

Established in 1974; an umbrella organization.

Activities: The EEB is a network of environmental citizens' groups, bringing together more than 185 civil society organizations from more than 40 European countries (mostly EU Member States, and accession and neighbouring countries). Includes a growing number of European networks, with a combined membership of an estimated 30m. people.

Geographical Area of Activity: Europe.

Restrictions: Not a grantmaking organization.

Publications: Annual Report; newsletter; briefings; position papers; reports.

Finance: Annual income €7.6m., expenditure €7.6m. (2023).

Board: Toni Vidan (Pres.); Andriy Andrusevych, Nuria Blazquez, Bjela Vossen, Bernhard Zlanabitnig (Vice-Pres); Axel Jansen (Treas.).

Principal Staff: Sec.Gen. Patrick Ten Brink.

Contact Details: 14–16 rue des Deux Eglises, 1000 Brussels; tel. (2) 289-10-90; e-mail eeb@eeb.org; internet www.eeb.org.

European Foundation for Management Development—EFMD

Founded in 1971; an international network of private and public organizations, educational institutions and individuals.

Activities: Organizes exchanges between companies and academic institutions through meetings, seminars, workshops and projects. The Foundation promotes the creation of member networks to facilitate the exchange of information nationally and development of transnational activities. It co-operates with management development associations in Africa, Central and Eastern Europe, and North, Central and South-East Asia; and administers management training programmes in Algeria, the Commonwealth of Independent States, the People's Republic of China, India and the Russian Federation. Comprises 991 member organizations, located in 95 countries; with offices in Geneva, Hong Kong, Miami and Prague.

Geographical Area of Activity: Worldwide.

Publications: Annual Report; *Global Focus—The EFMD Business Magazine* (3 a year, in English, Chinese and Spanish); *Bulletin* (newsletter, 3 a year); *Guide to the EC*; *Lobbying in the EU*; *European Directory on Executive Education*.

Finance: Total revenue €10.6m., expenditure €10.5m. (31 Dec. 2024).

Board: Alain Dominique Perrin (Chair.); Valery Katkalo, Rebecca Taylor (Vice-Chair.).

Principal Staff: Pres. Eric Cornuel; Vice-Pres. Helke Carvalho Hernandes.

Contact Details: 88 rue Gachard, bte 3, 1050 Brussels; tel. (2) 629-08-10; e-mail info@efmdglobal.org; internet www.efmdglobal.org.

European Foundation for Quality Management—EFQM

Founded in 1989 by 67 of Europe's largest companies; a non-profit membership foundation.

Activities: Supports sustainable economic development through providing a platform for members to share experiences and learn from others' excellence models. Activities include: training leaders and managers to use the models; assessing organizations' performance through peer-to-peer review; recognizing the good practices that leading organizations use; and sharing those practices. The Foundation comprises more than 450 member organizations from the private and public sectors. It offers the annual EFQM Global Excellence Award and maintains the EFQM Global Excellence Index.

Geographical Area of Activity: Worldwide.

Publications: Annual Report; newsletter (monthly); assessment tools; management documents; user guides; frameworks; guidelines; white papers.

Finance: Annual income €3.1m., expenditure €3.0m. (31 Dec. 2020).

Board of Directors: Dr Paul G. K. Little (Chair.).

Principal Staff: Exec. Dir Russell Longmuir.

Contact Details: Leonardo Da Vincilaan 19 A/8, 1831 Diegem; e-mail info@efqm.org; internet www.efqm.org.

European Roma Rights Centre—ERRC

Established in 1996 in Hungary; a Roma-led international public interest law organization; relocated to Belgium in 2019.

Activities: Combats anti-Romani racism and human rights abuses of Roma through strategic litigation, research and policy development, advocacy and human rights education. Priority areas include: states' response to violence and hate speech; access to education and housing; free movement and migration; identity documentation; and women's and children's rights. The Centre operates internationally, extending legal support in cases of human rights abuses of Roma. It disseminates legal findings and issues publications; maintains a documentation centre consisting of legal material; awards scholarships to Romani students pursuing law and public administration studies; and offers internships for Romani people to study human rights law.

Geographical Area of Activity: Europe, Türkiye (Turkey).

Publications: *ERRC News*; *Roma Rights Review* (formerly *Roma Rights Journal*); *Knowing Your Rights and Fighting for Them: A Guide for Romani Activists*; thematic and country reports; factsheets; position papers; Romani language translations; pamphlets.

Board: Ethel Brooks (Chair.).

Principal Staff: Pres. Đorđe Jovanović.

Contact Details: c/o Amnesty International, 71 ave de Cortenbergh, 4th Floor, 1000 Brussels; e-mail office@errc.org; internet www.errc.org.

Fondation Auschwitz—Mémoire d'Auschwitz (Auschwitz Foundation—Remembrance of Auschwitz)

Founded in 1980 by the Belgian Association of Former Political Prisoners in Auschwitz-Birkenau and Silesian Camps and Prisons to study the history and remembrance of the Holocaust and Nazi terror.

Activities: Operates nationally and internationally in the fields of education, the arts, law and human rights, and Holocaust studies, through organizing self-conducted programmes, conferences, study trips and training. The Foundation awards the annual Auschwitz Foundation Prize of €3,125 for an original and unpublished text that makes an important contribution to the political, economic, social or historical analysis of the world of the Nazi concentration camps and the processes leading to its creation; the Auschwitz Foundation Prize–Jacques Rozenberg Prize for original unpublished research on the processes that have given rise to mass crimes, crimes against humanity and genocides; and an annual Research Grant and two other awards, each worth €3,125. It maintains the Remembrance of Auschwitz Documentation Centre and a library containing more than 13,000 items.

Geographical Area of Activity: Europe.

Publications: Newsletter; *Témoigner: Entre Histoire et Mémoire* (journal); *Traces de mémoire*; *Bulletin Trimestriel de la Fondation Auschwitz/Driemaandelijks Tijdschrift*; *International Journal*; *Quarterly Bulletin*; *Sporen van herinnering* (educational bulletin); teaching materials.

Principal Staff: Pres. Henri Goldberg; Dir Frédéric Crahay.

Contact Details: 17 rue aux Laines, bte 50, 1000 Brussels; tel. (2) 512-79-98; e-mail info@auschwitz.be; internet www.auschwitz.be.

Fondation Bernheim (Bernheim Foundation)

Established in 1999 by the will of Emile Bernheim, the President of department store L'innovation and founder of the Fondation Belge de la Vocation (f. 1963), the Centre Emile Bernheim business school and the Prix Emile Bernheim.

Activities: Funds activities in Brussels for young people in the areas of self-confidence, socio-cultural capital, workforce development and citizenship. Main programmes are focused on personal development, professional integration and citizen integration, including themes of fight against discriminations, interculturality and solidarity. The Foundation mainly offers multi-year grants.

Geographical Area of Activity: Belgium (Brussels).

Restrictions: No grants to individuals.

Publications: Annual Report; newsletter; information brochures.

Finance: Annual budget €2.2m. (2024).

Board of Directors: Mathias Dewatripont (Pres.); Eric De Keuleneer (Vice-Pres. and Treas.); Caroline Mierop (Vice-Pres.).

Principal Staff: Man. Dir Anne-Catherine Chevalier.

Contact Details: 53 rue des Bouchers, 1000 Brussels; tel. (2) 213-14-99; e-mail info@fondationbernheim.be; internet www.fondationbernheim.be.

Fondation Boghossian (Boghossian Foundation)

Established in 1992 by Robert Boghossian and his sons Jean and Albert, Lebanese jewellers of Armenian origin, to provide a better life for young people in Armenia and Lebanon; supports the 'Hayastan' All-Armenian Fund in Armenia.

Activities: Operates projects for young people in Armenia and Lebanon in the areas of welfare, education, art and culture, and medicine. Annually, the Foundation offers the Boghossian Belgium Foundation Prize for young Belgian artists, which includes an award worth €2,000 and an artist residency at a partner Lebanese institution; the Boghossian Foundation Prize Lebanon for young Lebanese artists, awarded to artists from three different disciplines, which is worth up to US $10,000 and includes a residency at the Villa Empain in Brussels; and the Boghossian Foundation Prize Armenia (formerly known as the President of the Republic of Armenia Prize), worth $80,000, which is awarded to 13 laureates for achievements in the arts and humanities, science and technology and contributions to the recognition of the Armenian Genocide. It also offers a Youth Prize in Armenia, worth $2,500.

Geographical Area of Activity: Armenia, Belgium, Lebanon.

Board of Directors: Kathy van Keer-Boghossian (Chair.).

General Assembly: Ralph Boghossian (Chair.).

Principal Staff: Gen. Man Louma Salamé.

Contact Details: Villa Empain, 67 ave Franklin Roosevelt, 1050 Brussels; tel. (2) 627-52-30; e-mail info@boghossianfoundation.be; internet villaempain.com.

Fondation Evens Stichting (Evens Foundation)

Established in 1990 by Georges Evens, a diamond trader, and his wife Irena Evens-Radzymniska.

Activities: Promotes respect for individual and collective diversity through supporting projects that encourage citizens and nations to live together harmoniously. Areas of interest are: arts; democracy; education; history; journalism; media literacy; and science. Projects are organized under two main initiatives: Common Purpose through Differences; and Norms and Values within the European Reality. Every two years, it awards prizes in the fields of the arts, education, journalism and science. Has offices in Brussels, and Warsaw, Poland.

Geographical Area of Activity: Europe.

Restrictions: Does not accept unsolicited applications.

Publications: Annual Report; newsletter; booklets; learning materials; research reports; other publications.

Board of Directors: Corinne Evens (Hon. Pres. and Co-Founder); Jonathan Evens (Chair.); Déborah Flon (Vice-Chair.).

Principal Staff: Exec. Dir Joe Elborn.

Contact Details: Frankrijklei 37, bus 12, 2000 Antwerp; tel. (3) 231-39-70; e-mail antwerp@evensfoundation.be; internet www.evensfoundation.be.

Fondation Fernand Lazard Stichting (Fernand Lazard Foundation)

Founded in 1949 and administered by representatives of seven Belgian universities; promotes continuing education.

Activities: Provides interest-free loans to students graduated from Belgian universities to fund postgraduate studies and research worldwide. The Foundation offers around 50 awards worth up to €25,000 each. In partnership with Sofina, as part of the Sofina Boël Fund for Education and Talent, annually it awards some scholarships to study at a foreign university for one year.

Geographical Area of Activity: Worldwide.

Restrictions: Applicants must have studied in Belgium and be nationals of an EU country.

Board of Directors: François Glansdorff (Chair.); Pierre Lefebvre (Vice-Chair.).

Principal Staff: Sec.-Gen. Sophie Castelein.

Contact Details: 100 ave de Merode, 1330 Rixensart; tel. (2) 687-21-40; e-mail info@fernandlazard.com; internet fernandlazard.be.

Fondation Francqui (Francqui Foundation)

Founded in 1932 by Emile Francqui, a banker and diplomat, and US President Herbert Hoover to promote the development of scientific research and contacts in Belgium.

Activities: Operates in the field of higher education. The Foundation awards the annual Francqui Prize, worth €250,000, to a researcher in Belgium under 50 years of age; the prize rotates between exact sciences, the humanities or medicine. Annually, it awards around 20 Francqui Chairs, inviting top-level Belgian or international researchers to give a series of lectures in a Belgian university; International Francqui Chairs invite a small number of high-level foreign professors to lecture and work in Belgium under the Foundation's auspices for 3–6 months; and Francqui Research Professorships are given to eminent researchers active in Belgian universities for a period of three years. The Foundation collaborates with the Belgian-American Educational Foundation, awarding annual fellowships for young Belgian academics to study in the USA. In 2018 the Collen-Francqui Fund began financing the Foundation's biomedical activities, offering Start-Up Grants for research, worth €200,000.

Geographical Area of Activity: Belgium, USA.

Restrictions: Grants to researchers active in Belgium.

Board of Directors: Count Herman Van Rompuy (Chair.); Baron Jean-Pierre Hansen, Baron Mark Waer (Vice-Chair.).

Principal Staff: CEO Dr Marie-Claire Foblets; Sec.-Gen. Greet T'Jonck.

Contact Details: 11 rue d'Egmont, 1000 Brussels; tel. (2) 539-33-94; e-mail secretariat@francquifoundation.be; internet www.francquifoundation.be.

Fondation Marcel Hicter BELGIUM

Fondation Marcel Hicter (Marcel Hicter Foundation)
Established in 1980 to promote the sociocultural development of the French community in Belgium; and cultural co-operation at European and international level.

Activities: Operates in the field of the arts and culture. The Foundation organizes the European Diploma in Cultural Project Management, which operates in three countries; trains cultural managers from 36 countries; and manages mobility grants for cultural management experts and trainees on behalf of the Council of Europe. It also organizes conferences, carries out research and issues publications.

Geographical Area of Activity: Europe, Central Africa, Russian Federation.

Publications: Research reports; studies; analysis; books.

Principal Staff: Dir Frederic Jacquemin.

Contact Details: Association Marcel Hicter, 1 ave Maurice, 1050 Brussels; tel. (2) 641-89-80; e-mail contact@fondation-hicter.org; internet www.fondation-hicter.org.

Fondation P&V (P&V Foundation)
Established in 2000 by P&V Assurances, a co-operative insurance company.

Activities: Works with and for young people, supporting active citizenship and combating social exclusion. The Foundation offers an annual Citizenship Award to an individual or organization for promoting openness, democracy, tolerance and inclusivity.

Geographical Area of Activity: Europe.

Publications: Newsletter (quarterly); books.

Board: Olivier Servais, Jessy Siongers (Pres).

Principal Staff: Man. Dir Saskia De Groof.

Contact Details: 151 rue Royale, 1210 Brussels; tel. (2) 250-91-24; e-mail fondation@pv.be; internet www.fondationpv.be.

Fonds Baillet Latour (Baillet Latour Fund)
Established in 1974 by Count Alfred de Baillet Latour; formerly known as Fonds InBev-Baillet Latour.

Activities: Supports initiatives that use innovative approaches in the areas of health, education, culture and sport, providing financial support, awarding scholarships and endowing university chairs. The Foundation awards a thematic health prize, which each year covers in turn one of the following themes: metabolic diseases, infectious diseases, neurological diseases, cancer or cardiovascular diseases. It also awards two prizes annually for clinical research at a French- and a Dutch-speaking institution; and grants, worth €150,000 a year, for 3–5 years for medical research on the annual theme at a Belgian university or university hospital. Set up in 2022, the Baillet-Latour Biomedical Award, worth €1m., supports the development of young researchers for five years.

Geographical Area of Activity: Belgium.

Board of Directors: Thomas Leysen (Pres.).

Principal Staff: Gen. Man. Benoit Loore.

Contact Details: Brouwerijplein 1, 3000 Leuven; tel. (16) 27-61-59; internet www.fondsbailletlatour.com.

FRS-FNRS—Fonds de la Recherche Scientifique (Fund for Scientific Research)
Founded in 1928, as the Fonds National de la Recherche Scientifique (FNRS), by a group of industrialists and scientists; in 1992 it split into the FRS-FNRS and the FWO—Fonds Wetenschappelijk Onderzoek (q.v.).

Activities: Supports scientific research through remunerating researchers, funding research teams, offering grants and awarding scientific prizes. The Fund administers eight special funds: the Fund for Research Training in Industry and Agriculture (FRIA, f. 1994); the Fund for Research in Human Sciences (FRESH, f. 2012); the Interuniversity Institute for Nuclear Science (IISN, f. 1947); the Fund for Medical Scientific Research (FRSM, f. 1957); the Fund for Collective Fundamental Research (FRFC, f. 1965); the Fund for Fundamental Strategic Research (FRFS, f. 2013); the Excellence of Science (EOS) programme; and the Fund for Research in Art (FRArt, f. 2018).

Geographical Area of Activity: Belgium.

Publications: Annual Report; *La Lettre du FNRS*; *FNRS.news*; brochures; memoranda.

Finance: Annual income €228.4m., expenditure €229.5m. (31 Dec. 2022).

Board of Directors: Annemie Schaus (Pres.); Dr Véronique Halloin (Sec.-Gen.).

Contact Details: 5 rue d'Egmont, 1000 Brussels; tel. (2) 504-92-11; e-mail communication@frs-fnrs.be; internet frs-fnrs.be.

FWO—Fonds Wetenschappelijk Onderzoek (Scientific Research Foundation)
Established in 1992 by the division of the Fonds National de la Recherche Scientifique (FNRS; f. 1928), which also produced the FRS-FNRS—Fonds de la Recherche Scientifique (q.v.).

Activities: Supports fundamental and strategic scientific research in universities and research institutions in Flanders (Belgium) in all fields of science, including medicine, technology, environmental studies, social sciences and the humanities, including law. The Foundation offers doctoral and postdoctoral fellowships; and grants for national and international research. Every five years it awards FWO-Excellence Prizes to Flemish researchers, each worth €100,000; and also awards prizes sponsored by private companies.

Geographical Area of Activity: Belgium (Flanders).

Publications: Annual Report; newsletter; *FWO-nieuwsbrief* (newsletter); *Kennismakers Magazine*.

Finance: Annual income €507.5m., expenditure €507.5m. (31 Dec. 2023).

Board of Directors: Bruno Blondé (Pres.).

Principal Staff: Sec.-Gen. Dr Hans Willems.

Contact Details: Leuvenseweg 38, 1000 Brussels; tel. (2) 512-91-10; e-mail communicatie@fwo.be; internet www.fwo.be.

GAIA—Groupe d'Action dans l'Intérêt des Animaux (Global Action in the Interest of Animals)
Established in 1992 by Ann de Greef and Michel Vandenbosch.

Activities: Works for the cause of animal rights, through education, active campaigns, advocacy and publishing information. The Group promotes vegetarianism; and campaigns against experimentation on animals for the production of cosmetics and for medical research, and against maltreatment of animals in farming.

Geographical Area of Activity: Belgium.

Publications: *Animalibre*; *Vrijdier*; newsletter; educational material.

Board: Michel Vandenbosch (Pres.).

Principal Staff: Dir Ann De Greef.

Contact Details: 43 Hopstraat, 1000 Brussels; tel. (2) 245-29-50; e-mail info@gaia.be; internet www.gaia.be.

Îles de Paix (Islands of Peace)
Established in 1962 by Nobel Peace Prize winner Dominique Pire; officially founded in 1965.

Activities: Supports the development of sustainable family farming and decent living conditions for farmers; and promotes solidarity, human rights and environmental conservation. The organization improves access to and use of basic services through working with local authorities to build and refurbish schools and health centres; drinking water points; communication routes; and market buildings. In Belgium, it advocates for and raises awareness about the right to food and the need for sustainable food systems.

Geographical Area of Activity: Belgium, Benin, Bolivia, Burkina Faso, Peru, Tanzania, Uganda.

Publications: Annual Report; newsletter; *Transitions* (quarterly); reports; *Phosphore*.

BELGIUM

Finance: Annual revenue €6M., expenditure €6M.
Board: Freddy Meurs (Chair.).
Principal Staff: Man. Dir Marie Wuestenberghs.
Contact Details: 37 rue du Marché, 4500 Huy; tel. (85) 23-02-54; e-mail info@ilesdepaix.org; internet www.ilesdepaix.org.

Institute for European Environmental Policy—IEEP

Established in 1976, in Berlin, by the European Cultural Foundation (q.v.); a think tank.

Activities: Carries out evidence-based scientific research and public policy analysis, working with stakeholders in EU institutions, international bodies, academia and civil society. Main programme areas are: agriculture and land management; biodiversity and ecosystem services; climate change and energy; green economy; environmental governance; global challenges and the UN Sustainable Development Goals; industrial pollution and chemicals; natural resources and waste; and water, marine and fisheries. The Institute conducts research and promotes strategies and alternatives for dealing with environmental problems in Europe; and proposes solutions to national governments, the European Parliament and other institutions. It organizes conferences, seminars and training; and has an office in London (UK).
Geographical Area of Activity: Europe.
Publications: Annual Report; newsletter (monthly); policy briefs; reports.
Finance: Total assets €1.8m. (2024).
Board: Hans Wolters (Chair.).
Principal Staff: Interim Exec. Dir Antoine Oger.
Contact Details: 36 rue Joseph II, 1000 Brussels; tel. (2) 738-74-82; e-mail brussels@ieep.eu; internet www.ieep.eu.

Koning Boudewijnstichting/Fondation Roi Baudouin (King Baudouin Foundation)

Founded in 1976 to commemorate the 25th anniversary of King Baudouin's coronation.

Activities: Supports projects in the areas of justice, democracy and diversity, working in partnership with governmental and non-governmental organizations. Main programmes are: climate, the environment and biodiversity; education and talent development; Europe; health; heritage and culture; international philanthropy; social engagement; and social justice and poverty. The Foundation organizes roundtables, forums and seminars; and issues publications. The King Baudouin African Development Prize, worth €200,000, recognizes initiatives initiated and led by Africans that improve people's quality of life and empower them. It has branches in Montréal and New York.
Geographical Area of Activity: International.
Publications: Annual Report; *Blikveld/Champs* (newsletter in Dutch and French, 3 a year); *International Newsletter* (in English, 2 a year); regional reports.
Finance: Receives a grant from the Belgian National Lottery. Total assets €1,509.4m. (2023).
Board of Governors: Pierre Wunsch (Chair.); Lieze Cloots, Ralph Heck (Vice-Chair.).
Principal Staff: Man. Dir Brieuc Van Damme.
Contact Details: 21 rue Bréderode, 1000 Brussels; tel. (2) 500-45-55; e-mail info@kbs-frb.be; internet www.kbs-frb.be.

Open Society European Policy Institute—OSEPI

Established in 2004 as the EU policy arm of the Open Society Foundations (q.v.) network.

Activities: Advocates open society values. The Institute assists in collaboration between the Open Society Foundations network and the EU and other intergovernmental agencies. Main programmes within the EU include: democratic standards; human rights and rule of law; equality and anti-discrimination; migration and asylum; and transparency and accountability. Outside the EU, the Institute focuses on the EU and human rights and regional programmes.
Geographical Area of Activity: Eastern Europe, Russian Federation and Central Asia, EU, Middle East and North Africa, South-East Asia, sub-Saharan Africa, Western Balkans.
Principal Staff: Dir Heather Grabbe.
Contact Details: 5–6 square de Meeûs, 1000 Brussels; tel. (2) 505-46-46; e-mail osepi@opensocietyfoundations.org; internet www.opensocietyfoundations.org/who-we-are/programs/open-society-european-policy-institute.

Oxfam-Solidariteit/Solidarité

Established in 1964 as Oxfam-Belgique and renamed Oxfam-Solidarité in 1996; part of Oxfam-en-Belgique, with Oxfam-Wereldwinkels (Oxfam Worldshops) in Flanders and Brussels, which sits under the umbrella organization Oxfam Fair Trade; part of the Oxfam confederation of organizations (qq.v.).

Activities: Works to alleviate poverty through carrying out self-conducted programmes in areas including: active citizenship, holding governments, companies and international organizations to account; climate change; disasters and conflicts, providing aid and strengthening people's survivability and resilience; food sovereignty; healthcare and access to medicines; inequality; land grabbing; migration and asylum; and women's and girls' rights. The organization provides humanitarian aid and emergency assistance during conflicts and disasters in the form of clean water, hygiene kits, shelter, food and post-disaster recovery and development. It is present in 14 countries; and in Belgium organizes immersion workshops, provides teaching materials for schools and offers internships.
Geographical Area of Activity: International.
Restrictions: Does not make loans or grants to individuals.
Publications: Annual Report; newsletter; research reports; teaching materials.
Finance: Annual revenue €66.8m., expenditure €66.6m. (2023).
Board of Directors: Lodewijk De Witte (Chair.); Manoëlla Wilbaut (Vice-Chair.).
Principal Staff: Dir-Gen. Eva Smets.
Contact Details: 60 rue des Quatre-Vents, 1080 Sint-Jans-Molenbeek; tel. (2) 501-67-00; e-mail info@oxfambelgie.be; internet www.oxfamsol.be.

Peace Brigades International—PBI

Founded in 1981 by people and organizations with practical experience of non-violent action.

Activities: Works at local, regional and international level to protect human rights defenders and communities whose lives and work are threatened by political violence. An international political support network reinforces physical accompaniment by trained international volunteers to deter attacks against human rights defenders. The organization has 13 Country Groups in Australia, Canada, Europe and the USA; and works in Colombia, Guatemala, Honduras, Indonesia, Kenya, Mexico, Nepal and Nicaragua.
Geographical Area of Activity: International.
Restrictions: Does not fund groups or individuals.
Publications: Annual Review; newsletter; *The Protection Handbook for Human Rights Defenders*; project publications; toolkits.
Finance: Annual income €4.1m. (31 Dec. 2023).
International Council: Fathi Zabaar (Pres.); Marc Bontemps (Treas.); Shane Guthrie (Sec.).
Principal Staff: Int. Co-ordinator Sierra Schraff Thomas.
Contact Details: Village Partenaire, 15 rue Fernand Bernier, 1060 Brussels; tel. (2) 543-44-43; e-mail contact@peacebrigades.org; internet www.peacebrigades.org.

Pesticide Action Network Europe—PAN Europe

Established in 1987; a network of European environmental NGOs promoting a sustainable alternative to the use of pesticides; a regional centre of the PAN International network (f. 1982).

Activities: Works to eliminate hazardous pesticides, reduce use of pesticides and promote ecologically sound alternatives through advocacy, policy analysis, networking and campaigning. Areas of interest include: biodiversity; health; taxation; and water pollution. The Network works with representatives of the European Parliament, Commission and Council; as well as academics, farmers, retailers, scientists and trade unions. It commissions reports, disseminates information and takes part in public seminars. Comprises 49 member NGOs from 28 countries, of which 23 are in the EU.

Geographical Area of Activity: Europe.

Publications: Annual Report; newsletter; briefings; factsheets; reports; blog.

Finance: Annual budget €373,540 (2019).

Principal Staff: Exec. Dir Martin Dermine.

Contact Details: 67 rue de la Pacification, 1000 Brussels; tel. (2) 318-62-55; e-mail info@pan-europe.info; internet www.pan-europe.info.

Ruralité-Environnement-Développement—RED

(Rurality Environment Development)

Founded in 1980 to encourage communication between those involved in rural development throughout Europe.

Activities: Organizes conferences and seminars in the fields of economic development, planning and cultural heritage in rural areas. Project areas include: agriculture; cultural heritage; digital challenges; harmony and revitalization; heritage and energy; smart villages; and the Rurality Reference Centre. The organization chairs and co-ordinates the European Countryside Movement, and is President of the Advisory Committee on Rural Development of the European Commission of the EU. It has participatory status with the Council of Europe, with members in 15 countries.

Geographical Area of Activity: Europe.

Restrictions: Not a grantmaking organization.

Publications: *RED Dossier* (2 a year); brochures.

Board of Directors: Gérard Peltre (Pres.); Felipe González de Canales, Alfons Hausen, Istvan Bali (Vice-Pres); Alain Delchef (Treas.).

Principal Staff: Dir Marie Noël Neven.

Contact Details: 304 rue des Potiers, 6717 Attert; tel. (63) 23-04-90; e-mail info@ruraleurope.org; internet www.ruraleurope.org.

Service Civil International—SCI

Founded in 1920 by Pierre Cérésole, a Swiss humanitarian who established voluntary international 'workcamps' following the First World War.

Activities: Promotes a culture of peace, social justice and sustainable development through organizing international volunteering projects with a local and global impact. The organization arranges short-term projects, known as 'workcamps', in co-operation with local branches, partner organizations and local communities; and places volunteers on long-term volunteering projects abroad of 1–12 months. International projects address issues such as forced migration, peer learning in international volunteer work, tackling discrimination in the EU, environmental issues and antimilitarism. Has 40 branches worldwide.

Geographical Area of Activity: International.

Restrictions: Not a grantmaking organization; volunteers must be aged at least 18 years for most projects.

Publications: Annual Report; Impact Report; *SCI E-Zine* (newsletter); *Words About Deeds* (100th anniversary publication); toolkits; online learning platform.

Finance: Annual income €674,463, expenditure €615,807 (2023).

International Executive Committee: Antonella Di Matteo (Int. Pres.); Bert Verstappen (acting Int. Vice-Pres.); Nico Verzijden (Int. Treas.).

Principal Staff: Int. Coordinator Cristina Debu.

Contact Details: Belgiëlei 37, 2018 Antwerp; tel. (3) 266-57-27; e-mail info@sci.ngo; internet www.sci.ngo.

Solidar

Established in 1948 as International Workers Aid; present name adopted in 1995. Solidar Foundation is the organization's co-operation platform.

Activities: Works to advance social justice in Europe and worldwide. The network represents the concerns of its member organizations to the EU and international institutions across the policy sectors of social affairs, international co-operation and lifelong learning. In 2000 it launched the annual Silver Rose Awards, celebrating and awarding the work and commitment of individuals, Trade Unions and CSOs towards social justice and solidarity. This award is organized annually together with the Socialists and Democrats in the European Parliament. Includes more than 50 NGOs in 26 countries in Europe and worldwide.

Geographical Area of Activity: International.

Publications: Newsletter; *Economic & Social Rights Report*; *Social Rights Monitor*; Country Monitoring Reports; briefing notes; case studies; factsheets; position papers.

Finance: Annual income €296,079, expenditure €285,330 (2022).

Board of Directors: Anne Van Lancker (Pres.); Klaus Thieme (Vice-Pres.); Susanne Drake (Treas.).

Principal Staff: Sec.-Gen. Mikael Leyi.

Contact Details: 50 ave des Arts, bte 5, 2nd Floor, 1000 Brussels; tel. (2) 479-33-72; e-mail solidar@solidar.org; internet www.solidar.org.

Universitaire Stichting (University Foundation)

Founded in 1920 to promote scientific progress.

Activities: Works in the field of higher education, making grants to associations and individuals for the publication of scientific works and periodicals. The Foundation hosts Belgian and international academic associations, providing facilities for scientific and academic meetings and events. It organizes the annual Ethical Forum; and the Re-Bel (Rethinking Belgium) initiative to foster academic research and collaboration between Belgian universities on themes of general interest. The Fernand Collin Prize for Law, worth €7,500, is awarded every two years for a scholarly work in Dutch by a researcher at a Belgian academic institution. Also offers a Prize for English-language works (in odd years) for doctoral works or other research works carried out in universities in Flanders. The Club of the University Foundation is a meeting place for university professors and researchers from throughout Belgium as well as from abroad, where they also network with eminent members of civic society.

Geographical Area of Activity: Europe.

Publications: *Annual University Statistics for Belgium*; *Akkadica*; *Analecta Bollandiana*; *Annales d'histoire d'art et d'archéologie*; *Anthropologie et Préhistoire*; *Antiquité Classique*; *Augustiniana*; *Belgian Journal of Botany*; *Belgian Journal of English Language and Literature*; *Belgian Journal of Entomology*; *Belgian Journal of Linguistics*; *Belgian Journal of Zoology*.

Board of Directors: Prof. Jacques Willems (Chair.).

Principal Staff: Exec. Dir Eric De Keuleneer.

Contact Details: 11 rue d'Egmont, 1000 Brussels; tel. (2) 545-04-00; e-mail fu.us@universityfoundation.be; internet www.universitairestichting.be.

BENIN

FOUNDATIONS AND NON-PROFITS

Fondation Claudine Talon (Claudine Talon Foundation)
Established in 2016 by First Lady Claudine Talon.
Activities: Works to improve the wellbeing of vulnerable women and children by reducing the rate of maternal and infant mortality; and providing access to water and sanitation. Programmes include: expanding mother and child health services; preventing obstetric fistula; reducing mother-to-child HIV transmission, providing access to antiretroviral medicines and ending discrimination against people with HIV; and raising literacy rates and distributing school kits to pupils.
Geographical Area of Activity: Benin.
Publications: Annual Report; newsletter.
Finance: Annual revenue 2,894.4m. CFA francs, expenditure 2,091.5m. CFA francs (2023).
Principal Staff: Pres. Claudine Talon.
Contact Details: quartier Les Cocotiers, ave Jean Paul II, 05 BP 987, Cotonou; tel. 97-97-25-05; e-mail info@fondationclaudinetalon.org; internet fondationclaudinetalon.org.

Fondation MTN Bénin (MTN Foundation Benin)
Established in 2008 by MTN Bénin, a telecommunications company; part of the MTN Foundations network.
Activities: Carries out MTN Bénin's social investment programmes. The Foundation carries out activities to improve the lives of the disadvantaged and the most vulnerable people in the areas of education, the environment, health, rural women's empowerment and sport. Initiatives include: providing school kits to children; creating digital classrooms in schools; and providing hospitals with medical and technical equipment. In 2009 it set up the Yellow Line telephone hotline to provide information on HIV/AIDS and violence against women.
Geographical Area of Activity: Benin.
Principal Staff: Chair. Viviane Dalia Sissuh.
Contact Details: 360 Blvd de la Marina, 01 BP 5293, Cotonou; tel. 21-31-66-41; e-mail fondation@mtn.bj; internet www.mtn.bj/fondation.

Institut de Recherche Empirique en Économie Politique—IREEP (Institute for Empirical Research in Political Economy—IERPE)
Established in 2004; part of the African School of Economics.
Activities: Trains Master's-level researchers and government officials in empirical research and statistics. The Institute is the co-ordinating branch in francophone West Africa for the Afrobarometer (q.v.) network, carrying out research, collecting data and publishing information on Africans' views on democracy, governance, economic reforms, civil society and standards of living. Other areas of interest include: social mobility; education; and quality of public goods and services.
Geographical Area of Activity: Benin, francophone West Africa.
Publications: Working papers; studies; books; databases.
Principal Staff: Research Dir Dr Ian Heffernan.
Contact Details: Abomey-Calavi, Arconville, route de l'hôpital de zone, 02 BP 372, Cotonou; tel. 94-55-07-06; e-mail ireep@africanschoolofeconomics.com; internet africanschoolofeconomics.com/the-institute-for-empirical-research-in-political-economy.

BERMUDA

FOUNDATIONS AND NON-PROFITS

Bermuda Foundation
Established in 2013 as the Bermuda Community Foundation (BCF), later known as the Bermuda Foundation, with initial support from The Atlantic Philanthropies (q.v.), to build a central community endowment to fund non-profit organizations.
Activities: Funding areas are based on the *Bermuda Vital Signs Report*, outlining quality of life priorities for residents of Bermuda. The Foundation manages 69 endowed and non-endowed community funds, from which grants are made annually on the recommendation of donor-advisers or Grants Committees of the board to address emerging needs. It maintains GiveBermuda.org, an online directory of non-profit organizations in Bermuda.
Geographical Area of Activity: Bermuda.
Publications: Annual Report; *Bermuda Vital Signs Report*; *Bermuda Vital Signs Convening Reports*.
Finance: Annual income B $10.4m., expenditure B $1.3m. (30 June 2024).
Board of Directors: Amanda Outerbridge (Chair.).
Principal Staff: CEO and Man. Dir Myra Virgil.
Contact Details: Sterling House, 3rd Floor, 16 Wesley St, Hamilton HM 11; tel. 294-4959; e-mail admin@bermudafoundation.org; internet bermudafoundation.org.

The Peter Cundill Foundation
Established in Bermuda in 2012 following the death of Francis Peter Cundill, a Canadian value investment professional.
Activities: Supports a small number of organizations, with a focus on improving the lives of children. In 2008 the Cundill History Prize was established at McGill University, in Montreal, awarded to authors of any nationality who have published a book (written or translated into English) that has made an impact in the area of history; a grand prize, worth US $75,000, and two finalist prizes, each worth $10,000, are awarded.
Geographical Area of Activity: Bermuda, Canada, UK, East Africa.
Board of Directors: Richard W. J. Parry (Chair.).
Contact Details: FPC Philanthropies Ltd, Clarendon House, 2 Church St, Hamilton HM 11; e-mail admin@pcf.foundation; internet www.thepetercundillfoundation.com.

BOLIVIA

FOUNDATIONS AND NON-PROFITS

Fondo para el Desarrollo de los Pueblos Indígenas de América Latina y El Caribe—FILAC (Fund for the Development of Indigenous Peoples of Latin America and the Caribbean)

Established in 1992 at the second Ibero-American Summit of Heads of State and Government in Madrid, Spain.

Activities: Supports the self-development and promotes the rights of indigenous peoples, communities and organizations in Latin America and the Caribbean. Programmes focus on national and international dialogue and participation; economic development that respects and protects social, cultural, political and environmental rights of indigenous peoples; and education for equity for men and women, including through the flagship Indigenous Intercultural University (UII) initiative. The Fund comprises 22 member states (19 from Latin America and the Caribbean and the three others are Belgium, Portugal and Spain). It has Permanent Observer status at the UN.

Geographical Area of Activity: Belgium, Latin America and the Caribbean, Portugal, Spain.

Publications: Newsletter (monthly); reports; brochures.

Board of Directors: Sonja Guajajara (Pres.); Mirna Cunningham (First Vice-Pres.); Laura Oroz (Second Vice-Pres.).

Principal Staff: Technical Sec. Darío Mejía Montalvo.

Contact Details: Avda 20 de Octubre 2287, esq. Rosendo Gutiérrez, La Paz; tel. (2) 2423233; e-mail filac@filac.org; internet www.filac.org.

Fundación Amigos de la Naturaleza (Friends of Nature Foundation)

Founded in 1988 by a small group of naturalists located in Santa Cruz for the conservation of biodiversity in Bolivia.

Activities: Works to prevent environmental degradation and protect biodiversity in Bolivia and neighbouring countries. The Foundation runs conferences and self-conducted programmes, conducts research, and offers scholarships and fellowships. Programme areas include: bio-commerce; climate change and environmental services; science; communication; and conservation.

Geographical Area of Activity: South America.

Publications: Annual Report; *Infofan* (newsletter); *Síntesis Ambiental* (policy brief); factsheets; technical reports; books.

Board of Directors: Mario Foianini Landívar (Pres.); Walter Ridder Saucedo (Vice-Pres.); Hermes Justinian (Second Vice-Pres.).

Principal Staff: Exec. Dir Natalia Calderón.

Contact Details: Km 7 1/2 Doble Via la Guardia, Casilla 2241, Santa Cruz de la Sierra; tel. (3) 3556800; e-mail fan@fan-bo.org; internet www.fan-bo.org.

Fundación Jubileo (Jubilee Foundation)

Established in 2003 by the Bolivian Episcopal Conference and the German dioceses of Hildesheim and Trier to deepen ties between Bolivian and German branches of the Catholic Church.

Activities: Promotes a democratic and inclusive society and respect for human rights. The Foundation builds capacity and promotes leadership training for social and political actors; strengthens organizations, institutions and networks; and creates spaces for dialogue and public debate with social and political actors, to influence decisionmaking that contributes to efficient and transparent governance. Areas of interest include: development financing; budgets and taxation; hydrocarbons, mining and energy; human development; youth and leadership; participation and control; environment; Christian social ethics; and democracy and human rights.

Geographical Area of Activity: Bolivia.

Publications: *Revista Jubileo* (magazine); *Mujer y Minería* (magazine); posters; primers; reports.

Principal Staff: Exec. Dir Juan Carlos Núñez.

Contact Details: Calle Quintín Barrios 768, Sopocachi (media cuadra antes de Pl. España), Casilla 5870, La Paz; POB 5870, La Paz; tel. (2) 2125177; e-mail fundajub@jubileobolivia.org.bo; internet www.jubileobolivia.org.bo.

Fundación UNIR Bolivia (UNIR Bolivia Foundation)

Established in 2005.

Activities: Works in the fields of conflict management and development of intercultural citizenship and socioeconomic equity. The Foundation carries out research, analysis and conflict transformation activities; and develops capacities in democratic dialogue and communication. It comprises an Assembly of Institutes, with 13 representatives from different regions and sectors of the country. Has offices in La Paz, Santa Cruz and Cochabamba.

Geographical Area of Activity: Bolivia.

Publications: Periodicals; reports; books; posters.

Principal Staff: Exec. Dir Maria Soledad Quiroga.

Contact Details: Avda final Sánchez, Lima 2696; tel. (2) 2117069; e-mail conflictos@unirbolivia.org; internet unirbolivia.org.

Sembrar Sartawi

Established in 2009 following the merger of Fundación Sartawi (f. 1989) and Fundación Sembrar.

Activities: Promotes the inclusion of small-scale farmers in the financial system. The organization provides technical assistance to people who lack access to resources, with an emphasis on rural areas, facilitating economic initiatives and strengthening the artisanal sector to increase job opportunities for women. It runs programmes on agricultural forestation in valleys and the *altiplano* (high plateau), microenterprises and providing easier access to credit for those in need. Has four branches and 40 agencies in seven national departments.

Geographical Area of Activity: Bolivia.

Publications: Annual Report; *Boletín Trimestral de Educación Financiera* (quarterly newsletter).

Finance: Total assets 530.7m. bolivianos (30 June 2023).

Board of Directors: María Elena Querejazu Vidovic (Pres.); Elder Salazar Peredo (Vice-Pres.); Susana Moreno Velasco (Sec.).

Principal Staff: Man. Dir Marcelo Antonio Mallea Castillo.

Contact Details: Calle Pedro Salazar 509, Zona Sopocachi, La Paz; tel. (2) 419252; e-mail info@sembrarsartawi.org.

BOSNIA AND HERZEGOVINA

FOUNDATIONS AND NON-PROFITS

Analitika—Center for Social Research
Established in 2009 by Dr Edin Hodzić and Dr Tarik Jusić; a think tank.
Activities: Carries out public policy research and projects in the fields of the rule of law and human rights, public administration reform, media and public communication, and social policy. Organizes expert discussions, training and workshops.
Geographical Area of Activity: Western Balkans.
Publications: *Policy memo* (policy briefs); *Komentar* (commentaries); *Osvrt* (discussion papers); reports; conference reports.
Principal Staff: Dir Amra Nušinović.
Contact Details: 71000 Sarajevo, Avde Jabučice 12; tel. (33) 872306; e-mail info@analitika.ba; internet www.analitika.ba.

Međunarodnog foruma Bosna (International Forum Bosnia)
Established in 1997.
Activities: Promotes dialogue, trust and respect for human rights, the rule of law and democracy. Carries out research through 12 thematic research centres: cultural heritage; education; gender; history; inter-religious dialogue; linguistics; media; natural heritage; regional co-operation; strategic studies; student programmes; and technology and economic development. It organizes workshops, conferences, public lectures and exhibitions; and has three regional centres, in Banja Luka, Mostar and Tuzla.
Geographical Area of Activity: Bosnia and Herzegovina.
Publications: *Forum Bosnæ* (journal); working papers; books.
Principal Staff: Pres. Prof. Rusmir Mahmutćehajić.
Contact Details: 71000 Sarajevo, Sime Milutinovića 10; tel. (33) 217665; e-mail if_bosna@bih.net.ba; internet www.forumbosna.org.

Open Society Fund—Bosnia-Herzegovina
Founded in 1992; an independent foundation, part of the Open Society Foundations (q.v.) network.
Activities: Promotes social justice; respect for human rights; transparency and accountability in public institutions; and citizens' active participation in public life. Main programme areas are: providing universal access to quality education; protecting the rights of vulnerable people; supporting alternative voices in the public sphere; and fighting corruption. It operates grants programmes in the fields of: access to justice; the arts; civic engagement; health law and equality; inclusive education and education support; minority leadership; and public procurement. It has an office in Banja Luka.
Geographical Area of Activity: Bosnia and Herzegovina.
Publications: Reports, manuals and guides.
Finance: Annual income US $1.3m., expenditure $1.3m. (31 Dec. 2023).
Board of Directors: Eldan Mujanović (Chair.).
Principal Staff: Exec. Dir Mervan Mirascija.
Contact Details: 71000 Sarajevo, Marsala Tita 19/3; tel. (33) 444488; e-mail osf@osfbih.org.ba; internet osfbih.org.ba.

BOTSWANA

FOUNDATIONS AND NON-PROFITS

Botswana Institute for Development Policy Analysis—BIDPA

Established in 1995 by the Government of Botswana as an independent research institute.

Activities: Carries out policy research and analysis on the economy and social development; provides institutional capacity building through providing technical and financial assistance; and organizes training and public education in policy analysis. Programme areas include: the environment, agriculture and natural resources; governance and administration; human and social development; macroeconomics and development; and trade, industry and private sector development.

Geographical Area of Activity: Southern Africa.

Publications: Annual Report; newsletter; policy briefs.

Finance: Total assets 35m. pula (2023).

Board of Trustees: Daniel Molaode (Chair.).

Principal Staff: Acting Exec. Dir Dr Gloria Somolekae.

Contact Details: 134 Gaborone International Finance Park, Tshwene Dr., Kgale Hill, Private Bag BR29, Gaborone; tel. 3971750; e-mail info@bidpa.bw; internet bidpa.bw.

Lady Khama Charitable Trust
Established in 2002 in memory of Lady Ruth Khama, former First Lady and founding President of the Botswana Red Cross Society, the Botswana Council of Women, the Child to Child Foundation and SOS Children's Villages Association of Botswana.
Activities: Funds projects that improve the lives of vulnerable women and children, with a particular focus on early childhood development and disabilities.
Geographical Area of Activity: Botswana.
Publications: Newsletter.
Finance: Total disbursements since 2002 US $1.7m.
Board of Trustees: Lt-Gen. Dr Seretse K. I. Khama (Patron); Mpho Mothibatsela (Chair.); Ratang Icho-Molebatsi (Treas.).
Principal Staff: Trust Co-ordinator Laone Batshedi.
Contact Details: Plot 6109, The Farm, Forest Hill, 9-KO Gaborone; POB 45843, Riverwalk, Gaborone; tel. 72111128; e-mail info@ladykhamatrust.org; internet ladykhamatrust.org.

Orange Botswana Foundation
Established in 2011 by Orange, a telecommunications provider; part of the Fondation Orange (q.v.) network.
Activities: Promotes digital inclusion, in particular in the areas of education, women and start-ups. Provides digital education kits, including tablets and IT equipment, to primary schools; and has established Women's Digital Centres in Gantsi, Molepolole and Chobe to improve women's

employability through training in digital and entrepreneurship skills. Co-ordinates the national rounds of the annual international Orange Social Venture Prize, promoting social innovation through technology.

Geographical Area of Activity: Botswana.

Principal Staff: Foundation Man. Boga Chilinde-Masebu.

Contact Details: Plot 166, cnr Queens and Pilane Rd, Main Mall; Private Bag BO 64, Gaborone; tel. 3693700; internet www.orange.co.bw/en/orange-foundation.html.

BRAZIL

CO-ORDINATING BODIES

GIFE—Grupo de Institutos, Fundações e Empresas (Group of Institutes, Foundations and Enterprises)

Established in 1995 from an informal group of social investors that had existed since 1989.

Activities: Provides member organizations with information, and a centre where they can exchange knowledge and experience through meetings, seminars, courses and forums. The Group establishes links between similar local and national organizations to facilitate social investment in community development. It has a national reference centre, which contains materials on philanthropic knowledge and practices. Has more than 170 associates in its network.

Geographical Area of Activity: Brazil.

Publications: Annual Report; newsletter; *Censo GIFE* (biennial); books; guides; reports.

Finance: Annual income 6.6m. reais, expenditure 6.6m. reais (31 Dec. 2020).

Governing Board: Inês Lafer (Pres.).

Principal Staff: Sec.-Gen. Cassio França.

Contact Details: Av. Brigadeiro Faria Lima 2413, 1° andar, Conjunto 11, Jardim Paulistano, 01452-000 São Paulo, SP; tel. (11) 3816-1209; e-mail gife@gife.org.br; internet www.gife.org.br.

Instituto para o Desenvolvimento do Investimento Social—IDIS (Institute for the Development of Social Investment)

Established in 1999 by Marcos Kisil, a strategic consultant; in 2005 it became a member of the Global Alliance of the Charities Aid Foundation.

Activities: Supports social development and the reduction of social inequality through investing in financial, technical, managerial and human resources. The Institute carries out self-conducted programmes and provides technical and operational support to social investors and projects.

Geographical Area of Activity: Brazil, Latin America.

Publications: Annual Report; newsletter; guides; reports; research findings; technical notes; translations; event transcriptions.

Finance: Total assets 6.5m. reais; net annual income 526,409 reais (31 Dec. 2021).

Board of Directors: Luiz Sorge (Pres.); Maria Jose de Mula Cury (Vice-Pres.).

Principal Staff: CEO Paula Jancso Fabiani.

Contact Details: Rua Paes Leme 524, Cj 161, Pinheiros, 05424-904 São Paulo, SP; tel. (11) 3914-6700; e-mail comunicacao@idis.org.br; internet www.idis.org.br.

Rede Comuá (Common Network)

Established in 2012 as the Rede de Fundos Independentes para Justia Social; a network of community foundations and grantmakers. Name changed to Rede de Filantropia para a Justiça Social in 2017. Present name adopted in 2023.

Activities: Promotes social and community justice, human rights, racial and gender equality, social and environmental equity, and sustainable community development. Main programmes focus on support, strengthening member organizations' participation in the Network, and promoting knowledge exchange; and capacity building through peer learning, webinars and workshops in the areas of communication, resource mobilization, monitoring and evaluation, and safety and protection. Comprises 18 member organizations.

Geographical Area of Activity: Brazil.

Publications: Newsletter; consultation papers; guides; reports; studies; blog.

Principal Staff: Exec. Dir Jonathas Azevedo.

Contact Details: Rua Comendador Gervasio Seabra 690, 20531-470 Rio de Janeiro, RJ; tel. (21) 9641-8027; e-mail contato@redecomua.org.br; internet redecomua.org.br.

Rede Iberoamericana de Fundações Civicas ou Comunitárias—RIFC (Ibero-American Network of Community Foundations)

Established in 2013 by Fundación Bertelsmann (Spain); its Secretariat is ICOM—Instituto Comunitário Grande Florianópolis community foundation (f. 2005).

Activities: Promotes and strengthens community foundations. In 2016 the Network assisted around 262,000 people, directly and indirectly, and 1,445 organizations. It comprises 24 organizations from Brazil, Costa Rica, Mexico, Portugal, Puerto Rico, Spain and Uruguay.

Geographical Area of Activity: Portugal, South America, Central America and the Caribbean, Spain.

Publications: *Social Impact Report*.

Principal Staff: Exec. Co-ordinator Yana Lima.

Contact Details: Secretariat, c/o ICOM, Rua Felipe Schmidt, 835 Sl 08, Centro, 88010-001 Florianópolis, SC; tel. (48) 3222-5127; e-mail icomfloripa@icomfloripa.org.br.

WINGS—Worldwide Initiatives for Grantmaker Support

Established in 2000 by a group of philanthropy associations and support organizations.

Activities: Supports networking between, and development of, associations of grantmaking organizations and organizations serving philanthropy worldwide. The network carries out research, collecting and sharing data; offers capacity building and peer-learning events for members; organizes regional meetings, working groups and a global forum; and maintains a Knowledge Center and Global Philanthropy Resources Hub. It comprises more than 200 member organizations in over 50 countries, representing more than 15,000 foundations, grantmakers and social investors.

Geographical Area of Activity: Worldwide.

Publications: Annual Report; newsletter; *WINGS Updates*; *Global Landscape of Philanthropy*; *Community Foundation Atlas* (online); *Transparency and Accountability Toolkit*; grantmaker case studies; reports.

Finance: Total assets US $4.3m. (31 Dec. 2023).

Board of Directors: Chris Worman (Chair.); Barry Gaberman, Dr Atallah Kuttab (Chair. Emeriti).

Principal Staff: Exec. Dir Benjamin Bellegy.

Contact Details: Rua Cap. Antônio Rosa 409, Jardim Paulistano, São Paulo 01443-010; tel. (11) 3078-7299; e-mail info@wingsweb.org; internet www.wingsweb.org.

BRAZIL

FOUNDATIONS AND NON-PROFITS

BrazilFoundation
Established in 2000 by Leona Forman, former chief of Information Centers Services at the UN Department of Public Information.

Activities: Promotes equality, social justice and economic opportunity, connecting donors with social organizations to fund projects. The Foundation works in 21 states in Brazil, awarding grants in the fields of education and culture, human rights and civic engagement, health, socioeconomic development and the environment; and administering special funds for women, early childhood and young people, and the regions of Rio de Janeiro, São Paulo and Minas Gerais. It has chapters in Rio de Janeiro and São Paulo, and in New York, Los Angeles and Miami (USA).

Geographical Area of Activity: Brazil, USA.

Restrictions: Grants only in Brazil.

Publications: Annual Report; newsletter; evaluation reports.

Finance: Total assets US $10.1m. (31 Dec. 2021).

Board of Directors: Will Landers (Chair.); Pedro Lichtinger (Vice-Chair.); Ricardo Puggina (Treas.).

Principal Staff: Pres. and CEO Dr Rebecca Tavares.

Contact Details: Av. Nilo Peçanha 50, 20020-906 Rio de Janeiro, RJ; tel. (21) 2532-3029; e-mail info@brazilfoundation.org; internet www.brazilfoundation.org.

Centro Brasileiro de Relações Internacionais—CEBRI (Brazilian Center for International Relations)
Established in 1998 by a group of academics, business people and government authorities; a think tank.

Activities: Carries out public policy research and analysis in the field of international affairs. Programme areas include: South America; Asia; the USA; Europe; multilateralism; agribusiness; international trade; culture and international relations; energy; infrastructure; environment and climate change; and international security. The Center organizes conferences, debates, meetings, roundtables and seminars; and offers courses for students, executives, professionals and public sector employees.

Geographical Area of Activity: International.

Publications: Annual Report; newsletter; *CEBRI Dossier* (weekly); context notes; policy papers; reports; studies and surveys; books.

Finance: Annual income 12.6m. reais, expenditure 12.1m. reais (2023).

Board of Trustees: José Pio Borges (Pres.); Luiz Ildefonso Simões Lopes, José Alfredo Graça Lima (Vice-Pres.).

Principal Staff: CEO Julia Dias Leite.

Contact Details: Rua Marques de São Vicente 336, Gávea, 22451-044 Rio de Janeiro, RJ; tel. (21) 2206-4400; e-mail press@cebri.org.br; internet cebri.org.

Fundação Abrinq pelos Direitos da Criança e do Adolescente (Abrinq Foundation for the Rights of Children and Adolescents)
Established in 1990 by the Brazilian Association of Toy Manufacturers—Abrinq.

Activities: Supports projects that defend the basic rights of children and adolescents. The Foundation promotes inter-sector co-operation and offers technical assistance; and equips NGOs, government agencies and community groups with information and documentation. It operates the Observatory for Children and Adolescents, an online data and information resource.

Geographical Area of Activity: Brazil.

Publications: Annual Report; newsletter; technical notes; reports; brochures; guides.

Finance: Annual income 58.8m. reais, expenditure 39.4m. reais (31 Dec. 2023).

Executive Board: Synésio Batista da Costa (Pres.); Carlos Antonio Tilkian (Vice-Pres.).

Principal Staff: Exec. Sec. Victor Alcântara da Graça.

Contact Details: Rua Araguari 835, 14º andar, Vila Uberabinha, 04514-041 São Paulo, SP; tel. (11) 3848-8799; e-mail faleconosco@fadc.org.br; internet www.fadc.org.br.

Fundação ArcelorMittal Brasil (ArcelorMittal Brazil Foundation)
Established in 1988 as the Fundação Belgo-Mineira, by Belgo-Mineira, an iron and steel manufacturer; present name adopted in 2006.

Activities: Funds initiatives that support children and adolescents. Main programme areas are: culture, education, health, social inclusion and sport; with a focus on training artists, technicians and cultural managers. The Foundation operates in more than 40 cities throughout Brazil.

Geographical Area of Activity: Brazil.

Restrictions: Grants only to organizations registered with the Council for the Rights of Children and Adolescents.

Publications: Annual Report; *Revista Nota 10*; *Nota 10 online*.

Finance: Annual income 6.3m. reais, expenditure 6.1m. reais (31 Dec. 2022).

Board of Trustees: Wagner de Brito Barbosa (Pres.).

Principal Staff: Dir Pres. Tatiana Nolasco; Superintendent Dir Herik Pires Marques.

Contact Details: Av. Carandaí 1115, 17th Floor, Funcionários, 30130-915 Belo Horizonte, MG; tel. (31) 3219-1660; e-mail fundacao@arcelormittal.com.br; internet www.famb.org.br.

Fundação Armando Alvares Penteado (Armando Alvares Penteado Foundation)
Founded in 1947 by Armando Alvares Penteado, a coffee grower and business person, and his wife Annie.

Activities: Promotes culture and technological integration through teaching and related activities. The Foundation maintains a university, library, museum of fine arts, theatre and various centres and institutes. It offers courses in science and technology, the arts and humanities, economics, business management and international relations; and awards scholarships and has an academic exchange programme.

Geographical Area of Activity: Brazil.

Publications: *Revista FAAP* (6 a year); *Revista de Economia e Relações Internacionais*; *Revista Qualimetria*; *Revista Gerente de Cidade*; other magazines; newsletter; blog.

Board of Trustees: Celita Procopio de Carvalho (Pres.).

Principal Staff: CEO Dr Antonio Bias Bueno Guillon.

Contact Details: Rua Alagoas 903, Higienópolis, 01242-902 São Paulo, SP; tel. (11) 3662-7000; e-mail faleconosco@faap.br; internet www.faap.br.

Fundação Banco do Brasil (Banco do Brasil Foundation)
Founded in 1985 by Banco do Brasil.

Activities: Supports socioenvironmental investment through five main programmes: social assistance; education; social technologies; productive inclusion and income generation, combined with sustainable development and environmental awareness; and volunteering. The Foundation awards a social technology prize; and maintains a database of social technologies.

Geographical Area of Activity: Brazil.

Publications: Annual Report; newsletter; books; social and activities reports.

Finance: Annual income 178.2m. reais, expenditure 112.0m. reais (31 Dec. 2023).

Exec. Board: Kleytton Guimarães Morais (Pres.).

Principal Staff: CEO Gilson Adriano de Oliveira Lima; Exec. Dir Luciana Athaíde Brandão Bagno.

Fundação Getulio Vargas   BRAZIL

Contact Details: SCES, Trecho 02, lote 22, 70200-002 Brasília, DF; tel. (61) 3108-7000; e-mail fbb@fbb.org.br; internet fbb.org.br.

Fundação Getulio Vargas—FGV (Getulio Vargas Foundation)

Established in 1944 to stimulate Brazil's socioeconomic development; a think tank.

Activities: Carries out research in the fields of citizenship, education, history, justice, politics and the social sciences; and offers academic programmes in areas including: finance, health, law, macroeconomics, microeconomics, pollution, poverty and unemployment, social security and sustainable development. The Foundation's partner network comprises over 30 institutions, including the Brazilian Institute of Economics (IBRE; f. 1951) and the Applied Research and Knowledge Network (f. 2016). It provides technical assistance through FGV Projetos to organizations in the public, private and third sectors in Brazil and abroad; and undertakes exchanges with academic institutions worldwide. Has branches in São Paulo, Belohorizonte and Brasilia.

Geographical Area of Activity: International.

Publications: Annual Report; newsletter; journals; reports; studies; books.

Finance: Total assets 4.9m. reais (31 Dec. 2023).

Board of Trustees: João Alfredo Dias Lins (Acting Pres.).

Principal Staff: Pres. Carlos Ivan Simonsen Leal; Vice-Pres Clovis Jose Daudt Darrigue of Faro, Marcos Cintra Cavalcanti de Albuquerque.

Contact Details: Praia de Botafogo, nº 190, Botafogo, 22250-900 Rio de Janeiro; tel. (21) 3799-5938; e-mail contact@fgv.br; internet portal.fgv.br.

Fundação Grupo Boticário de Proteção à Natureza (Boticário Group Foundation)

Established in 1990 by Miguel G. Krigsner, founder of cosmetics company O Boticário; part of the Climate Observatory network.

Activities: Carries out activities and research in the fields of nature conservation and climate change; and supports the projects of other organizations. The Foundation protects more than 11,000 hectares of natural Atlantic Forest and Cerrado remnants, and surrounding areas. Runs the Oásis initiative, which makes financial awards to landowners who preserve natural areas and adopt soil management best practices.

Geographical Area of Activity: Brazil.

Publications: Annual Report; newsletter.

Board of Trustees: Miguel G. Krigsner (Pres.).

Supervisory Board: Américo Mattar (Pres.).

Principal Staff: CEO Artur N. Grynbaum; Exec. Dir Maria de Lourdes Nunes.

Contact Details: Gonçalves Dias 225, Batel, 80240-340 Curitiba, PR; tel. (41) 3318-2636; e-mail contato@fundacaogrupoboticario.org.br; internet www.fundacaogrupoboticario.org.br.

Fundação Iochpe (Iochpe Foundation)

Established in 1989 by Iochpe-Maxion SA, a manufacturer of vehicle parts.

Activities: Works in the field of children's and adolescents' development, through activities in the areas of art and vocational education. Main programmes are: Formare, which works with medium-sized and large companies to provide basic and technical skills training to young people from low-income backgrounds; and the Instituto Arte na Escola, which develops educational materials in partnership with universities for art teachers in schools. The Foundation operates in 17 states in Brazil.

Geographical Area of Activity: Brazil.

Publications: Activity Reports; monographs; books; educational kits.

Finance: Annual income 11.4m. reais, expenditure 6.0m. reais (31 Dec. 2024).

Board of Trustees: Marcos Sergio de Oliveira (Pres.); Solomon Ioschpe (Vice-Pres.).

Principal Staff: Pres., Exec. Board Luiz Claudio Correia dos Anjos.

Contact Details: Rua dos Pinheiros 870, 19th Floor, Pinheiros, 05422-001 São Paulo, SP; tel. (11) 3103-8088; e-mail contato@fiochpe.org.br; internet www.fiochpe.org.br.

Fundação Maria Cecilia Souto Vidigal (Maria Cecilia Souto Vidigal Foundation)

Established in 1965 by Gastão Eduardo de Bueno Vidigal and Maria Cecília Souto Vidigal to encourage research in the field of haematology, following the death of their daughter, Maria Cecília, from leukaemia; in 2007 the Foundation changed its focus to early childhood development.

Activities: Focuses on the development and education of children from birth to six years of age. Main programme areas include: access to pre-school and early childhood education; strengthening childcare and funding innovation; supporting, evaluating and systematizing public childhood policies and programmes; and raising public and media awareness. The Foundation offers grants; conducts research and disseminates publications; and organizes national and international courses, workshops and training. It is a partner with Fundación FEMSA and Open Society Foundations (qq.v.) in the Early Childhood Development Innovation Fund, which operates throughout Latin America and the Caribbean, co-ordinated and managed by the Inter-American Development Bank.

Geographical Area of Activity: Brazil.

Publications: Annual Report; *Boletim FMCSV* (newsletter, 6 a year); *Primeira Infância Em Pauta* (guidelines); data.

Finance: Total assets 631.4m. reais (31 Dec. 2024).

Board of Trustees: Tracy Francis (Chair.).

Supervisory Board: Adriana Katalan (Pres.).

Principal Staff: CEO Mariana Luz.

Contact Details: Rua Campos Bicudo 98, 1°andar, Cj 11 e 12, Edif. Itaquerê, Jardim Europa, 04536-010 São Paulo, SP; tel. (11) 3330-2888; e-mail contato@fmcsv.org.br; internet www.fmcsv.org.br.

Fundação Oswaldo Cruz—FIOCRUZ (Oswaldo Cruz Foundation)

Established in 1900 as the Federal Seropathy Institute; present name adopted in 1974, named after the first Director, bacteriologist Oswaldo Cruz. An independent agency under the Ministry of Health.

Activities: Promotes health and social development through carrying out scientific and technological research and providing health services. Programme areas include: teaching and research, offering postgraduate and vocational courses, conducting clinical research and maintaining 33 biological collections; undertaking medical innovation and vaccine production through the Drug Technology Institute (Farmanguinhos) and Immunobiological Technology Institute (Biomanguinhos); and providing primary healthcare services through the National Institute of Women, Children and Adolescents Health (IFF), Evandro Chagas Institute of Clinical Research (IPEC), Oswaldo Cruz Institute (IOC) and Germano Sinval Faria School Health Center. The Foundation comprises 16 technical and scientific units in 10 states in Brazil, with an office in Mozambique; four administrative units; and the Museum of Life. The Center for International Relations in Health (CRIS) was established in 2009 to co-ordinate and support international activities. The Fiocruz Libraries Network, which is co-ordinated by the Institute of Scientific and Technological Communication and Information in Health (ICICT, has 14 physical libraries and provides access to 10 thematic virtual libraries and three biographical ones; and the Arca institutional repository.

Geographical Area of Activity: International.

Publications: Annual Report; newsletter; *Cadernos de Saúde Pública* (monthly); *História, Ciências, Saúde-Manguinhos* (quarterly); *Memórias do Instituto Oswaldo Cruz* (12 a year); *Revista Eletrônica de Comunicação, Informação e Inovação em Saúde (Reciis)* (quarterly); *Fitos* (quarterly magazine); *Trabalho, Educação e Saúde* (magazine, 3 a year).

Finance: Annual income 26.1m. reais, expenditure 10,915.3m. reais (2024).

Principal Staff: Exec. Dir Juliano de Carvalho Lima; Deputy Exec. Dir Priscila Ferraz.

Contact Details: Av. Brasil 4365, Manguinhos, 21040-900 Rio de Janeiro, RJ; tel. (21) 2598-4242; e-mail portalfiocruz@icict.fiocruz.br; internet portal.fiocruz.br.

Fundação Roberto Marinho (Robert Marinho Foundation)

Established in 1977 by Roberto Pisani Marinho, who inherited the Grupo Globo media conglomerate.

Activities: Works primarily in the field of education, but also national heritage, and ecology and conservation. The Foundation collaborates with businesses, foundations and institutes, co-ordinating projects such as literacy programmes for adults and children, and teacher training; provides funding for music, dance and national museums; offers the Young Scientist Award for young researchers; and devises ecological campaigns for environment protection. It established the Casa da Cultura (f. 2003), the Museum of Portuguese Language (f. 2006) and the Football Museum (f. 2008) in São Paulo; the Paço do Frevo (f. 2012) in Recife; and the MAR—Rio Museum of Art (f. 2013) and the Museum of the Future (f. 2015) in Rio de Janeiro, where the new Museum of Image and Sound is also being built.

Geographical Area of Activity: Brazil.

Publications: Annual Report; newsletter; books; reports; teaching materials.

Board of Directors: José Roberto Marinho (Pres.).

Principal Staff: Sec.-Gen. João Alegria.

Contact Details: Rua Marques de Pombal 25, Centro, 20230-240 Rio de Janeiro, RJ; tel. (21) 3232-8090; e-mail imprensa@frm.org.br; internet www.frm.org.br.

Fundação SOS Mata Atlântica (Foundation for the Conservation of the Atlantic Forest)

Established in 1986 to protect the Atlantic Forest, which covers around 15% of the national territory, in 17 states.

Activities: Operates in the area of conservation, the environment and sustainable development. Programmes focus on: the climate emergency; forest restoration; establishing land and marine conservation areas; and ensuring clean water in rivers. The Foundation carries out environmental education activities for educators and students.

Geographical Area of Activity: Brazil.

Publications: Annual Report; newsletter; technical reports; factsheets; books.

Finance: Annual revenue 31.4m. reais, expenditure 29m. reais (31 Dec. 2024).

Board of Directors: Marcia Hirota (Chair.); Roberto Luiz Leme Klabin, Morris Safdié (Vice-Pres).

Principal Staff: CEO Luís Fernando Guedes Pinto.

Contact Details: Rodovia Marechal Rondon, KM 118, 13312-000 Bairro Porunduva, São Paulo, SP; tel. (11) 3262-4088; e-mail info@sosma.org.br; internet www.sosma.org.br.

Fundação Telefônica Vivo (Telefônica Vivo Foundation)

Established in 1999 by Telefônica Vivo, a telecommunications company; part of the Fundación Telefónica (q.v.) network.

Activities: Carries out activities in the areas of education, employability and volunteering. The Foundation offers educational resources and professional teacher training via the Pro-Futuro digital education programme, a joint initiative with Fundación Bancaria 'la Caixa' (q.v.), which incorporates the Aula Digital classroom technology project, Escolas Conectadas knowledge-sharing platform and Desafio Inova Escola pathway for teachers and other professionals in schools. Programmes aimed at young people include Pense Grande, which promotes social entrepreneurship and youth leadership; Programaê!, which teaches programming and digital skills; and the 42 coding academy, which offers peer-to-peer vocational training.

Geographical Area of Activity: Brazil.

Publications: Social Report; newsletter.

Finance: Annual revenue 50.8m. reais, expenditure 50.6m. reais (31 Dec. 2024).

Principal Staff: CEO Lia Glaz.

Contact Details: Av. Eng. Luís Carlos Berrini 1376, 16° andar, CEP 04571-936 São Paulo, SP; tel. (11) 3430-3501; e-mail fundacao.br@telefonica.com; internet fundacaotelefonicavivo.org.br.

Instituto Ayrton Senna (Ayrton Senna Institute)

Established in 1995 in memory of Ayrton Senna, a motor racing driver who died in 1994.

Activities: Promotes social transformation through comprehensive education. The Institute works with educators to prepare children and young people mentally, socially and emotionally for the world of work and to equip them with life skills. It carries out education research into new ideas and public policy through its eduLab21 innovation centre; and provides free online education courses for teachers through the Espaço Educador platform. The Ayrton Senna Foundation, based in the United Kingdom, operates internationally.

Geographical Area of Activity: Brazil.

Restrictions: No grants to individuals.

Publications: Annual Report; newsletter; research reports; studies; thematic guides; e-books.

Finance: Receives 100% of the profits obtained from the licensing of the Ayrton Senna brand and image, and is also financed through alliances with the Brazilian and multinational business community. Annual revenue 84.8m. reais, expenditure 45.0m. reais (2023).

Principal Staff: Pres. Viviane Senna.

Contact Details: Rua Dr Fernandes Coelho 85, 15° andar, Pinheiros, 05423-040 São Paulo, SP; tel. (11) 2974-3000; e-mail ias@ias.org.br; internet www.institutoayrtonsenna.org.br.

Oxfam Brasil

Established in 2014; part of the Oxfam confederation of organizations (qq.v.).

Activities: Works to eliminate the causes of poverty and inequality; and to allow citizens to exercise their rights and take part in political decisionmaking. Main programmes areas are: humanitarian aid; human rights and the private sector; social and economic justice; and youth, race and gender.

Geographical Area of Activity: Brazil.

Restrictions: Does not make loans or grants to individuals.

Publications: Annual Report; newsletter; guides; policy notes; blog.

Finance: Annual revenue 17.3m. reais, expenditure 16.5m. reais (31 Dec. 2023).

Board of Trustees: Helio Santos (Pres.).

Principal Staff: Exec. Dir Viviana Santiago.

Contact Details: Av. Pedroso de Morais 272, 8° andar, Pinheiros, 05432-040 São Paulo, SP; tel. (11) 3811-0408; e-mail doador@oxfam.org.br; internet www.oxfam.org.br.

REDEH—Rede de Desenvolvimento Humano (Network for Human Development)

Established in 1990 by Thais Corral, a social innovator.

Activities: Promotes gender, race and ethnic equality. The Network conducts training programmes for local leaders; and undertakes initiatives in areas including: digital inclusion; the environment; health, sexual and reproductive rights; non-discriminatory education; socioenvironmental entrepreneurship; sustainable development; youth and culture; and the Zero Tobacco Coalition. As part of the Mulher 500 Anos Atrás dos Panos project, it hosts the Acervo Centro de Memória Mulheres do Brasil e Pesquisa on the history and the role of women in Brazil.

Geographical Area of Activity: Brazil.

Publications: Annual Report; *Biography of Women* (online); books; posters.

Finance: Annual revenue 1.2m. reais, expenditure 1.5m. reais (31 Dec. 2020).

Principal Staff: Gen. Co-ordinator Thais Rodrigues Corral; Exec. Co-ordinator Maria Aparecida Schumaher.

Contact Details: Rua Álvaro Alvim 21, 16° andar, Centro, 20031-010 Rio de Janeiro, RJ; tel. (21) 3819-6616; e-mail redeh@redeh.org.br; internet www.redeh.org.br.

BULGARIA

CO-ORDINATING BODIES

BCause Foundation

Founded in 1995 by Evrika Foundation, Open Society Foundation—Sofia, St Cyril and Methodius International Foundation and the Union of Bulgarian Foundations and Associations to help to design and build a robust voluntary sector in Bulgaria; a member of the Global Alliance of the Charities Aid Foundation. Formerly known as BCAF—Bulgarian Charities Aid Foundation; present name adopted in 2016.

Activities: Manages seven charitable funds and runs grantmaking programmes. The Foundation promotes corporate giving, providing information to companies and helping them to organize their giving schemes effectively; and operates the platformata.bg online donation platform. It awards scholarships, worth up to 3,000 lev; and offers a range of grants for children with disabilities or in need of medical treatment, and to organizations that support disadvantaged young people, people with disabilities, social care for the elderly, women and their children who are victims of domestic violence, and environmental protection. Incorporates the Rinker Centre for Entrepreneurship and Training (f. 2014), which supports business development, education and lifelong learning; and co-ordinates the activities of the Social Enterprises in Bulgaria Forum (f. 2014).

Geographical Area of Activity: Bulgaria.

Publications: Annual Report; newsletter; reports.

Finance: Total assets 3.3m. lev (31 Dec. 2023).

Board of Directors: Mihail Boyadjiev (Chair.).

Principal Staff: Exec. Dir Elitsa Barakova.

Contact Details: 1000 Sofia, Vitosha Blvd 65, 2nd Floor; tel. (2) 981-19-01; e-mail office@bcause.bg; internet www.bcause.bg.

Black Sea NGO Network—BSNN

Established in 1998, and registered in 1999; a regional association of NGOs from all Black Sea countries.

Activities: Programmes include: regional, national and EU environmental policies; Black Sea issues and policies; international water management issues; Black Sea and international biodiversity protection; Natura 2000 sites; sustainable development; coastal zone management; data collection and management; production of databases of good practices; environmental governance; environmental education; youth involvement; civil society development; stakeholder involvement; advocacy and lobbying. Since 2001 the Network has been an observer at the Black Sea Commission and a member of the European Seas Environmental Cooperation network, co-ordinated by Seas at Risk, working mainly on Marine Strategy Framework Directive issues. It has more than 60 member organizations.

Geographical Area of Activity: Black Sea countries (Bulgaria, Georgia, Romania, Russian Federation, Türkiye—Turkey and Ukraine).

Publications: Newsletter; topical items; regional directories on Bulgaria, Georgia, Romania, Russia, Türkiye and Ukraine; numerous project publications.

Board of Directors: Prof. Dr Oleg Rubel (Chair.).

Principal Staff: Exec. Dir Emma Gileva.

Contact Details: 9000 Varna, POB 91, Dr L. Zamenhof St 2; 9000 Varna, Ivan Drasov St 11; tel. (52) 61-58-56; e-mail bsnn@bsnn.org; internet www.bsnn.org.

Bulgarian Donors' Forum

Established in 2003 by a group of 10 foundations.

Activities: Represents its members and works for the financial sustainability of the Bulgarian non-profit sector, including encouraging new donors. The Forum carries out research, lobbies government and provides information and advice to members and NGOs. It has 21 member foundations and 21 member companies; membership is open to donor organizations that provide annual grants greater than €5,000 and accept the Forum's Code of Ethics. Organizes annual Top Corporate Donor awards. Member of Philea (q.v.).

Geographical Area of Activity: Bulgaria.

Publications: Annual Report; newsletter; *Developing local grantmaking in Bulgaria*.

Finance: Annual income 3.1m. lev, expenditure 3.1m. lev (31 Dec. 2023).

Board of Directors: Tsetska Karadzhova (Chair.).

Principal Staff: CEO Teodora Bakardzhieva.

Contact Details: 1124 Sofia, Leonardo da Vinci St 4в, 2nd Floor; tel. (2) 951-59-78; e-mail info@dfbulgaria.org; internet www.dfbulgaria.org.

Bulgarian Platform for International Development—BPID

Established in 2009 under the TRIALOG project, in co-operation with CONCORD (q.v.) and the Ministry of Foreign Affairs, to facilitate dialogue between the EU and the global South.

Activities: Works in the fields of development co-operation, global education and the UN Sustainable Development Goals, through preparing policy documents and making recommendations. The Platform comprises 16 social justice NGOs. It is a member of CONCORD (q.v.).

Geographical Area of Activity: Bulgaria.

Publications: Newsletter; handbook; online educational resources.

Board of Directors: Petranka Fileva (Chair.).

Principal Staff: CEO Petar Buchkov.

Contact Details: 1000 Sofia, Tsar Simeon Str. 37, First Floor; tel. 878-910-075; e-mail office@bpid.bg; internet bpid.eu.

BULGARIA   *Open Society Institute*

FOUNDATIONS AND NON-PROFITS

America for Bulgaria Foundation
Established in 2009 as successor to the Bulgarian-American Enterprise Fund (f. 1991).
Activities: Promotes the development of economic prosperity and democracy through free market capitalism, legal justice and civic participation. Main programme areas are: business entrepreneurship, business skills, technology and innovation; cultural heritage and tourism; enabling business through improved legislation and regulation, government transparency and civic engagement; and focusing education on science, technology, engineering, English, and mathematics for future jobs. The Foundation administers the Borgatti Scholarship Fund for Bulgarian students at the American University in Bulgaria. Grants for the Economically Disadvantaged programme are administered by the Trust for Social Achievement (q.v.).
Geographical Area of Activity: Bulgaria, USA.
Restrictions: Does not fund political or exclusively religious activities; no grants to individuals.
Publications: Annual Report; newsletter.
Finance: Annual income US $67.3m., expenditure $39.3m. (31 Dec. 2023).
Board of Directors: Gail Buyske (Chair.).
Principal Staff: Pres. and CEO Nancy L. Schiller.
Contact Details: 1000 Sofia, Malyovica St 6; tel. (2) 806-38-00; e-mail ABF@us4bg.org; internet www.us4bg.org.

Bulgarian Fund for Women
Established in 2004 by the Gender Project for Bulgaria Foundation.
Activities: Funds projects in the areas of: political and economic empowerment of women and girls; elimination of violence against women; work with children and young people to overcome gender stereotypes; and empowering groups of women who experience multiple forms of discrimination. The Fund works to improve the quality of services provided by trainers, consultants and facilitators who work with NGOs on gender equality; and participates in international networks of women's funds.
Geographical Area of Activity: Bulgaria.
Publications: Annual Report; reports.
Finance: Annual income 1.1m. lev (2020).
Principal Staff: Co-Dirs Nadejda Dermendjieva, Gergana Kutseva.
Contact Details: 1000 Sofia, Solunska St 26; tel. (2) 426-92-02; e-mail office@bgfundforwomen.org; internet bgfundforwomen.org.

Elizabeth Kostova Foundation for Creative Writing
Established in 2007 by Elizabeth Kostova, a US author.
Activities: Supports creative writing in Bulgaria, especially in the field of translation. The Foundation offers the Krastan Dyankov Translation Award for translation from English into Bulgarian; and fellowships for Bulgarian literary translators working from Bulgarian into English. It organizes creative writing workshops, and public readings and lectures on literature; and runs a contest for contemporary Bulgarian writers and translators. A sister foundation operates in the USA.
Geographical Area of Activity: Bulgaria, UK, USA.
Publications: Lectures.
Board of Directors, Bulgaria: Milena Dileva (Chair.).
Board of Directors, USA: Elizabeth Kostova (Chair. and Pres.).
Principal Staff: Man. Dir Violeta Radkova.
Contact Details: 1510 Sofia, Vasil Petleshkov Str. 75; tel. (2) 988-81-88; e-mail info@ekf.bg; internet ekf.bg.

Evrika Foundation (Eureka Foundation)
Founded in 1990 to encourage and educate young people in the fields of science, economics, technology and management.
Activities: Operates nationally and internationally in the fields of economic and international affairs, education, medicine and health, and science and technology, through self-conducted programmes, grants to individuals and institutions, scholarships and fellowships, and conferences. The Foundation supports the education of talented young people; works towards implementing scientific and technological ideas and projects; provides equipment and material for creative work; and encourages international co-operation in the fields of science, technology and management. It organizes events; provides financial support for scientific research undertaken by talented young scholars; offers awards for young inventors, managers and farmers; and provides credit and loans to young inventors. In 2024/25 it awarded 44 scholarships, each worth up to 3,000 lev, to university and high school students.
Geographical Area of Activity: Bulgaria.
Restrictions: Supports young people up to the age of 35 years.
Publications: Annual Report; *EVRIKA* (monthly bulletin); *Computer* (magazine); *Do-it-Yourself* (magazine).
Finance: Annual revenue 556,779 lev (2024).
Governing Council: Kiril Boyanov (Chair.); Vasil Velev, Georgi Ivanov, Yachko Ivanov (Vice-Chair.).
Principal Staff: Exec. Dir Grigor Tzankov.
Contact Details: 1000 Sofia, Patriarch Evtimiy Blvd 1; tel. (2) 981-51-81; e-mail office@evrika.org; internet www.evrika.org.

Fondacija Cennosti (Values Foundation)
Founded in 1998 by Antonina Stoyanova, former First Lady of Bulgaria.
Activities: Promotes and supports the development of Bulgarian science, education and culture, collaborating with other Bulgarian organizations. The Foundation promotes European cultural values, while also preserving Bulgarian cultural values and diversity. It organizes projects on social integration and communication; and on education, awarding prizes and promoting exchanges between young people from European countries.
Geographical Area of Activity: Bulgaria.
Publications: *National History Competition* (biennial).
Principal Staff: Project Manager Ralitza Panteva.
Contact Details: 1000 Sofia, POB 1302, ul. 6th September 34; tel. (2) 988-12-04; e-mail foundationvalues@gmail.com; internet www.values.bg.

National Trust EcoFund
Established in 1995.
Activities: Operates in field of conservation and the environment. Main programmes focus on: climate microprogrammes; climate action education and training of trainers; climate mitigation and adaptation; electric cars; energy efficiency; and hydrothermal energy. The Fund offers annual Mimi Pramatarova Awards, ranging between 300 lev and 1,000 lev, for school projects on climate change.
Geographical Area of Activity: Bulgaria.
Publications: Annual Reports; newsletter.
Finance: Total assets 34.1m. lev (31 Dec. 2024).
Board of Directors: Penka Mollova-Smolenova (Chair.); Nikolay Kanchev, Nikola Malinovski (Deputy Chair.).
Principal Staff: Acting Exec. Dir Irena Pencheva.
Contact Details: 1574 Sofia, Shipchenski Prohod Blvd 67B; tel. (2) 973-36-37; e-mail ecofund@ecofund-bg.org; internet ecofund-bg.org.

Open Society Institute—Sofia
Founded in 1990; an independent foundation.

Activities: Works in the fields of democracy, the rule of law and human rights, European integration and regional co-operation. Main programmes areas are: European policies and civic participation; governance and public policies; law and justice; public debate; and Roma inclusion. The Institute is part of a consortium with the Workshop for Civic Initiatives Foundation and the Trust for Social Achievement Foundation (q.v.) that manages the Active Citizens Fund Bulgaria.

Geographical Area of Activity: Bulgaria; Western Balkans; EU.

Publications: Annual Report; The Catch Up Index (online); Media Literacy Index (online); data sets; reports.

Finance: Annual revenue €1.5m., expenditure €1.7m. (2023).

Board of Trustees: Pepka Boyadjieva (Chair.).

Principal Staff: Exec. Dir Georgi Stoytchev.

Contact Details: 1000 Sofia, Solunska St 56; tel. (2) 930-66-19; e-mail info@osi.bg; internet osis.bg.

Saint Cyril and Saint Methodius International Foundation

Founded in 1982 as the Lyudmila Zhivkova International Foundation.

Activities: Preserves and promotes the spiritual heritage of St Cyril and St Methodius. The Foundation encourages the creative and educational development of young people, and assists in the integration of Bulgaria into Europe and the world. It operates internationally in the fields of science, the arts and humanities and cultural education; arranges cultural and educational exchanges; promotes cultural and scientific exchange, international understanding and the creative development of young people; awards prizes and scholarships; and organizes conferences and exhibitions.

Geographical Area of Activity: International.

Publications: Annual Report; brochure.

Executive Committee: Prof. Stefan Stefanov (Pres.); Prof. Svetlin Russev, Boyko Vassilev, Dr Rumen Hristov, Prof. Alexander Fedotov (Vice-Pres).

Principal Staff: CEO Mikhail Tachev.

Contact Details: 1784 Sofia, Tsarigradsko Shose Blvd 113A; tel. (2) 943-41-85; e-mail cmfnd@cmfnd.org; internet www.cmfnd.org.

Trust for Social Achievement

Established in 2012.

Activities: Works to improve the educational and economic prospects of disadvantaged people, in particular Roma. Programme areas include: basic literacy skills for Roma youth; early childhood development; education for children aged 2–8 years; employment and entrepreneurship; family nurse visits; housing; and job skills and support for family businesses. The Trust offers coaching and mentoring and scholarships for participants in leadership programmes; and organizes conferences and training events. It also offers volunteering opportunities.

Geographical Area of Activity: Bulgaria.

Restrictions: Does not accept unsolicited applications.

Publications: Annual Report; handbooks; studies.

Finance: Annual revenue 6.2m. lev, expenditure 6.2m. lev (31 Dec. 2023).

Board of Directors: Jenna O'Keefe (Chair.).

Principal Staff: CEO Sarah Perrin.

Contact Details: 1000 Sofia, Patriarch Evtimiy Blvd 64; tel. (2) 424-66-80; e-mail info@tsa-bulgaria.org; internet socialachievement.org.

BURKINA FASO

FOUNDATIONS AND NON-PROFITS

CENOZO—Cellule Norbert Zongo pour le Journalisme d'Investigation en Afrique de l'Ouest (Norbert Zongo Cell for Investigative Journalism in West Africa)

Established in 2015 by the UN Office on Drugs and Crime and the Norbert Zongo National Press Centre; named in memory of Norbert Zongo (Henri Segbo), a Burkinabé investigative journalist killed in 1998.

Activities: Works to strengthen regional investigative journalism, with a focus on investigating transnational organized crime. The organization trains local journalists in data journalism and investigative techniques; carries out investigations; and collaborates with civil society. It offers training, mentoring and networking opportunities; and provides grants, scholarships, legal advice and technical support for investigations and a publication platform. Comprises a network of more than 50 journalists.

Geographical Area of Activity: West Africa.

Publications: Newsletter.

Board of Directors: David Dembélé (Pres.); Anas Aremeyaw Anas (Vice-Pres.); Sandrine Sawadogo (Gen. Sec.); Abdoulaye Diallo (Treas.).

Contact Details: Centre National de Presse Norbert Zongo (CNP-NZ), rue 9.113, Petit Paris, 04 BP 8524 Ouagadougou; tel. 50-34-41-89; e-mail contact@cenozo.org; internet cenozo.org.

Fondation Internationale Tierno et Mariam—FITIMA

Established in 2003 by Hawa Dramé, a biochemist and geneticist; comprises the West Africa Network for Myopathic Care—ROAMY (f. 2009) and the Club des Amis de FITIMA Guinée—CAFIT (f. 2014).

Activities: Supports human rights and the protection of women and children. Programmes focus on improving the lives of children and young people with disabilities; and promoting women's rights and autonomy, through training, awareness raising and developing income generating activities. The Foundation has centres in France (f. 2005) and Guinea (f. 2010).

Geographical Area of Activity: Burkina Faso, France, Guinea.

Publications: Annual Report; newsletter.

Principal Staff: Co-ordinator Aminata Diallo.

Contact Details: 11 BP 1189 CMS, Ouagadougou 11; tel. 25-37-49-56; e-mail fitima.burkina@fitima.org; internet www.fitima.org.

Fondation Jean-Paul II pour le Sahel (John Paul II Foundation for the Sahel)

Established in 1984 by Pope John Paul II.

Activities: Works in the fields of technical, social health, agricultural, socioeconomic and ecological development, supporting the training of local leaders to carry out micro-projects. Priority areas are combating desertification, supporting Sahelian peoples' autonomy, and contributing to peace and development.

CABO VERDE

Geographical Area of Activity: Sahel region (Burkina Faso, Cabo Verde, Chad, The Gambia, Guinea-Bissau, Mali, Mauritania, Niger, Senegal).

Restrictions: Grants made only within the nine Sahelian countries.

Finance: Receives donations from Catholics in Germany and Italy, through their Episcopal conferences. Total annual grants approx. US $3.5m.

Principal Staff: Pres. Cardinal Michael Czerny.

Contact Details: rue 28.43, Dassasgo, Ouagadougou; tel. 25-36-53-14; e-mail contact@fondationjp2sahel.org; internet www.fondationjp2sahel.org.

Fondation Orange Burkina Faso

Established in 2017.

Activities: Supports human development through initiatives in the areas of education, health and culture, in particular providing access to treatment for kidney-related illnesses and science education. The Foundation has set up several nephrology and haemodialysis units; and built and equipped 13 science-focused secondary schools around the country. In 2021 it established the Orange Digital Centre to strengthen youth employability, entrepreneurship and digital innovation. The Centre incorporates a computer coding school, a Solidarity FabLab digital manufacturing workshop, a start-up accelerator and support from the Orange Ventures Africa investment fund.

Geographical Area of Activity: Burkina Faso.

Finance: Initial endowment 400m. CFA francs.

Principal Staff: Sec.-Gen. Ibrahim Héma.

Contact Details: BP 6622, Ouagadougou 01; 771 ave du Président Aboubacar Sangoulé Lamizana, Ouagadougou; tel. 25-33-14-00; internet www.orange.bf/fr/fondation-orange.html.

IFRISSE Burkina

Established in 2015 as the Institute for Interdisciplinary Training and Research in Health and Education Sciences.

Activities: Works in the fields of health, education and technology through offering vocational training, undergraduate and postgraduate programmes and short courses; carrying out applied research; and providing expertise in the development of health and education services in Burkina Faso and across Africa. The Institute organizes conferences and maintains an online library.

Geographical Area of Activity: Burkina Faso.

Publications: Leaflets; dissertations.

Principal Staff: Gen. Man. Dr Dieudonné Soubeiga.

Contact Details: 09 BF 311, Ouagadougou 09; tel. 70-35-02-30; e-mail info@ifris-bf.org; internet www.ifris-bf.org.

BURUNDI

FOUNDATIONS AND NON-PROFITS

Fondation Stamm

Founded in 1999 by Verena Stamm, a trained nurse who was awarded the Order of Merit of the Federal Republic of Germany in 2017 for her work with the Foundation.

Activities: Fondation Stamm supports vulnerable populations in Burundi, including street children, former child soldiers, orphans, survivors of sexual violence, refugees, and socially excluded groups. Our work focuses on three key areas: protecting children's rights; ensuring access to quality education and healthcare for all; and promoting sustainable development that respects and protects the environment. Also provides education and vocational training opportunities, as well as microcredit to support local livelihoods. Programmes span 10 provinces in Burundi, working closely with communities to create lasting impact.

Geographical Area of Activity: Burundi.

Publications: Annual Reports.

Trustees: Verena Marion Stamm (Chair.); Daphné Ndorimana (Vice-Chair.); Doline Nyagatoma (Treas.); Béatrice Ndihobwayo (Sec.).

Principal Staff: Dir Verena Marion Stamm.

Contact Details: 5 ave Nyanza-Lac, quartier Asiatique, BP 2432, Bujumbura; tel. 22226138; e-mail info@fondation-stamm.org; internet www.fondation-stamm.org.

Tujenge Africa Foundation

Established in 2016 by Wendell Adjetey and Etienne Mashuli; registered in the USA.

Activities: Builds capacity among marginalized people, with a focus on education, dialogue and economic empowerment. The Foundation's main initiative is the 18-month Tujenge Scholars Program, providing college-level education and training in mathematics, English and leadership skills.

Geographical Area of Activity: Great Lakes Region.

Restrictions: Scholarship recipients must work in Burundi for at least two years after graduating from university.

Publications: Newsletter (quarterly).

Board: Stephen Peel (Chair.).

Principal Staff: Exec. Dir Etienne Mashuli.

Contact Details: Gihosha, 4 ave du Développement, Bujumbura; tel. 22279875; e-mail info@tujenge.org; internet www.tujenge.org.

CABO VERDE

FOUNDATIONS AND NON-PROFITS

Fundação Caboverdiana de Acção Social Escolar—FICASE (Cape Verdean Student Welfare Foundation)

Established in 2010 as a public foundation with administrative and financial autonomy; it assumed the responsibilities of the Cape Verdean Institute for Social Education (ICASE), the Education and Training Fund (FAEF) and the Independent Fund for Textbook Publishing (FAEME).

Activities: Promotes equality of opportunity in teaching and learning. Programmes include: providing school meals and building school canteens; arranging transport for students who live in remote locations; providing student accommodation; the National School Health Programme and child and adolescent health promotion; distributing school kits to 30,000 students annually; and funding the publication of textbooks and learning materials for primary and secondary education. The Foundation also administers grants and scholarships for secondary and tertiary education, postgraduate study, international exchanges and professional training.

Geographical Area of Activity: Cabo Verde.

Board of Directors: Dr Albertino Fernandes (Chair.).

Principal Staff: Exec. Admin. Dr Cristina Pina.

Fundação José Maria Neves para a Governança

Contact Details: Edif. Achada Santo António, next to the TCV, Achada Santo António CP 21A, Praia; tel. 2621545; e-mail info@ficase.gov.cv; internet www.ficase.cv.

Fundação José Maria Neves para a Governança (José Maria Neves Foundation for Governance)
Established in 2017 by former Prime Minister José Maria Pereira Neves.
Activities: Promotes democracy and the rule of law, good governance, effective public policy and the sustainable development of small island states, in particular Cabo Verde. Activities include capacity building and initiatives in the areas of climate change and environmental conservation, including support for the development of clean energy technologies. The Foundation carries out research and organizes debates, conferences and seminars.
Geographical Area of Activity: Cabo Verde.
Publications: Reports.
Principal Staff: Pres. José Maria Pereira Neves.
Contact Details: Av. OUA, Condomínio Comunidades, Bloco B, 4° andar, Apt. 11, Achada, Praia; tel. 2638814; e-mail fundacaojmn@gmail.com.

CAMBODIA

CO-ORDINATING BODY

Cooperation Committee for Cambodia—CCC (Comité de Coopération Pour le Cambodge)
Established in 1990; a professional association of NGOs.
Activities: Promotes the development of civil society in Cambodia. Strengthens co-operation and professionalism, accountability and good governance, and development effectiveness; maintains databases on NGOs and community-based organizations in Cambodia. Comprises 189 national and international non-governmental and civil society organizations.
Geographical Area of Activity: Cambodia.
Publications: Annual Report; e-newsletter; directories; guidelines; reports; research findings.
Executive Committee: Keng Bunchhoeuth (Chair.); Tum Vira (Treas.).
Principal Staff: Exec. Dir Putheary Sin.
Contact Details: House 9–11, St 476, Toul Tompung I, Phnom Penh; tel. (23) 214152; e-mail info@ccc-cambodia.org; internet www.ccc-cambodia.org.

FOUNDATIONS AND NON-PROFITS

Cambodia Development Resource Institute—CDRI
Established in 1990 by Eva Mysliwiec as an autonomous training and research institute.
Activities: Carries out policy research and provides training and capacity building to support macroeconomic management, development planning and aid management. Programmes areas include: agriculture, economics, education, the environment, governance and health. The Institute organizes the Cambodia Education Research Forum and co-ordinates the Cambodia Development Research Forum; offers research fellowships and internships for national and international graduates and young professionals; and has a public library containing more than 20,000 titles.
Geographical Area of Activity: South-East Asia.
Publications: Annual Report; newsletter; policy briefs; working papers.
Board of Directors: Dr Chea Serey (Chair.).
Principal Staff: Exec. Dir Netra Eng.
Contact Details: House 56, St 315, Tuol Kork, POB 622, 12152 Phnom Penh; tel. (23) 881701; e-mail cdri@cdri.org.kh; internet cdri.org.kh.

Don Bosco Foundation of Cambodia—DBFC
Established in 1991 by the Salesians of Don Bosco, a Roman Catholic religious congregation which had worked in Cambodian refugee camps in Thailand since 1988.
Activities: Focuses on supporting education and training initiatives in Cambodia, in particular helping orphans and vulnerable young people. It has funded the construction of six technical schools in Phnom Penh, Sihanoukville, Battambang, Poipet and Kep; also provides scholarships to young people aged 6–12 years, organizes literacy projects through the Don Bosco Children Fund and the Don Bosco Kep Children Fund, and runs a programme socially to reintegrate young prisoners.
Geographical Area of Activity: Cambodia.
Publications: Vocational technical manuals (in Khmer language).
Finance: International donations from countries including Germany, Italy, the Netherlands, the United Kingdom and the USA.
Principal Staff: Superior of the Cambodia Salesian Delegation Dir Fr Roel Soto; Gen. Sec. Dr Aun Soy.
Contact Details: House No. 203B, Phum Krung Thmey, Sangkat Kok Khleang, Khan Sen Sok, Phnom Penh; tel. 98709933; e-mail sdbdelegate@donboscocambodia.org; internet donboscocambodia.org.

Friends-International
Established in 1994 as Mith Samlanh ('Friends'), a local project helping 'street children'; Mith Samlanh became an affiliated independent national NGO in 1999.
Activities: Supports vulnerable children, young people and their families through providing social services and establishing social businesses. Main programmes include: Friends Alliance, offering drop-in, education and training centres; Saving Lives, providing social, prevention and protection services, including a holistic drug programme and support groups; Building Futures, ensuring sustainable access to education and employment, and preserving families. It also provides employment support to young people and adults through a network of Futures Offices, which offer careers advice, soft skills training, technical training for self-employment and work placements, with access to library and computer resources, and referrals to social services and professional training. Maintains an office in Siam Reap and is registered in France.
Geographical Area of Activity: Cambodia, France, Germany, Indonesia, Lao People's Dem. Repub., Switzerland, Thailand, USA.
Publications: Annual Report; newsletter; research reports; surveys.
Finance: Total income US $7.3m., expenditure $5.6m. (31 Dec. 2021).
Board: Olivier Farhi (Chair.); Olivier Veilhan (Treas.); Wilfried Schneider (Sec.).
Principal Staff: Exec. Dir Sébastien Marot.
Contact Details: House 89B, St 103, Phnom Penh; tel. (23) 986601; e-mail info@friends-international.org; internet friends-international.org.

CAMEROON

FOUNDATIONS AND NON-PROFITS

Fondation Chantal Biya—FCB (Chantal Biya Foundation)

Established in 1994 by First Lady Chantal Biya.

Activities: Works to alleviate poverty, disease and social exclusion in rural and urban areas. The Foundation supports the education, health and social welfare of mothers and their children, abandoned children and the elderly; and provides materials and drugs to hospitals in need. It has established a mother and child centre and a research and information centre on HIV/AIDS. Has special consultative status with ECOSOC.

Geographical Area of Activity: Cameroon.

Principal Staff: Pres. Chantal Biya.

Contact Details: c/o Centre Mère-Enfant de la Fondation Chantal Biya, BP 25121, Yaoundé-Messa; tel. 752432963; e-mail cellcom@prc.cm; internet www.prc.cm/fr/la-premiere-dame/fcb.

Fondation MTN Cameroun (MTN Cameroon Foundation)

Established in 2005 by MTN Cameroun, a telecommunications company; part of the MTN Foundations network.

Activities: Works in the fields of poverty alleviation and sustainable development. Foundation programmes focus on: health, carrying out rural health campaigns, preventing malaria and training hospital staff; local development, providing drinking water and helping young farmers; and education, building, refurbishing and providing equipment to secondary schools and science laboratories, and awarding scholarships to disadvantaged children.

Geographical Area of Activity: Cameroon.

Restrictions: Does not make grants to individuals; for capital projects; or for projects of a political or religious nature.

Principal Staff: Exec. Sec. Jean-Melvin Akam.

Contact Details: 360 rue Drouot, BP 15574, Douala; tel. 679009700; e-mail foundation.cm@mtn.com; internet mtn.cm/fr/foundation.

Fondation Orange Cameroun (Orange Foundation Cameroon)

Established in 2009 by Orange, a telecommunications provider; part of the Fondation Orange (q.v.) network.

Activities: Programmes focus on basic education, numeracy and vocational training; healthcare for mothers and children, and people with visual and hearing impairments, and autism; and culture and social inclusion. Since 2015 the Foundation has built six Orange Villages, renovating and building health facilities and schools, providing drinking water and toilets, and digital centres for women; and 20 'Digital Villages' to promote women's numeracy.

Geographical Area of Activity: Cameroon.

Board of Directors: Frédéric Debord (Chair.).

Principal Staff: Sec.-Gen. Elizabeth Ehabe.

Contact Details: blvd de la Liberté 1864, Douala; tel. 233-41-00-11; e-mail fondationorange.cameroun@orange.com; internet www.orange.cm/fondation.

CANADA

CO-ORDINATING BODIES

CanadaHelps

Established in 2000 by Aaron Pereira, Ryan Little and Matthew Choi; a public foundation and social enterprise.

Activities: Provides information to donors about charities; and technological and administrative services to charities. The organization operates an online giving platform that allows people to make donations to any of the more than 85,000 charities registered in Canada.

Geographical Area of Activity: Canada.

Publications: Annual Report; *The Giving Report*; newsletter; blog.

Finance: Annual revenue C $448.6m., expenditure $447.3m. (30 June 2024).

Board of Directors: Anita Ferrari (Chair.).

Principal Staff: Pres. and CEO Duke Chang.

Contact Details: 30 Adelaide St E, 12th Floor, Toronto, ON M5C 3G8; tel. (416) 628-6948; e-mail info@canadahelps.org; internet canadahelps.org.

Charitable Impact Foundation

Established in 2011 by John Bromley, an expert in charity entrepreneurship; formerly known as CHIMP.

Activities: Promotes charitable giving in Canada and facilitates making gifts to registered charities, operating as a donor-advised fund. The Foundation provides tools and information to help individuals, groups and companies to give to and fundraise for registered charities in Canada. It maintains a database of around 86,000 charities registered in Canada. Has an office in Bengaluru, India.

Geographical Area of Activity: Canada, India.

Publications: Annual Report; newsletter; blog.

Finance: Annual revenue C $247.1m., expenditure $110.3m. (31 July 2024).

Board: Josh Vander Vies (Sec.).

Principal Staff: CEO John Bromley.

Contact Details: 1500 West Georgia St, Suite 1250, Vancouver, BC V6G 2Z6; tel. (877) 531-0580; e-mail hello@charitableimpact.com; internet www.charitableimpact.com.

Community Foundations of Canada

Established in 1992 to act as an umbrella organization for community foundations in Canada.

Activities: Facilitates partnerships between organizations and provides resources to promote effective grantmaking. The network comprises 207 community foundations. It has an office in Toronto.

Geographical Area of Activity: Canada.

Publications: Annual Report; newsletter; factsheets; guidebooks; toolkits.

Finance: Annual revenue C $128.6m., expenditure $127.8m. (31 Dec. 2023).

Board of Directors: Gordon Holley (Chair.); Lisa Kolody (Past Chair.); Neil Parmar (Vice-Chair.).

Principal Staff: CEO Andrew Chunilall; Pres. Andrea Dicks.

Contact Details: 123 Slater St, Suite 600, Ottawa, ON K1P 5H2; tel. (613) 236-2664; e-mail info@communityfoundations.ca; internet www.communityfoundations.ca.

Cooperation Canada/Coopération Canada

Established in 1968 as the Canadian Council for International Cooperation—CCIC/Conseil Canadien pour la Coopération Internationale—CCCI; a coalition of NGOs and CSOs working in international development and humanitarian assistance. Present name adopted in 2021.

Activities: Carries out policy research and analysis in the fields of international development and the humanitarian sector, and overseas development assistance advocacy. The Asia Pacific Working Group and the Africa-Canada Forum bring together diaspora groups, faith-based organizations, labour unions, NGOs, research centres, solidarity groups and think tanks with a specific interest in development, human rights and social justice. The organization also hosts the Humanitarian Response Network, comprising 35 Canadian organizations; and the Emerging Leaders Network for young professionals involved in international development and the civil society community. Annually, it offers the Karen Takacs Award for women's leadership in international development; and jointly with the World University Service of Canada/Entraide Universitaire Mondiale du Canada—WUSC/EUMC (q.v.) and the trustees of the Lewis Perinbam Award offers Innovation and Impact Awards recognizing the work of Canadian individuals and CSOs in international development and/or humanitarian response. Has more than 100 member organizations.

Geographical Area of Activity: Canada.

Publications: Annual Report; newsletter (monthly).

Finance: Annual revenue C $3.1m., expenditure $3.3m. (31 March 2023).

Executive Committee: Eileen Alma, Christine Bui (Co-Chair.).

Principal Staff: CEO Kate Higgins.

Contact Details: 39 McArthur Ave, Ottawa, ON K1L 8L7; tel. (613) 241-7007; e-mail info@cooperation.ca; internet cooperation.ca.

Humanitarian Coalition

Established in 2005; a network of Canadian international aid agencies.

Activities: Co-ordinates among its members, government and the private sector to raise awareness of and funds for humanitarian disasters. The Coalition contributes to the Canadian Humanitarian Assistance Fund, with Global Affairs Canada (the government department of external affairs), to respond to small and medium-scale disasters. Current members are: Action Against Hunger; Canadian Foodgrains Bank (q.v.); Canadian Lutheran World Relief; CARE Canada; Doctors of the World; Humanity & Inclusion (q.v.); Islamic Relief Canada; Oxfam Canada (q.v.); Oxfam-Québec (q.v.); Plan International Canada; Save the Children Canada; and World Vision Canada. Operates in more than 140 countries.

Geographical Area of Activity: International.

Publications: Annual Report; newsletter; reports; factsheets.

Finance: Annual revenue C $43.1m., expenditure $43.2m. (31 Dec. 2023).

Principal Staff: Exec. Dir Richard Morgan.

Contact Details: 39 McArthur Ave, Ottawa, ON K1L 8L7; tel. (613) 239-2154; e-mail info@humanitariancoalition.ca; internet www.humanitariancoalition.ca.

Imagine Canada

Established in 2005 following the merger of the Canadian Centre for Philanthropy and the Coalition of National Voluntary Organizations.

Activities: Assists Canadian charitable and voluntary organizations through research, public affairs, information products and professional development. The organization researches the charitable and voluntary sector, issues publications, and organizes conferences and seminars. It works through a family of sub-sites, providing statistics and information on giving and volunteering; resources and tools for fund-raising, research and communications; and promotes corporate citizenship and community investment. Has offices in Ottawa and Québec.

Geographical Area of Activity: Canada.

Publications: Annual Report; *Grantseeker* (monthly newsletter); *Sector Monitor*; guides; handbooks; *360°* (blog).

Finance: Annual revenue C $5.1m., expenditure $5.4m. (31 Dec. 2023).

Board of Directors: Pascal Lépine (Chair.); Ninette Bishay (Treas.); Roger D. Ali (Sec.).

Principal Staff: Pres. and CEO Bruce MacDonald.

Contact Details: 2 St Clair Ave East, Suite 300, Toronto, ON M4T 2T5; tel. (416) 597-2293; e-mail info@imaginecanada.ca; internet www.imaginecanada.ca.

Philanthropic Foundations Canada—PFC (Fondations Philanthropiques Canada—FPC)

Established in 1999.

Activities: Promotes effective and responsible grantmaking among Canadian organizations, through providing services and resources to members. The organization comprises 134 member grantmakers. Has an office in Toronto.

Geographical Area of Activity: Canada.

Publications: Annual Report; briefs; guides; tools.

Finance: Annual revenue C $1.6m., expenditure $1.5m. (31 Dec. 2023).

Board: Simon Mallett (Chair.); Ina Gutium (Vice-Chair.); Amanda Mayer (Treas.); Cameron Miller (Sec.).

Principal Staff: Pres. and CEO Jean-Marc Mangin.

Contact Details: c/o Philanthropy House, 1095 St-Alexandre, Montréal, QC H2Z 1P8; tel. (514) 866-5446; e-mail info@pfc.ca; internet www.pfc.ca.

Rethink Charity

Established in 2014 as .impact; an umbrella body incorporating organizations including Rethink Charity USA and the Students for High-Impact Charity Foundation of Canada, with support from Effective Altruism UK. Present name adopted in 2017. In 2022 focus was turned to primarily the RC Forward platform.

Activities: The main project is RC Forward, an online platform that helps Canadian donors fund high-impact charities located inside and outside of Canada.

Geographical Area of Activity: International.

Publications: Annual Report; *Effective Altruism Survey* (annual); *Effective Altruism Newsletter* (with the Centre for Effective Altruism q.v.).

Finance: Annual revenue C $222,738, expenditure $2.7m. (31 Dec. 2023).

Principal Staff: Exec. Dir SK OwYong.

Contact Details: 997 Seymour St, Suite 250 #1338, Vancouver, BC V6B 3M1; e-mail donations@rethinkprojects.org; internet rethink.charity; rcforward.org.

FOUNDATIONS AND NON-PROFITS

Aga Khan Foundation Canada

Established in 1980 by HH Prince Karim Aga Khan; part of the Aga Khan Development Network (AKDN, q.v.).

Activities: Works to address the root causes of poverty and to improve the quality of life for poor communities through: building self-reliance; investing in the long term; working in partnership; fostering gender equality; and promoting pluralism. Main programme areas include: providing access to education and healthcare; ensuring food security; improving economic wellbeing; and developing resilient communities and societies. The Foundation annually offers 10–25 International Youth Fellowships to recent university graduates and young professionals to spend nine months working with AKDN agencies or partners in one of three streams: International Development Management; International Microfinance and Microenterprise; or Young Professionals in Media. It currently operates in 15 countries.

Geographical Area of Activity: Canada, Central Asia, Middle East and North Africa, South Asia, sub-Saharan Africa.

Restrictions: Youth Fellowships are open to Canadian citizens or residents of Canada aged 18–30 years.

Publications: Annual Report; newsletter; campaign reports.

Finance: Annual revenue C $100.6m., expenditure $111.7m. (31 Dec. 2023).

National Committee: Noordin Nanji (Chair.); Natasha Walji (Vice-Chair.).

Principal Staff: CEO Khalil Z. Shariff.

Contact Details: The Delegation of the Ismaili Imamat, 199 Sussex Dr., Ottawa, ON K1N 1K6; tel. (613) 237-2532; e-mail akfc.info@akdn.org; internet www.akfc.ca.

Alongside Hope/Auprès de l'espoir

Established in 1958 by the General Synod of the Anglican Church of Canada as the official relief and development agency of the Anglican Church of Canada. Formerly known as Primate's World Relief and Development Fund/Le Fonds du Primat Pour le Secours et le Développement Mondial—PWRDF; current name adopted in 2024. Member of the ACT Alliance (q.v.).

Activities: Works in the fields of international development and humanitarian response through advancing sustainable development, responding to emergencies and helping refugees. The Fund helps local partners in developing countries to provide long-term solutions to the causes of suffering and disaster. A percentage of funds is reserved for work with Canada's Indigenous peoples for land claims, self-determination and Aboriginal rights.

Geographical Area of Activity: International.

Publications: Annual Report; newsletter (monthly); *Under the Sun* (three times a year).

Finance: Total revenue C $8.9m., expenditure $8.9m. (31 March 2024).

Board of Directors: Mark Hauck (Pres.); Dr Lillian Scorrar-Olsen (Vice-Pres.); Shailene Caparas (Treas.); Rev. Barr Huether (Sec.).

Principal Staff: Exec. Dir Will Postma.

Contact Details: 80 Hayden St, Toronto, ON M4Y 3G2; tel. (416) 924-9199; e-mail info@alongsidehope.org; internet alongsidehope.org.

The Alva Foundation

Established in 1965.

Activities: Works in the fields of childhood development and the environment. The Foundation funds organizations that support children and young people aged 0–17 years, offering single-year grants worth up to C $50,000 and multi-year grants of $30,000 per year.

Geographical Area of Activity: Canada.

Restrictions: No grants to individuals.

Finance: Annual revenue C $1.1m., expenditure $627,142 (31 Dec. 2023).

Board of Directors: Alison Vilaca (Pres.); Matthew Holden (Treas.); Andrew McMartin (Sec.).

Contact Details: 138 Mainprize Cres., Mount Albert, ON L0G 1M0; e-mail info@alva.ca; internet alvafoundation.wordpress.com.

Arctic Institute of North America—AINA (Institut Arctique de l'Amérique du Nord—IAAN)

Founded in 1945 by an Act of Parliament in Canada and incorporated concurrently in the USA under the laws of the state of New York; the Canadian Corporation became an integral part of the University of Calgary in 1979.

Activities: Advances the study of Arctic and sub-Arctic conditions and problems. The Institute works in the fields of the physical, natural and social sciences and the humanities, mainly concerned with the North, but also Antarctica and Alpine environments. The Institute administers a small grants fund to assist student researchers on field projects, makes travel awards to enable researchers to travel to conferences, and awards scholarships. Maintains a library and an automated bibliographic database, the Arctic Science and Technology Information System.

Geographical Area of Activity: Canada, Greenland, USA (Alaska).

Restrictions: Not accepting applications for Fellows.

Publications: Annual Report; *ARCTIC* (quarterly journal); *Northern Lights* (book series); *Komatik* (book series); research papers; technical papers; monographs; occasional publications.

Finance: Annual revenue C $309,831, expenditure $97,924 (31 March 2020).

Board of Directors: George Lidgett (Chair.).

Principal Staff: Exec. Dir Maribeth Murray.

Contact Details: University of Calgary, 2500 University Dr. NW, ES-1040 Calgary, AB T2N 1N4; tel. (403) 220-7515; e-mail arctic@ucalgary.ca; internet arctic.ucalgary.ca.

Asia Pacific Foundation of Canada—APFCanada

Founded in 1984.

Activities: Hosts the Asia-Pacific Economic Co-operation (APEC) Study Centre in Canada, which promotes collaborative research and disseminates information. Thematic areas include: digital technologies; domestic networks; education and study abroad; surveys and polling; sustainable development; regional security; and trade and investment. The Foundation acts as the secretariat for the Asia Pacific Business Network, the Pacific Economic Co-operation Council, the Pacific Basin Economic Council and the APEC Business Advisory Council. In partnership with the Federal Government, it is developing a network of Canadian Education Centres in Asian cities, including Seoul, Taipei, Kuala Lumpur, Jakarta, Bangkok, Singapore, Hong Kong and New Delhi; and also has offices in Québec. The Grants Program offers postgraduate research, distinguished and media fellowships; and the John H. McArthur Distinguished Fellowship.

Geographical Area of Activity: Asia-Pacific, Canada.

Publications: Annual Report; *Asia Watch* (newsletter); *Canada/Asia Review; Canada Asia Commentary*; case studies; dispatches; policy briefs; research reports; surveys.

Finance: Annual revenue C $5.2m., expenditure $7.5m. (31 March 2024).

Board of Directors: Pierre Pettigrew (Chair.).

Principal Staff: Pres. and CEO Jeff Nankivell.

Contact Details: 680-1066 West Hastings St, Vancouver, BC V6E 3X2; tel. (604) 684-5986; e-mail info@asiapacific.ca; internet www.asiapacific.ca.

Calgary Foundation

Founded in 1955.

Activities: Helps connect community organizations and donors to develop philanthropic activity in Calgary and the surrounding area. Key priorities include mental health, poverty reduction, sustainability and strengthening relations with indigenous communities.
Publications: Annual Report; impact reports; *spur* magazine; Quality of Life report.
Finance: Total assets C $1,424.5m. (31 March 2024).
Board: Blaine Lennox (Chair.); Narmin Ismail-Teja (Vice-Chair.).
Principal Staff: Pres. and CEO Eva Friesen.
Contact Details: 1180–105 12 Ave SE, Calgary, AB T2G 1A1; tel. (403) 802-7700; e-mail info@calgaryfoundation.org; internet calgaryfoundation.org.

The Canada Council for the Arts/Conseil des Arts du Canada

Created in 1957 by the Parliament of Canada as an independent agency.
Activities: Fosters and promotes Canadian and Indigenous art in Canada and abroad through offering grants to artists, art groups and organizations. The Council's Art Bank rents contemporary Canadian art to the public and private sectors in Canada. The Council maintains the secretariat for the Canadian Commission for UNESCO; administers the Killam Program of research prizes and fellowships; and operates a range of targeted funds. Through the Public Lending Right Commission, it administers payments to Canadian writers for their books held in Canadian libraries.
Geographical Area of Activity: International.
Publications: Annual Report.
Finance: Funded by and reports to Parliament through the Minister of Canadian Heritage; its annual appropriation from Parliament is supplemented by endowment income, donations and bequests. Annual revenue C $399.3m., expenditure $388.0m. (31 March 2024).
Board of Directors: Jesse Wente (Chair.); Marie Pier Germain (Vice-Chair.).
Principal Staff: Dir and CEO Michelle Chawla.
Contact Details: 150 Elgin St, 2nd Floor, Ottawa, ON K2P 1L4; POB 1047, Ottawa, ON K1P 5V8; tel. (613) 566-4414; e-mail info@canadacouncil.ca; internet www.canadacouncil.ca.

Canada Foundation for Innovation (Fondation Canadienne pour l'Innovation)

Established in 1997 by the Federal Government.
Activities: Invests in research infrastructure to encourage innovation in universities, colleges, hospitals and other non-profit institutions, including funding the acquisition of state-of-the-art equipment, buildings, laboratories and databases required to conduct research, in particular in the Arctic and marine environments. The Foundation promotes the training of young Canadians for research and other careers; attracts and retains able research workers; and works to ensure the best results in innovation by promoting the sharing of information and resources among institutions. It also occasionally launches calls for proposals for international research projects.
Geographical Area of Activity: International.
Publications: Annual Report; newsletter; reports; blog.
Finance: Annual revenue C $511.9m., expenditure $511.9m. (31 March 2024).
Members: Sophie Bouffard, Joanne Gassman (Co-Chair.).
Board of Directors: Nancy Déziel (Chair.); Dr Cecilia Moloney (Vice-Chair.).
Principal Staff: Pres. and CEO Sylvain Charbonneau.
Contact Details: 55 Metcalfe St, Suite 1100, Ottawa, ON K1P 6L5; tel. (613) 947-6496; e-mail info@innovation.ca; internet www.innovation.ca.

Canadian Cancer Society

Founded in 1938; from 1947 the Society also funded research through its research partner, the National Cancer Institute of Canada, and more recently through the Canadian Cancer Society Research Institute.
Activities: A national, community-based organization of volunteers working to eliminate cancer and enhance the quality of life of people living with cancer. The Society funds and carries out research on all types of cancer; provides information about cancer care and treatment; supports people living with cancer; promotes healthy lifestyles and strategies for reducing cancer risk; and advocates public policies to prevent cancer and to help those affected by it. It offers a range of grants and awards to researchers.
Geographical Area of Activity: Canada.
Publications: Annual Report; newsletter; information on specific cancers, treatment, risk reduction, supportive care and tobacco control.
Finance: Annual revenue C $181.1m., expenditure $165.8m. (31 Jan. 2024).
Board of Directors: Robert Lawrie (Chair.).
Principal Staff: CEO Andrea Seale.
Contact Details: 55 St Clair Ave West, Suite 500, Toronto, ON M4V 2Y7; tel. (416) 961-7223; e-mail connect@cancer.ca; internet www.cancer.ca.

Canadian Feed The Children—CFTC

Established in 1986.
Activities: Works with local partners to support food security, poverty alleviation and children's education programmes. Programmes focus on: early childhood education and care, nutrition, and children and young people's rights in Bolivia; community-led food security among 26 Indigenous communities in Canada; agricultural training, self-help groups, early childhood care and education, alternative basic education and improved livelihoods in Ethiopia; sustainable agriculture, women's empowerment, children's education and income generation in Ghana; and school feeding, women and children at risk, agricultural training, microfinance, and early childhood and primary education in Uganda. The organization has offices in Ottawa and Winnipeg.
Geographical Area of Activity: Bolivia, Canada, Ethiopia, Ghana, Uganda.
Restrictions: Does not make grants.
Publications: Annual Report; Impact Report (annual); *Thrive!* (semi-annual magazine); *Childhood* (monthly newsletter); *Dream Season* (comic); *The Feed* (blog).
Finance: Annual income C $9.2m., expenditure $9.1m. (31 Dec. 2023).
Board of Directors: Marion Mackenzie (Chair.); Clare Ashbee (Immediate Past Chair.); Tony Malfara (Vice-Chair. and Treas.).
Principal Staff: Pres. and CEO Jacquelyn Wright.
Contact Details: 2 Lansing Sq., Suite 901, Toronto, ON M2J 4P8; tel. (416) 757-1220; e-mail contact@canadianfeedthechildren.ca; internet www.canadianfeedthechildren.ca.

Canadian Foodgrains Bank

Established in 1983 as a way for Christian international development agencies to work together to combat global hunger. From the begining, Canadian Foodgrains Bank has been strongly supported by farmers across Canada.
Activities: Operates in partnership with 15 Canadian churches and church-based organizations, representing more than 12,000 congregations. The Bank collects contributions in the form of money and agricultural produce including grains, to distribute them to hunger victims in developing countries. Other activities include: providing services and advice on food programming and related aspects; encouraging policy development; and educating people about hunger and food security. Operates in 37 countries; has an office in Ottawa.

Geographical Area of Activity: International.
Publications: Annual Report; *Table Talk* (newsletter, 6 a year); reports.
Finance: Annual revenue C $85.1m., expenditure $83.2m. (31 March 2024).
Board of Directors: Afua Adobea Mante (Vice-Chair.); Pamela Wilson McCormick (Treas.); Justine Shenher (Sec.).
Principal Staff: Exec. Dir Andy Harrington.
Contact Details: POB 767, Winnipeg, MB R3C 2L4; 400-393 Portage Ave, Winnipeg, MB R3B 3H6; tel. (204) 944-1993; e-mail cfgb@foodgrainsbank.ca; internet www.foodgrainsbank.ca.

Canadian International Council/Conseil International du Canada—CIC

Founded in 1928 as the Canadian Institute of International Affairs; a membership organization.
Activities: Carries out policy-relevant research on critical international issues and complex problems, such as threats from non-state actors and climate change. The Council organizes briefing missions, conferences, lectures and a publications programme; and offers two-year fellowships to academic and applied researchers. It has 18 branches across Canada. The Young Professionals Network connects members aged under 40 years, providing networking and career development opportunities.
Geographical Area of Activity: Mainly Canada.
Publications: Annual Report; newsletter; *International Journal* (quarterly); *International Security Series*; *International Insights*; *The Signal Board* (blog).
Finance: Annual revenue C $905,207, expenditure $673,008 (30 June 2024).
Board of Directors: William C. Graham (Chair. Emeritus); John English (Chair.); Nicolas M. Rouleau (Vice-Chair.).
Principal Staff: Pres. and Research Dir Ben Rowswell.
Contact Details: Mailing address: 6 Hoskin Ave, Toronto, ON M5S 1H8. Physical address: 15 Devonshire Pl., Rm 210, Toronto, ON M5S 1H8; tel. (416) 946-7209; e-mail info@thecic.org; internet thecic.org.

Canadian Urban Institute/Institut Urbain du Canada—CUI/IUC

Established in 1990 by the Municipality of Metropolitan Toronto and the City of Toronto.
Activities: Works to improve management and policymaking in urban areas, educating government, businesses and other significant institutions about urban issues. The Institute holds conferences and seminars; takes part in applied research and training; produces publications; and identifies emerging social and economic issues that can influence the urban sector in areas of social development, urban infrastructure, sustainability, housing, environment and economic development. It presents the annual Brownie Awards in recognition of leadership, environmental sustainability and innovation; and the Urban Leadership Awards to individuals and organizations that have contributed to the urban environment.
Geographical Area of Activity: International.
Publications: Annual Report; *The Urban Century* (quarterly newsletter); reports; report cards.
Finance: Annual revenue C $4.9m., expenditure $4.9m. (31 Dec. 2023).
Board of Directors: Cameron Charlebois (Chair.); Cynthia Dorrington (Vice-Chair.).
Principal Staff: Pres. and CEO Mary W. Rowe.
Contact Details: 30 St Patrick St, Suite 500, Toronto, ON M5T 3A3; tel. (416) 365-0816; e-mail cui@canurb.org; internet www.canurb.org.

Catalyste+

Founded in 1967 as CESO/SACO—Canadian Executive Service Organization/Service d'Assistance Canadienne aux Organismes; present name adopted in 2022.
Activities: Sends senior-level professional volunteers to work with partners in communities in Canada and overseas. The Organization builds capacity in governance and economic development through the transfer of knowledge and skills by volunteer advisers who work on short-term assignments, normally of two to four weeks' duration. It has an office in Montréal.
Geographical Area of Activity: Canada, Central Asia, South America, Central America and the Caribbean, South-East Asia, sub-Saharan Africa.
Restrictions: Applicants must be Canadian citizens.
Publications: Annual Report; *In Action!* (monthly newsletter); brochures; case studies.
Finance: Annual revenue C $20.7m., expenditure $20.6m. (31 March 2024).
Board of Directors: Darren Schemmer (Chair.).
Principal Staff: CEO and Pres. Wendy Harris.
Contact Details: 700 Bay St, Suite 800, Box 328, Toronto, ON M5G 1Z6; tel. (416) 961-2376; e-mail international@catalysteplus.org; internet www.catalysteplus.org.

CECI—Canadian Centre for International Studies and Co-operation/Centre d'Etudes et de Coopération Internationale

Founded in 1958, as the Centre d'Études Missionnaires, by Fr Jean Bouchard, a Jesuit priest; officially incorporated under its present name in 1968.
Activities: Works to eliminate poverty and exclusion through sustainable development and humanitarian aid. The Centre builds disadvantaged communities' development capacities; and supports gender equality, violence reduction, food security, resilience and adaptation to climate change. It offers international volunteering opportunities.
Geographical Area of Activity: South America, Central America and the Caribbean, South Asia, South-East Asia, sub-Saharan Africa.
Publications: Annual Report; newsletter (quarterly); *Capacity Building: A Manual for NGOs and Field Workers*.
Finance: Annual revenue C $44.1m., expenditure $43.9m. (31 March 2024).
Board of Directors: Marie-Claire Dumas (Pres.); Patricio Scaff (Exec. Vice-Pres.); Ekué Séssi Afanou (Treas.).
Principal Staff: Gen. Dir Philippe Dongier.
Contact Details: 3000 rue Omer-Lavallée, Montréal, QC H1Y 3R8; tel. (514) 875-9911; e-mail info@ceci.ca; internet www.ceci.ca.

Centre for International Governance Innovation—CIGI/Centre pour l'Innovation dans la Gouvernance Internationale

Founded as a not-for-profit institution in 2001 by Jim Balsillie, former co-CEO of Research in Motion (Blackberry).
Activities: CIGI is an independent, non-partisan think tank offering peer-reviewed research and analysis to encourage policy makers to innovate. It has a global network of multidisciplinary researchers and strategic partnerships to provide policy solutions for the digital era with one goal: to improve people's lives everywhere. CIGI's addresses significant global issues at the intersection of technology and international governance and builds upon existing expertise in the areas of security, trade, law and economics.
Geographical Area of Activity: International.
Publications: Annual Report; newsletter; conference reports; essays; papers; policy briefs; policy memos; special reports.
Finance: Annual revenue C $11.8m., expenditure $12.5m. (31 July 2024).

Board of Directors: Jim Balsillie (Chair.); Scott Burk (Treas.).

Principal Staff: Pres. Paul R. Samson.

Contact Details: 67 Erb St West, Waterloo, ON N2L 6C2; tel. (519) 885-2444; e-mail reception@cigionline.org; internet www.cigionline.org.

CNIB Foundation/Fondation INCA

Founded in 1918 as the Canadian National Institute for the Blind (CNIB), in response to the mass blinding caused by the Halifax Explosion (a maritime disaster) and the number of soldiers who suffered vision loss during the First World War.

Activities: CNIB is a non-profit organization that delivers innovative programmes and advocacy that empower people impacted by blindness to fulfill their potential and break down barriers to inclusion. It operates with a network of volunteers, donors and partners across Canada. CNIB programmes are free and available to Canadians who are blind or partially sighted, as well as their families, friends and caregivers.

Geographical Area of Activity: Canada.

Finance: Annual revenue C $100.9m., expenditure $88.1m. (31 March 2024).

National Board of Directors: Robert J. Fenton (Chair.).

Principal Staff: Pres. and CEO Angela Bonfanti.

Contact Details: 1929 Bayview Ave, Toronto, ON M4G 3E8; tel. (416) 486-2500; e-mail info@cnib.ca; internet www.cnib.ca.

Coady Institute

Founded in 1959 by the St Francis Xavier University; named in honour of Rev. Dr Moses Coady, a campaigner for social and economic justice and founder of the Antigonish Movement.

Activities: Works with partners in Canada and the global South to reduce poverty and transform societies by strengthening local economies, building resilient communities, and promoting social accountability and good governance. The Institute provides adult education programmes and carries out research, offering scholarships and Canadian youth fellowships. In 2011 it established the International Centre for Women's leadership; and in 2012, in collaboration with the Canadian Women's Foundation, the Canadian Women's Foundation Leadership Institute for mid-career women working in the charitable and non-profit sectors. The Marie Michael Library supports programmes with a collection of 12,000 books, focusing on social, community and economic development, in particular in countries of the global South.

Geographical Area of Activity: International.

Restrictions: An educational facility, not a grantmaking organization.

Publications: Annual Report; newsletter; reports; manuals; case studies; occasional papers; journal articles and books; conference presentations.

Finance: Annual revenue C $7.9m., expenditure $7.9m. (2024).

Principal Staff: Dir Eileen Alma.

Contact Details: St Francis Xavier University, 4780 Tompkins Lane, POB 5000, Antigonish, NS B2G 2W5; tel. (902) 867-3960; e-mail coady@stfx.ca; internet www.coady.stfx.ca.

CODE—Canadian Organization for Development through Education

Founded in 1959 by Dr Roby Kidd as Books for Developing Countries; present name adopted in 1982.

Activities: Supports literacy and education by distributing books from Canadian and US sources (usually new books from publishers) to countries in the developing world, primarily in Africa, but also to the Caribbean and the Pacific region. The Organization funds training of librarians, writers, illustrators and literacy workers. Comprises the CODE Foundation (f. 1992) and International Book Bank (f. 1987). In collaboration with the Literary Prizes Foundation, it offers Burt Literary Awards for young adult literature.

Geographical Area of Activity: Canada, Ethiopia, Ghana, Kenya, Liberia, Mali, Mozambique, Sierra Leone, Tanzania.

Publications: Annual Report; *The CODE Reader* (newsletter, 2 a year).

Finance: Annual revenue C $11.6m., expenditure $11.7m. (31 March 2024).

Board of Directors: Nathalie O'Neil (Chair.); Bruce Montador (Past Chair.); Pauline Port (Treas.).

Principal Staff: Exec. Dir Janice Ciavaglia.

Contact Details: RPO Bank & Heron, POB 39014, Ottawa, ON K1H 1A1; tel. (613) 232-3569; e-mail info@code.ngo; internet code.ngo.

Co-operative Development Foundation of Canada—CDF

Established in 1947; amalgamated with the Canadian Co-operative Association in 2017.

Activities: Promotes individuals' economic, cultural and social growth; and establishes and grows co-operatives, credit unions and community-based organizations to reduce poverty, build sustainable livelihoods and improve civil society in less-developed countries. Climate resilience and gender equality are cross-cutting priorities in all programmes. The Foundation works closely with Canadian co-operatives and credit unions to channel their knowledge and experience to partner organizations and co-operatives abroad that help communities to fight poverty and create more secure lives through community-owned co-operatives.

Geographical Area of Activity: Africa, Asia, Eastern Europe, Latin America.

Publications: Annual Report; *International Development Digest* (annual); *International Dispatch* (monthly e-newsletter); briefs; research papers and reports; videos.

Finance: Annual revenue C $7.3m., expenditure $7.3m. (31 March 2024).

Board of Directors: Ian McArthur (Chair.).

Principal Staff: Exec. Dir Ben André.

Contact Details: 350 Sparks St, Suite 906, Ottawa, ON K1R 7S8; tel. (613) 238-6711; e-mail info@cdfcanada.coop; internet www.cdfcanada.coop.

CPAR—Canadian Physicians for Aid and Relief

Established in 1984 in response to famine and poor health conditions suffered by Ethiopian refugees in Sudan.

Activities: Works to overcome poverty and build healthy communities for vulnerable people. The organization supports community efforts to address the determinants of health by ensuring sustainable access to clean water and adequate food, improving hygiene, sanitation and access to primary healthcare. Cross-cutting elements in all its programmes are: gender; people living with HIV; and the environment. Has offices in Ethiopia, Malawi and Tanzania.

Geographical Area of Activity: Canada, Ethiopia, Malawi, Tanzania.

Publications: Annual Report; newsletter; Special Health Reports.

Finance: Annual revenue C $2.4m., expenditure $2.3m. (31 March 2024).

Board of Directors: Dr Graeme McKillop (Chair.); George Vilili (Vice-Chair.); Claire Huxtable (Treas.).

Principal Staff: Exec. Dir and Sec. Kathrina Loeffler.

Contact Details: 240 Bank St, Suite 401, Ottawa, ON K2P 1X4; tel. (416) 369-0865; e-mail info@cpar.ca; internet www.cpar.ca.

The CRB Foundation/La Fondation CRB

Founded in 1988 by Charles R. Bronfman, Co-Chair. of Seagram's, a distillery.

Activities: Operates nationally and internationally through the Canadian heritage programme Historica; Project Involvement, an educational reform programme in Israel; and

Birthright Israel, which provides adults with their first living and learning experience in Israel. The Foundation prioritizes 'incubator' programmes in the areas of Jewish identity; relations between Israel and Jewish people worldwide; quality of life in Israel, especially in the area of educational reform; general and Jewish strategic philanthropy; and building networks of young Jewish people.

Geographical Area of Activity: Canada, Israel, USA.

Restrictions: Does not fund annual campaigns; capital works; general operating expenses; endowments, academic chairs or scholarships.

Publications: Information booklet.

Finance: Annual revenue C $703,197, expenditure $1.4m. (31 Dec. 2023).

Officers and Directors: Richard Doyle (Sec.); Ann Dadson (Treas.).

Contact Details: 1170 Peel St, 8th Floor, Montréal, QC H3B 4P2; tel. (514) 878-5250.

Crossroads International/Carrefour International

Established in 1960 as the Canadian Committee of Operations Crossroads, a counterpart to the US organization Operation Crossroads Africa, which was founded by Dr James H. Robinson in the 1950s; granted a charter as a separate organization in 1969.

Activities: A volunteer co-operation agency working in the fields of poverty alleviation and women's rights. Main programme areas focus on preventing sexual abuse and gender-based violence and providing access to justice for survivors; strengthening collective enterprises and small businesses led by women and young people; advancing women's and girls' rights; and supporting women in leadership roles in communities, businesses and government. The organization works with local partners in 10 countries. It has offices in Montréal and Toronto, in addition to offices in Senegal and Tanzania.

Geographical Area of Activity: Burkina Faso, Canada, Guinea, Ghana, Ivory Coast, Senegal, Eswatini, Tanzania, Togo, Uganda and Ethiopia.

Restrictions: Volunteering programmes are available only to Canadian citizens and to volunteers from African partner organizations.

Publications: Annual Report; Impact Report; Newsletter (bi-monthly).

Finance: Annual revenue C $11.8m., expenditure $11.9m. (2024–25).

Exec. Committee: Mariama Dramé (Chair.); Patricia Erb (Vice-Chair.); Janet Riehm (Treas.).

Principal Staff: Exec. Dir and Sec. Heather Shapter.

Contact Details: 49 Bathurst St, Suite 201, Toronto, ON M5V 2P2; tel. (416) 967-1611; e-mail info@cintl.org; internet cintl.org.

Cuso International

Established in 1961, as the Canadian University Service Overseas, by a group of Canadian university graduates; registered in the USA.

Activities: Works with governments, CSOs, multilateral agencies and the private sector to develop and deliver programmes to advance gender equality, empower women and girls, and improve young people's access to and quality of economic opportunities. The organization mobilizes volunteer professionals to work alongside local partners, sharing skills, perspectives and ideas.

Geographical Area of Activity: Benin, Cameroon, Canada (Northwest Territories), Colombia, Dem. Repub. of the Congo, Ethiopia, Honduras, Jamaica, Nigeria, Peru, Tanzania.

Publications: Annual Report; e-newsletter (6 a year); *Impact* (donor newsletter, 2 a year); *The Catalyst* (magazine).

Finance: Annual revenue C $25.5m., expenditure $28.1m. (31 March 2024).

Board of Directors: Darrell Gregersen, Lori Spadorcia (Co-Chair.); Rob Turpin (Treas.).

Principal Staff: CEO Nicolas Moyer.

Contact Details: 123 Slater St, Suite 800, Ottawa, ON K1P 5H2; tel. (613) 829-7445; e-mail info@cusointernational.org; internet www.cusointernational.org.

Cystic Fibrosis Canada (Fibrose Kystique Canada)

Founded in 1960 as the Canadian Cystic Fibrosis Foundation; present name adopted in 2011.

Activities: Raises and allocates funds to promote public awareness of cystic fibrosis; conducts research into improved care and treatment; and seeks a cure or control for the disorder. The organization promotes research on cystic fibrosis in Canadian universities and hospitals; funds research grants and major research development programmes; and gives special grants for training and research to fellows and visiting scientists skilled in such areas as respirology, paediatrics and behavioural sciences. It has more than 50 chapters throughout Canada.

Geographical Area of Activity: Canada.

Publications: Annual Report; newsletters; brochures and reports.

Finance: Annual revenue C $10.4m., expenditure $10.6m. (31 Jan. 2024).

Board of Directors: Barbara M. Hill (Chair.); Robert Deane (Vice-Chair.).

Principal Staff: Pres. and CEO Kelly Grover.

Contact Details: 20 Eglinton Ave W, Suite 1305, Toronto, ON M4R 1K8; tel. (416) 485-9149; e-mail info@cysticfibrosis.ca; internet www.cysticfibrosis.ca.

David Suzuki Foundation

Established in 1990 by Dr David Suzuki, a geneticist and broadcaster, and Dr Tara Cullis.

Activities: Works to address human-induced climate change through self-conducted programmes in three priority areas: asserting the environmental rights of Canadians; defending biodiversity, protecting and restoring species and habitats; and climate solutions, accelerating the transition to renewable energy. The Foundation annually awards nine one-year research fellowships, worth between C $30,000 and $50,000 each. It has offices in Toronto and Montréal.

Geographical Area of Activity: Canada, USA.

Publications: Annual Report; newsletter.

Finance: Annual revenue C $12.8m., expenditure $11.0m. (31 Aug. 2024).

Board of Directors: Dr Tara Cullis (Pres.); Jocelyn Joe-Strack (Chair.); Henry Annan (Vice-Chair.); Stephen Bronfman (Vice-Chair., Quebec); Dr Ginger Gibson (Sec.).

Principal Staff: Acting Exec. Dir Linda Nowlan; Exec. Dir Severn Cullis-Suzuki (on leave).

Contact Details: 340–1122 Mainland St, Vancouver, BC V6B 5L1; tel. (604) 732-4228; e-mail contact@davidsuzuki.org; internet davidsuzuki.org.

Development and Peace—Caritas Canada (Développement et Paix—Caritas Canada)

Established in 1967 by the Canadian Conference of Catholic Bishops; the official international development organization of the Catholic Church in Canada and a member of Caritas Internationalis (q.v.).

Activities: Works in the fields of community development in the global South and providing emergency humanitarian assistance. International programmes include: equality between men and women; citizen participation and democratic development; management and control of natural resources; ecological justice; peacebuilding and reconciliation; and emergency relief and reconstruction. It also educates

Disabled Peoples' International   CANADA

Canadians about the causes of poverty and the alternatives to unjust social, political and economic systems. Works in 34 countries, with more than 12,800 members in Canada.
Geographical Area of Activity: Middle East, South America, Central America and the Caribbean, South Asia, South-East Asia, sub-Saharan Africa.
Publications: Annual Report; newsletter; educational materials; graphic novels; guides; policies; religious leaflets; reports; blog.
Finance: Annual revenue C $18.3m., expenditure $12.4m. (31 Aug. 2024).
National Council: Gabrielle Dupuis (Pres.); Tasha Toupin (Vice-Pres.); Danny Gillis (Treas.); Frank Fohr (Sec.).
Principal Staff: Man. Dir Carl Hétu.
Contact Details: 555 René-Lévesque Blvd West, 8th Floor, Montréal, QC H2Z 1B1; tel. (514) 257-8711; e-mail info@devp.org; internet www.devp.org.

Disabled Peoples' International—DPI

Established in 1981, the International Year of Disabled Persons; a network of national organizations and assemblies of disabled people.
Activities: Promotes the human rights and economic and social integration of disabled people; and works to develop and support organizations of disabled people. The network comprises 139 National Assemblies (member organizations), and seven Regional Development Offices in Italy (Europe), Mauritania (Africa), Thailand (Asia-Pacific), Peru (Latin America), and Antigua and Barbuda (North America/Caribbean).
Geographical Area of Activity: International.
Publications: Position papers; newsletters.
Finance: Annual revenue C $104,290, expenditure $101,250 (31 March 2023).
Board: Henrietta Davis-Wray (Chair.); Shudarson Subedi (Treas.); Ayassou Komivi (Sec.).
Principal Staff: Information Officer Trevor Carroll.
Contact Details: Unit #1, 110 Didsbury Rd, Kanata, ON K2T 0C2; tel. (613) 563-2091; e-mail secretariat.dpi@gmail.com; internet disabledpeoplesinternational.org.

Echo Foundation/Fondation Écho

Established in 1983 as EJLB Foundation; present name adopted in 2012.
Activities: Operates in two main areas: Mental Health, with grants given to organizations in Montréal and Toronto that improve the quality of life of people suffering from mental health problems; and Environment, which focuses on Eastern Canada (Ontario, Québec and the Atlantic provinces) and prioritizes the protection of areas of ecological importance and the greening of urban areas, and supports the promotion of sustainable environmental practices.
Geographical Area of Activity: Canada, with limited international grantmaking.
Finance: Annual revenue C $31.4m., expenditure $13.0m. (31 Dec. 2023).
Board of Directors: Robert Alain (Pres.); Ann Parsons, Katherine Lewis (Vice-Pres).
Principal Staff: Gen. Man. Kevin Leonard.
Contact Details: 1350 Sherbrooke St West, Suite 1050, Montréal, QC H3G 1J1; tel. (514) 843-5112; e-mail general@fondationecho.ca; internet www.fondationecho.ca.

Equality Fund/Fonds Égalité

Established in 1976, as the MATCH International Centre, by Norma E. Walmsley and Suzanne Johnson-Harvor following the first UN women's conference in Mexico City; became the MATCH International Women's Fund in 2013; present name adopted in 2019. A collective of 11 organizations including the African Women's Development Fund and Oxfam Canada (qq.v.).
Activities: Operates in the fields of climate change, conflict, inequality and poverty, working with partner groups to improve conditions and quality of life for women. The Fund runs campaigns and awareness training, and carries out research on eliminating violence against women in Canada and abroad. It empowers women in developing countries by giving them the opportunity to improve their lives and enhance their roles, through training, community work and networking initiatives.
Geographical Area of Activity: Canada, Middle East and North Africa, South Asia, South America, Central America and the Caribbean, sub-Saharan Africa.
Restrictions: Not accepting new grant applications.
Publications: Annual Report; newsletter (monthly); briefs; reports; blog.
Finance: Annual revenue C $47.3m., expenditure $34.5m. (31 March 2024).
Board of Directors: Mebrat Beyene, Theo Sowa (Co-Chair.); Lianne Hannaway (Treas.).
Principal Staff: CEO Jess Tomlin.
Contact Details: 123 Slater St, Suite 600, Ottawa, ON K1P 5H2; tel. (855) 640-1872; e-mail hello@equalityfund.ca; internet equalityfund.ca.

ETC Group—Action Group on Erosion, Technology and Concentration

Founded in 1985 by Pat Mooney as the Rural Advancement Foundation International; reformed under the present name in 2001.
Activities: Addresses the socioeconomic and ecological impact of new technologies and corporate strategies on agriculture, nature and the human rights of the world's poorest and most vulnerable people. Areas of interest are: biodiversity, climate and geoengineering; corporate monopolies; sustainable development; synthetic biology; and technology assessment. The Group operates at global political level, working with partner CSOs and social movements, especially in Africa, Asia and Latin America. It has offices in Mexico and the Philippines.
Geographical Area of Activity: International.
Restrictions: Not a grantmaking organization.
Publications: Annual Report; newsletter; briefings; reports.
Finance: Total assets C $580,501 (31 Aug. 2021).
Board of Trustees: Niclas Hallström (Pres.).
Contact Details: 5961 Jeanne-Mance, Montréal, QC H4V 2K9; tel. (873) 649-2028; e-mail etc@etcgroup.org; internet etcgroup.org.

Focus Humanitarian Assistance—FOCUS

Founded in 1994 by the Ismaili Muslim community in Europe and North America; an international crisis response and disaster risk management agency, affiliated with the Aga Khan Development Network (q.v.).
Activities: Provides emergency humanitarian relief in areas affected by natural disasters or conflict and promotes disaster resilience in development and rehabilitation planning for local communities, refugees and internally displaced people. The organization has liaison offices in Afghanistan, India, Pakistan and the USA.
Geographical Area of Activity: Afghanistan, Canada, Europe, India, Middle East, Pakistan, Tajikistan, USA.
Restrictions: Not a grantmaking organization.
Publications: *FOCUS Global Newsletter*; *Emergency Kit Checklist* (English, Farsi, French); *Emergency Preparedness Tips*; *Family Emergency Plan* (English, Farsi, French); *Pandemic Preparedness Checklist*.
Board of Directors: Samir Manji (Chair.); Shailaz Dhalla (Vice-Chair.).
Principal Staff: Global Co-ordinator Shakeel Hirji.

CANADA

Contact Details: 49 Wynford Dr., Suite 200, Toronto, ON M3C 1K; tel. (416) 423-7988; e-mail focus.canada@focusha.org; internet focus-canada.org.

Fondation Baxter & Alma Ricard (Baxter & Alma Ricard Foundation)

Established in 1999 by Baxter and Alma Ricard, with the proceeds of broadcast media holdings.

Activities: Offers annual graduate and postgraduate scholarships to young minority French-speaking Canadians, for study in Canada or abroad for a period of up to three years. Scholarships are worth up to C $50,000 per year. Scholarship holders are invited to join the Association des Boursiers Ricard, a network of fellows.

Geographical Area of Activity: Canada (outside of Québec).

Restrictions: Scholarship applicants must be minority French-speaking Canadians who live in Canada outside of Québec.

Finance: Annual revenue C $4.2m., expenditure $2.4m. (30 June 2024).

Board of Trustees: Guy Desmarais (Pres.).

Principal Staff: Man. Dir Elia Eliev.

Contact Details: 435 Donald Street, Suite 205A, Ottawa, ON K1K 4X5; tel. (613) 880-8199; e-mail info@fondationricard.com; internet fondationricard.com.

Fondation J-Louis Lévesque (J-Louis Lévesque Foundation)

Established in 1961 by Jean-Louis Lévesque, a business person.

Activities: Operates in Québec, Ontario and the Atlantic Provinces of Canada in the fields of education, medical research and social welfare, through making grants for research and special projects.

Geographical Area of Activity: Canada.

Restrictions: Does not accept unsolicited applications.

Finance: Annual revenue C $8.8m., expenditure $6.3m. (31 Dec. 2023).

Board: Yanik Pagé (Pres.).

Contact Details: 468 Lakeshore Rd, Beaconsfield, QC H9W 4J5; tel. (514) 849-8606; internet fondationjllevesque.org.

Fondation Lucie et André Chagnon (Lucie et André Chagnon Foundation)

Established in 2000 by André Chagnon, founder of telecommunications company Le Groupe Vidéotron.

Activities: Works to prevent poverty and improve educational success by mobilizing CSOs and raising public awareness. Since 2017, 270 initiatives have been supported throughout quebec, with a total disburement of C $520m. between 2017 and 2023.

Geographical Area of Activity: Canada (Québec).

Restrictions: Grants only to organizations for projects in Québec.

Publications: Annual Report; newsletter; factsheets; surveys.

Finance: Annual revenue C $164.7m., expenditure $125.6m. (31 Dec. 2023).

Executive Committee: Claude Chagnon (Chair.).

Contact Details: 2001 McGill College Ave, Suite 1000, Montréal, QC H3A 1G1; tel. (514) 380-2001; e-mail info@fondationchagnon.org; internet www.fondationchagnon.org.

Fondation Marcelle et Jean Coutu (Marcelle et Jean Coutu Foundation)

Established in 1991 by the Groupe Jean Coutu pharmacy chain.

Activities: Operates in Canada, especially Québec, and internationally in the fields of community health, education, research and food security.

Geographical Area of Activity: Canada, Haiti, Mali.

Finance: Annual revenue C $43.3m., expenditure $36.5m. (28 Feb. 2024).

Board of Directors: Marie-Josée Coutu (Chair.).

Contact Details: 154 ave Laurier O, Suite 303, Montréal, QC H2T 2N7; tel. (514) 527-4510; e-mail info@fmjc.org; internet fmjc.org.

Fondation Pierre Elliott Trudeau/Pierre Elliott Trudeau Foundation

Established in 2001 by the family of former Prime Minister of Canada Pierre Trudeau in his memory and endowed by the Government of Canada with the Advanced Research in the Humanities and Human Sciences Fund.

Activities: Awards three-year doctoral scholarships, fellowships and mentorships to encourage reflection and action in human rights and dignity, responsible citizenship, Canada's role in the world, and people and their environment. Scholarships are worth up to a total of C $60,000 per year. Foundation scholars, fellows and mentors are invited to join the Pierre Elliott Trudeau Foundation Society, a network which fosters productive, long-term relationships.

Geographical Area of Activity: Canada.

Publications: Annual Report; newsletter; *The Trudeau Foundation Papers*.

Finance: Annual revenue C $23.3m., expenditure $10.1m. (31 Aug. 2024).

Board of Directors: Peter Sahlas (Chair.); Bruce McNiven (Vice-Chair. and Treas.).

Principal Staff: Pres. and CEO Bettina B. Cenerelli.

Contact Details: 1980 Sherbrooke St West, Suite 600, West Montréal, QC H3H 1E8; tel. (514) 938-0001; e-mail info@trudeaufoundation.ca; internet www.trudeaufoundation.ca.

Fraser Institute

Established in 1974 by T. Patrick Boyle, Vice-Pres. of MacMillan Bloedel forestry company, and Michael A. Walker, an economist; a think tank.

Activities: Carries out public policy research and measurement, and public education. Programme areas include: Aboriginal issues; democracy and governance; economic freedom; education; energy; healthcare; natural resources and the environment; poverty and inequality; taxation; and trade and US relations. The Institute organizes seminars and workshops; and offers the annual Founders' Award, which recognizes individuals' entrepreneurial achievements, philanthropic endeavours and dedication to the free market. It has offices in Calgary, Haliax, Montréal and Toronto.

Geographical Area of Activity: Canada, USA.

Publications: Annual Report; newsletter; *The Quarterly; Fraser Forum* (blog); *Economic Freedom Ranking*; *Essential Scholars* (website and e-book series); research studies.

Finance: Annual revenue C $15.1m., expenditure $14.9m. (31 Dec. 2023).

Board of Directors: Mark Scott (Chair.); Roderick Senft, Andrew Judson, Shaun Francis, Jonathan Wener (Vice-Chair.).

Principal Staff: Pres. Niels Veldhuis; Exec. Vice-Pres. Jason Clemens.

Contact Details: 4th Floor, 1770 Burrard St, Vancouver, BC V6J 3G7; tel. (604) 688-0221; e-mail info@fraserinstitute.org; internet www.fraserinstitute.org.

Gairdner Foundation

Founded in 1957 by James A. Gairdner, a stockbroker and business person.

Heart & Stroke   CANADA

Activities: Operates internationally in the fields of medicine, biomedical science and global health. The Foundation annually makes seven awards, each of C $100,000, to recognize and reward excellence in fundamental research that has an impact on human health: five Canada Gairdner International Awards for biomedical research; the John Dirks Canada Gairdner Global Health Award, for impact on global health issues; and the Canada Gairdner Wightman Award, for a Canadian scientist who has shown scientific excellence and leadership. It undertakes outreach programmes in Canada; and convenes meetings between the public, policymakers and others.
Geographical Area of Activity: International.
Restrictions: Awards only on the basis of nominations and peer review.
Publications: Annual Report; newsletter.
Finance: Annual revenue C $2.5m., expenditure $3.0m. (31 Dec. 2023).
Board of Directors: Dr Heather Munroe-Blum (Chair.); Elizabeth Cannon (Vice-Chair.).
Principal Staff: Pres. and Scientific Dir Dr Janet Rossant; Emeritus Pres. and Scientific Dir Dr John Dirks.
Contact Details: MaRS Centre, Heritage Bldg, 101 College St, Suite 335, Toronto, ON M5G 1L7; tel. (416) 596-9996; e-mail thegairdner@gairdner.org; internet gairdner.org.

Heart & Stroke

Established in 1952 by researchers and physicians; formerly known as the Heart and Stroke Foundation of Canada. Present name adopted in 2016.
Activities: Works to prevent the causes of heart disease, stroke and vascular cognitive impairment through promoting collaboration and innovation and funding research; closing the health gap that Indigenous people experience; supporting survivors and carers; and organizing fundraising campaigns. The Foundation provides grants in aid for basic biomedical and clinical research, and research on health systems and services and social, cultural, environmental and population health; seed/catalyst grants to translate knowledge into practice; and multidisciplinary, multi-institutional impact awards. It also offers a range of personnel awards, fellowships and scholarships; supports chairs and professorships; and provides access to continuing education for health professionals.
Geographical Area of Activity: Canada.
Publications: Annual Report; newsletter; health information publications; research e-newsletter (quarterly).
Finance: Annual revenue C $162.5m., expenditure $130.6m. (31 Aug. 2024).
Board of Directors: Charlene Ripley (Chair.); Clayton Norris (Vice-Chair.).
Principal Staff: CEO Doug Roth.
Contact Details: 2300 Yonge St, Suite 1200, Box 2414 Toronto ON M4P 1E4; e-mail webteam@heartandstroke.ca; internet heartandstroke.ca.

HOPE International Development Agency

Established in 1975 as Food for the Hungry, Canada, based on Christian values.
Activities: Helps underserved families living in extreme poverty through working with grassroots, community-based organizations to foster long-term sustainability and self-reliance. Main programmes focus on clean water and health, food security and nutrition, and livelihoods and learning. Activities are community led, gender inclusive, resilient and sustainable. The Agency is active in 14 countries.
Geographical Area of Activity: Canada, Central and South America and the Caribbean, South Asia, South-East Asia, sub-Saharan Africa.
Publications: Annual Report; newsletter; blog.
Finance: Annual revenue C $13.2m., expenditure $15.5m. (31 Dec. 2023).
Board of Directors: Ian Warkentin (Chair.); Dale Bowler (Vice-Chair.); Nancy Strong (Treas.); Anita Walker-Spiller (Sec.).
Principal Staff: Man. Dir Jon McKenzie; Int. Pres. David S. McKenzie.
Contact Details: 713 Columbia St, Suite 410, New Westminster, BC V3M 1B2; tel. (866) 525-4673; e-mail hope@hope-international.com; internet www.hope-international.com.

Horizons of Friendship

Established in 1973, as the Help Honduras Foundation, by Rev. Timothy Coughlan, Christine Stewart, a politician, and her husband David.
Activities: Works with people experiencing poverty in rural and urban communities. Main programme areas are: community health; food sovereignty and climate change; migration; rights of indigenous peoples and Afro-descendants; and violence against women and femicide. The organization runs development projects to provide clean water and sanitation, healthcare, housing and skills training.
Geographical Area of Activity: Canada, Costa Rica, El Salvador, Guatemala, Honduras, Nicaragua, Mexico, Panama.
Publications: Annual Report; newsletter (2 a year); blog.
Finance: Total revenue C $925,722, expenditure $868,467 (31 March 2024).
Board of Directors: Dr Paul Caldwell (Pres.); Dr Patti Tracy (Vice-Pres.); Mike Dupuis (Sec.).
Contact Details: 50 Covert St, POB 402, Cobourg, ON K9A 4L1; tel. (905) 372-5483; e-mail info@horizons.ca; internet www.horizons.ca.

IDRF—International Development and Relief Foundation

Founded in 1984 by a group of Canadian Muslims.
Activities: Aims to empower disadvantaged people through emergency relief and participatory development programmes based on the Islamic principles of human dignity, religious giving, self-reliance and social justice. The Foundation carries out projects in the fields of: economic development; education; emergency response; food security and nutrition; health; and water, sanitation and hygiene. In Canada, its focus is on providing access to education and youth leadership. Active in over 40 countries.
Geographical Area of Activity: International.
Publications: Annual Report; newsletter; *IDRF Reporter* (annual).
Finance: Annual revenue C $40.7m., expenditure $40.2m. (30 June 2024).
Board of Directors: Reza Rizvi, Yasmeena Mohamed (Co-Chair.); Muhammad Munshi, Marzia Habib-Hassan (Vice-Chair.); Nurhan Aycan (Gen. Sec.).
Principal Staff: CEO Mahmood Qasim.
Contact Details: 23 Lesmill Rd, Suite 300, North York, ON M3B 3P6; tel. (416) 497-0818; e-mail office@idrf.ca; internet idrf.com.

IMPACT Transforming Natural Resource Management (IMPACT Transformer la Gestion des Ressources Naturelles)

Established in 1986 as Partnership Africa Canada; present name adopted in 2018.
Activities: Works in the field of natural resource management in areas where security and human rights are at risk, conducting policy research, analysis and advocacy. Main programme areas are: environmental stewardship; gender equality; illicit trade and financing; regulatory and legal reform; and supply chain transparency. The organization has offices in the Democratic Republic of the Congo, Côte d'Ivoire and Uganda.

CANADA

Geographical Area of Activity: Canada, Burundi, Dem. Repub. of the Congo, Côte d'Ivoire, Guinea, Indonesia, Kenya, Liberia, Peru, Rwanda, Sierra Leone, Tanzania, Uganda, Zambia.

Restrictions: Not a grantmaking organization.

Publications: Annual Report; newsletter; Civil Society Toolkit on Supply Chain Risks; policy briefs; research reports.

Finance: Annual revenue C $4.1m., expenditure $4.1m. (31 March 2024).

Board of Directors: Nicole Piggot (Pres.); Shivani Kannabhiran (Vice-Pres.); Edward Blight (Treas.); Louise Ouimet (Sec.).

Principal Staff: Exec. Dir Joanne Lebert; Deputy Exec. Dir Yann Lebrat.

Contact Details: 135 ave Laurier W, Suite 100, Ottawa, ON K1P 5J2; tel. (613) 237-6768; e-mail info@impacttransform.org; internet impacttransform.org.

Innovators and Entrepreneurs Foundation/Fondation d'Innovateurs et d'Entrepreneurs—IEF/FIE

Established in 2019; a joint initiative of the Manning Foundation (f. 1982) and Startup Canada (f. 2012).

Activities: Promotes innovation and entrepreneurship among marginalized groups. The Foundation carries out research and publishes its findings; supports people from low-income and disadvantaged communities, providing them with access to educational resources; and funds educational programmes on business and financial skills, in particular for people from marginalized minorities, including Indigenous people, women, people with disabilities, newcomers to Canada, young people and people from socioeconomically disadvantaged backgrounds. It organizes the CANIE awards, which combine the Startup Canada Awards programme and the Ernest C. Manning Innovation Awards, to recognize excellence in innovation and entrepreneurship and promote social impact.

Geographical Area of Activity: Canada.

Restrictions: Award nominees must be Canadian citizens or living in Canada.

Publications: Newsletter.

Finance: Annual revenue C $192,100, expenditure $273,431 (31 Dec. 2023).

Board: Brenda Halloran (Pres. and Interim Exec. Dir).

Contact Details: 18 King St E., Toronto, Ontario M5C 1C4; tel. (613) 627-0787; e-mail info@ief-fie.ca; internet www.ief-fie.ca.

Inter Pares

Founded in 1975 by Timothy Brodhead and Ian Smillie, international development professionals.

Activities: Promotes international self-development through empowering communities and promoting equality, participation, solidarity and women's leadership. Main programmes areas include: control over resources; economic justice; food sovereignty; health; migration; peace and democracy; and women's rights and gender justice. The Peter Gillespie Social Justice Award is offered to organizations or groups in Canada for work in the areas of discrimination and social exclusion. The organization works with more than 75 social justice organizations in 22 countries.

Geographical Area of Activity: Canada, Latin America, South Asia, South-East Asia, sub-Saharan Africa.

Publications: Annual Report; e-newsletter (monthly); *Inter Pares Bulletin* (5 a year); briefs; occasional papers; reports.

Finance: Annual revenue C $9.3m., expenditure $9.1m. (31 Dec. 2023).

Board of Directors: Amanda Dale (Chair.).

Principal Staff: Exec. Dir Samantha McGavin.

Contact Details: 221 Laurier Ave East, Ottawa, ON K1N 6P1; tel. (613) 563-4801; e-mail info@interpares.ca; internet www.interpares.ca.

International Institute for Sustainable Development—IISD

Founded in 1990; a think tank.

Activities: Works towards achieving a stable climate, sustainable resources and fair economies. Main programmes include: supporting the transition to clean energy; economic law and policy development; managing climate- and conflict-related risks; protecting freshwater supplies; and tracking and analysis. The Institute collates and disseminates information on economic development; advises government agencies and national and international organizations involved in development work; develops business strategies and trade principles; and promotes community living and the creation of sustainable economies. It conducts research, produces educational materials and maintains a library. Has offices in Ottawa, Toronto and Geneva, Switzerland.

Geographical Area of Activity: International.

Publications: Annual Report; newsletter; books, brochures; handbooks; books; blog.

Finance: Annual revenue C $57.8m., expenditure $56.9m. (31 March 2024).

Board of Directors: Michelle Edkins (Chair.).

Principal Staff: Pres. and CEO Patricia Fuller.

Contact Details: 111 Lombard Ave, Suite 325, Winnipeg, MB R3B 0T4; tel. (204) 958-7700; e-mail info@iisd.org; internet www.iisd.org.

Ivey Foundation

Established in 1947 as The Richard Ivey Foundation by Richard G. Ivey, lawyer and business person, and his son Richard M. Ivey, who was also a lawyer.

Activities: Supports the transition to a sustainable economy through enhancing resource efficiency, fostering innovation and advancing sustainable finance. The Foundation offers grants to organizations in two main areas: economy and environment.

Geographical Area of Activity: Canada.

Restrictions: No unsolicited applications; grants only to organizations registered in Canada.

Publications: Annual Report; *Economy and Environment Framework*.

Finance: Annual revenue C $8.1m., expenditure $18.7m. (31 Dec. 2023).

Board of Directors: Rosamond A. Ivey (Chair.); Suzanne E. Ivey Cook (Vice-Chair.); Richard W. Ivey (Treas. and Sec.).

Principal Staff: Pres. Dr Bruce Lourie; Vice-Pres. Lorne Johnson.

Contact Details: 11 Church St, Suite 400, Toronto, ON M5E 1W1; tel. (416) 867-9229; e-mail info@ivey.org; internet www.ivey.org.

The J. W. McConnell Family Foundation

Established in 1937 by J. W. McConnell, an industrialist and newspaper publisher.

Activities: Works to address social, cultural, economic and environmental challenges through funding social innovation and creating a reconciliation economy for Indigenous and non-Indigenous peoples. Initiatives include the Social Innovation Fund, which makes grants to individuals and non-profit organizations; Innoweave, which provides funding and resources for professional development and coaching to leaders of community organizations; Cities for People, which supports inclusive urban innovation for resilient cities; Re-Code, which aims to achieve social impact through reforming post-secondary education; Sustainable Food Systems, with a focus on institutional food, regional food economies and community food security; and the Solutions Finance Accelerator, which supports innovation in social finance.

Geographical Area of Activity: Canada.

Restrictions: Does not make grants for conferences, seminars, scholarships, fellowships, bursaries, research, nor to individuals or projects in developing countries; no applications by email.

Publications: Newsletter; reports.

Finance: Annual revenue C $19.5m., expenditure $41.9m. (31 Dec. 2023).

Board of Directors: Graham Angus (Chair.).

Principal Staff: CEO Jane Rabinowicz; Exec. Sec. Sabrina Saint-Louis.

Contact Details: 1002 Sherbrooke St West, Suite 1800, Montréal, QC H3A 3L6; tel. (514) 288-2133; e-mail info@mcconnellfoundation.ca; internet www.mcconnellfoundation.ca.

Joseph Tanenbaum Charitable Foundation

Established in 1967 by Joseph Tanenbaum, an industrialist and real estate developer.

Activities: Makes grants primarily to Jewish organizations in the areas of education, care for disabled children, social and community services, and medical research.

Geographical Area of Activity: Canada, USA.

Finance: Annual revenue C $1,185, expenditure $101,791 (31 Jan. 2024).

Board of Directors: John Kaplan (Pres.).

Contact Details: 1600 Steeles Ave W, Suite 221, Concord, ON L4K 4M2; tel. (416) 298-0066.

Laidlaw Foundation

Established in 1949 by W. C. Laidlaw, R. A. Laidlaw, R. W. L. Laidlaw and Dr R. G. N. Laidlaw; the Foundation was funded by the R. Laidlaw Lumber Company, which was subsequently sold in 1972.

Activities: Works to make the non-profit sector more accessible to young people and youth-led community change. Main programmes focus on young people and Indigenous communities.

Geographical Area of Activity: Canada (mainly Ontario).

Publications: Annual Report; newsletter; briefing notes; occasional papers.

Finance: Annual revenue –C $12.4m., expenditure $5.6m. (31 Dec. 2023).

Board of Directors: Janine Manning (Chair.); Paul Nagpal (Vice-Chair.).

Principal Staff: Exec. Dir Jehad Aliweiwi.

Contact Details: 2 St Clair Ave East, 3rd Floor, Toronto, ON M4T 2T5; tel. (416) 964-3614; e-mail info@laidlawfdn.org; internet www.laidlawfdn.org.

The Lawson Foundation

Established in 1956 by Ray Lawson, a business person and Lt-Gov. of Ontario.

Activities: Focuses on the wellbeing of children and young people. The Foundation invests in four interconnected Impact Areas that it believes will have a lasting positive effect on development: early child development; child and youth diabetes; outdoor play; and youth and the environment. It offers grants to organizations for activities including community action, knowledge development, learning, monitoring and evaluation, leadership, capacity building and public policy.

Geographical Area of Activity: Canada.

Publications: Annual Report; newsletter; guides; reports; blog.

Finance: Annual revenue C $16.1m., expenditure $8.8m. (31 Dec. 2023).

Board of Directors: Wynne Young (Chair.); Tim Gardiner (Vice-Chair.); Vijay Venkatesan (Sec.-Treas.).

Principal Staff: Pres. and CEO Cathy Taylor.

Contact Details: c/o Foundation House, 2 St Clair Ave East, Suite 300, Toronto, ON M4T 2T5; tel. (416) 775-9458; e-mail info@lawson.ca; internet www.lawson.ca.

Light Up the World—LUTW

Founded in 1997 and formally incorporated as an NGO in 2002; merged with EnerGreen Foundation (f. 1994) in 2006.

Activities: Implements projects to provide 'off-grid' communities with sustainable energy and lighting using solar photovoltaic systems and LEDs. The organization trains local people to give them the necessary skills to install, maintain and repair renewable energy systems. It has a field office in Lima.

Geographical Area of Activity: Canada, Peru.

Publications: Annual Report; newsletter.

Finance: Annual revenue C $637,123, expenditure $557,009 (31 Dec. 2023).

Board of Directors: Michael Bate, Darren Malley (Co-Chair.).

Contact Details: POB 16039 Lower Mount Royal, Calgary, AB T2T 5H7; tel. (403) 266-5004; e-mail lutw@lutw.org; internet www.lutw.org.

Liver Canada

Established in 1969, as Canadian Liver Foundation/Fondation Canadienne du Foie—CLF/FCF, by a group of business leaders and doctors; present name adopted in 2024.

Activities: Promotes liver health through educating the public about liver disease; providing advocacy; supporting patients and their families; and raising funds for research. The Foundation offers studentships and operating grants to qualified individuals researching the causes, diagnosis, treatment and prevention of liver and biliary tract diseases.

Geographical Area of Activity: Canada.

Restrictions: Grants only to organizations registered in Canada.

Publications: Annual Report; newsletter; information sheets; pamphlets; blog.

Finance: Annual revenue C $5.0m., expenditure $7.6m. (31 Dec. 2023).

Board of Directors: Elliot M. Jacobson (Chair.); Gary Hokkanen (Sec./Treas.).

Principal Staff: Pres. and CEO Jennifer Nebesky.

Contact Details: 101-3100 Steeles Ave East, Markham, ON L3R 8T3; tel. (416) 491-3353; e-mail clf@liver.ca; internet www.liver.ca.

The Lotte and John Hecht Memorial Foundation

Established in 1962 as the 1945 Foundation by Lotte and John Hecht, owners of a sawmill and property investors.

Activities: Operates in two main areas: research and support of alternative and complementary medicine, specifically for the treatment of cancer; and economic education that furthers the principles of the free market, through offering grants to non-profit organizations. The Foundation funds the Dr Rogers Prize for Excellence in Complementary and Alternative Medicine, worth C $300,000, awarded every two years to researchers and practitioners.

Geographical Area of Activity: Canada.

Restrictions: Does not fund capital projects, endowments, scholarships or bursaries.

Finance: Annual revenue C $33.7m., expenditure $32.8m. (31 Dec. 2023).

Board of Directors: Patrick J. Julian (Chair.).

Principal Staff: Exec. Dir Alena Levitz.

Contact Details: 325 Howe St, Suite 502, Vancouver, BC V6C 1Z7; tel. (604) 683-7575; e-mail info@hecht.org; internet www.hecht.org.

Macdonald Stewart Foundation

Established in 1967 by David Macdonald Stewart, owner of Macdonald Tobacco Inc.

Activities: Operates in the fields of the arts and humanities; education, promoting new and innovative ideas; and medicine and health, supporting projects, short-term research and medical services.

Geographical Area of Activity: Canada.

Restrictions: No grants to individuals; projects supported must be Canadian or have Canadian content, and be carried out by registered charitable organizations.

Finance: Annual revenue C $4.9m., expenditure $3.2m. (31 Dec. 2023).

Principal Staff: Pres. Jean-Pierre Ouellet; Exec. Dir Thomas Leslie.

Contact Details: 1195 Sherbrooke St West, Montréal, QC H3A 1H9; tel. (514) 284-0723; internet www.msfoundation.org.

The McLean Foundation

Established in 1945 by James S. McLean, the owner of a meat packing company.

Activities: Supports projects for general social benefit that may initially lack broad public appeal, within the fields of the arts, education, conservation, health and social welfare.

Geographical Area of Activity: Canada.

Restrictions: Grants only to registered Canadian charities; no grants to individuals.

Finance: Annual revenue C $4.4m., expenditure $3.3m. (31 Dec. 2023).

Board of Directors: Simon Isdell-Carpenter (Chair.); Indira Stewart, Mark F. McLean (Vice-Chair.); Jonathan Carpenter (Treas.).

Principal Staff: Exec. Dir Ana Skinner Cervoni.

Contact Details: 2 St Clair Ave West, Suite 300, Toronto, ON M4V 1L5; tel. (416) 964-6802; e-mail info@mcleanfoundation.ca; internet mcleanfoundation.ca.

The MasterCard Foundation

Established in 2006 by MasterCard, a financial services company.

Activities: Promotes financial inclusion and provides education and skills training in developing countries, with a focus on youth employment. The Foundation works with partners in more than 45 countries to allow people living in poverty to access economic and educational opportunities, including scholarships. It has offices in Ethiopia, Ghana, Kenya, Nigeria, Senegal, Rwanda and Uganda.

Geographical Area of Activity: Canada, sub-Saharan Africa.

Publications: Newsletter.

Finance: Annual revenue US $14,470.1m., expenditure $1,533.5m. (31 Dec. 2023).

Board of Directors: Zein M. Abdalla (Chair.).

Principal Staff: Pres. and CEO Reeta Roy.

Contact Details: 250 Yonge St, Suite 2400, Toronto, ON M5B 2L7; tel. (647) 837-5787; e-mail info@mastercardfdn.org; internet www.mastercardfdn.org.

Max Bell Foundation

Founded in 1972 by George Maxwell Bell, a newspaper publisher.

Activities: Works to improve the wellbeing of Indigenous communities; and to help people to adapt to social, economic and technological changes. The Foundation supports projects that will have an impact on public policy and practice in the areas of health and wellness, the environment and education. The Foundation operates its own programmes, but mainly funds the work of partners through Project Grants and Development Grants.

Geographical Area of Activity: Canada.

Restrictions: Grants only to organizations registered in Canada.

Publications: Annual Report; newsletter.

Finance: Annual revenue C $7.2m., expenditure $4.4m. (31 Dec. 2023).

Board of Directors: Brenda Eaton (Chair.); Ken Marra (Vice-Chair.).

Principal Staff: Pres. Allan Northcott.

Contact Details: 105 12 Ave SE, Suite 970, Calgary, AB T2G 1A1; tel. (403) 215-7310; e-mail amccarry@maxbell.org; internet www.maxbell.org.

The Maytree Foundation

Established in 1982 by Alan Broadbent, the Chair. and CEO of Avana Capital Corporation, and his wife Judy, a social worker.

Activities: Promotes systemic solutions to eliminate poverty and strengthen civic communities. Programmes focus on: providing access to affordable, decent and suitable housing; the impact of poverty on human rights; income security and improving the social safety net; ensuring human rights in cities through advancing economic and social rights; and ensuring access to education. The Foundation carries out research and analysis on public policies. It makes grants for projects that address systemic causes of poverty and safeguard economic and social rights; develop leadership and skills capacity in civil society; and build a culture of rights.

Geographical Area of Activity: Canada.

Restrictions: No grants to individuals.

Publications: Reports; newsletter; backgrounders; briefs; commentaries; guides; toolkits; blog.

Finance: Annual revenue C $5.7m., expenditure $5.8m. (30 Nov. 2023).

Board of Directors: Alan Broadbent (Chair.); Matt Broadbent (Vice-Chair.); Vali Bennett (Vice-Pres. and Sec.); Jeff Szeto (Treas.).

Principal Staff: Pres. Elizabeth McIsaac.

Contact Details: 77 Bloor St West, Suite 1600, Toronto, ON M5S 1M2; tel. (416) 944-2627; e-mail info@maytree.com; internet www.maytree.com.

Molson Foundation

Established in 1958 by T. H. P. Molson, Hartland de Montarville Molson, E. H. Molson and S. T. Molson, whose family established the Molson brewery; formerly known as the Molson Family Foundation.

Activities: Operates in the fields of health and welfare, education, social development, national development and the humanities, through grants to charitable organizations for special projects. The Foundation funds the Molson Prize for the Arts, comprising two prizes of C $50,000 each awarded annually to distinguished Canadians, in the fields of the arts and the social sciences and humanities, and administered by the Canada Council for the Arts (q.v.) and the Social Sciences and Humanities Research Council.

Geographical Area of Activity: Canada.

Restrictions: No grants for conferences, seminars, publications, fellowships or scholarships; only registered Canadian charities are eligible.

Publications: Annual Report.

Finance: Annual revenue C $10.3m., expenditure $11.8m. (30 Sept. 2024).

Board of Directors: Andrew T. Molson (Pres.); Geoffrey E. Molson (Vice-Pres.); Dominique Paliotti (Exec. Dir/Treas.); Tim Anderson (Sec.).

Contact Details: 6125 route de l'Aéroport, St-Hubert, QC J3Y 0V9; tel. (514) 590-6335; e-mail info@themolsonfoundation.org; internet fondationmolson.org.

The Muttart Foundation

Founded in 1953 by Merrill and Gladys Muttart, business people and philanthropists.

Activities: Main activities focus on strengthening the charitable sector and early childhood education and care. The Foundation provides grants for infrastructure development and capacity building of not-for-profit organizations, community development, fellowships, training grants and bursaries; and grants to support the leadership capacity of organizations working with young children.
Geographical Area of Activity: Canada (primarily Alberta and Saskatchewan).
Restrictions: No unsolicited applications except for the Bursary Program and Training Program.
Publications: Muttart Fellowship publications; Board Development Workbooks; research studies; surveys; reports.
Finance: Annual revenue C $2.1m., expenditure $3.7m. (30 Nov. 2023).
Board: Bryan McLean (Pres.); Winnie Chow-Horn (Vice-Pres.); Karen MacDonald (Treas.).
Principal Staff: Exec. Dir Bob Wyatt; Assoc. Exec. Dir Dr Christopher Smith.
Contact Details: 1150 Rice Howard Pl., 10060 Jasper Ave, Edmonton, AB T5J 3R8; tel. (780) 425-9616; e-mail reception@muttart.org; internet www.muttart.org.

Myanmar/Burma Schools Project Foundation

Established in 2010 by Roger Brain, former Senior Vice-President of Teck Corporation, a mining company. Since 2012 MBSPF is a Canadian Registered Charity.
Activities: Funds the construction of new primary, middle and high schools and medical clinics in rural villages in Myanmar. The Foundation also renovates existing school buildings and installs outdoor toilets, water wells/storage and solar electricity.
Geographical Area of Activity: Canada, Myanmar.
Finance: Total assets C $190,511; Annual revenue C $175,000, expenditure C $315,000 (31 Dec. 2024).
Board: Roger Brain (Chair.).
Principal Staff: Exec. Dir Leslie Martin.
Contact Details: 1101-995 Roche Point Dr, North Vancouver, BC V7H 2X4; tel. (604) 202-5122; e-mail info@myanmarburmaschools.ca; internet myanmarburmaschools.ca.

The Neptis Foundation

Established in 1999 by Martha Shuttleworth, following the division of the assets of the Richard and Jean Ivey Fund, founded in 1947, which were shared with the Salamander Foundation.
Activities: Informs and improves policy and decisionmaking on regional urban growth and management in Canada. The Foundation carries out and publishes research, analysis and mapping on the design and function of national urban areas. It also runs the Neptis Geoweb online mapping and statistics service.
Geographical Area of Activity: Canada.
Restrictions: Does not accept unsolicited requests for financial support for research.
Publications: Newsletter; reports; analysis; briefing papers; books; posters.
Finance: Annual revenue C $751,922, expenditure $801,524 (31 Dec. 2023).
Board of Directors: Martha J. Shuttleworth (Pres.).
Contact Details: 39A Madison Ave, Toronto, ON M5R 2S2; tel. (416) 972-9199; e-mail publications@neptis.org; internet www.neptis.org.

Operation Eyesight Universal/Action Universelle de la Vue

Founded in 1963 by Arthur (Art) Jenkyns, a business person, and Dr Ben Gullison, who worked at a mission hospital in Sompeta, India.
Activities: Works to eliminate avoidable blindness. The organization operates in partnership with local medical professionals and community development teams, building resources for all people, especially the poor. It focuses on high-quality, comprehensive eye care that ensures a sustainable service for entire communities, with long-lasting results. Affiliated organizations operate in Bangladesh, Ethiopia, Ghana, India, Kenya, Nepal, the United Kingdom, the USA and Zambia.
Geographical Area of Activity: Canada, Ghana, India, Kenya, Nepal, UK, USA, Zambia.
Publications: Annual Report; *SightLines* (newsletter, 3 a year).
Finance: Annual revenue C $5.3m., expenditure $7.1m. (31 Dec. 2023).
Board of Directors: Dan Parlow (Chair.); Dr Diane A. Isabelle (Vice-Chair.); Byron Sonberg (Treas.); Shaad Oosman (Sec.).
Principal Staff: Pres. and CEO Kashinath Bhoosnurmath.
Contact Details: Suite 205, Campana Pl., 609-14 Street NW, Calgary, AB T2N 2A1; tel. (403) 283-6323; e-mail info@operationeyesight.com; internet www.operationeyesight.com.

Oxfam Canada

Established in 1967; part of the Oxfam confederation of organizations (qq.v.).
Activities: Focuses on women's rights. Main programmes include: ending violence against women and girls; gender in emergencies; sexual and reproductive health and rights; women's economic justice; and women's transformative leadership. The organization provides humanitarian assistance during emergency crises, including helping refugees.
Geographical Area of Activity: International.
Restrictions: Does not make loans or grants to individuals.
Publications: Annual Report; reports; educational materials.
Finance: Annual revenue C $42.6m., expenditure $43.3m. (31 March 2024).
Board of Directors: Amelia Martin, Karen Sander (Chair.); Iraz Soyalp (Vice-Chair.); Robert (Bob) Vandenberg (Treas.).
Principal Staff: Exec. Dir Lauren Ravon.
Contact Details: 39 McArthur Ave, Ottawa, ON K1L 8L7; tel. (613) 237-5236; e-mail info@oxfam.ca; internet www.oxfam.ca.

Oxfam-Québec

Established in 1973; part of the Oxfam confederation of organizations (qq.v.); in 2000 it merged with Club 2/3 (f. 1970), which subsequently became the organization's youth wing.
Activities: Works to end poverty and injustice. Main programme areas include: economic justice and respect for human rights, in particular women's rights; access to essential services, including education, healthcare, sanitation and water; rights during humanitarian crises; and gender equity and women's freedom from violence. The organization also provides emergency humanitarian assistance. It is advised on youth affairs by the Oxfam-Québec Youth Observatory.
Geographical Area of Activity: Benin, Bolivia, Burkina Faso, Canada, Colombia, Dem. Repub. of the Congo, El Salvador, Haiti, Honduras, Jordan, Mali, Niger, Palestinian Territories, Peru.
Restrictions: Does not make loans or grants to individuals.
Publications: Annual Report; newsletter; reports; studies; analysis; educational materials.
Finance: Annual revenue C $44.9m., expenditure $44.9m. (31 March 2024).
Board of Directors: Paul Buron (Pres.); Lylia Khennache (First Vice-Pres.); Roselyne Mavungu (Second Vice-Pres.); Michèle Gagné (Treas.); Isabelle Pasquet (Sec.).
Principal Staff: Gen. Man. Beatrice Vaugrante.

CANADA

Contact Details: 2330 rue Notre-Dame Ouest, Montréal, QC H3J 2Y2; tel. (514) 937-1614; e-mail info.oxfamqc@oxfam.org; internet oxfam.qc.ca.

Pacific Peoples' Partnership

Founded in 1975 as the South Pacific Peoples' Foundation of Canada.

Activities: Supports rights-based sustainable development initiatives that help communities to address poverty, environmental degradation and loss of culture. The Partnership supports Pacific Islanders' aspirations for peace, justice, environmental sustainability and development; and works to raise the profile of the Pacific island nations and territories internationally. It offers educational programmes; encourages links between Canadian and Pacific Islands organizations working in similar areas and between indigenous peoples in Canada and the Pacific region; and holds conferences and training courses.

Geographical Area of Activity: Canada, Pacific islands.

Restrictions: Grants only to specific organizations.

Publications: Annual Report; *Pasifik Currents* (newsletter); *Tok Blong Pasifik Journal* (every 5 years); videos.

Finance: Annual revenue C $45,282, expenditure $22,753 (30 June 2024).

Board of Directors: Dr James Boutilier (Pres. Emeritus); Muavae (Mua) Va'a (Pres.); Andy Telfer (Treas.); Kenneth Mackay (Sec.).

Principal Staff: Interim Exec. Dir Mere Sovick.

Contact Details: 620 View St, Suite 407, Victoria, BC V8W 1J6; tel. (250) 381-4131; e-mail info@pacificpeoplespartnership.org; internet www.pacificpeoplespartnership.org.

Presbyterian World Service & Development—PWS&D

Established in 1947; the development and relief agency of the Presbyterian Church in Canada and a member of the ACT Alliance (q.v.).

Activities: Supports people affected by poverty, injustice, disease and disasters. Main programme areas include: agriculture and food security; economic empowerment; education; health; HIV and AIDS; human rights; refugee sponsorship; and water and sanitation. The organization provides emergency humanitarian relief following natural disasters and conflicts; and works with the Canadian Foodgrains Bank (q.v.) to provide immediate and long-term food assistance. It also raises awareness about development issues within Canada.

Geographical Area of Activity: Canada, Central and South America and the Caribbean, Middle East, South Asia, South-East Asia, sub-Saharan Africa.

Publications: Annual Report; *PWSDevelopments* (quarterly newsletter); *e-news* (monthly e-newsletter); brochures; posters; religious materials.

Finance: Annual revenue C $3.7m., expenditure $3.9m. (31 Dec. 2023).

Principal Staff: Co-Conveners Shahrzad Kandalaft, Theresa McDonald-Lee.

Contact Details: 50 Wynford Dr., Toronto, ON M3C 1J7; tel. (416) 441-1111; e-mail pwsd@presbyterian.ca; internet presbyterian.ca/pwsd.

Prospera—International Network of Women's Funds

Established in 2016.

Activities: Prospera INWF is a global political network of 47 autonomous women's and feminist funds that nurture transformation by resourcing, supporting, and accompanying movements led by women, girls, trans, intersex, and non-binary people, and collectives primarily on the Global South and East.

Geographical Area of Activity: International.

Publications: Newsletter; Directory of Women's Funds Funders (online); *Collective Change Case Studies* (series).

Finance: Annual revenue US $3.2m., expenditure $3.2m. (31 Dec. 2021).

Board: Françoise Moudouthe, Virisila Buadromo (Co-Chair.); Nadejda Dermendjieva (Treas.), Joy Chia (Sec.).

Principal Staff: Exec. Dir Laila Alodaat.

Contact Details: 123 Slater St, Ottawa, ON K1P 5H2; e-mail info@prospera-inwf.org; internet www.prospera-inwf.org.

R. Howard Webster Foundation/Fondation R. Howard Webster

Established in 1967 by R. Howard Webster, an investor.

Activities: Makes grants to organizations working in the fields of the arts and culture, education, the environment, medicine and social services. Most grants are for 2–3 years.

Geographical Area of Activity: Canada.

Restrictions: Does not fund capital works or conferences and seminars; no grants to individuals.

Finance: Annual revenue C $16.3m., expenditure $13.6m. (31 Dec. 2023).

Board of Directors: Lucy Riddell (Chair.); Emily Webster (Vice-Chair.).

Principal Staff: Pres. Sacha Haque; Treas. Michael Svensson; Sec. Susan Lecouffe.

Contact Details: 1155 René-Lévesque blvd ouest, Suite 2912, Montréal, QC H3B 2L5; tel. (514) 866-2424; e-mail info@rhwfdn.ca; internet www.rhowardwebsterfoundation.ca.

RBC Foundation

Established in 1993 by the Royal Bank of Canada; formerly known as the Royal Bank of Canada Charitable Foundation.

Activities: Carries out the Bank's community and social impact programmes in the areas of: young people; the environment; diversity and inclusion; sustainable finance; and athletes and artists. Programmes include: Future Launch, preparing young people for the future of work; Youth Mental Well-being, supporting young people and their families; Emerging Artists, funding organizations that support artists aged 18–35 years with mentorships, apprenticeships and exposure to diverse audiences; and Tech for Nature, investing in technological innovation to address environmental challenges. The Foundation supports community initiatives through offering grants and sponsoring events.

Geographical Area of Activity: Canada, USA.

Restrictions: Does not make grants for conferences or seminars, nor to individuals.

Publications: *Corporate Social Responsibility Report*.

Finance: RBC Financial Group contributes 1% of its net income before tax. Annual revenue C $82.2m., expenditure $79.9m. (31 Oct. 2023).

Board of Directors: Mary Depaoli (Chair.); Karen McCarthy (Sec.).

Principal Staff: Exec. Dir Andrea Barrack.

Contact Details: 200 Bay St, 12th Floor, South Tower, Toronto, ON M5J 2J5; tel. (416) 974-1427; e-mail corporatecitizenship@rbc.com; internet www.rbc.com/community-social-impact.

SeedChange

Established in 1945, as the Unitarian Service Committe, by Dr Lotta Hirschmanova, a Czech refugee; formerly known as USC Canada.

Activities: Works in the fields of agroecology and food sovereignty, supporting 35,000 small-scale family farmers through helping to improve their incomes and defending their rights. Main programmes focus on: justice, health and sustainability. The organization saves, shares and breeds new seeds; restores degraded lands and soil; identifies local solutions to water shortages and climate change; establishes enterprises and co-operatives; shares and deepens farming knowledge, with a special focus on the knowledge of women farmers and Indigenous peoples; and advocates for farmers' rights at local, national and international level. In 2013 it launched the Bauta Family Initiative on Canadian Seed Security with Seeds of Diversity Canada. Has offices in Nepal, Timor-Leste and Mali.

Geographical Area of Activity: Bolivia, Burkina Faso, Canada, Cuba, Ethiopia, Guatemala, Honduras, Mali, Mexico, Nepal, Somaliland, Timor-Leste.

Publications: Annual Report; newsletter (weekly); *Jottings*; country sheets; educational materials.

Finance: Annual revenue C $742,252, expenditure $1m. (30 April 2024).

Board of Directors: Nicole McDonald (Chair.); Karim Salabi (Vice-Chair.); Cimoan Atkins (Treas.); Ericka Moerkerken (Sec.).

Principal Staff: Interim Exec. Dir Jessica Wood.

Contact Details: 56 Sparks St, Suite 600, Ottawa, ON K1P 5B1; tel. (613) 234-6827; e-mail info@weseedchange.org; internet weseedchange.org.

SickKids Foundation

Founded in 1972 by Duncan L. Gordon and John T. Law and others to provide funds for research, special programmes and public health education at the Hospital for Sick Children, Toronto, and throughout Canada.

Activities: Organizes educational and research programmes in two main areas: developing research skills; and knowledge generation and community action. The Foundation offers two main types of grants through its National Grants Program: New Investigator Research Grants, for research into childhood diseases and conditions; and Community Conference Grants, bringing together families, researchers, clinicians, and community organizations. It also supports the Canadian Child Health Clinician Scientist Training Program and the SickKids Research Institute (f. 1954).

Geographical Area of Activity: Canada.

Publications: Annual Report; newsletter (6 a year).

Finance: Total assets C $1,536.2m.; net annual revenue $161.3m. (31 March 2024).

Board of Directors: Walied Soliman (Chair.).

Principal Staff: Pres. and CEO Jennifer Bernard.

Contact Details: 525 University Ave, Suite 835, Toronto, ON M5G 2L3; tel. (416) 813-6166; e-mail donor.inquiries@sickkidsfoundation.com; internet www.sickkidsfoundation.com.

Steelworkers Humanity Fund/Le Fonds Humanitaire des Metallos

Established in 1985 by the United Steelworkers of America; a labour-based NGO.

Activities: Works with local trade unions and community organizations on international development projects that: support women's rights and gender equity; improve living standards; strengthen organizations through capacity building and organizing; and conduct research and analysis. The Fund has also provided emergency humanitarian aid during disaster; supported food banks in Canada; and offered an education programmes for Steelworker members.

Geographical Area of Activity: Africa, Central and South America, South Eastern Asia.

Publications: Annual Report; newsletter; brochure; posters; reports.

Finance: Annual revenue C $4.2m., expenditure $3.4m. (31 Dec. 2023).

Principal Staff: USW Int. Pres. David McCall; USW National Dir Marty Warren.

Contact Details: 234 Eglinton Ave East, 8th Floor, Toronto, ON M4P 1K7; tel. (416) 487-1571; e-mail humanityfund@usw.ca; internet www.usw.ca/humanityfund.

Terre Sans Frontières—TSF

Established in 1980 as Prodeva FIC by the Brothers of Christian Instruction; became Prodeva Tiers-Monde in 1986 and known as Terre Sans Frontières since 1994.

Activities: Works in the fields of community development, humanitarian aid and volunteer co-operation. The organization provides development and emergency assistance to communities in the global South, ensuring access to decent incomes, education and healthcare; cross-cutting themes include fair sharing, gender quality, respect for the environment and sound governance. It offers volunteers the opportunity to share their skills through the Professionals Without Borders programme, incorporating Dentistes Sans Frontières, Optométristes Sans Frontières, Physiothérapie Sans Frontières and the Office of Sound Management and Governance.

Geographical Area of Activity: Bolivia, Canada, Dem. Repub. of the Congo, Repub. of the Congo, Haiti, Mali, Senegal, Tanzania.

Publications: Annual Report; newsletter.

Finance: Annual revenue C $8.5m., expenditure $8.9m. (31 March 2024).

Board of Trustees and Executive Committee: Natacha Leclerc (Pres.); Richard Brisson (Vice-Pres.); Karine Arsenault-Pelletier (Treas.); Louise Marcoux (Sec.).

Principal Staff: Gen. Man. Jean L. Fortin.

Contact Details: 399 rue des Conseillers, Office 23, La Prairie, QC J5R 4H6; tel. (450) 659-7717; e-mail tsf@terresansfrontieres.ca; internet www.terresansfrontieres.ca.

Vancouver Foundation

Founded in 1943; formally established in 1950.

Activities: Works in areas including: arts and culture; education; children and young people's issues; the environment; animal welfare; community health and social development. The Foundation comprises 191 member community foundations and manages over 1,800 endowment funds. It awards Systems Change Grants for charitable projects in any sector (Develop Grants, of up to C $20,000 for a year and Test Grants worth up to $100,000 a year for three years); Participatory Action Research Grants for research co-led by community members and researchers (Convene Grants worth up to $20,000 for a year and Investigate Grants of up to $100,000 a year for three years); Fund for Gender Equality Grants, worth up to $40,000, to support to women, girls and gender-diverse people; LEVEL Youth Engagement Grants, of up to $20,000, with a focus on Indigenous, immigrant and refugee young people; LEVEL BIPOC Grants, worth up to $50,000, for BIPOC-led organizations working on racial equity and racial justice; Neighbourhood Small Grants of up to $500; and Downtown Eastside Small Arts Grants of up to $1,000 for local artists.

Geographical Area of Activity: Canada (mainly British Columbia).

Publications: Annual Report; *Vancouver Foundation Magazine*; *Vital Signs*; surveys; toolkits.

Finance: Annual revenue C $310.4m., expenditure $146.6m. (31 Dec. 2023).

Board of Directors: Susan Grossman (Chair.).

Principal Staff: Pres. and CEO Kevin McCort.

Contact Details: 475 West Georgia St, Suite 200, Vancouver, BC V6B 4M9; tel. (604) 688-2204; e-mail info@vancouverfoundation.ca; internet www.vancouverfoundation.ca.

Walter and Duncan Gordon Charitable Foundation

Established in 1965 by business person and politician Walter L. Gordon, his wife Elizabeth and brother Duncan L. Gordon.

Activities: Main initiatives are: the Jane Glassco Northern Fellowship, a policy and leadership programme for Northern Canadians, aged 25–35 years, who have an interest in public policy and activism and a history of community engagement and volunteering; DataStream, an open access platform on freshwater health across Canada; Northern Policy Hackathon, developing local recommendations on issues important to communities; the Understanding Our Treaties Initiative, helping Indigenous leaders learn from experts about the treaties in Canada and their impact on daily life; and the IBA (Impact and Benefit Agreement) Community Toolkit, a freely available resource for First Nations, Inuit and Métis communities involved in negotiating agreements with companies on natural resource extraction.

Geographical Area of Activity: Canada.

Restrictions: No grants to individuals.

Publications: Annual Report; newsletter; IBA Community Toolkit (in English and French); Northern Policy Hackathon Toolkit; reports; e-books; factsheets; infographics.

Finance: Annual revenue C \$7.6m., expenditure \$4.6m. (31 Dec. 2023).

Board of Directors: Adam Chamberlain (Chair.); Jaques Pinet (Treas.).

Principal Staff: Pres. and CEO Carolyn DuBois.

Contact Details: 11 Church St, Suite 400, Toronto, ON M5E 1W1; tel. (416) 601-4776; e-mail info@gordonfn.org; internet www.gordonfoundation.ca.

World University Service of Canada/Entraide Universitaire Mondiale du Canada—WUSC/EUMC

Established in 1939 as the Canadian committee of the International Student Service, which assisted Jewish students and other refugees fleeing Nazi persecution in Europe; present name adopted in 1950.

Activities: Works in the fields of women's and young people's education, employment and empowerment. The Service offers socioeconomic support to young people and their families to improve access to education, skills training and employment-related services. Initiatives include the Student Refugee Program in Canada, combining resettlement and access to higher education for more than 130 candidates each year. It works in 28 countries, with country offices in Burkina Faso, Ghana, Iraq, Jordan, Kenya, Malawi, Sri Lanka and Viet Nam.

Geographical Area of Activity: Canada, East Asia and South-East Asia, Middle East, South America, Central America and the Caribbean, South Asia, sub-Saharan Africa.

Restrictions: The Student Refugee Program is open to applicants aged 17–25 years, who are single and without dependents, and from one of the following countries of asylum: Jordan, Kenya, Lebanon, Malawi, Tanzania or Uganda.

Publications: Annual Report; *Monthly Development Review* (newsletter).

Finance: Annual revenue C \$50.6m., expenditure \$50.4m. (31 March 2024).

Board of Directors: Chris Whitaker (Chair.); Joy Johnson (Vice-Chair.); Dr Rahim Somani (Treas.).

Principal Staff: CEO Steve Mason.

Contact Details: 1404 Scott St, Ottawa, ON K1Y 4M8; tel. (613) 798-7477; e-mail wusc@wusc.ca; internet www.wusc.ca.

CENTRAL AFRICAN REPUBLIC

CO-ORDINATING BODY

Comité de Coordination des ONGI en RCA (International NGO Coordination Committee in CAR)

Established in 2014; an independent platform of international NGOs.

Activities: Provides humanitarian, recovery and development assistance to vulnerable people. The Committee co-ordinates between its members, the Government, international representatives and other partners; issues publications; and organizes roundtables. It has 36 member organizations.

Geographical Area of Activity: Central African Repub.

Publications: Newsletter; brochures; guides; magazines; reports.

Executive Committee: Michael Mbei (Pres.).

Contact Details: rue d'Uzès, Bangui; tel. 72-01-06-06; e-mail secretariat@ccorca.org; internet ccorca.org/comite-coordination-ongi.

FOUNDATIONS AND NON-PROFITS

Fondation Joseph Ichame Kamach

Established in 2007 by KGROUP, a business conglomerate, in memory of its founder, Joseph Ichame Kamach.

Activities: Works in the fields of health, education, the environment and vulnerable people. Initiatives include: promoting wellbeing and preventing disease; promoting girls' education, women's literacy and vocational training; protecting biodiversity and promoting renewable energy; and promoting microfinance and income-generating activities, especially among women, minorities, young people and disadvantaged people.

Geographical Area of Activity: Central African Repub.

Publications: Newsletter.

Principal Staff: Chair. Thérèse Kamach.

Contact Details: ave David Dacko, BP 804; tel. 21-61-18-05; e-mail contact@fondationkamach.org.

J'ai Rêvé Foundation

Established in 2013 by Zainab Djiwo Mansary (Liz Ellenz) and Moussa Deloose.

Activities: Carries out activities in the fields of community health, food security, protection and social development. Initiatives include: protecting children, young people and women from violence and discrimination; supporting rural communities; protecting the environment; preventing violence and radicalization; and preventing epidemics, HIV/AIDS and malaria.

Geographical Area of Activity: Central African Repub., Dem. Repub. of the Congo, Guinea.

Principal Staff: CEO Zainab Djiwo Mansary.

Contact Details: rue no. 2.065, Maison face au canal, Sica 3, BP 2864, Bangui; tel. 629-25-74-11; e-mail info@jairevefoundation.org; internet jairevefoundation.org.

CHAD

FOUNDATIONS AND NON-PROFITS

Fondation Grand Cœur—FGC (Big Heart Foundation)

Established in 2017, as Fondation Grand Cœur: Ta-Aoune pour le Bien-être Social et le Développement, by First Lady Hinda Déby Itno.

Activities: Works to eliminate social inequality and support vulnerable people. Main programme areas are: access to healthcare, organizing medical caravans, and building and equipping health facilities; schooling and training, supporting girls' education and youth entrepreneurship; sustainable rural development, training people in market gardening and establishing vegetable gardens; and solidarity, including providing vocational training to women and supporting income-generating activities. Also runs the Toumaï TV television channel.

Geographical Area of Activity: Chad.

Publications: Annual Report.

Principal Staff: Exec. Pres. Hinda Déby Itno; Sec.-Gen. Habiba Sahoulba Gontchomé; Deputy Sec.-Gen. Khadija Lamana.

Contact Details: Ave Gontchome Sahoulba, BP 1150, N'Djamena; tel. 22515055; e-mail contact@fondationgrandcoeur.td; internet fondationgrandcoeur.com.

CHANNEL ISLANDS

CO-ORDINATING BODIES

Association of Guernsey Charities—AGC

Established in 1984; an umbrella organization.

Activities: Supports and promotes non-profit organizations in the Bailiwick of Guernsey and disburses money raised by the Channel Island Christmas Lottery. Has approx. 300 members.

Geographical Area of Activity: Guernsey.

Publications: Newsletter.

Council: Peter Rose (Chair.); Malcolm Woodhams (Vice-Chair.); Mark O'Connor (Treas.); Maureen McLellan (Sec.).

Principal Staff: Exec. Dir Jo Le Poidevin.

Contact Details: c/o L'Heritage, Hougue du Pommier, Castel GY5 7FQ; tel. (7781) 433334; e-mail mail@charity.org.gg; internet charityt.w20.wh-2.com.

Association of Jersey Charities—AJC

Established in 1971.

Activities: Funds and supports non-profit organizations in Jersey. The Association provides information, advice and training; and disburses money raised by the Channel Island Lottery. It offers grants, worth up to £30,000, and small grants, worth up to £10,000. Has approx. 250 members.

Geographical Area of Activity: Jersey.

Restrictions: Grants and other services for AJC members, Jersey-registered charities and Foreign Excepted Charities whose work benefits Jersey residents.

Publications: Annual Report; newsletter.

Finance: Annual income £367k., expenditure £930k. (31 March 2024).

Executive Committee: Marcus Liddiard (Chair.); Robert Surcouf (Deputy Chair.); Sue Hamon (Treas.).

Principal Staff: Admin. Lyn Wilton.

Contact Details: POB 356, St Helier, Jersey, JE4 9YZ; tel. (1534) 840138; e-mail lyn@jerseycharities.org; internet www.jerseycharities.org.

CHILE

CO-ORDINATING BODY

Comunidad de Organizaciones Solidarios (Community of Solidarity Organizations)

Established in 2007.

Activities: Works to strengthen the role of CSOs in designing, implementing and evaluating public policy, offering training, development and technical support to members. The Community maintains an online directory of organizations. It comprises 254 CSOs, representing more than 11,000 workers and 17,000 volunteers; and has three regional offices.

Geographical Area of Activity: Chile.

Publications: Annual Report; Navegasocial.cl (online directory); blog.

Board of Directors: Alejandra Pizarro (Pres.); Catalina Littin (Vice-Pres.); Carola Rubia (Treas.).

Principal Staff: Exec. Dir Hans Rosenkranz.

Contact Details: General Bustamante 26, 4°, Providencia, Santiago; tel. (7) 476-3128; e-mail comunidad@comunidad-org.cl; internet www.comunidad-org.cl.

FOUNDATIONS AND NON-PROFITS

Centro de Estudios Públicos—CEP (Public Studies Centre)

Established in 1980; a private academic foundation.

Activities: Carries out research and analysis on public policy in support of personal freedoms, a social market economy and democracy. Areas of interest include: constitutional law; decentralization; democratic and political history; economic and political philosophy; education and higher education; electoral participation; energy; environment; free markets; health; immigration; inequality; legislation; macroeconomics and microeconomics; modernization of the state; pensions; political economy; poverty; and public opinion. The Centre organizes meetings, public seminars and working groups. It offers scholarships; and internships for Chilean and international students.

Geographical Area of Activity: Chile.

Publications: Annual Report; newsletter; *Estudios Públicos* (magazine); *Puntos de Referencia*; databases; studies; books.

Board of Directors: Juan Obach G. (Pres.); Juan Andrés Camus C. (Vice-Pres.).

CHILE

Principal Staff: Dir Dr Leonidas Montes L.
Contact Details: Monseñor Sótero Sanz 162, Providencia, Santiago 7500011; tel. (2) 2328-2400; e-mail escribanos@cepchile.cl; internet www.cepchile.cl.

Fundación Chile—FCH (Chile Foundation)

Established in 1976 by the Chilean Government and ITT Corpn, USA.

Activities: Fosters innovation in sustainability, human capital development, education, aquaculture, entrepreneurship and foods, developing local and international networks. The Foundation has created more than 65 companies, promoting new industries and innovative products in the main natural resource areas of the country. It also delivers high-impact technological solutions through transference, adaptation, research and development, working with more than 160 international organizations, companies, governments and technological centres in 35 countries.
Geographical Area of Activity: Chile.
Restrictions: No grants to individuals.
Publications: Annual Report; *Lignum* (trade magazine); *Aqua* (trade magazine); monographs.
Board of Directors: Pablo Zamora (Chair.).
Principal Staff: CEO Hernán Araneda.
Contact Details: Avda Parque Antonio Rabat Sur 6165, Vitacura, Santiago; tel. (2) 2240-0300; e-mail contacto@fch.cl; internet www.fch.cl.

Fundación Democracia y Desarrollo (Democracy and Development Foundation)

Established in 2006 by former President of Chile and founder of the Party for Democracy (PPD) Ricardo Lagos Escobar at the end of his term in office.

Activities: Uses digital technologies to foster civic engagement, sustainable economic development and greater social equality, with a particular focus on younger generations and under-represented groups. Main programmes are: #RedMujeres (#WomenNetwork), an online platform to provide mentoring and technology skills training to develop networks that promote women's leadership and participation; elquintopoder (The Fifth Power), an online platform for participative democracy; Bibliotecas para tu Acción Ciudadana (Public Libraries & Civic Engagement); Vecinos Conectados (Networked Neighbours), an online platform for reporting everyday problems to local councils; and #NuestraConstitución (#OurConstitution), an online platform that crowdsourced ideas for a new national Constitution. The Foundation also maintains Ricardo Lagos's personal archive of approx. 40,000 documents.
Geographical Area of Activity: Chile.
Publications: Reports; guides; e-books.
Finance: Mainly funded by the fees that the former President receives for conference appearances and talks internationally.
Principal Staff: Pres. Ricardo Lagos E.
Contact Details: La Concepción 141, off. 605, Providencia, Santiago; tel. (2) 2333-8098; e-mail contactenos@fdd.cl; internet www.fdd.cl.

Fundación Invica (Invica Foundation)

Established in 1959 by Cardinal Raúl Silva Henríquez; in 1977 it established the Cooperativa Abierta de Vivienda—PROVICOOP, a housing co-operative.

Activities: Works in the fields of urban planning, housing finance, development assistance, co-operatives and community development. The Foundation sponsors exhibitions; conducts research programmes and training courses; and maintains a database. It has built nearly 68,000 homes in 400 housing complexes.
Geographical Area of Activity: Chile.
Publications: *Boletín Construyendo*.

Red de Acción en Plaguicidas y sus Alternativas...

Board of Directors: Diego Vidal Sánchez (Pres.); Nicolas Parot Boragk (Vice-Pres.); Manuel Castillo Lea-Plaza (Sec.).
Principal Staff: Dir-Gen. Francisco Pinto Quappe.
Contact Details: Cienfuegos 67, Santiago; tel. (2) 690-0400; e-mail casapropia@invica.cl; internet www.invica.cl.

Fundación Pablo Neruda (Pablo Neruda Foundation)

Established in 1986 by the will of Matilde Urrutia, the widow of Chilean poet Pablo Neruda.

Activities: Operates in the fields of education and culture, through offering scholarships, fellowships and prizes; organizing conferences and cultural activities; and issuing publications. The Foundation maintains the Neruda Library and Archives in the Casa Museo La Chascona, including 5,000 vols from Neruda's personal collection. In 1987 it established the annual Pablo Neruda Award for poets aged under 40 years. In 2013, jointly with the Andrés Bello Archive at the Universidad de Chile, the Foundation created the Neruda Chair (Cátedra Neruda) to disseminate Neruda's work.
Geographical Area of Activity: Chile.
Publications: Newsletter; *Cuaderno* (magazine); *Nerudiana* (magazine); books.
Board of Directors: Alvaro Insunza Figueroa (Pres.); Claudia Morgana Rodríguez Larraín (Vice-Pres.); Claudio Herrera Jarpa (Sec.).
Principal Staff: Exec. Dir Fernando Sáez García.
Contact Details: Fernando Márquez de la Plata 0192, Barrio Bellavista, Providencia, POB 6640152, Santiago; tel. (2) 777-8741; e-mail info@fundacionneruda.org; internet www.fundacionneruda.org.

Fundación Telefónica Movistar Chile (Telefónica Movistar Chile Foundation)

Established in 1999 by Telefónica-Movistar, a telecommunications company; part of the Fundación Telefónica (q.v.) network.

Activities: Carries out activities in the areas of digital culture, education, employability and volunteering. As part of the ProFuturo digital education programme, a joint initiative with Fundación Bancaria 'la Caixa' (q.v.), the Foundation offers digital skills training through HUB Chile Programa. It offers free online training and digital tools via the Conecta Empleo platform; and has an exhibition space.
Geographical Area of Activity: Chile.
Publications: Annual Report.
Board: Roberto Muñoz (Pres.).
Principal Staff: Man. Olga Alarcón.
Contact Details: Av. Providencia 111, 28th Floor, Providencia, Santiago de Chile; tel. (2) 2691-3365; e-mail fundaciontelefonica.cl@telefonica.com; internet www.fundaciontelefonica.cl.

Red de Acción en Plaguicidas y sus Alternativas de América Latina—RAP-AL (Pesticide Action Network Latin America and the Caribbean)

Founded in 1982; subregional centre for the PAN International network.

Activities: Works to reduce and eliminate the use of harmful pesticides; campaigns against genetically modified crops; and promotes agriculture that is socially just, ecologically sustainable and economically viable as a means of achieving food security. The Network raises awareness about the effects of pesticide use in rural and urban areas; educates the public about the impacts of conventional agriculture on health and the environment; carries out political and legal action to eliminate pesticides and use alternatives; and promotes research and studies on the impacts of pesticides on, and their danger to, health and the environment. It is also involved in protecting heritage seeds. Has member organizations in 17 countries in Latin America and the Caribbean.
Geographical Area of Activity: Caribbean, Latin America.

SELAVIP

Publications: *Boletín Enlace* (quarterly newsletter); reports; guides.
Principal Staff: Co-ordinator Javier Souza Casadinho.
Contact Details: Compañía de Jesús 2540, Santiago; tel. (2) 699-7375; e-mail rap-al@terra.cl; internet www.rap-al.org.

SELAVIP—Services Latino-Américains, Africains et Asiatiques de Promotion de l'Habitation Populaire (Latin American, African and Asian Social Housing Service)

Founded in 1976 by Fr Josse van der Rest s.j. in Belgium and affiliated to Fondation van der Rest Emsens; the operational unit is based in Chile and the Advisory Board meets annually in Brussels at SELAVIP Belgium.
Activities: Provides shelter to very poor urban families in situations of extreme social emergency and supports organizations to initiate community-driven processes that will improve their shelter. The Service works with private and public institutions, NGOs, foundations and religious organizations. It insists on land title for the beneficiaries. The maximum amount granted per project is US $80,000.
Geographical Area of Activity: Africa, Asia, Latin America and the Caribbean.
Restrictions: Only funds projects in Asia, Africa and Latin America.
Publications: *SELAVIP Newsletter* (2 a year).
Board of Directors: Juan Cristobal Beytía (Pres.); Benito Baranda Ferrán (Vice-Pres.); Canio Corbo Lioi (Treas.).
Advisory Board: Jean Paul van der Rest (Pres.).
Principal Staff: Sec. Exec. Dir Henri Thijssen.
Contact Details: Casilla 597, Correos de Chile, Plaza de Armas, Santiago; tel. (2) 2581-3303; e-mail selavip.foundation@gmail.com; internet www.selavip.org.

THE PEOPLE'S REPUBLIC OF CHINA

CO-ORDINATING BODIES

China Charities Alliance
Founded in 2013 by 52 founding members.
Activities: Safeguards the public's interests and promotes transparency and professionalism in the philanthropic sector. Offers training for orgnaizations and practitioners across the charities sector and fosters co-operation with international organizations.
Geographical Area of Activity: People's Repub. of China.
Publications: Annual Report; brochures; reports.
Principal Staff: Sec.-Gen. Xiaojiu Jia.
Contact Details: Zhongcai Tower, 6th Floor, No. 48 Guang'anmen South St, Xicheng, Beijing 100054; tel. (10) 83523910; e-mail chuanbobu@charityalliance.org.cn; internet www.charityalliance.org.cn.

China Foundation Center—CFC
Established in 2010 by 35 Chinese foundations.
Activities: Promotes the transparency of philanthropic foundations in China. The Center maintains the Foundation Transparency Index, an online foundation database containing entries for more than 5,000 organizations; and an archive of information on China's foundation sector.
Geographical Area of Activity: People's Repub. of China.
Publications: Annual Report.
Board of Directors: Dezhi Lu (Chair.); Yongsheng Lei (Vice-Chair.).
Principal Staff: Pres. and Exec. Vice-Chair. Cheng Gang.
Contact Details: Room C, 12th Floor, Bldg B, Linda Bldg, No. 8 Dongtucheng Rd, Chaoyang District, Beijing 100028; tel. (10) 65691826; e-mail fti@foundationcenter.org.cn; internet www.foundationcenter.org.cn.

NPI Foundation
Established in 2006 by Zhao Lv; merged with China NPO Network in 2008. Formerly known as the Non-Profit Incubator and NPI Initiative. Present name adopted in 2016.
Activities: Supports social entrepreneurship and NGO capacity building. The Foundation provides training in accountability, develops networks, carries out research and issues publications. It has incubated more than 1,000 NGOs and social enterprises; in 2008 it established the Shanghai Wulixiang Community Service Center; and in 2009 it established the Shanghai United Foundation. Via the Duobaan learning management platform, courses are offered in community building, internet fundraising, public welfare, social entrepreneurship, project management and general skills. Has offices in 13 cities.
Geographical Area of Activity: People's Repub. of China.
Publications: Duobaan (online platform).
Board of Directors: Qingzhi Zhou (Chair.).
Principal Staff: Dir Wei He.
Contact Details: Room 223, Bldg 458, No. 535, Jinqiao Rd, Pudong New Area, Shanghai; tel. (21) 51879851; e-mail info@npi.org.cn; internet www.npi.org.cn.

FOUNDATIONS AND NON-PROFITS

Ai You Foundation
Established in 2004 by Wang Bing, an investor and social entrepreneur.
Activities: Carries out activities in the areas of child welfare and healthcare, in particular providing medical assistance to disadvantaged children; and providing philanthropy consultancy services to individuals. The Foundation has funded more than 100 organizations through the Philanthropy venture project; and provides training and professional development for charity workers through the Empowerment Community platform.
Geographical Area of Activity: People's Repub. of China.
Publications: Annual Report; newsletter.
Finance: Annual revenue 294.1m. yuan, expenditure 266.0m. yuan (31 Dec. 2020).
Board of Directors: Yuan Geng (Chair.); Shan Ding (Vice-Chair.).
Principal Staff: Sec.-Gen. Yibin Luan.
Contact Details: No. 1, Fu Tong East St, Wangjing SOHO-T3-B #609, Chaoyang District, Beijing 100102; tel. (10) 50948839; e-mail ay@ayfoundation.org; internet www.ayfoundation.org.

Amity Foundation
Established in 1985 by Chinese Christians under the leadership of Bishop K. H. Ting; a member of the ACT Alliance (q.v.).
Activities: Carries out activities in the areas of education, health, social welfare, community service, urban and rural community development, poverty alleviation, environmental conservation and disaster relief. The Education and International Exchange Program has co-ordinated the activities of more than 3,000 short- and long-term language teachers from overseas. The Foundation has offices in Hong Kong, Ethiopia, Kenya and Switzerland; a development centre in Guangzhou;

THE PEOPLE'S REPUBLIC OF CHINA

and in 2011 established the Rende Foundation in Shanghai, a grantmaking foundation which supports philanthropic innovation. Has special consultative status with ECOSOC.

Geographical Area of Activity: People's Repub. of China, Ethiopia, Hong Kong, Kenya, Switzerland.

Publications: Annual Report; *Amity Outlook* (newsletter); brochure.

Board of Directors: Zhonghui Qiu (Chair.); Chiuanyong Gu, Rev. Keyun Zhang (Vice-Chair.).

Principal Staff: Gen. Sec. Chunxiang Ling.

Contact Details: 71 Hankou Rd, Nanjing 210008; tel. (25) 83260800; e-mail amitynj@amity.org.cn; internet www.amityfoundation.org.

Center for China & Globalization—CCG

Established in 2008 by Dr Huiyao (Henry) Wang as an independent non-governmental think tank; a member of the Belt and Road Think Tank Alliance and a founding member of the US Research Think Tank Alliance established by the Chinese Ministry of Finance.

Activities: Carries out policy research and analysis in the field of Chinese globalization from an international perspective. Programme areas include: China-US relations; domestic policy; global governance; international economy and trade; international education; international relations; and global migration. The Center promotes the exchange of ideas between academia, business leaders experts and policymakers through platforms and events including international forums, roundtables and seminars. It comprises the CCG Belt and Road Institute, the CCG Chinese Entrepreneurs Research Center, the CCG Digital Economy Committee, the CCG Research Center, the CCG Northern Institute of International Talent and the CCG Southern Institute of International Talent. Has more than 10 national branches, with representatives overseas; and special consultative status with ECOSOC.

Geographical Area of Activity: International.

Publications: Annual Report; newsletter; policy recommendations; research reports; books.

Advisory Council: Yongtu Long (Chair.); Yafei He (Co-Chair.).

Principal Staff: Dir Dr Huiyao (Henry) Wang; Sec.-Gen. Dr Mable Lu Miao.

Contact Details: 12th Floor, West Wing, Hanwei Plaza, #7 Guanghua Rd, Chaoyang District, Beijing 100004; tel. (10) 65611038; e-mail ccg@ccg.org.cn; internet ccg.org.cn.

China Charities Aid Foundation for Children

Established in 2010.

Activities: Activities focus on the education and physical and mental health and wellbeing of children and adolescents. The Foundation supports NGOs, children's services projects and capacity building; carries out research; and organizes national and international exchanges for children.

Geographical Area of Activity: People's Repub. of China.

Publications: Annual Report; newsletter.

Finance: Donation income 5,899.3m. yuan, project expenditure 5,345.7m. yuan (22 May 2025).

Principal Staff: Chair. Xunchui Chen.

Contact Details: 9th Floor, Bldg 1, No. 24, Lize Rd, Fengtai District, Beijing; tel. (10) 88851687; e-mail ccafc@ccafc.org.cn; internet www.ccafc.org.cn.

China Children and Teenagers' Foundation

Established in 1981; affiliated to the All-China Women's Federation.

Activities: Cares for, fosters and educates children and teenagers. Activities include: the Spring Bud Project, helping girls living in poverty; the Safety and Health Plan, a large-scale public welfare programme; the Children's Happy Home project, addressing the physical and mental wellbeing of children who are separated from their parents for long periods; and HELLO Kids, providing care packages for children living in poverty or who have been affected by natural disasters.

Geographical Area of Activity: People's Repub. of China.

Publications: Annual Report.

Finance: Annual income 421.2m. yuan, expenditure 415.7m. yuan (31 Dec. 2020).

Principal Staff: Chair. Zhongxiao Cong; Sec.-Gen. Zhongming Li.

Contact Details: 10th Floor, Main Bldg, All-China Women's Federation Bldg, 15 Jianguomennei St, Dongcheng District, Beijing 100730; tel. (10) 65103493; e-mail cctf@cctf.org.cn; internet www.cctf.org.cn.

China Environmental Protection Foundation

Established in 1993 by Qu Geping.

Activities: Operates in the area of conservation and the environment. Encourages the development of eco-friendly manufacturing by aiding the development of eco-friendly products. The Foundation supports training, research, academic exchange and education in the field of environmental protection. It also sponsors eco-friendly businesses, organizations and individuals; issues publications; and implements environmental conservation projects.

Geographical Area of Activity: People's Repub. of China.

Publications: Annual Report; newsletter; briefings.

Principal Staff: Chair. Guang Xu; Sec.-Gen. Chunlong Liu.

Contact Details: No. 16 Guangqumennei St, Dongcheng District; tel. (10) 67113272; e-mail info@cepf.org.cn; internet www.cepf.org.cn.

China Foundation for Poverty Alleviation—CFPA

Established in 1989.

Activities: Works in the fields of poverty alleviation, healthcare, education and livelihoods development. Programmes include: reducing maternal and infant mortality and improving children's nutrition; providing affordable health insurance; improving the quality of education, building schools and offering scholarships; developing rural tourism and e-commerce; building rural infrastructure and providing small loans to farmers; and disaster relief, recovery and prevention. The Foundation also provides emergency humanitarian relief; and carries out international development programmes in areas including education and training, women's economic empowerment, refugee resettlement and community integration, and water, sanitation and hygiene. It works in 25 countries and regions; and has offices in Chengdu, as well as Ethiopia, Myanmar and Nepal.

Geographical Area of Activity: East and South-East Asia, South Asia, sub-Saharan Africa.

Publications: Annual Report; newsletter.

Finance: Total assets 2,248.5m. yuan (31 Dec. 2024).

Board of Directors: Wenkai Zheng (Chair.); Zhigang Chen, Wenkui Liu (Vice-Chair.); Hongtao Chen (Sec.-Gen.).

Contact Details: Room 101, 1st Floor, Bldg 4, No. 2 Huayuan Rd, Haidian District, Beijing 100191; tel. (10) 82872688; e-mail cfrd@cfrd.org.cn; internet www.cfpa.org.cn.

China Siyuan Foundation for Poverty Alleviation

Established in 2007.

Activities: Supports the socioeconomic development of disadvantaged groups. The Foundation carries out activities in the areas of education and training, healthcare, disaster relief, care of the elderly and environmental conservation. Projects include replacing wood-burning stoves with bio-gas in rural households; making grants and scholarships to primary and secondary school pupils; providing hearing tests and cochlear implants for children; setting up an ambulance service in under-served communities, benefiting around 400,000 people;

drilling wells and providing water storage facilities in drought-prone areas; and providing solar-powered electricity in mountainous rural areas.
Geographical Area of Activity: People's Repub. of China.
Publications: Annual Report.
Finance: Annual income 666.7m. yuan, expenditure 534.6m. yuan (2024).
Council: Weiping Li (Chair.).
Principal Staff: Sec.-Gen. Xizhen Cheng.
Contact Details: 208 Jixiangli, Chaowai St, Chaoyang District, Beijing 100020; tel. (10) 85698220; e-mail office@sygoc.org.cn; internet www.sygoc.org.cn.

China Youth Development Foundation
Established in 1989 by the All-China Youth Federation; a network of 38 local youth development foundations.
Activities: Works in the field of children and young people, promoting their work, education, culture and social welfare through projects and prizes; and encouraging relations between young people around the world with a view to safeguarding world peace. The Foundation's main programme is Project Hope, which improves underprivileged children's educational opportunities and provides financial aid to help children who do not attend school to return to education. The programme has funded the construction of more than 20,000 Hope Schools in remote rural areas. The Stars of Hope Award Fund supports further studies by Project Hope students; and the Hope Primary School Teacher-Training Fund enables teachers to develop their skills and expand their knowledge. Other initiatives include a river and wetlands protection programme; and joint programmes conducted with telecommunications company Nokia.
Geographical Area of Activity: People's Repub. of China.
Publications: Annual Report; *Hope Journal*; *News of CYDF*; *The Project Hope Public Announcement* (annual).
Council: Feng Mei (Chair.); Xuejun Wan (Vice-Chair. and Sec.-Gen.).
Contact Details: 51 Wangjing West Rd, Chaoyang District, Beijing 100102; tel. (10) 64035547; e-mail 64035547@cydf.org.cn; internet www.cydf.org.cn.

Dunhe Foundation
Established in 2012.
Activities: Activities fall into three main areas: promoting traditional Chinese culture; working with other foundations and organizations to support experts and research in charity culture; and funding the development of public welfare. Programmes include: the Seed Fund Program, funding the establishment of non-profit organizations; the Activate Program, funding newly established non-profit organizations; the Youtural Talent Program, developing the skills of charity professionals; and the Bamboo Fellow Program, supporting scholars and practitioners under the age of 40 years to carry out charity research. It has co-founded the China Global Philanthropy Institute, the Cross-Cultural Research Institute of Beijing Normal University and the Fuxing Academy of Zhejiang University and supports West Lake University (also known as Westlake Institute for Advanced Study); and sponsors events such as the Global Sinology Ceremony. Has an office in Beijing.
Geographical Area of Activity: People's Repub. of China.
Publications: Annual Report.
Finance: Donation income 8,202.1m. yuan, expenditure 4,942.1m. yuan (2024).
Council: Xuxin Shen (Chair.); Hong Lin (Sec.-Gen.).
Board of Supervisors: Gang Qiu (Chair.).
Contact Details: No. 57-1 Puyu Rd, Shangcheng District, Hangzhou City, Zhejiang Province; tel. (571) 87609810; e-mail info@dunhefoundation.org; internet www.dunhefoundation.org.

He Xiangjian Foundation
Established in 2013 by Xiangjian He, founder of Midea Group, a consumer appliance manufacturer.
Activities: Provides assistance to vulnerable people, including the elderly and people living in poverty; awards scholarships and provides capacity building for poor students and teachers at five colleges and universities in north-west and south-west China; supports Chinese culture and the arts and environmental conservation. The Foundation also funds other foundations and charitable organizations.
Geographical Area of Activity: People's Repub. of China.
Publications: Annual Report.
Finance: Annual income 690.5m. yuan, expenditure 293.1m. yuan (31 Dec. 2020).
Council: Situ Ying (Chair.).
Principal Staff: Sec.-Gen. Liu Chong.
Contact Details: 24th Floor, Yingfeng Business Center, No. 8, Yi Xing Rd, Beijiao Zhen, Shunde District, Foshan City 528311; e-mail hf@hefoundation.org; internet www.hefoundation.org.

Heren Philanthropic Foundation
Established in 2011 by Dewang Cao, Chair. and CEO of Fuyao Glass Industry Group Co Ltd.
Activities: Works in the fields of poverty alleviation, emergency assistance and education. Programmes include: expanding access to education and medical services for vulnerable people; supporting infrastructure development and environmental protection; emergency humanitarian relief and post-disaster recovery and reconstruction; social welfare and capacity building.
Geographical Area of Activity: People's Repub. of China.
Publications: Annual Report.
Board of Directors: Dewang Cao (First Chair.); Shuang Wu (Chair.).
Supervisory Board: Shi Chen (Chair.).
Principal Staff: Sec.-Gen. Yan Yan.
Contact Details: ICC Thanglong Global Center, 24th Floor, No. 23 Changting Rd, Taijiang District, Fuzhou 350000; e-mail heren_xiangmu@163.com; internet www.hcf.org.cn.

Heungkong Charitable Foundation
Established in 2005 by Meiqing Zhai, co-founder of Heungkong Group, a conglomerate; given charitable status in 2017.
Activities: Works in the fields of education, poverty alleviation, healthcare and disaster relief. Foundation initiatives include: building libraries; supporting poor families, disabled children and the elderly; sponsoring orphans; awarding scholarships to disadvantaged and outstanding university students; and building child-friendly community projects and houses for single mothers. Other programmes include: the Fund for Female Entrepreneurship; Heungkong Splendid Cultural Inheritance; and Public Welfare Training of Chinese Media Journalists.
Geographical Area of Activity: People's Repub. of China.
Finance: Total assets 98.1m. yuan (31 Dec. 2023).
Council: Taiwei Weng (Chair.); Gensen Liu (Vice-Pres.).
Principal Staff: Dir and Sec.-Gen. Yuping Hu.
Contact Details: 2nd Floor, Jinxiu Xiangjiang Garden Club, Yingbin Rd, Panyu District, Guangzhou 511442; tel. (20) 84566620; e-mail hkf@heungkong.com; internet www.hkf.org.cn.

Jack Ma Foundation—JMF
Established in 2014 by Jack Ma, co-founder and former Executive Chair. of Alibaba Group, an e-commerce company.
Activities: Carries out programmes in the areas of education, entrepreneurship, environmental protection, medical support and women's leadership. The Foundation cultivates future-orientated rural educators and entrepreneurs; helps rural children and young entrepreneurs; supports women's

development and growth; and works towards a greener, healthier, happier and more inclusive world. Main programmes include: the Rural Teacher Initiative, awarding grants worth 100,000 yuan to 100 rural teachers annually; the Rural Principals Initiative, awarding grants of 500,000 yuan to 20 headteachers to develop educational plans; and the Rural School Initiative, establishing pilot rural boarding schools. The Foundation set up the Hangzhou Normal University Jack Ma Education Fund with an endowment worth 100m. yuan; and the Ma & Morley Scholarship Program at the University of Newcastle, Australia, for Australian students, which annually offers 20 scholarships and 10 Lng Jūn Jn immersion experiences in China. The Africa Netpreneur Prize Initiative seeks to identify 100 outstanding African entrepreneurs in 10 years; each year, 10 entrepreneurs compete for a share of a US $1m. grant. In 2019 the Jack Ma Education Fund of Lhasa Normal University was endowed with 100m. yuan to provide subsidies and training for Tibetan teaching staff. Works closely with national and international organizations, in particular supporting the training of headteachers and development of an online learning platform to benefit learners in Jordan and neighbouring countries.

Geographical Area of Activity: Australia, People's Repub. of China, Jordan.

Publications: Annual Report; newsletter.

Finance: Annual income 745.2m. yuan, expenditure 205.1m. yuan (2019).

Board: Jack Ma (Chair.).

Principal Staff: Exec. Sec. Xiuhong Yu.

Contact Details: Bldg 8, Angel Village, Dream Town, 999 Xingcheng Rd, Yu Hang District, Hangzhou 311121; tel. (571) 86235021; e-mail info@jackmafoundation.org.cn; internet www.jackmafoundation.org.cn.

Ningxia Yanbao Charity Foundation

Established in 2011 by Yanbao Dang, Pres. of Ningxia Baofeng Energy Group Co Ltd, and his wife Bian Haiyan.

Activities: Works in the fields of social and economic development and poverty alleviation in remote areas. Main programmes focus on: access to education; community and rural health and welfare services for the elderly and disabled people; and disaster relief. The Foundation provides scholarships for college students and vocational learners; and has supported the building of primary schools and medical facilities in migrant communities. Established a chain of 100 community supermarkets which operate as social enterprises, funding community social projects.

Geographical Area of Activity: People's Repub. of China (primarily Ningxia).

Principal Staff: Chair. Yanbao Dang; Sec.-Gen. Dongmei Ma.

Contact Details: Bldg C, 3rd Floor, Lijing North St, Xingqing District, Ningxia, Yinchuan 750001; tel. (951) 6075007; e-mail nxybcsjjh@163.com.

One Foundation

Established in 2007 by Jet Li, an actor.

Activities: Carries out activities in the areas of disaster relief; children's health, welfare and education, in particular children living in poverty and disaster-prone areas or with other special needs; and building the capacity of NGOs through training, carrying out research, and project monitoring and evaluation. The Foundation has offices in Beijing, Chengdu, Shanghai and Ya-an City.

Geographical Area of Activity: People's Repub. of China.

Publications: Annual Report.

Finance: Annual income 565.4m. yuan, expenditure 477.1m. yuan (31 Dec. 2024).

Council: Weihua Ma (Chair.); Huateng Ma (Vice-Chair.).

Principal Staff: Sec.-Gen. Hong Li.

Contact Details: 15th Floor, Wanji Business Bldg, Fuhua Rd, Futian District, Shenzhen, Guangdong; tel. (400) 6902700; e-mail info@onefoundation.cn; internet www.onefoundation.cn.

Shanghai Soong Ching Ling Foundation

Founded in 1986, by the China Welfare Institute, in memory of Soong Ching Ling (Madame Sun Yat-sen), former Chinese Hon. Chair.

Activities: Carries out public welfare initiatives for people in need through self-conducted programmes in the areas of education, culture, health and medicine. Main programmes include: providing small loans to rural households to enable their children to go to school; improving maternal and infant healthcare in western regions; improving children's education in rural areas, providing grants and setting up libraries; providing science education in rural areas; organizing professional training in public welfare; and promoting transparent public welfare. The Foundation also carries out international exchanges and sister organizations have been established in Austria, Italy, Japan, South Africa and the USA.

Geographical Area of Activity: People's Repub. of China.

Publications: Annual Report; newsletter (quarterly).

Board of Supervisors: Xiaobao Miao (Chair.).

Board of Directors: Liang Jiang (Chair.); Xiaomin Zhang (Vice-Chair.).

Principal Staff: Sec.-Gen. Ming Zhang.

Contact Details: 369 North Shaanxi Rd, Shanghai 200040; tel. (21) 62530253; e-mail sclf@sclf.net; internet www.ssclf.net.

SOHO China Foundation

Established in 2005 by Zhang Xin, CEO of property development company SOHO China (f. 1995), and her husband Pan Shiyi, Chair. of SOHO China.

Activities: Programmes include: Teach for China, which trains university graduates from the USA and the People's Republic of China to teach at schools in Yunnan and Guangdong provinces; the Children's Virtues Project, promoting personal and communal responsibility in young children; the Bathroom Construction Campaign to improve school sanitation; and Futures Brightened through Helping Hands, which sponsors the university education of underprivileged students and encourages reciprocal volunteering. In 2014 the Foundation set up the SOHO China Scholarships, with an endowment of US $100m., for Chinese students to study at universities abroad.

Geographical Area of Activity: Principally People's Repub. of China.

Principal Staff: Chair. Yan Yan; Pres. Lu Wei.

Contact Details: c/o SOHO China Ltd, Chaowai SOHO, Bldg A, 11th Floor, 6B Chaowai St, Chaoyang District, Beijing 100020; tel. (10) 58788509.

State Grid Foundation for Public Welfare

Established in 2009 by State Grid Corpn of China, the state-owned electricity provider, as Grid Welfare Foundation; present name adopted in 2010.

Activities: Operates in the fields of poverty alleviation and disaster relief. The Foundation organizes social welfare programmes that support students from low-income backgrounds, the elderly and disabled people. It established the UHV Power Grid Scholarship Fund to encourage innovation by students in power research and development.

Geographical Area of Activity: People's Repub. of China.

Finance: Initial capital 100m. yuan.

Council: Xiaogang Pang (Chair.).

Principal Staff: Gen. Sec. Jiabin Ma.

Contact Details: 8 Xuanwumennei St, Xicheng District, Beijing 100031; tel. (10) 63413435; internet www.sgpwf.com.cn.

Tencent Foundation

Established in 2006 by Tencent Inc, an internet service provider.

Activities: Works to use the internet and information communications and technology for public benefit. The Foundation funds the construction of school buildings, dormitories and infrastructure, and provides teacher training, to improve education in disadvantaged areas. It raises awareness about welfare issues among university students; and runs the Tencent New Countryside Action public welfare programme in Guizhou and Yunnan. Other areas of interest include: culture; environmental protection; economic development; disaster relief and reconstruction; and scientific research.

Geographical Area of Activity: People's Repub. of China.

Publications: Annual Report.

Finance: Annual revenue 2,151.9m. yuan, expenditure 1,694.6m. yuan (31 Dec. 2020).

Council: Kaitian Guo (Chair.).

Principal Staff: Sec.-Gen. Yan Ge.

Contact Details: 33rd Floor, Tencent Bldg, Kejizhongyi Rd, High-Tech Park, Nanshan District, Shenzen, Guangdong; tel. (755) 86013388; internet www.tencentfoundation.org.

Yuan Lin Charity Fund

Established in 2012 by Yuanlin Ren, Pres. of Yangzijiang Shipbuilding Group.

Activities: Carries out activities in the areas of elderly people, technological innovation and disaster relief. The Foundation promotes respect for elderly people, building seniors' universities and activity centres; and undertaking the management of chronic diseases and rehabilitation of elderly people affected by them. Other activities include funding scientific research projects related to human health and environmental protection.

Geographical Area of Activity: People's Repub. of China.

Principal Staff: Chair. Jianguo Liu; Sec.-Gen. Yaqin Jia.

Contact Details: 10 Jiyang Rd, Jiangyin City, Jiangsu Province, Wuxi City; tel. (510) 86812600; e-mail cf@yuanlincf.com; internet yuanlincf.com.

COLOMBIA

CO-ORDINATING BODIES

Asociación de Fundaciones Familiares y Empresariales—AFE (Association of Family and Corporate Foundations)

Established in 2008 by a group of nine corporate foundations that had been working together since 2004; comprises the Alianza para el Desarollo Colectivo AFE Antioquia.

Activities: Acts as spokesperson for its associated foundations and promotes the improvement of their social management, facilitating articulation, co-operation, social innovation and knowledge exchange among the associates; acting with transparency to achieve a greater impact in their interventions and to contribute to equity and sustainable social development in Colombia.

Geographical Area of Activity: Colombia.

Publications: Annual Report; newsletter; discussion papers; reports; technical notes; books; blog.

Principal Staff: Exec. Dir Aura Lucía Lloreda Mera.

Contact Details: Calle 69 #4-48, Edif. Buró 501, Of. 501, Bogotá; tel. (314) 6103689; e-mail contacto@afecolombia.org; internet www.afecolombia.org.

Filantrópico (Philanthropic)

Established in 2010 under the name Filantropía Transformadora, with the help of Give to Colombia and Compartamos con Colombia.

Activities: Promotes long-term strategic philanthropy to improve social investment nationally. The organization hold conferences and workshops; facilitates training; and co-ordinates efforts and alliances between individuals, and the social, government and private sectors.

Geographical Area of Activity: Colombia.

Publications: Annual Report.

Board of Directors: Felipe Medina (Pres.).

Principal Staff: Exec. Dir Mariana Castro Dominguez.

Contact Details: Calle 77A, No. 12–32, Apto 501, Bogotá; tel. (317) 6472826; e-mail info@filantropico.co; internet www.filantropico.co.

FOUNDATIONS AND NON-PROFITS

Fundación Amanecer

Established in 1994 by Ecopetrol SA, BP, Total and Triton, oil and gas companies; in 2005 the Foundation became an independent organization.

Activities: Works in the fields of human development, business development and environmental protection. The Foundation works to alleviate extreme poverty and hunger; promote gender equality and women's empowerment; and guarantee environmental sustainability. It offers grants and financial support, including loans, to not-for-profit organizations and microcredit to individuals; and provides technical support in the field of agriculture and agricultural technology to co-operative enterprises and grassroots organizations. Has offices in six departments.

Geographical Area of Activity: Colombia.

Principal Staff: Dir-Gen. Dr César Iván Velosa Poveda.

Contact Details: Calle 24, No. 20A–27, Barrio Provivienda, Yopal, Casanare; tel. (310) 5872082; internet www.amanecer.org.co.

Fundación Capital

Established in 2009, as Fundación Capital—FundaK, by Yves Moury; a non-profit social enterprise.

Activities: Promotes 'economic citizenship' through financial literacy education and digital solutions. The Foundation carries out advocacy to improve public policy; and works with governments and the private sector to create large-scale programmes that will improve the lives and livelihoods of children and young people, women and girls, migrants and refugees, and vulnerable groups. It works in 20 countries; and has offices in Honduras, Mexico, Mozambique, Paraguay and Peru.

Geographical Area of Activity: Latin America, South Asia, South-East Asia, sub-Saharan Africa.

Publications: Annual Report; *Short Cuts* (factsheets); reports.

Principal Staff: Pres. and CEO Yves Moury.

Contact Details: Calle 86A Bis #15-31, Bogotá, 110221; tel. (1) 3847500; e-mail info@fundacioncapital.org; internet fundacioncapital.org.

COLOMBIA

Fundación Corona (Corona Foundation)

Established in 1963 by the Echavarría Olózaga family, founders of Corona, a manufacturer of ceramic products.

Activities: Works to reduce inequality through progress and social mobility. Main programmes focus on: education and training for employment; and education for citizens' participation through transparency, innovation and technology. The Foundation also works with Corona to provide clean water and sanitation and promote inclusive employment.

Geographical Area of Activity: Colombia.

Publications: Annual Report; *Intemperie* (2 a year); *Boletín Mensual* (monthly newsletter); briefing papers; reports; toolkits.

Finance: Annual income 21,472.4m. pesos, expenditure 28,091.3m. pesos (31 Dec. 2023).

Principal Staff: Exec. Dir Daniel Uribe Parra.

Contact Details: Calle 70, No. 7–30, Of. 1001, 11001000, Bogotá; tel. (1) 4000031; e-mail fundacion@fcorona.org; internet www.fundacioncorona.org.

Fundación para la Educación Superior y el Desarrollo—Fedesarrollo (Foundation for Higher Education and Development)

Founded in 1970 by Manuel Carvajal Sinisterra, Rodrigo Botero Montoya and Alberto Vargas Martínez.

Activities: Operates in the fields of social welfare, political science and administration, economic affairs and international relations; internationally through research, surveys, publications and lectures, and nationally through conferences and courses conducted in Colombia.

Geographical Area of Activity: Colombia.

Publications: *Tendencia Económica* (monthly); *Informe del Mercado Laboral* (monthly); *Informe del Mercado de Leasing*; *Coyuntura TIC*; *Prospectiva Económica* (3 a year); *Bitácora Semanal* (weekly); *Coyuntura Económica* (weekly); *Informe Mensual Macroeconómico* (monthly); reports; books; working papers.

Finance: Annual income 7.7m. pesos. expenditure 5.6m. pesos (2023).

Principal Staff: Exec. Dir Luis Fernando Mejía; Deputy Dir Ximena Cadena; Sec.-Gen. Marcela Pombo.

Contact Details: Calle 78, No. 9–91, AA75064 Bogotá; tel. (1) 3259777; e-mail comercial@fedesarrollo.org.co; internet www.fedesarrollo.org.co.

Fundación Escuela Nueva (New School Foundation)

Established in 1987 by Vicky Colbert, Beryl Levinger and Óscar Mogollónto, creators of the Escuela Nueva paedagogical model, to ensure its quality and continuing development.

Activities: Promotes active, collaborative and personalized learning. The Foundation provides technical assistance, facilitates networking and partnerships, and carries out research and evaluations. It also maintains the Renueva virtual community and the Rodrigo Escobar Nava documentation centre. Has worked in Latin American countries, India, Timor-Leste, Viet Nam and Zambia.

Geographical Area of Activity: International.

Publications: Annual Report; newsletter; learning guides; training manuals; research findings.

Finance: Annual income 4,364.5m. pesos (2022).

Principal Staff: Exec. Dir Vicky Colbert; Sec. Claudia Viviana Ruiz.

Contact Details: Calle 39, No. 21–57, Bogotá; tel. (1) 7432216; e-mail info@escuelanueva.org; internet escuelanueva.org.

Fundación Hábitat Colombia—FHC (Colombian Habitat Foundation)

Established in 1991 by Inés Useche de Brill, Lucelena Betancur Salazar and Mónica Ramírez.

Activities: Specializes in knowledge management on urban best practices, research, communication, technical assistance and co-operation for urban and regional development. The Foundation promotes a better quality of life for urban dwellers in collaboration with the Government, the private sector and social organizations. It supports initiatives that encourage environmental development, exchange of experience and information, and strategic alliances, and that promote sustainability.

Geographical Area of Activity: Colombia.

Publications: *Intercambios/Exchanges; Best Practices Transfer;* case studies; reports.

Principal Staff: Dir Lucelena Betancur Salazar.

Contact Details: Calle 127c, No. 6A–40, Bogotá; tel. (1) 2163606; e-mail direccion@fundacionhabitatcolombia.org; internet fundacionhabitatcol.wixsite.com/habitat-colombia.

Fundación Pies Descalzos

Established in 1997 by Shakira Mebarak, a pop singer.

Activities: Works to improve children's access to education. The Foundation builds schools and aims to improve the quality of teaching through innovation and technology.

Geographical Area of Activity: Latin America (mainly Colombia).

Publications: Annual Report.

Finance: Annual income 1,220.9m. pesos, expenditure 1,210.6m. pesos (31 Dec. 2024).

Board of Directors: Maria Emma Mejía (Pres.).

Principal Staff: Exec. Dir Patricia Sierra.

Contact Details: Calle 85, No. 18–32, Of. 401, Bogotá; tel. (315) 8242422; e-mail webmaster@fpd.ong; internet www.fundacionpiesdescalzos.com.

Fundación Telefónica Movistar Colombia (Telefónica Movistar Colombia Foundation)

Established in 2011 by Telefónica-Movistar, a telecommunications company; part of the Fundación Telefónica (q.v.) network.

Activities: Main programmes focus on digital culture, education, employability and volunteering, with a focus on digital education and women's empowerment.

Geographical Area of Activity: Colombia.

Publications: Newsletter.

Finance: Total assets 1,462.9m. pesos (31 Dec. 2024).

Principal Staff: Dir Mónica Hernández.

Contact Details: Transversal 60 (Av. Suba), No. 114A–55, Edif. Telefónica Colombia, Bogotá; e-mail fundaciontelefonica.co@telefonica.com; internet www.fundaciontelefonica.co.

Latimpacto—Red Latinoamericana de Inversión Social y Filantropía Estratégica (Latin American Venture Philanthropy Network)

Established in 2020; a non-profit organization; works closely with Impact Europe (q.v.), the Asian Venture Philanthropy Network and the African Venture Philanthropy Alliance (qq.v.).

Activities: Invests in social purpose organizations to support innovative solutions to social and environmental problems. Members include foundations, corporations and individuals. The Network also offers training, issues publications and organizes events.

Geographical Area of Activity: Latin America.

Publications: Newsletter; research reports; case studies.

Principal Staff: CEO María Carolina Suárez Visbal.

Contact Details: Cl 123 7-07, Of. 403, Bogotá; tel. (315) 6106491; e-mail comunidad@latimpacto.org; internet latimpacto.org.

DEMOCRATIC REPUBLIC OF THE CONGO

FOUNDATIONS AND NON-PROFITS

Centre d'Etudes Pour l'Action Sociale—CEPAS (Research Centre for Social Action)

Established in 1955 by the Society of Jesus, a Catholic Christian order.

Activities: Carries out socioeconomic research and promotes social justice and sustainable development though activities based on religious doctrine. Programmes include: leadership training and capacity building of NGOs; and carrying out studies on disadvantaged groups and supporting actions to resolve the problems they face. The Centre organizes conferences, seminars and training course; and maintains a research library containing more than 30,000 vols and 1,100 periodicals.

Geographical Area of Activity: Dem. Repub. of the Congo.

Publications: *Congo-Afrique* (journal, 10 a year); brochures; books; book catalogue; blog.

Principal Staff: Dir Fr Alain Nzadi-a-Nzadi.

Contact Details: 9 ave du Père Boka, en face du Ministère des Affaires Étrangères, BP 5717, Kinshasa/Gombe; tel. 822915688; e-mail congoadrique2@gmail.com; internet cepas.online.

Fondation Mapon

Established in 2007 by Matata Ponyo Mapon, former Minister of Finance.

Activities: Works to prevent poverty and malnutrition, with a focus on young people and families. Main programme areas are: education, health, agriculture and clean water. The Foundation operates a primary school and secondary school, Lumbu-Lumbu hospital and a pilot farm; and also Mapon University, which offers interdisciplinary courses in sciences, IT, engineering and economics for up to 3,500 students.

Geographical Area of Activity: Dem. Repub. of the Congo.

Publications: Newsletter.

Board of Directors: Matata Ponyo Mapon (Chair.).

Contact Details: 364 blvd du 30 juin, Immeuble Kiyo ya sita, 5ème étage, Local 501, Kinshasa/Gombe; tel. 812763003; e-mail contact@fondationmapon.org; internet www.fondationmapon.org.

Fondation Rawji

Established in 2003 as the philanthropic arm of Groupe Rawji, a conglomerate.

Activities: Carries out activities in the fields of education, health and wellbeing, and information media. The Foundation awards scholarships for primary, secondary and tertiary education; supports cross-cutting projects in education innovation; and encourages collaboration and partnerships with international organizations. It has built schools, hospitals, leisure centres and nursing homes, set up radio and television stations, and provided clean drinking water.

Geographical Area of Activity: Dem. Repub. of the Congo.

Publications: Newsletter.

Principal Staff: Deputy Gen. Man. Jean-Pierre Mutuale Mukadi Mpaka.

Contact Details: Bâtiment BELTEXCO, 1087 croisement ave du Marché et Bas-Congo, BP 8915, Kinshasa 1; tel. 810149144; e-mail info@rawjifondation.com; internet www.fondationrawji.org.

Fondation Vodacom RDC (Vodacom Foundation DRC)

Established in 2002 by Vodacom RDC, a telecommunications company; part of the Vodafone Foundation (q.v.) network.

Activities: Supports technology-based projects that address social and economic challenges in the areas of climate action, education, health, wellbeing and security. The Foundation provides access to online educational resources in English, French and Kiswahili for elementary and secondary schools through Vodaeduc platform; and for refugees through the Instant Schools Network, in partnership with UNHCR.

Geographical Area of Activity: Dem. Repub. of the Congo.

Publications: Social Achievements Report; *Vodanews*.

Principal Staff: Deputy Gen. Man. Paulin Ikwala.

Contact Details: 292 ave de la justice, Gombe; tel. 813131000; e-mail vodacom@vodacom.cd; internet www.vodacom.cd/apropos/rapport-de-la-fondation-vodacom.

HJ Foundation

Established in 2016 by Harish Jagtani, a business person who also founded HJ Hospitals, a healthcare provider.

Activities: Carries out activities in the areas of: health and wellbeing, building and operating hospitals and rural maternity wards, medical camps and vaccination drives, mobile clinics and soup kitchens, and offering free healthcare to underprivileged patients; child welfare and education, building schools and orphanages, training teachers and offering technical and medical training; and housing, sanitation and public infrastructure.

Geographical Area of Activity: Dem. Repub. of the Congo.

Publications: Newsletter; blog.

Principal Staff: Pres. Harish Jagtani; Vice-Pres. Sachin Gidwani; Co-ordinator Roshni Punjabi.

Contact Details: 8690 ave Kasavubu C/ Kasa Vubu, REF Boulangerie UPAK, Kinshasa; tel. 893444444; e-mail info@hjfoundations.org; internet www.hjfoundations.org.

KAF—Kataliko Actions for Africa

Established in 2001 by Barbara Bulambo-Marthaler and Ambroise Bulambo in memory of Emmanuel Kataliko, former Archbishop of Bukavu.

Activities: Promotes democracy and human rights. The organization works to prevent human rights abuses; rehabilitates victims of human rights abuses, providing medical and psychological assistance; and lobbies for change in national legislation and simplification of legal documents. It offers the Bulambo Wanyenga prize for encouraging education in South Kivu. Has an international office in Switzerland and observer status at the African Commission on Human and Peoples' Rights.

Geographical Area of Activity: Dem. Repub. of the Congo, Switzerland.

Publications: Annual Report; reports, books.

Board of Directors: Prof. Ambroise K. Bulambo (Chair.); Milenge Bulambo (Vice-Chair.).

Contact Details: 25 ave Matungulu, commune Mobale, Kamituga, South Kivu; tel. 998986786; e-mail ambroise.bulambo@gmail.com; internet www.kaf-africa.org.

Lukuru Wildlife Research Foundation

Established in 1992.

Activities: Conserves great apes, in particular bonobos, and other wildlife and their natural habitats. The Foundation locates and studies populations of great apes; identifies

regional threats; and works with local people to promote environmental security and social progress. It carries out its activities under the Lukuru Project and Tshuapa-Lomani-Lualaba (TL2) Project in Kasaï Occidental Province, and the Bili Project on the border with the Central African Republic. Has an office in the USA.
Geographical Area of Activity: Dem. Repub. of the Congo, USA.
Board of Directors: Jeff Harr (Treas.); Bibyche Llanga (Sec.).

Principal Staff: Pres. and Exec. Dir Dr Jo Thompson.

Contact Details: 1235 ave des Poids Lourds, quartier de Kingabois, Gombe/Kinshasa; e-mail lukuru@gmail.com; internet www.lukuru.org.

REPUBLIC OF THE CONGO

FOUNDATIONS AND NON-PROFITS

Fondation Congo Assistance
Established in 1984 by First Lady Antoinette Sassou N'Guesso.
Activities: Promotes health, development, education and professional training, with a particular focus on young children, women and the elderly. Has an office in Paris, France.
Geographical Area of Activity: Repub. of the Congo.
Board of Directors: Antoinette Sassou N'Guesso (Chair.).
Principal Staff: Sec.-Gen. Michel Mongo; Deputy Sec.-Gen. Rosalie Biangana Vouka.
Contact Details: 13 rue Behangle, BP 2720, Brazzaville; tel. 06-850-91-50; e-mail infocongoassistance@gmail.com; internet fondationcongoassistance.cg.

Fondation Mesmin Kabath—FOMEKA
Established in 2007 by Mesmin Kabath, founder of Keco Holding Group (f. 2006).
Activities: Programme areas include: education, awarding scholarships to secondary school pupils; health, providing access to quality healthcare for vulnerable people; poverty alleviation, giving people the means to improve their daily lives; and sustainable development, including combating climate change. The Foundation awards prizes, including the Prix Elu Bon, worth CFA 1m., for the best medical thesis nationally; the Prix Grand K for individual know-how; and the Grand Prix FOMEKA business awards.
Geographical Area of Activity: Repub. of the Congo.
Finance: Mainly financed by an annual 10% levy on Keco Group profits.
Principal Staff: Pres. Mesmin Kabath.
Contact Details: route de la frontière, arrêt ex-Mucodec, Imm. Fomeka, Tchimbamba; tel. 66-74-91-01; e-mail contact@fomeka.org.

Fondation MTN Congo (MTN Congo Foundation)
Established in 2007 by MTN Congo, a telecommunications company; part of the MTN Foundations network.
Activities: Carries out the social investment activities of MTN Congo. The Foundation supports communities through providing access to digital technologies. Programme areas include: arts and culture; access to education and sport in disadvantaged areas; the environment; sustainable development; and youth entrepreneurship.
Geographical Area of Activity: Repub. of the Congo.
Finance: Annual budget 1% of MTN Congo's annual turnover.
Principal Staff: Exec. Chair. Vanessa Tsouma.
Contact Details: 36 ave Amilcar Cabral, Centre Ville, BP 1150, Brazzaville; tel. 06-966-11-00; internet www.mtn.cg/fondation.

Fondation Mutuelles Congolaises d'Epargne et de Crédit—MUCODEC
Established in 2018 by MUCODEC, a microfinance provider.
Activities: Works to alleviate poverty and insecurity through providing access to essential services for marginalized people. The Foundation develops and supports programmes in the areas of health, education, sport and culture.
Geographical Area of Activity: Repub. of the Congo.
Publications: Newsletter.
Board of Directors: Florian Mounguengue Bitanda (Chair.).
Contact Details: blvd Denis Sassou Nguesso/rue Colbert, Centre Ville (Grande Gare), BP 13237, Brazzaville; tel. 06-987-90-27; e-mail communication@mucodec.com; internet mucodec.com/fondation/nq==.

Fondation Perspectives d'Avenir
Established in 2012 by Denis Christel Sassou Nguesso, Deputy Dir-Gen. of national oil company SNPC and son of President Denis Sassou Nguesso.
Activities: Focuses on education, youth training and employment, awarding scholarships for tertiary-level studies in science, technology and innovation. The Foundation also carries out activities in the areas of agriculture, culture and health.
Geographical Area of Activity: Repub. of the Congo.
Publications: Newsletter.
Principal Staff: Pres. Denis Christel Sassou Nguesso.
Contact Details: 35 ave des 3 Martyrs, Plateau des 15 ans, Moungali, Brazzaville; tel. 05-677-14-16; e-mail info@perspectivesavenir.org; internet perspectivesavenir.com.

COSTA RICA

FOUNDATIONS AND NON-PROFITS

Fundación Acceso (Access Foundation)
Established in 1992 by Stephen Cox, a conservationist, and Ana Elena Badilla, a women's rights advocate.
Activities: Works in the fields of digital security and human rights. The organization supports individuals and organizations working to defend human rights, carrying out research and offering security training and capacity building. In 2018, working with Hivos (q.v.) and the Embassy of the Netherlands, the Foundation co-founded Shelter City San José, part of the international Shelter City Network, to provide support and protection to human rights defenders from the neighbouring countries of Guatemala, Honduras, El Salvador and Nicaragua, and offering integral security (legal, physical, digital and psychosocial) training. Comprises the Central American Observatory for Digital Security.

Fundación Arias para la Paz y el Progreso Humano COSTA RICA

Geographical Area of Activity: Central America.
Publications: Country reports; booklets; directories.
Finance: Annual project income US $1.3m. (2023).
Board of Directors: Susana García Perdomo (Chair.); José Montero Peña (Treas.); Marcelo Gaete Astica (Sec.).
Contact Details: Sabanilla Montes de Oca, POB 288-2050, San José; tel. 2253-9860; e-mail info@acceso.or.cr; internet www.acceso.or.cr.

Fundación Arias para la Paz y el Progreso Humano (Arias Foundation for Peace and Human Progress)

Established in 1988 by Dr Oscar Arias Sánchez, former President of Costa Rica.
Activities: Promotes democracy, gender equality, disarmament and demilitarization. The Foundation carries out self-conducted programmes, research, workshops and training courses through three main centres: the Center for Human Progress, which carries out work on gender equality; the Center for Peace and Reconciliation, working in the field of demilitarization and conflict prevention; and the Center for Organized Participation, working in the field of civil society and democracy. The Foundation also administers the Museum of Peace and maintains a forest conservation area.
Geographical Area of Activity: Central America.
Publications: Manuals; reports; research findings; e-books.
Finance: Annual budget approx. US $1m.
Principal Staff: Exec. Dir Suzanne Fischel.
Contact Details: Costado noroeste Parque Francia, Barrio Escalante, San José; tel. 2222-9191; e-mail info@arias.or.cr; internet www.arias.or.cr.

Fundación DEMUCA—Fundación para el Desarrollo Local y el Fortalecimiento Municipal e Institucional de Centroamérica y el Caribe (Foundation for Local Development and the Municipal and Institutional Support of Central America and the Caribbean)

Founded in 1995, growing out of Programa DEMUCA, which began in the 1980s.
Activities: Strengthens the capacity of local governments to promote human development through supporting and representing all national associations of municipalities in Central America and the Caribbean. The Foundation promotes the exchange of knowledge and information, and international co-operation between Spain, Central America and the Caribbean to improve human development work. It works to improve municipal finances, and raise the level of efficiency in grantmaking and of basic public services in local government, including clean water supplies and sanitation, rubbish disposal and public transport. Has seven member associations, with offices in the Dominican Republic, El Salvador, Guatemala and Panama.
Geographical Area of Activity: Central America and the Caribbean.
Publications: Reports; research findings; books.
Principal Staff: Exec. Dir Daniel García González.
Contact Details: Apdo 697-1005, San José; Barrio Escalante, del Parque Francia 25 metros Sur, San José; tel. 2258-1813; e-mail info@demuca.org.

Fundación Mujer (Women's Foundation)

Founded in 1988; a continuation of a pilot programme of the Fondo Internacional para la Educación Extraterritorial.
Activities: Supports sustainable socioeconomic development through offering microfinance to individuals and organizations in urban and rural areas. Projects have focused on inclusion of refugees; and providing business and soft skills training to women to promote their financial independence and economic wellbeing. The Centro de Formación Integral offers training and technical assistance; and organizes talks and workshops on topics that include business management, employability, self-employment and formal employment. In 2000 the Foundation co-founded the Red Costarricense de Organizaciones para la Microempresa (RED-COM), a network of microfinance institutions; and co-founded the Red Latinoamericana para la Justicia de Género para el Desarrollo Económico (RED LADER). It has a branch in Limón.
Geographical Area of Activity: Costa Rica.
Publications: *Revista Informativa*.
Principal Staff: Exec. Dir Zobeida Moya Lacayo.
Contact Details: Calle 49A, San José Province, Mercedes, Betania; tel. 2253-1661; e-mail funmujer@fundacionmujer.org; internet www.fundacionmujer.org.

Fundación para la Paz y la Democracia—FUNPADEM

Established in 1988 by the Minister of Foreign Affairs, Rodrigo Madrigal Nieto.
Activities: Promotes sustainable human development. Main programme areas are: democratic governance; justice and labour compliance, including conflict resolution, environmental governance, eradication of child labour, health and safety at work and labour rights; peaceful conflict resolution; security and violence prevention. The Foundation supports access to education for children, young people and people at risk, offering training and teaching resources for educators and organizing seminars, symposia, talks and workshops. It offers internships of 3–12 months for students and young professionals in the areas of communication and languages, international relations, law and political science.
Geographical Area of Activity: Central America and the Caribbean.
Publications: *Mirador* (weekly newsletter); booklets; toolkits; blog.
Principal Staff: Exec. Dir and Chair. Carlos Rivera Bianchini.
Contact Details: WWHQ+R98, C. 37, Los Yoses, 12835-1000 San José; tel. 2283-9435; e-mail info@funpadem.org; internet funpadem.org.

FUNDES—Fundación para el Desarrollo Sostenible de la Pequeña y Mediana Empresa (Foundation for the Sustainable Development of Small and Medium-sized Enterprises—FUNDES International)

Established in 1984 in Panama to develop the region's private sector, based on the ideas of Swiss industrialist Stephan Schmidheiny; established in Costa Rica in 1986.
Activities: Works with multinational companies and governments to improve the competitiveness of micro, small and medium-sized enterprises through developing the business sector and value chains. The Foundation has regional offices in Bolivia, Chile, Mexico and Peru.
Geographical Area of Activity: Latin America.
Publications: Newsletter; reports.
Board of Directors: Andreas Eggenberg (Chair.).
Principal Staff: CEO Elfid Torres.
Contact Details: Apdo 798-4005, San Antonio de Belén; La Asunción de Belén, Heredia, San Antonio de Belén; tel. 2209-8300; e-mail contacto@fundes.org; internet www.fundes.org.

Instituto Interamericano de Derechos Humanos—IIDH (Inter-American Institute of Human Rights)

Founded in 1980 by Thomas Buergenthal, a judge.
Activities: Operates in the fields of education and human rights, working with other organizations and local governments. The Institute promotes human rights and social justice; and works to consolidate democracy through investigation, education, political mediation, technical assistance and the dissemination of relevant information through specialized publications. It organizes conferences; maintains a document centre; and has an office in Uruguay.
Geographical Area of Activity: Latin America.

Publications: *IIDH en las Américas* (newsletter); *Revista IIDH*; books; magazines; print, audiovisual and digital educational materials.

Board of Directors: Claudio Grossman (Pres.); Monica Pinto, Wendy Singh (Vice-Pres).

Principal Staff: Exec. Dir José Thompson J.

Contact Details: Apdo 10081-1000, San José; Avda 8, Calles 43-41, Casa No. 222, Barrio Los Yoses, Montes de Oca, San Pedro, San José; tel. 2234-0404; e-mail info@iidh.ed.cr; internet www.iidh.ed.cr.

Red de Mujeres para el Desarrollo (Women's Development Network)

Established in 1998; a strategic alliance of grassroots women's groups, NGOs, churches, development professionals and international agencies.

Activities: Operates in the field of women's rights through representing women at risk of exclusion. The Network promotes women's development and empowerment, and supports non-profit organizations searching for funding and training. It maintains a database of information and an online library, and has offices in Brazil, Colombia, Curaçao, Dominica, Haiti, Honduras, Puerto Rico, Trinidad and Tobago, and the USA.

Geographical Area of Activity: Central and South America and the Caribbean, USA.

Publications: *La Red* (quarterly newsletter); guides; manuals.

Principal Staff: Pres. Olga Parrado.

Contact Details: Apdo 447-2070, San José; Calle Cedros a 350m este del perimercado Vargas Araya Sabanilla, San Pedro Montes de Oca; tel. 2253-9003; e-mail info@redmujeres.org.

CÔTE D'IVOIRE

CO-ORDINATING BODY

Réseau des Fondations et Institutions de Recherche pour la Promotion d'un Culture de la Paix en Afrique—REFICA (Network of Foundations and Research Institutions for the Promotion of a Culture of Peace in Africa)

Established in 2013 at a meeting in Addis Ababa, Ethiopia, on the initiative of UNESCO and the Fondation Félix Houphouët-Boigny pour la Recherche de la Paix (q.v.).

Activities: Works towards implementing the African Union (AU) Agenda 2063 and UNESCO's Intersectoral Programme for a Culture of Peace, through co-ordinating the activities of member organizations. The Network seeks to establish a Community of Practice with a focus on four main themes: cultural resources for sustainable peace in Africa; natural resource management, conflict prevention and sustainable development; young people's role in peace and development; and creating a continent-wide movement under the aegis of the AU and UNESCO. It comprises 44 African and non-African organizations.

Geographical Area of Activity: Africa.

Publications: *CPNN—Culture of Peace News Network* (monthly newsletter).

Executive Board: João de Deus Gomes Pereira (Pres.); Fr Jean-Noël Loucou (Permanent Sec.); Abdon Sofonnou (Deputy Permanent Sec.).

Contact Details: c/o Fondation Félix Houphouët-Boigny pour la Recherche de la Paix, POB 1818, Yamoussoukro; tel. 30-64-31-04; e-mail info@reseaupaix.org.

FOUNDATIONS AND NON-PROFITS

Centre Ivoirien de Recherches Économiques et Sociales—CIRES (Ivorian Economic and Social Research Centre)

Established in 1971.

Activities: Carries out economic and social public policy research and projects. Programmes are organized under five research units: Rural Economy and Sociology; Macroeconomics and Modelling; Natural Resources and Environment; Human Resources and Poverty Reduction; and Institutional Economics and Applied Microeconomics. Three cells focus on applied research in the areas of gender and development, international economic relations and economic policy analysis. The Centre organizes monthly seminars and workshops; and offers academic programmes. It has a library.

Geographical Area of Activity: West Africa.

Publications: Notebooks.

Principal Staff: Dir Dr Ibrahim Diarra.

Contact Details: Blvd Latrille près du Lycée Classique d'Abidjan, 08 BP 1295, Abidjan 08; tel. 27-22-44-51-03; e-mail info@cires-ci.com; internet www.cires-ci.com.

Children of Africa Foundation

Established in 1998 by First Lady Dominique Ouattara.

Activities: Carries out activities in the areas of social welfare, health and education. Programmes focus on children and young people coping with social or family breakdown; children and young people living in precarious conditions and disadvantaged rural areas; mothers and children in health centres; and access to education for girls. Abroad, the Foundation has funded social centres in 10 African countries. Other initiatives include the Bibliobus mobile library, carrying around 2,500 books, computers with internet access and a video projector; the Case des Enfants reception centre for orphans and street children; and a hospital for mothers and children in the capital, Abidjan. It has offices in Paris, France, and Washington, DC, USA.

Geographical Area of Activity: Benin, Burkina Faso, Cameroon, Central African Repub., Côte d'Ivoire, Gabon, Guinea, Madagascar, Mali, Niger, Senegal, Togo.

Publications: Annual Report; newsletter; *Dîner Gala* (magazine).

Principal Staff: Pres. First Lady Dominique Ouattara; CEO Nadine Sangaré; Gen. Man. Elisabeth Gandon; Sec.-Gen. Nicole Affo.

Contact Details: rue Brooker Washington, Cocody Ambassades, 08 BP 1353, Abidjan 01; tel. 27-22-44-42-66; e-mail fondation.childrenofafrica@yahoo.fr; internet www.childrenofafrica.org.

Fondation Félix Houphouët-Boigny pour la Recherche de la Paix (Félix Houphouët-Boigny Foundation for Peace Research)

Established in 1973 by President Félix Houphouët-Boigny; works under the aegis of UNESCO.

Activities: Promotes a culture of peace nationally and internationally and carries out research. The Foundation offers training and citizenship training; establishes mechanisms and institutions to strengthen peace; provides a framework for research and dialogue; and organizes scientific, cultural and educational activities. It awards prizes annually for research in the fields of science and technology to postgraduate students, worth 500,000 CFA francs, and for a doctoral thesis, worth 1m. CFA francs. Has an office in Abidjan.

Geographical Area of Activity: International.

Fondation MTN Côte d'Ivoire

Publications: Newsletter (quarterly); *Dialogue & Paix* (annual journal); books.

Principal Staff: Sec.-Gen. Prof. Jean-Noël Loucou.

Contact Details: POB 1818, Yamoussoukro; POB 3941, Abidjan 01; tel. 30-64-31-04; e-mail info@fondation-fhb.org; internet www.fondation-fhb.org.

Fondation MTN Côte d'Ivoire (MTN Côte d'Ivoire Foundation)

Established in 2006 by MTN Côte d'Ivoire, a telecommunications company; part of the MTN Foundations network.

Activities: Programmes focus on three main areas: health, combating non-communicable diseases, HIV/AIDS and malaria; education, providing access to new information and communication technologies; and community development, building the capacity of women in rural areas.

Geographical Area of Activity: Côte d'Ivoire.

Board of Directors: Yigo Thiam (Chair.).

Principal Staff: Exec. Sec. Jocelyn Adjoby; Deputy Exec. Sec. Naminsita Bakayoko.

Contact Details: 12 ave Crosson Duplessis, 01 BP 3865, Abidjan-Plateau; tel. 20-31-63-18; e-mail fondationmtn.ci@mtn.com; internet www.mtn.ci/fondation.

Fondation Orange-Côte d'Ivoire Télécom—OCIT

Established in 2006 by Orange, a telecommunications provider; part of the Fondation Orange (q.v.) network.

Activities: Works in the fields of health, education and culture. The Foundation builds and refurbishes health and maternity centres, setting up awareness-raising campaigns and disease screening clinics; provides teaching in literacy and digital education, builds and renovates school canteens, and awards scholarships; and fosters artistic development and conserves cultural heritage. It has built 31 Orange Villages, providing access to education, healthcare and drinking water; 78 digital schools and 23 digital houses to provide digital skills training and financial literacy education for women; and three FabLab digital maker spaces for young people.

Geographical Area of Activity: Côte d'Ivoire.

Principal Staff: Chair. Mamadou Bamba.

Contact Details: Cocody Riviera Golf 'Orange Village', 4th Floor, 11 BP 20211, Abidjan; tel. 22-40-46-18; e-mail fondation.oci@orange.com; internet fondation.orange.ci.

CROATIA

CO-ORDINATING BODIES

CERANEO—Centar za razvoj neprofitnih organizacija (Centre for Development of Non-profit Organizations)

Established in 1995 by Dr Gojko Bežovan; a think tank.

Activities: Supports new initiatives and advocates a more important role for civil society. The Centre studies and works to influence public policies through organizing conferences, roundtables, seminars and workshops; connecting academics, researchers, decisionmakers in government and practitioners; and publishing results of projects and briefing articles. It offers resources to Croatian CSOs and promotes them to international donors.

Geographical Area of Activity: Croatia.

Publications: Annual Report; newsletter; research reports; books.

Finance: Annual income €25,000, expenditure €110,866 (2024).

Principal Staff: Pres. Prof. Dr Gojko Bežovan.

Contact Details: 10000 Zagreb, ul. Jakova Gotovca 1; tel. (1) 4812-384; e-mail ceraneo@ceraneo.hr; internet www.ceraneo.hr.

CROSOL—Platforma za međunarodnu građansku solidarnost Hrvatske (Croatian Platform for International Citizen Solidarity)

Established in 2014.

Activities: Represents CSOs working in the fields of international development co-operation and humanitarian aid. Priority areas include: civil society; development aid; development co-operation; EU policies; human rights; migration; development policy coherence; public policies; and sustainable development. The Platform has 29 members. It is a member of CONCORD Europe (q.v.).

Geographical Area of Activity: Croatia.

Publications: Annual Report.

Finance: Annual income 1.3m. kuna, expenditure 1.1m. kuna (2022).

Board of Directors: Cvijeta Senta (Pres.).

Principal Staff: Co-ordinator Branka Juran.

Contact Details: 10000 Zagreb, Selska cesta 112A; tel. (91) 529-1375; e-mail crosol@crosol.hr; internet crosol.hr.

Europska Zaklada za Filantropiju i Društveni Dazvoj (European Foundation for Philanthropy and Society Development)

Established in 2014.

Activities: Promotes social development based on philanthropy, social innovation and responsible governance. The Foundation provides technical and financial support to foundations and individuals in Croatia; fosters transnational financing, co-operation and exchange of knowledge and good practices; and represents the philanthropic sector at national and EU level. In 2016 it opened the Croatian Centre for Philanthropy with the Nacionalne Zaklade za Razvoj Civilnoga Društva (q.v.); and administers the Forum ZaDobro.BIT! (f. 2008 as the Croatian Foundations Forum), a platform of 38 foundations.

Geographical Area of Activity: EU.

Publications: Annual Report; newsletter; training manual.

Finance: Annual income €87,569, expenditure €94,694 (31 Dec. 2024).

Principal Staff: Man. Smiljana Rađa.

Contact Details: 10000 Zagreb, Dedići 83; tel. 916458949; e-mail info@europskazaklada-filantropija.hr; internet www.europskazaklada-filantropija.hr.

Nacionalne Zaklade za Razvoj Civilnoga Društva (National Foundation for Civil Society Development)

Founded in 2003 to promote and support civil society development.

Activities: Provides expert and financial support to innovative programmes that encourage the sustainability of the non-profit sector, inter-sector co-operation, civil initiatives, philanthropy, voluntary work and improvement of democratic institutions in society. The Foundation holds conferences, issues publications and offers prizes and scholarships. In 2016 it opened the Croatian Centre for Philanthropy with the Europska Zaklada za Filantropiju i Društveni Razvoj (q.v.).

Geographical Area of Activity: Croatia.

Publications: Annual Report; e-newsletter (monthly); *Civilno društvo* (journal); books; manuals; studies.

Finance: Total revenue €13.6m., expenditure €12.6m. (31 Dec. 2023).

Board of Directors: Prof. Dražen Vikić-Topić (Chair.); Martina Štefković (Vice-Chair.).

Principal Staff: Dir Cvjetana Plavša-Matić.

Contact Details: 10000 Zagreb, Štrigina 1A (entrance from the courtyard of the Bužanova 24a building); tel. (1) 2399-100; e-mail zaklada@civilnodrustvo.hr; internet zaklada.civilnodrustvo.hr.

FOUNDATIONS AND NON-PROFITS

BaBe—Budi aktivna, Budi emancipiran (Be Active, Be Emancipated)

Founded in 1994 by Vesna Kesic and nine activists, out of the Center for Women War Victims.

Activities: Operates in the field of human rights, through advocating for women's rights and gender equality, and supporting women who are marginalized and discriminated against. The organization works to eliminate violence against women; and promotes reproductive rights and adequate healthcare protection, and the right to equal and full participation in all areas of society.

Geographical Area of Activity: South-Eastern Europe.

Restrictions: Not a grantmaking organization.

Publications: Annual Report; books, documentaries, musical videos, social advertisements, installations, brochures, posters, leaflets.

Finance: Annual income €564,428, expenditure €585,641 (31 Dec. 2024).

Principal Staff: Pres. Petra Kontić.

Contact Details: 10000 Zagreb, Human Rights House, Selska cesta 112A; tel. (1) 4663-666; e-mail babe@babe.hr; internet www.babe.hr.

CURAÇAO

FOUNDATIONS AND NON-PROFITS

CARMABI Foundation (Foundation for Caribbean Research and Management of Biodiversity)

Founded in 1996. Originally established in 1955 as the Caribbean Marine Biological Institute; in 1996, it merged with the Stichting Nationale Parken—STINAPA (f. 1962).

Activities: Operates in the areas of conservation of the environment and applied marine natural resource research. The Foundation conducts marine biological research and conservation research with visiting scientists from the Netherlands and the USA. It manages nine protected areas; provides advice to local government; and runs an education programme for schoolchildren.

Geographical Area of Activity: Caribbean.

Publications: Annual Reports; online media; research findings; scholarly publications; e-handbooks; educational materials.

Finance: Total income 4.8m. gilders, expenditure 4.8m. gilders (2024).

Board: Odette Doest (Pres.); Karel van Haren (Vice-Pres.); Pieter van den Berg (Treas.).

Principal Staff: Dir Dr Manfred van Veghel; Deputy Dir Dr Mark Vermeij.

Contact Details: POB 2090, Piscaderabaai z/n, Willemstad; tel. (9) 462-42-42; e-mail carmabilog@gmail.com; internet www.carmabi.org.

CYPRUS

FOUNDATIONS AND NON-PROFITS

The A. G. Leventis Foundation

Established in 1979 by the will of Anastasios G. Leventis.

Activities: Promotes social welfare, environmental conservation and the preservation of Cyprus's cultural heritage, including supporting the establishment of new museums. The Foundation offers grants for study at the University of Cyprus and for postgraduate study abroad, especially in the fields of science and education. It also funds publications.

Geographical Area of Activity: Balkans, Central and Western Europe, Cyprus, Greece, North and West Africa, USA.

Restrictions: No support for projects outside of the Foundation's scope.

Publications: Publications in English, French and Greek on Cypriot and Greek art and civilization; archaeological reports and studies; Byzantine art; cartography; children's books; collections of essays; conference proceedings; lecture series.

Board of Trustees: Anastasios (Tasso) P. Leventis (Chair.).

Principal Staff: Exec. Dir Louisa Leventis; CEO Alexandros Papanastassiou.

Contact Details: 40 Gladstone St, POB 22543, 1095 Nicosia; tel. (22) 667706; e-mail info@leventis.org.cy; internet www.leventisfoundation.org.

Bank of Cyprus Cultural Foundation

Founded in 1984 by the Bank of Cyprus Group.

Activities: Promotes studies on Cyprus at professional and scholarly level and maintains five Cyprological collections: coins; maps; rare books and manuscripts, engravings, photographs and watercolours; contemporary Cypriot art; and archaeological artefacts. Each collection is linked to a long-term project involving research, publications, lectures, seminars, educational programmes, and temporary and permanent exhibitions. The Foundation opened the Museum of the History of Cypriot Coinage in 1995. The Museum of the Archaeological Collection of George and Nefeli Tziapra Rierides was inaugurated in 2002.

Geographical Area of Activity: Cyprus, Greece.

Publications: Annual Report; newsletters; information brochures; monographs; multi-year reports; publications catalogue.

Board of Directors: Efstratios Arapoglou (Chair.); Dr Charis Pouangare (Vice-Chair.); Irene Gregoriou (Sec.); Dr Yiannis Toumazis (Treas. and Man.).

Contact Details: 86–90 Phaneromenis St, 1011 Nicosia; POB 21995, 1515 Nicosia; tel. (22) 128157; e-mail info@cultural.bankofcyprus.com; internet www.boccf.org.

George and Thelma Paraskevaides Foundation

Founded in 1980 by George Paraskevaides, co-founder of the construction company Joannou & Paraskevaides, and his wife Thelma.

Activities: Carries out activities in the areas of medicine, education, culture and the arts. The Foundation funds medical treatment abroad for children and makes grants to medical institutions; and offers scholarships for higher education abroad. It makes grants for artistic and cultural purposes in Cyprus; and offers the Paraskevaides Award for individuals' contributions to the nations and peoples of Cyprus and the USA, and to Hellenism.

Geographical Area of Activity: Cyprus, USA.

Finance: Total disbursements since 1980 €16m.

Principal Staff: Exec. Dir Costas Paraskevaides.

Contact Details: Paraskevaides Foundation Bldg, 36 Griva Dighenis Ave, 1066 Nicosia; POB 2200, 1518 Nicosia; tel. (22) 445367; e-mail gnthparaskf@cytanet.com.cy; internet paraskevaidesfoundation.com.

Stelios Philanthropic Foundation (Philanthropikó Ídryma Stélios Chatzeioánnou stēn Kýpro)

Established by Sir Stelios Haji-Ioannou, founder of the EasyJet airline.

Activities: Supports charitable activities in countries where the founder has lived and worked. Main programmes include: distributing food to people experiencing economic hardship in Cyprus and Greece; promoting lasting peace on the island of Cyprus, offering bi-communal awards, worth €10,000, to teams comprising a Turkish Cypriot and a Greek Cypriot collaborating on projects in areas including the arts, business, NGO work and sport; in conjunction with Leonard Cheshire (q.v.), awarding cash prizes to disabled entrepreneurs in the United Kingdom; annually offering nine youth entrepreneur awards worth €10,000 and one worth €30,000 to people aged under 40 years in Greece; and funding school and university scholarships for young people. The Foundation also makes general charitable donations.

Geographical Area of Activity: Cyprus, Greece, Monaco, UK.

Principal Staff: Pres. Sir Stelios Haji-Ioannou.

Contact Details: Markou Drakou 5, 1102 Nicosia; tel. (98) 801010; internet steliosfoundation.com.cy.

CZECH REPUBLIC (CZECHIA)

CO-ORDINATING BODIES

Asociace komunitních nadací v České republice—Spolek AKN (Czech Association of Community Foundations—AKN Association)

Established in 2006 from trust funds administered by the VIA Foundation (q.v.).

Activities: Supports and promotes the development of community foundations and organizations striving to become community foundations, assisting in co-operation and communication between them. The Association comprises five community foundations and three support organizations which promote community foundations.

Geographical Area of Activity: Czech Repub.

Publications: Reports.

Principal Staff: Chair. Tomáš Krejčí.

Contact Details: Koněvova 1697/18, 400 01 Ústí nad Labem-město; tel. 602942728; e-mail info@akncr.cz; internet www.akncr.cz.

Česká rada sociálních služeb—CRSS (Czech Council of Social Services)

Established in 2011 as the successor to the Council of Humanitarian Associations, which was founded in 1990 as the Czechoslovak Council for Humanitarian Co-operation.

Activities: Work focuses on the elderly, disabled and homeless people, drug users, and abandoned and abused children. The Council provides a database of humanitarian organizations and training for members, and organizes seminars and workshops. It has around 35 member organizations.

Geographical Area of Activity: Czech Repub.

Publications: Monthly review; bulletin; newsletter; conference reports.

Board: Jiří Lodr (Pres.); Jan Vaněček, Pavel Janouškovec (Vice-Pres.).

Contact Details: Českobratrská 9, Žižkov, 130 00 Prague 3; tel. 222587455; e-mail kancelar@crss.cz; internet www.crss.cz.

Fórum Dárců (Czech Donors Forum)

Established in 1995 as an association of grantmakers; became a registered civic association in 1997.

Activities: Supports grantmaking organizations, focusing on the cultivation and development of the foundation sector and philanthropy; strengthening the co-operation and development of the foundation and private sectors; and playing an infrastructural role. Main programmes are: the Educational Training Programme; the Programme for the Development of Corporate Philanthropy; and the 1% of tax designation project. It operates Daruj Spravene (Donate Right), an online donation platform, and Dárcovské SMS (Donor SMA), a project to send donations by text message; jointly established Den dárců (Donor Day); and organizes annual awards to recognize the philanthropic work of non-profit organizations, companies and corporate foundations. Comprises the Association of Foundations, the Association of Endowment Funds, and the Association of Corporate Foundations and Funds, which represent 45 member organizations; and is a member of Philea (q.v.).

Geographical Area of Activity: Europe.

Restrictions: Not a grantmaking organization.

Publications: Annual Report; newsletter (quarterly); *Directory of Foundations*; manuals.

Finance: Annual revenue 4.9m. koruny, expenditure 5.2m. koruny (31 Dec. 2022).

Principal Staff: Exec. Dir Klára Šplíchalová.

Contact Details: Nám. Winstona Churchilla 1800/2, 130 00 Prague 3; tel. 725999103; e-mail donorsforum@donorsforum.cz; internet www.donorsforum.cz.

HESTIA

Established in 1993 by Dr Jiří Tošner and Olga Sozanská.

Activities: The organization promotes and develops the environment for volunteering in the Czech Republic. It raises awareness of the voluntary opportunities available to the public; offers training programmes for co-ordinators and organizations; and provides advice and information for volunteers, NGOs, companies and government. The national Five Ps/Pet P programme is a mentoring volunteer initiative to help children who have social or health problems. Also helps companies to introduce employee volunteering programmes, providing both individual and team corporate volunteering.

Geographical Area of Activity: Czechia.

Publications: Annual Report; books and articles on volunteer management.

Finance: Total assets 2.2m. koruny (31 Dec. 2023).

Board of Trustees: Marek Vozka (Chair.).

Principal Staff: Dir Hana Vosmíková.

Contact Details: Štefánikova 216/21, 150 00 Prague 5; tel. 257328901; e-mail info@hest.cz; internet www.hest.cz.

Nadace Neziskovky.cz

Established in 1992 as the ICN (Information Centre for Non-profit Organizations) Foundation and subsequently Nadace Auxilia; present name adopted in 2005.

Activities: Provides information for and about NGOs and the non-profit sector. The organization offers consultancy services to non-profit organizations; collates information about grants; and organizes courses, workshops and training.

Geographical Area of Activity: Czech Repub.

Publications: Annual Report; Svět neziskovek ('NGO World', online platform); Grantový diář ('Grant Diary', online platform).

Finance: Annual revenue 560,000 koruny, expenditure 370,000 koruny (31 Dec. 2023).

Board of Directors: Lukáš Novák (Chair.); Soňa Nebeská (Vice-Chair.).

Principal Staff: Dir Karolina Kratochvilova.

Contact Details: Dukelských hrdinů 500/25A, Letná, 170 00 Prague 7; tel. 730517966; e-mail nadace@neziskovky.cz; internet www.neziskovky.cz.

FOUNDATIONS AND NON-PROFITS

Česko-německý fond budoucnosti (Czech-German Fund for the Future)

Established in 1998, as an NGO based in the Czech Republic, by the Governments of the Czech Republic and Germany.

Activities: Operates in the field of social welfare, funding social projects for Czech survivors of atrocities committed during the country's occupation by German forces before and during the Second World War, including Jewish and Roma (Gypsy) people, Catholics, Jehovah's Witnesses, homosexuals and political prisoners. Since 1998 the Fund has provided approximately 2,300m. koruny to 15,000 projects in the areas of: young people and schools; culture; monument restoration; social projects and support for minority groups; and discussion forums and professional groups. It offers 10-month scholarships for Czech and German students in the fields of the humanities and social sciences who plan to work on a project with a Czech-German theme while studying in the partner country.

Geographical Area of Activity: Czech Repub.

Publications: Annual Report.

Finance: Annual income 176.5m. koruny, expenditure 282.6m. koruny (31 Dec. 2023).

Board of Directors: Jindřich Fryč (Chair.).

Principal Staff: Dirs Dr Tomáš Jelinek, Petra Ernstberger.

Contact Details: Železná 24, 110 00 Prague 1; tel. 283850512; e-mail info@fb.cz; internet www.fondbudoucnosti.cz.

Člověk v tísni (People in Need)

Established in 1992 by Jaromír Štětina and other journalists as Epicentrum, a humanitarian group raising money for Nagorno-Karabakh; it subsequently became part of the Lidové noviny foundation, which in 1994 merged with broadcaster České televize to become People in Need under the auspices of Czech Television.

Activities: Operates in the areas of human rights, humanitarian aid and development co-operation. The organization supports democratization processes and human rights protection. It also runs the annual One World human rights documentary film festival. Social integration programmes address poverty and social exclusion problems in the Czech Republic and Slovakia. Educational and informative programmes raise awareness on issues such as global problems and development co-operation, migration and multiculturalism among the public, the state administration and the media. Active in more than 60 cities in the Czech Republic and more than 25 countries.

Geographical Area of Activity: Africa, Asia, Europe.

Publications: Annual Report; newsletter.

Finance: Total assets 3.4m. koruny (31 Dec. 2023).

Board of Trustees: Jan Pergler (Pres.).

Supervisory Board: Václav Mazánek (Pres.).

Principal Staff: Pres., Exec. Bd Šimon Pánek.

Contact Details: Šafaříkova 635/24, 120 00 Prague 2; tel. 774819964; e-mail dary@clovekvtisni.cz; internet www.clovekvtisni.cz.

Nadace České spořitelny—Nadace ČS (Česká spořitelna Foundation)

Established in 2002 by Česká spořitelna, a bank, to help marginalized people and support social housing.

Activities: Works in the fields of education and civil society. The Foundation supports innovation in education, and professional and leadership development of teachers; and digital and financial literacy among children. Other programmes support social entrepreneurship in the areas of active ageing, care for the mentally disabled, and the treatment and prevention of drug addiction. Help is also offered to employees of the bank who are in need. It incorporates Nadace Depositum Bonum (f. 2012), which was established by the bank using unclaimed funds from dormant accounts and supports scientific and technical projects that have a social benefit; the two foundations formally merged in 2019.

Geographical Area of Activity: Czech Repub.

Publications: Annual Report; studies.

Finance: Total revenue 626.6m. koruny, expenditure 481.3m. koruny (2023).

Board of Directors: Dana Brandenburg (Chair.); Jakub Mareš (Vice-Chair.).

Supervisory Board: Tomáš Salomon (Chair.); Wolfgang Schopf (Vice-Chair.).

Contact Details: Olbrachtova 1929/64B, 140 00 Prague 4; e-mail info@nadacecs.cz; internet www.nadacecs.cz.

Nadace Český Hudebni Fond—NČHF (Czech Music Fund Foundation)

Founded in 1994 by the Czech Music Fund (f. 1954) to support and encourage the development of Czech musical culture.

Activities: Provides grants and scholarships to talented Czech musicians; supports musical activities, such as competitions for composers and performers, workshops and music education; and holds public composition competitions to stimulate new works. The Foundation has set up two beneficial institutions: the Music Information Centre; and the Czech Music Fund, which runs an instrument hire service with branches throughout the Czech Republic, and hires out musical scores and parts from other institutions all over the world.

Geographical Area of Activity: Czech Repub.

Publications: Annual Report.

Finance: Annual income 88.7m. koruny, expenditure 82.6m. koruny (31 Dec. 2023).

Board of Directors: Dr Pavel Fiedler (Chair.).

Supervisory Board: Dr Jana Vojtěšková (Chair.).

Principal Staff: Dir Radomír Kubík.

Nadace Český literární fond

Contact Details: Besední 3, 118 00 Prague 1; tel. 257320008; e-mail nadace@nchf.cz; internet www.nchf.cz.

Nadace Český literární fond—nčlf (Czech Literary Fund Foundation)

Founded in 1994 to promote literature in the Czech Republic; registered as a foundation in 1999.

Activities: Presents awards for prose, poetry, literary essays and literary research, including the K. H. Borovský Prize for Journalism; and the Josef Hlavka Prize for Scientific Books, which is jointly awarded with Nadání Josefa, Marie a Zdenky Hlávkových (the Hlávka Foundation). The Foundation awards grants and scholarships in the fields of: Czech literature and journalism, including translation into Czech; drama for theatre, radio and film, including translation into Czech, and translations of screenplays for documentary films; and also publication of scientific journals and travel fellowships for researchers aged under 35 years. It administers the Fond Boženy Němcové, which helps writers and translators in need; and the Fond Vratislava Effenbergera, which supports editorial and publishing work related to Wroclaw Effenberger, a surrealist artist.

Geographical Area of Activity: Czech Repub.

Restrictions: Grants only to specific organizations in the Czech Republic.

Publications: Annual Report.

Finance: Annual revenue 16.9m. koruny, expenditure 17.2m. koruny (31 Dec. 2021).

Board of Directors: Dr Jan Lukeš (Chair.).

Supervisory Board: Dr Jiří Bednář (Chair.).

Principal Staff: Dir Dr Ivo Purš; Deputy Dir Vratislav Keprt.

Contact Details: Pod Nuselskými schody 3, 120 00 Prague 2; tel. 222560081; e-mail nadace@nclf.cz; internet www.nclf.cz.

Nadace Charty 77 (The Charta 77 Foundation)

Established in 1990 by František Janouch, Karel Jan Schwarzenberg and George Soros; an autonomous branch of the Swedish Charta 77 Foundation.

Activities: Works in the fields of education, law and human rights, medicine and health and social welfare (especially for disabled citizens). The Foundation's longest-running project is Konto Bariéry (the Barriers Account), which began in 1992 and raises funds for Foundation activities through public fundraising from a base of approximately 40,000 donors. Annual Foundation awards are the literary Jaroslav Seifert Prize and Tom Stoppard Prize; the František Kriegel Prize for Civil Courage; the Josef Vavroušek Environmental Prize; and the Václav Havel Human Rights Prize.

Geographical Area of Activity: Europe.

Publications: Annual Report.

Finance: Annual income 127.4m. koruny, expenditure 29.0m. koruny (31 Dec. 2021).

Board of Directors: Bozena Jirků (Chair.); Evžen Lev Hart (Vice-Chair.).

Supervisory Board: Daniel Horák (Chair.).

Principal Staff: Dir Jolana Voldanová.

Contact Details: Melantrichova 5, 110 00 Prague 1; tel. 224214452; e-mail info@bariery.cz; internet www.kontobariery.cz/nadace-charty-77.

Nadace Občanského fóra—Nadace OF (Civic Forum Foundation)

Founded in 1990 by Dagmar Havlová and Dr Ivan M. Havel.

Activities: Works to protect and conserve national cultural heritage, with a focus on neglected monuments, by raising public awareness and promoting partnerships between the business, non-profit and government sectors. The Foundation carries out self-conducted projects; and offers grants to organizations within the Czech Republic and conservation awards. It works with international organizations and maintains a cultural heritage database.

CZECH REPUBLIC (CZECHIA)

Geographical Area of Activity: Czech Repub.

Publications: Annual Report; newsletter (3 a year); *Children's Guide Book to Třeboň Chateau*; *Cultural Programme Information Sheet*.

Finance: Annual income 1.6m. koruny, expenditure 2.4m. koruny (31 Dec. 2023).

Board of Trustees: Dagmar Havlová (Chair.).

Supervisory Board: Darja Zoubková (Chair.).

Contact Details: Štěpánská 704/61, 110 00 Prague 1; tel. 776575114; e-mail nadaceof@seznam.cz; internet www.nadaceof.cz.

Nadace Open Society Fund Praha (Open Society Fund Prague—OSF Prague)

Founded in 1992; an independent foundation, part of the Open Society Foundations (q.v.) network until 2012.

Activities: Supports the development of an open society and promotes systemic changes that strengthen democracy. Main programmes are: Living Democracy, which promotes openness and transparency in government, supports responsible citizens and the rule of law, and advocates for free access to information and quality journalism; and Fair Society, which supports mutual respect, understanding and equal opportunities for all people, including equal access to education and employment. The Fund offers grants and training. It administers the Nadační Fond Hyundai, supporting community projects in the areas of environmental conservation, government transparency and access to decisionmaking; and the Active Citizens Fund, jointly with the Committee of Goodwill—Olga Havel Foundation (q.v.) and the Scout Institute.

Geographical Area of Activity: Czech Repub.

Publications: Annual Report; newsletter (monthly).

Principal Staff: Exec. Dir Martina Břeňová.

Contact Details: Hradecká 92/18, 130 00 Prague 3; Prokopova 197/9, 130 00, Prague 3; tel. 222540979; e-mail osf@osf.cz; internet www.osf.cz.

Nadace Preciosa (Preciosa Foundation)

Founded in 1996 by Preciosa, a glass manufacturer, to support non-profit and publicly beneficial activities in the Czech Republic.

Activities: Supports organizations and civic initiatives in the region where the company was founded. The Foundation has set up funds in seven areas: public health; scientific research in universities and museums; physical education and sports, involving children and young people in particular; education, supporting universities and schools to purchase equipment and awarding scholarships; culture and the arts, funding choirs, music ensembles and exhibitions; ecology and the environment, supporting sustainable development and reforestation; and individual assistance, focusing on helping disabled people in need.

Geographical Area of Activity: Czech Repub. (mainly the Liberec region).

Finance: Annual revenue 102.3m. koruny, expenditure 96.8m. koruny (31 Dec. 2023).

Board of Directors: Stanislav Kadlec (Chair.); Lucie Karlová (Vice-Chair.).

Principal Staff: Dir Andrea Kroupová.

Contact Details: Opletalova 3197/17, 466 01 Jablonec nad Nisou; tel. 488115393; e-mail nadace@preciosa.com; internet www.nadacepreciosa.cz.

Nadace Vodafone Česká Republika (Vodafone Czech Republic Foundation)

Established in 2006 by Vodafone Česká Republika, a telecommunications company; part of the Vodafone Foundation (q.v.) network.

Activities: Supports the use of ICT for community development. Foundation programmes focus on creating, launching and developing social innovations, offering grants to NGOs, non-profit organizations and social enterprises. Vodafone employees can apply for grants, worth 15,000 koruny, to support organizations where they regularly volunteer; and there is a grant of 20,000 koruny for five people to work for five days on a project at a non-profit organization or social enterprise.

Geographical Area of Activity: Czech Repub.

Publications: Annual Report; newsletter.

Finance: Annual income 7.7m. koruny, expenditure 7.7m. koruny (31 March 2023).

Board of Trustees: Richard Stonavský (Chair.).

Principal Staff: Dir Zuzana Holá.

Contact Details: Náměstí Junkových 2, 155 00 Prague 5; tel. 776971677; e-mail nadace@vodafone.cz; internet www.nadacevodafone.cz.

VIA Foundation

Established in 1997 as the successor to the Prague office of the USA-based Foundation for a Civil Society (q.v.).

Activities: Operates in the Czech Republic in the fields of community development, the development of philanthropy and provision of institutional support for NGOs. The Foundation offers Fast Grants and Community Grants worth 40,000 koruny and 100,000 koruny, respectively, to community groups and volunteer-based non-profit organizations; grants worth up to 500,000 koruny to non-profit and civic bodies to create public meeting spaces; and Via Bona awards recognizing the work of philanthropic donors, businesses and individuals. It supports the Darujme.cz online donor platform, corporate giving and employee volunteering. Through the Community Alphabet programme, training is offered to programme managers and consultants from three community support organizations in the Czech Republic, Hungary and Serbia.

Geographical Area of Activity: Central and South-Eastern Europe.

Publications: Annual Report; newsletter; *Umění darovat* (quarterly supplement); *Filantropická ročenka* ('Philanthropic Year Book').

Finance: Annual revenue 66.4m. koruny, expenditure 64.8m. koruny (31 Dec. 2023).

Board of Directors: Petr Kasa (Chair.).

Principal Staff: Exec. Dir Zdeněk Mihalco.

Contact Details: Dejvická 306/9, 160 00 Prague 6; tel. 608538083; e-mail via@nadacevia.cz; internet www.nadacevia.cz.

Výbor dobré vůle—Nadace Olgy Havlové (Committee of Good Will—Olga Havel Foundation)

Established in 1992 by Olga Havel, founder of the Committee of Good Will (f. 1990) and first wife of President Václav Havel.

Activities: Raises awareness of the problems and challenges that people with disabilities and chronic illnesses face, particularly in the areas of employment, education and housing. The Foundation provides organizational and financial support to humanitarian projects and for disaster relief; and to help to create an integrated society. Programmes include: the Salzburg Medical Cornell Seminars; the Sasakawa Asthma Fund (which also operates in Slovakia), established to address the growing problem of asthma-related diseases; Ordinary Life, supporting civic associations in their programmes for homeless, excluded communities and mothers in difficult situations; and the Education Fund and the Nikola Tesla Scholarship, which award scholarships to students with social problems and disabilities. The Committee presents the annual Olga Havel Award to people who help others despite their own disability. The Active Citizens Fund is jointly administered in consortium with the Open Society Fund Prague—OSF Prague (q.v.) and the Scout Institute.

Geographical Area of Activity: Czech Repub.

Restrictions: Applications by post only.

Publications: Annual Report; books; *The Good News Magazine*.

Finance: Annual income 74.3m. koruny, expenditure 66.7m. koruny (31 Dec. 2023).

Board of Directors: Vojtěch Sedláček (Chair.); Dr Anna Šabatová (Vice-Chair.).

Supervisory Board: Zdenek Tuma (Chair.).

Principal Staff: Dir Monika Granja.

Contact Details: POB 240, 111 21 Prague 1; Senovážné náměstí č. 994/2, Prague 1; tel. 224217331; e-mail vdv@vdv.cz; internet www.vdv.cz.

Vzdělávací Nadace Jana Husa (Jan Hus Educational Foundation)

Founded in 1990 by Miroslav Pospíil, Jana Kuchtová and Julie Tastná to support the development of higher education in the arts, humanities and law in the Czech Republic and Slovakia; since 1993 the former branch office in Bratislava has operated as a sister foundation in Slovakia.

Activities: Operates in the Czech Republic in the fields of the development of education, and the development of civil society, through self-conducted programmes, training courses, grants to institutions and publication awards. The Foundation awards scholarships, each worth 60,000 koruny, for doctoral and postdoctoral research in non-applied humanities, social sciences and related fields; and annually awards up to three science fellowships, each worth 40,000 koruny, to study a degree course in mathematics, physics, chemistry, biology or medicine at a university anywhere in the world. Writing and publishing grants of up 100,000 koruny are also available to doctoral students and qualified doctors for essays in the fields of education, culture and freedom. It awards the Bronislava Müllerová Prize, worth 10,000 koruny to high school students for an essay on freedom of speech; and organizes a summer university exchange programme which alternates between the Czech Republic, Slovakia and France.

Geographical Area of Activity: Czech Repub., France, Slovakia.

Restrictions: Scholarships, fellowships and grants are only available to applicants from the Czech Republic and Slovakia.

Publications: Annual Report; reports; guides.

Finance: Annual revenue 14.6m. koruny, expenditure 11.4m. koruny (31 Dec. 2022).

Board of Directors: Lenka Pazdziorová, Dr Martin Šimsa (Vice-Chair.).

Supervisory Board: Jaromír Adamec (Chair.).

Principal Staff: Exec. Dir Jana Švábová; Sec. Miroslava Řehulková.

Contact Details: Cihlářská 15, 602 00 Brno; tel. 530331240; e-mail vnjh@vnjh.cz; internet www.vnjh.cz.

DENMARK

FOUNDATIONS AND NON-PROFITS

A. P. Møller og Hustru Chastine Mc-Kinney Møllers Fond til almene Formaal (The A. P. Møller and Chastine Mc-Kinney Møller Foundation)

Founded in 1953 by shipowner A. P. Møller and his wife Chastine Mc-Kinney Møller.

Activities: Supports Danish culture and heritage, Danish shipping and medical science; major institutions established with foundation funding include a new opera house in Copenhagen. The Foundation operates three funds: the A. P. Møller Fund, the Support Fund and the Fund for Medical Advancement; and also supports the A. P. Møller Fund for Icelandic Students in Denmark (f. 1936). In 2013 it established the holding company A. P. Møller Holding A/S.

Geographical Area of Activity: Denmark, Faroe Islands, Germany (South Schleswig), Greenland.

Restrictions: Does not make grants to individuals and only occasionally to non-Danish projects; does not accept applications by e-mail.

Publications: Newsletter.

Finance: Total assets 278.2m. Danish kroner (31 Dec. 2023).

Board of Directors: Ane Mærsk Mc-Kinney Uggla (Chair.).

Principal Staff: Dir Mads Ulrik Lebech; Sec.-Gen. Thomas Wohlert.

Contact Details: Esplanaden 50, 1263 Copenhagen K; tel. 33-63-35-00; e-mail kontakt@apmollerfonde.dk; internet www.apmollerfonde.dk.

Aktion Børnehjælp (Action Children's Aid)

Founded in 1965 as Abbé Pierres klunsere, S.O.S. Tørmælk; in 1986 it became Aktion Børnehjælp, Mother Teresas Medarbejdere i Danmark. Present name adopted in 1994.

Activities: Works in the fields of childcare and education. The organization funds projects in India in areas including: health and learning; children's rights; improving sanitation; and food security. It also supports orphanages, schools, kindergartens and vocational training for young people.

Geographical Area of Activity: India.

Publications: Annual Report; newsletter; *Aktion Børnehjælp Nyt* (magazine, 3 a year).

Finance: Total assets 5.7m. Danish kroner (31 Dec. 2023).

Board of Directors: Claus Skytt (Chair.); Tinne Midtgaard (Vice-Pres.).

Principal Staff: Programme Man. Mathilde Nielsen.

Contact Details: Fælledvej 12, C, 1, 2200 Copenhagen N; tel. 35-85-03-15; e-mail kontakt@aktionb.dk; internet www.aktionb.dk.

Alfred Benzons Fond (Alfred Benzon Foundation)

Founded in 1952 by Dr Bøje Benzon in memory of his paternal grandfather, Alfred Nicolai Benzon, founder of the first pharmaceutical company in Denmark.

Activities: Organizes the Benzon Symposia, which focus on medicine and pharmacy and related sciences. The Foundation offers fellowships to Danish research scientists undertaking study at foreign institutions; and to a limited number of foreign scientists wishing to conduct research in Denmark. It offers financial support for workshops to researchers based in Denmark; and under its clinical research programme awards grants of up to 1.5m. Danish kroner per year for projects of 1–3 years' duration. Grants are also made to Copenhagen Zoo for its research laboratory.

Geographical Area of Activity: Denmark.

Restrictions: Grant applications by foreign researchers must be forwarded by a Danish scientist.

Publications: *The Alfred Benzon Foundation 1952–2002.*

Board of Trustees: Prof. Mads Bryde Andersen (Chair.); Prof. Hanne Mørck Nielsen (Vice-Chair.).

Principal Staff: Admin Man. Leila Majdanac.

Contact Details: c/o Rigshospitalet—Copenhagen University Hospital, Centre for Genomic Medicine 4113, 2100 Copenhagen; tel. 22-97-87-52; e-mail mail@benzon-foundation.dk; internet www.benzon-foundation.dk.

Carlsbergfondet (Carlsberg Foundation)

Established in 1876 by Jacob Christian Jacobsen to contribute to the growth of science in Denmark.

Activities: Operates in the fields of basic research within natural science, social science, and the humanities. The Foundation carries out its activities through four departments: the Carlsberg Laboratory, which studies science with a view to improvements in malting, brewing and fermentation; the National History Museum at Frederiksborg Castle; Tuborgfondet (the Tuborg Foundation, f. 1931, merged with the Carlsberg Foundation in 1991), which works for socially beneficial purposes; and the New Carlsberg Foundation (q.v., f. 1902), which supports art and art history, and operates the Glyptotek museum. It offers a range of grants and fellowships.

Geographical Area of Activity: Denmark.

Publications: Annual Report; newsletter.

Finance: Total assets 43,540m. Danish kroner (31 Dec. 2024).

Board of Directors: Majken Schultz (Chair.); Prof. Susanne Mandrup (Deputy Chair.).

Principal Staff: Dir Lasse Horne Kjældgaard.

Contact Details: H. C. Andersens Blvd 35, 1553 Copenhagen V; tel. 33-43-53-63; e-mail info@carlsbergfoundation.dk; internet www.carlsbergfondet.dk.

Danmark-Amerika Fondet (Denmark-America Foundation)

Founded in 1914 to encourage understanding between the peoples of Denmark and the USA.

Activities: Encourages educational exchange between Denmark and the USA through the provision of grants to Danes. The Foundation organizes programmes; assists Danish academics in finding appointments in US institutions of higher education; and awards prizes to Danish citizens.

Geographical Area of Activity: Denmark, USA.

Restrictions: Grants only to Danish citizens.

Publications: Annual Report.

Foundation Executive Committee: Jørgen Bardenfleth (Chair.); Caroline Pontoppidan (Vice-Chair.).

Principal Staff: CEO Anders Obel.

Contact Details: Otto Mønsteds Gade 5, 1571 Copenhagen V; tel. 35-32-45-45; e-mail danmarkamerikafondet@bikubenfonden.dk; internet wemakeithappen.dk.

Danske Kulturinstitut—DKI (Danish Cultural Institute—DCI)

Founded in 1940 (originally as Danske Selskab—The Danish Institute) to stimulate cultural relations between Denmark and other countries.

Activities: Promotes dialogue and understanding across cultural differences and national borders. The Institute's work encompasses art, culture and society, focusing on: co-creation; education and research; welfare; sustainability; and children and young people. It facilitates networks and strengthens collaboration between Danish and international artists, cultural institutions and businesses; and creates platforms for knowledge sharing, exchanging ideas and experiences, and lasting cultural relations. Activities include: concerts, exhibitions, conferences, field trips, theatre, film, dance and, in some countries, Danish courses. Maintains international branches in Beijing, New Delhi, Riga, Rio de Janeiro and St Petersburg.

Geographical Area of Activity: Belarus, Brazil, People's Repub. of China, Denmark, Estonia, India, Latvia, Lithuania, Russian Federation, Türkiye (Turkey), Ukraine.

Publications: Annual Report; newsletter; reports.

Finance: Receives an annual grant from the Danish Ministry of Culture, which is supplemented by donations from foundations, business sponsors and local government organizations. Annual income 83m. Danish kroner, expenditure 81m. (31 Dec. 2023).

Board: Carsten Haurum (Chair.); Flemming Møller Mortensen (Deputy Chair.).

Principal Staff: CEO Camilla Mordhorst.

Contact Details: Vartov, Farvergade 27 L, 2nd Floor, 1463 Copenhagen K; tel. 33-13-54-48; e-mail mail@danishculture.com; internet www.danishculture.com.

Egmont Fonden (Egmont Foundation)

Established in 1920 in accordance with the wishes of Egmont Harald Petersen, printer to the Royal Danish Court, to operate the businesses established by him, to raise funds for charitable purposes; a commercial foundation, part of the Egmont media group.

Activities: Works to eliminate poverty through young people's education. Main programmes focus on: early childhood development and education; ensuring a good start to primary education; identifying and helping children with dyslexia; and supporting placed children and young people to complete youth education. The Foundation carries out research and offers grants. It comprises the Nordisk Film Fonden, which supports film-makers with Store Isbjørn and Lille Isbjørn travel scholarships, worth 25,000 Danish kroner, and Isbjørn Project Scheme grants for talent and skills development, worth 50,000 Danish kroner; organizes the PictureThis. film technology conference; and offers ISBJØRNEN film awards in Denmark, Finland and Norway.

Geographical Area of Activity: Denmark, Finland, Norway.

Restrictions: No grants to individuals.

Publications: Annual Report; *The Egmont Report.*

Finance: Total assets €340.8m.; annual income €31.4m. (31 Dec. 2024).

Board of Trustees: Merete Eldrup (Chair.); Tom Knutzen (Vice-Chair.).

Principal Staff: Man. Heidi Sorensen.

Contact Details: Vognmagergade 9, 5th Floor, 1120 Copenhagen K; tel. 70-24-00-00; e-mail fond@egmont.com; internet www.egmont.dk.

Folmer Wisti Fonden for International Forståelse (Folmer Wisti Foundation for International Understanding)

Founded in 1976 by Folmer Wisti, an academic.

Activities: Contributes to international understanding and co-operation on issues of importance in daily life at local and regional level; decentralization and regionalism; and the exchange of experiences and ideas primarily in the fields of culture and general education. The Foundation supports the activities of the Danske Kulturinstitut (q.v.) and has sponsored the 'Europe of Regions' conferences on decentralization and regional autonomy.

Geographical Area of Activity: Europe.

Restrictions: Grants only to apolitical non-profit NGOs; does not make grants to individuals.

Publications: *Industrial Life in Denmark*; *The Faroe Islands and Greenland*; *Danish Foundations*; *Regional Contact* (journal).

Board: Charlotte Flindt Pedersen (Chair.); Peter Carøe (Vice-Chair.).

Contact Details: c/o Det Udenrigspolitische Selskab, Amaliegade 40A, 1256 Copenhagen K; e-mail wistifond@gmail.com; internet wistifonden.dk.

Fonden Realdania (Realdania Foundation)

Established in 2000 following a merger between three financial institutions: RealDanmark A/S, Danske Bank and Foreningen RealDanmark.

Activities: Realdania is a fully self-endowed philanthropic association with about 190,000 members. Supports projects that aim to solve significant and complex societal problems and improve people's quality of life. The Foundation promotes sustainable cities; new community frameworks; improved housing; and healthy, efficient and sustainable construction. It comprises the Bolius Knowledge Center, which provides homeowners with impartial information about homes; and Realdania By & Byg, which operates in the fields of area development, property management, sustainable construction and restoration, investing in experimental construction designs and maintaining historic buildings.

Geographical Area of Activity: Denmark.

Publications: Annual Report; annual magazine.

Finance: Total assets 33,427.5m. Danish kroner; net annual income –279.6m. Danish kroner (31 Dec. 2024).

Board of Directors: Lars Krarup (Chair.); Mette Kynne Frandsen (Vice-Chair.).

Principal Staff: CEO Nina Kovsted Helk.

Contact Details: Jarmers Plads 2, 1551 Copenhagen V; tel. 70-11-66-66; e-mail realdania@realdania.dk; internet www.realdania.dk.

Foundation for Environmental Education—FEE

Founded in 1981 as the Foundation for Environmental Education in Europe to raise awareness of environmental issues; in 2001 became the Foundation for Environmental Education (FEE), with the addition of South Africa as the first non-European member country. An umbrella body, registered in the United Kingdom.

Activities: Co-ordinates international campaigns and creates awareness of environmental education. The Foundation's main programmes are: the Blue Flag eco-label scheme for clean beaches and marinas, and sustainable boating tourism; Eco-Schools, a sustainable schools programme; Learning About Forests (LEAF), promoting outdoor learning; Young Reporters for the Environment, promoting investigative environmental journalism by young people; and the Green Key eco-label scheme for hospitality accommodation. It also established the Global Forest Fund, a carbon offsetting scheme that funds tree planting and education. Has over 100 member organizations in 81 countries.

Geographical Area of Activity: Worldwide.

Publications: Annual Report; newsletter.

Finance: Annual income €1.5m., expenditure €1.3m. (2023).

Board of Directors: Lesley Jones (Pres.); Nikos Petrou (Vice-Pres.); Helena Atkinson (Treas.).

Principal Staff: CEO Daniel Schaffer.

Contact Details: Scandiagade 13, 2450 Copenhagen SV; tel. 70-22-24-27; e-mail info@fee.global; internet www.fee.global.

Friluftsrådet (Danish Outdoor Council)

Founded in 1942; an initiative of Prime Minister Thorvald Stauning.

Activities: Works in all areas of outdoor recreational facilities and conservation. The Council advocates for sustainable tourism and develops environmental education projects. It administers the distribution of funds from Det Danske Klasselotteri national lottery, awarding grants for outdoor activities and to support development of associations and local communities. It has more than 80 member organizations.

Geographical Area of Activity: Denmark.

Restrictions: Awards grants for projects and operating grants for organizations.
Publications: Annual Report; newsletter; leaflets, manuals and educational materials; blog.
Finance: Annual income 34,509.6m. Danish kroner, expenditure 34,748.8m. Danish kroner (31 Dec. 2024).
Board of Directors: Dorthe Molvig (Chair.).
Principal Staff: Acting Dir Torbjorn Eriksen.
Contact Details: Scandiagade 13, 2450 Copenhagen SV; tel. 33-79-00-79; e-mail fr@friluftsraadet.dk; internet www.friluftsraadet.dk.

Hempel Fonden (Hempel Foundation)

Established in 1948, as J. C. Hempel's Fond, by J. C. Hempel, a marine paint manufacturer; operates independently of the Hempels Kulturfond (f. 1964).
Activities: Supports children's access to education; biodiversity; and science. The Foundation carries out projects in 24 countries. In 2017 it established the Hempel Foundation Coatings Science and Technology Centre (CoaST) at the Technical University of Denmark.
Geographical Area of Activity: International.
Publications: Annual Report.
Finance: Total assets €848m. (31 Dec. 2022).
Board of Directors: Richard Sand (Chair.); Leif Jensen (Deputy Chair.).
Principal Staff: Man. Anders Holm.
Contact Details: Amaliegade 8, 1256 Copenhagen K; tel. 33-12-38-42; e-mail hempel.foundation@hempel.com; internet www.hempelfonden.dk.

Institut for Menneskerettigheder (Danish Institute for Human Rights)

Founded in 1987 by the Danish Parliament as the Danish Centre for Human Rights; present name adopted in 2002.
Activities: Operates in the field of human rights, engaging in research and education, and disseminating information and documentation regionally, nationally and internationally. The Institute co-operates with other human rights organizations in Denmark and abroad, carrying out research and monitoring across the broad range of human rights. It has a library that contains reference books and journals on international and European human rights policy, with access to e-resources.
Geographical Area of Activity: Burkina Faso, People's Repub. of China, Denmark, Egypt, Ethiopia, Ghana, Greenland, Jordan, Kenya, Kyrgyzstan, Mali, Morocco, Myanmar, Niger, Palestinian Territories, Tunisia, Ukraine, Zambia.
Publications: Annual Status Report; Annual Report to the Danish Parliament; newsletter (10 a year); working papers; review reports; research papers; e-resources.
Finance: Total budget 137.7m. Danish kroner (2022).
Board: Andreas Kamm (Chair.); Mette Boye (Vice-Chair.).
Principal Staff: Exec. Dir Louise Holck.
Contact Details: Wilders Plads 8K, 1403 Copenhagen K; tel. 32-69-88-88; e-mail info@humanrights.dk; internet humanrights.dk.

International Work Group for Indigenous Affairs—IWGIA

Established in 1968 by anthropologists concerned about the plight of indigenous peoples in the Amazon.
Activities: IWGIA is a non-governmental human rights organization. It promotes, protects and defends Indigenous Peoples' collective and individual rights, including the right to self-determination by virtue of which they can freely determine their political status and freely pursue their self-determined economic, social and cultural development. IWGIA works through a global network of partners, first and foremost Indigenous Peoples' own organizations and networks, but also supports NGOs, academia, international human rights bodies and alliances. Triangle of Change is IWGIA's key instrument for fostering change by: documenting the situation of Indigenous peoples and the human rights violations they experience; advocating for change at local, national and international levels; and empowering Indigenous peoples to claim and exercise their rights.
Geographical Area of Activity: International.
Restrictions: Grants only to partner organizations.
Publications: Annual Report; newsletter; *The Indigenous World* (annual); *Debates Indígenas* (digital magazine); Indigenous Navigator (online portal); books (mainly in English and Spanish); briefing papers; handbooks; manuals; reports.
Finance: Annual income 46.9m. Danish kroner, expenditure 46.5m. Danish kroner (31 Dec. 2023).
Board of Directors: Ida Theilade (Chair.); Rune Fjellheim (Vice-Chair.).
Principal Staff: Exec. Dir Kathrin Wessendorf.
Contact Details: Prinsessegade 29B, 3rd Floor, 1422 Copenhagen K; tel. 53-73-28-30; e-mail iwgia@iwgia.org; internet www.iwgia.org.

IUC International Education Center—IUC-Europe (Internationalt Uddannelsescenter)

Established in 1985 by Frits Korsgaard, Dr Jacob Christensen, Dr Tom Høyem, Dr Knud Overø, Bent le Févre and Ingolf Knudsen; a founding member of EUNET—European Network for Education and Training (f. 2004).
Activities: Supports long-term youth projects nationally and internationally, with a focus on cross-border co-operation. The Center carries out activities in the fields of teaching and learning, non-formal (political) education, citizenship and integration, culture and employment; and organizes study trips. At EUNET, it is the administrative co-ordinator for 10 countries in the Model European Parliament Baltic Sea Region organization.
Geographical Area of Activity: Europe, North America.
Restrictions: Does not sponsor individuals, groups or programmes outside the IUC network.
Publications: Newsletter (monthly).
Board: Nina Nørgaard (Chair. and Exec. Dir); Rasmus Stobbe (Vice-Chair.).
Contact Details: Kløverbladsgade 61, 2500 Valby; tel. 26-20-11-05; e-mail iuc@iuc-europe.dk; internet www.iuc-europe.dk.

LEGO Fonden (The LEGO Foundation)

Established in 2009 by the LEGO toy company.
Activities: Donates LEGO products worldwide; promotes children's education through new learning materials, research programmes and training of teachers in developing countries. The Foundation has offices in Mexico, South Africa, Ukraine and the USA. It also supports Ole Kirk's Foundation (f. 1964), established in memory of the founder of the LEGO Group.
Geographical Area of Activity: International.
Restrictions: Does not accept unsolicited applications.
Publications: Annual Report; activity cards; booklets; reports.
Finance: Total assets 19,983m. Danish kroner (31 Dec. 2022).
Board of Directors: Thomas Kirk Kristiansen (Chair.); Jørgen Vig Knudstorp (First Deputy Chair.); Agnete Kirk Kristiansen (Second Deputy Chair.).
Principal Staff: CEO Sidsel Marie Kristiansen.
Contact Details: Højmarksvej 8, 7190 Billund; tel. 79-50-60-70; e-mail legofoundation@lego.com; internet learningthroughplay.com.

Léonie Sonnings Musikfond (Léonie Sonning Music Foundation)

Established in 1959 by Léonie Sonning, the widow of writer and editor Carl Johan Sonning; operates independently of the Sonning-Fonden (q.v.).

Activities: Operates in the field of the arts and culture. The Foundation offers an annual prize of 1m. Danish kroner to an internationally acknowledged composer, conductor, singer or musician. Recent prizewinners include Pierre-Laurent Aimard (2022), Usuk Chin (2021) and Barbara Hannigan (2020). It also offers grants to support young musicians, composers, conductors and singers in the Nordic countries.

Geographical Area of Activity: Worldwide.

Restrictions: Does not offer scholarships.

Board of Directors: Esben Tange (Chair.).

Contact Details: c/o Aumento Advokatfirma, Ny Østergade 3, 1101 Copenhagen K; tel. 53-63-33-97; e-mail sekretariat@sonningmusik.dk; internet www.sonningmusik.dk.

Lundbeckfonden (Lundbeck Foundation)

Established in 1954 by Grete Lundbeck, whose late husband Hans founded the pharmaceutical company H. Lundbeck A/S; a business fund.

Activities: Operates in the field of science and technology. Annually, the Foundation offers grants amounting to around 600m. Danish kroner for basic, clinical applied or epidemiological research projects in biomedical sciences, particularly in the field of brain research; and in 2021 offered seven research fellowships, worth a total of 70m. Danish kroner. It also funds projects on science education and communication that aim to interest children and young people in science. The annual Brain Prize, worth 10m. Danish kroner, is awarded to scientists internationally for contributions to neuroscience.

Geographical Area of Activity: Mainly Denmark.

Restrictions: Does not fund students or tuition fees.

Publications: Annual Report; newsletter.

Finance: Net wealth 71,739m. Danish kroner; net annual income 6,567m. Danish kroner (2024).

Board of Directors: Steffen Kragh (Chair.); Soren Skou (Vice-Chair.).

Principal Staff: CEO Lene Skole.

Contact Details: Scherfigsvej 7, 2100 Copenhagen; tel. 39-12-80-00; e-mail application@lundbeckfonden.dk; internet www.lundbeckfonden.dk.

Mary Fonden (Mary Foundation)

Established in 2007 by HRH Crown Princess Mary.

Activities: Works to prevent social isolation, convening panels of international experts in the areas of bullying and wellbeing, domestic violence and loneliness.

Geographical Area of Activity: Denmark, Greenland.

Restrictions: Not a grantmaking organization.

Publications: Annual Report; newsletter.

Finance: Annual income 34.4 million Danish kroner (31 Dec. 2024); administrative costs are partly covered by the Hempel Foundation.

Board of Directors: Her Majesty The Queen of Denmark (Chair.).

Principal Staff: Dir Helle Østergaard.

Contact Details: Amaliegade 8B, 1256 Copenhagen K; tel. 45-27-30-20; e-mail info@maryfonden.dk; internet www.maryfonden.dk.

Nordisk Kulturfond (Nordic Culture Fund)

Founded in 1966 by the Nordic Council to encourage cultural co-operation in all its aspects among the Nordic countries (Denmark, Finland, Iceland, Norway and Sweden, incl. Greenland, Faroe Islands and Åland Islands).

Activities: Works to further artistic and cultural co-operation among the Nordic countries. The Fund supports projects through four main programmes: OPSTART, for projects in their start-up phase; Project Funding, awarding grants to projects three times a year; Globus, supporting artistic and cultural projects that extend beyond the Nordic Region; and Puls, a five-year funding programme supporting concert venues and festivals in the Nordic Region. It has a network of partners in Nordic countries: the Nordic Culture Point in Finland, which operates as a secretariat for Nordic Council programmes and has a culture centre and library; two Nordic House culture and knowledge centres in Iceland and the Faroe Islands; the Nordic Institute of Greenland; and the Nordic Institute in Åland.

Geographical Area of Activity: International.

Restrictions: A project is considered 'Nordic' if a minimum of three Nordic countries or self-governing areas are involved, either as participants, organizers or as subject areas.

Publications: Annual Report.

Finance: Annual budget 36m. Danish kroner (2023).

Board of Directors: Sigmundur Ernir Rúnarsson (Chair.); Arnbjörg María Danielsen (Deputy Chair.).

Principal Staff: Acting Dir Soren Merrild Staun.

Contact Details: Nordens Hus, Ved Stranden 18, 1061 Copenhagen K; tel. 33-96-02-42; e-mail kulturfonden@norden.org; internet www.nordiskkulturfond.org.

Novo Nordisk Foundation (Novo Nordisk Fonden)

Founded in 1989 following the merger of the Novo Foundation (f. 1951), the Nordisk Insulinfond (Nordic Insulin Foundation, f. 1926) and the Nordisk Insulinlaboratorium (Nordic Insulin Laboratory, f. 1923).

Activities: Supports a wide range of projects and initiatives with the overall aim of improving people's health and the sustainability of society and the planet. Within health, activities focus on progressing research and innovation in prevention and treatment of cardiometabolic and infectious diseases and on fighting inequity in health. In relation to sustainability, the Foundation aims to advance the development of sustainable agriculture and food production as well as climate change mitigating technologies. The Foundation also supports fundamental and translational research, education, innovation and technological development, as well as the establishment of new research infrastructures. In 2022 the Foundation awarded 751 grants and disbursed a total of 5,834m. Danish kroner. Has offices in Nairobi, Kenya and New Delhi, India.

Geographical Area of Activity: International.

Publications: Annual Report; newsletter; *Novo Nordisk Fond Magazine*.

Finance: Total assets 57,659m. Danish kroner; net annual income 4,500m. Danish kroner (31 Dec. 2023).

Board of Directors: Lars Rebien Sørensen (Chair.); Lars Munch (Vice-Chair.).

Principal Staff: CEO Mads Krogsgaard Thomsen.

Contact Details: Tuborg Havnevej 19, 2900 Hellerup; tel. 35-27-66-00; e-mail info@novonordiskfonden.dk; internet www.novonordiskfonden.dk.

Ny Carlsbergfondet (New Carlsberg Foundation)

Established in 1902 by Carl Jacobsen, owner of the New Carlsberg brewery, and his wife Ottilia; part of the Carlsbergfondet (q.v.).

Activities: Operates in the field of the arts and culture through offering grants in three main areas: work donations to museums; decoration assignments and art research; and a free pool containing funds for other art-relevant purposes. The Foundation supports museums in Denmark, including the Glyptoteket, which contains more than 10,000 works of art, mainly from ancient Mediterranean cultures, as well as 19th-century Danish and French sculpture and painting. It promotes the study of art and art history, offering grants for travel and for publications on art; and five annual Danish art awards, worth up to 300,000 Danish kroner. Teaching and learning materials are made freely available through the Tæt på Kunsten. In 2022 disbursements amounted to around 195m. Danish kroner.

Geographical Area of Activity: Denmark.

Restrictions: Does not accept unsolicited applications.

Publications: Annual Report; Ny Carlsbergfondet Årsblad (year book); Tæt på Kunsten (online).
Finance: Total assets 1,535.9m. Danish kroner; net annual result 404.4m. Danish kroner (31 Dec. 2024).
Board of Directors: Sanne Kofod Olsen (Chair.).
Principal Staff: Head of Secretariat Ditte Sig Kramer.
Contact Details: Brolæggerstræde 5, 1211 Copenhagen K; tel. 33-11-37-65; e-mail sekretariatet@ncf.dk; internet www.ny-carlsbergfondet.dk.

Otto Mønsteds Fond (Otto Mønsteds Foundation)

Founded in 1934 by Otto Mønsted, a margarine manufacturer, to contribute to the development of Danish trade and industry.
Activities: Awards grants to teachers and students at commercial and technical universities for study and training; internships and participation in congresses abroad; research stays and foreign visiting professorships. Annually, the Foundation offers The Bright Idea Award (Den Lyse Idé Prisen), worth a total of 500,000 Danish kroner, for ideas that combine research insight with commercial understanding. In 2025 it was expected to award grants amounting to 45m. Danish kroner.
Geographical Area of Activity: Denmark.
Restrictions: Does not fund degree programmes or research projects, general support or group tours for students; The Bright Idea Award is only open to students and researchers affiliated with a Danish university.
Publications: Annual Report.
Finance: Total assets 937.9m. Danish kroner; net annual income 78.1m. Danish kroner (31 Dec. 2024).
Board of Directors: Nis Alstrup (Chair.).
Principal Staff: Man. Dir Nina Movin.
Contact Details: Rathsacksvej 1, 3rd Floor, 1862 Frederiksberg C; tel. 39-62-08-11; e-mail omf@omfonden.dk; internet omfonden.dk.

Oxfam Denmark

Established in 1966; became part of the Oxfam confederation of organizations (qq.v.) in 2016.
Activities: Works for economic and social justice. Main programmes focus on: education; emergency relief; inequality; and peacebuilding. The organization also works to increase women's representation and participation in decisionmaking processes and to raise awareness about climate change.
Geographical Area of Activity: Bolivia, Burkina Faso, Ghana, Guatemala, Liberia, Mozambique, Nicaragua, Sierra Leone, South Sudan.
Publications: Annual Report; newsletter; *Oxfam Magasinet* (quarterly magazine).
Finance: Annual income 387m. Danish kroner, expenditure 385m. Danish kroner (31 Dec. 2023).
Board of Directors: Magnus Skovrind Pedersen (Chair.); Mette Lybye (Deputy Chair.).
Principal Staff: Sec.-Gen. Lars Koch.
Contact Details: Vesterbrogade 2B, 1620 Copenhagen V; tel. 35-35-87-88; e-mail oxfam@oxfam.dk; internet oxfam.dk.

Rockwool Fonden (Rockwool Foundation)

Founded in 1981 by the children of the late Gustav Kähler, founder of mineral wool manufacturer Rockwool.
Activities: Carries out research and work to strengthen the social and economic sustainability of the welfare state. Programmes areas include: young people at risk; marginalized groups and risky behaviour; immigration and integration; taxation and undeclared work; and family economics and the labour market. The Foundation supports social and humanitarian projects carried out by small organizations or by individuals; practical self-help projects in developing countries; and social capacity-building projects in Denmark.
Geographical Area of Activity: International.
Restrictions: Makes grants through Danish organizations.
Publications: Annual Report; books; newsletters; working papers.
Finance: Annual revenue 257m. Danish kroner (2023).
Board of Directors: Bo Kähler (Chair.); Gitte Pugholm Aabo (Vice-Chair.).
Principal Staff: Dir Elin Schmidt.
Contact Details: Ny Kongensgade 6, 1472 Copenhagen K; tel. 33-34-47-00; e-mail kontakt@rockwoolfonden.dk; internet rockwoolfonden.dk.

Sonning-Fonden (Sonning Foundation)

Founded in 1949 by the will of writer and editor Carl Johan Sonning to award a prize biennially for meritorious work in the promotion of European civilization; operates independently of the Léonie Sonnings Musikfond (q.v.).
Activities: Focuses on rehabilitation and restoration of historic buildings, and music research. The Foundation awards The Sonning Prize, usually biennially, which amounts to 1m. Danish kroner; European universities propose candidates who have benefited European culture, and the winner is selected by a committee established by the Rector of the University of Copenhagen.
Geographical Area of Activity: Europe.
Restrictions: Does not fund the purchase of musical instruments or scholarships.
Publications: Books.
Finance: Annual disbursements 1.3m. Danish kroner (2024).
Sonning Prize Committee: David Dreyer Lessen (Chair.).
Contact Details: c/o DEAS A/S, Dirch Passers Allé 76, 2000 Frederiksberg; tel. 39-46-62-21; e-mail ile@deas.dk; internet sonning-fonden.ku.dk.

Thomas B. Thriges Fond (Thomas B. Thrige Foundation)

Founded in 1933 by Thomas B. Thrige, an engineer and manufacturer.
Activities: Promotes scientific and educational projects that support Danish business and industry. The Foundation provides grants to Danish universities and research institutes for specialized equipment; and finances study tours abroad for Danish researchers and participation in international conferences by Danish experts. It also awards grants to visiting professors from abroad.
Geographical Area of Activity: Denmark.
Restrictions: Does not fund study in Denmark.
Publications: Annual Report.
Finance: Annual income 8.3m. Danish kroner, expenditure 2.3m. Danish kroner (29 Feb. 2020).
Board of Directors: Niels Jacobsen (Chair.); Jørgen Huno Rasmussen (Vice-Chair.).
Contact Details: c/o Terma A/S, Hovmarken 4, 8520 Lystrup; tel. 39-61-50-30; e-mail sekretariatet@thrigesfond.dk; internet thrigesfond.dk.

Vestnordenfonden (West-Nordic Foundation)

Founded in 1986 following an agreement signed by the Governments of Denmark, Finland, Iceland, Norway and Sweden, along with the autonomous Governments of the Faroe Islands and Greenland.
Activities: Provides funding for small and medium-sized enterprises in the Faroe Islands, Greenland and Iceland. The Foundation finances new and existing fishing businesses, works to expand the Greenland tourism industry and develops co-operative projects to include Icelandic businesses.
Geographical Area of Activity: Faroe Islands, Greenland, Iceland.
Publications: Annual Report.
Finance: Total assets 126.6m. Danish kroner; net annual income 34.3m. Danish kroner (31 Dec. 2023).

DOMINICAN REPUBLIC

CO-ORDINATING BODY

Solidarios—Consejo de Fundaciones Americanas de Desarrollo (Council of American Development Foundations)

Established in 1972 by 13 Latin American development foundations.

Activities: Provides technical assistance, training and microfinance services to members carrying out social and economic development programmes in their own countries. The Council has 14 member organizations in seven countries.

Geographical Area of Activity: Colombia, Dominican Repub., Ecuador, Guatemala, Honduras, Uruguay, Venezuela.

Publications: Annual Report; newsletter (monthly); *Solidarios de Primera Mano* (quarterly).

Finance: Annual income US $217,357, expenditure $191,958 (31 Dec. 2023).

Executive Committee: Juan Francisco Banegas (Pres.); Carlos Alberto Mejia (Vice-Pres.); Gonzalo Rodriguez (Treas.); Manuel Ricardo Canalda (Sec.).

Principal Staff: Exec. Dir Alexia Valerio Damirón.

Contact Details: Apdo 620, Calle Regina Koening, No. 10, Ensanche Paraíso, Santo Domingo; tel. 549-5111; e-mail info@redsolidarios.org; internet www.redsolidarios.org.

FOUNDATIONS AND NON-PROFITS

Fundación Dominicana de Desarrollo—FDD (Dominican Development Foundation)

Founded in 1966.

Activities: Provides access to basic goods and services through microfinance. It also offers microcredit, financial education, and training to help people start and improve their own businesses. It serves almost 20,000 people through a network of 15 offices.

Geographical Area of Activity: Dominican Republic.

Publications: Annual report; *Notas de Desarrollo*; *Catálogo de Organizaciones Voluntarias de Acción Social*.

Finance: Total assets 740.8m. Dominican pesos (31 Dec. 2024).

Board of Directors: María Virginia Elmúdesi (Pres.); Jean-Paul Quiroz (Vice-Pres.); María del Pilar Cañas (Treas.); María del Carmen Ramos (Sec.).

Principal Staff: Exec. Dir Mariano Frontera Martínez.

Contact Details: Calle Las Mercedes No. 4, Zona Colonial, Apdo 857, 10210 Santo Domingo; tel. 338-8101; e-mail info@fdd.org.do; internet www.fdd.org.do.

Fundación Global Democracia y Desarrollo—FUNGLODE (Global Democracy and Development Foundation)

Established in 2000; a think tank.

Activities: Promotes the development of the Dominican Republic. The Foundation comprises 10 study centres on: global multimedia; communication; future studies; urban planning and infrastructure; security and defence; public health; evironment, energy and sustainable development; francophone studies; education; and culture. It organizes film festivals; publishes books and magazines; and operates a radio station. The Juan Bosch Library hosts the Entrepreneurship and Innovation Observatory, the Dominican Judicial Observatory, the Dominican Political Observatory and a document centre; and contains 150,000 vols. A sister organization, the Global Foundation for Democracy and Development, operates in the USA; a Fellows exchange programme operates between the two organizations, promoting research and development in the Dominican Republic and the Caribbean. Has an office at the UNESCO headquarters in Paris, France.

Geographical Area of Activity: Dominican Repub., France, USA.

Publications: Annual Report; newsletter; periodicals; books.

Principal Staff: Pres. Leonel Fernández; Exec. Dir Marco Herrera.

Contact Details: Calle Capitán Eugenio de Marchena 26, La Esperilla, Santo Domingo; tel. 685-9966; e-mail info@funglode.org; internet funglode.org.

Fundación Solidaridad (Solidarity Foundation)

Established in 1990 by a group of community leaders, educators and members of co-operatives.

Activities: Offers education, capacity-building and development services to non-profit enterprises. The Foundation promotes CSOs and citizen participation; provides capacity building and tools to influence public policy; supports sustainable local development; and strengthens institutions. Gender equality and environmental sustainability are cross-cutting themes.

Geographical Area of Activity: Dominican Repub.

Publications: *Democracia Local* (newsletter); guides; magazines; reports; books; blog.

Board of Directors: Denis Mota Álvarez (Pres.); Guillermina Peña (Treas.); Miguel Ángel Cid (Sec.).

Principal Staff: Exec. Dir Juan Castillo.

Contact Details: Avda Francia 40, Apdo 129-2, 51021 Santiago; tel. 971-5400; e-mail fsolidaridad@gmail.com; internet solidaridad.do.

ECUADOR

CO-ORDINATING BODY

CERES—Consorcio Ecuatoriano Para La Responsabilidad Social (Ecuadorean Consortium for Social Responsibility)

Established in 2005; an association of Ecuadorean private, independent organizations.

Activities: Supports social responsibility and sustainability through building the capacity of social foundations. The Consortium facilitates networking and encourages dialogue between the private and public sectors. It has 86 members including public and private companies, NGOs and academic institutions.

Geographical Area of Activity: Ecuador.

Publications: Annual Report; bulletins (monthly); Campus Online (e-learning resources); reports; studies; guides; articles.

Board of Directors: Martín Vásconez (Pres.); Veronica Escobar (Vice-Pres.).

Principal Staff: Exec. Dir Evangelina Gómez-Durañona.

Contact Details: Edif. Metropolitan, Of. 1208, Avda Naciones Unidas y Núñez de Vela, Quito; tel. (2) 450-3366; e-mail comunicacion@redceres.org; internet www.redceres.com.

FOUNDATIONS AND NON-PROFITS

EcoCiencia—Fundación Ecuatoriana de Estudios Ecologicos (Ecuadorean Foundation of Ecological Studies)

Founded in 1989 by Danilo Silva, Patricio Mena, Roberto Ulloa, Mario Garcia, Luis Suarez, Juan Manuel Carrión and Miguel Vázquez.

Activities: Promotes the conservation of biodiversity, working with local NGOs and grassroots organizations to solve socioenvironmental problems. The Foundation works to: achieve ecological, economic and social sustainability; acknowledge and preserve the traditional knowledge of indigenous peoples and local communities; raise awareness about environmental problems; and promote equity between men and women and between generations. It carries out research; designs and implements activities for the management and sustainable use of natural resources; works with local governments to design public policy that promotes the conservation of biodiversity and sustainable development; and offers university scholarships.

Geographical Area of Activity: Ecuador.

Publications: Policy briefs; guides; leaflets; manuals; books.

Principal Staff: Pres. Miguel Vásquez; Exec. Dir Dr Carmen Josse.

Contact Details: Lizardo García E10-80 y 12 de Octubre, Edif. Alto Aragón, 170517 Quito; tel. (2) 323-0484; e-mail info@ecociencia.org; internet www.ecociencia.org.

Fondo Ecuatoriano de Cooperación para el Desarrollo—FECD (Ecuadorean Cooperation for Development Fund)

Established in 2005 as a successor to the Fondo Ecuatoriano Canadiense de Desarrollo.

Activities: Works to improve quality of life of the most vulnerable people in Ecuador, through involving them in self-sustaining productive activities. The Fund collaborates with NGOs and local organizations, governments and business to achieve long-term development at micro-regional level. Examples of projects include: peacebuilding; cocoa production; coffee management; marketing of agricultural produce; and responsible tourism.

Geographical Area of Activity: Ecuador.

Publications: Reports.

Finance: Total capital US $600,000.

Principal Staff: Exec. Dir William Hernández.

Contact Details: Prolongación de la Avda Granda Centeno, Urbanización el Alcázar, Pasaje 2, No. OE7-02, Casilla 17-21-1018, Quito; tel. (2) 246-8441; e-mail info-fecd@fecd.org.ec; internet www.fecd.org.ec.

Fundación Charles Darwin para las Islas Galápagos—FCD (Charles Darwin Foundation for the Galapagos Islands—CDF)

Founded in 1959 under the auspices of the Government of Ecuador, UNESCO and the World Conservation Union (IUCN, q.v.) to administer the Charles Darwin Research Station on the Galapagos Islands.

Activities: Provides knowledge and assistance through scientific research and complementary action to ensure the conservation of the environment and biodiversity in the Galapagos Archipelago. The Charles Darwin Research Station undertakes conservation measures for the unique fauna, flora and habitat of the archipelago; offers university scholarships to students from the Galapagos; and provides research facilities to visiting scientists. The Foundation supports the Galapagos National Park Directorate. It publishes the results of research and has a library of books, maps and photographs of the Galapagos Islands. Has an office in Quito.

Geographical Area of Activity: Ecuador, Galapagos Islands.

Publications: Annual Report; newsletter; research reports; databases; blog.

Finance: Annual income US $9.9m., expenditure $9.8m. (2024).

Board of Directors: Yolanda Kakabadse (Pres.).

Principal Staff: Exec. Dir and CEO Rakan A. Zahawi.

Contact Details: Avda Charles Darwin s/n, Puerto Ayora, Santa Cruz Island, Galapagos; Support Office: Francisco Andrade Marín E6-122 and Avda Eloy Alfaro, Pink Bldg, Apartment A, First Floor, La Carolina Park Sector, POB 17-1-3891, Quito; tel. (5) 252-6146; e-mail cdrs@fcdarwin.org.ec; internet www.darwinfoundation.org.

Fundación Futuro Latinoamericano (Latin American Future Foundation)

Established in 1993.

Activities: Fosters sustainable development in Latin America through promoting dialogue and strengthening civil society, political and institutional capacities. Programmes focus on: climate change, water and energy; the culture of peace and human mobility; and territorial and marine governance. The Foundation provides training and technical assistance; facilitates dialogue; and organizes regional forums on socioenvironmental conflict transformation.

Geographical Area of Activity: Latin America.

Publications: Annual Report; forum reports; bulletins.

Principal Staff: Exec. Dir Pablo Lloret.

Contact Details: Shyris N37-313 and The Telegraph, Quito; tel. (2) 226-6795; e-mail info@ffla.net; internet www.ffla.net.

Fundación Grupo Esquel—Ecuador (Esquel Group Foundation—Ecuador)

Established in 1990, building on the work of the Esquel Group, a network of Latin American NGOs.

Activities: Supports sustainable human development in Ecuador, improving the quality of life of poor people and building a democratic, responsible and supportive society. Main programme areas are: education and youth; health and development; and democracy and participation. The Foundation provides technical assistance and training; and acts as an intermediary between communities, businesses and other actors. It also works to strengthen the role of women, young people and LGBTI people.

Geographical Area of Activity: Ecuador.

Publications: Annual Report; *Esquela* (quarterly newsletter); handbooks; monographs; reports; working papers; books.

Finance: Annual income US $1.1m., expenditure $1.6m. (31 Dec. 2023).

Board of Directors: Pablo Rodolfo Better Grunbaun (Pres.); Grace Mónica Jaramillo Gutiérrez (Vice-Pres.).

Principal Staff: Exec. Dir Humberto Salazar.

Contact Details: Avda Colón E4-175 entre Amazonas y Foch, Edif. Torres de la Colón, Mezzanine Of. 12, Quito; tel. (2) 252-0001; e-mail fundacion@esquel.org.ec; internet www.esquel.org.ec.

Fundación Nobis (Nobis Foundation)

Established in 1996 by Consorcio Nobis, a holding company with interests in agro-industry, real estate, commerce and tourism.

Activities: Works to bring about sustainable change for vulnerable people and people from low-income backgrounds through education. Programmes include: education, work and entrepreneurship, with a focus on young people, providing educational opportunities in vulnerable areas and supporting the children of Nobis employees; and promoting impact investing in social innovation. The Foundation participates in the UN Global Pact to implement the Sustainable Development Goals; and organizes workshops.

Geographical Area of Activity: Ecuador.

Publications: COE Report; newsletter.

Board of Directors: Isabel Noboa (Pres.).

Principal Staff: Exec. Dir Juan Pablo Guerrero.

Contact Details: Edif. Executive Center, Avda Joaquín Orrantia y Avda Tanca Marengo, Guayaquil; tel. (4) 215-8000; e-mail info@fundacionnobis.com; internet www.fundacionnobis.com.

Fundación Telefónica Movistar Ecuador (Telefónica Movistar Ecuador Foundation)

Established in 2009 by Telefónica-Movistar, a telecommunications company; part of the Fundación Telefónica (q.v.) network.

Activities: Fundación Telefónica Ecuador promotes inclusive digital development through initiatives in education, employability, and corporate volunteering. It leads ProFuturo, a joint programme with Fundación Bancaria 'la Caixa' (q.v.), to bridge the educational gap using technology. The foundation offers free online training in digital skills, programming, and cybersecurity to enhance employability. Its corporate volunteering programme engages employees in impactful social initiatives, including digital inclusion efforts for vulnerable communities. With over 15 years of experience, it has invested more than US $60m., reaching all 24 provinces of Ecuador to drive digital education and professional development.

Geographical Area of Activity: Ecuador.

Publications: *Telos* (magazine); reports.

Board of Directors: Luis Benatuil Valls (Chair.).

Principal Staff: Exec. Dir Javier Alvarado; Gen. Sec. Blanca Isabel Egas.

Contact Details: Av. Simón Bolívar y Vía Nayón, Centro Corporativo Ekopark, Torre 3, Quito; tel. (2) 222-7700; e-mail fundacion.ec@telefonica.com; internet fundaciontelefonica.com.ec.

Grupo Social Fondo Ecuatoriano Populorum Progressio (Ecuadorean Social Group Fund Populorum Progressio)

Established in 1970, sponsored by the Ecuadorean Episcopal Conference; present name adopted in 2000.

Activities: Supports the development of marginalized groups in rural and urban areas of Ecuador through providing grants and technical assistance and raising awareness. Target groups include children and young people, with grants made to projects in the fields of health, social services, development, civil and human rights, and conflict resolution. The group comprises 10 regional offices and several enterprises: Codesarollo strengthens local financial markets through providing savings and credit facilities; Fundación Educativa Mons. Cándido Rada (Funder) provides vocational training for young people; Protierras provides legal services and mediation for indigenous groups and others in land and territorial matters; Camari provides export and marketing services for farmers and agricultural producers; Yurafepp supports conservation and the intelligent use of natural resources; FEPP Construcciones Aguavivienda builds social housing and infrastructure, including water supplies; Agroimportadora provides affordable agricultural equipment and supplies; Infofepp trains indigenous people and marginalized communities to use information technology; and Imprefepp is the Group's printing and publishing arm, producing a range of educational and commercial materials, including books, magazines, CDs and cassettes.

Geographical Area of Activity: Ecuador.

Publications: Annual Report; *La Bocina* (newsletter); leaflets; books.

Board of Directors: Bishop Néstor Herrera (Chair.); Luis Hinojosa (Exec. Dir).

Principal Staff: Sec.-Gen. Dr Sagrario Angulo.

Contact Details: Mallorca N24-275 y Avda La Coruña, La Floresta, Casilla 17-110-5202, Quito; tel. (2) 252-0408; e-mail fepp@fepp.org.ec; internet gsfepp.org.ec.

Red de Salud de las Mujeres Latinoamericanas y del Caribe—RSMLAC (Latin American and Caribbean Women's Health Network—LACWHN)

Established in 1984, during the first Regional Women and Health meeting in Colombia.

Activities: Links regional organizations that work in the area of women's health. The Network campaigns on health and rights for women of all ages, focusing particularly on sexual and reproductive health rights and the right to free and safe abortion. It offers training; strengthens regional co-ordination among organizations and individuals; supports and organizes regional and international events; and runs international campaigns on priority issues in women's health. Has more than 800 affiliates in 21 countries.

Geographical Area of Activity: Central and South America and the Caribbean, Pakistan, Spain.

Publications: Annual Report; newsletter; *Boletín Especial*; *Women's Health Journal* (magazine, quarterly); *Women's Health Collection* (annual).

Principal Staff: Gen. Co-ordinator Sandra Castañeda Martínez.

Contact Details: Alpallana 501 y Whimper Edif. Aramis, Dep. 03, Planta Baja, Quito; tel. 177069445; e-mail comunicaciones@reddesalud.org; internet www.reddesalud.org.

EGYPT

CO-ORDINATING BODY

Arab Network for Environment and Development—RAED

Established in 1990 as an umbrella body; the Arab Office for Youth and Environment operates as its Secretariat.

Activities: Member NGOs implement projects at regional and international level in: energy efficiency; protection of endangered species; renewable energy; safe disposal of hazardous waste; and waste recycling and water conservation. The Network comprises members from 17 countries.

Geographical Area of Activity: Mediterranean region, Middle East and North Africa.

Publications: *Montada Elbiah* (monthly newsletter).

Principal Staff: Gen. Co-ordinator Dr Emad El Din Adly; Deputy Gen. Co-ordinator Dr Mohamed Mahmoud.

Contact Details: 3A Masaken, Masr Lel-Taameer, Zahraa el-Maadi St, El Maadi, Cairo; tel. (2) 5161519; e-mail info@raednetwork.org; internet www.raednetwork.org.

FOUNDATIONS AND NON-PROFITS

Anna Lindh Euro-Mediterranean Foundation for Dialogue between Cultures

Established in 2004, building on the Euro-Mediterranean partnership; originally conceived as the Euro-Mediterranean Foundation for Dialogue between Cultures, but renamed in memory of Swedish Foreign Minister Anna Lindh, who was killed in 2003 in a hate crime.

Activities: Works in the field of intercultural dialogue through empowering young people and influencing policymakers. Main programmes focus on: countering growing mistrust and polarization among societies; creating more inclusive and empathetic societies; and building a culture based on dialogue and exchange. The Foundation offers Anna Lindh Grants to support projects in the fields of the arts and culture that promote intercultural dialogue, worth between €35,000 and €50,000 and lasting 8–11 months; and Intercultural Research Project Grants, worth between €20,000 and €30,000 for projects lasting 5–7 months. It co-ordinates the MedForum civil society gathering; hosts the Translation Platform, connecting academics, authors, foundations, libraries, private institutions and publishers; and organizes the Mediterranean Journalist Awards for cross-cultural reporting. Comprises more than 4,000 member civil organizations in 43 countries.

Geographical Area of Activity: EU and Southern Mediterranean countries.

Restrictions: Grants only to partnerships with at least one partner from a member Southern Mediterranean country and one from a partner European country; Intercultural Research Project Grants only to research institutes or universities.

Publications: Newsletter; *The Anna Lindh Education Handbook: Intercultural Citizenship Education in the Euro-Mediterranean Region*; reports; analysis.

Finance: Funded by the 43 member states of the Union for the Mediterranean and the European Commission.

Board of Governors: Dr Mari Neuvonen (Chair.).

Principal Staff: Pres. HRH Rym Ali; Exec. Dir Josep Ferré.

Contact Details: c/o Bibliotheca Alexandrina, 3rd Floor Conference Centre, POB 732, el-Mansheia, Alexandria 21111; tel. (3) 4831832; e-mail info@alfsecretariat.org; internet alf.website.

Arab Organization for Human Rights

Founded in 1983 to defend human rights.

Activities: Works to protect the human rights of people living in Arab countries and to defend those whose rights have been violated through conducting advocacy, research and training. The Organization provides legal assistance and advocates for people convicted without fair trial, supports improvements in conditions for prisoners of conscience; and campaigns for amnesty for political prisoners. It has 22 branches in member Arab countries and three European countries; has consultative status with ECOSOC; and observer status with the African Commission on Human and Peoples' Rights of the African Union, and the Arab Permanent Comittee on Human Rights of the League of Arab States. Maintains executive relations with the United Nations Educational, Scientific and Cultural Rights Organization, and with the UN Development Programme. Established the Social Justice Resources Center in 2014.

Geographical Area of Activity: Principally North Africa and the Middle East.

Publications: Annual Report; newsletter; *The Status of Human Rights in the Arab World* (annual); magazine; position papers; reports; studies.

Finance: Funded by members' dues and contributions.

Board of Trustees: Alaa Shalaby (Chair.); Issam Younes (Vice-Chair.); Maha Al-Barjas (Sec.-Gen.).

Principal Staff: Pres. Alaa Shalaby; Exec. Dir Mohamed Radi.

Contact Details: 91 al-Marghani St, Apts 7–8, Heliopolis, Cairo 11341; tel. (2) 4181396; e-mail info@aohr.net; internet aohrarab.com.

Mansour Foundation for Development—MFD

Established in 2001 by the Mansour family, as the Mansour Charity Foundation, to manage the philanthropic activities of the Mansour Group; present name adopted in 2009.

Activities: Priority areas of interest are: education, health and capacity building; with a focus on young people, women and girls, children with special needs, and residents of informal settlements. Programmes include: health; education; poverty alleviation; vocational training and employment; capacity building of vulnerable groups; and youth, entrepreneurship and volunteering. The Foundation provides research and development grants for social and business studies. Its programmes assist approximately 15,000 people annually. Has an office in Alexandria.

Geographical Area of Activity: Egypt.

Publications: Sustainability Report.

Principal Staff: Man. Dir Rania Hamoud.

Contact Details: Zahraa El Maadi, Industrial Zone, POB 97, New Maadi, Cairo; tel. (2) 25984600; e-mail info@mansourgroup.com; internet mmd.mansourgroup.com/mansour-foundation.

Mohamed Shafik Gabr Foundation for Social Development

Established in 2012 by Mohamed Shafik Gabr, Chair. and Man. Dir of the ARTOC Group for Investment and Development; the Shafik Gabr Foundation operates in the USA.

Activities: Areas of interest include: education, renovating and equipping schools and libraries, and sponsoring initiatives in partnership with the American University in Cairo, the Massachusetts Institute of Technology, the Lee Kuan Yew School of Public Policy in Singapore, and other educational programmes; health, operating a medical and social development centre in Mokattam, and mobile treatment centres; people trafficking; emergency aid; food; sports; culture; and women's issues. The Foundation's flagship initiative is East–West: The Art of Dialogue, promoting greater mutual understanding and closer relations between the peoples of the Arab world and the West, in particular the USA. The Gabr Fellowship is an international exchange programme, which arranges for around 20 participants to visit Egypt and the USA, spending two weeks in each country, and engaging in activities and discussions. It has an office in Washington, DC, USA.

Geographical Area of Activity: Egypt (with a particular focus on Mokattam, Mansouria and Greater Cairo).

Restrictions: Fellowship applicants must be aged 24–35 years and come from Egypt, France, Jordan, Lebanon, the UK or the USA.

Publications: Annual Report; newsletter; brochure.

Principal Staff: Chair. Mohamed Shafik Gabr.

Contact Details: Hassan al-Akbar St, Mokattam, Cairo 11571; tel. (2) 26673322; e-mail info@msgabrfoundation.org; internet www.msgabrfoundation.org.

Sawiris Foundation for Social Development—SFSD

Established in 2001 by the Sawiris family, who founded the Orascom Group companies.

Activities: Promotes social development through economic empowerment and participation in civil society. The Foundation supports job creation by providing training, education and access to microcredit; and better healthcare through improving infrastructure and access to basic services. It offers scholarships for study in Europe and abroad; and annually makes Sawiris Cultural Awards to Egyptian authors, screenwriters and playwrights. Has special consultative status with ECOSOC.

Geographical Area of Activity: Egypt.

Publications: Annual Report; newsletter; brochures.

Finance: Annual revenue 454.9m. Egyptian pounds, expenditure 427.7m. Egyptian pounds (31 Dec. 2023).

Board of Trustees: Yousriya Loza-Sawiris (Chair.); Naguib Sawiris (Vice-Chair.); Hazem Hassan (Second Vice-Chair.); Hala Hashem (Treas.); Taya Samih Sawiris (Sec.-Gen.).

Principal Staff: Exec. Dir Laila Hosny.

Contact Details: 10 El Diwan St, Garden City, Cairo; tel. (2) 27927660; e-mail info@sawirisfoundation.org; internet www.sawirisfoundation.org.

Syria Al-Gad Relief Foundation

Established formally in 2013 by a group of Syrian students in response to the conflict in the Syrian Arab Republic.

Activities: Supports Syrian refugees and their host communities in Egypt, providing access to education, vocational training, sustainable employment and healthcare. The Foundation arranges affordable housing, material and financial support; ensures gender equality, empowering women and girls through education, skills development and technical assistance; and fosters children's development, protecting their rights and providing psychosocial counselling. It has four implementation offices.

Geographical Area of Activity: Egypt, Syrian Arab Repub.

Publications: Reports; blog.

Board of Trustees: Dr Molham Muaz Al-Khan (Chair.).

Contact Details: 7 Essam El Daly St, Dokki, next to State Council, Cairo; tel. (10) 09597561; e-mail info@syria-algad.org; internet www.syria-algad.org.

Vodafone Egypt Foundation

Established in 2003 by Vodafone Egypt, a telecommunications company; part of the Vodafone Foundation (q.v.) network.

Activities: Supports non-governmental and civil society organizations and carries out activities in the areas of children's health and education, literacy, community development and use of mobile technology for development.

Geographical Area of Activity: Egypt.

Principal Staff: Sec.-Gen. May Yassin.

Contact Details: Vodafone Egypt Headquarters, 6th Horizon, 65/3 G Central Axis Rd, 6 October City; tel. (2) 25294769; e-mail csr@vodafone.com; internet web.vodafone.com.eg/en/social-engagement.

EL SALVADOR

FOUNDATIONS AND NON-PROFITS

Asociación Salvadoreña para el Desarrollo Económico y Social FUSADES (El Salvadoran Association for Economic and Social Development FUSADES)

Established in 1983; present name adopted in 2024; a think tank and research centre.

Activities: Promotes sustainable economic development and social progress under a democratic system through conducting policy research and advocacy. Research includes political, economic, social and legal studies on areas including: citizen safety; education and social cohesion; growth with opportunities; health and environment; infrastructure and connectivity; international relations; macroeconomic health; and strong institutions. The Association comprises a think tank, a research centre and a development centre.

Geographical Area of Activity: El Salvador, Central America and the Caribbean.

Publications: Annual Report; investigation series; newsletters; strategic and business reports; social, economic and political analysis; surveys and research.

Finance: Annual budget US $6.4m. (2024).

Board of Directors: Juan Daniel Alemán Gurdián (Pres.); Álvaro Ernesto Guatemala Cortez (Vice-Pres.); Rafael Arnoldo Gómez Salazar (Treas.); Carlos Mauricio Guzmán Segovia (Sec.).

Principal Staff: Exec. Dir Javier Castro De León.

Contact Details: Edif. FUSADES, Bulevar y Urbanización Santa Elena, Antiguo Cuscatlán, La Libertad; tel. 2248-5600; e-mail fusades@fusades.org; internet www.fusades.org.

Fundación Dr Guillermo Manuel Ungo—FUNDAUNGO (Dr Guillermo Manuel Ungo Foundation)

Established in 1992 in memory of Dr Guillermo Manuel Ungo, a politician; a think tank.

Activities: Promotes regional development and democratic governance through carrying out public policy research and capacity building. Main programme areas are: democratic governance, including the electoral system, citizens' security and prevention of violence, and participation, political culture and transparency; territorial management, citizenship and social inclusion; and public policy studies, covering demography, financing or development, inclusive education, and social protection systems and the labour market. The Foundation comprises the Centro de Estudios de Opinión Pública.

Geographical Area of Activity: Central America.

Publications: Institutional Profile; *Aportes al Debate* (series); *Boletín Estadístico* (newsletter); *Boletín de Monitoreo Electoral*; *Temas de Actualidad* (series); research reports; studies; working papers.

Board of Directors: José Guillermo Compte (Pres.); Víctor Antonio Orellana (Vice-Pres.); Mauricio E. Santamaría (Treas.); German Rivera (Sec.).

Principal Staff: Exec. Dir Dr Ricardo Córdova.

Contact Details: 83 Avda Norte y 15 Calle Poniente, Casa No. 830, Colonia Escalón, San Salvador; tel. 2264-5130; e-mail comunicaciones@fundaungo.org; internet www.fundaungo.org.sv.

Fundación Nacional para el Desarrollo (National Foundation for Development)

Established in 1992; a research institution.

Activities: Formulates socioeconomic policies, and advocates and promotes development for the most disadvantaged sectors of society. Programme areas include: macroeconomics and development; territorial development; violence prevention; and transparency. The Foundation provides funding for: development; integration and development; employment and growth; construction and development of territories; national public policies for territorial development; environmental management; and transparency.

Geographical Area of Activity: El Salvador.

Publications: Annual Report.

Finance: Annual revenue US $1.5m., expenditure $1.5m. (31 Dec. 2022).

Board of Directors: Flora Cecilia Guadalupe Blandón de Grajeda (Chair.); Amparo Marroquín Parducci (Vice-Chair.); José Antonio Basagoitia (Treas.); Julio Ramírez Murcia (Sec.).

Principal Staff: Exec. Dir Dr Roberto Rubio-Fabián.

Contact Details: Calle Arturo Ambrogi 411, entre 103 y 105 Avda Norte, Colonia Escalón, San Salvador; tel. 2209-5300; e-mail funde@funde.org; internet www.funde.org.

FUNDAMICRO

FUNDAMICRO—Fundación de Capacitación y Asesoría en Microfinanzas (Foundation for the Qualification and Consultancy in Microfinance)

Established in 1999 as part of a joint project between the EU and Banco Multisectorial de Inversiones.

Activities: Fosters and strengthens the development of microfinance institutions that provide financial services to micro and small businesses. The Foundation offers training, consultancy services and technology.

Geographical Area of Activity: El Salvador.

Board of Directors: Ana María Rodriguez Villalta (Pres.); Jacqueline Muñoz (Vice-Pres.).

Principal Staff: Gen. Man. Jesus Peña.

Contact Details: Calle Poniente 3856, 1º, Colonia Escalón, San Salvador; tel. 2511-7100; e-mail fundamicro@fundamicro.net; internet www.fundamicro.net.

ESTONIA

CO-ORDINATING BODIES

Arengukoostöö Ümarlaud—AKÜ (Development Cooperation Roundtable)

Established in 2007.

Activities: Represents Estonian NGOs active in the areas of: human rights; humanitarian aid; international development; nature conservation; sustainable development; and world education. The organization provides training and advice on sustainable development and global education to companies, organizations and educational institutions; and advocacy training for local NGOs and local government. It provides information on funding opportunities for members. Comprises 34 NGOs; a member of CONCORD (q.v.) and Eurodad networks.

Geographical Area of Activity: Estonia.

Publications: Annual Report; newsletter; reports; annual studies.

Finance: Annual revenue €114,014, expenditure €114,014 (2023).

Principal Staff: Dir Agne Kuimet.

Contact Details: Telliskivi 60A-3, 10412 Tallinn; tel. 56909722; e-mail info@terveilm.ee; internet www.terveilm.ee.

Eesti Mittetulundusühingute ja Sihtasutuste Liit (Network of Estonian Non-profit Organizations)

Established in 1991 by representatives of 26 Estonian foundations to promote co-operation between charitable, non-governmental and not-for-profit organizations; previously known as the Estonian Foundation Center.

Activities: Promotes active citizenship through strengthening the capacity of CSOs. The Network conducts research and advocacy; and organizes training courses and conferences. It comprises more than 100 member NGOs and foundations and approx. 4,000 organizations in its wider network.

Geographical Area of Activity: Estonia.

Restrictions: Not a grantmaking organization.

Publications: Annual Report; newsletter; *Hea Kodanik* (magazine).

Finance: Annual revenue €299,473, expenditure €288,358 (2024).

Principal Staff: Exec. Dir Triin Toomesaar.

Contact Details: Telliskivi Creative City, A3 Bldg, 3rd Floor, Telliskivi 60A, 10412 Tallinn; tel. 664-5077; e-mail info@heakodanik.ee; internet heakodanik.ee.

FOUNDATIONS AND NON-PROFITS

Balti Uuringute Instituut (Institute of Baltic Studies)

Established in 1996; a think tank.

Activities: Carries out public policy development and research and socioeconomic analysis in the areas of: economic and regional development, including innovation and technology, research and science, education and entrepreneurship; and social cohesion, including labour, migration, integration and fundamental rights. The Institute offers internships to students and graduates from Estonia and abroad.

Geographical Area of Activity: Baltic region (with a focus on Estonia).

Publications: Annual Report; newsletter (quarterly); impact assessments; evaluations; studies.

Finance: Total revenue €1.0m., expenditure €979,731 (2021).

Board: Marek Tiits (Chair.).

Contact Details: Lai 30, 51005 Tartu; tel. 6999-480; e-mail ibs@ibs.ee; internet www.ibs.ee.

Eestimaa Looduse Fond—ELF (Estonian Fund for Nature)

Established in 1991.

Activities: Operates in the fields of conservation and the environment through self-conducted programmes, research, conferences, training courses and publications. The Fund is an independent non-governmental organization that provides society with the necessary expertise for nature conservation. ELF helps unite the state and science institutions, businesses, and active citizens in their efforts to protect common natural resources.

Geographical Area of Activity: Estonia.

Publications: Annual Report; reports; handbooks.

Finance: Annual revenue €1.6m., expenditure €1.6m. (2024).

Council: Jüri Kaljundi (Chair.).

Board of Directors: Tarmo Tüür (Chair.); Silvia Lotman (Vice-Chair.).

Contact Details: Staadioni 67, 51008 Tartu; tel. 742-8443; e-mail elf@elfond.ee; internet www.elfond.ee.

Open Estonia Foundation (Avatud Eesti Fond)

Established in 1990; affiliated with the Open Society Foundations (q.v.) network.

Activities: Supports initiatives that advance openness and democratic practices in decisionmaking, inclusive civil dialogue and human dignity. The Foundation's priority is building capacity and advocacy skills in civil society. In a consortium with Network of Estonian Non-profit Organizations (Eesti Mittetulundusühingute ja Sihtasutuste Liit, q.v.), it is also the main operator of the Active Citizens' Fund in Estonia, supported by Iceland, Liechtenstein and Norway as part of the European Economic Area Grants 2014–21.

Geographical Area of Activity: EU, Russian Federation.

Publications: Annual Report; newsletter; reports; blog.

Finance: Annual grants disbursed €1.6m. (2023).

Supervisory Board: Siim Raie (Chair.).

Principal Staff: Exec. Dir Mall Hellam.

Contact Details: Kentmanni 10-18, 10116 Tallinn; tel. 615-5700; e-mail info@oef.org.ee; internet www.oef.org.ee.

Rahvusvaheline Kaitseuuringute Keskus—RKK (International Centre for Defence and Security—ICDS)
Established in 2006 by the Estonian Minister of Defence; an independent think tank.

Activities: Carries out policy research and analysis in the fields of international relations, foreign policy, security and defence in the Baltic and Nordic regions, in the context of NATO and EU relations. Programme areas include: Baltic-Nordic security in a transatlantic context; cybersecurity; Russian internal politics and external security policies; energy security in the Baltic-Nordic region and Eurasia; and security and internal reforms in Eastern Partnership and Balkan countries. The Centre organizes the annual Lennart Meri Conference on foreign policy, Tallinn Digital Summit and the Annual Baltic Conference on Defence. It organizes national defence courses and seminars; and includes the Estonian Foreign Policy Institute, which operates as an autonomous research unit.

Geographical Area of Activity: Baltic and Nordic regions.

Publications: Annual Report; *Diplomaatia* (magazine); reports; blogs.

Supervisory Board: Kaimo Kuusk (Chair.).

Principal Staff: Dir Kristi Raik; Chief Exec. Kadri Laar.

Contact Details: Narva mnt 63-4 East, 10120 Tallinn; e-mail info@icds.ee; internet www.icds.ee.

Sihtasutus Eesti Rahvuskultuuri Fond (Estonian National Culture Foundation)
Founded in 1991, as Eesti Kultuuri Päästefond (Estonian Cultural Rescue Fund), by the Supreme Council.

Activities: Supports Estonian national culture. The Foundation offers scholarships and grants to individuals and projects dedicated to developing aspects of Estonian culture; presents Lifetime Achievement Awards to people who have made significant contributions to national culture; and works in co-operation with a number of institutions and individuals that support Estonian culture. It administers 202 special sub-funds in areas including: architecture; art; cinematography; education and research; folk culture; journalism and literature; medicine; museums and libraries; music; sport; and theatre.

Geographical Area of Activity: Estonia.

Publications: Annual Report.

Finance: Annual income €230,592, expenditure €455,303 (30 June 2023).

Supervisory Board: Olav Ehala (Chair.).

Principal Staff: CEO Jüri Leiten.

Contact Details: A. Lauteri 7-13, 10145 Tallinn; tel. 601-3428; e-mail post@erkf.ee; internet www.erkf.ee.

Sihtasutus Poliitikauuringute Keskus Praxis (Praxis Centre for Policy Studies Foundation)
Established in 2000 by Tiina Randma-Liiv, Vello Andres Pettai, Heli Aru and Peter Lõhmus, with support from the Open Society Institute; a think tank.

Activities: Carries out applied socioeconomic research and analysis to assist policymakers and the third sector. Programme areas include: the economy; labour and social policy; innovation and education; health; gender equality; and governance and civil society. The organization provides training and consultancy services; and organizes policy dialogues. Has an office in Tartu.

Geographical Area of Activity: Estonia.

Publications: Annual Report; newsletter (monthly); case studies; surveys.

Principal Staff: CEO Urmo Kübar.

Contact Details: Ahtri 6A, VI Floor, 10151 Tallinn; tel. 640-8000; e-mail praxis@praxis.ee; internet www.praxis.ee.

ESWATINI

FOUNDATIONS AND NON-PROFITS

Swaziland Charitable Trust
Established in 1910.

Activities: Works in the areas of education, agriculture and social welfare. The Trust offers grants to schools, community groups and local branches of international charities. It runs an orphan support and sponsorship scheme. Has an office in the United Kingdom.

Geographical Area of Activity: Eswatini.

Publications: Newsletters.

Finance: Annual income £84,409, expenditure £139,226 (31 March 2020).

Board of Trustees: Victoria M. McDonaugh (Chair.); R. W. Mackenzie (Sec.).

Swaziland Board: Charles Gilbert (Chair.).

Principal Staff: Man. Phindile Ndabandaba.

Contact Details: Office No. 211, 2nd Floor, Liqhaga House, cnr Nkoseluhlaza and Masalesikhundleni St, POB 245 Manzini; tel. 505-2618; e-mail sct@africaonline.co.sz; internet www.swazilandcharitabletrust.org.

ETHIOPIA

FOUNDATIONS AND NON-PROFITS

Africa Humanitarian Action—AHA
Established in 1994 by Dr Dawit Zawde, a medical doctor, in response to ethnic cleansing in Rwanda.

Activities: Works in the fields of emergency relief and humanitarian assistance, supporting refugees, internally displaced people and local communities. Programme areas include: children's nutrition; water, sanitation and hygiene; preventive and curative healthcare; livelihoods training and support; protection of women and children; food security; shelter and rehabilitation of public infrastructure; and warehouse management and transportation. The organization currently operates in Cameroon, Ethiopia, Rwanda, South Sudan, Sudan and Uganda; with a presence in 20 countries in North Africa and sub-Saharan Africa and offices in Switzerland and the USA; and special consultative status with ECOSOC.

Geographical Area of Activity: North Africa, sub-Saharan Africa, Switzerland, USA.

Publications: Annual Report; newsletter.

Finance: Budget US $1.7m. (2022).

Centre for Dialogue, Research and Cooperation

Assembly of Trustees: Dr Salim Ahmed Salim (Chair.); Dr Sheikh M. H. Al-Amoudi (Co-Chair.).

Executive Board: Dr Dawit Zawde (Pres.); Asrat Betru (Treas.); Misikir Tilahun (Sec. and Exec. Dir).

Contact Details: Jambo Plaza, 1st Floor, 110 Lorenzo Tiezaz Rd, 1250 Addis Ababa; tel. (11) 6604800; e-mail info @africahumanitarian.org; internet www.africahumanitarian.org.

Centre for Dialogue, Research and Cooperation—CDRC

Established in 2016; successor to the Institute for Advanced Research (f. 2012).

Activities: Promotes development, democracy, and peace and security in the Horn of Africa region and beyond. The Centre carries out analysis and project evaluations and advises government agencies, businesses and organizations on national and international strategic issues. It organizes symposia and conferences on strategic, political, security, governance and development issues in Ethiopia, the Horn of Africa and across the African continent, facilitating critical scholarly dialogue and issuing publications; and is a forum for mediation and conflict resolution.

Geographical Area of Activity: Africa.

Publications: *CDRC Digest* (monthly).

Principal Staff: Exec. Dir Dr Abdeta Dribssa Beyene; Deputy Exec. Dir Kasahun Dender.

Contact Details: Ethio-China Friendship Rd, Medina Tower, 5th Floor, Kirkos Subcity, Kebele 03, Addis Ababa; tel. (11) 4700370; e-mail info@cdrcethiopia.com; internet cdrcethiopia.com.

Horn Economic and Social Policy Institute—HESPI

founded in 2006; an independent, non-profit think tank and consultancy firm established for the member countries of the Horn of Africa in particular and developing countries at large.

Activities: Carries out economic and social policy research and analysis; and provides institutional capacity building, training and advice. Areas of interest include promoting: accountability, transparency and anti-corruption measures in public finance management; public-private partnerships and financial reform; national and regional agricultural production and food security; conservation and sustainable use of natural resources; regional economic and social integration; and intra- and inter-state conflict prevention.

Geographical Area of Activity: Horn of Africa region.

Publications: Newsletter; studies; concept notes; working papers; conference proceedings; blogs.

Board of Directors: Wassihun Abate (Chair.).

Principal Staff: Man. Dir Dr Ali Issa Abdi.

Contact Details: Kirkos Sub City, Kebele 15, Teklu Desta Bldg H. No. 288/10-13, Addis Ababa; tel. (11) 5153262; e-mail contacthespi@hespi.org; internet www.hespi.org.

Organization for Social Science Research in Eastern and Southern Africa—OSSREA

Established in 1980.

Activities: Promotes dialogue and interaction between social science researchers and policymakers to enhance the impact of research on policymaking and development planning. The organization awards research grants and training fellowships. Members are individuals and institutions involved in teaching and research.

Geographical Area of Activity: East Africa, Southern Africa.

Publications: Annual Report; *OSSREA Bulletin*; *The EASSRR Journal*; *Gender Issues Research Report Series*; *Social Science Research Report Series*; policy briefs; training manuals; books.

Principal Staff: Exec. Dir Dr Truphena Mukuna.

Contact Details: Addis Ababa University, main campus at Sidist Kilo, POB 31971, Addis Ababa; tel. (11) 239484; e-mail info@ossrea.net; internet www.ossrea.net.

FIJI

FOUNDATIONS AND NON-PROFITS

FIJI Water Foundation

Established in 2007 by FIJI Water, a producer of bottled water.

Activities: Works in three main areas: providing access to clean water for rural communities; building educational facilities for children, young people and adults; and providing access to healthcare in under-served communities. The Foundation also provides emergency disaster relief; and collaborates with international partners on environmental conservation programmes. It awards grants of up to F$5,000 to teachers for projects that have a direct impact on student learning.

Geographical Area of Activity: Fiji.

Restrictions: Does not fund IT equipment or capital works.

Principal Staff: Dir Semi Lotawa.

Contact Details: POB 267, Lautoka; tel. 790-8706; e-mail grants@fijiwater.com; internet www.fijiwaterfoundation.com.

National Trust of Fiji—NTF

Established in 1970; part of the International National Trusts Organisation family.

Activities: Works to ensure that Fiji's natural, cultural and built heritage and traditional knowledge and local management systems are protected for their intrinsic value and studied for the role that they play in disaster risk reduction. Main programme areas include: heritage stewardship, looking after places; conservation, research and protection, addressing threats such as climate change; and providing places for people to enjoy. The Trust manages nine heritage sites: Garrick Forest Reserve; Laucala Ring Ditch Fortification; Levuka Historical Port Town; Momi Battery Historical Park; Nakanacagi Bat Sanctuary; Sigatoka Sand Dunes; Sovi Basin Key Biodiversity Area; Waisali Rainforest Reserve; and Yadua Taba Crested Iguana Sanctuary. It undertakes local capacity building and community heritage projects.

Geographical Area of Activity: Fiji.

Publications: Posters.

Council: Setoki Tuiteci (Acting Chair.).

Principal Staff: Dir Elizabeth Erasito.

Contact Details: 3 Ma'afu St, POB 2089, Government Bldgs, Suva; tel. 330-1807; e-mail info@nationaltrust.org.fj; internet nationaltrust.org.fj.

Vodafone ATH Fiji Foundation

Established in 2007 by Vodafone ATH Fiji, a telecommunications company; part of the Vodafone Foundation (q.v.) network.

Activities: Carries out social investment activities, promoting the use of mobile technology for development. Main programme areas are: agriculture; economic empowerment; education; environmental conservation; disaster response;

FINLAND

CO-ORDINATING BODIES

Säätiöiden post doc-poolin (Foundations' Post-Doc Pool)

Established in 2010 by eight foundations.

Activities: Offers grants for postdoctoral research abroad for at least one year. Current member foundations are the Emil Aaltosen Säätiö, Alfred Kordelinin Säätiö, Liikesivistysrahasto, Paulon Säätiö (q.v.), Päivikki ja Sakari Sohlbergin Säätiö, Suomalainen Tiedeakatemia, Suomen Kulttuurirahasto, Suomen Lääketieteen Säätiö, Svenska Kulturfonden (q.v.), Svenska Litteratursällskapet, Tekniikan Edistämissäätiö (q.v.), Jenny ja Antti Wihurin Rahasto (q.v.) and Ulla Tuomisen Säätiö. Around 70–80 grants are awarded each year.

Geographical Area of Activity: Finland.

Restrictions: Open to Finnish and non-Finnish citizens.

Finance: Annual pool investment €3.2m. (2025–27).

Board: Ari Sihvola (Chair.).

Principal Staff: Co-ordinator Mikko-Olavi Seppälä.

Contact Details: c/o Säätiöt ja rahastot ry Fredrikinkatu 61 A, 9 krs, 00100 Helsinki; tel. (400) 868006; e-mail info@postdocpooli.fi; internet postdocpooli.fi.

Säätiöt ja rahastot (Foundations and Funds Association)

Established in 1970, as Säätiöiden ja rahastojen neuvottelukunta—SRNK, by 23 foundations; an association of Finnish grantmaking foundations and associations. Present name adopted in 2021.

Activities: Assists member foundations and associations in exchanging information and ideas. The Council represents its members; advises members and grant seekers through its Foundation Service (Säätiöpalvelu), which also provides information on grants and foundations; maintains a database of grants; and issues publications. It comprises 240 member grantmaking organizations; is a member of Philea (q.v.) and WINGS (q.v.); and maintains the Aurora funding database.

Geographical Area of Activity: Finland.

Publications: *Good Governance of Foundations*; newsletter; research findings; guidelines; reports; studies; surveys.

Finance: Annual grants disbursed by member organizations €538m. (2023).

Board of Directors: Jannica Fagerholm (Chair.); Sirpa Jalkanen (Vice-Chair.).

Principal Staff: CEO Liisa Suvikumpu.

Contact Details: Fredrikinkatu 61A, 00100 Helsinki; tel. (9) 6818949; e-mail info@saatiotrahastot.fi; internet saatiotrahastot.fi.

Suomalaiset kehitysjärjestöt—Fingo (Finnish Development Organizations)

Established in 2018 by the merger of development organizations Kepa (formerly known as the Development Cooperation Service Center) and Kehys (EU Association of Development Cooperation Organizations); an umbrella organization, which co-ordinates the activities of CONCORD (q.v.) in Finland.

Activities: Supports organizations working in the fields of sustainable international development, global education and global justice through influencing policymaking in Finland, the EU and internationally. The organization supports teachers to integrate the themes of sustainable development and global education in primary and secondary education in Finland. It provides training, counselling and meeting facilities for organizations and individuals; and organizes events, including the Maailma kylässä -festivaali ('World in the Village Festival'). Has around 250 member organizations.

Geographical Area of Activity: International.

Publications: Annual Report; newsletter; *Maailman Kuvalehti* ('World Image Magazine'); analysis; blog; member database (online).

Finance: Annual income €4.5m., expenditure €4.5m. (2025).

Board of Directors: Eva Biaudet (Chair.); Ilkka Kantola, Elina Korhonen (Vice-Chair.).

Principal Staff: CEO Linda Konate.

Contact Details: Lintulahdenkuja 10, 2nd Floor, 00500 Helsinki; tel. (50) 3176690; e-mail info@fingo.fi; internet fingo.fi.

FOUNDATIONS AND NON-PROFITS

Abilis-säätiö (Abilis Foundation)

Established in 1998.

Activities: Supports grassroots disability organizations in developing countries, and funds projects promoting the human rights, participation, independent living, education and employment of people with disabilities. The Foundation gives special attention to girls and women with disabilities. Grants range from €1,000 to €20,000. It offers disability and development consulting through its subsidiary Abilis Consulting Oy; and has country offices in Ethiopia, Myanmar, Nepal, Tajikistan, Tanzania, Uganda and Viet Nam.

Geographical Area of Activity: Ethiopia, Malawi, Mozambique, Myanmar, Nepal, Tajikistan, Tanzania, Uganda, Ukraine, Viet Nam.

Publications: Annual Report; *Abilis Bulletin* (newsletter, 2 a year).

Finance: Total assets €2.7m. (31 Dec. 2022).

Board: Amu Urhonen (Chair.); Esa-Pekka Mattila (Vice-Chair.).

Principal Staff: COO Riina Paasio.

Contact Details: Lintulahdenkatu 10, 5th Floor, 00500 Helsinki; tel. (9) 61240300; e-mail abilis@abilis.fi; internet www.abilis.fi.

Hanaholmen—Swedish-Finnish Cultural Centre

Established in 1975 by the Governments of Finland and Sweden; overseen by the Swedish-Finnish Cultural Foundation (q.v.).

Activities: Develops co-operation between member countries across all areas of society, through carrying out projects and research, and organizing events, courses and seminars. The Centre has a conference hotel, gallery and art park. It administers four Nordic foundations: the Swedish-Finnish Cultural Foundation (Kulturfonden för Sverige och Finland, f. 1960); the Finnish-Norwegian Cultural Foundation (Norsk-finsk kulturfond, f. 1979); the Finnish-Danish Cultural Foundation (f. 1982); and the Icelandic-Finnish Cultural Foundation (f. 1975).

The Foundations offer grants and bursaries to individuals and non-profit organizations for projects that promote cultural exchange.

Geographical Area of Activity: Denmark, Finland, Iceland, Norway, Sweden.

Publications: Impact Report.

Finance: Part-funded by income from the Centre's conference, restaurant and hotel business, and government and other grants.

Executive Board: Elisabeth Nilsson (Chair.); Dean Timo Korkeamäki (Vice-Chair.).

Principal Staff: CEO Gunvor Kronman.

Contact Details: Hanasaarenranta 5, 02100 Espoo; tel. (9) 435020; e-mail info@hanaholmen.fi; internet www.hanaholmen.fi.

Helsingin Sanomain Säätiö (Helsingin Sanomat Foundation)

Formed in 2005 by the merger of the Helsingin Sanomat Centennial Foundation (f. 1990) and the Päivälehti Archive Foundation (f. 1984).

Activities: Supports free speech and research and training in the fields of communications and media through offering grants and scholarships. The Foundation maintains the Media Museum and Archives Merkki. It is a member of the Council of Finnish Foundations (q.v.).

Geographical Area of Activity: Finland.

Publications: Annual Report.

Finance: Annual income €4.8m., expenditure €3.7m. (2024).

Board of Trustees and Executive Council: Antero Mukka (Chair.); Pirjo Hiidenmaa, Pekka Aula (Vice-Chair.).

Principal Staff: Pres. Ulla Koski.

Contact Details: Korkeavuorenkatu 28, 00130 Helsinki; e-mail saatio@hssaatio.fi; internet www.hssaatio.fi.

Jenny ja Antti Wihurin Rahasto (Jenny and Antti Wihuri Foundation)

Founded in 1942 by Antti Wihuri, a shipowner, and his wife Jenny.

Activities: Established the Wihuri Research Institute for cardiovascular research in 1944; the Wihuri Foundation for International Prizes (q.v.) in 1953, with which it shares its administration; and in 1957 began collecting contemporary art, which became the basis of the Rovaniemi Art Museum (f. 1986). The Foundation awards grants to promote and support cultural and economic development in Finland. Grants awarded in 2024 amounted to €15m.

Geographical Area of Activity: Finland.

Publications: Annual Report.

Finance: Total assets €560m. (2024).

Board of Trustees: Dr h.c. Arto Hiltunen (Chair.); Tapani Väljä (Vice-Chair.).

Principal Staff: Exec. Dir Arto Mäenmaa.

Contact Details: Kalliolinnantie 4, 00140 Helsinki; tel. (9) 4542400; e-mail toimisto@wihurinrahasto.fi; internet www.wihurinrahasto.fi.

Kansainvälinen solidaarisuussäätiö (International Solidarity Foundation)

Established in 1970 to encourage co-operation between Finland and less-developed countries.

Activities: Promotes gender equality, the creation of sustainable livelihoods and strengthened civil liberties. Foundation projects aim to improve the living conditions of the very poor and encourage women to participate in developing their communities. Examples include: climate sustainability of agriculture; developing trade networks; food security; preventing female genital mutilation and violence against women; and promoting equality in small businesses.

Geographical Area of Activity: Finland, Ethiopia, Kenya, Somaliland.

Publications: Annual Report; newsletter; blog.

Finance: Annual budget approx. €3.8m. (2024).

Supervisory Board: Ilkka Kantola (Chair.); Tero Shemeikka (Vice-Chair.).

Delegation: Johannes Koskinen (Chair.); Nina Brask (Vice-Chair.).

Principal Staff: Exec. Dir Miia Nuikka.

Contact Details: Lintulahdenkatu 10, 00500 Helsinki; tel. (10) 5012120; e-mail solidaarisuus@solidaarisuus.fi; internet www.solidaarisuus.fi.

KAUTE-säätiö (KAUTE Foundation)

Founded in 1956 by Finnish business school and engineering graduate associations; formerly known as the Foundation for Commercial and Technical Sciences.

Activities: Supports and promotes scientific research in economics and technology. The Foundation promotes the renewal of Finnish industry and business through offering grants for research, teaching and study in commercial and technical sciences. It administers 17 special funds that were set up to support scholarships.

Geographical Area of Activity: Finland.

Restrictions: Supports individual or groups of researchers in business and engineering; does not award grants to companies.

Publications: Annual Report; newsletter; blog.

Board: Prof. Virpi Tuunainen (Chair.).

Delegation: Tuomo Haukkovaara (Chair.).

Principal Staff: Exec. Dir Tuomas Olkku.

Contact Details: c/o Sofia Helsinki, Sofiankatu 4C, 00170 Helsinki; e-mail info@kaute.fi; internet www.kaute.fi.

KIOS Foundation

Founded in 1998 by 11 Finnish NGOs working on human rights and development issues; formerly known as KIOS—Finnish NGO Foundation for Human Rights.

Activities: Promotes human rights as the foundation for sustainable peace and development. The Foundation supports projects that focus on the prevention of human rights abuses; human rights awareness raising and education; and advocacy or legal aid to victims of human rights abuses. It gives special consideration to projects promoting or protecting the rights of the most vulnerable groups, such as women, children, indigenous peoples, people with disabilities, sexual and gender minorities, human rights defenders and people living in extreme poverty. Currently present in seven countries.

Geographical Area of Activity: East Africa, South Asia.

Restrictions: Does not fund individuals, international NGOs or governmental bodies; development work, humanitarian aid or general socioeconomic support; scholarships, fellowships, conference participation or travel.

Publications: Annual Report; newsletter; evaluation and thematic reports; seminar publications.

Finance: Receives financial support from the Department for Development Policy at the Ministry for Foreign Affairs of Finland. Annual expenditure approx. €2m. (2023).

Executive Board: Kerttu Tarjamo (Chair.); Jenna Lähdemäki-Pekkinen (Vice-Chair.).

Principal Staff: Exec. Dir Kim Remitz.

Contact Details: Lintulahdenkatu 10, 00500 Helsinki; e-mail kios@kios.fi; internet kios.fi.

Maj ja Tor Nessling Säätiö (Maj and Tor Nessling Foundation)

Established in 1972 by Maj Nessling in memory of her husband Tor, former Man. Dir of Suomen Autoteollisuus Ab (Finnish Motors Ltd), to promote Finnish science and culture in the field of environmental protection.

Activities: Awards grants to individuals for postdoctoral research, worth €34,000 per year for up to two years, and for doctoral dissertation, worth €30,000 per year for up to four years; and to individuals and organizations for science based action projects. In 2024 the Foundation awarded grants amounting to approx. €2.3m.
Geographical Area of Activity: Finland and nearby countries.
Restrictions: Projects must relate to: climate change; loss of biodiversity; sustainable use of natural resources; water risks; or chemicalization and pollution.
Publications: Annual Report; newsletter.
Finance: Total assets €97.5m. (2024).
Board of Directors: Ilari Sääksjärvi (Chair.); Simo Honkanen (Vice-Chair.).
Principal Staff: Scientific and Exec. Dir Iina Koskinen.
Contact Details: Puistokatu 4, 00140 Helsinki; e-mail toimisto@nessling.fi; internet www.nessling.fi.

Paavo Nurmen Säätiö (Paavo Nurmi Foundation)
Established in 1968 by Paavo Nurmen, owner of a construction company, financier and former athlete.
Activities: Supports research into heart and vascular disease and promotes public welfare in Finland. The Foundation provides grants for postdoctoral research, and the acquisition of materials and equipment; and to Estonian cardiologists for visiting research tenures in Finland and Finnish scientists for visits to foreign research institutions. It offers the annual International Paavo Nurmi Foundation Award for medical research; runs an annual symposia programme; and publishes research results. Co-founded the *Tiede 2000* ('Science 2000') journal.
Geographical Area of Activity: Finland.
Finance: Annual disbursements approx. €200,000.
Board of Directors: Mika Nurmi (Chair.); Tuula Entelä (Vice-Chair.).
Principal Staff: Rep. Petri Manninen.
Contact Details: POB 330, 00121 Helsinki; tel. (41) 4617090; e-mail petri.manninen@paavonurmensaatio.fi; internet www.paavonurmensaatio.fi.

Östersjöfonden (Baltic Sea Foundation)
Founded in 1989 by Anders Wiklöf, founder of Wiklöf Holding.
Activities: Fosters economic, scientific and cultural relations among the countries of the Baltic Sea region. The foundation has the annual Baltic Sea Awards for individuals and organizations for significant and outstanding contributions to the Baltic Sea environment. The Awards are The Baltic Sea Award, the Lasse Wiklöf Award, the Åland Award and the Youth Award. Projects includes production of teaching material for schools in order to increase ocean literacy and the establishment of Wallins wetland, in Sund on Åland.
Geographical Area of Activity: Baltic Sea region.
Board of Trustees: Peter Lindbäck (Chair.); Johanna Mattila (Vice-Chair.).
Board: Peter Wiklöf (Chair.).
Principal Staff: CEO Sara Arons.
Contact Details: Hamngatan 5, 22100 Mariehamn, Åland; e-mail info@ostersjofonden.org; internet www.ostersjofonden.org.

Paulon Säätiö (Paulo Foundation)
Founded in 1966 by the wills of restaurateurs Reka and Hulda Paulo and their daughter Marja.
Activities: Focuses on medicine, business education, the visual arts and music. The Foundation supports research, offering grants to individuals and prizes nationally; and fellowships and scholarships internationally. It manages a number of trusts; runs a researcher exchange programme with Sapporo Medical University in Japan; organizes a biennial medical symposium; and is the main sponsor of the International Paulo Cello Competition, which is held every five years. Member of the Council of Finnish Foundations (q.v.).
Geographical Area of Activity: Finland.
Restrictions: Grants and prizes only to Finnish citizens and permanent residents of Finland.
Publications: Annual Report.
Finance: Total assets €14.6m. (31 Dec. 2020).
Board of Directors: Pekka Puustinen (Chair.).
Principal Staff: Man. Dir Risto Renkonen.
Contact Details: Kappelikuja 6B, 1st Floor, 02200 Espoo; tel. (45) 2463262; e-mail toimisto@paulo.fi; internet www.paulo.fi.

Signe och Ane Gyllenbergs stiftelse (Signe and Ane Gyllenberg Foundation)
Established in 1948 to support medical and scientific research, and the ideas of Rudolf Steiner, the founder of anthroposophy.
Activities: Supports medical and scientific research, especially in the area of psychosomatic illness and blood disorders, through awarding grants; and organizes symposia on interdisciplinary themes. The Foundation also maintains the Villa Gyllenberg Art Museum in Helsinki. It awards grants every two years.
Geographical Area of Activity: International.
Restrictions: Grants are not given for research that involves painful experiments on animals.
Publications: Annual Report; *Acta Gyllenbergiana*.
Finance: Annual income €5.1m., expenditure €4.7m. (31 Dec. 2024).
Board of Directors: Prof. Per-Henrik Groop (Chair.); Kaj Hedvall (Vice-Chair. and Treas.).
Principal Staff: CEO Jannica Fagerholm.
Contact Details: Georgsgatan 4 A 5, 00120 Helsinki; tel. (9) 647390; e-mail stiftelsen@gyllenbergs.fi; internet www.gyllenbergs.fi.

Sigrid Juséliuksen Säätiö (Sigrid Jusélius Foundation)
Founded in 1930 by the will of Fritz Arthur Jusélius, a politician and industrialist, in memory of his daughter Sigrid.
Activities: Operates in the fields of medicine, pharmacology, biochemistry and genetics. The Foundation supports research in those fields and awards grants to individuals and institutions, scholarships and fellowships. It organizes occasional symposia. Disbursed grants amounting to €26m. in 2024.
Geographical Area of Activity: Finland.
Restrictions: No direct grants for foreign medical research, studies or doctoral theses. Grants are made to medical research projects conducted by senior researchers in Finland and to foreign nationals carrying out research in Finland, and can cover living costs, equipment, materials and consumables.
Publications: Annual Report.
Finance: Annual income €96.7m., expenditure €51.9m. (31 Dec. 2024).
Board of Directors: Tom Böhling (Chair.).
Principal Staff: CEO Jussi Laitinen.
Contact Details: Aleksanterinkatu 48B, 00100 Helsinki; tel. (20) 7109083; e-mail info@sigridjuselius.fi; internet www.sigridjuselius.fi.

Suomen Kulttuurirahasto (Finnish Cultural Foundation)
Founded in 1939 by a national campaign to promote the development of cultural life in Finland.
Activities: Provides grants to science, research, art and culture. The activities cover the whole of Finland as the Foundation has established 17 regional funds to support cultural life throughout the country. The Foundation organises a comprehensive residency program for artists and runs the Kirpilä Art Collection, The Mirjam Helin International Singing Competition and the Mirjam Helin Academy for young, gifted

singers. The Foundation promotes a pluralistic and sustainable society throughout Finland by taking action and organising events. In 2024 it awarded grants amounting to over €50m.

Geographical Area of Activity: International (primarily Finland).

Publications: Annual Report; *Art & Science* quarterly magazine (In Finnish); reports; brochures.

Finance: Current assets €2,031m. (30 Sept. 2024).

Supervisory Board: Riitta Pyykkö (Chair.); Matti Kalliokoski (Vice-Chair.).

Board of Trustees: Mikko Niemi (Chair.); Anne Birgitta Pessi, Jukka Luostarinen (Vice-Chair.).

Principal Staff: CEO Dr Susanna Pettersson.

Contact Details: Bulevardi 5 A, 5 krs., 00120 Helsinki; POB 203, 00121 Helsinki; tel. (9) 612810; e-mail yleisinfo@skr.fi; internet www.skr.fi.

Svenska kulturfonden (The Swedish Cultural Foundation in Finland)

Founded in 1908 by the political party Svenska Folkpartiet (Swedish People's Party of Finland).

Activities: The Foundation's mission is to support and strengthen the culture and education of the Swedish-speaking minority in Finland, by supporting education, arts and culture and social cohesion through non-profit organizations. Annually the Foundation distributes around €45m. in funding. The Foundation provides grants for individuals, working groups and organizations for educational and cultural purposes and activities. The Foundation initiates projects and organizes conferences for key groups in the fields of education and arts and culture.

Geographical Area of Activity: Finland.

Publications: Annual report.

Finance: Total assets €850,049; annual income €22,731 (31 Dec. 2021).

Board of Directors: Mikaela Nylander (Chair.); Björn Vikström (Vice-Chair.).

Principal Staff: CEO Sören Lillkung.

Contact Details: Georgsgatan 27, PB 439, 00101 Helsingfors; e-mail kansliet@kulturfonden.fi; internet www.kulturfonden.fi.

Tekniikan Edistämissäätiö–Stiftelsen för teknikens främjande—TES (Finnish Foundation for Technology Promotion)

Founded in 1949 by 63 industrial and business institutions and individuals.

Activities: Operates in the fields of technology, education, international relations and the conservation of natural resources. The Foundation administers six Special Funds; and carries out programmes nationally, through research, grants to institutions, fellowships and scholarships, and nationally and internationally through grants to individuals, conferences, courses, publications and lectures. It offers grants for undergraduate and postgraduate study, and postdoctoral research; and makes awards to students and teachers to support technical research, training and education.

Geographical Area of Activity: Finland.

Publications: Report of operations and financial statement.

Finance: Total assets €586,287 (2023).

Board of Directors: Juho Malmberg (Chair.); Jorma Kyyrä (Vice-Chair.).

Principal Staff: Man. Dir Antti Aarnio.

Contact Details: c/o Navigator Partners Oy, Yrjönkatu 9 A, 00120 Helsinki; tel. (40) 5896263; e-mail tekniikanedistamissaatio@navigatorpartners.fi; internet www.tekniikanedistamissaatio.fi.

Väestöliitto (The Family Federation of Finland)

Founded in 1941.

Activities: Works in the fields of health and social welfare, supporting sexual health and people's responsible sexual well-being. The Federation carries out advocacy work and conducts research on sexual and reproductive health, sexuality, family and population policy, and global development issues, especially sexual and reproductive health rights. It distributes information and educational materials for young people, couples, single people and immigrants about sexuality, parenthood, and family and work; and provides counselling. Comprises 35 member organizations.

Geographical Area of Activity: Afghanistan, Cameroon, Finland, Kazakhstan, Kyrgyzstan, Malawi, Nepal, Tajikistan, Turkmenistan, Uzbekistan.

Publications: Annual Report; newsletter; reports; educational materials.

Board of Trustees: Hilkka Kemppi (Chair.); Eero Löytömäki, Hugo Paananen (Vice-Chair.); Laura Kormano (Sec.).

Principal Staff: Man. Dir Tiina Ristikari.

Contact Details: POB 849, 00101 Helsinki; Kalevankatu 16, 00101 Helsinki; e-mail viestinta@vaestoliitto.fi; internet www.vaestoliitto.fi.

Wihurin kansainvälisten palkintojen rahasto (Wihuri Foundation for International Prizes)

Founded in 1953 by Antti Wihuri, a shipowner.

Activities: Presents Wihuri International Prize, for contributions to intellectual and economic development, and the Wihuri Sibelius Prize, awarded to internationally acclaimed composers; prizes are worth between €30,000 and €150,000 and are awarded at least every three years. The Foundation shares its administration with the Jenny ja Antti Wihurin Rahasto (q.v.).

Geographical Area of Activity: International.

Finance: Total assets €3.5m. (2024).

Board of Trustees: Dr h.c. Arto Hiltunen (Chair.); Tapani Väljä (Vice-Chair.).

Principal Staff: Exec. Dir Arto Mäenmaa.

Contact Details: Kalliolinnantie 4, 00140 Helsinki; tel. (9) 4542400; e-mail toimisto@wihurinrahasto.fi; internet wihuriprizes.fi.

Yrjö Jahnssonin säätiö (Yrjö Jahnsson Foundation)

Founded in 1954 by lawyer Hilma Jahnsson in memory of her husband, Yrjö Jahnsson, a professor of economics.

Activities: Operates nationally in the field of education, and internationally in economic affairs, and science and medicine, through grants to Finnish institutions and individuals, and fellowships and scholarships for Finnish citizens; and through international research, conferences, courses, publications and lectures. The Foundation, with the European Economic Association, presents the Yrjö Jahnsson Award in Economics to a young European economist who has significantly advanced the field of economics research.

Geographical Area of Activity: Europe.

Publications: Annual Report.

Finance: Total assets €90.3m.; net annual income €1.1m. (31 Dec. 2024).

Board of Directors: Dr Jaakko Kiander (Chair.); Prof. Katriina Aalto-Setälä (Vice-Chair.).

Principal Staff: Exec. Dir Elli Dahl.

Contact Details: Yrjönkatu 11 D 19, 00120 Helsinki; e-mail toimisto@yjs.fi; internet www.yjs.fi.

FRANCE

CO-ORDINATING BODIES

Centre Français des Fonds et Fondations—CFF (French Foundation Centre)

Founded in 2002 as the Centre Français des Fondations by seven French foundations; present name adopted in 2011.

Activities: Promotes the development of foundations in France and their international representation. The Centre represents the interests of French foundations vis-à-vis public authorities whether national, European or international institutions. It advises individuals and corporations intending to create a foundation; is a source of information (database, research, studies and directories); and is a network of expertise, sharing and exchanging experiences. Has more than 500 member organizations and is a member of Philea (q.v.).

Geographical Area of Activity: Europe.

Publications: Annual Report; e-newsletter.

Finance: Annual revenue €1.7m., expenditure €1.9m. (31 Dec. 2023).

Board of Directors: Marion Lelouvier (Pres.); Dorothée Merville-Durand, François Romaneix (Vice-Pres); Cécile Cassin (Treas.); Jean-François Morin (Sec.-Gen.).

Principal Staff: Exec. Officer Benjamin Blavier.

Contact Details: 34 bis rue Vignon, 75009 Paris; tel. 1-83-79-03-52; e-mail info@centre-francais-fondations.org; internet www.centre-francais-fondations.org.

Coordination SUD

Established in 1994; an international solidarity organization.

Activities: Represents organizations working in the fields of citizenship advocacy and education, development aid, emergency humanitarian assistance, environmental protection and human rights. The organization advocates for international solidarity at national, European and international level; strengthens the professionalization of the sector through advice and training; and offers monitoring and evaluation services. It organizes thematic business clubs, commissions and working groups; and manages the Institutional and Organizational Strengthening Fund (FRIO) for co-financing external expertise on the organizational and institutional performance of NGOs. Has 183 members, mainly from six collectives: Centre de Recherche et d'Information Pour le Développement (CRID); CLONG-Volontariat; Comité pour les Relations Nationales et Internationales des Associations de Jeunesse et d'Éducation Populaire (CNAJEP); Coordination Humanitaire et Développement; Forum des Organisations de Solidarité Internationale Issues des Migrations (FORIM); and Groupe Initiatives.

Geographical Area of Activity: International.

Publications: Annual Report; *Les Notes du SUD* (newsletter); *Pratiques & Outils* (briefs); policy notes; reports; studies.

Finance: Annual income €2.5m., expenditure €2.5m. (2021).

Board of Directors: Olivier Bruyeron (Pres.); Anouchka Finker, Kevin Goldberg, Virginie Amieux (Vice-Pres); Catherine Giboin (Treas.).

Principal Staff: Exec. Dir Jérôme Fauré.

Contact Details: 14 passage Dubail, 75010 Paris; tel. 1-44-72-93-72; internet www.coordinationsud.org.

Fédération Internationale des Ligues des Droits de L'Homme—FIDH (International Federation of Human Rights)

Established in 1922 by French and German national associations.

Activities: Priority areas are: human rights defenders' freedom and capacity to act; universal human rights, particularly for women; promoting and protecting migrants' rights; ending impunity; and strengthening respect for human rights. The Federation organizes international campaigns; co-ordinates a human rights network; provides information services; and works to protect people suffering from human rights abuse. It comprises 188 member organizations in 116 countries, with a regional office in Tunisia and shared offices with member organizations in Guinea, Central African Republic, Côte d'Ivoire and Mali; and has permanent delegations to the UN in Geneva and New York, the EU in Brussels and the International Criminal Court in The Hague.

Geographical Area of Activity: International.

Publications: Annual Report; *La Lettre* (newsletter, 10 a year); *Mission Reports* (15 a year); comics.

Finance: Annual revenue €7.5m., expenditure €7.4m. (31 Dec. 2021).

International Board: Alice Mogwe (Pres.); Dominique Ledouble (Treas.).

Principal Staff: CEO Eléonore Morel; Deputy CEO Juliane Falloux.

Contact Details: 17 passage de la Main d'Or, 75011 Paris; tel. 1-43-55-25-18; e-mail contact@fidh.org; internet www.fidh.org.

Fondation de France

Founded in 1969 with an initial endowment made by the Caisse des Dépôts et Consignations (Bank of Security Deposits) and 17 major French banks.

Activities: Fosters the practice of charitable giving. The Foundation operates in three main areas: funding projects by organizations in the fields of social welfare, scientific and medical research, culture and the environment; helping individuals or companies to set up 'sheltered' foundations under the aegis of the Fondation de France; and developing associations, through helping them to raise funds. It manages 977 sheltered foundations, with six regional delegations.

Geographical Area of Activity: Europe.

Publications: Annual Report; newsletter; *Annuaire des Fondations Abritées* ('Directory of Sheltered Foundations', online); publications on social welfare, social work and philanthropy in France.

Finance: Annual revenue €376.6m., expenditure €423.0m. (31 Dec. 2020).

Board of Directors: Pierre Sellal (Pres.); René Ricol (Vice-Pres.); Yves Perrier (Treas.).

Principal Staff: Man. Dir Axelle Davezac.

Contact Details: 40 ave Hoche, 75008 Paris; tel. 1-44-21-31-00; e-mail fondations@fdf.org; internet www.fondationdefrance.org.

Network of Foundations Working for Development—netFWD

Established in 2012 as a platform for co-operation and exchange.

Activities: Works to improve the impact of philanthropy for development and engagement between foundations and governments. Working groups focus on education, gender and health, funding research projects through the OECD Centre on Philanthropy. The Network comprises more than 25 member and associate foundations.

Geographical Area of Activity: International.

Publications: *Guidelines for Effective Philanthropic Engagement*; studies; policy notes.

Principal Staff: OECD Development Centre Dir Ragnheiður Elín Árnadóttir.

Contact Details: OECD Development Centre, 2 rue André Pascal, 75775 Paris Cedex 16; tel. 1-45-24-82-00; e-mail dev.netfwd@oecd.org; internet www.oecd.org/development/networks.

FOUNDATIONS AND NON-PROFITS

Académie Goncourt—Société Littéraire des Goncourt (Goncourt Academy—Goncourt Literary Society)

Founded in 1896 by a legacy of Edmond de Goncourt, a writer and book publisher, to support literature, to give material assistance to particular writers and to strengthen the links between them.

Activities: Awards the annual Prix Goncourt for the best prose work of the year published in French, as well as scholarships in different fields of literature. The Academy has 10 members. Since 1973 the Academy has aimed to encourage francophone literature throughout the world and to support international cultural exchanges. It organizes conferences and lectures; and has an archive in Nancy.

Geographical Area of Activity: France and francophone countries.

Principal Staff: Pres. Philippe Claudel.

Contact Details: c/o Drouant, 16–18 pl. Gaillon, 75002 Paris; tel. 1-40-46-88-11; internet www.academiegoncourt.com.

Acting for Life

Established in 1973; formerly known as Groupe Développement; present name adopted in 2012.

Activities: Supports social and rural development projects in developing countries. Main programme areas are: agropastoralism; technical and vocational education and training, and social profesional integration; food systems and ecosystems. The organization supports long-term initiatives by local groups; and campaigns for human rights and social justice for all. Recognized as a public utility. It works with more than 50 local partner organizations in 12 countries.

Geographical Area of Activity: West Africa, Latin America.

Publications: Annual Report; Newsletter; Technical notes; Experience capitalization publications.

Finance: Annual income €8.7m. (31 Dec. 2024).

Board of Directors: Jean-Cyril Spinetta (Pres.); Philippe Calavia (Treas.); Xavier Boutin (Sec.).

Principal Staff: Dir Cédric Touquet.

Contact Details: 6 rue de la Haye, BP 11911 95731, Roissy Charles de Gaulle; tel. 1-49-34-83-13; e-mail contact@acting-for-life.org; internet acting-for-life.org.

Action contre la Faim—ACF France (Action Against Hunger)

Established in 1979 as part of French Doctors (f. 1968).

Activities: Works to eliminate hunger through emergency and post-emergency programs. Main areas of activity include: advocacy; food security and essential needs; mental health, gender and protection; nutrition and health; research; risk and disaster management; and water, sanitation and hygiene. Sister organizations operate in Canada, Germany, Italy, Spain, the United Kingdom and the USA. In 2013 the Fondation Action contre la Faim pour la Recherche et l'Innovation (Action Against Hunger Foundation for Research and Innovation) was established under the aegis of the Institut de France to strengthen the scientific expertise of the organizations.

Geographical Area of Activity: International.

Publications: Annual Report; newsletter (monthly); *Géopolitique de la Faim*; *Alimentation en Eau*; *La Faim dans le Monde*; *Souffles du Monde*; *La Malnutrition en Situation de Crise*.

Finance: Annual income US $330.2m., expenditure US $335.0m. (31 Dec. 2023).

Board of Directors: Aïcha Koraïchi (Chair.); Robert Sebbag (Vice-Chair.); Caroline Dib (Sec.-Gen.); Benjamin Nguyen (Treas.).

Principal Staff: CEO Chibuzo Okonta.

Contact Details: 102 rue de Paris, CS 10007, 93558 Montreuil Cedex; tel. 1-70-84-70-84; e-mail srd@actioncontrelafaim.org; internet www.actioncontrelafaim.org.

Action Education

Established in 1981 as Aide et Action by Pierre-Bernard Le Bas to improve standards of education in less-developed countries.

Activities: Operates in Africa, East and South-East Asia and the Caribbean in the area of education to enable children, young people and adults to access education, and works to improve the quality of education.

Geographical Area of Activity: International, in particular Africa, Asia and the Caribbean.

Publications: Annual Report; *Aide et Action* (quarterly); e-newsletter; reports; books.

Finance: Annual income €21.0m., expenditure €22.4m. (2023).

International Board of Directors: Aïcha Bah Diallo (Pres.); Rajiva Wijesinha (Sec.); Jean-Pierre Pichaut (Treas.).

Principal Staff: Dir-Gen. Gilles Delecourt.

Contact Details: 53 blvd de Charonne, 75545 Paris Cedex 11; tel. (1) 55-25-70-00; e-mail contact@action-education.org; internet action-education.org.

Afdi—Agriculteurs Français et Développement International (French Agriculturalists and International Development)

Founded in 1975.

Activities: Promotes sustainable rural development throughout the world; supports farmworkers internationally; arranges international exchanges; campaigns against the exploitation of agricultural workers; and works directly in rural areas in developing countries. The organization comprises a national office and 16 territorial organizations in France and seven overseas offices, in Burkina Faso, Chad, Côte d'Ivoire, Haiti, Madagascar and Mali; with 420 partner organizations. Carries out programmes in 18 countries.

Geographical Area of Activity: Middle East, South America, Central America and the Caribbean, South-East Asia, sub-Saharan Africa.

Publications: Annual Report.

Finance: Total assets €10.4m. (31 Dec. 2022).

Board of Directors: Cathy Faivre-Pierret (Pres.); Nicolas Assemat (First Vice-Pres.); Odile Dejean (Second Vice-Pres); Dominique Haegelen (Sec.-Gen.); René Collin (Treas.).

Principal Staff: Dir Samuel Diéval.

Contact Details: 11 rue de la Baume, 75008 Paris; tel. 1-45-62-25-54; e-mail afdi@afdi-opa.org; internet www.afdi-opa.org.

Agronomes et Vétérinaires sans Frontières—AVSF (Agronomists and Veterinarians Without Borders)

Established in 1977 by Bertrand Naegelen, Jean-Marie Abbès and Jean-Marie Lechevallier, as the Centre International de Coopération pour le Développement Agricole (CICDA); merged with Vétérinaires sans Frontières in 2004.

Activities: Operates in the field of aid to less-developed countries, through supporting agricultural development, to improve the quality of life of people living in rural areas. The organization provides technical and financial support, exchange of knowledge and information and training for land workers; and funds local development projects and publications focusing on local aid. It carries out activities under four core themes: improving agricultural production and sustainably managing natural resources; animal husbandry and health; adapting to climate change and natural disasters; and helping farmers' organizations to gain access to local and international markets. Runs projects in 22 countries, with an

FRANCE

office in Paris; and in 2016 established Groupe MOABI (formerly Groupe AVSF) with CESA in Ecuador and PROGRESO in Peru and TERO, comprising 450 member professionals in sustainable and equitable development. The inaugural Benoît Maria Prize for Peasant Agroecology was awarded in 2022.

Geographical Area of Activity: Central and South America and the Caribbean, East and South-East Asia, sub-Saharan Africa.

Restrictions: Grants only to specific countries and agricultural organizations.

Publications: Annual Report; newsletter; *Revue Habbanae*; *Editions Ruralter* (technical manuals); *Collection Traverses*.

Finance: Annual income €18.6m., expenditure €18.5m. (31 Dec. 2023).

Board of Directors: Barbara Dufour (Pres.); Jean-François Lamoureux (Vice-Pres.); Alain Yvergniaux (Secs-Gen.); Elisabeth Muller (Treas.).

Principal Staff: Exec. Dir Frédéric Apollin.

Contact Details: 14 ave Berthelot, Bâtiment F bis, 69007 Lyon; 45 bis, Ave de la Belle Gabrielle, 94736 Nogent-sur-Marne Cedex; tel. 4-78-69-79-59; e-mail avsf@avsf.org; internet www.avsf.org.

Alliance Israélite Universelle (Universal Jewish Alliance)

Founded in 1860 by Narcisse Leven, Charles Netter, Isidore Cahen, Eugène Manuel, Aristide Astruc and Jules Carvallo, to work for the emancipation and moral progress of Jewish people.

Activities: Operates in the fields of education and religion through self-conducted programmes, publications and lectures; and international human rights through the Consultative Council of Jewish Organizations. The Alliance has a network of schools in Belgium, Canada, France, Israel, Morocco and Spain, and a Hebrew teacher-training college in Morocco. It holds a Jewish library of around 150,000 vols; and runs the Collège des Études Juives and the Nadir publishing house.

Geographical Area of Activity: International.

Publications: Newsletter; *Les Cahiers de l'Alliance*; *Les Cahiers du judaisme*; *Traces* collection; *The Basics*.

Board of Directors: Marc Eisenberg (Chair.); Hubert Leven, Roger Cukierman, Paul Olivier Seligman (Vice-Chair.); Eric Sadoun (Treas.).

Principal Staff: Exec. Dir Dvorah Serrao.

Contact Details: 27 ave de Ségur, 75007 Paris; tel. 1-53-32-88-55; e-mail info@aiu.org; internet www.aiu.org.

Aviation Sans Frontières—ASF (Aviation Without Borders)

Established in 1980 by André Gréard, Gérald Similowski and Alain Yout.

Activities: Provides humanitarian relief through volunteer air services. The organization transports people in less-developed countries in need of medical aid. It dispatches medical supplies and transports medical personnel, offering emergency assistance following natural disasters and assisting other NGOs in their activities; its volunteers accompany children on flights to countries where they can be treated.

Geographical Area of Activity: International.

Publications: Annual Report; newsletter (quarterly, in French).

Finance: Annual income €4.0m., expenditure €3.8m. (31 Dec. 2021).

Board of Directors: Gérard Feldzer (Chair.); Jean-Yves Grosse (Vice-Chair.); Olivier Kudlikowski (Sec.-Gen.); Dominique Barbarin (Treas.).

Contact Details: Orly Fret 768, 94398 Orly Aérogares Cedex; tel. 1-49-75-74-37; e-mail communication@aviation-sans-frontieres-fr.org; internet www.asf-fr.org.

The Camargo Foundation

Founded in 1967 by American artist and philanthropist Jerome Hill, who also founded the Jerome Foundation (f. 1964 as the Avon Foundation).

Activities: Fosters creativity, research and experimentation through international residency programmes for artists, scholars and thinkers. The Foundation maintains a reference library containing 5,000 vols. The Jerome@Camargo programme offers residencies for research, study and/or creation of new work to artists who have been supported by the Jerome Foundation in the past five years. In 2018 the French Ministry of Culture designated the Foundation as a Landmark House (Maison des Illustres), recognizing its role in the political, scientific, social and cultural history of France.

Geographical Area of Activity: France.

Restrictions: Applications to the Jerome@Camargo programme by invitation only.

Publications: Newsletter.

Board of Trustees: Calogero Salvo, Christopher Apgar (Co-Chair.); Sara Maud Lydiatt (Treas.).

Board of Directors: Francis Maréchal (Pres.); Lili Chopra (Vice-Pres.); Anne Aghion (Treas.).

Principal Staff: Exec. Dir Julie Chénot.

Contact Details: 1 ave Maurice Jermini, 13260 Cassis; tel. 9-72-54-37-78; e-mail apply@camargofoundation.org; internet www.camargofoundation.org.

CEDIAS-Musée Social—Centre d'Etudes, de Documentation, d'Information et d'Action Sociales (Centre for Social Studies, Documentation, Information and Action)

Founded in 1963 by the merger of the Office Central des Oeuvres de Bienfaisance (f. 1890) and the Musée Social (f. 1894).

Activities: Works in the field of the social and solidarity economy. The Centre organizes conferences, courses and lectures; and hosts the Charles Gide Centre, which maintains information and resources on the social and solidarity economy, including a library of 12,000 items, including books, journals and reports, and the SYDES bibliographic database, which contains more than 15,000 references. In 2020, jointly with the Fondation Crédit Coopératif and Labo de l'Économie Sociale et Solidaire, it established the Institute for Social and Solidarity Economy.

Geographical Area of Activity: France.

Publications: *Revue Vie Sociale* (quarterly); *La Revue de l'ESS* (monthly); *Dictionnaire du Service Social*; reports.

Board of Directors: Dominique Demangel (Pres.); Michel Laroque (Vice-Pres.); Michel Dreyfus (Sec.-Gen.); Patrice Legrand (Treas.).

Contact Details: 5 rue Las Cases, 75007 Paris; tel. 1-45-51-99-51; e-mail cedias@cedias.org; internet www.cedias.org.

Centre International de Recherche sur le Cancer—CIRC (International Agency for Research on Cancer—IARC)

Founded in 1965 as a self-governing body within the framework of the WHO.

Activities: Operates internationally in the field of medical research, through self-conducted programmes and collaboration with other agencies, as well as with national institutions and laboratories. The Agency identifies causes of cancer and people at risk of developing cancer. Areas of research include: geographical incidence and time trends; environmental and occupational hazards; childhood cancer; nutrition and cancer; genetics and cancer; and carcinogenesis. It provides technical support in the form of computing services and statistical support, library and bibliographical services, banks of human biological material and common laboratory services; and awards research training fellowships and a visiting scientist award annually. Training courses on cancer epidemiology take place in various countries.

Geographical Area of Activity: Worldwide.

Publications: Biennial Report; newsletter; manuals; monographs; symposia proceedings.

Finance: Annual budget €48.7m. (2024/25).

Governing Council: Prof. Norbert Ifrah (Chair.).

Scientific Council: Dr Luis Felipe Ribeiro Pinto (Chair.).

Principal Staff: Dir Dr Elisabete Weiderpass.

Contact Details: 25 ave Tony Garnier, 69007 Lyon; tel. 4-72-73-84-85; e-mail com@iarc.who.int; internet www.iarc.who.int.

La Cimade—Service Oecuménique d'Entraide
(Cimade—Ecumenical Care Service)

Founded in 1939 as CIMADE (Inter-Movement Committee for Refugees) by members of the Youth Inter-Movement Committee (CIM), a Protestant organization, to help people displaced by the war.

Activities: Advocates for the right of migrants, asylum seekers and refugees concerning all aspects of immigration, helping them to access their legal rights, such as regularization requests and right of asylum, lodging appeals, registering addresses, and accessing care and education. The movement is organized into 90 local groups in 13 regions; and is present in several detention centres, where it provides legal assistance, and in more than 70 French prisons; as well as acting on behalf of migrants in their countries of origin and in transit, working with local associations and networks. Project Loujna Tounkaranké ('Migrant Committee' in Arabic and Soninké), which began in 2009, co-ordinates a network of 19 associations in eight countries in North Africa and West Africa, defending the rights of migrants and their families.

Geographical Area of Activity: Caribbean, Europe, Middle East and North Africa, sub-Saharan Africa.

Publications: Annual Report; newsletter; *Micracosme*; factsheets; reports on migration and detention centres.

Finance: Total assets €12.4m. (31 Dec. 2022).

Advisory Council: Henry Masson (Pres.); Monique Guyot-Berni (Vice-Pres.); Françoise Millot (Treas.); Anne-Sophie Astrup (Secs).

Contact Details: 91 rue Oberkampf, 75011 Paris; tel. 1-44-18-60-50; e-mail infos@lacimade.org; internet www.lacimade.org.

Emmaüs International

Established in 1971; an international federation of Emmaüs groups, part of the movement founded in 1949 by Abbé Pierre.

Activities: Works in the fields of social welfare, development and conservation of the environment. The organization helps people with disabilities, those with addictions, former prisoners, refugees and other underprivileged people, through the creation of communities for marginalized people. It promotes fair trade; develops networking between groups in less-developed countries; and supports recycling activities. Comprises 425 member organizations in 41 countries, with regional secretariats in Burkina Faso, India and Uruguay.

Geographical Area of Activity: International.

Publications: Annual Report; *Emmaus International Newsletter* (quarterly); reports; posters; flyers.

Finance: Annual income €4.5m., expenditure €3.6m. (31 Dec. 2023).

Board of Trustees: Patrick Atohoun (Chair.); Gloria Zuluaga (Second Vice-Chair.); Xavier Renard (Sec.).

Principal Staff: Chief Exec. Adrien Chaboche.

Contact Details: 47 ave de la Résistance, 93104 Montreuil; tel. 1-41-58-25-50; e-mail contact@emmaus-international.org; internet www.emmaus-international.org.

Enfance et Partage (Children and Sharing)

Established in 1977.

Activities: Intervenes to protect child victims of neglect and physical, psychological and sexual abuse. Abroad, the organization helps to tackle emergencies and invests in development programmes. It has 19 local committees.

Geographical Area of Activity: Africa, East Asia, France, South America and the Caribbean.

Restrictions: No public grants.

Publications: Annual Report; newsletter; *Enfance et Partage* (quarterly); *Agir contre la maltraitance* (legal guide).

Finance: Annual income €1.4m., expenditure €1.3m. (31 Dec. 2022).

Board of Directors: Claudine Jeudy (Pres.); Claude Bard (Vice-Pres.); Dominique Mermet (Sec.-Gen.); Richard Pawlikowski (Treas.).

Principal Staff: Dir Olivier Dejeufosse.

Contact Details: 5/7 rue Georges Enesco, 94000 Creteil; tel. 1-55-25-65-65; e-mail contacts@enfance-et-partage.org; internet www.enfance-et-partage.org.

Enfants du Mékong (Children of the Mekong)

Established in 1958 in Laos by René Péchard to assist children and families in South-East Asia.

Activities: Builds schools and medical centres and supports individual children and their families abroad. Priority areas are: disability and chronic diseases; isolated and rural populations; refugees and displaced people; slums; girls' education; and ethnic minorities. Nationally, the organization houses children from South-East Asia in France; and supports the French South-East Asian community. It has fundraising chapters in Belgium, Germany, Hong Kong, the United Kingdom and USA.

Geographical Area of Activity: Cambodia, France, Lao People's Dem. Repub., Myanmar, Philippines, Thailand, Viet Nam.

Publications: Annual Report; newsletter; *Enfants du Mékong* (magazine, 6 a year).

Finance: Annual revenue €18m., expenditure €18m. (2023).

Board of Directors: Alain Deblock (Chair.); Jean de Fumichon, Yves Meaudre (Vice-Chair.); Stanislas de Guigné (Sec.-Gen.); Hubert Paris (Deputy Sec.-Gen.); Tristan de Bodman (Treas.).

Principal Staff: CEO Guillaume d'Aboville; Deputy CEO Antoine Filloux.

Contact Details: 5 rue de la Comète, 92600 Asnières-sur-Seine; tel. 1-47-91-00-84; e-mail contact@enfantsdumekong.com; internet www.enfantsdumekong.com.

Fondation 30 Millions d'Amis (30 Million Friends Foundation)

Established in 1982 as the Association de Défense des Animaux de Compagnie by Jean-Pierre Hutin to promote respect for and protection of animals; present name adopted in 1995.

Activities: Operates nationally and internationally to protect animals. The Foundation makes grants to centres for abandoned animals; and provides food supplies and veterinary support for the treatment, vaccination and sterilization of animals. It campaigns against experimentation on animals and for the protection of animals in danger of extinction; and runs an online animal adoption service and database of animal protection organizations.

Geographical Area of Activity: International.

Publications: Annual Report; newsletter; magazine.

Principal Staff: Pres. Réha Hutin.

Contact Details: 40 cours Albert 1er, 75008 Paris Cedex 08; tel. 1-56-59-04-44; e-mail support@30millionsdamis.fr; internet www.30millionsdamis.fr.

Fondation Agir Contre l'Exclusion—FACE (Campaign Against Exclusion Foundation)

Founded in 1993 on the initiative of Martine Aubry, Deputy Director of aluminium producer Péchiney, by 13 French companies, including Casino, Club Méditerranée, Crédit Lyonnais, Renault and Péchiney, in collaboration with local authorities and partners.

Activities: A network of enterprise clubs, created in partnership with local communities, which contributes to the economic and social development of disadvantaged areas and promotes social inclusion. The Foundation works to reduce social exclusion in employment and local enterprise, through research and activities locally and nationally. Enterprise centres have been established in sectors including the environment, recreation, tourism, goods and services, support for local communities, and rehabilitation training and employment facilities. Its network comprises 5,650 businesses and 36 'sheltered' foundations, with branches in Belgium and Tunisia; and innovation partnerships in 21 European countries.

Geographical Area of Activity: International.

Publications: Annual Report; *FACE.infos* (newsletter); *Les Journaux de Face*; *Temoignages*.

Finance: Annual revenue €19.0m., expenditure €8.1m. (31 Dec. 2021).

Board of Directors: Jean Castex (Pres.); Gaëlle Tellier (Vice-Pres.); Romain Garcia (Treas.); Sofiane Kherarfa (Sec.).

Principal Staff: Dir Thomas Buberl.

Contact Details: 361 ave du Président Wilson, 93200 Saint-Denis La Plaine; tel. 1-49-22-68-68; e-mail contact@fondationface.org; internet www.fondationface.org.

Fondation Air France (Air France Foundation)

Established in 1992 by the Air France Group, an airline.

Activities: Works in the fields of children's education and welfare, and their access to sport, culture and leisure activities. The Foundation supports NGOs and associations' projects that help sick, disabled and vulnerable children and young people in France and in more than 80 countries. It awards the Prix Fondation Air France (f. 2009) every two years to individuals for their work with children and young people who are sick, handicapped or in need of assistance.

Geographical Area of Activity: International.

Restrictions: Does not fund special events, exchange programmes, transportation or medical projects; no grants to individuals.

Publications: Annual Report; *Le Mag* (magazine); newsletter; factsheets; news bulletins.

Principal Staff: Gen. Dir Estelle Brice Santos; Treas. Hubert de Dampierre.

Contact Details: 40 rue de Paris, 95747 Roissy Charles de Gaulle Cedex; tel. 1-41-56-57-27; e-mail mail.fondationaf@airfrance.fr; internet corporate.airfrance.com/fr/fondation-air-france.

Fondation Auchan (Auchan Foundation)

Established in 2021 by Auchan France, a retail group, under the aegis of the Fondation de France (q.v.), following the merger of the Fondation Auchan pour la Jeunesse (Auchan Foundation for Young People, f. 1996) and Fondation Weave Our Future (f. 2014).

Activities: Fondation Auchan promotes access to good food and encourages an understanding of the multiple dimensions of food, including food knowledge, social ties through food, and combating malnutrition.

Geographical Area of Activity: Bangladesh, France, Hungary, India, Luxembourg, Poland, Portugal, Romania, Senegal, Spain, Ukraine.

Publications: Annual Report.

Principal Staff: Gen. Man. Alain Reners.

Contact Details: 40 ave de Flandre, 59170 Croix; tel. 3-59-30-59-30; e-mail fondationauchan@auchan.fr; internet www.auchan-retail.com/fr/notre-fondation.

Fondation de l'Avenir pour la Recherche Médicale Appliquée (Foundation of the Future for Applied Medical Research)

Established in 1987 by the Mutualité Fonction Publique and the Association Française de Cautionnement Mutuel.

Activities: Works in the fields of medicine and health, through supporting applied medical research into new surgical techniques, and training. The Foundation awards scholarships for the development of nursing and paramedical research; and a national prize for Research in Nursing Science. Seven 'sheltered' foundations, which focus on medical advances and social innovation, operate under its auspices: Fondation Sandrine Castellotti; Fondation Matmut Paul Bennetot; Fondation Écouter Voir; Fondation Mutac; La Fondation Solimut Mutuelle de France; Fondation La Mutuelle des Motards; and Fondation Santé Environnement de La Mutuelle Familiale.

Geographical Area of Activity: France.

Publications: Annual Report; newsletter (monthly).

Finance: Annual revenue €13.8m., expenditure €14.4m. (31 Dec. 2023).

Board of Directors: Marion Lelouvier (Pres.); Guillaume Gardin (Treas.); Christelle Maltête (Sec.-Gen.).

Supervisory Board: Mattias Savignac (Chair.).

Contact Details: 10–14 rue Brancion, 75015 Paris; tel. 1-40-43-23-80; e-mail infocom@fondationdelavenir.org; internet www.fondationdelavenir.org.

Fondation Bettencourt Schueller (Bettencourt Schueller Foundation)

Founded in 1987 by Liliane Bettencourt, a business person and heiress to the L'Oréal cosmetics company fortune, and her family.

Activities: Active in the fields of life sciences, culture and social welfare. The Foundation devotes more than one-half of its budget to medical research and health programmes. The Foundation gives out five awards—three in science and two in culture—including the Liliane Bettencourt Life Sciences Award, worth €100,000, awarded to a European researcher under 45 years of age. In the field of culture, the Foundation supports talented artists or artisans and the development of new projects of exceptional quality, as well as awarding the annual Prix Liliane Bettencourt pour le Chant Choral and the Prix Liliane Bettencourt pour l'Intelligence de la Main.

Geographical Area of Activity: France and developing countries.

Publications: Annual Report; newsletter.

Finance: Annual revenue €71.4m., expenditure €116.9m. (31 Dec. 2020).

Board of Trustees: Françoise Bettencourt Meyers (Chair.); Jean-Pierre Meyers (Vice-Chair.).

Principal Staff: Man. Dir Nicolas Myers.

Contact Details: 18 rue Delabordère, 92522 Neuilly-sur-Seine Cedex; e-mail contact@fondationbs.org; internet www.fondationbs.org.

Fondation BNP Paribas (BNP Paribas Foundation)

Established in 1984, operating under the aegis of the Fondation de France (q.v.); one of 12 BNP Paribas foundations.

Activities: Works in the fields of culture, social support and the environment. The Foundation supports: museums and artists; specialized medical research; and initiatives that promote education, social inclusion and overcoming disabilities. It also develops and guides BNP Paribas Group's corporate sponsorship policy.

Geographical Area of Activity: Asia-Pacific, Central and South America, Europe, Middle East and North Africa, North America, sub-Saharan Africa.

Fondation Brigitte Bardot   FRANCE

Publications: Annual Report; *Sustainable Development Report*; press releases.
Finance: Annual budget €12.9m. (2023).
Executive Committee: Michel Pébereau (Chair.).
Principal Staff: Man. Isabelle Giordano.
Contact Details: 16 blvd des Italiens, 75009 Paris; tel. 1-40-14-45-46; e-mail fondation@bnpparibas.com; internet fondation.bnpparibas.

Fondation Brigitte Bardot (Brigitte Bardot Foundation)

Established in 1986 by Brigitte Bardot, an actress.
Activities: Operates in France and worldwide in the area of conservation and the environment, advocating for the rights of domestic, farmed and wild animals. The Foundation operates in 70 countries, with three refuges in France.
Geographical Area of Activity: International.
Publications: Newsletter; *Info Journal*.
Finance: Annual revenue €33.8m., expenditure €29.9m. (31 Dec. 2022).
Principal Staff: Pres. Brigitte Bardot; Man. Dir Ghyslaine Calmels-Bock.
Contact Details: 28 rue Vineuse, 75116 Paris; tel. 1-45-05-14-60; e-mail fbb@fondationbrigittebardot.fr; internet www.fondationbrigittebardot.fr.

Fondation Cartier pour l'Art Contemporain (Cartier Foundation for Contemporary Art)

Founded in 1984 by Alain Dominique Perrin, head of Cartier International and Cartier SA, designers and manufacturers of jewellery and watches.
Activities: Commissions works of art to exhibit at home and abroad; collects and exhibits the works of young artists; and stages exhibitions of its collection of contemporary art (it has a collection of almost 1,500 works of art by around 350 French and international artists). The Foundation commissions transitory or performance art for evening performances. It also organizes travelling exhibitions and promotes artistic exchange with foreign institutions; and organizes conferences, talks and workshops, as well as issuing publications.
Geographical Area of Activity: Asia, Europe, South America, USA.
Publications: Newsletter; artists' books and exhibition catalogues.
Finance: Financed by the Richemont Group.
Trustees: Alain Dominique Perrin (Pres.).
Principal Staff: Man. Dir Chris Dercon.
Contact Details: 261 blvd Raspail, 75014 Paris; tel. 1-42-18-56-50; e-mail info.reservation@fondation.cartier.com; internet www.fondation.cartier.com.

Fondation Casip-Cojasor

Established in 2000 by the merger of the Comité d'Action Sociale Israélite de Paris—CASIP (f. 1809) and the Comité Juif d'Action Sociale et de Reconstruction—COJASOR (f. 1945).
Activities: Assists children and disabled and older people, in particular members of the Jewish community. Foundation services include: culturally sensitive social welfare and employment advice; legal guardianship services; distribution of donated new or used clothes; a kosher food delivery service; and a community centre for the elderly. The Foundation also provides access to a number of charitable funds. It maintains an archive on the social history of the Jewish community in France and science communication in the sociomedical field.
Geographical Area of Activity: France.
Publications: Annual Report; newsletter.
Finance: Annual budget €52.4m. (2023).
Board of Directors: Henri Fiszer (Pres.); Eric de Rothschild (Hon. Pres.); Alain Riveline (Sec.-Gen.); Jean-Marc Choucroun (Treas.).
Principal Staff: CEO Karêne Fredj.
Contact Details: 8 rue Pali-Kao, 75020 Paris; tel. 1-44-62-13-13; e-mail fondation@casip-cojasor.fr; internet www.casip-cojasor.fr.

Fondation de la Cité internationale des arts

Initially conceived in 1937 by Eero Snellman, a Finnish artist, during a speech he gave for the Exposition Universelle in Paris; the idea of a residency for artists was taken up and developed by Mr and Mrs Felix Brunau, with the support of the Ministry of Culture, the Ministry of Foreign Affairs, the City of Paris and the Academy of Fine Arts. The first building was completed in 1965.
Activities: The Cité internationale des arts brings together over 300 international artists and creators each month, allowing them to arrange stays of between two months and one year to undertake a production or research project in all disciplines. French and foreign sponsors underwrite 70% of studios and designate their own artists-in-residence; 30% are reserved for direct applications. The Cité internationale des arts comprises two sites in Paris, one in the Marais and another in Montmartre. Several thematic and/or project-based open calls are held throughout the year.
Geographical Area of Activity: International.
Restrictions: Studio sponsors have their own application conditions (duration, scholarships, etc.).
Publications: Monthly newsletter (public).
Finance: Annual revenue €5.5m., expenditure €5.5m. (March 2023).
Board: Henri Loyrette (Pres.).
Principal Staff: CEO Bénédicte Alliot.
Contact Details: 18 rue de l'Hôtel de Ville, 75004 Paris; tel. 1-42-78-71-72; internet www.citedesartsparis.net.

Fondation de la Cité Internationale Universitaire de Paris (International University Centre of Paris Foundation)

Established in 1925.
Activities: Acts as a space for exchange, promoting tolerance and reflection. The Centre provides dedicated accommodation for approximately 12,000 students, researchers, artists and sportspeople each year in 47 halls of residence. It has sports facilities and a library holding 57,000 books, 365,000 e-books, 8,900 periodicals and 63 databases.
Geographical Area of Activity: France.
Publications: Annual Report; newsletter; *Citescope* (monthly cultural programme); *Le Guide* (residents' guide).
Finance: Annual revenue €48.4m., expenditure €46.6m. (2023).
Board of Directors: Jean-Marc Sauvé (Pres.); Claudine Pons (Second Vice-Pres.); Duncan Fairgrieve (Sec.); Patrice Henri (Treas.).
Principal Staff: Deputy CEO Catherine Ménézo-Méreur.
Contact Details: 17 blvd Jourdan, 75014 Paris; tel. 1-44-16-64-00; e-mail admissions.etudiants@ciup.fr; internet www.ciup.fr.

Fondation Claude Pompidou (Claude Pompidou Foundation)

Established in 1970 at the instigation of Claude Pompidou, wife of former President of France Georges Pompidou.
Activities: Supports projects helping children with disabilities, older people and people in hospital, as well as establishing 13 residential homes and centres. Other projects include an initiative to help elderly hospitalized people to return home. The Foundation awards the Claude Pompidou Prize, worth €100,000, for research into Alzheimer's disease.
Geographical Area of Activity: France.
Publications: Annual Report; newsletter.

FRANCE

Board of Directors: Claude Chirac (Chair.); David de Rothschild (Vice-Chair.); Dominique Graber (Treas.); Josselin de Rohan (Sec.).
Principal Staff: Man. Dir Richard Hutin.
Contact Details: 42 rue de Louvre, 75001 Paris; tel. 1-40-13-75-00; e-mail accueil@fondationclaudepompidou.fr; internet fondationclaudepompidou.org.

Fondation du Collège de France

Established in 2008 by the Collège de France.
Activities: Supports research in the sciences, social sciences and humanities and the dissemination of knowledge. Projects include renovating and modernizing the facilities of the Collège de France, including laboratories and 14 specialized libraries, and endowing chairs. In 2020 it established the Collège de France British Foundation to support the research carried out by the Collège de France and to encourage Franco-British co-operation.
Geographical Area of Activity: France.
Publications: Newsletter.
Finance: Annual income €2.1m., expenditure €2.2m. (31 Dec. 2023).
Board of Directors: Prof. Jean-François Joanny (Chair.); Mercedes Erra (Vice-Chair.); Prof. Pierre-Michel Menger (Sec.-Gen.); Philippe Lemoine (Treas.).
Principal Staff: Dir Marie Chéron.
Contact Details: 11 pl. de Marcelin-Berthelot, 75231 Paris Cedex 05; tel. 1-44-27-15-03; e-mail fondation@college-de-france.fr; internet www.fondation-cdf.fr.

Fondation de Coubertin (Coubertin Foundation)

Established in 1950 by Yvonne de Coubertin and Jean Bernard as the l'Association pour le développement d'un Compagnonnage rural; became a public foundation in 1973.
Activities: Operates in the area of education and training, offering courses of 11 months for around 30 young craftworkers annually, from France or abroad. The Foundation offers general courses and courses in crafts such as joinery, decorative metalwork, fine art foundry and stone masonry. It also organizes public concerts, and seminars for professionals; and maintains a library of around 3,000 vols. It is supported by Les Amis de la Fondation; the American Friends of Coubertin offer training fellowships.
Geographical Area of Activity: International.
Restrictions: Courses open to applicants aged 20–25 years.
Publications: Newsletter; books.
Board of Directors: Alain Rolland (Chair.); Michel Perret (Treas.); Sabine Angely-Manceau (Sec.).
Contact Details: Domaine de Coubertin, 78470 Saint-Rémy-les-Chevreuse; tel. 1-30-85-69-60; e-mail info@coubertin.fr; internet www.coubertin.fr.

Fondation Energies pour le Monde—Fondem (Energies for the World Foundation)

Founded in 1990 by Alain Liébard, an architect.
Activities: Promotes access to reliable, clean and affordable energy in rural areas, working with local partners to implement and monitor sustainable, long-term projects that contribute to economic and social development. The Foundation favours using a variety of renewable sources including photovoltaic and thermal solar energy, wind, hydropower and biomass. It trains migrants to France in rural electrification with a view to their reintegration and job creation in their countries of origin.
Geographical Area of Activity: Guinea, Madagascar, Mali, Senegal.
Publications: Annual Report; *Fondation Energies pour le Monde Infos* (2 a year); guides; technical documents.
Finance: Annual income €1.7m., expenditure €1.8m. (31 Dec. 2023).

Fondation d'Entreprise La Poste

Board of Directors: Jean-Louis Borloo (Pres.); Vincent Jacques le Seigneur (Vice-Pres.); Stephanie Rivoal (Treas.); Philippe Folliasson (Sec.).
Contact Details: 20 ter rue Massue, 94300 Vincennes; tel. 1-44-18-00-80; e-mail contact@fondem.ong; internet www.fondem.ong.

Fondation Ensemble

Established in 2004 by Gérard Brémond, a business person in the tourism sector, and his wife Jacqueline Délia Brémond.
Activities: Promotes sustainable human development that incorporates environmental protection. The Foundation supports the activities of organizations that operate within its four intervention sectors: sustainable agriculture; biodiversity conservation; sustainable fishing; and sustainable technologies.
Geographical Area of Activity: Ecuador, Europe, Lao People's Dem. Repub., Madagascar, Mozambique, Myanmar, Peru.
Restrictions: Not currently funding new projects.
Publications: Annual Report; newsletters; technical notes.
Finance: Annual revenue €1.5m., expenditure €1.5m. (31 Dec. 2020).
Board of Directors: Gérard Brémond (Chair.); Jacqueline Délia Brémond (Co-Chair.).
Principal Staff: Dir Olivier Braunsteffer.
Contact Details: 1 rue de Fleurus, 75006 Paris; tel. 1-45-51-18-82; e-mail contactfe@fondationensemble.org; internet www.fondationensemble.org.

Fondation d'Entreprise ENGIE (ENGIE Corporate Foundation)

Established in 2010, building on the work of the Fondation d'Entreprise GDF Suez (f. 1992 as Fondation d'Entreprise Gaz de France).
Activities: Main areas of focus are: social welfare, including children and young people and improving access to energy for disadvantaged people; and the environment, including biodiversity and cities, countering global warming and climate change, and sustainable architecture. The Foundation supports projects across 25 countries in the areas of: integrating children and young people into society; providing access to energy for sustainable development; and emergency aid.
Geographical Area of Activity: International.
Restrictions: Does not fund special events, publishing or film-making projects or advertising; no grants to individuals.
Publications: Annual Report; newsletter.
Board of Directors: Jean-Pierre Clamadieu (Pres.).
Principal Staff: Gen. Sec. Claire Waysand.
Contact Details: Tour T1, 1 pl. Samuel de Champlain, 92400 Courbevoie; internet fondation-engie.com.

Fondation d'Entreprise La Poste (Post Office Foundation)

Established in 1995 under the aegis of the Fondation de France (q.v.).
Activities: Operates nationally and in francophone countries in the area of the arts and culture, through financing festivals and literary prizes such as the Prix Wepler; promoting French songwriting through the Prix Timbres de Voix prize; and supporting publishing initiatives.
Geographical Area of Activity: France.
Publications: *FloriLettres* (monthly online magazine).
Finance: Annual revenue €960,000, expenditure €859,744 (31 Dec. 2020).
Executive Committee: Philippe Wahl (Pres.).
Principal Staff: CEO Anne-Marie Jean; Deputy CEO Maryline Girodias.
Contact Details: 9 rue du Colonel Pierre Avia, CP B 707, 75757 Paris Cedex 15; tel. 1-55-44-01-17; e-mail fondation.laposte@laposte.fr; internet www.fondationlaposte.org.

Fondation d'Entreprise Renault (Renault Foundation)

Established in 2001 by Renault, a motor vehicle manufacturer.

Activities: Collaborates with partner universities in France and abroad, designing and funding study programmes in three key areas: multicultural management; sustainable mobility; and road safety. The Foundation awards study grants of €1,050 per month. Local foundations operate in Argentina, Brazil, Columbia, Morocco, Spain and Romania.

Geographical Area of Activity: Algeria, Brazil, People's Repub. of China, France, India, Iran, Japan, Repub. of Korea, Lebanon, Morocco, Romania, Russian Federation, Türkiye (Turkey).

Publications: Annual Report; newsletter; brochure.

Principal Staff: Dir Catherine Gros; Deputy Dir Sophie Chazelle.

Contact Details: 13–15 quai Alphonse Le Gallo, FQLG V 15140, 92513 Boulogne-Billancourt Cedex; tel. 1-76-84-96-82; e-mail fondation.renault@renault.com; internet www.renaultgroup.com/groupe/mecenat-et-patrimoine/la-fondation.

Fondation d'Entreprise VINCI pour la Cité (VINCI Corporate Foundation for the City)

Established in 2002 by VINCI, a construction company.

Activities: Grant programmes help disadvantaged and socially excluded people to gain access to employment; and encourage citizens' initiatives focused on sustainable development and quality of life. The Foundation has a network of 11 affiliated foundations and funds in Europe.

Geographical Area of Activity: Belgium, Czech Repub. (Czechia), Denmark, Finland, France, Germany, Greece, Iceland, Netherlands, Portugal, Slovakia, Spain, Sweden, UK.

Restrictions: Projects from a country other than France must be submitted to the Foundation by a company employee; does not support temporary projects.

Publications: Annual Report; brochures.

Finance: Total grants disbursed since 2002 €68m.

Principal Staff: CEO Cecile Droux.

Contact Details: 1 cours Ferdinand de Lesseps, 92851 Rueil-Malmaison Cedex; tel. 1-47-16-30-63; e-mail fondation@vinci.com; internet www.fondation-vinci.com.

Fondation Euris (Euris Foundation)

Founded in 2000 by Jean-Charles Naouri, Chairman of holding company Euris SAS; under the aegis of Fondation de France (q.v.).

Activities: Provides university scholarships to French students from high schools classified as ZEP (Zones d'Education Prioritaire), ZS (Zones Sensibles) and underprivileged areas in need of financial support to acquire a university education. The maximum amount awarded is €8,000 per year, renewable once.

Geographical Area of Activity: France.

Board of Trustees: Pierre Sellal (Pres.); René Ricol (Vice-Pres.); Yves Perrier (Treas.).

Principal Staff: Gen. Man. Axelle Davezac.

Contact Details: 103 rue Boetie, 75008 Paris; tel. 1-44-71-14-90; e-mail fondationeuris@euris.fr; internet www.fondationdefrance.org/fr/fondation/fondation-euris.

Fondation FARM—Fondation pour l'Agriculture et la Ruralité dans le Monde (Foundation for World Agriculture and Rural Life)

Established in 2005.

Activities: Influences decisionmakers through conducting public policy research and advocacy. Areas of research include: agricultural policies and markets; value chain organization; agricultural financing and risk management; production systems; management of water for drinking, sanitation and agriculture; and training and advising agricultural producers. The Foundation undertakes pilot projects with local stakeholders; and provides training and education to build capacity and professionalize producer organizations.

Geographical Area of Activity: International.

Publications: Annual Report; newsletter (6 a year); *Point de Vue*; reports; studies; working papers; blog.

Board of Directors: Pascale l'Heureux (Pres.).

Principal Staff: Gen. Man. Catherine Migault.

Contact Details: s/c Crédit Agricole SA, 12 pl. des Etats Unis, 92127 Montrouge Cedex; tel. 1-57-72-07-19; e-mail contact@fondation-farm.org; internet www.fondation-farm.org.

Fondation France Chine—FFC (France China Foundation)

Established in 2014 as the Association Avenir France-Chine by Gérard Houa.

Activities: Promotes mutual understanding and dialogue between France and the People's Republic of China in the areas of politics, economics, finance, the environment and culture. The Foundation offers scholarships for the study of French and Chinese culture.

Geographical Area of Activity: People's Repub. of China, France.

Principal Staff: Pres. Gérard Houa.

Contact Details: 74 ave Kléber, 75116 Paris; e-mail contact@fondation-france-chine.org; internet fondation-france-chine.com.

Fondation France-Israël (France-Israel Foundation)

Launched in 2005 by the Governments of France and Israel to reinforce links and relations between the two countries at all levels.

Activities: Promotes the development of relations between the two countries through supporting educational, cultural, economic, scientific and technological projects. Activities include organizing symposia and student exchange trips; awarding every two years two Young Economist Prizes, worth €30,000 each, to a French economist under 40 years of age and an Israeli economist under 45 years of age; and awarding every year two prizes for information, organization of zooms between French regions and key decision makers in Israel.

Geographical Area of Activity: France, Israel.

Publications: Annual Report.

Board of Directors: Muriel Haim (Chair.); Alain Madar (Treas.).

Contact Details: BP 20024, 75008 Paris Cedex 08; tel. 1-82-28-95-85; e-mail contact@fondationfranceisrael.org; internet www.fondationfranceisrael.org.

Fondation Franco-Japonaise Sasakawa (Franco-Japanese Sasakawa Foundation)

Founded in 1990 by the Sasakawa Foundation (q.v.).

Activities: Fosters the long-term development of Franco-Japanese relations through offering scholarships, research grants and travel grants in the fields of the arts and humanities, education, and science and technology. The Foundation encourages projects that deal with contemporary rather than historical issues, including activities such as: the teaching of the French and Japanese languages; translation and publication of works; production of art; scientific research; promotion of exchanges of people and of knowledge; journalism; and exhibitions. It organizes conferences, runs self-conducted programmes and issues publications; and has an office in Tokyo, Japan.

Geographical Area of Activity: France, Japan.

Restrictions: No grants to individuals or for commercial ventures.

Publications: Annual Report; newsletter; *Cent Objets—Produits Artisanaux Traditionnels Japonais Commentés*; *Guide pour la promotion des objets d'artisanat traditionnel japonais*; cultural register of Japanese institutions located in France.

Finance: Total assets €35.4m. (2022).
Board of Directors: Masato Kitera (Chair.); Alain Boudou (Vice-Chair.); Pierre-Yves Carpentier (Treas.); Takashi Komori (Deputy Treas.); Bruno Gain (Sec.).
Principal Staff: Dir Eric Mollet.
Contact Details: 27 rue du Cherche-Midi, 75006 Paris; tel. 1-44-39-30-40; e-mail siegeparis@ffjs.org; internet www.ffjs.org.

Fondation Fyssen (Fyssen Foundation)
Established in 1979 by A. H. Fyssen, a business person.
Activities: Works in the fields of archaeology, anthropology, ethnology, ethology, human palaeontology, psychology and neurobiology. Postdoctoral study grants, of up to €40,000, are offered to scientists holding a French PhD for research abroad, and for foreign PhD holders wishing to work in French research centres. Research grants, worth between €15,000 and €100,000, are offered to support French or foreign scientists in establishing a research team for a collective scientific project in a laboratory in France. The Foundation organizes symposia and publishes research results; and awards an annual international scientific prize worth €100,000.
Geographical Area of Activity: Worldwide.
Restrictions: Makes study grants for a first postdoctorate only, less than two years after a PhD thesis, up to a maximum age of 35 years and research grants for French or foreign researchers, aged up to 35 for biological sciences and 40 for human sciences.
Publications: *Annales de la Fondation Fyssen*; posters.
Board of Directors: Daniel Lallier (Chair.); Bernard Zalc (Vice-Chair.); Jeanne-Marie Parly (Treas.).
Principal Staff: Man. Dir Franck Dufour.
Contact Details: 194 rue de Rivoli, 75001 Paris; tel. 1-42-97-53-16; e-mail secretariat@fondationfyssen.fr; internet www.fondationfyssen.fr.

Fondation Gan pour le Cinéma (Gan Foundation for the Cinema)
Established in 1987; one of two foundations belonging to Groupe Groupama, an insurance and finance company, along with Fondation Groupama pour la Santé.
Activities: Promotes French cinema and the audiovisual arts through film restoration; supporting the work of new filmmakers; offering financial assistance for the distribution of films; sponsoring French film festivals and awarding prizes. The Foundation also provides financial support to the Max Linder Panorama cinema in Paris.
Geographical Area of Activity: International.
Publications: Newsletter; brochure.
Principal Staff: Pres. Laurent Bouschon; Hon. Pres. and Dir Costa Gavras.
Contact Details: GroupAMA Campus, 3 pl. Marcel Paul, 92024 Nanterre; tel. 1-70-94-25-12; internet www.fondation-gan.com.

Fondation Groupe EDF (EDF Group Foundation)
Established in 1987 as Fondation Electricité de France (EDF); in 2016 incorporated the foundations of EDF subsidiaries Dalkia, EDF Energies Nouvelles and Enedis.
Activities: Funds initiatives in the areas of: the environment, preventing climate change and conserving nature; education, including culture and citizenship; and inclusion, in particular, improving standards of living and providing access to energy. The Foundation has an exhibition space in Paris, which hosts exhibitions of contemporary art, concerts, conferences, etc. It has 13 regional committees.
Geographical Area of Activity: International.
Restrictions: Grants only to NGOs or public institutions based in France.
Publications: Annual Report; newsletter; reports; catalogues; brochures.
Finance: Annual budget €10m. (2024).
Board of Directors: Luc Rémont (Chair.).
Principal Staff: CEO Alexandre Perra.
Contact Details: 6 rue Juliette Récamier, 75007 Paris; tel. 1-40-42-22-22; e-mail fondation-edf@edf.fr; internet fondation.edf.com.

Fondation Henri Cartier-Bresson (Henri Cartier-Bresson Foundation)
Established in 2003 to promote photography in general and in particular the work of Henri Cartier-Bresson.
Activities: Promotes the work of Henri Cartier-Bresson, through the establishment of a studio to house the photographer's works, books, films and designs; the studio is open to researchers. Every two years, the Foundation offers the €35,000 HCB Award. It organizes films, screenings and photography exhibitions; and conserves the archives of Cartier-Bresson and Martine Franck.
Geographical Area of Activity: Mainly Paris.
Restrictions: Does not make grants.
Publications: Newsletter; exhibition catalogues.
Board of Directors: Serge Toubiana (Pres.); François de Ricqlès (Vice-Pres.); Tatyana Franck (Treas.); Anne Cartier-Bresson (Sec.).
Principal Staff: Dir Clement Cheroux.
Contact Details: 79 rue des Archives, 75003 Paris; tel. 1-40-61-50-50; e-mail contact@henricartierbresson.org; internet www.henricartierbresson.org.

Fondation Jacques Chirac (Jacques Chirac Foundation)
Established in 2006 by former President of France Jacques Chirac to help build a peaceful international society.
Activities: Works in the fields of conflict prevention, dialogue of cultures, and access to healthcare and medicine. The Foundation awards the Prize for Conflict Prevention and Culture for Peace Prize.
Geographical Area of Activity: International.
Finance: Annual revenue €52.1m., expenditure €49.7m. (31 Dec. 2020).
Board of Directors: Françoise Beziat (Pres.); Patrick Gohet (Vice-Pres.); Matthieu Rambaud (Treas.); Bernard Fraysse (Sec.).
Contact Details: 16 blvd de la Sarsonne, 19200 Ussel; tel. 5-55-46-32-00; internet www.fondationjacqueschirac.fr.

Fondation Jean Dausset—Centre d'Etude du Polymorphisme Humain—CEPH (Jean Dausset Foundation—Centre for the Study of Human Polymorphism)
Established in 1984 by Prof. Daniel Cohen and Prof. Jean Dausset with a US $10m. bequest from a French art collector; became the Fondation Jean Dausset in 1993.
Activities: Works in the fields of medicine, health, science and technology, through self-conducted programmes, research and publications. The Centre conducts genetic research and produced the first genome map; and it maintains a database and the online Human BAC Library. It manages the CEPH CRB (the biological resources centre using human samples for research). Research is also carried out at its GENMED LabEx laboratory, which is an independent organization.
Geographical Area of Activity: International.
Publications: Research papers.
Board of Directors: André Syrota (Chair.).
Principal Staff: Dir Dr Jean-François Deleuze.
Contact Details: 27 rue Juliette Dodu, 75010 Paris; tel. 1-53-72-50-50; internet www.cephb.fr.

Fondation Jean Jaurès (Jean Jaurès Foundation)
Established by Pierre Mauroy.

Fondation Le Corbusier   FRANCE

Activities: A think tank aiming to promote ideas and debate towards increased democracy through conferences and public meetings. Maintains archives on social and labour history. Has 260 partners in 100 countries.
Geographical Area of Activity: International.
Finance: Annual income €2.6m., expenditure €2.6m. (2021).
Board of Directors: Henri Nallet (Hon. Pres.); Jen-Marc Ayrault (Pres.); Gerard Lindeperg (Vice-Pres.); Gilles Finchelstein (Sec.-Gen.).
Principal Staff: Co-CEO Laurent Cohen, Jérémie Peltier.
Contact Details: 12 cité Malesherbes, 75009 Paris; tel. 1-40-23-24-00; internet jean-jaures.org.

Fondation Le Corbusier—FLC (Le Corbusier Foundation)

Founded in 1968 according to the will of architect and designer Charles Edouard Jeanneret, known as 'Le Corbusier', to maintain and manage his architectural work, which is included on UNESCO's World Heritage List.
Activities: Works in the field of the arts and architecture. The Foundation maintains a permanent exhibition in the Villa La Roche of Le Corbusier's works (furniture, paintings and sculptures); loans original works for exhibitions; advises on and supervises the preservation of buildings designed by Le Corbusier; and maintains a library. It awards research scholarships; and in 2017 established a prize for young researchers worth €10,000.
Geographical Area of Activity: Argentina, Belgium, France, Germany, India, Japan, Switzerland.
Publications: Annual Report; *informations* (newsletter); *Masilia*; *Rencontres*; conference proceedings; guidebooks; catalogues; monographs.
Board of Directors: Phillippe Prost (Pres.); Wanda Diebolt (Vice-Pres.); Rémi Baudouï (Sec.-Gen.); Emmanuelle Brugerolles (Treas.).
Principal Staff: Dir Brigitte Bouvier.
Contact Details: 8–10 sq. du Docteur Blanche, 75016 Paris; tel. 1-42-88-41-53; e-mail info@fondationlecorbusier.fr; internet www.fondationlecorbusier.fr.

Fondation pour le Logement des Défavorisés (Foundation for Housing the Disadvantaged)

Established in 1987 as the Fondation Abbé Pierre pour le Logement des Défavorisés; formerly known as the Fondation Abbé Pierre until present name adopted in 2024. Part of the Emmaüs network (q.v.).
Activities: Works to give all disadvantaged people access to decent housing and a life with dignity. The Foundation has nine regional offices in France and development projects in 18 countries.
Geographical Area of Activity: Central America and the Caribbean, Central and South-Eastern Europe, East and South-East Asia, South Asia, sub-Saharan Africa, Western Europe.
Publications: *Focus* (report series); *L'État du mal-logement*.
Finance: Annual revenue €63.9m., expenditure €59.0m. (30 Sept. 2023).
Board of Directors: Marie-Hélène Le Nedic (Pres.); Dominique Ayrault (Vice-Pres.); Christian Alibay (Treas.); Patrick Rouyer (Sec.).
Principal Staff: CEO Christophe Robert; Deputy CEO Sonia Hurcet.
Contact Details: 3 rue de Romainville, 75019 Paris; tel. 1-55-56-37-00; e-mail contactape@fondationpourlelogement.fr; internet www.fondationpourlelogement.fr.

Fondation MACIF (MACIF Foundation)

Established in 1993 by MACIF, a non-profit insurance company, to support innovative French NGOs.
Activities: Supports projects in four areas: inclusive mobility; decent housing; healthcare access, including food issues, organic farming and short food supply chains; and solidarity finance.
Geographical Area of Activity: France.
Restrictions: Does not fund humanitarian projects or emergency aid, or projects outside the French metropolis.
Publications: Annual Report; newsletter.
Finance: Annual income €4.6m., expenditure €5.3m. (31 Dec. 2020).
Board of Directors: Françoise Lareur (Chair.).
Principal Staff: Sec.-Gen. Marcela Scaron.
Contact Details: 2 et 4 rue de Pied de Fond, 79037 Niort Cedex 09; tel. 1-51-31-63-14; e-mail fondation@macif.fr; internet www.fondation-macif.org.

Fondation MAIF pour la Recherche (MAIF Foundation for Research)

Established in 1989 by the Mutuelle Assurance des Instituteurs de France (mutual insurance company for primary school teachers).
Activities: Works in the field of safety and risk prevention, promoting collaboration between local government, universities and research institutions, NGOs and industry. Areas of research include: mobility risks; natural hazards; risks in daily life; and digital risks. The Foundation supports research; awards prizes and research grants; issues publications; and organizes conferences and meetings.
Geographical Area of Activity: International.
Publications: Annual Report; newsletter.
Finance: Annual income €249.342, expenditure €1.2m. (31 Dec. 2023).
Board of Directors: Christian Ponsolle (Pres.); Isabelle Neaud (Treas.).
Principal Staff: Sec.-Gen. Sandrine Spaeter-Loehrer.
Contact Details: 275 rue du Stade, 79180 Chauray; tel. 5-49-73-87-04; e-mail contact@fondation.maif.fr; internet www.fondation-maif.fr.

Fondation de la Maison de la Chimie (Chemistry Centre Foundation)

Founded in 1927 on the occasion of the centenary of the birth of Marcelin Berthelot, a chemist and politician.
Activities: Co-operates with other institutions in arranging scientific, cultural, professional and educational events. The Foundation makes a biennial award of €30,000 to recognize original work in chemistry of benefit to society, mankind or nature. Its Congress Centre provides lecture rooms, technical facilities and professional staff to French, foreign and international organizations to enable them to expand their mutual relations. It accommodates, on a permanent basis, institutions operating in the field of chemistry and provides accommodation for participants in the meetings and conferences that it sponsors.
Geographical Area of Activity: France.
Board of Directors: Philippe Goebel (Pres.); Danièle Olivier, Philippe Walter (Vice-Pres); Christian Bald (Treas.); Henri Dugert (Sec.).
Contact Details: 28 bis, rue Saint-Dominique, 75007 Paris; tel. 1-40-62-27-00; e-mail info@maisondelachimie.com; internet www.maisondelachimie.com.

Fondation Maison des Sciences de l'Homme—FMSH (House of the Human Sciences Foundation)

Founded in 1963.
Activities: Works in the fields of the humanities and social sciences. The Foundation carries out research and issues publications; organizes exchange of scientific information; and maintains a library containing approximately 500,000 vols. It awards the Prix Louis Dumont for research in social anthropology; the Prix d'Histoire Sociale Fondation Mattei Dogan &

FMSH for social history from the 19th to the 21st centuries; the Prix Herman Diederiks for writing on the history of criminality and criminal justice; the Prix Charles et Monique Morazé for research on science and society and education and society; and the Prix Ariane Deluz d'Ethnologie Africaine, worth €5,000, for research on African ethnology.

Geographical Area of Activity: International.

Publications: Annual Report; newsletter (quarterly).

Finance: Annual revenue €17.6m., expenditure €17.3m. (31 Dec. 2022).

Executive Board: Antonin Cohen (Pres.); Claire Borders, David Rochefort (Vice-Pres).

Supervisory Board: Caroline Ollivier-Yaniv (Pres.); Mohammed Benlahsen (Vice-Pres.).

Contact Details: 54 blvd Raspail, 75006 Paris; tel. 1-40-48-64-00; e-mail contact@msh-paris.fr; internet www.fmsh.fr.

Fondation Marc de Montalembert (Marc de Montalembert Foundation)

Established in 1994 in memory of Marc de Montalembert by Manuela and Marc René de Montalembert; operates under the aegis of the Fondation de France (q.v.).

Activities: Gives young people from 22 Mediterranean countries opportunities to experience other cultures in the fields of literature, architecture, music, photography and singing; and discussions on themes relating to peace and tolerance among Mediterranean countries. The Foundation awards grants of €7,000 each for projects on Mediterranean cultures or artistic crafts and trades; and, in partnership with the École du Louvre, Paris, awards the annual Marc de Montalembert Prize, worth €9,000, to holders of doctorates for research in Mediterranean history of art. It has a dialogue centre in the old town of Rhodes, Greece, where it hosts seminars and workshops and receives writers or artists in residence.

Geographical Area of Activity: Mediterranean region.

Restrictions: Grant applicants must come from countries bordering the Mediterranean; be under 28 years of age; and carry out projects in one or more countries of the Mediterranean, but not the applicant's country of origin. Prize applicants must come from countries bordering the Mediterranean, be under 35 years of age and hold a PhD in a subject related to art history.

Principal Staff: Pres. Marc René de Montalembert.

Contact Details: c/o Fondation de France, 40 ave Hoche, 75008 Paris; e-mail info@fondationmdm.com; internet www.fondationmdm.com.

Fondation Marcel Bleustein-Blanchet de la Vocation (Marcel Bleustein-Blanchet Vocational Foundation)

Established in 1960 by Marcel Bleustein-Blanchet, founder of Publicis Group, an advertising and public relations company; a sister foundation was established in Belgium.

Activities: Supports young people aged 18–30 years old to pursue their vocation. Each year it awards 20 Prix de la Vocation, each worth €10,000, to enable recipients to fulfil projects such as completing studies, buying materials or other essentials, taking up an internship abroad, performing a show, organizing an exhibition or buying a musical instrument. Hope Prizes worth awarded €5,000 are also awarded. The Prix Littéraire de la Vocation, worth €10,000, is awarded to young authors for their first or second novel, already published and written in French. The Prix de Poésie de la Vocation, worth €5,000, helps young poets writing in French to be published for the first or the second time.

Geographical Area of Activity: International.

Restrictions: No grants for religious or political vocations; scholarship applicants must be French or living in France.

Board: Elisabeth Badinter (Pres.); Leila Boudjennad (Treas.).

Principal Staff: CEO Sabine Van Vlaenderen Badinter.

Contact Details: 104 rue de Rennes, 75006 Paris; tel. 1-53-63-25-90; e-mail contact@fondationdelavocation.org; internet www.fondationvocation.org.

Fondation Marguerite et Aimé Maeght

Founded in 1964 by Aimé Maeght, an art collector and publisher, and his wife Marguerite to acquire, preserve and exhibit contemporary art.

Activities: Maintains a collection of paintings, sculptures and graphic works of art from the 20th century. The Foundation organizes retrospectives from its collection and exhibitions of contemporary art, in France and abroad. Founded a library in 1972, housing more than 35,000 items.

Geographical Area of Activity: International.

Publications: Newsletter; catalogue; exhibition posters.

Trustees: Adrien Maeght (Chair.).

Principal Staff: Admin. and Finance Dir Nicolas Gitton.

Contact Details: 623 chemin des Gardettes, quartier des Fumerates, 06570 Saint-Paul-de-Vence; tel. 4-93-32-81-63; e-mail info@fondation-maeght.com; internet www.fondation-maeght.com.

Fondation Mérieux (Mérieux Foundation)

Founded in 1967 by Dr Charles Mérieux, a virologist.

Activities: Works in the fields of medical and veterinary research, education, social welfare and aid to less-developed countries, through self-conducted programmes of research, grants to institutions and individuals, scholarships to overseas candidates, conferences and publications. The Foundation works closely with the Institut pour le Développement de l'Epidémiologie Appliquée (Annecy), the Association pour la Médecine Préventive and Bioforce (a training programme for polyvalent health auxiliaries); and also the Fondation Christophe et Rodolphe Mérieux (f. 2001), which carries out applied research on infectious diseases that affect mothers and children. It operates in more than 17 countries.

Geographical Area of Activity: Bangladesh, Benin, Brazil, Burkina Faso, Cambodia, Cameroon, People's Repub. of China, Guinea, Haiti, Iraq, Lao People's Dem. Repub., Lebanon, Madagascar, Mali, Niger, Senegal, Tajikistan, Togo.

Publications: Annual Report; newsletter; *Collection fondation Mérieux*.

Finance: Annual income €21.8m., expenditure €25.7m. (2023).

Board of Directors: Alain Mérieux (Pres.).

Scientific Advisory Board: Dr Marie-Paul Kieny (Pres.).

Principal Staff: Exec. Dir Jean-Pierre Bosser; Sec.-Gen. Clelia Lebayle.

Contact Details: 17 rue Bourgelat, 69002 Lyon; tel. 4-72-40-79-79; e-mail contact@fondation-merieux.org; internet www.fondation-merieux.org.

Fondation Nationale pour l'Enseignement de la Gestion des Entreprises (French National Foundation for Management Education)

Founded in 1968 by the Conseil National du Patronat Français, the Assemblée Permanente des Chambres de Commerce et d'Industrie and the Government.

Activities: Works in the field of management education, in five main areas: promoting stronger ties between education and industry; training and improvement of management teachers; updating curricula of management training institutions; developing management institutions; and promoting French management education abroad. The Foundation operates through research, grants to institutions and individuals, scholarships, conferences, courses, seminars and publications.

Geographical Area of Activity: International.

Publications: *Lettre FNEGE* (newsletter, 6 a year); *Baromètre FNEGE*; white papers; barometer.

Finance: Financed by French public authorities and businesses.

Board of Directors: Jean-Marc Janaillac (Pres.).

Principal Staff: CEO Prof. Jerome Caby; Exec. Dir Valérie Fourcade.

Contact Details: 2 ave Hoche, 75008 Paris; tel. 1-44-29-93-60; e-mail info@fnege.fr; internet www.fnege.org.

Fondation Nationale des Sciences Politiques—SciencesPo (National Foundation for Political Sciences)

Founded in 1945 by government ordinance to succeed the École Libre des Sciences Politiques (f. 1872).

Activities: Works in the fields of political, economic and social sciences, and international relations, through research, teaching, continuing professional development, publications and documentation services. The Foundation conducts research into: international relations; political life in France; economic activity; social affairs; contemporary European history; economic conditions; American studies; and social change. A range of scholarships and financial assistance are available. Its documentation services comprise a social science library of 1m. printed documents, 980,000 digitized documents, 570,000 online periodicals and 150,000 journals online, and compiling and keeping a documentation centre maintaining around 18,000 press-cuttings files since 1945. The Foundation also administers the Institut d'Études Politiques de Paris, assists the research and documentation activities of the Institutes of Political Studies at Grenoble and Bordeaux, and owns publisher Presses de Sciences Po.

Geographical Area of Activity: France.

Publications: Newsletter; *Revue française de science politique* (6 a year, jointly with the Association Française de Science Politique); *Critique Internationale* (quarterly); *Raisons Politique* (quarterly); *Revue économique* (6 a year); *Vingtième Siècle—Histoire* (quarterly); *Revue de l'OFCE* (quarterly); books; research monographs.

Board of Directors: Laurence Bertrand Dorleac (Pres.); Laurence Parisot (First Vice-Pres.); Sebastian Pimont (Second Vice-Pres.); Alexandre Mariani (Third Vice-Pres.).

Principal Staff: Admin. Jean Bassères.

Contact Details: 27 rue Saint-Guillaume, 75337 Paris Cedex 07; tel. 1-45-49-50-50; internet www.sciencespo.fr.

Fondation Nicolas Hulot pour la Nature et l'Homme—FNH (Nicolas Hulot Foundation for Nature and Humankind)

Established in 1990 by Nicolas Hulot, a journalist and environmentalist; a member of the International Union for Conservation of Nature and a non-governmental adviser to ECOSOC.

Activities: Works in the field of ecological transition. Programme areas include: biodiversity; climate deregulation; economy; food; democracy; globalization; and transport. The Foundation advocates for sustainable development through influencing political and economic decisionmakers; and working to change peoples' daily behaviours and attitudes. Grants of €1,000 are offered to organizations carrying out nature conservation projects in France. Three 'sheltered' foundations operate under its aegis: Fondation Breizh Biodiv, Fondation ETRE and Fondation Valorem.

Geographical Area of Activity: France, Madagascar, Morocco, Romania, Senegal.

Publications: Annual Report; newsletter (weekly).

Finance: Annual revenue €3.7m., expenditure €3.6m. (31 Dec. 2023).

Board of Directors: Gildas Bonnel (Pres.); Michèle Pappalardo (Vice-Pres.); Anne de Béthencourt (Treas.).

Principal Staff: Gen. Man. Stephanie Clement-Grandcourt.

Contact Details: 6 rue de l'Est, 92100 Boulogne-Billancourt; tel. 1-41-22-10-70; e-mail contact@fnh.org; internet www.fondation-nature-homme.org.

Fondation Orange (Orange Foundation)

Established in 1987, as Fondation d'Entreprise France Telecom, by France Telecom, a telecommunications company; part of the Fondation Orange (q.v.) network. Present name adopted in 2007.

Activities: Works in the fields of digital education and inclusion, health and disability, culture, and international emergency response. The Foundation operates through local foundations managed by Orange subsidiaries in Burkina Faso, Cameroon, Côte d'Ivoire, Guinea, Jordan, Liberia, Madagascar, Mali, Mauritius, Moldova, Morocco, Poland, Romania, Senegal, Sierra Leone, Slovakia and Spain. It has established a network of 449 Digital Houses in 24 countries, 300 Solidarity FabLab digital maker spaces in 24 countries and 1,400 digital schools in 17 countries.

Geographical Area of Activity: Africa, Europe, Middle East.

Publications: Annual Report; newsletter; brochures.

Board of Directors: Jacques Aschenbroich (Pres.); Caroline Guillaumin (Vice-Pres.).

Principal Staff: Man. Dir Hafida Guenfoud.

Contact Details: 111 Quai du President Roosevelt, 92130 Issy-les-Moulineaux; tel. 1-44-44-22-22; e-mail fondation.orange@orange.com; internet www.fondationorange.com.

Fondation Partage et Vie (Sharing and Life Foundation)

Created in 2001 as the Fondation Caisses d'Epargne pour la Solidarité by the Groupe Caisse d'Epargne; present name adopted in 2016.

Activities: Operates nationally in the field of social welfare. The Foundation manages 127 nursing homes for older people, establishments for disabled people and healthcare facilities. It has two 'sheltered' foundations under its aegis: Fondation Vivre Longtemps and Fondation Innovation et Handicap.

Geographical Area of Activity: France.

Publications: Annual Report; newsletter; booklets.

Board of Directors: Dominique Coudreau (Chair.).

Principal Staff: Man. Dir Delphine Langlet.

Contact Details: 11 rue de la Vanne, CS 20018, 92120 Montrouge; tel. 1-58-07-16-00; e-mail webmaster@fondationpartageetvie.org; internet www.fondationpartageetvie.org.

Fondation du Patrimoine (Heritage Foundation)

Established in 1996.

Activities: Acts as an umbrella organization, bringing together private and corporate funders to protect heritage sites in France, including unprotected heritage, natural or landscaped areas of interest, and architectural sites; and funding the restoration of buildings not covered by state subsidies. The Foundation has 21 regional delegations and 100 departmental delegations. It also has 9 'sheltered' foundations under its aegis: Fondation Ateliers d'Art de France; Fondation Belle Main; Fondation Essone Mécénat; Fondation Louis Cadic; Fondation Vernon Patrimoine; Fondation VMF; Fondation Gilles et Monique Cugnier; Fondation Rocamadour—Musique sacrée; and Fondation Fransylva.

Geographical Area of Activity: France.

Publications: Annual Report; newsletter; *Patrimoines en devenir* (2 a year).

Finance: Annual revenue €142.5m.m., expenditure €149.1m. (31 Dec. 2023).

Board of Directors: Guillaume Poitrinal (Chair.); Bertrand de Feydeau, Marie-Christine Labourdette (Vice-Chair.); Bernhardt Eichner (Treas.); Eric Jourde (Sec.).

Principal Staff: Man. Dir Alexandre Giuglaris.

Contact Details: 153 bis, ave Charles de Gaulle, 92200 Neuilly-sur-Seine; tel. 1-70-48-48-00; e-mail info@fondation-patrimoine.org; internet www.fondation-patrimoine.org.

Fondation pour la Recherche Médicale (Foundation for Medical Research)

Founded in 1947 by 13 researchers.

Activities: Operates exclusively in the field of medicine and the biological sciences through offering grants to individuals and institutions, especially in France, and disseminating information on medical research to the public. The Foundation subsidizes study abroad and assists the purchase of scientific equipment; organizes conferences, lectures and exhibitions; and maintains regional committees. Major annual awards include the Rosen Prize for Cancer Research, and other prizes for research in molecular biology, endocrinology, immunology, infectiology, clinical investigation, neurobiology, nephrology and cancer. It also awards special prizes in the field of scientific communication. Some 22 'sheltered' foundations operate under its aegis.

Geographical Area of Activity: International.

Publications: Annual Report; *E-Lettre* (newsletter); *Recherche & Santé* (quarterly).

Finance: Annual revenue €76.2m., expenditure €67.6m. (31 Dec. 2023).

Board of Directors: Benjamin Pruvost (Chair.).

Supervisory Committee: Denis Duverne (Chair.).

Contact Details: 54 rue de Varenne, 75007 Paris Cedex 07; tel. 1-44-39-75-75; e-mail avotreecoute@frm.org; internet www.frm.org.

Fondation pour la Recherche Stratégique (Foundation for Strategic Research)

Established in 1992 as the Fondation pour les Études de Défense to conduct research in the field of defence and international security studies; subsequently merged with the Centre de Recherches et d'Études sur les Stratégies et les Technologies.

Activities: Conducts research in the fields of defence policies, technology and security, and regional and international affairs. The Foundation organizes public events and closed seminars to foster debate on defence and security in France and abroad. Its documentation centre contains over 5,000 items, including books, periodicals and grey literature, in addition to more than 100 French and foreign magazines.

Geographical Area of Activity: Worldwide.

Publications: *Notes de la FRS*; *Recherches & Documents* (annual collection); *Défense & Industries* (quarterly magazine); *FRS Notes*; reports; books.

Finance: Annual income €4.0m., expenditure €4.1m. (31 Dec. 2023).

Board of Directors: Bruno Racine (Chair.); Laurent Collet-Billon (Vice-Chair.); Dahlia Kownator (Treas.).

Principal Staff: Dir Xavier Pasco; Deputy Dirs Isabelle Facon, Bruno Tertrais; Sec.-Gen. Alexandre Houdayer.

Contact Details: 55 rue Raspail, 92300 Levallois-Perret; tel. 1-43-13-77-77; e-mail contact@frstrategie.org; internet www.frstrategie.org.

Fondation Robert Schuman (Robert Schuman Foundation)

Founded in 1991 after the fall of the Berlin Wall; a reference research centre on Europe.

Activities: Promotes the construction of Europe and European ideals and values. The Foundation produces high-level studies on European policies. It organizes and participates in European and international meetings and conferences; and develops research programmes in co-operation with university centres and think tanks. Has an office in Brussels, Belgium.

Geographical Area of Activity: Europe.

Publications: *La Lettre de la Fondation Robert Schuman* (weekly newsletter); *Notes de la Fondation Robert Schuman*; *Observatoire des Elections en Europe*; *Schuman Report on Europe State of the Union* (annual); *EUscope* (digital app).

Finance: Annual income €1.2m, expenditure €1.2m. (2023).

Board of Directors: Jean-Dominique Giuliani (Pres.).

Principal Staff: Exec. Dir Pascale Joannin.

Contact Details: 203 bis blvd Saint-Germain, 75007 Paris; tel. 1-53-63-83-00; e-mail info@robert-schuman.eu; internet www.robert-schuman.eu.

Fondation S

Established in 2022 by the Sanofi Group, a healthcare provider, to replace the Fondation Sanofi Espoir (f. 2010) whose mandate expired in December 2021.

Activities: Operates in less-developed countries in the areas of childhood cancers, climate change, humanitarian aid and neglected tropical diseases, providing grants to partner organizations. The My Child Matters programme offers support and funding with the aim that all children with cancer can have access to treatment, and assists in the training of health workers. The Foundation funds projects and programmes that support health workers and provide humanitarian disaster assistance.

Geographical Area of Activity: International.

Publications: Annual Report.

Board of Directors: Frédéric Oudéa (Chair.).

Principal Staff: Exec. Dir Vanina Laurent-Ledru.

Contact Details: 46–48 ave de la Grande Armée, 75017 Paris; internet www.foundation-s.sanofi.com/fr.

Fondation Schneider Electric (Schneider Electric Foundation)

Established in 1998 by Schneider Electric SA, an energy supplier, under the aegis of the Fondation de France (q.v.); formerly known as Fondation Schneider Electric pour l'Insertion des Jeunes.

Activities: Main programmes focus on access to energy, fuel poverty and sustainable development. The Foundation supports projects that provide sustainable and practical training; help young people to find work, primarily in the energy sector; and provide sustainable development education. It also assists emergency operations following natural disasters; and encourages employee volunteering. Operates in 80 countries.

Geographical Area of Activity: International.

Publications: *Sustainability Report*.

Principal Staff: Senior Vice Pres., Corporate Citizenship and Institutional Affairs Gilles Vermot Desroches.

Contact Details: c/o Schneider Electric SA, 35 rue Joseph Monier, 92500 Rueil Malmaison; tel. 1-41-29-70-00; e-mail global-foundation@schneider-electric.com; internet www.se.com/fr/fr/about-us/sustainability/foundation.

Fondation Simone et Cino del Duca (Simone and Cino del Duca Foundation)

Founded in 1975 by Simone del Duca, the widow of publisher Cino del Duca; administered by the Institut de France since 2005.

Activities: Works in the fields of science and medicine, and the arts and humanities; and hosts conferences, seminars and other events organized by the Institut de France. In addition to social science grants, the Foundation annually awards three grants, each of €75,000, to teams of young French scientists for a year-long project in a scientific field defined each year. It also awards four prizes each year: a science prize to encourage research, alternating between European and international winners, worth €275,000; the Prix Mondial del Duca, worth €200,000 for writing in the French language; an archaeology prize worth €150,000; and an arts prize worth €100,000, given alternately in the fields of painting, sculpture or musical composition (winners in the other categories receiving €25,000). Each year, the Cancer Prize, of €15,000, is awarded to a young researcher working in France; and literary incentive prizes, of €5,000, are awarded to young French-speaking writers to enable them to continue their work.

Geographical Area of Activity: Worldwide.

Restrictions: Grant applicants must be aged under 45 years.

Publications: Annual Report.

Foundation Committee: Gabriel del Broglie (Chair.).

Contact Details: 10 rue Alfred de Vigny, 75008 Paris; tel. 1-47-66-01-21; e-mail fondation-del-duca@institutdefrance.fr; internet www.fondation-del-duca.fr.

Fondation Singer-Polignac (Singer-Polignac Foundation)

Founded in 1928 by Winnaretta Singer, Princess Edmond de Polignac.

Fondation TotalEnergies   FRANCE

Activities: Works in the fields of science, the arts, humanities and the conservation of nature, awarding grants, scholarships and prizes to individuals and institutions in France. The Foundation awards the Prix des Muses for writing about music and the Singer-Polignac Prize. It also publishes reports on works undertaken under its auspices and organizes lectures, conferences and concerts.

Geographical Area of Activity: France.

Publications: Letters.

Board of Directors: Pierre Corvol (Pres.); Michel Zink (Vice-Chair.); Gilbert Guillaume (Treas.).

Principal Staff: Dir Olivier Le Gal.

Contact Details: 43 ave Georges Mandel, 75116 Paris; tel. 1-47-27-38-66; e-mail infos@singer-polignac.org; internet www.singer-polignac.org.

Fondation TotalEnergies (TotalEnergies Foundation)

Founded in 1992 by TOTAL, an international oil and gas company.

Activities: Carries out activities in the area of civic responsibility. Main programme areas are: road safety; climate, coastal areas and oceans; youth inclusion and education; and cultural dialogue and heritage. Founded (f. 2020) and finances L'Industreet, a campus in Stains in Seine-Saint-Denis offering free training to young people to help them enter professions that are in short supply.

Geographical Area of Activity: International.

Publications: Annual Report; newsletter; books.

Board of Directors: Namita Shah (Chair.).

Principal Staff: CEO Jacques-Emmanuel Saulnier.

Contact Details: 2 pl. Jean Millier, La Défense 6, 92400 Courbevoie; internet www.foundation.totalenergies.com.

Fonds Européen pour la Jeunesse—FEJ (European Youth Foundation—EYF)

Established in 1972 by the Council of Europe; a division in the Youth Department of the Council of Europe's Directorate of Democratic Citizenship and Participation, Directorate General of Democracy.

Activities: Supports youth activities that promote democracy, human rights and the rule of law in accordance with the values of the Council of Europe. Priority areas include: access to rights; youth participation and youth work; and inclusive and peaceful societies. The Foundation offers four kinds of grants: annual work plans for NGOs or networks; international activities, for all apart from local NGOs; pilot activities for local or national NGOs and regional networks; and structural grants, for international NGOs or networks and regional networks. It funds activities on themes such as human rights education and education for democratic citizenship; peacebuilding and conflict transformation; intercultural dialogue; social exclusion, discrimination and xenophobia; young people's autonomy; and empowerment of vulnerable groups.

Geographical Area of Activity: 47 member European countries (European Cultural Convention), Belarus, Holy See, Kazakhstan.

Restrictions: No grants to individuals.

Publications: Annual Report; newsletter; leaflets.

Finance: Annual budget €3.5m. (2023).

Principal Staff: Head of Division Gordana Berjan.

Contact Details: European Youth Centre, 30 rue Pierre de Coubertin, 67000 Strasbourg; tel. 3-88-41-20-19; e-mail eyf@coe.int; internet eyf.coe.int.

Forum International de l'Innovation Sociale—FIIS (International Forum for Social Innovation—IFSI)

Founded in 1976.

Activities: Promotes social innovation and institutional transformation in private or public institutions. The Forum organizes conferences, workshops and training seminars for managers and consultants; and maintains an information centre on social innovation projects. It has developed an international network of consultants, which includes engineers, historians, psychologists, business leaders and designers. Funding is available for young professionals and professionals from the global South to attend seminars and conferences.

Geographical Area of Activity: International.

Publications: *FIIS-IFSI Annual Agenda*; books.

Board of Directors: Michael Gutmann (Pres.); David Gutmann (Vice-Pres.); Raphaël Gutmann (Sec.-Gen.); Sylvie Toral (Treas.).

Contact Details: 60 rue de Bellechasse, 75007 Paris; tel. 1-45-51-39-49; e-mail ifsi.fiis@orange.fr; internet www.ifsi-fiis-conferences.com.

France Amérique Latine—FAL (Latin America France)

Established in 1970 to show solidarity with Unidad Popular, a left-wing political alliance in Chile.

Activities: Works to protect the cultural heritage of and support the peoples of Central and South America. The organization defends human rights and condemns violations of regional indigenous peoples' rights; and fights discrimination towards the region throughout the rest of the world through holding conferences, debates, exhibitions and exchanges. It works to improve literacy and education, healthcare and sanitation, and provides emergency aid in Central and South America.

Geographical Area of Activity: Central and South America, France.

Publications: *Correo de la Semana* (weekly newsletter); *FAL-Mag* (quarterly); *One Culture*; brochure.

Management Committee: Franck Gaudichaud, Renata Molina (Co-Pres); Sophie Thonon-Wesfreid (Deputy Pres.); Fabien Cohen (Sec.-Gen.); Rodrigo Restrepo (Treas.).

Contact Details: 37 blvd Saint-Jacques, 75014 Paris; tel. 1-45-88-20-00; e-mail falnationale@franceameriquelatine.fr; internet www.franceameriquelatine.org.

France-Libertés Fondation Danielle Mitterrand (Danielle Mitterrand Foundation)

Founded in 1986 by Danielle Mitterrand, the widow of former President of France François Mitterrand.

Activities: Operates internationally in the fields of human rights and protecting common goods, raising awareness and building capacity in civil society. Projects focus on: the right to water; water and climate; intensive exploitation of natural resources ('extractivism'); privatization of biodiversity and traditional knowledge ('biopiracy'); indigenous peoples' rights; and programmes for young people in Kurdistan. The Foundation awards an annual prize for efforts to promote a fairer and more united world.

Geographical Area of Activity: International.

Publications: Annual Report; newsletter; *Olivier Unchained* (article).

Finance: Annual budget €1m. (2023).

Board of Directors: Gilbert Mitterrand (Pres.); Jacqueline Madrelle (Vice-Pres.); Emmanuel Poilane (Sec.-Gen.); Achille de Genestoux (Treas.).

Principal Staff: Co-Dir in Charge of Operations Agnès Golfier.

Contact Details: 5 rue Blanche, 75009 Paris; tel. 1-53-25-10-40; e-mail contact@france-libertes.fr; internet fondationdaniellemitterrand.org.

France Nature Environnement

Established in 1968 as the Fédération Française des Sociétés de Protection de la Nature by 18 associations.

Activities: Works to protect nature and the environment through preventing the erosion of biodiversity and overexploitation of resources; defending citizens' right to free expression; and promoting new modes of production and consumption. The organization disseminates information on the state of the environment in the areas of scientific research, conservation of fauna and flora and protection of biodiversity. It operates as a national federation of 46 member associations, with 6,206 affiliated associations.

Geographical Area of Activity: International.

Publications: Annual Report; newsletter; reports.

Finance: Annual revenue €8.7m., expenditure €7.9m. (31 Dec. 2023).

Board of Directors: Antoine Gatet (Pres.).

Principal Staff: CEO Bénédicte Hermelin.

Contact Details: Oasis 21, 2 rue de la Clôture, 75019 Paris; tel. 9-88-19-55-80; e-mail information@fne.asso.fr; internet www.fne.asso.fr.

Frères des Hommes—FDH (Brothers of Men)

Created in 1965; an organization for international solidarity, working in the area of global development.

Activities: Works to reduce poverty and achieve social and climate justice through supporting development projects initiated and implemented by local people. Programmes focus on community-supported farming, community-based economies and a democratic civil society. In France, the organization raises public awareness about sustainable international development.

Geographical Area of Activity: Africa, Asia, Latin America and the Caribbean.

Restrictions: Grants only to partner organizations.

Publications: Annual Report; *Agir*; *Témoignages et Dossiers* (quarterly); *Résonances* (newsletter).

Finance: Annual revenue €2.1m., expenditure €2.5m. (31 Dec. 2023).

Board of Directors: Louise Nimier (Pres.); Luc Michelon (Vice-Pres.); Claude Perseval (Treas.); Marc Fauveau (Sec.).

Principal Staff: Dir Audrey Noury.

Contact Details: 2 rue de Savoie, 75006 Paris; tel. 1-55-42-62-62; e-mail fdh@fdh.org; internet www.fdh.org.

Fulbright France—Commission Fulbright Franco-Américaine (Franco-American Fulbright Commission)

Established in 1948.

Activities: Awards scholarships to French citizens studying or undertaking academic research in the USA; and grants to US graduates and postgraduates with at least five years' professional experience to study, lecture or undertake research in France. The Commission also selects candidates for scholarships awarded by the Georges Lurcy Charitable and Educational Trust (q.v.).

Geographical Area of Activity: France, USA.

Publications: Newsletter.

Board of Directors: Lawrence Randolph, Emmanuel Lebrun-Damiens (Co-Chair.); Michael Turner (Treas.).

Principal Staff: Exec. Dir Martine Roussel.

Contact Details: 9 rue Chardin, 75016 Paris; tel. 1-44-14-53-60; internet fulbright-france.org.

Humanity & Inclusion

Founded in 1982, as Handicap International, by Jean-Baptiste Richardier and Claude Simonnot, two French doctors; present name adopted in 2018.

Activities: Supports programmes to meet the needs and defend the rights of people with disabilities. In countries affected by poverty, disasters and conflicts, the organization implements prevention, emergency relief and mine action projects; and provides long-term development support. National sections operate in Belgium, Canada, France, Germany, Luxembourg, Switzerland, the United Kingdom and the USA; depending on the country, these sections are known as Handicap International or Humanity & Inclusion. The organization has consultative status with ECOSOC; co-founded the International Campaign to Ban Landmines and was joint winner of the 1997 Nobel Peace Prize; and in 2014 established the Fondation Vivre Debout under the aegis of the Université de Lyon to help disabled or vulnerable people affected by conflict, natural disasters, health emergencies or chronic poverty. In 2015 the HI Institute for Humanitarian Action was established, reponsible for the ethical framework underpinning the network's actions. Present in more than 55 countries.

Geographical Area of Activity: International.

Publications: Annual Report; newsletter (quarterly); technical publications; videos.

Finance: Annual income €233.8m., expenditure €224.3m. (31 Dec. 2023).

Board of Directors: Jean-Noël Dargnies (Chair.); Christian Fuchs (Sec.); Claire Vaudray-Radisson (Treas.).

Principal Staff: Global Man. Dir Manuel Patrouillard.

Contact Details: 138 ave des Frères Lumière, CS 88379, 69008 Lyon, Cedex 08; tel. 4-78-69-79-79; e-mail contact@hi.org; internet www.hi.org.

Institut FMES—Institut Méditerranéen d'Etudes Stratégiques (Mediterranean Foundation for Strategic Studies Institute)

Established in 1990 as the Fondation Méditerranéenne d'Etudes Stratégiques; present name adopted in 2016.

Activities: As a think tank, the FMES Institute has two main missions: to educate and to communicate. The FMES carries out missions of general interest in the fields of education and information. It operates through a combination of research and the study of strategic thinking, the analysis of geopolitical issues and through a range of training opportunities on geostrategic issues, provided by the Mediterranean Sessions of Strategic Studies (SMHES).

Geographical Area of Activity: Mediterranean Region, Middle East.

Publications: *Strategic Atlas of the Mediterranean and the Middle East*; *Strategic Perspectives*; newsletter (*FMES News*); articles.

Board of Directors: Charles-Henri du Ché (Pres.); Jean-Michel Clouet (Sec.-Gen.).

Principal Staff: Dir-Gen. Pascal Ausseur.

Contact Details: Maison du Numérique et de l'Innovation, pl. Georges Pompidou, 83000 Toulon; tel. 4-94-05-55-55; e-mail info@fmes-france.org; internet www.fmes-france.org.

Institut Français des Relations Internationales—IFRI (French Institute of International Relations)

Established in 1979 by Thierry de Montbrial, the Director of the French Ministry of Foreign Affairs; an independent think tank.

Activities: Carries out policy-orientated research and analysis through some 15 regional and thematic programmes, including in the areas of: the economy; energy and climate; the geopolitics of technologies; global governance; health; migration and citizenship; security and defence; and space. The Institute hosts debates, organizing around 100 public and member-only events each year. It comprises the African Studies Center, the French-Austrian Center for European Convergence (CFA), the Russia/NIS Center and the Study Committee for French-German relations (CERFA).

Geographical Area of Activity: International.

Publications: Annual Report; newsletter; *Ramses* (annual strategic and economic report); *Politique étrangère* (quarterly journal); policy papers; reports; blogs.

Finance: Annual income €8.8m., expenditure €8.8m. (31 Dec. 2023).

Board of Directors: Dr Thierry de Montbrial (Exec. Chair.); Louis Schweitzer (Deputy Chair.); François Drouin (Treas.).

Principal Staff: Sec.-Gen. Valérie Genin; Dir Thomas Gomart.

Institut de Médecine et d'Epidémiologie Appliquée   FRANCE

Contact Details: 27 rue de la Procession, 75740 Paris Cedex 15; tel. 1-40-61-60-00; e-mail accueil@ifri.org; internet www.ifri.org.

Institut de Médecine et d'Epidémiologie Appliquée—Fondation Internationale Léon Mba (Institute of Applied Medicine and Epidemiology—International Foundation Léon Mba)

Founded in 1968 by the Governments of France and Gabon, according to the wishes of Léon Mba, then President of Gabon, to promote, within the framework of the activities of the Hôpital Claude-Bernard, the advancement of tropical medicine for the benefit of the populations of Black Africa.

Activities: Works in the field of public health in developing countries through conducting basic and clinical research, teaching and evaluation. Research areas include research covering all tropical diseases, with a focus on malaria, viral hepatitis, tuberculosis, sexually transmitted diseases and HIV/AIDS. The Institute provides training and support to health-care professionals and researchers who work in developing countries.

Geographical Area of Activity: Africa, Asia, France, South America.

Publications: Activity Report.

IMEA Board: Prof. François Simon (Chair.).

Supervisory Board: Prof. Olivier Bouchaud (Chair.).

Scientific Council: Prof. Marielle Bouyou Akotet (Chair.).

Contact Details: Hôpital Bichat, 46 rue Henri Huchard, 75018 Paris; tel. 1-40-25-69-58; e-mail imea.dpo@imea.fr; internet imea.fr/info/fondation-international-leon-mba.

Institut Océanographique—Fondation Albert 1er, Prince de Monaco (Oceanographic Institute—Albert I, Prince of Monaco Foundation)

Established in 1906 by Albert I, Prince of Monaco; comprises the Institut Océanographique in Paris and the Musée Océanographique in Monaco.

Activities: Promotes the study of and dissemination of knowledge about oceans and marine ecosystems, highlighting their importance to humans and working to protect them. The Institute organizes symposia, public conferences and exhibitions; and maintains libraries at both centres.

Geographical Area of Activity: France, Monaco.

Publications: Books on marine science.

Finance: Annual income €25.4m., expenditure €21.6m. (2023).

Board of Directors: Philippe Taquet (Pres.); Marie-Pierre Gramaglia (Vice-Pres.); Henri Peretti (Treas./Sec.).

Scientific Council: Dr François Houllier (Pres.); Dr Shubha Sathyendranath (Vice-Pres.); Dr Valérie Davenet (Sec.).

Principal Staff: Man. Dir Robert Calcagno.

Contact Details: Maison des Océans, 195 rue Saint-Jacques, 75005 Paris; tel. 1-44-32-10-70; e-mail institut@oceano.org; internet www.oceano.org.

Institut Pasteur (Pasteur Institute)

Founded in 1886 by Louis Pasteur and incorporated as a foundation in 1887 to promote research into infectious and parasitic diseases, including their prevention and treatment, and into immunity from disease.

Activities: Operates in the field of microbiology and its related disciplines, through research, teaching, prevention and diagnosis of infectious and parasitic diseases; and awarding grants, scholarships and fellowships. The Institute has its own medical centre, which provides international vaccinations as well as specialized consultations (including allergies, tropical diseases and HIV) and maintains a library. It operates through an international network of 33 facilities in 23 countries. WHO has accorded each of the Institute's laboratories the status of regional, national or international centre.

Geographical Area of Activity: Worldwide.

Publications: Annual Report; newsletter; *Research in Microbiology* (10 a year); *Lettre de l'Institut Pasteur* (quarterly); *Annales de l'Institut Pasteur: Actualités* (quarterly); *Microbes and Infection* (15 a year); *Collections des Laboratoires de Référénces et d'expertise* (11-title series of technical publications).

Board of Directors: Yves Saint-Geours (Chair.); Artur Scherf, Stéphanie Fougou (Vice-Chair.); Louis de Franclieu (Treas.); Sandrine Etienne-Manneville (Sec.).

Principal Staff: Dir Prof. Sir Stewart Cole.

Contact Details: 25–28 rue du Docteur Roux, 75015 Paris Cedex; tel. 1-45-68-80-00; e-mail info@pasteur.fr; internet www.pasteur.fr.

Institut Pasteur de Lille (Pasteur Institute of Lille)

Founded in 1899 by the City of Lille for biological and medical research, training and analysis.

Activities: Works in the field of public health through designing and developing treatments, diagnostics, vaccines and prevention protocols. The Institute carries out transdisciplinary and multisectoral research under two main programmes: infectious diseases in the context of emerging epidemic risks and antibiotic resistance; and lifestyle-related metabolic, degenerative and inflammatory diseases, including diabetes, cardiovascular and respiratory disease and neurodegenerative diseases, including senescence, fibrosis and cancer. It offers awards to French and foreign researchers, comprising an international network of 34 affiliated research institutes in 53 countries.

Geographical Area of Activity: International.

Publications: Annual Report; newsletter; *Vivre mieux, plus longtemps* (magazine); books.

Finance: Annual revenue €36.7m., expenditure €37.6m. (31 Dec. 2023).

Board of Directors: Jacques Richir (Pres.); Daniel Leca (Vice-Pres.); Patrick Vacossin (Treas.); Catherine Lefebvre (Sec.).

Principal Staff: Dir-Gen. Didier Bonneau; Gen. Man. Frédéric Batteux.

Contact Details: 1 rue du Professeur Calmette, BP 245, 59019 Lille Cedex; tel. 3-20-87-78-00; e-mail communication@pasteur-lille.fr; internet www.pasteur-lille.fr.

Médecins du Monde International (Doctors of the World International)

Established in 1980; the Fondation des Amis de Médecins du Monde International was founded in 2014 under the aegis of the Fondation de France (q.v.).

Activities: An international network of 17 associations, which provide general medical assistance to people excluded from care systems, including homeless people and rural communities in France and geographically or politically isolated people abroad. Main programmes include: crises and emergencies; sexual and reproductive health; risk reduction; migrants and displaced people; and health and environment. It carries out medical consultations, vaccinations and nutritional monitoring; dispenses medicines; detects diseases; provides pregnancy monitoring and contraception advice; organizes mobile clinics; strengthens local health systems; and trains staff. Present in 74 countries.

Geographical Area of Activity: International.

Publications: Annual Report; newsletter; *Médecins du Monde* (journal); *Revue humanitaire*; bulletins; reports.

Finance: Annual revenue €157.2m., expenditure €120.7m. (31 Dec. 2023).

Board of Directors: Jean-François Corty (Chair.); Dr Françoise Sivignon (Vice-Chair.); Anne Guilberteau (Sec.-Gen.); Dr Marc Tyrant (Treas.).

Principal Staff: Man. Dir Joël Weiler.

Contact Details: 84 ave du President Wilson, CS 20007, 93217 La Plaine Saint-Denis Cedex; tel. 1-44-92-15-15; e-mail medecinsdumonde@medecinsdumonde.net; internet www.medecinsdumonde.org.

Mouvement International ATD Quart-Monde (ATD Fourth World International)

Founded in 1957 by Joseph Wresinksi and families in an emergency homeless camp outside Paris.

Activities: Works to eliminate extreme poverty and exclusion worldwide. Priority areas are: human rights, including protecting families, housing, and health and employment; access to culture, knowledge and education; sustainable economies; participation, through People's Universities, the Tapori children's network, and processes such as Merging Knowledge and participatory research; and mobilizing civil society, through public campaigns, political engagement and international advocacy. ATD Fourth World International has consultative status with ECOSOC, UNICEF, the International Labour Organization and the Council of Europe; and has offices in Switzerland and the USA. It maintains the Joseph Wresinski Archives and Research Centre in Baillet-en-France.

Geographical Area of Activity: Africa, Asia, Europe, North, Central and South America and the Caribbean.

Publications: Newsletter; reports; books.

Finance: Budget approx. €22m. (2025).

Officers: Donald Lee (Australia, Pres.); Jacqueline Plaisir (France, Vice-Pres.); François Groh (France, Treas.).

Principal Staff: Dir-Gen. Mr Bruno Dabout; Exec. Sec. Jean-Charles Watiez.

Contact Details: 12 rue Pasteur, 95480 Pierrelaye; tel. 1-34-30-46-10; e-mail intl.comms@atd-fourthworld.org; internet www.atd-fourthworld.org.

Nitidæ

Established in 2017 by the merger of Rongead—Réseau d'ONG Européennes sur l'Agro-alimentaire, le Commerce, l'Environnement et le Développement (f. 1983) with Etc Terra (f. 2012).

Activities: Works to support economic development, reduce poverty and preserve natural capital in rural Africa, in particular providing technical assistance to agri-food and cosmetics companies. Initiatives include Nitidæ Lab, which carries out spatial and environmental research and analysis; N'kalô, an independent commercial consultancy service for the agri-food sector in Africa; and the Agrovalor Platform, which develops bioenergy projects. The organization has offices in France in Montpellier; and in Burkina Faso, Côte d'Ivoire, Madagascar, Mozambique and Senegal.

Geographical Area of Activity: sub-Saharan Africa.

Publications: Annual Report; brochure; briefings; scientific publications; technical documents; training and educational materials.

Finance: Annual revenue €8m., expenditure €8m. (31 Dec. 2023).

Board of Directors: Denis Loyer (Pres.); Olivier Langrand (Treas.); Emmanuel Gonon (Sec.).

Principal Staff: Co-Dirs Cédric Rabany, Matthieu Tiberghien.

Contact Details: 29 rue Imbert Colomès, 69001 Lyon; tel. 9-73-66-10-17; e-mail contact@nitidae.org; internet www.nitidae.org.

Office International de l'Eau—OiEau (International Office for Water)

Established in 1991 by the merger of the Association Française pour l'Étude des Eaux (f. 1949), the Centre de Formation International à la Gestion des Ressources en Eau (f. 1976) and the Institut de l'Eau (f. 1978).

Activities: Operates internationally in the areas of water conservation, basin management and environmental protection. The organization holds international conferences, training courses, exhibitions and symposia; produces water-related publications; manages water data; and is in charge of the French National Water Training Center. It is the world secretariat of the International Network of Basin Organizations and other institutions involved in water resources management and protection. Has offices in La Souterraine, Limoges and Sophia Antipolis. Has 150 partner organizations in 90 countries and territories.

Geographical Area of Activity: Worldwide.

Publications: Annual Report; *Aquaveille* (newsletter); *Les Nouvelles* (newsletter); *Information Eaux* (magazine); *La Lettre du RIOB* (newsletter); brochures; factsheets; handbooks; technical publications.

Finance: Annual revenue €15.4m. (31 Dec. 2022).

Board of Directors: Pascal Berteaud (Pres.); Eric De La Gueronniere, Guillaume Choisy (Vice-Pres); Arnaud Treguer (Treas.); Jean-Marc Philip (Sec.).

Principal Staff: Man. Dir Éric Tardieu.

Contact Details: 21 rue de Madrid, 75008 Paris; tel. 1-44-90-88-60; e-mail dg@oieau.fr; internet www.oieau.fr.

Organisation Panafricaine de Lutte pour la Santé—OPALS (Pan-African Organization for Health)

Founded in 1988 by Prof. Marc Gentilini as the Organisation Panafricaine de Lutte Contre le SIDA (Pan-African Organization for AIDS Prevention); present name adopted in 2011.

Activities: Works in the fields of maternal and child health and combating fake medicines. The Organisation improves the quality of life of sick people through providing access to comprehensive medical care and upholding their rights in society; supporting public health systems; and offering training to health workers to strengthen basic skills in managing disease of infants and children. It has offices in Guinea and Togo.

Geographical Area of Activity: France, Guinea, Togo.

Publications: Annual Report; newsletter; training materials.

Board of Directors: Prof. Marc Gentilini (Chair.); Prof. Dominique Richard-Lenoble (Sec.-Gen.); Jacques Vaysse (Treas.).

Principal Staff: Sec. Simone Legendre.

Contact Details: 56–58 rue des Morillons, 75015 Paris; e-mail programmes@opals.asso.fr; internet www.opals.asso.fr.

Oxfam France

Established in 1988 as Agir ici pour un monde solidaire; in 2003 it became part of the Oxfam confederation of organizations (qq.v.).

Activities: Works to eliminate injustice and poverty. Areas of interest include: inequalities and tax justice; climate and energy; agriculture and food security; finance for development; migration; and humanitarian and emergency relief. The organization conducts research and advocacy on human rights; organizes campaigns and mobilizes public action on particular issues; and makes policy and regulatory recommendations to authorities. Includes 12 local groups and six charity shops in France.

Geographical Area of Activity: International.

Restrictions: Does not make loans or grants to individuals.

Publications: Annual Report; newsletter; reports; e-books.

Finance: Annual income €16.0m., expenditure €15.6m. (31 March 2024).

Board of Directors: Emilia N'goadmy (Chair.); Frédéric Séguret, Anne Dupraz Poiseau (Vice-Chair.); Alice Moureau (Treas.); Jean-Pierre Petiteau, Titaua Chabanne (Co-Secs).

Principal Staff: Gen. Man. Cécile Duflot.

Contact Details: 62 bis ave Parmentier, 75011 Paris; tel. 1-56-98-24-40; e-mail info@oxfamfrance.org; internet www.oxfamfrance.org.

Partage

Established in 1973 as Comité de Soutien aux Orphelins du Viêtnam by Pierre Marchand to help orphans of the Viet Nam war; registered in 1976 as Partage avec les Enfants du Tiers-Monde. Present name adopted in 1998.

Activities: Works in the fields of education, health, nutrition and protection from abuse. The organization assists individual sponsors in helping children to access essential needs: food and shelter, care, clothing and education. It works with 25 partner organizations in 18 countries.

Geographical Area of Activity: Central and South America and the Caribbean, East Asia, Middle East and North Africa, South Asia, South-East Asia, South-Eastern Europe, sub-Saharan Africa.

Publications: Annual Report; news magazine (quarterly); newsletter (monthly).

Finance: Annual income €11.4m., expenditure €11.5m. (31 Dec. 2023).

Board of Directors: Dominique Bissuel (Chair.); Corinne Loverich-Bouvet (Vice-Chair.); Guillaume Sordet (Treas.); Bertrand Boisselet (Sec.).

Principal Staff: Dir-Gen. Yolaine Guérif.

Contact Details: 40 rue Vivenel, BP 70311, 60203 Compiègne; tel. 3-44-20-92-92; e-mail info@partage.org; internet www.partage.org.

Première Urgence Internationale

Formed in 2011 by the merger of Première Urgence (f. 1992) and Aide Médicale Internationale (f. 1979).

Activities: Works in the field of emergency response, providing humanitarian relief following natural disasters, conflict or economic collapse. Programmes cover: construction and rehabilitation; economic recovery; food security; health; nutrition; and water, sanitation and hygiene. The organization operates in 25 countries.

Geographical Area of Activity: Caribbean, East Asia and South-East Asia, Eastern Europe, France, Middle East and North Africa, sub-Saharan Africa.

Publications: Annual Report; newsletter; reports.

Finance: Annual budget €122.2m. (2023).

Board of Directors: Vincent Basquin (Pres.); Philippe Jouannet (Vice-Pres.); Jean-Philippe Horen (Treas.); Ernst van der Linden (Sec.).

Principal Staff: Gen. Man. Thierry Mauricet.

Contact Details: 2 rue Auguste Thomas, 92600 Asnières-sur-Seine; tel. 1-55-66-99-66; e-mail contact@premiere-urgence.org; internet www.premiere-urgence.org.

Santé Sud (Southern Health)

Founded in 1984 by health professionals; a member of Groupe SOS Santé.

Activities: Operates in the field of assistance to less-developed countries, through long-term projects which provide financial, technical and material aid, especially in the area of healthcare. The organization co-operates with local grassroots organizations. It runs 14 programmes in six countries and has offices in Madagascar, Mauritania, Mayotte, Morocco and Tunisia.

Geographical Area of Activity: Africa, Asia and the Middle East.

Publications: Annual Report; *Santé Sud Infos* (quarterly newsletter); reviews; articles; films.

Finance: Annual revenue €5.3m., expenditure €5.7m. (31 Dec. 2023).

Steering Committee: Marie-Josée Moinier (Chair.).

Principal Staff: Dir-Gen. Benjamin Soudier.

Contact Details: 200 blvd National, le Gyptis Bt N, 13003 Marseille; tel. (4) 91-95-63-45; e-mail contact@santesud.org; internet www.santesud.org.

Secours Catholique—Caritas de France (Catholic Help—Caritas France)

Founded in 1946 by Mgr Jean Rodhain as part of the Caritas Internationalis (q.v.) network.

Activities: Provides aid to developing countries and operates its own programmes in the fields of education, human rights, healthcare and social welfare. The organization offers grants to institutions and funds scholarships and fellowships; and also publishes annual statistical surveys of the extent of poverty in France. It has a network of 72 offices, which co-ordinate 3,500 local teams in France; and three specialized branches for vulnerable people in Paris, Jerusalem and Lourdes.

Geographical Area of Activity: Worldwide.

Publications: *Messages* (monthly); reports.

Finance: Annual revenue €141.5m., expenditure €153.7m. (31 Dec. 2023).

Board of Directors: Didier Duriez (Pres.).

Principal Staff: Dir-Gen. Adélaïde Bertrand.

Contact Details: 106 rue du Bac, 75341 Paris Cedex 7; tel. 1-45-49-73-00; e-mail info@secours-catholique.org; internet www.secours-catholique.org.

SEL—Service d'Entraide et de Liaison (Mutual Aid and Liaison Service)

Established in 1980 by the French Evangelical Alliance, a Christian (Protestant) organization; affiliated with SEL Projets (f. 1989) in Belgium and Alliance Évangélique Romande (f. 1847) in Switzerland.

Activities: Provides aid and assistance to less-developed countries, particularly to children, through local partners. The organization raises public awareness about poverty and aid to developing countries; supports child sponsorship programmes and development projects in the areas of agriculture, health, microcredit, nutrition, and water and sanitation; and offers emergency relief during crises. It works in 26 countries and has offices in Belgium and Switzerland.

Geographical Area of Activity: Worldwide (with a focus on French-speaking African countries and Madagascar).

Publications: Newsletter; *SEL–Informations* (periodical); brochures.

Finance: Annual income €12.3m., expenditure €12.2m. (18 months to 31 Dec. 2023).

Board of Directors: Daniel Babiak (Chair.); Muila Ikiessiba (Vice-Chair.); Jacques Bénétreau (Treas.); Jean-Pierre Bezin (Sec.).

Principal Staff: Gen. Dir Dr Patrick Guiborat.

Contact Details: 157 rue des Blains, 92220 Bagneux; tel. 1-45-36-41-51; e-mail contact@selfrance.org; internet www.selfrance.org.

UNESCO Centre du Patrimoine Mondial (UNESCO World Heritage Centre)

Established in 1992 within UNESCO as the focal point and co-ordinator for all matters relating to World Heritage.

Activities: Supports the identification and preservation of World Heritage sites in five specific areas: preparatory assistance; promotion and education; technical co-operation; emergency assistance; and training. The Centre maintains the World Heritage List, organizes annual sessions of the World Heritage Committee and arranges international assistance from the World Heritage Fund upon request. Other activities include: organizing technical seminars and workshops; updating the World Heritage List and database; and developing teaching materials for young people. Jointly with UNESCO, the United Nations Foundation (q.v.) and Fauna & Flora International, it also manages the Rapid Response Facility small grants programme to protect natural World Heritage sites during crises.

Geographical Area of Activity: International.

Publications: *World Heritage Review* (quarterly magazine); *World Heritage Newsletter* (2 a month); brochures; manuals; papers; reports.

Finance: The Centre receives its income essentially from compulsory contributions from the states parties to the 1972 World Heritage Convention (amounting to 1% of their UNESCO dues) and from voluntary contributions to the World Heritage Fund (around 1% of contributions or at least US $4m.).

Bureau of the World Heritage Committee: H.H. Princess Haifa Al Mogrin (Chair.); Shikha Jain (Rapporteur).

Principal Staff: Dir Lazare Eloundou Assomo; Deputy Dir Jyoti Hosagrahar.

Contact Details: c/o UNESCO, 7 pl. de Fontenoy, 75352 Paris 07 SP; tel. 1-45-68-11-04; e-mail wh-info@unesco.org; internet whc.unesco.org.

THE GAMBIA

CO-ORDINATING BODY

Association of Non-Governmental Organizations in The Gambia—TANGO

Established in 1983; an umbrella body of NGOs and CSOs.

Activities: Works to improve the lives of poor and marginalized people through poverty reduction and sustainable development initiatives. Five thematic working groups cover: gender, poverty and policy issues; climate, agriculture, land and environment; education and life skills; youth, child, health and population; and human rights and governance. The Association comprises more than 80 national and international organizations.

Geographical Area of Activity: The Gambia.

Publications: Reports.

Board: John Charles Njie (Chair.).

Principal Staff: Exec. Dir Ndey S. Bakurin.

Contact Details: c/o Fajara 'M' Section, PMB 392, Serekunda; tel. 9766660; e-mail info@tango.gm; internet www.tango.gm.

FOUNDATIONS AND NON-PROFITS

Fatoumatta Bah-Barrow Foundation—FaBB

Established in 2017 by First Lady Fatoumatta Bah-Barrow.

Activities: Works to reduce extreme poverty and support marginalized rural women, girls and vulnerable children, in particular widows and orphans. The Foundation carries out activities in the areas of women and children's health; women's welfare; vocational and skills training for young people; education; and social development to support people affected by poverty or natural disasters.

Geographical Area of Activity: The Gambia.

Publications: Newsletter.

Board: Fatoumatta Bah-Barrow (Chair.).

Principal Staff: CEO Betty Saine.

Contact Details: Marina Parade 1, Banjul; tel. 7883004; e-mail info@fabbfoundation.gm; internet www.fabbfoundation.gm.

GEORGIA

CO-ORDINATING BODY

Center for Training and Consultancy (Konsultatsiis da Treningis Tsentri)

Established in 1999.

Activities: Supports the institutional development of the not-for-profit sector. The Center offers training and consultancy services in institutional development, capacity building and strategic planning; and provides support through its resource centre. It promotes co-operation between Georgian NGOs and organizations from other Eastern and Western European countries; and has an office in Azerbaijan, with links to Armenia and Kyrgyzstan.

Geographical Area of Activity: Armenia, Azerbaijan, Georgia, Kyrgyzstan.

Publications: Annual Report; directories; reports.

Principal Staff: Exec. Dir Irina Khantadze.

Contact Details: 0186 Tbilisi, 5 Otar Chkheidze Str; tel. (32) 220-67-74; e-mail ctc@ctc.org.ge; internet www.ctc.org.ge.

FOUNDATIONS AND NON-PROFITS

Caucasus Institute for Peace, Democracy and Development—CIPDD (Mshvidobis, Demokratiisa, da Ganvit'arebis Kavkasiuri Instituti)

Established in 1992 as an independent policy research organization.

Activities: Primary areas of research are: regional security; state building; democratization; and civil integration. The Institute's main activities include: public policy research; publishing research results; and organizing debates and roundtable discussions. It hosts an online discussion forum and services for journalists and researchers.

Geographical Area of Activity: Mainly Georgia, but co-operates with organizations in the South Caucasus and Black Sea regions.

Publications: Annual Report; newsletter; periodicals; policy briefs and reports; discussion papers.

Board: Nino Tsintsadze (Chair.).

Principal Staff: Chair. Ghia Nodia; Exec. Dir Avtandil Jokhadze.

Contact Details: 0154 Tbilisi, 72 Tsereteli Ave, 2nd Floor; POB 101, 0108 Tbilisi; tel. (32) 235-51-54; e-mail info@cipdd.org; internet www.cipdd.org.

Civil Society Development Center—CSDC

Established in 2010.

Activities: Supports young people in Georgia and provides educational programmes for people such as those who are internally displaced, young people living in conflict zones, victims of violence, socially unprotected young people, homeless teenage girls and people with special needs. The Center defends women's rights and increases public awareness of women's rights and gender equality. It is a member of several international organizations, including Telecentre and the Eurasian Union, and receives technical and financial assistance from US NGO IREX.

Civil Society Foundation

Geographical Area of Activity: Georgia.

Principal Staff: Exec. Dir Nino Todua.

Contact Details: 0177 Tbilisi, 28/1 Al. Kazbegi Ave; tel. 509900; e-mail info@csdc.ge; internet csdc.ge.

Civil Society Foundation

Established in 1994 as OSGF—Open Society Georgia Foundation; an independent foundation.

Activities: Works to strengthen civil society and hold government accountable to citizens through grantmaking, advocacy, litigation and awareness-raising campaigns. Main programme areas are: EU integration; human rights; media; national integration; participatory democracy; and public health. The Foundation organizes conferences and issues publications.

Geographical Area of Activity: Georgia.

Restrictions: Grants only to NGOs registered in Georgia; does not award travel grants.

Publications: Annual Report; assessments; guidelines; reports; studies; blog.

Finance: Total investments since 1994 over US $100m. (2021).

Principal Staff: Exec. Dir Keti Khutsishvili; Deputy Exec. Dir Hatia Jinjikhadze.

Contact Details: 0108 Tbilisi, 4A Chovelidze Str; tel. (32) 225-04-63; e-mail Contact@csf.ge; internet csf.ge.

Europe Foundation—EPF (Evropis Pondis)

Established in 2008; part of the Eurasia Foundation (q.v.) network.

Activities: Works in the fields of social justice and economic prosperity, promoting co-operation between the Government, civil society and businesses. Main programme areas are: public accountability and civil monitoring of state, business and donor organizations; promotion of corporate and public philanthropy; evidence-based advocacy and public policy development; cross-border and intercommunity co-operation; gender equality; and youth integration. Through the Open Door Grant Program, it funds NGO projects that strengthen civic engagement; grants are typically in the range of 50,000 lari–60,000 lari.

Geographical Area of Activity: South Caucasus.

Restrictions: Grants only for long-term development projects, not emergency or short-term humanitarian assistance.

Publications: Annual Report; newsletter; reports; surveys.

Finance: Total assets US $2.1m. (31 Dec. 2022).

Principal Staff: Pres. Ketevan Vashakidze; Vice-Pres. Nino Khurtsidze.

Contact Details: 0179 Tbilisi, 2nd Floor, 3 Kavsadze St; tel. (32) 225-39-42; e-mail info@epfound.ge; internet www.epfound.ge.

Georgian Foundation for Strategic and International Studies (Rondeli Foundation)—GFSIS (Sakartvelos Strategiisa da Saertashoriso Urtiertobebis Kvlevis Pondi—Rondelis Pondi)

Established in 1998 by Alexander Rondeli, an international relations scholar, and Temuri Yakobashvili, a diplomat and founder and President of the New International Leadership Institute; a non-profit policy think tank.

Activities: Works to improve public policy decisionmaking, promoting democracy and regional co-operation. The Foundation carries out research and analysis; trains policymakers and policy analysts; and informs the public about the strategic issues affecting Georgia and the Caucasus. The Russia Monitor programme focuses on the foreign strategy of the Russian Federation. It organizes conferences and seminars in collaboration with other research institutions and government organizations; and carries out joint projects with research and educational institutions regionally and internationally. The Foundation broadens opportunities for young specialists from governmental and non-governmental organizations to participate in policy planning and decisionmaking, offering free evening classes in economics, foreign policy and international security, taught by international and local specialists. Has a branch in Akhalkakali.

Geographical Area of Activity: Caucasus region.

Publications: Annual Report; *China in the South Caucasus*; China Radar; *Georgian Economic Review*; *Middle East Review*; *North Caucasus Review*; *Russian Policies in the Post-Soviet Space*; *My World*; *Russian Military Digest*; *Russian Military Transformation Tracker*; *Security Review*; expert opinion papers; policy briefs; research; policy documents; blogs.

Finance: Total assets 4m. lari (31 Dec. 2023).

Board: Temuri Yakobashvili (Founder, Chair.).

Principal Staff: Pres. Ekaterine Metreveli.

Contact Details: 0108 Tbilisi, 3A Sh. Chitadze St; tel. (32) 247-35-55; e-mail info@gfsis.org; internet www.gfsis.org.

Media Development Foundation—MDF (Mediis Ganvitarebis Pondi)

Established in 2008 by a group of professional journalists.

Activities: Works to protect freedom of speech and expression. The Foundation advocates for human rights; promotes ethical journalism and media accountability; and supports media literacy, a diverse and inclusive society, gender equality, youth initiatives and civil activism. It maintains the fact-checking website Myth Detector, a partner of the Atlantic Council's DisinfoPortal online platform.

Geographical Area of Activity: Georgia.

Publications: Newsletter; reports.

Finance: Annual income €837,268, expenditure €1,340.9m. (2023).

Board: Tamar Khorbaladze (Chair.).

Principal Staff: Exec. Dir Tamar Kintsurashvili.

Contact Details: 0179 Tbilisi, Mtskheti Alley I, #6, 2nd Floor, Besik Burkiashvili Alley 1, #6; tel. (32) 211-20-26; e-mail info@mdfgeorgia.ge; internet www.mdfgeorgia.ge.

GERMANY

CO-ORDINATING BODIES

Bundesverband Deutscher Stiftungen eV (Association of German Foundations)

Established in 1948 by Prof. Dr Baron von Pölnitz, Ludwig Kastner and Prof. K. Franz.

Activities: Provides information about German foundations; publishes directories, books, reports, brochures and leaflets; organizes conferences, exhibitions and training for foundation staff. The Association maintains a database, with 25,777 entries for foundations in Germany, and works internationally with similar national and international organizations. It hosts the European Community Foundation Initiative (q.v.) and is a member of Philea (q.v.).

Geographical Area of Activity: Germany.

Restrictions: Not a grantmaking organization.

Publications: Annual Report; newsletter; *Verzeichnis Deutscher Stiftungen*; *StiftungsRatgeber*; *StiftungsReport*; *Stiftungsfokus*; *StiftungsWelt* (quarterly magazine).

Finance: Annual income €6.8m., expenditure €6.1m. (31 Dec. 2023).

Board of Directors: Annette Heuser (Chair.); Ansgar Wimmer (Deputy Chair.).

Principal Staff: Sec.-Gen. Friederike v. Bünau.

Contact Details: Karl-Liebknecht-Stra. 34, 10178 Berlin; tel. (30) 897947-0; e-mail post@stiftungen.org; internet www.stiftungen.org.

European Community Foundation Initiative—ECFI

Established in 2016 in partnership with the Centrum pre Filantropiu (q.v.) in Slovakia; hosted by the Bundesverband Deutscher Stiftungen (q.v.).

Activities: Promotes and strengthens community foundations and community foundation support organizations. The Initiative acts as a central point of contact, providing opportunities for peer learning and knowledge building; carrying out mapping and analysis of community foundation activities; and disseminating information. It maintains an atlas of community foundations.

Geographical Area of Activity: Europe.

Restrictions: Not a grantmaking organization.

Publications: Newsletter; guides.

Principal Staff: Co-ordinating Dir Kathrin Dombrowski.

Contact Details: c/o Bundesverband Deutscher Stiftungen, Karl-Liebknecht-Straße 34, 10178 Berlin; tel. (30) 897947-0; e-mail info@communityfoundations.eu; internet www.communityfoundations.eu.

F20 (Foundations Platform—F20)

Established in 2017 as a G20 platform of foundations.

Activities: Active in the fields of climate change and sustainability, working towards implementing the 2030 Agenda for Sustainable Development, its 17 Sustainable Development Goals and the 2015 Paris Agreement on climate change. Main programme areas include: climate action; resilient societies; and global responsibility. The platform comprises a network of more than 80 foundations and philanthropic organizations operating within and beyond the G20 countries.

Geographical Area of Activity: International.

Publications: Annual Report; reports; policy briefings.

Finance: Annual income €540,202, expenditure €512,330 (2024).

Steering Group: Raisa Cole (Chair.); Maria Netto (Co-Chair.).

Principal Staff: Sec.-Gen. Karina Harvey.

Contact Details: c/o Umweltstiftung Michael Otto, Glockengießerwall 26, 20095 Hamburg; tel. (667) 61934713; e-mail info@foundations-20.org; internet www.foundations-20.org.

Initiative Bürgerstiftungen (Alliance of Community Foundations Germany)

Established in 2001 to support new community foundations in Germany and professionalize existing ones; a project of the Bundesverband Deutscher Stiftungen (q.v.).

Activities: Promotes the development of community foundations in Germany. The Alliance provides mentoring, coaching, consultancy and advice to community foundations; an annual grants programme to support operating costs for selected community foundations; and a travel fund for community foundation practitioners. It organizes regional meetings, seminars and workshops; and carries out research, including an annual survey of the community foundation sector in Germany.

Geographical Area of Activity: Germany.

Publications: Newsletter (monthly); factsheets; information resources; books.

Board of Directors: Friederike von Bünau (Chair.); Ansgar Wimmer (Deputy Chair.).

Principal Staff: Dir Ulrike Reichart.

Contact Details: c/o Bundesverband Deutscher Stiftungen, Haus Deutscher Stiftungen, Mauerstr. 93, 10117 Berlin; tel. (30) 897947-90; e-mail info@buergerstiftungen.org; internet www.buergerstiftungen.org.

International Civil Society Centre

Established in 2007 by Peter Eigen and Burkhard Gnärig.

Activities: Works to achieve the UN's Sustainable Development Goals through carrying out research and capacity building, co-ordinating partnerships, incubating initiatives, and providing trend scanning and innovation. The Centre brings together the leaders of 30 international CSOs working in the fields of human rights, social justice, and humanitarian and environmental issues. It offers consultancy on management and leadership skills; and organizes conferences, meetings and retreats.

Geographical Area of Activity: International.

Publications: Newsletter; *Disrupt & Innovate* (blog); sector guide; research reports.

Finance: Annual income €1.7m., expenditure €1.6m. (31 Dec. 2021).

Board of Trustees: Caroline Harper (Chair.).

Principal Staff: Exec. Dir Dr Wolfgang Jamann.

Contact Details: Agricolastr. 26, 10555 Berlin; tel. (30) 2062469711; e-mail mail@icscentre.org; internet www.icscentre.org.

Maecenata Stiftung (Maecenata Foundation)

Established in 2010 as the legal representative for the Maecenata Institute (f. 1997) and the former Maecenata International (f. 2002).

Activities: A think tank for civil society and philanthropy. The main programmes comprise: the Maecenata Institute for Philanthropy and Civil Society, an independent academic research and policy centre; and the Transnational Giving programme, the German partner in the Transnational Giving Europe (q.v.) network, which facilitates cross-border giving worldwide by enabling donors to obtain tax breaks in their country of residence, and participates in debates on legal restrictions and combating money laundering and financing of terrorism. Other permanent programmes include the Tocqueville Forum, a programme for networking, support and dialogue between civil society and other players in society (also home to the Maecenata library and Europe Bottom-Up, a programme for European unification); and the MENA Study Centre. The foundation is active in publishing, teaching and lecturing on civil society and philanthropy issues.

Geographical Area of Activity: Worldwide.

Restrictions: Does not accept unsolicited applications for the Transnational Giving programme.

Publications: Annual Report; *Maecenata Newsletter* (monthly); *Maecenata Observatorium*; *Maecenata Schriften* (book series); *Opuscula*; *Europa Bottom-Up*.

Finance: 95% funded by donations from the Transnational Giving programme.

Supervisory Board: Stephanie Wahl (Chair.).

Principal Staff: Exec. Dir Ansgar Gessner.

Contact Details: Oberföhringerstr. 18, 81679 Munich; tel. (30) 28387909; e-mail mst@maecenata.eu; internet www.maecenata.eu.

Stifterverband für die Deutsche Wissenschaft eV (Donors' Association for the Promotion of Sciences and Humanities)

Founded in 1920 and re-established in 1949 by 61 national industrial and commercial organizations.

Activities: Operates nationally in the fields of: children and young people's education; science education and co-operation and exchange between science, business and civil society; and German innovation and setting research policy. The Association has around 3,500 members, comprising companies, associations and individuals making donations on an annual basis. Administers 680 trusts and foundations.

Geographical Area of Activity: International.

Publications: Annual Report; newsletter; *Wirtschaft und Wissenschaft* (quarterly); *Forschung & Entwicklung* (annual); reports.

Finance: Annual expenditure on programmes, initiatives and science funding €32.1m. (2023).

Board: Michael Kaschke (Pres.); Volker Meyer-Guckel (Sec.-Gen.).

Contact Details: Baedekerstr. 1, 45128 Essen; tel. (201) 84010; e-mail mail@stifterverband.de; internet www.stifterverband.de.

VENRO—Verband Entwicklungspolitik und Humanitäre Hilfe deutscher Nichtregierungsorganizationen (Association for Development Policy and Humanitarian Aid)

Established in 1995.

Activities: Works to overcome global inequality and poverty, to ensure human rights and preserve nature. Working groups monitor policy processes and develop joint positions in the areas of: 2030 Agenda; children's rights and development co-operation; climate change and development; co-financing; disability and development; fragile states; gender; global structural policy; health; humanitarian aid; impact orientation; local and global education; strengthening civil society; and transparency. The Association advocates for the interests of international development and humanitarian NGOs; strengthens the role of civil society in development policy; and raises public awareness about sustainable development. It has 144 members.

Geographical Area of Activity: Germany.

Publications: Newsletter; handouts; position papers; blog.

Finance: Annual income €2.5m., expenditure €2.4m. (2023).

Board: Michael Herbst (Chair.); Angela Bähr, Carsten Montag (Vice-Chair.).

Principal Staff: Man. Dir Åsa Månsson.

Contact Details: Geschäftsstelle Stresemannstr. 72, 10963 Berlin; tel. (30) 2639299-10; e-mail sekretariat@venro.org; internet www.venro.org.

Ziviler Friedensdienst—ZFD (Civil Peace Service—CPS)

Established in 1999.

Activities: Works to prevent violence and promote peace in regions in conflict; and resolve conflicts through non-violent means. The Service comprises the CPS Consortium, which co-ordinates the activities of member NGO and government agencies, including: Aktionsgemeinschaft Dienst für den Frieden; AGIAMONDO; Brot für die Welt; EIRENE—Internationaler Christlicher Friedensdienst; Forum Ziviler Friedensdienst (forumZFD); GIZ Deutsche Gesellschaft für Internationale Zusammenarbeit; KURVE Wustrow -Bildungs- und Begegnungsstätte für gewaltfreie Aktion; Peace Brigades International Deutschland; and Weltfriedensdienst. The organizations have about 380 international peace workers in conflict management working in 45 countries with 580 partner organizations.

Geographical Area of Activity: Central and South America, Central and South-Eastern Europe, East and South-East Asia, Eastern Europe, Middle East, sub-Saharan Africa.

Publications: Newsletter; reports; factsheets; manuals.

Finance: Funded by German peace and development organizations and the German Ministry for Economic Cooperation and Development; annual funding €60m. (2024).

Contact Details: Consortium CPS c/o Aktionsgemeinschaft Dienst für den Frieden (AGDF), Endenicher Str. 41, 53115 Bonn; tel. (228) 24999-0; e-mail kontakt@ziviler-friedensdienst.org; internet www.ziviler-friedensdienst.org.

FOUNDATIONS AND NON-PROFITS

Aid to the Church in Need—ACN International

Founded in 1947 by Fr Werenfried van Straaten; a Pontifical Foundation since 2011.

Activities: Provides assistance to the Catholic Church where its members are persecuted or in need, with a focus on helping local churches. Offers funding for the training of seminarians, and for nuns and lay people in areas lacking priests; for the Catholic media; for the distribution of religious material novices and clergy; for the construction of churches; and offers emergency assistance. The organization supports persecuted, oppressed and poor Catholics, members of the Russian Orthodox Church and refugees, regardless of religion. It works in nearly 138 countries and has national offices in 23 countries in Europe, North and South America, and Australia.

Geographical Area of Activity: International.

Restrictions: Grants for faith-related projects only.

Publications: Annual Report; *Religious Freedom Report Worldwide*.

Finance: Annual income €143.7m., expenditure €144.5m. (2023).

Supervisory Board: Cardinal Mauro Piacenza (Pres.).

Administrative Council: Regina Lynch (Exec. Pres.).

Principal Staff: Sec.-Gen. Philipp Ozores.

Contact Details: Postfach 1209, 61452 Königstein/Ts; tel. (6174) 2910; e-mail projects@acn-intl.org; internet www.acn-intl.org.

Alexander von Humboldt Stiftung (Alexander von Humboldt Foundation)

Established in 1860 as a private foundation in memory of the naturalist Alexander von Humboldt; re-established as a public foundation under private law in 1925 and again in 1953.

Activities: Promotes academic co-operation between scientists and scholars from abroad and from Germany. The Foundation maintains a network of more than 30,000 Humboldtians from all disciplines in over 140 countries worldwide, including Nobel Prize winners. Annually awards more than 800 research fellowships and awards for scientists and scholars from abroad to work on research projects with hosts and collaborative partners in Germany. Programmes include the Humboldt Research Fellowship, for postdoctoral and experienced researchers; the Georg Forster Research Fellowship, for postdoctoral and experienced researchers from developing countries; the Feodor Lynen Research Fellowship, for postdoctoral and experienced researchers in Germany going abroad; the Humboldt Research Award, for foreign researchers; the Alexander von Humboldt Professorship, for internationally recognized, innovative researchers; the Sofja Kovalevskaja Award, for outstanding junior researchers; and the Friedrich Wilhelm Bessel Research Award, for internationally renowned scientists and scholars.

Geographical Area of Activity: Worldwide.

Publications: Annual Report; newsletter; *Bibliographia Humboldtiana* (online); *Humboldt Kosmos* (magazine); *Profile and Services* (brochure); *Alexander von Humboldt Professorship* (brochure); *EURAXESS Germany—National Co-ordination Point at the Alexander von Humboldt Foundation* (flyer).

Finance: Total assets €27.2m.; net annual income €163.7m. (31 Dec. 2023).

Board of Trustees: Prof. Dr Robert Schlögl (Pres.).

Principal Staff: Acting Sec.-Gen. Dr Thomas Hesse.

Contact Details: Jean-Paul-Str. 12, 53173 Bonn; tel. (228) 833-0; e-mail info@avh.de; internet www.humboldt-foundation.de.

GERMANY

Alfred Toepfer Stiftung FVS (Alfred Toepfer Foundation FVS)

Founded in 1931 as the Stiftung F. V. S. zu Hamburg by Dr Alfred Toepfer, a business person and farmer, to promote European unity and understanding between nations.

Activities: Operates in Europe in the fields of the arts, science, humanities, young people, European relations and the conservation of natural resources, through self-conducted programmes, scholarships and grants to institutions. The Foundation makes four awards annually for achievements in the field of European relations. It also operates an extensive scholarship programme for students from Central and Eastern Europe.

Geographical Area of Activity: Europe.

Publications: Annual Report; newsletter; *Jahrbuch Alfred Toepfer Stiftung FVS* (yearbook); articles; essays; speeches; books on the Foundation's history and prizes.

Finance: Total assets €99.0m.; net annual income €786,275 (30 June 2023).

Board of Trustees: Marlehn Thieme (Chair.); Prof. Dr Georg Toepfer (Vice-Chair.).

Board of Directors: Ansgar Wimmer (Chair.).

Contact Details: Georgplatz 10, 20099 Hamburg; tel. (40) 33402-10; internet www.toepfer-stiftung.de.

Alfried Krupp von Bohlen und Halbach-Stiftung (Alfried Krupp von Bohlen und Halbach Foundation)

Founded in 1967 by the will of Dr Alfried Krupp von Bohlen und Halbach, owner of Friedrich Krupp AG, a heavy industry company.

Activities: Carries out self-conducted projects in the fields of scientific research and teaching (including the fostering of young scientific talent); education and training; health services; sport; and literature, music and the fine arts. The Foundation offers grants and fellowships (including an Internship Programme for students of Stanford University, CA, USA, to train in Germany, and a China Studies Programme for German students to spend a year of study in the People's Republic of China). It also awards an annual environmental prize. In 2023 annual grants disbursed amounted to approximately €8.5m.

Geographical Area of Activity: International.

Finance: Total assets €800m. (31 Dec. 2023).

Board of Trustees: Prof. Dr Dr Ursula Gather (Chair.); Prof. Dr Dr Christoph M. Schmidt (Deputy Chair.).

Contact Details: Hügel 15, 45133 Essen; POB 23 02 45, 45070 Essen; tel. (201) 188-1; e-mail info@krupp-stiftung.de; internet www.krupp-stiftung.de.

Allianz Foundation

Established in 2000 by Allianz AG (now Allianz SE), a financial services company as Allianz Kulturstiftung; merged with Allianz Umweltstiftung in 2022.

Activities: The Foundation aims to fight social discrimination, supporting particularly those in civil society in the fields of the environment, arts, culture, and local communities. Also supports people fleeing violence and seeking refuge in Europe. Offers grants in the range of €80,000 to €150,000 per year for a period of up to two years.

Geographical Area of Activity: Europe.

Restrictions: No grants to individuals.

Publications: Newsletter.

Finance: Initial capital €50m.

Board: Dr Werner Zedelius (Chair.); Prof. Dr Bénédicte Savoy (Deputy Chair.).

Principal Staff: CEO Christian Humborg.

Contact Details: Pariser Platz 6, 10117 Berlin; tel. (30) 20915731-30; internet allianzfoundation.org.

Arbeiterwohlfahrt Bundesverband eV—AWO (Federal Association of Social Welfare Organizations)

Founded in 1919.

Activities: Organizes and finances social welfare programmes, in particular counselling and advice services. The Foundation operates 18,000 facilities and services, including sheltered accommodation, dormitories for immigrants, healthcare facilities, women's shelters, day centres and counselling centres; and runs training courses for social workers and educational programmes for adults. It co-operates with social welfare organizations at national and international level, including development, aid and disaster relief projects in Eastern Europe, Asia, and Central and South America.

Geographical Area of Activity: Mainly Germany, some work carried out internationally.

Publications: Annual Report; newsletter; *Theorie und Praxis* (monthly); *Sozialprism* (monthly); directory; monographs; handbooks; yearbook; blog.

Board of Directors: Claudia Mandrysch (Chair.).

Principal Staff: Pres Kathrin Sonnenholzner, Michael Groß.

Contact Details: Heinrich-Albertz-Haus, Blücherstr. 62–63, 10961 Berlin; tel. (30) 26309-0; e-mail info@awo.org; internet www.awo.org.

ASKO Europa-Stiftung (ASKO Europe Foundation)

Established in 1990 by retail company ASKO Deutsche Kaufhaus AG; the Foundation became an independent entity in 1996 when ASKO Deutsche Kaufhaus AG merged with METRO AG.

Activities: Works to strengthen a united, democratic, sustainable, peaceful and free Europe through promoting scientific, educational or other institutions and organizations that focus on European integration. The Foundation supports training for junior and senior leaders, in particular from the commercial and service sectors; innovative projects in the fields of science, education and research; events, seminars and conferences; university studies and further education.

Geographical Area of Activity: Europe.

Restrictions: No scholarships to individuals.

Publications: Annual Report; *AES-Aktuell* (newsletter); *Denkart Europa*; discussion papers.

Board of Trustees: Dr med. Rainer G. Hanselmann (Chair.); David Lembert (Vice-Chair.).

Contact Details: Pestelstr. 2, 66119 Saarbrücken; tel. (681) 92674-0; e-mail info@asko-europa-stiftung.de; internet www.asko-europa-stiftung.de.

Aventis Foundation

Established in 1996 by life sciences company Hoechst AG and formerly known as the Hoechst Foundation; present name adopted in 2000.

Activities: Supports projects in areas including fine arts, civil society and science through offering grants to organizations. Special funds operate in the field of education, offering grants to gifted students in need, and for scientific research. It has an office in Berlin.

Geographical Area of Activity: International.

Restrictions: Does not accept individual scholarship applications.

Publications: Annual Report; newsletter.

Finance: Total assets €68.6m.; annual disbursements €1.9m. (31 Dec. 2023).

Board of Trustees: Prof. Dr Günther Wess (Chair.).
Board of Directors: Joachim Schwind (Chair.).

Principal Staff: Exec. Dir Ulrike Hattendorff.

Contact Details: Industriepark Höchst, 65926 Frankfurt am Main; tel. (69) 3057256; e-mail info@aventis-foundation.org; internet www.aventis-foundation.org.

Axel-Springer-Stiftung (Axel Springer Foundation)

Founded in 1953 by Axel Springer, a publishing company.

Activities: Supports all branches of learning through grants for research work; publications (printing of PhD theses, especially about German-Jewish history, the Third Reich, history of the media, international relations); conferences; and courses of further education. The Foundation supports poor elderly journalists and actors in need as a result of sickness; youth welfare; and restoration of monuments and religious buildings. It also encourages good relations between Germany and Israel by supporting youth and student exchanges.

Geographical Area of Activity: Eastern Europe, Germany, Israel.

Restrictions: Grants only for printing monographs or other publications in exceptional cases.

Board of Directors: Dr h.c. Friede Springer (Chair.).

Principal Staff: Exec. Dir Dr Erik Lindner.

Contact Details: Pacelliallee 55, 14195 Berlin; tel. (30) 8441410-50; e-mail erik.lindner@axelspringerstiftung.de; internet www.axelspringerstiftung.de.

Beisheim Stiftung (Beisheim Foundation)

Established in 1976, as the Professor Otto Beisheim-Stiftung, by Prof. Otto Beisheim, founder of Metro AG, a retail and wholesale group.

Activities: Funds projects in the fields of education, health, culture and sport. The Foundation promotes entrepreneurship and culture, particularly in Germany, by funding symposia and colloquia, donating art exhibits and funding chairs in entrepreneurship at German universities. It established the Otto Beisheim Graduate School of Management (WHU) in Vallendar, Germany; and promotes the use of new technologies, including funding the first Swiss Internet House. It has a sister foundation in Switzerland.

Geographical Area of Activity: Europe.

Executive Board: Dr Fredy Raas (Chair.); Hugo Trütsch (Vice-Chair.).

Principal Staff: Man. Dirs Ulf Matysiak, Max Wagner.

Contact Details: Maximilianstr. 35c, 80539 Munich; tel. (89) 215427-900; e-mail kontakt@beisheim-stiftung.com; internet www.beisheim-stiftung.com.

Berghof Stiftung für Konfliktforschung gGmbH (Berghof Foundation gGmbH)

Founded in 1971 by Prof. Dr Georg Zundel, a biophysicist and peace activist.

Activities: Works to move conflict away from violence and towards sustainable peace through self-conducted projects in the areas of: mediation and negotiation support; inclusivity and participation in peace processes; peace education; dialogue approaches; and collaborative research.

Geographical Area of Activity: International.

Publications: Annual Report; newsletter; *Berghof Papers*; *Berghof Handbook for Conflict Transformation*; *The Berghof Glossary on Conflict Transformation*; *Transitions Series*; handbooks; policy briefs; reports; books.

Finance: Total assets €8.3m. (31 Dec. 2023).

Board of Trustees: Johannes Zundel (Chair.).

Principal Staff: Exec. Dir Chris Coulter.

Contact Details: Lindenstr. 34, 10969 Berlin; tel. (30) 844154-0; e-mail info@berghof-foundation.org; internet www.berghof-foundation.org.

Bertelsmann Stiftung (Bertelsmann Foundation)

Established in 1977 by Reinhard Mohn, head of Bertelsmann AG, a publishing company.

Activities: Works in the fields of society, education, economy, culture, democracy and health. The Foundation awards the Reinhard Mohn Prize annually for social innovation. It has established several sister and subsidiary organizations: Bertelsmann Foundation North America (f. 2008) in Washington, DC, and Fundación Bertelsmann (f. 2014) in Barcelona; and, in Germany, the CHE Center for University Development, Founders Foundation, Liz Mohn Culture and Music Foundation, PHINEO, German Stroke Foundation, Reinhard Mohn Institute and Center for Digital Education and Schools.

Geographical Area of Activity: Europe, USA.

Restrictions: An operating foundation; does not accept unsolicited applications.

Publications: Annual Report; newsletter (3–4 a year); *change* (magazine); brochures; reports; blog; e-books.

Finance: Annual income €163.0m., expenditure €75.6m. (2023).

Board of Directors: Dr Hannes Ametsreiter (Chair.).

Contact Details: Carl-Bertelsmann-Str. 256, 33311 Gütersloh; tel. (5241) 810; e-mail info@bertelsmann-stiftung.de; internet www.bertelsmann-stiftung.de.

BMW Foundation Herbert Quandt

Founded in 1970 by BMW AG, a motor vehicle manufacturer, in recognition of engineer and industrialist Herbert Quandt, who secured the independence and succesful development of the company.

Activities: Promotes responsible leadership and advances the UN 2030 Agenda for Sustainable Development. The Foundation inspires leaders through international leadership programmes and connects them through its Responsible Leaders Network. It promotes venture philanthropy and impact investing as tools for social change. Has an office in Munich.

Geographical Area of Activity: International.

Restrictions: No unsolicited applications; no scholarships or other financial support.

Publications: Annual Report; newsletter; *TwentyThirty.com* (online magazine).

Finance: Annual income €13.5m., expenditure €13.4m. (31 Dec. 2021).

Board of Trustees: Dr Nicolas Peter (Chair.).

Contact Details: Reinhardtstr. 58, 10117 Berlin; tel. (30) 33963500; e-mail info@bmw-foundation.org; internet bmw-foundation.org.

Boehringer Ingelheim Fonds—Stiftung für medizinische Grundlagenforschung (Foundation for Basic Research in Biomedicine)

Established in 1983 by the companies C. H. Boehringer Sohn and Boehringer Ingelheim International; fully funded by the Boehringer Ingelheim Stiftung, a sister organization.

Activities: Funds biomedical research through four main programmes: PhD fellowships for pre-doctoral fellows working on projects in basic biomedical research; fellowships for medical students carrying out experimental research; travel grants for pre- and postdoctoral researchers who wish to learn new methods by visiting other laboratories or taking practical courses; and inviting researchers from different sub-disciplines to three-day International Titisee Conferences to discuss trends and new lines of research in the life sciences.

Geographical Area of Activity: Europe and overseas (supports Europeans in Europe and overseas; and scientists from overseas working in Europe).

Restrictions: Does not make grants to scientific institutions; nor for the payment of staff, overheads, equipment or materials.

Publications: *B.I.F.—FUTURA* (3 a year).

Finance: All funding comes from the Boehringer Ingelheim Foundation, an independent sister foundation. Annual expenditure €6.1m. (2023).

Executive Committee: Prof. Dr Jan-Michael Peters (Chair.); Prof. Dr Thomas Braun (Deputy Chair.).

Principal Staff: Man. Dirs Dr Stephan Formella, Marc Wittstock.

Contact Details: Schusterstr. 46–48, 55116 Mainz; tel. (6131) 27508-0; e-mail secretariat@bifonds.de; internet www.bifonds.de.

Bundeskanzler-Willy-Brandt-Stiftung (Federal Chancellor Willy Brandt Foundation)

Established in 1994 by the German Bundestag in honour of former Chancellor Willy Brandt.

Activities: Seeks to contribute to an understanding of the history of the 20th century and of the development of the Federal Republic of Germany. The Foundation promotes the ideals of Willy Brandt in the areas of the peace, freedom and unity of the German people; the safeguarding of democracy; and understanding and reconciliation between nations. It conducts research; organizes conferences and training courses; maintains two permanent exhibitions, in Berlin and Lübeck; and offers the Willy Brandt Prize for the Advancement of Rising Young Scholars, the biennial Willy Brandt Prize for Contemporary History and two short-term scholarships, awarded annually under the Willy Brandt Small Research Grant programme.

Geographical Area of Activity: International.

Publications: Annual Report; newsletter; *Edition Willy Brandt—Berliner Ausgabe; Willy-Brandt-Dokumente; Willy-Brandt-Studien; Schriftenreihe der Bundeskanzler-Willy-Brandt-Stiftung.*

Finance: Annual income €3.0m., expenditure €2.7m. (2023).

Board of Trustees: Dr h.c. Wolfgang Thierse (Chair.).

Board of Directors: Prof. Dr Ulrich Schöler (Chair.).

Principal Staff: Dir Dr Wolfram Hoppenstedt.

Contact Details: Wilhelmstr. 43, 10117 Berlin; tel. (30) 787707-0; e-mail info@willy-brandt.de; internet www.willy-brandt.de.

Brot für die Welt—Evangelisches Werk für Diakonie und Entwicklung (Bread for the World—Protestant Work for Social Welfare and Development)

Founded in 1959 by Protestant churches in Germany; in 2012, it merged with Diakonie Deutschland–Evangelischer Bundesverband.

Activities: Works in the fields of international development and relief. It supports local partners' projects to empower poor and marginalized people in 76 countries. Programmes include food security, health promotion and education, access to water, strengthening democracy, human rights and peace. Its sister organization Diakonie Katastrophenhilfe (f. 1954) provides emergency humanitarian assistance.

Geographical Area of Activity: International.

Publications: Annual Report.

Finance: Annual income €331.5m., expenditure €316.7m. (31 Dec. 2023).

Principal Staff: Chief Exec. Dr Dagmar Pruin.

Contact Details: Caroline-Michaelis-str.1, 10115 Berlin; tel. (30) 65211-0; e-mail kontakt@brot-fuer-die-welt.de; internet www.brot-fuer-die-welt.de.

Carl-Zeiss-Stiftung (Carl Zeiss Foundation)

Founded in 1889 by Dr Ernst Abbe, the Director of Carl Zeiss AG, a microscope manufacturer.

Activities: Funds research in the field of science and technology through self-conducted programmes; and supports young scientists and research projects at German universities. Funding of up to €200,000 for professorships is available to German universities to appoint international researchers; and, under the Transfer programme, awards of up to €1m. for basic research and application-oriented science.

Geographical Area of Activity: Germany.

Restrictions: Does not fund religious or political institutions.

Publications: Annual Report.

Finance: Total assets €1,273.9m.; net annual income €83.9m. (30 Sept. 2024).

Board of Trustees: Dr Michael Bolle (Chair.).

Management Board: Petra Olschowski (Chair.).

Principal Staff: Man. Dir Dr Felix Streiter; Deputy Man. Dir Hannes Banzhaf.

Contact Details: Kronprinzstr. 11, 70173 Stuttgart; tel. (711) 2793253; internet www.carl-zeiss-stiftung.de.

CBM-International

Founded in 1908 by Pastor Ernst Jakob Christoffel; a Christian international development organization, formerly known as Christoffel Blindenmission.

Activities: Works to improve the lives of people with disabilities in the world's poorest communities through strengthening the capacity of local services in the areas of healthcare, education, rehabilitation and livelihoods development. Main programmes are: disability inclusive development; community-based inclusive development; inclusive eye health; community mental health; and humanitarian action. The organization comprises 10 member associations, in Australia, Germany, Ireland, Italy, Kenya, New Zealand, South Africa, Switzerland, the United Kingdom and the USA. It has an office in Berlin.

Geographical Area of Activity: Africa, Asia, Latin America.

Publications: Annual Report; newspaper; toolkits; reports; policy papers; brochures; books.

Finance: Annual income €431m., expenditure €441m. (31 Dec. 2023).

Supervisory Board: Claus Duncker (Chair.); Dr Nina Roßmann (Vice-Chair.).

Principal Staff: CEOs Dr Peter Schießl, Dr Rainer Brockhaus.

Contact Details: Stubenwald-Allee 5, 64625 Bensheim; tel. (6251) 131131; e-mail contact@cbm.org; internet www.cbm.org.

Centre for Humanitarian Action—CHA

The Centre for Humanitarian Action (CHA) is a Berlin-based think tank founded in 2018.

Activities: CHA works to strengthen German and international humanitarian action by conducting research and analysis and raising public awareness of humanitarian principles. Its core areas of work include: humanitarian policy and strategy capacity of German actors; opportunities and risks of digitalization for German humanitarian actors; localization in practice—partnership in humanitarian projects and risk management; climate change and humanitarian change; the Triple Nexus; humanitarian innovation; and shrinking humanitarian space and European networking. The Centre serves as a forum for open discussions involving national and international actors and academic networks, as well as for sharing knowledge and expertise.

Geographical Area of Activity: International.

Publications: Newsletters; Reports; Blogs; Policy Briefs; Discussion/Working Papers; Research Papers; Executive Summaries; Humanitarian Topics To Go.

Principal Staff: Dir Ralf Südhoff.

Contact Details: Märkisches Ufer 34, 10179 Berlin; tel. (1590) 6818524; e-mail info@chaberlin.org; internet www.chaberlin.org.

Daimler und Benz Stiftung (Daimler and Benz Foundation)

Founded in 1986 by Daimler-Benz AG (then Daimler AG, now Mercedes-Benz Group AG and Daimler Truck AG), a motor vehicle manufacturer.

Activities: Supports research on the interaction between people, the environment and technology and publishes the results. Annually, the Foundation awards grants worth around €3.5m.

to individuals and institutions; and offers 12 scholarships, each worth €40,000, to post-doctoral candidates, junior professors and young heads of research. Also awards the annual Bertha-Benz Prize of €15,000 to a female engineer in honour of a dissertation that shows pioneering spirit and visionary character.

Geographical Area of Activity: International.

Restrictions: Scholarships are open to applicants from all scientific disciplines, including social and cultural sciences, and the humanities.

Publications: Annual Reports; Bertha Benz Lectures series; additional and recent publications are on the website.

Finance: Total assets €131.4m. (31 Dec. 2023).

Board of Trustees: Renata Jungo Brüngger (Chair.).

Principal Staff: Exec. Board Prof. Dr Julia Arlinghaus and Prof. Dr Lutz Gade; Man. Dir Dr Joerg Klein.

Contact Details: Dr Carl-Benz-Platz 2, 68526 Ladenburg; tel. (6203) 1092-0; e-mail info@daimler-benz-stiftung.de; internet www.daimler-benz-stiftung.de.

Deutsch-Russischer Austausch eV—DRA (German-Russian Exchange)

Established in 1992.

Activities: Operates in Germany, Ukraine and Belarus through local activities in large cities. Projects in the Russian Federation stopped in late 2021 following a court order banning the organization from working with partners or individuals there. The organization supports citizens' initiatives, human rights organizations and NGOs. It runs programmes in the fields of democracy, dialogue and conflict management, the environment and continuing education; organizes exchange initiatives; and helps in connecting with Western partners.

Geographical Area of Activity: Belarus, Germany, Ukraine.

Publications: Annual Report; newsletter.

Principal Staff: First Exec. Man. Igor Mitchnik.

Contact Details: Badstr. 44, 13357 Berlin; tel. (30) 4466800; e-mail info@austausch.org; internet www.austausch.org.

Deutsche AIDS-Stiftung (German AIDS Foundation)

Established in 1987.

Activities: Main activities include providing financial assistance and improved care for people with HIV; and assisting best practice projects in sub-Saharan Africa and the Ukraine. It awards every two years a Media Prize, worth €15,000, and a prize for students and young journalists, worth €3,000.

Geographical Area of Activity: Germany, sub-Saharan Africa, Ukraine.

Publications: Annual Report; newsletter (up to 12 a year); additional material for events; *Stiftung konkret*; blog.

Board: Anne von Fallois, Dr Florian Reuther.

Contact Details: Münsterstr. 18, 53111 Bonn; tel. (228) 604690; e-mail info@aids-stiftung.de; internet www.aids-stiftung.de.

Deutsche Bank Stiftung (Deutsche Bank Foundation)

Established in 2005 following the merger of Alfred Herrhausen Stiftung Hilfe zur Selbsthilfe (f. 1986) and Deutsche Bank Kulturstiftung.

Activities: Promotes talented young people; and supports projects in the areas of culture, equal opportunities, integration and disaster prevention.

Geographical Area of Activity: Germany.

Publications: Annual Report; newsletter.

Finance: Total assets €161.4m.; net annual income –€1.5m. (2024).

Board of Directors: Jürgen Fitschen (Chair.); Christof von Dryander (Deputy Chair.).

Principal Staff: Man. Dir Dr Kristina Hasenpflug.

Contact Details: Börsenplatz 5, 60313 Frankfurt am Main; tel. (69) 2475259-11; e-mail office@deutsche-bank-stiftung.de; internet www.deutsche-bank-stiftung.de.

Deutsche Bundesstiftung Umwelt—DBU (German Federal Foundation for the Environment)

Established in 1990 by the German Government using the proceeds from the privatization of state-owned steel company Salzgitter AG.

Activities: Supports innovative and sustainable projects in the fields of environmental protection and health, with special consideration for small and medium-sized businesses. The Foundation offers three scholarship programmes and an annual environmental prize worth €500,000. It comprises DBU Naturerbe GmbH, which manages 71 conservation areas that were formerly used for mining or military purposes in 10 federal states; and the DBU Centre for Environmental Communication.

Geographical Area of Activity: Germany, with occasional grants to other countries in Central and Eastern European countries and beyond.

Restrictions: No grants to state organizations.

Publications: Annual Report; *DBU aktuell* (newsletter); brochures.

Finance: Total assets €2,480m.; annual income €97.7m. (2023).

Board of Trustees: Prof. Dr Kai Niebert (Chair.); Dr Bettina Hoffmann, Elisabeth Kaiser, Prof. Dr Katharina Reuter (Vice-Chair.).

Principal Staff: Sec.-Gen. Alexander Bonde.

Contact Details: An der Bornau 2, 49090 Osnabrück; Postfach 1705, 49007; tel. (541) 9633-0; e-mail info@dbu.de; internet www.dbu.de.

Deutsche Gesellschaft für Auswärtige Politik—DGAP (German Council on Foreign Relations)

Founded in 1955; a national foreign policy network and an independent, non-partisan and non-profit organization.

Activities: Works to improve understanding of German foreign policy and international relations. Areas of interest are: the EU; geoeconomics; international order and democracy; migration; security and technology; and digitization. The Council conducts research and advises decisionmakers in politics, business and society. It organizes conferences and study groups, courses and lectures; issues publications; and maintains a research library specializing in foreign affairs, with more than 85,000 books and 200 specialist journals. Has more than 2,800 members. Young DGAP provides a forum for students and young professionals under the age of 35 to explore foreign policy issues. Founded in 2008, it has more than 900 members.

Geographical Area of Activity: People's Repub. of China, Europe, Eurasia, Russian Federation, USA.

Publications: *Jahrbuch Internationale Politik* (annual); *Internationale Politik* (bimonthly); *Berlin Policy Journal* (digital).

Finance: Funded by the German Federal Foreign Office, private corporations, foundations and others, as well as through the financial support of its members. Total assets €8.5m.; net annual income €35,580 (31 Dec. 2020).

Board: Dr Thomas Enders (Pres.); Rolf Nikel (Vice-Pres.); Dr Georg Graf Waldersee (Treas.).

Principal Staff: Dir Thomas Kleine-Brockhoff; Editor-in-Chief Martin Bialecki.

Contact Details: Rauchstr. 17–18, 10787 Berlin; tel. (30) 254231-0; e-mail info@dgap.org; internet www.dgap.org.

Deutsche Krebshilfe eV (German Cancer Aid)

Founded in 1974 by Dr Mildred Scheel, a radiologist and wife of Walter Scheel, former President of the Federal Republic of Germany.

Activities: Supports projects to improve prevention, early detection and diagnosis of all forms of cancer, therapy, medical follow-up and psychosocial care, including cancer self-help.

The organization offers grants to cancer patients in financial need; and funds clinical and basic research, patient care research, cancer therapy studies, innovative cancer detection projects and translational research. It also offers doctoral scholarships, postdoctoral fellowships and professorships.

Geographical Area of Activity: Germany.

Publications: Annual Report; newsletter; *Magazin der Deutschen Krebshilfe* (magazine); booklets; videos; CD-ROM; other publications.

Finance: Annual revenue €158m. (2023).

Board of Trustees: Prof. Dr Charlotte Niemeyer (Chair.).

Principal Staff: Pres. Anne-Sophie Mutter; Man. Dir Franz Kohlhuber.

Contact Details: Buschstr. 32, 53113 Bonn; tel. (228) 72990-0; e-mail deutsche@krebshilfe.de; internet www.krebshilfe.de.

Deutsche Nationalstiftung (German National Trust)

Established in 1993 by former Chancellor Helmut Schmidt and a group of his friends, including Herman J. Abs, Gerd Bucerius, Kurt Körber and Michael Otto.

Activities: Raises awareness of the mutual relationship between science, art and literature, law, politics and commerce; promotes and strengthens the process of German unity and German cultural identity within Europe; and examines pressing questions facing Germany at present and in the future. The Trust organizes annual meetings to consider urgent problems and discuss questions of national and European relevance. Annually, it offers up to 10 research scholarships, each worth up to €1,000; and awards a National Prize worth approximately €50,000 and the Richard von Weizsäcker Prize, formerly known as the Förderpreis (Sponsorship Award).

Geographical Area of Activity: EU.

Publications: Annual Report; newsletter; conference proceedings.

Senate: Prof. Dr Andreas Voßkuhle (Pres.).

Board of Trustees: Dr Rüdiger Grube (Chair.).

Board of Directors: Dr Thomas Mirow (Chair.).

Principal Staff: Exec. Dir Dr Agata Klaus.

Contact Details: Feldbrunnenstr. 56, 20148 Hamburg; tel. (40) 413367-53; e-mail info@nationalstiftung.de; internet www.nationalstiftung.de.

Deutsche Orient-Stiftung (German Orient Foundation)

Established in 1960 by the German Near and Middle East Association (NUMOV); comprises the German Orient-Institute (Deutsches Orient-Institut—DOI), the oldest private scientific institute in Germany.

Activities: Operates in the fields of science, culture, general knowledge and modern history, promoting dialogue between Germany and the countries of the Middle East. The Foundation carries out research into local political and social developments in the Middle East.

Geographical Area of Activity: Germany, Middle East and North Africa.

Restrictions: No grants to individuals.

Publications: *ORIENT* (magazine); *DOI-Kurzanalysen*; studies.

Board of Trustees: Thomas Bareiss (Chair.); Prof. Dr Mathias Rohe (Vice-Chair.).

Board of Directors: Philipp Lührs (Chair.); Prof. Dr O. Faruk Akyol, Helene Rang, Oliver Siebert (Vice-Chair.).

Contact Details: Kronenstr. 1, 10117 Berlin; tel. (30) 2064-10-21; e-mail doi@deutsches-orient-institut.de; internet deutsches-orient-institut.de.

Deutsche Sparkassenstiftung für Internationale Zusammenarbeit (German Savings Banks Foundation for International Co-operation)

Established in 1992 for the promotion of economic and social development in developing and transition countries and areas; formerly known as the Sparkassenstiftung für internationale Kooperation.

Activities: Works in the field of aid to developing countries. The Foundation supports retail banks and microfinance institutions through providing technical assistance in the areas of internal organization, human resource development and product development (especially lending to micro- and small entrepreneurs and attracting deposits).

Geographical Area of Activity: International, especially Asia, Africa, Central America, Central and Eastern Europe.

Restrictions: Does not accept unsolicited applications.

Publications: Annual Report.

Finance: Total assets €1,523m. (2022).

Board of Trustees: Ulrich Reuter (Chair.); Michael Breuer (Vice-Chair.).

Executive Board: Helmut Schleweis (Chair.).

Principal Staff: Man. Dir Niclaus Bergmann; Deputy Man. Dir Nicole Brand.

Contact Details: Simrockstr. 4, 53113 Bonn; tel. (228) 9703-0; e-mail office@sparkassenstiftung.de; internet www.sparkassenstiftung.de.

Deutsche Telekom Stiftung (Deutsche Telekom Foundation)

Established in 1993 by Deutsche Telekom, a telecommunications provider.

Activities: Works in the fields of research, technology and education, with a focus on science, technology, engineering and mathematics (STEM). Main programme areas are: education drivers; education opportunities; education innovations; and education dialogue.

Geographical Area of Activity: Mainly Germany.

Restrictions: Does not accept unsolicited applications.

Publications: Annual Report; newsletter; *Sonar* (magazine).

Finance: Annual income €15.9m., expenditure €8.6m. (31 Dec. 2023).

Board of Trustees: Timothy Höttges (Chair.).

Board of Directors: Prof. Dr Thomas de Maizière (Chair.); Prof. Dr Ulrike Cress (Deputy Chair.).

Principal Staff: Man. Dir Jacob Chammon.

Contact Details: Friedrich-Ebert-Allee 71–77 (Haus 3), 53113 Bonn; tel. (228) 181-92001; e-mail kontakt@telekom.de; internet www.telekom-stiftung.de.

Deutscher Akademischer Austauschdienst—DAAD (German Academic Exchange Service)

Founded in 1925 (re-established in 1950); a joint organization of institutions of higher education.

Activities: Offers long- and short-term scholarships in all fields of study to foreign students and young research workers, including 'sur place' scholarships to universities in developing countries; and to students from European countries for university summer vacation and language courses. The Service has bilateral agreements with German and foreign institutions; and promotes student exchange in connection with specific research projects. It supports a programme of exchanges of university teachers for short-term teaching and research visits on a reciprocal basis. Prizes are awarded for achievements in international academic exchange, German language and literature, German as a foreign language and German studies. Comprises an international network of 18 branch offices and 50 information centres and information points in more than 60 countries.

Geographical Area of Activity: International.

Publications: Annual Report; newsletter.

Finance: Annual budget €839.3m. (2023).

Executive Board and Board of Trustees: Prof. Dr Joybrato Mukherjee (Chair.); Dr Muriel Kim Helbig (Vice-Chair.).

Principal Staff: Sec.-Gen. Dr Kai Sicks; Deputy Secs-Gen. Dr Michael Harms, Rudolf Boden.

Contact Details: Kennedyallee 50, 53175 Bonn; POB 200404, 53134 Bonn; tel. (228) 882-0; e-mail postmaster@daad.de; internet www.daad.de.

Deutsches Rheuma-Forschungszentrum Berlin (German Rheumatism Research Centre Berlin)

Founded in 1988 by the City of Berlin and Immanuel Hospital; a member of the Leibniz Association (q.v.) of research institutes.

Activities: Works in the fields of immunology, experimental rheumatology and rheumatism epidemiology, carrying out biomedical and epidemiological research on the causes, diagnosis and treatment of inflammatory rheumatic diseases. Nationally and internationally, the Centre carries out self-conducted programmes; and internationally through conferences, training courses and publications.

Geographical Area of Activity: Mainly Germany.

Publications: Annual Report; *DRFZ NewsFlash* (newsletter); brochure.

Finance: Financed by the City of Berlin and other sources; annual expenditure approx. €3m.

Board of Trustees: Prof. Dr Thomas Krieg (Pres.).

Principal Staff: Scientific Dir Prof. Dr Eicke Latz; Administrative Dir Uta Bielfeldt.

Contact Details: Charitéplatz 1, 10117 Berlin; tel. (30) 28460-617; e-mail info@drfz.de; internet www.drfz.de.

Dietmar-Hopp-Stiftung (Dietmar Hopp Foundation)

Established in 1995 by Dietmar Hopp, a founder member of the computer software company SAP AG.

Activities: Offers grants to charities working in the fields of sport (football, handball, ice hockey and golf); education, with a focus on mathematics, computer science, science and technology; social affairs; and medical research, in particular neonatal screening and palliative care. Target groups include children and young, older and critically ill people. The Foundation funds and works closely with the Hopp Foundation for Computer Literacy & Informatics (f. 2013).

Geographical Area of Activity: Mainly the metropolitan Rhein-Neckar region.

Finance: Holds more than 15% of SAP AG shares.

Board: Dietmar Hopp, Daniel Hopp.

Principal Staff: Man. Dir Heike Bauer; Deputy Man. Dir Meike Leupold.

Contact Details: Opelstr. 28, 68789 St Leon-Rot; tel. (6227) 8608550; e-mail info@dietmar-hopp-stiftung.de; internet www.dietmar-hopp-stiftung.de.

DIPF—Leibniz-Institut für Bildungsforschung und Bildungsinformation (Leibniz Institute for Research and Information in Education)

Established in 1951 as the Deutsches Institut für Internationale Pädagogische Forschung—DIPF; a member of the Leibniz Association (q.v.) of research institutes.

Activities: Carries out research in the areas of: development of school and instructional practice; early childhood education; the history of education; digital education; and the effects of educational reforms. The Institute supports researchers, practitioners and policymakers; and participates in national and international networks and research alliances. It has an office in Berlin.

Geographical Area of Activity: Germany.

Restrictions: Does not accept unsolicited applications.

Board of Trustees: Prof. Dr Manfred Prenzel (Chair.); Dr Dorothee Lux (Deputy Chair.).

Scientific Advisory Board: Prof. Dr Tina Hascher (Chair.); Dr Michael Farrenkopf (Deputy Chair.).

Principal Staff: Exec. Dir Prof. Dr Kai Maaz; Deputy Exec. Dir Prof. Dr Marc Rittberger.

Contact Details: Rostockerstr. 6, 60323 Frankfurt am Main; POB 900 270, 60442 Frankfurt am Main; tel. (69) 24708-0; e-mail info@dipf.de; internet www.dipf.de.

Dr Rainer Wild-Stiftung—Stiftung für Gesunde Ernährung (Dr Rainer Wild Foundation for Healthy Nutrition)

Established in 1991 by Dr Rainer Wild.

Activities: Operates in the fields of nutritional education, consumer behaviour, food and culture, food sensory science, through networking, conventions and awarding prizes. Target groups are food scientists, nutritionists, dieticians, social scientists and educationalists. The Foundation hosts conventions; publishes books and journals; initiates research projects; and provides scholarships to young scientists. It also awards the Dr Rainer Wild Prize, worth €15,000, for outstanding accomplishments in the field of healthy nutrition.

Geographical Area of Activity: International.

Restrictions: Not a grantmaking organization.

Publications: Annual Report; *Healthy Nutrition* (book series); *Mitteilungen* (journal); booklets; briefings; blog; books.

Board of Directors: Dr Hans-Joachim Arnold (Chair.).

Board of Trustees: Prof. Dr Lucia A. Reisch (Chair.).

Principal Staff: CEO Dr Silke Lichtenstein.

Contact Details: Mittelgewannweg 10, 69123 Heidelberg; tel. (6221) 7511-200; e-mail info@gesunde-ernaehrung.org; internet www.gesunde-ernaehrung.org.

Dräger-Stiftung (Dräger Foundation)

Established in 1974 by Dr Heinrich Dräger, whose family founded Drägerwerk AG & Co KGaA, a manufacturer of medical, safety and diving equipment.

Activities: Works in a broad range of fields, including science and research, education, sport, arts and culture, monument and landscape conservation, international understanding and accident prevention. The Foundation carries out self-conducted programmes and organizes conferences. In the field of science and research, it supports basic medical research, certain research and health projects, and offers scholarships to a limited extent.

Geographical Area of Activity: Europe, USA.

Restrictions: No grants to individuals; no postgraduate scholarships.

Finance: Funded by a 9.6% shareholding in Drägerwerk AG & Co KGaA. Total assets approx. €6.1m.

Principal Staff: Dirs Stefan Dräger, Claudia Rohn.

Contact Details: Moislinger Allee 53–55, 23558 Lübeck; tel. (451) 882-2151; e-mail draeger-stiftung@draeger.com; internet www.draeger-stiftung.de.

DSW—Deutsche Stiftung Weltbevölkerung (German Foundation for World Population)

Established in 1991 by Dirk Rossmann, founder and CEO of health and beauty retail company Rossmann, and Erhard Schreiber, an entrepreneur.

Activities: Works to help young people out of poverty, especially girls and young women. Programmes focus on providing access to sexual and reproductive health rights services and eliminating gender-based discrimination. The Foundation supports community outreach initiatives to develop peer education, life skills, leadership, advocacy and economic empowerment. It has an office in Berlin; country offices in Ethiopia, Kenya and Tanzania; and an EU liaison office in Brussels.

Geographical Area of Activity: Ethiopia, EU, Kenya, Tanzania, Uganda.

Publications: Annual Report; *DSW Update*; German version of *UNFPA State of World Population* (annual); data report (annual); factsheets; newsletters; statistical reports.

Finance: Annual income €10.0m., expenditure €10.1m. (31 Dec. 2023).

Executive Board: Helmut Heinen (Chair.); Elmar Bingel (Deputy Chair.).

Principal Staff: Exec. Dir Jan Kreutzberg; Deputy Dir Angela Bähr.

Contact Details: Loebensteinstr. 25, 30175 Hannover; tel. (511) 94373-0; e-mail hannover@dsw.org; internet www.dsw.org.

Eberhard-Schöck-Stiftung (Eberhard Schöck Foundation)

Established in 1992 by Eberhard Schöck to promote the building trade in the former communist countries of Central and Eastern Europe; the Stiftung zur Förderung des Bauwesens is a subsidiary foundation based in Kyiv.

Activities: Works in the areas of aid, economic affairs and education. The Foundation carries out self-conducted programmes; awards grants, scholarships and fellowships; and organizes conferences and training courses. It runs practical programmes to train young building workers from the former communist countries of Europe to become self-employed builders in their own countries, and to contribute to stability and the principles of democracy and the market economy; and also runs practical programmes to train vocational teachers and managers of small and medium-sized enterprises in the building trade. Four prizes are offered: the Schöck Building Innovation Prize; the German Language Cultural Prize (in co-operation with the Dortmund Verein Deutsche Sprache); the Pre-Cast Concrete Parts Talent award (with Berufsförderungswerk für die Beton- und Fertigteilhersteller); and the German University Building award. Since 1998 the Foundation has run pilot projects to modernize vocational training in the Russian Federation, Ukraine and, since 2010, in Moldova.

Geographical Area of Activity: Central and Eastern Europe.

Restrictions: Grants only to the Foundation's own projects.

Publications: Annual Report; conference documentation.

Finance: Annual project expenditure approx. €3m. (2023).

Board of Trustees: Ursula Lazarus (Chair.); Hannes Ludwig (Vice-Chair.).

Board of Directors: Simone Schöck (Chair.); Dr Jürgen D. Wickert (Vice-Chair.).

Principal Staff: Man. Dir Peter Möller.

Contact Details: Schöckstr. 1, 76534 Baden-Baden; tel. (7223) 967-371; e-mail stiftung@schoeck.de; internet www.eberhard-schoeck-stiftung.de.

Else Kröner-Fresenius-Stiftung (Else Kröner-Fresenius Foundation)

Established in 1983 by Else Kröner, the founder of Fresenius, a global health company.

Activities: Focuses on medicine, health and science and technology through providing grants for research projects, in particular novel research in nutritional medicine, clinical research, infections and dialysis. The Foundation also finances humanitarian and educational initiatives, especially if they are conducive to development. It offers the Else Kröner Fresenius Prize for Medical Research, worth €2.5m. and the Else Kröner Fresenius Award for Development Cooperation in Medicine, worth €100,000.

Geographical Area of Activity: International.

Restrictions: Does not fund basic research.

Publications: Annual Report; newsletter.

Finance: Annual grants disbursed €71.9m. (2023).

Board of Trustees: Dr Dieter Schenk (Chair.); Dr Karl Schneider (Vice-Chair.).

Board of Directors: Prof. Dr Michael Madeja (Chair.).

Principal Staff: CEO Prof. Dr Michael Madeja.

Contact Details: Geschäftsstelle Bad Homburg v.d.H., Rathausplatz 3–7, 61348 Bad Homburg v.d.H; tel. (6172) 8975-0; e-mail kontakt@ekfs.de; internet www.ekfs.de.

Ernst-Schering-Stiftung (Ernst Schering Foundation)

Established in 2002 by Schering AG, Berlin, a pharmaceutical company.

Activities: Promotes science, in particular the natural sciences, and the arts, with a focus on the contemporary visual and performing arts, including dance and music; the scientific and cultural education of children and young people; and dialogue between science and society. The Foundation gives particular emphasis to projects in frontier areas, especially at the interface of art and science. It exhibits shows by young, experimental artists and organizes lectures and workshops, thus serving as a platform for interdisciplinary dialogue among science, culture and society. Every two years, an international art prize is awarded, worth €10,000, in collaboration with the KW Institute for Contemporary Art.

Geographical Area of Activity: International.

Publications: Project Report; newsletter (monthly); exhibition catalogues; brochures; publications of scientific symposia.

Finance: Total assets €35m. (2025).

Board of Trustees: Prof. Dr Max Löhning (Chair.); Prof. Dr Julia Fischer (Deputy Chair.).

Principal Staff: Man. Dir Dr Katja Naie.

Contact Details: Unter den Linden 32–34, 10117 Berlin; tel. (30) 206229-65; e-mail info@scheringstiftung.de; internet www.scheringstiftung.de.

EuroNatur

Established in 1987 as the Stiftung Europäisches Naturerbe (European Heritage Foundation).

Activities: Works in the fields of conservation and the environment and environmental policies. The organization carries out self-conducted programmes; makes grants to NGOs and other institutions; and organizes conferences and training courses. It offers the EuroNatur Environmental Award and European Stork Village prize.

Geographical Area of Activity: Europe.

Restrictions: Grants only for measures supporting self-conducted programmes.

Publications: *EuroNatur* (magazine); newsletter (monthly); papers on scientific and environmental issues.

Finance: Annual income €5.8m., expenditure €5.8m. (2023).

Board of Trustees: Peter Rüther (Chair.).

Board: Prof. Dr Thomas Potthast (Chair.); Dr Anna-Katharina Wöbse (Vice-Chair.).

Principal Staff: Exec. Dir Gabriel Schwaderer.

Contact Details: Westendstr. 3, 78315 Radolfzell; tel. (7732) 9272-0; e-mail info@euronatur.org; internet www.euronatur.org.

Europäische Rechtsakademie—ERA (Academy of European Law)

Established in 1992 on the initiative of the European Parliament by the governments of Luxembourg and the Rhineland-Palatinate, the City of Trier and the Association for the Promotion of the Academy.

Activities: Provides legal training and a forum for debate for lawyers throughout Europe. Activities include organizing conferences, seminars, language courses, e-learning courses and legal training projects. The Academy runs a scholarship programme to enable lawyers from new and future EU member states to attend its training courses in Trier. The ERA Jubilee Fund supports capacity building and training for legal practitioners in EU member states. Has an office in Brussels, Belgium.

Geographical Area of Activity: Europe.

Restrictions: Unsolicited applications for grants outside the framework of the Peter Caesar Scholarship Programme are not accepted.

Publications: Annual Report; newsletter; *ERA Forum* (quarterly review of European law, published in co-operation with Springer); handbooks; books.

Finance: Annual income €8.9m., expenditure €8.9m. (2023).

Governing Board: Jean-Claude Juncker (Pres.); Hendrik Hering (Vice-Pres.).

Executive Board: Sabine Verheyen (Chair.).

Principal Staff: Dir Jean-Philippe Rageade; Deputy Dir Vadász Viktor.

Contact Details: Metzer Allee 4, 54295 Trier; tel. (651) 937370; e-mail info@era.int; internet www.era.int.

European Center for Constitutional and Human Rights—ECCHR

Established in 2007 by Wolfgang Kaleck and other international human rights lawyers as an independent, non-profit legal and educational organization.

Activities: Works to uphold civil and legal rights in the fields of business and human rights, international crimes and accountability, legal intervention and migration. The Center uses legal means to hold accountable those responsible for corporate exploitation, fortress borders, sexual and gender-based violence, torture and war crimes. The Critical Legal Training programme offers training, networking and collaborative learning opportunities to young lawyers and legal activists.

Geographical Area of Activity: Worldwide.

Publications: Annual Report; newsletter; Glossary (online); books; brochures; policy papers; reports; studies.

Finance: Annual revenue €5m., expenditure €5m. (2023).

Council: Lotte Leicht (Chair.); Tobias Singelnstein (Vice-Chair.).

Principal Staff: Gen. Sec. Wolfgang Kaleck.

Contact Details: Zossener str. 55–58, Aufgang D, D-10961 Berlin; tel. (30) 40048590; e-mail info@ecchr.eu; internet www.ecchr.eu.

EYFA—European Youth For Action

Founded in 1986 as an activist network.

Activities: Works in Europe in the fields of conservation and the environment and promotes sustainable ways of living and working. The organization campaigns against ecologically and socially unsustainable systems, using cultural activism and alternative media, with a particular focus on youth-initiated activities and projects; and runs training and workshops on campaigning and social change. It helps other groups with their fundraising, as well as providing financial services, including bookkeeping assistance and the legal status to receive funds on behalf of other organizations. Has partner organizations in 26 European countries.

Geographical Area of Activity: Europe.

Publications: *Green Pepper*; newsletter; online resources; toolkits.

Finance: Receives funding from various organizations, including the EU.

Principal Staff: Co-ordinator Shannon Stephens.

Contact Details: New Yorck im Bethanien, Mariannenplatz 2A, 10997 Berlin; tel. (30) 61740102; e-mail eyfa@eyfa.org; internet eyfa.org.

Evangelisches Studienwerk eV (Protestant Study Foundation)

Founded in 1948 by several Protestant Churches to bring together and promote Protestant students of any faculty; now supported by all Protestant Churches in Germany.

Activities: Works in the fields of education and research through self-conducted programmes, grants to individuals, fellowships, scholarships, seminars, conferences, courses and advisory services. The Foundation mainly supports German Protestant university students and graduates in Germany and in other EU countries; and offers scholarships for refugees to study at German universities. In 2023 it supported around 1,500 students and 300 doctoral candidates at universities and technical colleges.

Geographical Area of Activity: Europe.

Publications: *Villigst Public* (newsletter); *Villigst Profile* (series); *Villigst Perspektiven* (dissertation series).

Finance: Total income €19.7m., expenditure €19.7m. (2023).

Board of Trustees: Dr Stephanie Springer (Chair.).

Board: Ulf Schlüter (Chair.); Hans-Rudolf von Campenhausen (Deputy Chair.).

Principal Staff: Dir Friederike Fass.

Contact Details: Iserlohner Str. 25, 58239 Schwerte; tel. (2304) 755196; e-mail info@evstudienwerk.de; internet www.evstudienwerk.de.

F. C. Flick-Stiftung gegen Fremdenfeindlichkeit, Rassismus und Intoleranz (F. C. Flick Foundation against Xenophobia, Racism and Intolerance)

Established in 2001 by Dr Friedrich Christian Flick, a business person and art collector.

Activities: Supports projects that focus on developing ways of combating xenophobia, racism and intolerance, in the focus areas of culture, sport and young people, aged 5–15 years. The Foundation focuses on work with children and young people in the eastern states of Germany, supporting existing projects, youth exchanges with Eastern Europe, assisting initiatives linking artistic ideas with political and contemporary enlightenment and promoting sport projects. Long-term projects include the German-Polish student exchange programme, Kopernikus; the Lindenstrasse Workshop for Youth in Potsdam; and the Rosa Luxemburg Elementary School in Potsdam.

Geographical Area of Activity: Germany, Israel, Poland, Russian Federation, Ukraine.

Publications: Annual Report.

Board of Trustees: Dr Charlotte von Koerber (Chair.); Günter Baaske (Deputy Chair.).

Principal Staff: Exec. Dir Susanne Krause-Hinrichs.

Contact Details: Schlossstr. 12, 14467 Potsdam; tel. (331) 2007770; e-mail info@stiftung-toleranz.de; internet www.stiftung-toleranz.de.

filia.die Frauenstiftung (filia—the Women's Foundation)

Established in 2001 to promote women playing a decisive role in all areas of society.

Activities: Works on behalf of women who are discriminated against because of their gender, skin colour, origins or sexual orientation. The Foundation provides grants to women's NGOs, community and grassroots organizations in Central and Eastern Europe (50% of budget), Germany and the global South. Grants are dedicated to projects in the focal areas of participation and freedom from violence for women and girls.

Geographical Area of Activity: Central and Eastern Europe, Germany and the global South.

Restrictions: Does not accept unsolicited applications; grants only to partners of Prospera—International Network of Women's Funds (q.v.); no grants to individuals or for scholarships.

Publications: Annual Report; *filianews* (e-newsletter).

Finance: Total capital €16.3m. (2023).

Board of Trustees: Dr Dana Jirous (Chair.); Dr Heike Pfitzner (Vice-Chair.).

Principal Staff: Exec. Dir Lizzy Wazinski.

Contact Details: Alte Königstr. 18, 22767 Hamburg; tel. (40) 38038199-0; e-mail info@filia-frauenstiftung.de; internet www.filia-frauenstiftung.de.

Frankfurter Stiftung für Deutsch-Italienische Studien (Frankfurt Foundation for German-Italian Studies)

Established in 1992 by the Deutsch-Italienische Vereinigung eV for the promotion of international understanding through the cultivation of academic, cultural and human relations between Germany and Italy.

Activities: Operates in the fields of the arts and humanities and education. Nationally and internationally the Foundation carries out self-conducted programmes and publications and funds other publications; and nationally it organizes conferences.

Geographical Area of Activity: Europe.

Publications: *Italienisch* (magazine of Italian language and literature); newsletter.

Board of Directors: Thanh Lan Nguyen-Gatti (Chair.); (Laura Melara-Dürbeck (Deputy Chair.).

Contact Details: Arndtstr. 12, 60325 Frankfurt am Main; tel. 69746752; e-mail info@italienstiftung.eu; internet www.italienstiftung.eu.

Fraunhofer-Gesellschaft (Fraunhofer Society)

Established in 1949 on the initiative of State Secretary Hugo Geiger; named after Joseph von Fraunhofer, a scientist, inventor and entrepreneur.

Activities: A society of 76 institutes and research institutions organized into thematic groups, including: energy technologies and climate protection; health; ICT technology; innovation research; light and surfaces; materials, components; microelectronics; production; and resource technologies and bioeconomy. The institutes undertake applied research to create innovative products and applications of use to private and public enterprise.

Geographical Area of Activity: International.

Publications: Annual Report.

Finance: Annual research budget €3,600m. (2025).

Principal Staff: Pres. Holger Hanselka.

Contact Details: Hansastraße 27c, 80686 Munich; Postfach 20 07 33, 80007 Munich; tel. (89) 1205-0; internet www.fraunhofer.de.

Freudenberg Stiftung (Freudenberg Foundation)

Founded in 1984 by partners of the Freudenberg & Co KG company.

Activities: Works to give all children and young people good educational opportunities. The Foundation develops practical, academic, medical and artistic approaches in two main programme areas: social inclusion, advancing the participation of people with mental impairments in the workplace; and democratic culture, working in schools and society more widely to promote democratic values and prevent denigration of other people.

Geographical Area of Activity: Germany.

Restrictions: Does not make grants to individuals; nor for scholarships, research or capital works.

Publications: *Journal* (annual).

Finance: Annual income €5.4m., expenditure €4.6m. (2023).

Board of Partners: Dr Mohsen Sohi (Chair.); Martin Wentzler (Vice-Chair.).

Board of Trustees: Stefanie Wahl (Chair.); Jonas König (Vice-Chair.).

Principal Staff: Man. Dirs Dr Pia Gerber, Dir Stefan Vogt.

Contact Details: Freudenbergstr. 2, 69469 Weinheim; tel. (6201) 49944330; e-mail info@freudenbergstiftung.de; internet www.freudenbergstiftung.de.

Friede Springer Stiftung (Friede Springer Foundation)

Founded in 2010 by Friede Springer, the widow of Axel Springer, a publisher, and Vice-Chair. of Axel Springer SE, a media conglomerate.

Activities: Supports scientific, artistic and cultural projects, meetings and symposia in scientific, artistic, cultural and educational areas. The Foundation funds scholarships and endowments and promotes scientific publications and research projects.

Geographical Area of Activity: Germany.

Finance: Initial endowment €80m.

Board of Trustees: Dr Eric Schweitzer (Chair.); Marianne Birthler (Vice-Chair.).

Principal Staff: CEO Dr h.c. Friede Springer; Deputy CEO Karin Arnold.

Contact Details: Pacelliallee 55, 14195 Berlin; tel. (30) 8441410-0; e-mail vorstand@friedespringerstiftung.de; internet www.friedespringerstiftung.de.

Friedensdorf International (Peace Village International)

Established in 1967 to care for children and adolescents injured as a result of the Vietnam War.

Activities: Operates worldwide in the areas of medicine, health and social welfare. Each year, the organization brings children from war zones to Germany for short-term medical care and rehabilitation; projects for the improvement of medical care have also been established in the native countries of the children and, where possible, children are treated there. It also promotes peace and carries out educational work, including at the Peace Village Bildungswerk educational centre, offering courses on non-violence, constructive resolution of conflicts and parenting skills. Has co-ordinating offices in Berlin, Nord and Sommerkahl.

Geographical Area of Activity: Afghanistan, Angola, Cambodia, The Gambia, Kyrgyzstan, Tajikistan, Uzbekistan, Iraq.

Publications: Annual Report; newsletter; *Peace Village Report* (2 a year).

Finance: Total assets €19.8m. (31 Dec. 2023).

Board of Directors: Dr Ralf Peppmüller (Chair.); Stefan Hennig (Deputy Chair.); Klaus Wieprecht (Treas.); Annegret Hübbers-Brechtmann (Sec.).

Principal Staff: Dir Birgit Stifter.

Contact Details: Lanterstr. 21, 46539 Dinslaken; tel. (2064) 49740; e-mail info@friedensdorf.de; internet www.friedensdorf.de.

Friedrich-Ebert-Stiftung eV

Founded in 1925 as a political legacy of Friedrich Ebert, the first President of the Weimar Republic, and re-established after the Second World War, to further the democratic education of the German people and build international co-operation towards democracy; a party-affiliated foundation.

Activities: Promotes freedom, justice and solidarity through carrying out self-conducted programmes and research; offering fellowships, scholarships and prizes; and organizing conferences, courses and lectures. Main programme areas include: democracy, civic engagement and local politics; economy, finance, ecology and social issues; education, work and digitization; flight, migration and integration; gender and youth; history, culture, media and internet politics; politics for Europe; shaping a just world; and trade unions and decent work. It maintains a specialized library of approximately 1m. items on the German and international labour movement and the Archive of Social Democracy. Has 18 national and regional offices in Germany and 104 overseas offices.

Geographical Area of Activity: International.

Restrictions: Not a grantmaking organization.

Publications: Annual Report; studies; briefing papers; analyses; political reviews.

Finance: Total budget €195m. (2022).

Board of Trustees: Hannelore Kraft (Chair.); Heike Taubert (Deputy Chair.).

Principal Staff: CEO Martin Schulz; Deputy CEOs Reiner Hoffmann, Anke Rehlinger; Exec. Dir Dr Sabine Fandrych.

Friedrich-Naumann-Stiftung für die Freiheit   GERMANY

Contact Details: Godesberger Allee 149, 53175 Bonn; tel. (228) 883-0; e-mail info@fes.de; internet www.fes.de.

Friedrich-Naumann-Stiftung für die Freiheit (Friedrich Naumann Foundation for Freedom)

Founded in 1958 by Dr Theodor Heuss, former President of the Federal Republic of Germany, as the Friedrich-Naumann-Stiftung; present name adopted in 2007.

Activities: Works in the fields of civic education, promoting an open society and a social market economy, through self-conducted programmes and research. The Foundation offers scholarships, fellowships and prizes; and organizes conferences and training courses. In developing countries, it assists co-operative associations, training institutes for journalism and organizations in the field of adult education. Has projects in more than 60 countries, with eight offices in Germany and regional offices in Europe, Africa, Asia and Central America; and maintains an archive on liberalism.

Geographical Area of Activity: International.

Restrictions: Does not support study or research trips abroad.

Publications: Annual Report; newsletter; *liberal* (quarterly); occasional papers.

Finance: Annual income €93m., expenditure €93m. (31 Dec. 2024).

Board of Trustees: Prof. Dr Ludwig Theodor Heuss (Chair.); Liane Knüppel (Deputy Chair.).

Board of Directors: Prof. Dr Karl-Heinz Paqué (Chair.); Sabine Leutheusser-Schnarrenberger (Deputy Chair.).

Principal Staff: CEO Annett Witte.

Contact Details: Karl-Marx-Str. 2, 14482 Potsdam-Babelsberg; tel. (30) 22012634; e-mail service@freiheit.org; internet www.freiheit.org.

Fritz Thyssen Stiftung (Fritz Thyssen Foundation)

Founded in 1959 by Amélie Thyssen and her daughter, Anita Countess Zichy-Thyssen, in memory of August and Fritz Thyssen, industrialists.

Activities: Funds research and scholarships in universities and research institutes in history, language and culture, the state, economy and society, and medicine. Special consideration is given to the rising generation of scientists and scholars.

Geographical Area of Activity: Mainly Germany.

Publications: Annual Report; newsletter; *FTS-Journal*; *Historia Scientiarum*; *Thyssen Lectures*; *THESEUS European Leadership in Challenging Times-Academia & Politics in Dialogue*.

Finance: Grants disbursed €12.5m. (2023).

Board of Trustees: Dr Karl-Ludwig Kley (Chair.); Rainer Neske (Vice-Chair.).

Principal Staff: Exec. Dir Dr Frank Suder.

Contact Details: Apostelnkloster 13–15, 50672 Cologne; tel. (221) 2774960; e-mail fts@fritz-thyssen-stiftung.de; internet www.fritz-thyssen-stiftung.de.

Gemeinnützige Hertie-Stiftung (Hertie Foundation)

Established in 1974 by Georg Karg, Managing Director of the Hermann Tietz (Hertie) department store company.

Activities: Main programmes are brain research and strengthening democracy. The Foundation funds clinical research on brain disease; and supports neuroscientific initiatives in innovative research, education and communication. It has an office in Berlin.

Geographical Area of Activity: Europe.

Publications: Annual Report; newsletter.

Finance: Total assets €970.6m.; Annual income €45.4m. (31 Dec. 2023).

Board of Trustees: Hans-Jörg Vetter (Chair.); Prof. Dr Maria Böhmer (Deputy Chair.).

Principal Staff: Dir Dr Grzegorz Nocko.

Contact Details: Grüneburgweg 105, 60323 Frankfurt am Main; tel. (69) 6607560; e-mail info@ghst.de; internet www.ghst.de.

Gerda Henkel Stiftung (Gerda Henkel Foundation)

Founded in 1976 by Lisa Maskell in memory of her mother Gerda Henkel; a private, non-profit, grantmaking organization.

Activities: Supports academic projects and PhD fellowships, primarily in the fields of history, art history, archaeology and the history of Islam. The Foundation supports research projects by national and international scholars on clearly defined, humanities-based topics; awards research and doctoral scholarships to national and international scholars; and supports measures in the field of historic preservation based on scholarly grounds. It focuses particularly on the advancement of young scholars. When awarding scholarships, special consideration is given to research projects that provide young scholars with the opportunity to be involved in research and to improve their professional qualifications. The Gerda Henkel Prize (f. 2006), worth €100,000, is awarded every two years to international researchers.

Geographical Area of Activity: International.

Restrictions: Only supports research projects with a clearly defined scope and time frame. Priority is given to research projects that are outstanding because of the nature of their results and that promise to make the greatest use of the funds available.

Publications: Annual Report; brochures.

Finance: Total assets €232.2m. (31 Dec. 2023).

Board of Trustees: Julia Schulz-Dornburg (Chair.); Prof. Andreas Beyer (Vice-Chair.).

Principal Staff: Chair. Dr Michael Hanssler.

Contact Details: Malkastenstr. 15, 40211 Dusseldorf; tel. (211) 936524-0; e-mail info@gerda-henkel-stiftung.de; internet www.gerda-henkel-stiftung.de.

German Institute of Development and Sustainability—IDOS

Established in 1964 in Berlin; a think tank; known as Deutsches Institut für Entwicklungspolitik until 2022.

Activities: Works in the fields of global public welfare policy and sustainable development, through carrying out interdisciplinary research and providing policy advice; and offering postgraduate and vocational training for university graduates and young leaders. Programme areas include: international and transnational cooperation; sustainable economic and social systems; environmental governance; and the impact of political transformation on institutions, values and peace. The Institute organizes conferences and workshops on development policy; and maintains a library of around 150,000 vols and 150 journals.

Geographical Area of Activity: International.

Publications: Discussion Papers; Policy Briefs; Studies; The Current Column; Annual Report.

Finance: Funded by the Federal Republic of Germany (75%) and the State of North Rhine-Westphalia/Germany (25%). Total assets €9.3m. (2022).

Board of Trustees: Jochen Flasbarth (Chair.).

Principal Staff: Dir Prof. Dr Anna-Katharina Hornidge; Acting Deputy Dir Dr Axel Berger.

Contact Details: Tulpenfeld 6, 53113 Bonn; tel. (228) 94927-0; e-mail idos@idos-research.de; internet www.idos-research.de.

German Institute for Global and Area Studies—GIGA (Leibniz-Institut für Globale und Regionale Studien)

Emerged in 2006 after the restructuring of the German Overseas Institute (f. 1964); a member of the Leibniz Association of Research Institutes.

GERMANY

Activities: Conducts analysis of political, social and economic developments in Africa, Asia, Latin America and the Middle East, as well as global issues. Main research areas include: political responsibility and participation; peace and security; growth and development; and power and ideas. The Institute comprises institutes for African, Asian, Latin American and Middle East studies. It offers visiting fellowships to postdoctoral researchers. The publicly accessible GIGA Library holds around 200,000 books, with access to around 130,000 journals. Has an office in Berlin.
Geographical Area of Activity: Africa, Asia, Latin America, Middle East.
Restrictions: Does not offer funded fellowships.
Publications: Publishes four academic open access journals: *Africa Spectrum, Journal of Current Chinese Affairs, Journal of Politics in Latin America, Journal of Current Southeast Asian Affairs* (all available online), *GIGA Focus, GIGA Working Papers,* Email alerts.
Finance: Annual revenue €15.1m., expenditure €15.1m. (31 Dec. 2023).
Board of Trustees: Dr Eva Gümbel (Chair.); Harald Herrmann (Deputy Chair.).
Principal Staff: Pres. Prof. Dr Sabine Kurtenbach; Vice-Pres. Prof. Dr Patrick Köllner.
Contact Details: Neuer Jungfernstieg 21, 20354 Hamburg; tel. (40) 42825593; e-mail info@giga-hamburg.de; internet www.giga-hamburg.de.

Goethe-Institut
Founded in 1951 as successor to the Deutsche Akademie.
Activities: Operates in the fields of the arts and humanities, international relations, language teaching and information brokerage, through self-conducted programmes, partnership programmes, grants to institutions and individuals, fellowships, scholarships, conferences, courses, publications and lectures. The Institute is particularly concerned with the teaching and promotion of the German language abroad and provides professional assistance to foreign teachers of German and students of German philology, and for the development and improvement of teaching methods and materials. It also provides information abroad about the cultural life of Germany and co-operates with cultural organizations abroad. Has 12 branches in Germany and 158 branches abroad, in 98 countries.
Geographical Area of Activity: Worldwide.
Publications: Annual Report; *das goethe* (magazine); newsletters; and other publications.
Finance: Annual income €416.4m., expenditure €413.3m. (31 Dec. 2023).
Presidium: Prof. Dr Carola Lentz (Chair.).
Principal Staff: Sec.-Gen. Johannes Ebert; Business Dir Rainer Pollack.
Contact Details: Oskar-von-Miller-Ring 18, 80333 Munich; tel. (89) 159210; e-mail info@goethe.de; internet www.goethe.de.

Haniel-Stiftung (Haniel Foundation)
Founded in 1988 by Franz Haniel & Cie GmbH, a holding company with interests in repair services, pharmaceuticals and recycling.
Activities: Promotes social entrepreneurship and supports children and young people from educationally disadvantaged backgrounds. The Foundation offers grants and funds scholarship programmes. It also awards the Haniel Prize for Economics, worth €5,000.
Geographical Area of Activity: International, especially Europe.
Publications: Annual Report; newsletter; project and conference reports.
Finance: Project spending since 1988 €50.7m. (2024).
Board of Trustees: Prof. Dr Kay Windthorst (Chair.); Kay Richard Landwers (Deputy Chair.).
Principal Staff: Exec. Dir Dr Rupert Antes.
Contact Details: Franz-Haniel-Platz 1, 47119 Duisburg; tel. (203) 806-368; e-mail stiftung@haniel.de; internet www.haniel-stiftung.de.

Hanns-Seidel-Stiftung eV (Hanns Seidel Foundation)
Founded in 1967.
Activities: Operates nationally in the fields of the arts and humanities and education; and internationally in the fields of education, international affairs, health and social welfare, through promoting self-sufficiency and individual initiatives, and through scholarships, travel grants, conferences and publications. The Foundation comprises: the Academy for Politics and Current Affairs; the Institute for Political Education; the Institute for Gifted Education, supporting around 1,600 scholarship holders; the Institute for International Co-operation, which promotes development and dialogue through around 97 projects in 71 countries; the Institute for European and Transatlantic Dialogue; and the Christian Social Policy Archive, with a library containing around 37,000 vols and 400 current periodicals. It has 14 project and liaison offices in Athens, Brussels, Moscow, Washington, DC, and throughout Europe. Prizes are awarded annually including 'Die Raute', for the best German school newspaper; the Franz Josef Strauss Prize for Christian values; and the Young Songwriters' Prize.
Geographical Area of Activity: International.
Publications: Annual Report; *Infobrief* (newsletter); political studies.
Finance: Annual income €71.1m., expenditure €71.1m. (31 Dec. 2020).
Board: Markus Ferber (Chair.).
Principal Staff: Gen. Sec. Dr Josef Widmann; Deputy Gen. Sec. Stefanie von Winning.
Contact Details: Lazarettstr. 33, 80636 Munich; tel. (89) 1258-0; e-mail info@hss.de; internet www.hss.de.

Hedwig und Robert Samuel-Stiftung (Hedwig and Robert Samuel Foundation)
Established in 1932 by Hedwig and Robert Samuel, business people.
Activities: Provides vocational training and lifelong learning for children and young people from disadvantaged backgrounds, including English language lessons and computer skills. The Foundation has offices in San José (Costa Rica), New Delhi (India) and Managua (Nicaragua); and jointly founded KiD—Kind in Düsseldorf (f. 1993) to care for children aged 4–12 years who are believed to have been mentally and physically abused or sexually abused.
Geographical Area of Activity: Costa Rica, Germany, India, Nicaragua.
Publications: Newsletter.
Finance: Annual revenue €2.8m., expenditure €1.8m. (2023).
Board: Martin Barth (Chair. and CEO).
Contact Details: Königsallee 14, 40212 Düsseldorf; tel. (211) 1386666; e-mail info@samuel.de; internet www.samuel.de.

Heinrich-Böll-Stiftung (Heinrich Böll Foundation)
Established in 1987 and associated with the German Green Party, to promote political education in the areas of ecology, solidarity, democracy, arms control and sexual equality; and preserve the works and thoughts of writer Heinrich Böll.
Activities: Works in the fields of education and culture, ecology, economic and social issues and international politics. Programmes include: globalization and sustainable development; climate and energy policy; strengthening civil society; gender policy; promoting democracy; European policy; transatlantic dialogue; political consulting; arts and culture; and promoting young talent. The Foundation runs a fellowship study programme, which is open to students and postgraduates in all fields and of all nationalities; and also founded the

Gunda Werner Institute (f. 2007). It offers the Peace Film Award, the Anne Klein Women's Award, the Hannah Arendt Prize and the biannual Petra Kelly Prize. Has more than 34 offices worldwide and co-operates with NGOs working in more than 60 countries.

Geographical Area of Activity: Central and South America, East and South-East Asia, Europe, Middle East and North Africa, North America, South Asia, sub-Saharan Africa.

Publications: Annual Report; newsletter; *Böll.Thema* (magazine); *Plastikatlas*; reports; blog; books.

Finance: Annual income €97.2m., expenditure €87.2m. (31 Dec. 2023).

Executive Board: Dr Imme Scholz, Jan Philipp Albrecht (Chair.).

Principal Staff: Man. Dir Steffen Heizman.

Contact Details: Schumannstr. 8, 10117 Berlin-Mitte; tel. (30) 28534-0; e-mail info@boell.de; internet www.boell.de.

Helmholtz-Gemeinschaft (Helmholtz Association)

Established in 1995; named after Hermann von Helmholtz, a natural scientist.

Activities: An association of 18 research scientific-technical and medical-biological research centres working on matters of critical importance to science, society and business, using large and highly complex infrastructures, such as accelerators, experimental facilities, research ships or supercomputers. The Association helps decisionmakers and the wider public in assessing risks and opportunities based on scientific evidence; and supports school laboratories and citizen science initiatives. Main programme areas include: aviation, space and transport; earth and environment; education; energy; health; information; matter; science and society; and science policy. Coronavirus SARS-CoV-2, cancer and hydrogen technologies are among the current research priorities. It has an office in Berlin; with international offices in Beijing (People's Repub. of China), Brussels (Belgium), Moscow (Russian Federation) and Tel Aviv (Israel).

Geographical Area of Activity: International.

Publications: Annual Report; newsletter; *Perspektiven* (quarterly magazine); brochures.

Finance: Distributes core funding from the German Federal Ministry of Education and Research. Annual budget €6,000m. (2023).

Board of Directors: Prof. Dr Dr h.c. Otmar D. Wiestler (Pres.).

Principal Staff: Man. Dir Franziska Broer.

Contact Details: Ahrstr. 45, 53175 Bonn; tel. (228) 30818-0; e-mail info@helmholtz.de; internet www.helmholtz.de.

Hirschfeld-Eddy-Stiftung (Hirschfeld-Eddy Foundation)

Established in 2007, as the human rights foundation of the Lesbian and Gay Federation (LSVD), named in honour of Dr Magnus Hirschfeld, a German sexual reformer and civil rights activist, and FannyAnn Eddy, a lesbian human rights activist from Sierra Leone.

Activities: Advocates for the human rights of homosexual, bisexual and transgender people. The Foundation supports human rights defenders and works to remove prejudice. It supports projects in the areas of: human rights education; capacity building and empowerment; anti-discrimination, anti-homophobia and acceptance work; science; public relations and educational materials; and congresses, conferences, workshops and campaigns.

Geographical Area of Activity: International.

Publications: Newsletter; country reports.

Board of Trustees: Philipp Braun (Chair.); Patrick Dörr (Vice-Chair.).

Principal Staff: Dirs Axel Hochrein, Alva Träbert.

Contact Details: Almstadtstr. 7, 10119 Berlin; Postfach 040165, 10061 Berlin; tel. (30) 78954778; e-mail info@hirschfeld-eddy-stiftung.de; internet www.hirschfeld-eddy-stiftung.de.

Humboldt Forum

Established in 2020; operated by the Stiftung Humboldt Forum im Berliner Schloss (f. 2009).

Activities: Comprises the Stiftung Preußischer Kulturbesitz (Prussian Cultural Heritage Foundation), the Ethnologisches Museum (Ethnological Museum), the Museum für Asiatische Kunst (Museum of Asian Art), the Staatlichen Museen zu Berlin (Berlin State Museums), the Stadtmuseum Berlin, the Kulturprojekte Berlin, the Humboldt-Universität zu Berlin and the Stiftung Humboldt Forum im Berliner Schloss. The Forum organizes exhibitions and educational events at its culture and science centre.

Geographical Area of Activity: Germany.

Publications: Magazine; books; catalogues.

Principal Staff: Dir and CEO Prof. Dr Hartmut Dorgerloh.

Contact Details: Schlossplatz, 10178 Berlin; POB 02 10 89, 10122 Berlin; tel. (30) 265950-0; e-mail info@humboldtforum.org; internet www.humboldtforum.org.

Institut für Weltwirtschaft—IfW Kiel (Kiel Institute for the World Economy)

Established in 1914 by Bernhard Harms, a professor of political science, as the Königliches Institut für Seeverkehr und Weltwirtschaft an der Universität Kiel (Royal Institute of Shipping and the World Economy at the University of Kiel); an independent public foundation and member of the Leibniz Association of research institutes.

Activities: Carries out applied and evidence-based research on economic policy and issues of globalization. Research centres focus on: macroeconomics; international finance; trade; international development; and global transformation. The Institute comprises the Kiel Centre for Globalization, the Kiel Institute Africa Initiative, the Kiel Institute China Initiative and the Kiel Geoeconomics Initiative. It offers the Advanced Studies Program in International Economic Policy Research and runs the Kiel Institute Summer School on Economic Policy; and organizes conferences, seminars, workshops and public lectures.

Geographical Area of Activity: International.

Publications: Newsletter; *Kiel Institute Economic Outlook*; *Kiel Focus*; *Review of World Economics* (quarterly journal); working papers; policy briefs.

Finance: Funded by the German Federal Government and the state of Schleswig-Holstein.

Board of Directors: Prof. Dr Moritz Schularick (Pres.); Prof. Dr Christoph Trebesch (Vice-Pres.).

Scientific Advisory Council: Isabelle Méjean (Head); Prof. Dr Gernot Müller (Co-Head).

Principal Staff: Exec. Admin. Dir Birgit Austen-Bosy.

Contact Details: Kiellinie 66, 24105 Kiel; tel. (431) 8814-1; e-mail info@ifw-kiel.de; internet www.ifw-kiel.de.

INTEGRATA—Stiftung für Humane Nutzung der Informationstechnologie (INTEGRATA Foundation)

Founded in 1999 by Prof. Dr Wolfgang Heilmann, a computer data-processing consultant and founder of INTEGRATA.

Activities: Funds research on the use of information technology in the fields of work, education, health, art and culture, in particular in working and professional life. Annually, the Foundation awards the Wolfgang Heilmann Prize, worth €10,000, in recognition of work in the social uses of information technology; and the eCare Prize for the humane use of IT in nursing, worth €3,000. Since 1999 it has disbursed more than €500,000.

Geographical Area of Activity: International.

Publications: Annual Report; *Humanithesia* (newsletter); *Thesis and Objectives on the Management of Tele-Processes*.

GERMANY

Board of Trustees: Dr Frank Schönthaler (Chair.); Christiane Eckardt (Vice-Chair.).
Principal Staff: Dirs Jürgen Bartling, Swen Heinemann.
Contact Details: Vor dem Kreuzberg 28, 72070 Tübingen; e-mail info@integrata-stiftung.de; internet www.integrata-stiftung.de.

International Society for Human Rights—ISHR

Established in 1972 by Iwan I. Agrusow, a former forced labourer, and 12 others to uphold the UN Universal Declaration of Human Rights.
Activities: Works in the field of law and human rights. The Society comprises national sections, national groups and working groups in 38 countries. Projects include: strengthening civil society in Central and Eastern Europe and the countries of the former USSR; promoting the International Criminal Court; and providing democracy and human rights training to the Ukrainian military. The Society holds consultative status with the Council of Europe, consultative status (Roster) with ECOSOC and associated status with the UN Department of Public Information. It has around 30,000 members in over 30 countries.
Geographical Area of Activity: Worldwide.
Restrictions: No grants available directly, except through co-financed international projects.
Publications: Newsletter; posters.
Executive Board: Prof. Dr Dr Thomas Paul Schirrmacher (Pres.); Dr Carmen Krusch-Grün (Treas.).
Principal Staff: Sec.-Gen. Matthias K. Boehning.
Contact Details: Reuterstr. 116, 53129 Bonn; tel. (228) 30426360; e-mail secretariat@ishr.org; internet www.ishr.org.

Internationale Jugendbibliothek (International Youth Library Foundation)

Established in 1995 by Christa Spangenberg, a publisher, to ensure the long-term existence of the International Youth Library, which was established after the end of the Second World War.
Activities: Operates nationally, providing training courses and issuing publications; and internationally, granting scholarships and fellowships. Other activities include: creating awareness among adults and educationists of the importance of books for children and young people through providing information to organizations involved in composing children's literature and their distribution; and advising illustrators, publishers, writers and translators. The Foundation supports organizations with similar objectives in Germany and abroad; promoting intercultural and international understanding through the acquisition and distribution of children's literature from Germany and abroad; and research on international literature for children, particularly within the scope of the International Youth Library, which has an estimated 600,000 vols. It offers scholarships for research on children's and youth literature.
Geographical Area of Activity: International.
Restrictions: Does not accept unsolicited applications; grants only to professionals working in the area of children's and youth literature.
Publications: Annual Report; newsletter; *Buecherschloss*; *The White Ravens* (annual catalogue); picture books; books for children and young adults.
Finance: Annual income €2.8m., expenditure €2.8m. (2023).
Board of Trustees: Rolf Griebel (Chair.); Dr Sabine Solf (Deputy Chair.).
Principal Staff: CEO Clara Fernández López.
Contact Details: Schloss Blutenburg, Seldweg 15, 81247 Munich; tel. (89) 891211-0; e-mail info@ijb.de; internet www.ijb.de.

Johanna-Quandt-Stiftung

IRZ (Deutsche Stiftung für Internationale Rechtliche Zusammenarbeit) eV (German Foundation for International Legal Co-operation)

Established in 1992 on the initiative of the then Federal Minister of Justice Dr Klaus Kinkel; initially, its work was largely promoted within the framework of the TRANSFORM consultation programme, and subsequently also by the Stability Pact for South-Eastern Europe, primarily from the budget of the Federal Ministry of Justice.
Activities: Supports partner states, on behalf of the German Federal Government, to reform their legal systems and judiciary. In providing legislative consultation, the Foundation undertakes discussions with experts, drafts expert reports and assists in drawing up draft bills. It promotes the implementation of reform statutes, in particular through basic and further training of judges, public prosecutors, attorneys, notaries, academics and young lawyers, including within the framework of the IPA and ENPI programmes of the EU; arranges seminars, workshops, lecture events and symposia in the partner states, as well as working visits, training periods and guest visits, primarily to Germany but also to other EU states. The focus is on German and European law, supplemented by a cross-border exchange of experience. Has an office in Berlin.
Geographical Area of Activity: Central and South-Eastern Europe, East and South-East Asia, Eastern Europe, Middle East and North Africa, Russian Federation, Central Asia, South Asia.
Restrictions: Does not accept unsolicited applications.
Publications: Annual Report; *WiRO—Wirtschaft und Recht in Osteuropa* (monthly); blog.
Finance: Funded by the German Federal Government and the EU.
Board of Trustees: Benjamin Strasser (Chair.); Ramona Pisal, Prof. Dr Stephan Wernicke (Vice-Chair.).
Principal Staff: Gen. Dir Alexandra Albrecht; Dir Dr Stefan Hülshörster.
Contact Details: Ubierstr. 92, 53173 Bonn; POB 200409, 53134 Bonn; tel. (228) 9555-0; e-mail info@irz.de; internet www.irz.de.

Japanisch-Deutsches Zentrum Berlin (Japanese-German Centre Berlin)

Founded in 1985 by the Governments of Germany and Japan.
Activities: Organizes academic conferences, seminars and workshops on a wide range of topics, and joint exhibitions and concerts of German, Japanese and international artists. The Centre offers Japanese language courses, manages the German side of the German-Japanese Forum and co-ordinates several programmes for German-Japanese Peoples Exchange. It maintains a library of around 13,000 items.
Geographical Area of Activity: Asia, Europe, North America.
Restrictions: Does not accept unsolicited applications.
Publications: *JDZB echo* (quarterly newsletter); documents and proceedings of the Centre's events; Directory of German-Japanese Co-operation.
Board of Trustees: Gerhard Wiesheu (Chair.); Masahiko Mori (Vice-Chair.).
Management Board: Takeshi Yagi (Pres.); Prof. Dr Werner Pascha (Vice-Pres.); Dr Julia Münch (Sec.-Gen.); Kenji Matsumoto (Deputy Sec.-Gen.).
Contact Details: Saargemünderstr. 2, 14195 Berlin; tel. (30) 839070; e-mail jdzb@jdzb.de; internet www.jdzb.de.

Johanna-Quandt-Stiftung (Johanna Quandt Foundation)

Founded in 1995 by Johanna Quandt, a business person and largest shareholder in car manufacturer BMW.

Klassik Stiftung Weimar GERMANY

Activities: Aims to promote the importance of private entrepreneurship as a contributor to economic development in the public and the media. The Foundation awards the Herbert Quandt Media Prize, worth €50,000.

Geographical Area of Activity: Germany.

Board of Trustees: Stefan Quandt (Chair.).

Contact Details: Günther-Quandt-Haus, Seedammweg 55, 61352 Bad Homburg v.d. Hohe; tel. (6172) 404342; e-mail info@johanna-quandt-stiftung.de; internet www.johanna-quandt-stiftung.de.

Klassik Stiftung Weimar (Foundation of Weimar Classics)

Founded in 1991 (becoming an independent foundation in 1994); the legal successor to the former non-independent National Research and Memorial Centre of Classical German Literature in Weimar. Formerly known as the Stiftung Weimarer Klassik; merged with the Kunstsammlungen zu Weimar in 2003.

Activities: Preserves and expands sites and collections of classical German literature in Weimar to make them available to the public; encourages the communication, research and dissemination of this cultural heritage; and maintains the sites and collections of the former National Research and Memorial Centre, as well as the collections of 19th- and 20th-century works. The Foundation maintains more than 27 museums, castles, historic houses and parks, as well as collections of literature and art. It conducts research; organizes conferences, exhibitions and other events; and maintains the Goethe and Schiller Archives, the Duchess Anna Amalia Library and a research database containing information on around 35,000 people and 1,000 corporations.

Geographical Area of Activity: Europe, USA.

Restrictions: Does not accept unsolicited applications.

Publications: Annual Report; newsletter; *so:fie* (research databse); online teaching resources; blog.

Finance: Financed by the Federal Government, the State of Thuringia and the City of Weimar; total contributions €30.6m. (2023).

Board of Trustees: Prof. Dr Benjamin-Immanuel Hoff (Chair.).

Scientific Advisory Board: Prof. Dr Johannes Grave (Chair.); Prof. Dr Jutta Müller-Tamm (Vice-Chair.).

Principal Staff: Pres. Dr Ulrike Lorenz.

Contact Details: Burgplatz 4, 99423 Weimar; tel. (3643) 545400; e-mail info@klassik-stiftung.de; internet www.klassik-stiftung.de.

Klaus Tschira Stiftung GmbH (Klaus Tschira Foundation)

Established in 1995 by Dr Klaus Tschira, co-founder of software company SAP AG.

Activities: Promotes natural sciences, mathematics and computer science. The Foundation funds initiatives in the areas of education, research, science communication and architecture for science. In 2012, with the Karlsruhe Institute of Technology, it founded the National Institute for Science Communication (NaWik); and annually offers the KlarText Award for Understandable Science, worth €7,500. The Heidelberg Laureate Forum, an annual networking conference, was established in 2013.

Geographical Area of Activity: International.

Restrictions: Does not normally make grants to individuals.

Principal Staff: Authorized signatory Dr Heribert Komarek.

Contact Details: Villa Bosch, Schloss-Wolfsbrunnenweg 33, 69118 Heidelberg; tel. (6221) 533-100; e-mail geschaeftsstelle@klaus-tschira-stiftung.de; internet klaus-tschira-stiftung.de.

Konrad-Adenauer-Stiftung eV—KAS (Konrad Adenauer Foundation)

Founded in 1964, emerging from the Society for Christian Democratic Education (f. 1956), and named after the first Chancellor of the Federal Republic, Konrad Adenauer. The Foundation is guided by the same principles that inspired Adenauer's work.

Activities: Operates in the fields of the humanities, development and international relations through: offering scholarships to gifted individuals; organizing public events; and supporting more than 200 projects in the field of international understanding in over 120 countries. The Foundation offers political education and research for political projects; researches the history of Christian Democracy; supports and encourages European unification; and operates a think tank on domestic policy and the social market economy, international understanding and co-operation on development policy. It has 18 political education forums in Germany, with 107 offices abroad; and maintains a library containing 190,000 items. Annually, it awards the KAS Literature Prize, a journalism prize and the Social Market Economy Award.

Geographical Area of Activity: Worldwide.

Publications: Annual Report; newsletter (10 a year); *KAS International* (3 a year); Country Reports series; conference, seminar and event proceedings; *Facts & Findings*; *KAS Auslandsinformationen* (periodical); books.

Finance: Total income €226.8m., expenditure €226.8m. (2024).

Board of Trustees: Prof. Dr Michael Baumann (Chair.).

Board: Prof. Dr Norbert Lammert (Chair.); Prof. Dr Verena Blechinger-Talcott, Hermann Gröhe, Dr Tamara Zieschang (Deputy Chair.); Michael Thielen (Sec.-Gen.); Dr Christoph Brand (Treas.).

Contact Details: Klingelhöferstr. 23, 10785 Berlin; tel. (30) 26996-0; e-mail zentrale@kas.de; internet www.kas.de.

Körber-Stiftung (Körber Foundation)

Founded in 1959 by Kurt A. Körber, an industrialist and entrepreneur.

Activities: Works in the fields of innovation in education and science, international understanding and civil society. Main programmes are: New Life in Exile, Technology Needs Society and Holding Europe Together. The Foundation organizes the Bergedorf Round Table on German and European foreign and security policy; and the annual Berlin Foreign Policy Forum. Annually, it offers the Körber European Science Award for research by individual scientists; and the German Study Award, which is open to doctoral students in all disciplines. Has an office in Berlin.

Geographical Area of Activity: Worldwide.

Restrictions: No grants to individuals.

Publications: *The Berlin Pulse* (magazine and survey, 1 a year); *MINT Nachwuchsbarometer* (report, 1 a year); *European Science Prize* (magazine, 1 a year); *Spurensuchen* (magazine, 1 a year); newsletters; Edition Körber (8 books per year).

Finance: Total assets €578.5m. (2023).

Executive Board: Dr Thomas Paulsen (Chair.).

Board of Directors: Dr Klaus Wehmeier (Chair.); Dr Peter Frey (Vice-Chair.).

Board of Trustees: Christian Wriedt (Chair.); Richard Bauer (Vice-Chair.).

Contact Details: Kehrwieder 12, 20457 Hamburg; tel. (40) 808192-0; e-mail info@koerber-stiftung.de; internet www.koerber-stiftung.de.

Kulturstiftung der Länder—KSL (Cultural Foundation of the German Länder)

Established in 1988 to promote and preserve national art and culture.

Activities: Operates nationally and internationally in the field of the arts, promoting and preserving cultural heritage of national importance. The Foundation supports the acquisition of works of art and cultural artefacts by German museums, libraries and archives.
Geographical Area of Activity: Germany.
Publications: Newsletter; *Arsprototo* (quarterly magazine); Patrimonia (book series).
Board of Trustees: Michael Kretschmer (Chair.).
Board: Prof. Dr Frank Druffner (Chair.).
Contact Details: Schloss Charlottenburg–Theaterbau, Spandauer Damm 10, 14059 Berlin; tel. (30) 8936350; e-mail kontakt@kulturstiftung.de; internet www.kulturstiftung.de.

Leibniz Gemeinschaft (Leibniz Association)

Established in 1990; named after Gottfried Wilhelm Leibniz, a philosopher, mathematician, scientist and inventor.
Activities: An association of 96 independent research institutes working in a range of fields, including economics, natural, engineering and environmental sciences, spatial and social sciences and the humanities. The Association works on issues of social, economic and ecological significance, transferring knowledge to policymakers, academia, business and the public. It promotes co-operation with universities through the ScienceCampi initiative; and participates in five German Science and Innovation Houses (DWIH) in Delhi (India), New York (USA), Moscow (Russian Federation), São Paulo (Brazil) and Tokyo (Japan). The Leibniz Founding Prize, worth €50,000, is awarded to member institutes in the start-up phase of innovative projects that show business potential.
Geographical Area of Activity: International.
Publications: Newsletter (monthly); blog.
Finance: Annual budget c. €2,300m. (2025).
Presidium: Prof. Dr Martina Brockmeier (Pres.); Prof. Dr Matthias Beller, Prof Dr Sebastian Lentz, Dr Martin Mittelbach, Barbara Sturm (Vice-Pres); Dr Bettina Böhm (Sec.-Gen.).
Contact Details: Chausseestr. 111, 10115 Berlin; tel. (30) 206049-0; e-mail info@leibniz-gemeinschaft.de; internet www.leibniz-gemeinschaft.de.

Leibniz-Institut für Agrarentwicklung in Transformationsökonomien—IAMO (Leibniz Institute of Agricultural Development in Transition Economies)

Established in 1994, as the Institut für Agrarentwicklung in Mittel- und Osteuropa, by the Federal State of Saxony-Anhalt as a public foundation; a member of the Leibniz Association (q.v.) of research institutes.
Activities: Conducts research and analysis in the areas of: agricultural policies; markets in the agricultural and food sector; and development of businesses and structures in rural areas. Main programmes include: policies and institutions; natural resource use; livelihoods in rural areas; organization of agriculture; and agricultural value chains. The Institute promotes international networking for research and dialogue between academia, governments and businesses. It offers fellowships and research residencies abroad; and maintains a library containing around 29,000 monographs and 176 journals and periodicals.
Geographical Area of Activity: International.
Restrictions: Does not accept unsolicited applications.
Publications: Annual Report; *IAMO Newsletter*; *IAMO Policy Briefs*; *IAMO Discussion Papers*; *IAMO Studies*; *Monographien*; magazines; studies.
Board of Trustees: Sebastian Graf von Keyserlingk (Chair.); Dr Michael Lehmann (Chair.).
Scientific Advisory Board: Prof. Dr Gertrud Buchenrieder (Chair.); Prof. Dr Jens-Peter Loy (Vice-Chair.).
Principal Staff: Dirs Prof. Dr Alfons Balmann, Prof. Dr Dr h. c. Thomas Glauben, Katja Guhr, Prof. Dr Thomas Herzfeld.
Contact Details: Theodor-Lieser-Str. 2, 06120 Halle (Saale); tel. (345) 2928-0; e-mail iamo@iamo.de; internet www.iamo.de.

Leibniz-Institut für Ost- und Südosteuropaforschung (Leibniz Institute for East and South-East European Studies)

Founded in 1930 by the German Government; formerly known as the Südost-Institut—Stiftung für wissenschaftliche Südosteuropaforschung (South-East Institute—Foundation for Academic Research into South-Eastern Europe) and one of four component institutions of the Wissenschaftszentrum Ost- und Südosteuropa Regensburg—WiOS (Research Centre for East and South-East Europe in Regensburg). A member of the Leibniz Association (q.v.) of research institutes.
Activities: Works in the fields of the history and current affairs of South-Eastern Europe. The Institute carries out research, organizes conferences and hosts guest researchers; offers scholarships and fellowships; and provides research services including supervising and publishing academic journals, book series, working papers and handbooks. It has a public research library containing more than 350,000 items.
Geographical Area of Activity: Europe.
Restrictions: Not a grantmaking organization.
Publications: Annual Report; *IOS-Informationen* (quarterly newsletter); journals: *Südost-Forschungen* (history); *Südosteuropa* (current affairs); series: *Südosteuropäische Arbeiten*; *Südosteuropa Bibliographie—Ergänzungsbände*; discussion papers; handbooks; periodicals.
Finance: Annual income €4.5m., expenditure €3.7m. (2020).
Board of Trustees: Florian Albert (Chair.); Dr Clemens Escher (Vice-Chair.).
Scientific Advisory Board: Prof. Dr Susan Zimmermann (Chair.).
Principal Staff: Academic Dir Prof. Dr Ulf Brunnbauer.
Contact Details: Landshuterstr. 4, 93047 Regensburg; tel. (941) 94354-10; e-mail info@ios-regensburg.de; internet www.suedost-institut.de.

Max-Planck-Gesellschaft zur Förderung der Wissenschaften eV (Max Planck Society for the Advancement of Science)

Founded in 1948 to succeed the Kaiser-Wilhelm-Gesellschaft (f. 1911) with the object of promoting basic research in the sciences.
Activities: Operates nationally and internationally in the fields of science, medicine, the social sciences and humanities, and the law and other professions. The Society maintains international relations through self-conducted projects, research, conferences, prizes, publications and lectures. Basic research, particularly in the fields of biology, medicine, chemistry, physics and the humanities, is carried out in 84 institutes and research facilities belonging to the Society, with the aim of complementing research conducted at universities. It presents the annual Max Planck Research Award to two internationally renowned scientists, one working in Germany and one abroad.
Geographical Area of Activity: International, centered in Germany.
Restrictions: Not a grantmaking organization.
Publications: Annual Report; *Max-Planck-Forschung* (research journal in German); *Max Planck Research* (research journal in English); information booklets.
Finance: Annual budget €2,100m. (2023).
Board of Directors: Prof. Dr Patrick Cramer (Pres.); Dr Asifa Akhtar, Prof. Dr Christian Doeller, Prof. Dr Claudia Felser, Sibylle Günter (Vice-Pres).
Principal Staff: Sec.-Gen. Simone Schwanitz.
Contact Details: Hofgartenstr. 8, 80539 Munich; tel. (89) 21080; e-mail post@gv.mpg.de; internet www.mpg.de.

Max-Planck-Institut für Neurobiologie des Verhaltens—caesar (Max Planck Institute for Neurobiology of Behavior—caesar)

Established in 1995 by the German Government and the Federal State of North-Rhine-Westphalia; a neuroscience research institute associated with the Max-Planck-Gesellschaft (q.v.). Formerly Stiftung CEASAR; present name adopted in 2022.

Activities: Works in the field of neuroethology, the study of how an animal's nervous system produces behaviour. Has two research departments and seven independent research groups. Current research advances technologies and develops experimental approaches to link neuronal activity to naturalistic behaviour in freely moving animals. Works with universities training researchers.

Geographical Area of Activity: International.

Restrictions: Not a grantmaking organization.

Publications: Annual Report; *Smart Materials*; *Proceedings of the First Caesarium* (1999); research materials and publications.

Finance: Annual income €20.1m., expenditure €18.6m. (31 Dec. 2019).

Board of Directors: Prof. Dr Jason Kerr (Chair.).

Principal Staff: Scientific Dir Prof. Dr Jason Kerr; Scientific Dir and Man. Dir Dr Kevin Brigmann.

Contact Details: Ludwig-Erhard-Allee 2, 53175 Bonn; tel. (228) 9656-0; e-mail office@mpinb.mpg.de; internet mpinb.mpg.de.

Max Weber Stiftung—MWS (Max Weber Foundation)

Established in 2002 as the Deutsche Geisteswissenschaftliche Institute im Ausland—DGIA; present name adopted in 2012.

Activities: Promotes research, particularly in the fields of history, cultural studies, economics and the social sciences, in selected countries; and mutual understanding between Germany and these countries. The Foundation is an umbrella organization, comprising 11 institutes, in France, Germany, Italy, Japan, Lebanon, Poland, Türkiye (Turkey), the United Kingdom and the USA. They carry out humanities research and promote co-operation between scholars and institutions within their own spheres by means of publications and academic conferences, providing academic information and advice, facilitating contacts between scholars, supporting the future generation of scholars, as well as setting up and maintaining libraries and collections of other media.

Geographical Area of Activity: International.

Publications: Annual Report; Monitoring Report; newsletter; *Weltweit vor Ort* (magazine); journals; monographs; blog.

Board of Trustees: Prof. Dr Ute Frevert (Chair.).

Principal Staff: Man. Dir Dr Harald Rosenbach; Assistant Man. Dir Georgia Mengelkoch.

Contact Details: Rheinallee 6, 53173 Bonn; tel. (228) 37786-0; e-mail info@maxweberstiftung.de; internet www.maxweberstiftung.de.

medica mondiale eV

Founded in 1993, medica mondiale provides support to women and girls who experienced sexualised wartime violence.

Activities: Working with local, female-led partner organizations, medica mondiale empowers women and girls by offering them medical and psychological assistance, legal advice, and programmes to help them generate their own income. At the same time the organization works at the political level to assert women's rights and raise awareness of the consequences of violence for the whole of society.

Geographical Area of Activity: Afghanistan, Central Africa, Germany, Iraq, South-Eastern Europe, West Africa.

Publications: Annual Report; donor magazine; newsletter.

Finance: Annual income €11.5m., expenditure €7.3m. (31 Dec. 2023).

Executive Board: Dr Monika Hauser (Chair.).

Principal Staff: Exec. Dirs Dr Monika Hauser, Elke Ebert, Sybille Fezer.

Contact Details: Hülchratherstr. 4, 50670 Cologne; tel. (221) 9318980; e-mail info@medicamondiale.org; internet www.medicamondiale.org.

Medico International

Established in 1968 to send medical supplies to countries in need; comprises the Stiftung Medico International (Medico International Foundation, f. 2004), which supports the development of psychosocial work and strengthens the rights of victims of torture, war and disasters.

Activities: Operates worldwide, in particular in less-developed countries or in countries where emergency relief is necessary, in the field of medicine and health, offering medicines and medical equipment, medical personnel, ambulances and other equipment. The organization runs campaigns against landmines, and various projects in the areas of asylum, rehabilitation, AIDS, human rights and basic healthcare. It carries out projects in 31 countries.

Geographical Area of Activity: Middle East and North Africa, South America, Central America and the Caribbean, South Asia, South-East Asia, sub-Saharan Africa.

Publications: Annual Report; newsletter; *medico-Reports*; leaflets; posters.

Finance: Annual income €24m., expenditure €21m. (31 Dec. 2023).

Board: Dr Anne Blum (Chair.); Helga Riebe, Rainer Berkert (Vice-Chair.).

Principal Staff: Exec. Dir Tsafrir Cohen.

Contact Details: Lindleystr. 15, 60314 Frankfurt am Main; tel. (69) 94438-0; e-mail info@medico.de; internet www.medico.de.

Michael-Otto-Stiftung für Umweltschutz (Michael Otto Foundation for Environmental Protection)

Established in 1993 by Dr Michael Otto, Chair. of the Otto Group, an online retail company.

Activities: Develops strategies and supports projects that conserve nature and the environment. The Foundation funds innovative environmental and major nature conservation projects; and helps young people to implement their own 'Aqua Projects', with a focus on the protection of flowing water and sustainable treatment of rivers and streams. The Foundation has set up academic chairs, including 'The Economics of Climate Change' (Berlin Technical University); and supports research and educational institutions. Beside educational and funding work, it mediates between different interest groups, initiating dialogue between influential representatives from the business sector, nature conservation, government and academia. Hosts the head office of the F20 (q.v.) foundations platform.

Geographical Area of Activity: Eastern Europe, Germany, USA.

Publications: Newsletter; Proceedings of the annual Hamburg Nature Conservation Forum; brochure.

Board of Trustees: Prof. Dr Michael Otto (Chair.).

Principal Staff: CEO Dr Johannes Merck.

Contact Details: Glockengiesserwall 26, 20095 Hamburg; tel. (40) 64617770; e-mail info@umweltstiftungmichaelotto.org; internet www.umweltstiftungmichaelotto.de.

Minna-James-Heineman-Stiftung (Minna James Heineman Foundation)

Founded in 1928 (to provide care for elderly Jewish women in Hanover) and re-established in 1951 by Dannie N. Heineman; administered by the Stifterverband für die Deutsche Wissenschaft (q.v.).

Activities: Offers grants to scientific institutions in Germany, the USA and Israel, in particular the Max-Planck-Gesellschaft (q.v.), the Weizmann Institute of Science (Israel) and the Heineman Medical Research Centre (USA), preferably for research in the life sciences. The Dannie Heineman Award, worth €30,000, is conferred biennially by the Academy of Sciences at Göttingen for outstanding work, mainly in the field of natural and life sciences. Dannie Heineman scholarships are awarded to students and doctoral students. The Foundation also offers the James Heineman Research Award, worth €60,000, which is overseen by the Minerva Stiftung, a subsidiary of the Max-Planck-Gesellschaft; the Dannie Heineman Grant for Doctoral Candidates, for German or foreign doctoral candidates at the University of Hannover working on research projects in the technological or natural sciences; Heineman Student Grants, for US students who wish to study science or technology courses at the University of Hannover; and the annual Chairman's Special Grant, worth €10,000, for non-profit institutions in the Hannover area.

Geographical Area of Activity: Germany, Israel, USA.

Publications: Brochure.

Finance: Assets approx. €9m.

Board of Directors: Anders Bergendahl (Chair.); Thomas Buhl (Vice-Chair.); Alexander Bergendahl (Treas.); Crista Bergendahl (Sec.).

Principal Staff: Gen. Man. Rainer Lüdtke.

Contact Details: c/o Deutsches Stiftungszentrum (DSZ), Barkhovenallee 1, 45239 Essen; tel. (201) 8401160; internet www.heinemanstiftung.org.

MISEREOR—Bischöfliches Hilfswerk Misereor eV (German Catholic Bishops' Organization for Development Co-operation)

Founded in 1958 by the Catholic Church in the Federal Republic of Germany.

Activities: Supports the weakest members of society. Programme areas include: peace; refugees; hunger; climate change, energy and natural resources; human rights; and fair trade. The organization works with local partners to implement long-term solutions to problems in developing countries through organizing and financing education and training programmes that emphasize self-help.

Geographical Area of Activity: International.

Publications: Annual Report; pamphlets.

Board: Andreas Frick (Chair.).

Principal Staff: Dir-Gen. Fr Primin Spiegel; Man. Dirs Dr Bernd Bornhorst, Annette Ptassek.

Contact Details: Mozartstr. 9, 52064 Aachen; POB 101545, 52015 Aachen; tel. (241) 4420; e-mail info@misereor.de; internet www.misereor.org.

Munich Re Foundation/Münchener Rück Stiftung

Established in 2005 to support innovative solutions to the challenges faced by people worldwide in areas such as population growth, globalization, diminishing natural resources, pollution and climate change.

Activities: Works in four principal fields: knowledge accumulation and implementation, through which it supports education and training, funds a chair at the United Nations University and supports publishing projects; clarification and dissemination of information, including through brochures, training programmes and exhibitions; networking; and direct help and support for disaster relief and local projects.

Geographical Area of Activity: International.

Publications: Annual Report; newsletter.

Board of Trustees: Dr Doris Höpke (Chair.); Prof. Dr Dr Peter Höppe (Vice-Chair.).

Principal Staff: Chair. Renate Bleich; Vice-Chair. Dirk Reinhard.

Contact Details: Eingang West 5 (Walking Man), Leopoldstr. 36, 80802 Munich; POB 80791, Munich; tel. (89) 38918888; e-mail info@munichre-foundation.org; internet www.munichre-foundation.org.

Naspa Stiftung (Naspa Foundation)

Established in 1989 by Nassauische Sparkasse, a savings bank; formerly known as Initiative und Leistung, Stiftung der Nassauischen Sparkasse für Kultur, Sport und Gesellschaft.

Activities: Operates in the fields of culture and the arts, sport, conservation and the environment, healthcare and support for young people.

Geographical Area of Activity: Germany.

Restrictions: Usually only funds recognized charities registered or carrying out projects in areas in which the bank operates.

Publications: Newsletter; blog.

Finance: Total assets €26.8m. (2025).

Principal Staff: Chair. Günter Högner; Vice-Chair. Frank Diefenbach; Man. Dir Rainer Pribbernow.

Contact Details: Nassauische Sparkasse, Anstalt des öffentlichen Rechts, Rheinstr. 42–46, 65185 Wiesbaden; tel. (611) 364-96606; e-mail naspa-stiftung@naspa.de; internet www.naspa-stiftung.de.

Niedersächsische Sparkassenstiftung (Lower Saxony Savings Bank Foundation)

Established in 1984 by the Niedersächsischer Sparkassen- und Giroverband savings bank.

Activities: Operates in the field of the arts, with an emphasis on visual arts, music, conservation of monuments and museums. The Foundation supports projects by other organizations, carries out its own activities, awards prizes and scholarships, including the €25,000 Kurt Schwitters Prize for contemporary art every two years; and the €12,500 Sprengel Prize for Fine Arts, which is connected with a scholarship to spend half a year in another European country. The Foundation works closely with the VGH Foundation (f. 2000), which promotes science and culture in areas where the VGH insurance company operates.

Geographical Area of Activity: Germany (Federal State of Lower Saxony), USA.

Restrictions: Grants only to individuals from and organizations in Lower Saxony.

Finance: Total endowment €63m.; annual disbursements approx. €5m.

Board: Thomas Mang (Pres.); Cord Bockhop, Johannes Hartig (Vice-Pres).

Principal Staff: Man. Dir Dr Johannes Janssen; Deputy Man. Dir Martina Fragge.

Contact Details: Schiffgraben 6–8, 30159 Hannover; Postfach 43 80, 30043 Hannover; tel. (511) 3603489; e-mail sparkassenstiftung@svn.de; internet www.nsks.de/nsks.

Novartis-Stiftung für therapeutische Forschung (Novartis Foundation for Therapeutical Research)

Established in 1969 by Sandoz AG Nuremberg, a pharmaceutical company, as the Sandoz-Stiftung für therapeutische Forschung; present name adopted in 1997 following the merger of Sandoz and Ciba-Geigy.

Activities: Operates in the field of medical research, organizing inter-disciplinary symposia. The Foundation offers grants, worth up to €100,000, made in the areas of the heart/circulation, anti-coagulation, dermatology, immunology, haematology, oncology, stem cell research, endocrinology, pulmonary diseases and neurology; and supports the establishment of endowed professorships. It also awards scholarships; graduate fellowships for junior researchers, worth €8,000 each; and every two years the Novartis Prize, worth €10,000, for pharmaceutical research.

Geographical Area of Activity: Germany.

Finance: Foundation capital approx. €10m.; annual income approx. €200,000 (2025).
Board of Directors: Dr Andreas Kreiss, Dr Andre Schmidt.
Contact Details: Roonstr. 25, Bldg 44, 90429 Nuremberg; tel. (911) 27312796; e-mail info@stiftung-tf.de; internet www.stiftung-tf.de.

Otto-Benecke-Stiftung eV (Otto Benecke Foundation)

Founded in 1965 by the Verband Deutscher Studentenschaften (Association of German Student Bodies).

Activities: Conducts education, counselling and scholarship programmes to integrate young asylum seekers, refugees and members of minority groups in Germany. The Foundation supports young immigrants to continue their studies; provides networking connections with local business people and vocational training opportunities; and promotes social acceptance of immigration to reduce xenophobia and prevent radicalization. In countries of origin, it works with local companies and industry associations to provide vocational training.
Geographical Area of Activity: Germany, Morocco.
Restrictions: Grants only to immigrants, refugees and asylum seekers.
Publications: *Schriftenreihe der Akademie für Migration und Integration*.
Finance: Annual expenditure approx. €20.5m.
Board of Trustees: Eberhard Diepgen (Chair.).
Board: Dr Lothar Theodor Lemper (Chair.); Gülistan Yüksel (Deputy Chair.).
Contact Details: Kennedyallee 105–107, 53175 Bonn; tel. (228) 8163-0; e-mail post@obs-ev.de; internet www.obs-ev.de.

Oxfam Deutschland eV

Established in 1995; became part of the Oxfam confederation of organizations (qq.v.) in 2003.

Activities: Supports women and girls through self-conducted programmes in partnership with local organizations in areas including: civil conflict management; emergency aid and reconstruction; gender equality; healthcare and education; HIV/AIDS and reproductive health; and securing livelihoods. The organization also provides emergency and disaster relief.
Geographical Area of Activity: Central America and the Caribbean, East Asia, EU, Middle East, South Asia, sub-Saharan Africa.
Restrictions: Does not make loans or grants to individuals.
Publications: Annual Report; newsletter; *EINS* (magazine).
Finance: Annual income €51.5m., expenditure €51.3m. (2022/23).
Board: Andrew Hammett (First Chair.); Maria von Borcke (Second Chair.); Eva Maria Ostendorf (Third Chair.).
Principal Staff: Exec. Chair. Serap Altinisik; Man. Dir Jan Heser.
Contact Details: Am Köllnischen Park 1, 10179 Berlin; tel. (30) 453069-0; e-mail info@oxfam.de; internet www.oxfam.de.

Prix Jeunesse Foundation

Established in 1964 by the Government of Bavaria, the City of Munich and Bayerischer Rundfunk, a public radio and television broadcaster.

Activities: Works in the field of children's and youth television. The Foundation awards Prix Jeunesse International Prizes for children's and youth television programmes; organizes conferences and training courses; conducts its own research and research in collaboration with its affiliate, the International Central Institute for Youth and Educational Television (IZI); and issues publications. It maintains a video library covering more than four decades of children's and youth television and organizes the Prix Jeunesse International Festival every two years.
Geographical Area of Activity: Europe, North Americe, Latin America.
Publications: *WATCHwords Online* (newsletter, 3 a year); *TeleVIZIon* (professional journal).
Finance: Financed by annual contributions from its founders.
Principal Staff: Man. Dir Dr Maya Götz.
Contact Details: c/o Bayerischer Rundfunk, Rudfunkpl. 1, 80335 Munich; tel. (89) 590042058; e-mail info@prixjeunesse.de; internet www.prixjeunesse.de.

Robert-Bosch-Stiftung GmbH (Robert Bosch Foundation)

Founded in 1964 by Bosch, an engineering and electronics company, in honour of its founder, Robert Bosch.

Activities: Offers grants in the areas of education, society, health, international relations and science and research. The Foundation focuses on migration, integration and inclusion; social cohesion in Germany and Europe; and sustainable living spaces. It has three foundations under its aegis: the Otto und Edith Mühlschlegel Stiftung and the Hans-Walz-Stiftung are dependent foundations and focus on specific issues such as the challenges of ageing and naturopathy; and the DVA-Stiftung supports the Foundation's activities in the field of German-French relations. The Foundation comprises seven health, research and higher education facilities: the Robert Bosch Hospital; the Dr Margarete Fischer-Bosch Institute for Clinical Pharmacology; the Institute for the History of Medicine; the Robert Bosch Academy; the German School Academy; the UWC Robert Bosch College; and the International Alumni Center. Jointly, with the Deutscher Übersetzerfonds (German Translator Fund, f. 1997), it also supports the TOLEDO translation programme, which offers scholarships and grants under its Mobility Fund for stays in European translation and literature centres. Has an office in Berlin.
Geographical Area of Activity: Asia, Europe, Middle East and North Africa, North America, sub-Saharan Africa.
Publications: Annual Report; newsletter.
Finance: Total assets €5,497.2m. (31 Dec. 2023).
Board of Trustees: Dr Christof Kübel (Chair.).
Principal Staff: CEO Berhnard Straub.
Contact Details: POB 100628, 70005 Stuttgart; Heidehofstr. 31, 70184 Stuttgart; tel. (711) 46084-850; e-mail info@bosch-stiftung.de; internet www.bosch-stiftung.de.

The Ronald S. Lauder Foundation

Founded in 1987 by Ronald S. Lauder, a business person and former US Ambassador to Austria.

Activities: Offers grants in the areas of Jewish welfare, religion, cultural programmes, conservation and education. The Foundation supports Jewish kindergartens, schools, youth centres and camps and higher education institutions; and non-sectarian international student exchanges. Along with the Joint Jewish Distribution Committee (q.v.), it sponsors Camp Szarvas, which takes place each summer in Hungary and is attended by Jews from more than 20 countries. Has an office in the USA.
Geographical Area of Activity: Austria, Belarus, Bulgaria, Croatia, Czech Repub. (Czechia), Greece, Germany, Hungary, Poland, Romania, Russia, Slovakia, Ukraine, USA.
Restrictions: Does not accept unsolicited applications.
Publications: Information brochure; newsletter.
Board of Directors: Ronald S. Lauder (Chair. and Pres.); Joseph F. Tuite, Jr (Treas.).
Principal Staff: Exec. Vice-Pres. and CEO Joshua I. Spinner.
Contact Details: Rykestr. 53, 10405 Berlin; tel. (30) 440131610; e-mail info@lauderfoundation.com; internet lauderfoundation.com.

Rosa-Luxemburg-Stiftung (Rosa Luxemburg Foundation)

Established in 1990 for the promotion of political education (associated with the Social Democratic Party—SPD), knowledge and research, culture and the arts, and international understanding.

Activities: Works in the fields of the arts and humanities, economic affairs, education, international affairs, law and human rights. The Foundation promotes research; issues publications; awards scholarships and the annual Rosa Luxemburg Prize; and maintains archives and a library. It administers several dependent foundations: Max-Lingner-Stiftung; Hermann-Henselmann-Stiftung; Erik-Neutsch-Stiftung; Harald-Breuer-Stiftung; Modrow-Stiftung; and Clara-Zetkin-Stiftung.

Geographical Area of Activity: International, in particular Africa, Asia, Central and Eastern Europe and the Russian Federation, Central and South America.

Publications: Annual Report; newsletter; *Utopie kreativ* (magazine); reports; books.

Finance: Annual income €76.0m., expenditure €74.7m. (31 Dec. 2023).

Executive Board: Prof. Dr Heinz Bierbaum (Chair.); Lena Saniye Güngör, Jan Korte (Vice-Chair.).

Principal Staff: Exec. Dir Daniela Trochowski.

Contact Details: Straße der Pariser Kommune 8A, 10243 Berlin; tel. (30) 44310-0; e-mail info@rosalux.de; internet www.rosalux.de.

Save Our Future Umweltstiftung—SOF (Save Our Future Environmental Foundation)

Founded in 1989 by Jürgen Oppermann, a business person.

Activities: Promotes education for sustainable development in early childhood education. The Foundation initiates and supports educational projects in day-care centres; and is involved in the education and training of teaching specialists.

Geographical Area of Activity: Germany.

Restrictions: Not a grantmaking organization.

Publications: *SOF-Newsletter* (1–2 a year); *Die Sonne und ihre Kinder* (children's publication); *Umweltschutz im Sportverein—Ein Praxisleitfaden* (video and brochures).

Finance: Total assets approx. €5m.

Board of Trustees: Jürgen Oppermann (Chair.); Sven Rothenbacher (Vice-Chair.).

Board: Burghard Solinsky (Chair.).

Principal Staff: Man. Dir Dirka Grießhaber.

Contact Details: Spaldingstr. 210, 20097 Hamburg; tel. (40) 240600; e-mail info@save-our-future.de; internet www.saveourfuture.de.

Schwarzkopf-Stiftung Junges Europa (Schwarzkopf Young Europe Foundation)

Founded in 1971 as the Heinz-Schwarzkopf Foundation.

Activities: Empowers young people aged 16–28 years to be active European citizens through developing a dialogue between young people and leaders from the fields of politics, economics and culture, providing information about the decision-making process in Europe. The Foundation organizes debates, lectures and seminars; visits to embassies and exhibitions; and EU Crash Courses at schools. Since 2004 it has been the international umbrella organization of the European Youth Parliament, a peer-to-peer educational debating programme; since 2009 it has hosted the Young Islam Conference, a pluralist dialogue forum for young adults, comprising a network of more than 500 former conference participants; and is part of the Competence Network 'Living together in a migration society', which promotes young people's political participation, offering advisory, training and dialogue services for educators and volunteers from the field of child and youth welfare. Travel grants are available to young people to explore Europe and exchange European perspectives. The Young European of the Year Award and the annual Schwarzkopf Europe Award recognize the commitment of young people or public figures to mutual international understanding and a peaceful Europe. The Margot Friedländer Award calls on young people and students to confront the history of the Holocaust and to combat current forms of anti-Semitism, racism and exclusion.

Geographical Area of Activity: Western, Central and Eastern Europe.

Publications: Annual Report; educational publications on youth pedagogy.

Finance: Annual budget €3.3m. (2024).

Board: Esra Kücük (Chair.).

Principal Staff: Man. Dir Tomas Sacher.

Contact Details: Sophienstr. 28–29, 10178 Berlin; tel. (30) 72621950; e-mail info@schwarzkopf-stiftung.de; internet www.schwarzkopf-stiftung.de.

Schweisfurth-Stiftung (Schweisfurth Foundation)

Founded in 1985 by Karl Ludwig Schweisfurth, founder of Herta, a meat-processing company.

Activities: Promotes sustainable agriculture and animal husbandry and identifies environmentally friendly methods of agriculture and how to improve the welfare standards of livestock. Other areas of interest are: food safety; safeguarding food quality; innovative organic food processing; and novel marketing. The Foundation supports rural development and multi-stakeholder dialogues between town and country; and proposes new forms of education and training in artisanal food processing, working closely with government agencies. It publishes guidelines for sustainable agriculture and food production.

Geographical Area of Activity: Europe.

Restrictions: Does not accept unsolicited applications or fund scholarships.

Publications: Newsletter; leaflets; books.

Supervisory Board: Anne Schweisfurth (Chair.); Dr Christa Mueller (Vice-Chair.).

Principal Staff: Dir Dr Niels Kohlschütter.

Contact Details: Rupprechtstr. 25, 80636 Munich; tel. (89) 179595-0; e-mail info@schweisfurth-stiftung.de; internet www.schweisfurth-stiftung.de.

Software AG Stiftung (Software AG Foundation)

Established in 1992 by Peter M. Schnell and Software AG, an enterprise computer software company.

Activities: Provides funding and technical support to non-profit organizations. Main programmes include: education; children and young people; disabled people; care for the elderly; science and research on complementary medicine, biodynamic agriculture and educational reform; and natural capital.

Geographical Area of Activity: Brazil, Europe.

Publications: Annual Report; *SAGST-Magazine*.

Finance: Total assets €1,067.0m.; net annual income €22.4m. (31 Dec. 2022).

Board of Trustees: Horst Kinzinger (Chair.); Hilmar Dahlem (Vice-Chair.).

Executive Board: Dr Peter M. Schnell (Chair.).

Contact Details: Am Eichwäldchen 6, 64297 Darmstadt; tel. (6151) 916650; e-mail stiftung@sagst.de; internet www.sagst.de.

Stiftung 'Erinnerung, Verantwortung und Zukunft'—EVZ (Foundation 'Remembrance, Responsibility and Future')

Established in 2000 to pay compensation to former forced labourers during the period of National Socialism (Nazism).

Activities: Promotes human rights and understanding between peoples. The Foundation supports international projects that critically examine history; work for human rights; and show a commitment to the victims of National

Socialism. Since 2001 it has also granted humanitarian aid to survivors; and strengthened civic involvement in Central and Eastern Europe.

Geographical Area of Activity: International.

Restrictions: No funding of commercial projects; projects geared exclusively towards a publication; or capital works.

Publications: Annual Report; newsletter; studies.

Finance: Of the initial total capital of 10,100m. Deutsche Marks, 9,400m. Deutsche Marks and the accumulated interest were used to compensate former forced labourers and other victims of the Nazi regime. Total assets €475.5m. (2023); annual project spending €7.6m. (2023).

Board of Trustees: Annette Schavan (Chair.); Dr Jörg Freiherr Frank von Fürstenwerth (Deputy Chair.).

Principal Staff: CEO Dr Andrea Despot.

Contact Details: Friedrichstr. 200, 10117 Berlin; tel. (30) 259297-0; e-mail info@stiftung-evz.de; internet www.stiftung-evz.de.

Stiftung Ettersberg (Ettersberg Foundation)

Established in 2002 on the initiative of Jorge Semprún, a Spanish author and Buchenwald concentration camp survivor.

Activities: Concerned with comparative research into European dictatorships in the 20th century, focusing on the reasons for their emergence, the form that they took and the ways in which they were overcome. The Foundation hosts international symposia and academic seminars, the results of which are presented in a series of publications and periodicals. It also conducts academic research into the socialist dictatorship in East Germany, to further the teaching of political history in schools and other contexts. In 2012 the Foundation took over the establishment and running of the Memorial and Study Centre Andreasstrasse in the former Stasi remand prison in Erfurt. Maintains a research library.

Geographical Area of Activity: Germany.

Publications: Annual Report; proceedings of international symposia and academic seminars.

Board of Trustees: Prof. Dr Teresa Pinheiro (Chair.); Tina Beer (Vice-Chair.).

Principal Staff: CEO Prof. Dr Jörg Ganzenmüller.

Contact Details: Jenaer Str. 4, 99425 Weimar; tel. (3643) 4975-0; e-mail weimar@stiftung-ettersberg.de; internet www.stiftung-ettersberg.de.

Stiftung zur Förderung der Hochschulrektorenkonferenz (Foundation for the Promotion of the German Rectors' Conference)

Founded in 1965 by Prof. Dr Julius Speer, Prof. Dr Rudolf Sieverts, Prof. Dr Helmut Witte, Prof. Dr Gerhard Kielwein and Prof. Dr Hans Leussink to support the Conference of Rectors, a voluntary association of higher/further education institutes in Germany.

Activities: Works within the fields of activity of the German Rectors' Conference: education, nationally and internationally, social welfare and international relations. The Foundation works to find common solutions to problems in higher education and makes recommendations; promotes co-operation among state, scientific and academic bodies; and provides information services. It organizes conferences and courses; issues publications; and maintains a library containing 70,000 monographs and 800 periodicals (including 350 university journals). The Corporate Communications Prize, worth €25,000, is awarded every two years in conjunction with ZEIT, a publishing company, and the Robert-Bosch-Stiftung GmbH (q.v.). Comprises 269 member institutions, with offices in Berlin and Brussels.

Geographical Area of Activity: International.

Publications: Annual Report.

Finance: Annual budget approx. €5.3m. (2022).

Board of Directors: Prof. Dr Walter Rosenthal (Pres.).

Principal Staff: Sec.-Gen. Jens-Peter Gaul; Deputy Sec.-Gen. Marijke Wahlers.

Contact Details: Ahrstr. 39, 53175 Bonn; tel. (228) 887-0; e-mail post@hrk.de; internet www.hrk.de/hrk/aufgaben-und-struktur/stiftung.

Stiftung Jugend forscht eV (Foundation for Youth Research)

Founded in 1965 by Henri Nannen, a magazine editor.

Activities: Promotes contests in science, technology, engineering and mathematics (STEM) for schoolchildren and young people aged under 21 years. Competition projects must fall into one of seven areas: work environment; biology; chemistry; geo- and space sciences; mathematics/IT; physics; or technology. The Foundation also provides support to participants after contests.

Geographical Area of Activity: Germany.

Restrictions: Does not accept unsolicited applications.

Publications: Annual Report; newsletter.

Finance: Annual revenue €3.1m., expenditure €3.1m. (31 Dec. 2021).

Principal Staff: Man. Dir Dr Jessica Bönsch; Deputy Man. Dir Dr Jennifer Plath.

Contact Details: Baumwall 3, 20459 Hamburg; tel. (40) 374709-0; e-mail info@jugend-forscht.de; internet www.jugend-forscht.de.

Stiftung Kinder in Afrika (Children in Africa Foundation)

Founded in 1984 by Horst W. Zillmer.

Activities: Works in Africa in the fields of education, and medicine and health, through grants to institutions. Since 1985 the Foundation has undertaken projects throughout sub-Saharan Africa. Its current focus is on East Uganda, supporting the building of schools.

Geographical Area of Activity: sub-Saharan Africa.

Trustees: Dr Hans-Dieter Höhnk (Chair.); Katharina Mitzlaff (Vice-Chair.).

Contact Details: Holsteiner Str. 12, 21465 Reinbek; tel. (40) 7229273; e-mail info@kinder-in-afrika.de; internet stiftung.kinder-in-afrika.de.

Stiftung Lesen (Reading Foundation)

Founded in 1988 to promote the joy of reading and literacy skills for children and young people.

Activities: Operates in the field of education for children and young people, supporting families, kindergartens, school teachers and volunteers. The Foundation also conducts research on reading and media.

Geographical Area of Activity: Germany.

Restrictions: No unsolicited applications.

Publications: Annual Report; reading recommendations; training materials and webinars; flyers; brochures; newsletters; articles and studies.

Finance: Total assets €9.9m. (2023).

Board of Trustees: Gerd Landsberg (Chair.); Thomas Rathnow (Vice-Chair.).

Principal Staff: CEO Dr Jörg F. Maas.

Contact Details: Römerwall 40, 55131 Mainz; tel. 6131-28890-0; e-mail mail@stiftunglesen.de; internet www.stiftunglesen.de.

Stiftung Meridian (Meridian Foundation)

Established in the 1990s by the Schmidt-Ruthenbeck family, which has interests in wholesale and retail.

Activities: Comprises: the Stiftung Mercator Deutschland, which carries out self-conducted programmes and offers grants in the thematic areas of Europe in the world, social participation and cohesion, climate protection, and digitized society; and the Stiftung Mercator Schweiz, which carries out activities in the areas of access to education, international understanding and dialogue, social participation and environmental conservation, with digital transformation as a crosscutting theme. The Foundations offer the Mercator Fellowship on International Affairs, which is run jointly with the Studienstiftung des deutschen Volkes (q.v.). The Stiftung Mercator Deutschland has offices in Beijing, People's Republic of China, and İstanbul, Türkiye (Turkey).

Geographical Area of Activity: International.

Restrictions: Grants only to non-profit organizations; Fellowships are open to German-speaking university graduates from all disciplines and young professionals.

Publications: Annual Report; newsletter.

Advisory Board: Frédéric Pflanz (Chair.).

Executive Board: Ralf Ruhrmann, Stefan Tieben.

Contact Details: Baedekerstr. 1, 45128 Essen; tel. (201) 811942-101; e-mail info@meridian.ruhr; internet www.meridian.ruhr.

Stiftung Nord-Süd-Brücken (North-South-Bridge Foundation)

Established in 1994 to promote co-operation in development and international understanding.

Activities: Promotes partnerships for development projects in less-developed regions, informing the public about the need for co-operation in development, especially through fostering tolerance and international understanding.

Geographical Area of Activity: Asia, Africa and Latin America.

Restrictions: Only supports NGOs based in the former German Democratic Repub. (East Germany) and East Berlin; no grants to individuals.

Finance: Total assets €21.1m.; annual project spending €3.9m. (31 Dec. 2023).

Board of Trustees: Dr Dawud Ansari (Chair.); Nadege Azafack, Anne Schicht (Vice-Chair.).

Principal Staff: CEO Ingrid Spiller; Deputy CEOs Dr Jürgen Varnhorn, Wilhelm Volks.

Contact Details: Greifswalder Str. 33A, 10405 Berlin; tel. (30) 92108410; e-mail info@nord-sued-bruecken.de; internet nord-sued-bruecken.de.

Stiftung für die Rechte zukünftiger Generationen—SRzG (Foundation for the Rights of Future Generations)

Established in 1997.

Activities: Raises awareness about intergenerational equity and sustainability in politics, business and society; and represents the rights of younger and future generations. The Foundation carries out research in the areas of artificial intelligence, the environment, finance, democracy, education, employment, pensions and youth policy; and awards prizes for research on generational justice and demography, and a legislative prize for laws that protect the interests of future generations. It has special consultative status with ECOSOC.

Geographical Area of Activity: International.

Publications: Annual Report; newsletter; *Intergenerational Justice Review* (journal); handbooks; position papers.

Board of Trustees: Prof. Dr Rolf Kreibich, Prof. Dr Dr h.c. Ortwin Renn (Co-Chair.).

Principal Staff: Man. Dir Jörg Tremmel.

Contact Details: Mannspergerstr. 29, 70619 Stuttgart; tel. (711) 28052777; e-mail kontakt@srzg.de; internet www.intergenerationaljustice.org.

Stiftung Weltethos (Global Ethic Foundation)

Established in 1995 by Hans Küng as the Stiftung Weltethos für interkulturelle und interreligiöse Forschung, Bildung und Begegnung (Foundation for Global Ethic for Intercultural and Interreligious Research, Education and Encounter) through a grant from Count K. K. von der Groeben.

Activities: Operates nationally and internationally in the areas of the humanities, intercultural and interreligious dialogue, education, international affairs and human rights. The Foundation carries out self-conducted programmes and research; organizes lectures, conferences and training courses; issues publications; and supports wider initiatives and projects. Programmes are guided by the 1993 Declaration Toward a Global Ethic endorsed by the Parliament of the World's Religions. In 2012 the Weltethos-Institut was jointly established with the Universität Tübingen and Karl Schlecht Stiftung. Other Global Ethic Foundations and Initiatives are present in Austria, Colombia, the Czech Republic (Czechia), Mexico, Slovenia, Switzerland; with projects in Bosnia and Herzegovina, the People's Republic of China, Hong Kong, Luxembourg and the USA.

Geographical Area of Activity: International.

Publications: Annual Report; newsletter; factsheets.

Principal Staff: Pres. Prof. Dr Bernd Engler; Man. Dir Lena Zoller.

Contact Details: Eisenbahnstr. 1, 72072 Tübingen; tel. (7071) 40053-0; e-mail office@weltethos.org; internet www.weltethos.org.

Stiftung West-Östliche Begegnungen (East-West Encounters Charitable Foundation)

Established in 1994 to support and promote contacts and exchange projects between the people of Germany and countries of the former Union of Soviet Socialist Republics (USSR).

Activities: Carries out activities in the fields of peace and friendship, culture, history, social networking, inclusion, the environment, sustainable development and civic engagement. The Foundation carries out its own projects in co-operation with public and private partners on town twinning and NGO networking. It provides grants for meetings and exchange projects between young people, schools, civil society actors, NGOs and municipalities.

Geographical Area of Activity: Armenia, Azerbaijan, Belarus, Estonia, Georgia, Germany, Kazakhstan, Kyrgyzstan, Latvia, Lithuania, Moldova, Russian Federation, Tajikistan, Turkmenistan, Ukraine, Uzbekistan.

Restrictions: Grants only to German institutions (e.g. registered NGOs, schools, municipalities, institutes, etc.); no grants to individuals or foundations; no stipends.

Publications: Activity Report; information brochures.

Finance: Total assets €19.1m. (2024).

Board of Trustees: Matthias Platzeck (Chair.); Jochen Rummenhöller (Vice-Chair.).

Board of Directors: Jelena V. Hoffmann (Chair.); Dr Martin Kummer (Vice-Chair.).

Principal Staff: Man. Anna Kaiser; Sec. Alina Vedmedyeva.

Contact Details: Nicolaihaus, Brüderstr. 13, 10178 Berlin; tel. (30) 2044840; e-mail info@stiftung-woeb.de; internet www.stiftung-woeb.de.

Stiftung Wissenschaft und Politik—Deutsches Institut für internationale Politik und Sicherheit—SWP (Science and Politics Foundation—German Institute for International and Security Affairs)

Founded in 1962; an independent research centre which advises the German Parliament and the German Federal Government on all matters relevant to German foreign and security policy.

Activities: Organized into eight research divisions, consisting of some 70 researchers. The Institute organizes conferences and workshops. It also maintains a library of around 85,000 vols and a computerized information system with around 900,000 bibliographical references in international relations and area studies. Has an office in Brussels, Belgium.

Geographical Area of Activity: Germany.

Restrictions: Does not offer grants or scholarships.

Publications: *SWP-Studien/SWP Research Paper*; *SWP-Aktuell/SWP Comment*; *SWP-Zeitschriftenschau/SWP Journal Review*; *Kurz gesagt/Point of View*; *Nomos Books Series*; *Internationale Politik und Sicherheit* (IPS); newsletter.

Finance: Funded mainly by the Federal Chancellery; institutional funding: €167.7m. (2023).

Board of Directors: Eckart von Klaeden (Pres.); Jens Hanefeld, Thomas Matussek (Vice-Pres).

Principal Staff: Dir Dr Stefan Mair.

Contact Details: Ludwigkirchplatz 3–4, 10719 Berlin; POB 311319, 10643 Berlin; tel. (30) 88007-0; e-mail swp@swp-berlin.org; internet www.swp-berlin.org.

Stiftungsfonds Deutsche Bank im Stifterverband für die Deutsche Wissenschaft (Deutsche Bank Endowment Fund at the Donors' Association for the Promotion of German Science)

Established in 1970 by Deutsche Bank AG, a financial services provider, under the aegis of the Stifterverband für die Deutsche Wissenschaft (q.v.).

Activities: Operates in the fields of science and technology, mainly through funding programmes at universities and other institutions. The Fund awards grants to universities to assist refugees and migrants in completing university studies at institutions in Germany. Grants disbursed in 2016 amounted to €158m.

Geographical Area of Activity: Europe.

Publications: Study courses.

Finance: Total endowment approx. €9m.

Board of Directors: Jörg Eigendorf (Senior Group Dir); Dr Volker Meyer-Guckel (Gen. Sec.).

Principal Staff: Man. Pia Heubgen.

Contact Details: c/o Stifterverband für die Deutsche Wissenschaft eV, Baedekerstr. 1, 45128 Essen; tel. (201) 8401-214; internet www.stiftungsfonds-deutsche-bank.de.

Studienstiftung des deutschen Volkes (German Academic Scholarship Foundation)

Founded in 1925; dissolved in 1934 and refounded in 1948.

Activities: Operates in the fields of science and medicine, the arts and humanities, law and other professions, through grants to individuals. Scholars may participate in summer schools arranged by the Foundation. Scholarship holders can apply for specific funding for study and research worldwide. Annually, the Foundation awards around 2,000 scholarships for undergraduate and postgraduate students, as well as about 300 scholarships for PhD candidates; also awards prizes for social or civic commitment as well as three awards for outstanding doctoral theses. It has an office in Berlin.

Geographical Area of Activity: Germany.

Publications: Annual Report.

Finance: Annual revenue €125.5m., expenditure €125.5m. (2023).

Board of Trustees: Dr Georg Schuette (Chair.); Prof. Dr Melanie Wald-Fuhrmann, Prof. Dr Cornelia Ruhe (Vice-Chair.).

Board: Prof. Dr Dr h.c. Michael Hoch (Pres.); Prof. Dr Ansgar Büschges (Vice-Pres.); Dr Detlef Hosemann (Treas.).

Principal Staff: Sec.-Gen. Dr Annette Julius.

Contact Details: Ahrstr. 41, 53175 Bonn; tel. (228) 82096-0; e-mail info@studienstiftung.de; internet www.studienstiftung.de.

Transparency International—TI

Established in 1993 by Peter Eigen and a group of former World Bank employees.

Activities: Promotes transparency and accountability in elections, in public administration, in procurement and in business through regional and national programmes. The organization carries out advocacy campaigns to lobby governments to implement anti-corruption reforms. More than 100 national chapters work in collaboration with CSOs, governments, companies and the media.

Geographical Area of Activity: International.

Publications: Annual Report; newsletter (weekly); *Corruption Perceptions Index* (annual); *Global Corruption Report*; *Policy Positions*; toolkits; working papers; blog.

Finance: Annual income €22.0m., expenditure €22.1m. (31 Dec. 2023).

Board of Directors: François Valérian (Chair.); Ketakandriana Rafitoson (Vice-Chair.).

Principal Staff: CEO Maíra Martini.

Contact Details: Alt-Moabit 96, 10559 Berlin; tel. (30) 3438200; e-mail ti@transparency.org; internet www.transparency.org.

Vodafone Stiftung Deutschland (Vodafone Foundation Germany)

Established in 2002 by Vodafone, a telecommunications company; part of the Vodafone Foundation (q.v.) network.

Activities: Focuses on teaching children and young people digital skills. Main programmes are: Coding For Tomorrow, which also provides training for teachers; and Klickwinkel, which offers tutorials for students and teachers on algorithms and fake news, fact-checking and online research, and using digital media. The Foundation has an office in Berlin.

Geographical Area of Activity: German-speaking countries.

Restrictions: Not currently funding new projects.

Publications: Annual Report; newsletter; reports; teaching materials.

Advisory Board: Philippe Rogge (Chair.).

Contact Details: Behrenstraße 18, 10117 Berlin; e-mail info@vodafone-stiftung.de; internet www.vodafone-stiftung.de.

VolkswagenStiftung (Volkswagen Foundation)

Founded in 1961 by the Federal Republic of Germany and the State of Lower Saxony.

Activities: Promotes science, technology and the humanities in research and university teaching. The Foundation offers grants to academic and technical institutions for research and teaching in any area of science, as well as the humanities, but has limited its funding programme to a range of specific fields; special programmes operate for sub-Saharan Africa and Central Asia/the Caucasus. In 2010 it took over fiduciary administration of the Cray Foundation (f. 1993), which promotes further training of engineers and scientists in Lower Saxony, offering scholarships in the fields of microelectronics and microtechnology.

Geographical Area of Activity: International.

Restrictions: Does not fund travel costs, congresses, capital works, schools, institutions with particular political or religious affiliations, profit-making activities or charitable causes; no grants to individuals. For applications from abroad, co-operation with German research workers or scholars is usually essential.

Publications: Annual Report; newsletter; *IMPULSE-Magazin*; brochures.

Finance: Total grants funding €611m. (2023); total capital €4,100m. (2025).

Supervisory Board: Falko Mohrs (Chair.).

Principal Staff: Sec.-Gen. Dr Georg Schütte.

Contact Details: Kastanienallee 35, 30519 Hannover; tel. (511) 8381-0; e-mail info@volkswagenstiftung.de; internet www.volkswagenstiftung.de.

WasserStiftung (Water Foundation)

Established in 2000 by Ernst Frost, a former magazine editor, and Henner Lang, who taught business administration.

Activities: Collaborates with local organizations to implement projects benefiting people who have limited or no access to water and sanitation, and whose lives are impacted by the environmental degradation, often women and girls. Activities promote water services, sanitation, reforestation and biodiversity projects in Africa and Latin America. The transfer of know-how and capacity building are cross-cutting aspects in all projects, to promote local sustainability. The Foundation awards the Hundertwasser Prize for contributions to the sustainable use of water resources and water supply to remote communities.
Geographical Area of Activity: Bolivia, Eritrea, Ethiopia, Morocco, Peru, Tanzania.
Finance: Annual budget €200,000–€400,000.
Board of Trustees: Wolf-Dietrich Pfaelzer (Chair.); Dr Beate Grotehans (Deputy Chair.).
Board of Directors: Monica Denomy (Chair.); Robert Balthasar (Deputy Chair.).
Contact Details: Pörtschacher Str. 27, 80687 München; tel. (1715) 601049; e-mail info@wasserstiftung.de; internet www.wasserstiftung.de.

Wilhelm-Sander-Stiftung (Wilhelm Sander Foundation)
Founded in 1974.
Activities: Works in the field of medicine and health. The Foundation sponsors medical research into preventing disease, in particular cancer, by means of grants to institutions and individuals.
Geographical Area of Activity: Germany, Switzerland.
Finance: Total assets US $650m. (31 Dec. 2024).
Board of Trustees: Harald Spiegel (Chair.); Prof. Dr Thomas Gudermann (Vice-Chair.).
Principal Staff: CEO Ernst G. Wittmann.
Contact Details: Zweigstr. 10, 80336 Munich; tel. (89) 544187-0; e-mail info@sanst.de; internet www.wilhelm-sander-stiftung.de.

ZEIT-Stiftung Ebelin und Gerd Bucerius (Ebelin and Gerd Bucerius ZEIT Foundation)
Established in 1971 by Gerd Bucerius, founder of weekly newspaper *Die Zeit* (f. 1946), and his wife Ebelin, former Man. Dir of the ZEIT publishing house.
Activities: Works in three fields: science and scholarships (including innovation in higher education, scholarship in the field of history and research); education and training (including press and journalism, dialogue in society, development of the Hamburg secondary school system); and art and culture (including literature, art and museums, cultural heritage, and music and theatre), through supporting research centres, scholarships and prizes. The Foundation also established the Bucerius Law School (f. 2000) and the Bucerius Art Forum (f. 2002).
Geographical Area of Activity: Germany, Central, Eastern and Western Europe, Israel.
Restrictions: Primarily funds its own initiatives, but considers innovative and cross-border proposals.
Publications: Report (biennially); newsletter; brochures.
Finance: Total assets €839.6m.; annual expenditure €18.1m. (2023).
Board of Trustees: Prof. Dr Burkhard Schwenker (Chair.).
Exec. Board: Manuel J. Hartung (Chair. and CEO).
Contact Details: Feldbrunnenstr. 56, 20148 Hamburg; tel. (40) 413366; e-mail post@zeit-stiftung.de; internet www.zeit-stiftung.de.

GHANA

FOUNDATIONS AND NON-PROFITS

African Women's Development Fund—AWDF
Established in 2000 by Bisi Adeleye-Fayemi, Hilda Tadria and Joana Foster.
Activities: Finances subregional, regional, local and national organizations that empower women; extends technical support to projects on women's development; and disseminates information on the work of organizations that benefit African women. Main programme areas are: body and health rights; women's economic security and justice; and leadership, participation and peace. In 2022 the Fund disbursed US $11.4m. in grants to 250 women's groups in 47 countries.
Geographical Area of Activity: Africa.
Publications: Annual Report; African Feminist Charter (in Wolof, Arabic and Kiswahili); blog.
Finance: Annual revenue US $12.8m., expenditure $12.5m. (31 Dec. 2021).
Executive Board: Taaka Awori (Chair.); Arielle Enniful (Treas.).
Principal Staff: CEO Françoise Moudouthe; Exec. Man. Patricia Rarriw.
Contact Details: Plot 78, AWDF House, Ambassadorial Enclave, East Legon, Accra; PMB CT 89 Cantonments, Accra; tel. (24) 2700881; e-mail awdf@awdf.org; internet www.awdf.org.

Afrobarometer
Established in 1999 by the merger of three survey research projects and registered as a non-profit organization in 2019; a pan-African research institution.
Activities: Carries out regular public attitude surveys in 43 African countries on democracy, governance, the economy and society. The organization makes its findings available for people involved or interested in policymaking, including policymakers, CSOs, academia, the media, donors, investors and the public. It organizes conferences and summer schools; and has regional offices in Accra, Cape Town and Nairobi. Part of the Global Barometer Surveys network.
Geographical Area of Activity: Africa.
Publications: Survey findings; datasets; briefing papers; dispatches; policy papers; working papers; books.
Finance: Annual revenue US $6.6m., expenditure $6.8m. (31 Dec. 2023).
Board: E. Gyimah-Boadi (Chair.).
Principal Staff: CEO Joseph Asunka.
Contact Details: 95 Nortei Ababio Loop, North Airport Residential Area, Accra; tel. (302) 776142; e-mail info@afrobarometer.org; internet www.afrobarometer.org.

Foundation for Security and Development in Africa—FOSDA
Established in 2001 by members of the West African diaspora concerned about conflicts in the region.
Activities: Promotes peace and human security through capacity building, research, documentation and advocacy. Main programmes focus on: gender equality; governance; and peace and security.
Geographical Area of Activity: West Africa.
Publications: Newsletter.
Principal Staff: Exec. Dir Afi Yakubu.

Media Foundation for West Africa

Contact Details: POB CT3140, Cantomment, Accra; 12 Shepherd Ave, Ogbojo, Mdina Rd, Accra; tel. (20) 0620935; e-mail info@fosda.org; internet fosda.org.

Media Foundation for West Africa (Fondation pour les Médias en Afrique de l'Ouest)
Established in 1997.
Activities: Promotes freedom of expression, media professionalism, media-led advocacy for peacebuilding and participatory governance. The Foundation works with national partner organizations in 16 countries. It is also the secretariat of the Africa Freedom of Expression Exchange Network.
Geographical Area of Activity: West Africa.
Publications: Newsletter; *West African Free Expression Monitor*; *Language Monitoring Report*; policy briefs; reports.
Board: Sophie K. Ly Sow (Chair.).
Principal Staff: Exec. Dir Sulemana Braimah.
Contact Details: Aar-Bakor St, Ogbojo, Accra; tel. (30) 2555327; e-mail info@mfwa.org; internet www.mfwa.org.

Rebecca Akufo-Addo Foundation—Rebecca Foundation
Established in 2017 by First Lady Rebecca Akufo-Addo.
Activities: Carries out activities that benefit women and children. Main programmes include: providing skills training, microloans and market access to help women to set up their own businesses; improving girls' access to education and reducing dropout rates from schools; and improving children's literacy through building libraries and using technology. The Foundation also builds community infrastructure; funds children's medical care and orphanages; improves access to clean water and sanitation; and creates green spaces in urban areas.
Geographical Area of Activity: Ghana.
Publications: Newsletter.
Principal Staff: Exec. Dir Rebecca Akufo-Addo.
Contact Details: PMB 000, Cantonments, Accra; tel. (26) 2640001; e-mail info@therebeccafoundation.org; internet therebeccafoundationghana.org.

SEND-West Africa
Established in 1998 by Siapha Kamara as the Social Enterprise Development Foundation of West Africa.
Activities: Main activities include: pro-poor advocacy and policy research; and monitoring of development programmes. The Foundation promotes good governance, gender equality and livelihoods security; and accountability, transparency and equity in resource allocation. It comprises three affiliated organizations, in Ghana, Liberia and Sierra Leone.
Geographical Area of Activity: Ghana, Liberia, Sierra Leone.
Publications: Annual Report; *Citizens' Watch* (newsletter); research reports; policy briefs; factsheets.
Principal Staff: CEO Siapha Kamara.
Contact Details: Box A28 Regimanuel Estates, Nungua Barrier, Sakumono, Accra; tel. (30) 2716830; e-mail info@sendwestafrica.org; internet www.sendwestafrica.org.

Vodafone Ghana Foundation
Established in 2009 by Vodafone, a telecommunications company; part of the Vodafone Foundation (q.v.) network.
Activities: Supports projects in the areas of: agriculture, promoting use of agrochemicals and farmer-based organizations; education, including reading clinics, vocational and digital skills training, and alternative livelihood skills; health, including HIV/AIDS counselling and screening, tuberculosis vaccination, malaria eradication, maternal health, drug addiction, disability, and supporting frontline health workers during the COVID-19 pandemic; and others, such as waste management, combating child labour, caring for the elderly and providing clean water. The Foundation awards university scholarships to underprivileged female students studying science, ICT and mathematics courses.
Geographical Area of Activity: Ghana.
Principal Staff: Head of Foundation Amaris Nana A. Perbi.
Contact Details: Telecom House, Nsawam Rd, PMB 221, Accra-North; tel. (30) 2782509; e-mail foundation.gh@vodafone.com; internet vodafone.com.gh/explore-vodafone/corporate-social-responsibilty/brain.

GIBRALTAR

FOUNDATIONS AND NON-PROFITS

Parasol Foundation Trust
Established in 2004 by Ruth Monicka Parasol, founder of PartyGaming, an online casino group.
Activities: The philanthropic division of Parasol International, focussing on creating opportunities for women to thrive and inspire future generations. Makes grants in the areas of medical research, education, culture and heritage.
Geographical Area of Activity: Gibraltar, India, Israel, Spain, UK, USA.
Finance: Total grantmaking since 2004 ammounting to more than £40m.
International Advisory Board: Ruth Monicka Parasol (Lead Member).
Contact Details: 10 John Mackintosh Sq., Gibraltar GX11 1AA; tel. 2000-2900; e-mail info@parasol.com; internet parasolfoundation.org.

GREECE

FOUNDATIONS AND NON-PROFITS

A. G. Leventis Foundation
Established in 1979 to preserve the cultural heritage of Greece and Cyprus.
Activities: Programmes include: protecting and promoting the cultural heritage of Cyprus and Greece; working to preserve the environment; granting postgraduate scholarships for postgraduate study abroad and at the University of Cyprus, and postdoctoral research grants; financing publications; working in the field of social welfare; and funding agricultural and technical education in West Africa. The Foundation has branch foundations in Cyprus (the Anastasios G. Leventis Foundation, q.v.) and Nigeria, as well as offices in the UK and Switzerland.
Geographical Area of Activity: Cyprus, Europe, Greece, West Africa.
Publications: Books; catalogues and other publications on the arts and culture.

Governing Board: Dr Anastasios (Tasso) P. Leventis (Chair.).
Principal Staff: Exec. Dir Louisa A. Leventis; CEO Alexandros Papanastassiou.
Contact Details: 9 Fragoklissias St, 151 25 Maroussi; tel. (21) 06165232; e-mail foundation@leventis.net; internet www.leventisfoundation.org.

Bodossaki Foundation

Founded in 1972 by Prodromos Bodossakis Athanassiades, an industrialist and shipowner.
Activities: To promote its vision of a society of equal opportunities and prospects for all, the Foundation funds, plans and implements activities around four strategic priority themes: promoting education; improving healthcare; protecting the environment; and empowering civil society. The Foundation offers grants to CSOs, schools, research centres and hospitals; awards scholarships and offers scientific awards; and manages third-party programmes. The Foundation's Social Dynamo initiative is a leading provider of capacity-building training, professional support and networking services to civil society groups and organizations in Greece. The Bodossaki Foundation also acts as a catalyst for fostering a broader culture of contribution in Greek society by managing resources on behalf of third parties—from international institutions, other foundations, corporations, and individuals—who wish to fund programmes in Greece with a significant social impact on Greek society that aim to address critical needs in education, healthcare, the protection of the environment and the empowerment of Civil Society.
Geographical Area of Activity: Mainly Greece.
Restrictions: Grants only to non-profit organizations, hospitals and schools based in Greece; applications must be in Greek. Applicants for Bodossaki Graduate Scholarships must be Greek citizens.
Publications: Bodossaki Lectures on Demand (online); e-learning resources.
Finance: Total assets €118.5m. (31 Dec. 2023).
Board of Directors: Athina Dessypri (Pres.).
Principal Staff: Dir Jennifer Clarke.
Contact Details: 14 Mourouzi Str., 106 74 Athens; tel. (21) 03237973; e-mail info@bodossaki.gr; internet www.bodossaki.gr.

ELEPAP—Rehabilitation for the Disabled

Established in 1937; formerly known as the Hellenic Society for Disabled Children.
Activities: Operates in the fields of medicine, social welfare, education and early childhood intervention. The organization provides rehabilitation for disabled children aged up to 16 years through physical, occupational and speech therapy, therapeutic swimming, music therapy, assistive technology and daily care units. There is a unique Neurohabilitation (Neuropsychology and Rehabilitation) Unit where vocational training for adults with disabilities, and facilities for supported living and independent living for persons with disabilities is also provided, in addition the Neuropsychology and Rehabilitation Unit for Brain Lesions co-operates with the Brain Injury Day Treatment Program of NYU Langone's Rusk Rehabilitation in the USA. ELEPAP organizes lectures and congresses for scientists to follow developments in their fields. Has branches in Agrinio, Chania, Ioannina, Thessaloniki and Volos.
Geographical Area of Activity: Europe.
Restrictions: Grants only within Greece; international grants are made through International Friends of ELEPAP, Inc, based in the USA.
Publications: Annual Reports; newsletter; scientific publications.
Finance: Total assets €6.9m., annual revenue €6.8m. (31 Dec. 2023).
Board of Directors: Eleni Skouteli (Chair.); Eta (Eftichia) Pagida-Samara (First Vice-Chair.); Fani Vouga-Mordo (Second Vice-Chair.); Isabella Covas (Gen. Sec.).
Principal Staff: Scientific Dir Dr Maria Pirgelli.
Contact Details: 16 Kononos St, 116 34 Athens; tel. (21) 07228360; e-mail epikoinonia@elepap.gr; internet www.elepap.gr.

Foundation of the Hellenic World

Established in 1993 by the family of Lazaros D. Efaimoglou, founder of Ergobank S.A. and Ergo Investment S.A.
Activities: Preserves Hellenic history and tradition, disseminating information and raising awareness about the universal dimension of Hellenism and its contribution to cultural evolution. At its cultural centre, 'Hellenic Cosmos', the Foundation organizes virtual reality tours, interactive exhibitions, educational programmes, conferences and theatrical performances.
Geographical Area of Activity: Mainly Greece.
Publications: Books; magazines; exhibition catalogues.
Board of Directors: Vasiliki Kounenaki (Chair.); Sofia Kounenaki-Efraimoglou, Elias Klis (Vice-Chair.); Ioannis Sakellariadis (Treas.); Natalia Efraimoglou (Sec.).
Principal Staff: CEO Dimitris Efraimoglou.
Contact Details: 38 Poulopoulou St, 118 51 Athens; tel. (21) 22545000; e-mail info@ime.gr; internet www.fhw.gr.

Foundation of Youth and Lifelong Learning—INEDIVIM

Established in 2011 by the merger of the Institute for Adult Continuing Education (IDEKE), the National Youth Foundation (EIN, f. 1947) and the Institute for Youth.
Activities: Supports lifelong learning through counselling, training and other services. The Foundation runs programmes for young people in mobility, innovation and entrepreneurship; and is the National Agency for the EU's Erasmus+ programme. It also manages students' educational welfare; and addresses the urgent social needs of working, unemployed and vulnerable people.
Geographical Area of Activity: Greece.
Publications: Annual Report; studies; promotional materials.
Finance: Annual income €97.8m., expenditure €97.7m. (31 Dec. 2023).
Board of Directors: Anna Rokofyllou Christos (Pres.); Anastasios Mandrapilias of Errikos (Vice-Pres.).
Contact Details: 417 Acharnon and Kokkinaki St, 111 43 Athens; tel. (21) 31314546; e-mail tm-kentrikisgrammateias@inedivim.gr; internet www.inedivim.gr.

Hellenic Foundation for Culture

Established in 1992.
Activities: Promotes Greek language learning and culture through organizing exhibitions, concerts, lectures, dramas and other cultural events in Greece and in other countries; and events to promote Greek artists and writers abroad, including cultural months and weeks, anniversary celebrations, film festivals and concerts. The Foundation plans and co-ordinates the participation and representation of Greece in international cultural events; and takes part in international cultural networks. It also collaborates with museums, universities, cultural centres and organizations, in Greece and abroad, to plan and develop cultural programmes. Has branches in Alexandria, Belgrade, Berlin, Bucharest, London, Nicosia, Odessa, Sofia, Tirana, Trieste, Washington, DC; and established the Cavafy Museum in Alexandria and the Philike Etairia Museum in Odessa.
Geographical Area of Activity: Albania, Bulgaria, Cyprus, Egypt, Germany, Italy, Greece, Romania, Serbia, UK, Ukraine, USA.
Restrictions: Institutions applying for sponsorship must come within the scope of the Foundation's interests.
Publications: Bulletin (2 a year); *Directory of Greek Publishers* (online); brochures; exhibition catalogues; newsletter.

Hellenic Foundation for European and Foreign Policy GREECE

Executive Board: Prof. Nikos A. Koukis (Pres.); Andreas Sideris (Vice-Pres.); Ilias Polymenidis (Treas.).

Contact Details: 50 Stratigou Kallari, Palaio Psychico, 154 52 Athens; tel. (21) 06776540; e-mail president@hfc.gr; internet hfc-worldwide.org.

Hellenic Foundation for European and Foreign Policy—ELIAMEP

Established in 1988; an independent, policy-orientated, non-profit research and training institute.

Activities: Operates in the field of international affairs. Programme areas include: European institutions and policies; security and foreign policy; culture, identity and religion; migration; the Greek and European Economy Observatory; and the South-East Europe Programme. The Foundation carries out self-conducted programmes and research on European integration, transatlantic relations, in addition to the Mediterranean, South-Eastern Europe, the Black Sea and other regions of particular interest to Greece. It awards scholarships and fellowships; and organizes conferences and training courses.

Geographical Area of Activity: Europe, Black Sea region, Mediterranean region, Middle East, South-Eastern Europe.

Publications: Annual Report; newsletter; *Journal of South-East European and Black Sea Studies*; ELIAMEP Thesis; books; policy papers; working papers.

Finance: Annual revenue €2.7m., expenditure €1.7m. (2023).

Board of Directors: Prof. Loukas Tsoukalis (Pres.); Thanos Veremis (Vice-Pres.); Effi Strataki (Treas.); Eleni Papakonstantinou (Sec.-Gen.).

Principal Staff: Dir-Gen. Maria Gavouneli.

Contact Details: 49 Vasilissis Sofias Ave, 106 76 Athens; tel. (21) 07257110; e-mail eliamep@eliamep.gr; internet www.eliamep.gr.

The J. F. Costopoulos Foundation

Established in 1979 by an endowment of the late Spyros and Eurydice Costopoulos.

Activities: Promotes Hellenic culture, supporting scientific, educational and cultural activities. The Foundation focuses on the fields of cultural heritage and tradition; society; science and research; education and studies; and the arts. It funds museums; libraries; holy dioceses and churches; public welfare societies; associations and unions; foundations and schools; research projects, seminars and conferences; studies; Chairs of Greek studies abroad; archaeological excavations and publications; theatre and dance companies; musical productions; and visual arts projects.

Geographical Area of Activity: Mainly Greece and Europe; some activity in the USA.

Restrictions: Subsidizes important initiatives that would not otherwise be funded; priority is given to Greek researchers or researchers of Greek origin. Not currently supporting doctoral and postdoctoral programmes and consequent publications. In the field of holy dioceses and churches, grants only for the restoration of Byzantine monuments, not contemporary churches. In the field of films, grants are given mainly for short films and documentaries.

Publications: Annual Report; catalogues of visual arts exhibitions.

Finance: Annual revenue €4.1m., expenditure €4.1m. (31 Dec. 2025, budget).

Board of Trustees: Demetrios P. Mantzounis (Pres.); Dafni G. Kostopoulou (Vice-Pres.); Thodoris N. Filaretos (Treas.).

Principal Staff: Dir Hector P. Verykios.

Contact Details: 9 Ploutarchou St, 106 75 Athens; tel. (21) 07293503; e-mail info@costopoulosfoundation.org; internet www.costopoulosfoundation.org.

Kokkalis Foundation

Established in 1998 by Sokratis Kokkalis, an information technology and telecommunications entrepreneur, in memory of his father, Petros Kokkalis, a surgeon and humanist, professor of medicine at the University of Athens and founder of the first neurosurgical clinic in Greece.

Activities: Promotes a peaceful, democratic and prosperous South-Eastern Europe, through supporting public, cultural and scientific life in the region. The Foundation sponsors initiatives in and relating to the region, including organizing public forums and international conferences. It supports scientific research, educational and humanitarian programmes; and the development of human networks that promote inter-ethnic understanding and regional co-operation, and strengthen democratic institutions and environmental protection.

Geographical Area of Activity: Greece, South-Eastern Europe, USA, Western Europe.

Publications: Books; newsletter; research publications and studies (in English and Greek); monographs; information brochures.

Board of Directors: Sokratis P. Kokkalis (Pres.); Petros S. Kokkalis (Vice-Pres.); Eleni S. Kokkali (Treas. and Sec.).

Contact Details: Nikis 33, 105 57 Athens; tel. (216) 8003090; e-mail kf@kokkalisfoundation.gr; internet www.kokkalisfoundation.gr.

Lambrakis Foundation

Established in 1991 by Christos D. Lambrakis, a newspaper publisher; formerly known as the Lambrakis Research Foundation.

Activities: Works in the areas of education, the arts and humanities, science and technology, and environmental conservation, through studies, projects and awareness activities; and addressing the increasing need for human resources policies and human capital development. The Foundation carries out self-conducted programmes and research; organizes conferences and training courses; and provides information and advice to schools in Greece on using modern technological tools and current educational issues. It offers Manolis Andronikos scholarships for archaeologists wishing to pursue postgraduate studies in archaeological computing; and the Christos Lambrakis Award to recognize achievements in addressing social inequality. Maintains the e-paideia.net portal, providing information and access to educational resources for teachers, students, researchers and parents; and the migrants.gr portal, serving immigrants, refugees, researchers and policymakers.

Geographical Area of Activity: Europe.

Restrictions: Grants only to specific organizations.

Publications: Newsletter (monthly); conference proceedings; multimedia publications; training manuals.

Finance: Total income €479,359, expenditure €530,662 (31 Dec. 2024).

Board of Directors: Manuel Savvidis (Chair.); Dimitrios Savvidis (Vice-Chair.); Dimosthenes Koressis (Treas.); Dimitrios Kastriotis (Sec.).

Principal Staff: CEO Sevasti-Sofia Anthopoulou.

Contact Details: 5 Anagnostopoulou St, 106 73 Athens; tel. (21) 03626150; e-mail info@lrf.gr; internet www.lrf.gr.

Marangopoulos Foundation for Human Rights

Established in 1977 by the bequest of George M. Marangopoulos, President of the Supreme Administrative Court of Greece.

Activities: Promotes human rights, focusing on human rights education, through organizing courses, lectures, seminars, symposia and conferences. The Foundation awards scholarships and prizes; provides financial support and sponsorship for specialized studies in human rights; lobbies governments and public authorities; provides free legal aid to people whose fundamental rights have been violated; and funds fact-finding missions in Greece and abroad. It conducts research, disseminates information and maintains a public library.

Geographical Area of Activity: Europe, USA.

Publications: The Foundation holds its own series of publications in two of the most reputable publishing houses in Greece (*Nomiki Bibliothiki*) and in France (*Pedone*). Publications include doctoral theses, edited volumes and monographs.

Governing Board: Professor Linos-Alexander Sicilianos (Pres.); Sotiris Mousouris (Vice-Pres. and Treas.); Petros Damianos (Gen.-Sec.).

Contact Details: 1c Lycavittou St, 106 72 Athens; tel. (21) 03637455; e-mail info@mfhr.gr; internet www.mfhr.gr/en.

National Bank of Greece Cultural Foundation

Established in 1966 by the National Bank of Greece.

Activities: Supports fine art, the humanities and sciences in Greece. The Foundation houses a collection of works of art and organizes exhibitions. It manages three cultural centres in Athens; maintains an archive of maps and a paper conservation laboratory; organizes seminars and workshops for editors; and issues publications that cannot be published commercially. The Board of Directors act as administrators for the Alex Minotas Legacy, which offers scholarships for undergraduate and postgraduate studies. The Panagiotis Moulas Prize is awarded to a postgraduate student for an essay on Greek or comparative literature.

Geographical Area of Activity: Greece.

Publications: Annual Report; newsletter; numerous publications in the fields of history, archaeology, anthropology, classical studies, art theory, law, philosophy, etc.

Finance: Total assets €4.6m. (31 Dec. 2023).

Board of Directors: Gikas Hardouvelis (Chair.); Christina Theophilidi (Treas.); Paschalis Kitromilidis (Gen. Sec.).

Principal Staff: Dir Kostas Kostis.

Contact Details: 13 Thoukydidou St, 105 58 Athens; tel. (21) 03221335; e-mail info@miet.gr; internet www.miet.gr.

State Scholarships Foundation—IKY (Idrima Kratikon Ipotrofion)

Founded in 1951 to offer grants to young scientists to study in Greece and abroad; since 1987 the Foundation has also administered funding under EU education programmes.

Activities: Offers scholarships annually for postgraduate and postdoctoral studies in Greece to nationals of any other country worldwide and to non-Greek nationals of Greek origin; and implements the EU's Erasmus+ programme for education, training youth and sport in Greece. The Foundation awards scholarships to teachers or researchers (foreigners or foreign nationals of Greek origin) working in Greek centres of studies abroad for further education in language, literature, philosophy, history and art. It awards scholarships for: postgraduate doctoral studies; postdoctoral research; further education in Greek language, literature, philosophy, history and art for professors of Greek language in foreign universities; further study in fine arts; and collection of research data for applicants who are conducting doctoral studies in their country.

Geographical Area of Activity: International.

Publications: Newsletter.

Board of Directors: Vasiliki Kinti (Pres.); Maria Erotokritou (Sec.).

Principal Staff: Dir-Gen. Angelos Ioubrekas.

Contact Details: 41 Ethnikis Antistaseos Ave, 142 34 Nea Ionia, Athens; tel. (21) 03726300; e-mail erasmusplus@iky.gr; internet www.iky.gr.

Stavros Niarchos Foundation—SNF

Established in 1996 by the will of Stavros S. Niarchos, a shipowner.

Activities: Operates worldwide in the areas of arts and culture, education, health and medicine, and social welfare. The Foundation funds projects within Greece and worldwide that promote and/or maintain Greek heritage and culture; and supports the Stavros Niarchos Foundation Cultural Center (f. 2017). It has offices in Athens, Monte Carlo (Monaco) and New York (USA).

Geographical Area of Activity: International.

Restrictions: No grants to individuals.

Publications: Newsletter.

Finance: Total grants disbursed since 1996 more than US $3,900m. (2024).

Board of Directors: Philip Niarchos, Spyros Niarchos, Andreas C. Dracopoulos (Co-Pres).

Principal Staff: COO Panos Papoulias.

Contact Details: 86A Vasilissis Sofias Ave, 115 28 Athens; tel. (21) 08778300; e-mail info@snf.org; internet www.snf.org.

Swedish Institute at Athens

Founded in 1948 by King Gustaf VI Adolf and others.

Activities: Operates internationally in the fields of the arts and humanities (mainly archaeology) and Greek-Swedish relations, through research, conferences, courses, publications and lectures. The Institute maintains a database and archive on Swedish archaeological research in Greece. Has an office in Kavala.

Geographical Area of Activity: Greece.

Restrictions: Grants only to students at Swedish universities.

Publications: Newsletter; *Skrifter utgivna av Svenska institutet i Athen* (monographs); collections of articles in *Opuscula Atheniensia*.

Board: Ruth Jacoby (Chair.); Staffan Bengtsson (Treas.); Dr Jenni Hjohlman (Sec.).

Principal Staff: Dir Dr Jenny Wallensten; Asst Dir Dr Georgia Galani.

Contact Details: 9 Mitseon, 117 42 Athens; tel. (21) 09232102; e-mail swedinst@sia.gr; internet www.sia.gr.

GUATEMALA

FOUNDATIONS AND NON-PROFITS

Antigua Forum

Established in 2012 by Giancarlo Ibárgüen, a business person and former President of Universidad Francisco Marroquín, as an invitation-only gathering of thought leaders.

Activities: Promotes free markets and personal liberty. The Forum organizes annual conferences of around 50 people, gathering international political leaders, entrepreneurs and experts to work on projects that advance human wellbeing and economic prosperity.

Geographical Area of Activity: Guatemala.

Publications: *Disruptor Series*; case studies.

Advisory Board: Brad Lips (Pres.).

Principal Staff: CEO Wayne Leighton; Exec. Dir Claudia Rosales Modenessi.

Contact Details: Universidad Francisco Marroquín, Calle Manuel F. Ayau (6 Calle Final), Zona 10, 01010 Ciudad de Guatemala; tel. 2413-3311; e-mail antiguaforum@ufm.edu; internet antiguaforum.ufm.edu.

FAFIDESS—Fundación de Asesoría Financiera a Instituciones de Desarrollo y Servicio Social (Foundation for the Financial Assessment of Social Service and Development Institutions)

Established in 1986 by members of the Rotary Club of Guatemala City.

Activities: Supports the economic and social development of Guatemala through offering sustainable microfinance, technical advice and support to microenterprises and small businesses, particularly those run by women.

Geographical Area of Activity: Guatemala.

Principal Staff: Exec. Dir Reynold O. Walter.

Contact Details: 5A Avda 16-68, Zona 10, 01010 Ciudad de Guatemala; tel. 2311-5800; e-mail fafidess@fafidess.org; internet www.fafidess.org.

Fundación Génesis Empresarial (Génesis Empresarial Foundation)

Founded in 1988.

Activities: Strengthens the development of microenterprises and small businesses, as well as communal banks in urban, marginal and rural areas of Guatemala; and provides credit, training and advice. The Foundation also helps poor rural communities to improve dwellings and introduce basic services. It has more than 150 branches throughout Guatemala.

Geographical Area of Activity: Guatemala.

Publications: Annual Report; *Libro de Transparencia*.

Finance: Annual income US $187.7m., expenditure $154.6m. (31 Dec. 2023).

Board of Directors: Dr Juan Niemann Enge (Chair.); Oscar Adolfo Salazar Perdomo (Vice-Chair.); Juan Andrés Torrebiarte Novella (Treas.); Fernando Mansilla Paetau (Sec.).

Principal Staff: Gen. Man. Edgardo Pérez Preciado.

Contact Details: 8ª Calle 7-11, Zona 9, Distrito Financiero, 01009 Ciudad de Guatemala; tel. 2383-9000; e-mail genesis@genesisempresarial.com; internet www.genesisempresarial.org.

Fundación Rigoberta Menchú Tum

Established in 1992 as the Fundación Vicente Menchú; renamed in 1995 following the awarding of the Nobel Peace Prize to Rigoberta Menchú Tum, an activist for indigenous peoples' rights.

Activities: Works in the field of human rights, especially of indigenous peoples, supporting education, community development and citizen participation.

Geographical Area of Activity: Guatemala, Mexico.

Publications: Reports.

Principal Staff: Pres. Dr Rigoberta Menchú Tum; Dir Dr Carlos Chocooj.

Contact Details: Avda Simeón Cañas 4-04, Zona 2, Ciudad de Guatemala; tel. 2230-2431; e-mail frmt.gt@gmail.com; internet rigobertamenchutum.weebly.com.

Fundación Tigo

Established in 2009 by Tigo Guatemala, a telecommunications company, as its social arm.

Activities: Works to improve quality of life through digital technology. Main programme areas are: education, improving school infrastructure and providing computers and teacher training; special projects, including recycling initiatives, corporate volunteering, supporting children's cancer care and providing clean water in schools; and transparency, promoting accountability in government and the private sector, and supporting media and CSOs with funding, training and technology.

Geographical Area of Activity: Guatemala.

Principal Staff: Pres. Mario López Estrada; Exec. Dir Melanie Reimers.

Contact Details: 6A Avda 9-00, 01001 Ciudad de Guatemala; tel. 2428-1000; e-mail fundaciontigo@tigo.com.gt; internet www.tigo.com.gt/conocenos/responsabilidad-corporativa.

FUNDAP—Fundación para el Desarrollo (Development Foundation)

Established in 1982 by a group of business people.

Activities: Focuses on developing low-income areas of western Guatemala through supporting small businesses and innovative projects that improve the quality of life of those communities. Programmes include: education; health; microcredit; craftwork; environmental forestry; agriculture and livestock.

Geographical Area of Activity: Guatemala.

Publications: Annual Report.

Board of Directors: Francisco Roberto Gutiérrez Martínez (Chair.); Jorge Arturo Gándara Gaborit (Vice-Chair.); Julio R. Bagur Cifuentes (Treas.); Eunice Cecilia Martinez de Alvarado (Sec.).

Principal Staff: CEO Jorge A. Gándara Gaborit.

Contact Details: 17 Avda 4-25, Zona 3, Quetzaltenango; tel. 7956-4400; e-mail info@fundap.com.gt; internet www.fundap.com.gt.

PRODESSA—Proyecto de Desarrollo Santiago (Santiago Development Project)

Established in 1989 by the Brothers de la Salle (Brothers of the Christian Schools), a Christian order.

Activities: Works in the field of development in rural communities. The Project works to build a just and multicultural society, with a particular focus on promoting the rights of indigenous peoples. It runs programmes in the fields of education, the environment and development.

Geographical Area of Activity: Guatemala.

Publications: Annual Report; *Bulletin*; educational materials and textbooks in Spanish and Maya languages; research papers.

Finance: Annual grant expenditure approx. US $500,000.

Board of Directors: Oscar Azmitia Barranco (Chair.); Benjamín Rivas (Treas.); Alberto Mairena (Sec.).

Contact Details: Km 15, Carretera Roosevelt, Zona 7, Mixco, Apdo 13-B, 01057 Ciudad de Guatemala; tel. 2501-1680; e-mail info@prodessa.edu.gt; internet prodessa.edu.gt.

GUINEA

FOUNDATIONS AND NON-PROFITS

Fondation Orange Guinée (Orange Foundation Guinea)
Established in 2015 by Orange, a telecommunications company; part of Fondation Orange (q.v.) network.
Activities: Works in the areas of education, health and social welfare. The Foundation has built seven Digital Houses and 97 Digital Schools, which provide internet access, tablet computers and training; and six Orange Villages, which provide access to education, healthcare and drinking water.
Geographical Area of Activity: Guinea.
Principal Staff: Pres. Ousmane Bole Traore.
Contact Details: Immeuble Orange Belle-Vue, BP 45 49, Commune de Dixinn, Conakry; tel. 626-64-43-0; e-mail fondation.ogc@orange-sonatel.com; internet www.orange-guinee.com/fondation.

Fondation Rio Tinto
Established in 2014 by Rio Tinto, a mining company.
Activities: Supports socioeconomic development and the funding of agricultural projects to improve food security and agricultural productivity; provides sponsorship for smaller requests.
Geographical Area of Activity: Guinea.
Restrictions: No grants to individuals.
Publications: Annual Report; *Spirit* (newsletter).
Principal Staff: Rio Tinto Country Dir Biro Diallo.
Contact Details: c/o Rio Tinto Guinée, Immeuble Belle vue, blvd Belle Vue, DI 536, Commune de Dixinn, BP 848, Conakry; tel. 624-21-30-23; e-mail fondationriotinto.guinee@riotinto.com.

HAITI

FOUNDATIONS AND NON-PROFITS

FOKAL—Open Society Foundation Haiti
Established in 1995, as the Fondation Connaissance et Liberté/Fondasyon Konesans Ak Libète, by Dr Michèle D. Pierre-Louis; an independent foundation, part of the Open Society Foundations (q.v.) network.
Activities: Operates in the fields of education, culture and strengthening of CSOs, especially land workers' and women's organizations. The Foundation runs programmes promoting debate, libraries, the internet, early childhood education, local production and water facilities in rural areas, and the rule of law; and providing technical and financial support to the judiciary. Through the community library project, it supports 20 community libraries and provides training in library management, finance and computers. Projects include: the creation and management of the Parc de Martissant national urban park, which includes a botanical garden specializing in traditional medicinal plants; the Katherine Dunham cultural centre; and the Monique Calixte Library.
Geographical Area of Activity: Haiti.
Publications: Annual Report; *Nouvèl FOKAL* (weekly newsletter); *Beyond Mountains More Mountains*.
Board of Directors: Maxime D. Charles (Pres.); Danièle Magloire (Vice-Pres.); Norma Powell (Sec.).
Principal Staff: Exec. Dir Lorraine Mangonès.
Contact Details: 143 ave Christophe, BP 2720, 6112 Port-au-Prince; tel. 2813-1694; e-mail studiofokal@fokal.org; internet fokal.org.

Fondation Digicel Haïti (Digicel Foundation Haiti)
Established in 2007 by Digicel, a telecommunications company; part of the Digicel Foundation network.
Activities: Main programmes focus on building schools, professional development of primary school teachers and school directors and supporting Digicel staff volunteering. The Foundation offers grants to organizations for community-based projects in the areas of education, culture, disaster prevention, inclusion and livelihoods. Total investment since 2007 was US $88.9m. at 2025.
Geographical Area of Activity: Haiti.
Publications: Annual Report; *Foundation Fundamentals* (newsletter, 2 a year).
Finance: Annual revenue US $3.3m., expenditure $3.5m. (31 March 2022).
Council: Maria Mulcahy (Global Pres.); Josefa Gauthier (Non-Exec. Pres.).
Contact Details: 151 ave Jean Paul II & Impasse Duverger, Port-au-Prince; tel. 3777-7710; e-mail fondation.projet@digicelgroup.com; internet www.fondationdigicelhaiti.org.

Fondation Rinaldi
Established in 2008 as the planning and development office of the Salesians of Don Bosco in Haiti, a Christian order.
Activities: Works for the sustainable social, economic and cultural development of poor and disadvantaged young people. Projects include: providing school meals; vocational training; preparation for work; reintegration of 'street children' into society; and violence reduction. The Foundation has nine education centres.
Geographical Area of Activity: Haiti.
Restrictions: Focuses on Ouest, Sud, Nord, Nord-Est, Artibonite departments.
Principal Staff: Superior of the Vice-Province Fr Morachel Bonhomme.
Contact Details: Tabarre 38, Impasse Audain, BP 13233 Delmas, Port-au-Prince; tel. 2940-0992; e-mail fondation.rinaldi@gmail.com; internet www.frinaldihaiti.org.

Haiti Development Institute—HDI
Established in 2017, a legacy of The Haiti Fund (f. 2010), which was created at The Boston Foundation in response to the 2010 earthquake.
Activities: Supports initiatives in the areas of livelihoods, education and health, providing funding to CSOs and capacity building to local community leaders. The Institute organizes Haiti Funders Conferences. Has an office in Boston, USA.
Geographical Area of Activity: Haiti, USA.
Publications: Newsletter.
Finance: Total grantmaking since 2010 approx. US $5m. (2025).
Board of Directors: Régine Desulmé Polynice (Chair.); Harry Dumay (Treas.).
Principal Staff: Exec. Dir Pierre Noel.
Contact Details: 130 route Coloniale, Corail, Arcahaie, Haiti; tel. 4047-0365; internet www.hdihaiti.org.

HONDURAS

FOUNDATIONS AND NON-PROFITS

Fundación BANHCAFE—FUNBANHCAFE (BANHCAFE Foundation)

Established in 1985; an initiative of Banco Hondureño del Café (BANHCAFE) and the Ministry of Home Affairs and Justice, to aid the development of coffee-producing communities in Honduras.

Activities: Works to develop social, economic and environmental elements of coffee-producing communities, through non-profit organizations in the local area. Programmes focus on environmental projects, sustainable agriculture, local economy and job opportunities for young people.

Geographical Area of Activity: Honduras.

Publications: Annual Report; guides; strategic reports; manuals; reports on different agricultural products.

Board of Directors: Miguel Alfonso Fernández Rápalo (Pres.); Guillermo Sagastume Perdomo (Sec.).

Principal Staff: Exec. Dir Ramón Arnold Sabillón Ortega.

Contact Details: Colonia Rubén Dario, Avda Las Minitas, Calle Cervantes 319, Apdo 3814, Tegucigalpa; tel. 2239-5211; e-mail direccion@funbanhcafe.hn; internet www.funbanhcafe.hn.

Fundación para la Inversión y Desarrollo de Exportaciones—FIDE (Foundation for Investment and Development of Exports—FIDE)

Established in 1984 by a group of business people.

Activities: Promotes sustainable development through strengthening investment and export by seeking to improve the international competitiveness of the country and its business sector. The Foundation organizes programmes and activities for investors and business owners, offering a wide range of services to develop exports and take advantage of emerging business opportunities. It has an office in Cortés.

Geographical Area of Activity: Honduras.

Publications: Annual Report; *Honduras Export Directory*; promotional brochures.

Board of Directors: Leonel Z. Bendeck (Pres.); Ramón Medina Luna (Vice-Pres.); Marco Tulio Mendieta (Treas.).

Principal Staff: Exec. Pres. and Sec. Teresa Maria Deras.

Contact Details: Colonia Lomas del Guijarro Sur, Calle Madrid, Bloque N, Lote 1, Apdo 2029, Tegucigalpa; tel. 2239-6417; e-mail info@fidehonduras.com.

Fundación Nacional para el Desarrollo de Honduras—FUNADEH (National Foundation for the Development of Honduras)

Founded in 1983 by José Antonio Bográn Paredes.

Activities: Works in the fields of human development and improving quality of life in vulnerable communities. Programmes focus on education, violence prevention, job opportunities and business skills. The Genesis project, developed jointly with the United States Agency for International Development (USAID), has established a network of 65 youth outreach centres to promote a culture of peace and provide income-generating opportunities for former gang members. The Foundation has offices in Chamelecon, La Ceiba and Tegucigalpa.

Geographical Area of Activity: Honduras.

Publications: Newsletter; blog.

Principal Staff: Exec. Pres. Arturo Aleman.

Contact Details: Colonia El Pedregal Bloque 31, 3 Calle, Blvd Las Torres, San Pedro Sula, Tegucigalpa; tel. 3194-5716; e-mail info@funadeh.org; internet www.funadeh.org.

HONG KONG

CO-ORDINATING BODIES

Community Chest of Hong Kong

Established in 1968; an independent non-profit organization.

Activities: Supports member social welfare agencies working in five main areas: children and young people; elderly, family and child welfare; medicine and health; rehabilitation and aftercare; and community development. The organization co-ordinates fundraising events and distributes donations among more than 167 member agencies. The Community Chest Rainbow Fund (f. 2004) provides emergency support to people in financial crisis, including victims and survivors of accidents and natural disasters.

Geographical Area of Activity: Hong Kong.

Restrictions: Grants only to non-profit organizations that have been registered in Hong Kong for at least three years.

Publications: Annual Report; *ChestLink* (quarterly newsletter).

Finance: Annual income HK $191.6m., expenditure $357.9m. (31 March 2023).

Board of Directors: Li Lin Lai Chan (Chair.); Raymund Chao Pak Ki (Treas.).

Executive Committee: Dr Simon Kwok (Chair.); Chan Tsz Ching, Kong Cheuk (Deputy Chair.).

Contact Details: Rm 1805, 18th Floor, Harcourt House, 39 Gloucester Rd, Wanchai; tel. 25996111; e-mail chest@commchest.org; internet www.commchest.org.

Hong Kong Council of Social Service—HKCSS

Established in 1947; a federation of NGOs.

Activities: Works in the field of social welfare, promoting equality, justice, social integration and a caring society. The Council promotes the development of social welfare through improving the performance and accountability of social welfare services. It comprises more than 520 member organizations; and has special consultative status with ECOSOC.

Geographical Area of Activity: Hong Kong.

Publications: Annual Report; policy bulletins; scenarios; brochure.

Finance: Total income HK $239.9m., expenditure $237.5m. (31 March 2024).

Executive Committee: Peter Douglas Koon Ho-ming (Chair.).

Principal Staff: Chief Exec. Grace Chan Man Lee.

Contact Details: 11th–13th Floors, Duke of Windsor Social Service Bldg, 15 Hennessy Rd, Wanchai; tel. 28642929; e-mail council@hkcss.org.hk; internet www.hkcss.org.hk.

HONG KONG

FOUNDATIONS AND NON-PROFITS

Croucher Foundation
Founded in 1979 by Noel Croucher, former Chairman of the Hong Kong Stock Exchange.

Activities: Offers scholarships and fellowships for doctoral or postdoctoral research outside Hong Kong. The Foundation makes grants to institutions and offers senior research fellowships and Innovation Awards to universities in Hong Kong; contributes to international scientific conferences in Hong Kong; supports advanced study institutes; funds international exchanges between scientific institutions in Hong Kong and abroad; and provides funds for scientists in mainland China to undertake placements at Hong Kong institutions. It also supports Summer Courses in local universities; co-sponsors Clinical Assistant Professorships at the two medical schools in Hong Kong; and offers a free festival exploring science and the world around us.

Geographical Area of Activity: Hong Kong.

Restrictions: Applicants for individual fellowships and scholarships for overseas studies must be permanent Hong Kong residents.

Publications: Reports.

Board of Governors: Prof. Timothy M. Cox (Chair.).

Principal Staff: Exec. Dir David Foster.

Contact Details: 501 Nine Queen's Rd Central, Hong Kong; tel. 27366337; e-mail info@croucher.org.hk; internet www.croucher.org.hk.

HER Fund
Established in 2004 by Chew Choo-Lin and Chung Yuen-Yi.

Activities: Works to improve social conditions, eliminate gender discrimination and safeguard the rights of women and transgender people. Main programmes are: eliminating violence against women; eliminating discrimination; eradicating poverty; and promoting female participation in civil society. The Fund offers General Grants, worth up to HK $50,000, to initiatives that fall within its main programme areas. The HER Hub organizes workshops, seminars, training and one-to-one peer guidance in areas including capacity building, leadership skills, governance and internal management skills.

Geographical Area of Activity: Hong Kong.

Publications: Annual Report; *HER Voice* (e-newsletter); research reports.

Finance: Annual income HK $3.5m., expenditure $2.9m. (31 March 2021).

Board of Directors: Terry Mui (Chair.); Feng Peiqi (Vice-Chair.).

Contact Details: Room A, 22/F, Skyline Tower, 18 Tong Mi Rd, POB 79890, Mong Kok Post Office; tel. 27941100; e-mail info@herfund.org.hk; internet www.herfund.org.hk.

Hong Kong Society for the Blind
Established in 1956 to investigate blindness and advance the science of ophthalmology.

Activities: Works to facilitate the equal participation of visually impaired people in society and to improve their quality of life, promoting social inclusion. The Society provides eye care and screening services; educational and community support; rehabilitation training; residential services; and career support. It also conducts and supports research in ophthalmology, through grants to institutions and individuals; and assists in the training of ophthalmic and multidisciplinary staff.

Geographical Area of Activity: South-East Asia.

Publications: Annual Report; newsletter; training manuals.

Finance: Annual income HK $326.1m., expenditure $326.3m. (31 March 2024).

Council: Nancy Law Tak Yin (Chair.); Winnie Kong Lai Wan (Vice-Chair.).

Principal Staff: Chief Exec. Maureen Tam Ching Yi.

Prudence Foundation

Contact Details: East Wing, 248 Nam Cheong St, Samshuipo, Kowloon; tel. 27788332; e-mail enquiry@hksb.org.hk; internet www.hksb.org.hk.

Li Ka Shing Foundation
Established in 1980 by Ka Shing Li, a business person.

Activities: Operates in the fields of education, and medicine and health through grants and sponsorships to schools, hospitals and universities; and considers projects that deal with emergency relief and capacity building. The Foundation established Shantou University in mainland China to engineer reforms in the higher education sector; and contributes to medical research at institutions worldwide, particularly in the area of cancer research. In mainland China it has undertaken programmes to improve rural healthcare and to provide free hospice care services.

Geographical Area of Activity: Australia, Canada, People's Repub. of China, Hong Kong, India, Indonesia, Israel, Japan, Nepal, New Zealand, Singapore, UK, USA.

Publications: *Sphere* (bulletin).

Finance: Total disbursements since 1980 over HK $30,000m.

Board of Directors: Sir Ka Shing Li (Chair.).

Principal Staff: Dir Solina Chau.

Contact Details: Cheung Kong Center, 7th Floor, 2 Queen's Rd, Central; tel. 21288888; e-mail general@lksf.org; internet www.lksf.org.

Oxfam Hong Kong
Established in 1976; part of the Oxfam confederation of organizations (qq.v.).

Activities: Works to eliminate poverty and injustice through carrying out self-conducted programmes in the fields of development, humanitarian response, advocacy and development education. Programme areas include: active citizenship; fairly sharing natural resources; financing for development and universal essential services; gender justice; girls' education; poverty among ethnic minorities and the elderly; poverty in Hong Kong and advocacy; reducing school dropout rates; saving lives and building back better; sustainable food; and working poverty and labour rights. The organization provides emergency humanitarian assistance following disasters. It works in nine countries and has offices in the People's Republic of China, Macao and Taiwan.

Geographical Area of Activity: Bangladesh, People's Repub. of China, Ethiopia, Hong Kong, India, Lao People's Dem. Repub., Macao, Myanmar, Nepal, Taiwan, Tanzania, Viet Nam, Zambia.

Restrictions: No loans or grants to individuals.

Publications: Annual Report; newsletter; blog.

Finance: Total income HK $198.2m., expenditure $202.3m. (31 March 2024).

Council: Wayne Porritt (Chair.); Hugh Kam (Vice-Chair.); Alex Setchina (Treas.).

Principal Staff: Dir-Gen. Dr Betty Pun.

Contact Details: China United Centre, 17th Floor, 28 Marble Rd, North Point; tel. 25202525; e-mail info@oxfam.org.hk; internet www.oxfam.org.hk.

Prudence Foundation
Established in 2011 by Prudential Corpn Asia, part of Prudential PLC, a financial services group.

Activities: Carries out activities in the areas of education, health and safety. Foundation programmes work to support the UN Sustainable Development Goals by reducing the number of deaths and minimizing their economic impact through increasing awareness of health and safety in life-threatening situations and teaching financial literacy.

Geographical Area of Activity: Cambodia, People's Repub. of China, Hong Kong, Indonesia, Malaysia, Philippines, Singapore, Taiwan, Thailand, Viet Nam.

Publications: *IMPACT* (newsletter).

Yidan Prize Foundation — HUNGARY

Principal Staff: Chair. Donald Kanak; Exec. Dir Marc Fancy.

Contact Details: 1 International Finance Centre, 13th Floor, 1 Harbour View St, Central; tel. 29186300; e-mail prudence.foundation@prudential.com.hk; internet www.prudentialcorporation-asia.com/corp/prudential-pca/en/our-foundation.

Yidan Prize Foundation

Established in 2016.

Activities: The Yidan Prize Foundation is a global philanthropic foundation, with a mission of creating a better world through education. Through its prizes and network of innovators, the Yidan Prize Foundation supports ideas and practices in education—specifically, ones with the power to positively change lives and society. The Yidan Prize recognizes individuals or teams who have contributed significantly to the theory and practice of education. It consists of two prizes: the Yidan Prize for Education Research and the Yidan Prize for Education Development. Laureates of each prize receive an unrestricted project fund of HK $15m. over three years, helping them scale up their work, as well as a gold medal and a cash prize of $15m.

Geographical Area of Activity: International.

Restrictions: The Yidan Prize accepts nominations globally. Nominators cannot put forward their immediate family members, nor any of Yidan Prize Foundation's current board directors, judges or advisers. Deceased people cannot be nominated.

Publications: Reports.

Board of Directors: Prof. Sir Leszek Borysiewicz (Chair.).

Principal Staff: Sec.-Gen. Bruce Au.

Contact Details: Level 28, 9 Queen's Rd Central; tel. 21554893; e-mail enquiry@yidanprize.org; internet yidanprize.org.

HUNGARY

CO-ORDINATING BODIES

Autonómia Alapítvány (Autonómia Foundation)

Founded in 1990; formerly known as the Hungarian Foundation for Self-Reliance.

Activities: Works in the fields of community development and strengthening civil society. The organization assists disadvantaged regions and excluded groups, in particular Roma people, through providing training and community initiatives in health and education. It also carries out research and makes policy recommendations.

Geographical Area of Activity: Bulgaria, Hungary, Romania, Serbia, Slovakia.

Publications: Annual Report; impact assessments; case studies; guides; training materials.

Finance: Financed mainly on an individual project basis by the EU; annual revenue 186.2m. forint, expenditure 186.0m. forint (2021).

Board of Trustees: Anna Csongor (Chair.).

Supervisory Board: István Varga (Chair.).

Principal Staff: Exec. Dir András Nun.

Contact Details: 1137 Budapest, Pozsonyi út 14, II/9; tel. (70) 491-1033; e-mail autonomia@autonomia.hu; internet www.autonomia.hu.

Effekteam Association

Established in 2006 as the Hungarian Donors Forum; an umbrella organization. Present name adopted in 2019.

Activities: Advocates for responsible community behaviour, to build a community that is willing and active, and to create the conditions for progressive social and environmental changes taking the viewpoints of business value creation and sustainability into account. The assocoation organizes conferences, workshops and working groups to share expertise, and carries out research. Effekteam provides services in the field of CSR and sustainablity. It has 34 members and is a member of Philea (q.v.).

Geographical Area of Activity: Hungary.

Publications: Annual Report; newsletter; research; surveys; studies.

Finance: Total assets 32.9m. forint (2024).

Supervisory Board: Csongor Hajna (Chair.).

Principal Staff: Pres. Orsolya Nyilas; Dir Dr Klára Molnár.

Contact Details: 1056 Budapest, Szerb út 17–19; tel. (1) 700-0020; e-mail info@effekteam.hu; internet effekteam.hu.

HAND—Hungarian Association of NGOs for Development and Humanitarian Aid

Established in 2003 by 12 organizations.

Activities: Represents Hungarian organizations and foundations working in the fields of international aid and development, conducting policy and advocacy work at national and EU level. The Association offers training and capacity building; raises public awareness of members' programmes and of humanitarian and development work more generally; promotes the development of multilateral projects and volunteering; and monitors and ensures the transparency of international development spending. Activities are organized under two working groups: Financing for Development and Global Education. It has 13 members; and is a member of CONCORD (q.v.).

Geographical Area of Activity: EU.

Publications: Annual Report; journalism handbooks; *AidWatch* reports.

Finance: Total assets 112.9m. forint (2023).

Board: Csaba Mezei (Pres.).

Principal Staff: Man. Dir Bálint Hamvas.

Contact Details: 1145 Budapest, Törökőr ut. 62. II. emelet; tel. (20) 483-7406; e-mail info@hand.org.hu; internet hand.org.hu.

NIOK Alapítvány—Nonprofit Információs és Oktató Központ Alapítvány—NIOK (NIOK Foundation—Non-Profit Information and Training Centre)

Established in 1994 by Nonprofit Kutatócsoport (Nonprofit Research Group).

Activities: Promotes the development of the third sector in Hungary, through building the capacity of NGOs. The Foundation campaigns on behalf of Hungarian NGOs, including organizing the 1% Campaign ('Give your 1% to a CSO'), promoting philanthropic giving in Hungary, and social dialogue. It maintains a Civil Service Centre and library; a website with details of more than 32,000 Hungarian NGOs; and an online crowdfunding platform.

Geographical Area of Activity: Hungary.

Publications: Annual Report; newsletter (weekly); reports.

Finance: Annual income 100.0m. forint, expenditure 97.7m. forint (2019).

Board of Trustees: Kornél Jellen (Chair.).

Principal Staff: Dir Balázs Gerencsér.

Contact Details: 1122 Budapest, Maros út 23. mfszt. 1; tel. (1) 315-3151; e-mail contact@niok.hu; internet www.niok.hu.

HUNGARY

FOUNDATIONS AND NON-PROFITS

Centre for Euro-Atlantic Integration and Democracy—CEID

Established in 2001 to promote Euro-Atlantic dialogue; a think tank.

Activities: Carries out policy research in the fields of foreign and security policy. Programme areas include: democratic transition and assistance to democracies; energy policy; the EU and the Eastern Partnership; energy policy; Euro-Atlantic integration and NATO; security and defence policy; Visegrád Group (V4) co-operation; and the Western Balkans. The Centre organizes conferences and panel discussions.

Geographical Area of Activity: Central Europe, Eastern Europe.

Publications: Policy briefs; reports; case studies.

Board: Dániel Bartha (Pres.).

Contact Details: 1029 Budapest, Dutka Ákos út 72; 1136 Budapest, Tátra út 6; tel. (20) 323-9443; e-mail info@ceid.hu; internet ceid.hu.

Danube Institute

Established in 2013 by the Batthyány Lajos Foundation (f. 1991); a think tank.

Activities: Conducts and supports research and activities in the fields of geopolitics, national sovereignty and Christianity and democracy. The Institute encourages the exchange of ideas and people within Central Europe, and between Central and other European countries and the English-speaking world. It organizes international conferences and workshops; and offers exchange fellowships in Hungary.

Geographical Area of Activity: International.

Publications: Reports; blog.

Principal Staff: Pres. John O'Sullivan; Exec. Dir István Kiss.

Contact Details: Lónyay-Hatvany Villa, 1015 Budapest, Csónak St 1; tel. (1) 269-1041; e-mail info@danubeinstitute.hu; internet danubeinstitute.hu.

DemNet—Demokratikus Jogok Fejlesztéséért Alapítvány (DemNet—Foundation for the Development of Democratic Rights)

Established in 1996 by Herbert Ascherman.

Activities: Supports civil society development. The Foundation advocates for better and more effective development co-operation policies; and fair financing for development. Main programme areas include: active citizenship; solidarity economy; and gender equality.

Geographical Area of Activity: Hungary, Eastern Partnership countries (EU, Armenia, Azerbaijan, Belarus, Georgia, Moldova, Ukraine), Western Balkans.

Publications: Annual Report; newsletters; reports; blog.

Board of Trustees: Thomas J. Donovan (Chair.).

Principal Staff: Man. Dir Dr Éva Bördős.

Contact Details: 1137 Budapest, Pozsonyi út 14 II/9, Kapucsengő 8; tel. (70) 775-5811; e-mail info@demnet.org.hu; internet www.demnet.hu.

Kárpátok Alapítvány (Carpathian Foundation)

Established in 1994 by the Institute for East–West Studies to support projects to improve the quality of life and the community in rural areas of the Carpathian Mountains, through integrated community development.

Activities: Supports local development initiatives by NGOs and communities; and disadvantaged rural areas, vulnerable groups and young people. Main programme areas are: improving early childhood development in marginalized Roma communities; the Carpathian Civil Society Platform, linking CSOs from Hungary, Poland, Slovakia and Ukraine; the Carpathian Equal Opportunities Scholarship Program, helping disadvantaged university students to complete their studies and remain in their home regions; and supporting community development in north-east Hungary. The Foundation also provides training for representatives from organizations and local government in obtaining and using EU funding.

Geographical Area of Activity: Carpathian region, bordering areas of Hungary, Poland, Romania, Slovakia and Ukraine. In Slovakia the Foundation concentrates its activities on the Košice and Presov regions in Eastern Slovakia.

Restrictions: No grants for investment activities, nor to businesses, state organizations or churches.

Publications: Annual Report; research; programme reports.

Finance: Total grantmaking since 1994 US $15m.

Board of Directors: Sándor Köles (Chair.).

Supervisory Board: Dr Benedek Varsányi.

Principal Staff: Exec. Dir Boglárka Bata.

Contact Details: 3300 Eger (Felnémet), Felvégi út 53; tel. (36) 516-750; e-mail cfhu@cfoundation.org; internet www.karpatokalapitvany.hu.

Ökumenikus Segélyszervezet (Interchurch Aid—HIA Hungary)

Established in 1991, as Magyar Ökumenikus Segélyszervezet, by a multifaith coalition; a member of the ACT Alliance (q.v.) of humanitarian church-based organizations.

Activities: Works to eliminate poverty in Hungary and the Carpathian Basin, supporting families and children, homeless people, addicts and survivors of abuse and promoting social solidarity. The organization provides emergency humanitarian assistance to victims of natural and human-made disasters; and implements international development programmes, including initiatives in education and vocational training, agriculture and rural development, strengthening local communities and building capacity in civil society.

Geographical Area of Activity: East and South-East Asia, Eastern Europe, Russian Federation and the Repubs of Central Europe, Ethiopia, Haiti, Middle East and North Africa, South Asia.

Publications: Annual Report; newsletter; reports.

Finance: Annual revenue 29.2m. forint, expenditure 22.1m. forint (2023).

Principal Staff: Chair. and Dir Rev. László Lehel.

Contact Details: 1221 Budapest, Kossuth Lajos út 64; tel. (1) 382-0700; e-mail segelyszervezet@segelyszervezet.hu; internet www.segelyszervezet.hu.

Regional Environmental Center

Established in 1990; legally based on a charter signed by the governments of over 30 countries and the European Commission.

Activities: Promotes co-operation among governments, NGOs, businesses and other environmental stakeholders; and supports free exchange of information and public participation in environmental decisionmaking. The Center participates in key global, regional and local processes; and contributes to environmental and sustainability solutions within and beyond its country office network, transferring transitional knowledge and experience to countries and regions.

Geographical Area of Activity: Albania, Bosnia and Herzegovina, Hungary, Kosovo, North Macedonia, Montenegro, Poland, Serbia, Türkiye (Turkey).

Publications: Annual Report; handbooks; toolkits; factsheets; leaflets; papers; periodicals; reports; posters.

Principal Staff: Head of Dept Kliment Mindjov.

Contact Details: 2000 Szentendre, Ady Endre út 9–11; tel. (26) 504-000.

Vodafone Magyarország Alapítvány (Vodafone Hungary Foundation)

Established in 2003 by Vodafone Hungary, a telecommunications company; part of the Vodafone Foundation (q.v.) network.

Activities: Funds initiatives in the areas of digital skills development and women's empowerment and safety. The Foundation provides children from underprivileged backgrounds with access to ICT through the Vodafone Digital School Programme and E-Skola e-learning platform. It has developed an emergency first aid digital app; and promotes volunteering. The Digital Award Competition offers a prize of 15m. forint for social innovation in the categories of Digital Children, Digital Family and Digital Social Organizations.

Geographical Area of Activity: Hungary.

Finance: Total disbursements since 2003 2,000m. forint.

Board of Trustees: Mártha Imre (Chair.).

Contact Details: 1112 Budapest, Boldizsár út 2; tel. (1) 288-3288; e-mail foundation.hu@vodafone.com; internet www.vodafone.hu/vodafonerol/vodafone-a-tarsadalomert.

ICELAND

FOUNDATIONS AND NON-PROFITS

Citizens Foundation

Established in 2008 by Robert Bjarnason, a technology entrepreneur, and Gunnar Grímsson, a diplomat.

Activities: Promotes digital democracy and civic engagement through developing open source platforms to connect citizens and governments, and organizing citizen engagement projects. Projects include: Your Priorities, a policy crowdsourcing initiative; Participatory Budgeting; and Empower Citizens with AI. The Foundation has offices in the Netherlands, the United Kingdom and the USA.

Geographical Area of Activity: International.

Publications: Blog.

Principal Staff: Pres and CEO Robert Bjarnason.

Contact Details: Vegmúli 2, 108 Reykjavík; tel. 694-4411; e-mail citizens@citizens.is; internet www.citizens.is.

International Arctic Science Committee—IASC

Founded in 1990; a membership organization comprising national science organizations covering all fields of Arctic research.

Activities: Encourages and facilitates co-operation in all aspects of Arctic research, in all countries engaged in Arctic research and in all areas of the Arctic region. The Committee acts as an information and communication forum for the Arctic science community, with 23 member countries, including 15 non-Arctic countries. It promotes Arctic research and develops research projects that require international and multidisciplinary co-operation. It offers fellowships of up to three years' duration; and also awards the IASC Medal annually for exceptional contributions to the understanding of the Arctic. Previously, Germany, Norway and Sweden have hosted the secretariat.

Geographical Area of Activity: Arctic region.

Publications: *IASC Bulletin*; *IASC Newsletter* (monthly); research findings.

Executive Committee: Henry Burgess (Pres.); Joao Canario, Matthew Druckenmiller, Hiroyuki Enomoto, Gabriela Schaepman-Strub (Vice-Pres); Gerlis Fugmann (Exec. Sec.).

Contact Details: IASC Secretariat, Borgir, Norðurslóð, 600 Akureyri; tel. 515-5824; e-mail info@iasc.info; internet www.iasc.info.

Mannréttindaskrifstofa Íslands (Icelandic Human Rights Centre)

Established in 1994 by 9 NGOs and organizations.

Activities: Promotes and raises awareness of human rights issues in Iceland and abroad. The Centre disseminates information and organizes public seminars; promotes research and legal reforms; comments on bills of law; and provides information to treaty bodies working on human rights issues in Iceland. It maintains a specialized library and conducts legal advice for immigrants and refugees in Iceland. Has 17 affiliates.

Geographical Area of Activity: Iceland.

Publications: Annual Report; newsletter; *Nordic Journal of Human Rights* (quarterly); *Yearbook of Human Rights in Development*; brochures; research reports; handbooks.

Board: Alma Ýr Ingólfsdóttir (Chair.).

Principal Staff: Dir Margrét Steinarsdóttir.

Contact Details: Túngata 14, 101 Reykjavík; tel. 552-2720; e-mail info@humanrights.is; internet www.humanrights.is.

INDIA

CO-ORDINATING BODIES

Centre for Social Impact and Philanthropy—CSIP

Established in 2016.

Activities: Conducts applied research on strategic philanthropy and civil society and disseminates knowledge to influence decisionmaking. The Centre convenes meetings and roundtables; offers training to non-profit organizations; and organizes the annual Social Innovation Summit. It offers nine-month research fellowships, with a stipend worth Rs 100,000 per month; and student volunteering opportunities through the year-long Jagriti programme.

Geographical Area of Activity: India.

Publications: Newsletter; case studies; policy briefs; research studies; surveys.

Principal Staff: Centre Dir Jinny Uppal.

Contact Details: Ashoka University, NH 44, Rajiv Gandhi Education City, Sonipat, Haryana 131 029; e-mail csip@ashoka.edu.in; internet csip.ashoka.edu.in.

Dasra

Established in 1999 as Impact Foundation India by Deval Sanghavi and Neera Nundy, who both worked in financial services in the USA.

Activities: Provides support and capacity building to non-profit organizations through strategic philanthropy. Main programmes focus on: adolescents; urban sanitation; democracy and governance; and knowledge creation and dissemination. Annually, the organization hosts the Dasra Philanthropy Forum in India and the USA.

Geographical Area of Activity: India, USA.

Publications: Annual Report; *COVID-19 Institutional Resilience and Impact Optimization Toolkit for Non-Profits and Funders.*

Finance: Annual income Rs 224.8m., expenditure Rs 272.2m. (31 March 2023).

Board: Deval Sanghavi, Neera Nundy (Co-Founders); Aditi Kothari Desai (Vice-Chair.).

Principal Staff: Team Lead Abhishek Nair.

Contact Details: F1, 1st Floor, opp. G5A, Laxmi Woollen Mills Estate, Shakti Mills Lane, off Dr E. Moses Rd, Jacob Circle, Mahalaxmi (West), Mumbai 400 011; tel. (22) 61200400; e-mail info@dasra.org; internet www.dasra.org.

GiveIndia

Established in 2000 by Venkat Krishnan, co-founder of Educational Initiatives, an educational research and assessment company.

Activities: Operates an online donation platform and co-ordinates workplace giving to more than 200 NGOs. Priority areas are: cancer care; children; education; women; and health. The organization has offices in the United Kingdom and the USA.

Geographical Area of Activity: India, UK, USA.

Restrictions: Not a grantmaking organization.

Publications: Newsletter.

Finance: Annual income Rs 1,116.9m., expenditure Rs 1,105.1m. (31 March 2024).

Principal Staff: CEO Atul Satija.

Contact Details: 1st floor, Rigel, No. 15-19 Doddanekkundi, Marathahalli Outer Ring Rd, Bengaluru, Karnataka 560037; tel. 7738714428; e-mail info@giveindia.org; internet www.giveindia.org.

GuideStar India

Established in 2009 by Pushpa Aman Singh, former COO of GiveIndia (q.v.).

Activities: Maintains a searchable database of philanthropic organizations registered in India. A programme of Civil Society Information Services India.

Geographical Area of Activity: India.

Publications: Studies.

Board of Trustees: Bishambar Nath Makhija (Chair.).

Contact Details: 707 Corporate Ave, A Wing Sonawala Rd, Goregaon (E), Mumbai 400 063; tel. 8356832329; e-mail info@guidestarindia.org; internet www.guidestarindia.org.

iPartner India

Established in 2008 by Bina Rani, a voluntary sector professional.

Activities: Co-ordinates philanthropic giving from within India and abroad to a network of grassroots organizations in 23 states in India, Nepal and the United Kingdom. Main programme areas are: vulnerable children; child trafficking; education; health; women and livelihoods; and the environment. The organization has offices in India and the United Kingdom.

Geographical Area of Activity: India, Nepal, UK.

Finance: Annual income Rs 1,192.8m., expenditure Rs 1,192.2m. (31 March 2023).

Board of Trustees, India: Sanjay Patra (Chair.).

Principal Staff: CEO Bina Rani; Country Co-Lead Eshant Kumar Rajput, Nisha Dubey.

Contact Details: 1-D/1, First Fl., Bharat Nagar, New Friends Colony, Near Mata Mandir, New Delhi 110 025; tel. 9971533099; e-mail info@ipartnerindia.org; internet www.ipartnerindia.org.

OneStage

Established in 1998 as CAF India; a member of the Global Alliance of the Charities Aid Foundation. Present name adopted in 2023.

Activities: Supports corporate organizations, individuals and charities to ensure greater impact of their philanthropic investments. Activities focus on the following themes: jobs, skills and livlihoods; the environment; early childhood development; healthcare; and education. The Foundation works to foster a culture of volunteering and giving through initiatives including the Give4Good online platform and Give As You Earn (GAYE).

Geographical Area of Activity: India.

Publications: Annual Report; newsletter (1–2 a year); *World Giving Index*; *India Giving*; reports.

Board: Dr Sanjay Patra (Chair.).

Principal Staff: CEO Dr Pratyush Kumar Panda.

Contact Details: Plot/Site No. 2, First Floor, Sector C (OFC Pocket), Nelson Mandela Marg, Vasant Kunj, New Delhi 110 070; tel. (11) 61424141; e-mail info@theonestage.org; internet theonestage.org.

Voluntary Action Network India—VANI

Established in 1990 as a platform for research, advocacy, capacity building and information exchange; an umbrella organization.

Activities: Active in the fields of volunteering and CSOs. An apex body of CSOs in India, the Network carries out research-based advocacy, capacity building, convening and knowledge creation. It has 624 members, reaching 10,000 non-profit organizations all over India.

Geographical Area of Activity: India.

Publications: Annual Report; *E-VANI* (newsletter, in Hindi and English); study reports; blog.

Finance: Annual income Rs 118.3m., expenditure Rs 116.1m. (31 March 2022).

Governing Body: Dattartray Shankar Patil (Chair.); Hemal Kamat (Co-Chair.); Jaswant Kaur (Treas.).

Principal Staff: CEO Harshvrat Jaitli.

Contact Details: VANI House, 7, PSP Pocket, Sector 8, Dwarka, New Delhi 110 077; tel. (11) 49148610; e-mail info@vaniindia.org; internet www.vaniindia.org.

FOUNDATIONS AND NON-PROFITS

African-Asian Rural Development Organization—AARDO

Founded in 1962 in Cairo, Egypt; formerly known as the Afro-Asian Rural Reconstruction Organization.

Activities: Works to restructure the economy of rural populations, promoting welfare and working to eradicate malnutrition, disease, illiteracy and poverty. The Organization conducts collaborative research on development issues; gives financial assistance for development projects and disseminates information; organizes international conferences and seminars; facilitates pilot projects; and awards more than 380 fellowships at training centres in Bangladesh, Egypt, India, the Republic of Korea, Malaysia, Nigeria, Pakistan, the Philippines, Taiwan, Thailand and Zambia. Membership comprises 32 countries, with three associate members.

Geographical Area of Activity: Africa, Asia.

Publications: Annual Report; *African-Asian Journal of Rural Development* (2 a year); *AARDO Newsletter* (2 a year, in Arabic and English); workshop and seminar reports.

Finance: Receives annual membership contributions from member countries. Annual income US $982,736, expenditure $826,993 (2022).

Principal Staff: Sec.-Gen. Dr Manoj Nardeosingh.

Contact Details: 2 State Guest Houses Complex, Chanakyapuri, New Delhi 110 021; tel. (11) 26877783; e-mail aardohq@aardo.org; internet www.aardo.org.

All India Disaster Mitigation Institute

Established in 1995.

Ambuja Cement Foundation INDIA

Activities: Works in a variety of areas of disaster management, including risk reduction, knowledge management, innovations in disaster response and recovery, and policy advocacy. The Institute promotes community-based disaster risk reduction through capacity building and facilitates the exchange of risk reduction strategies. It provides targeted relief to communities affected by disasters; and supports human security through shelter, livelihood, water and food projects, protecting and promoting rights, especially of women, children, Dalits and minorities.

Geographical Area of Activity: South Asia.

Restrictions: Supported efforts must reduce risks.

Publications: Annual Report; *NIDM Journal*; *India Disaster Report*; *Vipada Nivaran* (in Hindi); *Afat Nivaran* (in Gujarati); newsletter; online news; manuals.

Principal Staff: Dir Mihir R. Bhatt.

Contact Details: 411 Sakar Five, nr Old Natraj Cinema, Mithakhadi Railway Crossing, Ashram Rd, Ahmedabad 380 009; tel. (79) 26582962; e-mail bestteam@aidmi.org; internet www.aidmi.org.

Ambuja Cement Foundation—ACF

Established in 1993 by Narotam Sekhsaria, founder of Ambuja Cements Ltd, and Suresh Neotia, the company's Chair. Emeritus.

Activities: Aims to make people in India productive and prosperous and to improve their quality of life, through managing human and natural resources for sustainable development; through technical and financial support; and by serving as a catalyst for appropriate planning, implementation and post-implementation care. The Foundation works in the areas of: livelihoods (agricultural and skill based); natural resource management (water and energy); human development (health, education, women's empowerment and training); and rural infrastructure. It also provides disaster relief and long-term reconstruction support.

Geographical Area of Activity: India.

Publications: Annual Report; reports; blog.

Finance: Annual revenue, Rs 1,806.6m, expenditure Rs 1,793.1m. (31 March 2024).

Board of Directors: Narotam Sekhsaria (Chair.).

Principal Staff: Dir and CEO Pearl Tiwari.

Contact Details: Elegant Business Park, MIDC Cross Rd 'B', off Andheri-Kurla Rd, Andheri (East), Mumbai 400 059; tel. (22) 40667616; e-mail ceooffice@ambujafoundation.com; internet www.ambujacementfoundation.org.

Arghyam

Established in 2005 by Rohini Nilekani.

Activities: Supports the provision of safe and sustainable water and sanitation services across India. Its flagship project is the India Water Portal, an open resource facility for content, data and articles on water, supported by industry experts.

Geographical Area of Activity: India.

Finance: Total income Rs 93.3m., expenditure Rs 82.7m. (31 March 2024).

Board of Trustees: Rohini Nilekani, Sunita Nadhamuni (Chair.).

Principal Staff: CEO Anuj Sharma.

Contact Details: #599, ROHINI, 12th Main Rd, 7th Cross, HAL 2nd Stage, Indiranagar, Bengaluru, Karnataka 560068; tel. (80) 41698941; internet arghyam.org.

Asian Development Research Institute—ADRI

Established in 1991 by a group of social scientists in the eastern Indian state of Bihar.

Activities: Works in the fields of development and social science research, in the Bihar region and internationally, concentrating particularly on promoting literacy development and education. The Institute is also active in the area of cultural regeneration, including documenting Bihar's folk art tradition. It has established two financially independent research centres, in Ranchi and New Delhi, and works in collaboration with foreign universities and development organizations; and also holds conferences and the annual ADRI Foundation Lecture.

Geographical Area of Activity: Mainly India.

Publications: Newsletter; brochure; research reports; monographs; working papers; books.

Finance: Annual income Rs 146.9m., expenditure Rs 138.4m. (31 March 2023).

Board of Directors: Shri Dilip Sinha (Chair.); Dr Sunita Lall (Treas.); Dr Ashmita Gupta (Sec.).

Principal Staff: Dir Dr Ajit Sinha.

Contact Details: BSIDC Colony, off Boring Patliputra Rd, Patna 800 013; tel. (612) 2575649; e-mail adripatna@adriindia.org; internet www.adriindia.org.

Azim Premji Foundation

Established in 2000 by Azim Premji, Chair. of the Wipro Corporation; part of a group that includes Azim Premji Philanthropic Initiatives and Azim Premji University; it collaborates with Wipro Foundation, which is separate.

Activities: Funds teacher training and the development of primary education through using technology; and working with teachers, school leaders and education officials to improve processes and practices within schools, reform curricula and build professional networks. The Foundation offers two-year fellowships; organizes workshops teacher forums and seminars; and provides grants to NGOs to support disabled people and orphans, control drug abuse and prevent violence against women and people trafficking. It has Field Institutes in more than 59 districts, in seven states and in one union territory; and works closely with Azim Premji University.

Geographical Area of Activity: India.

Restrictions: Not a grantmaking organization; fellowship applicants must hold a postgraduate or professional degree, have 3–10 years' work experience and be proficient in local languages (Hindi, Kannada, Tamil or Telugu).

Publications: *Learning Curve* (newsletter); *Milestones* (newsletter); *Kindle* (newsletter, 6 a year); *Language Learning and Teaching* (2 a year); *I Wonder* (magazine, 2 a year); *At Right Angles* (2–3 a year); field newsletters; position papers; research studies; books; reports; papers and articles; CDs; online teaching and learning resources.

Board of Trustees: Azim Premji (Chair.).

Principal Staff: CEO Anurag Behar.

Contact Details: 134 Doddakannelli, next to Wipro Corporate Office, Sarjapur Rd, Bangalore 560 035; tel. (80) 66144900; e-mail fellowship@azimpremjifoundation.org; internet azimpremjifoundation.org.

Bharti Foundation

Established in 2000 by Sunil Bharti Mittal, founder of Bharti Enterprises, a conglomerate.

Activities: Works in the fields of education and sanitation through self-conducted programmes. In 2006 the Foundation began the Satya Bharti School Program, to provide primary education to children in rural areas, in particular girls. It has also established higher education learning centres and research partnerships with national and international institutions; these include the Bharti School of Telecommunication Technology & Management (IIT Delhi), the Bharti Center for Communication (IIT Bombay) and the Bharti Institute of Public Policy (Indian School of Business). In 2019 programmes were running in more than 750 government schools in 16 states.

Geographical Area of Activity: India.

Publications: Annual Report; newsletter.

Finance: Annual income Rs 1,229.2m., expenditure Rs 1,311.5m. (31 March 2024).

Board of Governors and Board of Trustees: Sunil Bharti Mittal (Chair.); Rakesh Bharti Mittal, Rajan Bharti Mittal (Vice-Chair.).

Principal Staff: CEO Mamta Saikia.

Contact Details: First Floor, B Wing, Plot No. 16, Udyog Vihar, Phase IV, Gurugram, Haryana 122 015; tel. (124) 4823500; e-mail bharti.foundation@bhartifoundation.org; internet bhartifoundation.org.

Biocon Foundation

Established in 2004 by Dr Kiran Mazumdar-Shaw, Chair. and Man. Dir of Biocon Ltd, a biotechnology company.

Activities: Promotes sustainable socioeconomic inclusion through innovation. Main programme areas are: education; healthcare; rural development; and grantmaking. Foundation activities include: strengthening preventive and primary healthcare; reducing hunger, poverty and malnutrition; providing safe water, sanitation and hygiene; providing access to equitable education; protecting the environment and natural resources; promoting rural development; reducing economic inequality; conserving traditional art and culture; fostering science and technology; and supporting sports.

Geographical Area of Activity: India (Karnataka, Nagaland, Rajasthan).

Publications: Annual Report; workbooks.

Board: Dr Kiran Mazumdar-Shaw (Man. Trustee).

Principal Staff: Mission Dir Dr Anupama Narayan Shetty.

Contact Details: 20th Km, Hosur Rd, Electronic City, Bengaluru 560 100; tel. (80) 28082808; e-mail info.biconfoundation@biocon.com; internet www.biocon.com/responsibility/biocon-foundation.

Centre for Civil Society—CCS

Established in 1997; an independent, non-profit, research and educational organization.

Activities: Works in the fields of education, livelihoods and policy training to promote choice and accountability and bring about social change through public policy. Programmes include: the School Choice Campaign, to improve education quality; Jeevika, which campaigns to make street vending a legal occupation; and the Viklap training voucher scheme. The Centre carries out policy training and outreach through the CCS Academy.

Geographical Area of Activity: India.

Publications: Annual Report; newsletter; research reports; brochures; books (in Hindi and English).

Finance: Annual income Rs 82.8m., expenditure Rs 106.2m. (31 March 2023).

Board of Advisers: Anirudha Dutta (Chair.).

Principal Staff: CEO Amit Chandra.

Contact Details: A-69 Hauz Khas Enclave, New Delhi 110 016; tel. (11) 26537456; e-mail ccs@ccs.in; internet ccs.in.

Concern India Foundation

Founded in 1991.

Activities: Supports grassroots NGOs across India in the areas of: access to education; preventive, remedial and rehabilitative healthcare; socioeconomic community development; sustainable livelihoods; girl children; women's empowerment and equality; care for elderly people; and special needs. Through financial and non-financial support to over 270 programmes, the Foundation helps destitute children, young people, differently abled people, women and elderly people. It has offices in New Delhi, Bengaluru, Chennai, Hyderabad, Kolkata and Pune.

Geographical Area of Activity: India.

Publications: Annual Report; blog.

Finance: Total assets Rs 3.8m. (31 March 2023).

Board of Trustees: Naheed H. Sorabjee (Chair. and Man. Trustee).

Principal Staff: CEO Kavita Shah.

Contact Details: Rampart House, 7th Floor, 6 K Dubash Marg, Mumbai 400 001; tel. (22) 35616653; e-mail concern@concernindia.org; internet www.concernindiafoundation.org.

Hinduja Foundation

Established in 1969 by Parmanand Deepchand Hinduja, founder of the Hinduja Group, a business conglomerate.

Activities: Works in the areas of poverty alleviation and sustainable rural development. Main programme areas include: arts and culture; education; healthcare; rural development; social welfare; and water. The Foundation promotes and preserves Indian heritage and culture. It has branches in the United Kingdom and the USA, which support Indian university students in those countries.

Geographical Area of Activity: India, UK, USA.

Publications: Annual Report.

Board of Trustees: Gopichand P. Hinduja (Chair.); Prakash P. Hinduja (Chair., Europe); Ashok P. Hinduja (Chair., India).

Contact Details: Hinduja House, 171 Dr Annie Besant Rd, Worli, Mumbai 400 018; tel. (22) 61360407; e-mail foundation@hindujagroup.com; internet www.hindujafoundation.org.

Indian Council for Cultural Relations

Founded in 1950 by Maulana Abul Kalam Azad, the first Education Minister of India following independence.

Activities: Operates through the reciprocal development of studies in Indian and foreign universities; awards scholarships and fellowships; exchanges cultural material with libraries and museums abroad; and promotes exchange visits of cultural delegations, scholars and artists. The Council organizes the Azad Memorial Lectures, international seminars, symposia and conferences; establishes chairs and centres of Indian studies abroad; looks after the welfare of foreign students in India; and compiles select bibliographies and publishes books and journals in English, French, Spanish and Arabic. It also administers the Jawaharlal Nehru Award for international understanding, instituted by the Government of India in 1964. Maintains 18 regional offices and 35 cultural centres worldwide; and a library containing more than 50,000 vols.

Geographical Area of Activity: International.

Publications: Annual Report; *Indian Horizons* (periodic, in English); *Gagananchal* (6 a year, in Hindi); *Thaqafat-ul-Hind* (quarterly, in Arabic); *Papeles de la India* (2 a year, in Spanish); *Rencontre avec l'Inde* (2 a year, in French); books on diplomacy, language and literature, and the arts, in particular Indian culture, philosophy and mythology, music, dance, theatre and translations of Sanskrit classics.

Finance: Annual expenditure Rs 2.9m. (31 March 2023).

Principal Staff: Dir-Gen. K. Nandini Singla.

Contact Details: Azad Bhawan Rd, Indraprastha Estate, New Delhi 110 002; tel. (11) 23379309; e-mail dg.iccr@mea.gov.in; internet iccr.gov.in.

Indian Council of Social Science Research—ICSSR

Founded in 1969 by the Government of India as an autonomous organization.

Activities: Funds research projects in social sciences. The Council conducts surveys of social science research; awards research fellowships, contingency grants, and grants for study and publication; gives financial support for conferences and seminars; and organizes or supports training courses in research methodology. It offers guidance and consultancy services in data processing and has a documentation centre, providing information support to social scientists; collaborates in international research and exchange programmes; and evaluates research proposals by foreign nationals for research in India. Part-finances 17 research institutes and has six regional offices. There are also five recognised institutes throughout India.

Inlaks Shivdasani Foundation INDIA

Geographical Area of Activity: India.

Publications: Annual Report; *ICSSR Journal of Abstracts and Reviews: Economics* (2 a year); *ICSSR Journal of Abstracts and Reviews: Geography* (2 a year); *ICSSR Journal of Abstracts and Reviews: Political Science* (2 a year); *ICSSR Newsletter* (quarterly); *ICSSR Research Abstracts* (quarterly); *Indian Psychological Abstracts and Reviews* (2 a year); NASSDOC research information series; ICSSR surveys of research; and various other publications of research reports, monographs, national and international seminar proceedings.

Council: Prof. Deepak Kumar Srivastava (Chair.).

Principal Staff: Member Sec. Prof. Dhananjay Singh.

Contact Details: Aruna Asaf Ali Marg, JNU Institutional Area, New Delhi 110 067; tel. (11) 26741849; e-mail cc@icssr.org; internet www.icssr.org.

Inlaks Shivdasani Foundation

Founded in 1976 by Indoo Shivdasani and his wife Laxmi.

Activities: Offers scholarships of up to US $100,000 to Indian students for study or research at universities and institutions in Europe and the USA. In the United Kingdom, the Foundation has joint scholarships with Imperial College London, the Royal College of Art, the School of Oriental and African Studies, the Cambridge Trust, and SciencesPo in Paris. The Foundation also offers research and travel grants for three months' doctoral research in the humanities and social sciences; assists young Indians through Take-Off Grants in India, which develop individual talent; and offers Inlaks Fine Arts Awards to help artists under 35 years of age in India. Awards are also available for studies in the fields of: ecology, conservation and field biology; theatre; Indian Classical and Western Classical music; film and television; and sports. Has an office in Mumbai.

Geographical Area of Activity: International.

Restrictions: Applicants must have been accepted for a course before applying for a scholarship and be aged under 30 years; no scholarships for courses in engineering, computer science, business studies, medicine and dentistry, public health, fashion design, music, film or film animation.

Publications: Annual Report; blog.

Principal Staff: Programme Dir Suchita Gokarn.

Contact Details: c/o ICGEB (International Centre for Genetic Engineering and Biotechnology), Aruna Asaf Ali Marg, New Delhi 110 067; POB 2108, Delhi 110 007; tel. (11) 26741260; e-mail info@inlaksfoundation.org; internet www.inlaksfoundation.org.

INTACH—Indian National Trust for Art and Cultural Heritage

Established in 1984 for the conservation and promotion of Indian heritage: architectural, natural, cultural and environmental.

Activities: Supports the preservation of man-made and natural heritage of India, including places of archaeological, historical, artistic and scientific value. The Trust also promotes public awareness of cultural issues and preservation of Indian heritage. It works through eight divisions: Art Conservation; Heritage Education and Communication Services; Architectural Heritage; Natural Heritage; Cultural Affairs; Intangible Heritage; Heritage Tourism; and Chapters. There are 228 Chapters across India and three Chapters in Belgium, the United Kingdom and the USA. The INTACH UK Trust offers scholarships and funding for British nationals to carry out research on India, and exchanges for young architects and planners in association with the Charles Wallace India Trust and the British Council (qq.v.). As part of the State of Built Heritage of India initiative, the Heritage at Risk Register database was established to record unprotected and endangered built heritage.

Geographical Area of Activity: Belgium, India, UK, USA.

Publications: Annual Report; *Virasat* (quarterly newsletter); *Young INTACH* (newsletter); environmental series; documentation on heritage properties; science in public policy series; studies in ecology and sustainable development; INTACH Southern Western Ghats environment series; Heritage at Risk Register.

Finance: Annual income Rs 127.6m., expenditure Rs 110.5m. (31 March 2021).

Governing Council and Executive Committee: Shri Ashok Singh Thakur (Chair.); Prof. Sukhdev Singh (Vice-Chair.).

Principal Staff: Mem. Sec. Ravindra Singh.

Contact Details: 71 Lodi Estate, New Delhi 110 003; tel. (11) 24631818; e-mail intach@intach.org; internet www.intach.org.

M. S. Swaminathan Research Foundation—MSSRF

Founded in 1988 by Prof. M. S. Swaminathan, with proceeds from the First World Food Prize, which he received in 1987.

Activities: Works in the areas of agriculture, food and nutrition. Main programmes include: biodiversity; biotechnology; climate change; coastal systems research; ecotechnology; food security; gender and grassroots institutions; geographical information systems; and information education communication. The Foundation promotes the use of modern science and technology for agricultural and rural development to improve people's quality of life and livelihoods, empowering poor people and women and conserving nature.

Geographical Area of Activity: India.

Restrictions: Not a grantmaking organization.

Publications: Annual Report; newsletter; brochures; research publications; blog; books.

Board of Trustees: Dr Soumya Swaminathan (Chair.).

Principal Staff: Exec. Dirs Dr G. N. Hariharan, Dr R. Rengalakshmi, Raman Srinivas.

Contact Details: 3rd Cross St, Institutional Area, Taramani, Chennai 600 113; tel. (44) 22541229; e-mail info@mssrf.res.in; internet mssrf.org.

M. Venkatarangaiya Foundation—MVF

Established in 1981 in memory of Prof. Mamidipudi Venkatarangaiya, an educationist and historian.

Activities: Seeks to abolish child labour through campaigning for a universal education system in India. The Foundation enrols children at school and provides support; and runs summer camps and extracurricular courses. It works to empower women through action in areas such as livelihoods and natural resource management. Has an office in the USA.

Geographical Area of Activity: India (Andhra Pradesh).

Publications: Annual Report; case studies; evaluations; research reports; blog.

Board of Trustees: M. Ravindra Vikram (Chair. and Man. Trustee); M. Savithri Sravanthi (Treas.); Shravan Karpuram (Sec.).

Principal Staff: Nat. Convener R. Venkat Reddy.

Contact Details: 201 Narayan Apartments, West Maredpally, Secunderabad 500 026; tel. (40) 27801320; e-mail mvfindia@gmail.com; internet www.mvfindia.in.

Naandi Foundation—A New Beginning

Established in 1998 by four businesses (Dr Reddy's Laboratories Ltd, Global Trust Bank, Satyam Computer Services Ltd and the Nagarjuna Group of companies) and a state government as a unique non-profit autonomous development organization.

Activities: Supports development initiatives in the fields of children and young people's rights, sustainable livelihoods for marginal and small farmers, and safe drinking water. The Foundation works directly with communities in partnership with the Government and CSOs.

Geographical Area of Activity: India (the states of Andhra Pradesh, Madhya Pradesh, Chhattisgarh, Nagaland, Rajasthan, Punjab, Haryana, Andaman and the Nicobar Islands).

Publications: Annual Report; *HUNGaMA Survey.*

Finance: Annual income Rs 1,004.7m., expenditure Rs 990.1m. (31 March 2021).

Board of Directors: Anand G. Mahindra (Chair.); Manoj Kumar (CEO and Sec.).

Contact Details: 502 Trendset Towers, Rd No. 2, Banjara Hills, Hyderabad 500 034; tel. (40) 23556491; e-mail info@naandi.org; internet www.naandi.org.

Nand & Jeet Khemka Foundation

Founded in 2005 by the Khemka family; in 2006 established the Global Education & Leadership Foundation (tGELF).

Activities: Seeks to develop multi-stakeholder, strategic, long-term initiatives in four main areas: social entrepreneurship; leadership and ethics; climate change; and governance and accountability. The Foundation jointly administers the Action to Improve Public Scheme Access and Delivery project in Bihar with the EU. The Nabha Foundation (f. 2003) is a sister organization which operates in Punjab.

Geographical Area of Activity: Mainly in India.

Restrictions: No unsolicited grant proposals.

Publications: *Jan Samvad* (newsletter, 6 a year); handbooks; podcasts; reports.

Trustees: Uday Khemka (Man. Trustee); Don Mohanlal (Vice-Chair.).

Principal Staff: CEO Shubhra Singh.

Contact Details: Khemka House, 1st Floor, 11 Community Centre, Saket, New Delhi 110 017; tel. (11) 46034800; e-mail info@khemkafoundation.net; internet www.khemkafoundation.net.

NFI—National Foundation for India

Established in 1992 under the aegis of the Ford Foundation, USA (q.v.).

Activities: Works with grassroots organizations in the areas of governance and health. The Foundation builds the capacity of CSOs that address gender and nutrition issues, and social justice; and supports emerging leaders from marginalized and disadvantaged communities. It promotes development journalism through its Media Awards; offers fellowships, worth Rs 30,000, for independent journalists who report in English and Malayalam; and organizes roundtable conferences with donors.

Geographical Area of Activity: India.

Restrictions: No grants for religious or political causes.

Publications: Annual Report; newsletter; reports; blog.

Finance: Annual income Rs 4,362.9m., expenditure Rs 3,277.5m. (31 March 2023).

Board: Satyananda Mishra (Chair.).

Principal Staff: Exec. Dir Biraj Patnaik.

Contact Details: India Habitat Centre, Core 4A, Upper Ground Floor, Lodhi Rd, New Delhi 110 003; tel. (11) 24641864; e-mail info@nfi.org.in; internet nfi.org.in.

Observer Research Foundation—ORF

Established in 1990 by Rishi Kumar Mishra, a journalist and former Member of the Indian Parliament; a think tank.

Activities: Conducts research and analysis on India's international political and economic relations. Main programmes areas include: climate change and sustainable development; economy and growth; energy; political economy; technology and media; and strategic studies. The Foundation hosts multi-sectoral and multidisciplinary forums for thought leaders from government, industry and academia; and roundtable discussions between international policymakers and audiences. It has offices in Kolkatta and Mumbai; and a sister organization, ORF Africa, is based in Morocco.

Geographical Area of Activity: International.

Publications: Annual Report; newsletter; *GP-ORF Series*; *ORF Discourse*; books and monographs; issue briefs and special reports; monitors; occasional papers; policy briefs; commentaries; event reports.

Finance: Annual income Rs 446.0m., expenditure Rs 434.7m. (31 March 2020).

Board of Trustees: Sunjoy Joshi (Chair.).

Principal Staff: Pres. Samir Saran.

Contact Details: 20 Rouse Ave, Institutional Area (nr Bal Bhavan, ITO), New Delhi 110 002; tel. (11) 35332000; e-mail contactus@orfonline.org; internet www.orfonline.org.

Oxfam India

Established in 2008 by a merger of Oxfam affiliates that had been working in India since 1951; became a fully affiliated member of the Oxfam confederation of organizations (qq.v.) in 2011.

Activities: Works to end discrimination, injustice and inequality. Main programme areas are: economic justice; essential services; gender justice; humanitarian response and disaster risk reduction; private sector engagement; and social inclusion. The organization provides humanitarian relief during crises and provides assistance to internally displaced people. It collaborates with 60 grassroots NGOs; and has eight programme and fundraising offices in India.

Geographical Area of Activity: India.

Restrictions: Does not make loans or grants to individuals.

Publications: Annual Report; factsheets; policy briefs; working papers; blog.

Governing Board: Shankar Venkateswaran (Chair.).

Contact Details: B-111, 1st Fl., Okhla Industrial Area, Phase-1, New Delhi 110 020; tel. 9958992255; e-mail friendsofoxfam@oxfamindia.org; internet www.oxfamindia.org.

Pratham Education Foundation

1995 by Dr Madhav Chavan and Farida Lambay.

Activities: Pratham is one of the largest education NGOs in India. It has won many prizes, including the Kravis Prize, the Skoll Award, the WISE Prize, the LUI Che Woo Prize and most recently the Yidan Prize. It focuses on high-quality, low-cost and replicable interventions to address gaps in the education system: teaching at the Right Level allows children who have reached classes 3–5 unable to read, write or do basic mathematics to catch up through 30 days of learning camps; Second Chance supports women of any age to prepare for their school-leaving exams, opening employment opportunities in the formal economy; vocational training targets youth from disadvantaged backgrounds, developing skills that the Indian labour market requires, through long and short courses; and the annual ASER Report measures learning outcomes across rural India and is used to drive change in educational policy to focus on learning outcomes, not inputs. Has international affiliates in Australia, Sweden, UK and USA.

Geographical Area of Activity: Africa, Asia, India, South America.

Publications: Annual Report; newsletter; *Annual Status of Education Report*; reports.

Finance: Annual revenue Rs 2,306.7m., expenditure Rs 2,398.4m. (31 March 2020).

Board: Ajay G. Piramal (Chair.); Dinyar (Dinny) Devitre (Vice-Chair.).

Principal Staff: CEO Dr Rukmini Banerji.

Contact Details: B-4/58, 2nd Floor, Safdarjung Enclave, New Delhi 110 029; tel. (11) 26716083; e-mail info@pratham.org; internet www.pratham.org.

Public Health Foundation of India—PHFI

Established in 2006 by the Government of India; an autonomously governed, independent public-private initiative.

Activities: Supports promotive, preventive and therapeutic public health services through self-conducted projects in areas including: epidemiology and control of infectious and chronic diseases; maternal and child health; health systems; and social determinants of health. The Foundation works to strengthen institutional capacity through training, research and policy development and has established four centres of excellence: the Centre for Chronic Conditions & Injuries; the Centre for Environmental Health; the Ramalingaswami Centre for Social Determinants of Health, Bengaluru; and the South Asia Centre for Disability Inclusive Development and Research, Hyderabad. It has also established Indian Institutes of Public Health in Gandhinagar, Hyderabad, Delhi, Bhubaneswar and Shillong, which offer postgraduate programmes and short courses on campus and via e-learning.

Geographical Area of Activity: India.

Publications: Annual Report; reports; journals; books; policy briefs.

Finance: Annual income Rs 7,161.4m., expenditure Rs 7,339.8m. (31 March 2023).

Executive Committee: S. Ramadorai (Chair.).

Principal Staff: Pres. Prof. Sanjay Zodpey.

Contact Details: 431A, Rectangle No. 1, 4th Floor, behind Saket Sheraton Hotel, Commercial Complex D4, Saket New Delhi 110 017; tel. (11) 40175500; e-mail contact@phfi.org; internet phfi.org.

Rajiv Gandhi Foundation

Established in 1991 by Sonia Gandhi, a politician, in honour of her late husband and former Prime Minister, Rajiv Gandhi.

Activities: Works in the areas of: natural resource management; libraries and education; health; welfare of the disabled; women and children's development; applied science and technology in rural areas; and the promotion of grassroots democracy through local self-government. The Foundation's largest programmes include establishing village libraries throughout India; implementing rainwater harvesting and environmental regeneration schemes in rural India using its own volunteers; supporting the education of child victims of terrorism; projects for the economic and educational empowerment of women; and AIDS control and awareness campaigns. These activities are implemented through self-conducted programmes, grants to institutions, scholarships, research, conferences and publications. The attached Rajiv Gandhi Institute for Contemporary Studies is a centre for interdisciplinary studies, including economic and legal reform, social issues and international relations. It organizes seminars and workshops, and issues publications.

Geographical Area of Activity: India.

Publications: Annual Report; reports.

Finance: Annual income Rs 76.5m., expenditure Rs 77.6m. (31 March 2021).

Board of Trustees and Executive Committee: Sonia Gandhi (Chair.).

Principal Staff: CEO and Sec. Vijay Mahajan.

Contact Details: Jawahar Bhavan, Dr Rajendra Prasad Rd, New Delhi 110 001; tel. (11) 23755117; e-mail info@rgfindia.org; internet www.rgfindia.com.

Reliance Foundation

Established in 2010 by Nita M. Ambani as the corporate social responsibility arm of Reliance Industries, a conglomerate.

Activities: Supports development through innovation and technology. The Foundation carries out self-conducted programmes in the areas of: arts, culture and heritage; disaster relief; education; health; rural transformation; sports for development; and urban renewal. Since 2010, it has assisted more than 86m. people across India, in over 91,500 villages and urban locations. The Dhirubhai Ambani Scholarship Programme offers scholarships for higher education in India and abroad.

Geographical Area of Activity: India.

Publications: Annual Report; newsletter.

Board: Nita M. Ambani (Chair.).

Contact Details: Reliance Corporate Park, 5 TTC Industrial Area, Thane-Belapur Rd, Ghansoli, Navi Mumbai 400701; e-mail contactus@reliancefoundation.org; internet www.reliancefoundation.org.

Rohini Nilekani Philanthropies

Established in 2003 by Rohini Nilekani.

Activities: Areas of interest include: active citizenship, access to justice, climate and biodiversity, gender equity, and mental health.

Geographical Area of Activity: India.

Publications: Books; reports.

Finance: Annual income Rs 892.9m., expenditure Rs 888.5m. (31 March 2024).

Principal Staff: Chair. Rohini Nilekani.

Contact Details: 1A101, WeWork Galaxy, 43 Residency Rd, Bangalore 560 025; e-mail contact@rohininilekaniphilanthropies.org; internet www.rohininilekaniphilanthropies.org.

Shiv Nadar Foundation Group

Established in 1994 by Shiv Nadar, founder of HCL, a technology company.

Activities: Carries out self-conducted programmes in the areas of leadership building, education and art. The Group comprises: the Shiv Nadar Foundation; VidyaGyan (f. 2009), a leadership academy for underprivileged rural students; the Shiksha Initiative to improve basic education in rural areas; Shiv Nadar School, for K-12 urban education; SSN Institutions (f. 1996), which include colleges of engineering, management, software engineering and career development, and research, incubation and innovation centres; Shiv Nadar University; and the Kiran Nadar Museum of Art (f. 2010), which exhibits contemporary South Asian art. SSN offers scholarships worth up to Rs 1m.

Geographical Area of Activity: India.

Publications: Annual Report; *The Foundation Post* (quarterly newsletter).

Finance: Annual income US $82.0m., expenditure $132.8m. (31 March 2024).

Principal Staff: Chair. Dr Shiv Nadar.

Contact Details: A-9, Sec. 3, Noida 201 301, Uttar Pradesh; tel. (120) 3667000; e-mail foundationconnect@shivnadarfoundation.org; internet www.shivnadarfoundation.org.

Tata Trusts

Established in 1892 by Jamsetji Tata.

Activities: India's oldest philanthropic organization. Tata Trusts' purpose is to catalyse development in the areas of health, nutrition, education, water, sanitation and hygiene, livelihood, digital transformation, migration and urban habitat, social justice and inclusion, environment and energy, skill development, sports, and arts and culture. The Trusts' programmes, achieved through direct implementation, partnerships and grant making, are marked by innovations, relevant to the country.

Geographical Area of Activity: India, USA.

Publications: Annual Report; *Hope-scape* (newsletter); *Horizons: The Tata Trusts Magazine*; Impact Stories; Publication, Policy recommendations; Surveys; Books.

Finance: Total disbursal of Sir Ratan Tata and Allied Trusts for 2023–24: US $69.3m.
Total disbursal of Sir Dorabji Tata and Allied Trusts for 2023–24: US $14.9m.

Board of Trustees: Noel N. Tata (Chair.); Vijay Singh, Venu Srinivasan (Vice-Chair.).

Principal Staff: CEO Siddharth Sharma.

INDONESIA

Contact Details: Bombay House, 24, Homi Mody St, Mumbai 400 001; tel. (22) 66658282; e-mail talktous@tatatrusts.org; internet www.tatatrusts.org.

Vivekananda International Foundation—VIF

Established in 2009; affiliated with the Hindu charitable organization Vivekananda Kendra.

Activities: Promotes the idea of a strong, secure and prosperous India through research and in-depth studies and is a platform for dialogue and conflict resolution. The Foundation comprises seven study centres: the Centre for National Security and Strategic Studies, which considers issues including terrorism, militancy and demographics; the Centre for International Relations and Diplomacy, which studies India's foreign policy; the Centre for Neighbourhood Studies, monitoring developments in Afghanistan, Bangladesh, the People's Republic of China, Myanmar, Nepal, Pakistan and Sri Lanka; the Centre for Economic Studies; the Centre for Historical and Civilisational Studies; the Centre for Governance and Political Studies, which encourages scholarships in constitutional and parliamentary studies; and the Centre for Technological and Scientific Studies. The Foundation organizes events including conferences, lectures, seminars and debates; in addition to exhibitions, cultural events, training workshops and yoga classes. It also maintains a library.

Geographical Area of Activity: East and South-East Asia, South Asia.

Publications: Annual Report; *Vivek* (digital magazine); VIF Briefs; VIF Papers; VIF Reports; VIF Viewpoint; monographs; books.

Finance: Annual income Rs 44.5m., expenditure Rs 44.5m. (31 March 2022).

Executive Committee: S. Gurumurthy (Chair.); Satish Chandra (Vice-Chair.).

Principal Staff: Sec. Anuttama Ganguly.

Contact Details: 3 San Martin Marg, Chanakyapuri, New Delhi 110 021; tel. (11) 24121764; e-mail info@vifindia.org; internet www.vifindia.org.

Vodafone Idea Foundation

Established in 1994 by Vodafone Idea, a telecommunications company; part of the Vodafone Foundation (q.v.) network.

Activities: Carries out activities in the areas of agriculture and livelihoods, education, financial literacy, healthcare, environment, poverty eradication and women's empowerment. Main programmes include: Smart Agri, improving sustainable farming practices through the use of technology; Jigyasa, training teachers in the use of digital tools, content and innovative teaching methods; Health Entrepreneurs–Diagnostic Tests, detecting anaemia in schoolchildren; Jaadu Ginni Ka, teaching people financial literacy; and Digital Village, establishing model villages and supporting rural women to use technology to set up food supply chains and improve their livelihoods. The Foundation offers grants and technology support to NGOs and civil society and community-based organizations through the Connecting for Good programme. It also established the online platforms Learning with Vodafone Idea, a multilingual website that curates information on scholarships; and Social App Hub, which curates mobile apps that have a social impact. Offers scholarships, and an award to mathematics and science teachers, to help overcome financial constraints.

Geographical Area of Activity: India.

CSR Committee: Neena Gupta (Chair.).

Principal Staff: Head of CSR and Foundation Dr Nilay Ranjan.

Contact Details: Suman Tower, Plot No. 18, Sector 11, Gandhinagar 382 011, Gujarat; tel. (79) 66714000; e-mail foundation.india@vodafoneidea.com; internet www.myvi.in/about-us/vodafoneidea-foundation.

INDONESIA

CO-ORDINATING BODY

International NGO Forum on Indonesian Development—INFID (Forum LSM Internasional untuk Pembangunan Indonesia)

Established in 1985 as the Inter-NGO Conference on IGGI Matters by CSOs in Indonesia and partners in the Netherlands.

Activities: Works to alleviate poverty in Indonesia through addressing the root causes thereof. Programmes focus on: promoting human rights and democracy; reducing inequality; and achieving the UN Sustainable Development Goals. The Forum INFID Conference takes place every three years. It has 88 members, and consultative status with ECOSOC.

Geographical Area of Activity: International.

Publications: Annual Report; newsletter; conference proceedings; factsheets; leaflets; working papers.

Committee: Khairani Arafin (Chair.); Muhammad Insur (Vice-Chair.); Listyowati (Treas.); Dina Mariana (Sec.).

Supervisory Board: Dwi Rubiyanti Kholifah (Chair.).

Principal Staff: Exec. Dir Siti Khoirun Ni'mah.

Contact Details: Jl. Sebret No.4 C, Jati Padang, Sunday St, South Jakarta 12540; tel. (21) 7819734; e-mail office@infid.org; internet www.infid.org.

FOUNDATIONS AND NON-PROFITS

ASEAN Foundation

Established in 1997 at the 30th Anniversary Summit of the Association of Southeast Asian Nations (ASEAN).

Activities: Works in the fields of education, arts and culture, media and community building, promoting awareness of ASEAN. The Foundation promotes community identity and solidarity, freedom of expression, participation in civic life and access to markets through capacity building and access to technology and skills, in particular for young people. The Foundation offers university scholarships and fellowships; and organizes academic exchanges, vocational training, apprenticeships and Foundation internships.

Geographical Area of Activity: ASEAN countries (Brunei Darussalam, Cambodia, Indonesia, Lao People's Dem. Repub., Malaysia, Myanmar, Philippines, Singapore, Thailand, Viet Nam).

Restrictions: Foundation internship applicants must be ASEAN national university students or recent graduates, and speak English fluently.

Publications: Annual Report; newsletter; *the ASEAN beat* (magazine); *Gazette*; curricula; factsheets; handbooks.

Board of Trustees: Sitsangkhom Sisaketh (Chair.); Sarah Al Bakri Devadason (Vice-Chair.).

Principal Staff: Exec. Dir Dr Piti Srisangnam.

Contact Details: Heritage Bldg, 1st Floor, Jl. Sisingamangaraja 70, Jakarta 12110; tel. (21) 31924828; e-mail secretariat@aseanfoundation.org; internet www.aseanfoundation.org.

ASEAN Institutes of Strategic and International Studies—ASEAN ISIS

Established in 1994 following a meeting in Bali convened by the Centre for Strategic and International Studies (CSIS Indonesia).

Activities: Aims to strengthen regional co-operation through joint studies and bilateral seminars between member institutions and with counterparts from outside the ASEAN region. The organization incorporates: the Brunei Darussalam Institute of Policy and Strategic Studies; Cambodian Institute for Cooperation & Peace; CSIS Indonesia; Institute of Foreign Affairs, Lao People's Democratic Republic; Institute of Strategic and International Studies (ISIS Malaysia); Myanmar Institute of Strategic and International Studies; Asia Pacific Pathways to Progress Foundation (Philippines); Singapore Institute of International Affairs; Institute of Strategic and International Studies (ISIS Thailand); and Diplomatic Academy of Vietnam. It takes part in the Annual Asia Pacific Roundtable on confidence building and conflict resolution, which is hosted in Malaysia; the annual Human Rights Colloquium in the Philippines; and the ASEAN People's Assembly, which involves CSOs, NGOs and people's organizations.

Geographical Area of Activity: International.

Publications: *Twenty-Two Years of ASEAN-ISIS: Origin, Evolution and Challenges of Track Two Diplomacy*.

Principal Staff: Chair. Prof Simon Tay.

Contact Details: ASEAN-ISIS Secretariat, Pakarti Centre Bldg, Jl. Tanah Abang 3 No. 23–27, Jakarta 10160; tel. (21) 386-5532; e-mail csis@csis.or.id.

Centre for Strategic and International Studies—CSIS

Established in 1971; a research and policy institution; comprises the CSIS Foundation.

Activities: Conducts policy-orientated research on economics, disaster management, international relations, and politics and social change. The Centre organizes public seminars, lectures and conferences; undertakes a programme of cultural events, including traditional, classical and modern music concerts, *wayang* (shadow puppet) performances, film screenings, and exhibitions of paintings and sculpture; and maintains a library of nearly 41,000 books and 400 scholarly journals, in English and Bahasa Indonesia. It was a founding member of the Council for Asia Europe Cooperation; a founding institution of the Council for Security Cooperation in Asia Pacific and the ASEAN Institutes of Strategic and International Studies; and is the secretariat for the ASEAN Economic Forum and the Indonesian National Committee of the Pacific Economic Cooperation Council.

Geographical Area of Activity: Asia-Pacific.

Publications: *CSIS Commentaries*; *Indonesian Quarterly*; *Analisis CSIS* (quarterly); *Bulletin of Indonesian Economic Studies*; *CSIS Commentaries*; blog.

Principal Staff: Exec. Dir Yose Rizal Damuri.

Contact Details: Pakarti Centre, 1st Floor, Jl. Tanah Abang 3, Nos 23–27, Jakarta 10160; tel. (21) 3865532; e-mail csis@csis.or.id; internet www.csis.or.id.

KEHATI—Yayasan Keanekaragaman Hayati Indonesia (Indonesia Biodiversity Foundation)

Founded in 1994.

Activities: Promotes biodiversity and the conservation of natural resources in local communities, through grants to projects in the fields of education and training, organizational development, environmental conservation, community development and research. Main programmes focus on agricultural, forest and marine ecosystems. The Foundation runs training courses and workshops, publishes information for the public and provides technical assistance to NGOs.

Geographical Area of Activity: Indonesia.

Publications: Annual Report; *Warta KEHATI* (newsletter); factsheets.

Finance: Annual revenue 107,939.9m. rupiah, expenditure 131,893.0m. rupiah (31 Dec. 2023).

Governing Board: Ismid Hadad (Chair.).

Supervisory Board: Amir Abadi Jusuf (Chair.).

Principal Staff: Exec. Dir Riki Frindos.

Contact Details: Jl. Benda Alam I No. 73, Cilandak Timur, Pasar Minggu, Jakarta Selatan; tel. (21) 78342866; e-mail kehati@kehati.or.id; internet kehati.or.id.

Tahir Foundation

Established by Prof. Dr Dato' Sri Tahir, Chair. and CEO of Mayapada Group; inspired by Christian values.

Activities: Main areas of activity are education, providing scholarships to universities in Indonesia and computers to disadvantaged students; healthcare, funding hospitals and health programmes; and research into legal reforms. The Foundation funds long-term projects that benefit disadvantaged and marginalized people. In 2014 it established the Indonesia Health Fund, in co-operation with the Bill & Melinda Gates Foundation (q.v.), to address issues such as HIV/AIDS, malaria, tuberculosis and polio, child mortality and family planning.

Geographical Area of Activity: Principally Indonesia.

Principal Staff: Chair. Prof. Dr Dato' Sri Tahir; Co-Chair. Jonathan Tahir.

Contact Details: Mayapada Tower, 3rd Floor, Jl. Jendral Sudirman Kav 28, Karet Setiabudi, Jakarta Selatan, Jakarta 12920; tel. (21) 5225503; e-mail info@tahirfoundation.or.id.

WALHI—Wahana Lingkungan Hidup Indonesia (Indonesian Forum for the Environment—Friends of the Earth Indonesia)

Established in 1980; part of the Friends of the Earth (q.v.) network.

Activities: Operates in the areas of conservation of natural resources, and civil and human rights, through advocacy, community empowerment, assisting community development and self-organization, and networking. The Forum comprises 487 member organizations and 203 individual members in 28 provinces.

Geographical Area of Activity: Indonesia.

Restrictions: Grants only to member organizations.

Publications: Annual Report; *Buletin Bumi* (newsletter); *Jurnal Walhi*; position papers; research reports; blog; books.

National Council: Raynaldo G. Sembiring (Chair.).

Principal Staff: Exec. Dir Zenzi Suhadi.

Contact Details: Jl. Tegal Parang Utara No. 14, Mampang Prapatan, Jakarta 12790; tel. (21) 79193363; e-mail informasi@walhi.or.id; internet www.walhi.or.id.

Yayasan Dian Desa—YDD (Light of the Village Foundation)

Founded in 1972 by Anton Soedjarwo.

Activities: Works to improve the welfare of rural communities in Indonesia. Programme areas include: clean water and sanitation; renewable energy; small-scale industry; waste treatment; and microfinance. The Foundation provides guidance, support and training to help people to help themselves. It has branch offices in Nusa Tenggara Timur and Bali.

Geographical Area of Activity: Indonesia.

Publications: *The Kotakatikotakita Urban Bulletin*; *ASAP* (magazine); *SODIS* (magazine).

Principal Staff: Exec. Dir Anton Soedjarwo.

Contact Details: Jl. Kaliurang Km 7, Gg Jurug Sari IV/19, POB 19, Yogyakarta; tel. (27) 4885247; e-mail secretariate.yogya@diandesa.org; internet diandesa.org.

Yayasan Geutanyoë (Our Foundation)

Established in 2015 by Aceh human rights activists.

Activities: Yayasan Geutanyoë seeks to empower and provide humanitarian assistance and protection of the rights of people in need, including disaster- and conflict-affected communities, refugees, migrants, and victims of trafficking; vulnerable and marginalized groups, including children, women, ethnic and religious minorities; and isolated communities. The vision of Yayasan Geutanyoë is to fight for sustainable communities in the ASEAN region founded on dignity, humanity, equality, ensuring peace and justice for all with democracy, human rights, and prosperity value at its core.
Geographical Area of Activity: Indonesia.
Publications: Reports; briefing notes; research.
Board: Hermanto (Chair.).
Principal Staff: Dir Al Fadhil.
Contact Details: Jalan T. Hasan Dek, Gang H. Hasan Ibrahim, Gampong Beurawe, Banda Aceh, Aceh 23124; tel. (811) 6899600; e-mail info@geutanyoe.id; internet www.geutanyoe.id.

Yayasan Insan Sembada (Self-Sufficient People Foundation)
Founded in 1974; formerly known as Yayasan Indonesia Sejahtera.
Activities: Works to reduce poverty through community-based programmes in the areas of: public health, sanitation and clean water; socioeconomic development; professional and technical training for community development; environmentally friendly farming; conflict management and peace building; and development of local civil society. The Foundation awards grants and small business development loans.
Geographical Area of Activity: Indonesia.
Publications: *Vibro* (newsletter in English); *Bergetar* (newsletter in Indonesian); brochures; factsheets; books.
Board of Trustees: Dr Joseph Gustama (Pres.).
Principal Staff: Chair. Dr H. Muki Reksoprojo; Treas. Lanny Hendrata; Sec. Fitrianti Roby.
Contact Details: Jl. Tanjung No. 96, Karangasem, Solo, Java 57145; tel. (271) 718506; e-mail yissolo@indo.net.id; internet yis.or.id.

Yayasan Pembinaan Masyarakat Desa—YADESA (Village Community Development Foundation)
Established in 1987.
Activities: Works to improve the quality of life of people in rural communities by helping to develop human resources and manage natural resources. Programmes include: research, training and education; environmental conservation; agricultural development; human rights; empowering marginalized people, including low-income groups and women; advocacy and consultation about family matters; technological development and home industry; rural co-operative development and private enterprises; and emergency humanitarian assistance.
Geographical Area of Activity: South-East Asia.
Restrictions: Does not make grants to individuals.
Publications: Publications on micro-credit and development issues.
Principal Staff: Man. Dir and Sec. Dr Martunis Yahya.
Contact Details: Jl. T. Nyak Arief 33A, Pasar Lamnyong, POB 137, Banda Aceh 2311; tel. (651) 7400911; e-mail yadesa_aceh@yahoo.co.id; internet yadesaaceh.org.

Yayasan Tifa (Tifa Foundation—Indonesia)
Established in 2000 by 13 civil society leaders; part of the Open Society Foundations (q.v.) network.
Activities: Works to address economic inequality and intolerance and injustice towards minority and marginalized groups through promoting inclusive economic growth and strengthening civil society. Main programme areas include: building an inclusive and tolerant civil society, with respect for human rights, freedom of expression and access to justice for all; achieving natural resource and environmental equity for marginalized communities and increasing the resilience and adaptation of vulnerable people to climate change; strengthening democracy through social movement innovation and increasing public participation; and fostering transparency and accountability on digital platforms. The Foundation makes grants to CSOs.
Geographical Area of Activity: Indonesia.
Publications: Annual Report; newsletter; books; reports; factsheets.
Finance: Total assets US $4.4m. (31 Dec. 2023).
Executive Board: Oslan Purba (Chair.); Dennis Tjandrasa (Treas.); Bernadetha Chelvi Yuliastuti (Sec.).
Contact Details: 18 Office Park, Lt. 15C-D, Jl. TB Simatupang No. 18, Jakarta 12520; tel. (21) 22701427; e-mail public@tifafoundation.org; internet www.tifafoundation.id.

IRAN

FOUNDATIONS AND NON-PROFITS

Institute for Iran-Eurasia Studies—IRAS

Established in 2004 by Dr Mehdi Sanaei, a diplomat; an independent think tank.
Activities: Promotes understanding of current affairs in Eurasia and the South Caucasus region. The Institute conducts research in the areas of: foreign policy; security and military policies; society and politics; economy and energy; regional organizations; history; and art and culture. It has a specialized library containing more than 3,000 books, scientific journals and databases.
Geographical Area of Activity: Afghanistan, Armenia, Azerbaijan, Belarus, People's Repub. of China, Georgia, Iran, Kazakhstan, Kyrgyzstan, Russian Federation, Tajikistan, Türkiye (Turkey), Turkmenistan, Ukraine, Uzbekistan.
Publications: Newsletter; policy notes; research papers.
Principal Staff: Dir Dr Mehdi Sanaei.
Contact Details: Unit 8, No. 2, Amini Alley, above Saei Park, Vali-e-Asr St, Tehran; tel. (21) 88770586; e-mail info@iras.ir; internet www.iras.ir.

Ravand Institute for Economic and International Studies

Established in 2005 by Dr Seyed Mohammad Hossein Adeli, an economist and diplomat.
Activities: Promotes deeper public understanding of international developments and macroeconomic and geopolitical trends. The Institute carries out research and issues policy reports on geopolitical, economic and environmental issues that affect politics and business in Iran and the wider region; and provides a forum for consultation, negotiation and co-operation for leaders from government, business and the third sector. It organizes the Ravand Conference; provides consulting and advisory services; and offers fellowships.
Geographical Area of Activity: International.
Publications: Newsletter; *Economic Trends* (periodical, English); *Ravand-e Eghtesadi* (periodical, Farsi); policy papers; research reports.

Saadi Foundation

Principal Staff: Dir Kia Tabatabaee.

Contact Details: Unit 18, 121 Boostan 10th Pasdaran Ave, Tehran 16669-17761; tel. (21) 22779270; e-mail info@ravandinstitute.com; internet ravandinstitute.com.

Saadi Foundation

Established in 2012.

Activities: Develops and supports Persian language and literature courses and resources abroad; supports foreign students to study in Iran; and awards scholarships and fellowships to foreign students, professors, and researchers in the fields of Persian language and literature. It has a Persian language and literature research centre in Tajikistan; and Persian language training Centres in Australia, Belarus, Nigeria and Serbia.

Geographical Area of Activity: Australia, Belarus, Iran, Nigeria, Serbia, Tajikistan.

Publications: Newsletter; textbooks.

Principal Staff: Dir Gholamali Haddad-Adel; Deputy Dir Hojatollah Ayoubi.

Contact Details: 17 East 15th St, Velenjak, Tehran; tel. (21) 22414393; e-mail info@saadifoundation.ir; internet saadifoundation.ir.

IRAQ

FOUNDATIONS AND NON-PROFITS

Al-Mortaqa Foundation for Human Development

Established in 2005 by a group of activists and academics; a founding member of the SILM (Peace) Network, funded by the United States Institute of Peace.

Activities: Promotes good governance and carries out development programmes to build capacity in civil society, in particular in the areas of leadership, awareness raising, monitoring and advocacy. The Foundation promotes human rights, justice and equality, in particular for women and disabled people; assists academic institutions by training staff and improving the learning environment; empowers people economically and socially; supports unemployed people to start or grow their own businesses, providing training and development and microfinance services; and improves the performance of the media through skills and leadership training. It has branches in most provinces; and has special consultative status with ECOSOC.

Geographical Area of Activity: Iraq.

Publications: Reports; brochures.

Contact Details: Al Mansour, Baghdad; tel. (772) 3682742; e-mail info@almortaqa.org; internet en.almortaqa.org.

Barzani Charity Foundation—BCF

Established in 2005 by Masrour Barzani, Prime Minister of the Kurdistan Regional Government; named after Kurdish leader Mustafa Barzani.

Activities: Works in the field of humanitarian relief, providing assistance to internally displaced people, refugees and host communities, and managing 14 camps. Programmes address: food; basic needs; WASH (water, sanitation and hygiene); education; livelihoods; cash assistance; protection; health; and shelter. The Foundation has consultative status with ECOSOC. It has branches in Duhok, Sulaymaniyah, Kirkuk, Nineveh, Sinjar and Garmiyan; and is registered in the USA.

Geographical Area of Activity: Australia, Bangladesh, Iraq, Saudi Arabia, Serbia, Syrian Arab Repub., Türkiye (Turkey), USA, Yemen.

Publications: Annual Report; newsletter; booklets; research reports.

Principal Staff: Pres. Musa Ahmed Agha; Vice-Pres. Ibrahim Samin.

Contact Details: Hawleri New Qtr, 120M Rd, next to Mass City Complex, Erbil; tel. (751) 5019400; e-mail info@bcf.krd; internet www.bcf.krd.

Democracy and Human Rights Development Centre

Established in 2005.

Activities: Promotes human rights and supports the development of civil society. The Centre advocates the independence of the courts and changes to the law in support of human rights; supports people whose rights the law does not protect; and compensates victims of miscarriages of justice. It co-operates with the Government and international organizations and takes part in regional forums; translates publications on torture and legal procedure; organizes lectures on human rights and advocacy training; and takes part in election monitoring.

Geographical Area of Activity: Iraq.

Publications: Reports; research papers; legal studies; books.

Principal Staff: Man. Sarwar Ali Jaffar Sarwar; Deputy Man. Omeed Amin Karim.

Contact Details: Bakhan 108/5/5, Sulaymaniyah, Iraqi Kurdistan; tel. (53) 3292431; e-mail info@dhrd.info; internet www.dhrd.info.

The General Kashif Al-Getaa Foundation

Established in 1993 by Dr Sheikh Abbas Kashif Al-Ghetaa.

Activities: Co-operates with Iraqi universities, libraries and religious institutions to preserve Iraq's cultural heritage, digitizing historical scientific and religious Arabic manuscripts to make them available to academic researchers. The Foundation organizes conferences, seminars and religious ceremonies and takes part in the International Book Fair in Tehran, Iran; and carries out charitable work, in particular supporting orphans. It has a public library containing 5,000 vols on religion, literature, language and history, 600 manuscripts and a digital library of 450 CDs.

Geographical Area of Activity: Iraq.

Publications: Books; educational religious leaflets; posters.

Principal Staff: Sec.-Gen. Dr Sheikh Abbas Kashif Al-Ghetaa; Dir Dhafer Satar.

Contact Details: Al-Tosi St, Najaf; tel. (780) 1006730; e-mail info@kashifalgetaa.com; internet www.kashifalgetaa.com.

Iraqi Institute for Economic Reform

Established in 2004.

Activities: Promotes and supports the country's transition to a market-based economy. The Institute carries out research, case studies and surveys; provides economic data and analysis; organizes training workshops, seminars and roundtable discussions; and publishes and disseminates information. It also periodically organizes a research competition.

Geographical Area of Activity: Iraq.

Publications: Newsletter; policy papers.

Principal Staff: Exec. Dir Dr Intisar Jawad Al Ramahi.

Contact Details: Jadriaya 913/31/54, Baghdad; tel. (1) 7788842; e-mail info@iier.org; internet www.iier.org.

Ruya Foundation for Contemporary Culture in Iraq

Established in 2012 by Tamara Chalabi, a historian and writer, to aid and enrich culture in Iraq and establish cultural ties internationally.

IRELAND

CO-ORDINATING BODIES

Charities Institute Ireland—Cii
Established in 2016 by the merger of Fundraising Ireland and Irish Charities Tax Research.

Activities: Supports charities through providing educational programmes and resources. The Institute conducts research and advocacy, advising members on best practice; and offering professional development and networking opportunities. It organizes the annual Charity Excellence Awards. Comprises 280 member organizations.

Geographical Area of Activity: Ireland.

Publications: Annual Report; newsletter; briefing notes; guidance notes; blog.

Finance: Annual income €872,330, expenditure €852,208 (31 Dec. 2023).

Board of Trustees: Susan O'Dwyer (Chair.).

Principal Staff: CEO Áine Myler.

Contact Details: 15–17 Leinster St S, Dublin, D02 CY95; tel. (1) 5414770; e-mail info@charitiesinstituteireland.ie; internet www.charitiesinstituteireland.ie.

Dóchas—Irish Association of Non-Governmental Development Organisations (Hope)
Established in 1993 as a co-ordinating body for the development of NGOs in Ireland, following the merger between CONGOOD (f. 1974) and the Irish National Assembly.

Activities: Works to achieve solidarity, respect for human rights and global justice. The organization promotes co-operation between development organizations in Ireland to increase the efficiency and effectiveness of programmes carried out in less-developed countries. It convenes working groups to share knowledge and influence decisionmakers; promotes development education; and provides a forum for member agencies to meet together. It has 46 full and 11 associate member organizations; and is a member of CONCORD (q.v.).

Geographical Area of Activity: Ireland.

Restrictions: Not a funding agency.

Publications: Annual Report; *DOCHAS Wednesday News* (weekly e-bulletin); Worldview Toolkit (online resources).

Finance: Annual income €619,846, expenditure €737,158 (31 Dec. 2021).

Board: Rosamond Bennett (Chair.); John Moffett (Vice-Chair.); Siobhán Cassidy (Treas. and Sec.).

Principal Staff: CEO Jane-Ann McKenna.

Contact Details: Suite 8, Olympic House, Pleasants St, Dublin 8; tel. (1) 4053801; e-mail anna@dochas.ie; internet www.dochas.ie.

Philanthropy Ireland
Established in 1998 as the Funders' Forum; present name adopted in 2004.

Activities: Aims to increase the level of philanthropy in Ireland and to expand the donor community. The organization supports research on giving and advocates for tax and policies that encourage philanthropy. It has more than 30 members; and is a member of Philea (q.v.).

Geographical Area of Activity: Ireland.

Publications: Annual Report; newsletter; *Philanthropy Scope* (journal, 2 a year); blog.

Finance: Annual income €246,216, expenditure €202,627 (31 Dec. 2022).

Board of Directors: Lorna Jennings (Chair.).

Principal Staff: Chief Exec. Éilis Murray.

Contact Details: 29 Mount St Upper, Dublin 2; tel. (1) 6768751; e-mail info@philanthropy.ie; internet www.philanthropy.ie.

The Wheel (Rotha)
Established in 1999 by Dr Mary Redmond, a lawyer and social entrepreneur.

Activities: The Wheel is Ireland's national association of community and voluntary organisations, charities and social enterprises. It represents, supports and connects individuals and organizations in the charity and non-profit sector. Main programmes focus on: public policy and advocacy; networking; skills training and leadership development; and information and advice. It maintains the Fundingpoint database of funding grants. The Wheel has more over 2,400 members.

Geographical Area of Activity: Ireland.

Publications: Annual Report; Director's Report; newsletter; briefings; factsheets; research reports; Sustainable Communities Toolkit (online).

Finance: Annual income €3m., expenditure €3m. (31 Dec. 2023).

Board: Vincent Keenan (Chair.).

Principal Staff: CEO Ivan Cooper.

Contact Details: 48 Fleet St (entrance Parliament Row), Dublin 2, D02 T883; tel. (1) 4548727; e-mail info@wheel.ie; internet www.wheel.ie.

FOUNDATIONS AND NON-PROFITS

Barretstown
Established in 1994 by the late actor and philantropist, Paul Newman.

Activities: Barretstown was established to help rebuild the lives of children and their families affected by cancer and other serious illnesses, through therapeutic Residential and Outreach programmes in a safe, fun and supportive environment. It offers free therapeutic programmes at a specially designed campus in County Kildare and through outreach programmes in hospitals and schools throughout Ireland, for children and their families living with a serious illness.

Geographical Area of Activity: Ireland.

Publications: Annual Report; newsletter (monthly).

Finance: Annual income €7.2m., expenditure €5.3m. (31 Dec. 2022).
Board of Directors: Anne Heraty (Chair.).
Principal Staff: CEO Dee Ahearn.
Contact Details: Barretstown Castle, Ballymore Eustace, Co Kildare W91 RDX6; tel. (45) 863100; e-mail info@barretstown.org; internet www.barretstown.org.

Bóthar

Established in 1991 by a group of farmers, business people and community and church leaders.
Activities: Helps people to overcome hunger and poverty and restore the environment through sustainable livestock production. The organization establishes livestock development projects, providing livestock and training; and supports the establishment of micro-farming enterprises. It has four additional offices in Ireland and Northern Ireland.
Geographical Area of Activity: Central America and the Caribbean, South Asia, South-East Asia, South-Eastern Europe, sub-Saharan Africa.
Publications: Annual Report; *The Bó Vine* (quarterly newsletter).
Finance: Annual income €527,998, expenditure €628,852 (30 June 2024).
Board: Shane McAuliffe (Chair.); Kenneth Arthur (Vice-Chair.); Patrick Manley (Sec.).
Principal Staff: Interim CEO Ailish O'Reilly.
Contact Details: c/o Regus Castletroy, Ducart Suite, Castletroy Park Commercial Centre, Limerick V94 AH28; tel. (61) 414142; e-mail info@bothar.ie; internet www.bothar.ie.

Concern Worldwide

Established in 1968; part of the Disasters Emergency Committee (q.v.).
Activities: Works to eliminate poverty, fear and oppression through advocacy, humanitarian response and development initiatives. Main programmes include: livelihoods; health and nutrition; education; emergencies; gender equality; and innovation. The organization funds development education on issues such as developing countries' debt, human rights, fair trade and refugees. It works in 26 countries and has offices in Belfast, Glasgow and London, with an affiliate in the USA.
Geographical Area of Activity: Caribbean, East Asia, Middle East, South Asia, sub-Saharan Africa.
Publications: Annual Report; newsletter.
Finance: Annual income €233.4m., expenditure €242.3m. (31 Dec. 2023).
Board of Directors: Donal D'Arcy (Chair.).
Principal Staff: CEO Dominic Crowley.
Contact Details: 52–55 Lower Camden St, Dublin 2, D02 H425; tel. (1) 4177700; e-mail info@concern.net; internet www.concern.net.

European Foundation for the Improvement of Living and Working Conditions—Eurofound

Founded in 1975 by the Council of Ministers of the European Community (now the EU) to contribute to the formulation of policies that would improve living and working conditions in member states.
Activities: Supports the policymaking activities of EU institutions, governments, employers, trade unions and CSOs through providing information, advice and expertise. Main topic areas are: working conditions and sustainable work; industrial relations and social dialogue; employment and labour markets; living conditions and quality of life; anticipating and managing the impact of change; and promoting social cohesion and convergence. The Foundation comprises three observatories: the European Observatory of Working Life (EurWORK); the European Monitoring Centre on Change (EMCC); and the European Observatory on Quality of Life (EurLIFE). Has an office in Brussels, Belgium.
Geographical Area of Activity: Europe (member states of the EU and candidate countries).
Restrictions: Not a grantmaking organization.
Publications: Annual Report; *Eurofound News* (newsletter); *Eurofound Yearbook*; databases; surveys; research reports; factsheets; information brochures and booklets.
Finance: Budget €23.8m. (2023).
Executive Board: Stefania Rossi (Chair.); Jan Kouwenberg, Jerzy Ciechański, Barbara Kauffmann (Vice-Chair.).
Principal Staff: Dir Ivailo Kalfin; Deputy Dir Maria Jepsen.
Contact Details: Wyattville Rd, Loughlinstown, Dublin D18 KP65; tel. (1) 2043100; e-mail information@eurofound.europa.eu; internet www.eurofound.europa.eu.

Front Line Defenders—FLD (International Foundation for the Protection of Human Rights Defenders)

Established in 2001, co-founded by Mary Lawlor, former director of the Irish section of Amnesty International (q.v.) and Denis O'Brien, Chair. of Digicel, a telecommunications company, who also established the Digicel Foundation (qq.v.) network.
Activities: Supports human rights defenders at risk and addresses protection needs they themselves have identified. The organization carries out advocacy on behalf of human rights defenders and provides emergency support, operating a multilingual 24-hour emergency phone line; offers grants, worth up to €7,500, for practical security needs; organizes risk analysis and protection training; issues materials on security, including digital security, and protection; and arranges rest and respite opportunities, lasting from one week to three months. It hosts the biennial Dublin Platform networking event; and offers the annual Front Line Defenders Award for Human Rights Defenders at Risk. Has an office in Brussels, Belgium, and leads ProtectDefenders.eu, the EU Human Rights Defenders mechanism, which comprises a consortium of 12 international and regional human rights organizations.
Geographical Area of Activity: International.
Restrictions: Rest and respite opportunities are by invitation only.
Publications: Annual Report; *Dispatches* (annual review); handbooks; training manuals; workbooks; blog.
Finance: Annual income €10.9m., expenditure €10.9m. (31 Dec. 2023).
Board of Directors: Kieran Mulvey (Chair.).
Principal Staff: Exec. Dir Alan Glasgow; Deputy Dir Olive Moore.
Contact Details: Avoca Ct, First Floor, Temple Rd, Blackrock, Co. Dublin A94 R7W3; tel. (1) 2123750; e-mail info@frontlinedefenders.org; internet www.frontlinedefenders.org.

GOAL

Founded in 1977 by John O'Shea, a sports journalist, following a visit to India.
Activities: Works in the fields of humanitarian relief and international development through strengthening systems, strategic partnerships and building resilience. Main programme areas are: emergency response; resilient health; food and nutrition security; sustainable livelihoods; and fostering global citizenship. The organization has offices in 14 countries, including London and Washington, DC.
Geographical Area of Activity: Central America and the Caribbean, Ireland, Middle East, sub-Saharan Africa.
Publications: Annual Report; newsletter; position papers.
Finance: Annual income €205.6m., expenditure €197.5m. (31 Dec. 2023).
Board: Barry O'Connell (Chair.).
Principal Staff: CEO Siobhan Walsh.

IRELAND

Contact Details: Carnegie House, Dun Laoghaire, Dublin A96 C7W7; tel. (1) 2809779; e-mail info@goal.ie; internet www.goalglobal.org.

Irish Youth Foundation

Established in 1985 as an independent development trust.

Activities: Works to meet the needs of vulnerable children and young people; and to address and reverse the social and personal impact of poverty, educational disadvantage, homelessness and social exclusion. The Foundation supports projects tackling problems of poverty, unemployment, drugs, alcohol abuse, crime, violence and vandalism; AIDS prevention programmes; and facilities and amenities for education and recreation. It seeks to identify, strengthen and expand existing programmes for Irish children and young people. The Foundation has Boards of Trustees in the United Kingdom and the USA, where it raises funds. It works in partnership with the International Youth Foundation (q.v.).

Geographical Area of Activity: Ireland, UK.

Restrictions: Grants only to registered voluntary or community groups that work with vulnerable and marginalized children and young people.

Publications: Annual Report; various papers and studies on youth and children's sector issues.

Finance: Annual income €1.1m., expenditure €1.3m. (31 Dec. 2022).

Board: Michael McLoughlin (Chair.).

Principal Staff: Chief Exec. Sarah Edmonds.

Contact Details: 16 Fitzwilliam Pl., Dublin 2; tel. (1) 6766535; e-mail info@iyf.ie; internet www.iyf.ie.

Katharine Howard Foundation—KHF

Founded in 1979 by Katharine Howard, a descendant of the Earls of Wicklow.

Activities: Katharine Howard Foundation (KHF) is an independent Foundation focused on improving the lives of young children and their families. The Foundation does this through working with others to identify needs, building on existing initiatives, formulating new initiatives, making strategic grants, gathering and sharing learning, contributing to the development of policy and practice and protecting the Foundation's endowment fund. Main programmes are the 'Children's Promise' Grants Programme and Strategic Grants. The Foundation supports several organizations and foundations that have a particular focus on early years. It works with others in identifying needs, building on existing programmes, making grants and sharing learning.

Geographical Area of Activity: Ireland.

Restrictions: Island of Ireland only.

Publications: Annual Report; research and evaluation reports.

Finance: Annual income €79,178, expenditure €591,364 (31 Dec. 2023).

Trustees: Willie Holmes (Chair.).

Principal Staff: CEO Dr Cliona Hannon.

Contact Details: 7 Red Cow Lane, Smithfield, Dublin D07 XN29; tel. (1) 6618963; e-mail info@khf.ie; internet www.khf.ie.

Oxfam Ireland

Founded in 1997; part of the Oxfam confederation of organizations (qq.v.).

Activities: Oxfam Ireland, as part of the global Oxfam movement, works to combat the inequalities that keep people poor, including unfair tax rules, the unequal distribution of wealth, discrimination against women and girls, and the worst impacts of the climate crisis. Ensures that the voices of people hardest hit by poverty and injustice are heard. Oxfam Ireland has four priority goals: a just economy, gender justice, climate justice and accountable governance.

Geographical Area of Activity: Democratic Republic of Congo, Malawi, Occupied Palestinian Territories, Israel, Somalia, Somaliland, South Sudan, Uganda, Zimbabwe and Zambia.

Restrictions: Does not make loans or grants to individuals.

Publications: Annual Report; newsletter.

Finance: Annual income €19.7m., expenditures €20.5m. (31 March 2024).

Board of Directors: Prof. Mary Murphy (Chair.).

Principal Staff: CEO Jim Clarken.

Contact Details: Portview House, Thorncastle St, Ringsend, Dublin 4 D04V9Y9; tel. (1) 6727662; e-mail irl-info@oxfam.org; internet www.oxfamireland.org.

Plan International Ireland

Founded in 1937 during the Spanish Civil War; established in Ireland in 2003, part of the Plan International (q.v.) network. Present name adopted in 2015.

Activities: Supports marginalized children and young people. Main programme areas are: children's rights and legal protection from abuse, neglect, exploitation and violence; improving access to and the quality of education; global emergency response and disaster risk management; household economic security, establishing village savings and loans associations to provide micro-credit; and development education in Ireland. The organization is active in more than 75 countries.

Geographical Area of Activity: Asia, Europe, North and South America, sub-Saharan Africa.

Publications: Annual Report; newsletter.

Finance: Annual income €19.3m., expenditure €18.2m. (30 June 2024).

Board of Trustees: Aoife Kelly-Desmond (Chair.); David O'Leary (Vice-Chair.); John Perry (Sec.).

Principal Staff: CEO Paul O'Brien.

Contact Details: 11 Harrington St, Dublin 8, D08 EK7D; tel. (1) 5685861; e-mail info@plan.ie; internet plan.ie.

RIA—Royal Irish Academy

Founded in 1785 to promote study in the sciences, humanities and social sciences.

Activities: Identifies and recognizes the achievements of researchers in Ireland; provides policy advice; and fosters international academic links, including membership of the International Council of Scientific Unions. The Academy manages a number of national research projects, gives grants, publishes books and journals, and maintains a library.

Geographical Area of Activity: Ireland.

Publications: Annual Review; *The Proceedings of the RIA* (three sections: mathematical proceedings of the RIA; biology and environment; archaeology, culture, history, and literature); *Ériu* (Irish philology and literature); *Irish Journal of Earth Sciences*; *Irish Studies in International Affairs*; conference proceedings; a range of books on Irish archaeology, history, folklore, science, Irish biographies, science and the arts.

Finance: Annual income €7.0m., expenditure €6.7m. (31 Dec. 2021).

Council: Mary Canning (Pres.); Patrick Honohan (Treas.); Mary O'Dowd (Sec.).

Principal Staff: Exec. Dir Dr Siobhan O'Sullivan.

Contact Details: 19 Dawson St, Dublin 2, D02 HH58; tel. (1) 6090600; e-mail info@ria.ie; internet www.ria.ie.

Self Help Africa—SHA

Established in 1965 by the Department of Agriculture. Formerly known as Gorta—Freedom from Hunger Council of Ireland; present name adopted following merger in 2014 with Self Help Africa. A member of the Gorta Group (f. 2018), which includes Partner Africa, TruTrade and Traidlinks.

Trócaire

Activities: Works with local NGOs to support development projects in sub-Saharan Africa. Main programmes include: agriculture and nutrition; gender; climate change; enterprise development; microfinance; and co-operatives. The organization works to eliminate hunger through long-term projects encouraging self-sufficiency, emphasizing the importance of local resources and offering training to local people to manage their own projects. It raises funds through public events and by running charity shops throughout Ireland; and hosts the annual World Food Day Conference. Has offices in the United Kingdom and the USA; with regional offices in Burkina Faso, Ethiopia, Kenya, Malawi, Uganda and Zambia.

Geographical Area of Activity: Benin, Burkina Faso, Ghana, Ethiopia, Kenya, Malawi, Togo, Uganda, Zambia.

Publications: Annual Report; newsletter.

Finance: Annual income €46.5m., expenditure €47.6m. (31 Dec. 2023).

Board of Directors: Geoff Meagher (Chair.).

Principal Staff: CEO Feargal O' Connell; Interim Co-Dirs Dee McMahon, Aoife Gleeson.

Contact Details: Joyce's Ct, 4th Floor, 38 Talbot St, Dublin 1, D01 C861; tel. (1) 6778880; e-mail info@selfhelpafrica.org; internet selfhelpafrica.org/ie.

Trócaire—Catholic Agency for World Development (Mercy)

Established in 1973 by the Catholic Bishops of Ireland.

Activities: Provides long-term support to people in extreme poverty in the Global South, enabling them to work their way out of poverty; assists people most in need in emergencies and enables communities to prepare for future emergencies; and tackles the structural causes of poverty. The Agency funds and provides expert technical support to programmes in the areas of: access to justice; empowering women; climate and environmental justice and access to resources; emergency humanitarian assistance; social justice; and localisation. It operates in more than 16 countries, with offices in Maynooth, Cork and Galway in the Republic of Ireland and Belfast in Northern Ireland (UK).

Geographical Area of Activity: Africa, Latin America, Asia, Middle East and Europe.

Restrictions: No grants to individuals.

Publications: Annual Report; newsletter.

Finance: Annual income €97.2m., expenditure €96.6m. (28 Feb. 2024).

Board of Trustees: Bishop William Crean (Chair.); Matt Walsh (Deputy Chair.).

Principal Staff: CEO Caoimhe de Barra.

Contact Details: South Campus, Maynooth, Co Kildare W23 NX63; tel. (1) 6293333; e-mail info@trocaire.org; internet www.trocaire.org.

Vita

Founded in 1989, as Refugee Trust International, by Fr Kevin Doheny and Fr Norman Fitzgerald; present name adopted in 2005.

Activities: Works to eliminate extreme poverty and reduce the vulnerability of poor people in Africa by building sustainable livelihoods. The organization improves the living conditions of poor and marginalized people in Ethiopia and Eritrea through supporting income-generating activities and improving family nutrition and access to affordable food. Goals include: facilitate thriving rural climate-smart economies with access to services, markets and livlihoods for all.

Geographical Area of Activity: Eritrea, Ethiopia.

Publications: Annual Report; Impact Report; newsletter.

Finance: Annual income €5.2m., expenditure €4.9m. (31 Dec. 2021).

Board of Directors: Ronan McCabe (Acting Chair.).

Principal Staff: CEO John Weakliam.

Contact Details: Equity House, 16–17 Upper Ormond Quay, Dublin 7; tel. (1) 8734303; e-mail info@vita.ie; internet www.vitaimpact.org.

Vodafone Ireland Foundation

Established in 2003 by Vodafone Ireland, a telecommunications company; part of the Vodafone Foundation (q.v.) network.

Activities: Supports Vodafone employee volunteering and matched funding; and projects that use technology to help children, young people and their families. The Foundation supports ISPCC Childline, a 24-hour charity listening service for children and young people in Ireland. It also provides emergency and post-disaster recovery assistance to aid agencies and affected people, working with UNHCR to provide digital educational content and internet access for refugee children in Africa through Instant Network schools and the Instant Classroom 'school in a box' programme.

Geographical Area of Activity: Dem. Repub. of the Congo, Ireland, Kenya, South Sudan.

Finance: Annual income €2.0m., expenditure €1.1m. (31 March 2022).

Trustees: Liam Brien (Chair.).

Contact Details: Mountainview, Leopardstown, Dublin 18; tel. (1) 2037000; e-mail vif.ie@vodafone.com; internet n.vodafone.ie/aboutus/foundation.html.

Women's Aid

Founded in 1974.

Activities: Women's Aid is a national organization working to prevent and address the impact of domestic violence and abuse. Advocates, influences, trains, and campaigns for effective responses to reduce the scale and impact of domestic abuse on women and children, and provides high-quality, specialized, integrated support services.

Geographical Area of Activity: Ireland.

Publications: Annual Report; Impact Report; Femicide Report; newsletter; briefings.

Finance: Annual income €4.6m., expenditure €3.5m. (31 Dec. 2022).

Board of Directors: Ailbhe Smyth (Chair.); Golda Hession (Sec.).

Principal Staff: CEO Sarah Benson.

Contact Details: 5 Wilton Pl., Dublin 2, D02 RR27; tel. (1) 6788858; e-mail info@womensaid.ie; internet www.womensaid.ie.

ISRAEL

FOUNDATIONS AND NON-PROFITS

Arthur Rubinstein International Music Society

Founded in 1980 by Yaakov (Yasha) Bistritzky in tribute to Arthur Rubinstein, a concert pianist.

Activities: Organizes and finances the Arthur Rubinstein International Piano Master Competition. The Society offers masterclasses and organizes a worldwide concert series, film shows and memorial festivals. It also organizes the Rubinstein Competition for pianists, awards prizes and makes grants.

Geographical Area of Activity: International.

ISRAEL

Publications: Newsletter.
Board of Directors: Arie Rapoport (Chair.).
Principal Staff: Chair. Nir Zuk.
Contact Details: 9 Bilu St, Tel Aviv 6522214; tel. (3) 6856684; e-mail competition@arims.org.il; internet www.arims.org.il.

Baha'i International Development Organization—BIDO

Established in 1983, by the Universal House of Justice, as the Office of Social and Economic Development, to co-ordinate the Baha'i community's social and economic development efforts; re-established in 2018.

Activities: Promotes and co-ordinates the activities of the Baha'i community in the fields of social and economic development. Programmes include: agriculture, local economies and village development; education and literacy; elimination of racial prejudice; the environment; health; support for refugees; women's advancement; and youth empowerment.
Geographical Area of Activity: International.
Board: Elisa Caney, Maame Brodwemaba Nketsiah, Lori McLaughlin Noguchi, Sina Rahmanian, George Soraya.
Contact Details: c/o Bahá'í World Centre, POB 155, Haifa, Israel 3100101; tel. (4) 8358339; e-mail serve@bwc.org; internet service.bwc.org.

Clore Israel Foundation

Established in 1965, as Keren Clore, by Sir Charles Clore; merged with the Charles Clore 1979 Israel Foundation in 1998.

Activities: Awards grants, scholarships fellowships and prizes. Main grantmaking programme areas are: the Arab Community, promoting coexistence between Jews and Arabs and supporting equal opportunities for Israeli Arabs; arts, culture and sports; diverse populations, particularly people from the Commonwealth of Independent States and Ethiopia, Bedouins and Druze; health and welfare, including young people at risk and older people; and science and education, supporting educational programmes and scholarships. Under the Clore Scholars Programme, the Foundation offers scholarships, worth 100,000 shekels a year for three years, to young doctoral students and researchers pursuing a career in the natural sciences, including agriculture, chemistry, computer science, earth sciences, engineering and technology, life sciences, mathematics and physics.
Geographical Area of Activity: Israel.
Restrictions: Does not accept unsolicited applications; grants only to non-profit organizations registered in Israel.
Board of Trustees: Dame Vivien Duffield (Chair.).
Principal Staff: Exec. Dir Rachel Lasry Zahavi.
Contact Details: 1 George Washington St, Jerusalem; tel. (2) 6250128; e-mail info@clorefoundation.org.il; internet clorefoundation.org.il.

Foundation for the Welfare of Holocaust Victims

Established in 1994 by Holocaust survivors, assisted by the Center for Organizations of Holocaust Survivors and the Conference on Jewish Material Claims Against Germany (Claims Conference).

Activities: Supports Holocaust survivors who are experiencing physical and health-related problems, emotional distress and loneliness and who lack social and financial support. The Foundation makes homes accessible and suitable for people with disabilities; funds short- and long-term nursing care; offers free eye examinations and glasses and subsidized dental treatment; arranges social service care and psychosocial support; and operates a telephone helpline for survivors, their families and carers. It matches survivors with visitors through the Lonely, But Not Alone Volunteer Program; and the Connected Program, which provides them with a computer and internet access, while volunteers teach them basic computer skills.
Geographical Area of Activity: Israel, USA.

Principal Staff: Chair. Limor Livnat; CEO Tamar Cohen Shamai.
Contact Details: The Craft 3, Tel Aviv; tel. (3) 6090866; e-mail info@k-shoa.org; internet www.k-shoa.org.

Fulbright Israel

Founded in 1956 as the United States–Israel Educational Foundation (USIEF) by the Governments of Israel and the USA.

Activities: Enables outstanding Israeli and US scholars and students to pursue research, lectures and study at leading institutes of higher learning in the USA and Israel. Main programmes include: the Fulbright Grant Program; the Fulbright Seminar for Advanced Studies; the USIEF Lecturer Program; and Alumni Activities. The Foundation offers a range of graduate and postgraduate fellowships, teaching awards and scholarships. Postdoctoral awards are worth from US $45,000 a year for two years for US students studying in Israel, and for Israeli students studying in the USA at accredited Universities.
Geographical Area of Activity: Israel, USA.
Restrictions: No grants to institutions or organizations.
Publications: *Alumni Newsletter*; *Fulbright Magazine*.
Finance: Annual budget approx. US $1.6m.
Board of Directors: Sender Cohen (Chair.).
Principal Staff: Exec. Dir Dr Anat Lapidot-Firilla.
Contact Details: Rothschild Blvd 74–76 (Moses House, First Floor), Tel Aviv-Yafo 6578517; tel. (3) 5213800; e-mail ILPrograms@fulbright.org.il; internet www.fulbright.org.il.

Henrietta Szold Institute—National Institute for Research in the Behavioural Sciences

Founded in 1941 by Henrietta Szold, founder of Hadassah, the Women's Zionist Organization of America.

Activities: Conducts research and experiments in the fields of education, psychometrics, sociology and psychology. The Institute conducts research and evaluation in the areas of education, wellbeing and identity formation; and organizes workshops and professional training courses. It has a digital information and knowledge centre for education and social sciences, which gathers research from Israel and maintains a database of more than 100,000 items and tools; and operates the National School for Information skills, which helps high school and college students with research papers and projects.
Geographical Area of Activity: Israel.
Publications: *Megamot* ('Trends', quarterly journal); newsletter; bibiliographies; monographs; research tools.
Exec. Committee: Shlomit Amichai (Chair.).
Principal Staff: CEO Dr Edith Mani-Aiken.
Contact Details: Columbia St, Kiryat Menachem 9, Jerusalem 9658326; tel. (2) 6494444; e-mail szold@szold.org.il; internet www.szold.org.il.

IsraAID

Established in 2001 by a coalition of Israeli disaster relief and international development organizations.

Activities: Supports people affected by humanitarian crises through working with local organizations. Main programmes are: emergency response; recovery and preparedness; and refugees and forced migration. The organization provides access to education; health and medical care; protection and safeguarding; and clean water, sanitation and hygiene. It has country offices in the Australia, Canada, Colombia, Dominica, Guatemala, Kenya, Malawi, South Sudan, Uganda and Vanuatu.
Geographical Area of Activity: International.
Publications: Annual Report; newsletter; brochure; blog.
Board of Trustees: Meira Aboulafia (Chair.).
Principal Staff: CEO Yotam Polizer.

Contact Details: Shaul Hamelech 8, Tel Aviv 6473307; e-mail info@israaid.org; internet www.israaid.org.

The Israel Democracy Institute—IDI

Established in 1991 by Dr Arye Carmon, a political reform expert; a think tank.

Activities: Works to strengthen democracy through carrying out applied research to educate decisionmakers and shape policy, legislation and public opinion. Programme areas include: Arab society; coronavirus; cyber; economy and governance; elections and parties; equality; governance; Judaism and democracy; the judiciary; legislation; media regulation; religion and state; rule of law; security and democracy; and the Ultra-Orthodox. The Institute comprises the Center for Democratic Values and Institutions; the Center for Governance and the Economy; the Center for Security and Democracy; the Center for Religion, Nation and State; and the Viterbi Family Center for Public Opinion and Policy Research (formerly known as the Guttman Center).

Geographical Area of Activity: Israel.

Publications: Annual Report; newsletter; books; datasets; surveys and polls.

Board of Directors: Bernard Marcus (Int. Chair.); Amir Elshtein (Chair. of the Board).

Principal Staff: Pres. Yohanan Plesner.

Contact Details: 4 Pinsker St, POB 4702 Jerusalem 9104602; tel. (2) 530-0888; e-mail info@idi.org.il; internet www.idi.org.il.

Jerusalem Foundation

Founded in 1966 by Teddy Kollek, a former mayor of Jerusalem, and Ruth Cheshin.

Activities: Aims to strengthen and enrich Jerusalem's cultural life and communities. Capital projects include: community centres; sports facilities and parks; libraries; theatres; museums; schools; neighbourhood and community facilities; and educational centres. The Foundation also funds social and educational activities for the benefit of all the city's residents; and maintains the Teddy Kollek Digital Archive. It has branches in Austria, Canada, Germany, Italy, Spain, Switzerland, the United Kingdom and the USA.

Geographical Area of Activity: International.

Publications: Annual Report; newsletter; brochures.

Finance: Annual income US $66.9m., expenditure $43.9m. (2024).

Board of Directors: Zvi Agmon (Chair.); Ruth Cheshin (Pres. Emerita).

Principal Staff: Pres. Arik Grebelsky; Gen. Dir Imry Ben-Ami.

Contact Details: 11 Rivka St, POB 53501, Jerusalem 9346117; tel. (2) 6751711; e-mail info@jfjlm.org; internet jerusalemfoundation.org.

Joseph S. and Caroline Gruss Memorial Fund for the Advancement of Veterans

Established in 1988 by Joseph S. Gruss, a US financier and business person.

Activities: Provides scholarships to former Israel Defense Forces personnel and members of minority communities, as well as providing assistance to projects that further their personal development in the fields of education and employment. The TELEM programme is aimed specifically at Ethiopian former service personnel. The Fund runs Centers for Young Adults in 32 cities, which offer education, employment and cultural services. Since its inception, the Fund has disbursed approximately 468m. shekels in scholarships.

Geographical Area of Activity: Israel.

Board of Trustees: Prof. Alex Stein (Chair.).

Principal Staff: Exec. Dir Naomi Fink-Gertner.

Contact Details: Boardwalk House, 2 Beitar St, Jerusalem 9338601; tel. (2) 5617176; e-mail gruss@gruss.org.il; internet www.gruss.org.il.

KIEDF—Koret Israel Economic Development Funds

Established in 1994.

Activities: Promotes philanthropy in the private sector and supports economic development and job creation through loans to small businesses. The organization operates revolving loan funds through commercial banks, providing bank guarantees and subsidizing interest rates to small business borrowers; offering microenterprise lending to home-based businesses; and operating a loan facility for not-for-profit organizations. Since its inception, it has provided more than 31,000 loans, amounting to 1,900m. shekels.

Geographical Area of Activity: Israel.

Publications: Annual Report.

Board of Directors: Adir Waldman (Chair.); Tal Keinan (Past Chair.).

Principal Staff: CEO Adi Azaria.

Contact Details: c/o Korat Israel Foundations Association, 18 Shankar, Herzliya; tel. (4) 6895287; e-mail info@kiedf.org; internet www.kiedf.com.

Lady Davis Fellowship Trust

Founded in 1973 by the Bloomfield Family in memory of Lady Davis, a philanthropist and benefactor of educational institutions in Canada.

Activities: Offers fellowships of 3–12 months to visiting professors, postdoctoral researchers and doctoral students at the Hebrew University of Jerusalem and at the Technion—Israel Institute of Technology in Haifa. Since its establishment, the Trust has supported more than 2,400 scholars.

Geographical Area of Activity: International.

Publications: Report of Operations; newsletter.

Principal Staff: Gen. Sec. Prof. Moshe Sidi.

Contact Details: Minhala Bldg, Rm 413, Hebrew University, Mt Sopus, Jerusalem 91904; tel. (2) 5882238; e-mail post_vp@savion.huji.ac.il; internet ldft.huji.ac.il.

Latet Israeli Humanitarian Aid (To Give)

Established in 1996 by Gilles Darmon as the local branch of French NGO Equilibre; an umbrella organization.

Activities: Helps disadvantaged people through eliminating poverty and food insecurity. The organization provides humanitarian aid and assistance internationally; and operates a national food bank, providing monthly assistance to 95,000 families and 1,450 Holocaust survivors. The three-year Latet Youth programme offers training in leadership and entrepreneurial skills to young people, while fostering social solidarity and encouraging volunteering. It comprises 210 local associations and around 27,000 volunteers.

Geographical Area of Activity: International.

Publications: Social Impact Report; newsletter.

Finance: Total income 187.7m. shekels, expenditure 175.2m. shekels (2023).

Board: Gilles Darmon (Pres.); Zvika Bar Nathan (Chair.).

Principal Staff: Exec. Dir Eran Weintraub.

Contact Details: Homa and Migdal 2, POB 20606-6120601, Tel Aviv; tel. (3) 6833388; e-mail latet@latet.org.il; internet www.latet.org.il.

Menomadin Foundation

Founded in 2019 by entrepreneur and philanthropist Haim Taib.

Activities: An international impact fund focused primarily enhancing social resilience in Israel, and addressing the impact of war and conflict. Projects in africa aim to empower children, young adults and women. Works internationally to establish philanthropic partnerships. Work areas include: the promotion of positive discourse between polarized populations; aiding individuals with disabilities; and the enhancement of art, culture and education.

Geographical Area of Activity: Israel, Africa, International.

Publications: Magazine (irregular).

Principal Staff: CEO Dr Merav Galili.

Contact Details: 14 Maskit St, 4673314 Herzliya Pituach; tel. 732582104; e-mail contact@menomadin.com; internet menomadinfoundation.com.

Peres Center for Peace and Innovation

Established in 1996 by Nobel Peace Laureate and former President of Israel Shimon Peres.

Activities: Focuses on common Arab and Israeli economic and social interests, with particular emphasis on Palestinian-Israeli relations. Main programme areas are: business and innovation; medicine and healthcare; sport; and youth leadership and entrepreneurship. The Center develops peacebuilding projects to address these interests, working with regional and international partners; and hosts the Innovation Center (f. 2019), which promotes Israeli technology and innovation.

Geographical Area of Activity: Middle East and North Africa.

Publications: Impact Report; *Peace in Progress* (newsletter); *Peres Blog*; e-bulletins (monthly); newsletter (2 a year); research and position papers.

International Board of Governors: Maurice Lévy (Chair.)

Board of Directors: Chemi Peres (Chair.).

Principal Staff: Dir-Gen. Efrat Duvdevani.

Contact Details: The Peres Peace House, 132 Kedem St, Tel Aviv-Jaffa 62745; tel. (3) 5680680; e-mail info@peres-center.org; internet www.peres-center.org.

Van Leer Jerusalem Institute

Established in 1959 by the family of Bernard van Leer, a Dutch industrialist; part of the Van Leer Group, which includes the Bernard van Leer Foundation (q.v.) and Jerusalem Film Center.

Activities: Undertakes projects in three main areas: globalization and sovereignty; sacredness, religion and secularization; and science, technology and civilization. Other areas of focus are Judaism, gender and the economy. The Institute organizes projects and discussion groups and encourages co-operation with CSOs, academia and government; and runs education and training programmes for educators and community leaders. It co-operates with Israeli and international research institutions, conducting joint projects with visiting scholars; hosts conferences and events; and has a library which focuses on philosophy, history, political science and religion.

Geographical Area of Activity: Israel.

Restrictions: Not a grantmaking organization.

Publications: Annual Review; newsletter; *Theory and Criticism* (2 a year); *Journal of Levantine Studies* (2 a year); position papers; studies; reports; books.

Finance: Annual income 23.8m. shekels, expenditure 25.8m. shekels (2022).

Board of Trustees: Faye Tversky (Chair.).

Principal Staff: Dir Uri Neuman.

Contact Details: 43 Jabotinsky St, Jerusalem 9214116; POB 4070, Jerusalem 9104001; tel. (2) 5605222; e-mail vanleer@vanleer.org.il; internet www.vanleer.org.il.

World Holocaust Forum Foundation—WHF

Established in 2005, by Moshe Kantor, Pres. of the European Jewish Congress (f. 1986), following the First International Holocaust Forum in Krakow, Poland.

Activities: Works to preserve the memory of the Holocaust, eliminate anti-Semitism, foster tolerance between religions and nationalities, and prevent nuclear war. Main programmes are: organizing international forums involving world leaders, to advance Holocaust education and commemoration; and the European Holocaust education programme, providing training and resources for educators.

Geographical Area of Activity: International.

Publications: Booklets; brochures; training materials.

Principal Staff: Pres. Dr Moshe Kantor.

Contact Details: c/o Yad Vashem, The World Holocaust Remembrance Center, Har Hazikaron, POB 3477, Jerusalem 9103401; tel. (2) 6443400; internet worldholocaustforum.org.

ITALY

CO-ORDINATING BODIES

Assifero—Associazione Italiana delle Fondazioni ed Enti della Filantropia Istituzionale (Italian Association of Foundations and Institutional Philanthropy Bodies)

Established in 2003; an association of grantmaking foundations and institutional philanthropy.

Activities: Promotes and consolidates institutional philanthropy in Italy through mobilizing private resources for the public good. The Association facilitates communication between members, exchange of expertise and skills, and formation of working groups. It organizes conferences, debates, seminars and webinars; offers legal, fiscal and strategic support; and promotes voluntary service among young people. Has 169 members; and is a member of Philea and WINGS (qq.v.). Has an office in Milan.

Geographical Area of Activity: Italy.

Publications: Annual Report; newsletter; *Alliance Magazine* (quarterly); map and directory of members (online).

Finance: Annual income €480,822, expenditure €554,807 (2022).

National Council: Stefania Mancini (Pres.).

Principal Staff: Gen. Sec. Carola Carazzone.

Contact Details: Via Pasquale Stanislao Mancini 2, 00196 Rome; tel. (06) 98230983; e-mail info@assifero.org; internet www.assifero.org.

Associazione di Fondazioni e di Casse di Risparmio SpA—ACRI (Association of Italian Foundations and Savings Banks)

Established in 1912 to represent and support the development of Italian savings banks and, since 1990, Italian banking foundations.

Activities: Provides support to Italian banking foundations and savings banks. Programme areas include: eliminating child poverty; promoting social cohesion and encouraging development in southern Italy; and supporting the national social housing programme. The Association has 102 member organizations; and is a member of Philea (q.v.).

Geographical Area of Activity: Italy.

Publications: Annual Report; *Il Risparmio* (monthly magazine); *Fondazioni* (magazine, 6 a year); reports; studies.

Executive Committee: Giovanni Azzone (Chair.).

Principal Staff: Gen. Man. Giorgio Righetti; Sec. Claudia Colletta.

Contact Details: Via del Corso 267, 00186 Rome; tel. (06) 681841; e-mail info@acri.it; internet www.acri.it.

FOUNDATIONS AND NON-PROFITS

Accademia Musicale Chigiana (Chigiana Musical Academy)

Founded in 1932 by Count Guido Chigi Saracini, a patron of music.

Activities: Operates internationally in the fields of education and the arts and humanities, through publications and courses, and awarding scholarships and fellowships. The Academy has a library of around 75,000 items, divided between music and literature, including musical scores and manuscripts, and audio materials; and holds the archives of the Chigi and Saracini families, which contain around 65,000 letters.

Geographical Area of Activity: International.

Publications: Annual Report; newsletter; *Chigiana* (annual magazine); music recordings; *Quaderni dell'Accademia Musicale Chigiana*; *Numeri Unici delle 'Settimane Musicali Senesi'*.

Finance: Total assets €10.5m. (2023).

Board of Directors: Carlo Rossi (Pres.); Angelica Lippi Piccolomini (Vice-Pres.).

Principal Staff: Man. Dir Angelo Armiento; Artistic Consultant Nicola Sani.

Contact Details: Via di Città 89, 53100 Siena; tel. (0577) 22091; e-mail accademia.chigiana@chigiana.it; internet www.chigiana.org.

Alliance of Bioversity International and the International Center for Tropical Agriculture—CIAT

Established in 1967 as the International Center for Tropical Agriculture (CIAT) by the Rockefeller Foundation and the Ford Foundation (qq.v.); part of the CGIAR (Consultative Group on International Agricultural Research) global network; present name adopted in 2019.

Activities: Works with farmers, policymakers and scientists to make agriculture in developing countries more competitive, profitable and resilient through sustainable resource management. Main research areas are: climate change; biodiversity loss; environmental degradation; and malnutrition. The Alliance carries out projects with government partners, national research organizations and universities, NGOs, civil society and farmers. It has offices and field operations sites in 32 countries.

Geographical Area of Activity: Central and South America, East and South-East Asia, South Asia, sub-Saharan Africa.

Publications: Annual Report; newsletter; *Growing Affinities* (2 a year); *CIAT in Perspective* (annual report); *Pasturas Tropicales* (*Tropical Pastures*, newsletter, 3 a year); brochures; information briefs; policy briefs; research reports; blog.

Finance: Total revenue US $33.0m., expenditure $33.5m. (31 Dec. 2023).

Board of Trustees: Julia Marton-Lefèvre (Chair.); Douglas van den Aardweg (Vice-Chair.).

Principal Staff: Dir-Gen. Juan Lucas Restrepo.

Contact Details: Via di San Domenico 1, 00153 Rome; tel. (66) 1181; e-mail bioversityweb@cgiar.org; internet alliancebioversityciat.org.

Biblioteca dell'Accademia Nazionale dei Lincei e Corsiniana (Library of the National Academy of Lincei and Corsiniana)

Founded in 1924 by Leone Caetani di Sermoneta, Prince of Teano, and formerly known as the Fondazione Leone Caetani.

Activities: Promotes knowledge of the ancient and contemporary Muslim world and Islamic culture, through organizing conferences and lectures and issuing publications. The Library maintains a specialized collection of 23,000 vols, 350 manuscripts (Arabic, Persian and Ethiopian) and 350 periodicals on Arab-Islamic classical civilization, which constitutes the Oriental Section. In 2004 the Museo Galileo digitized manuscripts and printed works from the Library relating to the founding period of the Academy.

Geographical Area of Activity: Italy.

Publications: Brochure.

Principal Staff: Pres. Prof. Roberto Antonelli; Vice-Pres. Prof. Carlo Doglioni.

Contact Details: Palazzo Corsini, Via della Lungara 10, 00165 Rome; tel. (06) 680271; e-mail segreteria@lincei.it; internet www.lincei.it.

CENSIS—Fondazione Centro Studi Investimenti Sociali (Foundation Centre for the Study of Social Investment)

Established in 1964 as a research institute; became a foundation in 1973.

Activities: Works in the fields of: communication and media; economy and local development, including transport and logistics, internationalization and consumption; education; public government; security and citizenship, including migration; territory, the environment, energy and urban development; welfare and health; and work. The Centre provides training and advice; and undertakes research commissioned by external groups and institutions, including the EU, chambers of commerce and private businesses. It publishes an annual report on the social situation in Italy.

Geographical Area of Activity: Europe.

Restrictions: Not a grantmaking organization.

Publications: Annual Report; *La rivista del CENSIS* (monthly); *Rapporto sulla situazione sociale del Paese* (annual); *Italy Today*; *Censis—Materiali di Ricerca*; *Forum per la Ricerca Biomedica (FBM)*; urban studies; research reports.

Finance: Annual budget US $5m.

Board of Directors: Giuseppe De Rita (Chair.); Giorgio De Rita (Sec.-Gen.).

Principal Staff: CEO Massimiliano Valerii.

Contact Details: Piazza di Novella 2, 00199 Rome; tel. (06) 860911; e-mail censis@censis.it; internet www.censis.it.

Centro Studi Internazionali—CSI (Centre for International Studies)

Established in 1992 in Naples.

Activities: Promotes research and analysis on political, economic and social issues through providing tools to institutions, companies, policymakers and private individuals. Programme areas include: Italian foreign policy; the EU Observatory; and the Elections Hub. The Centre organizes conferences, conventions, seminars and workshops; and supports cultural initiatives. It offers training courses for young people and professionals; and organizes activities for schools through the GeoLab project on geopolitics and international affairs.

Geographical Area of Activity: Italy.

Publications: *CSI Bulletin*; *CSI Review* (periodical); reports; scenarios; forecasts.

Principal Staff: Exec. Dir Francesco Gaudiosi; Deputy Exec. Dir Alexander Virgili.

Contact Details: Via Nomentana 251, 00137 Roma; e-mail segreteria@studi-internazionali.org; internet www.studi-internazionali.org.

Centro Studi e Ricerca Sociale Fondazione Emanuela Zancan (Emanuela Zancan Foundation Centre for Social Studies and Research)

Founded in 1964; works in the field of research, in particular educational, social and health services.

ITALY

Activities: Operates in the fields of education, health and social welfare through self-conducted programmes, research, conferences, publications and lectures. The Centre works in collaboration with other institutions and foreign experts.
Geographical Area of Activity: International.
Publications: *Studi Zancan: Politiche e servizi alle persone* (journal, 2 a month); research reports.
Board of Directors: Tiziano Vecchiato (Chair.).
Principal Staff: Dir Dr Cinzia Canali.
Contact Details: Via del Seminario 5A, 35122 Padova; tel. (049) 663800; e-mail segreteria@fondazionezancan.it; internet www.fondazionezancan.it.

Cooperazione Internazionale—COOPI (International Co-operation)
Founded in 1965 by Fr Vincenzo Barbieri; an independent and lay NGO.
Activities: Works in the fields of disaster recovery and long-term development. Main programme areas are: emergency education; the environment and disaster risk reduction; food security; nutritional security; protection; and water and hygiene. The organization helps people affected by natural disasters and promotes their civil, economic and social development; carries out development projects and emergency interventions abroad; and works to eliminate the causes of economic inequality between emerging countries of the global South and those of the North. It has three offices in Italy and one in Switzerland; and is present in more than 33 countries.
Geographical Area of Activity: Middle East, South America, Central America and the Caribbean, sub-Saharan Africa.
Publications: Annual Report; newsletter; brochure.
Finance: Annual income €70.1m., expenditure €70.1m. (31 Dec. 2023).
Board of Directors: Claudio Ceravolo (Chair.); Antonella Tagliabue (Vice-Chair.).
Principal Staff: Dir Giorgio Borea.
Contact Details: Via De Lemene 50, 20151 Milan; tel. (02) 3085057; e-mail coopi@coopi.org; internet www.coopi.org.

EMERGENCY
Established in 1994 by Gino Strada, a surgeon; an assembly of member organizations.
Activities: Provides medical and surgical care to the victims of war, through the provision of medical and technical personnel. The organization constructs and rehabilitates medical facilities; supports educational institutions; distributes medical and first aid supplies; and raises awareness about development and humanitarian needs. It has 107 members; special consultative status with ECOSOC; and offices in Rome and Venice.
Geographical Area of Activity: Afghanistan, Eritrea, Iraq, Italy, Sierra Leone, Sudan, Uganda.
Publications: Annual Report; newsletter; *Magazine* (quarterly).
Finance: Annual income €48.6m., expenditure €45.1m. (31 Dec. 2020).
Governing Council: Rossella Miccio (Chair.); Roberta Borroni (Vice-Chair. and Treas.); Gabriela Pardo (Sec.).
Principal Staff: Exec. Dir Gino Strada.
Contact Details: Via Santa Croce 19, 20122 Milan; tel. (02) 881881; e-mail info@emergency.it; internet www.emergency.it.

Eni Foundation
Established in 2006 by Eni, an oil and gas company.
Activities: Programmes focus on: providing medical services for mothers and children; vaccination and mothers' health; and supporting training for medical staff. The Foundation works in 13 countries and has offices in Milan.

European Training Foundation

Geographical Area of Activity: Algeria, Angola, Repub. of the Congo, Egypt, Ghana, Guinea Bissau, Indonesia, Italy, Libya, Mexico, Mozambique, Myanmar, Rwanda.
Publications: Annual Report.
Finance: Total assets €7.4m. (31 Dec. 2023).
Board of Directors: Domenico Giani (Chair.).
Board of Auditors: Marco Tani (Chair.).
Supervisory Board: Enrico del Prato (Chair.).
Principal Staff: Sec.-Gen. Filippo Uberti.
Contact Details: Piazzale Enrico Mattei 1, 00144 Rome; tel. (06) 59821; e-mail enifoundation@eni.com; internet www.eni.com/enifoundation/en-IT/home.html.

Ente Cassa di Risparmio di Firenze (Florence Savings Bank Foundation)
Founded in 1992 to continue the work of Cassa di Risparmio di Firenze (f. 1829).
Activities: Carries out self-conducted programmes and makes grants in Tuscany in the areas of: the arts and cultural heritage; volunteering and philanthropy; scientific and technological research and innovation; education and vocational training; and environmental conservation. The Foundation administers three smaller foundations; and maintains an art collection.
Geographical Area of Activity: Italy.
Publications: Newsletter; *I Fatti* (magazine); *OmA* (magazine).
Finance: Total income €472,985, expenditure €873,417 (31 Dec. 2023).
Board of Directors: Bernabo Bocca (Chair.); Maria Oliva Scaramuzzi (Vice-Chair.).
Supervisory Body: Prof. Francesco Corsi (Pres.).
Principal Staff: Gen. Man. Gabriele Gori.
Contact Details: Via Bufalini 6, 50122 Florence; tel. (055) 5384001; e-mail info@fondazionecrfirenze.it; internet www.fondazionecrfirenze.it.

European Training Foundation—ETF
Established in 1990 by the Council of Ministers of the European Community (now the EU); began its activities in 1995.
Activities: Supports vocational education and training reform in transition and developing countries in the context of the EU external relations programme. The Foundation provides technical assistance to the European Commission for the implementation of the Tempus programme in the field of higher education; and provides expertise in the areas of human resources, vocational training reform policies, skills development for enterprises, management and entrepreneurial training, and active labour market policies. It supports the European Commission's project cycle and contributes to the development and design of country strategy papers and programmes, including: country analyses; sector analyses; analyses of needs and feasibility studies; training needs assessment methodologies; key indicators and benchmarking; impact assessment, evaluation and peer reviews; and examples of good practice.
Geographical Area of Activity: Worldwide.
Restrictions: Not a training provider; no grants to individual students.
Publications: Annual Report; yearbook; reports; periodicals.
Finance: Annual revenue €20.1m., expenditure €20.1m. (31 Dec. 2020).
Governing Board: Mario Nava (Chair.).
Principal Staff: Dir Pilvi Torsti.
Contact Details: Villa Gualino, Viale Settimio Severo 65, 10133 Turin; tel. (011) 6302222; e-mail info@etf.europa.eu; internet www.etf.europa.eu.

FAI—Fondo per l'Ambiente Italiano (The National Trust for Italy)

Established in 1975 by Giulia Maria Crespi, an entrepreneur.

Activities: Works in the fields of natural and cultural heritage. The Trust carries out activities in three main areas: protecting artistic and natural heritage; raising people's awareness of the value of landscapes and monumental heritage through education and training; and protecting landscapes at risk. It acquires and restores special places, making them accessible to the public. Comprises 19 Regional Departments, organized into 131 Delegations; and 108 FAI Groups, 93 FAI Youth Groups and 8 FAI Bridging Groups of volunteers. FAI International has branches in Switzerland, the United Kingdom and the USA.

Geographical Area of Activity: International.

Publications: Annual Report; newsletter.

Finance: Annual income €55.1m., expenditure €34.2m. (2022).

Trustees: Marco Magnifico (Pres.); Ilaria Borletti Buitoni, Maurizio Rivolta (Vice-Pres.).

Principal Staff: Gen. Man. Davide Usai.

Contact Details: La Cavallerizza, Via Carlo Foldi 2, 20135 Milan; tel. (02) 4676151; e-mail info@fondoambiente.it; internet www.fondoambiente.it.

FEEM—Fondazione ENI Enrico Mattei (Enrico Mattei Eni Foundation)

Established in 1989.

Activities: Improves decisionmaking in public and private spheres through research. The Foundation conducts research on economic, environmental and energy issues; and fosters awareness of the interaction between businesses and the environment, the economy and energy scenarios, corporate responsibility and social conflict, and cultural responsibility. It maintains a network of international and multidisciplinary researchers who provide training in specialized areas of research through disseminating research results and presenting findings to policymakers at institutional forums. Has offices in Venice and Viggiano.

Geographical Area of Activity: International.

Publications: *Equilibri Magazine* (online magazine); *Note di Lavoro* (working papers series); policy briefs; reports; books; Annual Report.

Board of Directors: Giuseppe Zafarana (Chair.).

Principal Staff: Exec. Dir Alessandro Lanza.

Contact Details: Palazzo delle Stelline, Corso Magenta 63, 20123 Milan; tel. (02) 40336934; e-mail letter@feem.it; internet www.feem.it.

Fondazione 1563 per l'Arte e la Cultura (1563 Foundation for the Arts and Culture)

Founded in 1985; an initiative of the Istituto Bancario San Paolo di Torino; formerly known as the Fondazione San Paolo di Torino, established by the Compagnia di San Paolo (q.v.).

Activities: Operates in the fields of the arts and culture, through grants for the performing arts, exhibitions and restoration projects. The Foundation works in association with the Compagnia di San Paolo, with programmes focusing on the safeguarding, enrichment and enhancement of artistic heritage. Under its Baroque Programme, it awards scholarships and a prize for unpublished research.

Geographical Area of Activity: Europe.

Publications: Information brochures; books on art.

Finance: Annual income €3.2m., expenditure €1.9m. (31 Dec 2022).

Board of Directors: Dr Piero Gastaldo (Chair.); Prof. Blythe Alice Raviola (Vice-Chair.).

Supervisory Board: Dr Paolo Rizello (Pres.).

Principal Staff: Exec. Dir Elisabetta Ballaira; Sec. Gen. Dr Laura Fornara.

Contact Details: Piazza Gianlorenzo Bernini 5, 10138 Torino; tel. (011) 15630570; e-mail info@fondazione1563.it; internet www.fondazione1563.it.

Fondazione Adriano Olivetti (Adriano Olivetti Foundation)

Founded in 1962 in memory of Adriano Olivetti, an electrical engineer and industrialist, by members of his family, friends and colleagues.

Activities: Promotes, develops and co-ordinates research on in four main areas: institutional and public policies; economic and social development; cultural and social policies; and art, architecture and urban studies. The Foundation carries out self-conducted programmes, offering grants and issuing publications. It has an office in Rome.

Geographical Area of Activity: Europe, USA.

Publications: Annual Report; *Esiste un Diritto di Ingerenza?*; *Europa di fronte alla guerra*; *MoltepliCittà;* archive; other publications.

Finance: Total assets €4.6m. (31 Dec. 2024).

Board of Directors: Cinthia Bianconi (Chair.); Desire Olivetti (Vice-Chair.).

Principal Staff: Sec.-Gen. Beniamino de'Liguori Carino.

Contact Details: Strada Monte Bidasio 2, 10015 Ivrea (TO); tel. (0125) 627547; e-mail segreteria@fondazioneadrianolivetti.it; internet www.fondazioneadrianolivetti.it.

Fondazione Alessio Pezcoller (Alessio Pezcoller Foundation)

Founded in 1980 by Prof. Alessio Pezcoller, Chief Surgeon of Santa Chiara Hospital in Trento, to promote biomedical research.

Activities: Works in the fields of medicine and health through awarding fellowships and prizes: the Pezcoller Foundation—AACR International Award for Cancer Research, worth €75,000 and presented annually to a scientist who has made a major scientific discovery in the field of cancer; the Pezcoller Foundation–EACR Cancer Researcher Award for academic excellence and achievements in the field of cancer research, worth €10,000; the Pezcoller-Marina Larcher Fogazzaro—EACR Women in Cancer Research Award of €10,000, established in 2020; and the EACR—Mark Foundation—Pezcoller Foundation Rising Star award of up to €100,000. The Foundation organizes an annual symposium promoting interaction between international scientists working in basic oncological sciences, and a series of educational meetings for local medical doctors.

Geographical Area of Activity: International.

Restrictions: No grants to individuals.

Publications: *The Pezcoller Foundation Journal* (2 a year).

Board of Directors: Enzo Galligioni (Pres.); Gios Bernardi (Pres. Emeritus); Paolo Stefenelli (Vice-Pres.).

Principal Staff: Gen. Sec. Federica Mandato.

Contact Details: Via Malpaga 11, 38122 Trento; tel. (0461) 980250; e-mail pezcoller@pezcoller.it; internet www.pezcoller.it.

Fondazione Allianz Umana Mente (Allianz Umana Mente Foundation)

Established in 2001 by Allianz Group SpA, a financial services group.

Activities: Supports people with social and behavioural problems, through funding projects by non-profit organizations. The Foundation's activities focus on children with social and behavioural problems or people affected by congenital mental disabilities. It offers financial and managerial support to organizations.

Geographical Area of Activity: Italy.

Publications: Reports.

Finance: Annual revenue €1.1m., expenditure €316,769 (31 Dec. 2022).

Board of Directors: Maurizio Devescovi (Pres.); Monica Esposito (Vice-Pres.).

Principal Staff: Gen. Sec. Nicola Corti.

Contact Details: Piazza Tre Torri 3, 20145 Milan; tel. (02) 72162669; e-mail info@umana-mente.it; internet umanamente.allianz.it.

Fondazione Ambrosiana Paolo VI (Ambrosiana Paolo VI Foundation)

Founded 1976 by Archbishop Giovanni Colombo. Incorporated into the Istituto Superiore di Studi Religiosi (ISSR) Beato Paolo VI in 2017.

Activities: Funds research, conferences and studies primarily in the fields of faith and religion. The Foundation incorporates the Higher Institute of Religious Studies; and has a collection of studies on the religious history of Ireland.

Geographical Area of Activity: Europe.

Publications: Newsletter; *Quaderni della Gazzada*; *Storia religiosa della Lombardia*; *Europa ricerche*.

Principal Staff: Pres. Bishop Luigi Stucchi.

Contact Details: Villa Cagnola, Via Guido Cagnola 21, 21045 Gazzada Schianno; tel. (0332) 1614000; e-mail info@villacagnola.it; internet villacagnola.com.

Fondazione Angelo Della Riccia (Angelo Della Riccia Foundation)

Founded in 1939 by the will of Angelo Della Riccia, an engineer and pioneer of the electrical industry.

Activities: Supports research in microphysics. The Foundation awards prizes and scholarships for researchers resident in Italy. Both the Italian and Swiss branches award fellowships. In 2024/25 the total value of grants available was €190,800 from the Italian branch and €25,000 from the Swiss branch.

Geographical Area of Activity: Italy, Switzerland.

Restrictions: Grants only to Italian citizens resident in Italy for study in Italy or Switzerland.

Principal Staff: Pres. Prof. Roberto Casalbuoni.

Contact Details: Piazzale Donatello 2, 50132 Florence; tel. (05) 5212836; e-mail amministratoredelegato@fondazioneangelodellariccia.it; internet www.fondazioneangelodellariccia.it.

Fondazione AVSI (AVSI Foundation)

Established in 1972 as the Associazione Volontari per il Servizio Internazionale (AVSI); an NGO.

Activities: AVSI Foundation implements international development and humanitarian projects. Its projects support the UN's Sustainable Development Goals in the areas of: education and child protection; climate change, energy and environment; agriculture, food security and nutrition; economic strengthening and women empowerment; vocational training and job creation; sustainable cities and communities; human rights, democracy and peace; migration and integration; health and hygiene. Cross-cutting themes are migration, climate change, emergency, and women empowerment. The Foundation works in 42 countries through a network of 34 founding organizations and with 355 projects in Africa, Latin America and the Caribbean, Middle East, South-East Asia, Europe and the USA. AVSI has consultative status at the UN Economic and Social Council (ECOSOC). In Italy, the main offices of AVSI – ETS are in Milan and Cesena.

Geographical Area of Activity: International.

Publications: Social Report; Annual Report; newsletter.

Finance: Total revenue €114.6m., expenditure €114.5m. (2023).

Board of Directors: Patrizia Savi (Pres.); Alfredo Mantica (Vice-Pres.).

Supervisory Board: Benedetta Colombo (Pres.).

Principal Staff: Sec.-Gen. Giampaolo Silvestri.

Contact Details: Via Donatello 5B, 20131 Milan; tel. (02) 6749881; e-mail fondazione.avsi@avsi.org; internet www.avsi.org.

Fondazione Benetton Studi Ricerche (Benetton Foundation for Study and Research)

Founded in 1981; present name adopted in 1987.

Activities: Works to protect and promote natural and built heritage, through research on stewardship of landscapes, with special reference to Europe and the Mediterranean basin, and the history of games and sports. The Foundation carries out self-conducted programmes and research; offers scholarships; organizes conferences and training courses; and issues publications. It awards the annual International Carlo Scarpa Prize for Gardens to promote landscape management and the conservation of sites of natural and historical value; and has a public documentation centre, with a library, archives, and map and image collections.

Geographical Area of Activity: Mainly Europe.

Publications: Newsletter; annual booklet on Premio Internazionale Carlo Scarpa per il Giardino; *Ludica* (annual review of games and sport); *Studi veneti*.

Board of Directors: Luciano Benetton (Chair.).

Principal Staff: Dir Luigi Latini.

Contact Details: Via Cornarotta 7–9, 31100 Treviso; tel. (0422) 5121; e-mail fbsr@fbsr.it; internet www.fbsr.it.

Fondazione Cariplo (Cariplo Foundation)

Established in 1991 to continue the philanthropic activities previously carried out by the Cassa di Risparmio delle Provincie Lombarde (Savings Bank of the Lombard Provinces, f. 1823).

Activities: Works in four main areas: the environment, including conservation and energy efficiency; arts and culture, including education development in relation to migration and global citizenship; scientific research, including technology transfer and projects in areas such as neglected tropical diseases and agriculture; and services for people, including social welfare.

Geographical Area of Activity: International.

Restrictions: Does not make grants to individuals; trade union or patronage organizations; political parties or trade associations.

Publications: Annual Report; newsletter; monographs; conference reports; financial statements.

Finance: Total assets €8,407.1m.; net annual income €286.5m. (31 Dec. 2024).

Board of Directors: Giovanni Azzone (Pres.); Claudia Sorlini, Valeria Negrini (Vice-Pres).

Principal Staff: Gen. Man. Sergio Urbani.

Contact Details: Via Manin 23, 20121 Milan; tel. (02) 62391; e-mail comunicazione@fondazionecariplo.it; internet www.fondazionecariplo.it.

Fondazione Cassa di Risparmio di Padova e Rovigo (Cassa di Risparmio di Padova e Rovigo Foundation)

Established in 1991 as the continuation of the Cassa di Risparmio di Padova e Rovigo.

Activities: Works to improve the quality of life and promote sustainable development in the regions of Padova and Rovigo in Italy. The Foundation supports innovative projects in the fields of scientific research; education; arts and culture; health and the environment; social welfare; and other sectors (sport, civil protection, food safety, quality agriculture). It has an office in Rovigo.

Geographical Area of Activity: Italy (Padova and Rovigo).

Restrictions: Does not make grants to individuals, profit-seeking organizations, parties, political movements, trade unions, charitable institutions or trade associations.

Publications: Annual Report; newsletter; information brochures.

Fondazione Cassa di Risparmio di Torino — ITALY

Finance: Total assets €2,828.6m. (31 Dec. 2023).
Board of Directors: Gilberto Muraro (Pres.); Donato Nitti, Giuseppe Toffoli (Vice-Pres).
Supervisory Board: Antonio Guarnieri (Pres.).
Principal Staff: Sec.-Gen. Roberto Saro.
Contact Details: Piazza Duomo 15, 35141 Padova; tel. (049) 8234800; e-mail info@fondazionecariparo.it; internet www.fondazionecariparo.it.

Fondazione Cassa di Risparmio di Torino (Turin Savings Bank Foundation)

Established in 1991.
Activities: Promotes the economic and social development of the regions of Piemonte and Valle d'Aosta. The Foundation awards grants in the fields of: research and education; arts and culture and conservation of artistic heritage; and welfare and the environment.
Geographical Area of Activity: Italiy (mainly Piemonte and Valle d'Aosta).
Restrictions: No grants to individuals.
Publications: Annual Report; brochure; books; monographs; press releases; online magazine.
Finance: Total assets, €2,769.2m.; net annual income €65.3m. (31 Dec. 2020).
Board of Directors: Anna Maria Poggi (Pres.); Paola Casagrande, Claudio Albanese (Vice-Pres).
Principal Staff: Sec.-Gen. Patrizia Polliotto.
Contact Details: Via XX Settembre 31, 10121 Turin; tel. (011) 5065100; e-mail info@fondazionecrt.it; internet www.fondazionecrt.it.

Fondazione Cassa di Risparmio di Verona Vicenza Belluno e Ancona—Fondazione Cariverona

Originated in 1825 as the Cassa di Verona bank; became a private non-profit institution in 1991.
Activities: Offers grants to organizations working in the fields of scientific research, education, the arts and humanities, the environment, healthcare and social welfare.
Geographical Area of Activity: Italy.
Finance: Total assets €1,661.4m. (31 Dec. 2022).
Board of Directors: Bruno Giordano (Pres.); Giovanni Dolcetta Capuzzo (Vice-Pres.); Margherita Forestan (Deputy Vice-Pres.).
Principal Staff: Gen. Man. Filippo Manfredi.
Contact Details: Via A. Forti 3A, 37121 Verona; tel. (045) 8057311; e-mail segreteria@fondazionecariverona.org; internet www.fondazionecariverona.org.

Fondazione Cavaliere del Lavoro Carlo Pesenti (Carlo Pesenti Foundation)

Established in 2004 by Italcementi, a construction company, and Italmobiliare, a holding company, in honour of industrialist Carlo Pesenti; formerly known as the Fondazione Italcementi Cavaliere del Lavoro Carlo Pesenti.
Activities: Promotes innovation in the fields of education and scientific research and sustainable economic and social development, through supporting non-profit organizations. The Foundation carries out humanitarian projects, helping people affected by natural disasters and other emergencies; and also supports artistic and cultural events.
Geographical Area of Activity: International.
Publications: Brochure.
Board of Directors: Carlo Pesenti (Pres.); Giulia Pesenti (Vice-Pres.).
Principal Staff: Sec.-Gen. Sergio Crippa.
Contact Details: Via Borgonuovo 20, 20122 Milan; tel. (02) 29024251; e-mail segreteria@fondazionepesenti.it; internet www.fondazionepesenti.it.

Fondazione Centro Euro-Mediterraneo sui Cambiamenti Climatici—CMCC (Euro-Mediterranean Centre on Climate Change Foundation)

Established in 2005 with support from the Italian Ministry of Education, University and Research and the Ministry of the Environment, Land and Sea; became a foundation in 2015.
Activities: Carries out multidisciplinary scientific and policy research and analysis in the field of climate variability through: designing climate models; making forecasts and predictions; providing solutions and tools; offering training programmes; and organizing lectures and conferences. The Foundation has nine members and institutional partners: Istituto Nazionale di Geofisica e Vulcanologia; Università degli Studi del Salento; Centro Italiano Ricerche Aerospaziali; Università Ca' Foscari Venezia; Università di Sassari; Università della Tuscia; Politecnico di Milano; Resources for the Future; and Università di Bologna. Has offices in Bologna, Caserta, Milan, Sassari, Venice and Viterbo.
Geographical Area of Activity: Mediterranean region.
Publications: Annual Report; Foresight: The CMCC Observatory on Climate Policies and Futures (online forum); data sets; technical notes; books.
Finance: Total income €32.8m., expenditure €32.9m. (31 Dec. 2023).
Board of Directors: Antonio Navarra (Pres.).
Principal Staff: Exec. Dir Laura Panzera.
Contact Details: Via Marco Biagi 5, 73100 Lecce; tel. (832) 1902411; e-mail info@cmcc.it; internet www.cmcc.it.

Fondazione CIMA—Centro Internazionale in Monitoraggio Ambientale (CIMA Research Foundation—Centre for Environmental Monitoring)

Established in 2007; incorporates ACROTEC Technology Foundation, which specializes in technology transfer for disaster risk prevention and mitigation.
Activities: Promotes study, scientific research, technological development and advanced training in engineering and environmental sciences to safeguard public health, civil protection, and aquatic and terrestrial ecosystems. The Foundation carries out projects in more than 60 countries. It has a branch in Tirana, Albania (f. 2011).
Geographical Area of Activity: International.
Publications: Scientific papers and reports.
Finance: Annual income €9.5m., expenditure €9.2m. (31 Dec. 2020).
Board of Directors: Luca Ferraris (Pres.).
Principal Staff: Man. Dir Luisa Michela Colla.
Contact Details: Via Armando Magliotto 2, 17100 Savona; tel. (019) 230271; e-mail info@cimafoundation.org; internet www.cimafoundation.org.

Fondazione Compagnia di San Paolo

Established in 1563 as a religious brotherhood; now an independent grantmaking foundation.
Activities: Fosters civic, cultural and economic development through programmes in the areas of: scientific, economic and legal research; education; the arts and humanities; preservation of cultural heritage and activities, and of environmental assets; and health and welfare. Bodies that come under its institutional remit include: the Istituto Superiore Mario Boella, which operates in the field of information and communication technology, in association with the Politecnico di Torino; the Consorzio Collegio Carlo Alberto, which established a Centre for Advanced Training in Finance and Economics, also in association with the Politecnico di Torino; the Ufficio Pio, which has an active network of volunteers, helping people in need and offering grants for the vocational training of at-risk young people; and the Foundation for Schools (Educatorio Duchessa Isabella), which supports self-governing schools. It maintains a searchable grants database.
Geographical Area of Activity: Worldwide.

ITALY

Restrictions: Operates exclusively to the benefit of non-profit-making organizations; no grants to individuals.

Publications: Annual Report; newsletter (3 a year); *Quaderni della Compagnia*; *Quaderni dell'Archivio Storico* (monograph series, in Italian); reports; studies.

Finance: Total assets €7,575.2m. (31 Dec. 2024).

Management Committee: Marco Gilli (Chair.); Rosanna Ventrella Grimaldi (Vice-Pres.).

Principal Staff: Sec.-Gen. Alberto Francesco Anfossi.

Contact Details: Corso Vittorio Emanuele II 75, 10128 Turin; tel. (011) 15630100; e-mail communicazione@compagnia disanpaolo.it; internet www.compagniadisanpaolo.it.

Fondazione Edoardo Garrone (Edoardo Garrone Foundation)

Established in 2004 by energy company ERG SpA and San Quirico SpA, in memory of Edoardo Garrone, the founder of the ERG Group.

Activities: Carries out activities in the fields of young people and their regional environment, and education and social welfare. The Foundation supports young business entrepreneurs in Italy's mountain regions; and the teaching of regional cultural and environmental awareness in schools. Main programmes are: RestartAlp, fostering economic development and entrepreneurship in the areas of 'slow' tourism; and RestartApp, for Central Italy, an edition of the programme focusing on areas of the Apennine region that were affected by the 2016 earthquake.

Geographical Area of Activity: Italy (mainly Alpine and Apennine regions).

Publications: Newsletter.

Board of Directors: Alessandro Garrone (Pres.).

Principal Staff: Gen. Man. Francesca Campora.

Contact Details: Via San Luca 2, 16124 Genova; tel. (010) 8681530; e-mail info@fondazionegarrone.it; internet www.fondazionegarrone.it.

Fondazione Giangiacomo Feltrinelli (Giangiacomo Feltrinelli Foundation)

Established in 1949, as a library, by Giangiacomo Feltrinelli, a publisher.

Activities: Collects, preserves and makes available to scholars and the public materials documenting the history of ideas, in particular the development of the international labour and socialist movements. The library and archival holdings contain around 200,000 books, newspaper and periodical collections, and more than 1m. primary sources. The Foundation also promotes scholarly research initiatives; organizes seminars, conferences and exhibitions exploring historical and contemporary subjects; and issues publications.

Geographical Area of Activity: Italy.

Restrictions: Not a grantmaking organization.

Publications: Newsletter; *Movimento Operaio*; *Annali* (annual series featuring original research by international scholars of modern social history and historiography); *Biblioteca Europea* (collection of anastatic reprints of significant 17th- to 19th-century works); *Quaderni*; catalogues.

Board of Directors: Carlo Feltrinelli (Pres.).

Principal Staff: Dir Massimiliano Tarantino.

Contact Details: Viale Pasubio 5, 20154 Milano; tel. (02) 49583427; e-mail segreteria@fondazionefeltrinelli.it; internet www.fondazionefeltrinelli.it.

Fondazione Giorgio Cini (Giorgio Cini Foundation)

Founded in 1951 by Count Vittorio Cini in memory of his son Giorgio; the island of San Giorgio Maggiore, Venice, was entrusted to the Foundation for the purpose of restoring its historic buildings and supporting the development of social, cultural and artistic institutions.

Fondazione Giovanni Lorenzini

Activities: Organizes postgraduate courses, conferences and seminars on topics of historic, scientific, social or cultural interest. The Foundation comprises seven advanced study institutes and a research centre: the Institute of Art History; the Institute for the History of Venice; the Institute for Music; the Italian Antonio Vivaldi Institute; the Institute for Music; the Intercultural Institute of Comparative Music Studies; the Institute for Theatre and Melodrama; and the Comparative Civilization and Spirituality Study Centre (formerly the Venice and the East Institute). Each organizes and promotes exhibitions, study conferences and seminars. The Foundation also organizes the Egida Sartori and Laura Alvini Ancient Music Seminars.

Geographical Area of Activity: Italy.

Publications: Newsletter; *Lettera da San Giorgio* (weekly magazine); art catalogues; essays; periodicals.

Board of Directors: Gianfelice Rocca (Pres.).

Principal Staff: Sec.-Gen. Renata Codello.

Contact Details: Isola di San Giorgio Maggiore 1, 30124 Venice; tel. (041) 2710211; e-mail info@cini.it; internet www.cini.it.

Fondazione Giovanni Agnelli (Giovanni Agnelli Foundation)

Founded in 1966 by vehicle manufacturer Fiat SpA and the Istituto Finanziario Industriale on the 100th anniversary of Senator Giovanni Agnelli's birth.

Activities: Supports research in the field of education. Themes include school policies and education reform; teaching and learning practices; teacher training and career prospects; evaluation to improve the quality of teaching; equity and inclusion in schools; and university education. The Foundation established the Combo educational laboratory; and the Eduscopio online school and university comparison site.

Geographical Area of Activity: Italy.

Publications: Newsletter; *Eduscopio*.

Board of Directors: John P. Elkann (Chair.); Tiziana Nasi (Vice-Chair.).

Principal Staff: Dir Andrea Gavosto.

Contact Details: Via Giuseppe Giacosa 38, 10125 Turin; tel. (011) 6500504; e-mail segreteria@fondazioneagnelli.it; internet www.fondazioneagnelli.it.

Fondazione Giovanni Lorenzini (Giovanni Lorenzini Foundation)

Established in 1969 as a non-profit scientific organization by presidential decree; consists of two not-for-profit scientific organizations based in Milan (f. 1969) and New York (f. 1984).

Activities: Works in the fields of translational medicine and the health and wellbeing economy. Programme areas include: the first 1,000 days of children's lives; age-related hearing loss; vaccination and HPV; and nutrition and development. The Foundation organizes educational activities; and facilitates the exchange of multidisciplinary and interdisciplinary evidence-based findings to shape health policy and improve health literacy. It co-ordinates the activities of the International Society of Atherosclerosis.

Geographical Area of Activity: International.

Publications: Newsletter; brochure; conference proceedings; guidelines; position papers.

Board of Governors: Dr Giuseppe Novelli (Pres.); Dr Sergio Pecorelli (Vice-Chair.).

Principal Staff: Sec.-Gen. and CEO Dr Emanuela Folco.

Contact Details: Viale Piave 35, 20129 Milan; tel. (02) 29006267; e-mail info@lorenzinifoundation.org; internet www.lorenzinifoundation.org.

Fondazione Giulio Pastore—FGP (Giulio Pastore Foundation)

Founded in 1971 by the Associazioni Cristiane Lavoratori Italiani, Confederazione Italiana Sindacati dei Lavoratori, Democrazia Cristiana, Prof. Mario Romani, Prof. Vincenzo Saba, Vincenzo Scotti, Don Pierfranco Pastore and Idolo Marcone.

Activities: Researches the problems of labour and workers' experience of trade unions. The Foundation runs self-conducted programmes and offers grants, fellowships and scholarships. It also organizes conferences, courses and lectures. It has a library of around 30,000 vols and 300 periodicals.

Geographical Area of Activity: Worldwide.

Publications: *Annali* (annual report of operations); yearbooks; *Lavoro e Sindacato* (6 a year); *Quaderni della Fondazione Giulio Pastore*.

Board of Directors: Prof. Aldo Carera (Pres.); Dr Pierciro Galeone (Vice-Pres.); Prof. Michele Colasanto (Past Pres.).

Contact Details: Via Giovanni Maria Lancisi 25, 00161 Rome; tel. (06) 83960192; e-mail info@fondazionepastore.it; internet www.fondazionepastore.it.

Fondazione Internazionale Menarini (Menarini International Foundation)

Founded in 1976 by the Menarini Group, a pharmaceutical company, to promote research and knowledge in the fields of biology, pharmacology and medicine, but also, though more implicitly, in the fields of economic and human sciences.

Activities: Promotes research in the fields of biology, pharmacology and medicine, economics and the humanities. The Foundation organizes conferences and symposia. In 2020, in response to the COVID-19 pandemic, it established an online Coronavirus Library, collating the most significant and influential publications on the disease under the guidance of the Scientific Committee of the Foundation and making them freely available to healthcare professionals.

Geographical Area of Activity: Italy.

Publications: Newsletter; *Minuti Menarini* (monthly journal).

Principal Staff: Organizing Sec. Francesca Gaias.

Contact Details: Edif. L, Strada 6, Centro Direzionale Milanofiori, 20089 Rozzano, Milan; tel. (02) 55308110; e-mail milan@fondazione-menarini.it; internet www.fondazione-menarini.it.

Fondazione ISMU—Iniziative e Studi sulla Multietnicità (ISMU Foundation—Initiatives and Studies on Multiethnicity)

Established in 1991.

Activities: Promotes internationalism and multiculturalism, particularly within Europe; and study and research, especially in the field of immigration issues. The Foundation holds seminars, funds training and produces publications promoting multiethnicity. It has a library containing more than 12,600 titles, including 150 periodicals, and maintains an archive of national and international documentation.

Geographical Area of Activity: Mainly Europe.

Publications: Annual Report; *ISMU informa* (newsletter); *Annual Report on Migration*; factsheets; policy briefs.

Finance: Total assets €2.4m. (2023).

Board of Directors: Prof. Gian Carlo Blangiardo (Pres.).

Principal Staff: Sec.-Gen. Prof. Nicola Pasini.

Contact Details: Via Copernico 1, 20125 Milan; tel. (02) 6787791; e-mail ismu@ismu.org; internet www.ismu.org.

Fondazione per l'Istituto Svizzero di Roma (Foundation for the Swiss Institute of Rome)

Founded in 1947 for young Swiss scholars and artists to study in Rome.

Activities: Operates internationally in the fields of the arts and humanities and sciences. The Foundation organizes regular events in the artistic and scholarly fields to contribute to mutual understanding and to deepen intellectual and artistic relations between Switzerland and Italy, hosting 10–12 fellows each year. It has a Resource Centre with a library of 45,000 vols, and an office in Milan.

Geographical Area of Activity: International, with a special focus on Swiss-Italian relations.

Publications: Annual Report; newlsetter; *Bibliotheca Helvetica Romana*.

Finance: Funded by the Swiss Confederation, Pro Helvetia, BSI, the Swiss National Foundation and others.

Board of Directors: Mario Annoni (Pres.); Giovanna Masoni Brenni (Vice-Pres.).

Principal Staff: Dir Joëlle Comé.

Contact Details: Istituto Svizzero di Roma, Villa Maraini, Via Ludovisi 48, 00187 Rome; tel. (06) 420421; e-mail roma@istitutosvizzero.it; internet www.istitutosvizzero.it.

Fondazione ITS (ITS Foundation)

Founded in 2022 to continue the work of its predecessor the Eve Cultural Association Creativity Research Lab.

Activities: The Foundation's mission is to promote and cultivate creativity. Now runs the ITS Contest, which started in 2002 and recognises new creative talent in fashion, accessories and jewellery. Also home to the ITS Arcademy Museum of Art in Fashion which displays some 1,100 garments and preserves a collection of each of the former ITS Contest winners' work.

Geographical Area of Activity: Italy, International.

Principal Staff: Pres. Barbara Franchin; Vice-Pres. Sergio Drioli.

Contact Details: Via Cassa di Risparmio 10, 34121 Trieste; tel. (40) 300589; internet itsweb.org.

Fondazione Lelio e Lisli Basso Issoco—Sezione Internazionale (Lelio and Lisli Basso Foundation Onlus)

Founded in 2005 following the merger of the Fondazione Lelio e Lisli Basso-Issoco (f. 1974) and the Fondazione Internazionale Lelio Basso per il Diritto e la Liberazione dei Popoli.

Activities: Works in the fields of the environment, development studies and human rights. The Foundation promotes information exchange between politicians, academics and lawyers concerned with human rights issues; offers grants to individuals for research; operates training courses and workshops; and organizes seminars and conferences. It has a library containing more than 120,000 vols and 100 current journals, and an archive.

Geographical Area of Activity: Worldwide.

Publications: Newsletter (quarterly); catalogues; numerous publications on human rights issues.

Board of Directors: Franco Ippolito (Chair.); Fausto Tortora (Vice-Chair.).

Principal Staff: Sec.-Gen Germana Capellini.

Contact Details: Via della Dogana Vecchia 5, 00186 Rome; tel. (06) 6879953; e-mail basso@fondazionebasso.it; internet www.fondazionebasso.it.

Fondazione Luigi Einaudi (Luigi Einaudi Foundation)

Founded in 1964 by the family of Luigi Einaudi, former President of Italy, with the help of local financial institutions and the Italian Government.

Activities: Operates internationally, collaborating with the Colegio de México in Mexico and Cornell University in the USA, carrying out research into the effect of property on agricultural productivity in Europe and Central and South America; and develops projects on regional integration, conflict resolution, comparative models of employment and social policy, and contemporary political thought. The Foundation awards fellowships and research grants; organizes seminars and conferences; and sponsors publications in the fields of economics, politics and history. It also maintains the Luigi Einaudi Library, which contains more than 270,000 vols and 3,880 periodicals.

Geographical Area of Activity: Mainly Italy.

Publications: *Annali della Fondazione Luigi Einaudi*; *Scrittori italiani di politica, economia e storia* (collection of classics); *Studi* (collection of monographs).

Board of Directors: Prof. Domenico Siniscalco (Pres.).

Contact Details: Palazzo d'Azeglio, Via Principe Amedeo 34, 10123 Turin; tel. (011) 835656; e-mail informazioni@fondazioneeinaudi.it; internet www.fondazioneeinaudi.it.

Fondazione Nazionale Carlo Collodi (National Carlo Collodi Foundation)

Established in 1962 to disseminate the works of Carlo Lorenzini (Collodi), the author of *The Adventures of Pinocchio*.

Activities: Operates nationally through self-conducted programmes and grants to individuals, and nationally and internationally through conferences, courses, publications, exhibitions and lectures. The Foundation maintains a library of more than 6,000 works by and about Collodi, including translations; it maintains the Pinocchio Park in Collodi (Italy); and manages the Historical Garzoni Garden with the Collodi Butterfly House. It designs and implements national and European projects on educational and cultural subjects, and is a training provider.

Geographical Area of Activity: Worldwide.

Publications: *Quaderni della Fondazione Nazionale Carlo Collodi*; *Le Avventure di Pinocchio Official*; art catalogues; conference proceedings; research papers.

Council and Executive Committee: Dr Pier Francesco Bernacchi (Pres.); Dr Davide Battistini (Sec.-Gen.).

Contact Details: Via Pasquinelli 6, 51012 Collodi; tel. (0572) 429613; e-mail fondazione@pinocchio.it; internet www.fondazionecollodi.it.

Fondazione Piera, Pietro e Giovanni Ferrero (Piera, Pietro and Giovanni Ferrero Foundation)

Established in 1983, as Opera Sociale Ferrero, by Michele Ferrero, a business person and owner of Ferrero, a confectionery company; formally recognized as a foundation in 1991.

Activities: Promotes quality of life for older people and their mental and physical wellbeing, through supporting cultural and social activities and collaborating with a network of medical centres. The Foundation works with local, national and international foundations and institutions, supporting and organizing projects and conferences in the fields of science and research; arts and culture; economics and social sciences; and the cultural history of the Alba and Piedmont regions. It offers national and international scholarships to the children of Ferrero employees and pensioners for scientific and doctoral research; and hosts the Beppe Fenoglio Documentation Centre.

Geographical Area of Activity: France, Germany, Italy.

Publications: *Filodiretto* (magazine); and other publications.

Board of Directors: Maria Franca Ferrero (Pres.); Margherita Fenoglio (Vice-Pres.).

Principal Staff: Dir Bartolomeo Salomone.

Contact Details: Via Vivaro 49, 12051 Alba; tel. (0173) 295259; e-mail info@fondazioneferrero.it; internet www.fondazioneferrero.it.

Fondazione Prada (Prada Foundation)

Established in 1993 by fashion designer Miuccia Prada and her husband, Patrizio Bertelli.

Activities: Curates exhibitions and organizes cultural symposia; also produces visual art exhibitions. The Foundation maintains a collection of catalogues, monographs and artists' books. Has an office in Venice.

Geographical Area of Activity: Europe.

Publications: Newsletter; catalogues; books on architecture; conference proceedings.

Board of Trustees: Miuccia Prada (Pres. and Dir).

Principal Staff: Dir-Gen. Cristian Valsecchi.

Contact Details: Largo Isarco 2, 20139 Milan; tel. (02) 56662611; e-mail info@fondazioneprada.org; internet www.fondazioneprada.org.

Fondazione Querini Stampalia—FQS (Querini Stampalia Foundation)

Founded in 1869 by Count Giovanni Querini.

Activities: Operates in the field of the arts and humanities. The Foundation organizes seminars, conferences, training courses, exhibitions, educational activities and laboratories; and issues publications. It has a publicly accessible library of nearly 400,000 vols; and a museum containing 18th-century and neoclassical furniture, porcelain, bisque, sculpture, globes, and paintings from the 14th to the 20th centuries, mostly from the Venetian school.

Geographical Area of Activity: Europe.

Publications: Newsletter; historical and cultural publications.

Finance: Annual income €2.8m., expenditure €2.8m. (2022).

Board of Trustees: Paolo Molesini (Pres.); Donatella Calabi (Vice-Pres.).

Principal Staff: Dir Cristiana Collu.

Contact Details: Campo Santa Maria Formosa, Castello 5252, 30122 Venice; tel. (041) 2711415; e-mail fondazione@querinistampalia.org; internet www.querinistampalia.org.

Fondazione Rodolfo Debenedetti—FRDB (Foundation Rodolfo Debenedetti)

Established in 1998 by Carlo de Benedetti in memory of his father, an engineer and founder of several vehicle parts manufacturing companies.

Activities: Supports policy-orientated research on topics including: reform of public pension systems; causes of European unemployment; co-ordination of social and immigration policies in the EU; poverty, inequality and the role welfare systems play; and homelessness. The Foundation also organizes conferences and maintains a public documentation centre on social policy reforms and EU labour markets.

Geographical Area of Activity: Europe.

Publications: *Note Rapide* (online newsletter); conference proceedings; papers; reports; books.

Board: Carlo de Benedetti (Pres.).

Principal Staff: Co-ordinator Prof. Paolo Pinotti.

Contact Details: Via Roentgen 1, Room 5.C1-11, 20136 Milan; tel. (02) 58363342; e-mail info@frdb.org; internet www.frdb.org.

Fondazione Roma (Rome Foundation)

Established in 1836 as the Cassa di Risparmio di Roma.

Activities: Provides social benefits and promotes economic development through carrying out self-conducted programmes and supporting NGO initiatives in the areas of: health; fine arts and cultural heritage; education; scientific research; and aid to disadvantaged people. The Foundation funds hospitals and health centres; operates an exhibition space and has established a youth orchestra; supports a Master's Course in International Studies on Philanthropy; and sponsors the Centre for the Dissemination of the Results of Agricultural Research—CEDRA. It also operates through the Fondazione Italiana per il Volontariato (f. 1991), which promotes, encourages and supports voluntary service; and the Fondazione Europa Occupazione: Impresa e Solidarietà (f. 1995), which fosters occupational opportunities, through training activities for young people, disabled people and socially disadvantaged people.

Geographical Area of Activity: Italy (with focus on the province of Rome and the region of Lazio).

Restrictions: No funding for profit-making organizations, individuals and enterprises.

Publications: Newsletter; *NFR Notiziario Fondazione Roma* (quarterly magazine); TTR series (conference proceedings).

Finance: Total assets €1,923.5m. (31 Dec. 2024).

Board of Directors: Franco Parasassi (Pres.).

Contact Details: Palazzo Sciarra, Via Marco Minghetti 17, 00187 Rome; tel. (06) 697645100; e-mail info@fondazioneroma.it; internet www.fondazioneroma.it.

Fondazione Romaeuropa (Romaeuropa Foundation)

Established in 1986 as Associazione degli Amici di Villa Medici, a Franco-Italian initiative; present name adopted in 1990.

Activities: Administers and promotes the Romaeuropa Festival for contemporary culture.

Geographical Area of Activity: Italy.

Publications: Annual Report; newsletter.

Board of Directors: Guido Fabiani (Pres.); Claudia Fellus (Vice-Pres.).

Principal Staff: Artistic and Man. Dir Fabrizio Grifasi.

Contact Details: Opificio Romaeuropa, Via dei Magazzini Generali 20A, 00154 Rome; tel. (06) 45553000; e-mail romaeuropa@romaeuropa.net; internet romaeuropa.net/fondazione.

Fondazione RUI (RUI Foundation)

Established in 1959 by university teachers, professional workers and parents.

Activities: Promotes the further training of university students and intellectuals, and cultural activities for young people; awards scholarships to Italian and foreign students, collaborating with national and international organizations to these ends. The Foundation operates nationally in the field of the arts and humanities; and nationally and internationally in the fields of education, social welfare and studies. It is also active in the fields of international relations and aid to less-developed countries. Programmes are carried out internationally through self-conducted projects, and nationally and internationally through research, fellowships and scholarships, conferences, courses, publications and lectures. Has an office in Rome.

Geographical Area of Activity: Europe.

Publications: *Fondazione Rui* (magazine); *Universitas* (magazine); guides on higher education in Italy.

Board of Directors: Prof. Giuseppe Ghini (Pres.).

Principal Staff: Dir Francesca Travaglini.

Contact Details: Via Domenichino 16, 20149 Milan; tel. (02) 48010813; e-mail info@fondazionerui.it; internet www.fondazionerui.it.

Fondazione Salvatore Maugeri—Clinica del Lavoro e della Riabilitazione (Salvatore Maugeri Foundation—Occupational Health and Rehabilitation Clinic)

Founded in 1965, as the Fondazione Pro Clinica del Lavoro di Pavia, by Prof. Salvatore Maugeri; present name adopted in 1995. In 2013 it merged with the Fondazione Europea Riabilitazione e Sport.

Activities: Supports medical clinics and institutes that carry out research of international significance in the field of occupational diseases. The Foundation also supports five medical centres for cardio-respiratory and neurological rehabilitation. In total, it comprises 18 scientific institutes.

Geographical Area of Activity: Italy.

Publications: Newsletter; brochure.

Board of Directors: Dr Luca Damiani (Pres.); Chiara Maugeri (Vice-Pres.).

Contact Details: Via Salvatore Maugeri 4, 27100 Pavia; tel. (0382) 592504; e-mail comunicazione@fsm.it; internet www.fsm.it.

Fondazione Social Venture-Giordano Dell'Amore (Giordano Dell'Amore Social Venture Foundation)

Established in 2018 by the merger of the Fondazione Giordano Dell'Amore (f. 1977) and the Fondazione Social Venture (f. 1950s) within the Fondazione Cariplo (q.v.) Social Innovation programme.

Activities: Works in the fields of social impact investment and sustainable finance. The Foundation promotes and supports innovative and sustainable activities in the third sector that have social and environmental benefits; and the growth of skills and professionalism in the sector.

Geographical Area of Activity: Worldwide.

Publications: Newsletter; *Impact Weekly Report*; evaluations; reports.

Board of Directors: Prof. Cristian Chizzoli (Pres.).

Contact Details: Via Bernardino Zenale 8, 20123 Milan; tel. (02) 36683000; e-mail info@fsvgda.it; internet www.fondazionesocialventuregda.it.

Fondazione Terzo Pilastro – Internazionale

Founded in 2007 as the Fondazione Roma—Terzo Settore by the merger of the Fondazione Italiana per il Volontariato—FIVOL (f. 1991) and the Fondazione Europa Occupazione—Impresa e Solidarietà (f. 1995). Present name adopted in 2014 following merger with the Fondazione Roma-Mediterraneo (f. 2008); an initiative of the Fondazione Roma (q.v.).

Activities: Works in the fields of health; education and training; art and culture; scientific research; support for vulnerable groups; and job creation schemes. The Foundation promotes and supports social enterprise and voluntary work. It manages the Fondazione Miglioranzi, which supports people in financial need; and collaborates on medical research with the Biogem consortium, an initiative of the Italian National Research Council and several Italian universities and research centres. Has representative offices in Catania, Cosenza, Naples and Palermo; and abroad in Rabat, Morocco, and Madrid and Valencia, Spain.

Geographical Area of Activity: Italy, Mediterranean region, Middle East.

Publications: Newsletter; brochure; research reports; studies; books.

Board of Directors: Prof. Emmanuele F. M. Emanuele (Chair.).

Contact Details: Piazza di Monte Citorio 115, 00186 Rome; tel. (06) 97625591; e-mail fondazione@fondazioneterzopilastrointernazionale.it; internet www.fondazioneterzopilastrointernazionale.it.

Fondazione Ugo Bordoni (Ugo Bordoni Foundation)

Founded in 1952 by Cesare Albanese, Albino Antinori, Felice Calvanese, Antonio Carrelli, Romolo De Caterini, Andrea Ferrara-Toniolo, Alberto Fornò, Vittorio Gori, Ernesto Lensi, Algeri Marino, Enrico Medi, Michele Paris, Giuseppe Spataro and Scipione Treves; the Foundation was reconstituted in 2000.

Activities: Operates in the fields of electronics and communications, through research and publications, mainly in co-operation with the Istituto Superiore delle Comunicazioni e delle Tecnologie dell'Informazione (Advanced Institute for Communications and Information Technology). The Foundation works with national and international bodies.

Geographical Area of Activity: Italy.

Publications: Annual Report; magazines; conference proceedings; books.

Board of Directors: Dr Giovanna Bianchi Clerici (Pres.).

Principal Staff: Dir Gen. Alessio Zagaglia.

Contact Details: Viale del Policlinico 147, 00161 Rome; tel. (06) 54801; e-mail info@fub.it; internet www.fub.it.

ITALY

Fondazione Unipolis (Unipolis Foundation)

Established in 2007 by Unipol Gruppo Finanziario as successor to the Fondazione Cesarm (f. 1989), which was formerly known as the Centro Europeo di Ricerca dell'Economia Sociale e dell'Assicurazione per iniziativa dell'allora Unipol Assicurazioni.

Activities: Funds non-profit organizations in the areas of the arts and culture, social welfare, work and mobility. Under its 'Culturability' programme, the Foundation awards grants of up to €20,000 to co-operative start-ups in the culture sector.

Geographical Area of Activity: Italy.

Publications: Annual Report; newsletter.

Board of Directors: Carlo Cimbri (Pres.); Milo Pacchioni (Vice-Pres.); Alessandro Nerdi (Sec.).

Principal Staff: CEO Maria Luisa Parmigiani.

Contact Details: Via Stalingrado 53, 40128 Bologna; tel. (051) 6437601; e-mail info@fondazioneunipolis.org; internet www.fondazioneunipolis.org.

Fondazione di Venezia (Venice Foundation)

Established in 1992 by the Cassa di Risparmio di Venezia.

Activities: Active in the areas of education, training, scientific research, conservation and culture, through self-conducted programmes and projects, direct grants and co-operation with other organizations. The Foundation comprises M9 District Srl (f. 2000, formerly known as Polymnia Venezia), which carries out training and research in the fields of the arts and cultural heritage; and Fondazione M9, Museo del 900, which specializes in the history of Italy and Italians in the 20th century.

Geographical Area of Activity: Mainly Venice, Italy.

Publications: Annual Report; newsletter; conference reports; exhibition catalogues; studies.

Finance: Total assets €389.4m.; net annual income €2.6m. (31 Dec. 2022).

Board of Directors: Michele Bugliesi (Pres.); Vincenzo Marinese Maiola (Vice-Pres.).

Principal Staff: Gen. Sec. Giorgia Zanon; Gen. Man. Giovanni Dell'Olivo.

Contact Details: Dorsoduro 3488/U, 30123 Venice; tel. (041) 2201211; e-mail segreteria@fondazionedivenezia.org; internet www.fondazionedivenezia.org.

Fondazione Vodafone Italia (Vodafone Italy Foundation)

Established in 2002 by Vodafone Italia, a telecommunications company; part of the Vodafone Foundation (q.v.) network.

Activities: Promotes integration of the most vulnerable people through the use of digital technology. Main programmes are: Apps for Good, developing mobile apps for social participation; Connected Education, which supports initiatives to provide basic digital skills education to people aged 18–22 years not in education or employment; and Connected Health, which supports initiatives that improve the wellbeing of people with diseases and disabilities, and foster scientific research. The Foundation also supports community-based projects in the areas of territorial development, schools and the development of southern Italy.

Geographical Area of Activity: Italy.

Publications: Annual Report.

Finance: Total assets €1.7m. (31 March 2021).

Board of Directors: Marinella Soldi (Pres.).

Contact Details: Piazza SS Apostoli 81, 00187 Rome; tel. (06) 50921; e-mail info@fondazionevodafone.it; internet www.vodafone.it/portal/vodafone-italia/fondazione-vodafone.

Institute for Scientific Interchange Foundation—ISI

Established in 1983 to promote international co-operation in scientific research.

International Development Law Organization

Activities: Operates in the field of science and technology, through funding scientific programmes, and carrying out research to encourage and support science. The Institute is particularly interested in the study of complex systems and complexity science. Other research areas include: data science; computational social science; citizen science and smart cities; computational epidemiology and public health; collective phenomena in physics and materials science; quantum science and mathematics of networks; and mathematics and foundation of complex systems. In 2014 it established the ISI Global Science Foundation in New York, USA, with the Fondazione Sviluppo e Crescita CRT.

Geographical Area of Activity: International.

Principal Staff: Vice-Pres. Pierluigi Poggiolini.

Contact Details: Via Chisola 5, 10126 Turin; tel. (011) 6603090; e-mail isi@isi.it; internet www.isi.it.

International Balzan Prize Foundation (Fondazione Internazionale Premio Balzan)

Founded in 1956 by Angela Lina Balzan in memory of her father, Eugenio Balzan, an Italian journalist, who died in 1953.

Activities: Acts through two foundations jointly, the International Balzan Foundation 'Fund' in Zurich, under Swiss law, which manages the estate of Eugenio Balzan; and the International Balzan Foundation 'Prize' in Milan, under Italian law, whose General Prize Committee, composed of eminent European scholars and scientists, chooses the subject areas of the awards and makes the nominations each year. The Foundation awards four prizes annually, each worth 750,000 Swiss francs: two in the social sciences, literature and the arts; and two in physical, mathematical and natural sciences and medicine. At intervals of no less than three years, the Foundation also awards a prize for Humanity, Peace and Fraternity among Peoples, to a person or organization for outstanding humanitarian work. In 2023 the four prize categories are: World Literature; Evolution of Humankind: Paleoanthropology; Evolution of Humankind: Ancient DNA and Human Evolution; High resolution images: from planetary to cosmic objects.

Geographical Area of Activity: Worldwide.

Restrictions: Does not accept self-applications; one-half of each prize awarded must be used to finance research projects, carried out by young scholars or scientists.

Publications: Newsletter; annual *Premi Balzan*; *The Annual Balzan Lecture*.

Fund Board (Italy): Cristina Messa (Pres.); Laura Laera (Vice-Pres.).

Fund Board (Switzerland): Gisèle Girgis-Musy (Pres.).

Contact Details: Piazzetta Umberto Giordano 4, 20122 Milan; tel. (02) 76002212; e-mail balzan@balzan.it; balzan@balzan.ch; internet www.balzan.org.

International Development Law Organization—IDLO (Organisation Internationale de Droit du Développement—OIDD)

Established in 1983 by L. Michael Hager, Gilles Blanchi and William Loris.

Activities: Enables governments and empowers people to reform laws and strengthen institutions. Programme areas include: the rule of law; peace and democracy; access to justice; women and girls; public health; sustainability; and economic opportunity. The Organization works in a range of fields, including peace and institution building, and assisting economic recovery in countries emerging from conflict and striving towards democracy. It comprises a network of thousands of experts and alumni associations; with offices in The Hague (Netherlands), Geneva (Switzerland) and New York (USA), and observer status at the UN; and country offices in Burkina Faso, Honduras, Indonesia, Jordan, Kenya, Kyrgyzstan, Liberia, Mali, Moldova, Mongolia, Philippines, Tunisia, Uganda and Ukraine.

Geographical Area of Activity: International.

Publications: Annual Report; guides; guidelines; reports; toolkits.

Finance: Governments, multilateral development organizations, foundations and private companies contribute towards the Organization's budget, programme and fellowship requirements. Annual revenue €34.9m., expenditure €36.7m. (31 Dec. 2023).
Principal Staff: Dir-Gen. Jan Beagle.
Contact Details: Viale Vaticano 106, 00165 Rome; tel. (06) 40403200; e-mail info@idlo.int; internet www.idlo.int.

International Fund for Agricultural Development—IFAD

Founded in 1977; a specialized agency of the UN.
Activities: Works with poor rural people to enable them to grow and sell more food, increase their incomes and determine the direction of their own lives. The organization focuses on small, family farms and young people. Since 1978 it has invested more than US $18,500m. in grants and low-interest loans to developing countries. Operates as a partnership of 177 member countries.
Geographical Area of Activity: International.
Publications: *IFAD Annual Report* (in Arabic, English, French and Spanish); e-newsletters; *Rural Development Report*; *IFAD Research Series*; impact assessments; toolkits; blog; books.
Finance: Annual revenue US $440.1m., expenditure $695.0m. (31 Dec. 2023).
Principal Staff: Pres. Alvaro Lario.
Contact Details: Via Paolo di Dono 44, 00142 Rome; tel. (06) 54591; e-mail ifad@ifad.org; internet www.ifad.org.

INTERSOS

Established in 1992; has consultative status with ECOSOC.
Activities: Helps people at risk and victims of natural disasters and armed conflicts, providing first aid, food, shelter, medical assistance and basic goods. The organization has an office in Geneva, Switzerland. It has had projects in 52 countries.
Geographical Area of Activity: Italy, Greece, Middle East and North Africa, sub-Saharan Africa, Switzerland.
Publications: Annual Report.
Finance: Annual income €113.3m., expenditure €112.9m. (31 Dec. 2023).
Board of Directors: Nino Sergi (Pres. Emeritus).
Principal Staff: Gen. Man. and Interim Pres. Konstantinos Moschochoritis.
Contact Details: Via Aniene 26A, 00198 Rome; tel. (06) 8537431; e-mail intersos@intersos.org; internet www.intersos.org.

Istituto Affari Internazionali—IAI (Institute of International Affairs)

Founded in 1965 by Altiero Spinelli, a politician and political theorist.
Activities: Promotes research, often in collaboration with research institutes of other countries, and belongs to a number of international networks of research centres. Areas of interest include: defence; energy, climate and resources; EU, politics and institutions; international economy, global governance; Italian foreign policy; non-proliferation and disarmament; safety; technology and international relations; and young people. The Institute organizes national and international conferences in international relations. It has a library containing more than 27,000 books and periodicals.
Geographical Area of Activity: International.
Publications: *The International Spectator* (quarterly English language review); *IAI News* (newsletter); *IAI Research Papers* (series, irregular); *Quaderni IAI* (series, irregular); *AffarInternazionali* (webzine); books.
Board of Trustees: Michele Valensise (Pres.); Ettore Greco, Michele Nones, Pier Carlo Padoan (Vice-Pres); Simone Romano (Treas.).
Principal Staff: Dir Nathalie Tocci; Deputy Dir Federica Di Camillo.
Contact Details: Via dei Montecatini 17, 00186 Rome; tel. (06) 6976831; e-mail iai@iai.it; internet www.iai.it.

Istituto Carlo Cattaneo (Carlo Cattaneo Institute)

Founded in 1965 by a group of academic scientific publishers; granted foundation status in 1986.
Activities: Promotes democratic values through the dissemination of research findings on politics and social science. The Institute conducts research, studies and activities relating to culture and education, particularly in the fields of social and political science. It disseminates knowledge about Italian society, especially regarding its political system.
Geographical Area of Activity: Italy.
Publications: Newsletter; *Polis. Ricerche e studi su società e politica in Italia* (journal); *Politica in Italia/Italian Politics* (annual); *Polis* (quarterly); *Ricerche e studi dell-Istituto Cattaneo*; *Stranieri in Italia*; *Elezioni, Governi, democrazia*; *Cultura in Italia*; *Misure e Materiali di Ricerca dell'Istituto Cattaneo*.
Principal Staff: Pres. Asher Colombo; Dir Salvatore Vassallo.
Contact Details: Strada Maggiore 37, 40125 Bologna; tel. (351) 7851417; e-mail istitutocattaneo@cattaneo.org; internet www.cattaneo.org.

Istituto Luigi Sturzo (Luigi Sturzo Institute)

Founded in 1951 by a committee in honour of Luigi Sturzo, a priest and founder of the Italian Popular Party (PPI).
Activities: Works in the fields of history and the social sciences, through research, conferences and discussions, offering scholarships and issuing publications. The Institute works with European and international research institutes; and awards prizes to Italian and foreign scholars. It has a library, comprising 140,000 vols and 600 periodicals.
Geographical Area of Activity: Italy.
Publications: Annual Report; *Sociologia* (3 a year); scientific studies.
Board of Directors: Nicola Antonetti (Chair.).
Principal Staff: Sec.-Gen. Daniele Angelini.
Contact Details: Palazzo Baldassini, Via delle Coppelle 35, 00186 Rome; tel. (06) 6840421; e-mail infopoint@sturzo.it; internet www.sturzo.it.

Istituto di Ricerche Farmacologiche Mario Negri (Mario Negri Pharmacological Research Institute)

Founded in 1961 by the will of Mario Negri; formally recognized by the Italian Government in 2013 as a Scientific Institute for Research and Care, specializing in neurological, rare and environmental diseases.
Activities: Operates in the fields of education, science and medicine, through self-conducted biomedical research programmes. The Foundation offers research fellowships and scholarships; organizes conferences, courses and lectures; and issues publications. Research institutes are also situated in Bergamo and Ranica (Bergamo), comprising 50 laboratories.
Geographical Area of Activity: International.
Publications: *Negri News* (monthly); *Research and Practice* (6 a year); scientific reports; books; journals.
Finance: Total assets €74.2m. (2023).
Board of Directors: Prof. Silvio Angelo Garattini (Chair.); Dr Cristina Russo (Vice-Chair.).
Supervisory Board: Ida Gigliotti (Chair.).
Principal Staff: Dir Prof. Giuseppe Remuzzi.
Contact Details: Via Mario Negri 2, 20156 Milan; tel. (02) 390141; e-mail comunicazione@marionegri.it; internet www.marionegri.it.

ITALY

Istituto per gli Studi di Politica Internazionale—ISPI
(Italian Institute for International Political Studies)

Established in 1934 with the support of a group of business people led by Alberto Pirelli, the founder of tyre manufacturer Pirelli SpA.

Activities: Carries out sociopolitical and economic policy research and anlysis. Programme areas include: Africa; energy security; Latin America; global cities; migration; transatlantic relations; religions; and international relations; with specific desks for China, India and Iran. There are also observatories for: Asia; cybersecurity; Europe and global governance; geoeconomics; the Middle East and North Africa; radicalization and international terrorism; the Russian Federation, the Caucasus and Central Asia; and infrastructure. The Institute offers training and postgraduate and short courses through the ISPI School; and organizes conferences, seminars and research workshops.

Geographical Area of Activity: International.

Publications: *Daily Focus* (newsletter); *Dossier*; *Focus*; *Fact Checking*; *Watch* (business scenarios); *Commentaries*; reports; policy papers.

Finance: Total assets €5.3m. (31 Dec. 2022).

Presidency: Franco Bruni (Pres.); Carlo Altomonte, Emma Marcegaglia (Vice-Pres).

Principal Staff: Man. Dir Paolo Magri; Sec.-Gen. Francesco Rocchetti.

Contact Details: Palazzo Clerici, Via Clerici 5, 20121 Milan; tel. (02) 8633131; e-mail ispi@ispionline.it; internet www.ispionline.it.

Mani Tese (Outstretched Hands)

Established in 1964; became a federation in 2017.

Activities: Operates self-conducted programmes with local partners. Main programmes focus on food sovereignty, environmental justice, human rights for all and education for global citizenship. The organization also runs training courses in development studies; lobbies and campaigns on related issues; organizes conferences; and maintains a reference library of around 20,000 publications. It comprises 13 federated organizations in Italy; and has consultative status with ECOSOC.

Geographical Area of Activity: Benin, Burkina Faso, Guinea-Bissau, Italy, Kenya, Mozambique.

Publications: Newsletter; *Mani Tese* (monthly newspaper); audiovisual aids; brochures; educational materials; pamphlets; books.

Finance: Annual revenue €4.3m., expenditure €4.4m. (31 Dec. 2023).

Board of Directors: Giuseppe Stanganello (Pres.); Micol Dell'Oro (Vice-Pres.).

Principal Staff: Dir Marino Langiu.

Contact Details: Piazzale Rodolfo Morandi 2, 20121 Milan; tel. (02) 4075165; e-mail manitese@manitese.it; internet www.manitese.it.

Oxfam Italia

Established in 1970 as Ucodep; became part of the Oxfam confederation of organizations (qq.v.) in 2010.

Activities: Works to eliminate the causes of poverty, with a focus on inequality, discrimination against women and climate change. Nationally, programmes include: supporting asylum seekers and refugees, promoting autonomy, integration and social inclusion; helping vulnerable people living in poverty; and supporting educational activities in schools. Internationally, the organization responds to humanitarian emergencies; and carries out long-term programmes in the areas of sustainable agriculture and rural development, providing access to water, health and education. It comprises Cooperativa Oxfam Italia Intercultura, which promotes the integration and active citizenship of migrants through educational, social, health and cultural interventions; and Cooperativa Oxfam Italia Commercio Equo, which promotes fair trade and operates three charity shops.

Geographical Area of Activity: International.

Restrictions: Does not make loans or grants to individuals.

Publications: Annual Report; newsletter; case studies; immigration reports; research reports.

Finance: Annual income €18.6m., expenditure €18.5m. (31 March 2022).

Board of Directors: Emilia Romano (Chair.).

Principal Staff: Man. Dir Roberto Barbieri.

Contact Details: Via Pierluigi da Palestrina 26/r, 50144 Florence; tel. (055) 3220895; e-mail sostenitori@oxfamitalia.org; internet www.oxfamitalia.org.

SID—Society for International Development

Established in 1957; a global network.

Activities: The Society for International Development (SID) is an international network of individuals and organizations that promotes socioeconomic justice and fosters democratic participation in development. Through programmes and activities at national, regional, and global levels, SID strengthens collective knowledge and action on people-centered development strategies and promotes policy change towards inclusiveness, equity, and sustainability. SID has approximately 3,000 members and works with local chapters, institutional members, and partner organizations in more than 50 countries. SID's activities are facilitated by an International Secretariat with offices in Rome (headquarters) and Nairobi.

Geographical Area of Activity: International.

Publications: *Development* (quarterly journal); programme-based reports, books and other publications.

Governing Council: Larry Cooley (Pres.).

Principal Staff: Man. Dir Stefano Prato; Deputy Man. Dir Arthur Muliro.

Contact Details: Via degli Etruschi 7, 00185 Rome; tel. (06) 4872172; e-mail sidsec.rom@sidint.org; internet www.sidint.org.

Svenska Institutet i Rom/Istituto Svedese di Studi Classici a Roma (Swedish Institute in Rome)

Founded in 1925 by Crown Prince Gustaf Adolf and others.

Activities: Operates internationally in the fields of archaeology, philology, art and architecture. The Institute carries out excavations and research; offers fellowships, scholarships and travel grants; organizes conferences, courses and lectures; and issues publications. It has a research library containing around 70,000 vols and 200 periodicals; and also has an archaeological laboratory.

Geographical Area of Activity: International.

Publications: *Skrifter utgivna av Svenska Institutet i Rom*; *Opuscula: Annual of the Swedish Institutes at Athens and Rome*; *Suecoromana: Studia artis historiae Instituti Romani Regni Sueciae*.

Board of Directors: Göran Blomqvist (Pres.); Johan Eriksson (Vice-Pres.); Agneta Modig Tham (Treas.); Lovisa Brännstedt (Sec.).

Principal Staff: Dir Dr Ulf R. Hansson; Deputy Dir Sabrina Norlander Eliasson.

Contact Details: Via Omero 14, Valle Giulia, 00197 Rome; tel. (06) 3201596; e-mail info@isvroma.org; internet www.isvroma.org.

UniCredit Foundation

Established in 2003 by UniCredito Italiano, a banking and financial services group; in 2018 it merged with UniCredit & Universities Foscolo Foundation.

Activities: Works in the fields of health, the environment, training and education. Main programmes include: Solidarity, with a focus on supporting children and young people aged 0–18 years; Open Rehearsals, which allows audiences previews of Filarmonica della Scala orchestral concerts, with the proceeds from ticket sales being donated to non-profit organizations; and Call for Europe, which provides grants to non-

JAMAICA

FOUNDATIONS AND NON-PROFITS

Culture, Health, Arts, Sports and Education Fund—CHASE

Established in 2002 to administer, manage and distribute monetary contributions from the Jamaican lottery companies.

Activities: Supports initiatives in the areas of: arts and culture, improving libraries and archives, restoring and maintaining cultural heritage and offering scholarships in the visual performing and fine arts; early childhood education, building, renovating and equipping education and resource centres, supporting the development of educational materials, improving nutrition and offering scholarships for specialist training in early childhood education; health, building, renovating and equipping health facilities, providing healthcare training for staff and developing programmes for the prevention, detection, treatment and care of renal disease and cancer; and sport, supporting the Sports Development Foundation and administering the annual Courtney Walsh Award, worth US $500,000, offered to sportspeople who have represented Jamaica at senior level.

Geographical Area of Activity: Jamaica.

Publications: Annual Report.

Finance: Annual income J $194.1m., expenditure $173.5m. (31 March 2023).

Board of Directors: Omar Frith (Chair.).

Principal Staff: CEO W. Billy Heaven.

Contact Details: 8 Belmont Rd, Kingston 5; tel. 908-4134; e-mail chase12@cwjamaica.com; internet www.chase.org.jm.

Digicel Foundation Jamaica

Established in 2004 by Digicel, a telecommunications company; part of the Digicel Foundation network.

Activities: Programmes focus on: primary education; community development; social enterprise; and special needs. The Foundation offers grants and micro-grants for large projects and community initiatives, respectively. Independent foundations operate in Haiti, Papua New Guinea, and Trinidad and Tobago.

Geographical Area of Activity: Jamaica.

Publications: Annual Report.

Finance: Annual income US $2.2m., expenditure $2.1m. (31 March 2023).

Board of Directors: Maria Mulcahy (Global Chair.); Joy Clark (Chair.); Antonia Graham (Vice-Chair.).

Principal Staff: CEO Charmaine Daniels.

Contact Details: 14 Ocean Blvd, Kingston; tel. 619-5179; e-mail digicelfoundationja@digicelgroup.com; internet www.digicelfoundation.org/jm/en.

Environmental Foundation of Jamaica

Established in 1993 under a formal agreement between the Governments of Jamaica and the USA as an independent foundation.

Activities: Works in the fields of children's welfare and the environment. The Foundation helps children with special needs; supports at-risk children and adolescents, providing job and life skills training; and provides training in early childhood development for parents, teachers and caregivers. It established the Forest Conservation Fund to promote the protection and sustainable management of natural resources; and promotes innovation in research and development in the sustainable use of natural resources.

Geographical Area of Activity: Jamaica.

Publications: Annual Report; brochure; public lecture booklets (annual); blog brochures.

Board of Directors: Prof. Dale Webber (Chair.); Eleanor Jones (Vice-Chair.); Ian Watson (Treas.); Jennifer Scott (Sec.).

Principal Staff: CEO Barrington Lewis.

Contact Details: 1B Norwood Ave, Kingston 5; tel. 960-6744; e-mail support@efj.org.jm; internet www.efj.org.jm.

JN Foundation

Established in 1990 as the charitable arm of Jamaica National Group, a financial services provider.

Activities: Main programmes focus on: social empowerment; skills and personal development; education; and health and environment. The Foundation provides financial and technical support to projects and programmes at community and national level in the areas of rural development, health, housing, education, youth, community, and crime and safety. It also awards scholarships for secondary and tertiary education.

Geographical Area of Activity: Jamaica.

Publications: Annual Report.

Board: Parris A. Lyew-Ayee (Chair.).

Principal Staff: CEO Earl Jarrett; Gen. Man. Claudine Allen.

Contact Details: 17 Belmont Rd, Kingston 5; tel. 926-1344; e-mail jnfoundation@jngroup.com; internet www.jnfoundation.com.

Sandals Foundation

Established in 2009 by Gordon 'Butch' Stewart; the philanthropic arm of Sandals Resorts International.

Activities: Invests in initiatives that have a positive and sustainable impact in the areas of education, community and the environment. Main programme areas are: enhancing education through literacy, curriculum development, school renovation and scholarship grants for students and teachers; health and wellbeing, improving access to healthcare through providing medical equipment to health centres and training local staff; sustainable futures, empowering women and offering vocational and technical skills training to marginalized people; wildlife and marine conservation; and youth engagement, offering sport, music and communication programmes. The Foundation also funds disaster relief and recovery efforts.

Geographical Area of Activity: Canada, Caribbean, UK, USA.

Publications: Annual Report; newsletter.

Finance: Annual income US $13.6m., expenditure $13.3m. (30 June 2023).

Board of Directors: Adam Stewart (Pres.).

Principal Staff: Exec. Dir Heidi Clarke.

Contact Details: 38–42 Lady Musgrave Rd, Kingston 5; tel. 979-9130; e-mail foundation@grp.sandals.com; internet www.sandalsfoundation.org.

Usain Bolt Foundation

Established in 2011 by Usain Bolt, an athlete and Olympic and World Champion.

Activities: Activities focus on children's education and cultural development. The Foundation also funds health and sports initiatives and disaster relief.

Geographical Area of Activity: Caribbean (mainly Jamaica).

Board: Rev. Winsome Williams (Chair.); Nicole Foga (Sec.).

Contact Details: Unit 20, Ardenne Emirates, 7–9 Ardenne Rd, St Andrew; e-mail usainboltfoundation1@gmail.com; internet usainbolt.com/foundation.

JAPAN

CO-ORDINATING BODIES

JANIC—Japanese NGO Center for International Co-operation

Established in 1987.

Activities: Provides services for the development of NGOs. The Center promotes networking between domestic and international NGOs and related organizations; and dialogue between NGOs and other sectors of society. It fosters public understanding of and support for the activities of NGOs; conducts research on NGOs and international co-operation; maintains a library and database on NGOs; runs courses and training programmes and hosts meetings; lobbies the Japanese Government and business; and promotes educational activities, including the 'Global Citizenship Education Caravan'. Comprises more than 100 member organizations.

Geographical Area of Activity: Japan.

Restrictions: Not a grantmaking organization.

Publications: Annual Report; *Directory of Japanese NGOs Concerned with International Co-operation*; *NGO Correspondence: Global Citizens* (newsletter in Japanese, 10 a year); *Kokoro* (quarterly newsletter, in English); conference and symposia reports.

Finance: Annual revenue ¥117.4m., expenditure ¥117.2m. (31 March 2023).

Board of Trustees: Masaya Onimaru (Chair.); Yuichi Tanada, Yuka Iwatsuki (Vice-Chair.).

Principal Staff: Exec. Dir Megumi Mizusawa.

Contact Details: Nishiyama Bldg, 4th Floor, 4-7-1 Shiba, Minato-ku, Tokyo 108-0014; tel. (3) 5292-2911; e-mail global-citizen@janic.org; internet www.janic.org.

Japan Association of Charitable Organizations—JACO

Established in 1972 by Masao Watanabe.

Activities: Offers information, advice and support to the charity sector in Japan. The Association represents around 1,550 member organizations. Major activities include: consulting services, training programmes, public relations and publications, exchange of information, study and research, and advocacy.

Geographical Area of Activity: Japan.

Publications: *Koueki Houjin* (monthly magazine, in Japanese); books on management; commentaries on accounting standards, tax theories and practice; glossary of technical terms.

Finance: Total assets ¥162.4m. (31 March 2024).

Board of Directors: Tatsuo Ohta (Chair.).

Principal Staff: Pres. and CEO Takako Amemiya; Man. Dir Yoshiyuki Naganuma.

Contact Details: 2-27-15 Hon-komagome, Bunkyo-ku, Tokyo 113-0021; tel. (3) 3945-1017; e-mail info@kohokyo.or.jp; internet www.kohokyo.or.jp.

Japan Foundation Center

Founded in 1985.

Activities: Compiles and publishes information on grantmaking foundations in Japan; and provides assistance to member foundations. The Center maintains databases containing entries on around 1,500 organizations and the same number of grant programmes. It conducts research and publishes the results; sponsors seminars, lectures and symposia; and has a library of publications on Japanese and overseas foundations. Comprises 878 institutional and individual members.

Geographical Area of Activity: Japan.

Restrictions: Not a grantmaking organization.

Publications: *JFC Views* (in Japanese); newsletter; *Grant Organization Handbook* (Japanese); *Grant Foundation Grant Application Guide for Researchers* (in Japanese); *Directory of Grant-Making Foundations in Japan* (in English).

Finance: Annual income ¥55.3m., expenditure ¥59.9m. (31 March 2020).

Principal Staff: Pres. Yoshinori Yamaoka.

Contact Details: 1-26-9 Shinjuku, Believe Shinjuku Bldg, 4th Floor, Tokyo 160-0022; tel. (3) 3350-1857; e-mail office@jfc.or.jp; internet www.jfc.or.jp.

FOUNDATIONS AND NON-PROFITS

Akai Hane—Central Community Chest of Japan (Red Feather)

Established in 1947.

Activities: Annually supports around 50,000 non-governmental social welfare initiatives, including building care and nursing homes and increasing the number of vocational help centres for disabled people. In addition to its general fund, the organization operates the Community Impact Fund, which offers grants worth up to ¥10m. over 1–3 years to organizations working to find innovative solutions to social problems; and the Volsup Kyushu Fund for volunteers and NGOs supporting victims of natural disasters. It comprises 47 prefectural Community Chests and works in partnership with United Way Worldwide (q.v.).

Geographical Area of Activity: Japan.

Publications: Annual Report.

Finance: Total assets ¥5,467.6m. (31 March 2022).

Principal Staff: Pres. Muraki Atsuko; Man. Dir Yoichiro Abe.

Contact Details: Shin Kasumigaseki Bldg, 5th Floor, 3-3-2 Kasumigaseki, Chiyoda-ku, Tokyo 100-0013; tel. (3) 3581-3846; e-mail cccj@c.akaihane.or.jp; internet www.akaihane.or.jp.

Asahi Glass Foundation

Established in 1933 as the Asahi Foundation for Chemical Industry Promotion, by the Asahi Glass Company Ltd; present name adopted in 1990.

Activities: Funds research and commendation programmes that aim to solve the major challenges that humanity faces. The Foundation awards research grants and scholarships in the fields of life sciences, information sciences, environment, energy, humanity and the global environment; and also provides funding for overseas research at Chulalongkorn University, Thailand, and the Institut Teknologi Bandung, Indonesia. It awards the Blue Planet Prize to individuals and organizations that have made major contributions to solving global environmental problems. Each year, two nominees each receive a supplementary award of ¥50m.

Geographical Area of Activity: International.

Restrictions: Research grants generally made to university researchers in Japan.

Publications: Annual Report; *Conditions for Survival* (in Chinese, Japanese and Korean), *Results of the Questionnaire on Environmental Problems* and *The Survival of Humankind* (annual); *af News* (newsletter, 2 a year); *Blue Planet Prize Commemorative Lectures* (annual); research reports; brochure (updated annually).

Finance: Total assets ¥41,547m. (28 Feb. 2023).

Board of Directors and Councillors: Takuya Shimamura (Chair.).

Principal Staff: Man. Dir Naoki Sugimoto.

Contact Details: 2nd Floor, Science Plaza, 5-3 Yonbancho, Chiyoda-ku, Tokyo 102-0081; tel. (3) 5275-0620; e-mail post@af-info.or.jp; internet www.af-info.or.jp.

Asahi Group Foundation

Founded in 1989 by Asahi Breweries Ltd, as the Asahi Group Arts Foundation. Current name adopted in 2023 following the Merger of the Asahi Group Academic Foundation and the Asahi Group Arts and Culture Foundation.

Activities: The merged Foundation aims to address diversifying social issues through cultural, artisitc and creative projects as well as providing assistance for academic research. The Foundation also awards prizes and manages the Asahi Beer Oyamazaki Villa Museum of Art in Kyoto Oyamazaki.

Geographical Area of Activity: Japan.

Restrictions: Grants only for events held in Japan.

Publications: Annual Report; *Guide to the Foundation; Mécénat* (quarterly newsletter).

Board of Directors: Naoko Ishinaka (Representative Dir).

Principal Staff: Exec. Dir Junya Sakida.

Contact Details: 23-1 Azumabashi 1-chome, Sumida-ku, Tokyo 130-8602; tel. (3) 5608-5202; e-mail asahigroup-foundation@asahibeer.co.jp; internet www.asahigroup-foundation.com/art/index.html.

Asia Africa International Voluntary Foundation—AIV

Founded in 1989 by the Tsubosakadera Temple to support leprosy patients and their families.

Activities: Works in the field of sustainable development through providing technical and financial assistance. The Foundation promotes co-operation between Japan and developing countries; offers courses in Japanese language and culture; and organizes international exchanges.

Geographical Area of Activity: India, Japan, Uganda.

Publications: Annual Report; *Tsubosaka Tsubokokoro-kai* (newsletter); blog.

Board of Directors: Tokiwa Katsunori (Chair.).

Contact Details: 3 Tsubosaka Takatori-cho, Takaichi-gun, Nara 635-0102; tel. (7) 4452-3172; e-mail tbsk2@tsubosaka1300.or.jp; internet www.aivjapan.org.

Asia Crime Prevention Foundation—ACPF

Founded in 1982 by Atsushi Nagashima.

Activities: Organizes lectures on crime prevention and the treatment of offenders; carries out research; provides grants to institutions and individuals for relevant study programmes. The Foundation has members in 93 countries and general consultative status with ECOSOC. It has nine offices in Japan and international offices in Bangladesh, the People's Republic of China, Fiji, India, Indonesia, Kenya, the Republic of Korea, Malaysia, Mongolia, Nepal, Pakistan, the Philippines, Solomon Islands, Sri Lanka, Thailand, Tonga and Uganda.

Geographical Area of Activity: International.

Publications: *ACPF Today*; *ACPF News* (newsletter).

Finance: Annual income ¥41.4m., expenditure ¥45.6m. (31 March 2020).

Board of Directors: Toshiaki Hitoshi (Representative Dir); Kitada Mikinao (Chair.); Shimaoka Seiya, Yamashita Teruyoshi (Vice-Chair.).

Contact Details: International Legal Research Center, 2nd Floor, Ajiken/Hosoken Bldg, 2-1-18 Mokusei-no-mori, Akishima-shi, Tokyo 196-0035; tel. (4) 2543-7725; e-mail info@acpf.org; internet www.acpf.org.

Asia/Pacific Cultural Centre for UNESCO—ACCU

Founded in 1971.

Activities: Promotes cultural diversity, preservation of tangible and intangible cultural heritage, environmental protection and poverty alleviation, particularly among disadvantaged communities. The Centre develops educational materials and strategies for children's and adult learning in co-operation with governments, NGOs and educational institutions in the Asia-Pacific region; and facilitates exchanges, co-operation and information sharing among scholars, practitioners and students.

Geographical Area of Activity: Asia and the Pacific.

Restrictions: UNESCO member states in the Asia-Pacific region.

Publications: Activity Report; handbooks; periodicals; reports.

Finance: Annual income ¥254.5m., expenditure ¥266.8m. (31 March 2020).

Board of Directors: Fujio Cho (Chair.).

Principal Staff: Dir-Gen. Tetsuo Tamura.

Contact Details: 1-32-7F Publishers Club Bldg, Kanda Jimbocho, Chiyoda-ku, Tokyo 101-0051; tel. (3) 5577-2851; e-mail general@accu.or.jp; internet www.accu.or.jp.

Asian Community Trust—ACT

Founded in 1979 to promote social and economic development in Asian communities, and mutual understanding between people in Japan and in neighbouring Asian countries; since 2005 the Asian Community Centre 21 (ACC21) has acted as the Trust's steering committee and secretariat.

Activities: Provides financial assistance to institutions in South-East and South Asia for specific activities in rural development, education and youth development, health, environment and conservation, and the institutional development of NGOs. The Trust also administers a number of semi-independent trust funds and runs two resource desks in Indonesia and the Philippines.

Geographical Area of Activity: South Asia, South-East Asia.

Publications: Annual Report; *ACT Now* (2 a year).

Finance: Total assets ¥5m. (31 March 2023).

Principal Staff: Pres. and CEO Makoto Nagahata; Exec. Sec. Mari Suzuki.

Contact Details: Asian Culture House 1F, 2-12-13 Hon-komagome, Bunkyo-ku, Tokyo 113-8642; tel. (3) 3945-2615; e-mail info@acc21.org; internet www.acc21.org/act.

JAPAN

Asian Health Institute—AHI

Established in 1980 by Dr Hiromi Kawahara, a member of the Japan Christian Medical Doctors' Association.

Activities: Promotes accessible and affordable healthcare for marginalized people in Asia through human resource development among NGOs throughout Asia. The Institute funds courses to enhance the leadership skills of community-based health workers to develop their own organizations; and work to combat curable diseases in less-developed parts of Asia.

Geographical Area of Activity: Asia.

Restrictions: Not a grantmaking organization.

Publications: Annual Report; *Asian Health Institute* (newsletter, 3–4 a year); *AHI English Newsletter*; *Children of Asia* (newsletter for children, 1–2 a year); blog.

Finance: Total assets ¥926.5m. (31 March 2023).

Board: Hisafumi Saito (Chair.).

Principal Staff: Man. Dir Kyoko Shimizu.

Contact Details: 987-30 Minamiyama, Komenoki, Nisshin, Aichi 470-0111; tel. (561) 73-1950; e-mail info@ahi-japan.jp; internet www.ahi-japan.jp.

Bridge Asia Japan—BAJ

Established in 1993 as Indochina Co-operation Centre Japan; present name adopted in 1994.

Activities: Works in the areas of economic and skills development, infrastructure and environmental conservation. The organization carries out self-conducted projects, especially to assist vulnerable people, including refugees, disabled people and women and children. Projects include: supporting education and school construction; water and sanitation; afforestation; and training. Nationally, it supports exchanges and study tours, and issues publications. Has offices in Myanmar and Viet Nam.

Geographical Area of Activity: Japan, Myanmar, Viet Nam.

Publications: Annual Report; *BAJ Newsletter* (2 a month); books.

Finance: Annual revenue ¥92.0m., expenditure ¥89.2m. (31 Dec. 2023).

Principal Staff: Pres. Etsuko Nemoto; Sec. Gen. Masaharu Shinishi.

Contact Details: Shintoshin Mansion, Rm 303, 3-48-21 Honmachi, Shibuya-ku, Tokyo 151-0071; tel. (3) 3372-9777; e-mail info@baj-npo.org; internet www.baj-npo.org.

Canon Institute for Global Studies—CIGS

Established in 2008 to commemorate the 70th anniversary of Canon Inc, an optical and imaging technology manufacturer.

Activities: Carries out policy research and macroeconomic analysis in the areas of: energy and the environment, including climate change, nuclear safety and use of the sea; foreign affairs and national security; global economy, including agricultural policy and biotechnology, medical economics and the Fourth Industrial Revolution; finance and the social security system; and international exchange, including, Japan from a global perspective, Japan-US-China relations, academic exchanges with Russian institutions and economic exchanges with South-East Asian and international institutions.

Geographical Area of Activity: International.

Publications: Newsletter; leaflet; papers; event reports; books.

Board of Trustees: Fujio Mitarai (Chair.).

Principal Staff: Pres. Toshihiko Fukui.

Contact Details: Shin-Marunouchi, Shinmaru Bldg, 11th Floor, 1-5-1 Marunouchi, Chiyoda-ku, Tokyo 100-6511; tel. (3) 6213-0550; e-mail mail-info@canon-igs.org; internet cigs.canon.

Defense of Green Earth Foundation—DGEF

Founded in 1982 by Buishi Oishi, former Director of the Environment Agency.

Activities: Supports projects to protect the environment, including tree planting, the protection of the Oze swamp, and attempts to reduce desertification. The Foundation provides grants to organizations; sponsors environmental research and surveys; and raises awareness about environmental issues.

Geographical Area of Activity: People's Repub. of China, Japan, Viet Nam.

Publications: *Green Earth Newspaper* (quarterly newsletter); *Environmental Issues Research Report* (annual).

Finance: Annual income ¥22.2m., expenditure ¥34.7m. (2023).

Principal Staff: Chair. Mashamitsu Oishi; Vice-Chair. Saburo Mori.

Contact Details: 203 Baji Livestock Hall, 2-6-16 Shinkawa, Chuo-ku, Tokyo 104-0033; tel. (3) 3297-5505; e-mail defense@green.email.ne.jp; internet green-earth-japan.net.

Global Environmental Action—GEA

Established in 1991 to promote sustainable development and to help to solve global environmental problems.

Activities: Operates internationally in the field of conservation and the environment through organizing conferences and disseminating the results of conferences. Initiatives include an information resource for environmental NGOs in developing countries. The organization holds an international conference every two years.

Geographical Area of Activity: International.

Principal Staff: Chair. Shunichi Yamaguchi; Vice-Chair. Yuko Obuchi; Sec.-Gen. Kazuhiko Aoki.

Contact Details: Shinbashi SY Building Institute for Global Environmental Strategies, 4F, 1-14-2 Nishi-Shinbashi, Minato-ku, Tokyo 105-0003; tel. (3) 3595-1081; e-mail gea@gea.or.jp; internet www.gea.or.jp.

Hitachi Foundation

Set up in 1984 under the aegis of Hitachi Ltd, an electrical goods manufacturer.

Activities: Aims to develop human resources in South-East Asian universities to advance education, co-operation and collaboration among the universities in Japan and South-East Asia. The Foundation fosters a co-operative network among university personnel in Japan and South-East Asian countries and better cultural understanding, supporting research in Japan carried out by young faculty members and graduates from universities of Singapore, Indonesia, Malaysia, Thailand and the Philippines. It awards Kurata Grants and Hitachi International Scholarships for fundamental and applied research in natural science and natural science combined with social science in the areas of energy and the environment, urban traffic, and medicine and health.

Geographical Area of Activity: South-East Asia.

Restrictions: No grants to individuals.

Publications: Newsletter.

Finance: Total revenue ¥260.2m., expenditure ¥209.7m. (2023).

Principal Staff: Pres. Osamu Naito; Man. Dir Teruya Suzuki.

Contact Details: Marunouchi Center Bldg, 12th Floor, 1-6-1, Marunouchi, Chiyoda-ku, Tokyo 100-8220; tel. (3) 5221-6675; e-mail hitachizaidan@hdq.hitachi.co.jp; internet www.hitachi-zaidan.org.

Honda Foundation

Founded in 1977 by Soichiro Honda to support the development of environmentally friendly technology.

Activities: Supports annual international symposia, seminars and workshops for experts to discuss scientific and technological problems and how to improve society. The Foundation awards the annual Honda Prize, worth ¥10m., to an individual or organization for achievements in 'eco-technology'. In 2006 it established the Y-E-S Award programme in Viet

Nam for students who are developing science and eco-technology; the programme was subsequently extended to India, Cambodia, the Lao People's Democratic Republic and Myanmar.

Geographical Area of Activity: International.

Publications: Annual Report.

Finance: Total assets ¥6,120.7m. (31 March 2023).

Board of Directors: Hiroto Ishida (Pres.); Kazuko Matsumoto (Vice-Pres.).

Principal Staff: Man. Dir Masaki Tsunoda; Exec. Dir Prof. Tateo Arimoto.

Contact Details: 6F Yanmar Tokyo, 2-1-1 Yaesu, Chuo-ku, Tokyo 104-0028,; tel. (3) 3274-5125; e-mail h_info@hondafoundation.jp; internet www.hondafoundation.jp.

Hoso Bunka Foundation, Inc—HBF

Founded in 1974 by the Japan Broadcasting Corpn—NHK.

Activities: Provides financial assistance for: research in broadcasting technology; development of receiving equipment; international co-operation in broadcasting; and legal, socioeconomic and cultural studies related to broadcasting. The Foundation awards HBF Prizes annually for outstanding domestic television and radio programmes and broadcasting technology development.

Geographical Area of Activity: International.

Restrictions: Grants only to professional projects related to broadcasting culture.

Publications: Annual Research Report; *HBF* (annually, in Japanese).

Board of Directors: Junichi Hamada (Pres.).

Principal Staff: Gen. Man. Dir Hiroshi Umeoka.

Contact Details: Nihonkaikan2 Bldg, 2nd Floor, 9-6 Kamiyama-cho Shibuya-ku, Tokyo 150-0047; tel. (3) 5738-7151; e-mail kenkyu@hbf.or.jp; internet www.hbf.or.jp.

IMADR—The International Movement against All Forms of Discrimination and Racism

Founded in 1988 by the Burakumin in Japan, one of Japan's largest minority groups; an international, not-for-profit NGO.

Activities: Focuses on eliminating race- and gender-based discrimination. Main programmes are: Dalit met Buraku: Discrimination Based on Work and Descent; Racism and the UN; Upholding the Rights of Minorities and Indigenous Peoples; and Sri Lanka. The organization conducts research with academic institutions and NGOs on discrimination, exploitative migration and trafficking of women and children; develops grassroots movements and builds links between minority groups to promote solidarity and support; and advocates against discrimination through campaigns and at international conferences and UN meetings. It has regional committees and partners in Europe, North and South America, and Asia; maintains a UN liaison office in Geneva, Switzerland; and has consultative status with ECOSOC.

Geographical Area of Activity: Worldwide.

Restrictions: Grants awarded only to specific organizations that work with IMADR.

Publications: *E-Connect* (quarterly newsletter); *Peoples for Human Rights* (journal); *ICERD: A Guide for NGOs*; books.

Board of Directors: Shigeyuki Kumisaka, Nimalka Fernando (Co-Chair.).

Principal Staff: Sec.-Gen. Fujihiko Nishijima.

Contact Details: 6th Floor, 1-7-1, Irifune, Chuo-ku, Tokyo 104-0042; tel. (3) 6280-3101; e-mail imadr@imadr.org; internet www.imadr.org.

Inamori Foundation

Established in 1984 by Kazuo Inamori, founder of Kyoto Ceramic Co. (now Kyocera Corpn).

Activities: Supports creative activities in the fields of culture and the arts, science and contribution to society. The Foundation annually offers up to 50 grants, each worth ¥1m., for research in the natural sciences, humanities and social sciences; and two Inamori Research Institute for Science (InaRIS) fellowships, worth ¥10m. per year over 10 years. It also organizes the Children's Science Expo. The Kyoto Prize is awarded to individuals to recognize their achievements in the categories of advanced technology, basic sciences, and arts and philosophy; each prize is worth ¥100m.

Geographical Area of Activity: International.

Restrictions: Research grant applicants must reside in Japan; InaRIS fellowship applicants must be aged 50 years or younger.

Finance: Total net assets: ¥150,000m. (31 March 2024).

Board of Directors: Prof. Shigetada Nakanishi (Chair.); Hiroyuki Sakaki (Vice-Chair.).

Principal Staff: Pres. Shinobu Kanazawa; Exec. Man. Dir Shoichi Himono.

Contact Details: 620 Suiginya-cho, Shimogyo-ku, Kyoto 600-8411; tel. (75) 353-7272; e-mail media@inamori-f.or.jp; internet www.inamori-f.or.jp.

Institute of Developing Economies-Japan External Trade Organization—IDE-JETRO

Established in 1958 to improve economic co-operation and trade relations between Japan and developing countries; reorganized in 1960 as a semi-governmental body. In 1998 the Institute merged with the Japan External Trade Organization (JETRO), an Incorporated Administrative Agency under the supervision of the Ministry of Economy, Trade and Industry.

Activities: Around 100 researchers carry out self-conducted research projects on political, economic, social and other issues facing emerging and developing economies from national, regional and international perspectives. Every year, most of researchers conduct field surveys overseas; and around 10 are sent abroad for two years. The Institute has joint research projects with scholars in Japan and abroad; and a Visiting Research Fellows Programme, under which foreign researchers or experts are invited to work at the Institute. Other activities include: collecting books, government publications including statistical data, and other materials from emerging and developing economies; making awards to outstanding publications; holding international symposia; holding public seminars and lectures; and offering IDEAS Training Programme. It also maintains a library.

Geographical Area of Activity: Africa, Asia, Central Asia, Latin America, Middle East.

Publications: *The Developing Economies*; IDE Discussion Papers; periodicals; policy briefs; books.

Finance: Annual income ¥1.4m., expenditure ¥1.4m. (2022).

Principal Staff: Pres. Fukunari Kimura.

Contact Details: 3-2-2 Wakaba, Mihama-ku, Chiba-shi, Chiba 261-8545; tel. (4) 3299-9500; e-mail info@ide.go.jp; internet www.ide.go.jp/English.

The Institute of Energy Economics, Japan—IEEJ

Founded in 1966.

Activities: Carries out research activities in the field of energy as part of the economy as a whole, in order to contribute to the development of the Japanese energy supplying and consuming industries and to social improvement in Japan by analysing energy problems and providing data, information and reports necessary for the formulation of energy policies.

Geographical Area of Activity: Japan.

Publications: *EDMC Handbook of Energy & Economic Statistics in Japan*; *IEEJ Energy Journal* (quarterly, in English); *EDMC Energy Trend* (monthly, in Japanese); *Energy Economics* (quarterly, in Japanese); newsletter; research reports.

Finance: Annual income ¥2,464m., expenditure ¥2,400m. (31 March 2023).

Principal Staff: Chair. and CEO Tatsuya Terazawa.

Contact Details: Inui Bldg, 10th Floor, 13-1 Kachidoki, Chuo-ku, Tokyo 104-0054; tel. (3) 5547-0222; internet eneken.ieej.or.jp.

International Development Center of Japan

Founded in 1971 by Toshiwo Doko and Saburo Okita.

Activities: Organizes development training programmes in development economics, project analysis, project leaders' training, and language and cultural orientation. Main programme areas include: aid policy and governance; evaluation; industrial development; rural development; social development; rural development; and urban development and transport. The Center conducts basic research on problems of economic development, and undertakes research and surveys commissioned by other organizations. It sponsors international conferences, accepts overseas research associates; and sends Japanese scholars (5–6 a year) abroad for study connected with development problems.

Geographical Area of Activity: International.

Publications: Annual Report; *IDC Forum* (2 a year); regular series of working papers; occasional publications.

Finance: Total capital ¥80m. (2021).

Principal Staff: Chair. Masaya Futamiya; Pres. Hiromitsu Muta.

Contact Details: Shinagawa Crystal Sq., 12th Floor, 1-6-41 Konan, Minato-ku, Tokyo 108-0075; tel. (3) 6718-5932; e-mail inquiry@idcj.or.jp; internet www.idcj.or.jp.

International Lake Environment Committee Foundation

Founded in 1986 by the Shiga Prefectural Government; given legal status in 1987.

Activities: Operates nationally and internationally in the fields of aid to less-developed countries and conservation and the environment, through self-conducted programmes, research, conferences, training courses and publications. Main activities include: collecting and organizing data on the condition of lakes throughout the world; organizing training seminars and workshops on development issues and lake environment conservation in developing countries; promoting lake environment management with the UN Environment Programme; and holding the World Lake Conference. The Foundation also maintains a database surveying the condition of the world's lakes.

Geographical Area of Activity: International.

Publications: *ILEC Newsletter* (annually, in Japanese and English); *Lakes and Reservoirs: Research and Management* (quarterly journal); surveys and guidelines on lake management and workshop reports; *Lake Basin Management Initiative*; *World Lake Vision*.

Principal Staff: Pres. Kazuhiko Takemoto; Vice-Pres. Masahisa Nakamura.

Contact Details: 1091 Oroshimo-cho, Kusatsu-shi, Shiga 525-0001; tel. (77) 568-4567; e-mail infoilec@ilec.or.jp; internet www.ilec.or.jp.

Iwatani Naoji Foundation

Founded in 1973 by Naoji Iwatani, President of Iwatani & Co, Ltd, a distributor of chemicals and related products.

Activities: Works in the field of science and technology, through giving recognition to those whose work in these fields will make a lasting contribution to Japan; and promoting the international exchange of information in science and technology. The Foundation offers grants for research and development projects to improve national welfare. It presents the annual Naoji Iwatani Memorial Prize for research into gas and energy; and the Iwatani International Scholarships, which are awarded to foreign students from East or South-East Asian countries for postgraduate study in natural science and technology.

Geographical Area of Activity: Japan.

Restrictions: Grants for East and South-East Asian students (mainly from Japan).

Publications: Annual Report; *Kenkyu Hokokusho* (report on the research results funded by the Foundation, annually, in Japanese).

Finance: Total assets ¥26,605.8m. (31 Dec. 2023).

Councillors: Sadayuki Hayashi (Chair.).

Principal Staff: Pres. Takeshi Komura; Man. Dir Kazumichi Eda.

Contact Details: Tokyo Hibiya International Bldg, 18th Floor, 2-2-3 Uchisaiwaicho, Chiyoda-ku, Tokyo 100-0011; tel. (3) 6225-2400; e-mail information@iwatani-foundation.or.jp; internet www.iwatani-foundation.or.jp.

Japan Economic Research Institute Inc—JERI

Founded in 1962.

Activities: Operates in the fields of economic affairs and management, including urban and regional development, social infrastructure, energy and industry, through research, international co-operation and dissemination of material. Committees carry out economic research with experts from industry, government agencies and the academic world. Other activities include: organizing conferences, lectures and seminars; and advising on private finance initiative projects.

Geographical Area of Activity: International.

Finance: Total assets ¥2,476m. (2022).

Principal Staff: Pres. and CEO Akihito Shioya.

Contact Details: Otemachi Financial City Grand Cube, 15th Floor, 1-9-2 Otemachi, Chiyoda-ku, Tokyo 100-0004; tel. (3) 6214-4600; e-mail kokusai_e@jeri.co.jp; internet www.jeri.co.jp.

The Japan Foundation

Founded in 1972; supervised by the Ministry of Foreign Affairs, to promote international mutual understanding through the promotion of cultural exchange; reorganized as an independent administrative institution in 2003.

Activities: Carries out activities in three main fields: the arts and cultural exchange; Japanese language overseas; and Japanese studies and intellectual exchange, offering fellowships for research and through grant programmes for Japanese studies organizations. The Foundation hosts international conferences and symposia; and provides grants for conferences and other exchange programmes in and outside Japan. In addition to an office in Kyoto, it has two Japanese language institutes, in Urawa and Kansai, and 25 overseas offices in 24 countries.

Geographical Area of Activity: Worldwide.

Publications: Annual Report; *Japanese Book News* (quarterly); *Wochi Kochi* (online, 6 a year); bibliographical series; *Nihongo Kyoiku Tsushin* (journal, online).

Finance: Annual income ¥18,835.2m., expenditure ¥17,246.6m. (31 March 2023).

Governing Board: Shinya Kurosawa (Pres.).

Contact Details: Yotsuya Cruise, 1-6-1 Yotsuya, Shinjuku-ku, Tokyo 160-0004; tel. (3) 5369-6075; e-mail jf-toiawase@jpf.go.jp; internet www.jpf.go.jp.

Japan Foundation Center for Economic Research—JCER

Founded in 1963.

Activities: Conducts research on Japan's economy with particular emphasis on economic forecasting. The Center organizes joint economic research and undertakes research projects on a contractual basis. It sponsors economic study courses, seminars, lectures and symposia; and provides training for junior business people in advanced economics and research. It publishes the results of its research projects and operates a specialized library of more than 60,000 economic and statistical materials. At international level, the Center conducts joint research on specific problems with foreign institutions, organizes lectures and seminars for foreign economists; and sponsors an annual conference to which leading economists from advanced and developing countries are invited. Study facilities are made available to a limited number of foreign researchers, particularly from Asia. Has approximately 340 institutional members.

Geographical Area of Activity: International.

Publications: Annual Report; *Bulletin* (monthly); *Short-term Economic Forecast Series* (quarterly); *International Conference Series*; *Japan Financial Report* (2 a year, in Japanese); *Asia Research Report* (annually, in English); *China Research Report* (annually, in English); *Asian Economic Policy Review* (2 a year, in English).

Finance: Annual income ¥891.7m., expenditure ¥778.0m. (31 March 2020).

Board of Directors: Tsuneo Kita (Chair.).

Principal Staff: Pres. Kazumasa Iwata.

Contact Details: NIKKEI Inc Bldg, 11th Floor, 1-3-7 Otemachi, Chiyoda-ku, Tokyo 100-8066; tel. (3) 6256-7710; internet www.jcer.or.jp.

Japan Heart Foundation

Founded in 1970.

Activities: Offers grants to individuals, groups and research institutes engaged in research into heart and blood vessel diseases; and finances the publication of research findings. Internationally, the Foundation maintains contact and exchanges information with foreign institutions with similar interests.

Geographical Area of Activity: Mainly Japan and South-East Asia.

Publications: *Kenko Heart* (monthly).

Finance: Annual revenue ¥135.1m., expenditure ¥205.5m. (31 March 2024).

Principal Staff: Chair. Yoshio Yazaki; Man. Dir Yoshio Nakamura; Exec. Dir Kyohei Ameya.

Contact Details: Matsukusu Bldg, 6th Floor, 2-7-10 Uchikanda, Chiyoda-ku, Tokyo 101-0047; tel. (3) 5209-0810; e-mail info@jhf.or.jp; internet www.jhf.or.jp.

Japan International Volunteer Center—JVC

Established in 1980, originally to assist refugees from Indo-China; now an international NGO supporting development.

Activities: Works in the fields of aid to less-developed countries, education and agricultural development. The Center undertakes projects in collaboration with local people; and is also involved in disaster relief operations. It has overseas offices in Afghanistan, Cambodia, Israel, the Lao People's Democratic Republic, South Africa and Sudan.

Geographical Area of Activity: Japan, Repub. of Korea, Lao People's Dem. Repub., Palestinian Territories, South Africa, Sudan and South Sudan.

Publications: Annual Report.

Finance: Annual revenue ¥233.6m., expenditure ¥215.7m. (31 March 2022).

Board of Directors: Takaki Imai (Pres.).

Principal Staff: Sec.-Gen. Tokiko Ito.

Contact Details: Tourei Bldg, 4th Floor, 5-22-1 Ueno, Taito-ku, Tokyo 110-8605; tel. (3) 3834-2388; e-mail info@ngo-jvc.net; internet www.ngo-jvc.com.

Japan Society for the Promotion of Science—JSPS

Founded in 1932 through an endowment granted by Emperor Showa; re-established in 1967 by the Japanese Government to contribute to the advancement of science.

Activities: Nationally, offers research fellowships and grants for joint research activities among Japanese scientists from different institutions; promotes joint research by industrial concerns and universities; provides information services; publishes scientific works and produces films; and organizes lectures. The Society awards the International Prize for Biology annually for individual scientific achievement in the field of biology. Internationally, it offers research fellowships to foreign scientists and grants to Japanese scientists for travel abroad; supports international joint research projects, international research workshops and seminars; and administers bilateral programmes for scientific co-operation and exchange with foreign academic institutions. Has overseas liaison offices in Brazil, the People's Republic of China, Egypt, France, Germany, Kenya, Sweden, Thailand, the United Kingdom and the USA.

Geographical Area of Activity: International.

Publications: *JSPS Brochure*; *JSPS Quarterly*; *Gakujutsu Geppo (Japanese Science Monthly)* (magazine); *Life in Japan for Foreign Researchers*; information resources; scientific publications.

Finance: Approx. 99.8% of funds are provided by the Japanese Government, the rest by private sources. Annual budget ¥336,000m. (2024/25).

Principal Staff: Pres. Tsuyoshi Sugino; Exec. Dirs Tetsuya Mizumoto, Kazuhiro Kotani.

Contact Details: Kojimachi Business Center Bldg, 5-3-1 Kojimachi, Chiyoda-ku, Tokyo 102-0083; tel. (3) 3263-1722; e-mail invitation@jsps.go.jp; internet www.jsps.go.jp.

JEN

Established in 1994 as Japan Emergency NGOs; a network of Japanese relief organizations operating internationally to give emergency relief.

Activities: Provides assistance to less-developed countries, especially in the area of disaster relief. The organization works with local people, promoting self-reliance, with a focus on peoples and regions that receive little attention. Projects cover emergency supplies, reconstruction and rehabilitation, education, health and social welfare.

Geographical Area of Activity: Afghanistan, Iraq, Japan, Jordan, Pakistan, Sri Lanka.

Publications: Annual Report; newsletter; blog.

Finance: Annual revenue ¥582.6m., expenditure ¥563.5m. (31 Dec. 2022).

Board of Trustees: Kanae Kuwahara (Pres.); Koichi Saito, Mika Yamanokawa (Vice-Pres).

Principal Staff: Sec.-Gen. Keiko Kiyama.

Contact Details: #305, 7-5-27 Akasaka, Minato-ku, Tokyo 107-0052; tel. (3) 5114-6201; e-mail info@jen-npo.org; internet www.jen-npo.org.

JIIA—Japan Institute of International Affairs
(Nihon Kokusai Mondai Kenkyusho)

Founded in 1959 by Shigeru Yoshida, a former Prime Minister, as a national institution authorized by the Ministry of Foreign Affairs.

Activities: Encourages innovative thinking about major foreign policy issues. The Institute provides information on international affairs and foreign policy to its members; promotes wider public understanding of international affairs and foreign policy issues; provides a forum for discussion; and exchanges information with institutions abroad, organizing international conferences and seminars. Affiliated centres include the Center for Disarmament, Science and Technology (f. 1996); the Council for Security Cooperation in the Asia Pacific (f. 1993); and the Pacific Economic Cooperation Council (f. 1980) for which the Institute acts as secretariat. Maintains a library of 6,200 books and more than 600 periodicals; and an online database of organizations working for conflict prevention in the Asia-Pacific region. Comprises around 150 corporate members and 800 individual members.

Geographical Area of Activity: Japan.

Publications: Annual Brochure; *Kokusai Mondai (International Affairs)* (monthly, in Japanese); *Shoten (Focus)* (newsletter, 10 a year); *AJISS-Commentary* (occasional); books; policy reports.

Board of Trustees: Motoyuki Oka (Chair.); Yoshiji Nogami, Takashi Oyamada, Teisuke Kitayama (Vice-Chair.).

Principal Staff: Pres. Kenichiro Sasae.

Kajima Foundation

Established in 1976 by the family of Dr Morinosuke Kajima, former Chair. of Kajima Construction Co.

Activities: Offers grants to students, who are selected by their university or educational institution, to undertake research, especially in the fields of science and technology. The Foundation finances visits by overseas researchers, as well as long-term (spanning one year) and short-term (spanning three months) studies abroad for Japanese researchers; and supports international scientific conferences held in Japan, and joint co-operative research carried out by Japanese and foreign scholars.

Geographical Area of Activity: Mainly Japan.

Publications: Annual Report.

Finance: Total assets ¥23,187.1m (31 March 2024).

Principal Staff: Pres. and CEO Kimiko Kashima; Man. Dirs Hiroyoshi Koizumi, Norio Kamiho.

Contact Details: Kajima KI Bldg, 6-5-30 Akasaka, Minato-ku, Tokyo 107-8502; tel. (3) 3584-7418; e-mail kajima-gakuzai@ml.kajima.com; internet www.kajima-f.or.jp.

KDDI Foundation

Established in 2009 by the merger of the International Communications Foundation (f. 1988) and KDDI Engineering and Consulting, Inc.

Activities: Works in the field of ICT through offering research grants and scholarships; and fellowships for international graduate and postgraduate students. Foundation Awards, worth between ¥300,000 and ¥2m., are offered for research in any fields that contribute to sustainable development through using ICT.

Geographical Area of Activity: International.

Restrictions: Award applicants must be Japanese researchers or international researchers affiliated with a Japanese research institute, aged under 45 years, and who not have worked in the telecommunications sector.

Publications: Magazine; blog.

Finance: Total assets ¥241.1m. (31 March 2024).

Board of Directors: Shigehiro Ano (Chair.).

Contact Details: Garden Air Tower, 3-10-10, Iidabashi, Chiyoda-ku, Tokyo 102-8460; e-mail office@kddi-foundation.or.jp; internet www.kddi-foundation.or.jp.

Maison Franco-Japonaise

Established in 1924 by Paul Claudel and Eiichi Shibusawa to develop French and Japanese cultural and scientific research activities and exchanges.

Activities: Conducts simultaneous studies of French and Japanese culture; and organizes collections and exhibitions of study materials, meetings and conferences. The organization co-ordinates research exchanges between France and Japan; awards the Prix Shibusawa Claudel for research on the culture of the partner country; and also organizes a French competition in Japan. It hosts the French Institute for Research on Japan, which has a library.

Geographical Area of Activity: France, Japan.

Publications: Annual Report; newsletter; *Ebisu* (journal); *Nichifutsu Bunka;* brochure; monographs.

Finance: Annual revenue ¥166.0m., expenditure ¥186.5m. (31 March 2024).

Board of Directors: HIH Prince Hitachi (Pres.); Atsushi Nakajima (Chair.); Yoshikazu Nakaji, Mami Watanabe (Vice-Chair.).

Contact Details: 3-9-25 Ebisu, Shibuya-ku, Tokyo 150-0013; tel. (3) 5424-1141; e-mail bjmfj@mfjtokyo.or.jp; internet www.fmfj.or.jp.

Masason Foundation

Established in 2016 by Masayoshi Son, the Chair. and CEO of SoftBank Group Corpn, a technology company and founder of the Renewable Energy Council, the Great East Japan Earthquake Recovery Initiatives Foundation and the Renewable Energy Institute.

Activities: Seeks to contribute to the future of humankind by nurturing exceptionally talented young people with high aspirations and of differing abilities. The Foundation offers individual support grants for up to four years in any field for activities such as research and development of new technologies; start-up costs for business and social activities; and for higher-level studies and study abroad. It provides financial and managerial assistance to researchers, research institutes, and organizations that support young people and contribute to the development of civilization; and hosts networking events and lectures. Grantees also have access to Infinity facilities in Japan, the USA and the United Kingdom. Has 240 members.

Geographical Area of Activity: International.

Restrictions: Grant applicants must be aged 25 years or younger (current grantees are aged 9–29 years).

Principal Staff: Pres. Masayoshi Son; Vice-Pres. Shinya Yamanaka.

Contact Details: 1-7-1 Kaigan, Minato-Ku, Tokyo; internet masason-foundation.org.

The Matsumae International Foundation

Established in 1979 by Dr Shigeyoshi Matsumae, a politician and founder of Tokai University.

Activities: Works in the fields of medicine and health, and science and technology, through offering grants to individuals, and scholarships and fellowships, tenable for six months. The Foundation prioritizes fields of study in the areas of natural science, engineering and medicine.

Geographical Area of Activity: International.

Restrictions: Non-Japanese applicants must have a PhD, be under 45 years of age, have not been to Japan previously, and have established professions or positions in their home country.

Publications: *MIF Newsletter*.

Finance: Annual revenue ¥69.5m., expenditure ¥84.4m. (31 March 2023).

Board of Directors: Toshiaki Hashimoto (Chair.).

Principal Staff: Exec. Dir Prof. Dr Keiichi Katayama.

Contact Details: 4-14-46 Kamiogi, Suginami-ku, Tokyo 167-0043; tel. (3) 3301-7600; e-mail contact@mif-japan.org; internet www.mif-japan.org.

Moriya Scholarship Foundation

Established in 1995 by Masatoshi Moriya.

Activities: Offers two-year scholarships, worth ¥70,000 per month, to students from Asia enrolled in postgraduate courses in geography, history, education and related cultural sciences at designated universities in Tokyo.

Geographical Area of Activity: Asia.

Restrictions: Scholarship applicants must be aged under 35 years.

Principal Staff: Chair. Moriya Sono.

Contact Details: Ivy Sq. Bldg, 3rd Floor, 1-3-12 Minamichitose, Nagano City 380-0823; tel. (2) 6227-5804; internet moriyafoundation.com.

Naito Foundation

The Naito Foundation was established in 1969 with a financial contribution from Eisai Co. Ltd. and its founder, Toyoji Naito.

Activities: The Naito Foundation supports research with a variety of grants, including: the Naito Memorial Grant for Natural Science Researchers in Japan; the Naito Memorial Grant for Research Abroad; the Naito Grant for the advancement of natural science, to support expenses for scientists who are dedicated to the promotion of research; the Naito Grant

The Nippon Foundation   JAPAN

for female scientists after maternity leave; the Naito Grant for fostering scientific full bloom for the next generation, supporting a scientist who is within 10 years of their doctorate and is dedicated to the promotion of natural science research; the Naito Grant for studying overseas; and the Naito Grant for scientific international conferences, for organizing an international conference held in Japan, of which the total number of participants ranges from 50 to 500, and attendees come from more than two different countries. The Naito Foundation holds a conference every year where the top level researchers in the world make public their latest research results in the area of specific research areas. The Naito Memorial Award for the advancement of science for an outstanding advancement of science, worth ¥10m., is awarded annually.

Geographical Area of Activity: Japan.

Publications: Annual Report; *The Naito Foundation Report* (semi annually).

Finance: Annual revenue ¥728.8m., expenditure ¥786.2m. (31 March 2023).

Board of Trustees: Ryoji Noyori (Chair.).

Principal Staff: Pres. Haruo Naito; Exec. Dir Hiroyuki Mitsui.

Contact Details: NANKODO Bldg, 8th Floor, 3-42-6 Hongo, Bunkyo-ku, Tokyo 113-0033; tel. (3) 3813-3005; e-mail naitofound@naito-f.or.jp; internet www.naito-f.or.jp.

The Nippon Foundation

Founded in 1962 as the Sasakawa Foundation by Ryoichi Sasakawa, a business person and politician.

Activities: Operates nationally in supporting the development of shipbuilding technology, preventing marine disasters, and promoting physical training and social welfare. The Foundation provides international humanitarian assistance, particularly through the agencies of the UN, such as for programmes conducted by WHO, UNHCR, UNICEF and the UN Environment Programme. It supports the treatment of leprosy in a number of countries (through the Sasakawa Health Foundation); training in shipbuilding technology in developing countries; and activities aimed at strengthening links between Japan and the USA, the United Kingdom and Scandinavia. In Africa, the Foundation is conducting a project that aims to solve food shortages with improved agricultural methods; and in Asia and Central and South America it supports agricultural, crop research and training programmes.

Geographical Area of Activity: International.

Publications: Annual Report; brochure.

Finance: Mainly funded by the proceeds from Japanese motorboat racing. Annual revenue ¥68,832m., expenditure ¥71,935m. (31 March 2024).

Board of Trustees: Yohei Sasakawa (Chair.).

Principal Staff: Pres. Takeju Ogata; Vice-Pres. Jyunpei Sasakawa.

Contact Details: The Nippon Zaidan Bldg, 1-2-2 Akasaka, Minato-ku, Tokyo 107-8404; tel. (3) 6229-5111; e-mail cc@ps.nippon-foundation.or.jp; internet www.nippon-foundation.or.jp.

Niwano Peace Foundation

Established in 1978.

Activities: Works to achieve world peace and the betterment of culture through promoting research and other activities. The Foundation offers annual grants for activities on religion, ethics and peace; and sponsors symposia and lectures throughout Japan. It supports its counterparts in South Asia in improving human wellbeing by alleviating poverty in the region. The Niwano Peace Prize is awarded annually to an organization or individual contributing to the cause of peace through promotion of inter-religious tolerance.

Geographical Area of Activity: International.

Finance: Annual income ¥90.7m., expenditure ¥114.1m. (31 March 2023).

Trustees: Hiroshi Niwano (Chair.).

Contact Details: Shamvilla Catherina, 5th Floor, 1-16-9 Shinjuku, Shinjuku-ku, Tokyo 160-0022; tel. (3) 3226-4371; e-mail info@npf.or.jp; internet www.npf.or.jp.

OISCA International—Organization for Industrial, Spiritual and Cultural Advancement-International

Established in 1961 by Dr Yonosuke Nakano.

Activities: Promotes international co-operation through supporting environmentally, socially, culturally and economically sustainable development. Main programme areas include: capacity development, especially of young people; environmental education; rural development; and conservation and rehabilitation of forests and marine resources. The Organization sends volunteers to help indigenous groups with projects such as tree planting, agricultural development and the Children's Forest Programme. It works with local NGOs and indigenous populations in 41 countries and regions, with more than 20 training centres; and has consultative status with ECOSOC.

Geographical Area of Activity: International.

Publications: Annual Report; *OISCA* (monthly magazine).

Finance: Annual revenue ¥788.0m., expenditure ¥799.8m. (31 March 2020).

Principal Staff: Pres. Etsuko Nakano.

Contact Details: 17-5 Izumi 2-chome, Suginami-ku, Tokyo 168-0063; tel. (3) 3322-5161; e-mail oisca@oisca.org; internet www.oisca-international.org.

Osaka Community Foundation

Established in 1991.

Activities: Areas of interest include: medical research; education and scholarships; arts and culture; intercultural activities; overseas development aid; environmental protection; community development; disaster relief; and social welfare. The Foundation administers the Osaka Community Fund (f. 2006).

Geographical Area of Activity: Japan (principally Osaka and neighbouring areas).

Publications: Annual Report.

Finance: Annual revenue ¥88.8m., expenditure ¥89.2m. (31 March 2024).

Board of Directors: Setsuo Iuchi (Pres.).

Principal Staff: Man. Dir Takashi Hamoya.

Contact Details: Osaka Chamber of Commerce and Industry Bldg, 5th Floor, 2-8 Hommachibashi, Chuo-Ku, Osaka 540-0029; tel. (6) 6944-6260; e-mail info@osaka-community.or.jp; internet www.osaka-community.or.jp.

Peace Winds Japan—PWJ

Established in 1996; a non-political, non-religious organization.

Activities: Helps people in need, working with local organizations internationally. The organization provides emergency relief, medical assistance, scholarships and social services; promotes equal rights for women; and supports education, agriculture, housing and sanitation. Nationally, it promotes its work through symposia and lectures, and fair trade activities. Peace Winds America (f. 2009) operates in the USA. Has an office in Tokyo.

Geographical Area of Activity: Afghanistan, Iraq, Japan, Kenya, Mongolia, Myanmar, Nepal, South Sudan, Sri Lanka, Timor-Leste.

Publications: Annual Report; newsletter.

Finance: Total revenue ¥7,191m., expenditure ¥7,170m. (31 Jan. 2024).

Principal Staff: Chair. and CEO Kensuke Onishi.

Contact Details: 2nd Floor, 1161-2, Hiroshima Chikada, Jinsekikogen, Jinseki District, Yubinbango, Hiroshima 720-1622; tel. (3) 847-89-0885; e-mail pwj@peace-winds.org; internet peace-winds.org.

The PHD Foundation—Peace, Health and Human Development Foundation

Established in 1981 by Prof. Noboru Iwamura, a medical doctor who worked abroad for almost 20 years, mainly in Nepal.

Activities: Promotes peace and health through human development among people in Asia and the South Pacific. The Foundation fosters the exchange of values, knowledge and skills to improve the quality of life of those living in poverty in Asia and the South Pacific. It runs training programmes in Japan to provide long-term solutions for people suffering the effects of poverty, as well as follow-up programmes to consolidate technical and leadership skills; and strengthens links between the Japanese people and people in less wealthy neighbouring countries.

Geographical Area of Activity: Asia-Pacific, South Asia, South-East Asia.

Publications: *PHD Letter* (quarterly newsletter); project reports and other publications.

Finance: Annual income ¥42.9m., expenditure ¥46.3m. (31 March 2024).

Principal Staff: Pres. Yuji Mizuno; Sec.-Gen. Kenji Uematsu.

Contact Details: 3-7-4 Kagura-cho, Nagata-ku, Kobe-shi 653-0836; tel. (78) 414-7750; e-mail info@phd-kobe.org; internet www.phd-kobe.org.

Radiation Effects Research Foundation—RERF

Established in 1975 under the Ministries of Foreign Affairs and Health and Welfare, in accordance with an agreement between the Governments of Japan and the USA; succeeded the Atomic Bomb Casualty Commission (f. 1947).

Activities: Studies the effects, for peaceful purposes, of radiation on survivors of the atomic bombings of Hiroshima and Nagasaki in 1945, and contributes to their welfare and medical care. The Foundation collaborates with international organizations to establish global radiation protection standards; and trains physicians and researchers from countries where people have been exposed to radiation. It maintains laboratories in Hiroshima and Nagasaki, and a library.

Geographical Area of Activity: Japan, USA.

Publications: Annual Report; studies; research papers; radiation information.

Finance: Total assets ¥2,698.2m. (31 March 2024).

Board of Councilors: Yoshiharu Yonekura (Exec. Councilor); Joe W. Gray (Vice-Exec. Councilor).

Board of Directors: Kenji Kamiya (Chair.); Preetha Rajaraman (Vice-Chair.).

Principal Staff: Exec. Dir Kazunori Kodama.

Contact Details: 5-2 Hijiyama Park, Minami-ku, Hiroshima City; tel. (82) 261-3131; e-mail tour-info@rerf.jp; internet www.rerf.or.jp.

REI—Refugee Empowerment International

Established in 1979 as Refugees International Japan, in response to humanitarian crises in South-East Asia; present name adopted in 2021.

Activities: Supports projects for people who have been displaced by conflict, empowering them to rebuild their lives, restore their dignity and reconstruct their communities. The organization funds local projects that provide livelihood opportunities for refugees and internally displaced people through education and empowerment.

Geographical Area of Activity: Kenya, Lebanon, Myanmar, Thailand.

Publications: Annual Report; newsletter; factsheets; blog.

Finance: Annual income ¥11.1m., expenditure ¥10.0m. (30 June 2023).

Board of Directors: Simon Collins (Chair.).

Principal Staff: Exec. Dir Jane Best; Gen. Man. Yasuko Elison.

Contact Details: Mita Hillside Bldg 4F, 4-1-9 Mita, Minato-ku, Tokyo 108-0073; e-mail info@rei-npo.org; internet rei-npo.org.

Rohm Music Foundation

Established in 1991 by ROHM Semiconductor, an electronics manufacturer.

Activities: Supports young Japanese musicians, through organizing international music exchange activities; offering grants for music research; awarding scholarships; disseminating information; and carrying out research. The Foundation organizes the Kyoto International Music Students' Festival for young musicians from around the world.

Geographical Area of Activity: Japan.

Publications: *ROHM Music Friends* (magazine); blog.

Finance: Total assets ¥106,359m. (31 March 2024).

Principal Staff: Chair. Akitaka Idei; Man. Dir Keizo Ueda.

Contact Details: 44 Saiin Nishimizosaki-cho, Ukyo-ku, Kyoto 615-0046; tel. (75) 311-7710; e-mail rmf@rohm.co.jp; internet micro.rohm.com/en/rmf/index.html.

Rotary Yoneyama Memorial Foundation, Inc

Founded in 1967 by Rotarians (Rotary club members) in Japan.

Activities: Operates at international level, with a focus on education. The Foundation offers scholarships and fellowships to foreign students to study or pursue research at Japanese higher education institutions (including universities, junior colleges, colleges of technology and specialized training colleges). It is supported by 2,200 Rotary clubs in Japan, comprising 90,000 members.

Geographical Area of Activity: Worldwide.

Restrictions: Applicants must be enrolled in designated Japanese colleges or universities as undergraduates or graduates on a full-time basis.

Finance: Annual revenue ¥1,476.2m., expenditure ¥1,642.6m. (2025).

Board of Trustees: Norio Wakabayashi (Chair.).

Principal Staff: Exec. Dir Junko Mine.

Contact Details: Kokuryu-Shibakoen Bldg, 3rd Floor, 2-6-15, Shibakoen, Minato-ku, Tokyo 105-0011; tel. (3) 3434-8681; e-mail mail@rotary-yoneyama.or.jp; internet www.rotary-yoneyama.or.jp.

The Saison Foundation

Established in 1987 by Seiji Tsutsumi, head of the Saison Group retail chain.

Activities: Works in the field of the performing arts. The Foundation has two main grant programmes: Direct Support to Artists, which supports individual artists (e.g. playwrights, directors, choreographers) and their sabbatical (overseas travel/vacation) projects; and Partnership Programmes, which support individuals and organizations working to improve the infrastructure of contemporary performing arts in Japan or to enhance international artistic exchange. The Foundation also allows grantees to use its Morishita Studio in Tokyo.

Geographical Area of Activity: International.

Publications: Annual Report; *Viewpoint* (quarterly newsletter).

Finance: Total assets ¥13,187.7m. (31 March 2024).

Principal Staff: Pres Masao Katayama, Shinji Hojo; Vice-Pres. Asako Tsutsumi; Man. Dir Atsuko Kuno.

Contact Details: Kyobashi Yamamoto Building, 4th Floor, 3-12-7 Kyobashi, Chuo-ku, Tokyo 104-0031; tel. (3) 3535-5566; e-mail foundation@saison.or.jp; internet www.saison.or.jp.

Sanaburi Foundation

Established in 2011 under the auspices of the Sendai Miyagi NPO Center in response to the earthquake, tsunami and nuclear power plant accident that affected the Tohoku region in March of that year.

Activities: A community foundation, which disburses general and capital grants for reconstruction and community development in areas affected by disasters. The Foundation manages the Japan Society Tohoku Earthquake Relief Fund (Rose Fund) to support relief activities in the medium to long term in Iwate, Miyagi and Fukushima Prefectures. It also collaborates with Save the Children Japan in the Sanaburi Foundation Kodomo Hagukumi Fund (Fund for Foster Children), awarding grants for the protection, education and participation of children in community reconstruction.

Geographical Area of Activity: Japan (Tohoku region).

Publications: Annual Report.

Board of Directors: Prof. Seiichi Ohtaki (Chair.); Mitsutoshi Sasaki (Vice-Chair.).

Principal Staff: Sr Man. Dir and Sec.-Gen. Yuji Suzuki.

Contact Details: Sakura-Omachi Bldg, 3rd Floor, 1-2-23 Omachi, Aoba-Ward, Sendai 980-0804; tel. (22) 748-7283; e-mail info@sanaburifund.org; internet www.sanaburifund.org.

Sasakawa Health Foundation—SHF

Established in 1974 by Ryoichi Sasakawa, founder of the Nippon Foundation (q.v.), and Prof. Morizo Ishidate.

Activities: Works in three main areas: early detection and treatment of Hansen's disease (leprosy); community health, in particular home-care nursing and palliative care in Japan; and public health. The Foundation awards grants to tackle Hansen's disease, which are typically worth US $25,000–$30,000.

Geographical Area of Activity: People's Repub. of China, Japan, Malaysia, Nepal, Philippines, Portugal, Romania, Spain.

Restrictions: Grants only to non-profit organizations, educational and research institutions.

Publications: Annual Report; newsletter; *A New Atlas of Leprosy*; blog.

Finance: Total assets ¥784.4m. (31 March 2024).

Board: Dr Etsuko Kita (Chair.).

Principal Staff: Pres. Takahiro Nanzato; Man. Dir Tomoyuki Hashimoto.

Contact Details: Nippon Foundation Bldg, 5th Floor, 1-2-2 Akasaka, Minato-ku, Tokyo 107-0052; tel. (3) 6229-5377; e-mail hansen@shf.or.jp; internet www.shf.or.jp.

The Sasakawa Peace Foundation—SPF

Founded in 1986 by Ryoichi Sasakawa, founder of the Nippon Foundation (q.v.); in 2015 it merged with the Ocean Policy Research Foundation, which was subsequently renamed the Ocean Policy Research Institute, SPF.

Activities: Promotes international understanding, exchange and co-operation. The Foundation makes grants in five areas: strengthening Japan-USA relations; expanding Japan's presence in Asia; enhancing understanding of and relations with Islamic countries; establishing ocean governance; and empowering women. Grants are awarded for 1–3 years and typically range in value from US $20,000 to $100,000 per year. It established the Sasakawa Program Fund, which integrates several region-specific special funds: the Global Frontier Fund, which carries out and supports projects that build on the work of the Ocean Policy Research Institute, SPF; the Sasakawa Japan-China Friendship Fund Program, which strengthens relations between the two countries through exchanges, training and research projects that aim to introduce a market economy in China; the Sasakawa Pan Asia Fund Program, which works to stabilize rapid social change in Asia by providing assistance in education, agriculture, policymaking and networking; the India Exchange Program Fund; the Middle East and Islam Program, which works towards establishing peace in the Middle East; and the Pacific Island Nations Program, which promotes mutual understanding and co-operation, building links between government bodies, NGOs and other organizations working to improve people's quality of life in the region.

Geographical Area of Activity: Worldwide.

Restrictions: No grants to individuals or business corporations.

Publications: Annual Report; *Ocean Newsletter*; brochures; conference transcripts/minutes; survey reports; books.

Finance: Annual revenue ¥30,631.2m., expenditure ¥5,511.4m. (31 March 2024).

Principal Staff: Chair. Sunami Atsushi.

Contact Details: The Sasakawa Peace Foundation Bldg, 8th Floor, 1-15-16 Toranomon, Minato-ku, Tokyo 105-8524; tel. (3) 6229-5400; e-mail spfpr@spf.or.jp; internet www.spf.org.

Tokyu Foundation

Established in 2019 by the merger of the Tokyu Environment Foundation (f. 1974), the Tokyu International Scholarship Foundation (f. 1975) and the Gotoh Memorial Cultural Foundation (f. 1990).

Activities: Continues the work of the three formerly separate foundations. The Foundation supports basic and applied environmental research; awards travel expenses and scholarships for international exchange, worth ¥180,000 per month for up to two years; and offers awards and grants to talented newcomers in the fields of opera and the arts, and subsidies for opera productions.

Geographical Area of Activity: Asia and Pacific areas.

Restrictions: Applicants for scholarships for doctoral degrees must be aged under 34 years; and for Master's degrees, under 29 years.

Publications: *Tamagawa* (newsletter).

Finance: Total assets ¥38,000m. (March 2025).

Principal Staff: Chair. Kiyoshi Kanesashi; Man. Dir Shigeru Hayashi.

Contact Details: Tokyo Okasan Sakuragaoka Bldg, 4th Floor, Sakuragaokacho, Shibuya-ku, Tokyo 150-0031; tel. (3) 3477-6301; e-mail foundation@tkk.tokyu.co.jp; internet foundation.tokyu.co.jp.

Toshiba International Foundation—TIFO

Founded in 1989 by the Toshiba Corpn, a business conglomerate.

Activities: Promotes international understanding of Japan through cultural exchanges and organizing and sponsoring conferences and seminars. The Foundation supports exhibitions of Japanese arts and culture, funds research on Japan-related themes and promotes the study of Japan and the Japanese language. It also awards scholarships to overseas nationals to promote international understanding of Japan; and fellowships, worth up to €7,000, offered jointly with the European Association for Japanese Studies (EAJS) for doctoral candidates from European institutions to undertake research in Japan for three months.

Geographical Area of Activity: Worldwide.

Restrictions: No grants to individuals; fellowships only to EAJS members.

Publications: *TIFO Activities Report*; *TIFO News*; brochures.

Finance: Annual income ¥166.7m., expenditure ¥166.7m. (31 March 2022).

Board of Trustees: Satoshi Tsunakawa (Chair.); Shoei Utsuda, Shinji Fukukawa (Vice-Chair.).

Principal Staff: Pres. Hiroki Yamazaki.

Contact Details: Toshiba Bldg, 3rd Floor, 1-1 Shibaura 1-chome, Minato-ku, Tokyo 105-8001; tel. (3) 3457-2733; e-mail tifo@toshiba.co.jp; internet www.toshibafoundation.com.

Totto Foundation

Established in 1981 as a social welfare corporation by Tetsuko Kuroyanagi, an actress and television presenter.

Activities: Helps disabled people worldwide and lobbies for their equal rights. The Foundation manages the vocational Totto Cultural Institute (f. 1987) and the Japanese Theatre for the Deaf; and provides sign language training for volunteer workers.

Geographical Area of Activity: Mainly Japan.

Publications: Newsletter; blog.

Principal Staff: Chair. Tetsuko Kuroyanagi; Exec. Dir Hiroshi Kume.

Contact Details: 2-2-16 Nishishinagawa, Shinagawa-ku, Tokyo 141-0033; tel. (3) 3779-0233; e-mail jtd@japan.email.ne.jp; internet www.totto.or.jp.

The Toyota Foundation

Founded in 1974 by Toyota Motor Corpn.

Activities: Promotes sustainable development, community revitalization and coexistence. Grant programmes include: the Research Grant Programme, which supports research projects led by young researchers that will ambitiously address the transformation of social systems based on free-thinking perspectives unconstrained by conventional frameworks; the International Grant Programme, which supports cross-sectoral exchange projects in Asia; and the Grant Programme for Community Activities in Japan.

Geographical Area of Activity: Mainly Asia.

Restrictions: Does not make grants to individuals; for capital investment, plant or equipment; endowments; museum or library acquisitions; annual budgets of organizations or institutions, or of established programmes; propaganda or lobbying activities; or for religious activities.

Publications: *JOINT* (magazine, 3 a year).

Finance: Total assets ¥56,797.8m. (31 March 2024).

Principal Staff: Chair. Nobuyori Kodaira; Pres. Masashi Haneda; Man. Dir Akihiro Yamamoto.

Contact Details: Shinjuku Mitsui Bldg, 37th Floor, 2-1-1 Nishi Shinjuku, Shinjuku-ku, Tokyo 163-0437; tel. (3) 3344-1701; internet www.toyotafound.or.jp/english.

Yanai Tadashi Foundation

Established in 2015 by Yanai Tadashi, the founding Chair., Pres. and CEO of the Fast Retailing group of companies and Uniqlo, a clothing retailer.

Activities: Promotes leadership development and mutual cultural understanding through encouraging Japanese students to study undergraduate programmes at universities in the United Kingdom and the USA. The Foundation offers international scholarships and supports the Ryugaku Caravan, which promotes overseas study to students in underserved areas of Japan, offering the Global na Manabi no Community Ryugaku Fellowship.

Geographical Area of Activity: Japan, UK, USA.

Restrictions: Scholarship applicants must be Japanese citizens and preferably residents.

Finance: Annual income ¥1,300.1m., expenditure ¥1,552.7m. (31 Aug. 2022).

Principal Staff: Chair. Yanai Tadashi.

Contact Details: Midtown Tower, 9-7-1 Akasaka, Minato-ku, Tokyo; tel. (3) 6865-0496; e-mail office@yanaitadashi-foundation.or.jp; internet www.yanaitadashi-foundation.or.jp.

JORDAN

CO-ORDINATING BODY

Arab Foundations Forum

Established in 2011; a not-for-profit membership-based association of philanthropic foundations in the Arab region.

Activities: Works to establish an effective and strategic philanthropic sector in the region. The Forum serves as a hub for networking, knowledge sharing and capacity building for its members and partners, fostering dialogue and collaboration opportunities. It comprises 44 member organizations.

Geographical Area of Activity: Middle East and North Africa.

Publications: Annual Report; newsletter (quarterly); research reports; blog.

Principal Staff: CEO and Exec. Dir Naila Farouky.

Contact Details: POB 840888, Amman 11184; tel. 778867809; e-mail info@arabfoundationsforum.org; internet arabfoundationsforum.org.

FOUNDATIONS AND NON-PROFITS

Abdul Hameed Shoman Foundation—AHSF

Established in 1978 by the Arab Bank PLC; a non-profit cultural institution, in memory of the Bank's founder, the late Abdul Hameed Shoman.

Activities: Supports scientific research and Arab humanism, dialogue, cultural communication and the propagation of knowledge. Main programme areas are: thought leadership; literature and the arts; and social innovation. The Scientific Research Fund supports applied scientific research at higher education and scientific research institutions in Jordan; and collaborative research between international and national research centres. In collaboration with Massachusetts Institute of Technology (MIT), the MIT-Jordan Abdul Hameed Shoman Foundation Seed Fund offers grants worth US $30,000 for joint early-stage research projects between researchers and students in Jordan and their counterparts at MIT in the fields of: Arabic language automation; engineering; environment and climate change; food security and sustainable agriculture; health; innovation in education; manufacturing and innovation; planning and development; science, technology and society; and urban studies and planning. The Foundation makes annual awards for scientific research and offers grants for thought leadership in science and learning; and literature and arts grants to promote cultural diversity and preserve cultural heritage. In 1986 it established the Abdul Hameed Shoman Public Library; and the Abdul Hameed Shoman Cultural Forum, which hosts lectures on important public issues; and also runs cinema and music programmes.

Geographical Area of Activity: Jordan, USA.

Publications: Newsletter; proceedings from lectures, seminars and workshops; numerous works in Arabic and English.

Finance: Endowment based on 3% of net annual profits of the Arab Bank PLC.

Board of Directors: Sabih Taher Al-Masri (Chair.); Dr Mamdouh Al-Abbadi (Vice-Chair.).

Principal Staff: CEO Valentina Qussisiya.

Contact Details: POB 940255, Amman 11194; tel. (6) 4633627; e-mail ahsf@shoman.org.jo; internet www.shoman.org.

Arab Network for Civic Education

Established in 2008 by Refat Al-Sabbah as the Arab Network for Human Rights Education—ANHRE; present name adopted in 2015.

Activities: Promotes democratic citizenship and access to education through community advocacy campaigns and influencing government policy and legislation. The Network carries out civic and human rights education programmes for adults and children; and organizes training workshops. It co-ordinates the activities of 45 member CSOs across the Arab world.

Geographical Area of Activity: Algeria, Egypt, Iraq, Jordan, Lebanon, Morocco, Palestinian Territories, Tunisia, Yemen.

Publications: *ANHRE Newsletter*; brochures.

Co-ordinating committee: Rifaat Al-Sabah (Pres.); Karima Ibn Jelloun Touimi (Vice-Pres.); Arwa Khedr El-Borai (Treas.); Avian Rahim Sheikh Ali (Sec.).

Contact Details: Mecca St, Bldg No. 189, 3rd Floor, Amman; POB 4799 Amman 11953; tel. (6) 5560497; e-mail info@anhre.org; internet www.anhre.org.

JOHUD—Jordanian Hashemite Fund for Human Development

Established in 1977.

Activities: Promotes rights-based sustainable human development. Main programme areas are: learning for development, providing access to ICT equipment and education; community development, including economic empowerment and sustainable natural resource management; participation and rights, including good governance, women's empowerment and youth training and empowerment; and social support, including early childhood development and special needs, and working with refugees. The Fund operates through a network of 51 community development centres. The Goodwill Campaign (f. 1991) provides: emergency assistance to the most vulnerable people; medical assistance for uninsured people living in underserved areas; shelter, maintaining and restoring homes; and long-term development assistance, offering grants for small revenue-generating projects and providing academic assistance and skills training for undergraduate students to prepare them for the labour market.

Geographical Area of Activity: Jordan.

Publications: *Humanity* (quarterly newsletter); *Jordan National Human Development Report*; reports and case studies (in Arabic and English).

Board of Trustees: HRH Princess Basma bint Talal (Chair.); Dr Izzedin Kanakrieh (Deputy Chair.).

Principal Staff: Exec. Dir Farah Daghistani.

Contact Details: 127 Madina St, Amman; POB 5118, Amman 11183; tel. (6) 5560741; e-mail info@johud.org.jo; internet www.johud.org.jo.

Jordan River Foundation

Established in 1995 by HM Queen Rania al-Abdullah to empower local community members, alleviate poverty and ensure sustainable development.

Activities: Promotes the development of Jordanian society through sustainable social, economic and cultural programmes. Main programmes include: providing economic opportunities for people to improve their livelihoods; protecting children's rights and welfare, promoting a culture of sound parenting and child safety, and enforcing child protection laws; and building social enterprises through social and economic empowerment, creating opportunities for local and refugee women. The Foundation offers training, capacity building and consultancy services. It is registered in France, the United Kingdom and the USA; and affiliated with the Queen Rania Foundation (q.v.).

Geographical Area of Activity: France, Jordan, UK, USA.

Publications: Annual Report; newsletter; books; guides.

Board of Trustees: HM Queen Rania al-Abdullah (Chair.); Amin Khlifat (Vice-Chair.); Sa'ed Karajah (Sec.).

Principal Staff: Dir-Gen. Enaam Barrishi.

Contact Details: Masoud Ben Saad St, Amman; tel. (6) 5933211; e-mail info@jrf.org.jo; internet www.jordanriver.jo.

King Hussein Foundation—KHF

Established in 1999 by royal decree as a national and international NGO dedicated to the humanitarian vision of the late King Hussein of Jordan; incorporates the Noor Al Hussein Foundation (q.v.).

Activities: Works in the fields of security, social equity and peace. Programmes focus on: education and leadership; sustainable development; participatory decisionmaking; women's and girls' empowerment; and cross-cultural understanding. The Foundation has established a number of institutes in Jordan: the Jubilee Center for Excellence in Education (for teacher training); the Information and Research Center; the National Center for Culture and the Arts; the National Music Conservatory; and the Institute for Family Health. In 2001 the Foundation launched King Hussein Foundation International (KHFI) in Washington, DC, USA, to raise endowment funds for the Foundation. KHFI programmes include the King Hussein Leadership Prize and the Media and Humanity Program.

Geographical Area of Activity: Jordan, USA.

Publications: Newsletter (quarterly).

Board: HM Queen Noor Al Hussein (Chair.).

Contact Details: 17 Abdulmuttaleb St, Amman; POB 926687, Amman 11110; tel. (6) 5607460; e-mail khf-nhf@khf.org.jo; internet www.kinghusseinfoundation.org.

Queen Rania Foundation—QRF

Established in 2013 by HM Queen Rania Al Abdullah.

Activities: Works in the field of education through carrying out policy analysis and research and self-conducted programmes, providing access to learning for children and their families, and training teachers. Affiliated organizations include the Queen Rania Teacher Academy, which offers qualifications and professional development to teachers and educators; the Royal Health Awareness Society, which develops and implements public health and safety programmes, with a focus on non-communicable diseases, healthy schools, nutrition, and educating young people about the dangers of smoking and drugs; the Children's Museum Jordan, which offers programmes and activities for children aged 1–12 years and their families; the Queen Rania Al-Abdullah Association for Excellence in Education, which offers annual awards to teachers, principals and counsellors; Madrasati, which rehabilitates and improves the infrastructure of public schools and improves learning outcomes for Syrian refugee children; the Al-Aman Fund for the Future of Orphans, which provides higher education scholarships, vocational training, financial support and counselling to young people on leaving government-funded orphanages; and the Jordan River Foundation (q.v.). In 2014 the Edraak massive online learning platform was established to provide a wide range of free courses in Arabic to school-aged learners and teachers, promoting lifelong learning through higher education and professional development. The Queen Rania Award for Education Entrepreneurship in the Arab World offers grants to start-ups. Sister organizations operate in the United Kingdom and the USA.

Geographical Area of Activity: Arab region, UK, USA.

Publications: Newsletter; *A School's Guide to Parental Engagement* (in Arabic); children's stories; educational materials (in Arabic); factsheets; research reports; Teaching and Learning Toolkit; Edraak (online platform); blog; digital apps.

Board of Directors: Said Darwazah (Chair.); Randa Sadik (Vice-Chair.).

Principal Staff: CEO Bassem Saad.

Contact Details: Moh'd Al-Sa'd Al-Batayneh St, POB 140141 Amman 11814; tel. (6) 4016464; e-mail info@qrf.org; internet www.qrf.org.

Scientific Foundation of Hisham Adeeb Hijjawi

Established in 1981 in Liechtenstein by Hisham Hijjawi.

Activities: Operates in Jordan and the Palestinian Territories in the field of education, and in particular in the area of research in technical and applied sciences at universities and colleges. The Foundation supports scientific conferences and workshops, and the purchase of scientific equipment; makes annual awards, worth 5,000 dinars each, for research projects in the applied sciences; and funds a technical college in the Palestinian Territories. Training grants are available for students to take up six-month work placements internationally. It also operates in the field of social welfare and is a founding member of the Welfare Association, providing assistance in human resource development, institution building and the promotion of Palestinian culture and identity, in the Palestinian Territories and elsewhere. In 2018 the Hijjawi Tech Incubator was established at Yarmouk University.

Geographical Area of Activity: Jordan, Palestinian Territories.

Restrictions: Award candidates must be Arab nationals living in Jordan or the Palestinian Territories.

Board of Directors: Ayman Hisham Hijjawi (Chair.); Jaafar Hisham Hijjawi (Vice-Chair.).

Contact Details: Complex No. 190, 190 Zahran St, POB 1944, Amman 11821; tel. (6) 5500990; e-mail info@hijjawi.org; internet www.hijjawi.org.

KAZAKHSTAN

FOUNDATIONS AND NON-PROFITS

Nursultan Nazarbayev Educational Foundation

Established in 1998 by Pres. Nursultan Nazarbayev.

Activities: Operates in the fields of education and other charitable activities. The Foundation has established three kindergartens in Astana, Almatı and Atyrau; two international schools in Astana and Almatı, the International School of Almaty and Arystan specialized secondary school. It co-founded the University of International Business, the International Information Technology University and Astana IT University. In 2003 it founded the Institute of World Economics and Politics, which carries out research in the fields of economics, international relations and security, and the activities of the President.

Geographical Area of Activity: Kazakhstan.

Principal Staff: Dir Dr Dinara Kulibayeva.

Contact Details: Almatı, ul. Iskanderova 64A; tel. (727) 3131501; e-mail info@foundation.kz; internet foundation.kz.

Soros Foundation—Kazakhstan

Founded in 1995; an independent foundation, part of the Open Society Foundations (q.v.) network.

Activities: Operates in the fields of economic affairs, health and statistics, law and juvenile justice, media and information, and civil society. Main programme areas are: human rights; transparency and accountability; media; and civil society. The Foundation supports innovative projects focused on budget and extractive industry transparency at all levels. It supports NGOs and independent mass media; economic and law reform projects, including policymaking; dissemination of information and exchange of expertise; and awards travel grants.

Geographical Area of Activity: Kazakhstan.

Publications: Annual Report; newsletter; policy papers; books.

Board of Trustees: Juldyz Smagulova (Chair.).

Principal Staff: Chair. Exec. Council Aida Aidarkulova; Deputy Chair. Exec. Council Irina V. Koshkina.

Contact Details: 050000 Almatı, ul. Zheltoksan 111A-9; tel. (727) 2581354; e-mail sfk@soros.kz; internet www.soros.kz.

KENYA

CO-ORDINATING BODIES

African Venture Philanthropy Alliance—AVPA

Established in 2018; affiliated with the European Venture Philanthropy Association, the Asian Venture Philanthropy Network and Latimpacto (qq.v.).

Activities: Promotes and enables socially responsible investment in NGOs and social enterprises. The Alliance supports social investors, including foundations, government agencies and individuals.

Geographical Area of Activity: Africa.

Publications: Newsletter.

Finance: Total assets 28.9m. Kenyan shillings (2021).

Board: Adedotun Sulaiman (Chair.).

Principal Staff: CEO Dr Frank Aswani.

Contact Details: POB 764-00606, Nairobi; e-mail info@avpa.africa; internet avpa.africa.

East Africa Philanthropy Network—EAPN

Incorporated in 2003 as the East African Association of Grantmakers; present name adopted in 2016.

Activities: To promote local philanthropy and ethical grantmaking for development. The Network offers training and capacity building to member organizations in the areas of asset development, management, governance and grantmaking; and represents them in policy discussions with governments, the private sector and civil society. It also organizes conferences, national philanthropy forums and seminars. Currently has 136 members.

Geographical Area of Activity: Ethiopia, Kenya, Tanzania, Uganda, Rwanda.

Publications: Annual Report; monthly newsletter; *The State and Nature of Philanthropy in East Africa*; research reports.

Board of Directors: Eric Kimani (Chair.); Lulu Ng'wanakilala (Vice-Chair.); John Waimiri (Treas.).

Principal Staff: CEO and Sec. Evans Okinyi.

Contact Details: Rattansi Educational Trust Bldg, 4th Floor, Koinange St, POB 49626-00100, Nairobi; tel. (20) 3315773; e-mail info@eaphilanthropynetwork.org; internet www.eaphilanthropynetwork.org.

Ufadhili Trust

Established in 2001, building on the work of the Africa Philanthropy Initiative, which was commissioned by the East Africa office of the Ford Foundation (q.v.).

Activities: Promotes a culture of responsible, ethical and sustainable practices among businesses, governments and citizens in East Africa through conducting research, advocacy and capacity building. Activities include: building peaceful engagement between companies and communities; developing sustainable value chains; carrying out social and environmental audits; enhancing communities' economic wellbeing; mitigating the negative socioeconomic, political and environmental impacts of extractives, oil and gas projects; fostering social justice and good governance; and promoting sustainability and corporate social responsibility. The Trust facilitates partnerships between businesses, non-profit organizations, individuals and governments; provides technical assistance to East African foundations; runs community development projects; and campaigns on issues relating to the legal and fiscal status of NGOs and foundations. It maintains a resource centre; and has advisory boards in Uganda and Tanzania.

Geographical Area of Activity: East Africa.

Publications: *Corporate Concern* (quarterly newsletter); reports.

Board of Trustees: John H. Mramba (Chair.).

Principal Staff: Exec. Dir Elkanah Odembo.

Contact Details: Aqua Plaza, 3rd Floor, Murang'a Rd, opp. Kenya Institute of Curriculum Development, POB 14041-00100, Nairobi; tel. (73) 5171002; e-mail info@ufadhilitrust.org; internet www.ufadhilitrust.org.

FOUNDATIONS AND NON-PROFITS

The African Agricultural Technology Foundation—AATF

Established in 2002.

Activities: Promotes and facilitates public-private partnerships to provide smallholder farmers with access to appropriate proprietary agricultural technologies. Programme areas include: agricultural productivity; market systems for commercialization; mechanization and digital agriculture; nutrition, food quality and post-harvest management; and public policy and regulation. The Foundation provides advice and expertise, working towards food security and poverty reduction. It operates in 24 countries; and has an office in Abuja, Nigeria.

Geographical Area of Activity: Burkina Faso, Ethiopia, Ghana, Kenya, Malawi, Mozambique, Nigeria, Senegal, South Africa, Tanzania, Uganda, Zambia, Zimbabwe.

Publications: Annual Report; newsletters; factsheets; policy briefs; profiles; project briefs.

Finance: Annual income US $15.4m., expenditure $14.0m. (31 Dec. 2020).

Board of Trustees: Prof. Jennifer Ann Thomson (Chair. Emeritus); Dr Aggrey Ambali (Chair.); Dr Dahlia Garwe (Vice-Chair.).

Principal Staff: Exec. Dir Dr Canisius Kanangire.

Contact Details: ILRI Campus, Naivasha Rd, POB 30709-00100, Nairobi; tel. (20) 4223700; e-mail aatf@aatf-africa.org; internet www.aatf-africa.org.

African Wildlife Foundation—AWF

Founded in 1961 as the African Wildlife Leadership Foundation, Inc; present name adopted in 1982.

Activities: Promotes wildlife management and conservation in Africa. The Foundation operates projects in the areas of: wildlife conservation, training rangers and co-operating with communities; land and habitat protection, incentivizing governments, organizations and communities to set aside land in exchange for training in sustainable agriculture and ecotourism; community empowerment, providing jobs, conservation training and educational opportunities; and economic development, setting up economic enterprises and incentivizing conservation, allowing people to earn additional income and learn new job skills. It also organizes safaris. Has international offices in Cameroon, the Democratic Republic of the Congo, Niger, Switzerland, Tanzania, Uganda, the United Kingdom, the USA and Zimbabwe.

Geographical Area of Activity: sub-Saharan Africa, Switzerland, UK, USA.

Publications: Annual Report; *African Wildlife News* (quarterly newsletter); *African Heartland News* (newsletter); brochures; factsheets; reports; blog.

Finance: Annual revenue US $37.6m., expenditure $34.5m. (30 June 2024).

Board of Trustees: Larry Green (Chair.); Stephen Golden (Vice-Chair.).

Principal Staff: CEO Kaddu Sebunya.

Contact Details: Ngong Rd, Karen, POB 310, 00502 Nairobi; tel. 711063000; e-mail africanwildlife@awf.org; internet www.awf.org.

Amref Health Africa

Established in 1957 to provide healthcare services in East Africa; originally known as the Flying Doctors Service of East Africa and subsequently as the African Medical and Research Foundation. Present name adopted in 2014.

Activities: Works in the fields of medicine and health. Main programme areas are: expanding human resources for health, training health workers and providing continuing professional development; developing sustainable solutions to improve access to and use of quality preventive, curative and restorative health services; and investing in health to achieve universal health coverage by 2030. The Foundation runs a Flying Doctor Service in East Africa, which carries out emergency medical evacuations. It established the Institute of Capacity Development and the Amref International University for research and training in health sciences; and has offices in Europe, the USA and Canada.

Geographical Area of Activity: East Africa, South Africa, USA, West Africa, Western Europe.

Publications: Annual Report; newsletter; *AMREF News* (quarterly newspaper); manuals; position papers; research papers; technical and medical reports; toolkits.

Finance: Annual income US $254.7m., expenditure $254.0m. (31 Dec. 2023).

Board of Directors: Charles Okeahalam (Chair.).

Principal Staff: CEO Dr Githinji Gitahi.

Contact Details: Wilson Airport, Langata Rd, POB 27691-00506, Nairobi; tel. (20) 6994000; e-mail info@amref.org; internet www.amref.org.

Chandaria Foundation

Established in 1956 by Manilal ('Manu') Chandaria, former CEO and Chair. of the Comcraft Group, a steel and aluminium conglomerate.

Activities: Has funded hospital facilities in Nairobi and Mombasa, and a network of 15 rural clinics; and also established the Mabati Medical Centre (f. 2000) and the Mabati Technical Training Institute (f. 2004), a vocational training centre. In Nairobi, the Foundation supports the Chandaria School of Business at the United States International University and the Chandaria Business Innovation and Incubation Centre at Kenyatta University (f. 2013); and annually provides scholarships to more than 100 secondary school and university students through the Chandaria Foundation Education Scholarship Programme, in partnership with KCDF (q.v.). It also supports projects in countries where Chandaria Industries operates.

Geographical Area of Activity: Angola, Botswana, Burundi, Dem. Repub. of the Congo, Kenya, Rwanda, South Africa, Tanzania, Uganda, Zambia, Zimbabwe.

Publications: *Chandaria Education Scholarship Programme Newsletter*.

Principal Staff: Chair. Dr Manilal Chandaria.

Contact Details: c/o Comcraft Kenya Limited, 95 Limuru Rd, Nairobi City Sq. 200; tel. (20) 3742081; e-mail info@chandaria.com.

Equity Group Foundation—EGF

Established in 2008 as the social impact arm of Equity Bank.

Activities: Designs and delivers social development programmes in the fields of: education and leadership development; entrepreneurship and financial education; food and agriculture; health; energy and the environment; and social protection. The Foundation provides secondary schooling to students thorough the 'Wings to Fly' scholarships, offering 48,009 since 2010; offers internships across the group for secondary school graduates; and provides seed funding through Equity Innovators Awards. By 2030 it plans to extend its programmes to reach 100m. Africans in Equity Bank Group's markets in Rwanda, South Sudan, Tanzania and Uganda. Equity Group Foundation International operates in the USA.

Geographical Area of Activity: East Africa, USA.

Publications: Impact Reports; *The Mentor Magazine*.

Board of Directors: Dr James Mwangi (Exec. Chair.).

Principal Staff: Dir Joanne R. Korir.

Contact Details: Equity Center, 8th Floor, Hospital Rd, Upper Hill, POB 75104-00200, Nairobi; tel. (20) 2744000; e-mail support@equitygroupfoundation.com; internet equitygroupfoundation.com.

KCDF—Kenya Community Development Foundation

Established in 1997 by a group of Kenyan development workers.

Activities: Promotes social justice and community-led development. The Foundation works with poor, marginalized and disadvantaged communities. Focus areas include: education, youth and children; livelihoods, environment and climate change; policy, research and advocacy; and endowment fund and asset building. It manages 25 perpetual funds for community organizations and families. A member of the East Africa Philanthropy Network (q.v.).

Geographical Area of Activity: Kenya.

Restrictions: Grants only to community-based, civil society organizations and NGOs that mainly work with communities in need.

Publications: Annual Report; newsletters; *My Community Magazine*; factsheets; project reports.

Finance: Total grants disbursed since 1997 2,750m. Kenyan shillings; total assets 118.7m. Kenyan shillings (30 Sept. 2024).

Board of Trustees: Isaac Wanjohi (Chair.).

Board of Directors: Rose Mambo (Chair.); Gordon Otieno Odundo (Vice-Chair.).

Principal Staff: Exec. Dir Grace Wakesho Maingi.

Contact Details: Morning Side Office Park, 4th Floor, Ngong Rd, POB 10501-00100, Nairobi; tel. (20) 8067440; e-mail info@kcdf.or.ke; internet www.kcdf.or.ke.

Mawazo Institute (The Ideas Institute)

Established in 2017 by Dr Rose Mutiso and Rachel Strohm; a non-profit research institute.

Activities: The Mawazo Institute is a women-led organization supporting early career African women researchers to contribute important evidence-based solutions and a critical perspective to pressing development needs. Mawazo believes that African women conducting PhDs are driven, creative, analytical, and critical thinkers; and that as African women they bring a unique, and often forgotten, perspective and voice to research and development. Facilitates innovative, holistic, sustainable development on the continent and beyond.

Geographical Area of Activity: Africa.

Restrictions: In order to be eligible for the Mawazo Fellowship Programme, applicants must: be a woman (woman/women includes cisgender women, transgender women, Assigned Female At Birth individuals); be a citizen of an African country; be enrolled for a PhD at an accredited university in an African country; demonstrate that their PhD research is related to African development and is relevant to a global, regional, national or subnational policy priority.

Publications: Annual Report; Newsletter; reports and eBooks.

Finance: Total revenue US $1.9m., expenditure $1.1m (2024).

Board: Astrid R. N. Haas (Chair.).

Principal Staff: CEO Dr Fiona Wanjiku Moejes.

Contact Details: Kofisi Riverside Sq., 9th Floor, West Wing, Riverside Dr., Nairobi; POB 856-00606, Nairobi; tel. (20) 3673088; e-mail contact@mawazoinstitute.org; internet mawazoinstitute.org.

M-PESA Foundation

Established in 2010 by Safaricom, a mobile telecommunications provider; an independent charitable trust funded by M-Pesa Holdings and separate from Safaricom Foundation (q.v.).

Activities: Invests in large-scale health, conservation, education and water projects, integrating the use of mobile technology. In 2015 it established the M-PESA Foundation Academy, a co-educational, residential secondary school near Nairobi.

Geographical Area of Activity: Kenya.

Principal Staff: Chair. Michael Joseph; Exec. Dir Karen K. Basiye.

Contact Details: Safaricom House, POB 66872-00800, Westlands, Nairobi; tel. (72) 2001111; e-mail mpesafoundation@safaricom.co.ke; internet www.m-pesafoundation.org.

The Nourafchan Foundation—TNF

Established in 2005 in memory of Shahin Allen Nourafchan.

Activities: Promotes open-source, participatory philanthropy. The Foundation is headquartered and operates in Africa's largest slum, Kibera; and manages the Angel Center for Abandoned Children in Limuru and the Sheikh Mabarak Mohammad Al Nahayan Orphanage near Mombasa. In 2012 it established a strategic partnership with the Equity Group Foundation (q.v.) to explore offering joint programmes in the areas of: education and leadership; financial literacy and access; agribusiness; environment and sustainability; health; and innovation and entrepreneurship; and also to offer 'Wings to Fly' scholarships for secondary education. Has offices in Dubai (United Arab Emirates), Los Angeles (USA) and Shanghai (People's Repub. of China).

Geographical Area of Activity: Kenya (principally Kibera).

Publications: Newsletter.

Principal Staff: Hon. Chair. HH Sheikh Nahayan Mabarak Al Nahayan.

Contact Details: Karanja Rd, Kibera, Nairobi; e-mail info@nourafchan.com; internet nourafchan.com.

Open Society Initiative for Eastern Africa—OSIEA

Established in 2005; part of the Open Society Foundations (q.v.) network.

Activities: Works in the fields of human rights, the rule of law and equal access to justice. The Initiative makes grants in four programme areas: democratic governance and the rule of law; equality and non-discrimination, protecting the rights of the marginalized communities, in particular people with albinism, women, pastoralists, people with disabilities, people with addictions, and LGBTI people; health and rights; and economic governance, advancing accountability, fair distribution and sustainable use of resources. The Africa Regional Office (AfRO) works at pan-African level with other members of the Open Society Foundations network.

Geographical Area of Activity: Kenya, Rwanda, South Sudan, Sudan, Tanzania, Uganda.

Publications: Reports; factsheets.

Finance: Total grants disbursed since 2010 more than US $111.0m.

Board: Aliro Omara (Chair.).

Principal Staff: Exec. Dir George Kegoro; Deputy Dir Rita Nalunkuuma; AfRO Exec. Dir Muthoni Wanyeki.

Contact Details: ACS Plaza, Lenana Rd, Nairobi; POB 2193 00202, Nairobi; tel. (71) 5614126; e-mail info@osiea.org; internet www.osiea.org.

Oxfam International

Established in 1942 in the United Kingdom as the Oxford Committee of Famine Relief to provide relief for women and children in occupied Greece; an international confederation of 19 organizations, its International Secretariat was established in 1995 and moved to Kenya in 2018. Part of the Disasters Emergency Committee (q.v.).

Activities: Works to end poverty and responds to humanitarian and public health emergencies. Main programmes include: conflicts and disasters; extreme inequality and essential services; food, climate and natural resources; gender justice and women's rights; and water and sanitation. The organization provides assistance during and after crises, and campaigns for social justice. It has advocacy offices in Addis Ababa (Ethiopia), Brussels (Belgium), New York and Washington, DC (USA); and works with more than 3,500 partner organizations and local communities in 90 countries.

Geographical Area of Activity: International.

Restrictions: Not a funding body; affiliate organizations make grants; no grants to individuals.

Publications: Annual Report; newsletter; policy papers; reports; blog.

Board of Directors: Nisreen Alami (Interim Chair.); Michael Jongeneel (Treas.).

Principal Staff: Exec. Dir Gabriela Bucher.

Contact Details: ACS Plaza, 1st Floor, Lenana Rd, POB 40680, 00100 Nairobi; tel. (20) 2820000; e-mail kenyainfo@oxfam.org.uk; internet kenya.oxfam.org.

Safaricom Foundation

Established in 2003 by Safaricom, a telecommunications company, to help to build communities in Kenya; affiliated with the Vodafone Foundation (q.v.) network.

Activities: Supports organizations and institutions to improve people's lives through funding community-based projects. Main programmes focus on: education; economic empowerment; and health. Works in 47 countries.

Geographical Area of Activity: Kenya.

Publications: Annual Report.

Finance: Total investments since 2003 7,000m. Kenyan shillings.

Board of Trustees: Joseph Ogutu (Chair.).

Contact Details: Safaricom House, Waiyaki Way, Nairobi; tel. (79) 2989398; e-mail thefoundation@safaricom.co.ke; internet www.safaricomfoundation.org.

Zarina & Naushad Merali Foundation

Established in 2006 by Dr Naushad Merali, Exec. Chair. of Sameer Group, a business conglomerate, and his wife Zarina.

Activities: Funds hospitals, health centres, care homes for the elderly and mobile clinics; provides educational bursaries to orphans and disadvantaged students; and provides food aid and access to water in food-insecure and drought-affected regions.

Geographical Area of Activity: Kenya.

Contact Details: c/o Sameer Group, 49 Riverside Dr., POB 55358-00200 Nairobi; tel. (20) 4204000; e-mail info@sameer-group.co.ke; internet sameer-group.com/csr.

THE REPUBLIC OF KOREA

FOUNDATIONS AND NON-PROFITS

Arts Council Korea

Founded in 1973 as the Korean Culture and Arts Foundation; present name adopted in 2005.

Activities: Promotes Korean culture nationally and internationally. The Council supports creative activities in literature, the visual and performing arts; awards fellowships; finances research into aspects of Korean culture through institutions nationally and abroad; organizes courses, community outreach programmes and international exchanges; and maintains a library. Nationally, it invests in Korean artistic and cultural infrastructure; and in 1979 established the Arko Art Centre.

Geographical Area of Activity: Worldwide.

Publications: *Arco News* (2 a week); *Promotion of Arts and Culture* (monthly); *Almanac of Culture and Arts* (annual); Giving Korea Reports.

Finance: Annual income 489,650m. won, expenditure 489,650m. won (2022).

Council: Jeong Byeong-guk (Chair. and CEO).

Principal Staff: Sec.-Gen. Sikyung Song.

Contact Details: 640 Bitgaram-ro, Naju-si, Jeollanam-do 520-350; tel. (61) 900-2100; e-mail exchange@arko.or.kr; internet www.arko.or.kr/eng.

Ban Ki-Moon Foundation for a Better Future

Established in 2019 by Ban Ki-Moon, former Sec.-Gen. of the UN.

Activities: Promotes peace and security, sustainable development, human rights and conflict prevention. The Foundation supports domestic and international affairs and carries out policy research.

Geographical Area of Activity: Worldwide.

Board of Directors: Ban Ki-Moon (Chair.).

Principal Staff: Exec. Dir Sook Kim.

Contact Details: 5th Floor, Naeja Bldg, 33 Gyeonghuigung-gil, Jongno-gu, Seoul 03176; tel. (2) 739-9094; e-mail bkmfoundation@bf4bf.or.kr; internet bf4bf.or.kr.

The Beautiful Foundation (Areumdaun Jaedan)

Established in 2000.

Activities: Promotes the values of sharing and philanthropic culture, led by voluntary citizen participation, through supporting community and public-benefit activities. Programme areas include: culture; education; employment; environment; health; housing; safety; and social participation. The Foundation is an incubator for new ideas for sustainable public-benefit activities that creatively resolve social problems and improve people's lives. It hosts the Center on Philanthropy, which carries out research, surveys and educational programmes; and organizes Giving Korea, an international philanthropy symposium.

Geographical Area of Activity: Repub. of Korea.

Publications: Annual Report; newsletter; *Giving Korea* (conference proceedings); books on philanthropy (in translation); Research Series.

Finance: Annual revenue 9,956.7m. won, expenditure 10,185.1m. won (31 Dec. 2020).

Board of Directors: Park-Jongmun (Chair.).

Principal Staff: Sec.-Gen. Kwon Chan.

Contact Details: 6 Jahamun-ro 19-gil, Jongno-gu, Seoul 03035; tel. (2) 766-1004; e-mail given@bf.or.kr; internet beautifulfund.org/eng.

Community Chest of Korea—Fruit of Love

Established in 1998.

Activities: Organizes fundraising programmes and events and allocates donations to reduce poverty, illness and discrimination. The organization provides emergency support for individuals and families in crisis in the areas of basic needs and housing; medical treatment and healthcare; and disaster relief. Other programmes focus on: providing protection, nurturing and safety for minority groups including children, women, people with disabilities and older people; providing access to education and employment nationally and in developing countries; expanding cultural and leisure activities for vulnerable people; repairing and rehabilitating housing; and providing psychosocial support and expanding access to social services. It co-founded the Asia-Pacific Learning Center (f. 2010) in Seoul with United Way Worldwide (q.v.) as a regional hub for training in community capacity building. Has 17 provincial branches.

Geographical Area of Activity: Asia-Pacific region.

Finance: Annual income 1,661,617.2m. won, expenditure 1,661,617.2m. won (31 Dec. 2020).

Council: Kim Byung-jun (Chair.); Kim Hyung-cheol, Kim Yong-heon (Vice-Pres.).

Principal Staff: Sec.-Gen. Hwang In-sik.

Contact Details: 39 Sejong-daero, 21-gil, Jung-gu, Seoul 04519; tel. (2) 6262-3000; e-mail chest@chest.or.kr; internet chest.or.kr.

East Asia Institute—EAI

Established in 2002; a think tank.

Activities: Carries out interdisciplinary policy research in the promotion of respect for civil rights and human dignity, liberal democracy and a market economy. Programme areas include: education and human development; the economy and technology; and peace and security. The Institute comprises research centres specializing in: China studies; democracy co-operation; future innovation and governance; Japan studies; national security studies; North Korea studies; public opinion research; and trade, technology and transformation. It organizes conferences and seminars, and workshops on Korean society, culture and history; and offers fellowships, scholarships and internships. Educational programmes include: the EAI Academy, which offers seminars and an essay competition; and Sarabang, which offers weekly lectures and field trips to rising political experts and diplomats. The Asia Democracy Research Network was established in 2013, with EAI as its secretariat; the Network comprises 22 institutions from 14 countries and is part of the Asia Democracy Network.

Geographical Area of Activity: East Asia.

Publications: Annual Report; *Journal of East Asian Studies*; Global North Korea archival website; Commentaries; Issue Briefings; special reports; online seminars; working papers; books; brochures.

Finance: Annual revenue 1,726.7m won, expenditure 1,613.0m. won (2023).

Board of Trustees: Prof. Ha Young-Sun (Chair.).

Principal Staff: Pres. Prof. Sohn Yul; Dir Kang Hye-mi.

Contact Details: 1 Sajik-ro 7-gil, Jongno-gu, Seoul 03028; tel. (2) 2277-1683; e-mail eai@eai.or.kr; internet www.eai.or.kr.

Good Neighbors International

Established in 1991 by Yi Il-Ha, as Good Neighbors, Inc Korea, to provide humanitarian aid to people in less-developed countries; re-established in 1996 as Good Neighbors International.

Activities: Operates humanitarian and sustainable development projects throughout the world, providing emergency relief and funding long-term programmes in poor communities. Nationally, the organization funds social welfare projects that provide child protection and support low-income families. Internationally, the Community Development Project provides education and protection, emergency response, healthcare, improved livelihoods, water and sanitation; and in the Democratic People's Republic of Korea, agriculture and animal husbandry development, healthcare and welfare of orphans. It operates in 51 countries, with an International Cooperation Office in Switzerland, a Global Capacity Development Center in Thailand and a Global Partnership Center in the USA; and comprises the Global Impact Foundation, which designs and implements socioeconomic projects to reduce poverty.

Geographical Area of Activity: Africa, Asia-Pacific, Europe, Latin America and the Caribbean, North America.

Publications: Annual Report; *Partnership* (newsletter, 6 a year); *Good Neighbors* (newsletter).

Finance: Annual income US $295.6m., expenditure $295.6m. (2023).

Principal Staff: Chair. Yi Il-Ha; Sec.-Gen. Good Neighbors Int. Global Partnership Center Choi Min-Ho; Sec.-Gen. Good Neighbors Int. Kim Jung-Gon.

Contact Details: 13 Beodeunaru-ro, Yeongdeungpo-gu, Seoul 07253; tel. (2) 6717-4000; e-mail gpckorea@goodneighbors.org; internet www.goodneighbors.org.

Green Umbrella Children's Foundation—ChildFund Korea

Founded in 1948; renamed Korea Children's Foundation in 1979 and Korea Welfare Foundation in 1994. Joined the ChildFund International (q.v.) federation in 2002.

Activities: Helps children in need. Programmes include: preventing child abuse; supporting severely ill children; protecting children in local communities; and preventing child loss. The organization also runs a foster family programme. Overseas programmes focus on improving children's lives by tackling disease and poverty in developing countries, providing access to education, water and sanitation, health and livelihoods. The Child Welfare Research Center was established in 2011.

Geographical Area of Activity: Africa, East and South-East Asia, South America, South Asia.

Publications: Annual Report; *Danbee* (newsletter, 6 a year); *Apple Tree* (monthly magazine); books.

Finance: Annual revenue 288,067.5m. won, expenditure 288,067.5m. won (2024).

Principal Staff: Pres. Young-ki Hwang; CEO Byeong-deok Son.

Contact Details: Children's Foundation Bldg, 11th Floor, 20 Mugyo-ro, Jung-Gu, Seoul 100170; tel. 1588-1940; e-mail help@kwf.or.kr; internet www.childfund.or.kr.

IACD—Institute of Asian Culture and Development

Established in 1982.

Activities: Works to build peaceful and fair communities. The Institute offers long-term assistance to developing countries in the areas of education and training, community development and medical services. It participates in establishing and managing educational institutions; sends experts to oversee social and economic development projects; provides medical relief services; organizes academic, sports and cultural exchange programmes; hosts international academic conferences; provides training opportunities and scholarships; operates welfare programmes for children, women and the disabled; provides international peace volunteers; and provides business/investment consultancy services. Has special consultative status with ECOSOC.

Geographical Area of Activity: Asia, Central Asia, Middle East and North Africa.

Publications: *International Journal of Central Asian Studies*.

Finance: Annual income 11,952.6m. won, expenditure 11,813.6m. won (2023).

Principal Staff: Sec.-Gen. Dr Choi Han-Woo.

Contact Details: POB 180, Seoul 100-601; tel. (70) 77349410; e-mail iacd@iacd.or.kr; internet www.iacd.or.kr.

King Sejong Institute Foundation—KSIF

Established in 2012 under the Ministry of Culture, Sports and Tourism.

The Korea Foundation

Activities: Promotes and supports Korean language education and culture abroad through a network of 256 institutes in 88 countries and online resources. The Foundation organizes an annual Korean Speech Contest for King Sejong Institute language learners.
Geographical Area of Activity: International.
Publications: Newsletter (monthly); magazine (2 a year); textbooks; video materials.
Principal Staff: Pres. Kang Hyounhwa.
Contact Details: Arirang Tower, 11th and 13th Floors, 2351 Nambusunhwan-ro, Seocho-gu, Seoul 06716; tel. (2) 3276-0700; e-mail sejonghakdang@sejonghakdang.org; internet www.ksif.or.kr.

The Korea Foundation

Established in 1991.
Activities: Promotes Korean studies overseas, cultural exchange activities, and exchange and publication programmes. The Foundation makes grants to individuals and institutions; establishes professorships; awards scholarships and fellowships; supports museums, art galleries and other overseas organizations; distributes Korea-related books and materials to libraries; organizes international conferences; and sponsors international forums. It has eight overseas offices, in the People's Republic of China, the Russian Federation, Germany, Indonesia and Viet Nam, with two in the USA. The KF Public Diplomacy Academy was established in 2018.
Geographical Area of Activity: Worldwide.
Publications: Annual Report; newsletter (monthly, in English and Korean); *Koreana* (quarterly, in Arabic, German, English, French, Chinese, Russian, Spanish and Japanese).
Finance: Annual income 127,749m. won, expenditure 127,749m. won (2020).
Board of Directors: Kihwan Kim (Pres.).
Contact Details: 55 Sinjung-ro, Seogwipo-si, Jeju-do 63565; tel. (64) 804-1000; e-mail webmaster@kf.or.kr; internet www.kf.or.kr.

Samsung Foundation

Established in 1965 by Samsung, an electronics manufacturer.
Activities: Comprises the Samsung Foundation of Culture (f. 1965), which supports Korean arts, managing the Leeum, Samsung Museum of Art and Ho-Am Art Museum, and providing facilities for Korean artists internationally and maintaining a musical instrument bank; the Samsung Life Public Welfare Foundation (f. 1982), which carries out programmes in the areas of care for children and the elderly, medicine, women's empowerment and young people's mental health; the Samsung Welfare Foundation (f. 1989), which manages a network of domestic childcare centres; and the Ho-Am Foundation (f. 1997), which commemorates the life and work of Samsung's founder, Ho-Am Lee Byung-Chull, awarding the annual Ho-Am Prize for Koreans' achievements in the fields of science, engineering, medicine, the arts and community service.
Geographical Area of Activity: France, Germany, Japan, Repub. of Korea, UK, USA.
Principal Staff: Chair. of Samsung Foundation of Culture and Ho-Am Foundation Kim Hwang-sik; Chair. of Samsung Public Life Welfare Foundation Seo Jung-don; Chair. of Samsung Welfare Foundation Lee Seo-hyun.
Contact Details: 60-16, Itaewon-ro 55-gil, Yongsan-gu, Seoul 04348; tel. (2) 2014-6901; internet www.samsungfoundation.org.

SBS Cultural Foundation

Established in 1993 by Seoul Broadcasting System (SBS), a television and radio network; comprises the Seoam Yoon Se Young Foundation (f. 1989).
Activities: Conducts research in the areas of education, employment, social welfare, the environment, energy and national leadership. The Foundation funds projects in the media and the arts, including drama competitions and the Artist of the Year Award; and in 2014 established the Frontier Journalism School at Ewha Womans University. It offers scholarships for Master's and doctoral degrees.
Geographical Area of Activity: Repub. of Korea.
Publications: Newsletter.
Principal Staff: Chair. Yoon Se-Young.
Contact Details: SBS Public Hall, 3rd Floor, 442 Yangcheon-ro, Gangseo-gu, 157574 Seoul; tel. (2) 2113-5352; e-mail esprit7@sbs.co.kr; internet foundation.sbs.co.kr.

KOSOVO

CO-ORDINATING BODIES

Kosovar Civil Society Foundation—KCSF (Fondacioni Kosovar per Shoqeri Civile)

Established in 1998 as the Center for Development of Civil Society in Kosovo (CeDeCis). Present name adopted in 1999.

Activities: Supports the development of civil society and civic activism in Kosovo. KCSF carries out re-granting and capacity-building programmes; provides information and other support services related to civil society; conducts policy research; and engages in advocacy.
Geographical Area of Activity: Kosovo.
Publications: *Kosovo Civil Society Index*; *Monitoring Matrix for Enabling Environment for Civil Society*; policy briefs.
Finance: Annual budget approx. €2m. (31 Dec. 2022).
Board: Ardita Zejnullahu (Chair.).
Principal Staff: Exec. Dir Taulant Hoxha.
Contact Details: 10000 Prishtina, Lakrishtë, Musa Tolaj, Nartel Center, Lam A, H1, Kat. 12, No. 65-1; tel. (38) 600633; e-mail office@kcsfoundation.org; internet www.kcsfoundation.org.

Plataform CiviKos (CiviKos Platform)

Established in 2007.

Activities: Promotes co-operation between civil society and government authorities. Programmes focus on building the capacity of CSOs, government accountability and human rights. The platform monitors public procurement; organizes working groups and learning workshops; and issues publications. It has 301 members.
Geographical Area of Activity: Kosovo.
Publications: Annual Report; newsletter; *Human Rights Handbook for Parliamentarians*; Monitoring Matrix (online); manuals; reports.
Finance: Annual income €189,070, expenditure €189,070 (31 Dec. 2024).
Board: Nermin Mahmuti (Chair.).
Principal Staff: Exec. Dir Dardan Kryeziu.
Contact Details: 10000 Prishtina, Rr. Bedri Pejani 7/A; tel. (38) 224904; e-mail info@civikos.net; internet www.civikos.net.

KUWAIT

FOUNDATIONS AND NON-PROFITS

Kosovar Institute for Policy Research and Development—KIPRED (Instituti Kosovar për Kërkime dhe Zhvillim të Politikave)

Established in February 2002 by Lulzim Peci, Ilir Dugolli and Leon Malazogu.

Activities: Independent policy research in the following fields: foreign and security policies, European integration, administration and governance, inter-ethnic relations, and political parties. Runs capacity-building programmes for political parties and parliamentary oversight.

Geographical Area of Activity: Kosovo.

Publications: Policy reports; policy papers; policy briefs; books.

Board of Directors: Bekim Blakaj (Chair.).

Principal Staff: Exec. Dir Dr Lulzim Peci.

Contact Details: 10000 Prishtina, Str. Major Mehmet Bushi, H.III, No.1; tel. (38) 542 778; e-mail info@kipred.org; internet www.kipred.org.

Kosovo Foundation for Open Society—KFOS (Fondacioni i Kosovës për Shoqëri të Hapur)

Established in 1999; an independent foundation, part of the Open Society Foundations (q.v.) network. Formerly the Prishtina office of the Fund for an Open Society—Yugoslavia.

Activities: Provides humanitarian aid to refugees and supports small-scale projects in the fields of education, culture and the arts, information and the media, democratic institutions and human rights. Internationally, the Foundation cooperates with the East–East Beyond Borders Program, collaborating regionally on democracy programmes. Other programmes focus on transparency and accountability; European integration; and minority groups and Roma people.

Geographical Area of Activity: Kosovo.

Publications: Annual Report; newsletter; *European Magazine*; reports; books.

Finance: Annual expenditure €2.2m. (31 Dec. 2022).

Board: Lulzim Peci (Chair.).

Principal Staff: Exec. Dir Lura Limani.

Contact Details: Prishtina, Ulpiana, Imzot Nike Prela Vila 13; tel. (38) 542157; e-mail info@kfos.org; internet kfos.org.

KUWAIT

FOUNDATIONS AND NON-PROFITS

Kuwait Awqaf Public Foundation

Established in 1993 as a *waqf*, or community fund, to support private sector organizations in the promotion and development of society.

Activities: Operates nationally in the areas of religion and culture, the environment, community development, health and social welfare, science and technology and Islamic co-operation.

Geographical Area of Activity: Kuwait.

Publications: Annual Report; *Awqaf* (journal, 2 a year); *Journal of Endowments* (online); blog; books.

Principal Staff: Acting Sec.-Gen. Nasser Mohammed Al-Hamad.

Contact Details: Al-Dasma Plot 6, Hamoud Al-Raqaba St, POB 482, Al Safat 13005, Kuwait City; tel. 1804777; e-mail info@awqaf.org; internet www.awqaf.org.kw.

Kuwait Foundation for the Advancement of Sciences—KFAS

Established in 1976 by HH the Amir Sheikh Sabah Al-Ahmad Al-Jaber Al-Sabah; a private, non-profit scientific organization.

Activities: Supports pure and applied research of national importance in all disciplines, and promotes collaborative studies and deliberations with scientists internationally through conferences and symposia. The Foundation awards annual prizes to scientists and researchers in Kuwait and other Arab and Islamic countries; and scholarships and fellowships to Kuwaiti nationals. It has established and funds several subsidiaries: the Scientific Center; Dasman Diabetes Institute; Sabah Al-Ahmad Center for Giftedness and Creativity; Jaber Al Ahmad Center for Nuclear Medicine and Molecular Imaging; KFAS Academy; and the Advancement of Science Publishing and Distribution Company; and hosts the Kuwaiti branch of the Arab School for Science and Technology.

Geographical Area of Activity: Mainly Kuwait.

Publications: Annual Report; newsletter; *Atlas of the State of Kuwait from Satellite Images*; *Majallat Al-Oloom* (monthly, Arabic language edition of *Scientific American*); *Al-Taqaddum Al-Ilmi* (quarterly magazine); studies; white papers.

Finance: Funded by public Kuwaiti corporations (1% of their annual profits) and by other organizations and individuals.

Board of Directors: The Crown Prince Sheikh Meshal Al-Ahmad Al-Jaber Al-Sabah (Chair.).

Contact Details: Sharq, Ahmad Al Jaber St, POB 25263, 13113 Safat, Kuwait City; tel. 22278100; e-mail info@kfas.org.kw; internet www.kfas.org.

Kuwait Institute for Scientific Research—KISR

Founded in 1967 by the Arabian Oil Company Ltd (Japan) to develop the petroleum, desert agriculture and marine biology sectors.

Activities: Works to advance national industry and undertake studies to address significant challenges. Main research programmes encompass: petroleum, including oil recovery technology, petroleum chemistry and materials science; sustainable water resource management, desalination and wastewater recovery; the environment and life sciences, including agriculture and fisheries, restoring damaged ecosystems, preserving natural resources and lifestyle- and nutrition-related diseases; and sustainable energy, building materials and infrastructure. The Institute also researches ways of using technology to help people with special needs. It provides documentation and information services; and offers training schemes for scientific research workers. Has more than 100 laboratories in nine locations.

Geographical Area of Activity: Kuwait.

Publications: Annual Report; *Science & Technology Magazine*; conference proceedings; scientific reports; books.

Principal Staff: Acting Dir-Gen. Dr Faisal Al-Humaidani.

Contact Details: Al-Jaheth St, Shuwaikh, 13109 Kuwait City; POB 24885, Safat, 13109, Kuwait City; tel. 24989000; e-mail kisrdg@kisr.edu.kw; internet www.kisr.edu.kw.

Zakat House

Founded in 1982 for the Islamic practice of *zakat* (giving a fixed proportion of one's wealth to charity); an independent government authority.

Activities: Funds Islamic humanitarian programmes in Kuwait and abroad; and sponsors more than 17,000 orphans, mainly in Asia, and foreign students studying at Al Azhar University in Cairo, Egypt. The organization supports charitable projects to alleviate suffering and improve the quality of life

LATVIA

CO-ORDINATING BODY

LAPAS—Latvijas platforma attīstības sadarbībai (Latvian Platform for Development Cooperation)

Established in 2004.

Activities: Promotes NGOs' participation in development co-operation and co-ordinates national efforts in development education. Priority areas are: the UN Sustainable Development Goals; human security; policy coherence for development; and community resilience. The Platform provides advocacy, information exchange, training and capacity building. It comprises 43 member organizations; and maintains a member database. A member of CONCORD (q.v.).

Geographical Area of Activity: Latvia.

Publications: Newsletter; handbook; blog.

Board: Inga Belousa (Chair.); Ieva Jākobsone Bellomi, Gints Jankovskis (Deputy Chair.).

Principal Staff: Dir Inese Vaivare.

Contact Details: Pils iela 21, 1050 Rīga; tel. 2641-4862; e-mail info@lapas.lv; internet lapas.lv.

FOUNDATIONS AND NON-PROFITS

Fonds atvērtai sabiedrībai DOTS (Foundation for an Open Society DOTS)

Founded in 1992, as Soros Foundation—Latvia; an independent foundation, part of the Open Society Foundations (q.v.) network. Present name adopted in 2014.

Activities: Works in the fields of democracy, social economy and social entrepreneurship, and towards an inclusive society. The Foundation has supported the establishment of organizations including the Centre for Public Policy—PROVIDUS, Latvian Centre for Contemporary Art, Civic Alliance of Latvia, Education Development Centre, Latvian Judicial Training Centre, Society for Transparency—TI (Delna), Riga Graduate School of Law, Public Service Language Centre and several community foundations.

Geographical Area of Activity: Latvia.

Publications: Newsletter.

Finance: Total expenditure since 1992 over €65m.

Board of Directors: Maksims Jegorovs (Chair.).

Principal Staff: Exec. Dir Ieva Morica.

Contact Details: Alberta iela 13, 1010 Rīga; tel. 6703-9241; e-mail dots@fondsdots.lv; internet www.fondsdots.lv.

Latvijas Ārpolitikas Institūts—LAI (Latvian Institute of International Affairs—LIIA)

Established in 1992 as a non-profit foundation; a think tank.

Activities: The Latvian Institute of International Affairs (LIIA) conducts policy research and analysis on international affairs, regional security, and foreign policy. It runs dedicated research programmes on the EU, Asia, and the Middle East, and has published over 100 studies and books. LIIA informs both Latvian and international audiences, organizes high-level conferences such as the Riga Dialogue and the Riga Security Forum, and collaborates with national and global partners. It actively participates in EU-funded research projects and is a full member of networks such as the Trans European Policy Studies Association and EuroMeSCo—Euro-Mediterranean Research, Dialogue, Advocacy.

Geographical Area of Activity: Baltic region.

Publications: *Latvian Foreign and Security Policy Yearbook*; policy papers; reports.

Principal Staff: Dir Karlis Bukovskis; Deputy Dir Sintija Broka.

Contact Details: Pils iela 21, 1050 Rīga; tel. 2962-9269; e-mail liia@liia.lv; internet www.lai.lv.

Latvijas Bērnu fonds (Latvia Children's Fund)

Founded in 1988 to protect children's rights in Latvia; since 1991 it has been the official representative of the Christian Children's Fund International in Latvia and in 2003 became a member of the UNICEF regional network for children in Central Europe, Eastern Europe, the Russian Federation and the Baltic States.

Activities: Supports disadvantaged children and their families, developing programmes for children who have no parents, are in crisis situations or are severely ill; and funding the development of gifted children. Main activities include: implementing projects financed by the EU and other funds; organizing summer camps for children with special needs, victims of abuse and children in foster care; providing treatment for severely ill children; supporting large, low-income families; funding rehabilitation and crisis centres; and collecting and distributing humanitarian aid. The Fund also awards grants to winners of the 'Talent for Latvia' competition from children's music schools; and organizes the Christmas 'Don't Pass By!' charity campaign and concert; and offers scholarships jointly with the Latvian-American Association.

Geographical Area of Activity: Latvia.

Board: Andris Bērziņš (Pres.); Vaira Vucāne (Vice-Pres.).

Contact Details: Brīvības gatve 310-75, 1006 Rīga; tel. 6754-2072; e-mail bernufonds@lbf.lv; internet www.lbf.lv.

LEBANON

CO-ORDINATING BODY

ANND—Arab NGO Network for Development
Established in 1997.
Activities: Works to strengthen the role of civil society and enhance the values of democracy, respect for human rights and sustainable development. The Network advocates for socioeconomic reforms, organizing conferences, workshops and seminars. It comprises nine national networks, with an extended membership of 40 NGOs and 250 CSOs, working in 12 countries.
Geographical Area of Activity: Algeria, Bahrain, Egypt, Iraq, Jordan, Lebanon, Mauritania, Morocco, Palestinian Territories, Sudan, Tunisia, Yemen.
Publications: Annual Report; Progress Report; newsletter (monthly, in Arabic and English); *Arab Monitor for Economic and Social Rights*; *Arab Watch Report*; conference reports; guides; policy briefs; research papers.
Principal Staff: Exec. Dir Ziad Abdel Samad.
Contact Details: UNESCO 4191 Bldg, Block A, 7th Floor, UNESCO St, Beirut; POB 5792/14, Mazraa, Beirut 1105-2070; tel. (1) 808912; e-mail annd@annd.org; internet www.annd.org.

FOUNDATIONS AND NON-PROFITS

Adyan Foundation
Established in 2006.
Activities: Promotes diversity, solidarity and human dignity. The Foundation carries out activities in the areas of education, policymaking and intercultural and interfaith relations. It incorporates the Institute of Citizenship and Diversity Management, which conducts research and organizes conferences; and offers training and academic programmes in areas including: inclusive citizenship; interfaith dialogue; peacebuilding; religious and public affairs; religious diversity; resilience and reconciliation; and training of trainers.
Geographical Area of Activity: Middle East, Europe.
Publications: Biennial Report; newsletter; reports; training manuals; Teach Coexistence.com (e-learning platform); bihorriya.com; www.taadudiya.com.
Board: Dr Nayla Tabbara (Pres.); Adel Moubarak (Vice-Chair.); Fr Agapios Kfoury (Treas.); Dr Khouloud Al Khatib (Sec.).
Principal Staff: Exec. Dir Alexandre Adam.
Contact Details: Riverside Bldg, 6th–7th Floor, Charles Helou St, Sin el Fil, Beirut; POB 116, 5303 Mathaf, Beirut; tel. (1) 490406; e-mail contact@adyanfoundation.org; internet www.adyanfoundation.org.

Arab Fund for Arts and Culture—AFAC
Established in 2007 by Arab cultural activists.
Activities: Supports individual artists, writers, researchers and organizations in the Arab world working in the field of the arts and culture. Grantmaking programmes encompass: Arab documentary photography; arts and culture entrepreneurship; cinema; creative and critical writing; documentary film; music, training and regional events; performing arts; research on the arts; and visual arts. The Fund supports capacity building and training in the cultural sector; and facilitates cultural exchange, research and co-operation worldwide. It awards general grants, worth up to US $50,000 and also funds special programmes.
Geographical Area of Activity: International.
Restrictions: Grants to Arab individuals and institutions; and non-Arab institutions whose project content relates to Arab culture; does not grant scholarships.
Publications: Annual Report; newsletter; *Europa: An Illustrated Introduction to Europe for Migrants and Refugees* (e-book); brochures; catalogues; reports.
Finance: Total grant disbursment $6.2m. (2024).
Board of Trustees: Dr Nabil Qaddumi (Acting Chair.); Suzanne Wettenschwiler (Sec.).
Principal Staff: Exec. Dir Rima Mismar.
Contact Details: Charles Aoun Bldg, Sursock St, Saint Nicolas Stairs, Beirut; POB 13-5290, Beirut; tel. (1) 218901; e-mail info@arabculturefund.org; internet www.arabculturefund.org.

Arab Image Foundation—AIF (Fondation Arabe pour l'Image)
Established in 1997 to preserve and promote the photographic heritage in the Middle East, North Africa and the Arab diaspora.
Activities: Collects, preserves and studies photography and other related visual material from the Middle East, North Africa and the Arab diaspora. The Foundation produces exhibitions and issues publications in partnership with international museums, galleries, and cultural institutions. It holds a collection of more than 500,000 photographic objects dating from the mid-19th century to the present day; has a library, which contains approximately 1,300 books, monographs, catalogues and journals, and a video library; and organizes and participates in local and regional events related to the study of photography and its preservation.
Geographical Area of Activity: Middle East and North Africa.
Publications: Newsletter; books.
Principal Staff: Dir Heba Hage-Felder.
Contact Details: Zoghbi Bldg, 4th Floor, 337 Gouraud St, Gemmayzeh (opp. Byblos Bank), Beirut; tel. (1) 569373; e-mail communications@arabimagefoundation.org; internet arabimagefoundation.org.

Arab Thought Foundation—ATF
Established in 2000 on the initiative of HRH Prince Bandar bin Khalid Al-Faisal of Saudi Arabia.
Activities: Undertakes educational projects, research and youth programmes; and organizes the annual Fikr Conference. In 2010 the Foundation established the ATF Research and Studies Center, comprising a research unit and a translation unit; and also a Media Center, which collaborates with Arab media.
Geographical Area of Activity: Middle East.
Publications: Annual Report; *Ofoq* (newsletter); *Arab Report on Cultural Development*; *One Civilization* (book series); blog.
Board of Directors: HRH Prince Bandar bin Khalid Al-Faisal (Chair.).
Principal Staff: Gen. Dir Prof. Henri Al-Await.
Contact Details: Al-Omari Mosque St, Al Wasat Al Tejari, Beirut 52411; POB 524-11, Beirut; tel. (1) 997100; e-mail info@arabthought.org; internet www.arabthought.org.

Hariri Foundation for Sustainable Human Development
Founded in 1979 by former Prime Minister of Lebanon Rafik Hariri as the Islamic Foundation for Education and Higher Learning; present name adopted in 1990.
Activities: Established initially to improve the prospects of citizens in Lebanon suffering from the effects of the conflicts in the region through education. The Foundation offers loans and scholarships to students; funds academic institutions affected by conflict in the Middle East; and supports five schools, two of which are in Sidon and the others in Beirut, and the Hariri Canadian University (f. 1999). It offers career

guidance and support for educational organizations and programmes; promotes Lebanese heritage through the renovation and care of old buildings; and fosters relations with international organizations. In 1990 the newly renamed Foundation broadened its mandate to include the improvement of the social, cultural and economic situation of Lebanese citizens through sustainable human development.

Geographical Area of Activity: Middle East.

Publications: Books; conference proceedings.

Principal Staff: Pres. Bahia Hariri.

Contact Details: Emir Bechir Rd, Solidere 1301, 5th Floor, Nijme District, 11-2151 Beirut; tel. (1) 197223; e-mail info @hariri-foundation.org; internet hariri-foundation.org.

Institute for Palestine Studies—IPS

Founded in 1963 by a group of Arab scholars.

Activities: Specializes in research, documentation, analysis and publication on Palestinian affairs and the Arab–Israeli conflict, and possible ways of arriving at a peaceful resolution. The Institute organizes conferences, lectures, seminars, workshops and other events. The Beirut office houses the IPS Information and Documentation Center, which includes a library specializing in Palestinian affairs, the Arab–Israeli conflict, Judaica and Zionism. The library contains 78,000 vols and 248 current periodicals in Arabic, English, French, German, Italian and Hebrew. The Institute maintains offices in Ramallah and Washington, DC, USA.

Geographical Area of Activity: Middle East, USA.

Publications: *Journal of Palestine Studies* (quarterly, in English); *Jerusalem Quarterly* (in English); *Majallat al-Dirasat al-Filistiniyah* (quarterly, in Arabic); *IPS Papers*; *Palestinian Timeline* (online); occasional papers; monographs; books; blog.

Board of Trustees: Tarek Mitri (Chair.); Leila Shahid (Vice-Chair.); Ammar Aker (Treas.); Camille Mansour (Sec.).

Principal Staff: Gen. Dir Khaled Farraj.

Contact Details: Anis Nsouli St, Verdun, POB 11-7164, Beirut 1107-2230; tel. (1) 804959; e-mail ipsbeirut@palestine-studies .org; internet www.palestine-studies.org.

Kayany Foundation

Established in 2013 in response to the Syrian crisis.

Activities: Operates educational programmes for Syrian refugee children and young people in informal tented settlements. In partnership with the Center for Civic Engagement and Community Service at the American University of Beirut, as part of the Ghata project the Foundation established portable schools in the Bekaa valley to provide quality education to out-of-school refugees.

Geographical Area of Activity: Lebanon.

Publications: Brochure.

Board of Trustees: Nora Sharabati Joumblatt (Pres. and Dir); Nada Boulos (Vice-Pres.); Safa Saidi (Treas.).

Contact Details: Central Pharmacy Bldg, 2nd Floor, Taanayel; tel. (8) 542455; e-mail info@kayany-foundation.org; internet kayany-foundation.org.

Mouvement Social (Social Movement)

Established in 1958 by Grégoire Haddad, then general caretaker of the Greek Catholic Archbishopric of Beirut.

Activities: A citizen's platform to encourage community and active citizenship. Focuses on anti-violence and anti-discrimination. Supports socially challenged children, young people, women and their families through socioeconomic and educational programmes.

Geographical Area of Activity: Lebanon.

Finance: Annual income US $6.4m., expenditure $6.4m. (2024).

Principal Staff: Exec. Dir Tamam Mroueh; Treas. Roger Melki.

Contact Details: Mouvement Social Bldg, Badaro Main Rd, Beirut; tel. (1) 390335; e-mail msl@mouvementsocial.org; internet www.mouvementsocial.org.

René Moawad Foundation—RMF

Established in 1991, in memory of President René Moawad.

Activities: Works in the fields of agriculture, education, economic affairs, health and welfare, humanitarian relief and human rights through providing assistance to disadvantaged people. The Foundation operates the Agricultural Centre of the North (CAN), the Institut Technique René Moawad in Mejdlaya, the RMF Center for Education and Protection Services, the RMF Together initiative, a nursery, a community clinic and mobile dispensaries. It has offices in Mejdlaya, Tripoli and Washington, DC, USA.

Geographical Area of Activity: Lebanon.

Publications: Annual Report; newsletter; guides; manuals.

Finance: Annual budget approx. US $4m.

Principal Staff: Pres. Nayla René Moawad; Gen. Dir Nabil C. Moawad.

Contact Details: 844 rue Alfred Naccache, Achrafieh, Beirut; BP 468, Hazmieh; tel. (7) 0352230; e-mail together@rmf .org.lb; internet rmf.org.lb.

Samir Kassir Foundation

Established in 2006, in memory of Samir Kassir, a journalist and writer who was killed in Beirut in 2005.

Activities: Promotes a free press and the spread of democratic values and cultural freedom throughout the Arab world. The Foundation preserves, translates and spreads the work and legacy of Samir Kassir; and promotes cultural freedom and free thinking through organizing conferences, seminars and the annual Beirut Spring Festival (f. 2009). It also established the Samir Kassir Eyes (SKeyes) Center (f. 2007) to monitor violations of freedom of the press and culture, and to defend the rights and freedom of expression of journalists and intellectuals.

Geographical Area of Activity: Middle East.

Publications: Books by Samir Kassir; reports.

Board of Directors: Gisèle Al-Azzi Kassir (Pres.); Malek Mrowa (Vice-Pres.); Hind Darwish (Treas.); Jad Al-Akhaoui (Sec.).

Contact Details: Riverside Complex Bloc 6, 6th Floor, Charles Helou St, Sin el-Fil, Metn, Beirut; tel. (1) 499012; e-mail info@samirkassirfoundation.org; internet www .samirkassirfoundation.org.

LESOTHO

CO-ORDINATING BODY

Lesotho Council of Non-Governmental Organisations

Established in 1990 to provide support services to NGOs; an umbrella organization.

Activities: Promotes the development of civil society and democracy, providing advocacy, networking and leadership training and other support to NGOs. Areas of strategic focus are: economic justice and social development; empowering vulnerable and marginalized people; environmental protection and stewardship; governance and accountability; harnessing information and technology; responding to HIV and AIDS; and strengthening civil society. The Council incorporates thematic commissions for: agriculture, environment and natural resources; democracy and human rights; disaster management and humanitarian relief; economic justice; health and social development; and women and children.

Geographical Area of Activity: Lesotho.

Publications: Annual Report; project reports.

Board of Directors: Nkhasi Sefuthi (Pres.); Letsatsi Ntsibolane (Vice-Pres.); Ts'epo Masupha (Treas.).

Principal Staff: Exec. Dir Sekonyela Mapetja.

Contact Details: House No. 544, Hoohlo Extension, Private Bag A445, Maseru 100; tel. 22317205; e-mail admin@lcn.org.ls; internet www.lcn.org.ls.

FOUNDATIONS AND NON-PROFITS

Vodacom Lesotho Foundation

Established in 2009 by Vodacom Lesotho, a telecommunications company; part of the Vodafone Foundation (q.v.) network.

Activities: Invests in the fields of culture, education, gender equity and women's empowerment, health, social welfare, sports and youth empowerment. Main programmes include: the Vodacom Innovation Park, an incubator for young technology entrepreneurs; Vodacom iSchool Lesotho, promoting the use of digital technology in schools to improve educational outcomes; and Moyo Lesotho, providing access for women and children to HIV services, treatment and support.

Geographical Area of Activity: Lesotho.

Finance: Total investments since 2009 c. 8m. loti.

Principal Staff: Head of Legal, Regulatory and External Affairs Molemo Motseki.

Contact Details: Vodacom Park, 585 Mabile Rd, Maseru 100; POB 7387, Maseru 100; internet www.vodacom.co.ls/about-us/foundation.

LIBYA

FOUNDATIONS AND NON-PROFITS

Kafaa Development Foundation

Established in 2011.

Activities: Works in the field of humanitarian relief and development. Main programmes areas are: conflict management and human rights advocacy; management of migration, refugees and internally displaced people, providing food, shelter and advocacy; environment and post-war sustainable development, carrying out awareness raising and workshops; health, providing training for medical staff and improving the lives of people living with disabilities; education; relief and humanitarian aid during crises; and NGO and youth development, offering training and skills development.

Geographical Area of Activity: Libya.

Principal Staff: CEO Isa Barshushi.

Contact Details: Al Haji Bldg, Noufleen St, POB 80258, Tripoli; tel. (21) 8213409731; e-mail info@kafaa.ly; internet kafaa.ly.

LIECHTENSTEIN

CO-ORDINATING BODY

Vereinigung Liechtensteinischer gemeinnütziger Stiftungen eV (Association of Liechtenstein Charitable Foundations)

Established in 2010.

Activities: Promotes the foundation sector in Liechtenstein, and Liechtenstein as a base for foundations. The Association comprises 98 member foundations and three associate members, and is a member of Philea (q.v.). It has an office in Triesen.

Geographical Area of Activity: Liechtenstein.

Publications: Annual Report; newsletter.

Finance: Annual revenue 253,577 Swiss francs, expenditure 294,598 Swiss francs (2022).

Board of Directors: Dr Thomas Zwiefelhofer (Chair.).

Principal Staff: Dir Dagmar Bühler-Nigsch.

Contact Details: Kirchstrasse 5, 9494 Schaan; tel. 2223010; e-mail info@vlgst.li; internet www.vlgst.li.

FOUNDATIONS AND NON-PROFITS

Alexander S. Onassis Public Benefit Foundation

Established in 1975 in accordance with the will of Aristotle Onassis, a shipowner.

Activities: Works in the fields of education, culture and health. The Foundation support artists, scholars and scientists, funding Greek programmes in universities around the world, and granting scholarships and research fellowships for postgraduate and doctorate studies. In Athens, it established the Onassis Cardiac Surgery Center (and is building the Onassis National Transplant Center), and the Onassis Stegi cultural centre, which hosts performances and activities in the visual and performing arts, with an emphasis on contemporary cultural expression. Maintains the Cavafy Archive, with rare books collections in the Onassis Library. Onassis USA has branches in Los Angeles and New York.

Geographical Area of Activity: International.

Restrictions: No grants to individuals.

Publications: *Onassis Stegi Program Annual Guide*; *Onassis Educational Programs Annual Guide*; books.

Presidium: Dr Anthony S. Papadimitriou (Pres. and Treas.); Costas Grammenos, Dennis M. Houston, Florian Marxer (Vice-Pres); Marianna Moschou (Gen. Sec.).

Principal Staff: Exec. Dir Michael Gattenhof.

Contact Details: Heiligkreuz 2, 9490 Vaduz; tel. 2350220; e-mail contact.vaduz@onassis.org; internet www.onassis.org/foundation.

Hilti Foundation

Established in 1996 as the charitable arm of the Martin Hilti Family Trust.

Activities: Operates internationally in the fields of housing and community development, education, culture, disaster relief and social entrepreneurship.

Geographical Area of Activity: Worldwide.

Publications: Annual Report; newsletter.

Finance: Financed by 2% of the annual consolidated earnings of the Hilti Group and contributions from the Martin Hilti Family Trust.

Int. Board: Mathias Gillner (Chair.).

Liechtenstein Board: Michèle Frey-Hilti (Chair.).

Principal Staff: Int. Man. Dir Werner Wallner; Liechtenstein Man. Dir Michelle Kranz.

Contact Details: Feldkircherstr. 100, Postfach 550, 9494 Schaan; tel. 2343762; e-mail info@hiltifoundation.org; internet www.hiltifoundation.org.

International Music and Art Foundation

Established in 1988.

Activities: Works to preserve, facilitate the study of, and disseminate information on the arts and culture. The Foundation makes grants to recognized and established organizations in the performing arts; for architectural restorations and for the conservation of art; to museums; and for research and publication on the history of art. In 2024 the total donations paid was 1.3m. Swiss francs.

Geographical Area of Activity: International.

Restrictions: No grants to individuals.

Board: Brigitte Feger, Walter Feilchenfeldt, Kurt Kimmel.

Contact Details: Heiligkreuz 40, POB 39, 9490 Vaduz; e-mail board@imaf.li; internet www.imaf.li.

Kulturstiftung Liechtenstein (Liechtenstein Foundation for Culture)

Established in 2008 as a successor to a cultural and advisory council that advised the Government of Liechtenstein.

Activities: Supports activities in the fields of literature, music, performing and fine arts, audiovisual media, cultural studies and popular culture. The Foundation provides funding, project support and training to individuals and organizations.

Geographical Area of Activity: Liechtenstein.

Publications: Annual Report.

Finance: Annual income 3.6m. Swiss francs (31 Dec. 2023).

Board of Trustees: Hansjörg Büchel (Chair.); Rainer Gasser (Vice-Chair.).

Principal Staff: Man. Dir Elisabeth Stöckler.

Contact Details: Gamanderhof, Planknerstr. 39, 9494 Schaan; tel. 2366087; e-mail info@kulturstiftung.li; internet www.kulturstiftung.li.

Stiftung Zukunft.li (Future Foundation)

Established in 2014; a think tank.

Activities: Promotes national sustainable development through fostering exchange between science, business and politics. The Foundation conducts and commissions research on economic, scientific and sociopolitical issues.

Geographical Area of Activity: Liechtenstein.

Publications: Annual Report; newsletter.

Finance: Annual income 924,500 Swiss francs, expenditure 924,500 Swiss francs (31 Dec. 2020).

Board of Trustees: Dr Gerhard Schwarz (Pres.); Dr Martin Batliner (Vice-Pres.).

Principal Staff: CEO Dr Gerald Hosp.

Contact Details: Industriering 14, 9491 Ruggell; tel. 3900000; e-mail info@stiftungzukunft.li; internet www.stiftungzukunft.li.

LITHUANIA

CO-ORDINATING BODIES

Asociacija Litdea—Lithuanian Development Education and Awareness Raising Association (Litdea Association)

Established in 2004 as Naujos Jungtys, an informal coalition; present name adopted in 2010.

Activities: Supports organizations working in the fields of international development co-operation and education. The Association strengthens member organizations through providing advice and advocacy; organizes national and international conferences, debates, discussions and seminars; and, supported by the Ministry of Foreign Affairs, runs a development education programme nationally, organizing camps, consultations, lectures and seminars. It is a co-ordinating organization of the European Voluntary Service; and a member of CONCORD (q.v.). Has 10 members.

Geographical Area of Activity: International.

Finance: Annual income €86,178, expenditure €86,178 (31 Dec. 2021).

Principal Staff: Dir Tomas Kurapkaitis.

Contact Details: Raguvos g. 7, Kaunas 40207; tel. (6) 550-2233; e-mail info@litdea.eu; internet www.litdea.eu.

Nevyriausybinių organizacijų informacijos ir paramos centras (NGO Information and Support Centre—NISC)

Founded in 1995 by the Open Society Fund—Lithuania on the initiative of the UN Development Programme.

Activities: Facilitates co-operation between NGOs and government authorities. The Centre provides information, consultancy, training and support for NGOs; and maintains an online database of funding sources for Lithuanian NGOs and a library of more than 1,000 publications. It comprises 13 member organizations and two associate members; and is a member of CIVICUS (q.v.) and the Baltic Sea NGO Network.

Geographical Area of Activity: Lithuania.

Publications: Annual Report; *Partnership among NGOs and Local Governments*; *The Third Sector* (occasional newsletter); and other research publications.

Finance: Annual income €221,625, expenditure €216,567 (31 Dec. 2023).

Principal Staff: Dir Olia Žuravliova.

Contact Details: Odminių g. 12, Vilnius 01122; tel. (8) 670-36796; e-mail info@nisc.lt; internet www.nisc.lt.

FOUNDATIONS AND NON-PROFITS

Lietuvos vaikų fondas (Lithuanian Children's Fund)
Founded in 1988 by Romanas Burba, Romualda Navikaitė and Juozas Nekrošius.
Activities: Supports disadvantaged children, their families and caregivers. Programmes include: administering sponsorships for orphans and students; offering advice to caregivers on ensuring the welfare of foster children; organizing summer activities for children growing up in care institutions and families at risk; providing human rights and social skills training for Roma children; renovating children's care institutions; and preparing children in orphanages for independent living. The Fund also supports child care institutions, hospitals and other support organizations and individuals.
Geographical Area of Activity: Lithuania.
Publications: Annual Report.
Finance: Partly financed by the EU and the European Social Fund.
Principal Staff: Dir Romualda Navikaitė.
Contact Details: Laisvės pr. 125, Vilnius 06118; tel. (5) 262-8836; e-mail info@lvf.lt; internet www.lietuvosvaikufondas.eu.

Rytų Europos Studijų Centras—RESC (Eastern Europe Studies Centre—EESC)
Established in 2006 under the EU PHARE cross-border co-operation programme; an independent think tank.
Activities: Carries out policy research and analysis in the fields of international affairs, security and economic co-operation. The Centre promotes Euro-Atlantic co-operation and multilateral dialogue, an active civil society, democracy and the rule of law. It undertakes national and international projects, co-operating with state institutions and NGOs in Lithuania and abroad; and organizes public and private events, including discussions, seminars, roundtables and an annual foreign policy conference.
Geographical Area of Activity: Eastern Europe, EU, Russian Federation.
Publications: Annual Report; newsletter; *Vladimir Putin's Russia* (series); *Lithuanian Foreign Policy Review* (annual journal); studies.
Finance: Funded by Vilnius University and the Lithuanian Ministry of Foreign Affairs.
Principal Staff: Dir Linas Kojala.
Contact Details: D. Poškos g. 59, Vilnius 08114; tel. (6) 555-6836; e-mail info@eesc.lt; internet www.eesc.lt.

LUXEMBOURG

CO-ORDINATING BODY

Cercle de Coopération des ONGD du Luxembourg (Luxembourg Development NGO Co-operation Circle)
Established in 1979 by six development NGOs.
Activities: Supports development NGOs working to eliminate global poverty through humanitarian action, international solidarity and social change. Priority areas are policy coherence for development, global citizenship education and volunteering. The Circle strengthens, federates and represents member organizations, providing support and advice in development project planning; and advocacy to influence decision-makers in Luxembourg. It offers training in project management, evaluation and communication; co-ordinates working groups, sharing expertise and learning; and organizes activities and events. The Voluntary Cooperation Service (SVC) offers placements with development NGOs lasting between six months and one year, co-ordinated by the National Youth Service (SNJ). The Circle has 92 members and is a member of CONCORD (q.v.).
Geographical Area of Activity: Luxembourg.
Restrictions: SVC applicants must be Luxembourg residents aged 18–30 years.
Publications: Newsletter; brochure; checklists; position papers; reports; toolkits.
Board of Directors: Luc Siebenaller (Pres.); Véronique Weis, Richard Graf (Vice-Pres); Françoise Binsfeld (Treas.); Florence Burette (Sec.).
Principal Staff: Dir Nicole E. Ikuku.
Contact Details: 1–7 rue Saint Ulric, 2651 Luxembourg; tel. 26-02-09-11; e-mail info@cercle.lu; internet cercle.lu.

FOUNDATIONS AND NON-PROFITS

Action Solidarité Tiers Monde—ASTM (Third World Solidarity Action)
Established in 1969 by a group of student volunteers.
Activities: Collaborates with indigenous organizations in less-developed countries in the areas of education and sustainable development, concentrating on access to land, commercialization of agricultural production, microcredit, and health and women's rights. The organization also provides information on the cultures of the developing world; generates support for cultural activities; and develops cultural exchanges, initially through a programme linking Luxembourg with Algeria, India and Senegal. It maintains an information centre (CITIM), which provides access to more than 10,000 items and specialist information on countries of the global South, North–South relations and human development. Co-founded the Alliance pour le Climat Luxembourg (f. 1995), part of the Climate Alliance.
Geographical Area of Activity: Central and South America, Middle East, South and South-East Asia, West Africa.
Publications: Annual Report; *Brennpunkt Drëtt Welt* (newsletter); reports; brochures.
Finance: Annual revenue €3.6m., expenditure €3.6m. (2023).
Board of Directors: Richard Graf, Monique Langevin (Co-Chair.); Pierre Schmit (Treas.).
Contact Details: 136–138 rue Adolphe Fischer, 1521 Luxembourg; tel. 40-04-27-1; e-mail astm@astm.lu; internet astm.lu.

Fondation Follereau Luxembourg—FFL (Follereau Foundation Luxembourg)
Established in 1966 by Raoul Follereau, a French writer and journalist, to address the exclusion caused by leprosy.
Activities: Promotes solidarity and works to eliminate all forms of exclusion. Main programmes include education, emergency response, health and protection. The Foundation: improves public health, in particular of mothers and children, and works to end female genital mutilation (FGM); and helps children and young people in distress, providing vocational training and protecting them from human trafficking and child labour. It works in eight countries in sub-Saharan Africa.
Geographical Area of Activity: sub-Saharan Africa.
Publications: Annual Report; *Solidarité Follereau* (newsletter).
Finance: Annual income €3.8m., expenditure €4.5m. (2022).
Board of Directors: Jean Hilger (Pres.); Julio Nerin (Vice-Pres.).
Principal Staff: Exec. Officer Conny Reichling.

Contact Details: 204 route d'Arlon, 8010 Strassen; tel. 44-66-06-1; e-mail info@ffl.lu; internet www.ffl.lu.

IAESTE—International Association for the Exchange of Students for Technical Experience

Founded in 1948 by James Newby, following a conference at the Imperial College of Science and Technology, London (UK), with organizers from 10 European countries.

Activities: Promotes international understanding, co-operation and trust. The Association arranges reciprocal career-focused professional internships, and organizes social and intercultural programmes, mainly for students of engineering and technology, but also of agriculture, architecture, applied arts, biomedicine, business and management, and sciences. Students normally spend 8–12 weeks abroad; longer-term placements are also available. Each year, the Association exchanges more than 3,500 traineeships with 3,000 employers and 1,000 academic institutions in more than 100 countries.

Geographical Area of Activity: International.

Restrictions: Does not make grants; applicants must be enrolled in full-time Bachelor of Arts or Master of Arts courses.

Publications: Annual Review; newsletters.

Finance: Funded by member subscriptions.

Board: Thomas Faltner (Pres.); Dan Ewert (Treas.); Dr Karunakar A. Kotegar (Sec.).

Principal Staff: Head of Operations Olga Legacka.

Contact Details: 51 rue Albert I, 1st Floor, 1117 Luxembourg; tel. 20-33-16-99; e-mail info@iaeste.org; internet www.iaeste.org.

Unity Foundation

Established in 1980; an international development organization inspired by the Baha'i faith.

Activities: Empowers communities through education, working with local development organizations to meet the needs of local populations. The Foundation establishes community schools and training centres for teachers and local development organizations; and develops education programmes that build young people's skills in the areas of community development, community service and technology. In Luxembourg, it raises awareness about international development, offering training for teachers and organizations working in the socio-educational sector.

Geographical Area of Activity: Cambodia, Central African Repub., Colombia, Indonesia, Malawi, Uganda, Zambia.

Publications: Annual Report; newsletter; manuals.

Finance: Co-financed by the Ministry of Foreign and European Affairs (76%); project expenditure €857,108 (2023).

Administrative Council: Fernand Schaber (Pres.); Abbas Rafii (Vice-Pres.); Paola Dumet-Fusco (Treas.).

Contact Details: 29 blvd Prince Henri, 1724 Luxembourg; tel. 621-656-998; e-mail info@unityfoundation.lu; internet www.unityfoundation.lu.

Vodafone Foundation Luxembourg

Established in 2018.

Activities: Supports initiatives to prevent domestic abuse and violence against women using digital technology; and to provide access to sport for disabled athletes.

Geographical Area of Activity: Luxembourg.

Principal Staff: Head of Foundation Rhys Shegar-Astoralli.

Contact Details: Pixel Bldg, 15 rue Edward Steichen, 2540 Luxembourg; internet www.vodafone.com/vodafone-foundation/vodafone-luxembourg-foundation.

MADAGASCAR

FOUNDATIONS AND NON-PROFITS

Orange Solidarité Madagascar

Established in 2011 by Orange Madagascar, a mobile telecommunications company; part of the Fondation Orange (q.v.) network.

Activities: Supports equal opportunities and works to reduce the digital divide. The Foundation carries out activities in the fields of digital culture, education, health and socioeconomic development. It offers grants to NGOs and promotes corporate volunteering.

Geographical Area of Activity: Madagascar.

Principal Staff: Pres. Benja Arson.

Contact Details: La Tour, rue Ravoninahitriniarivo, Ankorondrano, BP 7754, 101 Antananarivo; tel. 32 34 567 89; e-mail orangesolidaritemadagascar.oma@orange.com; internet www.orange.mg/mecenat.

MALAWI

FOUNDATIONS AND NON-PROFITS

Joyce Banda Foundation International

Established in 1997 by Dr Joyce Banda, who was President of Malawi between 2012 and 2014.

Activities: Promotes women's mobilization and leadership. Main programme areas are: women, including MWAI Women, which empowers 400,000 members by giving them financial independence and business training; education, offering free primary and secondary education at two schools, in Domasi and Blantyre, and caring for orphans aged 3–5 years at 35 centres across the country; youth and sport, which also provides HIV/AIDS education; and village transformation, which provides smallholder farmers with seeds, fertilizers and training, runs the One Goat & One Cow Per Family Program, builds clinics in partnership with healthcare providers and helps local people to build homes. Runs the Joyce Banda Foundation Schools (f. 1997). Has an office in Washington, DC, USA.

Geographical Area of Activity: Malawi.

Principal Staff: Man. Dir Edith Akridge.

Contact Details: Chimwankhunda, Near Living Waters Church, Blantyre; POB 51321, Limbe; tel. 999090269; e-mail info@joycebandafoundation.org; internet joycebandafoundation.org.

Shaping Our Future Foundation—SOFF

Established in 2020 by First Lady Monica Chakwera.

Activities: Promotes the development of girls living in villages and 'street' children, advocates for menstrual health education and keeping girls in education, supports projects to improve agriculture and raises awareness of climate change.
Geographical Area of Activity: Malawi.
Board: Monica Chakwera (Chair.).
Contact Details: Plot 6/263, POB 3050, Lilongwe; e-mail info@shapingourfuturefoundation.org; internet soff.org.mw.

Tea Research Foundation of Central Africa—TRFCA
Founded in 1966.
Activities: Conducts research into aspects of tea and coffee production in Southern and Central Africa, with an emphasis on agronomy, plant breeding, plant propagation and crop management. The Foundation maintains two research stations in Malawi and one on-farm research centre in Chipinge, Zimbabwe. It runs a training programme for tea estate workers and managers.
Geographical Area of Activity: Malawi, Mozambique, Zambia, Zimbabwe.
Publications: Annual Report; newsletter (2 a year); manuals; handbooks; books.
Board of Management: Grant Bramsen (Chair.).
Principal Staff: CEO Tonda Chinangwa.
Contact Details: Mimosa Tea Research Station, 15 km from Mulanje Boma, along Muloza Border Rd; POB 51, Mulanje, Malawi; tel. 995187588; e-mail trfdirector@trfca.org.

MALAYSIA

FOUNDATIONS AND NON-PROFITS

Kuok Foundation Berhad
Established in 1970 by the Kuok family, who founded the Kuok Group, a conglomerate.
Activities: Works to alleviate poverty, foster self-reliance and empower disadvantaged people through education and training. Each year, the Foundation offers more than 1,800 scholarships and study loans for secondary and higher education in Malaysia and Singapore. It supports scientific research and teaching, providing facilities and services and endowing professorial chairs; organizes humanitarian and poverty relief, healthcare and social services for people in need and victims of disasters; and funds health institutions and therapeutic activities.
Geographical Area of Activity: Malaysia, Singapore.
Restrictions: Study awards for Malaysian students only; preference is given to students aged under 25 years for undergraduate awards and under 22 years for diploma-level awards.
Finance: Total annual disbursements 19m. ringgit.
Principal Staff: Chair. Robert Kuok Hock Nien.
Contact Details: Letter Box No. 110, 16th Floor, UBN Tower, No. 10, Jalan P. Ramlee, 50250 Kuala Lumpur; tel. (3) 27118428; e-mail general@kuokfoundation.com; internet www.kuokfoundation.com.

Perdana Global Peace Foundation—PGPF
Established in 2005 by Tun Dr Mahathir Mohamad, a former Prime Minister of Malaysia, at the launch of the Kuala Lumpur Initiative to Criminalise War, during the first Perdana Global Peace Forum.
Activities: Works in the fields of foreign aid and international relations. Main programmes and initiatives include: the Somalia Artesian Wells Project, building and refurbishing wells in and around the Somali capital, Mogadishu; the Enaya Physio & Rehab Centre in Gaza, building and equipping a modern facility for people in need; the Criminalise War Fund/War Disaster Fund Initiative, supporting NGOs and community development in countries affected by war; and the Rohingya Fund, raising funds to assist ethnic Rohingya people seeking refuge in foreign countries. The Foundation organizes international conferences and sponsors the Mahathir Award for Global Peace.
Geographical Area of Activity: Malaysia, Palestinian Territories, Somalia.
Board of Trustees: Tun Dr Mahathir Mohamad (Pres.); Tan Sri Norian Mai (Chair.); Dato' Haji Zaihal Hazri Abdul Halim (Treas.).
Contact Details: 5th Floor, No. 88, Jl. Perdana, Taman Tasek Perdana, 50480 Kuala Lumpur; tel. (3) 20927248; e-mail admin@perdana4peace.org; internet www.perdana4peace.org.

Pesticide Action Network Asia and the Pacific—PANAP
Established in 1992 as a regional centre of the PAN International network (f. 1982).
Activities: Works to protect people and the environment from Highly Hazardous Pesticides through monitoring communities and lobbying governments and international institutions. Activities include: promoting agroecology and food sovereignty; supporting people's movements to assert their rights to land and livelihoods; resisting corporate agriculture and control over seeds; opposing economic policies that harm people's interests; and empowering rural communities and strengthening women's leadership. The Network comprises 109 regional member organizations.
Geographical Area of Activity: Asia-Pacific region.
Publications: Annual Report; *Pesticide Monitor* (quarterly newsletter); books; booklets; e-books; factsheets; monographs.
Principal Staff: Exec. Dir Sarojeni V. Rengam.
Contact Details: 48 Persiaran Mutiara 1, Pusat Komersial Bandar Mutiara, 14120 Simpang Ampat, Penang; tel. (4) 5022337; e-mail info@panap.net; internet www.panap.net.

Third World Network—TWN
Founded in 1984; a non-profit international network of organizations and individuals.
Activities: Promotes the needs and rights of people in developing countries and the fair distribution of global resources through conducting policy research and advocacy. Thematic areas of interest include: biodiversity and indigenous knowledge; biotechnology and biosafety; climate change; finance and development; global financial and economic crises; health; human rights; intellectual property rights; sustainable development; tourism; the UN and UN reform; women and gender; and the World Trade Organization and free trade agreements. The Network organizes seminars and represents the interests of developing countries at international conferences. It has offices in Switzerland and India.
Geographical Area of Activity: Asia, Africa, Latin America, Western Europe.
Publications: *Third World Resurgence* (magazine, monthly); *Third World Economics* (magazine, 2 a month); *SUNS bulletin* (daily); *TWN Features Service* (media service, 3 a week); briefing papers; reports; books.
Finance: Funded by magazine subscription fees and sale of publications.
Board of Governors: Lim Mah Hui (Chair.).
Contact Details: 131 Jl. Macalister, 10400 Penang; tel. (4) 2266728; e-mail twn@twnetwork.org; internet www.twn.my.

Women's Aid Organisation—WAO (Pertubuhan Pertolongan Wanita)

Established in 1982 to promote women's rights in Malaysia, originally through the provision of women's refuges.

Activities: Provides free and confidential services to survivors of domestic violence and other forms of gender-based violence. The Organisation advocates for survivors' rights; conducts research; and improves public policies on discrimination and violence against women.

Geographical Area of Activity: Malaysia.

Publications: Annual Report; *Inroads* (quarterly newsletter); statistics; brochures.

Finance: Annual income 3.7m. ringgit, expenditure 4.0m. ringgit (31 Dec. 2022).

Executive Committee: Shanthi Dairiam (Pres.); Joyce Segajanantham (Vice-Pres.); Anitha Ramakrishnan (Treas.); Malligah Suppiah (Sec.).

Principal Staff: Exec. Dir Sumitra Visvanathan.

Contact Details: POB 493, Jalan Sultan, 46760 Petaling Jaya, Selangor Darul Ehsan; tel. (3) 79575636; e-mail info@wao.org.my; internet www.wao.org.my.

WorldFish

Established in 1975; an initiative of the Rockefeller Foundation (q.v.), previously known as the International Center for Living Aquatic Resources Management (ICLARM); part of the CGIAR (Consultative Group on International Agricultural Research) international network of research centres.

Activities: Conducts research on all aspects of aquatic food systems. Main programme areas are: climate change and climate-smart aquaculture; the blue economy and improved livelihoods; gender equity and improving economic opportunities for women and young people; nutrition, tackling hunger with aquatic foods; and enhancing sustainability through policy changes and building value chains. The Centre organizes conferences; and offers graduate and postgraduate studentships. It has country offices in Bangladesh, Cambodia, Egypt, India, Malawi, Myanmar, Nigeria, Solomon Islands, Tanzania, Timor-Leste and Zambia.

Geographical Area of Activity: Africa, Asia and the Pacific.

Publications: Annual Report; newsletter; *Coral Triangle Atlas*; FishBase; ReefBase; conference proceedings; reviews; studies; technical reports.

Finance: Annual revenue US $31.8m., expenditure $31.6m. (31 Dec. 2023).

Board of Trustees: Baba Yusuf Abubakar (Chair.); Alyssa Jade McDonald-Baertl (Vice-Chair.).

Principal Staff: Dir-Gen. Essam Yassin Mohammed.

Contact Details: POB 500, GPO 10670, Penang; Jl. Batu Maung, Batu Maung, 11960 Bayan Lepas, Penang; tel. (4) 6286888; e-mail worldfishcenter@cgiar.org; internet www.worldfishcenter.org.

Yayasan Azman Hashim (Azman Hashim Foundation)

Established in 1991 by Tan Sri Azman Hashim, founder and Exec. Chair. of Ambank Group, and his wife Tunku Arishah Tunku Maamor.

Activities: Works in the fields of education, social welfare and poverty alleviation, awarding scholarships and study grants. The Foundation has funded the construction of faculty and sports facilities, including at the International Islamic University of Malaysia, Universiti Sains Malaysia, Penang, and the University of Malaya.

Geographical Area of Activity: Malaysia.

Finance: The founders pledged US $300m. to the Foundation.

Principal Staff: Exec. Chair. Tan Sri Azman Hashim.

Contact Details: c/o Amcorp Group Berhad, 2-01 Amcorp Tower, 18 Persiaran Barat, 46050 Petaling Jaya, Selangor; tel. (3) 79662300; internet www.amcorp.com.my/html/corporate_social_responsibilities.aspx.

MALDIVES

FOUNDATIONS AND NON-PROFITS

Ali Fulhu Thuthu Foundation

Established in 2000 in memory of Moosa Ali (Ali Fulhu Thuthu).

Activities: Works in the fields of social and cultural development through making grants to grassroots community projects and offering scholarships for study abroad through the United World College. The Foundation collaborates with other NGOs on programmes that address issues such as drug abuse; the care and education of disabled children; and raising awareness about health and wellbeing in schools.

Geographical Area of Activity: International.

Publications: Annual Report.

Executive Board: Hussain Afeef (Chair.); Sarah Afeef (Sec.).

Contact Details: Champa Bldg, 3rd Floor, Kandidhonmaniku Goalhi, Malé 20187; tel. 3322475; e-mail info@aftfoundation.org.mv; internet www.aftfoundation.org.

Coastline Foundation

Established in 2013 by Coastline Investments, an investment company.

Activities: Provides access to medical care and education for vulnerable people and skills training for young people. The Foundation built the Hulhumalé Mosque; and established and manages the Technical and Vocational Education Center (TVEC) in Kihaadhoo, Baa Atoll, offering scholarships for trainee mechanics and engineers.

Geographical Area of Activity: Maldives.

Principal Staff: Chair. of Coastline Group Ahmed Umar Maniku.

Contact Details: Maaveyo Magu, Malé; tel. 3332822; e-mail secretary@coastlinefoundation.mv; internet www.coastlinegroup.com.mv/coastline-foundation.

Universal Foundation

Established in 2013 by Universal Enterprises, a leisure resort developer.

Activities: Works in the fields of education, health and community care through supporting community centres and schools, NGOs and local organizations. The Foundation awards grants and international scholarships; and supports the health sector, sponsoring doctors to study for medical qualifications.

Geographical Area of Activity: Maldives, Sri Lanka.

Principal Staff: Pres. Iyaz Waheed.

Contact Details: 39 Orchid Magu 20-02, Malé; tel. 3323080; e-mail info@universalfoundation.org.mv; internet www.universalfoundation.org.mv.

MALI

FOUNDATIONS AND NON-PROFITS

Association AGIR pour l'Environnement et la Qualité de la Vie (AGIR Association for the Environment and Quality of Life)
Established in 1994 as SOS Zoo by First Lady Keïta Aminata Maïga and the Association des Amis du Budo Club; present name adopted in 2003.
Activities: Works to improve people's quality of life. Main programme areas are: environmental education; health; hygiene and sanitation; and sustainable management of natural resources. The Foundation also carries out activities in the areas of: adolescent reproductive health; ending child marriage; and girls' and women's education and economic empowerment.
Geographical Area of Activity: Mali.
Publications: Annual Report; *AGIT infos* (weekly newsletter).
Principal Staff: Pres. Aminata Maïga Keïta.
Contact Details: ACI 2000 Hamdallaye, rue 234, Porte 92, BP E 3449, Bamako; tel. 20211556; e-mail contact@ong-agir.ml; internet ong-agir.ml.

Fondation CMDID—Centre Malien pour le Dialogue Interpartis et la Démocratie (CMDID Foundation—Malian Centre for Inter-Party Dialogue and Democracy)
Established in 2008, growing out of Projet Partenariat pour le Renforcement des Capacités des Partis Politiques (f. 2003).
Activities: Fosters democracy and political dialogue through strengthening the capacity of political parties and mediating in conflicts.
Geographical Area of Activity: Mali.
Board of Directors: Aboubacar Sandina Camara (Chair.).
Contact Details: rue 483, Porte 120, Bamako; tel. 20230610.

Fondation Orange Mali
Established in 2006 by Orange, a telecommunications company; part of the Fondation Orange (q.v.) network.
Activities: Runs programmes in the fields of health, education, culture and social welfare; and works with local organizations and NGOs. The Foundation's digital schools programme operates in 50 schools in and around Bamako. The Digital Houses programme uses digital tools to train women and girls in basic entrepreneurial skills such as managing income-generating activities, simplified accounting, financial management and marketing.
Geographical Area of Activity: Mali.
Principal Staff: Pres. Brelotte Ba.
Contact Details: Immeuble Mgr Jean-Marie Cissé, Hamdallaye ACI 2000, BP E 3991, Bamako; tel. 44999000; internet www.orangemali.com/fondation.

MALTA

FOUNDATIONS AND NON-PROFITS

DiploFoundation
Established in 2002 by the Governments of Malta and Switzerland, building on a project initiated in 1992 at the Mediterranean Academy of Diplomatic Studies.
Activities: Works to build the capacity of small and developing states in engaging in international policy processes, negotiations and diplomacy through: training officials and others working in the field of international relations; developing capacity in the areas of internet governance, data, artificial intelligence and emerging technologies; and promoting and developing digital tools for inclusive governance and policy-making. It has special consultative status with ECOSOC; and has offices in Belgrade (Serbia), Geneva (Switzerland) and Washington, DC (USA).
Geographical Area of Activity: International.
Publications: Annual Report; *Digital Watch* (newsletter); reports; research papers.
Finance: Annual income €2.9m., expenditure €2.6m. (31 Dec. 2023).
Board: Bernadino Ragazzoni (Chair.).
Principal Staff: Exec. Dir Dr Jovan Kurbalija.
Contact Details: Anutruf, Ground Floor, 5 Hriereb St, Msida MSD 1675; tel. 21333323; e-mail diplo@diplomacy.edu; internet www.diplomacy.edu.

Fondazzjoni Patrimonju Malti (Maltese Heritage Foundation)
Established in 1992 by a small group of Maltese cultural heritage enthusiasts with the backing of government.
Activities: Promotes Maltese cultural heritage through exhibitions of artefacts from private collections and public and non-profit institutions and organizations that would otherwise not be accessible to the public. The Foundation restored the 13th-century Palazzo Falson in Mdina, which houses the Historic House Museum (f. 2007). The Foundation also runs the Victor Pasmore Gallery.
Geographical Area of Activity: Malta.
Publications: Newsletter; *Treasures of Malta* (magazine, 3 a year); various publications about Melitensia.
Principal Staff: CEO Michael Lowell.
Contact Details: APS House, 275 St Paul St, Valletta VLT 1213; tel. 21244777; e-mail info@patrimonju.org; internet www.patrimonju.org.

Solidarity Overseas Service Malta—SOS Malta
Established in 1991 in response to the exodus of refugees from Albania.
Activities: Supports people who are experiencing times of crisis. Main programmes are: overseas development and emergency aid; social solidarity; research and training; and promoting volunteering. The organization is the Fund Operator for European Economic Area grants, managing the Active Citizens fund for NGOs.
Geographical Area of Activity: International.
Publications: Annual Report; newsletter; thematic country reports.
Principal Staff: CEO and Sec. Claudia Taylor-East.
Contact Details: 10 Triq il-Ward, Santa Venera SVR 1640; tel. 21244123; e-mail info@sosmalta.org; internet www.sosmalta.org.

Strickland Foundation
Established in 1979 by Mabel Strickland, a newspaper owner and politician.

Activities: Promotes democratic principles, human rights and freedom of the press. The Foundation supports projects in the areas of education, sport, religion, health, social and community services, arts and culture, national heritage and the environment. It awards scholarships; organizes and hosts seminars and conferences, supporting awards for Maltese journalists through the Malta–EU Information Centre; and funds publications, including *The Mediterranean Journal of Human Rights*, which is published by the University of Malta.

Geographical Area of Activity: Malta.

Council: Giovanni Bonello (Chair.); Peter Portelli (Exec. Sec.).

Contact Details: Villa Parisio 36, Mabel Strickland St, Lija; tel. 21435890; e-mail admin@thestricklandfoundation.org; internet thestricklandfoundation.org.

MAURITANIA

FOUNDATIONS AND NON-PROFITS

Fondation Noura
Established in 1988 in the Netherlands; present in Mauritania since 1997.

Activities: Supports disadvantaged people and their development. The Foundation offers courses including French literacy, computer and business skills, basic health and hygiene, and sewing through: the Training Center Project; Prison Projects; Juvenile Detention Center Projects; Women's Sewing Cooperative; and the Adult Literacy Project. It provides legal and psychosocial support to women in prison and women coming out of prison.

Geographical Area of Activity: Mauritania.

Principal Staff: Dir Alfred Mbemba.

Contact Details: Ksar A70, BP 1082, Nouakchott; tel. 620-0527; e-mail info@nouraprojects.com; internet www.noura.faithweb.com.

MAURITIUS

FOUNDATIONS AND NON-PROFITS

Mauritius Telecom Foundation—MTF
Established in 2009 by Mauritius Telecom; part of the Fondation Orange (q.v.) network.

Activities: Carries out activities in the fields of education, the environment, disability, ICT, and sport and wellness. The Foundation works with local NGOs and institutions; and oversees corporate social responsibility funds for several telecommunications companies.

Geographical Area of Activity: Mauritius.

Finance: Total disbursements since 2009 375m. rupees (2023).

Principal Staff: Chair. of Foundation Veemal Gungadin.

Contact Details: 5th Floor, Telecom Tower, Edith Cavell St, Port-Louis 11302; tel. 203-7522; e-mail mtfoundation@telecom.mu; internet www.telecom.mu/our-company/corporate-social-responsibility.html.

National Empowerment Foundation—NEF
Established in 2006 as a public non-profit company to carry out the Government's Empowerment Programme.

Activities: Works to eliminate extreme and chronic poverty and to create an inclusive and more equitable society. Main programmes are: fostering socioeconomic development to address poverty and social exclusion; providing technical and financial assistance to reduce unemployment among women; vocational and skills training; and fostering entrepreneurship. The Foundation also runs a child welfare programme for children's education and wellbeing. It works with local and international organizations and NGOs. Has an office on Île Rodrigues.

Geographical Area of Activity: Mauritius.

Principal Staff: Officer-in-Charge Trishna Jogessur.

Contact Details: Garden Tower, 8e étage, rue La Poudrière, Port-Louis; tel. 405-5100; e-mail contact@nef.mu; internet www.nef.mu.

MEXICO

CO-ORDINATING BODIES

Centro Mexicano para la Filantropía—CEMEFI (Mexican Centre for Philanthropy)

Established in 1988.

Activities: Promotes philanthropy and the socially responsible participation of citizens, social organizations and companies in building a more equitable, supportive and prosperous society. The Centre conducts research and advocacy; and organizes conferences and training courses. It comprises 1,538 institutional and individual members.

Geographical Area of Activity: Mexico.

Publications: Annual Report; *Vision con Futuro* (newsletter); *Cemefi Informa* (newsletter); *Directorio de Instituciones Filantrópicas*; *Mexican Civil Society Index*; guides.

Finance: Annual income 171.5m. pesos, expenditure 148.4m. pesos (31 Dec. 2024).

Board of Directors: Jorge Aguilar Valenzuela (Chair.); Javier de la Calle Pardo (Vice-Chair.); Javier Gavaldón Enciso (Treas.); Julio Copo Terrés (Sec.).

Principal Staff: CEO Ricardo Bucio Mujica.

Contact Details: Cerrada de Salvador Alvarado 7, Col. Escandón, Mayor Miguel Hidalgo, 11800 Ciudad de México; tel. (55) 5276-8530; e-mail cemefi@cemefi.org; internet www.cemefi.org.

Comunalia—Alianza de Fundaciones Comunitarias de México (Network of Mexican Community Foundations)

Established in 2011.

Activities: Focuses on local development and strategic social inversion, through amplifying the collective impact and reach of member foundations. The Alliance works to empower people; influence public policies; develop leadership; and replicate and strengthen the Mexican model of community foundations. It operates in 16 states.

Geographical Area of Activity: Mexico.

Publications: *El desarrollo de base en Comunalia*; *Glosario de las Fundaciones Comunitarias*; *Guía para las Fundaciones Comunitarias de México*; *Fortalecimiento de Redes*; *Las fundaciones comunitarias como un actor clave en el contexto de emergencia*; *Iniciativas de sociedad civil para la reactivación social y económica de las comunidades*.

Finance: Annual income US $7.8m., expenditure $8.0m. (31 Dec. 2023).

Board of Directors: Carlos Garcia (Pres.).

Principal Staff: Exec. Dir Daniella Undreiner.

Contact Details: YCo. Centro de Innovación e Impacto Social, Avda del Estado 208, Col. Tecnológico, 64700 Monterrey, Nuevo Leon; tel. (81) 2719 6670; e-mail direccion@comunalia.org.mx; internet www.comunalia.org.mx.

FOUNDATIONS AND NON-PROFITS

Centro Internacional de Mejoramiento de Maíz y Trigo—CIMMYT (International Maize and Wheat Improvement Center)

Founded in 1966 by the Government of Mexico and the Rockefeller Foundation (q.v.); part of the Consultative Group on International Agricultural Research (CGIAR) global network of research centres.

Activities: Operates internationally through self-conducted programmes, research, fellowships, scholarships, conferences, courses, publications and lectures. The Center supports the development and distribution worldwide of genetically modified wheat and maize; conservation and distribution of maize and wheat genetic resources; research on natural resource management in maize- and wheat-based cropping systems; documentation of new knowledge in the area of wheat and maize; development of more effective research methods; training; and technical consultation. Has offices in Benin, People's Repub. of China, Colombia, Ethiopia, India, Kenya, Malawi, Nepal, Pakistan, Senegal, Türkiye (Turkey), Zambia and Zimbabwe.

Geographical Area of Activity: Worldwide.

Publications: Annual Report; newsletter; reports; CIMMYT Academy (e-learning platform).

Finance: Annual revenue US $110.4m., expenditure $113.2m. (31 Dec. 2021).

Board of Trustees: Margaret Bath (Chair.).

Principal Staff: Dir-Gen. Bram Govaerts.

Contact Details: Edo. de México, Km 45, Carretera México-Veracruz, El Batán, 56237 Texcoco; tel. (55) 5804-2004; e-mail cimmyt@cgiar.org; internet www.cimmyt.org.

Fundación Carlos Slim (Carlos Slim Foundation)

Established in 1986 by Carlos Slim Helú, owner of Grupo Carso, a conglomerate.

Activities: Carries out self-conducted programmes in the fields of: culture; disaster relief; economic and social development; education; employment; the environment; health; human development; justice; migrants; research and innovation; road safety; and sport. The Foundation supports the Asociación de Superación por México (ASUME; f. 1980), which works in the field of human development in 15 Latin American countries; the Centro de Estudios de Historia de México Carso (CEHM; f. 1965), which archives materials on the history of Mexico; the Fundación del Centro Histórico de la Ciudad de México, which promotes socioeconomic development in central México, DF; and the Museo Soumaya (f. 1994), which houses a collection of Mesoamerican, Latin American and European art. The Salud Digital (Digital Health) programme offers scholarships to students of medicine, nursing and nutrition; the annual Premios Carlos Slim en Salud awards, each worth US $100,000, recognize Latin American health researchers and institutions.

Geographical Area of Activity: Latin America.

Publications: Annual Report.

Principal Staff: Pres. Carlos Slim.

Contact Details: Avda Paseo de las Palmas No. 781, Piso 03, Colonia Lomas de Chapultepec III Sección, CP 11000, Delegación Miguel Hidalgo, Ciudad de México; internet fundacioncarlosslim.org.

Fundación FEMSA (FEMSA Foundation)

Established in 2008 by Fomento Económico Mexicano, S.A.B. de C.V. (FEMSA), a multinational beverage and retail company.

Activities: Promotes sustainable social investment. Main programme areas are: early childhood development; water, sanitation and hygiene, and watershed conservation; and the arts and culture. In 2008, with the Inter-American Development Bank and Tecnológico de Monterrey, the Foundation established the Water Center for Latin America and the Caribbean, which carries out research on water sustainability and offers training courses for water professionals; and the FEMSA Biotechnology Center at Tecnológico de Monterrey, which carries out research on nutrigenomics and develops technologies for the measurement and early detection of diseases. In 2011, working with the Inter-American Development Bank, the Global Environment Facility, the International Climate Protection Initiative and the Nature Conservancy (q.v.), it established the Latin American Alliance for Water Funds, a network of 21 Water Funds. The FEMSA Collection comprises more than 1,200 works of modern and contemporary Latin American art, which have been loaned to exhibitions in 11 countries around the world; more than 100 works have been added to the collection through the FEMSA Biennial.

Geographical Area of Activity: Latin America and the Caribbean, Philippines.

Publications: Annual Report; newsletter; blog.

Finance: Programme expenditure US $44.4m. (2021).

Board of Directors: José Antonio Fernández Carbajal (Pres.); Alejandro Gil (Sec.).

Principal Staff: Dir Lorena Guillé-Laris.

Contact Details: Av. Gral. Anaya 601 Pte., Col. Bellavista, 64410 Monterrey, Nuevo Leon; tel. (81) 8328-6000; e-mail fundacion@femsa.com.mx; internet fundacionfemsa.org.

Fundación Miguel Alemán AC (Miguel Alemán Foundation)

Founded in 1984 by Miguel Alemán Valdés, former President of Mexico.

Activities: Works in the fields of health, innovation in agrifood, tourism, ecology and the environment, gender equality, and culture and education in the humanities. The Foundation carries out self-conducted programmes and research; awards grants to institutions and prizes; and organizes conferences and training courses.

Geographical Area of Activity: Mexico.

Publications: Annual Report; *Inform* (annual); several other publications.

Board of Trustees: Miguel Alemán Velasco (Chair.).

Principal Staff: Gen. Man. Dr Alejandro Carrillo Castro.

Contact Details: Rubén Darío 187, Col. Chapultepec Morales, 11570 Ciudad de México; tel. (55) 9126-0700; e-mail fundacionmiguelaleman@fma.com.mx; internet www.fundacionmiguelaleman.org.

Fundación Telefónica Movistar México (Telefónica Movistar México Foundation)

Established in 2003 by Telefónica Movistar México, a telecommunications company; part of the Fundación Telefónica (q.v.) network.

Activities: Main programmes focus on: digital culture, education, employability and volunteering. The Foundation offers free online training and digital tools via the Conecta Empleo platform; and educational resources and professional teacher training via the ProFuturo digital education programme, a joint initiative with Fundación Bancaria 'la Caixa' (q.v.).

Geographical Area of Activity: Mexico.

Finance: Total assets 19.4m. pesos (31 Dec. 2023).

Board of Directors: Camilo Aya Caro (Pres.); Delice Cristal Cruz Guzman (Treas.); Juan Manuel Haddad (Sec.).

Principal Staff: Dir Nidia Chavez.

Contact Details: Prol. Paseo de la Reforma 1200, Piso 19, Col. Cruz Manca Del. Cuajimalpa de Morelos, CP 05349, Ciudad de México; e-mail fundaciontelefonica.mx@telefonica.com; internet www.fundaciontelefonica.com.mx.

Fundación Teletón México (Teletón México Foundation)

Established in 1998.

Activities: Funds 22 rehabilitation centres for children with autism, disabilities and cancer. The Foundation set up the Fondo de Apoyo a Instituciones Teletón—FAI to support other organizations that help people with disabilities. In 2000, in collaboration with the Universidad Autónoma del Estado de México, the Foundation set up the Instituto Teletón de Estudios Superiores en Rehabilitación, which specialized in training rehabilitation professionals in occupational and physical therapy and was expanded to become the Universidad Teletón in 2013. A sister organization operates in the USA, which raises funds to operate the Children's Rehabilitation Institute of TeletonUSA.

Geographical Area of Activity: Mexico.

Finance: Annual income 2,862.7m. pesos, expenditure 2,201.7m. pesos (31 Dec. 2023).

Principal Staff: Pres. Dr Fernando Landeros Verdugo.

Contact Details: Av. Gustavo Baz No. 219, Col. San Pedro Barrientos, 54010 Tlalnepantla; tel. (55) 5321-2223; e-mail internet@teleton.org.mx; internet www.teleton.org.

Fundación Telmex Telcel (Telmex Telcel Foundation)

Established in 1995 by Telmex, a telecommunications company.

Activities: Carries out self-conducted programmes in the fields of culture and human development, education, health, and social justice. The Foundation offers scholarships and computer equipment to Mexican students for higher and postgraduate education.

Geographical Area of Activity: Mexico.

Finance: Endowment US $1,500m.

Principal Staff: CEO Arturo Elías Ayub.

Contact Details: Plaza Carso, Lago Zurich 245, Edif. Presa Falcón, Piso 20, Col. Ampliación Granada, 11529 Ciudad de México; tel. (55) 5244-2608; internet www.fundaciontelmextelcel.org.

Harp Helú Foundations

Established in 1994 by Alfredo Harp Helú, a business person and co-owner of the Diablos Rojos del México baseball team; operating as three foundations since 2000.

Activities: Comprising Fundación Alfredo Harp Helú (FAHH), Fundación Alfredo Harp Helú Oaxaca (FAHHO) and Fundación Alfredo Harp Helú para el Deporte (FAHHD). The Foundations broadly carry out activities in the fields of education, culture and sports, respectively; and also disaster relief, the environment, health, livelihoods and social welfare. They support events, exhibitions and academic research through a network of museums, cultural centres, archives and libraries; and the Alfredo Harp Helú Baseball Academy.

Geographical Area of Activity: Mexico.

Publications: Annual Report; newsletter.

Principal Staff: FAHH Pres. Dr María Isabel Grañén Porrúa; FAHO Pres. Sissi Harp Calderoni; FAHHD Dir Dr Daniel Aceves Villagrán.

Contact Details: Bosques de Alisos No. 45B, Of. B1-22, Col. Bosques de las Lomas, CP 05120, Ciudad de México; e-mail asistencia@fahh.com.mx; internet www.alfredoharphelu.com.

Oxfam Mexico

Founded in 1996 as Fundación Vamos and later renamed as Rostros y Voces; became part of the Oxfam confederation of organizations (qq.v.) in 2008.

Activities: Works to end inequality. Main programme areas include: disaster prevention, resilience and response; equitable access to natural resources for indigenous and rural people; humanitarian assistance during emergencies, providing access to safe water and sanitation; inclusive and sustainable economic development; and supporting CSOs working to prevent violence against women and girls.

Geographical Area of Activity: Africa, Central America and the Caribbean, South America.

Restrictions: Does not make loans or grants to individuals.

Publications: Annual Report; newsletter.

Finance: Annual income 70.7m., pesos, expenditure 84.3m. pesos (31 Dec. 2023).

Principal Staff: Exec. Dir Alexandra Haas.

Contact Details: Cda. Salvador Alvarado 7, Escandón I Secc, Miguel Hidalgo, 11800 Ciudad de México; tel. (55) 5687-3002; e-mail contacto@oxfammexico.org; internet www.oxfammexico.org.

MOLDOVA

CO-ORDINATING BODIES

Centrul Național de Asistență si Informare a Organizatiilor Neguvernamentale din Moldova—Centrul CONTACT (National Assistance and Information Centre for NGOs in Moldova—CONTACT Centre)

Established in 1995; an initiative of the Soros Foundation—Moldova (q.v.).

Activities: Promotes the development of civil society and promotes philanthropy and social responsibility through providing information, training, consultancy and technical assistance. The Centre works to increase the participation of community members to achieve regional and economic development and peaceful relations in conflict and post-conflict areas; and supports and strengthens cross-border and transnational co-operation through joint local and regional initiatives. It maintains an online database of training and organizational development service providers.

Geographical Area of Activity: Moldova.

Publications: Annual Report.

Principal Staff: Exec. Dir Serghei Neicovcen.

Contact Details: Bucuresti str. 83, 2012 Chișinău; tel. (22) 233946; e-mail info@contact.md; internet www.contact.md.

MONACO

CReDO—Centrul de Resurse pentru Drepturile Omului (Resource Centre for the Human Rights Nongovernmental Organizations of Moldova—CReDO)

Established in 1999; an initiative of three Moldovan human rights NGOs (the League for Defence of Human Rights of Moldova, the Moldovan Helsinki Committee for Human Rights and the Independent Society for Education and Human Rights), with financial and technical support from CordAid (Netherlands) and the Netherlands Helsinki Committee.

Activities: Supports human rights and the democratization of civil society through conducting public policy analysis and advocacy. The Centre strengthens the organizational and institutional capacities of NGOs, offering consultancy services and training on civic leadership, non-profit management and public policies.

Geographical Area of Activity: Eastern Europe (in particular Azerbaijan, Moldova and Ukraine).

Publications: Annual Report; reports.

Finance: Financial support through grants from international donors, provision of consultancy and individual contributions.

Principal Staff: Exec. Dir Serghei Ostaf.

Contact Details: str. Alexandru Hâjdeu 95A, 2005 Chișinău; tel. (22) 212816; e-mail credo@credo.md; internet www.credo.md.

FOUNDATIONS AND NON-PROFITS

Fundația Orange Moldova (Orange Moldova Foundation)

Established in 2009 by Orange, a telecommunications company; part of the Fondation Orange (q.v.) network.

Activities: Develops projects in four key areas: education and digital education, providing access to modern infrastructure, professional expertise and quality education in the field of information technologies; social aid, supporting young people from socially vulnerable families who wish to continue their vocational secondary education, providing grants, training women who have been victims of violence, and supporting families with many children; health and disabilities, facilitating access to quality medical services, improving healthcare, modernizing the public health system by investing in high-performance medical equipment; and culture, integrating children with limited access to cultural events, and promoting opera, ballet and choral music, as well as young talents in these fields.

Geographical Area of Activity: Moldova.

Publications: Annual Report.

Finance: Annual revenue 5.9m. lei, expenditure 5.1m. lei (31 Dec. 2024).

Board of Directors: Ludmila Nistorica (Pres.).

Contact Details: Alba Iulia str. 75, 2071 Chișinău; tel. (22) 975010; e-mail fundatia@orange.md; internet fundatia.orange.md.

Fundația Soros—Moldova (Soros Foundation—Moldova)

Established in 1992 to promote the development of open society; part of the Open Society Foundations (q.v.) network.

Activities: Supports the democratization of civil society through grantmaking and self-conducted programmes. Main programme areas are: supporting independent media by providing training and access to information; access to justice, the protection of human rights and criminal justice; universal access to public health and social services, and environmental protection; and good governance, working to increase the transparency, accountability and efficiency of public authorities.

Geographical Area of Activity: Moldova.

Restrictions: Grants only for specific projects, not for general support for organizations; no grants for humanitarian aid.

Publications: Annual Report; newsletter (monthly); policy briefs; public policy studies.

Finance: Annual expenditure US $2.5m. (2023).

Senate: Mariana Turcan (Pres.).

Principal Staff: Exec. Dir Daniela Vidaicu.

Contact Details: Bulgara str. 32, 2001 Chișinău; tel. (22) 274480; e-mail foundation@soros.md; internet www.soros.md.

MONACO

FOUNDATIONS AND NON-PROFITS

AMADE Mondiale—Association Mondiale des Amis de l'Enfance (World Association of Children's Friends)

Founded in 1963 by Princess Grace of Monaco.

Activities: Supports the protection and development of children worldwide. Main programmes include: providing access to menstrual hygiene for women and girls, preventing sexual abuse and providing medical and psychological care for victims of sexual violence, and promoting access to secondary education; providing access to solar lamps and digital education, and mobile apps for children's education, health and protection; promoting social capoeira (a Brazilian martial art combining dance and music) to accompany the demobilization and reintegration of child soldiers and in caring for vulnerable children, including 'street' children, young female victims of sexual violence, internally displaced children and refugees; and ensuring the rights of unaccompanied migrant children and providing them with psychosocial and legal support, promoting their vocational training and social integration in host communities, and preventing migration in countries of origin. The Association is the umbrella body for a network of local organizations in Belgium, Burundi, Chile, Italy, Monaco and the Netherlands.

Geographical Area of Activity: Europe, South-East Asia, sub-Saharan Africa.

Publications: Annual Report; newsletter; brochures; reports.

Finance: Operational costs are covered by an annual government grant.

Board of Directors: HRH The Princess of Hanover (Chair.); Jacques Boisson (Vice-Chair.); Vincent Bribosia (Treas.); Jérôme Froissart (Sec.-Gen.).

Contact Details: 4 rue des Iris, 98000 Monaco; tel. 97-70-52-60; e-mail philanthropie@amade.org; internet www.amade.org.

Fondation Prince Albert II de Monaco

Established in 2006 by HSH Prince Albert II of Monaco.

Activities: Works to protect the environment and encourage sustainable development through supporting the UN Sustainable Development Goals. Main grantmaking programmes are: The MedFund, improving the management of marine protected areas in the Mediterranean; Beyond Plastic Med: BeMed, eliminating plastic pollution in the Mediterranean; Monk Seal Alliance, protecting the Mediterranean monk seal; the Global Fund for Coral Reefs, protecting and restoring coral reef ecosystems; the Human-Wildlife Initiative (IHF), promoting human-wildlife cohabitation in Southern France;

Fondation Prince Pierre de Monaco

Because the Ocean, calling for oceans' inclusion in climate negotiations; Ocean Acidification and other ocean Changes—Impacts and Solutions (OACIS), which conducts and communicates scientific research; Mr Goodfish, promoting more responsible seafood consumption; the Pelagos Initiative, for the promotion and protection of the Pelagos Sanctuary; Donors' Initiative For Mediterranean Freshwater Ecosystems (DIMFE), founded in 2021 to conserve and restore freshwater ecosystems in the Mediterranean; and the Polar Initiative, to help better understand how changes in the polar regions affect global social, economic and envireonmental systems. It has branches in Canada, the People's Republic of China, France, Germany, Italy, Singapore, Spain, Switzerland, the United Kingdom and the USA.

Geographical Area of Activity: Worldwide (with particular emphasis on the Arctic and Antarctic, the Mediterranean and the least-developed countries of the world).

Publications: Annual Report; newsletter; brochures.

Board of Directors: HSH Prince Albert II (Pres.); Olivier Wenden (Vice-Pres. and CEO).

Principal Staff: Exec. Dir Romain Ciarlet.

Contact Details: Villa Girasole, 16 blvd de Suisse, 98000 Monaco; tel. 98-98-44-44; e-mail contact@fpa2.mc; internet fpa2.org.

Fondation Prince Pierre de Monaco

Established in 1966 by Prince Rainier III in memory of his father, Prince Pierre.

Activities: Promotes contemporary creativity through awarding prizes including: the Prince Pierre Literary Prize, worth €25,000, recognizing the achievements of young francophone writers; the annual Discovery Grant and High School Students' Favorite Choice, both for a young author's first work of fiction in French; the Musical Composition Prize, worth €75,000; the Young Musicians' Favorite Choice; the Musical Springboard, which supports a new project; and the International Prize for Contemporary Art, worth €75,000. The Foundation organizes a cycle of public conferences from January to June each year, with guest speakers from the fields including the arts, history, journalism, literature and science.

Geographical Area of Activity: International.

Council: HRH The Princess of Hanover (Chair.); Björn Dahlström (Vice-Chair.); Carole Laugier (Treas.).

Principal Staff: Artistic Dir Cristiano Raimondi.

Contact Details: Les Jardins d'Apolline, Bloc A, 1 promenade Honoré II, 98000 Monaco; tel. 98-98-85-15; e-mail info@fondationprincepierre.mc; internet www.fondationprincepierre.mc.

Fondation Princesse Charlène de Monaco (Princess Charlene of Monaco Foundation)

Established in 2012 by HSH Princess Charlene of Monaco.

Activities: Carries out activities in the areas of drowning prevention and sport. The Foundation raises public awareness about the dangers of water; and teaches children to swim, contributing to their wellbeing and development. Programmes include Learn to Swim, Water Safety, and Sport & Education. It has branches in South Africa and the USA.

Geographical Area of Activity: International.

Publications: Annual report.

Finance: Project spending €1.2m. (2023).

Board: HSH Princess Charlene (Pres.); HSH Prince Albert II (Vice-Pres.); Gareth Wittstock (Gen. Sec.); Anthony Stent Torriani (Dir).

Contact Details: 4 quai Antoine 1er, 98000 Monaco; tel. 98-98-99-99; e-mail contact@fpcm.mc; internet www.fondationprincessecharlene.mc.

Fondation Princesse Grace

Founded in 1964.

Activities: Main activities are supporting children in hospital, and providing financial aid for medical research. Projects include: the Boutiques du Rocher, which supports local craftspeople, the Académie de Danse, which funds training for talented young dancers, and the Princess Grace Irish Library. The Foundation also contributes to humanitarian projects related to children's healthcare and to cultural activities, providing scholarships to arts students. The Princess Grace Foundation—USA operates independently in the USA.

Geographical Area of Activity: Mainly Monaco and France.

Restrictions: No grants directly to students or children.

Board of Trustees: HRH Caroline, Princess of Hanover (Pres.); HSH Prince Albert (Vice-Pres.); Henri Riey (Treas./Sec.).

Principal Staff: Exec. Dir Caroline O'Conor.

Contact Details: 11 blvd Albert 1er, 98000 Monte Carlo; tel. 97-70-86-86; e-mail fpg@monaco.mc; internet www.fondation-psse-grace.mc.

MONGOLIA

FOUNDATIONS AND NON-PROFITS

Mongolian Women's Fund—MONES

Established in 2000 by N. Chinchuluun.

Activities: Operates in five areas: gender equality and discrimination; women and good governance; accountability and transparency; participation of women in decisionmaking; and empowering girls and young women. The Fund runs fundraising and grantmaking programmes to support women's organizations and groups that focus on issues such as tackling gender-based discrimination and violence; increasing the income capacity of women; increasing women's participation in civic life; and capacity building of women's organizations and groups.

Geographical Area of Activity: Mongolia.

Restrictions: Does not fund religious or political activities.

Publications: Annual Report; newsletter; research reports; books.

Board: Shuudertsetseg Baasansuren (Chair.).

Principal Staff: Exec. Dir Agni B.

Contact Details: 903 Centrum office 7/3 bldg, 1 khoroo, POB 280, Sukhbaatar district, 14240 Ulaanbaatar; tel. (11) 77119991; e-mail info@mones.org.mn; internet mones.org.mn.

Open Society Forum (Mongolia)

Established in 1996 as the Mongolian Foundation for Open Society—MFOS; an independent foundation, part of the Open Society Foundations (q.v.) network. Present name adopted in 2005.

Activities: Works in the fields of democratic governance, legal reform, education and civil society. Programmes include: enhancing citizen's legal capacity; improving government accountability and transparency mechanisms; inclusive education; preventing peer violence and bullying among young people; promoting good governance in the mineral sector; strengthening the independence of the judiciary; supporting law enforcement reform; and the election process and political financing.

Geographical Area of Activity: Mongolia.

Publications: Annual Report; reports; factsheets; research and policy briefs.

Finance: Annual budget 3.2m. tögrög (2023).

Board: D. Enkhjargal (Chair.).

Principal Staff: Exec. Dir Perenlei Erdenejargal.

Contact Details: Open Society Forum Bldg, Jamiyan Gun St 5/3, Sukhbaatar District, Ulaanbaatar 14240; tel. (76) 113207; e-mail osf@forum.mn; internet www.forum.mn.

Zorig Foundation

Established in 1998 in memory of Zorig Sanjaasuren, a politician, by friends, colleagues and members of his family.

Activities: Supports the development of informed and skilled young people who respect democratic values. The Foundation organizes educational and vocational programmes, generally lasting 6–8 months, for young professionals, including: Sustainable Youth Employment Support, providing classroom and soft skills training and internships for people aged under 26 years; the Women's Leadership Program, to improve professional and managerial skills, which includes two weeks' intensive training in Australia; the Environmental Fellowship Program (and 14-day Rural Environmental Fellowship Program); and the Young Leadership Program, developing self-management and leadership skills. It organizes the Democracy Summer Camp for university students; and the Young Scholars Program, to prepare high-school students for enrolment at international universities; and implements scholarship and exchange programmes funded by partner organizations. The Rural Women Changemakers Program develops leadership, communication, negotiation and time management skills in young women aged 22–30 years and deepens their knowledge of human rights, gender equality, project management and the environment.

Geographical Area of Activity: Australia, Mongolia, USA.

Publications: Handbooks; leaflets.

Principal Staff: Chair. Oyun Sanjaasuren; Exec. Dir Tsolmon Bayaraa.

Contact Details: Zorig Foundation Bldg, Peace Ave 17, Sukhbaatar District, Ulaanbaatar; tel. (11) 315444; e-mail admin@zorigfoundation.org; internet zorigfoundation.org.

MONTENEGRO

CO-ORDINATING BODY

Centre for the Development of Non-governmental Organizations

Established in 1999 to support the development of NGOs and build civil society.

Activities: Works to build the capacity of NGOs; improve co-operation between the state, NGOs and the private sector; increase understanding of the importance of the role that NGOs play in society; and contribute to the development of democracy, the rule of law and human rights. The Centre provides training and technical assistance to NGOs and acts as a policy advocate to government. It also organizes discussion meetings between donors and NGOs, and trains NGO leaders in policy advocacy and human rights issues.

Geographical Area of Activity: Montenegro.

Publications: Annual Report; *Citizen* (newsletter); guides.

Finance: Annual income €339,042 (31 Dec. 2021).

Principal Staff: Exec. Dir Zorana Marković.

Contact Details: Sima Barovića 24, lamela 2/I stan 18; tel. (81) 20219121; e-mail crnvo@crnvo.me; internet www.crnvo.me.

FOUNDATIONS AND NON-PROFITS

Centre for Democracy and Human Rights—CEDEM

Established in 1997.

Activities: Carries out policy research, analysis and public opinion surveys in the areas of civil, democratic, ecological and social justice. Programme areas include: Euro-Atlantic integration, including membership of the EU and NATO; human rights; the rule of law; security and defence; and social inclusion. The Centre organizes conferences, meetings, roundtables, seminars, training sessions and workshops. It offers internships.

Geographical Area of Activity: Western Balkans.

Publications: Annual Report; newsletter; *Political Public Opinion* (annual survey); reports.

Principal Staff: Dir Nevenka Kapičić.

Contact Details: 81000 Podgorica, Ul. Bulevar Džordža Vašingtona 92; tel. (20) 234114; e-mail info@cedem.me; internet www.cedem.me.

MOROCCO

FOUNDATIONS AND NON-PROFITS

Fondation Addoha (Addoha Foundation)

Established in 2011 by Anas Sefrioui, Chair. of Groupe Addoha, a property development company.

Activities: Funds apprenticeship programmes, in particular for young people who have dropped out of school. The Foundation operates three learning centres in Fez, Marrakesh and Rabat (Aïn Aouda), offering vocational training in sectors of the building trades, and has seven housing programmes in sub-Saharan Africa.

Geographical Area of Activity: Morocco, sub-Saharan Africa.

Principal Staff: Chair. Anas Sefrioui; Vice-Chair. Kenza Sefrioui.

Contact Details: c/o Groupe Addoha, Km 7, route de Rabat (Aïn Sebâa), Casablanca 20250; tel. (52) 2679900; e-mail contact@groupeaddoha.com; internet ir.groupeaddoha.com/la-fondation-addoha.

Fondation BMCE Bank (BMCE Bank Foundation)

Established in 1995 by Othman Benjelloun, Chair. and CEO of BMCE Bank Group.

Activities: Main programmes are: education; promotion of the Amazigh (Berber) language and culture; environmental conservation; and community development. The Foundation provides basic education for disadvantaged children in rural areas through a network of 69 schools under the Medersat.com programme; and provides microcredit to adults living in areas where Medersat.com schools are located, to improve households' living standards. It has built and manages schools in the Republic of the Congo, Djibouti, Mali, Rwanda and Senegal; and in Morocco co-operates with the Confucius Institute and the Institut Français on Chinese and French language tuition, respectively.

Geographical Area of Activity: Repub. of the Congo, Djibouti, Mali, Morocco, Rwanda, Senegal.

Publications: Annual Report.

Principal Staff: Pres. Dr Leïla Mezian Benjelloun.

Contact Details: Zénith Millénium, Immeuble 2 bis, BP 89, 4ème étage, Lot. Attaoufik, Sidi Mâarouf, Casablanca; tel. (52) 2977500; internet www.fondationbmce.org.

Fondation Hassan II pour les Marocains Résidant à l'Étranger (Hassan II Foundation for Moroccans Living Abroad)

Established in 1990 by HM King Hassan II.

Activities: Works to maintain links between Moroccans living abroad and Morocco, and helps them to overcome difficulties they may encounter while abroad. Activities include: cultural promotion, offering lessons on Arabic language, Moroccan culture and Islam to the children of Moroccan migrants; legal and social assistance, to safeguard migrants' rights and property; economic support, providing financial information and investment opportunities; international co-operation and partnership, working with the authorities and NGOs in Morocco and host countries of Moroccans living abroad; and the Observatory of the Moroccan Community Abroad, which collects and manages data on the Moroccan diaspora. The Foundation maintains e-taqafa.ma, a virtual cultural space; and the e-madrassa.ma children's e-learning platform.

Geographical Area of Activity: International.

Publications: Research reports; *Marhaba Infos*; *Marocains de l'extérieur*; reference publications; seminar proceedings.

Principal Staff: Chair. HRH Princess Lalla Meryem; Deputy Chair. Omar Azziman.

Contact Details: 67 blvd Ibn Sina, Agdal, BP 10090, Rabat; tel. (53) 7274650; e-mail info@fh2mre.ma; internet www.fh2mre.ma.

Fondation Miloud Chaâbi (Miloud Chaâbi Foundation)

Established in 1965 by Miloud Chaabi, Chair. of YNNA Holding.

Activities: Provides grants to projects in the areas of health, education, social welfare, the arts, sport and the environment; and scholarships for students to study in Morocco and abroad. The Foundation has funded the construction of university facilities in Morocco, including the Al Qalam Institute in Agadir (f. 1995), Essaouira Higher Institute of Technology (f. 2005) and Indiana State University of Morocco in Casablanca (f. 2008).

Geographical Area of Activity: Morocco.

Principal Staff: Chair. Asmaa Chaâbi.

Contact Details: c/o YNNA Holding, 233 blvd Mohammed V, 20000 Casablanca; internet www.ynna.ma/fr/fondation.

Fondation Mohammed V pour la Solidarité

Established in 1999 by HM King Mohammed VI.

Activities: Works in the fields of humanitarian aid and disaster response; supporting vulnerable people, in particular women, children, the elderly and people with disabilities, through training and integration, and providing them with shelter, healthcare and cultural activities; and sustainable development, improving basic infrastructure, supporting literacy, informal education and vocational training, and income-generating activities, particularly for women in rural areas. The Foundation also provides administrative and medical assistance to Moroccans living in Southern Europe. It has consultative status with ECOSOC.

Geographical Area of Activity: France, Italy, Spain, Morocco.

Publications: Annual Report; *Les annales de solidarité*; *Guide Marhaba*; brochures.

Principal Staff: Chair. HM King Mohammed VI; Co-ordinator Mohamed El Azami.

Contact Details: 3 rue Arrissani, Hassan, BP 4253, Rabat; tel. (53) 7263637; e-mail solidarite@fm5.ma; internet www.fm5.ma.

Fondation Orient-Occident—FOO (Orient-Occident Foundation)

Established in 1994 by Dr Yasmina Filali.

Activities: Aims to enhance dialogue between cultures by promoting mutual understanding. The Foundation works to integrate disadvantaged young people into Moroccan society, as well as migrants and refugees; and has established socio-educational and professional training centres in eight cities in Morocco, which offer programmes on educational reinforcement, psychological counselling, vocational training, solidarity economy and human rights. It established several migrant reception centres in Italy, working in partnership with UNHCR, and the Cooperativa Sociale Oriente-Occidente in Lecce, which operates the Atelier of Embroidery and Couture 'Migrants du Monde', a social enterprise involving migrant and refugee women and local people; and is also present in Paris and Meaux (France), where it has an experimental centre.

Geographical Area of Activity: France, Italy, Morocco.

Publications: Newsletter.

Principal Staff: Pres. and CEO Dr Yasmina Filali; Exec. Dir Nadia Tari.

Contact Details: ave des FAR El Massira, Commune de Yacoub el Mansour, BP 3210, Massira, Rabat; tel. (53) 7793637; e-mail contact@foo.ma; internet www.orient-occident.org.

Fondation du Roi Abdul-Aziz al-Saoud pour les Études Islamiques et les Sciences Humaines (King Abdul-Aziz al-Saoud Foundation for Islamic Study and the Humanities)

Established in 1985.

Activities: Operates in the fields of social sciences, the humanities and Arab-Islamic studies through conducting research and promoting cultural and scientific exchange. The Foundation organizes professional forums and training for researchers from Morocco and Maghreb; and hosts conferences, cultural meetings, lectures, roundtables, seminars, lectures and workshops. It has a research library of approximately 764,420 items in Arabic, Amazigh, French, English, Spanish and German; and maintains three databases: the Ibn Rushd database of more than 100,000 bibliographical references, with information on the Maghreb, Western European and West African Islamic communities; and the Mawsu'a database of more than 241,000 entries, containing bibliographical information on human and social sciences.

Geographical Area of Activity: Maghreb.

Publications: Annual Report; newsletter (twice a year); *Edition et Livre au Maroc* (annual); *Études Maghrébines* (monthly); *Actes de colloques* (series); *Dialogue des deux rives* (series); *Débats philosophiques* (series); *Chantiers de la recherche* (series); essays; reports; books; CD-ROMs.

Principal Staff: Dir-Gen. Ahmed Toufiq; Deputy Dir Mohamed-Sghir Janjar.

Contact Details: Marjan St, Ain Diab, Casablanca; BP 12585, Casablanca 20052; tel. (52) 2391027; e-mail secretariat@fondation.org.ma; internet www.fondation.org.ma.

MOZAMBIQUE

FOUNDATIONS AND NON-PROFITS

FDC—Fundação para o Desenvolvimento da Comunidade (Community Development Foundation)

Established in 1994 by Graça Machel, a former Minister of Education in Mozambique and wife of former President of South Africa Nelson Mandela; originally constituted in 1990 as the Association for the Development of the Community.

Activities: Helps communities to overcome poverty through promoting social justice and sustainable development. The Foundation carries out programmes in the areas of: nutrition for children, young people and women; health, improving life expectancy and quality of life through reducing the incidence of HIV/AIDS, tuberculosis and malaria; education, improving access to employment and vocational training; and girls, working to empower girls and reduce premature marriage.

Geographical Area of Activity: Mozambique.
Restrictions: Grants scholarships only to Mozambican women aged 17–25 years from low-income families.
Publications: Newsletter (weekly); brochures; guides; reports.
Administrative Council: Graça Simbine Machel (Chair.).
Principal Staff: Exec. Dir Diogo Milagre.
Contact Details: Av. 25 de Setembro, Edifício Times Sq., 3° andar, Bloco 2, CP 4206, Maputo; tel. (21) 355368; e-mail info@fdc.org.mz; internet www.fdc.org.mz.

MYANMAR

FOUNDATIONS AND NON-PROFITS

Brighter Future Myanmar Foundation—BFM

Established in 2008 by Daw Nang Lang Kham and Daw Nang Kham Noung as the philanthropic arm of the Kanbawza (KBZ) Group of Companies, a conglomerate.

Activities: Works to improve livelihoods and alleviate poverty. Activities fall into five main areas: community and health; disaster relief and recovery; water projects; women's empowerment; and youth development and education enhancement. Initiatives include funding post-disaster relief and providing essential items to displaced people; funding medical campaigns; supporting clean water projects; providing employment opportunities for disabled people; a microfinance project that empowers women; and assisting the return of migrant workers. In 2025 the foundation was undergoing a full external review to ensure the greatest impact was being made and that full accountability was implemented.

Geographical Area of Activity: Myanmar.
Principal Staff: Chair. Nang Lang Kham; Vice-Chair. Nang Kham Noung.
Contact Details: CSR Dept, KBZ Head Office, No. 615/1, Pyay Rd, Kamaryut Township, Yangon; tel. (1) 513849; e-mail info@kbzgroup.com.mm; internet www.brighterfuturemyanmar.org.

Daw Khin Kyi Foundation

Established in 2012 by civilian leader Aung San Suu Kyi, in memory of her mother, Khin Kyi.

Activities: Works with local and international partners to improve health, education and living standards, with a focus on the least-developed areas in the country. Projects include a mobile library and the Hospitality and Catering Training Academy. The Foundation also organizes teacher training in English language and civics, and literary and other talks on subjects such as health, education and job opportunities.

Geographical Area of Activity: Myanmar.
Executive Committee: Aung San Suu Kyi (Chair.).
Contact Details: No. 60, University Ave Rd, Bahan Township, Yangon; tel. (9) 254389959; e-mail info@dawkhinkyifoundation.org; internet www.dawkhinkyifoundation.org.

Myanmar Book Aid and Preservation Foundation—MBAPF

Established in 2002 by librarians, business and civic leaders, with a focus on book and manuscript preservation.

Activities: Works to create a knowledge-based society by transforming community libraries into community hubs. The Foundation works with the Government and local and international organizations to build librarians' capacity, improve library technology and infrastructure, and teach digital information and literacy skills. It has distributed international book donations to over 900 libraries throughout the country; and runs mobile schools in Yangon, Ayeyarwady, Mandalay and Magwe Division, providing training in basic ICT skills to aound 6,000 people. Reorganized in 2009, following Cyclone Nargis in 2008, to promote education of the poor and global knowledge.

Geographical Area of Activity: Myanmar.
Publications: Reports; surveys; training manuals.
Principal Staff: Exec. Dir Dr Thant Thaw Kaung.
Contact Details: No. 55, Baho Rd, cnr of Baho Rd and Ahlone Rd, Ahlone Township, Yangon; tel. (9) 70735331; e-mail info@mbapf.org.

New Myanmar Foundation

Established in 2008, initially to provide humanitarian aid after Cyclone Nargis and education programmes for orphans.

Activities: Promotes transparency, accountability and democratic culture. The Foundation encourages civil engagement in the political process by building citizens' capacity and national development through education. Activities include: national election observation and international election observation missions; voter education; and research and advocacy.

Geographical Area of Activity: South-East Asia, South Asia.
Publications: Newsletter; reports, surveys.
Principal Staff: Exec. Dir Dr Sann Aung.
Contact Details: Mae Sot Sub District, Mae Sot, Tak District, 63110; tel. (26) 874266; e-mail newmyanmaroffice@gmail.com; internet newmyanmarfoundation.info.

NAMIBIA

FOUNDATIONS AND NON-PROFITS

DRFN—Desert Research Foundation of Namibia
Established in 1990; incorporates the Desert Ecological Research Unit (f. 1963).

Activities: Works to further knowledge of and strengthen capacity to manage arid environments for sustainable development; and is the National Implementing Entity in Namibia for the Adaptation Fund. The Foundation works in all sectors involved in the management and use of natural resources, concentrating on the agriculture, water and energy sectors and collaborating with non-governmental and community-based organizations; works with the Ministry of Environment and Tourism in guiding the Gobabeb Namib Research Institute (q.v.); and undertakes commercial environmental work through its consulting arm, Environmental Evaluation Associates of Namibia (Pty) Ltd. It involves communities in participatory learning; engages managers and policymakers to improve the policy and regulatory framework; and builds a body of knowledge to improve understanding of arid and semi-arid lands.

Geographical Area of Activity: Southern Africa (particularly Namibia).

Publications: Annual Report; reports; factsheets; books.

Finance: Annual budget approx. N $10m.

Principal Staff: Exec. Dir Dr Martin B. Schneider.

Contact Details: Schoemans Bldg, cnr Sam Nujoma/Nelson Mandela Ave, 2nd Floor, Unit 11, POB 20232, Windhoek; tel. (61) 377500; e-mail drfn@drfn.org.na; internet www.drfn.org.na.

Gobabeb Namib Research Institute
Established in 1962 by the Southern African Museums Association as the Namib Desert Research Station; it became a joint venture between the Ministry of Environment and Tourism and the Desert Research Foundation of Namibia (q.v.) in 1998 after Namibia's independence. Formerly known as the Gobabeb Training and Research Centre, Desert Ecological Research Unit, Namib Research Station.

Activities: Situated in the central Namib Desert, it hosts international researchers and students from Namibia and regional universities working in fields including desert ecology and biodiversity, atmospheric sciences, aeolian geomorphology and EOS validation and calibration. The Institute also carries out research on the agricultural and herding practices of the indigenous ≠Aonin (Topnaar) Nama pastoralists. The Namib Ecological Restoration and Monitoring Unit provides scientific services to mining companies.

Geographical Area of Activity: Southern Africa.

Restrictions: Research permits and work visas required.

Publications: Research bibliographies.

Finance: Annual budget US $250,000.

Principal Staff: Exec. Dir Gillian Maggs-Kölling.

Contact Details: POB 953, Walvis Bay 13103; tel. (64) 205555; e-mail gobabeb@gobabeb.org; internet www.gobabeb.org.

Living Culture Foundation Namibia—LCFN
Established in 2007; has a partner association in Germany, Living Culture Namibia eV (f. 2006).

Activities: Works in the fields of cultural co-operation and poverty alleviation in rural areas. The Foundation establishes 'living museums' to: conserve and transfer traditional culture; generate income in local communities through sustainable tourism; and develop cultural and intercultural education, encouraging dialogue and tolerant relations between Namibians and non-Namibians and among Namibian language groups. To promote self-responsibility and avoid dependency, most support is indirect, providing assistance, education, marketing and advertising. There are museums at Damara, Ju/'Hoansi, Ovahimba, Mafwe and Mbunza.

Geographical Area of Activity: Germany, Namibia.

Publications: Newsletter.

Board of Directors: Sebastian Dürrschmidt, Kathrin Gebhardt, Werner Pfeifer.

Contact Details: Pienaar St 34, Pionierspark, POB 30627; tel. (61) 220563; e-mail contact@lcfn.info; internet www.lcfn.info.

One Economy Foundation
Established in 2016 by First Lady Monica Geingos.

Activities: Works to reduce inequality by unifying the formal and informal economies. Main programmes focus on: enterprise development and entrepreneurship; early childhood development; preventing and responding to gender-based violence; health, including adolescent reproductive health, communicable and non-communicable diseases; and strategic support for institutions. The Foundation offers microfinance, basic entrepreneurial training, coaching and mentorship to solidarity groups comprising at least four owners of small and medium-sized enterprises. Supported sectors include: agriculture; environment; exports; innovation and research; logistics and distribution; renewable energy; and retail.

Geographical Area of Activity: Namibia.

Publications: Newsletters; reports; booklets.

Board: Monica Geingos (Exec. Chair.).

Principal Staff: Exec. Dir Dr Veronica Rose Theron.

Contact Details: #BeFree Youth Campus, 9109 Bondel St, Katutura; tel. (83) 3726550; e-mail hello@1economy.org; internet www.oneeconomyfoundation.com.

Rössing Foundation
Established in 1978 by Rössing Uranium Ltd, Namibia and Rio Tinto Zinc, London (UK) to promote research and education in Namibia.

Activities: Supports social and economic transformation and environmental sustainability. Main programmes are in the areas of: education, supporting teachers and students in English, mathematics and the sciences, awarding scholarships and operating a mobile laboratory that visits rural schools; livelihoods and enterprise development, supporting small and medium-sized enterprises and providing access to microfinance; and community support, offering adult literacy courses and youth development activities. The Foundation has an office in Swakopmund and a training centre in Ondangwa.

Geographical Area of Activity: Namibia.

Publications: Annual Report.

Finance: Funded almost entirely by Rössing Uranium Ltd.

Board of Trustees: Gida Sekandi (Chair.); Clara Bohitile (Vice-Chair.).

Principal Staff: Exec. Dir Uparura Kuvare.

Contact Details: 360 Sam Nujoma St, POB 27046, Windhoek; tel. (61) 211721; e-mail info@rf.org.na; internet www.rossingfoundation.com.

NEPAL

FOUNDATIONS AND NON-PROFITS

INHURED International—International Institute for Human Rights, Environment and Development

Established in 1987 as Human Rights Information and Documentation Services; present name adopted in 1990.

Activities: Promotes the rule of law and respect for human rights through legal research and capacity building. Main programme areas are: community resilience; migration management; peace and transitional justice; and women, peace and security. The Institute has special consultative status with ECOSOC.

Geographical Area of Activity: Asia-Pacific region (with a focus on Nepal).

Publications: *Refugee Watch* (newsletter); issue briefs; periodicals; research reports; blog; books.

Board: Dr Gopal Krishna Siwakoti (Pres.); Hemanata Raj Dahal (Vice-Pres.); Ambika Bhandari (Treas.); Ganesh K. Ghimire (Gen. Sec.).

Contact Details: Kupondole, Lalitpur-10 (opp. Himalayan Hotel); POB 12684, Kathmandu; tel. (1) 5010536; e-mail info@inhuredinternational.org; internet inhuredinternational.org.

Tewa

Established in 1996 by Rita Thapa, a feminist educator and community activist.

Activities: Works in the field of women's development and empowerment through providing financial support and capacity building. The organization helps women to organize collectively to overcome poverty, marginalization, discrimination and injustice. It carries out activities in three main areas: grantmaking, fundraising and training of fundraising volunteers; and supports disaster relief and recovery efforts.

Geographical Area of Activity: Nepal.

Publications: Annual Report; *Tewa* (newsletter, 2 a year); *Volunteer Voice* (newsletter).

Finance: Annual income NRs 137.6m., expenditure NRs 136.6m. (15 July 2024).

Executive Board: Rama Laxmi Shrestha (Pres.); Dr Meeta S. Pradhan (Vice-Pres.); Sheetal Shakya Bajracharya (Gen. Sec.); Janaki Shah (Treas.); Usha Kiran Shrestha (Sec.).

Principal Staff: Exec. Dir Urmila Shrestha.

Contact Details: 23 Dhapakhel Rd, Laltipur; POB 750, Lalitpur; tel. (1) 5229054; e-mail info@tewa.org.np; internet www.tewa.org.np.

NETHERLANDS

CO-ORDINATING BODIES

FIN—Branchevereniging van Fondsen en Foundations (Association of Foundations in the Netherlands)

Established in 1988; members are private foundations established in the Netherlands.

Activities: Promotes the interests of member foundations through providing advocacy and advice. The Association organizes meetings, workshops and symposia; provides information about foundations in the Netherlands; maintains contact with public authorities, social organizations and the media; and advises members on matters concerning asset management and donations. It also promotes the establishment of new foundations and exchange of information between members. Comprises more than 350 member foundations; and is a member of Philea (q.v.).

Geographical Area of Activity: Netherlands.

Publications: Annual Report; newsletter; *FINieuws* (e-newsletter); brochures.

Finance: Financed by member subscriptions. Annual income €716,234, expenditure €738,609 (2024).

Board: Ronald van der Giessen (Chair.); Annette van Waning (Vice-Chair.); Sanne ten Bokkel Huinink (Treas.).

Principal Staff: Dir Siep Wijsenbeek.

Contact Details: Koninginnegracht 15, 2514 AB The Hague; tel. (70) 3262753; e-mail info@verenigingvanfondsen.nl; internet fondseninnederland.nl.

Partos

Established in 2004 by more than 60 CSOs.

Activities: Works in the field of sustainable development through connecting, strengthening and advocating for its members. The organizations offers activities and programmes in areas including innovation, learning and quality; and seeks opportunities to achieve cost benefits through shared services. Comprises 108 member organizations.

Geographical Area of Activity: Netherlands.

Publications: Annual Report; *Politieke Monitor* (weekly); reports; toolkits.

Finance: Annual income €1.4m., expenditure €1.5m. (2023).

Board: Andy Wehkamp (Chair.); Erik Ackerman (vice-Chair.); Hans Heijdra (Treas.).

Principal Staff: Dir Liana Hoornweg.

Contact Details: Fluwelen Burgwal 58, 2511 CJ The Hague; tel. (70) 2176229; e-mail info@partos.nl; internet partos.nl.

FOUNDATIONS AND NON-PROFITS

Adessium Foundation

Established in 2005 by the Van Vliet family.

Activities: Carries out activities in three main programme areas: public interest, which promotes a democratic society, funding investigative journalism, public awareness and advocacy initiatives; people and nature, which seeks to protect healthy ecological systems and promotes responsible use of natural resources; and social initiatives, which promotes equal opportunities, focusing on human dignity, self-sufficiency and solidarity to overcome poverty and isolation.

Geographical Area of Activity: Worldwide; social initiatives mainly in the Netherlands.

Restrictions: Projects must have a scientific basis; self-sustaining capacity; a focus on innovative and practical solutions; aim for structural and sustainable change; and have visible and quantifiable results. Does not accept unsolicited project proposals.

Publications: Annual Report.

Finance: Annual grant expenditure €18.3m. (2024).

Board of Directors: Rogier D. Van Vliet (Chair.).

Principal Staff: Man. Dir Rogier van der Weerd; Dir of Programmes Martijn Meijer.

Contact Details: Office Bldg 'het Baken', Reeuwijkse Poort 1, 2811 MV Reeuwijk; POB 76, 2810 AB Reeuwijk; tel. (182) 646100; e-mail info@adessium.org; internet www.adessium.org.

Anne Frank Stichting (Anne Frank Foundation)
Founded in 1957 to preserve the Anne Frank House and to propagate the ideals left to the world in Anne Frank's diary; and to fight against prejudice and discrimination in the world.

Activities: Works in the fields of education and international relations. The Foundation operates a museum in the house where Anne Frank and her family lived in hiding and maintains archives. It develops exhibitions and educational material on the Second World War and contemporary subjects, such as anti-Semitism, prejudice and stereotypes, discrimination and equal rights; and investigates far-right groups.

Geographical Area of Activity: International.

Publications: Annual Report; newsletter; reports; blog; books.

Finance: Annual income €17.8m., expenditure €17.9m. (2023).

Supervisory Board: Dr W. Koolmees (Chair.).

Principal Staff: Exec. Dir Ronald Leopold; Man. Dir Mireille Pondman.

Contact Details: Anne Frank House, Westermarkt 20, 1016 DK Amsterdam; POB 730, 1000 AS Amsterdam; tel. (20) 5567100; e-mail services@annefrank.nl; internet www.annefrank.org.

Canon Foundation in Europe
Founded in 1987 by Canon Europa NV, a camera manufacturer.

Activities: Fosters mutual understanding and the development of scientific expertise, in particular between Europe and Japan. Each year, the Foundation offers up to 15 Fellowships in all fields, for between three months and one year; European Fellows are expected to carry out research in Japan and Japanese Fellows to carry out research in Europe.

Geographical Area of Activity: Europe, Japan.

Restrictions: Applicants must already have obtained a Master's degree in order to apply.

Publications: *Bulletin* (annual).

Board of Directors: Jan-Ton Prinsze (Chair.); José Ignacio Rodrigo Fernandez (Treas. and Sec.).

Executive Committee: Dermot Moran (Chair.); Andrew Fisher (Vice-Chair.).

Contact Details: Bovenkerkerweg 59, 1185 XB Amstelveen; POB 2262, 1180 EG Amstelveen; tel. (20) 5458934; e-mail foundation@canon-europe.com; internet www.canonfoundation.org.

Carnegie-Stichting, Watelerfonds (Carnegie Foundation, Wateler Fund)
Founded in 1927 by J. G. D. Wateler, a banker; part of a network of 23 Carnegie organizations worldwide.

Activities: Awards the Wateler Peace Prize biennially to a person or institution for contributing to the cause of peace or to finding means of preventing war. The prize, worth €35,000, is given alternately to a Dutch or international person or organization. Previous winners are Rudi Vranckx (2018), Sigrid Kaag (2016) and Lakhdar Brahimi (2014). The Centre for Humanitarian Dialogue was awarded the prize in 2022, and the Netherlands Armed Forces received it in 2024. In 2018 the first Youth Carnegie Peace Prize was awarded to Fundación BogotArt, and the international youth organization 'World's Youth for Climate Justice' was awarded the Prize in 2023.

Geographical Area of Activity: International.

Publications: *The Peace Palace* (annual); *The Trusteeship of an Ideal*.

Board: J. P. H. Donner (Chair.); D. C. van Wassenaer (Treas.).

Principal Staff: Dir Iljan D. van Hardevelt.

Contact Details: Vredespaleis, Carnegieplein 2, 2517 KJ The Hague; tel. (70) 3024242; e-mail reception@peacepalace.org; internet www.vredespaleis.nl/carnegie/carnegie-wateler-peace-prize/?lang=en.

The Dr Denis Mukwege Foundation
Founded in 2015.

Activities: Works to support the victims and survivors of sexual violence in areas of conflict to support their activism and improve their access to holistic care. Facilitates the SEMA Global Network of survivors from more than 21 countries to provide opportunities for its members to come together and share their experiences and allow others to learn. Has an office in Bangui, Central African Republic.

Geographical Area of Activity: Burundi, Central African Repub., Iraq, Mali, Nepal, Nigeria, South Sudan, Uganda, Ukraine.

Restrictions: No grants are disbursed, funding is for own projects only.

Finance: Annual income €2.4m., expenditure €2.6m. (2021).

Supervisory Board: Marieke van Schaik (Chair.); Ellen Bien (Treas.).

Contact Details: Alexanderveld 5, 2585 DB The Hague; tel. (6) 16209560; e-mail info@mukwegefoundation.org; internet www.mukwegefoundation.org; www.semanetwork.org.

Europa Nostra (Pan-European Federation for Cultural Heritage)
Established in 1963 in response to the threat to Venice caused by rising floodwaters.

Activities: An umbrella network of heritage organizations working at local, regional, national or European level. The Federation raises awareness of cultural heritage; and advocates at local, national and international level for the preservation, rescue and rehabilitation of Europe's endangered heritage. It organizes the European Union Prize for Cultural Heritage/Europa Nostra Awards for services to cultural heritage, annually offering up to four monetary awards of €10,000 each to Grand Prix laureates. Comprises 239 member and 100 associate organizations, and more than 1,500 individual members; with an office in Brussels, Belgium, and representation in 19 countries.

Geographical Area of Activity: Europe (greater Europe as defined by the Council of Europe).

Restrictions: Member organizations must be approved by the Council; does not fund restorations, etc.

Publications: Annual Report; newsletter; *Heritage in Action* (annual magazine); *Scientific Bulletin* (discontinued); Learning Kits; Awards Publication.

Finance: Annual income €1.8m., expenditure €1.7m. (31 Dec. 2023).

Executive Board: Cecilia Bartoli (Pres.); Hermann Parzinger (Exec. Pres.); Guy Clausse (Exec. Vice-Pres.); Philippe de Cossé Brissac (Treas.); Plácido Domingo (Hon. Pres.).

Principal Staff: Gen. Man. Barbara Zander; Sec.-Gen. Sneška Quaedvlieg-Mihailovic.

Contact Details: Lange Voorhout 35, 2514 EC The Hague; tel. (70) 3024050; e-mail info@europanostra.org; internet www.europanostra.org.

European Climate Foundation
Established in 2008 by John McCall MacBain, founder of Pamoja Capital SA and the McCall MacBain Foundation.

Activities: Develops and implements climate and energy policies to reduce Europe's global greenhouse gas emissions in five priority areas: energy efficiency; climate diplomacy; low-carbon power generation; transportation; and EU climate policies. The Foundation has offices in Berlin (Germany), Brussels (Belgium), London (UK), Paris (France) and Warsaw (Poland).

Geographical Area of Activity: International (primarily EU).

Restrictions: Does not accept unsolicited proposals.
Publications: Annual Report; newsletter.
Finance: Annual national programme expenditure €35.6m. (2022).
Supervisory Board: Kate Hampton (Chair.); Sharan Burrow, Cornelia Quennet-Thielen, Jonathan Pershing (Vice-Chair.).
Principal Staff: CEO Laurence Tubiana.
Contact Details: Riviervismarkt 5, 2513 AM The Hague; tel. (70) 7119600; e-mail info@europeanclimate.org; internet www.europeanclimate.org.

European Cultural Foundation—ECF (Fondation Européenne de la Culture/Europese Culturele Stichting)

Founded in 1954 in Geneva, Switzerland, as an NGO; supported by Dutch charity lotteries and private sources to promote cross-cultural co-operation on a multilateral European level.
Activities: Promotes core values of democracy, diversity, trust, solidarity, interdependence, independence and equality, with a particular focus on young people and media. The Foundation develops and manages its own programmes and projects; and supports people and initiatives in 59 European and neighbouring countries through direct grants or regranting. Programmes include STEP Beyond Travel Grants, the Balkans Art and Culture Fund and Commissioning Grants; and also co-hosting events across Europe, including the ECF Princess Margaret Award for Culture, for artistic and cultural engagement that brings about social and political change.
Geographical Area of Activity: Europe and neighbouring countries.
Publications: Annual Report; newsletter; *Common Ground* (annual magazine).
Finance: Annual expenditure €8.1m. (31 Dec. 2023).
Supervisory Board: HRH Princess Laurentien of the Netherlands (Pres.); Gerry Salole (Chair.); Igno van Waesberghe (Vice-Chair.); Rob Defares (Treas.).
Principal Staff: Dir André Wilkens; Exec. Sec. Kati Visser-Telegdi.
Contact Details: Nieuwe Herengracht 14, 1018 DP Amsterdam; tel. (20) 5733868; e-mail ask@culturalfoundation.eu; internet culturalfoundation.eu.

Eurotransplant International Foundation

Founded in 1967 to facilitate the exchange of human organs to save lives.
Activities: Supports co-operation between transplant centres, donor hospitals, tissue-typing laboratories and national authorities. The Foundation matches donor organs and transplant candidates and organizes transplants. It funds programmes to improve the transplant system and maintains a database of patients.
Geographical Area of Activity: Austria, Belgium, Croatia, Germany, Hungary, Luxembourg, Netherlands, Slovenia.
Publications: Annual Report; brochures; factsheets; manuals.
Finance: Annual budget €11m. (31 Dec. 2023).
Council of Medicine and Science: Prof. Dr M. Guba (Chair.).
Council of Administration: Dr Jur. W. Abel (Chair.).
Contact Details: Haagse Schouwweg 6, 2332 KG Leiden; POB 2304, 2301 CH Leiden; tel. 715795800; e-mail communication@eurotransplant.org; internet www.eurotransplant.org.

FONDAD—Forum on Debt and Development

Established in 1987 by Jan Joost Teunissen, a social scientist and freelance journalist; an independent policy research centre and forum for international discussion.
Activities: A network of academics, experts and policymakers. The Forum conducts policy-orientated research on a range of global North-South issues, with particular emphasis on international financial issues. It provides factual background information and practical strategies for policymakers and other interested groups in industrial, developing and transition countries, organizing conferences and issuing publications.
Geographical Area of Activity: International.
Restrictions: Not a grantmaking organization.
Publications: Reports; papers; speeches.
Principal Staff: Dir Jan Joost Teunissen.
Contact Details: Nieuwendammerdijk 421, 1023 BM Amsterdam; tel. (20) 6371954; e-mail info@fondad.org; internet www.fondad.org.

Friends of the Earth International—FOEI

Established in 1971; a federation of environmental organizations and groups.
Activities: Campaigns on environmental and social issues. Main programme areas include: climate justice and energy; economic justice and resisting neoliberalism; food sovereignty; forests and biodiversity; and human rights defenders. The International Secretariat supports its member network through raising funds, co-ordinating campaigns, organizing workshops, disseminating information and maintaining databases. The federation comprises 70 grassroots member organizations.
Geographical Area of Activity: International.
Publications: Annual Report; newsletter; reports.
Finance: Annual income €3.2m., expenditure €3.6m. (31 Dec. 2023).
Executive Committee: Hemantha Withanage (Chair.); Anabela Lemos (Vice-Chair.); Bertrand Sansonnens (Treas.).
Principal Staff: Int. Co-ordinator Dave Hirsch.
Contact Details: Nieuwe Looiersstraat 31, 1017 VA Amsterdam; POB 19199, 1000 GD Amsterdam; tel. (20) 6221369; e-mail web@foei.org; internet www.foei.org.

Health Action International—HAI

Founded in 1981 by a group of medicine policy experts.
Activities: Works to increase access to essential medicines and improve their use through research and evidence-based advocacy. Projects include: equitable access to affordable medicines in Europe; providing access to insulin; raising community awareness about snakebite treatment and prevention; and researching the impact of artificial intelligence and automated decisionmaking in healthcare. The network comprises more than 200 health, consumer and development groups operating in more than 70 countries.
Geographical Area of Activity: Africa, Asia and the Pacific, Europe, the Americas.
Publications: Annual Report; Politics of Medicines Encyclopaedia (online); reports; briefing papers; factsheets; toolkits; blog.
Finance: Total income €4.8m., expenditure €4.7m. (31 Dec. 2023).
Board: Cecilia Sison (Chair.); Marcus Vreeburg (Treas.).
Principal Staff: Exec. Dir Dr Tim Reed; Asst Dir Renée Vasbinder.
Contact Details: Overtoom 60/II, 1054 HK Amsterdam; tel. (20) 4124523; e-mail info@haiweb.org; internet haiweb.org.

Heineken Prizes for Arts and Sciences (Heinekenprijzen voor kunst en wetenschap)

Established in 1963 by Heineken's Bierbrouwerij Maatschappij NV, a brewery.
Activities: Offered by the Dr A. H. Heineken Foundation for Art and the Alfred Heineken Fondsen Foundation. The Royal Netherlands Academy of Arts and Sciences (KNAW) appoints an independent jury of members of the Academy and

(international) experts to choose the prizewinners. Five international science prizes are awarded every two years and are worth US $250,000 each: the Dr H. P. Heineken Prize for Biochemistry and Biophysics (f. 1963); Dr A. H. Heineken Prize for Medicine (f. 1989); Dr A. H. Heineken Prize for History (f. 1990); Dr A. H. Heineken Prize for Environmental Sciences (f. 1990); and C. L. de Carvalho-Heineken Prize for Cognitive Science (f. 2006). The Dr A. H. Heineken Prize for Art (f. 1988) is presented to a visual artist working in the Netherlands and is worth €100,000, half of which is for a publication or an exhibition. In addition, four Heineken Young Scientists Awards, each worth €15,000, are presented to young researchers working in the Netherlands in the fields of the humanities, social sciences, (bio)medical sciences and natural sciences.

Geographical Area of Activity: International.

Principal Staff: Chair. Charlene L. de Carvalho-Heineken.

Contact Details: c/o Alfred Heineken Fondsen Foundation, Tweede Weteringplantsoen 5, 1017 ZD Amsterdam; KNAW, POB 19121, 1000 GC Amsterdam; tel. (20) 6263349; e-mail office@heinekenprizes.org; internet www.heinekenprizes.org.

Hivos—Humanistisch Instituut voor Ontwikkelings Samenwerking (Humanistic Institute for Co-operation with Developing Countries)

Founded in 1968; based on humanist values.

Activities: Supports activists, artists, entrepreneurs and journalists. Main programme areas are: civil rights and freedom of expression; climate justice; and gender equality, diversity and inclusion. The Institute works with 470 partner organizations in more than 40 countries. It has regional hubs in Costa Rica, Kenya and Zimbabwe, with country offices in Bolivia, Ecuador, Guatemala, Lebanon, Malawi, Tanzania, Timor-Leste and Zambia.

Geographical Area of Activity: International.

Restrictions: No unsolicited applications; grants only to specific projects.

Publications: Annual Review; *Hivos International* (newsletter).

Finance: Annual income €72.1m., expenditure €78.4m. (31 Dec. 2023).

Supervisory Council: Diana Monnisen (Chair.); Anja van Gorsel (Vice-Chair.).

Principal Staff: CEO Marco De Ponte.

Contact Details: Grote Marktstraat 47A, 2511 BH Den Haag; POB 85565, 2508 CG The Hague; tel. (70) 3765500; e-mail info@hivos.org; internet www.hivos.nl.

Institute of Social Studies—ISS (International Institute of Social Studies)

Founded in 1952; part of Erasmus University Rotterdam since 2009.

Activities: Conducts research and offers graduate and postgraduate courses in the areas of development studies and international co-operation. The Institute organizes and hosts conferences, public debates and seminars. It also manages a library containing 100,000 books and other print materials, 120,000 e-journals and provides access to over 300 online databases.

Geographical Area of Activity: Worldwide, focusing on developing countries and countries in transition.

Publications: Annual Report; newsletter; *Development and Change* (quarterly); *DevISSues* (magazine, once a year); brochures; journals; research reports; books.

Principal Staff: Rector Prof. Ruard Ganzevoort.

Contact Details: Kortenaerkade 12, 2518 AX The Hague; POB 29776, 2502 LT The Hague; tel. (70) 4260460; e-mail info@iss.nl; internet www.iss.nl.

Internationaal Instituut voor Sociale Geschiedenis—IISG (International Institute of Social History—IISH)

Founded in 1935 by Dr N. W. Posthumus and the Central Workers' Insurance Company; an institute of the Royal Netherlands Academy of Arts and Sciences (KNAW).

Activities: Operates as an international hub for social historians working on the origins, effects and consequences of social inequality, and the history of labour movements. The Institute provides historical sources and data and assists in research projects. It holds nearly 5,500 archives, more than 1m. printed vols; a similar number of audiovisual items, including posters; and 25 'dataverses'. Collections submitted to the Institute belong to the Stichting IISG (IISH Foundation), an independent foundation).

Geographical Area of Activity: International.

Publications: Annual Report; *International Review of Social History* (3 a year); *Sources for a History of the German and Austrian Working-class Movements* (series); *Studies in Social History* (series); *Contributions to the History of Labour and Society* (series); *Archives Michael Bakounine* (series); journals; blog; books.

Finance: Subsidized by an annual grant from the Dutch Ministry of Education and Science, and by contributions from various institutions and organizations.

Academic Advisory Board: Prof. Dr Jan Luiten van Zanden (Chair.).

Supervisory Board: Dr Henk Wals (Chair.); Agnes Jongerius (Sec.).

Principal Staff: Dir Prof. Dr Leo Lucassen.

Contact Details: Cruquiusweg 31, 1019 AT Amsterdam; POB 2169, 1000 CD Amsterdam; tel. (20) 6685866; e-mail info@iisg.nl; internet iisg.amsterdam.

International Penal and Penitentiary Foundation—IPPF (Fondation Internationale Pénale et Pénitentiaire—FIPP)

Founded in 1951 as successor to the Commission Internationale Pénale et Pénitentiaire.

Activities: Promotes the study of crime prevention, criminal procedure law and penitentiary law relating to detention and imprisonment, and treatment of offenders, especially by scientific research, publications and teaching. The Foundation has consultative status with the UN Commission on Crime Prevention and Criminal Justice, ECOSOC and the Council of Europe.

Geographical Area of Activity: International.

Publications: Books; reports.

Principal Staff: Pres. Prof. Véronique Erard; Sec.-Gen Prof. Dr Mary Rogan.

Contact Details: c/o Radboud University of Nijmegen, BP 9049, 6500 KK Nijmegen; tel. (24) 3615538; e-mail secretary.general@ippf-fipp.org; internet www.ippf-fipp.org.

Koninklijke Hollandsche Maatschappij der Wetenschappen (Royal Holland Society of Sciences and Humanities)

Founded in 1752 by seven leading Haarlem citizens for the promotion of science.

Activities: Operates nationally in the field of science through grants to institutions and individuals, conferences, publications and lectures. The Society awards annual prizes and subsidies for research and publication of scientific work; and comprises 450 societal members and more than 550 member professors. It manages several funds: the Pieter Langerhuizen Lambertszoon Fund, W. J. E. Voet Fund, Van der Knaap Fund, J. C. Baak Fund, Wim Drees Fund, Schouhamer Immink Fund, Jan Brouwer Foundation, Dr Saal van Zwanenberg Foundation and Eizenga-Van Oosten Foundation.

Geographical Area of Activity: Netherlands.

Publications: Books.

NETHERLANDS

Board: Dr Linda Hovius (Chair.); Dr Henk de Jong (Vice-Chair.); Didier Maclaine Pont (Treas.).
Principal Staff: Sec./Dir Dr Saskia van Manen.
Contact Details: Spaarne 17, 2011 CD Haarlem; tel. (23) 5321773; e-mail secretaris@khmw.nl; internet www.khmw.nl.

KWF Kankerbestrijding (KWF Dutch Cancer Society)

Founded in 1949 by Queen Wilhelmina as the Koningin Wilhelmina Fonds voor de Nederlandse Kankerbestrijding (Queen Wilhelmina Fund for the Dutch Cancer Society).
Activities: Operates nationally in the field of cancer control and promotes international scientific co-operation. The Society funds programmes at major specialized cancer hospitals; provides grants for projects on fundamental, epidemiological, clinical and psychosocial cancer research, and research on methods for cancer prevention; awards fellowships and scholarships; and organizes conferences and courses. It also runs a cancer information centre and free telephone helpline; publishes information brochures for patients and the public; and funds national support groups for cancer patients. A member of the International Union Against Cancer.
Geographical Area of Activity: Netherlands, its dependencies and former colonies.
Restrictions: There are limited funds for financial support of individual cancer patients.
Publications: Annual Report; newsletter; *Current Cancer Research in the Netherlands* (annual); *KWF Journal* (11 a year); *Kracht* (quarterly); brochures; progress reports.
Finance: Annual income €204.9m., expenditure €217.1m. (31 Dec. 2024).
Supervisory Board: Wiebe Draijer (Chair.).
Principal Staff: Dirs Dorine Manson, Carla van Gils.
Contact Details: Delflandlaan 17, 1062 EA Amsterdam; POB 75508, 1070 AM Amsterdam; tel. (20) 5700500; e-mail service@kwf.nl; internet www.kwf.nl.

Learning for Well-being Foundation—L4WB

Established in 2004 by Daniel Kropf, Corinne Evens and Marwan Awartani; formerly known as the Universal Education Foundation. Present name adopted in 2017.
Activities: Carries out activities in the areas of child participation, education, knowledge sharing, and research and assessment. The Foundation collaborates with partner organizations internationally; and organizes training workshops, community days and the annual Children as Actors Transforming Society (CATS) Conference. It has an office in Brussels, Belgium.
Geographical Area of Activity: International.
Publications: Annual Report; *Learning for Well-Being Magazine*; booklets; brochures; reports.
Finance: Annual revenue €1.5m., expenditure €1.5m. (31 Dec. 2023).
Board: Daniel Kropf (Exec. Chair.); Cova (Maria) Orejas (Vice-Chair.); Freek Noordman (Sec. and Treas.).
Principal Staff: Man. Dir Dominic Richardson.
Contact Details: Europaboulevard 57, 1083 AD Amsterdam; tel. (64) 2481361; e-mail info@learningforwellbeing.org; internet www.learningforwellbeing.org.

Nuffic

Formed in 2015 by the merger of the European Platform and the Netherlands Organization for International Co-operation in Higher Education—NUFFIC (f. 1952); formerly known as EP-Nuffic.
Activities: Works in the field of education. The organization's main activity areas are: development co-operation; internationalization of education from primary to higher level; international recognition and certification. It manages a range of scholarship and funding programmes on behalf of the Dutch and foreign governments, the European Commission and private donors; and houses the National Agency for Erasmus+, which provides Dutch organizations with funding for education, training, youth activities and sports through the EU's Erasmus+ programme. Has offices in Brazil, the People's Republic of China, India, Indonesia, the People's Republic of Korea, Mexico, the Russian Federation, South Africa and Viet Nam.
Geographical Area of Activity: Worldwide.
Publications: Annual Report.
Finance: Total assets €107.1m. (2023).
Supervisory Board: Bert van der Zwaan (Chair.).
Advisory Board: Tanja Jadnanansing (Chair.).
Principal Staff: Acting Man. Dir Imke Frijters.
Contact Details: Kortenaerkade 11, 2518 AX The Hague; POB 29777, 2502 LT The Hague; tel. (70) 4260260; e-mail info@nuffic.nl; internet www.nuffic.nl.

NWO Domain Applied and Engineering Sciences (Toegepaste en Technische Wetenschappen)

Formed in 2017 by the merger of the Technologiestichting (f. 1981) and the Netherlands Organisation for Scientific Research (Nederederlandse Organisatie voor Wetenschappelijk Onderzoek—NWO).
Activities: Operates nationally in the field of applied science and engineering, through research, travel grants, lectures and publications. The Foundation subsidizes research projects at universities and technological institutes in the Netherlands. Projects may be drawn from all technological fields, and are selected on the basis of both high scientific quality and applicability in industry.
Geographical Area of Activity: Netherlands.
Publications: Annual Report; project reports and others.
Finance: Annual revenue €1,176.2m., expenditure €1,332.6m. (31 Dec. 2023).
Supervisory Board: Dr Jan van den Berg (Pres.); Amandus Lundqvist (Vice-Pres.).
Board of Directors: Prof. Dr Dr Marcel Levi (Pres.); Prof. Hans Amman (Vice-Pres.).
Contact Details: POB 93138, 2509 AC The Hague; Laan van Nieuw Oost-Indië 300, 2593 CE The Hague; tel. (70) 3440640; e-mail nwo@nwo.nl; internet www.nwo.nl.

Oranje Fonds

Founded in 1948 to support social welfare at home and, in exceptional cases, abroad; formerly known as the Juliana Welzijn Fonds (Juliana Welfare Fund); present name adopted in 2002.
Activities: Works in the field of social welfare. The Fund annually supports around 10,000 social projects, such as small-scale community initiatives, mentoring projects for young people, and language programmes. Its priorities are: to enable development and innovation within its field of activity; to initiate or develop executive activity; and to address the shortage of available activities and organizations.
Geographical Area of Activity: Caribbean, Netherlands.
Restrictions: Does not make grants to individuals or in the areas of health, the arts, education, environment or development aid.
Publications: Annual Report; newsletter; brochure; blog.
Finance: Annual income €31.2m., total expenditure €32.9m. (31 Dec. 2024).
Board of Directors: Dr T. van Ark (Chair.); Prof. Z. C. B. Schellekens (Vice-Chair.).
Principal Staff: Man. Dir Sandra Jetten.
Contact Details: Maliebaan 18, 3581 CP Utrecht; POB 90, 3500 AB Utrecht; tel. (30) 6564524; e-mail info@oranjefonds.nl; internet www.oranjefonds.nl.

Oxfam NOVIB—Nederlandse Organisatie voor Internationale Ontwikkelingssamenwerking (Oxfam NOVIB—Netherlands Organization for International Development Co-operation)

Founded in 1956 as NOVIB to promote sustainable development by supporting the efforts of poor people in developing countries; became part of the Oxfam confederation of development agencies (qq.v.) in 1994.

Activities: Works to end poverty through: fighting inequality through system change; offering access to education, training and microcredit to women and young people; preventing disasters and providing emergency humanitarian assistance, helping migrants and assisting in reconstruction after disasters and conflicts; and providing security and protecting land rights. The organization works with local people in more than 80 countries. It offers academic and applied internships of 3–6 months in the fields of development and humanitarian assistance through the Oxfam Novib Academy.

Geographical Area of Activity: Africa, Asia, Central and South America, Eastern Europe and the countries of the former USSR.

Restrictions: Does not make loans or grants to individuals.

Publications: Annual Report; newsletter; case studies; reports; blog.

Finance: Annual revenue €188.7m., expenditure €193.2m. (31 March 2024).

Supervisory Board: Munish Ramlal (Chair.).

Principal Staff: Man. Dir Michiel Servaes.

Contact Details: Mauritskade 9, 2514 HD The Hague; POB 30919, 2500 GX The Hague; tel. (70) 3421621; e-mail info@oxfamnovib.nl; internet www.oxfamnovib.nl.

Prins Claus Fonds Voor Cultuur en Ontwikkeling (Prince Claus Fund for Culture and Development)

Established in 1996 by the Dutch Parliament as a tribute to HRH Prince Claus's dedication to culture and development.

Activities: Supports, connects and celebrates artists and cultural practitioners working under pressure. The Fund invests in exchanges as opportunities for encouragement, solidarity and professional networking. It offers awards that aim to achieve societal transformation through culture by creating space for new perspectives on social and/or political issues. The awards recognize transformative engagement and support talent, boost professional development and enable experimentation.

Geographical Area of Activity: Africa, Latin America, Asia and the Caribbean.

Publications: Annual Report; *The Prince Claus Awards Book*.

Finance: Annual income €5.0m., expenditure €5.2m. (31 Dec. 2023).

Board: Ila Kasem (Chair.); Mohamed Bouker (Treas.).

Principal Staff: Dir Marcus Desando.

Contact Details: Kingsfordweg 151, 1043 GR Amsterdam; tel. (20) 3449160; e-mail info@princeclausfund.nl; internet www.princeclausfund.org.

Rabo Foundation

Established in 1973 by Rabobank Group, a co-operative banking and financial services provider.

Activities: Offers financial support and advice in two fields: microfinance (and micro insurance); and developing sustainable supply chains in coffee, cocoa, fruit, cotton, nuts and sugar. The Foundation works in partnership with 375 local, national and international NGOs, supporting projects in 21 countries.

Geographical Area of Activity: International.

Publications: Annual Report.

Finance: Rabobank Nederland and its branches donate a percentage of their profit annually to the Foundation. Impact financing €42.8m. (2023).

Board and Supervisory Board: Netty Wakker (Chair.).

Principal Staff: Man. Dir Lidwien Schils.

Contact Details: Croeselaan 18, 3521 CB Utrecht; Postbus 17100, 3500 HG Utrecht; tel. (30) 2160000; e-mail rabobankfoundation@rabobank.nl; internet www.rabobank.com/about-us/rabo-foundation.

Rutgers

Founded in 1987, as the World Population Foundation; name changed to Rutgers WPF following merger with the Rutgers Nisso Group in 2010. Present name adopted in 2018. In 2021 Rutgers merged with Dance4Life.

Activities: Rutgers is the Netherlands' Centre on Sexuality, working with young people and women on sexual and reproductive health and rights (SRHR). Member Association of the International Planned Parenthood Federation and works in alliance with an extensive network of over 100 CSOs and NGO partners in approximately 30 countries. Committed to evidence-informed, rights-based, gender-transformative, inclusive, and positive approaches to sexuality and reproductive health programmes. Manages, coordinates and facilitates complex multi-country, multi-stakeholder and multi-million-euro consortium programmes. These include 'Right Here Right Now' and 'Generation Gender', Ado Avance Ensemble and She Makes Her Safe Choice. Has also facilitated online and face-to-face linking and learning programmes. Provides technical support and capacity building in the following areas: safe abortion and contraception; sex education; Youth-Friendly Services; sex- and gender-based violence; the Gender-Transformative Approach; meaningful and inclusive youth participation; prevention, mitigation and management of pushback to SRHR; advocacy; operational research; and sub-granting operations for NGOs and community-based organizations.

Geographical Area of Activity: Europe (especially the Netherlands), South and South-East Asia, Latin America and the Caribbean, sub-Saharan Africa, Middle East and North Africa.

Publications: Annual Report.

Finance: Annual turnover €24.9m. (2023).

Supervisory Board: Femke Aarts (Chair.).

Principal Staff: Exec. Dir Marieke van der Plas.

Contact Details: Arthur van Schendelstraat 696, 3511 MJ Utrecht; POB 9022, 3506 GA Utrecht; tel. (30) 2313431; e-mail office@rutgers.nl; internet rutgers.international.

SNV

Founded in 1965.

Activities: SNV is a mission-driven global development partner with the objective of strengthening capacities and fostering partnerships that transform the agri-food, energy, and water systems to enable sustainable and more equitable lives for all. Works in more than 20 countries in Africa and Asia.

Geographical Area of Activity: Asia, Africa.

Finance: Annual income €163.3m., expenditure €163.2m. (31 Dec. 2023).

Supervisory Board: Melanie Maas Geesteranus (Chair.).

Principal Staff: CEO Simon O'Connell.

Contact Details: Parkstraat 83, 2514 JG The Hague; tel. (70) 3440244; e-mail info@snv.org; internet www.snv.org.

Stichting Bellingcat (Bellingcat Foundation)

Established in 2018 by Eliot Higgins; an independent international collective of researchers, investigators and citizen journalists.

Activities: Works in the fields of journalism, information ecosystem, justice, transparency and accountability through conducting open-source investigations, evidence-based research and citizen journalism as well as using advanced technology to analyse publicly available data and social media. Areas of investigation include: conflicts and war crimes, state-actor wrongdoing, crimes against humanity; disinformation and misinformation; extremist groups; money laundering; transnational crime; and use of chemical weapons. The Foundation organizes training workshops on conducting open source and online investigations for journalists, activists, human rights defenders, etc. Bellingcat also started a program to teach media literacy in high schools. It has staff and contributors in more than 20 countries.

Geographical Area of Activity: International.

Publications: Annual Report; newsletter; case studies; guides; investigations; new research tools for free and how to use them.

Finance: Annual income €3m., expenditure €4m. (2023).

Executive Board: Eliot Higgins (Chair.); Dessilava Lange-Damianova (Treas.); Giancarlo Fiorella (Sec.).

Contact Details: Papaverweg 34, Unit B100, 1032 KJ Amsterdam; POB 15712, 1001 NE Amsterdam; e-mail contact@bellingcat.com; internet www.bellingcat.com.

Stichting Democratie en Media (Foundation for Democracy and Media)

Established in 2003 as the successor to Foundation Het Parool (f. 1944) to support the surviving relatives of the deceased staff of the newspaper *Het Parool*, which was covertly published during the German occupation of the Netherlands in the Second World War.

Activities: Works to stimulate independent, critical media; and maintain strong, comprehensive democratic rule of law. The Foundation offers subsidies, loans and investment to those promoting the Foundation's ideals, including support to institutions organizing debates and lectures, for publications, exhibitions, etc. In 2012 it co-founded the European Press Prize for quality journalism.

Geographical Area of Activity: Europe.

Finance: Total assets €152.9m.; net annual income €8.8m. (31 Dec. 2023).

Supervisory Board: Yvonne Zonderop (Chair.).

Principal Staff: Man. Dir Nienke Venema.

Contact Details: Singel 151, 1012 VK Amsterdam; Spuistraat 112-D, 1012 VA Amsterdam; tel. (20) 5300300; e-mail info@sdm.nl; internet sdm.nl.

Stichting Dioraphte (Dioraphte Foundation)

Established in 2002; in 2015 it merged with Stichting Liberty (f. 1995), Stichting Dijkverzwaring (f. 1997) and Stichting Continuendo MusartE Foundation (f. 2004).

Activities: Funds organizations carrying out projects in the areas of: Dutch cultural heritage; performing arts; science and research; social initiatives in the Netherlands and in East Africa.

Geographical Area of Activity: Netherlands, East Africa.

Publications: Annual Report.

Finance: Annual budget €14.5m. (2025).

Board: Prof. Dr Coen Teulings (Chair.); Roderik Los (Treas.).

Principal Staff: Dir Jasmijn Melse.

Contact Details: Rhijngeesterstraatweg 40D, 2341 BV Oegstgeest; internet www.dioraphte.nl.

Stichting DOEN (DOEN Foundation)

Established in 1991 by the Dutch Postcode Lottery to pursue the same objectives as the Lottery (i.e. people and nature) and to complement the Lottery's work.

Activities: Works in the areas of regenerative economy, social society and the power of imaginaton through promoting sustainable, cultural and socially minded pioneers. The Foundation defines pioneers as people who: take risks; have a creative or innovative approach; transform pioneering concepts into concrete projects; serve as an inspiring example to others; run sustainable and social business operations; put social and/or ecological objectives first; and/or create resourceful connections between sustainable, social and cultural interests.

Geographical Area of Activity: International.

Restrictions: Grants only to organizations.

Publications: Annual Report.

Finance: Receives funding from the Dutch Postcode Lottery and the Friends Lottery; Annual income €34.9m., expenditure €20.9m. (31 Dec. 2023).

Supervisory Board: Hester Maij (Chair.).

Principal Staff: Dir Carol Gribnau.

Contact Details: Beethovenstraat 200, 1077 JZ Amsterdam; POB 75621, 1070 AP Amsterdam; tel. (20) 5737333; e-mail doen@doen.nl; internet www.doen.nl.

Stichting Fonds 1818 (1818 Fund Foundation)

Founded in 1990 as the VSB Fonds Den Haag by the VSB Bank; present name adopted in 2001.

Activities: Supports projects in the areas of: the arts and culture; economic affairs; conservation and the environment; medicine and health; sport and recreation; animal welfare; and social welfare.

Geographical Area of Activity: Principally The Hague, Delft, Leiden and the Zoetermeer area of the Netherlands.

Restrictions: Grants only to projects that focus on the region in which the fund is established; no grants to individuals.

Publications: Annual Report; newsletter; information brochure; *Fonds 1818* (quarterly magazine); manuals.

Finance: Annual income €60.8m., expenditure €17.6m. (31 Dec. 2023).

Board: Pauline Kuipers (Chair.); Yvon van Houdt (Vice-Chair.).

Principal Staff: Dir Sanne ten Bokkel Huinink.

Contact Details: Riviervismarkt 5, 2513 AM The Hague; tel. (70) 3641141; e-mail info@fonds1818.nl; internet www.fonds1818.nl.

Stichting IKEA Foundation (IKEA Foundation)

Established in 1982 by Ingvar Kamprad, founder of the IKEA furniture and home furnishings company; the philanthropic arm of INGKA Foundation.

Activities: Supports rural communities, young people, women and refugees. Main programme areas are: agricultural livelihoods; climate action; employment and entrepreneurship; refugee livelihoods; renewable energy; and special initiatives and emergency response. In 2019 the Foundation established the Ingvar Kamprad Design Foundation at Lund University School of Industrial Design with an endowment of €33m.

Geographical Area of Activity: International, with a focus on Africa, the Middle East, South-East and South Asia (particularly India).

Restrictions: Does not accept unsolicited applications; no grants to individuals.

Publications: Annual Report; newsletter; factsheets.

Finance: Annual income €282.6m., expenditure €282.6m. (31 Dec. 2023).

Principal Staff: CEO Jessica Anderen.

Contact Details: Dellaertweg 9, 2316 WZ Leiden; tel. (71) 5240400; e-mail infor@ikeafoundation.org; internet www.ikeafoundation.org.

Stichting Liliane Fonds (Liliane Foundation)

Founded in 1980 by Liliane Brekelmans to provide aid for disabled children and young people up to the age of 25 years in less-developed countries.

Activities: Supports the participation of children with disabilities at home and in their communities. The Foundation offers grants to individuals for medical and social rehabilitation. It has an office in Belgium.

Geographical Area of Activity: Africa, Asia, Central and South America.

Publications: Annual Report; newsletter; brochures.

Finance: Annual income €29.6m., expenditure €26.9m. (31 Dec. 2023).

Supervisory Board: Thos Gieskes (Chair.).

Principal Staff: Man. Dir Erik Ackerman.

Contact Details: Havensingel 26, 5211 TX 's-Hertogenbosch; tel. (73) 5189420; e-mail voorlichting@lilianefonds.nl; internet www.lilianefonds.nl.

Stichting Mama Cash (Mama Cash Foundation)

Founded in 1983 by Marjan Sax, Dorelies Kraakman, Tania Leon, Patti Slegers and Lida van den Broek.

Activities: Promotes the human rights of women and girls through funding women-led organizations working in the thematic areas of body (safety from violence, sexual and reproductive rights, challenging harmful traditional practices); money (economic justice; workers' rights; property and inheritance rights); and voice (representation and participation, decision-making and leadership, and being seen and heard). The Foundation also helps local and regional women's funds, which support women's rights initiatives in their own communities.

Geographical Area of Activity: International.

Restrictions: Does not fund: organizations whose mission and primary focus are not the promotion of women's or girls' human rights; organizations that are led by men or based in the USA and Canada; organizations whose primary focus is development work, humanitarian assistance, poverty alleviation, or basic charity; organizations linked to political parties government agencies or religious institutions; businesses; individuals; academic research; scholarships; or travel grants.

Publications: Annual Report; *she has news* (newsletter); *she has e-news* (electronic newsletter).

Finance: Annual income €22.0m., expenditure €21.9m. (31 Dec. 2023).

Supervisory Board: Sara Vida Coumans, Oriana López Uribe (Co-Chair.).

Principal Staff: Co-Exec. Dirs Saranel Benjamin, Happy Mwende Kinyili.

Contact Details: Eerste Helmersstraat 17-III, 1054 CX Amsterdam; POB 15686, 1001 ND Amsterdam; tel. (20) 5158700; e-mail info@mamacash.org; internet www.mamacash.org.

Stichting Max Havelaar—Fairtrade Nederland (Max Havelaar Foundation—Fairtrade Netherlands)

Established in 1988 by Frans van der Hoff and Nico Roozen, named after a fictional character in a book by Dutch author Multatuli (Eduard Douwes Dekker).

Activities: Conducts policy research and advocacy on fair trade. Programme areas include: child labour; climate change; human rights; living income; living wage; and the UN Sustainable Development Goals. The organization works with small-scale producers in developing countries, Dutch importers and consumers; and carries out monitoring and evaluation, maintaining a register of producers and checking to ensure fair trade principles are observed.

Geographical Area of Activity: Africa, Asia, Central and South America, Netherlands.

Publications: Annual Report; commodity briefings; reports; toolkits; blog.

Finance: Annual income €4.0m., expenditure €4.8m. (31 Dec. 2023).

Supervisory Board: Martijn van Dam (Chair.); Erik Drok (Treas.).

Principal Staff: Exec. Dir Marloes Groenewegen.

Contact Details: Arthur van Schendelstraat 550, 3511 MH Utrecht; tel. (30) 2337070; e-mail info@fairtradenederland.nl; internet www.fairtradenederland.nl.

Stichting The Ocean Cleanup (The Ocean Cleanup Foundation)

Established in 2013 by Boyan Slat, an inventor.

Activities: Operates in the fields of the environment, the economy and health. The Foundation designs and develops technologies to remove plastic pollution from the world's oceans, focusing on ocean gyres such as 'The Great Pacific Garbage Patch' and rivers. It operates in the USA as the Ocean Cleanup North Pacific Foundation and has offices in New York and Kuala Lumpur.

Geographical Area of Activity: International.

Publications: Annual Report; newsletter; scientific reports.

Finance: Annual income €27.3m., expenditure €26.6m. (31 Dec. 2021).

Supervisory Board: Bert Bruggeman (Chair.).

Principal Staff: CEO Boyan Slat.

Contact Details: Coolsingel 6, 3011 AD Rotterdam; e-mail info@theoceancleanup.com; internet www.theoceancleanup.com.

Stichting Praemium Erasmianum (Praemium Erasmianum Foundation)

Founded in 1958 by HRH Prince Bernhard of the Netherlands, named after Dutch humanist scholar Desiderius Erasmus.

Activities: Operates internationally in the fields of education, social welfare and studies, the arts and humanities, law and other professions, through the awarding of the Erasmus Prize, worth €150,000, to a person or institution for 'an exceptional contribution to culture, society or social science'. Previous prizewinners include Trevor Noah (2023) and Grayson Perry (2021). The Foundation also awards up to five annual Research Prizes, worth €3,000 each, to young doctoral researchers in the humanities and social sciences.

Geographical Area of Activity: International.

Restrictions: Does not accept unsolicited applications.

Publications: Annual Report; series of publications in connection with the laureates or theme of the prize.

Governing Board: Andrée van Es (Chair.); Judi Mesman (Vice-Chair.); Peter Blom (Treas.).

Principal Staff: Dir Geertjan de Vugt.

Contact Details: Maliebaan 104, 3581 CZ Utrecht; tel. (65) 7594436; e-mail spe@erasmusprijs.org; internet www.erasmusprijs.org.

Stichting Prins Bernhard Cultuurfonds (Prince Bernhard Cultural Foundation)

Established in London (UK), in 1940 to raise money to buy war materials for the British and Dutch Governments; after the Second World War it was decided to continue the fund to rebuild cultural life in the Netherlands.

Activities: Manages more than 450 Designated Funds. The Foundation makes grants and awards for projects in the areas of culture, nature and science; awards scholarships for young artists and scholars to study abroad; and administers the Zilveren Anjer (Silver Carnation) Awards annually, which recognize individuals' contributions to Dutch cultural life and the environment. It has a local branch in each of the 12 Dutch provinces. The Prince Bernhard Cultural Fund Caribbean operates independently in the Caribbean (Aruba, Bonaire, Curaçao, Saba, Sint Eustatius and Sint Maarten).

Geographical Area of Activity: Netherlands.

Publications: Annual Report; newsletter.

Finance: Receives a share of the revenue of national lotteries, income from its own collections, and from assets and gifts. Total assets €425.7m. (31 Dec. 2023).

Supervisory Board: Prof. Dr Pauline L. Meurs (Chair.); Ronald Wuijster (Treas.).

Principal Staff: Dir and Man. Cathelijne Broers.

Contact Details: Da Costakade 102, 1053 WP Amsterdam; POB 19750, 1000 GT Amsterdam; tel. (20) 5206130; e-mail info@cultuurfonds.nl; internet www.cultuurfonds.nl.

Stichting Triodos Foundation (Triodos Foundation)

Established in 1971 by Lex Bos, Dieter Brüll, Rudolf Mees and Adriaan Deking Dura; after the establishment of Triodos Bank in 1980, the Foundation limited its role to granting gifts to institutions.

Activities: Supports national and international projects that initiate innovation in three main programme areas: development and health; equal opportunities; and food and biodiversity. Branches of Triodos Bank in Belgium, Spain and the United Kingdom each have a similar foundation.

Geographical Area of Activity: Worldwide.

Publications: Annual Report; newsletter; blog.

Finance: Annual income €1.4m., expenditure €1.9m. (31 Dec. 2023).

Executive Board: Daniël Köhler (Chair.); Patty Zuidhoek (Sec./Treas.).

Principal Staff: Dir Léonhard ten Siethoff.

Contact Details: Landgoed De Reehorst, Hoofdstraat 10, 3972 LA Driebergen-Rijsenburg; tel. (30) 6936535; e-mail triodos.foundation@triodos.nl; internet www.triodosfoundation.nl.

Stichting van Schulden naar Kansen (Debts to Opportunities Foundation)

Established in 2008 as Delta Lloyd Foundation by Delta Lloyd Bank; present name adopted in 2018.

Activities: Promotes financial self-reliance and the reduction of poverty caused by debt. The Foundation runs programmes in four cities in the Netherlands, strengthening people's skills and knowledge of personal administration, basic finance, income generation and controlling spending. It collaborates with CSOs and research institutes.

Geographical Area of Activity: Netherlands.

Publications: Annual Report.

Finance: Annual income €766,081, expenditure €1.2m. (2020).

Board: Peter Paul Boon (Treas.); Fleur Hudig (Sec.).

Principal Staff: Man. Miranda Visser-de Boer.

Contact Details: Schenkkade 65, 2595AS The Hague; tel. 611197951; e-mail vanschuldennaarkansen@nn-group.com; internet www.vanschuldennaarkansen.nl.

Stichting Vluchteling (Refugee Foundation)

Founded in 1976 by various churches and other groups in the Netherlands to provide assistance for refugees outside the Netherlands; in 2015 it merged with the International Rescue Committee (q.v.).

Activities: Provides emergency assistance to refugees and people displaced by conflict. Programmes focus on health, protection, education and economic wellbeing. Active in 32 countries.

Geographical Area of Activity: International.

Restrictions: Does not provide assistance to refugees in the Netherlands.

Publications: Annual Report; newsletter.

Finance: Annual income €37.8m., annual expenditure €38.9m. (2023).

Supervisory Board: Tineke Huizinga (Chair.); Thea Fierens (Vice-Chair.).

Principal Staff: Acting Dir Renske Boetje.

Contact Details: Laan van Nieuw Oost, Indië 131M, 3593 BM The Hague; tel. (70) 3468946; e-mail info@vluchteling.nl; internet www.vluchteling.nl.

Stichting Vodafone Netherlands (Vodafone Netherlands Foundation)

Established in 2002 by Vodafone Netherlands, a telecommunications provider; part of the Vodafone Foundation (q.v.) network.

Activities: Supports technology-based projects that improve the lives of vulnerable people. Main programmes are: Online Masters and Welkom Online, teaching digital skills to schoolchildren and elderly people, respectively; Experience Days, technology workshops for children from underprivileged backgrounds; Bondgenoten, a robot that helps children with long-term illnesses to keep in touch with school, friends and family; and Instant Network, building temporary networks to connect emergency services and local people. The Foundation also promotes employee volunteering and makes charitable donations.

Geographical Area of Activity: International.

Publications: Annual Report.

Finance: Annual income €840,325, expenditure €688,152 (31 March 2023).

Board: Robin Kroes (Chair.); Laura van Gestel (Treas.).

Contact Details: Boven Vredenburgpassage 128, 3511 WR Utrecht; tel. (43) 3555555; internet www.vodafoneziggo.nl/en/samenleving/vodafone-foundation.

Van Leer Foundation

The Van Leer Foundation was established in 1949 and was formerly known as the Bernard Van Leer Foundation.

Activities: An independent Dutch organization working globally to foster inclusive societies where all children and communities can flourish, bringing together people with different perspectives and support them to achieve large-scale impact. Support from the Foundation involves a combination of funding, networks, executive education, technical assistance and knowledge.

Geographical Area of Activity: Africa, Brazil, India, Israel, Jordan, Netherlands.

Restrictions: Does not accept unsolicited applications.

Publications: Annual Report; *Early Childhood Matters* (journal); *Diverse knowledge products from on early childhood development*.

Finance: Annual income €22.0m., expenditure €18.5m. (2023).

Board of Trustees: Nanno Kleiterp (Chair.).

Principal Staff: CEO Michael Feigelson.

Contact Details: Grote Marktstraat 43A, 2511 BH Den Haag The Hague; POB 82334, 2508 EH The Hague; tel. (70) 3312200; e-mail info@vanleerfoundation.org; internet www.vanleerfoundation.org.

ZOA

Founded in 1973 as Stichting Zuidoost Azië (South-East Asia Foundation); a Christian organization.

Activities: Works in the fields of emergency relief, rehabilitation and reintegration. The organization supports people affected by armed conflict or natural disasters. Main programmes include: livelihoods and food security; water, sanitation and hygiene (WASH); basic education; peacebuilding; shelter; and urban programming. Operates in 12 countries.

Geographical Area of Activity: Afghanistan, Burundi, Colombia, Dem. Repub. of the Congo, Ethiopia, Indonesia, Iraq (Kurdistan), Liberia, Myanmar, Netherlands, Nigeria, South Sudan, Sri Lanka, Sudan, Syrian Arab Repub., Uganda, Yemen.

Publications: Annual Report; *ZOA Magazine* (7 a year).

Finance: Annual income €92.6m., expenditure €92.6m. (31 Dec. 2023).

Supervisory Board: Dr K. (Niels) Hofstede (Chair.).

Principal Staff: CEO Chris Lukkien.

Contact Details: Sleutelbloemstraat 45, Apeldoorn; POB 4130, 7320 AC Apeldoorn; tel. (55) 3663339; e-mail info@zoa.nl; internet www.zoa.nl.

NEW ZEALAND

CO-ORDINATING BODIES

Community Foundations of New Zealand
Established in 2013 as a membership organization.

Activities: National body that supports 18 regional foundations, seeking to build strong communities, and fostering inclusivity where members can contribute to their community and thrive.

Geographical Area of Activity: New Zealand.

Publications: Newsletter (6 a year); Annual Impact Report.

Finance: Annual revenue NZ$607,000, expenditure NZ$630,000 (31 March 2024).

Board of Trustees: Raymond Key (Chair.); Lori Luke (Deputy Chair.).

Contact Details: POB 24-220, Manners St, Wellington 6142; tel. (27) 407-1073; e-mail admin@communityfoundations.org.nz; internet communityfoundations.org.nz.

Philanthropy New Zealand/Topūtanga Tuku Aroha o Aotearoa
Established in 1990 by Sir Roy McKenzie, a philanthropist.

Activities: Represents and supports philanthropy and grantmaking in New Zealand. Supports generosity, effective giving and a strong philanthropic eco-system. Provides training, sharing best practice, data and research, and connects members to enable collaboration. Offers guidance for anyone with an interest in giving to make the world a better place. Members include trusts, foundations, community groups, individuals, investors, corporates, local government, and iwi (Māori tribes).

Geographical Area of Activity: New Zealand.

Publications: Annual Report; *Giving Matters* (newsletter); *Philanthropy News* (magazine).

Finance: Annual income NZ$981,292, expenditure NZ$1.4m. (30 June 2023).

Board: Seumas Fantham (Chair.); Pulotu Tupe Solomon-Tanoa'i (Deputy Chair.).

Principal Staff: Chief Exec. Rahul Watson Govindan.

Contact Details: Level 2, 50 The Terrace, Wellington 6011; PO Box 1521, Wellington 6140; tel. (4) 499-4090; e-mail info@philanthropy.org.nz; internet www.philanthropy.org.nz.

FOUNDATIONS AND NON-PROFITS

All Good Foundation Charitable Trust
Founded in 2018 by New Zealand business owners Heather and Rod Claycomb.

Activities: All Good Ventures supports up to five early-stage social entrepreneurs each year through a one-year programme designed to help them launch and grow a business that improves the lives of people in need. Each entrepreneur receives: seed funding of between NZ$5,000 to NZ$20,000; mentoring for a full year; and practical help to fill resource or skill gaps as they start their social enterprise business, including access to online courses, expert advice, and hands-on support.

Geographical Area of Activity: New Zealand, Uganda, South Africa, United Kingdom, Australia, Kenya, Canada, Nepal, Ethiopia, Malawi, Rwanda, United States.

Restrictions: None.

Publications: Reports.

Trustees: Philip Mathew Renner, Heather Claycomb and Rodney Claycomb.

Principal Staff: Man. Beth Chapman.

Contact Details: Hamilton, New Zealand; e-mail info@allgood.ventures; internet www.allgood.ventures.

Antarctic Heritage Trust (NZ)
Established in 1987 to conserve expedition bases in the Antarctic.

Activities: Seeks to foster the spirit of exploration and encourage the next generation of explorers. The Trust conserves the expedition bases of polar explorers Capt. Robert Falcon Scott, Sir Ernest Shackleton, Carsten Borchgrevink and Sir Edmund Hillary.

Geographical Area of Activity: Antarctic regions.

Publications: Annual Report; newsletter.

Finance: Annual income NZ$5.0m., expenditure NZ$5.1m. (30 June 2024).

Trustees: Sir Jerry Mateparae (Chair.); Anthony Wright (Deputy Chair.); Wayne Munn (Treas.).

Principal Staff: Exec. Dir Francesca Eathorne.

Contact Details: 7 Ron Guthrey Road, Christchurch 8053; Private Bag 4745, Christchurch 8140; tel. (3) 358-0212; e-mail info@nzaht.org; internet www.nzaht.org.

Asia New Zealand Foundation/Te Whītau Tūhono
Established in 1994 to build New Zealanders' knowledge and understanding of Asia.

Activities: Promotes closer ties between New Zealand and Asia through cultural events, forums, professional development opportunities, international collaborations and school programmes. Main programme areas include: the arts and culture, organizing and supporting Asia-related events and festivals, and awarding grants and artist-in-residence places; business, offering seminars, grants and internships and networking opportunities; education, providing information, resources and professional development to teachers, study grants for high school students and undergraduates, and scholarships for undergraduate and postgraduate students; leadership networking, for young professionals; media, providing travel grants internships to journalists; research, commissioning social, economic and education research; Track II, on strategic, regional and security issues; sports, funding individual sportspeople and teams. The Foundation has offices in Auckland and Christchurch.

Geographical Area of Activity: East and South-East Asia, South Asia, New Zealand.

Publications: Annual Report; newsletter; surveys, reports, research and analysis.

Finance: Annual revenue NZ$6.6m., expenditure NZ$6.6m. (30 June 2024).

Board of Trustees: Dame Fran Wilde (Chair.); Te Poa Karoro (Paul) Morgan (Deputy Chair.).

Principal Staff: Exec. Dir Suzannah Jessep; Deputy Exec. Dir Adele Mason.

Contact Details: Level 16, Fujitsu Tower, 141 The Terrace, POB 10144, Wellington 6143; tel. (4) 471-2320; e-mail asianz@asianz.org.nz; internet www.asianz.org.nz.

Buchanan Charitable Foundation
Founded in 2011.

Activities: Offers grants and scholarships. Key interests include: young people; environmental issues; healthcare; optometry. Established the Buchanan Charitable Foundation Research Project Prize in 2020 at the University of Aukland for the optometry student with the best project in public eye health. The Buchanan Charitable Trust Scholarship is awarded to one student each year and covers tuition fees and additional expenses for a period of nine years, for education at King's School and later King's College.

Geographical Area of Activity: Australia, South Africa.

Finance: Annual income NZ$6.6m., expenditure NZ$1.5m. (31 March 2024).

Contact Details: c/o Perpetual Guardian, Level 8, 191 Queen St, Auckland 1010.

Cancer Society of New Zealand/Te Kāhui Matepukupuku o Aotearoa

Founded in 1929 by the British Empire Cancer Campaign Society.

Activities: Supports cancer research through grants to institutions and individuals in New Zealand; and through travelling fellowships enabling New Zealand graduates to travel abroad for study. The Society holds conferences with international participation, and disseminates the results of research. It also provides information and support services (including Living Well Programme and online forum, CancerChatNZ) to people affected by cancer.

Geographical Area of Activity: New Zealand.

Publications: Annual Report; Research Report; *Present State and Future Needs of Cancer Research in New Zealand;* information sheets.

Finance: Annual income NZ$7.4m., expenditure NZ$7.1m. (31 March 2022).

Principal Staff: CEO Nicola Coom.

Contact Details: Level 6, Ranchhod Tower, 39 The Terrace, Wellington; POB 651, Pipitea, Wellington 6140; tel. (4) 494-7270; e-mail info@cancersoc.org.nz; internet www.cancernz.org.nz.

ChildFund

Established in 1938.

Activities: Partners with local organizations worldwide to establish programmes and initiatives to help children and young people thrive and become self-reliant, free from poverty and violence.

Geographical Area of Activity: Australia, Kenya, Kiribati, Papua New Guinea, Solomon Islands, Timor-Leste, Viet Nam, Zambia.

Finance: Annual income NZ$11.0m., expenditure NZ$10.8m. (30 June 2024).

Principal Staff: Chair. Jay Stead.

Contact Details: 3/2 Kitchener St, Auckland 1010; POB 105630, Auckland 1143; tel. (9) 366-0333; e-mail info@childfund.org.nz; internet childfund.org.nz.

Forest & Bird Te Reo o te Taio

Established in 1923 as the Royal Forest and Bird Protection Society of New Zealand.

Activities: Operates nationally in the field of nature conservation, protecting natural areas, and plants and animals native to New Zealand. Main programmes focus on: land; fresh water; oceans; and climate and economy. The organization promotes sustainability in farming and land management; works as an advocate for conservation by lobbying the Government on environmental issues; and supports the protection of Antarctica. It offers Valder conservation grants, worth NZ$1,000–NZ$2,000 for conservation-focused research or advocacy; and administers the JS Watson Trust, which offers grants worth up to NZ$5,000 for restoration projects. Has over 100,000 members and more than 45 branches; and runs the Forest & Bird Youth network, for young people aged 14–25 years, and the Kiwi Conservation Club for children.

Geographical Area of Activity: Antarctica, New Zealand.

Restrictions: Grants only to member branches and networks.

Publications: Annual Report; newsletter; *Forest & Bird Magazine* (quarterly); *Best Fish Guide* (biennial consumer booklet); *Kiwi Conservation Club* (magazine, 4 a year); factsheets; blog.

Finance: Annual income NZ$16.7m., expenditure NZ$12.6m. (31 Dec. 2023).

Board: Kate Graeme (Pres.); Mark Hanger (Deputy Pres.); Nigel William Thomson (Treas.).

Principal Staff: Chief Exec. Nicola Toki.

Contact Details: Ground Floor, 205 Victoria St, Wellington 6011; POB 631, Wellington 6140; tel. (4) 385-7374; e-mail office@forestandbird.org.nz; internet www.forestandbird.org.nz.

Hagar NZ

Established in 2009.

Activities: Works to combat modern slavery and human trafficking, and to raise awareness of the issue. Provides counselling, case management, safe accommodation, legal support and economic empowerment advice to organizations worldwide in order to help survivors of human trafficking to overcome trauma and to re-enter their communities and thrive.

Geographical Area of Activity: Afghanistan, Australia, Cambodia, Myanmar, Singapore, Solomon Islands, Thailand, Viet Nam.

Finance: Annual income NZ$1.8m., expenditure NZ$2.0m. (31 Dec. 2022).

Principal Staff: Exec. Dir Kate Russell.

Contact Details: POB 6724, Upper Riccarton, Christchurch 8442; tel. (2) 145-2831; e-mail info@hagar.org.nz; internet hagar.org.nz.

J. R. McKenzie Trust

Founded in 1940 by Sir John Robert McKenzie, founder of the McKenzie department store chain and Rangatira Investments; part of the J. R. McKenzie Trust Group, which also includes the Jayar Charitable Trust.

Activities: Supports organizations working with people with special needs, especially children and young people, people at risk or at significant social disadvantage. The Trust also supports new and innovative approaches to social problems and organizations seeking to improve their services. The Te Kāwai Toro programme supports Māori development, incorporating the Pūtea Toro Fund, which offers small grants to rōpū (organizations).

Geographical Area of Activity: New Zealand.

Restrictions: Does not make grants to individuals, sports groups, schools and early childhood centres, out-of-school care programmes, rest homes and hospitals, environmental groups, or to religious or campaigning groups.

Publications: Annual Report; newsletter.

Finance: Annual income NZ$8.1m., expenditure NZ$9.8m. (31 March 2024).

Board of Trustees: Dr Chelsea Grootveld (Chair.).

Principal Staff: Exec. Dir Robyn Scott.

Contact Details: Level 7, Prime Property Tower, 88 Lambton Quay, 114 Lambton Quay, Wellington 6011; POB 10 006, The Terrace, Wellington 6140; tel. (4) 472-8876; e-mail info@jrmckenzie.org.nz; internet www.jrmckenzie.org.nz.

National Heart Foundation of New Zealand

Established in 1968.

Activities: Operates in the field of medicine and health, through research, providing grants for research projects, training fellowships for cardiology trainees to study overseas, senior fellowships and a Chair in Cardiovascular Studies; health promotion, through programmes to promote good health for all and reduce underlying causes of the disease; and medical care to prevent people at high risk from developing heart and blood vessel disease, and to improve the care and rehabilitation of people with heart disease. The Foundation has 16 branches.

Geographical Area of Activity: New Zealand.

Publications: Annual Report; newsletter; booklets; brochures; pamphlets; posters.

Finance: Annual revenue NZ$41.0m., expenditure NZ$37.2m. (30 June 2024).

Board of Directors: Michael Tomlinson (Chair.).

Principal Staff: Chief Exec. Clive Martin Nelson.

Contact Details: 9 Kalmia St, Ellerslie, Auckland 1051; POB 17-160, Greenlane, Auckland 1546; tel. (9) 571-9191; e-mail info@heartfoundation.org.nz; internet www.heartfoundation.org.nz.

NZIIA—New Zealand Institute of International Affairs

Founded in 1934.

Activities: Fosters understanding of international issues, trading partnerships and relations with other countries, particularly in relation to New Zealand, the Commonwealth, and the countries of South-East Asia and the Pacific. The Institute conducts research and organizes conferences and lectures. It has eight branches throughout New Zealand; and nearly 90 corporate and institutional members.

Geographical Area of Activity: International.

Publications: *New Zealand International Review* (6 a year); occasional papers; pamphlets; books.

Finance: Total assets NZ$621,456 (31 Dec. 2024).

Board: James Kember (Chair.); Serena Kelly (Vice-Chair.).

Principal Staff: Exec. Dir Hamish McDougall.

Contact Details: c/o Victoria University of Wellington, POB 600, Wellington 6140; RH325, Rutherford House, 23 Lambton Quay, Wellington 6011; tel. (4) 463-5356; e-mail nziia@vuw.ac.nz; internet www.nziia.org.nz.

Oxfam Aotearoa

Established in 1991 as part of the Oxfam confederation of organizations (qq.v.), fmrly known as Oxfam New Zealand.

Activities: Works to end poverty, injustice and inequality. Main programme areas include: aid and development; food and livelihoods; safe water and sanitation; and women's rights. The organization also provides emergency humanitarian assistance during crises.

Geographical Area of Activity: Asia-Pacific, South-East Asia.

Restrictions: Does not make loans or grants to individuals.

Publications: Impact Report; reports.

Finance: Annual income NZ$7.5m., expenditure NZ$8.5m. (31 March 2024).

Board of Trustees: Ngila Bevan (Chair.); Sarah Rennie (Deputy Chair.); Rohini Ram (Treas.).

Principal Staff: Kaiwhakahaere Exec. Dir Jason Myers.

Contact Details: Level 1, 14 West St, Eden Terrace, Auckland 1010; POB 68357, Victoria St West, Auckland 1142; tel. (9) 355-6500; e-mail oxfam@oxfam.org.nz; internet www.oxfam.org.nz.

Pacific Development and Conservation Trust

Established in 1989 by the Government of New Zealand with funds from the French Government in recognition of the events surrounding the destruction of the Greenpeace ship the *Rainbow Warrior,* which French secret service agents blew up and sank in Auckland Harbour in 1985.

Activities: Operates in New Zealand and the Pacific in the fields of conservation, cultural heritage, development and goodwill. The Trust promotes the enhancement, protection and conservation of the physical environment of the Pacific and of its natural and historic resources; the peaceful, economic, physical and social development of the Pacific and its peoples; peaceful conservation and development of the cultural heritage of the peoples of the Pacific; and peace, understanding and goodwill among the peoples of the Pacific. It offers grants to individuals and institutions, typically ranging from NZ$2,000 to NZ$50,000, which are administered by the Department of Internal Affairs.

Geographical Area of Activity: New Zealand and the Pacific.

Restrictions: Will not fund core salaries or ongoing organizational operating and related costs; the purchase of land or buildings; school trips; family reunions; research projects submitted by current or intending tertiary students that are primarily linked to a course of personal study.

Publications: Annual Report.

Finance: Annual income NZ$288,063, expenditure NZ$453,420 (30 June 2024).

Principal Staff: Trustee Peter David James.

Contact Details: Level 5, 45 Pipitea St, Wellington; POB 805, Wellington 6140; e-mail community.matters@dia.govt.nz; internet www.communitymatters.govt.nz/pacific-development-and-conservation-trust.

Pacific Leprosy Foundation

Established in 1939 by Patrick Twomey, who raised funds for leprosy patients on Makogai Island, Fiji; formerly known as the Makogai NZ Lepers' Trust Board.

Activities: Operates in the areas of medicine, health and social welfare. The Foundation works to eliminate leprosy as a threat to public health, through research and attention to sanitation and health issues; and provides medical and social assistance to those affected by leprosy and their families.

Geographical Area of Activity: Australasia and the Pacific.

Publications: Annual Report; newsletter.

Finance: Annual income NZ$883,964, expenditure NZ$1.4m. (30 June 2024).

Board: Richard C. Gray (Chair.); Andrew Tomlin (Treas.).

Principal Staff: Gen. Man. Jill Tomlinson.

Contact Details: 4 Anderson St, Addington, Christchurch 8140; Private Bag 4730, Christchurch 8140; tel. (3) 343-3685; e-mail admin@leprosy.org.nz; internet www.leprosy.org.nz.

Peace and Disarmament Education Trust—PADET

Established in 1988 by the Government of New Zealand with funds from the French Government in recognition of the events surrounding the destruction of the Greenpeace ship the *Rainbow Warrior,* which French secret service agents blew up and sank in Auckland Harbour in 1985.

Activities: Operates in the fields of education, international affairs, law and human rights, social studies and disarmament and arms control. The Trust promotes international peace, arms control and disarmament. It carries out self-conducted programmes and research and makes grants to individuals and institutions. It also offers scholarships for higher educational study in two categories: up to NZ$14,000 for one year's work towards a Master's thesis; and up to NZ$21,000 (plus up to NZ$5,000 for tuition fees) each year for up to three years' work towards a doctoral thesis. Grants are administered by the Department of Internal Affairs.

Geographical Area of Activity: New Zealand.

Restrictions: Does not fund capital costs; scholarship research must be relevant to New Zealand disarmament and arms control policy.

Publications: Annual Report; theses.

Finance: Annual income NZ$198,330, expenditure NZ$152,167 (31 March 2024).

Principal Staff: Trustee Paul David James.

Contact Details: 45 Pipitea St, Thorndon, Wellington 6011; POB 805, Wellington 6140; internet www.communitymatters.govt.nz/peace-and-disarmament-education-trust-2.

Queen Elizabeth II National Trust

Established in 1977 to protect open spaces in New Zealand through the protection of land and sites by means of covenants.

Activities: Operates in New Zealand, working with landowners to create protected areas. In 2023 the Trust's partner network comprised more than 5,000 protected areas, protecting 190,000 ha.

Geographical Area of Activity: New Zealand.

Publications: Annual Report; magazines; handbooks; guides.

Finance: Annual operating revenue NZ$8.7m., expenditure NZ$10.0m. (30 June 2023).

Board of Directors: Alan Livingston (Chair.).

Principal Staff: CEO Dan Coup.

Contact Details: Level 4, 138 The Terrace, POB 3341, Wellington 6140; tel. (4) 472-6626; e-mail info@qeii.org.nz; internet qeiinationaltrust.org.nz.

Sexual Wellbeing Aotearoa

Established in 1936, as the Sex Hygiene and Birth Regulation Society; name changed to the New Zealand Family Planning Association Inc in 1939. Present name adopted in 2024. In 1990 Te Puawai Tapu was formed by an autonomous group of Māori women from the Association.

Activities: Promotes a positive view of sexuality and enables people to make informed choices about their sexual and reproductive health and wellbeing. The organization offers clinical and health promotion services, clinical training, and community information and advocacy. It also makes submissions on proposed government legislation and works closely with government departments. The International Programmes team works on projects throughout the Pacific region.

Geographical Area of Activity: New Zealand, South-East Asia and the Pacific region.

Publications: Annual Report; newsletter (3 a year); *Forum* (annual).

Finance: Annual income NZ$19.9m., expenditure NZ$19.8m. (30 June 2024).

Council: Andreas Prager (Pres.); Dr Pualine Horrill (Deputy Pres.).

Principal Staff: Chief Exec. Jackie Edmond; Deputy Chief Exec. Kirsty Walsh.

Contact Details: Level 2, 205 Victoria St, Wellington 6011; POB 11515, Wellington 6142; tel. (4) 384-4349; e-mail national@familyplanning.org.nz; internet www.familyplanning.org.nz.

Sutherland Self Help Trust

Founded in 1941 with funds donated by Arthur F. H. Sutherland.

Activities: Provides capital and training/equipment grants to institutions in New Zealand operating in the fields of education, science and technology, medicine and health, and social welfare. The Trust carries out activities in the areas of care and advancement of physically disabled and disadvantaged children; community youth work; care of sick and older people; and alleviation of social problems, including alcohol and drug abuse and sexual abuse.

Geographical Area of Activity: New Zealand.

Restrictions: Does not make grants to individuals, or for administration costs, vehicles or overseas travel, nor for environmental, artistic, cultural or sporting purposes.

Publications: Case Studies.

Finance: Annual income NZ$1.6m., expenditure NZ$2.0m. (31 Dec. 2023).

Board of Trustees: John B. Sutherland (Chair.).

Principal Staff: Sec. David Gibbons.

Contact Details: 7 Kenwyn Terrace, Newtown, Wellington 6021; POB 193, Wellington 6140; tel. (4) 385-1563; e-mail office@sutherlandselfhelptrust.org.nz; internet sutherlandselfhelptrust.org.nz.

Tindall Foundation

Established in 1994 by Sir Stephen Tindall, founder and CEO of retail chain The Warehouse, and his wife Margaret, to help New Zealanders to reach their full potential.

Activities: Carries out activities in five main programme areas: family and social services; enterprise and employment; care of the environment and preservation of biodiversity; strengthening the community sector; and promoting philanthropy. Fund managers allocate a proportion of the Foundation's resources directly.

Geographical Area of Activity: New Zealand.

Publications: Annual Report.

Finance: Annual income NZ$12.3m., expenditure NZ$11.3m. (31 March 2024).

Principal Staff: Man. John McCarthy.

Contact Details: 1 Blomfield Spa, Takapuna, Auckland 0622; POB 33 181, Takapuna, Auckland 0740; tel. (9) 488-0170; e-mail admin@tindall.org.nz; internet www.tindall.org.nz.

The Todd Foundation

Established in 1972 by the Todd family's corporate interests, for charitable purposes within New Zealand.

Activities: Provides funding to New Zealand organizations that promote inclusive communities. The General Fund supports children, young people, their families and their communities. The Special Focus Fund is an invitation-only fund, which is designed to provide support for selected social, economic, environmental and cultural issues. The Foundation offers a doctoral scholarship in energy research; and awards for excellence for research projects that benefit New Zealand and its people, carried out in approved universities and polytechnics.

Geographical Area of Activity: New Zealand.

Restrictions: Does not fund: capital items; overseas organizations and travel; individuals (except for tertiary research scholarships); sports organizations; individual schools and early childhood centres or out-of-school care programmes; the promotion of religious beliefs; organizations that focus on specific conditions and disabilities.

Publications: Annual Report.

Finance: Annual income NZ$1.8m., expenditure NZ$922,501 (31 Dec. 2023).

Board: Charlotte Stellar (Chair.).

Principal Staff: Exec. Dir Seumas Fantham.

Contact Details: Level 15, Todd Bldg, 95 Customhouse Quay, Wellington 6011; POB 3142, Wellington 6140; tel. (4) 931-6189; e-mail info@toddfoundation.org.nz; internet www.toddfoundation.org.nz.

Trade Aid NZ Inc—TANZ

Established in 1973 to encourage sustainable development through fair trade; a social enterprise.

Activities: Operates in 30 developing countries, promoting self-reliance through fair trade. The organization imports products made by people from poor communities, offering a fair price for goods to provide a sustainable income.

Geographical Area of Activity: Africa, Asia, Australasia, Central and South America.

Publications: Annual Report; *Vital Magazine* (approx. 4 a year); *Pick of the Crop* (coffee-focused newsletter).

Finance: Annual gross profit NZ$26.8m., expenditure NZ$28.0m. (30 June 2024).

Principal Staff: CEO Geoff White.

Contact Details: 174 Gayhurst Rd, Dallington, Christchurch 8640; POB 35 049, Shirley, Christchurch 8640; tel. (3) 385-3535; e-mail customerservice@tradeaid.org.nz; internet www.tradeaid.org.nz.

Vodafone Foundation New Zealand

Established in 2002 by Vodafone New Zealand, a telecommunications company; part of the Vodafone Foundation (q.v.) network.

Activities: Funds projects that help excluded and disadvantaged children and young people. Main programme areas are: access to learning; care and protection; long-term beneficiaries; Rangatahi Māori (Maori Youth); and youth justice. Through its Innovation Fund, the Foundation awards grants for seed, pilot and scale funding, ranging from N$1,000 to

NZ$200,000. The Collaborative Fund offers funding to achieve positive systems change and disruption. Funding is also available through Alumni Grants and Alumni Development Grants, Extension Partnerships and Technology Development.
Geographical Area of Activity: New Zealand.
Restrictions: Grants only to charitable trusts registered with the Charities Commission.
Publications: Annual Report; Think Pieces; evaluations; research reports.
Finance: Annual income NZ$1.9m., expenditure NZ$1.8m. (31 March 2022).
Board of Directors: Juliet Jones (Chair.); Kamile Stankute (Sec.).
Principal Staff: Head of Foundation and Sustainability Lani Evans.
Contact Details: 68–76 Taharoto Rd, Takapuna, Auckland 0622; Private Bag 92161, Victoria St West, Auckland 1142; tel. (9) 355-2000; e-mail vodafonenzfoundation@vodafone.com; internet foundation.vodafone.co.nz.

Volunteer Service Abroad/Te Tūao Tāwāhi—VSA

Established in 1962 by Sir Edmund Hilary; comprises the VSA Foundation.
Activities: Connects volunteers from New Zealand with partner organizations in developing regions to assist local communities. Volunteers share knowledge and experience in a range of areas, including health, education and training, community development, economic development, enterprise, conservation and agriculture.
Geographical Area of Activity: Melanesia, Polynesia, Timor-Leste.
Publications: Annual Report; *VISTA* (magazine, 2 a year); *Talk Talk* (bimonthly e-newsletter); media releases.
Finance: Annual income NZ$10.2m., expenditure NZ$10.1m. (30 June 2024).
VSA Council: Dana MacDiarmid (Chair.); Simon Trotter (Deputy Chair.).
Contact Details: Level 2, 77 Thorndon Quay, Pipitea, Wellington 6011; POB 12246, Te Whanganui-a-Tara/Wellington 6144; tel. (4) 472-5759; e-mail info@vsa.org.nz; internet www.vsa.org.nz.

Winston Churchill Memorial Trust of New Zealand

Established in 1965 in memory of Sir Winston Churchill; administered by the Department of Internal Affairs.
Activities: Supports learning in the areas of the arts and culture, citizens and society, economy and enterprise, education and skills, environment and resources, health and wellbeing, science and technology. The Trust awards Churchill Fellowships to assist New Zealanders to travel overseas to visit other communities, learn from others and study topics that will help them to increase their contribution to the community, and advance their trade, industry, profession or business. Fellowships amount to up to 80% of costs for short-term travel and activity; grants average between NZ$7,000 and NZ$12,000.
Geographical Area of Activity: International.
Restrictions: Does not award grants for academic or professional qualifications.
Publications: Annual Report; Fellowship Reports.
Finance: Annual income NZ$570,962, expenditure NZ$163,222 (31 March 2024).
Board of Trustees: David Douglas Charles Ivory (Chair.).
Contact Details: 45 Pipitea St, Wellington 6011; POB 805, Wellington 6140; tel. (4) 495-9431; e-mail wcmt@dia.govt.nz; internet www.wcmt.co.nz.

NIGER

FOUNDATIONS AND NON-PROFITS

Fondation Guri Vie Meilleure

Established in 2011 by First Lady Aïssata Issoufou.
Activities: Works in the fields of health and nutrition, education and environmental conservation. Activities include: protecting mothers and children from HIV/AIDS; reproductive health of adolescents and young people; building and rehabilitating health facilities and providing medicines and equipment to hospitals; organizing mobile eye clinics for people in disadvantaged communities; advocating for children's rights, in particular girls' right to education; improving access to education and scientific training; awarding an annual prize for academic excellence and merit; improving sanitation in schools; distributing school kits to pupils; combating deforestation and desertification; and raising children's awareness of waterborne diseases.
Geographical Area of Activity: Niger.
Publications: Newsletter.
Principal Staff: Chair. Aïssata Issoufou.
Contact Details: BP 409, Niamey; tel. 74049263; e-mail contact@gourivm.com.

NIGERIA

CO-ORDINATING BODY

African Philanthropy Forum

Established in 2014, an affiliate of the Global Philanthropy Forum (q.v.).
Activities: Promotes inclusive and sustainable development in Africa through strategic giving and social investment. The Forum hosts regional meetings and conferences. It has an office in Johannesburg, South Africa.
Geographical Area of Activity: Africa.
Restrictions: Not a grantmaking organization.
Publications: Annual Report; newsletter; *Toolkit for African Philanthropists*.
Finance: Total assets 304.5m. naira; net operating income 147.3m. naira (31 Dec. 2022).
Board: Gbenga Oyebode (Chair.).
Principal Staff: Exec. Dir Mosun Layode.
Contact Details: 14 Chris Maduike St, Lekki Phase 1, Lagos; tel. (803) 7291889; e-mail apf@africanpf.org; internet africanpf.org.

NIGERIA

FOUNDATIONS AND NON-PROFITS

A. G. Leventis Foundation Nigeria
Established in 1988; a subsidiary foundation of the A. G. Leventis Foundation (q.v.) in Greece.

Activities: Works in the fields of agricultural training, education, the environment, healthcare and culture. The Foundation has established an Environmental Resource Centre, in collaboration with the Nigerian Conservation Foundation, as well as developing an agroforestry conservation programme; and providing equipment to technical colleges for vocational training.

Geographical Area of Activity: Ghana, Nigeria.

Publications: *The Millennium Farmer* (quarterly newsletter); *Small-scale Farming in West Africa*; *Agroforestry Guide: An Introductory Field Manual on Agroforestry Practices in Nigeria and Ghana*.

Board of Directors: Ahmed Kazalma Mantey (Chair.).

Principal Staff: Exec. Dir Dr Hope Ovie Usieta.

Contact Details: 2 Leventis Cl., Central Business District, POB 20351, F. C. T. Abuja; tel. (708) 5524233; e-mail info@leventisfoundation.org.ng; internet www.leventisfoundation.org.ng.

African Refugees Foundation—AREF
Established in 1993 by Chief Segun Olusola to assist refugees in Africa.

Activities: Helps refugees and displaced people, preparing for disasters and rehabilitating victims; promotes peace, organizing workshops on peace initiatives and conflict mediation, and seminars on conflict prevention and management; develops policy for governments; and promotes development and engagement with civil society. The Foundation offers voluntary medical corps services. Sister organizations operate in the United Kingdom and the USA. The Foundation has UN accreditation.

Geographical Area of Activity: Africa.

Publications: Newsletter (monthly); blog.

Principal Staff: CEO Olujimi Olusola, III; Hon. Pres. Chief Opral Benson.

Contact Details: Ajibulu-Moniya Gallery, Plot 49, Babs Animashaun Estate, Extension, Lagos; tel. (802) 354842; e-mail info@africanrefugeesfoundation.org; internet africanrefugeesfoundation.org.

Aisha Buhari Global Foundation
Established in 2014 by First Lady Aisha Buhari.

Activities: Supports the wellbeing of women, children and young people. The Foundation's flagship programme is Future Assured, which carries out activities in the areas of: health, including nutrition and screening for communicable and non-communicable diseases; women's and girls' education; women's economic empowerment, including providing seeds, fertilizer, livestock and other agricultural inputs to encourage women to take up farming, and providing microfinance services; protecting the rights of women and children, advocating against gender-based violence; and supporting people who have been displaced by violence to return to their homes, providing them with food, clothing and shelter, and building an orphanage and school for children in a camp for internally displaced people.

Geographical Area of Activity: Nigeria.

Finance: Initial endowment US $1m.

Principal Staff: Admin. Saidu Suleiman.

Contact Details: Office of the First Lady, Aso Rock Presidential Villa, Abuja; e-mail programs@futureassured.org.ng.

Aliko Dangote Foundation—ADF
Established in 1994 by Alhaji Aliko Dangote, Pres. of Dangote Group, an industrial conglomerate.

Activities: Operates internationally in the areas of health, education, economic empowerment and humanitarian relief. Alhaji Aliko Dangote endowed the Foundation with a gift of US $1,200m. in 2014.

Geographical Area of Activity: International.

Board of Directors: Alhaji Aliko Dangote (Pres. and Chief Exec.).

Contact Details: Dangote Group, Leadway Marble House, 1 Alfred Rewane Rd, PMB 40032, Falomo, Ikoyi, Lagos; tel. (1) 4480815; e-mail communications@dangote.com; internet www.dangote.com/foundation.

FATE Foundation
Founded in 2000 by Fola Adeola, a business person and politician, to tackle the high rate of unemployment and poverty in Nigeria.

Activities: Promotes wealth creation in Nigeria by providing Nigerian young people with the skills, tools, networks and financing needed to create successful businesses that will in turn offer employment to other people. The Foundation provides support and services to businesses; carries out research and advocacy; and organizes policy workshops. It also operates the FATE School of Entrepreneurship and makes annual awards to successful entrepreneurs. Has an office in Port Harcourt.

Geographical Area of Activity: Nigeria.

Publications: Annual Report; newsletter; factsheets; policy reports.

Finance: Annual revenue 874.7m. naira, expenditure 770.9m. naira (28 Feb. 2023).

Board: Fola Adeola (Chair.).

Principal Staff: Exec. Dir Adenike Adeyemi.

Contact Details: 16 Town Planning Way, Ilupeju, Lagos; tel. (701) 5300490; e-mail info@fatefoundation.org; internet www.fatefoundation.org.

International Institute of Tropical Agriculture—IITA
Founded in 1967 by the Ford and Rockefeller Foundations (qq.v.) to contribute to the improvement of tropical farming techniques; part of the CGIAR (Consultative Group on International Agricultural Research) international network of research centres.

Activities: A research-for-development organization which works to increase food security; reduce rural poverty and the incidence of under-nutrition; and introduce sustainable natural resource management. Main programmes are: Biotechnology and Genetic Improvement; Natural Resource Management; Social Science and Agribusiness; Plant Production and Plant Health; and Nutrition and Food Technology. The Institute has 15 stations, laboratories and field research sites across Africa.

Geographical Area of Activity: sub-Saharan Africa, USA.

Publications: Annual Report (in French and English); newsletter (monthly); *IITA Research* (2 a year, in French and English); brochures, conference proceedings, technical papers, training manuals.

Finance: Annual income US $126.8m., expenditure $126.1m. (31 Dec. 2023).

Board of Trustees: Precious Adebanjo (Sec.).

Contact Details: Oyo Rd, PMB 5320, Ibadan 200001, Oyo State; tel. 8034035281; e-mail iita@cgiar.org; internet www.iita.org.

MTN Nigeria Foundation
Established in 2004 by MTN Nigeria, a telecommunications company; part of the MTN Foundations network.

Activities: Carries out activities in the areas of health, education and economic empowerment. Main programmes are: the arts and culture; maternal and child health; and youth empowerment. Under the MTNF Science and Technology Scholarship

Scheme and the MTNF Scholarship Scheme for Blind Students, the Foundation awards scholarships worth 200,000 naira annually; and, under the MTNF MUSON Music Scholars Program, scholarships worth 250,000 naira annually.

Geographical Area of Activity: Nigeria.

Restrictions: Only funds non-profit organizations in Nigeria.

Publications: Annual Report.

Finance: Receives up to 1% of MTN Nigeria's annual profits; total disbursements since 2004 c. 25,700m. naira.

Board: Prince Julius Adelusi-Adeluyi (Chair.).

Principal Staff: Exec. Sec. Odunayo Sanya.

Contact Details: 2nd Floor, MTN Plaza, Falomo, Lagos; e-mail mtn.foundation@mtn.com; internet www.mtnonline.com/foundation.

Nigerian Conservation Foundation—NCF

Established in 1980 by Chief S. L. Edu; registered as a Charitable Trust in 1982.

Activities: Seeks to improve the quality of human life through preserving Nigeria's biodiversity; promoting the sustainable use of natural resources; and advocating to minimize pollution and the wasteful use of renewable and non-renewable resources. The Foundation runs participatory community-based projects; conducts research; and organizes conferences, seminars, training courses and workshops. It is an affiliate of the World Wide Fund for Nature (WWF) and a partner of Birdlife International. Has an office in Abuja and four regional offices.

Geographical Area of Activity: West Africa.

Publications: Newsletter (monthly).

Finance: Funded by donations, membership subscriptions and investment income.

Board of Trustees: Izoma Philip Asiodu (Pres.).

National Executive Council: Justice R.I.B. Adebiyi (Chair.).

Principal Staff: Dir-Gen. Dr Joseph Daniel Onoja.

Contact Details: Km 19, Lekki-Epe Expressway, POB 74638, Victoria Island, Lagos; tel. (906) 5460479; e-mail info@ncfnigeria.org; internet www.ncfnigeria.org.

Nigerian Institute of International Affairs—NIIA

Established in 1961 by Sir Tafawa Balewa and Sir Adetokunbo Ademola.

Activities: Provides advice and guidance for foreign policy development. Core areas of research are: African politics and integration; international economic relations; international politics; international law and organizations; and security and strategic studies. The Institute organizes conferences, lectures and roundtables on current foreign policy issues. It awards post-doctoral research fellowships; and has a library for the use of members and postdoctoral students.

Geographical Area of Activity: International.

Publications: *Nigerian Journal of International Affairs*; *Nigerian Forum*; *Nigerian Bulletin on Foreign Affairs*; *niianews* (newsletter).

Principal Staff: Dir-Gen. Prof. Eghosa E. Osaghae.

Contact Details: 13/15 Kofo Abayomi Rd, Victoria Island, POB 12750, Marina, Lagos; tel. (803) 3188011; e-mail info@niia.gov.ng; internet www.niia.gov.ng.

Orji Uzor Kalu Foundation

Established in 2011 by Orji Uzor Kalu, Chair. of SLOK Holding.

Activities: Works to improve the lives of underprivileged people through self-conducted programmes in the areas of health, education and economic empowerment. The Foundation organizes awareness-raising workshops on food security, nutrition for children and older people and environmental issues such as climate change and soil erosion; offers skills training for marginalized young people and women; and operates a microcredit scheme for small business owners. It has branch offices in Igbere, Abia State, Port Harcourt and Lagos; and special consultative status with ECOSOC.

Geographical Area of Activity: Nigeria.

Publications: Newsletters.

Board of Trustees: Dr Orji Uzor Kalu (Chair.); Rev. Jemaimah Ola Kalu (Exec. Sec.).

Contact Details: Orji Uzor Kalu House, Plot 322, Mabuchi, Abuja; tel. (806) 0399485; e-mail orjiuzorkalufoundation@gmail.com; internet www.orjiuzorkalufoundation.org.

Sir Ahmadu Bello Memorial Foundation

Established in 2009 by the Governors of 19 northern states of Nigeria in memory of Sir Ahmadu Bello, former Premier of Northern Nigeria.

Activities: Works to improve human and economic development through fostering good governance and leadership. Programmes focus on skills development and training for young people in business development, entrepreneurship and financial management; as well as providing youth mentorship and advocating against rape and other forms of gender-based violence. The Foundation awards scholarships, worth 100,000 naira, for tertiary-level studies in science or technology.

Geographical Area of Activity: Nigeria.

Finance: Funded mainly by the Northern Governors' Forum, donations and independently generated through investments.

Advisory Council: Alh Mohammed Munir Ja'afaru (Chair.).

Board of Trustees: Dr Mu'azu Babangida Aliyu (Chair.); Dr Gabriel Suswam (Deputy Chair.); Mallam Ibrahim Shekarau (Sec.).

Principal Staff: Dir-Gen. Abubakar Gambo Umar.

Contact Details: 21 Race Course Road, City Centre, Kaduna 800283; tel. 8068073783; e-mail info@ahmadubellofoundation.org; internet ahmadubellomemfoundation.org.

Sir Emeka Offor Foundation

Established in 2006 by Sir Emeka Offor, Chair. of the Chrome Group oil and gas company.

Activities: Fosters personal independence and self-sufficiency. Main programme areas include: education, offering scholarships to economically disadvantaged university students; ensuring access to healthcare; and human capacity development, providing microfinance grants and loans to young entrepreneurs and establishing co-operatives to help widows to achieve economic independence and provide for their children. The Foundation has a branch office in Oraifite.

Geographical Area of Activity: Africa.

Publications: Newsletter; brochure; blog.

Finance: Total disbursements since 2006 US $4.9m.

Principal Staff: Chair. Sir Emeka Offor.

Contact Details: 22 Lobito Cresc., Wuse II, Abuja; tel. (709) 8124159; e-mail info@sireofforfoundation.org; internet sireofforfoundation.org.

Tony Elumelu Foundation—TEF

Established in 2010 by Tony Elumelu, Chair. of investment company Heirs Holdings.

Activities: Promotes entrepreneurship in Africa. The Foundation invests in small and medium-sized enterprises, providing start-up funding worth US $5,000. Initiatives include: the pan-African TEF Entrepreneurship Programme to support 100,000 African entrepreneurs; and the Africapitalism Institute (f. 2014), which conducts research on the importance of economic prosperity and the private sector to social and economic development in Africa. It established TEFConnect, a digital networking platform for African entrepreneurs; and organizes the annual TEF Forum.

Geographical Area of Activity: Africa.

Publications: Newsletter; blog.

Principal Staff: CEO Somachi Chris-Asoluka.

Contact Details: Heirs Pl., 1 MacGregor Rd, Ikoyi, Lagos; tel. (1) 27746415; e-mail enquiries@tonyelumelufoundation.org; internet tonyelumelufoundation.org.

TY Danjuma Foundation

Established in 2008 by Theophilus Yakubu Danjuma, former Army Chief of Staff and founder and Chair. of South Atlantic Petroleum (SAPETRO).

Activities: Works in the fields of community health, education and income generation through working in partnership with Nigerian NGOs. The Foundation set up Community Funds in Taraba and Edo States to support community-based organizations and NGOs; and makes Discretionary Grants for humanitarian emergencies and short-term interventions. It has offices in Taraba and Edo.

Geographical Area of Activity: Nigeria (in particular, Taraba and Edo States).

Restrictions: Grants only to registered NGOs and community-based organizations working in Nigeria in the areas of community health and education and skills training.

Publications: Annual Report; newsletter (quarterly).

Finance: Total annual disbursements 253.7m. naira (2020).

Trustees: Lt Gen. Theophilus Yakubu Danjuma (Rtd) (Chair. Emeritus); Hannatu Gentles (Chair.).

Principal Staff: CEO Gima H. Forje.

Contact Details: 35 Fandriana Cl., off Oda Cresc., off Dar Es Salaam St, off Aminu Kanu Cresc., Wuse II, Abuja; tel. (906) 5447852; e-mail contact@tydanjumafoundation.org; internet tydanjumafoundation.org.

NORTH MACEDONIA

CO-ORDINATING BODIES

Association for Democratic Initiatives—ADI (Asotzijatzijata za Dyemokratska Initzijativa)

Established in 1994; a founding member of the Steering Committee of the Balkan Human Rights Network—BHRN (q.v.).

Activities: Promotes human rights, democracy and intercultural tolerance. Programme areas include: civic participation; good governance; civil society; decentralization; inter-ethnic relations; and media. The Association has established three NGO Resource Centres, in Gostivar, Stip and Tetovo, which offer advice and technical support to individuals and organizations on setting up civic initiatives; and has offices in Albania, Bosnia and Herzegovina, Kosovo and Metohija, and the USA. It has special consultative status with ECOSOC.

Geographical Area of Activity: North Macedonia.

Publications: Annual Report; *RETURN* (periodical); publications in the areas of human rights, refugees and migrants, democracy and civil society, and education and youth.

Assembly: Shpend Imeri (Pres.).

Principal Staff: First Exec. Dir Albert Musliu; Exec. Dir Lulzim Haziri.

Contact Details: Bul. Braka Ginoski 61/3, 1230 Gostivar; tel. (42) 221100; e-mail adi@adi.org.mk; internet www.adimacedonia.org.

Balkan Civil Society Development Network—BCSDN (Fondacija Balkanska Mreza za Razvoj na Gragjanskoto Opshtestvo)

Established in 2003; successor to a pilot programme by the Macedonian Center for International Co-operation (q.v.).

Activities: A regional network of 10 CSOs from nine countries that promotes the civic space and an enabling environment for CSOs, through evidence-based and collaborative policy influence on international, European, and national level. Goals are to advocate for the protection and expansion of civic space, securing more favourable donor practices for protection and expansion of the civic space, and to strengthen learning, coordination, and collaboration for stronger advocacy on civic space.

Geographical Area of Activity: Albania, Bosnia and Herzegovina, Kosovo, Montenegro, North Macedonia, Romania, Serbia, Slovenia, Türkiye (Turkey).

Publications: Annual Report on CSO enabling environment in WBT; newsletter (bi-monthly).

Finance: Annual revenue 29.4m. denars, expenditure 29.4m. denars (31 Dec. 2024).

Board: Taulant Hoxha (Chair.); Maja Stojanovic (Co-Chair.).

Principal Staff: Exec. Dir Biljana Spasovska.

Contact Details: Executive Office, bul. Mitropolit Teodosij Gologanov 59A-1/15, 1000 Skopje; tel. (2) 6144211; e-mail executiveoffice@balkancsd.net; internet www.balkancsd.net.

FOUNDATIONS AND NON-PROFITS

Foundation Open Society Macedonia—FOSIM (Fondatzija Otvoryeno Opshtyestvo Makyedonija)

Founded in 1992; an independent foundation, part of the Open Society Foundations (q.v.) network. Previously known as the Open Society Fund of Macedonia.

Activities: Promotes tolerance and accountability. Main programme areas are: civil society development and citizens' democratic participation; rule of law and good governance, with equal access to justice for all; access to education, enabling children and young people to think critically and respect diversity; healthcare and human rights; and providing legal services to marginalized citizens. The Foundation offers grants and scholarships for university students, doctoral candidates and university teaching staff.

Geographical Area of Activity: North Macedonia.

Publications: Annual Report; books; brochures; policy briefs; reports.

Finance: Annual revenue 233.3m. denars, expenditure 233.3m. denars (2020).

Executive Board: Santa Argirova (Chair.).

Principal Staff: Dir Andi Dobrushi; Deputy Dir Miodrag Milosavljevic.

Contact Details: Str. Chedomir Minderovikj 31, POB 378, 1000 Skopje; tel. (2) 2444488; e-mail fosm@fosm.mk; internet www.fosm.mk.

Macedonian Centre for International Co-operation—MCIC (Makyedonski Tzyentar za Myeroonarodna Sorabotka)

Established in 1993.

Activities: Carries out activities in the fields of civil society, good governance and anti-corruption, and social inclusion and cohesion, supporting European integration and strengthening regional co-operation. The Centre promotes cultural diversity, interdependence and dialogue; supports sustainable local and rural development; provides capacity development and training to CSOs; and carries out advocacy and research, issuing publications. It has consultative status with ECOSOC.

Geographical Area of Activity: North Macedonia.

Publications: Reports; e-newsletter; analysis; surveys.

Milieukontakt Macedonia   NORWAY

Finance: Annual revenue 101.8m. denars, expenditure 101.4m. denars (31 Dec. 2022).

Governance Board: Dr Sulejmani Rizvan (Chair.); Gabriela Micevska (Deputy Chair.).

Principal Staff: Dir Aleksandar Kržalovski.

Contact Details: Ul. Nikola Parapunov bb, POB 55, 1060 Skopje; tel. (2) 3065381; e-mail mcms@mcms.mk; internet www.mcms.mk.

Milieukontakt Macedonia—MKM

Founded in 2012 to take over programmes in Macedonia implemented by Netherlands-based organization Milieukontakt International (f. 1988).

Activities: Supports CSO initiatives in the areas of the environment, social justice and economic development. The organization promotes democracy, transparency and public participation in decisionmaking processes at local, national and international level; and co-operates with regional NGOs.

Geographical Area of Activity: Western Balkans.

Publications: Annual Report; newsletter; brochures; factsheets; manuals.

Principal Staff: Exec. Dir Maja Markovska.

Contact Details: Kukuska 4A, Skopje 1000; tel. (2) 2460876; e-mail info@mkm.mk; internet milieukontakt.mk.

NORWAY

CO-ORDINATING BODIES

Stiftelsesforeningen (Norwegian Donors Forum)

Established in 2003.

Activities: Promotes and strengthens the role of foundations in philanthropy in Norway, and acts as a forum for the exchange of information and ideas. The Forum has 356 members, including foundations managed by UNIFOR (q.v.); and is a member of Philea (q.v.).

Geographical Area of Activity: Norway.

Publications: Annual Report; research reports.

Finance: Annual income 2.6m. krone, expenditure 2.5m. krone (31 Dec. 2023).

Board: Hans Christian Lillehagen (Chair.); Ingrid Riddervold Lorange (Deputy Chair.).

Principal Staff: Man. Dir Karianne Bjellås Gilje.

Contact Details: Akersgata 28, 0158 Oslo; tel. 91-74-17-04; e-mail stiftelsesforeningen@gjensidigestiftelsen.no; internet stiftelsesforeningen.no.

UNIFOR—Forvaltningstiftelse for fond og legater (Fund and Endowment Management Foundation)

Established in 1993 by the University of Oslo.

Activities: Manages assets and provides business and accountancy services for more than 200 charitable foundations involved mainly in research and higher education.

Geographical Area of Activity: Norway.

Publications: Annual Report.

Finance: Total assets 3,500m. krone (2020).

Board: Leif H. Pedersen (Chair.); Stine M. Ulven (Deputy Chair.).

Principal Staff: CEO Hans Jørgen Stang.

Contact Details: Fridtjof Nansens vei 19, Majorstuen, 0369 Oslo; Postboks 1131, Blindern, 0317 Oslo; tel. 94-08-58-04; e-mail unifor@unifor.no; internet unifor.no.

FOUNDATIONS AND NON-PROFITS

Anders Jahres Humanitære Stiftelse (Anders Jahre's Foundation for Humanitarian Purposes)

Established in 1966 by Anders Jahre, a shipowner and business person; the Foundation is managed by UNIFOR (q.v.) at the University of Oslo.

Activities: Supports humanitarian, cultural and social activities with a focus on care for older people. The Foundation also funds medical and legal research, primarily at the University of Oslo; and research in the fields of chemistry and shipbuilding, primarily at the Norwegian University of Science and Technology in Trondheim. It awards the annual Anders Jahre Prize for Culture.

Geographical Area of Activity: Norway (mainly Sandefjord and Vestfold counties).

Publications: Annual Report.

Finance: Annual income 51.3m. krone, expenditure 6.1m. krone (31 Dec. 2024).

Board of Directors: Jon Gunnar Pedersen (Chair.).

Principal Staff: Dir Anne-Merethe Lie Solberg.

Contact Details: Postboks 440, Sentrum, 3201 Sandefjord; tel. 33-46-02-90; e-mail post@ajhs.no; internet ajhs.no.

Bellona Foundation

Established in 1986 by Frederic Hauge, an environmental activist; formerly known as Environmental Foundation Bellona.

Activities: Works in the field of the environment and climate change through programmes in the areas of: nuclear energy; fossil fuels; carbon capture and storage; renewable energy; energy efficiency; the Arctic; and the Russian Federation and human rights. Projects include: the Sahara Forest Project; the Ocean Forest; environmentally friendly packaging and reducing plastic waste; emission-free construction sites; and mapping countries' potential for cutting carbon dioxide emissions. The Foundation has offices in Brussels (Belgium), Murmansk, Kyiv, St Petersburg (Russian Federation) and Washington, DC (USA).

Geographical Area of Activity: International.

Publications: Reports; newsletter; *BellonaBrief* (briefing papers).

Principal Staff: Exec. Dir Jonas Helseth.

Contact Details: Rådhusgata 28, 0151 Oslo; tel. 23-23-46-00; e-mail info@bellona.no; internet www.bellona.org.

Children & War Foundation—CAW

Established in 2000; registered in the United Kingdom.

Activities: Works to improve the lives of children and their families and reduce the psychological after-effects of war and disasters. The Foundation conducts research on the effects and consequences of war, warlike situations and disasters. It provides training, advice and resources to practitioners.

Geographical Area of Activity: International.

Publications: Annual Report; newsletter (2–3 a year); *Teaching Recovery Manual*; *Children and War Manual*; *Children and Disasters*; *Children and Grief Manual*; *Writing for Recovery Manual*; *Manual for Children between 5 and 8 Years*; questionnaires.

Finance: Annual income 597,619 krone, expenditure 736,457 krone (31 Dec. 2022).

Board of Directors: Inger Hygen (Chair.); Svanhild Gjesdal (Sec.).
Contact Details: c/o Kluge Law Firm, Postboks 394 Sentrum, 5805 Bergen; tel. 92-00-09-20; e-mail contact@childrenandwar.org; internet www.childrenandwar.org.

CMI—Chr. Michelsen Institute for Science and Intellectual Freedom

Established in 1930 at the bequest of former Prime Minister Christian Michelsen.
Activities: An independent centre for research on international development and policy. The Institute conducts applied and theoretical research in 10 thematic research groups: aid; anti-corruption; culture and politics of faith; gender politics; global health and development; governance; natural resources; poverty dynamics; rights; and tax and public finance. It hosts the U4 Anti-Corruption Resource Centre (f. 2003).
Geographical Area of Activity: Latin America, Middle East, South Asia, sub-Saharan Africa.
Publications: Annual Report; newsletter; CMI Reports; CMI Working Papers; CMI Briefs; CMI Insights; monographs; reports; books.
Finance: Annual revenue 118.0m. krone, expenditure 121.7m. krone (31 Dec. 2023).
Board: Synnøve Kristine Nepstad Bendixsen, Alexander Cappelen (Chair.).
Principal Staff: Dir Espen Villanger.
Contact Details: Jekteviksbakken 31, Bergen; Postboks 6033, Bedriftssenteret, 5892 Bergen; tel. 47-93-80-00; e-mail cmi@cmi.no; internet www.cmi.no.

Fridtjof Nansens Institutt—FNI (Fridtjof Nansen Institute)

Founded in 1958 to conduct applied social science research on international issues in the fields of resource management, the environment and energy.
Activities: Carries out research on international environmental, energy and resource management politics. Programme areas include: global governance and sustainable development; marine affairs and law; biodiversity and biosafety; polar and Russian politics; European energy and environmental politics; and Chinese energy and environmental politics. The Institute also carries out academic studies, contract research, investigations and evaluations.
Geographical Area of Activity: International.
Restrictions: No grants to other organizations.
Publications: Annual Report; *FNI Newsletter* (2 a year); reports; books; brochure.
Finance: Annual income 48.6m. krone, expenditure 52.1m. krone (31 Dec. 2023).
Board: Prof. Ann Therese Lotherington (Leader); Nils Bøhmer (Deputy Leader).
Council: Christian Fredrik Michelet (Leader).
Principal Staff: Dir Iver B. Neumann; Deputy Dir Lars H. Gulbrandsen.
Contact Details: Fridtjof Nansens vei 17, 1366 Lysaker; POB 326, 1326 Lysaker; tel. 47-48-06-80; e-mail post@fni.no; internet www.fni.no.

Fulbright Norway—US-Norway Fulbright Foundation for Educational Exchange

Established in 1949.
Activities: Organizes educational exchanges between Norway and the USA. The Foundation annually awards grants for 40 Norwegians to study, teach and carry out research in the USA; and for some 30 US citizens to do the same in Norway. Grants are worth 100,000 krone–200,000 krone.
Geographical Area of Activity: Norway, USA.
Restrictions: Grants are awarded to postgraduate students and postdoctoral scholars.
Publications: Annual Report; Annual Rover Report.
Finance: Annual revenue 19.8m. krone, expenditure 21.6m. krone (30 Sept. 2023).
Board: Kristin Danielsen (Chair.).
Principal Staff: Exec. Dir Curt Rice.
Contact Details: Victoriapassasjen, Arbinsgate 2, 0253 Oslo; tel. 22-01-40-10; e-mail fulbright@fulbright.no; internet fulbright.no.

Henie Onstad Kunstsenter (Henie Onstad Art Centre)

Founded in 1968 by Sonja Henie, a figure skater and actress, and her husband Niels Onstad, a shipping magnate and art collector.
Activities: Arranges exhibitions of modern and contemporary art. The Centre houses a collection of modern and contemporary paintings. It is cross-disciplinary and engages international artists for commissioned works, exhibitions, concerts and performances.
Geographical Area of Activity: Norway.
Publications: Annual Report; catalogues.
Finance: Annual income 54m. krone (31 Dec. 2020).
Supervisory Board: Marianne H. Blystad (Chair.); Vibecke Hverven (Deputy Chair.).
Principal Staff: Dir Anne Hilde Neset.
Contact Details: Sonja Henies vei 31, 1311 Høvikodden; tel. 67-80-48-80; e-mail post@hok.no; internet www.hok.no.

Human Rights House Foundation—HRHF

Established in 1989.
Activities: Supports and protects human rights defenders and organizations through 16 Human Rights Houses in 11 countries, collaborative projects of NGOs working to promote and advance human rights nationally and internationally. The Foundation has offices in Brussels (Belgium) and Geneva (Switzerland), and representation in Tbilisi (Georgia); with consultative status at the UN and participatory status at the Council of Europe.
Geographical Area of Activity: Armenia, Azerbaijan, Belarus, Belgium, Croatia, Georgia, Norway, Poland, Russian Federation, Serbia, Switzerland, Ukraine, UK, Switzerland.
Publications: Newsletter.
Finance: Annual revenue 37.7m. krone, expenditure 37.3m. krone (2023).
Board: Bernt Hagtvet (Chair.); Christopher Hansteen (Deputy Chair.).
Principal Staff: Dir Maria Dahle.
Contact Details: Mariboes gate 13, 0183 Oslo; tel. 46-84-88-50; e-mail info@humanrightshouse.org; internet humanrightshouse.org.

Institusjonen Fritt Ord (Freedom Speech Foundation)

Established in 1974 to promote freedom of speech in Norway and internationally.
Activities: Operates in the field of the arts and culture through offering grants to projects that promote freedom of expression, public debate, arts and culture. Annually, the Foundation offers the Fritt Ords Prize for freedom of expression and the Fritt Ords Honorary Prize for free speech. It supports the Norwegian Institute of Journalism, offering the annual Freedom of Expression Prize; and, with the ZEIT-Stiftung (q.v.), offers Free Media Awards for journalism in Eastern Europe and the Russian Federation.
Geographical Area of Activity: International.
Publications: Annual Report; newsletter.
Finance: Total assets 3,674.5m. krone (31 Dec. 2023).
Board of Trustees: Prof. Grete Brochmann (Chair.); Bård Vegar Solhjell (Vice-Chair.).

Principal Staff: Exec. Dir Knut Olav Åmås.

Contact Details: Uranienborgveien 2, 0258 Oslo; tel. 23-01-46-46; e-mail post@frittord.no; internet www.frittord.no.

Janson Johan Helmich og Marcia Jansons Legat (Janson Johan Helmich and Marcia Jansons Endowment)

Founded in 1949 by Johan Helmich Janson, co-owner of Wolf & Janson, an iron and steel company, and his wife Marcia.

Activities: Works in the field of education. The organization awards scholarships to Norwegian postgraduate students for advanced study abroad in any field, including doctoral or post-graduate study, and professional development. Grants range from 75,000 krone to 150,000 krone for 3–12 months.

Geographical Area of Activity: Worldwide.

Restrictions: Studies should be of importance to business activities in Norway, including arts and crafts.

Board of Directors: Gro Brækken (CEO and Chair.).

Contact Details: Dronning Eufemias gate 11, 0150 Oslo; POB 2944, Solli, 0230 Oslo; tel. 23-27-27-00; e-mail post@jansonslegat.no; internet www.jansonslegat.no.

Minor Foundation for Major Challenges

Established in 2000 by Peter Opsvik, who designed the Tripp Trapp children's chair, and members of his family.

Activities: Supports climate communication projects that aim to limit human-created climate change, by influencing public opinion and changing attitudes to these problems. The Foundation prioritizes projects that are innovative, experimental and untested; look likely to have the greatest impact; and would be difficult to achieve without the Foundation's assistance. In 2019 the Foundation decided to spend out its capital over the next 10–15 years. Large grants typically range from €20,000 to €200,000; small grants are for amounts up to €10,000.

Geographical Area of Activity: International, but currently prioritizes European projects.

Restrictions: Does not support adaptation projects, mitigation technology, tree planting or museum exhibitions.

Publications: Project reports.

Finance: Total annual grant expenditure approx. 6m. krone.

Board of Trustees: Ingrid Lomelde (Chair.).

Principal Staff: Sec. Tore Brænd.

Contact Details: c/o Sørkedalsveien, 6 (KPMG-bygget) ⁰Share Spaces⁰£, 0369 Oslo; tel. 22-34-01-40; e-mail tore.braend@minor-foundation.no; internet www.minor-foundation.no.

Nordic International Support Foundation—NIS

Established in 2011.

Activities: Helps communities and institutions to recover from conflict through making grants to rebuild and rehabilitate social and economic infrastructure. The Foundation works with international donors, national governments, community leaders, national civil society groups and others. It designs programmes with a focus on gender and social inclusivity, which support peacebuilding and strengthen social cohesion.

Geographical Area of Activity: Mali, Myanmar, Somalia.

Publications: Annual Report.

Finance: Total assets 162.2m. krone; net annual income 7.9m. krone (31 Dec. 2023).

Principal Staff: Sr Partners Eric Sevrin, Christopher Eads.

Contact Details: Brenneriveien 5, 2nd Floor, 0182 Oslo; POB 9025 Grønland, 0133 Oslo; tel. 21-39-60-37; e-mail post@nis-foundation.org; internet www.nis-foundation.org.

Norsk Utenrikspolitisk Institutt—NUPI (Norwegian Institute of International Affairs)

Founded in 1959 by the Stortinget (Parliament); operates as an independent body under the Ministry of Education and Research.

Activities: Operates nationally in the field of information and research; and nationally and internationally in the fields of foreign affairs and international relations. Main programme areas are: defence and security; diplomacy and foreign policy; global economy; global governance; natural resources and climate; peace, crisis and conflict; and theory and methodology. The Institute carries out self-conducted programmes and research under four research groups: security and defence; Russian Federation, Asia and international trade; peace, conflict and development; and global order and diplomacy. It organizes conferences, courses and lectures; and maintains a library containing 90,000 items.

Geographical Area of Activity: Worldwide.

Publications: Annual Report; *Internasjonal politikk* (quarterly journal); *Forum for Development Studies* (journal, 2 a year); *NUPI-notat* (20–30 a year); *NUPI-rapport* (10–15 a year); *Nordisk Østforum* (quarterly); *Caspian Energy Politics*; conference proceedings; policy briefs; reports; books.

Finance: Annual income 165.0m. krone, expenditure 171.4m. krone (31 Dec. 2024).

Board of Directors: Karl Erik Haug (Chair.).

Principal Staff: Dir Kari Osland.

Contact Details: Rosenkrantz' gate 22, 0160 Oslo; POB 7024, Pilestredet Park 18, 0176 Oslo; tel. 22-99-40-00; e-mail post@nupi.no; internet www.nupi.no.

Norwegian Refugee Council—NRC

Founded in 1946 as Europahjelpen ('Aid to Europe'); present name adopted in 1953.

Activities: Operates to assist and protect people displaced due to conflict, climate change and natural disasters. Works across 40 countries worldwide. Has offices in Brussels, Berlin, Geneva, London and Washington, DC.

Geographical Area of Activity: Africa, Eastern Europe, Asia, Central and South America.

Finance: Annual income 8,097m. krone (2023).

Board: Kristin Skogen Lund (Chair.); Amira Malik Miller (Deputy Chair.).

Principal Staff: Sec.-Gen. Jan Egeland.

Contact Details: Prinsens gate 2, 0152 Oslo; tel. 23-10-98-00; e-mail nrc@nrc.no; internet nrc.no.

Olav Thon Stiftelsen (Olav Thon Foundation)

Established in 2013 by Olav Thon, founder of Olav Thon Gruppen AS, which has interests in property development and hotels.

Activities: Supports community-building initiatives in Norway; and funds research and teaching in the fields of mathematics, science and medicine. The Foundation annually awards up to 10 prizes for teaching in Norway, each worth up to 500,000 krone, and an international prize for research, worth 5m. krone.

Geographical Area of Activity: International.

Restrictions: Grants only to non-profit organizations; does not fund political or religious projects.

Finance: Annual disbursements up to 100m. krone.

Board: Kjetil Nilsen (Chair.); Ragnar Østensen (Deputy Chair.).

Principal Staff: Gen. Man. Geir Tore Thorvaldsen.

Contact Details: Postboks 489, Sentrum, 0105 Oslo; e-mail olavthonstiftelsen@olavthon.no; internet olavthonstiftelsen.no.

Peace Research Institute Oslo—PRIO

Founded in 1959; an independent research institution.

Activities: Conducts research on the conditions for peaceful relations between states, groups and people. The Institute works to identify new trends in and responses to global conflict; and studies how people are affected by and cope with armed conflict. Projects are organized within thematic research groups; in addition, researchers are organized into three administrative departments and the PRIO Cyprus Centre. It maintains a library containing approximately 30,000 vols and 430 journals. Global Fellowships are awarded to scholars from around the world nominated by PRIO staff; doctoral and research fellowships are also offered, and occasionally MA scholarships.

Geographical Area of Activity: Cyprus, Norway.

Publications: Annual Report; newsletter; *Journal of Peace Research*; *Security Dialogue*; PRIO Papers; PRIO Policy Briefs; PRIO Reports; blog; books.

Finance: Annual revenue 177.5m. krone, expenditure 171.7m. krone (31 Dec. 2023).

Board of Directors: Trine Skei Grande (Chair.); Elisabeth Heggelund Tørstad (Deputy Chair.).

Principal Staff: Dir Henrik Urdal; Deputy Dir Torunn L. Tryggestad.

Contact Details: Hausmanns Gate 3, 0186 Oslo; POB 9229, Grønland, 0134 Oslo; tel. 22-54-77-00; e-mail mail@prio.no; internet www.prio.org.

Raftostiftelsen for menneskerettigheter (Rafto Foundation for Human Rights)

Established in 1986 to commemorate the life of Prof. Thorolf Rafto, a human rights activist.

Activities: Works in the fields of human rights and democracy through advocacy and promoting corporate responsibility. Annually, the Foundation awards the Rafto Prize, worth US $20,000, to individuals and organizations fighting for human rights, freedom and democracy around the world. Previous winners include: the Egyptian Commission for Rights and Freedoms (2020); Rouba Mhaissen (2019); Adam Bodnar (2018); Parveena Ahangar and Parvez Imroz (2017); and Yanar Mohammed (2016). In Norway, it also offers educational programmes for students, teachers and other groups on issues related to democracy and citizenship, sustainable development, public health and life skills.

Geographical Area of Activity: International.

Publications: Newsletter; books.

Finance: Annual income 19.7m. krone, expenditure 21.8m. krone (31 Dec. 2021).

Board of Directors: Frode Elgesem (Chair.); Anders Skjævestad (Deputy Chair.).

Principal Staff: CEO Jostein Hole Kobbeltvedt.

Contact Details: Rafto House, Menneskerettighetenes plass 1, 5007 Bergen; tel. 55-21-09-30; e-mail rafto@rafto.no; internet www.rafto.no.

Regnskogfondet (Rainforest Foundation Norway)

Established in 1989 as part of the Rainforest Foundation network (qq.v.).

Activities: Operates in the field of conservation in rainforest areas in eight countries. The Foundation works to prevent the destruction of rainforests and to secure the rights of forest peoples, providing them with legal assistance and basic education. It also works to influence governments at local, national and international level, collaborating with more than 50 local organizations.

Geographical Area of Activity: The Amazon, Central Africa, Oceania, South-East Asia.

Publications: Annual Report; *News Magazine* (quarterly newsletter); *Regnskog* online magazine); reports.

Board: Kari Bucher (Chair.); Dagfrid Forberg (Deputy Chair.).

Principal Staff: Sec.-Gen. Tørris Jæger.

Contact Details: Mariboes gate 8, 0183 Oslo; tel. 23-10-95-00; e-mail regnog@regnskog.no; internet www.regnskog.no.

Sparebankstiftelsen DNB (DNB Savings Bank Foundation)

Established in 2002.

Activities: Makes grants to not-for-profit organizations in Norway in fields including the arts and culture, nature and outdoor life, local communities and cultural heritage, and sport and play.

Geographical Area of Activity: Norway.

Finance: Total assets 25,778.2m. krone (2024).

Board: Idar Kreutzer (Chair.); Birgitte Lange (Deputy Chair.).

Principal Staff: CEO Egil Matsen.

Contact Details: POB 555 Sentrum, 0105 Oslo; Sentralen, Øvre Slottsgate 3; tel. 90-24-41-00; e-mail post@sparebankstiftelsen.no; internet www.sparebankstiftelsen.no.

Stiftelsen Dam (Dam Foundation)

Established in 1993 by the Norwegian Cancer Society, the Norwegian Association of the Blind and the National Association for Public Health, funded by the profits from a nationwide computer game, Extra-spillet; renamed ExtraStiftelsen Helse og Rehabilitering in 2010. Present name adopted in 2019.

Activities: Carries out self-conducted programmes in the areas of health and volunteering. The Foundation funds health projects and health research and development in Norway; and supports member organizations and small projects with a focus on local activities and volunteering. The Foundation comprises 45 member organizations.

Geographical Area of Activity: Norway.

Publications: Annual Report; newsletter.

Finance: Total assets 639.7m. krone (31 Dec. 2024).

Board: Lilly Ann Elvestad (Chair.); Magne Wang Fredriksen (Deputy Chair.).

Principal Staff: Sec.-Gen. Hans Christian Lillehagen.

Contact Details: Akersgata 28, 0158 Oslo; tel. 22-40-53-70; e-mail post@dam.no; internet www.dam.no.

Strømmestiftelsen (Strømme Foundation)

Established in 1976.

Activities: Works to eliminate extreme poverty through self-conducted programmes in three main areas: creating livelihoods and job opportunities through savings groups and vocational training; children's and adults' education; and building a strong civil society. Has country offices in Bangladesh, Burkina Faso, Mali, Nepal, Niger, South Sudan, Tanzania, Uganda.

Geographical Area of Activity: Bangladesh, Burkina Faso, Kenya, Mali, Myanmar, Nepal, Niger, Norway, South Sudan, Tanzania, Uganda.

Publications: Annual Report; guidelines; policy documents.

Finance: Annual income 272.8m. krone, expenditure 264.2m. krone (2023).

Board of Directors: Kristin Tofte Andresen (Chair.).

Council: Lars Erik Lyngdal (Leader).

Principal Staff: Gen. Sec. Erik Lunde.

Contact Details: Tangen 8, 4th floor, Aquarama, 4608 Kristiansand; tel. 38-12-75-00; e-mail post@strommestiftelsen.no; internet strommestiftelsen.no.

OMAN

FOUNDATIONS AND NON-PROFITS

Al Jisr Foundation
Established in 2010 by Sheikh Saud bin Salim Bahwan Al Mukhaini.

Activities: Carries out sustainable development programmes in the areas of health, education and social welfare at local, regional and international level. The Foundation offers programmes to prepare school and university graduates for the job market and to foster a spirit of volunteering. It organizes training of trainers workshops to promote health education in schools; and organizes competitions to promote issues such as innovation in health and education, green building design and empowering people living with disabilities.

Geographical Area of Activity: International.

Board of Directors: Fawziya Saud Salim Bahwan Al Mukhaini (Chair.); Anisa Saud Salim Bahwan Al Mukhaini (Deputy Chair.).

Principal Staff: Head of Foundation Dina Al Khalili.

Contact Details: Al Harthy Complex, POB 332, 118 Muscat; tel. 2460-5708; e-mail info@aljisrfoundation.org; internet www.aljisrfoundation.org.

International Research Foundation
Established in 2005 by Dr Salim ben Nasser al Ismaily, the Minister for Investment; a non-profit think tank.

Activities: Carries out domestic and regional economic research, with a focus on the Arab region. The Foundation promotes wealth and job creation, entrepreneurship and the principle of economic freedom.

Geographical Area of Activity: Middle East and North Africa.

Publications: *Economic Freedom of the Arab World* (annual).

Board: Dr Salem ben Nasser al Ismaily (Chair.).

Contact Details: Al Wadi Al Kabir, POB 25, 117 Muscat; tel. 2462-3339; e-mail info@omanirf.org; internet www.omanirf.org.

Oman LNG Development Foundation—ODF
Established in 2015 by Oman LNG, a natural gas producer, as its corporate social responsibility arm.

Activities: Invests in sustainable projects. Main programmes include: the arts and cultural heritage; education, with a focus on science, technology, engineering and mathematics; environmental education and protection; entrepreneurship, vocational training and development; health, sports and young people; and social inclusion of marginalized and excluded groups. Three funds operate: the Community Fund, which provides financial support for communities living near the Oman LNG plant; the National Fund, which operates throughout Oman; and the Reserve Fund, which ensures the sustainability of Foundation programmes.

Geographical Area of Activity: Oman.

Finance: Administers 1.5% of Oman LNG's net income after tax; sponsorship and donations US $1.3m. (2023).

Principal Staff: CEO Khalid bin Abdullah Al-Massan.

Contact Details: Ghala, POB 560, CPO, 116 Muscat; tel. 2460-9999; e-mail info@omanlng.co.om; internet omanlng.co.om/en/Pages/csr.aspx.

PAKISTAN

CO-ORDINATING BODY

Pakistan Centre for Philanthropy—PCP

Established in 2001 as a membership organization serving grantmakers in Pakistan.

Activities: Provides a range of support services to foundations, philanthropists and corporate donors in Pakistan and promotes the development of philanthropy. Programmes include: the Enabling Environment Initiative, aiming to establish dialogue between government and CSOs; Creating Linkages, which boosts corporate support for the education sector; and the NPO Certification System, which sets sector-wide standards of good internal governance, transparent financial management and effective programme delivery. The Centre also carries out research into the nature and scope of diaspora and corporate philanthropy; and maintains a directory of certified non-profit and CSOs.

Geographical Area of Activity: Pakistan.

Publications: Annual Report; newsletter; *PCP Certified Network* (online directory of organizations); reports; studies.

Board of Directors: Zaffar A. Khan (Chair.); Badaruddin F. Vellani (Vice-Chair.).

Principal Staff: Exec. Dir Shazia Maqsood Amjad.

Contact Details: 31 RDF Centre, G9/1, Mauve Area, Islamabad 44000; tel. (51) 2286528; e-mail info@pcp.org.pk; internet www.pcp.org.pk.

FOUNDATIONS AND NON-PROFITS

Alkhidmat Foundation Pakistan—AKFP
Established in 1990.

Activities: Works in the field of humanitarian relief and development. The Foundation provides services to marginalized communities in the areas of: disaster management; health; education; orphan care and child protection; clean water; *mawakhat* (interest-free loans); and community development.

Geographical Area of Activity: Indonesia, Lebanon, Myanmar, Nepal, Pakistan, Sri Lanka, Syrian Arab Repub., Türkiye (Turkey).

Publications: Annual Report; *At A Glance*; flyers; brochures.

Board of Management: Prof. Dr Hafeez ur Rahman (Pres.); Syed Waqas Jafri (Sec.-Gen.).

Principal Staff: CEO Khubaib Bilal.

Contact Details: Alkhidmat Complex, 3km Khayaban-e-Jinnah, Lahore; tel. (42) 38020222; e-mail info@alkhidmat.org; internet alkhidmat.org.

Aman Foundation
Established in 2008 by Fayeeza Naqvi and Arif Naqvi; a social enterprise.

Activities: Advocates on behalf of underserved people, supporting initiatives in health and education. The Foundation runs an emergency medical and ambulance service, and a medical advice and diagnosis telephone service. It has a vocational training centre, which offers six-month training programmes in 13 different trades.

Geographical Area of Activity: Pakistan.

Publications: *Shanakht* (quarterly newsletter).
Board of Trustees: Fayeeza Naqvi (Chair.).
Principal Staff: CEO Shazina Masud.
Contact Details: Plot # 333, Korangi Township nr Pakistan Refinery Ltd, Karachi; tel. (21) 111111823; e-mail info @amanfoundation.org.

Ansar Burney Trust International

Established in 1980, as the Prisoners Aid Society, by Ansar Burney, a human rights advocate and adviser on human rights.
Activities: Works in the field of human rights, promoting peace and human dignity. The Trust works to prevent human trafficking; campaigns for women's and children's rights; and provides humanitarian assistance following natural disasters. It offers free legal advice and services; and has an office in the United Kingdom.
Geographical Area of Activity: International.
Publications: Blog.
Finance: Annual expenditure Rs 11.9m. (30 June 2022).
Board: Ansar Burney (Chair.); Shaheen Burney (Vice-Chair.).
Contact Details: 6 Hassan Manzil, Arambagh Rd, Karachi; Office #02, Mezzanine Floor, Noble Heights, Chandni Chowk nr Old Sabzi Mandi, New Town Karachi; tel. (21) 32623382; e-mail contact@ansarburney.org; internet ansarburney.org.

Aurat Publication & Information Service Foundation—AF

Established in 1986.
Activities: Works in the areas of women's empowerment, democratic governance and disaster relief. The Foundation offers grants to NGOs, community-based organizations, policy think tanks, and academic research and training institutions. It operates through five regional offices, 37 field offices and a network of volunteer groups, including Citizens' Action Committees, Resource Groups and AF Resource Centres, and Information Network Centres; and co-operates with regional and international partners.
Geographical Area of Activity: Pakistan.
Publications: Reports; newsletter; pamphlets; posters; books.
Board of Governors: Dr Masuma Hasan (Pres.); Dr Aliya H. Khan (Treas.).
Principal Staff: Exec. Dir Naeem Ahmed Mirza.
Contact Details: Plot No. 5, St No. 26, Said pur Market, Class-III Shopping centre, G-7/1, Islamabad; tel. (51) 2609596; e-mail headoffice@af.org.pk; internet www.af.org.pk.

Edhi Foundation

Established in 1951, as the Edhi Trust, by Abdul Sattar Edhi.
Activities: Works in the fields of social welfare, health and humanitarian assistance. The Foundation operates a network of 13 care homes for orphans, homeless children and disabled people. It cares for women and older people who have been neglected or abused; offers family planning, maternity services and medical assistance through mobile dispensaries and hospitals, and a diabetic centre in Karachi; and provides emergency aid during international humanitarian crises. Under the High Ways Project, 500 emergency medical centres were planned to provide first aid, ambulance, vaccination and dispensary services. Has six regional offices in Pakistan and international offices in the United Kingdom and the USA; and International Community Centers to provide welfare services for Asians abroad in Canberra (Australia), Dhaka (Bangladesh), Kabul (Afghanistan), Katmandu (Nepal), London (UK), New York (USA) and Tokyo (Japan).
Geographical Area of Activity: International.
Principal Staff: Chair. Faisal Edhi.
Contact Details: Sarafa Bazar, Boulton Market, Mithadar, Karachi; tel. (21) 32413232; e-mail info@edhi.org; internet edhi.org.

Hamdard Foundation Pakistan

Founded in 1969 to administer and control the charitable and philanthropic works arising from the financial support of Hamdard Laboratories (Waqf) Pakistan.
Activities: Supports the Pakistan Association of Eastern Medicine, Hamdard al-Majeed College of Eastern Medicine; and established the Madinat al-Hikmah (City of Education, Science and Culture) in Karachi, comprising a library (Bait-al-Hikmah) and institutes for education, medicine, science, Islamic studies and comparative religion, etc. The Foundation provides medicine and healthcare services in its clinics and through free mobile dispensaries; and initiated the Shura Hamdard (Hamdard Thinkers' Forum), a medico-scientific, educational and cultural service for the exchange of views on matters of national interest by leading intellectuals and business people, and the Naunehal Assembly for children and young people. It makes grants to individuals and institutions for research and education, particularly in the fields of medicine and pharmacy, and for general charitable purposes; awards fellowships and scholarships; and sponsors the publication of books.
Geographical Area of Activity: Pakistan.
Publications: Report of operations and financial statement; *Hamdard-i-Sehat* (monthly); *Hamdard Naunehal* (monthly); *Khaber Nama Hamdard* (monthly); *Hamdard Islamicus* (quarterly); *Hamdard Medicus* (quarterly); and other publications in Urdu and English.
Board of Trustees: Sadia Rashid (Pres.).
Principal Staff: Dir-Gen. Farrukh Imdad.
Contact Details: 16th Floor, Bahria Town Tower, Tariq Rd, opp. Allah Wali Chowrangi, Block 2 P.E.C.H.S, Karachi; tel. (21) 38244000; e-mail info@hamdardfoundation.org; internet www.hamdardfoundation.org.

Open Society Foundations in Pakistan

Established as Foundation Open Society Institute Pakistan—FOSIP—in 2003 as part of the Open Society Foundations (q.v.) network.
Activities: Works for tolerance, accountability and education to bring about major institutional reforms. Main programme areas are: early childhood and education; health and rights; human rights movements and institutions; information and digital rights; journalism; and justice reform and the rule of law. The Institute promotes equal access to primary and secondary education for all, encouraging libraries and introducing critical thinking; promotes free, independent and responsible media; promotes government transparency and accountability; supports CSOs that promote legal empowerment of poor people and the right to fair trial; and offers grants to support the right to information, budget transparency and community social audits. It also provides emergency relief funding after natural disasters.
Geographical Area of Activity: Pakistan.
Publications: Factsheet.
Finance: Annual budget US $3.6m. (2020).
Principal Staff: Acting Regional Dir Roque Raymundo.
Contact Details: N Wing, L3, Serena Office Complex, Plot 17, Islamabad G-5/1 Ramna 5; tel. (51) 2600192; internet www.opensocietyfoundations.org/explainers/open-society-foundations-pakistan.

Pakistan Institute of International Affairs—PIIA

Established in 1947; initially affiliated with the Royal Institute of International Affairs (q.v.) in London (UK), and the Institute of Pacific Relations.
Activities: Operates in the field of international affairs and the foreign policy of Pakistan. The Institute conducts research and issues publications; and organizes seminars, lectures, symposia and conferences. It has a specialized library, with more than 36,500 books and monographs, and 100 journals.
Geographical Area of Activity: South Asia.

Shahid Afridi Foundation

Publications: *Pakistan Horizon* (quarterly research journal); books; monographs.

Council: Dr Masuma Hasan (Hon. Chair.); Dr Tanweer Khalid (Hon. Sec.); Syed Mohammad Fazal (Treas.).

Contact Details: Aiwan-e-Sadar Rd, POB 1447, Karachi 74200; tel. (21) 35682891; e-mail info@piia.org.pk; internet www.piia.org.pk.

Shahid Afridi Foundation—SAF

Established in 2014 by Shahid ('Boom Boom') Afridi, former captain of the Pakistan cricket team.

Activities: Works to improve the lives of underprivileged people, and promote peace and goodwill. Main programmes focus on: education; emergency response; health; sports; and water. The Foundation has chapters in Australia, South Africa, the United Kingdom and the USA.

Geographical Area of Activity: Africa, Asia-Pacific, Europe, Middle East, North America.

Publications: Annual Report; newsletter; reports.

Finance: Annual income Rs 771.4m., expenditure Rs 630.4m. (30 June 2023).

Principal Staff: Global Chair. Shahid Khan Afridi.

Contact Details: Plot No. 6c, St No. 4, Zulfiqar Commercial Area, Phase 8, DHA, Karachi; tel. (21) 38881658; e-mail info@shahidafridifoundation.org; internet shahidafridifoundation.org.

Zuleikhabai Valy Mohamed Gany Rangoonwala Trust—ZVMG Rangoonwala Trust

Founded in 1967 by M. A. Rangoonwala, founder of Rangoonwala Group.

Activities: Operates nationally in the fields of education, social welfare, science and medicine, and the arts and humanities; and internationally in the fields of education, science and medicine, religion and the conservation of natural resources. The Trust makes grants to institutions in Pakistan and abroad and to individuals; awards fellowships and scholarships; and organizes conferences, courses, publications and lectures. It also establishes, supports and maintains community centres, educational institutions, hospitals, dispensaries, maternity homes, nursing homes, clinics, sanatoriums and medical research centres. Has affiliates in India and the United Kingdom.

Geographical Area of Activity: International.

Publications: Annual Report; brochures.

Finance: Annual revenue Rs 173.7m., expenditure Rs 142.8m. (30 June 2023).

Board of Trustees: Tariq Rangoonwala (Chair.); Afzal Nagaria (Managing Trustee).

Principal Staff: CEO Mustafa Bhaiwala; Gen. Man. Uzma Asim.

Contact Details: PB Block 4 and 5, K. D. A. Scheme No. 7, Dhoraji Co-operative Housing Society, Karachi 74800; tel. (21) 34938146; e-mail info@rangoonwalatrust.org; internet rangoonwalatrust.org.

PALESTINIAN TERRITORIES

CO-ORDINATING BODY

Palestinian NGO Network

Founded in 1993.

Activities: A civil society network focused on devloping a community that is independent, free of occupation and sustainable where Palestinians enjoy democracy, tolerance, dignity, social justice, rule of law and respect of human rights. 142 member NGOs.

Geographical Area of Activity: West Bank, Gaza Strip, East Jerusalem.

Publications: Annual Report; studies; factsheets; policy papers.

Principal Staff: Dir Shatha Odeh.

Contact Details: Ramallah; tel. (2) 297-5320; internet www.pngo.net.

FOUNDATIONS AND NON-PROFITS

Dalia Association

Established in 2007; a community foundation.

Activities: Promotes the sustainable development of an independent and accountable civil society, through community-controlled grantmaking, with a focus on ecological, economic, social and cultural dimensions. Supports civil society initiatives, especially grassroots efforts that seek to supplement local resources; fosters local networks, linking community activists to experts and resources; and encourages giving by local people, companies, Palestinian refugees and the Palestinian diaspora. It seeks to revive local traditions of philanthropy and volunteering and advocates for systemic change in the international aid system to respect Palestinian rights and respond to local priorities.

Geographical Area of Activity: Palestinian Territories.

Publications: Annual Report; newsletter.

Finance: Annual revenue US $761,221, expenditure $451,446 (31 Dec. 2021).

Board of Directors: Aisha Mansour (Chair.); Melia Tannous (Treas.); Fida Moussa (Sec.).

Principal Staff: Exec. Dir Nour Nusseibeh.

Contact Details: 4 Alsahel St, nr Darna Restaurant, Ramallah; POB 2394, Ramallah; tel. (2) 298-9121; e-mail info@dalia.ps; internet www.dalia.ps.

Taawon (Welfare Association)

Founded in 1983; registered in Switzerland.

Activities: Helps Palestinians' sustainable development through preserving their heritage and identity, supporting their living culture and building civil society. Programme areas include: access to education; culture and artistic expression; youth empowerment and preparation for work; and providing services and opportunities for orphans to lead healthy and productive lives. Other initiatives include revitalizing the Old City of Jerusalem, the Palestinian Museum and Taawon for Youth. The organization has offices in Gaza, Jerusalem, Beirut (Lebanon), Amman (Jordan), London (UK) and Geneva (Switzerland). A sister organization operates in the UK as the Welfare Association (f. 1993).

Geographical Area of Activity: Israel, Jordan, Lebanon, Palestinian Territories, Switzerland, UK, USA.

Restrictions: No grants to individuals; accepts unsolicited proposals for projects in the areas of education, culture and youth empowerment.

Publications: Annual Report; *Ta'awoun* (newsletter, in Arabic); Sustainability Report.

Finance: Total assets US $113.3m. (31 Dec. 2023).

Board of Trustees: Dr Nabil Hani Qaddumi (Chair.); Samer Khoury (Vice-Chair.); Abdulaziz Al Mulla (Treas.).

Principal Staff: Dir-Gen. Dr Aida Assem Al-Saeed.

Contact Details: Al Nahda Sq., Canada St, Ramallah; POB 658, Ramallah; tel. (2) 241-5130; e-mail info@taawon.org; internet www.taawon.org.

PANAMA

FOUNDATIONS AND NON-PROFITS

Fundación AVINA (AVINA Foundation)

Founded in 1994 by Stephan Schmidheiny, former President and owner of Swiss Eternit Group, a building materials company.

Activities: Funds activities that promote relations between civil society and private sector leaders. Main programme areas include: access to water; biomes; climate action; inclusive recycling; migration; political innovation; technology for social change; sustainable cities; and sustainable finance. The Foundation runs change-orientated projects in the fields of formal and non-formal education and training; citizen participation and grassroots social involvement; eco-efficiency and effective management of natural resources; economic and community development; and corporate social responsibility. It works in 11 countries in Latin America, with country offices in Argentina, Bolivia, Brazil, Chile, Colombia and Paraguay. The South-Global Initiative fosters bilateral learning and information exchange between Latin American and African countries. Avina Americas operates in the USA.

Geographical Area of Activity: Africa, Latin America, USA.

Publications: Annual Report; *Social Progress Index*; reports; books.

Finance: Annual revenue US $15.8m. (31 Dec. 2022).

Board of Directors: Sean McKaughan (Chair.).

Principal Staff: Exec. Dir Gabriel Baracatt.

Contact Details: Calle Evelio Lara, Casa 131B, Ciudad del Saber, Clayton, Panama City; tel. 317-1121; e-mail info.web@avina.net; internet www.avina.net.

Fundación Semah-Valencia

Established in 2018 by Semah Group, a real estate development and private investment company.

Activities: Supports initiatives to improve education and health in Panama and through carrying out self-conducted programmes to improve people's lives. Main programme areas include: access to the arts and culture; accessible healthcare; adequate infrastructure; decent housing; meaningful jobs that meet families' needs; and quality education. The Foundation established and manages Fundación Espacio Cívico, which works to strengthen citizens' participation and promote transparency and accountability in public institutions through providing access to information and digital tools.

Geographical Area of Activity: Panama.

Principal Staff: Pres. and CEO Claudio Valencia.

Contact Details: Torre de las Américas, Torre C, Officina 3301, Punta Pacifica, Panama City; tel. 216-8040; e-mail info@semah.com; internet www.semah.com/filantropia.

PAPUA NEW GUINEA

FOUNDATIONS AND NON-PROFITS

Digicel PNG Foundation

Established in 2008 by Digicel, a telecommunications company; part of the Digicel Foundation network.

Activities: Carries out activities in the areas of: access to basic health services; basic education; community building; and supporting people living with disabilities and special needs. The Foundation organizes the annual Men of Honour Awards to recognize role models and positive behaviour. It offers grants, worth up to 50,000 kina, and capacity building to community-based projects in the areas of: access to primary healthcare; inclusive education; improved water and sanitation; involving communities in decisionmaking; services for people with disabilities; and violence reduction for safer communities. Infrastructure funding is also available for elementary and primary schools. At 2025, total investments since 2008 were 176m. kina.

Geographical Area of Activity: Papua New Guinea.

Publications: Annual Report.

Finance: Total assets 3.9m. kina (31 March 2023).

Board: Michael Henao (Chair.); Ketan Mehta (Treas.).

Principal Staff: CEO Serena Sasingian.

Contact Details: Kennedy Rd, Gordons, POB 1618, Port Moresby, NCD; tel. 72222601; e-mail digicelpngfoundation@digicelpacific.com; internet foundation.digicelpacific.com.

Santos Foundation

Established as Oil Search Foundation in 2012 by Oil Search, an oil and gas company, as its corporate social responsibility arm; renamed in 2021 following the corporate merger with Australian company Santos.

Activities: Supports sustainable development through funding programmes in areas including: education; disaster relief; health; and women's empowerment and protection. The Foundation offers scholarships for university programmes related to health and education; and, through the PNG Partnership Fund with the Hela Provincial Health Authority and the Government of Australia, to provide training and qualifications for healthcare workers. It offers small grants, worth 3,000 kina–5,000 kina, to help Oil Search staff and contractors to prevent family and sexual violence in their communities; and to recover from and prepare for natural disasters. Headquartered in Adelaide, Australia.

Geographical Area of Activity: Alaska, Australia, Papua New Guinea, Timor-Leste.

Restrictions: Scholarship candidates must work for at least two years in rural areas of Gulf, Southern Highlands and Hela provinces on completing their studies.

Publications: Annual Report.

Finance: Annual funding US $13.6m. (2023).

Board: Kevin Gallagher (Chair.).

Principal Staff: CEO and Dir Jodie Hatherly.

Contact Details: Harbourside East, Stanley Esplanade, Port Moresby; tel. 3225599; internet www.santosfoundation.org.

PARAGUAY

FOUNDATIONS AND NON-PROFITS

Fundación Moisés Bertoni—FMB (Moisés Bertoni Foundation)

Established in 1988.

Activities: Works to improve people's quality of life through the protection of biodiversity, environmental conservation and promotion of sustainable development. Main programme areas include: conservation monitoring and research; education for sustainable development; management of protected areas; social enterprises; sustainable cities, climate change and resilience; sustainable production; sustainable tourism; sustainable water use; and territorial development. The Foundation offers scholarships for the development of graduate and undergraduate theses; organizes workshops; and operates ecotourism projects in managed nature reserves. It maintains an education centre and a document centre.

Geographical Area of Activity: Paraguay.

Publications: Annual Report; reports.

Finance: Annual revenue 11,253.3m. guaranis, expenditure 11,200.5m. guaranis (31 Dec. 2020).

Board of Directors: Raúl Gauto (Chair.).

Principal Staff: Exec. Dir Yan Speranza.

Contact Details: Prócer Carlos Argüello 208, entre Avda Mariscal López y Avda Guido Boggiani, POB 714, Asunción; tel. 985191000; e-mail mbertoni@mbertoni.org.py; internet www.mbertoni.org.py.

Fundación Paraguaya de Cooperación y Desarrollo (Paraguayan Foundation for Cooperation and Development)

Established in 1985 by Dr Martín Burt.

Activities: Works to eliminate global poverty, with a particular focus on young people and women, through providing microfinance, and promoting entrepreneurial education and a 'learning by doing, selling and earning' methodology. The Foundation's main programme is the Poverty Stoplight, which it has implemented in more than 20 countries, working with more than 200 organizations. It operates through 14 international hubs and has offices in Tanzania; a sister organization, Teach A Man to Fish (f. 2006), is based in the United Kingdom and operates the School Enterprise Challenge, awarding prizes to entrepreneurial schools, students and teachers.

Geographical Area of Activity: International.

Publications: Annual Report; research reports; studies; manuals.

Finance: Annual income US $16.9m., expenditure $16.0m. (2023).

Principal Staff: CEO Martín Burt; Man. Daniel Elicetche.

Contact Details: Manuel Blinder 5589 c/Tte Espinoza, Asunción; tel. (21) 729-3838; e-mail info@fundacionparaguaya.org.py; internet www.fundacionparaguaya.org.py.

PERU

CO-ORDINATING BODIES

Asociación Latinoamericana de Instituciones Financieras para el Desarrollo—ALIDE (Latin American Association of Development Financing Institutions)

Founded in 1968.

Activities: Strengthens banking institutions in Central and South America through supporting members to co-operate and contribute to the development and integration of the region's economies. The Association disseminates information; reports on investment projects; organizes training and seminars; and maintains an information network, documentation centre and online database. It also acts as an executive institution for projects and programmes being funded by international co-operation organizations and agencies. Comprises 61 member banks from 23 countries, as well as 21 associate members from Canada, France, Germany, India, Italy, Portugal, the Russian Federation and Spain.

Geographical Area of Activity: Central and South America and the Caribbean.

Restrictions: Works only with member organizations and institutions.

Publications: Annual Report; newsletter; *Banca & Desarollo* (magazine); technical papers.

Finance: Annual income US $1m., expenditure $1m. (31 Dec. 2024).

Board of Directors: Juan Cuattromo (Pres.); Luis Antonio Ramírez, Aloizio Mercadante (Vice-Pres).

Principal Staff: Sec.-Gen. Edgardo Álvarez Chávez.

Contact Details: Avda Paseo de la República 3211, San Isidro, Lima 27; POB 3988, Lima 100; tel. (1) 2035520; e-mail secretariageneral@alide.org; internet www.alide.org.

Latindadd—Red Latinoamericana por Justicia Económica y Social (Latin American Network for Economic and Social Justice)

Established in 2001, building on the work of the Red Estrategia Andina y Centroamericana frente a la Deuda.

Activities: Promotes the creation of an economy that serves the people and asserts their economic, social and cultural rights. The Network carries out research, lobbying, awareness-raising activities and training; monitors public policies; and mobilizes civil society and social movements. It comprises 31 member organizations.

Geographical Area of Activity: Argentina, Brazil, Colombia, Costa Rica, Ecuador, El Salvador, Guatemala, Honduras, Mexico, Nicaragua, Paraguay, Peru.

Publications: Reports; blog.

Board of Directors: Nathalie Beghin, Claudia Tamayo (Co-Chair.).

Principal Staff: Gen. Co-ordinator Carlos Bedoya.

Contact Details: Jr Mariscal Miller 2622, Lince, Lima; tel. (1) 7119914; e-mail latindadd@latindadd.org; internet www.latindadd.org.

FOUNDATIONS AND NON-PROFITS

CEDRO—Centro de Información y Educación para la Prevención del Abuso de Drogas (Information and Education Centre for the Prevention of Drug Abuse)

Established in 1986.

Activities: Works to prevent people's involvement in cultivating, producing, trafficking and using illegal drugs, especially children and adolescents. Programmes focus on early intervention and providing healthy and worthwhile alternatives through raising awareness and empowering leaders using a democratic and sustainable approach. The organization carries out monitoring evaluation and research; offers information, advice and psychosocial support for young people; and maintains a document centre and digital repository of publications on subjects including coca cultivation, drugs production, consumption and trafficking, prevention of risky behaviours and technology.

Geographical Area of Activity: Mainly Peru.

Finance: Budget approx. US $2m.

Board: Ursula Vega (Chair.); Oscar Caipo (Vice-Chair.).

Principal Staff: Exec. Dir Carmen Masias Claux.

Contact Details: Office 501, Ca. Enrique Palacios 335, Miraflores; tel. (1) 4467046; e-mail contacto@cedro.org.pe; internet www.cedro.org.pe.

CLADEM—Comité de América Latina y el Caribe para la Defensa de los Derechos de la Mujer (Latin American and Caribbean Committee for the Defence of Women's Rights)

Established in 1987 in Costa Rica; a regional network of individual women and women's organizations.

Activities: Works in the field of women's and girls' rights, promoting social justice and freedom from discrimination. Rights are divided into three thematic categories: the right to a life free from violence; sexual and reproductive rights; and economic, social and cultural rights. The Committee's main activities are: campaigning for women's and girls' rights; litigating rights violations; monitoring governments fulfilment of international commitments; and offering training to members, public officials, service providers and teachers. It has offices in 15 countries.

Geographical Area of Activity: Central and South America and the Caribbean.

Publications: Newsletter (monthly); national and regional reports.

Principal Staff: Regional Coordinator Milena Páramo Bernal.

Contact Details: Jirón Caracas 2624, Jesus Maria, Lima 15072; tel. (961) 234063; e-mail infocom@cladem.org; internet www.cladem.org.

Fundación Telefónica Movistar Perú (Telefónica Movistar Perú Foundation)

Established in 2001 by Telefónica, a telecommunications company; part of the Fundación Telefónica (q.v.) network.

Activities: Main programmes focus on digital culture, education, employability and volunteering. The Foundation offers free online training and digital tools via the Conecta Empleo platform; and educational resources and professional teacher training via the ProFuturo digital education programme, a joint initiative with Fundación Bancaria 'la Caixa' (q.v.). It also created the Educared online teaching and learning platform.

Geographical Area of Activity: Peru.

Principal Staff: Exec. Dir Luis Prendes.

Contact Details: Cal. Dean Valdivia 148, Dpto. 201 Urb. Jardín (centro empresarial Platinum, Torre 1), San Isidro, Lima; tel. (511) 2101020; e-mail fundacion.pe@telefonica.com; internet www.fundaciontelefonica.com.pe.

IIAP—Instituto de Investigaciones de la Amazonía Peruana (Institute for Research on the Peruvian Amazon)

Established in 1981; a research institution.

Activities: Operates in the fields of ecology and sustainable development. The Institute carries out scientific research and environmental impact evaluations; develops knowledge and technologies for the management and sustainable use of the region's forests and bodies of water; promotes the conservation of agro-biodiversity; and works to safeguard the biological diversity and traditional knowledge of indigenous peoples, and to improve their quality of life. It has five regional offices and six specialized research centres; and also comprises five research directorates for: Amazonian Terrestrial Biological Diversity (DBIO); Amazonian Aquatic Ecosystems (AQUAREC); Integrated Forest Management and Eco-System Service (BOSQUES); Amazonian Societies (SOCIODIVERSIDAD); and Information and Knowledge Management (GESCON). Maintains a library and digital repository; and a computer laboratory, with access to the MANATI supercomputer.

Geographical Area of Activity: Peru (Amazon Basin).

Publications: *Folia Amazónica* (journal, 2 a year).

Finance: Annual income 17.9m. soles, expenditure 14.9m. soles (31 Dec. 2021).

Principal Staff: Exec. Pres. Carmen Rosa García Dávila; Gen. Man. Marlon Javier Orbe Silva.

Contact Details: Alberto del Campo Av. 452, Of. 302, Magdalena del Mar, Lima; tel. (65) 480105; e-mail iiapli@iiap.gob.pe; internet www.gob.pe/iiap.

Instituto de Montaña (Mountain Institute)

Since 1995, Instituto de Montaña has been working closely with mountain people in the Andes to address their most critical challenges by focusing on conservation, community and culture.

Activities: Focuses on the challenges faced by remote communities and fragile environments. Main programmes include: advocacy and governance, influencing policymakers at national, regional and international level; conservation of biodiversity and stewardship of resources; ecosystem-based adaptation and using nature-based solutions to manage, conserve and restore nature; inclusive science and exploration, blending applied research with traditional knowledge; preserving and empowering cultural heritage; and sustainable community livelihoods and enterprise.

Geographical Area of Activity: Peru.

Publications: Annual Report; reports; handbooks; interactive GIS story maps; photo blogs.

Principal Staff: Exec. Dir Mirella Gallardo.

Contact Details: Calle Gral. Vargas Machuca 408, Miraflores, Lima; e-mail info@mountain.org; internet mountain.pe.

Pronaturaleza—Fundación Peruana para la Conservación de la Naturaleza (Peruvian Foundation for Nature Conservation)

Founded in 1984 by Manuel Ríos Rodriguez, Marc J. Dourojeanni Ricordi and Carlos Ponce del Prado.

Activities: Supports the conservation of soils, water resources, flora, fauna and other renewable natural resources in Peru. The Foundation promotes the development of environmental education and a culture of conservation; and provides technical advice on designing and implementing participatory environmental monitoring of natural resources extraction projects. It works in conjunction with the Tropical Rainforest Coalition.

Geographical Area of Activity: Peru.

Publications: *Biodiversifica-t* (newsletter, 10–11 a year); reports.

Finance: Budget US $2m. (2021).

Board of Directors: Josephine Takahashi Sato (Pres.); Marc Dourojeanni Ricordi (Vice-Pres.).

Contact Details: Calle Doña Juana 137, Urbanización Los Rosales, Santiago de Surco, Lima; tel. (1) 2712662; e-mail pronaturaleza@pronaturaleza.org; internet www.pronaturaleza.org.

PHILIPPINES

CO-ORDINATING BODIES

Association of Foundations
Founded in 1972 to foster broader public understanding of the nature of foundations as institutions in nation building; a member of the Caucus of Development NGO Networks (q.v.).

Activities: Works to strengthen and build trust in the NGO sector. The Association organizes conferences and workshops; liaises among members and between members and government agencies; and maintains a resource centre with a database of CSOs. It has more than 250 member foundations and NGOs; and is a founding member of the Philippine Council for NGO Certification.

Geographical Area of Activity: Philippines.

Publications: Annual Report; *AF Brochure*; *Foundation Bulletin*; *Directory of Philippine Foundations*; *CSO Database*; reports; books.

Board of Trustees: Austere Panadero (Chair.); Cecile Victoria Dominguez-Yujuico (Pres.); Arlyn Laroya, Jean Solidio, Liza Hora (Vice-Pres); Diane Romero (Treas.); Yasmin Mapua-Tang (Sec.).

Principal Staff: Exec. Dir Oman Jiao.

Contact Details: 3/F Cyberpark Tower 1, cnr Gen. Aguinaldo and Gen. McArthur Aves, Araneta City, Cubao, 1109 Quezon City; e-mail afsecretariat@afonline.org; internet www.afonline.org.

Caucus of Development NGO Networks—CODE-NGO
Established in 1990 by the 10 largest NGO networks in the Philippines.

Activities: Promotes the wellbeing of the Filipino people, human rights, social justice and equitable distribution of wealth. Caucus activities fall into four programmes: membership development; policy advocacy; knowledge development and management; and international networking. Priority areas include: transparency, anti-corruption and government accountability; people's participation in governance; asset reform; the environment; social services; good governance of CSOs; reform of official development aid; and federalism and constitutional reform. It has helped to establish NGO-managed fund mechanisms, including the Foundation for the Philippine Environment and the Foundation for Sustainable Society. Comprises 12 national and regional networks, representing 1,600 NGOs, people's organizations and co-operative groups.

Geographical Area of Activity: Philippines.

Publications: Annual Report; newsletter; reports.

Finance: Annual income 21.5m. pesos, expenditure 23.5m. pesos (31 Dec. 2022).

Principal Staff: Exec. Dir Sandino J. Soliman; Deputy Exec. Dir Anna Maria Socorro M. Abalahin.

Contact Details: 146-B, B. Gonzales St, Loyola Heights, 1108 Quezon City; tel. (2) 9202595; e-mail caucus@code-ngo.org; internet code-ngo.org.

League of Corporate Foundations—LCF
Established in 1991 within the Association of Foundations (q.v.); formally registered in 1996. A network of operating and grantmaking corporate foundations.

Activities: Promotes corporate social responsibility (CSR) in the private sector and serves as a forum for peer learning and exchanging ideas, information, experience and technology. The League is organized into programme-based committees for: the arts and culture; disaster resilience; education; enterprise development; environment; financial inclusion; and health. It organizes conferences and lectures; and provides capacity development and training through its CSR Institute. Comprises 96 member organizations.

Geographical Area of Activity: Philippines.

Publications: Newsletter; case studies; surveys; workbooks.

Board of Trustees: Shem Jose Garcia (Chair.); Edric Calma (Vice-Chair.); Ramon Derige (Treas.); Roberta Lopez-Feliciano (Sec.).

Principal Staff: Exec. Dir Celine Santillan.

Contact Details: Unit 6F Raha Sulayman, 108 Benavidez St, Legazpi Village, Makati, 1226 Metro Manila; tel. (2) 88929189; e-mail secretariat@lcf.org.ph; internet www.lcf.org.ph.

National Council of Social Development—NCSD
Established in 1949; formerly known as the Council of Welfare Agencies of the Philippines, Inc; a member of the Caucus of Development NGO Networks (q.v.).

Activities: A network of social welfare and development agencies. The Council carries out capacity-building, advocacy and social mobilization activities; and lobbies to change national policies on behalf of children, their families and the wider community. It is a member of the Caucus of Development NGO Networks and the Philippine Council for NGO Certification (q.v.).

Geographical Area of Activity: Philippines.

Board of Trustees: Rolando Cusi (Pres.).

Principal Staff: Exec. Dir Marian L. Opeña.

Contact Details: 2nd Floor, United Methodist Church Bldg, 900 United Nations Ave, Ermita, 1000 Manila; tel. (2) 85234846; e-mail ncsd_phils@yahoo.com.

Philippine Business for Social Progress—PBSP
Established in 1970 by 50 business leaders who shared a common vision of reducing poverty through social development programmes; a member of the Caucus of Development NGO Networks (q.v.).

Activities: Promotes strategic corporate citizenship and business sector leadership that contribute to sustainable development and poverty reduction. Main programme areas include: health; education; the environment; and livelihoods. The organization engages companies in social investment, responsible business practices and philanthropy. It comprises over 250 member companies; and has offices in Cebu City and Davao City.

Geographical Area of Activity: Philippines.

Publications: Annual Report; newsletter; *CHANGED Magazine*.

Finance: Annual income 3,056.0m. pesos, expenditure 3,011.5m. pesos (30 Sept. 2024).

Board of Trustees: Manuel V. Pangilinan (Chair.); Manolito T. Tayag (Vice-Chair.); Wilson P. Tan (Treas.); Carolina Francisca Racelis (Sec.).

Principal Staff: Exec. Dir Elvin Ivan Uy.

Contact Details: Unit 1, 7th Floor, Citynet Central, Sultan St Brgy. Highway Hills, Mandaluyong; tel. (2) 88010180; e-mail pbsp@pbsp.org.ph; internet www.pbsp.org.ph.

Philippine Council for NGO Certification
Established in 1999 by the Association of Foundations (q.v.), Bishops-Businessmen's Conference for Human Development, Caucus of Development NGO Networks, League of Corporate Foundations (q.v.), National Council of Social Development Foundations (q.v.) and Philippine Business for Social Progress (q.v.).

Activities: Promotes NGO transparency and accountability through a certification mechanism evaluating organizations' integrity, capability and effectiveness. The Council encourages private sector participation in social development; and greater collaboration between the Government and third sector organizations.

Geographical Area of Activity: Philippines.

Finance: Annual income 13.2m. pesos, expenditure 10.6m. pesos (31 Dec. 2023).

Board of Trustees: Fr. Manuel V. Francisco, SJ (Chair.); Dr Jaime Z. Galvez Tan (Vice-Chair.); Mario A. Deriquito (Treas.); Roberta Lopez Feliciano (Sec.).

Principal Staff: Exec. Dir Felix A. Tonog.

Contact Details: 6th Floor, SCC Bldg, CFA-MA Compound, 4427 Interior Old Santa Mesa, 1016 Manila; tel. (2) 87821568; e-mail pcnc@pcnc.com.ph; internet www.pcnc.com.ph.

FOUNDATIONS AND NON-PROFITS

ANGOC—Asian NGO Coalition for Agrarian Reform and Rural Development

Established in 1979 in Bangkok, Thailand; a regional association of national and regional NGO networks.

Activities: Works in two main areas: land and resource rights of the rural poor; and promoting smallholder agriculture for sustainable food systems and livelihoods. The Coalition comprises 20 national and regional NGO networks, representing around 3,000 CSOs. It has special consultative status with ECOSOC and the Food and Agricultural Organization of the UN.

Geographical Area of Activity: Bangladesh, Cambodia, People's Repub. of China, India, Indonesia, Kyrgyzstan, Nepal, Pakistan, Philippines, Sri Lanka.

Publications: Annual Report; newsletter; reports; toolkits.

Board of Trustees: Dewi Kartika (Chair.); Aneesh Kumar Thillenkery, Nhek Sarin (Vice-Chair.); Joy Demaluan (Treas.); Rowshan Jahan Moni (Sec.).

Principal Staff: Exec. Dir Nathaniel Don E. Marquez.

Contact Details: 33 Mapagsangguni St, Sikatuna Village, Diliman 1101, Quezon City; POB 3107, QCCPO 1101, Quezon City; tel. (2) 83510581; e-mail angoc@angoc.org; internet www.angoc.org.

AsiaDHRRA—Asian Partnership for the Development of Human Resources in Rural Asia

Established in 1975 as the Center for the Development of Human Resources in Rural Asia—CenDHRRA; present name adopted in 1994.

Activities: Promotes development projects in rural communities in Asia. Activities focus on: leadership and organizational development; regional advocacy and constituency building; resource development; and information management. The Partnership comprises 11 social development organizations. It has special consultative status with ECOSOC and is an affiliate of ASEAN.

Geographical Area of Activity: Cambodia, Indonesia, Japan, Rep. of Korea, Lao People's Dem. Repub., Malaysia, Myanmar, Philippines, Taiwan, Thailand, Viet Nam.

Publications: Biennial Report; brochures; blog; books.

Executive Committee: Dr Sung Lee (Chair.); Dwi Astuti (Vice-Chair., South-East Subregion); Kratae Petrat (Vice-Chair., Mekong Subregion); Dr Wen-Chi Huang (Vice-Chair., North-East Subregion).

Principal Staff: Sec.-Gen. Marlene D. Ramirez.

Contact Details: Rm 201, Partnership Center, 59C Salvador St, Loyola Heights, 1108 Quezon City; e-mail asiadhrra@asiadhrra.org; internet asiadhrra.org.

Ayala Foundation, Inc—AFI

Founded in 1961 by Col Joseph McMicking and his wife Mercedes Zobel; formerly known as the Filipinas Foundation, now the sociocultural development arm of the Ayala Group, a conglomerate.

Activities: Programme areas include: community development, leadership, arts and culture, corporate citizenship and volunteerism. As part of its arts and culture pillar, the Foundation runs the Ayala Museum and the Filipinas Heritage Library.

Geographical Area of Activity: Philippines.

Publications: Annual Report.

Finance: Annual revenue 312.9m. pesos, expenditure 396.1m. pesos (31 Dec. 2023).

Board of Trustees: Fernando Zobel de Ayala (Chair.); Jaime Z. Urquijo (Vice-Chair.); Antonio Joselito Lambino (Pres. and Treas.).

Contact Details: 4F Makati Stock Exchange Center, 6767 Ayala Triangle, Ayala Ave, Makati City; tel. (2) 77598288; e-mail info@ayalafoundation.org; internet www.ayalafoundation.org.

Childhope Philippines

Established in 1989 by Teresita L. Silva as a branch office of ChildHope International (f. 1986); became an independent NGO in 1995. Present name adopted in 2013.

Activities: Provides advocacy, capacity building and technical assistance, networking, and programme development and implementation. The organization's main programmes are the Baranggay Council for the Protection of Children and the Street Education Program. It also provides vocational/service skills training, psychosocial intervention, and health and medical services among street children in Metro Manila. Sister organizations are Families and Children for Empowerment and Development Foundation, Inc (f. 1987), which co-ordinates the activities of government, NGO and community-based organization services to promote social and economic development; and Tahanan Sta. Luisa, a crisis intervention centre for abandoned, neglected, physically and sexually abused or prostituted girls aged 7–17 years.

Geographical Area of Activity: Philippines (Metro Manila).

Publications: Annual Report; newsletter; directories; guidebooks; manuals narrative reports; research series; workshop proceedings; blog.

Finance: Funds raised 15.7m. pesos (2023).

Board of Directors: Samuel Guevara (Chair.); Sherwin C. O. (Vice-Chair.); Tricia Canapi-Monsod (Treas.); Aneth Ng-Lim (Sec.).

Principal Staff: Pres. Dr Jaime Z. Galvez Tan; Exec. Dir Herbert Q. Carpio; Asst Exec. Dir Helen M. Quinto.

Contact Details: 1640 Sulu St, cnr San Lazaro St, Brgy. 340, Zone 34, Santa Cruz, Manila; tel. (917) 1005303; e-mail igivehope@childhope.org.ph; internet www.childhope.org.ph.

Communication Foundation for Asia

Established in 1973, growing out of the Social Communication Center (f. 1968), which was founded by Dutch missionary Fr Cornelio Lagerwey, with journalist Genaro V. Ong and other lay Filipino communicators.

Activities: Works in the fields of development communication and citizenship education. The Foundation promotes Christian values and social transformation through producing video documentaries and TV programmes; and publishes educational comics and magazines, with an estimated readership of more than 1m. nationwide. It holds training workshops on communication skills and media education; and organizes media events such as film festivals, peace communication camps, environmental forums and travelling exhibitions.

Geographical Area of Activity: Asia.

Publications: *Gospel Notebook* (4 a year); *Gospel Komiks Edition for Young Readers* (4 a year); *Gospel Komiks* (4 a year, in English and Filipino); *Gospel K Magazine for High School* (4 a year); *Now* (5 a year); *The Comicbook Bible*; *Special Publications-Laudato Si*; *The Eucharist and You*.

Cultural Center of the Philippines—CCP (Sentrong Pangkultura ng Pilipinas)

Board of Trustees: Fr Leonardo M. Cabrera (Chair.); Lulu M. Virtusio (Vice-Chair.); Francisco Gonzalez V. (Sec.).

Principal Staff: Pres. Fr Filoteo C. Pelingon; Vice-Pres. Pie Mabanta-Fenomeno.

Contact Details: 4427 Old Santa Mesa St, 3rd Floor, Santa Mesa, 1016 Manila; tel. (2) 87132981; e-mail info@cfamedia.org; internet www.cfamedia.org.

Cultural Center of the Philippines—CCP (Sentrong Pangkultura ng Pilipinas)

Founded in 1969; mandated by Philippine law to preserve, promote and enhance the Filipino people's cultural heritage, and encourage the evolution of the national culture of the Philippines.

Activities: Operates as a national centre for the performing arts. The Center encourages, conserves and disseminates Filipino creativity and artistic experience, providing artistic programmes, services and facilities. It has a library; organizes international exchanges; and produces and presents music, dance, theatre, visual arts, literary, cinematic and design events.

Geographical Area of Activity: Philippines.

Publications: Annual Report; catalogues on dance, theatre and music; monographs.

Board of Trustees: Dr Jaime C. Laya (Chair.).

Principal Staff: Pres. Kaye C. Tinga; Vice-Pres. and Artistic Dir Dennis N. Marasigan.

Contact Details: CCP Complex, Roxas Blvd, Pasay City, 1300 Metro Manila; tel. (2) 88323704; e-mail cad@culturalcenter.gov.ph; internet culturalcenter.gov.ph.

Haribon Foundation for the Conservation of Natural Resources, Inc

Established in 1972 by Alicia Busser, Dr Robert Kennedy and Pedro Gonzales.

Activities: Works in the field of conservation and the environment, through self-conducted programmes, research, scholarships, conferences, training courses and community-based projects. Key programmes include the Philippine Eagle Project, Species of Hope and Communicating Biodiversity. The Foundation maintains links with local and international organizations such as BirdLife International and the International Union for Conservation of Nature (qq.v.).

Geographical Area of Activity: Asia-Pacific.

Publications: Annual Report; *Haring Ibon* (e-newsletter); brochures; guidelines; policy papers; primers; educational materials; books.

Board of Trustees: Marianne Quebral (Chair.); Rosallie A. Dimaano (Vice-Chair.); Philip Camara (Treas.); Jose Frandel-Recto (Sec.).

Principal Staff: COO Arlie Jo Endonila.

Contact Details: Rm 212, Manila Observatory Bldg, Ateneo de Manila University, Katipunan Avenue, Loyola Heights, Quezon City 1108; tel. (2) 84265921; e-mail hello@haribon.org.ph; internet www.haribon.org.ph.

IBON Foundation

Established in 1978 by Sr Soledad Perpiñan, Sally Bulatao and Antonio Tujan; in 2005 the international office became a separate organization, IBON International.

Activities: Promotes democratic social change and development through investigating socioeconomic and political issues. Topic areas include: construction and infrastructure; the COVID-19 pandemic; the environment; the international sphere; relations between the Philippines and the People's Republic of China; and social and economic reform. The Foundation conducts research, advocacy, education and information development; organizes seminars; and offers non-formal education to people's organizations. It comprises a databank and research centre, people's education and research centre and media centre; and established the Institute of Political Economy (f. 1997) and IBON Partnership for Education Development (f. 1998), working with more than 200 schools to design 'transformative education' programmes.

Geographical Area of Activity: Philippines.

Publications: *Birdtalk: Economic and Political Briefing*; *People Economics (booklet)*; policy notes; position papers.

Board of Trustees: Dr Francis Gealogo (Chair.); Dr Maria Corazon Jimenez-Tan (Vice-Chair.); Dr Mendiola Teng-Calleja (Treas.); Prof. Roland Simbulan (Sec.).

Principal Staff: Exec. Dir Jose Enrique Africa.

Contact Details: IBON Center, 114 Timog Ave, 1103 Quezon City; tel. (2) 9277060; e-mail admin@ibon.org; internet www.ibon.org.

Integrated Rural Development Foundation—IRDF

Established in 1989, as a livelihood support institution for farmer federations.

Activities: Works in the area of sustainable rural development through local community-based projects in natural resource management and food security. Main programme areas include: agricultural innovation and sustainable farming; capacity building and organizing; disaster risk reduction; policy research, advocacy and campaigns; women's empowerment and gender equality; and rural livelihoods and enterprise development.

Geographical Area of Activity: Philippines.

Publications: Annual Report; newsletter; policy papers; research reports.

Board: Rene Ofreneo (Chair.); Rev. Edwin Gariguez (Treas.); Eduardo More (Sec.).

Principal Staff: Exec. Dir Arze Glipo.

Contact Details: Unit 503 Fil Garcia Tower, 140 Kalayaan Ave, 1100 Quezon City; tel. (2) 89315452; e-mail irdfofficial@gmail.com; internet irdf.org.ph.

International Institute of Rural Reconstruction—IIRR

Established in 1960 by Dr Y. C. James Yen who founded the International Committee of the Mass Education Movement, a forerunner of IIRR.

Activities: Works to alleviate rural poverty and promotes people-led development through capacity building for poor people and their communities, development organizations and agencies. Main programme areas include: education for pastoralists and other marginalized communities; food security and wealth creation; disaster risk reduction and climate change adaptation; and applied learning. The Institute organizes training, including under the Global Learning Program, which offers short participatory and practice-based courses; and at the Yen Center, which has a conference centre and hosts Livelihood Learning Sites, including the George Sycip Bio Intensive Garden (BIG), Sustainable Livelihood Demonstration Sites, Youth Development Program Learning Center, International School for Sustainable Tourism and Philippine Rural Reconstruction Movement Farm. It maintains an Africa Regional Center in Kenya and country offices in Cambodia, Ethiopia, Kenya, Myanmar, South Sudan, Uganda and Zimbabwe; with an office in New York, USA.

Geographical Area of Activity: Cambodia, Ethiopia, Kenya, Myanmar, Philippines, South Sudan, Uganda, USA, Zimbabwe.

Publications: Annual Report; newsletter (quarterly); guidelines; policy briefs; toolkits; blog.

Finance: Annual revenue US $11.2m., expenditure $4.0m. (31 Dec. 2023).

Board of Trustees: Peter Williams (Pres.).

Contact Details: Y. C. James Yen Center, Biga 2, Km 39 Aguinaldo Highway, Silang, 4118 Cavite; tel. 9178696213; e-mail hq@iirr.org; internet www.iirr.org.

Philippine-American Educational Foundation—PAEF

Founded in 1948, as the US Educational Foundation in the Philippines, by the Governments of the USA and the Philippines; present name adopted in 1969. Also known as Fulbright Commission in the Philippines.

Activities: Promotes educational exchanges between the Philippines and the USA involving students, academics and professionals. The Foundation sponsors research, educational conferences, lectures and seminars; and administers scholarship and fellowship programmes, notably: the Philippine Fulbright Programme for study in the USA; the Hubert H. Humphrey North-South Fellowship Program for professional candidates; and the East-West Center student degree awards, providing financial assistance to students from the Philippines studying at the University of Hawaii. It also provides information and counselling services, and maintains an information resource library on US universities.

Geographical Area of Activity: Philippines, USA.

Restrictions: Fulbright Scholarship applicants must be Filipino citizens with an undergraduate degree and two years' work experience after college, with proficiency in English; Humphrey Fellowship applicants must have an undergraduate degree, five years' work experience and be fluent in English.

Finance: Funded by the Governments of the USA and the Philippines, private agencies and individuals.

Principal Staff: Exec. Dir Julio S. Amador, III.

Contact Details: 20th Floor, Greenfield Tower, Williams cnr Mayflower Sts, Greenfield District, 1550 Mandaluyong City; tel. (2) 88120919; e-mail fulbright@fulbright.org.ph; internet www.fulbright.org.ph.

Ramon Magsaysay Award Foundation

Founded in 1957 by Belen H. Abreu, Paz Marquez Benitez, Jaime N. Ferrer, Jesus Magsaysay, Francisco Ortigas, Jr, Pedro Tuason and Leopoldo Uichanco, in memory of former President of the Philippines Ramon Magsaysay.

Activities: Confers the Ramon Magsaysay Award: six annual awards of US $50,000 each are offered in the fields of government service; public service; community leadership; journalism, literature and creative communication arts; international understanding; and emergency leadership. The Foundation also runs the Programme for Asian Projects to enable awardees to develop their projects and runs an essay-writing competition. It maintains an Asian Library, with reference materials on contemporary Asia, as well as the Magsaysay Papers; organizes international seminars on issues affecting the Asian region; and offers presentations on the peoples and cultures of the region to secondary school pupils. The Foundation established the Ramon Magsaysay Transformative Leadership Institute (f. 2011) as a hub to foster dialogue and the exchange of ideas between awardees and global leaders, organizing conferences, lectures and online forums.

Geographical Area of Activity: Asia.

Restrictions: Grants only to people or institutions that operate in Asia.

Publications: Newsletter; *AwardeeLinks* (e-newsletter).

Finance: Funded by the Rockefeller Brothers Fund (q.v.) from 1958 to 1968, the Foundation is now supported by the income from the Ramon Magsaysay Center, which it owns. The Rockefeller Brothers Fund grants approx. US $150,000 annually to support the awards.

Board of Trustees: Edgar O. Chua (Chair.); Suzanne E. Siskel (Vice-Chair.); Susanna B. Afan (Pres.); Gizela M. Gonzalez-Montinola (Treas.).

Contact Details: Ground Floor, Ramon Magsaysay Center, 1680 Roxas Blvd, 1004 Malate, Manila; POB 3350, Manila; tel. 9544686513; e-mail info@rmaward.asia; internet rmaward.asia.

Tebtebba Foundation

Established in 1996 by Victoria Tauli-Corpuz.

Activities: Resolves conflicts and promotes sustainable development in indigenous communities. The Foundation advocates for law and human rights to achieve peace and social justice in indigenous territories around the world, and to promote indigenous rights. It provides training for indigenous leaders and consulting for indigenous organizations; and also disseminates information about issues affecting indigenous people, conducting research and holding conferences. Has an office in Manila.

Geographical Area of Activity: Worldwide.

Publications: *Tebtebba* (magazine); *Indigenous Perspectives* (magazine); brochure; guides; briefing papers; reports.

Board of Trustees: Fr Edwin Gariguez (Chair.); Prof. Jessica Carino (Vice-Chair.); Fr David Tabo-oy (Treas.); Dr Raymundo D. Rovillos (Sec.).

Principal Staff: Exec. Dir Victoria Tauli-Corpuz.

Contact Details: 1 Roman Ayson Rd, 2600 Baguio City; tel. (74) 4447703; e-mail tebtebba@tebtebba.org; internet www.tebtebba.org.

Villar Foundation, Inc

Established in 1995 by Manuel B. Villar, Jr, a property developer and politician.

Activities: Main programmes include: assistance to overseas Filipino workers; river rehabilitation programmes and social enterprises in Las Piñas City; entrepreneurship and livelihoods; health and social services; young people, education and sports; culture and the arts; tree planting; and church building and financial assistance to religious organizations. The Foundation established the Villar Social Institute for Poverty Alleviation and Governance (SIPAG); and annually offers 20 Villar SIPAG Awards on Poverty Reduction, each worth 250,000 pesos, which recognize the achievements of community enterprises.

Geographical Area of Activity: Philippines.

Publications: Annual Report; books.

Board of Trustees: Manuel B. Villar, Jr (Chair.); Mark A. Villar (Treas. and Sec.).

Principal Staff: Man. Dir Cynthia A. Villar.

Contact Details: C5 Extension Rd, Pulanglupa Uno, 1740 Las Piñas City; tel. (632) 85511871; e-mail villarfoundation95@gmail.com; internet www.villarfoundation.com.ph.

POLAND

CO-ORDINATING BODIES

Akademia Rozwoju Filantropii w Polsce—ARFP
(Academy for the Development of Philanthropy in Poland)

Established in 1998.

Activities: Promotes philanthropy in Poland and supports the third sector, through a local grants programme; a grant programme for organizations promoting Polish-Jewish dialogue; a local youth fund; senior citizen programmes; scholarships for young gifted people; and participation in international philanthropy networks. The Academy also organizes the Benefactor of the Year competition, which recognizes corporate philanthropists in Poland.

Geographical Area of Activity: Poland.

Publications: Annual Report; *The White Book of Philanthropy—Coalition for Better Law*.

Finance: Annual income 6.1m. new złotys, expenditure 6.2m. new złotys (31 Dec. 2019).

Board: Paweł Łukasiak (Chair.).

Contact Details: 00-590 Warsaw, ul. Marszałkowska 6/6; tel. (22) 6220122; e-mail arfp@filantropia.org.pl; internet www.filantropia.org.pl.

Federacja Funduszy Lokalnych w Polsce (Federation of Community Foundations in Poland)

Established in 2008.

Activities: Supports the development of community foundations. The Federation provides training, advisory, consulting and other services. It brings together 25 local funds and four partner organizations all over the country.

Geographical Area of Activity: Poland.

Publications: Annual Report.

Board of Directors: Dorota Komornicka (Pres.).

Contact Details: 57-500 Bystrzyca Kłodzka, ul. Wojska Polskiego 18; tel. (74) 8111880; e-mail biuro@ffl.org.pl; internet www.ffl.org.pl.

Forum Darczyńców (Polish Donors Forum)

Established in 2002; formally registered as an association in 2004.

Activities: Promotes transparency in philanthropic giving and strengthens the credibility of organizations in the sector, providing training to members, disseminating good practices and carrying out research. The Forum has 18 regular members, 22 supporting members, and is a member of Philea (q.v.).

Geographical Area of Activity: Poland.

Publications: Annual Report; reports; research reports; handbooks; brochures.

Finance: Annual income 679,465 new złotys, expenditure 500,644 new złotys (31 Dec. 2022).

Board: Marzena Atkielska (Chair.).

Principal Staff: Exec. Dir Magdalena Pękacka.

Contact Details: 00-533 Warsaw, ul. Mokotowska 65/7 (wejście w bramie); tel. (53) 5990910; e-mail poczta@forumdarczyncow.pl; internet www.forumdarczyncow.pl.

Grupa Zagranica (Zagranica Group)

Founded in 2001; a coalition of Polish NGOs operating outside Poland, originating from a conference held by the Stefan Batory Foundation (q.v.) in co-operation with the Ministry of Foreign Affairs.

Activities: Supports the exchange of information, experiences and common standards between Polish NGOs working abroad. The Group fosters co-operation between the NGOs and other sectors; advocates for Polish foreign and development aid policy in countries where the NGOs are engaged; facilitates contacts between NGOs and potential partners; establishes contacts and co-operation with similar groups of NGOs in other countries and with EU institutions, to exert influence on EU development aid policy and take part in its implementation; and disseminates information concerning the activities of Polish NGOs working abroad and campaigning for public support for their activities. Five working groups are currently active: Global Education, Polish AidWatch, Belarus, Eastern Partnership and Caucasus. The General Meeting of the Members of the Group comprises 59 organizations. It is a member of CONCORD (q.v.).

Geographical Area of Activity: Poland.

Publications: Annual Report; *Guiding Principles of Polish Non-governmental Organisations Working Abroad*.

Finance: Total assets 46,461 new złotys; net annual income 16,948 new złotys (31 Dec. 2022).

Principal Staff: Exec. Dir Jan Bazyl.

Contact Details: 00-215 Warsaw, ul. Sapieżyńska 10A; 00-637 Warsaw, Al. Armii Ludowej 6/137; tel. (22) 2990105; e-mail grupa@zagranica.org.pl; internet www.zagranica.org.pl.

Ogólnopolska Federacja Organizacji Pozarządowych—OFOP (National Federation of NGOs)

Established in 2003; a federation of civic and social organizations.

Activities: Supports the development of civil society and non-profit organizations. Main programmes include: monitoring and advocacy in relation to law and public policies to create favourable conditions for social and civic activity; European integration and monitoring of EU funds for social organizations; and animating discussions about the values and identity of the NGO sector and setting standards. The Federation organizes the Ogólnopolskie Forum Inicjatyw Pozarządowych (National Forum of Polish NGOs) every three years. It maintains a reference library containing more than 4,000 books and over 53,000 press clippings and online publications. Comprises 150 member organizations.

Geographical Area of Activity: Poland.

Publications: Annual Report; newsletter; leaflets; posters.

Finance: Total assets 557,625.7 new złotys (31 Dec. 2023).

Board: Karolina Dreszer-Smalec (Pres.); Weronika Czyżewska-Waglowska, Katarzyna Batko-Tołuć (Vice-Pres).

Contact Details: 00-031 Warsaw, ul. Szpitalna 5 lok. 3; tel. (22) 3702504; e-mail ofop@ofop.eu; internet ofop.eu.

OPUS—Centre for Promotion and Development of Civil Initiatives

Established in 1999.

Activities: Supports the development of civil society. The Centre provides advice and consulting services to NGOs and co-operates internationally in networks and with other organizations; and channels EU programme funds to local Polish NGOs. It has offices in Kutno and Piotrków Trybunalski.

Geographical Area of Activity: Poland.

Publications: Annual Report; newsletter.

Board of Directors: Łukasz Waszak (Pres.); Jolanta Woźnicka, Wioletta Gawrońska (Vice-Pres).

Contact Details: 90-135 Łódź, ul. Narutowicza 8/10; tel. (42) 2077339; e-mail opus@opus.org.pl; internet www.opus.org.pl.

Sieć Wspierania Organizacji Pozarządowych—SPLOT (Network of Information and Support for Non-governmental Organizations)

Established in 1994 by six organizations.

Activities: Supports the development of civil society and the social economy in Poland. The Network provides funding and advisory services to associations, foundations, support groups and other civil initiatives; and training and information. It operates through a network of 10 regional support centres; and has 10 member organizations.

Geographical Area of Activity: Poland.

Publications: Reports; manuals; studies.

Board: Zbigniew Wejcman (Pres.).

Contact Details: 00-031 Warsaw, ul. Szpitalna 5/5; tel. (22) 8275211; e-mail biuro@siecsplot.pl; internet www.siecsplot.pl.

Stowarzyszenie Klon/Jawor (Klon/Jawor Association)

Established in 1990 as part of the Regardless of the Weather Foundation; became independent in 2000.

Activities: Promotes the development of civil society. The Association conducts research, especially on the third sector in the EU and local government and NGOs, and issues publications; promotes European networking; and provides general assistance to NGOs. It maintains a database of Polish NGOs, containing around 190,000 profiles of associations and foundations.

Geographical Area of Activity: Poland.

Publications: Annual Report; guides; research reports; data.

Finance: Annual income 2.6m. new złotys, expenditure 2.6m. new złotys (31 Dec. 2023).

Board: Urszula Krasnodębska-Maciuła (Pres.); Renata Niecikowska (Treas.).

Contact Details: 00-031 Warsaw, ul. Szpitalna 5/5; tel. (22) 8289128; e-mail pozna@klon.org.pl; internet www.klon.org.pl.

FOUNDATIONS AND NON-PROFITS

CASE—Centrum Analiz Społeczno-Ekonomicznych (Center for Social and Economic Research)

Established in 1991 by a group of 10 economists as an independent non-profit foundation; a think tank.

Activities: Carries out research on policymaking and research and development. Main programme areas include: fiscal, monetary and financial policy; growth and trade; demography, the labour market and social policy; innovation, energy and climate; and sustainable development. The Center organizes conferences, seminars and workshops. It comprises a network of independent research institutes in Belarus, Georgia, Moldova, Kyrgyzstan and Ukraine.

Geographical Area of Activity: Central Asia, Central and South-Eastern Europe, Eastern Europe, EU, Middle East and North Africa.

Publications: Annual Report; newsletter; policy briefs; working papers; studies; reports; seminar papers.

Finance: Net annual income 439,527 new złotys (2023).

Supervisory Council: Ewa Balcerowicz (Chair.); Barbara Błaszczyk, Stanisława Golinowska (Vice-Chair.).

Principal Staff: Pres. Jan Hagemejer; Vice-Pres Marek Peda.

Contact Details: 01-065 Warsaw, ul. Zamenhofa 5/1B; tel. 798023759; e-mail case@case-research.eu; internet www.case-research.eu.

Fundacja Agory (Agora Foundation)

Established in 2004 to manage all charitable and social initiatives of the Agora and Agora Holding companies.

Activities: Supports educational and cultural initiatives. The Foundation offers financial support to disadvantaged individuals and families, and for healthcare development and initiatives to save people's lives.

Geographical Area of Activity: Poland.

Restrictions: Grants only to organizations.

Publications: Annual Report.

Finance: Total assets 111,073 new złotys (31 Dec. 2023).

Board of Directors: Wojciech Kamiński (Pres.); Joanna Kosmal (First Vice-Pres.); Anna Kołtunowicz (Vice-Pres.).

Contact Details: 00-732 Warsaw, ul. Czerska 8/10; tel. (22) 5555221; e-mail fundacja@agora.pl; internet fundacjaagory.pl.

Fundacja Auschwitz-Birkenau (Auschwitz-Birkenau Foundation)

Established in 2009 by Prof. Władysław Bartoszewski.

Activities: Preserves the site of the Auschwitz-Birkenau concentration and extermination camp and its maintenance as a memorial and museum. A number of governments have contributed funding, including those in Austria, Belgium, Germany, Israel, the Netherlands, New Zealand, Poland and the USA.

Geographical Area of Activity: Poland.

Publications: Annual Report; *Oś* (monthly magazine).

Finance: Total assets 812.9m. new złotys; net annual income –4.2m. new złotys (31 Dec. 2023).

Foundation Council: Marek Zając (Chair.).

Management Board: Piotr M. A. Cywiński (Pres.); Łukasz Rozdeiczer-Kryszkowski (Vice-Pres.).

Principal Staff: Dir-Gen. Wojciech Soczewica.

Contact Details: 00-533 Warsaw, ul. Mokotowska 65/3; tel. (22) 6204899; e-mail fundacja@fab.org.pl; internet www.fundacja.auschwitz.org.

Fundacja Citi Handlowy im. Leopolda Kronenberga (Citi Handlowy Leopold Kronenberg Foundation)

Established in 1996, in memory of the bank's founder Leopold Kronenberg, to mark the 125th anniversary of Bank Handlowy Warszawie SA.

Activities: Supports organizations and projects in the areas of education, science, the arts and humanities, healthcare and social welfare. The Foundation encourages employees to share their experience and skills to support social projects through its volunteering programme; and awards prizes for entrepreneurship.

Geographical Area of Activity: Poland.

Restrictions: Grants only to non-profit organizations in Poland.

Publications: Annual Report.

Advisory Council: Witold Zieliński (Chair.); Jenny Grey (Vice-Chair.).

Management Board: Paweł Zegarłowicz (Chair.).

Contact Details: 00-067 Warsaw, ul. R. Traugutta 7/9; tel. (22) 8268324; e-mail poczta@kronenberg.org.pl; internet www.kronenberg.org.pl.

Fundacja Dobroczynności Atlas (Atlas Charity Foundation)

Established in 1996 by the Atlas Group, a chemicals manufacturer.

Activities: Operates in the area of social welfare and poverty alleviation in Poland and Central and Eastern Europe, particularly children's welfare and Polish communities in Belarus, Kazakhstan, Lithuania, the Russian Federation and Ukraine. The Foundation supports four orphanages and two special schools.

Geographical Area of Activity: Eastern Europe.

Publications: Annual Report.

Finance: Total assets 25.9m. new złotys (31 Dec. 2022).

Board: Jerzy Blazy (Chair.); Piotr Pieczonka (Sec.).

Council: Roman Rojek (Chair.).

Principal Staff: Pres. Jolanta Rojek.

Contact Details: 80-252 Gdańsk, ul. Jaśkowa Dolina 17; tel. (58) 3421122; e-mail fundacja@atlas.com.pl; internet www.atlas.com.pl/atlas-pl/kontakt/fundacja-dobroczynnosci.

Fundacja Gospodarcza (Economic Foundation)

Established in 1990 by the National Commission (NSZZ) of Solidarność (Solidarity) to confront the problems of unemployment and education.

Activities: Main activities include providing business and skills training for start-ups and entrepreneurs; careers advice and services, and entrepreneurial training and guidance for school students, graduates, job seekers and others; and consulting, advice, coaching and mentoring for start-ups and entrepreneurs. The Foundation established the Gdynia Business Incubator, which hosts 16 start-ups.

Geographical Area of Activity: Poland.

Publications: *Economics*; *Career Skills*; *Labour Code*; publications for the unemployed and people in business.

Foundation Council: Grzegorz Adamowicz (Chair.); Krzysztof Woźniewski (Vice-Chair.).

Principal Staff: Pres. Mariusz Januć.

Contact Details: 81-538 Gdynia, ul. Olimpijska 2; tel. (58) 6226017; e-mail sekretariat@fungo.com.pl; internet fungo.com.pl.

Fundacja Orange (Orange Foundation)

Established in 2005 by Orange Polska SA, a telecommunications provider; part of the Fondation Orange (q.v.) network.

Fundacja Partnerstwo dla Środowiska POLAND

Activities: Focuses on the education of children and young people, in particular their use of new technologies in learning, culture and community building. The Foundation supports teachers and parents in developing digital skills. It has established FabLab digital maker spaces in Gdańsk and Warsaw.
Geographical Area of Activity: Poland.
Publications: Annual Report; newsletter; blog.
Finance: Total assets 4,373.2m. new złotys (31 Dec. 2023).
Board: Konrad Ciesiołkiewicz (Pres.).
Principal Staff: Gen. Man. Bozena Żołnierek.
Contact Details: 02-326 Warsaw, ul. Aleje Jerozolimskie 160; tel. (22) 5274014; e-mail fundacja@orange.com; internet fundacja.orange.pl.

Fundacja Partnerstwo dla Środowiska (Environmental Partnership Foundation)

Established in 1992 as a Programme Office of the German Marshall Fund of the USA; present name adopted in 1997 when it was registered as a foundation in Poland.
Activities: Supports sustainable development by building partnerships, strengthening civil society, proposing new solutions, disseminating good practice and promoting environmentally friendly lifestyles at local or community level. Programmes use a partnership approach to build more sustainable local food systems; improve the environmental performance of business, public agencies, schools, civil society groups; and make sustainability a part of everyday living in Poland.
Geographical Area of Activity: Poland.
Restrictions: Regranting programmes focus on community groups, schools, NGOs registered and operating in Poland.
Publications: Annual Report; newsletter; reports.
Principal Staff: CEO Rafał Serafin.
Contact Details: 31-005 Kraków, Bracka 6; tel. (12) 4225088; e-mail biuro@fpds.pl; internet www.fpds.pl.

Fundacja Pogranicze (Borderland Foundation)

Established in 1990.
Activities: Operates in the fields of the arts and culture, education, and law and human rights, through self-conducted programmes, conferences, training courses and publications. The Foundation maintains a library and an arts and cultural centre.
Geographical Area of Activity: Central and Eastern Europe.
Publications: Annual Report; *Krasnogruda* (quarterly, in Polish and English); newsletter; blog.
Principal Staff: Dir Krzysztof Czyżewski; Deputy Dir Wojciech Szroeder.
Contact Details: 16-500 Sejny, POB 15, ul. Piłsudskiego 37; tel. (87) 5162765; e-mail sekretariat@pogranicze.sejny.pl; internet www.pogranicze.sejny.pl.

Fundacja POLSAT (POLSAT Foundation)

Established in 1996 by POLSAT, a television company.
Activities: Operates in the areas of education and medicine and health, in particular for the benefit of children and young people. The Foundation offers grants to individuals for healthcare and equipment; and financial support to hospitals and medical centres, renovating them and providing modern medical equipment. It also takes part in ecological initiatives, such as combating pollution.
Geographical Area of Activity: Poland.
Publications: Annual Report; newsletter.
Finance: Total assets 19.0m. new złotys; annual income 14.6m. new złotys, expenditure 8.8m. new złotys (31 Dec. 2021).
Board: Krystyna Aldridge-Holc (Pres.).
Contact Details: 04-175 Warsaw, ul. Ostrobramska 77; tel. (22) 5145555; e-mail fundacja@polsat.com.pl; internet www.fundacjapolsat.pl.

Fundacja Pomocy Wzajemnej Barka (Barka Foundation for Mutual Assistance)

Founded in 1989 by Tomasz Sadowski, Maria Garwolińska and Barbara Sadowska.
Activities: Works in the field of social welfare, through self-conducted programmes, scholarships, prizes, conferences, training courses and publications. The Foundation runs four programmes: community; social education; employment opportunity; and housing. It assists homeless people through self-help projects throughout Poland and established the Poland-wide Confederation for Social Employment, which provides support to the long-term unemployed and homeless people. Comprises a network of 27 organizations, including affiliates in Canada, Iceland, Ireland, the Netherlands and the United Kingdom.
Geographical Area of Activity: Canada, Iceland, Ireland, Netherlands, Poland, UK.
Publications: *Gazeta Uliczna* (magazine); newsletter; books.
Finance: The Government of Poland provides 5% of the Foundation's funds.
Trustees: Barbara Sadowska (Vice-Pres.).
Contact Details: 61-003 Poznań, ul. św. Wincentego 6/9; tel. (61) 6682300; e-mail barka@barka.org.pl; internet www.barka.org.pl.

Fundacja Rozwoju Demokracji Loaklnej (Foundation in Support of Local Democracy)

Founded in 1989 by Prof. Jerzy Regulski, Andrzej Celiński, Aleksander Paszyński, Walerian Pańko and Jerzy Stępień to promote civic self-government at local level.
Activities: Works in the fields of education, and law and human rights, through self-conducted programmes, grants to institutions, conferences, training courses, publications, internet information systems and offering technical assistance. The Foundation's main activities are training and education programmes for local government officers, councillors, NGOs, community leaders and local business people; and consulting services in the technical areas of local government. It is also involved in sharing Poland's experience in building democracy with other countries of Central, Eastern and Southern Europe and Kazakhstan. Maintains national network of 14 regional centres and three branches.
Geographical Area of Activity: Armenia, Belarus, Bosnia and Herzegovina, Georgia, Kazakhstan, Latvia, Lithuania, Macedonia, Moldova, Montenegro, Poland, Romania, Russian Federation, Serbia, Tunisia, Ukraine.
Publications: Annual Report; newsletter; ressearch reports.
Finance: Net annual income 2.1m. new złotys (31 Dec. 2022).
Founders' Council: Jerzy Stępień (Chair.).
College of Directors: Michal Wojcik (Chair.).
Principal Staff: Chair., Exec. Bd Cezary Trutkowski; Vice-Chair. Marcin Smala.
Contact Details: 01-646 Warszawa, ul. Edwarda Jelineka 6; tel. (22) 3519321; e-mail zarzad@frdl.org.pl; internet www.frdl.org.pl.

Fundacja im. Stefana Batorego (Stefan Batory Foundation)

Founded in 1988 by George Soros and a group of Polish democratic opposition leaders.
Activities: Supports the development of a democratic and open society through strengthening civil society institutions; developing international co-operation and solidarity; and encouraging civic participation and public interest in local affairs. Grantmaking programmes include Active Citizens Fund—National, Batory Foundation Grants, Fund of Solidarity with Ukraine, and For Belarus. The Foundation conducts also research and advocacy, organizes debates and convenes expert groups in the fields of rule of law, good governance, civil society, electoral system and local democracy.
Geographical Area of Activity: Poland, Central Europe, Eastern Europe.

Restrictions: Grants to organizations based in Poland; in some programmes, also grants to organizations based in Belarus.

Publications: reports; manuals; analysis; books; newsletters.

Finance: Total assets 215.9m. new złotys; annual revenue 60.6m. new złotys, expenditure 68.7m. new złotys (31 Dec. 2021).

Governing Council: Andrzej Rychard (Chair.).

Board of Directors: Edwin Bendyk (Chair.).

Principal Staff: COO Maria Cywińska.

Contact Details: 00-215 Warsaw, ul. Sapiezynska 10A; tel. (22) 5360200; e-mail batory@batory.org.pl; internet www.batory.org.pl.

Fundacja Współpracy Polsko-Niemieckiej/Stiftung für Deutsch-Polnische Zusammenarbeit (Foundation for German-Polish Co-operation)

Established in 1991 by the Governments of Poland and Germany to sponsor non-commercial projects of German-Polish interest.

Activities: Works in the fields of the arts and humanities, conservation and the environment, education, international affairs, medicine and health, science and technology, and social welfare and social studies. The Foundation carries out research; awards grants to institutions, scholarships and fellowships; organizes conferences and training courses; and issues publications. It has an office in Berlin, Germany.

Geographical Area of Activity: Germany, Poland.

Publications: Annual Report; *Biuletyn Niemiecki*; Barometers; reports; analysis.

Finance: Total assets 435.0m. new złotys; net annual income 22.4m. new złotys (31 Dec. 2023).

Board of Trustees: Piotr Maciej Majewski, Cornelia Pieper (Co-Chair.).

Principal Staff: Dirs Dr. hab. Sebastian Płóciennik, Cornelius Ochmann.

Contact Details: 00-108 Warsaw, ul. Zielna 37; tel. (22) 3386200; e-mail fwpn@fwpn.org.pl; internet www.fwpn.org.pl.

Fundacja Wspomagania Wsi (Rural Development Foundation)

Established in 1999 as a result of the merger of the Water Supply Foundation and the Agricultural Foundation.

Activities: Promotes the sustainable development of rural Poland. The Foundation supports economic, social, cultural, educational and environmental initiatives, providing microloans and credit to businesses, local governments, public benefit agencies and individuals. It awards grants for infrastructural development; offers training for NGOs and programmes for local young people; and operates an exchange and partnership programme with European organizations.

Geographical Area of Activity: Poland.

Publications: Annual Report; newsletter; guides; toolkits; manuals; e-books.

Board: Piotr Szczepański (Pres.).

Contact Details: 01-022 Warsaw, ul. Bellottiego 1; tel. (22) 6362570; e-mail fww@fww.pl; internet www.fundacjawspomaganiawsi.pl.

Helsińska Fundacja Praw Człowieka (Helsinki Foundation for Human Rights)

Founded in 1982 by a group of intellectuals as the underground Helsinki Committee in Poland and formally established in 1989 as part of the International Helsinki Federation for Human Rights; a founding member of the Human Rights House Foundation (q.v.) network.

Activities: Carries out research and educational initiatives in the field of human rights. Main programmes include: providing education and training on human rights; and monitoring the legislative process and providing free legal assistance to Polish citizens, refugees and minority groups. The Foundation produces practical publications on rights in several languages for people dealing with Polish law enforcement agencies. It organizes the annual WATCH DOCS human rights film festival. Has consultative status with ECOSOC.

Geographical Area of Activity: International.

Publications: *Kwartalnik o Prawach Człowieka* ('Human Rights Quarterly'); newsletter; reports; guides; handbooks.

Finance: Total assets 10.4m. new złotys (31 Dec. 2023).

Management Board: Maciej Nowicki (Chair.); Dr Piotr Kładoczny (Deputy Chair.); Lenur Kerymov (Treas.); Małgorzata Szuleka (Sec.).

Council: Danuta Przywara (Chair.).

Contact Details: 00-490 Warsaw, ul. Wiejska 16; tel. (22) 5564440; e-mail hfhr@hfhr.pl; internet www.hfhr.pl.

Instytut Badań nad Demokracją i Przedsiębiorstwem Prywatnym (Institute for Private Enterprise and Democracy—IPED)

Established in 1993 by the Polish Chamber of Commerce.

Activities: Operates in the areas of economic affairs and social welfare. Programme areas include: the state of the private sector in Poland; tax reform; business ethics and social responsibility; Polish women in business; regional development and the promotion of entrepreneurship; legislative monitoring; and monitoring barriers to the development of small and medium-sized enterprises and their financing in Poland. The Institute conducts research, organizes conferences and supports the network of Chambers of Commerce in Poland.

Geographical Area of Activity: Poland.

Publications: Newsletter; brochure; reports.

Board: Dr Mieczysław Bąk (Chair. and CEO).

Principal Staff: Sec. Klaudia Urbaniak.

Contact Details: 00-074 Warsaw, ul. Trębacka 4; tel. (22) 6309801; e-mail iped@kig.pl; internet www.iped.pl.

Microfinance Centre—MFC

Established in 1997; a grassroots network.

Activities: Provides microfinance services, support and development to a wide range of financial institutions. The Centre promotes microfinance among policymakers, regulators, the formal banking sector and investors. It comprises more than 140 member organizations in 36 countries, with an office in Kyrgyzstan.

Geographical Area of Activity: Central Asia, Europe, Russian Federation.

Publications: Annual Report; *MFC Newsletter*; *Policy Monitor*.

Finance: Annual revenue 3.0m. new złotys, expenditure 2.3m. new złotys (31 Dec. 2023).

Council: Archil Bakuradze (Chair.); Gabriele Giuglietti (Vice-Chair.).

Principal Staff: Exec. Dir Katarzyna Pawlak.

Contact Details: 00-680 Warsaw, ul. Żurawia 47/49; tel. (22) 6223465; e-mail microfinance@mfc.org.pl; internet www.mfc.org.pl.

Polsko-Amerykańska Fundacja Wolności (Polish-American Freedom Foundation)

Established by the Polish-American Enterprise Fund in the USA in 1999; opened a Representative Office in Warsaw in 2000.

Activities: Supports the development of civil society, democracy and the market economy in Poland; and transformation processes in other countries of Central and Eastern Europe. Programmes include: Initiatives in Education, promoting English language teaching in Poland, offering grants to NGOs providing equal opportunities in access to education, professional and postgraduate teacher training, and corporate and doctoral scholarships for students, and supporting Third Age Universities; Development of Local Communities, supporting NGOs and civic initiatives through grants, and technical and

YORGHAS Foundation

leadership training; and Sharing the Polish Experiences in Transformation, offering scholarships to young leaders from Eastern Europe, the Caucasus and Central Asia to study in Poland, promoting development co-operation between NGOs in those regions and Poland, and organizing study tours of Poland.

Geographical Area of Activity: Armenia, Azerbaijan, Belarus, Georgia, Kazakhstan, Kyrgyzstan, Moldova, Poland, Russian Federation, Tajikistan, Ukraine, Uzbekistan.

Restrictions: Grants only to Polish NGOs; no grants for commercial projects.

Publications: Annual Report; newsletter.

Finance: Financed through revenues generated by its endowment, the source of which is the Polish-American Enterprise Fund. Total assets US $300.6m. (31 Dec. 2023).

Board of Directors: Andrew Nagorski (Chair.); Norman E. Haslun, III (Treas. and Sec.).

Principal Staff: Pres. and CEO Jerzy Koźmiński.

Contact Details: 02-954 Warsaw, ul. Królowej Marysienki 48; tel. (22) 5502800; e-mail paff@pafw.pl; internet www.pafw.pl.

YORGHAS Foundation

Established in 2018 by Alina Pelka.

Activities: YORGHAS Foundation is a non-profit, non-governmental organization headquartered in Warsaw, Poland, with its registered chapter and the Regional Office for Africa located in Lilongwe, Malawi. Its mission is to prevent maternal and newborn deaths caused by poverty, lack of access to healthcare, and education in developing countries across the African continent. Additionally, it aims to combat period poverty and advocate for the rights of women, girls, and children, ensuring their access to safe childbirth, proper healthcare, education, personal development, and a dignified life.

Geographical Area of Activity: Gambia, Kenya, Malawi, Nigeria, Poland, Sierra Leone, Tanzania, Uganda.

Board: Alina Pelka (Pres.); Malgorzata Pelka (Vice-Pres.).

Principal Staff: Regional Dir (Africa) Moses Busher.

Contact Details: 02-548 Warsaw, ul. Grazyny 15 lok. 221; tel. 501844438; e-mail yorghas@yorghas.org; internet yorghas.org.

PORTUGAL

CO-ORDINATING BODIES

Centro Português de Fundações—CPF (Portuguese Foundation Centre)

Established in 1993 by the Fundação Oriente (q.v.) in association with the Fundação Eng. António de Almeida and the Fundação Calouste Gulbenkian (qq.v.).

Activities: Promotes the interests of foundations in Portugal through co-operation and support, organizing meetings and conferences. The Centre has 151 members and is a member of Philea (q.v.).

Geographical Area of Activity: Portugal.

Publications: Annual Report; newsletter; *Portuguese Foundation Centre Directory*.

Finance: Total assets €301,987; net annual income €27,117 (31 Dec. 2024).

Board: João Luís Nunes (Pres.); Vasco do Canto Moniz (Vice-Pres.); Teresa Albuquerque (Sec.).

Principal Staff: Pres. José Manuel Nunes Liberato; Gen. Sec. Ricardo Garcia.

Contact Details: Rua Rodrigo da Fonseca 178, 7° Esq., 1070-239 Lisbon; tel. (21) 3538280; e-mail cpf@cpf.org.pt; internet www.cpf.org.pt.

Plataforma Portuguesa das Organizações Não-Governamentais para o Desenvolvimento—ONGD (Portuguese Platform of Non-Governmental Organizations for Development)

Established in 1985.

Activities: Represents and supports NGOs at national and international level through advocacy and capacity building. Members work in the fields of education for development and global citizenship, development co-operation, and humanitarian and emergency action. The Platform organizes activities into three working groups: AidWatch; Education for Development and Global Citizenship; and Ethics. It has 65 member organizations; and is a member of CONCORD (q.v.).

Geographical Area of Activity: Portugal.

Publications: Annual Repport; newsletter; *Revista da Plataforma Portuguesa das ONGD* (magazine, 2 a year); policy papers; position papers.

Finance: Total assets €154,589 (31 Dec. 2024).

General Assembly Board: Paulo Costa (Pres.); Teresa Paiva Couceiro (Vice-Pres.).

Supervisory Board: Victor Rosa (Pres.); Rachel Gomes (Vice-Pres.).

Principal Staff: Exec. Dir Rita Leote.

Contact Details: Rua Aprígio Mafra 17, 3rd dto, 1700-051 Lisbon; tel. (21) 8872239; e-mail info@plataformaongd.pt; internet www.plataformaongd.pt.

FOUNDATIONS AND NON-PROFITS

Fundação Arpad Szenes–Vieira da Silva (Arpad Szenes–Vieira da Silva Foundation)

Established in 1994 by the Portuguese Government, the Lisbon Municipal Council, the Luso-American Development Foundation, the Fundação Cidade de Lisboa and the Calouste Gulbenkian Foundation (qq.v.) to promote and study the work of Arpad Szenes and Maria Helena Vieira da Silva.

Activities: Operates in the fields of the arts and humanities, nationally through training courses, and nationally and internationally through research and conferences. The Foundation comprises a museum of contemporary art and a study and documentation centre. It organizes exhibitions and conferences on modern art and cultural development; issues publications in the field of art criticism and 20th-century art history; and promotes exchanges with similar national and international institutions.

Geographical Area of Activity: Mainly Portugal and South America.

Publications: Annual Report; catalogues of temporary exhibitions.

Finance: Financed by the Ministry of Culture and other sponsors. Total assets €8.3m.; net annual income €77,879 (31 Dec. 2024).

Board of Trustees: Vicente Pereira Gomes Marques (Chair.).

Board of Directors: António Gomes de Pinho (Chair.); João Corrêa Nunes (Vice-Chair.).

Principal Staff: Dir Nuno Faria.

Contact Details: Praça das Amoreiras 56, 1250-020 Lisbon; tel. (21) 3880044; e-mail fasvs@fasvs.pt; internet fasvs.pt.

Fundação Assistência Médica International—AMI (International Medical Assistance Foundation)

Established in 1984 by Dr Fernando José de La Vieter Ribeiro Nobre.

Activities: Works in the fields of development and emergency assistance through carrying out self-conducted programmes. Main programme areas are: citizenship; environment; health; and social inclusion. The Foundation offers grants to organizations; holds conferences and training courses; and runs information and awareness-raising sessions in schools on issues including citizenship and development, human rights, social solidarity, support for developing countries, the UN Sustainable Development Goals and volunteering; and organizes volunteering in Portugal and overseas. It operates a network of 9 Porta Amiga centres and two night shelters in Portugal that provide support to individuals and families experiencing economic vulnerability and social exclusion.

Geographical Area of Activity: International.

Restrictions: Grants only to organizations; volunteers must be aged 16 years or older.

Publications: *AMI Notícias* (quarterly newsletter); blog.

Finance: Total assets €34m.; net annual income –€421,567 (31 Dec. 2022).

Board of Directors: Prof. Dr Fernando José de La Vieter Ribeiro Nobre (Chair.); Maria Luísa Ferreira da Silva Nemésio (Vice-Chair.); Dr Isabel Focquet de La Vieter Nobre (Sec.-Gen.).

Contact Details: Rua José do Patrocínio, 49, 1959-003 Lisbon; tel. (21) 8362100; e-mail fundacao.ami@ami.org.pt; internet www.ami.org.pt.

Fundação Calouste Gulbenkian (Calouste Gulbenkian Foundation)

Founded in 1956 by Calouste Sarkis Gulbenkian, a business person and philanthropist, to operate in the general fields of charity, art, education and science, in Portugal and internationally.

Activities: The Foundation promotes wider access to culture, and the transformational power of art in the development of people and societies. It contributes to reducing inequalities in access to education and care for the most vulnerable. The Foundation promotes knowledge, scientific research, and greater participation and involvement of citizens and civil society in building more sustainable communities. It houses a museum, an arts centre, an orchestra and choir, an art library and archive, and a scientific research institute. The Foundation also develops innovative programmes and projects and supports, through scholarships and grants, social institutions and organizations in Portugal, the United Kingdom and France, as well as in Portuguese-speaking African countries and in Armenian communities.

Geographical Area of Activity: International.

Publications: Annual Report; annual activities and highlights reports; newsletter (monthly); *Colóquio-Letras* (periodical); Gulbenkian Editions.

Finance: Total assets €3,415.5m.; net annual income €372.3m. (31 Dec. 2022).

Board of Trustees: António Feijó (Pres.).

Principal Staff: Sec.-Gen. Rui Esgaio.

Contact Details: Av. de Berna 45A, 1067-001 Lisbon; tel. (21) 7823000; e-mail info@gulbenkian.pt; internet www.gulbenkian.pt.

Fundação da Casa de Mateus (Casa de Mateus Foundation)

Established in 1970 by Francisco de Sousa Botelho de Albuquerque, Count of Mangualde, Vila Real and Melo, to maintain the Casa de Mateus palace, a national monument since 1910.

Activities: Promotes scientific, cultural and pedagogical activities in the fields of the arts and humanities, including music, history and literature, and science. The Foundation organizes courses on theatre, sculpture, drawing and painting, exhibitions and seminars; hosts residences for artists from any country; awards the D. Dinis Prize and the Morgado de Mateus Prize in the field of literature; and maintains the archives of the Casa de Mateus. It also chairs the International Institute Casa de Mateus, which was established in 1986 by Portuguese public universities, academies and scientific institutes and organizes meetings of national and foreign scientists.

Geographical Area of Activity: Portugal.

Publications: Annual Report; newsletter.

Finance: Total assets €2.3m.; net annual income €558,192 (31 Dec. 2023).

Board of Directors: Teresa Margarida Gomez de Sousa Botelho de Albuquerque (Chair. and CEO).

Contact Details: 5000-291 Vila Real; tel. (259) 323121; e-mail casademateus@casademateus.pt; internet www.casademateus.pt/paginas/a-fundacao.

Fundação Centro Cultural de Belém (Belém Cultural Centre Foundation)

Established in 1991 by the Government of Portugal and Portuguese companies; formerly known as CCB—Belém Cultural Centre.

Activities: Promotes culture and the arts, especially Portuguese culture. The Foundation manages the Belém Cultural Centre, a conference centre, a performing arts centre and an exhibition centre; and facilitates exchanges with similar Portuguese and foreign institutions.

Geographical Area of Activity: Portugal.

Publications: Annual Report; newsletter.

Finance: Total assets €109.4m.; net annual income €1.2m. (31 Dec. 2023).

Board of Directors: Nuno Vassallo e Silva (Pres.).

Principal Staff: Dir Francisco Sacadura.

Contact Details: Praça do Império, 1449-003 Lisbon; tel. (21) 3612400; e-mail ccb@ccb.pt; internet www.ccb.pt.

Fundação Champalimaud (Champalimaud Foundation)

Established in 2004 by the will of António de Sommer Champalimaud, an industrialist and entrepreneur.

Activities: Supports work primarily in the areas of cancer and neuroscience, in particular research to benefit patients receiving clinical treatment. The Foundation also supports translational cancer research, with a particular focus on the prevention, diagnosis and treatment of metastatic diseases. The Champalimaud Cancer Clinic, housed in the Champalimaud Centre for the Unknown, Lisbon, began receiving patients in 2011. In addition to its in-house activities, the Foundation supports an outreach programme to aid the global fight against preventable blindness. The €1m. António Champalimaud Vision Award recognizes organizations' work to prevent blindness in the developing world and vision research.

Geographical Area of Activity: Worldwide.

Publications: Annual Report; newsletter.

Finance: Total assets €769.8m.; net annual income €2.4m. (31 Dec. 2023).

Board of Directors: Leonor Beleza (Pres.); João Silveira Botelho (Vice-Pres.).

General Council: Daniel Proença de Carvalho (Pres.).

Principal Staff: Dir of Champalimaud Centre Dr Zvi Fuks.

Contact Details: Champalimaud Centre for the Unknown, Av. Brasilia s/n, 1400-038 Lisbon; tel. (21) 0480200; e-mail info@fundacaochampalimaud.pt; internet www.fchampalimaud.org.

Fundação Cidade de Lisboa (City of Lisbon Foundation)

Founded in 1989 by Nuno Krus Abecasis, a former politician.

Activities: Promotes the protection of culture, the arts, monuments, tourism, ethnography, education and society in the city of Lisbon. The Foundation encourages the study of urban life in general and the development of relations and exchanges between Lisbon and other cities at national and international level, particularly with Portuguese and Portuguese-speaking communities.

Geographical Area of Activity: International.

Publications: Annual Report; books.
Finance: Total assets €1,918.5m. (31 Dec. 2024).
Board of Trustees: Eugénio Anacoreta Correia (Chair.).
Board of Directors: Prof. António Carmona Rodrigues (Pres.).
Principal Staff: Dir Vera Borges Pinto.
Contact Details: Campo Grande 380, 1700-097 Lisbon; tel. (21) 7568241; e-mail fclisboa@fundacaocidadedelisboa.pt; internet www.fundacaocidadedelisboa.pt.

Fundação Dom Manuel II (Dom Manuel II Foundation)

Established in 1966 by Dona Augusta Viktoria, the Duchess of Bragança, widow of King Dom Manuel II of Portugal, to help Portuguese emigrants.
Activities: Works in the fields of aid to less-developed countries, conservation and the environment, education and social welfare, through self-conducted programmes, awarding prizes, and organizing conferences and training courses. The Foundation provides help in the areas of housing, integration of Portuguese emigrants into local communities, and education. In conjunction with the University of Minho and the Municipality of Guimarães, it awards the Príncipe da Beira Prize for Biomedical Sciences, worth €15m. It has also established a subsidiary in Timor-Leste, the Timorese Cultural Foundation, which operates a printing factory.
Geographical Area of Activity: Angola (incl. Cabinda), Brazil, Canada, Guinea, India, Mozambique, Portugal, São Tomé and Príncipe, Timor-Leste.
Finance: Funded by donations and income from rented property.
Trustees: HRH Dom Duarte Pio, Duke of Bragança (Chair.).
Contact Details: Rua dos Duques de Bragança 10, 1200-162 Lisbon; tel. (21) 3423705; e-mail geral@fdommanuel.org; internet www.fdommanuel.org.

Fundação EDP (EDP Foundation)

Established in 2004.
Activities: Works in the fields of culture and the arts, and the preservation of historical heritage and the environment. The Foundation comprises the Central Tejo museum of electricity and energy production; and established the MAAT (Museum of Art, Architecture and Technology, f. 2016), which exhibits over 1,000 works by Portuguese artists. The EDP Social Hub programme works in communities with high levels of social exclusion in Portugal and São Paulo, Brazil, in the areas of education, mental and physical health, entrepreneurship, community empowerment and volunteering. Social enterprises are supported through the PPL crowdfunding platform. It also houses a documentation centre.
Geographical Area of Activity: Brazil (São Paulo), Portugal.
Publications: Annual Report.
Finance: Total assets €78.2m. (31 Dec. 2023).
Board of Trustees/Board of Trustees: Vera de Morais Pinto Pereira Carneiro (Pres.).
Fiscal Council: Felix Arribas Arias (Pres.).
Principal Staff: Gen. Dir Rui Miguel Coutinho Baptista.
Contact Details: Av. de Brasília, Central Tejo, 1300-598 Lisbon; tel. (21) 0028130; e-mail fundacaoedp@edp.pt; internet www.fundacaoedp.pt.

Fundação Eng. António de Almeida (António de Almeida Foundation)

Founded in 1969 by the will of António de Almeida, a civil engineer and banker.
Activities: Works in the fields of art and education through promoting Portuguese language and culture. The Foundation sponsors art exhibitions and musical recitals; offers grants to cultural institutions in Portugal and to Portuguese graduates for research work; awards the António de Almeida Prize annually to students from six universities for academic achievement; and organizes international conferences. It also maintains a museum of art to exhibit items collected by the founder, including furniture, textiles, porcelain, paintings, timepieces and a coin collection.
Geographical Area of Activity: Portugal.
Publications: Annual Report; periodicals.
Finance: Total assets €43.6m.; net annual income –€1.0m. (31 Dec. 2020).
Board of Directors: Dr Augusto Aguiar-Branco (Pres. and Exec. Dir).
Contact Details: Rua Tenente Valadim 231/325, 4100-479 Porto; tel. (22) 6067418; e-mail fundacao@feaa.pt; internet www.feaa.pt.

Fundação Luso-Americana para o Desenvolvimento—FLAD (Luso-American Development Foundation)

Founded in 1985 to assist Portugal in its development, mainly by building strong ties with the USA.
Activities: Works in the fields of technology and science, education, culture, transatlantic relations and public policy. The Foundation funds scholarships, internships and exchanges; conferences and publications; medical, scientific and technological research; and programms to test new approaches to public policies. Has a contemporary art collection, with more than 1,000 works. It is one of the main Portuguese private foundations.
Geographical Area of Activity: Portugal, USA.
Publications: Annual Report.
Finance: The Government of Portugal provided an initial fund of €85m. Total assets €152.5m.; net annual income €2.4m. (31 Dec. 2023).
Board of Trustees: Maria Gabriela (Pres.).
Board of Directors: Michael Alvin Baum, Jr (Pres.).
Contact Details: Rua do Sacramento à Lapa 21, 1249-090 Lisbon; tel. (21) 3935800; e-mail fladport@flad.pt; internet www.flad.pt.

Fundação Mário Soares e Maria Barroso (Mário Soares and Maria Barroso Foundation)

Founded in 1991 by Mário Soares, former President of Portugal.
Activities: Promotes civic and democratic culture inspired by the life and legacy of Mário Soares and Maria Barroso; and preserves historical memory and cultural heritage. The Foundation awards the Mário Soares Prize annually; and holds scientific and cultural events, providing training and debate programmes, co-operating with Portuguese-speaking countries, and encouraging the creation and dissemination of scientifically based knowledge. It has a library and archive; and also runs the João Soares Museum House in Cortes, Leiria. The Foundation houses a Portuguese political archive, comprising personal and political documentation that belonged to both Mário Soares and Maria Barroso, as well as several other collections.
Geographical Area of Activity: Portugal, Europe.
Publications: Annual Report.
Finance: Total assets €983,320; total income –€110,327 (31 Dec. 2023).
Board of Directors: Isabel Soares (Pres.).
Principal Staff: Exec. Dir Filipe Guimarães da Silva.
Contact Details: Rua de S. Bento 176, 1200-821 Lisbon; tel. (21) 3964179; e-mail geral@fmsoaresbarroso.pt; internet www.fmsoaresbarroso.pt.

Fundação Oriente (Orient Foundation)

Established in 1988 to maintain and strengthen historical and cultural ties between Portugal and Asia, particularly Macao; a founding member of the European Foundation Centre and the Portuguese Foundation Centre (qq.v.); in 2008 it opened the Museu do Oriente.

Activities: Supports cultural, educational, artistic and philanthropic activities; provides support for Macao communities; conducts research; awards scholarships and prizes; and co-operates with other organizations. The Foundation operates primarily in Portugal but also in Macao, the People's Republic of China, India, and Timor-Leste that have cultural and historic links with Portugal and where Macanese communities live. It maintains a documentation centre.

Geographical Area of Activity: Europe, East and South-East Asia.

Publications: Annual Report; publications relating to historical and cultural relations between Portugal and Asia; *Revista Oriente*.

Finance: Total assets €202.3m. (31 Dec. 2023).

Board of Trustees: Luís Filipe Marques Amado (Chair.).

Board of Directors: Carlos Augusto Pulido Valente Monjardino (Chair.); João António Morais da Costa Pinto (Vice-Chair.).

Contact Details: Edifício Pedro Álvares Cabral, Avda Brasília, Doca de Alcântara Norte, 1350-352 Lisbon; tel. (21) 3585200; e-mail info@foriente.pt; internet www.foriente.pt.

Fundação Ricardo do Espírito Santo Silva (Ricardo do Espírito Santo Silva Foundation)

Founded in 1953 by Ricardo do Espírito Santo Silva to preserve the tradition of decorative arts and crafts.

Activities: Maintains 18 workshops devoted to producing reproductions and to restoration in 21 traditional crafts, including cabinetmaking, marquetry, decorative and enamel paintings, Arraiolos carpets, bookbinding, book decoration, chiselling, handmade gold leaf, etc. The Foundation runs workshops and restoration projects in Brazil, and collaborates with other organizations to form cultural associations and run exhibitions. It also runs the Portuguese Museum-School for Decorative Arts, the High School of Decorative Arts and the Arts and Crafts Institute.

Geographical Area of Activity: Portugal.

Publications: Annual Report; newsletter; catalogues.

Finance: Total assets €27.0m.; net annual income €742,606 (31 Dec. 2023).

Board of Trustees: Paulo Sousa (Chair.).

Board of Directors: Gabriela Canavilhas (Chair. and Exec. Dir)

Contact Details: Rua de S. Tomé 90, 1100-564 Lisbon; tel. (21) 8814600; e-mail geral@fress.pt; internet www.fress.pt.

Fundação de Serralves (Serralves Foundation)

Established in 1989 as a partnership between the Government of Portugal and a group of companies.

Activities: Works in the fields of contemporary art and the humanities, conservation and the environment, through self-conducted programmes, conferences, environmental education programmes and publications. The Foundation organizes environmental conferences, seminars on the management of urban green areas and open-air classes and nature clubs; and promotes the arts through sponsorship of art exhibitions, conferences, dance, music and video production. In 1999 it established a museum of contemporary art in Porto.

Geographical Area of Activity: International.

Publications: Annual Report; newsletter; exhibition catalogues; information brochures.

Finance: Total assets €98.4m. (31 Dec. 2023).

Board of Founders: Emílio Rui Vilar (Pres.).

Board of Directors: Ana Pinho (Pres.); Manuel Ferreira da Silva, Isabel Pires de Lima, José Pacheco Pereira (Vice-Pres).

Contact Details: Rua D. João de Castro 210, 4150-417 Porto; tel. (22) 6156500; e-mail serralves@serralves.pt; internet www.serralves.pt.

Fundação Vodafone Portugal (Vodafone Portugal Foundation)

Established in 2001 by Vodafone Portugal, a telecommunications company; part of the Vodafone Foundation network.

Activities: Promotes the development of an Information Society and mobile telecommunications technology. The Foundation supports scientific and technological research; training and professional qualifications in the ICT sector; social integration projects; and internet-based initiatives that promote the Portuguese language and Portuguese culture. Other initiatives include using digital technology to prevent domestic abuse and violence against women.

Geographical Area of Activity: Portugal.

Publications: Annual Report.

Finance: Total assets €521,812 (31 March 2024).

Board of Directors: Dr Mario Vaz (Chair.).

Executive Committee: Luisa Pestana (Chair.).

Principal Staff: Man. Ana Mesquita Verissimo.

Contact Details: Av. de Dom João II, Lote 1.04.01 8, 1990-093 Lisboa; tel. (21) 0915000; e-mail fundacao.pt@vodafone.com; internet www.vodafone.pt/a-vodafone/fundacao.html.

PUERTO RICO

CO-ORDINATING BODY

Fundación Comunitaria de Puerto Rico—FCPR (Puerto Rico Community Foundation)

Established in 1984.

Activities: Promotes community development, funding and philanthropy to improve the socioeconomic development of Puerto Rico. Operates nationally, through community development programmes in areas including the arts; business–community relations; and youth programmes, such as providing alternative education to adolescents who have dropped out of formal education and a university-based programme of youth volunteer service. The Foundation supports other non-profit organizations in Puerto Rico, promoting charitable work to solve social problems on the island; and managing donor funds, which offer grants, scholarships and awards.

Geographical Area of Activity: South America, Central America and the Caribbean, USA.

Restrictions: Grants and scholarships for non-profit organizations and students only.

Publications: Annual Report; *Entrelazando/Interlacing* (magazine).

Finance: Annual income US $4.5m., expenditure $6.2m. (31 Dec. 2021).

Board of Directors: Miguel L. Vargas Jiménez (Pres.); Vivian I. Neptune Rivera (Vice-Pres.); Antonio Escudero Viera (Treas. and Sec.).

Principal Staff: Pres. and CEO Nelson I. Colón Tarrats.

Contact Details: 1719 Ave Ponce de León, San Juan 00909; POB 70362, San Juan, PR 00936-8362; tel. 721-1037; e-mail fcpr@fcpr.org; internet www.fcpr.org.

QATAR

FOUNDATIONS AND NON-PROFITS

Education Above All Foundation—EAA (Alet'Eleym Fewq Alejmey'e)

Established in 2012 by HH Sheikha Moza bint Nasser.

Activities: Works in the field of education for children, young people and women, with a particular focus on those affected by poverty, conflict and disaster. Stand-alone programmes include: Educate A Child, which provides primary education; Protect Education in Insecurity and Conflict; Al Fakhoora, which defends the right to education; Reach Out to Asia, which ensures access to education and training; the Innovation Development Directorate (IDD), an 'ideas lab'; and the Zero Out Of School Strategy. It supports projects in 73 countries.

Geographical Area of Activity: International.

Publications: Annual Report; reports; manuals; toolkits; online resources.

Board of Trustees: HH Sheikha Moza bint Nasser (Chair.).

Executive Committee: Dr Mazen Jassim Jaidah.

Principal Staff: Acting CEO Mohammed Saad Al Kubaisi.

Contact Details: POB 34173, Doha; tel. 44545868; e-mail info@eaa.org.qa.

Qatar Foundation

Established in 1995, as Qatar Foundation for Education, Science and Community Development, by HH Sheikh Hamad bin Khalifa Al Thani, Emir of Qatar, and HH Sheika Moza bint Nasser.

Activities: Operates in the fields of education, scientific research and community development. The Foundation comprises approximately 50 centres, including branches of nine international universities; three science and technology research institutes; and 'heritage centres', including the Qatar Philharmonic Orchestra, Qur'anic Botanic Garden, Mathaf: Arab Museum of Modern Art and the Qatar National Library. It provides pre-university education through seven academies and other educational programmes. Also incorporates Qatar Foundation International (f. 2009), based in the USA.

Geographical Area of Activity: Qatar.

Publications: *Qatar Foundation Telegraph*; *Think*; *The Foundation* (magazine); *QF Radio (93.7FM)* (radio station).

Board of Trustees and Board of Directors: HH Sheikha Moza bint Nasser (Chair.); HE Sheikha Hind bint Hamad Al Thani (Vice-Chair. and CEO).

Principal Staff: CEO of QF Int. Omran Hamad Al-Kuwari.

Contact Details: Education City, Al Huqoul St, Ar-Rayyan, Ad Dawhah, Doha; POB 5825, Doha; tel. 44540000; e-mail info@qf.org.qa; internet www.qf.org.qa.

RÉUNION

FOUNDATIONS AND NON-PROFITS

Apprentis d'Auteuil Océan Indien

Established in 2008 as Auteuil Océan Indien to carry out projects on behalf of Fondation d'Auteuil in Réunion; present name adopted in 2015.

Activities: Supports children, adolescents and young people, and their families, who are experiencing problems at home, socially or at school. The organization works with social services to protect children; and provides schooling and vocational training through four reception and training centres. It supports projects helping street children, out-of-school children and vulnerable families in Antananarivo, Madagascar; and organizes overseas projects for apprentices to practise their skills while volunteering. Has a branch in Mayotte. The Fondation Antenne Réunion operates under its aegis.

Geographical Area of Activity: Madagascar, Mayotte, Réunion (and the wider Indian Ocean region).

Publications: Annual Report.

Finance: Annual revenue €14.2m., expenditure €13.8m. (31 Dec. 2023).

Board of Directors: Christian Boyer de La Giroday (Pres.); David Titus (Vice-Pres.); Eric Ravaux (Treas.); Philippe Jean-Pierre (Sec.).

Principal Staff: Gen. Man. Guillaume Jeu.

Contact Details: 18 rue Nantier Didiée, 97400 Saint-Denis; tel. (262) 20-02-30; e-mail aaoi@apprentis-auteuil.org; internet ocean-indien.apprentis-auteuil.org.

Fondation d'Entreprise Crédit Agricole Réunion Mayotte

Established in 2013 by Crédit Agricole, a bank and insurance company.

Activities: Focuses on the development of a sustainable and socially responsible economy; and vocational training and youth employment. The Foundation supports projects of an educational or socioeconomic nature; those relating to sports; or which contribute to the enhancement of artistic heritage, the natural environment, language and scientific knowledge. Grants range between €10,000 and €50,000.

Geographical Area of Activity: French Southern and Antarctic Territories, Mayotte, Réunion.

Restrictions: Grants mainly for equipment and, in exceptional cases, services.

Publications: Annual Report.

Principal Staff: Gen. Man. Jean Marie Degard.

Contact Details: Parc Jean de Cambiaire, Cité des Lauriers, BP 84, 97462 Saint-Denis Cedex; tel. (262) 40-82-31; e-mail fondationreunionmayotte@ca-reunion.fr.

ROMANIA

CO-ORDINATING BODIES

Centras—Centrul de Asistenta pentru Organizatii Neguvernamentale (Centras—Assistance Centre for NGOs)

Established in 1995 by Dorin Tudoran, a journalist and political analyst.

Activities: Supports the development of civil society and promotes freedom of thought and creativity, education and free exchange of opinion and information based on democratic and humanitarian principles. The Centre carries out research and projects in the areas of conservation and the environment, economic affairs, education, law and human rights, NGO development and social welfare. It also organizes conferences and training courses.

Geographical Area of Activity: Romania.

Publications: *Attitudini* (magazine); *White Papers of the Romanian NGOs FORUM*.

Board of Trustees: Dorin Tudoran (Pres.).

Principal Staff: Exec. Dir Viorel Micescu.

Contact Details: 011454 Bucharest, blvd Mareșal Averescu 17, Pavilion F, et. 3, Sector 1; tel. (21) 2230010; e-mail office @centras.ro.

FOND—Federatia Organizatiilor Neguvernamentale pentru Dezvoltare din Romania (Federation of Non-Governmental Organizations for Development in Romania)

Established in 2006 by 34 NGOs.

Activities: Supports NGOs working in the field of international co-operation for development and humanitarian aid. Programme areas include: global education for development; humanitarian assistance; international volunteering; and policy coherence for development. The Federation conducts public policy research; offers training and networking opportunities; and provides advocacy and advice on project planning and implementation. It has 34 members; and is a member of CONCORD (q.v.).

Geographical Area of Activity: Romania.

Board of Directors: Stefan Cibian (Pres.); Anca Ciucă (Vice-Pres.).

Contact Details: Bucharest, str. Washington, nr. 38, Sector 1; tel. 734325662; e-mail fond.romania@gmail.com; internet www.fondromania.org.

Fundația pentru Dezvoltarea Societății Civile—FDSC (Civil Society Development Foundation)

Established in 1994.

Activities: Supports the development of CSOs. The Foundation conducts public policy research and advocacy; and offers technical and financial support, consulting and training. It maintains an NGO database; and in 2021 launched the Plataforma Donatorilor online donors' platform, containing information on 15 funders and 19 community foundations.

Geographical Area of Activity: Romania.

Publications: Annual Report; *Voluntar* (weekly magazine); studies; reports; white papers.

Finance: Annual income €3.0m., expenditure €2.6m. (2023).

Board of Directors: Cătălin R. Crețu (Chair.); Prof. Dr Simona-Nely Gherghina, Virginia-Elena Oțel (Vice-Chair.).

Principal Staff: Exec. Dir Ionuț Sibian.

Contact Details: 031044 Bucharest, blvd Nerva Traian 21, Sector 3; tel. 746280084; e-mail office@fdsc.ro; internet www.fdsc.ro.

FOUNDATIONS AND NON-PROFITS

Fundația Civitas pentru Societatea Civilă (Civitas Foundation for Civil Society)

Established in 1992 to improve and professionalize local administration following the 1989 revolution.

Activities: Increases the development capacity of local communities, designing and implementing local and regional development programmes. Main programme areas are: community development and good governance; entrepreneurship and social economy; rural economic development; and strengthening civil society. The Foundation supports local initiatives that build relations between local governments and people; provides specialist consultancy services for local governments; and runs training courses for local public officials. It also supports the establishment and functioning of NGOs. Has an office in Cluj-Napoca.

Geographical Area of Activity: Romania.

Publications: Annual Report.

Finance: Annual income 6.6m. lei, expenditure 6.1m. lei (2023).

Board of Trustees: Gábor Kolumbán (Chair.).

Principal Staff: Exec. Dir and Financial Dir Lajos-Geza Dénes (Odorheiu Szekler Office); Dir Marton Balogh (Cluj-Napoca Office).

Contact Details: 535600 Odorheiu Secuiesc, str. Solymossy nr. 29; tel. (26) 6218481; e-mail office.udv@civitas.ro; internet www.civitas.ro.

Fundația Orange (Orange Foundation)

Established in 2012 by Orange, a telecommunications company; part of the Fondation Orange (q.v.) network.

Activities: Focuses on digital education for disadvantaged groups, including projects for people with hearing and visual impairments. The Foundation provides tablets to students in financial need; and established the Digitaliada programme to provide rural middle schools with access to digital educational resources. It also supports NGO projects proposed by Orange employees with financial and technical assistance.

Geographical Area of Activity: Romania.

Publications: Annual Report; e-books.

Finance: Annual income 7.1m. lei, expenditure 6.8m. lei (31 Dec. 2020).

Board of Directors: Dana Deac (Pres.).

Contact Details: Bucharest, blvd Lascăr Cartagiu 47–53, ap. 10, et. 10, Birou E13; e-mail fundatia.orange@orange.com; internet www.fundatiaorange.ro.

Fundația Universitară a Mării Negre—FUMN (Black Sea University Foundation—BSUF)

Established in 1992 by 21 members of the Romanian scientific and cultural community, under the aegis of the Academiei Române.

Activities: Promotes and studies the economies, societies, education systems and governance of the Black Sea region, collaborating with international organizations, associations and similar institutions. The Foundation carries out scientific research and teaching programmes, in particular in the areas of: international relations and conflict prevention; science education and information technology; sustainable development; economic studies and management; management of international projects; ecology and marine resources; cultural policies and global problems; alternative and clean energy resources; and development of food production and non-agricultural activities. It considers the implications of regional economic co-operation and borderless and transnational co-operation; studies the ecological problems of the Black Sea, how to preserve its resources and combat pollution; promotes knowledge of regional cultural heritage, respect for diversity and a culture of peace; offers professional training courses; issues publications and organizes public events; and carries out consultancies.

Geographical Area of Activity: Romania.

Publications: Newsletter; reports; books.

Board of Directors: Liviu-Aurelian Bota (Chair.).

Principal Staff: Pres. Prof. Dan Dungaciu; Vice-Pres. Prof. Silviu Neguț; Exec. Dir Cosmin-Dragoș Dugan; Scientific Dir Prof. Dr Darie Cristea.

Contact Details: 761172 Bucharest, Sector 5, Calea 13 Septembrie 13, Casa Academiei Române; tel. (31) 4052542; e-mail office@fumn.eu; internet www.fumn.eu.

Fundația Vodafone România (Vodafone Romania Foundation)'

Established in 1998 by Vodafone Romania, a telecommunications company; part of the Vodafone Foundation (q.v.) network.

Activities: Carries out projects in the fields of education, health and social services. The Connecting for Good programme supports digital social innovation to help children and adults affected by serious diseases, transplant patients, people living in remote rural areas, and people with hearing and vision impairments. The Good Deeds Fund supports organizations that help disadvantaged children, adults and elderly people. Other initiatives include using digital technology to prevent domestic abuse and violence against women. The Foundation also promotes employee and local community volunteering.

Geographical Area of Activity: Romania.

Publications: Annual Report.

Finance: Total grants disbursed €2.2m. (2021).

Principal Staff: Hon. Pres. Irina-Margareta Nistor; Dir Angela Galeta.

Contact Details: 020276 Bucharest, Clădirea Globalworth Tower, str. Barbu Văcărescu 201, Sector 2; tel. (21) 3021000; e-mail fundatia.vodafone_ro@vodafone.com; internet www.fundatia-vodafone.ro.

Institutul Cultural Român—ICR (Romanian Cultural Institute)

Established in 2003 following the restructuring of the Romanian Cultural Foundation and the Romanian Cultural Foundation Publishing House.

Activities: Operates in the fields of the arts and humanities, education and science through self-conducted programmes, carrying out research and issuing publications; organizing training courses, international symposia, conferences and exhibitions; and awarding scholarships, fellowships and prizes. The Institute offers grants to overseas students wishing to study in Romania; supports Romanian cultural institutes abroad; and promotes relations with those interested in Romanian culture and civilization, and with Romanians living abroad. It has branches in Beijing (People's Repub. of China), Berlin (Germany), Brussels (Belgium), Budapest (Hungary), Chișinău (Moldova), İstanbul (Türkiye—Turkey), Lisbon (Portugal), London (UK), Madrid (Spain), New York (USA), Paris (France), Prague (Czech Republic), Rome (Italy), Stockholm (Sweden), Szeged (Hungary), Tel Aviv (Israel), Warsaw (Poland), Alien (USA) and Vienna (Austria).

Geographical Area of Activity: International.

Publications: Annual Report; *Curierul Românesc* (monthly); *Lettre Internationale* (quarterly); *Dilema* (weekly newspaper); *Transylvanian Review* (quarterly); *Contrafort* (monthly); *Destin Românesc* (quarterly); *Glasul Bucovinei* (quarterly); newsletter.

Finance: Partly self-financing; also receives government subsidies. Annual budget 43.7m. lei (2023).

Board of Directors: Liviu Sebastian Jicman (Pres.); Attila Iuliu Weinberger (Vice-Pres.).

Principal Staff: Dir Aura Woodward; Deputy Dir Raluca Cimpoiasu.

Contact Details: 011824 Bucharest, Aleea Alexandru 38, sector 1; Bucharest, Str. Amzei Church no. 21–23; tel. (31) 7100606; e-mail icr@icr.ro; internet www.icr.ro.

RUSSIAN FEDERATION

CO-ORDINATING BODIES

CAF Russia—Charities Aid Foundation Russia

Established in 1993 by CAF—Charities Aid Foundation (q.v.); a member of the Global Alliance of the Charities Aid Foundation.

Activities: Distributes grants provided by Russian and international donors; and provides support and advice to companies and private philanthropists who are planning charitable and social projects. The Foundation develops philanthropic programmes, including corporate giving, supporting community foundations and promoting payroll giving; and manages the Blago.ru online donor platform. It carries out research on charitable activity in the Russian Federation and promotes the development of civil society, advocating for changes to legislation on philanthropy and non-profit organizations; and offering consulting and training to civil initiatives.

Geographical Area of Activity: Russia.

Publications: Annual Report; *Filanthropa* (magazine); *Money and Charity* (magazine, 6 a year); *World Giving Index*; guidelines; reports.

Finance: Annual income 512.3m. roubles, expenditure 498.0m. roubles (2020).

Principal Staff: Dir Maria Chertok.

Contact Details: 119180 Moscow, ext. ter. Yakimanka Municipal District, st. Bolshaya Polyanka 7/10, Bldg 3; tel. (495) 989-41-00; e-mail cafrussia@cafrussia.ru; internet www.cafrussia.ru.

Community Foundation Partnership

Established in 2003 at the 4th Community Foundations Conference in Togliatti.

Activities: Works to strengthen civil society and improve people's quality of life through using technology for social stability. The Partnership advocates on behalf of community foundations; and ensures the effective and transparent use of funds. Through the Youth Bank programme, community foundations fund projects carried out by young people for young people, with Youth Banks in 14 cities. Comprises nine partner foundations.

Geographical Area of Activity: Russian Federation.

Publications: Partnership Report (annual); newsletter.

Board: Boris Albertovich Tsirulnikov (Chair.); Oleg Viktorovich Sharipkov (Vice-Chair.).

Contact Details: 445037 Samara region, Tolyatti, 3 'A' quarter, st. Yubileinaya 31-E, 4th Floor, Office 401; tel. (8482) 536-750; e-mail partnerstvo.fms@yandex.ru; internet www.p-cf.ru/2020.

NGO Development Centre

Established in 1994; formerly known as the Russian-German Exchange Society.

Activities: Works as an information centre for the non-profit sector in the Russian Federation. The Centre supports the development of a strong civil society in Russia through providing advice on forming an NGO and information and training on organizational development, including advice on management, fundraising, relations with the public and media, accountancy, taxation and legal matters. It also sponsors international, national and regional conferences on issues concerning non-profit sector development in Russia.

Geographical Area of Activity: Russian Federation.

Publications: Annual Report; *TsRNO* (e-newsletter); *Pchela* (magazine); bulletins, brochures and booklets.

Finance: Annual income 15.7m. roubles, expenditure 8.4m. roubles (31 Dec. 2020).

Principal Staff: Supervisor Anna Smirnova.

Contact Details: 191040 St Petersburg, pr. Ligovsky 87, Office 300; tel. (812) 718-37-94; e-mail crno@crno.ru; internet www.crno.ru.

Russian Donors Forum

Founded in 1996 as a membership organization of around 25 Russian and non-Russian grantmaking organizations.

Activities: Supports the development of a democratic civil society in the Russian Federation through effective organized grantmaking. The Forum conducts research; organizes the exchange of information between grantmakers and facilitating networks; provides information on grantmaking and services to support member organizations' development; and hosts the Top Corporate Philanthropist Award. It comprises 52 members, including corporate foundations and international organizations; and is a member of Philea (q.v.).

Geographical Area of Activity: Russian Federation.

Publications: Annual Report; brochures; reports.

Finance: Annual revenue 28.3m. roubles, expenditure 19.7m. roubles (31 Dec. 2020).

Council: Nikolay Slabzhanin (Chair.).

Principal Staff: Exec. Dir Alexandra Boldyreva; Deputy Exec. Dir Maria Mokina.

Contact Details: 127053 Moscow, ul. Sushevskaya 9, Bldg 4, Office 311; tel. (499) 978-59-93; e-mail dfinfo@donorsforum.ru; internet www.donorsforum.ru.

FOUNDATIONS AND NON-PROFITS

Anti-Corruption Foundation

Established in 2011 by Alexey Navalny, a lawyer, founder of anti-corruption projects RosPil, RosYama and RosZhKH, and head of the Progress Party.

Activities: Seeks to eliminate political and economic corruption. The Foundation investigates cases of corruption and illegal enrichment and prepares documents for legal action. It has an office in Moscow.

Geographical Area of Activity: Russian Federation.

Publications: Newsletter; reports.

Advisory Board: Yulia Navalnaya (Chair.).

Board of Directors: Maria Konstantinovna Pevchikh (Chair.).

Principal Staff: Exec. Dir Vladimir Ashurkov.

Contact Details: 190068 St Petersburg, av. Vosnesenskiy 33, Bldg A, Rm 13N; e-mail info@acf.international; internet acf.international.

Dmitry Likhachev Foundation

Established in 2001 in memory of Dmitry Likhachev, an editor and literary scholar.

Activities: Carries out activities in the fields of culture, education and the humanities, including protecting monuments; promoting local studies and civil society; studying the culture of the Russian diaspora; researching and disseminating information on philanthropy in the Russian Federation and organizing conferences and roundtables; awarding grants for the study, preservation and dissemination of Russian cultural heritage; and promoting the cultural integration of large and small Russian cities established by or otherwise connected with Peter the Great. Jointly with the Boris Yeltsin Presidential Center, the Foundation awards Cultural Fellowships in Russia, to promote cultural co-operation between Russia and other countries; and promote Russian culture and cultural institutions internationally. It awards the Likhachev Prize for the conservation of Russian cultural heritage; the Antsiferovskaya Prize for work on the history of St Petersburg; the Prize for Asceticism for work for the common good and contributions to the development of civil society; the Rauschenbach Scholarships for interdisciplinary research; and art history scholarships.

Geographical Area of Activity: International.

Restrictions: Applicants for fellowships must be specialists in culture, education or the humanities.

Publications: *Culture and Society* (annual almanac); *Encyclopaedia of St Petersburg*; art and history books; conference materials.

Board: Mikhail B. Piotrovsky (Chair.).

Principal Staff: Exec. Dir Alexander V. Kobak; Deputy Dir Oleg L. Leykind.

Contact Details: 191028 St Petersburg, ul. Mokhovaya 15 (right entrance); tel. (812) 272-29-12; e-mail ivanova@lfond.spb.ru; internet lfond.spb.ru.

Elena & Gennady Timchenko Foundation

Established in 2010 as the Ladoga Foundation by Gennady Timchenko, co-owner of gas company Novatek and founder of the Klyuch Foundation and Neva Foundation, which is based in Switzerland, and his wife Elena, President of the Neva Foundation; present name adopted in 2013.

Activities: Activities include: supporting older people, families and children; providing opportunities for people to take part in sport and culture; and restoring historical and religious monuments.

Geographical Area of Activity: Canada, People's Repub. of China, France, Israel, Italy, Latvia, Russian Federation, Switzerland, UK, USA.

Publications: Annual Report.

Finance: Annual expenditure 241.4m. roubles (2023).

Principal Staff: CEO Galina Laponova.

Contact Details: 119021 Moscow, ul. Timur Frunze 11, Bldg 1, Floor 1; tel. (495) 539-31-76; e-mail inform@timchenkofoundation.org; internet www.timchenkofoundation.org.

Glasnost Defence Foundation

Established in 1991 to provide legal support to the media in Russia and to monitor censorship.

Activities: Operates in the areas of the arts and humanities, and law and human rights through providing legal and advocacy services to the media; and conducts day-to-day monitoring of abuses of media rights in the Russian Federation. The Foundation carries out research and analysis; runs projects; and organizes seminars for journalists, lawyers and human rights activists. It maintains a monitoring network, which collates and maps information about media conflicts and violations of media rights in the Russian Federation.

Geographical Area of Activity: Russian Federation.

Publications: *Digest* (online, weekly, in Russian and English); *Vzglyad* (quarterly newsletter); Monitoring Results (monthly); books.

Finance: Receives funding from the MacArthur Foundation and the Norwegian Helsinki Committee.

Principal Staff: Pres. Alexey K. Simonov; CEO Nataliya Y. Maksimova.

Contact Details: 119021 Moscow, GSP-2, blvd Zubovsky 4 (RIA Novosti, entrance of the Union of Journalists), Rm 432, POB 536; tel. (495) 637-49-47; e-mail fond@gdf.ru.

Gorbachev Foundation

Founded in 1991 by Mikhail Gorbachev, President of the USSR, to conduct socioeconomic and political studies.

Activities: Operates in the fields of education, international affairs, medicine and health, welfare and social studies, through self-conducted programmes, research, conferences, training courses and publications. Research programmes include: the Twenty-First Century—a Century of Challenges and Responses (the principal international research project); Building a New Russia's Statehood; Russia, Greater Europe; the Asian Flank of the Commonwealth of Independent States (CIS); and Russia and Europe in a New World Order. The Foundation also undertakes humanitarian work, providing funds for medicines and equipment to treat children with blood diseases; and assists foreign businesses in finding partners in the countries of the former USSR. The Public Affairs Center maintains an archive of more than 30,000 items and a library, which contains around 6,000 publications. Has offices and partner organizations in the Russian Federation, Canada, Germany, Switzerland and the USA.

Geographical Area of Activity: Worldwide.

Publications: Annual Report; newsletter; books.

Finance: Annual expenditure 17.6m. roubles (2020).

Executive Board: Mikhail S. Gorbachev (Pres.); Irina M. Gorbacheva-Virganskaya (Vice-Pres.).

Principal Staff: Exec. Dir Andrey Vilenovich Ryabov.

Contact Details: 125167 Moscow, pr. Leningradsky Prospekt 39, Bldg 14; tel. (495) 945-59-99; e-mail gf@gorby.ru; internet www.gorby.ru.

International Historical, Educational, Charitable and Human Rights Society—International Memorial
(Mezhdunarodnyj Memorial)

Established in 1992; an umbrella organization.

Activities: Researches mass political repression in the former USSR, defends human rights, and promotes the development of civil society and the rule of law. The organization rehabilitates and supports victims of political repression and their families; publishes information and analysis on contemporary human rights violations; and carries out peacekeeping activities to resolve interethnic and interfaith conflicts. It comprises a network of more than 50 Memorial organizations in the Russian Federation, co-ordinated by Russian Memorial in Moscow. The Memorial Human Rights Centre has offices in four regions of Russia and 39 Migration and Law Network outlets. There are six Memorial organizations in Ukraine, and one each in Belgium, the Czech Republic (Czechia), France and Germany. The Moscow office houses an archive, a museum of life in Gulag forced labour camps, and a library containing more than 35,000 books and leaflets; and maintains archives and 15 databases, with access for researchers and journalists.

Geographical Area of Activity: Belarus, Belgium, Czechia, France, Germany, Italy, Russian Federation, Ukraine.

Publications: Annual Report.

Board: Jan Z. Raczynski (Chair.).

Contact Details: 127006, Moscow, ul. Karetny ryad, House 5/10; tel. (495) 650-78-83; e-mail nipc@memo.ru; internet www.memo.ru.

Non-Governmental Ecological Vernadsky Foundation

Established in 1995 by the OAO Gazprom Company, the OAO UKOIL Oil Company, RAO EES Russii, the Russian Federation Savings Bank, the Ministry of Public Health of the Russian Federation and the Russian Academy of Medical Sciences.

Activities: Works in the fields of environmental conservation, education and socially responsible business. The Foundation supports experts' efforts to strengthen environmental protection in the Russian Federation; sponsors international exhibitions and promotes partnerships with major foreign and domestic organizations; and supports events in Russia and abroad, including conferences, forums and roundtables on sustainable development. It awards scholarships and has established 14 regional competition committees at leading universities in Russia, Ukraine, Belarus and Bulgaria. The V. I. Vernadsky Medal for Contributions to Sustainable Development recognizes outstanding service in the area of sustainable economic, social and environmental development; and the V. I. Vernadsky Prize (f. 2003) is also awarded. Has branches in the Czech Republic (Czechia) and Kazakhstan (f. 2014).

Geographical Area of Activity: Russian Federation, Europe.

Restrictions: No grants to individuals.

Publications: Annual Report; *Noosphere* (journal); *The Ecological Encyclopedia*; scientific, educational, environmental and sustainable development literature.

Principal Staff: CEO Plyamina Olga Vladimirovna.

Contact Details: 119017 Moscow, POB 23, ul. B. Ordynka, 29, Bldg 1; tel. (495) 953-74-65; e-mail info@vernadsky.ru; internet www.vernadsky.ru.

Our Future—Foundation for Regional Social Programmes

Established in 2007 by Vagit Alekperov, President of LUKOIL, an oil and gas company.

Activities: Offers grants and interest-free loans to social entrepreneurs and for charitable causes, in particular for children and disabled people. The Foundation organizes events including: the annual 'A Force for Good' awards; the international Social Business Day; business fairs and exhibitions; and roundtables, seminars and training courses.

Geographical Area of Activity: Russian Federation.

Publications: Annual Report; brochures; booklets.

Finance: Annual revenue 672,786,000 roubles, expenditure 599,896,000 roubles (2020).

Public Council: Vagit Y. Alekperov (Chair.).

Principal Staff: Dir Natalia Zvereva.

Contact Details: 119019 Moscow, ul. Znamenka 8/13, Bldg 2; tel. (495) 780-96-71; e-mail fund@nb-fund.ru; internet www.nb-fund.ru.

Russian International Affairs Council—RIAC

Established in 2010 by the Ministry of Foreign Affairs, the Ministry of Education and Science, the Russian Academy of Sciences, the Russian Union of Industrialists and Interfax International Information Group, as a non-profit membership organization and think tank.

Activities: Works to strengthen international peace and solidarity and resolve conflicts through conducting research in the fields of international research, migration studies and politico-military studies. Research topics include: Asia-Pacific; ecology; economy; education and science; energy; global governance; international security; multipolar world; Russia's foreign policy; society and culture; and technology. The Council promotes co-operation between Russian and foreign institutions and scholars, organizing seminars, roundtable discussions, debates, public lectures and training sessions; hosting expert meetings; and participating in international conferences.

Geographical Area of Activity: International.

Publications: Annual Report; newsletter; *Handbook of the Russian International Affairs Council*; monographs; policy notes; reports; working papers; blog; books.

Finance: Annual budget 98.8m. roubles (2020).

Board of Trustees: Sergey Lavrov (Chair.).

Principal Staff: Pres. Igor Ivanov.

RUSSIAN FEDERATION

Contact Details: 119049 Moscow, 4th Dobryninsky Pereulok, Bldg 8; tel. (495) 225-62-83; e-mail welcome@russiancouncil.ru; internet russiancouncil.ru.

Russian LGBT Network

Established in 2006; an interregional human rights NGO.

Activities: Promotes equal rights and respect for human dignity, irrespective of sexual orientation or gender identity. The Network supports organizations that represent LGBTIQ+ people; develops regional initiatives, and national and international advocacy groups; monitors and documents violence and discrimination against LGBTIQ+ people; and provides emergency assistance, psychosocial support and legal services. It organizes conferences, roundtable discussions, seminars, trainings and an annual forum. Operates in 13 regions.

Geographical Area of Activity: Russian Federation.

Publications: Annual Report; brochures; reports.

Principal Staff: Chair. Igor Kochetkov.

Contact Details: 191040 St Petersburg, Ligovsky pr. 87; tel. (812) 454-64-52; e-mail info@lgbtnet.org; internet lgbtnet.org.

Sistema Charitable Foundation

Established in 2004 by Sistema PJSFC, a private investment company.

Activities: The foundation's programmes focus on innovative and impactful solutions in education, the arts and culture, and social affairs. The main project, 'Lift to the Future', aims to provide better career opportunities for young people. Social initiatives are represented by a comprehensive programme engaging the local community in regional social festivals, education, popularization of sports and development of the corporate volunteer movement. Also promotes ecological behaviour change in compliance with the environmental protection agenda.

Geographical Area of Activity: Russian Federation.

Restrictions: Not currently accepting applications for funding from organizations or individuals.

Publications: Annual Report.

Finance: Annual programme expenditure 405,718 roubles (2021).

Board: Svetlana Matveeva (Chair.).

Principal Staff: Pres. Larisa Pastukhova; Exec. Dir Shamil Alimkhanov.

Contact Details: Moscow, st. Malaya Dmitrovka, d.18, p.1; tel. (495) 737-44-19; e-mail info@bf.sistema.ru; internet bf.sistema.ru.

Skolkovo Foundation—Foundation for Development of the Center for the Development and Commercialization of New Technologies

Established in 2010 to manage the Skolkovo Innovation Center; a non-profit organization, part of the VEB.RF group of development institutions.

Activities: Fosters entrepreneurship and innovation in energy efficiency, biomedicine, computer, nuclear and space technologies. The Foundation oversees development of the Skolkovo Innovation Center, which also hosts sports and cultural events, the Technopark science and technology park, Skolkovo Institute of Technology (Skoltech) research university and Skolkovo City, incorporating a conference centre, and academic and residential buildings. It co-operates on scientific research and development with international academic institutions and technology companies; and has an office in Vladivostok.

Geographical Area of Activity: Russian Federation.

Publications: Annual Report.

Finance: Total revenue 508,000m. roubles (2023).

Council: Victor Vekselberg (Chair.), Prof. Dr Wolfgang A. Herrmann (Deputy Chair.).

Management Board: Igor Drozdov (Chair.); Viktor Dmitriev (Vice-Chair.).

Principal Staff: Chair. Arkady Dvorkovich.

Contact Details: 121205 Moscow, Mozhajskij region, ul. Nobelya 5, Skolkovo Innovation Center; tel. (495) 956-00-33; e-mail skfoundation@sk.ru; internet sk.ru/fund-skolkovo/about-skolkovo.

Victoria Children Foundation

Established in 2004 by Nikolai Alexandrovich Tsvetkov to ensure the wellbeing and sustainable future of, and equal opportunities for, disadvantaged children in the Russian Federation and the former USSR.

Activities: Programmes include: prevention of abandonment of children; support and family placement services for abandoned children; life skills development for children in care; and a supportive social environment for disadvantaged children. The Foundation runs programmes in 47 regions of the Russian Federation.

Geographical Area of Activity: Russian Federation.

Publications: Annual Report.

Finance: Annual income 46.3m. roubles, programme expenditure 91.0m. roubles (2021).

Board: Tatiana D. Letunova (Chair.); Valentina Vasilievna Roldugina (Deputy Chair.).

Contact Details: 125040 Moscow, 3rd Yamskogo Polya St, 24; tel. (495) 290-36-08; e-mail info@victoriacf.ru; internet victoriacf.ru; vk.com/cfvictoria.

Vladimir Potanin Foundation

Established in 1999 by Vladimir Potanin, CEO of Norilsk Nickel and founder of Interros Company.

Activities: Fosters the development of knowledge and professionalism, encourages volunteering and individual creativity, strengthens institutions, and promotes the development of philanthropy. The Foundation provides grants to innovative museum projects; promotes the development of young university faculty members who combine teaching and research; and offers scholarships for graduate students and faculty members at 75 universities in the Russian Federation. Scholarship holders are invited to join the Foundation School personal and professional development programme. In 2019 the Center for the Development of Philanthropy was established.

Geographical Area of Activity: Russian Federation.

Finance: Annual income 3,317.3m. roubles, expenditure 1,837.0m. roubles (2020).

Board of Trustees: Larisa Zelkova (Chair.).

Foundation Council: Marina Mikhailova (Chair.).

Principal Staff: CEO Oksana Oracheva; Sec. Polina Masenkova.

Contact Details: 125375 Moscow, ul. Tverskaya 16, Bldg 1; tel. (495) 149-30-18; e-mail info@fondpotanin.ru; internet www.fondpotanin.ru.

Volnoe Delo—Oleg Deripaska Foundation

Established in 2008 by Oleg Deripaska, Chairman of Basic Element, an industrial conglomerate, and President of UC RUSAL, an aluminium company.

Activities: Carries out activities in the fields of education and science, including a robotics engineering education programme for children and young people aged 6–26 years; PROFEST (formerly RoboFest), a festival of scientific and technical creativity; and a science competition for young science graduates and undergraduates of Moscow State University (MSU). The Foundation awards scholarships and grants for students and teachers of the MSU Physics and Mechanical Engineering Department. The Foundation also supports research carried out by the Institute of Archaeology and the Institute of General History of the Russian Academy of Sciences at Phanagoria in Greece, and in 2014 established the Phanagoria Scientific and Cultural Centre. Other initiatives include: sponsoring regional cultural events by the Moscow Art Theatre School-Studio; territorial development of urban infrastructure, support for education, culture, health and sports, volunteering

and local entrepreneurship in the Ust-Labinsk district; and the construction of 'Povodog' animal shelters for stray dogs. Operates in more than 50 regions in the Russian Federation.
Geographical Area of Activity: Greece, Russian Federation.
Finance: Total giving since 2008 10,600m. roubles.
Board of Trustees: Oleg Deripaska (Chair.).
Principal Staff: CEO Ekaterina Nikitina.
Contact Details: 121170 Moscow, Kutuzovskiy Prospekt 36, Bldg 23; tel. (495) 653-81-43; e-mail info@volnoe-delo.ru; internet www.volnoe-delo.ru.

RWANDA

FOUNDATIONS AND NON-PROFITS

Imbuto Foundation
Established in 2001 as Protection and Care of Families against HIV/AIDS—PACFA by First Lady Jeanette Kagame; present name adopted in 2007.
Activities: Priority programmes are: health, particularly in the areas of adolescent sexual and reproductive health rights, family planning and reducing rates of HIV infection; education, including early childhood development, literacy and digital literacy, and girls' education; and youth programmes, including preparing for university applications and support for survivors of the 1994 Genocide. Other initiatives include: ArtRwanda–Ubuhanzi, a talent search project to promote cultural and creative work; Imali, supporting vulnerable groups through teaching them agricultural skills; and the YouthConnekt and Celebrating Young Rwandan Achievers awards for personal and professional achievements. The Foundation offers scholarships for secondary education to students from economically vulnerable backgrounds; and under the Innovation Accelerator (iAccelerator) programme provides seed funding, training and skills development to young entrepreneurs working on population development challenges.
Geographical Area of Activity: Rwanda.
Publications: Annual Report; newsletter; reports.
Finance: Annual income US $18.0m., expenditure $22.5m. (30 June 2023).
Board: First Lady Jeanette Kagame (Chair.); Diana Louise Ofwona (First Vice-Chair.); Rose Rwabuhihi (Second Vice-Chair.).
Contact Details: Office of the First Lady, Kacyiru, Kigali; tel. 252552064; e-mail info@imbutofoundation.org; internet www.imbutofoundation.org.

SAINT LUCIA

FOUNDATIONS AND NON-PROFITS

The Do-Nation Foundation, Inc
Founded in 2018.
Activities: A non-profit organization that focuses on social issues, especially those impacting young people, including environmental awareness, poverty and education.
Geographical Area of Activity: St Lucia.
Principal Staff: CEO Diane Felicien.
Contact Details: Castries; tel. 727-8231; e-mail donationfoundationslu@gmail.com.

National Community Foundation
Established in 2002 by the National Insurance Corpn.
Activities: Promotes local philanthropy. The Foundation receives and distributes philanthropic funds; supports poor or disadvantaged people, and children's education. Main programmes include: Youth at Risk; Older Persons, providing food; Scholarship Program, for secondary school pupils; Health Care, for seriously ill people; Homeless, providing grants to victims of man-made and natural disasters; Persons with Disabilities, funding Special Education Centres; and Chess Program, promoting the game of chess in primary and secondary schools and the wider community.
Geographical Area of Activity: St Lucia.
Principal Staff: Exec. Dir Michelle Phillips; Deputy Chair. Dr Thecla Lewis.
Contact Details: Godfrey Hubert James Bldg, 1st Floor, 19–23 High St, POB CP 5390, Castries; tel. 453-6661; e-mail stluciancf@candw.lc; internet www.ncfstlucia.lc.

SAUDI ARABIA

FOUNDATIONS AND NON-PROFITS

Al Basar International Foundation

Established in 1989.

Activities: Provides therapeutic, preventative and educational programmes to manage blindness and visual impairment in developing countries. The Al Basar Caravans mobile outreach programme organizes free 'eye camps', which provide mass eye care in remote areas, including pre-operative evaluation, optical dispensing, medical and surgical management and post-operative care. The Foundation also maintains a network of eye hospitals and trains eye care personnel at a training institute in Pakistan and an ophthalmic technical college in Sudan. Maintains offices in Dubai (United Arab Emirates) and London (UK).

Geographical Area of Activity: Afghanistan, Bangladesh, Pakistan, Niger, Nigeria, Sudan, United Arab Emirates, UK, Yemen.

Publications: Annual Report.

Principal Staff: Sec.-Gen. Dr Adel Abdul Aziz Al-Rashoud; Exec. Dir Dr Farid Muhammad Al-Yagout.

Contact Details: POB 40030, Al-Khobar 31952; tel. (3) 895-5800; e-mail albasarint@yahoo.com; internet al-basar.com.

SAUDI ARABIA

Alwaleed Philanthropies

Established in 1996 by Prince Alwaleed Bin Talal as three Alwaleed Bin Talal Foundations operating in Saudi Arabia, Lebanon and internationally; the foundations were reorganized as the Alwaleed Philanthropies in 2015.

Activities: Operates internationally in the areas of community development; empowerment of women and young people; disaster relief; and intercultural and interfaith dialogue through higher education. The organization funds the Alwaleed Center for Muslim-Christian Understanding at Georgetown University and sponsors the Alwaleed Bin Talal Islamic Studies Program at Harvard University, USA. Alwaleed Philanthropies Lebanon provides philanthropic and humanitarian aid in Lebanon. It supports projects in 189 countries.

Geographical Area of Activity: International.

Restrictions: No grants to individuals.

Board of Trustees: Prince Alwaleed Bin Talal bin Abdulazia al Sa'ud (Chair.); Prince Khalid bin Alwaleed al Sa'ud (Vice-Chair.).

Contact Details: Kingdom Centre Tower, Riyadh; tel. (11) 211-0000; e-mail general@alwaleedphilanthropies.org; internet www.alwaleedphilanthropies.org.

Gulf Research Center—GRC

Established in 2000 by Dr Abdulaziz Sager, a business person, in Dubai, United Arab Emirates; an independent research institute.

Activities: Carries out research on Gulf Co-operation Council countries and the wider Gulf region. The Center promotes co-operation, disseminates information and issues publications. It has a branch in Riyadh.

Geographical Area of Activity: International.

Publications: Annual Report; *Gulf Yearbook*; *Araa Magazine*; GLMM Research Papers; Event Papers; Gulf Papers; Research Bulletins; books; sector reports.

Finance: Total revenue US $103.8m., expenditure $97.0m. (to 31 Dec. 2024).

Board: Dr Abdulaziz O. Sager (Chair.).

Principal Staff: Exec. Man. Dr Christian Koch.

Contact Details: 30 Rayat Al-Itihad St (19), POB 2134, Jeddah 21451; tel. (12) 651-1999; e-mail info@grc.net; internet www.grc.net.

International Organization for Relief, Welfare & Development—IORWD

Established in 1978, as the International Islamic Relief Organization of Saudi Arabia, by the Muslim World League.

Activities: Aids victims of natural disasters and war, and other displaced people, on an international scale. It runs programmes to provide religious teaching, vocational training and education, healthcare, social support and water infrastructure; and sponsors projects and small businesses whose work contributes to its objectives. Maintains offices in Saudi Arabia and worldwide.

Geographical Area of Activity: Worldwide.

Board of Directors: Dr Mohammed bin Abdulkarim bin Abdulaziz Al-Issa (Chair.).

Contact Details: Hail St, al-Ruwais District, opp. the Presidency of Meteorology and Environment, Jeddah; POB 14843, Jeddah 21434; tel. (2) 651-2333.

King Faisal Foundation

Founded in 1976 to use the estate of the late King Faisal bin Abdulaziz Al Sa'ud for charitable purposes.

Activities: Operates nationally and internationally in the fields of science and medicine, and the arts and humanities, chiefly by awarding the King Faisal International Prizes (for Arabic Language & Literature, Islamic Studies, Service to Islam, and Science), with prizes totalling approximately US $1m. The Foundation finances the King Faisal Centre for Research and Islamic Studies (f. 1983), the King Faisal School, the female-only Effat University and the Alfaisal University (a private university established in partnership with a US technology institute), and scholarships.

Geographical Area of Activity: Worldwide.

Restrictions: Nominations for the King Faisal International Prize are not acceptable from political institutes.

Finance: Total programme spending since 1976 approx. 2,400m. Saudi riyals (2020).

Board of Trustees: HRH Prince Muhammad al-Faisal (Chair.).

Principal Staff: CEO HRH Prince Khalid Al-Faisal; Sec.-Gen. HH Prince Bandar bin Sa'ud bin Khalid Al Sa'ud.

Contact Details: King Fahd Branch Rd, Al Olaya, Riyadh 12212; POB 352, Riyadh 11411; tel. (11) 465-2255; e-mail info@kff.com; internet www.kff.com.

King Khalid Foundation

Established in 2001 by the family of King Khalid bin Abdulaziz Al Sa'ud.

Activities: Promotes equality of opportunity through addressing the root causes of exclusion and empowering vulnerable people, such as low-income families, widows and divorced women, people with additional needs and the unemployed. The Foundation supports individuals, non-profit organizations, companies and initiatives working to solve social problems at scale. It offers Equal Opportunity Grants and Social Entrepreneurship Grants; and provides training, expertise and mentorship.

Geographical Area of Activity: Saudi Arabia.

Board of Trustees: HRH Prince Abdullah bin Khalid bin Abdulaziz Al Sa'ud (Pres.); HRH Prince Faisal bin Khalid bin Abdulaziz Al Sa'ud (Chair.); HRH Princess Moudi bint Khalid bin Abdulaziz Al Sa'ud (Gen. Sec.).

Principal Staff: CEO HH Princess Nouf bint Mohammed bin Abdullah Al Sa'ud.

Contact Details: POB 22, Riyadh 11333; tel. (11) 202-0202; e-mail info@kkf.org.sa; internet kkf.org.sa.

Mohammed bin Salman Foundation—Misk Foundation

Established in 2011 by HRH Prince Mohammed bin Salman.

Activities: Fosters learning and leadership among young people in Saudi Arabia, carrying out activities in four main areas: education, media, culture and technology. The Foundation offers fellowships to Saudi undergraduate and graduate students studying at universities in the United Kingdom and the USA. It convenes the Misk Global Forum (f. 2016), a global platform that focuses on future employment skills, entrepreneurship and global citizenship; and comprises the Misk Art Institute (f. 2017), which seeks to encourage the production and appreciation of Saudi and Arab art.

Geographical Area of Activity: Saudi Arabia.

Board: HRH Prince Mohammed bin Salman bin Abdulaziz (Chair.).

Principal Staff: CEO Dr Badr Al-Bader.

Contact Details: POB 10076, Riyadh 11433; e-mail contact@misk.org.sa; internet www.misk.org.sa.

Sulaiman Bin Abdul Aziz Bin Saleh Al Rajhi Foundation

Established in 1983 by Sulaiman Bin Abdul Aziz Bin Saleh Al Rajhi, a business person.

Activities: Supports around 1,200 charity projects in more than 130 towns and cities, operating through a network of 13 regional branches. The Foundation offers grants to community development organizations. Special projects include Haron, which builds the capacity of charitable and social institutions; Rushd, focusing on the health, welfare and education of orphans; the House of Expertise for Social Studies, which carries out research on building the capacity of family associations; Ataat Alilm Ltd, which invests in Islamic education; and International Curricula, which develops Arabic and Islamic curricula and teaching materials in Arabic and English.

Geographical Area of Activity: Saudi Arabia.

Publications: Newsletter.

Contact Details: POB 25759, Riyadh 11476; tel. (11) 241-1600; e-mail info@rf.org.sa; internet rf.org.sa.

Sultan bin Abdulaziz Al Sa'ud Foundation

Established in 1995 by HRH Prince Sultan bin Abdulaziz Al Sa'ud as a private non-profit organization.

Activities: Operates in the fields of healthcare, social welfare and education through four principal programmes: the Sultan Bin Abdulaziz Humanitarian City rehabilitation hospital and medical centre; the Science and Technology Centre; the Programme for Medical and Educational Telecommunications (Medunet); and the Special Education Programme. Awards the International Prize for Water, awarded every two years for scientific and technological solutions to water-related problems, comprising a prize for creativity worth 1m. Saudi riyals and four other prizes worth 500,000 Saudi riyals each.

Geographical Area of Activity: Saudi Arabia.

Board of Trustees: HRH Prince Khalid bin Sultan bin Abdulaziz (Chair.).

Principal Staff: Sec.-Gen. HRH Prince Faisal bin Sultan bin Abdulaziz.

Contact Details: POB 25759, Riyadh 11476; tel. (11) 482-7663; e-mail question@sultanfoundation.org.

SENEGAL

FOUNDATIONS AND NON-PROFITS

Enda Tiers Monde—Environnement et Développement du Tiers-Monde (Enda Third World—Environment and Development Action in the Third World)

Established in 1972.

Activities: An international network of 24 member organizations. Programme areas include: agriculture; gender; young people and education; natural resources; sustainable cities; energy and climate; trade and integration; solidarity finance; health; governance and democracy; leadership; and water and sanitation. The organization has branches in Africa, South America and Asia; and representative offices in Europe.

Geographical Area of Activity: Africa, Asia, Europe, South America.

Publications: Annual Report; reports.

Board of Directors: Marième Sow (Chair.).

Contact Details: Complexe SICAP Point E, Bâtiment B, 1er étage, ave Cheikh Anta Diop, BP 3370, Dakar 17000; tel. 33-869-9948; e-mail se@endatiersmonde.org; internet endatiersmonde.org.

Fondation Léopold Sédar Senghor (Léopold Sédar Senghor Foundation)

Founded in 1974 by Léopold Sédar Senghor, former President of Senegal, to preserve national heritage and support training and research, especially in the areas of culture and international co-operation.

Activities: Operates nationally and internationally in the fields of the arts and humanities, education, law and human rights, and science and technology, through self-conducted programmes, research, grants, literary prizes, conferences, training courses and publications. The Foundation maintains a library and museum. It has membership organizations in Brazil, Côte d'Ivoire, France, Switzerland and the USA; and a branch in Limoges, France.

Geographical Area of Activity: Worldwide.

Publications: *Éthiopiques* (2 a year); *Lettres Majeures* (bulletin).

Principal Staff: Chair. Moustapha Niasse; Exec. Dir Dr Alphonse Raphaël Ndiaye.

Contact Details: Rue Alpha Hachamiyou Tall X René Ndiaye, Dakar; tel. 33-849-1414; internet fondationleopoldsedarsenghor.org.

Fondation Rurale pour l'Afrique de l'Ouest—FRAO (West African Rural Foundation—WARF)

Established in 1993.

Activities: Operates internationally, supporting community organizations working in the fields of rural development, the environment and human rights. The Foundation promotes research and collaboration between researchers in the area of agricultural and rural development research; and provides training materials and technical and management advice. It also fosters links between organizations involved in rural development; and lobbies on behalf of rural organizations and individuals.

Geographical Area of Activity: West Africa.

Publications: Annual Report; reports.

Principal Staff: Exec. Dir Ngouye Fall.

Contact Details: 10103 rue MZ 25, Mermoz Pyrotechnic Extension Lot 12, BP 5177, Dakar; tel. 33-865-0060; e-mail secretary@frao.org; internet frao.org.

Fondation Sonatel

Established in 2002 by Sonatel, a telecommunications provider; part of the Fondation Orange (q.v.) group.

Activities: Runs three main programmes: health, including disease prevention, free medical care for the elderly education, care of children with disabilities, providing medical equipment, and support for medical education, training and research; education, with a focus on disadvantaged children and girls' education; and local culture and heritage conservation, providing training in cultural activities and organizing festivals.

Geographical Area of Activity: Senegal.

Principal Staff: Gen. Man. Coura Sow.

Contact Details: Villa 2, Cité Texaco, en face Librairie 4, Vents, Fann Mermoz, route de Ouakam, Dakar; tel. 33-865-1183; e-mail fondationsonatel@orange-sonatel.com; internet fondationsonatel.com.

Open Society Africa

Established in 2000; an independent foundation, part of the Open Society Foundations (q.v.) network.

Activities: Provides funding to organizations working in the areas of: the fight against corruption; civil society; elections and government; justice and the rule of law; media; minority rights; natural resources and governance; and provision of public services, including health and education. The organization supports national projects and those involving more than one country in Africa. Maintains offices in Kenya and South Africa.

Geographical Area of Activity: Benin, Côte d'Ivoire, Ghana, Guinea, Liberia, Mali, Niger, Nigeria, Senegal, Sierra Leone, Uganda.

Publications: Annual Report; discussion papers and reports.

PAN Africa—Pesticide Action Network Africa

Founded in 1996 as a regional centre of the PAN International network (f. 1982).

Activities: Promotes protection of the environment and pesticide-free sustainable agriculture through raising awareness of the problems and dangers of indiscriminate pesticide use in agriculture; and working to strengthen legislation in Africa on the use of toxic pesticides. The Network disseminates information on pesticides and their alternatives; and organizes workshops and training sessions. It maintains a Regional Documentation Centre and a database on pesticides, sustainable agriculture and agroecology.

Geographical Area of Activity: Africa.

Publications: Annual Report; newsletter; *Pesticides & Alternatives* (newsletter in French and English, 3 a year); briefings; studies; brochures; *PAN Africa* (bulletin).

Principal Staff: Regional Co-ordinator Abou Thiam.

Contact Details: 575 Cité El hadji Malick SY, Ouakam; POB 15938, Dakar-Fann; tel. 33-825-4914; e-mail panafrica@pan-afrique.org; internet pan-afrique.org.

SERBIA

CO-ORDINATING BODIES

Gradjanske inicijative—GI (Civic Initiatives)

Established in 1996 by a team of NGO activists who had contributed to non-nationalist democratic opposition and anti-war movements since 1990.

Activities: Strengthens civil society in Serbia through promotion of democracy, education and supporting active citizenship. The organization provides development, training and information to NGOs to enable them to develop the third sector in Serbia with enhanced sustainability. Activities include providing education, professional advice, technical assistance and information pertinent to the areas of interest of NGOs.

Geographical Area of Activity: Serbia.

Publications: *NGO Sector in Serbia*; *Civil Society and Democracy*; *Human Rights Monitoring*; *Little Dictionary of Parliamentary Terms*; *Market Democracy*; *Financing of the Political Parties in Europe*; *Membership in the Council of Europe*; *The Dictionary of Democracy*; *Trade Unions in Europe*; and other materials.

Finance: Annual income 95.4m. Serbian dinars, expenditure 94.6m. Serbian dinars (31 Dec. 2023).

Principal Staff: Exec. Dir Maja Stojanović.

Contact Details: 11000 Belgrade, Kneza Miloša 4; tel. (11) 3284188; e-mail civin@gradjanske.org; internet www.gradjanske.org.

Srpski Filantropski Forum (Serbian Philanthropy Forum)

Established in 2010 informally and registered in 2017; an umbrella organization of foundations and donors.

Activities: A platform for long-term social investment. In 2018 the Forum initiated National Giving Day. It has 37 member foundations, companies and CSOs.

Geographical Area of Activity: Serbia.

Publications: Newsletter.

Principal Staff: Exec. Dir Veran Matić; Co-ordinator Jelena Bratić.

Contact Details: 11000 Belgrade, Obilićev venac 2/I; tel. (11) 4057511; e-mail office@filantropskiforum.com; internet www.srpskifilantropskiforum.org.

FOUNDATIONS AND NON-PROFITS

Balkan Security Platform—BSP (Konzorcijum nezavisnih istraživačkih centara Zapadnog Balkana)

Established in 2009 as an initiative of the Belgrade Centre for Security Policy; formally established in 2016.

Activities: Works to strengthen the role of civil society through carrying out research and analysis on regional security sector reform. The platform comprises six CSOs: Belgrade Centre for Security Policy (Serbia); Centre for Security Studies (Bosnia and Herzegovina); Eurothink—Centre for European Strategies (North Macedonia); Institute Alternative (Montenegro); Institute for Democracy and Mediation (Albania); and the Kosovar Centre for Security Policy (Kosovo). Programme areas include: corruption; defence; democratic governance; intelligence; EU regional co-operation; police; security and human rights; and transparency. It maintains a digital library.

Geographical Area of Activity: Western Balkans.

Publications: Policy briefs; *Security Community in the Western Balkans*.

Contact Details: c/o Belgrade Center for Security Policy, 11000 Belgrade, Đure Jakšića 6/5; tel. (11) 3287226.

European Center for Peace and Development—ECPD

Established in 1985 following an agreement between the UN University for Peace and the Government of Yugoslavia.

Activities: Works towards finding solutions for acute and chronic problems of development and the quality of life in specific regions of Europe, particularly South-Eastern Europe, with an emphasis on countries in transition. The Center carries out interdisciplinary work across seven interconnected programmes: development of human resources; development of natural resources; social and economic development; scientific and technological development; sustainable development; cultural development; and management, international co-operation and development. It organizes and conducts post-graduate studies; runs projects in co-operation with universities and institutions in host countries, and with international organizations; carries out research; hosts international scientific meetings, conferences, symposia and seminars; provides consulting services; and disseminates information.

Geographical Area of Activity: Canada, Europe (in particular South-Eastern Europe), USA.

Publications: Research reports; conference proceedings; books.

Finance: Funded through donations from national and international organizations, tuition and registration fees.

Council: Frederico Mayor Zaragoza (Pres.); Prof. Dr Vlado Kambovski, Ouided Bouchamaoui (Vice-Pres).

Principal Staff: Exec. Dir Dr Negoslav P. Ostojić.

Contact Details: 11000 Belgrade, Terazije 41; tel. (11) 3246041; e-mail office@ecpd.org.rs; internet www.ecpd.org.rs.

Fondacija Braća Karić (Braća Karić Foundation)

Established in 1992, as the BK Foundation, by Milanka Karić, a politician, to help others and promote Serbian national culture and tradition.

Activities: Operates in the areas of: the arts and humanities; education; international affairs; law and human rights; medicine and health; and social welfare. The Foundation awards prizes (the Karić Brothers Awards) and supports humanitarian projects, international co-operation and family development; and issues publications.
Geographical Area of Activity: Europe, Montenegro, Serbia, USA.
Publications: *Bulletin* (newsletter); books.

Board of Directors: Danica B. Karić (Pres.).

Contact Details: 11040 Belgrade, Vase Pelagića 23; tel. (11) 63310606; e-mail kf@karicfoundation.com; internet www.karicfoundation.com.

SEYCHELLES

FOUNDATIONS AND NON-PROFITS

James Michel Foundation
Established in 2017 by James Michel, the former President of Seychelles.
Activities: Promotes the 'Blue Economy' nationally and internationally, through the James Michel Blue Economy Research Institute. The Foundation raises awareness about the impact of climate change; promotes environmental conservation, sustainable development, renewable energy, and maritime and food security; and advocates in support of small island states. Scholarships are offered for post-secondary school graduates and mid-career professionals in the Seychelles to undertake study on the Blue Economy. It houses a presidential library and museum, organizing public events and sponsoring research conferences.
Geographical Area of Activity: International.
Publications: Magazine.
Executive Committee: James Alix Michel (Exec. Chair.); Prof. Dennis Hardy (Vice-Chair.); David Savy (Treas.); Doreen Monthy (Sec.).
Contact Details: POB 1605, Bel Eau, Mahé; tel. 2599622; e-mail info@jamesmichelfoundation.org; internet www.jamesmichelfoundation.org.

Seychelles Islands Foundation—SIF
Established in 1979 by the Government of Seychelles as a public trust.
Activities: The Seychelles Islands Foundation (SIF) manages and protects the Seychelles' UNESCO World Heritage Sites of Aldabra Atoll in the far south of the archipelago and the Vallée de Mai on Praslin Island, as well as the Fond Ferdinand nature reserve. SIF has been a pioneer in nature conservation as the longest running environmental organization in Seychelles.
Geographical Area of Activity: Seychelles.
Publications: Annual Report; newsletter; scientific papers.
Trustees: Hon. Bernard Georges (Chair.).
Principal Staff: CEO Dr Frauke Fleischer-Dogley.
Contact Details: La Ciotat Bldg, Mont Fleuri, POB 853, Victoria; tel. 4321735; e-mail info@sif.sc; internet www.sif.sc.

SINGAPORE

CO-ORDINATING BODIES

Asia Philanthropy Circle—APC
Established in 2015 by Stanley Tan, Cherie Nursalim and Laurence Lien, Chair of the Lien Foundation (q.v.).
Activities: A membership platform for Asian philanthropists to collaborate on in-country and cross-border projects. The Circle has 59 members.
Geographical Area of Activity: Asia.
Restrictions: Membership by invitation only.
Publications: *APC Philanthropy Guide Series;* multisector partnership guides; talent development research for social sector.
Finance: Total assets S $2.4m.; Annual income S $1.9m., expenditure S $1.6m. (30 June 2022).
Board: Laurence Lien (Chair. and Acting CEO).
Principal Staff: Deputy CEO Carol Tan; Deputy Dir Lucy Tan.
Contact Details: Braddell House, #05-01, 1 Lorong 2 Toa Payoh, Singapore 319637; tel. 64710107; e-mail office@asiaphilanthropycircle.org; internet asiaphilanthropycircle.org.

Community Foundation of Singapore
Established in 2008.
Activities: Promotes local philanthropy, connecting donors to charitable organizations and non-profit organizations at community level. The Foundation has established 187 donor-advised funds, working with more than 400 charities; and makes grants in the areas of: animal welfare; the arts and heritage; children; education; the environment; families; health; people with disabilities; seniors; sport; and young people.
Geographical Area of Activity: Singapore.
Publications: Annual Report; *Change Matters* (quarterly newsletter); brochure.
Finance: Total income S $52.2m., expenditure S $22.9m. (31 March 2023).
Board of Directors: Christine Ong (Chair.); Lam Yi Young (Vice-Chair.).
Principal Staff: CEO Paul Tan.
Contact Details: 6 Eu Tong Sen St, #04-88 The Central, Singapore 059817; tel. 65509529; e-mail contactus@cf.org.sg; internet www.cf.org.sg.

FOUNDATIONS AND NON-PROFITS

Asian Venture Philanthropy Network—AVPN
Established in 2011 by Doug Miller, who also founded the European Venture Philanthropy Association (now Impact Europe, q.v.) and International Venture Philanthropy Center.
Activities: Promotes and enables socially responsible investment in non-profit organizations and social enterprises. Comprises more than 600 members, including foundations, impact funds, corporations and individuals. Has an office in Hong Kong.
Geographical Area of Activity: Asia, Australia.
Publications: Newsletter; reports; case studies; toolkits.
Board: Veronica Colondam (Chair.).
Principal Staff: CEO Naina Subberwal Batra.

SLOVAKIA

Contact Details: 171 Tras St, #10-179 Union Bldg, Singapore 079025; tel. 65361824; e-mail membership@avpn.asia; internet avpn.asia.

Community Chest

Established in 1983 by Dr Ee Peng Liang, under the Singapore Council of Social Service, which was restructured as the National Council of Social Service (NCSS); part of the NCSS Charitable Fund (f. 2003).

Activities: Operates as the fundraising and social engagement arm of the National Council of Social Services. The organization raises funds for around 300 social service agencies. Main programmes focus on: empowering children with special needs and young people at risk; integrating people with disabilities into society; caring for vulnerable elderly people; supporting families in need; and supporting people with mental health conditions.

Geographical Area of Activity: Singapore.

Finance: Annual disbursements S $33.9m. (2023).

Committee: Chew Sutat (Chair.); Chew Kwee San, Ted Tan Teck Koon, Yeoh Chee Yan, Danny Koh (Vice-Chair.); Lam Yi Young (Sec.).

Principal Staff: Man. Dir Jack Lim.

Contact Details: NCSS Centre, Ulu Pandan Community Bldg, 170 Ghim Moh Rd #01-02, Singapore 279621; tel. 62102500; e-mail ncss_comchest@ncss.gov.sg; internet www.comchest.gov.sg.

Lien Foundation

Established in 1980 by Dr George Lien Ying Chow, a banker and hotelier.

Activities: Works to achieve social change through research and advocacy. National programmes focus on improving the lives of older people, children with special needs and people from low-income backgrounds. Lien AID (f. 2006) implements international development programmes, with a focus on community-based approaches to improving access to clean water and sanitation. Other affiliates include: the Lien Centre for Palliative Care (f. 2008), which conducts research and education projects in the field of palliative cancer care; the Lien Centre for Social Innovation (f. 2006), which carries out applied research and capacity-building programmes; and the Lien Ying Chow Legacy Fellowship (f. 2007), which promotes social and economic development through fostering bilateral relations between academics, professionals and senior government officials from Singapore and the People's Republic of China.

Geographical Area of Activity: East and South-East Asia.

Board: Laurence Lien (Chair.); Margaret Lien (Governor Emeritus).

Principal Staff: CEO Lee Poh Wah.

Contact Details: 435 Orchard Rd, #22-06 Wisma Atria, Singapore 38877; tel. 68363033; e-mail george@lienfoundation.org; internet www.lienfoundation.org.

Singapore International Foundation—SIF

Established in 1991 by Prof. Chang Heng Chee, a diplomat.

Activities: Seeks to connect Singaporeans and world communities in areas including business development, the arts, culture and academia. Programmes focus on: international volunteering and networking, sharing skills, knowledge and expertise through Specialist Programmes for education and healthcare professionals; and Community Programmes for volunteers from all walks of life. The Foundation also offers Arts for Good (A4G) Fellowships for artists, art administrators and social-sector professionals; and the ASEAN Youth Fellowship, a leadership development programme for emerging young leaders.

Geographical Area of Activity: People's Repub. of China, Europe, Japan, Singapore, South Asia, South-East Asia.

Publications: Annual Report; *Singapore Magazine* (quarterly); research papers; reports.

Board of Governors: Janadas Devan (Chair.); Jean Tan, Lian Wee Cheow (Vice-Chair.).

Contact Details: International Involvement Hub, 60A Orchard Rd, #04-01 Tower 1, Singapore 238890; tel. 68378710; e-mail contactus@sif.org.sg; internet www.sif.org.sg.

Temasek Foundation

Established in 2007 by Temasek, an investment company.

Activities: Operates programmes and offers grants in the areas of: public health and the training of healthcare professionals; education and teacher training; cultural diversity, through regional student exchange programmes, professional networking and the Asia Journalism Fellowship; economic development through urban management and public administration; and disaster-preparedness and post-disaster rehabilitation programmes. The Foundation also manages the Singapore Technologies Endowment Programme (f. 1997), which provides social and cultural activities for young people across Asia under the themes of neuroscience, innovation and the environment.

Geographical Area of Activity: East and South-East Asia, South Asia.

Publications: Annual Report.

Finance: Cumulative funding committed S $1,080m. (2023/24).

Board of Directors: Jennie Chua (Chair.).

Principal Staff: CEO Boon Heong Ng; Deputy CEO Saet Nyoon Woon.

Contact Details: Temasek Shophouse, 28 Orchard Rd, Singapore 238832; tel. 68286030; e-mail tfadmin@temasekfoundation.org.sg; internet www.temasekfoundation.org.sg.

SLOVAKIA

CO-ORDINATING BODIES

Ambrela—Platforma rozvojových organizácií
(Ambrela Platform of Development Organizations)

Established in 2003, as Platforma Mimovládnych Rozvojových Organizácií—MVRO, by 15 organizations; present name adopted in 2019.

Activities: Works in the fields of development co-operation, humanitarian aid, international development cooperation, global citizenship education and sustainable development. The platform provides advocacy and capacity building to member organizations, and raises public awareness. It comprises 29 organizations (17 regular members and 12 observers); and is a member of CONCORD (q.v.).

Geographical Area of Activity: Slovakia.

Publications: Annual report.

Principal Staff: Exec. Sec. Daniel Kaba.

Contact Details: 821 08 Bratislava, Miletičova 7; tel. 907235511; e-mail media@ambrela.org; internet ambrela.org.

Asociácia komunitných nadácií Slovenska (Association of Slovakian Community Foundations)
Established in 2003 by eight Slovakian community foundations to promote the activities of its members and the concept of community philanthropy in Slovakia.
Activities: Promotes the community foundation movement in Slovakia, representing its members, and informing the public about the activities of community foundations in Slovakia. Grant programmes include: Young Philanthropists, promoting community youth philanthropy; and Help for Children, to improve children's health and support children who have serious and long-term illnesses. The Association lobbies the Government for legislation favourable to the development of philanthropy in Slovakia; and co-operates with similar organizations internationally. It comprises seven member foundations; and is a member of Fórum donorov (q.v.).
Geographical Area of Activity: Slovakia.
Principal Staff: Admin. Daniela Danihelová.
Contact Details: 811 03 Bratislava, Partizánska 2; tel. (2) 5441-9998; e-mail knzm@knzm.sk; internet www.asociaciakns.sk.

Centrum pre Filantropiu (Centre for Philanthropy)
Established in 1995 as the ETP (Environmental Training Project) Slovakia Foundation; in 2002 it split into ETP Slovensko—Centre for Sustainable Development and the Centre for Philanthropy.
Activities: Promotes philanthropy and strengthens civil society, fostering social change and inclusion, active citizenry, leadership and help for disadvantaged people. Grant programmes focused on: education; sports and culture; help for disadvantaged people; regional development; and environmental conservation. The Centre works with national and international partner organizations and NGOs.
Geographical Area of Activity: Slovakia.
Publications: Annual Report; Manuals.
Finance: Total annual income €705,314 (2024).
Board of Directors: Marcel Dávid Zajac (Chair.).
Principal Staff: Man. Zuzana Thullnerová.
Contact Details: Baštová 343/5, 811 03 Bratislava; e-mail cpf@changenet.sk; internet www.cpf.sk.

Fórum donorov (Slovak Donors Forum)
Established in 1996 by the Open Society Foundation, the Sasakawa Peace Foundation (q.v.) and other NGOs; an association of Slovak and foreign grantmaking organizations; officially registered in 2000.
Activities: Promotes effective grantmaking and supports not-for-profit organizations in Slovakia. The Forum carries out research and implements outreach initiatives focused on developing corporate and individual philanthropy in Slovakia. It has seven full members; and is a member of Philea (q.v.).
Geographical Area of Activity: Slovakia.
Publications: Annual Report; newsletter; manuals.
Principal Staff: Exec. Dir Soňa Lexmanová.
Contact Details: 811 03 Bratislava, Baštová 5; tel. 908592415; e-mail donorsforum@donorsforum.sk; internet donorsforum.sk.

Nadácia Pontis (Pontis Foundation)
Established in 1997 as the successor to the Bratislava office of the USA-based Foundation for a Civil Society (q.v.).
Activities: Encourages and supports the development and long-term financial sustainability of non-profit organizations nationally and internationally, providing grants and consulting. Main programmes focus on: corporate responsibility, education, transparency and inclusiveness; and arranging pro bono training and legal aid for NGOs. The Foundation awards the Via Bona Slovakia Award for philanthropy; and administers the Business Leaders Forum, an association of businesses which promotes corporate social responsibility in Slovakia. In 2012 it supported the establishment of the Fond pre transparentné Slovensko (Transparent Slovakia Fund), an initiative of seven companies to improve transparency and promote a healthy business environment; the Fund currently has 20 members.
Geographical Area of Activity: Slovakia.
Restrictions: Grants only to registered NGOs in Slovakia; restricted support is available for individuals, travel grants and internships abroad.
Publications: Annual Report; newsletter; reports; information brochures.
Finance: Annual revenue €6.0m., expenditure €5.9m. (31 Dec. 2022).
Principal Staff: Co-CEOs Martina Kolesárová, Michal Kišša.
Contact Details: 821 08 Bratislava, Zelinárska 2; tel. (2) 5710-8111; e-mail pontis@nadaciapontis.sk; internet www.nadaciapontis.sk.

SAIA—Slovak Academic Information Agency
Established in 1990 by Olga Šubeníková and Katarína Koštálová.
Activities: Provides training and advisory services for NGOs in Slovakia. The Agency issues publications; organizes conferences and seminars; runs volunteer projects and offers the Heart on Palm volunteer awards; and collaborates regionally and internationally with similar organizations on programmes. Educational services include providing information, scholarship competitions, seminars and workshops for those wishing to study abroad. It maintains a library on the third sector and a database of scholarships and grants; and has five branch offices throughout Slovakia.
Geographical Area of Activity: Slovakia.
Publications: Annual Report; *SAIA Bulletin* (monthly information journal); *NonProfit* (monthly magazine); *International Students' Guide to the Slovak Republic*.
Finance: Annual income €3m., expenditure €3m. (31 Dec. 2023).
Board of Directors: Prof. Dr Robert Redhammer (Chair.); Stanislav Čekovský (Vice-Chair.).
Principal Staff: Exec. Dir Michal Fedák; Deputy Exec. Dir Dr Karla Zimanová.
Contact Details: 812 20 Bratislava 1, Sasinkova 10; tel. (2) 5930-4700; e-mail saia@saia.sk; internet www.saia.sk.

Slovenská Humanitná Rada (Slovak Humanitarian Council)
Established in 1990 as the Czechoslovak Council for Humanitarian Co-operation, an independent non-governmental voluntary association; after the division of Czechoslovakia into the Czech Republic (Czechia) and Slovakia, it became the Czech Council for Humanitarian Co-operation (now the Council of Humanitarian Associations, q.v.) and the Slovak Humanitarian Council.
Activities: Promotes the interests of the voluntary sector and provides humanitarian assistance to refugees. The Council supports the projects of its member organizations; offers advice on management and fund distribution; organizes training courses; disseminates information; provides consultancy services; and issues publications. It comprises 116 member organizations.
Geographical Area of Activity: Slovakia.
Restrictions: Provides financial support, aid in kind and technical assistance only for projects in the social field.
Publications: Annual Report; *Humanita* (monthly newsletter); *Carissimi* (magazine); electronic/online information; information brochures.
Governing Board: Peter Devínsky (Pres.).
Contact Details: 831 03 Bratislava, Budyšínska 1; tel. (2) 5020-0500; e-mail shr@shr.sk; internet www.shr.sk.

FOUNDATIONS AND NON-PROFITS

Ekofond SPP
Established in 2021 as the successor to EkoFond (f. 2007), a non-investment fund created by national gas supplier SPP to implement the EU's energy efficiency policy.

Activities: Supports applied research and development of technologies based on natural gas or in combination with other types of energy; and carries out self-conducted programmes in the field of education to support innovative teaching practices.

Geographical Area of Activity: Slovakia.

Publications: Newsletter.

Board of Directors: Andrea Farkašová (Chair.).

Contact Details: 821 09 Bratislava-Ružinov, Mlynské nivy 4924/44A; tel. (2) 6262-2031; e-mail info@ekofondspp.sk; internet www.ekofondspp.sk.

GLOBSEC
Established in 2013 as the Central European Strategy Council, an umbrella organization comprising the Slovak Atlantic Commission (f. 1993), the Central European Policy Institute and the Centre for European Affairs; present name adopted in 2016.

Activities: Carries out research and analysis in the fields of foreign and security policy. Main programme areas include: cybersecurity; defence and security; democracy and resilience; energy security and sustainability; the Future of Europe Programme; and the European Neighbourhood Programme. The organization comprises the GLOBSEC Institute; and GLOBSEC Academy Centre, which provides training to future analysts. It organizes conferences, talks and seminars, including the annual Bratislava Forum and the Tatra Summit; and offers training workshops for NGOs. Has an office in Brussels, Belgium.

Geographical Area of Activity: International.

Publications: Annual Report; newsletter (monthly); *GLOBSEC Weekly Roundup* (newsletter); Countering Disinformation Online (online toolkit); policy papers; reports; studies.

Exec. Committee: Róbert Vass (Pres.); John Barter (Senior Vice-Pres.).

Contact Details: 831 04 Bratislava, Polus Tower II, Vajnorská 100/B; tel. (2) 3213-7800; e-mail info@globsec.org; internet www.globsec.org.

International Visegrad Fund—IVF
Established in 2000 by the countries of the Visegrad Group (V4): the Czech Republic (Czechia), Hungary, Poland and Slovakia.

Activities: Promotes regional co-operation among the V4 countries, as well as other regions in Central and Eastern Europe and the Western Balkans, through supporting common cultural, scientific and research projects, educational projects, youth exchanges and cross-border co-operation. The Fund awards grants; postdoctoral scholarships; short-term research fellowships; and individual and group artist residencies.

Geographical Area of Activity: Eastern Partnership countries: Armenia, Azerbaijan, Belarus, Georgia, Moldova, Ukraine; V4 countries: Czechia, Hungary, Poland, Slovakia; Western Balkans: Albania, Bosnia and Herzegovina, Kosovo, Montenegro, North Macedonia and Serbia.

Publications: Annual Report; newsletter; reports.

Finance: Annual budget €11m.

Principal Staff: Exec. Dir Linda Kapustová Helbichová; Deputy Exec. Dir Maja Wawrzyk.

Contact Details: 811 02 Bratislava, Hviezdoslavovo námestie 9; tel. (2) 5920-3811; e-mail visegradfund@visegradfund.org; internet www.visegradfund.org.

Nadácia pre Deti Slovenska (Children of Slovakia Foundation)
Established in 1995 by the International Youth Foundation (q.v.) as an independent NGO.

Activities: Operates in the fields of children and young people's education and social welfare, through self-conducted programmes, grants to institutions and training courses.

Geographical Area of Activity: Slovakia.

Restrictions: Projects are limited to Slovakia.

Publications: Annual Report; newsletter; research studies; reports.

Finance: Annual income €3.2m., expenditure €3.2m. (31 Dec. 2023).

Board of Directors: Matej Ribanský (Chair.).

Principal Staff: Admin. Ondrej Gallo.

Contact Details: 811 08 Bratislava, Heydukova 3; tel. (2) 5263-6471; e-mail nds@nds.sk; internet www.nds.sk.

Nadácia Ekopolis (Ekopolis Foundation)
Established in 1991 to promote sustainable development, civil society development and public participation.

Activities: Operates in Central Europe, making grants in the areas of civil society development, rural development, environmental protection, community foundation development and women's rights. The Foundation carries out a Tree of the Year (*Strom roka*) survey. Sister foundations operate in the Czech Republic (Czechia), Hungary, Poland and Romania. Jointly with the Open Society Foundation—Bratislava (q.v.) and Karpatskou Nadáciou, it administers the Active Citizens Fund, which strengthens civil society through promoting active citizenship and improves the situation of vulnerable groups.

Geographical Area of Activity: Central Europe.

Publications: Annual Report; newsletter; reports; studies.

Finance: Annual revenue €720,399, expenditure €701,743 (2024).

Principal Staff: Dir Peter Medved.

Contact Details: 974 01 Banská Bystrica, Komenského Ekopolis Foundation 21; tel. (48) 414-5259; e-mail ekopolis@ekopolis.sk; internet www.ekopolis.sk.

Nadácia Orange (Foundation Orange)
Established in 2007 by Orange Slovensko, a telecommunications company, as the successor to Konto Orange (f. 1998); part of the Orange Foundation (q.v.) network.

Activities: Carries out activities with a focus on the development of digital skills and internet safety. The Foundation has a long-term partnership with the Centre for Philantropy. It provides financial support through strategic partnerships with NGOs or grant programmes and the Orange Digital Center.

Geographical Area of Activity: Slovakia.

Publications: Annual Report.

Finance: Annual income €537,092, expenditure €547,293 (2023).

Board of Directors: Eve Bourdeau (Chair.).

Principal Staff: Trustee Andrea Ungvölgyi.

Contact Details: 811 03 Bratislava, Baštová 5; tel. 905313313; e-mail info@nadaciaorange.sk; internet www.nadaciaorange.sk.

Nadácia SPP (SPP Foundation)
Established in 2002 by SPP, a gas supplier.

Activities: Carries out programmes in the fields of: culture and heritage; education; health; regional development; support for disadvantaged people; and volunteering. The Foundation distributes 2% of SPP's annual tax allocation. It works in partnership with the Centrum pre Filantropiu and Ekofond SPP (qq.v.).

Geographical Area of Activity: Slovakia.

Publications: Annual Report; newsletter.

Nadácia Tatra Banky

Finance: Annual income €3.5m., expenditure €3.5m. (2023).
Administrative Council: Dr Vojtech Ferencz (Chair.).
Principal Staff: Administrator Zlatica Vargová.
Contact Details: 825 11 Bratislava, Mlynské nivy 44/a; tel. 908766833; e-mail zlatica.vargova@spp.sk; internet www.nadaciaspp.sk.

Nadácia Tatra Banky (Tatra Bank Foundation)

Established in 2004 by Tatra Bank.
Activities: Programmes focus on secondary and higher education, art and the promotion of digital technologies. The Foundation awards grants and an annual prize for the arts.
Geographical Area of Activity: Slovakia.
Restrictions: Grants only to students and non-profit organizations.
Publications: Annual Report.
Finance: Annual income €1.2m., expenditure €1.2m. (31 Dec. 2023).
Board: Michal Liday (Chair.).
Principal Staff: Man. Eva Šinková; Admin. Marcel Zajac.
Contact Details: 811 03 Bratislava, Baštová 5; tel. 918669214; internet www.nadaciatatrabanky.sk.

Open Society Foundation—Bratislava (Nadácia Otvorenej Spoločnosti)

Founded in 1992; an independent foundation, part of the Open Society Foundations (q.v.) network.
Activities: Supports and strengthens democratic and liberal values and an open society through self-conducted programmes. Main programme areas include: law, the judiciary and criminal justice; Roma people social integration and education; educational reform; publishing; media; co-operation among European countries; and civil society and European integration. Jointly with Nadácia Ekopolis (q.v.) and Karpatskou Nadáciou, the Foundation administers the Active Citizens Fund, which strengthens civil society through promoting active citizenship and improves the situation of vulnerable groups. Also supports Ukraine, with the distribution of material and financial aid. Advocates for democracy, equality, active civic space and other EU fundamental values.
Geographical Area of Activity: Slovakia.
Publications: Annual Report; newsletter; guides; manuals; reports; studies.
Finance: Annual income €18.3m. expenditure €18.4m. (31 Dec. 2023).
Board of Directors: Matej Ftáčnik (Chair.).
Principal Staff: Admin. Fedor Blaščák.
Contact Details: 811 03 Bratislava, Baštová 5; tel. (2) 5441-4730; e-mail osf@osf.sk; internet www.osf.sk.

Slovak Security Policy Institute (Slovenský inštitút pre bezpečnostnú politiku)

Established in 2015 by Dr Jaroslav Naď, a security specialist and politician, and Dr Marian Majer, a defence specialist and civil servant; and independent NGO.
Activities: Conducts research and analysis on security and defence; and raises public awareness about current security challenges. Programmes include: national cybersecurity and international cybercrime; countering misinformation, disinformation and foreign propaganda, in particular about the COVID-19 pandemic and the EU; the foreign policy of Slovakia; preparing for hybrid threats; strengthening defence capabilities; and young people against extremism and radicalization. The Institute organizes educational seminars for secondary school teachers on preventing the spread of misinformation and radicalization through strengthening students' critical thinking.
Geographical Area of Activity: International.
Publications: *Zabezpeč si vedomosti* ('Secure your Knowledge', e-textbook).
Principal Staff: Dir Monika Masariková.
Contact Details: 811 01 Bratislava, Na vŕšku 8; tel. (2) 4319-1592; e-mail info@slovaksecurity.org; internet slovaksecurity.org.

Slovak-Czech Women's Fund (Slovensko-český enský fond)

Founded in 2004 by the Open Society Fund Prague and the Open Society Foundation Bratislava (qq.v.).
Activities: Provides funding to NGOs and community organizations, targeting marginalized populations, including Roma women in Slovakia; young women who exceed the age for foster care in the Czech Republic (Czechia); and young women who could benefit from leadership skills training. A sister organization operates in Prague.
Geographical Area of Activity: Czechia, Slovakia.
Restrictions: Grants only to organizations based in the Czech Repub. dealing with gender equality and women's human rights.
Publications: Annual Report.
Finance: Total disbursements since 2004 US $1.4m.
Board of Directors: Markéta Hronková (Chair.).
Principal Staff: Exec. Dir Miroslava Bobáková.
Contact Details: 811 01 Bratislava, Na vŕšku 7008/10; tel. 948768920; e-mail info@womensfund.sk; internet www.womensfund.sk.

SLOVENIA

CO-ORDINATING BODIES

SLOGA—Platforma za Razvojno Sodelovanje in Humanitarno Pomoč (Platform for Development Cooperation and Humanitarian Aid)

Established in 2005, as Slovenian Global Action—SLOGA, by 19 NGOs; present name adopted in 2006.
Activities: Connects and represents Slovenian NGOs at European and international level working in the fields of global education, humanitarian aid, international development and policy coherence. The Platform monitors and participates in formulating, implementing and evaluating Slovenian and European international development co-operation policy; and offers training. Activities are organized under working groups for climate and development, global education, human rights in development co-operation, peacebuilding, and sexual and reproductive health and rights. In 2010, in co-operation with Ustanovo SKUPAJ (TOGETHER Foundation), it established the Humanitarian Response Centre (HOC). Comprises 37 organizations; a member of CONCORD (q.v.).
Geographical Area of Activity: Europe.
Publications: *Slogopsis* (newsletter); reports.
Board: Robert Križanič (Pres.); Tanja Leskovar (Vice-Pres.).
Expert Council: Aleksandra Gačić (Pres.).
Principal Staff: Dir Max Shonhiwa Zimani.
Contact Details: 1000 Ljubljana, Povšetova 37; 1000 Ljubljana, Kopitarjeva 4; tel. (1) 434 44 02; e-mail info@sloga-platform.org; internet sloga-platform.org.

Zavod Center za Informiranje, Sodelovanje in Razvoj Nevladnih Organizacije—CNVOS (Centre for the Information Service, Co-operation and Development of NGOs)

Established in 2001 by 27 NGOs to promote the development of civil society in Slovenia.

Activities: Offers services to NGOs and builds organizations' capacity to take on activities carried out by public sector bodies. The Centre provides networking opportunities for Slovenian NGOs with European institutions and organizations from other European countries; and legal assistance to NGOs. It comprises more than 1,600 member organizations; and is a member of the European Network of National Civil Society Associations, the European Civic Forum and the Balkan Civil Society Development Network (q.v.).

Geographical Area of Activity: Slovenia.

Publications: Annual Report; *NGO-ZINE = SEKTOR* (newsletter); guides; handbooks; toolkits.

Finance: Annual revenue €563,749, expenditure €562,400 (31 Dec. 2021).

Principal Staff: Dir Goran Forbici.

Contact Details: 1000 Ljubljana, Povšetova 37; tel. (1) 542 14 22; e-mail info@cnvos.si; internet www.cnvos.si.

FOUNDATIONS AND NON-PROFITS

Mirovni Inštitut—Inštitut za sodobne družbene in politične študije (Peace Institute—Institute for Contemporary Social and Political Studies)

Established in 1991 as a research institute.

Activities: Carries out interdisciplinary research, advocacy and educational activities in the fields of social science, the humanities, anthropology and law. Main programme areas are: cultural policies; gender; human rights and minorities; media; and politics. The Institute organizes conferences, lectures, roundtables, symposia and workshops; and has a library.

Geographical Area of Activity: Europe.

Publications: Annual Report; newsletter; *Maska* (magazine); *Intolerance Monitor Report* (annual); *Workers-Punks University* (lecture series); research reports; monographs; books.

Board of Directors: Dr Lev Kreft (Pres.).

Scientific Council: Tanja Rener (Chair.).

Principal Staff: Dir Dr Iztok Šori; Man. Dir Franja Arlič.

Contact Details: 1000 Ljubljana, Metelkova 6; tel. (1) 234 77 20; e-mail info@mirovni-institut.si; internet www.mirovni-institut.si.

Slovenska znanstvena fundacija—SZF (Slovenian Science Foundation)

Set up in 1994 by the Slovenian Government and prominent Slovenian organizations.

Activities: Operates in the areas of science and technology and education, offering professional training to develop research; conducting basic and applied research; extending scientific co-operation; and organizing programmes to deepen public understanding of technology and science, including the Slovene Science Festival. The Foundation supports scientific training by providing scholarships and fellowships; awards research grants; issues publications; conducts conferences; and promotes joint research projects and exchange of scientific knowledge.

Geographical Area of Activity: Slovenia.

Publications: *Glasnik ustanove Slovenska znanstvene fundacije* (Slovenian Science Foundation Courier).

Council: Prof. Dr Jože Grdadolnik (Pres.).

Principal Staff: Dir Dr Edvard Kobal.

Contact Details: 1000 Ljubljana, Štefanova ul. 15; tel. (1) 426 35 90; e-mail edvard.kobal@u-szf.si; internet www.u-szf.si.

SOMALIA

CO-ORDINATING BODY

Somalia NGO Consortium

Established in 1999; hosted by CARE International (q.v.).

Activities: Works to improve international aid co-ordination through exchanging, producing and providing information. Activities include advocacy and co-ordination; convening working groups on health, humanitarian communication, resilience and peacebuilding and community safety; and providing access to skills development resources. The Consortium comprises 110 national and international organizations that work in Somalia and Somaliland. It has offices in Garowe, Mogadishu and Nairobi (Kenya).

Geographical Area of Activity: Kenya, Somalia.

Publications: Brochure.

Principal Staff: Dir Nimo Hassan; Deputy Dir Abdulkadir Mohamed.

Contact Details: Jigjigayar, nr Darul-Iman Mosque, Ibrahim Koodbur District, Hargeisa; tel. 634442928; e-mail comms@somaliangoconsortium.org; internet somaliangoconsortium.org.

FOUNDATIONS AND NON-PROFITS

Heritage Institute for Policy Studies—HIPS

Established in 2013.

Activities: Works in the fields of peace, the rule of law and learning. Activities fall into two main programme areas: security, justice and rights; and aid and development. The Institute informs public policy by carrying out independent and impartial research and analysis, and organizing forums and roundtables. It is a member of the Somali Research and Education Network (SomaliREN) and works closely with the Somali Observatory of Conflict and Violence Prevention.

Geographical Area of Activity: Somalia.

Publications: Annual Report (in English and Somali); newsletter; policy briefs; research reports (in English and Arabic).

Principal Staff: Exec. Dir Mursal Saney; Deputy Dir Deka Abdullahi Moalim.

Contact Details: Mogadishu; tel. 612224247; e-mail info@heritageinstitute.org; internet www.heritageinstitute.org.

Hormuud Salaam Foundation

Established in 2012, as the Hormuud Telecom Foundation, by Hormuud Telecom Somalia Ltd.

Activities: Carries out activities in the areas of education, emergency response and healthcare. The Foundation supports Hormuud University and the Al-Nur School for the Blind; and offers scholarships for undergraduate university courses of 4–6 years' duration in agriculture, education, economics, engineering, health, management, and science and technology. It established and funds a fire-fighting service, and provides emergency response services during natural disasters; supports two dialysis centres in hospitals in the capital Mogadishu; and undertakes development programmes including offering microfinance to women and disabled people, and rehabilitating farmland and irrigation channels.

Geographical Area of Activity: Somalia.

Red Sea Cultural Foundation

Established in 2003 in Italy; formally registered in Hargeysa in 2010.

Activities: Promotes literature and literacy and civil society's access to information and communication technology, supporting local libraries, educational institutions and book shops; fosters a culture of reading and creative writing among Somali-speaking peoples. The Foundation set up the Hargeysa Cultural Center (f. 2014), which has a library containing 15,000 items; and organizes the annual Hargeysa International Book Fair (f. 2008). Has an office in Pisa, Italy.

Geographical Area of Activity: Italy, Somaliland/Somalia.

Publications: Newsletter; fiction and non-fiction books and audio books; magazines; online Somali-English-Italian dictionary.

Finance: Annual budget €350,000–€400,000.

Board: Amina Mohamud Warsame (Chair.); Cabdiraxmaan Yuusuf Cartan (Vice-Chair. and Treas.).

Principal Staff: Exec. Dir Dr Jama Musse Jama.

Contact Details: c/o Hargeysa Cultural Center, 26 June St No. 2, Sha'ab Area, Hargeysa, Somaliland; tel. 633628220; e-mail info@redsea-online.org; internet www.redsea-online.org.

SOUTH AFRICA

CO-ORDINATING BODIES

CIVICUS—World Alliance for Citizen Participation

Established in 1993 in the USA; in 2002 the global headquarters moved to Johannesburg from Washington, DC, USA.

Activities: Carries out activities in three main areas: defending civic freedoms and democratic values; strengthening the power of people to organize, mobilize and take action; and empowering a more accountable, effective and innovative civil society. The Alliance has more than 15,000 members in 189 countries; with hubs in Geneva, Switzerland, and New York, USA.

Geographical Area of Activity: Worldwide.

Publications: Annual Report; newsletter; *State of Civil Society Report*; *Compendium of International Legal Instruments and Other Intergovernmental Commitments Concerning Core Civil Society Rights*; Policy Action Briefs; guidelines; reports; toolkits.

Board of Directors: Dylan Mathews (Chair.); Sonia Kwami (Vice-Chair.); Patricia Tatis (Treas.).

Principal Staff: Interim Sec.-Gen. Claire Nylander, Mandeep Tiwana.

Contact Details: 25 Owl St, 6th Floor, Johannesburg 2092; tel. (11) 8335959; e-mail info@civicus.org; internet www.civicus.org.

Global Fund for Community Foundations—GFCF

Established in 2006, with funding from the World Bank, the Ford Foundation, the Mott Foundation and other US and European funders (qq.v.).

Activities: Provides grants and technical support to community foundations and other local philanthropy institutions and to support organizations in low- and middle-income countries. Grants are typically for one year and are worth up to US $20,000. The Fund is registered as a charitable organization in the United Kingdom and South Africa.

Geographical Area of Activity: Low- and middle-income countries and occasionally in disadvantaged communities in the global North.

Restrictions: Grants only to more-established community foundations, philanthropy support organizations and community foundation networks and associations.

Finance: Annual income £2.4m., expenditure £3.1m. (31 March 2024).

Board of Trustees: Ian Bird (Chair.).

Principal Staff: Exec. Dir Jenny Hodgson.

Contact Details: 50 Oxford Rd, Parktown, Johannesburg 2193; tel. (11) 4474396; e-mail info@globalfundcf.org; internet www.globalfundcommunityfoundations.org.

South Africa Philanthropy Foundation

Established in 1997 and CAF Southern Africa; a member of the Global Alliance of the Charities Aid Foundation (q.v.). Present name adopted in 2024.

Activities: Supports and strengthens the effectiveness of the non-profit sector. The organization helps with corporate social investment and employee community involvement strategy development; and encourages and facilitates investment of money, in-kind resources and time in the NGO sector by corporate entities, companies, institutions and individuals.

Geographical Area of Activity: South Africa.

Publications: *Isiphala Online Newsletter*; reports.

Finance: Total assets 18.6m. rand; total comprehensive income 3.5m. rand (31 March 2022).

Board of Directors: Jo-Ann Pohl (Chair.).

Principal Staff: CEO Gill Bates.

Contact Details: Studio 16, Arts on Main, Maboneng Precinct, 264 Fox St, City and Suburban, Johannesburg 2094; Postnet Suite #37, Private Bag X9, Melville 2109, Johannesburg; tel. (11) 3340404; e-mail info@sa-pf.org.za; internet www.sa-pf.org.za.

FOUNDATIONS AND NON-PROFITS

ActionAid International

Founded in 1972 by Cecil Jackson Cole; moved its head office from the United Kingdom to South Africa in 2003. Part of the Disasters Emergency Committee (q.v.).

Activities: Works to achieve social justice and gender equality and to eradicate poverty. Main programmes focus on: women's rights; politics and economics; land and climate; and emergencies. Comprises 48 national organizations.

Geographical Area of Activity: International.

Restrictions: Grants only to approved partner organizations.

Publications: Annual Report; reports; books.

Finance: Total income €228.6m., expenditure €254.6m. (31 Dec. 2023).

International Board: Manzoor Hasan (Chair.); Imoni Mac Amarere (Vice-Chair.).

Principal Staff: Sec.-Gen. Arthur Laroc.

Contact Details: 28 Bath St, Heritage Bldg, Rosebank, Johannesburg; PostNet Suite No. 248, Private Bag X31, Saxonwold 2132, Johannesburg; tel. (11) 7314500; e-mail mail.jhb@actionaid.org; internet www.actionaid.org.

Africa Foundation

Founded in 1992.

Activities: Works to conserve nature and wildlife through training and in consultation with community leaders and people living in rural communities near core conservation areas. The Foundation provides support in the areas of: education, funding infrastructure development in rural schools and providing bursaries for rural young people to access higher education; healthcare, clinic development and provision of accommodation for doctors and nurses; access to water, providing boreholes, water reticulation systems and tanks, and water transportation rollers; rural business, assisting with financial literacy training, mentoring and support with achieving compliance and legal registrations; and development and conservation, engaging in conservation lessons with schoolchildren, and supporting land and marine conservation activities. Independent organizations operating in the United Kingdom and the USA.
Geographical Area of Activity: Botswana, Kenya, Mozambique, Namibia, South Africa, Tanzania, UK, USA.
Publications: Newsletter.
Board of Trustees: Sheila Surgey (Chair.).
Principal Staff: CEO Dr Andrew Venter.
Contact Details: Block F, Pinmill Farm, 164 Katherine St, Sandown, Gauteng; POB 784826, Sandton 2146; tel. (11) 8094300; e-mail contactus@africafoundation.org.za; internet www.africafoundation.org.za.

AISA—Africa Institute of South Africa
Founded in 1960 by the South African Academy of Arts and Science and the University of South Africa; in 2014 it officially became a division of the Human Sciences Research Council.
Activities: Collects, interprets and disseminates information and analyses on African affairs, with a focus on Southern Africa; and the political, socioeconomic, international and developmental issues Africa faces as a whole. The Institute conducts research; issues publications; organizes seminars and conferences; and maintains a specialized reference library of around 60,000 vols and 480 journals and a monitoring service. It collaborates with other institutions and with researchers and academics in the field of African studies worldwide; and has co-operation agreements with centres of African studies abroad (including joint research projects).
Geographical Area of Activity: Africa.
Publications: Annual Report; *AISA Newsletter*; *AISA Brochure*; *Africa Insight* (journal); concept notes; policy briefs; reports.
Principal Staff: Exec. Dir Prof. Cheryl Hendricks.
Contact Details: HSRC Bldg, 134 Pretorious St, Pretoria 0002; Bag X41, Pretoria 0001; tel. (12) 3169700; e-mail anematandani@hsrc.ac.za.

Cyril Ramaphosa Foundation
Established in 2004 as Shanduka Foundation by Shanduka Group, an investment holding company founded by Cyril Ramaphosa, a business person and politician who was elected President of South Africa in 2018; present name adopted in 2015.
Activities: Works to develop education, social cohesion and the growth of small businesses. Main programmes include: Adopt-a-School, organizing private sector support for disadvantaged schools; Kagiso Shanduka Trust, providing infrastructure development, curriculum support, social welfare and leadership training for schools at district level; Cyril Ramaphosa Education Trust, providing bursaries and mentoring for students of business degrees; and Shanduka Black Umbrellas, promoting entrepreneurship and fostering 100% black-owned businesses.
Geographical Area of Activity: South Africa.
Publications: *The ESD Handbook*; *Shanduka Blackpages* (online); blog.
Board: Cyril Ramaphosa (Chair.).
Principal Staff: CEO Mmabatho Maboya.
Contact Details: CRF House, 18 Acacia Rd, Chislehurston, Sandton; Postnet Suite 167, Private Bag X9924, Sandton 2146; tel. (11) 5926580; e-mail info@cyrilramaphosa.org; internet www.cyrilramaphosafoundation.org.

Desmond & Leah Tutu Legacy Foundation
Established in 2013 as an umbrella organization for all the initiatives that bear the names of Desmond Tutu and Leah Tutu.
Activities: Promotes peace through conflict resolution and fosters reconciliation; cultivates accountable leadership; promotes mutual respect and tolerance nationally and internationally; and enhances the health and wellbeing of people and the planet. Maintains a museum.
Geographical Area of Activity: International.
Publications: Books; newsletter.
Board of Directors: Niclas Kjellström-Matseke (Chair.).
Principal Staff: CEO Janet Jobson.
Contact Details: The Old Granary Bldg, 11 Buitenkant St, Cape Town 8001; tel. (21) 5527524; e-mail info@tutu.org.za; internet www.tutu.org.za.

Eskom Development Foundation
Established in 1998.
Activities: Contributes to the wellbeing of disadvantaged South Africans, supporting social projects and providing grants for economic development. The Foundation focuses on poverty alleviation, income generation, job creation and social wellbeing. It is active in underdeveloped areas, particularly rural regions and new urban settlements, in all the provinces of South Africa.
Geographical Area of Activity: South Africa.
Publications: Annual Report.
Principal Staff: Acting CEO Mologadi Motshele.
Contact Details: Eskom Megawatt Park, 2 Maxwell Dr., Sunninghill, Sandton, Johannesburg 2000; POB 1091, Johannesburg 2000; tel. (11) 8008111; e-mail csi@eskom.co.za; internet www.eskom.co.za/about-eskom/corporate-social-investment.

EWT—Endangered Wildlife Trust
Established in 1973; a member of the International Union for Conservation of Nature—IUCN.
Activities: The Endangered Wildlife Trust is driven by a team of conservationists working through 13 specialized programmes across Southern and East Africa, each falling under one of three key strategic pillars: saving species; conserving habitats; and benefiting people. The Trust conducts applied research; supports community-led conservation, training and building capacity; addresses human–wildlife conflict; monitors threatened species; and establishes safe spaces for wildlife range expansion. The Trust works alongside key partners, including communities, business, landowners, academic institutions and governments, to create a sustainable future for wildlife and people.
Geographical Area of Activity: East Africa, Southern Africa.
Publications: Integrated Report (annual); *Conservation Matters* (digital magazine, 11 a year); species factsheets; human–wildlife conflict guidelines; environmental and natural resource management guidelines.
Finance: Annual revenue 79.7m. rand, expenditure 78.6m. rand (30 June 2023).
Board of Trustees: Muhammad Seedat (Chair.); Dirk Ackerman (Vice-Chair.); Paul John Smith (Treas.).
Principal Staff: CEO Yolan Friedmann.
Contact Details: 27 and 28 Austin Rd, Glen Austin AH, Midrand, 1685 Gauteng; Postnet Suite 002, Private Bag X08, Wierda Park 0149, Gauteng; tel. (11) 3723600; e-mail ewt@ewt.org.za; internet www.ewt.org.za.

FirstRand Foundation

Established in 1998 by FirstRand, a financial services provider; it is separate from FirstRand Empowerment Foundation (f. 2005).

Activities: Activities fall into four main areas: education (early childhood development, primary and tertiary education, and maths); health (hospices); social development (community care, the arts, culture and heritage, environment, food security and agricultural livelihoods); and strategic leadership and skills development. The Foundation supports mathematics education research, jointly funding the South African Maths Education Chairs (with the Dept of Science and Technology and the RMB Fund) and South African Numeracy Chairs (with the Dept of Science and Technology and the Anglo American Chairman's Fund). It awards bursaries for education under the FirstRand Laurie Dippenaar and Momentum Dippenaar Scholarship programmes.

Geographical Area of Activity: South Africa.

Publications: Annual Report.

Finance: Receives an annual contribution of 1% from the after-tax profits of the FirstRand group companies (First National Bank—FNB, Momentum, FirstRand, Wesbank and Rand Merchant Bank—RMB). Total corporate social responsibility investment since 1998 approx. 1,000m. rand.

Board of Trustees: Nolulamo (Lulu) Gwagwa (Chair.).

Contact Details: FirstRand, 4 Merchant Pl., cnr Fredman Dr. and Rivonia Rd, Sandton 2196; POB 650149, Benmore 2010; tel. (11) 2821808; internet www.firstrand.co.za/foundations/firstrand-foundation.

Gift of the Givers Foundation

Established in 1992 by Dr Imtiaz Sooliman, a medical doctor; the largest disaster response NGO of African origin in the African continent.

Activities: Builds relations between peoples of different cultures and religions, fostering goodwill, harmonious co-existence, tolerance and mutual respect. Main programme areas include: disaster response; education; healthcare; hunger alleviation; socioeconomic development; and water provision. The Foundation offers bursaries for international study; and organizes HIV/AIDS workshops and anti-drug campaigns in South Africa. Campaigns have included the Millions for Africa Campaign and South Africans Helping South Africans, which promotes corporate social responsibility. It has branches in Johannesburg, Cape Town, Lenasia and Durban; with offices in Malawi, the Palestinian Territories, Somalia, the Syrian Arab Republic, Yemen and Zimbabwe.

Geographical Area of Activity: Worldwide.

Finance: Total disbursements since 1992 3,200m. rand.

Principal Staff: Chair. and Dir Dr Imtiaz Sooliman.

Contact Details: 290 Prince Alfred St, Pietermaritzburg; tel. (33) 3450175; e-mail info@giftofthegivers.org; internet www.giftofthegivers.org.

Graça Machel Trust

Established in 2010 by Graça Machel, a former politician and First Lady in Mozambique and South Africa, and co-convener of international NGO The Elders (f. 2007).

Activities: Carries out activities in the areas of: children's health and nutrition; education; women's economic and financial empowerment; and leadership and good governance. The Trust supports networks involved in women's and children's rights across the continent. Current priorities are ending child marriage violence against children and female genital mutilation, and promoting children's rights, with a particular focus on Malawi, Mozambique, Tanzania and Zambia. It awards scholarships for professional women to study at universities in South Africa, Spain and the United Kingdom.

Geographical Area of Activity: Africa.

Publications: Annual Report; newsletter; blog.

Board of Trustees: Graça Machel (Chair.).

Principal Staff: CEO Melizsa Mugyenyi.

Contact Details: Investment Pl., Block C, 10th Rd, Hyde Park, Johannesburg 2196; tel. (11) 3250501; e-mail info@gracamacheltrust.org; internet gracamacheltrust.org.

Ichikowitz Family Foundation—IFF

Established in 2010 by Ivor Ichikowitz, founder and Exec. Chair. of Paramount Group, a defence, aerospace and shipbuilding company.

Activities: Supports young people's development through educational, environmental and cultural programmes. Initiatives include: #IAMCONSTITUTION, which promotes citizenship and democracy; sustainable use of natural resources, development of renewable energy and conservation of biodiversity; the online African Oral History Archive; and promoting computer literacy. The Foundation funds scholarships and awards for excellence in business, culture, music and sports.

Geographical Area of Activity: Africa.

Publications: *African Youth Survey* (annual).

Principal Staff: Chair. Ivor Ichikowitz.

Contact Details: Private Bag X10042 Sandton, Johannesburg 2146; tel. (11) 0866800; e-mail info@ichikowitzfoundation.com; internet ichikowitzfoundation.com.

Institute for Security Studies—ISS

Established in 1991, as the Institute for Defence Policy, by Dr Jakkie Cilliers and P. B. Mertz; present name adopted in 1996.

Activities: Promotes security, peace and prosperity in Africa through carrying out research, analysis and training, and providing technical assistance to governments and civil society. Programme areas include African futures, transnational crimes, climate change, migration, maritime security and development, peacekeeping, peacebuilding, crime prevention and criminal justice, and the analysis of conflict and governance. The Institute organises briefings, seminars and workshops. It has offices in South Africa, Ethiopia, Kenya and Senegal.

Geographical Area of Activity: Africa.

Publications: Annual Review; *ISS Today* (daily analysis); *ISS Weekly* (newsletter); *Peace and Security Council Report*; *Africa Report*; *Enact Observer*; *Organised Crime Index*; guides; handbooks; manuals; policy briefs; reports.

Finance: Total assets 218.8m. rand (31 Dec. 2023).

Board of Trustees: Dr Jakkie Cilliers (Chair.).

Principal Staff: Exec. Dir Fonteh Akum.

Contact Details: Block C, Brooklyn Ct, 361 Veale St, New Muckleneuk, Pretoria 0181; POB 1787, Brooklyn Sq., Pretoria 0075; tel. (12) 3469500; e-mail iss@issafrica.org; internet issafrica.org.

Lifeline Energy

Established in 1999 by Rory Stear in the United Kingdom as Freeplay Foundation; present name adopted in 2010.

Activities: Designs, manufactures and distributes solar-powered and wind-up radios and media players for education and information initiatives. The organization supports vulnerable women, children and other groups in sub-Saharan Africa; and also responds to emergencies worldwide. Has offices in London, UK, and New York, USA.

Geographical Area of Activity: Less-developed countries.

Publications: Newsletter; marketing brochures; blog.

Finance: Established Lifeline Technologies Trading Ltd in 2010 as a for-profit company which designs and manufactures products for the charity and humanitarian sector only; company profits accrue to the charity in the form of dividend payments.

Board: Arthur Johnson (SA Chair.); Kristine Pearson (US Chair.); Edmund Burns (US Sec.).

Contact Details: 1st Floor, Block D, The Terraces, 1 Silverwood Cl., Steenberg Office Park, Westlake, Cape Town 7945; tel. (21) 8139522; e-mail hello@lifelineenergy.org; internet www.lifelineenergy.org.

Mandela Institute for Development Studies—MINDS

Established by Dr Nkosana Moyo.

Activities: Carries out research to inform policymaking and practice in the fields of governance, integrated economic development and institutional growth. Main programme areas are: African heritage; economic and regional integration; and youth. The Institute offers scholarships.

Geographical Area of Activity: Africa.

Board of Trustees: Graça Machel (Chair.).

Contact Details: Investment Pl., Block C, 10th Rd, Hyde Park, Johannesburg 2196; tel. (11) 3250501; e-mail info @minds-africa.org; internet minds-africa.org.

The Mandela Rhodes Foundation

Established in 2002 by Nelson Mandela, former President of South Africa, in partnership with the Rhodes Trust (q.v.), to build exceptional leadership capacity in Africa.

Activities: Offers scholarships for Master's and Honours degrees at accredited South African tertiary education institutions. The Mandela Rhodes Scholarship is open to applicants of any gender, race, culture, religion, class and field of academic study, aged 19–30 years and a citizen of an African country. Three annual supplementary residential leadership courses and a mentoring system promote and support leadership development.

Geographical Area of Activity: Africa.

Publications: Yearbook; newsletter; *Young African Magazine*; blog.

Finance: Total assets 794.3m. rand; annual comprehensive income 60.1m. rand (31 Dec. 2020).

Board of Trustees: Justice Catherine O'Regan (Chair.).

Principal Staff: CEO Judy Sikuza.

Contact Details: The Mandela Rhodes Bldg, 150 St George's Mall, Cape Town 8001; POB 15897, Vlaeberg 8018; tel. (21) 4243346; e-mail info@mrf.org.za; internet www.mandelarhodes.org.

Motsepe Foundation

Established in 1999 by Patrice Motsepe, founder and Exec. Chair. of African Rainbow Minerals (f. 1994), a mining company, and his wife Dr Precious Moloi Motsepe.

Activities: Promotes social and economic welfare at the community level through education and better health, working with community- and faith-based organizations. The Foundation's main fields of interest are economic empowerment, women's empowerment, education and leadership, and sports. It provides scholarships for higher education and business grants to young entrepreneurs; and also awards grants in the areas of the arts and music, education and sport.

Geographical Area of Activity: South Africa.

Restrictions: Grants only to traditional councils; women- or youth-owned businesses and co-operatives; workers' organizations; public benefit organizations, religious organizations and NGOs.

Finance: In 2013 Patrice Motsepe signed Bill Gates' and Warren Bufett's Giving Pledge to give one-half of the income from his assets to philanthropic causes. Total disbursements since 2013 US $50m.

Principal Staff: Co-Chair. Patrice Motsepe, Dr Precious Moloi-Motsepe.

Contact Details: 29 Impala Rd, Chislehurston, Johannesburg; POB 782058, Sandton, Johannesburg; tel. (11) 3241500; e-mail info@motsepefoundation.org; internet motsepefoundation.org.

MTN SA Foundation

Established in 2001 by MTN, a telecommunications company; part of the MTN Foundations network.

Activities: Carries out activities in the areas of education, health and enterprise. Main programmes are: Education, with a focus on connectivity and helping learners with special needs; Community Programmes, supporting community-based e-health and entrepreneurship projects; Arts & Culture, through the MTN Art Collection, which contains over 1,400 traditional and contemporary works by African artists; and Special Projects, funding initiatives that fall outside the Foundation's areas of focus.

Geographical Area of Activity: South Africa.

Publications: Annual Report.

Finance: Annual income 54m. rand, expenditure 54m. rand (31 Dec. 2021).

Board: Prof. Njabulo S. Ndebele (Chair.).

Principal Staff: Gen. Man. Kusile Mtunzi-Hairwadzi.

Contact Details: MTN Group Ltd, Innovation Centre, 216 14th Ave, Fairland, Roodepoort 2170; Private Bag 9955, Cresta, Johannesburg 2118; tel. (11) 9123000; e-mail foundation@mtn.com; internet www.mtn.co.za/pages/mtn-foundation.aspx.

Music in Africa Foundation—MIAF

Established in 2013 in Kenya; a membership organization.

Activities: Promotes African music and music education. Initiatives include Instrument Building and Repair, encouraging the professionalization of instrument making and repair, particularly in relation to indigenous African instruments; and Music in Africa Connects–Artist Mobility Programme, supporting national, regional and international tours by musicians from countries affected by conflict. The Foundation provides information about musicians and the music sector in Africa through the online Music in Africa Portal; and organizes mentoring workshops for musicians and conferences. It has regional offices in the Democratic Republic of the Congo, Kenya, Nigeria and Senegal. Members comprise music professionals, businesses and non-profit organizations.

Geographical Area of Activity: International.

Publications: Annual Report; newsletter.

Finance: Total assets €1.0m. (30 June 2023).

Board of Management: Marcus Tawanda Gora (Chair.); Julz Ossom (Deputy Chair.); William Chirinda (Treas.).

Contact Details: 3rd Floor, 158 Jan Smuts Ave, Johannesburg; tel. (10) 1401317; e-mail info@musicinafrica.net; internet www.musicinafrica.net.

Nelson Mandela Children's Fund

Established in 1994 by Nelson Mandela, who contributed one-third of his salary to the Fund during his tenure as President of South Africa until 1999.

Activities: Works to address problems that children and young people face in the areas of housing and sanitation, malnutrition, child abuse, youth unemployment and disability. Programme areas include: child safety and protection; child survival and development; sustainable livelihoods; and youth leadership. The Foundation funds projects in South Africa that empower disadvantaged children and young people. It has offices in the United Kingdom and the USA; operates in association with the Nelson Mandela Children's Fund in Canada, an independently registered welfare organization; and initiated the Nelson Mandela Children's Hospital Trust (f. 2009), which was established as a specialized paediatric hospital for children in sub-Saharan Africa.

Geographical Area of Activity: South Africa.

Restrictions: Does not fund capital works; conferences or seminars; exchange programmes; school fees, scholarships or tertiary bursaries; or medical expenses.

Publications: Annual Report; newsletter.

Finance: Total assets 1,040.2m. rand (31 March 2024).

Board of Trustees: Nana Magomola (Chair.).

Principal Staff: CEO Dr Linda Ncube-Nkomo.

Contact Details: 21 Eastwold Way, Saxonwold 2196, Gauteng; POB 797, Highlands North, Johannesburg 2037; tel. (11) 2745600; e-mail fundraising@nmcf.co.za; internet www.nelsonmandelachildrensfund.com.

Nelson Mandela Foundation

Established in 1999 by former President Nelson Mandela.

Activities: Core business is memory and dialogue work, principally conducted by the Nelson Mandela Centre of Memory and Dialogue (f. 2013). In 2009, with its sister charities, the Foundation initiated Mandela Day, which takes place on 18 July every year, to encourage public community service; the UN has since declared it Nelson Mandela International Day.

Geographical Area of Activity: South Africa.

Publications: Annual Report; newsletter; policy papers; educational publications on the life and times of Nelson Mandela; publications on ongoing memory and dialogue work.

Finance: Total assets 499.1m. rand; annual comprehensive income 1.9m. rand (29 Feb. 2024).

Board of Trustees: Dr Grace Naledi Mandisa Pandor (Chair.).

Principal Staff: CEO Mbongiseni Buthelezi.

Contact Details: 107 Central St, Houghton 2198; Private Bag X70000, Houghton 2041; tel. (11) 5475600; e-mail nmf @nelsonmandela.org; internet www.nelsonmandela.org.

NRF—National Research Foundation

Established in 1999 by the South African Government, replacing the former Foundation for Research Development.

Activities: Offers research grants, scholarships and bursaries to researchers and students at the country's higher education institutions. All support programmes prioritize the development of black and women researchers and building research capacity at previously disadvantaged institutions. The Foundation focuses on developing skills and research related to South Africa's indigenous knowledge systems. Research and research skills are promoted across many disciplines, including: natural sciences and engineering; agricultural and environmental sciences; health sciences; social sciences and the humanities. Seven national research facilities also offer opportunities for research, advanced training and international collaboration.

Geographical Area of Activity: South Africa.

Restrictions: Training of human resources through grants essential.

Publications: Annual Report; newsletter; research publications of national facilities; manuals and guidelines.

Finance: Annual revenue 4,537.2m. rand, expenditure 4,384.0m. rand (31 March 2024).

Board of Directors: Prof. Mosa Moshabela (Chair.).

Principal Staff: CEO Prof. Fulufhelo Nelwamondo.

Contact Details: NRF Bldg, South Gate, CSIR Complex, Meiring Naudé Rd, Brummeria, Pretoria; Box 2600, Pretoria 0001; tel. (12) 4814000; e-mail info@nrf.ac.za; internet www.nrf.ac.za.

Open Society Foundation South Africa—OSF-SA

Founded in 1993; an independent foundation, part of the Open Society Foundations (q.v.) network.

Activities: Operates in the fields of civil society, law and criminal justice, public health, youth and women, democracy building, economic reform, and information and the media. The Foundation offers scholarships and fellowships.

Geographical Area of Activity: South Africa.

Publications: Annual Report; notes; factsheets; policy briefs.

Finance: Total budget US $3.6m. (2020).

Board of Directors: Nkateko Nyoka (Chair.).

Principal Staff: Exec. Dir Bulelwa Ngewana.

Contact Details: Open Society–Africa, 1 Hood Ave, 148 Jan Smuts, Rosebank, Johannesburg, GP 2196; tel. (11) 5875000; e-mail info@osfsa.org.za; internet www.opensocietyfoundations.org/newsroom/open-society-foundations-south-africa.

Open Society Initiative for Southern Africa—OSISA

Founded in 1997; an independent foundation, part of the Open Society Foundations network and affiliated with the Open Society Foundation for South Africa—OSF-SA (qq.v.).

Activities: Promotes open, vibrant societies, the elimination of poverty, and civic and democratic participation. Programme areas include: democracy and governance; economic and social justice; human rights, the rule of law and access to justice; and women's rights. The organization operates in 11 countries in Southern Africa funding civil society projects and advocacy activities in the areas of education, human rights, democracy, HIV/AIDS, women's rights, media, economic justice, law, language rights, and information and communication technology.

Geographical Area of Activity: Southern Africa (Angola, Botswana, Dem. Repub. of the Congo, Lesotho, Madagascar, Malawi, Mozambique, Namibia, Eswatini—fmrly Swaziland, Zambia, Zimbabwe).

Restrictions: Does not typically fund individual scholarships or fellowships.

Publications: Annual Report; newsletter; *Openspace* (3 a year); *Buwa!* (2 a year); reports; studies; yearbooks.

Principal Staff: Exec. Dir Siphosami Malunga; Deputy Dir/Head of Programmes Tiseke Kasambala.

Contact Details: 1 Hood Ave/148 Jan Smuts Ave, Rosebank, Johannesburg 2196; tel. (11) 5875000; e-mail info@osisa.org; internet www.osisa.org.

Oppenheimer Generations Foundation

Established by the Oppenheimer family.

Activities: Comprises the Oppenheimer Memorial Trust (f. 1958), which funds initiatives in the areas of early childhood development, basic and higher education, the arts, policy research and advocacy, awarding scholarships for higher education and the annual Harry Oppenheimer Fellowship Award for research; and the Brenthurst Foundation (f. 2004), which provides policy advice in the fields of economic development, youth employment, urban planning, and peace and security in the African continent, convening high-level meetings on development and security under the Tswalu Dialogue series every three years. Oppenheimer Generations also awards grants for research in the areas of medicine and conservation.

Geographical Area of Activity: Africa.

Board: Nicky Oppenheimer (Chair.); Jonathan Oppenheimer (Exec. Chair.).

Contact Details: c/o The Brenthurst Foundation, St Andrew's House, 6 St Andrew's Rd, Parktown, Johannesburg; POB 61631, Marshalltown 2107; tel. (82) 6588831; e-mail media@opp-gen.com; internet opp-gen.com.

Oxfam South Africa

Established in 2014; part of the Oxfam confederation of organizations (qq.v.).

Activities: Works to end poverty and inequality. Main programme areas include: building resilience to economic, social and environmental shocks; democracy and governance; economic justice; women's rights and gender justice; and strengthening civil society networks in global development.

Geographical Area of Activity: Southern Africa.

Restrictions: Does not make loans or grants to individuals.

Publications: Annual Inequality Report; briefing papers; research reports.

Principal Staff: Acting Exec. Dir Nkateko Chauke.

Contact Details: 32 Princess of Wales St, 4th Floor, Block D, Sunnside Office Park, Johannesburg 2091; tel. (11) 1004610; e-mail info@oxfam.org.za; internet www.oxfam.org.za.

Peace Parks Foundation

Established in 1997 by Dr Anton Rupert, Prince Bernhard of the Netherlands and President Nelson Mandela.

Activities: Works to re-establish and preserve landscapes and rebuild functioning ecosystems, providing advocacy and planning and project management support for 'peace parks' (transfrontier conservation areas straddling the boundaries of two or more countries). The Foundation supports community-based agriculture, conservation and tourism-related projects for local communities living next to the parks, and conducts research on animal disease control. It works with two colleges to train students in the hospitality sector, conservation management and wildlife tracking; and also assists transfrontier conservation areas in combating wildlife crime.

Geographical Area of Activity: Southern Africa.

Publications: Annual Review; brochure.

Finance: Annual income 416.5m. rand, expenditure 337.1m. rand (31 Dec. 2023).

Board of Directors: J. P. Rupert (Chair.); J. A. Chissano (Vice-Chair.).

Principal Staff: CEO Werner Myburgh.

Contact Details: 11 Termo Rd, Techno Park, Stellenbosch, 7600; POB 12743, Die Boord, Stellenbosch 7613; tel. (21) 8805100; e-mail ppfcomms@peaceparks.org; internet www.peaceparks.org.

Reeva Rebecca Steenkamp Foundation

Established in 2016 by June Steenkamp, in memory of her daughter Reeva, to campaign against the abuse of women and children.

Activities: Raises awareness about violence and abuse against women and children. The Foundation distributes educational materials about domestic violence to victims, government and private institutions; provides legal support and advocacy to individuals; and annually awards a bursary to one third-year law student with an interest in family law. It also organizes fundraising events and takes part in national and international campaigns.

Geographical Area of Activity: International.

Principal Staff: CEO Kim Martin.

Contact Details: 39 Sunningdale Dr., Sunningdale, Cape Town, Western Cape; tel. (41) 4502932; e-mail info@reevasteenkampfoundation.org; internet www.reevasteenkampfoundation.org.

Rupert Family Foundations

Established in 1984 by Johann Rupert, a former merchant banker, Chair. of Compagnie Financière Richemont and co-founder of the Michelangelo Foundation for Creativity and Craftsmanship (f. 2015) in Switzerland.

Activities: Comprising the Rupert Art Foundation, which supports visual and applied arts and the Rupert Museum (f. in the 1940s by Anton and Huberte Rupert), a private art collection of paintings, sculptures and tapestries; the Rupert Education Foundation (f. 1985), a special fund for education and training; the Rupert Music Foundation, to promote and support classical music; the Rupert Nature Foundation, which supports conservation of wildlife; and the Rupert Historical Homes Foundation, which buys and restores threatened historic buildings. In 2001 the Foundations financed the establishment of the South African Tourism College to support local economic development and train unemployed young people from impoverished, rural communities in hospitality and skills such as tracking and herding.

Geographical Area of Activity: South Africa.

Principal Staff: Dir Robyn Cedras-Tobin.

Contact Details: Stellentia Rd, Stellenbosch, Western Cape; tel. (21) 8883344; e-mail info@rupertmuseum.org; internet www.rupertmuseum.org.

SAASTA—South African Agency for Science and Technology Advancement

Established in 1955; known as the Foundation for Education, Science and Technology—FEST until 2002 after its incorporation into the National Research Foundation (q.v.).

Activities: Promotes understanding of and engagement with science, engineering and technology among all South Africans; encourages young people into careers in science, technology and innovation; interacts with the public on issues of science, engineering and technology; and communicates advances in science and technology to the public, organizing competitions and festivals. The Agency also operates an astronomical observatory in Johannesburg.

Geographical Area of Activity: South Africa.

Publications: Annual Report; *GetSETgo* (quarterly e-newsletter); brochures; leaflets; posters.

Principal Staff: Man. Dir Dr Mamoeletsi Mosia.

Contact Details: Didacta Bldg, 211 Nana Sita (Skinner) St, Pretoria 0001; POB 1758, Pretoria 0001; tel. (12) 3929300; e-mail info@saasta.ac.za; internet www.saasta.ac.za.

South African Institute of International Affairs

Founded in 1934 as an independent NGO.

Activities: Key research areas are: South African foreign policy and African driver countries; governance and the African Peer Review Mechanism; governance of Africa's resources; economic diplomacy; relations of existing and emerging powers to Africa; and current global challenges. The Institute's activities include: empirical research; granting fellowships and internships; organizing study and discussion groups, public addresses, conferences and symposia; and producing publications. It maintains a library and information service, and runs several youth programmes with high school and university students. Has branches in East London, Pietermaritzburg and the Western Cape.

Geographical Area of Activity: Majority of research work conducted across Africa.

Publications: Annual Report; *South African Journal of International Affairs* (4 a year); Africa Portal; policy briefings; policy insights; occasional papers; special studies; reports; videos; podcasts; newsletters.

Finance: Total assets 47.3m. rand (30 June 2022).

National Council: Moeletsi Mbeki (Chair.).

Principal Staff: Chief Exec. Elizabeth Sidiropoulos.

Contact Details: East Campus, University of the Witwatersrand, Johannesburg; POB 31596, Braamfontein 2017; tel. (11) 3392021; e-mail info@saiia.org.za; internet www.saiia.org.za.

South African Institute of Race Relations—IRR

Founded in 1929 as a national multiracial organization; a think tank.

Activities: Conducts policy research, public education and advocacy programmes. The Institute examines macroeconomic, socioeconomic, labour, constitutional and political trends, as well as race relations in South Africa. It oversees a bursary programme for students at universities; and provides a consultancy service.

Geographical Area of Activity: South Africa.

Publications: Annual Report; *South Africa Survey* (annual); *Free Facts* (monthly); *@Liberty Reports* (occasional); research reports; policy briefs; books.

Finance: Annual income 22.4m. rand, expenditure 27.1m. rand (31 Dec. 2023).

Board of Directors: Roger Crawford (Chair.).

Principal Staff: Chief Exec. Dr John Endres; Pres. Mark Oppenheimer.

Contact Details: 222 Smit St, 21st Floor, Braamfontein, Johannesburg 2000; POB 291722, Melville 2109; tel. (11) 4827221; e-mail info@irr.org.za; internet www.irr.org.za.

Southern Africa Trust

Established in 2005.

Activities: Works to strengthen regional integration to benefit poor people through making grants to organizations and brokering dialogue between the public, private and civil society sectors. The Trust supports projects in areas including agriculture, climate resilience, migration, social development, trade and workers' rights. It offers conference and meeting facilities to NGOs and small, medium- and micro-sized enterprises.

Geographical Area of Activity: Southern African Development Community region.

Publications: Research reports; policy briefs; case studies; *Society Talks* (weekly webinar series).

Finance: Total grants disbursed since 2005 US $17.2m. (2024).

Board of Trustees: Sazini Mojapelo (Chair.).

Principal Staff: CEO Alice D. Kanengoni.

Contact Details: 45 Kyalami Business Park, Kyalami 1684; Postnet Suite 379, Private Bag X121, Halfway House, Midrand 1685; tel. (11) 3181012; e-mail info@southernafricatrust.org; internet www.southernafricatrust.org.

Thabo Mbeki Foundation

Established in 2008 by former President Thabo Mbeki.

Activities: Promotes political, social, economic and cultural development in Africa and the African diaspora. Main programmes include: the Thabo Mbeki African Leadership Institute (f. 2010), established in partnership with the University of South Africa, to develop good governance and provide leadership training; the South African Democracy Education Trust, researching and analysing the anti-apartheid movement; the Thabo Mbeki Presidential Library and Museum, containing the papers of Thabo Mbeki and other African leaders; the African Centre on Conflict Management, in partnership with the University of the Witwatersrand (Wits), researching and analysing conflict management and governance in Africa and assisting in mediation; and the Thabo Mbeki African School of Public and International Affairs, a gradaute school to advance public sector education.

Geographical Area of Activity: International.

Board of Trustees: Geraldine Fraser-Moleketi (Chair.); Dr Vincent Maphai (Deputy Chair.).

Principal Staff: CEO Max Boqwana.

Contact Details: No. 7 North Ave, Riviera, Killarney, Johannesburg; Private Bag X444, Houghton 2041; tel. (11) 4861560; e-mail info@mbeki.org; internet www.mbeki.org.

Transnet Foundation

Established in 1994 by Transnet, South Africa's government-owned transport and logistics organization.

Activities: Carries out self-conducted programmes in four main areas: education; health; sport; and socioeconomic infrastructure development. The Foundation also promotes employee volunteering.

Geographical Area of Activity: South Africa.

Restrictions: Does not make grants to individuals, political parties or groups with partisan political affiliations, professional fundraising institutions, religious organizations for sectarian activities, institutions or bodies that are racially exclusive, profit-making concerns, trade unions, research projects or for travel.

Publications: *Transnet Cares* (monthly newsletter); factsheets.

Principal Staff: CEO Portia Darby.

Contact Details: Carlton Centre, 24th Floor, 150 Commissioner St, Johannesburg 2001; tel. (11) 3083000; e-mail tfsponsorshipsanddonations@transnet.net; internet www.transnet.net/aboutus/pages/transnet-foundation.aspx.

Vodacom Foundation

Established in 1999 as the corporate social investment arm of Vodacom South Africa, a telecommunications company; part of the Vodafone Foundation (q.v.) network.

Activities: Supports projects in the areas of agriculture, education, gender empowerment, health, safety and security, and youth development, promoting the use of technology for development. The Foundation: equips Early Childhood Development Centres, Schools of Excellence and Teacher Centres with digital equipment and training, provides free access to digital educational content through the Vodacom e-School platform and offers bursaries for disadvantaged university students; develops stock management systems for health clinics to track and trace medications; and established the Gender Based Violence Command Centre and MeMeZa Shout Crime Prevention Initiative. It promotes volunteering among Vodacom employees; and operates the Red Alert emergency fundraising SMS (text messaging) platform.

Geographical Area of Activity: South Africa.

Restrictions: Grants only to non-profit organizations registered and operating in South Africa.

Finance: Total disbursements since 1999 approx. 1,600m. rand.

Principal Staff: Chair. Sakumzi (Saki) Justice Macozoma.

Contact Details: Vodacom Corporate Park, 082 Vodacom Blvd, Vodavalley, Midrand 1635; Private Bag X9904, Sandton 2146; tel. (11) 6535229; e-mail foundation@vodacom.co.za; internet www.vodacom.com/vodacom-foundation.

Wilderness Foundation Global—WFG

Established in 2015; a global network comprising Wilderness Foundation Africa, Wilderness Foundation UK (f. 1976), WILD Foundation (q.v.) and the Wilderness Leadership School (f. 1957).

Activities: Works in the field of nature conservation, through protecting wilderness and connecting it to people's needs. Main initiatives are: the World Wilderness Congress, a public environmental forum which convenes every four years; the Wilderness Conservation Fund, which establishes and expands protected areas, ecological corridors and biodiversity hotspots; the Wilderness Specialist Group, which liaises between the World Commission for Protected Areas of the International Union for the Conservation of Nature (q.v.) and the World Wilderness Congress; and Survival Revolution, the global campaign for the Nature Needs Half movement. Projects include: Forest, Culture, Future, protecting the sovereignty of the Yawanawá people and their stewardship of the rainforest in Brazil; Forever Wild Rhino, a counter-poaching initiative in Southern Africa and Asia; the Mali Elephant Project, promoting community-centred conservation; Turn-Around, supporting vulnerable young people in the United Kingdom through Outward Bound courses; Umzi Wethu, which supports displaced and vulnerable young people in South Africa through education and vocational training in the hospitality and ecotourism sectors; and the Wildlife Operations Group, a multi-agency partnership to combat wildlife crime.

Geographical Area of Activity: International.

Trustees: Todani Moyo (Chair.).

Principal Staff: Pres. Vance G. Martin; CEO Andrew Muir.

Contact Details: 11 Newington St, Central, Port Elizabeth 6001; POB 12509, Centrahil, Port Elizabeth 6006; tel. (41) 3730293; e-mail info@wildernessfoundation.org; internet www.wildernessfoundationglobal.org.

SOUTH SUDAN

FOUNDATIONS AND NON-PROFITS

South Sudan Center for Strategic and Policy Studies—CSPS

Established in 2011 by Dr John Gai Yoh as an independent research centre; a think tank.

Activities: Carries out policy research and analysis in the areas of: governance, democracy and institution building; national security, regional strategy and international geopolitics; the economy, natural resources, sustainable development and environmental conservation; ethnicity studies, including culture, religion, traditional justice and leadership; and science, technology and innovation. The Center maintains a reference library for university students, faculty members and researchers; and offers translation services.

Geographical Area of Activity: South Sudan.

Publications: Reports; *Policy Analysis*; *Juba Trends*; *Notes and Records*.

Board of Directors: Dr John Gai Yoh (Chair.).

Principal Staff: Acting Exec. Dir Prof. Dr Melha Rout Biel.

Contact Details: CSPS House, POB 619, Hai Jebrona, next to Martyrs Primary School, Juba; tel. 920310415; e-mail info@csps.org.ss; internet csps.org.ss.

Sudd Institute

Established by 2012 by policy analysts and social scientists; a think tank.

Activities: Carries out evidence-based policy research and analysis and training. Programme areas include: achieving and sustaining national stability and peace; addressing external and internal security, including tribal conflicts, youth and gender-based violence and the criminal justice system; and building government accountability and transparency, including resource generation and allocation and constitutional development. The Institute offers Visiting Research Fellowships.

Geographical Area of Activity: South Sudan.

Publications: *Weekly Review*; policy briefs; dialogue briefs; special reports.

Board of Directors: Dr Pauline Riak (Chair.); Atem Garang (Deputy Chair.); Dr Leben Moro (Treas.).

Principal Staff: Man. Dir Luka Biong Deng Kuol.

Contact Details: POB 34, Kolo Rd, Juba; tel. 921766194; e-mail info@suddinstitute.org; internet www.suddinstitute.org.

SPAIN

CO-ORDINATING BODIES

Asociación Española de Fundaciones (Spanish Association of Foundations)

Established in 2003 following the merger of the Confederación Española de Fundaciones and the Centro de Fundaciones.

Activities: Provides a forum for foundations, co-ordinates initiatives and represents their interests to the public, media and Government. The Association promotes co-operation between foundations nationally and internationally, sharing experience and allowing co-ordinated work. It advises foundations on a range of legal, fiscal, economic, financial and telecommunication issues; organizes training courses, conferences and seminars; and maintains a database of foundations and other funding sources. Comprises more than 900 member organizations and is a member of Philea (q.v.).

Geographical Area of Activity: Spain.

Publications: Annual Report; newsletter; *Cuadernos de la Asociación Española de Fundaciones* (quarterly); *Tribuna de las Fundaciones* (monthly newsletter); monographs.

Finance: Total assets €1.1m.; net annual income €269,886 (31 Dec. 2022).

Board of Directors: Pilar García Ceballos-Zúñiga (Pres.); Alberto Durán López (First Vice-Pres.); Vicente José Montes Gan (Second Vice-Pres.); Luis González Martín (Third Vice-Pres); Carmen García de Andrés (Treas.); Adolfo Menéndez Menéndez (Sec.).

Principal Staff: Gen. Man. Silverio Agea Rodríguez.

Contact Details: Impact Hub Barceló, Calle Serrano Anguita 13, 28004 Madrid; tel. 913106309; e-mail info@fundaciones.org; internet www.fundaciones.org.

Coordinadora de ONGD España (Development NGO Coordinator Spain)

Established in 1986 with the assistance of Ayuda en Acción, Cáritas, CIC, IEPALA, Intermón, Justice and Peace, Manos Unidas, Medicus Mundi and Movimiento 0.7%.

Activities: A network of organizations and social platforms that work in the fields of development, international solidarity, humanitarian action, education for global citizenship and the defence of human rights. The organization carries out policy research and analysis; and provides advocacy and training for international co-operation. Member organizations participate in thematic working groups in the areas of: the Autonomous NGO Coordinators' Network; childhood and co-operation; development and co-operation financing; development policies; feminism; global citizenship; humanitarian action; security management in organizations; transparency and good governance; volunteering; and water and sanitation. It comprises 73 development NGOs, six associate entities and 17 regional coordinators, which in turn represent more than 600 organizations working in 100 countries; and is a member of CONCORD (q.v.).

Geographical Area of Activity: Spain.

Publications: Annual Report; newsletter; reports.

Finance: Total assets €730,897 (2023).

Governing Board: Javier Ruiz Gaitán (Pres.); Penelope Berlamas Orquín, Irene Molero Gurrutxaga (Vice-Pres); Jose Luis Postigo Sierra (Treas.); Felix Gonzalez Lopez (Sec.).

Principal Staff: Dir Maite Serrano Oñate.

Contact Details: Calle De la Reina 17, 3°, 28004 Madrid; tel. 915210955; e-mail informacion@coordinadoraongd.org; internet coordinadoraongd.org.

Fundación Lealtad (Loyalty Foundation)

Established in 2001 by a group of civic-minded business people.

Activities: Monitors the compliance of NGOs with nine standards of transparency and best practices; provides self-assessment and improvement workshops for NGOs that are not yet being monitored. The Foundation works with companies and corporate foundations with an interest in financing or working with NGOs in the framework of their social commitment strategy. It supports two projects in Mexico and Chile involving the adaptation of Spanish NGO analysis methodology in those countries. A member of the International Committee on Fundraising Organizations.

Geographical Area of Activity: Chile, Mexico, Spain.

Publications: Annual Report; newsletter; *Solidarity Transparency*; *Transparency and Best Practices Guide to Spanish NGOs* (online); guides and other publications.

Finance: Total assets €423,533; net annual income –€110,851 (31 Dec. 2023).

Board of Trustees: Salvador García-Atance Lafuente (Chair.); Rufino García-Quirós García (Vice-Chair.); Cecilia Plañiol Lacalle (Treas.).

Principal Staff: Gen. Dir Ana Benavides Gonzlez-Camino.

Contact Details: Plaza de Manuel Becerra 16, 5ª Izda, 28028 Madrid; tel. 917890123; e-mail fundacion@fundacionlealtad.org; internet www.fundacionlealtad.org.

Lafede.cat—Federació d'Organitzacions per a la Justícia Global (Lafede.cat—Federation of Organizations for Global Justice)

Established in 2013 by the Catalan Federation of NGOs for Development (FCONGD), Catalan Federation of NGOs for Human Rights (FCONGDH) and Catalan Federation of NGOs for Peace (FCONGPAU).

Activities: Promotes economic, environmental, feminist and antiracist justice; and the transformational change of organizational culture within member NGOs. The Federation provides advice, services and training to members; and information to the public. It organizes events and roundtables, including the annual #TornaCanviada international volunteering fair. Comprises 131 organizations.

Geographical Area of Activity: France, Spain.

Publications: Annual Report; *InterCom-PDH Agenda* (weekly newsletter).

Finance: Annual income €722,754, expenditure €707,818 (2023).

Board of Directors: Núria Carulla, Àlex Guillamón, Ares Perceval (Co-Pres); Mariano Flores (Treas.); Laura Riba (Sec.).

Contact Details: Calle Tàpies 1–3, 08001 Barcelona; tel. 934422835; e-mail informacio@lafede.cat; internet www.lafede.cat.

FOUNDATIONS AND NON-PROFITS

Acción Contra el Hambre–ACH (Action Against Hunger)

Established in 1979 in France; an international network; merged with the Fundación Luis Vives (f. 1987) in 2013.

Activities: Works to eliminate direct and indirect causes of malnutrition. Programme areas include: advocacy; employability; food security and livelihoods; humanitarian emergencies; nutrition and health; and water, sanitation and hygiene. The organization operates in more than 50 countries.

Geographical Area of Activity: International.

Publications: Annual Report; manuals; policy briefings; studies; technical briefings; blog.

Finance: Total assets €297.2m. (31 Dec. 2023).

Board of Trustees: José Luis Leal (Chair.); Emilio Aragón, Luis Escauriaza Ibáñez, María Jarai (Vice-Chair.); Francisco Javier Ruiz Paredes (Sec.).

Principal Staff: Exec. Dir Olivier Longué.

Contact Details: Calle Duque de Sevilla 3, 28002 Madrid; tel. 913915300; e-mail ach@achesp.org; internet www.accioncontraelhambre.org.

Anesvad

Founded in 1968.

Activities: Focuses on eradicating neglected tropical diseases (NTDs) in sub-Saharan Africa and providing access to healthcare. Projects also address: nutrition; water and sanitation; training; energy; and decent work.

Geographical Area of Activity: Benin, Côte d'Ivoire, Ghana, Nigeria, Spain, Togo.

Publications: Annual Report; newsletter; magazines; leaflets; brochures.

Finance: Total assets €61.9m. (31 Dec. 2022).

Board of Trustees: Garbiñe Biurrun Mancisidor (Pres.); Antonio González Martín (Vice-Pres.); Alfonso Davalillo Aurrekoetxea (Sec.).

Principal Staff: Gen. Dir Iñigo Lasa.

Contact Details: Henao 29-31 (1º planta), 48009 Bilbao; tel. 944418008; e-mail anesvad@anesvad.org; internet www.anesvad.org.

Educo

Established in 2013 by the merger of Fundación Intervida (f. 1995) and Educación Sin Fronteras (f. 1988); part of ChildFund Alliance.

Activities: Works in the fields of children's welfare and rights, and access to quality education. Programmes encompass education, child protection, development, health and humanitarian action. The organization has six regional offices in Spain.

Geographical Area of Activity: Central and South America, South Asia and South-East Asia, West Africa.

Publications: Annual Report; Accountability Report; newsletter; blog.

Finance: Annual income €45.4m., expenditure €45.4m. (31 Dec. 2023).

Board of Trustees: Antoni Isac Aguilar (Chair.); Hector Litvan Suquieni (Vice-Chair.); Ferran Olmedo Cano (Sec.).

Principal Staff: CEO Pilar Orenes.

Contact Details: Calle Guillem Tell 47, 08006 Barcelona; tel. 933001101; e-mail educo@educo.org; internet www.educo.org.

FUHEM—Fundación Benéfico-Social Hogar del Empleado

Established in 1965.

Activities: Activities come under two main programmes: education, operating through the Foundation's three schools; and 'ecosocial', encompassing sustainability, social cohesion and democracy. The Foundation conducts research; publishes research findings; and organizes conferences and seminars, and training courses for schoolteachers. It has a documentation centre with 5,000 publications.

Geographical Area of Activity: Spain.

Publications: Annual Report; *Boletín ECOS* (digital); *El Estado del poder* (digital); *Papeles de Relaciones Ecosociales y Cambio Global*; *La Situación del Mundo*; *Economía Crítica & Ecologismo Social*; *Boletín FUHEM Intercentros* (digital); *Noticias FUHEM Intercentros* (magazine); surveys; papers; books; magazines.

Finance: Total assets €23.7m. (31 Dec. 2023).

Board of Trustees: Juan Carlos Estepa (Chair.); Yayo Herrero López (Vice-Chair.); María José Román (Sec.).

Contact Details: Avda de Portugal 79 (posterior), 28011 Madrid; provisional address: calle O'Donnell 18, 5th Floor, 28009 Madrid; tel. 914310280; e-mail fuhem@fuhem.es; internet www.fuhem.es.

Fundació Agrupació AMCI (Agrupació AMCI Foundation)

Established in 1993 by Agrupació AMCI, an insurance company, to promote social welfare.

Activities: Offers support to older people, children, young people and disabled people; promotes healthy living and personal autonomy through prevention strategies. The Foundation awards the Infancy Prize, worth €15,000, for research into the prevention, diagnosis and treatment of childhood illness and accidents; and scholarships, worth €30,000 each, for postgraduate study at European universities.

Geographical Area of Activity: Spain.

Publications: Annual Report; *El Boletín* (newsletter, 6 a year); books.

Finance: Total assets €714,103 (31 Dec. 2020).

Board of Trustees: Josep Alfonso Caro (Pres.); Rodrigo Fuentes Gómez (First Vice-Pres.); Ferran Gonzalvo Martí (Treas.); Francisco Tomas Bellido (Sec.).

Contact Details: Gran Via de les Corts Catalanes 652, Eixample, Barcelona; tel. 934826700; e-mail fundacio@agrupcio.es; internet www.fundacioagrupacio.es.

Fundació CIDOB (CIDOB Foundation—Barcelona Centre for International Affairs)

Established in 1973 by Josep Ribera as a non-profit organization; became a private foundation in 1979.

Activities: Research priorities are largely based on previous research carried out, but also aim to analyse and respond to global challenges that have a particular impact on global governance and multilateralism. Interdisciplinary working groups consider strategic subjects, including: the EU in the world; supranationality, sovereignties and European integration; global cities and metropolises; diversity, solidarity and inclusion; mobility, migration policies and human rights; global geopolitics; and sustainable development and equality of opportunities.

Geographical Area of Activity: International.

Publications: Annual Report; *CIDOB News* (monthly newsletter); *Revista Carta Internacional CIDOB* (monthly newsletter); *CIDOB d'Afers Internacionals*; *Notes Internacionals CIDOB*; *Opinión CIDOB*; *Documents CIDOB (Nueva época)*; *Anuario Internacional CIDOB*; *Anuario de la Inmigración en España*; monographs; reports; books.

Finance: Total assets €2.5m. (31 Dec. 2023).

Board of Trustees: Antoni Segura i Mas (Acting Pres.).

Principal Staff: Pres. Josep Borrell; Dir Pol Morillas; Man. María José Rodriguez.

Contact Details: Calle Elisabets 12, 08001 Barcelona; tel. 933026495; e-mail cidob@cidob.org; internet www.cidob.org.

Fundació Futbol Club Barcelona (Barça Foundation)

Established in 1994 by Catalan football club FC Barcelona (Barça).

Activities: Carries out activities in the fields of sports, education, social inclusion and violence prevention to improve the lives of marginalized children and young people. Carries out projects in Catalonia and 34 countries around the world.

Geographical Area of Activity: Africa, Middle East, South America, Central America and the Caribbean, South Asia, South-East Asia.

Publications: Annual Report.

Finance: Total assets €9.5m.; net annual income €1.3m. (30 June 2022).

Board of Trustees: Joan Laporta i Estruch (Pres.); Xavier Sala i Martín (First Vice-Pres.); Joan Boix i Sans (Second Vice-Pres.); Jordi Llauradó i Conejero (Third Vice-Pres.); Ferran Olivé i Cànovas (Treas.); Josep Cubells i Ribé (Sec.).

Principal Staff: Dir-Gen. Marta Segú.

Contact Details: Travessera de les Corts 51–55, Planta 2a, Puerta 5B, 08028 Barcelona; tel. 934967551; e-mail fundacio@fcbarcelona.cat; internet foundation.fcbarcelona.com.

Fundació Gala–Salvador Dalí (Salvador Dalí Foundation)

Created in 1983 by the will of Salvador Dalí, an artist.

Activities: Promotes the work of Dalí through the study and dissemination of his works, publishing books and articles and organizing conferences. The Foundation provides research grants and organizes international events such as the International Salvador Dalí Symposium, and temporary exhibitions. It holds and conserves the collections that the painter bequeathed to the Spanish Government on his death, including manuscripts, letters, photographs, books and films, all of which are made available to students and researchers. The Foundation also administers three museums dedicated to the artist's work; and a library at the Centre d'Estudis Dalinians, which contains 19,019 vols.

Geographical Area of Activity: Spain.

Publications: Annual Report; catalogues; books.

Finance: Total assets approx. €114.4m. (2022).

Board of Directors: Jordi Mercader (Pres.); Isabella Kleinjung (Sec.-Gen.).

Principal Staff: Man. Dir Fèlix Roca Batllori.

Contact Details: Torre Galatea, Pujada del Castell 28, 17600 Figueres; tel. 972677505; e-mail comunicacio@fundaciodali.org; internet www.salvador-dali.org/fundacio-dali.

Fundació Jaume Bofill (Foundation Bofill)

Established in 1969.

Activities: Bofill Foundation is a think-and-do-tank that promotes research, debates and initiatives to generate educational opportunities and combat social inequalities. It focuses on five strategic areas: creating educational community-based opportunities, and activities outside school for all vulnerable groups; combating school segregation; preventing school drop-out; transforming disadvantaged schools and advocate for policymakers to invest more so vulnerable schools can achieve that transformation; and creating more and better digital opportunities, forging alliances to drive digital equity initiatives and promote public policies aimed primarily at the most vulnerable people and groups.

Geographical Area of Activity: Catalonia (Spain).

Publications: Research, public policy papers, blog, books.

Finance: Average annual budget €4m.

Board of Trustees: Isabel Vilaseca Roca (Chair.); Ignasi Carreras Fisas (Vice-Chair.); Joan Majo Cruzate (Vice-Chair.); Joan Abella Barril (Sec.).

Principal Staff: CEO Ismael Palacín Giner.

Contact Details: Carrer Girona 34, B, 08010 Barcelona; tel. 934588700; e-mail fbofill@fundaciobofill.org; internet fundaciobofill.cat.

Fundación AFIM—Ayuda, Formación e Integración del Discapacitado (Foundation for Assistance, Training and Integration of Disadvantaged People)

Established in 1992 as Fundación AFIM—Ayuda, Formación e Integración del Minusválido.

Activities: Promotes the inclusion of economically disadvantaged people or people with mental disabilities through self-conducted and funded programmes in the fields of training, rehabilitation and cultural visits. The Foundation offers scholarships for study. It has delegations in Malaga, Murcia, Salamanca, Santander, Valdepeñas and Valencia.

Geographical Area of Activity: International.

Restrictions: Scholarships are available to students from Spain and Latin America and Spanish-speakers worldwide.

Publications: Annual Report; newsletter (quarterly); *Revista AFIM* (magazine).

Principal Staff: Pres. Alicia González Sanz.

Contact Details: Ctra de La Coruña km 17,800, Edif. FL Smidth, 1º C, 28231 Las Rozas, Madrid; tel. 917105858; e-mail afim@fundacionafim.org; internet www.fundacionafim.org.

Fundación de los Agentes Comerciales de España (Foundation of Spanish Commercial Agents)

Established in 1989.

Fundación Albéniz   SPAIN

Activities: Operates in the areas of economic affairs, education, international affairs and social welfare, nationally and internationally through self-conducted programmes and conferences, and nationally through grants to individuals and institutions, prizes and publications.

Geographical Area of Activity: Worldwide.

Publications: Newsletter; *La Gaceta del Agente Comercial* (journal, 6 a year).

Board of Trustees: Francisco Manuel Maestre Barrajón (Pres.); Valentín Batalla Magariño (Vice-Pres.); Carlos Dominguez Santander (Treas.); Juan Francisco Zamora Gomila (Sec.).

Contact Details: Calle Goya 55, 1° piso, 28001 Madrid; tel. 914363670; e-mail fundacion.ac@cgac.es; internet www.cgac.es.

Fundación Albéniz (Albéniz Foundation)

Established in 1986 by Federico Sopeña, Paloma O'Shea, Elena G. Botín, J. L. Martínez Marauri, Pedro Robles and Luis Revenga; named after composer and pianist Isaac Albéniz (1860–1909).

Activities: Promotes music and the teaching of music, through self-conducted programmes, research, scholarships and fellowships, publications and training courses. The Foundation's principal activities are the Concurso Internacional de Piano de Santander Paloma O'Shea, supporting a music school, maintaining an archive and documentation centre and funding a music academy in Santander. It also awards the Yehudi Menuhin Prize (f. 1999) for the Integration of the Arts and Education. Maintains a library containing more than 25,000 documents and an audiovisual archive. Has an office in Santander.

Geographical Area of Activity: Spain.

Publications: Annual Report; newsletter; *Rubinstein y España; Albénez; Imágenes de la Música Iberoamericana; Imágenes de Isaac Albéniz.*

Finance: Total assets €38.6m. (31 Aug. 2023).

Board of Trustees: Paloma O'Shea (Pres.); Alberto Ruiz-Gallardon (Vice-Pres.); Luis Briones (Sec.).

Principal Staff: CEO Julia Sánchez Abeal.

Contact Details: c/o Escuela Superior de Música Reina Sofía, Calle Requena 1, 28013 Madrid; tel. 913511060; e-mail esmrs@albeniz.com; internet www.escuelasuperiordemusicareinasofia.es/fundacion-albeniz.

Fundación Almine y Bernard Ruiz-Picasso (Almine y Bernard Ruiz-Picasso Foundation)

Founded in 2002.

Activities: Houses a significant collection of Pablo Picasso's work, as well as work from other contemporary artists. Works to study the work of Pablo Picasso from a historical, scientific and technological perspective. Contributes pieces to numerous exhibitions. Has a conservation and restoration departments focussed on preserving works of art.

Geographical Area of Activity: Spain.

Board of Trustees: Almine Ruiz-Picasso, Bernard Ruiz-Picasso (Co-Chair.).

Principal Staff: Registrar Sophie Bravo-Morales.

Contact Details: c/o LEXXEL, Servicios Empresariales, S.L., Calle de Diego Leon 59, 28036 Madrid; e-mail contact@fabarte.org; internet www.fabarte.org.

Fundación Alzheimer España—FAE (Alzheimer Spain Foundation)

Established in 1994 to support and train families and carers of those suffering from Alzheimer's disease and to carry out research.

Activities: Operates in the fields of medicine and health and social welfare and social studies, through training courses, consultancy, publications and international conferences. The Foundation is a founding member of Alzheimer Europe. It works in partnership with the Spanish Ministry of Health to develop policies for neurodegenerative illnesses; provides training for carers; and works to increase non-pharmacological therapies. Also operates Radio Alzheimer FAE online, designed by and for carers.

Geographical Area of Activity: Spain.

Publications: Newsletter (quarterly); reports; guides.

Finance: Annual income approx. €500,000.

Junta Directiva: Micheline Antoine Selmes (Pres.); Adolfo Toledano Gasca (Vice-Pres.); Alfonso López-Ibor Aliño (Sec.).

Principal Staff: Pres. Dr Micheline Antoine Selmés; Vice-Pres Dr Adolfo Toledano Gasca, Nohemí Martínez; Sec. Dr Alfonso López-Ibor Aliño.

Contact Details: Avda Daroca 80, 28017 Madrid; tel. 913431165; e-mail fae@alzfae.org; internet alzfae.org.

Fundación Amancio Ortega (Amancio Ortega Foundation)

Founded in 2001 by Amancio Ortega Gaona, the founder of the Inditex fashion group.

Activities: Main fields of interest are education and social welfare. The Foundation designs, manages and evaluates its own initiatives, supporting pilot projects orientated towards the modernization of civil society, through public and private co-operation. It offers scholarships for Spanish high school students to study in Canada or the USA.

Geographical Area of Activity: Canada, Spain (Galicia), USA.

Finance: Total assets €75.2m. (31 Dec. 2023).

Board of Trustees: Flora Pérez Marcote (Chair.); Marta Ortega Pérez (First Vice-Pres.); José Arnau Sierra (Second Vice-Pres.); Jaime Carro Merchan (Sec.).

Principal Staff: Dir-Gen. Oscar Ortega Chávez.

Contact Details: Cantón Grande no. 4, 15003 La Coruña; tel. 981185596; e-mail contacto@faortega.org; internet www.faortega.org.

Fundación para el Análisis y los Estudios Sociales—FAES (Foundation for Analysis and Social Studies)

Established in 1989.

Activities: Carries out policy research and analysis in the promotion of political, intellectual and economic freedom, democracy, the rule of law, free market economy and Western humanism. The Foundation organizes conferences, seminars, summer schools and leadership training programmes.

Geographical Area of Activity: Europe, Latin America, USA.

Publications: Annual Report; newsletter; *Cuadernos de Pensamiento Político* (journal); *FAES Papers* (series); strategic reports; books.

Finance: Total assets €301,243; net annual income €104,272 (2023).

Board of Trustees: José María Aznar (Pres.); Manuel Pizarro (Vice-Pres.).

Principal Staff: Dir Javier Zarzalejos.

Contact Details: Calle Ruiz de Alarcón 13, 2°, 28014 Madrid; tel. 915766857; e-mail info@fundacionfaes.org; internet fundacionfaes.org.

Fundación Bancaria 'la Caixa' ('La Caixa' Banking Foundation)

Established in 1991 following the merger of Fundació Caixa de Barcelona and Fundació Caixa de Pensions; present name adopted in 2013.

Activities: Works to address social needs unaddressed by other organizations in the areas of social aid, education, healthcare, science and culture, and emergency humanitarian aid through its own programmes and with other organizations in Spain, as well as in other countries where La Caixa savings bank operates. The Foundation manages Obra Social, a social welfare organization, and also funds allotted for social

SPAIN

welfare by Caja de Ahorros y Pensiones de Barcelona. It runs two proprietary science museums, an art gallery exhibiting a collection of contemporary art, and a school of nursing.

Geographical Area of Activity: Spain and internationally in countries where La Caixa operates.

Publications: Annual Report; Annual Corporate Governance Report; *Estrella* (6 a year); brochures.

Finance: Total assets €11,685.5m. (31 Dec. 2023).

Board of Trustees: Isidro Fainé Casas (Chair.); Javier Godó Muntañola (Vice-Chair.); Josep Maria Coronas Guinart (Man. Dir and Sec.).

Contact Details: Avda Diagonal 621, 08028 Barcelona; tel. 934046000; e-mail info@fundacionlacaixa.org; internet www.fundacionlacaixa.org.

Fundación Banco Bilbao Vizcaya Argentaria—Fundación BBVA (BBVA Foundation)

Founded in 1988 by Banco Bilbao Vizcaya; merged with the Fundación Argentaria in 2000.

Activities: Funds scientific research in five key areas: the environment; biomedicine and health; economy and society; basic sciences and technology; and culture. The Foundation encourages analysis, reflection and debate through programmes, conferences, publications and courses in collaboration with other groups and organizations. It awards scholarships for the continued professional development of medical specialists from Latin America; and prizes in recognition of artistic and scientific achievements that advance the frontiers of knowledge. Has an office in Madrid.

Geographical Area of Activity: Central and South America, Europe, Spain, USA.

Publications: Annual Report; newsletter; working papers; books; monographs; reports.

Finance: Annual income €26.1m., expenditure €26.1m. (31 Dec. 2023).

Board of Trustees: Carlos Torres Vila (Pres.); Domingo Armengol Calvo (Sec.).

Principal Staff: Dir Rafael Pardo Avellaneda.

Contact Details: San Nicolás Bldg, Plaza de San Nicolás 4, 48005 Bilbao; tel. 944875626; e-mail informacion@fbbva.es; internet www.fbbva.es.

Fundación Barceló (Barceló Foundation)

Established in 1989 by the Barceló Oliver family, founders of the Barceló tourism group.

Activities: Operates in the areas of education, development and health. The Foundation offers microloans; provides equipment and assistance for medical training; extends financial support to housing projects and initiatives for agricultural development; hosts art exhibitions; and supports educational projects in developing countries. It has worked in 44 countries; and in 2004 opened a cultural centre in Felanitx, Mallorca.

Geographical Area of Activity: Central and South America, Spain (Mallorca), sub-Saharan Africa.

Publications: Annual Report; newsletter (monthly).

Finance: Total assets €59.7m. (31 Dec. 2023).

Board of Trustees: Antonia Barceló Tous (Pres.); Francisca Barceló Vadell (Vice-Pres.); Francisco Barceló Ordinas (Treas.); Jose de Juan Orlandis (Sec.).

Principal Staff: Dir-Gen. José Maria Navarro; Sec. Patricia Cebrian.

Contact Details: Casa del Marqués de Reguer-Rullán, Calle San Jaime 4, 07012 Palma de Mallorca; tel. 971721837; e-mail fundacion@barcelo.com; internet fundacionbarcelo.org.

Fundación Barenboim-Said (Barenboim-Said Foundation)

Established in 2004 by the Andalusian regional government with composer Daniel Barenboim and critical thinker Edward Said.

Activities: Advocates peace and reconciliation through music; promotes music education; and operates and promotes music education projects in Andalusia, Israel, the Palestinian Territories and Arab countries. Initiatives include: the West-Eastern Divan Orchestra of musicians from Israel, the Middle East and Spain; the Academy of Orchestral Studies; a music education project in the Palestinian Territories; and an early childhood music education project which operates in Andalusian primary schools. The Foundation has representative offices in Germany and the Palestinian Territories.

Geographical Area of Activity: Middle East, Spain.

Publications: Annual Report; newsletter; *Parallels and Paradoxes*; *Humanism and Democratic Criticism*; *Musical Elaborations*; *Representations of the Intellectual*; *Music and Literature against the grain;* DVDs.

Board of Trustees: Juan Fernández Pantoja (Sec.).

Principal Staff: Man. Dir Muriel Páez Rasmussen.

Contact Details: Patio de Banderas 14, 41004 Seville; tel. 955037385; e-mail info.fbs@juntadeandalucia.es; internet www.barenboim-said.org.

Fundación de las Cajas de Ahorros—FUNCAS (Foundation of Banks and Savings Banks of CECA)

Founded in 1968 by the Confederación Española de Cajas de Ahorros.

Activities: Conducts research on economics and financial systems, fiscal and tax law, contemporary history and statistics, with special emphasis on their relation to the field of savings, and to similar European institutions. The Foundation maintains close links with economic ministries and financial centres. It has an extensive library, a publishing fund and a small grants fund for sustainable development projects in Spain. Awards four annual Enrique Fuentes Quintana Prizes, each worth €4,000, for the best doctoral thesis in social sciences, health sciences, humanities, and engineering, maths, architecture and physics.

Geographical Area of Activity: Spain.

Publications: Annual Report; working papers; reports; studies; *Papeles de Economía Española* (quarterly journal); *Cuadernos de Información Económica* (journal, 6 a year); *Papeles de Energía* (weekly magazine); *Panorama Social* (journal); *Focus on Spanish Society*; *Fronteras del conocimiento*.

Finance: Annual income €4.9m., expenditure €4.9m. (2022).

Board of Trustees: Isidro Fainé Casas (Pres.); José Maria Méndez Álvarez-Cedrón (Vice-Pres.); Fernando Conlledo Lantero (Sec.).

Principal Staff: Dir-Gen. Carlos Ocaña Pérez de Tudela.

Contact Details: Edif. Foro, Calle Caballero de Gracia 28, 28013 Madrid; tel. 915965718; e-mail funcas@funcas.es; internet www.funcas.es.

Fundación Carlos de Amberes (Carlos de Amberes Foundation)

Established in 1594 by Carlos de Amberes, a Flemish merchant living in Madrid, to support pilgrims from the then Spanish Low Countries; in 1988 the Foundation refocused its mission on cultural activities, aiming to build a united Europe.

Activities: Conducts research into the history of cultural and artistic relations between Spain, the Hispanic world and Europe, in particular the Low Countries. The Foundation acts as a cultural link between Spain, Belgium, Luxembourg, France and the Netherlands, organizing exhibitions, courses, seminars, conferences and music concerts, held at the Foundation's headquarters. It has a research centre and a library specializing in EU issues; and organizes courses and seminars on the construction of a new Europe.

Geographical Area of Activity: Spain.

Publications: Newsletter; books.

Board of Trustees: Miguel Ángel Aguilar Tremoya (Pres.); Daniel de Busturia y Jimeno (Sec.).

Principal Staff: Man. Dir Elena Alonso Casillas.

Contact Details: Calle Claudio Coello 99, 28006 Madrid; tel. 914352201; e-mail fca@fcamberes.org; internet www.fcamberes.org.

Fundación Carolina

Established in 2000 by the Spanish Government to commemorate the 25th year of the rule of HH King Juan Carlos I and the 500th anniversary of the birth of Spain.

Activities: Promotes cultural, educational and scientific co-operation between Spain and countries of the Organization of Ibero-American States. The Foundation awards scholarships and grants to students and researchers from Latin America and Spain to study in Spain. It also organizes and international programme for professionals, thought leaders and emerging figures in politics and civil society to visit and learn about Spain and Europe from an international and socioeconomic perspective. The beneficiaries make up the Carolina Communication Network, comprising more than 20,000 former scholars, leaders, researchers and professionals; in addition to 10 Carolina Associations in Latin America.

Geographical Area of Activity: South America, Central America and the Caribbean, Spain.

Publications: Annual Report; books; working papers; analyses.

Governing Board: Eva Granados (Chair.).

Principal Staff: Sec.-Gen. Purification Causapié.

Contact Details: Plaza del Marqués de Salamanca 8, 4th floor, 28006 Madrid; tel. 913796771; e-mail informacion@fundacioncarolina.es; internet www.fundacioncarolina.es.

Fundación Científica de la Asociación Española Contra el Cáncer—AECC (Scientific Foundation of the Spanish Cancer Association)

Established in 1971 to manage the funds that the Spanish Cancer Association devotes to cancer research to promote and advance oncological research.

Activities: Promotes and advances oncological research, offers funding under the following programmes: stable research groups; child cancer research project; advanced cancer training programme; and assistance for researchers.

Geographical Area of Activity: Mainly Spain.

Publications: Annual Report; *Estadística* (annual); monographs; guides.

Finance: Annual income €31.2m., expenditure €27.9m. (31 Dec. 2023).

Board: Dr Ramón Reyes Bori (Pres.); Dr Nieves Mijimolle Cuadrado (First Vice-Pres.); Carmen Recio (Second Vice-Pres.); Laura de Rivera García de Leaniz (Sec.).

Principal Staff: CEO Isabel Orbe.

Contact Details: Calle Teniente Coronel Noreña 30, 28045 Madrid; tel. 913194138; e-mail fundacion.cientifica@contraelcancer.es; internet www.aecc.es/es/investigacion/fundacion-cientifica-aecc.

Fundación CODESPA (CODESPA Foundation)

Established in 1985 by diplomat Laureano López Rodó and a group of business people and university professors concerned about poverty.

Activities: Works in the fields of economic and social development. Programmes include: community-managed rural tourism; professional training and integration; microfinance for development; rural markets development; food security and food sovereignty; social entrepreneurship and micro-enterprise; and environmental sustainability and energy. The NGO awards grants to institutions; organizes conferences and training courses; and issues publications. It has offices in Angola, the Democratic Republic of the Congo, Morocco, the Philippines, the Dominican Republic, Colombia, Ecuador, Guatemala, Nicaragua, Peru and Bolivia; with separate delegations operating in Catalonia and the USA.

Geographical Area of Activity: Africa, South America, Central America and the Caribbean, Philippines, Spain.

Publications: Annual Report; newsletter; blog.

Finance: Annual income €191,897, expenditure €78,301 (31 Dec. 2023).

Board of Trustees: Andrés Fontenla Contreras (Pres.); Eduardo Conde Muntadas-Prim (Vice-Pres.); Miriam Herrando Deprit (Sec.).

Principal Staff: Dir-Gen. José Ignacio González-Aller Gross.

Contact Details: Calle Rafael Bergamín 12, Bajo, 28043 Madrid; tel. 917444240; e-mail codespa@codespa.org; internet www.codespa.org.

Fundación Empresa-Universidad de Zaragoza (University of Zaragoza Business Foundation)

Founded in 1982 by the Universidad y Cámara de Comercio e Industria de Zaragoza.

Activities: Manages the Leonardo Da Vinci Programme and Erasmus+ programmes for graduates of the University of Zaragoza to undertake workplace internships in EU countries. The Foundation offers technical and vocational training for students and graduates, including in employability and workplace integration, and English language certification. Regionally, it promotes and supports ideas entrepreneurship among teachers; conducts research and promotes the transfer of technology and innovation from university to public and private enterprise and society more broadly; and offers organizational needs identification services to companies.

Geographical Area of Activity: EU.

Publications: Newsletter.

Finance: Total assets €2.2m. (31 Dec. 2023).

Trustees: Dr Manuel López Pérez (Pres.); Dr Manuel Teruel Izquierdo (Vice-Pres.); Dr José Miguel Sánchez Muñoz (Sec.).

Principal Staff: Dir-Gen. Dr José Javier Sánchez Asín.

Contact Details: Paseo Fernando el Católico 59, escalera dcha, 1° izq., 50006 Zaragoza; tel. 976351508; e-mail feuz@feuz.es; internet www.feuz.es.

Fundación Felipe González

Established in 2013 to manage the archive of former Prime Minister Felipe González.

Activities: Works to address political and social challenges through modernization and promotion of equality; and encourages increased knowledge of Spanish and international politics and contemporary issues. Main programmes include: Genera, a forum for intergenerational dialogue; Palancas, a citizen platform for co-creating micro-reforms in areas including building insulation, art and memory, forest fire management, medical prescriptions, election manifesto audits and alternative indicators to GDP; and the Opportunities Atlas, mapping social mobility in Spain.

Geographical Area of Activity: Colombia, Ecuador, Spain.

Publications: Annual Report; newsletter.

Finance: Total assets €443,543; net annual income €70,084 (31 Dec. 2022).

Board of Trustees: Felipe González Márquez (Chair.).

Principal Staff: Dir Rocío Martínez-Sampere.

Contact Details: Calle Fuenterrabía 2, 28014 Madrid; tel. 915134945; e-mail info@fundacionfelipegonzalez.org; internet www.fundacionfelipegonzalez.org.

Fundación Fernando Rielo (Fernando Rielo Foundation)

Founded in 1981 by poet and philosopher Fernando Rielo to promote understanding between different cultures and traditions, and mysticism.

Activities: Organizes international conferences, seminars and concerts; and poetry, music, education and philosophy courses. The Foundation awards prizes, scholarships and grants to promote culture, in particular literature, including the Fernando Rielo Prize for Mystical Poetry (worth €7,000), and the International Prize for Sacred Music (worth €5,000). It has close links with foundations and universities in Spain and abroad and has established the Fernando Rielo Chair in

Spanish Literature and Thought at the University of the Philippines; and in Spain has organized the World Conference on Mysticism at the Universidad Pontificia de Salamanca and courses at the Universidad Internacional Menéndez Pelayo. Has 53 offices around the world.

Geographical Area of Activity: Worldwide.

Publications: *La Revista Internacional de Poesía Equivalencias/Equivalencias y diverssas* (magazine); publications on the humanities, pedagogy and philosophy, and collections of poetry; also publishes the winners of the Fernando Rielo Prize for Mystical Poetry.

Principal Staff: CEO Ascensión Escamilla Valera.

Contact Details: Calle Hermosilla 5, 3rd Floor, 28001 Madrid; tel. 915754091; e-mail fundacion@rielo.com; internet rielo.com.

Fundación IE (IE Foundation)

Established in 1997 as the Fundación Instituto de Empresa.

Activities: Promotes entrepreneurship, diversity, inclusivity and innovation, with a particular emphasis on the humanities in higher education. The Foundation works to improve the quality of education at IE and foster a culture of social awareness and community engagement. It supports applied research projects with high social and educational impact; and offers scholarships.

Geographical Area of Activity: Primarily Spain, but also Europe, the Middle East and North Africa, North and South America.

Publications: Annual Report; *IDEAS* (quarterly magazine); *advanced series* (report).

Finance: Total assets €19m. (31 Dec. 2023).

Board of Governors: Gonzalo Garland (Exec. Vice-Pres.).

Principal Staff: Dir-Gen. Geoffroy Gérard.

Contact Details: Calle María de Molina 13, 28006 Madrid; Paseo de la Castellana 259, 29th Floor, 28046 Madrid; tel. 915689600; e-mail iefoundation@ie.edu; internet www.ie.edu/es/fundacion-ie.

Fundación José Miguel de Barandiarán (José Miguel de Barandiarán Foundation)

Established in 1988 by the Sociedad de Estudios Vascos–Eusko Ikaskuntza in conjunction with José Miguel de Barandiarán Ayerbe, an anthropologist and ethnographer.

Activities: Organizes and funds programmes and awards research grants in the fields of prehistory, archaeology, anthropology and ethnology. The Foundation also organizes courses, seminars, conferences and other related activities, and disseminates their results.

Geographical Area of Activity: Spain.

Publications: *Colección Sara*; *Colección Barandiaran*; *Yearbook of Eusko Folklore*; catalogues.

Board: Abel Ariznabarreta Zubero (Pres.); Jexux Aizpurua Barandiaran (Sec.).

Contact Details: Secretariat: Pedro Asua 2, 2º piso, of. 60, 01008 Vitoria-Gasteiz; tel. 945143066; e-mail gasteiz@barandiaranfundazioa.eus; internet www.barandiaranfundazioa.eus.

Fundación José Ortega y Gasset—Gregorio Marañón (José Ortega y Gasset—Gregorio Marañón Foundation)

Established in 1978 by Soledad Ortega Spottorno as a private, non-profit-making academic research institute to further the cultural legacy of philosopher and essayist José Ortega y Gasset; it comprises the Fundación Gregorio Marañón (f. 1988), which conserves the works of Gregorio Marañón, a doctor and historian.

Activities: Operates in the fields of the humanities and social sciences, through research and study activities, including postgraduate and doctoral research projects, seminars, lectures, exhibitions, and cultural and scientific meetings that cover unlimited topics. Emphasis is placed on subjects covering Iberia, Europe and Central and South America. In 1986 the Foundation established the Instituto Universitario de Investigación Ortega y Gasset for postgraduate training and research in the social sciences and humanities, part of the Universidad Complutense de Madrid. The Foundation runs an International Programme of Spanish Language, Latin American and European Studies at its centre in Toledo, providing study opportunities for undergraduate and graduate students, as well as the annual Young Hispanic Leaders Programme, providing young US citizens of Hispanic origin with the opportunity to familiarize themselves with Spain's political, economic, social and cultural environment. It also has a centre in Buenos Aires, Argentina; and has established relations with several international universities. The Foundation also maintains the private library and archives of José Ortega y Gasset, comprising approximately 72,000 vols.

Geographical Area of Activity: Argentina, Colombia, Mexico, Peru, Dominican Rep., Spain, USA.

Publications: Annual Report; newsletter; *Revista de Occidente* (monthly); Revista de Estudios Orteguianos, papers and series.

Finance: Total assets €21.0m.; net annual income –€2.4m. (31 Aug. 2021).

Board of Trustees: Gregorio Marañón and Bertrán de Lis (Pres.); Juan Pablo Fusi Aizpúrua (First Vice-Pres.); Inés López-Ibor Alcocer (Second Vice-Pres.).

Principal Staff: Dir-Gen. Lucía Sala Silveira.

Contact Details: Calle Fortuny 53, 28010 Madrid; tel. 917004100; e-mail comunicacion@fogm.es; internet www.ortegaygasset.edu.

Fundación Juan March (Juan March Foundation)

Founded in 1955 by Juan March Ordinas, a financier.

Activities: Organizes science courses and workshops, awards prizes, and makes grants for fellowships and group research programmes in the fields of scientific and technical research. The Centre for International Meetings on Biology, established in 1991, promotes collaboration between Spanish and foreign scientists working in the field of biology. A Centre for Advanced Study in the Social Sciences opened in 1987, within the Juan March Institute, to promote and conduct research and offer postgraduate courses; in 2013 it was integrated into the Universidad Carlos III and renamed IC3JM. Grants are made to institutions devoted to social welfare. The Foundation awards scholarships to artists and researchers in the visual arts undertaking work nationally and abroad. It maintains a library, and a research and documentation centre. Its Madrid headquarters serve as a cultural centre and the Foundation also directs the Museum of Spanish Abstract Art in Cuenca and Juan March Foundation Museum in Palma de Mallorca.

Geographical Area of Activity: International.

Publications: Annual Report; *Noticias y propuestas de la Fundación* (e-newsletter); *Anales* (annual report); *Revista Informativa*; (monthly); *Calendario de actos* (monthly); *Biografías de Españoles eminentes* (series); brochures; catalogues and other publications.

Finance: Annual expenditure €13m. (2023).

Board of Trustees: Juan March Delgado (Pres.); Carlos March Delgado (Vice-Pres.).

Principal Staff: Dir Javier Gomá Lanzón.

Contact Details: Castelló 77, 28006 Madrid; tel. 914354240; e-mail fundacion@march.es; internet www.march.es.

Fundación Juanelo Turriano (Juanelo Turriano Foundation)

Established in 1987 by José Antonio García-Diego, a civil engineer, in honour of Juanelo Turriano, a 16th-century watchmaker and engine builder from Lombardy.

Activities: Focuses on the study of history of science, technology and engineering. Every two years, the Foundation offers the International García-Diego Prize, worth €9,000, for research on the history of technology; and also offers the

Pedro Navascués Prize worth €6,000 for PhD thesis, read in the previous year. It organizes exhibitions and courses; publishes books; and maintains a specialized library.

Geographical Area of Activity: International.

Restrictions: Submissions for the International García-Diego Prize must be in Spanish.

Publications: Annual Report; newsletter; books.

Finance: Total assets €22.2m. (31 Dec. 2023).

Board of Trustees: José María Goicolea Ruigómez (Pres.); José Antonio González Carrión (Vice-Pres.); Claudio Olalla y Marañón (Sec.).

Advisory Committee: David Fernández-Ordóñez Hernández (Pres.).

Principal Staff: CEO Bernardo Revuelta Pol.

Contact Details: Calle Zurbano 41, 1°, 28010 Madrid; tel. 915313005; e-mail fundacion@juaneloturriano.com; internet www.juaneloturriano.com.

Fundación Leo Messi (Leo Messi Foundation)

Established in 2007 by Lionel Messi, an Argentinian footballer.

Activities: Carries out activities to benefit children in the fields of health, education and sport.

Geographical Area of Activity: Middle East and North Africa, South America, Central America and the Caribbean, South-East Asia, Southern Africa, Spain, West Africa, USA.

Publications: Annual Report.

Finance: Total assets €2.1m.; net annual income −€193,653 (2021).

Board of Trustees: Rodrigo Martín Messi (Chair.); María Florencia Parisi (Sec.).

Contact Details: Av. Diagonal 682, 9è pis A, 08034 Barcelona; tel. 932055648; e-mail info@messi.com; internet messi.com/fundacion-leo-messi.

Fundación Loewe (Loewe Foundation)

Established in 1988 by Enrique Loewe Lynch, head of Loewe, a fashion company.

Activities: Promotes creativity and education, promoting and sponsoring poetry, dance, photography, architecture and design in Spain. In 1988 the Foundation established the Loewe Foundation International Poetry Prize for poetry in Spanish; and in 2016 the Loewe Craft Prize, worth €50,000, for artisanal excellence.

Geographical Area of Activity: Spain.

Publications: Newsletter; poetry collections.

Board of Trustees: Sheila Loewe (Chair.); Pascale Lepoivre (Vice-Chair.).

Contact Details: Calle Goya 4, 28001 Madrid; tel. 912041300; e-mail fundacion@loewe.es; internet www.loewe.com/eur/en/stories-loewe-foundation/loewe-foundation.html.

Fundación MAPFRE (MAPFRE Foundation)

Activities: Fundación MAPFRE organizes a wide range of activities worldwide in five key areas that all share a common objective: ethical commitment to society. The five key areas of activity are: social action, culture, health promotion, road safety, and insurance and social protection. Also manages a Documentation Center that offers a free information service for the general public on insurance, risk management and social security, as well as related subjects such as economics and law; and the Ageingnomics Research Center that aims to promote a positive view of demographic change based on the economic and social opportunities that come with an ageing population.

Geographical Area of Activity: International.

Publications: Annual Report; newsletters; *La Fundación* (print); brochures; blog; books.

Finance: Total assets €76.8m.; annual income €4.6m., expenditure €3.7m. (2023).

Board of Trustees: Antonio Huertas Mejías (Pres.); José Manuel Inchausti (First Vice-Pres.); Antonio Miguel-Romero de Olano (Second Vice-Pres.).

Principal Staff: Man. Dir Julio Domingo Souto.

Contact Details: Paseo de Recoletos 23, 28004 Madrid; internet www.fundacionmapfre.org.

Fundación Marcelino Botín (Botín Foundation)

Established in 1964 by Marcelino Botin Sanz de Sautuola, a financier, to promote social development in the province of Cantabria.

Activities: Aims to stimulate the economic, social and cultural development of society. Main programmes are: Science and Technology Transfer; Education; Rural Development and Heritage; and Social Action. The Trend Observatory works on education, science and technology transfer, water and energy; and oversees a talent development programme and a programme to strengthen the civil service in Latin America. The Foundation offers grants in the areas of visual arts, museum management, music, higher education and civil service. It operates the Centro Botín arts centre and has a library, containing 28,000 items, specializing in art since the 19th century and music; and maintains several historic properties around Santander where the Foundation hosts exhibitions and workshops. Has an office in Madrid.

Geographical Area of Activity: Europe, Latin America.

Publications: Annual Report; newsletter; catalogues; publications on education, art, rural development and music.

Finance: Annual expenditure €16.2m. (2021).

Board of Trustees: Javier Botín-Sanz de Sautuola y O'Shea (Pres.).

Principal Staff: Man. Dir and Sec. Iñigo Saenz de Miera Cárdenas.

Contact Details: Calle Pedrueca 1, 39003 Santander; tel. 942226072; e-mail prensa@fundacionbotin.org; internet www.fundacionbotin.org.

Fundación María Francisca de Roviralta (María Francisca de Roviralta Foundation)

Established in 1959 by José María Roviralta and Manuel Roviralta Alemany, industrialists.

Activities: Carries out activities under four main programmes: social development; medicine and health; education and science; and other activities. In 2009 the Asociación Española de Fundaciones awarded it the Medal of Honour.

Geographical Area of Activity: International.

Publications: Annual Report.

Finance: Total assets €39.9m.; net annual income €1.3m. (2023).

Board of Trustees: Gerardo Salvador (Pres.); Tomás Testor (Vice-Pres. and Sec.).

Principal Staff: Dir Javier Serra.

Contact Details: Calle Tuset 20–24, 08006 Barcelona; Calle Sauceda 10, 2°, 28050 Madrid; tel. 915560228; e-mail fundacion@roviralta.org; internet www.roviralta.org.

Fundación Montemadrid (Montemadrid Foundation)

Established in 1991 by the Caja Madrid savings bank to operate in the fields of the arts and humanities; formerly known as the Fundación Caja Madrid.

Activities: Main programme areas are culture, education, environment and social action. The Foundation operates four nursery schools; two education centres; two facilities for older people; two libraries; a sports centre; an employment centre; and 35 social institution management centres. It awards scholarships for study abroad; supports emerging artists; and runs a heritage conservation programme.

Geographical Area of Activity: Spain.

Publications: Annual Report.

Finance: Total assets €388.0m.; net annual income €1.8m. (31 Dec. 2023).

Board of Trustees: Jesús Núñez Velázquez (Pres.).
Principal Staff: Gen. Man. Amaya Miguel.
Contact Details: Ronda de Valencia 2, 28012 Madrid; tel. 913685999; e-mail consultas@montemadrid.es; internet www.fundacionmontemadrid.es.

Fundación Mujeres (Foundation for Women)

Established in 1994.

Activities: Promotes equal opportunities for women and the prevention of violence against women. The Foundation carries out self-conducted programmes and research; and organizes conferences and training courses. It has regional delegations in Andalucia, Extremadura, Asturias and Galicia.

Geographical Area of Activity: International.

Publications: Annual Report; *Monográfico* (newsletter); *El Libro del Buen Hablar: Una Apuesta por un Lenguaje no Sexist*; blog.

Finance: Annual income €5.7m., expenditure €5.5m. (31 Dec. 2023).

Board of Trustees: María Elena Valenciano Martínez-Orozco (Pres.); María Luisa Soleto Ávila (Exec. Vice-Pres.).

Principal Staff: Sec.-Gen. Cristina García Comas.

Contact Details: Calle San Bernardo 64, 2ª planta, 28015 Madrid; tel. 915912420; e-mail mujeres@fundacionmujeres.es; internet www.fundacionmujeres.es.

Fundación ONCE (ONCE—Spanish National Organization for the Blind—Foundation)

Founded in 1988 by ONCE, the Spanish National Organization for the Blind.

Activities: Helps people with disabilities to integrate into society. The Foundation works with government agencies; offers grants and low-interest loans for job creation, education, rehabilitation and training; and helps to break down barriers to communication. It promotes sport for its role in the personal and social development of people with disabilities; and has a library which specializes in disability, containing more than 4,900 titles, and a digital library of more than 50,000 audiobooks.

Geographical Area of Activity: Mainly Spain.

Publications: Annual Report; *Así Somos* (newsletter); *Manual de Accesibilidad Global para la Formación;* information brochures; books on disability and social issues.

Finance: Receives 3% of revenue from lottery tickets sold by ONCE, equivalent to 20% of the Foundation's operating revenue. Total assets €715.9m.; net annual income €17.5m. (31 Dec. 2022).

Board of Trustees: Miguel Carballeda Piñeiro (Chair.); Alberto Durán López (Exec. Vice-Chair.).

Principal Staff: Dir-Gen. José Luis Martínez Donoso; Sec.-Gen. Virginia Carcedo Illera.

Contact Details: Calle Sebastián Herrera 15, 28012 Madrid; tel. 915068888; e-mail fundaciononce@fundaciononce.es; internet www.fundaciononce.es.

Fundación Orange (Orange Foundation)

Established in 1998 as Fundación Retevisión, a telecommunications provider; part of the Fondation Orange (q.v.) network.

Activities: Promotes use of technology for communication and social inclusion, particularly for young people with autism or at risk of exclusion; and to improve the autonomy of vulnerable women and their access to employment. The Foundation offers an annual prize, worth €4,000, for women working in the fields of technology and social innovation.

Geographical Area of Activity: Spain.

Publications: Newsletter (monthly).

Finance: Initial endowment €60,101.

Principal Staff: Pres. Jean-François Fallacher.

Contact Details: Parque Empresarial La Finca, Paseo del Club Deportivo 1, Edif. 7, Planta 2, 28223 Pozuelo de Alarcón, Madrid; tel. 911785024; e-mail fundacion.es@es.orange.com; internet www.fundacionorange.es.

Fundación Oxfam Intermón

Established in 1956 as the secretariat for missions and development of the Compañía de Jesús; part of the Oxfam confederation of organizations (qq.v.).

Activities: Works to end poverty worldwide through reducing social and economic inequality. Main programmes focus on: access to food and decent work; the rights of women and girls; providing water, sanitation food and shelter during humanitarian crises; and reducing inequality through redistributing power and wealth. The organization supports 13 smaller organizations in Spain working in the areas of migration and women's rights; and collaborates with a network of 18,900 educators to produce resources on global citizenship.

Geographical Area of Activity: International.

Restrictions: Does not make loans or grants to individuals.

Publications: Annual report; newsletter (monthly); *Revista Oxfam Intermón* (3 a year); books, studies and reports.

Finance: Annual income €114.7m., expenditure €113.6m. (31 March 2024).

Board of Trustees: Ignasi Fisas Carreras (Chair.); Sylvia Koniecki (Vice-Chair.); Anna Xicoy Cruells (Treas.); Maria Vidal (Sec.).

Principal Staff: Man. Dir Franc Cortada.

Contact Details: DMOURA4 Bldg, Calle Treball 100, 08019 Barcelona; tel. 900223300; e-mail info@oxfamintermon.org; internet www.oxfamintermon.org.

Fundación Paideia Galiza (Paideia Galiza Foundation)

Founded in 1986 by Rosalía Mera Goyenechea, co-founder of Zara, a fashion retailer.

Activities: Promotes social innovation, using an interdisciplinary approach, through innovative and sustainable projects that promote employment of disadvantaged groups, equal opportunities and economic development. Programme areas include: disability and employment, preventing and avoiding social exclusion and building self-sufficiency; young people and mobility, promoting opportunities for young Galicians through stays in other countries through the European Voluntary Service programme, La Ida transnational training placements and non-formal education programmes; entrepreneurship in areas including new technologies, services, audiovisual, cultural and/or social; territorial development, in the Sar, Barbanza, Noia and Muros regions; and education and research. Its facilities include a Business Initiatives Centre (MANS), a co-working space, and a music and media recording studio. Has an office in Padrón.

Geographical Area of Activity: Spain.

Publications: Annual Report; reports; legal guides.

Finance: Annual budget €2.7m. (2022).

Board of Trustees: Sandra Ortega Mera (Chair.); Guillermo Vergara Muñoz (Vice-Chair.); María Cotón Fernández (Sec.).

Contact Details: Plaza de María Pita 17, 15001 A Coruña; tel. 981223927; e-mail paideia@paideia.es; internet www.paideia.es.

Fundación Pedro Barrié de la Maza (Pedro Barrié de la Maza Foundation)

Founded in 1966 by Pedro Barrié de la Maza, Conde de Fenosa.

Activities: Operates mainly in Galicia in the fields of education, social welfare and studies, science, medicine and the arts and humanities, through self-conducted programmes, research, grants to individuals and institutions, conferences, courses and publications. The Foundation awards scholarships, prizes and research grants, and has financed the construction and equipment of technical schools and cultural and social institutions. In 1994 it established the Galician Institute of Economic Studies.

Fundación Princesa de Asturias SPAIN

Geographical Area of Activity: Spain (Galicia).
Publications: Annual Report; newsletter; books; dictionaries.
Finance: Total assets €167m. (31 Dec. 2023).
Board of Trustees: Pilar Romero Vázquez-Gulías (Chair.); Pilar Arias Romero, Joaquin Arias Romero (Vice-Chair.); Carlos Lema Devesa (Sec.).
Principal Staff: Dir Carmen Arias Romero.
Contact Details: Cantón Grande 9, 15003 A Coruña; tel. 981221525; e-mail info@fbarrie.org; internet www.fundacionbarrie.org.

Fundación Princesa de Asturias (Princess of Asturias Foundation)

Founded in 1980 as the Príncipe de Asturias Foundation; present name adopted in 2014 following the proclamation of HM King Felipe VI as King of Spain.
Activities: Promotes scientific, cultural and humanist values. The Foundation presents the annual Princess of Asturias Awards in communication and the humanities, social sciences, arts, literature, technical and scientific research, international co-operation, concord and sport. The Awards recognize scientific, technical, cultural, social and humanist achievements by individuals or organizations at an international level. In 1983 the Foundation created a music department, which has three choirs and an international music school.
Geographical Area of Activity: International.
Publications: Annual Report.
Finance: Annual income €6.7m., expenditure €6.3m. (31 Dec. 2023).
Board of Trustees: Ana Isabel Fernández Álvarez (Pres.).
Principal Staff: Gen. Sec. Adolfo Menéndez Menéndez.
Contact Details: Plácido Arango Arias 2, 33004 Oviedo; tel. 985258755; e-mail info@fpa.es; internet www.fpa.es.

Fundación Promi (Promi Foundation)

Founded in 1998.
Activities: Works to improve the quality of life of mentally disabled people throughout Europe, through projects, conferences and training programmes, concentrating on integration in work and society, and the rehabilitation of people with mental disabilities. The Foundation assists NGOs and other organizations with similar aims and lends its support to businesses employing people with mental disabilities. It has two research and information centres.
Geographical Area of Activity: Europe.
Publications: Annual Report; newsletter; *Deficiencia, Enfermedad Mental y Senilidad: Mecanismos Legales de Protección*; publications relating to disability.
Finance: Total assets €13.1m. (2021).
Board of Trustees: Juan Antonio Pérez Benítez (Pres.); Juan de Dios Serrano González (Vice-Pres.); José María Castilla Martínez (Sec.).
Contact Details: Avda Fuente de las Piedras s/n, 14940 Cabra, Córdoba; tel. 900777111; e-mail informacion@promi.es; internet fundacionpromi.es.

Fundación Rafa Nadal (Rafa Nadal Foundation)

Established in 2008 by Rafael Nadal, a tennis player, and his mother Ana María Parera.
Activities: Carries out activities in the fields of sports, education and social integration for marginalized children and young people; and awards educational grants for tennis players and scholarships to study at universities in the USA. In 2010 the Foundation established the Anantapur Educational Centre in Andhra Pradesh, India, in collaboration with Fundación Vicente Ferrer. It also operates the Rafa Nadal Foundation Centre (f. 2014) in Palma de Mallorca. The Rafa Nadal Foundation Inc operates in the USA.
Geographical Area of Activity: India, Spain, USA.
Publications: Annual Report; newsletter; blog.
Finance: Total assets €8.1m.; net annual income €17,228 (31 Aug. 2023).
Board of Trustees: Ana María Parera (Pres.); Sebastián Nadal (Vice-Pres.).
Principal Staff: Dir and Sec. Maria Francisca Perelló; Deputy Dir Jose Antonio Ruiz.
Contact Details: Rafa Nadal Sports Center, Ctra. Cales de Mallorca, km 1.2, 07500 Manacor; tel. 971171679; e-mail info@fundacionrafanadal.org; internet www.fundacionrafanadal.org.

Fundación Rafael del Pino (Rafael del Pino Foundation)

Established in 1999 by Rafael del Pino y Moreno, a business person.
Activities: Provides leadership training; promotes individual initiative and free market and free enterprise principles; improves the health and living standards of citizens; fosters entrepreneurship; and promotes and conserves Spanish culture and heritage. The Foundation offers scholarships to Spanish students; funds research programmes and management training for NGOs; and organizes seminars, lectures and meetings, including the Free Enterprise Forum. It also offers grants to projects aiming to protect and develop Spain's cultural heritage; and a series of awards and prizes, recognizing Spanish literature, dissertations in the fields of economics, law, business, politics, international relations, mass media and education, and initiatives aiming to eliminate inefficient regulations or foster market competition.
Geographical Area of Activity: Spain.
Publications: Annual Report; publications on economics, business, law, history and other subjects.
Finance: Total assets €130.6m. (31 Dec. 2023).
Board of Trustees: María del Pino y Calvo-Sotelo (Pres.); Ana Mª Cebrián del Pino (Vice-Pres.); José Ignacio Ysasi-Ysasmendi y Pemán (Sec.).
Principal Staff: Dir Vicente José Montes Gan.
Contact Details: Rafael Calvo 39, 28010 Madrid; tel. 913968600; e-mail info@frdelpino.es; internet www.frdelpino.es.

Fundación Ramón Areces (Ramón Areces Foundation)

Founded in 1976 by Ramón Areces Rodríguez, former President of El Corte Inglés, a department store chain.
Activities: Co-operates with other organizations to promote and preserve Spanish culture and scientific research. The Foundation awards research grants for projects in the fields of life and earth sciences and social sciences; and scholarships for postgraduate study at universities and research centres abroad. Its cultural programme includes lectures, symposia, conferences and inter-university courses.
Geographical Area of Activity: Spain.
Publications: Annual Report.
Board of Trustees: Marta Álvarez Guil (Chair.); Cristina Álvarez Guil (Vice-Chair.); José Ramón de Hoces (Sec.).
Principal Staff: Dir Raimundo Pérez-Hernández y Torra.
Contact Details: Calle Vitruvio 5, 28006 Madrid; tel. 915158980; e-mail info@fundacionareces.es; internet www.fundacionareces.es.

Fundación Real Instituto Elcano (Royal Elcano Institute Foundation)

Established in 2001, named after Juan Sebastián de Elcano, the navigator of the first maritime expedition to circumnavigate the globe; a think tank.
Activities: Works in the field of strategic and international studies, promoting knowledge of international affairs and Spain's foreign relations. The Institute carries out research and analysis in four main areas: Spanish foreign policy, new threats to security and global governance; the future of the EU; the global agenda from a Spanish and European

perspective; and tools for analysing international relations. Other areas of interest include: energy and climate change; demography and migration; digitization of the economy; the global economy; international terrorism; security and defence; and Spain's image abroad. It organizes conferences, seminars and working groups; and has an office in Brussels, Belgium.

Geographical Area of Activity: International.

Publications: Annual Report; *Boletín/Newsletter* (monthly, in Spanish and English); *Revista Elcano*; *Comentarios Elcano*; *Análisis del Real Instituto Elcano (ARI)*; *Novedades en la RED* (weekly newsletter); working papers; reports; monographs; books; Elcano Global Presence Index; Spain's Image Barometer (BIE).

Finance: Total assets €3.0m.; net annual income €3.0m. (31 Dec. 2023).

Board of Trustees and Executive Committee: José Juan Ruiz (Chair.); María Dolores de Cospedal (Deputy Chair.).

Principal Staff: Dir Charles Powell.

Contact Details: Príncipe de Vergara 51, 28006 Madrid; tel. 917816770; e-mail info@rielcano.org; internet www.realinstitutoelcano.org.

Fundación Real Madrid (Real Madrid Foundation)

Established in 1997 by football club Real Madrid.

Activities: Carries out activities in the fields of sports, with a focus on football and basketball; children and young people's education and cultural awareness; social welfare; and international co-operation. The Foundation awards scholarships to marginalized children to attend its network of social sports schools; and carries out projects in prisons, detention centres, hospitals and for the elderly. It also manages the club's Historical Heritage Centre.

Geographical Area of Activity: International.

Publications: Annual Report; *Revista Fundación* (magazine).

Finance: Total assets €5.0m.; net annual income –€122.4m. (30 June 2021).

Board of Trustees: Florentino Pérez Rodríguez (Pres.); Enrique Sánchez González (Vice-Pres. and Sec.).

Principal Staff: Man. Dir Julio González Ronco; Gen. Man. Manuel Redondo Sierra.

Contact Details: Calle Concha Espina 1, Estadio Santiago Bernabéu, 28036 Madrid; tel. 913984300; e-mail correo.fundacion@corp.realmadrid.com; internet www.realmadrid.com/sobre-el-real-madrid/fundacion.

Fundación Repsol (Repsol Foundation)

Established in 1995 by Repsol, an oil and gas company.

Activities: Main programme areas include: supporting entrepreneurs to bring technological innovations in the fields of energy and mobility to market; working for the inclusion of people with disabilities and other vulnerable groups, through sport, culture, training and raising awareness; and raising awareness among young children about responsible energy use through organizing projects, workshops and science weeks. The Foundation offers scholarships and study grants for university courses and vocational training.

Geographical Area of Activity: Bolivia, Colombia, Ecuador, Morocco, Peru, Portugal, Senegal, Spain, Trinidad and Tobago.

Publications: Annual Report.

Finance: Total assets €56.3m.; net annual income –€1.8m. (31 Dec. 2023).

Board of Trustees: Antonio Brufau Niubó (Pres.); António Calçada de Sá (Vice-Pres. and Gen. Dir); Iñigo Alonso de Noriega Satrústegui (Sec.).

Contact Details: Calle Mendez Alvaro 44, 28045 Madrid; tel. 917539079; e-mail fundacion@fundacion.repsol.org; internet www.fundacionrepsol.com.

Fundación SM (SM Foundation)

Founded in 1977 as Fundación Santa María by the Compañía de María (Marianistas), a religious order.

Activities: Works in four main areas: education, technology and learning; transformative leadership in education; literacy and childhood development; and young people in Ibero-America. The Foundation offers grants for educational, social and cultural development programmes; organizes conferences and seminars; and annually awards prizes, worth €200,000, for children and young people's literature and illustration.

Geographical Area of Activity: Brazil, Chile, Dominican Repub., Ecuador, Mexico, Puerto Rico, Spain.

Restrictions: Grants only to people who work or study in Spain.

Publications: Annual Report; brochures; monographs; blog.

Finance: Funded by annual contributions from Ediciones SM. Total assets €71.2m.; net annual income –€4.1m. (31 Dec. 2023).

Board of Trustees: Iñaki Sarasua Maritxalar (Pres.); Miguel Angel Dieste Pontaque (Vice-Pres.); Miguel Agustí Martínez-Arcos (Sec.).

Principal Staff: Gen. Dir Mayte Ortiz Vélez.

Contact Details: Calle Impresiones 15, 28660 Boadilla del Monte, Madrid; tel. 914228800; e-mail comunicacion.fsm@fundacion-sm.com; internet www.fundacion-sm.org.

Fundación Telefónica (Telefónica Foundation)

Established in 1998 by Telefónica, a telecommunications company.

Activities: Carries out activities in the areas of digital culture, education, employability and volunteering. The Foundation offers free online training and digital tools via the Conecta Empleo platform and peer-to-peer vocational training at the 42 coding academy; has an exhibition space in Madrid; and organizes the annual Foro Telos, with interviews, dialogues and roundtables on themes that include cities and health, the climate emergency, the future of work and companies, geopolitics and international affairs, and science in the humanities. The ProFuturo digital education programme, a joint initiative with Fundación Bancaria 'la Caixa' (q.v.), aims to improve the education of vulnerable children in Africa, Asia, Latin America and the Caribbean. The Annual enlightED awards are offered to educational technology start-ups. It promotes corporate volunteering among its employees in 41 countries; and comprises a network of affiliated foundations in Argentina, Brazil, Chile, Colombia, Ecuador, Mexico, Peru, Uruguay and Venezuela.

Geographical Area of Activity: International.

Publications: Annual Report; newsletter; *Telos* (magazine); exhibition guides; reports.

Finance: Total assets €72.0m.; net annual income –€7.6m. (31 Dec. 2023).

Board of Trustees: José María Álvarez-Pallete López (Chair.); Pablo de Carvajal González (Sec.).

Principal Staff: Man. Dir Luis A. Prendes.

Contact Details: Calle Gran Vía 28, 7ª Planta, 28013 Madrid; tel. 914823800; e-mail contacto@fundaciontelefonica.com; internet www.fundaciontelefonica.com.

Fundación Universidad-Empresa—UE (University-Industry Foundation)

Founded in 1973 by the universities of Madrid and the Chamber of Commerce and Industry to promote co-operation between the universities and industries of Madrid.

Activities: Works to address the challenges and opportunities generated in the framework of university-business relations, with a special focus on: education; employment and career development; entrepreneurship; and research and innovation.

Geographical Area of Activity: Worldwide, with a particular focus on Europe.

Fundación Víctimas del Terrorismo SPAIN

Publications: *Guía de Empresas que Ofrecen Empleo* (annual job opportunities guide); newsletter; reports; blog; books.

Finance: Total assets €14.7m.; net operating income €108,539 (31 Dec. 2023).

Board of Trustees: Antonio Angel Asensio Laguna (Pres.); Miguel Garrido de la Cierva (First Vice-Pres.); Amaya Mendikoetxea Pelayo (Second Vice-Pres.); Fernando Martínez Gómez (Exec. Vice-Pres.); Alfonso Calderon Yebra (Sec.).

Contact Details: Calle Alberto Aguilera 62, 1ª planta, 28015 Madrid; tel. 915489860; e-mail info@fue.es; internet www.fundacionuniversidadempresa.es.

Fundación Víctimas del Terrorismo (Foundation for the Victims of Terrorism)

Established in 2001.

Activities: Works in the fields of democracy and human rights. The Foundation co-operates with other organizations in the third sector and the Spanish Government to support victims of terrorism and persecution, providing direct welfare aid to victims and their families.

Geographical Area of Activity: Spain.

Publications: Annual Report; newsletter; *Fundación* (magazine); books.

Board of Trustees: Juan Francisco Benito Valenciano (Pres.); Ángeles Pedraza Portero, Francisco Javier López Ruiz (Vice-Pres).

Principal Staff: Sec. Isabel Moya Pérez.

Contact Details: Apdo 46.453, 28080 Madrid; tel. 913952377; e-mail fundacionvt@fundacionvt.org; internet www.fundacionvt.org.

Fundación Vodafone España (Vodafone Spain Foundation)

Established in 1995 by Vodafone, a telecommunications company; part of the Vodafone Foundation (q.v.) network.

Activities: Invests in improving communities through the use of digital technology. It's main program is DigiCraft, teaching children aged 6–12 years digital skills; Youth 4 Good, promoting social change and volunteering among young people; and Espacio Innova, a community space for digital social innovation. In 2002, in partnership with the Spanish Red Cross, the Foundation established the Fundación Tecnologías Sociales (TECSOS) to address social challenges and assist vulnerable people through the use of ICT. Vodafone Spain Foundation works in coordination with other foundations within Vodafone Group; in this context, Digicraft is part of Skills Upload Jr, an initiative to empower teachers and students across 10 European countries to build the digital skills they need to thrive in a digital society.

Geographical Area of Activity: Spain.

Publications: Newsletter; reports.

Finance: Total assets €715,264; net annual income –€316,202 (31 March 2023).

Board of Trustees: Remedios Orrantia Pérez (Pres.).

Principal Staff: Gen. Man. Gloria Placer.

Contact Details: Avda de América 115, 28042 Madrid; tel. 607133333; e-mail infofve@vodafone.com; internet www.fundacionvodafone.es.

Institut Europeu de la Mediterrània—IEMed (European Mediterranean Institute)

Founded in 1989; a consortium comprising the Catalan Government, the Spanish Ministry of Foreign Affairs and Co-operation, and Barcelona City Council.

Activities: Promotes mutual understanding, peace, stability, shared prosperity and dialogue in the Mediterranean region. Main programmes focus on: Euro-Mediterranean policies and Euromed regional programmes; socioeconomic development; the Arab and Mediterranean world; and Mediterranean cultures and cultural activities. The Institute carries out multi-disciplinary research; issues publications; and organizes seminars, debates, conferences and cultural events. It awards grants and prizes for work on Mediterranean-related subjects; and funds postdoctoral research and doctoral theses. Has a library, comprising more than 14,100 items and more than 80 periodicals.

Geographical Area of Activity: Mediterranean region.

Publications: Annual Report; newsletter; *IEMed Mediterranean Yearbook*; *Afkar/Ideas* (quarterly journal); *Quaderns de la Mediterrània*; *Mediterranean Monographies*; *Euromed Survey*; *PapersIEMed*; *DocumentsIEMed*; *PapersIEMed/EuroMeSCo*; *Focus*; Joint Policy Studies; catalogues; monographs.

Board of Governors: Salvador Illa i Roca (Pres.); José Manuel Albares Bueno (First Vice-Pres.); Jaume Collboni Cuadrado (Second Vice-Pres.); Jaume Duch Guillot (Third Vice-Pres.).

Principal Staff: Exec. Pres. Senén Florensa Palau; Man. Dir Roger Albinyana.

Contact Details: Calle Girona 20, 5º, 08010 Barcelona; tel. 932449850; e-mail info@iemed.org; internet www.iemed.org.

Instituto Europeo de Salud y Bienestar Social (European Institute of Health and Social Welfare)

Established in 1996 to encourage health, social welfare and environmental protection through multiple co-operation.

Activities: Focuses on educating health professionals, patient satisfaction, social responsibility and development co-operation. The Institute offers more than 2,000 accredited training activities in areas including: health management; emergencies; quality of care; geriatrics; mental health; pneumology; cardiology; neuroscience; public health; and primary care. It organizes congresses, conferences and seminars; and supports research in the area of environment and social issues.

Geographical Area of Activity: Europe.

Publications: Newsletter; monographs; reports; blog.

Principal Staff: Pres. Dr Manuel de la Peña Castiñeira.

Contact Details: Calle Joaquín Costa 16, El Viso, 28002 Madrid; tel. 914118090; e-mail contacto@institutoeuropeo.es; internet www.institutoeuropeo.es.

Paz y Cooperación (Peace and Co-operation)

Founded in 1982 by Joaquin Antuña, a publicist and author; became a foundation in 1998.

Activities: Organizes and manages co-operative projects in 27 countries around the world that are involved in the fields of human rights, co-operative development, children and young people, women and development, microcredit, education, health, agriculture and the environment, and integral development with local communities and authorities. The organization funds the annual International Peace and Co-operation School Award, which promotes education for peace and global solidarity. It has consultative status with ECOSOC.

Geographical Area of Activity: Worldwide (in particular, Africa, Asia, Central and South America and the Middle East).

Principal Staff: Pres. Rosa Olazábal.

Contact Details: Calle Meléndez Valdés 68, 4º izq., 28015 Madrid; tel. 915496156; e-mail pazycooperacion@pazycooperacion.es; internet www.peaceandcooperation.org.

SRI LANKA

FOUNDATIONS AND NON-PROFITS

A. M. M. Sahabdeen Trust Foundation

Founded in 1991 by Dr Abdul Majeed Mohamed Sahabdeen, a business person and former public servant.

Activities: Works in the fields of education and social development through awarding scholarships, particularly to students in need; and making grants to organizations to build and maintain orphanages, care homes, clinics, hospitals, welfare centres, places of worship, educational institutes and vocational training centres. The Foundation offers Sri Lankan International Awards to scholars and scientists in the Asian region and others for contributions to human progress in the fields of international understanding, science, literature and human development. In 1998 it established the Mohamed Sahabdeen Institute for Advanced Studies and Research at Pahamune in the Kurunegala District; and in 2005 it established Pahamune House to rehabilitate destitute children affected by the tsunami in December 2004.

Geographical Area of Activity: Asia.

Principal Staff: Man. Dir and Chair. Rizvan Sahabdeen.

Contact Details: 4th Floor, 86 Galle Rd, Colombo 3; tel. (11) 2399601; e-mail ammstrust@gmail.com.

International Water Management Institute—IWMI

Established in 1985; formerly known as the International Irrigation Management Institute; part of the CGIAR (Consultative Group on International Agricultural Research) international network of research centres.

Activities: Conducts research in the fields of sustainable management of land and water resources for food, livelihoods and the environment. Main programmes focus on: food, managing water for resilient food systems; climate, adapting to water disparities and disasters; and growth, inclusive water governance and sustainable economic development. The Institute has offices in 15 countries.

Geographical Area of Activity: Africa, Asia.

Publications: Annual Report; newsletter; brochures; issue briefs; policy briefs; research report series; working papers; blog; books.

Finance: Annual revenue US $39.2m., expenditure $40.7m. (31 Dec. 2023).

Board of Governors: Simi Kamal (Vice-Chair.).

Principal Staff: Dir-Gen. Mark Smith; Deputy Dir-Gen. Rachael McDonnell.

Contact Details: 127 Sunil Mawatha, Pelawatte, Battaramulla; POB 2075, Colombo; tel. (11) 2880000; e-mail iwmi@cgiar.org; internet www.iwmi.org.

Regional Centre for Strategic Studies—RCSS

Established in 1992; a think tank.

Activities: Operates in the field of international affairs, carrying out research into issues relating to South Asia, including regional security, conflict and co-operation. The Centre facilitates communication between organizations and individuals; organizes seminars and workshops; promotes research; and issues publications. It presents Kodikara Awards to scholars from Bangladesh, Bhutan, India, the Maldives, Nepal, Pakistan and Sri Lanka; Mahbub ul Haq Research Awards for Non-Traditional Security Issues in South Asia, sponsoring collaborative research projects in the fields of governance in plural societies and security, environment and security, globalization and security, and conflict resolution; and the Mahbub ul Haq Award for collaborative research on non-traditional security issues that are relevant to contemporary South Asia, within the themes of Governance in Plural Societies and Security, Environment and Security, Globalization and Security, and Conflict Resolution.

Geographical Area of Activity: South Asia.

Publications: *RCSS Newsletter*; occasional papers; books.

Principal Staff: Exec. Dir Dr George Cooke.

Contact Details: 20/73 Fairfield Gardens, Colombo 8; tel. (11) 2690913; e-mail rcss@rcss.org; internet www.rcss.org.

Women's Fund Asia

Established in 2004 as the South Asia Women's Fund; present name adopted in 2018; a member of Prospera—International Network of Women's Funds (q.v.).

Activities: Promotes feminist philanthropy, supporting women and transgender peoples' access to human rights and financial and technical resources. The organization has three main grantmaking programmes: Strengthening Feminist Movements in Asia, including individuals, groups and networks; Leading from the South, supporting activism designed and led by organizations in the global South; and Linking and Learning, offering awards travel and workshop grants of up to US $1,000 to women's rights activists and organizations. It has offices in India.

Geographical Area of Activity: Afghanistan, Bangladesh, Bhutan, Cambodia, India, Indonesia, Lao People's Dem. Repub., Malaysia, Maldives, Mongolia, Myanmar, Nepal, Pakistan, Philippines, Sri Lanka, Thailand, Timor-Leste, Viet Nam.

Publications: Annual Report; newsletter.

Finance: Total assets US $13.7m.; net annual income $659,381 (31 March 2024).

Principal Staff: Exec. Dir Anisha Chugh.

Contact Details: 30/62A Longden Pl., Colombo 7; tel. (11) 4324541; e-mail info@wf-asia.org; internet womensfundasia.org.

SUDAN

FOUNDATIONS AND NON-PROFITS

Al-Zubair Charity Foundation

Established in 1998 in memory of Vice-President Zubair Mohammed Saleh, who was killed in a military plane crash.

Activities: Promotes humanitarian co-operation, *takaful* (solidarity), national unity and a culture of peace. The Foundation works in the fields of humanitarian relief, health, social welfare, education and culture. It has special consultative status with ECOSOC.

Geographical Area of Activity: Sudan.

Principal Staff: Sec.-Gen. Dr Ibrahim Abdul Halim; Deputy Sec.-Gen. Tarig Abdel-Fattah.

Contact Details: POB 10359, Khartoum; tel. (183) 434484; e-mail zcfsudan@gmail.com.

Sudan Foundation (M'essh al Sudan)

Established in 2015.

Activities: Promotes justice and social security through the development of civil society. The Foundation carries out projects in the areas of agriculture, economic development, education, health, and water and water harvesting; provides training and capacity building to NGOs; and organizes seminars and conferences. Its annual Excellence Award recognizes civil society and national organizations' achievements in adopting creative and innovative processes, activities and services.

Geographical Area of Activity: Sudan.

Board of Directors: Osama Abdullah Mohammed Al-Hassan (Chair.).

Principal Staff: Exec. Dir Mohammed Sulaiman Jodabi.

Contact Details: Elammarat, St 33, Block No. 12, Bldg No. 15, 11111 Khartoum; tel. (183) 583517; e-mail info@sudanfoundation.net.

SWEDEN

CO-ORDINATING BODY

Stiftelser i Samverkan (Association of Swedish Foundations)

Established in 1989.

Activities: Supports and promotes the work of Swedish foundations, enabling the exchange of information and ideas, and monitoring changes to relevant legislation in Sweden and abroad. The Association has four working groups: Civil Law, Accounting, Tax, and Research and International Affairs. It has more than 300 members; and is a member of Philea (q.v.).

Geographical Area of Activity: Sweden.

Publications: Annual Report.

Finance: Annual income €174,200, expenditure €90,698 (31 Dec. 2020).

Board of Directors: Kerstin Fagerberg (Pres.); Wilhelm Reuterswärd (Treas.).

Contact Details: Box 3615, 103 59 Stockholm; e-mail info@stiftelserisamverkan.se; internet www.stiftelserisamverkan.se.

FOUNDATIONS AND NON-PROFITS

Air Pollution and Climate Secretariat—AirClim

Established in 1982, as the Swedish NGO Secretariat on Acid Rain, a collaborative venture between Friends of the Earth Sweden, Nature and Youth Sweden, the Swedish Society for Nature Conservation and the World Wide Fund for Nature Sweden; present name adopted in 2008.

Activities: Raises awareness about, and campaigns to reduce, air pollution, including greenhouse gases. The Secretariat operates primarily in the EU and Central and Eastern Europe, disseminating information, lobbying, supporting environmental organizations in other countries, and issuing publications.

Geographical Area of Activity: Worldwide (primarily in the EU and Central and Eastern Europe).

Publications: *Acid News* (magazine); factsheets; guides; policy briefs; reports (in the Air Pollution & Climate series).

Secretariat: Rikard Rudolfsson (Chair.).

Contact Details: Första Långgatan 18, 413 28 Gothenburg; tel. (31) 711 45 15; e-mail info@airclim.org; internet www.airclim.org.

Cancerfonden (Swedish Cancer Society)

Founded in 1951 by Morri Nidén and Ebba Andersson, cancer survivors.

Activities: Awards grants and fellowships to individuals of any nationality to carry out cancer research, or research in a related science, including biochemistry, cell biology, pathology, virology, immunology, etc. Grants range from 600,000 Swedish kronor to 2.3m. Swedish kronor. The Society also disseminates information on cancer for public education purposes. It is a member of the Swedish Fundraising Council.

Geographical Area of Activity: Sweden.

Restrictions: No grants to individuals. Awards for Swedish researchers are tenable in countries outside Sweden; foreign recipients must carry out their research in Sweden.

Publications: Annual Report; *Rädda Livet* (quarterly); reports; newsletter; brochure.

Finance: Annual income 982.8m. Swedish kronor, expenditure 1,231.2m. Swedish kronor (2022).

Board of Directors: Göran Hägglund (Pres.); Kjell Asplund (Vice-Pres.).

Principal Staff: Sec.-Gen. Ulrika Årehed Kågström.

Contact Details: David Bagares gata 5, 101 55 Stockholm; tel. (10) 199 10 10; e-mail info@cancerfonden.se; internet www.cancerfonden.se.

Crafoordska stiftelsen (The Crafoord Foundation)

Estblished in 1980 by Holger Crafoord, a co-founder of Gambro, a medical technology company.

Activities: Focuses on geosciences, mathematics and astronomy, biosciences (particularly ecology), and medicine (rheumatoid arthritis); awards grants to individuals and organizations in Sweden pursuing scientific research; awards Nobel prizes in chemistry and physics totalling 9m. Swedish kronor each; and may also support the education of, and assistance to, disadvantaged children and youngsters. Each year, the King of Sweden presents the Crafoord Prize, worth 6m. Swedish kronor, for basic research in mathematics and astronomy, geosciences, biosciences (with an emphasis on ecology) and polyarthritis (rheumatoid arthritis).

Geographical Area of Activity: Worldwide.

Publications: Annual Report.

Finance: Annual revenue 182.8m. Swedish kronor, expenditure 8.5m. Swedish kronor (31 Dec. 2024).

Board of Trustees: Ebba Fischer (Chair.).

Principal Staff: CEO Leif Andersson.

Contact Details: Malmövägen 8, 222 25 Lund; tel. (46) 38 58 80; e-mail crafoord@crafoord.se; internet www.crafoord.se.

Diakonia

Established in 1966 by five Swedish churches; a non-profit development organization.

Activities: Comprises two principal organizations: the Swedish Alliance Mission and the Uniting Church in Sweden. The organization works in the areas of democratization and human rights, gender equality, social and economic justice, and peace and reconciliation. It supports approximately 350 local partner organizations in 26 countries.

Geographical Area of Activity: Central and South America, Middle East and North Africa, South and South-East Asia, sub-Saharan Africa.

Restrictions: Does not make grants to individuals, nor to organizations in Europe, the USA or countries of the former USSR.

Publications: Annual Report; newsletter.

Finance: The Swedish Government provides 80% of the budget (through the Swedish International Development Co-operation Agency). EuropeAid, other governments, UN agencies and private donors provide the rest. Annual revenue 523.7m. Swedish kronor, expenditure 531.0m. Swedish kronor (31 Dec. 2023).
Board: Pether Nordin (Chair.); Anette Drewitz (Vice-Chair.).
Principal Staff: Sec.-Gen. Mattias Brunander.
Contact Details: Alsnögatan 7, 116 44 Stockholm; tel. (8) 453 69 00; e-mail diakonia@diakonia.se; internet www.diakonia.se.

Dr Marcus Wallenbergs Stiftelse för Utbildning i Internationellt Industriellt Företagande (Dr Marcus Wallenberg Foundation for Further Education in International Industry)

Founded in 1982 in memory of Dr Marcus Wallenberg, an industrialist; part of the Wallenberg Foundations.
Activities: Awards scholarships for Master's studies abroad in all areas for up to two years.
Geographical Area of Activity: Sweden.
Restrictions: Grants are available to Swedish citizens with a university degree and two years' experience in business or public administration; only accepts electronic applications made online.
Finance: Annual scholarships awarded 41m. Swedish kronor (2024).
Board of Directors: Peter Wallenberg, Jr (Chair.).
Principal Staff: Exec. Dir Ingrid Sundström.
Contact Details: POB 16066, 103 22 Stockholm; tel. (8) 54 50 17 77; e-mail tmw@wallenbergfoundations.se; internet tmw.wallenberg.org.

Ekhagastiftelsen (Ekhaga Foundation)

Founded in 1944 by Gösta Videgård, a construction engineer and owner of refrigerated ships.
Activities: Promotes human health through supporting development of better food and natural medicines and healing practices. The Foundation makes grants to Scandinavian institutions and individuals, and for the provision of fellowships and scholarships. Total annual disbursements range from 20m. Swedish kronor to 25m. Swedish kronor to projects in agriculture and medicine.
Geographical Area of Activity: Worldwide.
Restrictions: Applicants from outside Europe must be in co-operation with a European institution; does not sponsor basic education at university level; does not accept applications by e-mail.
Finance: Total funds disbursed since 1999 270m. Swedish kronor.
Board: Helena Dandenell (Chair.); Hubertus Videgård (Sec.).
Scientific Council: Prof. Walter Osika (Chair.).
Contact Details: POB 113, 182 12 Danderyd; tel. (70) 240 81 81; e-mail info@ekhagastiftelsen.se; internet www.ekhagastiftelsen.se.

Erik Philip-Sörensens Stiftelse (Erik Philip-Sörensen Foundation)

Established in 1976 by Erik Philip-Sörensens, the founder of the Securitas security group.
Activities: Supports basic and specialized research in the fields of genetics and the humanities. The Foundation makes grants in the field of the humanities on the recommendation of Lund University. Grants range from 50,000 to 400,000 Swedish kronor.
Geographical Area of Activity: Sweden.
Restrictions: No grants for research work outside Sweden; accepts applications only from Swedish universities.
Finance: Capital 200m. Swedish kronor; annual grants disbursed 4m. Swedish kronor (2020).
Board of Directors: Lennart Nilsson (Chair.).
Principal Staff: Dir Sven Philip-Sorensen.
Contact Details: SEB Kapitalförvaltning, Institutioner & Stiftelser, 205 20 Malmö; tel. (40) 667 64 17; e-mail stiftelsesupport.malmo@seb.se; internet www.epss.se.

Folke Bernadottes Minnesfond (Folke Bernadotte Memorial Foundation)

Founded in 1948 by the Swedish Relief Committee for Europe, in memory of Count Folke Bernadotte af Wisborg, a diplomat and UN mediator who was killed in Jerusalem in 1948.
Activities: Offers scholarships to young people living in Sweden, aged 11–26 years, for travel outside Scandinavia to experience other cultural conditions; and also to those taking part in camps and volunteering. The Foundation co-ordinates the activities of organizations abroad that commemorate Count Folke Bernadotte.
Geographical Area of Activity: Worldwide.
Restrictions: No scholarships for study or for travel within Sweden or to Denmark, Finland or Norway; some kind of exchange must be included, and the social aspect is important.
Board: Folke Bernadotte af Wisborg (Chair.).
Contact Details: Malmgårdsvägen 63, 2tr, 116 38 Stockholm; tel. (8) 662 25 05; e-mail ansokan@fbminne.se; internet www.folkebernadottesminnesfond.se.

Föreningen Svenska Atheninstitutets Vänner (Association of the Friends of the Swedish Institute at Athens)

Founded in 1976 by Anders Sundberg and 13 others to support the Swedish Institute at Athens (q.v.).
Activities: Offers grants to institutions and individuals, and awards prizes and scholarships within Scandinavia. The Association also organizes conferences and lectures.
Geographical Area of Activity: Scandinavia.
Publications: Annual Report; *Hellenika* (quarterly); books.
Finance: Annual income 240,953 Swedish kronor, expenditure 362,716 Swedish kronor (31 Dec. 2021).
Board of Directors: Dag Mattsson (Chair.); Lars Nordgren (Vice-Chair.); Martina Björk (Chair. of South Swedish Dept); Helene Whittaker (Chair. of West Swedish Dept); Ingrid Markovits (Treas.).
Contact Details: Skeppargatn 8, 3 tr, 114 52 Stockholm; tel. (8) 667 64 55; e-mail info@athenvannerna.se; internet www.athenvannerna.se.

FREE Network—Forum for Research on Eastern Europe and Emerging Economies

Established in 2011; a research institute network.
Activities: Conducts public policy research in economics, development, and emerging economies. Encompasses various institutions including the Baltic International Centre for Economic Policy Studies (BICEPS) in Latvia, the Center for Economic Research (BEROC) in Belarus, the Centre for Economic Analysis (CenEA) in Poland, the Center for Economic and Financial Research and Development (CEFIR) in the Russian Federation, the ISET Policy Institute (ISET-PI) in Georgia, the Kyiv School of Economics (KSE) in Ukraine, and the Stockholm Institute of Transition Economics (SITE) in Sweden. Facilitates conferences, seminars, and workshops, and in 2019 introduced the Forum for Research on Gender Economics (FROGEE), concentrating on gender inequality in Central and Eastern Europe. Additionally, in 2021, the FREE Network launched the Forum for Research on Eastern Europe: Climate and Environment (FREECE), dedicated to fostering environmentally sustainable economic development. Furthermore, in the same year, the FREE Network inaugurated the Forum for Research on Media and Democracy in Eastern Europe (FROMDEE), with a specific focus on media and democracy within the region.
Geographical Area of Activity: Baltic region, Central and Eastern Europe, Russian Federation, South Caucasus region.
Publications: Newsletter; *FREE Policy Brief Series* (weekly).

Contact Details: c/o SITE, Sveavägen 65, POB 6501, 113 83 Stockholm; tel. (8) 736 96 0; internet freepolicybriefs.org.

Gapminder (Stiftelsen Gapminder)

Established in 2005 by Ola Rosling, Anna Rosling Rönnlund and Prof. Hans Rosling; an independent foundation.

Activities: Seeks to counter misconceptions about global social, economic and environmental development through increasing the use and understanding of statistics and other information. The Foundation carries out research and conducts surveys; and develops and makes freely available digital visualization tools. It works with NGOs, public agencies, universities and UN organizations.

Geographical Area of Activity: International.

Restrictions: Not a grantmaking organization.

Publications: Newsletter; *Dollar Street* (online tool); *Factfulness* (book); *Worldview Upgrader* (online tool); datasets; data visualizations; educational materials; frameworks; posters; slide decks; videos.

Principal Staff: Pres. Ola Rosling; Vice-Pres. Anna Rosling Rönnlund.

Contact Details: Tantogatan 71, 118 42 Stockholm; e-mail info@gapminder.org; internet www.gapminder.org.

Globetree Association

Founded in 1982 by Kajsa Dahlström and Ben van Bronckhorst.

Activities: Operates nationally and internationally in the fields of aid to less-developed countries, the arts and humanities, conservation and the environment, education, medicine and health. The Association runs self-conducted programmes, organizes training courses, conferences and research programmes; offers grants to individuals; and awards scholarships and fellowships.

Geographical Area of Activity: Kenya, Sweden, Tanzania.

Publications: Newsletter; *Meeting in the Globetree*; reports; books and teaching aids.

Principal Staff: Chair. Kajsa B. Dahlström; Vice-Chair. Peroy Kirchner; Treas. Sam Samuelsson.

Contact Details: POB 2048, 103 11 Stockholm; tel. (73) 997 17 88; e-mail info@globetree.org; internet globetree.info.

The Greta Thunberg Foundation

Established in 2019 by climate activist Greta Thunberg and her parents, Malena Ernman and Svante Thunberg (as Greta was a minor at the time), with prize money awarded by the Right Livelihood Award Foundation (q.v.) and the Gulbenkian Prize for Humanity awarded by the Fundação Calouste Gulbenkian (q.v.).

Activities: Promotes a sustainable climate, a socially sustainable society, environmentalism, preservation of biodiversity, human rights and animal rights. The Foundation funds humanitarian and environmental initiatives.

Geographical Area of Activity: International.

Finance: Annual income 3.8m. Swedish kronor, expenditure 2.4m. Swedish kronor (31 Dec. 2022).

Board: Lina Burnelius (Chair.).

Principal Staff: Dir Erika Jangen.

Contact Details: c/o Von Euler & Partners, Cardellgatan 1, 114 36 Stockholm; e-mail info@thegretathunbergfoundation.org; internet thegretathunbergfoundation.org.

Hjärt-Lungfonden (The Swedish Heart-Lung Foundation)

Established in 1904 as the Svenska Nationalföreningen mot Tuberkulos (Swedish National Anti-tuberculosis Association); a charitable fundraising organization.

Activities: Collects and distributes money for heart, lung and vascular research. The Foundation provides information about heart and lung diseases and risks, including angina, cardiac arrhythmias, chronic obstructive pulmonary disease, hypertension, myocardial infarction and stroke. It has around 1,500 members.

Geographical Area of Activity: Mainly Sweden.

Publications: Annual Report; newsletter; *Hjärtrapporten*; *Lungrapporten*.

Finance: Annual income 480.5m. Swedish kronor, expenditure 776.1m. Swedish kronor (2023).

Research Council: Prof. John Pernow (Chair.); Prof. Gunilla Westergren-Thorsson (Vice-Chair.).

Board: Thomas Rolén (Chair.).

Principal Staff: Sec.-Gen. Kristina Sparreljung.

Contact Details: Stora Nygatan 27, 111 27 Stockholm; POB 2167, 103 14 Stockholm; tel. (8) 566 242 00; e-mail info@hjart-lungfonden.se; internet www.hjart-lungfonden.se.

H&M Foundation

Established in 2007, as a closed foundation, privately funded by the Stefan Persson family, main owners of the H&M Group.

Activities: Main programme areas are: children's education and inclusion; clean water and sanitation; equality, in particular women's empowerment, refugee integration and youth employment; and recycling clothes. The Foundation also provides emergency relief. It operates in 33 countries where the company is present. Made annually, the Global Change Award (f. 2015) recognizes innovation in transforming the fashion industry from a linear to a circular industry.

Geographical Area of Activity: International.

Publications: Annual Report.

Finance: Total investment since 2013 1,900m. Swedish kronor (2024).

Principal Staff: Global Man. Anna Gedda.

Contact Details: Drottninggatan 57, 106 38 Stockholm; tel. (8) 796 55 00; e-mail info@hmfoundation.com; internet www.hmfoundation.com.

Institut Mittag-Leffler (Mittag-Leffler Foundation of the Royal Swedish Academy of Sciences)

Founded in 1916 by Magnus Gösta Mittag-Leffler, a professor of mathematics, and his wife Signe.

Activities: Conducts research in pure mathematics. The Foundation offers grants and scholarships to researchers who have recently obtained a doctorate; and to advanced graduate students researching within the topic of the year.

Geographical Area of Activity: International.

Restrictions: Grants restricted to the annual theme.

Publications: Annual Report; *Acta Mathematica* (journal); *Arkiv för Matematik* (journal); books; research papers.

Finance: Funded by the research councils of Denmark, Norway and Sweden, the Ministry of Education of Finland, the Icelandic Mathematical Society and foundations. Annual income 16.5m. Swedish kronor, expenditure 22.1m. Swedish kronor (2024).

Scientific Board: Bo Berndtsson (Chair.).

Principal Staff: Dir Tobias Eckholm; Deputy Dir Hans Ringström.

Contact Details: Auravägen 17, 182 60 Djursholm; tel. (8) 622 05 60; e-mail administration@mittag-leffler.se; internet www.mittag-leffler.se.

International Foundation for Science—IFS

Founded in 1972 by the national academies or research councils of 12 countries.

Activities: Provides young scientists and technologists of outstanding merit from developing countries with financial and other support in their work. The sharing of scientific information between researchers and advisers is encouraged by regional meetings and visits to project sites. The Foundation has 92 member organizations (scientific academies, research councils and national and international organizations) mainly in low- and middle-income countries.

Geographical Area of Activity: International.

Restrictions: Researchers must carry out the work in their own country, and research is restricted to biological and agricultural sciences, and the chemistry of natural resources.

Publications: Annual Report; e-newsletter; *IFS Impact Studies (MESIA)*; *External Evaluations of IFS*; *IFS Strategic Plans*; *IFS Work Plans*; briefings; reports; blog.

Finance: Core contributions to the budget come from France, Germany, the Netherlands, Norway, Sweden, Switzerland and the USA; restricted contributions are made by several other organizations. Annual revenue 12.3m. Swedish kronor, expenditure 19.3m. Swedish kronor (31 Dec. 2023).

Board of Trustees: Dr Patrick Van Damme (Chair. and Interim Dir); Dr Mónica Moraes (Vice-Chair.).

Contact Details: IFS Secretariat, Karlavägen 108, 8th Floor, 115 26 Stockholm; tel. (8) 545 818 00; e-mail info@ifs.se; internet www.ifs.se.

KK-stiftelsen (Knowledge Foundation)

Established in 1994 by the Swedish Government, using capital from former wage-earner investment funds.

Activities: Increases communication between academic and business sectors through developing research in Sweden's universities and colleges. The Foundation invests resources in postgraduate programmes to promote competence in business; supports advancement in Swedish schools; and develops new technologies to improve healthcare.

Geographical Area of Activity: Sweden.

Publications: Annual Report; research papers; feasibility studies.

Finance: Annual income 101.4m. Swedish kronor, expenditure 38.2m. Swedish kronor (31 Dec. 2024).

Board of Directors: Elisabeth Nilsson (Chair.).

Principal Staff: Man. Dir Eva Schelin.

Contact Details: Kungsträdgårdsgatan 18, 111 47 Stockholm; tel. (8) 566 481 00; e-mail info@kks.se; internet www.kks.se.

Knut och Alice Wallenbergs Stiftelse (Knut and Alice Wallenberg Foundation)

Founded in 1917 by Knut Agathon Wallenberg, Chairman of Stockholms Enskilda Bank, and Alice O. Wallenberg; part of the Wallenberg Foundations.

Activities: Supports basic research and education, primarily in medicine, technology and the natural sciences, in particular funding high-value equipment and laboratories. Annually, the Foundation offers grants, scholarships and fellowships.

Geographical Area of Activity: Sweden.

Restrictions: Does not make grants to private individuals without connection to a research institution, except for scholarship programmes established by or supported by the Foundation; only considers Swedish applications.

Finance: Annual grants awarded c. 2,400m. Swedish kronor (2024).

Board of Directors: Peter Wallenberg, Jr (Chair.); Marcus Wallenberg (Vice-Chair.).

Principal Staff: Exec. Dir Sara Mazur.

Contact Details: Box 16066, 22 Stockholm; tel. (8) 545 017 80; e-mail kaw@kaw.se; internet kaw.wallenberg.org.

Konung Gustaf V's 90-Årsfond (King Gustaf V's 90th Birthday Foundation)

Founded in 1949 by the Swedish people, in honour of King Gustaf's 90th birthday, to support voluntary youth activities.

Activities: Awards grants to Swedish organizations run by, with or for young people. The Foundation particularly emphasizes leadership training programmes in Europe. It awards the annual Ernst Killander Scholarship, recognized as the foremost award to a voluntary Swedish youth leader. Grants typically range from 2,000 to 150,000 Swedish kronor. Member of the International Youth Foundation (q.v.).

Geographical Area of Activity: Mainly Europe.

Restrictions: No grants to individuals, schools or companies.

Finance: Annual grantmaking 5m. Swedish kronor (2021).

Board of Trustees: Fredrik Wersäll (Chair.); Eva Önnesjö (Vice-Chair.).

Principal Staff: Sec. Suzanne Fredborg.

Contact Details: Kungliga Slottet, Högvaktsterrassen 1, 111 30 Stockholm; tel. (735) 89 62 89; internet www.gv90.a.se.

Kulturfonden för Sverige och Finland (Swedish-Finnish Cultural Foundation)

Established in 1960; the largest bilateral foundation in Scandinavia, it oversees the work of Hanaholmen—Swedish-Finnish Cultural Centre (q.v.).

Activities: Provides project subsidies, scholarships and travel grants for a broad range of activities that aim to increase contact and understanding between the people of Sweden and Finland, especially in the fields of culture, the environment, industry and media. The Foundation also works to promote the Finnish language in Sweden. Has an office in Finland.

Geographical Area of Activity: Finland, Sweden.

Restrictions: Does not make grants to municipalities, counties or state agencies.

Publications: Annual Report.

Finance: Total assets €61.3m. (2023).

Finnish Committee: Anneli Jäätteenmäki (Chair.).

Swedish Committee: Lotta Finstorp (Chair.).

Principal Staff: CEO Anne-Mari Virolainen.

Contact Details: Banérgatan 27, Box 20429, 104 51 Stockholm; tel. (73) 50 22 110; e-mail info@fondensverigefinland.org; internet fondensverigefinland.org.

Kvinna till Kvinna (Woman to Woman Foundation)

Founded in 1993 in response to the war in the Balkans and the atrocities committed against women.

Activities: Works for women's rights and peace in regions affected by war and armed conflict, carrying out advocacy, research, training and fieldwork in six main areas: creating safe meeting places; empowering defenders of women's rights; increasing women's power; increasing the number of women in peace processes; giving women power over their own bodies; and providing security for all. The Foundation also seeks to build networks among women's groups across conflict borders and raise awareness on developing issues. It supports more than 100 women's organizations in 20 countries, with regional offices in the Balkans, South Caucasus and Middle East.

Geographical Area of Activity: Central Africa, Middle East, South Caucasus, Sweden, Western Africa, Western Balkans.

Restrictions: Does not accept unsolicited proposals.

Publications: Annual Report; newsletter; handbooks; thematic reports.

Finance: Funding from the Swedish International Development Agency (Sida) and other trusts and foundations. Public fundraising activities. Total assets 552m. Swedish kronor (31 Dec. 2024).

Board of Directors: Devrim Mavi (Chair.); Malin Almroth (Deputy Chair.); Carina Andersson (Sec.).

Principal Staff: Sec.-Gen. Petra Tötterman Andorff.

Contact Details: Hammarby fabriksväg 65, 120 30 Stockholm; tel. (73) 95 00 325; e-mail info@kvinnatillkvinna.se; internet www.kvinnatillkvinna.se.

Nobelstiftelsen (Nobel Foundation)

Founded in 1900 by the will of Alfred Nobel.

Activities: Operates internationally in the fields of science and medicine, literature and peace promotion, through prizes to individuals, a peace prize to institutions or individuals, conferences and publications. Prizewinners are chosen by the Royal Academy of Sciences, Stockholm (Physics, Chemistry), the Nobel Assembly at the Karolinska Institutet, Stockholm (Physiology or Medicine), the Swedish Academy, Stockholm (Literature) and the Norwegian Nobel Committee (Peace). In 1968 the Central Bank of Sweden instituted an Alfred Nobel Memorial Prize in Economic Sciences of the same value as the Nobel Prize—the prizewinner of this award is chosen by the Royal Swedish Academy of Sciences.

Geographical Area of Activity: International.

Publications: Annual Report; Annual Review; *Les Prix Nobel*; *Nobel Lectures*; books and journals.

Finance: Total assets 4,172m. Swedish kronor (31 Dec. 2024).

Trustees: Gunilla Karlsson Hedestam (Chair.).

Board of Directors: Prof. Astrid Söderbergh Widding (Chair.); Thomas Perlmann (Vice-Chair.).

Contact Details: Sturegatan 14, Stockholm; POB 5232, 102 45 Stockholm; tel. (8) 663 09 20; e-mail info@nobel.se; internet www.nobelprize.org/the-nobel-prize-organisation/the-nobel-foundation.

Nordiska Afrikainstitutets Stipendier (Nordic Africa Institute Scholarships)

Founded in 1962; a Swedish public authority funded also by the Finnish and Icelandic Governments.

Activities: Provides grants for those preparing and conducting research projects concerned with development issues in Africa. The Institute emphasizes the social sciences and closely related fields. It awards scholarships for PhD students and researchers based in Africa; for students and researchers based in Sweden, Finland, Denmark and Iceland; and the Claude Ake Visiting Chair in collaboration with the Department of Peace and Conflict Research at Uppsala University.

Geographical Area of Activity: Africa, Sweden, Finland, Iceland, Denmark.

Publications: Annual Report; newsletter; more than 600 academic titles on African politics, development, economics, human rights, social issues and modern history.

Contact Details: Villavägen 6, SE-752 36 Uppsala; POB 1703, SE-751 47 Uppsala; tel. (18) 471 52 00; e-mail nai@nai.uu.se; internet nai.uu.se/opportunities/scholarships.html.

NORDITA—Nordiska Institutet för Teoretisk Fysik (Nordic Institute for Theoretical Physics)

Founded in 1957 by the Governments of Denmark, Finland, Iceland, Norway and Sweden to promote co-operation between institutes in member countries; in 2007 moved to Sweden from Denmark.

Activities: Conducts research and strengthens Nordic collaboration within the basic areas of theoretical physics. The main research areas are: astrophysics and astrobiology; condensed matter and statistical and biological physics; and subatomic physics. The Institute is run jointly by the Royal Institute of Technology (KTH) and Stockholm University, and is located on the premises of AlbaNova University Center in Stockholm. It also has an office at the Niels Bohr Institute in Copenhagen, Denmark.

Geographical Area of Activity: Scandinavia.

Publications: *Nordita News* (online newsletter, four a year); research reports; brochure.

Finance: Funded by the Nordic Council of Ministers, Swedish Research Council, KTH Royal Institute of Technology, Stockholm University and Uppsala University.

Governing Board: Prof. Susanne Viefers (Chair.).

Principal Staff: Dir Prof. Mikael Fogelström; Deputy Dir Prof. Axel Brandenburg.

Contact Details: Hannes Alfvéns väg 12, 106 91 Stockholm; tel. (8) 5537 8473; e-mail info@nordita.org; internet www.nordita.org.

Olof Palmes Minnesfond för internationell förståelse och gemensam säkerhet (Olof Palme Memorial Fund for International Understanding and Common Security)

Established in 1986 by the family of Prime Minister Olof Palme, who was killed that year, and the Social Democratic Party to honour his memory.

Activities: Awards the annual Olof Palme prize, worth US $100,000, for outstanding achievement; and scholarships worth in total US $1m.–$2m. in the fields of peace and disarmament, anti-racism and opposition to hostility to foreigners. The Fund supports projects that range from advanced research to simple individual projects, including trade union and cultural exchanges between young people from different countries, and studies and research, principally for young people in Sweden. It also supports initiatives by schools and youth organizations at national and local level; and promotes international understanding in other ways, actively seeking out and funding projects in Sweden and elsewhere.

Geographical Area of Activity: International.

Publications: Newsletter.

Finance: Capital 70m. Swedish kronor.

Board: Stefan Löfven (Chair.); Joakim Palme (Vice-Chair.); Björn Wall (Treas.).

Contact Details: POB 836, 101 36 Stockholm; tel. (8) 677 57 90; e-mail info@palmefonden.se; internet www.palmefonden.se.

Reumatikerförbundet (Swedish Rheumatism Association)

Founded in 1945 by the Swedish Confederation of Trade Unions, the Co-operative Union and Wholesale Society, the Federation of Swedish Farmers' Associations, the Federation of Swedish Trade Unions and workers' social welfare associations.

Activities: Funds research on the diagnosis and treatment of rheumatic diseases. Operates nationally, running a hospital for rheumatic patients; enables information to be exchanged among members and others interested; makes grants for research in rheumatology, and participates in international conferences. The Association has over 38,000 members, divided into 172 local associations.

Geographical Area of Activity: Sweden.

Publications: Annual Report; *Reumatikervärlden* (periodical); diagnosis sheets and disease brochures.

Board of Directors: Lotta Håkansson (Chair.); Tommy Olsson (First Vice-Chair.); Pia Lennberg (Second Vice-Chair.).

Principal Staff: Sec.-Gen. Stina Nordström.

Contact Details: Arenavägen 47, 121 77 Johanneshov; POB 90337, 120 25 Stockholm; tel. (8) 505 805 00; e-mail info@reumatiker.se; internet www.reumatiker.se.

Right Livelihood Award Foundation

Established in 1980 by Jakob von Uexküll as an 'Alternative Nobel Prize'.

Activities: Presents the Right Livelihood Awards annually to honour and support courageous people solving global problems, continuing to support Laureates in various ways and organizing public lectures, seminars and other events. The Foundation has partner organizations in Germany and Switzerland; and in 2009 established the Right Livelihood College, a network of nine campuses at universities in Argentina, Chile, Ethiopia, Germany, India, Nigeria, Sweden, Thailand and the USA. The Global Campus of Human Rights is also a partner. Has special consultative status with ECOSOC. There are 198 Laureates in 77 countries.

Geographical Area of Activity: International.

Restrictions: Anyone can propose any individual or organization, apart from themselves, close relatives or their own organization.

Publications: Annual Reports; bibliographies and stories of Laureates (mainly digital).

Finance: Funded mainly by private donations.

Board: Gunilla Hallonsten (Chair.); Juliane Kronen (Vice-Chair.).
Principal Staff: Exec. Dir Ole von Uexküll; Deputy Dir Jenny Jansson Pearce.
Contact Details: Stockholmsvägen 23, 122 62 Enskede; tel. (8) 702 03 40; e-mail info@rightlivelihood.org; internet rightlivelihood.org.

Stiftelsen Blanceflor Boncompagni Ludovisi, född Bildt (Blanceflor Boncompagni Ludovisi, née Bildt Foundation)

Founded in 1955 by the will of Blanceflor Boncompagni Ludovisi, née Bildt.
Activities: Awards grants worth between 50,000 and 170,000 Swedish kronor to individuals usually under the age of 33 years for study abroad in life sciences: physics, chemistry, odontology, medical science, engineering, computer science, geophysics, geochemistry, astrophysics and related areas. Grants are awarded for higher education (at university or equivalent) to those not eligible for state or community grants.
Geographical Area of Activity: International.
Restrictions: No grants to groups or associations, nor for undergraduate study; only Italian and Swedish citizens are eligible for scholarships. Grants are made for study in certain disciplines only and in certain countries: Canada, Germany, Italy, Japan, Sweden, Switzerland, the UK or the USA. Does not accept applications by e-mail; all written communications should be in English.
Publications: Newsletter (3–4 a year); blog.
Finance: Total grants awarded c. 1.9m. Swedish kronor (2023).
Board: Anders Flodström (Pres.).
Principal Staff: Admin. Lars Bildt.
Contact Details: POB 145, 686 23 Sunne; tel. (70) 791 87 00; e-mail info@blanceflor.se; internet blanceflor.se.

Stiftelsen Dag Hammarskjölds Minnesfond (Dag Hammarskjöld Foundation)

Established in 1962 in memory of Dag Hammarskjöld, the second Sec.-Gen. of the UN.
Activities: Aims to advance dialogue and policy for sustainable development and peace. The Foundation organizes workshops and training and an annual Dag Hammarskjöld Lecture; and produces a series of publications. Has an office in New York, USA.
Geographical Area of Activity: International.
Restrictions: Not a grantmaking foundation.
Publications: Annual Report; newsletter; *Development Dialogue*; *Development Dialogue Papers*; reports; seminar papers; blog.
Finance: Annual income 17m. Swedish kronor, expenditure 21m. Swedish kronor (2023).
Board of Trustees: Hans Wallmark (Chair.).
Principal Staff: Exec. Dir Björn Holmberg.
Contact Details: Övre Slottsgatan 2, 753 10 Uppsala; tel. (18) 410 10 00; e-mail secretariat@daghammarskjold.se; internet www.daghammarskjold.se.

Stiftelsen Ingmar Bergman (Ingmar Bergman Foundation)

Established in 2002 on the initiative of film-maker Ingmar Bergman.
Activities: Preserves and disseminates information on Ingmar Bergman and his works; and promotes interest in and knowledge about Swedish film and culture. The Foundation maintains the Ingmar Bergman Archives, which consist of documents and some 10,000 letters to and from Bergman, and are registered on the UNESCO World Heritage List. It holds the rights to Bergman's scripts; and works with, but is separate from, the Stiftelsen Bergmancenter visitor centre and Stiftelsen Bergmangårdarna retreat for artists and scholars, both on Fårö.
Geographical Area of Activity: International.
Board of Directors: Christer Nylander (Chair.).
Principal Staff: CEO Jan Homberg.
Contact Details: Borgvägen 1–5, Box 27178, 102 52 Stockholm; tel. (8) 665 11 00; e-mail info@ingmarbergman.se; internet www.ingmarbergman.se.

Stiftelsen för Miljöstrategisk Forskning—Mistra (Mistra—Foundation for Strategic Environmental Research)

Established in 1994 by the Swedish Government using capital from former wage-earner investment funds.
Activities: Supports environmental research programmes in the area of sustainable development, and promotes co-operation between universities, industry and international centres of research.
Geographical Area of Activity: International.
Publications: Annual Report; background papers; feasibility studies; brochures; conference reports.
Finance: Total assets 1,832.7m. Swedish kronor (31 Dec. 2024).
Board: Anna Jakobsson (Chair.); Anders Tunlid (Vice-Chair.).
Principal Staff: CEO Anna Jöborn.
Contact Details: Sveavägen 25, 111 34 Stockholm; tel. (8) 791 10 20; e-mail mail@mistra.org; internet www.mistra.org.

Stiftelsen Riksbankens Jubileumsfond

Established in 1964 by the Swedish Parliament and the Bank of Sweden (Sveriges Riksbank) to commemorate the 300th anniversary of the bank, and to support scientific research.
Activities: Supports research and outreach in the humanities and social sciences through grants.
Geographical Area of Activity: International, but must have a clear base in Swedish research and Swedish research institutions.
Restrictions: Grants to postgraduates only, with a Swedish connection.
Publications: Annual Report; yearbook; newsletter; occasional research reports and books.
Finance: Annual income 651.7m. Swedish kronor, expenditure 83.9m. Swedish kronor (31 Dec. 2022).
Board of Directors: Prof. Anders Malmberg (Chair.); Dennis Dioukarev (Deputy Chair.).
Principal Staff: Chief Exec. Marika Hedin.
Contact Details: Kungsträdgårdsgatan 18, POB 5675, 114 86 Stockholm; tel. (8) 506 264 00; e-mail rj@rj.se; internet www.rj.se.

Stockholm Environment Institute

Founded in 1989 by the Swedish Parliament.
Activities: Conducts scientific research and policy analysis on environmental and development issues including climate change, energy systems, food security, water and urbanization; and specific problems, such as air pollution, at local level. The Institute develops modelling tools that help practitioners around the globe to make decisions about water and energy use. It has offices in Stockholm; and in Colombia, Estonia, Kenya, Thailand, the United Kingdom and the USA.
Geographical Area of Activity: International.
Publications: Annual Report; newsletter; discussion briefs; factsheets; policy briefs; project reports; research reports; working papers.
Finance: Total assets 260.4m. Swedish kronor; net annual income –1.1m. Swedish kronor (31 Dec. 2023).
Board: Lennart Båge (Chair.); Kristin Halvorsen (Vice-Chair.).
Principal Staff: Exec. Dir Måns Nilsson.
Contact Details: Linnégatan 87D, 115 23 Stockholm; POB 24218, 104 51 Stockholm; tel. (8) 30 80 44; e-mail info-hq@sei.org; internet www.sei.org.

Stockholm International Peace Research Institute—SIPRI

Established in 1966 by the Swedish Parliament as an independent international institute.

Activities: Conducts research and policy analysis in the fields of armament and disarmament; conflict, peace and security; and peace and development. The Institute maintains several databases on international arms transfers, military expenditure, multilateral peace operations and international arms embargoes. It organizes seminars and conferences; and provides advice and consulting.

Geographical Area of Activity: International.

Publications: Annual Review; newsletter (monthly); *SIPRI Yearbook*; monographs; research reports; policy papers; peace and security policy briefs; factsheets; special reports; handbooks.

Finance: The Swedish Government provides a substantial part of the Institute's funding through an annual grant. The Institute also seeks financial support from other organizations. Annual income 104.5m. Swedish kronor, expenditure 111.7m. Swedish kronor (2024).

Governing Board: Stefan Löfven (Chair.).

Principal Staff: Dir Dan Smith; Deputy Dir Charlotta Sparre.

Contact Details: Signalistgatan 9, 169 72 Solna; tel. (8) 655 97 00; e-mail sipri@sipri.org; internet www.sipri.org.

Sverige-Amerika Stiftelsen (Sweden-America Foundation)

Established in 1919.

Activities: Promotes the exchange of scientific, cultural and practical experiences. The Foundation awards scholarships to Swedish citizens for advanced study and research in the USA or Canada.

Geographical Area of Activity: Canada, Sweden, USA.

Restrictions: Applicants must be Swedish citizens.

Publications: Annual Report.

Finance: Total assets 202.7m. Swedish kronor (31 Dec. 2024).

Board of Directors: Christian Salamon (Chair.); Henrik Ekelund (First Vice-Chair.); Linn Edström Larsson (Second Vice-Chair.).

Principal Staff: Exec. Dir Anna Rosvall Stuart.

Contact Details: Grev Turegatan 14, S-102 46 Stockholm; tel. (8) 611 46 11; e-mail info@sweamfo.se; internet www.sweamfo.se.

Sweden-Japan Foundation—SJF

Founded in 1971 to increase understanding between the peoples of Sweden and Japan.

Activities: Operates in the fields of research and development, industry, science, commerce and culture. The Foundation organizes courses, seminars and study trips; publishes documentation; and encourages cultural exchange and co-operation between Sweden and Japan. Each year, it awards around 50 scholarships to students at Swedish universities who wish to study or conduct research in Japan.

Geographical Area of Activity: Japan, Sweden.

Publications: Reports.

Board of Directors: Prof. Harriet Wallberg (Chair.).

Principal Staff: Sec.-Gen. Hans G. Rhodiner.

Contact Details: Grev Turegatan 14, 114 46 Stockholm; tel. (8) 611 68 73; e-mail info@swedenjapan.se; internet swedenjapan.se.

TFF–Transnational Foundation for Peace and Future Research (TFF–Transnationella Stiftelsen för Freds- och Framtidsforskning)

Founded in 1986 by Dr Christina Spännar and Dr Jan Oberg to promote the UN Charter norm to create peace by peaceful means.

Activities: Promotes conflict mitigation and reconciliation. The Foundation carries out research, advocacy, training, media commentary and education under the themes of: non-violence, reconciliation and forgiveness; media, war and peace; world order and governance; nuclear abolition, peace culture, values and theories; and pro-peace inspiration. Since 2016 it has focused on the People's Republic of China, the Syrian Arab Republic, Iran and the Silk Peace Art Road Project (SPAR), but also publishes articles, reports and videos about the changing world order, the Belt & Road Initiative, the new Cold War, Ukraine and the West's decine and slide into irrational militarism.

Geographical Area of Activity: People's Republic of China, EU, Iran, Iraq, Silk Road (Belt and Road Initiative) region.

Restrictions: Not a grantmaking organization.

Publications: *TFF PressInfo* (e-newsletter); *The TFF Peace Affairs* and *Bootprint–Militarism & Environment* (online magazines); research reports; occasional papers; blogs.

Board of Directors: Dr Jan Oberg (Chair. and Research Dir).

Contact Details: Vegagatan 25, 224 57 Lund; tel. 738525200; e-mail tff@transnational.org; internet transnational.live.

Wenner-Gren Foundations

Established in 1955; comprises the Wenner-Gren Centre Foundation for Scientific Research, the Axel-Wenner-Gren Foundation for International Research Exchange and the Wenner-Gren Society Foundation.

Activities: Provides guest accommodation for foreign researchers in Stockholm; awards fellowships to Swedish researchers wanting to go abroad, and to guest scientists who wish to visit Sweden; supports the invitation of foreign guest lecturers; organizes international symposia; and facilitates the exchange of knowledge between researchers in different countries. Fellows receive a one-off research grant of 600,000 Swedish kronor.

Geographical Area of Activity: International.

Restrictions: All applications for fellowships must come through Swedish institutions.

Publications: Annual Report; research reports.

Finance: Total capital approx. 1,330m. Swedish kronor.

Board of Directors: Kerstin Eliasson (Chair.); Agneta Nordberg (Vice-Chair.).

Principal Staff: Scientific Sec. Britt-Marie Sjöberg; Admin. Dir Katarina Andersson.

Contact Details: Sveavägen 166, 23rd Floor, 113 46 Stockholm; tel. (8) 736 98 00; e-mail reception@swgc.org; internet www.swgc.org.

SWITZERLAND

CO-ORDINATING BODIES

Alliance Sud—Swiss Alliance of Development Organizations

Established in 1971 to pursue development projects common to the six member organizations: SWISSAID (q.v.), Fastenopfer—Swiss Catholic Lenten Fund, Bread for All, HEKS Swiss Church Aid, Helvetas (q.v.) and Caritas (q.v.).

Activities: Focuses on development policy, advocating within Switzerland for disadvantaged social classes in the global South. The Alliance works through a combination of lobbying, public relations works and grassroots mobilization in activities designed to be politically effective. It maintains information and documentation centres in Bern and Lausanne; and a lending library in Bern, with more than 3,000 vols and over 160 periodicals.

Geographical Area of Activity: Worldwide.

Restrictions: Not a grantmaking organization.

Publications: Annual Report; *Global* (quarterly); *Alliance Sud News* (newsletter); *Social Watch Report*; *The Reality of Aid Report*.

Finance: Annual expenditure 2.2m. Swiss francs (2023).

Board: Markus Allemann (Pres.); Bernd Nilles (Vice-Pres.).

Principal Staff: Man. Dir Andreas Missbach.

Contact Details: Monbijoustr. 31, 3001 Bern; tel. 313909330; e-mail mail@alliancesud.ch; internet www.alliancesud.ch.

Christoph-Merian-Stiftung (Christoph Merian Foundation)

Established in 1886 at the bequest of Christoph Merian (1800–58) and Margaretha Merian-Burckhardt (1806–86); an umbrella organization.

Activities: Helps people in need; and promotes a healthy environment, quality of life and culture in Basel. The Foundation manages more than 30 foundations and funds, providing advice, administrative services and asset management.

Geographical Area of Activity: Switzerland (Basel).

Restrictions: Grants only to individuals and organizations in Basel.

Publications: Annual Report.

Finance: Total assets 1,785.1m. Swiss francs (31 Dec. 2022).

Principal Staff: Dir Baschi Dürr.

Contact Details: St Alban-Vorstadt 12, 4052 Basel; tel. 612263333; e-mail info@cms-basel.ch; internet www.cms-basel.ch.

International Council of Voluntary Agencies—ICVA

Founded in 1962 by a group of NGOs that focused on refugees and migration.

Activities: Functions as a platform for co-ordination and collaboration between NGOs and humanitarian actors. The Council's objectives include alleviating human suffering in disaster areas, and protecting and promoting the human rights of refugees, internally displaced people, stateless people and vulnerable migrants. It acts as a liaison with UNHCR and participates in the UN Inter-Agency Standing Committee. Has over 160 NGO members in 160 countries.

Geographical Area of Activity: International.

Restrictions: Does not make grants.

Publications: Annual Report; *ICVA Bulletin* (monthly newsletter); briefing papers.

Finance: Total assets 2.5m. Swiss francs; net annual income 67,819 Swiss francs (31 Dec. 2024).

Board: Nimo Hassan (Chair.).

Principal Staff: Exec. Dir Dr Jamie Munn.

Contact Details: NGO Humanitarian Hub, 16 La Voie-Creuse, 1202 Geneva; tel. 229509600; e-mail secretariat@icvanetwork.org; internet www.icvanetwork.org.

proFonds

Established in 1990 to support the development and activities of foundations and associations in Switzerland; an umbrella organization.

Activities: Promotes the rights and activities of foundations and associations in Switzerland, through networking at national and international levels; conducting policy research and advocacy on legal and fiscal issues relating to the non-profit sector; and promoting and facilitating the exchange of information between non-profit organizations. The organization has around 500 members.

Geographical Area of Activity: Switzerland.

Publications: Annual Report; *Stiftungsland Schweiz*; *proFonds-Info* (quarterly newsletter); publications on management, law and tax issues related to the non-profit sector.

Finance: Annual income 571,906 Swiss francs, expenditure 496,397 Swiss francs (31 Dec. 2024).

Board of Directors: François Geinoz (Pres.); Dr Harold Grüninger (Vice-Pres.).

Principal Staff: Man. Dir Dr Christoph Degen.

Contact Details: Dufourstr. 49, 4052 Basel; tel. 612721080; e-mail info@profonds.org; internet www.profonds.org.

Sphere

Established in 1997 as the Sphere Project by humanitarian professionals who drafted the Humanitarian Charter and the first edition of the Sphere Minimum Standards. Became an independent NGO in 2016.

Activities: Sphere is a global network of international, national and local NGOs; UN agencies; donors; national and sub-national disaster management agencies; civil society and civil protection actors; community-based organizations; standards development organizations; universities and academic institutes; foundations; private companies; and individuals. The network aims to improve the quality and accountability of humanitarian assistance. Sphere's flagship publication is *The Sphere Handbook* which includes The Humanitarian Charter, the Protection Principles, the Core Humanitarian Standard (CHS), and minimum standards in four life-saving areas. The Handbook is used in the humanitarian sector during preparation, response and recovery phases. It is also used for humanitarian advocacy and by the development sector.

Geographical Area of Activity: Worldwide.

Restrictions: Not a grantmaking organization.

Publications: Annual Report; *The Sphere Handbook*; newsletter (monthly); *The Humanitarian Charter*; reports; case studies; training materials; e-learning courses.

Finance: Annual budget 1m. Swiss francs (2023).

Governing Board: Alper Küçük (Pres.); Jess Camburn (Vice-Pres.).

Principal Staff: Exec. Dir William Anderson.

Contact Details: Humanitarian Hub, La Voie-Creuse 16, 1202 Geneva; tel. 225225911; e-mail info@spherestandards.org; internet www.spherestandards.org.

Swiss Philanthropy Foundation

Established in 2006; a non-profit hosting foundation; part of the Transnational Giving Europe (q.v.) network.

Activities: Creates, hosts and manages philanthropic funds, advising private donors and foundations, and allocating grants to projects internationally. The Foundation has 55 'sheltered' funds under its aegis, which had distributed 430m. Swiss francs since 2006.
Geographical Area of Activity: International.
Publications: Annual Report; newsletter; *Practical Guide to Cross-Border Donations*; brochure blog.
Finance: Annual donations 31.6m. Swiss francs (31 Dec. 2023).
Council: Etienne Eichenberger (Chair.); Bernard Vischer (Vice-Chair.); Xavier Isaac (Treas.).
Contact Details: 2 pl. de Cornavin, POB 2097, 1211 Geneva 1; tel. 227325554; e-mail contact@swissphilanthropy.ch; internet www.swissphilanthropy.ch.

SwissFoundations—Verband der Schweizer Förderstiftungen/Association des Fondations Donatrices Suisses (Association of Grantmaking Foundations in Switzerland)
Established in 2001; an initiative of 11 large Swiss grant-making foundations.
Activities: A platform for inter-foundation collaboration. The Association shares technical expertise and experience, promotes transparency and encourages the involvement of new foundations. It has 231 members and is a member of Philea (q.v.), with an office in Geneva.
Geographical Area of Activity: Switzerland.
Publications: Annual Report; newsletter; *Swiss Foundation Code*.
Finance: Annual income 1.5m. Swiss francs, expenditure 992,005 Swiss francs (31 Dec. 2020).
Board of Directors: Sabrina Grassi (Pres.); Lisa Meyerhans (Vice-Pres.).
Principal Staff: Man. Dir Katja Schönenberger.
Contact Details: Kirchgasse 42, 8001 Zürich; tel. 444400010; e-mail info@swissfoundations.ch; internet www.swissfoundations.ch.

FOUNDATIONS AND NON-PROFITS

Abegg-Stiftung (Abegg Foundation)
Founded in 1961 by Werner Abegg for the collection, conservation and study of historical textiles and other works of art.
Activities: Supports textile restoration projects and students of textile restoration, through creating and running a degree course in textile art at the University of Applied Science, Bern. The Foundation maintains a research library and museum. It promotes scientific exchange in textile art by maintaining a research institute, organizing conferences and issuing publications.
Geographical Area of Activity: Switzerland.
Publications: *Riggisberger Berichte*; *Schriften*; monographs; collection catalogues and other specialist publications.
Board: Dominik Keller (Chair.).
Principal Staff: Dir Dr Regula Schorta.
Contact Details: Werner Abeggstr. 67, 3132 Riggisberg; tel. 318081201; e-mail info@abegg-stiftung.ch; internet www.abegg-stiftung.ch.

ACT Alliance
Established in 2010 by the merger of ACT International (f. 1995) and ACT Development (f. 2007), a coalition of Protestant and Orthodox churches and related organizations.
Activities: Works in the fields of humanitarian aid and development. The Alliance addresses systemic poverty; supports survivors of disasters, wars and conflicts; trains rural communities in sustainable agriculture; helps people adapt to environmental change; and influences governments and decisionmakers to safeguard human rights. Communities of Practice work on cross-cutting themes. It has 145 members, comprising member churches of the World Council of Churches and the Lutheran World Federation (q.v.), working in 127 countries.
Geographical Area of Activity: International.
Publications: ACT Alerts; Humanitarian Templates; Emergency Preparedness and Response Plan (EPRP) Templates; online resources.
Finance: Annual income US $33.1m., expenditure $33.3m. (31 Dec. 2023).
Governing Board: Erik Lysén (Moderator); Minnie Anne Mata-Calub (Vice-Moderator); Simangaliso Hove (Treas.).
Principal Staff: Gen. Sec. Rudelmar Bueno de Faria.
Contact Details: Global Secretariat, Ecumenical Center, Kyoto Bldg, 42 Chemin Du Pommier, 1218 Le Grand Saconnex; tel. 227916434; e-mail actcom@actalliance.org; internet actalliance.org.

Aga Khan Development Network—AKDN
Established by HH Prince Karim Aga Khan, after he became 49th Hereditary Imam and spiritual leader of the Shi'a Ismaili Muslims in 1957.
Activities: Operates in the field of international development, promoting self-reliance and improving quality of life. Programmes cover four main areas: developing human capacity; building resilient communities; generating economic growth; and honouring cultural heritage. The Network comprises: the Aga Khan Foundation (AKF, f. 1967), which offers grants to institutions, fellowships and scholarships; the Aga Khan Fund for Economic Development (AKFED, f. 1984), an international development agency that promotes entrepreneurship and local ownership; the Aga Khan Trust for Culture (AKTC, f. 1988), which runs the Historic Cities Support Program and the Aga Khan Music Initiative, offers the triennial Aga Khan Award for Architecture (worth a total of US $1m.) and maintains the Aga Khan Museum in Canada; and the Aga Khan Agency for Microfinance (AKAM, f. 2005). Other agencies include: Aga Khan Academies; Aga Khan Agency for Habitat; Aga Khan Education Services; Aga Khan Health Services; Aga Khan University; University of Central Asia (f. 2000); and Aga Khan Planning and Building Services. The Network employs around 96,000 people in more than 30 countries.
Geographical Area of Activity: International (primarily Africa and Asia).
Restrictions: No grants to individuals, for research or capital works; grants only in specific countries or regions. Scholarships are open to applicants from Afghanistan, Bangladesh, Egypt, India, Kenya, Kyrgyzstan, Madagascar, Mozambique, Pakistan, Syrian Arab Repub., Tajikistan, Tanzania and Uganda.
Publications: *AKDN Overview* (factsheet); newsletter (quarterly); reports; brochures; bulletins; factsheets.
Finance: Funded by individual agencies. Annual budget approx. US $1,000m.
Board of Directors: HH the Aga Khan (Chair.).
Contact Details: POB 2049, 1–3 ave de la Paix, 1202 Geneva 2; tel. 229097200; e-mail info@akdn.org; internet the.akdn.

Anne Frank-Fonds (Anne Frank Fund)
Founded in 1963 by Otto H. Frank, father of Anne Frank, to promote charitable, social and cultural activities and tolerance in the spirit of Anne Frank and protect the literary heritage and rights of the author.
Activities: Operates in the fields of the arts and humanities and human rights, raising funds for its charitable purposes through the licensing of Anne Frank's diary and other work.
Geographical Area of Activity: International, usually through Swiss organizations or the New Israel Fund in Israel.
Publications: Annual Report.
Board of Trustees: John D. Goldsmith (Pres.); Daniel Fürst (Vice-Pres.).

Contact Details: Steinengraben 18, 4051 Basel; tel. 612741174; e-mail info@annefrank.ch; internet www.annefrank.ch.

C. G. Jung-Institut Zürich

Founded in 1948 by Prof. C. G. Jung, C. A. Meier, K. Binswanger, L. Frey-Rohn and J. Jacobi.

Activities: Operates internationally in the fields of analytical psychology, education, science and medicine, through research, courses, public lectures and events, and the publication of scientific works. The Institute also maintains a library which houses some 15,000 volumes and periodicals.

Publications: Newsletter; books.

Advisory Board: Evy Tausky (Pres.); Dr Andreas Michel (Vice-Pres.).

Principal Staff: Head of Admin. Petra Brem.

Contact Details: Hornweg 28, 8700 Küsnacht; tel. 449141040; e-mail cg@junginstitut.ch; internet www.junginstitut.ch.

CARE International—CI

Founded in 1945 in Washington, DC, USA, as the Co-operative for American Remittances to Europe; present name adopted in 1981.

Activities: Provides humanitarian assistance and aims to improve social and economic conditions in developing countries, in particular for women and girls. Projects focus on: responding to emergencies; education; food security and climate change; women's economic empowerment; and reproductive and sexual heath. Its network comprises 16 national member organizations and five candidate and affiliated organizations. Maintains offices in Brussels (Belgium), London (UK) and New York (USA).

Geographical Area of Activity: Asia and the Pacific, Eastern Europe, Middle East and North Africa, South America, Central America and the Caribbean, sub-Saharan Africa.

Restrictions: Does not normally award grants; funds its own programmes.

Publications: Annual Report; member publications.

Principal Staff: Pres. and CEO Michelle Nunn.

Contact Details: 7–9 chemin de Balexert, 1219 Chatelaine, Geneva; tel. 227951020; e-mail cisecretariat@careinternational.org; internet www.care-international.org.

Centre Ecologique Albert Schweitzer—CEAS (Albert Schweitzer Ecological Centre)

Founded in 1980 to promote ecological solutions to agricultural problems.

Activities: Encourages ecologically sound practices in agriculture through the application of appropriate technology. Programmes include: Handicrafts and Renewable Energy; Water and Waste Management; and Sustainable Agriculture. It organizes training, compiles documentation and maintains a library. Has offices in Burkina Faso, Madagascar and Senegal.

Geographical Area of Activity: Burkina Faso, Madagascar, Senegal.

Publications: Annual Report; *DECLIC* (quarterly); books.

Finance: Annual income 3.6m. Swiss francs, expenditure 3.5m. Swiss francs (2023).

Board: Luc Meylan (Pres.); Roland Stähli (Vice-Pres.); Sandra Gibbons (Sec.).

Principal Staff: Co-Dirs Patrick Kohler, Jean-François Houmard, Niels Bourquin.

Contact Details: 21 rue des Beaux-Arts, 2000 Neuchâtel; tel. 327250836; e-mail info@ceas.ch; internet www.ceas.ch.

Centre Européen de la Culture—CEC (European Cultural Centre)

Founded in 1950 by Denis de Rougemont, a Swiss writer and philosopher, and Salvador de Madariaga, a Spanish writer, diplomat and historian.

Activities: Conducts cultural and educational activities in order to promote peace through a federal Europe and cultural dialogue. In 2015 the Centre inaugurated the Geneva Hub for Democracy to carry out activities in the areas of democracy, security and democratic culture, working in close coordination with the Geneva Centre for Security Policy, Geneva Centre for the Democratic Control of Armed Forces and the Foraus (Swiss Forum on Foreign Policy).

Geographical Area of Activity: Europe.

Publications: books, policy papers; periodicals.

Board: Prof. Dusan Sidjanski, Prof. Charles Méla (Co-Chair.); Micheline Calmy-Rey (Hon. Chair.).

Principal Staff: Sec.-Gen. François Saint-Ouen.

Contact Details: 40 rue Le-Corbusier, 1208 Geneva; tel. 227106600; e-mail info@ceculture.org; internet www.ceculture.org.

Centre for Humanitarian Dialogue—HD (Centre pour le Dialogue Humanitaire)

Established in 1999 as a private diplomacy organization; a non-profit foundation.

Activities: Carries out public and confidential international peace and mediation initiatives. Jointly with the Norwegian Ministry of Foreign Affairs, the Centre co-hosts the Oslo Forum, a series of retreats for international conflict mediators, decisionmakers and others involved in peace processes. It has regional offices in Kenya and Singapore, with country offices in the Central African Republic, Lebanon, Mali, Niger, Nigeria, the Philippines, Senegal and Sudan.

Geographical Area of Activity: International.

Publications: Meeting reports.

Finance: Annual income 46.0m. Swiss francs, expenditure 45.5m. Swiss francs (2021).

Board: Joanne Liu (Chair.); Markus Ederer (Vice-Chair.).

Principal Staff: Exec. Dir David Harland; Deputy Exec. Dir Katie Sams.

Contact Details: Villa Plantamour, 114 rue de Lausanne, 1202 Geneva; tel. 229081130; e-mail info@hdcentre.org; internet www.hdcentre.org.

Defence for Children International—DCI

Founded in 1979 by Nigel Cantwell, a consultant on child protection, to provide practical help to children internationally, and to promote and protect the rights of the child.

Activities: Works to improve children's rights internationally in the areas of: justice for children; violence against children; children affected by armed conflict; children on the move; child trafficking; child labour; and child participation. The organization publishes information about children's rights, and monitors the implementation of laws that should protect children. It has national sections in more than 37 countries.

Geographical Area of Activity: International.

Publications: Annual Report; newsletter; *Child Rights Observer* (newsletter); reports; factsheets; guides; handbooks.

Finance: Annual income 447,741 Swiss francs, expenditure 499,529 Swiss francs (31 Dec. 2022).

International Executive Council: Khaled Quzmar (Pres.); Mirjam Blaak (Treas.).

Principal Staff: Exec. Dir Alex Kamarotos.

Contact Details: 1 rue de Varembé, CP 88, 1211 Geneva 20; tel. 227340558; e-mail info@defenceforchildren.org; internet www.defenceforchildren.org.

Earthworm Foundation

Established in 1999, as the Tropical Forest Trust (subsequently, the Forest Trust—TFT), by Scott Poynton; in 2019, most of TFT's assets and staff were transferred to Earthworm Foundation, TFT becoming a subsidiary.

Activities: Works with brands, retailers and producers to make supply chains benefit people and nature, and change how raw materials are sourced. Main programmes are:

Healthy Forests; Teeming Oceans; Living Soils; Thriving Communities; Respected Workers; and Resilient Farmers. In 2008 the Foundation established the Centre of Social Excellence to offer training in social management practices in Africa and subsequently Indonesia and Brazil. In 2017, in partnership with with Airbus and SarVision, the Starling satellite initiative was launched to monitor deforestation. Has overseas offices including in France, the USA and the United Kingdom.

Geographical Area of Activity: Brazil, Cameroon, Côte d'Ivoire, Ecuador, France, Ghana, India, Indonesia, Malaysia, Peru, Switzerland, Türkiye, UK, USA, Viet Nam.

Publications: Annual Report; newsletter; brochures; Tools for Transformation (online).

Finance: Annual income US $24.7m., expenditure $24.5m. (31 Dec. 2023).

Board: Eric Bouchet (Chair.).

Principal Staff: CEO Bastien Sachet.

Contact Details: route de Divonne 50A, 1260 Nyon; tel. 225652095; e-mail info@earthworm.org; internet www.earthworm.org.

Edmond de Rothschild Foundations

Established in 2005; a philanthropic network.

Activities: Foundations within the network operate in Europe, Israel, Africa and the USA in the arts, entrepreneurship and health and by sharing best practices in philanthropy.

Geographical Area of Activity: Europe, Israel, USA.

Restrictions: Does not accept unsolicited proposals.

Finance: Total assets US $17m. (2023).

Board of Directors: Ariane de Rothschild (Pres.).

Principal Staff: CEO Firoz Ladak.

Contact Details: 18 rue de Hesse, 1204 Geneva; e-mail info@edrfoundations.org; internet www.edmondderothschildfoundations.org.

Fondation Charles Léopold Mayer pour le Progrès de l'Homme—FPH (Charles Léopold Mayer Foundation for the Progress of Humankind)

Founded in 1982 at the bequest of Charles Léopold Mayer (1881–1971), a chemist and financier.

Activities: Focuses on three main areas: new forms of governance; common ethical principles; and the transition towards more sustainable modes of living and societies. The Foundation funds civil society initiatives that will contribute to a global society and develop, reinforce and globalize networks. It has an office in Paris, France, with partners in more than 150 countries; and established the publishing company Éditions Charles Léopold Mayer. Is a member of Philea (q.v.).

Geographical Area of Activity: International.

Restrictions: Does not accept unsolicited individual applications for scholarships, fellowships or travel grants.

Publications: Annual Report; newsletter; books.

Finance: Budget €27m. (2021–23).

Board of Trustees: Claudia Genier (Chair.).

Principal Staff: Dir Matthieu Calame.

Contact Details: Vortex, 29 route de Praz-Véguey, BP 907, 1002 Chavannes-près-Renens; tel. 213425010; e-mail contact.fph@fph.ch; internet www.fph.ch.

Fondation Charles Veillon

Established in 1972 in memory of Charles Veillon, an entrepreneur and philanthropist; until 2009 it also administered the Veillon Research Fund for Malignant Lymphoma.

Activities: Works in the fields of international relations and culture, through promoting dialogue covering European culture, philosophy, federalism and interdisciplinary studies. The Foundation offers the Prix Européen de l'Essai Charles Veillon to European writers for an essay dealing with contemporary society. The award is worth 20,000 Swiss francs, and is offered annually in collaboration with the Université de Lausanne.

Geographical Area of Activity: Europe.

Council: Cyril Veillon (Chair.); Francesco Panese (Vice-Chair.).

Principal Staff: Sec.-Gen. Élise David.

Contact Details: 18 ave Église-Anglaise, 1006 Lausanne; tel. 795350053; e-mail info@fondation-veillon.ch; internet www.fondation-veillon.ch.

Fondation pour l'Economie et le Développement Durable des Régions d'Europe—FEDRE (European Foundation for the Sustainable Development of the Regions)

Established in 1996 as an offshoot of the Congress of Local and Regional Authorities of the Council of Europe (CLRAE).

Activities: Promotes the sustainable development of the regions of Eastern, Central and Western Europe, and of the South-Western Mediterranean Basin. The Foundation carries out activities in the fields of: renewable energy and climate policy; regional mobility; forestry in border regions; taxation in cross-border areas; and culture, co-operating with the Centre Européen de la Culture (q.v.) and the Denis de Rougemont Foundation for Europe.

Geographical Area of Activity: Europe.

Publications: Annual Report; magazines; *Directory of European Regions*.

Board of Directors: Claude Haegi (Chair.).

Principal Staff: Sec.-Gen. François Saint-Ouen.

Contact Details: 17 rue François-Dussaud, 1227 Acacias-Geneva; tel. 228071710; e-mail info@fedre.org; internet www.fedre.org.

Fondation Espace Afrique (Africa Space Foundation)

Established in 1996 by Samuel Dossou-Aworet, founder of the Petrolin Group; registered in Benin in 2004.

Activities: Carries out self-conducted programmes in the areas of agriculture, education, entrepreneurship, health and culture. Activities include: building infrastructure, including schools and health centres; equipping schools and education centres, offering scholarships and supporting vocational training; providing access to drinking water, improving nutrition and funding research into plant-based medicine; promoting self-sufficiency and food security through organic agriculture and food processing; encouraging private sector participation in development programmes and other co-operative partnerships; and preserving and promoting African traditions, knowledge and know-how. The Foundation established the International Centre for Experimentation and the Development of African Resources (CIEVRA) near Cotonou, Benin.

Geographical Area of Activity: Benin, Burkina Faso, Dem. Repub. of the Congo, Côte d'Ivoire, Ethiopia, Gabon, Namibia, Niger, Nigeria, The Gambia, Switzerland.

Publications: Annual Report.

Principal Staff: Pres. Samuel Dossou-Aworet.

Contact Details: CP 1921, 1211 Geneva 01; e-mail info@espaceafrique.org; internet espaceafrique.org.

Fondation Franz Weber—FFW

Established in 1975 by Franz Weber, an ecologist.

Activities: Conserves natural habitats, protects wildlife and defends animal rights. The Foundation runs national and international campaigns; fights the destruction of natural habitats; and campaigns for the rights of indigenous species and to obtain legal status for animals. It has established sanctuaries for horses and other animals in Argentina and Australia; a conservation area in southern France; and formerly managed the Fazao-Malfakassa National Park in Togo.

Geographical Area of Activity: International.

Publications: Newsletter; *Journal Franz Weber;* Briefing Notes.
Finance: Funded by contributions, donations and legacies. Annual expenditure approx. 2m. Swiss francs.
Board: Vera Weber (Pres.).
Contact Details: Postfach 257, 3000 Bern 13; tel. 219642424; e-mail ffw@ffw.ch; internet www.ffw.ch.

Fondation Hans Wilsdorf (Hans Wilsdorf Foundation)
Established in 1945; the sole owner of the share capital of Montres Rolex SA.
Activities: Works in the fields of social welfare, training and culture. The Foundation supports social institutions in Geneva and organizations helping people in financial need; offers scholarships to students in financial need and supports initiatives helping people find or return to work; and funds institutions involves in music, theatre and the visual arts.
Geographical Area of Activity: Mainly Switzerland.
Finance: Total assets approx. €9,000m.
Board: Costin van Berchem (Chair.).
Contact Details: 20 pl. d'Armes, POB 1432, 1227 Carouge; tel. 227373000; e-mail info@hanswilsdorf.ch; internet hanswilsdorf.ch.

Fondation Hirondelle: Media for Peace and Human Dignity
Established in 1995.
Activities: Produces and broadcasts information to people affected by crises using different media channels. The Foundation provides training and editorial, managerial and structural support to partner organizations. Programme areas include: elections and democratic processes; parliaments and media; justice and reconciliation; giving women a voice; youth participation; climate change adaptation; peacebuilding; migration and humanitarian crises.
Geographical Area of Activity: International.
Restrictions: Not a grantmaking organization.
Publications: Annual Report; newsletter; studies.
Finance: Total assets 8.7m. Swiss francs (2023).
Foundation Council: Tony Burgener (Pres.).
Principal Staff: Exec. Dir Caroline Vuillemin.
Contact Details: 19c ave du Temple, 1012 Lausanne; tel. 216542020; e-mail info@hirondelle.org; internet www.hirondelle.org.

Fondation Internationale Florence Nightingale (Florence Nightingale International Foundation)
Founded in 1934 in memory of Florence Nightingale (1820–1910), a social reformer and pioneer of modern nursing; the charitable arm of the International Council of Nurses (ICN).
Activities: Supports the advancement of nursing education, research and services for the public good. Initiatives include the Girl Child Education Fund, which supports primary and secondary education of girls in developing countries whose nurse parent or parents have died; its expansion is supported by the FNIF Endowment Fund. The Foundation offers the International Achievement Award every two years to a mid-career practising nurse working in the field of direct care, education, research or management. Other awards include: the Kim Mo Im Policy Innovation and Impact Award; Christiane Reimann Prize; Health and Human Rights Award; Partners in Development Award; and ICN Membership Awards. The International Council of Nurses carries out the Foundation's day-to-day administration.
Geographical Area of Activity: International.
Publications: Biennial Report; project publications.
Board of Directors: Pamela Cipriano (Pres.); Lisa Little (First Vice-Pres.); Karen Bjøro (Second Vice-Pres.); Lian-Hua Huang (Third Vice-Pres.).
Contact Details: International Council of Nurses, 3 pl. Jean-Marteau, 1201 Geneva; tel. 229080100; e-mail fnif@icn.ch; internet www.icn.ch/who-we-are/foundations.

Fondation ISREC (ISREC Foundation)
Established in 1964 by G. Candardjis, J.-L. de Coulon, H. Isliker, P. Mercier, A. de Muralt, A. Sauter, P. Schumacher, R. Stadler and F. Zumstein; formerly known as the Fondation Institut Suisse de Recherche Expérimentale sur le Cancer (Swiss Institute for Experimental Cancer Research/Schweizerisches Institut für Experimentelle Krebsforschung).
Activities: Carries out research and teaching in three areas: translational research, supporting projects that promote knowledge transfer and collaborations between basic research and clinical applications; young scientists and academics, awarding scholarships to doctoral students and researchers in the areas of biology, technology or medicine who work on immunology and oncology; and development of the AGORA Cancer Centre in Lausanne.
Geographical Area of Activity: Switzerland.
Publications: Annual Report; brochures.
Foundation Council: Pierre-Marie Glauser (Pres.); Claudine Amstein (Vice-Pres.).
Principal Staff: Pres. of Scientific Council Dr Michael N. Hall; Dir Susan M. Gasser.
Contact Details: 25A rue du Bugnon, 1005 Lausanne; tel. 216530716; e-mail info@isrec.ch; internet www.isrec.ch.

Fondation Jean Monnet pour l'Europe (Jean Monnet Foundation for Europe)
Founded in 1978 by Jean Monnet, a French economist and public official, who gave the organization his archives; a think tank.
Activities: Seeks to build a united Europe in accordance with Jean Monnet's thoughts, methods and actions. The Foundation maintains the archives of several protagonists of European unification, conducts research, and holds international conferences on topics related to European political and economic unity; publishes the results of research; and organizes an introductory course on European integration at the University of Lausanne. It also awards the Jean Monnet Medal; and the Henri Rieben Scholarship for advanced doctoral research for 1–6 months.
Geographical Area of Activity: Europe.
Publications: Activity Report; *Cahiers rouges* (series); *Collection débats et documents* (series); *Un changement d'espérance*; books on European topics.
Finance: Annual revenue 1.4m. Swiss francs, expenditure 1.4m. Swiss francs (31 Dec. 2023).
Executive Council: Pat Cox (Pres.); Jacques de Watteville, Pascal Fontaine (Vice-Pres).
Principal Staff: Dir Dr Gilles Grin.
Contact Details: Ferme de Dorigny, 1015 Lausanne; tel. 216922090; e-mail secr@fjme.unil.ch; internet www.jean-monnet.ch.

Fondation Latsis Internationale (International Latsis Foundation)
Established in 1975 by John S. Latsis, a Greek shipowner.
Activities: Operates in the field of science and technology. The Foundation funds four University Latsis Prizes (worth 25,000 Swiss francs each), which are awarded by the Université de Genève et de Saint-Gall and the Ecoles Polytechniques Fédérales de Zurich (EPFZ) and Lausanne (EPFL). It also funds the annual National Latsis Prize (worth 100,000 Swiss francs), which the Fonds National Suisse de la Recherche Scientifique awards to an individual aged under 40 years or to an organization's contribution to research in a particular scientific field. EPFZ and EPFL organize two annual symposia with the Foundation's financial support, worth 50,000 Swiss francs each.
Geographical Area of Activity: Europe.

Fondation Louis-Jeantet de Médecine — SWITZERLAND

Board: Recteur Yves Flückiger (Pres.).
Principal Staff: Sec. Eva-Maria Martin-Troy.
Contact Details: 40 rue Le Corbusier, 1208 Geneva; tel. 229590580; e-mail info@fondationlatsis.org; internet www.fondationlatsis.org.

Fondation Louis-Jeantet de Médecine (Louis-Jeantet Foundation for Medicine)

Established in 1982 by the will of Loius Jeantet, a French business person.
Activities: Awards the annual Prix Louis-Jeantet de Médecine to experienced researchers who have distinguished themselves in the field of biomedical research in Europe. The Foundation also encourages teaching and research development at the Faculty of Medicine of the University of Geneva.
Geographical Area of Activity: Europe.
Publications: Brochures; books; audio and video publications.
Finance: Annual research budget 2.5m. Swiss francs (2025).
Board: Prof. Denis Duboule (Pres.).
Principal Staff: Sec.-Gen. Elodie van Hove.
Contact Details: Maison des Fondations, 17 chemin Rieu, 1208 Geneva; tel. 227043636; e-mail info@jeantet.ch; internet www.jeantet.ch.

Fondation Nestlé pour l'Etude des Problèmes de l'Alimentation dans le Monde (Nestlé Foundation for the Study of the Problems of Nutrition in the World)

Founded in 1966 by Nestlé, a food and drink manufacturer, to improve nutrition.
Activities: Develops and sponsors nutrition-related research projects, awarding research grants to individuals and institutions, ranging from US $20,000 to $300,000; and awarding scholarships for postgraduate studies in nutrition to candidates from selected nutrition units. The Foundation also organizes scientific conferences; and publishes and disseminates scientific literature. It has supported projects in more than 50 countries.
Geographical Area of Activity: Low- and middle-income countries.
Publications: Annual Report; newsletter; scientific publications.
Council: Dr Petra S. Hüppi (Pres.).
Principal Staff: Dir Dr Paolo M. Suter.
Contact Details: 4 pl. de la Gare, POB 581, 1001 Lausanne; tel. 213203351; e-mail nf@nestlefoundation.org; internet www.nestlefoundation.org.

Fondation Simón I. Patiño (Simón I. Patiño Foundation)

Established in 1958 in memory of Simón I. Patiño, a Bolivian industrialist, by his heirs.
Activities: Works in the fields of education, culture, health and agriculture, through self-conducted programmes and research. In Bolivia, the Foundation operates a paediatric centre, which provides medical care, carries out training and research and runs a nutritional centre for malnourished children; a pedagogical and cultural centre, which offers literacy programmes through a network of village-based libraries, a central library and cultural events; an agricultural research and seed centre, and model farm; a centre for applied ecology; and a cultural centre, which houses the Documentation Centre for Latin American Arts and Literature. Internationally, in particular in Switzerland, the Foundation provides university scholarships for Bolivian students who will return to help in Bolivian development. It is also active in the field of the arts and culture, through organizing visual arts exhibitions and musical events, and offering scholarships for young artists. Comprises 20 centres, museums, parks and libraries in Geneva and Bolivia, where it carries out its activities as the Fundación Universitaria Simón I. Patiño.
Geographical Area of Activity: Belgium, Bolivia, Costa Rica, Spain, Switzerland.
Restrictions: Awards grants to Bolivian graduates who wish to study for a Master's; and Bolivian students who wish to study at universities in Bolivia designated by the Foundation or to specialize in tropical agricultural techniques at the Escuela Agrícola de la Región del Trópico Húmedo, Universidad EARTH de Costa Rica.
Publications: Annual Report; *Contacto* (annual newsletter); Latin American Literatures and Cultures (book series).
Governing Board: Benoît Merkt (Chair. and Sec.); Nicolas du Chastel (Vice-Chair.); Grégoire de Sartiges (Sec.).
Principal Staff: Man. Dir Frédéric Debray.
Contact Details: 8 rue Giovanni-Gambini, 1206 Geneva; tel. 223470211; e-mail info@patino.org; internet patino.org.

Franciscans International

Established in 1989; has general consultative status with the UN (ECOSOC).
Activities: Advocates for the protection of human dignity and environmental justice. Main programmes focus on: development and human rights; environmental justice; and human rights vs security. The organization builds the capacity of grassroots partners to monitor and prevent human rights violations; and works to influence governments through key UN mechanisms, human rights experts and diplomats.
Geographical Area of Activity: Africa, Asia-Pacific, the Americas, Europe.
Publications: Reports; toolbox; newsletters.
Finance: Annual income 1.2m. Swiss francs, expenditure 1.2m. Swiss francs (2023).
International Board of Directors: Michael Perry (Pres.); Charity Lydia Katongo Nkandunu (Vice-Pres.); James Donnegan (Treas.); Joseph Blay (Sec.).
Principal Staff: Exec. Dir Blair Matheson.
Contact Details: 37–39 rue de Vermont, POB 104, 1211 Geneva 20; tel. 227794010; e-mail geneva@franciscansinternational.org; internet www.franciscansinternational.org.

FXB International—Association François-Xavier Bagnoud

Established in 1989 in memory of François-Xavier Bagnoud, a helicopter pilot, by his mother Countess Albina du Boisrouvray; an umbrella organization.
Activities: Main programme areas include: economic and community development (FXBVillage), bringing people from extreme poverty to self-sufficiency within three years; health, improving access to health services, disease prevention, antiretroviral therapy, counselling and WASH (water, sanitation and hygiene); education, providing young people with formal and informal education, life skills and vocational skills; and protection and climate change, including reducing gender-based violence and insecurity towards women and children. In 1993 the organization established the FXB Center for Health and Human Rights at Harvard University; and it has offices in France and the USA. Sister organizations operate in India and Rwanda.
Geographical Area of Activity: Burkina Faso, Burundi, People's Repub. of China, Colombia, France, India, Mongolia, Myanmar, Rwanda, South Africa, Switzerland, Uganda, USA.
Restrictions: No unsolicited applications or grants to individuals.
Publications: Annual Report; newsletter; *FXB Toolkit and Planning Guide*; evaluations; factsheets; handouts.
Finance: Global annual income US $6.1m., expenditure $5.1m. (2023).
Board: Albina du Boisrouvray (Pres. Emerita); Didier Cherpitel, Albina du Boisrouvray (Co-Pres.); Jacques Vollenweider (Treas.); Céline Guillet-Dauphine (Sec.).
Principal Staff: Gen. Dir Christine Eggs.

Contact Details: 44 rue de Lausanne, 1201 Geneva; tel. 227410030; e-mail info@fxb.org; internet fxb.org.

Gebert Rüf Stiftung

Established in 1997 by Heinrich Gebert in memory of his first wife Paula Rüf.

Activities: Supports scientific research projects at institutions of higher education in Switzerland related to innovation and transfer of science. The Foundation directs its funding towards young entrepreneurs in four target areas: science and entrepreneurship, focusing on research and innovation in Switzerland; education and entrepreneurship, supporting new forms of teaching using digital tools; science and the public, promoting science communication and 'scientainment' and funding development in the South Caucasus region; and professionalizing the foundation sector in Switzerland. Since its inception, it has disbursed approximately 308m. Swiss francs.

Geographical Area of Activity: South Caucasus, Switzerland.

Publications: Annual Report; *Rapport sur les fondations*.

Finance: Total assets 65.8m. Swiss francs; annual disbursements 12.2m. Swiss francs (31 Dec. 2024).

Board of Trustees: Prof. Dr Roland Siegwart (Pres.); Prof. Dr Monika Bütler (Deputy Pres.).

Principal Staff: CEO and Dir Dr Pascale Vonmont; Deputy Dir Dr Marco Vencato.

Contact Details: Haus der Stiftungen, St Alban-Vorstadt 12, 4052 Basel; tel. 612708822; e-mail info@grstiftung.ch; internet www.grstiftung.ch.

HEKS—Hilfswerk der Evangelischen Kirchen Schweiz (Swiss Church Aid)

Established in 1946 by the Federation of Swiss Protestant Churches (FSPC) to contribute to the reconciliation and reconstruction of Europe in co-operation with the Protestant churches of the respective partner countries; became a foundation in 2004.

Activities: Promotes self-determination and the right to live in dignity, supporting access to land and natural resources and equal opportunities for all. Internationally, the organization focuses on rural development and eliminating poverty and hunger; and emergency humanitarian assistance, providing aid and routes to safety. Programmes include: providing access to education, healthcare and social services for all; sustainable agriculture and access to markets; vocational training in rural areas; defending security and rights; promoting good governance and civil society; fighting discrimination against minorities; peacebuilding through advocacy; preparing for disasters and environmental change; and gender equality. Nationally, it focuses on helping refugees and other socially disadvantaged people through building sociopolitical commitment and the support of civil society; and integration projects, which provide legal advice and build self-confidence and self-responsibility, organizing language classes, education and information workshops and job opportunities. Five regional offices carry out programmes in Switzerland, with co-ordination offices in 17 priority regions abroad, overseeing work in more than 30 countries; and co-operating with Reformed Churches in Italy, Eastern Europe and the Middle East through the Kirchliche Zusammenarbeit (KiZA) network.

Geographical Area of Activity: Central and South-Eastern Europe, Italy, Middle East, South America, Central America and the Caribbean, sub-Saharan Africa.

Publications: Annual Report; *HEKS Newsletter*.

Finance: Annual income 137.3m. Swiss francs, expenditure 138.5m. Swiss francs (31 Dec. 2023).

Board of Trustees: Walter Schmid (Pres.); Michèle Künzler (Vice-Pres.).

Principal Staff: CEO Karolina Frischkopf.

Contact Details: Seminarstr. 28, Postfach, 8042 Zürich; tel. 443608800; e-mail info@heks.ch; internet www.heks.ch.

Helmut-Horten-Stiftung (Helmut Horten Foundation)

Established in 1971 by Helmut Horten, the founder of Horten AG, a chain of German department stores.

Activities: Supports the healthcare system in Switzerland through financial contributions to medical research facilities, hospitals and other healthcare institutions, as well as to individuals in need of medical care. The Foundation gives priority to large-scale research projects, particularly where it is the sole funder. Significant initiatives include the Horten Center for Applied Research and Science and the Institute for Research in Biomedicine in Bellinzona, Switzerland. It also occasionally awards scholarships for young researchers at Swiss universities.

Geographical Area of Activity: Mainly Switzerland.

Board of Trustees: Alain Robert (Pres.).

Principal Staff: Man. Dir Corina Albertini.

Contact Details: Via B. Lambertenghi 5, 6900 Lugano; tel. 916102280; e-mail info@helmut-horten-stiftung.org; internet www.helmut-horten-stiftung.org.

Helvetas Swiss Intercooperation

Established in 2011 following merger of Helvetas (f. 1955) and Intercooperation (f. 1982); a network of independent affiliates.

Activities: Co-ordinates development projects, offers advisory services to governmental organizations and NGOs, and raises awareness concerning the problems faced by people in developing countries. Main programme areas are: gender and social equity; humanitarian response; skills, jobs and income; urban engagement; voice, inclusion and cohesion; water, food and climate; and youth. The organization is active in 35 countries; and has offices in Germany and the USA.

Geographical Area of Activity: Africa, Asia, Eastern Europe, Latin America.

Restrictions: No grants to individuals.

Publications: Annual Report; newsletter; position papers; blog.

Finance: Annual income 156.1m. Swiss francs, expenditure 161.8m. Swiss francs (31 Dec. 2023).

Board of Directors: Regula Rytz (Pres.); Peter Niggli (Vice-Pres.).

Principal Staff: Exec. Dir Melchior Lengsfeld.

Contact Details: Weinbergstr. 22A, 8021 Zürich; tel. 443686500; e-mail info@helvetas.org; internet www.helvetas.ch.

Institut de Hautes Études Internationales et du Développement—IHEID (Graduate Institute of International Studies and Development Studies)

Founded in 1927 as l'Institut Universitaire de Hautes Études Internationales by Prof. W. Rappard and Prof. P. Mantoux; in 2008, it merged with the Institut Universitaire du Développement (f. 1961).

Activities: Carries out interdisciplinary research through centres specializing in: conflict, development and peacebuilding; finance and development; international environmental studies; global migration; trade and economic integration; health; governance; democracy; and gender. The Institute disseminates its findings through publications, roundtables and executive education courses. It maintains a library, which contains approximately 350,000 vols, 650 journals and 685 monographic series. Every two years, the Edgar de Picciotto International Prize, worth 100,000 Swiss francs, is awarded for research that has enhanced understanding of global challenges and influenced policymakers. In 2014 the annual Advancing Development Goals Contest (the Geneva Challenge) was launched, open to teams of 3–5 Master's students, worth 25,000 Swiss francs in total.

Geographical Area of Activity: International.

Publications: Annual Report; newsletter; *Globe—the Graduate Institute Review* (2 a year); factsheets; working papers; books.

Finance: Annual revenue 111.2m. Swiss francs (2023).
Foundation Board: Rolf Soiron (Chair.); Beth Krasna (Vice-Chair.).
Principal Staff: Dir Marie-Laure Salles.
Contact Details: Maison de la Paix, 2A rue Eugène-Rigot, 1202 Geneva; CP 1672, 1211 Geneva 1; tel. 229085700; e-mail info@graduateinstitute.ch; internet graduateinstitute.ch.

Institut International des Droits de l'Enfant (International Institute for the Rights of the Child)

Founded in 1995 by Dr Bernard Comby and Jean Zermatten, through the merger of the International Association of Youth and Family Judges and Magistrates.

Activities: Works in the field of children's law and human rights. The Institute holds international seminars, provides training nationally and internationally, and issues publications. It has consultative status with ECOSOC; hosts the Sarah Oberson Foundation (f. 1998), which is particularly concerned with the disappearance and separation of children from their parents; and the headquarters of the Veillard-Cybulski Fund Association (f. 1986), which makes an award every two years, worth 5,000 Swiss francs, for advancing treatment of children and adolescents and their families in difficulty. Has an office in Geneva.
Geographical Area of Activity: International.
Publications: Annual Report; books.
Finance: Funded by the Swiss Confederation and by private funding.
Foundation Council: Jean-Dominique Vassalli (Pres.).
Principal Staff: Co-Dirs Yann Colliou, Steven Fricaud.
Contact Details: 18 chemin de l'Institut, 1967 Bramois; tel. 586110666; e-mail ide@childsrights.org; internet www.childsrights.org.

International Baccalaureate—IB

Founded in 1968 as the International Baccalaureate Organization, following the recommendation of an International Schools Association conference of teachers of social studies to create an International Passport to Higher Education; present name adopted in 2014.

Activities: Promotes multilingualism, an international outlook and action through community service; and fosters critical thinking, study across disciplines and lifelong learning. Courses comprise: the Primary Years Programme for students aged 3–11 years; the Middle Years Programme (11–16 years); and the Diploma Programme and Career-related Programme (16–19 years). The organization carries out education research; and offers short-term grants for schools in temporary financial difficulty or that are expanding access to IB programmes. It operates through three regional offices, serving the Americas; Africa, Europe and the Middle East; and the Asia-Pacific region. Programmes are offered in more than 5,000 schools in over 150 countries.
Geographical Area of Activity: International.
Publications: Annual Review; *IB World*; *Statistical Bulletin*; newsletter; curriculum support materials; blog.
Finance: Annual income US $208.8m., expenditure $130.5m. (30 June 2022).
Board of Governors: Dr Helen Drennen (Chair.); Cyrille NKontchou (Vice-Chair.).
Principal Staff: Dir-Gen. Olli-Pekka Heinonen.
Contact Details: 1 rue du Pré-de-la-Bichette, 1202 Genève; tel. 223092540; e-mail support@ibo.org; internet www.ibo.org.

International Red Cross and Red Crescent Movement—ICRC

Comprises the National Red Cross and Red Crescent Societies, the International Committee of the Red Cross (ICRC), founded in 1863 to help soldiers wounded on the battlefield, and the International Federation of Red Cross and Red Crescent Societies (the Federation), founded in 1919 (as the League of Red Cross and Red Crescent Societies) to promote humanitarian activities in peacetime.

Activities: Protects the lives and dignity of victims of war, violence and humanitarian emergencies, in particular vulnerable civilian groups such as women, children and displaced people. Programmes include: Addressing sexual violence; Building respect for the law; Co-operating with National Societies; Economic security; Enabling people with disabilities; Forensic science and humanitarian action; Health; Health care in danger; Helping detainees; Humanitarian; Migrants, refugees, asylum seekers; Mine action; Restoring family links; Water and habitat; and Working with the corporate sector. The Movement directs and co-ordinates international relief activities in situations of conflict; advocates strengthening humanitarian law and universal humanitarian principles; administers philanthropic funds; and offers the Humanitarian Visa d'or award, worth €8,000, for photojournalism in armed conflict. It is a permanent body for liaison, co-ordination and study, advising members on development of their services; and comprising 196 National Red Cross and Red Crescent Societies. Works in over 100 countries.
Geographical Area of Activity: International.
Publications: Annual Report; *International Review of the Red Cross* (quarterly); *Red Cross, Red Crescent* (quarterly magazine); discussion papers; handbooks; guides; manuals; toolkits.
Finance: Annual income 2,520m. Swiss francs, expenditure 2,270m. (31 Dec. 2023).
Assembly: Mirjana Spoljaric Egger (Pres.); Gilles Carbonnier (Vice-Pres.).
Principal Staff: Dir-Gen. Pierre Krähenbühl.
Contact Details: 19 ave de la Paix, 1202 Geneva; tel. 227346001; internet www.icrc.org.

International Service for Human Rights—ISHR

Established in 1984 by Adrien-Claude Zoller, a former management consultant and founder of the Ecumenical Research Exchange Centre.

Activities: Supports human rights defenders, strengthens human rights systems and leads and participates in coalitions for human rights change. The organization provides training, information, advice and advocacy to ensure that national-level human rights defenders can use international and regional human rights mechanisms; and works with decisionmakers and diplomats within the UN and regional systems to make human rights systems more accessible, effective and protective for human rights defenders and the people they represent, promoting justice and accountability for violations. It focuses on those human rights defenders who are most at risk, including women human rights defenders; defenders of LGBTI rights; those who work on business and human rights; and those who promote democratic freedoms and work to end impunity, particularly in countries in transition. Has an office in New York, USA.
Geographical Area of Activity: International.
Restrictions: Not a grantmaking organization; does not campaign on individual cases.
Publications: Annual Report; *Human Rights Monitor*; manuals; handbooks; reports; briefing papers; factsheets.
Finance: Annual income 3.9m. Swiss francs, expenditure 3.9m. Swiss francs (31 Dec. 2023).
Board of Directors: Vrinda Grover (Chair.); Bruno Stagno Ugarte (Deputy Chair.); Florian Pollner (Treas.).
Principal Staff: Exec. Dir Phil Lynch; Deputy Exec. Dir Marina Dailly.
Contact Details: 1 rue de Varembé, 5th Floor, CP 16, 1211 Geneva 20; tel. 229197100; e-mail information@ishr.ch; internet www.ishr.ch.

SWITZERLAND

Internationale Stiftung Hochalpine Forschungsstationen Jungfraujoch und Gornergrat (International Foundation of the High-Altitude Research Stations Jungfraujoch and Gornergrat)

Founded in 1930 by representatives of scientific institutions in Belgium, Germany, Austria, France, the United Kingdom and Switzerland to promote high-altitude research.

Activities: Supports the research station and Sphinx laboratory on the Jungfraujoch, and the two astronomical observatories, Gornergrat South and Gornergrat North. The Foundation does not itself carry out research, but provides the necessary infrastructure and administrative support for researchers in the fields of physiology, physics, environment, astronomy and astrophysics. It has 11 member institutions from Austria, Belgium, the People's Repub. of China, Finland, Germany, Switzerland and the United Kingdom.

Geographical Area of Activity: International.

Publications: Annual Report; white papers.

Board of Trustees: Prof. Dr Silvio Decurtins (Pres.).

Principal Staff: Dir Dr Eliza Harris; Sec. Claudine Frieden.

Contact Details: Sidlerstr. 5, 3012 Bern; tel. 316844052; e-mail claudine.frieden@unibe.ch; internet www.hfsjg.ch/de/stiftung.

IUCN/UICN (International Union for Conservation of Nature and Natural Resources)

Founded in 1948 as the International Union for the Protection of Nature (IUPN); present full name adopted in 1956.

Activities: Works in the areas of biodiversity, climate change, livelihoods, energy and green markets. It supports scientific research; manages field projects all over the world; and brings governments, NGOs, businesses, the UN, international conventions and community organizations together to develop policy, legislation and best practice. The Union comprises more than 1,400 government and non-government member organizations, and 17,000 volunteer scientists in more than 160 countries. In addition, it works with companies, academic institutions, social and indigenous groups, and UN organizations; and runs the IUCN Conservation Centre, which hosts conferences and provides services to member and partner organizations. Awards the John C. Phillips Memorial Medal for services to conservation and the Harold Jefferson Coolidge Memorial Medal for conservation of nature and natural resources.

Geographical Area of Activity: International.

Publications: Annual Report; *World Conservation/Planète conservation/Conservacíon mundial* (3 a year); *The Red List of Threatened Species*; *Best Practice Guidelines on Protected Areas series*; *Environmental Policy and Law Papers*; *Species Conservation and Action Plans*; brochures; reports; blog.

Finance: Annual income 164.5m. Swiss francs, expenditure 156.2m. Swiss francs (31 Dec. 2023).

Council: Razan Al Mubarak (Pres.); Nihal Welikala (Treas.).

Principal Staff: Dir-Gen. Dr Grethel Aguilar.

Contact Details: 28 rue Mauverney, 1196 Gland; tel. 229990000; e-mail mail@iucn.org; internet www.iucn.org.

Jacobs Foundation

Established in 1988 by Klaus J. Jacobs, a chocolate and confectionery manufacturer.

Activities: Supports research and intervention projects in the field of child and youth development. Main programme areas include: the science of learning, funding innovative research into how individual children can learn better; early childhood education and care, developing best practices in Switzerland and Germany and disseminating this to other European countries; and rural livelihoods, focusing on Côte d'Ivoire and sharing its benefits with other West African countries. The Foundation awards Fellowships for early and mid-career researchers; and prizes for research and best practice. The Jacobs Foundation Marbach Castle Residence Program, in Germany, offers the opportunity for collaborative work; the castle also hosts an annual conference.

Geographical Area of Activity: Europe, West Africa.

Restrictions: Does not accept unsolicited applications.

Publications: Annual Report; newsletter.

Finance: Annual income 41.6m. Swiss francs, expenditure 18.0m. Swiss francs (2020).

Principal Staff: Co-CEOs Fabio Segura, Simon Sommer.

Contact Details: Seefeldquai 17, 8034 Zürich; tel. 443886123; e-mail jf@jacobsfoundation.org; internet www.jacobsfoundation.org.

Kofi Annan Foundation

Established in 2010 by former Sec.-Gen. of the UN Kofi Annan.

Activities: Promotes better global governance and strengthening the capacities of people and countries to achieve a fairer, more secure world. Main programme areas are: reconciliation and transitional justice; mediation and crisis resolution; electoral integrity and democracy; eliminating hunger; changing drug policy; and promoting youth leadership.

Geographical Area of Activity: International.

Restrictions: Does not make grants or award scholarships.

Publications: Annual Report; newsletter (quarterly).

Finance: Annual income 2.8m. Swiss francs, expenditure 2.8m. Swiss francs (2023).

Board: Elhadj As Sy (Chair.).

Principal Staff: Exec. Dir Corinne Momal-Vanian.

Contact Details: POB 157, 1211 Geneva 20; tel. 229197520; e-mail info@kofiannanfoundation.org; internet www.kofiannanfoundation.org.

Landis & Gyr Stiftung (Landis & Gyr Foundation)

Established in 1971, as the Zuger Kulturstiftung Landis & Gyr, by Landis & Gyr, a manufacturer of energy meters.

Activities: Supports artistic and cultural projects to integrate people from foreign cultures. The Foundation offers studio scholarships to Swiss artists and cultural workers in London (UK), Budapest (Hungary), Bucharest (Romania), Sofia (Bulgaria) and Zug in the fields of visual arts, literature, composition and cultural criticism; and supplementary project-related travel grants to the Balkans and Türkiye (Turkey). The Foundation also supports the New Europe College in Bucharest and promotes exchange in the humanities with Eastern Europe. Every two years, it awards the Landis & Gyr Stiftung Prize, worth 100,000 Swiss francs, to an individual or group for services of social benefit.

Geographical Area of Activity: Switzerland (in particular Zug), Europe.

Restrictions: Scholarship applicants must be Swiss citizens or have been resident in Switzerland for at least three years; applicants for Zug must be from Ticino or French-speaking Switzerland. Does not support educational projects or programmes or social welfare.

Publications: Annual Report; newsletter.

Board of Trustees: Dr Brigit Eriksson-Hotz (Pres.); Ulrich Straub (Vice-Pres.).

Principal Staff: Dir Nela Bunjevac.

Contact Details: Chamerstr. 10 (entrance via Bundesstrasse 17), 6300 Zug; POB 7838, 6302 Zug; tel. 7252358; e-mail info@lg-stiftung.ch; internet www.lg-stiftung.ch.

Laudes Foundation

Established in 2020 by the Brenninkmeijer family business owners as an independent foundation responding to the crises of climate breakdown and deepening inequality.

Activities: Supports action that challenges and inspires industry, in particular the fashion and built environment industries, which have a negative impact on emissions and social inclusion, and finance and capital markets, which impact decisions and corporate action throughout the real economy. Its focus in the fashion industry is on scaling next-generation materials and building more regenerative business models, while supporting collective action and social protection for workers, and incentives for accountability. In the built environment, it works on decarbonising the built environment, accelerating bio-based construction and ensuring a just transition for construction workers. In finance and capital markets, it focuses on mobilising investment to accelerate industry transition through its influence, policies, practices and valuations.

Geographical Area of Activity: International.

Restrictions: Does not, in general, accept unsolicited applications; no grants to individuals.

Publications: Annual reports; research reports; evaluations.

Finance: Grants disbursed €225.6m. (active, in 2022).

Board: Eric Lawrence Brenninkmeijer (Chair.).

Principal Staff: CEO Leslie Johnston.

Contact Details: Grafenauweg 10, 6300 Zug; e-mail communications@laudesfoundation.org; internet www.laudesfoundation.org.

Limmat Stiftung (Limmat Foundation)

Founded in 1972 by Toni Zweifel and Dr Arthur Wiederkehr to promote initiatives for the common good in Switzerland and abroad.

Activities: An umbrella foundation, comprising 14 sub-foundations that operate in the fields of education, health, advancement of the poor (especially women) and vocational training. Programmes are instruction orientated and encourage self-help.

Geographical Area of Activity: International.

Publications: Annual Report; articles; brochure.

Finance: Total income 4.0m. Swiss francs, expenditure 5.1m. Swiss francs (31 Dec. 2023).

Board: Elisabeth András (Pres.).

Principal Staff: Exec. Dir François Geinoz.

Contact Details: Rosenbühlstr. 32, 8044 Zürich; tel. 442662030; e-mail limmat@limmat.org; internet www.limmat.org.

The Lutheran World Federation (Lutherischer Weltbund/Fédération Luthérienne Mondiale/Federación Luterana Mundial)

Founded in 1947 to serve Lutheran churches as an instrument for humanitarian assistance, mission and development, ecumenism, communication and theological study.

Activities: Promotes theological reflection and study, and campaigns for human rights, gender justice and youth participation under three main programmes: Theology and Dialogue, working with groups from other faith groups and Christian traditions for peace, justice and reconciliation; Holistic Mission and Relationships, fostering equitable participation and leadership within and between churches; and Diakonia ('service to those in need'), which addresses human suffering, injustice and emergencies. The Department for World Service is the Federation's humanitarian and development arm, which works for human rights, impartiality, accountability, gender justice, climate justice and environmental protection. Has 150 member churches in 99 countries.

Geographical Area of Activity: International.

Publications: *Lutheran World Information* (newsletter); *LWF Annual Report*; *LWF Documentation/LWB Dokumentation*; *LWF Studies/LWB-Studien*; *LWF Women*; *LWF Youth*; frameworks; reports; blog.

Finance: Annual income €178m., expenditure €176m. (31 Dec. 2022).

Executive Committee: Bishop Henrik Stubkjær (Pres.).

Contact Details: 2 Chemin du Pavillon, 1218 Le Grand Saconnex, Geneva; tel. 227916000; e-mail info@lutheranworld.org; internet www.lutheranworld.org.

Max Schmidheiny-Stiftung an der Universität St Gallen (Max Schmidheiny Foundation at the University of St Gallen)

Established in 1978 at the University of St Gallen by Max Schmidheiny, an industrialist and financier.

Activities: Promotes the preservation and further development of a free market economy and society, especially initiatives to safeguard individual freedom, individuals' responsibility for their own welfare and the guaranteed maintenance of social security. The Foundation focuses on entrepreneurship and risk and on business in a socioeconomic context; and is a strategic partner of the Global Trade Alert information platform, which monitors state trade policy measures. It promotes exchanges and collaboration between younger entrepreneurs, business people and politicians; organizes forums in Bad Ragaz and Max Schmidheiny Lectures at the St Gallen Symposium; and has endowed the Max Schmidheiny Foundation Professorship for Entrepreneurship and Risk at the University of St Gallen. Has an office in Zurich.

Geographical Area of Activity: International.

Board of Trustees: Dr h.c. Thomas Schmidheiny (Chair.).

Principal Staff: Pres. Andreas R. Kirchschläger; Deputy Man. Dir Adrian Ackert.

Contact Details: Dufourstr. 83, CP 1045, 9001 St Gallen; Wiesenstrasse 7, 8008 Zurich; tel. 434667743; e-mail info@max-schmidheiny.foundation; internet www.max-schmidheiny.foundation.

Médecins Sans Frontières International—MSF International (Doctors Without Borders International)

Founded in 1971 in Paris, France, by a group of doctors and journalists.

Activities: Provides emergency medical assistance to people affected by conflict, epidemics or disasters or who have been excluded from healthcare; and speaks out against violence and neglect. The organization conducts research into the treatment of infectious diseases, including tuberculosis (TB), HIV/AIDS and neglected tropical diseases; and carries out training and development based on analysis of and reflection on humanitarian operations. It has 24 national and regional associations worldwide and works in more than 70 countries.

Geographical Area of Activity: International.

Publications: Annual Report; newsletter; Speaking Out Case Studies; factsheets; reports; studies.

Finance: Annual income €2,365.1m., expenditure €2,308.8m. (31 Dec. 2023).

International Board: Dr Christos Christou (Pres.); Yvan Legris (Treas.).

Principal Staff: Sec.-Gen. Christopher Lockyear.

Contact Details: 140 route de Ferney, 1202 Geneva; tel. 228498484; e-mail office-gva@geneva.msf.org; internet www.msf.org.

Novartis Foundation

Established in 1973 as a department within the Novartis company for relations with developing countries; name changed in 1979 to the Ciba-Geigy Foundation for Co-operation with Developing Countries and subsequently to the Novartis Foundation for Sustainable Development. Present name adopted in 2015.

Activities: Supports the implementation of health initiatives financially and technically. The Foundation operates in three overlapping areas: developing and supporting healthcare projects that focus on people in low-income settings and improve access to healthcare, strengthening human resources and empowering vulnerable groups; serving as a think tank on international health and corporate responsibility; and fostering dialogue between the private sector, government and civil society regarding global development and corporate responsibility.

Geographical Area of Activity: India, South America; sub-Saharan Africa.

SWITZERLAND

Restrictions: Does not make grants; does not normally accept unsolicited applications.
Publications: Annual Report; newsletter; symposium reports; factsheets.
Board of Trustees: Dr Joerg Reinhardt (Chair.).
Principal Staff: Head of Foundation Dr Ann Aerts.
Contact Details: Novartis Campus, Forum 1-3.97, 4002 Basel; tel. 616962300; e-mail info@novartisfoundation.org; internet www.novartisfoundation.org.

Oak Foundation

Established in 1983 by Alan Parker, a business person; a group of charitable and philanthropic organizations.
Activities: Works to address matters of global, social and environmental concern. Main programmes focus on: environment; prevention of child abuse; housing and homelessness; international human rights; issues that affect women; and learning differences. There are also national programmes for Brazil, Denmark, India and Zimbabwe; and a Special Interest Programme, which funds causes that fall outside the other programmes, such as health, humanitarian relief, education and the arts. Grants typically range from US $25,000 to $10m. The Foundation works in around 40 countries, with offices in Denmark, India, the United Kingdom, USA and Zimbabwe.
Geographical Area of Activity: International.
Restrictions: Does not fund religious or political causes; no grants to individuals or for scholarships.
Publications: Annual Report; newsletter; policy papers; guidelines.
Finance: Total annual grantmaking US $474m. (2023).
Board of Trustees: Natalie Shipton (Chair.); Kristian Parker, Caroline Turner (Vice-Chair.).
Principal Staff: Pres. Douglas Griffiths.
Contact Details: 58 ave Louis Casaï, CP 115, 1216 Cointrin, Geneva; tel. 223188640; e-mail info@oakfnd.ch; internet www.oakfnd.org.

Pro Helvetia (Swiss Arts Council)

Founded in 1939.
Activities: The Swiss Arts Council Pro Helvetia fosters contemporary art production in Switzerland and helps disseminate and promote Swiss arts at home and abroad. Pro Helvetia is active in all arts disciplines with the exception of film, and contributes to national and international cultural exchange and to innovation in the field of cultural promotion. Pro Helvetia has its head office in Zurich and maintains an international network abroad, which cultivates close ties with local partners and provides opportunities for residencies and cultural exchange.
Geographical Area of Activity: International.
Restrictions: Grants only for projects connected to Switzerland, which are of nationwide importance, publicly accessible and co-financed by public or private sponsors.
Publications: Newsletters; information sheets.
Finance: As a public-law foundation, Pro Helvetia is funded by the Swiss Confederation.
Board of Trustees: Michael Brändle (Pres.).
Principal Staff: Dir Philippe Bischof; Deputy Dir Jérôme Benoit.
Contact Details: Schweizer Kulturstiftung, Hirschengraben 22, 8024 Zürich; tel. 442677171; e-mail info@prohelvetia.ch; internet www.prohelvetia.ch.

Pro Juventute

Established in 1912 by Dr Carl Horber.
Activities: Focuses on protecting children and adolescents and improving their quality of life in families and in society in general. The organization works in the fields of education, human rights, healthcare and social welfare. It funds projects, makes grants to individuals, organizes conferences and develops its own programmes. Has five regional offices.
Geographical Area of Activity: Switzerland.
Publications: Annual Report; newsletter; *Futura* (quarterly magazine); brochures; factsheets.
Finance: Annual income 21.3m. Swiss francs, expenditure 23.7m. Swiss francs (31 Dec. 2024).
Board of Trustees: Roselien Huisman (Pres.).
Principal Staff: Dir Nicole Platel.
Contact Details: 24 pl. Chauderon, 1003 Lausanne; tel. 216220817; e-mail info.sr@projuventute.ch; internet www.projuventute.ch.

Pro Victimis

Established in 1988; a private foundation.
Activities: Supports: survivors of gender-based violence, including sexual violence; the integration and inclusion of people living with a disability (physical and/or mental); ending the violation of fundamental rights against vulnerable people due to a specific situation.
Geographical Area of Activity: International.
Restrictions: Does not fund emergency relief operations; projects related to widely publicized situations; organizations without previous experience with international grants, unless the project is conducted in partnership with a more experienced organization; activities entirely dependent on permanent international funding, at a cost disproportionate to the context; political or religious groups; or individual needs (care, housing, scholarships, etc.).
Board: Jasmine Caye (Pres.); Prof. Alexis Keller (Vice-Pres.).
Principal Staff: Dir Ariane Waldvogel.
Contact Details: 7 rue Versonnex, 1207 Geneva; e-mail contact@provictimis.org; internet www.provictimis.org.

Roger Federer Foundation

Established in 2003 by Roger Federer, a tennis player.
Activities: Improves the lives of young children living in poverty by supporting services in early childhood, preschool and primary education. Works in Switzerland and countries in southern Africa. Has an office in South Africa.
Geographical Area of Activity: Lesotho, Malawi, Namibia, South Africa, Switzerland, Zambia, Zimbabwe.
Publications: Annual Report.
Finance: Annual income 12.5m. Swiss francs, expenditure 9.0m. Swiss francs (31 Dec. 2024).
Board of Trustees: Roger Federer (Pres.).
Principal Staff: CEO Maya Ziswiler; Exec. Dir York Lunau.
Contact Details: Wiesenstr. 9, 8008 Zürich; e-mail foundation@rogerfederer.com; internet www.rogerfedererfoundation.org.

Rroma Foundation (Rromani Fundacija)

Established in 1993 to support Roma people in Central and Eastern Europe; initially part of the Soros network of foundations, but now a fully independent foundation.
Activities: Supports programmes in the fields of education, civil society, human rights, healthcare and culture. The Foundation provides financial support and advice to Roma NGOs and awards scholarships to Roma students. It also provides free legal advice and representation to Roma refugees, mainly in Switzerland.
Geographical Area of Activity: Central and Eastern Europe, Switzerland.
Restrictions: Only supports projects that are established and run by Roma for Roma.
Publications: Background reports.
Board of Trustees: Cristina Kruck (Chair.).
Principal Staff: Exec. Dir Dr Stéphane Laederich.

Contact Details: Gladbachstr. 67, 8044 Zürich; tel. 2550856; e-mail admin@rroma.org; internet rroma.org/the-foundation.

Schwab Foundation for Social Entrepreneurship

Established in 1998 by Hilde and Prof. Klaus Schwab as a complementary foundation to the World Economic Foundation (q.v.), which Prof. Schwab founded in 1971.

Activities: Provides platforms at regional and global level to promote leading models of sustainable social innovation. The Foundation identifies 10–15 social entrepreneurs from a pool of applicants each year and engages them in shaping global, regional and industry agendas that improve the state of the world. More than 330 social entrepreneurs, intrapreneurs—social and business innovators in the public and private sectors—and thought leaders make up the Foundation community; they participate in meetings of the World Economic Forum and work with the Forum of Young Global Leaders.

Geographical Area of Activity: Switzerland.

Restrictions: Does not make grants.

Publications: Annual Report; guides; manuals; reports.

Board: Hilde Schwab (Chair.).

Principal Staff: Dir Prof. François Bonnici.

Contact Details: 91–93 route de la Capite, 1223 Cologny/Geneva; tel. 228691212; e-mail info@schwabfound.org; internet www.schwabfound.org.

Schweizerisch-Liechtensteinische Stiftung für Archäologische Forschungen im Ausland—SLSA (Swiss-Liechtenstein Foundation for Archaeological Research Abroad—SLFA)

Established in 1986 with the participation of HSH Prince Hans-Adam II of Liechtenstein.

Activities: Funding of Swiss institutions to carry out archaeological research in the field. Helps developing countries to preserve their national heritage and contributes to international solidarity in the field of archaeological research. The Foundation collaborates with local organizations and universities in the areas of archaeological, ethnographical and cultural research.

Geographical Area of Activity: Albania, Bhutan, Ecuador, Ghana, Iraq, Jordan, Lebanon, Madagascar, Morocco, Peru, Senegal, Switzerland.

Restrictions: Supports only its own research.

Publications: Annual Report; Terra Archaeologica (monograph series); research publications.

Finance: Funding from Prince Hans-Adam II of Liechtenstein, private sponsors and the Swiss state. Total assets 2.5m. Swiss francs (2024).

Board of Trustees: Albert Lutz (Chair.); Jean Terrier, Gian-Pietro Rossetti (Vice-Chair.).

Principal Staff: Exec. Dir Daniel Schneiter.

Contact Details: c/o Museum Rietberg Zürich, Gablerstr. 15, 8002 Zürich; tel. 442017669; e-mail postfach@slsa.ch; internet www.slsa.ch.

Schweizerische Akademie der Medizinischen Wissenschaften (Swiss Academy of Medical Sciences)

Founded in 1943.

Activities: Supports advanced medical research. The Academy awards a limited number of grants and scholarships for research and several prizes, including the Robert Bing Prize, worth 60,000 Swiss francs, for work in the field of neurological diseases; and the Théodore Ott Prize, also worth 60,000 Swiss francs, for basic research in neurosciences. The Stern-Gattiker Prize was launched in 2018, worth 15,000 Swiss francs, and to promote female role models in academia. In addition, it administers the Käthe Zingg Schwichtenberg Fund, which provides financial support for research in bioethics and medical ethics; and the Théodore Ott Fund, which provides research grants for basic neurological research. The Academy organizes scientific meetings and symposia, and produces medico-scientific publications.

Geographical Area of Activity: Switzerland.

Restrictions: Support restricted to Switzerland.

Publications: Annual Report; newsletter; *Ethical Guidelines for Physicians*; *SAMW Bulletin* (quarterly, in German and French); brochures; guides; position papers.

Finance: Annual income 13.6m. Swiss francs, expenditure 6.7m. Swiss francs (2023).

Executive Board: Prof. Arnaud Perrier (Pres.); Prof. Henri Bounameaux (Vice-Pres.).

Principal Staff: Sec.-Gen. Valérie Clerc; Deputy Sec.-Gen. Franziska Egli.

Contact Details: Haus der Akademien, Laupenstr. 7, Postfach 3001 Bern; tel. 313069270; e-mail mail@samw.ch; internet www.samw.ch.

Schweizerische Herzstiftung (Swiss Heart Foundation)

Established in 1967 by a group of Swiss doctors concerned about the increase in cardiovascular diseases.

Activities: Works to reduce the number of people suffering from cardiovascular diseases or remaining disabled by them and help those affected to cope. The Foundation's main activities are promoting scientific research; informing patients and the public about cardiovascular diseases; diagnosis; treatment; life-saving (HELP programme); heart groups; and prevention.

Geographical Area of Activity: Switzerland.

Publications: Annual Report; newsletter; information brochures; magazine for donors.

Finance: Annual income 7.3m. Swiss francs, expenditure 8.0m. Swiss francs (31 Dec. 2023).

Board of Trustees: Prof. Dr Stefan Osswald (Pres.); Prof. Dr Marcel Arnold (Vice-Pres.).

Principal Staff: Chief Exec. Dr Robert C. Keller.

Contact Details: Dufourstr. 30, POB 368, 3000 Bern 14; tel. 313888080; e-mail info@swissheart.ch; internet www.swissheart.ch.

Schweizerische Stiftung für Alpine Forschungen—SSAF (Swiss Foundation for Alpine Research—SFAR)

Founded in 1939 to organize, finance and equip expeditions to mountains outside Europe and to the Arctic and Antarctic regions, and for Alpine research.

Activities: Operates internationally in the fields of science, mountaineering and alpine safety (high-altitude medicine, glaciology, geology, avalanches, ecological deterioration of high-altitude regions, etc.). The Foundation carries out self-conducted programmes and research; and issues publications and topographical maps. Awards the Prix de Quervain to young scientists for research into polar and high-altitude studies; and the ProMontesPrize for work on the study of the future of the Alpine region's cultural landscape.

Geographical Area of Activity: International.

Publications: Brochure; newsletter; maps; brochures; books.

Board of Trustees: Thomas Weber-Wegst (Pres.).

Contact Details: Stadelhoferstr. 42, 8001 Zürich; tel. 442531200; e-mail mail@alpinfo.ch; internet www.alpinfo.ch.

Schweizerischer Nationalfonds zur Förderung der Wissenschaftlichen Forschung/Fonds National Suisse de la Recherche Scientifique—SNF (Swiss National Science Foundation—SNSF)

Founded in 1952 by the Schweizerische Naturforschende Gesellschaft, the Akademie der Medizinischen Wissenschaften, the Schweizerische Geisteswissenschaftliche Gesellschaft, the Schweizerischer Juristenverein and the Schweizerische Gesellschaft für Statistik und Volkswirtschaft.

Activities: Works in the fields of education, science and medicine, the arts and humanities, law and other professions. The Foundation offers grants to individuals and institutions, as well as fellowships and scholarships; conducts research; and organizes conferences, courses and lectures. It is responsible for several national research programmes and implements the National Centres of Competence in Research (NCCR); and maintains a database of more than 6,000 funded projects.

Geographical Area of Activity: Mainly Switzerland.

Restrictions: Research grant candidates must be resident in Switzerland (regardless of citizenship); fellowship candidates must be resident in Switzerland or have Swiss or Liechtenstein nationality.

Publications: Annual Report; newsletter; *SNSF Profile including Facts and Figures*; *Horizonte/Horizons* (quarterly); guides; reports.

Finance: Total assets 917.8m. Swiss francs (31 Dec. 2023).

Board: Jürg Stahl (Pres. of the Foundation Council); Matthias Egger (Pres. of the Research Council); Angelika Kalt (Man. Dir).

Contact Details: Wildhainweg 3, POB 8232, 3001 Bern; tel. 313082222; e-mail desk@snf.ch; internet www.snf.ch.

Secours Dentaire International (Dental Aid International)

Founded in 1981 by Dr Jean-François Guignard, Adrien Jemelin and Franz Plattner.

Activities: Supports co-operation and development in medical dentistry in developing countries. The organization teaches and trains staff for dental clinics; and provides technical skills and trains school teachers. A sister organization operates in Germany.

Geographical Area of Activity: Benin, Burkina Faso, Cameroon, Dem. Repub. of the Congo, Côte d'Ivoire, Gabon, Haiti, Madagascar, Peru, Tanzania, Uganda, Zimbabwe.

Restrictions: No grants to individuals.

Publications: Annual Report; statistics; posters; leaflets.

Board of Directors: Dr Giuseppe Botte (Chair.); Christel Métrailler (Vice-Pres.).

Contact Details: c/o Q. Voellinger, Le Bourg 11, 1610 Oron-la-Ville; tel. 219462532; e-mail info@secoursdentaire.ch; internet www.secoursdentaire.ch.

Stanley Thomas Johnson Foundation

Established in 1969 by the will of June Johnson, in memory of her husband Stanley Johnson, who founded Avdel, a manufacturer of aircraft parts.

Activities: Main programme areas are: culture, supporting works in theatre, dance, music and the visual arts; conflict and violence, funding projects that protect displaced people and refugees, in particular children and young people, and provide psychosocial assistance to and rehabilitation of victims of war and armed conflict; medical research in palliative care, and healthcare for refugees and displaced people; and educational grants for residents of the Canton of Bern with special educational needs or who are in financial need, and for projects in Bern schools. Grants typically range between 5,000 and 100,000 Swiss francs. Every two years, the Foundation awards the June Johnson Dance Prize, worth 25,000 Swiss francs.

Geographical Area of Activity: Afghanistan, Angola, Central African Repub., Chad, Ethiopia, Mali, Myanmar, Nigeria, Pakistan, Somalia, South Sudan, Switzerland, Syrian Arab Repub., UK, Yemen.

Restrictions: Grants only to British or Swiss artists and non-profit organizations registered in Switzerland or the UK.

Publications: Annual Report.

Finance: Annual disbursements 3.8m. Swiss francs (2023).

Board: Mirjam Eglin (Pres.); Ursula Frauchiger (Vice-Pres.).

Contact Details: Schwanengasse 6, 3001 Bern; tel. 313722595; e-mail info@johnsonstiftung.ch; internet www.johnsonstiftung.ch.

Stiftung Kinderdorf Pestalozzi (Pestalozzi Children's Foundation)

Founded in 1946 by Walter Robert Corti, a philosopher and publicist, in response to the humanitarian crisis following World War II.

Activities: Works to improve access to quality education for children and young people. Programmes promote participatory forms of learning and encourage the training and education of teaching and support staff, while including a focus on children's rights. The Foundation operates a children's village in Trogen, where children and young people from different backgrounds meet during camps and project weeks. Topics include robotics, media literacy, critical thinking and diversity. They acquire conflict resolution skills and learn about democracy and policy.

Geographical Area of Activity: Central America, East Africa, South-East Asia, South-Eastern Europe and Switzerland.

Restrictions: Not a grantmaking organization.

Publications: Annual Report; newsletter; magazine (French, German, Italian).

Finance: Annual revenue 20m. Swiss francs, expenditure 20m. Swiss francs (2023).

Board: Rosmarie Quadranti (Pres.).

Principal Staff: CEO Martin Bachofner.

Contact Details: Kinderdorfstr. 20, 9034 Trogen; tel. 713437343; e-mail service@pestalozzi.ch; internet www.pestalozzi.ch.

Stiftung Klimarappen (Climate Cent Foundation)

Established in 2005; a voluntary initiative of four major Swiss business associations.

Activities: Aims to contribute to Switzerland's fulfilment of its climate policy targets as set by the Swiss CO_2 Law and the Kyoto Protocol. Between 2013 and 2022 the Foundation intended to mainly carry out activities abroad. Projects include providing microfinance for clean energy in India; treatment of drinking water in Kenya and Malawi; and landfill gas projects in Brazil, Colombia and Mexico.

Geographical Area of Activity: International.

Publications: Annual Report; newsletter.

Foundation Council: Dr Rolf Hartl (Chair.); Georges Spicher (Vice-Chair.).

Principal Staff: Man. Dir Dr Marco Berg.

Contact Details: Streulistr. 19, 8032 Zurich; tel. 443879900; e-mail info@climatecent.ch; internet www.klimarappen.ch.

Stiftung Vivamos Mejor (Vivamos Mejor Foundation)

Established in 1981 by Dr Rupert Spillman, a medical doctor.

Activities: Co-finances and supervises development projects in the fields of: education (preschool and school advancement, fostering of caring, responsible and non-violent behaviour); training (adult education, professional training and advancement, organizational development and gender); employment (nutritional safety, earnings promotion and sustainable handling of natural resources); and health (hygiene, healthcare, pregnancy, AIDS, combat of maternal and infant mortality, and a balanced diet). The Foundation has an office in Zurich.

Geographical Area of Activity: Brazil, Colombia, Guatemala, Honduras, Nicaragua, Switzerland.

Publications: Annual Report; newsletter (2 a year); brochures and leaflets.

Finance: Annual income 2.7m. Swiss francs, expenditure 2.6m. Swiss francs (31 Dec. 2020).

Board of Trustees: Franziska Kristensen-Rohner (Chair.).

Principal Staff: Man. Sabine Maier.

Contact Details: Thunstr. 17, 3005 Bern; tel. 313313929; e-mail info@vivamosmejor.ch; internet www.vivamosmejor.ch.

SWISSAID Foundation

Established in 1947 as Schweizer Spende; subsequently renamed Schweizer Europahilfe; an umbrella organization providing humanitarian assistance in post-war Europe. Renamed Schweizer Auslandhilfe in 1956; present name adopted in 1969.

Activities: Provides aid and promotes justice and independence. The Foundation collaborates with local partners in the fields of social and economic development. Projects include: equal participation of women; food sovereignty; preventing and finding peaceful solutions to conflict; respect for human rights; and sustainable use of natural resources. It has offices in Geneva and Zurich. Sister organizations operate in Colombia and Ecuador.

Geographical Area of Activity: Chad, Colombia, Ecuador, Guinea-Bissau, India, Myanmar, Nicaragua, Niger, Switzerland, Tanzania.

Publications: Annual Report; newsletter; *SWISSAID Spiegel/Le Monde* (quarterly).

Finance: Annual revenue 23.3m. Swiss francs, expenditure 24.7m. Swiss francs (31 Dec. 2023).

Board of Trustees: Fabian Molina (Pres.); Martin Sommer (Vice-Pres.).

Principal Staff: Exec. Dir Markus Alleman.

Contact Details: Lorystr. 6A, 3008 Bern; tel. 313505353; e-mail info@swissaid.ch; internet www.swissaid.ch.

Swisscontact—Swiss Foundation for Technical Co-operation

Established in 1959 by scientists and business people.

Activities: Promotes economic, social and ecological development by supporting people to integrate successfully into local commercial life and improve their living conditions through their own efforts. The Foundation focuses on four core areas: skills development, providing vocational training and access to productive employment; enterprise promotion, strengthening businesses through interventions in the value chain and local economy; inclusive finance, improving access to financial products and services; and climate-smart economy, creating green jobs. Present in 36 countries.

Geographical Area of Activity: Central and South America, Central and South-Eastern Europe, North Africa, South Asia, South-East Asia, sub-Saharan Africa.

Restrictions: No grants to individuals.

Publications: Annual report; newsletter; regional reports.

Finance: Annual income 108.2m. Swiss francs, expenditure 94.9m. Swiss francs (2024).

Executive Committee: Thomas D. Meyer (Pres.); Dr Isabelle Welton (Vice-Pres.).

Principal Staff: CEO and Exec. Dir Philippe Schneuwly.

Contact Details: Hardturmstr. 134, 8005 Zurich; tel. 444541717; e-mail info@swisscontact.ch; internet www.swisscontact.ch.

Terre des Hommes International Federation—TDHIF

Founded in 1960 in Switzerland by Edmond Kaiser, who also founded Sentinelles (q.v), to support children in distress; in 1966 it joined with groups established in Germany, the Netherlands and France.

Activities: Provides short- and long-term help to children in need. The Foundation conducts projects in five priority intervention areas: improving the health of children during their first 1,000 days of life and those requiring specialist medical care; protecting migrant children; protecting children from exploitation; promoting restorative justice for children in conflicts; and providing emergency humanitarian assistance to children and their families. It has member organizations in Denmark, France, Germany, Italy, Luxembourg, the Netherlands, Spain and Switzerland; and also incorporates the Terre des Hommes Foundation. The International Secretariat is based in Geneva, with an EU Liaison Office in Brussels, Belgium.

Geographical Area of Activity: International.

Publications: Annual Report; guides; handbooks; policy papers; position papers.

Finance: Annual global income €228.7m. (2023); International Secretariat (Geneva) annual income 349,100 Swiss francs, expenditure 652,806 Swiss francs (2022).

International Board: Franziska Lauper (Chair.); Beat Wehrle (Vice-Chair.); Paolo Ferrera (Treas.).

Principal Staff: Sec.-Gen. Valérie Ceccherini.

Contact Details: 3 chemin du Pré-Picot, 1223 Cologny/Geneva; tel. 227363372; e-mail info@terredeshommes.org; internet www.terredeshommes.org.

Tibet-Institut Rikon

Founded in 1967 by Henri Kuhn-Ziegler and Jacques Kuhn.

Activities: Aims to take care of the spiritual and religious needs of Tibetans living in exile in Switzerland; to enable Tibetan scholars and learned priests to teach compatriots the values of their ancient culture; and to enable Tibetan scholars and priests to learn Western sciences and languages to become informed about the Western way of living and thinking. The Institute operates internationally in the fields of education, social welfare and studies, science and the arts, and humanities, through research carried out in Switzerland and in co-operation with European and US institutions, and conferences, courses, publications and lectures. It undertakes research in the fields of history of religion, literature, cultural anthropology, linguistics and related disciplines. Courses are held on Tibetan religion, history, script and language, and basic instruction is given in the techniques of meditation. Formal opinions and reports on Tibetan affairs are prepared by the monks. Maintains a library of more than 12,000 titles; and film and photograph archives.

Geographical Area of Activity: International.

Publications: Annual Report; *Opuscula Tibetana* (series of publications); books on Tibetan language, culture, history, literature and music.

Governing Board: Dr Karma Lobsang (Pres.); Dr Werner Nater (Vice-Pres.).

Principal Staff: Man. Dir Peter Oberholzer; Sec. Barbara Ziegler.

Contact Details: Wildbergstr. 10, 8486 Rikon im Tösstal; tel. 523831729; e-mail info@tibet-institut.ch; internet www.tibet-institut.ch.

UEFA Foundation for Children

Established in 2015 by the Union of European Football Associations—UEFA.

Activities: Supports children with disabilities and their carers; and promotes children's personal development and empowerment through sociocultural activities and sports. The Foundation has supported projects in 109 countries.

Geographical Area of Activity: Worldwide.

Publications: Annual Report; newsletter.

Finance: Annual income 8.1m. Swiss francs, expenditure 8.1m. (30 June 2024).

Board of Trustees: Aleksander Čeferin (Chair.).

Principal Staff: Gen. Sec. Urs Kluser.

Contact Details: 46 route de Genève, 1260 Nyon; e-mail contact@uefafoundation.org; internet uefafoundation.org.

Union for International Cancer Control—UICC

(Union Internationale Contre le Cancer)

Founded in 1933 as a world federation of non-governmental agencies and organizations.

Activities: Promotes collaboration between cancer organizations, among cancer investigators, physicians and allied health professionals and experts. Programmes include: the

Global Access to Pain Relief Initiative; Cervical Cancer Initiative; Childhood Cancer; Global Education and Training Initiative; and Global Initiative for Cancer Registries. The Union convenes World Cancer Day, the World Cancer Congress and World Cancer Leaders' Summit; and organizes international conferences, study groups and courses, and leadership development activities. It also administers fellowships, including: UICC Technical Fellowships; UICC Fellowships for Francophone Africa; Yamagiwa-Yoshida Memorial International Cancer Study Grants; the Chinese Fellowship Programme; UICC-IARC Development Fellowships; McCabe Centre for Law and Cancer Fellowships; and Asia-Pacific Cancer Society Training Grants. Comprises more than 1,100 member organizations in over 170 countries.

Geographical Area of Activity: International.

Publications: Annual Report; *International Journal of Cancer*; *Journal of Global Oncology*; handbooks; information summaries; toolkits; blog.

Finance: Income from membership dues, national subscriptions, grants and donations. Annual income US $13.0m., expenditure $12.3m. (31 Dec. 2023).

Board of Directors: Ulrika Årehed Kågström (Pres.); Zainab Shinkafi-Bagudu (Pres.-elect).

Principal Staff: CEO Dr Cary Adams.

Contact Details: 31–33 ave Giuseppe Motta, 1202 Geneva; tel. 228091811; e-mail info@uicc.org; internet www.uicc.org.

Volkart-Stiftung (Volkart Foundation)

Founded in 1951 on the 100th anniversary of the foundation of the Gebrüder Volkart trading company; in 2014 it merged with Volkart Vision and also took over the activities of the George Foundation.

Activities: Supports cultural, social and environmental projects. Programme areas include: development co-operation in the areas of water resource management and women's empowerment; and social engagement with cultural, environmental and social organizations.

Geographical Area of Activity: Latin America, sub-Saharan Africa, Switzerland.

Restrictions: Does not accept unsolicited applications.

Publications: Annual Report.

Finance: Annual disbursements 3m. Swiss francs (2023).

Foundation Council: Marc Reinhart (Chair.).

Principal Staff: Man. Dir Judith Schläpfer.

Contact Details: 1 Turnerstr., Postfach, 8400 Winterthur; tel. 522686868; e-mail info@volkart.ch; internet www.volkartstiftung.ch.

WHO Foundation

Established in 2020 by Prof. Dr Thomas Zeltner to support the work of WHO; an independent grantmaking foundation.

Activities: Funds initiatives that address critical global health challenges. Main programmes focus on: health emergencies; climate and health; mental health; women's health; and digital health care. As part of the global response to the coronavirus pandemic, the Foundation manages the COVID-19 Solidarity Response Fund with the UN Foundation (q.v.) and a global network of fiduciary partners.

Geographical Area of Activity: Worldwide.

Finance: Annual disbursements US $18.8m. (2024).

Board: Prof. Dr Thomas Zeltner (Chair.); Rebecca Enonchong (Vice-Chair.).

Principal Staff: CEO Anil Soni.

Contact Details: Sécheron, 2 chemin des Mines, 1202 Geneva; e-mail info@who.foundation; internet www.who.foundation.

WILPF—Women's International League for Peace and Freedom

Founded in 1915 in The Hague, Netherlands.

Activities: Campaigns and conducts advocacy in three main programme areas: disarmament; human rights; and women, peace and security; with Feminist Political Economy, Feminism, Peace and Environment and Mobilising Men for Feminist Peace as thematic work. The League lobbies governments at international, national and local level; connects communities with the international sphere, through a local-global-local approach; and participates in and collaborates with international institutions and global movements. It develops reference, education and action tools through websites, conferences, publications, panel discussions, seminars and webinars; and monitors and contributes to the work of the UN to ensure a gender perspective. Has an office in Geneva (Switzerland) and one in New York (USA) with 42 Sections and 6 Groups worldwide.

Geographical Area of Activity: International.

Restrictions: Not a grant-making organization.

Publications: Annual Report; newsletters; reports; brochures; guidelines; advocacy documents.

International Board: Sylvie Jacqueline Ndongmo (Int. Pres.); Jamila Afghani, Melissa Torres (Vice-Pres); Janette McLeod (Treas.).

Principal Staff: Sec.-Gen. Amrita Kapur.

Contact Details: 1 rue de Varembé, CP 28, 1211, Geneva 20; tel. 229197080; e-mail secretariat@wilpf.org; internet www.wilpf.org.

The Womanity Foundation

Established in 2005, as the Smiling Children Foundation, by Yann Borgstedt, an entrepreneur; present name adopted in 2012.

Activities: Works towards full, equal social, economic and political rights for women and men through innovative investment. The Foundation supports: access for girls and women to education and training; the creation of income-earning and professional opportunities for women; the promotion of women's voices in society and challenges gender stereotypes; and the prevention of violence against women and girls. Initiatives include Girls Can Code, which provides coding training; land rights for women in India; the Womanity Award, which provides funding, capacity building and access to networks for organizations combatting violence against women; Disruptive Media, supporting Radio Nisaa, the first women's Arabic-speaking radio station in the Middle East; and a programme that creates progressive media platforms and pioneering content to create fairer societies in the Middle East and North Africa region where women can play an equal role. A sister organization operates in the United Kingdom.

Geographical Area of Activity: Afghanistan, India, Middle East and North Africa, Switzerland.

Publications: Annual Report; newsletter; blog.

Finance: Annual revenue 1.5m. Swiss francs, expenditure 1.5m. Swiss francs (2023).

Board: Yann Borgstedt (Pres.).

Principal Staff: Co-CEO Shivani Gupta, Laura Somoggi.

Contact Details: 55 route des Jeunes, 1212 Grand-Lancy; tel. 225443960; e-mail info@womanity.org; internet womanity.org.

World Alliance of YMCAs—Young Men's Christian Associations

Founded in 1844 in England by George Williams, a draper, as a Christian movement. The first World Alliance of YMCAs conference took place in Paris, France, in 1855, establishing the Central International Committee; a formal Committee structure and headquarters were created in Geneva in 1878.

Activities: Promotes economic empowerment, social justice and peace for young people and their communities, through activities in the areas of civic engagement, employment, environment and health, which cover all areas of the UN Sustainable Development Goals. The Alliance strengthens the capacity of national YMCAs and advocates for young people at international level. It holds consultative status with ECOSOC and represents 120 national YMCAs.

Geographical Area of Activity: Africa, Asia and the Pacific, Europe, Middle East, North and South America.

Restrictions: Does not make grants.

Publications: Annual Report; newsletter; *YMCA World* (magazine); *YMCA Blue Book*; *World Week of Prayer; Living in Hope;* directory; reports.

Finance: Annual income 3.5m. Swiss francs, expenditure 4.1m. Swiss francs (31 Dec. 2024).

Executive Committee: Soheila Hayek (Pres.); Ronald Tak Fai Yam (Deputy Pres.); Cici Rojas (Treas.); Carlos Madjri Sanvee (Sec.-Gen.).

Contact Details: 1 chemin de Mouille-Galand, 1214 Vernier; tel. 228495100; e-mail office@ymca.int; internet www.ymca.int.

World Economic Forum

Founded in 1971 by Prof. Klaus M. Schwab; supervised by the Swiss Federal Council, with consultative status with the UN.

Activities: Encourages the direct exchange of information between world leaders in business, politics and the academic sphere, to promote worldwide prosperity, particularly through engaging its corporate members in global citizenship. Platforms offer the opportunity to aggregate efforts in defining and combating global issues in the areas of: Cybersecurity; Nature and Climate; the New Economy and Society; Climate Action; Advanced Manufacturing and Value Chains; Consumption; Digital Economy; Energy, Materials and Infrastructure; Financial and Monetary Systems; Health; Media, Entertainment and Sport; Mobility; Technology Governance; Trade and Investment; and Urban Transformation. The Forum holds an annual meeting, the World Business Summit, in Davos, and arranges Industry Summits and conferences geared to the requirements of the specific needs of individual countries or regions. It has offices in New York (USA), Beijing (People's Repub. of China) and Tokyo (Japan); and works in close partnership with the Schwab Foundation for Social Entrepreneurship (q.v.). In 2020 the 1t.org initiative was launched to support the UN Decade on Ecosystem Restoration 2021–2030 in planting 1,000,000m. trees.

Geographical Area of Activity: International.

Publications: Annual Report; *Global Competitiveness Report* (annually, in collaboration with the International Monetary Fund—IMF); *World Link* (magazine, 6 a year); Annual Meeting and Summit Reports; white papers; institutional brochure; newsletters.

Managing Board: Peter Brabeck-Letmathe (Interim Chair.).

Principal Staff: Pres. Børge Brende; Man. Dir Mirek Dušek.

Contact Details: 91–93 route de la Capite, 1223 Cologny/Geneva; tel. 228691212; e-mail contact@weforum.org; internet www.weforum.org.

World Scout Foundation—Fondation du Scoutisme Mondial—WSF/FSM

Established in 1969.

Activities: Funds scouting activities and provides support to the World Organization of the Scout Movement; and awards the World Baden-Powell Fellowship, which recognizes individuals' contributions to the WSF. The Foundation comprises 176 National Scout Organizations.

Geographical Area of Activity: Worldwide.

Publications: Annual Report; Baden-Powell's writings; catalogue.

Finance: Total assets US $63.1m., annual grants disbursed $6.2m. (2023).

Board: HRH King Carl XVI Gustaf of Sweden (Hon. Chair.); Rob Woolford (Chair.); Beat Wenger (Chair.-elect); Fredrik Gottlieb (Treas.); Norbert Becker (Treas.-elect); Lars Kolind (Sec.).

Principal Staff: CEO Mark Knippenberg.

Contact Details: 5 rue Henri-Christiné, 1205 Geneva; tel. 227051090; e-mail info@worldscoutfoundation.org; internet worldscoutfoundation.org.

WWF International

Established in 1961 by Sir Peter Scott and others, originally known as the World Wildlife Fund; in 2013, with the Fondation MAVA (q.v.), it co-founded the Luc Hoffmann Institute, an independent research hub.

Activities: Works to stop the degradation of natural environment, maintain biodiversity and reduce the impact of negative human activity. Main programme areas are: climate and energy; food; forests; freshwater; oceans; people and conservation; and wildlife. The organization works in partnership with local people and multinational corporations, governments and NGOs, financial institutions and development agencies, consumers and researchers. It offers scholarships and grants; and runs the WWF Young Adult Volunteer & Intern Programme, for young people aged 19–27 years. Comprises 33 national organizations, with offices in around 100 countries.

Geographical Area of Activity: Worldwide.

Publications: Annual Review; *WWF News* (quarterly); *Living Planet Report* (periodically updated).

Finance: Annual income €1,109m., expenditure €776m. (2021).

International Board of Trustees: Adil Najam (Pres.); Elaine J. Cheung (Treas.).

Principal Staff: Dir-Gen. Kirsten Schuijt.

Contact Details: 28 rue Mauverney, 1196 Gland; tel. 223649111; e-mail donations@wwfint.org; internet wwf.panda.org.

WWSF—Women's World Summit Foundation (Fondation Sommet Mondial des Femmes)

Established in 1991 by Elly (Maria Elfriede) Pradervand, a teacher and social educator, after attending the UN 1990 World Summit for Children in New York, USA.

Activities: Annually convenes multiple empowerment programmes: the Women's Section includes the new 75% campaign—WWSF Leadership Training for Women and Youth, claiming a seat at the Table; the annual Prize for women's creativity in rural Life (481 prizes awarded to date); the International Day of Rural Women (15 Oct.); and the annual 17 Days of Activism campaign for the Empowerment of Rural Women Leaders & their Communities (1–17 Oct.); the Children/Youth Section runs the annual 19 Days of Activism for the Prevention of Violence against Children and Youth (1–19 Nov.), and the Swiss White Ribbon campaign, advocating for the end of violence against women and young people in Switzerland by 2030. The Foundation organizes regular roundtables, advocacy alerts, training sessions and campaigns, and participates in civil society working groups. It has UN ECOSOC, UNFPA, and DPI status.

Geographical Area of Activity: International.

Publications: Annual Activity Report; *Empowering Women and Children* (newsletter); brochures; posters; flyers; postcards; Empowerment tool kits; Prevention of child abuse tool kits.

Finance: Annual budget US $400,000.

Principal Staff: Pres. Elly Pradervand; Vice-Pres. Gulzar Samji.

Contact Details: POB 1504, 1211 Geneva 1; tel. 227386619; e-mail info@wwsf.ch; internet www.woman.ch.

TAIWAN

FOUNDATIONS AND NON-PROFITS

Chang Yung-fa Foundation
Established in 1985 by Chang Yung-fa, the founder and Chair. of Evergreen Group, a shipping and logistics company.

Activities: Provides maritime education and training to personnel, and scholarships to study in Taiwan and abroad; supports social welfare initiatives and public health programmes; and funds disaster relief. The Foundation has its own classical symphony orchestra (f. 2002), which performs approximately 100 times a year; runs the Evergreen Maritime Museum (f. 2008); and maintains an international conference centre.

Geographical Area of Activity: East Asia.

Publications: Annual Report; newsletter (monthly); *Morals* (monthly magazine).

Finance: Annual income NT $506.0m., expenditure $423.2m. (31 Dec. 2020).

Principal Staff: Exec. Dir Chung Demie.

Contact Details: 11 Zhongshan South Rd, Zhongzheng District, Taipei City 10048; tel. (2) 2351-6699; e-mail cyff@cyff.org.tw; internet www.cyff.org.tw.

Chia Hsin Foundation
Founded in 1963 by Dr Chang Min-yu and Oung Ming-chong, Chair. of the Board of Directors and Man. Dir, respectively, of the Chia Hsin Cement Corporation, for the promotion of culture in Taiwan; present name adopted in 1994.

Activities: Operates in the fields of the arts and humanities, social studies, science and medicine, law and education, through research projects, courses, conferences, lectures, publications, fellowships and scholarships, and grants to individuals and institutions. The Foundation offers the Chia Hsin Technology Award, the Distinguished Contribution Award, the Chia Hsin Prize for Journalism and the Chia Hsin Sports Award. It also awards scholarships and finances study abroad for a limited number of students.

Geographical Area of Activity: Taiwan.

Publications: Corporate Social Responsibility Report.

Board of Directors: Zhang Ganglun (Chair.).

Principal Staff: Dir Pan Howard Wei-Hao.

Contact Details: c/o Jiaxin Enterprise Group, 104 Jiaxin Bldg, No. 96, Section 2, Zhongshan North Rd, Zhongshan District, Taipei City; tel. (2) 2551-5211; e-mail ch_found@chcgroup.com.tw; internet www.chcgroup.com.tw/index.php?route=chiahsin/chiahsin/csrorganization.

Chiang Ching-kuo Foundation for International Scholarly Exchange—CCKF
Founded in 1989 by the Government of Taiwan and the private sector in memory of President Chiang Ching-kuo.

Activities: Works in the fields of the arts and humanities, economic affairs, education, international affairs, law and human rights, medicine and health, and social welfare and social studies. Programmes cover the American Region (including North, Central and South America), the Asian/Pacific Region, the European Region and the Republic of China. The Foundation conducts research; and offers grants to institutions and individuals, scholarships and fellowships. It has an office in the USA and overseas centres at universities in the Czech Republic (Czechia), Germany, Hong Kong and the USA.

Geographical Area of Activity: International.

Publications: Annual Report (in Chinese and English); newsletter (quarterly); books.

Board of Directors: Qian Fu (Chair.).

Principal Staff: CEO Prof. Chen Chunyi.

Contact Details: 303 Bei'an Rd, Zhongshan District, Taipei City 104037; tel. (2) 2704-5333; e-mail cckf@ms1.hinet.net; internet cckf.org.tw.

Himalaya Research and Development Foundation—Himalaya Foundation
Established in 1990 by Zhong Yu, an economist and former Gen. Man. of Deltec Bank, as Himalaya Foundation.

Activities: Works in the fields of Chinese studies, economic affairs and civil society, through research, grants, exchanges, publications and involvement in international philanthropic associations. The Foundation is also involved in the development of civil society and the third sector, setting up the Taiwan Philanthropy Information Center (later renamed the Taiwan NPO Information Platform), which provides information about the non-profit sector in Taiwan and elsewhere; and maintaining a database of foundations, as well as a library on philanthropy and the third sector. It established the NPO Development Center for not-for-profit organization IT capacity building and the NPO book website, providing publications relating to the third sector or published by not-for-profit organizations.

Geographical Area of Activity: Asia.

Restrictions: Prefers to fund projects that have tangible and far-reaching benefits for society.

Publications: *Directory of Foundations in Taiwan*; *Handbook on Good Practices for Laws Relating to Non-Governmental Organizations* (Chinese translation); case studies; handbooks; law books (series).

Principal Staff: Chair. Chen Jinlong.

Contact Details: 167 Fuxing North Rd, 6F-3, Songshan District, Taipei City 105; tel. (2) 2718-7061; e-mail hmfdtion@himalaya.org.tw; internet www.himalaya.org.tw.

Straits Exchange Foundation—SEF
Established in 1991 as a private intermediary in relations between Taiwan and the People's Republic of China, which is represented by the Association for Relations Across the Taiwan Strait as a counterpart to the SEF.

Activities: Promotes friendly relations and mutual understanding between Taiwan and China, and the rights and welfare of people on both sides of the Taiwan Strait. The Foundation provides economic and trade, legal and cultural and educational exchange services, and runs a Service and Information Centre.

Geographical Area of Activity: People's Repub. of China, Taiwan.

Publications: Annual Report; newsletter; research reports.

Finance: Annual income NT $284.7m., expenditure $261.8m. (31 Dec. 2023).

Board of Directors: Wu Fengshan (Chair.); Xu Shengxiong, Liang Wenjie (Vice-Chair.).

Principal Staff: Sec.-Gen. and Vice-Chair. Luo Wenjia.

Contact Details: 536 Beian Rd, Zhongshan District, Taipei City 10465; tel. (2) 2175-7000; e-mail service@sef.org.tw; internet www.sef.org.tw.

Syin-Lu Social Welfare Foundation
Founded in 1976, as the Syin-Lu Foundation, by Zong Jing-yi; present name adopted in 1998.

Activities: Campaigns for the rights of physically and mentally disabled people to ensure their entitlement to social benefits. The Foundation funds education, rehabilitation, housing, leisure and counselling services for physically and mentally disabled people; trains professionals to mobilize community services on behalf of people with disabilities; and publishes relevant information. It has branches in Hsinchu, Kaohsiung and Taoyuan.

Tang Prize Foundation

Geographical Area of Activity: Taiwan.
Publications: Annual Report; newsletter.
Finance: Total assets NT $819.2m. (31 Dec. 2024).
Principal Staff: Chair. Feng Bi-hua; CEO Zong Jing-yi.
Contact Details: 364 Jilin Rd, (104) 4th Floor, Zhongshan District, Taipei City 104; tel. (2) 2592-9778; e-mail syinlu@syinlu.org.tw; internet www.syinlu.org.tw.

Tang Prize Foundation

Established in 2012 by Samuel (Yen-Liang) Yin, Chair. of Ruentex Group and founder of Kwang-Hua Education Foundation (f. 1989 in the People's Repub. of China), Yin Xun-Ruo Educational Foundation, Yin Shu-Tien Medical Foundation and Kwang-Hua Education Foundation.

Activities: Awards prizes to individuals and organizations for achievements in the fields of: biopharmaceutical science, including biomedical research; Rule of Law, encompassing legal theory and practice and peace and human rights; Sinology, for research on China and related fields; and Sustainable Development, in particular for innovations in science and technology. Awards are made every two years and are worth NT $40m.; recipients in each category also receive research grants of up to NT $10m.
Geographical Area of Activity: International.
Publications: Newsletter; Biennial Book.
Board: Chung-Yao Yin (Chair.).
Principal Staff: CEO Jenn-Chuan Chern.
Contact Details: 2nd Floor, No. 308, Section 2, Bade Rd, Taipei City 104498; tel. (2) 8772-5188; e-mail tang-prize@tang-prize.org; internet www.tang-prize.org.

World Vegetable Center

Founded in 1971 as the Asian Vegetable Research and Development Center.

Activities: Conducts research on and develops safe vegetable farming in the tropics and subtropics; and improves the nutrition, health, employment and income of small-scale farmers in developing countries. The Center maintains the world's largest public sector gene bank of vegetable germplasm, with more than 65,000 accessions; holds training workshops, seminars and conferences; and operates regional vegetable research and development networks. It maintains the HARVEST (Holistic Access to Research on Vegetables, Economies, Societies and Technology) open access document and data archive, which contains more than 54,000 entries. Has regional offices in Benin, India, the Republic of Korea, Mali, Tanzania and Thailand.
Geographical Area of Activity: International (with an emphasis on developing countries).
Publications: Annual Report; *FRESH! Newsletter*; seminar proceedings; technical bulletins; production manuals; field guides.
Finance: Annual revenue US $29.4m., expenditure $30.6m. (31 Dec. 2023).
Board: Dr Chen Junne-jih (Chair.); Gordon Rogers (Vice-Chair.).
Principal Staff: Dir-Gen. Dr Marco Wopereis; Deputy Dir-Gen. Wang Yun Ping.
Contact Details: 60 Yin-Min Liao, Shanhua, Tainan 74151; POB 42, Shanhua, Tainan 74199; tel. (6) 583-7801; e-mail info@worldveg.org; internet avrdc.org.

YongLin Charity Foundation

Established in 2000 by Taiming (Terry) Guo, founder and former CEO of Hon Hai Technology Group (Foxconn).

Activities: Carries out initiatives in the areas of social welfare, education, public health, women's empowerment, arts and culture, and physical education; and operates an organic farm. The YongLin Healthcare Foundation focuses on cancer treatment through funding research promoting co-operation between industry and academia. The YongLin Education Foundation provides access to learning and promotes science and technology education, offering online resources and teacher training; and awards scholarships to college and postgraduate students worth NT $100,000.
Geographical Area of Activity: Taiwan.
Contact Details: No. 2 Zihyou St Tucheng District, Taipei City 236; tel. (2) 2268-3466; e-mail info@yonglin.org.tw; internet www.yonglin.org.tw.

TANZANIA

CO-ORDINATING BODY

Foundation for Civil Society—FCS

Established in 2002.

Activities: Provides grants and capacity-building services to CSOs and promotes good governance, citizen empowerment and engagement in the democratic process. Strategic grants are worth up to 750m. Tanzanian shillings over three years; medium grants are worth up to 360m. Tanzanian shillings over three years; and innovative grants are worth between 20m. and 50m. Tanzanian shillings for one year. The Foundation comprises the FCS Trust, a development agency which offers consulting services for CSOs; and the FCS Resource Centre, which offers information and advisory services to CSOs and others involved in the civil society sector. It maintains a directory of CSOs in Tanzania.
Geographical Area of Activity: Tanzania.
Restrictions: Does not make grants for activities outside of Tanzania or scolarships.
Publications: Annual Report; *FCS Newsletter* (quarterly); *Habari Jamii Bulletin* (COVID-19 news); *Tanzania Directory of Civil Society Organisations*; leaflets; reports; blog.
Finance: Annual revenue 10,983.8m. Tanzanian shillings, expenditure 10,956.6m. Tanzanian shillings (31 Dec. 2022).
Board of Directors: Ally Laay (Chair.).
Principal Staff: Exec. Dir and Sec. Justice Rutenge.
Contact Details: 7 Madai Cresc., Ada Estate, Plot No. 154, Kinondoni, POB 7192, Dar es Salaam; tel. (22) 2664890; e-mail information@thefoundation.or.tz; internet www.thefoundation.or.tz.

FOUNDATIONS AND NON-PROFITS

Economic and Social Research Foundation—ESRF

Established in 1992 as an independent research institute; a think tank.

Activities: Carries out policy research and capacity development. Programme areas include: globalization and regional integration; governance and accountability; implementing the UN Sustainable Development Goals; inclusive growth, employment and industrialization; knowledge management and social innovation; natural resource and environmental management; and social service delivery and social protection. The Foundation offers training to NGO researchers and policy analysts; and organizes policy dialogues, vocational training courses and workshops. It maintains an information centre and library; and has an office in Dodoma.
Geographical Area of Activity: East Africa.

Publications: Annual Report; newsletter; *Quarterly Economic Review*; *Region Investment Guides* (series); discussion papers; policy briefs; research reports.

Finance: Annual income US $2.3m., expenditure $2.1m. (31 Dec. 2022).

Board of Trustees: Abdulmajid Mussa Nsekela (Chair.); Dr Stigmata Tenga (Vice-Chair.).

Principal Staff: Exec. Dir Prof. Fortunata Songora Makene.

Contact Details: 51 Uporoto St, Ursino Estate, POB 31226, Dar es Salaam; tel. (22) 2926084; e-mail info@esrf.or.tz; internet esrf.or.tz.

Mo Dewji Foundation

Established in 2014 by Mohammed Dewji, CEO of MeTL Group, building on the work of Singida Yetu (f. 2006).

Activities: Active in the fields of: education, building and equipping schools, training teachers and supporting literacy initiatives; healthcare, building hospitals, providing subsidized healthcare and cataract operations, raising awareness about contraception and HIV/AIDS, and donating mosquito nets; and community development, including infrastructure development, financial inclusion and access to markets, and promoting gender equality. The Foundation runs the Mo Entrepreneurs Competition for young people in collaboration with local NGO Darecha (f. 2008); and offers scholarships for four years of undergraduate study at the University of Dar es Salaam or University of Dodoma. Other areas of interest include sports and access to water.

Geographical Area of Activity: Tanzania.

Finance: Initial endowment US $2m.

Board of Directors: Mohammed Dewji (Chair.).

Principal Staff: Head of Foundation Imran Sherali.

Contact Details: PSPF Golden Jubilee Tower, 20th Floor, Ohio St, POB 22196, Dar es Salaam; tel. (22) 2122830; e-mail info@modewjifoundation.org; internet www.modewjifoundation.org.

Vodacom Tanzania Foundation—VTF

Established in 1999 by Vodacom, a telecommunications company; part of the Vodafone Foundation (q.v.) network.

Activities: Carries out activities in the fields of economic empowerment, education, health and social welfare. Main programmes are: Connected Learning, equipping students with digital skills, and incorporating the Smart Schools and Instant Schools programmes, which provide computers, internet access and digital educational materials to primary and secondary schools; and Our Planet, supporting conservation organizations to implement sustainable nature-based solutions to climate change, such as tree planting in the Dodoma region. The Foundation supports NGOs, non-profit and community-based organizations working with girls and women in the fields of education, financial inclusion and health. The Pamoja na Vodacom employee volunteering programme carries out charitable activities such as youth mentoring and coaching, and donating to hospitals, children's homes and underprivileged groups.

Geographical Area of Activity: Tanzania.

Publications: Social Impact Report.

Finance: Total investments since 2004 12,500m. Tanzanian shillings.

Principal Staff: Chair. Thomas Mihayo.

Contact Details: 7th Floor, Vodacom Tower, Ursino Estate, Plot 23, Bagamoyo Rd, POB 2369, Dar es Salaam; tel. 754705000; internet vodacom.co.tz/foundation.

WAMA Foundation (Women in Development Foundation)

Established in 2006 by First Lady Salma Kikwete.

Activities: Improves the wellbeing of women, girls and other vulnerable children, including orphans. The Foundation carries out activities in the fields of: education, awarding scholarships for secondary and higher education, providing educational materials, improving water and sanitation, and building boarding facilities for students who have to travel far; health services, including adolescent sexual and reproductive health and maternal and infant health; and economic empowerment, providing skills training and capacity building.

Geographical Area of Activity: Tanzania.

Publications: Newsletter; reports.

Board: Salma Kikwete (Chair.); Zakia Hamdan Meghji (Vice-Chair.).

Contact Details: Luthuli St, POB 10641, Dar es Salaam; tel. (22) 2126516; e-mail info@wamafoundation.or.tz; internet www.wamafoundation.or.tz.

THAILAND

FOUNDATIONS AND NON-PROFITS

AIT—Asian Institute of Technology

Founded in 1959 as the SEATO Graduate School of Engineering; present name adopted in 1967.

Activities: Provides advanced (postgraduate) education in engineering, science and allied fields, through academic programmes and research; and organizes conferences, seminars and short courses. The Institute comprises three schools, for engineering and technology, the environment, resources and development, and management; AIT Extension, for executive and professional training; a language centre; and 24 research and outreach centres. It maintains databases and a library of more than 230,000 items. A range of scholarships are available. Has a centre in Viet Nam.

Geographical Area of Activity: Africa, Asia, Europe, USA.

Publications: Annual Report; *AIT Newsletter* (monthly).

Finance: Annual income 1,378.8m. baht, expenditure 1,389.0m. baht (31 Dec. 2023).

Board of Trustees: Dr Anat Abhabirama (Chair.); Dr Suwit Khunkitti, Somprasong Boonyachai, Prof. David Mclean (Vice-Chair.).

Principal Staff: Pres. Prof. Pai-Chi Li.

Contact Details: POB 4, 58 Moo 9, Km 42, Paholyothin Hwy, Klong Luang, Pathum Thani 12120; tel. (2) 524-5000; e-mail opa@ait.ac.th; internet ait.ac.th.

DTGO Group of Foundations

Established by Khun Thippaporn Ariyawararom, founder of DTGO Group, a conglomerate.

Activities: Comprises: the Buddharaksa Foundation (f. 2002), which supports Buddhist religious initiatives and helps underprivileged children in Thailand, providing access to welfare and education, and scholarships for secondary education in India and short-term study in the People's Repubublic of China and the USA; the Buddharaksa Family Association (f. 2018); the Blue Carbon Society (f. 2018), which conserves and restores coastal and marine ecosystems; the Dhanin Tawee Chearavanont Foundation (f. 2018 as DT Families Foundation), which improves the livelihoods and living conditions of vulnerable people in Thailand and abroad through providing access to healthcare and education; and the Givers Network (f. 2018), a regional network comprising charities, NGOs, social enterprises and individual philanthropists.

Geographical Area of Activity: International.

Principal Staff: Group Chair. Khun Thippaporn Ariyawararomp.

Contact Details: 695 Sukhumvit 50, Prakanong Klongtoey, Bangkok 10260; tel. (2) 742-9141; e-mail pr@dtgo.com; internet www.dtgo.com/csr.

ECPAT International

Established in 1991 as End Child Prostitution in Asian Tourism; became an international NGO in 1996 and expanded to have a global focus. Present name adopted in 2017.

Activities: Works to protect children from sexual exploitation, including trafficking, early and forced marriage, prostitution, online and by travellers and tourists. Activities include conducting research and advocacy; facilitating an enabling legal environment; training frontline practitioners such as hotel workers and law enforcement; providing a voice for survivors; and direct action. The organization maintains a database of domestic legal frameworks. It has 134 member CSOs in 110 countries.

Geographical Area of Activity: International.

Publications: Annual Report; newsletter; country overview reports; regional overviews; journals; training resources and toolkits.

Finance: Annual revenue US $5.3m., expenditure $5.1m. (30 June 2024).

Board: Cornelius Williams (Chair.); Michel Rioux (Treas.).

Principal Staff: Exec. Dir Guillaume Landry.

Contact Details: 328/1 Phaya Thai Rd, Rachathewi, Bangkok 10400; tel. (2) 215-3388; e-mail info@ecpat.org; internet www.ecpat.org.

The Education for Development Foundation—EDF

Established in 1987; part of the EDF Group with EDF Lao (f. 1997), EDF Japan (f. 1997) and EDF Cambodia (f. 2008).

Activities: Works in the socioeducational field, with a focus on poverty reduction, education development and international peacebuilding. The Foundation provides educational opportunities to children in countries in the Greater Mekong region. Activities include a scholarship programme, which enables students to continue their education beyond primary school; educational development projects, which aim to improve students' agricultural knowledge, vocational skills and health education, and improve school infrastructure and facilities; and helping schools to become community learning centres that promote innovation and self-reliance.

Geographical Area of Activity: Cambodia, Lao People's Dem. Repub., Myanmar, Thailand, Viet Nam.

Restrictions: Scholarships available only for poor students.

Publications: Annual Report; newsletter; brochure.

Finance: Annual revenue 38.2m. baht, expenditure 38.0m. baht (31 March 2024).

Board of Directors: Terumasa Akio (Chair.).

Principal Staff: Man. Dir Sunphet Nilrat.

Contact Details: 594/22 Patio Residence Ratchayothin, Phaholyothin 32 Alley, Chandrakasem, Chatuchak District, Bangkok 10900; tel. (2) 579-9209; e-mail info@edfthai.org; internet www.edfthai.org.

Foundation for Women

Founded in 1984 as an information centre for Thai women going to work abroad.

Activities: Offers grants to projects promoting women's rights and equality, and to organizations helping marginalized women, particularly in the North and North-East of Thailand. The Foundation provides training for women and young people in the areas of violence against young people and women's rights; provides assistance and temporary accommodation to women who have experienced violence; co-ordinates assistance from agencies and provides information to Thai women travelling abroad to work; and helps foreign women and children coming to work in Thailand who are victims of exploitation and abuse. It carries out research and data-collection activities on problems affecting women, including female trafficking; and disseminates information to government and private organizations.

Geographical Area of Activity: Thailand.

Publications: *Voices of Thai Women* (newsletter).

Finance: Annual income approx. 3m. baht.

Board: Siriporn Sakronbanek (Chair.); Amara Phongsapich (Vice-Chair.).

Principal Staff: Sec.-Gen. Rangsima Limpisawat.

Contact Details: 295 Soi Charansanitwong, 62 Bangphet, Bangkok 10700; POB 47 Bangkoknoi, Bangkok 10700; tel. (2) 433-5149; e-mail libraryffw@gmail.com.

Seub Nakhasathien Foundation

Founded in 1990, in memory of Seub Nakhasathien, a conservationist who was killed in Huai Kha Khaeng forest.

Activities: Builds and works with networks to conserve and monitor forest ecology and mitigate climate change. The Foundation works to establish mechanisms to manage natural resources in the Western Forests and support local communities to live in balance with ecosystems.

Geographical Area of Activity: Western Thailand.

Publications: Situation Reports; books.

Finance: Annual revenue approx. 3m. baht.

Board of Directors: Panudet Kerdmali (Chair.); Ratiya Chantaratian, Rangsarit Kanchanavanich, Wanchai Tantiwittayapitak (Vice-Chair.); Waraporn Serttikul (Treas.); Aryupa Sangkhaman (Sec.).

Contact Details: 140 Tiwanon Rd, Bang Kraso Subdistrict, Mueang Nonthaburi District, Nonthaburi Province 11000; tel. (2) 580-4381; e-mail snf@seub.or.th; internet www.seub.or.th.

Siam Society

Founded in 1904 to investigate and encourage the arts and sciences in relation to Thailand and its neighbouring countries.

Activities: Operates internationally in the fields of education, economic affairs, the arts and humanities, religion, international relations and the conservation of natural resources, through self-conducted programmes, carrying out research; offering grants to institutions and individuals, fellowships and scholarships; and organizing conferences, courses and lectures. In 2011 the Society established the Siamese Heritage Trust, which carries out activities in the fields of advocacy, education, knowledge and networking, organizing conferences, lectures, seminars and study trips. It has a library of approx. 50,000 vols; and nearly 1,800 members.

Geographical Area of Activity: South-East Asia.

Publications: Annual Report; *Journal of the Siam Society* (2 a year); *Natural History Bulletin of the Siam Society* (2 a year); books; monographs.

Council: Bilaibhan Sampatisiri (Pres.); Dr Weerachai Nankorn, Somlak Charoenpot, Suraya Supanwanich (Vice-Pres.).

Principal Staff: Man. Dir Kanitha Kasina-Ubol.

Contact Details: 131 Asoke Montri Rd, Sukhumvit 21, Bangkok 10110; tel. (2) 661-6470; e-mail info@thesiamsociety.org; internet thesiamsociety.org.

Thai Rath Foundation

Founded in 1979 by Kampol Vacharaphol, former director of the daily newspaper *Thai Rath*; approved as a public charitable organization in 1999.

Activities: Works in the fields of education and newspaper research. Programmes include renovating school buildings, providing sports and classroom equipment, and developing libraries. The Foundation oversees and supports a network of

111 Thai Rath Witthaya schools in 13 regions. It offers scholarships to underprivileged children and provides management and teacher training.

Geographical Area of Activity: Thailand.

Finance: Current capital 470.9m. baht.

Board of Directors: Khunying Praneetsilp Watcharapol (Chair.); Yingluck Wacharapol (Vice-Chair. and Treas.); Wichian Pochanukul (Sec.).

Contact Details: Bldg 1, 2nd Floor, 1 Vibhavadi Rangsit, Chom Phon, Chatuchak, Bangkok 10900; tel. (2) 127-1064; e-mail Thairath.found@gmail.com; internet www.thairath-found.or.th.

TISCO Foundation

Founded in 1982 by the TISCO Financial Group.

Activities: Provides financial assistance to people in need in the areas of education, self-employment and medical treatment. The Foundation annually awards around 50,000 student scholarships at all levels from primary school to university, worth from 1,000 baht to 15,000 baht. It provides start-up funding to disadvantaged people to set up small businesses; and funds medical treatment and prosthetics for disabled people.

Geographical Area of Activity: Thailand.

Publications: *Daily Knowledge Poster*; blog.

Finance: Endowment fund 333m. baht.

Advisory Board: Gen. Somchai Uboldejpracharak (Chair.).

Foundation Committee: Siwaporn Thattaranon (Chair.); Pliu Mangkornkanok (Vice-Chair.); Chutinthorn Waikasi (Treas.); Wanee Ubondejpracharak (Sec.).

Principal Staff: Man. Phatthanit Phantharaphong; Asst Man. Rachat Yubolwat.

Contact Details: TISCO Tower, 1st Floor, 48/4 North Sathorn Rd, Silom Subdistrict, Bang Rak District, Bangkok 10500; tel. (2) 633-7501; e-mail tiscofoundation@tiscofoundation.org; internet www.tiscofoundation.org.

TTF—Toyota Thailand Foundation

Established in 1992 by the Toyota Thailand Company, a motor vehicle manufacturer.

Activities: Active in the fields of education, social welfare and community development in Thailand, through funding NGOs and training schemes. Projects include an initiative to teach primary school children in remote areas about nutrition and hygiene; offering scholarships in engineering at the Institute of Traffic and Transport Engineering at Chulalongkorn University; supporting orphans whose parents have died from AIDS; and a programme to empower young women. The Foundation co-operates with other organizations on projects in areas such as sustainable development and equitable use of natural resources.

Geographical Area of Activity: Thailand.

Board: Pramon Suthiwong (Chair.); Noriaki Yamashita (Vice-Chair.); Tomohiko Deguchi (Treas.); Nantawat Sriwarat-atchakul (Sec.).

Contact Details: 186/1 Moo 1, Old Railway Rd, Samrong Tai, Phrapadaeng, Samut Prakarn, Province 10130; tel. (2) 386-1393; internet www.toyota.co.th/ttf.

TIMOR-LESTE

FOUNDATIONS AND NON-PROFITS

Fundasaun Alola (Alola Foundation)

Founded in 2001 by First Lady Kirsty Sword Gusmão.

Activities: Fosters leadership of women; raises awareness about sexual violence against women and girls; and lobbies for women's and children's rights. Programmes support National Development Goals: improving the health of mothers and children; promoting human rights, strengthening community development and women's economic participation, improving quality of and access to education, and improving women's status. The Foundation works in partnership with Alola Australia (f. 2008).

Geographical Area of Activity: Timor-Leste.

Publications: Annual Report; newsletter.

Board of Directors: Dr Kirsty Sword Gusmão (Chair.).

Principal Staff: CEO Maria Imaculada Guterres.

Contact Details: Av. Bispo de Medeiros, Mascarenhas, Mercado Lama, Dili; POB 3, Dili, Timor-Leste via Darwin, Australia; tel. 332-3855; e-mail info@alolafoundation.org; internet www.alolafoundation.org.

Fundasaun Haburas (Haburas Foundation)

Founded in 1998 by Demetrio do Amaral de Carvalho to promote and protect the environment in Timor-Leste; a member of Friends of the Earth International (q.v.).

Activities: Initiates and funds projects designed to help Timor-Leste develop sustainably and equitably. The Foundation promotes reforestation and the establishment of the country's first national park; educates people about environmental issues; and mediates in environmental disputes.

Geographical Area of Activity: Timor-Leste.

Publications: *Verde* (monthly bulletin); brochures.

Principal Staff: Dir Pedrito Vieira.

Contact Details: Rua dos Direitos Humanos No. 16, Aldeia Halibur, Suco Motael Posto Administrativo, Verra Cruz, Dili; tel. 331-0103; e-mail haburaslorosae@yahoo.com; internet haburasfoundation.org.

Fundasaun Mahein (Guardian Foundation)

Established in 2009 by Nélson Belo, founder of the Judicial System Monitoring Programme, and Edward Rees, a peace and development specialist.

Activities: Aims to increase the legitimacy and capacity of the Timorese security sector through citizen participation in developing legislation, policies and procedures.

Geographical Area of Activity: Timor-Leste.

Publications: Newsletter; blog.

Principal Staff: Pres. Joao Da Silva Sarmento.

Contact Details: Rua da Felicidade, Aldea Central, Suku Gricenfor, Postu Administrativu Nain Feto, Dili; tel. 78316075; e-mail direktor.mahein@gmail.com; internet www.fundasaunmahein.org.

Rede ba Rai (Land Network)

Established in 2001.

Activities: Works to address land conflict and large-scale population displacement. The Network monitors land laws and government policies; and supports and advocates for local communities. It promotes equality, social and justice, fair and sustainable ecology, good governance, and transparency and accountability. Comprises 25 national and international NGOs and CSOs.

Geographical Area of Activity: Timor-Leste.

Publications: Research reports.

Principal Staff: Nat. Co-ordinator Hortencio Pedro Vieira.

Contact Details: Rua dos direitos humanos 16, Aldeia Halibur, Suco Motael, Posto Administrativo Verra Cruz, Dili; tel. 77163059; e-mail redebarai@gmail.com; internet redebarai.org.

TRINIDAD AND TOBAGO

FOUNDATIONS AND NON-PROFITS

Digicel Trinidad and Tobago Foundation

Established in 2012 by Digicel, a telecommunications company; part of the Digicel Foundation network.

Activities: The Digicel Foundation focuses on three main areas: community Development—through strategic partnerships it empowers community-based organizations to transform their community spaces for underserved and marginalized groups like women and children who are victims of domestic violence; special needs—implementing interventions and supporting initiatives that improve opportunities for persons with disabilities; and digital citizenship—increasing access to the internet and techology for youth and vulnerable groups.

Geographical Area of Activity: Trinidad and Tobago.

Restrictions: Partnerships are limited to reigistered groups working in Trinidad and Tobago.

Publications: Annual Report.

Finance: Total investment US $9.2m. (at 2025).

Board of Directors: Maria Mulcahy (Global Chair.); Desha Clifford (Chair.); Sacha Thompson (Sec.).

Principal Staff: CEO Penny Gomez.

Contact Details: 11c Ansa Centre, Maraval Rd, Port of Spain, Trinidad; tel. 399-9998; e-mail digicelfoundationtt@digicelgroup.com; internet www.digicelfoundation.org/trinidad-and-tobago/en/home.html.

TUNISIA

FOUNDATIONS AND NON-PROFITS

Fondation BIAT pour la Jeunesse (BIAT Youth Foundation)

Established in 2014 by Ismaïl Mabrouk, Chair. of Banque Internationale Arabe de Tunisie (BIAT).

Activities: Supports the reduction of social and regional inequality and creation of cultural diversity. Activities fall into three main areas: education, awarding scholarships for higher education, providing opportunities for internships, and organizing visits to companies and sites of historic and cultural significance; culture, promoting cultural heritage, helping to renovate works of art and listed monuments, organizing conferences and the publication of books and articles; and the promotion of entrepreneurship among young people aged 12–18 years and, through the Foundation's SPARK Ideation Workshops programme, aged 15–20 years, with a view to participating in regional and international markets, also setting up and funding a start-up incubator platform and a networking initiative. In 2017 the Foundation launched the Bloom Masters entrepreneurship competition with the MIT Enterprise Forum Pan-Arab, awarding nine prizes totalling 400,000 Tunisian dinars to Tunisian innovators, start-ups and social enterprises.

Geographical Area of Activity: Tunisia.

Board of Directors: Ismaïl Mabrouk (Pres.); Malek Ellouze (Vice-Chair.); Mohamed Agrebi (Treas.); Thameur Derbel (Sec.-Gen.).

Contact Details: 70–72 ave Habib Bourguiba, Tunis; tel. (31) 311519; e-mail fondation@biat.com.tn; internet www.fondationbiat.org.tn.

Fondation Jasmin pour la Recherche et la Communication (Jasmine Foundation for Research and Communication)

Established in 2013; a think tank and research institute.

Activities: Programmes focus on engaging vulnerable and marginalized women and young people in local decisionmaking and civic life. Areas of interest are: citizen participation; constitution and elections; democracy; local governance; public policy; rule of law; and transitional justice. The Foundation organizes conferences and seminars; and works with CSOs and international institutions.

Geographical Area of Activity: Tunisia.

Publications: Newsletter (weekly); policy briefs; research reports.

Principal Staff: Dir Dr Tasnim Chirchi.

Contact Details: 17 Ave Mustapha Abdessalem, 2nd Floor, Menzah V, 2037 Ariana; tel. (71) 751858; e-mail info@jasminefoundation.org; internet www.jasminefoundation.org.

Fondation Orange Tunisie (Orange Foundation Tunisia)

Established in 2010 by Orange, a telecommunications company; part of the Fondation Orange (q.v.) network.

Activities: Carries out activities in the fields of culture, digital education and health. Main programmes are Orange Villages and Digital Schools. Under the Innovation programme, the Orange Developer Center offers training and workshops on coding for students and young professionals. Since 2015, in collaboration with local NGOs, the Foundation has established 10 FabLab Solidaire digital maker spaces, and a mobile FabLab.

Geographical Area of Activity: Tunisia.

Publications: *Digitall* (magazine); newsletter.

Principal Staff: Dir of External Relations, CSR and Innovation Asma Ennaifer.

Contact Details: c/o Immeuble Orange, Centre Urbain Nord, 1003 Tunis; tel. 30013001; internet www.orange.tn/actualites/actus/la-fondation-orange-tunisie.

Fondation Rambourg (Rambourg Foundation)

Established in 2011 by Guillaume Rambourg and Olfa Terras.

Activities: Facilitates public access to the arts and culture, promoting education, sports and handicrafts. Foundation programmes encourage the development of a knowledge and creative economy to create economic benefits, while preserving cultural heritage and supporting innovative initiatives and practices. It works internationally, with a special focus on Tunisia; and awards a prize for contemporary art. Has a fundraising office in Paris, France.

Geographical Area of Activity: France, Tunisia.

Publications: Newsletter.

Principal Staff: Pres. Sarah Ben Hsouna.

Contact Details: 26 ave 1er juin 1955, Mutuelleville, 1002 Tunis; tel. (71) 781467; e-mail contact@fondationrambourg.tn.

Fondation Tunisie pour le Développement (Tunisia Development Foundation)

Established in 2016 by Badreddine Ouali, founder of Vermeg, an insurance and banking software publisher.

Activities: Promotes socioeconomic development, and the political and economic development of young people in Tunisia; and carries out social welfare projects to support disadvantaged people in Tunisia and abroad. The Foundation promotes young people's employment, working to correct regional imbalances and ensure gender equality. Programmes focus on health, culture and economic innovation. The Elife programme plans to establish 10 technology centres for the training of up to 5,000 young people a year in marginalized and disadvantaged regions.

Geographical Area of Activity: International.

Finance: Initial endowment €20m.

Board of Directors: Badreddine Ouali (Pres.); Sleheddine Hmadi (Treas.).

Principal Staff: Exec. Dir Hassen Manai.

Contact Details: Zone d'activité Kheireddine (lac3), 13 rue Socrate, 2015 Lagoulette; 21 rue el Qods, 1002 Tunis; tel. (71) 130160; e-mail contact@fondation-tunisie.org; internet fondationtunisie.org.

Kamel Lazaar Foundation—KLF

Established in 2005 in Geneva, Switzerland, by Kamel Lazaar, a financier and art collector; present in Tunisia since 2016.

Activities: Supports artistic and cultural projects, in particular contemporary visual arts, and promotes arts and artists from the Arab world. The Foundation funds research on visual culture; awards grants of 10,000–40,000 Tunisian dinars and fellowships to artists, and artistic and cultural events and projects; and supports the creation of cultural and artistic spaces. It has a library and documentation centre containing more than 1,000 vols; in 2011 the Foundation launched the Ibraaz online platform and critical forum on visual culture. Has an office in London (UK).

Geographical Area of Activity: Middle East and North Africa, UK.

Publications: Newsletter; academic works; exhibition catalogues; children's books.

Principal Staff: Pres. Lina Lazaar.

Contact Details: rue de l'Ile de Malte, Immeuble Lira, Les jardins du Lac, Les berges du Lac II, 1053 Tunis; tel. (70) 147165; e-mail contact-tunis@kamellazaarfoundation.org; internet www.kamellazaarfoundation.org.

TÜRKIYE (TURKEY)

CO-ORDINATING BODIES

Sivil Toplum Geliştirme Merkezi—STGM (Association of Civil Society Development Center)

Formed in 2004 by a group of thought leaders and civil activists.

Activities: The fundamental purpose of STGM is to support civil society organizations towards being capable of realizing more effective actions. Therefore, although providing assistance to all structures within civil society, STGM gives priority to the organizations that employ rights-based approach. The priority target group of STGM comprises civil society organizations in the fields of gender, children, human rights, youth, environment, disabled rights and cultural rights. Priorities are capacity building and policy advocacy. STGM also prepares monitoring reports on freedom of association. Carries out communication studies to increase the visibility of civil society organizations as well as aiming to publicize the efforts of STGM.

Geographical Area of Activity: Türkiye.

Publications: *Siviliz* (bulletin, 2 a month, in Turkish and English); brochure; guides; handbooks; reports; blog.

Board of Directors: Dr Yakup Levent Korkut (Chair.).

Principal Staff: Gen. Co-ordinator Tezcan Eralp Abay.

Contact Details: Buğday Sok. 2/5, Çankaya, 06680 Kavaklıdere, Ankara; tel. (312) 4424262; e-mail bilgi@stgm.org.tr; internet www.stgm.org.tr.

TÜSEV—Türkiye Üçüncü Sektör Vakfı (Third Sector Foundation of Turkey)

Established in 1993 by 23 CSOs.

Activities: A network of more than 100 associations and foundations that work to strengthen the legal, fiscal and operational infrastructure of the third (non-profit) sector in Türkiye. Programmes include civil society law reform, social investment, international relations, networking and research. The Foundation is a member of Philea and WINGS (qq.v.).

Geographical Area of Activity: Türkiye.

Publications: Annual Report; *TUSEV e-newsletter* (quarterly); *Directory of Member Foundations and Associations of the Third Sector Foundation of Turkey*; information brochures; monographs; periodicals.

Finance: Annual income 20.9m. Turkish liras, expenditure 17.4m. Turkish liras (31 Dec. 2024).

Board of Representatives: Erdal Yıldırım (Chair.); Nevgül Bilsel Safkan (Vice-Chair.).

Supervisory Board: Sait Tosyalı (Chair.).

Principal Staff: Sec.-Gen. Rana Kotan; Deputy Sec.-Gen. Birce Altay.

Contact Details: Bankalar Cad. No. 2, Minerva Han Kat 5, 34420 Karaköy, İstanbul; tel. (212) 2438307; e-mail info@tusev.org.tr; internet www.tusev.org.tr.

FOUNDATIONS AND NON-PROFITS

Anne Çocuk Eğitim Vakfı—AÇEV (Mother Child Education Foundation)

Established in 1993.

Activities: Supports early childhood education and family literacy programmes to provide equal access to education for all, with a focus on disadvantaged communities. Education programmes are aimed at mothers and children, supporting fathers and empowering women through functional literacy. The Foundation organizes training courses, seminars and awareness-raising programmes. It works with government agencies, local and international NGOs, universities and private businesses; and has international programmes in 14 countries.

Geographical Area of Activity: Bahrain, Belgium, Bosnia and Herzegovina, Brazil, Cyprus, France, Germany, Jordan, Lao People's Dem. Repub., Lebanon, Mexico, Netherlands, Saudi Arabia, Switzerland, Türkiye.

Publications: Annual Report; newsletter; evaluations; guides; reports.

Finance: Annual revenue 32.9m. Turkish liras, expenditure 28.0m. Turkish liras (2022).

Board of Trustees: Ayşen Özyeğin (Chair.).

Board of Directors: Ayşecan Özyeğin Oktay (Chair.); Ayla Göksel (Vice-Chair.).

Principal Staff: Gen. Man. Senem Basyurt.

Contact Details: Merkez Mah. Cendere Cad. 22, 7th Floor, 34406 Kagithane, İstanbul; tel. (212) 2134220; e-mail acev@acev.org; internet www.acev.org.

Aydın Doğan Vakfı — TÜRKIYE (TURKEY)

Aydın Doğan Vakfı (Aydın Doğan Foundation)

Established in 1996 by Aydın Doğan, a business person.

Activities: Works in the fields of culture and education, with a focus on girls' education. The Foundation has built schools and dormitories, libraries, and sports and cultural centres; and maintains an art gallery. It makes a number of awards, including the Aydın Doğan Award for individuals' contributions to culture, the arts, literature and science; the Aydın Doğan International Cartoon Prize; Young Communicators' awards; and various awards in the areas of architecture, social services, literature and music.

Geographical Area of Activity: Türkiye.

Board of Directors: Arzuhan Doğan Yalçındağ (Chair.); Vuslat Doğan Sabanci (Deputy Chair.).

Principal Staff: Exec. Dir Candan Fetvaci.

Contact Details: Burhaniye Mah. Kısıklı Cad. No. 65, PK 34676 Üsküdar, İstanbul; tel. (216) 5569176; e-mail advakfi@advakfi.org; internet aydindoganvakfi.org.tr.

Beyaz Nokta Gelişim Vakfı (White Point Development Foundation)

Established in 1994 by Ishak Alaton, M. Tinaz Titiz, Faruk Ekinci, Yuksel Domaniç, Mümin Erkunt and Ibrahim Kocabas to promote problem solving in society.

Activities: Works in the field of education innovation through self-conducted programmes. Programmes promote science education and increasing learners' problem-solving capabilities. The Foundation conducts research; organizes conferences, seminars and training courses; and offers scholarships. It has an office in Ankara.

Geographical Area of Activity: Türkiye.

Restrictions: Grants only to foundation members.

Publications: Annual Report; *Beyaz Bülten* (newsletter); white papers.

Finance: Total assets 875,419 Turkish liras (31 Dec. 2022).

Board of Directors: Dr Necati Saygılı (Chair.); Ayhan Yıldızel (Sec.-Gen.).

Supervisory Board: Hüseyin Cimşit (Chair.).

Contact Details: Fulya Mah. Büyükdere Cad., No. 74/A Torun Center, Kat B-1, Garden Ofis No. 171, 34394 Mecidiyeköy-Şişli, İstanbul; tel. (212) 8038397; e-mail bilgi@beyaznokta.org.tr; internet www.beyaznokta.org.tr.

Çevre Koruma ve Ambalaj Atıkları Değerlendirme Vakfı—ÇEVKO (Environmental Protection and Packaging Waste Recovery and Recycling Foundation)

Established in 1991 by 14 national and multinational companies to promote and organize economically efficient and environmentally friendly packaging, waste recovery and recycling based on the principle of co-responsibility.

Activities: Works in the field of conservation and the environment. The Foundation conducts research and advocacy; and organizes training courses and national and international conferences. It co-ordinates implementation of the European Green Dot packaging recycling initiative in Türkiye.

Geographical Area of Activity: Türkiye.

Publications: Annual Report; newsletter; *ÇEVKO Donusum* ('Transformation', magazine).

Finance: Total assets approx. US $400,000.

Board of Directors: Okyar Yayalar (Chair.); Figan Soykut, Melike Özener, Mehmet H. Erbak (Vice-Chair.).

Principal Staff: Gen. Sec. Mete İmer.

Contact Details: Cenap Şahabettin Sok. 94, 31748 Koşuyolu, Kadıköy, İstanbul; tel. (216) 4287890; e-mail cevko@cevko.org.tr; internet www.cevko.org.tr.

Hisar Education Foundation—HEV

Established in 1970 by a group of education volunteers.

Activities: Works in the field of education through self-conducted programmes. The Foundation organizes conferences and training courses; and offers scholarships and fellowships. It comprises centres for culture, fitness, information strategies, innovation, university counselling and careers, and writing; and operates a school in İstanbul, offering preschool to high school education.

Geographical Area of Activity: Türkiye.

Publications: *Educating Young Children*.

Board of Directors: Prof. Dr Üstün Ergüder (Chair.); Prof. Dr Gülsün Sağlamer (Deputy Chair.); İpek Erduran (Gen. Sec.).

Principal Staff: Founders' Rep. and Gen. Man. Prof. Dr Gülay Barbarosoğlu.

Contact Details: Göktürk Merkez Mah. İstanbul Cad. No. 3, 34077 Eyüpsultan, İstanbul; tel. (212) 3640000; e-mail info@hisarschool.k12.tr; internet www.hisarschool.k12.tr.

İktisadi Kalkınma Vakfı (Economic Development Foundation)

Founded in 1965 by the İstanbul Chamber of Commerce and the İstanbul Chamber of Industry.

Activities: Conducts research on Türkiye-EU relations; formulates and expresses opinions and proposals on behalf of the Turkish private sector on EU and Türkiye-EU relations; carries out projects that address general and technical issues related to Türkiye-EU integration, and inform and involve businesses, NGOs, media and the public. The Foundation organizes conferences, panels and seminars; informs the European Commission and Parliament, as well as European NGOs and the media about activities undertaken by Türkiye in the harmonization process; and carries out lobbying activities promoting Türkiye. It maintains a library, which is the depository library of EU publications in Türkiye, and has permanent representation in Brussels, Belgium.

Geographical Area of Activity: EU member states, Türkiye.

Publications: *IKV Monthly* (newsletter); *IKV Brief Notes*; annual almanac; brochure; research studies.

Finance: Fully financed by the private sector; does not receive financial support from the Government.

Board of Directors: Ayhan Zeytinoğlu (Pres.); Prof. Dr Halûk Kabaalioğlu, Sedat Zincirkıran (Vice-Pres.).

Principal Staff: Sec.-Gen. Assoc. Prof. Çiğdem Nas; Deputy Sec.-Gen. Gökhan Kilit; Brussels Rep. Haluk Nuray.

Contact Details: Esentepe Mah. Harmann Sok., TOBB Plaza No. 10, K 7–8 Şişli, İstanbul; tel. (212) 2709300; e-mail ikv@ikv.org.tr; internet www.ikv.org.tr.

İnsan Hak ve Hürriyetleri İnsani Yardım Vakfı—IHH (IHH Humanitarian Relief Foundation)

Established in 1995 by Bulent Yildirim, a lawyer, and Mehmet Kose in response to the war in Bosnia.

Activities: Provides humanitarian relief and emergency aid to people affected by conflict and human-made or natural disasters; promotes human rights and the rule of law; and carries out humanitarian diplomacy. The Foundation also cares for the welfare and education of orphans; carries out cataract surgery in 13 sub-Saharan African countries and established an eye hospital in Niger; and provides access to clean water by building wells. It works in 123 countries and has offices in Gaza, Morocco, Niger and Somalia.

Geographical Area of Activity: Africa, Central and South America, Central and South Asia, Far East, Middle East, South-Eastern Europe.

Publications: Annual Report; newsletter; *İnsani Yardım* ('Humanitarian Aid', magazine); reports; books.

Finance: Annual income 1,202.1m. Turkish liras, expenditure 1,369.5m. Turkish liras (31 Dec. 2021).

Board of Trustees: Fehmi Bülent Yıldırım (Chair.); Huseyin Oruç (Deputy Chair.).

Principal Staff: Sec.-Gen. Durmuş Aydın.

TÜRKIYE (TURKEY)

Contact Details: Büyük Karaman Cad. Taylasan Sok., No. 3 Pk, 34083 Fatih, İstanbul; tel. (212) 6312121; e-mail info@ihh.org.tr; internet www.ihh.org.tr.

İnsan Kaynağını Geliştirme Vakfı—IKGV (Human Resource Development Foundation)

Founded in 1988 by a group of academics and business people.

Activities: Works to empower people, especially women and children, through advocacy, training and service provision in the areas of population and sustainable development. Programmes include: promoting reproductive health and rights; community development and women's empowerment; irregular migration; combating human trafficking; and development of civil society.

Geographical Area of Activity: Türkiye.

Publications: Reports; manuals; surveys.

Board of Directors: Hasip Buldanlıoğlu (Chair.); Prof. Dr Ayşen Bulut (Vice-Chair.); Dr Demet Güral (Treas.).

Principal Staff: Gen. Man. Dr Muhtar Çokar.

Contact Details: Yeniçarşı Cad. 34, 34425 Beyoğlu, İstanbul; tel. (212) 2931605; e-mail ikgv@ikgv.org; internet www.ikgv.org.

International Blue Crescent Relief and Development Foundation—IBC

Established in 1999 in Albania to provide emergency food aid to Kosovan refugees; officially registered in Türkiye (Turkey) in 2000.

Activities: Works in the fields of humanitarian aid and sustainable development. Programmes include: disaster relief and rehabilitation; post-emergency housing and reconstruction; rural social and economic development; supporting civil society and community development through technical and financial capacity building; formal and informal education and training; and renovating, building and managing public health facilities. The Foundation works in more than 20 countries, with offices in Iran, Iraq, Pakistan, Somalia, the Syrian Arab Republic, Uganda and Yemen. It has special consultative status with ECOSOC.

Geographical Area of Activity: Central and South-Eastern Europe, Middle East, South Asia, South-East Asia, sub-Saharan Africa.

Publications: Annual Report; newsletter; booklets; brochures; directories; manuals; posters; reports.

Board of Directors: Recep Üker (Chair.); Muzaffer Baca (Deputy Chair.).

Principal Staff: Gen. Man. Mustafa Ekici.

Contact Details: 19 Mayıs Mahallesi Sinan Ercan Caddesi Paşa Korusu Sitesi No:18/2, B2 Blok, 34736 Kadıköy, İstanbul; tel. (216) 3841486; e-mail info@ibc.org.tr; internet www.ibc.org.tr.

Kadın Emeğini Değerlendirme Vakfı—KEDV (Foundation for the Support of Women's Work)

Established in 1986 to help low-income women's groups to improve the quality of their lives, their communities and their leadership.

Activities: Works in the field of women's empowerment through creating an egalitarian, inclusive and resilient society. The Foundation supports women's organizations and co-operatives working to eliminate poverty; promotes women's leadership and economic empowerment; and strengthens the role of women in disaster and migration management. In 2002 it established the MAYA microfinance initiative to make loans to women to enable them to establish small businesses; and also operates four craft shops.

Geographical Area of Activity: Türkiye.

Publications: Handbooks; reports.

Finance: Total assets 314.4m. Turkish liras (31 Dec. 2024).

Board of Directors: Zehra Coşkun (Chair.).

Principal Staff: Gen. Dir Şengül Akcar.

Contact Details: Istiklal Cad. Bekar Sok. No. 17, Beyoğlu, İstanbul; tel. (212) 2922672; e-mail kedv@kedv.org.tr; internet www.kedv.org.tr.

Sabanci Vakfı—Haci Omer Sabanci Foundation

Established in 1974 by the Sabanci family.

Activities: The Sabanci Foundation's mission is to contribute to the educational, cultural and social development of Türkiye and make a difference in the lives of individuals. The vision of the Foundation is to advance social development by promoting an equitable environment in which women, youth and persons with disabilities have access and equal opportunities to actively participate in society. It continues its activities for women, youth and persons with disabilities in the fields of arts and culture, education and social change. The Foundation has established a network of more than 120 institutions all around Türkiye in 78 cities; these include schools, dormitories, teachers' centres, medical and sports facilities, cultural centres and social facilities, and the Sabanci University. The Foundation supports students and artists by offering scholarships and grants; it empowers CSOs that promote equality and active participation for young people, women and people with disabilities by making grants and sharing expertise; it inspires society by increasing visibility of changemakers who contribute to the social development and share knowledge and experience with the aim of strengthening philanthropy by engaging in international collaborations and organizing philanthrophy seminars.

Geographical Area of Activity: International.

Restrictions: Grants only to organizations based in Türkiye.

Publications: Annual Report; newsletter; brochure.

Finance: Total assets 2,300m. Turkish liras (31 Dec. 2024).

Board of Trustees and Executive Committee: Güler Sabanci (Chair.); Hayri Çulhacı (Vice-Chair.).

Contact Details: Sabanci Center, 4 Levent, 34330 İstanbul; tel. (212) 3858800; e-mail info@sabancivakfi.org; internet www.sabancivakfi.org.

Tarih Vakfı (History Foundation of Turkey)

Established in 1991, as the Economic and Social History Foundation of Turkey, by 264 members of the scientific and cultural community.

Activities: Works in the areas of history and the preservation of historical heritage, and the development of NGOs, through self-conducted programmes. The Foundation conducts research and organizes conferences, co-operating with similar national and international organizations. It maintains an information and documentation centre, containing 20,000 vols and around 900 periodicals, and an online database of Turkish NGOs. Has a liaison office in Ankara.

Geographical Area of Activity: Türkiye.

Publications: Newsletter; *Tarih Vakfı'ndan Haberler* (monthly bulletin); *Toplumsal Tarih* (monthly magazine); *Istanbul* (magazine, 2 a year); books.

Finance: Annual income 848,706 Turkish liras, expenditure 848,706 Turkish liras (2021).

Board of Directors: Nurşen Gürboğa (Chair.); Ali Sipahi, Neslişah Başaran Lotz (Vice-Chair.); Yaşar Tolga Cora (Gen. Sec.); Sırrı Emrah Üçer (Treas.).

Principal Staff: Gen. Co-ordinator Ali Eryüzlü.

Contact Details: Sarıdemir Mah. Ragıp Gümüşpala Cad. Değirmen Sok. No. 10 Eminönü, Fatih, Istanbul; tel. (212) 5220202; e-mail tarihvakfi@tarihvakfi.org.tr; internet www.tarihvakfi.org.tr.

TESEV—Türkiye Ekonomik ve Sosyal Etüdler Vakfı (Turkish Economic and Social Studies Foundation)

Established in 1961 as the Economic and Social Studies Conference Committee; became a think tank in 1994.

Activities: Carries out public policy research and advocacy in the fields of democratization, good governance and transparency, foreign policy, social inequality and inclusion.

Programme areas include: child policy; digital policy tools; empowering civil society; gender equality; migration policy; transparency and accountability; and urban governance and sustainability. The Foundation organizes panel discussions, roundtables, training and workshops.

Geographical Area of Activity: Türkiye.

Publications: Annual Report; briefs; reports; studies.

Finance: Annual income 4.4m. Turkish liras, expenditure 4.2m. Turkish liras (31 Dec. 2022).

Executive Board: Prof. Dr Ali Çarkoğlu (Chair.); Necla Zarakol, Devrim Çubukçu (Vice-Chair.).

Principal Staff: Exec. Dir Dr Özge Aktaş Mazman.

Contact Details: Halaskargazi Mah. Halaskargazi Cad. No:38/66E, İç Kapı No:215, 34371 Şişli, İstanbul; tel. (212) 2928903; e-mail info@tesev.org.tr; internet www.tesev.org.tr.

Türkiye Aile Sağlığı ve Planlaması Vakfı—TAPV (Turkish Family Health and Planning Foundation)

Established in 1985 by Vehbi Koç, the founder of the Koç Group, an industrial conglomerate.

Activities: Promotes sustainable and equitable development through improving women's and girls' access to education and quality of life for all. Main programme areas are: gender equality; safe motherhood training and counselling; safe sexuality and youth studies; sexual health education; and women's empowerment. The Foundation organizes seminars, meetings and training courses.

Geographical Area of Activity: Türkiye.

Publications: Annual Report; *Görünüm* (quarterly newsletter); booklets; brochures; posters; reports; books.

Finance: Total assets 17.8m. Turkish liras; net annual result 237,460 Turkish liras (31 Dec. 2022).

Board of Directors: Temel Kamil Atay (Pres.); Nevzat Tüfekçioğlu (Vice-Pres.).

Board of Trustees: Temel Atay (Chair.); Nevzat Tüfekçioğlu (Deputy Chair.).

Principal Staff: Gen. Co-ordinator Nurcan Müftüoğlu.

Contact Details: Adnan Saygun Cad., Güzel Konutlar Sitesi, A Blok, D3–4, Kültür Mah., 34340 Beşiktaş, İstanbul; tel. (212) 2577941; e-mail info@tapv.org.tr; internet www.tapv.org.tr.

Türkiye Çevre Vakfı (Environment Foundation of Turkey)

Founded in 1978 by Dr Cevdet Aykan, Serbülent Bingöl, Muslih Fer, Ertugrul Soysal, Prof. Dr Necmi Sönmez, Engin Ural and Altan Zeki Ünver.

Activities: Operates in the field of conservation and the environment through conducting research and advocacy. The Foundation organizes national and international conferences and seminars; and maintains a library. It offers grants and scholarships to Turkish university students studying in Türkiye through the Hâle-Nail Oraman and Necdet Öztüzün Scholarship Funds.

Geographical Area of Activity: Central Asia and the Black Sea region, Türkiye.

Restrictions: Grants only to specific NGOs working in Central Asia and the Black Sea region.

Publications: Newsletter (quarterly); books.

Board of Trustees: Prof. Dr Mehmet Somuncu (Pres.); Prof. Dr M. Hakan Yiğitbaşıoğlu (Sec.-Gen.).

Contact Details: Fidanlık Mah. Ataç-1 Sokak/20 No. 20/6, 06420 Kızılay, Ankara; tel. (312) 4255508; e-mail cevre@cevre.org.tr; internet www.cevre.org.tr.

Türkiye Erozyonla Mücadele Ağaçlandırma ve Doğal Varlıkları Koruma Vakfı—TEMA (Turkish Foundation for Combating Soil Erosion, for Reforestation and the Protection of Natural Habitats)

Established in 1992 by Hayrettin Karaca and Nihat Gökyiğit to draw attention to soil erosion and land degradation and their associated effects.

Activities: Works in the field of nature conservation through self-conducted programmes, public policy research and advocacy. Main programme areas are: policy advocacy on climate, ecopolitics, energy and mining, land use and water; afforestation, planting and protecting forests and combating erosion; education, promoting children's nature projects and environmental education in schools and offering scholarships for graduate and doctoral research; and rural development, promoting sustainable agriculture and agroforestry and protecting soil and soil-related ecosystems. The Economic Enterprise Landscape Department offers garden maintenance, landscape design and project planning, promoting the use of ecologically sound practices and planting of species that use organic fertilizers and less water. The Foundation works in 81 provinces, with more than 900,000 volunteers.

Geographical Area of Activity: Türkiye.

Publications: Annual Report; policy notes; scientific reports.

Finance: Total assets 259.0m. Turkish liras (31 Dec. 2023).

Board of Trustees: A. Doğan Arikan (Chair.).

Board of Directors: Deniz Ataç (Pres.); Hatice Meral Gezgin (Vice-Pres.).

Principal Staff: Gen. Man. Reyhan Biberci.

Contact Details: Halaskargazi Mah. Halaskargazi Cad. No. 22, Floors 5–8, 34371 Sisli, İstanbul; tel. (212) 2919090; e-mail tema@tema.org.tr; internet www.tema.org.tr.

Türkiye İnsan Hakları Vakfı—TİHV (Human Rights Foundation of Turkey)

Established in 1990 by the İnsan Hakları Derneği (Human Rights Association) and human rights activists.

Activities: Operates in Türkiye in the field of human rights. The Foundation supports measures against torture; protects the rights of refugees and asylum seekers; and runs treatment and rehabilitation centres. It maintains a documentation centre; and has offices in Diyarbakır, İstanbul and Izmir, with reference centres in Cizre and Van.

Geographical Area of Activity: Türkiye.

Publications: Working Report (annual); Human Rights Report (annual); Treatment and Rehabilitation Centres Reports; special reports; studies.

Executive Committee: Dr Metin Bakkalci (Pres.); Coşkun Üsterci (Sec.-Gen.); Saadet Erdem Kalyoncugil (Treas.).

Contact Details: Mithatpaşa Cad. 49/11, 6. Kat 06420 Kızılay, Ankara; tel. (312) 3106636; e-mail tihv@tihv.org.tr; internet www.tihv.org.tr.

Türkiye Kalkinma Vakfi (Development Foundation of Turkey)

Founded in 1969, building on the success of small-scale pilot income-generating projects around the city of Tarsus.

Activities: Works to raise income levels and improve quality of life in poor rural communities through economic, social and human development programmes. The Foundation develops income-generating activities and provides administrative and technical training. It also builds the capacity of farming communities and organizations to manage natural resources; raises awareness of environmental issues and increases environmental protection; improves access to and management of water resources and builds public washing facilities; establishes fuelwood forests; promotes solar energy; develops skills to enable women to participate in social organizations; and arranges rural loans. Programmes respect local values, are gender-balanced and environmentally friendly, emphasizing food quality and safety. Operates in 14 regions.

Geographical Area of Activity: Eastern and South-Eastern Türkiye.

Publications: Annual Report; *Mellifera* (annual); reports; books.

UGANDA (Türkiye section continued)

Finance: Funds are derived from the Turkish Government, institutions and individuals in Türkiye, Europe and the USA, bilateral technical assistance programmes with Germany and Switzerland, and loans from national and international agencies.

Board of Trustees: Prof. Dr Aziz Ekşi (Pres.); Süleyman Şeyhnebi (Vice-Pres.).

Contact Details: Çukurambar Mah. Malcolm X Cad., Bayındır Apt No. 24, Daire 14, Çukurambar-Çankaya, 06510 Ankara; tel. (312) 8145388; e-mail tkv@tkv-dft.org.tr; internet www.tkv-dft.org.tr.

Türkiye Vodafone Vakfı (Vodafone Türkiye Foundation)

Established in 2007 by Vodafone Türkiye, a telecommunications company; part of the Vodafone Foundation (q.v.) network.

Activities: Supports technology-based projects in the fields of education and women's empowerment, children and people with disabilities. Main programmes are: Coding Tomorrow, teaching children aged 7–14 years digital skills; and Connected Women First, promoting women's inclusion through digital skills. The Foundation also promotes volunteering; and develops digital apps with a social benefit in areas including: early childhood development; fostering women's economic and social empowerment; helping disabled people integrate into society through art; and preventing violence against women. The Support Fund for the Families of Martyrs offers scholarships to children of people killed in terrorist attacks.

Geographical Area of Activity: Türkiye.

Finance: Total investment since 2007: 41m. Turkish liras.

Board: Dr Hasan Süel (Chair.).

Contact Details: Büyükdere Cad. 251, Vodafone Pl., 34398 Maslak Sarıyer, İstanbul; tel. (212) 3670000; e-mail vodafonevakfi@vodafone.com; internet www.turkiyevodafonevakfi.org.tr.

Umut Vakfı (Hope Foundation)

Established in 1993 as Umut Onurlu Önderler Vakfı by the Dedeman and Önal families, in memory of four of their children.

Activities: Works to empower young people through promoting the rule of law, peaceful conflict resolution and individual disarmament. The Foundation conducts research in the areas of conflict resolution and reconciliation; and organizes meetings and training. It includes the Gurkaynak Citizenship Institute, which conducts research on participatory citizenship.

Geographical Area of Activity: Middle East, South-Eastern Europe, Türkiye.

Publications: Newsletter; manuals; reports; studies; books.

Board of Directors: Özben Önal (Chair.).

Contact Details: Yıldız Posta Cad. 52/1, 34340 Esentepe, İstanbul; tel. (212) 2160670; e-mail vakif@umut.org.tr; internet www.umut.org.tr.

Vehbi Koç Vakfı (Vehbi Koç Foundation)

Founded in 1969 by Vehbi Koç, the founder of the Koç Group, an industrial conglomerate.

Activities: Operates nationally in the fields of education, healthcare, the arts and culture, and civil society, through research, conferences, courses, seminars, lectures, awards, scholarships and travel grants. The Foundation provides grants for social welfare, buildings and medical equipment for hospitals in Türkiye. It supports public museums, including the Sadberk Hanım Müzesi, which exhibits collections in the fields of ethnography, archaeology and artistic cultural traditions; the Rahim H. Koç Museum of the history of technology and industry; and the Suna-Inan Kıraç Research Institute on Mediterranean Civilisations, which researches archaeology and indigenous cultures. The Foundation established Koç University and funds the building of schools, as well as the Vehbi Koç Professorship of Turkish Studies at Harvard University. The Vehbi Koç Prize is awarded annually to individuals or institutions that have contributed to the development of Türkiye and the Turkish people in the fields of education, health or culture. In 1990 the Tofaş Fiat Fund was created in conjunction with the Turkey Fiat Group to provide scholarships to students in Italy and Türkiye to support conservation work and to sponsor bilingual (Italian and Turkish) art publications.

Geographical Area of Activity: EU, Türkiye, United Arab Emirates, USA.

Publications: Annual Report; newsletter; catalogues; journals; magazines; books.

Finance: Total assets 7,303.4m. Turkish liras; annual expenditure 1,495.1m. Turkish liras (2020).

Board of Directors: Semahat Arsel (Chair.); Rahmi M. Koç (Vice-Chair.).

Executive Committee: Semahat Arsel (Chair.).

Principal Staff: Gen. Man. Oguz Toprakoglu.

Contact Details: Nakkaştepe, Azizbey Sok. 1, Kuzguncuk, 81207 İstanbul; tel. (216) 5310858; e-mail info@vkv.org.tr; internet www.vkv.org.tr.

UGANDA

FOUNDATIONS AND NON-PROFITS

African Youth Initiative Network—AYINET

Established in 2005 by Victor Ochen, a peace and human rights activist.

Activities: Carries out activities in three main areas: health and psychosocial rehabilitation of those who have suffered injuries during conflict and crimes; transitional justice for communities recovering from civil war and insurgency; and youth empowerment and skills training. The Network runs programmes in four main areas: youth leadership development; medical and psychosocial rehabilitation for war victims; sexual reproductive health; and sports, arts and cultural activities for advocacy. It conducts research, working with national and international partners, and also organizes sports and other events, including the national and regional War Victims Conference.

Geographical Area of Activity: Uganda.

Publications: Annual Report; newsletter; programme reports.

Principal Staff: Exec. Dir Victor Ochen.

Contact Details: Plot 11, Onapa Rd Barogole, POB 981, Lira; tel. (789) 622661; e-mail uganda@ayinet.org; internet ayinet.org.

Kulika Charitable Trust Uganda

Founded in 1981 by Patricia Brenninkmeyer in the United Kingdom; in 2005 the operational management of Kulika was transferred to the Uganda office.

Activities: Operates in the fields of education, sustainable agriculture and development in Uganda. The Trust offers scholarships; runs a training programme on organic agriculture; and supports community development and social business projects.

Geographical Area of Activity: East Africa (mainly Uganda).

Publications: Annual Report; newsletter.

Principal Staff: Chief Exec. Magdalene Amujal.

Mara Foundation

Established in 2009 by Ashish J. Thakkar, CEO of conglomerate Mara Group.

Activities: Fosters local entrepreneurship, mentoring and funding business people, and providing business training facilities. The Foundation runs the Mara Mentor online social network and organizes Mara One on One 'speed mentoring' events.

Geographical Area of Activity: Kenya, Nigeria, South Africa, Tanzania, Uganda.

Publications: *Ashish J. Thakkar Global Entrepreneurship Index*.

Finance: Receives a percentage of Mara Phone's revenue.

Principal Staff: Chair. Jagdish Thakkar.

Contact Details: 3rd Floor, Ham Towers, Makerere Hill Rd, Kampala; tel. (756) 707224; e-mail uganda@mara-foundation.org.

MTN Uganda Foundation

Established in 2007 by MTN Uganda, a telecommunications company; part of the MTN Foundations network.

Activities: Carries out the social investment activities of MTN Uganda in the areas of: education; health; and national priority areas, including water and sanitation. The Foundation provides ICT training to learners, teachers and other community members; offers scholarships to girls for university courses in science, technology, engineering and mathematics; and builds and furnishes primary school classrooms. It also contributes materially and financially to health projects and healthcare facilities. Other initiatives include digital skills training for young people and sport. A youth-focused initiative, MTN Skills Academy, was launched in 2023.

Geographical Area of Activity: Uganda.

Principal Staff: Snr Man. Bryan Mbasa.

Contact Details: Plot 69–71 Jinja Rd, Kampala; POB 24624 Kampala; tel. (31) 2120333; e-mail mtnfoundation.ug@mtn.com; internet www.mtn.co.ug/impact/foundation.

Ruparelia Foundation

Established in 2012 by Dr Sudhir Ruparelia, founder of Crane Bank Ltd (f. 1995) and Goldstar Insurance Co Ltd (f. 1996), and Jyotsna Rupareli.

Activities: Carries out activities in the fields of: education, funding school infrastructure and students' fees; environmental conservation, protecting wildlife and forests; health, funding medical research, primary and maternal and child healthcare, and subsidizing medical bills; social welfare, through poverty alleviation and sustainable livelihoods initiatives; religion, supporting multifaith activities; and sports, sponsoring local and national teams and sportspeople.

Geographical Area of Activity: Uganda.

Publications: Annual Report.

Board of Trustees: Dr Sudhir Ruparelia (Chair.).

Contact Details: c/o Ruparelia Group, Crane Chambers, 4th Floor, Plot 38, Kampala Rd, Kampala; POB 3673, Kampala; tel. (702) 711271; e-mail info@rupareliafoundation.org; internet www.rupareliafoundation.com.

UKRAINE

CO-ORDINATING BODIES

Ednannia—Initiative Centre to Support Social Action

Established in 1997 by Ukrainian NGOs and ISAR: Initiative for Social Action and Renewal in Eurasia; officially registered in 1999.

Activities: Supports local philanthropy and develops civil society through providing micro-grants, consultation, training, information, networking, research and other services to NGOs and other interested parties. The Centre organizes the Civil Society Development Forum; and runs the online Marketplace Civil Society Development Platform and NGO.Studio, which produces video interviews, articles and podcasts about CSOs' activities.

Geographical Area of Activity: Ukraine.

Publications: Annual Report; *Bulletin for NGOs* (monthly); *NGO Success Stories*.

Finance: Annual budget US $16.0m., expenditure $10.9m. (2024).

Advisory Board: Andrii Pavlovych (Chair.).

Principal Staff: CEO Volodymyr Sheyhus.

Contact Details: str. Esplanadna 17, Kyiv; tel. (44) 201-01-60; e-mail office@ednannia.ua; internet ednannia.ua.

GURT Resource Centre for NGO Development

Established in 1995; a network of CSO managers and community leaders.

Activities: Contributes to democratic social transformation through strengthening civil society. Main programme areas include: promoting volunteering and small business development; amplifying civil society's voice; developing local communities and sharing best practices; and reshaping Ukraine through policymaking. The Centre provides access to information on civil society, training and networking opportunities.

Geographical Area of Activity: Ukraine.

Publications: Annual Report; *GURT Bulletin* (weekly e-mail newsletter); manuals; reports; toolkits; blog.

Finance: Annual income 18.5m. hryvnias, expenditure 27.6m. hryvnias (31 Dec. 2023).

Board: Oleksiy Meleschuk (Chair.).

Contact Details: 01001 Kyiv, POB 126, str. Esplanadna 28, Office 7; tel. (44) 300-24-10; e-mail info@gurt.org.ua; internet global.gurt.org.ua; www.gurt.org.ua.

Ukrainian Philanthropists Forum

Established in 2005; a professional association of charitable and philanthropic organizations.

Activities: Supports civil society and social prosperity through fostering a responsible, transparent and accountable charitable community and improving efficiency of the Ukrainian charitable sector. Main activities include: developing and implementing standards for charitable organizations; encouraging reform of Ukraine's social services sector; and advancing the charitable sector. The Forum has 39 members; and is itself a member of Philea and WINGS (qq.v.).

Geographical Area of Activity: Ukraine.

Publications: Annual Report; *Chronicles of Philanthropy* (weekly e-digest); *Philanthroscop* (monthly newsletter).

Finance: Annual income 5.7m. hryvnias (2020).

Supervisory Board: Oksana Kulish (Chair.).

Principal Staff: Dir Polina Nyukhina.

UKRAINE

Contact Details: Kyiv, Mykhailivskyi Lane 9A, Apt. 51; tel. (44) 279-12-62; e-mail info@ufb.org.ua.

FOUNDATIONS AND NON-PROFITS

International Charitable Fund 'Concord 3000'
Established in 2001 by Victor Yushchenko, opposition leader and subsequently President of Ukraine.

Activities: Operates in three main areas: history and culture, with programmes on developing museum business and conservation of monuments, and supporting historical, archaeological and cultural studies; medicine and health, implementing programmes for mothers and children, to improve patient care and rehabilitation, look after children with special needs, and build hospitals for critically ill children; and education, focusing on medicine and supporting talented young people. From February 2022 the Foundation focused on supporting those affected by the conflict with Russia.

Geographical Area of Activity: Ukraine.

Restrictions: Does not accept applications by email.

Publications: Annual Report; newsletter.

Board of Directors: Maryna Antonova (Chair.); Oleksandr Maksymchuk (Vice-Chair.).

Contact Details: 04080 Kyiv, Kyrylivska St, Bldg 1–3; tel. (67) 547-25-97; e-mail cf.concord3000@gmail.com; internet concord3000.com.ua.

International Renaissance Foundation—IRF
Established in 1990; part of the Open Society Foundations (q.v.) network, founded by George Soros.

Activities: Supports the development of an active, diverse and open civic society. Main programme areas are: public health; democratic practice; environment; Europe; human rights and justice; Roma; social capital; and support for think tanks. The Foundation works to build the capacity of civil society to implement and monitor reforms; promote decentralization and development of local democracy; and strengthen European integration and transatlantic co-operation.

Geographical Area of Activity: Primarily Ukraine.

Restrictions: Does not fund commercial projects, humanitarian aid projects or projects from individuals, political parties or religious organizations.

Publications: Annual Report; *IRF Newsletter*; research reports.

Finance: Annual income US $20m., expenditure $20m. (31 Dec. 2023).

Executive Board: Olga Ayvazovska (Chair.).

Principal Staff: Exec. Dir Oleksandr Sushko; Deputy Exec. Dir Inna Pidluska.

Contact Details: 04053 Kyiv, str. Sichovyh Striltsiv 46; tel. (44) 461-97-09; e-mail irf@irf.ua; internet www.irf.ua.

Razumkov Centre
Established in 1994 as the Ukrainian Center for Economic and Political Studies, a non-governmental think tank; present name adopted in 2000, in memory of Oleksandr Razumkov, a civil servant and former Chair. of the Centre.

Activities: Promotes democracy and the rule of law; protection of human rights and freedoms; government accountability; effective public policy; citizens' active participation in public policy; democratic civilian control of the military; and the market economy. The Centre carries out public policy research and analysis in the fields of: domestic policy; economic policy; energy; foreign policy; governance; international and regional security; national security and defence; social and gender policy. It conducts nationwide public opinion surveys; organizes and takes part in international events, including conferences, expert discussions roundtables and summits.

Geographical Area of Activity: International.

Publications: Annual Report; newsletter; *Index of Economic Capacity of Households* (quarterly); *National Security & Defence* (journal); reports; papers.

Finance: Annual revenue 13.3m. hryvnias, expenditure 19.9m. hryvnias (2020).

Board: Yuriy Yakymenkon (Pres.).

Principal Staff: Dir-Gen. Pavlo Pynzenyk.

Contact Details: 01032 Kyiv, 33B Taras Shevchenko Blvd, 7th Floor; tel. (44) 201-11-98; e-mail info@razumkov.org.ua; internet razumkov.org.ua.

Ukrainian Women's Fund
Founded in 2000 to provide financial and consultative support and information to public organizations, particularly women's organizations, from Ukraine, Moldova and Belarus.

Activities: Supports women's organizations through providing grants, information and training. The Fund supports projects to expand economic opportunities for women, developing businesses run by women, reducing unemployment among women, and increasing women's political participation and gender equality. It promotes information exchange between women's organizations to build NGO networks; and aims to increase the activity of young women in civil society, preparing future female leaders.

Geographical Area of Activity: Belarus, Moldova, Ukraine.

Publications: Annual Report; brochures; case studies; books.

Finance: Annual budget 214.5m. hryvnias (2024).

Board of Directors: Marta Kolomayets (Chair.).

Principal Staff: Dir Olesya Bondar.

Contact Details: 04116 Kyiv, str. Marshala Rybalka 5B, Office 331; tel. (44) 507-06-10; e-mail uwf@uwf.org.ua; internet www.uwf.org.ua.

Victor Pinchuk Foundation
Established in 2006 by Victor Pinchuk, an industrialist and founder of EastOne Ltd, an investment company.

Activities: Works in the fields of education, healthcare and contemporary art; and promotes closer ties with the EU. The Foundation offers scholarships through the Zavtra.UA programme to students wishing to study in Ukraine and abroad; organizes a programme of public lectures by international leaders; and supports the development of the Kyiv School of Economics. It has established a network of neonatal centres throughout the country; and the PinchukArtCentre, which awards an art prize every two years to artists aged 35 years or under. In 2018 the Veteran Hub was launched, in collaboration with the Elena Pinchuk Foundation, providing psychosocial, legal and educational support to war veterans and their families. RECOVERY is a network of rehabilitation centres, a project founded in 2022 to support the Ukranian armed forces.

Geographical Area of Activity: International.

Publications: Annual Report.

Board: Benjamin Loring (Chair.).

Principal Staff: Exec. Dir Victoria Chernyavska.

Contact Details: 01024 Kyiv, str. Shovkovychna 42–44; tel. (44) 490-48-35; e-mail info@pinchukfund.org; internet www.pinchukfund.org.

UNITED ARAB EMIRATES

FOUNDATIONS AND NON-PROFITS

Abdulla Al Ghurair Foundation for Education
Established in 2015 by Abdulla Al Ghurair, founder and Chair. of Mashreq Bank.

Activities: Provides support and skills training to students from across the Arab region; and awards scholarships for study at partner universities abroad. Main programmes are: the Young Thinkers Program, an online platform to prepare Emirati students for higher education; STEM Scholars, providing financial and non-financial support for Bachelor's and Master's degrees in science, technology, engineering and mathematics; and Open Learning Scholars, supporting online and blended learning through accredited massive online open courses.

Geographical Area of Activity: Middle East and North Africa.

Restrictions: STEM Scholars are expected to live in the Arab world after graduation.

Publications: Newsletter.

Finance: Initial capital US $1,100m.

Board of Directors: HE Abdul Aziz Al Ghurair (Chair.).

Principal Staff: CEO Dr Sonia Ben Jaafar.

Contact Details: POB 6999, Dubai; e-mail info@alghurairfoundation.org; internet www.alghurairfoundation.org.

Al Jalila Foundation
Established in 2013 by HH Sheikh Muhammed bin Rashid Al Maktoum, Vice-President and Prime Minister of the United Arab Emirates and Ruler of Dubai; part of the Mohamed Bin Rashid Al Maktoum Global Initiatives (q.v.).

Activities: Works in the fields of medical education and research. The Foundation awards Seed Grants, worth up to 300,000 Emirati dirhams, for health and disease research in the UAE; Fellowship Grants, worth up to 200,000 Emirati dirhams, for Emirati medical students and professionals to study for three months at institutions of international repute; and scholarships for postgraduate study in the UAE and abroad. Other programmes include parenting skills, teacher training, raising awareness of breast cancer and providing access to affordable healthcare. It has established the Al Jalila Foundation Research Centre to carry out multidisciplinary research with a focus on cancer, cardiovascular diseases, diabetes, obesity and mental health; and in 2020 inaugurated the Mohammed Bin Rashid Medical Research Institute.

Geographical Area of Activity: International.

Publications: Newsletter; reports.

Scientific Advisory Committee: Prof. Yousef Mohamed Abdulrazzaq Al Bastaki (Chair.).

Board of Directors: Dr Raja Easa Saleh Al Gurg (Chair.); Essam Al Tamimi (Vice-Chair.).

Principal Staff: CEO Dr Abdulkareem Sultan Al Olama.

Contact Details: Bldg 12, First Floor, Dubai Healthcare City, POB 300100, Dubai; e-mail info@aljalilafoundation.ae; internet www.aljalilafoundation.ae.

Barjeel Art Foundation
Established in 2010 by Sultan Sooud Al-Qassemi to contribute to the intellectual development of art in the Arab world.

Activities: Manages, preserves and exhibits modern and contemporary Arab art. The Foundation curates and mounts exhibitions locally, regionally and internationally, to contribute to a greater understanding of the Arab region and its diaspora. It issues print and online publications; organizes public programmes and the Barjeel Poetry Prize; supports scholarly conferences and symposia; and has established partnerships with artistic, cultural and educational institutions globally to raise public awareness of the presence, importance and history of art in the Arab region.

Geographical Area of Activity: International.

Principal Staff: Curator Suheyla Takesh.

Contact Details: Al Saud Head Office Bldg, Level 2, Block B, Sheikh Khalifa Bin Zayed Al Nahyan Rd, Muwailih Commercial, Sharjah; POB 2, Sharjah; tel. (6) 569-1112; e-mail info@barjeelartfoundation.org; internet www.barjeelartfoundation.org.

Emirates Foundation
Established in 2005, and funded by the United Arab Emirates Government and the private sector in the UAE, to improve the quality of life in the country.

Activities: Main programmes are: Takatof, promoting volunteering among young people; Sanid, training volunteers to support the emergency services in the event of local or national emergencies; Kafa'at, providing leadership and business skills to young people through training, mentoring and internships; Think Science, working with academic institutions and industry to foster young people's interest in science, technology and innovation; Esref Sah, developing financial literacy among young people; Dawamee, an unemployment support programme for young people aged 15–35 years, with a focus on people from low-income backgrounds or who live in remote areas; and the mental support line—800Hope. Has offices in Dubai and Ras al-Khaimah.

Geographical Area of Activity: United Arab Emirates.

Publications: Sustainability Report; newsletter.

Board of Directors: HH Sheikh Abdullah bin Zayed Al Nahyan (Chair.); HH Sheikh Theyab bin Mohamed bin Zayed Al Nahyan (Chair. of Exec. Cttee); HE Sheikh Sultan bin Tahnoon Al Nahyan (Man. Dir).

Principal Staff: CEO Maytha Al Habsi.

Contact Details: POB 111445, Mezzanine Floor, Al Mamoura Bldg, 4th and 15th Sts, Abu Dhabi; tel. (2) 404-2994; e-mail information@emiratesfoundation.ae; internet www.emiratesfoundation.ae.

Khalifa Bin Zayed Al Nahyan Foundation
Established in 2007 by HH Khalifa Bin Zayed Al Nahyan.

Activities: Works in the fields of health and education at national, regional and global level. The Foundation supports projects on vocational education, malnutrition, mother and child protection and care, and the provision of safe water. It also supports scientific research into fatal diseases, and provides humanitarian aid and disaster relief. Has worked in more than 87 countries worldwide.

Geographical Area of Activity: International.

Principal Staff: Chair. Sheikh Mansour Bin Zayed Al Nahyan.

Contact Details: Al Khalidiya area, intersection of Mubarak bin Mohammed St and Zayed the First St, POB 28, Abu Dhabi; tel. (2) 885-5555; e-mail info@khalifafoundation.ae; internet www.khalifafoundation.ae.

Legatum Foundation
Established in 1999 as the development arm of the Legatum Group, a private investment company.

Activities: Uses investment expertise to award grants to small, community-based organizations in developing countries. Main programme areas include: human liberty, combating slavery, human trafficking and forced labour; disaster recovery, addressing the basic needs of victims of war, famine and other disasters; education, through the Speed School accelerated learning programme in Ethiopia and West Africa; economic empowerment, providing grants to create markets

UNITED KINGDOM

and provide goods and services; health, with a focus on HIV/AIDS, clean water and neglected tropical diseases; and environment, preventing loss of habitat and species diversity. The Foundation established the END Fund (f. 2012) to address Neglected Tropical Diseases; the Freedom Fund (f. 2013) to combat human slavery; and the Luminos Fund (f. 2015), focusing on primary school education. It also funds the Legatum Institute (UK), a libertarian think tank; and Legatum Center for Development and Entrepreneurship at the Massachusetts Institute of Technology—MIT (USA).

Geographical Area of Activity: International.

Publications: Newsletters.

Principal Staff: Pres. Guy Cave; Chair. Christopher Chandler.

Contact Details: Legatum Plaza, Level 2, Dubai International Financial Centre, POB 506625, Dubai; tel. (4) 317-5800; e-mail info@legatum.com; internet www.legatum.org.

Mohammed bin Rashid Al Maktoum Global Initiatives—MBRGI

Established in 2015 by HH Sheikh Mohammed bin Rashid Al Maktoum, Vice-President and Prime Minister of the United Arab Emirates and Ruler of Dubai; successor to the Mohammed bin Rashid Al Maktoum Foundation (f. 2007).

Activities: Carries out programmes in five main areas: humanitarian aid and relief; healthcare and disease control; education and knowledge; innovation and entrepreneurship; and empowering communities. The Foundation carries out more than 1,400 programmes through 33 institutions and initiatives in over 100 countries. It includes, *inter alia*: Dubai Humanitarian, formerly the International Humanitarian City (f. 2003); UAE Food Bank (f. 2017); UAE Water Aid Foundation—Suqia (f. 2015); 1 Billion Meals Endowment (f. 2023); Mohammed Bin Rashid Global Centre for Endowment Consultancy (f. 2016); Noor Dubai Foundation (f. 2008); Al Jalila Foundation (f. 2012, q.v.); Fathers' Endowment (f. 2025); Mohammed Bin Rashid Library Foundation (f. 2016); Mohammed Bin Rashid Al Maktoum Knowledge Foundation (f. 2007); Dubai Future Foundation (f. 2015); Mohammed Bin Rashid School of Government (f. 2005); International Institute for Tolerance (f. 2017); Arab Media Forum (f. 2001); Arab Social Media Influencers Summit (f. 2015); Mohammed Bin Rashid Center for Leadership Development (f. 2003); Arab Hope Makers (f. 2017); Middle East Exchange (f. 2016); and the Food Innovation Hub UAE (f. 2022).

Geographical Area of Activity: International.

Publications: Annual Report; Madrasa.org (e-learning platform).

Finance: Annual expenditure 2,200m. Emirati dirhams (2024).

Board of Trustees: HH Sheikh Muhammad bin Rashid Al Maktoum (Chair.); Hamdan bin Mohammed bin Rashid Al Maktoum (Vice-Chair.).

Principal Staff: Sec.-Gen. Mohammad Al Gergawi; Asst Sec.-Gen. Saeed Al Eter.

Contact Details: POB 21444, 32nd Floor, Dubai World Trade Center 1, Dubai; tel. (14) 423-3444; e-mail info@almaktouminitiatives.org; internet www.almaktouminitiatives.org.

UNITED KINGDOM

CO-ORDINATING BODIES

Association of Charitable Foundations—ACF

Established in 1989 as a member-led association.

Activities: A membership organization for foundations and grantmaking charities based in the United Kingdom. The Association helps members to use their resources effectively, providing expertise, practical advice and advocacy; and offering opportunities for networking and professional development. It has 450 members.

Geographical Area of Activity: UK.

Restrictions: Not a grantmaking organization; does not give individual advice to grantseeking organizations or individuals.

Publications: Annual Report; *Trust & Foundation News*; *Good Practice Guide for Corporate Foundations*.

Finance: Annual income £1.5m., expenditure £1.5m. (31 Dec. 2023).

Board of Trustees: Jessica Brown (Chair.).

Principal Staff: Chief. Exec. Carol Mack.

Contact Details: Toynbee Hall, 28 Commercial St, London E1 6LS; tel. (20) 7255-4499; e-mail acf@acf.org.uk; internet www.acf.org.uk.

Association of Medical Research Charities—AMRC

Established in 1987; a national membership organization.

Activities: Supports medical and health research charities through developing best practice guides, offering training and audit services, and promoting networking and collaboration. The Association has more than 150 members.

Geographical Area of Activity: UK.

Restrictions: UK only; does not fund medical research itself, or assist grant applicants in obtaining grants from member charities.

Publications: Annual Report; newsletter; briefings; policy papers; guidelines; reports.

Finance: Annual income £1.3m., expenditure £1.1m. (31 March 2024).

Executive Council: Dr Louise Wood (Chair.).

Principal Staff: CEO Nicola Perrin.

Contact Details: Churchill House, 35 Red Lion Sq., London WC1R 4SG; tel. (20) 8078-6042; e-mail ceoffice@amrc.org.uk; internet www.amrc.org.uk.

Bond

Established in 1993, as British Overseas NGOs for Development—Bond, by 61 organizations; a network of international development and humanitarian organizations.

Activities: Supports the world's poorest people through promoting the efficiency and effectiveness of voluntary organizations and other institutions. The network: offers networking opportunities for individuals to share expertise and develop their skills; carries out advocacy to influence governments and policymakers; and strengthens member organizations through training, resources and support services. Activities are organized into 31 working groups with almost 3,000 members. It comprises over 350 member organizations; and is a member of the UK Alliance of National Networks for International Development.

Geographical Area of Activity: UK.

Publications: Annual Report; *Network News* (newsletter); briefings; case studies; manuals; reports; toolkits; webinars; blog.

Finance: Annual income £2.7m., expenditure £3.2m. (31 March 2024).

Board of Trustees: Kirsty Smith (Chair.); Nick Waring (Treas.).

Contact Details: Society Bldg, 8 All Saints St, London N1 9RL; tel. (20) 7837-8344; e-mail info@bond.org.uk; internet www.bond.org.uk.

CAF—Charities Aid Foundation

Established in 1924, as part of the National Council of Social Service (NCSS); launched as an independent foundation in 1974, under a Declaration of Trust between the NCSS (now the National Council for Voluntary Organisations, q.v.) and the Trustees of the Foundation. Serves as headquarters for the Global Alliance of the Charities Aid Foundation.

Activities: Works to increase resources available to the voluntary sector. The Foundation operates donor-advised funds for private and corporate donors; manages a payroll deduction scheme; and provides financial, fundraising and advisory services to charities. It runs grantmaking programmes on behalf of other foundations and businesses; publishes research findings and statistics about the voluntary sector; and incorporates the Giving Thought think tank. All surpluses are distributed throughout the sector in grants and loans. Has an office in London and maintains several overseas offices. Operates CAF Bank, which offers banking services for charities and non-profit organizations.

Geographical Area of Activity: Australia, Europe, India, North and South America, Southern Africa, UK.

Restrictions: No grants to individuals.

Publications: Annual Report; *World Giving Index*; *Charity Landscape*; country reports; blog.

Finance: Annual income £1,194.8m., expenditure £1,160.6m. (30 April 2024).

Trustees: Sir Edward Braham (Chair.); Sir Ernest Ryder (Vice-Chair.).

Principal Staff: Chief Exec. Neil Heslop.

Contact Details: 25 Kings Hill Ave, Kings Hill, West Malling ME19 4TA; 30 Old Broad St, London EC2N 1HT; tel. (3000) 123000; e-mail enquiries@cafonline.org; internet www.cafonline.org.

Charities Advisory Trust

Established in 1979 by Dame Hilary Blume as the Charity Trading Advisory Group.

Activities: Aims to redress injustice and inequality through practical approaches. The Trust conducts research on all aspects of charity trading to provide authentic information on the sector and provides information on proposals made by governments, as well as by NGOs, on third sector reform and income generation. It makes charitable donations in areas including: peace and reconciliation projects; medical research, including diabetic prevention and control, prevention of blindness and early detection of cancer; urban tree-planting; and tackling homelessness. Fundraising initiatives include: Card Aid, the Good Gifts Catalogue, Knit for Peace, Peace Oil and the Green Hotel in India.

Geographical Area of Activity: India, UK.

Restrictions: No grants to individuals, large fundraising organizations or to missionary charities; considers grants for any charitable purpose; rarely responds to unsolicited applications.

Publications: Annual Report; *The Charity Shops Handbook*; *Charities, Trading and the Law*; *Trading by Charities: A Statistical Analysis*; blog.

Finance: Annual income £546,506, expenditure £747,471 (30 June 2023).

Trustees: Dame Hilary S. B. Blume (Sec.).

Contact Details: Radius Works, Back Lane, London NW3 1HL; tel. (20) 7794-9835; e-mail people@charitiesadvisorytrust.org.uk; internet www.charitiesadvisorytrust.org.uk.

DEC—Disasters Emergency Committee

Established in 1963 to provide support for relief sector charities in the United Kingdom dealing with the effects of major overseas disasters.

Activities: Proves an accredited national forum for fundraising and a focal point for public response, facilitating co-operation, co-ordination and communication, and ensuring that funds are used effectively and properly. The Committee has a Rapid Response Network of partners, which provides free facilities as and when required, comprising broadcasters, banks, the Post Office, regional and national telephone companies, and a range of organizations in the corporate sector. The 15 organizations that meet the Committee's membership criteria are Action Against Hunger, ActionAid UK, Age International, British Red Cross Society, CAFOD—Catholic Agency for Overseas Development, CARE International, Christian Aid, Concern Worldwide, International Rescue Committee, Islamic Relief, Oxfam, Plan, Save the Children, Tearfund and World Vision (qq.v.).

Geographical Area of Activity: International.

Publications: Annual Report; *DEC Policy Handbook*.

Finance: Annual income £32.9m., expenditure £53.7m. (31 March 2024).

Board of Trustees: Michael Jermey (Chair.); Farmida Bi (Vice-Chair.); Melanie Hind (Hon. Treas.).

Principal Staff: Chief Exec. Saleh Saeed.

Contact Details: 17–21 Wenlock Rd, London N1 7GT; e-mail info@dec.org.uk; internet www.dec.org.uk.

Directory of Social Change

Established in 1975 by Michael Norton, founder of YouthBank UK and co-founder of Changemakers and UnLtd.

Activities: An independent source of information and advocate for international recognition of the voluntary and community sectors worldwide. The organization promotes the voluntary sector through: conducting research; organizing briefings, seminars and conferences, including Charityfair; encouraging voluntary groups to communicate and share information; and campaigning on behalf of the voluntary sector. It conducts training courses on management, fundraising, organizational and personal development, finance, law and communication; and maintains the Funds Online database, containing more than 8,000 entries.

Geographical Area of Activity: UK.

Publications: Annual Report; newsletter; *The Directory of Grant Making Trusts*; *The Guide to New Trusts*; books; guides; handbooks; blog.

Finance: Annual income £1.5m., expenditure £1.6m. (31 Dec. 2023).

Board of Trustees: William Butler (Chair.).

Principal Staff: Chief Exec. Debra Allcock Tyler.

Contact Details: 1st floor, 10 Queen St Pl., London EC4R 1BE; tel. (20) 4526-5995; e-mail cs@dsc.org.uk; internet www.dsc.org.uk.

Global Dialogue

Established in 2006, as Global Dialogue for Human Rights & Social Change, by Andrew Puddephatt, former Gen. Sec. of Liberty, a civil liberties and human rights advocacy group.

Activities: Promotes human rights worldwide. Main initiatives include: Ariadne (f. 2009), a European network of funders and philanthropists in 22 countries who support human rights and social change; the Funders' Initiative for Civil Society, which in 2021 established the Global Initiative on Civic Space and Security; Migration Exchange, an informal network of funders working to improve the lives of immigrants and host communities in the UK; the Philanthropy for Social Justice and Peace hub; and International Education Funders' Group, a network of funders focused on basic education in low- and middle- income countries.

Geographical Area of Activity: International.

Publications: Annual Report; newsletters; *Rethinking Civic Space*; policy briefings; reports; blog.

Finance: Annual income £6.1m., expenditure £5.2m. (30 April 2024).

Board of Trustees: Rob Abercrombie (Chair.); Gabriel Ng (Vice-Chair.).
Principal Staff: Exec. Dir Esther Hughes.
Contact Details: First Floor, 10 Queen St Pl., London EC4R 1BE; tel. (7494) 152877; e-mail info@global-dialogue.org; internet global-dialogue.org.

INTRAC
Established in 1991; formerly known as the International NGO Training and Research Centre.
Activities: Strengthens the effectiveness of civil society to tackle poverty and inequality, helping people to organize in forms that are effective, sustainable and legitimate in their own societies. The organization develops practical solutions and promotes critical thinking, combining consultancy, capacity development, training, research, monitoring, evaluation and learning.
Geographical Area of Activity: Worldwide.
Restrictions: Not a grantmaking organization.
Publications: Annual Report; *INTRAC News* (newsletter); *Praxis Series Papers*; dialogue papers; reports; blog.
Finance: Annual income £1.6m., expenditure £1.4m. (31 March 2024).
Board of Trustees: Yvonne Taylor (Chair.); David-Huw Owen (Deputy Chair.); Ashley Green-Thompson (Treas.).
Principal Staff: Chief Exec. Dr Kate Newman.
Contact Details: The Wheelhouse, Angel Ct, 81 St Clements St, Oxford OX4 1AW; tel. (1865) 201851; e-mail info@intrac.org; internet www.intrac.org.

NCVO—National Council for Voluntary Organisations
Established in 1919 as the National Council of Social Services with a £1,000 legacy from Edward Vivian Birchall, who was killed during the First World War.
Activities: Represents and supports voluntary organizations, charities, community groups and social enterprises. The Council researches and analyses the voluntary sector; and campaigns on issues affecting the sector, such as the role of voluntary organizations in public service delivery and the future of local government. It provides information, advice and consultancy to people and organizations working in or with the voluntary sector; organizes networking and training events; and manages and facilitates a wide range of forums and networks for staff and volunteers working in specific areas such as policy, planning, ICT, membership, publishing and public service delivery. Has more than 17,000 members.
Geographical Area of Activity: UK.
Publications: Annual Report; e-newsletter; *UK Civil Society Almanac*; reports; briefing papers; toolkits; books.
Finance: Annual income £12.3m., expenditure £8.1m. (31 March 2024).
Trustee Board: Dr Priya Singh (Chair.); Emily Agius (Vice-Chair.); Paul Breckell (Hon. Treas.).
Principal Staff: Dir Sarah Elliott.
Contact Details: Society Bldg, 8 All Saints St, London N1 9RL; tel. (20) 7713-6161; e-mail ncvo@ncvo.org.uk; internet www.ncvo.org.uk.

Scotland's International Development Alliance
Established in 2000 as the Network of International Development Organisations in Scotland (NIDOS); present name adopted in 2017.
Activities: Supports members to build capacity, represents their interests and raises awareness in Scotland about international development. Members include over 100 NGOs, academic institutions, companies, social enterprises and public sector bodies operating in more than 100 countries.
Geographical Area of Activity: Scotland.
Restrictions: Members must be based or work in Scotland.
Publications: Annual Report; newsletter.
Finance: Annual income £418,014, expenditure £405,512 (31 March 2024).
Board of Trustees: Cathy Ratcliff (Chair.); Fiona Greig (Treas.).
Principal Staff: Chief Exec. Frances Guy.
Contact Details: CBC House, 24 Canning St, Edinburgh EH3 8EG; tel. (131) 281-0897; e-mail admin@intdevalliance.scot; internet www.intdevalliance.scot.

Scottish Council for Voluntary Organisations—SCVO
Established in 1944.
Activities: Members comprise 3,768 Scottish charities, voluntary organizations and social enterprises. The Council supports member organizations, lobbies the Government on policy issues, promotes digital skills and offers training. It operates the Funding Scotland service, providing information on grants, loans, prizes and other funding support; and Community Jobs Scotland, an employability programme creating job opportunities in the voluntary sector for young people aged 16–29 years.
Geographical Area of Activity: Scotland.
Publications: Annual Report; members' bulletin; *Third Force News*; *Coronavirus Third Sector Bulletin*.
Finance: Annual income £7.5m., expenditure £13.1m. (31 March 2024).
Board of Trustees: Richard Jennings (Convener); Farha Jamadar (Treas.).
Principal Staff: Chief Exec. Anna Fowlie.
Contact Details: Caledonian Exchange, 19A Canning St, Edinburgh EH3 8EG; tel. (131) 474-8000; e-mail enquiries@scvo.org.uk; internet www.scvo.org.uk.

South West International Development Network—SWIDN
Established in 2017; an umbrella organization.
Activities: Supports members working to prevent or relieve poverty worldwide and to achieve the UN Sustainable Development Goals. The Network builds the capacity of charitable and voluntary organizations through organizing working groups, training sessions and networking events. It has more than 80 members, comprising non-profit organizations, businesses, foundations, academic institutions and consultants.
Geographical Area of Activity: UK (primarily South-West).
Restrictions: Not a grantmaking organization.
Publications: Annual Report; newsletter; funding sources update.
Finance: Annual income £38,904, expenditure £48,616 (31 Dec. 2023).
Board of Trustees: Frances Hill, Rachel Haynes (Co-Chair.); Stuart Davis (Treas.).
Principal Staff: Exec. Dir Hannah Stevenson Doornbos.
Contact Details: c/o Future Leap, The Old Chapel, 16 Oakfield Rd, Clifton, Bristol BS8 2AP; tel. 7805363772; e-mail info@swidn.org.uk; internet www.swidn.org.uk.

Start Network
Established in 2010, as the Consortium of British Humanitarian Agencies, by 15 agencies; present name adopted in 2012.
Activities: Comprises the Start Network charity and Start Programmes team. Programmes include: the Start Fund (f. 2014), which fills gaps in humanitarian funding for small- to medium-scale crises and during spikes in chronic emergencies; Start Fund Bangladesh (f. 2017) for local and national NGOs; and anticipation and risk financing for civil society responders. Five Start Network Hubs, comprising local, national and international organizations, operate in the Democratic Republic of the Congo, Guatemala, India, the

Pacific region and Pakistan. Network members include 134 national and international NGOs, with 7,000 partner organizations, operating in more than 200 countries.

Geographical Area of Activity: International.

Publications: Annual Report; newsletter; Crisis Response Summaries; Network Directory (online); *Start Fund Handbook*; learning materials.

Finance: Annual income £22.0m., expenditure £16.5m. (31 Dec. 2023).

Board of Trustees: Sanjayan Srikanthan (Chair.); Glyn Isherwood (Treas.).

Principal Staff: CEO Christina Bennett.

Contact Details: Albert House, 256–260 Old St, London EC1V 9DD; tel. (20) 3848-3937; e-mail info@startnetwork.org; internet startnetwork.org.

UK Community Foundations—UKCF

Established in 1991 as the Community Foundation Network (CFN); present name adopted in 2013.

Activities: Membership body supporting 47 accredited Community Foundations operating in the United Kingdom. The organization partners with the Government, large charities, businesses and infrastructure companies.

Geographical Area of Activity: UK.

Restrictions: Not a grantmaking organization.

Publications: Annual Report; newsletter; *Philanthropy Advice Framework*; case studies.

Finance: Annual income £13.0m., expenditure £13.1m. (31 March 2024).

Board of Trustees: Lord Dr Michael Hastings of Scarisbrick (Pres.); Andrew Tuggey (Chair.); Tom Van Oss, Michelle Cooper (Co-Vice-Chair.).

Principal Staff: CEO Emma de Closset.

Contact Details: Northgate Business Centre, 38–40 Northgate, Newark NG24 1EZ; tel. (20) 7713-9326; e-mail info@ukcommunityfoundations.org; internet www.ukcommunityfoundations.org.

FOUNDATIONS AND NON-PROFITS

A. M. Qattan Foundation

Established in 1993 by Abdel Mohsin Al-Qattan, co-founder of the Al-Hani Construction and Trading company, the Institute for Palestine Studies and Taawon (qq.v).

Activities: Advances the education and cultural development of, and about, Arabs in general and Palestinians in particular, with a focus on children, teachers and young artists. The Foundation carries out activities in four main areas: educational research and development; culture and the arts; the Child Centre in Gaza, which offers information and recreational services, culture and science activities for children and their families, and has a library containing more than 100,000 books; and a public programme of curated cultural events. Activities are mainly carried out in Palestine, but also in Lebanon through Selat: Links Through the Arts, and in the United Kingdom through the Mosaic Rooms non-profit bookshop and art gallery. It has offices in London, Ramallah and Gaza City (Palestinian Territories).

Geographical Area of Activity: Lebanon, Palestinian Territories, UK.

Publications: Annual Report; e-newsletter (6 a year); *Young Artist of the Year Award* (catalogue); research reports; translations in the field of education; children's books; *Rua Tarbawiyyah* ('Educational Outlooks', quarterly journal); Arabic literary books resulting from the Young Writer of the Year Award; other publications.

Finance: Annual income £2.4m., expenditure £8.3m. (31 Dec. 2023).

Board of Trustees: Dr Najwa Al-Qattan (Chair.).

Principal Staff: Gen. Man. Fidaa Touma.

Contact Details: Tower House, 226 Cromwell Rd, London SW5 0SW; tel. (20) 7370-9990; e-mail info@qattanfoundation.org; internet www.qattanfoundation.org.

A. S. Hornby Educational Trust

Founded in 1961 for the advancement of the English language, and its teaching and learning as a foreign language.

Activities: Provides scholarships (approximately 10 a year) for international students to study Master's degree courses at British universities and for senior English language specialists from outside the United Kingdom to study teaching English as a foreign language; and funds regional workshops for teachers of English. The Trust collaborates with the British Council (q.v.).

Geographical Area of Activity: International.

Finance: Annual income £312,370, expenditure £534,093 (31 March 2024).

Trustees: Harry Kuchah Kuchah (Chair.); John Whitehead (Deputy Chair.); Anita Manek (Treas.).

Contact Details: c/o Moore Kingston Smith LLP, Orbital House, 20 Eastern Rd, Romford RM1 3PJ; tel. (1708) 759759; e-mail enquiries@hornby-trust.org.uk; internet www.hornby-trust.org.uk.

Action for Children

Founded in 1869 by Thomas Bowman Stephenson, a Methodist minister, and formerly known as NCH (National Children's Home); works in partnership with the Methodist Church. Present name adopted in 2008.

Activities: Helps children and young people suffering because of poverty, disability, abuse, neglect and social exclusion. The organization campaigns for policy changes to benefit children and young people. Activities include: ending child poverty and social exclusion; providing safeguards for children and young people at risk of abuse; promoting education and health; preventing youth crime and homelessness; improving the quality of life for children in care; foster care; family centres and residential homes; mediation services; and ensuring safe use of the internet for children. It runs short-break projects, residential centres and community centres. Has offices in Belfast, Cardiff, Edinburgh and London.

Geographical Area of Activity: UK.

Publications: Annual Report; newsletter; information guides; policy briefings; research reports; blog.

Finance: Annual income £155.3m., expenditure £161.0m. (31 March 2024).

Council of Trustees: Sarika Patel (Chair.).

Principal Staff: Chief Exec. Paul Carberry.

Contact Details: 3 The Boulevard, Ascot Rd, Watford WD18 8AG; tel. (1923) 361500; e-mail ask.us@actionforchildren.org.uk; internet www.actionforchildren.org.uk.

Aga Khan Foundation UK

Established in 1973 by HH the Aga Khan to promote social development in less-developed countries of Asia and Africa; an agency of the Aga Khan Development Network (q.v.).

Activities: Funds organizations and programmes, principally in less-developed countries. The Foundation offers grants to institutions, promoting community self-help projects, scholarships and fellowships, conferences and publications. It operates programmes in agriculture and food security; civil society strengthening; climate resilience; early childhood development; education; health and nutrition; and work and enterprise to improve the quality of life. It also promotes skills development, training and technical exchanges internationally. Active in 18 countries.

Geographical Area of Activity: International.

Restrictions: Does not accept unsolicited applications.

Publications: Annual Report; newsletter; project briefings; information sheets; project evaluation reports.

UNITED KINGDOM

Finance: Annual income £58.8m., expenditure £58.1m. (31 Dec. 2023).

National Committee: Mahmood H. Ahmed (Chair.), Abyd Karmali (Vice-Chair.); Habib Motani (Sec.).

Principal Staff: CEO Dr Matt Reed.

Contact Details: Aga Khan Centre, 10 Handyside St, London N1C 4DN; tel. (20) 7383-9085; e-mail front.office@akdn.org; internet www.akf.org.uk.

Age International

Established in 2012 as a subsidiary of Age UK (f. 2009) to carry out its international work; a member of the HelpAge International network and Disasters Emergency Committee (qq.v.).

Activities: Supports older people and their families in developing countries. The organization works to provide older people with appropriate healthcare; offers free cataract operations; supports independence at home by providing free prescription glasses, adjustable walking sticks and hearing aids; protects older people's rights, combating ageism, violence and abuse; empowers older women; and ensures older people receive age-appropriate humanitarian relief during conflicts, crises and natural disasters. It establishes pension schemes; supports older people to start their own businesses or re-establish livelihoods after emergencies; and provides direct cash transfers to the most vulnerable. Works in more than 25 countries.

Geographical Area of Activity: East and South-East Asia, Central and South-Eastern Europe, Eastern Europe, Middle East, Russian Federation and Central Asia, South Asia, sub-Saharan Africa.

Publications: Annual Report; Annual Review; *Older Citizen Monitoring Report*; factsheets.

Finance: Annual income £22.0m., expenditure £21.8m. (31 March 2023).

Board of Trustees: Ann Keeling (Chair.).

Principal Staff: Man. Dir Alison Marshall.

Contact Details: 1 America Sq., 7th Floor, 17 Crosswall, London EC3N 2LB; tel. (800) 032-0699; e-mail contact@ageinternational.org.uk; internet www.ageinternational.org.uk.

AKO Foundation

Established in 2013 by Nicolai Tangen, founder and CEO of AKO Capital, an investment advisory firm.

Activities: Supports charities working in the fields of the arts, education, wellbeing of young people, and climate change mitigation through provision of grants. AKO Capital staff may nominate charities to support through the AKO Give Back initiative. The Foundation supported the establishment of the AKO Kunststiftelse (f. 2016), a foundation that collects Nordic modern art for display in the Kunstsilo in Kristiansand, Norway (opened in 2024).

Geographical Area of Activity: Developing nations, Norway, UK.

Restrictions: Does not accept unsolicited applications.

Publications: Annual Report.

Finance: Total income £117.4m., expenditure £46.7m. (31 Dec. 2023).

Principal Staff: Chief Exec. Philip Lawford.

Contact Details: 1 Newman St, London W1T 1PB; tel. (20) 7070-2400; e-mail enquiries@akofoundation.org; internet www.akofoundation.org.

The Al-Khoei Benevolent Foundation

Established in 1989 by Grand Ayatullah (marj'a) Sayyid Abul Qasim Musawi Al-Khoei, a Shi'a Islamic scholar.

Activities: Aims to advance the Islamic religion and prevent or relieve poverty through collecting and distributing religious dues. The Foundation operates schools, a nursery, a mosque and a library; organizes religious and social meetings, and interfaith activities; and provides advice on good practice and capacity building to mosques and Islamic teaching institutions. Has an office in New York.

Geographical Area of Activity: England, Wales, Iraq.

Publications: Annual Report; *Dialogue* (in English); *Al-Ghadeer* (in Arabic).

Finance: Annual income £2.4m., expenditure £2.7m. (31 Aug. 2023).

Principal Staff: Sec.-Gen. Seyed Saheb Khoei.

Contact Details: Stone Hall, Chevening Rd, London NW6 6TN; tel. (20) 7372-4049; e-mail info@al-khoei.org; internet www.al-khoei.org.

The Alan Turing Institute

Established in 2015 by five universities and the UK Engineering and Physical Sciences Research Council as the national institute for data science and subsequently artificial intelligence; a collaborative hub for 13 universities.

Activities: Undertakes applied cross-disciplinary research in data science and artificial intelligence to address major challenges in science, society and the economy. Main programme areas include: advancing knowledge in science and the humanities; climate action; data-centric engineering; data ethics; fostering innovation in government; high-performance computing and cybersecurity; optimizing healthcare; smart cities; and understanding the economy. The Institute offers teaching and training, doctoral studentships and various fellowships. It organizes Interest Groups to share ideas and knowledge and foster research collaboration and projects.

Geographical Area of Activity: UK.

Publications: Annual Report; newsletter (monthly).

Finance: Annual income £45m., expenditure £53m. (31 March 2024).

Board of Trustees: Douglas Gurr (Chair.).

Principal Staff: CEO Jean Innes.

Contact Details: 1st Floor, British Library, 96 Euston Rd, London NW1 2DB; tel. (20) 3862-3352; e-mail info@turing.ac.uk; internet www.turing.ac.uk.

Allen Lane Foundation

Established in 1966 by Sir Allen Lane, the founder of Penguin Books publishers.

Activities: Supports organizations that work with: asylum seekers and refugees; gypsies and travellers; migrant communities; offenders and former offenders; older people; people experiencing mental health problems; and people experiencing violence or abuse. The Foundation gives priority to projects that will make a long-term difference. Grants are typically of between £5,000 and £6,000, up to a maximum of £15,000.

Geographical Area of Activity: UK.

Restrictions: Does not make grants where other sources of funding are more likely to be available than for the Foundation's priority areas; or where small grants are unlikely to make a significant difference.

Publications: Annual Report.

Finance: Annual income £707,162, expenditure £964,892 (31 March 2024).

Trustees: Fredrica Teale (Chair.).

Principal Staff: Dir Gill Aconley.

Contact Details: 90 The Mount, York YO24 1AR; tel. (1904) 613223; e-mail info@allenlane.org.uk; internet www.allenlane.org.uk.

Alzheimer's Society

Founded in 1979 by Dr Anne Hunter and Brian Hunter.

Activities: Provides advice and guidance to patients and carers dealing with Alzheimer's and dementia. Funds research and runs fundraising campaigns. Sister organizations Alzheimer Scotland and Alzheimer's Society of Ireland are also in operation.

Geographical Area of Activity: England, Wales, Northern Ireland.

Finance: Total income £131.4m., expenditure £138.2m. (31 March 2024).

Trustees: Suzi Leather (Chair.); Prof. Hugh McKenna (Vice-Chair.).

Principal Staff: Chief Exec. Kate Lee.

Contact Details: Plumer House, Suite 2, 1st Floor, East Wing, Tailyour Rd, Plymouth PL6 5FS; tel. (330) 3330804; e-mail governance@alzheimers.org.uk; internet www.alzheimers.org.uk.

Amnesty International

Founded in 1961 by lawyer Peter Benenson and others to secure throughout the world the provisions of the UN Universal Declaration of Human Rights (1948) and other internationally recognized human rights instruments; the International Secretariat is organized into two legal entities: Amnesty International Ltd and Amnesty International Charity Limited.

Activities: Promotes the protection and advancement of human rights. The organization carries out, commissions and publishes research on human rights around the world; raises awareness about human rights issues; lobbies governments to change oppressive laws; provides relief to victims of human rights abuses and violations; and supports human rights education and activism. It operates through a network of regional offices in Hong Kong, Iran, Israel/Palestinian Territories, Kenya, Lebanon, Mexico, Senegal, South Africa, Thailand and Tunisia; and has Sections in more than 60 countries.

Geographical Area of Activity: International.

Publications: Annual Report; *Amnesty International Report* (annual); *Wire Magazine* (2 a month); thematic and regional reports on human rights issues; Human Rights Academy (online learning resources).

Finance: Annual income €370m., expenditure €383m. (2023).

International Board: Bernadita Bock (Vice-Chair.); Dawana Wright (Int. Treas.).

Principal Staff: Sec.-Gen. Agnès Callamard; Deputy Sec.-Gen. Kathryn Tomlinson.

Contact Details: c/o Amnesty International Charity, Peter Benenson House, 1 Easton St, London WC1X 0DW; tel. (20) 7413-5500; e-mail contactus@amnesty.org; internet www.amnesty.org.

Andrews Charitable Trust—ACT

Founded in 1965 by Cecil Jackson-Cole, co-founder of commercial property group Andrews & Partners and Oxfam International (q.v.); formerly known as the Phyllis Trust and later World in Need.

Activities: Supports initiatives that are innovative, replicable and sustainable. The Trust supports activities in three main areas: housing and poverty, providing safe, decent and affordable housing that promotes inclusive communities and, following disasters or conflict, to bridge the gap between emergency shelter and permanent housing; Christian community grants, offering small grants to individuals and organizations; and providing accommodation for young people looking for work. The Christian Book Promotion Trust is a sister organization.

Geographical Area of Activity: International.

Restrictions: Does not accept unsolicited applications.

Publications: Annual Report.

Finance: Annual income £20.3m., expenditure £22.4m. (31 Dec. 2023).

Board of Trustees: Ami Davis (Chair.).

Principal Staff: Exec. Dir Siân Edwards.

Contact Details: The Clockhouse, Bath Hill, Keynsham, Bristol BS31 1HL; tel. (117) 9461834; e-mail info@andrewscharitabletrust.org.uk; internet www.andrewscharitabletrust.org.uk.

Anglo American Foundation

Established in 2005 by Anglo American PLC, a mining company.

Activities: Promotes sustainable livelihoods in the communities where the company operates. The Foundation funds projects in the areas of education and training, international and London-based community development, HIV/AIDS and welfare, and the environment. It is affiliated with the Anglo American Chairman's Fund in South Africa.

Geographical Area of Activity: Australia, Botswana, Brazil, Canada, Chile, Colombia, Peru, South Africa, UK, Zimbabwe.

Restrictions: Grants only to registered charities; no unsolicited applications.

Publications: Trustees' Report.

Finance: Annual income £3.8m., expenditure £5.9m. (31 Dec. 2023).

Board of Trustees: Jon Samuel (Chair.).

Principal Staff: CEO Michael Mapstone.

Contact Details: 17 Charterhouse St, London EC1N 6RA; tel. (20) 7968-8888; e-mail aagf@angloamerican.com; internet www.angloamericangroupfoundation.org.

Anti-Slavery International

Founded in 1839; known as the Anti-Slavery Society for the Protection of Human Rights until 1990.

Activities: Aims to eliminate slavery and forced labour in all their forms through: research and publishing information about all forms of slavery throughout the world; advocacy and generating greater awareness of such abuses; campaigning nationally and internationally; and working with local partners to help the victims of human rights injustices. The organization has consultative status with ECOSOC, and has members worldwide. The annual Anti-Slavery Award was established in 1991.

Geographical Area of Activity: International.

Restrictions: Not a grantmaking organization.

Publications: Annual Review; *Anti-Slavery Reporter* (newsletter, 2 a year); various other publications on issues including bonded, forced and child labour.

Finance: Annual income £5.0m., expenditure £4.4m. (31 March 2024).

Board of Trustees: Sunil Sheth (Chair.); Peter Freedman (Treas.).

Principal Staff: CEO Helen Moulinos.

Contact Details: The Foundry, 17 Oval Way, London SE11 5RR; tel. (20) 7737-9434; e-mail supporter@antislavery.org; internet www.antislavery.org.

Archie Sherman Charitable Trust

Founded in 1967, by property developer Archie Sherman, to support Israeli causes, in particular Holocaust survivors; shares an administration with the Archie Sherman Cardiff Foundation.

Activities: Operates nationally and internationally, making small and large grants in the areas of education and training, overseas aid, arts and culture, health and for general charitable purposes.

Geographical Area of Activity: International.

Publications: Annual Report.

Finance: Annual income £1.4m., expenditure £1.2m. (5 April 2024).

Trustees: Michael J. Gee (Chair.).

Contact Details: 274A Kentish Town Rd, London NW5 2AA; tel. (20) 7493-1904; e-mail trust@sherman.co.uk.

Ark

Established in 2002, as ARK—Absolute Return for Kids, by Arpad Busson, a financier.

Activities: Operates a network of 39 academy schools in the United Kingdom. Through Ark Ventures, the organization incubates initiatives that address issues affecting education and society. Examples include the Education Partnerships Group, a non-profit consultancy that supports governments in low- and middle-income countries to strengthen education systems; and the Global Schools Forum, a network of nonprofit, for-profit and faith-based organizations involved in education, comprising 61 members in 50 countries. Has an office in New York, USA.

Geographical Area of Activity: Côte d'Ivoire, Ghana, India, Kenya, South Africa, Uganda, UK, USA.

Publications: Annual Report; newsletter.

Finance: Annual income £22.1m., expenditure £28.7m. (31 Aug. 2023).

Board of Trustees: Tina Alexandrou (Chair.).

Principal Staff: Chief Exec. Lucy Heller.

Contact Details: 1EdCity, EdCity Walk, London W12 7TF; tel. (20) 3116-0800; e-mail info@arkonline.org; internet arkonline.org.

Art Fund—National Art Collections Fund

Founded in 1903 by a group of artists and patrons.

Activities: Operates in the field of the arts, through grants or bequests to regional and national institutions for the acquisition of works of art of national and historical importance. The Fund campaigns on behalf of museums and galleries, particularly on issues such as free admission to national collections and funding for acquisitions, as well as promoting art to a wider audience through initiatives such as the National Art Pass and the multi-platform Art Guide. The Art Fund Museum of the Year prize awards £100,000 to an outstanding winner and £15,000 to each finalist.

Geographical Area of Activity: UK.

Publications: Annual Report; newsletter; *Review* (annual); *Art Quarterly* (magazine).

Finance: Annual income £16.3m., expenditure £19.4m. (31 Dec. 2023).

Board of Trustees: Sandy Nairne (Chair.); Jeremy Palmer (Treas.).

Principal Staff: Dir Dr Jenny Waldman.

Contact Details: 2 Granary Sq., King's Cross, London N1C 4BH; POB 4387, Chippenham SN15 9NY; tel. (20) 7225-4800; e-mail info@artfund.org; internet www.artfund.org.

Arts Council England

Established in 1946 by Royal Charter; the national development agency for the arts in England.

Activities: Operates in the field of the arts. The Council distributes national lottery and government funds to artists, arts organizations, museums and libraries. Funding programmes include Artsmark, a national arts award for schools; and National Lottery Project Grants, an open access programme for arts, museums and libraries projects, supporting individual artists and community and cultural organizations.

Geographical Area of Activity: England.

Publications: Annual Report; newsletter (monthly); information sheets; advice and guidance publications; blog.

Finance: Annual income £803.1m., expenditure £756.3m. (31 March 2024).

National Council: Sir Nicholas Serota (Chair.).

Principal Staff: Chief Exec. Darren Henley; Deputy Chief Execs Laura Dyer, Simon Mellor.

Contact Details: 21 Stephen St, London W1T 1LN; tel. (161) 9344317; e-mail enquiries@artscouncil.org.uk; internet www.artscouncil.org.uk.

Asthma + Lung UK

Asthma + Lung UK was established in February 2022, following the merger of Asthma UK and the British Lung Foundation in 2020 to form the Asthma UK and British Lung Foundatoin Partnership. Asthma UK was established in 1989 by the merger of the Asthma Research Council (f. 1927) and the Friends of Asthma Research Council (f. 1972).

Activities: Asthma + Lung prioritize lung health through better understanding, research, treatment and support. Activities include research, campaigning, and offering advice and support to those suffering with asthma or lung diseases. It advocates for reducing asthma prescription prices and for controlling pollution levels. It researches the impact of COVID-19 on the lungs. It also raises awareness to reduce healthcare inequalities that can have an effect on lung health.

Geographical Area of Activity: UK.

Publications: Annual Report.

Finance: Annual income £14.7m., expenditure £14.9m. (30 June 2023).

Board of Trustees: Tamara Ingram (Chair.); Prof. Ian Hall (Vice-Chair.).

Principal Staff: CEO Sarah Sleet.

Contact Details: The White Chapel Building, 10 Whitechapel High Street, London, E1 8QS; tel. (300) 222-5800; e-mail info@asthmaandlung.org.uk; internet www.asthmaandlung.org.uk.

Aurora Trust

Established in 1989 as the Ashden Trust for general charitable purposes; one of the Sainsbury Family Charitable Trusts (q.v.), which share a common administration.

Activities: Makes grants in five priority areas: sustainable farming; connecting people with nature; avoiding deforestation; people at risk of homelessness; and divestment from fossil fuels. The Trust collaborates with the Mark Leonard Trust, the J. J. Charitable Trust and the Tedworth Trust on the Climate Change Collaboration, supporting projects to reduce carbon dioxide emissions. It also supports Ashden—climate solutions in action, a separate charity that works in the fields of sustainable energy and climate change.

Geographical Area of Activity: Africa, Asia, UK.

Restrictions: Does not accept unsolicited applications.

Publications: Annual Report; *The Ashden Directory*; reports.

Finance: Annual income £2.1m., expenditure £2.7m. (5 April 2024).

Board of Trustees: Sarah Butler-Sloss (Chair.).

Principal Staff: Trust Exec. Sian Ferguson; Deputy Trust Exec. Darren Chin.

Contact Details: c/o Sainsbury Family Charitable Trusts, The Peak, 5 Wilton Rd, London SW1V 1AP; tel. (20) 7410-0330; e-mail auroratrust@sfct.org.uk; internet auroratrust.org.uk.

Baring Foundation

Established in 1969 as a corporate foundation of Barings Bank, which was bought by ING in 1995.

Activities: Works to protect human rights and promote inclusion. The Foundation makes grants in three main areas: arts (arts and creativity for people with mental health problems); international development (supporting LGBTI civil society in sub-Saharan Africa); and strengthening UK civil society (supporting the use of the law and human rights based approaches by civil society organisations to bring about positive social change).

Geographical Area of Activity: sub-Saharan Africa, UK.

Restrictions: Does not accept unsolicited applications.

Publications: Annual Report; newsletter; reports; blogs.

Finance: Total income £4.0m., expenditure £5.4m. (31 Dec. 2023).

Trustees: Lucy de Groot (Chair.).

Principal Staff: Dir and Sec. David Cutler; Deputy Dir David Sampson.

Contact Details: 8–10 Moorgate, London EC2R 6DA; e-mail baring.foundation@ing.com; internet www.baringfoundation.org.uk.

Barnardo's

Established in 1867 by Dr Thomas Barnardo, a doctor who set up a 'ragged school' in the East End of London.

Activities: Provides guidance, support and care to young people and their families. Programmes include: fostering and adoption; providing social welfare services for families; offering young people practical and emotional support; protecting children from harm; and empowering young people and involving them in decisionmaking. The organization carries out research and advocacy. It has regional offices throughout the United Kingdom. Independent affiliates operate in Australia, Ireland and New Zealand.

Geographical Area of Activity: UK.

Publications: Annual Report; newsletter; What Works? (series); policy and research documents; teaching and training publications; toolkits.

Finance: Annual income £326.1m., expenditure £335.7m. (31 March 2024).

Board of Trustees: Mark Wood (Chair.); Penny Thompson (Deputy Chair.).

Principal Staff: CEO Lynn Perry.

Contact Details: Tanners Lane, Barkingside, Ilford IG6 1QG; tel. (20) 8550-8822; e-mail info@barnardos.org.uk; internet www.barnardos.org.uk.

Bat Conservation Trust

Established in 1990; an umbrella organization.

Activities: Works locally and across Europe to secure bat populations, carrying out monitoring and scientific research programmes. The Trust's activities include: the National Bat Monitoring Programme; biodiversity policy, consultation and advocacy; investigating bat-related crime; and providing guidance and training on bat conservation for professionals such as builders, landowners and woodland managers. Annually, it offers the Vincent Weir Scientific Award to new researchers at UK institutions for research on bat conservation biology; the Kate Barlow Award to postgraduate students anywhere in the world for research on bat conservation; and the Pete Guest Award for practical contributions to bat conservation. Supports over 100 local groups and 6,000 members; runs the National Bat Helpline; and maintains a photographic and sound library.

Geographical Area of Activity: Europe.

Restrictions: Award applicants must be PhD or MSc students.

Publications: Annual Review; leaflets (in English and Welsh); e-bulletin; teaching materials; guidelines; technical guides.

Finance: Annual revenue £2.7m., expenditure £2.3m. (31 March 2024).

Board of Trustees: Jean Matthews (Chair.); Steve Roe (Vice-Chair.); Helen Slinger (Treas.); Annika Binet (Hon. Sec.).

Principal Staff: Pres. Chris Packham; Chief Exec. Kit Stoner.

Contact Details: Cloisters House, Studio 15, Cloisters Business Centre, 8 Battersea Park Rd, London SW8 4BG; tel. (20) 7820-7171; e-mail enquiries@bats.org.uk; internet www.bats.org.uk.

BBC Children in Need

Established in 1980 as a telethon.

Activities: Works to give children a safe, happy and secure childhood and the opportunity to reach their full potential. The organization makes grants to projects that focus on disadvantaged children and young people. Programmes include: Main Grants, worth more than £10,000 per year for up to three years; Small Grants of up to £10,000 per year for up to three years; and Emergency Essentials, meeting the basic needs of children, young people and families with children who are living with financial, health and social difficulties, and providing other items and services that are critical to their wellbeing.

Geographical Area of Activity: UK.

Restrictions: Grants only to not-for-profit organizations working with disadvantaged children and young people aged under 18 years living in the UK.

Publications: Annual Report; newsletters.

Finance: Annual income £54.9m., expenditure £49.2m. (30 June 2024).

Trustees: James Fairclough (Interim Chair.).

Principal Staff: Chief Exec. Simon Antrobus.

Contact Details: 4th Floor, Dock House, Greater Manchester M50 2LH; tel. (345) 609-0015; e-mail pudsey@bbc.co.uk; internet www.bbcchildreninneed.co.uk.

BBC Media Action

Established in 1992 by the BBC (British Broadcasting Corporation) as the BBC Marshall Plan of the Mind Trust; name changed to the BBC World Service Trust in 1999. Present name adopted in 2011.

Activities: Uses television and radio programmes, digital media and face-to-face dialogue to build knowledge and change behaviour, working with development policymakers, academics and practitioners. Main programme areas include: addressing the needs and voices of women and girls, people living with disabilities and young people; boosting the resilience and economic security of people affected by climate change; helping people to make informed decisions about their health, supporting health workers and building more effective health systems; providing accurate, balanced and trusted information for people to understand their rights and freedoms and hold leaders to account; strengthening editorial, production and management capacity in public-interest media; and supporting people affected by emergencies, providing information and humanitarian training. The organization works in more than 30 countries.

Geographical Area of Activity: Central Asia, Eastern Europe, Middle East and North Africa, South Asia, South-East Asia, sub-Saharan Africa.

Publications: Annual Report; newsletter; approach papers; brochures; case studies; conference reports; policy briefings; working papers; *My Media Action* films.

Finance: Annual income £32.0m., expenditure £33.8m. (31 March 2024).

Board of Trustees: Francesca Unsworth (Chair.); Sir Myles Wickstead (Vice-Chair.).

Principal Staff: CEO Simon Bishop.

Contact Details: Broadcasting House, Portland Pl., London W1A 1AA; tel. (20) 8008-2026; e-mail media.action@bbc.co.uk; internet www.bbc.co.uk/mediaaction.

Beit Trust

Founded in 1906 by the will of Alfred Beit, a financier and director of the British South Africa Company.

Activities: Works in the fields of conservation, education, healthcare and emergency relief. The Trust operates a secondary school bursary scheme and postgraduate scholarships scheme for students from Malawi, Zambia and Zimbabwe to study at universities in the United Kingdom or South Africa; and awards bursaries to medical students from the UK to spend 6–8 weeks at hospitals in Malawi, Zambia and Zimbabwe. It offers infrastructure grants, worth up to £50,000, to schools, health centres and hospitals; and funded the establishment of two nature conservancies in Southern Zimbabwe. In 2009 the Beit Memorial Fellowships for Medical Research transferred all its undertakings to the Wellcome Trust (q.v.). The Trust has an office in Harare, Zimbabwe.

UNITED KINGDOM

Geographical Area of Activity: Malawi, Zambia, Zimbabwe.
Restrictions: No grants to undergraduates.
Publications: Annual Report.
Finance: Annual income £3.0m., expenditure £3.9m. (31 Dec. 2023).
Trustees: Alex Duncan (Chair.).
Contact Details: Beit House, Grove Rd, Woking GU21 5JB; tel. (1483) 772575; e-mail enquiries@beittrust.org.uk; internet www.beittrust.org.uk.

BirdLife International

Founded in 1922 as the International Council for Bird Preservation; renamed BirdLife International in 1993.
Activities: A worldwide partnership of organizations working for the diversity of all life through the conservation of birds and their habitats. The organization carries out surveys, studies and conservation and education programmes; provides expert advice to governments on bird conservation; supports local societies and their projects; convenes international conferences; and publishes information. It supports more than 123 partner organizations through regional offices in Belgium, Ecuador, Fiji, Ghana, Japan, Jordan, Kenya and Singapore. Maintains a reference library of 5,000 vols.
Geographical Area of Activity: International.
Publications: Annual Report; newsletter; *BirdLife: The Magazine*; conference proceedings; technical publications; study reports; surveys.
Finance: Annual income £35.8m., expenditure £29.8m. (31 Dec. 2023).
Board: Dr Mike Rands (Chair.); Martin Birch (Treas.).
International Advisory Group: John S. Adams, Piyush Gupta (Co-Chair.).
Principal Staff: CEO Martin Harper.
Contact Details: The David Attenborough Bldg, Pembroke St, Cambridge CB2 3QZ; tel. (1223) 277318; e-mail birdlife@birdlife.org; internet www.birdlife.org.

Blood Cancer UK—Bloodwise

Founded in 1960 as Leukaemia Research; subsequently renamed Leukaemia and Lymphoma Research. Current name adopted in 2015.
Activities: Dedicated exclusively to researching blood cancers and disorders including leukaemia, Hodgkin's and other lymphomas, and myeloma. The organization offers professional development and online nursing courses; and funds laboratory-based research projects, training and career development and clinical trials. It awards research project grants worth up to £250,000 and up to three years; programme continuity grants worth up £300,000 for up to three years; and Early Phase Clinical Trial grants worth up to £400,000.
Geographical Area of Activity: UK.
Restrictions: Grants for research only.
Publications: Annual Report; newsletter; information for health professionals; patient information booklets; webinars.
Finance: Annual income £18.5m., expenditure £16.8m. (31 March 2024).
Board of Trustees: Matthew Wilson (Chair.); Jules Hillier (Vice-Chair.).
Principal Staff: Chief Exec. Helen Rowntree.
Contact Details: Suite 31 Bonnington Bond, 2 Anderson Pl., Edinburgh EH6 5NP; tel. (808) 2080888; e-mail hello@bloodcancer.org.uk; internet bloodcancer.org.uk.

Blue Marine Foundation—BLUE

Established in 2010 by Chris Gorell Barnes, a new media entrepreneur, George Duffield, a film producer, and Charles Clover, an author and environmental journalist.
Activities: Works to address overfishing by: promoting the creation of large-scale marine reserves; developing new models of sustainable fishing; protecting biodiversity and endangered species; and raising awareness of overfishing and potential solutions. The Foundation comprises several units: BLUE Carbon, which conducts research into marine habitats' potential to sequester and store carbon; BLUE Economics, which examines the economics of the use and abuse of the oceans; BLUE Investigations, which works to expose and prevent unsustainable practices, such as overfishing, deep-sea mining and human rights abuses; and BLUE Legal, which mounts legal cases for the proper creation and enforcement of law at sea. It organizes the Ocean Awards, which recognize the contributions of individuals, community groups, organizations and businesses in the areas of marine health, environment, sustainable management of marine resources and public engagement.
Geographical Area of Activity: Aeolian Islands, Caspian Sea, Maldives, Menorca, Namibia, Patagonia, UK, UK Overseas Territories.
Publications: Annual Report; newsletter; Blue Digital Education (online educational resources).
Finance: Annual income £12.3m., expenditure £12.5m. (31 March 2024).
Trustees: Dr Arlo Brady (Chair.).
Principal Staff: CEO Clare Brook.
Contact Details: 3rd Floor, South Bldg, Somerset House, Strand, London WC2R 1LA; tel. (20) 7845-5850; e-mail info@bluemarinefoundation.com; internet www.bluemarinefoundation.com.

Book Aid International—BAI

Founded in 1954 by Hermione, Countess of Ranfurly as the Ranfurly Library Service; present name adopted in 1994.
Activities: Provides books for all, encouraging children to read, supporting education, improving access to healthcare information and providing books during conflicts. The organization sends more than 1m. new and up-to-date books to libraries, schools, hospitals, prisons and refugee camps. It refurbishes libraries and establishes rural Community Container libraries; and trains teachers and librarians. The UK book trade donates most of the books and professional librarians ensure that they meet the needs of local people. Works with partners in 22 countries.
Geographical Area of Activity: Bhutan, Caribbean, Greece, Iraq, Jordan, Lebanon, Nepal, Palestinian Territories, sub-Saharan Africa, Syrian Arab Repub.
Publications: Annual Review; *BookMark* (newsletter); *Book-Links* (newsletter).
Finance: Annual income £22.6m., expenditure £20.0m. (31 Dec. 2023).
Board of Trustees: Nigel Newton (Pres.); Dr Alice Prochaska (Chair.).
Principal Staff: Chief Exec. Alison Tweed.
Contact Details: 39–41 Coldharbour Lane, Camberwell, London SE5 9NR; tel. (20) 7733-3577; e-mail info@bookaid.org; internet www.bookaid.org.

Born Free Foundation

Founded in 1984 by Virginia McKenna and Bill Travers, the leading actors in the wildlife film *Born Free* (1966).
Activities: Works in the fields of animal protection and wildlife conservation. Priority areas are: preventing the exploitation of captive wild animals; eliminating trophy and canned hunting; fighting to end the illegal wildlife trade; rescuing and rehabilitating captive animals; human/wildlife co-existence and compassionate conservation; integrated wildlife protection and law enforcement; transboundary programmes, principally in West Africa and the Horn of Africa; protecting wildlife in the United Kingdom; and educating people to respect wildlife and natural habitats. The Foundation works in 13 countries, with sister organizations in Ethiopia, Kenya,

British Academy

South Africa and the USA. The McKenna-Travers Award for Compassionate Conservation recognizes conservationists, researchers and practitioners who prioritize animal welfare in field conservation, conservation policy and environmental education; the award confers a project grant worth up to £10,000.

Geographical Area of Activity: International.

Publications: Annual Report; newsletter.

Finance: Annual income £6.1m., expenditure £6.1m. (31 March 2024).

Trustees: Michael Reyner (Chair.).

Principal Staff: Exec. Pres. Will Travers; Man. Dir Karen Botha.

Contact Details: 2nd Floor, Frazer House, 14 Carfax, Horsham RH12 1ER; tel. (1403) 240170; e-mail info@bornfree.org.uk; internet www.bornfree.org.uk.

British Academy

Established in 1902 as the British Academy for the Promotion of Historical, Philosophical and Philological Studies.

Activities: The Academy operates nationally and internationally in the fields of academic research in the humanities and social sciences; and provides grants to British scholars for a wide range of personal research projects, conference attendance and international collaboration, including BA/Leverhulme Small Research Grants, worth up to £10,000 over a period of up to two years, to support primary research. It supports research posts (postdoctoral and senior level) and a series of scholarly projects; funds a number of British institutes abroad and in the United Kingdom; organizes and publishes papers from lectures, conferences and symposia; and maintains links with international partners (academies and research councils). Every year, up to 52 UK-based scholars are elected to the Academy's Fellowship, which comprises around 1,400 national and international academics. Visiting Fellowships and Newton International Fellowships enable researchers from overseas to spend two years working at UK institutions for up to six months and two years, respectively; and Global Professorships for four years. Awards include: annually, the British Academy Book Prize for Global Cultural Understanding (formerly known as the Nayef Al-Rodhan Prize), worth £25,000, for a non-fiction book; the Brian Barry Prize, worth £500, for political science; the Derek Allen Prize, worth £400, for musicology, numismatics and Celtic studies, in rotation; various medals, including the British Academy Medal and British Academy President's Medal; every two years, the Peter Townsend Prize, worth £2,000, for policy-relevant work on poverty and inequality, health inequalities, disability or older people; and, every three years, the Leverhulme Medal and Prize, worth £5,000, for the humanities and social sciences. The Academy is a member of the European Science Foundation (q.v.), ALLEA and the Union Académique Internationale.

Geographical Area of Activity: International.

Restrictions: In most cases, only offers awards for postdoctoral research in the humanities and social sciences undertaken by scholars normally resident in the UK.

Publications: Annual Report; newsletter; *British Academy Review*; *Journal of the British Academy* (online); *Proceedings of the British Academy*; monographs and other scholarly publications; catalogues; conference proceedings, lectures and biographies.

Finance: Annual income £78.7m., expenditure £74.4m. (31 March 2024).

Council: Prof. Julia Black (Pres.); Prof. April McMahon (Treas.).

Principal Staff: Chief Exec. Prof. Hetan Shah.

Contact Details: 10–11 Carlton House Terrace, London SW1Y 5AH; tel. (20) 7969-5200; e-mail enquiries@thebritishacademy.ac.uk; internet www.britishacademy.ac.uk.

The British Council

Established in 1934 to promote educational and cultural relations between the United Kingdom and other countries worldwide; incorporated by Royal Charter in 1940.

Activities: Works with governments and partners in the fields of arts and culture, education and English language teaching. The British Council operates in over 200 countries and territories around the world and contributes to international development aims by helping to enable an environment for trade in education and culture. It works directly with individuals to help them build networks and explore creative ideas, to learn English, to get a high-quality education and to gain internationally recognised qualifications. It influences international students to come to the UK and creates opportunities for the UK English sector and awarding bodies. It works to extend English around the world, as the principal language of business, science, academia and collaboration. It has offices and teaching centres in more than 100 countries.

Geographical Area of Activity: International.

Publications: Annual Report; newsletters; *Voices Magazine*; publications in the fields of English language, education and the arts & culture.

Finance: Gross annual income £873.3m., expenditure £925.2m. (31 March 2023).

Board of Trustees: Dr Paul Thompson (Chair.).

Principal Staff: Chief Exec. Scott McDonald.

Contact Details: 1 Redman Place, Stratford, London E20 1JQ; tel. (161) 957-7755; e-mail general.enquiries@britishcouncil.org; internet www.britishcouncil.org.

British Gas Energy Trust

Established in 2004; independent from, but solely funded by, British Gas.

Activities: The Trust's objective is to alleviate the detrimental impact of poverty, with a focus on fuel poverty. Support is delivered through four programmes: debt relief grants, which can help households with up to £2,000 in fuel debt; a small grants programme that provides emergency energy vouchers and payments; a white goods scheme through trusted partners; and a programme that funds over 40 money and energy advice projects throughout Britain.

Geographical Area of Activity: England, Scotland, Wales.

Publications: Annual Report.

Finance: Annual income £24.2m., expenditure £18.6m. (31 March 2024).

Board of Trustees: Arvinda Gohil (Chair.); Mark McGillicuddy (Treas.).

Principal Staff: CEO Jessica Taplin.

Contact Details: 65–66 Lincoln's Inn Fields, London WC2A 3LH; tel. (12) 1348-7797; e-mail contact@britishgasenergytrust.org.uk; internet www.britishgasenergytrust.org.uk.

British Heart Foundation—BHF

Founded in 1961 by a group of medical professionals.

Activities: Funds medical research into the causes, prevention, diagnosis and treatment of heart disease. The Foundation provides support and information to sufferers and their families, through its own nurses, rehabilitation programmes and support groups. It educates the public and health professionals about heart disease prevention and treatment; promotes training in emergency life-support skills for the public and health professionals; and provides equipment to hospitals and other healthcare providers. A range of grants, chairs, awards, studentships and fellowships are available to researchers.

Geographical Area of Activity: UK.

Publications: Annual Review; newsletters; *Heart Matters* (magazine); factsheets; statistics.

Finance: Annual income £398.9m., expenditure £416.7m. (31 March 2024).

UNITED KINGDOM

Board of Trustees: Dr Sarah Clarke (Deputy Chair.).
Principal Staff: Chief Exec. Dr Charmaine Griffiths.
Contact Details: Compton House, 2300 The Cres., Birmingham Business Park, Birmingham B37 7YE; tel. (300) 3303322; e-mail heretohelp@bhf.org.uk; internet www.bhf.org.uk.

British Institute at Ankara (Ankara İngiliz Arkeoloji Enstitüsü)

Established in 1947 at the instigation of John B. E. Garstang, founder of the Institute of Archaeology at the University of Liverpool.
Activities: Supports, promotes and publishes British research focused on Türkiye (Turkey) and the Black Sea littoral in all academic disciplines within the arts, humanities and social sciences. Areas of interest include: habitat and settlement through time; human movement and cultural exchange; climate change and environment; legacy data and digital humanities; cultural heritage, society and economy; and culture, modernity and changing identities. The Institute maintains a centre of excellence in Ankara, focused on archaeology and related subjects, with a library of more than 65,000 items and research collections. It offers a range of project funding, scholarships and fellowships, support for academic trips and facilitation support.
Geographical Area of Activity: Türkiye and the Black Sea region, UK.
Publications: Annual Report; newsletter; *Anatolian Studies* (annual); *Heritage Turkey* (annual); monograph series.
Finance: Total income £1m., expenditure £850,536 (31 March 2024).
Council of Management: Prof. Jim Crow (Chair.).
Principal Staff: Dir Dr Lutgarde Vandeput; Asst Dirs Dr Peter Cherry, Dr Işılay Gürsu.
Contact Details: 10 Carlton House Terrace, London SW1Y 5AH; Atatürk Bulvarı 154, Çankaya, 06700 Ankara, Türkiye; tel. (20) 7969-5204; e-mail biaa@britac.ac.uk; internet www.biaa.ac.uk.

British Institute of International and Comparative Law—BIICL

Founded in 1958 by the merger of the Society of Comparative Legislation (f. 1895) and the Grotius Society (f. 1915).
Activities: Promotes the rule of law in national and international affairs through conducting applied legal research in four areas: public international law; private international law; European law; and comparative law. Programmes include: business and human rights; citizenship and the rule of law; climate change law; cultural heritage law; international investment law and dispute resolution; international trade law; the law of the sea; public international law in practice; and rule of law and democracy in Europe. The Institute offers in-person and online teaching and training to government officials, practitioners, civil society representatives and others; and organizes conferences, discussion and working groups (Forums), lectures and seminars. It offers Visiting Research Fellowships to international legal academics and scholars; and a number of Honorary Fellowships by invitation. Incorporates the Bingham Centre for the Rule of Law.
Geographical Area of Activity: International.
Publications: Annual Report; newsletter (monthly); *International and Comparative Law Quarterly*; reports; monographs; blog.
Finance: Annual income £5.6m., expenditure £5.5m. (31 Dec. 2023).
Board of Trustees: Eva Salomon (Chair.).
Principal Staff: Pres. The Rt Hon. the Lord Neuberger of Abbotsbury; Vice-Pres The Rt Hon the Lord Collins of Mapesbury, The Rt Hon Sir David Edward, Judge Joan Donoghue, Sir Christopher Greenwood.
Contact Details: Charles Clore House, 17 Russell Sq., London WC1B 5JP; tel. (20) 7862-5151; e-mail info@biicl.org; internet www.biicl.org.

British Red Cross Society

Established in 1870 as the British National Society for Aid to the Sick and Wounded in War; renamed in 1905 and incorporated by Royal Charter in 1908.
Activities: Provides emergency services and skilled care for those in need and crisis in their local community and overseas. The organization operates through local branches and centres to provide a full range of services in the community, which include: ambulance support; commode and wheelchair hire; emergency response; event first aid; fire and emergency support services; grants in the United Kingdom for people affected by terrorism overseas; help with loneliness; home support after leaving hospital; international family tracing services; medical loans; support for asylum seekers, refugees and trafficked people; therapeutic care; training in first aid and preparing for emergencies; and youth and schools services. It raises funds to provide aid in the form of money, materials or personnel to disaster-affected areas in the UK and abroad. Part of the International Red Cross and Red Crescent movement (q.v.).
Geographical Area of Activity: International.
Restrictions: No grants to individuals.
Publications: Annual Report; research reports; evaluations.
Finance: Annual income £330.6m., expenditure £322.7m. (31 Dec. 2023).
Board of Trustees: Elizabeth J. Padmore (Chair.); Louise Halpin, Geeta Nargund (Vice-Chair.).
Principal Staff: CEO Béatrice Butsana-Sita.
Contact Details: 44 Moorfields, London EC2Y 9AL; tel. (20) 7138-7900; e-mail contactus@redcross.org.uk; internet www.redcross.org.uk.

CABI

Established in 1913 as the Commonwealth Agricultural Bureaux (CAB); became an international non-profit organization with a new constitution in 1986, called the Centre for Agricultural Bioscience International. Present name adopted in 2006.
Activities: Promotes sustainable development and human welfare through disseminating scientific knowledge and responding to emerging threats. The organization operates in four principal areas: scientific research, international development, knowledge management and publishing; and comprises SciDev.Net, an independent news network, which publishes news and analysis on science and technology for global development. It comprises 48 member countries, with centres in Brazil, the People's Republic of China, Ghana, India, Kenya, Malaysia, Pakistan, Switzerland, Trinidad and Tobago, the United Kingdom, the USA and Zambia.
Geographical Area of Activity: International.
Publications: Annual Review; newsletter; *CABI Agriculture and Bioscience* (journal); PlantwisePlus (online); abstracts; books; compendia; datasheets; e-books; textbooks; toolkits; blog.
Finance: Annual income £42.8m., expenditure £42.8m. (31 Dec. 2023).
Board: Chileshe Kapwepwe (Chair.).
Executive Council: Fatou Bensouda (Chair.).
Principal Staff: CEO Dr Daniel Elger.
Contact Details: Nosworthy Way, Wallingford OX10 8DE; tel. (1491) 832111; e-mail enquiries@cabi.org; internet www.cabi.org.

CAFOD—Catholic Agency for Overseas Development

Established in 1962 as the official organization of the Roman Catholic Bishops' Conference of England and Wales; the official aid agency of the Catholic Church in England and Wales.
Activities: Shares resources with sister churches and other partners throughout the world to combat poverty, hunger, ignorance, disease and suffering. Main programme areas include: children and young people; civil society and

Cambridge Commonwealth, European and International Trust UNITED KINGDOM

governance; climate change and energy; debt cancellation; economic justice; emergencies and conflict; fossil fuels and poverty; HIV and AIDS; housing justice; the private sector and accountability; and the UN Sustainable Development Goals. The Agency conducts campaigns in the United Kingdom to raise awareness of the causes of poverty and injustice worldwide; and co-funds projects with the EU. Operates in 165 countries; part of Caritas Internationalis and the Disasters Emergency Committee (qq.v.). A gap year programme offers opportunities for volunteer placements in the UK, with 2–3 weeks spent visiting partner organizations in the global South.

Geographical Area of Activity: International.

Restrictions: Does not fund primary or secondary education nor projects involving heavy construction costs.

Publications: Annual Report; e-newsletter (monthly); *Side by Side*; *CAFOD Bulletin*; briefings; reports.

Finance: Annual income £47.9m., expenditure £59.2m. (31 March 2024).

Board of Trustees: Bishop John Arnold (Chair.).

Principal Staff: Dir Christine Allen.

Contact Details: Romero House, 55 Westminster Bridge Rd, London SE1 7JB; tel. (20) 7733-7900; e-mail cafod@cafod.org.uk; internet www.cafod.org.uk.

Cambridge Commonwealth, European and International Trust

Formed in 2013 by a merger of the Cambridge Commonwealth Trust (f. 1982) and the Cambridge Overseas Trust (f. 1989), which were established to give financial support to international students studying at the University of Cambridge.

Activities: Awards grants and scholarships to students of outstanding merit to pursue study or research courses. The Trust awards approximately 500 scholarships each year and supports around 1,400 students in residence.

Geographical Area of Activity: International.

Restrictions: Awards scholarships based on academic merit.

Publications: Annual Review.

Finance: Annual income £41.6m., expenditure £41.4m. (31 July 2024).

Trustees: Loretta Minghella (Chair.); Prof. Loraine Gelsthorpe (Deputy Chair.).

Principal Staff: Dir Helen Pennant; Deputy Dirs Dr Rachel Coupe (Awards), Williamson (Partnerships and Communications).

Contact Details: Student Services Centre, Bene't St, Cambridge CB2 3PT; tel. (1223) 338498; e-mail TrustCommunications@admin.cam.ac.uk; internet www.cambridgetrust.org.

CAMFED International

Founded in 1993 by Ann Cotton OBE, former English teacher and philanthropist.

Activities: A grassroots-led movement tackling poverty, inequality and injustice through girls' education and women's leadership. Addresses the challenges that lead to girls dropping out of school, such as a lack of income for food, transport, school fees, uniforms, and essentials like menstrual products; and early marriage, early pregnancy, and abuse. Ensuring every child is has access to a quality education in a safe environment, and to a life as an independent adult, girls and women can go on to launch climate-smart businesses, become health workers, run schools, and lead governments, contributing to their communities and to wider society. Works across Africa with offices in Australia, Canada, Ghana, Malawi, Switzerland, Tanzania, the USA, Zambia and Zimbabwe.

Geographical Area of Activity: Africa.

Publications: Annual Review; reports.

International Board: Anne-Birgitte Albrectsen (Chair.).

Principal Staff: CEO Angeline Murimirwa.

Contact Details: 20 Station Rd, Cambridge CB1 2JD; tel. (1223) 362648; e-mail info@camfed.org; internet camfed.org.

Cancer Research UK

Formed in 2002 by the merger of the Cancer Research Campaign and the Imperial Cancer Research Fund.

Activities: Supports and undertakes research in institutes, hospitals, universities and medical schools throughout Britain and Northern Ireland. The organization works in anti-cancer drug development and to ensure cancer sufferers receive new treatments as quickly as possible; carries out research into the psychological impact of cancer and improving communication between doctors and patients; publishes authoritative cancer information and guidelines for general practitioners; and runs a helpline. It promotes cancer prevention through education and research; and trains cancer scientists, nurses and doctors, offering a wide range of awards, fellowships, grants and studentships.

Geographical Area of Activity: UK.

Publications: Annual Review; scientific report; brochures; leaflets; factsheets; accounts.

Finance: Annual income £684.2m., expenditure £692.4m. (31 March 2024).

Council of Trustees: Lord Simon Stevens of Birmingham (Chair.); Prof. Pamela Kearns (Deputy Chair.); Dr Robert Easton (Treas.).

Principal Staff: CEO Michelle Mitchell.

Contact Details: POB 1561, Oxford OX4 9GZ; tel. (300) 1231022; e-mail supporter.services@cancer.org.uk; internet www.cancerresearchuk.org.

Carnegie Trust for the Universities of Scotland

Founded in 1901 by Andrew Carnegie, a US industrialist and philanthropist, to promote the development of Scottish universities; part of a network of 23 Carnegie organizations worldwide.

Activities: Provides vacation scholarships and grants to Scottish undergraduates to help with university fees, to postgraduates in the form of PhD scholarships and to staff of Scottish universities to fund research. It awards Research Incentive Grants worth between £1,500 and £15,000 to early career researchers for short projects over 12 months; and Research Workshop Grants, of up to £50,000 over 24 months, to address emerging scientific, technological, environmental, intellectual, cultural or societal developments.

Geographical Area of Activity: Scotland.

Publications: Annual Report.

Finance: Annual income £2.9m., expenditure £2.6m. (30 Sept. 2024).

Board of Trustees: Ronnie Bowie (Chair.); Prof. Andrea Nolan (Vice-Chair.).

Contact Details: Andrew Carnegie House, Pittencrieff St, Dunfermline KY12 8AW; tel. (1383) 724990; e-mail admin@carnegie-trust.org; internet www.carnegie-trust.org.

Carnegie UK Trust

Founded in 1913 by Andrew Carnegie, a US industrialist and philanthropist; part of a network of 23 Carnegie organizations worldwide.

Activities: Carnegie UK's purpose is to foster better wellbeing for people in the UK and Ireland. Works on research and practice to expand the knowledge of wellbeing. Advocates for action to improve the quality of people's lives now and in the future.

Geographical Area of Activity: Mainly UK and Ireland; also works with international partners on issues of a more global nature that affect the UK and Ireland.

Restrictions: Does not accept unsolicited requests; mainly operates through partnerships.

UNITED KINGDOM

Publications: Annual Review; newsletter (2 a month); consultation responses; project leaflets; policy and practice reports; blog.

Finance: Annual income £1.1m., expenditure £2.0m. (31 Dec. 2023).

Board: David Emerson (Chair.).

Principal Staff: CEO Sarah Davidson.

Contact Details: Andrew Carnegie House, Pittencrieff St, Dunfermline KY12 8AW; tel. (1383) 721445; e-mail info@carnegieuk.org; internet www.carnegieuktrust.org.uk.

The Charles Wallace India Trusts

Founded in 1981 by the will of Charles Wallace, a business person and entrepreneur, to help nationals of Bangladesh, Burma (Myanmar), India and Pakistan to obtain education and professional development in the United Kingdom.

Activities: Comprises four trusts: the Charles Wallace Bangladesh Trust; the Charles Wallace Burma Trust; the Charles Wallace India Trust; and the Charles Wallace Pakistan Trust. The Trusts work closely with the British Council, awarding grants for residents of the respective countries for education and professional development in the United Kingdom. The India Trust is the largest of the four, working in the fields of the arts, heritage conservation and the humanities; awarding scholarships for creative artists in visual arts, music, drama and dance, and for Indian postgraduate students in the UK; Visiting Fellowships of 2–3 months' duration in specified areas at British universities or other institutions; and 15–20 grants for short-term research, worth £1,400 each. It also makes awards for the conservation of architectural and structural materials and works of arts, and the training of museum conservators; awards for the training of museum and art gallery curators; and for research and short-term professional visits in the UK.

Geographical Area of Activity: Bangladesh, India, Myanmar, Pakistan, UK.

Principal Staff: Sec. Tim Butchard.

Contact Details: Charles Wallace Pakistan, Bangladesh, and Burma Trusts, 4 Dorville Cresc., London W6 0HJ; e-mail timbutchard@wallace-trusts.org.uk; internet www.wallace-trusts.org.uk.

Charles Wolfson Charitable Trust

Founded in 1960; shares objectives and a joint administration with the Wolfson Family Charitable Trust and the Wolfson Foundation (q.v.). The Wolfson Jewish Education Fund sits alongside them, but has a separate administration.

Activities: Provides funds to registered charities to support medical research, education and welfare. The Trust derives most of its funds from Benesco (f. 1970), a registered charity and company with investments in property.

Geographical Area of Activity: Israel, UK.

Restrictions: No grants to individuals; grants only to UK-based charities.

Publications: Annual Report.

Finance: Annual income £5.5m., expenditure £7.1m. (5 April 2024).

Board of Trustees: Andrew Wolfson (Chair.).

Principal Staff: Correspondent Joanne Cowan.

Contact Details: c/o Metrus Ltd, 8–10 Hallam St, London W1W 6NS; tel. (20) 7079-2506; e-mail admin@cwctcharity.org.uk.

Child Migrants Trust

Established in 1987 by Margaret Humphreys as an advisory and support organization for former child migrants who were sent abroad from the United Kingdom between the end of the Second World War and 1970.

Activities: Operates as a counselling and advisory organization in the UK, Australia, Canada, New Zealand, South Africa, the USA and Zimbabwe for former child migrants and their families. The Trust provides family research and social work services to help former child migrants from the UK to reclaim their identities and reunite with their families. It manages the Family Restoration Fund, which is funded by the UK Department of Health and Social Care. Has offices in Perth and Melbourne, Australia.

Geographical Area of Activity: Australia, Canada, New Zealand, South Africa, UK, USA, Zimbabwe.

Publications: Annual Report; *Empty Cradles/Oranges & Sunshine*; *Lost Children of the Empire*.

Finance: Annual income £545,554, expenditure £1m. (31 March 2024).

Board of Trustees: Joan Taylor (Chair.).

Principal Staff: Int. Dir Margaret Humphreys.

Contact Details: 124 Musters Rd, West Bridgford, Nottingham NG2 7PW; tel. (115) 9822811; e-mail enquiries@childmigrantstrust.com; internet www.childmigrantstrust.com.

The Children's Investment Fund Foundation

Established in 2004 by Sir Chris Hohn, a financier, and Jamie Cooper, a charity sector professional.

Activities: Works to transform the lives of children and young people. Main programmes include: child health and development, improving the wellbeing of children and mothers, through health, nutrition, education, de-worming and welfare initiatives; adolescence, in particular sexual and reproductive health; climate change, to provide a healthy and sustainable, low-carbon future for children; girl capital, addressing gender inequality through ensuring girls are able to complete their education, averting child marriage and increasing women's participation in the labour force; and child protection, working to end child labour and sexual exploitation. The Foundation offers grants to cost-effective and evidence-based projects that will bring about long-term transformational change at scale, monitoring and evaluating their progress. It has offices in Nairobi, Kenya, and New Delhi, India.

Geographical Area of Activity: East and South-East Asia, Europe, Latin America, South Asia, sub-Saharan Africa.

Publications: Annual Report; newsletter (quarterly).

Finance: Annual revenue £239.0m., expenditure £449.1m. (31 Dec. 2023).

Board of Trustees: Chris Hohn (Chair.).

Principal Staff: CEO Kate Hampton.

Contact Details: 7 Clifford St, London W1S 2FT; tel. (20) 3740-6100; e-mail info@ciff.org; internet ciff.org.

Childwick Trust

Founded in 1985 by H. J. (Jim) Joel, a racehorse owner and breeder.

Activities: Funds charities that help people with disabilities, elderly people in need, and seriously ill adults and children; and also supports the welfare of people in horse racing. The Trust funds several Jewish charities in the United Kingdom; and preschool education projects in South Africa through the Jim Joel Fund (South Africa).

Geographical Area of Activity: UK (mainly South and South-East England), South Africa.

Restrictions: Does not fund certain health and social welfare charities or applicants who have received a donation in the previous two years; grants only within the UK or South Africa.

Publications: Annual Report.

Finance: Annual income £2.0m., expenditure £4.1m. (31 March 2024).

Board of Trustees: Peter D. Anwyl-Harris (Chair.).

Principal Staff: Trust Admin. Kirsty Jones.

Contact Details: 9 The Green, Childwickbury, St Albans AL3 6JJ; tel. (1727) 844666; e-mail kirsty@childwicktrust.org; internet www.childwicktrust.org.

Christian Aid

Founded in 1945 as Christian Reconstruction in Europe to assist refugees; became a department of the British Council of Churches and was subsequently renamed the Department of Interchurch Aid and Refugee Service; present name adopted in 1964. The official relief, development and advocacy agency of 41 Sponsoring Churches in Great Britain and Ireland; part of the ACT Alliance and Disasters Emergency Committee (qq.v.).

Activities: Works to end poverty and social injustice through tackling their root causes. Programmes include: addressing the deeper causes of malnutrition; citizen-led accountability and ensuring delivery of basic services; the Climate Justice Resilience Fund for pastoralist communities; combating corruption and promoting transparency; emergency humanitarian response, providing food, shelter, clean water, and security and protection from gender-based violence; improving the livelihoods and economic resilience of women and marginalized groups through agribusiness; inclusive development, reducing poverty, achieving rights and improving the wellbeing of the most marginalized people; improving jobs and incomes for rural women in sustainable energy; increasing vaccination demand for young children; protecting indigenous people's territories and increasing their access to land; supporting orphans and vulnerable children; and providing young people's education in crisis-affected countries. The organization operates in 29 countries.

Geographical Area of Activity: Africa, Asia, Latin America and the Caribbean, Middle East, UK.

Publications: Annual Report; Annual Review; *Christian Aid News*; frameworks; policy documents; reports; blog.

Finance: Annual income £83.3m., expenditure £82.4m. (31 March 2024).

Trustees: Maggie Swinson (Interim Chair.).

Principal Staff: CEO Patrick Watt.

Contact Details: 35–41 Lower Marsh, Waterloo, London SE1 7RL; tel. (20) 7620-4444; e-mail info@christian-aid.org; internet www.christianaid.org.uk.

The Churchill Fellowship

Founded in 1965 as the Winston Churchill Memorial Trust, a memorial to Sir Winston Churchill, the former Prime Minister. Present name adopted in 2021.

Activities: Awards up to 150 Churchill Fellowships annually for a stay overseas of 4–8 weeks to research a practical topic that has a wider public benefit. Award categories address 'universal themes' in society, including: the arts and culture; community and citizenship; economy and enterprise; education and skills; environment and resources; health and wellbeing; governance and public provision; and science and technology. There is also an open category for other ideas. The Trust offers an Archive By-Fellowship at the Churchill Archives Centre. It maintains an online reports library; and Fellows' online local and thematic networks.

Geographical Area of Activity: International.

Restrictions: Applicants must be UK resident citizens aged over 18 years.

Publications: Annual Report; newsletter; leaflet and brochure; project reports.

Finance: Annual income £1.3m., expenditure £3.0m. (30 Sept. 2023).

Board of Trustees: Jeremy Soames (Chair.); James Willims (Vice-Chair.).

Principal Staff: Chief Exec. Julia Weston.

Contact Details: Church House (South Door), 29 Great Smith St, London SW1P 3BL; tel. (20) 7799-1660; e-mail office@churchillfellowship.org; internet www.churchillfellowship.org.

The City Bridge Trust

Established in 1995 through a scheme to distribute surplus funds from Bridge House Estates, an ancient charity which maintains five of the bridges that cross the River Thames.

Activities: Distributes the majority of its funds through traditional grantmaking, with an open application process against published funding criteria. Each year, the Trust awards around £30m. in grants. It occasionally runs one-off grant programmes to tackle specific issues, which may be by invitation only. Up to 20% of the annual budget may be used for Strategic Initiatives, pieces of work initiated by the Trust that respond to learning or to emerging areas of need.

Geographical Area of Activity: London, UK.

Restrictions: Grants are made for the benefit of London only. No grants to individuals, statutory bodies, political parties, for medical or academic research, to churches or religious bodies for religious purposes or maintenance of religious buildings, or to educational establishments.

Publications: Annual Review; Trustees Annual Report; *The Knowledge: Learning From London*.

Finance: Annual income £40.1m., expenditure £118.9m. (31 March 2024).

Board: Paul Nicholas Martinelli (Chair.); Dr Giles Robert Evelyn Shilson (Deputy Chair.).

Principal Staff: Man. Dir David Farnsworth.

Contact Details: City of London, POB 270, Guildhall, London EC2P 2EJ; tel. (20) 7332-3710; e-mail funding@citybridgefoundation.org.uk; internet www.citybridgetrust.org.uk.

Comic Relief

Established in 1985 by Richard Curtis, a screenwriter, Jane Tewson, a charity worker, and friends; has the operating name of Charity Projects.

Activities: Works nationally and internationally in the fields of poverty alleviation and social change. Programmes focus on: early childhood development, encompassing nutrition, health, safety and protection, care and early stimulation; identifying and treating mental health problems; gender justice, empowering women and girls; and providing safe and secure shelter for vulnerable people, including access to food, clothes and housing. The organization runs the Red Nose Day fundraising campaign biennially and in 2002 launched the Sport Relief fundraiser.

Geographical Area of Activity: International (mainly sub-Saharan Africa and the UK).

Publications: Annual Report; newsletter; information leaflet.

Finance: Annual income £53.8m., expenditure £46.2m. (31 July 2024).

Board of Trustees: Tom Shropshire (Interim Chair.).

Principal Staff: Chief Exec. Samir Patel.

Contact Details: The White Chapel Bldg, 6th Floor, 10 Whitechapel High St, London E1 8QS; tel. (20) 7820-2000; e-mail info@comicrelief.com; internet www.comicrelief.com.

Commonwealth Foundation

Founded in 1965 as an intergovernmental organization to support the work of the non-governmental sector within the Commonwealth; works alongside alongside the Commonwealth Secretariat and the Commonwealth of Learning.

Activities: Develops the capacity of CSOs and promotes diversity, collaboration, integrity and ingenuity. Main programme areas include: participatory governance and gender; learning and communications; and Commonwealth Writers, organizing the Commonwealth Short Story Prize, with regional prizes of £2,500 and an overall prize of £5,000. The Foundation offers grants worth up to £200,000 for sustainable development projects that contribute to effective, responsive and accountable governance in the areas of: citizen education; civil society empowerment; creative expression; economic development; environment; gender equality and women's empowerment; health; and human rights.

Geographical Area of Activity: Commonwealth countries.

Publications: Annual Report; newsletter (monthly); *Commonwealth Insights*; *Commonwealth Perspectives*; toolkits; frameworks; blog.

Finance: Annual assessed contributions £3.6m., expenditure £3.1m. (30 June 2024).

Board of Governors: Winnie Anna Kiap (Chair.).

Principal Staff: Dir-Gen. Anne Therese Gallagher; Deputy Dir-Gen. Shem Ochola.

Contact Details: Marlborough House, Pall Mall, London SW1Y 5HY; tel. (20) 7930-3783; e-mail info@commonwealthfoundation.com; internet www.commonwealthfoundation.com.

Community Foundation for Northern Ireland

Founded in 1979 as the Northern Ireland Voluntary Trust; present name adopted in 2003.

Activities: Encourages local philanthropy in Northern Ireland and promotes community empowerment and social justice. The Foundation supports projects that deal with social problems in urban and rural areas, such as those with a focus on young people, women's groups, unemployed people, community care, the arts, education, welfare rights and inter-community activity. It administers more than 65 funds. Has an office in Derry-Londonderry.

Geographical Area of Activity: Northern Ireland.

Publications: Annual Report; *Vital Signs* (policy updates); Policy Briefings; *Vision in Philanthropy Research*; reports; evaluations; case studies.

Finance: Annual income £6.7m., expenditure £17.0m. (31 March 2024).

Board of Trustees: Adrian Johnston (Chair.).

Principal Staff: Chief Exec. Róisín Wood.

Contact Details: Community House, City Link Business Park, 6A Albert St, Belfast BT12 4HQ; tel. (28) 9024-5927; e-mail info@communityfoundationni.org; internet www.communityfoundationni.org.

The Confederation of Service Charities—Cobseo

Established in 1984 as the Confederation of British Service and Ex-Service Organisations, a non-profit organization; present name adopted in 2012.

Activities: The Confederation of Service Charities provides a single point of contact for interaction with the Government, including local government and the Devolved Administrations; with the Royal Household; with the Private Sector; and with other members of the Armed Forces Community. This allows Cobseo members to interact with all interested parties and especially to co-operate and collaborate with others in order to provide the best possible level of support to beneficiaries.

Geographical Area of Activity: UK and Commonwealth countries.

Publications: Annual Report; Member Directory (online).

Finance: Annual income £677,533, expenditure £623,262 (31 Dec. 2023).

Executive Committee: Lt-Gen. Sir Nicholas Pope (Chair.); Alistair Halliday (Vice-Chair.).

Principal Staff: Dir of Operations Kate McCullough.

Contact Details: Mountbarrow House, 12 Elizabeth St, London SW1W 9RB; tel. (20) 7811-3200; e-mail enquiries@cobseo.org.uk; internet www.cobseo.org.uk.

Co-op Foundation

Established in 2002 by the Co-operative Group (Co-op), a consumer co-operative.

Activities: Helps disadvantaged communities and works to prevent loneliness among young people by working co-operatively and providing digital capacity building.

Geographical Area of Activity: UK.

Publications: Annual Report.

Finance: Annual income £5.7m., expenditure £8.8m. (31 Dec. 2023).

Board of Trustees: Jamie Ward-Smith (Chair.); Sharon Jones (Vice-Chair.); Saleem Chowdhery (Treas.).

Principal Staff: Chief Exec. Nick Crofts.

Contact Details: 8th Floor, 1 Angel Sq., Manchester M60 0AG; tel. (161) 6921877; e-mail foundation@coop.co.uk; internet www.coopfoundation.org.uk.

Coram

Originally established as the Foundling Hospital in 1739 by Thomas Coram, now a group of charities focused on improving the lives of vulnerable children and young people in the United Kingdom.

Activities: Coram includes a number of organizations working in children's rights, safety and welfare, including: the Coram Children's Legal Centre, Coram Ambitious for Adoption, Coram Voice, Coram Life Education and Coram International.

Geographical Area of Activity: Worldwide.

Finance: Annual income £25.6m., expenditure £25.1m. (31 March 2024).

Trustees: Jenny Coles (Vice-Chair.); Geoff Berridge (Treas.).

Principal Staff: Pres. Sir Ivor Crewe.

Contact Details: Coram Campus, 41 Brunswick Sq., London WC1N; tel. (20) 7520-0300; internet coram.org.uk.

Corra Foundation

Established in 1985 as Lloyds TSB Foundation for Scotland; present name adopted in 2017.

Activities: Corra Foundation is a Scottish grantmaking charity that is about strengthening and amplifying people's voices and their power to make change. It gives grants to charities and grassroots groups that make a day-to-day difference to people's lives. Some is through funding managed for others, like the Scottish Government. Corra also works alongside communities where people come together to find their own solutions to things like poverty, isolation, loneliness, and health issues. The Foundation provides funding, through participatory grant programmes; and opportunities to build and share skills, and connect with other communities. The Henry Duncan Grants programme offers Organisation Grants and Black, Asian and Minority Ethnic Project Grants, worth up to £8,000, and Micro Grants, worth £1,000 for community-based organizations. The programme's theme changes each year; in 2025 it is to focus on human rights and racial equity.

Geographical Area of Activity: Developing countries, Scotland.

Publications: Annual Report; *eNews*; *Insight Briefings*; policy responses; research reports; blogs.

Finance: Annual income £38.0m., expenditure £41.6m. (31 March 2024).

Trustees: Luke McCullough (Chair.); Jude Turbyne (Deputy Chair.).

Principal Staff: CEO Carolyn Sawers.

Contact Details: Office Suite 30, Pure Offices, 4 Lochside Way, Edinburgh EH12 9DT; tel. (131) 444-4020; e-mail hello@corra.scot; internet www.corra.scot.

The Cure Parkinson's Trust

Founded in 2005 by Tom Isaacs, Sir Richard Nichols, Air Vice Marshal Michael Dicken and Sir David Jones, all of whom were living with Parkinson's and wanted to focus on finding a treatment to slow, stop or reverse the progression of the disease.

Activities: Provides leadership and funding for neuroscientists and neurologists worldwide working on researching and developing new drugs for clinical trials. Offers support and information to people living with Parkinson's and their carers. Organizes fundraising campaigns and encourages participation in events to collect donations.

Geographical Area of Activity: Worldwide.

Publications: Annual Report; monthly e-newsletter.

Finance: Total income £9.4m., expenditure £7.8m. (31 March 2024).

Board of Trustees: Mike Ashton (Chair.).

Principal Staff: CEO Helen Matthews.

Contact Details: 120 New Cavendish St, London W1W 6XX; tel. (20) 7487-3892; e-mail info@cureparkinsons.org.uk; internet cureparkinsons.org.uk.

Cystic Fibrosis Trust

Founded in 1964 as the Cystic Fibrosis Research Foundation Trust.

Activities: Funds research to find a cure for cystic fibrosis and to improve symptom control; ensures appropriate clinical care for those with cystic fibrosis; and helps those affected by cystic fibrosis by providing information and support. The Trust offers various grants: emergency grants for transplant-related travel costs up to £250, financial difficulties up to £150 and funeral expenses up to £750; health and wellbeing grants up to £250; grants for exercise equipment up to £200; and holiday grants, for people over 18 years of age, up to £300. The Edward W. Joseph Cystic Fibrosis Home Care programme offers grants worth up to £500 for home care in times of acute illness or personal crisis. The Joseph Levy Education Fund, which is part of the Trust but administered by the Joseph Levy Foundation (q.v.), offers grants towards the costs of higher education, professional qualifications and vocational training.

Geographical Area of Activity: Mainly UK.

Publications: Annual Review; *CF Today* (5 a year); *CF Talk*; *Focus on Fundraising;* booklets; factsheets.

Finance: Annual income £14.7m., expenditure £15.1m. (31 March 2024).

Board of Trustees: Richard Hunt (Chair.).

Principal Staff: Chief Exec. David Ramsden.

Contact Details: 1 Aldgate, 2nd Floor, London EC3N 1RE; tel. (20) 3795-1555; e-mail enquiries@cysticfibrosis.org.uk; internet www.cysticfibrosis.org.uk.

Daiwa Anglo-Japanese Foundation

Established in 1988 with a benefaction from Daiwa Securities, an investment bank.

Activities: Makes grants to individuals and organizations; awards scholarships to British graduates to study Japan and its language; and organizes events to increase understanding of Japan in the United Kingdom. The Foundation offers small grants of between £2,000 and £7,000 for individuals or organizations in the UK and Japan to promote links between the two countries; and awards of between £7,000 and £15,000 for collaborative projects. It offers scholarships to support 18 months in Japan (12 months' language study and six months' work placement) to British nationals who have not completed a degree in Japanese; and scholarships in Japanese Studies for British nationals who have a degree in Japanese, for postgraduate studies related to Japan in either the UK or Japan. The London headquarters are a centre for academic and cultural activities relating to Japan.

Geographical Area of Activity: Japan, UK.

Restrictions: Grants only for UK–Japan exchanges; projects must involve British and Japanese partners.

Publications: Annual Review.

Finance: Annual income £623,670, expenditure £1.9m. (31 March 2024).

Trustees: Sir Tim Hitchens (Chair.); Keiko Tashiro (Vice-Chair.).

Principal Staff: Dir-Gen. Jason James.

Contact Details: Daiwa Foundation Japan House, 13–14 Cornwall Terrace (Outer Circle), London NW1 4QP; tel. (20) 7486-4348; e-mail office@dajf.org.uk; internet www.dajf.org.uk.

David Nott Foundation

Established in 2015 and founded by consultant vascular and trauma surgeon, Prof. David Nott, and his wife, Elly Nott, now CEO of the Foundation.

Activities: The David Nott Foundation trains medical professionals to provide safe, skilled surgical care in countries impacted by conflict and catastrophe. The Foundation also offers scholarships and grants to medical professionals who wish to further their medical careers, education or training. By April 2025 the Foundation had trained 2,158 doctors and run 68 courses worldwide.

Geographical Area of Activity: International.

Publications: Annual Reports; impact reports; newsletters.

Finance: Annual income £2.0m. expenditure £1.3m. (31 March 2024).

Board of Trustees: Graham Hodgkin (Chair.); Caitlin Hughes (Hon. Treas.).

Principal Staff: Chief Exec. James Gough.

Contact Details: 193 Hercules Rd, London SE1 7LD; tel. (300) 5610050; e-mail enquiries@davidnottfoundation.com; internet davidnottfoundation.com.

DHL UK Foundation

Established in 2000, as the Excel Foundation, by the merger of the National Freight Corporation Foundation (f. 1988) and the Philip Holt Benevolent Fund (f. 1880); present name adopted in 2008.

Activities: Supports projects in the areas of education, employability and community engagement, with a particular focus on children and young people from disadvantaged backgrounds. The Foundation promotes road safety initiatives; and offers hardship grants to current and retired DHL employees and their dependents. In 2015 it established a £750,000 scholarship fund at the University of Edinburgh for undergraduate study in science, technology, engineering or mathematics; 14–15 scholarships are awarded annually, each worth £2,000 a year for up to five years.

Geographical Area of Activity: UK.

Restrictions: Scholarships are open to students from around the world.

Finance: Annual income £544,094, expenditure £2.4m. (31 March 2024).

Board of Trustees: Susan Robinson (Chair.).

Principal Staff: CEO Caroline Courtois.

Contact Details: Eastworth House, Eastworth Rd, Chertsey, Surrey KT16 8SH; tel. (1285) 841914; e-mail GoTeachUK@dhl.com; internet www.dhlukfoundation.org.

Diabetes UK

Founded in 1934, as the Diabetic Association, by author H. G. Wells and Dr R. D. Lawrence; in 1954 it became the British Diabetic Association. Present name adopted in 2000.

Activities: Funds research into the prevention, treatment and cure of diabetes. The organization provides information and support to people living with diabetes and to healthcare professionals; campaigns against discrimination; promotes improved services for people with diabetes; and awards medals to people who have lived with the condition for more than 50, 60, 70 or 80 years. Research awards offered include: research project grants for up to five years; early career small grants for research projects or pilot studies of up to 12 months and a maximum amount of £75,000; Harry Keen Intermediate Clinical Fellowships, for medically or clinically qualified professionals to establish themselves as independent researchers; Sir George Alberti Research Training Fellowships, for graduates working in the National Health Service to study for a PhD or MD in diabetes research; NIHR/Diabetes UK Doctoral Fellowships, to fund a PhD in diabetes-related research; RD Lawrence Fellowships, to support postdoctoral researchers in establishing their independence in diabetes research; and PhD Studentships, for experienced researchers to recruit science graduates to study for a PhD in diabetes-related research.

Geographical Area of Activity: UK.

Publications: Annual Report; e-newsletter; *Diabetes Update* (quarterly journal); *Balance* (magazine, 2 a month).

Finance: Annual income £42.7m., expenditure £49.4m. (31 Dec. 2023).

Board of Trustees: Dr Carol Homden (Chair.); Alexandra Lewis (Treas.).

Principal Staff: Chief Exec. Colette Marshall.

Contact Details: Wells Lawrence House, 126 Back Church Lane, Whitechapel, London E1 1FH; tel. (20) 7424-1001; e-mail helpline@diabetes.org.uk; internet www.diabetes.org.uk.

Ditchley Foundation

Founded in 1958 by Sir David Wills; affiliated with the American Ditchley Foundation (f. 1964) and Canadian Ditchley Foundation (f. 1981).

Activities: Carries out activities that advance education and improve public policymaking in North America and the United Kingdom. The Foundation maintains Ditchley Park as a conference centre and supports the Ditchley conference programme. It organizes invitation-only conferences on topics of international concern to the British and American peoples, with the participation of other nationalities, particularly from member states of the EU.

Geographical Area of Activity: UK.

Restrictions: No grants to individuals or groups unless at Ditchley.

Publications: Annual Report; newsletters; conference reports.

Finance: Annual income £76.7m., expenditure £4.5m. (31 March 2024).

Council of Management: Lady Wills (Hon. Life Pres.); Lord Hill of Oareford (Chair.).

Principal Staff: Dir James Arroyo.

Contact Details: Lower House, Ditchley Park, Enstone, Chipping Norton OX7 4ER; tel. (1608) 677346; e-mail info@ditchley.co.uk; internet www.ditchley.co.uk.

Dulverton Trust

Founded in 1949 by Sir Gilbert Wills, the first Lord Dulverton, a politician and President of the Imperial Tobacco Company.

Activities: Supports UK charities and charitable incorporated organizations. The Trust makes grants in the areas of: environmental conservation; general welfare of disadvantaged people and communities; heritage and traditional craftsmanship; peace and humanitarian support; and providing life skills for disadvantaged children and young people.

Geographical Area of Activity: Kenya, Uganda, UK.

Restrictions: Does not make grants in area of medicine and health; to organizations based in Greater London or Northern Ireland; nor to museums, arts organizations, expeditions, schools, colleges or universities. Grants only to registered charities and never to individuals.

Publications: Annual Report.

Finance: Annual income £2.7m., expenditure £3.8m. (31 March 2024).

Trustees: Christopher Wills (Chair.); Richard Fitzalan Howard (Vice-Chair.).

Principal Staff: CEO and Dir Binda Patel.

Contact Details: 5 St James's Pl., London SW1A 1NP; tel. (20) 7495-7852; e-mail grants@dulverton.org; internet www.dulverton.org.

Education and Training Foundation—ETF

Established in 2013 by the Association of Colleges, Association of Employment and Learning Providers and Holex, a professional body for adult community education and learning; the expert body for professional development and standards in further education and training in England.

Activities: Works to improve education and training for learners aged 14 years and over, through designing, developing and delivering continuous professional development for teachers, education leaders and trainers. The Foundation is developing initiatives to support the adoption of education for sustainable development nationally and internationally. Professional development grants are available for mentors and coaches, worth up to £6,000; and for 'edtech' and digital skills mentors and coaches, worth up to £1,000. It comprises the Society for Education and Training, a membership body for professionals working in further education, vocational teaching and training, with approx. 20,000 members.

Geographical Area of Activity: England, Wales.

Publications: Annual Report; newsletter; *inTuition* (quarterly journal); Excellence Gateway (practitioner research and evidence portal); case studies; research reports; thought pieces; blog.

Finance: Annual income £23.6m., expenditure £25.3m. (31 March 2024).

Board of Trustees: Sir Frank McLoughlin (Chair.).

Principal Staff: CEO Katerina Kolyva.

Contact Details: 157–197 Buckingham Palace Rd, London SW1W 9SP; tel. (20) 3740-8280; e-mail enquiries@etfoundation.co.uk; internet www.et-foundation.co.uk.

Educational Opportunity Foundation

Established in 1808, as British & Foreign School Society—BFSS, by Christian social reformers to continue the work of Joseph Lancaster, a public education innovator; name changed in 2024.

Activities: Supports non-profit organizations working to improve access to or the quality of education for disadvantaged children and young people who are experiencing poverty or suffering from conflict, natural disaster, neglect, abuse or other very difficult circumstances. The charity awards funding ranging from £5,000 to £60,000 for up to three years both internationally and in the United Kingdom. It also administers a number of restricted subsidiary trusts, which award small grants for education and training to individuals and organizations in the UK.

Geographical Area of Activity: International, UK.

Restrictions: Grants only to UK-based charities for new projects; does not fund bursaries, scholarships or adult education for people aged over 25 years.

Publications: Annual Report.

Finance: Annual income £620,440, expenditure £1.6m. (31 Dec. 2023).

Council: Jane Creasy (Chair.); Charlotte Cashman (Vice-Chair.); Robert Spencer (Treas.).

Principal Staff: Pres. Estelle Morris; Vice-Pres. John Furlong; Dir Joanne Knight.

Contact Details: Canopi, 82 Tanner St, London SE1 3GN; e-mail grants@educationalopportunity.org.uk; internet educationalopportunity.org.uk.

Edward Cadbury Charitable Trust

Founded in 1945 by Edward Cadbury, the grandson of the founder of the Cadbury chocolate company; shares an administration with the William A. Cadbury Trust (q.v.).

Activities: Principally supports the voluntary sector in the Midlands region, including Herefordshire, Shropshire, Staffordshire, Warwickshire and Worcestershire. The Trust makes grants in six areas: arts and culture, encompassing heritage and science; community projects and integration, to advance citizenship or community development; compassionate

The Elders Foundation   UNITED KINGDOM

support, for people in need; conservation and the environment; education and training; and research in health and to save lives. Grants usually range between £500 and £10,000.

Geographical Area of Activity: UK (West Midlands).

Restrictions: Grants to registered charities only; no grants to students or individuals.

Publications: Annual Report.

Finance: Annual income £1.5m., expenditure £1.1m. (5 April 2024).

Trustees: Dr William Southall (Chair.).

Principal Staff: Trust Man. and Clerk Sue Anderson.

Contact Details: Woodbrooke, 1046 Bristol Rd, Birmingham B29 6LJ; tel. (121) 4721838; e-mail sue.anderson@edwardcadburytrust.org.uk; internet www.edwardcadburytrust.org.uk.

The Elders Foundation

Established in 2007 by Nelson Mandela, former President of South Africa; a network of independent global leaders.

Activities: Uses the collective experience and influence of independent global leaders to work for peace, justice and human rights. The Foundation carries out activities under six main programmes: Ethical Leadership & Multilateral Cooperation; Conflict Countries & Regions; Universal Health Coverage; Climate Change; Access to Justice; and Refugees & Migration.

Geographical Area of Activity: Worldwide.

Publications: Annual Report; newsletter; reports; blog.

Finance: Annual income £3.5m., expenditure £3.1m. (31 Dec. 2023).

The Elders: Juan Manuel Santos (Chair.); Ban Ki-Moon, Graça Machel (Deputy Chair.).

Principal Staff: Chief Exec. Alistair Fernie.

Contact Details: 3 Tilney St, London W1K 1BJ; tel. (20) 7013-4646; e-mail info@theelders.org; internet theelders.org.

Elrahma Charity Trust

Established in 1993 as Charity Islamic Trust Elrahma; shares an administration with El Farouq Foundation.

Activities: Operates in the fields of education and training, poverty alleviation and humanitarian aid, through grants for the building of schools, charitable institutions, mosques, orphanages and nurseries for Muslims in the United Kingdom and abroad.

Geographical Area of Activity: Egypt, Jordan, Malaysia, Thailand, Tunisia, UK, USA.

Restrictions: Grants only to registered charitable institutions and students in full-time education at officially recognized universities.

Publications: Annual Report.

Finance: Annual income £649,212, expenditure £1.1m. (31 Dec. 2023).

Trustees: Abubaker Megerisi (Chair.).

Principal Staff: Charity Correspondent Abdulkadir A. Naib.

Contact Details: Suite 201, Stanmore Business & Innovation Centre, Stanmore Pl., Howard Rd, Stanmore HA7 1BT; tel. (20) 3026-3397; e-mail projects@elrahma.org.uk; internet www.elrahma.org.uk.

Elrha

Established in 2009 as Enhancing Learning and Research for Humanitarian Assistance—ELRHA, initially as hosted entity of Save the Children (UK) (q.v.); became an independent organization in 2018.

Activities: Works with humanitarian organizations, researchers and the private sector, funding humanitarian innovation projects and research studies. Main programmes are the Humanitarian Innovation Fund (f. 2010), an independent grantmaking programme; and Research for Health in Humanitarian Crises (R2HC), providing evidence for public health initiatives. The organization provides technical support and capacity building. It has an office in Cardiff.

Geographical Area of Activity: Worldwide.

Restrictions: Does not fund individuals.

Publications: Annual Report; newsletter; *Humanitarian Innovation Guide* (online); *WASH Innovation Catalogue*; briefing notes; case studies; toolkits.

Finance: Annual revenue £12.7m., expenditure £12.5m. (31 Dec. 2023).

Board of Trustees: Dr Jane Cocking (Chair.).

Principal Staff: Intreim CEO Fiona McSheehy.

Contact Details: 1 St John's Lane, London EC1M 4AR; tel. (29) 2105-2546; e-mail info@elrha.org; internet www.elrha.org.

Elton John AIDS Foundation

Established in 1992 in the USA and 1993 in the United Kingdom by Sir Elton John, a pop musician, and Robert Key, the founding Exec. Dir.

Activities: Funds services and research that focus on the most disadvantaged groups and those most at risk from HIV/AIDS. Priority areas are: children and young people in Africa aged 10–24 years; supporting treatment for LGBT people and confronting homophobia; challenging criminalization of drug use and discrimination against people who use drugs; investing in community-led HIV prevention in Eastern Europe and Central Asia through the RADIAN initiative; and overcoming bias, stigma and racism that prevent people from accessing essential services in the USA.

Geographical Area of Activity: Central Asia, Eastern Europe, India, Myanmar, Russian Federation, sub-Saharan Africa, UK, USA.

Restrictions: No grant applications by e-mail; grants only to organizations working in listed countries.

Publications: Annual Report; newsletter.

Finance: Annual income £26.5m., expenditure £26.5m. (31 Dec. 2023).

Board of Trustees: David Furnish (Chair.); Emma Kane (Deputy Chair.); Tracy Blackwell (Treas.); Jared Cranney (Sec.).

Principal Staff: Global CEO Anne Aslett.

Contact Details: 88 Old St, London EC1V 9HU; tel. (20) 7603-9996; e-mail admin@eltonjohnaidsfoundation.org; internet www.eltonjohnaidsfoundation.org.

Embrace the Middle East

Founded in 1854 as the Turkish Missions Aid Society to support Christian missions in the lands of the Bible; also formerly known as the Bible Lands Society. Present name adopted in 2012.

Activities: Works in the fields of education, healthcare and community development to address poverty and injustice. The organization supports transformational projects that help vulnerable and marginalized people to achieve their potential, principally in historic Christian communities in the Middle East region. It offers volunteering opportunities in the United Kingdom and the Middle East.

Geographical Area of Activity: Egypt, Israel and Palestinian Territories, Iraq, Lebanon, Syrian Arab Repub.

Restrictions: No grants to individuals.

Publications: Annual Report; *Re:Action* (newsletter); *Embrace* (quarterly magazine); study guides; blog.

Finance: Annual income £4.6m., expenditure £4.7m. (31 Dec. 2023).

Council of Trustees: John Mitchell (Chair.); Anne Clayton (Vice-Chair.); Victoria Smith (Treas.).

Principal Staff: CEO Jamie Eyre.

UNITED KINGDOM

Contact Details: Old Library Bldg, Queen Victoria Rd, High Wycombe HP11 1BG; tel. (1494) 897950; e-mail info@embraceme.org; internet www.embraceme.org.

Emunah (Faith)

Established in 1933 by a group of British women to assist children escaping Nazi persecution.

Activities: Promotes the welfare of underprivileged and vulnerable children in Israel; provides funds for education and therapy; and helps dysfunctional families. In Israel, the organization funds special needs centres, residential homes, schools, after-school activities, community centres, sports centres and day-care centres. It is part of World Emunah (f. 1935), which has more than 180,000 members in nearly 30 countries.

Geographical Area of Activity: Israel, UK.

Publications: Annual Report; newsletter (quarterly).

Finance: Annual revenue £958,913, expenditure £913,042 (31 Dec. 2023).

Trustees: Rochelle Selby (Chair.); Rosalyn Liss (Sec.).

Principal Staff: Chair Hilary Lewis; Co-Vice Chair. Sharon Dewinter, Sara Greenfield; CEO Julia Kay.

Contact Details: Unit 2, 74 Grove Park, London NW9 0DD; tel. (20) 8203-6066; e-mail info@emunah.org.uk; internet www.emunah.org.uk.

The English-Speaking Union—ESU

Founded in 1918 by writer and journalist Sir Evelyn Wrench, to promote the mutual advancement of the education of the English-speaking peoples of the world; formerly known as the English-Speaking Union of the Commonwealth.

Activities: Promotes oracy and the development of young people's speaking and listening through education and cultural exchange programmes. The Union organizes the International Public Speaking Competition for students aged 16–20 years; a summer school Debate Academy; and an annual national Shakespeare competition for secondary school students. It offers scholarships and fellowships for British graduates and teachers to pursue research at US universities and institutions, and for study trips to the USA; and awards for British graduates or holders of professional qualifications to work on projects in developing countries. Has groups in 54 countries.

Geographical Area of Activity: International.

Publications: Annual Report; newsletter; *Dialogue*; *ESU Newsletter*; blog.

Finance: Annual income £2.8m., expenditure £3.3m. (31 March 2024).

Board of Trustees: Miles Young (Chair.); Becca Preen, Richard Humphreys (Deputy Chair).

Contact Details: Dartmouth House, 37 Charles St, London W1J 5ED; tel. (20) 7529-1550; e-mail esu@esu.org; internet www.esu.org.

Environmental Justice Foundation—EJF

Established in 1999 by Steve Trent and Juliette Williams, environmental advocates.

Activities: Works in the fields of environmental security and environmental and human rights abuses. Main campaigns focus on climate, cotton, forests, the ocean, and wildlife and biodiversity. The Foundation carries out investigations and makes films; and provides training to organizations and activists on advocacy, communications, desk research, field investigations, and using photography and video. It offers opportunities to volunteer with fundraising, marketing and design; and has staff in Belgium, Brazil, Cameroon, France, Germany, Ghana, Indonesia, Liberia, Senegal, South Korea, Spain, Taiwan, Thailand, the Philippines, Japan and the United Kingdom.

Geographical Area of Activity: Central and South America, East Africa, East and South-East Asia, EU, South Asia, West Africa, UK.

Publications: Annual Report; reports; *EJF Newsletter*.

Finance: Annual income £5.6m., expenditure £5.9m. (31 Dec. 2023).

Board of Trustees: Steve McIvor (Chair.); Bob Lutgen (Treas.).

Principal Staff: CEO Steve Trent.

Contact Details: 2nd Floor, Gensurco House, 3–5 Spafield St, Farringdon, London EC1R 4QB; tel. (20) 7239-3310; e-mail info@ejfoundation.org; internet ejfoundation.org.

Ernest Kleinwort Charitable Trust

Founded in 1963 by Ernest Kleinwort, the former Chair of Kleinwort, Sons & Co. banking house.

Activities: Makes grants under three programmes: to charities in the United Kingdom county of Sussex for care of the elderly, disability, general welfare, hospices, youth, wildlife and environmental conservation; in the UK and internationally for wildlife and environmental conservation; and internationally only for reproductive health and family planning work in Africa and Asia that has a clear and intentional impact on the environment. The Trust awards small grants (up to £10,000), medium-sized grants (from £10,001 to £20,000) and large grants (for £20,001 and over).

Geographical Area of Activity: International, UK (in particular, Sussex).

Restrictions: No grants to individuals; grants only to charities registered in the UK that have been registered for at least a year. Does not fund large charities or animal rescue or animal welfare organizations. Large grants are restricted to existing and long-term grantees; funding is normally only for 12 months.

Publications: Annual Report.

Finance: Annual income £1.3m., expenditure £2.5m. (31 March 2024).

Board: Mark Tyndall (Chair.).

Principal Staff: Dir Sally Case.

Contact Details: EKCT, c/o Andrina Murrell, 1 Bell Lane, Lewes BN7 1JU; tel. (7960) 057742; e-mail admin@ekct.org.uk; internet www.ekct.org.uk.

Esmée Fairbairn Foundation

Founded in 1961 by Ian Fairbairn, a financier, as the Esmée Fairbairn Charitable Trust, in memory of his wife; present name adopted in 2001.

Activities: The Foundation aims to improve the natural world, secure a fairer future and strengthen the bonds in communities in the United Kingdom. The Foundation seeks to unlock change by working with people and organizations that share its goals.

Geographical Area of Activity: UK.

Restrictions: Only funds work that is of direct benefit to the UK and is legally charitable; no grants to individuals, for capital costs, academic research (unless it can demonstrate real potential for practical outcomes), healthcare with a clinical basis, independent education, work that is primarily the responsibility of statutory authorities, or the advancement of religion.

Publications: Annual Report; reports.

Finance: Annual income £8.4m., expenditure £66.5m. (31 Dec. 2023).

Trustees: Beatrice Hollond (Chair.).

Principal Staff: Chief Exec. Dame Caroline Mason.

Contact Details: 210 Pentonville Rd, London N1 9JY; tel. (20) 7812-3700; e-mail info@esmeefairbairn.org.uk; internet www.esmeefairbairn.org.uk.

European Association for Cancer Research—EACR

Established in 1968 by researchers.

Activities: Advances cancer research, from basic research to prevention, treatment and care. The Association organizes conferences and sponsors researchers. It offers Travel Fellowships worth up to €3,000; Meeting Bursaries worth up to

€1,300 to fund attendance at conferences; the Mike Price Gold Medal, every two years, to senior researchers for their contribution to cancer research in Europe; and the Pezcoller Foundation-EACR Cancer Researcher Award. Has over 13,000 members from more than 100 countries within and outside Europe; including 14 affiliated National Societies in Belgium, Croatia, Denmark, France, Germany, Hungary, Ireland, Israel, Italy, Portugal, Serbia, Spain, Türkiye (Turkey) and the United Kingdom.

Geographical Area of Activity: International (mainly Europe).

Publications: *EACR Yearbook* (annual); *European Journal of Cancer* (18 a year); *The Cancer Researcher* (online magazine).

Finance: Annual income £2.2m., expenditure £2.4m. (31 Dec. 2023).

Board: Yardena Samuels (Pres.); René Bernards (Past Pres.); Alberto Bardelli (Sec.-Gen.); Caroline Dive (Treas.).

Principal Staff: CEO Jane Smith.

Contact Details: EACR Secretariat, Sir Colin Campbell Bldg, University of Nottingham Innovation Park, Triumph Rd, Nottingham NG7 2RD; tel. (115) 9515114; e-mail hello@eacr.org; internet www.eacr.org.

Farm Africa

Established in 1985 by Sir Michael Wood and David Campbell in response to famine in Ethiopia.

Activities: Reduces poverty through promoting effective, 'climate-smart' agricultural development. The organization provides business training for farmers; sets up farmers' groups; and promotes innovation, using mobile technology to reach the most farmers possible, improve production and connect farmers with business. It has regional offices in Ethiopia, Kenya, Tanzania and Uganda.

Geographical Area of Activity: Dem. Repub. of the Congo, Ethiopia, Kenya, Tanzania, Uganda.

Restrictions: Does not accept unsolicited applications.

Publications: Annual Review; newsletter; reports; studies; surveys.

Finance: Annual income £11.0m., expenditure £14.2m. (31 Dec. 2023).

Board of Trustees: John Reizenstein (Chair.); Nick Allen (Vice-Chair.); Kieth Pickard (Treas.).

Principal Staff: Chief Exec. Dan Collison.

Contact Details: 1 St John's Lane, London EC1M 4BL; tel. (20) 7430-0440; e-mail info@farmafrica.org; internet www.farmafrica.org.

Feed the Minds

Founded in 1964 by Lord Coggan, who was Archbishop of Canterbury from 1974 to 1980.

Activities: Works in the field of international development. The organization runs practical education projects, supporting adults living in poverty to have a new start. Projects reach people, especially women, who missed out on school or training opportunities due to extreme poverty, conflict and/or discrimination. Adult education projects focus on three themes, each of which includes an element of literacy skills training. The three themes are: citizenship, economic empowerment and health education. Manages the day-to-day activities of the United Society for Christian Literature—USCL (f. 1799), which makes grants to Feed the Minds to support practical education projects worldwide; serving communities of all faiths and none.

Geographical Area of Activity: Africa, Asia, Oceania.

Publications: Annual Review.

Finance: Annual income £779,617, expenditure £754,346 (30 April 2024).

Board of Trustees: Sandy Sneddon (Chair.); Rev. Canon Mark Oxbrow (Pres.); Garry Beech (Treas.).

Principal Staff: Interim CEO Lucy Moore.

Contact Details: The Foundry, 17 Oval Way, London SE11 5RR; tel. (20) 3752-5797; e-mail together@feedtheminds.org; internet www.feedtheminds.org.

Finnish Institute in the UK and Ireland Trust

Founded in 1991; one of 17 Finnish cultural and academic institutes.

Activities: Works with artists, researchers, experts and policymakers to promote networks in the fields of culture and social studies, funding artists and researchers. The Institute awards the Below Zero contemporary art prize, worth £15,000; and offers Finnish language lessons through its Finnish School. It offers internships of 4–12 months to Finnish students of administration, arts and culture, social sciences and communication.

Geographical Area of Activity: Finland, Ireland, UK.

Publications: Annual Report; newsletter; reports; working papers; Reaktio (book series); blog.

Finance: Finnish Ministry of Education and Culture annual funding €780,000 (2022).

Executive Board: Malin Groop (Chair.).

Principal Staff: Dir Jaakko Nousiainen.

Contact Details: Somerset House, New Wing, Strand, London WC2R 1LA; tel. (20) 3701-7660; e-mail info@fininst.uk; internet www.fininst.uk.

FORWARD—Foundation for Women's Health Research and Development

Founded in 1983 by Efua Dorkenoo, a campaigner against female genital mutilation (FGM).

Activities: Promotes gender equality and safeguards the rights of African girls and women. The Foundation works to end FGM, child marriage and obstetric fistula. Activities include community engagement programmes and lobbying governments. It runs programmes in Africa and among the African diaspora in the United Kingdom and the EU; and is part of a consortium that oversees the TuWezeshe Akina Dada Africa–UK Young Women's Leadership and Empowerment Movement, which offers one-year fellowships to those who are interested in or are currently working in the field of sexual and gender-based rights advocacy.

Geographical Area of Activity: Ethiopia, EU, Kenya, Sierra Leone, Somaliland, Tanzania, Uganda, UK.

Restrictions: Does not make grants; the TuWezeshe Fellowship is open to black British and African women, aged 18–26 years, who live in the UK.

Publications: Annual Report; newsletters; reports; guides.

Finance: Annual income £706,211, expenditure £871,507 (31 March 2024).

Board of Trustees: Dr Titilola Banjoko (Chair.); Dr Lisa Smith (Treas.).

Principal Staff: Exec. Dir Naana Otoo-Oyortey.

Contact Details: Suite 4.8, Chandelier Bldg, 8 Scrubs Lane, London NW10 6RB; tel. (20) 8960-4000; e-mail forward@forwarduk.org.uk; internet www.forwarduk.org.uk.

Freedom from Torture (Medical Foundation for the Care of Victims of Torture)

Founded in 1985 by Helen Bamber and Amnesty International volunteers for the Care of Victims of Torture.

Activities: Freedom from Torture provides a holistic programme of therapeutic and practical support for survivors of torture (asylum seekers and refugees), encompassing psychological therapy; stabilization groups; pain self-management; social group activities; legal and welfare advice; and medico-legal reports across five treatment centres in London, Birmingham, Manchester, Newcastle and Glasgow. Also undertakes research, policy and advocacy, campaigning, and survivor activism work to protect the rights of torture survivors as well as delivering training and capacity-building to statutory and voluntary organizations. Supports hundreds of survivors through therapy and care co-ordination work,

UNITED KINGDOM

helping them to process and recover from their trauma and reintegrate into their communities. Alongside this, Survivors Speak OUT—SSO (f. 2007) is a national network of torture survivors and former clients of Freedom from Torture, nested within and supported by the organization to advocate for the rights of survivors.

Geographical Area of Activity: UK.

Publications: Annual Review; *Supporter* (e-newsletter); thematic reports.

Finance: Annual income £9.9m., expenditure £12.1m. (31 Dec. 2023).

Principal Staff: CEO Sonya Sceats.

Contact Details: 111 Iseldon Rd, Islington, London N7 7JW; tel. (20) 7697-7777; e-mail info@freedomfromtorture.org; internet www.freedomfromtorture.org.

The Gaia Foundation

Founded in 1985 by Liz Hosken and Ed Posey; began its work in the Amazon region.

Activities: Works to restore resilience in ecosystems and local communities, through reviving and protecting cultural and biological diversity. Programmes include: Food, Seed and Climate Change Resilience, supporting small farmers, in particular women, and promoting regenerative agriculture; Earth Jurisprudence, which recognizes nature as the primary source of law and ethics; Beyond Extractivism, helping local, indigenous and traditional communities and organizations to protect water, land and life, and create alternatives to natural resource extraction; and Sacred Lands and Wilderness, protecting the rights of traditional custodians. The Foundation provides training and peer-to-peer learning exchanges for community and civil leaders; provides legal and policy advice and advocacy; and manages a Small Grants Fund.

Geographical Area of Activity: International.

Restrictions: Does not make grants to individuals.

Publications: Annual Report; reports; briefings; papers.

Finance: Annual income £1.5m., expenditure £1.3m. (31 Dec. 2023).

Principal Staff: Dir Liz Hosken; Deputy Dir Rowan Phillimore.

Contact Details: 44 Grand Parade, Brighton BN2 9QA; tel. (7483) 950855; e-mail info@gaianet.org; internet www.gaiafoundation.org.

Garden Organic

Founded in 1958 by Lawrence Hills, a journalist, as the Henry Doubleday Research Association, named after the 19th-century Quaker smallholder who brought comfrey to the United Kingdom; adopted Garden Organic as its working name in 2005.

Activities: Works in the fields of conservation and the environment, science and education, through self-conducted programmes nationally and internationally. The organization conducts research; organizes conferences and training courses; runs an education and conference centre; and has a consultancy department on organic waste disposal. It maintains organic gardens, a Heritage Seed Library and the Vegetable Kingdom visitor centre; and trades through Organic Enterprises Ltd.

Geographical Area of Activity: International.

Publications: Annual Report; *Organic Matters* (monthly newsletter); *The Organic Way* (2 a year); step-by-step guides; organic gardening books; composting manuals.

Finance: Annual income £2.1m., expenditure £2.1m. (31 Dec. 2023).

Council of Trustees: Angela Wright (Chair.); Joe McIndoe, Mark Mitchell (Vice-Chair.); Keith Arrowsmith (Treas.).

Principal Staff: Chief Exec. Fiona Taylor.

Contact Details: Ryton Gardens, Wolston Lane, Ryton on Dunsmore, Coventry CV8 3LG; tel. (24) 7630-3517; e-mail enquiry@gardenorganic.org.uk; internet www.gardenorganic.org.uk.

Garfield Weston Foundation

Established in 1958 by Willard Garfield Weston, a Canadian business person who founded Associated British Foods, a food processing and retailing company.

Activities: Makes grants to charities in the areas of: the arts; community projects; education and lifelong learning; the environment; faith-based activities; health information services and capital projects; museums and heritage; welfare, supporting vulnerable and disadvantaged people; and young people. The Foundation offers Regular Grants for applications up to £100,000 and Major Grants for applications of £100,000 or more.

Geographical Area of Activity: Mainly UK, with limited funding available overseas.

Restrictions: Grants only to registered charities (with the exception of applications from churches); no grants for animal welfare projects.

Publications: Annual Report; blog.

Finance: Annual income £110.3m., expenditure £102.0m. (5 April 2024).

Trustees: Sir Guy H. Weston (Chair.); Sophia Weston (Deputy Chair.).

Principal Staff: Interim Dir Flora Craig.

Contact Details: Weston Centre, 10 Grosvenor St, London W1K 4QY; tel. (20) 7399-6565; e-mail admin@garfieldweston.org; internet www.garfieldweston.org.

The Gatsby Charitable Foundation

Established in 1967 by David Sainsbury; one of the Sainsbury Family Charitable Trusts (q.v.), which share a common administration.

Activities: Currently active in: plant science research; neuroscience research; science and engineering education; economic development in Africa; public policy research and advice; and the arts. The Foundation acts as an enabler for projects, designing, developing, overseeing and, in some cases, delivering activities. In partnership with the Wellcome Trust (q.v.) it established the Sainsbury Wellcome Centre for Neural Circuits and Behaviour.

Geographical Area of Activity: sub-Saharan Africa, UK.

Restrictions: Does not accept unsolicited applications; no grants to individuals.

Publications: Annual Review.

Finance: Annual income £61.2m., expenditure £82.1m. (5 April 2024).

Principal Staff: CEO Peter Hesketh.

Contact Details: The Peak, 5 Wilton Rd, London SW1V 1AP; tel. (20) 7410-0330; e-mail contact@gatsby.org.uk; internet www.gatsby.org.uk.

Global Health Partnerships

Established in 1988, as the Tropical Health and Education Trust, by Prof. Sir Eldryd Parry, a physician; formerly known as THET, name changed in 2024.

Activities: Trains healthcare workers and supports capacity development of health systems and through self-conducted programmes, grant management and policy work. The organization supports Health Partnerships between hospitals, universities, research centres and other health institutions in the United Kingdom and overseas.

Geographical Area of Activity: Ethiopia, Myanmar, Somalia (Somaliland), Tanzania, Uganda, UK, Zambia.

Restrictions: Grants only to established Health Partnerships.

Publications: Annual Report; newsletter; case studies; reports; toolkits; blog.

Global Innovation Fund   UNITED KINGDOM

Finance: Annual income £5.3m., expenditure £5.3m. (31 Dec. 2023).

Trustees: Justin Ash (Chair.); John Headley (Treas.).

Principal Staff: CEO Ben Simms.

Contact Details: 3rd Floor, 86–90 Paul St, London EC2A 4NE; tel. (7399) 621271; e-mail info@thet.org; internet www.globalhealthpartnerships.org.

Global Innovation Fund

Established in 2013.

Activities: Invests in innovative new business models, policy practices, technologies, behavioural insights and means of delivering products and services that have great potential for large-scale social impact and will benefit poor people in developing countries. The Fund offers grants, loans and equity investments, with funding ranging from US $50,000 to $15m. Has offices in Nairobi, Kenya, and Washington, DC, USA.

Geographical Area of Activity: Central America, Middle East, South Asia, South-East Asia, sub-Saharan Africa, UK, USA.

Publications: Annual Report; newsletter; manuals; reports; toolkits; blog.

Finance: Annual income £5.4m., expenditure £8.2m. (31 Dec. 2023).

Board: James Clark (Chair.).

Principal Staff: CEO Joseph Ssentongo.

Contact Details: WeWork/Spice Bldg, 8 Devonshire Sq., London EC2M 4PL; tel. (20) 7971-1078; e-mail hello@globalinnovation.fund; internet www.globalinnovation.fund.

Good Things Foundation

Established in 2011 as the Online Centres Foundation; subsequently renamed Tinder Foundation in 2013. Present name adopted in 2016.

Activities: Promotes social change through digital inclusion. Programmes focus on health and wellbeing, financial inclusion, employability, and essential digital skills including AI literacy and digital media literacy. Good Things provides a free learning platform: Learn My Way, which has over 100 topics on essential digital skills; supports the National Digital Inclusion Network, comprising more than 5,000 grassroots organizations that provide people with skills to use digital technology. In Australia it manages the national Be Connected Network, comprising 3,000 community organizations that provide older people with digital skills.

Geographical Area of Activity: Australia, UK.

Publications: Newsletter (monthly).

Finance: Annual income £8.9m., expenditure £10.1m. (31 July 2024).

Board of Trustees: Liz Williams (Chair.).

Principal Staff: Group Chief Exec. Helen Milner.

Contact Details: Showroom Workstation, 15 Paternoster Row, Sheffield S1 2BX; tel. (114) 3491666; e-mail hello@goodthingsfoundation.org; internet www.goodthingsfoundation.org.

Goodenough College

Established in 1930 by Frederick Craufurd Goodenough, Chairman of Barclays Bank, as the Dominions Students' Hall Trust; present name adopted in 2001.

Activities: An independent residential community of international postgraduate students. The College organizes workshops, seminars, conferences and public events, cultural, artistic, community volunteering and sporting activities; and offers scholarships and bursaries. It owns 'The Burn' country house in the Scottish Highlands, which is used for study retreats and holidays, and by reading groups from universities in Scotland during term time.

Geographical Area of Activity: UK.

Restrictions: Open to postgraduate students by application.

Publications: Annual Review; newsletter (2 a year); brochures.

Finance: Annual income £16.7m., expenditure £15.5m. (31 August 2023).

Board of Trustees: Stuart Shilson (Chair.); Andrew Brown, Dame Maura McGowan (Vice-Chair.).

Principal Staff: Dir Alice Walpole; Dean Alan McCormack.

Contact Details: Mecklenburgh Sq., London WC1N 2AB; tel. (20) 7837-8888; e-mail reservations@goodenough.ac.uk; internet www.goodenough.ac.uk.

Great Britain Sasakawa Foundation

Founded in 1985 by Ryoichi Sasakawa, a business person and politician, with a £10m. donation from what is now named the Nippon Foundation (q.v.).

Activities: Supports reciprocal projects between Japan and the United Kingdom in the fields of: the arts and culture; the humanities and social issues; Japanese language; medicine and health; science, technology and the environment; sport; and youth and education. The Foundation offers Butterfield Awards for collaboration in medicine and health, worth up to £10,000 a year for a maximum of three years; and the Japan Experience Study Tour Programme for sixth formers from the UK. It administers the Sasakawa Japanese Studies Postgraduate Studentship Programme, which is fully funded by the Nippon Foundation, providing up to 30 studentships annually, each worth £15,000. Has an office in Tokyo, Japan.

Geographical Area of Activity: Japan, UK.

Restrictions: Grants to institutions and organizations of the UK or Japan.

Publications: Annual Report.

Finance: Annual income £1.4m., expenditure £1.5m. (31 Dec. 2023).

Board of Trustees: The Earl of St Andrews (Chair.); Joanna Pitman (Vice-Chair.); Jeremy Scott (Treas.).

Principal Staff: Chief Exec. Charles Bodsworth; Dir of Japan Office Kyoko Haruta.

Contact Details: Lower Ground Floor, 24 Bedford Row, London WC1R 4TQ; tel. (20) 7436-9042; e-mail gbsf@gbsf.org.uk; internet www.gbsf.org.uk.

Great Ormond Street Hospital Children's Charity

Founded in 1998 as a separate legal entity from Great Ormond Street Hospital (GOSH).

Activities: Supports GOSH and its patients in four key areas: building maintenance and refurbishment; help and support for the families of children going through live-saving treatment; funding clinical research into children's health and childhood diseases; and funding the provision of the latest medical equipment.

Geographical Area of Activity: England.

Finance: Total income £131.2m., expenditure £93.2m. (31 March 2024).

Trustees: Anne Bulford (Chair.).

Principal Staff: Chief Exec. Louise Parkes.

Contact Details: 40 Bernard St, London WC1N 1LE; tel. (20) 3841-3841; e-mail supporter.care@gosh.org; internet www.gosh.org.

The Guardian Foundation

Established in 1992 as the Scott Trust Foundation, the charitable arm of the Scott Trust, the sole shareholder in the Guardian Media Group; present name adopted in 2013.

Activities: The Foundation works directly with journalists, news organizations, audiences and educators, in schools and across communities to: build news and media literacy skills for the next generation; champion more diverse voices and perspectives in the media; and support at-risk independent media to continue their work and engage audiences with fact based journalism. Programmes include: NewsWise, which teaches news literacy for children aged 7–11; Behind the Headlines, which focuses on opening up the world of news for young people; the Emerging Voices Awards recognizing young talent in political opinion writing; the Scott Trust Bursary, which supports journalists from underrepresented backgrounds; the Incubator for Independent Media, which aims to build capacity for journalists from across Turkey; and the GNM Archive for preserving and sharing Guardian and Observer history.

Geographical Area of Activity: Worldwide.

Restrictions: Not primarily a grant-giving organization; works with and sub-grants to partners on joint projects.

Publications: Annual Report.

Finance: Annual income £1.9m., expenditure £1.8m. (31 March 2024).

Board of Trustees: Keith Magee (Chair.).

Principal Staff: Exec. Dir Kelly Walls.

Contact Details: POB 68164, Kings Pl., 90 York Way, London N1 9GU; tel. (20) 3353-3759; e-mail info@theguardianfoundation.org; internet theguardianfoundation.org.

The Guide Dogs for the Blind Association

Founded in 1931 by Muriel Crooke and Rosamund Bond.

Activities: Breeds and trains working dogs to provide assistance to blind and partially sighted people in the United Kingdom. Carries out research to determine the needs of guide dog users as well as understanding how best to cater to the welfare and training needs of working dogs. Advocates for policy change. Raises awareness of eye conditions and runs fundraising campaigns.

Geographical Area of Activity: UK.

Publications: Annual Report; reports.

Finance: Total income £144.7m., expenditure £145.0m. (31 Dec. 2023).

Board of Trustees: Isabel Hudson (Chair.).

Principal Staff: Chief Exec. Andrew Lennox.

Contact Details: Hillfields, Burghfield Common, Reading RG7 3YG; tel. (118) 9835555; e-mail guidedogs@guidedogs.org.uk; internet www.guidedogs.org.uk.

HALO Trust

Established in 1989, as the Hazardous Area Life-Support Organization—HALO, by Guy Willoughby and Colin Mitchell, former soldiers.

Activities: Specializes in removing the debris of war, particularly mine clearance. The Trust works with local and national governments, as well as aid and development organizations; and builds capacity in local communities, training local teams of managers, mine clearers, mechanics, medical staff, technicians and drivers. It works in 24 countries and territories, with an office in Salisbury, England. HALO Trust US is based in Washington, DC, USA.

Geographical Area of Activity: Eastern Europe and the Caucasus, Latin America, Middle East, South Asia, South-Eastern Europe, sub-Saharan Africa.

Restrictions: Not a grantmaking organization.

Publications: Annual Report; newsletter.

Finance: Annual income £147.6m., expenditure £145.1m. (31 March 2024).

UK Board of Trustees: Jonathan Evans (Chair.).

US Board of Trustees: Rexon Ryu (Chair.); Jamie M. Morin (Vice-Chair.).

Principal Staff: CEO James Cowan.

Contact Details: Carronfoot, Thornhill, Dumfries DG3 5BF; tel. (1848) 331100; e-mail mail@halotrust.org; internet www.halotrust.org.

Headley Trust

Founded in 1973; one of the Sainsbury Family Charitable Trusts (q.v.), which share a common administration.

Activities: Areas of interest include arts and heritage in the United Kingdom and overseas; restoration or repair of cathedrals; bursaries for British graduate/postgraduate students in dance and music, primary school music tuition, vocational training in conservation and heritage skills; health and social welfare, support for older people to live independently for as long as possible, improve older people's quality of life in residential care homes including supporting people with dementia; support for disadvantaged families and young people. Work overseas including sub-Saharan Anglophone Africa, development projects on education and employment interventions for women and girls, sanitation and hygiene and community health programmes. Arts and Heritage work in South-Eastern Europe. In 2010 the Trust established the Headley Museums Archaeological Acquisition Fund.

Geographical Area of Activity: South-Eastern Europe, sub-Saharan Anglophone Africa, UK.

Restrictions: does not fund parish churches; does not fund individuals, expeditions or fees.

Publications: Annual Report.

Finance: Annual income £2.2m., expenditure £6.5m. (5 April 2024).

Principal Staff: Lead Exec. Helen McLeod.

Contact Details: c/o The Sainsbury Family Charitable Trusts, The Peak, 5 Wilton Rd, London SW1V 1AP; tel. (20) 7410-0330; e-mail headley.trust@sfct.org.uk; internet www.sfct.org.uk/the-headley-trust.

The Health Foundation

Established in 1983 as the PPP Medical Trust; became fully independent in 1998, following the sale of the PPP Healthcare group to Guardian Royal Exchange. Present name adopted in 2003.

Activities: Works for better health and healthcare for people in the United Kingdom. The Foundation awards grants for research and policy analysis, to inform effective policymaking, and fellowships.

Geographical Area of Activity: UK.

Restrictions: No grants for capital works.

Publications: Annual Report; newsletter; briefings; learning reports; policy analysis; quick guides; blog.

Finance: Annual income £18.6m., expenditure £62.7m. (31 Dec. 2023).

Board of Governors: Sir Hugh Taylor (Chair.).

Principal Staff: Chief Exec. Dr Jennifer Dixon.

Contact Details: Salisbury Sq. House, 8 Salisbury Sq., London EC4Y 8AP; tel. (20) 7257-8000; e-mail info@health.org.uk; internet www.health.org.uk.

HelpAge International

Founded in 1983 by Help the Aged (Canada), HelpAge (India), HelpAge (Kenya), Help the Aged (UK) and Pro Vida Colombia.

Activities: Works to improve the lives of disadvantaged older people through providing expertise and grants to organizations serving the needs of older people. The organization promotes a positive image of older people worldwide; provides advocacy, training and research, disaster relief, refugee resettlement and rehabilitation; and develops and supports programmes designed to meet the financial, material, medical and social needs of older people worldwide. Has 199 member organizations in 98 countries; with regional centres in Amman (Jordan), Bogotá (Colombia), Chiang Mai (Thailand), Nairobi (Kenya) and London.

Geographical Area of Activity: International.

Restrictions: Grants only to older people and those working with them; mainly funds its own projects.

Publications: Annual Report; newsletter; briefings; guidelines; reports; studies.

Finance: Annual income £34.3m., expenditure £42.2m. (31 March 2024).

Governing Board: Sarah Harper (Chair.); Helen Mealins (Treas.).
Principal Staff: Chief Exec. Cherian Matthews.
Contact Details: POB 78840, London SE1 7RL; tel. (20) 7278-7778; e-mail info@helpage.org; internet www.helpage.org.

The Henry Moore Foundation

Founded in 1977 by Henry Moore, a sculptor, and his family to encourage public appreciation of the visual arts and in particular the works of Henry Moore.
Activities: Operates nationally and internationally through self-conducted programmes; and nationally through research, funding for institutions, scholarships, bursaries and fellowships (with grants of up to £20,000 a year), and publications. The Foundation maintains Henry Moore's former home and studios in Hertfordshire, United Kingdom; and funds exhibitions and research at the Henry Moore Institute in Leeds. It maintains an archive.
Geographical Area of Activity: International.
Publications: Annual Report; *Henry Moore Foundation Review*; bibliographies; catalogues; books.
Finance: Annual income £8.9m., expenditure £6.7m. (31 March 2024).
Board of Trustees: David Isaac (Chair.).
Principal Staff: Dir Godfrey Worsdale.
Contact Details: Dane Tree House, Perry Green, Much Hadham SG10 6EE; tel. (1279) 843333; e-mail admin@henry-moore.org; internet www.henry-moore.org.

The Henry Smith Charity

Established in 1628 for the relief of the poor kindred of Henry Smith, the relief and maintenance of 'Godly preachers', and limited charitable purposes.
Activities: Operates locally in the areas of medicine and health and social welfare through two main programmes, Improving Lives and Strengthening Communities. Grants range from £20,000 to £60,000 for 1–3 years. The Charity also awards County Grants, worth between £500 and £20,000, usually for 1–2 years, for small organizations working with people from disadvantaged backgrounds; and Holiday Grants, worth between £500 and £2,500, for recreational trips for disabled or disadvantaged children under 13 years of age.
Geographical Area of Activity: UK.
Restrictions: Grants are usually made to community-led charities and social enterprises.
Publications: Annual Report.
Finance: Annual income £14.4m., expenditure £65.5m. (31 Dec. 2023).
Board of Trustees: William Sieghart (Chair.).
Principal Staff: CEO Anand Shukla.
Contact Details: Caledonia House, 3rd Floor, 223 Pentonville Rd, London N1 9NG; tel. (20) 7264-4970; internet www.henrysmithcharity.org.uk.

Historic Environment Scotland (Àrainneachd Eachdraidheil Alba)

Established in 2015 by the merger of the merger of Historic Scotland, a government agency, with the Royal Commission on the Ancient and Historical Monuments of Scotland; a non-departmental public body with charitable status, governed by a Board of Trustees appointed by Scottish Ministers.
Activities: Investigates, cares for and promotes Scotland's historic environment, including more than 300 buildings, monuments and places of national importance. The body funds national and local organizations through making grants to support ancient monuments, archaeological work, building repairs, coastal and waterway heritage, the Conservation Area Regeneration Scheme and voluntary sector. It provides guidance, training and technical research on Scotland's built environment; and promotes community and individual learning about national heritage. Maintained collections include more than 5m. drawings, photographs and manuscripts; and 20m. aerial images of international locations.
Geographical Area of Activity: Scotland.
Publications: Annual Report; *The Keystone* (newsletter); teaching resources (online); Gaelic learning resources; Canmore (online heritage catalogue); Scran (digital heritage resources); blog.
Finance: Annual income £137.0m., expenditure £129.1m. (31 March 2024).
Board: Hugh Hall (Chair.).
Principal Staff: Chief Exec. Katerina Brown.
Contact Details: Longmore House, Salisbury Pl., Edinburgh EH9 1SH; John Sinclair House, 16 Bernard Terrace, Edinburgh EH8 9NX; tel. (131) 668-8600; e-mail website@hes.scot; internet www.historicenvironment.scot.

Hodge Foundation

Founded in 1962 as the Jane Hodge Foundation by Sir Julian Hodge, an entrepreneur and banker, in memory of his mother.
Activities: Main programme areas are: welfare, supporting vulnerable or disadvantaged people; education, both learning in formal school settings and vocational training; medical, with a focus on local hospices, children's care and university-based research on cancer and mental health; and religion, funding projects including facilities in church buildings and activities that involve the wider community. The Foundation funded the establishment of the Julian Hodge Institute of Applied Macroeconomics and the Hodge Centre for Neuropsychiatric Immunology at Cardiff University.
Geographical Area of Activity: Worldwide.
Restrictions: Grants only to charities registered in the UK or exempt charities.
Publications: Annual Report; *Annual Memorial Lecture*.
Finance: Annual income £3.7m., expenditure £1.9m. (30 Sept. 2023).
Trustees: J. Jonathan Hodge (Chair.).
Contact Details: 1 Central Sq., Cardiff CF10 1FS; tel. (29) 2078-7674; e-mail contact@hodgefoundation.org.uk; internet www.hodgefoundation.org.uk.

Homeless World Cup Foundation—HWCF

Established in 2001 by Mel Young, a social entrepreneur, and Harald Schmied, Editor-in-Chief of Austrian street newspaper *Das Megaphon*.
Activities: Supports people who are homeless; and works to change perceptions of and attitudes towards people experiencing homelessness. The Foundation operates through a network of Street Football Partners in almost 70 countries; and organizes an annual international football tournament.
Geographical Area of Activity: International.
Publications: Annual Report.
Finance: Annual income £342,657, expenditure £327,637 (31 Dec. 2023).
Board of Trustees: Mel Young (Chair.).
Principal Staff: COO James McMeekin.
Contact Details: 2nd Floor, 48 Palmerston Pl., Edinburgh EH12 5DE; e-mail info@homelessworldcup.org; internet www.homelessworldcup.org.

Hope not Hate Charitable Trust—HNHCT

Established in 1992 as the charitable arm of Hope not Hate (f. 1986 as Searchlight Information Services).
Activities: Hope not Hate monitors, exposes and challenges the far right, engages with the communities who are susceptibble to them, and adresses the issues and policies which give rise to them. HNHCT promotes inclusive, resilient communities and challenges mistrust and racism through research, education and public engagement. The Trust supports education and training programmes in schools for pupils and

teachers. It also offers community training workshops; and workplace training on challenging prejudice and supporting workers. The Hope Education Fund supports education outreach in schools.

Geographical Area of Activity: UK.

Publications: Annual Report.

Finance: Annual income £418,237, expenditure £794,578 (31 Dec. 2023).

Trustees: Gurinder Singh Josan (Chair.).

Principal Staff: CEO Nick Lowles; Deputy Dir and Sec. Jemma Levene.

Contact Details: 5th Floor, 167–169 Great Portland St, London W1W 5PF; tel. (20) 7952-1181; e-mail info@hopenothate.org.uk; internet hopenothate.org.uk/hnh-charitable-trust.

Human Dignity Trust

Established in 2011.

Activities: Defends the rights of LGBT+ people by offering legal support. In collaboration with a network of 25 law firms worldwide, the Trust supports cases seeking to decriminalize same-sex marriage, uphold freedoms for LGBT+ people, ensure protections against discrimination and challenge degrading treatment of LGBT+ people, particularly in cases of medical care.

Geographical Area of Activity: International.

Finance: Total income £1.8m., expenditure £1.4m. (31 March 2024).

Board: Dr Conway Blake (Chair.); Patrick Doris (Deputy Chair.); Matthew Robinson (Treas.).

Principal Staff: CEO Téa Braun.

Contact Details: Quality House, 4th Floor West, 5–9 Quality Court, Chancery Lane, London WC2A 1HP; tel. (20) 7419-3770; e-mail info@humandignitytrust.org; internet www.humandignitytrust.org.

Humanitarian Academy for Development—HAD

Established in 2013 as the learning and development arm of Islamic Relief Worldwide—IRW (q.v.); became an independent organization in 2018.

Activities: Carries out training and consultancy in the fields of humanitarian and international development through capacity building of non-governmental and CSOs, applied research, and leadership and management development. The organization offers short-term visiting fellowships for Academic Fellows with an interest in faith-literate development; and for Postgraduate Fellows conducting research on international development and humanitarian aid. It also runs workplace and field-based internships and a one-year graduate programme. Works in partnership with IRW through more than 40 field offices.

Geographical Area of Activity: International.

Publications: Annual Report; newsletter; fact sheets; policy papers; reports; studies; blog.

Board: Dr Mohamed Amr Attawia (Chair.).

Principal Staff: Man. Dir Dr Hossam Said.

Contact Details: 22–24 Sampson Rd North, Birmingham B11 1BL; tel. (121) 309-0290; e-mail info@had-int.org; internet had-int.org.

The Hunter Foundation—THF

Established in 1998 by Sir Tom Hunter, a business person, and Lady Marion Hunter.

Activities: Operates through venture philanthropy, promoting entrepreneurship, investing in education and funding partnerships to provide opportunity for all. The Foundation works overseas in partnership with the Clinton Foundation (q.v.) through the Clinton Hunter Development Initiative and has also funded scholarship programmes. In 2018 it launched the 100 Disrupters competition for young people aged under 26 years, awarding 100 grants of £1,000 to individuals or groups to fund innovation in Scotland.

Geographical Area of Activity: Rwanda, UK (especially Scotland).

Publications: Annual Report; *Britain's Decision: Facts and Impartial Analysis.*

Finance: Annual income £1.1m., expenditure £3.9m. (31 March 2024).

Trustees: Sir Tom Hunter (Chair.).

Principal Staff: CEO Ewan Hunter.

Contact Details: Marathon House, Olympic Business Park, Drybridge Rd, Dundonald KA2 9AE; e-mail info@thehunterfoundation.co.uk; internet www.thehunterfoundation.co.uk.

Inclusion International

Established in 1960.

Activities: Inclusion International is the global federation of organizations of persons with disabilities (OPDs) representing people with intellectual disabilities and their families. Inclusion International campaigns on behalf of the human rights of people with intellectual disabilities worldwide. The organization hosts regional forums for families and self-advocates to learn from each other about initiatives in different countries that promote and implement aspects of the UN Convention on the Rights of Persons with Disabilities. It draws on the knowledge and expertise of its volunteers and member organizations to support country-level initiatives; and collaborates with the International Disability Alliance, UN agencies and development agencies to identify opportunities to include and promote the rights of people with intellectual disabilities in their work, campaigning to promote their right to live within the community. Represents more than 200 member federations in 115 countries.

Geographical Area of Activity: Asia-Pacific, Europe, Middle East and North Africa, North and South America, sub-Saharan Africa.

Publications: Annual Report; Global Reports; position statements; *Inclusion Around the World* (newsletter).

Finance: Annual income £814,992, expenditure £824,421 (31 Dec. 2023).

Officers of the Council: Sue Swenson (Pres.); Luis Gabriel Villarreal (Vice-Pres.); Nagase Osamu (Sec.-Gen.); Lloyd Lewis (Treas.).

Principal Staff: Interim Exec. Dir Manuela Hasselknippe.

Contact Details: Office 1.6, The Foundry, 17 Oval Way, London SE11 5RR; tel. (20) 3752-5653; e-mail info@inclusion-international.org; internet www.inclusion-international.org.

Institute of Economic Affairs—IEA

Established in 1955 by Sir Antony Fisher, who introduced factory farming to the United Kingdom and founded the Atlas Network (q.v.) in the USA, and Lord Harris of High Cross, an economist; a free market think tank.

Activities: Carries out research on economic and social problems and promotes markets' role in solving them without government interference. The Institute organizes conferences, seminars and lectures; runs an educational and international outreach programme; and issues publications. For an essay on a contemporary public policy question it offers a student Monetary Policy Essay Prize, worth a total of £4,500; and the Dorian Fisher Memorial Prize for schools, worth a total of £750.

Geographical Area of Activity: International (mainly UK).

Publications: Annual Report; newsletter; *Economic Affairs* (journal, 3 a year); *EA Magazine* (2 a year); policy papers; consultation responses; reports; books.

Finance: Annual income £5.9m., expenditure £3.0m. (31 March 2024).

Board of Trustees: Linda Edwards (Chair.).

Principal Staff: Exec. Dir Tom Clougherty.

International Alert—Alert

Founded in 1986 by Martin Ennals, Archbishop Desmond Tutu and other human rights advocates.

Activities: Their vision is a world where conflicts can be resolved without violence and people work together to support and sustain peace. Works with people around the world to support a sustainable and inclusive end to violence by: working with people directly affected by violence to support lasting solutions; advocating with them for the changes to policies, practices and behaviours that are required for peace to be inclusive and sustainable; and collaborating openly and in solidarity with all those striving for peace, to strengthen the common cause.

Geographical Area of Activity: Africa, Asia, the Middle East, Europe.

Restrictions: Not a grantmaking organization.

Publications: Research papers; policy briefs; guidance notes; toolkits.

Finance: Annual income £19.2m., expenditure £20.7m. (31 December 2023).

Board of Trustees: David Nussbaum (Chair.); Emma Hillyard (Treas.).

Principal Staff: Exec. Dir Nic Hailey.

Contact Details: 10 Salamanca Pl., London, SE1 7HB; e-mail info@international-alert.org; internet www.international-alert.org.

International Institute for Environment and Development—IIED

Founded in 1971 by economist and policy adviser Barbara Ward.

Activities: Works to build a fairer, more sustainable world, using evidence, action and influence, working in partnership with others. Promotes sustainable development to improve livelihoods and protect the environment. The Institute carries out research, policy studies, networking and information dissemination through four research groups: Climate Change; Human Settlements; Natural Resources; and Shaping Sustainable Markets. It works in partnership with individuals and organizations internationally to ensure that policy reflects the agendas of marginalized people. Has an office in Edinburgh, Scotland.

Geographical Area of Activity: Africa, Asia, Central and South America, Middle East.

Publications: Annual Report; newsletters; journals; reports; briefing papers; podcasts; videos.

Finance: Total revenue £26.1m., expenditure £26.3m. (31 March 2024).

Board of Trustees: Tara Shine (Chair.); Paul George (Deputy Chair.); Les Campbell (Treas.).

Principal Staff: Exec. Dir Tom Mitchell.

Contact Details: 44 Southampton Bldgs, London, WC2A 1AP; tel. (20) 3463-7399; e-mail inforequest@iied.org; internet www.iied.org.

The International Institute for Strategic Studies—IISS

Established in 1958 by Prof. Sir Michael Howard, a military historian, Denis Healey, a politician, and Alastair Buchan, the defence correspondent for *The Observer* newspaper, growing out of a study group at the Royal Institute of International Affairs—RIIA—Chatham House (q.v.); a research institute and membership organization.

Activities: Promotes, on a non-party basis, the study and discussion of, and exchange of information on, military strategy, weapons control, regional security and conflict resolution. Thematic research programmes include: defence and military analysis; conflict, security and development; non-proliferation and nuclear policy; geoeconomics, geopolitics and strategy; and cyber, space and future conflict. The Institute organizes conferences, discussion meetings and seminars; and the Alastair Buchan Memorial Lecture. It offers Research Fellowships and Visiting Research Fellowships; and maintains a library and information centre. Has offices in Bahrain, Berlin, Singapore and Washington, DC, USA.

Geographical Area of Activity: Worldwide.

Publications: Annual Report; newsletter (bimonthly); *The Military Balance* (annual); *Strategic Survey: The Annual Review of World Affairs* (annual); *Survival* (bimonthly); *Adelphi Papers* (monographs, 8–10 a year); *Strategic Comments* (10 a year); *Strategic Dossier*; blog.

Finance: Annual income £20.0m., expenditure £25.2m. (30 Sept. 2023).

Trustees: Bill Emmott (Chair. of IISS Trustees); Dr Chung Min Lee (Chair. of IISS Advisory Council).

Principal Staff: Dir-Gen. and Chief Exec. Bastian Giegerich; Exec. Chair Sir John Chipman.

Contact Details: Arundel House, 6 Temple Pl., London WC2R 2PG; tel. (20) 7379-7676; e-mail iiss@iiss.org; internet www.iiss.org.

IPPF—International Planned Parenthood Federation

Established in 1952 at the Third International Conference on Planned Parenthood by eight national family planning associations.

Activities: Works in the field of sexual and reproductive health, choice and rights. The Federation promotes family planning and addresses subjects including human rights, HIV/AIDS, gender, young people, refugees, violence against women and poverty. It funds programmes and services; and provides training on issues relating to adolescents, abortion, access to contraception and global advocacy. The Federation's International Medical Panel, which comprises leading medical experts, provides guidelines on current medical and scientific thinking and the best practices. A Youth Working Group ensures that programmes are accessible to young people and promote young people's rights. Comprises 150 member associations working in over 146 countries; and has offices in Belgium, India, Kenya, Malaysia, Thailand, Tunisia and the USA.

Geographical Area of Activity: Africa, the Americas and the Caribbean, Arab world, East and South-East Asia and Oceania, Europe, South Asia.

Restrictions: Only funds member associations.

Publications: Annual Report; newsletter; factsheets; handbooks; reports; blog.

Finance: Annual income £97.3m., expenditure £98.9m. (31 Dec. 2023).

Board of Trustees: Kate Gilmore (Chair.).

Principal Staff: Dir-Gen. Dr Alvaro Bermejo.

Contact Details: 4 Newhams Row, London SE1 3UZ; tel. (20) 7939-8200; e-mail info@ippf.org; internet www.ippf.org.

Islamic Relief Worldwide

Established in 1984 by Dr Hany El Banna; a humanitarian and development organization inspired by the Islamic faith. Part of the Disasters Emergency Committee (q.v.).

Activities: Operates in the areas of social welfare, disaster management and sustainable development. Programme areas include: child protection; climate change; forced migration; gender justice; inclusion; and peacebuilding. The organization works in more than 30 countries, with partner organizations in 15 countries. In 2013 it established the Islamic Relief Academy, which became the Humanitarian Academy for Development (q.v.); and owns a subsidiary fundraising company, TIC International (f. 1993).

Geographical Area of Activity: International.

Publications: Annual Report; guidance; learning papers; policy documents; reports; toolkits.

Finance: Annual income £275.1m., expenditure £235.1m. (31 Dec. 2023).

Board of Trustees: Dr Ihab Saad (Chair.); Nurhayati Hassan (Vice-Chair.).

Principal Staff: CEO Waseem Ahmad.

Contact Details: 19 Rea St South, Digbeth, Birmingham B5 6LB; tel. (121) 6055555; e-mail irw@irworldwide.org; internet www.islamic-relief.org.

Japan Foundation Endowment Committee—JFEC

Founded in 1974 by the University Grants Committee (UGC) to administer an endowment made by the Japanese Government through the Japan Foundation (q.v.) for the promotion of Japanese studies within universities in the United Kingdom.

Activities: Provides small grants to support academic research in Japanese studies by staff and doctoral research students in higher education institutions in the United Kingdom, covering research on any aspect of Japan within the humanities and social sciences (including comparative studies where Japan is a major element). Applications are considered for funding for fieldwork in Japan, other forms of research support, and the partial support of doctoral students. Grants typically range between £1,000–£2,000 and upwards, depending on research needs; and up to £850 towards the cost of a return airfare for Japan-related research.

Geographical Area of Activity: UK.

Restrictions: Applications must be made by staff of UK higher education institutions; applications may not be made directly by students. Funding is not available for coursework or Master's dissertations.

Publications: Annual Report.

Finance: Grants disbursed approx. £50,000 per year.

Trustees: Dr Helen Parker (Chair.).

Principal Staff: Exec. Sec. Dr Sharleen Estampador Hughson.

Contact Details: 39 Scald Law Drive, Edinburgh EH13 0FE; tel. (7580) 178960; e-mail admin@jfec.org.uk; internet www.jfec.org.uk.

JCA Charitable Foundation

Founded in 1891, as the Jewish Colonization Association, by the will of Baron Maurice de Hirsch to assist Jews in need, particularly in those countries where they are oppressed.

Activities: Works in the fields of economic development and education in rural areas. The Foundation offers grants for agricultural research and rural tourism and for educational purposes at all levels to institutions in or serving rural areas.

Geographical Area of Activity: Israel, UK.

Restrictions: No grants to individuals; does not usually accept applications from bodies not currently linked to the Foundation.

Publications: Annual Report; *Centenary Brochure*.

Finance: Annual income £757,207, expenditure £2.7m. (31 Dec. 2023).

Council of Administration: Sir Stephen Waley-Cohen (Pres.).

Principal Staff: Sec. Timothy R. Martin.

Contact Details: 14 Hillbury Rd, London SW17 8JT; e-mail thejcafoundation@gmail.com; internet ica-israel.org.

The Jerusalem Trust

Founded in 1982; one of the Sainsbury Family Charitable Trusts (q.v.), which share a common administration.

Activities: Operates internationally in the areas of Christian evangelism and relief work overseas; and Christian media, education and art. Within the United Kingdom, the Trust operates in the areas of Christian evangelism and social responsibility work with children and young people, and prisoners and former prisoners.

Geographical Area of Activity: Anglophone sub-Saharan Africa, Egypt, Ethiopia, Jordan, Iran, Iraq, Lebanon, Syrian Arab Repub.

Restrictions: Unsolicited applications are unlikely to be successful; no grants to individuals.

Publications: Annual Report.

Finance: Annual income £3.2m., expenditure £5.6m. (5 April 2024).

Principal Staff: Lead Trust Exec. Vikki McLachlan.

Contact Details: c/o The Sainsbury Family Charitable Trusts, The Peak, 5 Wilton Rd, London SW1V 1AP; tel. (20) 7410-0330; e-mail info@sfct.org.uk; internet www.sfct.org.uk/the-jerusalem-trust.

JNF UK—JNF Charitable Trust

Founded in 1905 as the Jewish National Fund Commission for England; also known as the JNF Charitable Trust.

Activities: Active in all areas of people's lives in the Negev region in southern Israel. The organization supports schools and hospitals; fosters the development of the technology industry in remote desert towns; promotes cultural life through community development; advances environmental protection; and provides relief to vulnerable or marginalized people. It also offers educational grants to Jewish schools in the United Kingdom to improve pupils' connection to Israel. Grants are made over four years for up to £10,000 for primary schools and up to £50,000 for secondary schools.

Geographical Area of Activity: Israel (Negev, Galilee), UK.

Restrictions: No grants to individuals.

Publications: Annual Report; newsletter; books.

Finance: Annual income £19.3m., expenditure £18.0m. (31 Dec. 2023).

Executive Board: Samuel Hayek (Chair.); Dr Alan Mendoza (Pres.); Belinda Oakland, Gideon Falter (Vice-Chair.); Laurence Julius (Treas.).

Principal Staff: CEO Elan Gorji.

Contact Details: 95 Church Rd, London NW4 4FE; tel. (20) 8732-6100; e-mail info@jnf.co.uk; internet www.jnf.co.uk.

John Ellerman Foundation

Formed in 1992 by the merger of the Moorgate Trust Fund (f. 1970) and New Moorgate Trust Fund (f. 1971), which were beneficiaries of a transfer of shares in Ellerman Lines, a shipping company, by Sir John Ellerman.

Activities: Works to benefit the wellbeing of people, society and the natural world. Main programme areas are: arts, focusing on the performing arts, and museums and galleries outside London; environment, protecting marine environments and building healthier urban and rural ecosystems; and social action, using policy, advocacy and campaigning to improve systems, and involving people with direct experience of issues being addressed. The Foundation offers grants for core costs or projects to organizations that have a national reach. Grants typically range between £10,000 and £50,000 for up to 3 years. It makes an annual contribution to the Rachel Swart Fund in South Africa, co-founded by Sir John in 1960, which helps people living with physical disabilities.

Geographical Area of Activity: UK and Overseas Territories.

Restrictions: Grants only to organizations registered in the UK.

Publications: Annual Report.

Finance: Annual income £3.2m., expenditure £6.5m. (31 March 2024).

Trustees: Geraldine Blake (Chair.); Tufyal Choudhury (Vice-Chair.).

Principal Staff: Dir Sufina Ahmad.

Contact Details: Aria House, 23 Craven St, London WC2N 5NS; tel. (20) 7930-8566; e-mail enquiries@ellerman.org.uk; internet www.ellerman.org.uk.

John Innes Foundation—JIF

Established in 1909 as the John Innes Horticultural Institution, following a bequest from John Innes, a landowner in the City of London.

Activities: Works in the fields of research and teaching in plant science, offering grants to students in agriculture, horticulture and biotechnology, and an agricultural bursary; and supports Emeritus Fellows and studentships under the Rotation PhD programme in plant and microbial sciences at the John Innes Centre (JIC), the Sainsbury Laboratory and Earlham Institute. It provides land and buildings for research at the JIC in Norwich; and supports the Norwich Research Park and Rutlish Science School, Merton; the Food & Farming Discovery Trust; and the John Innes Foundation Food & Farming Challenge, a competition for schools centred on the Royal Norfolk Show. Maintains a library on the history of genetics and rare botanical books.

Geographical Area of Activity: UK.

Publications: Annual Report.

Finance: Annual income £1.5m., expenditure £5.9m. (31 March 2024).

Trustees: Peter D. Innes (Chair.).

Principal Staff: Clerk Samantha Fox.

Contact Details: John Innes Centre, Colney Lane, Norwich, Norfolk NR4 7UH; tel. (1362) 685502; e-mail clerk @johninnesfoundation.org.uk; internet www.johninnesfoundation.org.uk.

John Moores Foundation

Established in 1964 by Sir John Moores, founder of Littlewoods, a retail company.

Activities: Offers grants to voluntary organizations in Northern Ireland and Merseyside, giving preference to projects in target areas, which include: local community groups; black and minority ethnic organizations; women and girls; second chance learning; poverty alleviation advice and information; grassroots social health initiatives; training for voluntary organizations; joint working and trust-building initiatives; and equality and diversity. In Merseyside, target areas also include: refugees; children and young people; family support; homeless people; and carers. Has an office in Carnlough, Northern Ireland.

Geographical Area of Activity: Merseyside, Northern Ireland.

Restrictions: Mainly awards grants to new and/or small, local organizations.

Finance: Annual income £595,502, expenditure £1.5m. (5 April 2023).

Trustees: Barnaby Moores (Chair.).

Principal Staff: Grants Dir Lenka Vidamour.

Contact Details: 1st Floor, Front Office, 96 Bold St, Liverpool, Merseyside L1 4HY; tel. (151) 707-6077; e-mail info @johnmooresfoundation.com; internet www.jmf.org.uk.

Joseph Levy Foundation

Founded in 1965 by Joseph Levy, a property developer; formerly known as the Joseph Levy Charitable Foundation.

Activities: Supports children and young people through offering grants to organizations. The Foundaiton has a long term interest in supporting people with cystic fibrosis through its partnership with the Cystic Fibrosis Trust. In 2024 the Foundation's focus was on youth disadvantage, offering grants of up to £30,000 to organizations supporting people aged between 16 and 25 who face challenges due to ill health, poverty or disability.

Geographical Area of Activity: UK.

Restrictions: Does not accept unsolicited applications.

Finance: Annual income £760,309, expenditure £656,344 (31 March 2024).

Board of Trustees: Jane Jason (Chair.).

Principal Staff: Exec. Dir Denise Ramsey.

Contact Details: 1 Bell St, London NW1 5BY; tel. (20) 7616-1200; e-mail info@jlf.org.uk; internet www.jlf.org.uk.

Joseph Rowntree Charitable Trust—JRCT

Founded in 1904 by Joseph Rowntree, owner of Rowntree's, a confectionery company; a Quaker organization which is independent of the Joseph Rowntree Foundation and the Joseph Rowntree Reform Trust (qq.v.).

Activities: Supports individuals and organizations that address the root causes of conflict and injustice. Priority programme areas are: Peace and Security; Power and Accountability; Rights and Justice; Sustainable Future; and Northern Ireland. The Trust funds work at national level in the United Kingdom; and makes a few grants for work at a pan-European level if it relates to international institutions or affects the UK.

Geographical Area of Activity: Europe (mainly UK).

Restrictions: Has a number of general exclusions and specific exclusions that apply to each area of interest.

Publications: Annual Report.

Finance: Annual income £2.9m., expenditure £24.6m. (31 Dec. 2023).

Trustees: Jonathan Heawood (Chair.); Alison Breadon (Vice-Chair.).

Principal Staff: Acting Chief Exec. Nicola Purdy.

Contact Details: The Garden House, Water End, York YO30 6WQ; tel. (1904) 627810; e-mail enquiries@jrct.org.uk; internet www.jrct.org.uk.

Joseph Rowntree Foundation—JRF

Founded in 1904 by Joseph Rowntree, owner of Rowntree's, a confectionery company; a Quaker organization which is independent of the Joseph Rowntree Charitable Trust and the Joseph Rowntree Reform Trust (qq.v.).

Activities: Works to eliminate poverty through social change. The Foundation conducts research on underlying causes of poverty and disadvantage; and demonstrates solutions through developing and running services, managing land and buildings, and supporting innovation. It also includes, and shares, trustees and directors with the Joseph Rowntree Housing Trust (JRHT), a registered housing association and provider of care services, which manages around 2,620 homes and local amenities in Yorkshire.

Geographical Area of Activity: UK.

Restrictions: Not a grantmaking organization.

Publications: Annual Report; newsletter (weekly); research reports; blog.

Finance: Annual income £36.0m., expenditure £49.2m. (31 Dec. 2023).

Board of Trustees: Prof. Carol Tannahill (Chair.); Terrie Alafat (Chair. of JRHT Board).

Principal Staff: Group Chief Exec. Paul Kissack; JRHT Exec. Dir Chris Simpson.

Contact Details: The Homestead, 40 Water End, York YO30 6WP; tel. (1904) 629241; e-mail info@jrf.org.uk; internet www.jrf.org.uk; www.jrht.org.uk.

Joseph Rowntree Reform Trust Ltd (including the JRSST Charitable Trust)

Founded in 1904 by Joseph Rowntree, owner of Rowntree's, a confectionery company; a Quaker organization which is independent of the Joseph Rowntree Charitable Trust and the Joseph Rowntree Foundation (qq.v.).

Activities: Funds political campaigns in the United Kingdom to promote democratic reform and speak truth to power. The Joseph Rowntree Reform Trust works with an independent but connected charity, the JRSST Charitable Trust.

Geographical Area of Activity: UK.

Restrictions: Does not fund work that can be funded from charitable sources.

Publications: Annual Report.

UNITED KINGDOM

Directors: Andrew Neal (Chair.); Alison Goldsworthy (Vice-Chair.).
Principal Staff: Chief Exec. Fiona Weir.
Contact Details: The Garden House, Water End, York YO30 6WQ; tel. (1904) 625744; e-mail info@jrrt.org.uk; internet www.jrrt.org.uk.

Karuna Trust

Established in 1980 as Aid for India, inspired by Buddhist values.

Activities: Supports community-based organizations and builds their capacity to address discrimination, poverty and inequality arising from the traditional caste system. Programmes focus on: education of Dalit (the lowest caste) and tribal children; gender equality and the establishment of a strong Dalit women's movement; and livelihoods, providing people from Dalit and tribal communities with vocational skills that will give them access to dignified and better-paid employment. Approx. 5% of funding goes towards providing facilities for people from marginalized Buddhist communities to practise their religion.
Geographical Area of Activity: India, Nepal, UK.
Publications: Annual Report; newsletter; blog.
Finance: Annual income £2.2m., expenditure £2.2m. (31 March 2024).
Trustees: Peter David White (Chair.).
Principal Staff: CEO Ciaran Maguire.
Contact Details: 72 Holloway Rd, London N7 8JG; tel. (20) 7700-3434; e-mail info@karuna.org; internet www.karuna.org.

Kennedy Memorial Trust

Founded in 1966 from the proceeds of a National Memorial Appeal launched by the Lord Mayor of London following the assassination of US President John F. Kennedy in 1963.

Activities: Preserves the Kennedy Memorial at Runnymede, in association with the National Trust, and administers the Kennedy Memorial Fund. The Trust awards about 10 Kennedy Scholarships annually to British citizens to study at Harvard University or the Massachusetts Institute of Technology for one year; and administers awards of the Frank Knox Memorial Fellowships (q.v.) to study at Harvard. It also funds a Special Studentship for general, non-degree study. Scholarships are tenable in all areas of the arts, sciences, social sciences and political studies.
Geographical Area of Activity: UK, USA.
Publications: Annual Report.
Finance: Kennedy Memorial Fund: annual income £292,366, expenditure £691,526 (30 April 2024).
Trustees: Prof. Sir Mark Walport (Chair.).
Principal Staff: Dir Tim Farrow-House.
Contact Details: 3 Birdcage Walk, Westminster, London SW1H 9JJ; tel. (20) 7222-1151; e-mail info@kennedytrust.org.uk; internet www.kennedytrust.org.uk.

The King's Foundation

Established as the Prince's Trust in 2018 by the merger of the Prince's Foundation for Building Community, the Prince's Regeneration Trust, the Great Steward of Scotland's Dumfries House Trust and the Prince's School of Traditional Arts. Became the King's Foundation when HRH King Charles III acceeded to the throne in 2022.

Activities: Operates nationally and internationally in education and training programmes in areas including crafts, architecture, heritage, horticultre and hospitality, at Dumfries House in Scotland and elsewhere.
Geographical Area of Activity: Scotland and international.
Finance: Total income £26.1m., expenditure £25.9m. (31 March 2024).
Trustees: Dame Ann Limb (Chair.); Michael Jarry (Deputy Chair.).
Principal Staff: CEO Kristina Murrin; Deputy Chief Exec. Emily Cherrington.
Contact Details: Dumfries House, Cumnock, KA18 2NJ; tel. (12) 9042-5959; e-mail enquiries@kings-foundation.org; internet kings-foundation.org.

The King's Fund

Founded in 1897 (as King Edward's Hospital Fund for London) by King Edward VII, then Prince of Wales, originally for the support, benefit and extension of the hospitals of London, now interpreted broadly to include all the health services in Greater London.

Activities: Supports the health of people in England through policy analysis, service development and education. Strategic priorities are: promoting health and wellbeing, and reducing health inequalities, across places and communities; improving health and healthcare for groups with the worst health outcomes; and supporting the health and healthcare workforce. The Fund manages GSK IMPACT Awards, which provide funding, training and development for organizations working to improve people's health and wellbeing.
Geographical Area of Activity: England.
Publications: Annual Report; newsletter (weekly); briefings; commissioned reports; blog.
Finance: Annual income £14.6m., expenditure £19.5m. (31 Dec. 2022).
Board of Trustees: Prof. the Lord Ajay Kakkar (Chair.).
Principal Staff: Chief Exec. Sarah Woolnough.
Contact Details: 11–13 Cavendish Sq., London W1G 0AN; tel. (20) 7307-2400; e-mail enquiry@kingsfund.org.uk; internet www.kingsfund.org.uk.

The King's Trust

Founded in 1976 as the Prince's Trust by HRH King Charles III, then HRH The Prince of Wales—current name adopted in 2024.

Activities: Operates in the United Kingdom to help disadvantaged young people aged 11–30 years into employment, education, training or volunteering. Particular emphasis is placed on projects to aid the community, education, training and employment programmes; and helping young offenders and people experiencing homelessness. The Trust operates through a network of national and regional offices. Part of the King's Trust Group, which comprises the King's Trust International (f. 2015) and King's Trust Australia (f. 2017).
Geographical Area of Activity: UK.
Restrictions: Not a grantmaking organization.
Publications: Annual Report; newsletter; research reports.
Finance: Annual income £71.1m., expenditure £71.0m. (31 March 2024).
Council: Tom Ilube (Chair.); Suzy Neubert (Vice-Chair.).
Principal Staff: Pres. HRH King Charles III; Chief Exec. Jonathan Townsend.
Contact Details: South London Centre, 8 Glade Path, London SE1 8EG; tel. (20) 7543-1234; e-mail customer.services@kingstrust.org.uk; internet www.kingstrust.org.uk.

Kusuma Trust UK

Established in 2008 by Anurag Dikshit and Dr Soma Pujari.

Activities: Carries out self-conducted programmes through making grants to organizations in the areas of access to opportunity, community and the environment, and health and wellbeing; and commissions scientific and educational research. The Trust awards Excellence Prize grants, worth £3,000, to Gibraltarian undergraduates; and Gibraltar Professional Development Awards, worth £5,000. A sister organization operates in Gibraltar.
Geographical Area of Activity: Gibraltar, India, UK.
Restrictions: No unsolicited applications.

Publications: Annual Report.

Finance: Annual income £4.9m., expenditure £7.0m. (31 Dec. 2023).

Trustees: Dr Soma Pujari (Exec. Trustee).

Contact Details: 5th Floor, 55 New Oxford St, London WC1A 1BS; tel. (20) 7420-0650; e-mail info@kusumatrust.org; internet www.kusumatrust.org.

Laidlaw Foundation

Established in 2017 by Lord Laidlaw of Rothiemay, founder of the Institute for International Research Ltd.

Activities: Invests in the education of underprivileged and underrepresented people to break the cycle of poverty, reduce inequality and develop a new generation of leaders. Main programmes are: the Laidlaw Schools Trust, a multi-academy trust incorporating eight schools in the north-east of England; the Laidlaw Schoalrs Leadership and Research Programme, which funds undergraduate students at 17 universities around the world to develop ethical leaders who are skilled researchers and use data-based decisionmaking; the Laidlaw Women's Business Education Scholarship, which funds MBA degrees of women with leadership potential at London Business School and Oxford Saïd Business School; and Laidlaw Scholars Ventures, a venture capital fund that invests in businesses founded and led by Laidlaw Scholars.

Geographical Area of Activity: International.

Restrictions: Not a grantmaking organization.

Publications: Annual Report.

Board of Trustees: Lord Laidlaw of Rothiemay (Chair.).

Principal Staff: CEO Susanna Kempe.

Contact Details: 27 Furnival St, London EC4A 1JQ; tel. (0191) 6622400; e-mail contact@laidlawfoundation.com; internet www.laidlawfoundation.com.

Laing Family Trusts

Established in 1979 by Sir Martin Laing, who became Chair. of John Laing & Sons, a construction company.

Activities: Comprises four grantmaking trusts, which promote the Christian faith, caring for people in need and young people's education (especially in science and engineering). The Beatrice Laing Trust (f. 1952) supports charities working in deprived areas of the United Kingdom. The Kirby Laing Foundation (f. 1972) supports education, social and medical welfare, and overseas development. The Martin Laing Foundation (f. 1979) supports environmental and conservation work, and community projects for disadvantaged young people and the elderly. The Maurice & Hilda Laing Charitable Trust (f. 1996) supports poverty alleviation and people with disabilities. Grants range from £500 to £25,000.

Geographical Area of Activity: International.

Restrictions: No unsolicited applications; no grants to individuals or charities registered overseas.

Publications: Annual Report.

Principal Staff: Trusts Dir Elizabeth A. Harley.

Contact Details: 33 Bunns Lane, Mill Hill, London NW7 2DX; tel. (20) 8238-8890; e-mail info@laingfamilytrusts.org; internet www.laingfamilytrusts.org.uk.

Laureus Sport for Good

Established in 2000 by Johann Rupert, Exec. Chair. of Compagnie Financière Richemont, and Dr Dieter Zetsche, Chair. of Daimler AG and Head of Mercedes-Benz Cars.

Activities: Funds and promotes the use of sport as a tool for social change and the establishment of institutes and sports academies. The Foundation has supported more than 300 programmes in over 40 countries that bring about social change. Key project areas are: social exclusion; gun and gang violence; discrimination; community integration and cohesion; peace and reconciliation; and education and health. The Foundation has subsidiaries in Argentina, Germany, Italy, the Netherlands, South Africa, Spain, Switzerland and the USA.

Geographical Area of Activity: Worldwide.

Restrictions: Grants only to community-based organizations or legally registered NGOs; does not fund certain types of organizations or activities.

Publications: Annual Report; newsletter.

Finance: Annual income £3.6m., expenditure £5.4m. (31 Dec. 2023).

Trustees: Dr Edwin Moses (Chair.).

Principal Staff: Chief Exec. Adam Fraser; Sec. Nicholas Garside.

Contact Details: 15 Hill St, London W1J 5QT; tel. (20) 7514-2898; e-mail foundation@laureus.com; internet www.laureus.com/sport-for-good.

Leonard Cheshire Disability

Founded in 1948 by Group Capt. Leonard Cheshire, a former Royal Air Force officer in Bomber Command; part of the Leonard Cheshire Disability Global Alliance, a network of more than 200 independently managed organizations in 54 countries.

Activities: Works with disabled people worldwide. The organization provides support and guidance to locally run programmes for disabled people and their families. Programmes include rehabilitation centres, community-based support services and residential homes; inclusive education projects to help children with disabilities to attend mainstream schools; and livelihood projects to support people with disabilities in finding paid or self-employment, providing skills training and career guidance. It also advises local communities on obtaining grants for new developments; and carries out research on disability and inclusive development. Has an offices in Northern Ireland.

Geographical Area of Activity: East Asia and South-East Asia, South Asia, sub-Saharan Africa, UK.

Publications: Annual Report; newsletter; *Disability and Inclusive Development*; *Compass* (quarterly); Impact Report.

Finance: Annual income £151.8m., expenditure £151.3m. (31 March 2024).

Trustees: Neil Goulden (Chair.).

Principal Staff: Chief Exec. Dr Ruth Owen.

Contact Details: The News Bldg, 3rd Floor, 3 London Bridge St, London SE1 9SG; tel. (20) 3242-0200; e-mail info@leonardcheshire.org; internet www.leonardcheshire.org.

The Leprosy Mission International

Established in 1874 in India, as the Mission to Lepers, by Christian missionaries Wellesley and Alice Bailey.

Activities: Works with national governments and other organizations to improve the quality of life of people affected by leprosy, by dealing with detection of the disease and their treatment, care, rehabilitation and reintegration. The Mission raises awareness of leprosy in all areas, removing the stigma attached to the disease and reducing discrimination. It runs centres to provide suitable treatment and carry out surgery; engages in research into leprosy and its treatment; provides socioeconomic assistance to patients in developing countries and supports community-based rehabilitation and self-help initiatives. A Global Fellowship of member organizations operates in more than 30 countries. The Board of the Leprosy Mission International is also the governing board for the Leprosy Mission Global Fellowship.

Geographical Area of Activity: Projects in Africa, Asia and South-East Asia; national support offices in the UK, Europe, South Africa, Australia and New Zealand.

Publications: Annual Report; *Ask Prayer Guide*; blog.

Finance: Annual income £20.2m., expenditure £19.2m. (31 Dec. 2023).

Board of Trustees: Colin Osborne (Chair.); Helen Fernandes (Vice-Chair.); Gordon Brown (Treas.).

Principal Staff: Int. Dir and Sec. Brent J. Morgan.

Leverhulme Trust

Founded in 1925 by the will of William Hesketh Lever, first Viscount Leverhulme, who co-founded manufacturing company Lever Brothers (subsequently Unilever).

Activities: Offers grants to institutions and charitable organizations in the United Kingdom and abroad for specific research projects, educational innovations and Trust-approved schemes of academic interchange between the UK and other countries. A number of smaller individual awards of research fellowships and grants, emeritus fellowships, visiting professorships and studentships for study abroad are made annually; and 30 Philip Leverhulme Prizes, each worth £100,000 over 2–3 years, for early-stage researchers.

Geographical Area of Activity: Mainly UK.

Restrictions: Does not give support in the areas of medicine or social policy.

Publications: Annual Report; Annual Review; newsletter (3 a year); funding e-bulletin.

Finance: Annual income £98.9m., expenditure £127.5m. (31 Dec. 2023).

Trust Board: Alan Jope (Chair.).

Principal Staff: Dir Prof. Anna Vignoles.

Contact Details: 1 Pemberton Row, London EC4A 3BG; tel. (20) 7042-9888; e-mail grants@leverhulme.ac.uk; internet www.leverhulme.ac.uk.

LifeArc—MRC Technology

Established 1992 by the Medical Research Council, which is part of UK Research and Innovation (q.v.); an independent medical charity.

Activities: Carries out and funds research and experimental development in the fields of biotechnology and biomedicine, working with charities, industry, public bodies and universities. The organization offers grants through: the Philanthropic Fund, for rare disease research; Seed Fund, for promising early-stage therapeutics, diagnostics and biological research; Lifearc & MND Association Translational Research Fund, for research into treatments for motor neurone disease; Development Gap Fund, administered by LifeArc to support small-scale studies by Medical Research Council researchers; Gene Therapy Innovation Hubs, for rapid development of novel gene therapies in the United Kingdom; and LifeArc-CSO Fund for Scottish researchers, for research led by Scottish institutes or the National Health Service. It has offices in Stevenage and Edinburgh (Scotland).

Geographical Area of Activity: UK.

Publications: Annual Report.

Finance: Generates income from the royalties from marketed treatments. Annual income £169.6m., expenditure £73.5m. (31 Dec. 2023).

Board of Trustees: Dr Ian Gilham (Chair.); Lynne Robb (Vice-Chair.).

Principal Staff: CEO Sam Barrell; Deputy CEO Stéphane Maikovsky.

Contact Details: Lynton House, 7–12 Tavistock Sq., London WC1H 9LT; tel. (20) 7391-2700; e-mail info@lifearc.org; internet www.lifearc.org.

Linbury Trust

Founded in 1973 by Lord Sainsbury of Preston Candover, and his wife Lady Sainsbury, the former ballerina Anya Linden; one of the Sainsbury Family Charitable Trusts (q.v.), which share a common administration.

Activities: Funds projects in the fields of the arts and education, including: arts education; the environment; medical research; museums and heritage; and social welfare, improving the lives of disadvantaged people, including young and older people, and people experiencing homelessness. The Trust occasionally funds overseas emergency relief operations. The Linbury Prize is awarded every two years in partnership with the National Theatre for excellence in theatre stage design.

Geographical Area of Activity: International (mainly UK).

Restrictions: Does not make grants directly to individuals.

Publications: Annual Report.

Finance: Annual income £8.0m., expenditure £9.9m. (5 April 2024).

Trustees: Mark Sainsbury (Chair.).

Principal Staff: Dir Karen Everett.

Contact Details: c/o The Sainsbury Family Charitable Trusts, The Peak, 5 Wilton Rd, London SW1V 1AP; tel. (20) 7410-0330; e-mail linbury@sfct.org.uk; internet www.linburytrust.org.uk.

Lloyds Bank Foundation for England and Wales

Founded in 1985; part of a group of charitable foundations that also comprises the Bank of Scotland Foundation, the Halifax Foundation for Northern Ireland and the Lloyds Bank Foundation for the Channel Islands, all funded by the profits of Lloyds Banking Group.

Activities: The Foundation provides unrestricted funding, support to develop and influences policy and practice to help small and local charities thrive, communities grow stronger, and people overcome complex issues and barriers so they can transform their lives. The Foundation makes grants to specialist charities supporting people in the areas of: addiction; asylum seekers and refugees; care leavers; domestic abuse; homelessness; offending; sexual abuse; trafficking and modern slavery. The Foundation also makes grants to charities and community interest companies working with people experiencing inequity because of their race or ethnicity, and d/Deaf and disabled-led organizations. The Foundation seeks to influence policy and practice around accommodation, social security and refugee and asylum seeker support, part of which is achieved through national and regional grants.

Geographical Area of Activity: England, Wales.

Restrictions: Supports charities with an annual income of £25,000–£500,000; no upper limit for National Influencing Programme grants.

Publications: Impact Report; newsletter; research publications.

Finance: Annual income £19.2m., expenditure £24.2m. (31 Dec. 2023).

Board of Trustees: Dame Ann Limb (Chair.).

Principal Staff: Chief Exec. Paul Streets.

Contact Details: Society Bldg, 8 All Saints St, London N1 9RL; tel. (370) 4111223; e-mail enquiries@lloydsbankfoundation.org.uk; internet www.lloydsbankfoundation.org.uk.

Lloyd's Register Foundation

Established in 2012 by Lloyd's Register, a shipping classification society.

Activities: Lloyd's Register Foundation's mission is engineering a safer world. It aims to reduce risk and enhance the safety of the critical infrastructure that modern society relies upon in areas such as energy, transport and food by supporting high quality research, accelerating technology to application and through education and public outreach.

Geographical Area of Activity: International.

Publications: *Foresight Reviews* (reports); Annual Review; *World Risk Poll* (report); *A Safer World* (book); Lloyd's Register historical publications (online resources).

Finance: Annual income £560.4m., total expenditure £550.1m. (30 June 2023).

Board of Trustees: Thomas Thune Andersen (Chair.).

Principal Staff: Chief Exec. Dr Ruth Boumphrey.

Lullaby Trust UNITED KINGDOM

Contact Details: 71 Fenchurch St, London EC3M 4BS; tel. (20) 7709-9166; e-mail info@lrfoundation.org.uk; internet www.lrfoundation.org.uk.

Lullaby Trust

Founded in 1971, as the Foundation for the Study of Infant Deaths, by Mrs J. Hunter-Gray; present name adopted in 2013.

Activities: Operates in the fields of medicine and health, and social welfare and studies, through self-conducted programmes, research, grants to institutions and individuals, conferences, training courses and publications. The Trust provides support to families whose babies have died suddenly and unexpectedly, and disseminates information about sudden infant death syndrome (SIDS—cot death) and baby care among professionals and the public. It supports research programmes, including epidemiology, immunology, pathology, statistics and infection; and offers research grants.

Geographical Area of Activity: England, Northern Ireland, Wales.

Publications: Annual Report; newsletters; leaflets; posters.

Finance: Annual income £1.5m., expenditure £1.5m. (30 June 2024).

Board of Trustees: Dr Stephanie Henderson-Begg (Chair.); Pete Thomas (Treas.).

Principal Staff: Chief Exec. Jenny Ward.

Contact Details: 10–18 Union St, London SE1 1SZ; tel. (20) 7802-3200; e-mail office@lullabytrust.org.uk; internet www.lullabytrust.org.uk.

Lumos Foundation

Established in 2005 by J. K. Rowling, an author.

Activities: Works to end the systematic institutionalization of children worldwide and provide family- and community-based alternatives to orphanages. The Foundation has offices in Colombia, Moldova and Ukraine, and a sister organization in the USA.

Geographical Area of Activity: Colombia, Moldova, Ukraine, UK, USA.

Publications: Annual Report.

Finance: Annual income £7.9m., expenditure £5.0m. (31 Dec. 2023).

Board of Trustees: Kenneth Ian Towle (Chair.).

Principal Staff: CEO Howard Taylor.

Contact Details: 3–7 Temple Ave, London EC4Y 0DA; tel. (20) 7253-6464; e-mail communications@wearelumos.org; internet www.wearelumos.org.

The Mackintosh Foundation

Founded in 1988 by Sir Cameron Mackintosh, a theatre producer.

Activities: Works nationally and internationally in the areas of: education, making grants to schools and assisting disadvantaged students; funding poverty relief; promoting theatre, music and drama, funding education and theatre refurbishment/restoration initiatives; funding medical research; making grants to nature conservation projects; and funding community-based projects.

Geographical Area of Activity: Greece, Malta, UK, USA.

Restrictions: No grants for individuals nor for political or religious causes.

Publications: Annual Report.

Finance: Annual income £633,896, expenditure £1.3m. (31 March 2024).

Trustees: Sir Cameron Mackintosh (Chair.).

Principal Staff: Appeals Dir Nicholas Mackintosh.

Contact Details: 1 Bedford Sq., London WC1B 3RB; tel. (20) 7637-8866; e-mail info@camack.co.uk.

Macmillan Cancer Support

Founded in 1911, as the Society for the Prevention and Relief of Cancer, by Douglas Macmillan, a civil servant, whose father died of cancer.

Activities: Offers emotional, physical and financial support to people diagnosed with cancer. The organization: runs training courses for doctors and nurses in the care of patients, particularly pain control; funds specialist Macmillan nurses and doctors; provides care in the home and, through special units, within hospitals; and operates a telephone helpline. It offers cash grants to patients in need, grants and scholarships for study and academic appointments; funds academic and clinical research at universities and hospitals; and supports certain charities that offer support and information to cancer sufferers.

Geographical Area of Activity: UK.

Publications: Annual Review; newsletter; *Macmillan News* (quarterly); booklets; cancer-related publications.

Finance: Annual income £232.5m., expenditure £265.2m. (31 Dec. 2023).

Board of Trustees: Richard Murley (Chair.); Iain Cornish (Treas.).

Principal Staff: CEO Gemma Peters.

Contact Details: 3rd Floor, Bronze Bldg, The Forge, 105 Sumner St, London SE1 9HZ; tel. (20) 7840-7840; e-mail contact@macmillan.org.uk; internet www.macmillan.org.uk.

MAG—Mines Advisory Group

Established in 1989 by Rae McGrath, a former British army engineer, and his brother Lou.

Activities: Removes and destroys landmines and unexploded ordnance (UXO), improving communities' access to food, livelihoods, health services and education; and providing access to NGOs and other humanitarian and development organizations. The organization runs risk education programmes, helping people—particularly the most vulnerable, such as children—to live alongside the danger of landmines and UXO until land can be cleared, reducing the risk of death and injury. It also offers expertise and training to national authorities in storing and managing arms to prevent them ending up on the black market; and where unsafe or insecure storage of weapons and explosives poses a threat to communities. The Group has supported more than 20m. people in 70 countries. It currently works in 26 countries.

Geographical Area of Activity: Worldwide.

Publications: Annual Summary; *Insight*; *Impact*; newsletters.

Finance: Annual income £91.9m., expenditure £92.4m. (31 Dec. 2023).

Board of Trustees: Julia Palca (Chair.); Peter Jones (Vice-Chair.); Angela Mulholland-Wells (Treas.).

Principal Staff: Chief Exec. Darren Cormack.

Contact Details: Suite 3A, South Central, 11 Peter St, Manchester M2 5QR; tel. (161) 2364311; e-mail info@maginternational.org; internet www.maginternational.org.

Marie Curie

Founded in 1948, as the Marie Curie Memorial Foundation, by former committee members of the Marie Curie Hospital in Hampstead, London; in 1995 it became Marie Curie Cancer Care. Present name adopted in 2014.

Activities: Cares for terminally ill people and improves their quality of life, through its caring services, cancer research and education. The organization operates hospices throughout the United Kingdom and provides a network of nurses, giving practical nursing care at home to terminally ill people, free of charge. It carries out research into palliative care, finding better ways to care for terminally ill people and their families; and has Palliative Care Research Centres at Cardiff University and University College London. Maintains an office in Scotland.

Geographical Area of Activity: UK.

Publications: Annual Report; newsletter; *Shine On* (magazine); leaflets; brochures.

Finance: Annual income £169.7m., expenditure £199.2m. (31 March 2024).

Principal Staff: Chief Exec. Matthew Reed.

Contact Details: 1 Embassy Gardens, 8 Viaduct Gardens, London SW11 7BW; tel. (20) 7599-7777; e-mail supporter.relations@mariecurie.org.uk; internet www.mariecurie.org.uk.

Medical Aid for Palestinians—MAP

Founded in 1982 by orthopaedic surgeon Dr Swee Chai Ang and other fellow medical professionals.

Activities: MAP's primary goal is the realisation of the health and wellbeing potential of Palestinians, supported by a sustainable, high-quality, readily accessible and locally-led health care system. Works in collaboration with Palestinian communities and local partners to attend to a wide range of health and social needs, including providing medical aid in emergencies, and supporting the development of better health services in the long term. Currently, the focus is on providing health care for Palestinians impacted by occupation, displacement and conflict.

Geographical Area of Activity: Lebanon, Palestinian Territories.

Publications: Annual Reports; reviews; factsheets; *Witness* (magazine, 2 a year).

Board of Trustees: Richard Makepeace (Interim Chair.); Shireen Jayyusi (Vice-Chair.); Hilary Wild (Treas.).

Principal Staff: Interim Chief Exec. Steve Cutts; Dirs Aisha Mansour (West Bank), Fikr Shalltoot (Gaza), Wafa Dakwar (Lebanon).

Contact Details: 50 Featherstone St, London EC1Y 8RT; tel. (20) 7226-4114; e-mail info@map.org.uk; internet www.map.org.uk.

Mencap—Royal Mencap Society

Founded in 1946 by Judy Fryd as the National Association of Parents of Backward Children and subsequently renamed as the National Society for Mentally Handicapped Children; present name adopted in 1969.

Activities: Works to improve the lives of people with learning disabilities. The organization provides residential, educational and employment services, leisure opportunities, and support and advice for people with learning disabilities, their families and carers. It works with more than 300 independent Network Partners; and runs a helpline for questions relating to benefits, employment, housing and other issues.

Geographical Area of Activity: Mainly England, Northern Ireland, Wales.

Publications: Annual Report; *Viewpoint* (newspaper); campaign reports.

Finance: Annual income £228m., expenditure £226m. (31 March 2024).

Board of Trustees: Dame Carolyn Fairbairn (Chair.).

Principal Staff: Chief Exec. Jon Sparkes.

Contact Details: 6 Cyrus Way, Peterborough PE7 8HP; tel. (1733) 873700; e-mail supportercare@mencap.org.uk; internet www.mencap.org.uk.

Mental Health Foundation

Founded in 1949 to support research into mental health problems.

Activities: The Foundation's vision is for a world with good mental health for all. Aims to find and address the sources of mental health problems so that people and communities can thrive. The Foundation drives Mental Health Awareness Week, offering advice to those in need and most at risk. The Foundation tests and evaluates the best approaches to improving mental health in communities and then rolls them out as widely as possible. Publishes studies and reports on what protects mental health and the causes of poor mental health and how to tackle them. Proposes solutions and campaigns for change to address the underlying causes of poor mental health.

Geographical Area of Activity: UK.

Publications: Annual Report; newsletter (monthly); bulletins; information booklets; policy briefings; research reports; blog.

Finance: Annual income £7.7m., expenditure £8.9 (31 March 2024).

Board of Trustees: Aisha Sheikh-Anene (Chair.).

Principal Staff: Chief Exec. Mark Rowland.

Contact Details: Studio 2, 197 Long Lane, London SE1 4PD; tel. (20) 7803-1100; e-mail info@mentalhealth.org.uk; internet www.mentalhealth.org.uk.

The Mercers' Charitable Foundation

Founded in 1983 by the Worshipful Company of Mercers (City of London) to make grants for charitable purposes according to English law.

Activities: Main programmes focus on young people and education, older people and housing, and church and communities. Most grants are for less than £10,000 but may range up to £100,000 or more. The Foundation shares its administration with the Mercers' Educational Trust Fund, which provides grants to individuals for educational purposes; and the Whittington Charity and the Earl of Northampton's Charity, which fund welfare projects.

Geographical Area of Activity: UK.

Restrictions: No grants to individuals.

Publications: Annual Report.

Finance: Annual income £8.0m., expenditure £3.4m. (31 March 2024).

Principal Staff: Clerk Rob Abernethy; Deputy Clerk Serena Hedley-Dent.

Contact Details: 6 Frederick's Pl., London EC2R 8AB; tel. (20) 7726-4991; e-mail info@mercers.co.uk; internet www.mercers.co.uk/philanthropy.

Mercury Phoenix Trust

Established in 1992 in memory of Freddie Mercury, principal singer of the pop group Queen, by the remaining members of the group and the group's manager.

Activities: Operates in the areas of medicine and health and social welfare. The Trust funds programmes in education and to raise awareness of HIV/AIDS among young people in and out of school; and to support children orphaned by AIDS. Has supported projects in 57 countries.

Geographical Area of Activity: Developing countries.

Restrictions: Grants only to charities registered in the UK; does not make grants to individuals or fund travel grants.

Publications: Annual Report; blog.

Finance: Annual income £500,838, expenditure £1m. (31 March 2024).

Principal Staff: Admin. Janice Page.

Contact Details: c/o Dale Evans & Co Ltd, 2nd Floor, 88–90 Baker St, London W1U 6TQ; tel. (20) 7298-1899; e-mail mercuryphoenixtrust@idrec.com; internet www.mercuryphoenixtrust.org.

Mind

Founded in 1946 as the National Association for Mental Health.

Activities: Provides information and support to people experiencing mental health problems: Infoline offers confidential support via telephone; the Legal Line gives access to advice on mental health-related law; there is a network of more than 130 local branches across England and Wales. Mind Cymru sets its own agenda and prioritises campaigns to lead initiatives across Wales to support communities.

Minhaj Welfare Foundation UNITED KINGDOM

Geographical Area of Activity: England, Wales.
Finance: Total income £62.7m., expenditure £79.8m. (31 March 2024).
Trustees: Stephanie Spring (Chair.).
Principal Staff: Pres. Stephen Fry.
Contact Details: Mind, 2 Redman Pl., London E20 1JQ; Mind Cymru, Suite 1, 9th Floor, Brunel House, 2 Fitzalan Rd, Cardiff, CF24 0EB; tel. (20) 8215-2243; (29) 2039-5123; e-mail info@mind.org.uk; internet www.mind.org.uk.

Minhaj Welfare Foundation

Established in 1989, a worldwide humanitarian aid organization.

Activities: Supports the poor and people in need in marginalized communities by securing their basic human rights. The Foundation provides access to education for children; access to basic healthcare for poor people; and means of generating sustainable socioeconomic development for communities. Maintains an office in Pakistan. Minhaj Welfare Canada was established in 2017.
Geographical Area of Activity: Africa, Australia, Bangladesh, Canada, Europe, India, Middle East, Pakistan, Nepal, Türkiye (Turkey), UK, USA.
Publications: Annual Report; newsletter.
Finance: Annual income £4.1m., expenditure £4.8m. (31 March 2024).
Principal Staff: Man. Dir Faisal Hussain.
Contact Details: 5 Christie Way, Manchester M21 7QY; tel. (300) 3030777; e-mail info@minhajwelfare.org; internet minhajwelfare.org.

Minority Rights Group International—MRG

Established in 1969 by David Astor, a newspaper editor and proprietor; an international human rights organization.

Activities: Works to ensure the rights of ethnic, religious and linguistic minorities and indigenous people. MRG conducts research, lobbies the UN, international organizations and governments on behalf of minority groups, and trains minority and indigenous leaders on advocacy and human rights. It maintains an online Directory of minorities and indigenous peoples and works with almost 300 partners in 60 countries, with regional offices in Hungary and Uganda. MRG has consultative status with ECOSOC and observer status with the African Commission for Human and Peoples' Rights.
Geographical Area of Activity: International.
Publications: *Minority and Indigenous Trends*; newsletters; *World Directory of Minorities and Indigenous Peoples* (online); briefings; reports; training manuals.
Finance: Annual income £6.2m., expenditure £6.7m. (31 Dec. 2023).
Council: Anastasia Crickley (Chair.); Mahdis Keshavarz (Vice-Chair.); Bill Samuel (Treas.).
Principal Staff: Co-Exec. Dirs Joshua Castellino, Claire Thomas.
Contact Details: 54 Commercial St, London E1 6LT; tel. (20) 7422-4200; e-mail minority.rights@minorityrights.org; internet minorityrights.org.

The Mission to Seafarers

Established in 1856 by Anglican ministries as the Mission to Seamen Afloat, at Home and Abroad; renamed the Missions to Seamen in 1858; present name adopted in 2000.

Activities: Works in 200 ports in over 50 countries, caring for seafarers of all ranks, nationalities and beliefs. Through its global network of chaplains, staff and volunteers, the Mission offers practical, emotional and spiritual support to seafarers through ship visits, drop-in centres and a range of welfare and emergency support services.
Geographical Area of Activity: International.
Publications: Annual Report; newsletter; *Flying Angel News* (magazine); *The Sea* (bimonthly newsletter); *Prayer Diary* (annual); Seafarers Happiness Index (quarterly).
Finance: Annual income £5.8m., expenditure £5.8m. (31 Dec. 2023).
Board of Trustees: Tom Boardley (Chair.); Rt Rev. David Williams (Vice-Chair.).
Principal Staff: Sec.-Gen. Peter Rouch.
Contact Details: 1st Floor, 6 Bath Place, Rivington St, London EC2A 3JE; tel. (20) 7248-5202; e-mail info@missiontoseafarers.org; internet www.missiontoseafarers.org.

Mo Ibrahim Foundation

Established in 2006 by Mo Ibrahim, the founder of Celtel International, a mobile telecommunications company; incorporated in Jersey, Channel Islands.

Activities: Focuses on governance and leadership in Africa. The Foundation maintains the *Ibrahim Index of African Governance*; awards the Ibrahim Prize for Achievement in African Leadership, worth US $5m. over 10 years and $200,000 annually for life thereafter. It organizes the Ibrahim Forum and Ibrahim Governance Weekend; offers Leadership Fellowships, mentoring future African leaders, with an annual stipend of $100,000; and also awards Ibrahim Scholarships. Fellows and scholars are invited to join the pan-African Now Generation Network. Has an office in Dakar, Senegal.
Geographical Area of Activity: Africa, UK.
Restrictions: Scholarships are open to African nationals who have a Master's degree and 7–10 years' relevant work experience and are aged under 40 years (or 45 for women with children).
Publications: *Ibrahim Index of African Governance*; *African Governance Report* (annual); *Ibrahim Forum Report* (annual); research reports.
Council: Dr Mo Ibrahim (Chair.).
Principal Staff: Exec. Dir Nathalie Delapalme.
Contact Details: 3rd Floor North, 35 Portman Sq., London W1H 6LR; tel. (20) 7535-5063; e-mail info@moibrahimfoundation.org; internet mo.ibrahim.foundation.

MS Society—Multiple Sclerosis Society of Great Britain and Northern Ireland

Founded in 1953 by Sir Richard Cave, an industrialist, and his wife Mary, who had multiple sclerosis (MS).

Activities: Promotes research into the cause and cure of MS; and provides welfare and support services for people with MS and their friends, families and carers. The Society conducts and supports research within the United Kingdom, offering project grants, innovative awards, PhD studentships and junior fellowships. It holds international conferences, disseminates information and runs a national helpline for people affected by MS.
Geographical Area of Activity: UK.
Restrictions: Only funds research grant applications where the principal investigator is based in the UK; collaborative applications by UK-based research groups with genuine participation of research groups outside the UK are encouraged.
Publications: Annual Report; e-newsletter (2 a month); *MS Matters* (members' magazine, 6 a year); factsheets; information booklets.
Finance: Annual income £27.7m., expenditure £30.4m. (31 Dec. 2023).
Board of Trustees: Sir Paul Curran (Chair.); Emily Revess (Vice-Chair.); Nick Keveth (Treas.).
Principal Staff: Chief Exec. Nick Moberly.
Contact Details: Carriage House, 8 City North Pl., London N4 3FU; tel. (20) 8438-0700; e-mail supportercare@mssociety.org.uk; internet www.mssociety.org.uk.

UNITED KINGDOM

MSI Reproductive Choices

Established in 1976 by Tim Black, Jean Black and Phil Harvey; formerly known as Marie Stopes International.

Activities: Supports the right to have children by choice, through the provision of information and services. The organization lobbies governments and international organizations to influence policy and allocation of resources in the areas of family-planning services and reproductive healthcare. It provides information and family-planning and healthcare services in 36 countries, working in collaboration with local organizations. Each programme is managed and run by a local team and meets the specific needs of the country, with a focus on building the capacity of indigenous organizations.

Geographical Area of Activity: Worldwide.

Publications: Annual Report; Global Impact Report; *First People* (newsletter); handbooks; reports; factsheets.

Finance: Annual income £414.4m., expenditure £313.8m. (31 Dec. 2023).

Board of Trustees: Frank Braeken (Chair.).

Principal Staff: CEO Simon Cooke.

Contact Details: 1 Conway St, Fitzroy Sq., London W1T 6LP; tel. (20) 7636-6200; e-mail info@msichoices.org.uk; internet msichoices.org.

Muscular Dystrophy UK

Founded in 1959 as the Muscular Dystrophy Group of Great Britain and Northern Ireland and subsequently known as the Muscular Dystrophy Campaign; present name adopted in 1999.

Activities: Works to prevent more than 60 rare and very rare progressive muscle-weakening and -wasting conditions. The organization supports research to find treatments and cures; supports health and education professionals, offering training and e-learning courses on neuromuscular conditions; and provides information and access to services, resources and specialist care to help people to live independently. It includes the Joseph Patrick Trust (f. 1986), the organization's welfare trust, which part-funds equipment costs; and is a member of the company forum of the European Neuromuscular Centre, working with and promoting the exchange of information between similar associations in other countries.

Geographical Area of Activity: UK.

Publications: Annual Report; *Target MD* (quarterly magazine); *Campaign* (newsletter); factsheets; impact reports.

Finance: Annual income £9.5m., expenditure £8.0m. (31 March 2024).

Board of Trustees: Prof. Michael Hanna (Chair.); Joseph Gorden (Treas.).

Principal Staff: CEO Andy Fletcher.

Contact Details: 32 Ufford St, London SE1 8QD; tel. (20) 7803-4800; e-mail info@musculardystrophyuk.org; internet www.musculardystrophyuk.org.

Muslim Aid

Established in 1985 by community leaders from 17 Islamic organizations, in response to drought in the Horn of Africa region; a faith-based international relief and development agency.

Activities: Programmes include: emergency response, relief and rehabilitation; securing sustainable livelihoods for marginalized and very poor communities; providing access to primary education, for girls in particular; and improving access to mother and child healthcare and primary healthcare services. The organization operates overseas programmes working with partner organizations. In the United Kingdom, it focuses on homeless and elderly people, and prisoner rehabilitation.

Geographical Area of Activity: Bangladesh, Bosnia and Herzegovina, Myanmar, Pakistan, Palestinian Territories, Somalia, Sri Lanka, Sudan, UK.

Restrictions: Aid distributed through partner and local community organizations only.

Publications: Annual Review; newsletter; *Harvest Booklet*; *Zakat Guide*; blog.

Finance: Annual income £21.2m., expenditure £18.5m. (31 Dec. 2023).

Board of Trustees: Mustafa Faruqi (Chair.); Faria Ali (Deputy Chair.).

Principal Staff: CEO Khalid Javid.

Contact Details: POB 3, London E1 1WP; LMC Business Wing, 4th Floor, 38–44 Whitechapel Rd, Tower Hamlets, London E1 1JX; tel. (20) 7377-4200; e-mail mail@muslimaid.org; internet www.muslimaid.org.

National Emergencies Trust

Established in 2019; convened by the Charity Commission, in response to terrorist attacks in London and Manchester and the Grenfell Tower fire in 2017; independent of the Government.

Activities: Supports the physical and mental health and well-being of people affected by national emergencies, including survivors and their loved ones. The Trust works with charities and other bodies to raise and distribute funds fast and fairly and delivers projects that improve outcomes for future disaster survivors.

Geographical Area of Activity: United Kingdom.

Publications: Annual Report; newsletter.

Finance: Annual income £481,270, expenditure £772,575 (31 March 2024).

Board of Trustees: John Barradell (Chair.); Gerald Oppenheim (Deputy Chair.).

Principal Staff: Pres. Gen. the Lord Richard Dannatt; CEO Mhairi Sharp.

Contact Details: London Scottish House, 95 Horseferry Rd, London SW1P 2DX; e-mail info@nationalemergenciestrust.org.uk; internet nationalemergenciestrust.org.uk.

National Foundation for Educational Research—NFER

Founded in 1946 as an independent education and children's services research body.

Activities: Conducts research and evaluations of education systems and communicates findings to decisionmakers in government, the third sector, private and public companies, and other interested organizations. Key themes include: accountability and school performance; assessment and benchmarking; classroom practice and quality of teaching; the transition from education to employment; social mobility, educational outcomes and careers; school funding models; school workforce engagement and retention; and reform of systems and structures. The Foundation offers a full range of support services, including library, national and international information services and an in-house publishing unit; and works internationally with overseas partner organizations. It has an office in York.

Geographical Area of Activity: International.

Publications: Annual Report; *NFER Direct* (monthly newsletter); *NFER Direct for Schools* (monthly newsletter); *Assessment Digest* (monthly newsletter); *Educational Research* (journal); research reports; blog.

Finance: Annual income £21.8m., expenditure £25.2m. (31 March 2024).

Board of Trustees: Lorna Cocking (Chair.); Melvyn Keen (Hon. Treas.).

Principal Staff: Chief Exec. Carole Willis.

Contact Details: The Mere, Upton Park, Slough SL1 2DQ; tel. (1753) 574123; e-mail enquiries@nfer.ac.uk; internet www.nfer.ac.uk.

The National Lottery Community Fund

Founded in 1994, as the National Lottery Charities Board; name changed in 2001 to the Community Fund, then in 2004 to the Big Lottery Fund, following its merger with the New Opportunities Fund. Present name adopted in 2019; a non-departmental public body.

Activities: Offers grants to community-based organizations worth from £300 up to £10,000; and above £10,000 for longer-term funding. Grantmaking is organized into five portfolios for England, Northern Ireland, Scotland and Wales, and the United Kingdom as a whole.

Geographical Area of Activity: UK.

Restrictions: Only funds UK-based charities and voluntary groups.

Publications: Annual Report; *eBulletin*; *Big Times* (magazine); research reports.

Finance: Annual income £906m., expenditure £953m. (31 March 2024).

Board: Dame Julia Cleverdon (Chair.).

Principal Staff: CEO David Knott.

Contact Details: Apex House, 3 Embassy Dr., Edgbaston, Birmingham B15 1TR; tel. (345) 4102030; e-mail general.enquiries@tnlcommunityfund.org.uk; internet www.tnlcommunityfund.org.uk.

The National Lottery Heritage Fund

Established in 1994, under the National Lottery etc. Act 1993; the Trustees of the National Heritage Memorial Fund (f. 1980) became responsible for the distribution of that proportion of the National Lottery proceeds allocated to heritage in the United Kingdom; formerly known as the Heritage Lottery Fund.

Activities: Distributes funds allocated to heritage by its parent body the National Heritage Memorial Fund. Grants range between £3,000 and £1m. for a wide range of heritage projects, including countryside, parks and gardens; objects and sites that are linked to industrial, transport and maritime history; records such as local history archives, photographic collections or oral history; historic buildings; museum and gallery collections; and places of worship.

Geographical Area of Activity: UK.

Publications: Annual Report; e-bulletin; research and evaluation reports.

Finance: Annual income £361.6m., expenditure £368.0m. (31 March 2024).

Board of Trustees: Simon Thurley (Chair.); Ray MacFarlane, Mukesh Sharma (Deputy Chair.).

Principal Staff: Chief Exec. Eilish McGuinness.

Contact Details: 4th Floor, Cannon Bridge House, 25 Dowgate Hill, London EC4R 2YA; tel. (20) 7591-6000; e-mail enquire@heritagefund.org.uk; internet www.heritagefund.org.uk.

National Trust

Established in 1895, as the National Trust for Places of Historic Interest or Natural Beauty, by Octavia Hill and Sir Robert Hunter, leading members of the Commons Preservation Society, and Canon Hardwicke Rawnsley, a social reformer and conservationist.

Activities: Maintains more than 500 historically or architecturally important buildings, as well as ancient monuments, coast, gardens, parks and nature reserves, to which the Trust may provide public access. An independent research organization recognized by UK Research and Innovation (q.v.), it sponsors and conducts collections conservation, curatorial and environmental research; and offers historical and environmental learning programmes, and conservation skills courses. Has 5m. members; and an office in London.

Geographical Area of Activity: England, Northern Ireland, Wales.

Restrictions: Does not normally make grants.

Publications: Annual Reports; newsletter; magazine (3 a year); *National Trust Handbook for Members and Visitors* (annual); *Information for Visitors with Disabilities* (annual); *Interim Report on the Connections between Colonialism and Properties now in the Care of the National Trust, Including Links with Historic Slavery*.

Finance: Annual income £723.8m., expenditure £767.7m. (28 Feb. 2024).

Board of Trustees and Council: René Olivieri (Chair.); Sandy Nairne (Deputy Chair.).

Principal Staff: Dir-Gen. Hilary McGrady.

Contact Details: Heelis, Kemble Dr., Swindon SW2 2NA; tel. (1793) 817400; e-mail enquiries@nationaltrust.org.uk; internet www.nationaltrust.org.uk.

Nesta—National Endowment for Science, Technology and the Arts

Established in 1998 as a national endowment under the National Lottery Act 1998; a non-departmental body and Trustee of the Nesta Trust.

Activities: Works to eliminate childhood disadvantage, increase life expectancy and reduce health inequalities, decarbonize household activities and improve productivity. The Endowment provides practical and financial support to individuals, charities, social enterprises, businesses and public organizations. It established the Innovation Growth Lab, a global collaboration for experimental innovation and entrepreneurship; and the Alliance for Useful Evidence, a network that promotes more effective use of evidence in social policy and practice; and offers Challenge Prizes to solve public problems, including the £8m. Longitude Prize challenge fund, which was launched to tackle the threat of antibiotic resistance. The Discovery Hub explores emerging trends, and promising technologies and interventions.

Geographical Area of Activity: International.

Publications: Annual Report; newsletter (weekly); *DIY Toolkit* (in 12 languages); *Innovation for International Development*; policy briefings; reports; working papers; blog.

Finance: Annual income £52.4m., expenditure £65.7m. (31 March 2024).

Board of Trustees: Ed Richards (Chair.).

Principal Staff: CEO Ravi Gurumurthy; Deputy CEO Emily Bushby.

Contact Details: 58 Victoria Embankment, London EC4Y 0DS; tel. (20) 7438-2500; e-mail information@nesta.org.uk; internet www.nesta.org.uk.

Network for Social Change Charitable Trust—NSCCT

Founded in 1986 as the Network Foundation by Dr Frederick Mulder, an art dealer and founder of the Frederick Mulder Foundation (f. 1986) and the Funding Network (f. 2000), and others.

Activities: Funds projects to bring about progressive social change through research and education. Topic-based project pools are: Arts & Education for Change; Economic Justice; Green Planet; Health & Wellbeing; Human Rights; and Peace. The network has over 100 members.

Geographical Area of Activity: International.

Restrictions: Funding applications must be sponsored by a Network member; does not accept unsolicited applications. Members must contribute at least £4,000 a year.

Publications: Annual Report; funding reports.

Finance: Annual income £1.7m., expenditure £1.8m. (31 Aug. 2023).

Principal Staff: Sec. Carol Freeman.

Contact Details: BM 2063, London WC1N 3XX; tel. (1647) 61106; e-mail nfscct@gmail.com; internet thenetworkforsocialchange.org.uk.

UNITED KINGDOM

New Economics Foundation—NEF
Established in 1986 by the leaders of the Other Economic Summit (f. 1983), a counter-summit to annual meetings of the Group of Seven (G7) nations.

Activities: Promotes economic transformation through social and environmental justice. Main programme areas are: a new social settlement, sharing economic wealth and resources so that everyone enjoys a good quality of life; a Green New Deal, addressing climate change and inequality at the same time; and democratic economy, devolving power to city and regional authorities and improving living standards. The Foundation conducts public policy research and advocacy, working with academics, campaigners, community-based organizations, progressive businesses, trade unions and women's groups. NEF Consulting offers strategic consulting, training and impact evaluation services.

Geographical Area of Activity: UK.

Publications: Annual Review; newsletter; reports; blog.

Finance: Annual income £4.9m., expenditure £4.9m. (30 June 2024).

Board of Trustees: Adam Sharples (Chair.); Richard Bryars (Treas.).

Principal Staff: Chief Exec. Danny Sriskandarajah.

Contact Details: 10 Salamanca Pl., London SE1 7HB; tel. (20) 7820-6300; e-mail info@neweconomics.org; internet www.neweconomics.org.

NHS Charities Together
Founded in 2000.

Activities: A national independent charity working with a network of more than 230 charitable organizations to provide support to staff, patients and communities across the United Kingdom.

Geographical Area of Activity: United Kingdom.

Finance: Total income £9.5m., expenditure on £24.2m. (31 Dec. 2023).

Trustees: Ian Lush (Chair.); Tim Diggle, Kirsty Thomson (Joint Deputy Chair.).

Principal Staff: Chief Exec. Ellie Orton.

Contact Details: Suite 68, Lake View House, Wilton Dr., Warwick, CV34 6RG; tel. (300) 3035748; e-mail hello@anhsc.org.uk; internet nhscharitiestogether.co.uk.

NSPCC—National Society for the Prevention of Cruelty to Children
Established in 1884, as the London Society of Prevention of Cruelty to Children, by Rev. Benjamin Waugh; name changed to the National Society of Prevention of Cruelty to Children in 1889. Incorporated by Royal Charter in 1895.

Activities: Works to eliminate child abuse and neglect. The Society conducts policy, lobbying, influencing and campaigning work; undertakes and funds research on child health and development and children and families at risk; and provides training in child protection and safeguarding. It provides local services to help children and families to recover from their experiences; carries out activities in schools; and runs a national helpline, offering advice and support on children's welfare, ChildLine, a free helpline for children and young people, and the Report Abuse in Education helpline.

Geographical Area of Activity: UK, Jersey.

Publications: Annual Report; *CASPAR* (weekly safeguarding child protection newsletter); *NSPCC Learning Newsletter*; *Safeguarding in Education Update* (monthly newsletter); *New in the Library* (weekly); *Case Reviews Update* (monthly); briefings; case reviews; factsheets; information leaflets; research reports; statistics.

Finance: Annual income £124.7m., expenditure £118.2m. (31 March 2024).

Board of Trustees: Neil Berkett (Chair.); Pippa Gough, Ife Grillo (Vice-Chair.); Mark Corbridge (Treas.).

Principal Staff: CEO Chris Sherwood.

Contact Details: Weston House, 42 Curtain Rd, London EC2A 3NH; tel. (20) 7825-2505; e-mail supporter@nspcc.org.uk; internet www.nspcc.org.uk.

Nuffield Foundation
Founded in 1943 by William Morris, Lord Nuffield, the founder of Morris Motors, the Nuffield Trust (f. 1940) and Nuffield College, Oxford (f. 1949); comprises the Nuffield Council on Bioethics (f. 1991) and the Nuffield Family Justice Observatory (f. 2019).

Activities: Awards grants through institutions in the United Kingdom. Major grants are for experimental or development projects in education, justice and social welfare; small grants and fellowships in science and social science are also offered under research grant schemes, which are open to members of universities and other research institutions in the UK; and more than 1,000 Nuffield Research Placements are open annually to students on science, technology, engineering and mathematics courses. The Foundation established the Nuffield Council on Bioethics (f. 1991), which it co-funds with the Wellcome Trust and the Medical Research Council (part of UK Research and Innovation, qq.v.); and the Nuffield Family Justice Observatory (f. 2019). It also administers the Oliver Bird Fund (f. 1948), for research into musculoskeletal conditions, including arthritis, back and neck pain, and autoimmune diseases; and the Commonwealth Relations Trust (f. 1937). In 2018, it established the Ada Lovelace Institute to study the impact of using data, algorithms and artificial intelligence.

Geographical Area of Activity: UK.

Restrictions: No grants to individuals for financial assistance.

Publications: Annual Report; newsletter; reports; blog.

Finance: Annual revenue £8.5m., expenditure £23.1m. (31 Dec. 2023).

Trustees: Prof. Sir Keith Burnett (Chair.).

Principal Staff: Chief Exec. Gavin Kelly.

Contact Details: 100 St John St, London EC1M 4EH; tel. (20) 7631-0566; e-mail info@nuffieldfoundation.org; internet www.nuffieldfoundation.org.

ODI
Founded in 1960 as the Overseas Development Institute; rebranded as ODI in 2020. A global affairs think tank.

Activities: Works in developed as well as developing countries. Main programme areas are: climate and sustainability; development and public finance; digital societies; gender equality and social inclusion; global risks and resilience; humanitarian policy; international economic development; and politics and governance. The Institute manages international networks of practitioners, policymakers and researchers, including the Humanitarian Practice Network (f. 1994) and Evidence-based Policy in Development Network; and also hosts the Secretariat of the Active Learning Network for Accountability and Performance in Humanitarian Action (f. 1997), a network of NGOs, UN agencies and the Red Cross/Red Crescent Movement. It undertakes policy-related research and evaluations, provides advisory services and organizes public events. ODI Fellowships, worth up to £23,000 a year, allow postgraduate economists and statisticians to spend two years in developing countries working as civil servants in the public sector.

Geographical Area of Activity: International.

Publications: Annual Report; newsletter; *Development Policy Review* (quarterly); *Disasters* (quarterly); *Natural Resources Perspectives;* briefing papers; journals; reports; toolkits; working papers.

Finance: Annual income £29.9m., expenditure £32.3m. (31 March 2024).

Board: Suma Chakrabarti (Chair.).

Principal Staff: Chief Exec. Sara Pantuliano; Deputy Chief Exec. and Man. Dir Hans Peter Lankes.

The Officers' Association

Contact Details: 203 Blackfriars Rd, London SE1 8NJ; tel. (20) 7922-0300; e-mail odi@odi.org.uk; internet odi.org.

The Officers' Association

Founded in 1920 by Admiral of the Fleet Earl Beatty, Field Marshal Earl Haig and Air Marshal Sir Hugh Trenchard for the relief of financial distress among male or female former officers of HM Naval, Military or Air Forces, their widows/widowers and dependants; incorporated under Royal Charter in 1921.

Activities: Operates in the United Kingdom and abroad in the field of social welfare, through grants to individuals. The Association provides advice on finding accommodation in homes for the elderly; and its Employment Department helps officers leaving the armed services and former officers to find employment in civilian life.

Geographical Area of Activity: International.

Publications: Annual Report; Impact Report.

Finance: Annual income £1.3m., expenditure £1.6m. (30 Sept. 2023).

Executive Committee: Alex Spofforth (Chair.).

Principal Staff: Pres Lt-Gen. Andrew Figgures, Air Marshal Sir Baz North, Vice-Admiral Peter Hudson; CEO Lee Holloway.

Contact Details: Third Floor, 40 Caversham Rd, Reading RG1 7EB; tel. (20) 7808-4175; e-mail help@officersassociation.org.uk; internet www.officersassociation.org.uk.

Open Society Foundation—London

Established in 2002 as IUF Ltd; an independent foundation, part of the Open Society Foundations (q.v.) network. Present name adopted in 2003.

Activities: Supports good governance, democracy and CSOs; and the advancement of education about human rights and in journalism and other media. Main programme areas include: Africa; climate priorities; early childhood; economic justice; education and higher education support; Eurasia; Europe; human rights; independent journalism and information; justice; and international migration. The Foundation offers scholarships; and makes grants institutions.

Geographical Area of Activity: Africa, Eurasia, Europe.

Publications: *Section 172 Report*.

Finance: Annual income £70.0m., expenditure £70.5m. (31 Dec. 2023).

Principal Staff: Dir Michael Vachon.

Contact Details: 4th Floor, Herbal House, 8 Back Hill, London EC1R 5EN; tel. (20) 7031-0200; e-mail mbox_london@opensocietyfoundations.org; internet www.opensocietyfoundations.org/about/offices-foundations/open-society-foundation-london.

Opportunity International UK

Founded in 1992 as the Opportunity Trust, based on Christian values.

Activities: Empowers people in developing countries to create small businesses and strengthen communities. The organization is part of the Opportunity network, comprising more than 40 organizations, most of which are local microfinance organizations, which provide financial services and training to remote and marginalized communities. It works in more than 20 countries, with fundraising offices in Australia, Canada, Germany, Hong Kong, Switzerland and the USA.

Geographical Area of Activity: International.

Restrictions: Only makes grants to Opportunity International implementing partner organizations.

Publications: Annual Report; *Impact* (newsletter); blog.

Finance: Annual income £2.7m., expenditure £2.8m. (31 Dec. 2023).

Board of Trustees: Cliff Hampton (Chair.); David Burndred (Treas.).

Principal Staff: CEO Mary Oakes.

Contact Details: Angel Ct, 81 St Clements St, Oxford OX4 1AW; tel. (1865) 725304; e-mail ukinfo@opportunity.org; internet www.opportunity.org.uk.

Orangutan Foundation

Established in 1990.

Activities: Works with local communities, grassroots NGOs, local businesses and regional governments to protect orangutans, conserve their tropical forest habitat, and promote research and education. Programme areas include: habitat protection and reforestation; orangutan translocation and release; capacity building and sustainable livelihoods; education and awareness; and scientific research. The Foundation's small research grants programme makes awards of up to £500 for the study of orangutan behaviour and ecology or related rainforest field research in Indonesia. In 2016 the Foundation inaugurated the Terry Pratchett 'Oook' Award for the Conservation of Orangutans and their Habitat.

Geographical Area of Activity: Indonesia (Borneo, Sumatra), Malaysia, UK.

Publications: *Red Ape* (newsletter, 2 a year); factsheets; reports.

Finance: Annual income £805,770, expenditure £709,124 (31 Dec. 2023).

Board of Trustees: Ashley Leiman (Chair.); Guy Sanders (Treas.).

Principal Staff: Dir and Founder Ashley Leiman.

Contact Details: 7 Kent Terrace, London NW1 4RP; tel. (20) 7724-2912; e-mail info@orangutan.org.uk; internet www.orangutan.org.uk.

Orbis Charitable Trust

Established in 1982 as a mobile teaching eye hospital (the Flying Eye Hospital).

Activities: Works to prevent and treat avoidable blindness. The organization carries out specialized training programmes for healthcare workers and community health projects to improve further the standard of eye care in less-developed countries. In 2003 it launched the Cybersight telemedicine initiative, using the internet to connect local doctors and volunteer opthamologists for training and mentoring. Works in 19 countries, with fundraising offices in Canada, the People's Republic of China, Hong Kong, Ireland, Macao, Singapore and the United Kingdom.

Geographical Area of Activity: International.

Publications: Annual Report; *Observer* (newsletter); factsheets; brochures; posters.

Finance: Annual revenue £6.5m., expenditure £6.1m. (31 Dec. 2023).

Board of Directors: Nick Fox (Chair.).

Principal Staff: CEO Rebecca Cronin.

Contact Details: 41-42 Craven St, London WC2N 5NG; tel. (20) 7608-7260; e-mail info@orbis.org.uk; internet gbr.orbis.org.

Oxfam GB

Founded in 1942, as the Oxford Committee for Famine Relief; part of the Oxfam confederation (qq.v.).

Activities: Supports poor people who face hunger, disease, exploitation and poverty worldwide. Main programme areas include: beating hunger; climate change preparation, adaptation and response; fighting coronavirus; providing free quality healthcare and education; responding to humanitarian emergencies; women's rights and gender justice; and providing safe, clean water for all. The organization offers professional development for teachers in the field of global citizenship; and maintains an online library of resources and free activities for schools. It works in over 80 countries with more than 2,500 partner organizations; and operates a network of c. 600 charity shops in the United Kingdom.

Geographical Area of Activity: International.

UNITED KINGDOM

Publications: Annual Report; *Inside Oxfam* (quarterly); briefing papers; evaluation reports; blog.

Finance: Annual income £368.0m., expenditure £396.4m. (31 March 2024).

Board of Trustees: Charles Gurassa (Chair.); Annie Hudson (Deputy Chair.); Les Campbell (Treas.).

Principal Staff: CEO Halima Begum.

Contact Details: Oxfam House, John Smith Dr., Cowley, Oxford OX4 2JY; tel. (300) 200-1300; e-mail heretohelp@oxfam.org.uk; internet www.oxfam.org.uk.

Paul Hamlyn Foundation—PHF

Founded in 1987 by Paul Hamlyn, a publisher, incorporating an earlier Paul Hamlyn Foundation (f. 1972).

Activities: Helps people to fulfil their potential and improve their quality of life, particularly children and young people, and disadvantaged people. The Foundation's work in the United Kingdom focuses on six priority areas: nurturing ideas and imaginative people; widening access to and deepening participation in the arts; improving education and learning through the arts; showing that the arts make a difference to people's lives; supporting organizations that invest in young people; and improving support for young people who migrate and their integration into local communities. In India, it works with local NGOs that enable vulnerable people in the poorest regions of the country to improve their lives. The Ideas and Pioneers Fund offers grants of up to £15,000 for innovative ideas and new approaches to social change. Individual awards and grants through the Breakthrough Fund are made to visual artists and composers.

Geographical Area of Activity: India, UK.

Restrictions: Prioritizes support to people who have been most affected by systemic oppression and/or discrimination; and young people aged 18–30 years.

Publications: Annual Report; newsletter; *PHF Yearbook*; evaluations; research reports; teaching resources.

Finance: Annual income £72.0m., expenditure £72.1m. (31 March 2024).

Trustees: Jane Hamlyn (Chair.); Tom Wylie (Vice-Chair.).

Principal Staff: Chief Exec. Halima Khan.

Contact Details: 5–11 Leeke St, London WC1X 9HY; tel. (20) 7812-3300; e-mail information@phf.org.uk; internet www.phf.org.uk.

Peace Direct

Founded in 2002.

Activities: Peace Direct works in partnership with local peacebuilders and other allies to shift power and resources for sustainable peace. It supports locally-led peacebuilding initiatives through advocacy, monitoring and research. The organization supports programmes in areas including: building livelihoods; conflict prevention; justice and human rights; helping former fighters; supporting women; and vocational training as an alternative to violence. It works through a network of 25 partner organizations in 14 countries. Has offices in London, UK, New York and Washington, DC, USA, and Brussels, Belgium.

Geographical Area of Activity: East and South-East Asia, Middle East, South Asia, sub-Saharan Africa, UK, USA.

Restrictions: No unsolicited applications.

Publications: Annual Report; newsletter; *Peace Insight* (online platform); case studies; toolkits.

Finance: Annual income US $4.5m., expenditure $4.1m. (31 Dec. 2023).

UK Board of Trustees: Anthony Smith (Chair.).

US Board of Trustees: Anthony Smith (Chair.); Colleen Smith (Treas.).

Principal Staff: Chief Exec. Dylan Mathews; US Man. Dir Vahe Mirikian.

Contact Details: Dynamis House, 1st Floor, 6–8 Sycamore St, London EC1Y 0SW; tel. (20) 3422-5549; e-mail info@peacedirect.org; internet www.peacedirect.org.

Penal Reform International—PRI

Founded in 1989 by an international group of criminal justice and human rights activists; registered in the Netherlands, with headquarters in the United Kingdom.

Activities: Promotes the right of detainees to fair and humane treatment. The organization campaigns for the prevention of torture and abolition of the death penalty; and works to ensure just and appropriate responses to children and women in their interactions with the law. It works with intergovernmental organizations to enact reforms that balance the rights of offenders and victims; and provides practical assistance to policymakers, criminal justice authorities and civil society to reform legislation, policy and practice. Has headquarters in London and The Hague (Netherlands), with regional offices in Amman (Jordan), Bishkek (Kyrgyzstan), Kampala (Uganda), Nur-Sultan (Kazakhstan) and Tbilisi (Georgia); and consultative status with ECOSOC, the Inter-Parliamentary Union, the African Commission on Human and Peoples' Rights, the African Committee of Experts on the Rights and Welfare of the Child, and the Council of Europe.

Geographical Area of Activity: Worldwide.

Publications: Annual Report; newsletter (monthly); *Global Prison Trends*; reports; briefings; international standards; models for reform; blog.

Finance: Annual income £3.8m., expenditure £3.3m. (2023).

Membership Council: David Fathi (Chair.); Dr Roselyn Karugonjo-Segawa (Sec.-Gen.); Erika Marseille (Treas.).

Principal Staff: Exec. Dir Olivia Rope.

Contact Details: The Green House, 244–254 Cambridge Heath Rd, London E2 9DA; tel. (203) 559-6752; e-mail info@penalreform.org; internet www.penalreform.org.

Pesticide Action Network UK—PAN UK

Founded in 1987, a member of PAN Europe (q.v.) and part of the PAN International network (f. 1982).

Activities: Works to eliminate the use of Highly Hazardous Pesticides, promoting ecologically sound alternatives, healthy food and sustainable farming. The Network supports projects with partner organizations in developing countries; researches related issues; engages with retailers and producers on supply chain issues; and undertakes policy advocacy. It provides information through publishing briefings, books and journals.

Geographical Area of Activity: International.

Restrictions: Not a grantmaking organization.

Publications: Annual Report; *Pesticides News*; factsheets; guides; journals; leaflets; manuals; posters; reports; toolkits.

Finance: Annual income £1.4m., expenditure £1.4m. (31 Dec. 2023).

Board of Trustees: Barbara Dinham (Chair.); Edward Moore (Treas.).

Contact Details: The Brighthelm Centre, North Rd, Brighton BN1 1YD; tel. (1273) 964230; e-mail admin@pan-uk.org; internet www.pan-uk.org.

Pilgrim Trust

Founded in 1930 by Edward Stephen Harkness, a US philanthropist.

Activities: Supports social welfare projects, with a focus on vulnerable women and girls; preservation of architecturally or historically important buildings, artefacts or documents, and countryside; and the promotion of scholarship, art and learning. The Main Grant Fund makes awards for sums above £5,000, and the Small Grant Fund for sums below that amount, for up to three years.

Geographical Area of Activity: UK.

Restrictions: Does not make grants to individuals nor to organizations and projects outside the UK.
Publications: Annual Report; guidelines.
Finance: Annual income £1.6m., expenditure £2.8m. (31 Dec. 2023).
Trustees: Lord James Sassoon (Chair.).
Principal Staff: Dir Sue Bowers.
Contact Details: New Wing, Somerset House, Strand, London WC2R 1LA; tel. (20) 7834-6510; e-mail info@thepilgrimtrust.org.uk; internet www.thepilgrimtrust.org.uk.

PLAN International—PI

Established in 1937 by John Langdon-Davies, a journalist, and Eric Muggeridge, an aid worker, as Foster Parents Plan for Children in Spain to help refugee children affected by the Spanish Civil War. Part of the Disasters Emergency Committee (q.v.).
Activities: Promotes children's rights and equality for girls. The organization works locally, nationally and internationally to empower children, young people and communities to eliminate discrimination against girls, exclusion and vulnerability; and to prepare for and respond to crises and overcome adversity. Programme areas include: early childhood; education; ending violence; emergency response; sexual health and rights; skills and work; and youth activism. It comprises 20 national organizations and Plan International, Inc, which organizes field operations; and has more than 50 country offices, with four liaison offices in Geneva (Switzerland), New York (USA), Addis Ababa (Ethiopia) and Brussels (Belgium). Active in over 80 countries.
Geographical Area of Activity: Worldwide.
Publications: Annual Review; Impact Reports; newsletter; case studies; evaluations; manuals; policy briefs; reports; toolkits; blog.
Finance: Annual income €65.0m., expenditure €32.7m. (30 June 2024, UK only).
International Board of Directors: Gunvor Kronman (Chair.); Madhukar Kamath (Vice-Chair.); Axel Berger (Treas.).
Principal Staff: CEO Reena Ghelani.
Contact Details: Global Hub, Dukes Court, Block A, Duke St, Woking GU21 5BH; tel. (1483) 755155; e-mail info@plan-international.org; internet www.plan-international.org.

Plunkett Foundation

Founded in 1919 by Sir Horace Curzon Plunkett, who promoted agricultural co-operatives internationally.
Activities: Works to relieve rural poverty and social exclusion through helping rural communities to establish and run enterprises that provide essential services. The Foundation undertakes training courses, consultancy projects and research studies on co-operative development and management in the United Kingdom and developing countries. It awards fellowships in recognition of individuals' support to the Foundation over a number of years.
Geographical Area of Activity: UK.
Publications: Annual Report; newsletter; *Better Business Reports;* Community Business Map (online); case studies; impact report.
Finance: Annual income £1.1m., expenditure £1.3m. (31 Dec. 2023).
Board of Trustees: Stephen Nicol (Chair.); Helen Aldis (Vice-Chair.).
Principal Staff: Chief Exec. James Alcock; Deputy Chief Exec. Harriet English.
Contact Details: The Quadrangle, Banbury Rd, Woodstock OX20 1LH; tel. (1993) 630022; e-mail info@plunkett.co.uk; internet www.plunkett.co.uk.

Practical Action

Established in 1966, as the Intermediate Technology Development Group, by the economist Dr E. F. 'Fritz' Schumacher; present name adopted in 2005.
Activities: Reduces poverty through working with communities to develop solutions in agriculture, water and waste management, climate resilience and access to clean energy. The organization undertakes consultancy and provides publishing, educational and technical information services. It works in more than 45 countries and has offices in Bangladesh, Bolivia, India, Kenya, Nepal, Peru, Senegal and Zimbabwe.
Geographical Area of Activity: South America, Central America and the Caribbean, South Asia, sub-Saharan Africa, UK.
Restrictions: Not a grantmaking organization; only funds identified project partners.
Publications: Annual Reports; *Small Talk* (newsletter); *Waterlines* (journal); *Enterprise Development & Microfinance* (journal); *Food Chain* (journal); briefing papers; handbooks; manuals; reference works; toolkits.
Finance: Annual income £30.0m., expenditure £30.5m. (31 March 2024).
Board of Trustees: Sazini Mojapelo (Chair.); Martin Tyler (Vice-Chair.).
Principal Staff: CEO Sarah Roberts.
Contact Details: The Robbins Bldg, 25 Albert St, Rugby CV21 2SD; tel. (1926) 634400; e-mail enquiries@practicalaction.org.uk; internet www.practicalaction.org.

Project Trust

Founded in 1967 by Nicholas Maclean-Bristol; in 1998 the Trust co-founded the Year Out Group, an association of gap year organizations.
Activities: Sends around 300 individuals abroad for 8–12 months to take part in voluntary work with overseas partners in education, social care and Outward Bound projects. The Project Trust Community enables volunteers to share their experiences and knowledge within their own communities in the United Kingdom and to mentor new volunteers. Volunteers are encouraged to fundraise to support their costs; the Access Bursary Fund offers subsidies for up to half the costs for young people in the UK from low-income backgrounds.
Geographical Area of Activity: East and South-East Asia, Latin America, South Asia, sub-Saharan Africa, UK.
Restrictions: Open to young people aged 17–25 years; volunteers must hold a passport from the UK or a EU member state and have a minimum education standard of six grade C GCSEs (or equivalent).
Publications: Annual Report; Annual Guide; fundraising toolkits.
Finance: Annual income £790,105, expenditure £1.1m. (30 Sept. 2023).
Board of Directors: Steve Price-Thomas (Interim Chair.).
Principal Staff: CEO Ingrid Emerson.
Contact Details: The Hebridean Centre, Isle of Coll, Argyll PA78 6TE; tel. (1879) 230444; e-mail info@projecttrust.org.uk; internet www.projecttrust.org.uk.

PRS for Music Foundation

Established in 1999 by PRS (Performing Right Society) for Music, a membership organization for songwriters, composers and music publishers.
Activities: Aims to stimulate and support the creation and performance of new British music in the United Kingdom and overseas. Funding falls into two programmes: Funding for Organisations, including the Talent Development Network, which offers grants worth up to £25,000, and Beyond Borders, which offers grants worth up to £15,000 for cross-border collaborations; and Funding for Music Creators, which includes the Open Fund and offers grants worth up to £5,000.
Geographical Area of Activity: Ireland, UK.

UNITED KINGDOM

Restrictions: Does not fully fund projects.
Publications: Annual Report; newsletter (monthly); blog.
Finance: Annual income £4.2m., expenditure £4.2m. (31 Dec. 2023).
Trustees: Jane Dyball (Chair.).
Principal Staff: CEO Joe Frankland.
Contact Details: Tea Auction House, 1st Floor, Hays Galleria, Counter St, London SE1 2HD; e-mail info@prsfoundation.com; internet www.prsfoundation.com.

The Rainforest Foundation UK—RFUK

Founded in 1989 by Gordon Sumner (Sting), a musician, and Trudie Styler, an actress and film producer.
Activities: Supports indigenous people and traditional populations of the world's rainforests to protect their environment and establish community rights to land, life and livelihoods. The Foundation assists marginalized people and women to secure the natural resources that they need for their long-term wellbeing and to manage these resources in ways that do not harm their environment, violate their culture or compromise their future; and to protect their individual and collective rights and ensure access to basic services from the state. Projects include participatory land use planning, community mapping, real-time monitoring, sustainable livelihoods and community forest management. It works with affiliate foundations in Austria, Japan, Norway and the USA, and partner organizations in Brazil.
Geographical Area of Activity: Cameroon, Central African Repub., Dem. Repub. of the Congo, Repub. of the Congo, Gabon, Ghana, Peru, UK.
Publications: Annual Report; *Forest in Focus* (newsletter, 2 a year); Mapping for Rights (online tools and resources); country reports; studies; educational materials.
Finance: Annual income £2.8m., expenditure £2.6m. (31 Dec. 2023).
Board of Trustees: Lucy Katherine Napier Claridge (Chair.); David Morgan (Vice-Chair.).
Principal Staff: Exec. Dir Joe Eisen.
Contact Details: Suite 201, Pill Box Studios, 115 Coventry Rd, London E2 6GG; tel. (20) 7485-0193; e-mail info@rainforestuk.com; internet www.rainforestfoundationuk.org.

The Rank Foundation

Founded in 1953 by J. Arthur Rank (Baron Rank), a flour miller and film-maker.
Activities: Works to improve the lives of people by: encouraging and developing leadership; promoting enterprise and innovation; caring for disadvantaged and marginalized people; and promoting the Christian faith. Programmes include: Time to Shine, offering 12-month paid leadership and development placements in charities; Pebble Grants, small grants for unsolicited applications, which account for 5% of the Foundation's total giving; and School Leadership Awards, which provide financial assistance for young people to complete their education. The Rank Fellowship network is open to past and present award holders. Anyone linked with the Foundation's programmes may be invited to join the Rank Network (RankNet). The Foundation also offers the Memorial Award, worth £8,000, to individuals linked with the Foundation or RankNet who have designed their own programme of learning in leadership and enterprise.
Geographical Area of Activity: UK.
Restrictions: Only funds charities registered in the UK and recognized churches, for projects that are for the benefit of people in the UK; does not accept overseas applications.
Publications: Annual Report.
Finance: Annual income £10.7m., expenditure £15.4m. (31 Dec. 2023).
Trustees: William Wyatt (Chair.).
Principal Staff: Chief Exec. David J. Sanderson; Deputy Chief Exec. Caroline Broadhurst.
Contact Details: 19–21 Garden Walk, London EC2A 3EQ; tel. (20) 4583-4572; e-mail contactus@rankfoundation.co.uk; internet www.rankfoundation.com.

RE:ACT

Established as Team Rubicon UK in 2015 to assist in disaster relief.
Activities: Works with ex-military personnel, first responders and civilians to use their skills to repond to disasters in the United Kingdom and internationally.
Geographical Area of Activity: International.
Finance: Total income £992,019, expenditure £2.5m. (31 March 2024).
Board of Trustees: Gen. Sir Nick Parker (Chair.).
Principal Staff: CEO Toby Wicks.
Contact Details: Bldg 8, Chilmark Estates, Salisbury SP3 5DU; tel. (300) 330-9488; e-mail info@re-act.org.uk; internet www.re-act.org.uk.

Reall—Real Equity for All

Established in 1989, as Homeless International, following the 1987 UN International Year of Shelter for the Homeless; present name adopted in 2014.
Activities: Builds and invests in affordable homes through supporting community-led housing and infrastructure-related development. The organization conducts research and analysis; and works with local partners on long-term development, offering grants, specialist technical assistance, and advisory and financial services. It has established Housing Development Enterprises in more than 15 countries.
Geographical Area of Activity: sub-Saharan Africa, South Asia, South-East Asia.
Publications: Annual Report; newsletter; Data Dashboard (online); Impact Summary Briefs; case studies; reports; blog.
Finance: Annual income £5.5m., expenditure £12.7m. (30 Sept. 2023).
Board: Vivienne Yeda (Incoming Chair.); Steven Troop (Interim Chair.).
Principal Staff: Chief Exec. Ian Shapiro.
Contact Details: 6th Floor, Friars House, Manor House Dr., Coventry CV1 2TE; tel. (24) 7509-3340; e-mail info@reall.net; internet www.reall.net.

RedR UK

Founded in 1980 by Peter Guthrie, an engineer, as an international disaster relief charity, following his experiences working in a refugee camp during the Vietnamese Boat People crises; part of the RedR International federation, which includes organizations in Australia, India, Indonesia and Malaysia.
Activities: Trains and supports aid workers and humanitarian organizations to deliver practical, life-saving skills that enable people to prepare for, respond to and recover from natural disaster and conflict. The organization works in partnership with NGOs, governments and academic institutions to improve the effectiveness of humanitarian action and build technical capacity. It comprises 1,800 member humanitarian professionals, including a network of more than 150 technical experts who provide expertise via the KnowledgePoint online forum. Has a regional office in Jordan.
Geographical Area of Activity: Europe, Middle East, South Asia, South-East Asia, sub-Saharan Africa.
Publications: Annual Report; newsletter (monthly); *Red Alert* (magazine, once a year); Knowledge Point (online forum); guides; handbooks; reports; blog.
Finance: Annual income £1.7m., expenditure £1.8m. (31 March 2024).
Board of Trustees: Sophie Gillibert (Chair.); Heather McKinlay (Treas.); Sally Sudworth (Sec.).

Principal Staff: CEO Bernadette Sexton.

Contact Details: 8 Fitzroy St, London W1T 4BJ; tel. (20) 3996-1743; e-mail info@redr.org.uk; internet www.redr.org.uk.

Resolution Foundation

Established in 2005 by Clive Cowdery, founder of the Resolution Group, a financial services investor.

Activities: Carries out research and analysis in the field of social and economic policy, with a focus on improving living standards of people on low-to-middle incomes. Areas of interest include: incomes and inequality; jobs, skills and pay; housing, wealth and debt; tax and welfare; public finance and the economy. In 2019 the Foundation established the Intergenerational Centre to carry out policy research and analysis on fairness and how living standards challenges affect different generations in different ways.

Geographical Area of Activity: UK.

Publications: Annual Report; Spotlight (series); *Earnings Outlook* (quarterly); *Housing Outlook* (quarterly); *Macro Outlook* (quarterly); *Living Standards Audit* (annual); *Living Standards Outlook* (annual); briefing notes; reports.

Finance: Annual income £3.7m., expenditure £3.4m. (30 Sept. 2023).

Board of Trustees: Clive Cowdery (Chair.).

Principal Staff: Chief Exec. Ruth Curtice; Deputy Chief Exec. and Chief Economist Mike Brewer.

Contact Details: 2 Queen Anne's Gate, London SW1H 9AA; tel. (20) 3372-2960; e-mail info@resolutionfoundation.org; internet www.resolutionfoundation.org.

Rhodes Trust

Founded in 1902 by the will of Cecil John Rhodes, the former Prime Minister of Cape Colony and co-founder of De Beers Consolidated Mines; comprises four charitable funds: the Public Purposes Fund, the Cecil Rhodes Scholarship Fund, the New Scholarship Fund and the Rhodes Trust Horizon Fund.

Activities: Awards 104 Rhodes Scholarships annually to overseas graduates from all around the world to study a full-time postgraduate degree at the University of Oxford for 2–3 years, with an annual stipend of £19,800 (2024/25). Scholars are invited to join a fellowship of nearly 8,000 current and Senior Scholars. In 2003, with Nelson Mandela, former President of South Africa, the Trust established the Mandela Rhodes Foundation (q.v.) in South Africa; and in 2016, with the Atlantic Philanthropies, the Atlantic Institute (part of the Rhodes Trust Horizon Fund), working with seven international fellowship programmes for brain equity in brain health and health, social and racial equity. Working with the Schmidt Futures philanthropic initiative, in 2017 it established Schmidt Science Fellows, to develop leadership in science to address the world's most challenging problems; and the Rise partnership, a global talent development programme for young people aged 15–17 years. The Rhodes Trust's most recent initiative, Oxford Next Horizon, was launched in January 2024 with Oxford's Harris Manchester College and offers a six-month experience designed for mid- to late career participants.

Geographical Area of Activity: International.

Restrictions: Scholarship applicants must be aged 18–27 years.

Publications: Annual Report; newsletter.

Finance: Annual income £45.8m., expenditure £55.3m. (30 June 2024).

Board of Trustees: Prof. Sir John Bell (Chair.).

Principal Staff: Warden and CEO Prof. Sir Rick Trainor.

Contact Details: Rhodes House, South Parks Rd, Oxford OX1 3RG; tel. (1865) 270901; e-mail admin@rhodeshouse.ox.ac.uk; internet www.rhodeshouse.ox.ac.uk.

Rivers Trust

Established in 2004 as the Association of River Trusts; an umbrella organization.

Activities: Works to protect and improve river environments for people and wildlife. Activities include: building and restoring wetlands; helping communities at risk from flooding; planting trees to provide shade and slow river flow; removing and easing barriers that prevent fish migration; monitoring the quality of water and levels of fish stocks; and working with farmers to reduce pollution and run-off. The organization comprises 65 local member Trusts.

Geographical Area of Activity: Ireland, UK.

Publications: Annual Report.

Finance: Annual income £6.7m., expenditure £6.9m. (31 Dec. 2023).

Board of Trustees: Graham Thomas (Chair.); Bella Davies (Vice-Chair.).

Principal Staff: CEO Mark Lloyd.

Contact Details: Rain Charm House, Kyl Cober Parc, Stoke Climsland, Callington PL17 8PH; tel. (1579) 372142; e-mail info@theriverstrust.org; internet www.theriverstrust.org.

The Robertson Trust

Established in 1961 by sisters Elspeth, Agnes and Ethel Robertson with shares in family businesses founded by their father and grandfather, which became Edrington, a distillery owner.

Activities: Works to improve the lives of people experiencing poverty, trauma or both. Priority groups include: asylum seekers and refugees; certain family groups (larger families, single parents, those with children who have experience of being in care); older people; people experiencing severe and multiple disadvantages; people from a black, Asian or ethnic minority background; people living in certain geographical locations (particularly remote and rural ones); people with a disability; women; and young people aged under 25 years. It offers Wee Grants, Small Grants, Large Grants, Community Vehicle Grants and Community Building Grants ranging from £2,000 to £75,000; Partners in Change project-restricted funding worth £50–£150,000 per year for up to three years; and Robertson Trust Scholarships, worth up to £4,000 per year for undergraduate study at a Scottish university.

Geographical Area of Activity: Scotland.

Restrictions: Grants only to constituted community groups and registered charities.

Publications: Reports; blog.

Finance: Annual income £1,361.6m., expenditure £983.0m. (31 March 2024).

Trustees: Morag McNeill (Chair.); Gerry McLaughlin (Vice-Chair.).

Principal Staff: Chief Exec. Jim McCormick.

Contact Details: Robertson House 152, Bath St, Glasgow G2 4TB; tel. (141) 3537300; e-mail trtcomms@therobertsontrust.org.uk; internet www.therobertsontrust.org.uk.

Royal Aeronautical Society—RAeS

Founded in 1866, as the Aeronautical Society of Great Britain, for the general advancement of aeronautical art, science and engineering; incorporates the Royal Aeronautical Society Foundation (f. 2006).

Activities: Promotes professional standards in all aerospace disciplines, acting as a central forum for the exchange of ideas and influencing opinion on aerospace-related matters. The Society offers career guidance, professional and skills development and networking opportunities; organizes conferences, lectures, seminars and technical visits; and maintains the National Aerospace Library in Farnborough. It has more than 25,000 members from the aerospace, aviation and space industries and related sectors.

Geographical Area of Activity: International.

Publications: Annual Report; *The Aeronautical Journal* (monthly); *AEROSPACE* (monthly); conference proceedings.

Finance: Annual income £5.9m., expenditure £4.9m. (31 Dec. 2023).

UNITED KINGDOM

Board of Trustees: Peter Round (Chair.).
Council: David Chinn (Pres.).
Principal Staff: Chief Exec. David Edwards.
Contact Details: 4 Hamilton Pl., London W1J 7BQ; tel. (20) 7670-4300; e-mail raes@aerosociety.com; internet www.aerosociety.com.

Royal Air Force Benevolent Fund

Founded in 1919 by Lord Trenchard, Chief of Staff of the Royal Air Force (RAF).
Activities: Operates internationally, providing financial, practical and emotional support to all RAF members and their dependants, from childhood through to old age. External grants are available to organizations that support it's welfare aims, worth up to £5,000 for Small Grants; and in excess of £5,000 for Large Grants. The organization manages the Royal Air Force Benevolent Fund Housing Trust and in 2017 absorbed the Royal Observer Corps Benevolent Fund. It also maintains the RAF Memorial on Victoria Embankment, London, and Bomber Command Memorial in Green Park, London.
Geographical Area of Activity: International.
Restrictions: Only serving or former members of the RAF or their family members may be eligible.
Publications: Annual Report; Impact Report; newsletter.
Finance: Annual income £19.0m., expenditure £24.1m. (31 Dec. 2023).
Board of Trustees and Advisory Council: Richard Daniel (Chair.).
Principal Staff: Controller Air Vice-Marshal Chris Elliot.
Contact Details: 67 Portland Pl., London W1B 1AR; tel. (20) 7580-8343; e-mail mail@rafbf.org.uk; internet www.rafbf.org.

Royal Anthropological Institute of Great Britain and Ireland—RAI

Founded in 1871 by the merger of the Ethnological Society and the Anthropological Society.
Activities: Promotes the public understanding of anthropology, and the contribution of anthropology to public affairs through: issuing publications; organizing conferences, lectures and the RAI Film Festival; and offering research grants, scholarships and fellowships. The Institute awards international prizes, including: annually, the Marsh Award for Anthropology in the World (worth £1,000); the Amaury Talbot Prize for African Anthropology (£750); the Curl Essay Prize (£1,100); the Arthur Maurice Hocart Prize and the RAI Student Essay Prize (£250 each); and every two years, the Wellcome Medal for Anthropology as Applied to Medical Problems (£600), the J. B. Donne Essay Prize on the Anthropology of Art (£700) and a number of film prizes. It maintains the Anthropology Library and Research Centre, located within the British Museum, which contains 120,000 books and pamphlets and 4,000 journals, of which 1,500 are current; and the Anthropological Index Online.
Geographical Area of Activity: International.
Restrictions: Grants and scholarships are open only to those replying to published advertisements.
Publications: Annual Report; *The Journal of the Royal Anthropological Institute* (quarterly journal, incorporating *Man*); *Anthropology Today* (6 a year); *Anthropological Index Online* (internet service); *Teaching Anthropology* (open access journal); *Discovering Anthropology;* occasional papers.
Finance: Annual income £1.5m., expenditure £1.1m. (31 Dec. 2023).
Council: Prof. Deborah Swallow (Pres.); Prof. Emma Gilberthorpe, Prof. Ann MacLarnon, Prof. Maya Unnithan (Hon. Vice-Pres.).
Principal Staff: Dir Dr David Shankland.
Contact Details: 50 Fitzroy St, London W1T 5BT; tel. (20) 7387-0455; e-mail info@therai.org.uk; internet www.therai.org.uk.

The Royal Commonwealth Society

Royal British Legion

Founded in 1921, bringing together four national organizations of former service personnel that had been established after the First World War; in 2011 it merged with Poppyscotland (f. 1921 as the Earl Haig Fund Scotland).
Activities: Provides assistance to those serving, or who have served in the armed forces, and to their dependants. The Legion assists former service personnel and their dependants who are in need, by running residential homes; providing sheltered employment and special housing; proving entitlement to pensions and assisting individual cases of hardship; advising on small businesses; and providing resettlement training. It also arranges visits to war graves abroad. Has 180,000 members, with approx. 2,500 branches in the United Kingdom and more than 50 overseas. Includes the National Memorial Arboretum (f. 1997).
Geographical Area of Activity: International.
Publications: Annual Report; *Legion* (magazine); reports; leaflets; factsheets; newsletters.
Finance: Annual income £147.1m., expenditure £180.6m. (30 Sept. 2023).
Board of Trustees: Lt-Gen. James Bashall (Nat. Pres.); Jason Coward (Nat. Chair.); Lynda Atkins (Nat. Vice-Chair.).
Principal Staff: Dir-Gen. Charles Byrne.
Contact Details: 199 Borough High St, London SE1 1AA; tel. (20) 3207-2100; e-mail info@britishlegion.org.uk; internet www.britishlegion.org.uk.

Royal Commission for the Exhibition of 1851

Founded in 1850 to organize the Great Exhibition; a supplementary charter was granted in 1851 to use surplus funds of the Exhibition to extend industrial education and the influence of science and art on productive industry.
Activities: Operates in the fields of science, engineering, the built environment and design. Annually, the Commission makes around 35 postgraduate awards, which include: eight Research Fellowships, including the Brunel Fellowship for qualified engineering researchers; nine Industrial Fellowships, including the ERA (Electrical Research Association) Foundation Fellowship for the electro-technology sector; around 10 Industrial Design Studentships and scholarships in science and engineering; the RAEng 1851 Enterprise Fellowship, with professional mentoring and worth up to £50,000; and one Design Fellowship and one Built Environment Fellowship, each worth £50,000 per year, for individuals or informal partnerships. It also offers Special Awards to worthy causes or individuals, including ETF Technical Teaching Fellowships, in partnership with the Education and Training Foundation (q.v.), worth £5,000–£15,000, for further education practitioners; Smallpiece Trust Arkwright Engineering Scholarships for less-advantaged and underrepresented students aged 16–18 years; and Sir Misha Black Awards for Distinguished Services to Design Education (f. 1977).
Geographical Area of Activity: UK.
Restrictions: Research Fellowships are open to applicants of all nationalities, usually for research at UK institutions; Industrial Fellowship applicants must be employed by a company; Studentship applicants must be UK residents.
Publications: Annual Report.
Finance: Annual income £2.6m., expenditure £5.7m. (31 Dec. 2023).
Commission: HRH The Princess Royal (Pres.); The Rt Hon. Prof. Lord Kakkar (Chair.).
Principal Staff: Sec. John Lavery.
Contact Details: 453 Sherfield Bldg, Imperial College, London SW7 2AZ; tel. (20) 7594-8790; e-mail royalcom1851@imperial.ac.uk; internet www.royalcommission1851.org.uk.

The Royal Commonwealth Society—RCS

Founded in 1868.

Activities: The Royal Commonwealth Society is a network of individuals and organizations committed to improving the lives and prospects of Commonwealth citizens across the world. Areas of focus include literacy, equality and inclusion, the environment and connected communities.

Geographical Area of Activity: International.

Restrictions: Not a grantmaking organization.

Publications: *Commonwealth Voices* (magazine).

Finance: Annual income £323,775, expenditure £238,714 (31 March 2024).

Board of Trustees: Dr Linda Yueh (Exec. Chair.); Paul Green (Treas.).

Contact Details: 65 Basinghall St, London EC2V 5DZ; tel. (20) 3727-4300; e-mail communications@royalcwsociety.org; internet www.royalcwsociety.org.

The Royal Foundation of the Prince and Princess of Wales

Established in 2009 to fund charitable work undertaken by the Duke and Duchess of Cambridge and the Duke and Duchess of Sussex; formerly known as the Royal Foundation of The Duke and Duchess of Cambridge and Prince Harry.

Activities: Operates in the areas of conservation, early childhood, emergency responders, homelessness and mental health. The Foundation established the United for Wildlife Transport Taskforce (f. 2016) to tackle the illegal wildlife trade; and in 2019 co-founded the Earthshot Prize, to award five prizes each year over 10 years to individuals and organizations to stimulate innovative solutions to global environmental problems.

Geographical Area of Activity: UK.

Publications: Annual Report; newsletter; cookbook.

Finance: Annual revenue £8.0m., expenditure £8.7m. (31 Dec. 2023).

Trustees: Simon Patterson (Chair.).

Principal Staff: CEO Amanda Berry.

Contact Details: c/o Kensington Palace, Palace Green, London W8 4PU; tel. (20) 7101-2963; e-mail info@royalfoundation.com; internet www.royalfoundation.com.

Royal Geographical Society (with the Institute of British Geographers)—RGS-IBG

Founded in 1830 by Sir John Barrow, an explorer and Second Secretary to the Admiralty, and others for the 'advancement of geographical science'; merged with the Institute of British Geographers in 1995. Learned society and professional body for geography.

Activities: Supports and promotes geographical research, expeditions and fieldwork, education, public engagement and geography input to policy. The Society aims to foster an understanding and informed enjoyment of our world and maintains the world's largest private geographical collection. It makes grants to support geographical research, fieldwork and teaching, in the United Kingdom and overseas; offers medals and awards for achievements in geographical research, fieldwork and teaching, photography and public engagement; and also awards prizes and honorary fellowships. Has 16,000 members.

Geographical Area of Activity: International.

Publications: Annual Review; Trustees' Report; *The Geographical Journal*; *Geographical Magazine*; *Area*; *Transactions*; *WIRES Climate Change* (online); guides; books.

Finance: Annual income £5.8m., expenditure £6.1m. (31 Dec. 2023).

Council: Prof. Dame Jane Francis (Pres.).

Principal Staff: Dir and Sec. Prof. Joe Smith.

Contact Details: 1 Kensington Gore, London SW7 2AR; tel. (20) 7591-3000; e-mail foh@rgs.org; internet www.rgs.org.

Royal Institute of International Affairs—RIIA—Chatham House

Founded in 1920 as the British Institute of International Affairs, a sister institute to the Council on Foreign Relations in the USA; a think tank. Present name adopted when it received its Royal Charter in 1926; the Charter precludes the Institute from expressing opinions of its own.

Activities: Operates as an independent centre for the study of international political and economic affairs, through self-conducted research, discussion and publication programmes. Research themes include: defence and security; economics and trade; environment; health; institutions; major powers; politics and law; society; and technology. The Institute maintains a library and information service; and organizes conferences, meetings and seminars. It encompasses the Queen Elizabeth II Academy for Leadership in International Affairs, which offers several international fellowships. Has 3,000 individual and institutional members.

Geographical Area of Activity: International.

Restrictions: Not a grantmaking organization.

Publications: Annual Review; *The World Today* (monthly); *International Affairs* (6 a year); *Chatham House Reports*; briefing papers; programme papers; books.

Finance: Annual income £21.5m., expenditure £23.5m. (31 March 2024).

Council: Sir Simon Fraser (Chair.); Joanna Cound (Deputy Chair.); Keith Harrington (Hon. Treas.).

Principal Staff: Pres Baroness Manningham-Buller, Helen Clark, Sir John Major; Dir and Chief Exec. Bronwen Maddox.

Contact Details: Chatham House, 10 St James's Sq., London SW1Y 4LE; tel. (20) 8713-0313; e-mail contact@chathamhouse.org; internet www.chathamhouse.org.

Royal Literary Fund—RLF

Established in 1790 by Rev. David Williams; granted a Royal Charter in 1842.

Activities: Provides grants and pensions to professional published authors and translators experiencing financial difficulty; and carries out work in the social sector under its public education programme. Through the Fellowship Scheme, professional writers provide writing support to university students across disciplines; and to secondary school students in Scotland through the Bridge project. Fellows may also form reading groups that are part of the RLF Reading Round network.

Geographical Area of Activity: UK.

Restrictions: No loans or grants for work in progress or publication costs; does not generally fund external organizations.

Publications: Annual Report; writing guides.

Finance: Annual income £4.2m., expenditure £8.3m. (31 March 2024).

Trustees: Sir Ian Blatchford (Pres. and Chair.); Hilary Hale (Deputy Pres.).

Principal Staff: Chief Exec. Edward Kemp.

Contact Details: 3 Johnson's Ct, off Fleet St, London EC4A 3EA; tel. (20) 7353-7150; internet www.rlf.org.uk.

Royal National Institute of Blind People—RNIB

Founded in 1868, as the British and Foreign Blind Association for Improving the Embossed Literature of the Blind, by Dr Thomas Armitage; in 1914 it became the National Institute for the Blind and subsequently the Royal National Institute for the Blind in 1953. Present name adopted in 2002 when it became a membership organization.

Activities: Provides advice, information and services to blind and partially sighted people, and campaigns for them to enjoy the same rights, freedoms and responsibilities as fully sighted people. The Institute funds research into the prevention and treatment of eye disease; offers grants for technology that allow registered blind or partially sighted people to live independently; offers computer training; and maintains a library, containing more than 60,000 items, including Braille, giant print books and music, and over 32,000 'talking' books. Subsidiary organizations include RNIB Charity, Cardiff Institute for Blind People and Bucks Vision; with a related charity, RNIB Specialist Learning Trust, which operates an academy. The group operates schools and a college; a children's home and care homes; supported housing and living services; day support and assessment centres; and holiday schemes.

Geographical Area of Activity: UK.

Publications: Annual Report; newsletter; *RNIB Connect Magazine*.

Finance: Annual income £89.7m., expenditure £90.5m. (31 March 2024).

Board of Trustees: Anna Tylor (Chair.); Sir Martin Davidson (Vice-Chair.).

Principal Staff: Chief Exec. Matt Stringer.

Contact Details: The Grimaldi Bldg, 154A Pentonville Rd, London N1 9JE; tel. (20) 7388-1266; e-mail helpline@rnib.org.uk; internet www.rnib.org.uk.

The Royal Society

Founded in 1660 to promote natural knowledge; granted a Royal Charter by King Charles II in 1662.

Activities: Operates nationally and internationally in the fields of education, natural and applied science (including mathematics, engineering and medicine), international scientific relations and the conservation of natural resources; and provides an independent source of advice on scientific matters, notably to the British Government. The Society carries out self-conducted programmes and research; offers grants to institutions and individuals; awards fellowships, scholarships and prizes; organizes conferences and lectures; and issues publications. Each year, up to 52 Fellows and 10 Foreign Members are elected by the Fellowship, which comprises nearly 1,600 scientists, engineers and technologists from the United Kingdom and the Commonwealth.

Geographical Area of Activity: International.

Publications: Trustees' Report (annual); *Royal Society Open Science*; *Proceedings of the Royal Society A: Mathematical, Physical & Engineering Sciences*; *Proceedings of the Royal Society B: Biological Sciences*; *Philosophical Transactions of the Royal Society A: Mathematical, Physical & Engineering Sciences*; *Philosophical Transactions of the Royal Society B: Biological Sciences*; *Biology Letters*; *Journal of the Royal Society Interface*; *Interface Focus*; *Notes & Records of the Royal Society*; *Open Biology*; *Biographical Memoirs of Fellows of the Royal Society*; *Year Book of the Royal Society*.

Finance: Annual income £396.3m., expenditure £146.0m. (31 March 2024).

Council: Sir Adrian Smith (Pres.); Prof. Jonathan Keating (Treas.).

Principal Staff: Exec. Dir Dr Dame Julie Maxton.

Contact Details: 6–9 Carlton House Terrace, London SW1Y 5AG; tel. (20) 7451-2500; e-mail info@royalsociety.org; internet royalsociety.org.

The Royal Society of Medicine—RSM

Founded in 1805 as the Medical and Chirurgical Society of London; granted a Royal Charter by King William IV in 1834.

Activities: Provides postgraduate medical education. The Society operates nationally and internationally in medicine and science, through organizing conferences, meetings, public lectures, webinars and e-learning courses. It provides members (those involved in medicine, science and healthcare-related professions) with access to its library, online journals and databases, and use of facilities in central London; and offers a variety of awards, bursaries and prizes for members and non-member doctors and healthcare professionals, students and trainees across 55 specialities. Has more than 18,000 members in the United Kingdom and internationally.

Geographical Area of Activity: International.

Publications: Annual Report; *The Journal of the Royal Society of Medicine*; *JRSM Open* (online journal).

Finance: Annual income £12.2m., expenditure £14.6m. (30 Sept. 2023).

Council: Prof. Gillian Leng (Pres.); Prof. Henrietta Bowden-Jones, Prof. Paul O'Flynn (Vice-Pres); Sanjay Shah (Hon. Treas.).

Principal Staff: Dean Prof. Gillian Leng.

Contact Details: 1 Wimpole St, London W1G 0AE; tel. (20) 7290-2900; e-mail info@rsm.ac.uk; internet www.rsm.ac.uk.

RSA—Royal Society for the Encouragement of Arts, Manufactures and Commerce

Established in 1754 by William Shipley, a drawing master, to award premiums for inventions and discoveries in six areas: agriculture, manufacturing, chemistry, mechanics, polite arts, colonies and trade; granted a Royal Charter in 1847.

Activities: Works to remove barriers to social progress; and drives ideas, innovation and social change through research projects, public events and lectures. Runs the Future of Work and Regenerative Futures programmes, with projects spanning a broad range of themes including: crises and change; deliberative democracy; economic security; education; healthcare; heritage; and Universal Basic Income. The Society comprises three affiliated non-profit organizations—the Royal Charter Company in the United Kingdom, RSA US and RSA Oceania—and has a network of 30,000 Fellows in over 90 countries. The Catalyst Awards programme offers Fellows £2,000 seed and £10,000 scaling grants for social innovations. It also offers Student Design Awards and Pupil Design Awards (for pupils aged 11–18 years); and the annual Albert Medal for creativity and innovation. In 2011 RSA Academies was established as an umbrella trust for a group of nine schools in the West Midlands region, with around 5,000 pupils aged 4–18 years.

Geographical Area of Activity: International.

Restrictions: Not a grantmaking organization.

Publications: Annual Report; Impact Report; *RSA Journal* (quarterly); *RSA Future Change Framework*; reports; blog.

Finance: Annual income £12.5m., expenditure £13.2m. (31 March 2024).

Trustee Board: Loyd Grossman (Chair.); Charlotte Oades (Deputy Chair.); Ian Ailles (Co-Treas); Shaifali Puri (Chair., US Board).

Principal Staff: Chief Exec. Andy Haldane.

Contact Details: RSA House, 8 John Adam St, London WC2N 6EZ; tel. (20) 7930-5115; e-mail general@rsa.org.uk; internet www.thersa.org.

RSPB—Royal Society for the Protection of Birds

Founded in 1889 by Emily Williamson as the Society for the Protection of Birds; in 1904 it was granted a Royal Charter.

Activities: Promotes the conservation of birds and wildlife throughout the United Kingdom and worldwide, working with farmers, landowners, policymakers, scientists and teachers. Programmes include: birds and biodiversity: biodiversity and sustainability: and working with local communities on issues of national importance. The Society protects and recreates habitats for endangered birds and wildlife; and seeks to influence national and international government policy. It acquires land and manages many nature reserves; campaigns for better protection and management of wildlife sites not in conservation ownership; works in partnership with conservation organizations, including BirdLife International (q.v.); and raises awareness of conservation issues through education in agriculture, planning and other key professions. It offers awards in the area of conservation science; and makes small grants through the Birdfair/RSPB Research Fund for Endangered Birds.

Geographical Area of Activity: Africa, Asia, Europe, Middle East, UK.

Publications: Annual Report; Annual Review; *Birds* (members' magazine).

Finance: Annual income £169.9m., expenditure £168.0m. (31 March 2024).

Council: Andrew Cahn (Chair.); Robert Cubbage (Treas.).

Principal Staff: Pres. Dr Amir Khan.

Contact Details: The Lodge, Potton Rd, Sandy SG19 2DL; tel. (1767) 693680; e-mail membership@rspb.org.uk; internet www.rspb.org.uk.

RSPCA—Royal Society for the Prevention of Cruelty to Animals

Founded in 1824 as the Society for the Prevention of Cruelty to Animals; present name adopted in 1840.

Activities: Investigates, prevents and prosecutes cruelty to animals and alleviates their suffering; encourages responsible pet care; and supports animal welfare projects. It campaigns to change animal welfare laws; improve the welfare of pets and wild animals; and improve the lives and reduce the suffering of farm animals through the RSPCA Assured scheme; and reduce the suffering of animals used in scientific research. The Society promotes animal welfare education in schools and the wider community; conducts scientific and technical research on all aspects of farm, wild, laboratory and companion animal welfare; and operates three animal hospitals, four wildlife centres, a network of rehoming centres and a telephone advice line. RSPCA International works at the multilateral level to engage with the Quadripartite (UN agencies WHO, FAO, UNEP, plus WOAH – the World Organisation for Animal Health). The RSPCA is a member of Eurogroup for Animals and other important animal welfare coalitions, and has established an RSPCA Europe office in Brussels. Additionally the organization has programmes in the Balkans, Caucasus, Central Asia and East Asia.

Geographical Area of Activity: International.

Publications: Annual Review; Science Group Review; newsletter; *Animal Life* (magazine); *Animal Action* (magazine); leaflets; posters.

Finance: Annual income £151.6m., expenditure £149.5m. (31 Dec. 2023).

Board of Trustees: Claire Horton (Chair.); David Thomas (Vice-Chair.); Karen Harley (Treas.).

Principal Staff: Interim CEO Shan Nicholas.

Contact Details: Parkside, Chart Way, Horsham RH12 1GY; tel. (300) 123-0100; e-mail supportercare@rspca.org.uk; internet www.rspca.org.uk.

The Rufford Foundation

Established in 2013 by the merger of the Rufford Small Grants Foundation, which was founded in 2007, and the Rufford Foundation, founded in 1982 by John Hedley Laing.

Activities: Supports nature conservation projects, predominantly in developing countries. The main area of giving is through the Foundation's Small Grants programme, for amounts up to £6,000, which is aimed at individuals and small organizations in developing countries; the Foundation has awarded grants to more than 5,100 projects in 155 countries. Booster Grants and Completion Grants are also available, worth £10,000 and £15,000, respectively. Through the General Grants programme the Foundation funds small or medium-sized organizations, with a particular focus on the wildlife trade; grants range from below £10,000 to over £30,000.

Geographical Area of Activity: Mainly developing countries.

Restrictions: Only funds nature/biodiversity conservation projects; rarely funds projects in developed countries.

Publications: Annual Report.

Finance: Annual income £4.2m., expenditure £3.8m. (5 April 2024).

Board of Trustees: John H. Laing (Chair.); R. K. Reilly (Vice-Chair.).

Principal Staff: Dir Terry Kenny.

Contact Details: 6th Floor, 250 Tottenham Court Rd, London W1T 7QZ; tel. (20) 7436-8604; internet www.rufford.org.

Saïd Foundation

Founded in 1982, as the Karim Rida Saïd Foundation, by Wafic Saïd, a business person, who also founded the Saïd Business School at the University of Oxford, and his wife Rosemary, in memory of their son; present name adopted in 2008.

Activities: Operates in the fields of education and disability through grants to institutions working with disadvantaged children and young people. Grants are usually made to experienced NGOs in Jordan, Lebanon, the Palestinian Territories and the Syrian Arab Republic; and around 20 scholarships annually to students from the Middle East for postgraduate study in the United Kingdom. The Foundation supports the Saïd Business School Foundation (f. 1998).

Geographical Area of Activity: Middle East (in particular Syrian Arab Repub., as well as Jordan, Lebanon and the Palestinian Territories), UK.

Publications: Annual Report; newsletter; brochure.

Finance: Annual income £8.9m., expenditure £8.5m. (31 Aug. 2023).

Board of Trustees: Wafic R. Saïd (Chair.); Dr Rasha Saïd (Deputy Chair.).

Principal Staff: CEO Hani Jesri.

Contact Details: College House, 272 King's Rd, Chelsea, London SW3 5AW; e-mail admin@saidfoundation.org; internet www.saidfoundation.org.

Sainsbury Family Charitable Trusts

Established in 2001 as the operating office of 20 independent grantmaking trusts set up by members of the Sainsbury family.

Activities: Manages the activities of its member trusts. The Alan and Babette Sainsbury Charitable Fund, Headley Trust (q.v.), Jerusalem Trust (q.v.), J J Charitable Trust and Three Guineas Trust consider proposals that meet their specific areas of interest. The Ashden Trust, Gatsby Charitable Foundation (qq.v.), Glass-House Trust, Indigo Trust, Linbury Trust (q.v.), Mark Leonard Trust, Staples Trust (q.v.) and Tedworth Charitable Trust do not accept unsolicited applications. The Kay Kendall Leukaemia Fund, True Colours Trust and Woodward Charitable Trust have their own procedure for grant applications in defined areas. The Ashden Trust, J J Charitable Trust, Mark Leonard Trust and Tedworth Trust work together as the Climate Change Collaboration (f. 2011). The Frankopan Fund (f. 1999) is an initiative of the Staples Trust that offers scholarships, worth up to £2,000, to Croatian students to pursue higher education in the United Kingdom or at international institutions.

Geographical Area of Activity: Middle East, South-Eastern Europe, sub-Saharan Africa, UK.

Finance: Does not make grants as a single entity; only the individual component trusts do so.

Principal Staff: Sec. Karen Everett.

Contact Details: The Peak, 5 Wilton Rd, London SW1V 1AP; tel. (20) 7410-0330; e-mail info@sfct.org.uk; internet www.sfct.org.uk.

St John Ambulance

Established in 1877, as the St John Ambulance Brigade, to offer free medical care; its parent charity is the Priory of England and the Islands of the Order of St John, which is governed by St John International.

Activities: Provides first aid and care training to more than 400,000 people every year in the United Kingdom. Care programmes include: primary healthcare for the homeless; training courses for those working with the homeless; conferences to promote healthy lifestyles, aimed at young people; care courses; and young carers' support groups. The organization runs first aid courses for young people in co-operation with schools; and provides first aid cover at sporting and entertainment events, at national and local level. It also provides dental and ophthalmic care; relief and disaster planning; primary healthcare; and ambulance services. Sister organizations operate in the UK and Ireland; St John International has members in more than 40 countries.

Geographical Area of Activity: England.

Publications: Annual Report; Impact Report; *SJA Newsletter*; handbooks; resource packs.

Finance: Annual income £107.9m., expenditure £124.1m. (31 Dec. 2023).

Board of Trustees: Rear Adm. Simon Williams (Prior); Rev. Canon Dr Paul Williams (Dean); Carole Lawrence-Parr (Chief Commander).

Principal Staff: Chief. Exec. Shona Dunn.

Contact Details: St John House, 5 Broadfield Cl., Sheffield S8 0XN; tel. (370) 010-4950; e-mail info@sja.org.uk; internet www.sja.org.uk.

The Salvation Army International Trust

Founded in 1865 by William Booth for the advancement of the Christian religion, the advancement of education, the relief of poverty and other charitable objects; a quasi-military command structure was introduced in 1878.

Activities: Promotes the advancement of the Christian religion. The organization also carries out specific projects around the world, including providing emergency shelter, food and clothing; medical and educational work; agricultural training and social welfare programmes. The International College for Officers offers a short-term residential course for officers of the organization selected by their leaders, providing opportunities for training, development, personal reflection and spiritual renewal. The Learning Pathways online platform offers certificate-, diploma- and degree-level content in the areas of community engagement, community development and community project management for anyone connected with the Salvation Army; the platform is administered by Booth University College in Winnipeg, Canada. Individual Salvation Army territories offer gap year and shorter-term programmes for young people. Operates in 134 countries.

Geographical Area of Activity: International.

Publications: Annual Report; *All the World* (magazine); *Words of Life* (3 a year); books.

Finance: Annual income £280.4m., expenditure £269.8m. (31 March 2023).

Principal Staff: World Leader Gen. Lyndon Buckingham.

Contact Details: 1 Champion Park, London SE5 8FJ; tel. (20) 7367-4500; e-mail info@salvationarmy.org.uk; internet www.salvationarmy.org.

Samaritans

Founded in 1953.

Activities: A suicide prevention charity. Samaritans provides emotional support, free, 24/7 by phone, email, online chat, letter, face-to-face and further programmes

Geographical Area of Activity: UK, Ireland.

Publications: reports; policy briefings.

Finance: Total income £24.6m., expenditure £25.9m. (31 March 2024).

Board of Trustees: Keith Leslie (Chair.); Rory Girvan, Dr Hester Wain (Co-Vice-Chair.).

Principal Staff: CEO Julie Bentley.

Contact Details: The Upper Mill, Kingston Rd, Ewell KT17 2AF; tel. (20) 8394-8300; e-mail admin@samaritans.org; internet www.samaritans.org.

Save the Children (UK)

Established in 1919, as the Save the Children Fund, by Eglantyne Jebb and her sister Dorothy Buxton, for famine relief in post-war Europe; part of a network of national organizations in 29 countries, centrally co-ordinated by Save the Children International (q.v.).

Activities: Committed to the rights of children, as enshrined in the UN Convention on the Rights of the Child. The organization runs programmes nationally and internationally to help children under the three key themes of education, food and medicine; these include health, hunger, poverty, protection and rights. Policy areas include: conflict and humanitarian response; education; health; inclusive development; nutrition; and poverty in the United Kingdom. It provides emergency relief, as well as long-term development, working with local, national and international organizations and governments to support projects in around 118 countries; and hosts the Secretariat of the Scaling Up Nutrition (SUN) Civil Society Network to end malnutrition, which has approx. 4,000 member organizations.

Geographical Area of Activity: International.

Restrictions: No grants to individuals.

Publications: Annual Report; reports; blog.

Finance: Annual income £296.0m., expenditure £295.4m. (31 Dec. 2023).

Board of Trustees: Dr Tsitsi Chawatama-Kwambana (Chair.); Dr Arabella Duffield, Richard Winter (Vice-Chair.).

Principal Staff: CEO Gwen Hines.

Contact Details: 1 St John's Lane, London EC1M 4AR; tel. (20) 7012-6400; e-mail supporter.care@savethechildren.org.uk; internet www.savethechildren.org.uk.

Save the Children International

Established in 1919, as the Save the Children Fund, by Eglantyne Jebb and her sister Dorothy Buxton; subsequently known as International Save the Children Alliance. In 2013 it merged with MERLIN—Medical Emergency Relief International (f. 1993). Part of the Disasters Emergency Committee (q.v.).

Activities: Works in the field of emergency humanitarian aid based on a child-rights approach. The organization assists children, their families and communities affected by natural or human-made disasters, disease outbreaks, armed conflict and migration. Main programme themes: are survival; learning; protection; emergencies; and climate crisis. It operates internationally through 30 member organizations, with projects in 116 countries; regional offices in Amman (Jordan), Dakar (Senegal), Nairobi (Kenya), Panama and Singapore; and advocacy offices in Brussels (Belgium), Addis Ababa (Ethiopia), Geneva (Switzerland) and New York (USA).

Geographical Area of Activity: International.

Publications: Annual Report; reports.

Finance: Annual income £1,216.3m., expenditure £1,222.6m. (31 Dec. 2023).

International Board: Angela Ahrendts (Chair.).

Principal Staff: CEO Inger Ashing.

Contact Details: St Vincent House, 30 Orange St, London WC2H 7HH; tel. (20) 3272-0300; e-mail info@savethechildren.org; internet www.savethechildren.net.

Scope

Established in 1952 as the Spastics Society; present name adopted in 1994.

Activities: Works with disabled people—especially those with cerebral palsy, autism spectrum disorders, communication and learning difficulties, and hearing and visual impairment—and their families. The charity campaigns for fairness and equality, to give disabled people the same opportunities as everyone else, based on the social model of disability. It makes recommendations to politicians and policymakers; offers emotional and practical support, from information services to education and everyday care; and runs a helpline.

Scottish Catholic International Aid Fund—SCIAF

Geographical Area of Activity: England, Wales.
Publications: Annual Report; reports; policy briefings; research briefings.
Finance: Annual income £47.2m., expenditure £48.7m. (31 March 2024).
Board of Trustees: Sir Robin Millar (Chair.).
Principal Staff: Chief Exec. Mark Hodgkinson.
Contact Details: 2nd Floor, Here East Press Centre, 14 East Bay Lane, London E15 2GW; tel. (20) 7619-7200; e-mail helpline@scope.org.uk; internet www.scope.org.uk.

Scottish Catholic International Aid Fund—SCIAF

Founded in 1965 as the overseas relief development agency of the Scottish Catholic Church.

Activities: Supports poor communities in developing countries through carrying out self-conducted programmes in education, livelihoods, and peace and justice. The Fund raises awareness about the underlying causes of poverty and campaigns for a fairer world. It works with Catholic network Caritas Internationalis (q.v.); and, working with Trócaire Malawi on behalf of the Scottish Government, administers the Climate Challenge Programme Malawi, improving people's access to food, water and energy. Works with partners in more than 160 countries.
Geographical Area of Activity: Asia, Latin America, Middle East, sub-Saharan Africa.
Publications: Annual Report; newsletter; *Review* (magazine).
Finance: Annual income £8.6m., expenditure £9.2m. (31 Dec. 2023).
Board: Bishop Brian McGee (Bishop Pres.).
Principal Staff: Chief Exec. Lorraine Currie.
Contact Details: 196 Clyde St, Glasgow G1 4JY; tel. (141) 3545555; e-mail sciaf@sciaf.org.uk; internet www.sciaf.org.uk.

The Seafarers' Charity

Founded in 1917 by HM King George V to raise funds to support Marine Benevolent and Welfare Institutions throughout the United Kingdom and the Commonwealth; granted a Royal Charter in 1920; formerly known as the King George's Fund for Sailors, present name adopted in 2021.

Activities: Supports people working across the Merchant Navy, Fishing Fleets, Royal Navy and Royal Marines through conducting research and advocacy; and offering grants to maritime welfare organizations that help seafarers experiencing hardship, their families and carers. The Charity co-founded the Merchant Navy Fund (f. 2012) for Merchant Navy seafarers from the United Kingdom and their families; and co-ordinates the Seafarers International Relief Fund, which was established in 2021.
Geographical Area of Activity: UK and Commonwealth countries.
Restrictions: No grants to individuals.
Publications: Annual Report; *Seapost* (newsletter); *Nautical Welfare Guide* (every 2–3 years).
Finance: Annual income £2.8m., expenditure £4.3m. (31 Dec. 2023).
General Council: Paul Butterworth (Chair.); William Reid (Deputy Chair.).
Principal Staff: CEO Deborah Layde.
Contact Details: 8 Hatherley St, London SW1P 2YY; tel. (20) 7932-0000; e-mail help@theseafarerscharity.org; internet www.theseafarerscharity.org.

Sentebale

Established in 2006 by Prince Harry, the Duke of Sussex, and HRH Prince Seeiso of Lesotho.

Activities: Provides psychosocial support to vulnerable children and adolescents in extreme poverty to find solutions to the challenges of health and mental health, inequality and climate change. The Foundation runs a network of clubs and camps; organizes peer educator workshops; and provides HIV testing, counselling and prevention services. It has offices in Gaborone, Botswana, and Maseru, Lesotho. A sister organization, American Friends of Sentebale, operates in the USA.
Geographical Area of Activity: Botswana, Lesotho.
Publications: Annual Report.
Finance: Annual income £3.4m., expenditure £3.8m. (31 Aug. 2023).
Board of Trustees: Dr Sophie Chandauka (Chair.).
Principal Staff: Interim Chief Exec. Carmel Gaillard.
Contact Details: 17 Gresse St, 6 Evelyn Yard Entrance, London W1T 1QL; tel. (20) 7462-1450; e-mail info@sentebale.org; internet sentebale.org.

Shell Foundation—SF

Established in 2000 by the Shell Group, a multinational oil and gas company.

Activities: Works in the fields of access to energy, social mobility and sustainable job creation. The Foundation provides entrepreneurs with grant funding, business support and access to networks; and forms strategic partnerships. Its Incubator programme focuses on identifying new products and services to provide social and environmental benefits to low-income consumers.
Geographical Area of Activity: International.
Restrictions: Does not accept unsolicited proposals.
Publications: Annual Report; newsletter.
Finance: Annual income £23.0m., expenditure £30.2m. (31 Dec. 2023).
Board of Trustees: Gail Klintworth (Chair.).
Principal Staff: CEO Jonathan Berman.
Contact Details: Embassy Tea House, 195–205 Union St, London SE1 0LN; tel. (20) 7934-2727; e-mail info@shellfoundation.org; internet www.shellfoundation.org.

Shelter—National Campaign for Homeless People

Established in 1966 by Rev. Bruce Kenrick and Des Wilson, social activists.

Activities: Supports people affected by homelessness, including young people, people escaping domestic abuse or who have been evicted, care and prison leavers, refugees and asylum seekers, people from the traveller community, and EU and European Economic Area nationals. Programmes and services include: Shelterline, a free national telephone helpline; homelessness and housing advice consultancy services; Homeless to Home Projects, which aim to resettle families; the National Homelessness Advice Service; Shelter Legal, an online law resource; and the Shelter Housing Databank, which collates government data. The organization carries out policy research; co-ordinates events and fundraising campaigns; and provides training and online learning programmes in housing and homelessness law.
Geographical Area of Activity: UK.
Publications: Annual Report; newsletter; policy reports; briefings; factsheets; guides; reports; blog; books.
Finance: Annual income £81.3m., expenditure £82.7m. (31 March 2024).
Board of Trustees: Helen MacNamara (Chair.); John McQuade (Vice-Chair.).
Principal Staff: Interim Chief. Exec. Tim Gutteridge.
Contact Details: 88 Old St, London EC1V 9HU; tel. (344) 515-2000; e-mail info@shelter.org.uk; internet www.shelter.org.uk.

Sightsavers International

Founded in 1950, as the British Empire Society for the Blind, by Sir John Wilson; in 1958 it became the Royal Commonwealth Society for the Blind. Present name adopted in 1986.

UNITED KINGDOM

Activities: Works to eliminate avoidable blindness and promotes the rights of people living with disabilities. Main programmes focus on: protecting sight; fighting disease; and disability rights. The organization supports research on eye health and neglected tropical diseases; funds operations and trains eye care workers and surgeons; and finances scholarships, training programmes, university student placements and information exchange initiatives. It also undertakes capacity-building activities with international NGOs and academic institutions. Active in more than 30 countries, with regional and support offices in 12 countries.
Geographical Area of Activity: Middle East, South Asia, sub-Saharan Africa, USA, Western Europe.
Publications: Annual Report; newsletter (monthly); evidence gap maps; reports; reviews.
Finance: Annual income £338.2m., expenditure £340.5m. (31 Dec. 2023).
Global Board: Sir Clive Jones (Chair.); Margaret Gyapong (Vice-Chair.); Bill Kendall (Hon. Treas.).
Principal Staff: CEO Dr Caroline Harper.
Contact Details: Bumpers Way, Bumpers Farm, Chippenham SN14 6NG; tel. (1444) 446600; e-mail info@sightsavers.org; internet www.sightsavers.org.

Sigrid Rausing Trust—SRT

Established in 1995 by Dr Sigrid Rausing, a publisher.
Activities: Promotes human rights, equality and the rule of law, and seeks to preserve nature. Programme areas are: the arts; conservation; defending civic space; detention, torture and the death penalty; LGBTI rights; strengthening human rights; transitional justice; transparency and accountability; women's rights; and xenophobia and intolerance. Individual trustees may sponsor small, one-off awards to organizations they know well; projects that fall outside the remit of the thematic programmes may occasionally receive support from the Miscellaneous Fund.
Geographical Area of Activity: Central and South-Eastern Europe, Eastern Europe and the former USSR, Egypt, Kenya, Morocco, Tunisia, Türkiye (Turkey), South Africa, Zimbabwe.
Restrictions: Does not accept unsolicited applications; does not normally make grants that are worth more than 25% of an organization or project's budget.
Publications: Annual Report.
Finance: Annual income £82.6m., expenditure £55.1m. (31 Dec. 2023).
Board of Trustees: Dr Sigrid Rausing (Chair. and Co-Dir); Andrew Puddephatt (Deputy Chair. and Co-Dir).
Contact Details: 12 Penzance Pl., London W11 4PA; tel. (20) 7313-7720; e-mail info@srtrust.org; internet www.sigrid-rausing-trust.org.

Sino-British Fellowship Trust—SBFT

Established in 2017, taking over the work of the charity of the same name founded in 1948.
Activities: Provides travel grants for academic staff and postgraduate students from, and for British academic staff and postgraduate students to visit, Hong Kong and mainland China. Grants are mainly to allied institutions and made on a three-year basis; if funds become available individual grants may be made in exceptional circumstances.
Geographical Area of Activity: People's Repub. of China, Hong Kong, UK.
Restrictions: Candidates must usually be over 25 years of age; applications are made through supported institutions.
Publications: Annual Report.
Finance: Annual revenue £437,241, expenditure £574,588 (31 Dec. 2023).
Council: Peter Ely (Chair.).
Principal Staff: Sec. Debbie Haine.
Contact Details: c/o 23 Bede House, Manor Fields, London SW15 3LT; tel. (20) 8788-6252; e-mail enquiries@sbft.org.uk; internet www.sbft.org.uk.

Sir Halley Stewart Trust

Established in 1924 by Sir Halley Stewart, a business person and politician, based on Christian values.
Activities: Supports innovative and groundbreaking social, medical and religious development projects that prevent suffering and allow people to achieve their full potential. Grants span 1–3 years; main grants range from over £5,000 and up to £60,000, while small grants are for amounts less than £5,000.
Geographical Area of Activity: UK.
Restrictions: Does not make grants to individuals; grants for international projects must be made through charities based in the UK.
Publications: Annual Report.
Finance: Annual income £1.2m., expenditure £1.6m. (31 March 2024).
Trustees: Theresa Bartlett (Chair.); Louisa Elder (Vice-Chair.).
Principal Staff: Pres. Celia Atherton.
Contact Details: BM Sir Halley Stewart Trust, London WC1N 3XX; tel. (20) 8144-0375; e-mail email@sirhalleystewart.org.uk; internet www.sirhalleystewart.org.uk.

The Sir Jules Thorn Charitable Trust

Founded in 1964 by Sir Jules Thorn, the founder of Thorn Electrical Industries.
Activities: Supports the prevention and treatment of disease and care of sick and disadvantaged people. The Trust funds biomedical and translational biomedical research in universities and National Health Service organizations. It also supports organizations working in the fields of serious illness and disability; and charities that address disability, disadvantage and overcoming adversity. Two four-year doctoral scholarships, of up to £112,000 each, are offered to institutions each year.
Geographical Area of Activity: UK.
Restrictions: No grants to individuals or to applicants from countries other than the UK.
Publications: Annual Report.
Finance: Annual income £2.0m., expenditure £3.9m. (31 Dec. 2023).
Board of Trustees: Elizabeth Charal (Chair.).
Principal Staff: Dir Richard Benson.
Contact Details: 24 Manchester Sq., London W1U 3TH; tel. (20) 7487-5851; e-mail info@julesthorntrust.org.uk; internet www.julesthorntrust.org.uk.

Skinners' Charity Foundation

Established in 2022 by the Skinners' Company, which also runs the Skinners' Education Foundation (f. 2023) and the Skinners' Almshouse Charity (f. 2009).
Activities: Offers grants for projects focusing on three key areas: young people's vocational development; relief of poverty and hardship; and arts, heritage and communities.
Geographical Area of Activity: United Kingdom.
Finance: Annual income £24.1m., expenditure £49,970 (30 June 2024).
Board of Trustees: Lord Evans of Weardale (Chair.).
Principal Staff: Man Andy Matthews.
Contact Details: 8 Dowgate Hill, London EC4R 2SP; tel. (20) 7236-5629; e-mail charities@skinners.org.uk; internet www.skinners.org.uk/our-grants.

Smallwood Trust

Established in 1886 by Edith Smallwood as the Society for the Assistance of Ladies in Reduced Circumstances; present name adopted in 2017.

Activities: Works to enable women to be financially resilient. The Trust offers grants in three main areas: to support low-income women in need; for women-led and women-focused third sector organizations providing services locally; and for policy initiatives to end gender poverty. In 2021, working with Rosa—The UK Fund for Women and Girls, it established the Women Thrive Fund (endowed with money from the Government's Tampon Tax Fund), offering grants of up to £40,000 to women's organizations working to improve the mental health, wellbeing and financial resilience of women and girls.

Geographical Area of Activity: UK.

Publications: Annual Report.

Finance: Annual income £2.1m., expenditure £3.9m. (31 Dec. 2023).

Board of Trustees: D'Arcy Myers (Chair.); Maureen Margerie (Deputy Chair.).

Principal Staff: CEO Paul Carbury.

Contact Details: Lancaster House, 25 Hornyold Rd, Malvern WR14 1QQ; tel. (300) 365-1886; e-mail info@smallwoodtrust.org.uk; internet www.smallwoodtrust.org.uk.

The Sobell Foundation

Founded in 1977 by Sir Michael Sobell, a business person and racehorse breeder.

Activities: Supports charities working in the fields of medical care and treatment; care and education of mentally and physically disabled people; and care of and support for the elderly and disadvantaged children. In Israel, the Foundation also supports projects on coexistence and immigration.

Geographical Area of Activity: England and Wales, Israel.

Restrictions: Grants only to charities registered in the UK that the Foundation has supported within the past five years.

Publications: Annual Report.

Finance: Annual income £1.2m., expenditure £2.3m. (5 April 2024).

Principal Staff: Admin. Penny Newton.

Contact Details: POB 5402, Wincanton BA9 0BH; tel. (20) 8922-9097; e-mail enquiries@sobellfoundation.org.uk; internet www.sobellfoundation.org.uk.

Souter Charitable Trust

Established in 1992 by Sir Brian Souter, co-founder of the Stagecoach Group of bus and rail operators, and his wife Lady Souter.

Activities: Supports initiatives that prevent or relieve human suffering and poverty, and promote spiritual welfare, through social investments and offering grants. The Trust supports evangelical and social welfare initiatives of Christian churches and organizations; and charitable projects inspired by the Christian gospel. It offers grants to organizations that share the same or similar objectives. Small grants are available for gap year or short-term projects that last at least one calendar year. There are no minimum or maximum amounts, but grants typically range between £1,000 and £3,000.

Geographical Area of Activity: International.

Restrictions: Grants only to organizations registered in the UK; does not fund capital works.

Finance: Annual income £11.4m., expenditure £12.0m. (30 June 2024).

Principal Staff: Admin. Dion Judd; Sec. John Berthinussen.

Contact Details: POB 7412, Perth, PH1 5YX; tel. (1738) 450408; e-mail enquiries@soutercharitabletrust.org.uk; internet www.soutercharitabletrust.org.uk.

Spinal Research

Established in 1980 as International Spinal Research Trust.

Activities: Operates nationally and internationally in the field of traumatic spinal cord injury through funding medical research in treatments for paralysis. Spinal Research sets the standard for spinal cord research across the world, and is at the forefront of developing research strategies and priorities for regenerative repair. Funds world-class research across the world. Committed to continuing to find effective treatments that improve the quality of life, participation and integration of those paralysed after spinal cord injury.

Geographical Area of Activity: International.

Publications: Annual Review; newsletter; *Annual Research Review*; research updates.

Finance: Annual income £4m., expenditure £5m. (31 March 2024).

Board of Trustees: Tara Howell (Chair.).

Principal Staff: CEO Louisa McGinn.

Contact Details: 201 Borough High St, London SE1 1JA; tel. (20) 3824-7400; e-mail info@spinal-research.org; internet www.spinal-research.org.

Stewards Company Limited

Founded in 1898 to support Christian organizations.

Activities: Provides grants to Christian organizations throughout the world, particularly those furthering the Christian gospel. The Company acts as administrative trustee for a number of Christian trusts, including the J.W. Laing Trust and J.W. Laing Biblical Scholarship Trust.

Geographical Area of Activity: International.

Restrictions: All applications should be for Gospel-focused projects.

Publications: Annual Report.

Finance: Annual income £5.0m. expenditure £8.2m. (31 Dec. 2024).

Board of Trustees: Stephen Shaw (Chair.); Simon Tomlinson (Vice-Chair.).

Contact Details: 122 Wells Rd, Bath BA2 3AH; tel. (1225) 427236; e-mail stewardsco@stewards.co.uk.

Street Child

Africa Educational Trust was founded in 1958 by Rev. Michael Scott, an opponent of colonial rule; merged with Street Child in Nov. 2020.

Activities: Operates in sub-Saharan Africa, Asia and Europe in the field of education. Main programmes focus on: non-formal education and skills training; primary and secondary education; and development of local NGOs.

Geographical Area of Activity: sub-Saharan Arfica, Asia, Europe.

Restrictions: Not a grantmaking organization.

Publications: Annual Report.

Finance: Annual income £21.5m., expenditure £22.1m. (31 March 2024).

Board of Trustees: Dr Anthony Wallersteiner (Chair.); Marcel Van Den Berg (Treas.).

Principal Staff: CEO Tom Dannatt.

Contact Details: 33 Creechurch Lane, London EC3A 5EB; tel. (20) 7614-7696; e-mail info@street-child.org; internet street-child.org.

Stroke Association

Established in 1899 as the National Association for the Prevention of Consumption and other forms of Tuberculosis; became the Chest, Heart and Stroke Association in 1974. Present name adopted in 1992.

Activities: Supports people who have had strokes, people suffering from dysphasia and their families; and raises public awareness of stroke. The Association provides community services; runs a network of regional information centres and the Stroke Helpline; offers welfare and research grants; and

UNITED KINGDOM

provides training and resources for healthcare professionals. It is a member of the World Stroke Organization and Stroke Alliance for Europe.

Geographical Area of Activity: International.

Publications: Annual Report; *Stroke News* (quarterly); information leaflets; toolkits.

Finance: Annual income £42.1m., expenditure £43.8m. (31 March 2024).

Board of Trustees: Stephen King (Chair.).

Principal Staff: Chief Exec. Juliet Bouverie.

Contact Details: Stroke Association House, 240 City Rd, London EC1V 2PR; tel. (20) 7566-0300; e-mail supporter.relations@stroke.org.uk; internet www.stroke.org.uk.

Survival International

Founded in 1969 in response to the plight of indigenous peoples in the Amazon.

Activities: Campaigns for tribal peoples' rights, working with them to defend their lives, protect their lands and determine their own futures. Programmes include: decolonizing conservation, through preventing human rights abuses and putting indigenous peoples in control of protecting wildlife; stopping the extermination of uncontacted tribes and securing their lands; and eliminating 'factory schools', which erase children's indigenous identity, through putting tribal and indigenous peoples' education under their control. The organization has branches in France, Germany, Italy, Spain and the USA.

Geographical Area of Activity: Botswana, Brazil, Democratic Repub. of the Congo, Repub. of the Congo, Ethiopia, India, Paraguay, Peru, UK.

Publications: Annual Report; Tribal Voice (video platform); guidelines for film-makers; books.

Finance: Annual income £1.6m., expenditure £1.5m. (31 Dec. 2023).

Principal Staff: Chief Exec. Caroline Pearce.

Contact Details: 6 Charterhouse Bldgs, London EC1M 7ET; tel. (20) 7687-8700; e-mail info@survivalinternational.org; internet www.survivalinternational.org.

Tearfund

Founded in 1968 by the Evangelical Alliance to serve churches in the United Kingdom and Ireland; a Christian relief and development agency, part of the Disasters Emergency Committee (q.v.).

Activities: Works to address poverty and injustice through sustainable development. Main programmes include: mobilizing the Church to help the poor; churches spearheading national advocacy campaigns; food security; livelihoods; water, sanitation and hygiene; and disaster response and resilience. The organization works with partner churches in more than 50 countries.

Geographical Area of Activity: International.

Publications: Annual Report; newsletter; policy reports; research papers; toolkits.

Finance: Annual income £82.6m., expenditure £82.7m. (31 March 2024).

Board of Directors: Anna Laszlo (Chair.); David Wesson (Vice-Chair.); John Davidson (Interim Treas.).

Principal Staff: Chief Exec. Nigel Harris.

Contact Details: 100 Church Rd, Teddington TW11 8QE; tel. (20) 3906-3906; e-mail info@tearfund.org; internet www.tearfund.org.

Terrence Higgins Trust—THT

Founded in 1982, in memory of Terrence Higgins, by his partner Rupert Whitaker, Martyn Butler and other friends.

Activities: Provides HIV support and prevention services, as well as sexual health services across England, Scotland and Wales. The Trust aims to reduce transmission of HIV and promote good sexual health; provides services and support for those living with HIV; and campaigns for greater public understanding of HIV and AIDS, and sexual health in general. It runs a national helpline, an online community of people living with HIV in the United Kingdom, and has local centres which provide a range of services.

Geographical Area of Activity: UK.

Publications: Annual Report; publications about living with HIV and promoting sexual health; research reports; policy briefings.

Finance: Annual income £12.0m., expenditure £14.8m. (31 March 2024).

Trustees: Jonathan McShane (Chair.).

Principal Staff: Chief Exec. Richard Angell.

Contact Details: 439 Caledonian Rd, London N7 9BG; tel. (20) 7812-1600; e-mail info@tht.org.uk; internet www.tht.org.uk.

Thomson Foundation

Founded in 1962 by Roy Thomson, later Lord Thomson of Fleet.

Activities: Provides skills training, consultancy and advice to raise standards in journalism and communication in developing countries. Areas of focus are: training; media development; and e-learning through the Journalism Now online platform. The Foundation works with media, governments, NGOs, civil society and commercial organizations. It also organizes the Mobile Journalist Award, the Young Journalist Award, the Commonwealth Digital Challenge, and the Journalism Now Scholar programme (offering a five-week course and one-week work-study trip in London).

Geographical Area of Activity: International.

Restrictions: Grants only for Thomson courses.

Publications: Annual Report; Annual Review; newsletter; journalism guides.

Finance: Annual income £2.4m., expenditure £3.4m. (31 Dec. 2023).

Board of Trustees: Lord (Tom) Chandos of Aldershot (Chair.).

Principal Staff: Chief Exec. Caro Kriel.

Contact Details: 6 Greenland Pl., London NW1 0AP; tel. (20) 3440-2438; e-mail enquiries@thomsonfoundation.org; internet www.thomsonfoundation.org.

Thomson Reuters Foundation

Founded in 1982 by Reuters, an international news and information organization; registered as an independent charity in the United Kingdom and the USA.

Activities: Carries out activities under three main programmes in the areas of media freedom, inclusive economies and human rights. The Foundation works with journalists, law firms, social enterprises, NGOs and human rights leaders. Initiatives include: journalism, covering under-reported issues such as aid and development, women's rights, human trafficking, property rights, climate change and resilience; media development, creating news platforms, providing journalism training and funding the Reuters Institute for the Study of Journalism at Oxford University; training, delivering media and communications training to companies and government officials; and TrustLaw, which provides free legal assistance to NGOs and social enterprises in more than 175 countries. It organizes the annual Trust Conference on fighting slavery, empowering women and advancing human rights worldwide, awarding scholarships to fund the attendance of frontline activists and human rights defenders at the conference; and funds research fellowships for journalists, lasting three or six months, at the Reuters Institute. Has offices in New York, USA, and Mumbai, India.

Geographical Area of Activity: International.

Restrictions: Not a grantmaking organization.

Publications: Annual Report; newsletter.

Finance: Annual income £18.4m., expenditure £19.1m. (31 Dec. 2023).

Board of Trustees: Jim Smith (Chair.).

Tony Blair Institute for Global Change

Principal Staff: CEO Antonio Zappulla.
Contact Details: 5 Canada Sq., Canary Wharf, London E14 5AQ; tel. (20) 7542-7015; e-mail foundation@thomsonreuters.com; internet www.trust.org.

Tony Blair Institute for Global Change—TBI

Established in 2016 by former British Prime Minister Tony Blair; took over the work of the Tony Blair Faith Foundation (f. 2008).

Activities: Works to address the challenges of globalization through two main programmes: Policy Futures, equipping leaders to combat populism, with a focus on renewing the centre ground in politics, technology and public policy, and counter-extremism; and Government Advisory, strengthening the effectiveness of governments and leaders in carrying out plans the areas of economic reform, the private sector and business, foreign investment, infrastructure and public services.
Geographical Area of Activity: Middle East, sub-Saharan Africa, UK.
Publications: Annual Report; newsletter.
Finance: Net assets £37.4m. (31 Dec. 2023).
Principal Staff: Exec. Chair. Sir Tony Blair; CEO Catherine Rimmer.
Contact Details: 1 Bartholomew Cl., London EC1A 7BL; tel. (20) 3370-1959; e-mail info@institute.global; internet institute.global.

The Trussell Trust

Established in 1997 by Carol and Paddy Henderson with a legacy left by Betty Trussell, Carol Henderson's mother; projects initially focused on helping children in Bulgaria, before establishing the Salisbury Foodbank in 2000.

Activities: Supports people living in poverty through a network of 1,300 food bank centres, providing nutritionally balanced emergency food and guidance; and campaigns to change structural causes of poverty. The Trussell Trust Social Enterprise operates 11 community shops and a warehouse, and offers volunteering opportunities.
Geographical Area of Activity: UK.
Publications: Annual Report; newsletter.
Finance: Annual income £54.1m., expenditure £62.0m. (31 March 2024).
Board of Trustees: Natalie Campbell (Chair.).
Principal Staff: Chief Exec. Emma Revie.
Contact Details: Unit 9 Ashfield Trading Estate, Ashfield Rd, Salisbury SP2 7HL; tel. (1722) 580180; e-mail enquiries@trussell.org.uk; internet www.trussell.org.uk.

Trust for London

Founded in 1891 as the City Parochial Foundation for general charitable purposes in the Metropolitan Police District of London and the City of London; present name adopted in 2010 following merger with Trust for London.

Activities: Works within all London boroughs and the City of London to address poverty and inequality. Programmes fund activities such as advocacy and legal advice in the areas of: affordable housing, providing access to good-quality and secure homes; better work, providing low-paid workers with training and support; decent living standards, creating an inclusive and responsive welfare and support system; supporting migrants, protecting their rights and ensuring their participation; sharing wealth, addressing income inequality; and community-based organizations, supporting disadvantaged groups to improve their quality of life and help them find work. The Trust convenes several networks, including the Employment Legal Advice Network, Commission on Social Security led by Experts by Experience, London Housing Panel and Better Work Network.
Geographical Area of Activity: London Boroughs and City of London.
Restrictions: Does not support applications that do not benefit Londoners or that directly replace public funds; are from individuals or organizations with fewer than three people on their governing body; or for mainstream educational activity, promotion of religion, large capital appeals or general appeals.
Publications: Annual Report; research reports; learning reports; evaluations.
Finance: Annual income £11.4m., expenditure £23.0m. (31 Dec. 2023).
Board of Trustees: Dr Omar Khan (Chair.).
Principal Staff: Chief Exec. Manny Hothi.
Contact Details: 4th Floor, 4 Chiswell St, London EC1Y 4UP; tel. (20) 7606-6145; e-mail info@trustforlondon.org.uk; internet www.trustforlondon.org.uk.

Trusthouse Charitable Foundation

Established in 1997 following the merger between Forte Group and Granada, both hotel and restaurant companies.

Activities: Works in the areas of extreme urban deprivation, and remote and fragile rural communities. The Foundation supports small, well-established organizations in the areas of community support and the arts, education and heritage. For core, project or capital costs, under the Major Grants programme it awards single-year grants worth between £10,000 and £100,000, and multi-year grants up to a maximum of £100,000; and under the Small Grants programme, one-off grants worth between £2,000 and £10,000. The Henry Smith Charity (q.v.) carries out day-to-day management of the Foundation.
Geographical Area of Activity: UK.
Restrictions: Does not fund individuals; organizations and projects outside the UK; ecological projects; medical research; or unsolicited applications from hospices.
Publications: Annual Report.
Finance: Annual income £1.5m., expenditure £3.4m. (30 June 2024).
Board of Trustees: Olga Polizzi (Chair.).
Principal Staff: Grants Dir Jessica Brown.
Contact Details: Ground Floor East, Kings Bldgs, 16 Smith Sq., London SW1P 3HQ; tel. (20) 3150-4431; e-mail grants@trusthousecharitablefoundation.org.uk; internet trusthousecharitablefoundation.org.uk.

Turquoise Mountain Foundation

Established in 2006 by Rory Stewart, a British diplomat, at the request of President Hamid Karzai and HRH Prince of Wales; Turquoise Mountain Foundation is the operational name of Turquoise Mountain Trust.

Activities: Works to preserve historic buildings and culture through training artisans and reviving traditional crafts. The Foundation has restored the Murad Khani district (Kabul) and established a primary school, health clinic and the internationally accredited Institute for Afghan Arts and Architecture. Other projects include: in Yangon, regenerating urban heritage and revitalizing traditional crafts in jewellery, textiles and woodwork; in Saudi Arabia, training artisans, who are predominantly women; and in 2017 a project began in Jordan, focusing on culture, heritage and artisans, working with refugees from the Syrian Arab Republic and Jordanians. A separate foundation operates in the USA.
Geographical Area of Activity: Afghanistan, Jordan, Myanmar, Saudi Arabia, UK.
Publications: Annual Report; newsletter; catalogues; newsletter.
Finance: Annual income £17.0m., expenditure £15.7m. (31 Dec. 2023).
Principal Staff: Pres. Shoshana Stewart.
Contact Details: Princes Exchange, 1 Earl Grey St, Edinburgh EH3 9EE; tel. (131) 2100040; e-mail contact@turquoisemountain.org; internet www.turquoisemountain.org.

Tusk

Established in 1990 in response to poaching in Africa; the working name of the Tusk Trust Ltd.

Activities: Works in the fields of wildlife conservation and community development through self-conducted programmes in habitat protection, human-wildlife coexistence and environmental education. Recognizes individuals for their work with the Tusk Conservation Awards. The organization supports 50 projects in 22 countries. It has an office in Kenya.

Geographical Area of Activity: sub-Saharan Africa, UK.

Publications: Annual Report; newsletter; *Tusk Talk* (annual magazine); fundraising toolkit.

Finance: Total annual income £12.4m., expenditure £12.4m. (31 Dec. 2023).

Trustees: Alexander Rhodes (Chair.).

Principal Staff: Chief Exec. Nick Rubb; Pres. Charles Mayhew.

Contact Details: 4 Cheapside House, High St, Gillingham SP8 4AA; tel. (1747) 831005; e-mail info@tusk.org; internet www.tusk.org.

UJIA—United Jewish Israel Appeal

Established in 1996 as the Joint Jewish Charitable Trust; present name adopted in 2000.

Activities: Operates school and after-school programmes for pupils and teachers; and runs Jewish youth movements and the UJIA Israel Experience. The organization supports educational and sports initiatives for young people in Israel; and the Union of Jewish Students and young people in the United Kingdom; and organizes gap years and internships in Israel. In 2016 it established the Centre for Israel Engagement and the Reshet network for informal Jewish educators. Has offices in Manchester, Glasgow and Leeds; and a sister organization in Israel, UJIA Israel (formerly, the British Olim Society Charitable Trust). UJIA Women operates its own projects and programmes in the areas of women's education, employment and empowerment; integrating vulnerable immigrants; and co-existence between Arab and Jewish children.

Geographical Area of Activity: Israel, UK.

Publications: Annual Report; newsletter; *Episodes* (magazine).

Finance: Annual income £6.4m., expenditure £8.3m. (30 Sept. 2023).

Trustees: Zvi Noé (Chair.); Simon Wagman (Treas.).

Principal Staff: Chief Exec. Mandie Winston.

Contact Details: 4th Floor, Amelie House, 221 Golders Green Rd, London NW11 9DQ; tel. (20) 7424-6400; e-mail info@ujia.org; internet www.ujia.org.

UK Research and Innovation—UKRI

Established in 2018 to replace Research Councils UK (f. 2002); a non-departmental public body sponsored by the Department for Science, Innovation and Technology.

Activities: Supports research, innovation and postgraduate training through offering grants and fellowships to research organizations and businesses. The body comprises Research England (f. 2018), which supports research and knowledge exchange at higher education institutions, the national innovation agency Innovate UK (f. 2007), and seven research councils, which offer funding in their respective fields: the Arts and Humanities Research Council (f. 2005; including histories, cultures and heritage, creative and performing arts, languages and literature); Biotechnology and Biological Sciences Research Council (f. 1994; bioscience and bioeconomy); Economic and Social Research Council (f. 1965; economic, social, behavioural and human data science); Engineering and Physical Sciences Research Council (f. 1994; including artificial intelligence, chemistry, computer science, mathematics and physics); Medical Research Council (f. 1913; science that prevents illness, develops therapies and improves human health); Natural Environment Research Council (f. 1965; environmental science); and Science and Technology Facilities Council (f. 2007; including astronomy, nuclear physics, particle physics and space science). Main funds include: the Fund for International Collaboration, strengthening global partnerships; Future Leaders Fellowships, developing research and innovation leaders; Global Challenges Research Fund, creating opportunities in developing countries; Industrial Strategy Challenge Fund, addressing big societal challenges; Strategic Priorities Fund, supporting government priorities across 34 inter- and multidisciplinary research themes; and Strength in Places Fund, driving regional economic growth in the United Kingdom. It has offices in Bristol and London; and international offices in Beijing (People's Repub. of China), Brussels (Belgium), New Delhi (India) and Washington, DC, USA. Maintains the Gateway to Research (GtR) portal.

Geographical Area of Activity: UK.

Publications: Annual Report; newsletter; Gateway to Research (online); blog.

Finance: Total income £10.0m., expenditure £9.1m. (31 March 2024).

Board: Sir Andrew Mackenzie (Chair.).

Principal Staff: Chief Exec. Prof. Sir Ian Chapman.

Contact Details: Polaris House, North Star Ave, Swindon SN2 1ET; tel. (1793) 444000; e-mail communications@ukri.org; internet www.ukri.org.

United Purpose

Founded in 1976; formerly known as Concern Universal. Present name adopted in 2017.

Activities: Promotes justice, dignity and respect for all. The organization uses innovative, community-led approaches to achieve the UN Sustainable Development Goals. The organization operates through a number of subsidiaries: Village Aid (f. 2014), an international development charity; International Inspiration (f. 2007), a legacy charity of the London 2012 Olympics and Paralympics, which integrates sports into development programmes; and CUMO, a microfinance organization serving more than 81,000 people in rural communities. It has country offices in Bangladesh, Brazil, Ghana, Guinea, Malawi, Mozambique, Nigeria, The Gambia and Senegal.

Geographical Area of Activity: Brazil, India, sub-Saharan Africa.

Restrictions: Not a grantmaking organization.

Publications: Annual Report.

Finance: Annual income £12.7m., expenditure £14.4m. (31 Dec. 2023).

Trustees: Mary Robinson (Chair.).

Principal Staff: CEO Ray Jordan.

Contact Details: W2, 1st Floor, Wellington House, Wellington St, Cardiff CF11 9BE; tel. (2920) 220066; e-mail supporter.care@united-purpose.org; internet www.united-purpose.org.

USPG—United Society Partners in the Gospel

USPG was founded in 1701 as the Society for the Propagation of the Gospel in Foreign Parts (SPG); it then merged with the Universities' Mission to Central Africa (f. 1857) in 1965.

Activities: USPG strives to make connections between the churches of the Anglican Communion to deepen bonds of affection and learn from each other in rich exchange. It promotes education and leadership and strengthen the unity and capacity of the Anglican Church. It also accompanies Anglican churches across the world as they form communities of hope and resistance in the struggles associated with climate change, migration, gender, the human rights of indigenous people and inter-religious living.

Geographical Area of Activity: International.

Publications: Annual Report; e-newsletter; *Revive* (magazine); *Pray With the World Church* (booklet).

Finance: Annual income £3.7m., expenditure £3.9m. (31 Dec. 2023).

Varkey Foundation   UNITED KINGDOM

Board of Trustees: Rt Rev. Prof. David Walker (Chair.).
Principal Staff: Gen. Sec. Rev. Dr Duncan Dormor.
Contact Details: 5 Trinity St, London SE1 1DB; tel. (20) 7921-2200; e-mail info@uspg.org.uk; internet www.uspg.org.uk.

Varkey Foundation

Established in 2011 by Sunny Varkey, founder and Chair. of GEMS Education, an education management company; affiliated to Fundación Varkey Argentina (f. 2016).

Activities: Works to ensure that every child has a good teacher. The Foundation promotes excellence in teaching practice, builds the capacity of school leaders, and provides new research on education. It organizes the Global Education series of conferences, as well as the annual Global Teacher Prize, worth US $1m. and the annual Global Student Prize worth £100,000. Has offices in Argentina and the United Kingdom.
Geographical Area of Activity: International.
Restrictions: Not a grantmaking organization.
Finance: Annual income £3.2m., expenditure £3.5m. (31 March 2024).
Principal Staff: Exec. Dir Nicole Lui.
Contact Details: 1st Floor, 10 Queen St Pl., London EC4R 1BE; tel. (20) 7593-4040; e-mail info@varkeyfoundation.org; internet www.varkeyfoundation.org.

Versus Arthritis

Founded in 1936 as the Empire Rheumatism Council; previously known as Arthritis Research Campaign. In 2017 it merged with Arthritis Care; formerly known as Arthritis Research UK.

Activities: Funds high-quality research into the cause, treatment and cure of all types of arthritis and musculoskeletal conditions; and advocates for government policy changes that help sufferers. The organization offers a range of awards, fellowships, internships, project grants and scholarships.
Geographical Area of Activity: UK.
Publications: Annual Report; quarterly research magazine; information booklets.
Finance: Annual income £31.7m., expenditure £32.6m. (31 March 2024).
Board of Trustees: Kate Tompkins (Chair.); Prof. Martijn Steultjens (Vice-Chair.).
Principal Staff: CEO Deborah Alsina.
Contact Details: Copeman House, St Mary's Ct, St Mary's Gate, Chesterfield S41 7TD; tel. (300) 7900400; e-mail enquiries@versusarthritis.org; internet www.versusarthritis.org.

Vodafone Foundation

Established in 2001 by Vodafone, a telecommunications company; part of the Vodafone Foundation network.

Activities: Works in the fields of disaster response, education, gender equality and health, supporting projects that use digital and mobile technology. Main programmes are: Connected Learning, including Instant Network Schools, in partnership with UNHCR, giving young refugees and teachers access to the internet, and supporting NGOs in Europe to offer digital skills training; Connected Health, including m-mama, connecting mothers in rural areas of Lesotho and Tanzania to healthcare; and Connected Living, supporting people with learning disabilities in assisted care homes in the United Kingdom. Other initiatives include: providing mobile services to vulnerable girls in; using technology to assist victims of domestic abuse and gender-based violence. The Foundation supports a network of 27 local foundations in countries where the company has a presence and works with partners in 22 countries.
Geographical Area of Activity: International.
Publications: Annual Report.
Finance: Annual income £22.0m., expenditure £18.4m. (31 March 2024).

Board of Trustees: Nick Land (Chair.).
Principal Staff: Foundation Dir Lisa Felton.
Contact Details: 1 Kingdom St, London W2 6BY; tel. (7824) 342833; e-mail groupfoundation@vodafone.com; internet www.vodafone.com/start/foundation.html.

VSO—Voluntary Service Overseas

Established in 1958 by Alec and Mora Dickson, who recruited volunteer English teachers in response to a request from the Bishop of Portsmouth.

Activities: Works to alleviate poverty through recruiting professional volunteers to share their skills and experience with people in Africa and Asia. The organization collaborates with local partners to improve: education, annually training more than 40,000 teachers; health, training health practitioners and providing access to better quality healthcare, with a focus on mother and child health, young people's sexual health and HIV/AIDS; and livelihoods, ensuring access to reliable sources of food and income. It has operated in over 90 countries, with recruitment offices in the Netherlands and the United Kingdom, and regional hubs in South Africa and Thailand.
Geographical Area of Activity: South and South-East Asia, sub-Saharan Africa.
Restrictions: Not a grantmaking organization; volunteers must hold a degree or equivalent qualification and have at least three years' experience in their field.
Publications: Annual Report; newsletter; education and development publications for development practitioners; advocacy papers; working papers.
Finance: Annual income £32.1m., expenditure £34.5m. (5 April 2024).
International Board: Julia Lalla-Maharajh (Chair.).
Principal Staff: Co-CEOs Donné Cameron, Kathryn Gordon.
Contact Details: 100 London Rd, Kingston upon Thames KT2 6QJ; tel. (20) 8780-7500; e-mail enquiry@vsoint.org; internet www.vsointernational.org.

War Child

Established in 1993 by film-makers David Wilson and Bill Leeson.

Activities: Protects, educates and asserts the rights of children affected by war. The organization helps children to access education; rehabilitates former child soldiers; and seeks justice for young people who have been detained. It campaigns against the causes of conflict and works to put children at the centre of humanitarian response efforts. The Youth Advocates Panel in the United Kingdom is made up of young people aged 16–24 years from conflict-affected backgrounds who influence the public and decisionmakers through representing and amplifying the voices of children affected by war.
Geographical Area of Activity: Afghanistan, Central African Repub., Dem. Repub. of the Congo, Iraq, UK, Yemen.
Publications: Annual Report.
Finance: Annual income £18.9m., expenditure £19.7m. (31 Dec. 2023).
Board of Trustees: John Fallon (Chair.); Caroline Browne (Treas.).
Principal Staff: CEO Helen Pattinson.
Contact Details: Dunn's Hat Factory, 4th Floor, 106–110 Kentish Town Rd, London NW1 9PX; tel. (20) 7112-2555; e-mail info@warchild.org.uk; internet www.warchild.org.uk.

War on Want

Founded in 1951, as the Association for World Peace, by Victor Gollancz, a publisher.

Activities: Works to eliminate the root causes of global poverty, inequality and injustice in partnership with community-based movements, trade unions and workers' organizations. Main programmes focus on: climate justice and a Global Green New Deal that protects people and the planet; food sovereignty and the rights of rural communities; garment workers' rights; fast-food workers' demands for a living wage and job security; militarized conflicts, the arms trade and natural resources; justice for the Palestinian people; and dangerous trade deals that undermine environmental, social and labour standards.

Geographical Area of Activity: International.

Restrictions: Does not accept unsolicited applications.

Publications: Annual Report; newsletter; *Upfront* (magazine); briefings; reports.

Finance: Total income £2.1m., expenditure £2.5m. (31 March 2024).

Council of Management: Alia Al-Ghussain (Chair.).

Contact Details: 44–48 Shepherdess Walk, London N1 7JP; tel. (20) 7324-5040; e-mail support@waronwant.org; internet www.waronwant.org.

WaterAid

Founded in 1981 at the start of the UN International Drinking Water Decade (1981–90); became an international federation in 2010, co-ordinated by WaterAid International.

Activities: Provides access to clean water, decent toilets and knowledge about good hygiene. The organization provides local partners with skills and support to help communities to set up and manage practical and sustainable projects; and works locally and internationally to change policy and practice to ensure recognition of the role that WASH (water, sanitation and hygiene) plays in reducing poverty. Works in 28 countries, with member organizations in Australia, Canada, India, Japan, Sweden, the United Kingdom and the USA.

Geographical Area of Activity: Asia and Pacific, Central and South America, South and South-East Asia, sub-Saharan Africa, Sweden, UK, USA.

Restrictions: Grants only to specific (partner) organizations.

Publications: Annual Report; newsletter; *Oasis* (journal, 2 a year); country information sheets; issue sheets; blog.

Finance: Annual income £90.0m., expenditure £93.6m. (31 March 2024).

Board of Trustees: Andrew James Green (Chair.).

Principal Staff: Exec. Dir Tim Wainwright.

Contact Details: 6th Floor, 20 Canada Sq., London E14 5NN; tel. (20) 7793-4500; e-mail wateraid@wateraid.org; internet www.wateraid.org.

The Waterloo Foundation—TWF

Established in 2007 by Heather and David Stevens, co-founders of Admiral, an insurance company.

Activities: Funds projects that address gaps in opportunities and wealth, and the unsustainable use of natural resources. Main grant programme areas are: world development, comprising education, water, sanitation and hygiene, sexual and reproductive health, and nutrition; the environment, in particular, tropical rainforests and marine habitats; children's development, primarily funding research on psychological and behavioural development; and Wales, addressing care for the elderly, job creation and education. Grants typically range from £10,000 to £100,000.

Geographical Area of Activity: Worldwide.

Restrictions: Unlikely to fund individuals.

Publications: Annual Report.

Finance: Annual income £10.3m., expenditure £13.7m. (31 Dec. 2023).

Board of Trustees: Heather Stevens (Chair.).

Contact Details: Tudor House, 4th Floor, 16 Cathedral Rd, Cardiff CF11 9LJ; tel. (29) 2083-8980; e-mail info@waterloofoundation.org.uk; internet www.waterloofoundation.org.uk.

Wellbeing of Women

Established in 1964 as the Childbirth Research Centre by Prof. Will Nixon as the Childbirth Research Centre. Renamed Birthright in 1972. The charity expanded to all areas of women's reproductive health, becoming Wellbeing of Women in 2004.

Activities: Wellbeing of Women is a women's health charity saving and changing the lives of women, girls and babies. Led by women's voices, it improves health and wellbeing through research, education and advocacy. Wellbeing of Women is the only UK charity working across all of women's gynaecological and reproductive health. Various grants, ranging from £20,000 up to £300,000, are available for research projects, scholarships and fellowships in basic science, clinical or translational research. Research must be focused on women's reproductive or gynaecological health and addressing areas of clinical or patient need. Wellbeing of Women funds world-class research and supports the next generation of talented researchers.

Geographical Area of Activity: United Kingdom.

Restrictions: Grants only for research based in the UK and related to women's reproductive and gynaecological health.

Publications: Annual Report; health information.

Finance: Annual income £2.8m., expenditure £2.7m. (31 Dec 2023).

Board of Trustees: Prof. Dame Lesley Regan (Chair.).

Principal Staff: Chief Exec. Janet Lindsay.

Contact Details: 10–18 Union St, London SE1 1SZ; tel. (20) 3697-7000; e-mail hello@wellbeingofwomen.org.uk; internet www.wellbeingofwomen.org.uk.

Wellcome Trust

Founded in 1936 by the will of Sir Henry Wellcome, a pharmacist and medical entrepreneur.

Activities: Works to understand health and disease, improve health, engage the public and influence policy. Main programmes focus on: climate and health; infectious diseases; and mental health. The Trust supports individuals, teams and major initiatives in the areas of: biomedical science; population health; product development and applied research; humanities and social science; public engagement and creative industries; and education. It offers clinical and non-clinical research fellowships and postgraduate studentships; scholarships and bursaries; and programme, travel, project, refurbishment and equipment grants. In 2009 the Beit Memorial Fellowships for Medical Research transferred all its undertakings to the Trust. Maintains the Wellcome Library and Wellcome Collection museum.

Geographical Area of Activity: International.

Publications: Annual Report; newsletter; *Wellcome News* (quarterly magazine); *Mosaic* (digital); *Big Picture*; *Wellcome History*; books.

Finance: Total income £541.8m., expenditure £1,660.8m. (30 Sept. 2023).

Board of Governors: Julia Gillard (Chair.); Prof. Fiona Powrie (Deputy Chair.).

Principal Staff: CEO John-Arne Røttingen.

Contact Details: Gibbs Bldg, 215 Euston Rd, London NW1 2BE; tel. (20) 7611-8888; e-mail communication@wellcome.org; internet www.wellcome.org.

Westminster Foundation for Democracy—WFD

Founded in 1992; an independent public body sponsored by the Foreign and Commonwealth Office (FCO).

Activities: Specializes in parliamentary strengthening and political party development. The Foundation draws directly on parliamentary and political party expertise, working on a party-to-party and cross-party basis to develop the capacity of political parties and politicians at national and subnational level. Work themes include: accountability and transparency; elections; environmental democracy; inclusion;

participation and openness; and women's political leadership. Works in more than 30 countries; a member of the European Partnership for Democracy.

Geographical Area of Activity: Asia, Central Asia, Eastern Europe, Middle East and North Africa, South Asia, sub-Saharan Africa.

Publications: Annual Report; Annual Review; *WFD Newsletter* (monthly); handbooks; reports; blog.

Finance: Receives core funding from the FCO, as well as funding for specific programmes from the UK Department for International Development, the EU and the British Council. Annual income £8.8m., expenditure £15.7m. (31 March 2024).

Board of Governors: Yasmin Qureshi (Chair.).

Principal Staff: CEO Anthony Smith.

Contact Details: Clive House, 70 Petty France, London SW1H 9EX; tel. (20) 7799-1311; e-mail comms@wfd.org; internet www.wfd.org.

The Whitley Fund for Nature—WFN

Established in 1994 by Edward Whitley, founder of Whitley Asset Management.

Activities: Offers funding and training to proven grassroots conservation leaders in the Global South. Whitley Awards are worth £40,000 in project funding over one year. Further funding is available for previous winners for up to two years through the WFN Continuation Funding programme. The Whitley Gold Award, worth up to £100,000, is offered annually to a previous Whitley Award winner for their outstanding contribution to conservation.

Geographical Area of Activity: International.

Restrictions: Grants given to countries in the Global South only.

Publications: Annual Report; newsletter.

Finance: Annual income £2.6m., expenditure £2.7m. (30 June 2024).

Trustees: Edward Whitley (Chair.).

Principal Staff: Dir Danni Parks.

Contact Details: 23A Berghem Mews, Blythe Rd, London W14 0HN; tel. (20) 7221-9752; e-mail info@whitleyaward.org; internet www.whitleyaward.org.

The Wildlife Trusts

Established in 1912 as the Royal Society of Wildlife Trusts.

Activities: Promotes the conservation and recovery of wildlife; and brings people closer to nature by providing access to nature reserves, outdoor learning and education, and training and volunteering opportunities. The Wildlife Trusts comprise 46 independent organisations, which manage around 2,300 nature reserves and 100 coastal and marine conservation projects. Every Wildlife Trust works within its local community to inspire people to create a wilder future—including advising thousands of landowners on how to manage their land to benefit wildlife. The movement is supported by more than 900,000 members.

Geographical Area of Activity: UK.

Publications: Impact Report; Annual Review; reports; policies and position statements.

Finance: Annual income £32.7m., expenditure £28.7m. (31 March 2024).

Council: Duncan Ingram (Chair.).

Principal Staff: Pres. Liz Bonnin.

Contact Details: The Kiln, Mather Rd, Newark NG24 1WT; tel. (1636) 677711; e-mail enquiry@wildlifetrusts.org; internet www.wildlifetrusts.org.

William Adlington Cadbury Charitable Trust

Founded in 1923 by William C. Cadbury, a chocolate manufacturer and former Lord Mayor of Birmingham; shares an administration with the Edward Cadbury Charitable Trust (q.v.).

Activities: Main grant programmes focus on: Birmingham and the West Midlands (Herefordshire, Staffordshire, Warwickshire and Worcestershire), in the fields of community action, vulnerable groups, advice and mediation, education and training, environment and conservation, medical and healthcare, the arts and penal affairs; United Kingdom, supporting projects connected to the Quakers and supporting the work of the Religious Society of Friends; Ireland and Northern Ireland, in the field of peace and reconciliation; and international development, in particular poverty alleviation and children's education in West Africa. The Trust awards small grants monthly up to £2,000; and approx. 20 large grants, normally ranging between £10,000 and £20,000, up to £50,000.

Geographical Area of Activity: Asia and Eastern Europe, Ireland, South America, sub-Saharan Africa, UK.

Restrictions: Grants only to charities registered in the UK; no funding for individuals. International grants currently to organizations known to the Trust.

Publications: Annual Report.

Finance: Annual income £1.5m., expenditure £1.3m. (31 March 2024).

Trustees: Sophy Juliet Blandy (Chair.).

Principal Staff: Trust Administrator Ruth Payn.

Contact Details: Woodbrooke, 1046 Bristol Rd, Birmingham B29 6LJ; tel. (121) 4721464; e-mail info@wa-cadbury.org.uk; internet www.wa-cadbury.org.uk.

Windle Trust International

Established in 1986 as the Hugh Pilkington Charitable Trust, by the will of Dr Hugh Pilkington, who supported refugees' access to higher education; present name adopted in 2002.

Activities: Supports teaching and learning in communities affected by conflict, including refugees and internally displaced people. The Trust awards undergraduate and postgraduate scholarships for students from Central and Eastern Africa to study at universities and colleges in Sudan and the United Kingdom. It has offices in Sudan and South Sudan; and forms part of Windle International, an umbrella organization that also comprises Windle International Kenya, which provides education to refugees and host communities in Kenya, and Windle International Uganda, which operates the DAFI (Albert Einstein German Academic Refugee Initiative) Tertiary Scholarship Programme in Uganda on behalf of UNHCR.

Geographical Area of Activity: Kenya, South Sudan, Sudan, Somaliland, Uganda, UK.

Publications: Annual Report.

Finance: Annual income £5.6m., expenditure £5.6m. (31 Dec. 2023).

Board of Trustees: Sam Bickersteth (Chair.); Alistair Mack (Deputy Chiar.); Stuart Wilson (Treas.).

Principal Staff: CEO Dr David Masua.

Contact Details: 37A Oxford Rd, Cowley, Oxford OX4 2EN; tel. (1865) 712900; e-mail info@windle.org.uk; internet www.windle.org.uk.

The Wolfson Foundation

Founded in 1955; shares objectives and a joint administration with the Charles Wolfson Charitable Trust (q.v.) and the Wolfson Family Charitable Trust. The Wolfson Jewish Education Fund sits alongside them, but has a separate administration.

Activities: Supports excellence in science and medicine, health and disability, education, and arts and humanities, usually through the provision of infrastructure. The Foundation awards the Wolfson History Prize (f. 1972) annually for the best historical writing produced in the United Kingdom; the winner receives £40,000 and each shortlisted author £4,000. In 2018 it launched the Royal Society Wolfson Fellowship Scheme, worth up to £300,000 over five years, for universities and research institutions to recruit research scientists from overseas.

UNITED KINGDOM

Geographical Area of Activity: Commonwealth countries, Israel, UK.

Restrictions: No grants to individuals.

Publications: Annual Report.

Finance: Annual income £25.8m., expenditure £46.7m. (31 March 2024).

Board of Trustees: Dame Janet Wolfson de Botton (Chair.).

Principal Staff: Chief Exec. Paul Ramsbottom.

Contact Details: 8 Queen Anne St, London W1G 9LD; tel. (20) 7323-5730; e-mail grants@wolfson.org.uk; internet www.wolfson.org.uk.

The Wood Foundation—TWF

Established in 2007, by Sir Ian Wood, former Chair. of the Wood Group oil company, as the Wood Family Trust; present name adopted in 2014. It is the parent charity of TWF Africa.

Activities: Main programmes are: Venture Philanthropy in Africa, investing in smallholder tea farmers in Rwanda and Tanzania and sugar farmers in Kenya; Developing Young People in Scotland, alleviating child and youth poverty, promoting science, technology, engineering and mathematics, proving professional development for educators, with overseas placements in Rwanda and Uganda, raising awareness of philanthropy and social issues, and offering overseas volunteering opportunities for young people from north and north-east Scotland; and Economic & Education Development, to support the transition in north-east Scotland away from an economy based on North Sea oil extraction. The Wood Foundation Africa is a subsidiary, with an office in Nairobi and regional offices in Rwanda and Tanzania.

Geographical Area of Activity: Kenya, Rwanda, Scotland, Tanzania, Uganda.

Restrictions: No unsolicited applications.

Publications: Annual Report.

Finance: Annual income £21.5m., expenditure £7.6m. (31 March 2024).

Trustees: Sir Ian Wood (Pres.); Gareth Wood (Chair.).

Principal Staff: Africa Dir David Knopp; UK Dir Alison MacLachlan.

Contact Details: Blenheim House, Fountainhall Rd, Aberdeen AB15 4DT; tel. (1224) 619862; e-mail info@thewoodfoundation.org.uk; internet www.thewoodfoundation.org.uk.

World Animal Protection

Founded in 1981 by the merger of the World Federation for the Protection of Animals (f. 1950) and the International Society for the Protection of Animals (f. 1959). Present name adopted in 2014; formerly know as the World Society for the Protection of Animals.

Activities: Promotes effective means for the protection of animals, and for the prevention of cruelty to and the relief from suffering and exploitation of animals. The organization operates to protect animals internationally in four main areas: disasters, communities, the wild and farming. Programmes cover education, international relations and international law, through self-conducted programmes, education campaigns, research, conferences and courses, publications and lectures. Projects include campaigns in the areas of whaling, disaster management, bullfighting, working horses, bears, stray animals and factory farming. It has offices in 14 countries and has consultative status at the Council of Europe.

Geographical Area of Activity: International.

Publications: Annual Report; newsletter; blog.

Finance: Annual income £29.6m., expenditure £36.1m. (31 Dec. 2023).

Board of Trustees: Sarah Ireland (Chair.).

Principal Staff: CEO Tricia Croasdell.

Contact Details: 5th Floor, 222 Grays Inn Rd, London WC1X 8HB; tel. (20) 7239-0500; e-mail info@worldanimalprotection.org; internet www.worldanimalprotection.org.

World Jewish Relief

Established in 1933 as the Central British Fund for German Jewry (CBF) to rescue Jews from persecution in Germany; an international humanitarian agency; present name adopted in 1995.

Activities: Supports the poorest Jewish communities. The organization meets the essential basic needs needs of older people and their families; and works to eliminate poverty by helping people to find meaningful employment through livelihood and job skills programmes. It responds to international emergencies, providing emergency aid and supporting longer-term recovery; and helps Jewish refugees and internally displaced people into employment.

Geographical Area of Activity: East Africa, Eastern Europe, UK.

Publications: Annual Report; *Reach Out* (newsletter, 2 a year); brochure.

Finance: Annual income £17.3m., expenditure £21.3m. (30 June 2024).

Trustees: Maurice Helfgott (Chair.); Henry Grunwald (Pres.); Jeremy Newman (Treas.).

Principal Staff: Chief Exec. Paul Anticoni.

Contact Details: Oscar Joseph House, 54 Crewys Rd, London NW2 2AD; tel. (20) 8736-1250; e-mail info@worldjewishrelief.org; internet www.worldjewishrelief.org.

World Land Trust—WLT

Established in 1989 by John Burton, a conservationist.

Activities: Concerned with conservation initiatives, including land purchase and protection of threatened areas in partnership with overseas project partner organizations. The Trust raises funds and public awareness to support its conservation aims and objectives; and acts as a platform to develop an international network of like-minded organizations. The Carbon Balanced Programme seeks to offset carbon dioxide emissions by restoring ecology and avoiding deforestation; other programmes include the Action Fund and Buy An Acre.

Geographical Area of Activity: International.

Restrictions: Support projects focused on protecting threatened biodiversity worldwide; projects are usually in developing countries. Does not usually accept unsolicited applications; no grants to individuals.

Publications: Annual Review; *WLT News* (2 a year); e-bulletins (monthly).

Finance: Annual income £10.2m., expenditure £7.8m. (31 Dec. 2023).

Board of Trustees: Myles Archibald (Chair.).

Principal Staff: CEO Dr Catherine Barnard.

Contact Details: Blyth House, Bridge St, Halesworth IP19 8AB; tel. (1986) 874422; e-mail info@worldlandtrust.org; internet www.worldlandtrust.org.

World Vision International

Established in 1950 in the USA as World Vision by Dr Robert Pierce, a Baptist minister and founder of Samaritan's Purse (q.v.); restructured in 1977 to take into account its international development work. A Christian relief, development and advocacy organization.

Activities: Works to improve the lives of vulnerable children. Programmes include: child participation and protection; clean water; climate change; disaster management; economic development; education; emergency response; faith and development; food assistance; health and nutrition; peacebuilding; and social accountability. The organization works in nearly 100 countries, with headquarters in the United Kingdom and the USA, with liaison offices in Belgium and Switzerland, and is part of the Disasters Emergency Committee (q.v.).

Geographical Area of Activity: International.

Publications: Annual Report; newsletter; *World Vision Magazine* (quarterly); *World Vision News* (quarterly); *World Vision eNews* (monthly); factsheets; reports; research papers; books; blog.

Finance: Annual revenue US $3,460m., expenditure $3,479m. (30 Sept. 2023).

Board of Directors: Dr Ivan Satyavrata (Chair.); Suanne Miedema (Vice-Chair.); Rosa E. Santizo (Sec.).

Principal Staff: Pres. and CEO Andrew Morley.

Contact Details: Romero House, 55 Westminster Bridge Rd, London SE1 7JB; 800 W Chestnut Ave, Monrovia, CA 91016; tel. (20) 7758-2900; 1 (626) 303-8811; e-mail info@wvi.org; internet www.wvi.org.

Worldwide Cancer Research

Founded in 1979; formerly known as the Association for International Cancer Research.

Activities: Supports discovery research to improve the prevention, diagnosis and treatment of cancers. The organization awards projects grants of up to £275,000 over 1–3 years; and, jointly with the European Association for Cancer Research (q.v.), offers Travel Fellowships and Travel Grants. It has funded over 2,000 projects in 35 countries since 1979.

Geographical Area of Activity: International.

Restrictions: Does not fund clinical research, including clinical trials, patient care, nursing or healthcare delivery research; nor other types of applied cancer research, such as policy, public health or psychosocial research.

Publications: Annual Review; newsletter; leaflets; impact report.

Finance: Annual income £10.1m., expenditure £11.5m. (31 Dec 2023).

Principal Staff: Chief Exec. Dr Helen Rippon.

Contact Details: Third Floor South, 121 George St, Edinburgh EH2 4YN; tel. (300) 7777910; e-mail enquiries@worldwidecancerresearch.org; internet www.worldwidecancerresearch.org.

YMCA—Young Men's Christian Association

Founded in 1844 by George Williams, a draper; a Christian federation, part of the World Alliance of YMCAs (q.v.).

Activities: Helps young people and communities. Main programmes include: supplying around 8,800 beds nightly, ranging from emergency accommodation to longer-term housing and youth hostels; offering family services, including nurseries, out-of-school clubs and relationship services; promoting health and wellbeing through sports and activity programmes; providing education, skills-based training, placements and apprenticeship schemes; and offering support and advice in all areas to young people. The Association conducts research and organizes campaigns, and jointly with the British Youth Council runs the Secretariat for the All-Party Parliamentary Group (APPG) on Youth Affairs. The federation comprises 84 YMCAs in England and Wales.

Geographical Area of Activity: England, Wales.

Publications: Annual Report; booklets; reports.

Finance: Each of the YMCAs in England and Wales is an independent charity. YMCA England & Wales (National Council of YMCAs) annual income £22.8m., expenditure £22.7m. (31 March 2024).

Board of Trustees: Roy O'Shaughnessy (Chair.); Emma Osmundsen (Vice-Chair.).

Principal Staff: CEO and Nat. Sec. Denise Hatton.

Contact Details: YMCA England & Wales, 10–11 Charterhouse Sq., London EC1M 6EH; tel. (20) 7186-9500; e-mail enquiries@ymca.org.uk; internet www.ymca.org.uk.

Young Citizens—Citizenship Foundation

Founded in 1989, developing out of the Law in Education Project (f. 1984); in 2008 it merged with the Council for Education in World Citizenship (f. 1939).

Activities: Promotes a fair and inclusive society, based on a strong and secure democracy and active citizen participation. The Foundation supports citizenship education in primary and secondary schools in the United Kingdom, teaching young people about 'British values', citizenship, law and social action. It offers teaching resources and training to teachers and other educational professionals.

Geographical Area of Activity: United Kingdom.

Publications: Annual Report; newsletter; teaching materials; blog.

Finance: Annual income £865,909, expenditure £1m. (31 March 2024).

Board of Trustees: Ashley Wheaton (Chair.); Orlá McKeon-Carter (Treas.).

Principal Staff: Chief Exec. Ashley Hodges.

Contact Details: 37 Heneage St, London E1 5LJ; tel. (20) 7566-4141; e-mail info@youngcitizens.org; internet www.youngcitizens.org.

Young Lives vs Cancer

Formed in 2005 as CLIC Sargent after a merger between CLIC (Cancer and Leukaemia in Childhood (f. 1976) and Sargent Cancer Care for Children (f. 1968); present name adopted in 2021.

Activities: Provides practical, financial and emotional support to children and young people, and their families, who are affected by cancer. The organization offers registration grants to cover immediate logistical and household costs associated with diagnosis. Other grants are also available.

Geographical Area of Activity: UK.

Restrictions: Registration grants only to young people diagnosed between the ages of 16 and 24 years; and parents of children aged 0–15 years.

Publications: Annual Report; Impact Summary; newsletter; storybooks; guides; booklets; leaflets.

Finance: Annual income £23.1m., expenditure £26.1m. (31 March 2024).

Board of Trustees: Prof. Sir David Haslam (Chair.); Anna Hancock (Treas.).

Principal Staff: Chief Exec. Rachel Kirby-Rider.

Contact Details: 4th Floor, Whitefriars, Lewins Mead, Bristol BS1 2NT; tel. (300) 3300803; e-mail supporter.services@younglivesvscancer.org.uk; internet www.younglivesvscancer.org.uk.

Zochonis Charitable Trust

Founded in 1977 on the settlement of property by the late Sir John Basil Zochonis, the former Chair. of PZ Cussons, a consumer products group.

Activities: Operates nationally and internationally through making grants to local charities, with a particular emphasis on education and children's welfare.

Geographical Area of Activity: International.

Restrictions: Grants only to registered charities.

Publications: Annual Report.

Finance: Annual income £3.3m., expenditure £3.5m. (5 April 2024).

Principal Staff: Contact Marie E. Gallagher.

Contact Details: c/o PZ Cussons PLC, Manchester Business Park, 3500 Aviator Way, Manchester M22 5TG; tel. (161) 435-1005; e-mail enquiries@zochonischaritabletrust.com; internet www.pzcussons.com/about-us/the-zochonis-charitable-trust.

Zurich Community Trust—ZCT

Founded in 1973, as Hambro Life Charitable Trust, by Hambro Life, an insurance company; present name adopted in 1998.

Activities: Supports the most vulnerable people. Programme areas include: tackling loneliness experienced by older people; addressing the impact on families of parental substance abuse;

helping children and young people with their mental health; and organizing exercise and activities to bring together isolated elderly people and young people not in education, employment or training. The Foundation promotes volunteering, including mentoring and skillsharing, among Zurich UK employees. It incorporated the Openwork Foundation, which provides financial advice in the United Kingdom and which became an independent organization in 2019.

Geographical Area of Activity: UK.

Restrictions: No grants to individuals, for research, animal welfare, emergency or disaster appeals, nor to political, religious or mainstream educational institutions (unless directly benefiting people with disabilities).

Publications: Annual Report; factsheets; *The Fortieth* (special anniversary newspaper).

Finance: Annual income £3.4m., expenditure £3.9m. (31 Dec. 2023).

Board of Trustees: Steve Collinson (Chair.).

Principal Staff: Acting Head of Trust Samantha Owen.

Contact Details: Unity Pl., 1 Carfax Cl., Swindon, SN1 1AP; tel. (1793) 502450; e-mail zct@zct.org.uk; internet www.zct.org.uk.

UNITED STATES OF AMERICA

CO-ORDINATING BODIES

Accountable Now
Established in 2008 by a small group of passionate CSOs.

Activities: Works with organizations to ensure their actions are aligned with their values and commitments. Aims to create better and stronger enabling environments for civil society; advocates for civil society self-regulation, shifting power, and locally led change. Members are non-profits, networks, and other CSOs and partnerships who work in a range of sectors including human rights, international development and humanitarian interventions. Runs an Independent Review Panel to examine members' actions and reporting and offer advice. Accountable Now offers training, policy design and access to peer advice groups; members can also gain tailored insights, skills, and practical tools for their programmes, operations, governance and impact. Also offers a range of support and services for non-members and key enablers of civil society like philanthropies, multilaterals, and multisectoral partnerships. Provides research, tools, peer guidance, and professional development support for civil society advocates and practitioners around the world through the Good Practice Library. Registered as International NGO Accountability Charter gUG in Germany.

Geographical Area of Activity: Worldwide.

Publications: Annual Report; newsletter.

Finance: Total revenue US $623,399 (2025).

Board of Trustees: Rachel Smith (Chair.); Vanessa Goas (Acting Treas.).

Principal Staff: Exec. Dir Megan Colnar.

Contact Details: c/o Accountability Lab, 110 13th Street NW, Suite 800, Washington, DC 20005; e-mail info@accountablenow.org; internet accountablenow.org.

Africa Grantmakers' Affinity Group—AGAG
Established in 2000, growing out of the informal networks that supported the anti-apartheid movement; previously known as the South Africa Grantmakers' Affinity Group, then the Southern Africa Grantmakers' Affinity Group.

Activities: Operates as a membership network of funders, practitioners, scholars and grantmaking organizations. The Group promotes greater foundation interest and funding to benefit African communities; and offers opportunities for networking, professional development, and sharing knowledge and experience. It is a project of the Tides Center, part of the Tides Network (q.v.). Announced in 2022 that it would be concluding its work and in 2025 was entering its final phase of operations.

Geographical Area of Activity: Africa, Europe, North America.

Restrictions: Membership open to funders only; not a grant-making organization.

Publications: Newsletter; research findings.

Principal Staff: Exec. Dir Niamani Mutima.

Contact Details: POB 150, Warrenton, VA 20188-0150; tel. (540) 935-1307; e-mail contactus@agag.org; internet www.africagrantmakers.org.

Candid
Established in 2019 by the merger of the Foundation Center (f. 1956) and GuideStar, a non-profit information provider.

Activities: Researches and provides information and data on non-profit organizations, foundations and grants. The organization maintains the Foundation Directory Online database, which contains information on 300,000 US foundations. It has offices in Oakland, CA, Atlanta, GA, Cleveland, OH, Washington, DC, and Williamsburg, VA; and operates the Funding Information Network, comprising more than 400 libraries, community foundations and non-profit resource centres.

Geographical Area of Activity: USA.

Restrictions: Does not direct applications for funds to particular foundations, nor does it arrange introductions to foundation officials or assist persons seeking positions in foundations.

Publications: Annual Report; newsletter; *Foundation Directory Online*; blog.

Finance: Annual revenue US $51.8m., expenditure $39.9m. (31 Dec. 2022).

Board of Trustees: Melissa A. Berman (Chair.); Donna Murray-Brown (Vice-Chair.); Brian Trelstad (Treas.).

Principal Staff: CEO Ann Mei Chang.

Contact Details: 32 Old Slip, 24th Floor, New York, NY 10005; POB 22799, New York, NY 10087-2799; tel. (212) 620-4230; e-mail support@candid.org; internet candid.org.

Charities Aid Foundation of America—CAF America
Established in 1992; a member of the Global Alliance of the Charities Aid Foundation.

Activities: Helps North American donors to create effective philanthropy nationally and internationally. The Foundation serves thousands of foreign non-profit organizations in more than 135 countries and grants directly to 1.9m. charities worldwide. It has two subsidiaries: CAF Canada and the CAF American Donor Fund in the United Kingdom. Has offices in San Francisco, CA, Miami, FL, Toronto, Vancouver (Canada) and London (UK).

Geographical Area of Activity: International.

Publications: Annual Report; newsletter; *Cross-Border Giving: A Legal and Practical Guide*; *World Giving Index*.

Finance: Annual revenue US $816.4m., expenditure $748.1m. (30 April 2023).

Council on Foundations

Board of Directors: Martin Riant (Chair.); Audrey L. Jacobs (Vice-Chair.); Anna Hofmeiste (Treas.); rAndras Kosaras (Sec.).

Principal Staff: Pres. and CEO Jessie Krafft
Pres. and CEO Jessie Krafft.

Contact Details: King St Station, 225 Reinekers Lane, Suite 375, Alexandria, VA 22314; tel. (202) 793-2232; e-mail info@cafamerica.org; internet www.cafamerica.org.

Council on Foundations—COF

Established in 1949 as the National Committee on Foundations and Trusts for Community Welfare.

Activities: Advocates on behalf of members and promotes public policy that strengthens the philanthropic sector. The Council offers technical and advisory services to guide members on including legal and tax issues, investment management, programme development and grantmaking. It liaises with other parts of the philanthropic sector, including the Foundation Center (q.v.); organizes conferences and meetings; and sponsors research and educational programmes. Awards offered include the Wilmer Shields and Distinguished Grantmaker Awards. Has more than 900 members, including private, community- and company-sponsored foundations and corporate contributors; regional associations of grantmakers are also affiliates.

Geographical Area of Activity: USA.

Publications: Annual Report; *Council Columns*; *Foundation News and Commentary Magazine*; *Principles and Practices for Effective Grantmaking*; blog.

Finance: Annual revenue US $11.5m., expenditure $10.7m. (31 Dec. 2022).

Board of Directors: Jay Williams (Chair.); Jennifer Ford Reedy (Vice-Chair.); Srikanth Gopal (Sec.).

Principal Staff: Pres. and CEO Kathleen P. Enright.

Contact Details: 1255 23rd St NW, Suite 200, Washington, DC 20037; tel. (202) 991-2225; e-mail info@cof.org; internet www.cof.org.

Council of Michigan Foundations—CMF

Established in 1972.

Activities: Promotes philanthropy in Michigan and supports charitable organizations. Members include community, corporate, family, independent and public foundations. The Council offers Consulting Services Grants and Technology Grants. It comprises nearly 300 member organizations; and has offices in Grand Rapids, MI, Lansing, MI, and Detroit, MI.

Geographical Area of Activity: USA (Michigan).

Restrictions: Not a grantmaking organization.

Publications: Research, data and reports; toolkits.

Finance: Total revenue US $5.7m., expenditure $7.8m. (31 March 2023).

Board of Trustees: David Mengebier (Chair.); Lizabeth Ardisana (Chair.-elect); Maha Freij (Treas.); Camille Gerville-Reache (Sec.).

Principal Staff: Pres. and CEO Kyle Caldwell.

Contact Details: 3101 East Grand Blvd, Suite 300, Detroit, MI 48202; tel. (313) 566-2444; e-mail info@michiganfoundations.org; internet www.michiganfoundations.org.

EDGE Funders Alliance

Formed in 2012 by a merger of the Funders Network on Transforming the Global Economy and Grantmakers without Borders.

Activities: Works in the fields of social justice and environmental sustainability. The Alliance operates in three main areas: organizing and networking; philanthropic learning and advocacy; and information services. It produces social justice films, organizes an annual conference and has an affinity group in Europe. The FundAction (f. 2017) initiative is a participatory fund that makes grants to European activists for social transformation, offering grants worth from €5,000 to €20,000. Comprises almost 500 members in more than 40 countries, supporting 130 diverse institutions.

Geographical Area of Activity: International.

Restrictions: FundAction grants only to individuals who are active in progressive social movements.

Publications: *Leading EDGE* (newsletter); white papers; conference reports; climate justice reports; webinar series.

Finance: Annual revenue US $1.5m., expenditure $1.1m. (31 Dec. 2021).

Board of Directors: Maartje Eigman, Michael Kourabas (Co-Chair.); Sharon Anderson Damelio (Treas.); Eva Rehse (Sec.).

Contact Details: 2021 Fillmore St #66, San Francisco, CA 94115; tel. (415) 577-1177; e-mail contactus@edgefunders.org; internet edgefunders.org.

Florida Philanthropic Network—FPN

Established in 2001 by seven Florida foundation leaders; merged with Community Foundations of Florida in 2009.

Activities: Promotes local philanthropy, and connects donors with community foundations. The Network comprises private independent, corporate and family foundations, community foundations, public charity grantmakers and corporate giving programmes, which hold more than US $6,500m. in charitable assets. It organizes conferences, webinars and training for members; and hosts a number of affinity groups and networks. Has an office in Miami, FL.

Geographical Area of Activity: Florida.

Publications: Briefings; meeting notes; webinar recordings.

Finance: Annual revenue US $2.4m., expenditure $2.0m. (31 Dec. 2023).

Board of Directors: Grace Sacerdote (Chair.); Theresa Grimison (Vice-Chair.); Allison Chase (Treas.); Roshell Rinkins (Sec.).

Principal Staff: Pres. and CEO Ashley Heath Dietz.

Contact Details: 12191 W Linebaugh Ave, Suite 626, Tampa, Florida 33626; tel. (813) 983-7399; e-mail info@fpnetwork.org; internet www.fpnetwork.org.

Give2Asia

Established in 2011 by the Asia Foundation (q.v.), following the acquisition of the Asia Pacific Philanthropy Consortium; became a separate organization in 2012.

Activities: Funds initiatives in the areas of: the arts and culture; civil society; disaster relief; education; environment; health; livelihoods; social services; and women and girls. The organization works with individual donors, family and corporate foundations, and non-profit and community-based organizations, offering technical support, training, research and information services, and opportunities for networking and exchange; and organizes conferences. It works in more than 23 countries, with a representative office in Beijing, People's Republic of China. Subsidiaries operate in Hong Kong (f. 2012) and Australia (f. 2021).

Geographical Area of Activity: Australasia, East and South-East Asia, South Asia, USA.

Publications: Newsletter; reports.

Finance: Annual revenue US $46.0m., expenditure $44.9m. (31 Dec. 2022).

Board of Directors: George SyCip (Chair.); Naren Agrawal (Vice-Chair.).

Principal Staff: Pres. and CEO Birger Stamperdahl.

Contact Details: 2 Embarcadero Center, 8th Floor, San Francisco, CA 94111; tel. (415) 967-6300; e-mail info@give2asia.org; internet www.give2asia.org.

Giving USA Foundation

Founded in 1985 by the Giving Institute.

Activities: Advances the research, education and public understanding of philanthropy. The Foundation publishes data and trends about charitable giving and reports on topics related to the field of philanthropy.

Geographical Area of Activity: USA.

Publications: *Giving USA Annual Report* (annual); *Giving USA Special Reports* (quarterly).

Finance: Annual revenue US $1.4m., expenditure $1.1m. (31 July 2022).

Board of Directors and Executive Committee: Wendy McGrady (Chair.); Gabe Cooper (Vice-Chair.); Don Souhrada (Treas./Sec.); Joshua Birkholz (Immediate Past Chair.).

Contact Details: 1660 International Dr., Suite 600, McLean, VA 22102; tel. (312) 981-6794; e-mail info@givingusa.org; internet www.givingusa.org.

Global Health Council

Established in 1972, as the National Council for International Health; a membership organization. Present name adopted in 1999.

Activities: Supports and connects organizations and individuals involved in global health programmes and research; and engages decisionmakers to influence health policy. Members include academic institutions and think tanks, associations and NGOs, consultants, corporations and corporate foundations. The Council comprises more than 100 member organizations and 250 individual members operating in more than 150 countries.

Geographical Area of Activity: International.

Publications: Annual Report; newsletter (monthly); blog.

Finance: Annual revenue US $863,828, expenditure $1.3m. (31 Dec. 2022).

Board of Directors: Kate Dodson (Chair.).

Principal Staff: Pres. and CEO Elisha Dunn-Georgiou.

Contact Details: 2300 N St, NW Suite 501A, Washington, DC 20037; tel. (703) 659-6480; e-mail membership@globalhealth.org; internet www.globalhealth.org.

Global Impact

Established in 1956 as International Service Agencies; present name adopted in 2002.

Activities: Raises funds for causes such as disaster relief and global development through working on charitable ventures as an adviser, intermediary and implementing partner across the private, non-profit and public sectors. Areas of expertise include: fundraising and partnerships; employee engagement and corporate social responsibility; finance and business services; and in-country programme design and delivery. The organization works with almost 300 public and private sector workplace giving campaigns to fund an alliance of 100 international charities. It has a subsidiary, Geneva Global, based in Pennsylvania, PA; and has established several counterpart organizations: Global Impact UK (f. 2016); Global Impact Canada (f. 2020); and Global Impact Australia (f. 2021).

Geographical Area of Activity: International.

Restrictions: No grants to organizations or financial assistance to individuals.

Publications: Annual Report; *Greater Giving Weekly* (newsletter); *COVID-19 Regulatory and Response Matrix; 2018 Giving Global Matrix: Tax, Fiduciary and Philanthropic Requirements; Spotlight on Giving; Donor Advised Funds: Democratizing Philanthropy to Change the World*.

Finance: Annual revenue US $145.2m., expenditure $81.6m. (30 June 2023).

Board of Directors: Anita Whitehead (Chair.); Sarah Degnan Kambou (Vice-Chair.); James B. Kanuch (Treas.); David Wu (Sec.).

Principal Staff: Pres. and CEO Scott Jackson.

Contact Details: 2300 N St NW, Suite 501A, Washington, DC 20037; tel. (800) 836-4620; e-mail info@charity.org; internet charity.org.

Global Philanthropy Forum

Established in 2001; a project of the World Affairs Council of Northern California.

Activities: A peer-learning network of philanthropists, social investors, grantmakers and foundation executives working internationally. It has members in 98 countries and has helped to establish the Dasra Philanthropy Forum, with a focus on India, and Filantropía Transformadora (q.v.) in Colombia. The Brazilian Philanthropy Forum, established with the Instituto para o Desenvolvimento do Investimento Social, and the African Philanthropy Forum (q.v.), based in Nigeria, are affiliates.

Geographical Area of Activity: International.

Restrictions: Not a grantmaking organization.

Publications: Blog.

Steering Committee: Philip Yun (Chair.).

Principal Staff: Man. Dir Sarah Howard.

Contact Details: 110 The Embarcadero, San Francisco, CA 94108; tel. (415) 293-4633; e-mail info@philanthropyforum.org; internet www.philanthropyforum.org.

Human Rights Funders Network—HRFN

Established in 1994 as the International Human Rights Funders Group by human rights grantmakers.

Activities: A peer-led network that fosters new initiatives and increases attention on particular human rights issues. The Network offers resources and networking opportunities, organizing working groups, workshops and conferences; and, in partnership with Candid (q.v.), created the Advancing Human Rights online research tool, which maps the field of human rights philanthropy. In 2003 it established the Fund for Global Human Rights; and in 2008 the Disability Rights Fund. Comprises almost 450 institutions in 70 countries, with more than 1,800 individual and institutional members.

Geographical Area of Activity: Worldwide.

Publications: Annual Report; newsletter; reports; Advancing Human Rights (online research tool); blogs.

Principal Staff: Exec. Dir Kellea Miller.

Contact Details: 500 7th Ave, 8th Fl., New York, 10018 New York; e-mail community@hrfn.org; internet www.hrfn.org.

Independent Sector

Founded in 1980; a national coalition of foundations, non-profit organizations and corporations.

Activities: Acts as a forum for member organizations, as a source of information and as a mediator between the grantmaking and grantseeking communities. The organization also works to encourage volunteer work and community action in society. It supports non-profit initiatives in areas such as public policy, research and communications; and organizes the annual Innovate for Good Challenge to advance the use of technology for the common good.

Geographical Area of Activity: Puerto Rico, USA.

Publications: Annual Report; *Facts and Findings Series*; reports; factsheets; policy briefs; toolkits; blog.

Finance: Annual revenue US $5.5m., expenditure $9.3m. (31 Dec. 2023).

Exec. Committee: Fred Blackwell (Chair.); Sarah Kastelic (Vice-Chair.); Jen Ford Reedy (Treas.); Michael McAfee (Sec.).

Principal Staff: Pres. and CEO Dr Akilah Watkins.

Contact Details: 1602 L St NW, Suite 900, Washington, DC 20036; tel. (202) 467-6100; e-mail info@independentsector.org; internet www.independentsector.org.

InterAction

Formed in 1984 by the merger of the American Council of Voluntary Agencies for Foreign Service and Private Agencies Collaborating Together.

Activities: Enhances the effectiveness and professional capacities of NGOs working in the field of international development, fostering partnership, collaboration and leadership among member organizations. Members' activities include disaster relief, refugee protection, assistance and resettlement, sustainable development, public policy and educating the US public on global development issues. The organization comprises more than 180 US-based private and voluntary organizations working in more than 130 countries.

Geographical Area of Activity: USA.

Publications: Annual Report; newsletter; NGO Aid Map.

Finance: Annual revenue US $8.4m., expenditure $9.9m. (31 Dec. 2022).

Board of Directors: Janti Soeripto (Chair.); Christine Squires (Vice-Chair.); Rabih Torbay (Treas.).

Principal Staff: Pres. and CEO Tom Hart.

Contact Details: 1400 16th St NW, Suite 210, Washington, DC 20036; tel. (202) 667-8227; e-mail ia@interaction.org; internet www.interaction.org.

International Center for Not-for-Profit Law—ICNL

Established in 1992.

Activities: The International Center for Not-for-Profit Law (ICNL) works to improve the legal environment for civil society, philanthropy, and public participation around the world. ICNL works in more than 100 countries, developing long-term relationships with partners in civil society, government, and the international community to advance reforms. It provides technical legal assistance, training, and educational materials for stakeholders; publishes research and analyses on key issues and trends; and maintains a website with over 4,500 resources in more than 60 languages. ICNL is based in Washington, DC, has offices in Jordan, Kyrgyzstan and Tajikistan, and is affiliated with the Bulgarian Center for Not-for-Profit Law and the European Center for Not-for-Profit Law in the Netherlands. ICNL is part of the Lifeline Consortium, led by Freedom House (q.v.), which supports CSOs under threat because of their human rights work.

Geographical Area of Activity: Worldwide.

Restrictions: Does not provide legal services.

Publications: Civic Freedom Monitor; Digital Legal Library; US Protest Law Tracker; COVID-19 Civic Freedom Tracker.

Finance: Annual revenue US $10.7m., expenditure $13.4m. (31 Dec. 2022).

Board of Directors: Bindu Sharma (Chair.); Mary Beth Goodman (Vice-Chair.); Oyebisi B. Oluseyi (Sec.); Mark Sidel (Treas.).

Principal Staff: Pres. Douglas Rutzen.

Contact Details: 1126 16th St NW, Suite 400, Washington, DC 20036; tel. (202) 452-8600; e-mail info@icnl.org; internet www.icnl.org.

League of California Community Foundations

Established in 1994; a statewide partnership of community foundations.

Activities: Promotes the development of community foundations. Comprises more than 40 member foundations, with combined assets of more than US $22,000m.

Geographical Area of Activity: USA (California).

Finance: Annual revenue US $5.0m., expenditure $2.9m. (31 Dec. 2020).

Board: Susan True (Chair.); Marian Kaanon (Vice-Chair.); Terence Mulligan (Treas.); Mark Stuart (Sec.).

Principal Staff: CEO Laura Seaman.

Contact Details: POB 402275, Hesperia, CA 92345; tel. (209) 984-3955; e-mail info@lccf.org; internet lccf.org.

Peace and Security Funders Group—PSFG

Established in 2000 by a group of foundations.

Activities: A network that promotes communication and collaboration among funders working in the field of international peace and security. Main activities include capacity-building programmes and establishing partnerships with policymakers. The organization also hosts expert briefings, working groups and webinars; carries out research; and issues publications. Members include grant-giving and operating foundations, individual philanthropists and investors.

Geographical Area of Activity: International.

Publications: *Peace and Security Funding Index*; *Peace and Security Funding Map*.

Finance: Members' approx. annual giving US $357m.

Principal Staff: Exec. Dir Alexandra I. Toma.

Contact Details: 1625 K St NW, Suite 1050, Washington, DC 20006; tel. (202) 351-6821; e-mail info@peaceandsecurity.org; internet www.peaceandsecurity.org.

Synergos—The Synergos Institute

Established in 1986 as the Synergos' Global Philanthropists Circle by Peggy Dulany and her father, David Rockefeller.

Activities: Promotes collective learning and systems thinking to solve complex problems to poverty. The organization fosters collaboration among businesses, governments, CSOs and marginalized communities. Main programmes focus on agriculture, health, nutrition, youth employment, social entrepreneurship and philanthropy. It offers three-year fellowships to civil society leaders as part of the Senior Fellows Network; and has also established the Global Philanthropists Circle and Leadership and Innovation Network for Collaboration in South Africa's children's sector. The David Rockefeller Bridging Leadership Award is made annually to honour leaders who cross traditional boundaries. Has supported initiatives in more than 30 countries.

Geographical Area of Activity: Middle East, Bangladesh, Brazil, People's Repub. of China, Ethiopia, India, Mexico, Namibia, Nigeria, South Africa.

Publications: Annual Report; newsletter.

Finance: Annual revenue US $6.4m., expenditure $8.0m. (31 Dec. 2022).

Board of Directors: Peggy Dulany (Chair.); Elliott Donnelly, II (Vice-Chair.).

Principal Staff: Pres./CEO Camille Massey; Senior Dir Chong-Lim Lee.

Contact Details: 1 East 53rd St, 7th Floor, New York, NY 10022; tel. (646) 963-2100; e-mail synergos@synergos.org; internet www.synergos.org.

FOUNDATIONS AND NON-PROFITS

Abdorrahman Boroumand Center for Human Rights in Iran—ABC

Established in 2002 as the Abdorrahman Boroumand Foundation, in memory of Dr Abdorrahman Boroumand, an Iranian lawyer and pro-democracy activist, who was killed in 1991; present name adopted in 2020.

Activities: Promotes human rights and democracy in Iran through research and education, documenting human rights violations in Iran and issuing publications. The Center maintains the dual language Omid ('Hope') Memorial database of victims of persecution; and a digital archive, containing books, articles, memoirs, letters, documents and other information.

Geographical Area of Activity: USA.

Publications: Newsletter; reports and interviews (in Farsi and English).

Finance: Annual revenue US $1.9m., expenditure $997,688 (31 Dec. 2022).

Board of Directors: Shéhérazade Semsar-de Boisséson (Chair.).

Principal Staff: Exec. Dir and Sec. Roya Boroumand.

Contact Details: 3220 N St, NW, Suite 357 Washington, DC 20007; tel. (202) 465-7184; e-mail info@boroumandcenter.org; internet www.iranrights.org.

UNITED STATES OF AMERICA

Accion
Founded in 1961; formerly known as ACCION International.

Activities: Provides financial services to underserved communities through microfinance and financial technology (fintech) impact investing. The organization supports fintech start-ups and microfinance institutions to provide financial services for 350m. people. It works with more than 267 partners in 75 countries, with offices in Washington, DC, Bogotá (Colombia), and Bangalore and Mumbai (India).

Geographical Area of Activity: East and South-East Asia, Middle East and North Africa, North America, South America, Central America and the Caribbean, South Asia, sub-Saharan Africa.

Restrictions: Neither lends to nor funds individuals directly.

Publications: Annual Report; *Accion Insights* (bulletin); research reports; blog.

Finance: Annual revenue US $36.5m., expenditure $38.3m. (31 Dec. 2023).

Board of Directors: Diana L. Taylor (Chair.); Ron Hoge, Barbara Lucas (Vice-Chair.); Phillip Riese (Treas.); Thomas C. Barry (Sec.).

Principal Staff: Pres. and CEO Michael Schlein.

Contact Details: 1101 15th St NW, Suite 400, Washington DC 20005; tel. (202) 393-5113; e-mail info@accion.org; internet www.accion.org.

ACDI/VOCA
Established in 1963 as the International Cooperative Development Association by major US farm co-operatives; present name adopted following the merger in 1997 with Volunteers in Overseas Co-operative Assistance (VOCA).

Activities: Designs and implements global development programmes, providing technical assistance and expertise. The organization promotes food security through helping farmers and agribusinesses; strengthens community and household resilience to shocks and stresses; and encourages economic growth through building inclusive market systems. It incorporates an affiliated international non-profit organization, Tanager (formerly known as Agribusiness Systems International). Works in more than 60 countries, with an office in Accra, Ghana.

Geographical Area of Activity: International.

Publications: Annual Report; *Global Connections* (monthly e-newsletter); reports; guides.

Finance: Annual revenue US $111.0m., expenditure $109.7m. (2022).

Board of Directors: Timothy Beans (Chair.); Asif M. Shaikh (Vice-Chair.).

Principal Staff: Pres. and CEO Sylvia Megret.

Contact Details: 50 F St, NW, Suite 1000, Washington, DC 20001; tel. (202) 469-6000; e-mail partnerwithus@acdivoca.org; internet www.acdivoca.org.

Acumen
Founded in 2001 as the Acumen Fund by Jacqueline Novogratz, a social entrepreneur, with seed capital from the Rockefeller Foundation (q.v.) and Cisco Systems Foundation.

Activities: Invests 'patient' (philanthropic) capital in start-ups that provide access to water and sanitation, health, energy, housing, education, financial inclusion and agricultural services to people with low incomes. The Acumen Academy offers courses related to social change; and a one-year leadership development Fellows Program for candidates in Bangladesh, Colombia, East Africa, India, Malaysia, Spain, the United Kingdom and West Africa. It has offices in San Francisco, as well as Colombia, India, Nigeria, Kenya, Pakistan and the UK.

Geographical Area of Activity: East and West Africa, Latin America, South Asia, UK, USA.

Restrictions: Does not award scholarships, stipends or funding for the Fellows Program.

Publications: Annual Report; *Lean Data* (monthly newsletter); reports.

Finance: Annual revenue US $58.1m., expenditure $39.6m. (31 Dec. 2023).

Principal Staff: CEO Jacqueline Novogratz; Pres. Carlyle Singer.

Contact Details: 40 Worth St, Suite 303, New York, NY 10013; tel. (212) 566-8821; internet acumen.org.

The Adolph and Esther Gottlieb Foundation, Inc
Founded in 1976 by Esther Gottlieb in memory of her husband Adolph, an abstract expressionist artist.

Activities: Runs two grant programmes that assist painters, sculptors and printmakers in a mature phase of their art who are in current financial need: the Emergency Grant Programme, available throughout the year, is typically worth US $5,000; and the Individual Support Grant, is awarded annually. In 2024 the Foundation awarded support grants worth $25,000 each to 20 artists.

Geographical Area of Activity: USA.

Restrictions: No grants to organizations, students, educational institutions, to those working in crafts, graphic artists or for projects.

Publications: Newsletter; Catalogue Raisonné.

Finance: Annual revenue US $865,331, expenditure $1.5m. (30 June 2022).

Board of Directors: Robert Mangold (Pres.); Sanford Hirsch (Exec. Dir, Treas. and Sec.).

Contact Details: 380 West Broadway, New York, NY 10012-5115; tel. (212) 226-0581; e-mail office@gottliebfoundation.org; internet www.gottliebfoundation.org.

Advance
Founded in 1970, as Esperança, Inc, to support the work of Fr Luke Tupper; affiliated with Fundação Esperança in Brazil; present name adopted in 2023.

Activities: Operates in the field of medicine and health in developing countries, working to improve healthcare, particularly focusing on reducing child mortality. Programmes include: ensuring food security, investing in food-related micro-businesses; improving water and sanitation, building community wells, water systems and toilets; preventing the spread of communicable diseases; providing secure housing, building and repairing homes; and the Volunteer Surgical Program, which organizes teams of medical volunteers from the USA for surgical missions. In the USA, the organization addresses the health needs of low-income and underserved families in the Phoenix Metropolitan area.

Geographical Area of Activity: Bolivia, Ecuador, Mozambique, Nicaragua, Peru, USA (Phoenix, AZ).

Restrictions: Does not make grants.

Publications: Annual Report; newsletter; blog.

Finance: Annual revenue US $1.8m., expenditure $2.3m. (30 Sept. 2023).

Board of Directors: Dawn Marie Buckland (Chair.); Al Marquiss (Vice-Chair.); Mark Nichols (Treas.); Concepcion Gallegos Henderson (Sec.).

Principal Staff: Pres. and CEO Jeri Royce.

Contact Details: 1911 West Earll Dr., Phoenix, AZ 85015; tel. (602) 252-7772; e-mail info@advancecommunity.org; internet advancecommunity.org.

Adventist Development and Relief Agency International—ADRA
Formed in 1956 by the Seventh-day Adventist Church as an independent humanitarian agency.

Activities: Works in the fields of humanitarian relief and development assistance. Main programme areas are: emergency response; livelihoods; education; and health. Student scholarships are available for ADRA Connections, a short-term voluntary service programme. The agency is present in 120 countries.

Geographical Area of Activity: International.

Restrictions: ADRA Connections scholarship applicants must be aged under 25 years and enrolled in secondary or higher education in Canada or the USA.

Publications: Annual Report; *Villages & Voyages* (quarterly newsletter).

Finance: Annual revenue US $98.5m., expenditure $105.4m. (31 Dec. 2022).

Board of Directors: Geoffrey Mbwana (Chair.); Paul H. Douglas (First Vice-Chair.); Audrey E. Andersson (Second Vice-Chair.).

Principal Staff: Pres. and Sec. Michael Kruger.

Contact Details: 12501 Old Columbia Pike, Silver Spring, MD 20904; tel. (800) 424-2372; e-mail info@adra.org; internet www.adra.org.

Africa-America Institute—AAI

Founded in 1953 to help to further development in Africa, improve African-American understanding and inform Americans about Africa.

Activities: Promotes engagement between African countries and the USA through education, training and dialogue. Main initiatives include: Pathways to Livelihood, which focuses on instructional reform at African universities; Africa Illuminated, which aims to improve the quality of information available about Africa and the African diaspora; the African Diplomatic Orientation and Engagement Program, which convenes African ambassadors and sectoral experts at peer-learning events twice a year; and the Transformational Leadership Program, which offers leadership development opportunities for African nationals working in the social sector. The Institute offers graduate scholarships, jointly with the East African Development Bank (EADB), for teachers and lecturers from EADB member countries (Kenya, Tanzania, Rwanda and Uganda) to pursue a Master's degree in science, technology, engineering and mathematics at Rutgers University, USA; and co-founded the Jim Ovia Foundation Leaders Scholarship for youth leaders from disadvantaged backgrounds to study at Ashesi University in Ghana or Covenant University in Nigeria. It organizes the Annual State of Education on Africa Conference; and the AAI Annual Awards Gala, recognizing the achievements of Africans and Afro-descendants.

Geographical Area of Activity: Eastern Africa, Ghana, Nigeria, Southern Africa, USA.

Restrictions: Scholarship applicants must be African citizens, residing in Africa.

Publications: Biennial Report; newsletter; *AAIONLINE* (quarterly newsletter); *African Perspectives*; *Africa Report* (magazine); policy forum, symposium and conference reports; art exhibition catalogues; bulletins; educational materials.

Finance: Annual revenue US $2.2m., expenditure $2.1m. (31 Dec. 2021).

Board of Trustees: Christal Jackson (Chair.); Bob McCarthy (Vice-Chair.).

Principal Staff: Pres. and CEO Kofi Appenteng.

Contact Details: 1 Grand Central Pl., 60 E 42nd St, Suite 1700, New York, NY 10165; tel. (212) 655-7686; e-mail info@aaiafrica.org; internet www.aaiafrica.org.

Alavi Foundation

Founded in 1973; formerly known as the Mostazafan Foundation of New York.

Activities: Supports young people's education, to prevent their radicalization and violent extremism. The Foundation promotes the teaching of Persian history, culture and religion, including Islamic studies; and supports primary and secondary schools, free health clinics, Farsi language schools, summer camps, and mosques. It awards scholarships and interest-free loans to graduates and postgraduates; makes grants to universities and colleges and for museum and art exhibitions; and in 2004 established the Disaster Relief Fund to provide humanitarian aid worldwide.

Geographical Area of Activity: Mainly USA.

Publications: Farsi language and religious materials.

Finance: Annual revenue US $2.1m., expenditure $6.0m. (31 March 2023).

Board of Trustees: Dr Hamid Yazdi (Pres.).

Contact Details: 650 Fifth Ave, Suite 1101, New York, NY 10019; tel. (212) 944-8333; e-mail info@alavifoundation.org; internet www.alavifoundation.org.

Alcoa Foundation

Established in 2016, with Arconic Foundation, out of Legacy Alcoa Foundation (f. 1952 as Alcoa Foundation by the Aluminum Company of America—Alcoa).

Activities: Operates where Alcoa Corpn has a presence, working with local communities. Main programmes focus on the environment; and education, jobs and economic development. The Foundation supports research programmes and initiatives that preserve biodiversity, particularly in relation to mining and refining activities, and mitigate climate change.

Geographical Area of Activity: Australia, Brazil, Canada, Hungary, Iceland, Norway, Spain, Suriname, USA.

Restrictions: Does not accept unsolicited applications.

Publications: Annual Report.

Finance: Annual revenue US $13.2m., expenditure $7.6m. (31 Dec. 2022).

Board: Caroline Rossignol (Pres.).

Contact Details: 201 Isabella St, Suite 500, Pittsburgh, PA 15212-5858; tel. (412) 315-2900; e-mail alcoa.foundation@alcoa.com; internet www.alcoa.com/foundation.

Alfred P. Sloan Foundation

Established in 1934 by Alfred Pritchard Sloan, Jr, Pres. and CEO of General Motors Co.

Activities: Operates through self-conducted programmes and grants to institutions within five areas: basic scientific research; higher education in science, technology, mathematics and engineering; digital technology; public understanding of science and technology; and the New York City Program. The Foundation sponsors the Sloan Fellowships for Basic Research, worth US $75,000 over two years, for young chemists, physicists, mathematicians, neuroscientists and economists in institutions in the USA and Canada.

Geographical Area of Activity: USA.

Restrictions: Rarely supports activities outside the USA; does not normally support projects in areas of religion, creative or performing arts, elementary or secondary education, the humanities, medical research or healthcare. No grants for endowments or capital works.

Publications: Annual Report; information brochure.

Finance: Annual income US $118.5m., expenditure $110.8m. (31 Dec. 2022).

Board of Trustees: Frederick A. Henderson (Chair.).

Principal Staff: Pres. Adam F. Falk.

Contact Details: 630 Fifth Ave, Suite 2200, New York, NY 10111-0242; tel. (212) 649-1649; e-mail frontdesk@sloan.org; internet www.sloan.org.

Alicia Patterson Foundation—APF

Founded in 1965 in memory of Alicia Patterson, editor and publisher of *Newsday*, by members of the Albright and Patterson families.

Activities: Awards one-year and six-month fellowships, worth US $40,000 and $20,000, respectively, to print journalists with at least five years' experience. Fellowship recipients pursue independent projects of significant interest in the

USA or overseas. Since 2016 the Foundation has also offered the Cissy Patterson Fellowship for Science and Environmental Writers. It maintains a database of Fellows.

Geographical Area of Activity: USA.

Restrictions: Fellowships open only to US citizens, or non-US citizens who work on US print publications; no grants are made for academic study.

Publications: Annual Report; *The APF Reporter* (quarterly); online magazine; information brochure; blog.

Finance: Annual revenue US $182,221, expenditure $454,732 (31 Dec. 2022).

Board of Directors: Robert Lee Hotz (Pres.).

Principal Staff: Exec. Dir Margaret Engel.

Contact Details: 1100 Vermont Ave NW, Suite 900, Washington, DC 20005; tel. (202) 393-5995; e-mail info @aliciapatterson.org; internet www.aliciapatterson.org.

Alight

Alight was founded in 1979 as the American Refugee Committee; renamed in 2019.

Activities: Alight humanitarians, of whom there are some 2,300, serve more than 4m. people in over 20 countries every year. In addition to addressing essential needs such as health care, clean water, shelter and protection, Alight provides livelihood programming and education. It focuses on women and girls, the population most affected by displacement, while also creating innovative solutions for those displaced due to climate or emergencies.

Geographical Area of Activity: International.

Publications: Annual report; 5-year strategy; blog.

Finance: Annual revenue US $72.7m., expenditure $77.7m. (31 March 2024).

Board of Directors: Lynn Hiestand (Chair.); Brenda Cassellius (Vice-Chair.); Mark Dayton (Treas.); Martha (Muffy) MacMillan (Sec.).

Principal Staff: CEO Jocelyn Wyatt.

Contact Details: 1325 Quincy St, NE, Suite A1, Minneapolis, MN 55413; tel. (612) 872-7060; e-mail info@wearealight.org; internet wearealight.org.

Alliance for International Exchange

Formed in 1992 as the Alliance for International Educational and Cultural Exchange by a group of US international exchange organizations.

Activities: Supports and promotes the interests of international exchange organizations in the USA through advocacy, information services and networking. The Alliance organizes a programme of government relations activities and provides a discussion forum for leaders of international exchange groups. The McCarry Leadership Award supports the development of exchange professionals in the USA, waiving their registration fee for the Annual Alliance Meeting and reimbursing them up to US $1,000 for travel expenses. Comprises 88 member organizations.

Geographical Area of Activity: USA.

Restrictions: Award applicants must be aged under 35 years and have at least three years' experience in the exchange field.

Publications: *The Policy Monitor* (quarterly journal); *News News News* (bulletin); *Action Alerts*; factsheets; reports.

Finance: Annual revenue US $843,601, expenditure $1.1m. (31 Dec. 2022).

Board of Directors: Jennifer Clinton (Chair.); Tara Hofmann (Vice-Chair.); Goran T. Rannefors (Treas.).

Principal Staff: Exec. Dir Mark Overmann.

Contact Details: 1828 L St, NW, Suite 1150, Washington, DC 20036; tel. (202) 293-6141; e-mail info@alliance-exchange.org; internet www.alliance-exchange.org.

The Ambrose Monell Foundation

Established in 1953 by Maude Monell Vetlesen in honour of her first husband, Ambrose Monell, a business person and financier; shares an administration with the G. Unger Vetlesen Foundation (q.v.).

Activities: Supports scientific, cultural, educational and other charitable initiatives through funding early-stage research and social initiatives. The Foundation's signature programme is funding the Monell Chemical Senses Center at the University of Pennsylvania.

Geographical Area of Activity: USA.

Restrictions: Does not accept unsolicited applications.

Publications: Annual Report; case studies.

Finance: Annual revenue US $20.3m., expenditure $21.2m. (31 Dec. 2022).

Board of Directors: Ambrose K. Monell (Pres. and Treas.); Maurizio J. Morello (Exec. Vice-Pres. and Asst Treas.); Maia Maude Monell (Vice-Pres.).

Principal Staff: Dir Gary K. Beauchamp.

Contact Details: c/o Fulton Vittoria, LLP, 1 Rockefeller Plaza, Suite 301, New York, NY 10020-2002; tel. (212) 586-0700; e-mail contact@monellfoundation.org; internet www.monellfoundation.org.

American Association of University Women—AAUW Educational Foundation

Established in 1959 by the American Association of University Women (AAUW) to encourage the continuation of education beyond college.

Activities: Operates nationally and internationally in the field of education. The association provides one-year American Fellowships (worth US $6,000–$30,000) for US women for dissertation writing and postdoctoral research, as well as short-term publications fellowships. Career Development Grants ($2,000–$12,000) support women who hold a Bachelor's degree and who are preparing to advance or change their careers, or re-enter the workforce. Community Action Grants ($3,000–$10,000) are offered to individuals, branches of the Association and state organizations, as well as community-based non-profit organizations for innovative programmes or non-degree research that promote education and equality for women and girls; and one-year International Fellowships ($18,000–$30,000) to non-US citizens or permanent residents of the USA for study in the USA at Master's, PhD or postdoctoral level. International Fellowships alumnae may apply for International Project Grants ($5,000–$7,000) for community-based projects in their home countries. Research Publication Grants in Engineering, Medicine, and Science ($10,000–$35,000) are available to women conducting basic research. The Foundation also offers Selected Professions Fellowships ($5,000–$18,000) and scholarships; and makes several prestigious national awards recognizing excellence in achievement. The AAUW Action Fund focuses on educating and registering women voters.

Geographical Area of Activity: International.

Restrictions: Grants only to women.

Publications: Annual Report; newsletter; *AAUW Outlook* (magazine).

Finance: Annual fellowships and grants awarded US $6.2m. (30 June 2024).

Board of Directors: Cheryl Sorokin (Chair.); Gloria Bañuelos (Vice-Chair.).

Principal Staff: CEO Gloria L. Blackwell; Man. Dir and Chief of Staff Shannon Wolfe.

Contact Details: 1310 L St NW, Suite 1000, Washington, DC 20005; tel. (202) 785-7700; e-mail connect@aauw.org; internet www.aauw.org/resources/programs/fellowships-grants.

American Council of Learned Societies—ACLS

Established in 1919 by representatives of 13 learned societies.

Activities: Comprises 81 scholarly organizations concerned with the humanities and related social sciences. The Council offers grants and fellowships to US citizens or permanent residents to carry out postdoctoral research in the humanities. Programmes are concerned with digital humanities, collaborative research and scholars working outside the academy. Internationally, it supports various research and planning activities to encourage research on specific countries or regions of the world, as well as comparative and transnational research projects. Key initiatives include the African Humanities Program, Center for Educational Exchange with Viet Nam and the Robert H. N. Ho Family; and administration of the Henry Luce Foundation (q.v.)/ACLS Program in China Studies.

Geographical Area of Activity: International.

Restrictions: No funding for fellowships or scholarships for undergraduate study; no grants for creative work.

Publications: Annual Report; newsletter; *ACLS Reports*; *ACLS Centennial Vol.*; *ACLS Occasional Papers*; *ACLS Humanities E-Book*; *East European Politics and Societies and Cultures—EEPS* (journal); *American National Biography*.

Finance: Annual revenue US $48.0m., expenditure $37.8m. (30 June 2022).

Board of Directors: Marwan M. Kraidy (Chair.); Jimena Canales (Vice-Chair.); Melani McAlister (Treas.); Dana A. Williams (Sec.).

Principal Staff: Pres. Joy Connolly; Vice-Pres. and COO James Shulman.

Contact Details: 633 Third Ave, 8th Floor, New York, NY 10017-6706; tel. (212) 697-1505; e-mail fellowships@acls.org; internet www.acls.org.

American Councils for International Education

Established in 1974; comprises the American Council of Teachers of Russian (ACTR), American Councils for Collaboration in Education and Language Study (ACCELS), American Center for Education and Research (ACER), American Center for Education and Testing (ACET) and American Councils Research Center.

Activities: Works in the fields of cultural exchange, language training and professional development. The Council administers 5,000 scholarships and fellowships annually in 148 countries of significance to US national security, prosperity and peace. Alumni include national and business leaders, ministers, legislators and ambassadors.

Geographical Area of Activity: International.

Restrictions: Not a grantmaking organization in its own right; administers funding from US government agencies, charitable foundations and foreign ministries of education.

Publications: Annual Report; newsletter; journals; articles; presentations; textbooks.

Finance: Annual revenue US $110.9m., expenditure $109.4m. (30 June 2023).

Board of Trustees: Amb. John Ordway (Chair.); Edith Falk (Vice-Chair.).

Principal Staff: Pres. and CEO Lisa Choate.

Contact Details: 1828 L St NW, Suite 1200, Washington, DC 20036; tel. (202) 833-7522; e-mail info@americancouncils.org; internet www.americancouncils.org.

American Enterprise Institute—AEI

Established in 1938, as the American Enterprise Association, by Lewis H. Brown, Pres. of Johns Manville, an asbestos manufacturer; a think tank.

Activities: Carries out public policy research and educational outreach in the promotion of democracy, free enterprise and entrepreneurial culture, social solidarity and strong international US leadership. Programme areas include: the economy; education; foreign and defence policy; healthcare; politics and public opinion; poverty; society and culture; and technology and innovation. The Institute organizes academic programmes; and offers leadership training and internships. It hosts the Open Source Policy Center (f. 2013), an incubator for open source projects, models and digital apps.

Geographical Area of Activity: USA.

Publications: Annual Report; *National Affairs* (quarterly journal); *AEI Today* (daily newsletter); *AEI This Week* (weekly newsletter); reports; working papers; books; surveys.

Finance: Annual revenue US $53.8m., expenditure $66.8m. (30 June 2023).

Board of Trustees: Daniel A. D'Aniello (Chair.).

Principal Staff: Pres. Robert Doar.

Contact Details: 1789 Massachusetts Ave, NW, Washington, DC 20036; tel. (202) 862-5800; internet www.aei.org.

American Express Foundation

Established in 1954 by the American Express Co, a financial services company.

Activities: Offers grants to initiatives through three main programmes: developing personal, business and leadership skills of social purpose leaders and social entrepreneurs through the American Express Leadership Academy; promoting stewardship of historic places and preserving cultural heritage; and encouraging community volunteering, and supporting disaster preparedness, relief and recovery programmes.

Geographical Area of Activity: International.

Restrictions: Grants only to non-profit organizations; Historic Preservation grants by invitation only; does not fund scholarships for leadership training.

Publications: *CSR Report*; *Grant List*.

Finance: Annual revenue US $704,482, expenditure $21.2m. (31 Dec. 2022).

Board of Directors: Mike O'Neil (Chair.); Jeff Campbell (Treas.); Mary Ellen Craig (Sec.).

Principal Staff: Pres. Tim McClimon.

Contact Details: 200 Vesey St, 48th Floor, New York, NY 10285; tel. (212) 640-4648; e-mail corporate.social.responsibility@aexp.com; internet www.americanexpress.com/en-us/company/corporate-sustainability/community-impact.

American Foundation for the Blind—AFB

Founded in 1921, with the support of M. C. Migel, Pres. of the Allied Silk Trading Corp, who wanted to help soldiers who were blinded during the First World War.

Activities: Provides educational, vocational, advisory and social services, and publications (including 'talking books') related to blindness; and conducts public policy research and advocacy. Priority areas are education, employment and ageing. In partnership with the American Council of the Blind, the Foundation awards scholarships for visually impaired and blind undergraduate and graduate students, ranging from US $2,000 to $7,500. It also offers the Stephen Garff Marriott Award to a blind or visually impaired individual for remarkable mentorship or success in their career; and Helen Keller Achievement Awards to individuals who are role models or improve the quality of life of individuals with visual impairment.

Geographical Area of Activity: USA.

Publications: Annual Report; *AFB Newsletter*; *Journal of Visual Impairment & Blindness* (10 a year); *AccessWorld* (magazine, 6 a year); *AFB Directory of Services for Blind and Visually Impaired Persons in the US and Canada*; blog.

Finance: Annual revenue US $1.9m., expenditure $7.5m. (30 June 2024).

Board of Trustees: Debbie Dennis (Chair.).

Principal Staff: Pres. and CEO Eric Bridges.

Contact Details: River Tower, 1108 Third Ave, Suite 200, Huntington, WV 25701; 2900 S Quincy St, Suite 200, Arlington, VA 22206; tel. (202) 502-7600; e-mail info@afb.org; internet www.afb.org.

UNITED STATES OF AMERICA

American Foundation for Pharmaceutical Education—AFPE

Established in 1942 by leaders of the National Drug Trade Conference.

Activities: Funds research and offers grants, fellowships and scholarships in the field of pharmaceutical sciences, particularly pharmaceutics, pharmacology, manufacturing pharmacy, pharmaco-economics and medicinal chemistry. Awards include: Student Gateway Research Scholarships; First Year Graduate School Scholarships; Pre-Doctoral Graduate Scholarships in the Pharmaceutical Sciences; Clinical Pharmacy Post-Pharmaceutical Doctoral Fellowships in the Biomedical Research Sciences; and Pharmacy Faculty Investigator Grants.

Geographical Area of Activity: USA.

Restrictions: Grants are usually open only to those studying in the USA.

Publications: Brochure.

Finance: Annual revenue US $1.1m., expenditure $771,260 (31 Dec. 2021).

Board of Directors: Dr Calvin H. Knowlton (Chair.); Dr Lucinda L. Maine (Vice-Chair.); John M. Couric, Jr (Treas.).

Principal Staff: Pres. and Sec. Ellen L. Woods.

Contact Details: 11325 Random Hills Rd, Suite 360A-105 Fairfax, VA 22030; tel. (571) 404-0471; e-mail woods@afpepharm.org; internet www.afpepharm.org.

American Friends Service Committee—AFSC

Established in 1917; a Quaker organization that aims to overcome poverty, injustice and strife in the world through practical aid and non-violent means, based on the belief in the good of every person, regardless of race or religion.

Activities: Addresses the root causes of poverty, injustice and conflict, working for relief through immediate aid and long-term development projects. Main programmes focus on: building economic justice; creating inclusive communities; defending immigrants' rights; ending mass incarceration; international peacebuilding; and justice in the Palestinian Territories and Israel.

Geographical Area of Activity: East and South-East Asia, Latin America, Middle East, North America, sub-Saharan Africa, USA.

Publications: Annual Report; *Quaker Action* (magazine, 3 a year); *Wage Peace* (newsletter); blog.

Finance: Annual revenue US $48.2m., expenditure $38.4m. (30 Sept. 2023).

Board of Directors: Álvaro Alvarado (Presiding Clerk); Steve Fortuna (Asst Clerk); Frederick Dettmer (Recording Clerk); Dave Wells (Treas.).

Principal Staff: Gen. Sec. Joyce Ajlouny; Deputy Gen. Sec. Hector Cortez.

Contact Details: 1501 Cherry St, Philadelphia, PA 19102; tel. (215) 241-7000; e-mail ask@afsc.org; internet www.afsc.org.

American Heart Association—AHA

Founded in 1924 by six cardiologists; the American Stroke Association—ASA—was created as a division in 1997. Comprises the Institute for Precision Cardiovascular Medicine.

Activities: Works in the field of public health, carrying out research into basic, clinical and population science. The Association carries out cardiopulmonary resuscitation (CPR) education and training and provides science-based treatment guidelines for healthcare professionals; educates legislators, policymakers and the public, advocating changes to protect and improve people's health. It funds several research networks in the USA: the ASA/Bugher Foundation Centers of Excellence in Hemorrhagic Stroke; and thematic Strategically Focused Research Networks (arrhythmias and sudden cardiac death; atrial fibrillation; cardiometabolic health and Type 2 diabetes; children; diversity in clinical trials; health technologies and innovation; obesity; and vascular disease), which offer postdoctoral fellowships. Volunteer experts select the scientific research most worthy of funding. AHA/CHF Congenital Heart Defect Research Awards are made in partnership with the Children's Heart Foundation. Research Partnership Programs identify and support specific science areas. Global programmes in collaboration with partner organizations include those targeting women, children, hospital care improvement and bystander CPR. Has 144 local offices nationwide.

Geographical Area of Activity: International.

Restrictions: Awards only to non-profit institutions in Canada, Mexico and the USA; awards for research outside the USA are limited to principal investigators who are US citizens.

Publications: Annual Report; *Stroke Connection* (magazine, 2 a month); *Research Insider* (newsletter); *Heart & Stroke Encyclopedia* (online); journals; medical guidelines; scientific reports; e-books.

Finance: Annual revenue US $1,305.9m., expenditure $1,346.3m. (30 June 2024).

Board of Directors: Marsha Jones (Chair.); Lee Shapiro (Chair.-elect); Raymond P. Vara (Immediate Past Chair.); Linda Gooden (Treas.).

Principal Staff: Pres. Dr Keith Churchwell; Pres.-elect Stacey E. Rosen; Immediate Past Pres. Dr Joseph C. Wu; CEO Nancy Brown.

Contact Details: National Center, 7272 Greenville Ave, Dallas, TX 75231-4596; tel. (214) 570-5943; e-mail inquiries@heart.org; internet www.heart.org.

American Historical Association—AHA

Established in 1884 by Herbert Baxter Adams and other historians attending the annual meeting of the American Social Science Association.

Activities: Advocates history education, the professional work of historians and historical thinking in public life; and promotes new approaches in history education and scholarship. The Association offers fellowships and a range of awards for: publications (including books, articles, film and digital formats) and scholarly and professional distinction; research; and to attend annual meetings. It maintains the *Directory of History Departments and Organizations* and the *Directory of History Dissertations*, containing more than 57,000 dissertations from the USA and Canada; and compiles materials and tools to help historians with remote teaching and learning. Has more than 11,500 individual and institutional members. The National History Center (f. 2002) was established with a focus on the relationship between history and public policy, providing historical perspectives on current issues and organizing programmes for policymakers, journalists, educators and the public.

Geographical Area of Activity: USA.

Restrictions: Research grants to members only.

Publications: Annual Report; *American Historical Review*; *Perspectives on History* (magazine); *Directory of History Departments and Organizations* (online); *Directory of History Dissertations*; Remote Teaching Resources (online); doctoral dissertations; essays; studies.

Finance: Annual revenue US $5.8m., expenditure $6.2m. (30 June 2023).

Council: Suzanne Marchand (Pres.-elect); Ben Vinson, III (Pres.); Thavolia Glymph (Past Pres.); William F. Wechsler (Treas.).

Principal Staff: Exec. Dir Jim Grossman; Deputy Dir Dana Schaffer.

Contact Details: 400 A St SE, Washington, DC 20003-3889; tel. (202) 544-2422; e-mail info@historians.org; internet www.historians.org.

American Institute of Pakistan Studies

Founded in 1973 by Dr Hafeez Malik, a political scientist and social activist.

Activities: Promotes academic study of Pakistan in the USA and encourages scholarly exchange between the USA and Pakistan. The Institute offers pre- and postdoctoral research fellowships, summer research grants and conference travel grants to scholars who are affiliated to US academic institution(s) and are engaged in research on Pakistan, in all fields of the humanities and social sciences. It administers lectureships and organizes and/or supports academic conferences. It has an office in Islamabad, Pakistan.

Geographical Area of Activity: Pakistan, USA.

Restrictions: Grants only to scholars affiliated to US academic institutions.

Publications: Annual Report; *AIPS Newsletter*; *The Annual of Urdu Studies; Modern Asian Studies*.

Finance: Annual revenue US $647,178, expenditure $739,297 (30 Sept. 2022).

Executive Committee: Dr Matthew A. Cook (Pres.); Daniel Majchrowicz (Vice-Pres.); Michael Hirsch (Treas.); Sameetah Agha (Sec.).

Principal Staff: US Dir Laura Hammond; Pakistan Dir Aalia Sohail Khan.

Contact Details: 702 Langdon St, Madison, WI 53706; tel. (608) 265-1471; e-mail aips@pakistanstudies-aips.org; internet www.pakistanstudies-aips.org.

American Jewish Joint Distribution Committee—JDC

Founded in 1914; a Jewish humanitarian organization.

Activities: JDC is the leading global Jewish humanitarian organization, working in 70 countries. JDC rescues Jewish people in danger, provides aid to vulnerable Jewish communities, develops innovative solutions to Israel's most complex social challenges, cultivates a Jewish future, and leads the Jewish community's response to global crises like natural disasters and public health emergencies. The Entwine initiative offers young adults overseas volunteering, travel and educational experiences through a Jewish lens.

Geographical Area of Activity: International.

Restrictions: Does not accept unsolicited funding requests. Entwine accepts applications for its programmes.

Publications: Annual Report; newsletter; reports.

Finance: Annual revenue US $393.8m., expenditure $390.3m. (31 Dec. 2024).

Board of Trustees: Annie Sandler (Pres.); Mark B. Sisiky (Chair.); Geoffrey Colvin (Treas.); Stuart Kurlander (Sec.).

Principal Staff: CEO Ariel Zwang; Deputy CEO Pablo Weinsteiner.

Contact Details: POB 4124, New York, NY 10163; tel. (212) 687-6200; e-mail info@jdc.org; internet www.jdc.org.

American Jewish World Service—AJWS

Established in 1985 by American Jews to help poor and oppressed people globally.

Activities: Works to end poverty and defend human human dignity and rights through providing financial support to more than 500 social justice organizations in 18 countries; and advocating for laws and policies in the USA that will improve people's lives worldwide. Main programmes areas are: civil and political rights; humanitarian and disaster response; land, water and climate justice; ending child marriage and achieving gender equality; and sexual health and rights. The organization leads overseas study tours lasting 7–10 days; and offers six-month Global Justice Fellowships to train rabbis in the USA to become global justice activists. In the USA, young professionals are invited to join the Global Circle of donors, which has chapters in Los Angeles, New York, San Francisco and Washington, DC.

Geographical Area of Activity: Africa, Asia, Latin America and the Caribbean, USA.

Publications: Annual Report; newsletter; *AJWS Reports* (magazine); briefings; brochures; factsheets; blog.

Finance: Annual revenue US $44.8m., expenditure $46.8m. (30 April 2024).

Board of Trustees: Jill Minneman (Chair.); Scott Waxman (Vice-Chair.); Bruce Rosenblum (Treas.); Shuli Karkowsky (Sec.).

Principal Staff: Pres. and CEO Robert Bank.

Contact Details: 45 West 36th St, New York, NY 10018-7904; tel. (212) 792-2900; e-mail ajws@ajws.org; internet www.ajws.org.

American Near East Refugee Aid—Anera

Established in 1968 to assist Palestinian refugees after the Arab–Israeli War of 1967.

Activities: Works in the fields of humanitarian assistance and sustainable development. The organization runs long-term health, education and economic development programmes; and provides humanitarian and emergency relief to Palestinians and other marginalized communities, including refugees from the Syrian Arab Republic. The organization has 11 offices and warehouses in Gaza, the West Bank, Lebanon and Jordan.

Geographical Area of Activity: Jordan, Lebanon, Palestinian Territories, USA.

Publications: Annual Report; newsletter (quarterly); capacity statements; health education materials; situation reports; blog.

Finance: Annual revenue US $204.9m., expenditure $182.6m. (31 May 2024).

Board of Directors: Joseph P. Saba (Chair.); Grace Tompkins (Vice-Chair.); Lawrence A. Hamdan (Treas.); Dr Alfred N. Khoury (Sec.).

Principal Staff: Pres. and CEO Sean Carroll.

Contact Details: 1111 14th St NW, Suite 400, Washington, DC 20005; tel. (202) 266-9700; e-mail anera@anera.org; internet www.anera.org.

American Philosophical Society—APS

Founded in 1743 by Benjamin Franklin, a printer, scientist and diplomat.

Activities: Promotes scholarly research in the sciences and humanities. The Society offers about 185 awards and prizes each year which are open to US citizens and to foreign nationals for research in the USA. Grants range from US $1,000 to $6,500 and programmes include: Blumberg Grants in Astrobiology; Franklin Research Grants; the Lewis and Clark Fund; Lewis and Clark Fund in Astrobiology; Library David Center Fellowship; Library Digital Humanities Fellowship; Library Digital Knowledge Sharing Fellowship; Library Short-Term Fellowship; Library NASI Undergraduate Internship; and Phillips Fund for Native American Research. Other fellowship programmes offer larger amounts ranging from $28,000 to $60,000; these include: the Daland Fellowship in Clinical Investigation; John Hope Franklin Dissertation Fellowship; Library Long-Term Post-Doctoral Fellowship; Library Long-Term Pre-Doctoral Fellowship; and Mellon Curatorial Post-Doctoral Fellowship. The APS Library and Museum offer short- and long-term resident Library Fellowships for subject-specific research and digital humanities; and postdoctoral Museum Curatorial Fellowships for PhD graduates to experience curatorial work while undertaking an independent research project. The Society holds two annual conferences or symposia. It has a library of 300,000 vols and around 11m. manuscripts, specializing in the history of science and early American history; it comprises the David Center for the American Revolution, Center for Native American and Indigenous Research and Center for Digital Scholarship.

Geographical Area of Activity: USA.

Restrictions: Grants to residents of the USA or to US citizens abroad; foreign nationals whose research is to be carried out in the USA may also apply; institutions are not eligible.

Publications: *News* (1 a year); *Proceedings* (quarterly); *Transactions* (5 a year); *Mendel Newsletter* (annual); memoirs; yearbook; blog.

Finance: Annual revenue US $12.3m., expenditure $13.2m. (31 Dec. 2022).

Council: Roger S. Bagnall (Pres.); Jacqueline K. Barton, Harvey Fineberg, Nina G. Jablonski (Vice-Pres); Marna C. Whittington (Treas.); David Skorton (Sec.).

Principal Staff: Exec. Officer Patrick Spero.

Contact Details: 104 South Fifth St, Philadelphia, PA 19106-3387; tel. (215) 440-3400; e-mail libfellows@amphilsoc.org; internet www.amphilsoc.org.

American-Scandinavian Foundation—ASF

Founded in 1910 (incorporated in the State of New York in 1911) to promote international understanding through educational and cultural exchange between the USA and Denmark, Finland, Iceland, Norway and Sweden.

Activities: Promotes intellectual and creative exchanges between the USA and Nordic countries through awarding fellowships and grants; and sponsoring cultural programmes and internships/training. The Foundation offers several prizes, including an annual Translation Prize, Gold Medal and Cultural Awards. It operates Scandinavia House: the Nordic Center in America, which presents exhibitions, films, concerts, lectures, and has a gallery, auditorium and library.

Geographical Area of Activity: Denmark, Finland, Iceland, Norway, Sweden, USA.

Publications: Biannual Report; *Scandinavian Review* (3 a year); *Scan* (quarterly newsletter); *The Longboat* (newsletter).

Finance: Annual revenue US $6.8m., expenditure $4.6m. (30 June 2022).

Board of Trustees: Dr Terje Lande (Chair.); Anders Iversen (Deputy Chair.); Lizanne Kindler (Vice-Chair. for Denmark); Dr Aili Flint (Vice-Chair. for Finland); Sigríður Benediktsdóttir (Vice-Chair. for Iceland); Bente Svensen Frantz (Vice-Chair. for Norway); Monika Heimbold (Vice-Chair. for Sweden); Steven B. Peri (Vice-Chair. for the USA); Henrik Steffensen (Treas.); Lynn Carter (Sec.).

Principal Staff: Pres. and CEO Edward P. Gallagher.

Contact Details: Scandinavia House, 58 Park Ave, between 37th and 38th Sts, New York, NY 10016-3007; tel. (212) 779-3587; e-mail info@amscan.org; internet www.amscan.org.

American Schools of Oriental Research—ASOR

Founded in 1900 by the Society of Biblical Literature, the Archaeological Institute of America and the American Oriental Society.

Activities: Operates internationally in the fields of education and the humanities by conducting and supporting research into Middle Eastern culture, especially through archaeological, anthropological and historical projects. The organization has three affiliated research centres—the W. F. Albright Institute of Archaeological Research in Jerusalem, American Center of Oriental Research in Amman, and Cyprus American Archaeological Research Institute in Nicosia—and also the Baghdad Committee (Committee on Mesopotamian Civilization); collectively, they offer a range of summer stipends, research fellowships, dig scholarships and excavation grants for archaeologists and students, ranging from US $1,500 to $10,000. It has more than 2,200 individual members and 53 institutional members.

Geographical Area of Activity: Middle East, USA.

Publications: *Bulletin of the American Schools of Oriental Research*; *News@ASOR* (2 a month); *The Ancient Near East Today* (weekly newsletter); *Near Eastern Archaeology*; *Journal of Cuneiform Studies; Archaeological Report Series*; books; journals; monographs.

Finance: Annual revenue US $3.8m., expenditure $2.0m. (30 June 2024).

Board of Trustees: Sheldon Fox (Chair.); Sharon Herbert (Pres.); Jane DeRose Evans (Pres.-elect); Charles Ellwood Jones (Vice-Pres.); Emily Miller Bonney (Treas.); Sarah Jarmer Scott (Sec.).

Principal Staff: Exec. Dir Dr Andrew G. Vaughn.

Contact Details: The James F. Strange Center, 209 Commerce St, Alexandria, VA 22314; tel. (703) 789-9229; e-mail info@asor.org; internet www.asor.org.

AmeriCares Foundation, Inc

Officially established in 1982, having been initiated in 1975 by Robert C. Macauley, a paper broker, and his wife Alma Jane (Leila) Macauley.

Activities: Operates in the fields of emergency relief and development, with a focus on health. The organization provides healthcare, medicines and medical supplies to people affected by poverty or disaster, helping to rebuild communities and restore health services. In the USA, it supplies more than 1,000 clinics for uninsured or underinsured people, including four free clinics in Connecticut. Works in more than 85 countries, with health programmes in over 30 countries; and has offices in Texas, Colombia, El Salvador, Haiti, India, Liberia, Malawi, the Philippines, Puerto Rico and Tanzania.

Geographical Area of Activity: Central Asia, Central and South-Eastern Europe, Latin America and the Caribbean, Middle East, North America, South Asia, South-East Asia, sub-Saharan Africa.

Publications: Annual Report.

Finance: Annual revenue US $1,560.8m., expenditure $1,512.9m. (30 June 2023).

Board of Directors: Susan Grossman (Chair.); Jeffrey T. Becker (Vice-Chair.).

Principal Staff: Pres. and CEO Christine Squires.

Contact Details: 88 Hamilton Ave, Stamford, CT 06902; tel. (203) 658-9500; e-mail info@americares.org; internet www.americares.org.

Amerind Foundation, Inc

Founded in 1937 by William Shirley Fulton, an archaeologist.

Activities: Works in the fields of anthropological field research and collections study. The Foundation organizes advanced research seminars and visiting scholar programmes; and co-operates with organizations and individuals engaged in similar work. It maintains an anthropological research centre; an archaeological, ethnographic and fine arts museum complex; archaeological site files, photographic collections and a research library containing 22,000 vols.

Geographical Area of Activity: Mexico, USA.

Restrictions: Grants are made only for advanced seminars.

Publications: Annual Report; *Amerind Notebook* (newsletter); Amerind Technical Reports; *Amerind New World Studies Series*; *Amerind Studies in Archaeology*.

Finance: Annual revenue US $2.0m., expenditure $1.5m. (31 Dec. 2022).

Board of Directors: Laura Brown (Chair.); Christine Szuter (Vice-Chair.); Arch M. Brown, Jr (Treas.); Marilyn J. Fulton (Sec.).

Principal Staff: Pres. and CEO Dr Eric Kaldahl.

Contact Details: POB 400, 2100 North Amerind Rd, Dragoon, AZ 85609; tel. (520) 586-3666; e-mail amerind@amerind.org; internet www.amerind.org.

amfAR—The Foundation for AIDS Research

Founded in 1985 by the merger of the AIDS Medical Foundation and the National AIDS Research Foundation.

Activities: Supports AIDS research, AIDS prevention and treatment education; and advocates for sound AIDS-related public policy. The Foundation offers grants to non-profit institutions for basic biomedical and clinical research in fields related to HIV/AIDS and for postdoctoral investigators to study at other institutions. In 2001 it established TREAT Asia

AMIDEAST   UNITED STATES OF AMERICA

(Therapeutics Research, Education, and AIDS Training in Asia), a network including 21 adult and 20 paediatric clinical sites in 12 countries, and various regional, national and community organizations. Has an office in Washington, DC.

Geographical Area of Activity: International.

Restrictions: Grants only to non-profit organizations.

Publications: Annual Report; *amfAR e-News* (monthly newsletter); *amfAR News* (biannual newsletter); *TREAT Asia Report* (quarterly); *Ending the AIDS Epidemic*.

Finance: Annual revenue US $31.0m., expenditure $29.6m. (30 Sept. 2024).

Board of Trustees: T. Ryan Greenawalt, Kevin McClatchy (Co-Chair.); Jeffrey Schoenfeld (Treas.); Dr Robert L. Traynham II (Sec.).

Principal Staff: CEO Kevin Robert Frost; CEO-elect Kyle Clifford.

Contact Details: 120 Wall St, 13th Floor, New York, NY 10005-3908; tel. (212) 806-1600; e-mail Information@amfar.org; internet www.amfar.org.

AMIDEAST—America-Mideast Educational and Training Services, Inc

Founded in 1951 by Dorothy Thompson to strengthen mutual understanding and co-operation between Americans and peoples of the Middle East and North Africa.

Activities: Fosters mutual understanding through international educational and cultural exchanges. The organization administers publicly and privately sponsored programmes in the Middle East and North Africa, including: employability skills for women; professional training and development; English language training; institutional development; and educational advising and testing. It also administers overseas study programmes for US citizens; and develops and distributes educational resources on the Middle East and North Africa to US schools and libraries. Has more than 20 offices in 11 countries.

Geographical Area of Activity: Egypt, Iraq, Jordan, Kuwait, Lebanon, Libya, Morocco, Palestinian Territories, Saudi Arabia, Tunisia, United Arab Emirates, USA, Yemen.

Restrictions: Not a grantmaking organization.

Publications: Annual Report; newsletter; *The Advising Quarterly*.

Finance: Annual revenue US $48.3m., expenditure $48.8m. (30 Sept. 2021).

Board of Directors: Deborah K. Jones (Chair.); Antoine N. Frem (Vice-Chair.); Amjad Ahmad (Treas.); Hon. Michael Pelletier (Sec.).

Principal Staff: Pres. and CEO Greta C. Holtz.

Contact Details: 2025 M St, NW, Suite 600, Washington, DC 20036-3363; tel. (202) 776-9600; e-mail inquiries@amideast.org; internet www.amideast.org.

The Andrew W. Mellon Foundation

Founded in 1969 by the merger of the Avalon Foundation (f. 1940 by Ailsa Mellon Bruce) and the Old Dominion Foundation (f. 1941 by Paul Mellon).

Activities: Operates four programmes nationally in the areas of: the arts and culture; higher learning and humanities education; scholarly communications; equitable access to deep public knowledge; and humanities in place, including the Monuments Project. The Foundation offers Distinguished Achievement in the Humanities awards annually to academics holding tenured positions at US universities.

Geographical Area of Activity: International (mainly USA).

Restrictions: Rarely makes grants to non-US organizations; no grants to individuals.

Publications: Annual Report; newsletter; blog.

Finance: Total assets US $8,028.0m.; annual expenditure $617.1m. (31 Dec. 2023).

Principal Staff: Pres. Elizabeth Alexander.

Contact Details: 140 East 62nd St, New York, NY 10065; tel. (212) 838-8400; e-mail inquiries@mellon.org; internet www.mellon.org.

The Andy Warhol Foundation for the Visual Arts, Inc

Founded in 1987 by the will of artist Andy Warhol.

Activities: Works to advance the visual arts. The Foundation makes grants to institutions that support artists, through funding curatorial programmes and exhibitions in museums, universities and other organizations; and initiatives that promote the health, welfare and freedom of expression of artists. It offers the Wynn Kramarsky Freedom of Artistic Expression Award to recognize the work of organizations for preserving and defending the First Amendment rights of artists. Curatorial Research Fellowships are offered for research in the field of contemporary art.

Geographical Area of Activity: USA.

Restrictions: Does not make grants to individuals; mainly grants to organizations in the USA.

Publications: Annual Report; Catalogue Raisonné.

Finance: Annual revenue US $23.5m., expenditure $26.5m. (30 April 2023).

Board of Directors: Deborah Willis (Chair.); Kathleen C. Maurer (Treas.).

Principal Staff: Pres. Joel Wachs.

Contact Details: 65 Bleecker St, 7th Floor, New York, NY 10012; tel. (212) 387-7555; e-mail info@warholfoundation.org; internet warholfoundation.org.

The Annenberg Foundation

Founded in 1989 by Walter H. Annenberg, a publisher and broadcaster.

Activities: Works in the fields of the arts, community, education, global humanitarian efforts and leadership development in non-profit organizations through awarding grants and providing technical assistance. The Foundation gives priority to non-profit organizations serving the counties of Los Angeles, Ventura, Orange, Riverside and San Bernardino in California. It has established university schools for communications, journalism and public policy; in 2013 established the Wallis Annenberg Center for the Performing Arts in Beverly Hills, CA; with an office in Conshohocken, PA.

Geographical Area of Activity: International.

Restrictions: Only accepts unsolicited applications through the Community Grantmaking programme; does not accept unsolicited requests from organizations outside the USA; no grants to individuals, for scholarships or publication of books.

Publications: Application Guidelines; online educational resources.

Finance: Annual revenue US $149.0m., expenditure $99.5m. (31 Dec. 2022).

Board of Directors: Wallis Annenberg (Chair., Pres. and CEO).

Principal Staff: Exec. Dir Cinny Kennard.

Contact Details: 2000 Ave of the Stars, Suite 1000S, Los Angeles, CA 90067; tel. (310) 209-4560; e-mail info@annenberg.org; internet annenberg.org.

The Annie E. Casey Foundation

Established in 1948 by Jim Casey, founder of United Parcel Service, and his siblings in honour of their mother; part of the Casey Philanthropies, including Casey Family Programs (f. 1966) and the Marguerite Casey Foundation (f. 2001).

Activities: Works to improve the lives of children at risk of poor educational, economic, social and health outcomes through strengthening families and communities and ensuring access to opportunity. Main programmes focus on: child welfare and foster care; community development; employment education and training; and juvenile justice. The Foundation funds activities including policy advocacy and analysis, community and youth engagement, research and evaluation; and

UNITED STATES OF AMERICA

initiatives in the areas of leadership development and racial and ethnic equity and inclusion. The average grant size is around US $76,000. Has an office in Baltimore, MD.

Geographical Area of Activity: USA, Puerto Rico, US Virgin Islands.

Restrictions: Does not accept unsolicited applications or make grants to individuals; does not fund projects outside the USA.

Publications: Annual Report; newsletter; *Kids Count Data Book*; case studies; reports; blog.

Finance: Annual revenue US $208.3m., expenditure $162.5m. (31 Dec. 2023).

Board of Trustees: Michael L. Eskew (Chair.).

Principal Staff: Pres. and CEO Lisa Lawson.

Contact Details: 701 St Paul St, Baltimore, MD 21202; tel. (410) 547-6600; internet www.aecf.org.

Anti-Defamation League—ADL

Established in 1913 to counter the defamation of Jewish people; comprises the Anti-Defamation League Foundation. Formerly known as the Anti-Defamation League of B'nai B'rith.

Activities: Works to prevent the defamation of the Jewish people and to secure justice and fair treatment for all through combating discrimination extremism and hate. The League serves as a resource for governments, media and the public; runs educational programmes on the Holocaust, anti-Semitism and anti-Israel bias and bullying prevention; maintains a hate symbols database; and works to safeguard religious liberty. It carries out an annual audit of anti-Semitic incidents in the USA; and supports peace talks in the Middle East. Has offices throughout the USA and in Jerusalem, Israel.

Geographical Area of Activity: International.

Publications: Annual Report; newsletter; Hate on Display Hate Symbols Database (online); *Antisemitism Uncovered: A Guide to Old Myths in a New Era* (online); backgrounders; factsheets; reports; toolkits; blog.

Finance: Annual revenue US $171.1m., expenditure $134.2m. (31 Dec. 2024).

Board of Directors: Nicole Mutchnik (Chair.); Dr Sharon S. Nazarin, Rob Stavis (Vice-Chair.); Barry Curtiss-Lusher (Treas.); Jonathan Neman (Sec.).

Principal Staff: CEO and Nat. Dir Jonathan Greenblatt.

Contact Details: 605 Third Ave, New York, NY 10158-3655; tel. (212) 885-7700; e-mail adlmedia@adl.org; internet www.adl.org.

Arab American Institute Foundation—AAIF

Established in 1985 by James Zogby, Director of Zogby Research Services.

Activities: Represents and promotes greater awareness of Arab Americans in the USA; and carries out demographic research and policy formation to counter anti-Arab and anti-Muslim xenophobia. Programmes include professional mentoring, voter registration and international outreach. The Foundation offers scholarships; and Helen Abbott Community Service Awards for youth leadership, each worth US $1,000, to Arab American students aged under 30 years. It organizes regional internships in the USA for Arab American students and recent graduates interested in civic engagement, civil rights advocacy and public policy.

Geographical Area of Activity: Middle East, USA.

Publications: Newsletter; opinion polls.

Finance: Annual revenue US $1.2m., expenditure $1.3m. (31 Dec. 2021).

Board of Directors: George R. Salem (Chair.).

Principal Staff: Pres. Dr James Zogby; Exec. Dir Maya Berry.

Contact Details: 1600 K St, NW, Suite 601, Washington, DC 20006; tel. (202) 429-9210; e-mail communications@aaiusa.org; internet www.aaiusa.org.

Arca Foundation

Founded in 1952 as the Nancy Susan Reynolds Foundation by Nancy Susan Reynolds, a philanthropist; present name adopted in 1958.

Activities: Works in the fields of social equity and justice. Nationally, the Foundation supports educational and charitable activities in the areas of economic and racial justice, inclusive democracy, peace and security, human rights and the environment. Internationally, it supports organizations working for a more just US foreign policy that prioritizes human rights, peace and security over militarization. Grants are available for general organizational support; specific projects within organizations; and fiscally sponsored projects. The average grant is around US $50,000. The Smith Bagley Memorial Grant Award to organizations for speaking the truth to those in power is offered annually.

Geographical Area of Activity: Central and South America and the Caribbean, USA.

Restrictions: No unsolicited applications; only funds organizations registered in the USA.

Publications: Annual Report.

Finance: Annual revenue US $3.0m., expenditure $5.2m. (31 Dec. 2022).

Board of Trustees: Nicole Bagley (Pres.); Margery Tabankin (Vice-Pres.); Janet Shenk (Treas.); Mike Lux (Sec.).

Principal Staff: Exec. Dir Jennifer S. Pae.

Contact Details: 1730 Rhode Island Ave, NW, Suite 606, Washington, DC 20036; tel. (202) 822-9193; e-mail info@arcafoundation.org; internet www.arcafoundation.org.

Archewell Foundation

Established in 2020 by the Duke and Duchess of Sussex to promote cultural change through compassion.

Activities: Works with communities to bring about systemic cultural change. Initiatives include support for: research and education on developing compassion and promoting altruism; changing digital infrastructure to create safer online communities; and providing access to mental health resources for black women and girls. The Foundation established the Fund for the University of California, Los Angeles (UCLA) Center for Critical Internet Inquiry (C2I2), supporting racial and economic justice in the technology sector; and, in partnership with World Central Kitchen, financed the establishment of four Community Relief Centers in the Dominican Republic and Puerto Rico to provide humanitarian response services in times of high need or disaster, operating as food distribution hubs, schools, health clinics and community spaces at other times.

Geographical Area of Activity: Caribbean, South America, USA.

Finance: Annual income US $5.7m., expenditure $3.3m. (31 Dec. 2023).

Principal Staff: Co-Exec. Dirs James Holt, Shauna Nep.

Contact Details: 9665 Wilshire Blvd, Suite 500, Los Angeles, CA 90212; tel. (310) 385-9300; e-mail info@archewell.com; internet archewell.org.

Arcus Foundation

Established in 2000 by Jon Stryker, a social and environmental activist.

Activities: Promotes respect for diversity among peoples and in nature. The Foundation makes grants to organizations through two main programmes: Social Justice, supporting interfaith initiatives and the integration of sexual orientation and gender identity into shared conceptions of human rights; and Great Apes & Gibbons, working to conserve and protect the primates in sustainably managed habitats and integrating economic development. It has supported projects in more than 50 countries; most grants range between US $100,000 and $150,000. Has an office in the United Kingdom.

Arthritis Foundation — UNITED STATES OF AMERICA

Geographical Area of Activity: East and South-East Asia, North America, South America, Central America and the Caribbean, sub-Saharan Africa, UK, USA.

Restrictions: Does not support political activities or lobbying; no grants to individuals.

Publications: Annual Report; *Politics of Species, Culture and Conservation*; *State of the Apes* (series); *Diverse Humanity* (photography book series); blog.

Finance: Annual revenue US $33.5m., expenditure $39.4m. (2022).

Board of Directors: Jon Stryker (Pres.).

Principal Staff: CEO Annette Lanjouw.

Contact Details: 445 5th Ave, 7th Floor, New York, NY 10016; tel. (212) 488-3000; e-mail contact@arcusfoundation.org; internet www.arcusfoundation.org.

Arthritis Foundation

Founded in 1948 to improve lives through leadership in the prevention, control and cure of arthritis and related diseases.

Activities: Operates nationally in the fields of education, science and medicine, through self-conducted programmes, research, grants to institutions and individuals, fellowships, scholarships, conferences, courses, publications and lectures. The Foundation works in five key areas: increasing funding to arthritis-related research; building awareness; empowering health actions, through involving everyone in healthy behaviour; influencing national health policy; and exploring all possible research angles. It awards the Russell L. Cecil Arthritis Medical Journalism Awards, the Arthritis Investigator Award and the Segal Clinical Scientist Grants for Osteoarthritis Biomarkers.

Geographical Area of Activity: USA.

Publications: Annual Report; *Arthritis Today* (magazine, 6 a year); blog.

Finance: Annual revenue US $68.3m., expenditure $61.8m. (31 Dec. 2023).

Board of Directors: Dennis Ehling (Chair.); Matt Mooney (Immediate Past Chair.); Winell Belfonte (Vice-Chair.); Carlos Carasco (Treas.); Helen King (Sec.).

Principal Staff: Pres. and CEO Steven Taylor.

Contact Details: 1355 Peachtree St NE, Suite 600, Atlanta, GA 30309; tel. (404) 872-7100; e-mail arthritisfoundation@arthritis.org; internet www.arthritis.org.

Asia Foundation

Established in 1954 to foster mutual respect and understanding between Asia and the West.

Activities: Works in the field of international development. Main programme areas are: empowering women; expanding economic opportunity; increasing environmental resilience; promoting international co-operation; and strengthening governance and law. The Foundation works with partner organizations from the public and private sectors to support institutional development, exchanges and dialogue, technical assistance, research and policy engagement; and also makes grants to organizations based in Asia. Since 1954 its Books for Asia initiative has distributed books and digital content to students, educators and leaders in 20 countries; and in 2001 the Give2Asia (q.v.) fundraising initiative was launched. Has offices in 17 countries as well as in Washington, DC and New York.

Geographical Area of Activity: Asia-Pacific, East Asia and South-East Asia, South Asia.

Restrictions: No grants to individuals or organizations based in the USA.

Publications: Annual Report; newsletter; Asian Perspectives (series); brochures; handouts; reports; surveys.

Finance: Annual revenue US $119.5m., expenditure $117.2m. (30 Sept. 2024).

Board and Exec. Committee: S. Timothy Kochis (Chair.); Janet Montag, Kathleen Stephens (Vice-Chair.); Patricia M. Loui (Treas.); Michael J. Green (Sec.).

Principal Staff: Pres. and CEO Laurel E. Miller.

Contact Details: 465 California St, 9th Floor, San Francisco, CA 94104-1804; tel. (415) 982-4640; e-mail info.sf@asiafoundation.org; internet asiafoundation.org.

Asia Society

Founded in 1956 by John D. Rockefeller, III, a philanthropist and art collector.

Activities: Promotes mutual understanding and strengthens partnerships among peoples, leaders and institutions in Asia and the USA. Main programme areas include the arts, business, culture, education and policy. The Society comprises the Asia Society Policy Institute, Center for Global Education and Center on US–China Relations. It has public buildings in New York, Hong Kong and Houston; and offices in Los Angeles, San Francisco and Washington, DC, as well as in Manila (Philippines), Melbourne, Sydney (Australia), Mumbai (India), Seoul (Republic of Korea), Shanghai (People's Repub. of China), Tokyo (Japan) and Zurich (Switzerland).

Geographical Area of Activity: Australia, People's Repub. of China, Hong Kong, India, Japan, Repub. of Korea, Philippines, Switzerland, USA.

Publications: Annual Report; *ChinaFile* (online magazine); *Asia Blog*.

Finance: Annual revenue US $30.4m., expenditure $32.1m. (30 Sept. 2023).

Board of Trustees: Chan Heng Chee, John L. Thornton (Co-Chair.); Betsy Z. Cohen, Hamid Biglari, Lulu C. Wang (Vice-Chair.).

Principal Staff: Pres. and CEO Dr Kyung-wha Kang; Exec. Vice-Pres. Debra Eisenman.

Contact Details: 725 Park Ave/East 70th St, New York, NY 10021; tel. (212) 288-6400; e-mail info@asiasociety.org; internet www.asiasociety.org.

Asian Cultural Council—ACC

Founded in 1963 by John D. Rockefeller, III, a philanthropist and art collector; originally known as the JDR 3rd Program; it has been formally affiliated to the Rockefeller Brothers Fund (q.v.) since 1991.

Activities: Fosters international dialogue, understanding and respect through cultural exchange. The Council offers individual fellowship awards to artists, scholars, students and specialists in the visual and performing arts for research, travel, study and creative work involving cultural exchange between Asia and the USA; and makes a limited number of grants to arts organizations and educational institutions for specific projects of Asian-American cultural exchange. Priority is given to individuals in East and South-East Asia seeking grant assistance for research, travel, study, training or creative activity in the USA. It also offers the John D. Rockefeller 3rd Award to individuals from Asia or the USA for their contribution to the international understanding, practice or study of the visual or performing arts of Asia; and the Blanchette Hooker Rockefeller Award to individuals for their contribution to international cultural exchange and Council programmes. Has offices in Hong Kong, Japan, the Philippines and Taiwan.

Geographical Area of Activity: Mainly Asia, from Pakistan eastwards to Japan.

Restrictions: No grants to individuals for lecture programmes, personal exhibitions, individual performance tours, undergraduate studies, nor for activities within their home countries; no grants to organizations for publications, film and video productions, capital works or general programme or administrative costs.

Publications: Annual Report; e-newsletter; information brochure.

UNITED STATES OF AMERICA   *The Barack Obama Foundation*

Finance: Annual revenue US $4.5m., expenditure $3.5m. (31 Dec. 2023).

Board of Trustees: Josie Cruz Natori (Chair.); Hans Michael Jebsen, Susan Rockefeller (Vice-Chair.); John R. Witt (Treas.); Anne Straton Pierson (Sec.).

Principal Staff: Exec. Dir Judy Kim.

Contact Details: 1 Rockefeller Plaza, Room 2500, New York, NY 10020; tel. (212) 843-0403; e-mail acc@accny.org; internet www.asianculturalcouncil.org.

Aspen Institute

Established in 1949 by Walter Paepcke, Chair. of Container Corpn of America, a box manufacturer.

Activities: Runs a series of Seminar Programs and Policy Programs to encourage corporate leaders to act responsibly and provide a forum for debates on domestic and international issues. Thematic areas include: business and society; communications and culture; education; energy and environment; health and sport; justice and civic identity; opportunity and development; and security and global affairs. The philanthropy and social enterprise programme offers fellowships and co-ordinates the work of the Artist-Endowed Foundations Initiative. The Institute's flagship leadership programme is the Henry Crown Fellowship; other fellowship programmes are grouped within the Aspen Global Leadership Network. Has 14 offices in Asia, Europe and North America; and a conference centre in Aspen, CO.

Geographical Area of Activity: International.

Restrictions: Not a grantmaking organization.

Publications: Annual Report; Impact Report; newsletter; *IDEAS* (magazine, 2–3 a year); research reports; guides.

Finance: Annual revenue US $232.1m., expenditure $225.7m. (31 Dec. 2023).

Board of Trustees: Margot L. Pritzker (Chair.).

Principal Staff: Pres. and CEO Dr Daniel R. Porterfield; Exec. Vice-Pres. Maria Laura Acebal.

Contact Details: 2300 N St NW, Suite 700, Washington, DC 20037; tel. (202) 736-5800; internet www.aspeninstitute.org.

Atlas Network

Founded in 1981 by Sir Antony Fisher, who introduced factory farming of chickens to the United Kingdom; formerly known as the Atlas Economic Research Foundation. Present name adopted in 2013.

Activities: Provides opportunities for training, support and international recognition. The Foundation makes grants to think tanks in the USA and abroad for projects in the areas of public policy and deregulation; start-up grants for think tanks, international student groups and other organizations; and the Illiberalism Grant for countering the new authoritarianism, worth up to US $10,000. It also offers awards including the Templeton Freedom Award for contributions to the understanding of free enterprise and the public policies that encourage prosperity, innovation and human fulfilment through free competition. Comprises the Center for Latin America, Center for African Prosperity and almost 500 free market organizations in nearly 100 countries.

Geographical Area of Activity: International.

Publications: Annual Report; *World10* (newsletter); *Freedom's Champion* (quarterly); books.

Finance: Annual revenue US $29.5m., expenditure $22.5m. (31 Dec. 2023).

Board of Directors: Montgomery Brown (Chair.); Dan Grossman (Treas.).

Principal Staff: Pres. Matt Warner; CEO Brad Lips.

Contact Details: 2 Liberty Center, 4075 Wilson Blvd, Suite 310, Arlington, VA 22203; tel. (202) 449-8449; e-mail development@atlasnetwork.org; internet www.atlasnetwork.org.

AT&T Foundation

Founded in 1984 by AT&T Corpn, a telecommunications provider.

Activities: Funds programmes in two main areas: environment, including investing in a carbon neutral future, helping to reduce emissions, building climate resilience and developing an Internet of Things for good; and society, including disaster response, education and economic opportunity, promoting diversity in media and entertainment, employee volunteering, and supporting military personnel and first responders. The Aspire Accelerator programme offers US $100,000 and ongoing support to educational technology start-ups.

Geographical Area of Activity: International.

Restrictions: Grants only to organizations.

Publications: Biennial Report; newsletters.

Finance: Annual revenue US $207,934, expenditure $17.6m. (31 Dec. 2022).

Board of Trustees: David McAtee (Chair.); Charlene Lake (Vice-Pres.); George Goeke (Vice-Pres. and Treas.); Thomas R. Giltner (Vice-Pres. and Sec.).

Principal Staff: Pres. Nicole Anderson.

Contact Details: 208 S. Akard, 12th Floor, Dallas, TX 75202-4206; tel. (800) 591-9663; e-mail foundation@att.com; internet sustainability.att.com.

Bank of America Charitable Foundation

Established in 1998 by Bank of America Corporation.

Activities: The Foundation supports non-profit alliances around the world, which include grants and sponsorships to local organizations that help improve financial lives and entire communities. Areas of focus include: workforce development and education, basic needs like food and housing, and community development. Support focuses both on programmes that address immediate needs as well as on ones that offer longer-term solutions that give people the tools to achieve economic mobility.

Geographical Area of Activity: Asia-Pacific, Europe, Latin America, Middle East and Africa, USA.

Publications: Annual Report; newsletter (quarterly).

Finance: Annual revenue US $77m., expenditure $315m. (31 Dec. 2022).

Trustees: Anne M. Finucane (Chair.); Susan A. Campbell (Treas.); Colleen O. Johnson (Sec.).

Principal Staff: Pres. Kerry H. Sullivan.

Contact Details: 401 N. Tryon St, NC1-021-06-01, Charlotte, NC 28255; tel. (980) 386-9127; e-mail foundation@bankofamerica.com; internet www.bankofamerica.com/foundation.

The Barack Obama Foundation

Established in 2014 by President Barack Obama, the 44th President of the USA, to develop the next generation of citizens.

Activities: Seeks to empower people with skills and tools to create change in their communities. Main programmes are: the Girls Opportunity Alliance, which supports adolescent girls' education worldwide; Leaders: Africa, a year-long leadership development and skill-building programmes for emerging changemakers; the Community Leadership Corps, offering leadership skills training for young people aged 18–25 years in Chicago, IL, and Hartford, CT; the Scholars Program, providing academic, skills-based, and hands-on learning to MA students at the University of Chicago Harris School of Public Policy; and My Brother's Keeper Alliance to support boys and young men of colour. The Foundation offers two-year, non-residential fellowships to civic innovators; and collaborates with organizations to hold training days on putting civics into action. It maintains the Obama Presidential Center and archives.

Geographical Area of Activity: Worldwide.

Barbra Streisand Foundation   UNITED STATES OF AMERICA

Publications: Annual Report.
Finance: Annual revenue US $144.0m., expenditure $88.7m. (31 Dec. 2023).
Board: Martin H. Nesbitt (Chair.).
Principal Staff: CEO Valerie Jarrett.
Contact Details: 5235 South Harper Ct, Suite 1140, Chicago, IL 60615; tel. (773) 420-1700; e-mail info@obama.org; internet www.obama.org.

Barbra Streisand Foundation

Founded in 1986 by Barbra Streisand, a singer and actress.
Activities: Makes grants to US-based organizations working at national level to support: environmental initiatives; women's sexual and reproductive health; civil liberties and democratic values; civil rights and race relations; economically disadvantaged children and young people; nuclear disarmament; and AIDS research, advocacy, service and litigation. Awards range from US $1,000 to $25,000.
Geographical Area of Activity: USA.
Restrictions: No grants to individuals, or to local organizations, except for programmes for disadvantaged youth in Los Angeles, CA; no unsolicited applications.
Publications: Application guidelines.
Finance: Annual revenue US $2.0m., expenditure $2.3m. (31 Dec. 2022).
Trustees: Barbra Streisand (Pres.); Margery Tabankin (Exec. Dir and Treas./Sec.).
Contact Details: 21731 Ventura Blvd, Suite 206, Woodland Hills, CA 91364; tel. (818) 592-3000; e-mail sfinquiries @streisandfoundation.org; internet www.barbrastreisand .com/streisand-foundation.

Batonga

Founded in 2006 by singer-songwriter Angélique Kidjo to invest in the futures of girls and young women in Africa.
Activities: The Batonga Foundation aims to equip underprivileged girls and young women aged 14 to 30 in Africa with the tools they need to change their own lives and that of their communities. Through various initiatives, the Foundation mentors and supports young people in areas of: leadership; economic empowerment; business coaching; community engagement; and gender equality. The Men and Boys Engagement initiative helps train male champions in the community to ensure girls and young women can work and thrive in an equitable environment.
Geographical Area of Activity: Benin, Senegal.
Finance: Annual income US $623,333, expenditure $1.4m. (31 Dec. 2022).
Board: Aleta J. Williams (Chair.).
Principal Staff: Exec. Dir Codou Diaw.
Contact Details: 2202 18th St NW, #123, Washington, DC 20009; tel. (202) 670-7313; e-mail info@batongafoundation .org; internet www.batongafoundation.org.

Better World Campaign—BWC

Established in 1997 as the Better World Fund along with its sister organization, the UN Foundation (q.v.), following a gift of US $1,000m. to the UN by R. E. (Ted) Turner, III, the founder of the Cable News Network (CNN) and the Turner Foundation (q.v.).
Activities: Conducts and funds projects to educate the public about the work and role of the UN in addressing global issues; and build public support for the organization, in particular highlighting the UN's work to strengthen international security through global co-operation. In conjunction with the UN Foundation, it sponsors the daily *UN Wire* news summary on UN and global affairs. Promotes US engagement with the UN and educates the public about its benefits, working with its sister organization the UN Association of the United States of America, which has more than 20,000 members in over 200 chapters.
Geographical Area of Activity: International.
Publications: Newsletter; *Congressional Briefing Book*; factsheets; white papers.
Finance: Annual revenue US $3.9m., expenditure $4.5m. (31 Dec. 2021).
Global Leadership Council: Thomas Pickering (Chair.).
Principal Staff: Pres. Peter Yeo; Exec. Dir Jordie Hannum.
Contact Details: 1750 Pennsylvania Ave, NW, Suite 300, Washington, DC 20006; tel. (202) 462-4900; e-mail info_bwc @unfoundation.org; internet betterworldcampaign.org.

Bezos Earth Fund

Established in 2020 by Jeff Bezos, founder of Amazon (f. 1995), an e-commerce and technology company.
Activities: Funds scientists, activists and non-governmental organizations working to mitigate the impact of climate change. In 2020 the Fund awarded US $791m. in grants to 16 environmental organizations. It planned to give away US $10,000m. within a decade.
Geographical Area of Activity: International.
Finance: Initial capital US $10,000m.
Principal Staff: Exec. Chair. Jeff Bezos; Vice-Chair. Lauren Sánchez.
Contact Details: c/o Fellowship Ventures LLC, 1201 Third Ave, Suite 4900, Seattle, WA 98101; tel. (206) 266-1000; internet www.bezosearthfund.org.

Black Lives Matter Global Network Foundation—BLM Global Network Foundation

Established in 2013 by Patrisse Cullors, Alicia Garza and Opal Tometi as Black Lives Matter, a decentralized grassroots movement.
Activities: Works to eliminate the culture of white supremacy through building local capacity to counter institutional racism and advocating against police violence. In 2020, the Foundation established a fund worth US $12m. to support anti-racist organizations and black-led grassroots organizing groups; and a fund worth $6.5m. to support affiliated network chapters with multi-year grants worth up to $500,000. The BLM Arts Culture programme promotes emerging black artists. The Tides Foundation (q.v.) is the fiscal sponsor of the BLM Support Fund. Comprises up to 30 local affiliates.
Geographical Area of Activity: Canada, UK, USA.
Publications: Newsletter; toolkits.
Finance: Total revenue US $4.7m., expenditure $10.8m. (30 June 2023).
Board: Cicley Gay (Chair.).
Contact Details: 248 Third St, Oakland, CA 94607; tel. (510) 509-1603; e-mail press@blacklivesmatter.com; internet blacklivesmatter.com.

Blakemore Foundation

Established in 1990 by Thomas and Frances Blakemore, who lived and worked in Japan for more than 50 years.
Activities: Awards grants for college graduates and young professionals to study East and South-East Asian languages abroad, with the support of the Freeman Foundation (q.v.); and also Blakemore Freeman Fellowships for advanced language study abroad of Chinese, Japanese, Korean, Burmese, Indonesian, Khmer, Thai and Vietnamese. The Foundation also awards Frances Blakemore & Griffith Way Asian Art Grants to improve understanding of East Asian fine arts.
Geographical Area of Activity: East Asia, South-East Asia, USA.
Restrictions: Blakemore Freeman Fellowship applicants must be US citizens or permanent residents of the USA; Frances Blakemore Asian Art Grants are made by invitation only to a few organizations in the USA.
Finance: Annual revenue US $518,568, expenditure $839,365 (2023).

UNITED STATES OF AMERICA

Board of Managers: Mimi Gardner Gates (Chair.).

Contact Details: POB 50347, Bellevue, WA 98015; tel. (206) 427-4838; e-mail contactus@blakemorefoundation.org; internet www.blakemorefoundation.org.

Blavatnik Family Foundation

Established in the 1990s by Len Blavatnik, the Chair. and founder of Access Industries, a global investment group.

Activities: Supports early-stage scientific research and discovery into the treatment of disease. The Foundation also funds international schools of business and government; local organizations supporting underserved communities; and art and cultural institutions, including the Blavatnik Archive Foundation (f. 2005), which holds a collection of Judaica. In 2007 it created the Blavatnik Awards for Young Scientists with the New York Academy of Sciences; in 2010 the Blavatnik School of Government at the University of Oxford; and in 2013 the Blavatnik Fellowship in Life Science Entrepreneurship at Harvard Business School.

Geographical Area of Activity: International.

Finance: Annual revenue US $87.4m., expenditure $40.2m. (31 Dec. 2022).

Principal Staff: Co-Chair. Sir Leonard Blavatnik, Lady Emily Blavatnik.

Contact Details: c/o Access Inc, 40 West 57th St, New York, NY 10019; tel. (203) 622-7400; internet blavatnikfoundation.org.

Bloomberg Philanthropies

Established in 2006 by Michael R. Bloomberg, founder of data and media company Bloomberg LP and Mayor of New York City at that time; comprises the Bloomberg Family Foundation (f. 2006).

Activities: Works in five main areas: the arts; education; the environment; government innovation; and public health. The organization also has several Founder's Projects, including: the American Cities Initiative, strengthening leadership and problem solving, and supporting artists; the Bloomberg American Health Initiative at Johns Hopkins University; and Women for Women International, empowering victims of conflict in Africa. It funds activities in more 700 cities in 150 countries; and is part of the Partnership for Healthy Cities with Vital Strategies (q.v.) and WHO, which works to prevent non-communicable diseases and injuries in 70 cities.

Geographical Area of Activity: Worldwide.

Restrictions: Does not accept unsolicited applications.

Publications: Annual Report.

Finance: Annual revenue US $1,510m., expenditure $1,430m. (2023).

Principal Staff: CEO Patricia E. Harris.

Contact Details: 25 East 78th St, New York, NY 10075; tel. (212) 205-0100; e-mail communications@bloomberg.org; internet www.bloomberg.org.

Born This Way Foundation

Established in 2012 by Lady Gaga (Stefani Germanotta), a pop singer, and her mother, Cynthia Germanotta.

Activities: Supports young people's mental health through conducting research and advocacy. The Foundation works to provide young people with kinder communities, improved mental health resources and more positive online and offline environments. The Channel Kindness digital platform promotes heroic acts of kindness, training youth reporters.

Geographical Area of Activity: USA.

Publications: Impact Report; *Channel Kindness: Stories of Kindness*; international surveys.

Finance: Annual revenue US $3.5m., expenditure $3.3m. (31 Dec. 2021).

Board of Directors: Cynthia Germanotta (Pres.); Tamika L. Tremaglio (Treas.); Charles Smith (Sec.).

Principal Staff: Exec. Dir Maya Enista Smith.

Contact Details: 261 5th Ave, New York, NY 10016-7701; tel. (212) 685-4300; e-mail info@bornthisway.foundation; internet bornthisway.foundation.

BP Foundation, Inc

Established in 1953 by British Petroleum (BP), an international oil and gas company; operates separately from BP.

Activities: Supports disaster and humanitarian relief efforts in areas where BP has a significant local employee and business presence. The Foundation operates the BP Foundation Employee Matching Fund, which includes grants and donations of time.

Geographical Area of Activity: International.

Restrictions: No unsolicited applications.

Finance: Annual revenue US $8.1m., expenditure $6.8m. (31 Dec. 2022).

Board of Directors: Mary Streett (Chair.).

Principal Staff: Exec. Dir Tara Harrison.

Contact Details: 501 Westlake Park Blvd, Fl 24, Houston, TX 77079; tel. (281) 892-7301; internet www.bp.com/en_us/united-states/home/community/bp-foundation.html.

Breakthrough T1D

Established in 1970 as the Juvenile Diabetes Foundation; formerly Juvenile Diabetes Research Foundation International—JDRF; present name adopted in 2025.

Activities: Funds research on type 1 diabetes (T1D). The Foundation offers grants and awards, including: the Career Development Award in diabetes research for postdoctoral study in any country; the New Training for Established Scientist Award for visiting scholars carrying out research in any country, in a field different from, but related to, the area in which they normally work; the Summer Student Program in diabetes research, to assist colleges, universities, medical schools, etc., in supporting student research work; and fellowships and research awards tenable in any country for research into diabetes and its complications. The Foundation has affiliates in Australia, Canada, Israel, the Netherlands and the United Kingdom. In 2016 it established the T1D Fund to invest in therapeutics, devices, vaccines and diagnostics.

Geographical Area of Activity: International.

Publications: Annual Report; *Online Countdown*; *Emerging Technologies E-Newsletter*; *Life with Diabetes E-Newsletter*; factsheets; blog.

Finance: Annual revenue US $33.7m., expenditure $212.1m. (30 June 2023).

International Board of Directors: Lisa F. Wallack (Chair.); Matt Varey (Vice-Chair.).

Principal Staff: Pres. and CEO Dr Aaron J. Kowalski.

Contact Details: 200 Vesey St, 28th Floor, New York, NY 10281; POB 5021, Hagerstown, MD 21741-5021; tel. (800) 533-2873; e-mail info@BreakthroughT1D.org; internet www.breakthroughtld.org.

BrightFocus Foundation

Established in 1973 as American Health Assistance Foundation; present name adopted in 2013.

Activities: Supports scientific investigation of Alzheimer's disease, glaucoma and macular degeneration; and raises awareness about age-related, degenerative diseases. The Foundation grants awards to peer-reviewed and selected researchers around the world through three programmes: Alzheimer's Disease Research; National Glaucoma Research; and Macular Degeneration Research.

Geographical Area of Activity: International.

Publications: Annual Report; newsletter; brochures; factsheets; disease toolkit.

Finance: Annual revenue US $43.9m., expenditure $48.5m. (31 March 2023).

Board of Directors: Patricia McGlothlin Stewart (Chair.); Scott Kaiser (Vice-Chair.); Thomas Freddo (Sec.).

Bristol-Myers Squibb Foundation

Principal Staff: Pres. and CEO Stacy Pagos Haller.
Contact Details: 22512 Gateway Center Dr., Clarksburg, MD 20871; tel. (800) 437-2423; e-mail info@brightfocus.org; internet www.brightfocus.org.

Bristol-Myers Squibb Foundation

Established in 1982, successor to the Bristol-Myers Fund (f. 1955), by Bristol-Myers, a biopharmaceuticals manufacturer.

Activities: Promotes health equity and works to improve the health outcomes of populations disproportionately affected by serious diseases through strengthening healthcare worker capacity, integrating medical care and community-based support services, and mobilizing communities to fight disease. Main programmes include: community-based cancer awareness, screening, care and support programmes for high-risk populations in Central and Eastern Europe, sub-Saharan Africa and the USA; improving access to cardiovascular disease care in the USA; raising awareness about hepatitis B and C in the Asia-Pacific region; providing care and support for people in sub-Saharan Africa affected by HIV, tuberculosis, non-communicable diseases and AIDS-related cancers; improving the health of people with diabetes in the USA; and supporting returning soldiers and their families in the USA. The Foundation works with academic, community and faith-based organizations to address non-clinical barriers to care; and offers mentoring partnerships between primary care providers and local and remote specialists.
Geographical Area of Activity: International.
Restrictions: No funding requests for diabetes, mental health or breast cancer.
Publications: Annual Report; Global Citizenship Report; *Life & Science Magazine*.
Finance: Annual revenue US $46,784, expenditure $54.4m. (31 Dec. 2021).
Board of Directors: Dr Chris Boerner (Chair. and CEO).
Contact Details: Bristol-Myers Squibb Corporate Headquarters, Route 206 & Province Line Rd, Princeton, NJ 08543; e-mail bms.foundation@bms.com; internet www.bms.com/foundation.

British Schools and Universities Foundation, Inc—BSUF

Founded in 1961 by a group led by Thomas E. Ward, Sr, to promote closer relations between the USA and the British Commonwealth.

Activities: Makes grants to educational institutions in the United Kingdom and the British Commonwealth and supports reciprocal Anglo-American education. The Foundation manages the Thomas E. Ward Fund, Richard A. and Kathleen B. May Memorial Fund and Alan C. Root Fund, which fund scholarship grants for British scholars to pursue studies or research in the USA. It works in partnership with the Marshall Scholarship and Fulbright Scholarship Program.
Geographical Area of Activity: British Commonwealth countries, UK, USA.
Restrictions: Grants only for study at institutions in the British Commonwealth or USA.
Publications: Annual Report; newsletter.
Finance: Annual revenue US $12.0m., expenditure $11.7m. (31 Dec. 2022).
Board of Directors: David Lipson (Chair.); Patrick M. Russell (Treas.); Sara Kendrick Moose (Sec.).
Principal Staff: Exec. Dir Dr Roger H. Martin.
Contact Details: 641 Lexington Ave, 15th Floor, New York, NY 10022-4503; e-mail exec@bsuf.org; internet www.bsuf.org.

The Broad Foundation

Established in 1999 by Eli Broad, owner of insurance company SunAmerica, and his wife Edythe.

Activities: Carries out activities in the fields of education, science and the arts. The Foundation comprises Eli and Edythe Broad Foundation (f. 1967); the Broad Center, which develops school leadership; and the Broad Institute, which specializes in genomics. The Broad Art Foundation (f. 1984) is a pioneering lending library, dedicated to increasing public access to contemporary art.
Geographical Area of Activity: International.
Publications: Reports.
Finance: Annual revenue US $135.8m., expenditure $87.3m. (31 Dec. 2022).
Principal Staff: Pres. of the Eli and Edythe Broad Foundation Gerun Riley.
Contact Details: 300 South Grand Ave, Suite 1800, Los Angeles, CA 90071; tel. (310) 954-5000; e-mail info@broadfoundation.org; internet broadfoundation.org.

Brookings Institution

Founded in 1927 by Robert S. Brookings, a business person, Chairman of the Institute for Government Research and co-founder of the Institute of Economics and the Brookings Graduate School of Economics and Government; these merged into one institution, which was named in Brookings' honour.

Activities: Carries out public policy research on issues at local, national and global level. Research programmes include: economic studies; foreign policy; global economy and development; governance studies; and the metropolitan policy. The Institution organizes educational conferences for leaders in business and government professions. It offers research fellowships in support of policy-orientated pre-doctoral research in national security policy, government and economics; and appoints 10 early- and mid-career scholars and experts to serve for two years at the Institution as David M. Rubenstein Fellows. Maintains a library and archives; with a research centre in Qatar and partnerships with the University of Nevada, Las Vegas and Washington University in St Louis.
Geographical Area of Activity: International.
Publications: Annual Report; newsletter; Brookings Essays; *Brookings Papers on Economic Activity* (2 a year); *Economia* (2 a year); *Behavioral Science & Policy*; *Brookings Review* (quarterly); periodic journals; policy briefs; research and commentary; books.
Finance: Annual revenue US $98.7m., expenditure $100.1m. (30 June 2024).
Board of Trustees: Glenn Hutchins, Suzanne Nora Johnson (Co-Chair.); Pete Higgins, Kenneth M. Jacobs, Leonard D. Shaeffer (Vice-Chair.); Victor L. Hymes (Treas.); Tracy R. Wolstencroft (Sec.).
Principal Staff: Pres. Cecilia Elena Rouse.
Contact Details: 1775 Massachusetts Ave, NW, Washington, DC 20036-2188; tel. (202) 797-6000; e-mail media@brookings.edu; internet www.brookings.edu.

Brother's Brother Foundation

Established in 1958 by Dr Robert A. Hingson, a professor of public health and anaesthesiologist.

Activities: Works in the fields of humanitarian aid and sustainable development. The organization supports localized initiatives through providing essential resources in the areas of disaster response, education, healthcare and infrastructure. It operates in 42 countries.
Geographical Area of Activity: International.
Publications: Annual Report; newsletter; blog.
Finance: Annual revenue US $99.6m., expenditure $86.8m. (31 Dec. 2023).
Board of Trustees: Eric Saks (Chair.); Dr Svetlana Faktorovich (Vice-Chair.); Bryant Mitchell (Treas.); Michael Maselli (Sec.).
Principal Staff: Pres. Ozzy Samad.

UNITED STATES OF AMERICA

Contact Details: 1200 Galveston Ave, Pittsburgh, PA 15233-1604; tel. (412) 321-3160; e-mail info@brothersbrother.org; internet brothersbrother.org.

Burroughs Wellcome Fund—BWF

Established in 1955 by the Burroughs Wellcome Co, USA, the US branch of Wellcome, a British pharmaceutical company.

Activities: Supports early career biomedical scientists and undervalued and underfunded areas of science. The Fund offers awards in areas including: primary and secondary science, technology, engineering and mathematics education in North Carolina, offering awards of up to US $60,000 over three years; innovation in teaching in science and mathematics, offering up to $3,000 for equipment and materials and $1,500 for professional development; graduate diversity, offering $5,000 to under-represented minority PhD students over two years; career guidance for trainees, offering grants worth $15,000–$25,000 over one year for demonstration projects; and career awards for postdoctoral fellows, offering up to $500,000 over five years to bridge advanced training. Awards are also available in areas such as infectious disease, regulatory science, reproductive science and translational research.

Geographical Area of Activity: Canada, USA.

Restrictions: No grants to individuals.

Publications: Annual Report; *FOCUS* (newsletter); programme brochures; special reports.

Finance: Annual revenue US $23.4m., expenditure $32.4m. (31 Aug. 2023).

Board of Directors: Dr Brenda Andrews (Chair.).

Principal Staff: Pres. and CEO Dr Louis J. Muglia; Vice-Pres. Ken Browndorf.

Contact Details: POB 13901, 21 T. W. Alexander Dr., Research Triangle Park, NC 27709-3901; tel. (919) 991-5100; e-mail info@bwfund.org; internet www.bwfund.org.

California Community Foundation

Established in 1915, as the Los Angeles Community Foundation, by Joseph Sartori, a banker.

Activities: Provides financial, technical and managerial support to non-profit organizations. Priority areas are: the arts; civic engagement; community building; education; health; housing and economic opportunity; integration of immigrants; sustainability of non-profit organizations; public transport; and youth empowerment. The Foundation offers scholarships to students in need; and provides conference facilities for non-profit organizations through the Joan Palevsky Center for the Future of Los Angeles. It administers more than 1,900 charitable funds.

Geographical Area of Activity: Mainly Los Angeles County.

Publications: Annual Report; *CCF News* (newsletter); factsheets.

Finance: Annual revenue US $373.6m., expenditure $369.0m. (30 June 2023).

Principal Staff: Pres and CEO Miguel A. Santana.

Contact Details: 717 W. Temple St, Los Angeles, CA 90012; tel. (213) 413-4130; e-mail info@calfund.org; internet www.calfund.org.

The Camille and Henry Dreyfus Foundation, Inc

Founded in 1946 by Camille E. Dreyfus, a chemist and inventor, in memory of his brother Henry.

Activities: Helps academic institutions to foster research and train students for graduate study for doctoral degrees in chemistry; other qualifying organizations, such as research institutes with similar goals, are also eligible for grant consideration. The Foundation sponsors the Camille Dreyfus and the Henry Dreyfus Teacher-Scholar Awards Programs, the Postdoctoral Program in Environmental Chemistry, the Senior Scientist Mentor Program, and the Jean Dreyfus Boissevan Lectureship for Undergraduate Institutions. It also sponsors awards administered by the American Chemical Society: the ACS Award for Encouraging Women into Careers in the Chemical Sciences and ACS Award for Encouraging Disadvantaged Students into Careers in the Chemical Sciences. The Dreyfus Prize in the Chemical Sciences, worth US $250,000, is awarded every two years for exceptional and original research.

Geographical Area of Activity: USA.

Restrictions: Does not make grants to individuals.

Publications: Annual Report; newsletter (annual); programme brochures.

Finance: Annual revenue US $5.2m., expenditure $5.6m. (31 Dec. 2021).

Board of Directors: H. Scott Walter (Pres.); Paul Woitach (Vice-Pres.); Mary Eileen Dowling Walter (Treas./Sec.).

Principal Staff: Man. Dir Gerard L. Brandenstein.

Contact Details: 405 Lexington Ave, Suite 909, New York, NY 10174; tel. (212) 753-1760; e-mail info@dreyfus.org; internet www.dreyfus.org.

Carnegie Corporation of New York

Founded in 1911 by Andrew Carnegie, an industrialist and philanthropist; part of a network of 23 Carnegie organizations worldwide.

Activities: Undertakes grantmaking programmes in four main areas: democracy, integrating immigrants into civil society and protecting voting rights, building diverse alliances and supporting community-based organizations; education, preparing students to participate in democracy and succeed in the global economy, and strengthening teaching and school leadership; international peace, including conflict in the Middle East, geopolitical trends, nuclear security, peacebuilding in Africa, and technology and social change; and higher education and research in sub-Saharan Africa, improving the training of academics and capacity in the sector. The Corporation offers Fellowships of up to two years, worth US $200,000, to scholars nominated by university presidents, leaders of think tanks and publishers. It awards the Carnegie Medal of Philanthropy in recognition of individuals' achievements; and every two years, jointly with the Carnegie Endowment for International Peace (q.v.), the Nunn-Lugar Award for Promoting Nuclear Security, worth $50,000.

Geographical Area of Activity: International.

Restrictions: No grants to individuals, for fundraising or political activities, scholarships or religious organizations; rarely funds unsolicited applications. Fellows must be US citizens or resident in the USA.

Publications: Annual Report; newsletter; *Carnegie Reporter* (magazine); *Carnegie Results*; books; reports; meeting papers; essays.

Finance: Annual revenue US $553.7m., expenditure $225.2m. (30 Sept. 2022).

Board of Trustees: Janet L. Robinson (Chair.); Kurt L. Schmoke (Vice-Chair.).

Principal Staff: Pres. Dame Louise Richardson.

Contact Details: 437 Madison Ave, New York, NY 10022; tel. (212) 371-3200; e-mail externalaffairs@carnegie.org; internet www.carnegie.org.

Carnegie Endowment for International Peace

Established in 1910 by Andrew Carnegie, an industrialist and philanthropist; part of a network of 23 Carnegie organizations worldwide.

Activities: Conducts research, publishes information, holds meetings, and occasionally creates new institutions and international networks. Main programme areas include: Asia; climate and energy; defence and security; democracy and governance; economy; foreign policy; global governance; nuclear weapons; political reform; society and culture; and technology. Its interests are international and concentrate on relations between governments, businesses, international organizations and civil society, focusing on the economic, political and technological forces driving global change. Around

Carnegie Hero Fund Commission   UNITED STATES OF AMERICA

12 James C. Gaither Junior Fellows spend one year as research assistants to senior Carnegie scholars. Has centres in Beijing (People's Repub. of China), Beirut (Lebanon), Brussels (Belgium), Moscow (Russian Federation) and New Delhi (India), with more than 150 scholars in over 20 countries.

Geographical Area of Activity: Australasia, East and South-East Asia, Eastern Europe, Russian Federation and Central Asia, South Asia, USA, Western Europe.

Restrictions: Not a grantmaking organization.

Publications: Annual Report; newsletter; *Foreign Policy* (6 a year); monographs; reports; working papers; blog; books.

Finance: Annual revenue US $51.1m., expenditure $45.4m. (30 June 2023).

Board of Trustees: Catherine James Paglia (Chair.); Steven A. Denning (Vice-Chair.).

Principal Staff: Pres. Mariano-Florentino 'Tino' Cuéllar.

Contact Details: 1779 Massachusetts Ave NW, Washington, DC 20036-2103; tel. (202) 483-7600; e-mail info@ceip.org; internet www.carnegieendowment.org.

Carnegie Hero Fund Commission

Founded in 1904 by Andrew Carnegie, an industrialist and philanthropist, to recognize heroism voluntarily performed by civilians in the USA and Canada, in saving or attempting to save the lives of others; part of a network of 23 Carnegie organizations worldwide.

Activities: Works in the field of civilian life, through awarding the Carnegie Medal and grants to individuals, including scholarship assistance and continuing aid to those disabled in their attempts to save others, and grants to the dependants of those who died in such attempts. National Carnegie Hero Fund Foundations were established in 1908 in the United Kingdom; in 1909 in France; and in 1911 in Belgium, Denmark, Italy, the Netherlands, Norway, Sweden and Switzerland. These foundations also award medals and diplomas to individuals in those countries who have risked or lost their lives, as well as cash grants.

Geographical Area of Activity: Canada, USA.

Restrictions: Acts of heroism must have occurred in Canada or the USA and the Commission must be notified within two years.

Publications: Biennial Report; newsletter; leaflets.

Finance: Annual revenue US $2.7m., expenditure $2.4m. (31 Dec. 2023).

Commission: Thomas L. Wentling, Jr (Chair.); Eric P. Zahren (Pres. and Sec.); Arthur M. Scully, III (Treas.).

Contact Details: 436 Seventh Ave, Suite 1101, Pittsburgh, PA 15219-1841; tel. (412) 281-1302; e-mail carnegiehero@carnegiehero.org; internet www.carnegiehero.org.

The Carter Center

Established in 1982 by Jimmy Carter, the 39th President of the USA, and Rosalynn Carter, the former First Lady, to work in partnership with Emory University.

Activities: Seeks to prevent and resolve conflicts, enhance freedom and democracy, and improve health worldwide. The Center operates peace programmes in the areas of democracy, human rights, conflict resolution, the Americas and the People's Republic of China; and health programmes to fight six preventable diseases (Guinea worm, river blindness, trachoma, schistosomiasis, lymphatic filariasis and malaria) by using health education and simple, low-cost methods.

Geographical Area of Activity: Less-developed countries worldwide.

Publications: Annual Report; newsletter (2 a year); programme publications; brochure.

Finance: Annual revenue US $413.6m., expenditure $412.3m. (31 Aug. 2023).

Board of Trustees: Jason Carter (Chair.); C. D. Glin (Vice-Chair.).

Board of Councilors: Clark H. Dean (Chair.).

Principal Staff: CEO Paige Alexander.

Contact Details: 453 John Lewis Freedom Parkway, Atlanta, GA 30307-1406; tel. (404) 420-5100; e-mail info@cartercenter.org; internet www.cartercenter.org.

Caterpillar Foundation

Established in 1952 by Caterpillar, a manufacturer of agricultural and construction machinery.

Activities: Main programmes focus on: workforce readiness and science, technology, engineering and mathematics education; building sustainable community infrastructure, including natural ecosystems, and access to basic services (water and energy); and employee volunteering and donations.

Geographical Area of Activity: International.

Restrictions: Does not accept unsolicited applications; no grants to individuals.

Publications: *State of the Foundation*.

Finance: Annual revenue US $72.9m., expenditure $44.1m. (31 Dec. 2022).

Principal Staff: Pres. Asha Varghese.

Contact Details: 100 NE Adams St, Peoria, IL 61629-1480; tel. (309) 675-1000; internet www.caterpillar.com/en/company/caterpillar-foundation.html.

CDC Foundation

Established in 1992 by the US Congress as an independent non-profit organization.

Activities: Builds partnerships between the US Centers for Disease Control and Prevention (CDC), philanthropic organizations and the private sector. The Foundation carries out public health protection and safety programmes in areas including healthy lifestyle promotion, disease research and injury prevention. It also offers fellowships and internships. Has managed over 1,450 programmes in more than 90 countries.

Geographical Area of Activity: International.

Restrictions: Does not accept unsolicited applications.

Finance: Annual revenue US $123.9m., expenditure $207.6m. (30 June 2024).

Board: Dr Raymond J. Baxter (Chair.); David Aldridge (Treas.); Dr Raymond J. Baxter (Sec.).

Principal Staff: Pres. and CEO Judy Monroe.

Contact Details: 600 Peachtree St, NE, Suite 1000, Atlanta, GA 30308; POB 748645, Atlanta, GA 30374-8645; tel. (404) 653-0790; e-mail info@cdcfoundation.org; internet www.cdcfoundation.org.

Center for Inquiry—CFI

Established in 1991 as an umbrella organization for the Committee for Skeptical Inquiry (CSI) and the Council for Secular Humanism (CODESH).

Activities: Works in the fields of science and religion through the application of critical thinking, evidence, science and compassion in public policy. The Center promotes atheism, secular humanism, secularism and scepticism. Main initiatives include: Secular Rescue, which provides emergency assistance to activists, bloggers, publishers and writers facing threats because of their beliefs or statements on religion; the Campaign for Free Expression, which raises public awareness about human rights and the right to freedom of expression, and International Blasphemy Rights Day; the Teacher Institute for Evolutionary Science, which trains schoolteachers on teaching evolution; Quackwatch, a network of websites focusing on health fads, fallacies, frauds, misconduct and myths; the Translations Project, which translates scientific texts into local languages where access may be restricted; the CFI Investigations Group, which investigates paranormal claims; Openly Secular, a coalition of organizations that seek to eliminate discrimination against secular people; and the CFI Libraries, for visiting scholars and researchers. It has 13 branches in the USA, with international branches in

Argentina, Canada, the People's Republic of China, France, Kenya, Peru, Poland and Spain. The Richard Dawkins Foundation for Reason and Science (f. 2006) became a division in 2016.

Geographical Area of Activity: International.

Publications: Annual Report; *The Morning Heresy* (newsletter); blog; toolkits.

Finance: Annual revenue US $8.5m., expenditure $5.0m. (31 Dec. 2021).

Board of Directors: Eddie Tabash (Chair.).

Principal Staff: Pres. and CEO Robyn E. Blumner.

Contact Details: POB 741, Amherst, NY 14226; tel. (716) 636-4869; e-mail info@centerforinquiry.org; internet centerforinquiry.org.

Center for Victims of Torture—CVT

Founded in 1985 by Rudy Perpich, former Governor of Minnesota.

Activities: Provides direct care for victims of politically motivated torture and their families. The Center evaluates and monitors the progress of survivors in its care programmes; runs training programmes for healthcare, education and social work professionals in the USA and abroad; and works towards the elimination of torture through public policy initiatives and education campaigns. The New Tactics in Human Rights programme brings together an online community of 3,500 human rights defenders in over 120 countries, organizing monthly Tactical Dialogues and providing access to a database of more than 220 human rights tactics. It has offices in Ethiopia, Jordan and Kenya.

Geographical Area of Activity: International.

Publications: Annual Report; *Storycloth* (newsletter); *Tactical Notebooks*; training materials; *Healing and Human Rights* (blog).

Finance: Annual revenue US $31.4m., expenditure $32.1m. (30 Sept. 2023).

Board of Directors: Julia Classen (Chair.); Connie Magnuson (Vice-Chair.); Charles P. Henry (Past Chair.); Kate Barr (Treas.).

Principal Staff: Pres. and CEO Dr Simon Adams.

Contact Details: 2356 University Ave West, Suite 430, St Paul, MN 55114; tel. (612) 436-4800; e-mail cvt@cvt.org; internet www.cvt.org.

The Century Foundation—TCF

Founded in 1919 by Edward A. Filene as the Co-operative League; formerly known as the Twentieth Century Fund, Inc.

Activities: Conducts research nationally and internationally in the fields of communications, international affairs and economic development, and on major political, economic and social institutions. Main programme areas are: economics and inequality; retirement security; education; healthcare; homeland security; election reform; media and politics; and international affairs. The Foundation awards the Leonard Silk Journalism Fellowship to an established journalist producing a book on a topic that the Foundation considers an important contemporary issue. In 2019 it launched Next100, a policy think tank. Has an office in Washington, DC.

Geographical Area of Activity: International.

Restrictions: Not a grantmaking foundation.

Publications: Annual Report; newsletter; studies; paperback series.

Finance: Annual revenue –US $1.2m., expenditure $10.0m. (30 June 2022).

Trustees: Bradley Abelow (Chair.).

Principal Staff: Pres. Julie Margetta Morgan.

Contact Details: 1 Whitehall St, 15th Floor, New York, NY 10004; tel. (917) 512-3806; e-mail info@tcf.org; internet www.tcf.org.

Cetana Educational Foundation

Established in 1993.

Activities: Promotes leadership development, supporting local institutions with educational resources and professional development. The Foundation provides English language courses and develops critical thinking skills to prepare students for study abroad. It has learning centres in Kyaing Tong which offer courses in English language, professional development and teacher training; operates a scholarship programme for study abroad; and distributes book and journal donations to college-level institutions and medical schools, and to university and other libraries throughout the country. Learning centre in Yangon was temporarily closed in 2025.

Geographical Area of Activity: Malaysia, Myanmar, Thailand, USA.

Publications: Newsletter; trilingual dictionaries (in English, Myanmar/Burmese and either Karen, Kachin, Shan or Chin); Teacher's Guide.

Board of Directors: Susan C. Jennings (Pres.); Dr Myat Myat Mon (Vice-Pres.); Michael Jennings (Treas.); Chenault Spence (Sec.).

Contact Details: 487 Jefferson Rd, Princeton, NJ 08540; tel. (609) 865-5644; internet www.cetana.org.

Charles and Lynn Schusterman Family Philanthropies

Established in 1987, as Charles and Lynn Schusterman Family Foundation, by Charles Schusterman, founder of oil and gas company Samson Resources, and his wife Lynn; present name adopted in 2021.

Activities: Works to improve lives of marginalized people and communities, strengthen communities advance equity, based on Jewish values. Main programmes areas are: criminal justice; democracy and voting rights; education; gender and reproductive equity; the local Tusla community; Jewish community affairs; and funding projects in Israel. The REALITY programme organizes week-long visits to Israel for people aged 25–45 years who are recognized leaders in their field. The ROI ('Return On Investment') Community is an international social change network of young Jewish activists, entrepreneurs and innovators, which organizes an annual summit and offers microgrants for personal and professional development. The Schusterman Fellowship is an 18-month programme for emerging leaders in Jewish and Israeli organizations, with 8–12 years' experience. The Foundation offers the Schusterman Fellowship for training in leadership roles at Jewish or Israeli organizations and funds education reform within and outside of US school systems to improve opportunities and outcomes for all students. Has offices in Tulsa, Washington, DC, Atlanta, GA, San Francisco, GA; and Jerusalem, Israel.

Geographical Area of Activity: Israel, USA.

Restrictions: No grants to individuals; non-sectarian groups or local Jewish programmes outside Tulsa; Schusterman Fellows by nomination only.

Publications: *Impact Magazine*; *Leadership Development Guide*; playbooks; toolkits; blogs.

Finance: Annual revenue US $230.8m., expenditure $405.0m. (31 Dec. 2022).

Board of Trustees: Lynn Schusterman (Chair. Emerita); Stacy Schusterman (Chair.).

Principal Staff: Co-Pres Lisa Eisen, Julie Mikuta, David Weil; CEO Ohad Reifen.

Contact Details: 110 West 7th St, Suite 2000, Tulsa, OK 74119; tel. (918) 879-0290; e-mail information@schusterman.org; internet www.schusterman.org.

Charles Koch Foundation

Established in 1980, as the Charles G. Koch Charitable Foundation, by Charles Koch, Chair. and CEO of Koch Industries, to advance social wellbeing through economic freedom.

Activities: Works with social entrepreneurs to advance societal progress through innovation and academic research. Programme areas include: criminal justice; economic opportunity; entrepreneurship; foreign policy; free speech and peace; immigration; primary and secondary education; and technology and innovation. The Foundation offers grants to universities and non-profit organizations for research in its areas of interest; and graduate student grants and fellowships. It supports the Charles Koch Institute, which carries out public policy research on societal problems.

Geographical Area of Activity: International (mainly USA).

Publications: Newsletter.

Finance: Annual revenue US $1.3m., expenditure $83.0m. (31 Dec. 2023).

Board: Charles G. Koch (Chair.).

Principal Staff: Pres. Brian Hooks; Exec. Dir Ryan Stowers.

Contact Details: 4201 Wilson Blvd, Suite 0800, Arlington, VA 22203; tel. (703) 875-1600; internet www.charleskochfoundation.org.

Charles Stewart Mott Foundation—CSMF

Founded in 1926 by Charles Stewart Mott, head of Weston-Mott Company, an automotive parts manufacturer.

Activities: Promotes a just, equitable and sustainable society. Main grantmaking programmes focus on: civil society, strengthening the non-profit sector and increasing civic engagement; education, alleviating poverty through expanding educational opportunities in low-income communities; environment, supporting stewardship of natural resources in North America and globally; and Flint, MI, supporting the local community in the areas of education, employment and arts and culture. The Foundation has offices in Troy, MI, London (UK) and Johannesburg (South Africa).

Geographical Area of Activity: North America, Central and Eastern Europe, South Africa, UK.

Restrictions: Does not make grants to individuals nor to religious organizations for religious purposes; the Education programme only funds projects in the USA.

Publications: Annual Report; occasional reports.

Finance: Annual income US $109.6m., expenditure $221.7m. (31 Dec. 2022).

Board of Trustees: Ridgway H. White (Pres., CEO and Chair.); Frederick S. Kirkpatrick (Vice-Chair.).

Contact Details: Mott Foundation Bldg, 503 S Saginaw St, Suite 1200, Flint, MI 48502-1851; tel. (810) 238-5651; e-mail info@mott.org; internet www.mott.org.

The Chatlos Foundation, Inc

Established in 1953 by William F. Chatlos, who founded a construction company.

Activities: Funds Bible colleges and seminaries, religious causes, medicine and health, liberal arts colleges; and social welfare, including child welfare, vocational training, alternatives to prison, concerns for elderly people and people living with disabilities, and people and families in crisis. Grants range from US $2,000 to $20,000.

Geographical Area of Activity: Worldwide.

Restrictions: Grants only to charities registered in the USA; does not fund medical research, individual church congregations, education below college level, the arts or individuals.

Publications: Information brochure; application guidelines.

Finance: Annual revenue –US $242,536, expenditure $3.5m. (31 Dec. 2022).

Board of Trustees: Kathryn A. Randle (Chair.).

Principal Staff: Pres., CEO and Chief Investment Officer William J. Chatlos.

Contact Details: POB 915048, Longwood, FL 32791-5048; tel. (407) 862-5077; e-mail info@chatlos.org; internet www.chatlos.org.

The Chicago Community Trust

Founded in 1915 to assist the inhabitants of Cook County, IL.

Activities: Works to address racial and ethnic wealth inequity through offering grants for general operating support and specific programmes in the areas of the arts and humanities, basic human needs, community development, education and health. Affinity Trust giving groups include: African American Legacy; Asian Giving Circle; Disabilities Fund; LGBT Community Fund; Nuestro Futuro (for Latinx philanthropy); Pillars Fund (for US Muslims); and Young Leaders Fund. The Trust organizes the annual On the Table forum; and, with the Knight Foundation, created the On the Table National Learning Network online platform for foundations, civic institutions and non-profit leaders.

Geographical Area of Activity: USA (Greater Chicago).

Restrictions: No grants to individuals.

Publications: Annual Report; *Trust in Action* (quarterly newsletter); grant guidelines; financial statement.

Finance: Annual revenue US $1,720.1m., expenditure $1,613.1m. (30 Sept. 2023).

Executive Committee: Bryan Traubert (Chair.); Renetta McCann (Vice-Chair.).

Principal Staff: Pres. and CEO Andrea Sáenz.

Contact Details: 33 South State St, Suite 750, Chicago, IL 60603; tel. (312) 616-8000; e-mail info@cct.org; internet www.cct.org.

ChildFund International

Founded in 1938 by Dr J. Calvitt Clarke, a Presbyterian minister; previous names include Christian Children's Fund and China's Children Fund; an international child development and protection organization.

Activities: Helps children who live in poverty and promotes societies that value, protect and advance the wellbeing and rights of children. Programmes focus on: child protection, preventing violence, exploitation and abuse; early childhood development, meeting young children's emotional, mental and physical needs; education, providing access to schools and educating families about early childhood development, livelihood training and saving money; economic strengthening, helping families build sustainable livelihoods; emergencies, safeguarding children during crises, providing emergency response and psychosocial support; health, making healthcare accessible to children and their families. The organization works in 23 countries, including the USA.

Geographical Area of Activity: South America and Central America, South Asia, South-East Asia, sub-Saharan Africa, USA.

Restrictions: No grants to individuals.

Publications: Annual Report; newsletter; booklets; studies.

Finance: Annual revenue US $242.5m., expenditure $222.3m. (30 June 2024).

Board of Directors: Tamar Manuelyan Atinc (Chair.); Helen Thompson (Vice-Chair.); Terry Peigh (Sec.).

Principal Staff: Pres. and CEO Isam Ghanim.

Contact Details: 2821 Emerywood Parkway, Richmond, VA 23294; POB 1911, Merrifield, VA 22116-1911; tel. (804) 756-2700; e-mail questions@childfund.org; internet www.childfund.org.

Children International—CI

Established in 1936 to care for disabled children and provide outreach to widows and orphans.

Activities: Works in the fields of children's health, welfare and education. The organization provides enrollees in its programmes with access to local doctors, dentists, tutors and sponsors; a safe place (such as a community centre); and a path out of poverty that includes youth development programmes to strengthen life skills, increase social responsibility, and prepare the enrollees to join the workforce. It also organizes sponsorship of children by supporters.

Geographical Area of Activity: Colombia, Dominican Repub., Ecuador, Guatemala, Honduras, India, Mexico, Philippines, USA, Zambia.

Publications: Annual Report; *Journeys* (magazine).

Finance: Annual revenue US $109.3m., expenditure $105.5m. (30 Sept. 2022).

Board of Directors: Adam Newsome (Chair.); Marvin Irby (Treas.).

Principal Staff: Pres. and CEO Susana Eshleman.

Contact Details: 2000 E Red Bridge Rd, Kansas City, MO 64131; POB 219055, Kansas City, MO 64121; tel. (816) 942-2000; e-mail children@children.org; internet www.children.org.

China Medical Board—CMB

Established in 1928 by the Rockefeller Foundation (q.v.) to provide financial support to the Peking Union Medical College and similar institutions in East Asia.

Activities: Supports health institutions in enhancing educational and research activities in medicine, nursing and public health. The organization targets its grantmaking at key Chinese and other Asian universities and encourages international groups to collaborate directly with them. It has offices in Bangkok (Thailand) and Beijing (People's Repub. of China).

Geographical Area of Activity: People's Repub. of China (including Tibet), Repub. of China (Taiwan), Hong Kong, Indonesia, Repub. of Korea, Lao People's Dem. Repub., Malaysia, Myanmar, Philippines, Singapore, Thailand.

Restrictions: Does not accept unsolicited applications.

Publications: Biennial Report.

Finance: Annual revenue US $13.7m., expenditure $10.2m. (31 Dec. 2022).

Principal Staff: Pres. Dr Roger I. Glass; Exec. Vice-Pres. Barbara Stoll.

Contact Details: 2 Arrow St, Cambridge, MA 02138; tel. (617) 979-8000; e-mail info@cmbfound.org; internet www.chinamedicalboard.org.

Christopher & Dana Reeve Foundation

Established in 1999 following the merger of the American Paralysis Association (f. 1982) and the Christopher Reeve Paralysis Foundation.

Activities: Works to cure spinal cord injury through funding innovative research. The Foundation improves quality of life for people living with paralysis, offering financial support, information and advocacy. In the USA, it supports a network of five Clinical Rehabilitation Centres and five Community Fitness and Wellness Facilities; and through the Quality of Life Grants Program supports non-profit organizations in the USA and internationally with awards ranging from US $25,000 to $50,000.

Geographical Area of Activity: International.

Restrictions: No grants to individuals.

Publications: Annual Report; newsletter.

Finance: Annual revenue US $16.8m., expenditure $14.4m. (31 Dec. 2021).

Board of Directors: James Calbi (Chair.); John E. McConnell (Vice-Chair.); Tania Lynn Taylor (Treas.); Helen V. Cantwell (Sec.).

Principal Staff: Pres. and CEO Maggie Goldberg.

Contact Details: 636 Morris Turnpike, Suite 3A, Short Hills, NJ 07078; tel. (973) 379-2690; e-mail TeamReeve@Reeve.org; internet www.christopherreeve.org.

CIEE—Council on International Educational Exchange

Founded in 1947 by organizations active in the fields of international education and student travel to improve understanding and co-operation between countries, and help to re-establish student exchanges after the Second World War.

Activities: Represents educational institutions in developing educational exchange policy; provides consultation services and evaluation of exchange programmes; and acts as a clearing house for information. The Council awards a range of scholarships and grants; organizes conferences and seminars, and administers programmes to work, study, teach, carry out research, undertake professional development and volunteer abroad. It comprises the Ping Foundation (f. 2004). Operates in more than 30 countries and has branches in Boston, MA, Germany and the United Kingdom.

Geographical Area of Activity: International.

Publications: *Journal of Studies in International Education* (2 a year); *Council–ISP News* (monthly newsletter); *Update* (monthly); guides; handbook; blog.

Finance: Annual revenue US $7.6m., expenditure $6.6m. (31 Aug. 2023).

Board of Directors: Laura A. Brege (Chair.); Francis X. Taylor (Vice-Chair.).

Principal Staff: Pres. and CEO Dr James P. Pellow.

Contact Details: 600 Southborough Dr., Suite 104, South Portland, ME 04106; tel. (207) 553-4000; e-mail contact@ciee.org; internet www.ciee.org.

Citi Foundation

Established in 1995, as Citigroup Foundation, by Citigroup, an investment bank and financial services provider.

Activities: Promotes economic progress and works to improve the lives of people in low-income communities. Programmes focus on increasing financial inclusion, creating job opportunities for young people and building economically vibrant cities. The Foundation leads the bank's international Pathways to Progress initiative, supporting programmes that help young people aged 16–24 years to develop an entrepreneurial mindset, acquire leadership, financial and workplace skills and start their first job; employee volunteers provide professional advice, serving as mentors and coaches. The Community Progress Makers Fund supports innovative approaches by non-profit organizations to solving longstanding urban problems in six cities: Chicago, Los Angeles, Miami, New York City, San Francisco and Washington, DC. Has partner organizations in more than 80 countries and territories.

Geographical Area of Activity: International.

Restrictions: Does not fund individuals, political causes, religious organizations or fundraising events; rarely accepts unsolicited applications.

Publications: Environmental, Social and Governance Report.

Finance: Annual revenue US $82.5m., expenditure $108.0m. (31 Dec. 2022).

Board of Directors: Vis Raghavan (Exec. Vice-Chair.).

Principal Staff: Pres. Brandee McHale.

Contact Details: 388 Greenwich St, New York, NY 10013; tel. (212) 793-8451; e-mail citizenship@citi.com; internet www.citigroup.com/global/foundation.

Clara Lionel Foundation—CLF

Established in 2012 by Robyn Fenty (Rihanna), a singer, in honour of her grandparents, Clara and Lionel Braithwaite.

Activities: Supports organizations working in education and humanitarian response. Main programmes focus on: emergency response and climate resilience, including strengthening school and reproductive and sexual health clinic infrastructure; and education, providing scholarships for girls' secondary education and, through the Global Scholarship Program, for young women from the Caribbean and South America to pursue higher education in the USA. Legacy projects include supporting the Clara Braithwaite Center for Oncology and Nuclear Medicine at the Queen Elizabeth Hospital in Barbados; and funding organizations in the USA working for racial justice and systemic change.

CLEAR Global UNITED STATES OF AMERICA

Geographical Area of Activity: Caribbean, North America, sub-Saharan Africa.
Publications: Newsletter.
Finance: Annual revenue US $28.7m., expenditure $20.3m. (31 Dec. 2022).
Board of Directors: Tamara Larsen (Pres.).
Principal Staff: Exec. Dir Jessie Schutt-Aine.
Contact Details: c/o FFO, 545 Fifth Ave, New York, NY 10017; tel. (212) 202-3230; e-mail info@claralionelfoundation.org; internet claralionelfoundation.org.

CLEAR Global

Originally founded in 2011 as Translators without Borders—TWB; CLEAR Global is a non-profit that also comprises CLEAR Tech and CLEAR Insights.
Activities: CLEAR Global helps people get vital information and be heard, whatever language they speak. Provides research and scalable language technology solutions that improve two-way communication with communities that speak marginalized languages. With its innovative language technology solutions, research, and the TWB community of over 100,000 language volunteers, CLEAR Global supports its partner organizations working around the world.
Geographical Area of Activity: Worldwide.
Publications: Annual Report; research reports, summaries and recommendations; language and communication resources; language-use data and maps; CLEAR Global Blog; TWB Blog.
Finance: Annual revenue US $15.3m., expenditure $16.5m. (2022).
Board of Directors: Andrew Bredenkamp (Chair.); Donna Parrish (Sec.).
Principal Staff: CEO Aimee Ansari.
Contact Details: 9169 W State St #3055, Garden City, ID 83714; tel. (203) 794-6698; e-mail info@clearglobal.org; internet clearglobal.org.

Cleveland Foundation

Founded in 1914 by Frederick Harris Goff, a lawyer and philanthropist, as the world's first community foundation.
Activities: Serves the Greater Cleveland area, providing community leadership, making grants and awarding scholarships. Priority areas are: the arts and culture; economic and workforce development; education; environment; health and human services; leadership development; neighbourhood revitalization and engagement; and youth and social services. The Foundation offers Public Service Fellowships to prepare young leaders from across the country for a career in public service; and Homer C. Wadsworth Awards, recognizing local civic leaders. It also presents the annual Anisfield-Wolf Book Awards, for works that address racism or expand the appreciation of human diversity. Comprises more than 1,300 funds.
Geographical Area of Activity: USA.
Restrictions: No grants for religious purposes, and not normally for endowments, membership drives, fundraising projects, travel, publications or videos.
Publications: Annual Report; newsletter (monthly); information brochures.
Finance: Annual revenue US $418.1m., expenditure $148.0m. (31 Dec. 2023).
Board of Directors: Randell McShepard (Chair.); Richard Stovsky (Vice-Chair.).
Principal Staff: Pres. and CEO Lillian A. Kuri.
Contact Details: 6601 Euclid Ave, Cleveland, OH 44103; tel. (216) 861-3810; e-mail hello@clevefdn.org; internet www.clevelandfoundation.org.

Cleveland H. Dodge Foundation, Inc

Founded in 1917 by Cleveland H. Dodge, an industrialist and philanthropist.
Activities: Funds projects that support underprivileged young people and early years education. The Foundation gives priority to organizations based in New York City.
Geographical Area of Activity: Middle East, USA.
Restrictions: Does not make grants to individuals, for healthcare or medical research.
Publications: Annual Report; programme policy statement.
Finance: Annual revenue US $2.4m., expenditure $3.8m. (31 Dec. 2022).
Board of Directors: William D. Rueckert (Pres.); Johnson Garrett (Vice-Pres.); Catherine Olmsted Kerr (Treas.); Louis E. Black (Sec.).
Principal Staff: Exec. Dir Sarah Barnett.
Contact Details: 515 Madison Ave, Suite 1125, New York, NY 10022; tel. (212) 972-2800; e-mail connect@chdodgefoundation.org; internet www.chdodgefoundation.org.

Clinton Foundation

Founded in 2002 by Bill Clinton, 42nd President of the USA.
Activities: Operates internationally in the areas of climate change, economic development, women and girls, global health, and health and wellness. Programmes include: the Clinton Climate Initiative, developing renewable energy in the Caribbean; Clinton Development Initiative, helping smallholder farmers in Malawi, Rwanda and Tanzania; Clinton Global Initiative leadership forum and Clinton Global Initiative University higher education programme; Clinton Health Matters Initiative, with a focus on preventing prescription drug abuse in the USA; and Too Small to Fail early years intervention. Independent and associated programmes include: Acceso (f. 2007 as the Clinton Giustra Enterprise Partnership), which supports agribusiness in Latin America and the Caribbean; the Clinton Foundation in Haiti, promoting economic development and empowerment of women and girls; and No Ceilings: The Full Participation Project, empowering women and girls and countering gender-based violence. The Foundation also maintains the Clinton Presidential Center, in Little Rock, AR, which organizes educational programmes and events, and jointly runs the Presidential Leadership Scholars programme with the George W. Bush Presidential Center, George H. W. Bush Presidential Library Foundation and Lyndon Baines Johnson Foundation (q.v.).
Geographical Area of Activity: International.
Restrictions: Does not usually make grants to outside organizations.
Publications: Annual Report; blog.
Finance: Annual revenue US $9.1m., expenditure $55.3m. (31 Dec. 2022).
Board of Directors: Bill Clinton (Chair.); Chelsea Clinton (Vice-Chair.).
Principal Staff: Pres. Bari Lurie; Interim CEO Robert S. Harrison; Exec. Dir Stephanie S. Streett.
Contact Details: 55 West 125th St, 14th Floor, New York, NY 10027; tel. (212) 397-2255; e-mail development@clintonfoundation.org; internet www.clintonfoundation.org.

Clooney Foundation for Justice—CFJ

Established in 2016 by Amal Clooney, an international human rights lawyer, and George Clooney, an actor and co-founder of The Sentry (f. 2015) investigative and policy team and Enough Project (f. 2007) human rights organization.
Activities: Advocates for justice for marginalized and vulnerable people, including refugees, and accountability for hate crimes and human rights abuses. Initiatives include TrialWatch, representing people who have been unfairly targeted by oppressive governments through the courts; The Sentry, which works to expose financial corruption; and The Docket, which aims to bring individual and corporate beneficiaries of war crimes and human rights abuses to trial.
Geographical Area of Activity: International.

UNITED STATES OF AMERICA   *Consuelo Zobel Alger Foundation*

Finance: Annual revenue US $10.0m., expenditure $8.6m. (31 Dec. 2022).
Board: Amal Clooney, George Clooney (Co-Chair.).
Principal Staff: Co-CEOs Emma Lindsay, David Sagal.
Contact Details: 169 Madison Ave Suite 11436, New York, NY 10016; tel. (347) 735-8944; e-mail info@cfj.org; internet cfj.org.

The Coca-Cola Foundation, Inc

Founded in 1984 by the Coca-Cola Co, a soft drinks manufacturer; part of a global network of 20 local and regional foundations.
Activities: Supports sustainable community initiatives. Main programmes include: access to clean water, its conservation and recycling; and emergency relief during natural disasters. The Foundation supports local community programmes in the USA that focus on activities such as arts and culture and economic development; and HIV/AIDS prevention and awareness programmes in sub-Saharan Africa and Latin America.
Geographical Area of Activity: International.
Restrictions: No grants to individuals.
Publications: Annual Report.
Finance: Annual revenue US $128.6m., expenditure $96.7m. (31 Dec. 2023).
Board: Beatriz Perez (Chair.); Kathy N. Waller (Treas.); Inal Finan (Sec.).
Principal Staff: Pres. Saadia Madsbjerg.
Contact Details: 1 Coca-Cola Plaza, Atlanta, GA 30313-2420; tel. (404) 689-7363; e-mail cocacolacommunityrequest@na.ko.com; internet www.coca-colacompany.com/social/coca-cola-foundation.

The Commonwealth Fund

Founded in 1918 by Anna M. Harkness, widow of oil investor Stephen V. Harkness, and others.
Activities: Works in the field of healthcare through supporting research and funding improvements in healthcare practice and policy. Major programme areas include: improving health insurance coverage and access to medical care; improving the quality of healthcare services; promoting ways for elderly Americans to participate more fully in community life; developing the capacities of children and young people; and improving the health of minorities. The Harkness Fellowships Program offers health policy fellowships to researchers and practitioners from Australia, Canada, France, Germany, the Netherlands, New Zealand, Norway and the United Kingdom to spend up to a year in the USA. The Fund also makes grants to enhance quality of life in New York City. It has an office in Washington, DC.
Geographical Area of Activity: International.
Publications: Annual Report; *Transforming Care* (newsletter); *To the Point* (blog); briefs; case studies; reports.
Finance: Annual revenue US $22.3m., expenditure $52.4m. (30 June 2023).
Board of Directors: Michael V. Drake (Chair.); Sheila P. Burke (Vice-Chair.).
Principal Staff: Pres. Joseph R. Betancourt.
Contact Details: 1 E 75th St, New York, NY 10021; tel. (212) 606-3800; e-mail info@cmwf.org; internet www.commonwealthfund.org.

Conrad N. Hilton Foundation

Founded in 1944 by Conrad N. Hilton, founder of Hilton Hotels; not connected to Hilton Worldwide.
Activities: Priority areas are: providing safe water in sub-Saharan Africa; supporting transition-age young people in foster care; ending chronic homelessness; helping children affected by HIV/AIDS; extending the Catholic Sisters Initiative; disaster relief and recovery; and providing development opportunities for employees in the hospitality sector. Following selection by an independent international jury, the Foundation annually awards the US $2m. Hilton Humanitarian Prize to a non-profit organization that reduces human suffering.
Geographical Area of Activity: Worldwide.
Restrictions: Does not accept unsolicited proposals; no grants to individuals.
Publications: Annual Report; newsletter.
Finance: Annual revenue US $787.6m., expenditure $269.0m. (31 Dec. 2023).
Board of Directors: Linda Hilton (Chair.); Justin McAuliffe (Vice-Chair.).
Principal Staff: Pres. and CEO Peter Laugharn.
Contact Details: 1 Dole Dr., Westlake Village, CA 91362; tel. (818) 851-3700; e-mail communications@hiltonfoundation.org; internet www.hiltonfoundation.org.

Conservation International Foundation

Founded in 1987 by Peter Seligmann, a conservationist.
Activities: Works with governments and other organizations to promote sustained biological diversity and ecosystems and prevent species extinction, along with basic economic and social requirements. The Foundation runs international programmes; carries out research; promotes educational projects and eco-tourism; researches and markets rain forest products; and assists in policymaking. It makes grants to individuals and local not-for-profit organizations in all countries or regions that are hot spots or wilderness areas; and offers fellowships to innovators, scientists and indigenous leaders. Incorporates the Betty and Gordon Moore Center for Science and the Center for Global Policy and Government Affairs; and has offices in more than 24 countries.
Geographical Area of Activity: International.
Publications: Annual Report; Impact Report; newsletters; reports; scientific papers; brochures; blog; books and other publications; Trends.Earth (Land Degradation Monitoring Toolbox).
Finance: Annual revenue US $246.7m., expenditure $247.4m. (30 June 2023).
Board of Directors: Peter A. Seligmann (Chair.).
Executive Committee: Wes Bush (Chair.); Harrison Ford (Vice-Chair.).
Leadership Council: Daniel A. Shaw (Chair.); Kristina Brittenham (Vice-Chair.).
Principal Staff: CEO Dr M. Sanjayan.
Contact Details: 2011 Crystal Dr., Suite 500, Arlington, VA 22202; tel. (703) 341-2400; e-mail inquiry@conservation.org; internet www.conservation.org.

Consuelo Zobel Alger Foundation

Established in 1988, as the Consuelo Zobel Alger Foundation, by Consuelo Zobel de Ayala y Montojo Terrentegui Zambrano Alger, whose family founded the Ayala Group, a conglomerate; formerly known as the Children and Youth Foundation of the Philippines. Present name adopted in 2004.
Activities: A private, US-based foundation that works for the prevention and treatment of abuse, neglect, and exploitation of children, women, and their families in the Philippines and in Hawai'i. Through programmess in the Philippine branch, the Foundation collaborates closely with like-minded institutions for evidence-based and context-sensitive initiatives that advance children's rights.
Geographical Area of Activity: Hawaii, Philippines.
Restrictions: Supports partner organizations only.
Publications: Reports.
Finance: Annual revenue US $8.2m., expenditure $9.0m. (31 Dec. 2022).
Board of Directors: Constance H. Lau (Chair.); Hoyt H. Zia (Sec.).
Principal Staff: President and CEO Gregory T. Auberry.

Corus International

Contact Details: 110 N Hotel St, Honolulu, HI 96817; tel. (808) 532 3939; e-mail info@consuelo.org; internet www.consuelo.org.

Corus International

Established in 2020 as a joint initiative of Lutheran World Relief (f. 1945) and IMA World Health (f. 1960); an ensemble of faith-based non-profit and for-profit organizations, which also incorporates CGA Technologies, Farmers Market Coffee and Ground Up Investing.

Activities: Works with local partners and governments to build capacity, provide access to resources, improve public health and build economic resilience in communities experiencing poverty conflict and other hardships. Main programme areas are: health, including disease prevention and treatment, global health security, health systems strengthening, maternal and child health, nutrition, sexual and gender-based violence and water, sanitation and hygiene; rural economic development, including agricultural value chain strengthening, climate-smart improved agriculture, enterprise capacity-building, livelihood diversification, market systems analysis, rural financing and water and land management; and technology for development, using smartphones and other technologies to provide digital tools, geospatial satellite imagery, information sharing and education via SMS (text messages), mobile banking and cash transfers. Cross-cutting themes are gender equity, resilience and youth development. The organization invests in enterprises that add value to small-scale farmers' crops, reinvesting profits in local communities; and offering complementary social services, marketing, organizational management training and technical assistance. It also provides emergency humanitarian assistance during crises and helps communities to recover.

Geographical Area of Activity: International.

Publications: Newsletter; blog.

Finance: Annual revenue US $126,977, expenditure $24.6m. (30 Sept. 2023).

Board of Directors: Kenneth Jones, II (Chair.); Dr Kathi Tunheim (Vice-Chair.); Philip Atkins-Pattenson (Sec.).

Principal Staff: Pres. and CEO Daniel V. Speckhard.

Contact Details: 1730 M St, NW, Suite 1100, Washington, DC 20036; tel. (202) 888-6200; e-mail info@imaworldhealth.org; internet corusinternational.org.

Council for International Exchange of Scholars—CIES

Founded in 1947 to assist the US Government in administering the Fulbright Scholar Program; the scholar division of the Institute of International Education (IIE).

Activities: Aims to increase mutual understanding between the people of the USA and those of other nations; to strengthen the ties that unite the USA with other nations; and promote international co-operation for educational and cultural advancement. The Council administers the Fulbright Scholar Program, working with a network of binational Fulbright Commissions in 49 countries and 90 US diplomatic posts. The Program offers more than 400 teaching, research or combination teaching/research awards in over 130 countries.

Geographical Area of Activity: Worldwide.

Restrictions: Fulbright Scholar Awards are open to US citizens who hold a doctorate or comparable professional qualification, along with university or college teaching experience, for research or teaching in any discipline; Awards are also open to nationals of those countries to conduct research or lecture in the USA.

Publications: Annual Report; *Fulbright Online Awards Catalog*; *Fulbright Scholar Program: Grants for Faculty and Professionals*; blog.

Finance: Funded by the US Dept of State, Bureau of Educational and Cultural Affairs.

Advisory Board: Joan Gabel (Chair.).

Contact Details: Institute of International Education, 1350 Eye St NW, Washington, DC 20005; tel. (202) 686-4000; e-mail scholars@iie.org; internet fulbrightscholars.org.

Counterpart International

Founded in 1965 by Betty Bryant Silverstein, an Australian actress, and Fr Stan Hosie, a Christian Marist priest; comprises the WomenLead Institute.

Activities: Works in the fields of international development. The organization helps people in need in the areas of civil society, food security, private enterprise, environmental resource management, humanitarian relief and healthcare. It builds the capacity of local leaders, organizations and social sector networks to solve their own self-defined economic, ecological, political and social problems in ways that are sustainable, practical and independent. Operates in 67 countries.

Geographical Area of Activity: International.

Publications: Annual Report; *Counterpart Connections* (newsletter).

Finance: Annual revenue US $51.6m., expenditure $51.6m. (30 Sept. 2023).

Board of Directors: Mary Karen Wills (Chair.); Hilda M. Arellano (Vice-Chair.); Roldan Trujillo (Sec.).

Principal Staff: Pres. and CEO Ann Huddock.

Contact Details: 1919 Pennsylvania Ave NW, 425, Washington, DC 20006; tel. (571) 447-5700; e-mail communications@counterpart.org; internet www.counterpart.org.

Covenant Foundation

Established in 1990 by the Crown Family Foundation in partnership with the Jewish Education Service of North America; a programme of the Crown Family Philanthropies (q.v.).

Activities: Perpetuates the identity and cultural heritage of Jewish people through strengthening Jewish education. The Foundation supports programmes in Jewish schools and institutions and funds Jewish educators; issues information about effective programmes; and organizes conferences. It awards Signature Grants, for innovative programmes in Jewish schools and community organizations, typically worth up to US $150,000 over three years; and Ignition Grants, for new or untested ideas, worth up to $20,000 for one year.

Geographical Area of Activity: Canada, USA.

Restrictions: Only funds programmes in North America; no funding for endowments, building funds or tuition fees.

Publications: *The First 10 Years*; *Grant Impact and Sustainability Report 2000–2007*; *Covenant of Dreams*.

Finance: Annual revenue US $6.4m., expenditure $6.0m. (31 Dec. 2022).

Board of Directors: Deborah S. Meyer (Chair.).

Principal Staff: Exec. Dir Joni Blinderman.

Contact Details: 45 Rockefeller Plaza, Suite 2300, New York, NY 10111; tel. (212) 245-3500; e-mail info@covenantfn.org; internet www.covenantfn.org.

The Craig and Susan McCaw Foundation

Established in 1998 by Craig McCaw, a former telecommunications executive, and Susan McCaw, former US ambassador to Austria.

Activities: Focuses on access to education, international economic development and environmental conservation. The Foundation makes grants to organizations that have an entrepreneurial and innovative approach.

Geographical Area of Activity: Africa, South-East Asia.

Restrictions: No unsolicited applications.

Finance: Annual revenue US $3.8m., expenditure $8.9m. (31 Dec. 2019).

Board of Directors: Craig O. McCaw (Pres.); Susan R. McCaw, Amit Mehta (Vice-Pres); Teresa Mason (Sec.).

Contact Details: POB 2908, Kirkland, WA 98083-2908; tel. (425) 828-8000; internet mccawfoundation.org.

UNITED STATES OF AMERICA

CRDF Global
Established in 1995 by the National Science Foundation (q.v.); formerly known as the US Civilian Research & Development Foundation.

Activities: Promotes peace and prosperity through international scientific collaboration and exchanges. Main programme areas are: agriculture and food security; chemical, biological, radiological, nuclear, and explosive security; cybersecurity; global health; innovation ecosystems; strategic trade and border security; and women in science and security. The Foundation offers fellowships, research grants, technical resources and training, to promote scientific and technical collaboration. It works in more than 120 countries, with offices in Jordan and Ukraine.

Geographical Area of Activity: Asia, Eurasia, Middle East and North Africa.

Restrictions: Does not fund unsolicited proposals; companies or individuals; early childhood, primary or secondary education initiatives; or projects related to military or weapons research and development.

Publications: Annual Report; newsletter; factsheets.

Finance: Annual revenue US $70.8m., expenditure $72.5m. (31 Dec. 2022).

Board of Directors: Dr Tomas Diaz de la Rubia (Chair.);.

Principal Staff: CEO Mike Dignam.

Contact Details: 1776 Wilson Blvd, Suite 300, Arlington, VA 22209; tel. (703) 526-9720; e-mail info@crdfglobal.org; internet www.crdfglobal.org.

Crown Family Philanthropies
Founded in 1947 as the Arie and Ida Crown Memorial by members of the Crown family; present name adopted in 2009.

Activities: Supports positive social change. The organization offers grants in the areas of: access to high-quality education in Chicago schools, including arts and civics education; improving the ecological health of watersheds in the Midwest and Great Lakes region and supporting forest health in the Western United States; increasing access to high-quality healthcare in the Chicagoland region; improving the health of poor people in developing countries through community-based healthcare, including mother and child health, nutrition and psychosocial support in areas recovering from conflict; improving quality of life for people and families in low-income communities, providing safe housing and employment stability; and supporting and strengthening the Jewish community in the greater Chicago area through education and social services, and providing targeted support in Israel in the areas of medical care, poverty alleviation and higher education.

Geographical Area of Activity: Israel, sub-Saharan Africa, USA.

Restrictions: No grants to individuals; does not accept unsolicited applications.

Finance: Annual revenue US $26.4m., expenditure $46.3m. (31 Dec. 2023).

Board of Directors: Barbara Goodman Manilow (Chair.); A. Steven Crown (Vice-Chair.); James S. Crown (Treas.).

Principal Staff: Pres. Evan Hochberg.

Contact Details: 30 S Wells St 4049, Chicago, IL 60606; tel. (312) 750-6671; e-mail granthelp@crown-chicago.com; internet www.crownfamilyphilanthropies.org.

CURE International
Established in 1996; in 2019 it merged with International Aid, Inc (f. 1980), a Christian relief and development agency.

Activities: Works to improve the health and spiritual well-being of disabled children through a network of seven hospitals, in Ethiopia, Kenya, Malawi, Niger, the Philippines, Uganda, Zambia and Zimbabwe. The CURE Neuro programme carries out training, treatment and research into hydrocephalus and spina bifida, and offers fellowships. The Global Outreach (GO) programme organizes short-term missions for volunteers. Through International Aid it distributes hygiene kits, health products, and new and refurbished medical equipment and supplies to hospitals and clinics in developing countries, including Lab-In-A-Suitcase portable laboratories; collaborates with academia, businesses and NGOs to develop and implement training programmes for health professionals; and provides disaster relief.

Geographical Area of Activity: International.

Publications: Annual Report; newsletter.

Finance: Annual revenue US $45.5m., expenditure $40.6m. (30 June 2023).

Board of Directors: Jerry Tubergen (Chair.); Joe Stowell (Vice-Chair.); Peter Schulze (Treas.); Mike Houskamp (Sec.).

Principal Staff: Pres. and CEO Justin Narducci.

Contact Details: 70 Ionia Ave SW, Suite 200, Grand Rapids, MI 49503; tel. (616) 512-3105; e-mail info@cure.org; internet www.cure.org.

Cystic Fibrosis Foundation
Established in 1955 by a group of parents whose children had cystic fibrosis.

Activities: Works to cure cystic fibrosis and support people living with the disease. The Foundation funds research and drug development through grants and scholarships, promotes individualized treatment and provides access to high-quality, specialized care. It offers awards for research, training and career development. Has 70 chapters and branch offices in the USA.

Geographical Area of Activity: USA.

Publications: Annual Report; newsletters.

Finance: Annual revenue US $115.7m., expenditure $427.3m. (31 Dec. 2023).

Board of Trustees: Bryan White (Chair.); Teresa L. Elder, Dr Eric R. Olson (Vice-Chair.).

Principal Staff: Pres. and CEO Dr Michael Boyle.

Contact Details: 4550 Montgomery Ave, Suite 1100 N, Bethesda, MD 20814; tel. (301) 951-4422; e-mail info@cff.org; internet www.cff.org.

Dalio Foundation
Established in 2003 by Ray Dalio, founder of investment firm Bridgewater Associates, and Barbara Dalio; part of Dalio Philanthropies, which also includes the Beijing Dalio Foundation.

Activities: Main programmes are: Education; Ocean Exploration and Awareness; Investing in Technology Access and Education; Mental Health and Wellness; Financial Inclusion and Social Entrepreneurship; Community and the Arts; and China: Child Welfare and Capacity Building.

Geographical Area of Activity: International.

Restrictions: Does not accept unsolicited applications.

Finance: Annual revenue US $131.3m., expenditure $19.1m. (31 Dec. 2022).

Board: Ray Dalio (Pres.).

Principal Staff: Exec. Dir Janine Racanelli.

Contact Details: 1 Glendenning Pl., Westport, CT 06880; tel. (203) 291-5000; e-mail inquiries@daliophilanthropies.org; internet www.daliophilanthropies.org.

Damon Runyon Cancer Research Foundation
Founded in 1946 by Walter Winchell in memory of Damon Runyon, a sportswriter and journalist.

Activities: Awards up to 60 postdoctoral research fellowships a year for basic scientists and physician scientists, allowing scientists and medical practitioners beginning full-time post-doctoral research to carry out cancer research.

Geographical Area of Activity: USA.

Restrictions: US citizens may study in any country; foreign researchers' study must be carried out in the USA.

Publications: Annual Report; newsletter.

Finance: Annual revenue US $21.9m., expenditure $21.9m. (30 June 2023).
Board of Directors: Andrew S. Rachleff (Chair.).
Principal Staff: Pres. and CEO Dr Yung S. Lie.
Contact Details: 1 Exchange Plaza, 55 Broadway, Suite 302, New York, NY 10006; tel. (212) 455-0500; e-mail info@damonrunyon.org; internet www.damonrunyon.org.

Daniele Agostino Derossi Foundation

Founded in 1991 by Flavia Robinson Derossi in memory of her father, an Italian business person and innovator.
Activities: Promotes the wellbeing of indigenous women and children through grants to support projects active in the fields of education, health and women's co-operatives. In 2015 the Foundation began a pilot project in Ponderano, Italy, helping women and children who were victims of domestic violence and war.
Geographical Area of Activity: Guatemala, Italy, Mexico.
Restrictions: Does not accept unsolicited applications.
Finance: Annual revenue US $425,417, expenditure $650,752 (30 June 2022).
Board of Directors: Daniele C. Derossi (Pres.); Joan D. Robinson (Vice-Pres.); David J. Pollack (Treas.); Sarah M. Saalfield (Sec.).
Principal Staff: Dir Armando J. Alfonzo.
Contact Details: 25 Drummer Boy Way, Lexington, MA 02420; tel. (703) 627-6385; internet dadfound.org.

David and Lucile Packard Foundation

Founded in 1964 by David Packard, co-founder of information technology company Hewlett-Packard, and his wife Lucile.
Activities: Works with partners to bring about social, cultural and environmental change. Programmes focus on: improving children's lives; improving reproductive health; promoting creative science; and restoring natural ecosystems. Annually, the Foundation offers 20 science and engineering fellowships, worth US $875,000 each over five years, to nominated early career professors from 50 US universities.
Geographical Area of Activity: International.
Restrictions: No grants to individuals or religious organizations.
Publications: Annual Report; newsletter; reports; information brochures.
Finance: Annual revenue US $496.6m., expenditure $540.6m. (31 Dec. 2022).
Board of Trustees: Jason K. Burnett (Chair.); Julie E. Packard (Vice-Chair.).
Principal Staff: Pres. and CEO Nancy Lindborg.
Contact Details: 343 Second St, Los Altos, CA 94022; tel. (650) 948-7658; e-mail info@packard.org; internet www.packard.org.

Deutsche Bank Americas Foundation

Established in 1999 by Deutsche Bank.
Activities: Promotes social responsibility, a just society, equity and inclusion through making loans, grants and investments. Main programme areas include: community development; education; and social and creative enterprise. The Foundation also funds emerging artists, musicians and cultural institutions; and encourages employee volunteering.
Geographical Area of Activity: Canada, Latin America, USA.
Restrictions: Does not accept unsolicited applications.
Publications: Annual Report; *Community Focus* (newsletter); brochures.
Finance: Annual revenue US $9.5m., expenditure $8.6m. (31 Dec. 2023).
Principal Staff: Exec. Dir Alessandra Digiusto.
Contact Details: 60 Wall St, NYC60–2112, New York, NY 10005; tel. (212) 250-0538; e-mail corporate.responsibility@db.com; internet country.db.com/usa/responsibility.

Development Gateway—DG

Established in 2000 in partnership with the International Bank for Reconstruction and Development (World Bank).
Activities: Development Gateway: an IREX Venture researches data ecosystems to identify incentives and barriers to data use; builds technical tools to support data analysis, visualization, and management; and advises on data strategy and policy to strengthen data-driven decisionmaking. In 2021 DG formed a strategic partnership with IREX, which positions DG as a subsidiary of IREX. DG works with more than 80 organizations worldwide.
Geographical Area of Activity: International.
Publications: Annual Report; blog; white papers; and other publications.
Finance: Annual revenue US $11.6m., expenditure $9.2m. (30 June 2023).
Board of Directors: Santiago Sedaca (Chair.); George Kogola (Acting Chair.).
Principal Staff: CEO Josh Powell.
Contact Details: 1100 13th St, NW, Suite 800, Washington, DC 20005; tel. (202) 572-9200; e-mail info@developmentgateway.org; internet www.developmentgateway.org.

Direct Relief

Established in 1948 as the William Zimdin Foundation, a former financier; renamed the Direct Relief Foundation in 1957 and Direct Relief International in 1982.
Activities: Works with community-based organizations to provide appropriate, specifically requested medical resources and healthcare to underserved and uninsured people. The organization provides disaster relief during humanitarian emergencies, safeguarding healthcare workers and responding to the needs of refugees. Operates in more than 90 countries, including the USA.
Geographical Area of Activity: International.
Publications: Annual Report; news alerts; maps.
Finance: Annual revenue US $2,266.8m., expenditure $2,071.2m (30 June 2023).
Board of Directors: Mark Linehan (Chair.); Harry McMohan (Vice-Chair.); Thomas Sturgess (Treas.); Siri Marshall (Sec.).
Principal Staff: Pres. and CEO Thomas Tighe.
Contact Details: 6100 Wallace Becknell Rd, Santa Barbara, CA 93117; tel. (805) 964-4767; e-mail info@directrelief.org; internet www.directrelief.org.

Dollywood Foundation

Established in 1988 by Dolly Parton to assist in the education of children in her home county; its book gifting programme was subsequently expanded nationally and internationally, to Australia, Canada, Ireland and the United Kingdom.
Activities: Operates the Dolly Parton Imagination Library book gifting programme for pre-school children. By the end of April 2025 the programme had gifted more than 277m. books.
Geographical Area of Activity: Australia, Canada, Ireland, UK, USA.
Finance: Annual revenue US $55.0m., expenditure $52.4m. (31 Dec. 2022).
Board of Directors (USA): Dolly Parton (Chair.).
Principal Staff: Pres. Jeff Conyers.
Contact Details: 111 E Main St, 2nd Floor, Sevierville, TN 37862; tel. (865) 428-9606; internet imaginationlibrary.com.

Doris Duke Charitable Foundation—DDCF

Established in 1996 by the will of Doris Duke, the only child of James Buchanan (J. B.) Duke, a founder of the American Tobacco Company, Duke Energy Company and the Duke Endowment (q.v.).

Activities: Works to improve people's lives through four national grantmaking programmes in the areas of the performing arts (in particular, jazz, theatre and contemporary dance), environmental conservation, medical research and children's wellbeing. Grants typically range between US $100,000 and $1m. The Foundation supports the African Health Initiative (f. 2007), which works to strengthen health systems in sub-Saharan Africa; and the Doris Duke Foundation for Islamic Art, which operates the Building Bridges Program to increase understanding between Muslims and non-Muslims. It also manages three properties that belonged to Doris Duke as museums and educational centres in New Jersey, Hawaii and Rhode Island.

Geographical Area of Activity: sub-Saharan Africa, USA.

Finance: Annual revenue US $174.3m., expenditure $139.9m. (31 Dec. 2023).

Board of Trustees: William H. Wright, II (Chair.); Dr Anthony S. Fauci (Vice-Chair.).

Principal Staff: Pres. and CEO Sam Gill.

Contact Details: 444 Madison Ave, 10th Floor, New York, NY 10022; tel. (908) 243-3619; e-mail webmaster@ddcf.org; internet www.ddcf.org.

Dr Scholl Foundation

Founded in 1947 by William M. Scholl, a podiatrist and designer of foot care products; formerly known as the William M. Scholl Foundation.

Activities: Operates in the fields of education, civil society and culture, healthcare, social service and the environment. Grant amounts typically range from US $5,000 to $25,000.

Geographical Area of Activity: Mainly the USA.

Restrictions: Does not fund individuals, endowments or capital campaigns, political organizations, political action committees or general support; only one request from the same organization in the same year.

Finance: Annual revenue US $13.2m., expenditure $12.0m. (31 Dec. 2023).

Board of Directors: Pamela Scholl (Chair. and Pres.); Anne Mosely (Dir and Vice-Pres.); Lea Slahor (Treas.).

Contact Details: 1033 Skokie Blvd, Suite 230, Northbrook, IL 60062; tel. (847) 559-7430; internet www.drschollfoundation.com.

Drug Policy Alliance—DPA

Established in 2000 by a merger between the Lindesmith Center (f. 1994) and the Drug Policy Foundation (f. 1987).

Activities: Advocates for drug policy reform based on science, compassion, health, and human rights. The Drug Policy Alliance's Advocacy Grants programme disbursed $425,000 to 18 grantees in grants in FY 2023. Primarily funds grassroots allies.

Geographical Area of Activity: USA.

Restrictions: Does not fund organizations outside the USA; individuals; or punitive abstinence-only treatment programmes.

Publications: Annual Report; journal articles; reports; testimonies; factsheets; working papers; bibliographies; research briefs; monographs.

Finance: Annual income US $13.4m., expenditure $13.3m. (31 May 2024).

Board: Derek Hodel (Pres.).

Principal Staff: Exec. Dir Kassandra Frederique.

Contact Details: 131 W 33rd St, 15th Floor, New York, NY 10001; tel. (212) 613-8020; e-mail contact@drugpolicy.org; internet www.drugpolicy.org.

Duke Endowment

Founded in 1924 by James B. Duke, a founder of the American Tobacco Company and Duke Energy Company.

Activities: Makes grants in North and South Carolina in the fields of childcare, healthcare, higher education and rural United Methodist church initiatives. The Endowment also operates a fellowship programme, which cultivates emerging leaders in philanthropy. Since its inception, it has awarded more than US $4,000m. in grants, including more than $1,500m. to Duke University.

Geographical Area of Activity: USA (North and South Carolina).

Restrictions: No awards are made outside the states of North and South Carolina or outside the four established grant programmes.

Publications: Annual Report; *Issues* (newsletter); reports; evaluations.

Finance: Annual revenue US $497.7m., expenditure $255.1m. (31 Dec. 2022).

Board of Trustees: Charles C. Lucas, III (Chair.); Jean G. Spaulding, Dennis M. Campbell (Vice-Chair.).

Principal Staff: Pres. Rhett N. Mabry.

Contact Details: 800 East Morehead St, Charlotte, NC 28202; tel. (704) 376-0291; e-mail infotde@tde.org; internet www.dukeendowment.org.

Dumbarton Oaks

Founded in 1940 by Mildred Barnes Bliss, an art collector, and her husband, Robert Woods Bliss, a diplomat; a research institute and museum.

Activities: The Dumbarton Oaks Research Library and Collection houses important research and study collections in Byzantine, Garden and Landscape, and Pre-Columbian studies; it is administered by the Trustees for Harvard University. The institute offers residential summer fellowships, as well as one-year junior and postdoctoral fellowships. It also makes grants to assist scholarly projects in the three fields with which it is concerned, and organizes conferences and symposia.

Geographical Area of Activity: USA and Canada.

Restrictions: Grants are limited to applicants holding a doctorate or the equivalent for research purposes or to fund a suitable project.

Publications: Annual Report; newsletter; *Dumbarton Oaks Papers* (annual); books and journal articles.

Trustees for Harvard University: Alan Garber (Pres.).

Principal Staff: Dir Prof. Thomas B. F. Cummins; Exec. Dir Yota Batsaki.

Contact Details: 1703 32nd St, NW, Washington, DC 20007; tel. (202) 339-6400; e-mail visit@doaks.org; internet www.doaks.org.

E. O. Wilson Biodiversity Foundation

Established in 2005 by Dr Jay M. Short, Neil Patterson and Charles J. Smith.

Activities: Area-based scientific conservation research, youth education and outreach, international advocacy for global biodiversity protection.

Geographical Area of Activity: International.

Publications: Newsletter; *Life on Earth* digital textbook and online materials.

Finance: Annual revenue US $3.6m., expenditure $5.0m. (2022).

Board of Directors: David J. Prend (Chair.).

Principal Staff: Pres. and CEO Dr Paula J. Ehrlich.

Contact Details: 300 Blackwell St, Suite 102, Durham, NC 27701; tel. (984) 219-2279; e-mail info@eowilsonfoundation.org; internet www.eowilsonfoundation.org.

Earth Island Institute—EII

Established in 1982 by David Brower, founder of Friends of the Earth (q.v.), to develop conservation and environment projects.

Activities: Works in the field of conservation, preservation and restoration of the environment through promoting citizen action and incubating global projects. Project areas include: agriculture; energy and climate; conservation; education; international and indigenous communities; leadership development; ocean and water; pollution and toxic materials; sustainability and community resilience; wildlife protection; women's environmental leadership; and youth empowerment. The Institute provides mentoring, training and support for more than 75 projects in over 25 countries. It presents annual Brower Youth Awards for environmental leadership.

Geographical Area of Activity: International.

Publications: Annual Report; *Earth Island Journal*; *Island-Wire* (e-bulletin, 6 a year); *Borneo Wire*; *ECO*; *Global Service Corps*; *INLAKECH!*; *Kids for the Bay*; *Late Friday* (newsletter); electronic publications.

Finance: Annual revenue US $32.1m., expenditure $35.9m. (30 June 2024).

Board of Directors: Francisco Martinez (Chair.); Ariela St. Pierre (Vice-Chair.).

Principal Staff: Exec. Dir Sumona Majumdar.

Contact Details: 2150 Allston Way, Suite 460, Berkeley, CA 94704-1375; tel. (510) 859-9100; e-mail donorinquiry @earthisland.org; internet www.earthisland.org.

Earthrights International—ERI

Founded in 1995, on the Thailand–Myanmar border, by human rights activist Ka Hsaw Wa and law students Katie Redford and Tyler Giannini.

Activities: Represents and works with individuals and communities around the world who are victims, survivors, or at risk of human rights and environmental abuses that occur during natural resource extraction projects, such as oil and gas development, water diversion projects, logging and mining. The organization uses legal actions, media campaigns, public education and organizing strategies to hold corporations and governments to account. It runs the EarthRights School, Mekong Legal Advocacy Institute and Indigenous Legal Advocates Seminar; and co-ordinates the Mekong Legal Network and the Myanmar Environmental Lawyers Network. Has offices in Peru and Thailand.

Geographical Area of Activity: Latin America, South-East Asia, USA.

Publications: Annual Report; Report Cards; reports; blog.

Finance: Annual revenue US $6.5m., expenditure $7.5m. (31 Jan. 2023).

Board of Directors: Shalini Nataraj, Aaron Eske (Co-Chair.); Fernanda Hopenhaym (Treas.).

Principal Staff: Exec. Dir Bobbie Sta. Maria.

Contact Details: 1612 K St, NW, Suite 800, Washington, DC 20006; tel. (202) 466-5188; e-mail infousa@earthrights.org; internet www.earthrights.org.

East-West Center—EWC

Founded in 1960, as the Center for Cultural and Technical Interchange Between East and West in Hawaii, by the US Congress; a public, non-profit national and international research and education institution, incorporating the East-West Center Foundation.

Activities: Receives most of its financial support from the US Congress, with contributions from Asian and Pacific governments, private agencies and corporations. The Center's staff co-operate in study, research and training with research fellows, graduates and professionals in business and government in the areas of: economic change; international co-operation; national economic development strategies; energy policy; politics and security; environmental issues; behaviour and health; and Pacific island development. Scholarship-fellowships are offered to scholars from the People's Republic of China, journalists from the Republic of Korea, early career Arctic researchers and tourism industry professionals from the Pacific Islands; and graduate degree fellowships to Master's and doctoral students from the USA, Asia, the Pacific region and the Russian Federation. Has an office in Washington, DC.

Geographical Area of Activity: Pacific region, South-East, East and South Asia, USA.

Restrictions: Grants only for degree and non-degree scholarships, workshop participants and visiting fellowships.

Publications: Annual Report; *East-West Center Observer* (quarterly newsletter); reports; conference proceedings.

Finance: Annual revenue US $1.1m., expenditure $1.3m. (30 Sept. 2022).

Board of Governors: John Waihe'e (Chair.); Teddy B. Taylor (Vice-Chair.).

Principal Staff: Interim Pres. James K. Scott; Vice-Pres. Satu P. Limaye.

Contact Details: John A. Burns Hall, 1601 East-West Rd, Honolulu, HI 96848; tel. (808) 944-7111; e-mail EWCcontact @eastwestcenter.org; internet www.eastwestcenter.org.

eBay Foundation

Founded in 1998 by Pierre Omidyar, founder of e-commerce company eBay and the Omidyar Group (q.v.).

Activities: Supports innovative entrepreneurship to build economically vibrant and sustainable communities. Supports employees with meaningful giving and volunteering opportunities. Leads local giving and volunteering in communities, and matches employees' donations and volunteer hours. In 2024 it awarded nearly US $18m. in grants.

Geographical Area of Activity: International.

Restrictions: Does not accept unsolicited proposals.

Finance: Annual revenue US $32.9m., expenditure $24.3m. (31 Dec. 2022).

Principal Staff: Pres. Allie Ottoboni.

Contact Details: 60 South Market St, Suite 1000, San Jose, CA 95113; tel. (650) 450-5400; e-mail impact@ebay.com; internet www.ebayinc.com/global-impact/ebay-foundation.

EcoHealth Alliance

Established in 1971 by Gerald M. Durrell, a British naturalist, as Wildlife Trust; present name adopted in 2010 following its merger with the Consortium for Conservation Medicine.

Activities: Works in the field of environmental health, protecting wildlife and people from emerging diseases. Main programmes are: Biosurveillance; Deforestation; One Health; Pandemic Prevention; and Wildlife Conservation. The Alliance carries out research and training in the USA and more than 30 other countries.

Geographical Area of Activity: International.

Publications: Annual Report; *Emerging Infectious Disease Repository* (online); reports; bulletins; blog.

Finance: Annual revenue US $13.9m., expenditure $15.0m. (30 June 2022).

Board of Directors: Carlota Vollhardt (Chair.); Nancy Griffin (Vice-Chair.); Dr Frederick Baum (Treas.); Steven Wils (Sec.).

Principal Staff: Pres. Dr Peter Daszak.

Contact Details: 520 Eighth Ave, Suite 1200, New York, NY 10018; tel. (212) 380-4460; e-mail homeoffice @ecohealthalliance.org; internet www.ecohealthalliance .org.

The Edna McConnell Clark Foundation

Established in 1969 by Edna McConnell Clark, daughter of the founder of Avon Products, David H. McConnell.

Activities: Seeks to transform the life prospects of economically disadvantaged children and young people. The Foundation invests in organizations that help vulnerable young people to become successful adults through three principal strategies: the Youth Development Fund, which helps young people (aged 9–24 years) from low-income backgrounds; Blue Meridian Partners, an independent collaboration of 12 philanthropic institutions and individuals, incubated at the Foundation, serving young people from birth to 30 years of age; and Propel-Next, which helps non-profit organizations to serve disadvantaged young people through fostering a culture of continuous learning and improvement. In 2018 the Foundation planned to spend its remaining assets within a decade, moving staff and operations to Blue Meridian Partners.

Geographical Area of Activity: USA.

Restrictions: Not making new grants.

Publications: Annual Reports; *EMCF News* (newsletter); evaluation reports; programme assessments.

Finance: Annual revenue –US $9.3m., expenditure $295.1m. (30 June 2022).

Board of Trustees: H. Lawrence Clark (Chair.).

Principal Staff: Pres. and CEO Nancy Roob.

Contact Details: c/o Blue Meridian Partners, Inc, 477 Madison Ave, 6th Floor, New York, NY 10022; tel. (212) 551-9100; e-mail emcf-info@bluemeridian.org; internet www.emcf.org.

Electronic Frontier Foundation—EFF

Established in 1990 by Mitch Kapor, founder of software company Lotus Development Corporation, John Perry Barlow, a writer, and John Gilmore, a technologist.

Activities: Defends civil liberties in the digital world through grassroots activism, litigation, policy analysis and technology development. Areas of global interest are: free speech and use of the internet for free expression; fair use and intellectual property; protection for innovation; respect for individuals' privacy; and government transparency. The Foundation works with organizations, individuals and companies worldwide to oppose international treaties and agreements that weaken civil liberties; encourages governments and internet intermediaries to oppose online censorship; and advocates balanced intellectual property laws. It undertakes legal action and provides legal assistance; carries out software development and technology research projects; and publishes white papers on law and technology. Pioneer Awards are offered annually; and EFF Cooperative Computing Awards to encourage internet users to contribute to solving scientific problems.

Geographical Area of Activity: Worldwide.

Restrictions: Not a grantmaking organization.

Publications: Annual Report; *EFFector* (weekly newsletter); toolkits; white papers; blog.

Finance: Annual revenue US $16.6m., expenditure $16.7m. (30 June 2022).

Board of Directors: Gigi Sohn (Chair.); Brian Behlendorf (Vice-Chair.).

Principal Staff: Exec. Dir Cindy Cohn.

Contact Details: 815 Eddy St, San Francisco, CA 94109; tel. (415) 436-9333; e-mail info@eff.org; internet www.eff.org.

Elizabeth Glaser Pediatric AIDS Foundation—EGPAF

Founded in 1988 by Elizabeth Glaser, Susie Zeegen and Susan DeLaurentis as the Pediatric AIDS Foundation; renamed in 1994 to honour the legacy of Elizabeth Glaser.

Activities: Works to eradicate paediatric AIDS through advocating for public policies that support children's health and funding research. Main programmes focus on: adolescents and HIV; adult HIV care and treatment; community engagement; maternal, newborn and child health; preventing mother-to-child transmission; reaching newly infected children and their mothers; strategic information, evaluation and research; strengthening health systems; and working to prevent the spread of tuberculosis. The Foundation provides care and treatment for people with HIV and AIDS; and aims to accelerate the discovery of new treatments for other serious and life-threatening paediatric illnesses. It works in 30 countries.

Geographical Area of Activity: India, sub-Saharan Africa, Switzerland, USA.

Publications: Annual Report; newsletter; factsheets; issue briefs; technical briefs; technical bulletins; technical reports; toolkits.

Finance: Annual revenue US $172.5m., expenditure $172.1m. (31 Dec. 2022).

Board of Directors: Jack Leslie (Chair.); Kathleen Cravero-Kristofferson (Vice-Chair.).

Principal Staff: Pres. and CEO Charles Lyons.

Contact Details: 1350 Eye St NW, Suite 400, Washington, DC 20005; tel. (202) 296-9165; e-mail info@pedaids.org; internet www.pedaids.org.

The ELMA Group of Foundations

Established in 2005 by Clive Calder, co-founder of Zomba Recordings, a music company; ELMA Philanthropies Services is the foundations' service arm.

Activities: Comprises: the ELMA Foundation, which funds organizations working to improve the education, health and wellbeing of children in Africa, offering community grants and paediatric fellowships; the ELMA Relief Foundation, which supports disaster response and post-disaster recovery operations worldwide, with a focus on children in Africa, and includes the ELMA Grantee Relief Fund and the Syria Crisis Drawdown Fund; the ELMA Growth Foundation, which supports organizations working to improve the lives of people in low-income African communities and develop social entrepreneurship; the ELMA Music Foundation, which supports organizations working with children and young people in South Africa and the USA; the ELMA Vaccines & Immunization Foundation, which invests in expanding children's immunization coverage; the ELMA South Africa Foundation, which supports CSOs and the response to COVID-19; the ELMA Caribbean Foundation, which focuses on climate resilience, healthcare and disaster response; and the ELMA Climate Foundation, which worls to combat climate change. Has offices in Cape Town, Johannesburg (South Africa) and Kampala (Uganda).

Geographical Area of Activity: International (with a focus on sub-Saharan Africa).

Publications: Biennial Report.

Finance: Annual revenue US $350,006, expenditure $10,929 (31 Dec. 2022).

Principal Staff: ELMA Philanthropies Exec. Dir Robyn Calder; CEO Tom McPartland.

Contact Details: 1345 Ave of the Americas, Suite 2302, New York, NY 10105; tel. (212) 697-1000; internet www.elmaphilanthropies.org.

Enchanted Peach Children's Foundation—EPCF

Founded in 1985 as the Children's Wish Foundation by Linda Dozoretz, whose daughter Susan died from bone cancer; present name adopted in 2023.

Activities: Works to distract critically ill children from the anxieties of treatment and empower them to face the difficulties ahead. Programmes include once-in-a-lifetime wish fulfilment; and hospital enrichment, sending educational and entertainment gift packages to paediatric hospitals, and organizing in-patient events to help to counter feelings of isolation and build a natural support group for children and their families. Has worked in 53 countries.

Geographical Area of Activity: International.

Restrictions: No minimum age, but if children's health allows, the Foundation tries to wait to fulfil wishes until they are old enough to enjoy fully and remember the experience. Children must be under 18 years of age.

Publications: Newsletter.

Finance: Annual revenue US $1.1m., expenditure $1.9m. (30 June 2023).

Principal Staff: Chair. Linda Dozoretz.

Contact Details: 8615 Roswell Rd, Atlanta, GA 30350; tel. (678) 449-9749; e-mail info@enchantedpeach.org; internet enchantedpeach.org.

endPoverty.org

Established in 1985; a Christian organization.

Activities: Creates jobs and economic opportunities through granting small loans to poor people in remote areas to start microenterprises. The organization's partner network includes indigenous non-profit organizations working in over 47 countries.

Geographical Area of Activity: Bangladesh, Cameroon, Guatemala, India, Kenya, Philippines, Uganda, USA, Zambia.

Publications: Annual Report; field reports; blog.

Finance: Annual revenue US $770,781, expenditure $708,926 (30 June 2023).

Board of Directors: Paul Vinogradov (Chair.); Richard Dean (Vice-Chair.); Jon-Michael Johnson (Treas.).

Principal Staff: Exec. Dir Peter Fry.

Contact Details: 1930 Isaac Newton Sq., Suite 203, Reston, VA 20190; tel. (571) 278-6061; e-mail info@endpoverty.org; internet endpoverty.org.

EngenderHealth

Established in 1943; name changed from AVSC International in 2001.

Activities: Operates in the field of sexual and reproductive health and rights, improving family planning and maternal healthcare, working with governments, health institutions and clinic staff to develop services where none currently exist and improving care in existing facilities. The organization provides technical assistance and training; training seminars and on-site help for healthcare workers on safe medical techniques; management and supervision; research on family planning issues and attitudes; and accessible technical reference publications for reproductive healthcare workers. It is also involved in women's general healthcare, including HIV, AIDS and sexually transmitted infections, obstetric fistula, maternity services and gender equity. Works in 10 countries.

Geographical Area of Activity: South Asia, sub-Saharan Africa, USA.

Publications: Annual Report; *EngenderHealth Connect* (e-newsletter, monthly); training curricula; clinical guidelines; instructional videos; brochures; working papers; articles.

Finance: Annual revenue US $37.1m., expenditure $34.8m. (30 June 2023).

Board of Directors: Linda Rosenstock (Chair.); Sarah Cairns-Smith (Chair., Exec. Cttee); Robert D. Petty (Treas.); Rosemary Ellis (Sec.).

Principal Staff: Pres. and CEO Traci L. Baird.

Contact Details: 505 9th St, NW, Suite 601, Washington, DC 20004; tel. (202) 902-2000; e-mail info@engenderhealth.org; internet www.engenderhealth.org.

Epilepsy Foundation

Founded in 1968 by merger of the Epilepsy Foundation (f. 1954) and the Epilepsy Association of America (f. 1965) as the national, voluntary health organization for epilepsy; supported by the Epilepsy Research Foundation.

Activities: Supports individuals and families affected by epilepsy and seizures. The Foundation provides assistance in overcoming the challenges of living with epilepsy and to accelerate therapies to stop seizures, find cures and save lives. Activities include providing services locally, online and through a 24/7 helpline; educating people affected by epilepsy, caregivers and healthcare providers, and the public; conducting federal and local advocacy; and supporting research into new treatments and therapies. It comprises a network of nearly 50 local organizations.

Geographical Area of Activity: USA.

Publications: Annual Report; newsletter; brochures; specialist publications.

Finance: Annual revenue US $19.7m., expenditure $19.4m. (30 June 2022).

Board of Directors: Jeffrey Parent (Chair.); Courtney Genosi Watson (Vice-Chair.); Daniel Moore (Treas.); Mark Theeuwes (Sec.).

Principal Staff: Bernice (Bee) Martin Lee.

Contact Details: 3540 Crain Hwy, Suite 675, Bowie, MD 20716; tel. (301) 459-3700; internet www.epilepsy.com.

Equal Justice Initiative—EJI

Founded in 1989 by Bryan Stevenson, a lawyer and author.

Activities: Campaigns to end mass incarceration and excessive punishment in the USA; challenges racial and economic injustice; and protects the basic human rights of marginalized people. Main programmes are: Criminal Justice Reform, encompassing children in adult prisons, the death penalty, excessive punishment, prison conditions and wrongful convictions; and Racial Justice, encompassing the legacy of slavery, presumption of guilt, racial segregation and racial terror lynching. The Initiative carries out research; provides legal representation; documents racial terror lynchings; and organizes educational tours and presentations. In 2018 the Initiative established the Legacy Museum and National Memorial for Peace and Justice in Montgomery, AL.

Geographical Area of Activity: USA.

Publications: Annual Report; reports; discussion guides; educational materials; wall calendar; short films.

Finance: Annual income US $91.9m., expenditure $28.4m. (30 Sept. 2022).

Board of Directors: Kim Taylor-Thompson (Chair.).

Principal Staff: Exec. Dir Bryan Stevenson; Deputy Dir Tera DuVernay.

Contact Details: 122 Commerce St, Montgomery, AL 36104; tel. (334) 269-1803; e-mail contact_us@eji.org; internet eji.org.

Eurasia Foundation–EF

Founded in 1992 with funds from the US Agency for International Development (USAID) to promote the advancement of democratic institutions and private enterprise in the countries of the former USSR.

Activities: Empowers citizens to build resilient communities, with a focus on marginalized groups, including women, young people and minority populations. The Foundation provides training to build local leadership and expertise; and organizes international exchanges and peer-to-peer dialogues. Since 1992 it has invested more than US $400m. to build civil society through the Eurasia Foundation Network, comprising locally registered organizations in the Russian Federation, Central Asia, the South Caucasus, Ukraine and Moldova; and, through the Caucasus Research Resource Center (q.v.) programme, creating research and training centres in social science and public policy analysis in Baku (Azerbaijan), Tbilisi (Georgia) and Yerevan (Armenia). The Bill Maynes Fellowship fosters professional connections between emerging civil society leaders from Asia, Eurasia and the Middle East and North Africa and their counterparts in the USA. The Fellowship for Women Changemakers supports women activists and civic leaders.

Geographical Area of Activity: Canada, People's Repub. of China, Eastern Europe and Central Asia, Middle East and North Africa, Russian Federation, USA.

Restrictions: Does not fund political parties or movements and activities of a religious nature.

Publications: Annual Report; newsletter; information brochure; application guidelines.

Finance: Annual revenue US $21.4m., expenditure $21.5m. (30 Sept. 2023).

Board of Trustees: Pamela L. Spratlen (Chair.); Leif Ulstrup (Vice-Chair.); Brad Stevenson (Treas.).

Principal Staff: Pres. Lisa Coll; Senior Vice-Pres. Robert O'Donovan.

Contact Details: 1990 K St, NW, Suite 615, Washington, DC 20006; tel. (202) 234-7370; e-mail info@eurasia.org; internet www.eurasia.org.

Ewing Marion Kauffman Foundation

Established in 1966 by Ewing Marion Kauffman, founder of Marion Laboratories, a pharmaceutical company, and the Kansas City Royals baseball team; in 1987 the Muriel McBrien Kauffman Foundation became a separate entity, with a focus on the visual and performing arts.

Activities: Works to build inclusive prosperity through a prepared workforce and entrepreneur-focused economic development. Main programmes include: improving education, from preschool readiness to postsecondary level; strengthening entrepreneurship, by empowering people to start and grow their own businesses; and helping young people and families to thrive culturally, economically and socially. The Foundation campus includes a conference centre and public memorial garden and park. It established the Ewing Marion Kauffman School (f. 2011), a pre-college charter school; and the Kauffman Scholars postsecondary education programme.

Geographical Area of Activity: USA (Greater Kansas City).

Publications: *Kauffman Currents Newsletter* (weekly); *Start Us Up* (biweekly newsletter); *Insights to Entrepreneurship* (bimonthly newsletter); *Entrepreneurial Ecosystems* (monthly newsletter); *Rethink Education* (monthly newsletter); *Kauffman Indicators of Entrepreneurship* (occasional newsletter).

Finance: Annual income US $112.7m., expenditure $192.8m. (31 Dec. 2022).

Principal Staff: Pres. and CEO DeAngela Burns-Wallis.

Contact Details: 4801 Rockhill Rd, Kansas City, MO 64110; tel. (816) 932-1000; internet www.kauffman.org.

ExxonMobil Foundation

Established in 1955 by Esso, an oil and gas company, as the Esso Education Foundation; name changed to Exxon Education Foundation in 1972. Present name adopted in 1999.

Activities: Main programmes focus on: education, with an emphasis on mathematics and science in the USA; promoting women's economic development; combating malaria; and ExxonMobil employee volunteering and gift matching. The Foundation supports non-profit organizations, investing in social and economic projects.

Geographical Area of Activity: Worldwide.

Restrictions: Rarely funds unsolicited applications.

Publications: *Worldwide Giving Report*.

Finance: Annual revenue –US $4.1m., expenditure $22.0m. (31 Dec. 2021).

Principal Staff: Pres. Kevin Murphy.

Contact Details: 22777 Springwoods Vlg Pkwy, Spring, TX 77389-1425; tel. (832) 648-5548; internet corporate.exxonmobil.com/sustainability/community-engagement/worldwide-giving.

Feed the Children

Founded in 1979; a Christian, non-profit charitable organization.

Activities: Works internationally to improve the food and nutrition security of mothers and children through child-focused community development programmes. Other programme areas include: education; disaster response; health and water; and livelihoods. In the USA, the organization distributes corporate food donations through a network of local community partners. It operates in nine countries.

Geographical Area of Activity: El Salvador, Guatemala, Haiti, Honduras, Kenya, Malawi, Philippines, Tanzania, Uganda, USA.

Publications: Annual Report.

Finance: Annual revenue US $415.2m., expenditure $432.5m. (30 June 2024).

Board of Directors: Mike Hogan (Chair.); Rhonda Hooper (Vice-Chair.); C. E. Crouse (Treas.).

Principal Staff: Pres. and CEO Emily Callahan.

Contact Details: 333 N. Meridian, Oklahoma City, OK 73107; tel. (405) 942-0228; e-mail info@feedthechildren.org; internet feedthechildren.org.

FHI 360

Established in 2011 as a global development organization following the takeover of the Academy for Educational Development (f. 1961) by Family Health International—FHI (f. 1971).

Activities: Works with local and national partner organizations to address complex human development needs in areas including civil society, economic development, education, the environment, gender, health, nutrition and young people. The organization operates in more than 60 countries including the USA, with offices in Washington, DC, New York, Bangkok and Pretoria. The FHI Foundation (f. 1990) was established to support the work of FHI 360 and other partners; it offers Catalyst Fund awards for innovation.

Geographical Area of Activity: International.

Publications: Annual Report; *Inside FH I360* (newsletter); *Degrees* (blog); *R&E Search for Evidence* (blog); research reports.

Finance: Annual revenue US $867.7m. expenditure $872.8m. (30 Sept. 2023).

Board of Directors: Louise B. (Holly) Wise (Chair.); Dr Paul R. De Lay (Vice-Chair.).

Principal Staff: CEO Tessie San Martin.

Contact Details: 359 Blackwell St, Suite 200, Durham, NC 27701; tel. (919) 544-7040; e-mail info@fhi360.org; internet www.fhi360.org.

The Film Foundation

Established in 1990 by film-maker Martin Scorsese; aligned with the Directors Guild of America.

Activities: Protects and preserves motion picture history. The Foundation works with archives and studios to restore films, making them publicly available through festivals, museums and educational institutions; and, through its free educational curriculum, teaches young people about film literacy. It has restored over 1,000 films in total, including 64 films from Africa, Asia, Eastern Europe, Central America, South America, and the Middle East under its World Cinema Project. Has an office in New York.

Geographical Area of Activity: International.

Publications: Annual Report; lesson plans.

Finance: Annual revenue US $1.4m., expenditure $1.9m. (31 Dec. 2021).

Board of Directors: Martin Scorsese (Chair.); Lesli Linka Glatter (Pres.); Paris Barclay (Sec.-Treas.).

Principal Staff: Exec. Dir Margaret Bodde; Man. Dir Jennifer Ahn.

Contact Details: 7920 Sunset Blvd, 6th Floor, Los Angeles CA 90046; tel. (323) 436-5060; e-mail tff_asst@film-foundation.org; internet www.film-foundation.org.

FINCA International (Foundation for International Community Assistance)

Established in 1984 by John Hatch, the creator of Village Banking.

Activities: Works to end global poverty through sustainable and scalable solutions that are driven by the insights and needs of people in the communities where they live and work. Programmes include: FINCA Impact Finance, a network of

Firelight Foundation

banks and microfinance institutions that deliver responsible financial services to more than 3m. low-income customers across the world and consistently delivers a double-bottom line of financial and social performance; and FINCA Ventures, which provides patient capital to innovative, high-impact social enterprises that spark household and MSME labour productivity. FINCA International has sister organizations in Canada (FINCA Canada) and the United Kingdom (FINCA UK).

Geographical Area of Activity: Worldwide.

Publications: Annual Report; *FINCA News* (quarterly newsletter); white papers; case studies; one-pagers; factsheets.

Finance: Annual revenue US $273.4m., expenditure $266.3m. (31 Dec. 2023).

Principal Staff: Pres. and CEO Andrée Simon.

Contact Details: 1201 15th St, NW, 8th Floor, Washington, DC 20005; tel. (202) 682-1510; e-mail info@finca.org; internet www.finca.org.

Firelight Foundation

Established in 1999 by Kerry Olson, an educator and co-founder of the Faith to Action Initiative, and her husband David Katz.

Activities: Supports vulnerable children and families in sub-Saharan Africa by funding community-based organizations that support the fundamental needs and rights of children orphaned or otherwise affected by poverty and HIV and AIDS. The Foundation prioritizes grassroots projects that respond to local community needs, particularly community-based organizations which raise resources from within the local community, bringing together clusters of 4–12 geographically and thematically linked organizations. It offers grants ranging from US $5,000 to $50,000 for up to seven years.

Geographical Area of Activity: sub-Saharan Africa.

Restrictions: Does not accept unsolicited applications.

Publications: Annual Report; newsletter; *Protecting Our Children: How African Community Organizations Improve Child Protection Systems* (e-book); blog.

Finance: Annual revenue US $3.7m., expenditure $4.2m. (30 June 2023).

Board of Directors: Sibongile (Bongi) Mkhabela (Chair.); Mike Lorey (Vice-Chair. and Sec.); Elisa de Martel (Treas.).

Principal Staff: Exec. Dir Marième Daff.

Contact Details: 216 Mount Hermon Rd, Box 103-E, Scotts Valley, CA 95066; tel. (831) 429-8750; e-mail info@firelightfoundation.org; internet www.firelightfoundation.org.

First Nations Development Institute

Established in 1980.

Activities: Strengthens and revitalizes Native American, Alaska Native and Native Hawaiian economies and communities. Main programme areas include: achieving native financial empowerment; advancing household and community asset-building strategies; investing in native young people; nourishing native foods and health; and strengthening tribal and community institutions. The Institute conducts advocacy, technical assistance and training. It offers grants through the Eagle Staff Fund and awards scholarships to study agriculture and related subjects. Has field offices in Albuquerque, NM, and Pasadena, CA.

Geographical Area of Activity: USA.

Publications: Annual Report; newsletter.

Finance: Annual revenue US $38.4m., expenditure $27.8m. (30 June 2024).

Board of Directors: Benny Shendo, Jr (Chair.); Marguerite Smith (Vice-Chair.); Susan Jenkins (Treas.); Shyla Sheppard (Sec.).

Principal Staff: Pres. and CEO Michael E. Roberts.

Contact Details: 2432 Main St, Longmont, CO 80501; tel. (303) 774-7836; e-mail info@firstnations.org; internet www.firstnations.org.

Flight Safety Foundation

Founded in 1947, as Engineering for Safety, by Jerome F. 'Jerry' Lederer, an aeronautical engineer and former Director of the Bureau of Flight Safety.

Activities: Provides impartial, independent, expert safety guidance and resources for the aviation and aerospace industry. The Foundation conducts specialized research and flight safety analyses for operators, publishing bulletins on aviation safety and accident prevention; and organizes annual business air safety seminars and awards. Its members include more than 1,000 organizations, individuals, companies, etc. in 150 countries. Maintains the SKYbrary, an online repository of aviation safety knowledge, and has regional offices in Brussels, Belgium, and Melbourne, Australia.

Geographical Area of Activity: Worldwide.

Publications: *AeroSafety World* (digital only); special reports; toolkits.

Finance: Annual revenue US $3.7m., expenditure $3.3m. (31 Dec. 2022).

Board of Governors and Governance Council: Bobbi Wells (Chair.); Capt. Conor Nolan (Immediate Past Chair.); Kenneth P. Quinn (Gen. Counsel and Sec.); Dr John R. Watret (Treas.).

Principal Staff: Pres. and CEO Dr Hassan Shahidi.

Contact Details: 1920 Ballenger Ave, 4th Floor, Alexandria, VA 22314; tel. (703) 739-6700; e-mail events@flightsafety.org; internet www.flightsafety.org.

Food for the Hungry—FH

Founded in 1971 by Dr Larry Ward; a Christian relief and development organization.

Activities: Works in the fields of community development, emergency relief, healthcare and nutrition. The organization provides an information and education service; organizes seminars and workshops; provides training for farmers; promotes child sponsorship; and gives financial assistance to other development organizations. It has subsidiaries in Canada, the Republic of Korea, Switzerland and the United Kingdom; and operates programmes in 18 countries, with offices in Albert Lea, MN, Franklin, TN, and Washington, DC.

Geographical Area of Activity: Asia, Africa, Latin America, USA.

Publications: Annual Report; *Food for the Hungry Story* (newsletter); factsheets; blog.

Finance: Annual revenue US $203.4m., expenditure $217.9m. (30 Sept. 2024).

Board of Directors: Larry Jones (Chair.); Peter Mogan (Vice-Chair.).

Principal Staff: Pres. and CEO Mark Viso.

Contact Details: 2 N Central Ave, Suite 200, Phoenix, AZ 85004; tel. (866) 307-3259; e-mail donorhelp@fh.org; internet www.fh.org.

Food for the Poor, Inc

Established in 1982 by Robin Mahfood; an interdenominational Christian relief and development organization.

Activities: Serves people living in extreme poverty in developing countries. The organization provides access to clean water, education, emergency relief, food, healthcare and secure housing; and supports micro-enterprises. It works with partner organizations to raise funding and develop projects in 15 countries. Has a subsidiary in Canada.

Geographical Area of Activity: Canada, Central and South America and the Caribbean, USA.

Publications: Annual Report; e-newsletter; *Blog for the Poor*.

Finance: Annual revenue US $411.4m., expenditure $417.6m. (31 Dec. 2024).

UNITED STATES OF AMERICA

Board of Directors: P. Todd Kennedy (Chair.); William G. Benson (Vice-Chair. and Treas.); Gail Hamaty-Bird (Sec.).

Principal Staff: Pres. and CEO Ed Raine.

Contact Details: 6401 Lyons Rd, Coconut Creek, FL 33073; tel. (954) 427-2222; e-mail webmaster@foodforthepoor.com; internet www.foodforthepoor.org.

Ford Foundation

Founded in 1936 by Edsel B. Ford, son of Henry Ford, the founder of the Ford Motor Company.

Activities: Works to reduce inequality through investing in individuals, leadership and innovation. The Foundation offers grants to institutions within eight interconnected programme areas: civic engagement and government; cities and states; creativity and free expression; disability inclusion; the future of work and workers; gender, racial and ethnic justice; natural resources and climate change; and technology and society. The Building Institutions and Networks (BUILD) initiative strengthens the resilience of social justice organizations through grantmaking. Ford Foundation Fellowships are offered through the National Academy of Sciences, including: the Ford Global Fellowship, for social justice leaders; Ford-Mozilla Open Web Fellows, ensuring the internet remains a force for good; and Disability Futures Fellows, for disabled artists, film-makers and journalists. Foundation offices maintain Good Neighbor Committees to strengthen ties with immediate neighbours and connect with local organizations.

Geographical Area of Activity: Central and South America, East and South-East Asia, Middle East and North Africa, South Asia, sub-Saharan Africa, USA.

Restrictions: Does not make grants for personal needs, religious activities or building construction; fellowship applicants must be US citizens, nationals or permanent residents.

Publications: Annual Report; newsletter; magazine (quarterly); *Current Interest* (biennially); International Fellowships Program Archive (online).

Finance: Annual revenue US $1,232.9m., expenditure $808.5m. (30 Sept. 2023).

Board of Trustees: Prof. Francisco G. Cigarroa (Chair.).

Principal Staff: Pres. Darren Walker.

Contact Details: Ford Foundation Center for Social Justice, 320 E 43rd St, New York, NY 10017; tel. (212) 573-5000; e-mail office-secretary@fordfoundation.org; internet www.fordfoundation.org.

Foreign Policy Association

Founded in 1918, as the League of Free Nations Association, to support President Woodrow Wilson; present name adopted in 1923.

Activities: Educates the public about US foreign policy and global affairs, principally through its Great Decisions programme, which consists of an annual impartial briefing of eight key foreign policy issues, discussed by groups, and at seminars and public forums. The Association organizes an annual Great Decisions Teacher Training Institute for secondary school teachers; and Global Career Bootcamps for internationally minded professionals.

Geographical Area of Activity: Worldwide, but mainly USA.

Restrictions: Does not make grants.

Publications: Annual Report; *FPA Today* (newsletter); *Great Decisions* (briefing book, updates and teachers' guides); educational publications on global affairs and foreign policy; blogs; books.

Finance: Annual revenue US $4.7m., expenditure $4.3m. (30 June 2022).

Board of Directors: Jillian Sackler (Chair.); Robert Miller (Vice-Chair.); Reede Phillips (Treas.); Jeane Olivier (Sec.).

Principal Staff: Pres. and CEO Noel V. Lateef.

Contact Details: 551 Fifth Ave, 30th Floor, New York, NY 10176; tel. (212) 481-8100; e-mail info@fpa.org; internet www.fpa.org.

Florence Gould Foundation

Founded in 1957 by Florence J. Gould, an art collector and opera singer, and daughter-in-law of railway magnate Jay Gould.

Activities: Promotes French-US exchange. The Foundation offers fellowships for research to be carried out in France; and a prize for translation from French to English in fiction and non-fiction.

Geographical Area of Activity: France, USA.

Restrictions: Fellowship applicants must be US citizens.

Finance: Annual revenue US $40,328, expenditure $2.8m. (31 Dec. 2023).

Principal Staff: Pres. and Dir Anne H. Young; Vice-Pres. and Treas. Mary Young; Vice-Pres. and Sec. Joan Murtagh Frankel.

Contact Details: c/o Cahill, 32 Old Slip, New York City, NY 10005; tel. (212) 701-3292.

Fòs Feminista

Founded in 2021 by the merger of the International Women's Health Coalition (f. 1984, building on the work of the National Women's Health Coalition—f. 1980), and the Center for Health and Gender Equity (CHANGE, f. 1994), under the umbrella of IPPFWHR (International Planned Parenthood Federation Western Hemisphere Region).

Activities: An intersectional organization focusing on sexual and reproductive health and the rights of women, girls and gender-diverse people. Offers sexual and reproductive healthcare services; education programmes; and care to survivors of gender-based violence. An alliance of more than 250 organizations in more than 40 countries. 'Fòs' means strength in Haitian Creole.

Geographical Area of Activity: International.

Publications: Annual Report; newsletter.

Finance: Annual revenue US $32.6m., expenditure $32.8m. (31 Dec. 2023).

Board of Directors: Pamela Barnes (Chair.); María Consuelo Mejía (Vice-Chair.); Jacques Max Maura (Treas.); Lusungu Kalanga (Sec.).

Principal Staff: Dir/CEO Giselle Carino.

Contact Details: 333 Seventh Ave, 6th Floor, New York, NY 10001; tel. (212) 248-6400; e-mail online@fosfeminista.org; internet fosfeminista.org.

Foundation for Defense of Democracies—FDD

Established in 2001 by Clifford D. May, a former journalist; a research institute.

Activities: Carries out research and policy analysis to identify illicit activities and threats posed by adversaries and enemies of the USA. Programmes include: the Center on Cyber and Technology Innovation; Center on Economic and Financial Power; Center on Military and Political Power; Iran; the Transformative Cyber Innovation Lab; and Türkiye (Turkey). The Foundation sponsors the one-year National Security Fellows Program for mid-career US national security leaders, organizing monthly networking opportunities, expert roundtables and skill-building workshops.

Geographical Area of Activity: International.

Restrictions: Fellowship applicants must be US citizens based in Washington, DC, aged 30–40 years, with at least seven years' experience in national security or foreign policy.

Publications: *FDD's Long War Journal*; policy briefs; reports; podcasts; books.

Finance: Annual revenue US $16.1m., expenditure $17.7m. (31 Dec. 2021).

Board: Mark Pruzanski (Chair.).

Principal Staff: Pres. Clifford D. May; Chief Exec. Mark Dubowitz.

Foundation for Middle East Peace

Contact Details: POB 33249, Washington, DC 20033; tel. (202) 207-0190; e-mail info@fdd.org; internet www.fdd.org.

Foundation for Middle East Peace—FMEP

Founded in 1979 by Merle Thorpe, Jr, a lawyer.

Activities: Works towards a just and lasting resolution to the Israeli–Palestinian conflict through research and supporting organizations working to end Israel's occupation of the West Bank, Gaza Strip and East Jerusalem. Grants have supported educational, humanitarian, public affairs, civil rights and Palestinian-Israeli reconciliation activities, as well as small-scale economic projects that meet the needs of victims of the current conflict.

Geographical Area of Activity: Israel, Palestinian Territories, USA.

Restrictions: Grants only to organizations and projects that contribute to Israeli–Palestinian peace.

Publications: *Report on Israeli Settlement in the Occupied Territories* (6 a year); news summary (daily); Settlement Reports (weekly); Legislative Round-up (weekly, when US Congress is in session).

Finance: Annual revenue US $1.1m., expenditure $1.5m. (31 Dec. 2022).

Principal Staff: Pres. Lara Friedman.

Contact Details: 2025 M St, NW, Suite 600, Washington, DC 20036; tel. (202) 835-3650; e-mail info@fmep.org; internet www.fmep.org.

Frank Knox Memorial Fellowships

Founded in 1945, as the Frank Knox Memorial, by Annie Reid Knox, in memory of her husband, a former newspaper publisher and Secretary of the Navy.

Activities: Annually awards fellowships to around 27 newly admitted students from Australia, Canada, New Zealand and the United Kingdom to undertake graduate study at Harvard University for up to two years. In the United Kingdom, awards are administered by the Kennedy Memorial Trust (q.v.). The Frank Knox Committee is developing the Knox Alumni network.

Geographical Area of Activity: Australia, Canada, New Zealand, UK, USA.

Restrictions: Awards fellowships only to citizens of Australia, Canada, New Zealand and the UK; preference is given to degree applicants.

Principal Staff: Asst Dir Rebecca Lock.

Contact Details: Committee on General Scholarship, Harvard University, 14 Story St, 3rd Floor, Cambridge, MA 02138; tel. (617) 496-9367; internet frankknox.harvard.edu.

Free Russia Foundation

Established in 2015.

Activities: Promotes democracy and transparency. The Foundation represents members of the Russian and Ukrainian diaspora in the USA; and informs and educates US and European policymakers and foreign policy institutions about the situation in the Russian Federation. Main programmes focus on: documenting and analysing cyberattacks; supporting and building the capacity of CSOs in Russia; advocating for rights and dignity through training seminars; promoting global dialogue, in particular between Russia and the USA and Russia and Ukraine; and the political and economic future of Russia. It has regional offices in Berlin (Germany), Brussles (Belgium), Kyiv and Lviv (Ukraine), Talinn (Estonia), Tbilisi (Georgia), and Vilnius (Lithuania).

Geographical Area of Activity: Belarus, Canada, Central Asia, Czech Repub. (Czechia), Georgia, Germany, Russian Federation, South Caucasus, Ukraine, USA.

Publications: Newsletter; research reports.

Finance: Annual revenue US $3.4m., expenditure $3.0m. (31 Dec. 2022).

Board: David J. Kramer (Chair.); Paige Alexander (Vice-Chair.).

Principal Staff: Pres. Natalia Arno.

Contact Details: 1015 15 St, NW, Suite 600, Washington DC 20005; e-mail hello@4freerussia.org; internet www.4freerussia.org.

Freedom House, Inc

Founded in 1941 by journalists, business and labour leaders, academics and former government officials; in 1997 it incorporated the programmes of the National Forum Foundation.

Activities: Fosters the development of democracy. The organization conducts US and overseas research, advocacy, education and training initiatives that promote human rights, democracy, free market economics, the rule of law, independent media and US engagement in international affairs. Regional programmes include supporting independent local media, reducing violence against women, torture treatment and prevention, and human rights training; and provide emergency assistance to frontline activists, including journalists, human rights defenders, CSOs and survivors of religious persecution. It leads the Lifeline Consortium in implementing the Lifeline Embattled CSO Assistance Fund, which provides emergency assistance, advocacy grants and resiliency grants to CSOs under threat because of their human rights work. Has offices in New York and Johannesburg, South Africa.

Geographical Area of Activity: Worldwide.

Publications: Annual Report; newsletter (monthly); *China Media Bulletin*; *Freedom in the World* (annual); *Freedom on the Net* (annual); *Nations in Transit*; *Countries at the Crossroads*; studies; surveys.

Finance: Annual revenue US $90.0m., expenditure $88.8m. (30 June 2024).

Board of Trustees: Norman Wilcox (Chair.); Mark D. Goodman, Rachel Kleinfeld (Vice-Chair.); Tom Kahn (Treas.), Cater Lee (Sec.).

Principal Staff: Interim Co-Pres. Annie Wilcox Boyajian, Gerardo Berthin; Vice-Pres. Adrian Shahbaz.

Contact Details: 1850 M St, NW, Floor 11, Washington, DC 20036; tel. (202) 296-5101; e-mail info@freedomhouse.org; internet www.freedomhouse.org.

Freedom Together Foundation

Established in 2011 as the JPB Foundation, with an endowment bequeathed by Jeffry M. Picower, an investor; present name adopted in 2024.

Activities: Works to advance opportunity. Main programmes focus on: democracy, gender and racial justice; community and worker power; movement infrastructure and explorations; faith, bridging and belonging; and reproductive health, medical research, and community grants.

Geographical Area of Activity: USA.

Restrictions: Does not accept unsolicited applications; grants only to organizations based in the USA.

Finance: Annual revenue US $158.0m., expenditure $385.4m. (31 Dec. 2022).

Board of Directors: Barbara Picower (Pres. Emerita and Chair.); Deepak Bhargava (Pres. and Vice-Chair.).

Contact Details: 875 Third Ave, 29th Floor, New York, NY 10022; tel. (212) 935-9860; e-mail info@freedomtogether.org; internet www.freedomtogether.org.

The Freeman Foundation

Established in 1994 by Houghton 'Buck' Freeman, with funds from the estate of his father, Mansfield Freeman; both men worked for Shanghai-based insurance company American International Underwriters.

Activities: Promotes international understanding, with a focus on Asia, and supports farmland preservation projects in the state of Vermont and special projects in Hawaii. The Foundation established the Undergraduate Asian Studies Funding Initiative to make grants to US colleges to expand

Asian studies programmes. It also sponsors programmes to study and work abroad. These include the Blakemore Freeman Fellowship for Advanced Asian Language Study, awarded by the Blakemore Foundation (q.v.); and the Freeman Foundation International Internship Program in East and Southeast Asia at Furman University, which awards up to US $8,000 each to 16 students to live and work abroad for at least six weeks. Has offices in Stowe, VT.

Geographical Area of Activity: East and South-East Asia, South Asia, USA.

Finance: Annual revenue US $10.6m., expenditure $23.6m. (31 Dec. 2022).

Principal Staff: Exec. Dir and Pres. Graeme Freeman.

Contact Details: c/o Rockefeller Trust Co, POB 5016, New York, NY 10185-5016; tel. (212) 549-5544.

French-American Foundation

Established in 1976 by James G. Lowenstein, a diplomat, and James Chace and Nicholas Wahl, historians.

Activities: Acts as a platform for leaders, policymakers and professionals from France and the USA to discuss matters of concern to both countries, share opinions and establish relationships. The Foundation's flagship initiative is the Young Leaders programme, which provides networking opportunities for emerging leaders in government, business, media, the military, and the cultural and non-profit sectors. It organizes Policy Breakfasts to discuss economic, social and political topics; and the Transatlantic Forum for members. Immigration Journalism Fellowships are available to journalists of any nationality who are interested in immigration and integration; the Immigration Journalism Prize and Prix Cercle des Médias are offered for work on immigration in English and French, respectively. Also awarded is an annual prize for the best translation from French to English in fiction and non-fiction. Has a sister organization in France.

Geographical Area of Activity: France, USA.

Restrictions: Not a grantmaking organization; fellowship applicants must have at least three years' professional experience as journalists and be fluent in English or French.

Publications: Annual Report; project reports; newsletter (annual).

Finance: Annual revenue US $1.4m., expenditure $932,899 (31 Dec. 2021).

Board of Directors: Edward C. Wallace (Chair.).

Principal Staff: Co-Exec. Dir Jennifer Walden Weprin, Elizabeth McGehee.

Contact Details: 28 West 44th St, Suite 912, New York, NY 10036; tel. (212) 829-8800; e-mail info@frenchamerican.org; internet www.frenchamerican.org.

G. Unger Vetlesen Foundation

Founded in 1955 by Georg Unger Vetlesen, a Norwegian shipbuilder and founder of Scandinavian Airlines System, an air travel consortium; shares an administration with the Ambrose Monell Foundation (q.v.).

Activities: Supports academic, economic and environmental innovation. The Foundation makes grants mainly in the areas of oceanography, climate studies and other earth sciences. It also makes grants for biological, geophysical and environmental scientific research, higher education and cultural activities, with an emphasis on Norwegian-US relations and maritime issues; and supports public policy research and libraries. The Vetlesen Foundation Prize (f. 1959), worth US $250,000, is awarded for scientific achievement in the field of earth sciences.

Geographical Area of Activity: International.

Restrictions: No grants to individuals.

Publications: Annual Report.

Finance: Annual revenue US $12.7m., expenditure $8.6m. (31 Dec. 2021).

Board of Directors: Ambrose K. Monell (Pres. and Treas.); Maurizio J. Morello (Exec. Vice-Pres. and Asst Treas.); Maia Maude Monell (Vice-Pres.).

Contact Details: c/o Fulton, Rowe & Hart, 1 Rockefeller Plaza, Suite 301, New York, NY 10020-2002; tel. (212) 586-0700; e-mail contact@monellfoundation.org; internet www.vetlesenfoundation.org.

Gates Foundation

Established in 1994 by William (Bill) Gates, co-founder of Microsoft, and his wife Melinda; the Gates Learning Foundation (f. 1997 as the successor to the Microsoft/American Library Association) and the William H. Gates Foundation (f. 1994) were integrated into the Bill & Melinda Gates Foundation in 1999; present name adopted in 2024.

Activities: Works to eliminate poverty, disease and inequity. In developing countries, the Foundation focuses on helping people to overcome hunger and extreme poverty; and in the USA, on ensuring access to education and livelihoods opportunities. Main programme areas include: charitable sector support; gender equality; global development; global health; global growth and opportunity; global policy and advocacy; and the USA. The Strategic Investment Fund makes programme-related investments of more than US $5m. in private sector innovation. In 2003 it launched the Grand Challenges in Global Health initiative—subsequently renamed Grand Challenges—to foster innovation to solve major global health and development problems. Has offices in Washington, DC, the People's Republic of China, Ethiopia, Germany, India, Nigeria, South Africa and the United Kingdom; and a Discovery Center in Seattle, WA. Works in more than 130 countries.

Geographical Area of Activity: International.

Restrictions: Does not make grants outside its funding priorities; to individuals; or to projects addressing health problems in developed countries.

Publications: Annual Report; Annual Letter; newsletter.

Finance: Annual revenue US $19.8m., expenditure US $8,257.0m. (31 Dec. 2023).

Board of Trustees: Bill Gates (Chair.).

Principal Staff: CEO Mark Suzman.

Contact Details: 500 Fifth Ave North, Seattle, WA 98109; POB 23350, Seattle, WA 98102; tel. (206) 709-3100; e-mail info@gatesfoundation.org; internet www.gatesfoundation.org.

GE Aerospace Foundation

Founded in 1952 as the General Electric Foundation for the support of education in the USA; adopted GE Foundation name in 1994 following the merger of the General Electric Foundation and General Electric Foundation, Inc; present name adopted in 2024.

Activities: Main programmes include: education for students aged 14–24 years, developing skills in science, technology, engineering and mathematics; increasing access to community healthcare for marginalized people; and disaster response and recovery, providing humanitarian relief, technology and other resources.

Geographical Area of Activity: International.

Restrictions: Does not accept unsolicited applications.

Publications: Annual Report; archives.

Finance: Annual revenue US $27.5m., expenditure $26.3m. (31 Dec. 2021).

Board of Directors: Kevin Cox (Chair.); Kathleen Mayglothling (Sec.).

Principal Staff: Pres. Linda Boff.

Contact Details: 901 Main Ave (Internal Mail Drop: 801-4), Norwalk CT 06851; tel. (617) 443-3080; e-mail philanthropy.inquiries@ge.com; internet www.geaerospace.com/company/philanthropy.

General Service Foundation—GSF

Founded in 1946 by Clifton R. Musser, an industrialist, and his wife Margaret.

Activities: Works in the fields of human rights, social justice and democracy. Main programmes are: Building Voice and Power, supporting organizations working for gender and racial justice and income equity, with grants ranging from US $20,000 to $35,000; and the annual Lani Shaw Movement Award, recognizing campaigns and leadership in social justice. The Foundation has an office in Aspen, CO.

Geographical Area of Activity: North and Central America and the Caribbean.

Restrictions: Prioritizes multiyear grants for long-term partners.

Publications: Newsletter.

Finance: Annual revenue US $7.5m., expenditure $5.4m. (31 Dec. 2022).

Board of Directors: Robin Snidow (Chair.).

Principal Staff: Exec. Dir Desiree Flores.

Contact Details: 3001 Bishop Dr., Suite 300, San Ramon, CA 94583; tel. (510) 679-3876; e-mail info@generalservice.org; internet www.generalservice.org.

The George A. and Eliza Gardner Howard Foundation

Founded in 1952 by Nicea Howard, a Providence resident, to aid the personal development of individuals at the middle stage of their careers.

Activities: Awards a limited number of one-year fellowships for independent projects in a five-year rotation of categories: creative non-fiction, literary translation into English, literary studies, film studies; photography, anthropology, archaeology; painting, sculpture, history of art and architecture; playwriting, music, musicology, theatre studies, history; and creative writing in English, including fiction, poetry and philosophy. In 2026 the Foundation will award 14 fellowships in the fields of fiction and poetry and literary studies, worth US $40,000 each.

Geographical Area of Activity: USA.

Restrictions: Fellowships are tenable anywhere in the world, but are restricted to candidates who, regardless of their country of citizenship, are professionally based in the USA; fellowships are not given to support degree candidates.

Finance: Annual revenue US $356,049, expenditure $562,938 (31 Dec. 2022).

Board of Trustees: William W. Kenyon (Chair.).

Principal Staff: Dir Joseph Meisel.

Contact Details: Brown University, Box 1857, Providence, RI 02912; tel. (401) 863-2429; e-mail howard_foundation@brown.edu; internet www.brown.edu/howard-foundation/george-and-eliza-gardner-howard-foundation.

The George I. Alden Trust

Founded in 1912 by George I. Alden, a teacher of mechanical engineering and inventor.

Activities: Involved in the fields of higher and vocational education in the USA. The Trust makes grants in five areas: Higher Education; Secondary Schools; Educationally Related Community Organizations; YMCAs; and Unsolicited Special Worcester grants. It offers scholarships and endowment funds; and carries out research and organizes conferences.

Geographical Area of Activity: USA.

Publications: Annual Report; information brochure.

Finance: Annual revenue US $34.4m., expenditure $12.8m. (31 Dec. 2023).

Board of Trustees: Warner S. Fletcher (Chair.); Gail T. Randall (Vice-Chair.); Jim Collins (Treas.); Douglas Q. Meystre (Clerk).

Contact Details: 100 Front Street, 5th Floor, Worcester, MA 01608; tel. (508) 459-8005; e-mail trustees@aldentrust.org; internet www.aldentrust.org.

Georges Lurcy Charitable and Educational Trust

Founded in 1985 by the will of Georges Lurcy, a French banker who emigrated to the USA, to support educational purposes.

Activities: Provides grants to students of French nationality for educational exchanges; and supports professorial university chairs, conferences, cultural organizations and secondary education. The Trust awards fellowships, worth US $20,000, for students enrolled at a US university to pursue a degree or, in some cases, to conduct doctoral research. Candidates from France are selected by the Franco-American Fulbright Commission (q.v.).

Geographical Area of Activity: France, USA.

Finance: Annual revenue US $1m., expenditure $2m. (30 June 2023).

Principal Staff: Contact Seth E. Frank.

Contact Details: 1633 Broadway, 32nd Floor, New York, NY 10019; tel. (212) 660-3000; internet www.lurcy.org.

German Marshall Fund of the United States—GMF

Established in 1972 by Dr Guido Goldman, an academic and co-founder of the Center for European Studies at Harvard University, through a gift from the German people as a permanent memorial to the Marshall Plan.

Activities: Works to strengthen transatlantic co-operation in the areas of: policy, through research and analysis; leadership, providing professional training and fellowships; and civil society, supporting democratic initiatives. The Fund established the Balkan Trust for Democracy in 2003 in partnership with the US Agency for International Development (USAID) and the Charles Stewart Mott Foundation (q.v.), supporting projects in the areas of democracy and good governance, policy dialogue and networking, and regional co-operation and European integration; the Fund for Belarus Democracy in 2005; and in 2007 the Black Sea Trust for Regional Cooperation (BST), offering grants to civic activists, citizen and grassroots initiatives, and NGOs in Belarus. The Fund houses the Alliance for Securing Democracy, which works in the fields of cybersecurity, disinformation, economic coercion, elections integrity, emerging technologies and malign finance. It has offices in Ankara (Türkiye), Belgrade (Serbia), Berlin (Germany), Brussels (Belgium), Bucharest (Romania), Paris (France) and Warsaw (Poland).

Geographical Area of Activity: Albania, Armenia, Azerbaijan, Belarus, Bosnia and Herzegovina, EU, Georgia, Kosovo, Macedonia, Moldova, Montenegro, Serbia, Türkiye, Ukraine, USA.

Restrictions: Projects must address issues important to European countries and the USA and involve people or institutions on both sides of the Atlantic.

Publications: Annual Report; newsletter; policy papers; special reports; toolkits.

Finance: Annual revenue US $29.8m., expenditure $40.0m. (31 May 2022).

Board of Trustees: J. Robinson West (Chair.); Christopher Schroeder (Vice-Chair.).

Principal Staff: Pres. Heather A. Conley.

Contact Details: 1744 R St, NW, Washington, DC 20009; tel. (202) 683-2650; e-mail info@gmfus.org; internet www.gmfus.org.

GiveWell—The Clear Fund

Established in 2007 by a group of donors.

Activities: Researches and publishes analysis on making effective charitable donations. The organization develops criteria and processes for identifying charities that do the most good in terms of saving or improving people's lives, considering their effectiveness and transparency. It offers incubation grants to support the development of future top charities.

Priority areas include distributing insecticide-treated nets to prevent malaria, treating children for parasites and direct cash transfers. Works closely with the Open Philanthropy Project (f. 2014), which it established with Good Ventures (q.v.) and which became an independent limited liability company in 2017.

Geographical Area of Activity: USA.

Publications: *List of Top Charities*; newsletter.

Finance: Annual revenue US $10.1m., expenditure $10.2m. (31 Dec. 2023).

Board of Directors: Timothy Ogden (Chair.).

Principal Staff: CEO and Pres. Elie Hassenfeld.

Contact Details: 1714 Franklin St #100335, Oakland, CA 94612; tel. (415) 689-5803; e-mail info@givewell.org; internet www.givewell.org.

Global Communities

Founded in 1952 as the Foundation for Cooperative Housing; subsequently known as the Cooperative Housing Foundation and CHF International; in 2020 it merged with PCI—Project Concern International (f. 1961). Part of the Vitas Group, which it founded in 2004, a network of financial services companies.

Activities: Helps people in low- and moderate-income communities around the world to improve their economic circumstances, environment and infrastructure. The organization carries out programmes to improve health and hygiene, provide food security and strengthen communities' resilience to shocks. It provides technical expertise and leadership in international development, including development finance, housing and entrepreneurship, collaborating with local organizations and governments. Works in more than 30 countries. Has an office in San Diego, CA.

Geographical Area of Activity: International.

Restrictions: Grants only to project-specific local organizations; does not accept unsolicited applications; no grants to individuals.

Publications: Annual Report; newsletter; *Building a Better World* (annual); bulletins; country profiles; factsheets; manuals; research reports; toolkits; white papers.

Finance: Annual revenue US $190.8m., expenditure $175.7m. (30 Sept. 2022).

Board of Trustees: John Potter (Chair.); John Duong (Vice-Chair.); Joseph Abbate (Treas.); Dr Hillary Thomas-Lake (Sec.).

Principal Staff: Pres. and CEO Carrie Hessler-Radelet.

Contact Details: 7700 Wisconsin Ave, Suite 1100, Bethesda, MD 20814; tel. (301) 587-4700; e-mail mailbox@globalcommunities.org; internet www.globalcommunities.org.

The Global Foodbanking Network—GFN

Established in 2006.

Activities: Works to eliminate hunger by supporting, uniting and strengthening food banks. Main programme areas include: partnering with new local food banks; peer-to-peer training and knowledge exchange; offering capacity-building grants to food banks; and assuring safety through certification. It has partners in more than 50 countries.

Geographical Area of Activity: International.

Publications: Annual Report; newsletter; *The Global Food Donation Policy Atlas*; *The State of Global Food Banking* (annual).

Finance: Annual revenue US $14.5m., expenditure $17.5m. (30 June 2024).

Board of Directors: Sachin Gupta (Chair.).

Principal Staff: Pres. and CEO Lisa Moon.

Contact Details: 70 E. Lake St, Suite 1200, Chicago, IL 60601; tel. (312) 782-4560; e-mail info@foodbanking.org; internet www.foodbanking.org.

Global Fund for Children

Founded in 1993 by Maya Ajmera.

Activities: Offers funding to local organizations working with children and young people worldwide in the areas of education, gender equity, youth rights and combating violence and exploitation. Has a sister organization in the UK, Global Fund for Children UK Trust (f. 2006).

Geographical Area of Activity: sub-Saharan Africa, Central and South America, South Asia, Europe, Türkiye (Turkey), USA.

Restrictions: No funding for int. organizations, political or religious organizations requiring conversion.

Finance: Annual revenue US $36.4m., expenditure $14.2m. (30 June 2023).

Global Board of Directors: Swatee Deepak, Greg Wallig (Co-Chair.); Lila Rymer (Treas.).

Principal Staff: Exec. Dir Steina Bjorgvinsdottir.

Contact Details: 1411 K St, NW, Suite 1200, Washington, DC 20005; tel. (202) 331-9003; e-mail info@globalfundforchildren.org; internet globalfundforchildren.org.

Global Fund for Women—GFW

Founded in 1987 by Anne Firth Murray, a scholar and activist; in 2014 it merged with the International Museum of Women (f. 1997).

Activities: Supports women and girls, working for the elimination of sexual and gender-based violence, economic and political empowerment, and sexual and reproductive health and rights. The Fund carries out programmes in the areas of economic affairs, education, human rights, medicine and health, and social welfare and studies. It supports grassroots women's organizations outside the USA. Has an office in Atlanta, Georgia and a subsidiary in the United Kingdom.

Geographical Area of Activity: International.

Restrictions: Operates internationally, but does not support individuals or groups based in the USA.

Publications: Annual Report; *Raising Our Voices* (newsletter); reports; handbooks; information brochure.

Finance: Annual revenue US $41.5m., expenditure $33.4m. (30 June 2024).

Board of Directors: Layli Maparyan (Chair.); Caroline Barlerin (Vice-Chair.); Theresa Preston-Werner (Sec.).

Principal Staff: Pres. and CEO PeiYao Chen.

Contact Details: 505 Montgomery St, 11th Floor, San Francisco, CA 94111; tel. (415) 248-4800; e-mail info@globalfundforwomen.org; internet www.globalfundforwomen.org.

Global Greengrants Fund

Established in 1993 by Chet Tchozewski, a former regional director for Greenpeace USA and co-founder of the Rocky Mountain Peace and Justice Center.

Activities: Supports environmental and social justice projects led by local people through participatory grantmaking. Main programme areas are: climate justice; healthy ecosystems and communities; livelihoods; land, water and resource rights; and environmental action led by women. The Fund awards small grants, typically worth around US $5,000, to grassroots NGOs. It has an office in London (UK).

Geographical Area of Activity: International.

Restrictions: Does not accept unsolicited applications.

Publications: Annual Report; newsletter; blog.

Finance: Annual revenue US $40.3m., expenditure $17.6m. (30 June 2022).

Board of Directors: Katharine Pease (Chair.); Chinesom Ejiasa (Treas.); Kimberly Hult (Sec.).

Principal Staff: Pres. and CEO Laura García.

Contact Details: 2840 Wilderness Pl., Suite A, Boulder, CO 80301; tel. (303) 939-9866; e-mail info@greengrants.org; internet www.greengrants.org.

Goldman Sachs Foundation

Established in 1999 by Goldman Sachs, a banking and securities firm; formerly known as the Goldman Sachs Charitable Fund.

Activities: Supports projects in the field of education through promoting partnerships between the public, private and non-profit sectors. Programmes include: 10,000 Women, providing women entrepreneurs with business and management education, mentoring and networking opportunities, financial capital and Growth Fellowships; 10,000 Small Businesses, helping to create jobs and economic opportunities; Community TeamWorks, a volunteer scheme for Goldman Sachs employees to work with local non-profit organizations for at least one day a year; and Supporting Veterans, helping former military service personnel to reintegrate into civilian life through training and mentoring.

Geographical Area of Activity: International.

Publications: Annual Report.

Finance: Annual revenue US $19.2m., expenditure $82.0m. (31 Dec. 2022).

Board of Directors: John F. W. Rogers (Chair.).

Principal Staff: Pres. Asahi Pompey.

Contact Details: c/o Office of Corporate Engagement, 200 West St, 29th Floor, New York, NY 10282; tel. (212) 902-4223; internet www.goldmansachs.com/our-commitments/community-engagement.

Good360

Established in 1984, as Gifts in Kind International; present name adopted in 2011.

Activities: A global network that co-ordinates and distributes donated products from the private sector, providing quality services and goods for poorer communities in different countries and as part of post-disaster recovery efforts. Donations include computers for education, clothing for the homeless, products for disaster relief and construction materials for the rehabilitation of residential areas.

Geographical Area of Activity: International.

Publications: Annual Report; newsletter; catalogue; blog.

Finance: Annual revenue US $3,062.5m., expenditure $2,971.3m. (31 Dec. 2023).

Board of Directors: John Grugan (Chair.); Rosemarie Ryan (Vice-Chair.).

Principal Staff: CEO Cinira Baldi.

Contact Details: 675 N Washington St, Suite 330, Alexandria, VA 22314; tel. (703) 836-2121; e-mail press@good360.org; internet good360.org.

Goodwill Industries International, Inc—GII

Established in 1902 by Rev. Edgar Helms, a Methodist minister and social innovator.

Activities: Works to ensure that all people have the opportunity to achieve their fullest potential as individuals and to participate and contribute fully in all aspects of a productive life. The organization runs employment and training programmes to increase the self-sufficiency of people with barriers to work, including young people, military veterans, older people and people with disabilities, criminal backgrounds and other particular needs; and offers vocational training and employment through its network of more than 150 autonomous, community-based agencies in the USA and Canada and in collaboration with other NGOs, foundations and companies. It is affiliated with 12 organizations in countries around the world; and operates a chain of more than 3,300 Goodwill charity shops in the USA and Canada to raise funds. Goodwill Global, with an office in Washington, DC, fosters the organization's entrepreneurial efforts outside the USA and Canada.

Geographical Area of Activity: International.

Publications: Annual Report; newsletter; *Working!* (quarterly magazine); blog.

Finance: Annual revenue US $71.0m., expenditure $67.7m. (31 Dec. 2023).

Board of Directors: Anne Richards (Chair.); Ken Diekroeger (Treas.); Chris Hess (Sec.).

Principal Staff: Pres. and CEO Steven C. Preston.

Contact Details: 15810 Indianola Dr., Rockville, MD 20855; tel. (301) 530-6500; e-mail contactus@goodwill.org; internet www.goodwill.org.

Google.org—Google Foundation

Established in 2004 by Google, a technology company, part of Alphabet, Inc.

Activities: Supports non-profit organizations working to address inequities and solve complex problems, providing funding, technology and Google volunteers. Main programme areas are: knowledge, skills and learning; scientific advancement; and building resilient communities. It established the Global Environmental Insights Explorer Action Fund for data-driven climate action. The organization manages and funds a portion of its grants through the Google Foundation. It organizes an annual Impact Challenge competition for innovative projects with community impact that have the potential to be scaled up; winners receive funding and Google volunteers' support.

Geographical Area of Activity: Worldwide.

Board of Directors: Jacquelline Fuller (Pres.); Kristin Reinke (Treas.).

Contact Details: 1600 Amphitheatre Parkway, Mountain View, CA 94043-1351; tel. (650) 253-0000; e-mail press@google.com; internet www.google.org.

Gordon and Betty Moore Foundation

Established in 2000 by Gordon Moore, the co-founder of technology company Intel, and his wife Betty.

Activities: Seeks to improve the quality of life for future generations. Main programme areas are: science, advancing basic science through developing new technologies and supporting research; environmental conservation, protecting critical ecosystems worldwide; patient care, improving patient safety and serious illness care; and the San Francisco Bay Area, with a focus on conservation and supporting science and technology museums. The Foundation has an office in San Francisco, CA.

Geographical Area of Activity: International.

Restrictions: No grants for religious purposes; the arts and cultural activities; civil disobedience; buildings and endowments not directly related to Foundation programmes; or for emergency and disaster relief efforts. Does not accept unsolicited proposals.

Publications: Annual Report.

Finance: Annual revenue US $371.8m., expenditure $485.6m. (31 Dec. 2023).

Board of Trustees: Ken Moore (Chair.); Dr John Hennessy (Vice-Chair.).

Principal Staff: Pres. Dr Harvey V. Fineberg.

Contact Details: 1661 Page Mill Rd, Palo Alto, CA 94304-1209; tel. (650) 213-3000; e-mail info@moore.org; internet www.moore.org.

Graham Foundation for Advanced Studies in the Fine Arts—GF

Founded in 1956 by the will of Ernest R. Graham, an architect.

Activities: Fosters the development and exchange of ideas about architecture and its role in the arts, culture and society. The Foundation supports investigations into architecture; architectural history, theory and criticism; design; engineering; landscape architecture; urban planning; urban studies; visual arts; and related fields of inquiry. Its interests also extend to work being done in the fine arts, humanities and sciences that expands the boundaries of thinking about architecture and space. Grantmaking focuses on the public dissemination of ideas and supports individuals and organizations.

UNITED STATES OF AMERICA

Geographical Area of Activity: International.

Finance: Annual revenue US $541,336, expenditure $2.4m. (31 Dec. 2022).

Board of Trustees: David Brown (Pres.); Eric T. McKissack (Treas.); Monica Chadha (Sec.).

Principal Staff: Dir Sarah Herda.

Contact Details: Madlener House, 4 West Burton Pl., Chicago, IL 60610-1416; tel. (312) 787-4071; e-mail info@grahamfoundation.org; internet www.grahamfoundation.org.

Grameen Foundation—GF

Founded in 1997 by Alex Counts, who was inspired by the work of Grameen Bank in Bangladesh; merged with Freedom from Hunger (f. 1946 as Meals for Millions) in 2016.

Activities: Works in countries with large populations that experience extreme poverty and chronic hunger, in particular in rural areas. The Foundation operates six main programmes: AccelHERate: Supporting Young Women; InvestHER: Supporting Entrepreneurs; TogetHER, We Grow: Supporting Farmers; Program SAFE: Safeguarding women from Abuse in the Financial Ecosystem; GAIT LAB: Grameen's AI and Technology Lab; and Sparks For Change: Building Stronger Families. It offers fellowships and internships through its Bankers Without Borders initiative. Has offices in Ghana, India, Kenya, the Philippines and Uganda.

Geographical Area of Activity: South America, Central America and the Caribbean, South Asia, South-East Asia, sub-Saharan Africa.

Publications: Annual Report; newsletters; brochure; blog; books.

Finance: Annual revenue US $12.9m., expenditure $13.9m. (30 June 2023).

Board of Directors: Elisabeth Rhyne (Chair.).

Principal Staff: Pres. and CEO Zubaida Bai.

Contact Details: 2001 L St NW, Suite 500, Washington, DC 20036; c/o EarthClass, 9450 SW Gemini Dr., PMB 13977, Beaverton, Oregon 97008-7105; tel. (202) 628-3560; e-mail info@grameenfoundation.org; internet www.grameenfoundation.org.

The Grass Foundation

Founded in 1955 by Albert and Ellen Grass, physiologists.

Activities: Operates in the fields of medicine and science through offering summer fellowships for young researchers conducting independent research at the Marine Biological Laboratory, Woods Hole, MA. The Foundation supports courses in neuroscience, funds lectureships, awards prizes and organizes annual lectures.

Geographical Area of Activity: USA.

Restrictions: Applicants from overseas are eligible for fellowships, but work must be carried out at a North American institution. No support for ongoing research, full-time students, symposia or conferences.

Publications: Application guidelines; programme policy statement; information brochure.

Board of Trustees: Matthew B. McFarlane (Pres.); Bernice Grafstein (Vice-Pres.); Joshua Grass (Treas.).

Contact Details: POB 11342, Takoma Park, MD 20913; tel. (424) 832-4188; e-mail info@grassfoundation.org; internet www.grassfoundation.org.

Grassroots International—GRI

Established in 1983 by members of Oxfam America (q.v.) after it closed its operations in Lebanon.

Activities: Active in the fields of social justice and human rights. The organization supports community development by providing grants through partner NGOs to bring about positive social change. Grants fall into three categories: sustainable livelihoods, providing basics such as seeds and tools; movement building, nurturing leadership, in particular among women and young people; and defending human rights, protecting activists' civil and human rights. It carries out advocacy and educational activities on behalf of its partner organizations; and raises public awareness about issues of power, social change and poverty.

Geographical Area of Activity: Africa (Horn), Asia, Latin America and the Caribbean, Middle East.

Restrictions: Grants are only made to specific organizations in specific regions.

Publications: Annual Report; *Insights* (newsletter); *GrassrootsONLINE*; factsheets; reports and summaries.

Finance: Annual revenue US $13.3m., expenditure $12.2m. (31 Oct. 2023).

Board of Directors: Maria Aguiar (Chair.); Kalila Barnett (Treas.).

Principal Staff: Co-Exec. Dirs Chung-Wha Hong, Sara Mersha.

Contact Details: 867 Boylston St, Suite 500, #1721, Boston, MA 02116; tel. (617) 524-1400; e-mail info@grassrootsonline.org; internet www.grassrootsonline.org.

Greater Kansas City Community Foundation

Established in 1978.

Activities: Aims to improve the quality of life in Greater Kansas City, through offering grants and scholarships. Programme areas include: art, culture and the humanities; education; environment and animals; health; human services; international; public and societal benefit; and religion. The Foundation administers more than 7,000 charitable funds. Regional affiliates include the Black Community Fund, Hispanic Development Fund, Northland Community Foundation and Regional Advisory Council. It maintains a database of more than 700 non-profit organizations.

Geographical Area of Activity: USA (Greater Kansas City).

Publications: Annual Report; blog.

Finance: Annual revenue US $540.7m., expenditure $475.9m. (31 Dec. 2022).

Board of Directors: Jeff Hargroves (Chair.); Ann F. Konecny (Vice-Chair.); William M. Lyons (Immediate Past Chair.); Ken Williams (Treas.); Gayle Packer (Sec.).

Principal Staff: Pres. and CEO Debbie Wilkerson.

Contact Details: 1055 Broadway, Suite 130, Kansas City, MO 64105; tel. (816) 842-0944; e-mail info@growyourgiving.org; internet www.gkccf.org.

Habitat for Humanity International

Founded in 1976 by Millard and Linda Fuller; a global non-profit, ecumenical Christian housing organization.

Activities: Operates in the field of social welfare, in particular safe affordable shelter and housing. The organization provides volunteers to work alongside those in need of shelter to build adequate basic houses, which are then sold to families at no profit or interest. It promotes sustainable building, providing education and training to local affiliates, and conducts programmes in more than 70 countries. Has offices in Atlanta, GA; and Costa Rica, the Philippines and Slovakia.

Geographical Area of Activity: International.

Publications: Annual Report; newsletter (monthly); *Habitat World Magazine*.

Finance: Annual revenue US $329.2m., expenditure $330.6m. (30 June 2023).

Board of Directors: Mary Cameron (Chair.); Bill Brand, Christiana Smith Shi (Vice-Chair.); Kimberlee Cornett (Treas.); Olivia Wong (Sec.).

Principal Staff: CEO Jonathan Reckford.

Contact Details: 322 West Lamar St, Americus, GA 31709-3543; tel. (229) 924-6935; e-mail publicinfo@habitat.org; internet www.habitat.org.

Harold Grinspoon Foundation

Established in 1991 by Harold Grinspoon, a property developer.

Activities: Supports Jewish civic and educational institutions and organizations through fostering Jewish culture and learning. Main programmes are: PJ Library, providing books, music and other resources to children in more than 20 countries in languages including Russian, Spanish and Ukrainian; Sifriyat Pajama ('Pajama Library'), based in Israel, which distributes literary books in Hebrew; JCamp 180, offering consulting services and professional development to more than 115 overnight and day camps in North America; and Life & Legacy, promoting philanthropic giving. In the USA, the Foundation offers grants to individuals and organizations in Western Massachusetts, including local initiatives in education, energy, entrepreneurship, farming and *Havurot* shared-interest community groups.

Geographical Area of Activity: International.

Restrictions: Does not accept unsolicited applications for national grants.

Publications: Annual Report; *Voices & Visions* (poster series).

Finance: Annual revenue US $197.2m., expenditure $57.7m. (31 Dec. 2022).

Principal Staff: Pres. Winnie Sandler Grinspoon.

Contact Details: 67 Hunt St, Suite 100, Agawam, MA 01001; tel. (413) 276-0700; e-mail info@hgf.org; internet hgf.org.

The Harry Frank Guggenheim Foundation—HFG

Founded in 1929 by Harry Frank Guggenheim, a business person, diplomat and newspaper publisher.

Activities: Promotes the creation and dissemination of knowledge about the causes and spread of violence and how to address it. Research subjects include: war; terrorism; crime; family and intimate-partnership relationships; climate instability and natural resource competition; racial, ethnic and religious conflict; and political extremism and nationalism. The Foundation supports basic research in the social, behavioural and biological sciences, offering grants and fellowships; and organizing the annual HFG Symposium on Crime in America, offering 20–30 fellowships to enable journalists to attend. It offers Distinguished Scholar Awards of between US $15,000 and $75,000 per year for 1–2 years; Emerging Scholars Awards, worth $25,000 during the writing phase of a PhD dissertation; and two-year African Fellows Awards, which include fieldwork research grants worth $10,000.

Geographical Area of Activity: International.

Restrictions: No grants to institutions, nor for programmes; research must be relevant to understanding human problems.

Publications: Annual Report; *HFG Review*; *Occasional Papers of the HFG*; conference reports; policy briefs; research reports.

Finance: Annual revenue US $1.4m., expenditure $4.3m. (31 Dec. 2022).

Board of Trustees: Peter Lawson-Johnston (Chair.).

Principal Staff: Pres. Daniel F. Wilhelm.

Contact Details: 120 West 45th St, New York, NY 10036; tel. (646) 428-0971; e-mail info@hfg.org; internet www.hfg.org.

Harry and Jeanette Weinberg Foundation, Inc

Established in 1959 by Harry Weinberg, a real estate investor and owner of a mass transit bus company, and his wife Jeanette.

Activities: Focuses on alleviating poverty. The Foundation offers capital, operating and programme grants to organizations working in the areas of housing, health, jobs, education and community services for the elderly, at-risk women and children, people living with disabilities, military veterans and the Jewish community in the USA and Israel. The Small Grants Program offers grants of up to US $50,000 a year for two years to small non-profit organizations in Baltimore, Chicago, Hawaii, New York City, North-Eastern Pennsylvania, San Francisco and rural areas. The Baltimore City Community Grants Program offers grants of up to $10,000 for one year to small non-profit organizations in Baltimore City. Has an office in Honolulu, HI.

Geographical Area of Activity: Israel, USA.

Restrictions: No grants to individuals; neither solicits, nor accepts, any type of donation.

Publications: Annual Report; newsletter; Community Grants Overview; blog.

Finance: Annual revenue US $107.3m., expenditure $177.5m. (31 Dec. 2022).

Board of Trustees: Paula B. Pretlow (Chair.).

Principal Staff: Pres. and CEO Rachel Garbow Monroe.

Contact Details: 7 Park Center Ct, Owings Mills, MD 21117-4200; tel. (410) 654-8500; internet hjweinbergfoundation.org.

Hasbro Foundation

Established in 2006 by Hasbro, Inc, a toy and games manufacturer; continues programmes formerly carried out by Hasbro Children's Foundation (f. 1984) and Hasbro Charitable Trust; formerly known as the Hasbro Children's Fund.

Activities: Works in the fields of children's education and social welfare; and supports programmes that help disadvantaged and seriously ill children. The Foundation provides local community grants where Hasbro has operating facilities in the USA (Boulder, CO, Los Angeles, CA, Miami, FL, Renton, WA, and Rhode Island).

Geographical Area of Activity: International.

Restrictions: No grants to individuals, religious or political organizations, or schools; does not accept unsolicited applications.

Publications: Annual Report.

Finance: Annual revenue US $5.0m., expenditure $3.1m. (31 Dec. 2021).

Board of Directors: Kevin Colman (Pres.); Deborah Thomas (Treas.); Sibley Tarrant (Sec.).

Principal Staff: Pres. Kevin Colman.

Contact Details: 200 Narragansett Park Dr., Suite C-9, Pawtucket, RI 02862-0200; tel. (401) 431-8151; e-mail hcfinfo@hasbro.com; internet globalphilanthropy.hasbro.com.

Health Volunteers Overseas—HVO

Established in 1986, building on the work of Orthopaedics Overseas.

Activities: Operates in the fields of healthcare and international development, working to improve access to and quality of healthcare in resource-scarce countries. The organization recruits health professionals to work directly with health workers in resource-scarce countries to provide education, training and professional opportunity. Staff and volunteers collaborate with health institutions to design, develop and implement projects to improve trauma care, child and maternal health, essential surgical care, cancer care, rehabilitation and nursing. It offers the Warfield Scholarship for Anesthesia Professionals and the Wyss Scholarship for Future Leaders in Global Health.

Geographical Area of Activity: Africa, Asia, Central and South America.

Restrictions: Does not make grants.

Publications: Annual Report; *Net Connection* (monthly e-newsletter); *Volunteer Connection* (biannual newsletter); *A Guide to Volunteering Overseas*.

Finance: Annual income US $815,416, expenditure $1.1m. (31 Dec. 2022).

Board of Directors: Dr Carla Smith (Chair.).

Principal Staff: Exec. Dir April Pinner.

Contact Details: 1900 L St, NW, Suite 310, Washington, DC 20036; tel. (202) 296-0928; e-mail info@hvousa.org; internet www.hvousa.org.

Hearst Foundations

Founded in by William Randolph Hearst, a newspaper publisher, politician and art collector, comprising the Hearst Foundation, Inc (f. 1946) and the William Randolph Hearst Foundation (f. 1949 as the California Charities Foundations); managed as one entity, sharing the same leadership and mission.

Activities: Funds programmes in the fields of culture, higher and private secondary education, healthcare and social service; first grants are typically worth US $75,000. The Foundations offer scholarships through the US Senate Youth Program, worth $10,000, for students who wish to pursue a career in public service; and the Hearst Journalism Awards Program, which comprises a series of competitions for writing, photojournalism, radio, television and multimedia, with a total prize fund of $700,000. The New York office supports organizations located east of the Mississippi River and the San Francisco office, those to the west.

Geographical Area of Activity: USA and its dependencies.

Restrictions: No grants to individuals.

Finance: Annual revenue –US $10.3m., expenditure $23.0m. (31 Dec. 2022).

Board of Directors: Virginia H. Randt (Pres.); James M. Asher (Sec.).

Principal Staff: Co-Exec. Dirs Donna Kalajian Lagani (NY), Paul 'Dino' Dinovitz (CA).

Contact Details: 300 West 57th St, 26th Floor, New York, NY 10019-3741; 90 New Montgomery St, Suite 1212, San Francisco, CA 94105; tel. (212) 649-3750; (415) 908-4500; e-mail hearst.ny@hearstfdn.org; hearst.sf@hearstfdn.org; internet www.hearstfdn.org.

Heart to Heart International—HHI

Founded in 1992 by Gary Morsch, a family and emergency physician, and Jim Kerr, a pharmacist, to distribute aid to Russian hospitals and orphanages.

Activities: Improves access to healthcare. Main programmes include: delivering essential medicines, medical supplies and hygiene kits to healthcare facilities and people during humanitarian emergencies and in refugee camps; distributing medicine and equipment to clinics in the USA and equipping international medical teams; improving laboratory services through training; and engaging volunteers. It has worked in 131 countries.

Geographical Area of Activity: International.

Publications: Annual Report; *The Link* (quarterly newsletter); special reports; brochure.

Finance: Annual revenue US $430.1m., expenditure $406.2m. (31 Dec. 2023).

Executive Committee: Wendy Blackburn (Chair.); Austin Bickford (Treas.); Dan McClain (Sec.).

Principal Staff: Pres. and CEO Kim Carroll.

Contact Details: 11550 Renner Blvd, Lenexa, KS 66219; tel. (913) 764-5200; e-mail info@hearttoheart.org; internet www.hearttoheart.org.

Heifer Foundation

Founded in 1991 to support the work of Heifer International (f. 1944), which Dan West, a farmer, set up to provide long-term solutions to hunger and poverty.

Activities: Manages an endowment to support the work of Heifer International through providing trusts, annuities and other financial instruments. Since 2003 the Foundation has made an annual Dan West Fellow Award for individuals' humanitarian work.

Geographical Area of Activity: International.

Publications: Annual Report; e-newsletter (weekly).

Finance: Annual revenue US $17.4m., expenditure $7.9m. (30 June 2024).

Board of Trustees: Elizabeth Bawden (Chair.); Stephanie Buckley (Sec.).

Principal Staff: Pres. and CEO Kim Dempsey.

Contact Details: 1 World Ave, Little Rock, AR 72202; tel. (833) 904-4483; e-mail legacyinfo@heiferfoundation.org; internet www.heiferfoundation.org.

Helen Keller International—HKI

Founded in 1915 by Helen Keller, an author and educator, and George Kessler, a survivor of the sinking of the *RMS Lusitania*.

Activities: Works to eliminate preventable vision loss, malnutrition and neglected tropical diseases, and addresses gender equality. Main programmes are: eye health, to prevent and treat cataracts, onchocerciasis (river blindness), trachoma and diabetic retinopathy by providing equipment and training; and nutrition, providing Vitamin A supplements and leading food fortification initiatives, and promoting homestead food production, consumption of orange-fleshed sweet potatoes (OFSPs), and community management of malnutrition. The organization focuses on the major causes of blindness in the world that have been identified as priority eye diseases by the VISION 2020 global initiative to eliminate avoidable blindness. It works in 20 countries; HKI Europe, with headquarters in Paris, France, is an affiliate.

Geographical Area of Activity: Asia, sub-Saharan Africa, USA.

Restrictions: Not a grantmaking organization.

Publications: Annual Report; bulletins and reports; research, resources and publications on: anaemia; food fortification; general health and nutrition; eye health; homestead food production; micronutrients; nutrition surveillance; and onchocerciasis.

Finance: Annual revenue US $94.9m., expenditure $124.1m. (30 June 2024).

Board of Trustees: Bill Toppeta (Chair.); Desmond G. FitzGerald, Henry C. Barkhorn, III (Vice-Chair.); David Glassman (Treas.); Peirce Moser (Sec.).

Principal Staff: Pres. and CEO Sarah Bouchie.

Contact Details: 1 Dag Hammarskjold Plaza, Floor 2, New York, NY 10017; tel. (212) 532-0544; e-mail infoeurope@hki.org; internet www.hki.org.

Henry J. Kaiser Family Foundation—KFF

Established in 1948 by Henry J. Kaiser, an industrialist and shipbuilder; restructured in 1991.

Activities: Operates in the areas of national healthcare and the role of the USA in global health policy through self-conducted programmes in the areas of policy analysis, polling, journalism and communications. The Foundation offers media fellowships in health reporting in the USA; and the Rowland Fellowship for Policy Research on Coverage and Access to Care for Low Income People, worth up to US $15,000 for two Master's or doctoral students to carry out innovative research. It has an office in Washington, DC.

Geographical Area of Activity: USA.

Restrictions: Not a grantmaking foundation.

Publications: Annual Report; *The Latest* (newsletter, 2 a week); research; reports; polls; data.

Finance: Annual income US $111.0m., expenditure $66.7m. (31 Dec. 2021).

Board of Trustees: Olympia Snowe (Chair.); James E. Canales (Vice-Chair.).

Principal Staff: Pres. and CEO Dr Drew E. Altman.

Contact Details: 185 Berry St, Suite 2000, San Francisco, CA 94107; tel. (650) 854-9400; e-mail kffhelp@kff.org; internet www.kff.org.

Henry Luce Foundation, Inc

Founded in 1936 by Henry Robinson Luce, co-founder and Editor-in-Chief of Time Inc.

Activities: Grantmaking programmes include: American Art; Asia; Religion and Theology; Religion in International Affairs; Public Policy; the Clare Boothe Luce Program for Women in Science, Mathematics and Engineering; and Higher Education. Under the Luce Scholars Program, annually 15–18 college seniors, graduate students and young professionals with limited experience of Asia spend one year in East and South-East Asia; the programme provides stipends, language training and individualized professional placements.

Geographical Area of Activity: East and South-East Asia, USA.

Restrictions: Luce Scholars applicants must be US citizens aged under 30 years and hold at least a Bachelor's degree; grants only to institutions for other programmes.

Publications: Annual Report.

Finance: Annual revenue US $77.1m., expenditure $58.4m. (31 Dec. 2023).

Board of Directors: Terrence B. Adamson, Debra S. Knopman (Co-Chair.); Margaret Boles Fitzgerald (Immediate Past Chair.).

Principal Staff: Interim Pres. Sean Buffington; Pres. Emeritus Michael Gilligan.

Contact Details: 41 Madison Ave, 27th Floor, New York, NY 10010; tel. (212) 489-7700; e-mail info@hluce.org; internet www.hluce.org.

The Heritage Foundation

Established in 1973 by Paul M. Weyrich, a Republican political activist, Edwin Feulner, a Republican congressional aide, and Joseph Coors, Pres. of Coors Brewing Co; a conservative think tank.

Activities: Carries out public policy research and educational outreach in the promotion of free enterprise, limited government, personal liberty, traditional American values and strong national defence. Programme areas include: culture; domestic policy; the economy; energy and environment; government spending; healthcare; infrastructure and technology; international relations; legal and judicial; national security; political thought; and poverty and welfare. The Foundation's Young Leaders Program offers internships. The Academy programme provides online leadership training and learning in the areas of US foreign, domestic and economic policy aimed at students, young professionals and civic leaders.

Geographical Area of Activity: International.

Publications: Annual Report; reports; research papers; issue briefs; backgrounders; guides; books.

Finance: Annual revenue US $106.3m., expenditure $93.7m. (31 Dec. 2022).

Board of Trustees: Barb Van Andel-Gaby (Chair.); Michael W. Gleba (Vice-Chair.).

Principal Staff: Pres. Dr Kevin Roberts; Exec. Vice-Pres. Derrick Morgan.

Contact Details: 214 Massachusetts Ave NE, Washington, DC 20002-4999; tel. (202) 546-4400; e-mail info@heritage.org; internet www.heritage.org.

HIAS—Hebrew Immigrant Aid Society

Founded in 1881 to help Jews fleeing pogroms in Russia and Eastern Europe; in the 2000s it expanded its work to include non-Jewish refugees.

Activities: Protects and campaigns on behalf of refugees on a non-sectarian basis. The Society helps refugees to integrate in countries of asylum by providing legal services, trauma counselling and livelihood programmes; and resettles the most vulnerable refugees to the USA. It also reunites refugee families separated during migration; campaigns for increased refugee protection and funding; and engages the Jewish community in its mission. Works in 24 countries and has an office in New York City.

Geographical Area of Activity: Aruba, Austria, Belgium, Chad, Colombia, Costa Rica, Ecuador, Greece, Guyana, Israel, Kenya, Mexico, Panama, Peru, Ukraine, USA.

Publications: Annual Report; reports; policy papers.

Finance: Annual revenue US $127m., expenditure $148m. (30 Sept. 2023).

Board of Directors: Jeffrey Blattner (Chair.); Marc L. Silberberg (Vice-Chair.); Leon Rodriguez (Treas./Sec.).

Principal Staff: Pres. and CEO Mark Hetfield.

Contact Details: 1300 Spring St, Suite 500, Silver Spring, MD 20910; tel. (301) 844-7300; e-mail info@hias.org; internet www.hias.org.

Holt International

Established in 1956 in Korea, by Harry and Bertha Holt and David Kim, as the Holt Adoption Program; subsequently known as Holt International Children's Services.

Activities: Operates in the field of child welfare, specifically national and international adoption and family preservation, based on Christian principles. The organization supports adopting families; funds staff training in child welfare; and recommends policies related to children's rights and those of adoptive and birth parents to national governments and the UN. It runs sponsorship programmes in 17 locations across five continents, maintaining a network of its own offices, agencies and affiliated organizations around the world.

Geographical Area of Activity: Bulgaria, Cambodia, People's Repub. of China, Colombia, Ethiopia, Haiti, India, Repub. of Korea, Mongolia, Thailand, Uganda, USA, Viet Nam.

Publications: Annual Report; *Holt International Magazine*; *Gifts of Hope Catalog*; *E-News Updates* (quarterly).

Finance: Annual revenue US $26.4m., expenditure $24.8m. (30 Sept. 2024).

Board of Directors: Derek Parker (Chair.); Dan Dietrich (Vice-Chair.); Linda Voelsch (Treas.); Tom Feely (Sec.).

Principal Staff: Pres. and CEO Dan Smith.

Contact Details: 250 Country Club Rd, Eugene, OR 97401; POB 2880, Eugene, OR 97402; tel. (541) 687-2202; e-mail info@holtinternational.org; internet www.holtinternational.org.

The Home Depot Foundation

Founded in 2011.

Activities: Works to improves the living conditions of US veterans; and to provide opportunities for returning military personnel to retrain in new trades to help fill the labour gap through the Path to Pro Program. The Foundation supports communities impacted by natural disasters. The Veteran's Housing Grants Program offers funding to non-profit organizations to support the contruction or renovation of supportive housing for veterans with awards ranging from US $100,000–$500,000. Has branches in Canada and Mexico.

Geographical Area of Activity: Canada, Mexico, USA.

Board: Erin Izen (Chair. and Exec. Dir); John Dennison (Treas.); Peter Muniz (Sec.).

Contact Details: 258 E Milwaukee Ave, Detroit, MI 48202; tel. (770) 384-4646; e-mail public_relations@homedepot.com; internet corporate.homedepot.com/page/home-depot-foundation.

Horace W. Goldsmith Foundation

Founded in 1955 by Horace W. Goldsmith, a stockbroker.

Activities: Provides support for cultural activities; Jewish welfare funds and temple support; hospitals, particularly for the elderly; and education, especially higher education. In 2009 the Foundation endowed the Horace W. Goldsmith Foundation Fund at Yale Law School. It also offers Horace W. Goldsmith Fellowships, each worth US $10,000, to 7–10 incoming MBA students at Harvard Business School.

Geographical Area of Activity: Israel, USA.

Restrictions: No grants to individuals.

Finance: Annual revenue US $28.8m., expenditure $40.2m. (31 Dec. 2022).

Principal Staff: Man. Dir William A. Slaughter.

Contact Details: 375 Park Ave, Suite 1601, New York, NY 10152-1600; tel. (212) 319-8700.

The Howard G. Buffett Foundation

Established in 1999 by Howard G. Buffet, President of Buffet Farms.

Activities: Works to improve the lives of very poor and marginalized people. The Foundation funds activities in three main areas: food and water security; conflict mitigation; and public safety. It also makes smaller investments in local projects and environmental conservation initiatives. The Foundation plans to dissolve all its assets by the end of 2045.

Geographical Area of Activity: Colombia, El Salvador, Guatemala, Honduras, Mexico, Rwanda, USA.

Restrictions: Does not accept unsolicited requests for funding.

Publications: Annual Report; books; databooks; reports.

Finance: Annual revenue US $462.5m., expenditure $307.8m. (31 Dec. 2022).

Trustees: Howard G. Buffett (Chair. and CEO); Devon G. Buffet (Exec. Vice-Pres. and Sec.); Trisha A. Cook (Treas.).

Principal Staff: Pres. Ann Kelly Bolten.

Contact Details: 145 N. Merchant St, Decatur, IL 62523-1442; tel. (217) 423-9286; internet www.thehowardgbuffettfoundation.org.

Howard Hughes Medical Institute—HHMI

Founded in 1953 by Howard R. Hughes, an industrialist and film producer.

Activities: Conducts biomedical research in the USA in fields such as cell biology, genetics, immunology, neuroscience, structural biology and bioinformatics/computational biology. The Institute makes grants to promote education in the biological sciences in the USA and supports research abroad. Main programmes are the HHMI Investigator Program and science education; in 2006 the Institute established the Janelia Research Campus in Ashburn, VA, for research. The Institute awards grants for research training for medical students.

Geographical Area of Activity: Worldwide.

Restrictions: Grants are made primarily within defined competitive programmes; rarely funds unsolicited proposals.

Publications: Annual Report; newsletter; occasional reports; HHMI BioInteractive (online teaching resources).

Finance: Annual revenue US $2,470.0m., expenditure $1,054.1m. (31 Aug. 2024).

Board of Trustees: Dr Clayton S. Rose (Chair.).

Principal Staff: Pres. Dr Erin O'Shea.

Contact Details: 4000 Jones Bridge Rd, Chevy Chase, MD 20815-6789; tel. (301) 215-8500; e-mail webmaster@hhmi.org; internet www.hhmi.org.

Howard Karagheusian Commemorative Corporation—HKCC

Founded in 1921 by Mihran and Zabel Karagheusian, in memory of their son Howard, who died in 1918.

Activities: Helps vulnerable Armenian communities. Priority areas include: children's and community healthcare; distribution of medical equipment and medication; afterschool programmes for at-risk youths; vocational training and recreational programmes; social and housing assistance, including for families of soldiers; and funding for social and medical institutions.

Geographical Area of Activity: Armenia, Azerbaijan (Karabagh), Lebanon, Syrian Arab Repub.

Restrictions: No grants to individuals or organizations.

Publications: Annual Report.

Finance: Annual revenue US $834,266, expenditure $3.1m. (31 Dec. 2022).

Board of Directors: Harry S. Cherken, Jr (Pres.); Dennis Tarzian (Vice-Pres.); Richard J. Varadian (Treas./Sec.).

Principal Staff: Man. Dir Irina Lazarian.

Contact Details: 381 Park Ave S, Suite 617, New York, NY 10016-8804; tel. (212) 725-0973; e-mail info@thkcc.org; internet www.thkcc.org.

Hudson Institute

Established in 1961 in Croton-on-Hudson by Herman Kahn, Max Singer and Oscar Ruebhausen; a think tank.

Activities: Carries out public policy research and analysis in the areas of: culture and social policy; drug policy; economics; energy and environmental policy; government and politics; healthcare and obesity; international relations; legal affairs and criminal justice; national security; religion and human rights; and technology and applied science. The Institute incorporates several policy centres and thematic programmes, including in the areas of: coronavirus; defence and technology; the economics of the internet; food policy; intellectual property; Islamist ideology; Japan; kleptocracy; political studies; religious freedom; South Asia; substance abuse; and US sea power. It offers Summer Fellowships to undergraduates in political theory and practice, strategic thinking and public policy; and internships.

Geographical Area of Activity: USA.

Publications: Annual Report; newsletter (monthly); policy briefings; event transcripts.

Finance: Annual revenue US $25.2m., expenditure $22.3m. (31 Dec. 2022).

Board of Trustees: Sarah May Stern (Chair.); Richard S. Emmet, Russell Pennoyer (Vice-Chair.).

Principal Staff: Pres. and CEO John P. Walters.

Contact Details: 1201 Pennsylvania Ave, NW, 4th Floor, Washington, DC 20004; tel. (202) 974-2400; e-mail info@hudson.org; internet www.hudson.org.

Human Rights Watch—HRW

Established in 1978 as Helsinki Watch to support civil rights groups in the USSR and Eastern Europe in monitoring government compliance with the 1975 Helsinki Accords.

Activities: Activities focus on systematic investigation of human rights abuses and providing human rights education. The organization advocates for changes in policy and practice that promote human rights and justice; and address underlying causes of poverty, such as discrimination, armed conflict and displacement. It monitors human rights in around 100 countries and has offices in Chicago, IL, Los Angeles, Palo Alto, San Francisco, Silicon Valley, CA, Washington, DC; and in Amsterdam (Netherlands), Beirut (Lebanon), Berlin (Germany), Brussels (Belgium), Geneva (Switzerland), Johannesburg (South Africa), London (UK), Nairobi (Kenya), Oslo (Norway), Paris (France), São Paulo (Brazil), Stockholm (Sweden), Sydney (Australia), Tokyo (Japan), Toronto (Canada) and Zurich (Switzerland). Administers the Hellman/Hammett grant programme for writers who have been victims of political persecution and are in financial need.

Geographical Area of Activity: Worldwide.

Publications: Annual Report; newsletter (weekly); produces more than 100 reports and briefings each year on human rights in around 100 countries.

Finance: Annual revenue US $111.1m., expenditure $116.0m. (30 June 2023).

Board of Directors: Amy Rao, Neil Rimer (Co-Chair.); Akwasi Aidoo, Kimberly Marteau Emerson, Bruce Simpson, Joseph Skrzynski (Vice-Chair.); Bruce Rabb (Sec.).

Principal Staff: Interim Exec. Dir Federico Borello; Acting Deputy Exec. Dir Lama Fakih.

Contact Details: 350 Fifth Ave, 34th Floor, New York, NY 10118-3299; tel. (212) 290-4700; e-mail hrwnyc@hrw.org; internet www.hrw.org.

Humanity United
Established in 2008 by Pam Omidyar; part of the Omidyar Group (q.v.).

Activities: Makes grants for specific interventions and activities to change the systems that contribute to specific global problems, in particular those which suppress human rights and contribute to human suffering. The organization carries out activities under two main portfolios: forced labour and human trafficking; and locally led peacebuilding. It leads and supports the Alliance to End Slavery and Trafficking (ATEST), a coalition of organizations based in the USA; and has an office in Washington, DC.

Geographical Area of Activity: International, especially Asia and Africa.

Restrictions: Does not accept unsolicited applications.

Publications: Performance Report (annual); newsletter; blog.

Finance: Annual income US $47.7m., expenditure $42.7m. (31 Dec. 2022).

Board: Pam Omidyar (Chair.).

Principal Staff: Pres. and Man. Partner Srik Gopal.

Contact Details: 456 Montgomery St, Suite 500, San Francisco, CA 94104; tel. (415) 426-6300; e-mail info@humanityunited.org; internet www.humanityunited.org.

The Hunger Project
Established in 1977, as the Global Hunger Project, following the first Rome World Food Conference.

Activities: Works to eliminate hunger and poverty. Programmes incorporate three core elements: empowering women as key change agents; mobilizing communities for self-reliant action; and fostering effective partnerships with local governments. The organization works in nearly 15,000 communities in 22 countries; and has an office in Washington, DC.

Geographical Area of Activity: Australasia, Latin America, North America, South Asia, sub-Saharan Africa, Western Europe.

Publications: Annual Report; newsletter (monthly).

Finance: Annual revenue US $23.9m., expenditure $19.1m. (31 Dec. 2023).

Board of Directors: Sheree S. Stomberg (Chair.).

Principal Staff: Pres. and CEO Rowlands Kaotcha.

Contact Details: 110 W 30th St, 6th Floor, New York, NY 10001; tel. (212) 251-9100; e-mail info@thp.org; internet www.thp.org.

IBM International Foundation
Founded in 1985, as the IBM South Africa Projects Fund, by IBM, an information technology company; in 1992 the Foundation's charter was amended to allow charitable giving worldwide.

Activities: Main programme areas are: education and skills, focusing on education equity and workforce inclusion; and using technology for social impact, addressing the world's biggest challenges, such as climate change, pandemic preparedness and human trafficking. The Foundation supports non-profit and educational organizations, including the IBM UK Trust, and awards postdoctoral fellowships. Since 2011 it has established 200 Pathways in Technology Early College High (P-TECH) schools in 18 countries, offering science, engineering, engineering and mathematics education to students from disadvantaged backgrounds.

Geographical Area of Activity: Worldwide.

Restrictions: No grants to individuals.

Publications: Corporate Responsibility Report; Activity Kits (online); *Open P-Tech* (online educational tools); *Good Tech IBM Blog*.

Finance: Annual revenue US $35.9m., expenditure $16.3m. (31 Dec. 2022).

Board of Directors: Virginia Rometty (Chair.); Guillermo Miranda (Pres. and Vice-Chair.); Simon J. Beaumont (Treas.); Frank Sedlarcik (Sec.).

Contact Details: c/o IBM Tax Dept, North Castle Dr., Armonk, NY 10504; tel. (914) 499-4690; internet ibm.org.

IFAW—International Fund for Animal Welfare
Founded in 1969.

Activities: A global non-profit helping animals and people to thrive together. Working in more than 40 countries around the world, the Fund rescues, rehabilitates and releases animals, and restores and protects their natural habitats. Partners with local communities, governments, NGOs and businesses.

Geographical Area of Activity: Worldwide.

Publications: Annual Report; *Our Shared World* (quarterly magazine); factsheets; policy briefings; programme publications; white papers.

Finance: Annual revenue US $68.5m., expenditure $75.5m. (30 June 2023).

Board of Directors: Mark Beaudouin (Chair.); Joyce Doria (Vice-Chair.).

Principal Staff: Pres. and CEO Azzedine Downes.

Contact Details: International Headquarters, 1400 16th St NW, Suite 330, Washington, DC 20036; tel. (202) 536-1900; e-mail info@ifaw.org; internet www.ifaw.org.

Improving Economies for Stronger Communities—IESC
Founded in 1964 as Improving Economies for Stronger Communities by a group of US business leaders, entrepreneurs and philanthropists led by David Rockefeller, the President of Chase Manhattan Bank. Present name adopted in 2023.

Activities: Catalyzes private sector growth and creates economic opportunity for people and communities throughout the economically developing world. IESC delivers lasting solutions across 139 countries by sharing proven business skills and experience with entrepreneurs, jobseekers, businesses, farmers, cooperatives, and governments. IESC also offer resources—human, technological, and financial—that sustainably strengthen capacity and empower communities.

Geographical Area of Activity: Worldwide.

Publications: Annual Report; *IESC Update Newsletter*; brochures; toolkits.

Finance: Annual revenue US $23.8m., expenditure $23.9m. (31 Dec. 2022).

Board of Directors: Wing Keith (Chair.).

Principal Staff: Pres. and CEO David Hartingh.

Contact Details: 2000 M St NW, Suite 250, Washington, DC 20036; tel. (202) 589-2600; e-mail iesc@iesc.org; internet www.iesc.org.

India Partners
Founded in 1984; an evangelical Christian organization.

Activities: Works with indigenous Christian partner organizations to seek long-term solutions to poverty for every individual, regardless of race, religion, caste or sex. The organization carries out its activities in the areas of: caring for orphans and widows; disaster relief; economic development; education; health and nutrition; human trafficking; safe water; and vocational training.

Geographical Area of Activity: India.

Publications: Annual Report; newsletter.

Finance: Annual revenue US $3.5m., expenditure $3.4m. (30 June 2022).

Board of Directors: S. King (Chair.); B. Spotts (Vice-Chair.).

Principal Staff: Pres. and CEO John Sparks.

Contact Details: POB 5470, Eugene, OR 97405; tel. (541) 683-0696; e-mail info@indiapartners.org; internet www.indiapartners.org.

UNITED STATES OF AMERICA

Institute for Citizens & Scholars

Founded in 1945 as the Woodrow Wilson Fellowships at Princeton University and subsequently known as the Woodrow Wilson National Fellowship Foundation; present name adopted in 2020.

Activities: Works to strengthen education in the USA and rebuild civil society through supporting young people and connecting civic leaders. Fellowships support the development of future leaders at a variety of career stages in the fields of: access and opportunity; American history; education; faculty development; religion and ethics; teaching; and women and gender. The Institute has conferred more than 27,000 Fellowships.

Geographical Area of Activity: USA.

Publications: Annual Report; newsletter (2 a year); policy reports.

Finance: Annual revenue US $6.8m., expenditure $11.1m. (30 June 2023).

Board of Trustees: Stefanie Sanford (Chair.); Jeffrey A. Goldstein (Vice-Chair.); Jane Phillips Donaldson (Chair. Emerita).

Principal Staff: Pres. Rajiv Vinnakota; Exec. Vice-Pres. Beverly Sanford.

Contact Details: 104 Carnegie Center, Suite 301, Princeton, NJ 08540; POB 826031, Philadelphia, PA 19182-6031; tel. (609) 452-7007; e-mail communications@woodrow.org.org; internet citizensandscholars.org.

Institute of International Education—IIE

Founded in 1919 by Nobel Peace Prize winners Dr Nicholas Murray Butler, President of Columbia University, and Elihu Root, former Secretary of State; and Stephen Duggan, Sr, a professor of political science.

Activities: Works to increase people's capacity to think and work globally. The Institute manages over 200 international exchange programmes in more than 180 countries; and administers the Fulbright US Student Program (f. 1947) for students, professionals and artists. It provides testing and advisory services, scholarships, information on opportunities for international study, and emergency assistance to students and scholars. Key programmes include the Carnegie African Diaspora Fellowship, Higher Education Readiness (HER), USAID Democracy Fellows and Grants and the Julia Stasch-IIE Scholarship for Refugees. Comprises a network of 18 offices and affiliates; the IIE Network membership programme links colleges and universities worldwide.

Geographical Area of Activity: International.

Publications: Annual Report; newsletter (monthly); *IIE Global News Newsletter*; *Open Doors* (annual); *Funding for U.S. Study* (annual); *IIE Passport Study Abroad Directory* (annual); *IIE Network Membership Directory* (annually); evaluation and impact studies; handbooks; surveys; toolkits; blog.

Finance: Annual revenue US $326.5m., expenditure $310.6m. (30 Sept. 2022).

Board of Trustees: Thomas S. Johnson, Henry Kaufman (Chair. Emeriti); Mark A. Angelson (Chair.); Calvin G. Butler, Jr, Linda Vester (Vice-Chair.); Hartley R. Rogers (Vice-Chair. and Treas.).

Principal Staff: Pres. Jason Czyz.

Contact Details: 1 World Trade Center, 36th Floor, New York, NY 10007; tel. (212) 883-8200; e-mail info@iie.org; internet www.iie.org.

Institute for Sustainable Communities—ISC

Established in 1991 by former Governor of Vermont Madeleine M. Kunin; merged with the Advocacy Institute in 2006.

Activities: Works in the fields of climate change, income equality and social justice. The organization works to address the challenges of urbanization, manufacturing and reducing harmful emissions through working with government agencies, businesses, universities and other organizations. Programme areas include: community economic development; clean energy transition; green finance; urban systems; and water. It operates in 30 countries, with offices in Washington, DC, Bangladesh, the People's Republic of China and India.

Geographical Area of Activity: International.

Publications: Annual Report; newsletter.

Finance: Annual revenue US $9.2m., expenditure $9.1m. (30 Sept. 2023).

Board of Directors: Rev. Eugene Taylor Sutton (Chair.); Derek Walker (Vice-Chair.); Dr Susan M. Pepin (Sec.).

Principal Staff: Pres. Rebecca Kaduru.

Contact Details: 535 Stone Cutters Way, Montpelier, VT 05602; tel. (802) 229-2900; e-mail isc@sustain.org; internet sustain.org.

Inter-American Foundation—IAF

Founded in 1969 by the US Congress as an independent agency.

Activities: Provides grants of between US $25,000 and $400,000 to non-governmental and community-based organizations in Latin America and the Caribbean for innovative, sustainable and participatory self-help programmes. The Foundation primarily funds partnerships among grassroots and non-profit organizations, businesses and local governments, to improve the quality of life of poor people and strengthen participation, accountability and democratic practices.

Geographical Area of Activity: Central and South America and the Caribbean.

Restrictions: Funding in the Caribbean is currently restricted to the Dominican Republic, Haiti and Jamaica. Does not accept grant applications from individuals, governments, political parties, organizations based outside the region or that do not contribute their own resources to projects; or projects for welfare or purely religious or research purposes.

Publications: *Grassroots Development* (journal, 2 a year in English, Spanish and Portuguese); annual review; factsheets.

Finance: Receives about 60% of its annual budget from the US Congress; also receives funding from the Social Progress Trust Fund of the Inter-American Development Bank.

Board of Directors: Eddy Arriola (Chair.); Juan Carlos Iturregui (Vice-Chair.).

Advisory Council: Alexander F. Watson (Chair.); Kay K. Arnold (Vice-Chair.).

Principal Staff: Pres. and CEO Sarah Aviel.

Contact Details: 1331 Pennsylvania Ave, NW, Suite 1200, North Washington, DC 20004; tel. (202) 360-4530; e-mail inquiries@iaf.gov; internet www.iaf.gov.

International Center for Research on Women—ICRW

Founded in 1976; in 2016 merged with Re:Gender (formerly known as the National Council for Research on Women, f. 1981).

Activities: Works with governments and partner organizations worldwide to reduce poverty, promote development and improve the lives of women. Through research, direct action and advocacy, the Center supports work on issues that affect women everywhere, including HIV/AIDS; economic growth; poverty reduction; reproductive health and nutrition; policy and communications; population and social transition; and social struggle and transformation. It has regional offices in Amsterdam (Netherlands), Kampala (Uganda) and New Delhi (India).

Geographical Area of Activity: International.

Publications: Annual Report; *ICRW News* (newsletter); background papers; case studies; factsheets; policy briefs; position papers; reports; technical briefs; toolkits; workbooks; working papers; blog.

Finance: Annual revenue US $11.3m., expenditure $10.8m. (30 Sept. 2023).

Board of Directors: Tara Abrahams (Global Chair.).

Principal Staff: Interim CEO Ann Warner.

Contact Details: 601 Pennsylvania Ave NW, South Bldg, Suite 900, Washington, DC 20004; tel. (202) 797-0007; e-mail info@icrw.org; internet www.icrw.org.

International Center for Transitional Justice—ICTJ

Established in 2001 at the suggestion of the Ford Foundation (q.v.).

Activities: Works for justice in countries that have experienced large-scale and systematic human rights abuses under repression and in conflict. The Center carries out research and advises victims, civil society groups, and national and international organizations to ensure redress and prevent atrocities. It has offices in Belgium, Colombia, Kenya, the Netherlands, Tunisia and Uganda.

Geographical Area of Activity: International.

Publications: Annual Report; newsletter (monthly); briefing papers; case studies; factsheets; handbooks; reports; research briefs and papers.

Finance: Annual revenue US $9.9m., expenditure $10.2m. (31 March 2023).

Board of Directors: Robert Cusumano (Chair.).

Principal Staff: Exec. Dir Fernando Travesí; Deputy Exec. Dir Anna Myriam Roccatello.

Contact Details: 50 Broadway, 23rd Floor, New York, NY 10004; tel. (917) 637-3800; e-mail info@ictj.org; internet www.ictj.org.

International College of Surgeons—ICS

Founded in 1935 in Geneva, Switzerland, by Dr Max Thorek, co-founder of the American Hospital in Chicago, IL; a worldwide federation of organizations.

Activities: Encourages surgical excellence through training, humanitarian work, education and fellowship. The College promotes the exchange of surgical knowledge and techniques, and assists in surgical missions in developing countries around the world, including disaster relief work and providing surgical care alongside other humanitarian agencies. It offers scholarships for surgical training and funds surgical research and lectureships. Comprises six international federations and 60 national sections, of which ICS–USA is the largest; and maintains the International Museum of Surgical Science in Chicago, IL.

Geographical Area of Activity: Worldwide.

Publications: *International Surgery* (6 a year); newsletter.

Finance: Annual revenue US $1.3m., expenditure $1.2m. (31 Dec. 2022).

International Executive Council: Dr Guido Parquet Villagra (World Pres.); Thav Thambi-Pillai (Pres.-elect); Prof. Aij-Lie Kwan (Immediate Past World Pres.); Prof. Karel Novak (World First Vice-Pres.); Dr Elias Tam (World Treas.); Dr Nelson Mitsui (World Corp. Sec.).

Principal Staff: Exec. Dir Max. C. Downham.

Contact Details: 1524 N Lakeshore Dr., Chicago, IL 60610; tel. (312) 642-3555; e-mail info@icsglobal.org; internet www.icsglobal.org.

International Education Research Foundation, Inc—IERF

Established in 1969 as a public benefit, non-profit agency.

Activities: Founded as the first credentials evaluation service in the USA. Evaluates international education credentials in terms of US equivalence for purposes of employment, further education, professional licensure, visa certification and enlistment in the armed services. The Foundation conducts and publishes research; and, under the Sepmeyer Research Grant Program, offers grants worth US $1,000.

Geographical Area of Activity: Worldwide.

Finance: Annual revenue US $2.5m., expenditure $2.3m. (30 June 2023).

Board of Directors: Elaine Wheeler (Chair.).

Principal Staff: Exec. Dir Dr Lin Reed.

Contact Details: 10736 Jefferson Blvd, Suite 532, Culver City, CA 90230; tel. (310) 258-9451; e-mail info@ierf.org; internet www.ierf.org.

International Eye Foundation—IEF

Founded in 1961 as the International Eye Bank by Dr John Harry King, Jr; present name adopted in 1969.

Activities: Operates internationally in the fields of medicine, public health and education, through co-operative programmes with health ministries and private indigenous organizations, fellowships for ophthalmic training and scientific conferences. The Foundation restores eyesight and prevents blindness, treating conditions such as onchocerciasis (river blindness), xerophthalmia, glaucoma, cataracts and other major eye diseases. It established SightReach Surgical, a social enterprise that provides low-cost equipment and supplies for eye care surgery.

Geographical Area of Activity: Worldwide.

Publications: Annual Report; *International Eye Foundation Newsletter*; *SightReach Surgical Newsletter*; factsheets; scientific publications.

Finance: Annual revenue US $1.9m., expenditure $1.7m. (30 June 2023).

Governing Board: Kathryn D. Leckey (Chair.); Frances R. Pierce (Vice-Chair.); Ann M. Hilpert (Treas.); Ralph J. Helmsen (Sec.).

Principal Staff: Pres. and CEO John Barrows.

Contact Details: 10801 Connecticut Ave, Kensington, MD 20895; tel. (240) 290-0263; e-mail contact@iefusa.org; internet www.iefusa.org.

The International Foundation

Founded in 1948.

Activities: Makes grants to non-profit organizations engaged in aid to developing countries. The Foundation prioritizes agricultural research and production; medicine and health (including sanitation and nutrition); education and research; and the environment.

Geographical Area of Activity: Asia and the South Pacific, Central and South America, Middle East, sub-Saharan Africa.

Restrictions: Grants only to non-profit organizations based in the USA.

Finance: Annual revenue US $740,350, expenditure $1.4m. (31 Dec. 2022).

Board of Directors: John D'A. Tyree, Douglas P. Walker (Co-Chair./Treas.); Matthew Hurlock (Endowment Chair.); Fernando Soto (Sec.).

Contact Details: 55 Lane Rd, Suite 300, Fairfield, NJ 07004; tel. (973) 406-3970; e-mail info@intlfoundation.org; internet www.intlfoundation.org.

International Foundation for Electoral Systems—IFES

Established in 1987 by F. Clifton White, an international affairs and political consultant.

Activities: Promotes democracy, good governance and democratic rights. The Foundation provides technical assistance to election officials; empowers under-represented people to participate in political processes; and uses field-based research to improve the electoral cycle. It issues publications on topics including: election security; political finance; gender equality; standards for conducting election audits and ensuring electoral integrity and transparency; public opinion on elections and democracy; and providing equal access for persons with disabilities to electoral and political processes. Democracy Studies Fellowships are offered to graduate students to undertake democracy development research at the Center for Applied Research and Learning for 6–10 weeks.

Geographical Area of Activity: Worldwide.

Restrictions: Not a grantmaking organization.

Publications: Annual Report; white papers; books; reports; manuals; FAQs; primers.

Finance: Annual revenue US $76.4m., expenditure $76.0m. (30 Sept. 2021).

Board of Directors: M. Peter McPherson, William C. Eacho (Co-Chair.); Sarah Tinsley, Theodore Sedgwick (Vice-Chair.); Garvin Brown (Treas.); Randall Teague, Sr (Sec.).

Principal Staff: Pres. and CEO Anthony Banbury.

Contact Details: 2011 Crystal Dr., 10th Floor, Arlington, VA 22202; tel. (202) 350-6700; e-mail media@ifes.org; internet www.ifes.org.

International Orthodox Christian Charities—IOCC

Established in 1992.

Activities: IOCC is the official humanitarian and development agency of the Assembly of Canonical Orthodox Bishops of the United States of America. It provides emergency relief and international development assistance to people in need worldwide. Programme areas include emergency preparedness and response; water, sanitation, and hygiene (WASH); sustainable livelihoods; agriculture and food security; and health. IOCC assists families, refugees, people displaced in their own country, the elderly, school children, people with disabilities, and those facing or recovering from natural or human-caused disasters. All aid is provided based on need alone.

Geographical Area of Activity: Balkans, Ethiopia, Georgia, Greece, Haiti, Jordan, Lebanon, Palestinian Territories, Poland, Romania, Syrian Arab Repub., Uganda, Ukraine, USA.

Restrictions: Does not support church mission programmes.

Publications: Annual Report; *News and Needs* (newsletter); *Year in Review*; *IOCC in Brief*; *Priest to Priest* (clergy newsletter).

Finance: Total revenue US $39.0m., expenditure $35.8m. (31 Dec. 2023).

Officers of the Board of Directors: Jasmina T. Boulanger (Chair.); Frank B. Cerra (Vice-Chair.); Dimitri Zgourides (Treas.); Gayle F. Malone (Sec.).

Principal Staff: Exec. Dir and CEO Constantine (Dean) M. Triantafilou.

Contact Details: 110 West Rd, Suite 360, Baltimore, MD 21204; tel. (410) 243-9820; e-mail relief@iocc.org; internet www.iocc.org.

International Relief Teams—IRT

Established in 1988 as Southwest Medical Teams by Barry La Forgia, a former air force pilot and lawyer, following church mission visits to the Amazon and Mexico City.

Activities: Provides health services and humanitarian assistance to victims of disaster, neglect and extreme poverty. The organization focuses on two core activities: disaster relief, which includes deploying medical and reconstruction teams, providing relief supplies, and financing the restoration of livelihoods and infrastructure; and building healthy communities, by providing medical training to save babies' lives, surgeries for the poor, eyeglasses to improve sight, medicines for rural hospitals and clinics, and nutrition and education support for abused, abandoned and homeless children.

Geographical Area of Activity: International.

Publications: Annual Report; newsletter.

Finance: Annual revenue US $51.7m., expenditure $52.4m. (30 June 2023).

Board of Directors: Richard Yousko (Chair.).

Principal Staff: CEO David Murphy.

Contact Details: 3545 Camino del Rio, S., Suite A, San Diego, CA 92108; tel. (619) 284-7979; e-mail info@irteams.org; internet www.irteams.org.

International Rescue Committee—IRC

Founded in 1933 as a voluntary organization at the suggestion of Albert Einstein to help Germans suffering under the Nazi regime in Germany.

Activities: Works internationally to help those fleeing victimization, oppression and conflict. The Committee resettles and rehouses refugees; and provides emergency shelter and supplies for homeless and displaced people. Areas of focus are economic wellbeing, education, health, rights and safety. It works in partnership with Stichting Vluchteling (q.v.) in the Netherlands, and with IRC-UK, an affiliate in the United Kingdom. Awards the annual IRC Freedom Award for contributions to the cause of refugees and human freedom. Present in more than 40 countries and 29 US cities.

Geographical Area of Activity: International.

Publications: Annual Report.

Finance: Annual revenue US $1,580.0m., expenditure $1,619.7m. (30 Sept. 2024).

Board of Directors: Mona Sutphen, Victoria Long Foley (Co-Chair.); Martin Bratt (Sec.).

Board of Advisors: Liv Ullman (Chair.).

Principal Staff: Pres. and CEO David Miliband.

Contact Details: 122 East 42nd St, New York, NY 10168-1289; tel. (212) 551-3000; e-mail communications@rescue.org; internet www.rescue.org.

International Rhino Foundation—IRF

Established in 1989 as the Black Rhino Foundation; present name adopted in 1993.

Activities: Works to preserve the five rhino species through carrying out conservation activities and scientific research; and supports anti-poaching initiatives. The Foundation offers grants for work to manage, propagate and conserve rhinos in the wild and in captive breeding centres. It has more than 1,000 members, comprising individuals, zoos, foundations, businesses and government agencies; with an office in Fort Worth, TX.

Geographical Area of Activity: India, Indonesia, South Africa, Eswatini, Viet Nam, Zimbabwe.

Publications: Annual Report; blog.

Finance: Annual revenue US $3.8m., expenditure $4.0m. (31 Dec. 2022).

Board of Directors: John Lukas (Pres.); Lee Bass (Treas.).

Principal Staff: Exec. Dir Nina Fascione; Deputy Dir Margaret Moore.

Contact Details: 201 Main St, Suite 2600, Fort Worth, TX 76102; tel. (540) 465-9595; e-mail info@rhinos.org; internet www.rhinos.org.

International Rivers

Founded in 1985, as International Rivers Network, by a small group of volunteers.

Activities: Works with environmental and human rights organizations around the world to campaign for community-based river development; and with people directly affected by dams and other large-scale water projects. The organization fosters greater understanding of rivers, and participates in research and project analyses. It makes recommendations for alternative solutions to international environmental problems caused by governments' environmental policies.

Geographical Area of Activity: Africa, Latin America, South Asia, South-East Asia.

Publications: Annual Report; special reports; factsheets; working papers; information resources.

Finance: Annual revenue US $2.2m., expenditure $1.9m. (31 Dec. 2023).

Board of Directors: Melina Selverston (Chair.); Chance Cutrano (Sec.).

Principal Staff: Co-Exec. Dirs Isabella Winkler, Josh Klemm.

International Youth Foundation

Contact Details: 344 20th St, Oakland, CA 94612; tel. (510) 848-1155; e-mail contact@internationalrivers.org; internet www.internationalrivers.org.

International Youth Foundation—IYF

Founded in 1990 by Rick Little, a social entrepreneur.

Activities: Empowers young people to be healthy, productive and engaged citizens through building and maintaining a worldwide community of businesses, governments and CSOs. The Foundation runs programmes that help young people to obtain a quality education, gain employability skills, make healthy choices and improve their communities. It works with partners in more than 100 countries; and has offices in Jordan, Kazakhstan, Mexico, Morocco, Mozambique, South Africa, Tanzania and Zimbabwe.

Geographical Area of Activity: International.

Restrictions: Does not accept unsolicited applications.

Publications: Annual Report; newsletter; case studies; assessments; reports; factsheets.

Finance: Annual revenue US $13.6m., expenditure $19.1m. (31 Dec. 2023).

Board of Directors: Joseph M. Matalon (Chair.); Umran Beba, Katie Beirne Fallon (Vice-Chair.); Douglas L. Becker (Chair. Emeritus).

Principal Staff: Pres. and CEO Christina Sass.

Contact Details: 841 E Fort Ave, #105, Baltimore, MD 21230; tel. (410) 951-1500; internet www.iyfnet.org.

The Ireland Funds America

Established in 1976 as the Ireland Fund by Dan Rooney, former US Ambassador to Ireland and owner of the Pittsburgh Steelers American football team, and Anthony J.F. O'Reilly, a business person; in 1987 merged with the American Irish Foundation, founded by Irish President Eamonn De Valera and US President John F. Kennedy. Registered as a charity in Ireland.

Activities: Promotes and supports the arts and culture, education, community development, and peace and reconciliation in the island of Ireland and among Irish communities internationally; and awards grants to non-profit organizations in Ireland and Northern Ireland. The organization has chapters in 10 US cities; and operates internationally as the Ireland Funds, with chapters in Australia, Canada, the People's Republic of China, France, Germany, Great Britain, Ireland, Japan, Monaco, New Zealand and Singapore.

Geographical Area of Activity: International (mainly the island of Ireland).

Restrictions: No grants to individuals.

Publications: Annual Report; newsletter; *Connect* (magazine).

Board of Directors: Eugene M. McQuade (Chair.); Shaun T. Kelly, Angela H. Moore (Vice-Chair.); Christopher Kondron (Treas.); Sheila O'Malley (Sec.).

Principal Staff: Pres. and CEO Catriona Fottrell.

Contact Details: 200 Park Ave, 17th Floor, New York, NY 10166; tel. (212) 689-3100; internet irelandfunds.org.

IREX—International Research & Exchanges Board

Established in 1968 by a group of US universities, with support from the Ford Foundation, American Council of Learned Societies (qq.v.), Social Science Research Council and US Department of State.

Activities: Carries out activities in the fields of civil society, education, gender equality and inclusion, governance, leadership, media, technology and young people. The Board administers programmes in academic research, professional training, institution building, technical assistance and policymaking. It offers fellowships, grants and opportunities for international exchanges and mentorship, working with partners in more than 100 countries.

Geographical Area of Activity: Asia, Central and Eastern Europe, Eurasia, Middle East and North Africa, North and South America, sub-Saharan Africa.

Publications: Annual Report; *Frontline* (newsletter); policy papers; newsletter; conference reports.

Finance: Annual revenue US $146.5m., expenditure $146.5m. (30 June 2023).

Board of Governors: David Gross (Chair.); Liliana Ayalde (Vice-Chair.).

Principal Staff: Pres. and CEO Kristin M. Lord.

Contact Details: 1275 K St NW, Suite 600, Washington, DC 20005; tel. (202) 628-8188; e-mail communications@irex.org; internet www.irex.org.

Isabel Allende Foundation

Established in 1996 by the author Isabel Allende, in memory of her daughter Paula Frias.

Activities: Supports reproductive rights, economic independence and freedom from violence for women and girls. The Foundation makes Esperanza Grants of between US $1,000 and $10,000 to non-profit organizations and NGOs working in its fields of interest, mainly for programmes in California or Chile. In 2001 the Foundation established the Espiritu Awards, worth between US $25,000 and $80,000, for exemplary work in the same fields.

Geographical Area of Activity: Chile, USA.

Restrictions: Does not accept unsolicited applications; grants mainly to organizations with headquarters in California or Chile; no grants to individuals.

Finance: Annual revenue US $1.2m., expenditure $2.8m. (31 Dec. 2022).

Board of Trustees: Isabel Allende (Pres.); Nicolas Frias (Sec.).

Principal Staff: Exec. Dir Lori Barra.

Contact Details: 116 Caledonia St, Sausalito, CA 94965; tel. (415) 289-0992; e-mail assistant@isabelallende.org; internet www.isabelallende.org.

Izumi Foundation

Established in 1998 by the lay Buddhist order Shinnyo-en.

Activities: Focuses on the alleviation of human suffering through improved healthcare, in particular for the poorest and most vulnerable members of society. The Foundation runs programmes in five areas: infectious diseases that cause high morbidity and mortality; neglected tropical diseases; nutrition; maternal and infant health; and healthcare infrastructure. Grants are typically between US $50,000 and $100,000 over two years. It has supported 300 projects in 32 countries.

Geographical Area of Activity: Central and South America, sub-Saharan Africa.

Restrictions: No unsolicited proposals. No funding for medical research or other research-related activities; endowments, capital costs or fundraising activities; ongoing general operating expenses or existing deficits; lobbying of any kind; individuals; religious activities; or indirect costs. Maximum grant available US $100,000.

Finance: Annual revenue US $2.8m., expenditure $3.0m. (31 Dec. 2020).

Board of Directors: Shinrei Ito (Pres.); Ko Yamamoto (Treas.); Yuko Yoshida (Clerk).

Contact Details: 1 Financial Center, Boston, MA 02111; tel. (617) 292-2333; e-mail info@izumi.org; internet www.izumi.org.

J. Paul Getty Trust

Founded in 1954, as the J. Paul Getty Museum, by J. Paul Getty, a business person and art collector.

Activities: Preserves, conserves and interprets the world's artistic legacy and promotes civil society through an understanding of the visual arts. The Trust comprises the Getty

Conservation Institute, Getty Foundation, J. Paul Getty Museum and Getty Research Institute. Collectively, they organize public performances and readings; host professional and educational events for local, national and international organizations; and make their resources available to scholars and art institutions.

Geographical Area of Activity: International.

Publications: Annual Report; *Getty Foundation* (e-newsletter); scholarly publications; blog.

Finance: Annual revenue US $926.7m., expenditure $344.4m. (30 June 2022).

Board of Trustees: Robert W. Lovelace (Chair.).

Principal Staff: Pres. and CEO Katherine Elizabeth Fleming.

Contact Details: 1200 Getty Center Dr., Los Angeles, CA 90049-1679; tel. (310) 440-7360; e-mail communications@getty.edu; internet www.getty.edu.

The James Irvine Foundation

Founded in 1937 by James Irvine, an agricultural grower and landowner.

Activities: Advances the economic and political opportunities of poor working families and young people; and protects immigrants' rights. The Foundation works with employers to improve training for lower-skilled workers and provide higher-quality jobs; help students to transition to and through post-secondary education; and strengthen the voice and influence of low-income workers. It also offers exploratory grants to programmes that may become priorities for the Foundation; grants for housing affordability; and Leadership Awards worth US $350,000. Has an office in Los Angeles, CA.

Geographical Area of Activity: California, USA.

Restrictions: Does not accept unsolicited applications.

Publications: Annual Report; *Irvine Quarterly* (newsletter); information brochure; blog.

Finance: Annual revenue US $298.0m., expenditure $210.6m. (31 Dec. 2023).

Board of Directors: Tim Rios (Chair.).

Principal Staff: Pres. and CEO Don Howard.

Contact Details: 1 Bush St, Suite 800, San Francisco, CA 94104; tel. (415) 777-2244; e-mail communications@irvine.org; internet www.irvine.org.

James S. McDonnell Foundation

Founded in 1950 by James S. McDonnell, founder of McDonnell Aircraft, a manufacturer of military and commercial aircraft.

Activities: Operates in the fields of biological and behavioural sciences. The Foundation makes grants through its 21st Century Science Initiative, which supports individual and collaborative research in two areas: Understanding Human Cognition, including the Teachers as Learners education research programme, which provides up to US $2.5m. over five years, and up to 10 Opportunity Awards for research on human cognition, each worth $250,000; and Understanding Dynamic and Multi-scale Systems, which offers a postdoctoral fellowship in complex systems science, worth $200,000 over 2–3 years.

Geographical Area of Activity: International.

Publications: Newsletter; *Clothing the Emperor* (online discussion forum).

Finance: Annual revenue US $30.2m., expenditure $33.3m. (31 Dec. 2022).

Board of Directors: John F. McDonnell (Treas.); James S. McDonnell, III (Sec.).

Principal Staff: Pres. Dr Jason Q. Purnell.

Contact Details: 4565 McRee Ave, #120, St Louis, MO 63110; tel. (314) 721-1532; e-mail contact@jsmf.org; internet www.jsmf.org.

Jane Coffin Childs Memorial Fund for Medical Research—JCC Fund

Founded in 1937 in memory of Jane Coffin Childs by her husband Starling W. Childs and sister Alice S. Coffin.

Activities: Operates nationally and internationally in the field of basic research, biomedical research and cancer research, through postdoctoral fellowships. The basic fellowship stipend increases from US $70,000 to $74,000 over three years, with additional funds for research and travel expenses. Fellows are also offered stipends for childcare costs through the Joan A. Steitz Fund of the Community Foundation for Greater New Haven.

Geographical Area of Activity: Worldwide.

Restrictions: US citizens may hold fellowships in any country; non-US citizens must study in the USA.

Publications: Blog.

Finance: Annual revenue US $2.0m., expenditure $5.7m. (30 June 2023).

Board of Scientific Advisers: Dr Sue Biggins (Dir).

Principal Staff: Exec. Dir Dr Anita Pepper.

Contact Details: Yale University, POB 208037, New Haven, CT 06520-8037; 333 Cedar St, SHM L300, New Haven, CT 06510; tel. (203) 785-4612; e-mail jccfund@yale.edu; internet www.jccfund.org.

Jazz Foundation of America—JFA

Established in 1989 by Herb Storfer, Ann Ruckert, Cy Blank, Phoebe Jacobs and Dr Billy Taylor.

Activities: Supports professional blues, jazz and roots musicians in need. Main programmes are: the Musicians' Emergency Fund, providing housing and emergency assistance, free medical care and disaster relief; and Creating Employment, which comprises the Jazz and Blues in the Schools programme, the Gig Fund, Jazz & Blues in Nursing Homes and Lessons from the Legends.

Geographical Area of Activity: Puerto Rico, USA.

Publications: Newsletter.

Finance: Annual revenue US $3.1m., expenditure $3.9m. (30 June 2022).

Executive Board: Jarrett Lilien (Chair.); Dr Daveed D. Frazier (Pres.); Michael Devins (Treas.).

Principal Staff: Exec. Dir Joseph Petrucelli.

Contact Details: 247 West 37 St, Suite 201, New York, NY 10018; tel. (212) 245-3999; e-mail info@jazzfoundation.org; internet www.jazzfoundation.org.

The John A. Hartford Foundation—JAHF

Founded in 1929 by brothers John and George Hartford, executives of the A&P retail store chain.

Activities: Works in the field of ageing and health. Priority areas are: building age-friendly health systems; supporting family caregivers; and improving serious illness and end of life care. The Foundation provides grants to US organizations to improve the efficacy and affordability of healthcare for the increasingly ageing population in the USA.

Geographical Area of Activity: USA.

Restrictions: No grants to individuals.

Publications: Annual Report; newsletter; blog.

Finance: Annual revenue US $86.4m., expenditure $35.4m. (31 Dec. 2023).

Board of Trustees: John R. Mach, Jr (Chair.); Elizabeth A. Palmer, Earl A. Samson, III (Co-Vice-Chair.).

Principal Staff: Pres. Dr Terry Fulmer.

Contact Details: 55 E 59th St, 16th Floor, New York, NY 10022-1713; tel. (212) 832-7788; e-mail mail@johnahartford.org; internet www.johnahartford.org.

The John D. and Catherine T. MacArthur Foundation

Founded in 1978 by John D. MacArthur, owner of Bankers Life and Casualty Co, a financial services company, and his wife Catherine.

Activities: Supports creative people, effective institutions and influential networks. Main programme areas include: climate solutions; criminal justice; nuclear challenges; and Nigeria. The Foundation also supports civic, cultural and community projects in Chicago, IL, and invests in independent journalism and media to strengthen democracy in the USA. Through the MacArthur Fellows Program, each year the Foundation awards 20–30 fellowships (informally known as 'Genius Grants'), worth US $625,000 over five years, for creative work in any field. It also makes awards for journalism and media. The 100&Change competition offers a $100m. grant to fund a single proposal to solve a current critical problem. Has supported organizations and individuals in 117 countries; has offices in India and Nigeria.

Geographical Area of Activity: International.

Restrictions: Fellows must be citizens or residents of the USA. Does not support political activities or attempts to influence action on specific legislation; does not offer scholarships or tuition assistance for undergraduate, graduate or postgraduate studies.

Publications: Annual Report.

Finance: Annual revenue US $613.8m., expenditure $415.3m. (31 Dec. 2023).

Board of Directors: Martha Minnow (Chair.).

Principal Staff: Pres. John Palfrey.

Contact Details: Office of Grants Management, 140 S. Dearborn St, Chicago, IL 60603-5285; tel. (312) 726-8000; e-mail 4answers@macfound.org; internet www.macfound.org.

John S. and James L. Knight Foundation

Established in 1950 by brothers John S. and James L. Knight, newspaper publishers.

Activities: Invests in the cities where the Knight brothers published newspapers. Main programme areas include: the arts and culture; equitable and inclusive communities; and sustainable journalism. The Foundation operates in 26 communities, with offices in eight and works through community foundations in the remaining 18.

Geographical Area of Activity: USA.

Restrictions: Primarily funds organizations based in the USA.

Publications: Research reports.

Finance: Annual income US $66.9m., expenditure $109.0m. (31 Dec. 2022).

Board of Trustees: Christopher M. Austen (Chair.).

Principal Staff: Pres. and CEO Maribel Pérez Wadsworth.

Contact Details: 2850 Tigertail Ave, Suite 600, Miami, FL 33133; tel. (305) 908-2600; e-mail media@kf.org; internet knightfoundation.org.

John Simon Guggenheim Memorial Foundation

Established in 1925 by Senator Simon Guggenheim and his wife Olga in memory of their son, who died in 1922.

Activities: Operates nationally and internationally in all fields of science, the humanities and the creative arts, through 'mid-career' fellowships and grants to individuals who have demonstrated exceptional capacity for productive scholarship or exceptional creative ability in the arts. The Foundation annually awards around 175 fellowships.

Geographical Area of Activity: North, Central and South America and the Caribbean.

Restrictions: No grants to organizations or institutions; nor for the performing arts. Fellowships are open to citizens and permanent residents of the USA, Canada, Central and South America and the Caribbean.

Publications: Annual Report; newsletter; brochures.

Board of Trustees: Dwight E. Lee (Chair.).

Principal Staff: Pres. Edward Hirsch.

Contact Details: 90 Park Ave, 33rd Floor, New York, NY 10016; tel. (212) 687-4470; e-mail fellowships@gf.org; internet www.gf.org.

John Templeton Foundation

Founded in 1987 by Sir John Templeton, an investor and fund manager; part of the Templeton Philanthropies, with the Templeton World Charity Foundation and Templeton Religion Trust (q.v.), which are based in the Bahamas.

Activities: Supports research on subjects ranging from complexity, evolution, and emergence to creativity, forgiveness and free will. The Foundation encourages civil, informed dialogue among scientists, philosophers, and theologians, as well as between such experts and the public at large. It provides grants for independent research that advances the mission of the Foundation and public engagement. The Templeton Prize (f. 1972), worth £1m., is awarded for scientific insights about religion.

Geographical Area of Activity: International.

Publications: *The Templeton Report* (e-newsletter, 2 a month); books.

Finance: Annual revenue –US $48.9m., expenditure $212.4m. (31 Dec. 2022).

Trustees: Leigh Cameron (Chair.).

Principal Staff: Pres. Heather Templeton Dill.

Contact Details: 300 Conshohocken State Rd, Suite 500, West Conshohocken, PA 19428; tel. (610) 941-2828; e-mail info@templeton.org; internet www.templeton.org.

The Johnson Foundation at Wingspread

Founded in 1958 by Herbert F. Johnson, Jr, head of SC Johnson, a manufacturer of household cleaning products and consumer chemicals.

Activities: Supports the development of more resilient communities which are socially, economically and environmentally sustainable. The Foundation convenes small face-to-face meetings of leaders and experts; and also organizes conferences at Wingspread, its educational conference centre in Racine, WI.

Geographical Area of Activity: USA.

Restrictions: Supports conference-related activities by nonprofit organizations.

Publications: Annual Report; *Wingspread Journal*; *Conversations from Wingspread*; reports.

Finance: Annual revenue US $3.8m., expenditure $5.2m. (30 June 2023).

Board: Helen Johnson-Leipold (Chair.).

Principal Staff: Pres. Marcus White; Gen. Man. Eric Bates.

Contact Details: 33 E Four Mile Rd, Racine, WI 53402-2621; tel. (262) 639-3211; e-mail info@johnsonfdn.org; internet www.johnsonfdn.org.

Johnson & Johnson Foundation US—JJF

Established in 1953 by Johnson & Johnson, a healthcare company; Johnson & Johnson Scotland (f. 2007) operates in the United Kingdom.

Activities: Works in the fields of primary healthcare and disaster relief. The Foundation supports frontline healthcare workers, including nurses, midwives and community health workers through funding training and education, and promoting digital technology. In 2019 it established the Johnson & Johnson Center for Health Worker Innovation, which has 10 regional Impact Hubs and comprises Johnson & Johnson Impact Ventures for impact investing. Has partners in 27 countries.

Geographical Area of Activity: Worldwide.

Restrictions: Does not accept unsolicited applications; no grants to individuals.

Publications: Annual Report; newsletter.

Finance: Annual revenue US $136.2m., expenditure $55.4m. (2023).

Principal Staff: Pres. Howard Reid.

Contact Details: 1 Johnson & Johnson Plaza, New Brunswick, NJ 08933; tel. (732) 524-2892; internet www.jnjfoundation.com.

Josiah Macy Jr Foundation

Founded in 1930 by Kate Macy Ladd, a philanthropist, in memory of her father.

Activities: Operates nationally and internationally in the fields of science and medicine, through health programmes, grants to institutions, conferences and publications. The Foundation's main interest is in medical education, including: preparing medical professionals for dealing with ethical questions; increasing teamwork between and among multiple health professions; educational strategies to increase access and use of healthcare facilities by underserved communities; and increasing diversity among healthcare professionals. It is particularly concerned with African American, Latino and Native American health issues. Up to 40 Board Grants are awarded each year for 1–3 years; President's Grants may be awarded at any time, for one year or less, and are worth up to US $35,000. The Macy Faculty Scholars Program identifies up to five educational innovators each year, awarding them up to $100,000 a year over two years to implement change projects in their institutions.

Geographical Area of Activity: USA.

Restrictions: No grants to individuals or for capital works, endowments or activities outside the USA.

Publications: Annual Report; newsletter; reports; research findings.

Finance: Annual revenue US $8.4m., expenditure $7.5m. (30 June 2023).

Board of Directors: Meredith B. Jenkins (Chair.).

Principal Staff: Pres. Holly J. Humphrey.

Contact Details: 44 East 64th St, New York, NY 10065; tel. (212) 486-2424; e-mail info@macyfoundation.org; internet macyfoundation.org.

Joyce Foundation

Established in 1948 by Beatrice Joyce Kean, the sole heiress of the Joyce family, which built a fortune in the lumber industry.

Activities: Supports policies to advance racial equity and economic mobility for the next generation in the Great Lakes region. The Foundation focuses most of its grantmaking on six states: Illinois, Indiana, Michigan, Minnesota, Ohio and Wisconsin. Programmes areas include: culture; democracy; education and economic mobility; the environment; and gun violence prevention and justice reform.

Geographical Area of Activity: Canada, USA.

Finance: Total assets US $1,243.3m. (31 Dec. 2023).

Board of Directors: Margot M. Rogers (Chair.); José B. Alvarez (Vice-Chair.).

Principal Staff: Pres. Ellen S. Alberding.

Contact Details: 321 N. Clark St, Suite 1500, Chicago, IL 60654; tel. (312) 782-2464; e-mail info@joycefdn.org; internet www.joycefdn.org.

JPMorgan Chase Foundation

Established in 1956 as the Manufacturers Hanover Foundation, becoming the Chemical Bank Foundation in 1993; merged with the J. P. Morgan Charitable Trust, following the merger of J. P. Morgan and Chase Manhattan Bank in 2000.

Activities: Works to increase economic opportunity. The Foundation invests in five priority areas: business growth and entrepreneurship; careers and skills; community development; environmental sustainability; and financial health and wealth creation. It funds non-profit organizations and provides employee volunteers in more than 100 countries.

Geographical Area of Activity: International.

Restrictions: Does not accept unsolicited applications.

Publications: Annual Report; *Global Strength, Local Impact* (quarterly newsletter).

Finance: Annual revenue US $52.0m., expenditure $203.2m. (31 Dec. 2022).

Board of Directors: Peter Scher (Chair.); Karen Keogh (Vice-Chair.); David Salaverry (Treas.); Ingrid Miller (Sec.).

Principal Staff: Pres. Janis Bowdler.

Contact Details: 383 Madison Ave, 41st Floor, New York, NY 10017; tel. (212) 270-3685; internet www.jpmorganchase.com/impact.

Jubilee USA Network

Established in 1997 by faith-based groups.

Activities: A coalition of religious, development and advocacy groups that campaigns for debt relief to end poverty and to build an economy that serves and protects the world's most vulnerable people. Areas of interest include: debt and lending; tax, corruption and transparency; banks and financial institutions; trade; bankruptcy and financial crises; and debt and disaster relief in Puerto Rico. The Network comprises more than 75 US organizations, more than 750 faith communities and 50 international partners.

Geographical Area of Activity: International.

Finance: Annual revenue US $1.1m., expenditure $849,073 (31 Dec. 2022).

Board: Rabbi Matthew Cutler, Sobia Ijaz (Co-Chair.); Rev. Caleb Lines (Treas.).

Principal Staff: Exec. Dir Eric LeCompte.

Contact Details: 110 Maryland Ave, NE, Suite 210, Washington, DC 20002; tel. (202) 783-3566; e-mail coord@jubileeusa.org; internet www.jubileeusa.org.

Kettering Foundation—KF

Established in 1927 by Charles F. Kettering, co-founder of the Dayton Engineering Laboratories Company—DELCO.

Activities: Works in the fields of governance, education and science. The Foundation works on five focus areas: defending inclusive democracy; information for a democratic society; democracy and community; democracy and the arts; and democracy around the world. It holds training workshops in the USA and abroad; and has an office in Washington, DC.

Geographical Area of Activity: Mainly USA.

Restrictions: Does not make grants.

Publications: *Connections* (annual journal); *Higher Education Exchange* (annual periodical); *Kettering Review* (journal); brochures; issue guides; occasional papers; reports; books.

Finance: Annual income US $15.4m., expenditure $17.7m. (31 Dec. 2022).

Board of Directors: Sherry Magill (Chair.).

Principal Staff: Pres. and CEO Sharon L. Davies; Exec. Vice-Pres. John R. Dedrick.

Contact Details: 200 Commons Rd, Dayton, OH 45459; tel. (937) 434-7300; e-mail info@kettering.org; internet www.kettering.org.

King Philanthropies

Established in 2016 by Bob and Dottie King, who founded investment management firm R. Eliot King & Associates.

Activities: Works to overcome global poverty through self-conducted programmes and grants to organizations. Main programmes include King Essentials, which focuses on meeting essential needs in the areas of agriculture, early childhood development, land rights and primary healthcare; the Global Scholars initiative, providing access to higher education in the USA to scholars from low-income countries; and the Climate + Poverty initiative, comprising the work of the King Climate Action Initiative (K-CAI), a joint venture with the Abdul Latif Jameel Poverty Action Lab (J-PAL) at MIT. Working with

Kiwanis Children's Fund

the Stanford Institute for Innovation in Developing Economies (Stanford Seed) the organization invests in high-impact interventions. It also supports the Stanford King Center on Global Development, a joint venture between Stanford Seed and the Stanford Institute for Economic Policy Research (SIEPR).

Geographical Area of Activity: International.

Restrictions: Does not accept unsolicited proposals.

Publications: Newsletter; toolkits.

Finance: Annual revenue US $651.6m., expenditure $20.5m. (31 Dec. 2022).

Principal Staff: Pres. and CEO Kim Starkey.

Contact Details: POB 1119, Menlo Park, CA 94025; tel. (650) 600-5395; e-mail info@kingphilanthropies.org; internet kingphilanthropies.org.

Kiwanis Children's Fund

Established in 1939 as the Kiwanis International Foundation, the fundraising and grantmaking arm of Kiwanis International (f. 1915); present name adopted in 2016.

Activities: Supports Kiwanis International children's and youth programmes. The Fund awards grants for Kiwanis Service Leadership Programs, club and district service projects, disaster relief; and to eliminate maternal and neonatal tetanus, and iodine deficiency disorders. It also offers university scholarships for members of the Key Club International and Circle K International youth community service organizations. Works in 80 countries and territories.

Geographical Area of Activity: International.

Publications: Annual Report; Impact Report.

Finance: Annual revenue US $18.4m., expenditure $20.6m. (30 Sept. 2021).

Board of Trustees: Robert S. Maxwell (Pres.); Lenora Hanna (Pres.-elect); Amy Zimmerman (Immediate Past Pres.); Richard A. Poulton (Vice-Pres.).

Principal Staff: Exec. Dir Paul Palazzolo.

Contact Details: 3636 Woodview Trace, Indianapolis, IN 46268-3196; tel. (317) 875-8755; e-mail childrensfund@kiwanis.org; internet www.kiwanis.org/who-we-are/kiwanis-childrens-fund.

Koch Foundation, Inc

Established in 1979 by Carl E. Koch, founder of the American Beauty Products Co, and Paula Koch to promote Roman Catholicism.

Activities: Awards grants to Catholic organizations, nationally and internationally, that propagate the Catholic faith. Grants are made for different evangelization programmes; educational and spiritual formation of evangelists; resource-poor Catholic schools, which are the principal means of evangelization in the community; a Catholic presence in the media; and capital expenditures. The Foundation gives priority to situations involving financially distressed, underdeveloped areas.

Geographical Area of Activity: International.

Restrictions: No grants to individuals, loans or scholarships.

Publications: Annual Report.

Finance: Annual revenue US $2.4m., expenditure $7.1m. (31 March 2023).

Officers and Directors: William A. Bomberger (Pres.); Inge L. Vraney (Vice-Pres.); Carolyn L. Bomberger (Treas.); Rachel A. Bomberger (Sec.).

Principal Staff: Exec. Dir Carolyn A. Young.

Contact Details: 4421 NW 39th Ave, Bldg 1, Suite 1, Gainesville, FL 32606-7211; tel. (352) 373-7491; e-mail staff@thekochfoundation.org; internet www.thekochfoundation.org.

Koret Foundation

Established in 1979 by Joseph Koret and Stephanie Koret, who founded Koret of California, a women's clothing company.

UNITED STATES OF AMERICA

Activities: Operates in the fields of community development and Jewish life and culture. The Foundation's initiatives include the Koret Israel Economic Development Funds, Koret Jewish Studies Publications Program, Koret Jewish Book Awards, Koret Israel Emergency Fund, Koret Synagogue Initiative, Routes to Learning and the Koret Prize.

Geographical Area of Activity: Israel, Poland, USA (mainly San Francisco Bay Area).

Restrictions: Does not fund private foundations or individuals.

Publications: *Catalyst* (newsletter); community reports; *Perspectives*.

Finance: Annual revenue US $29.8m., expenditure $54.7m. (31 Dec. 2022).

Board of Directors: Michael J. Boskin, Anita Friedman (Pres.).

Principal Staff: CEO Jeffrey A. Farber.

Contact Details: 611 Front St, San Francisco, CA 94111; tel. (415) 882-7740; internet koret.org.

The Kosciuszko Foundation, Inc

Founded in 1925 to promote closer ties between Poland and the USA; named in honour of Thaddeus Kosciuszko, a military strategist and engineer.

Activities: Operates nationally and internationally in the fields of education, science and medicine, and the arts and humanities, through grants to institutions and individuals, fellowships, scholarships, conferences, courses, publications and lectures. The Foundation awards grants for Polish Americans to enter medical schools in Poland; and to enable writers, artists and students to complete scholarly, artistic or literary projects that would serve to implement the purposes of the Foundation. It also awards scholarships for Polish Americans to go on to higher education, and for Americans of non-Polish background to undertake Polish studies. The Chopin Piano Competition and the Marcella Sembrich Competition in Voice are held annually, as well as the Metchie J. E. Budka Award for outstanding scholarly work. Has offices in Washington, DC, and Warsaw.

Geographical Area of Activity: Poland, USA.

Publications: Annual Report; newsletter.

Finance: Annual revenue US $5.9m., expenditure $3.9m. (30 June 2023).

Board of Trustees: Alex Storozynski (Chair.); Cynthia Rosicki, Stephen Kusmierczak (Vice-Chair.); Andrzej Rojek (Vice-Chair./Treas.); Joseph E. Gore (Chair. Emeritus).

Principal Staff: Pres. and Exec. Dir Marek Skulimowski.

Contact Details: 15 East 65th St, New York, NY 10065; tel. (212) 734-2130; e-mail info@thekf.org; internet www.thekf.org.

Kresge Foundation

Established in 1924 by Sebastian S. Kresge, the founder of S. S. Kresge Co (subsequently Kmart Corpn), a retail company.

Activities: Focuses on improving the lives of low-income, vulnerable and underserved adults and children in US cities, in particular Detroit. The Foundation makes grants and social investments in the areas of American cities, the arts and culture, education, the environment, health and human services. Has an office in Detroit, MI.

Geographical Area of Activity: USA.

Publications: Annual Report; newsletter; brochure.

Finance: Annual revenue US $234.5m., expenditure $224.4m. (31 Dec. 2023).

Board of Trustees: Cecilia Muñoz (Chair.).

Principal Staff: Pres. and CEO Rip Rapson.

Contact Details: 3215 W. Big Beaver Rd, Troy, MI 48084; tel. (248) 643-9630; e-mail info@kresge.org; internet www.kresge.org.

UNITED STATES OF AMERICA

Landesa—Rural Development Institute

Established in 1981, as the Rural Development Institute, by Roy Prosterman, a lawyer and land rights advocate.

Activities: Works to alleviate poverty through securing land rights for marginalized people, in particular women. The Institute collaborates with governments and regional and CSOs to help poor rural people to gain secure land tenure and improve livelihoods; address problems including women's lack of control over assets, weak land management and conflict resolution institutions, and gaps and contradictions between customary and formal law; and make sure communities, land users and smallholders are informed about and consulted on land-related investments and equitably share in benefits. It maintains the Center for Women's Land Rights; and has offices in Cambodia, China, India, Indonesia, Kenya, Liberia, Rwanda and Tanzania.

Geographical Area of Activity: Asia, sub-Saharan Africa.

Publications: Annual Report; *Plotlines* (monthly newsletter); brochures; case studies; country guidebooks; factsheets; infographics; issue briefs; research reports; books.

Finance: Annual revenue US $36.9m., expenditure $11.9m. (30 June 2022).

Board of Directors: Titi Liu (Chair.).

Principal Staff: Pres. and CEO Chris Jochnick.

Contact Details: 1424 Fourth Ave, Suite 430, Seattle, WA 98101; tel. (206) 528-5880; e-mail info@landesa.org; internet www.landesa.org.

Lannan Foundation

Established in 1960 by J. Patrick Lannan, Sr, a financier and collector of contemporary and modern American and European art.

Activities: Promotes cultural freedom, diversity and creativity. The Foundation supports contemporary artists and writers; and Native activists in rural indigenous communities for the revival and preservation of Native languages, legal rights and environmental protection. It makes grants to non-profit organizations in the areas of contemporary visual art, literature, indigenous communities and cultural freedom; and offers awards and fellowships to writers of poetry, fiction and non-fiction and in the area of cultural freedom.

Geographical Area of Activity: USA.

Restrictions: Does not accept unsolicited applications; grants only to organizations registered in the USA and federally recognized tribes.

Publications: Audio and bookworm archives; programme statements.

Finance: Annual revenue US $21.8m., expenditure $25.0m. (31 Dec. 2022).

Board of Directors: Lawrence P. Lannan, Jr (Pres.); Frank C. Lawler (Vice-Pres.).

Principal Staff: Dir Emeritus John R. Lannan.

Contact Details: 369 Montezuma Ave, Suite 312, Santa Fe, NM 87501; tel. (505) 986-8160; e-mail info@lannan.org; internet www.lannan.org.

Latter-day Saint Charities—LDSC

Established in 1996; the humanitarian arm of the Church of Jesus Christ of Latter-day Saints.

Activities: Works to relieve suffering, foster self-reliance and provide opportunities for service. The organization collaborates with NGOs, government ministries and local organizations to provide emergency relief and implement programmes, including: providing food security; clean water and sanitation; establishing community projects; disaster relief; supporting immunization campaigns; maternal and newborn care; refugee response; improving eye care and preventing avoidable blindness; and providing appropriate manual wheelchairs to people with mobility problems. Sponsors relief and development projects in 192 countries and territories.

Geographical Area of Activity: Worldwide.

Restrictions: No grants to individuals.

Publications: Annual Report; blog.

Finance: Funded by public donations and the Church of Jesus Christ of Latter-day Saints; total assistance since 1985 US $2,300m.

Principal Staff: Pres. Russel M. Nelson.

Contact Details: 50 E. North Temple St, Floor 7, Salt Lake City, UT 84150-6890; tel. (801) 240-1201; e-mail lds-charities@ldschurch.org; internet www.ldscharities.org.

The Leakey Foundation

Founded in 1968 as the L. S. B. Leakey Foundation for Research Related to Man's Origins, Behavior & Survival; inspired by the work of Dr Louis S. B. Leakey, an anthropologist.

Activities: Supports postgraduate research (principally doctoral candidates and scientists with professional qualifications and demonstrated capability) in human origins and evolution, and human behaviour and survival. The Foundation offers research grants, up to US $20,000 for doctoral students and up to $30,000 for senior scientists and postdoctoral researchers. It awards Franklin Mosher Baldwin Memorial Fellowships, worth up to $15,000 annually, to students from developing countries for advanced education and training in palaeoanthropology and primatology. Scholarships are available to students or researchers of East African heritage through the Francis H. Brown African Scholarship Fund, worth up to $30,000; and to students from countries where academic resources are limited through the Joan Donner Field School Scholarship, worth up to $2,000. Emergency funding for long-term primate field research sites, worth up to $25,000, is available through the Primate Research Fund.

Geographical Area of Activity: International.

Restrictions: Fellowship applicants must be enrolled in a postgraduate programme related to the study of human origins or evolution and plan to work in their home country on completing their training.

Publications: *AnthroQuest* (newsletter, 2 a year); research reports; blog.

Finance: Annual revenue US $6.7m., expenditure $3.7m. (31 Aug. 2023).

Board of Trustees: Gordon P. Getty (Chair.); Jeanne Newman (Pres.); J. Diana McSherry, William P. Getty (Vice-Pres); Duggan Jensen (Treas.); Dana Lajoie (Sec.).

Scientific Executive Committee: Dr Robert Seyfarth, Dr Carol Ward (Co-Chair.).

Principal Staff: Exec. Dir Sharal Camisa Smith.

Contact Details: 1003B O'Reilly Ave, San Francisco, CA 94129-1359; tel. (415) 561-4646; e-mail info@leakeyfoundation.org; internet www.leakeyfoundation.org.

The Leona M. and Harry B. Helmsley Charitable Trust

Established in 1999 by Leona Helmsley, the widow of Harry Helmsley, a real estate developer.

Activities: Works to improve people's lives and improve health outcomes for individuals and communities. Main programme areas are: conservation, addressing environmental threats and ensuring the wellbeing of local people, sustaining natural resources and biodiversity; Crohn's disease, searching for a cure and providing better treatments; Israel, funding scientific, technological and medical research; New York City, ensuring people's economic security and improving their quality of life; rural healthcare, using telemedicine and other information technologies to connect people in remote areas of the USA to medical care; Type 1 diabetes, improving care for people with the condition and working towards prevention; and vulnerable children in sub-Saharan Africa, providing access to education, improved food and nutrition, and clean water and sanitation. Has an office in Sioux Falls, SD.

Geographical Area of Activity: Israel, sub-Saharan Africa, USA.

Publications: Workshop and programme reports; e-news; brochures.

Finance: Annual revenue US $385.2m., expenditure $600.1m. (31 March 2024).

Principal Staff: CEO Sarah Paul.

Contact Details: 230 Park Ave, Suite 659, New York, NY 10169-0698; tel. (212) 679-3600; e-mail grants@helmsleytrust.org; internet helmsleytrust.org.

Levi Strauss Foundation

Founded in 1952 by Levi Strauss & Co, a clothing manufacturer; operates independently of the Red Tab Foundation (f. 1981), which supports Levi's employees in need.

Activities: Supports non-governmental and community-focused organizations in the areas of HIV/AIDS, workers rights and wellbeing, and social justice and human rights. The Foundation has more than 100 partnerships in over 40 countries and supports highly vulnerable groups through the Rapid Response Fund.

Geographical Area of Activity: Worldwide.

Restrictions: No grants to individuals; does not accept unsolicited applications.

Publications: Annual Report; case studies.

Finance: Annual revenue US $6.1m., expenditure $11.7m. (30 Nov. 2023).

Principal Staff: CEO Fatima Angeles.

Contact Details: Levi's Plaza, 1155 Battery St, San Francisco, CA 94111-1230; tel. (415) 501-6579; e-mail mbxlsfoundation@levi.com; internet www.levistrauss.com/values-in-action/levi-strauss-foundation.

Liberty Fund, Inc

Founded in 1960 by Pierre F. Goodrich, a lawyer and business person.

Activities: Publishes print and electronic scholarly resources, including new editions of classic works in American constitutional history, European history, law, political philosophy and theory, economics and education. The Fund organizes more than 150 conferences annually throughout the USA, Canada, Central and South America and Europe; and maintains a library.

Geographical Area of Activity: Worldwide.

Restrictions: Does not make grants.

Publications: Newsletter (quarterly); books.

Finance: Annual revenue US $40.4m., expenditure $18.0m. (30 April 2022).

Board of Directors: Nathan J. Feltman (Chair.); Sandra J. Schaller (Treas./Sec.).

Principal Staff: Pres. and CEO Sean R. Shelby.

Contact Details: 11301 N. Meridian St, Carmel, IN 46032-4564; tel. (800) 866-3520; e-mail info@libertyfund.org; internet www.libertyfund.org.

Life Sciences Research Foundation—LSRF

Founded in 1983 by Dr Donald D. Brown, a professor of developmental biology.

Activities: Operates in the field of life sciences. The Foundation provides early career funding to young scientists in all areas of basic life sciences; and a peer-review service to individuals or organizations wishing to sponsor a fellow who shares their research vision. Postdoctoral fellowships are worth US $77,000 a year for three years.

Geographical Area of Activity: USA.

Restrictions: Applications from non-US citizens must be for study in the USA.

Publications: Annual Report; information brochure.

Finance: Annual revenue US $3.9m., expenditure $3.1m. (31 May 2024).

Principal Staff: Pres. Douglas E. Koshland; Exec. Dir Susan Davidson.

Contact Details: 3020-I Prosperity Church Rd, PMB 267, Charlotte, NC 28269; e-mail admin@lsrf.org; internet www.lsrf.org.

Lilly Endowment, Inc

Founded in 1937 by J. K. Lilly, Sr, Chair. of pharmaceutical firm Eli Lilly and Co., and his sons Eli and J. K., Jr.

Activities: Operates in the fields of community development (including social welfare and the arts and humanities), education and religion. The Endowment gives special attention to programmes in Indianapolis and Indiana. It prioritizes projects that depend on private support, but a limited number of grants are made to governmental institutions and tax-supported programmes. Support for international projects is limited to a few emergency relief and public policy programmes, mostly in Canada and Mexico.

Geographical Area of Activity: Canada, Mexico, USA (mainly Indiana).

Restrictions: No grants to individuals; does not usually fund projects in healthcare, biological and physical science research, housing, transport, environment and population.

Publications: Annual Report; newsletters; occasional reports.

Finance: Annual income US $465.4m., expenditure $1,434.1m. (31 Dec. 2022).

Board of Directors: N. Clay Robbins (Chair. and CEO); Jennett M. Hill (Pres.); Diane M. Stenson (Vice-Pres. and Treas.); Ben W. Blanton (Vice-Pres. and Sec.).

Contact Details: 2801 N Meridian St, POB 88068, Indianapolis, IN 46208-0068; tel. (317) 924-5471; e-mail communications@lei.org; internet lillyendowment.org.

Livestrong Foundation

Established in 1997 by Lance Armstrong, a road-racing cyclist; present name adopted in 2003.

Activities: Improves the lives of people affected by cancer through self-conducted programmes. The Foundation supports cancer survivors, caregivers and healthcare professionals, providing information and resources; and grants to organizations in the areas of post-treatment care, patient and caregiver education, comprehensive quality of life services, streamlining systems and care, and overlooked cancer problems. Acceleration grants are worth US $5,000–$20,000; Transformation Grants are worth $25,000–$100,000. It established the Livestrong Cancer Institutes of the Dell Medical School at the University of Texas.

Geographical Area of Activity: USA.

Restrictions: Grants only to organizations and projects in the USA; no grants to individuals.

Publications: *Livestrong Guidebook*; brochures.

Finance: Annual revenue US $2.8m., expenditure $4.5m. (31 Dec. 2023).

Board of Directors: Candice Aaron (Chair.); Joseph C. Aragona (Vice-Chair.).

Principal Staff: Pres. and CEO Suzanne Stone.

Contact Details: 623 W 38th St, Suite 300, Austin, TX 78705; tel. (877) 236-8820; e-mail livestrong@livestrong.org; internet www.livestrong.org.

Liz Claiborne & Art Ortenberg Foundation

Founded in 1984 by fashion designer Liz Claiborne and her husband, Art Ortenberg.

Activities: Works to conserve nature and alleviate human distress. Programmes focus on species extinction, habitat destruction and resource depletion. The Foundation supports work that directly benefits local communities, while protecting species and wildlands.

Geographical Area of Activity: Asia, Central and South America, sub-Saharan Africa, USA (Rocky Mountains).

Restrictions: No unsolicited applications.
Finance: Annual revenue US $4.2m., expenditure $14.1m. (31 Dec. 2022).
Principal Staff: Exec. Dir Kent W. Wommack.
Contact Details: 1385 Broadway, 23rd Floor, New York, NY 10018; tel. (212) 333-2536; e-mail lcaof@lcaof.org; internet www.lcaof.org.

The Long Now Foundation
Established in 1996 by Stewart Brand, the creator and editor of the *Whole Earth Catalogue*, and Danny Hillis, a physicist and computer scientist.
Activities: Aims to build a coherent and compelling body of ideas to make long-term thinking automatic and common. Initiatives include: the 10,000 Year Old Clock project; the Rosetta Project, a publicly accessible online resource which contains material in more than 2,300 languages; PanLex, which aims to create a collection of every word in every language; the Organizational Continuity Project, studying long-lived institutions to build long-lasting companies and governments; Long Bets, making predictions about future events; and Long Server, a digital continuity software project. The Foundation organizes seminars and other events for members and the public.
Geographical Area of Activity: USA.
Publications: Newsletter; essays; seminar transcripts; blog; books.
Finance: Annual revenue US $7.2m., expenditure $3.9m. (31 Dec. 2022).
Board of Directors: Patrick Dowd (Pres.); Joe Speicher (Treas.); Danica Remy (Sec.).
Principal Staff: Exec. Dir Rebecca Lendl.
Contact Details: 2 Marina Blvd, Bldg A, Fort Mason Center, San Francisco, CA 94123; tel. (415) 561-6582; e-mail services@longnow.org; internet longnow.org.

Lucius N. Littauer Foundation, Inc
Founded in 1929 by Lucius Littauer, an industrialist and politician.
Activities: Makes grants in the areas of education, social welfare, Jewish communal life and Jewish studies. The Foundation's Jewish studies work mainly focuses on large-scale digitization and processing projects in Judaica libraries and archives.
Geographical Area of Activity: Israel, USA (mainly New York metropolitan area).
Restrictions: No grants to individuals, or for religious activities or publishing of monographs and exhibition catalogues; grants only to non-profit organizations in the USA.
Publications: Guidelines.
Finance: Annual revenue US $2.8m., expenditure $3.7m. (31 Dec. 2022).
Board of Trustees: Robert D. Frost (Pres. and CEO); Geula R. Solomon (Treas.); Noah B. Perlman (Sec.).
Contact Details: 200 Madison Ave, Suite 1910, New York, NY 10016; tel. (646) 237-5158; e-mail adivack@littauerfoundation.org; internet littauerfoundation.org.

Ludwig Cancer Research
Established in 1971, as Ludwig Institute for Cancer Research, by Daniel K. Ludwig, a shipowner and financier.
Activities: Funds clinical and laboratory research on preventing and controlling cancer. In 2006 the organization established Ludwig Centers and professorships at Johns Hopkins University, Harvard Medical School, Massachusetts Institute of Technology, the Memorial Sloan-Kettering Cancer Center, Stanford University and the University of Chicago. It also has branches in Switzerland and the United Kingdom.
Geographical Area of Activity: Europe, USA.
Publications: Annual Report; *Ludwig Link* (newsletter); research highlights.
Finance: Annual revenue US $89.3m., expenditure $90.0m. (31 Dec. 2021).
Board of Directors: Edward A. McDermott, Jr (Chair.).
Principal Staff: CEO and Scientific Dir Dr Chi Van Dang.
Contact Details: 600 Third Ave, 32nd Floor, New York, NY 10016; tel. (212) 450-1500; e-mail communications@ludwigcancerresearch.org; internet www.ludwigcancerresearch.org.

Lynde and Harry Bradley Foundation, Inc
Founded in 1942 by brothers Lynde and Harry Bradley, co-founders of electronics manufacturer the Allen-Bradley Company, as the Allen-Bradley Foundation, Inc; present name adopted in 1985 following the company's sale to Rockwell International.
Activities: Promotes US exceptionalism through four main programmes: Constitutional Order; Free Markets; Civil Society; and Informed Citizens. The Foundation offers graduate and postgraduate fellowships; and up to four Bradley Prizes, each worth US $250,000, to individuals for their contribution in areas of the Foundation's interest. It organizes Bradley Forum events; sponsors the Bradley Impact Fund, a network of conservative philanthropic donors; and supports Encounter Books, the publishing arm of Encounter for Culture and Education, Inc.
Geographical Area of Activity: USA (with a focus on Milwaukee, WI).
Restrictions: No grants to individuals.
Publications: Annual Report; newsletter.
Finance: Annual revenue US $1.0m., expenditure $63.8m. (31 Dec. 2022).
Board of Directors: Patrick J. English (Chair.); James T. Barry, III (Vice-Chair.).
Principal Staff: Sec. Cleta Mitchell.
Contact Details: 1400 N. Water St, Suite 300, Milwaukee, WI 53202; tel. (414) 291-9915; internet www.bradleyfdn.org.

Lyndon Baines Johnson Foundation
Founded in 1969; manages gifts that benefit two institutions at the University of Texas at Austin—the Lyndon B. Johnson Library and Museum and the Lyndon B. Johnson School of Public Affairs.
Activities: Offers grants for living and travel expenses incurred by researchers of any nationality while conducting research on the life and career of Lyndon B. Johnson at the Johnson Library. The Foundation also awards fellowships for work to be done in National Archives facilities, including Presidential Libraries. Grants and initiatives include: the Presidential Timeline Project, an interactive online project; the Lady Bird Johnson Environmental Award; the D. B. Hardeman Prize for the best book on the US Congress; the LBJ Liberty & Justice for All Award; and lectureships and fellowships.
Geographical Area of Activity: USA.
Finance: Annual revenue US $12.7m., expenditure $8.7m. (31 Aug. 2022).
Board of Trustees: Larry E. Temple (Chair.); Ben Barnes, Elizabeth Christian (Vice-Chair.).
Principal Staff: Pres. and CEO Mark K. Updegrove.
Contact Details: 2313 Red River St, Austin, TX 78705; tel. (512) 721-0265; e-mail info@lbjfoundation.org; internet www.lbjlibrary.org/foundation.

McKnight Foundation
Established in 1953 by William L. McKnight, Chair. of the Minnesota Mining and Manufacturing Co, and his wife Maude.
Activities: Works to improve people's quality of life through policy and systems change. Main grantmaking programme areas include: arts, supporting artists in Minnesota; international, funding crop research in 12 countries; Midwest climate and energy, promoting a carbon-neutral regional economy;

Maclellan Foundation, Inc   UNITED STATES OF AMERICA

neuroscience, supporting research through the McKnight Endowment Fund for Neuroscience, which administers three annual awards; and vibrant and equitable communities, investing in civil society, culture and the economy in Minnesota.

Geographical Area of Activity: Andes, sub-Saharan Africa, USA (Minnesota).

Restrictions: Each programme has its own criteria; some are by invitation only.

Publications: Annual Report; newsletter; occasional reports; information brochures.

Finance: Annual revenue US $165.0m., expenditure $200.9m. (31 Dec. 2022).

Board of Directors: Ted Staryk (Chair.); Kathy Tunheim (Vice-Chair.); Erika L. Binger (Treas.).

Principal Staff: Pres. Tonya Allen.

Contact Details: 710 South Second St, Suite 400, Minneapolis, MN 55401; tel. (612) 333-4220; e-mail communications@mcknight.org; internet www.mcknight.org.

Maclellan Foundation, Inc

Incorporated in 1945 by Robert J. Maclellan, Chair. of Provident Insurance Co, and his family. Part of the Maclellan Family Foundations group, which includes the Robert L. and Kathrina H. Maclellan Foundation (f. 1972) and the Christian Education Charitable Trust (f. 1974).

Activities: Provides financial and leadership support to faith-based ministries to foster biblical Christian values.

Geographical Area of Activity: Worldwide.

Restrictions: No grants to individuals or scholarships.

Finance: Annual revenue US $13.6m., expenditure $32.0m. (31 Dec. 2022).

Board of Trustees: Christopher H. Maclellan (Chair.); Robert H. Maclellan (Vice-Chair.); Hugh O. Maclellan, Jr (Treas.); Catherine M. Heald (Sec.).

Principal Staff: Exec. Dir David G. Denmark.

Contact Details: 820 Broad St, Suite 300, Chattanooga, TN 37402; tel. (423) 755-8142; e-mail support@maclellan.net; internet www.maclellan.net.

MADRE

Established in 1983 by Kathy Engel and Vivian Stromberg, women's rights advocates.

Activities: Collaborates with grassroots women's groups to advance women's human rights and create social change in contexts of war, disaster and injustice. Main programme areas are: ending gender violence; advancing climate justice; and building a just peace; and the No Borders on Gender Justice campaign. The organization provides advocacy and practical skills training. It funds women-led organizations that focus on the leadership of women and girls, in particular from minority or marginalized groups.

Geographical Area of Activity: Colombia, Guatemala, Haiti, Iraq, Kenya, Nicaragua, Palestinian Territories, Syrian Arab Repub., USA.

Restrictions: Grants only to partner organizations.

Publications: Annual Report; newsletter; human rights reports; position papers.

Finance: Annual revenue US $30.7m., expenditure $10.7m. (30 Sept. 2022).

Board of Directors: Anne H. Hess, Blaine Bookey (Co-Chair.).

Principal Staff: Exec. Dir Yifat Susskind.

Contact Details: 26 Broadway, 3rd Floor, Office 390, New York, NY 10004; tel. (212) 627-0444; e-mail madrespeaks@madre.org; internet www.madre.org.

MAP International—Medical Assistance Programs

Established in 1954 by Dr J. Raymond Knighton; a Christian relief and development organization.

Activities: Operates in the field of medicine and health, collaborating with other organizations to provide essential medicines to those in need; prevent and eradicate diseases (particularly addressing the problem of HIV/AIDS); and promote community health development in less-developed countries. The organization also provides emergency healthcare in areas affected by natural and human-made disasters. It offers scholarships to medical students from North America to travel to developing countries to work at hospitals helping people in financial need. Maintains overseas offices in Bolivia, Côte d'Ivoire, Kenya and Liberia.

Geographical Area of Activity: International.

Publications: Annual Report; newsletter.

Finance: Annual revenue US $935.4m., expenditure $926.3m. (30 Sept. 2024).

Board of Directors: Michael Knighton (Chair.); Zoe Hicks (Treas.); James Leonard (Sec.).

Principal Staff: Pres. and CEO Chris Palombo.

Contact Details: 4700 Glynco Pkwy, Brunswick, GA 31525; tel. (912) 265-6010; e-mail map@map.org; internet www.map.org.

March of Dimes Foundation

Founded in 1938 by US President Franklin Roosevelt as the National Foundation for Infantile Paralysis to combat polio; later renamed March of Dimes Birth Defects Foundation.

Activities: Promotes the continuing education of professionals in the field of perinatal care, and the expansion of public education programmes. The Foundation makes grants to organizations for research in aspects of birth defects; and various research awards for research in the USA, including Clinical Research Grants, Predoctoral Graduate Research Training Fellowships, Social and Behavioral Sciences Research Grants, the Summer Science Research Program for Medical Students, the Basil O'Connor Starter Scholar Research Award Program, and the Research Support Program on Reproductive Hazards in the Workplace, Home, Community and Environment.

Geographical Area of Activity: Africa, Asia, Central and Eastern Europe, Latin America.

Publications: Annual Report; newsletter.

Finance: Annual revenue US $88.5m., expenditure $94.9m. (31 Dec. 2023).

Board of Trustees: Ellen Kelsay (Chair.); Dr Phyllis A. Dennery, Amy L. Casseri (Vice-Chair.); Andrew (Andy) J. Dahle (Treas.); Sue Schick (Sec.).

Principal Staff: Pres. and CEO Cindy Rahman.

Contact Details: 1550 Crystal Dr, Suite 1300, Arlington, VA 22202; tel. (914) 428-7100; internet www.marchofdimes.org.

Margaret A. Cargill Philanthropies—MACP

Established in 1995 as the Akaloa Resource Foundation; an umbrella organization comprising the Anne Ray Foundation (f. 1996) and the Margaret A. Cargill Foundation (f. 2006), which was established following the death of Margaret Cargill, heiress to the Cargill Corpn fortune.

Activities: Supports initiatives in the areas of: Native American and Scandinavian-American folk arts and cultures; disaster preparedness, relief and recovery; environmental conservation; improving quality of life for vulnerable people; teacher training and development; welfare of domestic and injured wild animals; and specific organizations in the Upper Midwest and Southern California. The organization focuses on underserved areas and causes, preferring community-based programmes on the ground over policy initiatives or endowments. The Anne Ray Foundation makes grants only to specified organizations.

Geographical Area of Activity: International.

Restrictions: Does not accept unsolicited applications.

Finance: Annual revenue –US $13.0m., expenditure $163.8m. (31 Dec. 2022).

Board: Christine M. Morse (Chair.).
Principal Staff: Pres. Heather Kukla.
Contact Details: 6889 Rowland Rd, Eden Prairie, MN 55344; tel. (952) 540-4050; e-mail info@macphil.org; internet www.macphilanthropies.org.

Marisla Foundation

Founded in 1986, as the Homeland Foundation, by Anne G. Earhart, heiress to the Getty Oil fortune.

Activities: Makes grants under three main programmes: Human Services, supporting women's physical, mental and financial wellbeing, with a particular focus on Los Angeles and Orange counties in California; Environment, promoting biological diversity and sustainable management of ecosystems, focusing on the conservation of marine resources in western North America, Chile and the Western Pacific, and also providing solutions to the threats to health that toxic chemicals pose; and Special Interests, as determined by the Foundation's Board of Directors. Grants typically range from US $20,000 to $100,000.
Geographical Area of Activity: Chile, western North America, USA, Western Pacific.
Restrictions: Does not accept unsolicited applications.
Finance: Annual revenue US $35.6m., expenditure $37.0m. (31 Dec. 2022).
Board of Directors: Anne G. Earhart (Pres.); Oliver N. Crary (Treas.); Sara M. Lowell (Sec.).
Principal Staff: Exec. Dir Herbert M. Bedolfe, III.
Contact Details: 668 N Coast Hwy, PMB 1400, Laguna Beach, CA 92651; tel. (800) 839-5316; internet online.foundationsource.com/ws/index.jsp?site=marisla.

Markle Foundation

Founded in 1927 by John Markle, an inventor, industrialist and financier, and his wife Mary, a philanthropist.

Activities: Focuses on the potential of mass communications and information technology to address problems in the areas of economic security, health and national security. The Foundation operates throughout the USA through self-conducted programmes, carries out research and makes grants to institutions.
Geographical Area of Activity: USA.
Restrictions: No grants to individuals.
Publications: Reports; essays; briefs; white papers; surveys.
Finance: Annual revenue –US $803,771, expenditure $14.6m. (30 June 2023).
Board of Directors: Suzanne Nora Johnson (Chair.).
Principal Staff: Interim Pres. Ellen V. Futter.
Contact Details: 1270 Ave of the Americas, 12th Floor, New York, NY 10020; tel. (212) 713-7600; e-mail info@markle.org; internet www.markle.org.

The Max Foundation

Established in 1997 by Pedro José Rivarola, in memory of his son Maximiliano (Max) Rivarola, who died of chronic myeloid leukaemia.

Activities: Operates in the field of medicine and health, with a focus on cancer. The Foundation provides information about treatment options; offers advice and emotional and financial support to sufferers of blood-related diseases; and raises awareness of the importance of becoming a bone marrow donor. It has regional offices in 20 countries and works with more than 500 partner healthcare organizations.
Geographical Area of Activity: International.
Restrictions: Not a grantmaking organization.
Publications: Newsletter.
Finance: Annual revenue US $312.1m., expenditure $296.0m. (31 Dec. 2023).
Board of Directors: Curt Malloy (Pres.); Edgar Thomas (Treas.); Graciela Mabel Woloj Rothstein (Sec.).
Principal Staff: CEO Pat Garcia-Gonzalez.
Contact Details: 1416 NW 46th St, Suite 105, #146, Seattle, WA 98107; tel. (425) 778-8660; e-mail info@themaxfoundation.org; internet www.themaxfoundation.org.

Max Kade Foundation, Inc

Established in 1944 by Max Kade, founder of Seeck and Kade, Inc, a pharmaceutical company.

Activities: Promotes Germanic studies and transatlantic exchange, to encourage positive relations between German-speaking countries and the USA. The Foundation sponsors exchange programmes between Austria and Germany and the USA in medicine and in the natural and physical sciences. It makes grants to educational institutions for exchange programmes for postdoctoral researchers and visiting faculty members ('Distinguished Visiting Professorships'); for the training of language teachers, undergraduate and graduate study abroad and international conferences; and to maintain equipment and facilities at residential language centres (Max Kade Houses) in universities and colleges in Germany and the USA.
Geographical Area of Activity: Austria, Germany, USA.
Restrictions: Grants only to publicly supported charitable organizations; no grants to individuals.
Finance: Annual revenue US $1.7m., expenditure $5.6m. (31 Dec. 2022).
Board of Directors: Lya Friedrich Pfeifer (Pres. and Treas.).
Contact Details: 6 E. 87th St, 5th Floor, New York, NY 10128-0505; tel. (646) 672-4354; internet www.maxkadefoundation.org.

MDA—Muscular Dystrophy Association

Founded in 1950 by business person Paul Cohen and a group of people affected by muscular dystrophy.

Activities: Invests in research on neuromuscular diseases and provides care and support for people living with such diseases and their families. The Association funds more than 150 research projects worldwide and operates a network of more than 150 Care Centers in hospitals and health centres in the USA and Puerto Rico. It provides medical equipment; organizes support groups, educational seminars and a children's summer camp; and maintains the Muscular Dystrophy Association Art Collection. In 2016 the National Resource Center was launched. Research grants and development grants are offered to advance basic science through discovery, translational and clinical research; create new therapies through researcher-initiated projects; and for infrastructure and conferences.
Geographical Area of Activity: Conducts research worldwide; services available only in the USA.
Restrictions: Grants to individual scientific investigators affiliated with academic institutions or qualified research facility.
Publications: Annual Report; *ALS Newsletter*; *Quest Magazine*; *MDA/ALS Newsmagazine*; factsheets.
Finance: Annual revenue US $60.4m., expenditure $66.0m. (31 Dec. 2024).
Board of Directors: Brad Henry (Chair.); Dr Christopher Rosa (Vice-Chair.).
Principal Staff: Pres. and CEO Dr Donald S. Wood.
Contact Details: 1016 W Jackson Blvd #1073, Chicago, IL 60607; tel. (800) 572-1717; e-mail resourcecenter@mdausa.org; internet www.mda.org.

Mercatus Center

Established in 1980; a university-based research centre.

Activities: Carries out research in the areas of: corporate welfare; financial markets; government spending; healthcare; monetary policy; regulation; technology and innovation; trade and immigration; and urban economics. The Center offers a range of fellowships for students from graduate to postdoctoral level. In 2018 the Emergent Ventures fellowship and grant programme was established with a US $1m. grant from the Thiel Foundation (q.v.) to fund 'moonshot' ideas for transformational social change.

Geographical Area of Activity: International.

Publications: Newsletter; books; policy briefings; research papers; *Marginal Revolution* (blog).

Finance: Annual income US $47.4m., expenditure $49.3m. (31 Aug. 2023).

Board: Dr Tyler Cowen (Chair.); Gary Leff (Treas.); Jennifer Zambone (Sec.).

Principal Staff: Exec. Dir Benjamin Klutsey.

Contact Details: George Mason University, 3434 Washington Blvd, 4th Floor, Arlington, VA 22201; tel. (703) 993-4930; e-mail mercatus@mercatus.gmu.edu; internet www.mercatus.org.

Mercy Corps

Founded in 1981 by Dan O'Neill and Ellsworth Culver, aid workers; merged with Scottish European Aid in 1996.

Activities: Works to help vulnerable people. Programmes cover: agriculture; cash and voucher assistance; climate, environment and energy; emergency response; financial inclusion; food security and nutrition; gender equality; governance; market development; peace and conflict; resilience; social ventures; technology; water, sanitation and hygiene; and youth. Works in more than 40 countries, with offices in Washington, DC, and in London (UK) and the Hague (Netherlands).

Geographical Area of Activity: International.

Publications: Annual Report; case studies; impact evaluations; reports; blog.

Finance: Annual revenue US $522.0m., expenditure $523.3m. (30 June 2023).

Board of Directors: Vijaya Gadde (Chair., Global); Ludovic Subran (Chair., Netherlands).

Principal Staff: CEO Tjada D'Oyen McKenna.

Contact Details: Dept. W, National Processing Center, POB 37800, Boone, IA 50037-4800; tel. (888) 842-0842; e-mail info@mercycorps.org; internet www.mercycorps.org.

Mercy For Animals—MFA

Established in 1999 by Nathan (Milo) Runkle.

Activities: Works to build a compassionate food system by reducing animals' suffering and their exploitation for food through enforcing legislation, regulations and corporate policies, and strengthening the animal protection movement. The organization carries out investigations to expose animal abuse in factory farms and slaughterhouses, working with policymakers and food companies to eliminate the worst industrial farming practices, protect animals, and promote plant- and cell-based foods. It supports and trains animal advocates, community leaders and undercover investigators; and helps farmers change from animal agriculture to growing crops through the Transfarmation Project. Has an office in Brazil.

Geographical Area of Activity: Asia, India, Latin America, North America.

Publications: Annual Report; *Compassionate Living* (magazine); Farmed Animal Opportunity Index (online); blog.

Finance: Annual income US $11.8m., expenditure $23.9m. (31 Dec. 2023).

Board: Neysa Colizzi (Chair.); Michael Pellman Rowland (Treas.).

Principal Staff: Pres. Leah Garcés.

Contact Details: 8033 Sunset Blvd, Suite 864, Los Angeles, CA 90046; tel. (866) 632-6446; e-mail info@mercyforanimals.org; internet mercyforanimals.org.

Mercy-USA for Aid and Development

Incorporated in 1988; an international relief and development organization.

Activities: Operates in the areas of aid to less-developed countries, education, medicine and health, and social welfare, through projects that include promoting economic and educational growth, disaster relief, reconstruction and rehabilitation, and international development projects. A partner organization operates in Canada.

Geographical Area of Activity: Albania, Bangladesh, Bosnia and Herzegovina, Ethiopia, Kenya, Lebanon, Pakistan, Palestinian Territories, Somalia, Türkiye (Turkey), USA, Yemen.

Restrictions: No grants are made to individuals.

Publications: Annual Report; *Mercy-USA* (newsletter).

Finance: Annual revenue US $54.1m., expenditure $57.0m. (31 Dec. 2023).

Board of Directors: Dr Ali El-Menshawi (Chair.); Samar Mady (Vice-Chair.); Othman Altalib (Treas.).

Principal Staff: Pres., CEO and Sec. Umar al-Qadi.

Contact Details: 44450 Pinetree Dr., Suite 201, Plymouth, MI 48170-3869; tel. (734) 454-0011; e-mail info@mercyusa.org; internet www.mercyusa.org.

Mertz Gilmore Foundation

Established in 1959, as the Mertz Foundation, by Joyce Mertz Gilmore and her parents, LuEsther and Harold, who founded Publishers Clearing House, a direct marketing company; present name adopted in 2002 in honour of Joyce's husband, Robert Gilmore.

Activities: Makes grants to non-profit organizations. Main programmes are: Climate Change Solutions, funding alternatives to coal, projects in New York City and new approaches to developing a national climate movement; Democratic Values; New York City Communities, funding community-based organizations, technical assistance providers and collaborative campaigns; and New York City Dance, funding presenters of small to medium-sized dance companies and improvements in conditions for individual dance artists.

Geographical Area of Activity: USA.

Restrictions: Does not make grants for individuals, sectarian religious concerns, conferences, film or media projects, endowments, publications or single-country projects.

Publications: Report (biennially); information brochure; grants list; staff departures.

Finance: Annual revenue US $10.8m., expenditure $16.8m. (31 Dec. 2022).

Board of Directors: Andrea Sholler (Chair.); Ciara Torres-Spelliscy (Vice-Chair.); Rini Banerjee (Treas.); Robin Krause (Sec.).

Principal Staff: Pres. Aditi Vaidya.

Contact Details: 218 East 18th St, New York, NY 10003-3694; tel. (212) 475-1137; e-mail info@mertzgilmore.org; internet www.mertzgilmore.org.

MFJC—Memorial Foundation for Jewish Culture

Founded in 1965 by Dr Nahum Goldmann, co-founder and President of the World Jewish Congress.

Activities: Encourages and assists Jewish scholarship and contributes to the preservation, enhancement and transmission of Jewish culture throughout the world. The Foundation awards scholarships to doctoral candidates pursuing degrees in areas of Jewish culture and fellowship grants to postdoctoral candidates. It also sponsors the Nahum Goldmann Fellowship Program, a week-long immersive Jewish communal leadership programme for people aged 25–40 years.

Geographical Area of Activity: Worldwide.

Publications: Newsletter.

Finance: Annual revenue US $1.9m., expenditure $1.5m. (30 Sept. 2021).

Principal Staff: Exec. Dir Rabbi Jennifer Friedman.

Contact Details: 45 Broadway, Suite 2350, New York, NY 10006; tel. (212) 425-6606; e-mail office@mfjc.org; internet www.mfjc.com.

Michael J. Fox Foundation for Parkinson's Research—MJFF

Established in 2000 by Michael J. Fox, an actor, and Deborah W. Brooks to find a cure for Parkinson's disease; merged with the Michael Stern Foundation in 2015.

Activities: Funds research to find a cure for Parkinson's disease and develop improved therapies for people living with the disease. The Foundation provides advice and information for patients, their families and medical practitioners; and makes tools available to researchers. It offers research grants for translational and clinical research and also high-risk/high-reward discovery work; and sponsors and awards prizes.

Geographical Area of Activity: Canada, USA.

Publications: Annual Report; *The Fox Focus on Parkinson's* (newsletter, 2 a year); clinician articles; study documents.

Finance: Annual revenue US $316.1m., expenditure $386.2m. (31 Dec. 2023).

Board of Directors: Andrew J. O'Brien (Chair.); Skip Irving (Vice-Chair.).

Principal Staff: CEO Deborah W. Brooks.

Contact Details: Grand Central Station, POB 4777, New York, NY 10163-4777; tel. (212) 509-0995; e-mail info@michaeljfox.org; internet www.michaeljfox.org.

Michael & Susan Dell Foundation

Established in 1999 by Michael Dell, founder of ICT company Dell Technologies, and his wife Susan.

Activities: Programmes focus on improving the lives of children living in urban poverty and their families through education, health and economic stability (including livelihoods and financial stability). The Foundation offers grants to social enterprises; and scholarships for undergraduates in South Africa and the USA. It has offices in New Delhi (India) and Cape Town (South Africa).

Geographical Area of Activity: India, South Africa, USA (Central Texas and Greater Boston).

Publications: Annual Report; newsletter.

Finance: Annual revenue US $143.2m., expenditure $183.6m. (31 Dec. 2022).

Board of Directors: Susan Dell (Chair.).

Principal Staff: Exec. Dir Janet Mountain.

Contact Details: 4417 Westlake Dr., Austin, TX 78746; POB 16387, Austin, TX 78716-3867; tel. (512) 600-5500; e-mail info@dell.org; internet www.dell.org.

Milbank Memorial Fund

Founded in 1905 by philanthropist Elizabeth Milbank Anderson.

Activities: The Milbank Memorial Fund is an endowed operating foundation that works to improve population health and health equity by collaborating with leaders and decision makers and connecting them with experience and sound evidence. The Fund advances its mission by identifying, informing, and inspiring current and future state and local health policy leaders to enhance their effectiveness as population health and health equity leaders; convening and supporting state health policy decision makers to advance progress in selected areas important to population health and health equity, including primary care and sustainable health care costs; and publishing evidence-based publications and The Milbank Quarterly, an editorially independent, peer-reviewed journal of population health and health policy.

Geographical Area of Activity: USA.

Publications: *The Milbank Quarterly*; reports; issue briefs; case studies; toolkits; blogs.

Finance: Annual revenue US $6.2m., expenditure $5.5m. (31 Dec. 2021).

Board of Directors: John M. Colmers (Chair.); Lashawn Richburg-Hayes (Vice-Chair.); Robert E. Harvey (Treas.).

Principal Staff: Pres. Christopher F. Koller.

Contact Details: 645 Madison Ave, 15th Floor, New York, NY 10022-1095; tel. (212) 355-8400; e-mail info@milbank.org; internet www.milbank.org.

MIUSA—Mobility International USA

Founded in 1981 by Susan Sygall and Barbara Williams, graduate students at the University of Oregon; a disability-led non-profit organization.

Activities: Works to advance the human rights of people with disabilities through international exchanges and international development. Programmes include: advocacy; coalition building; bridging communities; inclusive education and employment; training and technical assistance; capacity building for disability organizations; leadership training for women and girls; inclusive recreation and adaptive sports; developing higher education courses on inclusive development; and accessibility guidance. The organization manages the National Clearinghouse on Disability and Exchange, a project of the Bureau of Educational and Cultural Affairs in the US Department of State which aims to increase participation by people with disabilities in international exchanges between the USA and other countries.

Geographical Area of Activity: Worldwide.

Publications: *A World Awaits You* (magazine); newsletter; manuals; guides.

Finance: Annual revenue US $1.7m., expenditure $1.9m. (31 Dec. 2022).

Principal Staff: CEO Susan Sygall.

Contact Details: 132 E. Broadway, Suite 343, Eugene, OR 97401; tel. (541) 343-1284; e-mail clearinghouse@miusa.org; internet www.miusa.org.

Morehead-Cain Foundation

Established in 1945 as the John Motley Morehead Foundation by John Motley Morehead, III, a chemist; renamed in 2007 following a US $100m. grant from the Gordon and Mary Cain Foundation.

Activities: Awards merit scholarships for undergraduate study at the University of North Carolina at Chapel Hill (UNC-CH). In addition to covering the full cost of attending UNC-CH, the scholarship includes four summer enrichment programmes across the country and around the world. Morehead-Cain Scholars are selected from North Carolina high schools, British and Canadian secondary schools, and selected high schools across the USA. Certain international secondary schools may also nominate candidates.

Geographical Area of Activity: International.

Restrictions: Scholarships only for undergraduate study at the University of North Carolina at Chapel Hill.

Publications: Annual Report; electronic newsletters; online resources for scholars, prospective scholars and program alumni.

Finance: Annual revenue US $9.5m., expenditure $14.8m. (30 June 2022).

Board of Trustees: Tim Sullivan (Chair.); Walker Poole (Vice-Chair.).

Principal Staff: Pres. Chris Bradford.

Contact Details: POB 690, Chapel Hill, NC 27514-0690; tel. (919) 962-1201; e-mail info@moreheadcain.org; internet www.moreheadcain.org.

Morgan Stanley Foundation

Established in 1963 by Morgan Stanley, an investment bank.

Activities: Operates nationally through Community Affairs grants and programmes; and nationally and internationally, through the Morgan Stanley Global Alliance for Children's Health. The Foundation provides scholarships to university students from minorities through the Richard B. Fisher Scholarship programme. Affiliated with the Morgan Stanley International Foundation (f. 1994), which operates in Europe, the Middle East and Africa.

Geographical Area of Activity: International.

Restrictions: Community Affairs grants are mainly limited to charities based in the USA for national initiatives and those serving multiple cities across the USA; no grants to individuals, political causes, religious or sports organizations or for special events or performances.

Finance: Annual revenue US $7.6m., expenditure $4.4m. (31 Dec. 2022).

Board: James P. Gorman (Exec. Chair.).

Principal Staff: Pres. Joan Steinberg.

Contact Details: Morgan Stanley Community Affairs, 1585 Broadway, 23rd Floor, New York, NY 10036; tel. (212) 296-3600; e-mail whatadifference@morganstanley.com; internet www.morganstanley.com/about-us/giving-back.

Morningside Foundation

Established in 1997 by Dr Gerald Chan, Chair. and CEO of Morningside Group, and Ronnie C. Chan, Chair. of Huang Lung Group, founder of the China Heritage Fund and Centre for Asian Philanthropy and Society, and co-founder of the Forbidden City Cultural Heritage Conservation Foundation; the charitable arm of the Morningside Group, a private equity and venture capital firm.

Activities: Funds activities in the fields of education, medical research, classical music and architectural conservation. The Foundation supports non-profit organizations in the USA and charities in the People's Republic of China; offers scholarships to disadvantaged students at Chinese universities; and supports the Morningside Scholars programme at Zhejiang University. It established the Morningside Center of Mathematics (f. 1996) in Beijing and Morningside College (f. 2010) at the Chinese University of Hong Kong; funded the establishment of the Morningside Center for Innovative and Affordable Medicine (f. 2019) at Emory University, promoting research into cost-effective treatments for cancer and other diseases; and has endowed the Locarnini-Morningside Fellowship in Virology at the University of Melbourne and professorships in the USA. Morningside Music Bridge (f. 1996) offers summer masterclasses at the New England Conservatory in Boston, MA, to young classical musicians. Has offices in Monaco and Hong Kong.

Geographical Area of Activity: Australia, People's Repub. of China, Hong Kong, Monaco, USA.

Finance: Annual revenue US $64.3m., expenditure $61.5m. (2023).

Principal Staff: Pres. Ronnie Chan.

Contact Details: 1188 Centre St, Newton Centre, MA 02459; tel. (617) 244-2800; e-mail enquiries@morningside.com; internet morningside.com/philanthropy.

Motorola Solutions Foundation

Established in 1953 by Motorola Solutions, a communication and electronics company.

Activities: Offers grants and carries out activities in the areas of education, with a focus on engineering and information technology; public safety education and professional development for first responders; disaster relief, working with international humanitarian organizations; and employee volunteering and gift matching. The Foundation helps local communities where the company is present and is affiliated with more than 170 organizations in 21 countries. It awards grants to organizations of up to US $50,000 and scholarships for young people.

Geographical Area of Activity: International.

Publications: Info sheets.

Finance: Annual revenue US $12.7m., expenditure $12.4m. (31 Dec. 2022).

Board: Gino Bonanotte (Pres. and Treas.); Deborah J. McMillan (Sec.).

Principal Staff: Exec. Dir Karem Perez.

Contact Details: 500 W. Monroe St, 43rd Floor, Chicago, IL 60661; tel. (847) 576-7895; e-mail foundation@motorolasolutions.com; internet www.motorolasolutions.com/en_us/about/motorola-solutions-foundation.html.

Ms. Foundation for Women

Founded in 1973 by Patricia Carbine, Letty Cottin-Pogrebin, Gloria Steinem, Marlo Thomas and Marie C. Wilson.

Activities: Operates in three project areas: women's health, including reproductive rights; safety, safeguarding women and children from sexual and gender-based violence; and economic justice, including affordable childcare and good-quality jobs. The Foundation conducts advocacy and public education campaigns, provides technical assistance, and directs resources to organizations operating in these project areas. In 1992 it established Take Our Daughters To Work Day (expanded to include boys in 2003).

Geographical Area of Activity: USA.

Restrictions: Grants only to non-profit organizations registered in the USA; does not fund individuals, scholarships, capital or endowment requests, fundraising events, university-based research or government agencies; does not accept unsolicited applications.

Publications: Annual Report; newsletter; handbooks; reports.

Finance: Annual revenue US $14.1m., expenditure $12.2m. (30 June 2022).

Board of Directors: Charline Gipson (Chair.); Diane M. Manuel (Treas.); James White (Sec.).

Principal Staff: Pres. and CEO Teresa C. Younger; Deputy CEO Ruth McFarlane.

Contact Details: 1 Willoughby Sq., Suite 2000, Brooklyn, NY 11201; tel. (212) 742-2300; e-mail info@ms.foundation.org; internet forwomen.org.

Musk Foundation

Established in 2001 by Elon Musk, founder and CEO of SpaceX, a space exploration technologies company, and CEO of Tesla, a manufacturer of electric vehicles and batteries.

Activities: Makes grants in the areas of: research and advocacy in renewable energy and human space exploration; paediatric research; science and engineering education; and artificial intelligence. The Foundation also supports post-disaster recovery.

Geographical Area of Activity: International.

Finance: Total assets US $9,400m. (2021).

Principal Staff: Pres. Elon Musk; Treas. and Sec. Kimbal Musk.

Contact Details: POB 341886, Austin, TX 78734; tel. (737) 235-6956; internet www.muskfoundation.org.

NAACP Legal Defense and Educational Fund, Inc—LDF

Established in 1940 by Thurgood Marshall, a lawyer and civil rights activist, as the legal arm of the US civil rights movement; became independent from the National Association for the Advancement of Colored People (NAACP) in 1957.

Activities: Works for racial justice in the USA through litigation, advocacy and public education in the areas of capital punishment, criminal justice, education, fair employment, poverty and voting rights; and supports international human rights campaigns. It offers fellowships, scholarships and internships; and in 2021 launched the US $40m. Marshall-Motley Scholars Program (MMSP) to support and develop civil rights lawyers in the South of the USA. Has an office in Washington, DC; and incorporates the Thurgood Marshall Institute (f. 2015), a multidisciplinary research and advocacy centre.

Geographical Area of Activity: USA.

Restrictions: MMSP scholarship applicants must be eligible to work in the USA and commit to working in civil rights law in a Southern US state for eight years.

Publications: Annual Report; Issue Reports; factsheets; brochures; flyers.

Finance: Annual revenue US $83.8m., expenditure $48.7m. (30 June 2022).

National Officers: Kim Koopersmith, Angela Vallot (Co-Chair.); James Castillo (Treas.); Steven B. Pfeiffer (Sec.).

Principal Staff: Pres. and Dir-Counsel Janai Nelson.

Contact Details: 40 Rector St, 5th Floor, New York, NY 10006; tel. (212) 965-2200; internet www.naacpldf.org.

National Fish and Wildlife Foundation—NFWF

Chartered in 1984 by US Congress.

Activities: NFWF is dedicated to sustaining, restoring, and enhancing the nation's fish, wildlife, plants and habitats for current and future generations. The Foundation operates nationally and internationally, but with a strong focus on the USA, through matching grant and special grant programmes.

Geographical Area of Activity: Mainly USA.

Restrictions: Does not fund lobbying, political activism or litigation.

Publications: Annual Report.

Finance: Annual revenue US $386.3m., expenditure $374.0m. (30 Sept. 2022).

Board of Directors: Jennifer Mull Neuhaus (Chair.); Patsy Ishiyama, John A. Tomke (Vice-Chair.).

Principal Staff: Exec. Dir and CEO Jeffrey Trandahl.

Contact Details: 1625 Eye Street NW, Suite 300, Washington, DC 20006; tel. (202) 857-0166; e-mail info@nfwf.org; internet www.nfwf.org.

National Geographic Society

Established in 1888; a non-profit organization.

Activities: Supports research, exploration and conservation through making grants for projects in the areas of science, technology, education and storytelling. The Society offers Early Career Grants (worth US $5,000–$10,000), Exploration Grants ($10,000–$30,000) and Requests for Proposals; Fellowships, worth up to $170,000; and runs an Innovation Challenge competition, with a prize purse of $390,000. It offers professional development programmes and classroom resources for school educators through digital resources and online networks. Has regional offices in the Asia-Pacific region, East Africa, Europe and Latin America; and operates the National Geographic Museum in Washington, DC.

Geographical Area of Activity: International.

Publications: Impact Report (annual); newsletter; *National Geographic* (monthly magazine); *Explorer Magazine* (monthly); blog.

Finance: Annual revenue US $157.6m., expenditure $188.9m. (31 Dec. 2022).

Board of Trustees: Jean M. Case (Chair.); Katherine Bradley, Kevin J. Maroni (Vice-Chair.).

Principal Staff: CEO Jill Tiefenthaler.

Contact Details: 1145 17th St NW, Washington, DC 20036; tel. (202) 857-7000; internet www.nationalgeographic.org.

National Humanities Center—NHC

Established in 1978 by the American Academy of Arts and Sciences to foster the influence of the humanities in the USA.

Activities: Operates in the field of humanities research and education. The Center awards up to 40 fellowships annually for mid-career and senior scholars in the humanities, including history, philosophy, languages, literature, classics, religion, history of art, etc. Fellowships are open to scholars of any nationality for study in the USA. It offers online resources as part of its education programme along with interactive webinars, online courses, and other professional development experiences. The Center also hosts public events and implements a variety of pubilc initiatives to raise awareness and appreciation for the humanities and humanities scholarship.

Geographical Area of Activity: USA.

Restrictions: Grants only for study in the USA.

Publications: Annual Report; *News of the National Humanities Center* (newsletter); conference reports; occasional papers; online resources.

Finance: Annual revenue US $5.9m., expenditure $6.8m. (30 June 2023).

Trustees: Rishi Jaitly (Chair.); Raymond J. Wiacek (Treas.); Karen R. Lawrence (Sec.).

Principal Staff: Interim Pres. and Dir J. Porter Durham.

Contact Details: 7 T. W. Alexander Dr., POB 12256, Research Triangle Park, NC 27709-2256; tel. (919) 549-0661; e-mail info@nationalhumanitiescenter.org; internet nationalhumanities center.org.

National Kidney Foundation—NKF

Established in 1950, as the National Nephrosis Foundation, by Ada and Harry DeBold, whose son had nephrosis (kidney disease); present name adopted in 1964.

Activities: Supports those at risk of and diagnosed with chronic kidney disease through education, programmes and support services. The Foundation develops accredited medical education programmes and clinical decisionmaking materials for healthcare professionals. It also awards grants for nephrology research, including clinical scientist grants and young investigator grants; a Research Award Committee reviews applications and selects awardees on an annual basis.

Geographical Area of Activity: USA.

Restrictions: Grants only for study in the USA.

Publications: Annual Report; newsletters; journals; *NKF Blog*.

Finance: Annual revenue US $45.8m., expenditure $46.6m. (31 March 2023).

Board of Directors: Anne Davidson Barr (Chair.); Tracy McKibben (Immediate Past Chair.); Dr Kirk Campbell (Pres.); Sylvia Rosas (Immediate Past Pres.); Michele Estrella (Pres.-elect); Art P. Pasquarella (Chancellor).

Principal Staff: CEO Kevin Longino.

Contact Details: 30 East 33rd St, New York, NY 10016; tel. (800) 622-9010; e-mail info@kidney.org; internet www.kidney.org.

National Park Foundation

Established in 1967 by Congressional Charter of the US Congress to support the National Park Service (f. 1916).

Activities: Supports national parks in the USA. The Foundation raises and allocates funds; and promotes programmes and projects that protect landscapes and wilderness and places of historic and cultural significance, and encourage healthy lifestyles.

Geographical Area of Activity: USA.

Restrictions: Provides support to US National Parks only.

Publications: Annual Report; newsletter.

Finance: Annual revenue US $184.5m., expenditure $162.1m. (30 Sept. 2023).

Board of Directors: Rhoda L. Altom (Chair.); Richard P. Malloch (Treas.); Charles F. Sams, III (Sec.).

National Council: Linda Fisher, Randi Fisher, David Marchick (Co-Chair.).

Principal Staff: Pres. and CEO Will Shafroth.

Contact Details: 1500 K St NW, Suite 700, Washington, DC 20005; tel. (202) 796-2500; e-mail parkpartners@nationalparks.org; internet www.nationalparks.org.

National Science Foundation—NSF

Established in 1950 as an independent US government agency.

Activities: Funds research in the areas of: biological sciences; computers; information science and computer engineering; education; engineering; environmental research; geosciences; mathematics; physical sciences; polar research;

and social, behavioural and economic sciences. The Foundation funds co-operative research between US scientists and those in other countries; supporting around 200,000 scientists, engineers, educators and students at universities, laboratories and field sites each year.

Geographical Area of Activity: International.

Publications: *Budget Request to Congress*; reports; surveys; statistics; toolkits.

Finance: Total assets US $19,978.5m.; net cost of operations $9,432.5m. (30 Sept. 2024).

National Science Board: Dr Dan Reid (Chair.); Dr Victor McCrary (Vice-Chair.).

Principal Staff: Dir Dr Sethuraman Panchanathan.

Contact Details: 2415 Eisenhower Ave, Alexandria, VA 22314; tel. (703) 292-5111; e-mail info@nsf.gov; internet www.nsf.gov.

National Wildlife Federation—NWF

Established in 1936, as the General Wildlife Federation, by J. N. 'Ding' Darling, a cartoonist; present name adopted in 1938.

Activities: Works in the field of habitat protection, restoration and management. The Federation's activities include hands-on programmes, policy work and community outreach. It runs educational programmes and provides internships for students and recent graduates; and offers EcoLeader Fellowships to graduate students working on research with Federation staff to expand the EcoLeaders programme, an online community of conservation leaders, comprising pre-college young leaders, college students and young professionals. Has 52 state and territory affiliates.

Geographical Area of Activity: USA.

Publications: Annual Report; e-newsletter; *National Wildlife* (6 a year); reports; case studies.

Finance: Annual revenue US $124.9m., expenditure $126.6m. (31 Aug. 2023).

Board of Directors: John Robbins (Chair.); Bill Houston (Past Chair.); Frederick Kowal (Chair.-elect).

Principal Staff: Pres. and CEO Collin O'Mara.

Contact Details: 11100 Wildlife Center Dr., Reston, VA 20190-5362; POB 1583, Merrifield VA 22116-1583; tel. (703) 438-6000; e-mail info@nwf.org; internet www.nwf.org.

The Nature Conservancy—TNC

Established in 1946 as the Ecologists Union by a small group of scientists; present name adopted in 1950 and officially incorporated as an NGO in 1951.

Activities: Works in the field of international conservation with governments, businesses, landowners and local people to save and preserve land, including forests, aquatic areas, prairies and deserts, and the communities that live there. Programme areas include: climate change; protecting land and water; food and water sustainability; and building healthy cities. Operates in more than 80 countries.

Geographical Area of Activity: Asia and the Pacific, Australia, Europe, India, North, Central and South America and the Caribbean, sub-Saharan Africa, USA.

Publications: Annual Report; *Nature Conservancy* (magazine); e-newsletter; reports.

Finance: Annual revenue US $1,346.0m., expenditure $1,274.3m. (30 June 2023).

Board of Directors: Dr William Frist (Chair.); Amy Batchelor (Vice-Chair.); Sally Jewell (Treas.); Shirley Ann Jackson (Sec.).

Principal Staff: CEO Jennifer Morris.

Contact Details: 4245 North Fairfax Dr., Suite 100, Arlington, VA 22203-1606; tel. (703) 841-5300; e-mail member@tnc.org; internet www.nature.org.

NDI—National Democratic Institute for International Affairs

Created as part of the 1984 statute that set up the National Endowment for Democracy; affiliated to the US Democratic Party and established as an independent organization to expand and strengthen democracy worldwide.

Activities: Provides practical assistance and training to civic and political leaders advancing democratic values, practices and institutions. Programmes focus on: citizen participation; civil-military relations; election and political processes; democratic governance; political party development and women's participation. The Institute has more than 50 field offices.

Geographical Area of Activity: International.

Restrictions: Not a grantmaking organization.

Publications: NDI brochure; *NDI Reports: A review of political developments in new democracies* (newsletter); *DemTools* (digital tools); manuals; reports; toolkits.

Finance: Annual revenue US $141m., expenditure $139m. (30 Sept. 2022).

Board of Directors: Thomas A. Daschle (Chair.); Madeleine K. Albright (Immediate Past Chair.); Harriet C. Babbitt (Vice-Chair.); Robert G. Liberatore (Treas.); Frank M. Conner, III (Sec.).

Principal Staff: Pres. Tamara Wittes.

Contact Details: 455 Massachusetts Ave, NW, 8th Floor, Washington, DC 20001-2621; tel. (202) 728-5500; e-mail info@ndi.org; internet www.ndi.org.

NEF—Near East Foundation

Founded in 1915 as the American Committee for Syrian and Armenian Relief, responding to the massive humanitarian crisis that followed the dissolution of the Ottoman Empire.

Activities: Works to build sustainable, prosperous and inclusive communities in the Middle East and Africa through education, community organizing and economic development. Main programme areas include: agriculture and natural resource management, helping smallholder farmers and communities that rely on natural resources to improve food security and incomes; peacebuilding through economic co-operation and development, promoting conflict mitigation and reconciliation through poverty reduction and sustainable development; women's microenterprise development, helping women to overcome social barriers and develop skills; and youth civic engagement, investing in underserved young people. The Foundation is affiliated with Syracuse University, offering internships and NEF fellowships to recent graduates. It shares technical and management capabilities with NEF UK (f. 2012) and NEF Belgium (f. 2019), which are independent organizations. Has offices in Belgium, the UK and Washington, DC.

Geographical Area of Activity: Armenia, Iraq, Jordan, Lebanon, Mali, Morocco, Palestinian Territories, Sudan, Syrian Arab Repub.

Publications: Annual Report; *Near East Relief Digital Museum* (online resource); case studies; country reviews; factsheets; literature reviews; program briefs; toolkits; training manuals; working papers.

Finance: Annual revenue US $20.5m., expenditure $19.2m. (30 June 2023).

Board of Directors: Nina Bogosian Quigley (Chair.); Emily Rosenberg (Vice-Chair.); Mona Eraiba (Treas.).

Principal Staff: CEO John Ashby.

Contact Details: 110 W. Fayette St, Suite 710, Syracuse, NY 13202; tel. (315) 428-8670; e-mail info@neareast.org; internet www.neareast.org.

New World Foundation—NWF

Founded in 1954 by Anita McCormick Blaine, a supporter of civil rights and unionization.

Activities: Promotes inclusive democracy through environmental safety, economic equality, immigrants' rights, access to education and democratic participation. The Foundation

strengthens community-based organizations and local leadership, offering: general support grants; regional and cluster grants; technical assistance for capacity development; small discretionary grants; inquiry grants for new work and to develop long-term sustainability; and special project grants.
Geographical Area of Activity: Worldwide.
Restrictions: No grants to individuals; does not accept unsolicited applications.
Publications: Biennial Report; articles; books; reports.
Finance: Annual revenue US $12.5m., expenditure $16.1m. (30 Sept. 2022).
Board of Directors: Fred Azcarate (Chair.); Jonathan Glionna (Vice-Chair.); Linda Colon (Treas.); Cynthia Choi (Sec.).
Principal Staff: Pres. Dr Colin Greer.
Contact Details: 627 West End Ave, New York, NY 10024; tel. (212) 249-1023; e-mail reception@newwf.org; internet www.newwf.org.

The New York Community Trust—NYCT
Established in 1924; comprises the New York Company Trust, an association of charitable trusts, and Community Funds, Inc, a non-profit corpn.
Activities: Administers more than 2,000 charitable funds. The Trust makes grants to organizations through three programmes: Thriving Communities, supporting affordable housing, equity in the arts, civic engagement and the environment; Promising Futures, helping young people, providing job training and placements, alleviating hunger and homelessness, and improving family and child welfare services; and Healthy Lives, providing efficient, cost-effective healthcare services. It focuses its grantmaking within New York City and has two divisions: the Westchester Community Foundation and the Long Island Community Foundation.
Geographical Area of Activity: New York City.
Restrictions: Scholarships by invitation only.
Publications: Annual Report; newsletter; biographical brochures; guidelines and planning notes.
Finance: Annual revenue US $528.1m., expenditure $216.2m. (31 Dec. 2023).
Board of Directors: Jamie Drake (Chair.).
Principal Staff: Pres. Amy Freitag.
Contact Details: 909 Third Ave (between 54th and 55th Sts), 22nd Floor, New York, NY 10022; tel. (212) 686-0010; e-mail info@thenytrust.org; internet thenytrust.org.

Newberry Library
Founded in 1887 at the bequest of Walter Loomis Newberry, a business person and former President of the Galena and Chicago Union Railroad; an independent research library, which includes the division of Research and Education.
Activities: Promotes the effective use of its collections for research, teaching and publication; the collections contain more than 1.5m. books, 5m. manuscript pages and 600,000 historic maps on the civilizations of Europe and the Americas. The Newberry offers long- and short-term research fellowships for scholars, of 4–9 months' and 1–2 months' duration, artist-in-residence fellowships, and publication subventions; and short-term fellowships to graduate students and scholars, lasting one month, with a stipend of US $3,000. It organizes a Scholarly Seminars series and Summer Seminars and Institutes programme; and provides professional development for teachers. Three research centres—the Center for Renaissance Studies Programs, D'Arcy McNickle Center for American Indian and Indigenous Studies and the Hermon Dunlap Smith Center for the History of Cartography—sponsor consortia, seminars and other programmes, collaborating with scholars from around the world.
Geographical Area of Activity: International.
Publications: Annual Report; *The Newberry Magazine*; *Newberry Blogs*; catalogues; guides; research guides.
Finance: Annual revenue US $14.6m., expenditure $13.8m. (30 June 2023).
Board of Trustees: Robert A. Holland (Chair.); Lisa J. Pattis (Vice-Chair.); David B. Smith, Jr (Treas.); Nancy Spain, (Sec.).
Principal Staff: Pres. and Librarian Astrida Tantillo.
Contact Details: 60 West Walton St, Chicago, IL 60610; tel. (312) 943-9090; e-mail research@newberry.org; internet www.newberry.org.

NFCR—National Foundation for Cancer Research
Founded in 1973 by Nobel Prize winner Albert Szent-Györgyi to provide seed funding for basic scientific research towards the better understanding of and cures for cancer.
Activities: Funds cancer research laboratories in a variety of scientific disciplines. The Foundation holds conferences and symposia; and awards the annual Szent-Györgyi Prize for Progress in Cancer Research, worth US $30,000, to a researcher who has made an outstanding contribution in the field of cancer research. It has provided more than $420m. for basic cancer research science and education.
Geographical Area of Activity: Asia-Pacific, Canada, Europe, USA.
Publications: Annual Report; *Research for a Cure* (newsletter); e-newsletter.
Finance: Annual revenue US $9.8m., expenditure $9.7m. (31 Dec. 2023).
Board of Directors: Dr Alfred Slanetz (Chair.).
Principal Staff: Pres. and CEO Dr Sujuan Ba; CFO and Sec. Kwok Leung.
Contact Details: 5515 Security Lane, Suite 1105, Rockville, MD 20852; tel. (800) 321-2873; e-mail info@nfcr.org; internet www.nfcr.org.

Nonprofit Enterprise and Self-sustainability Team—NESsT
Founded in 1997 in Hungary by Lee Davis, a social entrepreneur, and Nicole Etchart, an international development professional.
Activities: Works to eliminate poverty and provide dignified work through investing in social enterprises in emerging markets. The organization provides social entrepreneurs with financing, through grants, capital and loans; and business development support. It has offices in Brazil, Chile, Hungary, Peru, Poland and Romania and an affiliate in the United Kingdom.
Geographical Area of Activity: Brazil, Chile, Colombia, Ecuador, Peru, Poland, Romania, UK, USA.
Restrictions: Only supports social enterprises in Central and Eastern Europe and Latin America.
Publications: Annual Report; newsletter; *Learning Series*; case studies; legal guides; online tools; blog.
Finance: Annual revenue US $5.7m., expenditure $3.8m. (31 Dec. 2023).
International Board: Lord Davies of Abersoch (Chair.).
Principal Staff: CEO Kirsten Dueck.
Contact Details: 5917 Jordan Ave, El Cerrito, CA 94530; tel. (503) 704-9195; e-mail nesst@nesst.org; internet www.nesst.org.

Novartis US Foundation
Established in 1997 by Novartis Corporation, a global healthcare company.
Activities: Works to improve the health of underserved communities. Main programmes are: building health system capacity, improving access to healthcare using digital and innovative solutions, and supporting a diverse healthcare workforce; and supporting local communities, improving social determinants of health, supporting access to higher education and ensuring preparedness for disaster response. The Foundation offers grants and scholarships.
Geographical Area of Activity: USA.

NoVo Foundation UNITED STATES OF AMERICA

Restrictions: Grants only to non-profit organizations in the USA; does not accept unsolicited applications.
Finance: Annual revenue US $11.7m., expenditure $6.8m. (31 Dec. 2022).
Board of Trustees: Tom Kendris (Chair.).
Principal Staff: Pres. Patrice Matchaba.
Contact Details: 1 Health Plaza, East Hanover, NJ 07936-1080; tel. (862) 778-8300; e-mail uscorporate.responsibility@novartis.com; internet www.novartis.com/us-en/esg/corporate-responsibility/novartis-us-foundation.

NoVo Foundation

Established in 2006 by Peter Buffet, a musician, and his wife Jennifer.
Activities: Promotes social justice based on mutual respect, collaboration and civic participation. The Foundation funds projects in the areas of: adolescent girls' rights; ending violence against girls and women; social and emotional learning; supporting indigenous communities in North America; and thriving local economies.
Geographical Area of Activity: International.
Restrictions: Does not accept unsolicited applications.
Finance: Annual revenue US $332.6m., expenditure $273.2m. (31 Dec. 2022).
Principal Staff: Co-Pres Jennifer Buffet, Peter Buffet.
Contact Details: 43 Crown St, POB 3971, Kingston, NY 12401; tel. (212) 808-5400; e-mail info@novofoundation.org; internet novofoundation.org.

NOW Foundation

Established in 1986; an education and litigation organization allied with the National Organization for Women—NOW (f. 1966).
Activities: Operates in the field of women's rights. The Foundation runs projects in areas including: economic justice; pay equity; racial discrimination; women's health and body image; women with disabilities; reproductive rights and justice; family law; marriage and family formation rights of same-sex couples; representation of women in the media; global feminist issues; and voter mobilization. It organizes conferences, seminars and training programmes; and issues educational materials. Has more than 600 local chapters.
Geographical Area of Activity: Worldwide.
Publications: Annual Report.
Finance: Annual revenue US $2.3m., expenditure $1.7m. (31 Dec. 2022).
Board of Directors: Christian F. Nunes (Pres.); Bear Atwood (Vice-Pres.).
Contact Details: 1100 H St NW, Washington, DC 20005; tel. (202) 628-8669; internet now.org/now-foundation.

The Ocean Foundation

Established in 2002 as the Coral Reef Foundation; a community foundation.
Activities: The foundation's mission is to improve global ocean health, climate resilience, and the blue economy. Creates partnerships to connect communities to the informational, technical, and financial resources needed to achieve their ocean stewardship goals. Distributes grants, donations, and other funds to projects that will directly benefit coastal communities and restore ocean health and abundance. Since 2002 the Foundation has raised US $114m. for ocean projects. The Foundation also offers services to organizations, including fiscal sponsorship and advised funds hosting, and carries out consultancies and research.
Geographical Area of Activity: International.
Restrictions: Does not accept unsolicited applications.
Publications: Annual Report; newsletter; *Seven Seas Magazine*.
Finance: Annual revenue US $18.9m., expenditure $18.8m. (30 June 2024).
Board of Directors: Dr Joshua Ginsberg (Chair.); Tom Brigandi (Treas.); Russell Smith (Sec.).
Principal Staff: Pres. Mark J. Spalding.
Contact Details: 1320 19th St, NW, Suite 401, Washington, DC 20036; tel. (202) 887-8996; e-mail info@oceanfdn.org; internet oceanfdn.org.

Omidyar Group

Established in 2010 by Pam Omidyar and Pierre Omidyar, the founder of e-commerce platform eBay and the eBay Foundation (q.v.).
Activities: Promotes courageous leadership, good governance, informed and engaged citizens, and thriving communities. The Group comprises: the Democracy Fund (f. 2014), strengthening democracy in the USA; Hopelab (f. 2001), designing science-based technologies to improve young people's health and wellbeing; Humanity United (q.v.), supporting efforts to eliminate human trafficking, mass atrocities and violent conflict; Omidyar Network (q.v.), investing in innovative for-profit companies and non-profit organizations; Luminate (f. 2018), working in the fields of civic empowerment, data and digital rights, financial transparency and independent media; First Look Media (f. 2013), a for-profit investigative media company, which comprises the Press Freedom Defense Fund; and impact investment firms, including Ulupono Initiative (f. 2009), improving the quality of life in Hawaii, Flourish (f. 2019), investing in financial technology entrepreneurs, and Imaginable Futures (f. 2020), investing in education internationally.
Geographical Area of Activity: International.
Restrictions: Does not accept unsolicited applications.
Principal Staff: Man. Dir Pat Christen.
Contact Details: 1991 Broadway St, Suite 200, Redwood City, CA 94063; tel. (650) 364-8801; e-mail info@omidyargroup.com; internet www.omidyargroup.com.

Omidyar Network Fund

Established in 2004 by Pam Omidyar and Pierre Omidyar, the founder of e-commerce platform eBay; part of the Omidyar Group (q.v.).
Activities: Works to bring about social change through structural and systemic change. Main programmes are: Responsible Technology, ensuring that technological innovation promotes wellbeing and individual liberty, while safeguarding against risks and unintended consequences; Reimagining Capitalism, addressing economic, racial, and geographic inequities; and Pluralism, creating a more open society that empowers diversity. Omidyar Network also operates a separate limited liability company (LLC) which invests in for-profit companies. The Fund has offices in Washington, DC, South Africa and the United Kingdom; a sister organization, Omidyar Network India (f. 2009), is based in Mumbai, with an office in Bengaluru.
Geographical Area of Activity: Worldwide.
Restrictions: Does not accept unsolicited applications.
Finance: Annual revenue US $25.2m., expenditure $30.5m. (31 Dec. 2022).
Board of Trustees: Pat Christen (Chair.).
Principal Staff: CEO Mike Kubzansky.
Contact Details: 1991 Broadway St, Suite 200, Redwood City, CA 94063; tel. (650) 482-2500; e-mail info@omidyar.com; internet www.omidyar.com.

Open Society Action Fund

Established in 1997 as the Research and Policy Reform Center, renamed Open Society Policy Center in 2002; an independent foundation, part of the Open Society Foundations (q.v.) network.

UNITED STATES OF AMERICA

Activities: Works to influence US government policy on domestic and international issues. Programmes focus on: promoting open societies; courts and elections; criminal justice reform and racial equality; immigration; international human rights and overseas aid; public health; transparency and accountability; and US national security and human rights. The Center offers grants to support policy advocacy and provide organizational support.
Geographical Area of Activity: International.
Publications: *OSPC Summary of Lobbying Activities*.
Finance: Annual revenue US $240.0m., expenditure $205.5m. (2022).
Board of Directors: Maija Arbolino (Treas.); Debbie Fine (Sec.).
Principal Staff: Exec. Dir Laleh Ispahani.
Contact Details: 1730 Pennsylvania Ave, NW, 7th Floor, Washington, DC 20006; tel. (202) 721-5600; internet opensocietyactionfund.org.

Open Society Foundations

Founded in 1993 by George Soros as the Open Society Institute; an international grantmaking network; present name adopted in 2011.
Activities: Works to strengthen the rule of law; respect for human rights, minorities and a diversity of opinions; democratically elected governments; and an empowered civil society. Main programme areas include: culture and the arts; economic justice; education and higher education; global drug policy; information; international migration; journalism; public health; and women's rights. The organization works through conducting in-depth research into the thematic and geographic areas of its work; making grants to organizations; advocacy; litigation; educational initiatives; issuing publications; organizing conferences; and offering fellowships and university scholarships. In 2008 it established the Open Society Fellowship, for research on economic inequality; and in 2016 the Leadership in Government Fellowship Program, to support former senior-level government staff in the USA who have significantly advanced social change from within government. Present in more than 120 countries.
Geographical Area of Activity: Africa, Asia-Pacific, Eurasia, Europe, Latin America and the Caribbean, Middle East, North Africa, South-West Asia, USA.
Restrictions: Fellowships for individuals only; grants mainly to organizations, by direct invitation.
Publications: Annual Report; *Open Society News* (quarterly newsletter); leaflets, articles and other publications.
Finance: Annual expenditure US $1,700m. (2023).
Global Board: Alexander Soros (Chair.).
Principal Staff: Pres. Binaifer Nowrojee.
Contact Details: 224 West 57th St, New York, NY 10019; tel. (212) 548-0600; e-mail contact@opensocietyfoundations.org; internet www.opensocietyfoundations.org.

Operation USA

Established in 1979 as Operation California, to provide emergency relief to people in South-East Asia.
Activities: Works to mitigate the effects of poverty and the results of natural and human-made disasters in the USA and abroad, with a focus on education and health. The organization provides emergency medical, nutritional and shelter supplies to victims of poverty and disaster. It also builds schools and libraries; supports long-term projects to provide education, healthcare and advocacy; and promotes sustainable development, income-generating activities and leadership building.
Geographical Area of Activity: International.
Publications: Annual Report.
Finance: Annual revenue US $2.8m., expenditure $3.0m. (30 June 2024).
Board of Directors: Michael Mahdesian (Chair.); Bob L. Johnson, Gary Larsen (Co-Treas.).
Principal Staff: Pres. and CEO Richard M. Walden.
Contact Details: 7421 Beverly Blvd, Los Angeles, CA 90036; tel. (323) 413-2353; e-mail info@opusa.org; internet www.opusa.org.

Oprah Winfrey Leadership Academy Foundation—OWLAF

Established in 2007 by Oprah Winfrey, a talk show host and founder of Harpo Productions, a multimedia production company, and the Oprah Winfrey Network, a television network; separate from the Oprah Winfrey Charitable Foundation (f. 2010), which succeeded the Angel Network (f. 1998), a charitable organization.
Activities: Provides services to underserved women, children and families. The Foundation's main purpose is to support the operation of the Oprah Winfrey Leadership Academy for Girls near Johannesburg, South Africa.
Geographical Area of Activity: South Africa, USA.
Finance: Annual revenue US $6.7m., expenditure $9.6m. (31 Dec. 2022).
Principal Staff: Pres. Dir Oprah Winfrey; Pres. Rebecca Sykes.
Contact Details: 1041 N Formosa Ave, West Hollywood, CA 90046; tel. (323) 284-7095; internet www.oprahfoundation.org/portfolio-item/oprah-leadership-academy.

Orentreich Foundation for the Advancement of Science, Inc—OFAS

Founded in 1961; classified as an operating private foundation in 1972.
Activities: Carries out biomedical research into preventing, halting or reversing disorders that decrease the quality or length of life. The Foundation collaborates with other institutions; organizes conferences and seminars; and offers occasional research grants.
Geographical Area of Activity: Mainly USA.
Restrictions: Grant recipients are typically at or above postgraduate level in science or medicine at accredited universities or research institutions in the USA.
Publications: Annual Directors' Report; *VitaLongevity* (newsletter); blog.
Finance: Annual revenue US $2.4m., expenditure $4.5m. (31 Dec. 2022).
Board: Norman Orentreich (Chair.).
Principal Staff: Pres. and Dir Dr David Orentreich.
Contact Details: 855 NY301, Cold Spring, NY 10516; tel. (845) 265-4200; e-mail info@orentreich.org; internet www.orentreich.org.

Outreach International

Established in 1979 by Charles Neff, a Christian minister.
Activities: Works to eliminate poverty, hunger and disease through its community-led Participatory Human Development Process, which helps people collectively to identify and collaborate on sustainable solutions. Programmes areas include: agriculture; economic and social services; education; environment; health and sanitation; housing and infrastructure; livelihood; nutrition; organizational development; and water. The organization operates in 10 countries.
Geographical Area of Activity: Bolivia, Cambodia, Dem. Repub. of the Congo, Haiti, India, Malawi, Nepal, Nicaragua, Philippines, USA, Zambia.
Publications: Annual Report; *Outreach Developments* (quarterly newsletter); brochure; case studies; field notes; blog.
Finance: Annual revenue US $4.0m., expenditure $3.5m. (30 Sept. 2024).
Board of Directors: Laura Clark (Chair.); Michele McGrath (Vice-Chair.); Tim Connealy (Treas.); Mark Wildermuth (Sec.).

OutRight Action International

Principal Staff: Pres. and CEO Dr John Herron.
Contact Details: 112 W 18th St, Kansas City, MO 64108; tel. (816) 833-0883; e-mail info@outreachmail.org; internet www.outreach-international.org.

OutRight Action International

Established in 1990, as the International Gay and Lesbian Human Rights Commission, by Julie Dorf, a human rights advocate.
Activities: Provides human rights advocacy for people who experience discrimination or abuse based on their actual or perceived sexual orientation or gender. The organization provides capacity building and training; carries out research; and has consultative status with ECOSOC. Has staff in six countries.
Geographical Area of Activity: International.
Publications: Newsletter; research reports; blog.
Finance: Annual revenue US $15.5m., expenditure $9.6m. (30 June 2022).
Board: Aalap Shah, Jenny Pizer (Co-Chair.).
Principal Staff: Exec. Dir Maria Sjödin.
Contact Details: 216 East 45th St, 17th Floor, New York, NY 10017; tel. (212) 430-6054; e-mail hello@outrightinternational.org; internet outrightinternational.org.

Oxfam America

Established in 1970; part of the Oxfam confederation of organizations (qq.v.).
Activities: Works to eliminate poverty, hunger and social injustice; and assists people affected by emergencies, conflicts and natural disasters worldwide. The organization campaigns on issues including access to clean water and basic infrastructure; overcoming gender discrimination towards women and girls; the right to earn a decent living; natural resources and rights; and climate change adaptation. It works in more than 80 countries; and has an office in Washington, DC.
Geographical Area of Activity: International.
Publications: Annual Report; newsletter; *Oxfam CloseUp* (magazine, 3 a year); briefing papers; brochures; evaluation reports; factsheets; books.
Finance: Annual revenue US $83.0m., expenditure $85.5m. (31 March 2024).
Board of Directors: N. James Shachoy (Chair.); Sherine Jayawickrama (Vice-Chair.); Tara L. Torrens (Treas.); Jack Regan (Sec.).
Principal Staff: Pres. and CEO Abby Maxman.
Contact Details: 77 North Washington St, Suite 500, Boston, MA 02114; tel. (800) 776-9326; e-mail info@oxfamamerica.org; internet www.oxfamamerica.org.

Pact

Established in 1971 as Private Agencies Collaborating Together, a membership organization for registered US private voluntary organizations.
Activities: Operates in the field of international development through working with local organizations, businesses and governments to build systemic solutions to poverty and marginalization. Main programme areas include: capacity development of local NGOs; environment and building resilience, sustainably managing natural resources; governance and citizens' initiatives; health and social services; livelihoods, with a focus on women; and markets, strengthening local economies and eliminating exploitation. The organization works in nearly 40 countries; and also operates through Pact UK, the Pact Ventures impact investing unit and the Pact Institute (f. 1998).
Geographical Area of Activity: Eastern Europe, South America, South Asia, South-East Asia, sub-Saharan Africa.
Publications: Annual Report; *Inside Our Promise* (e-newsletter); *All In* (e-magazine); handbooks; reports; factsheets.
Finance: Annual revenue US $158.4m., expenditure $156.3m. (30 Sept. 2023).
Board of Directors: Jeremy Ngunze (Chair.).
Principal Staff: Pres. and CEO Caroline Anstey.
Contact Details: 1140 3rd St NE, Suite 400, Washington, DC 20002; tel. (202) 466-5666; e-mail info@pactworld.org; internet www.pactworld.org.

PADF—Pan American Development Foundation

Founded in 1962 to promote regional social and economic development.
Activities: Works to bring technical expertise and resources to Central and South America and the Caribbean. Programmes include: building and rehabilitating schools, homes and public infrastructure; capacity building of communities and institutions; children's education; empowering girls and women; environmental conservation; helping displaced people and vulnerable groups; improving the lives of Afro-descendants and indigenous peoples; job creation; looking after young people; promoting South-South co-operation; reducing maternal mortality; responding to and preparing for disasters; strengthening communities and civil society; and supporting human rights. The Foundation works with local organizations, multinational corporations, private businesses and NGOs in the region, along with the US Government and inter-American NGOs. It has offices in Colombia, El Salvador, Guatemala, Haiti, Honduras and Mexico.
Geographical Area of Activity: Central and South America and the Caribbean, USA.
Publications: Annual Report; newsletter; technical publications.
Finance: Annual revenue US $101.9m., expenditure $102.1m. (30 Sept. 2021).
Board of Trustees: Luis Almagro Lemes (Chair.); Nestor Mendez (Vice-Chair.); Alexandra Aguirre (Pres.); Mina Pacheco Nazemi (First Vice-Pres.); German Herrera (Second Vice-Pres); Niel Parsan (Treas.); Stephen Donehoo (Sec.).
Principal Staff: Exec. Dir Katie Taylor.
Contact Details: 1889 F St, NW, Second Floor, Washington, DC 20006; tel. (202) 458-3969; e-mail connect@padf.org; internet www.padf.org.

PAI—Population Action International

Founded in 1965; an independent policy advocacy group.
Activities: Strengthens political and financial support worldwide for population programmes and individual rights. The organization advances universal access to family planning and related health services, and to educational and economic opportunities, especially for girls and women. It links population, reproductive health, the environment and development; fosters the development of US and international policy on population and reproductive health issues through an integrated programme of research, advocacy and communications; issues research publications; participates in and sponsors conferences, meetings and seminars; and works to educate and inform policymakers and international colleagues in related fields. In 2015 the CSO GFF Hub was launched to support CSOs' engagement with the multilateral Global Financing Facility for Every Woman Every Child through capacity building, grants and technical assistance.
Geographical Area of Activity: International.
Publications: Annual Report; newsletter; factsheets; policy briefs; case studies.
Finance: Annual revenue US $5.2m., expenditure $9.9m. (31 Dec. 2023).
Board of Directors: Neeraja Bhavaraju (Chair.); James Siegal (Vice-Chair.); Luis Guardia (Treas.); Barbara Sapin (Sec.).
Principal Staff: Pres. and CEO Nabeeha Kazi Hutchins.
Contact Details: 1300 19th St NW, Suite 200, Washington, DC 20036-1624; tel. (202) 557-3400; e-mail info@pai.org; internet pai.org.

UNITED STATES OF AMERICA

PANZI Foundation

Established in 2008 by Dr Denis Mukwege, 2018 Nobel Peace Prize Laureate.

Activities: Panzi Foundation provides survivors of sexual violence in the Democratic Republic of Congo the services and resources they need to rebuild their lives. The foundation's four-pillar holistic healing model includes medical care provided at Panzi Hospital, psychosocial support, socioeconomic reintegration opportunities, and access to legal services. The foundation also conducts outreach via mobile clinics and deploys rapid response missions to treat mass rapes in last-mile communities. Lastly, the organization participates in strategic advocacy to draw attention to the societal and systemic issues contributing to sexual violence, including the role of conflict minerals and transitional justice in ending impunity in DRC.

Geographical Area of Activity: Dem. Repub. of the Congo.

Restrictions: No grants are disbursed, funding is for own projects only.

Finance: Annual revenue US $2.8m., expenditure $3.7m. (31 Dec. 2023).

Board: Edward Sullivan (US Chair.); Fred Kramer (US Treas.).

Principal Staff: Pres. Dr Denis Mukwege; Vice-Pres. Christine Schuler Deschryver; Exec. Dir (DRC Office) Vanessa Goscinny; Exec. Dir (USA Office) Emily Warne.

Contact Details: 5185 MacArthur Blvd, NW, Suite 708, Washington, DC 20016; tel. (301) 541-8375; e-mail info@panzi.org; internet panzifoundation.org.

The Papal Foundation

Founded in the USA in 1988.

Activities: Collaborates with laity, clergy and the hierarchy of the Church to provide faith-based support and financial resources to those in need. Each year the Trustees designate funding to projects and programmes which may be a one-time donation or multi-year initiatives to support communities and parishes and ensure the future of the Church. In 2024 nearly $15m. was distributed in grants, scholarships and charitable aid to fund projects including providing access to clean water, renovations and repairs to schools and seminaries, and providing transportation for students in remote areas.

Geographical Area of Activity: Worldwide.

Finance: Annual revenue US $31.8m., expenditure $2.8m. (30 June 2024).

Principal Staff: Pres. Ward Fitzgerald; Exec. Dir Dave Savage.

Contact Details: 2501 Seaport Dr., Suite SH300, Chester, PA 19013; tel. (610) 535-6340; e-mail contact@thepapalfoundation.com; internet www.thepapalfoundation.org.

Parkinson's Foundation

Established in 2016 by the merger of the National Parkinson Foundation (f. 1957) and the Parkinson Disease Foundation (f. 1957).

Activities: Supports people living with Parkinson's disease and their carers. The Foundation funds research on treatment and care through four main programmes: the Centers of Excellence Network; Parkinson's Outcomes Project; Research Centers; and PD GENEration: Mapping the Future of Parkinson's Disease. It offers grants and fellowships to institutions, investigators and researchers.

Geographical Area of Activity: USA.

Publications: Annual Report; newsletter; *Parkinson Report* (online magazine); factsheets; blog.

Finance: Annual revenue US $56m., expenditure $52m. (30 June 2023).

Board of Directors: J. Gordon Beckham, Jr (Chair.); Andrew B. Albert (Vice-Chair.); Paul Nathan (Treas.); Dr Constance Atwell (Sec.).

Principal Staff: Pres. and CEO John L. Lehr.

Contact Details: 1359 Broadway, Suite 1509, New York, NY 10018; tel. (212) 923-4700; e-mail contact@parkinson.org; internet parkinson.org.

Partners in Health

Established in 1987 by a group of health advocates and medical professionals.

Activities: Works in the field of primary healthcare. The organization collaborates with local governments and international academic and medical institutions to build capacity and strengthen health systems. Main programme areas are: cancer and chronic diseases; child health; emergency response; HIV/AIDS; maternal health; mental health; and tuberculosis. It has a sister organization in Canada.

Geographical Area of Activity: Haiti, Kazakhstan, Lesotho, Liberia, Malawi, Mexico, Peru, Russian Federation, Rwanda, Sierra Leone, USA (Navajo Nation).

Publications: Annual Report.

Finance: Annual revenue US $238.3m., expenditure $239.5m. (30 June 2024).

Executive Committee: Ophelia Dahl (Chair.).

Principal Staff: CEO Sheila Davis.

Contact Details: 800 Boylston St, Suite 300, Boston, MA 02199; tel. (857) 880-5100; e-mail info@pih.org; internet www.pih.org.

PATH

Established in 1977 as PIACT, the Program for the Introduction and Adaptation of Contraceptive Technology; known as PATH—Program for Appropriate Technology in Health since 1980.

Activities: Works in the fields of healthcare and health equity, across five platforms: vaccines for children; drugs to treat diseases more effectively and for less; diagnostics to detect and track diseases; devices, such as household water filters and prefilled, non-reusable syringes; and system and service innovations to make sure that these tools reach the people who need them. The organization maintains an online Vaccine Resource Library; and has offices in more than 20 countries.

Geographical Area of Activity: International.

Restrictions: Not a grantmaking organization.

Publications: Annual Report; newsletters; factsheets; briefs; policy reports; specialized websites on global health topics.

Finance: Annual revenue US $352.7m., expenditure $351.8m. (31 Dec. 2023).

Board of Directors: Beth Galetti (Chair.); Dr Fredrick Namenya Were (Vice-Chair.); Dr Sanford M. Melzer (Treas.); Carole T. Faig (Sec.).

Principal Staff: Pres. and CEO Nikolaj Gilbert.

Contact Details: 437 N 34th St, Seattle, WA 98103; tel. (206) 285-3500; e-mail info@path.org; internet www.path.org.

Pathfinder International

Established in 1957 as the Pathfinder Fund by Dr Clarence Gamble.

Activities: A global health organization with locally led, community-driven programmes that support women to make their own reproductive health decisions. Works with local partners to advance contraceptive services, comprehensive abortion care, and young people's sexual and reproductive rights in communities around the world—including those affected by poverty, conflict, climate change and natural disasters. Has offices in Burkina Faso and Pakistan.

Geographical Area of Activity: Africa, South-East Asia.

Publications: Annual Report; *Pathways* (newsletter); factsheets; technical guidelines; toolkits; training publications; blog.

Finance: Annual revenue US $117.9m., expenditure $120.0m. (30 June 2023).

Board: Collin Mothupi (Chair.).

The Paul G. Allen Family Foundation

Principal Staff: Pres. and CEO Lois Quam.

Contact Details: 1015 15th St NW, Suite 1100, Washington, DC 20005; tel. (617) 924-7200; e-mail info@pathfinder.org; internet www.pathfinder.org.

The Paul G. Allen Family Foundation

Established in 1990 by Paul G. Allen, co-founder of computer software company Microsoft, the Allen Institute for Brain Science and Allen Institute for Artificial Intelligence, and his sister Jody Allen.

Activities: Funds organizations that use technology and conduct applied research to advance knowledge and influence policy change. Main programme areas are: arts and culture; environment and ecosystems; bioscience; and empowering young changemakers. In the USA, the Foundation focuses activities on the Pacific North-West regions. It supports the Paul G. Allen Frontiers Group at the Allen Institute, which funds bioscience research.

Geographical Area of Activity: International.

Restrictions: Does not accept unsolicited applications.

Publications: Research reports.

Finance: Annual revenue US $18.3m., expenditure $55.4m. (31 Dec. 2022).

Board of Directors: Jody Allen (Chair. and Pres.).

Contact Details: 505 Fifth Ave South, Suite 900, Seattle, WA 98104; tel. (206) 342-2030; e-mail info@pgafamilyfoundation.org; internet pgafamilyfoundation.org.

Pearl S. Buck International

Established in 1964 by Pearl S. Buck, a Nobel and Pulitzer prize-winning author and humanitarian.

Activities: Works to improve quality of life and opportunities for children who suffer discrimination related to the circumstances of their birth through humanitarian aid and intercultural education. The organization promotes access to opportunity, dignity and human rights; and mitigates the effects of injustices suffered by children. It also promotes the legacy of the founder and awareness of the mission through historical tours of the Pearl S. Buck House, a National Historic Landmark.

Geographical Area of Activity: People's Repub. of China, Repub. of Korea, Philippines, Taiwan, Thailand, Viet Nam, USA.

Restrictions: Grants to affiliated and partner organizations.

Publications: Annual Report; *Mission Matters* (monthly newsletter); *News from the Field* (annual).

Finance: Annual revenue US $1.4m., expenditures $1.9m. (30 June 2023).

Board of Directors: Falesha Grasty (Chair.); Maxine Romano (Treas.); Susan Berrodin (Sec.).

Principal Staff: Pres. and CEO Cheryl Castro.

Contact Details: 520 Dublin Rd, Perkasie, PA 18944; tel. (215) 249-0100; e-mail info@pearlsbuck.org; internet www.pearlsbuck.org.

PepsiCo Foundation, Inc

Founded in 1962 by PepsiCo, Inc and Frito-Lay, Inc, food, snack and beverage manufacturers.

Activities: Works to improve access to nutrition and safe water, reduce and eliminate plastic waste and drive prosperity, in particular among women and girls. The Foundation provides financial support to non-profit organizations primarily where employees of PepsiCo are involved as volunteers. It is also involved in disaster response and humanitarian assistance.

Geographical Area of Activity: Worldwide.

Restrictions: Does not accept unsolicited applications.

Finance: Annual revenue US $81.8m., expenditure $58.0m. (31 Dec. 2022).

Board of Directors: Roberto Azvedo (Chair.).

Principal Staff: Pres. C. D. Glin.

Contact Details: c/o PepsiCo, Inc, 700 Anderson Hill Rd, Purchase, NY 10577; tel. (914) 253-2000; internet www.pepsico.com/our-impact/philanthropy/pepsico-foundation.

Pesticide Action Network North America—PANNA

Established in 1982 as a regional centre of the PAN International network (f. 1982).

Activities: Promotes healthier and more effective methods of pest control to replace harmful pesticides, through research, policy development, media coverage, education and international advocacy campaigns. Areas of interest include: agroecology and farming; genetically modified organisms, pesticides and corporate agriculture; food democracy; and food policy. The Network provides activists, researchers and policymakers with technical information, analysis, training, campaign support and policy guidance. It works with health, consumer, agricultural and environmental groups throughout North America; and has an office in Minneapolis, MN.

Geographical Area of Activity: Canada, Mexico, USA.

Publications: Annual Report; *PAN Newsletter*; issue briefs; reports; toolkits; blog.

Finance: Annual revenue US $3.2m., expenditure $3.7m. (31 March 2023).

Board of Directors: Jennifer Lamson (Pres.); Iris Figueroa (Vice-Pres.); Jodi Angelo (Treas.); Kyle Powys Whyte (Sec.).

Principal Staff: Exec. Dir Allison Davis.

Contact Details: 2029 University Ave, Suite 200, Berkeley, CA 94704; tel. (510) 788-9020; e-mail panna@panna.org; internet www.panna.org.

The Pew Charitable Trusts

Comprising the Pew Memorial Trust (f. 1948), the J. N. Pew, Jr Charitable Trust (f. 1956), the J. Howard Pew Freedom Trust, the Mabel Pew Myrin Trust and the Mary Anderson Trust (all f. 1957), the Knollbrook Trust (f. 1965) and the Medical Trust (f. 1979).

Activities: Supports non-profit activities in three main areas: using data-based research to inform the public, through the Pew Research Center, based in Washington, DC, which explores important issues and trends that affect public opinion; improving public policy nationally and globally by helping to find non-partisan solutions to the problems affecting communities; and stimulating civic life, including by supporting organizations in Philadelphia that encourage local citizens' participation in the city's arts and culture community. Key topics are: communities; conservation; finance and the economy; governing; health; and trends. The organization has an office in Washington, DC.

Geographical Area of Activity: International.

Restrictions: No grants to individuals; nor for scholarships, endowment funds, non-applied research, land acquisition, equipment purchases, capital projects or debt reduction.

Publications: *Program Resource Guide*; *The Rundown* (weekly newsletter); *Trust Magazine* (quarterly); factsheets; issue briefs; reports.

Finance: Annual revenue US $415.2m., expenditure $361.4m. (30 June 2023).

Board of Directors: Christopher Jones (Chair.).

Principal Staff: Pres. and CEO Dr Susan K. Urahn.

Contact Details: 1 Commerce Sq., 2005 Market St, Suite 2800, Philadelphia, PA 19103-7077; tel. (215) 575-9050; e-mail info@pewtrusts.org; internet www.pewtrusts.org.

Pfizer Foundation

Founded in 1953 by Pfizer Inc, a pharmaceuticals company.

Activities: Operates in areas where the Pfizer company has offices, through providing grants and investments. The Foundation funds initiatives in the areas of: health delivery and social innovation; women and children's health; and reducing non-communicable diseases. It also provides disaster and humanitarian relief; and supports employee volunteering in local communities.

Geographical Area of Activity: Worldwide.

Restrictions: Does not accept unsolicited applications.

Finance: Annual revenue US $37.9m., expenditure $52.1m. (31 Dec. 2022).

Board of Directors: William C. Steere, Jr (Chair.); Brian Byala (Treas.); Dezarie Mayers (Sec.).

Principal Staff: Pres. Caroline Roan; Exec. Dir Oonagh Puglisi.

Contact Details: 235 East 42nd St, New York, NY 10017-5703; tel. (212) 733-4250; internet www.pfizer.com/about/responsibility/global-impact/the-pfizer-foundation.

PH International

Established in 1985, as Project Harmony, by Charles Hosford, an architect and community leader, and Kathy Caldwell, a teacher.

Activities: Co-ordinates cultural, educational and professional exchanges to enhance international understanding, strengthen communities and nurture personal friendships. The organization also carries out programmes in: civic participation; combating domestic violence; digital literacy; economic development; reparative justice; social media for social change; and youth leadership. It has offices in Ukraine, Georgia and Armenia.

Geographical Area of Activity: Armenia, Bosnia and Herzegovina, Georgia, Moldova, Ukraine, USA.

Publications: Annual Report; *PH International News*.

Finance: Annual revenue US $6.5m., expenditure $6.6m. (30 June 2023).

Board: Lynn McNair (Chair.); Nahela Hadi (Vice-Chair.); Ali Jalili (Treas.); Beth Humstone (Sec.).

Principal Staff: Exec. Dir Meg Harris.

Contact Details: 5197 Main St, Unit 6, Waitsfield, VT 05673; tel. (802) 496-4545; e-mail info@ph-int.org; internet www.ph-int.org.

Physicians for Human Rights—PHR

Established in 1986 by a group of medical doctors; shared the 1997 Nobel Peace Prize as a founding member of the International Campaign to Ban Landmines.

Activities: Works in the fields of medicine, science, law and human rights. The organization trains and supports physicians, nurses, psychologists, lawyers, police officers, judges and others in conflict and post-conflict regions to document human rights and humanitarian law violations using forensic techniques, promoting prevention, protection, justice and redress. It defends medical professionals when they are attacked or jailed by authorities for carrying out their professional obligations; corroborates human rights abuse claims of asylum seekers in the USA through a network of more than 1,900 volunteer medical professionals, trained primarily through partnerships with medical schools; and uses what it learns through research, investigations, trainings and examinations of victims to advocate human rights policy reforms internationally and to prompt robust responses to humanitarian emergencies and human rights violations from state governments, regional bodies and the UN. Has an office in Washington, DC.

Geographical Area of Activity: Worldwide.

Publications: Annual Report; newsletter; factsheets; reports; blog.

Finance: Annual revenue US $5.9m., expenditure $9.0m. (30 June 2023).

Board of Directors: Gerson H. Smoger (Chair.); Raymond P. Happy (Vice-Chair.); Darren Thompson (Treas.); Dr Gail Saltz (Sec.).

Advisory Council: Kerry J. Sulkowicz (Chair.).

Principal Staff: Exec. Dir Saman Zia-Zarifi.

Contact Details: 520 8th Ave, Suite 2301, 23rd Floor, New York, NY 10018; tel. (646) 564-3720; e-mail info@phr.org; internet www.phr.org.

Ploughshares Fund

Founded in 1981 by Sally Lillenthal, a sculptor and human rights activist.

Activities: Promotes the elimination of nuclear weapons and works to prevent the emergence of new nuclear powers and build regional peace. The Fund operates internationally in the fields of weapons control and conflict resolution, particularly in the USA, Europe, Asia, the Middle East, the Russian Federation, the Democratic People's Republic of Korea and Japan. It conducts research; organizes the annual Chain Reaction gala; and makes grants for projects, research, conferences and to individuals; discretionary grants are worth up to US $25,000. Comprises a network of 85 organizations and 200 individuals; and has an office in Washington, DC.

Geographical Area of Activity: International.

Restrictions: Does not fund films, books, art projects, research or the writing of academic dissertations; does not provide scholarships.

Publications: Annual Report; newsletter.

Finance: Annual revenue $9.1m., expenditure $9.0m. (30 June 2023).

Board of Directors: Terry Gamble Boyer (Chair.); Gretchen Hund (Treas.); Philip Ames (Sec.).

Principal Staff: Pres. Dr Emma Belcher; Exec. Dir Elizabeth Warner.

Contact Details: 315 Bay St, Suite 400, San Francisco, CA 94133; tel. (415) 668-2244; e-mail ploughshares@ploughshares.org; internet www.ploughshares.org.

Pollock-Krasner Foundation, Inc

Founded by Lee Krasner, one of the foremost abstract expressionist painters, the Pollock-Krasner Foundation was established in 1985 to provide financial resources to individual visual artists internationally.

Activities: Offers organization grants to institutions; and three-year Lee Krasner Awards to older artists working in the fields of sculpture, painting, works on paper, printmaking and fine art photography. Since 1985 the Foundation has awarded more than 5,100 grants totalling more than US $90m. to artists in 80 countries. It also offers emergency relief grants; and in 2016 instituted the Pollock Prize for Creativity. The Foundation awarded US $2.7m. to 93 artists and non-profit organizations during its July 2022–June 2023 grant cycle, providing essential support to US-based and international artists.

Geographical Area of Activity: Worldwide.

Restrictions: The Foundation does not accept applications from commercial artists, graphic artists, video artists, performance artists, filmmakers, crafts-makers, or any artist whose work primarily falls into these categories. The Foundation does not have an open photography grant programme. The Foundation does not make grants to students or fund academic study. The Foundation does not make grants to pay for past debts, legal fees or personal travel. The Foundation does not have research facilities.

Finance: Annual revenue US $8.3m., expenditure $6.6m. (30 June 2023).

Board of Directors: Ronald D. Spencer (Chair. and CEO); Samuel Sachs II (Pres.); Caroline Black (Exec. Dir).

Contact Details: 863 Park Ave, New York, NY 10075; tel. (212) 517-5400; e-mail grants@pkf.org; internet www.pkf.org.

Population Council

Founded in 1952 by John D. Rockefeller, III, a philanthropist.

Activities: Transforms global thinking on critical health and development issues through social science, public health, and biomedical research, with a current focus on sexual and reproductive health, rights, and choices; adolescents and young people; gender equality and equity; and climate and environmental changes.

Geographical Area of Activity: Africa, Asia, Latin America, Middle East, USA.

Restrictions: Not a grant-making organization.

Publications: Annual Report; *Studies in Family Planning* (quarterly journal); *Population and Development Review* (quarterly journal); reports; briefs; peer-reviewed articles; curricula; toolkits; guides; books.

Finance: Annual revenue $67.2m., expenditure $79.5m. (31 December 2023).

Board: Nyovani Madise (Chair.); Jonathan Shakes (Vice-Chair.).

Principal Staff: Pres. Dr Rana Hajjeh.

Contact Details: 1 Dag Hammarskjöld Plaza, New York, NY 10017; tel. (212) 339-0500; e-mail pubinfo@popcouncil.org; internet www.popcouncil.org.

Pro Mujer International (Pro Women International)

Established in 1990 in Bolivia by school teachers Lynne Patterson and Carmen Velasco.

Activities: Works in the field of development for marginalized women, who experience gender-based violence, chronic health problems and discrimination. The organization promotes: security, providing access to microfinance for economic independence; health, delivering local primary healthcare services; solidarity, supporting women through communal groups of female entrepreneurs; and leadership, through empowerment and business training. It has a local chapter in the United Kingdom.

Geographical Area of Activity: Latin America, UK, USA.

Publications: Annual Report; newsletter; blog.

Finance: Annual revenue US $44.9m., expenditure $41.4m. (31 Dec. 2021).

Board of Directors: Ana Demel (Chair.); Vanessa Dager (Vice-Chair.); Camilio Mendez (Treas.); Mark Roy McMahon (Sec.).

Principal Staff: CEO Carmen Correa.

Contact Details: 515 Madison Ave, 8th Floor, New York, NY 10022; tel. (646) 626-7000; e-mail communications@promujer.org; internet www.promujer.org.

Project HOPE

Established in 1958 as an inititative of the People-to-People Health Foundation, founded by Dr William B. Walsh.

Activities: Improves the health and wellbeing of people and communities by placing power in the hands of healthcare workers. Main programme areas include: distributing personal protective equipment and providing training for healthcare and frontline workers; disasters and health crises, distributing essential medicines and supplies; infectious diseases, including tuberculosis and HIV; global health security, strengthening public health systems; health equity, working towards universal access to basic health services for all; maternal, neonatal and child health, providing healthcare support, education, nutrition and immunization; non-communicable diseases, such as diabetes, obesity and cardiovascular disease; and public health policy. The organization works in more than 25 countries and maintains a volunteer roster.

Geographical Area of Activity: Africa, the Americas and the Caribbean, Asia, Central Asia, Central and Eastern Europe, People's Repub. of China, Middle East, USA.

Publications: Annual Report; newsletter; *Health Affairs* (journal); brochures.

Finance: Annual revenue US $182.3m., expenditure $179.7m. (31 Dec. 2023).

Board of Directors: Reynold W. Mooney (Chair.); Dr Peter Wilden, Anne M. Simonds (Vice-Chair.); Raphael Marcello (Treas.); Viren Mehta (Sec.).

Principal Staff: Pres. and CEO Rabih Torbay; Exec. Vice-Pres. Chris Skopec.

Contact Details: 1101 Connecticut Ave, NW, Suite 500, Washington, DC 20036; tel. (844) 349-0188; e-mail hope@projecthope.org; internet www.projecthope.org.

ProLiteracy

Formed in 2002 by the merger of Laubach Literacy International and Literacy Volunteers of America.

Activities: Increases the capacity and quality of adult literacy programmes through technical assistance, professional development, training and content development. Programmes focus on: basic literacy in reading, writing and mathematics; English language learning; preparation for the High School Equivalency Degree; and financial, digital and health literacy. The Expanding Access to Adult Literacy programme supports social services in the USA; and the International programme provides training, capacity building and grants for literacy instruction and skills to address socioeconomic issues, reduce poverty, improve health and advance human rights. The organization supports public libraries and, through the National Book Fund, provides grants for educational materials to adult literacy and education programmes. Other programmes focus on financial literacy for women and low-income immigrants with limited English skills. Comprises a network of more than 1,000 member organizations in the USA and 28 developing countries.

Geographical Area of Activity: Worldwide.

Publications: Annual Report; newsletter (monthly); *Adult Literacy Education: The International Journal of Literacy, Language, and Numeracy* (journal); *Workforce Atlas* (e-learning platform); brochures; factsheets; research briefs; white papers; blog.

Finance: Annual revenue US $13.0m., expenditure $12.2m. (30 June 2024).

Board of Directors: Kate Costello-Sullivan (Chair.); Kathleen A. Hinchman (Vice-Chair.); Jack Burke (Treas.); Maria Bartoszewicki (Sec.).

Principal Staff: Pres. and CEO Mark Vineis.

Contact Details: 308 Maltbie St, Suite 100, Syracuse, NY 13204; tel. (315) 422-9121; e-mail info@proliteracy.org; internet www.proliteracy.org.

Pulitzer Center on Crisis Reporting

Established in 2006 by Jon Sawyer, a newspaper editor.

Activities: Supports engagement with under-reported global affairs through sponsorship of high-quality international journalism and photojournalism across all media platforms. The Center runs an outreach and education programme for schools, colleges and universities. It awards Global Reporting Grants, worth between US $5,000 and $10,000; and grants for data journalism, local reporting and themes including climate change, gender equality and property seizures. The Persephone Miel Fellowship, worth $5,000, is open to journalists and other media professionals from outside the USA and Western Europe for reporting from their home countries; and the Richard C. Longworth Media Fellowship, worth $10,000, promotes international reporting by journalists from Chicago and the US Midwest. The Rainforest Journalism Fund was established in 2018 for reporting on tropical rainforests in the Brazil and Congo Basins, and in South-East Asia.

Geographical Area of Activity: Worldwide.

Publications: Annual Report; newsletter; print series; documentaries; data interactives; e-books.

Finance: Annual revenue US $15.6m., expenditure $11.8m. (31 Dec. 2023).

Board of Directors: Emily Rauh Pulitzer (Chair. Emeritus); Richard Moore (Chair.); William Bush (Treas.); Linda Winslow (Sec.).

Principal Staff: CEO Lisa Gibbs.

UNITED STATES OF AMERICA

Contact Details: 2000 Pennsylvania Ave NW, Suite 7000, Washington, DC 20006; tel. (202) 332-0982; e-mail contact@pulitzercenter.org; internet www.pulitzercenter.org.

PwC Charitable Foundation

Established in 2001 by PwC, a multinational professional services network, revitalizing a legacy foundation.

Activities: Main programmes are: People of PwC, supporting employees who are experiencing financial hardship and funding charities where they volunteer; Education, investing in innovative organizations that increase access for underserved communities; and Humanitarianism, supporting long-term global disaster response. Special initiatives support former US military service personnel and their families, and social entrepreneurs. The Foundation awards grants and scholarships.

Geographical Area of Activity: USA.

Restrictions: Does not accept unsolicited applications.

Publications: Annual Report.

Finance: Annual revenue US $35.1m., expenditure $26.6m. (30 Sept. 2022).

Board of Trustees: Michael Sutphin (Pres.); Christine Freyermuth (Treas.); Stacey Empson (Sec.).

Principal Staff: Exec. Dir Charlotte Coker Gibson.

Contact Details: 300 Madison Ave, New York, NY 10017; tel. (813) 348-7725; e-mail us_foundation@pwc.com; internet www.pwc.com/us/en/about-us/corporate-responsibility/foundation.html.

Quincy Institute for Responsible Statecraft–QI

Established in 2019 by Andrew Bacevich, Stephen Wertheim and Eli Clifton; a think tank named after the sixth President of the USA, John Quincy Adams.

Activities: Promotes diplomacy and the pursuit of international peace through conducting research and advocacy on US foreign policy. Main programmes are: East Asia; Ending Endless War; Democratizing Foreign Policy; and the Middle East.

Geographical Area of Activity: USA.

Publications: Newsletter (weekly); *Responsible Statecraft*; briefs; papers; special reports.

Finance: Annual revenue US $8.9m., expenditure $6.2m. (31 Dec. 2023).

Board: Stephen Heintz (Chair.); Sally Donnelly (Treas./Sec.).

Principal Staff: Exec. Vice-Pres. Trita Parsi; CEO Lora Lumpe.

Contact Details: 2000 Pennsylvania Ave NW, Washington, DC 20006; tel. (202) 800-4662; e-mail info@quincyinst.org; internet quincyinst.org.

Rainforest Action Network—RAN

Founded in 1985 by Randy Hayes, a film-maker, and Mike Roselle, an environmental activist.

Activities: Supports leadership and human rights in indigenous and frontline communities to confront profit-driven systems of injustice. Main programmes focus on forests, climate and community. The Network offers Community Action Grants to organizations and communities in rainforest regions through the Protect-an-Acre programme, typically worth up to US $5,000; and the Climate Action Fund, supporting community groups to prevent fossil fuel extraction with grants worth up to $2,500. It is also involved in negotiation, research and education; and organizes conferences and seminars.

Geographical Area of Activity: International.

Publications: Annual Report; *The Panther* (yearly newsletter); research reports; case studies; policy briefs; factsheets; information packs.

Finance: Annual revenue US $11.9m., expenditure $12.4m. (30 June 2024).

Board of Directors: Andre Carothers (Pres. and Chair. Emeritus); Avi Mahaningtyas (Chair.); Anna Lappé (Vice-Chair.); Scott B. Price (Treas.); Marsela Pecanac (Sec.).

Principal Staff: Exec. Dir Ginger Cassidy.

Contact Details: 425 Bush St, Suite 300, San Francisco, CA 94108; POB 3563, Seattle, WA 98124-3563; tel. (415) 398-4404; e-mail membership@ran.org; internet www.ran.org.

Rainforest Foundation US—RFUS

Established in 1988 by Sting and Trudie Styler.

Activities: RFUS works with Indigenous peoples and local communities in South America, Central America, and Mexico at the global, regional, national, and community levels to support human rights, land rights, land management, and forest-protection efforts. The mission of RFUS is to support Indigenous and traditional peoples of the world's rainforests in their efforts to protect their environment and uphold their rights by assisting them in: securing and controlling the natural resources necessary for their long-term well-being and managing these resources in ways that do not harm their environment, violate their culture, or compromise their future; and developing the means to protect their individual and collective rights and to obtain, shape, and control basic services from the state. RFUS advances three programme areas: Land Rights—securing and defending rights to Indigenous peoples' lands and forests; Territorial Governance—protecting Indigenous lands and forests through land management plans and tech-enabled forest monitoring; and Institutional Strengthening—building partners' capacity to leverage financial resources and administer programmes.

Geographical Area of Activity: Brazil, Guatemala, Guyana, Honduras, Mexico, Panama, Peru.

Publications: Annual Report; reports; studies; audited financials.

Finance: Annual budget US $9.3m. (2025).

Board of Directors: John W. Copeland (Chair.); S. Todd Crider (Vice-Chair.); Brett Odom (Treas.).

Principal Staff: Exec. Dir Suzanne Pelletier.

Contact Details: 50 Court St, Suite 712, Brooklyn, NY 11201; tel. (212) 431-9098; e-mail giving@rainforestus.org; internet www.rainforestfoundation.org.

RAND Corporation

Established in 1945 as Project RAND under the Douglas Aircraft Company; became an independent non-profit organization in 1948.

Activities: Carries out research and analysis to inform public policy- and decisionmaking. Current research areas include: children, families and communities; cyber and data sciences; domestic security and public safety; education and literacy; energy and the environment; health, healthcare and ageing; infrastructure and transportation; international affairs; law and business; national security and terrorism; science and technology; and workers and the workplace. In addition to thematic research divisions and regional centres, the organization incorporates two wholly owned subsidiaries, RAND Australia and RAND Europe; the Pardee RAND Graduate School, a doctoral public policy programme; and the RAND Innovation network of research centres. The RAND Center to Advance Racial Equity Policy was established in 2020. Fellowships are offered to professionals, postdoctoral candidates and members of the military. Operates in 30 countries, with offices in Boston, MA, Pittsburgh, PA, and Washington, DC; and Brussels (Belgium), Cambridge (UK), The Hague (Netherlands), and Canberra (Australia).

Geographical Area of Activity: International.

Publications: Annual Report; *Policy Currents* (weekly newsletter); *Forward* (newsletter); *RAND Journal of Economics*; research briefs; research reports; databases and tools; conference proceedings; books.

Finance: Annual revenue US $501.7m., expenditure $427.0m. (30 Sept. 2023).

Board of Trustees: Michael E. Leiter (Chair.); Teresa Wynn Roseborough (Vice-Chair.).
Principal Staff: Pres. and CEO Jason Matheny.
Contact Details: 1776 Main St, POB 2138, Santa Monica, CA 90407-2138; tel. (310) 393-0411; e-mail giving@rand.org; internet www.rand.org.

Rare

Established in 1973, as Rare Animal Relief Effort, by David Hill, an ornithologist; formerly part of WWF International (q.v.).
Activities: Designs conservation programmes through its Center for Behavior & the Environment (BE.Center) based on behaviour change and social marketing techniques. The organization works across 60 countries and has offices in Brazil, Colombia, Germany, Indonesia, Mexico, Mozambique and the Philippines. The Meloy Fund for Sustainable Community Fisheries is a wholly owned subsidiary that invests in fishing and seafood-related enterprises in Indonesia and the Philippines.
Geographical Area of Activity: Worldwide.
Publications: Annual Report; e-newsletter; brochures; factsheets; toolkit.
Finance: Annual revenue US $25.3m., expenditure $31.0m. (30 Sept. 2022).
Board of Directors: Bruce W. Boyd, Lizanne Galbreath (Co-Chair.); Dorothy Batten (Vice-Chair.); Randy Brown (Treas.); Sarah Stein Greenberg (Sec.).
Principal Staff: CEO Brett Jenks.
Contact Details: 1310 N Courthouse Rd, Suite 110, Arlington, VA 22201; tel. (703) 522-5070; e-mail info@rare.org; internet www.rare.org.

Re:wild

Founded in 2021 by the merger of the Leonardo DiCaprio Foundation (LDF), established in 1998, and Global Wildlife Conservation (GWC), which had co-founded Earth Alliance in 2019 with LDF and Emerson Collective.
Activities: Supports projects that build climate resiliency, protect vulnerable wildlife and restore balance to ecosystems and communities under threat. Main programme areas are: climate change and the transition to renewable energy; defending indigenous rights, cultures and lands; oceans conservation, including expanding marine protected areas and constraining overfishing; and wildlands conservation, protecting critical ecoregions and restoring threatened species.
Geographical Area of Activity: International.
Restrictions: Does not accept unsolicited applications.
Publications: Newsletter; reports; blog; books.
Finance: Total revenue US $55.6m., expenditure $54.0m. (30 June 2023).
Principal Staff: CEO and Board Chair Dr Wes Sechrest; Exec. Vice-Pres. Dr Penny Langhammer.
Contact Details: POB 129, Austin, TX 78767; tel. (512) 686-6062; e-mail hello@rewild.org; internet www.rewild.org.

Refugees International—RI

Established in 1979 by Sue Morton as a citizens' movement to protect Indo-Chinese refugees.
Activities: Operates in areas of war and crisis, providing direct aid to refugees and people who have been displaced from their homes, including emergency relief, repatriation and protection. The organization also provides on-site field assessments and reports to policymakers worldwide to mobilize help for the victims. Main programme areas include: climate displacement, which promotes funding for programmes to reduce disaster risk and build communities' resilience; labour market access, researching innovative programmes with the Center for Global Development; and women and girls, which works to prevent gender-based violence and ensure that displaced women and girls have access to medical, psychological, legal and security assistance.
Geographical Area of Activity: International.
Publications: Annual Report; newsletter (monthly); reports; blog.
Finance: Annual revenue US $4.9m., expenditure $5.2m. (31 Dec. 2023).
Board of Directors: Jeffrey Tindell, Maureen White (Co-Chair.); Darya Nasr (Vice-Co-Chair.); L. Craig Johnstone (Treas.); Sophal Ear (Sec.).
Principal Staff: Pres. Jeremy Konyndyk.
Contact Details: 1800 M St, NW, Suite 405N, Washington, DC 20036; POB 33036, Washington, DC 20033; tel. (202) 828-0110; e-mail ri@refugeesinternational.org; internet www.refugeesinternational.org.

Rehabilitation International—RI

Founded in 1922 as the International Society for Crippled Children and subsequently the International Society for the Welfare of Cripples and the International Society for the Rehabilitation of the Disabled; present name adopted in 1972. A federation of national and international organizations and aid agencies.
Activities: Promotes and implements the rights and inclusion of people with disabilities through the exchange of information and experience on research and practice. Commissions of specialists and experts undertake work in the areas of: assistive technology and accessibility; education for children and young people; health and wellbeing, including gender-sensitive rehabilitation; leisure, recreation and physical activity; participation in society and inclusiveness; policy and service, aligning work with the implementation of the UN Convention on the Rights of People with Disabilities and organizing outreach at the National Rehabilitation Conference in Helsinki, Finland; and work and employment. The organization offers grants through the Africa Fund and Global Disability Development Fund; and organizes an annual World Congress. It comprises more than 1,000 organizations in 100 countries, with regional offices in Africa, the Middle East, Asia, Europe, North America, South America and Central America.
Geographical Area of Activity: International.
Publications: Annual Report; newsletter; *Rehabilitation Review* (annual); *One in Ten*; bulletins; factsheets; catalogues.
Finance: Annual revenue US $1.3m., expenditure $493,736 (31 Dec. 2021).
Board of Directors: Prof. Dr Christoph Gutenbrunner (Pres.); Haidi Zhang (Immediate Past Pres.); Susan Parker (Treas.).
Principal Staff: Sec.-Gen. Teuta Rexhepi.
Contact Details: 866 UN Plaza, Office 422, New York, NY 10017; tel. (212) 420-1500; e-mail info@riglobal.org; internet www.riglobal.org.

Relief International

Founded in 1990 to reduce suffering worldwide; merged with Schools Online in 2006 and Enterpriseworks/VITA in 2009.
Activities: Promotes self-reliance in fragile settings and empowers communities by maximizing local resources. Main programme areas are: economic opportunity; education; health and nutrition; and water, sanitation and hygiene. Cross-cutting themes are climate change, refugees and internally displaced people and cash assistance. It works in 16 countries, with offices in London (UK) and Lyon (France).
Geographical Area of Activity: Asia, France, Middle East and North Africa, sub-Saharan Africa, UK, USA.
Publications: Annual Report; newsletter; reports; toolkits.
Finance: Annual revenue US $63.3m., expenditure $61.4m. (31 Dec. 2022).
Board of Directors: Chip Levengood (Chair.).
Principal Staff: CEO Craig Redmond.
Contact Details: 1101 14th St NW, Suite 710, Washington, DC 20005; tel. (202) 639-8660; e-mail info@ri.org; internet www.ri.org.

Research Corporation for Science Advancement—RCSA

Established in 1912 by Frederick Gardner Cottrell, a professor of chemistry, and others.

Activities: Funds scientific research (in physics, chemistry, astronomy and closely related fields) proposed by US and Canadian colleges and university faculties. Programmes include: the Cottrell Scholars programme, which funds basic research and innovative science teaching; and the Scialog Award, which supports research, intensive dialogue and community building to address scientific challenges of global significance. Within each multi-year initiative, Scialog Fellows collaborate in high-risk discovery research on untested ideas and communicate their progress in annual closed conferences.

Geographical Area of Activity: USA.

Publications: Annual Report; newsletter; occasional reports; books.

Finance: Annual revenue US $42.3m., expenditure $12.7m. (31 Dec. 2023).

Board of Directors: Peter K. Dorhout (Chair.); Eugene Flood, Jr (Immediate Past Chair.); James DeNaut (Treas.); Danielle D. Johnson (Sec.).

Principal Staff: Pres. and CEO Dr Daniel Linzer.

Contact Details: 4703 East Camp Lowell Dr., Suite 201, Tuscon, AZ 85712; tel. (520) 571-1111; e-mail contactus@rescorp.org; internet www.rescorp.org.

The Resource Foundation—TRF

Established in 1987 by Dr Loren Finnell, an international development consultant and co-founder of Private Agencies Collaborating Together (Pact, q.v.).

Activities: Works to give people in low-income communities skills, knowledge and opportunities to improve their lives. Programme areas include: affordable housing; capacity building; culture; disaster relief; education and vocational training; environmental conservation; financial inclusion; healthcare and HIV/AIDS; impact investing; potable water and sanitation; sustainable agriculture; and women's empowerment. The Foundation supports seven Greatest Needs Funds, which focus on pressing issues including education, healthcare, food security and potable water; and manages Hosted Funds and Fiscal Sponsorship Funds on behalf of individual, corporate and foundation donors, and non-profit organizations. It comprises a network of more than 370 local non-profit organizations in 34 countries; and was a founding member of the Alliance for International Giving (f. 2007).

Geographical Area of Activity: Latin America and the Caribbean, USA.

Publications: Annual Report; newsletter; blog.

Finance: Annual revenue US $2.8m., expenditure $2.6m. (31 Dec. 2023).

Board of Directors: Pedro Lichtinger (Chair.).

Principal Staff: Exec. Dir Beatriz Guillén.

Contact Details: 244 Fifth Ave, Suite 1428, New York, NY 10001; tel. (212) 675-6170; e-mail inquiries@resourcefnd.org; internet resourcefnd.org.

Richard King Mellon Foundation

Founded in 1947 by Richard King Mellon, Pres. and Chair. of Mellon Bank.

Activities: Invests in economic development, education and human services in South-Western Pennsylvania; and in the protection, preservation and restoration of environmental heritage in the USA. Main programmes are Regional Economic Development and Conservation, Education and Human Services, and Nonprofit Capacity Building.

Geographical Area of Activity: USA (primarily South-Western Pennsylvania).

Restrictions: No grants to individuals or for applications from outside the USA; funding is mainly restricted to South-Western Pennsylvania.

Publications: Annual Report; information brochure.

Finance: Annual income US $288.9m., expenditure $125.1m. (31 Dec. 2023).

Trustees: Richard A. Mellon (Chair. and CEO); Lynne Ventress (Sec.).

Principal Staff: Pres. Catharine Mellon Cathey; Vice-Pres. and Treas. Douglas L. Sisson; Dir Sam Reiman.

Contact Details: The Auction House, 42 21st St, Suite 201, Pittsburgh, PA 15222; tel. (412) 392-2800; e-mail rkmf@rkmf.org; internet www.rkmf.org.

Righteous Persons Foundation

Established in 1994 by film-maker Steven Spielberg, initially with his profits from the films *Schindler's List* and subsequently *Munich* and *Lincoln*.

Activities: Supports efforts that build a vibrant, just and inclusive Jewish community in the USA. The Foundation has invested in organizations and efforts working to: revitalize Jewish arts, culture and identity; preserve Jewish history and traditions and engage the next generation; strengthen a commitment to social justice; promote understanding between Jews and those of other faiths and backgrounds; and ensure that the Holocaust is not forgotten.

Geographical Area of Activity: Mainly USA.

Restrictions: Does not generally fund programmes outside of the USA, individuals or scholarships.

Finance: Annual revenue US $3.4m., expenditure $3.4m. (31 Dec. 2022).

Principal Staff: Exec. Dir Shayna Triebwasser.

Contact Details: 400 S Beverly Dr., Suite 420, Beverly Hills, CA 90212; tel. (310) 314-8393; e-mail grants@righteouspersons.org; internet www.righteouspersons.org.

Rising Impact

Founded in 1985 as Population Communications International (PCI); formerly PCI Media Impact, current name adopted in 2025.

Activities: Works with media and other organizations to influence population trends. Programmes focus on health, the environment and social justice. The organization promotes sustainable development through the research, production and broadcast of locally run and culturally appropriate radio and television serial dramas. These productions inform and educate local communities about population and development issues through popular entertainment, and work to enhance communications between NGOs. Issues covered include violence against women, HIV/AIDS prevention, reproductive health, human rights and democracy. It also acts as the Secretariat for the NGO Committee on Population and Development, which encourages co-operation between the UN and NGOs. Operates in 70 countries, with offices in Africa, Latin America and the Caribbean.

Geographical Area of Activity: International.

Restrictions: Does not make grants.

Publications: Annual Report; newsletter; brochure.

Finance: Annual revenue US $7.2m., expenditure $3.9m. (31 Dec. 2022).

Board of Directors: Tony Lee (Chair.); Luis Orozco (Treas.); Judy Friedman (Sec.).

Principal Staff: Pres. Meesha Brown.

Contact Details: 26 Broadway, Suite 934, New York, NY 10004; tel. (212) 457-7566; e-mail info@pcimedia.org; internet risingimpactglobal.org.

Robert Wood Johnson Foundation—RWJF

Founded in 1936, as the Johnson New Brunswick Foundation, by Robert Wood Johnson, II, the Pres. and Gen. Man. of Johnson & Johnson, a manufacturer of pharmaceutical and medical supplies.

Activities: Works to improve health, equity and wellbeing through conducting policy and systems research and evaluations. The Foundation funds research and initiatives in the areas of: healthy children and families, including early childhood, obesity and wellbeing; healthy communities, including the built environment, disease prevention, health disparities and social determinants; health systems, including public and community healthcare access, coverage, quality and value; and leadership for better health, including nurses and nursing. It has offices in New York and Washington, DC.

Geographical Area of Activity: USA.

Restrictions: Does not fund basic biomedical research or research on drug therapies or devices.

Publications: Annual Report; *Advance* (newsletter); occasional reports; blog; books.

Finance: Annual revenue US $1,119.2m., expenditure $877.6m. (31 Dec. 2022).

Board of Trustees: Starsky D. Wilson (Chair.).

Principal Staff: Pres. and CEO Richard E. Besser.

Contact Details: 50 College Rd East, Princeton, NJ 08540-6614; tel. (609) 627-6000; e-mail mail@rwjf.org; internet www.rwjf.org.

Robertson Foundation for Government—RFG

Established in 2010 by the family of the late Charles and Marie Robertson, who had inherited the A&P retail chain fortune.

Activities: Promotes careers with the Federal Government. The Foundation prepares US graduate students for careers in foreign policy, national security and international affairs. Its flagship Robertson Fellows Program offers scholarships and stipends to students at five universities.

Geographical Area of Activity: USA.

Restrictions: Robertson Fellows must work for the Federal Government for three of the first seven years after graduation and become proficient in a foreign language upon graduation.

Publications: Newsletter.

Finance: Annual revenue –US $203,544, expenditure $1.5m. (31 Dec. 2022).

Board of Directors: Carmen Iezzi Mezzera (Chair.); Nils Moe (Treas.); Olivia Robertson-Moe (Sec.).

Principal Staff: Pres. Julia Robertson.

Contact Details: 1455 Pennsylvania Ave, NW, Suite 400, Washington, DC 20004; tel. (202) 489-0825; e-mail info@rfg.org; internet rfg.org.

Rockefeller Brothers Fund—RBF

Founded in 1940 as a vehicle through which the five sons and daughter of John D. Rockefeller, Jr, a financier and philanthropist, could share advice and research on charitable activities and combine philanthropies to better effect. John D. Rockefeller, Jr, made a substantial gift to the Fund in 1951, and in 1960 the Fund received a major bequest from his estate. In 1999 it merged with the Charles E. Culpepper Fund.

Activities: Supports social change for a more just, sustainable and peaceful world through grantmaking, convening and investing. Main programmes include: Democratic Practice; Peacebuilding; Sustainable Development; China; Western Balkans; and Culpepper Arts and Culture. The Fund works worldwide, but concentrates cross-programmatic attention on specific 'RBF pivotal places': subnational areas, nation-states or cross-border regions that have special importance with regard to the Fund's substantive concerns, and whose future will have disproportionate significance for the future of a surrounding region, ecosystem or the world. It manages the Pocantico Center in Tarrytown, NY, a venue for conferences, public lectures and cultural events.

Geographical Area of Activity: Worldwide.

Restrictions: No grants to individuals or for capital works.

Publications: Annual Review; newsletter.

Finance: Annual revenue US $118.2m., expenditure $83.2m. (31 Dec. 2021).

Board of Trustees: Joseph Pierson (Chair.).

Principal Staff: Pres. and CEO Stephen B. Heintz.

Contact Details: 475 Riverside Dr., Suite 900, New York, NY 10115; tel. (212) 812-4200; e-mail communications@rbf.org; internet www.rbf.org.

Rockefeller Foundation

Founded in 1913 by John D. Rockefeller, Sr, founder of the Standard Oil Co.

Activities: Operates nationally and internationally through offering grants. Main programmes include: agriculture, food security and healthy diets; improving medical outcomes for people in need and supporting Universal Health Coverage; ending energy poverty through providing reliable renewable electricity; expanding equity and economic opportunity for US working families; and using impact investing, data science, technology and innovation. The Foundation organizes international conferences and residencies for artists and scholars at its Bellagio Study and Conference Center (f. 1959) on Lake Como in northern Italy. It has offices in Washington, DC; and Bangkok, Thailand and Nairobi, Kenya.

Geographical Area of Activity: International.

Restrictions: No grants are made for personal aid to individuals, nor for general institutional support or fund endowments, nor for building or operating funds.

Publications: Annual Report; newsletter.

Finance: Annual revenue US $335.7m., expenditure $352.6m. (31 Dec. 2022).

Board of Trustees: Adm. (Ret.) James Stavridis (Chair.).

Principal Staff: Pres. Dr Rajiv J. Shah.

Contact Details: 420 Fifth Ave, New York, NY 10018; tel. (212) 869-8500; internet www.rockefellerfoundation.org.

Rogosin Institute

Founded in 1983; an independent, non-profit institution affiliated with the New York-Presbyterian Hospital (NYPH) and Weill Cornell Medical College.

Activities: Researches, treats and prevents kidney disease, carrying out dialysis and transplantation; and also conducts clinical research on diabetes, cancer and cardiovascular disease. The Institute includes the Rogosin Kidney Center, the Dreyfus Health Foundation (f. 1965), the Susan R. Knafel Polycystic Kidney Disease Center (f. 2002); and the Maurice R. & Corinne P. Greenberg Center for Integrative Health (f. 2015), comprising the Jack J. Dreyfus Center for Health Action and Policy (CHAP), which provides community and professional healthcare education and training, community outreach, and data analysis and policy advocacy on contemporary health problems.

Geographical Area of Activity: USA.

Finance: Annual revenue US $116.5m., expenditure $123.9m. (31 Dec. 2022).

Principal Staff: Pres. David A. Wyman; Exec. Vice-Pres. Allyson Pifko.

Contact Details: 504–506 E. 74th St, New York, NY 10021; tel. (212) 746-1551; e-mail info-rogosin@nyp.org; internet www.rogosin.org.

The Rotary Foundation

Founded in 1917 by the Rotary International civilian service network.

Activities: Works to advance world understanding, goodwill and peace through improving health, supporting education and eliminating poverty. Grantmaking themes include: basic education and literacy; community economic development; disease prevention and treatment; maternal and child health; peacebuilding and conflict prevention; water, sanitation and hygiene; and the environment. The Foundation offers district grants for small-scale, short-term activities at community level; global grants, through the World Fund, of between US $30,000 and $400,000; and grants for large-scale, longer-term programmes, of up to $2m. over 3–5 years. It also offers disaster response grants of up to $25,000 to Rotary districts that have been affected by natural disasters. There are associate foundations in Australia, Brazil, Canada, Germany, India, Japan and the United Kingdom.

Geographical Area of Activity: International.

Restrictions: Grants only to Rotary club members.

Publications: Annual Report; programme brochures; reports.

Finance: Annual revenue US $467.1m., expenditure $347.2m. (30 June 2024).

Board of Trustees: Mark Daniel Maloney (Chair.); Holger Knaack (Chair.-elect).

Board of Directors: Stephanie A. Urchick (Pres.); Mário César Martins de Camargo (Pres.-elect); Hans-Hermann Kasten (Vice-Pres.); Rhonda 'Beth' Stubbs (Treas.).

Principal Staff: Gen. Sec. and CEO John Hewko.

Contact Details: 1 Rotary Center, 1560 Sherman Ave, Evanston, IL 60201; tel. (847) 866-3000; e-mail rotarysupportcenter@rotary.org; internet www.rotary.org/en/about-rotary/rotary-foundation.

Russell Sage Foundation—RSF

Established in 1907 by Margaret Olivia Sage, in memory of her husband Russell Sage, a financier.

Activities: Works to strengthen the methods, data and theory of social sciences. Main programme areas are: behavioural economics; the future of work; race, ethnicity and immigration; and social, political and economic equality. The Visiting Scholars Program allows social scientists to carry out research while in residence at the Foundation, which also offers shorter-term residencies for Visiting Researchers and Visiting Journalists. It offers Project Grants, typically worth up to US $175,000; and supports data analysis and the writing up of results.

Geographical Area of Activity: USA.

Restrictions: No grants to programmes that do not focus on the USA, for pre-doctoral study or research; no scholarships or other types of grants for support of college funding.

Publications: *RSF: The Russell Sage Foundation Journal of the Social Sciences;* newsletter; working papers; books.

Finance: Annual revenue US $12.8m., expenditure $16.3m. (31 Aug. 2022).

Board of Trustees: Jennifer Richeson (Chair.); Leana Chatrath (Sec.).

Principal Staff: Pres. Sheldon Danziger.

Contact Details: 112 E. 64th St, New York, NY 10065; tel. (212) 750-6000; e-mail info@rsage.org; internet www.russellsage.org.

Rutherford Institute

Founded in 1982 by John Whitehead, a lawyer and author.

Activities: Dedicated to the defence of civil and human rights. The Institute provides lawyers to help people whose civil rights or human rights have been violated. It also provides educational opportunities to improve standards of social justice in the USA.

Geographical Area of Activity: International.

Publications: *Insider* (e-mail newsletter); Freedom Resource Bank (briefs and pamphlets); books.

Finance: Annual revenue US $745,109, expenditure $821,822 (30 June 2023).

Board of Directors: John W. Whitehead (Pres. and Chair.); Mike Masters (Vice-Chair.); Thomas S. Neuberger (Treas./Sec.).

Principal Staff: Exec. Dir Nisha N. Whitehead.

Contact Details: POB 7482, Charlottesville, VA 22906-7482; tel. (434) 978-3888; e-mail staff@rutherford.org; internet www.rutherford.org.

Sakena Fund

Founded in 1982 by Carolyn 'Toc' Dunlap, an educator and lawyer, and Dr Sakena Yacoobi, founder and CEO of the Afghan Institute of Learning. Formerly known as Creating Hope International.

Activities: Helps victims of war, political unrest and natural disasters through grassroots programmes so that they can rebuild their lives for a better future. The organization provides technical and financial assistance to raise the level of education, health and economy throughout parts of the world where people, particularly women and children, are underprivileged, poor, oppressed or generally in need. It fosters worldwide interest in these causes to increase funding for those who lack basic healthcare, and educational and training opportunities. Currently concentrates on assisting women and children in Afghanistan, through the Afghan Institute of Learning, and Tibetan refugees in India.

Geographical Area of Activity: Afghanistan, India, Pakistan.

Publications: Newsletter.

Finance: Annual revenue US $1.3m., expenditure $1.2m. (31 Dec. 2022).

Board of Directors: Dr Sakena Yacoobi (Pres., Chair. and Exec. Dir); Behzad Boroumand (Treas.); Liela Yacoobi (Sec.).

Contact Details: POB 1058, Dearborn, MI 48121; tel. (313) 278-5806; e-mail contact@sakena.org; internet www.sakena.org.

Samaritan's Purse

Founded in 1970 by Dr Robert Pierce, a Baptist minister and founder of World Vision (q.v.); an international non-denominational Christian organization.

Activities: Provides aid and assistance to victims of war, disasters, disease, famine and poverty and promotes Christianity worldwide. Programmes include: emergency healthcare and improving existing medical facilities; providing emergency supplies, including food and clothing; funding community development projects; and providing shelters for abandoned children. The organization also holds evangelical Christian festivals throughout the world. It has offices in Australia, Canada, Germany and the United Kingdom.

Geographical Area of Activity: International.

Publications: Annual Report; newsletter; factsheets.

Finance: Annual revenue US $1,201.9m., expenditure $1,037.5m. (31 Dec. 2023).

Board: Franklin Graham (Chair., Pres. and CEO); Brian Pauls (Vice-Chair.); Sterling Carroll (Treas.); Donna Pierce (Sec.).

Contact Details: POB 3000, Boone, NC 28607; tel. (828) 262-1980; e-mail info@samaritan.org; internet www.samaritanspurse.org.

Samuel H. Kress Foundation

Established in 1929 by Samuel H. Kress, a business person and art collector.

Activities: Offers grants and professional development fellowships to advance the understanding and conservation of European art, architecture and archaeology from antiquity to the early 19th century. The Foundation has partnerships with the International Center of Medieval Art, the Renaissance Society of America and the Archaeological Institute of America.

Geographical Area of Activity: Europe, North America.

Restrictions: Grants only to US non-profit organizations; no grants to individuals or to purchase art; fellowship applicants must be nominated by academic departments or host institutions.

Publications: Annual Report.

Finance: Annual revenue US $5.1m., expenditure $3.9m. (30 June 2022).

Board of Trustees: Carmela Vircillo Franklin (Chair.).

The San Diego Foundation UNITED STATES OF AMERICA

Principal Staff: Pres. Julia M. Alexander.
Contact Details: 174 East 80th St, New York, NY 10075; tel. (212) 861-4993; e-mail info@kressfoundation.org; internet www.kressfoundation.org.

The San Diego Foundation
Established in 1975, with support from the Gildred Foundation, United Way (q.v.) and the Ed and Mary Fletcher and Willis and Jane Fletcher Foundations.
Activities: Supports communities and individuals in San Diego, and increases effective philanthropy, managing more than 2,100 funds. The Foundation awards grants to individuals and organizations in areas including education, the environment, civic engagement, health and human services, and the arts. It contributes to charitable causes; awards scholarships; lends organizational support to projects; and facilitates communication among San Diego's communities. The San Diego Women's Foundation (f. 2000) is a supporting foundation.
Geographical Area of Activity: USA.
Publications: Annual Report; *SDF News – Nonprofit Newsletter* (monthly).
Finance: Annual revenue US $294.9m., expenditure $144.1m. (30 June 2023).
Board of Governors: Dr Pamela Luster (Chair.); Steven Klosterman (Immediate Past Chair. and Vice-Chair.); Elvin Lai (Treas.); Dr Becky Petitt (Sec.).
Principal Staff: Pres. and CEO Mark Stuart.
Contact Details: 2508 Historic Decatur Rd, Suite 200, San Diego, CA 92106; tel. (619) 235-2300; e-mail info@sdfoundation.org; internet www.sdfoundation.org.

San Francisco Foundation—SFF
Founded in 1948 for the support of philanthropic undertakings in the San Francisco Bay Area, CA.
Activities: Advances racial equity and economic inclusion through strengthening communities, fostering civic leadership and promoting philanthropy. Main grantmaking programmes are: People, expanding access to opportunity, funding projects to improve access to jobs, education and community services; Place, providing affordable housing, fostering arts and culture and supporting community-based organizations; and Power, building the capacity of community organizers and increasing political participation and voter turnout among marginalized groups. It offers Arts Awards and Community Leadership Awards to individuals and organizations; and administers the Daniel E. Koshland Civic Unity Program (f. 1982), which makes investments in neighbourhood initiatives of up to US $300,000 over five years.
Geographical Area of Activity: USA (San Francisco Bay area).
Restrictions: Grants only to non-profit organizations in Alameda, Contra Costa, Marin, San Francisco and San Mateo counties.
Publications: Annual Report; *Enews*; *Koshland Connect* (annual); research reports.
Finance: Annual revenue US $235.2m., expenditure $228.9m. (30 June 2024).
Board of Trustees: Robert (Bob) Friedman (Chair.); David ibnAle (Vice-Chair.).
Principal Staff: CEO Fred Blackwell.
Contact Details: 1 Embarcadero Center, Suite 1400, San Francisco, CA 94111; tel. (415) 733-8500; e-mail info@sff.org; internet www.sff.org.

Sarah Scaife Foundation, Inc
Founded in 1941 by Sarah Mellon Scaife, daughter of Richard B. Mellon, a banker and industrialist; present name adopted in 1974. Merged with the Carthage Foundation (f. 1966) in 2015; shares administration with the Allegheny Foundation (f. 1958); and is related to the Scaife Family Foundation (f. 1983), which mainly operates in Florida and Pennsylvania.
Activities: Supports public policy programmes that address major domestic and international issues, in areas such as education, government, economics, international law, crime and law enforcement, and international affairs. Makes grants for fellowships, research, projects, conferences and publications.
Geographical Area of Activity: USA.
Restrictions: No grants to individuals or national fund-raising groups.
Publications: Annual Report.
Finance: Annual revenue US $40.8m., expenditure $49.8m. (31 Dec. 2023).
Board: Michael W. Gleba (Chair, CEO and Treas.); Linda M. Buckley Bly (Sec.).
Contact Details: 1 Oxford Centre, 301 Grant St, Suite 3900, Pittsburgh, PA 15219-6401; tel. (412) 392-2900; internet www.scaife.com/sarah.html.

Schlumberger Foundation
Established in 1954 in the USA by Schlumberger, an oilfield services company; includes Schlumberger Stichting Fund in the Netherlands.
Activities: Operates in the field of science, technology, engineering and mathematics (STEM) education. The Foundation focuses on strengthening university faculties and mitigating obstacles faced by women scientists through its Faculty for the Future grant programme, which offers fellowships to women from developing and emerging economies preparing for a PhD, of up to US $50,000 per year, or postdoctoral study, of up to $40,000 per year, in the physical sciences, engineering or related disciplines to pursue study at top universities abroad. Grant recipients are selected for their leadership capabilities in addition to their scientific talents and are expected to return to their home countries to continue their academic careers and inspire other young women.
Geographical Area of Activity: Worldwide.
Restrictions: Does not accept unsolicited applications; Faculty for the Future applicants must be citizens of developing countries.
Publications: Annual Report; conference proceedings.
Finance: Annual revenue US $1.4m., expenditure $948,533 (31 Dec. 2022).
Board of Directors: Gerard Martellozo (Chair.); Capella Festa (Pres.); Roseline Chapel (Treas.).
Contact Details: c/o BDO USA PC, 100 Park Ave, New York, NY 10017; tel. (212) 885-8000; e-mail foundation@slb.com; internet schlumbergerfoundation.com.

Seeds of Peace
Founded in 1993 by John Wallach, a journalist.
Activities: Inspires and cultivates new generations of leaders in communities divided by conflict by providing them with the skills and relationships to accelerate social, economic and political change. The organization organizes a summer camp on Pleasant Lake in Maine for delegates aged 14–16 years. Its network includes more than 8,000 alumni in 27 countries, with staff in Amman (Jordan), Cairo (Egypt), Gaza (Palestinian Territories), Jerusalem (Israel), Lahore (Pakistan), London (UK) and Mumbai (India).
Geographical Area of Activity: Europe, Middle East, South Asia, USA.
Restrictions: Camp applicants are nominated by schools and must be proficient in English.
Publications: Annual Report; newsletter; brochures.
Finance: Annual revenue US $5.3m., expenditure $7.6m. (31 Dec. 2022).
Board of Directors: Sandra S. Wijnberg (Chair.); Jordan Solomon, Tiziana Sousou (Vice-Chair.); Anna Tunkel (Sec.).
Contact Details: 370 Lexington Ave, Suite 201, New York, NY 10017; tel. (212) 573-8040; e-mail info@seedsofpeace.org; internet www.seedsofpeace.org.

Serrv International, Inc

Established in 1949, as Sales Exchange for Refugee Rehabilitation and Vocation (SERRV), by the Church of the Brethren to help refugees in Europe after the Second World War; present name adopted in 1999.

Activities: Promotes the economic and social progress of people living in developing countries and aims to alleviate poverty through fair trade. The organization acts as a fair trade, non-profit organization, advancing money to low-income artisans in developing countries to buy raw materials to make crafts, which it sells through more than 3,000 churches, non-profit groups and retail outlets. Works with more than 8,000 artisans in 23 countries.

Geographical Area of Activity: International.

Publications: Annual Report; newsletter (quarterly); *SERRV Catalogue*; blog.

Finance: Annual revenue US $4.7m., expenditure $5.4m. (31 Dec. 2023).

Board of Directors: Ron Kruczynski (Chair. and Treas.); Joseph Lewzcak (Sec.).

Principal Staff: Pres. and CEO Serena Sato.

Contact Details: 532 Baltimore Blvd, No. 409, Westminster, MD 21157; tel. (608) 255-0440; internet www.serrv.org.

Sesame Workshop

Established in 1969 by Joan Ganz Cooney and Lloyd Morrisett as the Children's Television Workshop, the creator of *Sesame Street*, a children's TV series; incorporates the Yellow Feather Fund.

Activities: Supports the developmental, physical and emotional needs of children aged 0–6 years through research-based media, social impact programmes and formal education. Areas of focus are: autism; gender equity; health and hygiene; military families; racial justice; refugee response; and traumatic experiences. The organization: produces educational children's TV programmes; invests in social impact initiatives; convenes educators, producers and entrepreneurs to advance digital learning; and researches emerging technologies through the Joan Ganz Cooney Center. It invests in and supports mission-aligned start-ups through Sesame Ventures. Sesame Street in Communities, funded by the Joan Ganz Cooney Fund for Vulnerable Children and the Robert Wood Johnson Foundation (q.v.), provides free educational resources for parents and caregivers; and offers professional development and training to community providers.

Geographical Area of Activity: East Asia and Oceania, Europe, Latin America, Middle East and North Africa, North America, South Asia, sub-Saharan Africa.

Publications: Annual Report; newsletter; educational resources; blog.

Finance: Annual revenue US $258.3m., expenditure $224.3m. (30 June 2022).

Board of Trustees: Jane D. Hartley (Chair.).

Principal Staff: Exec. Chair. Jeffrey D. Dunn; CEO Steve Youngwood; Pres. Sherrie Westin.

Contact Details: 1 Lincoln Plaza, 1900 Broadway, New York, NY 10023; tel. (212) 595-3456; e-mail Web.CorpComm@sesame.org; internet www.sesameworkshop.org.

Seva Foundation

Established in 1978 by Dr Larry Brilliant, an epidemiologist and founder of Ending Pandemics (q.v.), and his wife Girija Brilliant, a public health specialist, among others.

Activities: Works with partners in under-served countries to prevent avoidable blindness and establish self-sustaining, community-based programmes to preserve and restore sight. Priority areas are care for children, gender equity, sustainability, training and universal access. The Foundation builds capacity in hospitals and institutions; and provides medical treatment, surgery and glasses. It works in more than 20 countries, with offices in Cambodia and Nepal.

Geographical Area of Activity: Worldwide.

Restrictions: Does not accept unsolicited applications.

Publications: Annual Report; *Spirit of Service* (newsletter); special programme reports; blog.

Finance: Annual revenue US $11.8m., expenditure $13.5m. (30 June 2024).

Board of Directors: Mariano Yee (Chair.); Claudio Privetera (Vice-Chair.); Lisa Laird (Treas.); Vaughan Acton (Sec.).

Principal Staff: Exec. Dir and CEO Kate Moynihan.

Contact Details: 1786 Fifth St, Berkeley, CA 94710; tel. (510) 845-7382; e-mail info@seva.org; internet www.seva.org.

The Sierra Club Foundation

Founded in 1960 to support the Sierra Club (f. 1982), an environmental organization.

Activities: Works in the fields of environmental quality and social justice. The Foundation supports the Sierra Club and other non-profit organizations that protect and restore the environment; and carries out advocacy in environmental litigation. It offers international partnership grants to organizations working to prevent the expansion of coal and fossil fuel development; and, through the Forward Faster Fund, invests in community-based clean energy projects.

Geographical Area of Activity: International.

Restrictions: Does not accept unsolicited proposals.

Publications: Annual Report; factsheets.

Finance: Annual revenue US $104.1m., expenditure $113.5m. (31 Dec. 2023).

Board of Directors: Robin Mann (Chair.); Joel Sanders (Vice-Chair.); Jessica Sarowitz (Treas.); Rebekah Saul Butler (Sec.).

Principal Staff: Exec. Dir Dan Chu.

Contact Details: 2101 Webster St, Suite 1250, Oakland, CA 94612; tel. (415) 995-1780; e-mail foundation@sierraclubfoundation.org; internet www.sierraclubfoundation.org.

Silicon Valley Community Foundation—SVCF

Established in 2007 by the merger of the Peninsula Community Foundation and Community Foundation Silicon Valley.

Activities: Provides leadership, expertise and capital to address social, economic and environmental challenges. The Foundation commissions research to identify and analyse emerging trends; holds public discussions to solve problems and stimulate new insights; advocates policy changes; and collaborates with other organizations on initiatives and special projects. Strategic grants are awarded covering five areas: civic participation; common core education; financial stability; housing and transportation; and immigration. It also administers open competitive grantmaking programmes for corporate partners locally, nationally and internationally; and awards around 600 scholarships to high-school, community college and university students from or studying in California and from outside the USA. Manages more than 1,500 charitable funds.

Geographical Area of Activity: International.

Restrictions: Makes strategic grants to non-profit organizations serving San Mateo and/or Santa Clara Counties, CA.

Publications: Annual Report; newsletter (monthly); *SVCF Magazine*; reports; blog.

Finance: Annual revenue US $3,304.5m., expenditure $4,728.5m. (31 Dec. 2023).

Board of Directors: Greta S. Hansen (Chair.).

Principal Staff: Pres. and CEO Nicole Taylor.

Contact Details: 444 Castro St, Suite 140, Mountain View, CA 94041; tel. (650) 450-5400; e-mail info@siliconvalleycf.org; internet www.siliconvalleycf.org.

Simons Foundation

Established in 1994 by Dr Jim Simons, a mathematician and hedge fund manager, and Dr Marilyn Simons, an economist.

Activities: Supports research in mathematics and the basic sciences. The Foundation offers grants in the areas of: autism research (through the Simons Foundation Autism Research Initiative); life sciences, mathematics and physical sciences (and Simons Collaborations, which span these three fields); and outreach and education, including the Science Sandbox and Math for America initiatives to encourage interest in scientific thinking and science, technology, engineering and mathematics among secondary school students, and public Simons Foundation Lectures. In 2016 it established the Flatiron Institute, which comprises: the Center for Computational Biology (f. 2013 as the Simons Center for Data Analysis); Center for Computational Astrophysics (f. 2016); Center for Computational Quantum Physics (f. 2017); Center for Computational Mathematics (f. 2018); Center for Computational Neuroscience (f. 2020); and the Scientific Computing Core.

Geographical Area of Activity: USA.

Publications: Annual Report; newsletter; *Spectrum* (online magazine); *Quanta Magazine* (online).

Finance: Annual income US $192.8m., expenditure $579.1m. (31 Dec. 2023).

Board of Directors: Dr Marilyn H. Simons (Chair.); Dr Shirley M. Tilghman (Vice-Chair.); Dr James H. Simons (Chair. Emeritus).

Principal Staff: Pres. Dr David N. Spergel.

Contact Details: 160 Fifth Ave, 7th Floor, New York, NY 10010; tel. (646) 654-0066; e-mail info@simonsfoundation.org; internet www.simonsfoundation.org.

Skoll Foundation

Established in 2002 by Jeff Skoll, former President of e-commerce company eBay; incorporates the Skoll Fund (f. 1999), associated with the Silicon Valley Community Foundation (q.v.). Part of the Jeff Skoll Group, which incorporates Participant Media, an entertainment company, and Capricorn Investment Group, a sustainable investment firm.

Activities: Invests in social entrepreneurs and creates networks to bring about social transformation through disrupting social and political forces. Main portfolio areas are: climate action; democracy; economic inclusion; and racial justice. The Foundation established the Skoll Awards for Social Entrepreneurship, each worth US $1.5m. over three years, in the areas of economic opportunity, education, environmental sustainability, health, peace and human rights, and sustainable markets. It convenes the annual Skoll World Forum in Oxford, United Kingdom; and in 2003 established the Skoll Centre for Social Entrepreneurship at the Saïd Business School, Oxford University. The Skoll Global Threats Fund (f. 2008) closed in 2017, its Climate Advocacy Lab and the Ending Pandemics Initiative becoming independent organizations.

Geographical Area of Activity: UK, USA.

Publications: Annual Report; newsletter.

Finance: Annual revenue US $109.5m., expenditure $71.5m. (31 Dec. 2023).

Board of Directors: Jeffrey S. Skoll (Chair.); James DeMartini, III (Vice-Chair.).

Principal Staff: Pres. and COO Marla Blow; CEO Don Gips.

Contact Details: 250 University Ave, Suite 200, Palo Alto, CA 94301; tel. (650) 331-1031; e-mail info@skoll.org; internet www.skoll.org.

Smith Richardson Foundation, Inc

Founded in 1935 by H. S. Richardson, Sr, head of Richardson-Vicks, Inc, a pharmaceutical company, and his wife Grace Jones Richardson.

Activities: Informs public policy debates through supporting pragmatic, policy-relevant research, analysis and writing. The Foundation provides grants in two main programme areas: international security and foreign policy, which supports research and policy projects on issues central to the strategic interests of the USA; and domestic public policy, researching the development of US economic, social and governmental institutions.

Geographical Area of Activity: USA.

Restrictions: Does not usually accept unsolicited applications; no grants to individuals nor for projects in the arts and humanities, physical sciences or historic restoration.

Publications: Annual Report.

Finance: Annual revenue US $7.7m., expenditure $40.0m. (31 Dec. 2023).

Trustees: Peter L. Richardson (Chair.); W. Winburne King, III (Vice-Chair.); Dr Arvid R. Nelson (Sec.).

Principal Staff: Pres. Dr Marin Strmecki; Vice-Pres. Ross F. Hemphill.

Contact Details: 60 Jesup Rd, Westport, CT 06880; tel. (203) 222-6222; e-mail info@srf.org; internet www.srf.org.

Smithsonian Institution

Created in 1846 by an Act of Congress in accordance with the terms of the will of James Smithson of England.

Activities: Operates nationally and internationally in the fields of education, science, the arts and humanities, and the conservation of natural resources. The Institution conducts basic research; publishes results of studies, explorations and investigations; maintains study and reference collections in the sciences, culture and history; and exhibitions in the arts, American history, technology, aeronautics, space exploration and natural history. It administers 21 museums, 21 specialized research libraries, the National Zoo, and several education and research centres, including the Smithsonian Astrophysics Observatory, Smithsonian Tropical Research Institute, Smithsonian Environmental Research Center and Smithsonian Science Education Center. Fellowships are offered to students of all nationalities to study at Smithsonian Institution facilities. Through the National Museum Act, grants are made to museum professionals for museum studies. The Smithsonian Institution Travelling Exhibition Service organizes exhibitions which circulate to museums around the USA, while the Smithsonian Affiliates Program establishes links and affiliations across the country.

Geographical Area of Activity: USA.

Publications: Annual Report; *Smithsonian Opportunities for Research and Study*; *Smithsonian Magazine*; *Air and Space Magazine*; *American Art*; *Zooger*; factsheets; research centre publications and books; blog.

Finance: Annual revenue US $1,662m., expenditure $1,661m. (30 Sept. 2023).

Board of Regents: Chief Justice John G. Roberts, Jr (Chancellor); Risa J. Lavizzo-Mourey (Chair.); John Fahey (Vice-Chair.).

Principal Staff: Sec. Lonnie G. Bunch, III.

Contact Details: 1000 Jefferson Drive S.W., Washington, DC 20013-7012; tel. (202) 633-1846; e-mail info@si.edu; internet www.si.edu.

Snow Leopard Trust

Established in 1981, as the International Snow Leopard Trust, by Helen Freeman, Curator of Education at the Woodland Park Zoo in Seattle, WA.

Activities: Dedicated to the conservation of the snow leopard and its mountain ecosystem, through conservation, research, education and information exchange. The Trust works with partner organizations in the People's Republic of China, India, Kyrgyzstan, Mongolia and Pakistan. It also carries out certain environmental education, captive breeding and research programmes outside Central Asia.

Geographical Area of Activity: People's Repub. of China, India, Kyrgyzstan, Mongolia, Pakistan.

UNITED STATES OF AMERICA

Publications: Annual Report; *Snow Leopard Tracks Newsletter* (monthly); *Conservation Handbook*; symposia proceedings; scholarly articles; pamphlets; annual reports; annual conservation reports.

Finance: Annual revenue US $3.3m., expenditure $2.9m. (2023).

Board of Directors: Rhetick Sengupta (Pres.); Gayle Podrabsky (Vice-Pres.); Gary Podrabsky (Treas./Sec.).

Principal Staff: Executive Dir Dr Charudutt (Charu) Mishra; Deputy Dir Marissa Niranjan.

Contact Details: 4649 Sunnyside Ave North, Suite 325, Seattle, WA 98103; tel. (206) 632-2421; e-mail info@snowleopard.org; internet www.snowleopard.org.

Solomon R. Guggenheim Foundation

Established in 1937 to operate museums to display the art collection of Solomon Guggenheim, an industrialist, and his wife Irene Rothschild.

Activities: Funds the Solomon R. Guggenheim Museum, New York; the Peggy Guggenheim Collection, Venice, Italy; the Guggenheim Museum Bilbao, Spain; and the Guggenheim Abu Dhabi, United Arab Emirates. The Foundation supports international partnerships and the development of new museums in other regions of the world, special exhibitions, conservation efforts, educational initiatives and research. It maintains a library and archives.

Geographical Area of Activity: International.

Publications: Books; exhibition catalogues.

Finance: Annual revenue US $67.5m., expenditure $46.6m. (31 Dec. 2023).

Trustees: J. Thomilson Hill (Chair.); Wendy Fisher (Pres.); Stephen Robert (Treas.); Sarah G. Austrian (Sec.).

Contact Details: Solomon R. Guggenheim Museum, 1071 Fifth Ave (at 89th St), New York, NY 10128-0173; tel. (212) 423-3500; e-mail foundation@guggenheim.org; internet www.guggenheim.org/about-us/foundation.

Sorenson Legacy Foundation

Established in 2002 by James LeVoy Sorenson, a biotechnology executive and entrepreneur, and his wife Beverley Taylor Sorenson, an education philanthropist.

Activities: Operates in the fields of: arts education; technological innovation; healthcare; and community development, including environmental conservation, helping disenfranchised people, and promoting understanding and tolerance.

Geographical Area of Activity: USA.

Restrictions: Preference is given to initiatives in Utah.

Finance: Annual revenue US $16.0m., expenditure $28.8m. (31 Dec. 2022).

Principal Staff: Pres. Joseph Sorenson.

Contact Details: 6900 S. 900 E., Suite 230, Midvale, UT 84047; tel. (801) 461-9771; e-mail lisa@sdihq.com; internet www.sorensonlegacyfoundation.org.

Spencer Foundation

Established in 1962 by Lyle M. Spencer, founder of Science Research Associates, an educational publisher.

Activities: Supports academic research on education, with an emphasis on behavioural sciences. The Foundation awards research grants of up to US $1m. It also offers postdoctoral fellowships worth $70,000, administered through the National Academy of Education; and journalism fellowships for journalists to spend a year's multidisciplinary study at Columbia University, with the aim of making education research more accessible.

Geographical Area of Activity: USA.

Publications: Newsletter.

Finance: Annual revenue US $42.0m., expenditure $28.3m. (31 March 2023).

Board of Directors: Cecilia Rios-Aguilar (Chair.); Doris Fischer (Sec.).

Principal Staff: Pres. Na'ilah Suad Nasir.

Contact Details: 625 N Michigan Ave, Suite 1600, Chicago, IL 60611; tel. (312) 337-7000; e-mail dfischer@spencer.org; internet www.spencer.org.

Stanley Center for Peace and Security

Founded in 1956, as the Stanley Foundation, by C. Maxwell Stanley, an engineer, and his wife Elizabeth; present name adopted in 2019.

Activities: Advocates principled multilateralism and supports global governance based on laws and norms that uphold peace and security. Main programme areas are: climate change; nuclear weapons; and mass violence and atrocities. The Center organizes strategic policy forums, commissions analysis and publishes policy recommendations; and also journalism workshops, reporting fellowships and investigative reporting projects. It offers Catherine Miller Explorer Awards for teachers from Muscatine, IA, to study abroad.

Geographical Area of Activity: Worldwide.

Restrictions: Not a grantmaking organization.

Publications: *Courier* (magazine, 3 a year); newsletter (6 a year); conference reports; policy briefs; analysis; reports.

Finance: Annual revenue US $5.6m., expenditure $6.8m. (31 Dec. 2022).

Board of Directors: Lori Zook-Stanley (Chair.); Georgina Dodge (Vice-Chair.).

Principal Staff: Pres. and CEO Keith Porter.

Contact Details: 304 Iowa Ave, Muscatine, IA 52761; tel. (563) 264-1500; e-mail info@stanleycenter.org; internet stanleycenter.org.

The Starr Foundation

Founded in 1955 by Cornelius V. Starr, an insurance entrepreneur.

Activities: Makes grants largely in the area of education, particularly secondary and higher education, and to encourage international exchanges. The Foundation is also active in the areas of: culture and community arts; environmental conservation; human needs (including emergency food programmes, job training, literacy programmes, programmes for disabled people and emergency or transitional housing; and grants abroad to refugee and relief efforts, and to provide medical care and support microenterprise development); and public policy in international relations. It offers funding for scholarships, professorships, fellowships and endowment funds.

Geographical Area of Activity: International (but with a focus on New York).

Restrictions: No grants to individuals; does not accept unsolicited applications.

Publications: Annual report; books.

Finance: Annual revenue US $76.8m., expenditure $125.3m. (31 Dec. 2023).

Board of Directors: Jeffrey W. Greenberg (Chair.); L. Scott Greenberg (Treas.).

Principal Staff: Pres. Courtney O'Malley; Senior Vice-Pres. and Sec. Martha Livingston.

Contact Details: 399 Park Ave, 3rd Floor, New York, NY 10022; tel. (212) 909-3600; e-mail info@starrfoundation.org; internet www.starrfoundation.org.

Stewardship Foundation

Founded in 1962 by C. Davis Weyerhaeuser, a director of the Weyerhaeuser Timber Company.

Activities: Funds evangelical Christian organizations whose ministries operate over a wide area. The Foundation's areas of interest include Christian leadership, poverty, justice and reconciliation, faith and discipleship, and children at risk. It makes grants to international development organizations, foreign missions and youth ministries.

Surdna Foundation, Inc

Geographical Area of Activity: Worldwide.

Restrictions: Grants only to US public non-profit organizations; no grants to individuals.

Finance: Annual revenue US $1.9m., expenditure $7.5m. (31 Dec. 2022).

Board of Trustees: Dr William T. Weyerhaeuser (Chair.); Dr Gail T. Weyerhaeuser (Vice-Chair. and Treas.).

Principal Staff: Pres. Jon J. Beighle.

Contact Details: 1145 Broadway, Suite 1500, Tacoma, WA 98402; POB 1278, Tacoma, WA 98401-1278; tel. (253) 620-1340; e-mail contact@stewardshipfdn.org; internet www.stewardshipfdn.org.

Surdna Foundation, Inc

Established in 1917 by John E. Andrus, founder and CEO of the Arlington Chemical Company.

Activities: Carries out activities under three main programmes: Inclusive Economies, investing in businesses owned by people of colour, in particular African-Americans and Latinos; Sustainable Environments, supporting grassroots movements in the areas of environmental and social justice; and Thriving Cultures, offering grants to artists and communities of colour.

Geographical Area of Activity: USA.

Restrictions: No grants to individuals.

Publications: Annual Report; reports; announcements; commissioned reports.

Finance: Annual revenue US $6.1m., expenditure $102.7m. (30 June 2023).

Board of Directors: Caitlin Boger-Hawkins (Chair.); Shari Wilson (Vice-Chair.); Peter Voorhees (Treas./Sec.).

Principal Staff: Pres. Don Chen.

Contact Details: 200 Madison Ave, 25th Floor, New York, NY 10016; tel. (212) 557-0010; e-mail grants@surdna.org; internet www.surdna.org.

Susan G. Komen Breast Cancer Foundation

Established in 1982 by Nancy G. Brinker, in memory of her sister Susan G. Komen, who died from breast cancer.

Activities: Aims to eradicate breast cancer as a life-threatening disease. The organization funds breast cancer research, education, screening and treatment programmes, as well as operating a community-based grants programme; and funding breast cancer health education and screening projects for disadvantaged people. Funding is provided to non-profit organizations, educational institutions and government agencies. It also funds fellowships designed to improve the quality of care for breast cancer patients; and operates a national telephone helpline and International Grant Fund. International affiliates operate in Germany, Italy and Puerto Rico.

Geographical Area of Activity: International.

Publications: Annual Report; newsletter; blog.

Finance: Annual revenue US $130.5m., expenditure $148.5m. (31 March 2023).

Board of Directors: Ed Dandridge (Chair.).

Principal Staff: Pres. and CEO Paula Schneider.

Contact Details: 13770 Noel Rd, Suite 801889, Dallas TX 75380; tel. (972) 855-1600; e-mail info@komen.org; internet www.komen.org.

The Susan Thompson Buffett Foundation—STBF

Established in 1964 by Warren Buffett, Chair. and CEO of investment firm Berkshire Hathaway; renamed in memory of his wife Susan Buffett, who died in 2004.

Activities: Supports international initiatives on women and girls' sexual and reproductive health. The Foundation awards scholarships to college students from Nebraska; and offers annual Alice Buffett Outstanding Teacher Awards to 15 educators at public schools in Omaha, NE, each worth US $10,000.

Geographical Area of Activity: International.

Restrictions: Does not accept unsolicited applications other than for scholarships.

Finance: Annual revenue US $958.1m., expenditure $547.7m. (31 Dec. 2022).

Board: Susan A. Buffett (Chair.).

Contact Details: 808 Conagra Dr., Suite 300, Omaha, NE 68102-5025; tel. (402) 943-1383; e-mail scholarships@stbfoundation.org; internet buffettscholarships.org.

TechnoServe

Founded in 1968 by Ed Bullard, a business person who spent a year doing voluntary service in Ghana.

Activities: Works in the fields of agriculture and entrepreneurship through helping people to build farms, businesses and industries. Critical areas are: corporate and environmental sustainability; food security; women's economic empowerment; youth economic opportunity; and technology. The organization develops business solutions to poverty by linking people to information, capital and markets. It gives advice, shares technical expertise, and provides marketing and capital to create prosperity and sustainable long-term solutions to poverty. The Fellows Program gives business professionals the opportunity to participate in 12-month international development projects. Works in 35 countries; with offices in Norwalk, CT, and the United Kingdom.

Geographical Area of Activity: India, Latin America, Puerto Rico, sub-Saharan Africa, USA.

Restrictions: Does not make grants.

Publications: Annual Report; newsletter; case studies; factsheets; reports; white papers; blog.

Finance: Annual revenue US $116.0m., expenditure $117.5m. (31 Dec. 2023).

Board of Directors: Michael J. Bush, Rachel Hines (Co-Chair.); Peter A. Flaherty (Vice-Chair.); Michael Spies (Treas.); Jennifer Bullard Broggini (Sec.).

Principal Staff: Pres. and CEO William Warshauer.

Contact Details: 1777 N Kent St, Suite 1100, Arlington, VA 22209; tel. (202) 785-4515; e-mail info@technoserve.org; internet www.technoserve.org.

Thiel Foundation

Established in 2006 by Peter Thiel, founder of PayPal, an online money transfer system.

Activities: Promotes political, personal and economic freedoms. The Foundation supports science, technology and long-term thinking about the future. It runs two main programmes: the Thiel Fellowship, worth US $100,000 over two years, provides an opportunity for young people who do not finish school to build things; and Imitatio, which supports research and application of René Girard's mimetic theory in the social sciences.

Geographical Area of Activity: International.

Restrictions: Fellowship applicants must be aged under 22 years.

Finance: Annual revenue US $5.7m., expenditure $7.4m. (31 Dec. 2022).

Board of Directors: Peter Thiel (Chair. and CEO).

Principal Staff: Pres. Brian Rowen.

Contact Details: 9200 W. Sunset Blvd, Suite 1110, West Hollywood, CA 90069; tel. (323) 990-2000; e-mail info@thielfoundation.org; internet thielfoundation.org.

Thrasher Research Fund

Founded in 1977 by E. W. 'Al' Thrasher, an inventor in the lumber industry.

Activities: Funds applied medical research with the potential to benefit large numbers of children and find sustainable solutions to major problems of child health and wellbeing. The Fund focuses on gaps in paediatric medical research most likely to have an impact on the treatment of children with critical illnesses and major health problems. It awards two kinds of research grant: E. W. 'Al' Thrasher Awards are typically worth around US $350,000 over three years; and Early Career Awards are limited to a maximum of $25,000 for up to two years.

Geographical Area of Activity: International.

Restrictions: No grants for research on human foetal tissue; behavioural science research; educational programmes; general operating expenses; capital works; general donations; loans, student aid, scholarships; nor to other funding organizations.

Publications: Biennial Report; brochure.

Principal Staff: Pres. R. Justin Brown.

Contact Details: 68 S. Main St, Suite 400, Salt Lake City, UT 84101; tel. (801) 240-4753; internet www.thrasherresearch.org.

Tibet Fund

Established in 1981 by a small group of US citizens and Tibetan immigrants living in the USA.

Activities: Supports community and economic development projects in Tibetan refugee communities; and provides emergency relief and resettles new refugees who have fled Tibet (Xizang Autonomous Region of the People's Repub. of China). Main programme areas include: community and economic development; cultural and religious preservation; educational and vocational training; healthcare and sanitation; and humanitarian aid; and in Tibet, the Khawachen Assistance Program to address medical, educational and economic needs. It awards higher education scholarships to Tibetan students and professionals; and administers the Ngawang Choephel Fellowship Program, funded by the US State Department's Office of Citizen Exchanges, for scholars and professionals from Tibet to visit the USA. Has a Field Office in India.

Geographical Area of Activity: Bhutan, India, Nepal, Tibet (the Xizang Autonomous Region of the People's Repub. of China), USA.

Publications: Annual Report; newsletter; brochures.

Finance: Annual revenue US $12.8m., expenditure $11.8m. (31 Dec. 2023).

Board of Directors: Michael Lemle (Chair.); Geoffrey Menin (Vice-Pres.); Tenzin T. Lama (Treas.); Tsewang Namgyal (Sec.).

Principal Staff: Pres. Bob Ankerson.

Contact Details: 241 East 32nd St, New York, NY 10016; tel. (212) 213-5011; e-mail info@tibetfund.org; internet www.tibetfund.org.

Tides Organizations

Founded in 1976; comprises the Tides Network, Tides Center, Tides Foundation (a grantmaking organization), Tides Two Rivers Fund and Tides Inc.

Activities: Mediates between donors and charitable organizations in need of resources, promoting human rights, social justice and a healthy environment. Programmes include: the Healthy Democracy Fund, which works to increase voter turnout and defends the voting rights of communities of colour, and young and economically disadvantaged voters; and the Women's Environmental Leadership Fund (WE LEAD), which invests in women's leadership in climate, gender and racial justice movements. The Network strengthens community non-profit organizations through awarding grants; and offers services to donors including flexible and personalized grantmaking programmes, expert advice and networking opportunities. It has an office in New York.

Geographical Area of Activity: USA.

Restrictions: Does not accept unsolicited applications; no grants to individuals except for scholarships.

Publications: Annual Report; newsletter; brochures; donor guides.

Finance: Annual revenue US $627.3m., expenditure $1,013.3m. (31 Dec. 2023).

Board of Directors: Roslyn Dawson Thompson (Chair.); Brickson Diamond (Vice-Chair.).

Principal Staff: CEO Janiece Evans-Page; Tides Center Exec. Dir Ayesha Khanna.

Contact Details: The Presidio, 1012 Torney Ave, San Francisco, CA 94129-1755; POB 889389, Los Angeles, CA 90088-9389; tel. (415) 561-6400; e-mail info@tides.org; internet www.tides.org.

Tiffany & Co Foundation

Established in 2000 by Tiffany & Co, a luxury goods company.

Activities: Supports large-scale ocean and coral conservation efforts and blue carbon exploration initiatives.

Geographical Area of Activity: International.

Restrictions: Only supports organizations registered in the USA, but may fund international work; not currently accepting new applications.

Finance: Annual revenue US $6.2m., expenditure $6.0m. (31 Dec. 2022).

Board: Annika Dubrall (Pres. and Chair.); Jennifer Kweon (Sec.); Angelos Kontopanagiotis (Treas.).

Contact Details: 200 Fifth Ave, New York, NY 10010; tel. (212) 230-6591; e-mail foundation@tiffany.com; internet www.tiffanyandcofoundation.org.

Tinker Foundation, Inc

Founded in 1959 by Edward Larocque Tinker, a lawyer, author, and collector, in memory of his wife Frances McKee Tinker, his father Henry Champlin Tinker and his grandfather Edward Greenfield Tinker.

Activities: Works in the fields of democratic governance, education and sustainable management of natural resources. The Foundation supports initiatives of CSOs and institutions and promotes collaboration between organizations in the USA and Latin America. It also makes grants to US universities for graduate student research in Spanish- and Portuguese-speaking countries of Latin America.

Geographical Area of Activity: Latin America, USA.

Restrictions: No grants to individuals.

Finance: Annual revenue US $15.1m., expenditure $3.1m. (31 Dec. 2023).

Board of Directors: Shannon K. O'Neil (Chair.); Susal L. Segal (Treas.); Katherine Lorenz (Sec.).

Principal Staff: Pres. Caroline B. Kronley.

Contact Details: 55 East 59th St, New York, NY 10022; tel. (212) 421-6858; e-mail tinker@tinker.org; internet www.tinker.org.

TOSA Foundation

Established in 1992 by John Morgridge, former Chair. and CEO of technology company Cisco Systems, and Tashia Morgridge, a special education teacher.

Activities: Supports initiatives in the fields of the arts, education, the environment, human services and medical research. The Foundation established the Wisconsin Technology Initiative, providing grants to schools and other educational institutions to integrate technology into their teaching; and the Morgridge Institute for Research (f. 2004) for biomedical research. It funds the Morgridge Family Foundation, which supports education, the wellbeing of low-income families, the arts and conservation.

Geographical Area of Activity: USA.

Restrictions: Does not accept unsolicited applications.

Finance: Annual revenue US $45.1m., expenditure $47.9m. (31 Dec. 2022).

Principal Staff: Pres. and Dir Tashia F. Morgridge.

Contact Details: 3130 Alpine Rd, Suite 288, PMB 705, Portola Valley, CA 94028; tel. (650) 851-6922.

Trust for Mutual Understanding—TMU

Founded in 1984 by an anonymous US philanthropist.

Activities: Promotes culture and ecology through funding professional exchanges in the arts and environmental sciences for projects that respond to social contexts and engage local communities. The Trust supports a broad range of activities involving exchanges between professionals from the USA and 28 partner countries.

Geographical Area of Activity: Baltic States, Central Asia, Central and South-East Europe, Eastern Europe, Mongolia, Russian Federation.

Restrictions: Grants only to US non-profit organizations; does not support exchanges where the primary participants or beneficiaries are young people or students.

Publications: Annual Report; *Grantee Voices* (newsletter).

Finance: Annual revenue US $2.6m., expenditure $4.2m. (31 Dec. 2022).

Board of Trustees: Sarah Berresford (Chair.).

Principal Staff: Exec. Dir Barbara Lanciers.

Contact Details: 1 Rockefeller Plaza, Room 2500, New York, NY 10020; tel. (212) 649-5776; e-mail tmu@tmuny.org; internet www.tmuny.org.

Tulsa Community Foundation—TCF

Founded in 1998 as a community-owned institution.

Activities: Promotes personal and corporate charitable giving. The Foundation offers grants and scholarships for higher education; and provides disaster relief and medical assistance to people in emergencies or who are experiencing financial hardship. It organizes the Funders Roundtable, composed of representatives from foundations in Tulsa; the Planned Giving Partnership, which comprises 60 non-profit agencies; and the Women Impacting Tulsa giving circle. Administers more than 1,500 funds.

Geographical Area of Activity: USA (Tulsa and Eastern Oklahoma).

Publications: Annual Report; brochures.

Finance: Annual revenue US $329.5m., expenditure $216.7m. (31 Dec. 2023).

Principal Staff: CEO Phil Lakin, Jr.

Contact Details: 7030 South Yale Ave, Suite 600, Tulsa, OK 74136; tel. (918) 494-8823; e-mail info@tulsacf.org; internet tulsacf.org.

Turner Foundation, Inc

Founded in 1990 by R. E. (Ted) Turner, III, the founder of the Cable News Network (CNN) and the UN Foundation (q.v.).

Activities: Carries out self-conducted programmes to protect and restore natural systems through conserving land and wildlife diversity, promoting clean energy technologies and managing surface and groundwater resources.

Geographical Area of Activity: USA.

Restrictions: Does not accept unsolicited applications; no grants to individuals.

Publications: Annual Report.

Finance: Annual revenue US $2.6m., expenditure $2.7m. (31 Dec. 2022).

Board of Trustees: R. E. (Ted) Turner, III (Chair.); Robert Edward Turner IV (Co-Chair.); Rutherford Seydel (Sec.); Christine Hung (Treas.).

Principal Staff: Exec. Dir Troy Ettel.

Contact Details: 133 Luckie St NW, 2nd Floor, Atlanta, GA 30303; tel. (404) 681-9900; internet www.turnerfoundation.org.

Unbound Philanthropy

Established in 2003; a private grantmaking foundation.

Activities: Supports social justice through investing in leaders and organizations in the United Kingdom and the USA. Priority areas are: ensuring legal rights and protections; strengthening community integration; and building public understanding. The organization builds grantees' capacity; organizes meetings, roundtables and retreats; and supports learning exchanges between the UK and the USA. It has an office in London, UK.

Geographical Area of Activity: UK, USA.

Restrictions: Does not accept unsolicited applications.

Publications: Newsletter; reports; cases studies; evaluations.

Finance: Annual income US $46.4m., expenditure $16.4m. (31 Dec. 2021).

Board of Directors: Debbie Berger (Chair. and Sec.); Hilary Weinstein (Vice-Pres.); Bill Reeves (Treas.).

Principal Staff: Exec. Dir Taryn Higashi.

Contact Details: 101 Ave of the Americas, Suite 1400, New York, NY 10013-1941; tel. (212) 219-1009; e-mail mail@unboundphilanthropy.org; internet unboundphilanthropy.org.

Unitarian Universalist Service Committee—UUSC

Established in 1963 by the merger of the Unitarian Service Committee (f. 1940) and the Universalist Service Committee (f. 1945), which were both founded to provide humanitarian relief in Europe during and after the Second World War.

Activities: A human rights organization, based on grassroots collaboration. The Committee works specifically with people and communities who are denied their rights because of who they are—women, people of colour, religious minorities, and others—and who are not served by mainstream human rights organizations. It promotes economic and environmental justice; protects civil liberties; and delivers aid to advance the rights of people left behind during humanitarian crises, including forgotten conflicts and natural disasters.

Geographical Area of Activity: International.

Publications: Annual Report; *Toward Justice* (quarterly e-newsletter); *Rights Now* (2 a year); *Stories of Hope*; research reports.

Finance: Annual revenue US $10.8m., expenditure $12.4m. (30 June 2024).

Board of Trustees: Rev. Manish Mishra-Marzetti, Lynn Miyamoto (Co-Chair.); Jim Smith (Treas.); Cynthia Totten (Sec.).

Principal Staff: Pres. and CEO Rev. Mary Katherine Morn.

Contact Details: 689 Massachusetts Ave, Cambridge, MA 02139-3302; tel. (617) 868-6600; e-mail info@uusc.org; internet www.uusc.org.

United Nations Foundation

Established in 1997 along with its sister organization, the Better World Campaign (q.v.), following a gift of US $1,000m. to the UN by R. E. (Ted) Turner, III, the founder of the Cable News Network (CNN) and the Turner Foundation (q.v.).

Activities: Supports the goals and objectives of the UN Sustainable Development Goals and the Paris Climate Agreement, working in the interconnected areas of: climate and environment; girls and women; global health; data technology; UN reform and innovation; peace, human rights and humanitarian response; and emerging issues, such as antimicrobial resistance, cybersecurity and artificial intelligence. The Foundation works in partnership with the private sector, civil society and governments; and with its sister organizations, the Better World Campaign and the UN Association of the United States of America. Has an office in New York.

Geographical Area of Activity: International.

Restrictions: Grants only to support UN priorities, including the Sustainable Development Goals.

Publications: Annual Report; *UN Wire* (e-mail news briefing); factsheets; report; blog.

Finance: Annual revenue US $113.4m., expenditure $127.5m. (31 Dec. 2023).

Board of Directors: R. E. (Ted) Turner, III (Chair.); Marc-André Blanchard (Co-Chair.).

Principal Staff: Pres. and CEO Elizabeth Cousens.

Contact Details: 1750 Pennsylvania Ave NW, Suite 300, Washington, DC 20006; tel. (202) 887-9040; e-mail info @unfoundation.org; internet unfoundation.org.

United States African Development Foundation—USADF

Established in 1980 by the US Congress as an independent agency to provide economic assistance to grassroots communities in Africa.

Activities: Provides economic and technical development assistance in the areas of agriculture, off-grid energy and youth-led enterprises, in fragile states and frontier markets. Target groups include: social entrepreneurs; smallholder farmers; young people; women and girls; nomadic and pastoralist populations; ethnic and religious minorities; and people with disabilities. The Foundation awards grants to community enterprises ranging from US $50,000 to $250,000.

Geographical Area of Activity: Great Lakes region, Horn of Africa; Sahel.

Restrictions: Grants only to registered African NGOs and community-based organizations in countries where the Foundation is active; does not provide funding for individuals.

Publications: Annual Report; *USADF Messenger* (online); *USADF e-news*; *USADF Approach* (online); issue papers; project briefs; reports.

Finance: Annual revenue US $40.4m., expenditure $36.4m. (30 Sept. 2020).

Board of Directors: Carol Moseley Braun (Chair.).

Principal Staff: Pres. and CEO Ward Brehm.

Contact Details: 1400 I St NW, Suite 1000, Washington, DC 20005-2248; tel. (202) 673-3916; e-mail info@usadf.gov; internet www.usadf.gov.

United States-Japan Foundation

Founded in 1980 by Ryoichi Sasakawa, a business person and founder of the Nippon Foundation and the Sasakawa Peace Foundation (qq.v.).

Activities: Promotes stronger ties between Americans and Japanese through supporting projects that foster mutual knowledge and education and deepen understanding. The Foundation offers grants to organizations for projects and programmes in the areas of pre-college education, communications and public opinion and US-Japan policy studies. Has an office in Tokyo, Japan.

Geographical Area of Activity: Japan, USA.

Restrictions: Does not accept unsolicited full applications; only funds organizations based in Japan or the USA.

Publications: Annual Report.

Finance: Annual revenue US $2.4m., expenditure $4.4m. (31 Dec. 2022).

Board of Trustees: Lawrence K. Fish (Chair.); Kohei Itoh (Vice-Chair.).

Principal Staff: CEO Jacob M. Schlesinger.

Contact Details: 10045 Red Run Blvd, Suite 250, Owing Mills, MD 21117; tel. (212) 481-8753; e-mail info@us-jf.org; internet www.us-jf.org.

United Way Worldwide

Established in 1887 to collect funds for local charities, coordinate relief services and make emergency assistance grants; formerly known as United Way International.

Activities: Works in the areas of education, financial stability, health and disaster recovery, leading and supporting a network of around 1,800 community-based United Ways. The organization runs the Center on Human Trafficking & Slavery (f. 2015). Present in more than 37 countries and territories.

Geographical Area of Activity: International.

Publications: Annual Report; newsletter; blog.

Finance: Annual revenue US $51.6m., expenditure $65.7m. (31 Dec. 2023).

Worldwide Board of Trustees: Yuri Fulmer (Chair.); Michael K. Hayde (Treas.); Mark S. Howard (Sec.).

Worldwide Leadership Council: Cathy McRae (Chair.); Jenny Holsman Tetreault (Vice-Chair.).

Principal Staff: Pres. and CEO Angela F. Williams.

Contact Details: 701 North Fairfax St, Alexandria, VA 22314-2045; tel. (703) 836-7112; e-mail worldwide@unitedway.org; internet www.unitedway.org.

UPS Foundation

Established in 1951 by James E. Casey, founder of United Parcel Service (UPS).

Activities: Offers grants to local charitable organizations. Main programmes are: community safety, improving people's wellbeing through combating human trafficking, road safety, and humanitarian relief and resilience; environmental sustainability, reducing carbon and supporting reforestation; equity and inclusion, creating opportunities for underserved and under-represented people; and volunteering, building global volunteer capacity and promoting volunteering among UPS employees in support of the UN Sustainable Development Goals.

Geographical Area of Activity: International.

Restrictions: Does not accept unsolicited applications.

Publications: Social Impact Report; *UPS Horizons* (newsletter).

Finance: Annual revenue US $53.5m., expenditure $48.4m. (31 Dec. 2022).

Board of Trustees: Laura Lane (Chair.).

Principal Staff: CEO Carol B. Tomé.

Contact Details: 55 Glenlake Parkway NE, Atlanta, GA 30328; tel. (404) 828-6000; e-mail sustainability@ups.com; internet about.ups.com/ae/en/our-impact/community.html.

USC Shoah Foundation—The Institute for Visual History and Education

Established in 1994, as the Survivors of the Shoah Visual History Foundation, by film-maker Steven Spielberg.

Activities: Records and preserves the testimonies of Holocaust (Shoah) survivors and other witnesses; and works to overcome prejudice, ignorance and bigotry, and the suffering they cause, through the educational use of visual history testimonies. The Foundation has collected more than 57,400 recorded testimonies of Holocaust survivors and other witnesses in 65 countries and in 45 languages. It develops partnerships to support three main strategic goals: to use the archive to create educational projects for classrooms and broader dissemination; to build and support educational programmes; and to preserve the archive and provide access to it. Under its Witnesses for Humanity programme, the Foundation collects and publishes testimonies of survivors and witnesses of other genocides including: the Armenian Genocide, which coincided with the First World War; the 1994 Genocide against the ethnic Tutsi in Rwanda; the 1937 Nanjing Massacre in China; the Cambodian Genocide of 1975–79; the Guatemalan Genocide of 1978–83; continuing conflicts in the Central African Republic and South Sudan; violence against ethnic Kurds in Northern Syria; mass violence against ethnic Rohingyas in Myanmar; and contemporary anti-Semitism. It incorporates the Center for Advanced Genocide Research (f. 2014), which awards research fellowships to doctoral candidates, and USC undergraduates, graduates and faculty members.

Geographical Area of Activity: Worldwide.

Restrictions: Not a grantmaking organization.

Publications: Annual Impact Report; newsletter (monthly); Visual History Archive Online; documentary films; study guides; books.

Board of Councilors: Joel Citron (Chair.).

Principal Staff: Exec. Dir Dr Robert Williams.

Vital Strategies

Contact Details: Leavey Library, 650 West 35th St, Suite 114, Los Angeles, CA 90089-2571; tel. (213) 740-6001; e-mail vhi-web@usc.edu; internet sfi.usc.edu.

Vital Strategies

Established in 2016 by the merger of the World Lung Foundation (f. 2004) and the North American branch of the International Union Against Tuberculosis and Lung Disease (f. 1920).

Activities: Works with governments and civil society to design and implement public health initiatives, especially in low- and middle-income countries. Programmes cover: air pollution; cardiovascular health; childhood lead poisoning; drug overdose; epidemics; food policy; road safety; and tobacco control. The organization is part of the Partnership for Healthy Cities with Bloomberg Philanthropies (q.v.) and WHO, which works to prevent non-communicable diseases and injuries in 70 cities. Operates in 73 countries, with offices in Brazil, the People's Republic of China, Ethiopia and France; and a regional hub in Singapore.

Geographical Area of Activity: International.

Publications: Annual Report; newsletter; economic reports; factsheets; technical guides; white papers.

Finance: Annual revenue US $104.1m., expenditure $117.0m. (31 Dec. 2022).

Board of Trustees: Bruce Mandell (Chair.); Dr Mary-Ann Etiebet, Dr Masae Kawamura (Vice-Chair.); Marc Sznajderman (Treas.); Meron Makonnen (Sec.).

Principal Staff: Pres. and CEO José Luis Castro.

Contact Details: 100 Broadway, 4th Floor, New York, NY 10005; tel. (212) 500-5720; e-mail info@vitalstrategies.org; internet www.vitalstrategies.org.

Vital Voices Global Partnership

Established in 1997 by Donna Cochran McLarty, Alyse Nelson, Melanne Verveer and Mary Daley Yerrick; a global network.

Activities: Carries out targeted training and mentoring programmes and invests in women leaders. Main programme areas are: economic empowerment and entrepreneurship; human rights and ending gender-based violence; political leadership; and women's leadership development and mentoring. The organization administers grants through its Global Investment Portfolio. It has a network of 47,000 changemakers in 188 countries.

Geographical Area of Activity: Worldwide.

Publications: Annual Report.

Finance: Annual revenue US $30.8m., expenditure $23.9m. (31 Dec. 2023).

Board of Directors: Kate James (Chair.); Geraldine Laybourne (Vice-Chair.).

Principal Staff: Pres. and CEO Alyse Nelson.

Contact Details: 1509 16th St, NW, Washington, DC 20039; tel. (202) 861-2625; e-mail events@vitalvoices.org; internet www.vitalvoices.org.

Vodafone Americas Foundation

Established in 2007 by Vodafone, a telecommunications company; part of the Vodafone Foundation (q.v.) network.

Activities: Funds projects that use technology to foster social change through empowering women and girls. The Foundation supports employee volunteering; and awards community support grants in the areas that include strengthening families, supporting children and young people, leadership development, civic participation and urban issues, and the arts.

Geographical Area of Activity: International.

Restrictions: No unsolicited applications; no grants to individuals, political or religious organizations, fraternal, veterans or labour groups.

Publications: Blog.

Finance: Annual revenue US $142,373, expenditure $1.1m. (31 Dec. 2022).

Board of Directors: David Joosten (Pres.); Megan Doberneck (Sec.).

Principal Staff: Dir Andrew de la Torre.

Contact Details: 275 Shoreline Dr., Suite 400, Redwood City, CA 94065; tel. (650) 832-6611; e-mail project@vodafone.com; internet vodafone-us.com.

W. K. Kellogg Foundation—WKKF

Founded in 1930 by W. K. Kellogg, a food manufacturer and industrialist; primarily funded by the W. K. Kellogg Foundation Trust.

Activities: Operates three grantmaking programmes: Thriving Children, supporting a healthy start and good-quality learning for all children; Working Families, helping families to obtain stable, high-quality jobs; and Equitable Communities, promoting vibrant, engage and equitable communities. Cross-cutting themes are racial equity, developing leaders and engaging communities in solving their own problems. The Foundation concentrates two-thirds of its grantmaking in priority areas: Michigan, Mississippi, New Mexico and New Orleans in the USA; Chiapas and the Yucatán Peninsula in Mexico; and in Central and South Haiti. It has offices in Detroit, MI, Grand Rapids, MI, Jackson, MS, Albuquerque, NM, New Orleans, LA and Mexico City.

Geographical Area of Activity: Brazil, Haiti, Mexico, USA (including with sovereign tribes).

Restrictions: Does not support research or endowment projects; does not award grants for operational phases of established programmes, capital works, equipment, conferences, films, television or radio programmes (unless as an integral phase of a project that the Foundation already supports), planning and studies, religious purposes, nor to individuals except for fellowships in specific areas of Foundation programming.

Publications: Annual Report; newsletter; brochures; reports.

Finance: Annual revenue US $381.2m., expenditure $367.0m. (31 Aug. 2024).

Board: Dr Khan Nedd (Chair.).

Principal Staff: Pres. and CEO La June Montgomery Tabron.

Contact Details: 1 Michigan Ave E, Battle Creek, MI 49017-4012; tel. (269) 968-1611; e-mail int@wkkf.org; internet www.wkkf.org.

The Wallace Foundation

Established in 2003 by the merger of the DeWitt Wallace—Reader's Digest Fund, Inc and the Lila Wallace—Reader's Digest Fund, Inc, both established by the founders of the Reader's Digest Association.

Activities: Seeks to improve and expand access to learning and enrichment for disadvantaged children and to the arts. The Foundation focuses on exploring knowledge gaps in seven programme areas: strengthening school leadership; after-school programmes; out of school learning; stemming summer learning loss; social and emotional learning; improving arts education for children; and building audiences for the arts. Grants are typically worth around US $400,000. It maintains an online Knowledge Center.

Geographical Area of Activity: USA.

Restrictions: Rarely funds unsolicited applications.

Publications: Annual Report; reports; online knowledge products.

Finance: Annual revenue US $147.8m., expenditure $84.9m. (31 Dec. 2023).

Board of Directors: Mary Beth West (Chair.); Will I. Miller (Pres.).

Contact Details: 140 Broadway, 49th Floor, New York, NY 10005; tel. (212) 251-9700; e-mail info@wallacefoundation.org; internet www.wallacefoundation.org.

Walmart Foundation

Established in 1982 by Walmart, a retail company.

UNITED STATES OF AMERICA

Activities: Activities fall into three main areas: fostering economic opportunity; sustainability of global supply chains; and strengthening community cohesion and resilience. The Foundation awards grants to organizations, ranging from US $250 to $5,000 for community grants; and offers scholarships for post-secondary education to Walmart employees and their dependents. In 2021 Walmart pledged to invest $100m. in the Center for Racial Equity to fund research and advocacy on eliminating systematic disparities in the areas of criminal justice, education, finance and healthcare experienced by black and African American communities in USA. Separate charitable foundations operate in Mexico and the United Kingdom.
Geographical Area of Activity: International.
Restrictions: Scholarship applicants must be US citizens or permanent legal residents of the USA.
Publications: Newsletter.
Finance: Annual revenue US $133.6m., expenditure $132.4 (31 Jan. 2023).
Board of Directors: Kathleen McLaughlin (Chair.); Jacquelyn Brigance (Treas.); Bryan Del Rosario (Sec.).
Principal Staff: Pres. Julie Gehrki.
Contact Details: 702 SW 8th St, Bentonville, AK 72716-8611; tel. (800) 530-9925; internet walmart.org.

Walton Family Foundation

Established in 1988 by Sam Walton, the founder of retail chain Walmart, and his wife Helen; operates separately from the Walmart Foundation (q.v.).
Activities: Main programmes include: Environment, securing healthy fisheries, freshwater conservation initiatives in the Mississippi and Colorado River Basins, and restoring wetlands and coastal ecosystems; Home Region, improving quality of life in north-west Arkansas and the Delta region of Arkansas and Mississippi, with investments in the arts and culture, entrepreneurship and access to green spaces; and K-12 Education, supporting innovation, research and reforms in pre-primary, primary and secondary education. In 2024 the Foundation awarded grants amounting to nearly US $548.8m. It has offices in Denver, CO, and Washington, DC.
Geographical Area of Activity: Chile, Gulf of California, Gulf of Mexico, Indonesia, Japan, Peru, Spain, USA.
Restrictions: Does not accept unsolicited proposals.
Publications: Annual Report.
Finance: Annual revenue US $872.2m., expenditure $801.2m. (31 Dec. 2023).
Principal Staff: Exec. Dir Stephanie Cornell.
Contact Details: POB 2030, Bentonville, AK 72712; tel. (479) 464-1570; e-mail info@wffmail.com; internet www.waltonfamilyfoundation.org.

Water for Good

Founded as Lifewater International in 1977 by William A. Ashe; a Christian non-profit organization; present name adopted in 2024.
Activities: We are Christians providing access to safe water, and improved sanitation and hygiene, one village at a time. Lifewater's grassroots approach to solving the global water and sanitation crisis is called 'Vision of a Healthy Village'.
Geographical Area of Activity: Cambodia, Ethiopia, Tanzania, Uganda.
Publications: Annual Report; *Lifewater International Newsletter* (quarterly); research reports; programme reports; blog.
Finance: Total assets US $8.5m.; total revenue $7.7m. (31 Dec. 2023).
Board of Directors: John Drechny (Chair.); Sue Hostetler (Vice-Chair.); Tim Culp (Treas.); Ted Song (Sec.).
Principal Staff: CEO Dave LeVan.
Contact Details: POB 2868, Bentonville, AR 72712; tel. (479) 360-5030; e-mail info@waterforgood.org; internet waterforgood.org.

Water for People

Established in 1991 by the American Water Works Association.
Activities: Promotes universal access to reliable and safe water and sanitation services. The organization supports the development of high-quality drinking water and sanitation services for families, clinics and schools. A separate organization operates in Canada.
Geographical Area of Activity: Bolivia, Guatemala, Honduras, India, Malawi, Nicaragua, Peru, Rwanda, Uganda.
Publications: Annual Report; newsletter.
Finance: Annual revenue US $32.6m., expenditure $36.9m. (30 Sept. 2023).
Board of Directors: Eleanor Allen (Chair.); Irene Lofland (Vice-Chair.); Debra Coy (Treas.); Greg McIntyre (Sec.).
Principal Staff: Co-CEOs Samson Hailu Bekele, Mark Duey.
Contact Details: 7100 E Belleview Ave, Suite 310, Greenwood Village, CO 80111; tel. (720) 488-4590; e-mail info@waterforpeople.org; internet www.waterforpeople.org.

Water.org, Inc

Established in 2009 by Gary White and actor Matt Damon through a merger between WaterPartners and the H2O Africa Foundation.
Activities: Provides access to safe water and sanitation through affordable financing. Programmes include: WaterCredit, providing microfinance and small, affordable loans for water and sanitation solutions; Global Engagement, working with financial institutions, governments and others to expand access to affordable financing for water and sanitation. The organization has programmes in 15 countries.
Geographical Area of Activity: International.
Publications: Annual Report; newsletter; position papers.
Finance: Annual revenue US $51.3m., expenditure $35.8m. (30 Sept. 2023).
Board of Directors: Hilary Schneider (Chair.); Larry Tanz (Vice-Chair.); Terry Trayvick (Treas.); Jack Leslie (Sec.).
Principal Staff: CEO Gary White.
Contact Details: 117 West 20th St, Suite 203, Kansas City, MO 64108; tel. (816) 877-8400; e-mail info@water.org; internet water.org.

Weeden Foundation

Founded in 1963 by Frank Weeden, an investment banker.
Activities: Operates nationally and internationally in the field of conservation and the environment. Programmes focus on: protecting diversity, including old-growth forests; expanding habitats for endangered species and linking key wildlife corridors; addressing the adverse impact of growing human populations and overuse of natural resources; and advocacy for family planning and reducing birth rates. Grants typically range between US $15,000 and $25,000 for one year.
Geographical Area of Activity: Chile (Patagonia), USA (Alaska, High Divide in the Rockies, Northern California).
Restrictions: No grants to individuals, for endowment or capital fund projects, for large organizations unless for new projects, or for general support.
Finance: Annual revenue US $991,882, expenditure $2.6m. (31 Dec. 2022).
Board of Directors: Leslie Weeden (Pres.); Barbara Daugherty (Vice-Pres.); Nick Leibowitz (Treas.); John Weeden (Sec.).
Principal Staff: Foundation Administrator Peggy Kennedy.
Contact Details: POB 606, Bedford Hills, NY 10507-0606; tel. (914) 864-1375; e-mail info@weedenfoundation.org; internet www.weedenfoundation.org.

The Welch Foundation

Founded in 1954 by the will of Robert A. Welch, who made his fortune in oil and minerals.

Activities: Funds basic research in chemistry, with research grants to full-time faculty members at educational institutions in Texas for a minimum of US $100,000 per year; departmental grants for chemistry faculties in small and medium-sized educational institutions; postdoctoral fellowships; and programme grants. The Foundation also supports endowed chairs; sponsors a conference; and awards the Welch Award in Chemistry, worth $500,000; and the Norman Hackerman Award in Chemical Research, worth $100,000.

Geographical Area of Activity: USA.

Restrictions: Only full-time faculty members at educational institutions in Texas are eligible to apply.

Publications: Annual Report.

Finance: Annual revenue US $23.8m., expenditure $19.4m. (31 Aug. 2023).

Board of Directors: Frederick W. Brazelton (Chair.); Gina A. Luna (Vice-Chair.); Carin M. Barth (Treas.); Carolyn C. Sabat (Sec.).

Principal Staff: Pres. Adam Kuspa.

Contact Details: POB 27944, Houston, TX 77227; tel. (713) 961-9884; e-mail info@welch1.org; internet www.welch1.org.

Wenner-Gren Foundation for Anthropological Research, Inc

Founded in 1941 as the Viking Fund, Inc, by Dr Axel L. Wenner-Gren.

Activities: Operates an individual research grants programme, awarding up to US $25,000 for fieldwork and basic research in anthropology to holders of a doctorate degree and doctoral candidates undertaking dissertation projects; and offers a number of awards and scholarships, including the Hunt postdoctoral fellowship worth up to $40,000; conference and workshop grants worth up to $20,000; and Global Initiatives Grants ranging from $5,000 to $20,000. The Foundation organizes conferences, seminars and symposia; and sponsors the publication of the journal *Current Anthropology*.

Geographical Area of Activity: International.

Publications: Annual Report; *Viking Fund Publications in Anthropology* (monograph series); *Sapiens* (online magazine); research reports; symposia publications; blog.

Finance: Annual revenue US $18.3m., expenditure $11.5m. (31 Dec. 2023).

Board of Trustees: Dr Danilyn Rutherford (Pres.); Barbara Rockenbach (Chair.); Dr Justin Zaremby (Vice-Chair.); Kiele Neas (Treas.).

Contact Details: 655 Third Ave, 23rd Floor New York, NY 10017; tel. (212) 683-5000; e-mail inquiries@wennergren.org; internet www.wennergren.org.

Weyerhaeuser Family Foundation, Inc

Founded in 1950; formerly known as the Weyerhaeuser Foundation.

Activities: Main programmes are: International Initiative, which helps women, girls and their families to overcome violence, poverty and other hardships (working with organizations in the USA, with a particular focus on programmes in education, health and economic development); Youth Initiative, supporting young people who have experienced (witnessed) traumatic events (working with organizations in the Pacific Northwest, Minnesota and Wisconsin); and the Sustainable Forest and Communities Initiative, which mainly focuses on the forested regions of Idaho, Oregon, Washington, northern California, western Montana, Minnesota and Wisconsin. Grants are typically in the range of US $25,000–$30,000.

Geographical Area of Activity: International.

Restrictions: Does not normally make grants for projects with limited geographical emphasis, operating budgets, annual campaigns, building and equipment, elementary and secondary education, lobbying or propaganda; nor does it make grants to individuals, for scholarships, fellowships or for travel. No fiscal agents or fiscal sponsorships.

Publications: Annual Report.

Board: Margaret W. G. Carr (Pres.); Cody N. Reiter (Vice-Pres.); Gretchen Sprafke (Treas.); Catherine M. Davis (Sec.).

Contact Details: 30 Seventh St East, Suite 2000, St Paul, MN 55101-4930; tel. (303) 506-3127; e-mail wff@fidcouns.com; internet www.wfamilyfoundation.org.

Whirlpool Foundation

Founded in 1951 by Louis and Frederick Upton, co-founders of the Whirlpool Corpn, a home appliances manufacturer.

Activities: Carries out activities in locations where the Whirlpool Corpn has a presence. Activities focus on employee-directed programmes to support non-profit organizations based in the USA and disaster relief. The Foundation offers university scholarships to employees' children.

Geographical Area of Activity: International.

Restrictions: No grants to religious or labour organizations.

Finance: Annual revenue US $9.7m., expenditure $9.8m. (31 Dec. 2022).

Principal Staff: Man. Sarah Rogers.

Contact Details: 2000 North M-63, Benton Harbor, MI 49022; tel. (269) 923-5000; e-mail whirlpool_foundation@whirlpool.com; internet www.whirlpoolcorp.com/our-impact/social-impact/whirlpool-foundation.html.

Whitehall Foundation, Inc

Founded in 1937.

Activities: Assists scholarly work in the life sciences, primarily areas of basic biological research not generally supported by federal agencies or other foundations with specialized missions. The Foundation focuses on basic research in neurobiology: invertebrate and vertebrate neurobiology, exclusive of human beings, including investigation into the neural mechanisms involved in sensory, motor and other complex functions of the whole organism as these relate to behaviour. Research grants are for up to three years, awarded to established scientists working at accredited institutions in the USA. Grants-in-aid are for one year and are designed especially for young postgraduate investigators who have not yet established themselves, as well as for senior scientists. Research grants of up to US $100,000 per year for two or three years; grants-in-aid do not exceed $30,000 for one year.

Geographical Area of Activity: USA.

Publications: Report of operations.

Finance: Annual revenue US $4.7m., expenditure $7.1m. (30 Sept. 2023).

Contact Details: POB 3423, Palm Beach, FL 33480; 220 Sunrise Ave, Suite 211, Palm Beach, FL 33480; tel. (561) 655-4474; e-mail email@whitehall.org; internet www.whitehall.org.

Wikimedia Foundation

Established in 2003 by Jimmy Wales, co-founder of the Wikipedia online encyclopedia.

Activities: Encourages the growth, development and distribution of wiki-based (collaboratively edited) free, multilingual, educational content, and its provision to the public free of charge. The Foundation supports internet reference projects, including Wikipedia, and community-based initiatives worldwide. Projects include Wikibooks, providing open content textbooks; Wikiversity, which offers learning resources for all levels of education; and Wikimedia Commons, a repository of free media files. It conducts research and advocacy; and offers grants for projects to develop existing Wikimedia websites, including Rapid Grants (worth from US $500 to $2,000), Project Grants, Conference Grants and Annual Plan Grants. Has more than 130 affiliates, including thematic organizations, user groups and 39 chapters worldwide.

Geographical Area of Activity: Worldwide.

Publications: Annual Report; fundraising reports.

Finance: Annual revenue US $180.2m., expenditure $169.1m. (30 June 2023).

Board of Trustees: Nataliia Tymkiv (Chair.); Lorenzo Losa (Chair.-elect and Vice-Chair.); Kathy Collins (Vice-Chair.).

Principal Staff: CEO Maryana Iskander.

Contact Details: 1 Sansome St, Suite 1895, San Francisco, CA 94104; tel. (415) 839-6885; e-mail info@wikimedia.org; internet wikimediafoundation.org; meta.wikimedia.org.

The WILD Foundation—International Wilderness Leadership Foundation

Founded in 1974 by Dr Ian Player, a South African conservationist; a founding member of Wilderness Foundation Global (q.v.).

Activities: Operates in the field of conservation and the environment at grassroots, national and international level, collaborating with local peoples, organizations, businesses and governments. The Foundation runs programmes on wilderness and wildlife, ecotourism, and education and training; the World Wilderness Congress is its flagship programme. It promotes the wise use of wildland resources and provides environmental education and training. CoalitionWILD (f. 2013) mobilizes young conservation changemakers, offering leadership and capacity training and cross-generational mentoring opportunities.

Geographical Area of Activity: International.

Publications: Annual Report; newsletter; *International Journal of Wilderness*; handbooks; report; blog.

Finance: Annual revenue US $6.8m., expenditure $5.5m. (31 Dec. 2023).

Board of Directors: Joel D. Holtrop (Chair.); Clay Stranger (Vice-Chair.); Jonathan Miller (Treas.).

Principal Staff: Man. Dir Amy Lewis.

Contact Details: 717 Poplar Ave, Boulder, CO 80304; tel. (303) 442-8811; e-mail info@wild.org; internet www.wild.org.

The William and Flora Hewlett Foundation

Founded in 1966 by William R. Hewlett, an engineer, his wife Flora Lamson Hewlett and their son Walter B. Hewlett.

Activities: Supports organizations that promote a better world and improve people's lives. Main programme areas include: economy and society, seeking to replace neoliberalism with a new paradigm based on economic justice; education, increasing access to open educational resources worldwide; environment, addressing global climate change, expanding clean energy, and conserving landscapes and waterways in the Western USA and Canada; global development and population, giving women greater reproductive and economic choice, increasing citizen participation and improving evidence-based policymaking; performing arts, with a focus on the San Francisco Bay Area; effective philanthropy, informing and improving decisionmaking; cyber, with a focus on cybersecurity; and US democracy, strengthening democratic norms, values and institutions.

Geographical Area of Activity: International.

Restrictions: Makes grants to non-profit charitable organizations; no grants to individuals or for scholarships.

Publications: Annual Report; brochures and programme reports; newsletter.

Finance: Annual revenue US $1,204.6m., expenditure $665.5m. (31 Dec. 2023).

Board of Directors: Mariano-Florentino Cuéllar (Chair.).

Principal Staff: Pres. Amber D. Miller.

Contact Details: 2121 Sand Hill Rd, Menlo Park, CA 94025; tel. (650) 234-4500; internet www.hewlett.org.

The William H. Donner Foundation, Inc

Established in 1961 with funds originally donated by William Donner, an industrialist and philanthropist.

Activities: Supports activities in areas including: animal welfare; the arts and culture; at-risk children; development; domestic public policy; education; the environment; foreign and defence policy; human rights; science; veterans' affairs; and women's issues.

Geographical Area of Activity: Canada, USA.

Restrictions: Does not accept unsolicited applications.

Publications: Annual Report.

Finance: Annual revenue US $12.9m., expenditure $15.4m. (14 months to 31 Dec. 2023).

Board: David Donner (Pres.); Christopher Roosevelt (Vice-Pres.); Kaila Spencer (Treas.); Suzanne Spencer (Sec.).

Principal Staff: Exec. Dir Helen McLean.

Contact Details: 520 White Plains Rd, Suite 500, Tarrytown, NY 10591; tel. (914) 524-0404; internet whdonner.org.

William T. Grant Foundation

Established in 1936 by William T. Grant, founder of Grants, a mass-merchandise retail chain.

Activities: Promotes the value of young people and enables them to reach their full potential. Main programmes focus on reducing inequality and improving the use of research evidence. The Foundation funds research and projects that use evidence-based approaches; and offers grants to organizations providing services to children and young people aged 5–25 years in New York City. The Scholars Program offers grants to early careers researchers worth up to US $350,000 over five years.

Geographical Area of Activity: Mainly USA.

Restrictions: Research must address an issue or question affecting a large number of young people aged 5–25 years in the USA or a particularly vulnerable subgroup of young people.

Publications: Annual Report; *The Digest* (newsletter, 2 a year); brochures; blog.

Finance: Annual revenue US $17.1m., expenditure $21.9m. (31 Dec. 2022).

Board of Trustees: Scott Evans (Chair.).

Principal Staff: Pres. Adam Gamoran.

Contact Details: 60 East 42nd St, 43rd Floor, New York, NY 10165; tel. (212) 752-0071; e-mail info@wtgrantfdn.org; internet www.wtgrantfoundation.org.

Winrock International

Formed in 1985 by the merger of the Agricultural Development Council (f. 1953 by John D. Rockefeller, III), the International Agricultural Development Service (f. 1975 by the Rockefeller Foundation, q.v.) and the Winrock International Livestock Research and Training Center (f. 1975 by the bequest of Winthrop Rockefeller).

Activities: Works to reduce poverty and hunger through sustainable agricultural and rural development. The organization conducts integrated programmes in areas that include: agriculture and sustainability; human and social capital; economic development; energy and environment; services to provide research-based solutions to complex problems; a social enterprise incubator; and access to and development of leadership networks. It works in more than 46 countries, with offices in Arlington, VA, Kenya and the Philippines; European Cooperative for Rural Development in Belgium is an affiliate.

Geographical Area of Activity: International.

Publications: Annual Report; newsletter; project factsheets; research papers; project and capability brochures; project reports; blog.

Finance: Annual revenue US $111.0m., expenditure $104.5m. (31 Dec. 2022).

Board of Directors: Jude Kearney (Chair.); Suzanne E. Siskel (Vice-Chair.).

Principal Staff: Pres. and CEO Rodney Ferguson.

Winston Churchill Foundation of the United States

Founded in 1959 by American friends of Sir Winston Churchill.

Activities: Annually, offers up to 18 Churchill Scholarships for postgraduate courses in science, mathematics and engineering, and two Kanders Churchill Scholarship in science policy, at the University of Cambridge in the United Kingdom. The Foundation also offers an annual Churchill Adviser Award to people who support scholarship nominees.

Geographical Area of Activity: USA.

Restrictions: Scholarship applications are open to US citizens aged 19–26 years, holding a Bachelor's degree from a US university or college, and enrolled at a US institution that participates in the programme.

Publications: Newsletter.

Finance: Annual revenue US $2.0m., expenditure $1.9m. (31 Dec. 2022).

Board of Trustees: Patrick A. Gerschel (Chair.); David A. Burrows (Treas.); James A. FitzPatrick, Jr (Sec.).

Principal Staff: Pres. Elizabeth D. Mann.

Contact Details: 600 Madison Ave, Suite 1601, New York, NY 10022-1737; tel. (212) 752-3200; e-mail info@churchillscholarship.org; internet www.churchillscholarship.org/the-foundation.

Women's Environment & Development Organization—WEDO

Established in 1990 by Bella Abzug, a former US member of Congress, and Mim Kelber, a feminist activist; an international advocacy network.

Activities: Promotes women's rights, social, economic and environmental justice, and sustainable development through gender equality and diversity in leadership. Main programme areas include: biodiversity; disaster risk reduction; global climate policy; international finance and trade; peace, conflict and natural resources; and sustainable cities and transport. The Women Delegates Fund was established to ensure women's equal participation in climate change decisionmaking through providing travel support, technical knowledge and capacity building on negotiations, regional training, advocacy and networking. Working with Women in Europe for a Common Future, the Organization established the Empower Women–Benefit (for) All (EWA) programme to improve gender equality in legislation, policies and programmes at national and international levels. It is also an Organizing Partner in the Women's Major Group, which facilitates women's participation in UN processes on sustainable development and the environment.

Geographical Area of Activity: International.

Restrictions: Not a grantmaking organization.

Publications: Annual Report; newsletters; briefs; factsheets; reports; toolkits.

Finance: Annual revenue US $2.7m., expenditure $2.9m. (31 Dec. 2022).

Board of Directors: Annabella Rosemberg (Chair.); Ed Harrington (Treas.); Kristin Hetle (Sec.).

Principal Staff: Exec. Dir Bridget Burns.

Contact Details: 147 Prince St, Brooklyn, NY 11201; tel. (212) 973-0325; e-mail wedo@wedo.org; internet www.wedo.org.

Woodrow Wilson International Center for Scholars

Founded in 1968 by the US Congress as a living memorial to President Woodrow Wilson in the form of a non-partisan foreign affairs think tank bridging the worlds of academia and policymaking.

Activities: Researches security and governance issues and other dynamics that affect the USA and the world at large. The Center comprises the Brazil Institute, Canada Institute, Hyundai Motor-Korea Foundation Center for Korean History and Public Policy, China Environment Forum, Kennan Institute, Kissinger Institute on China and the US, Mexico Institute and Polar Institute. Programme areas encompass: congressional relations; geopolitical regional programmes; global risk and resilience, including environmental change and security, maternal health and urban sustainability; history and public policy, including Cold War international history, North Korea and nuclear proliferation; and science and technology innovation, including computer gaming and digital futures. The Wilson Center Fellowship is an international programme, offering nine-month residential fellowships to scholars, practitioners, journalists and public intellectuals to work alongside programme experts. Other fellowship opportunities include: the Foreign Policy Fellowship Program and Wilson Center's Technology Labs, both of which are six-week seminar series for congressional and policymakers' staff.

Geographical Area of Activity: Worldwide.

Publications: Annual Report; newsletter; *Wilson Quarterly* (online magazine); reports; analyses; policy briefs; research papers; reports; Woodrow Wilson Center Press (peer-reviewed books).

Finance: Annual revenue US $13.1m., expenditure $41.2m. (30 Sept. 2022).

Principal Staff: Pres. and CEO Natasha Jacome.

Contact Details: 1 Woodrow Wilson Plaza, 1300 Pennsylvania Ave NW, Washington, DC 20004-3027; tel. (202) 691-4000; e-mail wwics@wilsoncenter.org; internet www.wilsoncenter.org.

World Central Kitchen—WCK

Founded in 2010 by José Andrés.

Activities: Provides meals in response to humanitarian, climate and community crises. Helps communities develop resiliency in their food systems by partnering with local organizations as well as co-ordinating resources from local restaurants and community kitchens to provide solutions quickly in response to local needs in times of crisis.

Geographical Area of Activity: Worldwide.

Finance: Total revenue US $241.5m., expenditure $277.0m. (2023).

Board: Rob Wilder (Co-Chair. and Co-Founder); Javier Garcia (Exec. Co-Chair. and Treas.); Lizette Corro (Sec.).

Principal Staff: Chief Feeding Officer José Andrés; CEO Erin Gore.

Contact Details: 200 Massachusetts Ave NW, 7th Floor, Washington, DC 20001; POB 96538, Washington, DC 20090-6538; tel. (202) 844-6330; e-mail hello@wck.org; internet wck.org.

World Concern

Founded in 1955 as Medicine for Missions, a Christian international relief organization; incorporates World Concern Development Organization—WCDO (f. 1981). Since 1970 it has been part of CRISTA Ministries (f. 1948).

Activities: Works in the fields of poverty alleviation aid to less-developed countries, through emergency relief, rehabilitation and long-term development programmes. Projects have included vocational training to equip people with the skills to support themselves; providing emergency food supplies to famine victims; training farmers in improved agricultural methods of food production; and supplying survivors of disasters with food, clothing and critical aid.

Geographical Area of Activity: Africa, Asia, the Americas.

Restrictions: Not a grantmaking organization.

Publications: Annual Report.

Finance: Annual revenue US $16.4m., expenditure $17.2m. (30 June 2024).

WCDO Board: Francisca Engmann (Chair.); Seth Harper (Vice-Chair.); Tracy LaBossier (Sec.).

Principal Staff: Pres. and WCDO Exec. Dir Nick Archer.

Note: Contact Details at top of page: 204 E 4th St, North Little Rock, AR 72114; tel. (501) 280-3000; e-mail communications@winrock.org; internet www.winrock.org.

UNITED STATES OF AMERICA

Contact Details: 19303 Fremont Ave North, Seattle, WA 98133; tel. (206) 546-7201; e-mail info@worldconcern.org; internet www.worldconcern.org.

World Emergency Relief—WER

Established in 1985; merged with Rescue Task Force in 2009.

Activities: Works to address children's critical needs, providing access to water, food, healthcare, education and child safety, as well as the needs of their families and surrounding communities. The organization provides humanitarian assistance to people affected by natural disasters, armed conflict, physical or mental abuse and exploitation, or poverty. Programmes include Native American Emergency Relief and the Children's Food Fund.

Geographical Area of Activity: Africa, Asia, North, Central and South America and the Caribbean, South-Eastern Europe, Russian Federation.

Restrictions: No unsolicited applications; no grants to individuals.

Publications: Annual Report.

Finance: Annual revenue US $38.0m., expenditure $38.1m. (31 Dec. 2022).

Board of Directors: Gary Becks (Chair.); Lawrence E. Cutting (Sec.).

Principal Staff: CEO Kristy Scott.

Contact Details: 425 W Allen Ave #111, San Dimas, CA 91773; POB 218, San Dimas, CA 91773-9998; tel. (909) 593-7140; e-mail info@wer-us.org; internet www.wer-us.org.

World Learning

Founded in 1932, as the Experiment in International Living, by Dr Donald Watt, the personnel director of Syracuse University.

Activities: Works in the fields of sustainable development and education through organizing international academic and professional exchanges. Main programme areas are: people-to-people exchanges; virtual exchanges; social emotional learning; global education; capacity strengthening; youth workforce and entrepreneurship; and English as a second language techer training. The organization comprises the Experiment in International Living, which organizes thematic programmes for high school students to spend summer overseas, in homestays or virtually; and the School for International Training, which offers overseas undergraduate programmes and Master's degrees on pressing global issues. It works in more than 150 countries; and has an office in Washington, DC, and field offices in Algeria, Lebanon, Myanmar, Mongolia, Pakistan and the United Kingdom.

Geographical Area of Activity: Worldwide.

Publications: Annual Report; newsletter (monthly); capacity statements; research reports; toolkits; blog.

Finance: Annual revenue US $91.4m., expenditure $91.8m. (30 June 2022).

Board of Trustees: Allen B. Cutler (Chair.); Jenny Backus, Jack Benson (Vice-Chair.).

Principal Staff: Pres. and CEO Carol Jenkins.

Contact Details: 1015 15th St, NW, 7th Floor, Washington, DC 20005; 1 Kipling Rd, POB 676, Brattleboro, VT 05302-0676; tel. (202) 408-5420; e-mail info@worldlearning.org; internet www.worldlearning.org.

World Monuments Fund—WMF

Established in 1965 by individuals concerned about the destruction of artistic treasures.

Activities: Works to preserve architectural and cultural sites in 112 countries. The World Monuments Watch programme identifies sites at risk from social, political and economic change, conflict or natural disasters, and provides technical and financial assistance for their preservation. Affiliate organizations are based in India, Peru, Portugal, Spain and the United Kingdom.

Geographical Area of Activity: Worldwide.

World Resources Institute

Publications: Annual Report; newsletter (monthly); *Watch* (annual magazine); project reports.

Finance: Annual revenue US $20.3m., expenditure $15.4m. (30 June 2023).

Board of Trustees: Lorna B. Goodman (Chair.); John J. Kerr, Jr (Vice-Chair.); Peter Kimmelman (Treas.); Susan de Menil (Sec.).

Principal Staff: Pres. and CEO Bénédicte de Montlaur; Exec. Vice-Pres. Jeffrey Reinke.

Contact Details: Rockefeller Center, 600 Fifth Ave, 25th Floor, New York, NY 10020; tel. (646) 424-9594; e-mail wmf@wmf.org; internet wmf.org.

World Neighbors

Founded in 1952 by Dr John L. Peters, a Methodist minister and former soldier.

Activities: Aims to improve the lives of those living in rural communities in developing countries through long-term development and the elimination of hunger, disease and poverty. Main programme areas are: community and reproductive health; community-based natural resources management; gender equity; and sustainable agriculture and rural livelihoods. The organization works with local partner organizations in 14 countries in Asia, Africa, Latin America and the Caribbean.

Geographical Area of Activity: Latin America and the Caribbean, South Asia, South-East Asia, sub-Saharan Africa, USA.

Restrictions: Not a grantmaking organization; works directly with regional partners.

Publications: Annual Report; newsletter (monthly); *Neighbors* (magazine); books, videos and papers.

Finance: Annual revenue US $4.3m., expenditure $4.4m. (30 June 2023).

Board of Trustees: Beth McLaughlin (Chair.); Anita Kendrick (Vice-Chair.); Mindy Galoob (Treas.); Ujjwal Pradhan (Sec.).

Principal Staff: Pres. and CEO Dr Kate Schecter.

Contact Details: 5600 N. May Ave, Suite 160, Oklahoma City, OK 73112-4222; tel. (405) 752-9700; e-mail info@wn.org; internet www.wn.org.

World Peace Foundation—WPF

Established in 1910 by Edwin Ginn, a Boston-based publisher of educational texts and an advocate for international peace as the International School of Peace; in 2011 the Foundation established a programme at the Fletcher School at Tufts University.

Activities: Concerned with peace, justice and security. The Foundation carries out activities in the areas of education and policy engagement; and research under three main programmes: Peace and Global Trends; Protecting Vulnerable Groups; and African Peace Research. It offers grants to support student group initiatives and PhD research.

Geographical Area of Activity: International.

Restrictions: Support only for its self-initiated projects and for students enrolled at the Fletcher School.

Publications: Annual Report; books; seminar briefings; occasional papers; reports.

Finance: Annual revenue US $1.1m., expenditure $1.3m. (30 June 2023).

Governing Board: Peter Blum (Chair.); Anat Biletzki (Vice-Chair.); Andy Evans (Treas.).

Principal Staff: Exec. Dir Alex de Waal.

Contact Details: 114 Curtis St, Second Floor, Somerville, MA 02144; tel. (617) 627-2255; e-mail worldpeacefoundation@tufts.edu; internet worldpeacefoundation.org.

World Resources Institute—WRI

Founded in 1982 with a grant from the John D. and Catherine T. MacArthur Foundation (q.v.).

Activities: Works to reduce poverty, grow economies and protect natural systems through conducting policy research and analysis and influencing decisionmakers. Major programme areas are: cities; climate; energy; food; forests; oceans and water. The Institute operates through four cross-cutting centres for business, economics, finance and governance; and organizes conferences and seminars. It works in more than 50 countries with international offices in Brazil, the People's Republic of China, India, Indonesia and Mexico; regional hubs in Ethiopia and the Netherlands; and programme offices in the Democratic Republic of the Congo, Türkiye (Turkey) and the United Kingdom.

Geographical Area of Activity: International.

Publications: Annual Report; newsletter; *World Resources Report*; *WRI Digest* (weekly); data; handbooks; maps; reports; studies; blog; books.

Finance: Annual revenue US $365.9m., expenditure $235.2m. (30 Sept. 2023).

Board of Directors: David Blood (Chair.); Susan Tierney, Pamela P. Flaherty (Vice-Chair.).

Principal Staff: Pres. and CEO Ani Dasgupta.

Contact Details: 10 G St, NE, Suite 800, Washington, DC 20002; tel. (202) 729-7600; internet www.wri.org.

World Telehealth Initiative

Founded in 2017.

Activities: Uses state-of-the-art technology to provide medical expertise to vulnerable communities and helps them build sustainable healthcare services. Operates programmes in Argentina, Bangladesh, Cambodia, Ethiopia, Guinea, Malawi, Nigeria and Ukraine.

Geographical Area of Activity: Worldwide.

Finance: Total income US $946,985, expenditure $1.1m. (31 Dec. 2022).

Board: Dr Yulun Wang (Exec. Chair.).

Principal Staff: Exec. Dir Sharon Allen.

Contact Details: 7406 Hollister Ave, Santa Barbara, CA 93117; e-mail inquiry@worldtelehealthinitiative.org; internet www.worldtelehealthinitiative.org.

The Wyss Foundtion

Established in 1998 by Hansjörg Wyss, founder of Synthes USA, a medical device manufacturer, and the Wyss Medical Foundation (formerly called the Wyss Peace Foundation).

Activities: Invests in innovation in the fields of the arts, conflict resolution, economic opportunity, education, medicine, land conservation and social justice. The Foundation offers scholarships for graduate and postgraduate study in land conservation in the American West and law; and offers two-year fellowships for future conservation leaders to work in Arizona, California, Colorado, Idaho, Montana, Nevada, New Mexico, Oregon, Utah, Washington, DC, and Wyoming. In 2008 the Wyss Institute for Biologically Inspired Engineering was established at Harvard University. The Wyss Campaign for Nature is a US $1,500m. initiative to conserve 30% of the planet's natural state by 2030.

Geographical Area of Activity: International (mainly USA).

Restrictions: No unsolicited applications.

Finance: Annual revenue US $55.2m., expenditure $180.0m. (31 Dec. 2022).

Board: Hansjörg Wyss (Chair.); Joseph Fisher (Treas.); Patricia Kohl Davis (Sec.).

Principal Staff: Pres. Molly McUsic.

Contact Details: 1759 R St, NW, Washington, DC 20009; tel. (202) 232-4418; e-mail wyss@wyssfoundation.org; internet www.wyssfoundation.org.

XPRIZE Foundation

Established in 1999 by Dr Peter H. Diamandis, an engineer and physician, and Gregg Maryniak, former CEO of the Space Studies Institute of Princeton.

Activities: Awards prizes for innovating and developing technologies that address global problems that are currently without solution in the areas of exploration, global development, energy and environment, learning and life sciences. Current prizes include awards for: technologies to remove carbon dioxide from the atmosphere and oceans technologies, awarded jointly with the Musk Foundation (q.v.) (US $100m.); protein alternatives to meat ($15m.); rapid reskilling of workers to prepare for the digital revolution ($5m.); technologies to assess rainforest biodiversity ($10m.); 'breakthrough' technologies to turn carbon dioxide emissions into usable items ($20m.); artificial intelligence to solve global challenges ($5m.); and developing an 'avatar' system to carry a human's sense, actions and presence to a remote location in real time ($10m.). The Foundation hosts an annual summit.

Geographical Area of Activity: Worldwide.

Publications: Annual Report; newsletter.

Finance: Annual revenue US $16.1m., expenditure $24.2m. (31 Dec. 2022).

Board of Directors: Peter H. Diamandis (Exec. Chair.); Robert K. Weiss (Vice-Chair.); Gregg E. Maryniak (Sec.).

Principal Staff: CEO Anousheh Ansari.

Contact Details: 10736 Jefferson Blvd, Suite 406, Culver City, CA 90230; tel. (310) 741-4880; e-mail individualgiving@xprize.org; internet www.xprize.org.

Zonta Foundation for Women

Founded in 1984 as Zonta International—present name adopted in 2020; a leading global organization of professionals empowering women worldwide through service and advocacy.

Activities: Supports the charitable and educational programmes of Zonta International (f. 1919) through effective fundraising, investment of funds, and the distribution of proceeds. Zonta Foundation for Women has 26,000 members in 62 countries, supporting and advocating key issues impacting women's empowerment on local, national and interntional levels. In the last 100 years, Zonta has provided more than US $45.9m. to empower women and their access to education, healthcare, economic opportunities and safe living conditions.

Geographical Area of Activity: International.

Restrictions: No grants to individuals except for established scholarships and awards; international development projects for women primarily through UN agencies.

Publications: Annual Report; newsletter; quarterly magazine.

Finance: Annual revenue US $5.3m., expenditure $3.3m. (31 May 2024).

Board of Directors: Salla Tuominen (Pres.); Fernanda Gallo-Freschi (Pres.-elect); Sandy Venn-Brown (Vice-Pres.); Souella Cumming (Treas./Sec.).

Principal Staff: Exec. Dir Megan Radavich.

Contact Details: 1200 Harger Rd, Suite 330, Oak Brook, IL 60523; tel. (630) 928-1400; e-mail zontaintl@zonta.org; internet www.zonta.org/web/your_support/the_foundation.aspx.

URUGUAY

FOUNDATIONS AND NON-PROFITS

Fundación Astur (Astur Foundation)
Established in 2009 by Enrique V. Iglesias, former President of the Inter-American Development Bank (IDB).
Activities: Carries out self-conducted programmes to improve the quality of life of the elderly, through training caregivers and companions. The Foundation also organizes conferences, seminars and workshops on global political, economic and social challenges under the theme of 'Thinking the Future'. It funds prizes and national and international scholarships.
Geographical Area of Activity: Uruguay.
Publications: Brochure; *Revista Nuestr@s Mayores* (magazine); *Cuadernos de Astur*; studies.
Board of Directors: Enrique V. Iglesias (Pres.); Gunther Rotzinger (Vice-Pres.); Graciela Catañy (Sec.).
Advisory Board: Juan José Taccone (Pres.); José Cesar Iglesias (Vice-Pres.).
Contact Details: Iturriaga 3379, CP 11300, Montevideo; tel. (2) 6223096; e-mail info@fundacionastur.org; internet www.fundacionastur.org.

Fundación Circulo de Montevideo (Montevideo Circle Foundation)
Established in 1996 by Julio María Sanguinetti, then President of Uruguay, to convene international meetings between leaders from Europe and Latin America; became an academic foundation in 2000.
Activities: Promotes democracy, competitive and open markets, equitable and cohesive societies and good governance throughout Latin America. The Foundation convenes annual international meetings between policymakers, business leaders and academics.
Geographical Area of Activity: Latin America, Spain.
Publications: Meeting Reports.
Board: Julio María Sanguinetti (Pres.); Felipe Gonzalez (Vice-Pres.); Enrique Iglesias (Sec.).
Principal Staff: Gen. Man. Isabel Vázquez D'Elía.
Contact Details: José Luis Zorrilla de San Martín 248, CP 11300 Montevideo; tel. (2) 7123115; e-mail circulodemontevideo@gmail.com; internet circulodemontevideo.org.

Fundación Telefónica Movistar Uruguay (Telefónica Movistar Uruguay Foundation)
Established in 2013 by Telefónica-Movistar, a telecommunications company; part of the Fundación Telefónica (q.v.) network.
Activities: Carries out activities in the areas of digital culture, education, employability and volunteering. The Foundation offers online educational resources for children and teachers; offers free online training and digital tools via the Conecta Empleo platform to improve the skills and employability of young people; and supports corporate volunteering. Its educational training and innovation centre in Maldonado offers courses for teachers, including in computational thinking, robotics and programming, and digital literacy workshops for older people.
Geographical Area of Activity: Uruguay.
Publications: Reports.
Board of Trustees: Jose Luis Aiello (Pres.).
Principal Staff: Dir Leticia Lago; Man. María Noel Orellano.
Contact Details: Avda. San Martín 2842, esquina Ceibal, Montevideo; tel. 95704040; e-mail fundacion.uy@telefonica.com; internet www.fundaciontelefonica.uy.

Fundación UPM (UPM Foundation)
Established in 2006 by UPM, a forestry company.
Activities: Promotes the development of communities where the company is present, working with local organizations in more than 150 rural communities to support education and entrepreneurship. The Foundation awards project development grants worth up to US $20,000; and scholarships for primary and secondary school teachers.
Geographical Area of Activity: Uruguay.
Principal Staff: Pres. Magdalena Ibañez.
Contact Details: Avda Italia 7519, 2nd Floor, Edif. Blue, Art Carrasco Business, 11500 Montevideo; tel. 45620100; e-mail fundacion@upm.com; internet www.upm.uy/fundacion.

UZBEKISTAN

FOUNDATIONS AND NON-PROFITS

Sog'lom Avlod Uchun (For a Healthy Generation)

Founded in 1993 by presidential decree to promote improved health for future generations.

Activities: Carries out activities in five programme areas: medicine; humanitarian aid; education; culture; and sports. The organization operates through a network of 14 regional branches and more than 100 support centres, distributing donated medicines and humanitarian assistance, and conducting health and other programmes. It works in co-operation with international partners. Also owns two journals and three newspapers.
Geographical Area of Activity: Uzbekistan.
Finance: Owns five commercial companies. Net assets US $70m.; annual revenue approx. $20m.
Board of Directors: Svetlana Tursunkhodzhaevna Inamova (Chair.); Nazimjan Ergashevich Muminov (Vice-Chair.).
Principal Staff: Hon. Pres. Tatyana Akbarovna Karimova.
Contact Details: Istiqbol str. 15, 100047 Tashkent; tel. (71) 233-21-75; e-mail maktub@sau.uz; internet sau.uz.

VATICAN CITY

CO-ORDINATING BODY

Caritas Internationalis—CI

Established in 1950, in Rome, Italy, as International Caritas Conference (ICC), a global umbrella organization for the various national Catholic humanitarian assistance, social service and development organizations worldwide, many of which, but not all, used the name 'Caritas'. Incorporated the already-existing Caritas Internationalis based in Lucerne, Switzerland; present name adopted in 1954. Full title is Caritas Internationalis—International Confederation of Catholic Organizations for Charitable and Social Action (Confédération Internationale d'Organismes Catholiques d'Action Charitable et Sociale—Confederación Internacional de Organizaciones Católicas de Acción Caritativa y Social).

Activities: Supports national Caritas organizations to assist the development of the most underprivileged people through active charity, in keeping with the teachings and traditions of the Catholic Church. The organization studies problems of poverty; fosters the establishment of national Catholic charitable organizations and contributes to their development; promotes collaboration among member organizations and co-ordinates international activities; assists communities in improving their standard of living; encourages and co-ordinates humanitarian assistance by member organizations during emergencies; and promotes co-operation with other international aid and development organizations. It has consultative status with various international organizations, including ECOSOC, UNHCR, the Food and Agriculture Organization of the UN, the World Food Programme, WHO, UNICEF and the International Labour Organization; and maintains offices at the UN in New York, USA, and Geneva, Switzerland. Comprises more than 160 member organizations.

Geographical Area of Activity: Worldwide.

Publications: Annual Report; Four-Year Report; information sheets; brochures; reports and monographs.

Finance: Annual income €6.3m., expenditure €6.2m. (2023).

Bureau: Bishop Tarcisius Isao Kikuchi (Pres.).

Principal Staff: Sec.-Gen. Alistair Dutton.

Contact Details: Palazzo San Calisto, 00120 Vatican City; tel. (06) 69879799; e-mail caritas.internationalis@caritas.va; internet www.caritas.org.

FOUNDATIONS AND NON-PROFITS

Fondazione Centesimus Annus—Pro Pontifice

Established in 1993.

Activities: Promotes informed knowledge of the teachings of the Catholic Church and the Holy See. Areas of interest include: social welfare; poverty; the environment; and the common good. The Foundation organizes courses and conferences to promote the teachings of the Catholic Church. It holds courses and an annual conference in the Vatican City.

Geographical Area of Activity: Belgium, Germany, Italy, Malta, Netherlands, Slovakia, Spain, Switzerland, USA.

Publications: Annual Report; *Focus: Flash News*.

Finance: Total assets €5.9m.; net annual income €43,460 (31 Dec. 2024).

Board of Directors: Prof. Paolo Garonna (Pres.).

Principal Staff: Sec.-Gen. Dr Oliver Galea.

Contact Details: 00120 Vatican City; tel. (06) 69885752; e-mail centannus@foundation.va; internet www.centesimusannus.org.

Fondazione Fratelli Tutti (Fratelli Tutti Foundation)

Established by Pope Frances in 2021 for cultural and spiritual education.

Activities: The Foundation has two main aims: to allow tourists to experience the spirituality of art; and to develop a community around St Peter's to offer educational experiences through seminars, lectures and cultural events.

Geographical Area of Activity: Vatican City.

Board of Directors: Cardinal Mauro Gambetti (Chair.).

Principal Staff: Sec.-Gen. Francesco Occhetta.

Contact Details: Largo della Sagrestia, 00120 Vatican City; e-mail fondazioneft@fondazionefratellitutti.va; internet www.fondazionefratellitutti.org.

Fondazione Populorum Progressio (Populorum Progressio Foundation)

Established in 1992, as the Fondazione Populorum Progressio per l'America Latina, by Pope John Paul II to promote solidarity with poor and marginalized peoples, in accordance with the social teachings of the Church.

Activities: Operates in the field of aid to less-developed countries. The Foundation finances projects nominated by national sociopastoral institutions that conform to the aims of the Foundation. In particular, it supports micro-projects through one-off donations; the average contribution is approximately US $10,000. Areas of interest include: agriculture and livestock; crafts and micro-enterprises; infrastructure for drinking water; training and educational facilities; health; construction; etc. The Foundation's secretariat is based in Colombia.

Geographical Area of Activity: Latin America.

Restrictions: Grants only to projects approved by the local ecclesiastical authority.

Publications: Annual Report; newsletter; *Motu Proprio*.

Finance: Grants awarded 1992–2025 US $52m.

Principal Staff: Pres. Cardinal Michael Zcerny.

Contact Details: Dicastero per il Servizio dello Sviluppo Umano Integrale, Palazzo San Calisto, 00120 Vatican City; tel. (06) 69892711; internet populorum.celam.org.

Fondazione Vaticana Giovanni Paolo I (John Paul I Vatican Foundation)

Established in 2020 by Pope Francis.

Activities: Promotes and disseminates the thoughts, words and example of Pope John Paul I. Main areas of activity include: protecting and preserving the cultural and religious heritage of Pope John Paul I; promoting initiatives dedicated to him, such as conferences and seminars; publishing studies and research on Pope John Paul I; and establishing awards and scholarships.

Geographical Area of Activity: International.

Board of Directors: Cardinal Pietro Parolin (Pres.); Dr Stefania Falasca (Vice-Pres.).

Contact Details: Via della Conciliazione 3, 00120 Vatican City; tel. (06) 69885925; e-mail fondazione@fondazionevaticanagpi.va; internet www.fondazionevaticanagpi.va.

VENEZUELA

CO-ORDINATING BODY

Sinergia—Red Venezolana de OSC (Venezuelan Network of Civil Society Organizations)

Founded in 1996 as the Asociación Nacional de Organizaciones de la Sociedad Civil.

Activities: Promotes freedom of expression and association, democracy, active and responsible civic participation, and human rights. The Foundation provides training, technical assistance and information on setting up CSOs and takes part in international networks.

Geographical Area of Activity: Venezuela.

Restrictions: Not a grantmaking organization.

Publications: *Voces de la Sociedad Civil* (monthly newsletter); reports.

Operating Committee: Luisa Rodríguez Táriba (Pres.); Marianela Bañbi (Vice-Pres.); Rocío Guijarro (Treas.).

Principal Staff: Exec. Dir Morella Ramírez A.

Contact Details: Centro Rental de la Universidad Metropolitana (CENTROMET), Entrada Sur, Edif. Andrés Germán Otero, 2°, Of. 4, Urb. Terrazas del Ávila, Caracas 1071; tel. (212) 241-1559; e-mail info@sinergia.org.ve.

FOUNDATIONS AND NON-PROFITS

Fundación Bigott

Established in 1963 by Cigarerra Bigott, the Venezuelan subsidiary of British American Tobacco.

Activities: Carries out educational, cultural and environmental programmes to promote and protect Venezuela's traditional cultural heritage. The Foundation carries out research; and organizes courses and workshops on popular culture and cultural entrepreneurship. It offers free online courses on vocal technique, traditional dances, imagery and clothing, musical instruments, cultural theory and gastronomy; and maintains a document centre.

Geographical Area of Activity: Venezuela.

Publications: *Revista Bigott* (magazine); *Revista Veintiuno* (magazine); notebooks; teaching manuals; books.

Principal Staff: Gen. Man. Giannina Rodríguez.

Contact Details: Centro Histórico de Petare, Calle Vigía, Casa 10–11, Caracas; tel. (212) 203-7511; e-mail info@fundacionbigott.org; internet www.fundacionbigott.org.

Fundación para la Defensa de la Naturaleza—FUDENA (Foundation for the Defence of Nature)

Established in 1975.

Activities: Promotes conservation of the environment through the preservation of natural resources and sustainable development. The Foundation: conducts research; organizes the planning and management of protected areas and endangered species; runs environmental education and community participation projects; promotes co-operation between environmental groups; and disseminates information to the public.

Geographical Area of Activity: Venezuela.

Publications: Newsletters; research reports; technical reports.

Principal Staff: Exec. Dir Déborah Bigio.

Contact Details: Edif. Centro Empresarial Senderos, 5°, Of. 505, Avda Principal Los Cortijos de Lourdes con 2ª Transversal, Apdo 77076, Caracas 1071; tel. (212) 238-2930; e-mail comunicacionesfudena@gmail.com; internet fudena.org.ve.

Fundación Empresas Polar (Empresas Polar Foundation)

Founded in 1977 by Empresas Polar, a food and drink conglomerate, to contribute to the social development of Venezuela.

Activities: Operates in the fields of education, community development and health, collaborating with public and private development institutions. Since 1983 the Foundation has awarded the Lorenzo Mendoza Fleury Prize every two years to Venezuelan scientists working in the fields of biology, physics, mathematics and chemistry. It has a library that is open to the public and maintains three other sites: the Casa Alejo Zuloaga conference and training centre in San Joaquín; the 'Lorenzo A. Mendoza Quintero' Study Centre on the History of Venezuela; and the Center for Training and Promotion of Crafts.

Geographical Area of Activity: Venezuela.

Publications: Annual Report; *BiblioFEP*.

Principal Staff: Pres. Leonor Giménez de Mendoza; Vice-Pres. Rafael Antonio Sucre Matos; Gen. Man. Alicia Pimentel Benzo.

Contact Details: Segunda Avda, Los Cortijos de Lourdes, Edif. Fundación Polar, 1°, Los Ruices Municipio Sucre, Caracas 1071; tel. (212) 202-7530; e-mail maria.mijares@fundacionempresaspolar.org; internet www.fundacionempresaspolar.org.

Fundación Eugenio Mendoza—FEM (Eugenio Mendoza Foundation)

Founded in 1951 by Eugenio Mendoza Goiticoa, founder of Grupo Mendoza, and Luisa R. de Mendoza to promote social development, education, agriculture and culture.

Activities: Carries out self-conducted programmes in the areas of education, social development and culture. The Foundation provides microfinance for community development and entrepreneurial training for low-income families; and trains teachers and day care providers in low-income communities with tools to improve primary education. In co-operation with other organizations, it created Bangente, the first private Venezuelan microfinance bank; and, with Grupo Santander, the Bancrecer development bank (f. 2005). It includes the Fundación Sala Mendoza exhibition space for contemporary art.

Geographical Area of Activity: Venezuela.

Restrictions: Does not make grants to individuals or organizations.

Publications: Annual Report.

Board of Directors: Luisa Elena Mendoza de Pulido (Pres.); Luisa Mariana Pulido de Sucre (Exec. Vice-Pres.).

Principal Staff: Gen. Man. Antonio Fonseca.

Contact Details: Urb. Terrazas del Avila, Universidad Metropolitana, CENTROMET, Edif. Andrés Germán Otero Piso 1, Of. 101, Caracas; tel. (212) 241-1905; e-mail contacto@fundacioneugeniomendoza.org.ve; internet www.fundacioneugeniomendoza.org.ve.

Fundación La Salle de Ciencias Naturales—FLASA (La Salle Foundation for Natural Sciences)

Founded in 1957 as a Lasallian institution by Pablo Mandazen Soto ('Hermano Ginés'), a Christian Brother and zoologist.

Activities: Promotes national development in the areas of science and technology, education, social welfare, conservation and the environment. The Foundation carries out applied research in and provides environmental and social impact services for the Government and industry in the fields of: environmental and socioenvironmental studies; marine biology; terrestrial biology; oceanography and limnology; geographic-environmental information systems; assessment of fishery resources; quality control of food; marine farming; sociocultural evaluations; museum studies and science

Fundación de la Vivienda Popular   VIET NAM

communication; and continuing professional development in socioenvironmental subjects. It organizes conferences, courses and lectures; and has a network of 11 campuses across the country. The Caracas campus is the site of the Foundation's national headquarters, the Caribbean Institute of Anthropology and Sociology (ICAS), La Salle Natural History Museum (MHNLS), the Venezuelan Museum of Mankind and the Environment (MHoVA) and La Salle Society Natural Science. The Margarita campus hosts the Benigno Román Oceanological Museum; and the Tumeremo campus incorporates the Instituto Universitario de Tecnología del Mar (IUTEMAR), which offers courses in mining technology, industrial security, finance and accountancy, and electricity. Has a branch in Colombia.

Geographical Area of Activity: Colombia, Venezuela.

Publications: Newsletter; *Antropológica* (review); Memoria (monographic series); *Natura*; books on science and technology.

Finance: Funded by the Ministry of Education and corporate donations.

Board of Directors: Francer Alberto Goenaga (Chair.).

Contact Details: Edif. Fundación La Salle, Avda Boyacá, Sector Maripérez, Apdo 1930, Caracas 1010-A; tel. (212) 709-5803; e-mail communications@fundacionlasalle.org.ve.

Fundación de la Vivienda Popular (Foundation for Social Housing)

Established in 1958 by Eugenio Mendoza Goiticoa, founder of Grupo Mendoza, an industrial conglomerate, with the support of public figures, companies and foundations.

Activities: Works in the field of sustainable housing. The Social Action programme promotes community self-management, supporting low-income families and helping them to improve their housing and surroundings by starting housing associations; it also advises businesses wishing to help with their workers' housing problems, and trains public and private institutions interested in setting up housing associations. The Research and Development programme carries out research in areas associated with housing, especially families with few economic resources; its support programmes seek to advance knowledge of housing and the environment, and it offers the Eugenio Mendoza Chair in Housing at national universities, and the Eugenio Mendoza Prize for Research in Housing. Also maintains a documentation and information centre, which offers information on housing and the environment.

Geographical Area of Activity: Venezuela.

Publications: Annual Report.

Board of Directors: Eugenio A. Mendoza Rodríguez (Chair.); Dr Pablo A. Pulido Musche, Dr Manuel Azpúrua Arreaza, Oswaldo Carrillo Jiménez (Vice-Chair.).

Principal Staff: Gen. Man. R. Alexis Delgado Silva.

Contact Details: Avda Diego Cisneros (Principal de Los Ruices), Edif. Centro Empresarial Autana, 1°, Urb. Los Ruices, Municipio Sucre, Estado Maranda, Caracas; tel. (212) 239-4936; e-mail info@viviendaenred.net; internet viviendaenred.net.

VIET NAM

FOUNDATIONS AND NON-PROFITS

Quỹ Thiện Tâm (Kind Heart Foundation)

Established in 2006 by Phạm Nhật Vượng, Chair. of Vingroup, a conglomerate, and founder of the VinFuture Foundation (q.v.).

Activities: The corporate social responsibility arm of Vingroup. Activities include: supporting disadvantaged families and recipients of social welfare benefits; offering scholarships to underprivileged students; providing financial assistance for healthcare and medicines; fostering economic development in low-income areas; funding charitable projects to build cultural, educational and public health centres; and assisting people affected by natural disasters. In 2008 the Football Talent Development and Investment Fund was set up to train young professional football players. In 2010, working with the Buddhist Sangha of Viet Nam, the Foundation established Phat Tich Custodian Care and Talent Development Facility, which provides care and housing for older people, orphans, disadvantaged people and those receiving social welfare benefits.

Geographical Area of Activity: Viet Nam.

Finance: Funded by Vingroup.

Principal Staff: Chair. Phạm Nhật Vượng.

Contact Details: c/o Vingroup JSC, No. 7, Bang Lang 1 St, Viet Hung Ward, Long Bien District, Ha Noi; tel. (24) 39749999; e-mail info@vingroup.net; internet vingroup.net/vi/phat-trien-ben-vung/20/environment-and-community.

Toyota Vietnam Foundation—TVF

Established in 2005 by Toyota Motor Vietnam Co Ltd.

Activities: Aims to contribute to the development of Vietnamese society through supporting initiatives in traffic safety, education and training, healthcare, and the environment. The Toyota Scholarship Program (f. 1997) awards more than 100 scholarships each year to students in the fields of technology and the environment; and the Toyota Scholarship for Vietnamese Young Music Talents (f. 2009) awards between 85 and 100 music scholarships. The Foundation also supports the Vietnamese National Symphony Orchestra and since 1998 has organized the annual Toyota Concert Tour.

Geographical Area of Activity: Viet Nam.

Finance: Established with an initial donation from Toyota Motor Vietnam Co Ltd of US $4m.

Principal Staff: Chair. Do Thu Hoang; Dir Shinjiro Kajikawa.

Contact Details: c/o Toyota Motor Vietnam Co Ltd, Phuc Thang Ward, Phuc Yen Town, Vinh Phuc Province; tel. 916001524; e-mail tmv_cs@toyotavn.com.vn; internet www.toyota.com.vn/quy-toyota-tvf.

TYM Fund

Established in 1992 by the Vietnamese Women's Union (f. 1930) as a microfinance institution, to implement the Government's poverty alleviation programme; officially renamed Tinh Thuong One Member Limited Liability Microfinance Institution in 2013.

Activities: Seeks to improve women's economic development, welfare and equality, providing low-interest loans, financial services, and basic business and financial training. The Institution operates in 13 provinces and cities, serving more than 200,000 women and their families; and working with international organizations.

Geographical Area of Activity: Viet Nam (Central and Northern regions).

Publications: Annual Report; newsletter.

Members' Council: Do Thi Thu Thao (Chair.).

Principal Staff: Gen. Dir Nguyen Thi Thu Hien.

Contact Details: Bldg B, 3rd Floor, 20 Thuy Khue, Tay Ho, Hanoi; tel. (4) 37281003; e-mail tymfund@tymfund.org.vn; internet www.tymfund.org.vn.

VinFuture Foundation

Established in 2020 by Phạm Nhật Vượng, Chair. of Vingroup, a conglomerate, and founder of Quỹ Thiện Tâm (q.v.), and his wife Phạm Thu Hương.

Activities: Promotes positive change through science and technology by supporting research and innovation. The main programme is the VinFuture Prize. The Foundation annually awards one Grand Prize, worth US $3m. for breakthrough research and technological innovation that improves people's quality of life and creates a more equitable and sustainable future. It also awards three prizes, each worth $500,000, to innovators from developing countries, women innovators and for research and innovation in emerging fields.

Geographical Area of Activity: International.

Finance: Initial capital US $100m.

VinFuture Prize Council: Sir Richard Friend (Chair.).

Principal Staff: Chair. Phạm Nhật Vượng.

Contact Details: Administration Bldg, VinUniversity Campus, Vinhomes Ocean Park, Gia Lam, Ha Noi; e-mail info@vinfutureprize.org; internet vinfutureprize.org.

YEMEN

FOUNDATIONS AND NON-PROFITS

Civic Democratic Initiative Support Foundation—CDF

Established in 1993 as an umbrella organization for affiliated NGOs and local associations.

Activities: Works in the fields of governance, democracy, women's rights, public policy, tribal conflict resolution, and young people. The Foundation comprises five centres: the Centre for the Support of Women's Issues; the Youth Care Centre; the Youth Support Centre; the Centre for the Care of the Marginalized; and the Health and Environment Control Centre. Programmes and activities include decentralization; the judiciary; civic education; increasing democratic participation; elections monitoring; advocacy and lobbying on behalf of women; preventing violence against women; and promoting economic empowerment of women.

Geographical Area of Activity: Yemen.

Publications: Bulletins (democratic trends, local development, culture, volunteering); research reports; studies; books.

Principal Staff: Exec. Dir Sultana Al-Jeham.

Contact Details: POB 22 257, 55 Hadda St, Sana'a; tel. (1) 500304; e-mail info@cdf-ye.org; internet www.cdf-ye.org.

Human Rights Information and Training Center—HRITC

Founded in 2015 by Ezzaddin Al Asbahi, former Minister for Human Rights.

Activities: Non-partisan civil organization founded to promote human rights values in Yemen and the Arab world. Holds a consultative status with the UN. Main work areas are: to raise awareness of human rights issues; collaborate with other NGOs; developing tools and mechanisms to help monitor human rights violations and defending those who are victim to abuse.

Geographical Area of Activity: Yemen, Middle East.

Principal Staff: Pres. Abdulaziz Al-Maqeleh;.

Contact Details: Al-Majalliya neighborhood, Taiz; tel. 9674216277; e-mail hritc@yemen.net.ye; internet hritc.co.

Wujoh Foundation for Media and Development

Established in 2012 by Mansoor Al-Garadi.

Activities: Supports professional media and promotes freedom of opinion and expression, institutional transparency, democracy, and the rights of women and children. Programmes include: media rights and freedoms; peacebuilding and good governance; protection and gender; environment and renewable energy; humanitarian response (food); and sustainable development.

Geographical Area of Activity: Yemen.

Principal Staff: Dir Mansoor Al-Garadi; Deputy Dir Maliha Al-Asaadi.

Contact Details: North 60th St, next to Yahya Suhail Company, Sana'a; tel. 733893894; e-mail wujoh.f@gmail.com.

Yemen Polling Center—YPC

Established in 2004 by Hafez Albukari, a journalist.

Activities: Works to strengthen the advocacy skills of women, CSOs and youth activists. Projects include the Yemen Parliament Watch, the Civil Society Forum, and mapping state and non-state security providers. The Center carries out policy research and analysis through local enumerators in every governorate in Yemen and consultants based abroad; and organizes workshops. It has a branch in Aden. A sister organization, the Yemen Policy Center, was established in 2020 by a group of Yemeni and German researchers to conduct research and advocacy and to influence national and international policymaking.

Geographical Area of Activity: Egypt, Germany, Yemen.

Publications: Policy reports; policy briefs; data.

Principal Staff: CEO Rana Jarhum; Pres. Hafez Albukari; Vice-Pres. Kamal Muqbil.

Contact Details: 2nd Floor, in front of the Central Bank of Yemen, Jamal St, Taiz; tel. (1) 505647; e-mail contact@yemenpolling.org; internet www.yemenpolling.org.

Youth Leadership Development Foundation—YLDF

Established in 2005 by Dr Antelak Almutawakel, Dr Gabool Almutawakel and Carin Meerburg; incorporates the Girls World Communication Center (f. 1998) and the Youth Economic Development Center (f. 2005).

Activities: A youth- and women-led NGO. The Foundation's vision is for a Yemen in which skilled, well-qualified and active young women and men play leadership roles in all domains of society and enable Yemenis to contribute to a better world. The Foundation aims to contribute to the efforts of economic empowerment of the most vulnerable low-income young men and women, providing all types of its assistance in a neutral and transparent manner. It promotes the equality of both youth and women and protects the rights of such groups through programmes that empower them to meet their own needs; participate in and express their ideas, creativity and needs; and encourage their engagement in decisionmaking processes in their own lives, as well as in development and humanitarian contexts. Programmes prioritize continual improvement in management systems and impact, while focusing on learning outcomes for staff, beneficiaries and key stakeholders.

Geographical Area of Activity: Yemen.

Publications: Annual Report; programme reports; guidelines; studies; films and documentaries.

Board of Directors: Dr Antelak Almutawakel (Chair.).

Contact Details: Western Ring Rd, Behind Qasr Al-Dhifafah Restaurants, Sana'a 27705; tel. (1) 215537; e-mail info@yldf.org; internet www.yldf.org.

ZAMBIA

FOUNDATIONS AND NON-PROFITS

Copperbelt Development Foundation

Established in 2004 by Anglo American Corporation, a mining company; became operational in 2009.

Activities: Works to alleviate poverty and empower local people through infrastructure development, and business and skills training. The Foundation builds and equips school facilities; invests in health infrastructure; provides access to clean water and sanitation in rural areas and informal settlements; provides skills training centres and income-generating activities for women and young people; works to diversify the region's economy and reduce its reliance on mining; and protects and promotes regional cultures.

Geographical Area of Activity: Zambia (Copperbelt Province and Shibuyunji District).

Publications: Brochure.

Board of Directors: Edward Zulu (Chair.).

Principal Staff: Man. Kebby Mukalo Mushili.

Contact Details: 32A Pamo Ave, POB 20917, Parklands, Kitwe; tel. (21) 2227480; e-mail cdfl@cdfl.co.zm; internet www.cdfl.co.zm.

ZIMBABWE

FOUNDATIONS AND NON-PROFITS

African Capacity Building Foundation—ACBF (Fondation pour le Renforcement des Capacités en Afrique)

Established in 1991 through a collaboration between the African Development Bank, the World Bank and the UN Development Programme; a specialized agency of the African Union.

Activities: Promotes and supports the improvement of human and institutional capacities in the areas of policy analysis and development management. The Partnership for Capacity Building in Africa (PACT) initiative funds: projects and programmes to strengthen the public sector and its interface with the private sector and civil society; regional policy-related initiatives in the areas of advocacy, analysis, research and training; and institutional frameworks for country ownership of capacity-building activities. The Foundation awards fellowships to improve research and training skills and expand in-service training for professionals. It maintains a library of more than 10,000 publications; and has regional offices in Ghana and Kenya.

Geographical Area of Activity: sub-Saharan Africa.

Publications: Annual Report; *African Capacity Bulletin* (monthly); workshop reports; blog; books.

Finance: Annual revenue US $7.9m., expenditure $10.5m. (31 Dec. 2022).

Executive Board: Mohamed Beavogui (Interim Chair.).

Principal Staff: Exec. Sec. Mamadou Biteye.

Contact Details: 2 Fairbairn Dr., Mount Pleasant, Harare; tel. (242) 304663; e-mail root@acbf-pact.org; internet www.acbf-pact.org.

African Forum and Network on Debt and Development—AFRODAD

Established in 1996 by Opa Kapijimpanga, an economist, and CSOs in sub-Saharan Africa; part of a network comprising Eurodad, Latindadd and Jubilee USA Network (qq.v.).

Activities: Lobbies and advocates for debt cancellation and on other issues related to debt, development aid and economic governance issues in Africa. Main areas of research include: domestic and external loan contraction processes; debt profiles; legal and institutional frameworks of government debt systems; fair and transparent arbitration of sovereign debts; emerging lenders to Africa; responsible lending and borrowing; development effectiveness; transparency and accountability in extractive industries; development finance and financial flows; and fiscal issues in Africa. The Forum comprises a network of African NGOs, organizations, churches and individuals.

Geographical Area of Activity: Africa.

Publications: Annual Report; newsletter; concept notes; discussion papers; occasional papers; policy briefs; research reports; blog.

Board of Trustees: Barbara Kalima-Phiri (Chair.).

Principal Staff: Exec. Dir Jason Rosario Braganza.

Contact Details: 31 Atkinson Dr., Hillside, POB CY1517, Causeway, 9995 Harare; tel. (242) 778531; e-mail info@afrodad.org; internet www.afrodad.org.

Angel of Hope Foundation

Established in 2018 by First Lady Auxillia Mnangagwa, a former Member of Parliament.

Activities: Supports children and women from disadvantaged backgrounds and minority groups and through lobbying and advocacy and implementing programmes. Main programmes include: health and nutrition, offering cancer screening, rehabilitating health facilities and providing medical equipment and medicines, distributing nutrition packs to pregnant and lactating women, and setting up gardens in orphanages, schools and health facilities, and drilling and refurbishing boreholes; social protection and emergency response, countering forced and child marriages and gender-based violence, and promoting access to sanitary towels; and women's economic empowerment, improving livelihoods and employment through providing loans and mentoring. The Foundation organizes focus groups discussions and conferences with authorities and experts; and disseminates information.

Geographical Area of Activity: Zimbabwe.

Publications: Newsletter.

Board: Molly Dingani (Chair.); Chipo Mtasa (Vice-Chair.).

Contact Details: 16 Wakefield Rd, Avondale, Harare; tel. (242) 709934; e-mail info@angelofhopezim.org; internet angelofhopezim.org.

Community Foundation for the Western Region of Zimbabwe—CFWRZ

Established in 1997 by 50,000 community members who contributed to the Foundation's initial endowment.

Activities: Promotes sustainable socioeconomic development of remote and rural regions, facilitatiing the creation of funds for self-empowerment and poverty reduction and offering micro-credit to social enterprises and grants for community projects. The Foundation improves quality of life in economically disadvantaged communities using the Community Endowment Fund created using the Qogelela (saving little amounts for future use) Approach. Main programmes focus on: women's empowerment; youth development; health development; education; and water and agriculture.

ZIMBABWE

Geographical Area of Activity: Western Zimbabwe (Matebeleland North, Matebeleland South and Midlands Provinces).

Finance: Initial funding provided by a 'Qogelela' endowment, a community savings programme worth approx. US $100,000.

Board of Trustees: Rev. Tomson Dube (Chair.); Felicity V. C. Gangada (Vice-Chair.); Mirirayi M. S. Huni (sec.).

Principal Staff: Exec. Dir Stewart M. Mantula.

Contact Details: 21 Walter Howard Rd, Northend, 00263 Bulawayo; POB 1799, Bulawayo; tel. (292) 209617; e-mail westfund@mweb.co.zw; internet www.comfoundzim.org.zw.

Higherlife Foundation

Established in 1996 by Strive Masiyiwa, founder and Exec. Chair. of Econet Wireless International, a telecommunications company, and his wife Tsitsi Masiyiwa.

Activities: Areas of focus are: education; health; disaster relief and preparedness; and rural transformation and sustainable livelihoods. The Foundation is an umbrella organization, which comprises: the Capernaum Trust (f. 1996) and Capernaum Trust International, providing education for vulnerable children; Christian Community Partnership Trust (f. 2005), supporting evangelical Christian organizations; the Joshua Nkomo Scholarship Fund (f. 2005), sponsoring secondary- and tertiary-level students in Zimbabwe; and the National Healthcare Trust Zimbabwe (f. 2008), which provides emergency healthcare, refurbishes hospitals, trains health workers and offers scholarships to medical students. Education initiatives include the Yale Young African Scholars Program, preparing gifted students for university; and Ruzivo Smart Learning, an online digital learning platform for primary and secondary school students. Operates in five countries and has an office in Lesotho.

Geographical Area of Activity: sub-Saharan Africa.

Publications: Newsletter (monthly); brochures; research reports.

Board: Dr Tsitsi Masiyiwa (Exec. Chair.).

Principal Staff: CEO Dr Kennedy Mubaiwa; Exec. Dir Elizabeth Tanya Masiyiwa.

Contact Details: 58 Alpes Rd, Vainona, Harare; tel. 772222922; e-mail info@higherlifefoundation.org; internet www.higherlifefoundation.com.

J. F. Kapnek Zimbabwe

Established in as the J. F. Kapnek Trust Zimbabwe in 1966 in the USA from the estate of James F. Kapnek, who made his fortune in mining in Southern Africa; registered in Zimbabwe in 1986.

Activities: Works to improve family health, reduce child mortality and create educational opportunity for children. Main programme areas are: children and young people with disabilities, supporting sign language training, providing access to rehabilitation and protection services, and promoting access to inclusive sexual reproductive health and rights and sexual gender-based violence information and services; HIV and family health, reducing new infections and improving quality of life; integrated early childhood development and health, renovating and refurbishing rural schools, providing community-supported school feeding programmes, conducting health assessments and teaching parenting skills; and orphans and vulnerable children, providing protection and access to education. The Strengthening Sciences for Women programme offers scholarships for women to study science-related degrees and attend medical school. A sister organization operates in the USA.

Geographical Area of Activity: Zimbabwe.

Publications: Annual Report.

Principal Staff: Exec. Dir Hillary Tanyanyiwa.

Contact Details: 33 Harvey Brown Ave, Milton Park, Harare; tel. (242) 792153; e-mail info@jfkapnek.org; internet www.jfkapnek.org.

Self Help Development Foundation—SHDF

Established in 1963 by Francis Waddelove, a Jesuit priest, to reduce poverty through food security; the NGO arm of the SHDF Trust.

Activities: Promotes the development of women and communities through self-reliance and savings clubs. The Foundation runs capacity-building programmes in the areas of business and agriculture, including marketing and financial literacy; and offers business development services to small- and medium-scale farmers, farmer associations, commodity associations, women's clubs and associations, leaders of community projects, agro-dealers and communities at large. It has 20,000 savings club members and works in 30 districts in Zimbabwe, with offices in Bulawayo, Buhera, Gweru and Seke.

Geographical Area of Activity: Zimbabwe.

Principal Staff: Exec. Dir Muchanyara Mukamuri.

Contact Details: 17 Nirvana Rd, Hatfield, POB 4576, Harare; tel. 777821579; e-mail shdftas@africaonline.co.zw; internet www.shdf.org.zw.

Uluntu Community Foundation—UCF

Established in 2008 by Inviolatta Mpuli Moyo, a community activist.

Activities: Works to eliminate poverty and hunger through self-reliance and sustainable development. Main programme areas are: education, improving infrastructure and reducing school dropout; food security and sustainable livelihoods; and social entrepreneurship, offering grants and supporting skills development. The Foundation provides advocacy and financial and technical assistance; conducts research and disseminates information; and promotes local philanthropy.

Geographical Area of Activity: Zimbabwe (Bulawayo, Matabeleland North and South Provinces).

Publications: Annual Report; newsletter; research surveys.

Principal Staff: Exec. Dir Sibusisiwe Sithole.

Contact Details: 11 Coghlan Ave, Kumalo, Bulawayo; POB 3055, 00263 Bulawayo; tel. (9) 231294; e-mail info@uluntu.org; internet uluntufoundation.org.

Select Bibliography

Acs, Zoltan J. *Why Philanthropy Matters: How the Wealthy Give, and What It Means for Our Economic Well-Being.* Princeton University Press, Princeton, NJ, 2013.

Adam, T. *American Philanthropy in Its Global Context.* Policy Press, Bristol, 2025.

Alliance Publishing Trust. *Alliance* (quarterly journal).

Andreoni, J. *The Economics of Philanthropy and Fundraising.* Edward Elgar, Cheltenham, 2015.

Anheier, H. K. *Non-Profit Organizations: Theory, Management, Policy* (3rd edn). Routledge, Abingdon, 2023.

Anheier, H. K., and Daly, S. *The Roles and Visions of Foundations in Europe.* London School of Economics, London, 2004. (Eds) *The Politics of Foundations: Comparative Perspectives from Europe and Beyond.* Routledge, Abingdon, 2006.

Anheier, H. K., and Hammack, D. *American Foundations: Roles and Contributions.* Brookings Institution, Washington, DC, 2010. *A Versatile American Institution: The Changing Ideals and Realities of Philanthropic Foundations.* Brookings Institution Press, Washington, DC, 2013.

Anheier, H. K., and Leat, D. *From Charity to Creativity: Philanthropic Foundations in the 21st Century: Perspectives from Britain and Beyond.* Comedia, Stroud, 2002. *Creative Philanthropy: Toward a New Philanthropy for the Twenty-First Century.* Routledge, Abingdon, 2006.

Anheier, H. K., and List, R. A. *A Dictionary of Civil Society, Philanthropy and the Non-Profit Sector.* Routledge, London, 2005.

Anheier, H. K., and Toepler, S. (Eds). *Private Funds, Public Purpose: Philanthropic Foundations in International Perspective.* Kluwer Academic/Plenum Publishers, USA, 1999. *The Routledge Companion to Nonprofit Management.* Routledge, Abingdon, 2020.

Avenell, S., and Ogawa, A. *Transnational Civil Society in Asia: The Potential of Grassroots Regionalization.* Routledge, Abingdon, 2022.

Baker, G., and Chandler, D. *Global Civil Society: Contested Futures.* Routledge, Abingdon, 2006.

Bebbington, A. J., Hickey, S., and Mitlin, D. (Eds). *Can NGOs Make a Difference? The Challenge of Development Alternatives.* Zed Books, London, 2007.

Bennett, Roger. *Fundraising and Nonprofit Marketing: A Research Overview.* Routledge, Abingdon, 2023.

Boesso, G., and Cerbioni, F. *Governance and Strategic Philanthropy in Grant-Making Foundations: How to Improve the Effectiveness of Nonprofit Boards.* Palgrave Macmillan, London, 2019; *Governance, Nonprofit Organizations and Strategy: The Network Philanthropy Model.* Routledge, Abingdon, 2024.

Bolling, Landrum R., and Smith, C. *Private Foreign Aid: US Philanthropy for Relief and Development.* Routledge, Abingdon, 2019.

Brass, J. *Allies or Adversaries: NGOs and the State in Africa.* Cambridge University Press, New York, 2016.

Breeze, B., Lafferty, D. D., and Wiepking, P. (Eds). *The Fundraising Reader.* Routledge, Abingdon, 2023.

Bremner, R. H. *Giving: Charity and Philanthropy in History.* Rutgers University Press, New Brunswick, NJ, 1995.

Brest, P., and Harvey, H. *Money Well Spent: A Strategic Plan for Smart Philanthropy* (2nd edn). Stanford Business Books. Stanford, CA, 2018.

Briguglio, L., Briguglio, M., Bunwaree, S., and Slatter, C. (Eds). *Handbook of Civil Society and Social Movements in Small States.* Routledge, Abingdon, 2023.

Brown, R. A., and Pierce, J. *Charities in the Non-Western World: The Development and Regulation of Indigenous and Islamic Charities.* Routledge, Abingdon, 2013.

Buchanan, P., Feuerstein, M., and Walker, D. *Giving Done Right: Effective Philanthropy and Making Every Dollar Count.* PublicAffairs, New York, 2019.

Callahan, D. *The Givers: Wealth, Power, and Philanthropy in a New Gilded Age.* Vintage Books, New York, 2018.

Candid. *Philanthropy News Digest* (weekly, by e-mail).

Cavatorta, F., and Durac, V. *Civil Society and Democratization in the Arab World.* Routledge, Abingdon, 2010.

Chevalier-Watts, J. *Charity Law: International Perspectives.* Routlege, Abingdon, 2017.

Chew, C. *Strategic Positioning in Voluntary and Charitable Organizations.* Routledge, Abingdon, 2009.

Christie, R. *Peacebuilding and NGOs: State-Civil Society Interactions.* Routledge, Abingdon, 2013.

Claeyé, F. *Managing Nongovernmental Organizations: Culture, Power and Resistance.* Routledge, Abingdon, 2014.

Cornforth, C., and Brown, W. A. *Nonprofit Governance: Innovative Perspectives and Approaches.* Routledge, Abingdon, 2013.

Cuninggim, M. *Private Money and Public Service: The Role of Foundations in American Society.* Herder & Herder, New York, 1972.

Cunningham, H. *The Reputation of Philanthropy Since 1750: Britain and Beyond.* Manchester University Press, Manchester, 2020.

Davies, T. *NGOs: A New History of Transnational Civil Society.* Oxford University Press, New York, 2014. (Ed.) *Routledge Handbook of NGOs and International Relations.* Routledge, Abingdon, 2019.

de Lauri, A. *The Politics of Humanitarianism: Power, Ideology and Aid.* I. B. Tauris, London, 2014.

Directory of Social Change. *The Directory of Grant Making Trusts,* London, annual; *The Guide to Major Trusts,* London, annual; *The Guide to New Trusts,* London, annual.

Dogra, N. *Representations of Global Poverty: Aid, Development and International NGOs.* I. B. Tauris, London, 2012.

Donnelly-Cox, G., Meyer, M., and Wijkström, F. (Eds). *Research Handbook on Nonprofit Governance.* Edward Elgar Publishing, Cheltenham, 2021.

Editions Ruyant. *GAFA: Guide Annuaire des Fondations et des Associations.* Cosne sur Loire, 2009.

Edwards, M. *Civil Society* (4th edn). Polity, Cambridge, 2019. (Ed.) *The Oxford Handbook of Civil Society.* Oxford University Press, New York, 2011.

Elson, P. R., Lefvre S. A., and Fontan J.-M. (Eds). *Philanthropic Foundations in Canada: Landscapes, Indigenous Perspectives and Pathways to Change.* Tellwell, Victoria, BC, 2020.

Enjolras, B., Salamon, L. M., et al. *The Third Sector as a Renewable Resource for Europe: Concepts, Impacts, Challenges and Opportunities*. Palgrave Macmillan, Cham, 2018.

Fejerskov, A. M. *The Gates Foundation's Rise to Power: Private Authority in Global Politics*. Routledge, Abingdon, 2018.

Filep, B. *The Politics of Good Neighbourhood: State, Civil Society and the Enhancement of Cultural Capital in East Central Europe*. Routledge, Abingdon, 2016.

Fridell, G., and Konings, M. *Age of Icons: Exploring Philanthrocapitalism in the Contemporary World*. University of Toronto Press, Toronto, 2014.

Fundación Arias para la Paz y el Progreso Humano. *Directorio de organizaciones para la promoción de la micro, pequeña y mediana empresa en Centroamérica*. San José, 2006.

Gabay, C. *Civil Society and Global Poverty: Hegemony, Inclusivity, Legitimacy*. Routledge, Abingdon, 2012.

Gale Cengage Learning. *Encyclopedia of Associations: International Organizations* (63rd edn). Detroit, MI, 2024.

Garcia-Rodriguez, I., and Romero-Merino, M. E. *Financing Nonprofit Organizations*. Routledge, Abingdon, 2020.

Gates, M. *Moment of Lift: How Empowering Women Changes the World*. Flatiron Books, New York, 2019.

Gevorgyan, V. *Civil Society and Government Institutions in Armenia: Leaving Behind the 'Post-Soviet' Title*. Routledge, Abingdon, 2024.

Glasius, M., Lewis, D. and Seckinelgin, H. (Eds). *Exploring Civil Society: Political and Cultural Contexts*. Routledge, Abingdon, 2004.

Goldseker, S., and Moody, M. P. *Generation Impact: How Next Gen Donors Are Revolutionizing Giving*. John Wiley & Sons, Hoboken, NJ, 2021.

Gonçalves, G., and Oliveira, E. (Eds). *The Routledge Handbook of Nonprofit Communication*. Routledge, Abingdon, 2023.

Hammack, D. C., and Smith, S. R. (Eds). *American Philanthropic Foundations: Regional Difference and Change*. Indiana University Press, Bloomington, 2018.

Hanson, Craig. *An Introduction to Ethics for Nonprofits and NGOs*. Palgrave Macmillan, Cham, 2023.

Hilton, M. *A Historical Guide to NGOs in Britain: Charities, Civil Society and the Voluntary Sector since 1945*. Palgrave Macmillan, Basingstoke, 2012.

Hoelscher, H., List, R., Ruser, A., and Toepler, S. *Civil Society: Concepts, Challenges, Contexts: Essays in Honor of Helmut K. Anheier*. Springer, Cham, 2022.

Horton Smith, D. and Stebbins, R. A. *A Dictionary of Nonprofit Terms and Concepts*. Indiana University Press, Bloomington, IN, 2006.

Hsu, C. L. *Social Entrepreneurship and Citizenship in China: The Rise of NGOs in the PRC*. Routledge, Abingdon, 2017.

Information Today. *Annual Register of Grant Support*. Medford, NJ (annual).

International Society for Third-Sector Research—ISTR. *Voluntas* (journal); *Inside ISTR*; *ISTR Report*.

James, H. (Ed.). *Civil Society, Religion and Global Governance*. Routledge, Abingdon, 2007.

Jegers, M. *Managerial Economics of Non-Profit Organizations*. Routledge, Abingdon, 2009.

Jobert, B., and Kohler-Koch, B. (Eds). *Changing Images of Civil Society: From Protest to Governance*. Routledge, Abingdon, 2008.

Joseph, J. A. (Ed.). *The Charitable Impulse: Wealth and Social Conscience in Communities and Cultures Outside the United States*. Foundation Center, New York, 1989.

Jung, T., Phillips, S., and Harrow, J. *The Routledge Companion to Philanthropy*. Routledge, Abingdon, 2016.

Kaldor, M., Selchow, S., and Moore, H. L. (Eds). *Global Civil Society 2012: Ten Years of Critical Reflection*. Palgrave Macmillan, Basingstoke, 2012.

Kalm, S., and Uhlin, A. *Civil Society and the Governance of Development*. Palgrave Macmillan, New York, 2015.

Kamruzzaman, P. *Civil Society in the Global South*. Routledge, Abingdon, 2018.

Kenniscentrum Filantropie. *Fondsenboek* (online).

Keohane, G. L. *Social Entrepreneurship for the 21st Century: Innovation Across the Nonprofit, Private, and Public Sectors*. McGraw-Hill, New York, 2013.

Keppel, F., and Lagemann, E. *The Foundation: Its Place in American Life*. Routledge, Abingdon, 2017.

Kiger, J. *Philanthropists and Foundation Globalization*. Routledge, Abingdon, 2017.

Kilby, Patrick. *Philanthropic Foundations in International Development: Rockefeller, Ford and Gates*. Routledge, Abingdon, 2021.

Lambin, R., Roberts, J., and Surender, R. *Handbook on Philanthropy and Social Policy*. Edward Elgar Publishing, Cheltenham, 2025.

Lang, S. *NGOs, Civil Society, and the Public Sphere*. Cambridge University Press, Cambridge, 2013.

Laville, J.-L., Young, D. R., and Eynaud, P. *Civil Society, the Third Sector and Social Enterprise: Governance and Democracy*. Routledge, Abingdon, 2015.

Littleberry Press LLC. *Directory of Research Grants; Directory of Grants in the Humanities; Directory of Biomedical and Health Care Grants; Operating Grants for Nonprofit Organizations; Directory of Research Grants; Funding Sources for Community and Economic Development*. West Lafayette, IN.

MacAskill, W. *Doing Good Better: Effective Altruism and a Radical New Way to Make a Difference*. Guardian Books, Faber & Faber, London, 2016.

McGregor-Lowndes, M., and Wyatt, B. *Regulating Charities: The Inside Story*. Routledge, Abingdon, 2017.

Mckeever, B. S., Dietz, N. E., and Fyffe, S. D. *The Nonprofit Almanac: The Essential Facts and Figures for Managers, Researchers, and Volunteers* (9th edn). Rowman & Littlefield/Urban Institute, Lanham, MD, 2016.

Magat, R. (Ed.). *An Agile Servant: Community Leadership by Community Foundations*. Foundation Center, New York, 1989.

Maurrasse, D. J. *Philanthropy and Society*. Routledge, Abingdon, 2020.

Michelson, E. S. *Philanthropy and the Future of Science and Technology*. Routledge, Abingdon, 2022.

Mitchell, K., and Pallister-Wilkins, P. (Eds). *The Routledge International Handbook of Critical Philanthropy and Humanitarianism*. Routledge, Abingdon, 2023.

Mitchell, S. *Charity Management: Leadership, Evolution, and Change*. Routledge, Abingdon, 2021.

Moody, M., and Breeze, B. *The Philanthropy Reader*. Routledge, Abingdon, 2016.

Moore, C. *Strategic FUEL for Nonprofits: How to Create a Strategy that is Focused, Understandable, Embedded, and Living*. Routledge, Abingdon, 2024.

Moran, M. *Private Foundations and Development Partnerships: American Philanthropy and Global Development Agendas*. Routledge, Abingdon, 2014.

Morvaridi, B. *New Philanthropy and Social Justice: Debating the Conceptual and Policy Discourse*. Policy Press, Chicago, IL, 2015.

SELECT BIBLIOGRAPHY

Nagai, A., Lerner, R., and Rothman, R. (Eds). *Giving for Social Change: Foundations, Public Policy, and the American Political Agenda*. Praeger Publishers, Westport, CT, 1994.

Natil, I. (Ed.). *New Leadership of Civil Society Organisations: Community Development and Engagement*. Routledge, Abingdon, 2022. *Public Diplomacy and Civil Society Organisations*. Routledge, Abingdon, 2024.

NCVO. *UK Civil Society Almanac*. London, annual.

Nejima, S. *NGOs in the Muslim World: Faith and Social Services*. Routledge, Abingdon, 2016.

Neri-Castracane, and Ugazio, G. (Eds). *Philanthropy: Multidisciplinary Perspectives*. Routledge, Abingdon, 2025.

Osborne, S. P. *The Third Sector in Europe: Prospects and Challenges*. Routledge, Abingdon, 2008. *Innovation in Public Services: Theoretical, Managerial, and International Perspectives*. Routledge, Abingdon, 2017.

O'Sullivan, Kevin. *The NGO Moment: The Globalisation of Compassion from Biafra to Live Aid*. Cambridge, Cambridge University Press, 2021.

Ott, J. S., and Dicke, L. *The Nature of the Nonprofit Sector* (4th edn). Routledge, Abingdon, 2021.

Palgrave Macmillan (Ed.). *The Grants Register 2025: The Complete Guide to Postgraduate Funding Worldwide* (43rd edn). Springer Nature, London, 2024.

Peter, H., and Huber, G. L. (Eds). *The Routledge Handbook of Taxation and Philanthropy*. Routledge, Abingdon, 2022.

Pétric, B.-M. *Democracy at Large: NGOs, Political Foundations, Think Tanks, and International Organizations*. Palgrave Macmillan, New York, 2012.

Phillips, K. *Trust, Impact, and Fundraising for Nonprofits: How Meaningful Ethics and Strategic Evaluation can Multiply your Revenue and Expand your Program*. Routledge, Abingdon, 2023.

Phillips, S., and Rathgeb Smith, S. *Governance and Regulation in the Third Sector*. Routledge, Abingdon, 2011.

Pifer, A. *Philanthropy in an Age of Transition*. Foundation Center, New York, 1984.

Pomey, M. *Traité des Fondations d'Utilité Publique*. Presse Universitaire de France, Paris, 1980.

Powell, W. W., and Bromley, P. (Eds). *The Nonprofit Sector: A Research Handbook* (3rd edn). Stanford University Press, Stanford, CA, 2020.

Pratt, B., and Hayman, R. *Civil Society Sustainability: New Challenges in Organisational Legitimacy, Credibility, and Viability*. Routledge, Abingdon, 2017.

Qiaoan, R. *Civil Society in China: How Society Speaks to the State*. Routledge, Abingdon, 2021.

Randel, J., German, T., and Ewing, D. *The Reality of Aid 2000* (7th edn). Routledge, Abingdon, 2013.

Reich, R. *Just Giving: Why Philanthropy Is Failing Democracy and How It Can Do Better*. Princeton University Press, Princeton, NJ, 2020.

Rostis, A. *Organizing Disaster: The Construction of Humanitarianism*. Emerald Publishing, Bingley, 2017.

Routledge. *Journal of Civil Society* (journal, 3 a year). Routledge, Abingdon.

Roza, L., Bethmann, S., Meijs, L., and von Schnurbein, G. (Eds). *Handbook on Corporate Foundations: Corporate and Civil Society Perspectives*. Springer, 2020.

Sahoo, S. *Civil Society and Democratization in India: Institutions, Ideologies and Interests*. Routledge, Abingdon, 2013.

Salamon, L. M. *The Global Associational Revolution: The Rise of the Third Sector on the World Scene*. Johns Hopkins University, Institute for Policy Studies, Baltimore, MD, 1993. *Leverage for Good: An Introduction to the New Frontiers of Philanthropy and Social Investment*. Oxford University Press, Oxford, 2014. *New Frontiers of Philanthropy: A Guide to the New Tools and Actors Reshaping Global Philanthropy and Social Investing*. Oxford University Press, Oxford, 2014.

Salamon, L. M., and Anheier, H. K. *The Emerging Sector: The Nonprofit Sector in Comparative Perspective: An Overview*. Johns Hopkins University, Institute for Policy Studies, Baltimore, MD, 1994. *The Emerging Nonprofit Sector: An Overview*. Manchester University Press, Manchester, 1996. (Eds) *Defining the Nonprofit Sector: A Cross-National Analysis*. Manchester University Press, Manchester, 1997.

Salamon, L. M., Anheier, H. K., Toepler, S., Sokolowski, S. W., List, R., et al. *Global Civil Society: Dimensions of the Nonprofit Sector*. Kumarian Press, Boulder, CO, 2006.

Salamon, L. M., Sokolowski, S. W., and Haddock, M. A. *Explaining Civil society Development: A Social Origins Approach*. Johns Hopkins University Press, Baltimore, MD, 2017.

Salamon, L. M., Sokolowski, S. W., and List, R. *Global Civil Society: An Overview*. Johns Hopkins University, Institute for Policy Studies, Baltimore, MD, 2003.

Salvatici, S. *A History of Humanitarianism, 1755–1989: In the Name of Others*. Manchester University Press, Manchester, 2019.

Sanchez Salgado, R. *Europeanizing Civil Society: How the EU Shapes Civil Society Organizations*. Palgrave Macmillan, Basingstoke, 2014.

Sargeant, A., and George, J. *Fundraising Management: Analysis, Planning and Practice* (4th edn). Routledge, Abingdon, 2022.

Sarukkai, S. *JRD Tata and the Ethics of Philanthropy*. Routledge India, New Delhi, 2020 (ebook).

Schneiker, A. *Humanitarian NGOs, (In)Security and Identity: Epistemic Communities and Security Governance*. Routledge, Abingdon, 2015.

Schramme, A., Müller, U., Verboven, N., and D'hoore, L. (Eds). *Cultural Philanthropy and Entrepreneurship*. Routledge, Abingdon, 2024.

Schuyt, T. N. M. *Philanthropy and the Philanthropy Sector: An Introduction*. Routledge, Abingdon, 2016.

Schwittay, A. *New Media and International Development: Representation and Affect in Microfinance*. Routledge, New York, 2015.

Siegel, D., and Yancey, J. *The Rebirth of Civil Society: The Development of the Nonprofit Sector in East Central Europe and the Role of Western Assistance*. Rockefeller Brothers Fund, New York, 1992.

Sievers, B. R. *Civil Society, Philanthropy, and the Fate of the Commons*. Tufts University Press, Medford, MA, 2010.

Silber, N. *A Corporate Form of Freedom: The Emergence of the Nonprofit Sector*. Routledge, Abingdon, 2019.

Simsa, R., Meyer, M., and Badelt, C. (Eds). *Handbuch der Nonprofit-Organisationen*. Schäffer-Poeschel Verlag, Stuttgart, 2013.

Sklair, Jessica. *Brazilian Elites and their Philanthropy: Wealth at the Service of Development*. Routledge, Abingdon, 2022.

Srinivas, Nidhi. *Against NGOs: A Critical Perspective on Civil society, Management and Development*. Cambridge University Press, Cambridge, 2022.

Stoesz, E. *Doing Good Better: How to Be an Effective Board Member of a Nonprofit Organization*. Good Books, New York, 2015.

Sudetic, C. *The Philanthropy of George Soros: Building Open Societies*. PublicAffairs, Perseus Books Group, New York, 2011.

Sundar, P. *Foreign Aid for Indian NGOs: Problem or Solution?* Routledge, Abingdon, 2009.

Thümler, E. *Philanthropy in Practice: Pragmatism and the Impact of Philanthropic Action.* Routledge, Abingdon, 2017.

Ugazio, G., and Maricic, M. (Eds). *The Routledge Handbook of Artificial Intelligence and Philanthropy.* Routledge, Abingdon, 2024.

Ungsuchaval, T. *NGOs and Civil Society in Thailand: Metagovernance and the Politics of NGO Funding.* Routledge, Abingdon, 2022.

Ural, E. (Ed.). *Foundations in Turkey.* Development Foundation of Turkey, Ankara, 1978.

Vallely, P. *Philanthropy: From Aristotle to Zuckerberg.* Bloomsbury Continuum, London, 2020.

Van den Bulck, H. *Celebrity Philanthropy and Activism: Mediated Interventions in the Global Public Sphere.* Routledge, Abingdon, 2018.

van Wessel, M., Kontinen, T., and Bawole, J. N. (Eds). *Reimagining Civil Society Collaborations in Development: Starting from the South.* Routledge, Abingdon, 2023.

Weaver, W. *U.S. Philanthropic Foundations: Their History, Structure, Management and Record.* Harper & Row, New York, 1967.

Wee, B. G. *Managing Social Purpose Driven Organizations: Looking at the Third Sector.* Routledge, Abingdon, 2017.

Wei, Qian. *The Governance of Philanthropic Foundations in Authoritarian China: A Power Perspective.* Routledge, Abingdon, 2023.

Weiss, T., and Wilkinson, R. *International Organization and Global Governance.* Routledge, London and New York, 2014.

Wiepking, P., and Handy, F. (Eds). *The Palgrave Handbook of Global Philanthropy.* Palgrave Macmillan, Basingstoke, 2015.

Witesman, E., and Child, C. *Reimagining Nonprofits: Sector Theory in the Twenty-First Century.* Cambridge University Press, Cambridge, 2024.

Worth, M. J. *Nonprofit Management: Principles and Practice* (7th edn). Sage Publishing, Thousand Oaks, CA, 2024.

Zunz, O. *Philanthropy in America: A History.* Princeton University Press, Princeton, NJ, 2014.

Indexes

Index of Foundations

1563 Foundation for the Arts and Culture, Italy, 174
1818 Fund Foundation, Netherlands, 229
30 Million Friends Foundation, France, 102

The A. G. Leventis Foundation, Cyprus, 77
A. G. Leventis Foundation Nigeria, Nigeria, 237
A. M. M. Sahabdeen Trust Foundation, Sri Lanka, 297
A. M. Qattan Foundation, UK, 338
The A. P. Møller and Chastine Mc-Kinney Møller Foundation, Denmark, 82
A. P. Møller og Hustru Chastine Mc-Kinney Møllers Fond til almene Formaal, Denmark, 82
A. S. Hornby Educational Trust, UK, 338
AARDO—African-Asian Rural Development Organization, India, 155
AAUW Educational Foundation, USA, 399
Abdorrahman Boroumand Center for Human Rights in Iran—ABC, USA, 396
Abdul Hameed Shoman Foundation—AHSF, Jordan, 195
Abdulla Al Ghurair Foundation for Education, United Arab Emirates, 334
Abegg Foundation, Switzerland, 306
Abegg-Stiftung, Switzerland, 306
Abilis Foundation, Finland, 95
Abilis-säätiö, Finland, 95
Abjadnany Sliach, Belarus, 25
Abrinq Foundation for the Rights of Children and Adolescents, Brazil, 39
Académie Goncourt—Société Littéraire des Goncourt, France, 100
Academy for the Development of Philanthropy in Poland, Poland, 253
Academy of European Law, Germany, 127
Accademia Musicale Chigiana, Italy, 172
Access Foundation, Costa Rica, 73
Accion, USA, 397
Acción Contra el Hambre–ACH, Spain, 286
Accountable Now, USA, 393
ACDI/VOCA, USA, 397
ACF—Association of Charitable Foundations, UK, 335
ACFID—Australian Council for International Development, Australia, 12
Acíndar Foundation, Argentina, 6
ACLS—American Council of Learned Societies, USA, 399
ACRF—Australian Cancer Research Foundation, Australia, 11
ACROTEC Technology Foundation, Italy, 176
ACT Alliance, Switzerland, 306
Acting for Life, France, 100
Action Against Hunger, Spain, 286
Action for Children, UK, 338
Action Children's Aid, Denmark, 82
Action contre la Faim—ACF France, France, 100
Action Damien/Damiaanactie, Belgium, 28
Action Education, France, 100
Action Group on Erosion, Technology and Concentration, Canada, 54
Action on Poverty, Australia, 10
Action Solidarité Tiers Monde—ASTM, Luxembourg, 209
ActionAid International, South Africa, 278
Active for People in Need Austria, Austria, 20
Acumen, USA, 397
Addoha Foundation, Morocco, 219
Adenauer (Konrad) Stiftung eV, Germany, 134
Adessium Foundation, Netherlands, 223
The Adolph and Esther Gottlieb Foundation, Inc, USA, 397
ADRA—Adventist Development and Relief Agency International, USA, 397
Adriano Olivetti Foundation, Italy, 174
Advance, USA, 397
Adventist Development and Relief Agency International—ADRA, USA, 397

Adyan Foundation, Lebanon, 205
Afdi—Agriculteurs Français et Développement International, France, 100
Afghan Women's Network, Afghanistan, 3
Afghanistan Institute for Civil Society—AICS, Afghanistan, 3
Afghanistan Research and Evaluation Unit, Afghanistan, 3
AFPE—American Foundation for Pharmaceutical Education, USA, 401
Africa-America Institute—AAI, USA, 398
Africa Foundation, South Africa, 278
Africa Grantmakers' Affinity Group—AGAG, USA, 393
Africa Humanitarian Action—AHA, Ethiopia, 93
Africa Institute of South Africa—AISA, South Africa, 279
Africa Space Foundation, Switzerland, 308
The African Agricultural Technology Foundation—AATF, Kenya, 198
African-Asian Rural Development Organization—AARDO, India, 155
African Capacity Building Foundation—ACBF, Zimbabwe, 490
African Forum and Network on Debt and Development—AFRODAD, Zimbabwe, 490
African Philanthropy Forum, Nigeria, 236
African Refugees Foundation—AREF, Nigeria, 237
African Venture Philanthropy Alliance—AVPA, Kenya, 197
African Wildlife Foundation—AWF, Kenya, 198
African Women's Development Fund—AWDF, Ghana, 143
African Youth Initiative Network—AYINET, Uganda, 331
Afrobarometer, Ghana, 143
AFRODAD—African Forum and Network on Debt and Development, Zimbabwe, 490
Aga Khan Development Network—AKDN, Switzerland, 306
Aga Khan Foundation, Switzerland, 306
Aga Khan Foundation Canada, Canada, 49
Aga Khan Foundation UK, UK, 338
AGAG—Africa Grantmakers' Affinity Group, USA, 393
Age International, UK, 339
AGIR Association for the Environment and Quality of Life, Mali, 213
Agnelli (Giovanni), Fondazione, Italy, 177
Agora Foundation, Poland, 255
Agriculteurs Français et Développement International, France, 100
Agronomes et Vétérinaires sans Frontières—AVSF, France, 100
Agronomists and Veterinarians Without Borders, France, 100
Agrupació AMCI Foundation, Spain, 286
AHA—American Historical Association, USA, 401
Ai You Foundation, China (People's Republic), 66
AIC—Association Internationale des Charités, Belgium, 28
Aid to the Church in Need—ACN International, Germany, 120
Aid for Development Club, Austria, 20
AID Foundation, Bangladesh, 24
AIIA—Australian Institute of International Affairs, Australia, 12
AINA—Arctic Institute of North America, Canada, 49
Air France Foundation, France, 103
Air Pollution and Climate Secretariat—AirClim, Sweden, 298
AirClim—Air Pollution and Climate Secretariat, Sweden, 298
AISA—Africa Institute of South Africa, South Africa, 279
Aisha Buhari Global Foundation, Nigeria, 237
AIT—Asian Institute of Technology, Thailand, 323

Akademia Rozwoju Filantropii w Polsce—ARFP, Poland, 253
Akai Hane—Central Community Chest of Japan, Japan, 185
AKO Foundation, UK, 339
Aktion Børnehjælp, Denmark, 82
Al Basar International Foundation, Saudi Arabia, 268
Al Jalila Foundation, United Arab Emirates, 334
Al Jisr Foundation, Oman, 244
The Al-Khoei Benevolent Foundation, UK, 339
Al-Mortaqa Foundation for Human Development, Iraq, 164
Al-Zubair Charity Foundation, Sudan, 297
The Alan Turing Institute, UK, 339
Alavi Foundation, USA, 398
Albanian Disability Rights Foundation, Albania, 4
Albanian Institute for International Studies—AIIS, Albania, 4
Albéniz Foundation, Spain, 288
Albert Schweitzer Ecological Centre, Switzerland, 307
Alcoa Foundation, USA, 398
Alden (George I.) Trust, USA, 430
Alemán (Miguel), Fundación, Mexico, 215
Alert—International Alert, UK, 360
Alessio Pezcoller Foundation, Italy, 174
Alet'Eleym Fewq Alejmey'e, Qatar, 262
Alexander von Humboldt Foundation, Germany, 120
Alexander von Humboldt Stiftung, Germany, 120
Alexander S. Onassis Public Benefit Foundation, Liechtenstein, 207
Alfred Benzon Foundation, Denmark, 82
Alfred Benzons Fond, Denmark, 82
Alfred P. Sloan Foundation, USA, 398
Alfred Toepfer Foundation FVS, Germany, 121
Alfred Toepfer Stiftung FVS, Germany, 121
Alfried Krupp von Bohlen und Halbach Foundation, Germany, 121
Alfried Krupp von Bohlen und Halbach-Stiftung, Germany, 121
Ali Fulhu Thuthu Foundation, Maldives, 212
Alicia Patterson Foundation—APF, USA, 398
ALIDE—Asociación Latinoamericana de Instituciones Financieras para el Desarrollo, Peru, 248
Alight, USA, 399
Aliko Dangote Foundation—ADF, Nigeria, 237
Alkhidmat Foundation Pakistan—AKFP, Pakistan, 244
All Good Foundation Charitable Trust, New Zealand, 232
All India Disaster Mitigation Institute, India, 155
Allen Lane Foundation, UK, 339
Allen (Paul G.) Family Foundation, USA, 462
Allende (Isabel) Foundation, USA, 442
Alliance of Bioversity International and the International Center for Tropical Agriculture—CIAT, Italy, 172
Alliance of Community Foundations Germany, Germany, 119
Alliance for International Exchange, USA, 399
Alliance Israélite Universelle, France, 101
Alliance for Securing Democracy, USA, 430
Alliance Sud—Swiss Alliance of Development Organizations, Switzerland, 305
Allianz Foundation, Germany, 121
Allianz Umana Mente Foundation, Italy, 174
Almeida (Eng. António de), Fundação, Portugal, 260
Almine y Bernard Ruiz-Picasso Foundation, Spain, 288
Alola Foundation, Timor-Leste, 325
Alongside Hope/Auprès de l'espoir, Canada, 49
The Alva Foundation, Canada, 49
Alvares Penteado (Armando), Fundação, Brazil, 39
Alwaleed Philanthropies, Saudi Arabia, 269
Alzheimer Spain Foundation, Spain, 288

Alzheimer's Society, UK, 339
AMADE Mondiale—Association Mondiale des Amis de l'Enfance, Monaco, 217
Aman Foundation, Pakistan, 244
Amancio Ortega Foundation, Spain, 288
Amberes (Carlos de), Fundación, Spain, 289
Ambrela Platform of Development Organizations, Slovakia, 273
Ambrela—Platforma rozvojových organizácií, Slovakia, 273
The Ambrose Monell Foundation, USA, 399
Ambrosiana Paolo VI Foundation, Italy, 175
Ambuja Cement Foundation—ACF, India, 156
America for Bulgaria Foundation, Bulgaria, 43
America–Mideast Educational and Training Services Inc, USA, 404
American Association of University Women—AAUW Educational Foundation, USA, 399
American Council of Learned Societies—ACLS, USA, 399
American Councils for International Education, USA, 400
American Enterprise Institute—AEI, USA, 400
American Express Foundation, USA, 400
American Foundation for the Blind—AFB, USA, 400
American Foundation for Pharmaceutical Education—AFPE, USA, 401
American Friends Service Committee—AFSC, USA, 401
American Heart Association—AHA, USA, 401
American Historical Association—AHA, USA, 401
American Institute of Pakistan Studies, USA, 401
American Jewish Joint Distribution Committee—JDC, USA, 402
American Jewish World Service—AJWS, USA, 402
American Near East Refugee Aid—Anera, USA, 402
American Philosophical Society—APS, USA, 402
American-Scandinavian Foundation—ASF, USA, 403
American Schools of Oriental Research—ASOR, USA, 403
AmeriCares Foundation, Inc, USA, 403
Amerind Foundation, Inc, USA, 403
amfAR—The Foundation for AIDS Research, USA, 403
AMIDEAST—America-Mideast Educational and Training Services, Inc, USA, 404
Amigos de la Tierra, Netherlands, 225
AMINA—aktiv für Menschen in Not Austria, Austria, 20
Les Amis de la Terre, Netherlands, 225
Amity Foundation, China (People's Republic), 66
Amnesty International, UK, 340
AMP Foundation, Australia, 10
Amref Health Africa, Kenya, 198
Analitika—Center for Social Research, Bosnia and Herzegovina, 37
Anders Jahre's Foundation for Humanitarian Purposes, Norway, 240
Anders Jahres Humanitære Stiftelse, Norway, 240
Andrew W. Mellon Foundation, USA, 404
Andrews Charitable Trust—ACT, UK, 340
The Andy Warhol Foundation for the Visual Arts, Inc, USA, 404
Anera—American Near East Refugee Aid, USA, 402
Anesvad, Spain, 286
Angel of Hope Foundation, Zimbabwe, 490
Angelo Della Riccia Foundation, Italy, 175
Anglo American Foundation, UK, 340
ANGOC—Asian NGO Coalition for Agrarian Reform and Rural Development, Philippines, 251
Anguilla Community Fund, Anguilla, 5
Anguilla National Trust—ANT, Anguilla, 6
Ankara İngiliz Arkeoloji Enstitüsü, UK, 345
Anna Lindh Euro-Mediterranean Foundation for Dialogue between Cultures, Egypt, 90
ANND—Arab NGO Network for Development, Lebanon, 205
Anne Çocuk Eğitim Vakfı—AÇEV, Türkiye, 327
Anne Frank-Fonds, Switzerland, 306
Anne Frank Foundation, Netherlands, 224
Anne Frank Fund, Switzerland, 306
Anne Frank Stichting, Netherlands, 224
Anne Ray Foundation, USA, 450
The Annenberg Foundation, USA, 404
The Annie E. Casey Foundation, USA, 404
Ansar Burney Trust International, Pakistan, 245
Antarctic Heritage Trust (NZ), New Zealand, 232
Anti-Corruption Foundation, Russian Federation, 265
Anti-Defamation League—ADL, USA, 405

Anti-Slavery International, UK, 340
Antigua Forum, Guatemala, 147
António de Almeida Foundation, Portugal, 260
Apex Foundation, Australia, 10
APHEDA—Union Aid Abroad, Australia, 19
Apprentis d'Auteuil Océan Indien, Réunion, 262
Arab American Institute Foundation—AAIF, USA, 405
Arab Foundations Forum, Jordan, 195
Arab Fund for Arts and Culture—AFAC, Lebanon, 205
Arab Image Foundation—AIF, Lebanon, 205
Arab Network for Civic Education, Jordan, 195
Arab Network for Environment and Development—RAED, Egypt, 89
Arab Office for Youth and Environment, Egypt, 89
Arab Organization for Human Rights, Egypt, 90
Arab Thought Foundation—ATF, Lebanon, 205
Arainneachd Eachdraidheil Alba, UK, 358
Arbeiterwohlfahrt Bundesverband eV—AWO, Germany, 121
Arca Foundation, USA, 405
ArcelorMittal Brazil Foundation, Brazil, 39
Archewell Foundation, USA, 405
Archie Sherman Charitable Trust, UK, 340
Arctic Institute of North America—AINA, Canada, 49
Arcus Foundation, USA, 405
Areces (Ramón), Fundación, Spain, 294
Arengukoostöö Ümarlaud—AKÜ, Estonia, 92
Areumdaun Jaedan, Korea (Republic), 200
Argentine Council for International Relations, Argentina, 6
Arghyam, India, 156
Ariadne—European Funders for Social Change and Human Rights, UK, 336
Arias Foundation for Peace and Human Progress, Costa Rica, 74
Ark, UK, 341
Armando Alvares Penteado Foundation, Brazil, 39
Armanshahr Foundation—OPEN ASIA, Afghanistan, 3
Arpad Szenes-Vieira da Silva Foundation, Portugal, 258
Art Fund—National Art Collections Fund, UK, 341
Arthritis Australia, Australia, 10
Arthritis Foundation, USA, 406
Arthur Rubinstein International Music Society, Israel, 168
Arts Council England, UK, 341
Arts Council Korea, Korea (Republic), 200
Asahi Glass Foundation, Japan, 186
Asahi Group Foundation, Japan, 186
ASEAN Foundation, Indonesia, 161
ASEAN Institutes of Strategic and International Studies—ASEAN ISIS, Indonesia, 162
Asia Africa International Voluntary Foundation—AIV, Japan, 186
Asia Crime Prevention Foundation—ACPF, Japan, 186
Asia Foundation, USA, 406
Asia New Zealand Foundation/Te Whītau Tūhono, New Zealand, 232
Asia/Pacific Cultural Centre for UNESCO—ACCU, Japan, 186
Asia Pacific Foundation of Canada—APFCanada, Canada, 49
Asia Philanthropy Circle—APC, Singapore, 272
Asia Society, USA, 406
AsiaDHRRA—Asian Partnership for the Development of Human Resources in Rural Asia, Philippines, 251
Asian Community Trust—ACT, Japan, 186
Asian Cultural Council—ACC, USA, 406
Asian Development Research Institute—ADRI, India, 156
Asian Health Institute—AHI, Japan, 187
Asian Institute of Technology—AIT, Thailand, 323
Asian Partnership for the Development of Human Resources in Rural Asia, Philippines, 251
Asian Venture Philanthropy Network—AVPN, Singapore, 272
ASKO Europa-Stiftung, Germany, 121
ASKO Europe Foundation, Germany, 121
Asociace komunitních nadací v České republice—Spolek AKN, Czech Republic, 78
Asociácia komunitných nadácií Slovenska, Slovakia, 274
Asociacija Litdea—Lithuanian Development Education and Awareness Raising Association, Lithuania, 208
Asociación Española de Fundaciones, Spain, 285
Asociación de Fundaciones Familiares y Empresariales—AFE, Colombia, 70

Asociación Latinoamericana de Instituciones Financieras para el Desarrollo—ALIDE, Peru, 248
Asociación Salvadoreña para el Desarrollo Económico y Social FUSADES, El Salvador, 91
Asotzijatzjata za Dyemokratska Initzijativa, North Macedonia, 239
Aspen Institute, USA, 407
Assifero—Associazione Italiana delle Fondazioni ed Enti della Filantropia Istituzionale, Italy, 171
Association AGIR pour l'Environnement et la Qualité de la Vie, Mali, 213
Association of Charitable Foundations—ACF, UK, 335
Association of Civil Society Development Center, Türkiye, 327
Association for Democratic Initiatives—ADI, North Macedonia, 239
Association for Development Policy and Humanitarian Aid, Germany, 120
Association of Family and Corporate Foundations, Colombia, 70
Association des Fondations Donatrices Suisses, Switzerland, 306
Association of Foundations, Philippines, 250
Association of Foundations in the Netherlands, Netherlands, 223
Association of the Friends of the Swedish Institute at Athens, Sweden, 299
Association of German Foundations, Germany, 118
Association of Grantmaking Foundations in Switzerland, Switzerland, 306
Association of Guernsey Charities—AGC, Channel Islands, 64
Association Internationale des Charités—AIC, Belgium, 28
Association of Italian Foundations and Savings Banks, Italy, 171
Association of Jersey Charities—AJC, Channel Islands, 64
Association of Liechtenstein Charitable Foundations, Liechtenstein, 207
Association of Medical Research Charities—AMRC, UK, 335
Association of Non-Governmental Organizations in The Gambia—TANGO, Gambia, 117
Association for Public Benefit Foundations, Austria, 20
Association of Slovakian Community Foundations, Slovakia, 274
Association of Swedish Foundations, Sweden, 298
Associazione di Fondazioni e di Casse di Risparmio SpA—ACRI, Italy, 171
Associazione Italiana delle Fondazioni ed Enti della Filantropia Istituzionale, Italy, 171
Asthma + Lung UK, UK, 341
ASTM—Action Solidarité Tiers Monde, Luxembourg, 209
Astur Foundation, Uruguay, 485
AT&T Foundation, USA, 407
ATD Fourth World International, France, 115
Atlas Charity Foundation, Poland, 255
Atlas Network, USA, 407
Auchan Foundation, France, 103
Aurat Publication & Information Service Foundation—AF, Pakistan, 245
Aurora Trust, UK, 341
Auschwitz-Birkenau Foundation, Poland, 255
Auschwitz Foundation—Remembrance of Auschwitz, Belgium, 30
Australian Academy of the Humanities, Australia, 11
Australian Academy of Science, Australia, 11
Australian Academy of Technological Sciences and Engineering, Australia, 11
Australian-American Fulbright Commission, Australia, 11
Australian Cancer Research Foundation—ACRF, Australia, 11
Australian Communities Foundation, Australia, 12
Australian Conservation Foundation—ACF, Australia, 12
Australian Council for International Development—ACFID, Australia, 12
Australian Foundation for the Peoples of Asia and the Pacific—AFAP, Australia, 10
Australian Institute of International Affairs—AIIA, Australia, 12
Australian Multicultural Foundation—AMF, Australia, 12
Australian Volunteers International—AVI, Australia, 13
Austrian Foundation for Development Research, Austria, 22

INDEX OF FOUNDATIONS

Austrian Science Fund, Austria, 21
Autonómia Alapítvány, Hungary, 152
Autonómia Foundation, Hungary, 152
Avatud Eesti Fond, Estonia, 92
Aventis Foundation, Germany, 121
AVI—Australian Volunteers International, Australia, 13
Aviation Sans Frontières—ASF, France, 101
Aviation Without Borders, France, 101
AVINA Foundation, Panama, 247
AVSI Foundation, Italy, 175
Axel Springer Foundation, Germany, 122
Axel-Springer-Stiftung, Germany, 122
Ayala Foundation, Inc—AFI, Philippines, 251
Aydın Doğan Foundation, Türkiye, 328
Aydın Doğan Vakfı, Türkiye, 328
Ayrton Senna Institute, Brazil, 41
Azim Premji Foundation, India, 156
Azman Hashim Foundation, Malaysia, 212

BaBe—Budi aktivna, Budi emancipiran, Croatia, 77
Bagnoud (François-Xavier) Association, Switzerland, 310
Baha'i International Development Organization—BIDO, Israel, 169
Baillet Latour Fund, Belgium, 32
Baker Heart & Diabetes Institute, Australia, 13
Balkan Civil Society Development Network—BCSDN, North Macedonia, 239
Balkan Security Platform—BSP, Serbia, 271
Balti Uuringute Instituut, Estonia, 92
Baltic Sea Foundation, Finland, 97
Balzan Fonds, Internationale Stiftung, Italy, 181
Ban Ki-Moon Foundation for a Better Future, Korea (Republic), 200
Banco do Brasil Foundation, Brazil, 39
Banda (Joyce) Foundation International, Malawi, 210
Bangladesh Freedom Foundation—BFF, Bangladesh, 24
BANHCAFE Foundation, Honduras, 150
Bank of America Charitable Foundation, USA, 407
Bank of Cyprus Cultural Foundation, Cyprus, 77
The Barack Obama Foundation, USA, 407
Barandiarán (José Miguel de), Fundación, Spain, 291
Barbados Entrepreneurship Foundation Inc, Barbados, 25
Barbra Streisand Foundation, USA, 408
Barça Foundation, Spain, 287
Barceló Foundation, Spain, 289
Barcelona Centre for International Affairs, Spain, 287
Bardot (Brigitte), Fondation, France, 104
Barenboim-Said Foundation, Spain, 289
Bariloche Foundation, Argentina, 7
Baring Foundation, UK, 341
Barjeel Art Foundation, United Arab Emirates, 334
Barka Foundation for Mutual Assistance, Poland, 256
Barnardo's, UK, 342
Barretstown, Ireland, 165
Barrié de la Maza (Pedro, Conde de Fenosa), Fundación, Spain, 293
Barzani Charity Foundation—BCF, Iraq, 164
Basso Issoco (Leilio e Lisli), Fondazione, Italy, 178
Bat Conservation Trust, UK, 342
Batonga, USA, 408
Baxter & Alma Ricard Foundation, Canada, 55
BBC Children in Need, UK, 342
BBC Media Action, UK, 342
BBVA Foundation, Spain, 289
BCause Foundation, Bulgaria, 42
Be Active, Be Emancipated, Croatia, 77
The Beautiful Foundation, Korea (Republic), 200
Beisheim Foundation, Germany, 122
Beisheim Stiftung, Germany, 122
Beit Trust, UK, 342
Belém Cultural Centre Foundation, Portugal, 259
Belgian Federation of Philanthropic Foundations, Belgium, 26
Belgische Federatie van Filantropische Stichtingen, Belgium, 26
Bell (Max) Foundation, Canada, 59
Bellingcat Foundation, Netherlands, 228
Bello (Sir Ahmadu) Memorial Foundation, Nigeria, 238
Bellona Foundation, Norway, 240
Benaad Enetkhabat Shafaf Afghanistan, Afghanistan, 4
Benecke (Otto) Stiftung eV, Germany, 138
Benesco, UK, 347
Benetton Foundation for Study and Research, Italy, 175
Benzon (Alfred) Foundation, Denmark, 82

Berghof Foundation gGmbH, Germany, 122
Berghof Stiftung für Konfliktforschung gGmbH, Germany, 122
Bergman (Ingmar), Stiftelsen, Sweden, 303
Bermuda Foundation, Bermuda, 35
Bernadottes (Folke) Minnesfond, Sweden, 299
Bernheim Foundation, Belgium, 31
Bertelsmann Foundation, Germany, 122
Bertelsmann Stiftung, Germany, 122
Bertoni (Moisés) Foundation, Paraguay, 248
Bettencourt Schueller Foundation, France, 103
Better World Campaign—BWC, USA, 408
Beyaz Nokta Gelişim Vakfı, Türkiye, 328
Bezos Earth Fund, USA, 408
Bharti Foundation, India, 156
BIAT Youth Foundation, Tunisia, 326
Biblioteca dell'Accademia Nazionale dei Lincei e Corsiniana, Italy, 172
Big Heart Foundation, Chad, 64
Biocon Foundation, India, 157
BirdLife International, UK, 343
Bischöfliches Hilfswerk Misereor eV, Germany, 137
Black Lives Matter Global Network Foundation—BLM Global Network Foundation, USA, 408
Black Sea NGO Network—BSNN, Bulgaria, 42
Black Sea Trust for Regional Cooperation, USA, 430
Black Sea University Foundation—BSUF, Romania, 263
Blair (Tony) Institute for Global Change, UK, 386
Blakemore Foundation, USA, 408
Blancefor Boncompagni Ludovisi, née Bildt Foundation, Sweden, 303
Blavatnik Family Foundation, USA, 409
Bleustein-Blanchet (Marcel), Fondation de la Vocation, France, 109
BLM Global Network Foundation, USA, 408
Blood Cancer UK—Bloodwise, UK, 343
Bloomberg Philanthropies, USA, 409
Blue Marine Foundation—BLUE, UK, 343
BMCE Bank Foundation, Morocco, 219
BMW Foundation Herbert Quandt, Germany, 122
BNP Paribas Foundation, France, 103
Bodossaki Foundation, Greece, 145
Boehringer Ingelheim Fonds—Stiftung für medizinische Grundlagenforschung, Germany, 122
Bofill (Jaume), Fundació, Spain, 287
Boghossian Foundation, Belgium, 31
Böll (Heinrich) Stiftung, Germany, 131
Boltzmann (Ludwig) Gesellschaft, Austria, 21
Bond, UK, 335
Book Aid International—BAI, UK, 343
Borderland Foundation, Poland, 256
Bordoni (Ugo), Fondazione, Italy, 180
Born Free Foundation, UK, 343
Born This Way Foundation, USA, 409
Bosch (Robert) Stiftung GmbH, Germany, 138
Bóthar, Ireland, 166
Boticário Group Foundation, Brazil, 40
Botín Foundation, Spain, 292
Botín (Marcelino), Fundación, Spain, 292
Botswana Institute for Development Policy Analysis—BIDPA, Botswana, 37
BP Foundation, Inc, USA, 409
Braća Karić Foundation, Serbia, 271
BRAC, Bangladesh, 25
Bradley (Lynde and Harry) Foundation, Inc, USA, 449
Brandt (Bundeskanzler Willy) Stiftung, Germany, 123
BrazilFoundation, Brazil, 39
Brazilian Center for International Relations, Brazil, 39
Bread for the World—Protestant Work for Social Welfare and Development, Germany, 123
Breakthrough T1D, USA, 409
Brenthurst Foundation, South Africa, 282
Bridge Asia Japan—BAJ, Japan, 187
Bridge House Estates, UK, 348
Brighter Future Myanmar Foundation—BFM, Myanmar, 221
BrightFocus Foundation, USA, 409
Brigitte Bardot Foundation, France, 104
Bristol-Myers Squibb Foundation, USA, 410
British & Foreign School Society—BFSS, UK, 351
British Academy, UK, 344
The British Council, UK, 344
British Gas Energy Trust, UK, 344
British Heart Foundation—BHF, UK, 344
British Institute at Ankara, UK, 345
British Institute of International and Comparative Law—BIICL, UK, 345
British Overseas NGOs for Development, UK, 335

British Red Cross Society, UK, 345
British Schools and Universities Foundation, Inc—BSUF, USA, 410
The Broad Foundation, USA, 410
Brookings Institution, USA, 410
Brot für die Welt—Evangelisches Werk für Diakonie und Entwicklung, Germany, 123
Brother's Brother Foundation, USA, 410
Brothers of Men, France, 113
Bruegel—Brussels European and Global Economic Laboratory, Belgium, 28
Bruno Kreisky Forum for International Dialogue, Austria, 20
Bruno Kreisky Forum für internationalen Dialog, Austria, 20
Buchanan Charitable Foundation, New Zealand, 232
Buck (Pearl S.) International, USA, 462
Buckland (William) Foundation, Australia, 19
Buddharaksa Foundation, Thailand, 323
Buffett (Howard G.) Foundation, USA, 437
Buffett (Susan Thompson) Foundation, USA, 474
Bulgarian Donors' Forum, Bulgaria, 42
Bulgarian Fund for Women, Bulgaria, 43
Bulgarian Platform for International Development—BPID, Bulgaria, 42
Bundeskanzler-Willy-Brandt-Stiftung, Germany, 123
Bundesverband Deutscher Stiftungen eV, Germany, 118
Bunge y Born Foundation, Argentina, 7
Burroughs Wellcome Fund—BWF, USA, 411

C. G. Jung-Institut Zürich, Switzerland, 307
CABI, UK, 345
Cadbury (Edward) Charitable Trust, UK, 351
Cadbury (William Adlington) Charitable Trust, UK, 390
CAF America, USA, 393
CAF—Charities Aid Foundation, UK, 336
CAF India, India, 155
CAF Russia—Charities Aid Foundation Russia, Russian Federation, 264
CAFOD—Catholic Agency for Overseas Development, UK, 345
Calgary Foundation, Canada, 49
California Community Foundation, USA, 411
Calouste Gulbenkian Foundation, Portugal, 259
The Camargo Foundation, France, 101
Cambodia Development Resource Institute—CDRI, Cambodia, 46
Cambodian Salesian Delegation, Cambodia, 46
Cambridge Commonwealth, European and International Trust, UK, 346
CAMFED International, UK, 346
The Camille and Henry Dreyfus Foundation, Inc, USA, 411
Campaign Against Exclusion Foundation, France, 103
The Canada Council for the Arts/Conseil des Arts du Canada, Canada, 50
Canada Foundation for Innovation, Canada, 50
CanadaHelps, Canada, 47
Canadian Cancer Society, Canada, 50
Canadian Centre for International Studies and Co-operation, Canada, 51
Canadian Council for International Co-operation—CCIC/Conseil Canadien pour la Coopération Internationale—CCCI, Canada, 48
Canadian Feed The Children—CFTC, Canada, 50
Canadian Foodgrains Bank, Canada, 50
Canadian International Council/Conseil International du Canada—CIC, Canada, 51
Canadian Liver Foundation/Fondation Canadienne du Foie, Canada, 58
Canadian Organization for Development through Education—CODE, Canada, 52
Canadian Physicians for Aid and Relief—CPAR, Canada, 52
Canadian Urban Institute/Institut Urbain du Canada—CUI/IUC, Canada, 51
Cancer Council Australia, Australia, 13
Cancer Research UK, UK, 346
Cancer Society of New Zealand/Te Kāhui Matepukupuku o Aotearoa, New Zealand, 233
Cancerfonden, Sweden, 298
Candid, USA, 393
Canon Foundation in Europe, Netherlands, 224
Canon Institute for Global Studies—CIGS, Japan, 187
Cape Verdean Student Welfare Foundation, Cabo Verde, 45
CARE International—CI, Switzerland, 307
Cargill (Margaret A.) Philanthropies, USA, 450
Caribbean Policy Development Centre—CPDC, Barbados, 25
Cariplo Foundation, Italy, 175

Caritas Canada, Canada, 53
Caritas de France—Secours Catholique, France, 116
Caritas Internationalis—CI, Vatican City, 486
Carl Zeiss Foundation, Germany, 123
Carl-Zeiss-Stiftung, Germany, 123
Carlo Cattaneo Institute, Italy, 182
Carlo Pesenti Foundation, Italy, 176
Carlos de Amberes Foundation, Spain, 289
Carlos Slim Foundation, Mexico, 215
Carlsberg Foundation, Denmark, 82
Carlsbergfondet, Denmark, 82
CARMABI Foundation, Curaçao, 77
Carnegie Corporation of New York, USA, 411
Carnegie Endowment for International Peace, USA, 411
Carnegie Foundation, Wateler Fund, Netherlands, 224
Carnegie Hero Fund Commission, USA, 412
Carnegie-Stichting, Watelerfonds, Netherlands, 224
Carnegie Trust for the Universities of Scotland, UK, 346
Carnegie UK Trust, UK, 346
Carpathian Foundation, Hungary, 153
Carrefour International, Canada, 53
The Carter Center, USA, 412
Cartier-Bresson (Henri), Fondation, France, 107
Cartier Foundation for Contemporary Art, France, 104
Casa de Mateus Foundation, Portugal, 259
CASE—Centrum Analiz Społeczno-Ekonomicznych, Poland, 255
Casey (Annie E.) Foundation, USA, 404
Cassa di Risparmio di Padova e Rovigo Foundation, Italy, 175
Catalyste+, Canada, 51
Caterpillar Foundation, USA, 412
Catholic Agency for Overseas Development—CAFOD, UK, 345
Catholic Agency for World Development—Trócaire, Ireland, 168
Catholic Help—Caritas France, France, 116
Cattaneo (Carlo), Istituto, Italy, 182
Caucasus Institute for Peace, Democracy and Development—CIPDD, Georgia, 117
Caucasus Research Resource Center Armenia Foundation—CRRC, Armenia, 9
Caucus of Development NGO Networks—CODE-NGO, Philippines, 250
CBM-International, Germany, 123
CCKF—Chiang Ching-kuo Foundation for International Scholarly Exchange, Taiwan, 321
CDC Foundation, USA, 412
CEAS—Centre Ecologique Albert Schweitzer, Switzerland, 307
CECI—Canadian Centre for International Studies and Co-operation/Centre d'Etudes et de Coopération Internationale, Canada, 51
CEDIAS-Musée Social—Centre d'Etudes, de Documentation, d'Information et d'Action Sociales, France, 101
CEDRO—Centro de Información y Educación para la Prevención del Abuso de Drogas, Peru, 248
CENOZO—Cellule Norbert Zongo pour le Journalisme d'Investigation en Afrique de l'Ouest, Burkina Faso, 44
CENSIS—Fondazione Centro Studi Investimenti Sociali, Italy, 172
Center for China & Globalization—CCG, China (People's Republic), 67
Center for Economic & Social Development—CESD, Azerbaijan, 23
Center for Inquiry—CFI, USA, 412
Center for Social and Economic Research, Poland, 255
Center for Training and Consultancy, Georgia, 117
Center for Victims of Torture—CVT, USA, 413
Centras—Assistance Centre for NGOs, Romania, 263
Centras—Centrul de Asistenta pentru Organizatii Neguvernamentale, Romania, 263
Centre for Civil Society—CCS, India, 157
Centre for Democracy and Human Rights—CEDEM, Montenegro, 219
Centre for the Development of Non-governmental Organizations, Montenegro, 219
Centre for Development of Non-profit Organizations, Croatia, 76
Centre pour le Dialogue Humanitaire, Switzerland, 307
Centre for Dialogue, Research and Cooperation—CDRC, Ethiopia, 94
Centre Ecologique Albert Schweitzer—CEAS, Switzerland, 307

Centre d'Etude du Polymorphisme Humain, France, 107
Centre d'Etudes Pour l'Action Sociale—CEPAS, Congo (Democratic Republic), 72
Centre for Euro-Atlantic Integration and Democracy—CEID, Hungary, 153
Centre Européen de la Culture—CEC, Switzerland, 307
Centre Français des Fonds et Fondations—CFF, France, 99
Centre for Humanitarian Action—CHA, Germany, 123
Centre for Humanitarian Dialogue—HD, Switzerland, 307
Centre for the Information Service, Co-operation and Development of NGOs, Slovenia, 277
Centre for International Governance Innovation—CIGI/Centre pour l'Innovation dans la Gouvernance Internationale, Canada, 51
Centre International de Recherche sur le Cancer—CIRC, France, 101
Centre for International Studies, Italy, 172
Centre Ivoirien de Recherches Economiques et Sociales—CIRES, Côte d'Ivoire, 75
Centre for Philanthropy, Russia, 274
Centre for Promotion and Development of Civil Initiatives—OPUS, Poland, 254
Centre for Social Impact and Philanthropy—CSIP, India, 154
Centre for Social Studies, Documentation, Information and Action, France, 101
Centre for Strategic and International Studies—CSIS, Indonesia, 162
Centro Brasileiro de Relações Internacionais—CEBRI, Brazil, 39
Centro de Estudios Públicos—CEP, Chile, 64
Centro de Información y Educación para la Prevención del Abuso de Drogas—CEDRO, Peru, 248
Centro Internacional de Mejoramiento de Maíz y Trigo—CIMMYT, Mexico, 215
Centro Mexicano para la Filantropía—CEMEFI, Mexico, 214
Centro Português de Fundações—CPF, Portugal, 258
Centro Studi Internazionali—CSI, Italy, 172
Centro Studi e Ricerca Sociale Fondazione Emanuela Zancan, Italy, 172
Centrul Naţional de Asistenţă şi Informare a Organizaţiilor Neguvernamentale din Moldova—Centrul CONTACT, Moldova, 216
Centrul de Resurse pentru Drepturile Omului—CReDO, Moldova, 217
Centrum pre Filantropiu, Slovakia, 274
The Century Foundation—TCF, USA, 413
Cera, Belgium, 28
CERANEO—Centar za razvoj neprofitnih organizacija, Croatia, 76
Cercle de Coopération des ONGD du Luxembourg, Luxembourg, 209
CERES—Consorcio Ecuatoriano Para La Responsabilidad Social, Ecuador, 87
Česká rada sociálních služeb—CRSS, Czech Republic, 78
Česká spořitelna Foundation, Czech Republic, 79
Česko-německý fond budoucnosti, Czech Republic, 79
CESO/SACO—Canadian Executive Service Organization/Service d'Assistance Canadienne aux Organismes, Canada, 51
Cetana Educational Foundation, USA, 413
Çevre Koruma ve Ambalaj Atıkları Değerlendirme Vakfı—ÇEVKO, Türkiye, 328
Chaabi (Miloud), Fondation, Morocco, 220
Chagnon (Lucie et André), Fondation, Canada, 55
Champalimaud Foundation, Portugal, 259
Chandaria Foundation, Kenya, 198
Chang Yung-fa Foundation, Taiwan, 321
Chantal Biya Foundation, Cameroon, 47
Charitable Impact Foundation, Canada, 47
Charities Advisory Trust, UK, 336
Charities Aid Foundation of America—CAF America, USA, 393
Charities Aid Foundation—CAF, UK, 336
Charities Aid Foundation Russia—CAF Russia, Russian Federation, 264
Charities Institute Ireland—Cii, Ireland, 165
Charity Islamic Trust Elrahma, UK, 352
Charity Projects, UK, 348
Charles Darwin Foundation for the Galapagos Islands—CDF, Ecuador, 88
Charles Koch Foundation, USA, 413
Charles Léopold Mayer Foundation for the Progress of Humankind, Switzerland, 308
Charles and Lynn Schusterman Family Philanthropies, USA, 413

Charles Stewart Mott Foundation—CSMF, USA, 414
The Charles Wallace India Trusts, UK, 347
Charles Wolfson Charitable Trust, UK, 347
The Charta 77 Foundation, Czech Republic, 80
Chatham House, UK, 378
The Chatlos Foundation, Inc, USA, 414
Chemistry Centre Foundation, France, 108
Cheshire (Leonard) Foundation, UK, 364
Chia Hsin Foundation, Taiwan, 321
Chiang Ching-kuo Foundation for International Scholarly Exchange—CCKF, Taiwan, 321
The Chicago Community Trust, USA, 414
Chigiana Musical Academy, Italy, 172
Child Migrants Trust, UK, 347
ChildFund, New Zealand, 233
ChildFund International, USA, 414
Childhope Philippines, Philippines, 251
Children & War Foundation—CAW, Norway, 240
Children in Africa Foundation, Germany, 140
Children International—CI, USA, 414
Children of the Mekong, France, 102
Children and Sharing, France, 102
Children of Slovakia Foundation, Slovakia, 275
The Children's Investment Fund Foundation, UK, 347
Children's Medical Research Institute—CMRI, Australia, 13
Childs (Jane Coffin) Memorial Fund for Medical Research, USA, 443
Childwick Trust, UK, 347
Chile Foundation, Chile, 65
China Charities Aid Foundation for Children, China (People's Republic), 67
China Charities Alliance, China (People's Republic), 66
China Children and Teenagers' Foundation, China (People's Republic), 67
China Environmental Protection Foundation, China (People's Republic), 67
China Foundation Center—CFC, China (People's Republic), 66
China Foundation for Poverty Alleviation—CFPA, China (People's Republic), 67
China Medical Board—CMB, USA, 415
China Siyuan Foundation for Poverty Alleviation, China (People's Republic), 67
China Youth Development Foundation, China (People's Republic), 68
Chirac (Jacques), Fondation, France, 107
Chr. Michelsen Institute for Science and Intellectual Freedom—CMI, Norway, 241
Christian Aid, UK, 348
Christoph Merian Foundation, Switzerland, 305
Christoph-Merian-Stiftung, Switzerland, 305
Christopher & Dana Reeve Foundation, USA, 415
Churches' Commission for Migrants in Europe, Belgium, 28
The Churchill Fellowship, UK, 348
Churchill (Winston) Foundation of the United States, USA, 482
Churchill (Winston) Memorial Trust, Australia, 19
Churchill (Winston) Memorial Trust of New Zealand, New Zealand, 236
CIAT—Centro Internacional de Agricultura Tropical, Italy, 172
CIDOB Foundation—Barcelona Centre for International Affairs, Spain, 287
CIDSE—Together for Global Justice, Belgium, 29
CIEE—Council on International Educational Exchange, USA, 415
CIMA Research Foundation—Centre for Environmental Monitoring, Italy, 176
Cimade—Ecumenical Care Service, France, 102
La Cimade—Service Oecuménique d'Entraide, France, 102
Cini (Giorgio), Fondazione, Italy, 177
Citi Foundation, USA, 415
Citi Handlowy Leopold Kronenberg Foundation, Poland, 255
Citizens Foundation, Iceland, 154
Citizenship Foundation, UK, 392
The City Bridge Trust, UK, 348
City of Lisbon Foundation, Portugal, 259
Civic Democratic Initiative Support Foundation—CDF, Yemen, 489
Civic Forum Foundation, Czech Republic, 80
Civic Initiatives, Serbia, 271
CIVICUS—World Alliance for Citizen Participation, South Africa, 278
CiviKos Platform, Kosovo, 202
Civil Peace Service—CPS, Germany, 120
Civil Society Development Center—CSDC, Georgia, 117
Civil Society Development Foundation, Romania, 263
Civil Society Foundation, Georgia, 118

INDEX OF FOUNDATIONS

Civil Society and Human Rights Network, Afghanistan, 3
Civil Society and Human Rights Organization—CSHRO, Afghanistan, 3
Civitas Foundation for Civil Society, Romania, 263
Civitates, Belgium, 27
CLADEM—Comité de América Latina y el Caribe para la Defensa de los Derechos de la Mujer, Peru, 249
Claiborne (Liz) & Art Ortenberg Foundation, USA, 448
Clara Lionel Foundation—CLF, USA, 415
Claude Pompidou Foundation, France, 104
Claudine Talon Foundation, Benin, 35
Clean Up Australia, Australia, 13
CLEAR Global, USA, 416
Cleveland Foundation, USA, 416
Cleveland H. Dodge Foundation, Inc, USA, 416
CLIC Sargent, UK, 392
Climate Cent Foundation, Switzerland, 317
Clinton Foundation, USA, 416
Clooney Foundation for Justice—CFJ, USA, 416
Clore Israel Foundation, Israel, 169
Člověk v tísni, Czech Republic, 79
CMDID Foundation—Malian Centre for Inter-Party Dialogue and Democracy, Mali, 213
CMI—Chr. Michelsen Institute for Science and Intellectual Freedom, Norway, 241
CNIB Foundation/Fondation INCA, Canada, 52
CNVOS—Zavod Center za Informiranje, Sodelovanje in Razvoj Nevladnih Organizacije, Slovenia, 277
Coady Institute, Canada, 52
Coastline Foundation, Maldives, 212
The Coca-Cola Foundation, Inc, USA, 417
Çocuk (Anne) Eğitim Vakfı, Türkiye, 327
CODE—Canadian Organization for Development through Education, Canada, 52
CODESPA Foundation, Spain, 290
Collier Charitable Fund, Australia, 13
Collodi (Carlo), Fondazione Nazionale, Italy, 179
Colombian Habitat Foundation, Colombia, 71
Comic Relief, UK, 348
Comité de América Latina y el Caribe para la Defensa de los Derechos de la Mujer—CLADEM, Peru, 249
Comité de Coopération Pour le Cambodge, Cambodia, 46
Comité de Coordination des ONGI en RCA, Central African Republic, 63
Commission des Eglises auprès des Migrants en Europe/Kommission der Kirchen für Migranten in Europa, Belgium, 28
Committee of Good Will—Olga Havel Foundation, Czech Republic, 81
Common Network, Brazil, 38
Commonwealth Foundation, UK, 348
The Commonwealth Fund, USA, 417
Communication Foundation for Asia, Philippines, 251
Community Chest, Singapore, 273
Community Chest of Hong Kong, Hong Kong, 150
Community Chest of Korea—Fruit of Love, Korea (Republic), 200
Community Development Foundation, Mozambique, 221
Community Foundation for Northern Ireland, UK, 349
Community Foundation Partnership, Russian Federation, 264
Community Foundation of Singapore, Singapore, 272
Community Foundation for the Western Region of Zimbabwe—CFWRZ, Zimbabwe, 490
Community Foundations of Canada, Canada, 47
Community Foundations of New Zealand, New Zealand, 232
Community of Solidarity Organizations, Chile, 64
Comunalia—Alianza de Fundaciones Comunitarias de México, Mexico, 215
Comunidad de Organizaciones Solidarios, Chile, 64
Concawe—Oil Companies' European Association for Environment, Health and Safety in Refining and Distribution, Belgium, 29
Concern India Foundation, India, 157
Concern Worldwide, Ireland, 166
CONCORD—European NGO Confederation for Relief and Development, Belgium, 26
The Confederation of Service Charities—Cobseo, UK, 349
Conrad N. Hilton Foundation, USA, 417
Conseil des Arts du Canada, Canada, 50
Consejo Argentino para las Relaciones Internacionales—CARI, Argentina, 6
Consejo Latinoamericano de Ciencias Sociales—CLACSO, Argentina, 6

Conservation International Foundation, USA, 417
Consuelo Zobel Alger Foundation, USA, 417
Co-op Foundation, UK, 349
Cooperation Canada/Coopération Canada, Canada, 48
Cooperation Committee for Cambodia—CCC, Cambodia, 46
Co-operative Community Investment Foundation, UK, 349
Co-operative Development Foundation of Canada—CDF, Canada, 52
Cooperazione Internazionale—COOPI, Italy, 173
Coordinadora de ONGD España, Spain, 285
Coordination SUD, France, 99
Copperbelt Development Foundation, Zambia, 490
Coram, UK, 349
Le Corbusier Foundation, France, 108
Corona Foundation, Colombia, 71
Corra Foundation, UK, 349
Corus International, USA, 418
Costopoulos (J. F.) Foundation, Greece, 146
Coubertin Foundation, France, 105
Council of American Development Foundations, Dominican Republic, 87
Council on Foundations—COF, USA, 394
Council for International Exchange of Scholars—CIES, USA, 418
Council of Michigan Foundations—CMF, USA, 394
Counterpart International, USA, 418
Coutu (Marcelle et Jean), Fondation, Canada, 55
Covenant Foundation, USA, 418
CPAR—Canadian Physicians for Aid and Relief, Canada, 52
The Crafoord Foundation, Sweden, 298
Crafoordska stiftelsen, Sweden, 298
The Craig and Susan McCaw Foundation, USA, 418
The CRB Foundation/La Fondation CRB, Canada, 52
CRDF Global, USA, 419
CReDO—Centrul de Resurse pentru Drepturile Omului, Moldova, 217
Croatian Platform for International Citizen Solidarity, Croatia, 76
CROSOL—Platforma za međunarodnu građansku solidarnost Hrvatske, Croatia, 76
Crossroads International/Carrefour International, Canada, 53
Croucher Foundation, Hong Kong, 151
Crown Family Philanthropies, USA, 419
Cruz (Oswaldo), Fundação, Brazil, 40
Cultural Center of the Philippines—CCP, Philippines, 252
Cultural Foundation of the German Länder, Germany, 134
Culture, Health, Arts, Sports and Education Fund—CHASE, Jamaica, 184
Cundill (Peter) Foundation, Bermuda, 35
CURE International, USA, 419
The Cure Parkinson's Trust, UK, 349
Cuso International, Canada, 53
CVT—Center for Victims of Torture, USA, 413
Cyril Ramaphosa Foundation, South Africa, 279
Cystic Fibrosis Canada, Canada, 53
Cystic Fibrosis Foundation, USA, 419
Cystic Fibrosis Trust, UK, 350
Czech Association of Community Foundations—AKN Association, Czech Republic, 78
Czech Council of Social Services, Czech Republic, 78
Czech Donors Forum, Czech Republic, 78
Czech-German Fund for the Future, Czech Republic, 79
Czech Literary Fund Foundation, Czech Republic, 80
Czech Music Fund Foundation, Czech Republic, 79

DAAD—Deutscher Akademischer Austauschdienst, Germany, 125
Dag Hammarskjöld Foundation, Sweden, 303
Daimler and Benz Foundation, Germany, 123
Daimler und Benz Stiftung, Germany, 123
Daiwa Anglo-Japanese Foundation, UK, 350
Dalia Association, Palestinian Territories, 246
Dalio Foundation, USA, 419
Dam Foundation, Norway, 243
Damon Runyon Cancer Research Foundation, USA, 419
Daniele Agostino Derossi Foundation, USA, 420
Danielle Mitterrand Foundation, France, 112
Danish Cultural Institute—DCI, Denmark, 82
Danish Institute for Human Rights, Denmark, 84
Danish Outdoor Council, Denmark, 83
Danmark-Amerika Fondet, Denmark, 82
Danske Kulturinstitut—DKI, Denmark, 82

Danube Institute, Hungary, 153
Darwin (Charles) Foundation for the Galapagos Islands, Ecuador, 88
Dasra, India, 154
David and Lucile Packard Foundation, USA, 420
David Nott Foundation, UK, 350
David Suzuki Foundation, Canada, 53
Davis (Lady) Fellowship Trust, Israel, 170
Daw Khin Kyi Foundation, Myanmar, 221
Debenedetti (Rodolfo), Fondazione, Italy, 179
Debts to Opportunities Foundation, Netherlands, 231
DEC—Disasters Emergency Committee, UK, 336
Defence for Children International—DCI, Switzerland, 307
Defense of Green Earth Foundation—DGEF, Japan, 187
Dell (Michael & Susan) Foundation, USA, 453
del Pino (Rafael), Fundación, Spain, 294
DemNet—Demokratikus Jogok Fejlesztéséért Alapítvány, Hungary, 153
DemNet—Foundation for the Development of Democratic Rights, Hungary, 153
Democracy and Development Foundation, Chile, 65
Democracy Fund, USA, 458
Democracy and Human Rights Development Centre, Iraq, 164
Denmark-America Foundation, Denmark, 82
Dental Aid International, Switzerland, 317
Deripaska (Oleg) Foundation, Russian Federation, 267
Derossi (Daniele Agostino) Foundation, USA, 420
Desmond & Leah Tutu Legacy Foundation, South Africa, 279
Deutsch-Russischer Austausch eV—DRA, Germany, 124
Deutsche AIDS-Stiftung, Germany, 124
Deutsche Bank Americas Foundation, USA, 420
Deutsche Bank Endowment Fund at the Donors' Association for the Promotion of German Science, Germany, 142
Deutsche Bank Foundation, Germany, 124
Deutsche Bank Stiftung, Germany, 124
Deutsche Bundesstiftung Umwelt—DBU, Germany, 124
Deutsche Gesellschaft für Auswärtige Politik—DGAP, Germany, 124
Deutsche Krebshilfe eV, Germany, 124
Deutsche Nationalstiftung, Germany, 125
Deutsche Orient-Stiftung, Germany, 125
Deutsche Sparkassenstiftung für Internationale Zusammenarbeit, Germany, 125
Deutsche Telekom Foundation, Germany, 125
Deutsche Telekom Stiftung, Germany, 125
Deutscher Akademischer Austauschdienst—DAAD, Germany, 125
Deutsches Institut für internationale Politik und Sicherheit, Germany, 141
Deutsches Rheuma-Forschungszentrum Berlin, Germany, 126
Development Cooperation Roundtable, Estonia, 92
Development Foundation, Guatemala, 148
Development Foundation of Turkey, Türkiye, 330
Development Gateway—DG, USA, 420
Development NGO Coordinator Spain, Spain, 285
Development and Peace—Caritas Canada, Canada, 53
Développement et Paix—Caritas Canada, Canada, 53
Dewji (Mo) Foundation, Tanzania, 323
DHL UK Foundation, UK, 350
Diabetes UK, UK, 350
Diakonia, Sweden, 298
Dietmar Hopp Foundation, Germany, 126
Dietmar-Hopp-Stiftung, Germany, 126
Digicel Foundation Haiti, Haiti, 149
Digicel Foundation Jamaica, Jamaica, 184
Digicel PNG Foundation, Papua New Guinea, 247
Digicel Trinidad and Tobago Foundation, Trinidad and Tobago, 326
Dioraphte Foundation, Netherlands, 229
DIPF—Leibniz-Institut für Bildungsforschung und Bildungsinformation, Germany, 126
DiploFoundation, Malta, 213
Direct Relief, USA, 420
Directory of Social Change, UK, 336
Disability Rights Fund, USA, 395
Disabled Peoples' International—DPI, Canada, 54
Disasters Emergency Committee—DEC, UK, 336
Ditchley Foundation, UK, 351
Dmitry Likhachev Foundation, Russian Federation, 265
DNB Savings Bank Foundation, Norway, 243
The Do-Nation Foundation, Inc, Saint Lucia, 268

Dóchas

Dóchas—Irish Association of Non-Governmental Development Organisations, Ireland, 165
Doctors Without Borders International, Switzerland, 314
Doctors of the World International, France, 114
Dodge (Cleveland H.) Foundation, Inc, USA, 416
DOEN Foundation, Netherlands, 229
Doğan (Aydın) Vakfı, Türkiye, 328
Dokolo (Sindika), Fundação, Angola, 5
Dollywood Foundation, USA, 420
Dom Manuel II Foundation, Portugal, 260
Dominican Development Foundation, Dominican Republic, 87
Don Bosco Foundation of Cambodia—DBFC, Cambodia, 46
Donner (William H.) Foundation, Inc, USA, 481
Donors' Association for the Promotion of Sciences and Humanities, Germany, 119
Doris Duke Charitable Foundation—DDCF, USA, 421
The Dr Denis Mukwege Foundation, Netherlands, 224
Dr Guillermo Manuel Ungo Foundation, El Salvador, 91
Dr Marcus Wallenberg Foundation for Further Education in International Industry, Sweden, 299
Dr Marcus Wallenbergs Stiftelse för Utbildning i Internationellt Industriellt Företagande, Sweden, 299
Dr Rainer Wild Foundation for Healthy Nutrition, Germany, 126
Dr Rainer Wild-Stiftung—Stiftung für Gesunde Ernährung, Germany, 126
Dr Scholl Foundation, USA, 421
Dräger Foundation, Germany, 126
Dräger-Stiftung, Germany, 126
Dreyfus (Camille and Henry) Foundation, USA, 411
Dreyfus Health Foundation, USA, 468
DRFN—Desert Research Foundation of Namibia, Namibia, 222
Drug Policy Alliance—DPA, USA, 421
DSW—Deutsche Stiftung Weltbevölkerung, Germany, 126
DTGO Group of Foundations, Thailand, 323
del Duca (Simone et Cino), Fondation, France, 111
Duke Endowment, USA, 421
Dulverton Trust, UK, 351
Dumbarton Oaks, USA, 421
Dunhe Foundation, China (People's Republic), 68
Dutch-Bangla Bank Foundation, Bangladesh, 25

E. O. Wilson Biodiversity Foundation, USA, 421
Earth Island Institute—EII, USA, 422
Earthrights International—ERI, USA, 422
Earthworm Foundation, Switzerland, 314
East Africa Philanthropy Network—EAPN, Kenya, 197
East Asia Institute—EAI, Korea (Republic), 201
East-West Center—EWC, USA, 422
East-West Encounters Charitable Foundation, Germany, 141
Eastern Europe Studies Centre—EESC, Lithuania, 209
eBay Foundation, USA, 422
Ebelin and Gerd Bucerius ZEIT Foundation, Germany, 143
Eberhard Schöck Foundation, Germany, 127
Eberhard-Schöck-Stiftung, Germany, 127
Ebert (Friedrich) Stiftung, Germany, 129
Echo Foundation/Fondation Echo, Canada, 54
EcoCiencia—Fundación Ecuatoriana de Estudios Ecologicos, Ecuador, 88
EcoHealth Alliance, USA, 422
Economic Development Foundation, Türkiye, 328
Economic Foundation, Poland, 255
Economic and Social Research Foundation—ESRF, Tanzania, 322
ECPAT International, Thailand, 324
Ecuadorean Consortium for Social Responsibility, Ecuador, 87
Ecuadorean Cooperation for Development Fund, Ecuador, 88
Ecuadorean Foundation of Ecological Studies, Ecuador, 88
Ecuadorean Social Group Fund Populorum Progressio, Ecuador, 89
EDF Group Foundation, France, 107
EDGE Funders Alliance, USA, 394
Edhi Foundation, Pakistan, 245
Edmond de Rothschild Foundations, Switzerland, 308
The Edna McConnell Clark Foundation, USA, 422
Ednannia—Initiative Centre to Support Social Action, Ukraine, 332
Edoardo Garrone Foundation, Italy, 177

EDP Foundation, Portugal, 260
Education Above All Foundation—EAA, Qatar, 262
The Education for Development Foundation—EDF, Thailand, 324
Education and Training Foundation—ETF, UK, 351
Educational Opportunity Foundation, UK, 351
Educo, Spain, 286
Edward Cadbury Charitable Trust, UK, 351
EEB—European Environmental Bureau, Belgium, 30
Eesti Mittetulundusühingute ja Sihtasutuste Liit, Estonia, 92
Eestimaa Looduse Fond—ELF, Estonia, 92
Effekteam Association, Hungary, 152
EFQM—European Foundation for Quality Management, Belgium, 30
Egmont Fonden, Denmark, 83
Egmont Foundation, Denmark, 83
EGMONT—Institut Royal des Relations Internationales, Belgium, 29
Einaudi (Luigi), Fondazione, Italy, 178
Ekhaga Foundation, Sweden, 299
Ekhagastiftelsen, Sweden, 299
Ekofond SPP, Slovakia, 275
Ekopolis Foundation, Slovakia, 275
The Elders Foundation, UK, 352
Electronic Frontier Foundation—EFF, USA, 423
Elena & Gennady Timchenko Foundation, Russian Federation, 265
ELEPAP—Rehabilitation for the Disabled, Greece, 145
ELIAMEP—Hellenic Foundation for European and Foreign Policy, Greece, 146
Elizabeth Glaser Pediatric AIDS Foundation—EGPAF, USA, 423
Elizabeth Kostova Foundation for Creative Writing, Bulgaria, 43
Ellerman (John) Foundation, UK, 361
The ELMA Group of Foundations, USA, 423
Elrahma Charity Trust, UK, 352
Elrha, UK, 352
Else Kröner-Fresenius Foundation, Germany, 127
Else Kröner-Fresenius-Stiftung, Germany, 127
Elton John AIDS Foundation, UK, 352
Elumelu (Tony) Foundation, Nigeria, 238
Emanuela Zancan Foundation Centre for Social Studies and Research, Italy, 172
Embrace the Middle East, UK, 352
EMERGENCY, Italy, 173
Emirates Foundation, United Arab Emirates, 334
Emmaüs International, France, 102
Empresas Polar Foundation, Venezuela, 487
Emunah, UK, 353
Enchanted Peach Children's Foundation—EPCF, USA, 423
Enda Third World—Environment and Development Action in the Third World, Senegal, 270
Enda Tiers Monde—Environnement et Développement du Tiers-Monde, Senegal, 270
endPoverty.org, USA, 424
Energies for the World Foundation, France, 105
Enfance et Partage, France, 102
Enfants du Mékong, France, 102
EngenderHealth, USA, 424
ENGIE Corporate Foundation, France, 105
The English-Speaking Union—ESU, UK, 353
Eni Foundation, Italy, 173
Enough Project, USA, 416
Enrico Mattei Eni Foundation, Italy, 174
Ente Cassa di Risparmio di Firenze, Italy, 173
Entraide Protestante Suisse, Switzerland, 311
Entraide Universitaire Mondiale du Canada, Canada, 63
Entwicklungshilfe-Klub, Austria, 20
Environment Foundation of Turkey, Türkiye, 330
Environment and Natural Resources Foundation, Argentina, 7
Environmental Foundation of Jamaica, Jamaica, 184
Environmental Justice Foundation—EJF, UK, 353
Environmental Partnership Foundation, Poland, 256
Environmental Protection and Packaging Waste Recovery and Recycling Foundation, Türkiye, 328
Epilepsy Foundation, USA, 424
Equal Justice Initiative—EJI, USA, 424
Equality Fund/Fonds Égalité, Canada, 54
Equity Group Foundation—EGF, Kenya, 198
ERA—Europäische Rechtsakademie, Germany, 127
Erik Philip-Sörensen Foundation, Sweden, 299
Erik Philip-Sörensens Stiftelse, Sweden, 299
Ernest Kleinwort Charitable Trust, UK, 353

INDEX OF FOUNDATIONS

Ernst Schering Foundation, Germany, 127
Ernst-Schering-Stiftung, Germany, 127
ERSTE Foundation, Austria, 21
ERSTE Stiftung—Die ERSTE Österreichische Spar-Casse Privatstiftung, Austria, 21
Eskom Development Foundation, South Africa, 279
Esmée Fairbairn Foundation, UK, 353
Esquel Group Foundation—Ecuador, Ecuador, 88
Estonian Foreign Policy Institute, Estonia, 93
Estonian Fund for Nature, Estonia, 92
Estonian National Culture Foundation, Estonia, 93
ETC Group—Action Group on Erosion, Technology and Concentration, Canada, 54
Ettersberg Foundation, Germany, 140
Eugenio Mendoza Foundation, Venezuela, 487
Eurasia Foundation—EF, USA, 424
Eurasia Partnership Foundation-Armenia—EPF-Armenia, Armenia, 9
Eureka Foundation, Bulgaria, 43
Euris Foundation, France, 106
Euro-Mediterranean Centre on Climate Change Foundation, Italy, 176
EURODAD—European Network on Debt and Development, Belgium, 29
EuroNatur, Germany, 127
Europa Nostra, Netherlands, 224
Europäische Rechtsakademie—ERA, Germany, 127
Europe Foundation—EPF, Georgia, 118
European Anti-Poverty Network—EAPN, Belgium, 29
European Association for Cancer Research—EACR, UK, 353
European Center for Constitutional and Human Rights—ECCHR, Germany, 128
European Center for Peace and Development—ECPD, Serbia, 271
European Centre for Social Welfare Policy and Research, Austria, 21
European Climate Foundation, Netherlands, 224
European Community Foundation Initiative—ECFI, Germany, 119
European Cultural Centre, Switzerland, 307
European Cultural Foundation—ECF, Netherlands, 225
European Environmental Bureau—EEB, Belgium, 30
European Federation of National Organisations Working with the Homeless, Belgium, 26
European Food Banks Federation—EFBF, Belgium, 26
European Foundation for the Improvement of Living and Working Conditions—Eurofound, Ireland, 166
European Foundation for Management Development—EFMD, Belgium, 30
European Foundation for Philanthropy and Society Development, Croatia, 76
European Foundation for Quality Management—EFQM, Belgium, 30
European Foundation for the Sustainable Development of the Regions, Switzerland, 308
European Institute of Health and Social Welfare, Spain, 296
European Mediterranean Institute, Spain, 296
European Network on Debt and Development—EURODAD, Belgium, 29
European NGO Confederation for Relief and Development—CONCORD, Belgium, 26
European Roma Rights Centre—ERRC, Belgium, 30
European Think Tanks Group—ETTG, Belgium, 26
European Training Foundation—ETF, Italy, 173
European Youth For Action—EYFA, Germany, 128
European Youth Foundation—EYF, France, 112
Europese Culterele Stichting, Netherlands, 225
Europska Zaklada za Filantropiju i Društveni Dazvoj, Croatia, 76
Eurotransplant International Foundation, Netherlands, 225
Evangelisches Studienwerk eV, Germany, 128
Evens Foundation, Belgium, 31
EVPA—European Venture Philanthropy Association, Belgium, 27
Evrika Foundation, Bulgaria, 43
Evropis Pondis, Georgia, 118
Ewing Marion Kauffman Foundation, USA, 425
EWT—Endangered Wildlife Trust, South Africa, 279
ExxonMobil Foundation, USA, 425
EYFA—European Youth For Action, Germany, 128

INDEX OF FOUNDATIONS

F. C. Flick Foundation against Xenophobia, Racism and Intolerance, Germany, 128
F. C. Flick-Stiftung gegen Fremdenfeindlichkeit, Rassismus und Intoleranz, Germany, 128
F20, Germany, 119
FAFIDESS—Fundación de Asesoría Financiera a Instituciones de Desarrollo y Servicio Social, Guatemala, 148
FAI—Fondo per l'Ambiente Italiano, Italy, 174
Fairbairn (Esmée) Foundation, UK, 353
Fairtrade Nederland, Netherlands, 230
Faith, UK, 353
The Family Federation of Finland, Finland, 98
Family Restoration Fund, UK, 347
Farm Africa, UK, 354
FARN—Fundación Ambiente y Recursos Naturales, Argentina, 7
FATE Foundation, Nigeria, 237
Fatoumatta Bah-Barrow Foundation—FaBB, Gambia, 117
FDC—Fundação para o Desenvolvimento da Comunidade, Mozambique, 221
FEANTSA—Fédération Européenne des Associations Nationales Travaillant avec les Sans-Abri, Belgium, 26
Federacja Funduszy Lokalnych w Polsce, Poland, 254
Federal Association of Social Welfare Organizations, Germany, 121
Federal Chancellor Willy Brandt Foundation, Germany, 123
Fédération Belge des Fondations Philanthropiques, Belgium, 26
Federation of Community Foundations in Poland, Poland, 254
Fédération Européenne des Associations Nationales Travaillant avec les Sans-Abri—FEANTSA, Belgium, 26
Fédération Européenne des Banques Alimentaires—FEBA, Belgium, 26
Fédération Internationale des Ligues des Droits de L'Homme—FIDH, France, 99
Federation of Non-Governmental Organizations for Development in Romania, Romania, 263
Fedesarrollo—Fundación para la Educación Superior y el Desarrollo, Colombia, 71
FEDRE—European Foundation for the Sustainable Development of the Regions, Switzerland, 308
Feed the Children, USA, 425
Feed the Minds, UK, 354
FEEM—Fondazione ENI Enrico Mattei, Italy, 174
FEIM—Fundación para Estudio e Investigación de la Mujer, Argentina, 7
Félix Houphouët-Boigny Foundation for Peace Research, Côte d'Ivoire, 75
Feltrinelli (Giangiacomo), Fondazione, Italy, Italy, 177
FEMSA Foundation, Mexico, 215
Fernand Lazard Foundation, Belgium, 31
Fernando Rielo Foundation, Spain, 290
Ferrero (Piera, Pietro e Giovanni), Fondazione, Italy, 179
FHI 360, USA, 425
Fibrose Kystique Canada, Canada, 53
FIJI Water Foundation, Fiji, 94
Filantrópico, Colombia, 70
filia.die Frauenstiftung, Germany, 128
filia—the Women's Foundation, Germany, 128
The Film Foundation, USA, 425
FIN—Branchevereniging van Fondsen en Foundations, Netherlands, 223
FINCA International, USA, 425
Finnish Cultural Foundation, Finland, 97
Finnish Development Organizations, Finland, 95
Finnish Foundation for Technology Promotion, Finland, 98
Finnish Institute in the UK and Ireland Trust, UK, 354
FIPP—Fondation Internationale Pénale et Pénitentiaire, Netherlands, 226
Firelight Foundation, USA, 426
First Nations Development Institute, USA, 426
FirstRand Foundation, South Africa, 280
Flatiron Institute, USA, 472
Flick (F. C.) Stiftung gegen Fremdenfeindlichkeit, Rassismus und Intoleranz, Germany, 128
Flight Safety Foundation, USA, 426
Florence Gould Foundation, USA, 427
Florence Nightingale International Foundation, Switzerland, 309
Florence Savings Bank Foundation, Italy, 173
Florida Philanthropic Network—FPN, USA, 394
Focus Humanitarian Assistance—FOCUS, Canada, 54
FOKAL—Open Society Foundation Haiti, Haiti, 149

Folke Bernadotte Memorial Foundation, Sweden, 299
Folke Bernadottes Minnesfond, Sweden, 299
Follereau Foundation Luxembourg, Luxembourg, 209
Folmer Wisti Fonden for International Forståelse, Denmark, 83
Folmer Wisti Foundation for International Understanding, Denmark, 83
FOND—Federatia Organizatiilor Neguvernamentale pentru Dezvoltare din Romania, Romania, 263
Fondacija Balkanska Mreza za Razvoj na Gragjanskoto Opshtestvo, North Macedonia, 239
Fondacija Braća Karić, Serbia, 271
Fondacija Cennosti, Bulgaria, 43
Fondacioni Kosovar per Shoqeri Civile, Kosovo, 202
Fondacioni i Kosovës për Shoqëri të Hapur, Kosovo, 203
Fondacioni Shqiptar për të Drejtat e Personave me Aftësi të Kufizuar—FSHDPAK, Albania, 4
FONDAD—Forum on Debt and Development, Netherlands, 225
Fondation 30 Millions d'Amis, France, 102
Fondation Abbé Pierre, France, 108
Fondation Addoha, Morocco, 219
Fondation Africaine pour les Technologies Agricoles, Kenya, 198
Fondation Agir Contre l'Exclusion—FACE, France, 103
Fondation pour l'Agriculture et la Ruralité dans le Monde—Fondation FARM, France, 106
Fondation Air France, France, 103
Fondation Arabe pour l'Image, Lebanon, 205
Fondation Auchan, France, 103
Fondation Auschwitz—Mémoire d'Auschwitz, Belgium, 30
Fondation de l'Avenir pour la Recherche Médicale Appliquée, France, 103
Fondation Baxter & Alma Ricard, Canada, 55
Fondation Bernheim, Belgium, 31
Fondation Bettencourt Schueller, France, 103
Fondation BIAT pour la Jeunesse, Tunisia, 326
Fondation BMCE Bank, Morocco, 219
Fondation BNP Paribas, France, 103
Fondation Boghossian, Belgium, 31
Fondation Brigitte Bardot, France, 104
Fondation Canadienne pour l'Innovation, Canada, 50
Fondation Cartier pour l'Art Contemporain, France, 104
Fondation Casip-Cojasor, France, 104
Fondation Chantal Biya—FCB, Cameroon, 47
Fondation Charles Léopold Mayer pour le Progrès de l'Homme—FPH, Switzerland, 308
Fondation Charles Veillon, Switzerland, 308
Fondation de la Cité internationale des arts, France, 104
Fondation de la Cité Internationale Universitaire de Paris, France, 104
Fondation Claude Pompidou, France, 104
Fondation Claudine Talon, Benin, 35
Fondation CMDID—Centre Malien pour le Dialogue Interpartis et la Démocratie, Mali, 213
Fondation du Collège de France, France, 105
Fondation Congo Assistance, Congo (Republic), 73
Fondation Le Corbusier—FLC, France, 108
Fondation de Coubertin, France, 105
Fondation Digicel Haïti, Haiti, 149
Fondation pour l'Economie et le Développement Durable des Régions d'Europe—FEDRE, Switzerland, 308
Fondation Energies pour le Monde—Fondem, France, 105
Fondation Ensemble, France, 105
Fondation d'Entreprise Crédit Agricole Réunion Mayotte, Réunion, 262
Fondation d'Entreprise ENGIE, France, 105
Fondation d'Entreprise La Poste, France, 105
Fondation d'Entreprise Renault, France, 106
Fondation d'Entreprise VINCI pour la Cité, France, 106
Fondation Espace Afrique, Switzerland, 308
Fondation Euris, France, 106
Fondation Européenne de la Culture/Europese Culturele Stichting, Netherlands, 225
Fondation Evens Stichting, Belgium, 31
Fondation FARM—Fondation pour l'Agriculture et la Ruralité dans le Monde, France, 106
Fondation Félix Houphouët-Boigny pour la Recherche de la Paix, Côte d'Ivoire, 75
Fondation Fernand Lazard Stichting, Belgium, 31
Fondation Follereau Luxembourg—FFL, Luxembourg, 209

Fondation du Patrimoine

Fondation de France, France, 99
Fondation France Chine—FFC, France, 106
Fondation France-Israël, France, 106
Fondation Franco-Japonaise Sasakawa, France, 106
Fondation Francqui, Belgium, 31
Fondation Franz Weber—FFW, Switzerland, 308
Fondation Fyssen, France, 107
Fondation Gan pour le Cinéma, France, 107
Fondation Grand Cœur—FGC, Chad, 64
Fondation Groupe EDF, France, 107
Fondation Guri Vie Meilleure, Niger, 236
Fondation Hans Wilsdorf, Switzerland, 309
Fondation Hassan II pour les Marocains Résidant à l'Étranger, Morocco, 220
Fondation Henri Cartier-Bresson, France, 107
Fondation Hirondelle: Media for Peace and Human Dignity, Switzerland, 309
Fondation Internationale Florence Nightingale, Switzerland, 309
Fondation Internationale Pénale et Pénitentiaire—FIPP, Netherlands, 226
Fondation Internationale Tierno et Mariam—FITIMA, Burkina Faso, 44
Fondation ISREC, Switzerland, 309
Fondation J-Louis Lévesque, Canada, 55
Fondation Jacques Chirac, France, 107
Fondation Jasmin pour la Recherche et la Communication, Tunisia, 326
Fondation Jean Dausset—Centre d'Etude du Polymorphisme Humain—CEPH, France, 107
Fondation Jean Jaurès, France, 107
Fondation Jean Monnet pour l'Europe, Switzerland, 309
Fondation Jean-Paul II pour le Sahel, Burkina Faso, 44
Fondation Joseph Ichame Kamach, Central African Republic, 63
Fondation Latsis Internationale, Switzerland, 309
Fondation Léopold Sédar Senghor, Senegal, 270
Fondation pour le Logement des Défavorisés, France, 108
Fondation Louis-Jeantet de Médecine, Switzerland, 310
Fondation Lucie et André Chagnon, Canada, 55
Fondation MACIF, France, 108
Fondation MAIF pour la Recherche, France, 108
Fondation de la Maison de la Chimie, France, 108
Fondation Maison des Sciences de l'Homme—FMSH, France, 108
Fondation Mapon, Congo (Democratic Republic), 72
Fondation Marc de Montalembert, France, 109
Fondation Marcel Bleustein-Blanchet de la Vocation, France, 109
Fondation Marcel Hicter, Belgium, 32
Fondation Marcelle et Jean Coutu, Canada, 55
Fondation Marguerite et Aimé Maeght, France, 109
Fondation pour les Médias en Afrique de l'Ouest, Ghana, 144
Fondation Mérieux, France, 109
Fondation Mesmin Kabath—FOMEKA, Congo (Republic), 73
Fondation Miloud Chaâbi, Morocco, 220
Fondation Mohammed V pour la Solidarité, Morocco, 220
Fondation MTN Bénin, Benin, 35
Fondation MTN Cameroun, Cameroon, 47
Fondation MTN Congo, Congo (Republic), 73
Fondation MTN Côte d'Ivoire, Côte d'Ivoire, 76
Fondation Mutuelles Congolaises d'Epargne et de Crédit—MUCODEC, Congo (Republic), 73
Fondation Nationale pour l'Enseignement de la Gestion des Entreprises, France, 109
Fondation Nationale des Sciences Politiques—SciencesPo, France, 110
Fondation Nestlé pour l'Etude des Problèmes de l'Alimentation dans le Monde, Switzerland, 310
Fondation Nicolas Hulot pour la Nature et l'Homme—FNH, France, 110
Fondation Noura, Mauritania, 214
Fondation Orange, France, 110
Fondation Orange Burkina Faso, Burkina Faso, 45
Fondation Orange Cameroun, Cameroon, 47
Fondation Orange-Côte d'Ivoire Télécom—OCIT, Côte d'Ivoire, 76
Fondation Orange Guinée, Guinea, 149
Fondation Orange Mali, Mali, 213
Fondation Orange Tunisie, Tunisia, 326
Fondation Orient-Occident—FOO, Morocco, 220
Fondation P&V, Belgium, 32
Fondation Partage et Vie, France, 110
Fondation du Patrimoine, France, 110

505

INDEX OF FOUNDATIONS

Fondation Perspectives d'Avenir, Congo (Republic), 73
Fondation Pierre Elliott Trudeau/Pierre Elliott Trudeau Foundation, Canada, 55
Fondation Prince Albert II de Monaco, Monaco, 217
Fondation Prince Pierre de Monaco, Monaco, 218
Fondation Princesse Charlène de Monaco, Monaco, 218
Fondation Princesse Grace, Monaco, 218
Fondation Rambourg, Tunisia, 326
Fondation Rawji, Congo (Democratic Republic), 72
Fondation pour la Recherche Médicale, France, 110
Fondation pour la Recherche Stratégique, France, 111
Fondation pour le Renforcement des Capacités en Afrique, Zimbabwe, 490
Fondation Rinaldi, Haiti, 149
Fondation Rio Tinto, Guinea, 149
Fondation Robert Schuman, France, 111
Fondation du Roi Abdul-Aziz al-Saoud pour les Études Islamiques et les Sciences Humaines, Morocco, 220
Fondation Roi Baudouin, Belgium, 33
Fondation Rurale pour l'Afrique de l'Ouest—FRAO, Senegal, 270
Fondation S, France, 111
Fondation Schneider Electric, France, 111
Fondation du Scoutisme Mondial, Switzerland, 320
Fondation Simón I. Patiño, Switzerland, 310
Fondation Simone et Cino del Duca, France, 111
Fondation Singer-Polignac, France, 111
Fondation Sommet Mondial des Femmes, Switzerland, 320
Fondation Sonatel, Senegal, 270
Fondation Stamm, Burundi, 45
Fondation Suisse-Liechtenstein pour les Recherches Archéologiques à l'Étranger, Switzerland, 316
Fondation Suisse pour Recherches Alpines—FSRA, Switzerland, 316
Fondation TotalEnergies, France, 112
Fondation Tunisie pour le Développement, Tunisia, 326
Fondation Vodacom RDC, Congo (Democratic Republic), 72
Fondations Philanthropiques Canada—FPC, Canada, 48
Fondatzija Otvoryeno Opshtyestvo Makyedonija, North Macedonia, 239
Fondazione 1563 per l'Arte e la Cultura, Italy, 174
Fondazione Adriano Olivetti, Italy, 174
Fondazione Alessio Pezcoller, Italy, 174
Fondazione Allianz Umana Mente, Italy, 174
Fondazione Ambrosiana Paolo VI, Italy, 175
Fondazione Angelo Della Riccia, Italy, 175
Fondazione AVSI, Italy, 175
Fondazione Benetton Studi Ricerche, Italy, 175
Fondazione Cariplo, Italy, 175
Fondazione Cassa di Risparmio di Padova e Rovigo, Italy, 175
Fondazione Cassa di Risparmio di Torino, Italy, 176
Fondazione Cassa di Risparmio di Verona Vicenza Belluno e Ancona—Fondazione Cariverona, Italy, 176
Fondazione Cavaliere del Lavoro Carlo Pesenti, Italy, 176
Fondazione Centesimus Annus—Pro Pontifice, Vatican City, 486
Fondazione Centro Euro-Mediterraneo sui Cambiamenti Climatici—CMCC, Italy, 176
Fondazione Centro Studi Investimenti Sociali—CENSIS, Italy, 172
Fondazione CIMA—Centro Internazionale in Monitoraggio Ambientale, Italy, 176
Fondazione Compagnia di San Paolo, Italy, 176
Fondazione Edoardo Garrone, Italy, 177
Fondazione Fratelli Tutti, Vatican City, 486
Fondazione Giangiacomo Feltrinelli, Italy, 177
Fondazione Giorgio Cini, Italy, 177
Fondazione Giovanni Agnelli, Italy, 177
Fondazione Giovanni Lorenzini, Italy, 177
Fondazione Giulio Pastore—FGP, Italy, 178
Fondazione Internazionale Menarini, Italy, 178
Fondazione Internazionale Premio Balzan, Italy, 181
Fondazione ISMU—Iniziative e Studi sulla Multietnicità, Italy, 178
Fondazione per l'Istituto Svizzero di Roma, Italy, 178
Fondazione ITS, Italy, 178
Fondazione Lelio e Lisli Basso Issoco—Sezione Internazionale, Italy, 178
Fondazione Luigi Einaudi, Italy, 178

Fondazione Nazionale Carlo Collodi, Italy, 179
Fondazione Piera, Pietro e Giovanni Ferrero, Italy, 179
Fondazione Populorum Progressio, Vatican City, 486
Fondazione Prada, Italy, 179
Fondazione Querini Stampalia—FQS, Italy, 179
Fondazione Rodolfo Debenedetti—FRDB, Italy, 179
Fondazione Roma, Italy, 179
Fondazione Romaeuropa, Italy, 180
Fondazione RUI, Italy, 180
Fondazione Salvatore Maugeri—Clinica del Lavoro e della Riabilitazione, Italy, 180
Fondazione Social Venture-Giordano Dell'Amore, Italy, 180
Fondazione Terzo Pilastro – Internazionale, Italy, 180
Fondazione Ugo Bordoni, Italy, 180
Fondazione Unipolis, Italy, 181
Fondazione Vaticana Giovanni Paolo I, Vatican City, 486
Fondazione di Venezia, Italy, 181
Fondazione Vodafone Italia, Italy, 181
Fondazzjoni Patrimonju Malti, Malta, 213
Fonden Realdania, Denmark, 83
Fondo para el Desarrollo de los Pueblos Indígenas de América Latina y El Caribe—FILAC, Bolivia, 36
Fondo Ecuatoriano de Cooperación para el Desarrollo—FECD, Ecuador, 88
Fonds atvērtai sabiedrībai DOTS, Latvia, 204
Fonds Baillet Latour, Belgium, 32
Fonds Égalité, Canada, 54
Fonds Européen pour la Jeunesse—FEJ, France, 112
Fonds National Suisse de la Recherche Scientifique, Switzerland, 316
Food for the Hungry—FH, USA, 426
Food for the Poor, Inc, USA, 426
For a Healthy Generation, Uzbekistan, 485
Ford Foundation, USA, 427
Foreign Policy Association, USA, 427
Foreign Policy and United Nations Association of Austria—UNA-AUSTRIA, Austria, 22
Föreningen Svenska Atheninstitutets Vänner, Sweden, 299
Forest & Bird Te Reo o te Taio, New Zealand, 233
The Forest Trust, Switzerland, 307
Fórum Dárců, Czech Republic, 78
Forum Darczyńców, Poland, 254
Forum on Debt and Development—FONDAD, Netherlands, 225
Fórum donorov, Slovakia, 274
Forum International de l'Innovation Sociale—FIIS, France, 112
Forum LSM Internasional untuk Pembangunan Indonesia, Indonesia, 161
Forum ZaDobro.BIT!, Croatia, 76
FORWARD—Foundation for Women's Health Research and Development, UK, 354
Fòs Feminista, USA, 427
Foundation for AIDS Research—amfAR, USA, 403
Foundation for Analysis and Social Studies, Spain, 288
Foundation for Assistance, Training and Integration of Disadvantaged People, Spain, 287
Foundation of Banks and Savings Banks of CECA, Spain, 289
Foundation for Basic Research in Biomedicine, Germany, 122
Foundation Bofill, Spain, 287
Foundation for Caribbean Research and Management of Biodiversity, Curaçao, 77
Foundation Center, USA, 393
Foundation Centre for the Study of Social Investment, Italy, 172
Foundation for Civil Society—FCS, Tanzania, 322
Foundation for the Conservation of the Atlantic Forest, Brazil, 41
Foundation for Culture and Civil Society—FCCS, Afghanistan, 3
Foundation for the Defence of Nature, Venezuela, 487
Foundation for Defense of Democracies—FDD, USA, 427
Foundation for Democracy and Media, Netherlands, 229
Foundation for Environmental Education—FEE, Denmark, 83
Foundation for the Financial Assessment of Social Service and Development Institutions, Guatemala, 148
Foundation of the Future for Applied Medical Research, France, 103

Foundation for German-Polish Co-operation, Poland, 257
Foundation of the Hellenic World, Greece, 145
Foundation for Higher Education and Development, Colombia, 71
Foundation for Housing the Disadvantaged, France, 108
Foundation for International Community Assistance, USA, 425
Foundation for Investment and Development of Exports—FIDE, Honduras, 150
Foundation for Latin American Economic Research, Argentina, 7
Foundation for Local Development and the Municipal and Institutional Support of Central America and the Caribbean, Costa Rica, 74
Foundation for Medical Research, France, 110
Foundation for Middle East Peace—FMEP, USA, 428
Foundation for National Parks & Wildlife, Australia, 14
Foundation for an Open Society DOTS, Latvia, 204
Foundation Open Society Institute Pakistan, Pakistan, 245
Foundation Open Society Macedonia—FOSIM, North Macedonia, 239
Foundation Orange, Slovakia, 275
Foundation for the Promotion of the German Rectors' Conference, Germany, 140
Foundation for the Qualification and Consultancy in Microfinance, El Salvador, 92
Foundation 'Remembrance, Responsibility and Future', Germany, 139
Foundation for the Rights of Future Generations, Germany, 141
Foundation Rodolfo Debenedetti, Italy, 179
Foundation for Rural & Regional Renewal—FRRR, Australia, 14
Foundation for Security and Development in Africa—FOSDA, Ghana, 143
Foundation for Social Housing, Venezuela, 488
Foundation of Spanish Commercial Agents, Spain, 287
Foundation for Strategic Research, France, 111
Foundation in Support of Local Democracy, Poland, 256
Foundation for the Support of Women's Work, Türkiye, 329
Foundation for the Sustainable Development of Small and Medium-sized Enterprises—FUNDES International, Costa Rica, 74
Foundation for the Swiss Institute of Rome, Italy, 178
Foundation for the Victims of Terrorism, Spain, 296
Foundation of Weimar Classics, Germany, 134
Foundation for the Welfare of Holocaust Victims, Israel, 169
Foundation for Women, Spain, 293
Foundation for Women's Health, Research and Development—FORWARD, UK, 354
Foundation for Women's Research and Studies, Argentina, 7
Foundation for World Agriculture and Rural Life, France, 106
The Foundation for Young Australians—FYA, Australia, 14
Foundation of Youth and Lifelong Learning—INEDIVIM, Greece, 145
Foundation for Youth Research, Germany, 140
Foundations and Funds Association, Finland, 95
Foundations Platform—F20, Germany, 119
Foundations' Post-Doc Pool, Finland, 95
Fox (Michael J.) Foundation for Parkinson's Research, USA, 453
France Amérique Latine—FAL, France, 112
France China Foundation, France, 106
France-Israel Foundation, France, 106
France-Libertés Fondation Danielle Mitterrand, France, 112
France Nature Environnement, France, 112
Franciscans International, Switzerland, 310
Franco-American Fulbright Commission, France, 113
Franco-Japanese Sasakawa Foundation, France, 106
Francqui Foundation, Belgium, 31
Frank (Anne)-Fonds, Switzerland, 306
Frank (Anne) Stichting, Netherlands, 224
Frank Knox Memorial Fellowships, UK, 363
Frankfurt Foundation for German-Italian Studies, Germany, 129
Frankfurter Stiftung für Deutsch-Italienische Studien, Germany, 129
Fraser Institute, Canada, 55
Fratelli Tutti Foundation, Vatican City, 486

INDEX OF FOUNDATIONS

Fraunhofer-Gesellschaft, Germany, 129
Fraunhofer Society, Germany, 129
The Fred Hollows Foundation, Australia, 14
FREE Network—Forum for Research on Eastern Europe and Emerging Economies, Sweden, 299
Free Russia Foundation, USA, 428
Freedom from Torture (Medical Foundation for the Care of Victims of Torture), UK, 354
Freedom House, Inc, USA, 428
Freedom Speech Foundation, Norway, 241
Freedom Together Foundation, USA, 428
The Freeman Foundation, USA, 428
French Agriculturalists and International Development, France, 100
French-American Foundation, USA, 429
French Foundation Centre, France, 99
French Institute of International Relations, France, 113
French National Foundation for Management Education, France, 109
Frères des Hommes—FDH, France, 113
Freudenberg Foundation, Germany, 129
Freudenberg Stiftung, Germany, 129
Fridtjof Nansen Institute, Norway, 241
Fridtjof Nansens Institutt—FNI, Norway, 241
Friede Springer Foundation, Germany, 129
Friede Springer Stiftung, Germany, 129
Friedensdorf International, Germany, 129
Friedrich-Ebert-Stiftung eV, Germany, 129
Friedrich Naumann Foundation for Freedom, Germany, 130
Friedrich-Naumann-Stiftung für die Freiheit, Germany, 130
Friends of the Earth International—FOEI, Netherlands, 225
Friends-International, Cambodia, 46
Friends of Nature Foundation, Bolivia, 36
Friluftsrådet, Denmark, 83
Fritz Thyssen Foundation, Germany, 130
Fritz Thyssen Stiftung, Germany, 130
Front Line Defenders—FLD, Ireland, 166
FRS-FNRS—Fonds de la Recherche Scientifique, Belgium, 32
FUHEM—Fundación Benéfico-Social Hogar del Empleado, Spain, 286
Fulbright Commission Philippines, Philippines, 253
Fulbright France—Commission Fulbright Franco-Américaine, France, 113
Fulbright Israel, Israel, 169
Fulbright Norway—US-Norway Fulbright Foundation for Educational Exchange, Norway, 241
Fulbright Scholar Program, USA, 418
Fund for the Development of Indigenous Peoples of Latin America and the Caribbean, Bolivia, 36
Fund and Endowment Management Foundation, Norway, 240
Fund for Global Human Rights, USA, 395
Fund for Scientific Research, Belgium, 32
Fundação Abrinq pelos Direitos da Criança e do Adolescente, Brazil, 39
Fundação ArcelorMittal Brasil, Brazil, 39
Fundação Armando Alvares Penteado, Brazil, 39
Fundação Arpad Szenes–Vieira da Silva, Portugal, 258
Fundação Assistência Médica International—AMI, Portugal, 258
Fundação Banco do Brasil, Brazil, 39
Fundação Caboverdiana de Acção Social Escolar—FICASE, Cabo Verde, 45
Fundação Calouste Gulbenkian, Portugal, 259
Fundação da Casa de Mateus, Portugal, 259
Fundação Centro Cultural de Belém, Portugal, 259
Fundação Champalimaud, Portugal, 259
Fundação Cidade de Lisboa, Portugal, 259
Fundação Dom Manuel II, Portugal, 260
Fundação EDP, Portugal, 260
Fundação Eng. António de Almeida, Portugal, 260
Fundação Getulio Vargas—FGV, Brazil, 40
Fundação Grupo Boticário de Proteção à Natureza, Brazil, 40
Fundação Iochpe, Brazil, 40
Fundação José Maria Neves para a Governança, Cabo Verde, 46
Fundação Luso-Americana para o Desenvolvimento—FLAD, Portugal, 260
Fundação Maria Cecilia Souto Vidigal, Brazil, 40
Fundação Mário Soares e Maria Barroso, Portugal, 260
Fundação Oriente, Portugal, 260
Fundação Oswaldo Cruz—FIOCRUZ, Brazil, 40
Fundação Ricardo do Espírito Santo Silva, Portugal, 261

Fundação Roberto Marinho, Brazil, 41
Fundação de Serralves, Portugal, 261
Fundação Sindika Dokolo, Angola, 5
Fundação SOS Mata Atlântica, Brazil, 41
Fundação Telefônica Vivo, Brazil, 41
Fundação Vodafone Portugal, Portugal, 261
Fundació Agrupació AMCI, Spain, 286
Fundació CIDOB, Spain, 287
Fundació Futbol Club Barcelona, Spain, 287
Fundació Gala–Salvador Dalí, Spain, 287
Fundació Jaume Bofill, Spain, 287
Fundación Acceso, Costa Rica, 73
Fundación Acindar, Argentina, 6
Fundación AFIM—Ayuda, Formación e Integración del Discapacitado, Spain, 287
Fundación de los Agentes Comerciales de España, Spain, 287
Fundación Albéniz, Spain, 288
Fundación Almine y Bernard Ruiz-Picasso, Spain, 288
Fundación Alzheimer España—FAE, Spain, 288
Fundación Amancio Ortega, Spain, 288
Fundación Amanecer, Colombia, 70
Fundación Ambiente y Recursos Naturales—FARN, Argentina, 7
Fundación Amigos de la Naturaleza, Bolivia, 36
Fundación para el Análisis y los Estudios Sociales—FAES, Spain, 288
Fundación Arias para la Paz y el Progreso Humano, Costa Rica, 74
Fundación Astur, Uruguay, 485
Fundación AVINA, Panama, 247
Fundación Bancaria 'la Caixa', Spain, 288
Fundación Banco Bilbao Vizcaya Argentaria—Fundación BBVA, Spain, 289
Fundación BANHCAFE—FUNBANHCAFE, Honduras, 150
Fundación Barceló, Spain, 289
Fundación Barenboim-Said, Spain, 289
Fundación Bariloche, Argentina, 7
Fundación BBVA, Spain, 289
Fundación Bigott, Venezuela, 487
Fundación Bunge y Born, Argentina, 7
Fundación de las Cajas de Ahorros—FUNCAS, Spain, 289
Fundación Capital, Colombia, 70
Fundación Carlos de Amberes, Spain, 289
Fundación Carlos Slim, Mexico, 215
Fundación Carolina, Spain, 290
Fundación Charles Darwin para las Islas Galápagos—FCD, Ecuador, 88
Fundación Chile—FCH, Chile, 65
Fundación Científica de la Asociación Española Contra el Cáncer—AECC, Spain, 290
Fundación Circulo de Montevideo, Uruguay, 485
Fundación CODESPA, Spain, 290
Fundación Comunitaria de Puerto Rico—FCPR, Puerto Rico, 261
Fundación Corona, Colombia, 71
Fundación para la Defensa de la Naturaleza—FUDENA, Venezuela, 487
Fundación Democracia y Desarrollo, Chile, 65
Fundación DEMUCA—Fundación para el Desarrollo Local y el Fortalecimiento Municipal e Institucional de Centroamérica y el Caribe, Costa Rica, 74
Fundación para el Desarrollo Local y el Fortalecimiento Municipal e Institucional de Centroamérica y el Caribe, Costa Rica, 74
Fundación Dominicana de Desarrollo—FDD, Dominican Republic, 87
Fundación Dr Guillermo Manuel Ungo—FUNDAUNGO, El Salvador, 91
Fundación para la Educación Superior y el Desarrollo—Fedesarrollo, Colombia, 71
Fundación Empresa-Universidad de Zaragoza, Spain, 290
Fundación Empresas Polar, Venezuela, 487
Fundación Escuela Nueva, Colombia, 71
Fundación Espacio Cívico, Panama, 247
Fundación para Estudio e Investigación de la Mujer—FEIM, Argentina, 7
Fundación Eugenio Mendoza—FEM, Venezuela, 487
Fundación Felipe González, Spain, 290
Fundación FEMSA, Mexico, 215
Fundación Fernando Rielo, Spain, 290
Fundación Futuro Latinoamericano, Ecuador, 88
Fundación Génesis Empresarial, Guatemala, 148
Fundación Global Democracia y Desarrollo—FUNGLODE, Dominican Republic, 87
Fundación Grupo Esquel—Ecuador, Ecuador, 88
Fundación Hábitat Colombia—FHC, Colombia, 71
Fundación IE, Spain, 291
Fundación para la Inversión y Desarrollo de Exportaciones—FIDE, Honduras, 150
Fundación de Investigaciones Económicas Latinoamericanas—FIEL, Argentina, 7

Fundacja Rozwoju Demokracji Loaklnej

Fundación Invica, Chile, 65
Fundación José Miguel de Barandiarán, Spain, 291
Fundación José Ortega y Gasset—Gregorio Marañón, Spain, 291
Fundación Juan March, Spain, 291
Fundación Juanelo Turriano, Spain, 291
Fundación Jubileo, Bolivia, 36
Fundación Lealtad, Spain, 285
Fundación Leo Messi, Spain, 292
Fundación Loewe, Spain, 292
Fundación MAPFRE, Spain, 292
Fundación Marcelino Botín, Spain, 292
Fundación María Francisca de Roviralta, Spain, 292
Fundación Mediterránea—IERAL, Argentina, 7
Fundación Miguel Alemán AC, Mexico, 215
Fundación Moisés Bertoni—FMB, Paraguay, 248
Fundación Montemadrid, Spain, 292
Fundación Mujer, Costa Rica, 74
Fundación Mujeres, Spain, 293
Fundación Mujeres en Igualdad—MEI, Argentina, 8
Fundación Nacional para el Desarrollo, El Salvador, 91
Fundación Nacional para el Desarrollo de Honduras—FUNADEH, Honduras, 150
Fundación Nobis, Ecuador, 88
Fundación ONCE, Spain, 293
Fundación Orange, Spain, 293
Fundación Oxfam Intermón, Spain, 293
Fundación Pablo Neruda, Chile, 65
Fundación Paideia Galiza, Spain, 293
Fundación Paraguaya de Cooperación y Desarrollo, Paraguay, 248
Fundación para la Paz y la Democracia—FUNPADEM, Costa Rica, 74
Fundación Pedro Barrié de la Maza, Spain, 293
Fundación Pies Descalzos, Colombia, 71
Fundación Princesa de Asturias, Spain, 294
Fundación Promi, Spain, 294
Fundación Rafa Nadal, Spain, 294
Fundación Rafael del Pino, Spain, 294
Fundación Ramón Areces, Spain, 294
Fundación Real Instituto Elcano, Spain, 294
Fundación Real Madrid, Spain, 295
Fundación Repsol, Spain, 295
Fundación Rigoberta Menchú Tum, Guatemala, 148
Fundación La Salle de Ciencias Naturales—FLASA, Venezuela, 487
Fundación Semah-Valencia, Panama, 247
Fundación SES—Sustentabilidad, Educación, Solidaridad, Argentina, 8
Fundación SM, Spain, 295
Fundación Solidaridad, Dominican Republic, 87
Fundación Tecnologías Sociales—TECSOS, Spain, 296
Fundación Telefónica, Spain, 295
Fundación Telefónica Movistar Argentina, Argentina, 8
Fundación Telefónica Movistar Chile, Chile, 65
Fundación Telefónica Movistar Colombia, Colombia, 71
Fundación Telefónica Movistar Ecuador, Ecuador, 89
Fundación Telefónica Movistar México, Mexico, 216
Fundación Telefónica Movistar Perú, Peru, 249
Fundación Telefónica Movistar Uruguay, Uruguay, 485
Fundación Teletón México, Mexico, 216
Fundación Telmex Telcel, Mexico, 216
Fundación Tigo, Guatemala, 148
Fundación Torcuato Di Tella—FTDT, Argentina, 8
Fundación UNIR Bolivia, Bolivia, 36
Fundación Universidad-Empresa—UE, Spain, 295
Fundación UPM, Uruguay, 485
Fundación Víctimas del Terrorismo, Spain, 296
Fundación de la Vivienda Popular, Venezuela, 488
Fundación Vodafone España, Spain, 296
Fundacja Agory, Poland, 255
Fundacja Auschwitz-Birkenau, Poland, 255
Fundacja Citi Handlowy im. Leopolda Kronenberga, Poland, 255
Fundacja Dobroczynności Atlas, Poland, 255
Fundacja Gospodarcza, Poland, 255
Fundacja im. Stefana Batorego, Poland, 256
Fundacja Orange, Poland, 255
Fundacja Partnerstwo dla Srodowiska, Poland, 256
Fundacja Pogranicze, Poland, 256
Fundacja POLSAT, Poland, 256
Fundacja Pomocy Wzajemnej Barka, Poland, 256
Fundacja Rozwoju Demokracji Loaklnej, Poland, 256

Fundacja Współpracy Polsko-Niemieckiej/ Stiftung für Deutsch-Polnische Zusammenarbeit, Poland, 257
Fundacja Wspomagania Wsi, Poland, 257
FundAction, USA, 394
FUNDAMICRO—Fundación de Capacitación y Asesoría en Microfinanzas, El Salvador, 92
FUNDAP—Fundación para el Desarrollo, Guatemala, 148
Fundasaun Alola, Timor-Leste, 325
Fundasaun Haburas, Timor-Leste, 325
Fundasaun Mahein, Timor-Leste, 325
Fundația Civitas pentru Societatea Civilă, Romania, 263
Fundația pentru Dezvoltarea Societății Civile—FDSC, Romania, 263
Fundația Orange, Romania, 263
Fundația Orange Moldova, Moldova, 217
Fundația Soros—Moldova, Moldova, 217
Fundația Universitară a Mării Negre—FUMN, Romania, 263
Fundația Vodafone România, Romania, 264
FUNDAUNGO—Fundación Dr Guillermo Manuel Ungo, El Salvador, 91
FUNDES—Fundación para el Desarrollo Sostenible de la Pequeña y Mediana Empresa, Costa Rica, 74
Future Foundation, Liechtenstein, 208
Future in Our Hands Youth NGO—FIOH, Armenia, 9
FWF—Österreichischer Wissenschaftsfonds, Austria, 21
FWO—Fonds Wetenschappelijk Onderzoek, Belgium, 32
FXB International—Association François-Xavier Bagnoud, Switzerland, 310
Fyssen Foundation, France, 107

G. Unger Vetlesen Foundation, USA, 429
The Gaia Foundation, UK, 355
GAIA—Groupe d'Action dans l'Intérêt des Animaux, Belgium, 32
Gairdner Foundation, Canada, 55
Gan Foundation for the Cinema, France, 107
Gapminder, Sweden, 300
Garden Organic, UK, 355
Garfield Weston Foundation, UK, 355
Garrone (Edoardo), Fondazione, Italy, 177
Gates (Bill & Melinda) Foundation, USA, 429
Gates Foundation, USA, 429
The Gatsby Charitable Foundation, UK, 355
GE Aerospace Foundation, USA, 429
Gebert Rüf Stiftung, Switzerland, 311
Gemeinnützige Hertie-Stiftung, Germany, 130
The General Kashif Al-Getaa Foundation, Iraq, 164
General Service Foundation—GSF, USA, 430
Génesis Empresarial Foundation, Guatemala, 148
The George A. and Eliza Gardner Howard Foundation, USA, 430
The George I. Alden Trust, USA, 430
George and Thelma Paraskevaides Foundation, Cyprus, 78
Georges Lurcy Charitable and Educational Trust, USA, 430
Georgian Foundation for Strategic and International Studies (Rondeli Foundation)—GFSIS, Georgia, 118
Gerda Henkel Foundation, Germany, 130
Gerda Henkel Stiftung, Germany, 130
German Academic Exchange Service, Germany, 125
German Academic Scholarship Foundation, Germany, 142
German AIDS Foundation, Germany, 124
German Cancer Aid, Germany, 124
German Catholic Bishops' Organization for Development Co-operation, Germany, 137
German Council on Foreign Relations, Germany, 124
German Federal Foundation for the Environment, Germany, 124
German Foundation for International Legal Co-operation, Germany, 133
German Foundation for World Population, Germany, 126
German Institute of Development and Sustainability—IDOS, Germany, 130
German Institute for Global and Area Studies—GIGA, Germany, 130
German Marshall Fund of the United States—GMF, USA, 430
German National Trust, Germany, 125
German Orient Foundation, Germany, 125
German Rheumatism Research Centre Berlin, Germany, 126
German-Russian Exchange, Germany, 124

German Savings Banks Foundation for International Co-operation, Germany, 125
Getty (J. Paul) Trust, USA, 442
Getulio Vargas Foundation, Brazil, 40
Ghazanfar Foundation, Afghanistan, 4
Giangiacomo Feltrinelli Foundation, Italy, 177
GIFE—Grupo de Institutos, Fundações e Empresas, Brazil, 38
Gift of the Givers Foundation, South Africa, 280
Giordano Dell'Amore Social Venture Foundation, Italy, 180
Giorgio Cini Foundation, Italy, 177
Giovanni Agnelli Foundation, Italy, 177
Giovanni Lorenzini Foundation, Italy, 177
Giovanni Paolo I, Fondazione Vaticana, Vatican City, 486
Giulio Pastore Foundation, Italy, 178
To Give, Israel, 170
Give Foundation, India, 155
Give2Asia, USA, 394
GiveIndia, India, 155
GiveWell—The Clear Fund, USA, 430
Giving USA Foundation, USA, 394
Glaser (Elizabeth) Pediatric AIDS Foundation, USA, 423
Glasnost Defence Foundation, Russian Federation, 265
Global Action in the Interest of Animals, Belgium, 32
Global Communities, USA, 431
Global Democracy and Development Foundation, Dominican Republic, 87
Global Dialogue, UK, 336
Global Environmental Action—GEA, Japan, 187
Global Ethic Foundation, Germany, 141
The Global Foodbanking Network—GFN, USA, 431
Global Forest Fund, Denmark, 83
Global Fund for Children, USA, 431
Global Fund for Community Foundations—GFCF, South Africa, 278
Global Fund for Women—GFW, USA, 431
Global Greengrants Fund, USA, 431
Global Health Council, USA, 395
Global Health Partnerships, UK, 355
Global Impact, USA, 395
Global Innovation Fund, UK, 356
Global Philanthropy Forum, USA, 395
Global Schools Forum, UK, 341
Globetree Association, Sweden, 300
GLOBSEC, Slovakia, 275
GOAL, Ireland, 166
Gobabeb Namib Research Institute, Namibia, 222
Goethe-Institut, Germany, 131
Goldman Sachs Foundation, USA, 432
Goldsmith (Horace W.) Foundation, USA, 436
Goncourt Academy—Goncourt Literary Society, France, 100
Good Neighbors International, Korea (Republic), 201
Good Things Foundation, UK, 356
Good2Give, Australia, 10
Good360, USA, 432
Goodenough College, UK, 356
Goodwill Industries International, Inc—GII, USA, 432
Google.org—Google Foundation, USA, 432
Gorbachev Foundation, Russian Federation, 266
Gordon and Betty Moore Foundation, USA, 432
Gordon (Walter and Duncan) Charitable Foundation, Canada, 62
Gottlieb (Adolph and Esther) Foundation, Inc, USA, 397
Gould (Florence) Foundation, USA, 427
Graça Machel Trust, South Africa, 280
Gradjanske inicijative—GI, Serbia, 271
Graduate Institute of International Studies and Development Studies, Switzerland, 311
Graham Foundation for Advanced Studies in the Fine Arts—GF, USA, 432
Grameen Foundation—GF, USA, 433
Grant (William T.) Foundation, USA, 481
The Grass Foundation, USA, 433
Grassroots International—GRI, USA, 433
Great Britain Sasakawa Foundation, UK, 356
Great Ormond Street Hospital Children's Charity, UK, 356
Greater Kansas City Community Foundation, USA, 433
Green Umbrella Children's Foundation—ChildFund Korea, Korea (Republic), 201
The Greta Thunberg Foundation, Sweden, 300
Grinspoon (Harold) Foundation, USA, 434
Group of Foundations and Businesses, Argentina, 6
Group of Institutes, Foundations and Enterprises, Brazil, 38

Groupe d'Action dans l'Intérêt des Animaux—GAIA, Belgium, 32
Grupa Zagranica, Poland, 254
Grupo de Fundaciones y Empresas, Argentina, 6
Grupo Social Fondo Ecuatoriano Populorum Progressio, Ecuador, 89
Gruss (Joseph S. and Caroline) Memorial Fund, Israel, 170
Guardian Foundation, Timor-Leste, 325
Guggenheim (Harry Frank) Foundation, USA, 434
Guggenheim (John Simon) Memorial Foundation, USA, 444
Guggenheim (Solomon R.) Foundation, USA, 473
The Guide Dogs for the Blind Association, UK, 357
GuideStar, USA, 393
GuideStar India, India, 155
Gulbenkian (Calouste), Fundação, Portugal, 259
Gulf Research Center—GRC, Saudi Arabia, 269
GURT Resource Centre for NGO Development, Ukraine, 332

H&M Foundation, Sweden, 300
Habitat for Humanity International, USA, 433
Haburas Foundation, Timor-Leste, 325
Hagar NZ, New Zealand, 233
Haiti Development Institute—HDI, Haiti, 149
HALO Trust, UK, 357
Hamdard Foundation Pakistan, Pakistan, 245
Hamlyn (Paul) Foundation, UK, 373
Hammarskjölds (Dag) Minnesfond, Stiftelsen, Sweden, 303
Hanaholmen—Swedish-Finnish Cultural Centre, Finland, 95
HAND—Hungarian Association of NGOs for Development and Humanitarian Aid, Hungary, 152
Haniel Foundation, Germany, 131
Haniel-Stiftung, Germany, 131
Hanns Seidel Foundation, Germany, 131
Hanns-Seidel-Stiftung eV, Germany, 131
Hans Wilsdorf Foundation, Switzerland, 309
Haribon Foundation for the Conservation of Natural Resources, Inc, Philippines, 252
Hariri Foundation for Sustainable Human Development, Lebanon, 205
Harold Grinspoon Foundation, USA, 434
Harp Helú Foundations, Mexico, 216
The Harry Frank Guggenheim Foundation—HFG, USA, 434
Harry and Jeanette Weinberg Foundation, Inc, USA, 434
Hartford (John A.) Foundation, Inc, USA, 443
Hasbro Childrens Trust, USA, 434
Hasbro Foundation, USA, 434
Hassan II Foundation for Moroccans Living Abroad, Morocco, 220
Havelaar (Max) Foundation, Netherlands, 230
Hawaii Resilience Fund, USA, 458
He Xiangjian Foundation, China (People's Republic), 68
Headley Trust, UK, 357
Health Action International—HAI, Netherlands, 225
The Health Foundation, UK, 357
Health Volunteers Overseas—HVO, USA, 434
Hearst Foundations, USA, 435
Heart & Stroke, Canada, 56
Heart to Heart International—HHI, USA, 435
Hecht (Lotte and John) Memorial Foundation, Canada, 58
Hedwig and Robert Samuel Foundation, Germany, 131
Hedwig und Robert Samuel-Stiftung, Germany, 131
Heifer Foundation, USA, 435
Heineken Prizes for Arts and Sciences, Netherlands, 225
Heinekenprijzen voor kunst en wetenschap, Netherlands, 225
Heineman (Minna-James) Stiftung, Germany, 136
Heinrich Böll Foundation, Germany, 131
Heinrich-Böll-Stiftung, Germany, 131
HEKS—Hilfswerk der Evangelischen Kirchen Schweiz, Switzerland, 311
Helen Keller International—HKI, USA, 435
Hellenic Foundation for Culture, Greece, 145
Hellenic Foundation for European and Foreign Policy—ELIAMEP, Greece, 146
Helmholtz Association, Germany, 132
Helmholtz-Gemeinschaft, Germany, 132
Helmich (Janson Johan og Marcia) Legat, Norway, 242
Helmsley (Leona M. and Harry B.) Charitable Trust, USA, 447
Helmut Horten Foundation, Switzerland, 311
Helmut-Horten-Stiftung, Switzerland, 311

INDEX OF FOUNDATIONS

HelpAge International, UK, 357
Helsińska Fundacja Praw Człowieka, Poland, 257
Helsingin Sanomain Säätiö, Finland, 96
Helsingin Sanomat Foundation, Finland, 96
Helsinki Foundation for Human Rights, Poland, 257
Helvetas Swiss Intercooperation, Switzerland, 311
Hempel Fonden, Denmark, 84
Hempel Foundation, Denmark, 84
Henie Onstad Art Centre, Norway, 241
Henie Onstad Kunstsenter, Norway, 241
Henkel (Gerda) Stiftung, Germany, 130
Henri Cartier-Bresson Foundation, France, 107
Henrietta Szold Institute—National Institute for Research in the Behavioural Sciences, Israel, 169
Henry Doubleday Research Association, UK, 355
Henry J. Kaiser Family Foundation—KFF, USA, 435
Henry Luce Foundation, Inc, USA, 435
The Henry Moore Foundation, UK, 358
The Henry Smith Charity, UK, 358
HER Fund, Hong Kong, 151
Heren Philanthropic Foundation, China (People's Republic), 68
Heritage Foundation, France, 110
Heritage Institute for Policy Studies—HIPS, Somalia, 277
Hertie Foundation, Germany, 130
HESTIA, Czech Republic, 78
Heungkong Charitable Foundation, China (People's Republic), 68
Hewlett (William and Flora) Foundation, USA, 481
Heydar Aliyev Fondu, Azerbaijan, 23
Heydar Aliyev Foundation, Azerbaijan, 23
HIAS—Hebrew Immigrant Aid Society, USA, 436
Hicter (Marcel), Fondation, Belgium, 32
Higgins (Terrence) Trust, UK, 385
Higherlife Foundation, Zimbabwe, 491
Hilti Foundation, Liechtenstein, 208
Hilton (Conrad N.) Foundation, USA, 417
Himalaya Research and Development Foundation—Himalaya Foundation, Taiwan, 321
Hinduja Foundation, India, 157
HIPS—Heritage Institute for Policy Studies, Somalia, 277
Hirschfeld-Eddy Foundation, Germany, 132
Hirschfeld-Eddy-Stiftung, Germany, 132
Hisar Education Foundation—HEV, Türkiye, 328
Historic Environment Scotland, UK, 358
History Foundation of Turkey, Türkiye, 329
Hitachi Foundation, Japan, 187
Hivos—Humanistisch Instituut voor Ontwikkelings Samenwerking, Netherlands, 226
HJ Foundation, Congo (Democratic Republic), 72
Hjärt-Lungfonden, Sweden, 300
Hodge Foundation, UK, 358
Hollows (Fred) Foundation, Australia, 14
Holt International, USA, 436
The Home Depot Foundation, USA, 436
Homeless World Cup Foundation—HWCF, UK, 358
Honda Foundation, Japan, 187
Hong Kong Council of Social Service—HKCSS, Hong Kong, 150
Hong Kong Society for the Blind, Hong Kong, 151
Hope, Ireland, 165
Hope Foundation, Türkiye, 331
HOPE International Development Agency, Canada, 56
Hope not Hate Charitable Trust—HNHCT, UK, 358
Hopp (Dietmar) Stiftung, Germany, 126
Horace W. Goldsmith Foundation, USA, 436
Horizons of Friendship, Canada, 56
Hormuud Salaam Foundation, Somalia, 277
Horn Economic and Social Policy Institute—HESPI, Ethiopia, 94
Hornby (A. S.) Educational Trust, UK, 338
Horten (Helmut) Stiftung, Switzerland, 311
Hoso Bunka Foundation, Inc—HBF, Japan, 188
Houphouët-Boigny (Félix), Fondation, Côte d'Ivoire, 75
House of the Human Sciences Foundation, France, 108
The Howard G. Buffett Foundation, USA, 437
Howard (George A. and Eliza Gardner) Foundation, USA, 430
Howard Hughes Medical Institute—HHMI, USA, 437
Howard Karagheusian Commemorative Corporation—HKCC, USA, 437
Howard (Katharine) Foundation, Ireland, 167
Hudson Institute, USA, 437

Hulot (Nicolas), Fondation, France, 110
Human Dignity Trust, UK, 359
Human Resource Development Foundation, Türkiye, 329
Human Rights Foundation of Turkey, Türkiye, 330
Human Rights Funders Network—HRFN, USA, 395
Human Rights House Foundation—HRHF, Norway, 241
Human Rights Information and Training Center—HRITC, Yemen, 489
Human Rights Watch—HRW, USA, 437
Humanistic Institute for Co-operation with Developing Countries, Netherlands, 226
Humanitarian Academy for Development—HAD, UK, 359
Humanitarian Coalition, Canada, 48
Humanity & Inclusion, France, 113
Humanity United, USA, 438
von Humboldt (Alexander) Stiftung, Germany, 120
Humboldt Forum, Germany, 132
Hungarian Donors Forum, Hungary, 152
The Hunger Project, USA, 438
The Hunter Foundation—THF, UK, 359

IACD—Institute of Asian Culture and Development, Korea (Republic), 201
IAESTE—International Association for the Exchange of Students for Technical Experience, Luxembourg, 210
IAI—Istituto Affari Internazionali, Italy, 182
Ian Potter Foundation, Australia, 14
IARC—International Agency for Research on Cancer, France, 101
Ibero-American Network of Community Foundations, Brazil, 38
IBM International Foundation, USA, 438
IBON Foundation, Philippines, 252
Ibrahim (Mo) Foundation, UK, 368
Icelandic Human Rights Centre, Iceland, 154
Ichikowitz Family Foundation—IFF, South Africa, 280
ICRC—International Red Cross and Red Crescent Movement, Switzerland, 312
ICVA—International Council of Voluntary Agencies, Switzerland, 305
The Ideas Institute, Kenya, 199
IDLO—International Development Law Organization, Italy, 181
IDRF—International Development and Relief Foundation, Canada, 56
Idrima Kratikon Ipotrofion, Greece, 147
IE Foundation, Spain, 291
IFAD—International Fund for Agricultural Development, Italy, 182
IFAW—International Fund for Animal Welfare, USA, 438
IFES—International Foundation for Electoral Systems, USA, 440
IFRISSE Burkina, Burkina Faso, 45
IHH Humanitarian Relief Foundation, Türkiye, 328
IIAP—Instituto de Investigaciones de la Amazonía Peruana, Peru, 249
IIED—International Institute for Environment and Development, UK, 360
IISD—International Institute for Sustainable Development, Canada, 57
IJ4EU—Investigative Journalism for Europe, Austria, 21
IKEA Foundation, Netherlands, 229
IKGV—İnsan Kaynağını Geliştirme Vakfı, Türkiye, 329
İktisadi Kalkınma Vakfı, Türkiye, 328
IKY—State Scholarships Foundation, Greece, 147
Îles de Paix, Belgium, 32
IMADR—The International Movement against All Forms of Discrimination and Racism, Japan, 188
Imagine Canada, Canada, 48
Imbuto Foundation, Rwanda, 268
Impact Europe, Belgium, 27
IMPACT Transformer la Gestion des Ressources Naturelles, Canada, 56
IMPACT Transforming Natural Resource Management, Canada, 56
Improving Economies for Stronger Communities—IESC, USA, 438
Inamori Foundation, Japan, 188
Inclusion International, UK, 359
Independent Sector, USA, 395
India Partners, USA, 438
Indian Council for Cultural Relations, India, 157
Indian Council of Social Science Research—ICSSR, India, 157

Institute of Social Studies

Indian National Trust for Art and Cultural Heritage—INTACH, India, 158
Indonesia Biodiversity Foundation, Indonesia, 162
Indonesian Forum for the Environment—Friends of the Earth Indonesia, Indonesia, 162
INEDIVIM—Foundation of Youth and Lifelong Learning, Greece, 145
Information and Education Centre for the Prevention of Drug Abuse, Peru, 248
Ingmar Bergman Foundation, Sweden, 303
INHURED International—International Institute for Human Rights, Environment and Development, Nepal, 223
Initiative Bürgerstiftungen, Germany, 119
Inlaks Shivdasani Foundation, India, 158
Innovators and Entrepreneurs Foundation/Fondation d'Innovateurs et d'Entrepreneurs—IEF/FIE, Canada, 57
İnsan Hak ve Hürriyetleri İnsani Yardım Vakfı—IHH, Türkiye, 328
İnsan Kaynağını Geliştirme Vakfı—IKGV, Türkiye, 329
Institusjonen Fritt Ord, Norway, 241
Institut Arctique de l'Amérique du Nord—IAAN, Canada, 49
Institut Europeu de la Mediterrània—IEMed, Spain, 296
Institut FMES—Institut Méditerranéen d'Etudes Stratégiques, France, 113
Institut Français des Relations Internationales—IFRI, France, 113
Institut de Hautes Études Internationales et du Développement—IHEID, Switzerland, 311
Institut International des Droits de l'Enfant, Switzerland, 312
Institut de Médecine et d'Epidémiologie Appliquée—Fondation Internationale Léon Mba, France, 114
Institut for Menneskerettigheder, Denmark, 84
Institut Mittag-Leffler, Sweden, 300
Institut Océanographique—Fondation Albert 1er, Prince de Monaco, France, 114
Institut Pasteur, France, 114
Institut Pasteur de Lille, France, 114
Institut de Recherche Empirique en Économie Politique—IREEP, Benin, 35
Institut Royal des Relations Internationales—EGMONT, Belgium, 29
Institut für Weltwirtschaft—IfW Kiel, Germany, 132
Institute of Applied Medicine and Epidemiology—International Foundation Léon Mba, France, 114
Institute of Asian Culture and Development—IACD, Korea (Republic), 201
Institute of Baltic Studies, Estonia, 92
Institute of British Geographers, UK, 378
Institute for Citizens & Scholars, USA, 439
Institute of Developing Economies-Japan External Trade Organization—IDE-JETRO, Japan, 188
Institute for the Development of Social Investment, Brazil, 38
Institute of Economic Affairs—IEA, UK, 359
Institute for Empirical Research in Political Economy—IERPE, Benin, 35
The Institute of Energy Economics, Japan—IEEJ, Japan, 188
Institute for European Environmental Policy—IEEP, Belgium, 33
Institute of International Affairs, Italy, 182
Institute of International Education—IIE, USA, 439
Institute of International Law, Argentina, 6
Institute for International Security and Strategic Affairs—ISIAE, Argentina, 6
Institute for Iran-Eurasia Studies—IRAS, Iran, 163
Institute for Latin American and Caribbean Integration, Argentina, 8
Institute for Palestine Studies—IPS, Lebanon, 206
Institute for Policy and Legal Studies—IPLS, Albania, 4
Institute for Precision Cardiovascular Medicine, USA, 401
Institute for Private Enterprise and Democracy—IPED, Poland, 257
Institute for Research on the Peruvian Amazon, Peru, 249
Institute for Scientific Interchange Foundation—ISI, Italy, 181
Institute for Security Studies—ISS, South Africa, 280
Institute of Social Studies—ISS, Netherlands, 226

Institute for Sustainable Communities—ISC, USA, 439
Instituti Kosovar për Kërkime dhe Zhvillim të Politikave, Kosovo, 203
Instituto Ayrton Senna, Brazil, 41
Instituto para o Desenvolvimento do Investimento Social—IDIS, Brazil, 38
Instituto Europeo de Salud y Bienestar Social, Spain, 296
Instituto para la Integración de América Latina y el Caribe—BID-INTAL, Argentina, 8
Instituto Interamericano de Derechos Humanos—IIDH, Costa Rica, 74
Instituto de Montaña, Peru, 249
Institutul Cultural Român—ICR, Romania, 264
Instytut Badań nad Demokracją i Przedsiębiorstwem Prywatnym, Poland, 257
INTACH—Indian National Trust for Art and Cultural Heritage, India, 158
INTEGRATA Foundation, Germany, 132
INTEGRATA—Stiftung für Humane Nutzung der Informationstechnologie, Germany, 132
Integrated Rural Development Foundation—IRDF, Philippines, 252
Inter-American Foundation—IAF, USA, 439
Inter-American Institute of Human Rights, Costa Rica, 74
Inter Pares, Canada, 57
InterAction, USA, 395
Interchurch Aid—HIA Hungary, Hungary, 153
Internationaal Instituut voor Sociale Geschiedenis—IISG, Netherlands, 226
International Agency for Research on Cancer—IARC, France, 101
International Alert—Alert, UK, 360
International Arctic Science Committee—IASC, Iceland, 154
International Association of Charities, Belgium, 28
International Baccalaureate—IB, Switzerland, 312
International Balzan Prize Foundation, Italy, 181
International Blue Crescent Relief and Development Foundation—IBC, Türkiye, 329
International Center for Not-for-Profit Law—ICNL, USA, 396
International Center for Research on Women—ICRW, USA, 439
International Center for Transitional Justice—ICTJ, USA, 440
International Centre for Defence and Security—ICDS, Estonia, 93
International Charitable Fund 'Concord 3000', Ukraine, 333
International Civil Society Centre, Germany, 119
International College of Surgeons—ICS, USA, 440
International Confederation Catholic Organizations Charitable Social Action, Vatican City, 486
International Co-operation, Italy, 173
International Council of Voluntary Agencies—ICVA, Switzerland, 305
International Development Center of Japan, Japan, 189
International Development Law Organization—IDLO, Italy, 181
International Development and Relief Foundation—IDRF, Canada, 56
International Education Research Foundation, Inc—IERF, USA, 440
International Eye Foundation—IEF, USA, 440
International Federation of Human Rights, France, 99
International Forum Bosnia, Bosnia and Herzegovina, 37
International Forum for Social Innovation—IFSI, France, 112
The International Foundation, USA, 440
International Foundation for Electoral Systems—IFES, USA, 440
International Foundation of the High-Altitude Research Stations Jungfraujoch and Gornergrat, Switzerland, 313
International Foundation for the Protection of Human Rights Defenders, Ireland, 166
International Foundation for Science—IFS, Sweden, 300
International Foundation for Socio-economic and Political Studies, Russian Federation, 266
International Fund for Agricultural Development—IFAD, Italy, 182
Internationaal Fund for Animal Welfare—IFAW, USA, 438
International Historical, Educational, Charitable and Human Rights Society—International Memorial, Russian Federation, 266

International Institute for Applied Systems Analysis—IIASA, Austria, 21
International Institute for Environment and Development—IIED, UK, 360
International Institute for Human Rights, Environment and Development, Nepal, 223
International Institute for the Rights of the Child, Switzerland, 312
International Institute of Rural Reconstruction—IIRR, Philippines, 252
International Institute of Social History—IISH, Netherlands, 226
International Institute of Social Studies, Netherlands, 226
The International Institute for Strategic Studies—IISS, UK, 360
International Institute for Sustainable Development—IISD, Canada, 57
International Institute of Tropical Agriculture—IITA, Nigeria, 237
International Lake Environment Committee Foundation, Japan, 189
International Latsis Foundation, Switzerland, 309
International Maize and Wheat Improvement Center, Mexico, 215
International Medical Assistance Foundation, Portugal, 258
International Memorial, Russian Federation, 266
International Music and Art Foundation, Liechtenstein, 208
International NGO Charter of Accountability, USA, 393
International NGO Coordination Committee in CAR, Central African Republic, 63
International NGO Forum on Indonesian Development—INFID, Indonesia, 161
International Office for Water, France, 115
International Organization for Relief, Welfare & Development—IORWD, Saudi Arabia, 269
International Orthodox Christian Charities—IOCC, USA, 441
International Penal and Penitentiary Foundation—IPPF, Netherlands, 226
International Planned Parenthood Federation—IPPF, UK, 360
International Press Institute—IPI, Austria, 21
International Red Cross and Red Crescent Movement—ICRC, Switzerland, 312
International Relief Teams—IRT, USA, 441
International Renaissance Foundation—IRF, Ukraine, 333
International Rescue Committee—IRC, USA, 441
International Research & Exchanges Board—IREX, USA, 442
International Research Foundation, Oman, 244
International Rhino Foundation—IRF, USA, 441
International Rivers, USA, 441
International Service for Human Rights—ISHR, Switzerland, 312
International Society for Human Rights—ISHR, Germany, 133
International Solidarity Foundation, Finland, 96
International Union for Conservation of Nature and Natural Resources, Switzerland, 313
International University Centre of Paris Foundation, France, 104
International Visegrad Fund—IVF, Slovakia, 275
International Water Management Institute—IWMI, Sri Lanka, 297
International Women's Health Coalition, USA, 427
International Work Group for Indigenous Affairs—IWGIA, Denmark, 84
International Youth Foundation—IYF, USA, 442
International Youth Library Foundation, Germany, 133
Internationale Jugendbibliothek, Germany, 133
Internationale Stiftung Hochalpine Forschungsstationen Jungfraujoch und Gornergrat, Switzerland, 313
Internationale Stiftung Preis E. Balzan-Fonds, Italy, 181
Internationalt Uddannelsescenter, Denmark, 84
INTERSOS, Italy, 182
INTRAC, UK, 337
Invica Foundation, Chile, 65
IOCC—International Orthodox Christian Charities, USA, 441
Iochpe Foundation, Brazil, 40
iPartner India, India, 155
IPPF—International Planned Parenthood Federation, UK, 360
Iraqi Institute for Economic Reform, Iraq, 164
IRC—International Rescue Committee, USA, 441
The Ireland Funds America, USA, 442
IREX—International Research & Exchanges Board, USA, 442

Irish Youth Foundation, Ireland, 167
Irvine (James) Foundation, USA, 443
IRZ (Deutsche Stiftung für Internationale Rechtliche Zusammenarbeit) eV, Germany, 133
Isabel Allende Foundation, USA, 442
Islamic Relief Worldwide, UK, 360
Islands of Peace, Belgium, 32
ISMU Foundation—Initiatives and Studies on Multi-ethnicity, Italy, 178
ISPI—Istituto per gli Studi di Politica Internazionale, Italy, 183
IsraAID, Israel, 169
The Israel Democracy Institute—IDI, Israel, 170
ISREC Foundation, Switzerland, 309
Istituto Affari Internazionali—IAI, Italy, 182
Istituto Carlo Cattaneo, Italy, 182
Istituto Luigi Sturzo, Italy, 182
Istituto di Ricerche Farmacologiche Mario Negri, Italy, 182
Istituto per gli Studi di Politica Internazionale—ISPI, Italy, 183
Istituto Svedese di Studi Classici a Roma, Italy, 183
Italian Association of Foundations and Institutional Philanthropy Bodies, Italy, 171
Italian Institute for International Political Studies, Italy, 183
ITS Foundation, Italy, 178
IUC International Education Center—IUC-Europe, Denmark, 84
IUCN/UICN, Switzerland, 313
Ivey Foundation, Canada, 57
Ivorian Economic and Social Research Centre, Côte d'Ivoire, 75
Iwatani Naoji Foundation, Japan, 189
Izumi Foundation, USA, 442

The J. F. Costopoulos Foundation, Greece, 146
J. F. Kapnek Zimbabwe, Zimbabwe, 491
J-Louis Lévesque Foundation, Canada, 55
J. Paul Getty Trust, USA, 442
J. R. McKenzie Trust, New Zealand, 233
The J.W. McConnell Family Foundation, Canada, 57
Jack Ma Foundation—JMF, China (People's Republic), 68
Jacobs Foundation, Switzerland, 313
Jacques Chirac Foundation, France, 107
Jahnsson (Yrjö) Foundation, Finland, 98
Jahres (Anders) Humanitære Stiftelse, Norway, 240
J'ai Rêvé Foundation, Central African Republic, 63
The James Irvine Foundation, USA, 443
James Michel Foundation, Seychelles, 272
James S. McDonnell Foundation, USA, 443
Jan Hus Educational Foundation, Czech Republic, 81
Jane Coffin Childs Memorial Fund for Medical Research—JCC Fund, USA, 443
JANIC—Japanese NGO Center for International Co-operation, Japan, 185
Janson Johan Helmich and Marcia Jansons Endowment, Norway, 242
Janson Johan Helmich og Marcia Jansons Legat, Norway, 242
Japan Association of Charitable Organizations—JACO, Japan, 185
Japan Economic Research Institute Inc—JERI, Japan, 189
The Japan Foundation, Japan, 189
Japan Foundation Center, Japan, 185
Japan Foundation Center for Economic Research—JCER, Japan, 189
Japan Foundation Endowment Committee—JFEC, UK, 361
Japan Heart Foundation, Japan, 190
Japan International Volunteer Center—JVC, Japan, 190
Japan Society for the Promotion of Science—JSPS, Japan, 190
Japanese-German Centre Berlin, Germany, 133
Japanisch-Deutsches Zentrum Berlin, Germany, 133
Jasmine Foundation for Research and Communication, Tunisia, 326
Jaurès (Jean), Fondation, France, 107
Jazz Foundation of America—JFA, USA, 443
JCA Charitable Foundation, UK, 361
Jean Dausset Foundation—Centre for the Study of Human Polymorphism, France, 107
Jean Jaurès Foundation, France, 107
Jean Monnet Foundation for Europe, Switzerland, 309
Jeans for Genes, Australia, 13
JEN, Japan, 190
Jenny and Antti Wihuri Foundation, Finland, 96
Jenny ja Antti Wihurin Rahasto, Finland, 96

INDEX OF FOUNDATIONS

JERI—Japan Economic Research Institute Inc, Japan, 189
Jerusalem Foundation, Israel, 170
The Jerusalem Trust, UK, 361
JFEC—Japan Foundation Endowment Committee, UK, 361
JIIA—Japan Institute of International Affairs, Japan, 190
JN Foundation, Jamaica, 184
JNF UK—JNF Charitable Trust, UK, 361
Johanna Quandt Foundation, Germany, 133
Johanna-Quandt-Stiftung, Germany, 133
The John A. Hartford Foundation—JAHF, USA, 443
The John D. and Catherine T. MacArthur Foundation, USA, 444
John Ellerman Foundation, UK, 361
John Innes Foundation—JIF, UK, 362
John Moores Foundation, UK, 362
John Paul I Vatican Foundation, Vatican City, 486
John Paul II Foundation for the Sahel, Burkina Faso, 44
John S. and James L. Knight Foundation, USA, 444
John Simon Guggenheim Memorial Foundation, USA, 444
John Templeton Foundation, USA, 444
Johnson & Johnson Foundation US—JJF, USA, 444
The Johnson Foundation at Wingspread, USA, 444
Johnson (Lyndon Baines) Foundation, USA, 449
Johnson (Stanley Thomas) Foundation, Switzerland, 317
JOHUD—Jordanian Hashemite Fund for Human Development, Jordan, 196
Jordan River Foundation, Jordan, 196
José Maria Neves Foundation for Governance, Cabo Verde, 46
José Miguel de Barandiarán Foundation, Spain, 291
José Ortega y Gasset—Gregorio Marañón Foundation, Spain, 291
Joseph Levy Foundation, UK, 362
Joseph Patrick Trust, UK, 369
Joseph Rowntree Charitable Trust—JRCT, UK, 362
Joseph Rowntree Foundation—JRF, UK, 362
Joseph Rowntree Reform Trust Ltd (including the JRSST Charitable Trust), UK, 362
Joseph S. and Caroline Gruss Memorial Fund for the Advancement of Veterans, Israel, 170
Joseph Tanenbaum Charitable Foundation, Canada, 58
Josiah Macy Jr Foundation, USA, 445
Joyce Banda Foundation International, Malawi, 210
Joyce Foundation, USA, 445
JPB Foundation, USA, 428
JPMorgan Chase Foundation, USA, 445
JRSST Charitable Trust, UK, 362
Juan March Foundation, Spain, 291
Juanelo Turriano Foundation, Spain, 291
Jubilee Foundation, Bolivia, 36
Jubilee USA Network, USA, 445
Jung (C. G.) Institut Zürich, Switzerland, 307
Jusélius (Sigrid) Stiftelse, Finland, 97
Juvenile Diabetes Research Foundation International, USA, 409

Kade (Max) Foundation, Inc, USA, 451
Kadın Emeğini Değerlendirme Vakfı—KEDV, Türkiye, 329
KAF—Kataliko Actions for Africa, Congo (Democratic Republic), 72
Kafaa Development Foundation, Libya, 207
Kaiser (Henry J.) Family Foundation, USA, 435
Kajima Foundation, Japan, 191
Kamel Lazaar Foundation—KLF, Tunisia, 327
Kansainvälinen solidaarisuussäätiö, Finland, 96
Kapnek (J. F.) Charitable Trust Zimbabwe, Zimbabwe, 491
Karagheusian (Howard) Commemorative Corporation, USA, 437
Kárpátok Alapítvány, Hungary, 153
Karuna Trust, UK, 363
Katharine Howard Foundation—KHF, Ireland, 167
KAUTE Foundation, Finland, 96
KAUTE-säätiö, Finland, 96
Kayany Foundation, Lebanon, 206
KCDF—Kenya Community Development Foundation, Kenya, 199
KDDI Foundation, Japan, 191
KEHATI—Yayasan Keanekaragaman Hayati Indonesia, Indonesia, 162
Keller (Helen) International, USA, 435
Kellogg (W. K.) Foundation, USA, 478

Kennedy Memorial Trust, UK, 363
Kettering (Charles F.) Foundation, USA, 445
Kettering Foundation—KF, USA, 445
Khalifa Bin Zayed Al Nahyan Foundation, United Arab Emirates, 334
Khemka (Nand & Jeet) Foundation, India, 159
KIEDF—Koret Israel Economic Development Funds, Israel, 170
Kiel Institute for the World Economy, Germany, 132
Kind Heart Foundation, Viet Nam, 488
King Abdul-Aziz al-Saoud Foundation for Islamic Study and the Humanities, Morocco, 220
King Baudouin Foundation, Belgium, 33
King Faisal Foundation, Saudi Arabia, 269
King Gustaf V's 90th Birthday Foundation, Sweden, 301
King Hussein Foundation—KHF, Jordan, 196
King Khalid Foundation, Saudi Arabia, 269
King Philanthropies, USA, 445
King Sejong Institute Foundation—KSIF, Korea (Republic), 201
The King's Foundation, UK, 363
The King's Fund, UK, 363
The King's Trust, UK, 363
KIOS Foundation, Finland, 96
Kiwanis Children's Fund, USA, 446
KK-stiftelsen, Sweden, 301
Klassik Stiftung Weimar, Germany, 134
Klaus Tschira Foundation, Germany, 134
Klaus Tschira Stiftung GmbH, Germany, 134
Kleinwort (Ernest) Charitable Trust, UK, 353
Klon/Jawor Association, Poland, 254
Knight (John S. and James L.) Foundation, USA, 444
Knowledge Foundation, Sweden, 301
Knox (Frank) Memorial Fellowships, USA, 428
Knut and Alice Wallenberg Foundation, Sweden, 301
Knut och Alice Wallenbergs Stiftelse, Sweden, 301
Koç (Vehbi), Vakfı, Türkiye, 331
Koch (Charles) Foundation, USA, 413
Koch Foundation, Inc, USA, 446
Kofi Annan Foundation, Switzerland, 313
Kokkalis Foundation, Greece, 146
Komen (Susan G.) Breast Cancer Foundation, USA, 474
Koning Boudewijnstichting/Fondation Roi Baudouin, Belgium, 33
Koninklijke Hollandsche Maatschappij der Wetenschappen, Netherlands, 226
Konrad Adenauer Foundation, Germany, 134
Konrad-Adenauer-Stiftung eV—KAS, Germany, 134
Konsultatsiis da Treningis Tsentri, Georgia, 117
Konung Gustaf V's 90-Årsfond, Sweden, 301
Konzorcijum nezavisnih istraživačkih centara Zapadnog Balkana, Serbia, 271
Körber Foundation, Germany, 134
Körber-Stiftung, Germany, 134
The Korea Foundation, Korea (Republic), 202
Koret Foundation, USA, 446
Koret Israel Economic Development Funds—KIEDF, Israel, 170
The Kosciuszko Foundation, Inc, USA, 446
Kosovar Civil Society Foundation—KCSF, Kosovo, 202
Kosovar Institute for Policy Research and Development—KIPRED, Kosovo, 203
Kosovo Foundation for Open Society—KFOS, Kosovo, 203
Kostova (Elizabeth) Foundation for Creative Writing, Bulgaria, 43
Kresge Foundation, USA, 446
Kress (Samuel H.) Foundation, USA, 469
Kronenberg (Leopold) Foundation, Poland, 255
Kröner-Fresenius (Else) Stiftung, Germany, 127
Krupp von Bohlen und Halbach (Alfried) Stiftung, Germany, 121
Kulika Charitable Trust Uganda, Uganda, 331
Kulturfonden för Sverige och Finland, Sweden, 301
Kulturstiftung der Länder—KSL, Germany, 134
Kulturstiftung Liechtenstein, Liechtenstein, 208
Kuok Foundation Berhad, Malaysia, 211
Kusuma Trust UK, UK, 363
Kuwait Awqaf Public Foundation, Kuwait, 203
Kuwait Foundation for the Advancement of Sciences—KFAS, Kuwait, 203
Kuwait Institute for Scientific Research—KISR, Kuwait, 203

Kvinna till Kvinna, Sweden, 301
KWF Dutch Cancer Society, Netherlands, 227
KWF Kankerbestrijding, Netherlands, 227

'La Caixa' Banking Foundation, Spain, 288

Li Ka Shing Foundation

La Salle Foundation for Natural Sciences, Venezuela, 487
Lady Davis Fellowship Trust, Israel, 170
Lady Khama Charitable Trust, Botswana, 37
Lafede.cat—Federació d'Organitzacions per a la Justícia Global, Spain, 286
Lafede.cat—Federation of Organizations for Global Justice, Spain, 286
Laidlaw Foundation, UK, 364
Laing Family Trusts, UK, 364
Laing (J. W.) Trust, UK, 384
Lambrakis Foundation, Greece, 146
Land Network, Timor-Leste, 325
Landesa—Rural Development Institute, USA, 447
Landis & Gyr Foundation, Switzerland, 313
Landis & Gyr Stiftung, Switzerland, 313
Lannan Foundation, USA, 447
LAPAS—Latvijas platforma attīstības sadarbībai, Latvia, 204
Latet Israeli Humanitarian Aid, Israel, 170
Latimpacto—Red Latinoamericana de Inversión Social y Filantropía Estratégica, Colombia, 71
Latin America France, France, 112
Latin American, African and Asian Social Housing Service, Chile, 66
Latin American Association of Development Financing Institutions, Peru, 248
Latin American and Caribbean Committee for the Defence of Women's Rights, Peru, 249
Latin American and Caribbean Women's Health Network—LACWHN, Ecuador, 89
Latin American Council of Social Sciences, Argentina, 6
Latin American Future Foundation, Ecuador, 88
Latin American Network for Economic and Social Justice, Peru, 248
Latin American Venture Philanthropy Network, Colombia, 71
Latindadd—Red Latinoamericana por Justicia Económica y Social, Peru, 248
Latter-day Saint Charities—LDSC, USA, 447
Latvia Children's Fund, Latvia, 204
Latvian Institute of International Affairs—LIIA, Latvia, 204
Latvian Platform for Development Cooperation, Latvia, 204
Latvijas Ārpolitikas Institūts—LAI, Latvia, 204
Latvijas Bērnu fonds, Latvia, 204
Lauder (Ronald S.) Foundation, Germany, 138
Laudes Foundation, Switzerland, 313
Laureus Sport for Good, UK, 364
The Lawson Foundation, Canada, 58
Lazard (Fernand), Fondation, Belgium, 31
LBJ Foundation, USA, 449
League of California Community Foundations, USA, 396
League of Corporate Foundations—LCF, Philippines, 250
The Leakey Foundation, USA, 447
Learning for Well-being Foundation—L4WB, Netherlands, 227
Legatum Foundation, United Arab Emirates, 334
LEGO Fonden, Denmark, 84
The LEGO Foundation, Denmark, 84
Leibniz Association, Germany, 135
Leibniz Gemeinschaft, Germany, 135
Leibniz-Institut für Agrarentwicklung in Transformationsökonomien—IAMO, Germany, 135
Leibniz-Institut für Globale und Regionale Studien, Germany, 130
Leibniz-Institut für Ost- und Südosteuropaforschung, Germany, 135
Leibniz Institute of Agricultural Development in Transition Economies, Germany, 135
Leibniz Institute for East and South-East European Studies, Germany, 135
Leibniz Institute for Research and Information in Education, Germany, 126
Lelio and Lisli Basso Foundation Onlus, Italy, 178
Leo Messi Foundation, Spain, 292
The Leona M. and Harry B. Helmsley Charitable Trust, USA, 447
Leonard Cheshire Disability, UK, 364
Léonie Sonning Music Foundation, Denmark, 84
Léonie Sonnings Musikfond, Denmark, 84
Léopold Sédar Senghor Foundation, Senegal, 270
The Leprosy Mission International, UK, 364
Lesotho Council of Non-Governmental Organisations, Lesotho, 207
Leventis (A. G.) Foundation, Cyprus, 77
Leventis (A. G.) Foundation Nigeria, Nigeria, 237
Leverhulme Trust, UK, 365
Levesque (Jean-Louis), Fondation, Canada, 55
Levi Strauss Foundation, USA, 448
Levy (Joseph) Foundation, UK, 362
Li Ka Shing Foundation, Hong Kong, 151

INDEX OF FOUNDATIONS

Liberty Fund, Inc, USA, 448
Library of the National Academy of Lincei and Corsiniana, Italy, 172
Liechtenstein Foundation for Culture, Liechtenstein, 208
Lien Foundation, Singapore, 273
Lietuvos vaikų fondas, Lithuania, 209
Life Sciences Research Foundation—LSRF, USA, 448
LifeArc—MRC Technology, UK, 365
Lifeline Consortium, USA, 428
Lifeline Energy, South Africa, 280
Lifewater International, USA, 479
Light Up the World—LUTW, Canada, 58
Light of the Village Foundation, Indonesia, 162
Likhachev (Dmitry) Foundation, Russian Federation, 265
Liliane Foundation, Netherlands, 229
Lilly Endowment, Inc, USA, 448
Limmat Foundation, Switzerland, 314
Limmat Stiftung, Switzerland, 314
Linbury Trust, UK, 365
Lindh (Anna) Euro-Mediterranean Foundation for Dialogue between Cultures, Egypt, 90
Litdea Association, Lithuania, 208
Lithuanian Children's Fund, Lithuania, 209
Littauer (Lucius N.) Foundation, Inc, USA, 449
Liver Canada, Canada, 58
Livestrong Foundation, USA, 448
Living Culture Foundation Namibia—LCFN, Namibia, 222
Liz Claiborne & Art Ortenberg Foundation, USA, 448
Lloyds Bank Foundation for England and Wales, UK, 365
Lloyd's Register Foundation, UK, 365
Loewe Foundation, Spain, 292
The Long Now Foundation, USA, 449
Lord Mayor's Charitable Foundation, Australia, 14
Lorenzini (Giovanni), Fondazione, Italy, 177
The Lotte and John Hecht Memorial Foundation, Canada, 58
Louis-Jeantet Foundation for Medicine, Switzerland, 310
Lower Saxony Savings Bank Foundation, Germany, 137
Lowy Institute for International Policy, Australia, 15
Loyalty Foundation, Spain, 285
Luce (Henry) Foundation, Inc, USA, 435
Lucie et André Chagnon Foundation, Canada, 55
Lucius N. Littauer Foundation, Inc, USA, 449
Ludwig Boltzmann Gesellschaft, Austria, 21
Ludwig Cancer Research, USA, 449
Luigi Einaudi Foundation, Italy, 178
Luigi Sturzo Institute, Italy, 182
Lukuru Wildlife Research Foundation, Congo (Democratic Republic), 72
Lullaby Trust, UK, 366
Lumos Foundation, UK, 366
Lundbeck Foundation, Denmark, 85
Lundbeckfonden, Denmark, 85
Lurcy (Georges) Charitable and Educational Trust, USA, 430
Luso-American Development Foundation, Portugal, 260
The Lutheran World Federation, Switzerland, 314
Lutherischer Weltbund/Fédération Luthérienne Mondiale/Federación Luterana Mundial, Switzerland, 314
Luxembourg Development NGO Co-operation Circle, Luxembourg, 209
Luxemburg (Rosa) Stiftung, Germany, 139
Lyford Cay Foundations, Bahamas, 24
Lynde and Harry Bradley Foundation, Inc, USA, 449
Lyndon Baines Johnson Foundation, USA, 449

M. S. Swaminathan Research Foundation—MSSRF, India, 158
M. Venkatarangaiya Foundation—MVF, India, 158
MacArthur (John D. and Catherine T.) Foundation, USA, 444
McCaw (Craig and Susan) Foundation, USA, 418
McConnell Clark (Edna) Foundation, USA, 422
McConnell (J. W.) Family Foundation, Canada, 57
Macdonald Stewart Foundation, Canada, 59
McDonnell (James S.) Foundation, USA, 443
Macedonian Centre for International Co-operation—MCIC, North Macedonia, 239
Machel (Graça) Trust, South Africa, 280
MACIF Foundation, France, 108
McKenzie (J. R.) Trust, New Zealand, 233
The Mackintosh Foundation, UK, 366
McKnight Foundation, USA, 449
The McLean Foundation, Canada, 59

Maclellan Foundation, Inc, USA, 450
Macmillan Cancer Support, UK, 366
Macquarie Group Foundation, Australia, 15
Macy (Josiah), Jr Foundation, USA, 445
MADRE, USA, 450
Maecenata Foundation, Germany, 119
Maecenata Stiftung, Germany, 119
Maeght (Marguerite et Aimé), Fondation, France, 109
MAG—Mines Advisory Group, UK, 366
MAIF Foundation for Research, France, 108
Maison Franco-Japonaise, Japan, 191
Maj ja Tor Nessling Säätiö, Finland, 96
Maj and Tor Nessling Foundation, Finland, 96
Makyedonski Tzyentar za Myeroonarodna Sorabotka, North Macedonia, 239
Maltese Heritage Foundation, Malta, 213
Mama Cash Foundation, Netherlands, 230
Mandela Institute for Development Studies—MINDS, South Africa, 281
Mandela (Nelson) Children's Fund, South Africa, 281
Mandela (Nelson) Foundation, South Africa, 282
The Mandela Rhodes Foundation, South Africa, 281
Mani Tese, Italy, 183
Mannréttindaskrifstofa Íslands, Iceland, 154
Mansour Foundation for Development—MFD, Egypt, 90
MAP International—Medical Assistance Programs, USA, 450
MAPFRE Foundation, Spain, 292
Mara Foundation, Uganda, 332
Marangopoulos Foundation for Human Rights, Greece, 146
Marc de Montalembert Foundation, France, 109
Marcel Bleustein-Blanchet Vocational Foundation, France, 109
Marcel Hicter Foundation, Belgium, 32
Marcelle et Jean Coutu Foundation, Canada, 55
March of Dimes Foundation, USA, 450
March (Juan), Fundación, Spain, 291
Margaret A. Cargill Philanthropies—MACP, USA, 450
Maria Cecilia Souto Vidigal Foundation, Brazil, 40
María Francisca de Roviralta Foundation, Spain, 292
Marie Curie, UK, 366
Marinho (Roberto), Fundação, Brazil, 41
Mario Negri Pharmacological Research Institute, Italy, 182
Mário Soares and Maria Barroso Foundation, Portugal, 260
Marisla Foundation, USA, 451
Markle Foundation, USA, 451
Mary Fonden, Denmark, 85
Mary Foundation, Denmark, 85
Masason Foundation, Japan, 191
The MasterCard Foundation, Canada, 59
The Matsumae International Foundation, Japan, 191
Mattei (Enrico), Fondazione ENI, Italy, 174
Maugeri (Salvatore), Fondazione, Italy, 180
Mauritius Telecom Foundation—MTF, Mauritius, 214
Mawazo Institute, Kenya, 199
Max Bell Foundation, Canada, 59
The Max Foundation, USA, 451
Max Havelaar Foundation—Fairtrade Netherlands, Netherlands, 230
Max Kade Foundation, Inc, USA, 451
Max-Planck-Gesellschaft zur Förderung der Wissenschaften eV, Germany, 135
Max-Planck-Institut für Neurobiologie des Verhaltens—caesar, Germany, 136
Max Planck Institute for Neurobiology of Behavior—caesar, Germany, 136
Max Planck Society for the Advancement of Science, Germany, 135
Max Schmidheiny Foundation at the University of St Gallen, Switzerland, 314
Max Schmidheiny-Stiftung an der Universität St Gallen, Switzerland, 314
Max Weber Foundation, Germany, 136
Max Weber Stiftung—MWS, Germany, 136
Mayer (Charles Léopold Mayer), Fondation, Switzerland, 308
The Maytree Foundation, Canada, 59
Mbeki (Thabo) Foundation, South Africa, 284
MDA—Muscular Dystrophy Association, USA, 451
Medunarodnog foruma Bosna, Bosnia and Herzegovina, 37
Médecins du Monde International, France, 114
Médecins Sans Frontières International—MSF International, Switzerland, 314

Media Development Foundation—MDF, Georgia, 118
Media Foundation for West Africa, Ghana, 144
medica mondiale eV, Germany, 136
Medical Aid for Palestinians—MAP, UK, 367
Medico International, Germany, 136
Mediis Ganvitarebis Pondi, Georgia, 118
Mediterranean Foundation, Argentina, 7
Mediterranean Foundation for Strategic Studies Institute, France, 113
Mellon (Richard King) Foundation, USA, 467
Menarini International Foundation, Italy, 178
Mencap—Royal Mencap Society, UK, 367
Mendoza (Eugenio), Fundación, Venezuela, 487
Menomadin Foundation, Israel, 170
Mental Health Foundation, UK, 367
Menzies Foundation, Australia, 15
Menzies (Sir Robert) Foundation, Australia, 15
Mercatus Center, USA, 451
The Mercers' Charitable Foundation, UK, 367
Merchant Navy Fund, UK, 382
Mercury Phoenix Trust, UK, 367
Mercy, Ireland, 168
Mercy For Animals—MFA, USA, 452
Mercy Corps, USA, 452
Mercy-USA for Aid and Development, USA, 452
Merian (Christoph) Stiftung, Switzerland, 305
Meridian Foundation, Germany, 140
Mérieux Foundation, France, 109
Mertz Gilmore Foundation, USA, 452
M'essh al Sudan, Sudan, 297
Messi (Leo), Fundación, Spain, 292
Mexican Centre for Philanthropy, Mexico, 214
Mezhdunarodnyj Memorial, Russian Federation, 266
MFJC—Memorial Foundation for Jewish Culture, USA, 452
Michael & Susan Dell Foundation, USA, 453
Michael J. Fox Foundation for Parkinson's Research—MJFF, USA, 453
Michael Otto Foundation for Environmental Protection, Germany, 136
Michael-Otto-Stiftung für Umweltschutz, Germany, 136
Michel (James) Foundation, Seychelles, 272
Microfinance Centre—MFC, Poland, 257
Miguel Alemán Foundation, Mexico, 215
Milbank Memorial Fund, USA, 453
Milieukontakt Macedonia—MKM, North Macedonia, 240
Miloud Chaâbi Foundation, Morocco, 220
Mind, UK, 367
Minderoo Foundation, Australia, 15
Mines Advisory Group—MAG, UK, 366
Minhaj Welfare Foundation, UK, 368
Minna James Heineman Foundation, Germany, 136
Minna-James-Heineman-Stiftung, Germany, 136
Minor Foundation for Major Challenges, Norway, 242
Minority Rights Group International—MRG, UK, 368
Mirovni Inštitut—Inštitut za sodobne družbene in politične študije, Slovenia, 277
MISEREOR—Bischöfliches Hilfswerk Misereor eV, Germany, 137
The Mission to Seafarers, UK, 368
Mistra—Foundation for Strategic Environmental Research, Sweden, 303
Mith Samlanh, Cambodia, 46
Mittag-Leffler Foundation of the Royal Swedish Academy of Sciences, Sweden, 300
Mitterrand (Danielle), Fondation, France, 112
MIUSA—Mobility International USA, USA, 453
Mo Dewji Foundation, Tanzania, 323
Mo Ibrahim Foundation, UK, 368
Moawad (René) Foundation, Lebanon, 206
Mobility International USA—MIUSA, USA, 453
Mohamed Shafik Gabr Foundation for Social Development, Egypt, 90
Mohammed bin Rashid Al Maktoum Global Initiatives—MBRGI, United Arab Emirates, 335
Mohammed bin Salman Foundation—Misk Foundation, Saudi Arabia, 269
Moisés Bertoni Foundation, Paraguay, 248
Møller (A.P.) and Chastine Mc-Kinney Møller Foundation, Denmark, 82
Molson Foundation, Canada, 59
Monell (Ambrose) Foundation, USA, 399
Mongolian Women's Fund—MONES, Mongolia, 218
Monnet (Jean), Fondation pour l'Europe, Switzerland, 309
Mønsteds (Otto) Fond, Denmark, 86
de Montalembert (Marc), Fondation, France, 109
Montemadrid Foundation, Spain, 292
Montevideo Circle Foundation, Uruguay, 485

INDEX OF FOUNDATIONS

Moore (Gordon and Betty) Foundation, USA, 432
Moore (Henry) Foundation, UK, 358
Moores (John) Foundation, UK, 362
Morehead-Cain Foundation, USA, 453
Morgan Stanley Foundation, USA, 453
Moriya Scholarship Foundation, Japan, 191
Morningside Foundation, USA, 454
Mother Child Education Foundation, Türkiye, 327
Motorola Solutions Foundation, USA, 454
Motsepe Foundation, South Africa, 281
Mountain Institute, Peru, 249
Mouvement International ATD Quart-Monde, France, 115
Mouvement Social, Lebanon, 206
M-PESA Foundation, Kenya, 199
Ms. Foundation for Women, USA, 454
MS Society—Multiple Sclerosis Society of Great Britain and Northern Ireland, UK, 368
MSF International—Médecins Sans Frontières International, Switzerland, 314
Mshvidobis, Demokratiisa, da Ganvit'arebis Kavkasiuri Instituti, Georgia, 117
MSI Reproductive Choices, UK, 369
MTN Afghanistan Foundation, Afghanistan, 4
MTN Cameroon Foundation, Cameroon, 47
MTN Congo Foundation, Congo (Republic), 73
MTN Côte d'Ivoire Foundation, Côte d'Ivoire, 76
MTN Foundation Benin, Benin, 35
MTN Nigeria Foundation, Nigeria, 237
MTN SA Foundation, South Africa, 281
MTN Uganda Foundation, Uganda, 332
Mukwege (Dr Denis) Foundation, Netherlands, 224
Multiple Sclerosis Society of Great Britain and Northern Ireland, UK, 368
Munich Re Foundation/Münchener Rück Stiftung, Germany, 137
Murdoch Children's Research Institute—MCRI, Australia, 15
Muriel McBrien Kauffman Foundation, USA, 425
Muscular Dystrophy UK, UK, 369
Music in Africa Foundation—MIAF, South Africa, 281
Musk Foundation, USA, 454
Muslim Aid, UK, 369
The Muttart Foundation, Canada, 59
Mutual Aid and Liaison Service, France, 116
Myanmar Book Aid and Preservation Foundation—MBAPF, Myanmar, 221
Myanmar/Burma Schools Project Foundation, Canada, 60
Myer Foundation, Australia, 18
Myer (Sidney) Fund, Australia, 18

NAACP Legal Defense and Educational Fund, Inc—LDF, USA, 454
Naandi Foundation—A New Beginning, India, 158
Nacionalne Zaklade za Razvoj Civilnoga Društva, Croatia, 76
Nadace České spořitelny—Nadace ČS, Czech Republic, 79
Nadace Český Hudební Fond—NČHF, Czech Republic, 79
Nadace Český literární fond—nčlf, Czech Republic, 80
Nadace Charty 77, Czech Republic, 80
Nadace Neziskovky.cz, Czech Republic, 79
Nadace Občanského fóra—Nadace OF, Czech Republic, 80
Nadace Open Society Fund Praha, Czech Republic, 80
Nadace Preciosa, Czech Republic, 80
Nadace Vodafone Česká Republika, Czech Republic, 80
Nadácia Ekopolis, Slovakia, 275
Nadácia Orange, Slovakia, 275
Nadácia Otvorenej Spoločnosti, Slovakia, 276
Nadácia Pontis, Slovakia, 274
Nadácia pre Deti Slovenska, Slovakia, 275
Nadácia SPP, Slovakia, 275
Nadácia Tatra Banky, Slovakia, 276
Naito Foundation, Japan, 191
Nand & Jeet Khemka Foundation, India, 159
Nansen (Fridtjof) Institute, Norway, 241
Naspa Foundation, Germany, 137
Naspa Stiftung, Germany, 137
National Assistance and Information Centre for NGOs in Moldova—CONTACT Centre, Moldova, 216
National Bank of Greece Cultural Foundation, Greece, 147
National Carlo Collodi Foundation, Italy, 179
National Community Foundation, Saint Lucia, 268
National Council of Social Development—NCSD, Philippines, 250

National Council for Voluntary Organisations, UK, 337
National Emergencies Trust, UK, 369
National Empowerment Foundation—NEF, Mauritius, 214
National Endowment for Science, Technology and the Arts—Nesta, UK, 370
National Federation of NGOs, Poland, 254
National Fish and Wildlife Foundation—NFWF, USA, 455
National Foundation for Civil Society Development, Croatia, 76
National Foundation for Development, El Salvador, 91
National Foundation for the Development of Honduras, Honduras, 150
National Foundation for Educational Research—NFER, UK, 369
National Foundation for Political Sciences, France, 110
National Geographic Society, USA, 455
National Heart Foundation of Australia, Australia, 15
National Heart Foundation of New Zealand, New Zealand, 233
National Heritage Memorial Fund, UK, 370
National Humanities Center—NHC, USA, 455
National Institute for Research in the Behavioural Sciences—Szold (Henrietta) Institute, Israel, 169
National Kidney Foundation—NKF, USA, 455
The National Lottery Community Fund, UK, 370
The National Lottery Heritage Fund, UK, 370
National Organization for Women Foundation, USA, 458
National Park Foundation, USA, 455
National Science Foundation—NSF, USA, 455
National Society for the Prevention of Cruelty to Children—NSPCC, UK, 371
National Trust, UK, 370
National Trust EcoFund, Bulgaria, 43
National Trust of Fiji—NTF, Fiji, 94
The National Trust for Italy, Italy, 174
National Wildlife Federation—NWF, USA, 456
The Nature Conservancy—TNC, USA, 456
Naumann (Friedrich) Stiftung, Germany, 130
NCVO—National Council for Voluntary Organisations, UK, 337
NDI—National Democratic Institute for International Affairs, USA, 456
Near East Foundation—NEF, USA, 456
Nederlandse Organisatie voor Internationale Ontwikkelingssamenwerking—Stichting NOVIB, Netherlands, 228
NEF—National Empowerment Foundation, Mauritius, 214
NEF—Near East Foundation, USA, 456
Negri (Mario), Istituto di Ricerche Farmacologiche, Italy, 182
Neighbour in Need, Austria, 22
Nelson Mandela Children's Fund, South Africa, 281
Nelson Mandela Foundation, South Africa, 282
The Neptis Foundation, Canada, 60
Neruda (Pablo), Fundación, Chile, 65
Nesr Art Foundation, Angola, 5
Nessling (Maj and Tor) Foundation, Finland, 96
Nesta—National Endowment for Science, Technology and the Arts, UK, 370
Nestlé Foundation for the Study of the Problems of Nutrition in the World, Switzerland, 310
Network of Estonian Non-profit Organizations, Estonia, 92
Network of European Foundations—NEF, Belgium, 27
Network of Foundations and Research Institutions for the Promotion of a Culture of Peace in Africa, Côte d'Ivoire, 75
Network of Foundations Working for Development—netFWD, France, 99
Network for Human Development, Brazil, 41
Network of Information and Support for Non-governmental Organizations, Poland, 254
Network of Mexican Community Foundations, Mexico, 215
Network for Social Change Charitable Trust—NSCCT, UK, 370
Neves (José Maria), Fundação para a Governança, Cabo Verde, 46
Nevyriausybinių organizacijų informacijos ir paramos centras, Lithuania, 208
New Carlsberg Foundation, Denmark, 85
New Economics Foundation—NEF, UK, 371
New Myanmar Foundation, Myanmar, 221
New School Foundation, Colombia, 71
New World Foundation—NWF, USA, 456
The New York Community Trust—NYCT, USA, 457

Observer Research Foundation

New Zealand Institute of International Affairs—NZIIA, New Zealand, 234
Newberry Library, USA, 457
NFCR—National Foundation for Cancer Research, USA, 457
NFER—National Foundation for Educational Research, UK, 369
NFI—National Foundation for India, India, 159
NGO Center—NGOC, Armenia, 9
NGO Development Centre, Russian Federation, 265
NGO Information and Support Centre—NISC, Lithuania, 208
NHS Charities Together, UK, 371
Niarchos (Stavros) Foundation, Greece, 147
Nicolas Hulot Foundation for Nature and Humankind, France, 110
Niedersächsische Sparkassenstiftung, Germany, 137
Nigerian Conservation Foundation—NCF, Nigeria, 238
Nigerian Institute of International Affairs—NIIA, Nigeria, 238
Nightingale (Florence), Fondation Internationale, Switzerland, 309
Nihon Kokusai Mondai Kenkyusho, Japan, 190
Ningxia Yanbao Charity Foundation, China (People's Republic), 69
NIOK Alapítvány—Nonprofit Információs és Oktató Központ Alapítvány—NIOK, Hungary, 152
NIOK Foundation—Non-Profit Information and Training Centre, Hungary, 152
The Nippon Foundation, Japan, 192
Nitidæ, France, 115
Niwano Peace Foundation, Japan, 192
Nobel Foundation, Sweden, 301
Nobelstiftelsen, Sweden, 301
Nobis Foundation, Ecuador, 88
Non-Governmental Ecological Vernadsky Foundation, Russian Federation, 266
Nonprofit Enterprise and Self-sustainability Team—NESsT, USA, 457
Norbert Zongo Cell for Investigative Journalism in West Africa, Burkina Faso, 44
Nordic Africa Institute Scholarships, Sweden, 302
Nordic Culture Fund, Denmark, 85
Nordic Institute for Theoretical Physics, Sweden, 302
Nordic International Support Foundation—NIS, Norway, 242
Nordisk Kulturfond, Denmark, 85
Nordiska Afrikainstitutets Stipendier, Sweden, 302
NORDITA—Nordiska Institutet för Teoretisk Fysik, Sweden, 302
Norsk Utenrikspolitisk Institutt—NUPI, Norway, 242
North-South-Bridge Foundation, Germany, 141
Norwegian Donors Forum, Norway, 240
Norwegian Institute of International Affairs, Norway, 242
Norwegian Refugee Council—NRC, Norway, 242
Nott (David) Foundation, UK, 350
The Nourafchan Foundation—TNF, Kenya, 199
Novartis Foundation, Switzerland, 314
Novartis Foundation for Therapeutical Research, Germany, 137
Novartis-Stiftung für therapeutische Forschung, Germany, 137
Novartis US Foundation, USA, 457
NOVIB (Oxfam Netherlands), Netherlands, 228
NoVo Foundation, USA, 458
Novo Nordisk Fonden, Denmark, 85
Novo Nordisk Foundation, Denmark, 85
NOW Foundation, USA, 458
NPI Foundation, China (People's Republic), 66
NRF—National Research Foundation, South Africa, 282
NSPCC—National Society for the Prevention of Cruelty to Children, UK, 371
Nuffic, Netherlands, 227
Nuffield Foundation, UK, 371
Nursultan Nazarbayev Educational Foundation, Kazakhstan, 197
NWO Domain Applied and Engineering Sciences, Netherlands, 227
Ny Carlsbergfondet, Denmark, 85
NYCT—The New York Community Trust, USA, 457
NZIIA—New Zealand Institute of International Affairs, New Zealand, 234

Oak Foundation, Switzerland, 315
Obama (Barack) Foundation, USA, 407
Observer Research Foundation—ORF, India, 159

The Ocean Cleanup Foundation, Netherlands, 230
The Ocean Foundation, USA, 458
Oceanographic Institute—Albert I, Prince of Monaco Foundation, France, 114
ODI, UK, 371
OeAD, Austria, 22
Office International de l'Eau—OiEau, France, 115
The Officers' Association, UK, 372
Offor (Sir Emeka) Foundation, Nigeria, 238
Ogólnopolska Federacja Organizacji Pozarządowych—OFOP, Poland, 254
Oil Search Foundation, Papua New Guinea, 247
OISCA International—Organization for Industrial, Spiritual and Cultural Advancement-International, Japan, 192
Ökumenikus Segélyszervezet, Hungary, 153
Olav Thon Foundation, Norway, 242
Olav Thon Stiftelsen, Norway, 242
Olivetti (Adriano), Fondazione, Italy, 174
Olof Palme Memorial Fund for International Understanding and Common Security, Sweden, 302
Olof Palmes Minnesfond för internationell förståelse och gemensam säkerhet, Sweden, 302
Oman LNG Development Foundation—ODF, Oman, 244
Omidyar Group, USA, 458
Omidyar Network Fund, USA, 458
Onassis (Alexander S.) Public Benefit Foundation, Liechtenstein, 207
ONCE—Spanish National Organization for the Blind—Foundation, Spain, 293
One Economy Foundation, Namibia, 222
One Foundation, China (People's Republic), 69
OneStage, India, 155
Onstad (Henie) Kunstsenter, Norway, 241
OPALS—Organisation Panafricaine de Lutte pour la Santé, France, 115
OPEN ASIA—Armanshahr Foundation, Afghanistan, 3
Open Estonia Foundation, Estonia, 92
Open Society Action Fund, USA, 458
Open Society Africa, Senegal, 270
Open Society European Policy Institute—OSEPI, Belgium, 33
Open Society Forum (Mongolia), Mongolia, 218
Open Society Foundation for Albania, Albania, 5
Open Society Foundation—Bratislava, Slovakia, 276
Open Society Foundation Haiti, Haiti, 149
Open Society Foundation—London, UK, 372
Open Society Foundation South Africa—OSF-SA, South Africa, 282
Open Society Foundation—Western Balkans, Albania, 5
Open Society Foundations, USA, 459
Open Society Foundations—Armenia, Armenia, 9
Open Society Foundations in Pakistan, Pakistan, 245
Open Society Fund—Bosnia-Herzegovina, Bosnia and Herzegovina, 37
Open Society Fund Prague—OSF Prague, Czech Republic, 80
Open Society Initiative for Eastern Africa—OSIEA, Kenya, 199
Open Society Initiative for Southern Africa—OSISA, South Africa, 282
Open Society Institute—Sofia, Bulgaria, 43
Open Society Policy Center, USA, 458
Operation Eyesight Universal/Action Universelle de la Vue, Canada, 60
Operation USA, USA, 459
Oppenheimer Generations Foundation, South Africa, 282
Opportunity International UK, UK, 372
Oprah Winfrey Leadership Academy Foundation—OWLAF, USA, 459
OPUS—Centre for Promotion and Development of Civil Initiatives, Poland, 254
Orange Botswana Foundation, Botswana, 37
Orange Foundation, Romania, 263
Orange Foundation Cameroon, Cameroon, 47
Orange Foundation Guinea, Guinea, 149
Orange Foundation Tunisia, Tunisia, 326
Orange Moldova Foundation, Moldova, 217
Orange Solidarité Madagascar, Madagascar, 210
Orangutan Foundation, UK, 372
Oranje Fonds, Netherlands, 227
Orbis Charitable Trust, UK, 372
Orentreich Foundation for the Advancement of Science, Inc—OFAS, USA, 459
ORF Nachbar in Not, Austria, 22
Organisation Internationale de Droit du Développement—OIDD, Italy, 181

Organisation Panafricaine de Lutte pour la Santé—OPALS, France, 115
Organization for Social Science Research in Eastern and Southern Africa—OSSREA, Ethiopia, 94
Orient Foundation, Portugal, 260
Orient-Occident Foundation, Morocco, 220
Orji Uzor Kalu Foundation, Nigeria, 238
Ortega (Amancio), Fundación, Spain, 288
Ortega y Gasset (José), Fundación, Spain, 291
Osaka Community Foundation, Japan, 192
Österreichische Forschungsstiftung für Internationale Entwicklung—OFSE, Austria, 22
Österreichische Gesellschaft für Aussenpolitik und Internationale Beziehungen—ÖGAVN, Austria, 22
Österreichischer Wissenschaftsfonds—FWF, Austria, 21
Östersjöfonden, Finland, 97
Oswaldo Cruz Foundation, Brazil, 40
Otto Benecke Foundation, Germany, 138
Otto-Benecke-Stiftung eV, Germany, 138
Otto (Michael) Stiftung, Germany, 136
Otto Mønsteds Fond, Denmark, 86
Otto Mønsteds Foundation, Denmark, 86
Our Foundation, Indonesia, 162
Our Future—Foundation for Regional Social Programmes, Russian Federation, 266
Outreach International, USA, 459
OutRight Action International, USA, 460
Outstretched Hands, Italy, 183
Oxfam America, USA, 460
Oxfam Aotearoa, New Zealand, 234
Oxfam Australia, Australia, 16
Oxfam Brasil, Brazil, 41
Oxfam Canada, Canada, 60
Oxfam Denmark, Denmark, 86
Oxfam Deutschland eV, Germany, 138
Oxfam France, France, 115
Oxfam GB, UK, 372
Oxfam Hong Kong, Hong Kong, 151
Oxfam India, India, 159
Oxfam International, Kenya, 200
Oxfam Ireland, Ireland, 167
Oxfam Italia, Italy, 183
Oxfam Mexico, Mexico, 216
Oxfam NOVIB—Nederlandse Organisatie voor Internationale Ontwikkelingssamenwerking, Netherlands, 228
Oxfam NOVIB—Netherlands Organization for International Development Co-operation, Netherlands, 228
Oxfam-Québec, Canada, 60
Oxfam-Solidariteit/Solidarité, Belgium, 33
Oxfam South Africa, South Africa, 282
OzChild—Children Australia Inc, Australia, 16

P&V Foundation, Belgium, 32
Paavo Nurmen Säätiö, Finland, 97
Paavo Nurmi Foundation, Finland, 97
Pablo Neruda Foundation, Chile, 65
Pacific Development and Conservation Trust, New Zealand, 234
Pacific Leprosy Foundation, New Zealand, 234
Pacific Peoples' Partnership, Canada, 61
Packard (David and Lucile) Foundation, USA, 420
Pact, USA, 460
PADF—Pan American Development Foundation, USA, 460
PAI—Population Action International, USA, 460
Paideia Galiza Foundation, Spain, 293
Pakistan Centre for Philanthropy—PCP, Pakistan, 244
Pakistan Institute of International Affairs—PIIA, Pakistan, 245
Palestinian NGO Network, Palestinian Territories, 246
Palme (Olof) Minnesfond fr Internationell Frstelse och Gemensam Skerhet, Sweden, 302
PAN Africa—Pesticide Action Network Africa, Senegal, 271
Pan-African Organization for Health, France, 115
Pan American Development Foundation—PADF, USA, 460
PAN Europe—Pesticide Action Network Europe, Belgium, 34
Pan-European Federation for Cultural Heritage, Netherlands, 224
PAN UK—Pesticide Action Network UK, UK, 373
PANAP—Pesticide Action Network Asia and the Pacific, Malaysia, 211
Pancare Foundation, Australia, 16
PANNA—Pesticide Action Network North America, USA, 462
PANZI Foundation, USA, 461
The Papal Foundation, USA, 461

Paraguayan Foundation for Cooperation and Development, Paraguay, 248
Paraskevaides (George and Thelma) Foundation, Cyprus, 78
Parasol Foundation Trust, Gibraltar, 144
Parkinson's Foundation, USA, 461
Partage, France, 116
Partners for Equity, Australia, 16
Partners in Health, USA, 461
Partos, Netherlands, 223
Pasteur Institute, France, 114
Pasteur Institute of Lille, France, 114
Pastore (Giulio), Fondazione, Italy, 178
PATH, USA, 461
Pathfinder International, USA, 461
Patiño (Simón I.), Fondation, Switzerland, 310
Patterson (Alicia) Foundation, USA, 398
The Paul G. Allen Family Foundation, USA, 462
Paul Hamlyn Foundation—PHF, UK, 373
The Paul Ramsay Foundation, Australia, 16
Paulo Foundation, Finland, 97
Paulon Säätiö, Finland, 97
Paz y Cooperación, Spain, 296
PCI Media Impact, USA, 467
PCI—Project Concern International, USA, 431
Peace Brigades International—PBI, Belgium, 33
Peace and Co-operation, Spain, 296
Peace Direct, UK, 373
Peace and Disarmament Education Trust—PADET, New Zealand, 234
Peace, Health and Human Development Foundation—PHD Foundation, Japan, 193
Peace Institute—Institute for Contemporary Social and Political Studies, Slovenia, 277
Peace Parks Foundation, South Africa, 282
Peace Research Institute Oslo—PRIO, Norway, 242
Peace and Security Funders Group—PSFG, USA, 396
Peace Village International, Germany, 129
Peace Winds Japan—PWJ, Japan, 192
Pearl S. Buck International, USA, 462
Pedro Barrié de la Maza Foundation, Spain, 293
Penal Reform International—PRI, UK, 373
People in Need, Czech Republic, 79
PepsiCo Foundation, Inc, USA, 462
Perdana Global Peace Foundation—PGPF, Malaysia, 211
Peres Center for Peace and Innovation, Israel, 171
Perpetual Foundation, Australia, 16
Pertubuhan Pertolongan Wanita, Malaysia, 212
Peruvian Foundation for Nature Conservation, Peru, 249
Pestalozzi Children's Foundation, Switzerland, 317
Pesticide Action Network Africa—PAN Africa, Senegal, 271
Pesticide Action Network Asia and the Pacific—PANAP, Malaysia, 211
Pesticide Action Network Europe—PAN Europe, Belgium, 34
Pesticide Action Network Latin America and the Caribbean, Chile, 65
Pesticide Action Network North America—PANNA, USA, 462
Pesticide Action Network UK—PAN UK, UK, 373
The Peter Cundill Foundation, Bermuda, 35
The Pew Charitable Trusts, USA, 462
Pezcoller (Alessio), Fondazione, Italy, 174
Pfizer Foundation, USA, 462
PH International, USA, 463
The PHD Foundation—Peace, Health and Human Development Foundation, Japan, 193
Philanthropic, Colombia, 70
Philanthropic Foundations Canada—PFC, Canada, 48
Philanthropikó Ídryma Stélios Chatzeioánnou stēn Kýpro, Cyprus, 78
Philanthropy Australia, Australia, 10
Philanthropy Europe Association—Philea, Belgium, 27
Philanthropy Ireland, Ireland, 165
Philanthropy New Zealand/Topūtanga Tuku Aroha o Aotearoa, New Zealand, 232
Philanthropy for Social Justice and Peace, UK, 336
Philea—Philanthropy Europe Association, Belgium, 27
Philip-Sörensens (Erik) Stiftelse, Sweden, 299
Philippine-American Educational Foundation—PAEF, Philippines, 253
Philippine Business for Social Progress—PBSP, Philippines, 250
Philippine Council for NGO Certification, Philippines, 250
PHR—Physicians for Human Rights, USA, 463
Physicians for Human Rights—PHR, USA, 463

INDEX OF FOUNDATIONS

Piera, Pietro and Giovanni Ferrero Foundation, Italy, 179
Pilgrim Trust, UK, 373
Pinchuk (Victor) Foundation, Ukraine, 333
Ping Foundation, USA, 415
Plan International Ireland, Ireland, 167
PLAN International—PI, UK, 374
Planck (Max) Gesellschaft zur Förderung der Wissenschaften eV, Germany, 135
Plataform CiviKos, Kosovo, 202
Plataforma Portuguesa das Organizações Não-Governamentais para o Desenvolvimento—ONGD, Portugal, 258
Platform for Development Cooperation and Humanitarian Aid, Slovenia, 276
Platforma Mimovládnych Rozvojových Organizácií, Slovakia, 273
Ploughshares Fund, USA, 463
Plunkett Foundation, UK, 374
Polish-American Freedom Foundation, Poland, 257
Polish Donors Forum, Poland, 254
Pollock-Krasner Foundation, Inc, USA, 463
POLSAT Foundation, Poland, 256
Polsko-Amerykańska Fundacja Wolności, Poland, 257
Pompidou (Claude), Fondation, France, 104
Pontis Foundation, Slovakia, 274
Population Action International—PAI, USA, 460
Population Council, USA, 463
Populorum Progressio Foundation, Vatican City, 486
Portuguese Foundation Centre, Portugal, 258
Portuguese Platform of Non-Governmental Organizations for Development, Portugal, 258
Post Office Foundation, France, 105
Potanin (Vladimir) Foundation, Russian Federation, 267
Potter (Ian) Foundation, Australia, 14
Practical Action, UK, 374
Prada Foundation, Italy, 179
Praemium Erasmianum Foundation, Netherlands, 230
Pratham Education Foundation, India, 159
Pratt Foundation, Australia, 17
Praxis Centre for Policy Studies Foundation, Estonia, 93
Preciosa Foundation, Czech Republic, 80
Première Urgence Internationale, France, 116
Premji (Azim) Foundation, India, 156
Presbyterian World Service & Development—PWS&D, Canada, 61
Primate's World Relief and Development Fund/Le Fonds du Primat Pour le Secours et le Développement Mondial—PWRDF, Canada, 49
Prince Bernhard Cultural Foundation, Netherlands, 230
Prince Claus Fund for Culture and Development, Netherlands, 228
Prince's Trust, UK, 363
Princess of Asturias Foundation, Spain, 294
Princess Charlene of Monaco Foundation, Monaco, 218
Prins Bernhard Culturfonds, Stichting, Netherlands, 230
Prins Claus Fonds Voor Cultuur en Ontwikkeling, Netherlands, 228
PRIO—Peace Research Institute Oslo, Norway, 242
Prix Jeunesse Foundation, Germany, 138
Pro Helvetia, Switzerland, 315
Pro Juventute, Switzerland, 315
Pro Mujer International, USA, 464
Pro Victimis, Switzerland, 315
Pro Women International, USA, 464
PRODESSA—Proyecto de Desarrollo Santiago, Guatemala, 148
proFonds, Switzerland, 305
Project Harmony, USA, 463
Project HOPE, USA, 464
Project Trust, UK, 374
ProLiteracy, USA, 464
Promi Foundation, Spain, 294
Pronaturaleza—Fundación Peruana para la Conservación de la Naturaleza, Peru, 249
Prospera—International Network of Women's Funds, Canada, 61
Protestant Study Foundation, Germany, 128
PROVICOOP, Chile, 65
PRS for Music Foundation, UK, 374
Prudence Foundation, Hong Kong, 151
Public Health Foundation of India—PHFI, India, 159
Public Studies Centre, Chile, 64
Puerto Rico Community Foundation, Puerto Rico, 261
Pulitzer Center on Crisis Reporting, USA, 464

PwC Charitable Foundation, USA, 465

Qatar Foundation, Qatar, 262
Qattan (A. M.) Foundation, UK, 338
Quỹ Thiện Tâm, Viet Nam, 488
Quandt (Herbert) Stiftung, Germany, 122
Quandt (Johanna) Stiftung, Germany, 133
Queen Elizabeth II National Trust, New Zealand, 234
Queen Rania Foundation—QRF, Jordan, 196
Querini Stampalia Foundation, Italy, 179
Quincy Institute for Responsible Statecraft—QI, USA, 465

R. Howard Webster Foundation/Fondation R. Howard Webster, Canada, 61
Rabo Foundation, Netherlands, 228
Radiation Effects Research Foundation—RERF, Japan, 193
Rafa Nadal Foundation, Spain, 294
Rafael del Pino Foundation, Spain, 294
Rafto Foundation for Human Rights, Norway, 243
Raftostiftelsen for menneskerettigheter, Norway, 243
Rahvusvahelne Kaitseuuringute Keskus—RKK, Estonia, 93
Rainforest Action Network—RAN, USA, 465
Rainforest Foundation Norway, Norway, 243
The Rainforest Foundation UK—RFUK, UK, 375
Rainforest Foundation US—RFUS, USA, 465
Rainforest Journalism Fund, USA, 464
Rajiv Gandhi Foundation, India, 160
Ramaciotti Foundations, Australia, 17
Rambourg Foundation, Tunisia, 326
Ramón Areces Foundation, Spain, 294
Ramon Magsaysay Award Foundation, Philippines, 253
Ramsay (Paul) Foundation, Australia, 16
RAN—Rainforest Action Network, USA, 465
RAND Corporation, USA, 465
The Rank Foundation, UK, 375
Rare, USA, 466
Rausing (Ruben and Elisabeth) Trust, UK, 383
Ravand Institute for Economic and International Studies, Iran, 163
Razumkov Centre, Ukraine, 333
RBC Foundation, Canada, 61
RC Forward, Canada, 48
RE:ACT, UK, 375
Re:wild, USA, 466
Reading Foundation, Germany, 140
Real Madrid Foundation, Spain, 295
Realdania Foundation, Denmark, 83
Reall—Real Equity for All, UK, 375
Rebecca Akufo-Addo Foundation—Rebecca Foundation, Ghana, 144
Red de Acción en Plaguicidas y sus Alternativas de América Latina—RAP-AL, Chile, 65
Red Feather, Japan, 185
Red de Mujeres para el Desarrollo, Costa Rica, 75
RED—Ruralité-Environnement-Développement, Belgium, Belgium, 34
Red de Salud de las Mujeres Latinoamericanas y del Caribe—RSMLAC, Ecuador, 89
Red Sea Cultural Foundation, Somalia, 278
Rede ba Rai, Timor-Leste, 325
Rede Comuá, Brazil, 38
Rede Iberoamericana de Fundações Cívicas ou Comunitárias—RIFC, Brazil, 38
REDEH—Rede de Desenvolvimento Humano, Brazil, 41
RedR UK, UK, 375
Reeva Rebecca Steenkamp Foundation, South Africa, 283
Reeve (Christopher and Dana) Foundation, USA, 415
Refugee Empowerment International—REI, Japan, 193
Refugee Foundation, Netherlands, 231
Refugees International—RI, USA, 466
Regional Centre for Strategic Studies—RCSS, Sri Lanka, 297
Regional Environmental Center, Hungary, 153
Regnskogfondet, Norway, 243
Rehabilitation for the Disabled—ELEPAP, Greece, 145
Rehabilitation International—RI, USA, 466
REI—Refugee Empowerment International, Japan, 193
Reliance Foundation, India, 160
Relief International, USA, 466
Renault Foundation, France, 106
René Moawad Foundation—RMF, Lebanon, 206
Repsol Foundation, Spain, 295
Research Centre for Social Action, Congo (Democratic Republic), 72

Research Corporation for Science Advancement—RCSA, USA, 467
Réseau Européen des Associations de Lutte contre la Pauvreté et l'Exclusion Sociale, Belgium, 29
Réseau des Fondations et Institutions de Recherche pour la Promotion d'un Culture de la Paix en Afrique—REFICA, Côte d'Ivoire, 75
Resolution Foundation, UK, 375
Resource Centre for the Human Rights Nongovernmental Organizations of Moldova—CReDO, Moldova, 217
The Resource Foundation—TRF, USA, 467
Rethink Charity, Canada, 48
Reumatikerförbundet, Sweden, 302
Rhodes Trust, UK, 376
RIA—Royal Irish Academy, Ireland, 167
Ricard (Baxter & Alma), Fondation, Canada, 55
Ricardo do Espírito Santo Silva Foundation, Portugal, 261
Richard Dawkins Foundation for Reason and Science, USA, 412
Richard King Mellon Foundation, USA, 467
Rielo (Fernando), Fundación, Spain, 290
Right Livelihood Award Foundation, Sweden, 302
Righteous Persons Foundation, USA, 467
Rising Impact, USA, 467
Rivers Trust, UK, 376
RNIB Charity, UK, 378
Robert Bosch Foundation, Germany, 138
Robert-Bosch-Stiftung GmbH, Germany, 138
Robert Marinho Foundation, Brazil, 41
Robert Schuman Foundation, France, 111
Robert Wood Johnson Foundation—RWJF, USA, 467
Robertson Foundation for Government—RFG, USA, 468
The Robertson Trust, UK, 376
Rockefeller Brothers Fund—RBF, USA, 468
Rockefeller Foundation, USA, 468
Rockwool Fonden, Denmark, 86
Rockwool Foundation, Denmark, 86
Roger Federer Foundation, Switzerland, 315
Rogosin Institute, USA, 468
Rohini Nilekani Philanthropies, India, 160
Rohm Music Foundation, Japan, 193
Romaeuropa Foundation, Italy, 180
Romanian Cultural Institute, Romania, 264
Rome Foundation, Italy, 179
The Ronald S. Lauder Foundation, Germany, 138
Rosa Luxemburg Foundation, Germany, 139
Rosa-Luxemburg-Stiftung, Germany, 139
Rosetta Foundation, USA, 416
Ross (R. E.) Trust, Australia, 17
The Ross Trust, Australia, 17
Rössing Foundation, Namibia, 222
The Rotary Foundation, USA, 468
Rotary Yoneyama Memorial Foundation, Inc, Japan, 193
Rotha, Ireland, 165
Rothschild (Edmond de) Foundations, Switzerland, 308
Roviralta (María Francisca de), Fundación, Spain, 292
Rowntree (Joseph) Charitable Trust, UK, 362
Rowntree (Joseph) Foundation, UK, 362
Rowntree (Joseph) Reform Trust, UK, 362
Royal Aeronautical Society—RAeS, UK, 376
Royal Air Force Benevolent Fund, UK, 377
Royal Anthropological Institute of Great Britain and Ireland—RAI, UK, 377
The Royal Australasian College of Physicians—RACP, Australia, 17
Royal British Legion, UK, 377
Royal Commission for the Exhibition of 1851, UK, 377
The Royal Commonwealth Society—RCS, UK, 377
Royal Elcano Institute Foundation, Spain, 294
Royal Flying Doctor Service of Australia—RFDS, Australia, 17
The Royal Foundation of the Prince and Princess of Wales, UK, 378
Royal Geographical Society (with the Institute of British Geographers)—RGS-IBG, UK, 378
Royal Holland Society of Sciences and Humanities, Netherlands, 226
Royal Institute of International Affairs—RIIA—Chatham House, UK, 378
Royal Institute of International Relations—Egmont Institute, Belgium, 29
Royal Literary Fund—RLF, UK, 378
Royal National Institute of Blind People—RNIB, UK, 378
The Royal Society, UK, 379
The Royal Society of Medicine—RSM, UK, 379
Royal Society for the Prevention of Cruelty to Animals—RSPCA, UK, 380

INDEX OF FOUNDATIONS

Royal Society for the Protection of Birds—RSPB, UK, 379
Rroma Foundation, Switzerland, 315
Rromani Fundacija, Switzerland, 315
RSA—Royal Society for the Encouragement of Arts, Manufactures and Commerce, UK, 379
RSPB—Royal Society for the Protection of Birds, UK, 379
RSPCA—Royal Society for the Prevention of Cruelty to Animals, UK, 380
Rubinstein (Arthur) International Music Society, Israel, 168
Rüf (Gebert) Stiftung, Switzerland, 311
The Rufford Foundation, UK, 380
RUI Foundation, Italy, 180
Ruiz-Picasso (Almine y Bernard), Fundación, Spain, 288
Runyon (Damon) Cancer Research Foundation, USA, 419
Ruparelia Foundation, Uganda, 332
Rupert Family Foundations, South Africa, 283
Rural Development Foundation, Poland, 257
Rural Development Institute—Landesa, USA, 447
Ruralité-Environnement-Développement—RED, Belgium, 34
Rurality Environment Development, Belgium, 34
Russell Sage Foundation—RSF, USA, 469
Russian Donors Forum, Russian Federation, 265
Russian International Affairs Council—RIAC, Russian Federation, 266
Russian LGBT Network, Russian Federation, 267
Rutgers, Netherlands, 228
Rutherford Institute, USA, 469
Ruya Foundation for Contemporary Culture in Iraq, Iraq, 164
Rytų Europos Studijų Centras—RESC, Lithuania, 209

Saadi Foundation, Iran, 164
SAASTA—South African Agency for Science and Technology Advancement, South Africa, 283
Säätiöiden post doc-poolin, Finland, 95
Säätiöt ja rahastot, Finland, 95
Sabanci Vakfı—Haci Omer Sabanci Foundation, Türkiye, 329
Safaricom Foundation, Kenya, 200
Sahabdeen (A. M. M.) Trust Foundation, Sri Lanka, 297
SAIA—Slovak Academic Information Agency, Slovakia, 274
Saïd Foundation, UK, 380
Sainsbury Family Charitable Trusts, UK, 380
Saint Cyril and Saint Methodius International Foundation, Bulgaria, 44
The Saison Foundation, Japan, 193
Sakartvelos Strategiisa da Saertashoriso Urtiertobebis Kvlevis Pondi—Rondelis Pondi, Georgia, 118
Sakena Fund, USA, 469
Salvador Dalí Foundation, Spain, 287
El Salvadoran Association for Economic and Social Development FUSADES, El Salvador, 91
The Salvation Army International Trust, UK, 381
Salvatore Maugeri Foundation—Occupational Health and Rehabilitation Clinic, Italy, 180
Salzburg Global Seminar, Austria, 22
Samaritans, UK, 381
Samaritan's Purse, USA, 469
Samir Kassir Foundation, Lebanon, 206
Samsung Foundation, Korea (Republic), 202
Samuel H. Kress Foundation, USA, 469
Samuel (Hedwig und Robert) Stiftung, Germany, 131
The San Diego Foundation, USA, 470
San Francisco Foundation—SFF, USA, 470
Sanaburi Foundation, Japan, 193
Sandals Foundation, Jamaica, 184
Sander (Wilhelm) Stiftung, Germany, 143
Santé Sud, France, 116
Santiago Development Project, Guatemala, 148
Santos Foundation, Papua New Guinea, 247
Sarah Scaife Foundation, Inc, USA, 470
Sasakawa, Fondation Franco-Japonaise, France, 106
Sasakawa Health Foundation—SHF, Japan, 194
The Sasakawa Peace Foundation—SPF, Japan, 194
Save the Children International, UK, 381
Save the Children (UK), UK, 381
Save Our Future Environmental Foundation, Germany, 139
Save Our Future Umweltstiftung—SOF, Germany, 139
Sawiris Foundation for Social Development—SFSD, Egypt, 90
SBS Cultural Foundation, Korea (Republic), 202

Scaife (Sarah) Foundation, Inc, USA, 470
Schering (Ernst) Stiftung, Germany, 127
Schlumberger Foundation, USA, 470
Schmidheiny (Max) Stiftung, Switzerland, 314
Schneider Electric Foundation, France, 111
Schöck (Eberhard) Stiftung, Germany, 127
Schuman (Robert), Fondation, France, 111
Schusterman (Charles and Lynn) Family Foundation, USA, 413
Schwab Foundation for Social Entrepreneurship, Switzerland, 316
Schwarzkopf-Stiftung Junges Europa, Germany, 139
Schwarzkopf Young Europe Foundation, Germany, 139
Schweisfurth Foundation, Germany, 139
Schweisfurth-Stiftung, Germany, 139
Schweizerisch-Liechtensteinische Stiftung für Archäologische Forschungen im Ausland—SLSA, Switzerland, 316
Schweizerische Akademie der Medizinischen Wissenschaften, Switzerland, 316
Schweizerische Herzstiftung, Switzerland, 316
Schweizerische Stiftung für Alpine Forschungen—SSAF, Switzerland, 316
Schweizerischer Nationalfonds zur Förderung der Wissenschaftlichen Forschung/Fonds National Suisse de la Recherche Scientifique—SNF, Switzerland, 316
Science and Politics Foundation—German Institute for International and Security Affairs, Germany, 141
Scientific Foundation of Hisham Adeeb Hijjawi, Jordan, 196
Scientific Foundation of the Spanish Cancer Association, Spain, 290
Scientific Research Foundation, Belgium, 32
Scope, UK, 381
Scotland's International Development Alliance, UK, 337
Scott Trust Foundation, UK, 356
Scottish Catholic International Aid Fund—SCIAF, UK, 382
Scottish Council for Voluntary Organisations—SCVO, UK, 337
SCVO—Scottish Council for Voluntary Organisations, UK, 337
The Seafarers' Charity, UK, 382
Seafarers International Relief Fund, UK, 382
Secours Catholique—Caritas de France, France, 116
Secours Dentaire International, Switzerland, 317
SeedChange, Canada, 61
Seeds of Affinity, Australia, 17
Seeds of Peace, USA, 470
SEEMO—South East Europe Media Organisation, Austria, 23
Seidel (Hanns) Stiftung, Germany, 131
SEL—Service d'Entraide et de Liaison, France, 116
SELAVIP—Services Latino-Américains, Africains et Asiatiques de Promotion de l'Habitation Populaire, Chile, 66
Self Help Africa—SHA, Ireland, 167
Self Help Development Foundation—SHDF, Zimbabwe, 491
Self-Sufficient People Foundation, Indonesia, 163
Sembrar Sartawi, Bolivia, 36
SEND-West Africa, Ghana, 144
Senna (Ayrton), Instituto, Brazil, 41
Sentebale, UK, 382
Sentrong Pangkultura ng Pilipinas, Philippines, 252
Seoam Yoon Se Young Foundation, Korea (Republic), 202
Serbian Philanthropy Forum, Serbia, 271
Serralves Foundation, Portugal, 261
Serrv International, Inc, USA, 471
Service Civil International—SCI, Belgium, 34
SES Foundation—Sustainability, Education, Solidarity, Argentina, 8
Sesame Workshop, USA, 471
Seub Nakhasathien Foundation, Thailand, 324
Seva Foundation, USA, 471
Sexual Wellbeing Aotearoa, New Zealand, 235
Seychelles Islands Foundation—SIF, Seychelles, 272
Shafik Gabr (Mohamed) Foundation, Egypt, 90
Shahid Afridi Foundation—SAF, Pakistan, 246
Shanghai Soong Ching Ling Foundation, China (People's Republic), 69
Shaping Our Future Foundation—SOFF, Malawi, 210
Sharing and Life Foundation, France, 110
Shell Foundation—SF, UK, 382
Shelter—National Campaign for Homeless People, UK, 382
Sherman (Archie) Charitable Trust, UK, 340

Shiv Nadar Foundation Group, India, 160
Shoman (Abdul Hameed) Foundation, Jordan, 195
Siam Society, Thailand, 324
Siamese Heritage Trust, Thailand, 324
SickKids Foundation, Canada, 62
SID—Society for International Development, Italy, 183
Sidney Myer Fund & The Myer Foundation, Australia, 18
Sieć Wspierania Organizacji Pozarządowych—SPLOT, Poland, 254
The Sierra Club Foundation, USA, 471
Sightsavers International, UK, 382
Signe and Ane Gyllenberg Foundation, Finland, 97
Signe och Ane Gyllenbergs stiftelse, Finland, 97
Sigrid Juséliuksen Säätiö, Finland, 97
Sigrid Jusélius Foundation, Finland, 97
Sigrid Rausing Trust—SRT, UK, 383
Sihtasutus Eesti Rahvuskultuuri Fond, Estonia, 93
Sihtasutus Poliitikauuringute Keskus Praxis, Estonia, 93
Silicon Valley Community Foundation—SVCF, USA, 471
Silva (Ricardo do Espírito Santo), Fundação, Portugal, 261
Simón I. Patiño Foundation, Switzerland, 310
Simone and Cino del Duca Foundation, France, 111
Simons Foundation, USA, 472
Sindika Dokolo Foundation, Angola, 5
Sinergia—Red Venezolana de OSC, Venezuela, 487
Singapore International Foundation—SIF, Singapore, 273
Singer-Polignac Foundation, France, 111
Sino-British Fellowship Trust—SBFT, UK, 383
SIPRI—Stockholm International Peace Research Institute, Sweden, 304
Sir Ahmadu Bello Memorial Foundation, Nigeria, 238
Sir Emeka Offor Foundation, Nigeria, 238
Sir Halley Stewart Trust, UK, 383
The Sir Jules Thorn Charitable Trust, UK, 383
Sistema Charitable Foundation, Russian Federation, 267
Sivil Toplum Geliştirme Merkezi—STGM, Türkiye, 327
Skinners' Charity Foundation, UK, 383
Skolkovo Foundation—Foundation for Development of the Center for the Development and Commercialization of New Technologies, Russian Federation, 267
Skoll Foundation, USA, 472
Slim (Carlos), Fundación, Mexico, 215
Sloan (Alfred P.) Foundation, USA, 398
SLOGA—Platforma za Razvojno Sodelovanje in Humanitarno Pomoč, Slovenia, 276
Slovak Academic Information Agency—SAIA, Slovakia, 274
Slovak-Czech Women's Fund, Slovakia, 276
Slovak Donors Forum, Slovakia, 274
Slovak Humanitarian Council, Slovakia, 274
Slovak Security Policy Institute, Slovakia, 276
Slovenian Science Foundation, Slovenia, 277
Slovenská Humanitná Rada, Slovakia, 274
Slovenska znanstvena fundacija—SZF, Slovenia, 277
Slovensko-český enský fond, Slovakia, 276
Slovenský inštitút pre bezpečnostnú politiku, Slovakia, 276
SM Foundation, Spain, 295
Smallwood Trust, UK, 384
Smith (Henry) Charity, UK, 358
Smith Richardson Foundation, Inc, USA, 472
Smithsonian Institution, USA, 472
The Snow Foundation, Australia, 18
Snow Leopard Trust, USA, 472
SNV, Netherlands, 228
Soares (Mário), Fundação, Portugal, 260
The Sobell Foundation, UK, 384
Social Movement, Lebanon, 206
Society for Education and Training, UK, 351
Society for International Development—SID, Italy, 183
Software AG Foundation, Germany, 139
Software AG Stiftung, Germany, 139
Sog'lom Avlod Uchun, Uzbekistan, 485
SOHO China Foundation, China (People's Republic), 69
Solidaarisuus, Finland, 96
Solidar, Belgium, 34
Solidarios—Consejo de Fundaciones Americanas de Desarrollo, Dominican Republic, 87
Solidarity Foundation, Dominican Republic, 87
Solidarity Overseas Service Malta—SOS Malta, Malta, 213
Solomon R. Guggenheim Foundation, USA, 473

INDEX OF FOUNDATIONS

Somalia NGO Consortium, Somalia, 277
Sonning-Fonden, Denmark, 86
Sonning Foundation, Denmark, 86
Sonning (Léonie) Musikfond, Denmark, 84
Sorenson Legacy Foundation, USA, 473
Soros Foundation—Kazakhstan, Kazakhstan, 197
Soros Foundation—Moldova, Moldova, 217
SOS Atlantic Forest Foundation, Brazil, 41
SOS Malta—Solidarity Overseas Service, Malta, 213
Souter Charitable Trust, UK, 384
South Africa Philanthropy Foundation, South Africa, 278
South African Agency for Science and Technology Advancement—SAASTA, South Africa, 283
South African Institute of International Affairs, South Africa, 283
South African Institute of Race Relations—IRR, South Africa, 283
South East Europe Media Organisation—SEEMO, Austria, 23
South Sudan Center for Strategic and Policy Studies—CSPS, South Sudan, 285
South West International Development Network—SWIDN, UK, 337
Southern Africa Trust, South Africa, 283
Southern Health, France, 116
Souto Vidigal (Maria Cecilia), Fundação, Brazil, 40
Spanish Association of Foundations, Spain, 285
Sparebankstiftelsen DNB, Norway, 243
Sparkassenstiftung für internationale Kooperation, Germany, 125
Spencer Foundation, USA, 473
Sphere, Switzerland, 305
Spinal Research, UK, 384
SpinalCure Australia, Australia, 18
SPP Foundation, Slovakia, 275
Springer (Axel) Stiftung, Germany, 122
Springer (Friede) Stiftung, Germany, 129
Srpski Filantropski Forum, Serbia, 271
St John Ambulance, UK, 380
Stanley Center for Peace and Security, USA, 473
Stanley Thomas Johnson Foundation, Switzerland, 317
The Starr Foundation, USA, 473
Start Network, UK, 337
State Grid Foundation for Public Welfare, China (People's Republic), 69
State Scholarships Foundation—IKY, Greece, 147
Stavros Niarchos Foundation—SNF, Greece, 147
Steelworkers Humanity Fund/Le Fonds Humanitaire des Metallos, Canada, 62
Steenkamp (Reeva Rebecca) Foundation, South Africa, 283
Stefan Batory Foundation, Poland, 256
Stelios Philanthropic Foundation, Cyprus, 78
Stewards Company Limited, UK, 384
Stewardship Foundation, USA, 473
Stewart (Sir Halley) Trust, UK, 383
Stichting Bellingcat, Netherlands, 228
Stichting Democratie en Media, Netherlands, 229
Stichting Dioraphte, Netherlands, 229
Stichting DOEN, Netherlands, 229
Stichting Fonds 1818, Netherlands, 229
Stichting IKEA Foundation, Netherlands, 229
Stichting Liliane Fonds, Netherlands, 229
Stichting Mama Cash, Netherlands, 230
Stichting Max Havelaar—Fairtrade Nederland, Netherlands, 230
Stichting The Ocean Cleanup, Netherlands, 230
Stichting Praemium Erasmianum, Netherlands, 230
Stichting Prins Bernhard Cultuurfonds, Netherlands, 230
Stichting van Schulden naar Kansen, Netherlands, 231
Stichting Triodos Foundation, Netherlands, 231
Stichting Vluchteling, Netherlands, 231
Stichting Vodafone Netherlands, Netherlands, 231
Stiftelsen Blanceflor Boncompagni Ludovisi, född Bildt, Sweden, 303
Stiftelsen Dag Hammarskjölds Minnesfond, Sweden, 303
Stiftelsen Dam, Norway, 243
Stiftelsen Gapminder, Sweden, 300
Stiftelsen Ingmar Bergman, Sweden, 303
Stiftelsen för Miljöstrategisk Forskning—Mistra, Sweden, 303
Stiftelsen Riksbankens Jubileumsfond, Sweden, 303
Stiftelsen Teknikens Främjande—Tekniikan Edistämissäätiö, Finland, 98
Stiftelser i Samverkan, Sweden, 298
Stiftelsesforeningen, Norway, 240

Stifterverband für die Deutsche Wissenschaft eV, Germany, 119
Stiftung 'Erinnerung, Verantwortung und Zukunft'—EVZ, Germany, 139
Stiftung Ettersberg, Germany, 140
Stiftung zur Förderung der Hochschulrektorenkonferenz, Germany, 140
Stiftung Jugend forscht eV, Germany, 140
Stiftung Kinder in Afrika, Germany, 140
Stiftung Kinderdorf Pestalozzi, Switzerland, 317
Stiftung Klimarappen, Switzerland, 317
Stiftung Lesen, Germany, 140
Stiftung Mercator, Germany, 140
Stiftung Meridian, Germany, 140
Stiftung Nord-Süd-Brücken, Germany, 141
Stiftung Prix Jeunesse, Germany, 138
Stiftung für die Rechte zukünftiger Generationen—SRzG, Germany, 141
Stiftung Vivamos Mejor, Switzerland, 317
Stiftung Weltethos, Germany, 141
Stiftung West-Östliche Begegnungen, Germany, 141
Stiftung Wissenschaft und Politik—Deutsches Institut für internationale Politik und Sicherheit—SWP, Germany, 141
Stiftung Zukunft.li, Liechtenstein, 208
Stiftungsfonds Deutsche Bank im Stifterverband für die Deutsche Wissenschaft, Germany, 142
Stockholm Environment Institute, Sweden, 303
Stockholm International Peace Research Institute—SIPRI, Sweden, 304
Stowarzyszenie Klon/Jawor, Poland, 254
Straits Exchange Foundation—SEF, Taiwan, 321
Street Child, UK, 384
Streisand (Barbra) Foundation, USA, 408
Strickland Foundation, Malta, 214
Stroke Association, UK, 384
Strømme Foundation, Norway, 243
Strømmestiftelsen, Norway, 243
Studienstiftung des deutschen Volkes, Germany, 142
Sturzo (Luigi), Istituto, Italy, 182
Sudan Foundation, Sudan, 297
Sudd Institute, South Sudan, 285
Südosteuropäische Medienorganisation, Austria, 23
Sulaiman Bin Abdul Aziz Bin Saleh Al Rajhi Foundation, Saudi Arabia, 269
Sultan bin Abdulaziz Al Sa'ud Foundation, Saudi Arabia, 270
SUN Civil Society Network, UK, 381
Suomalaiset kehitysjärjestöt—Fingo, Finland, 95
Suomen Kulttuurirahasto, Finland, 97
Surdna Foundation, Inc, USA, 474
Survival International, UK, 385
Susan G. Komen Breast Cancer Foundation, USA, 474
The Susan Thompson Buffett Foundation—STBF, USA, 474
Sutherland Self Help Trust, New Zealand, 235
Suzuki Foundation (David), Canada, 53
Svenska Institutet i Rom/Istituto Svedese di Studi Classici a Roma, Italy, 183
Svenska kulturfonden, Finland, 98
Sverige-Amerika Stiftelsen, Sweden, 304
Swaminathan (M. S.) Research Foundation, India, 158
Swaziland Charitable Trust, Eswatini, 93
Sweden-America Foundation, Sweden, 304
Sweden-Japan Foundation—SJF, Sweden, 304
Swedish Cancer Society, Sweden, 298
The Swedish Cultural Foundation in Finland, Finland, 98
Swedish-Finnish Cultural Foundation, Sweden, 301
The Swedish Heart-Lung Foundation, Sweden, 300
Swedish Institute at Athens, Greece, 147
Swedish Institute in Rome, Italy, 183
Swedish Rheumatism Association, Sweden, 302
Swiss Academy of Medical Sciences, Switzerland, 316
Swiss Alliance of Development Organisations, Switzerland, 305
Swiss Arts Council, Switzerland, 315
Swiss Church Aid, Switzerland, 311
Swiss Foundation for Alpine Research—SFAR, Switzerland, 316
Swiss Foundation for Technical Co-operation, Switzerland, 318
Swiss Heart Foundation, Switzerland, 316
Swiss-Liechtenstein Foundation for Archaeological Research Abroad—SLFA, Switzerland, 316
Swiss National Science Foundation—SNSF, Switzerland, 316
Swiss Philanthropy Foundation, Switzerland, 305
SWISSAID Foundation, Switzerland, 318

Swisscontact—Swiss Foundation for Technical Co-operation, Switzerland, 318
SwissFoundations—Verband der Schweizer Förderstiftungen/Association des Fondations Donatrices Suisses, Switzerland, 306
Syin-Lu Social Welfare Foundation, Taiwan, 321
Sylvia and Charles Viertel Charitable Foundation, Australia, 18
Synergos—The Synergos Institute, USA, 396
Syria Al-Gad Relief Foundation, Egypt, 91
Szenes (Arpad)–Vieira da Silva, Fundação, Portugal, 258

Taawon, Palestinian Territories, 246
Tahir Foundation, Indonesia, 162
Taiwan NPO Information Platform, Taiwan, 321
Talk Out Loud, Australia, 18
Talon (Claudine), Fondation, Benin, 35
Tanager, USA, 397
Tanenbaum (Joseph) Charitable Foundation, Canada, 58
Tang Prize Foundation, Taiwan, 322
TANZ—Trade Aid NZ Inc, New Zealand, 235
Tarih Vakfı, Türkiye, 329
Tata Trusts, India, 160
Tatra Bank Foundation, Slovakia, 276
Tea Research Foundation of Central Africa—TRFCA, Malawi, 211
Tearfund, UK, 385
Tearfund Australia, Australia, 18
Tebtebba Foundation, Philippines, 253
TechnoServe, USA, 474
Tekniikan Edistämissäätiö—Stiftelsen för teknikens främjande—TES, Finland, 98
Telefónica Foundation, Spain, 295
Telefónica Movistar Argentina Foundation, Argentina, 8
Telefónica Movistar Chile Foundation, Chile, 65
Telefónica Movistar Colombia Foundation, Colombia, 71
Telefónica Movistar Ecuador Foundation, Ecuador, 89
Telefónica Movistar México Foundation, Mexico, 216
Telefónica Movistar Perú Foundation, Peru, 249
Telefónica Movistar Uruguay Foundation, Uruguay, 485
Telefónica Vivo Foundation, Brazil, 41
Teletón México Foundation, Mexico, 216
Telmex Telcel Foundation, Mexico, 216
Temasek Foundation, Singapore, 273
Templeton (John) Foundation, USA, 444
Templeton Philanthropies, USA, 444
Templeton Religion Trust, Bahamas, 24
Tencent Foundation, China (People's Republic), 70
Terre des Hommes International Federation—TDHIF, Switzerland, 318
Terre Sans Frontières—TSF, Canada, 62
Terrence Higgins Trust—THT, UK, 385
TESEV—Türkiye Ekonomik ve Sosyal Etüdler Vakfı, Türkiye, 329
Tewa, Nepal, 223
TFF—Transnational Foundation for Peace and Future Research, Sweden, 304
TFF—Transnationella Stiftelsen för Freds- och Framtidsforskning, Sweden, 304
Thabo Mbeki Foundation, South Africa, 284
Thai Rath Foundation, Thailand, 324
THET, UK, 355
Thiel Foundation, USA, 474
Third Sector Foundation of Turkey, Türkiye, 327
Third World Network—TWN, Malaysia, 211
Third World Solidarity Action, Luxembourg, 209
Thomas B. Thrige Foundation, Denmark, 86
Thomas B. Thriges Fond, Denmark, 86
Thomson Foundation, UK, 385
Thomson Reuters Foundation, UK, 385
Thorn (The Sir Jules) Charitable Trust, UK, 383
Thrasher Research Fund, USA, 474
Thriges (Thomas B.) Fond, Denmark, 86
Thunberg (Greta) Foundation, Sweden, 300
Thurgood Marshall Institute, USA, 454
Thyssen (Fritz) Stiftung, Germany, 130
TI—Transparency International, Germany, 142
Tibet Fund, USA, 475
Tibet-Institut Rikon, Switzerland, 318
Tides Organizations, USA, 475
Tifa Foundation—Indonesia, Indonesia, 163
Tiffany & Co Foundation, USA, 475
Timchenko (Elena & Gennady) Foundation, Russian Federation, 265
Tindall Foundation, New Zealand, 235
Tinh Thuong One Member Limited Liability Microfinance Institution, Viet Nam, 488
Tinker Foundation, Inc, USA, 475
TISCO Foundation, Thailand, 325
TK Foundation, Bahamas, 24
The Todd Foundation, New Zealand, 235

INDEX OF FOUNDATIONS

Toegepaste en Technische Wetenschappen, Netherlands, 227
Toepfer (Alfred) Stiftung, Germany, 121
Together for Global Justice—CIDSE, Belgium, 29
Tokyu Foundation, Japan, 194
Tony Blair Institute for Global Change—TBI, UK, 386
Tony Elumelu Foundation—TEF, Nigeria, 238
Topūtanga Tuku Aroha o Aotearoa, New Zealand, 232
Torcuato Di Tella Foundation, Argentina, 8
TOSA Foundation, USA, 475
Toshiba International Foundation—TIFO, Japan, 194
TotalEnergies Foundation, France, 112
Totto Foundation, Japan, 194
The Toyota Foundation, Japan, 195
Toyota Vietnam Foundation—TVF, Viet Nam, 488
TPG Telecom Foundation, Australia, 19
Trade Aid NZ Inc—TANZ, New Zealand, 235
Translators without Borders, USA, 416
Transnational Giving Europe—TGE, Belgium, 27
Transnet Foundation, South Africa, 284
Transparency International—TI, Germany, 142
Transparent Election Foundation of Afghanistan—TEFA, Afghanistan, 4
The Trawalla Foundation, Australia, 19
Triodos Foundation, Netherlands, 231
Trócaire—Catholic Agency for World Development, Ireland, 168
Trudeau (Pierre Elliott) Foundation, Canada, 55
The Trussell Trust, UK, 386
Trust for London, UK, 386
Trust for Mutual Understanding—TMU, USA, 476
Trust for Social Achievement, Bulgaria, 44
Trustees for Harvard University, USA, 421
Trusthouse Charitable Foundation, UK, 386
Tschira (Klaus) Stiftung, Germany, 134
TTF—Toyota Thailand Foundation, Thailand, 325
Tujenge Africa Foundation, Burundi, 45
Tulsa Community Foundation—TCF, USA, 476
Tunisia Development Foundation, Tunisia, 326
Turin Savings Bank Foundation, Italy, 176
Turing (Alan) Institute, UK, 339
Turkish Economic and Social Studies Foundation, Türkiye, 329
Turkish Family Health and Planning Foundation, Türkiye, 330
Turkish Foundation for Combating Soil Erosion, for Reforestation and the Protection of Natural Habitats, Türkiye, 330
Türkiye Aile Sağlığı ve Planlaması Vakfı—TAPV, Türkiye, 330
Türkiye Çevre Vakfı, Türkiye, 330
Türkiye Erozyonla Mücadele Ağaçlandırma ve Doğal Varlıkları Koruma Vakfı—TEMA, Türkiye, 330
Türkiye İnsan Hakları Vakfı—TİHV, Türkiye, 330
Türkiye Kalkınma Vakfı, Türkiye, 330
Türkiye Vodafone Vakfı, Türkiye, 331
Turner Foundation, Inc USA, 476
Turquoise Mountain Foundation, UK, 386
Turriano (Juanelo) Fundación, Spain, 291
TÜSEV—Türkiye Üçüncü Sektör Vakfı, Türkiye, 327
Tusk, UK, 387
Tutu (Desmond & Leah) Legacy Foundation, South Africa, 279
TY Danjuma Foundation, Nigeria, 239
TYM Fund, Viet Nam, 488

U4 Anti-Corruption Resource Centre, Norway, 241
UAI—Union des Associations Internationales, Belgium, 27
Ucom Foundation, Armenia, 9
UEFA Foundation for Children, Switzerland, 318
Ufadhili Trust, Kenya, 197
Ugo Bordoni Foundation, Italy, 180
UJIA—United Jewish Israel Appeal, UK, 387
UK Community Foundations—UKCF, UK, 338
UK Research and Innovation—UKRI, UK, 387
Ukrainian Philanthropists Forum, Ukraine, 332
Ukrainian Women's Fund, Ukraine, 333
Uluchay Social-Economic Innovation Center, Azerbaijan, 23
Uluntu Community Foundation—UCF, Zimbabwe, 491
Umut Vakfı, Türkiye, 331
Unbound Philanthropy, USA, 476
UNESCO Centre du Patrimoine Mondial, France, 116
UNESCO World Heritage Centre, France, 116
UniCredit Foundation, Italy, 183
UNIFOR—Forvaltningsstiftelse for fond og legater, Norway, 240
Union Aid Abroad—APHEDA, Australia, 19
Union des Associations Internationales—UAI, Belgium, 27
Union of International Associations—UIA/Unie van de Internationale Vereinigingen—UIV, Belgium, 27
Union for International Cancer Control—UICC, Switzerland, 318
Union Internationale Contre le Cancer, Switzerland, 318
Unipolis Foundation, Italy, 181
UNIR Bolivia Foundation, Bolivia, 36
Unitarian Universalist Service Committee—UUSC, USA, 476
United Jewish Israel Appeal—UJIA, UK, 387
United Nations Foundation, USA, 476
United Purpose, UK, 387
United States African Development Foundation—USADF, USA, 477
United States-Japan Foundation, USA, 477
United Way—Belarus/NGO Development Centre, Belarus, 25
United Way Worldwide, USA, 477
Unity Foundation, Luxembourg, 210
Universal Foundation, Maldives, 212
Universal Jewish Alliance, France, 101
Universitaire Stichting, Belgium, 34
University Foundation, Belgium, 34
University-Industry Foundation, Spain, 295
University of Zaragoza Business Foundation, Spain, 290
UPM Foundation, Uruguay, 485
UPS Foundation, USA, 477
US Civilian Research & Development Foundation, USA, 419
Usain Bolt Foundation, Jamaica, 185
USC Shoah Foundation—The Institute for Visual History and Education, USA, 434
USPG—United Society Partners in the Gospel, UK, 387
UUSC—Unitarian Universalist Service Committee, USA, 476

Väestöliitto, Finland, 98
Values Foundation, Bulgaria, 43
Vancouver Foundation, Canada, 62
VANI—Voluntary Action Network India, India, 155
Van Leer Foundation, Netherlands, 231
Van Leer Jerusalem Institute, Israel, 171
Vargas (Getulio), Fundação, Brazil, 40
Varkey Foundation, UK, 388
Vehbi Koç Foundation, Türkiye, 331
Vehbi Koç Vakfı, Türkiye, 331
Veillon (Charles), Fondation, Switzerland, 308
Venezuelan Network of Civil Society Organizations, Venezuela, 487
Venice Foundation, Italy, 181
Venkatarangaiya (M.) Foundation, India, 158
VENRO—Verband Entwicklungspolitik und Humanitäre Hilfe deutscher Nichtregierungsorganizationen, Germany, 120
Verband für Gemeinnütziges Stiften, Austria, 20
Vereinigung Liechtensteinischer gemeinnütziger Stiftungen eV, Liechtenstein, 207
Versus Arthritis, UK, 388
Vestnordenfonden, Denmark, 86
Vetlesen (G. Unger) Foundation, USA, 429
VIA Foundation, Czech Republic, 81
Victor Pinchuk Foundation, Ukraine, 333
Victoria Children Foundation, Russian Federation, 267
VIDC—Vienna Institute for International Dialogue and Co-operation, Austria, 23
Vienna Institute for International Dialogue and Co-operation—VIDC, Austria, 23
Viertel (Sylvia and Charles) Charitable Foundation, Australia, 18
Village Community Development Foundation, Indonesia, 163
Villar Foundation, Inc Philippines, 253
Vincent Fairfax Family Foundation—VFFF, Australia, 19
VINCI Corporate Foundation for the City, France, 106
VinFuture Foundation, Viet Nam, 489
Vita, Ireland, 168
Vital Strategies, USA, 478
Vital Voices Global Partnership, USA, 478
Vivamos Mejor Foundation, Switzerland, 317
Vivekananda International Foundation—VIF, India, 161
Vladimir Potanin Foundation, Russian Federation, 267
Vodacom Foundation, South Africa, 284
Vodacom Foundation DRC, Congo (Democratic Republic), 72
Vodacom Foundation South Africa, South Africa, 284
Vodacom Lesotho Foundation, Lesotho, 207
Vodacom Tanzania Foundation—VTF, Tanzania, 323
Vodafone Albania Foundation, Albania, 5
Vodafone Americas Foundation, USA, 478
Vodafone ATH Fiji Foundation, Fiji, 94
Vodafone Czech Republic Foundation, Czech Republic, 80
Vodafone Egypt Foundation, Egypt, 91
Vodafone Foundation, UK, 388
Vodafone Foundation Germany, Germany, 142
Vodafone Foundation India, India, 161
Vodafone Foundation Luxembourg, Luxembourg, 210
Vodafone Foundation New Zealand, New Zealand, 235
Vodafone Ghana Foundation, Ghana, 144
Vodafone Hungary Foundation, Hungary, 153
Vodafone Idea Foundation, India, 161
Vodafone Ireland Foundation, Ireland, 168
Vodafone Italy Foundation, Italy, 181
Vodafone Magyarország Alapítvány, Hungary, 153
Vodafone Netherlands Foundation, Netherlands, 231
Vodafone Portugal Foundation, Portugal, 261
Vodafone Romania Foundation, Romania, 264
Vodafone Spain Foundation, Spain, 296
Vodafone Stiftung Deutschland, Germany, 142
Vodafone Türkiye Foundation, Türkiye, 331
Volkart Foundation, Switzerland, 319
Volkart-Stiftung, Switzerland, 319
Volkswagen Foundation, Germany, 142
VolkswagenStiftung, Germany, 142
Volnoe Delo—Oleg Deripaska Foundation, Russian Federation, 267
Voluntary Action Network India—VANI, India, 155
Voluntary Service Overseas, UK, 388
Volunteer Service Abroad/Te Tūao Tāwāhi—VSA, New Zealand, 236
VSO—Voluntary Service Overseas, UK, 388
Výbor dobré vůle—Nadace Olgy Havlové, Czech Republic, 81
Vzdělávací Nadace Jana Husa, Czech Republic, 81

W. K. Kellogg Foundation—WKKF, USA, 478
Wahana Lingkungan Hidup Indonesia—WALHI, Indonesia, 162
WALHI—Wahana Lingkungan Hidup Indonesia, Indonesia, 162
Walk Free, Australia, 15
Wallace (Charles) Trusts, UK, 347
The Wallace Foundation, USA, 478
Wallenberg (Knut och Alice) Stiftelse, Sweden, 301
Walmart Foundation, USA, 478
Walter and Duncan Gordon Charitable Foundation, Canada, 62
Walton Family Foundation, USA, 479
WAMA Foundation, Tanzania, 323
War Child, UK, 388
War on Want, UK, 388
WasserStiftung, Germany, 142
Water for Good, USA, 479
Water.org, Inc, USA, 479
Water for People, USA, 479
WaterAid, UK, 389
WaterFoundation, Germany, 142
The Waterloo Foundation—TWF, UK, 389
Weber (Franz), Fondation, Switzerland, 308
Weber (Max) Stiftung, Germany, 136
Webster (R. Howard) Foundation, Canada, 61
Weeden Foundation, USA, 479
Weinberg (Harry and Jeanette) Foundation, USA, 434
The Welch Foundation, USA, 479
Welfare Association, Palestinian Territories, 246
Wellbeing of Women, UK, 389
Wellcome Trust, UK, 389
Wenner-Gren Foundation for Anthropological Research, Inc, USA, 480
Wenner-Gren Foundations, Sweden, 304
West African Rural Foundation—WARF, Senegal, 270
West-Nordic Foundation, Denmark, 86
Westminster Foundation for Democracy—WFD, UK, 389
Weston (Garfield) Foundation, UK, 355
Weyerhaeuser Family Foundation, Inc, USA, 480
The Wheel, Ireland, 165
Whirlpool Foundation, USA, 480
White Point Development Foundation, Türkiye, 328
Whitehall Foundation, Inc, USA, 480
The Whitley Fund for Nature—WFN, UK, 390
WHO Foundation, Switzerland, 319

INDEX OF FOUNDATIONS

Wihuri Foundation for International Prizes, Finland, 98
Wihuri (Jenny and Antti) Foundation, Finland, 96
Wihurin kansainvälisten palkintojen rahasto, Finland, 98
Wikimedia Foundation, USA, 480
Wild (Dr Rainer) Stiftung, Germany, 126
The WILD Foundation—International Wilderness Leadership Foundation, USA, 481
Wilderness Foundation Global—WFG, South Africa, 284
The Wildlife Trusts, UK, 390
Wilhelm Sander Foundation, Germany, 143
Wilhelm-Sander-Stiftung, Germany, 143
William Adlington Cadbury Charitable Trust, UK, 390
William Buckland Foundation, Australia, 19
The William and Flora Hewlett Foundation, USA, 481
The William H. Donner Foundation, Inc, USA, 481
William Randolph Hearst Foundation, USA, 435
William T. Grant Foundation, USA, 481
WILPF—Women's International League for Peace and Freedom, Switzerland, 319
Wilsdorf (Hans), Fondation, Switzerland, 309
Wilson (E. O.) Biodiversity Foundation, USA, 421
Wilson (Woodrow) International Center for Scholars, USA, 482
Windle Trust International, UK, 390
Winfrey (Oprah) Leadership Academy Foundation, USA, 459
WINGS—Worldwide Initiatives for Grantmaker Support, Brazil, 38
Winrock International, USA, 481
Winston Churchill Foundation of the United States, USA, 482
Winston Churchill Memorial Trust, Australia, 19
Winston Churchill Memorial Trust of New Zealand, New Zealand, 236
Wisti (Folmer) Foundation for International Understanding, Denmark, 83
The Wolfson Foundation, UK, 390
Woman to Woman Foundation, Sweden, 301
The Womanity Foundation, Switzerland, 319
Women in Development Foundation, Tanzania, 323
Women in Equality Foundation, Argentina, 8
Women Thrive Fund, UK, 384
WomenLead Institute, USA, 418
Women's Aid, Ireland, 168
Women's Aid Organisation—WAO, Malaysia, 212
Women's Development Network, Costa Rica, 75
Women's Environment & Development Organization—WEDO, USA, 482
Women's Foundation, Costa Rica, 74
Women's Fund Asia, Sri Lanka, 297
Women's International League for Peace and Freedom, Switzerland, 319
Women's World Summit Foundation—WWSF, Switzerland, 320
The Wood Foundation—TWF, UK, 391
Woodrow Wilson International Center for Scholars, USA, 482
World Alliance for Citizen Participation—CIVICUS, South Africa, 278
World Alliance of YMCAs—Young Men's Christian Associations, Switzerland, 319
World Animal Protection, UK, 391
World Association of Children's Friends, Monaco, 217
World Central Kitchen—WCK, USA, 482
World Concern, USA, 482
World Economic Forum, Switzerland, 320
World Emergency Relief—WER, USA, 483
World Holocaust Forum Foundation—WHF, Israel, 171
World Jewish Relief, UK, 391
World Land Trust—WLT, UK, 391
World Learning, USA, 483
World Monuments Fund—WMF, USA, 483
World Neighbors, USA, 483
The World of NGOs, Austria, 20
World Peace Foundation—WPF, USA, 483
World Resources Institute—WRI, USA, 483
World Scout Foundation—Fondation du Scoutisme Mondial—WSF/FSM, Switzerland, 320
World Telehealth Initiative, USA, 484
World University Service of Canada/Entraide Universitaire Mondiale du Canada—WUSC/EUMC, Canada, 63
World Vegetable Center, Taiwan, 322
World Vision International, UK, 391
WorldFish, Malaysia, 212
Worldwide Cancer Research, UK, 392
Worldwide Initiatives for Grantmaker Support—WINGS, Brazil, 38
Wujoh Foundation for Media and Development, Yemen, 489
WWF International, Switzerland, 320
WWSF—Women's World Summit Foundation, Switzerland, 320
The Wyss Foundtion, USA, 484

Xiangjiang Social Relief Fund, China (People's Republic), 68
XPRIZE Foundation, USA, 484

YADESA—Yayasan Pembinaan Masyarakat Desa, Indonesia, 163
Yanai Tadashi Foundation, Japan, 195
Yanbao Charity Foundation, China (People's Republic), 69
Yayasan Azman Hashim, Malaysia, 212
Yayasan Dian Desa—YDD, Indonesia, 162
Yayasan Geutanyoë, Indonesia, 162
Yayasan Insan Sembada, Indonesia, 163
Yayasan Pembinaan Masyarakat Desa—YADESA, Indonesia, 163
Yayasan Tifa, Indonesia, 163
Year Out Group, UK, 374
Yellow Feather Fund, USA, 471
Yemen Policy Center, Yemen, 489
Yemen Polling Center—YPC, Yemen, 489
Yidan Prize Foundation, Hong Kong, 152
YMCA—Young Men's Christian Association, UK, 392
YongLin Charity Foundation, Taiwan, 322
YORGHAS Foundation, Poland, 258
Young Citizens—Citizenship Foundation, UK, 392
Young Lives vs Cancer, UK, 392
Youth Leadership Development Foundation—YLDF, Yemen, 489
Yrjö Jahnsson Foundation, Finland, 98
Yrjö Jahnssonin säätiö, Finland, 98
Yuan Lin Charity Fund, China (People's Republic), 70

Zagranica Group, Poland, 254
Zakat House, Kuwait, 203
Zancan (Emanuela), Fondazione Centro Studi e Ricerca Sociale, Italy, 172
Zarina & Naushad Merali Foundation, Kenya, 200
Zavod Center za Informiranje, Sodelovanje in Razvoj Nevladnih Organizacije—CNVOS, Slovenia, 277
Zeiss (Carl) Stiftung, Germany, 123
ZEIT-Stiftung Ebelin und Gerd Bucerius, Germany, 143
Ziviler Friedensdienst—ZFD, Germany, 120
ZOA, Netherlands, 231
Zochonis Charitable Trust, UK, 392
Zonta Foundation for Women, USA, 484
Zorig Foundation, Mongolia, 219
Zuleikhabai Valy Mohamed Gany Rangoonwala Trust—ZVMG Rangoonwala Trust, Pakistan, 246
Zurich Community Trust—ZCT, UK, 392
ZVMG Rangoonwala Trust, Pakistan, 246

Index of Main Activities

Co-ordinating bodies	520
Aid to less-developed countries	522
Arts and humanities	526
Conservation and the environment	532
Economic affairs	538
Education	546
International affairs	557
Law, civil society and human rights	561
Medicine and health	571
Science and technology	578
Social welfare	585

CO-ORDINATING BODIES

Abjadnany Šliach, Belarus, 25
Academy for the Development of Philanthropy in Poland, Poland, 253
Accountable Now, USA, 393
ACF—Association of Charitable Foundations, UK, 335
Afghanistan Institute for Civil Society—AICS, Afghanistan, 3
Africa Grantmakers' Affinity Group—AGAG, USA, 393
African Philanthropy Forum, Nigeria, 236
African Venture Philanthropy Alliance—AVPA, Kenya, 197
AGAG—Africa Grantmakers' Affinity Group, USA, 393
Akademia Rozwoju Filantropii w Polsce—ARFP, Poland, 253
ALIDE—Asociación Latinoamericana de Instituciones Financieras para el Desarrollo, Peru, 248
Alliance of Community Foundations Germany, Germany, 119
Alliance Sud—Swiss Alliance of Development Organizations, Switzerland, 305
Ambrela Platform of Development Organizations, Slovakia, 273
Ambrela—Platforma rozvojových organizácií, Slovakia, 273
ANND—Arab NGO Network for Development, Lebanon, 205
Arab Foundations Forum, Jordan, 195
Arab Network for Environment and Development—RAED, Egypt, 89
Arab Office for Youth and Environment, Egypt, 89
Arengukoostöö Ümarlaud—AKÜ, Estonia, 92
Ariadne—European Funders for Social Change and Human Rights, UK, 336
Asia Philanthropy Circle—APC, Singapore, 272
Asociace komunitních nadací v České republice—Spolek AKN, Czech Republic, 78
Asociácia komunitných nadácií Slovenska, Slovakia, 274
Asociacija Litdea—Lithuanian Development Education and Awareness Raising Association, Lithuania, 208
Asociación Española de Fundaciones, Spain, 285
Asociación de Fundaciones Familiares y Empresariales—AFE, Colombia, 70
Asociación Latinoamericana de Instituciones Financieras para el Desarrollo—ALIDE, Peru, 248
Asotzijatzijata za Dyemokratska Initzijativa, North Macedonia, 239
Assifero—Associazione Italiana delle Fondazioni ed Enti della Filantropia Istituzionale, Italy, 171
Association of Charitable Foundations—ACF, UK, 335
Association of Civil Society Development Center, Türkiye, 327
Association for Democratic Initiatives—ADI, North Macedonia, 239
Association for Development Policy and Humanitarian Aid, Germany, 120
Association of Family and Corporate Foundations, Colombia, 70

Association des Fondations Donatrices Suisses, Switzerland, 306
Association of Foundations, Philippines, 250
Association of Foundations in the Netherlands, Netherlands, 223
Association of German Foundations, Germany, 118
Association of Grantmaking Foundations in Switzerland, Switzerland, 306
Association of Guernsey Charities—AGC, Channel Islands, 64
Association of Italian Foundations and Savings Banks, Italy, 171
Association of Jersey Charities—AJC, Channel Islands, 64
Association of Liechtenstein Charitable Foundations, Liechtenstein, 207
Association of Medical Research Charities—AMRC, UK, 335
Association of Non-Governmental Organizations in The Gambia—TANGO, Gambia, 117
Association for Public Benefit Foundations, Austria, 20
Association of Slovakian Community Foundations, Slovakia, 274
Association of Swedish Foundations, Sweden, 298
Associazione di Fondazioni e di Casse di Risparmio SpA—ACRI, Italy, 171
Associazione Italiana delle Fondazioni ed Enti della Filantropia Istituzionale, Italy, 171
Autonómia Alapítvány, Hungary, 152
Autonómia Foundation, Hungary, 152
Balkan Civil Society Development Network—BCSDN, North Macedonia, 239
BCause Foundation, Bulgaria, 42
Belgian Federation of Philanthropic Foundations, Belgium, 26
Belgische Federatie van Filantropische Stichtingen, Belgium, 26
Black Sea NGO Network—BSNN, Bulgaria, 42
Bond, UK, 335
British Overseas NGOs for Development, UK, 335
Bulgarian Donors' Forum, Bulgaria, 42
Bulgarian Platform for International Development—BPID, Bulgaria, 42
Bundesverband Deutscher Stiftungen eV, Germany, 118
CAF America, USA, 393
CAF—Charities Aid Foundation, UK, 336
CAF India, India, 155
CAF Russia—Charities Aid Foundation Russia, Russian Federation, 264
CanadaHelps, Canada, 47
Canadian Council for International Co-operation—CCIC/Conseil Canadien pour la Coopération Internationale—CCCI, Canada, 48
Candid, USA, 393
Caribbean Policy Development Centre—CPDC, Barbados, 25
Caritas Internationalis—CI, Vatican City, 486
Caucus of Development NGO Networks—CODE-NGO, Philippines, 250
Center for Training and Consultancy, Georgia, 117
Centras—Assistance Centre for NGOs, Romania, 263

Centras—Centrul de Asistenta pentru Organizatii Neguvernamentale, Romania, 263
Centre for the Development of Non-governmental Organizations, Montenegro, 219
Centre for Development of Non-profit Organizations, Croatia, 76
Centre Français des Fonds et Fondations—CFF, France, 99
Centre for the Information Service, Co-operation and Development of NGOs, Slovenia, 277
Centre for Philanthropy, Slovakia, 274
Centre for Promotion and Development of Civil Initiatives—OPUS, Poland, 254
Centre for Social Impact and Philanthropy—CSIP, India, 154
Centro Mexicano para la Filantropía—CEMEFI, Mexico, 214
Centro Português de Fundações—CPF, Portugal, 258
Centrul Naţional de Asistenţă și Informare a Organizaţiilor Neguvernamentale din Moldova—Centrul CONTACT, Moldova, 216
Centrul de Resurse pentru Drepturile Omului—CReDO, Moldova, 217
Centrum pre Filantropiu, Slovakia, 274
CERANEO—Centar za razvoj neprofitnih organizacija, Croatia, 76
Cercle de Coopération des ONGD du Luxembourg, Luxembourg, 209
CERES—Consorcio Ecuatoriano Para La Responsabilidad Social, Ecuador, 87
Česká rada sociálních služeb—CRSS, Czech Republic, 78
Charitable Impact Foundation, Canada, 47
Charities Advisory Trust, UK, 336
Charities Aid Foundation of America—CAF America, USA, 393
Charities Aid Foundation—CAF, UK, 336
Charities Aid Foundation Russia—CAF Russia, Russian Federation, 264
Charities Institute Ireland—Cii, Ireland, 165
China Charities Alliance, China (People's Republic), 66
China Foundation Center—CFC, China (People's Republic), 66
Christoph Merian Foundation, Switzerland, 305
Christoph-Merian-Stiftung, Switzerland, 305
Civic Initiatives, Serbia, 271
CIVICUS—World Alliance for Citizen Participation, South Africa, 278
CiviKos Platform, Kosovo, 202
Civil Peace Service—CPS, Germany, 120
Civil Society Development Foundation, Romania, 263
Civil Society and Human Rights Network, Afghanistan, 3
Civil Society and Human Rights Organization—CSHRO, Afghanistan, 3
Civitates, Belgium, 27
CNVOS—Zavod Center za Informiranje, Sodelovanje in Razvoj Nevladnih Organizacije, Slovenia, 277
Comité de Coopération Pour le Cambodge, Cambodia, 46
Comité de Coordination des ONGI en RCA, Central African Republic, 63
Common Network, Brazil, 38
Community Chest of Hong Kong, Hong Kong, 150

INDEX OF MAIN ACTIVITIES
Co-ordinating bodies

Community Foundation Partnership, Russian Federation, 264
Community Foundation of Singapore, Singapore, 272
Community Foundations of Canada, Canada, 47
Community Foundations of New Zealand, New Zealand, 232
Community of Solidarity Organizations, Chile, 64
Comunalia—Alianza de Fundaciones Comunitarias de México, Mexico, 215
Comunidad de Organizaciones Solidarios, Chile, 64
CONCORD—European NGO Confederation for Relief and Development, Belgium, 26
Cooperation Canada/Coopération Canada, Canada, 48
Cooperation Committee for Cambodia—CCC, Cambodia, 46
Coordinadora de ONGD España, Spain, 285
Coordination SUD, France, 99
Council of American Development Foundations, Dominican Republic, 87
Council on Foundations—COF, USA, 394
Council of Michigan Foundations—CMF, USA, 394
CReDO—Centrul de Resurse pentru Drepturile Omului, Moldova, 217
Croatian Platform for International Citizen Solidarity, Croatia, 76
CROSOL—Platforma za međunarodnu građansku solidarnost Hrvatske, Croatia, 76
Czech Association of Community Foundations—AKN Association, Czech Republic, 78
Czech Council of Social Services, Czech Republic, 78
Czech Donors Forum, Czech Republic, 78
Dasra, India, 154
DEC—Disasters Emergency Committee, UK, 336
Development Cooperation Roundtable, Estonia, 92
Development NGO Coordinator Spain, Spain, 285
Directory of Social Change, UK, 336
Disability Rights Fund, USA, 395
Disasters Emergency Committee—DEC, UK, 336
Dóchas—Irish Association of Non-Governmental Development Organisations, Ireland, 165
Donors' Association for the Promotion of Sciences and Humanities, Germany, 119
East Africa Philanthropy Network—EAPN, Kenya, 197
Ecuadorean Consortium for Social Responsibility, Ecuador, 87
EDGE Funders Alliance, USA, 394
Ednannia—Initiative Centre to Support Social Action, Ukraine, 332
Eesti Mittetulundusühingute ja Sihtasutuste Liit, Estonia, 92
Effekteam Association, Hungary, 152
European Community Foundation Initiative—ECFI, Germany, 119
European Federation of National Organisations Working with the Homeless, Belgium, 26
European Food Banks Federation—EFBF, Belgium, 26
European Foundation for Philanthropy and Society Development, Croatia, 76
European NGO Confederation for Relief and Development—CONCORD, Belgium, 26
European Think Tanks Group—ETTG, Belgium, 26
Europska Zaklada za Filantropiju i Društveni Dazvoj, Croatia, 76
EVPA—European Venture Philanthropy Association, Belgium, 27
F20, Germany, 119
FEANTSA—Fédération Européenne des Associations Nationales Travaillant avec les Sans-Abri, Belgium, 26
Federacja Funduszy Lokalnych w Polsce, Poland, 254
Fédération Belge des Fondations Philanthropiques, Belgium, 26
Federation of Community Foundations in Poland, Poland, 254
Fédération Européenne des Associations Nationales Travaillant avec les Sans-Abri—FEANTSA, Belgium, 26
Fédération Européenne des Banques Alimentaires—FEBA, Belgium, 26
Fédération Internationale des Ligues des Droits de L'Homme—FIDH, France, 99
Federation of Non-Governmental Organizations for Development in Romania, Romania, 263
Filantrópico, Colombia, 70
FIN—Branchevereniging van Fondsen en Foundations, Netherlands, 223
Finnish Development Organizations, Finland, 95
Florida Philanthropic Network—FPN, USA, 394

FOND—Federatia Organizatiilor Neguvernamentale pentru Dezvoltare din Romania, Romania, 263
Fondacija Balkanska Mreza za Razvoj na Gragjanskoto Opshtestvo, North Macedonia, 239
Fondacioni Kosovar per Shoqeri Civile, Kosovo, 202
Fondation de France, France, 99
Fondations Philanthropiques Canada—FPC, Canada, 48
Fórum Dárců, Czech Republic, 78
Forum Darczyńców, Poland, 254
Fórum donorov, Slovakia, 274
Forum LSM Internasional untuk Pembangunan Indonesia, Indonesia, 161
Forum ZaDobro.BIT!, Croatia, 76
Foundation Center, USA, 393
Foundation for Civil Society—FCS, Tanzania, 322
Foundations and Funds Association, Finland, 95
Foundations Platform—F20, Germany, 119
Foundations' Post-Doc Pool, Finland, 95
French Foundation Centre, France, 99
Fund and Endowment Management Foundation, Norway, 240
Fund for Global Human Rights, USA, 395
Fundación Comunitaria de Puerto Rico—FCPR, Puerto Rico, 261
Fundación Lealtad, Spain, 285
FundAction, USA, 394
Fundația pentru Dezvoltarea Societății Civile—FDSC, Romania, 263
GIFE—Grupo de Institutos, Fundações e Empresas, Brazil, 38
Give Foundation, India, 155
Give2Asia, USA, 394
GiveIndia, India, 155
Giving USA Foundation, USA, 394
Global Dialogue, UK, 336
Global Fund for Community Foundations—GFCF, South Africa, 278
Global Health Council, USA, 395
Global Impact, USA, 395
Global Philanthropy Forum, USA, 395
Good2Give, Australia, 10
Gradjanske inicijative—GI, Serbia, 271
Group of Foundations and Businesses, Argentina, 6
Group of Institutes, Foundations and Enterprises, Brazil, 38
Grupa Zagranica, Poland, 254
Grupo de Fundaciones y Empresas, Argentina, 6
GuideStar, USA, 393
GuideStar India, India, 155
GURT Resource Centre for NGO Development, Ukraine, 332
HAND—Hungarian Association of NGOs for Development and Humanitarian Aid, Hungary, 152
HESTIA, Czech Republic, 78
Hong Kong Council of Social Service—HKCSS, Hong Kong, 150
Hope, Ireland, 165
Human Rights Funders Network—HRFN, USA, 395
Humanitarian Coalition, Canada, 48
Hungarian Donors Forum, Hungary, 152
Ibero-American Network of Community Foundations, Brazil, 38
ICVA—International Council of Voluntary Agencies, Switzerland, 305
Imagine Canada, Canada, 48
Impact Europe, Belgium, 27
Independent Sector, USA, 395
Initiative Bürgerstiftungen, Germany, 119
Institute for the Development of Social Investment, Brazil, 38
Instituto para o Desenvolvimento do Investimento Social—IDIS, Brazil, 38
InterAction, USA, 395
International Center for Not-for-Profit Law—ICNL, USA, 396
International Civil Society Centre, Germany, 119
International Confederation Catholic Organizations Charitable Social Action, Vatican City, 486
International Council of Voluntary Agencies—ICVA, Switzerland, 305
International Federation of Human Rights, France, 99
International NGO Charter of Accountability, USA, 393
International NGO Coordination Committee in CAR, Central African Republic, 63
International NGO Forum on Indonesian Development—INFID, Indonesia, 161
INTRAC, UK, 337
iPartner India, India, 155

Italian Association of Foundations and Institutional Philanthropy Bodies, Italy, 171
JANIC—Japanese NGO Center for International Co-operation, Japan, 185
Japan Association of Charitable Organizations—JACO, Japan, 185
Japan Foundation Center, Japan, 185
Klon/Jawor Association, Poland, 254
Konsultatsiis da Treningis Tsentri, Georgia, 117
Kosovar Civil Society Foundation—KCSF, Kosovo, 202
Lafede.cat—Federació d'Organitzacions per a la Justícia Global, Spain, 286
Lafede.cat—Federation of Organizations for Global Justice, Spain, 286
LAPAS—Latvijas platforma attīstības sadarbībai, Latvia, 204
Latin American Association of Development Financing Institutions, Peru, 248
Latin American Network for Economic and Social Justice, Peru, 248
Latindadd—Red Latinoamericana por Justicia Económica y Social, Peru, 248
Latvian Platform for Development Cooperation, Latvia, 204
League of California Community Foundations, USA, 396
League of Corporate Foundations—LCF, Philippines, 250
Lesotho Council of Non-Governmental Organisations, Lesotho, 207
Litdea Association, Lithuania, 208
Loyalty Foundation, Spain, 285
Luxembourg Development NGO Co-operation Circle, Luxembourg, 209
Maecenata Foundation, Germany, 119
Maecenata Stiftung, Germany, 119
Merian (Christoph) Stiftung, Switzerland, 305
Mexican Centre for Philanthropy, Mexico, 214
Nacionalne Zaklade za Razvoj Civilnoga Društva, Croatia, 76
Nadace Neziskovky.cz, Czech Republic, 79
Nadácia Pontis, Slovakia, 274
National Assistance and Information Centre for NGOs in Moldova—CONTACT Centre, Moldova, 216
National Council of Social Development—NCSD, Philippines, 250
National Council for Voluntary Organisations, UK, 337
National Federation of NGOs, Poland, 254
National Foundation for Civil Society Development, Croatia, 76
NCVO—National Council for Voluntary Organisations, UK, 337
Network of Estonian Non-profit Organizations, Estonia, 92
Network of European Foundations—NEF, Belgium, 27
Network of Foundations and Research Institutions for the Promotion of a Culture of Peace in Africa, Côte d'Ivoire, 75
Network of Foundations Working for Development—netFWD, France, 99
Network of Information and Support for Non-governmental Organizations, Poland, 254
Network of Mexican Community Foundations, Mexico, 215
Nevyriausybinių organizacijų informacijos ir paramos centras, Lithuania, 208
NGO Center—NGOC, Armenia, 9
NGO Development Centre, Russian Federation, 265
NGO Information and Support Centre—NISC, Lithuania, 208
NIOK Alapítvány—Nonprofit Információs és Oktató Központ Alapítvány—NIOK, Hungary, 152
NIOK Foundation—Non-Profit Information and Training Centre, Hungary, 152
Norwegian Donors Forum, Norway, 240
NPI Foundation, China (People's Republic), 66
Ogólnopolska Federacja Organizacji Pozarządowych—OFOP, Poland, 254
OneStage, India, 155
OPUS—Centre for Promotion and Development of Civil Initiatives, Poland, 254
Pakistan Centre for Philanthropy—PCP, Pakistan, 244
Palestinian NGO Network, Palestinian Territories, 246
Partos, Netherlands, 223
Peace and Security Funders Group—PSFG, USA, 396
Philanthropic, Colombia, 70
Philanthropic Foundations Canada—PFC, Canada, 48
Philanthropy Australia, Australia, 10

521

Aid to less-developed countries

Philanthropy Europe Association—Philea, Belgium, 27
Philanthropy Ireland, Ireland, 165
Philanthropy New Zealand/Topūtanga Tuku Aroha o Aotearoa, New Zealand, 232
Philanthropy for Social Justice and Peace, UK, 336
Philea—Philanthropy Europe Association, Belgium, 27
Philippine Business for Social Progress—PBSP, Philippines, 250
Philippine Council for NGO Certification, Philippines, 250
Plataform CiviKos, Kosovo, 202
Plataforma Portuguesa das Organizações Não-Governamentais para o Desenvolvimento—ONGD, Portugal, 258
Platform for Development Cooperation and Humanitarian Aid, Slovenia, 276
Platforma Mimovládnych Rozvojových Organizácií, Slovakia, 273
Polish Donors Forum, Poland, 254
Pontis Foundation, Slovakia, 274
Portuguese Foundation Centre, Portugal, 258
Portuguese Platform of Non-Governmental Organizations for Development, Portugal, 258
proFonds, Switzerland, 305
Puerto Rico Community Foundation, Puerto Rico, 261
RC Forward, Canada, 48
Rede Comuá, Brazil, 38
Rede Iberoamericana de Fundações Civicas ou Comunitárias—RIFC, Brazil, 38
Réseau des Fondations et Institutions de Recherche pour la Promotion d'un Culture de la Paix en Afrique—REFICA, Côte d'Ivoire, 75
Resource Centre for the Human Rights Nongovernmental Organizations of Moldova—CReDO, Moldova, 217
Rethink Charity, Canada, 48
Rotha, Ireland, 165
Russian Donors Forum, Russian Federation, 265
Säätiöiden post doc-poolin, Finland, 95
Säätiöt ja rahastot, Finland, 95
SAIA—Slovak Academic Information Agency, Slovakia, 274
Scotland's International Development Alliance, UK, 337
Scottish Council for Voluntary Organisations—SCVO, UK, 337
SCVO—Scottish Council for Voluntary Organisations, UK, 337
Serbian Philanthropy Forum, Serbia, 271
Sieć Wspierania Organizacji Pozarządowych—SPLOT, Poland, 254
Sinergia—Red Venezolana de OSC, Venezuela, 487
Sivil Toplum Geliştirme Merkezi—STGM, Türkiye, 327
SLOGA—Platforma za Razvojno Sodelovanje in Humanitarno Pomoč, Slovenia, 276
Slovak Academic Information Agency—SAIA, Slovakia, 274
Slovak Donors Forum, Slovakia, 274
Slovak Humanitarian Council, Slovakia, 274
Slovenská Humanitná Rada, Slovakia, 274
Solidarios—Consejo de Fundaciones Americanas de Desarrollo, Dominican Republic, 87
Somalia NGO Consortium, Somalia, 277
South Africa Philanthropy Foundation, South Africa, 278
South West International Development Network—SWIDN, UK, 337
Spanish Association of Foundations, Spain, 285
Sphere, Switzerland, 305
Srpski Filantropski Forum, Serbia, 271
Start Network, UK, 337
Stiftelser i Samverkan, Sweden, 298
Stiftelsesforeningen, Norway, 240
Stifterverband für die Deutsche Wissenschaft eV, Germany, 119
Stowarzyszenie Klon/Jawor, Poland, 254
Suomalaiset kehitysjärjestöt—Fingo, Finland, 95
Swiss Alliance of Development Organisations, Switzerland, 305
Swiss Philanthropy Foundation, Switzerland, 305
SwissFoundations—Verband der Schweizer Förderstiftungen/Association des Fondations Donatrices Suisses, Switzerland, 305
Synergos—The Synergos Institute, USA, 396
Third Sector Foundation of Turkey, Türkiye, 327
Topūtanga Tuku Aroha o Aotearoa, New Zealand, 232
Transnational Giving Europe—TGE, Belgium, 27
TÜSEV—Türkiye Üçüncü Sektör Vakfı, Türkiye, 327
UAI—Union des Associations Internationales, Belgium, 27
Ufadhili Trust, Kenya, 197

UK Community Foundations—UKCF, UK, 338
Ukrainian Philanthropists Forum, Ukraine, 332
UNIFOR—Forvaltningstiftelse for fond og legater, Norway, 240
Union des Associations Internationales—UAI, Belgium, 27
Union of International Associations—UIA/Unie van de Internationale Verenigingen—UIV, Belgium, 27
United Way—Belarus/NGO Development Centre, Belarus, 25
VANI—Voluntary Action Network India, India, 155
Venezuelan Network of Civil Society Organizations, Venezuela, 487
VENRO—Verband Entwicklungspolitik und Humanitäre Hilfe deutscher Nichtregierungsorganizationen, Germany, 120
Verband für Gemeinnütziges Stiften, Austria, 20
Vereinigung Liechtensteinischer gemeinnütziger Stiftungen eV, Liechtenstein, 207
Voluntary Action Network India—VANI, India, 155
The Wheel, Ireland, 165
WINGS—Worldwide Initiatives for Grantmaker Support, Brazil, 38
World Alliance for Citizen Participation—CIVICUS, South Africa, 278
The World of NGOs, Austria, 20
Worldwide Initiatives for Grantmaker Support—WINGS, Brazil, 38
Zagranica Group, Poland, 254
Zavod Center za Informiranje, Sodelovanje in Razvoj Nevladnih Organizacije—CNVOS, Slovenia, 277
Ziviler Friedensdienst—ZFD, Germany, 120

AID TO LESS-DEVELOPED COUNTRIES

AARDO—African-Asian Rural Development Organization, India, 155
Acción Contra el Hambre–ACH, Spain, 286
Accountable Now, USA, 393
ACDI/VOCA, USA, 397
ACFID—Australian Council for International Development, Australia, 12
ACT Alliance, Switzerland, 306
Acting for Life, France, 100
Action Against Hunger, Spain, 286
Action Children's Aid, Denmark, 82
Action contre la Faim—ACF France, France, 100
Action Damien/Damiaanactie, Belgium, 28
Action Education, France, 100
Action Group on Erosion, Technology and Concentration, Canada, 54
Action on Poverty, Australia, 10
Action Solidarité Tiers Monde—ASTM, Luxembourg, 209
ActionAid International, South Africa, 278
Active for People in Need Austria, Austria, 20
Acumen, USA, 397
ADRA—Adventist Development and Relief Agency International, USA, 397
Advance, USA, 397
Adventist Development and Relief Agency International—ADRA, USA, 397
Afdi—Agriculteurs Français et Développement International, France, 100
Africa-America Institute—AAI, USA, 398
Africa Foundation, South Africa, 278
Africa Grantmakers' Affinity Group—AGAG, USA, 393
Africa Institute of South Africa—AISA, South Africa, 279
African-Asian Rural Development Organization—AARDO, India, 155
African Capacity Building Foundation—ACBF, Zimbabwe, 490
African Forum and Network on Debt and Development—AFRODAD, Zimbabwe, 490
African Women's Development Fund—AWDF, Ghana, 143
AFRODAD—African Forum and Network on Debt and Development, Zimbabwe, 490
Aga Khan Development Network—AKDN, Switzerland, 306
Aga Khan Foundation, Switzerland, 306
Aga Khan Foundation Canada, Canada, 49
Aga Khan Foundation UK, UK, 338
AGAG—Africa Grantmakers' Affinity Group, USA, 393
Age International, UK, 339
Agriculteurs Français et Développement International, France, 100
Agronomes et Vétérinaires sans Frontières—AVSF, France, 100

INDEX OF MAIN ACTIVITIES

Agronomists and Veterinarians Without Borders, France, 100
AIC—Association Internationale des Charités, Belgium, 28
Aid to the Church in Need—ACN International, Germany, 120
Aid for Development Club, Austria, 20
AISA—Africa Institute of South Africa, South Africa, 279
AIT—Asian Institute of Technology, Thailand, 323
Aktion Børnehjælp, Denmark, 82
The Al-Khoei Benevolent Foundation, UK, 339
Alavi Foundation, USA, 398
Albert Schweitzer Ecological Centre, Switzerland, 307
ALIDE—Asociación Latinoamericana de Instituciones Financieras para el Desarrollo, Peru, 248
Alight, USA, 399
Aliko Dangote Foundation—ADF, Nigeria, 237
Alkhidmat Foundation Pakistan—AKFP, Pakistan, 244
All Good Foundation Charitable Trust, New Zealand, 232
All India Disaster Mitigation Institute, India, 155
Alliance Sud—Swiss Alliance of Development Organizations, Switzerland, 305
Alongside Hope/Auprès de l'espoir, Canada, 49
AMADE Mondiale—Association Mondiale des Amis de l'Enfance, Monaco, 217
Aman Foundation, Pakistan, 244
Amberes (Carlos de), Fundación, Spain, 289
Ambrela Platform of Development Organizations, Slovakia, 273
Ambrela—Platforma rozvojových organizácií, Slovakia, 273
American Friends Service Committee—AFSC, USA, 401
American Jewish Joint Distribution Committee—JDC, USA, 402
American Jewish World Service—AJWS, USA, 402
American Near East Refugee Aid—Anera, USA, 402
AmeriCares Foundation, Inc, USA, 403
AMINA—aktiv für Menschen in Not Austria, Austria, 20
Amref Health Africa, Kenya, 198
Andrews Charitable Trust—ACT, UK, 340
Anera—American Near East Refugee Aid, USA, 402
Anesvad, Spain, 286
ANGOC—Asian NGO Coalition for Agrarian Reform and Rural Development, Philippines, 251
Anne Ray Foundation, USA, 450
APHEDA—Union Aid Abroad, Australia, 19
Apprentis d'Auteuil Océan Indien, Réunion, 262
Arbeiterwohlfahrt Bundesverband eV—AWO, Germany, 121
Archewell Foundation, USA, 405
Archie Sherman Charitable Trust, UK, 340
Arengukoostöö Ümarlaud—AKÜ, Estonia, 92
Asia Africa International Voluntary Foundation—AIV, Japan, 186
Asia Foundation, USA, 406
Asia/Pacific Cultural Centre for UNESCO—ACCU, Japan, 186
Asia Philanthropy Circle—APC, Singapore, 272
AsiaDHRRA—Asian Partnership for the Development of Human Resources in Rural Asia, Philippines, 251
Asian Community Trust—ACT, Japan, 186
Asian Institute of Technology—AIT, Thailand, 323
Asian Partnership for the Development of Human Resources in Rural Asia, Philippines, 251
Asociacija Litdea—Lithuanian Development Education and Awareness Raising Association, Lithuania, 208
Asociación Latinoamericana de Instituciones Financieras para el Desarrollo—ALIDE, Peru, 248
Association for Development Policy and Humanitarian Aid, Germany, 120
Association Internationale des Charités—AIC, Belgium, 28
ASTM—Action Solidarité Tiers Monde, Luxembourg, 209
ATD Fourth World International, France, 115
Australian Communities Foundation, Australia, 12
Australian Council for International Development—ACFID, Australia, 12
Australian Foundation for the Peoples of Asia and the Pacific—AFAP, Australia, 10

INDEX OF MAIN ACTIVITIES

Aid to less-developed countries

Australian Volunteers International—AVI, Australia, 13
Austrian Foundation for Development Research, Austria, 22
AVI—Australian Volunteers International, Australia, 13
Aviation Sans Frontières—ASF, France, 101
Aviation Without Borders, France, 101
AVINA Foundation, Panama, 247
AVSI Foundation, Italy, 175
Bagnoud (François-Xavier) Association, Switzerland, 310
Baha'i International Development Organization—BIDO, Israel, 169
Bank of America Charitable Foundation, USA, 407
Bariloche Foundation, Argentina, 7
Baring Foundation, UK, 341
Basso Issoco (Leilio e Lisli), Fondazione, Italy, 178
BBC Media Action, UK, 342
Beit Trust, UK, 342
Berghof Foundation gGmbH, Germany, 122
Berghof Stiftung für Konfliktforschung gGmbH, Germany, 122
Bertoni (Moisés) Foundation, Paraguay, 248
Bischöfliches Hilfswerk Misereor eV, Germany, 137
Bond, UK, 335
Book Aid International—BAI, UK, 343
Bóthar, Ireland, 166
BP Foundation, Inc, USA, 409
BRAC, Bangladesh, 25
Bread for the World—Protestant Work for Social Welfare and Development, Germany, 123
Bridge Asia Japan—BAJ, Japan, 187
British Overseas NGOs for Development, UK, 335
British Red Cross Society, UK, 345
Brot für die Welt—Evangelisches Werk für Diakonie und Entwicklung, Germany, 123
Brother's Brother Foundation, USA, 410
Brothers of Men, France, 113
Buck (Pearl S.) International, USA, 462
Buffett (Howard G.) Foundation, USA, 437
Bulgarian Platform for International Development—BPID, Bulgaria, 42
CABI, UK, 345
Cadbury (William Adlington) Charitable Trust, UK, 390
CAF America, USA, 393
CAFOD—Catholic Agency for Overseas Development, UK, 345
California Community Foundation, USA, 411
Calouste Gulbenkian Foundation, Portugal, 259
Cambodian Salesian Delegation, Cambodia, 46
Canadian Centre for International Studies and Co-operation, Canada, 51
Canadian Council for International Co-operation—CCIC/Conseil Canadien pour la Coopération Internationale—CCCI, Canada, 48
Canadian Feed The Children—CFTC, Canada, 50
Canadian Foodgrains Bank, Canada, 50
Canadian Physicians for Aid and Relief—CPAR, Canada, 52
CARE International—CI, Switzerland, 307
Cargill (Margaret A.) Philanthropies, USA, 450
Caritas Canada, Canada, 53
Caritas de France—Secours Catholique, France, 116
Caritas Internationalis—CI, Vatican City, 486
Carlos de Amberes Foundation, Spain, 289
Carlos Slim Foundation, Mexico, 215
Carnegie Corporation of New York, USA, 411
Carrefour International, Canada, 53
The Carter Center, USA, 412
Cassa di Risparmio di Padova e Rovigo Foundation, Italy, 175
Catalyste+, Canada, 51
Caterpillar Foundation, USA, 412
Catholic Agency for Overseas Development—CAFOD, UK, 345
Catholic Agency for World Development—Trócaire, Ireland, 168
Catholic Help—Caritas France, France, 116
CBM-International, Germany, 123
CEAS—Centre Ecologique Albert Schweitzer, Switzerland, 307
CECI—Canadian Centre for International Studies and Co-operation/Centre d'Etudes et de Coopération Internationale, Canada, 51
Centras—Assistance Centre for NGOs, Romania, 263
Centras—Centrul de Asistenta pentru Organizatii Neguvernamentale, Romania, 263
Centre Ecologique Albert Schweitzer—CEAS, Switzerland, 307

Centre for Humanitarian Action—CHA, Germany, 123
Cera, Belgium, 28
Cercle de Coopération des ONGD du Luxembourg, Luxembourg, 209
CESO/SACO—Canadian Executive Service Organization/Service d'Assistance Canadienne aux Organismes, Canada, 51
Charities Advisory Trust, UK, 336
Charities Aid Foundation of America—CAF America, USA, 393
Charity Islamic Trust Elrahma, UK, 352
Charity Projects, UK, 348
Charles Stewart Mott Foundation—CSMF, USA, 414
The Chatlos Foundation, Inc, USA, 414
ChildFund International, USA, 414
Children in Africa Foundation, Germany, 140
Children International—CI, USA, 414
Children of the Mekong, France, 102
The Children's Investment Fund Foundation, UK, 347
China Foundation for Poverty Alleviation—CFPA, China (People's Republic), 67
Christian Aid, UK, 348
CIDSE—Together for Global Justice, Belgium, 29
Civil Peace Service—CPS, Germany, 120
Civitates, Belgium, 27
Clara Lionel Foundation—CLF, USA, 415
CLEAR Global, USA, 416
Clinton Foundation, USA, 416
Člověk v tísni, Czech Republic, 79
Coady Institute, Canada, 52
CODESPA Foundation, Spain, 290
Comic Relief, UK, 348
Comité de Coordination des ONGI en RCA, Central African Republic, 63
Commonwealth Foundation, UK, 348
Community Chest of Korea—Fruit of Love, Korea (Republic), 200
Concern Worldwide, Ireland, 166
CONCORD—European NGO Confederation for Relief and Development, Belgium, 26
Conrad N. Hilton Foundation, USA, 417
Cooperation Canada/Coopération Canada, Canada, 48
Co-operative Development Foundation of Canada—CDF, Canada, 52
Cooperazione Internazionale—COOPI, Italy, 173
Coordinadora de ONGD España, Spain, 285
Corra Foundation, UK, 349
Corus International, USA, 418
Council of American Development Foundations, Dominican Republic, 87
Counterpart International, USA, 418
Coutu (Marcelle et Jean), Fondation, Canada, 55
CPAR—Canadian Physicians for Aid and Relief, Canada, 52
Croatian Platform for International Citizen Solidarity, Croatia, 76
CROSOL—Platforma za međunarodnu građansku solidarnost Hrvatske, Croatia, 76
Crossroads International/Carrefour International, Canada, 53
Crown Family Philanthropies, USA, 419
Cundill (Peter) Foundation, Bermuda, 35
CURE International, USA, 419
Cuso International, Canada, 53
Dag Hammarskjöld Foundation, Sweden, 303
Dalia Association, Palestinian Territories, 246
Daniele Agostino Derossi Foundation, USA, 420
Danielle Mitterrand Foundation, France, 112
DEC—Disasters Emergency Committee, UK, 336
Democracy Fund, USA, 458
Derossi (Daniele Agostino) Foundation, USA, 420
Deutsche AIDS-Stiftung, Germany, 124
Deutsche Bank Americas Foundation, USA, 420
Deutsche Sparkassenstiftung für Internationale Zusammenarbeit, Germany, 125
Development Cooperation Roundtable, Estonia, 92
Development Foundation of Turkey, Türkiye, 330
Development Gateway—DG, USA, 458
Development NGO Coordinator Spain, Spain, 285
Development and Peace—Caritas Canada, Canada, 53
Développement et Paix—Caritas Canada, Canada, 53
Diakonia, Sweden, 298
Direct Relief, USA, 420
Disasters Emergency Committee—DEC, UK, 336
Doctors Without Borders International, Switzerland, 314
Doctors of the World International, France, 114
DOEN Foundation, Netherlands, 229
Dom Manuel II Foundation, Portugal, 260
Don Bosco Foundation of Cambodia—DBFC, Cambodia, 46

DSW—Deutsche Stiftung Weltbevölkerung, Germany, 126
Dulverton Trust, UK, 351
Earth Island Institute—EII, USA, 422
Eberhard Schöck Foundation, Germany, 127
Eberhard-Schöck-Stiftung, Germany, 127
Ebert (Friedrich) Stiftung, Germany, 129
Ecuadorean Social Group Fund Populorum Progressio, Ecuador, 89
Edhi Foundation, Pakistan, 245
Educo, Spain, 286
The Elders Foundation, UK, 352
Elizabeth Glaser Pediatric AIDS Foundation—EGPAF, USA, 423
The ELMA Group of Foundations, USA, 423
Elrahma Charity Trust, UK, 352
Elrha, UK, 352
EMERGENCY, Italy, 173
Emmaüs International, France, 102
Enda Third World—Environment and Development Action in the Third World, Senegal, 270
Enda Tiers Monde—Environnement et Développement du Tiers-Monde, Senegal, 270
endPoverty.org, USA, 424
Energies for the World Foundation, France, 105
Enfants du Mékong, France, 102
The English-Speaking Union—ESU, UK, 353
Eni Foundation, Italy, 173
Entraide Protestante Suisse, Switzerland, 311
Entraide Universitaire Mondiale du Canada, Canada, 63
Entwicklungshilfe-Klub, Austria, 20
Equality Fund/Fonds Égalité, Canada, 54
ETC Group—Action Group on Erosion, Technology and Concentration, Canada, 54
Eugenio Mendoza Foundation, Venezuela, 487
Eurasia Foundation—EF, USA, 424
EURODAD—European Network on Debt and Development, Belgium, 29
European Center for Peace and Development—ECPD, Serbia, 271
European Network on Debt and Development—EURODAD, Belgium, 29
European NGO Confederation for Relief and Development—CONCORD, Belgium, 26
European Think Tanks Group—ETTG, Belgium, 26
Fairtrade Nederland, Netherlands, 230
The Family Federation of Finland, Finland, 98
Farm Africa, UK, 354
Federal Association of Social Welfare Organizations, Germany, 121
Feed the Children, USA, 425
Feed the Minds, UK, 354
FEIM—Fundación para Estudio e Investigación de la Mujer, Argentina, 7
Fernando Rielo Foundation, Spain, 290
FHI 360, USA, 425
FINCA International, USA, 425
Finnish Development Organizations, Finland, 95
Focus Humanitarian Assistance—FOCUS, Canada, 54
Follereau Foundation Luxembourg, Luxembourg, 209
FONDAD—Forum on Debt and Development, Netherlands, 225
Fondation Abbé Pierre, France, 108
Fondation pour l'Agriculture et la Ruralité dans le Monde—Fondation FARM, France, 106
Fondation Energies pour le Monde—Fondem, France, 105
Fondation Ensemble, France, 105
Fondation FARM—Fondation pour l'Agriculture et la Ruralité dans le Monde, France, 106
Fondation Follereau Luxembourg—FFL, Luxembourg, 209
Fondation de France, France, 99
Fondation Jean-Paul II pour le Sahel, Burkina Faso, 44
Fondation pour le Logement des Défavorisés, France, 108
Fondation Marc de Montalembert, France, 109
Fondation Marcelle et Jean Coutu, Canada, 55
Fondation Mérieux, France, 109
Fondation Nestlé pour l'Etude des Problèmes de l'Alimentation dans le Monde, Switzerland, 310
Fondation Noura, Mauritania, 214
Fondation Prince Albert II de Monaco, Monaco, 217
Fondation Princesse Charlène de Monaco, Monaco, 218
Fondation pour le Renforcement des Capacités en Afrique, Zimbabwe, 490
Fondation Roi Baudouin, Belgium, 33
Fondation Rurale pour l'Afrique de l'Ouest—FRAO, Senegal, 270

523

Aid to less-developed countries

Fondation S, France, 111
Fondation Sommet Mondial des Femmes, Switzerland, 320
Fondazione AVSI, Italy, 175
Fondazione Cassa di Risparmio di Padova e Rovigo, Italy, 175
Fondazione ISMU—Iniziative e Studi sulla Multietnicità, Italy, 178
Fondazione Lelio e Lisli Basso Issoco—Sezione Internazionale, Italy, 178
Fondazione Populorum Progressio, Vatican City, 486
Fondazjone RUI, Italy, 180
Fonds Égalité, Canada, 54
Food for the Hungry—FH, USA, 426
Food for the Poor, Inc, USA, 426
Forum on Debt and Development—FONDAD, Netherlands, 225
Foundation for Housing the Disadvantaged, France, 108
Foundation for International Community Assistance, USA, 425
Foundation for Local Development and the Municipal and Institutional Support of Central America and the Caribbean, Costa Rica, 74
Foundation for Women, Spain, 293
Foundation for Women's Research and Studies, Argentina, 7
Foundation for World Agriculture and Rural Life, France, 106
France Amérique Latine—FAL, France, 112
France-Libertés Fondation Danielle Mitterrand, France, 112
French Agriculturalists and International Development, France, 100
Frères des Hommes—FDH, France, 113
Friedensdorf International, Germany, 129
Friedrich-Ebert-Stiftung eV, Germany, 129
Friedrich Naumann Foundation for Freedom, Germany, 130
Friedrich-Naumann-Stiftung für die Freiheit, Germany, 130
Front Line Defenders—FLD, Ireland, 166
Fundação Assistência Médica Internacional—AMI, Portugal, 258
Fundação Calouste Gulbenkian, Portugal, 259
Fundação Dom Manuel II, Portugal, 260
Fundación Amanecer, Colombia, 70
Fundación AVINA, Panama, 247
Fundación Bariloche, Argentina, 7
Fundación Carlos de Amberes, Spain, 289
Fundación Carlos Slim, Mexico, 215
Fundación CODESPA, Spain, 290
Fundación DEMUCA—Fundación para el Desarrollo Local y el Fortalecimiento Municipal e Institucional de Centroamérica y el Caribe, Costa Rica, 74
Fundación para el Desarrollo Local y el Fortalecimiento Municipal e Institucional de Centroamérica y el Caribe, Costa Rica, 74
Fundación para Estudio e Investigación de la Mujer—FEIM, Argentina, 7
Fundación Eugenio Mendoza—FEM, Venezuela, 487
Fundación Fernando Rielo, Spain, 290
Fundación Moisés Bertoni—FMB, Paraguay, 248
Fundación Mujeres, Spain, 293
Fundación Oxfam Intermón, Spain, 293
Fundación Paraguaya de Cooperación y Desarrollo, Paraguay, 248
FXB International—Association François-Xavier Bagnoud, Switzerland, 310
The Gatsby Charitable Foundation, UK, 355
GE Aerospace Foundation, USA, 429
German AIDS Foundation, Germany, 124
German Catholic Bishops' Organization for Development Co-operation, Germany, 137
German Foundation for World Population, Germany, 126
German Savings Banks Foundation for International Co-operation, Germany, 125
Gift of the Givers Foundation, South Africa, 280
Give2Asia, USA, 394
Glaser (Elizabeth) Pediatric AIDS Foundation, USA, 423
Global Communities, USA, 431
The Global Foodbanking Network—GFN, USA, 431
Global Fund for Children, USA, 431
Global Fund for Community Foundations—GFCF, South Africa, 278
Global Greengrants Fund, USA, 431
Global Health Council, USA, 395
Global Impact, USA, 395
Globetree Association, Sweden, 300
GOAL, Ireland, 166

Good Neighbors International, Korea (Republic), 201
Good360, USA, 432
Google.org—Google Foundation, USA, 432
Grameen Foundation—GF, USA, 433
Grassroots International—GRI, USA, 433
Green Umbrella Children's Foundation—ChildFund Korea, Korea (Republic), 201
Grupa Zagranica, Poland, 254
Grupo Social Fondo Ecuatoriano Populorum Progressio, Ecuador, 89
Gulbenkian (Calouste), Fundação, Portugal, 259
H&M Foundation, Sweden, 300
Habitat for Humanity International, USA, 433
Haiti Development Institute—HDI, Haiti, 149
HALO Trust, UK, 357
Hamlyn (Paul) Foundation, UK, 373
Hammarskjölds (Dag) Minnesfond, Stiftelsen, Sweden, 303
HAND—Hungarian Association of NGOs for Development and Humanitarian Aid, Hungary, 152
Havelaar (Max) Foundation, Netherlands, 230
Hawaii Resilience Fund, USA, 458
Headley Trust, UK, 357
Health Action International—HAI, Netherlands, 225
Health Volunteers Overseas—HVO, USA, 434
Heart to Heart International—HHI, USA, 435
Hedwig and Robert Samuel Foundation, Germany, 131
Hedwig und Robert Samuel-Stiftung, Germany, 131
Heifer Foundation, USA, 435
HEKS—Hilfswerk der Evangelischen Kirchen Schweiz, Switzerland, 311
Helen Keller International—HKI, USA, 435
HelpAge International, UK, 357
Helvetas Swiss Intercooperation, Switzerland, 311
Hilti Foundation, Liechtenstein, 208
Hilton (Conrad N.) Foundation, USA, 417
Hivos—Humanistisch Instituut voor Ontwikkelings Samenwerking, Netherlands, 226
Holt International, USA, 436
HOPE International Development Agency, Canada, 56
Horizons of Friendship, Canada, 56
The Howard G. Buffett Foundation, USA, 437
Howard Karagheusian Commemorative Corporation—HKCC, USA, 437
Humanistic Institute for Co-operation with Developing Countries, Netherlands, 226
Humanitarian Academy for Development—HAD, UK, 359
Humanitarian Coalition, Canada, 48
Humanity & Inclusion, France, 113
The Hunger Project, USA, 438
IACD—Institute of Asian Culture and Development, Korea (Republic), 201
IBM International Foundation, USA, 438
ICRC—International Red Cross and Red Crescent Movement, Switzerland, 312
ICVA—International Council of Voluntary Agencies, Switzerland, 305
IDRF—International Development and Relief Foundation, Canada, 56
IFAD—International Fund for Agricultural Development, Italy, 182
IHH Humanitarian Relief Foundation, Türkiye, 328
IIED—International Institute for Environment and Development, UK, 360
IISD—International Institute for Sustainable Development, Canada, 57
IKEA Foundation, Netherlands, 229
Iles de Paix, Belgium, 32
Improving Economies for Stronger Communities—IESC, USA, 438
Inclusion International, UK, 359
India Partners, USA, 438
Indonesia Biodiversity Foundation, Indonesia, 162
İnsan Hak ve Hürriyetleri İnsani Yardım Vakfı—IHH, Türkiye, 328
Institut de Médecine et d'Epidémiologie Appliquée—Fondation Internationale Léon Mba, France, 114
Institute of Applied Medicine and Epidemiology—International Foundation Léon Mba, France, 114
Institute of Asian Culture and Development—IACD, Korea (Republic), 201
Institute of Developing Economies-Japan External Trade Organization—IDE-JETRO, Japan, 188
Institute of Economic Affairs—IEA, UK, 359

INDEX OF MAIN ACTIVITIES

Institute for Security Studies—ISS, South Africa, 280
Institute of Social Studies—ISS, Netherlands, 226
Integrated Rural Development Foundation—IRDF, Philippines, 252
Inter-American Foundation—IAF, USA, 439
Inter Pares, Canada, 57
InterAction, USA, 395
Interchurch Aid—HIA Hungary, Hungary, 153
International Association of Charities, Belgium, 28
International Blue Crescent Relief and Development Foundation—IBC, Türkiye, 329
International Center for Research on Women—ICRW, USA, 439
International Confederation Catholic Organizations Charitable Social Action, Vatican City, 486
International Co-operation, Italy, 173
International Council of Voluntary Agencies—ICVA, Switzerland, 305
International Development Center of Japan, Japan, 189
International Development and Relief Foundation—IDRF, Canada, 56
International Eye Foundation—IEF, USA, 440
The International Foundation, USA, 440
International Foundation for the Protection of Human Rights Defenders, Ireland, 166
International Foundation for Science—IFS, Sweden, 300
International Fund for Agricultural Development—IFAD, Italy, 182
International Institute for Environment and Development—IIED, UK, 360
International Institute of Rural Reconstruction—IIRR, Philippines, 252
International Institute of Social Studies, Netherlands, 226
International Institute for Sustainable Development—IISD, Canada, 57
International Institute of Tropical Agriculture—IITA, Nigeria, 237
International Lake Environment Committee Foundation, Japan, 189
International Medical Assistance Foundation, Portugal, 258
International NGO Charter of Accountability, USA, 393
International NGO Coordination Committee in CAR, Central African Republic, 63
International Orthodox Christian Charities—IOCC, USA, 441
International Planned Parenthood Federation—IPPF, UK, 360
International Red Cross and Red Crescent Movement—ICRC, Switzerland, 312
International Relief Teams—IRT, USA, 441
International Rescue Committee—IRC, USA, 441
International Water Management Institute—IWMI, Sri Lanka, 297
International Youth Foundation—IYF, USA, 442
INTERSOS, Italy, 182
INTRAC, UK, 337
IOCC—International Orthodox Christian Charities, USA, 441
IPPF—International Planned Parenthood Federation, UK, 360
IRC—International Rescue Committee, USA, 441
Islamic Relief Worldwide, UK, 360
Islands of Peace, Belgium, 32
ISMU Foundation—Initiatives and Studies on Multi-ethnicity, Italy, 178
IsraAID, Israel, 169
Japan International Volunteer Center—JVC, Japan, 190
JEN, Japan, 190
The Jerusalem Trust, UK, 361
John Paul II Foundation for the Sahel, Burkina Faso, 44
Johnson & Johnson Foundation US—JJF, USA, 444
Johnson (Stanley Thomas) Foundation, Switzerland, 317
Jubilee USA Network, USA, 445
KAF—Katalike Actions for Africa, Congo (Democratic Republic), 72
Karagheusian (Howard) Commemorative Corporation, USA, 437
Karuna Trust, UK, 363
KEHATI—Yayasan Keanekaragaman Hayati Indonesia, Indonesia, 162
Keller (Helen) International, USA, 435
King Baudouin Foundation, Belgium, 33
King Philanthropies, USA, 445
Kiwanis Children's Fund, USA, 446
Kofi Annan Foundation, Switzerland, 313

INDEX OF MAIN ACTIVITIES

Aid to less-developed countries

Koning Boudewijnstichting/Fondation Roi Baudouin, Belgium, 33
Kulika Charitable Trust Uganda, Uganda, 331
Kvinna till Kvinna, Sweden, 301
Lafede.cat—Federació d'Organitzacions per a la Justícia Global, Spain, 286
Lafede.cat—Federation of Organizations for Global Justice, Spain, 286
Laing Family Trusts, UK, 364
LAPAS—Latvijas platforma attīstības sadarbībai, Latvia, 204
Latin America France, France, 112
Latin American, African and Asian Social Housing Service, Chile, 66
Latin American Association of Development Financing Institutions, Peru, 248
Latter-day Saint Charities—LDSC, USA, 447
Latvian Platform for Development Cooperation, Latvia, 204
Legatum Foundation, United Arab Emirates, 334
LEGO Fonden, Denmark, 84
The LEGO Foundation, Denmark, 84
Lelio and Lisli Basso Foundation Onlus, Italy, 178
Lifeline Energy, South Africa, 280
Lifewater International, USA, 479
Light Up the World—LUTW, Canada, 58
Light of the Village Foundation, Indonesia, 162
Liliane Foundation, Netherlands, 229
Lilly Endowment, Inc, USA, 448
Limmat Foundation, Switzerland, 314
Limmat Stiftung, Switzerland, 314
Linbury Trust, UK, 365
Litdea Association, Lithuania, 208
Lowy Institute for International Policy, Australia, 15
The Lutheran World Federation, Switzerland, 314
Lutherischer Weltbund/Fédération Luthérienne Mondiale/Federación Luterana Mundial, Switzerland, 314
Luxembourg Development NGO Co-operation Circle, Luxembourg, 209
MAG—Mines Advisory Group, UK, 366
Mani Tese, Italy, 183
MAP International—Medical Assistance Programs, USA, 450
Marc de Montalembert Foundation, France, 109
Marcelle and Jean Coutu Foundation, Canada, 55
Margaret A. Cargill Philanthropies—MACP, USA, 450
The MasterCard Foundation, Canada, 59
Max Havelaar Foundation—Fairtrade Netherlands, Netherlands, 230
Médecins du Monde International, France, 114
Médecins Sans Frontières International—MSF International, Switzerland, 314
medica mondiale eV, Germany, 136
Medical Aid for Palestinians—MAP, UK, 367
Medico International, Germany, 136
Mendoza (Eugenio), Fundación, Venezuela, 487
Menomadin Foundation, Israel, 170
Mercury Phoenix Trust, UK, 367
Mercy, Ireland, 168
Mercy Corps, USA, 452
Mercy-USA for Aid and Development, USA, 452
Mérieux Foundation, France, 109
Mines Advisory Group—MAG, UK, 366
Minhaj Welfare Foundation, UK, 368
MISEREOR—Bischöfliches Hilfswerk Misereor eV, Germany, 137
Mitterrand (Danielle), Fondation, France, 112
MIUSA—Mobility International USA, USA, 453
Mobility International USA—MIUSA, USA, 453
Mohammed bin Rashid Al Maktoum Global Initiatives—MBRGI, United Arab Emirates, 335
Moisés Bertoni Foundation, Paraguay, 248
de Montalembert (Marc), Fondation, France, 109
Motorola Solutions Foundation, USA, 454
Mouvement International ATD Quart-Monde, France, 115
MSF International—Médecins Sans Frontières International, Switzerland, 314
Munich Re Foundation/Münchener Rück Stiftung, Germany, 137
Mutual Aid and Liaison Service, France, 116
Myanmar/Burma Schools Project Foundation, Canada, 60
National Endowment for Science, Technology and the Arts—Nesta, UK, 370
The National Lottery Community Fund, UK, 370
Naumann (Friedrich) Stiftung, Germany, 130
Near East Foundation—NEF, USA, 456
Nederlandse Organisatie voor Internationale Ontwikkelingssamenwerking—Stichting NOVIB, Netherlands, 228
NEF—Near East Foundation, USA, 456
Neighbour in Need, Austria, 22

Nesta—National Endowment for Science, Technology and the Arts, UK, 370
Nestlé Foundation for the Study of the Problems of Nutrition in the World, Switzerland, 310
Network of European Foundations—NEF, Belgium, 27
Network for Social Change Charitable Trust—NSCCT, UK, 370
The Nippon Foundation, Japan, 192
Nitidæ, France, 115
Niwano Peace Foundation, Japan, 192
Nonprofit Enterprise and Self-sustainability Team—NESsT, USA, 457
Nordic Africa Institute Scholarships, Sweden, 302
Nordiska Afrikainstitutets Stipendier, Sweden, 302
North-South-Bridge Foundation, Germany, 141
Norwegian Refugee Council—NRC, Norway, 242
NOVIB (Oxfam Netherlands), Netherlands, 228
NoVo Foundation, USA, 458
Novo Nordisk Fonden, Denmark, 85
Novo Nordisk Foundation, Denmark, 85
Nuffic, Netherlands, 227
Nuffield Foundation, UK, 371
ODI, UK, 371
OISCA International—Organization for Industrial, Spiritual and Cultural Advancement-International, Japan, 192
Ökumenikus Segélyszervezet, Hungary, 153
Omidyar Group, USA, 458
OPALS—Organisation Panafricaine de Lutte pour la Santé, France, 115
Open Society Action Fund, USA, 458
Open Society Foundation—London, UK, 372
Open Society Initiative for Southern Africa—OSISA, South Africa, 282
Open Society Policy Center, USA, 458
Operation Eyesight Universal/Action Universelle de la Vue, Canada, 60
Operation USA, USA, 459
Opportunity International UK, UK, 372
Orbis Charitable Trust, UK, 372
ORF Nachbar in Not, Austria, 22
Organisation Panafricaine de Lutte pour la Santé—OPALS, France, 115
Osaka Community Foundation, Japan, 192
Österreichische Forschungsstiftung für Internationale Entwicklung—ÖFSE, Austria, 22
Outreach International, USA, 459
Outstretched Hands, Italy, 183
Oxfam America, USA, 460
Oxfam Aotearoa, New Zealand, 234
Oxfam Australia, Australia, 16
Oxfam Brasil, Brazil, 41
Oxfam Canada, Canada, 60
Oxfam Denmark, Denmark, 86
Oxfam Deutschland eV, Germany, 138
Oxfam France, France, 115
Oxfam GB, UK, 372
Oxfam India, India, 159
Oxfam International, Kenya, 200
Oxfam Ireland, Ireland, 167
Oxfam Italia, Italy, 183
Oxfam Mexico, Mexico, 216
Oxfam NOVIB—Nederlandse Organisatie voor Internationale Ontwikkelingssamenwerking, Netherlands, 228
Oxfam NOVIB—Netherlands Organization for International Development Co-operation, Netherlands, 228
Oxfam-Québec, Canada, 60
Oxfam-Solidariteit/Solidarité, Belgium, 33
Oxfam South Africa, South Africa, 282
Pacific Development and Conservation Trust, New Zealand, 234
Pact, USA, 460
PADF—Pan American Development Foundation, USA, 460
Pan-African Organization for Health, France, 115
Pan American Development Foundation—PADF, USA, 460
Paraguayan Foundation for Cooperation and Development, Paraguay, 248
Partage, France, 115
Partners for Equity, Australia, 16
Partners in Health, USA, 461
PATH, USA, 461
Pathfinder International, USA, 461
Paul Hamlyn Foundation—PHF, UK, 373
Paz y Cooperación, Spain, 296
PCI Media Impact, USA, 467
PCI—Project Concern International, USA, 431
Peace and Co-operation, Spain, 296
Peace Direct, UK, 373
Peace, Health and Human Development Foundation—PHD Foundation, Japan, 193

Peace Village International, Germany, 129
Peace Winds Japan—PWJ, Japan, 192
Pearl S. Buck International, USA, 462
People in Need, Czech Republic, 75
PepsiCo Foundation, Inc, USA, 462
Perdana Global Peace Foundation—PGPF, Malaysia, 211
Perpetual Foundation, Australia, 16
Pestalozzi Children's Foundation, Switzerland, 317
The Peter Cundill Foundation, Bermuda, 35
Pfizer Foundation, USA, 462
The PHD Foundation—Peace, Health and Human Development Foundation, Japan, 193
Plan International Ireland, Ireland, 167
PLAN International—PI, UK, 374
Plataforma Portuguesa das Organizações Não-Governamentais para o Desenvolvimento—ONGD, Portugal, 258
Platform for Development Cooperation and Humanitarian Aid, Slovenia, 276
Platforma Mimovládnych Rozvojových Organizácií, Slovakia, 273
Populorum Progressio Foundation, Vatican City, 486
Portuguese Platform of Non-Governmental Organizations for Development, Portugal, 258
Practical Action, UK, 374
Pratham Education Foundation, India, 159
Première Urgence Internationale, France, 116
Presbyterian World Service & Development—PWS&D, Canada, 61
Primate's World Relief and Development Fund/Le Fonds du Primat Pour le Secours et le Développement Mondial—PWRDF, Canada, 49
Prince Claus Fund for Culture and Development, Netherlands, 228
Princess Charlene of Monaco Foundation, Monaco, 218
Prins Claus Fonds Voor Cultuur en Ontwikkeling, Netherlands, 228
Pro Mujer International, USA, 464
Pro Victimis, Switzerland, 315
Pro Women International, USA, 464
PRODESSA—Proyecto de Desarrollo Santiago, Guatemala, 148
Project HOPE, USA, 464
Project Trust, UK, 374
ProLiteracy, USA, 464
PwC Charitable Foundation, USA, 465
Rabo Foundation, Netherlands, 228
Rainforest Action Network—RAN, USA, 465
RAN—Rainforest Action Network, USA, 465
RE:ACT, UK, 375
Reall—Real Equity for All, UK, 375
RedR UK, UK, 375
Refugee Foundation, Netherlands, 231
Refugees International—RI, USA, 466
Rehabilitation International—RI, USA, 466
Relief International, USA, 466
The Resource Foundation—TRF, USA, 467
Rielo (Fernando), Fundación, Spain, 290
Rising Impact, USA, 467
Rockefeller Brothers Fund—RBF, USA, 468
Rockefeller Foundation, USA, 468
Rosetta Foundation, USA, 416
The Rotary Foundation, USA, 468
The Royal Society, UK, 379
RUI Foundation, Italy, 180
Rutgers, Netherlands, 228
Saïd Foundation, UK, 380
Sainsbury Family Charitable Trusts, UK, 380
Sakena Fund, USA, 469
The Salvation Army International Trust, UK, 381
Samaritan's Purse, USA, 469
Samuel (Hedwig und Robert) Stiftung, Germany, 131
Santé Sud, France, 116
Santiago Development Project, Guatemala, 148
Save the Children International, UK, 381
Save the Children (UK), UK, 381
Schlumberger Foundation, USA, 470
Schöck (Eberhard) Stiftung, Germany, 127
Scotland's International Development Alliance, UK, 337
Scottish Catholic International Aid Fund—SCIAF, UK, 382
Secours Catholique—Caritas de France, France, 116
SeedChange, Canada, 61
SEEMO—South East Europe Media Organisation, Austria, 23
SEL—Service d'Entraide et de Liaison, France, 116
SELAVIP—Services Latino-Américains, Africains et Asiatiques de Promotion de l'Habitation Populaire, Chile, 66

Arts and humanities

Self Help Africa—SHA, Ireland, 167
Sembrar Sartawi, Bolivia, 36
Serrv International, Inc, USA, 471
Sexual Wellbeing Aotearoa, New Zealand, 235
Sherman (Archie) Charitable Trust, UK, 340
SID—Society for International Development, Italy, 183
Sightsavers International, UK, 382
Singapore International Foundation—SIF, Singapore, 273
SIPRI—Stockholm International Peace Research Institute, Sweden, 304
Skoll Foundation, USA, 472
Slim (Carlos), Fundación, Mexico, 215
SLOGA—Platforma za Razvojno Sodelovanje in Humanitarno Pomoč, Slovenia, 276
Society for International Development—SID, Italy, 183
Solidar, Belgium, 34
Solidarios—Consejo de Fundaciones Americanas de Desarrollo, Dominican Republic, 87
Solidarity Overseas Service Malta—SOS Malta, Malta, 213
Somalia NGO Consortium, Somalia, 277
SOS Malta—Solidarity Overseas Service, Malta, 213
Souter Charitable Trust, UK, 384
South East Europe Media Organisation—SEEMO, Austria, 23
South West International Development Network—SWIDN, UK, 337
Southern Africa Trust, South Africa, 283
Southern Health, France, 116
Sparkassenstiftung für internationale Kooperation, Germany, 125
Sphere, Switzerland, 305
Stanley Thomas Johnson Foundation, Switzerland, 317
The Starr Foundation, USA, 473
Start Network, UK, 337
Steelworkers Humanity Fund/Le Fonds Humanitaire des Metallos, Canada, 62
Stewardship Foundation, USA, 473
Stichting DOEN, Netherlands, 229
Stichting IKEA Foundation, Netherlands, 229
Stichting Liliane Fonds, Netherlands, 229
Stichting Max Havelaar—Fairtrade Nederland, Netherlands, 230
Stichting Triodos Foundation, Netherlands, 231
Stichting Vluchteling, Netherlands, 231
Stichting Vodafone Netherlands, Netherlands, 231
Stiftelsen Dag Hammarskjölds Minnesfond, Sweden, 303
Stiftung Kinder in Afrika, Germany, 140
Stiftung Kinderdorf Pestalozzi, Switzerland, 317
Stiftung Nord-Süd-Brücken, Germany, 141
Stiftung Vivamos Mejor, Switzerland, 317
Stockholm Environment Institute, Sweden, 303
Stockholm International Peace Research Institute—SIPRI, Sweden, 304
Street Child, UK, 384
Strømme Foundation, Norway, 243
Strømmestiftelsen, Norway, 243
Südosteuropäische Medienorganisation, Austria, 23
SUN Civil Society Network, UK, 381
Suomalaiset kehitysjärjestöt—Fingo, Finland, 95
Swiss Alliance of Development Organisations, Switzerland, 305
Swiss Church Aid, Switzerland, 311
Swiss Foundation for Technical Co-operation, Switzerland, 318
SWISSAID Foundation, Switzerland, 318
Swisscontact—Swiss Foundation for Technical Co-operation, Switzerland, 318
Synergos—The Synergos Institute, USA, 396
Syria Al-Gad Relief Foundation, Egypt, 91
Taawon, Palestinian Territories, 246
Tanager, USA, 397
TANZ—Trade Aid NZ Inc, New Zealand, 235
Tearfund, UK, 385
Tearfund Australia, Australia, 18
Tebtebba Foundation, Philippines, 253
TechnoServe, USA, 474
Terre des Hommes International Federation—TDHIF, Switzerland, 318
Terre Sans Frontières—TSF, Canada, 62
Third World Network—TWN, Malaysia, 211
Third World Solidarity Action, Luxembourg, 209
Thomson Foundation, UK, 385
Thomson Reuters Foundation, UK, 385
TI—Transparency International, Germany, 142
Tibet Fund, USA, 475
Together for Global Justice—CIDSE, Belgium, 29
Trade Aid NZ Inc—TANZ, New Zealand, 235
Translators without Borders, USA, 416
Transparency International—TI, Germany, 142

Triodos Foundation, Netherlands, 231
Trócaire—Catholic Agency for World Development, Ireland, 168
Türkiye Kalkinma Vakfi, Türkiye, 330
UK Research and Innovation—UKRI, UK, 387
Union Aid Abroad—APHEDA, Australia, 19
Unitarian Universalist Service Committee—UUSC, USA, 476
United Nations Foundation, USA, 476
United Purpose, UK, 387
United States African Development Foundation—USADF, USA, 477
United Way Worldwide, USA, 477
Unity Foundation, Luxembourg, 210
UPS Foundation, USA, 477
USPG—United Society Partners in the Gospel, UK, 387
UUSC—Unitarian Universalist Service Committee, USA, 476
Väestöliitto, Finland, 98
VANI—Voluntary Action Network India, India, 155
Van Leer Foundation, Netherlands, 231
VENRO—Verband Entwicklungspolitik und Humanitäre Hilfe deutscher Nichtregierungsorganizationen, Germany, 120
Village Community Development Foundation, Indonesia, 163
VinFuture Foundation, Viet Nam, 489
Vita, Ireland, 168
Vivamos Mejor Foundation, Switzerland, 317
Vodafone Americas Foundation, USA, 478
Vodafone Foundation, UK, 388
Vodafone Netherlands Foundation, Netherlands, 231
Volkart Foundation, Switzerland, 319
Volkart-Stiftung, Switzerland, 319
Voluntary Action Network India—VANI, India, 155
Voluntary Service Overseas, UK, 388
Volunteer Service Abroad/Te Tūao Tāwāhi—VSA, New Zealand, 236
VSO—Voluntary Service Overseas, UK, 388
War on Want, UK, 388
WasserStiftung, Germany, 142
Water for Good, USA, 479
Water.org, Inc, USA, 479
Water for People, USA, 479
WaterAid, UK, 389
WaterFoundation, Germany, 142
Welfare Association, Palestinian Territories, 246
West African Rural Foundation—WARF, Senegal, 270
Westminster Foundation for Democracy—WFD, UK, 389
Whirlpool Foundation, USA, 480
WHO Foundation, Switzerland, 319
William Adlington Cadbury Charitable Trust, UK, 390
Winrock International, USA, 481
Woman to Woman Foundation, Sweden, 301
WomenLead Institute, USA, 418
Women's World Summit Foundation—WWSF, Switzerland, 320
World Alliance of YMCAs—Young Men's Christian Associations, Switzerland, 319
World Animal Protection, UK, 391
World Association of Children's Friends, Monaco, 217
World Central Kitchen—WCK, USA, 482
World Concern, USA, 482
World Emergency Relief—WER, USA, 483
World Jewish Relief, UK, 391
World Neighbors, USA, 483
World Telehealth Initiative, USA, 484
World University Service of Canada/Entraide Universitaire Mondiale du Canada—WUSC/EUMC, Canada, 63
World Vegetable Center, Taiwan, 322
World Vision International, UK, 391
WorldFish, Malaysia, 212
WWSF—Women's World Summit Foundation, Switzerland, 320
YADESA—Yayasan Pembinaan Masyarakat Desa, Indonesia, 163
Yayasan Dian Desa—YDD, Indonesia, 162
Yayasan Pembinaan Masyarakat Desa—YADESA, Indonesia, 163
Year Out Group, UK, 374
YORGHAS Foundation, Poland, 258
Youth Leadership Development Foundation—YLDF, Yemen, 489
Zagranica Group, Poland, 254
Zakat House, Kuwait, 203
Ziviler Friedensdienst—ZFD, Germany, 120
ZOA, Netherlands, 231

INDEX OF MAIN ACTIVITIES

ARTS AND HUMANITIES

1563 Foundation for the Arts and Culture, Italy, 174
1818 Fund Foundation, Netherlands, 229
The A. G. Leventis Foundation, Cyprus, 77
A. G. Leventis Foundation Nigeria, Nigeria, 237
A. M. Qattan Foundation, UK, 338
The A. P. Møller and Chastine Mc-Kinney Møller Foundation, Denmark, 82
A. P. Møller og Hustru Chastine Mc-Kinney Møllers Fond til almene Formaal, Denmark, 82
Abdul Hameed Shoman Foundation—AHSF, Jordan, 195
Abegg Foundation, Switzerland, 306
Abegg-Stiftung, Switzerland, 306
Académie Goncourt—Société Littéraire des Goncourt, France, 100
Accademia Musicale Chigiana, Italy, 172
ACLS—American Council of Learned Societies, USA, 399
Adenauer (Konrad) Stiftung eV, Germany, 134
Adessium Foundation, Netherlands, 223
The Adolph and Esther Gottlieb Foundation, Inc, USA, 397
Adriano Olivetti Foundation, Italy, 174
Africa-America Institute—AAI, USA, 398
Africa Space Foundation, Switzerland, 308
African Youth Initiative Network—AYINET, Uganda, 331
Aga Khan Development Network—AKDN, Switzerland, 306
Aga Khan Foundation, Switzerland, 306
Agora Foundation, Poland, 255
AHA—American Historical Association, USA, 401
Air France Foundation, France, 103
AKO Foundation, UK, 339
Al-Zubair Charity Foundation, Sudan, 297
The Alan Turing Institute, UK, 339
Alavi Foundation, USA, 398
Albanian Institute for International Studies—AIIS, Albania, 4
Albéniz Foundation, Spain, 288
Alemán (Miguel), Fundación, Mexico, 215
Alexander von Humboldt Foundation, Germany, 120
Alexander von Humboldt Stiftung, Germany, 120
Alexander S. Onassis Public Benefit Foundation, Liechtenstein, 207
Alfred Toepfer Foundation FVS, Germany, 121
Alfred Toepfer Stiftung FVS, Germany, 121
Alfried Krupp von Bohlen und Halbach Foundation, Germany, 121
Alfried Krupp von Bohlen und Halbach-Stiftung, Germany, 121
Ali Fulhu Thuthu Foundation, Maldives, 212
Alicia Patterson Foundation—APF, USA, 398
Alight, USA, 399
Allianz Foundation, Germany, 121
Almeida (Eng. António de), Fundação, Portugal, 260
Almine y Bernard Ruiz-Picasso Foundation, Spain, 288
Alvares Penteado (Armando), Fundação, Brazil, 39
Alwaleed Philanthropies, Saudi Arabia, 269
AMADE Mondiale—Association Mondiale des Amis de l'Enfance, Monaco, 217
Amberes (Carlos de), Fundación, Spain, 289
The Ambrose Monell Foundation, USA, 399
Ambrosiana Paolo VI Foundation, Italy, 175
America for Bulgaria Foundation, Bulgaria, 43
American Council of Learned Societies—ACLS, USA, 399
American Enterprise Institute—AEI, USA, 400
American Express Foundation, USA, 400
American Foundation for the Blind—AFB, USA, 400
American Historical Association—AHA, USA, 401
American Institute of Pakistan Studies, USA, 401
American Philosophical Society—APS, USA, 402
American-Scandinavian Foundation—ASF, USA, 403
American Schools of Oriental Research—ASOR, USA, 403
Amerind Foundation, Inc, USA, 403
Anders Jahre's Foundation for Humanitarian Purposes, Norway, 240
Anders Jahres Humanitære Stiftelse, Norway, 240
Andrew W. Mellon Foundation, USA, 404
The Andy Warhol Foundation for the Visual Arts, Inc, USA, 404
Ankara İngiliz Arkeoloji Enstitüsü, UK, 345

INDEX OF MAIN ACTIVITIES

Arts and humanities

Anna Lindh Euro-Mediterranean Foundation for Dialogue between Cultures, Egypt, 90
Anne Frank-Fonds, Switzerland, 306
Anne Frank Fund, Switzerland, 306
Anne Ray Foundation, USA, 450
The Annenberg Foundation, USA, 404
António de Almeida Foundation, Portugal, 260
Apex Foundation, Australia, 10
Arab Fund for Arts and Culture—AFAC, Lebanon, 205
Arab Image Foundation—AIF, Lebanon, 205
Arab Thought Foundation—ATF, Lebanon, 205
Arainneachd Eachdraidheil Alba, UK, 358
ArcelorMittal Brazil Foundation, Brazil, 39
Archie Sherman Charitable Trust, UK, 340
Arcus Foundation, USA, 405
Areces (Ramón), Fundación, Spain, 294
Areumdaun Jaedan, Korea (Republic), 200
Argentine Council for International Relations, Argentina, 6
Armando Alvares Penteado Foundation, Brazil, 39
Armanshahr Foundation—OPEN ASIA, Afghanistan, 3
Arpad Szenes–Vieira da Silva Foundation, Portugal, 258
Art Fund—National Art Collections Fund, UK, 341
Arthur Rubinstein International Music Society, Israel, 168
Arts Council England, UK, 341
Arts Council Korea, Korea (Republic), 200
Asahi Group Foundation, Japan, 186
ASEAN Foundation, Indonesia, 161
Asia Africa International Voluntary Foundation—AIV, Japan, 186
Asia New Zealand Foundation/Te Whītau Tūhono, New Zealand, 232
Asia/Pacific Cultural Centre for UNESCO—ACCU, Japan, 186
Asia Pacific Foundation of Canada—APFCanada, Canada, 49
Asia Philanthropy Circle—APC, Singapore, 272
Asia Society, USA, 406
Asian Cultural Council—ACC, USA, 406
Aspen Institute, USA, 407
Association of the Friends of the Swedish Institute at Athens, Sweden, 299
Association for Public Benefit Foundations, Austria, 20
AT&T Foundation, USA, 407
ATD Fourth World International, France, 115
Aurora Trust, UK, 341
Auschwitz-Birkenau Foundation, Poland, 255
Auschwitz Foundation—Remembrance of Auschwitz, Belgium, 30
Australian Academy of the Humanities, Australia, 11
Australian-American Fulbright Commission, Australia, 11
Australian Communities Foundation, Australia, 12
Australian Multicultural Foundation—AMF, Australia, 12
Australian Volunteers International—AVI, Australia, 13
Austrian Science Fund, Austria, 21
Aventis Foundation, Germany, 121
AVI—Australian Volunteers International, Australia, 13
Axel Springer Foundation, Germany, 122
Axel-Springer-Stiftung, Germany, 122
Ayala Foundation, Inc—AFI, Philippines, 251
Aydın Doğan Foundation, Türkiye, 328
Aydın Doğan Vakfı, Türkiye, 328
Baillet Latour Fund, Belgium, 32
Baltic Sea Foundation, Finland, 97
Balzan Fonds, Internationale Stiftung, Italy, 181
Bank of America Charitable Foundation, USA, 407
Bank of Cyprus Cultural Foundation, Cyprus, 77
Barandiarán (José Miguel de), Fundación, Spain, 291
Barça Foundation, Spain, 287
Barenboim-Said Foundation, Spain, 289
Baring Foundation, UK, 341
Barjeel Art Foundation, United Arab Emirates, 334
Barrié de la Maza (Pedro, Conde de Fenosa), Fundación, Spain, 293
BBC Media Action, UK, 342
BBVA Foundation, Spain, 289
The Beautiful Foundation, Korea (Republic), 200
Beisheim Foundation, Germany, 122
Beisheim Stiftung, Germany, 122
Belém Cultural Centre Foundation, Portugal, 259
Benetton Foundation for Study and Research, Italy, 175

Bergman (Ingmar), Stiftelsen, Sweden, 303
Bernadottes (Folke) Minnesfond, Sweden, 299
Bertelsmann Foundation, Germany, 122
Bertelsmann Stiftung, Germany, 122
Bettencourt Schueller Foundation, France, 103
BIAT Youth Foundation, Tunisia, 326
Biblioteca dell'Accademia Nazionale dei Lincei e Corsiniana, Italy, 172
Biocon Foundation, India, 157
Black Lives Matter Global Network Foundation—BLM Global Network Foundation, USA, 408
Black Sea University Foundation—BSUF, Romania, 263
Blakemore Foundation, USA, 408
Blavatnik Family Foundation, USA, 409
Bleustein-Blanchet (Marcel), Fondation de la Vocation, France, 109
BLM Global Network Foundation, USA, 408
Bloomberg Philanthropies, USA, 409
BMCE Bank Foundation, Morocco, 219
BNP Paribas Foundation, France, 103
Boghossian Foundation, Belgium, 31
Böll (Heinrich) Stiftung, Germany, 131
Boltzmann (Ludwig) Gesellschaft, Austria, 21
Book Aid International—BAI, UK, 343
Borderland Foundation, Poland, 256
Bosch (Robert) Stiftung GmbH, Germany, 138
Botín Foundation, Spain, 292
Botín (Marcelino), Fundación, Spain, 292
Braća Karić Foundation, Serbia, 271
Bradley (Lynde and Harry) Foundation, Inc, USA, 449
Brandt (Bundeskanzler Willy) Stiftung, Germany, 123
BrazilFoundation, Brazil, 39
Brenthurst Foundation, South Africa, 282
Bridge House Estates, UK, 348
British Academy, UK, 344
The British Council, UK, 344
British Institute at Ankara, UK, 345
British Institute of International and Comparative Law—BIICL, UK, 345
The Broad Foundation, USA, 410
Buck (Pearl S.) International, USA, 462
Buddharaksa Foundation, Thailand, 323
Bundeskanzler-Willy-Brandt-Stiftung, Germany, 123
Bunge y Born Foundation, Argentina, 7
Cadbury (Edward) Charitable Trust, UK, 351
Cadbury (William Adlington) Charitable Trust, UK, 390
CAF America, USA, 393
Calgary Foundation, Canada, 49
California Community Foundation, USA, 411
Calouste Gulbenkian Foundation, Portugal, 259
The Camargo Foundation, France, 101
The Canada Council for the Arts/Conseil des Arts du Canada, Canada, 50
Canadian Organization for Development through Education—CODE, Canada, 52
Canon Foundation in Europe, Netherlands, 224
Cargill (Margaret A.) Philanthropies, USA, 450
Cariplo Foundation, Italy, 175
Carlo Cattaneo Institute, Italy, 182
Carlo Pesenti Foundation, Italy, 176
Carlos de Amberes Foundation, Spain, 289
Carlos Slim Foundation, Mexico, 215
Carlsberg Foundation, Denmark, 82
Carlsbergfondet, Denmark, 82
Carnegie Endowment for International Peace, USA, 411
Carnegie Trust for the Universities of Scotland, UK, 346
Cartier-Bresson (Henri), Fondation, France, 107
Cartier Foundation for Contemporary Art, France, 104
Casa de Mateus Foundation, Portugal, 259
Cassa di Risparmio di Padova e Rovigo Foundation, Italy, 175
Cattaneo (Carlo), Istituto, Italy, 182
CCKF—Chiang Ching-kuo Foundation for International Scholarly Exchange, Taiwan, 321
CENSIS—Fondazione Centro Studi Investimenti Sociali, Italy, 172
Center for Inquiry—CFI, USA, 412
Centre for Civil Society—CCS, India, 157
Centre Européen de la Culture—CEC, Switzerland, 307
Centre for International Studies, Italy, 172
Centre for Philanthropy, Slovakia, 274
Centre for Strategic & International Studies—CSIS, Indonesia, 162
Centro de Estudios Públicos—CEP, Chile, 64
Centro Studi Internazionali—CSI, Italy, 172
Centrum pre Filantropiu, Slovakia, 274
The Century Foundation—TCF, USA, 413

Çera, Belgium, 28
Česko-německý fond budoucnosti, Czech Republic, 79
Chaabi (Miloud), Fondation, Morocco, 220
Chang Yung-fa Foundation, Taiwan, 321
Charities Advisory Trust, UK, 336
Charities Aid Foundation of America—CAF America, USA, 393
Charles and Lynn Schusterman Family Philanthropies, USA, 413
Charles Stewart Mott Foundation—CSMF, USA, 414
The Charles Wallace India Trusts, UK, 347
The Charta 77 Foundation, Czech Republic, 80
The Chatlos Foundation, Inc, USA, 414
Chia Hsin Foundation, Taiwan, 321
Chiang Ching-kuo Foundation for International Scholarly Exchange—CCKF, Taiwan, 321
The Chicago Community Trust, USA, 414
Chigiana Musical Academy, Italy, 172
Chirac (Jacques), Fondation, France, 107
Christoph Merian Foundation, Switzerland, 305
Christoph-Merian-Stiftung, Switzerland, 305
The Churchill Fellowship, UK, 348
Churchill (Winston) Memorial Trust of New Zealand, New Zealand, 236
Cini (Giorgio), Fondazione, Italy, 177
Citi Handlowy Leopold Kronenberg Foundation, Poland, 255
The City Bridge Trust, UK, 348
City of Lisbon Foundation, Portugal, 259
Civic Democratic Initiative Support Foundation—CDF, Yemen, 489
Civic Forum Foundation, Czech Republic, 80
Civil Society Foundation, Georgia, 118
Clara Lionel Foundation—CLF, USA, 415
Cleveland Foundation, USA, 416
The Coca-Cola Foundation, Inc, USA, 417
CODE—Canadian Organization for Development through Education, Canada, 52
Collodi (Carlo), Fondazione Nazionale, Italy, 179
Commonwealth Foundation, UK, 348
Communication Foundation for Asia, Philippines, 251
Community Chest of Korea—Fruit of Love, Korea (Republic), 200
Community Foundation for Northern Ireland, UK, 349
Conseil des Arts du Canada, Canada, 50
Consejo Argentino para las Relaciones Internacionales—CARI, Argentina, 6
Consejo Latinoamericano de Ciencias Sociales—CLACSO, Argentina, 6
Copperbelt Development Foundation, Zambia, 490
Coram, UK, 349
Le Corbusier Foundation, France, 108
Costopoulos (J. F.) Foundation, Greece, 146
Coubertin Foundation, France, 105
Covenant Foundation, USA, 418
The Crafoord Foundation, Sweden, 298
Crafoordska stiftelsen, Sweden, 298
The CRB Foundation/La Fondation CRB, Canada, 52
Crown Family Philanthropies, USA, 419
Cultural Center of the Philippines—CCP, Philippines, 252
Cultural Foundation of the German Länder, Germany, 134
Culture, Health, Arts, Sports and Education Fund—CHASE, Jamaica, 184
Czech-German Fund for the Future, Czech Republic, 79
Czech Literary Fund Foundation, Czech Republic, 80
Czech Music Fund Foundation, Czech Republic, 79
DAAD—Deutscher Akademischer Austauschdienst, Germany, 125
Dag Hammarskjöld Foundation, Sweden, 303
Daiwa Anglo-Japanese Foundation, UK, 350
Dalio Foundation, USA, 419
Danish Cultural Institute—DCI, Denmark, 82
Danske Kulturinstitut—DKI, Denmark, 82
Davis (Lady) Fellowship Trust, Israel, 170
Deripaska (Oleg) Foundation, Russian Federation, 267
Desmond & Leah Tutu Legacy Foundation, South Africa, 279
Deutsche Bank Americas Foundation, USA, 420
Deutsche Bank Foundation, Germany, 124
Deutsche Bank Stiftung, Germany, 124
Deutsche Nationalstiftung, Germany, 125
Deutsche Orient-Stiftung, Germany, 125
Deutscher Akademischer Austauschdienst—DAAD, Germany, 125
Dietmar Hopp Foundation, Germany, 126
Dietmar-Hopp-Stiftung, Germany, 126

Arts and humanities

Digicel Foundation Haiti, Haiti, 149
Dioraphte Foundation, Netherlands, 229
Dmitry Likhachev Foundation, Russian Federation, 265
DNB Savings Bank Foundation, Norway, 243
DOEN Foundation, Netherlands, 229
Doğan (Aydın) Vakfı, Türkiye, 328
Dokolo (Sindika), Fundação, Angola, 5
Donner (William H.) Foundation, Inc, USA, 481
Doris Duke Charitable Foundation—DDCF, USA, 421
Dr Scholl Foundation, USA, 421
DTGO Group of Foundations, Thailand, 323
del Duca (Simone et Cino), Fondation, France, 111
Dulverton Trust, UK, 351
Dumbarton Oaks, USA, 421
Dunhe Foundation, China (People's Republic), 68
East Asia Institute—EAI, Korea (Republic), 201
East-West Center—EWC, USA, 422
East-West Encounters Charitable Foundation, Germany, 141
Ebelin and Gerd Bucerius ZEIT Foundation, Germany, 143
EDF Group Foundation, France, 107
Edmond de Rothschild Foundations, Switzerland, 308
Edoardo Garrone Foundation, Italy, 177
EDP Foundation, Portugal, 260
Edward Cadbury Charitable Trust, UK, 351
Egmont Fonden, Denmark, 83
Egmont Foundation, Denmark, 83
Einaudi (Luigi), Fondazione, Italy, 178
Electronic Frontier Foundation—EFF, USA, 423
Elena & Gennady Timchenko Foundation, Russian Federation, 265
Elizabeth Kostova Foundation for Creative Writing, Bulgaria, 43
Ellerman (John) Foundation, UK, 361
The ELMA Group of Foundations, USA, 423
Emirates Foundation, United Arab Emirates, 334
Empresas Polar Foundation, Venezuela, 487
The English-Speaking Union—ESU, UK, 353
Ente Cassa di Risparmio di Firenze, Italy, 173
Erik Philip-Sörensen Foundation, Sweden, 299
Erik Philip-Sörensens Stiftelse, Sweden, 299
Ernst Schering Foundation, Germany, 127
Ernst-Schering-Stiftung, Germany, 127
ERSTE Foundation, Austria, 21
ERSTE Stiftung—Die ERSTE Österreichische Spar-Casse Privatstiftung, Austria, 21
Esmée Fairbairn Foundation, UK, 353
Estonian National Culture Foundation, Estonia, 93
Ettersberg Foundation, Germany, 140
Eugenio Mendoza Foundation, Venezuela, 487
Eurasia Partnership Foundation-Armenia—EPF-Armenia, Armenia, 9
Europa Nostra, Netherlands, 224
European Center for Constitutional and Human Rights—ECCHR, Germany, 128
European Center for Peace and Development—ECPD, Serbia, 271
European Cultural Centre, Switzerland, 307
European Cultural Foundation—ECF, Netherlands, 225
European Foundation for the Sustainable Development of the Regions, Switzerland, 308
European Institute of Health and Social Welfare, Spain, 296
European Mediterranean Institute, Spain, 296
European Youth For Action—EYFA, Germany, 128
Europese Culterele Stichting, Netherlands, 225
Evens Foundation, Belgium, 31
Ewing Marion Kauffman Foundation, USA, 425
ExxonMobil Foundation, USA, 425
EYFA—European Youth For Action, Germany, 128
FAI—Fondo per l'Ambiente Italiano, Italy, 174
Fairbairn (Esmée) Foundation, UK, 353
Federal Chancellor Willy Brandt Foundation, Germany, 123
FEDRE—European Foundation for the Sustainable Development of the Regions, Switzerland, 308
Félix Houphouët-Boigny Foundation for Peace Research, Côte d'Ivoire, 75
Feltrinelli (Giangiacomo), Fondazione, Italy, 177
FEMSA Foundation, Mexico, 215
Fernand Lazard Foundation, Belgium, 31
Fernando Rielo Foundation, Spain, 290
Ferrero (Piera, Pietro e Giovanni), Fondazione, Italy, 179
The Film Foundation, USA, 425
Finnish Cultural Foundation, Finland, 97
Finnish Development Organizations, Finland, 95

Finnish Institute in the UK and Ireland Trust, UK, 354
First Nations Development Institute, USA, 426
Florence Gould Foundation, USA, 427
Florence Savings Bank Foundation, Italy, 173
FOKAL—Open Society Foundation Haiti, Haiti, 149
Folke Bernadotte Memorial Foundation, Sweden, 299
Folke Bernadottes Minnesfond, Sweden, 299
Folmer Wisti Fonden for International Forståelse, Denmark, 83
Folmer Wisti Foundation for International Understanding, Denmark, 83
Fondacija Braća Karić, Serbia, 271
Fondacija Cennosti, Bulgaria, 43
Fondacioni i Kosovës për Shoqëri të Hapur, Kosovo, 203
Fondation Air France, France, 103
Fondation Arabe pour l'Image, Lebanon, 205
Fondation Auschwitz—Mémoire d'Auschwitz, Belgium, 30
Fondation Bettencourt Schueller, France, 103
Fondation BIAT pour la Jeunesse, Tunisia, 326
Fondation BMCE Bank, Morocco, 219
Fondation BNP Paribas, France, 103
Fondation Boghossian, Belgium, 31
Fondation Cartier pour l'Art Contemporain, France, 104
Fondation Casip-Cojasor, France, 104
Fondation Charles Veillon, Switzerland, 308
Fondation de la Cité internationale des arts, France, 104
Fondation du Collège de France, France, 105
Fondation Le Corbusier—FLC, France, 108
Fondation de Coubertin, France, 105
Fondation Digicel Haïti, Haiti, 149
Fondation pour l'Economie et le Développement Durable des Régions d'Europe—FEDRE, Switzerland, 308
Fondation d'Entreprise Crédit Agricole Réunion Mayotte, Réunion, 262
Fondation d'Entreprise La Poste, France, 105
Fondation Espace Afrique, Switzerland, 308
Fondation Européenne de la Culture/Europese Culturele Stichting, Netherlands, 225
Fondation Evens Stichting, Belgium, 31
Fondation Félix Houphouët-Boigny pour la Recherche de la Paix, Côte d'Ivoire, 75
Fondation Fernand Lazard Stichting, Belgium, 31
Fondation de France, France, 99
Fondation France Chine—FFC, France, 106
Fondation France-Israël, France, 106
Fondation Franco-Japonaise Sasakawa, France, 106
Fondation Gan pour le Cinéma, France, 107
Fondation Groupe EDF, France, 107
Fondation Hans Wilsdorf, Switzerland, 309
Fondation Hassan II pour les Marocains Résidant à l'Étranger, Morocco, 220
Fondation Henri Cartier-Bresson, France, 107
Fondation Hirondelle: Media for Peace and Human Dignity, Switzerland, 309
Fondation Jacques Chirac, France, 107
Fondation Jean Jaurès, France, 107
Fondation Jean Monnet pour l'Europe, Switzerland, 309
Fondation Léopold Sédar Senghor, Senegal, 270
Fondation Maison des Sciences de l'Homme—FMSH, France, 108
Fondation Marc de Montalembert, France, 109
Fondation Marcel Bleustein-Blanchet de la Vocation, France, 109
Fondation Marcel Hicter, Belgium, 32
Fondation Marguerite et Aimé Maeght, France, 109
Fondation Miloud Chaäbi, Morocco, 220
Fondation Mohammed V pour la Solidarité, Morocco, 220
Fondation MTN Congo, Congo (Republic), 73
Fondation Mutuelles Congolaises d'Epargne et de Crédit—MUCODEC, Congo (Republic), 73
Fondation Orange, France, 110
Fondation Orange Burkina Faso, Burkina Faso, 45
Fondation Orange Cameroun, Cameroon, 47
Fondation Orange-Côte d'Ivoire Télécom—OCIT, Côte d'Ivoire, 76
Fondation Orange Mali, Mali, 213
Fondation Orient-Occident—FOO, Morocco, 220
Fondation du Patrimoine, France, 110
Fondation Perspectives d'Avenir, Congo (Republic), 73
Fondation Prince Pierre de Monaco, Monaco, 218
Fondation Princesse Grace, Monaco, 218
Fondation Rambourg, Tunisia, 326
Fondation Rinaldi, Haiti, 149

INDEX OF MAIN ACTIVITIES

Fondation du Roi Abdul-Aziz al-Saoud pour les Études Islamiques et les Sciences Humaines, Morocco, 220
Fondation Roi Baudouin, Belgium, 33
Fondation Simón I. Patiño, Switzerland, 310
Fondation Simone et Cino del Duca, France, 111
Fondation Singer-Polignac, France, 111
Fondation Sonatel, Senegal, 270
Fondation Suisse-Liechtenstein pour les Recherches Archéologiques à l'Etranger, Switzerland, 316
Fondation TotalEnergies, France, 112
Fondation Tunisie pour le Développement, Tunisia, 326
Fondazione 1563 per l'Arte e la Cultura, Italy, 174
Fondazione Adriano Olivetti, Italy, 174
Fondazione Ambrosiana Paolo VI, Italy, 175
Fondazione Benetton Studi Ricerche, Italy, 175
Fondazione Cariplo, Italy, 175
Fondazione Cassa di Risparmio di Padova e Rovigo, Italy, 175
Fondazione Cassa di Risparmio di Torino, Italy, 176
Fondazione Cassa di Risparmio di Verona Vicenza Belluno e Ancona—Fondazione Cariverona, Italy, 176
Fondazione Cavaliere del Lavoro Carlo Pesenti, Italy, 176
Fondazione Centro Studi Investimenti Sociali—CENSIS, Italy, 172
Fondazione Compagnia di San Paolo, Italy, 176
Fondazione Edoardo Garrone, Italy, 177
Fondazione Fratelli Tutti, Vatican City, 486
Fondazione Giangiacomo Feltrinelli, Italy, 177
Fondazione Giorgio Cini, Italy, 177
Fondazione Internazionale Premio Balzan, Italy, 181
Fondazione per l'Istituto Svizzero di Roma, Italy, 178
Fondazione ITS, Italy, 178
Fondazione Luigi Einaudi, Italy, 178
Fondazione Nazionale Carlo Collodi, Italy, 179
Fondazione Piera, Pietro e Giovanni Ferrero, Italy, 179
Fondazione Prada, Italy, 179
Fondazione Querini Stampalia—FQS, Italy, 179
Fondazione Roma, Italy, 179
Fondazione Romaeuropa, Italy, 180
Fondazione RUI, Italy, 180
Fondazione Unipolis, Italy, 181
Fondazione Vaticana Giovanni Paolo I, Vatican City, 486
Fondazione di Venezia, Italy, 181
Fondazzjoni Patrimonju Malti, Malta, 213
Fonden Realdania, Denmark, 83
Fonds atvērtai sabiedrībai DOTS, Latvia, 204
Fonds Baillet Latour, Belgium, 32
Fonds National Suisse de la Recherche Scientifique, Switzerland, 316
For a Healthy Generation, Uzbekistan, 485
Ford Foundation, USA, 427
Foreign Policy and United Nations Association of Austria—UNA-AUSTRIA, Austria, 21
Föreningen Svenska Atheninstitutets Vänner, Sweden, 299
Foundation for Analysis and Social Studies, Spain, 288
Foundation Centre for the Study of Social Investment, Italy, 172
Foundation for Culture and Civil Society—FCCS, Afghanistan, 3
Foundation for Democracy and Media, Netherlands, 229
Foundation for German-Polish Co-operation, Poland, 257
Foundation of the Hellenic World, Greece, 145
Foundation for an Open Society DOTS, Latvia, 204
Foundation for Rural & Regional Renewal—FRRR, Australia, 14
Foundation for the Swiss Institute of Rome, Italy, 178
Foundation of Weimar Classics, Germany, 134
Foundation of Youth and Lifelong Learning—INEDIVIM, Greece, 145
Foundations' Post-Doc Pool, Finland, 95
France China Foundation, France, 106
France-Israel Foundation, France, 106
Franco-American Fulbright Commission, France, 113
Franco-Japanese Sasakawa Foundation, France, 106
Frank (Anne)-Fonds, Switzerland, 306
Frank Knox Memorial Fellowships, USA, 428
Frankfurt Foundation for German-Italian Studies, Germany, 129
Frankfurter Stiftung für Deutsch-Italienische Studien, Germany, 129

INDEX OF MAIN ACTIVITIES

Arts and humanities

Fratelli Tutti Foundation, Vatican City, 486
Freedom Speech Foundation, Norway, 241
French-American Foundation, USA, 429
Freudenberg Foundation, Germany, 129
Freudenberg Stiftung, Germany, 129
Friede Springer Foundation, Germany, 129
Friede Springer Stiftung, Germany, 129
Fritz Thyssen Foundation, Germany, 130
Fritz Thyssen Stiftung, Germany, 130
Fulbright Commission Philippines, Philippines, 253
Fulbright France—Commission Fulbright Franco-Américaine, France, 113
Fulbright Norway—US-Norway Fulbright Foundation for Educational Exchange, Norway, 241
Fund and Endowment Management Foundation, Norway, 240
Fundação ArcelorMittal Brasil, Brazil, 39
Fundação Armando Alvares Penteado, Brazil, 39
Fundação Arpad Szenes–Vieira da Silva, Portugal, 258
Fundação Calouste Gulbenkian, Portugal, 259
Fundação da Casa de Mateus, Portugal, 259
Fundação Centro Cultural de Belém, Portugal, 259
Fundação Cidade de Lisboa, Portugal, 259
Fundação EDP, Portugal, 260
Fundação Eng. António de Almeida, Portugal, 260
Fundação Getulio Vargas—FGV, Brazil, 40
Fundação Iochpe, Brazil, 40
Fundação Luso-Americana para o Desenvolvimento—FLAD, Portugal, 260
Fundação Mário Soares e Maria Barroso, Portugal, 260
Fundação Oriente, Portugal, 260
Fundação Ricardo do Espírito Santo Silva, Portugal, 261
Fundação Roberto Marinho, Brazil, 41
Fundação de Serralves, Portugal, 261
Fundação Sindika Dokolo, Angola, 5
Fundação Vodafone Portugal, Portugal, 261
Fundació Futbol Club Barcelona, Spain, 287
Fundació Gala–Salvador Dalí, Spain, 287
Fundación Albéniz, Spain, 288
Fundación Almine y Bernard Ruiz-Picasso, Spain, 288
Fundación para el Análisis y los Estudios Sociales—FAES, Spain, 288
Fundación Bancaria 'la Caixa', Spain, 288
Fundación Banco Bilbao Vizcaya Argentaria—Fundación BBVA, Spain, 289
Fundación Barenboim-Said, Spain, 289
Fundación BBVA, Spain, 289
Fundación Bigott, Venezuela, 487
Fundación Bunge y Born, Argentina, 7
Fundación Carlos de Amberes, Spain, 289
Fundación Carlos Slim, Mexico, 215
Fundación Carolina, Spain, 290
Fundación Comunitaria de Puerto Rico—FCPR, Puerto Rico, 261
Fundación Empresas Polar, Venezuela, 487
Fundación Espacio Cívico, Panama, 247
Fundación Eugenio Mendoza—FEM, Venezuela, 487
Fundación Felipe González, Spain, 290
Fundación FEMSA, Mexico, 215
Fundación Fernando Rielo, Spain, 290
Fundación Global Democracia y Desarrollo—FUNGLODE, Dominican Republic, 87
Fundación José Miguel de Barandiarán, Spain, 291
Fundación José Ortega y Gasset—Gregorio Marañón, Spain, 291
Fundación Juan March, Spain, 291
Fundación Juanelo Turriano, Spain, 291
Fundación Leo Messi, Spain, 292
Fundación Loewe, Spain, 292
Fundación MAPFRE, Spain, 292
Fundación Marcelino Botín, Spain, 292
Fundación Miguel Alemán AC, Mexico, 215
Fundación Montemadrid, Spain, 292
Fundación Orange, Spain, 293
Fundación Pablo Neruda, Chile, 65
Fundación Pedro Barrié de la Maza, Spain, 293
Fundación Princesa de Asturias, Spain, 294
Fundación Rafa Nadal, Spain, 294
Fundación Ramón Areces, Spain, 294
Fundación Real Madrid, Spain, 295
Fundación Repsol, Spain, 295
Fundación Semah-Valencia, Panama, 247
Fundación SM, Spain, 295
Fundación Telmex Telcel, Mexico, 216
Fundacja Agory, Poland, 255
Fundacja Auschwitz-Birkenau, Poland, 255
Fundacja Citi Handlowy im. Leopolda Kronenberga, Poland, 255

Fundacja Pogranicze, Poland, 256
Fundacja Współpracy Polsko-Niemieckiej/Stiftung für Deutsch-Polnische Zusammenarbeit, Poland, 257
Fundația Orange Moldova, Moldova, 217
Fundația Soros—Moldova, Moldova, 217
Fundația Universitară a Mării Negre—FUMN, Romania, 263
FWF—Österreichischer Wissenschaftsfonds, Austria, 21
FWO—Fonds Wetenschappelijk Onderzoek, Belgium, 32
G. Unger Vetlesen Foundation, USA, 429
Gan Foundation for the Cinema, France, 107
Garfield Weston Foundation, UK, 355
Garrone (Edoardo), Fondazione, Italy, 177
The Gatsby Charitable Foundation, UK, 355
The General Kashif Al-Getaa Foundation, Iraq, 164
The George A. and Eliza Gardner Howard Foundation, USA, 430
Georges Lurcy Charitable and Educational Trust, USA, 430
Gerda Henkel Foundation, Germany, 130
Gerda Henkel Stiftung, Germany, 130
German Academic Exchange Service, Germany, 125
German Academic Scholarship Foundation, Germany, 142
German National Trust, Germany, 125
German Orient Foundation, Germany, 125
Getty (J. Paul) Trust, USA, 442
Getulio Vargas Foundation, Brazil, 40
Giangiacomo Feltrinelli Foundation, Italy, 177
Giorgio Cini Foundation, Italy, 177
Giovanni Paolo I, Fondazione Vaticana, Vatican City, 486
Give2Asia, USA, 394
Glasnost Defence Foundation, Russian Federation, 265
Global Democracy and Development Foundation, Dominican Republic, 87
Global Ethic Foundation, Germany, 141
Globetree Association, Sweden, 300
Goethe-Institut, Germany, 131
Goldsmith (Horace W.) Foundation, USA, 436
Goncourt Academy—Goncourt Literary Society, France, 100
Good Things Foundation, UK, 356
Goodenough College, UK, 356
Gottlieb (Adolph and Esther) Foundation, Inc, USA, 397
Gould (Florence) Foundation, USA, 427
Graham Foundation for Advanced Studies in the Fine Arts—GF, USA, 432
Great Britain Sasakawa Foundation, UK, 356
Greater Kansas City Community Foundation, USA, 433
Guggenheim (John Simon) Memorial Foundation, USA, 434
Guggenheim (Solomon R.) Foundation, USA, 473
Gulbenkian (Calouste), Fundação, Portugal, 259
Hamlyn (Paul) Foundation, UK, 373
Hammarskjölds (Dag) Minnesfond, Stiftelsen, Sweden, 303
Hanaholmen—Swedish-Finnish Cultural Centre, Finland, 95
Hanns Seidel Foundation, Germany, 131
Hanns-Seidel-Stiftung eV, Germany, 131
Hans Wilsdorf Foundation, Switzerland, 309
Hariri Foundation for Sustainable Human Development, Lebanon, 205
Harp Helú Foundations, Mexico, 216
Hassan II Foundation for Moroccans Living Abroad, Morocco, 220
He Xiangjian Foundation, China (People's Republic), 68
Headley Trust, UK, 357
Hearst Foundations, USA, 435
Heineken Prizes for Arts and Sciences, Netherlands, 225
Heinekenprijzen voor kunst en wetenschap, Netherlands, 225
Heinrich Böll Foundation, Germany, 131
Heinrich-Böll-Stiftung, Germany, 131
Hellenic Foundation for Culture, Greece, 145
Helmich (Janson Johan og Marcia) Legat, Norway, 242
Helsińska Fundacja Praw Człowieka, Poland, 257
Helsingin Sanomain Säätiö, Finland, 96
Helsingin Sanomat Foundation, Finland, 96
Helsinki Foundation for Human Rights, Poland, 257
Henie Onstad Art Centre, Norway, 241
Henie Onstad Kunstsenter, Norway, 241
Henkel (Gerda) Stiftung, Germany, 130
Henri Cartier-Bresson Foundation, France, 107
Henry Luce Foundation, Inc, USA, 435

The Henry Moore Foundation, UK, 358
Heritage Foundation, France, 110
Heungkong Charitable Foundation, China (People's Republic), 68
Hewlett (William and Flora) Foundation, USA, 481
Heydar Aliyev Fondu, Azerbaijan, 23
Heydar Aliyev Foundation, Azerbaijan, 23
Hicter (Marcel), Fondation, Belgium, 32
Hinduja Foundation, India, 157
Historic Environment Scotland, UK, 358
History Foundation of Turkey, Türkiye, 329
Hitachi Foundation, Japan, 187
Hivos—Humanistisch Instituut voor Ontwikkelings Samenwerking, Netherlands, 226
Homeless World Cup Foundation—HWCF, UK, 358
Hopp (Dietmar) Stiftung, Germany, 126
Horace W. Goldsmith Foundation, USA, 436
Hoso Bunka Foundation, Inc—HBF, Japan, 188
Houphouët-Boigny (Félix), Fondation, Côte d'Ivoire, 75
House of the Human Sciences Foundation, France, 108
Howard (George A. and Eliza Gardner) Foundation, USA, 430
Howard (Katharine) Foundation, Ireland, 167
Hudson Institute, USA, 437
Humanistic Institute for Co-operation with Developing Countries, Netherlands, 226
von Humboldt (Alexander) Stiftung, Germany, 120
Humboldt Forum, Germany, 132
IACD—Institute of Asian Culture and Development, Korea (Republic), 201
Ian Potter Foundation, Australia, 14
Ichikowitz Family Foundation—IFF, South Africa, 280
The Ideas Institute, Kenya, 199
Idrima Kratikon Ipotrofion, Greece, 147
IKY—State Scholarships Foundation, Greece, 147
Imbuto Foundation, Rwanda, 268
Inamori Foundation, Japan, 188
Indian Council for Cultural Relations, India, 157
Indian National Trust for Art and Cultural Heritage—INTACH, India, 158
INEDIVIM—Foundation of Youth and Lifelong Learning, Greece, 145
Ingmar Bergman Foundation, Sweden, 303
Inlaks Shivdasani Foundation, India, 158
Institusjonen Fritt Ord, Norway, 241
Institut Europeu de la Mediterrània—IEMed, Spain, 296
Institute of Asian Culture and Development—IACD, Korea (Republic), 201
Institute of British Geographers, UK, 378
Institute for Citizens & Scholars, USA, 439
Institute of International Law, Argentina, 6
Institute for International Security and Strategic Affairs—ISIAE, Argentina, 6
Institute for Iran-Eurasia Studies—IRAS, Iran, 163
Institute for Palestine Studies—IPS, Lebanon, 206
Instituto Europeo de Salud y Bienestar Social, Spain, 296
Instituto de Montaña, Peru, 249
Institutul Cultural Român—ICR, Romania, 264
INTACH—Indian National Trust for Art and Cultural Heritage, India, 158
Internationaal Instituut voor Sociale Geschiedenis—IISG, Netherlands, 226
International Balzan Prize Foundation, Italy, 181
International Charitable Fund 'Concord 3000', Ukraine, 333
International Forum Bosnia, Bosnia and Herzegovina, 37
International Institute for Applied Systems Analysis—IIASA, Austria, 21
International Institute of Social History—IISH, Netherlands, 226
International Music and Art Foundation, Liechtenstein, 208
International Renaissance Foundation—IRF, Ukraine, 333
International Visegrad Fund—IVF, Slovakia, 275
International Youth Library Foundation, Germany, 133
Internationale Jugendbibliothek, Germany, 133
Internationale Stiftung Preis E. Balzan-Fonds, Italy, 181
Internationalt Uddannelsescenter, Denmark, 84
Iochpe Foundation, Brazil, 40
The Ireland Funds America, USA, 442
The Israel Democracy Institute—IDI, Israel, 170
Istituto Carlo Cattaneo, Italy, 182

Arts and humanities

Istituto Luigi Sturzo, Italy, 182
Istituto Svedese di Studi Classici a Roma, Italy, 183
ITS Foundation, Italy, 178
IUC International Education Center—IUC-Europe, Denmark, 84
The J. F. Costopoulos Foundation, Greece, 146
J. Paul Getty Trust, USA, 442
Jack Ma Foundation—JMF, China (People's Republic), 68
Jacques Chirac Foundation, France, 107
Jahres (Anders) Humanitære Stiftelse, Norway, 240
Janson Johan Helmich and Marcia Jansons Endowment, Norway, 242
Janson Johan Helmich og Marcia Jansons Legat, Norway, 242
The Japan Foundation, Japan, 189
Japan Foundation Endowment Committee—JFEC, UK, 361
Japanese-German Centre Berlin, Germany, 133
Japanisch-Deutsches Zentrum Berlin, Germany, 133
Jaurès (Jean), Fondation, France, 107
Jazz Foundation of America—JFA, USA, 443
Jean Jaurès Foundation, France, 107
Jean Monnet Foundation for Europe, Switzerland, 309
Jenny and Antti Wihuri Foundation, Finland, 96
Jenny ja Antti Wihurin Rahasto, Finland, 96
Jerusalem Foundation, Israel, 170
The Jerusalem Trust, UK, 361
JFEC—Japan Foundation Endowment Committee, UK, 361
JNF UK—JNF Charitable Trust, UK, 361
The John D. and Catherine T. MacArthur Foundation, USA, 444
John Ellerman Foundation, UK, 361
John Paul I Vatican Foundation, Vatican City, 486
John S. and James L. Knight Foundation, USA, 444
John Simon Guggenheim Memorial Foundation, USA, 444
Johnson (Lyndon Baines) Foundation, USA, 449
Johnson (Stanley Thomas) Foundation, Switzerland, 317
Jordan River Foundation, Jordan, 196
José Miguel de Barandiarán Foundation, Spain, 291
José Ortega y Gasset—Gregorio Marañón Foundation, Spain, 291
Joseph Levy Foundation, UK, 362
Joseph Tanenbaum Charitable Foundation, Canada, 58
Joyce Foundation, USA, 445
Juan March Foundation, Spain, 291
Juanelo Turriano Foundation, Spain, 291
Kade (Max) Foundation, Inc, USA, 451
Kamel Lazaar Foundation—KLF, Tunisia, 327
Katharine Howard Foundation—KHF, Ireland, 167
KCDF—Kenya Community Development Foundation, Kenya, 199
Khemka (Nand & Jeet) Foundation, India, 159
Kind Heart Foundation, Viet Nam, 488
King Abdul-Aziz al-Saoud Foundation for Islamic Study and the Humanities, Morocco, 220
King Baudouin Foundation, Belgium, 33
King Faisal Foundation, Saudi Arabia, 269
King Hussein Foundation—KHF, Jordan, 196
King Sejong Institute Foundation—KSIF, Korea (Republic), 201
The King's Foundation, UK, 363
Klassik Stiftung Weimar, Germany, 134
Knight (John S. and James L.) Foundation, USA, 444
Knox (Frank) Memorial Fellowships, USA, 428
Knut and Alice Wallenberg Foundation, Sweden, 301
Knut och Alice Wallenbergs Stiftelse, Sweden, 301
Koç (Vehbi), Vakfı, Türkiye, 331
Koning Boudewijnstichting/Fondation Roi Baudouin, Belgium, 33
Konrad Adenauer Foundation, Germany, 134
Konrad-Adenauer-Stiftung eV—KAS, Germany, 134
Körber Foundation, Germany, 134
Körber-Stiftung, Germany, 134
The Korea Foundation, Korea (Republic), 202
Koret Foundation, USA, 446
The Kosciuszko Foundation, Inc, USA, 446
Kosovo Foundation for Open Society—KFOS, Kosovo, 203
Kostova (Elizabeth) Foundation for Creative Writing, Bulgaria, 43
Kresge Foundation, USA, 446
Kress (Samuel H.) Foundation, USA, 469

Kronenberg (Leopold) Foundation, Poland, 255
Krupp von Bohlen und Halbach (Alfried) Stiftung, Germany, 121
Kulturfonden för Sverige och Finland, Sweden, 301
Kulturstiftung der Länder—KSL, Germany, 134
Kulturstiftung Liechtenstein, Liechtenstein, 208
Kuwait Awqaf Public Foundation, Kuwait, 203
Kuwait Foundation for the Advancement of Sciences—KFAS, Kuwait, 203
'La Caixa' Banking Foundation, Spain, 288
Lady Davis Fellowship Trust, Israel, 170
Lambrakis Foundation, Greece, 146
Landis & Gyr Foundation, Switzerland, 313
Landis & Gyr Stiftung, Switzerland, 313
Lannan Foundation, USA, 447
Latin American Council of Social Sciences, Argentina, 6
Latter-day Saint Charities—LDSC, USA, 447
Lauder (Ronald S.) Foundation, Germany, 138
Lazard (Fernand), Fondation, Belgium, 31
LBJ Foundation, USA, 449
League of Corporate Foundations—LCF, Philippines, 250
Leibniz Association, Germany, 135
Leibniz Gemeinschaft, Germany, 135
Leibniz-Institut für Ost- und Südosteuropaforschung, Germany, 135
Leibniz Institute for East and South-East European Studies, Germany, 135
Leo Messi Foundation, Spain, 292
Léonie Sonning Music Foundation, Denmark, 84
Léonie Sonning Musikfond, Denmark, 84
Léopold Sédar Senghor Foundation, Senegal, 270
Leventis (A. G.) Foundation, Cyprus, 77
Leventis (A. G.) Foundation Nigeria, Nigeria, 237
Leverhulme Trust, UK, 365
Levy (Joseph) Foundation, UK, 362
Library of the National Academy of Lincei and Corsiniana, Italy, 172
Liechtenstein Foundation for Culture, Liechtenstein, 208
Likhachev (Dmitry) Foundation, Russian Federation, 265
Lilly Endowment, Inc, USA, 448
Linbury Trust, UK, 365
Lindh (Anna) Euro-Mediterranean Foundation for Dialogue between Cultures, Egypt, 90
Living Culture Foundation Namibia—LCFN, Namibia, 222
Lloyd's Register Foundation, UK, 365
Loewe Foundation, Spain, 292
The Long Now Foundation, USA, 449
Lower Saxony Savings Bank Foundation, Germany, 137
Luce (Henry) Foundation, Inc, USA, 435
Ludwig Boltzmann Gesellschaft, Austria, 21
Luigi Einaudi Foundation, Italy, 178
Luigi Sturzo Institute, Italy, 182
Lurcy (Georges) Charitable and Educational Trust, USA, 430
Luso-American Development Foundation, Portugal, 260
Luxemburg (Rosa) Stiftung, Germany, 139
Lynde and Harry Bradley Foundation, Inc, USA, 449
Lyndon Baines Johnson Foundation, USA, 449
MacArthur (John D. and Catherine T.) Foundation, USA, 444
Macdonald Stewart Foundation, Canada, 59
The Mackintosh Foundation, UK, 366
McKnight Foundation, USA, 449
The McLean Foundation, Canada, 59
Maecenata Foundation, Germany, 119
Maecenata Stiftung, Germany, 119
Maeght (Marguerite et Aimé), Fondation, France, 109
Maison Franco-Japonaise, Japan, 191
Maltese Heritage Foundation, Malta, 213
Mandela (Nelson) Foundation, South Africa, 282
MAPFRE Foundation, Spain, 292
Marc de Montalembert Foundation, France, 109
Marcel Bleustein-Blanchet Vocational Foundation, France, 109
Marcel Hicter Foundation, Belgium, 32
March (Juan), Fundación, Spain, 291
Margaret A. Cargill Philanthropies—MACP, USA, 450
Marinho (Roberto), Fundação, Brazil, 41
Mário Soares and Maria Barroso Foundation, Portugal, 260
Masason Foundation, Japan, 191
Mawazo Institute, Kenya, 199
Max Kade Foundation, Inc, USA, 451
Max-Planck-Gesellschaft zur Förderung der Wissenschaften eV, Germany, 135
Max Planck Society for the Advancement of Science, Germany, 135

INDEX OF MAIN ACTIVITIES

Max Weber Foundation, Germany, 136
Max Weber Stiftung—MWS, Germany, 136
Mbeki (Thabo) Foundation, South Africa, 284
MDA—Muscular Dystrophy Association, USA, 451
Medunarodnog foruma Bosna, Bosnia and Herzegovina, 37
Mencap—Royal Mencap Society, UK, 367
Mendoza (Eugenio), Fundación, Venezuela, 487
Menomadin Foundation, Israel, 170
Menzies Foundation, Australia, 15
Menzies (Sir Robert) Foundation, Australia, 15
The Mercers' Charitable Foundation, UK, 367
Merian (Christoph) Stiftung, Switzerland, 305
Meridian Foundation, Germany, 140
Mertz Gilmore Foundation, USA, 452
Messi (Leo), Fundación, Spain, 292
MFJC—Memorial Foundation for Jewish Culture, USA, 452
Miguel Alemán Foundation, Mexico, 215
Miloud Chaâbi Foundation, Morocco, 220
Mirovni Inštitut—Inštitut za sodobne družbene in politične študije, Slovenia, 277
Mohammed bin Rashid Al Maktoum Global Initiatives—MBRGI, United Arab Emirates, 335
Mohammed bin Salman Foundation—Misk Foundation, Saudi Arabia, 269
Møller (A.P.) and Chastine Mc-Kinney Møller Foundation, Denmark, 82
Monell (Ambrose) Foundation, USA, 399
Monnet (Jean), Fondation pour l'Europe, Switzerland, 309
de Montalembert (Marc), Fondation, France, 109
Montemadrid Foundation, Spain, 292
Moore (Henry) Foundation, UK, 358
Moriya Scholarship Foundation, Japan, 191
Morningside Foundation, USA, 454
Motsepe Foundation, South Africa, 281
Mountain Institute, Peru, 249
Mouvement International ATD Quart-Monde, France, 115
MTN Congo Foundation, Congo (Republic), 73
MTN Nigeria Foundation, Nigeria, 237
MTN SA Foundation, South Africa, 281
Muriel McBrien Kauffman Foundation, USA, 425
Music in Africa Foundation—MIAF, South Africa, 281
Myer Foundation, Australia, 18
Myer (Sidney) Fund, Australia, 18
Nadace Český Hudební Fond—NCHF, Czech Republic, 79
Nadace Český literární fond—nčlf, Czech Republic, 80
Nadace Charty 77, Czech Republic, 80
Nadace Občanského fóra—Nadace OF, Czech Republic, 80
Nadace Preciosa, Czech Republic, 80
Nadácia Otvorenej Spoločnosti, Slovakia, 276
Nadácia SPP, Slovakia, 275
Nadácia Tatra Banky, Slovakia, 276
Nand & Jeet Khemka Foundation, India, 159
Naspa Foundation, Germany, 137
Naspa Stiftung, Germany, 137
National Bank of Greece Cultural Foundation, Greece, 147
National Carlo Collodi Foundation, Italy, 179
National Community Foundation, Saint Lucia, 268
National Endowment for Science, Technology and the Arts—Nesta, UK, 370
National Geographic Society, USA, 455
National Heritage Memorial Fund, UK, 370
National Humanities Center—NHC, USA, 455
The National Lottery Community Fund, UK, 370
The National Lottery Heritage Fund, UK, 370
National Park Foundation, USA, 455
National Trust, UK, 370
National Trust of Fiji—NTF, Fiji, 94
The National Trust for Italy, Italy, 174
Nelson Mandela Foundation, South Africa, 282
Neruda (Pablo), Fundación, Chile, 65
Nesr Art Foundation, Angola, 5
Nesta—National Endowment for Science, Technology and the Arts, UK, 370
Network for Human Development, Brazil, 41
Network for Social Change Charitable Trust—NSCCT, UK, 370
New Carlsberg Foundation, Denmark, 85
The New York Community Trust—NYCT, USA, 457
Newberry Library, USA, 457
NGO Center—NGOC, Armenia, 9
Niarchos (Stavros) Foundation, Greece, 147
Niedersächsische Sparkassenstiftung, Germany, 137
Nobel Foundation, Sweden, 301
Nobelstiftelsen, Sweden, 301

INDEX OF MAIN ACTIVITIES

Arts and humanities

Nordic Africa Institute Scholarships, Sweden, 302
Nordic Culture Fund, Denmark, 85
Nordisk Kulturfond, Denmark, 85
Nordiska Afrikainstitutets Stipendier, Sweden, 302
Novo Nordisk Fonden, Denmark, 85
Novo Nordisk Foundation, Denmark, 85
Ny Carlsbergfondet, Denmark, 85
NYCT—The New York Community Trust, USA, 457
Oak Foundation, Switzerland, 315
OeAD, Austria, 22
Olav Thon Foundation, Norway, 242
Olav Thon Stiftelsen, Norway, 242
Olivetti (Adriano), Fondazione, Italy, 174
Oman LNG Development Foundation—ODF, Oman, 244
Onassis (Alexander S.) Public Benefit Foundation, Liechtenstein, 207
Onstad (Henie) Kunstsenter, Norway, 241
OPEN ASIA—Armanshahr Foundation, Afghanistan, 3
Open Society Foundation—Bratislava, Slovakia, 276
Open Society Foundation Haiti, Haiti, 149
Open Society Foundations, USA, 459
Open Society Initiative for Southern Africa—OSISA, South Africa, 282
Oppenheimer Generations Foundation, South Africa, 282
Orange Foundation, Spain, 293
Orange Foundation Cameroon, Cameroon, 47
Orange Moldova Foundation, Moldova, 217
Orange Solidarité Madagascar, Madagascar, 210
Orient Foundation, Portugal, 260
Orient-Occident Foundation, Morocco, 220
Orji Uzor Kalu Foundation, Nigeria, 238
Ortega y Gasset (José), Fundación, Spain, 291
Osaka Community Foundation, Japan, 192
Österreichische Gesellschaft für Aussenpolitik und Internationale Beziehungen—ÖGAVN, Austria, 22
Österreichischer Wissenschaftsfonds—FWF, Austria, 21
Östersjöfonden, Finland, 97
Our Foundation, Indonesia, 162
Pablo Neruda Foundation, Chile, 65
Pacific Peoples' Partnership, Canada, 61
Pan-European Federation for Cultural Heritage, Netherlands, 224
Parasol Foundation Trust, Gibraltar, 144
Patiño (Simón I.), Fondation, Switzerland, 310
Patterson (Alicia) Foundation, USA, 398
Paul Hamlyn Foundation—PHF, UK, 373
Paulo Foundation, Finland, 97
Paulon Säätiö, Finland, 97
PCI Media Impact, USA, 467
Peace Institute—Institute for Contemporary Social and Political Studies, Slovenia, 277
Pearl S. Buck International, USA, 462
Pedro Barrié de la Maza Foundation, Spain, 293
Peres Center for Peace and Innovation, Israel, 171
Perpetual Foundation, Australia, 16
The Pew Charitable Trusts, USA, 462
PH International, USA, 463
Philanthropikó Ídryma Stélios Chatzeioánnou stēn Kýpro, Cyprus, 78
Philip-Sörensens (Erik) Stiftelse, Sweden, 299
Philippine-American Educational Foundation—PAEF, Philippines, 253
Piera, Pietro and Giovanni Ferrero Foundation, Italy, 179
Pilgrim Trust, UK, 373
Pinchuk (Victor) Foundation, Ukraine, 333
Planck (Max) Gesellschaft zur Förderung der Wissenschaften eV, Germany, 135
Pollock-Krasner Foundation, Inc, USA, 463
Post Office Foundation, France, 105
Potanin (Vladimir) Foundation, Russian Federation, 267
Potter (Ian) Foundation, Australia, 14
Prada Foundation, Italy, 179
Praemium Erasmianum Foundation, Netherlands, 230
Pratt Foundation, Australia, 17
Preciosa Foundation, Czech Republic, 80
Prince Bernhard Cultural Foundation, Netherlands, 230
Prince Claus Fund for Culture and Development, Netherlands, 228
Princess of Asturias Foundation, Spain, 294
Prins Bernhard Cultuurfonds, Stichting, Netherlands, 230
Prins Claus Fonds Voor Cultuur en Ontwikkeling, Netherlands, 228
Prix Jeunesse Foundation, Germany, 138
Pro Helvetia, Switzerland, 315

Pro Victimis, Switzerland, 315
Project Harmony, USA, 463
PRS for Music Foundation, UK, 374
Public Studies Centre, Chile, 64
Puerto Rico Community Foundation, Puerto Rico, 261
Qatar Foundation, Qatar, 262
Qattan (A. M.) Foundation, UK, 338
Quỹ Thiện Tâm, Viet Nam, 488
Querini Stampalia Foundation, Italy, 179
R. Howard Webster Foundation/Fondation R. Howard Webster, Canada, 61
Rafa Nadal Foundation, Spain, 294
Rajiv Gandhi Foundation, India, 160
Rambourg Foundation, Tunisia, 326
Ramón Areces Foundation, Spain, 294
Ramon Magsaysay Award Foundation, Philippines, 253
Rausing (Ruben and Elisabeth) Trust, UK, 383
RBC Foundation, Canada, 61
Reading Foundation, Germany, 140
Real Madrid Foundation, Spain, 295
Realdania Foundation, Denmark, 83
RED—Ruralité-Environnement-Développement, Belgium, Belgium, 34
Red Sea Cultural Foundation, Somalia, 278
REDEH—Rede de Desenvolvimento Humano, Brazil, 41
Reliance Foundation, India, 160
Repsol Foundation, Spain, 295
The Resource Foundation—TRF, USA, 467
RIA—Royal Irish Academy, Ireland, 167
Ricardo do Espírito Santo Silva Foundation, Portugal, 261
Richard Dawkins Foundation for Reason and Science, USA, 412
Rielo (Fernando), Fundación, Spain, 290
Right Livelihood Award Foundation, Sweden, 302
Righteous Persons Foundation, USA, 467
Rising Impact, USA, 467
Robert Bosch Foundation, Germany, 138
Robert-Bosch-Stiftung GmbH, Germany, 138
Robert Marinho Foundation, Brazil, 41
Rockefeller Brothers Fund—RBF, USA, 468
Rohini Nilekani Philanthropies, India, 160
Rohm Music Foundation, Japan, 193
Romaeuropa Foundation, Italy, 180
Romanian Cultural Institute, Romania, 264
Rome Foundation, Italy, 179
The Ronald S. Lauder Foundation, Germany, 138
Rosa Luxemburg Foundation, Germany, 139
Rosa-Luxemburg-Stiftung, Germany, 139
Rössing Foundation, Namibia, 222
Rothschild (Edmond de) Foundations, Switzerland, 308
Royal Anthropological Institute of Great Britain and Ireland—RAI, UK, 377
Royal Commission for the Exhibition of 1851, UK, 377
The Royal Commonwealth Society—RCS, UK, 377
Royal Geographical Society (with the Institute of British Geographers)—RGS-IBG, UK, 378
Royal Literary Fund—RLF, UK, 378
Rroma Foundation, Switzerland, 315
Rromani Fundacija, Switzerland, 315
RSA—Royal Society for the Encouragement of Arts, Manufactures and Commerce, UK, 379
Rubinstein (Arthur) International Music Society, Israel, 168
RUI Foundation, Italy, 180
Ruiz-Picasso (Almine y Bernard), Fundación, Spain, 288
Rupert Family Foundations, South Africa, 283
Ruralité-Environnement-Développement—RED, Belgium, 34
Rurality Environment Development, Belgium, 34
Russian International Affairs Council—RIAC, Russian Federation, 266
Ruya Foundation for Contemporary Culture in Iraq, Iraq, 164
Saadi Foundation, Iran, 164
Säätiöiden post doc-poolin, Finland, 95
Sabanci Vakfı—Haci Omer Sabanci Foundation, Türkiye, 329
Saïd Foundation, UK, 380
Sainsbury Family Charitable Trusts, UK, 380
Saint Cyril and Saint Methodius International Foundation, Bulgaria, 44
The Saison Foundation, Japan, 193
Salvador Dalí Foundation, Spain, 287
Salzburg Global Seminar, Austria, 22
Samir Kassir Foundation, Lebanon, 206
Samsung Foundation, Korea (Republic), 202
Samuel H. Kress Foundation, USA, 469
The San Diego Foundation, USA, 470
San Francisco Foundation—SFF, USA, 470
Sandals Foundation, Jamaica, 184

Sasakawa, Fondation Franco-Japonaise, France, 106
Sawiris Foundation for Social Development—SFSD, Egypt, 90
SBS Cultural Foundation, Korea (Republic), 202
Schering (Ernst) Stiftung, Germany, 127
Schusterman (Charles and Lynn) Family Foundation, USA, 413
Schwab Foundation for Social Entrepreneurship, Switzerland, 316
Schwarzkopf-Stiftung Junges Europa, Germany, 139
Schwarzkopf Young Europe Foundation, Germany, 139
Schweizerisch-Liechtensteinische Stiftung für Archäologische Forschungen im Ausland—SLSA, Switzerland, 316
Schweizerischer Nationalfonds zur Förderung der Wissenschaftlichen Forschung/Fonds National Suisse de la Recherche Scientifique—SNF, Switzerland, 316
Scientific Research Foundation, Belgium, 32
SEEMO—South East Europe Media Organisation, Austria, 23
Seidel (Hanns) Stiftung, Germany, 131
Sentrong Pangkultura ng Pilipinas, Philippines, 252
Seoam Yoon Se Young Foundation, Korea (Republic), 202
Serralves Foundation, Portugal, 261
Serrv International, Inc, USA, 471
Shahid Afridi Foundation—SAF, Pakistan, 246
Sherman (Archie) Charitable Trust, UK, 340
Shiv Nadar Foundation Group, India, 160
Shoman (Abdul Hameed) Foundation, Jordan, 195
Siam Society, Thailand, 324
Siamese Heritage Trust, Thailand, 324
Sidney Myer Fund & The Myer Foundation, Australia, 18
Sigrid Rausing Trust—SRT, UK, 383
Sihtasutus Eesti Rahvuskultuuri Fond, Estonia, 93
Silva (Ricardo do Espírito Santo), Fundação, Portugal, 261
Simón I. Patiño Foundation, Switzerland, 310
Simone and Cino del Duca Foundation, France, 111
Sindika Dokolo Foundation, Angola, 5
Singapore International Foundation—SIF, Singapore, 273
Singer-Polignac Foundation, France, 111
Sistema Charitable Foundation, Russian Federation, 267
Skinners' Charity Foundation, UK, 383
Skolkovo Foundation—Foundation for Development of the Center for the Development and Commercialization of New Technologies, Russian Federation, 267
Slim (Carlos), Fundación, Mexico, 215
Slovak Humanitarian Council, Slovakia, 274
Slovenská Humanitná Rada, Slovakia, 274
SM Foundation, Spain, 295
Smithsonian Institution, USA, 472
Soares (Mário), Fundação, Portugal, 260
Sog'lom Avlod Uchun, Uzbekistan, 485
Solomon R. Guggenheim Foundation, USA, 473
Sonning-Fonden, Denmark, 86
Sonning Foundation, Denmark, 86
Sonning (Léonie) Musikfond, Denmark, 84
Sorenson Legacy Foundation, USA, 473
Soros Foundation—Moldova, Moldova, 217
South East Europe Media Organisation—SEEMO, Austria, 23
South Sudan Center for Strategic and Policy Studies—CSPS, South Sudan, 285
Sparebankstiftelsen DNB, Norway, 243
SPP Foundation, Slovakia, 275
Springer (Axel) Stiftung, Germany, 122
Springer (Friede) Stiftung, Germany, 129
Stanley Thomas Johnson Foundation, Switzerland, 317
The Starr Foundation, USA, 473
State Scholarships Foundation—IKY, Greece, 147
Stavros Niarchos Foundation—SNF, Greece, 147
Stelios Philanthropic Foundation, Cyprus, 78
Stichting Democratie en Media, Netherlands, 229
Stichting Dioraphte, Netherlands, 229
Stichting DOEN, Netherlands, 229
Stichting Fonds 1818, Netherlands, 229
Stichting Praemium Erasmianum, Netherlands, 230
Stichting Prins Bernhard Cultuurfonds, Netherlands, 230
Stichting Triodos Foundation, Netherlands, 231
Stichting Vodafone Netherlands, Netherlands, 231
Stiftelsen Dag Hammarskjölds Minnesfond, Sweden, 303

Conservation and the environment

Stiftelsen Ingmar Bergman, Sweden, 303
Stiftelsen Riksbankens Jubileumsfond, Sweden, 303
Stiftung Ettersberg, Germany, 140
Stiftung Lesen, Germany, 140
Stiftung Mercator, Germany, 140
Stiftung Meridian, Germany, 140
Stiftung Prix Jeunesse, Germany, 138
Stiftung Weltethos, Germany, 141
Stiftung West-Östliche Begegnungen, Germany, 141
Strickland Foundation, Malta, 214
Studienstiftung des deutschen Volkes, Germany, 142
Sturzo (Luigi), Istituto, Italy, 182
Südosteuropäische Medienorganisation, Austria, 23
Suomalaiset kehitysjärjestöt—Fingo, Finland, 95
Suomen Kulttuurirahasto, Finland, 97
Surdna Foundation, Inc, USA, 474
Svenska Institutet i Rom/Istituto Svedese di Studi Classici a Roma, Italy, 183
Svenska kulturfonden, Finland, 98
Sweden-Japan Foundation—SJF, Sweden, 304
The Swedish Cultural Foundation in Finland, Finland, 98
Swedish-Finnish Cultural Foundation, Sweden, 301
Swedish Institute at Athens, Greece, 147
Swedish Institute in Rome, Italy, 183
Swiss Arts Council, Switzerland, 315
Swiss-Liechtenstein Foundation for Archaeological Research Abroad—SLFA, Switzerland, 316
Swiss National Science Foundation—SNSF, Switzerland, 316
Szenes (Árpád)-Vieira da Silva, Fundação, Portugal, 258
Taawon, Palestinian Territories, 246
Tanenbaum (Joseph) Charitable Foundation, Canada, 58
Tang Prize Foundation, Taiwan, 322
Tarih Vakfı, Türkiye, 329
Tata Trusts, India, 160
Tatra Bank Foundation, Slovakia, 276
Telmex Telcel Foundation, Mexico, 216
Templeton Religion Trust, Bahamas, 24
TFF—Transnational Foundation for Peace and Future Research, Sweden, 304
TFF—Transnationella Stiftelsen för Freds- och Framtidsforskning, Sweden, 304
Thabo Mbeki Foundation, South Africa, 284
Thiel Foundation, USA, 474
Thyssen (Fritz) Stiftung, Germany, 130
Tibet Fund, USA, 475
Tibet-Institut Rikon, Switzerland, 318
Tides Organizations, USA, 475
Timchenko (Elena & Gennady) Foundation, Russian Federation, 265
The Todd Foundation, New Zealand, 235
Toepfer (Alfred) Stiftung, Germany, 121
Tokyu Foundation, Japan, 194
TOSA Foundation, USA, 475
Toshiba International Foundation—TIFO, Japan, 194
TotalEnergies Foundation, France, 112
Totto Foundation, Japan, 194
The Toyota Foundation, Japan, 195
Toyota Vietnam Foundation—TVF, Viet Nam, 488
Transnet Foundation, South Africa, 284
Triodos Foundation, Netherlands, 231
Trust for Mutual Understanding—TMU, USA, 476
Trustees for Harvard University, USA, 421
Trusthouse Charitable Foundation, UK, 386
Tunisia Development Foundation, Tunisia, 326
Turin Savings Bank Foundation, Italy, 176
Turing (Alan) Institute, UK, 339
Türkiye Vodafone Vakfı, Türkiye, 331
Turquoise Mountain Foundation, UK, 386
Turriano (Juanelo) Fundación, Spain, 291
Tutu (Desmond & Leah) Legacy Foundation, South Africa, 279
Ucom Foundation, Armenia, 9
UEFA Foundation for Children, Switzerland, 318
UJIA—United Jewish Israel Appeal, UK, 387
UK Research and Innovation—UKRI, UK, 387
UNESCO Centre du Patrimoine Mondial, France, 116
UNESCO World Heritage Centre, France, 116
UniCredit Foundation, Italy, 183
UNIFOR—Forvaltningstiftelse for fond og legater, Norway, 240
Unipolis Foundation, Italy, 181
United Jewish Israel Appeal—UJIA, UK, 387
United Purpose, UK, 387
Universitaire Stichting, Belgium, 34
University Foundation, Belgium, 34

Usain Bolt Foundation, Jamaica, 185
USC Shoah Foundation—The Institute for Visual History and Education, USA, 477
Values Foundation, Bulgaria, 43
Vancouver Foundation, Canada, 62
Van Leer Foundation, Netherlands, 231
Van Leer Jerusalem Institute, Israel, 171
Vargas (Getulio), Fundação, Brazil, 40
Vehbi Koç Foundation, Türkiye, 331
Vehbi Koç Vakfı, Türkiye, 331
Veillon (Charles), Fondation, Switzerland, 308
Venice Foundation, Italy, 181
Verband für Gemeinnütziges Stiften, Austria, 20
Vetlesen (G. Unger) Foundation, USA, 429
Victor Pinchuk Foundation, Ukraine, 333
Villar Foundation, Inc, Philippines, 253
Vivekananda International Foundation—VIF, India, 161
Vladimir Potanin Foundation, Russian Federation, 267
Vodafone Foundation Germany, Germany, 142
Vodafone Netherlands Foundation, Netherlands, 231
Vodafone Portugal Foundation, Portugal, 261
Vodafone Stiftung Deutschland, Germany, 142
Vodafone Türkiye Foundation, Türkiye, 331
Volkart Foundation, Switzerland, 319
Volkart-Stiftung, Switzerland, 319
Volkswagen Foundation, Germany, 142
VolkswagenStiftung, Germany, 142
Volnoe Delo—Oleg Deripaska Foundation, Russian Federation, 267
Wallace (Charles) Trusts, UK, 347
The Wallace Foundation, USA, 478
Wallenberg (Knut och Alice) Stiftelse, Sweden, 301
Walton Family Foundation, USA, 479
Weber (Max) Stiftung, Germany, 136
Webster (R. Howard) Foundation, Canada, 61
Welfare Association, Palestinian Territories, 246
Wellcome Trust, UK, 389
Weston (Garfield) Foundation, UK, 355
Weyerhaeuser Family Foundation, Inc, USA, 480
Whirlpool Foundation, USA, 480
Wihuri Foundation for International Prizes, Finland, 98
Wihuri (Jenny and Antti) Foundation, Finland, 96
Wihuri kansainvälisten palkintojen rahasto, Finland, 98
Wikimedia Foundation, USA, 480
William Adlington Cadbury Charitable Trust, UK, 390
The William and Flora Hewlett Foundation, USA, 481
The William H. Donner Foundation, Inc, USA, 481
William Randolph Hearst Foundation, USA, 435
Wilsdorf (Hans), Fondation, Switzerland, 309
Wilson (Woodrow) International Center for Scholars, USA, 482
Winston Churchill Memorial Trust of New Zealand, New Zealand, 236
Wisti (Folmer) Foundation for International Understanding, Denmark, 83
The Wolfson Foundation, UK, 390
Woodrow Wilson International Center for Scholars, USA, 482
World Association of Children's Friends, Monaco, 217
World Economic Forum, Switzerland, 320
World Learning, USA, 483
World Monuments Fund—WMF, USA, 483
The Wyss Foundtion, USA, 484
Xiangjiang Social Relief Fund, China (People's Republic), 68
Yayasan Geutanyoë, Indonesia, 162
Youth Leadership Development Foundation—YLDF, Yemen, 489
ZEIT-Stiftung Ebelin und Gerd Bucerius, Germany, 143
Zuleikhabai Valy Mohamed Gany Rangoonwala Trust—ZVMG Rangoonwala Trust, Pakistan, 246
Zurich Community Trust—ZCT, UK, 392
ZVMG Rangoonwala Trust, Pakistan, 246

CONSERVATION AND THE ENVIRONMENT

1818 Fund Foundation, Netherlands, 229
30 Million Friends Foundation, France, 102
The A. G. Leventis Foundation, Cyprus, 77
A. G. Leventis Foundation Nigeria, Nigeria, 237
Abdul Hameed Shoman Foundation—AHSF, Jordan, 195
Accountable Now, USA, 393

INDEX OF MAIN ACTIVITIES

ACROTEC Technology Foundation, Italy, 176
Acting for Life, France, 100
Action Group on Erosion, Technology and Concentration, Canada, 54
Action on Poverty, Australia, 10
Action Solidarité Tiers Monde—ASTM, Luxembourg, 209
ActionAid International, South Africa, 278
Adessium Foundation, Netherlands, 223
Adriano Olivetti Foundation, Italy, 174
Afghanistan Institute for Civil Society—AICS, Afghanistan, 3
Afghanistan Research and Evaluation Unit, Afghanistan, 3
Africa Foundation, South Africa, 278
Africa Institute of South Africa—AISA, South Africa, 279
The African Agricultural Technology Foundation—AATF, Kenya, 198
African Venture Philanthropy Alliance—AVPA, Kenya, 197
African Wildlife Foundation—AWF, Kenya, 198
Aga Khan Development Network—AKDN, Switzerland, 306
Aga Khan Foundation, Switzerland, 306
Aga Khan Foundation UK, UK, 338
AGIR Association for the Environment and Quality of Life, Mali, 213
Agronomes et Vétérinaires sans Frontières—AVSF, France, 100
Agronomists and Veterinarians Without Borders, France, 100
AID Foundation, Bangladesh, 24
AINA—Arctic Institute of North America, Canada, 49
Air Pollution and Climate Secretariat—AirClim, Sweden, 298
AirClim—Air Pollution and Climate Secretariat, Sweden, 298
AISA—Africa Institute of South Africa, South Africa, 279
AKO Foundation, UK, 339
The Alan Turing Institute, UK, 339
Albert Schweitzer Ecological Centre, Switzerland, 307
Alcoa Foundation, USA, 398
Alemán (Miguel), Fundación, Mexico, 215
Alert—International Alert, UK, 360
Alexander S. Onassis Public Benefit Foundation, Liechtenstein, 207
Alfred Toepfer Foundation FVS, Germany, 121
Alfred Toepfer Stiftung FVS, Germany, 121
Alicia Patterson Foundation—APF, USA, 398
All India Disaster Mitigation Institute, India, 155
Allen (Paul G.) Family Foundation, USA, 462
Alliance of Bioversity International and the International Center for Tropical Agriculture—CIAT, Italy, 172
The Alva Foundation, Canada, 49
Ambuja Cement Foundation—ACF, India, 156
America for Bulgaria Foundation, Bulgaria, 43
American Express Foundation, USA, 400
American Jewish World Service—AJWS, USA, 402
American Philosophical Society—APS, USA, 402
Amigos de la Tierra, Netherlands, 225
Les Amis de la Terre, Netherlands, 225
Amity Foundation, China (People's Republic), 66
Andrews Charitable Trust—ACT, UK, 340
Anglo American Foundation, UK, 340
ANGOC—Asian NGO Coalition for Agrarian Reform and Rural Development, Philippines, 251
Anguilla National Trust—ANT, Anguilla, 6
Ankara İngiliz Arkeoloji Enstitüsü, UK, 345
Anne Ray Foundation, USA, 450
The Annenberg Foundation, USA, 404
Antarctic Heritage Trust (NZ), New Zealand, 232
APHEDA—Union Aid Abroad, Australia, 19
Arab Network for Environment and Development—RAED, Egypt, 89
Arab Office for Youth and Environment, Egypt, 89
Àrainneachd Eachdraidheil Alba, UK, 358
Arca Foundation, USA, 405
Arctic Institute of North America—AINA, Canada, 49
Arcus Foundation, USA, 405
Arengukoostöö Ümarlaud—AKÜ, Estonia, 92
Areumdaun Jaedan, Korea (Republic), 200
Argentine Council for International Relations, Argentina, 6
Arghyam, India, 156
Asahi Glass Foundation, Japan, 186
Asia Foundation, USA, 406
Asia Pacific Foundation of Canada—APFCanada, Canada, 49
Asia Philanthropy Circle—APC, Singapore, 272

INDEX OF MAIN ACTIVITIES

Conservation and the environment

Asian Venture Philanthropy Network—AVPN, Singapore, 272
Asociacija Litdea—Lithuanian Development Education and Awareness Raising Association, Lithuania, 208
Asociación Salvadoreña para el Desarrollo Económico y Social FUSADES, El Salvador, 91
Aspen Institute, USA, 407
Association AGIR pour l'Environnement et la Qualité de la Vie, Mali, 213
Association for Development Policy and Humanitarian Aid, Germany, 120
Association of Non-Governmental Organizations in The Gambia—TANGO, Gambia, 117
Association for Public Benefit Foundations, Austria, 20
ASTM—Action Solidarité Tiers Monde, Luxembourg, 209
AT&T Foundation, USA, 407
ATD Fourth World International, France, 115
Aurora Trust, UK, 341
Australian Academy of Science, Australia, 11
Australian Academy of Technological Sciences and Engineering, Australia, 11
Australian-American Fulbright Commission, Australia, 11
Australian Communities Foundation, Australia, 12
Australian Conservation Foundation—ACF, Australia, 12
Australian Foundation for the Peoples of Asia and the Pacific—AFAP, Australia, 10
Australian Volunteers International—AVI, Australia, 13
Austrian Science Fund, Austria, 21
AVI—Australian Volunteers International, Australia, 13
AVINA Foundation, Panama, 247
AVSI Foundation, Italy, 175
Ayala Foundation, Inc—AFI, Philippines, 251
Bagnoud (François-Xavier) Association, Switzerland, 310
Baha'i International Development Organization—BIDO, Israel, 169
Baillet Latour Fund, Belgium, 32
Baltic Sea Foundation, Finland, 97
Balzan Fonds, Internationale Stiftung, Italy, 181
Ban Ki-Moon Foundation for a Better Future, Korea (Republic), 200
Banco do Brasil Foundation, Brazil, 39
BANHCAFE Foundation, Honduras, 150
Barbra Streisand Foundation, USA, 408
Bardot (Brigitte), Fondation, France, 104
Bariloche Foundation, Argentina, 7
Basso Issoco (Leilio e Lisli), Fondazione, Italy, 178
Bat Conservation Trust, UK, 342
BBC Media Action, UK, 342
BCause Foundation, Bulgaria, 42
The Beautiful Foundation, Korea (Republic), 200
Beit Trust, UK, 342
Bell (Max) Foundation, Canada, 59
Bellona Foundation, Norway, 240
Benetton Foundation for Study and Research, Italy, 175
Bertoni (Moisés) Foundation, Paraguay, 248
Bezos Earth Fund, USA, 408
Big Heart Foundation, Chad, 64
Biocon Foundation, India, 157
BirdLife International, UK, 343
Black Sea NGO Network—BSNN, Bulgaria, 42
Black Sea University Foundation—BSUF, Romania, 263
Bleustein-Blanchet (Marcel), Fondation de la Vocation, France, 109
Bloomberg Philanthropies, USA, 409
Blue Marine Foundation—BLUE, UK, 343
BMCE Bank Foundation, Morocco, 219
BNP Paribas Foundation, France, 103
Bodossaki Foundation, Greece, 145
Böll (Heinrich) Stiftung, Germany, 131
Bond, UK, 335
Born Free Foundation, UK, 343
Bosch (Robert) Stiftung GmbH, Germany, 138
Bóthar, Ireland, 166
Boticário Group Foundation, Brazil, 40
Botín Foundation, Spain, 292
Botín (Marcelino), Fundación, Spain, 292
Botswana Institute for Development Policy Analysis—BIDPA, Botswana, 37
BRAC, Bangladesh, 25
BrazilFoundation, Brazil, 39
Brazilian Center for International Relations, Brazil, 39
Brenthurst Foundation, South Africa, 282
Bridge Asia Japan—BAJ, Japan, 187
Bridge House Estates, UK, 348

Brighter Future Myanmar Foundation—BFM, Myanmar, 221
Brigitte Bardot Foundation, France, 104
British Institute at Ankara, UK, 345
British Institute of International and Comparative Law—BIICL, UK, 345
British Overseas NGOs for Development, UK, 335
Brookings Institution, USA, 410
Brothers of Men, France, 113
Bruegel—Brussels European and Global Economic Laboratory, Belgium, 28
Buddharaksa Foundation, Thailand, 323
Buffett (Howard G.) Foundation, USA, 437
Bulgarian Platform for International Development—BPID, Bulgaria, 42
CABI, UK, 345
Cadbury (Edward) Charitable Trust, UK, 351
Cadbury (William Adlington) Charitable Trust, UK, 390
CAF America, USA, 393
CAFOD—Catholic Agency for Overseas Development, UK, 345
Calgary Foundation, Canada, 49
California Community Foundation, USA, 411
Calouste Gulbenkian Foundation, Portugal, 259
Cambodia Development Resource Institute—CDRI, Cambodia, 46
Canadian Centre for International Studies and Co-operation, Canada, 51
Canadian Physicians for Aid and Relief—CPAR, Canada, 52
Canadian Urban Institute/Institut Urbain du Canada—CUI/IUC, Canada, 51
Canon Foundation in Europe, Netherlands, 224
Canon Institute for Global Studies—CIGS, Japan, 187
CARE International—CI, Switzerland, 307
Cargill (Margaret A.) Philanthropies, USA, 450
Caribbean Policy Development Centre—CPDC, Barbados, 25
Cariplo Foundation, Italy, 175
Caritas Canada, Canada, 53
Carlos Slim Foundation, Mexico, 215
Carlsberg Foundation, Denmark, 82
Carlsbergfondet, Denmark, 82
CARMABI Foundation, Curaçao, 77
Carnegie Endowment for International Peace, USA, 411
Carnegie Trust for the Universities of Scotland, UK, 346
CASE—Centrum Analiz Społeczno-Ekonomicznych, Poland, 255
Cassa di Risparmio di Padova e Rovigo Foundation, Italy, 175
Caterpillar Foundation, USA, 412
Catholic Agency for Overseas Development—CAFOD, UK, 345
Catholic Agency for World Development—Trócaire, Ireland, 168
Caucasus Research Resource Center Armenia Foundation—CRRC, Armenia, 9
Caucus of Development NGO Networks—CODE-NGO, Philippines, 250
CEAS—Centre Ecologique Albert Schweitzer, Switzerland, 307
CECI—Canadian Centre for International Studies and Co-operation/Centre d'Etudes et de Coopération Internationale, Canada, 51
CENSIS—Fondazione Centro Studi Investimenti Sociali, Italy, 172
Center for Social and Economic Research, Poland, 255
Centre for Democracy and Human Rights—CEDEM, Montenegro, 219
Centre Ecologique Albert Schweitzer—CEAS, Switzerland, 307
Centre for International Studies, Italy, 172
Centre Ivoirien de Recherches Économiques et Sociales—CIRES, Côte d'Ivoire, 75
Centre for Philanthropy, Slovakia, 274
Centro Brasileiro de Relações Internacionais—CEBRI, Brazil, 39
Centro de Estudios Públicos—CEP, Chile, 64
Centro Internacional de Mejoramiento de Maíz y Trigo—CIMMYT, Mexico, 215
Centro Studi Internazionali—CSI, Italy, 172
Centrum pre Filantropiu, Slovakia, 274
Cera, Belgium, 28
Cercle de Coopération des ONGD du Luxembourg, Luxembourg, 209
Çevre Koruma ve Ambalaj Atıkları Değerlendirme Vakfı—ÇEVKO, Türkiye, 328
Chaabi (Miloud), Fondation, Morocco, 220
Charities Advisory Trust, UK, 336
Charities Aid Foundation of America—CAF America, USA, 393

Charles Darwin Foundation for the Galapagos Islands—CDF, Ecuador, 88
Charles Léopold Mayer Foundation for the Progress of Humankind, Switzerland, 308
Charles Stewart Mott Foundation—CSMF, USA, 414
Chatham House, UK, 378
Chemistry Centre Foundation, France, 108
The Children's Investment Fund Foundation, UK, 347
Chile Foundation, Chile, 65
China Environmental Protection Foundation, China (People's Republic), 67
China Siyuan Foundation for Poverty Alleviation, China (People's Republic), 67
China Youth Development Foundation, China (People's Republic), 68
Christian Aid, UK, 348
Christoph Merian Foundation, Switzerland, 305
Christoph-Merian-Stiftung, Switzerland, 305
The Churchill Fellowship, UK, 348
Churchill (Winston) Memorial Trust of New Zealand, New Zealand, 236
CIAT—Centro Internacional de Agricultura Tropical, Italy, 172
CIDSE—Together for Global Justice, Belgium, 29
CIMA Research Foundation—Centre for Environmental Monitoring, Italy, 176
Cini (Giorgio), Fondazione, Italy, 177
Citi Foundation, USA, 415
Citi Handlowy Leopold Kronenberg Foundation, Poland, 255
The City Bridge Trust, UK, 348
Civic Democratic Initiative Support Foundation—CDF, Yemen, 489
Civic Forum Foundation, Czech Republic, 80
Civil Peace Service—CPS, Germany, 120
Claiborne (Liz) & Art Ortenberg Foundation, USA, 448
Clean Up Australia, Australia, 13
CLEAR Global, USA, 416
Cleveland Foundation, USA, 416
Climate Cent Foundation, Switzerland, 317
Clinton Foundation, USA, 416
The Coca-Cola Foundation, Inc, USA, 417
Colombian Habitat Foundation, Colombia, 71
Common Network, Brazil, 38
Commonwealth Foundation, UK, 348
Communication Foundation for Asia, Philippines, 251
Community Development Foundation, Mozambique, 221
Community Foundation for the Western Region of Zimbabwe—CFWRZ, Zimbabwe, 490
Concawe—Oil Companies' European Association for Environment, Health and Safety in Refining and Distribution, Belgium, 29
Consejo Argentino para las Relaciones Internacionales—CARI, Argentina, 6
Consejo Latinoamericano de Ciencias Sociales—CLACSO, Argentina, 6
Conservation International Foundation, USA, 417
Co-op Foundation, UK, 349
Co-operative Community Investment Foundation, UK, 349
Cooperazione Internazionale—COOPI, Italy, 173
Coordination SUD, France, 99
Corus International, USA, 418
Counterpart International, USA, 418
CPAR—Canadian Physicians for Aid and Relief, Canada, 52
The Craig and Susan McCaw Foundation, USA, 418
CRDF Global, USA, 419
Crown Family Philanthropies, USA, 419
Cuso International, Canada, 53
Dalio Foundation, USA, 419
Danielle Mitterrand Foundation, France, 112
Danish Institute for Human Rights, Denmark, 84
Danish Outdoor Council, Denmark, 83
Darwin (Charles) Foundation for the Galapagos Islands, Ecuador, 88
David and Lucile Packard Foundation, USA, 420
David Suzuki Foundation, Canada, 53
Defense of Green Earth Foundation—DGEF, Japan, 187
Democracy Fund, USA, 458
Deutsch-Russischer Austausch eV—DRA, Germany, 124
Deutsche Bundesstiftung Umwelt—DBU, Germany, 124
Development Cooperation Roundtable, Estonia, 92
Development Foundation, Guatemala, 148
Development Foundation of Turkey, Türkiye, 330
Development Gateway—DG, USA, 420
Development and Peace—Caritas Canada, Canada, 53

Conservation and the environment

Développement et Paix—Caritas Canada, Canada, 53
Diakonia, Sweden, 298
Digicel Trinidad and Tobago Foundation, Trinidad and Tobago, 326
DNB Savings Bank Foundation, Norway, 243
The Do-Nation Foundation, Inc, Saint Lucia, 268
DOEN Foundation, Netherlands, 229
Dom Manuel II Foundation, Portugal, 260
Donner (William H.) Foundation, Inc, USA, 481
Doris Duke Charitable Foundation—DDCF, USA, 421
Dr Scholl Foundation, USA, 421
Dräger Foundation, Germany, 126
Dräger-Stiftung, Germany, 126
DRFN—Desert Research Foundation of Namibia, Namibia, 222
DTGO Group of Foundations, Thailand, 323
Dulverton Trust, UK, 351
Dutch-Bangla Bank Foundation, Bangladesh, 25
E. O. Wilson Biodiversity Foundation, USA, 421
Earth Island Institute—EII, USA, 422
Earthrights International—ERI, USA, 422
Earthworm Foundation, Switzerland, 307
Ebert (Friedrich) Stiftung, Germany, 129
Echo Foundation/Fondation Écho, Canada, 54
EcoCiencia—Fundación Ecuatoriana de Estudios Ecologicos, Ecuador, 88
EcoHealth Alliance, USA, 422
Economic and Social Research Foundation—ESRF, Tanzania, 322
Ecuadorean Cooperation for Development Fund, Ecuador, 88
Ecuadorean Foundation of Ecological Studies, Ecuador, 88
Ecuadorean Social Group Fund Populorum Progressio, Ecuador, 89
EDGE Funders Alliance, USA, 394
Edoardo Garrone Foundation, Italy, 177
EDP Foundation, Portugal, 260
Edward Cadbury Charitable Trust, UK, 351
EEB—European Environmental Bureau, Belgium, 30
Eestimaa Looduse Fond—ELF, Estonia, 92
Ekhaga Foundation, Sweden, 299
Ekhagastiftelsen, Sweden, 299
Ekofond SPP, Slovakia, 275
Ekopolis Foundation, Slovakia, 275
The Elders Foundation, UK, 352
ELIAMEP—Hellenic Foundation for European and Foreign Policy, Greece, 146
Ellerman (John) Foundation, UK, 361
Emirates Foundation, United Arab Emirates, 334
Enda Third World—Environment and Development Action in the Third World, Senegal, 270
Enda Tiers Monde—Environnement et Développement du Tiers-Monde, Senegal, 270
Energies for the World Foundation, France, 105
ENGIE Corporate Foundation, France, 105
Ente Cassa di Risparmio di Firenze, Italy, 173
Environment Foundation of Turkey, Türkiye, 330
Environment and Natural Resources Foundation, Argentina, 7
Environmental Foundation of Jamaica, Jamaica, 184
Environmental Justice Foundation—EJF, UK, 353
Environmental Partnership Foundation, Poland, 256
Environmental Protection and Packaging Waste Recovery and Recycling Foundation, Türkiye, 328
Equity Group Foundation—EGF, Kenya, 198
Ernest Kleinwort Charitable Trust, UK, 353
Esmée Fairbairn Foundation, UK, 353
Esquel Group Foundation—Ecuador, Ecuador, 88
Estonian Fund for Nature, Estonia, 92
ETC Group—Action Group on Erosion, Technology and Concentration, Canada, 54
Eureka Foundation, Bulgaria, 43
Euro-Mediterranean Centre on Climate Change Foundation, Italy, 176
EuroNatur, Germany, 127
Europa Nostra, Netherlands, 224
European Center for Peace and Development—ECPD, Serbia, 271
European Climate Foundation, Netherlands, 224
European Cultural Foundation—ECF, Netherlands, 225
European Environmental Bureau—EEB, Belgium, 30
European Foundation for the Sustainable Development of the Regions, Switzerland, 308
European Institute of Health and Social Welfare, Spain, 296
European Think Tanks Group—ETTG, Belgium, 26

European Youth For Action—EYFA, Germany, 128
Europese Culterele Stichting, Netherlands, 225
Evrika Foundation, Bulgaria, 43
EWT—Endangered Wildlife Trust, South Africa, 279
ExxonMobil Foundation, USA, 425
EYFA—European Youth For Action, Germany, 128
F20, Germany, 119
FAI—Fondo per l'Ambiente Italiano, Italy, 174
Fairbairn (Esmée) Foundation, UK, 353
Fairtrade Nederland, Netherlands, 230
Farm Africa, UK, 354
FARN—Fundación Ambiente y Recursos Naturales, Argentina, 7
FDC—Fundação para o Desenvolvimento da Comunidade, Mozambique, 221
FEDRE—European Foundation for the Sustainable Development of the Regions, Switzerland, 308
FEIM—Fundación para Estudio e Investigación de la Mujer, Argentina, 7
FEMSA Foundation, Mexico, 215
Fernando Rielo Foundation, Spain, 290
FHI 360, USA, 425
FIJI Water Foundation, Fiji, 94
FINCA International, USA, 425
Finnish Development Organizations, Finland, 95
Florence Savings Bank Foundation, Italy, 173
FOKAL—Open Society Foundation Haiti, Haiti, 149
Fondation 30 Millions d'Amis, France, 102
Fondation Africaine pour les Technologies Agricoles, Kenya, 198
Fondation pour l'Agriculture et la Ruralité dans le Monde—Fondation FARM, France, 106
Fondation BMCE Bank, Morocco, 219
Fondation BNP Paribas, France, 103
Fondation Brigitte Bardot, France, 104
Fondation Charles Léopold Mayer pour le Progrès de l'Homme—FPH, Switzerland, 308
Fondation pour l'Economie et le Développement Durable des Régions d'Europe—FEDRE, Switzerland, 308
Fondation Energies pour le Monde—Fondem, France, 105
Fondation Ensemble, France, 105
Fondation d'Entreprise Crédit Agricole Réunion Mayotte, Réunion, 262
Fondation d'Entreprise ENGIE, France, 105
Fondation Européenne de la Culture/Europese Culturele Stichting, Netherlands, 225
Fondation FARM—Fondation pour l'Agriculture et la Ruralité dans le Monde, France, 106
Fondation de France, France, 99
Fondation France Chine—FFC, France, 106
Fondation Franz Weber—FFW, Switzerland, 308
Fondation Grand Cœur—FGC, Chad, 64
Fondation Guri Vie Meilleure, Niger, 236
Fondation Hans Wilsdorf, Switzerland, 309
Fondation Hirondelle: Media for Peace and Human Dignity, Switzerland, 309
Fondation Jean-Paul II pour le Sahel, Burkina Faso, 44
Fondation Joseph Ichame Kamach, Central African Republic, 63
Fondation MACIF, France, 108
Fondation MAIF pour la Recherche, France, 108
Fondation de la Maison de la Chimie, France, 108
Fondation Marcel Bleustein-Blanchet de la Vocation, France, 109
Fondation Mesmin Kabath—FOMEKA, Congo (Republic), 73
Fondation Miloud Chaâbi, Morocco, 220
Fondation Mutuelles Congolaises d'Epargne et de Crédit—MUCODEC, Congo (Republic), 73
Fondation Nicolas Hulot pour la Nature et l'Homme—FNH, France, 110
Fondation du Patrimoine, France, 110
Fondation Prince Albert II de Monaco, Monaco, 217
Fondation pour la Recherche Stratégique, France, 111
Fondation Rinaldi, Haiti, 149
Fondation Roi Baudouin, Belgium, 33
Fondation Rurale pour l'Afrique de l'Ouest—FRAO, Senegal, 270
Fondation S, France, 111
Fondation Schneider Electric, France, 111
Fondation Singer-Polignac, France, 111
Fondation Stamm, Burundi, 45
Fondation Suisse-Liechtenstein pour les Recherches Archéologiques à l'Etranger, Switzerland, 316
Fondation Suisse pour Recherches Alpines—FSRA, Switzerland, 316
Fondation TotalEnergies, France, 112

INDEX OF MAIN ACTIVITIES

Fondation Vodacom RDC, Congo (Democratic Republic), 72
Fondazione Adriano Olivetti, Italy, 174
Fondazione AVSI, Italy, 175
Fondazione Benetton Studi Ricerche, Italy, 175
Fondazione Cariplo, Italy, 175
Fondazione Cassa di Risparmio di Padova e Rovigo, Italy, 175
Fondazione Cassa di Risparmio di Verona Vicenza Belluno e Ancona—Fondazione Cariverona, Italy, 176
Fondazione Centesimus Annus—Pro Pontifice, Vatican City, 486
Fondazione Centro Euro-Mediterraneo sui Cambiamenti Climatici—CMCC, Italy, 176
Fondazione Centro Studi Investimenti Sociali—CENSIS, Italy, 172
Fondazione CIMA—Centro Internazionale in Monitoraggio Ambientale, Italy, 176
Fondazione Compagnia di San Paolo, Italy, 176
Fondazione Edoardo Garrone, Italy, 177
Fondazione Fratelli Tutti, Vatican City, 486
Fondazione Giorgio Cini, Italy, 177
Fondazione Internazionale Premio Balzan, Italy, 181
Fondazione Lelio e Lisli Basso Issoco—Sezione Internazionale, Italy, 178
Fondazione Social Venture-Giordano Dell'Amore, Italy, 180
Fonden Realdania, Denmark, 83
Fondo para el Desarrollo de los Pueblos Indígenas de América Latina y El Caribe—FILAC, Bolivia, 36
Fondo Ecuatoriano de Cooperación para el Desarrollo—FECD, Ecuador, 88
Fonds Baillet Latour, Belgium, 32
Ford Foundation, USA, 428
Forest & Bird Te Reo o te Taio, New Zealand, 233
The Forest Trust, Switzerland, 307
Forum LSM Internasional untuk Pembangunan Indonesia, Indonesia, 161
Foundation for Caribbean Research and Management of Biodiversity, Curaçao, 77
Foundation Centre for the Study of Social Investment, Italy, 172
Foundation for the Conservation of the Atlantic Forest, Brazil, 41
Foundation for the Defence of Nature, Venezuela, 487
Foundation for Environmental Education—FEE, Denmark, 83
Foundation for German-Polish Co-operation, Poland, 257
Foundation for International Community Assistance, USA, 425
Foundation for Latin American Economic Research, Argentina, 7
Foundation for National Parks & Wildlife, Australia, 14
Foundation for the Rights of Future Generations, Germany, 141
Foundation for Rural & Regional Renewal—FRRR, Australia, 14
Foundation for Strategic Research, France, 111
Foundation for Women's Research and Studies, Argentina, 7
Foundation for World Agriculture and Rural Life, France, 106
The Foundation for Young Australians—FYA, Australia, 14
Foundation of Youth and Lifelong Learning—INEDIVIM, Greece, 145
Foundations Platform—F20, Germany, 119
France China Foundation, France, 106
France-Libertés Fondation Danielle Mitterrand, France, 112
France Nature Environnement, France, 112
Franciscans International, Switzerland, 310
Fraser Institute, Canada, 55
Fratelli Tutti Foundation, Vatican City, 486
Fraunhofer-Gesellschaft, Germany, 129
Fraunhofer Society, Germany, 129
Freedom Together Foundation, USA, 428
French Institute of International Relations, France, 113
Frères des Hommes—FDH, France, 113
Fridtjof Nansen Institute, Norway, 241
Fridtjof Nansens Institutt—FNI, Norway, 241
Friedrich-Ebert-Stiftung eV, Germany, 129
Friends of the Earth International—FOEI, Netherlands, 225
Friends of Nature Foundation, Bolivia, 36
Friluftsrådet, Denmark, 83
FUHEM—Fundación Benéfico-Social Hogar del Empleado, Spain, 286
Fund for the Development of Indigenous Peoples of Latin America and the Caribbean, Bolivia, 36

INDEX OF MAIN ACTIVITIES

Fund and Endowment Management Foundation, Norway, 240
Fundação Assistência Médica International—AMI, Portugal, 258
Fundação Banco do Brasil, Brazil, 39
Fundação Calouste Gulbenkian, Portugal, 259
Fundação Dom Manuel II, Portugal, 260
Fundação EDP, Portugal, 260
Fundação Getulio Vargas—FGV, Brazil, 40
Fundação Grupo Boticário de Proteção à Natureza, Brazil, 40
Fundação José Maria Neves para a Governança, Cabo Verde, 46
Fundação Luso-Americana para o Desenvolvimento—FLAD, Portugal, 260
Fundação Roberto Marinho, Brazil, 41
Fundação de Serralves, Portugal, 261
Fundação SOS Mata Atlântica, Brazil, 41
Fundación Amanecer, Colombia, 70
Fundación Ambiente y Recursos Naturales—FARN, Argentina, 7
Fundación Amigos de la Naturaleza, Bolivia, 36
Fundación AVINA, Panama, 247
Fundación Bancaria 'la Caixa', Spain, 288
Fundación BANHCAFE—FUNBANHCAFE, Honduras, 150
Fundación Bariloche, Argentina, 7
Fundación Carlos Slim, Mexico, 215
Fundación Charles Darwin para las Islas Galápagos—FCD, Ecuador, 88
Fundación Chile—FCH, Chile, 65
Fundación Comunitaria de Puerto Rico—FCPR, Puerto Rico, 261
Fundación para la Defensa de la Naturaleza—FUDENA, Venezuela, 487
Fundación para Estudio e Investigación de la Mujer—FEIM, Argentina, 7
Fundación Felipe González, Spain, 290
Fundación FEMSA, Mexico, 215
Fundación Fernando Rielo, Spain, 290
Fundación Futuro Latinoamericano, Ecuador, 88
Fundación Global Democracia y Desarrollo—FUNGLODE, Dominican Republic, 87
Fundación Grupo Esquel—Ecuador, Ecuador, 88
Fundación Hábitat Colombia—FHC, Colombia, 71
Fundación de Investigaciones Económicas Latinoamericanas—FIEL, Argentina, 7
Fundación Jubileo, Bolivia, 36
Fundación MAPFRE, Spain, 292
Fundación Marcelino Botín, Spain, 292
Fundación Miguel Alemán AC, Mexico, 215
Fundación Moisés Bertoni—FMB, Paraguay, 248
Fundación Montemadrid, Spain, 292
Fundación Nacional para el Desarrollo, El Salvador, 91
Fundación Nobis, Ecuador, 88
Fundación para la Paz y la Democracia—FUNPADEM, Costa Rica, 74
Fundación Princesa de Asturias, Spain, 294
Fundación Real Instituto Elcano, Spain, 294
Fundación Repsol, Spain, 295
Fundación La Salle de Ciencias Naturales—FLASA, Venezuela, 487
Fundación Solidaridad, Dominican Republic, 87
Fundación Tecnologías Sociales—TECSOS, Spain, 296
Fundación Telefónica, Spain, 295
Fundación Tigo, Guatemala, 148
Fundación Torcuato Di Tella—FTDT, Argentina, 8
Fundación UNIR Bolivia, Bolivia, 36
Fundación Vodafone España, Spain, 296
Fundacja Citi Handlowy im. Leopolda Kronenberga, Poland, 255
Fundacja Partnerstwo dla Srodowiska, Poland, 256
Fundacja POLSAT, Poland, 256
Fundacja Współpracy Polsko-Niemieckiej/Stiftung für Deutsch-Polnische Zusammenarbeit, Poland, 257
FundAction, USA, 394
FUNDAP—Fundación para el Desarrollo, Guatemala, 148
Fundasaun Haburas, Timor-Leste, 325
Fundația Soros—Moldova, Moldova, 217
Fundația Universitară a Mării Negre—FUMN, Romania, 263
Future in Our Hands Youth NGO—FIOH, Armenia, 9
FWF—Österreichischer Wissenschaftsfonds, Austria, 21
FWO—Fonds Wetenschappelijk Onderzoek, Belgium, 32
FXB International—Association François-Xavier Bagnoud, Switzerland, 310
G. Unger Vetlesen Foundation, USA, 429
The Gaia Foundation, UK, 355

GAIA—Groupe d'Action dans l'Intérêt des Animaux, Belgium, 32
Gapminder, Sweden, 300
Garden Organic, UK, 355
Garfield Weston Foundation, UK, 355
Garrone (Edoardo), Fondazione, Italy, 177
George and Thelma Paraskevaides Foundation, Cyprus, 78
Gerda Henkel Foundation, Germany, 130
Gerda Henkel Stiftung, Germany, 130
German Federal Foundation for the Environment, Germany, 124
German Institute of Development and Sustainability—IDOS, Germany, 130
German-Russian Exchange, Germany, 124
Getulio Vargas Foundation, Brazil, 40
Giordano Dell'Amore Social Venture Foundation, Italy, 180
Giorgio Cini Foundation, Italy, 177
Give2Asia, USA, 394
Global Action in the Interest of Animals, Belgium, 32
Global Communities, USA, 431
Global Democracy and Development Foundation, Dominican Republic, 87
Global Environmental Action—GEA, Japan, 187
Global Forest Fund, Denmark, 83
Global Greengrants Fund, USA, 431
Globetree Association, Sweden, 300
Gobabeb Namib Research Institute, Namibia, 222
Good Neighbors International, Korea (Republic), 201
Google.org—Google Foundation, USA, 432
Gordon and Betty Moore Foundation, USA, 432
Graduate Institute of International Studies and Development Studies, Switzerland, 311
Great Britain Sasakawa Foundation, UK, 356
Greater Kansas City Community Foundation, USA, 433
The Greta Thunberg Foundation, Sweden, 300
Groupe d'Action dans l'Intérêt des Animaux—GAIA, Belgium, 32
Grupo Social Fondo Ecuatoriano Populorum Progressio, Ecuador, 89
Guggenheim (Harry Frank) Foundation, USA, 434
Gulbenkian (Calouste), Fundação, Portugal, 259
H&M Foundation, Sweden, 300
Haburas Foundation, Timor-Leste, 325
Hanaholmen—Swedish-Finnish Cultural Centre, Finland, 95
HAND—Hungarian Association of NGOs for Development and Humanitarian Aid, Hungary, 152
Hans Wilsdorf Foundation, Switzerland, 309
Haribon Foundation for the Conservation of Natural Resources, Inc, Philippines, 252
Harp Helú Foundations, Mexico, 216
The Harry Frank Guggenheim Foundation—HFG, USA, 434
Havelaar (Max) Foundation, Netherlands, 230
Hawaii Resilience Fund, USA, 458
He Xiangjian Foundation, China (People's Republic), 68
Headley Trust, UK, 357
Heineken Prizes for Arts and Sciences, Netherlands, 225
Heinekenprijzen voor kunst en wetenschap, Netherlands, 225
Heinrich Böll Foundation, Germany, 131
Heinrich-Böll-Stiftung, Germany, 131
Hellenic Foundation for European and Foreign Policy—ELIAMEP, Greece, 146
Helmholtz Association, Germany, 132
Helmholtz-Gemeinschaft, Germany, 132
Helmich (Janson Johan og Marcia) Legat, Norway, 242
Helmsley (Leona M. and Harry B.) Charitable Trust, USA, 447
Helvetas Swiss Intercooperation, Switzerland, 311
Hempel Fonden, Denmark, 84
Hempel Foundation, Denmark, 84
Henkel (Gerda) Stiftung, Germany, 130
Henry Doubleday Research Association, UK, 355
Heren Philanthropic Foundation, China (People's Republic), 68
Heritage Foundation, France, 110
Hewlett (William and Flora) Foundation, USA, 481
Heydar Aliyev Fondu, Azerbaijan, 23
Heydar Aliyev Foundation, Azerbaijan, 23
Historic Environment Scotland, UK, 358
Hivos—Humanistisch Instituut voor Ontwikkelings Samenwerking, Netherlands, 226
Honda Foundation, Japan, 187
Horizons of Friendship, Canada, 56

Conservation and the environment

Hormuud Salaam Foundation, Somalia, 277
Horn Economic and Social Policy Institute—HESPI, Ethiopia, 94
The Howard G. Buffett Foundation, USA, 437
Hudson Institute, USA, 437
Hulot (Nicolas), Fondation, France, 110
Human Rights Watch—HRW, USA, 437
Humanistic Institute for Co-operation with Developing Countries, Netherlands, 226
IACD—Institute of Asian Culture and Development, Korea (Republic), 201
IAI—Istituto Affari Internazionali, Italy, 182
Ian Potter Foundation, Australia, 14
IBM International Foundation, USA, 438
IBON Foundation, Philippines, 252
Ichikowitz Family Foundation—IFF, South Africa, 280
The Ideas Institute, Kenya, 199
IFAD—International Fund for Agricultural Development, Italy, 182
IFAW—International Fund for Animal Welfare, USA, 438
IIAP—Instituto de Investigaciones de la Amazonía Peruana, Peru, 249
IIED—International Institute for Environment and Development, UK, 360
IISD—International Institute for Sustainable Development, Canada, 57
IKEA Foundation, Netherlands, 229
Îles de Paix, Belgium, 32
IMPACT Transformer la Gestion des Ressources Naturelles, Canada, 56
IMPACT Transforming Natural Resource Management, Canada, 56
Indian Council of Social Science Research—ICSSR, India, 157
Indian National Trust for Art and Cultural Heritage—INTACH, India, 158
Indonesia Biodiversity Foundation, Indonesia, 162
Indonesian Forum for the Environment—Friends of the Earth Indonesia, Indonesia, 162
INEDIVIM—Foundation of Youth and Lifelong Learning, Greece, 145
Inlaks Shivdasani Foundation, India, 158
Institut Arctique de l'Amérique du Nord—IAAN, Canada, 49
Institut FMES—Institut Méditerranéen d'Etudes Stratégiques, France, 113
Institut Français des Relations Internationales—IFRI, France, 113
Institut de Hautes Etudes Internationales et du Développement—IHEID, Switzerland, 311
Institut for Menneskerettigheder, Denmark, 84
Institut Océanographique—Fondation Albert Ier, Prince de Monaco, France, 114
Institut für Weltwirtschaft—IfW Kiel, Germany, 132
Institute of Asian Culture and Development—IACD, Korea (Republic), 201
Institute of British Geographers, UK, 378
Institute of Economic Affairs—IEA, UK, 359
Institute for European Environmental Policy—IEEP, Belgium, 33
Institute of International Affairs, Italy, 182
Institute of International Law, Argentina, 6
Institute for International Security and Strategic Affairs—ISIAE, Argentina, 6
Institute for Research on the Peruvian Amazon, Peru, 249
Institute of Social Studies—ISS, Netherlands, 226
Institute for Sustainable Communities—ISC, USA, 439
Instituto Europeo de Salud y Bienestar Social, Spain, 296
Instituto de Montaña, Peru, 249
INTACH—Indian National Trust for Art and Cultural Heritage, India, 158
Integrated Rural Development Foundation—IRDF, Philippines, 252
Inter Pares, Canada, 57
Internationaal Instituut voor Sociale Geschiedenis—IISG, Netherlands, 226
International Alert—Alert, UK, 360
International Arctic Science Committee—IASC, Iceland, 154
International Balzan Prize Foundation, Italy, 181
International Civil Society Centre, Germany, 119
International Co-operation, Italy, 173
International Development Center of Japan, Japan, 189
International Forum Bosnia, Bosnia and Herzegovina, 37
The International Foundation, USA, 440
International Foundation of the High-Altitude Research Stations Jungfraujoch and Gornergrat, Switzerland, 313

Conservation and the environment

International Fund for Agricultural Development—IFAD, Italy, 182
International Fund for Animal Welfare—IFAW, USA, 438
International Institute for Applied Systems Analysis—IIASA, Austria, 21
International Institute for Environment and Development—IIED, UK, 360
International Institute of Rural Reconstruction—IIRR, Philippines, 252
International Institute of Social History—IISH, Netherlands, 226
International Institute of Social Studies, Netherlands, 226
The International Institute for Strategic Studies—IISS, UK, 360
International Institute for Sustainable Development—IISD, Canada, 57
International Institute of Tropical Agriculture—IITA, Nigeria, 237
International Lake Environment Committee Foundation, Japan, 189
International Maize and Wheat Improvement Center, Mexico, 215
International Medical Assistance Foundation, Portugal, 258
International NGO Charter of Accountability, USA, 393
International NGO Forum on Indonesian Development—INFID, Indonesia, 161
International Office for Water, France, 115
International Renaissance Foundation—IRF, Ukraine, 333
International Rhino Foundation—IRF, USA, 441
International Rivers, USA, 441
International Solidarity Foundation, Finland, 96
International Union for Conservation of Nature and Natural Resources, Switzerland, 313
International Visegrad Fund—IVF, Slovakia, 275
International Water Management Institute—IWMI, Sri Lanka, 297
Internationale Stiftung Hochalpine Forschungsstationen Jungfraujoch und Gornergrat, Switzerland, 313
Internationale Stiftung Preis E. Balzan-Fonds, Italy, 181
iPartner India, India, 155
Islamic Relief Worldwide, UK, 360
Islands of Peace, Belgium, 32
Istituto Affari Internazionali—IAI, Italy, 182
IUCN/UICN, Switzerland, 313
Ivey Foundation, Canada, 57
Ivorian Economic and Social Research Centre, Côte d'Ivoire, 75
Iwatani Naoji Foundation, Japan, 189
The J. W. McConnell Family Foundation, Canada, 57
Jack Ma Foundation—JMF, China (People's Republic), 68
J'ai Rêvé Foundation, Central African Republic, 63
James Michel Foundation, Seychelles, 272
Janson Johan Helmich and Marcia Jansons Endowment, Norway, 242
Janson Johan Helmich og Marcia Jansons Legat, Norway, 242
The Japan Foundation, Japan, 189
Japan International Volunteer Center—JVC, Japan, 190
Japanese-German Centre Berlin, Germany, 133
Japanisch-Deutsches Zentrum Berlin, Germany, 133
JN Foundation, Jamaica, 184
JNF UK—JNF Charitable Trust, UK, 361
The John D. and Catherine T. MacArthur Foundation, USA, 444
John Ellerman Foundation, UK, 361
John Paul II Foundation for the Sahel, Burkina Faso, 44
The Johnson Foundation at Wingspread, USA, 444
Johnson (Lyndon Baines) Foundation, USA, 449
JOHUD—Jordanian Hashemite Fund for Human Development, Jordan, 196
José Maria Neves Foundation for Governance, Cabo Verde, 46
Joseph Levy Foundation, UK, 362
Joseph Rowntree Charitable Trust—JRCT, UK, 362
Joyce Foundation, USA, 445
JPB Foundation, USA, 428
Jubilee Foundation, Bolivia, 36
KAF—Kataliko Actions for Africa, Congo (Democratic Republic), 72
Kafaa Development Foundation, Libya, 207
Kansainvälinen solidaarisuussäätiö, Finland, 96
KCDF—Kenya Community Development Foundation, Kenya, 199

KDDI Foundation, Japan, 191
KEHATI—Yayasan Keanekaragaman Hayati Indonesia, Indonesia, 162
Khemka (Nand & Jeet) Foundation, India, 159
Kiel Institute for the World Economy, Germany, 132
King Baudouin Foundation, Belgium, 33
King Hussein Foundation—KHF, Jordan, 196
King Philanthropies, USA, 445
Kleinwort (Ernest) Charitable Trust, UK, 353
Kokkalis Foundation, Greece, 146
Koning Boudewijnstichting/Fondation Roi Baudouin, Belgium, 33
Kresge Foundation, USA, 446
Kronenberg (Leopold) Foundation, Poland, 255
Kulika Charitable Trust Uganda, Uganda, 331
Kusuma Trust UK, UK, 363
Kuwait Awqaf Public Foundation, Kuwait, 203
Kuwait Institute for Scientific Research—KISR, Kuwait, 203
'La Caixa' Banking Foundation, Spain, 288
La Salle Foundation for Natural Sciences, Venezuela, 487
Lafede.cat—Federació d'Organitzacions per a la Justícia Global, Spain, 286
Lafede.cat—Federation of Organizations for Global Justice, Spain, 286
Laing Family Trusts, UK, 364
Lambrakis Foundation, Greece, 146
Land Network, Timor-Leste, 325
Landesa—Rural Development Institute, USA, 447
LAPAS—Latvijas platforma attīstības sadarbībai, Latvia, 204
Latimpacto—Red Latinoamericana de Inversión Social y Filantropía Estratégica, Colombia, 71
Latin American Council of Social Sciences, Argentina, 6
Latin American Future Foundation, Ecuador, 88
Latin American Venture Philanthropy Network, Colombia, 71
Latvian Platform for Development Cooperation, Latvia, 204
Lauder (Ronald S.) Foundation, Germany, 138
Laudes Foundation, Switzerland, 313
The Lawson Foundation, Canada, 58
LBJ Foundation, USA, 449
League of Corporate Foundations—LCF, Philippines, 250
Legatum Foundation, United Arab Emirates, 334
Leibniz Association, Germany, 135
Leibniz Gemeinschaft, Germany, 135
Leibniz-Institut für Agrarentwicklung in Transformationsökonomien—IAMO, Germany, 135
Leibniz Institute of Agricultural Development in Transition Economies, Germany, 135
Lelio and Lisli Basso Foundation Onlus, Italy, 178
The Leona M. and Harry B. Helmsley Charitable Trust, USA, 447
Lesotho Council of Non-Governmental Organisations, Lesotho, 207
Leventis (A. G.) Foundation, Cyprus, 77
Leventis (A. G.) Foundation Nigeria, Nigeria, 237
Leverhulme Trust, UK, 365
Levy (Joseph) Foundation, UK, 362
Lien Foundation, Singapore, 273
Lifewater International, USA, 479
Light Up the World—LUTW, Canada, 58
Light of the Village Foundation, Indonesia, 162
Linbury Trust, UK, 365
Litdea Association, Lithuania, 208
Living Culture Foundation Namibia—LCFN, Namibia, 222
Liz Claiborne & Art Ortenberg Foundation, USA, 448
The Long Now Foundation, USA, 449
Lukuru Wildlife Research Foundation, Congo (Democratic Republic), 72
Luso-American Development Foundation, Portugal, 260
The Lutheran World Federation, Switzerland, 314
Lutherischer Weltbund/Fédération Luthérienne Mondiale/Federación Luterana Mundial, Switzerland, 314
Luxembourg Development NGO Co-operation Circle, Luxembourg, 209
Lyndon Baines Johnson Foundation, USA, 449
M. S. Swaminathan Research Foundation—MSSRF, India, 158
M. Venkatarangaiya Foundation—MVF, India, 158
MacArthur (John D. and Catherine T.) Foundation, USA, 444
McCaw (Craig and Susan) Foundation, USA, 418
McConnell (J. W.) Family Foundation, Canada, 57
MACIF Foundation, France, 108
The Mackintosh Foundation, UK, 366

INDEX OF MAIN ACTIVITIES

McKnight Foundation, USA, 449
The McLean Foundation, Canada, 59
MADRE, USA, 450
MAIF Foundation for Research, France, 108
Maj ja Tor Nessling Säätiö, Finland, 96
Maj and Tor Nessling Foundation, Finland, 96
MAPFRE Foundation, Spain, 292
Marangopoulos Foundation for Human Rights, Greece, 146
Marcel Bleustein-Blanchet Vocational Foundation, France, 109
Margaret A. Cargill Philanthropies—MACP, USA, 450
Marinho (Roberto), Fundação, Brazil, 41
Marisla Foundation, USA, 451
Masason Foundation, Japan, 191
Mauritius Telecom Foundation—MTF, Mauritius, 214
Mawazo Institute, Kenya, 199
Max Bell Foundation, Canada, 59
Max Havelaar Foundation—Fairtrade Netherlands, Netherlands, 230
Mayer (Charles Léopold Mayer), Fondation, Switzerland, 308
Medunarodnog foruma Bosna, Bosnia and Herzegovina, 37
Mediterranean Foundation for Strategic Studies Institute, France, 113
Mellon (Richard King) Foundation, USA, 467
Menzies Foundation, Australia, 15
Menzies (Sir Robert) Foundation, Australia, 15
Mercy, Ireland, 168
Mercy For Animals—MFA, USA, 452
Mercy Corps, USA, 452
Merian (Christoph) Stiftung, Switzerland, 305
Meridian Foundation, Germany, 140
Mertz Gilmore Foundation, USA, 452
Michael Otto Foundation for Environmental Protection, Germany, 136
Michael-Otto-Stiftung für Umweltschutz, Germany, 136
Michel (James) Foundation, Seychelles, 272
Miguel Alemán Foundation, Mexico, 215
Milieukontakt Macedonia—MKM, North Macedonia, 240
Miloud Chaâbi Foundation, Morocco, 220
Minderoo Foundation, Australia, 15
Minor Foundation for Major Challenges, Norway, 242
Minority Rights Group International—MRG, UK, 368
Mistra—Foundation for Strategic Environmental Research, Sweden, 303
Mitterrand (Danielle), Fondation, France, 112
Mohammed bin Rashid Al Maktoum Global Initiatives—MBRGI, United Arab Emirates, 335
Moisés Bertoni Foundation, Paraguay, 248
Montemadrid Foundation, Spain, 292
Moore (Gordon and Betty) Foundation, USA, 432
Mountain Institute, Peru, 249
Mouvement International ATD Quart-Monde, France, 115
M-PESA Foundation, Kenya, 199
MTN Uganda Foundation, Uganda, 332
Munich Re Foundation/Münchener Rück Stiftung, Germany, 137
Muslim Aid, UK, 369
Myer Foundation, Australia, 18
Myer (Sidney) Fund, Australia, 18
Naandi Foundation—A New Beginning, India, 158
Nadace Občanského fóra—Nadace OF, Czech Republic, 80
Nadace Open Society Fund Praha, Czech Republic, 80
Nadace Preciosa, Czech Republic, 80
Nadácia Ekopolis, Slovakia, 275
Nadácia SPP, Slovakia, 275
Nand & Jeet Khemka Foundation, India, 159
Nansen (Fridtjof) Institute, Norway, 241
Naspa Foundation, Germany, 137
Naspa Stiftung, Germany, 137
National Endowment for Science, Technology and the Arts—Nesta, UK, 370
National Fish and Wildlife Foundation—NFWF, USA, 455
National Foundation for Development, El Salvador, 91
National Geographic Society, USA, 455
National Heritage Memorial Fund, UK, 370
The National Lottery Community Fund, UK, 370
The National Lottery Heritage Fund, UK, 370
National Park Foundation, USA, 455
National Science Foundation—NSF, USA, 455
National Trust, UK, 370
National Trust EcoFund, Bulgaria, 43
National Trust of Fiji—NTF, Fiji, 94

INDEX OF MAIN ACTIVITIES

The National Trust for Italy, Italy, 174
National Wildlife Federation—NWF, USA, 456
The Nature Conservancy—TNC, USA, 456
Near East Foundation—NEF, USA, 456
Nederlandse Organisatie voor Internationale Ontwikkelingssamenwerking—Stichting NOVIB, Netherlands, 228
NEF—Near East Foundation, USA, 456
The Neptis Foundation, Canada, 60
Nessling (Maj and Tor) Foundation, Finland, 96
Nesta—National Endowment for Science, Technology and the Arts, UK, 370
Network of Foundations and Research Institutions for the Promotion of a Culture of Peace in Africa, Côte d'Ivoire, 75
Network for Human Development, Brazil, 41
Network for Social Change Charitable Trust—NSCCT, UK, 370
Neves (José Maria), Fundação para a Governança, Cabo Verde, 46
New Economics Foundation—NEF, UK, 371
The New York Community Trust—NYCT, USA, 457
NGO Center—NGOC, Armenia, 9
Nicolas Hulot Foundation for Nature and Humankind, France, 110
Nigerian Conservation Foundation—NCF, Nigeria, 238
Nitidæ, France, 115
Niwano Peace Foundation, Japan, 192
Nobis Foundation, Ecuador, 88
Non-Governmental Ecological Vernadsky Foundation, Russian Federation, 266
Nordic Africa Institute Scholarships, Sweden, 302
Nordiska Afrikainstitutets Stipendier, Sweden, 302
Norsk Utenrikspolitisk Institutt—NUPI, Norway, 242
Norwegian Institute of International Affairs, Norway, 242
NOVIB (Oxfam Netherlands), Netherlands, 228
Novo Nordisk Fonden, Denmark, 85
Novo Nordisk Foundation, Denmark, 85
NYCT—The New York Community Trust, USA, 457
Oak Foundation, Switzerland, 315
Observer Research Foundation—ORF, India, 159
The Ocean Cleanup Foundation, Netherlands, 230
The Ocean Foundation, USA, 458
Oceanographic Institute—Albert I, Prince of Monaco Foundation, France, 114
ODI, UK, 371
Office International de l'Eau—OiEau, France, 115
OISCA International—Organization for Industrial, Spiritual and Cultural Advancement-International, Japan, 192
Olivetti (Adriano), Fondazione, Italy, 174
Oman LNG Development Foundation—ODF, Oman, 244
Omidyar Group, USA, 458
Onassis (Alexander S.) Public Benefit Foundation, Liechtenstein, 207
One Economy Foundation, Namibia, 222
Open Society Foundation Haiti, Haiti, 149
Open Society Foundation—London, UK, 372
Open Society Fund Prague—OSF Prague, Czech Republic, 80
Oppenheimer Generations Foundation, South Africa, 282
Orangutan Foundation, UK, 372
Organization for Social Science Research in Eastern and Southern Africa—OSSREA, Ethiopia, 94
Orji Uzor Kalu Foundation, Nigeria, 238
Osaka Community Foundation, Japan, 192
Österreichischer Wissenschaftsfonds—FWF, Austria, 21
Östersjöfonden, Finland, 97
Otto (Michael) Stiftung, Germany, 136
Our Foundation, Indonesia, 162
Outreach International, USA, 459
Oxfam Australia, Australia, 16
Oxfam Denmark, Denmark, 86
Oxfam France, France, 115
Oxfam GB, UK, 372
Oxfam Hong Kong, Hong Kong, 151
Oxfam International, Kenya, 200
Oxfam Italia, Italy, 183
Oxfam Mexico, Mexico, 216
Oxfam NOVIB—Nederlandse Organisatie voor Internationale Ontwikkelingssamenwerking, Netherlands, 228
Oxfam NOVIB—Netherlands Organization for International Development Co-operation, Netherlands, 228
Oxfam-Solidariteit/Solidarité, Belgium, 33

Oxfam South Africa, South Africa, 282
Pacific Development and Conservation Trust, New Zealand, 234
Pacific Peoples' Partnership, Canada, 61
Packard (David and Lucile) Foundation, USA, 420
Pact, USA, 460
PADF—Pan American Development Foundation, USA, 460
PAI—Population Action International, USA, 460
PAN Africa—Pesticide Action Network Africa, Senegal, 271
Pan American Development Foundation—PADF, USA, 460
PAN Europe—Pesticide Action Network Europe, Belgium, 34
Pan-European Federation for Cultural Heritage, Netherlands, 224
PAN UK—Pesticide Action Network UK, UK, 373
PANAP—Pesticide Action Network Asia and the Pacific, Malaysia, 211
PANNA—Pesticide Action Network North America, USA, 462
Paraskevaides (George and Thelma) Foundation, Cyprus, 78
Partos, Netherlands, 223
Patterson (Alicia) Foundation, USA, 398
The Paul G. Allen Family Foundation, USA, 462
PCI Media Impact, USA, 467
PCI—Project Concern International, USA, 431
Peace Parks Foundation, South Africa, 282
Peace Winds Japan—PWJ, Japan, 192
PepsiCo Foundation, Inc, USA, 462
Perpetual Foundation, Australia, 16
Peruvian Foundation for Nature Conservation, Peru, 249
Pesticide Action Network Africa—PAN Africa, Senegal, 271
Pesticide Action Network Asia and the Pacific—PANAP, Malaysia, 211
Pesticide Action Network Europe—PAN Europe, Belgium, 34
Pesticide Action Network Latin America and the Caribbean, Chile, 65
Pesticide Action Network North America—PANNA, USA, 462
Pesticide Action Network UK—PAN UK, UK, 373
The Pew Charitable Trusts, USA, 462
Philanthropy New Zealand/Topūtanga Tuku Aroha o Aotearoa, New Zealand, 232
Philippine Business for Social Progress—PBSP, Philippines, 250
Pilgrim Trust, UK, 373
Plataforma Portuguesa das Organizações Não-Governamentais para o Desenvolvimento—ONGD, Portugal, 258
POLSAT Foundation, Poland, 256
Population Action International—PAI, USA, 460
Population Council, USA, 463
Portuguese Platform of Non-Governmental Organizations for Development, Portugal, 258
Potter (Ian) Foundation, Australia, 14
Practical Action, UK, 374
Pratt Foundation, Australia, 17
Preciosa Foundation, Czech Republic, 80
Prince Bernhard Cultural Foundation, Netherlands, 230
Princess of Asturias Foundation, Spain, 294
Prins Bernhard Cultuurfonds, Stichting, Netherlands, 230
PRODESSA—Proyecto de Desarrollo Santiago, Guatemala, 148
Pronaturaleza—Fundación Peruana para la Conservación de la Naturaleza, Peru, 249
Public Studies Centre, Chile, 64
Puerto Rico Community Foundation, Puerto Rico, 261
Queen Elizabeth II National Trust, New Zealand, 234
R. Howard Webster Foundation/Fondation R. Howard Webster, Canada, 61
Rafto Foundation for Human Rights, Norway, 243
Raftostiftelsen for menneskerettigheter, Norway, 243
Rainforest Action Network—RAN, USA, 465
Rainforest Foundation Norway, Norway, 243
The Rainforest Foundation UK—RFUK, UK, 375
Rainforest Foundation US—RFUS, USA, 465
Rajiv Gandhi Foundation, India, 160
RAN—Rainforest Action Network, USA, 465
RAND Corporation, USA, 465
Rare, USA, 466
Rausing (Ruben and Elisabeth) Trust, UK, 383
RBC Foundation, Canada, 61
Re:wild, USA, 466
Realdania Foundation, Denmark, 83

Conservation and the environment

Rebecca Akufo-Addo Foundation—Rebecca Foundation, Ghana, 144
Red de Acción en Plaguicidas y sus Alternativas de América Latina—RAP-AL, Chile, 65
RED—Ruralité-Environnement-Développement, Belgium, Belgium, 34
Rede ba Rai, Timor-Leste, 325
Rede Comuá, Brazil, 38
REDEH—Rede de Desenvolvimento Humano, Brazil, 41
Regional Environmental Center, Hungary, 153
Regnskogfondet, Norway, 243
Relief International, USA, 466
Repsol Foundation, Spain, 295
Réseau des Fondations et Institutions de Recherche pour la Promotion d'un Culture de la Paix en Afrique—REFICA, Côte d'Ivoire, 75
The Resource Foundation—TRF, USA, 467
RIA—Royal Irish Academy, Ireland, 167
Richard King Mellon Foundation, USA, 467
Rielo (Fernando), Fundación, Spain, 290
Right Livelihood Award Foundation, Sweden, 302
Rising Impact, USA, 467
Rivers Trust, UK, 376
Robert Bosch Foundation, Germany, 138
Robert-Bosch-Stiftung GmbH, Germany, 138
Robert Marinho Foundation, Brazil, 41
Rockefeller Brothers Fund—RBF, USA, 468
Rockefeller Foundation, USA, 468
Rohini Nilekani Philanthropies, India, 160
The Ronald S. Lauder Foundation, Germany, 138
Rosetta Foundation, USA, 416
Ross (R. E.) Trust, Australia, 17
The Ross Trust, Australia, 17
Rössing Foundation, Namibia, 222
Rowntree (Joseph) Charitable Trust, UK, 362
Royal Anthropological Institute of Great Britain and Ireland—RAI, UK, 377
The Royal Commonwealth Society—RCS, UK, 377
Royal Elcano Institute Foundation, Spain, 294
The Royal Foundation of the Prince and Princess of Wales, UK, 378
Royal Geographical Society (with the Institute of British Geographers)—RGS-IBG, UK, 378
Royal Institute of International Affairs—RIIA—Chatham House, UK, 378
The Royal Society, UK, 379
Royal Society for the Prevention of Cruelty to Animals—RSPCA, UK, 380
Royal Society for the Protection of Birds—RSPB, UK, 379
RSA—Royal Society for the Encouragement of Arts, Manufactures and Commerce, UK, 379
RSPB—Royal Society for the Protection of Birds, UK, 379
RSPCA—Royal Society for the Prevention of Cruelty to Animals, UK, 380
The Rufford Foundation, UK, 380
Ruparelia Foundation, Uganda, 329
Rupert Family Foundations, South Africa, 283
Rural Development Institute—Landesa, USA, 447
Ruralité-Environnement-Développement—RED, Belgium, 34
Rurality Environment Development, Belgium, 34
Russian International Affairs Council—RIAC, Russian Federation, 266
Sabanci Vakfi—Haci Omer Sabanci Foundation, Türkiye, 329
Sainsbury Family Charitable Trusts, UK, 380
El Salvadoran Association for Economic and Social Development FUSADES, El Salvador, 91
Salzburg Global Seminar, Austria, 22
The San Diego Foundation, USA, 470
Sandals Foundation, Jamaica, 184
Santiago Development Project, Guatemala, 148
Save the Children International, UK, 381
Save Our Future Environmental Foundation, Germany, 139
Save Our Future Umweltstiftung—SOF, Germany, 139
SBS Cultural Foundation, Korea (Republic), 202
Schneider Electric Foundation, France, 111
Schwab Foundation for Social Entrepreneurship, Switzerland, 316
Schweisfurth Foundation, Germany, 139
Schweisfurth-Stiftung, Germany, 139
Schweizerisch-Liechtensteinische Stiftung für Archäologische Forschungen im Ausland—SLSA, Switzerland, 316
Schweizerische Stiftung für Alpine Forschungen—SSAF, Switzerland, 316
Scientific Research Foundation, Belgium, 32
Scottish Catholic International Aid Fund—SCIAF, UK, 382
SeedChange, Canada, 61

Economic affairs

Self Help Africa—SHA, Ireland, 167
Self-Sufficient People Foundation, Indonesia, 163
Seoam Yoon Se Young Foundation, Korea (Republic), 202
Serralves Foundation, Portugal, 261
Serrv International, Inc, USA, 471
Service Civil International—SCI, Belgium, 34
Seub Nakhasathien Foundation, Thailand, 324
Seychelles Islands Foundation—SIF, Seychelles, 272
Shell Foundation—SF, UK, 382
Shoman (Abdul Hameed) Foundation, Jordan, 195
Siam Society, Thailand, 324
Siamese Heritage Trust, Thailand, 324
SID—Society for International Development, Italy, 183
Sidney Myer Fund & The Myer Foundation, Australia, 18
The Sierra Club Foundation, USA, 471
Sigrid Rausing Trust—SRT, UK, 383
Silicon Valley Community Foundation—SVCF, USA, 471
Singapore International Foundation—SIF, Singapore, 273
Singer-Polignac Foundation, France, 111
Sistema Charitable Foundation, Russian Federation, 267
Skoll Foundation, USA, 472
Slim (Carlos), Fundación, Mexico, 215
Smithsonian Institution, USA, 472
Snow Leopard Trust, USA, 472
Society for International Development—SID, Italy, 183
Software AG Foundation, Germany, 139
Software AG Stiftung, Germany, 139
Solidaarisuus, Finland, 96
Solidarity Foundation, Dominican Republic, 87
Sorenson Legacy Foundation, USA, 473
Soros Foundation—Moldova, Moldova, 217
SOS Atlantic Forest Foundation, Brazil, 41
South Sudan Center for Strategic and Policy Studies—CSPS, South Sudan, 285
South West International Development Network—SWIDN, UK, 337
Southern Africa Trust, South Africa, 283
Sparebankstiftelsen DNB, Norway, 243
Sphere, Switzerland, 305
SPP Foundation, Slovakia, 275
Stanley Center for Peace and Security, USA, 473
The Starr Foundation, USA, 473
Stichting DOEN, Netherlands, 229
Stichting Fonds 1818, Netherlands, 229
Stichting IKEA Foundation, Netherlands, 229
Stichting Max Havelaar—Fairtrade Nederland, Netherlands, 230
Stichting The Ocean Cleanup, Netherlands, 230
Stichting Prins Bernhard Cultuurfonds, Netherlands, 230
Stichting Triodos Foundation, Netherlands, 231
Stiftelsen Gapminder, Sweden, 300
Stiftelsen för Miljöstrategisk Forskning—Mistra, Sweden, 303
Stiftung Klimarappen, Switzerland, 317
Stiftung Mercator, Germany, 140
Stiftung Meridian, Germany, 140
Stiftung für die Rechte zukünftiger Generationen—SRzG, Germany, 141
Stiftung Vivamos Mejor, Switzerland, 317
Stockholm Environment Institute, Sweden, 303
Streisand (Barbra) Foundation, USA, 408
Strickland Foundation, Malta, 214
Sudd Institute, South Sudan, 285
Suomalaiset kehitysjärjestöt—Fingo, Finland, 95
Surdna Foundation, Inc, USA, 474
Survival International, UK, 385
Suzuki Foundation (David), Canada, 53
Swaminathan (M. S.) Research Foundation, India, 158
Sweden-Japan Foundation—SJF, Sweden, 304
Swiss Foundation for Alpine Research—SFAR, Switzerland, 316
Swiss Foundation for Technical Co-operation, Switzerland, 318
Swiss-Liechtenstein Foundation for Archaeological Research Abroad—SLFA, Switzerland, 316
SWISSAID Foundation, Switzerland, 318
Swisscontact—Swiss Foundation for Technical Co-operation, Switzerland, 318
Tang Prize Foundation, Taiwan, 322
Tata Trusts, India, 160
Tearfund Australia, Australia, 18
TechnoServe, USA, 474
Telefónica Foundation, Spain, 295
Temasek Foundation, Singapore, 273
Tencent Foundation, China (People's Republic), 70
Third World Network—TWN, Malaysia, 211
Third World Solidarity Action, Luxembourg, 209

Thomson Reuters Foundation, UK, 385
Thunberg (Greta) Foundation, Sweden, 300
TI—Transparency International, Germany, 142
Tides Organizations, USA, 475
Tifa Foundation—Indonesia, Indonesia, 163
Tiffany & Co Foundation, USA, 475
Tindall Foundation, New Zealand, 235
Tinker Foundation, Inc, USA, 475
The Todd Foundation, New Zealand, 235
Toepfer (Alfred) Stiftung, Germany, 121
Together for Global Justice—CIDSE, Belgium, 29
Tokyu Foundation, Japan, 194
Topūtanga Tuku Aroha o Aotearoa, New Zealand, 232
Torcuato Di Tella Foundation, Argentina, 8
TOSA Foundation, USA, 475
TotalEnergies Foundation, France, 112
The Toyota Foundation, Japan, 195
Translators without Borders, USA, 416
Transparency International—TI, Germany, 142
Triodos Foundation, Netherlands, 231
Trócaire—Catholic Agency for World Development, Ireland, 168
Trust for Mutual Understanding—TMU, USA, 476
TTF—Toyota Thailand Foundation, Thailand, 325
Turing (Alan) Institute, UK, 339
Turkish Foundation for Combating Soil Erosion, for Reforestation and the Protection of Natural Habitats, Türkiye, 330
Türkiye Çevre Vakfı, Türkiye, 330
Türkiye Erozyonla Mücadele Ağaçlandırma ve Doğal Varlıkları Koruma Vakfı—TEMA, Türkiye, 330
Türkiye Kalkınma Vakfı, Türkiye, 330
Turner Foundation, Inc, USA, 476
Turquoise Mountain Foundation, UK, 386
Tusk, UK, 387
Ufadhili Trust, Kenya, 197
UK Research and Innovation—UKRI, UK, 387
Uluntu Community Foundation—UCF, Zimbabwe, 491
UNESCO Centre du Patrimoine Mondial, France, 116
UNESCO World Heritage Centre, France, 116
UniCredit Foundation, Italy, 183
UNIFOR—Forvaltningstiftelse for fond og legater, Norway, 240
Union Aid Abroad—APHEDA, Australia, 19
UNIR Bolivia Foundation, Bolivia, 36
Unitarian Universalist Service Committee—UUSC, USA, 476
United Nations Foundation, USA, 476
United Purpose, UK, 387
United States African Development Foundation—USADF, USA, 477
United States-Japan Foundation, USA, 477
UPS Foundation, USA, 477
US Civilian Research & Development Foundation, USA, 419
USPG—United Society Partners in the Gospel, UK, 387
UUSC—Unitarian Universalist Service Committee, USA, 476
Vancouver Foundation, Canada, 62
Van Leer Jerusalem Institute, Israel, 171
Vargas (Getulio), Fundação, Brazil, 40
Venkatarangaiya (M.) Foundation, India, 158
VENRO—Verband Entwicklungspolitik und Humanitäre Hilfe deutscher Nichtregierungsorganizationen, Germany, 120
Verband für Gemeinnütziges Stiften, Austria, 20
Vetlesen (G. Unger) Foundation, USA, 429
VIA Foundation, Czech Republic, 81
Village Community Development Foundation, Indonesia, 163
Villar Foundation, Inc, Philippines, 253
VinFuture Foundation, Viet Nam, 489
Vita, Ireland, 168
Vivamos Mejor Foundation, Switzerland, 317
Vodacom Foundation DRC, Congo (Democratic Republic), 72
Vodacom Tanzania Foundation—VTF, Tanzania, 323
Vodafone ATH Fiji Foundation, Fiji, 94
Vodafone Foundation India, India, 161
Vodafone Idea Foundation, India, 161
Vodafone Spain Foundation, Spain, 296
Volkart Foundation, Switzerland, 319
Volkart-Stiftung, Switzerland, 319
Wahana Lingkungan Hidup Indonesia—WALHI, Indonesia, 162
WALHI—Wahana Lingkungan Hidup Indonesia, Indonesia, 162
Walk Free, Australia, 15
Walton Family Foundation, USA, 479
War on Want, UK, 388

INDEX OF MAIN ACTIVITIES

WasserStiftung, Germany, 142
Water for Good, USA, 479
Water.org, Inc, USA, 479
WaterFoundation, Germany, 142
The Waterloo Foundation—TWF, UK, 389
Weber (Franz), Fondation, Switzerland, 308
Webster (R. Howard) Foundation, Canada, 61
Weeden Foundation, USA, 479
Wellcome Trust, UK, 389
West African Rural Foundation—WARF, Senegal, 270
Weston (Garfield) Foundation, UK, 355
The Whitley Fund for Nature—WFN, UK, 390
Wihuri Foundation for International Prizes, Finland, 98
Wihurin kansainvälisten palkintojen rahasto, Finland, 98
The WILD Foundation—International Wilderness Leadership Foundation, USA, 481
Wilderness Foundation Global—WFG, South Africa, 284
The Wildlife Trusts, UK, 390
William Adlington Cadbury Charitable Trust, UK, 390
The William and Flora Hewlett Foundation, USA, 481
The William H. Donner Foundation, Inc, USA, 481
WILPF—Women's International League for Peace and Freedom, Switzerland, 319
Wilsdorf (Hans), Fondation, Switzerland, 309
Wilson (E. O.) Biodiversity Foundation, USA, 421
Wilson (Woodrow) International Center for Scholars, USA, 482
Winrock International, USA, 481
Winston Churchill Memorial Trust of New Zealand, New Zealand, 236
WomenLead Institute, USA, 418
Women's Environment & Development Organization—WEDO, USA, 484
Women's International League for Peace and Freedom, Switzerland, 319
The Wood Foundation—TWF, UK, 391
Woodrow Wilson International Center for Scholars, USA, 482
World Alliance of YMCAs—Young Men's Christian Associations, Switzerland, 319
World Animal Protection, UK, 391
World Economic Forum, Switzerland, 320
World Land Trust—WLT, UK, 391
World Learning, USA, 483
World Monuments Fund—WMF, USA, 483
World Neighbors, USA, 483
World Resources Institute—WRI, USA, 483
World Vision International, UK, 391
WorldFish, Malaysia, 212
Wujoh Foundation for Media and Development, Yemen, 489
WWF International, Switzerland, 320
The Wyss Foundtion, USA, 484
XPRIZE Foundation, USA, 484
YADESA—Yayasan Pembinaan Masyarakat Desa, Indonesia, 163
Yayasan Dian Desa—YDD, Indonesia, 162
Yayasan Geutanyoë, Indonesia, 162
Yayasan Insan Sembada, Indonesia, 163
Yayasan Pembinaan Masyarakat Desa—YADESA, Indonesia, 163
Yayasan Tifa, Indonesia, 163
YORGHAS Foundation, Poland, 258
Yuan Lin Charity Fund, China (People's Republic), 70
Ziviler Friedensdienst—ZFD, Germany, 120
Zorig Foundation, Mongolia, 219
Zuleikhabai Valy Mohamed Gany Rangoonwala Trust—ZVMG Rangoonwala Trust, Pakistan, 246
ZVMG Rangoonwala Trust, Pakistan, 246

ECONOMIC AFFAIRS

1818 Fund Foundation, Netherlands, 229
A. G. Leventis Foundation Nigeria, Nigeria, 237
Accion, USA, 397
ACDI/VOCA, USA, 397
ACFID—Australian Council for International Development, Australia, 12
ACT Alliance, Switzerland, 306
Action Children's Aid, Denmark, 82
Action Damien/Damiaanactie, Belgium, 28
Action Group on Erosion, Technology and Concentration, Canada, 54
Action on Poverty, Australia, 10
ActionAid International, South Africa, 278
Active for People in Need Austria, Austria, 20
Acumen, USA, 397
Adenauer (Konrad) Stiftung eV, Germany, 134

INDEX OF MAIN ACTIVITIES

Economic affairs

ADRA—Adventist Development and Relief Agency International, USA, 397
Advance, USA, 397
Adventist Development and Relief Agency International—ADRA, USA, 397
Afghanistan Institute for Civil Society—AICS, Afghanistan, 3
Afghanistan Research and Evaluation Unit, Afghanistan, 3
Africa-America Institute—AAI, USA, 398
Africa Foundation, South Africa, 278
Africa Humanitarian Action—AHA, Ethiopia, 93
Africa Institute of South Africa—AISA, South Africa, 279
Africa Space Foundation, Switzerland, 308
The African Agricultural Technology Foundation—AATF, Kenya, 198
African Capacity Building Foundation—ACBF, Zimbabwe, 490
African Forum and Network on Debt and Development—AFRODAD, Zimbabwe, 490
African Venture Philanthropy Alliance—AVPA, Kenya, 197
African Wildlife Foundation—AWF, Kenya, 198
African Women's Development Fund—AWDF, Ghana, 143
Afrobarometer, Ghana, 143
AFRODAD—African Forum and Network on Debt and Development, Zimbabwe, 490
Aga Khan Development Network—AKDN, Switzerland, 306
Aga Khan Foundation, Switzerland, 306
Aga Khan Foundation Canada, Canada, 49
Aga Khan Foundation UK, UK, 338
Age International, UK, 339
AGIR Association for the Environment and Quality of Life, Mali, 213
AID Foundation, Bangladesh, 24
AIIA—Australian Institute of International Affairs, Australia, 12
AISA—Africa Institute of South Africa, South Africa, 279
Aisha Buhari Global Foundation, Nigeria, 237
Akai Hane—Central Community Chest of Japan, Japan, 185
Aktion Børnehjælp, Denmark, 82
Al-Mortaqa Foundation for Human Development, Iraq, 164
The Alan Turing Institute, UK, 339
Albanian Disability Rights Foundation, Albania, 4
Albanian Institute for International Studies—AIIS, Albania, 4
Alcoa Foundation, USA, 398
Alemán (Miguel), Fundación, Mexico, 215
Alert—International Alert, UK, 360
Alfred P. Sloan Foundation, USA, 398
ALIDE—Asociación Latinoamericana de Instituciones Financieras para el Desarrollo, Peru, 248
Alight, USA, 399
Aliko Dangote Foundation—ADF, Nigeria, 237
Alkhidmat Foundation Pakistan—AKFP, Pakistan, 244
All Good Foundation Charitable Trust, New Zealand, 232
Allende (Isabel) Foundation, USA, 442
Alliance for Securing Democracy, USA, 430
Alongside Hope/Auprès de l'espoir, Canada, 49
Aman Foundation, Pakistan, 244
Ambrela Platform of Development Organizations, Slovakia, 273
Ambrela—Platforma rozvojových organizácií, Slovakia, 273
Ambuja Cement Foundation—ACF, India, 156
America for Bulgaria Foundation, Bulgaria, 43
American Enterprise Institute—AEI, USA, 400
American Foundation for the Blind—AFB, USA, 400
American Friends Service Committee—AFSC, USA, 401
Amigos de la Tierra, Netherlands, 225
AMINA—aktiv für Menschen in Not Austria, Austria, 20
Les Amis de la Terre, Netherlands, 225
Andrews Charitable Trust—ACT, UK, 340
Anesvad, Spain, 286
Angel of Hope Foundation, Zimbabwe, 490
Anglo American Foundation, UK, 340
ANGOC—Asian NGO Coalition for Agrarian Reform and Rural Development, Philippines, 251
Ankara İngiliz Arkeoloji Enstitüsü, UK, 345
The Annie E. Casey Foundation, USA, 404
Anti-Slavery International, UK, 340
Antigua Forum, Guatemala, 147
Arca Foundation, USA, 405
Archewell Foundation, USA, 405

Arcus Foundation, USA, 405
Arengukoostöö Ümarlaud—AKÜ, Estonia, 92
Areumdaun Jaedan, Korea (Republic), 200
Argentine Council for International Relations, Argentina, 6
ASEAN Foundation, Indonesia, 161
Asia Foundation, USA, 406
Asia New Zealand Foundation/Te Whītau Tūhono, New Zealand, 232
Asia Pacific Foundation of Canada—APFCanada, Canada, 49
Asia Philanthropy Circle—APC, Singapore, 272
Asia Society, USA, 406
AsiaDHRRA—Asian Partnership for the Development of Human Resources in Rural Asia, Philippines, 251
Asian Partnership for the Development of Human Resources in Rural Asia, Philippines, 251
Asian Venture Philanthropy Network—AVPN, Singapore, 272
Asociacija Litdea—Lithuanian Development Education and Awareness Raising Association, Lithuania, 208
Asociación de Fundaciones Familiares y Empresariales—AFE, Colombia, 70
Asociación Latinoamericana de Instituciones Financieras para el Desarrollo—ALIDE, Peru, 248
Asociación Salvadoreña para el Desarrollo Económico y Social FUSADES, El Salvador, 91
Asotzijatzijata za Dyemokratska Initzijativa, North Macedonia, 239
Aspen Institute, USA, 407
Association AGIR pour l'Environnement et la Qualité de la Vie, Mali, 213
Association for Democratic Initiatives—ADI, North Macedonia, 239
Association for Development Policy and Humanitarian Aid, Germany, 120
Association of Family and Corporate Foundations, Colombia, 70
Association of Italian Foundations and Savings Banks, Italy, 171
Associazione di Fondazioni e di Casse di Risparmio SpA—ACRI, Italy, 171
AT&T Foundation, USA, 407
ATD Fourth World International, France, 115
Atlas Network, USA, 407
Australian Academy of Technological Sciences and Engineering, Australia, 11
Australian Communities Foundation, Australia, 12
Australian Conservation Foundation—ACF, Australia, 12
Australian Council for International Development—ACFID, Australia, 12
Australian Foundation for the Peoples of Asia and the Pacific—AFAP, Australia, 10
Australian Institute of International Affairs—AIIA, Australia, 12
Australian Volunteers International—AVI, Australia, 13
Autonómia Alapítvány, Hungary, 152
Autonómia Foundation, Hungary, 152
AVI—Australian Volunteers International, Australia, 13
AVINA Foundation, Panama, 247
AVSI Foundation, Italy, 175
Ayrton Senna Institute, Brazil, 41
Azim Premji Foundation, India, 156
Azman Hashim Foundation, Malaysia, 212
BaBe—Budi aktivna, Budi emancipiran, Croatia, 77
Bagnoud (François-Xavier) Association, Switzerland, 310
Baha'i International Development Organization—BIDO, Israel, 169
Balti Uuringute Instituut, Estonia, 92
Baltic Sea Foundation, Finland, 97
Ban Ki-Moon Foundation for a Better Future, Korea (Republic), 200
Banco do Brasil Foundation, Brazil, 39
Banda (Joyce) Foundation International, Malawi, 210
BANHCAFE Foundation, Honduras, 150
Bank of America Charitable Foundation, USA, 407
Barbados Entrepreneurship Foundation Inc, Barbados, 25
Barbra Streisand Foundation, USA, 408
Barceló Foundation, Spain, 289
Barcelona Centre for International Affairs, Spain, 287
Bariloche Foundation, Argentina, 7
Barka Foundation for Mutual Assistance, Poland, 256

Barzani Charity Foundation—BCF, Iraq, 164
BBVA Foundation, Spain, 289
BCause Foundation, Bulgaria, 42
Be Active, Be Emancipated, Croatia, 77
The Beautiful Foundation, Korea (Republic), 200
Bell (Max) Foundation, Canada, 59
Bello (Sir Ahmadu) Memorial Foundation, Nigeria, 238
Benecke (Otto) Stiftung eV, Germany, 138
Bernheim Foundation, Belgium, 31
Bertelsmann Foundation, Germany, 122
Bertelsmann Stiftung, Germany, 122
Bertoni (Moisés) Foundation, Paraguay, 248
BIAT Youth Foundation, Tunisia, 326
Big Heart Foundation, Chad, 64
Biocon Foundation, India, 157
Bischöfliches Hilfswerk Misereor eV, Germany, 137
Black Sea Trust for Regional Cooperation, USA, 430
Black Sea University Foundation—BSUF, Romania, 263
Blair (Tony) Institute for Global Change, UK, 386
Bleustein-Blanchet (Marcel), Fondation de la Vocation, France, 109
BMCE Bank Foundation, Morocco, 219
BMW Foundation Herbert Quandt, Germany, 122
Böll (Heinrich) Stiftung, Germany, 131
Bond, UK, 335
Bóthar, Ireland, 166
Botswana Institute for Development Policy Analysis—BIDPA, Botswana, 37
BRAC, Bangladesh, 25
BrazilFoundation, Brazil, 39
Brazilian Center for International Relations, Brazil, 39
Brenthurst Foundation, South Africa, 282
Bridge Asia Japan—BAJ, Japan, 187
Brighter Future Myanmar Foundation—BFM, Myanmar, 221
British Gas Energy Trust, UK, 344
British Institute at Ankara, UK, 345
British Institute of International and Comparative Law—BIICL, UK, 345
British Overseas NGOs for Development, UK, 335
Brookings Institution, USA, 410
Brothers of Men, France, 113
Bruegel—Brussels European and Global Economic Laboratory, Belgium, 28
Bruno Kreisky Forum for International Dialogue, Austria, 20
Bruno Kreisky Forum für internationalen Dialog, Austria, 20
Buckland (William) Foundation, Australia, 19
Buddharaksa Foundation, Thailand, 323
Bulgarian Fund for Women, Bulgaria, 43
CABI, UK, 345
CAF America, USA, 393
CAF—Charities Aid Foundation, UK, 336
CAFOD—Catholic Agency for Overseas Development, UK, 345
Cambodia Development Resource Institute—CDRI, Cambodia, 46
Campaign Against Exclusion Foundation, France, 103
Canadian Centre for International Studies and Co-operation, Canada, 51
Canadian Council for International Co-operation—CCIC/Conseil Canadien pour la Coopération Internationale—CCCI, Canada, 48
Canadian Feed The Children—CFTC, Canada, 50
Canadian Urban Institute/Institut Urbain du Canada—CUI/IUC, Canada, 51
Canon Foundation in Europe, Netherlands, 224
Canon Institute for Global Studies—CIGS, Japan, 187
Caribbean Policy Development Centre—CPDC, Barbados, 25
Caritas Canada, Canada, 53
Caritas Internationalis—CI, Vatican City, 486
Carl Zeiss Foundation, Germany, 123
Carl-Zeiss-Stiftung, Germany, 123
Carlos Slim Foundation, Mexico, 215
CARMABI Foundation, Curaçao, 77
Carnegie Corporation of New York, USA, 411
Carnegie Endowment for International Peace, USA, 411
Carnegie UK Trust, UK, 346
Carpathian Foundation, Hungary, 153
Carrefour International, Canada, 53
CASE—Centrum Analiz Społeczno-Ekonomicznych, Poland, 255
Casey (Annie E.) Foundation, USA, 404
Catalyste+, Canada, 51
Caterpillar Foundation, USA, 412

539

Economic affairs

Catholic Agency for Overseas Development—CAFOD, UK, 345
Catholic Agency for World Development—Trócaire, Ireland, 168
Caucasus Research Resource Center Armenia Foundation—CRRC, Armenia, 9
Caucus of Development NGO Networks—CODE-NGO, Philippines, 250
CBM-International, Germany, 123
CCKF—Chiang Ching-kuo Foundation for International Scholarly Exchange, Taiwan, 321
CECI—Canadian Centre for International Studies and Co-operation/Centre d'Etudes et de Coopération Internationale, Canada, 51
CEDIAS-Musée Social—Centre d'Etudes, de Documentation, d'Information et d'Action Sociales, France, 101
CENSIS—Fondazione Centro Studi Investimenti Sociali, Italy, 172
Center for China & Globalization—CCG, China (People's Republic), 67
Center for Economic & Social Development—CESD, Azerbaijan, 23
Center for Social and Economic Research, Poland, 255
Centras—Assistance Centre for NGOs, Romania, 263
Centras—Centrul de Asistenta pentru Organizatii Neguvernamentale, Romania, 263
Centre for Democracy and Human Rights—CEDEM, Montenegro, 219
Centre for Dialogue, Research and Cooperation—CDRC, Ethiopia, 94
Centre for Euro-Atlantic Integration and Democracy—CEID, Hungary, 153
Centre for International Governance Innovation—CIGI/Centre pour l'Innovation dans la Gouvernance Internationale, Canada, 51
Centre for International Studies, Italy, 172
Centre Ivoirien de Recherches Economiques et Sociales—CIRES, Côte d'Ivoire, 75
Centre for Social Studies, Documentation, Information and Action, France, 101
Centre for Strategic and International Studies—CSIS, Indonesia, 162
Centro Brasileiro de Relações Internacionais—CEBRI, Brazil, 39
Centro de Estudios Públicos—CEP, Chile, 64
Centro Studi Internazionali—CSI, Italy, 172
The Century Foundation—TCF, USA, 413
Cera, Belgium, 28
Cercle de Coopération des ONGD du Luxembourg, Luxembourg, 209
CESO/SACO—Canadian Executive Service Organization/Service d'Assistance Canadienne aux Organismes, Canada, 51
Charities Advisory Trust, UK, 336
Charities Aid Foundation of America—CAF America, USA, 393
Charities Aid Foundation—CAF, UK, 336
Charles Koch Foundation, USA, 413
Charles Léopold Mayer Foundation for the Progress of Humankind, Switzerland, 308
Charles and Lynn Schusterman Family Philanthropies, USA, 413
Charles Stewart Mott Foundation—CSMF, USA, 414
Chatham House, UK, 378
Cheshire (Leonard) Foundation, UK, 364
Chiang Ching-kuo Foundation for International Scholarly Exchange—CCKF, Taiwan, 321
The Chicago Community Trust, USA, 414
ChildFund International, USA, 414
Children International—CI, USA, 414
The Children's Investment Fund Foundation, UK, 347
Chile Foundation, Chile, 65
China Foundation for Poverty Alleviation—CFPA, China (People's Republic), 67
China Siyuan Foundation for Poverty Alleviation, China (People's Republic), 67
Chr. Michelsen Institute for Science and Intellectual Freedom—CMI, Norway, 241
Christian Aid, UK, 348
The Churchill Fellowship, UK, 348
Churchill (Winston) Memorial Trust of New Zealand, New Zealand, 236
CIDOB Foundation—Barcelona Centre for International Affairs, Spain, 287
CIDSE—Together for Global Justice, Belgium, 29
Citi Foundation, USA, 415
Citizens Foundation, Iceland, 154
Civic Democratic Initiative Support Foundation—CDF, Yemen, 489
Civitas Foundation for Civil Society, Romania, 263

Civitates, Belgium, 27
CLADEM—Comité de América Latina y el Caribe para la Defensa de los Derechos de la Mujer, Peru, 249
Claiborne (Liz) & Art Ortenberg Foundation, USA, 448
Cleveland Foundation, USA, 416
Clinton Foundation, USA, 416
CMI—Chr. Michelsen Institute for Science and Intellectual Freedom, Norway, 241
Coady Institute, Canada, 52
The Coca-Cola Foundation, Inc, USA, 417
CODESPA Foundation, Spain, 290
Collier Charitable Fund, Australia, 13
Comité de América Latina y el Caribe para la Defensa de los Derechos de la Mujer—CLADEM, Peru, 249
Commonwealth Foundation, UK, 348
Community Chest of Korea—Fruit of Love, Korea (Republic), 200
Community Development Foundation, Mozambique, 221
Community Foundation for the Western Region of Zimbabwe—CFWRZ, Zimbabwe, 490
Concern India Foundation, India, 157
Concern Worldwide, Ireland, 166
CONCORD—European NGO Confederation for Relief and Development, Belgium, 26
The Confederation of Service Charities—Cobseo, UK, 349
Consejo Argentino para las Relaciones Internacionales—CARI, Argentina, 6
Conservation International Foundation, USA, 417
Consuelo Zobel Alger Foundation, USA, 417
Cooperation Canada/Coopération Canada, Canada, 48
Co-operative Development Foundation of Canada—CDF, Canada, 52
Cooperazione Internazionale—COOPI, Italy, 173
Coordinadora de ONGD España, Spain, 285
Coordination SUD, France, 99
Copperbelt Development Foundation, Zambia, 490
Corona Foundation, Colombia, 71
Corra Foundation, UK, 349
Corus International, USA, 418
Counterpart International, USA, 418
The Craig and Susan McCaw Foundation, USA, 418
CRDF Global, USA, 419
Croatian Platform for International Citizen Solidarity, Croatia, 76
CROSOL—Platforma za medunarodnu gradansku solidarnost Hrvatske, Croatia, 76
Crossroads International/Carrefour International, Canada, 53
Crown Family Philanthropies, USA, 419
Cuso International, Canada, 53
Cyril Ramaphosa Foundation, South Africa, 279
Dag Hammarskjöld Foundation, Sweden, 303
Dalio Foundation, USA, 419
Danielle Mitterrand Foundation, France, 112
Danish Institute for Human Rights, Denmark, 84
Davis (Lady) Fellowship Trust, Israel, 170
Daw Khin Kyi Foundation, Myanmar, 221
Debenedetti (Rodolfo), Fondazione, Italy, 179
Debts to Opportunities Foundation, Netherlands, 231
Dell (Michael & Susan) Foundation, USA, 453
del Pino (Rafael), Fundación, Spain, 294
DemNet—Demokratikus Jogok Fejlesztéséért Alapítvány, Hungary, 153
DemNet—Foundation for the Development of Democratic Rights, Hungary, 153
Democracy and Development Foundation, Chile, 65
Democracy Fund, USA, 458
Deutsche Bank Americas Foundation, USA, 420
Deutsche Bundesstiftung Umwelt—DBU, Germany, 124
Deutsche Gesellschaft für Auswärtige Politik—DGAP, Germany, 124
Deutsche Sparkassenstiftung für Internationale Zusammenarbeit, Germany, 125
Deutsches Institut für internationale Politik und Sicherheit, Germany, 141
Development Cooperation Roundtable, Estonia, 92
Development Foundation, Guatemala, 148
Development Foundation of Turkey, Türkiye, 330
Development Gateway—DG, USA, 420
Development NGO Coordinator Spain, Spain, 285
Development and Peace—Caritas Canada, Canada, 53
Développement et Paix—Caritas Canada, Canada, 53
Dewji (Mo) Foundation, Tanzania, 323
DHL UK Foundation, UK, 350

INDEX OF MAIN ACTIVITIES

Digicel Foundation Haiti, Haiti, 149
Digicel Foundation Jamaica, Jamaica, 184
Digicel Trinidad and Tobago Foundation, Trinidad and Tobago, 326
Dioraphte Foundation, Netherlands, 229
Ditchley Foundation, UK, 351
Dominican Development Foundation, Dominican Republic, 87
Donner (William H.) Foundation, Inc, USA, 481
Dr Guillermo Manuel Ungo Foundation, El Salvador, 91
Dr Scholl Foundation, USA, 421
Dräger Foundation, Germany, 126
Dräger-Stiftung, Germany, 126
DRFN—Desert Research Foundation of Namibia, Namibia, 222
DSW—Deutsche Stiftung Weltbevölkerung, Germany, 126
DTGO Group of Foundations, Thailand, 323
Dutch-Bangla Bank Foundation, Bangladesh, 25
Earth Island Institute—EII, USA, 422
Earthworm Foundation, Switzerland, 307
East Asia Institute—EAI, Korea (Republic), 201
East-West Center—EWC, USA, 422
Eastern Europe Studies Centre—EESC, Lithuania, 209
eBay Foundation, USA, 422
Eberhard Schöck Foundation, Germany, 127
Eberhard-Schöck-Stiftung, Germany, 127
Ebert (Friedrich) Stiftung, Germany, 129
EcoCiencia—Fundación Ecuatoriana de Estudios Ecologicos, Ecuador, 88
Economic Development Foundation, Türkiye, 328
Economic Foundation, Poland, 255
Economic and Social Research Foundation—ESRF, Tanzania, 322
Ecuadorean Cooperation for Development Fund, Ecuador, 88
Ecuadorean Foundation of Ecological Studies, Ecuador, 88
Ecuadorean Social Group Fund Populorum Progressio, Ecuador, 89
EDF Group Foundation, France, 107
Edoardo Garrone Foundation, Italy, 177
EDP Foundation, Portugal, 260
The Education for Development Foundation—EDF, Thailand, 324
EFQM—European Foundation for Quality Management, Belgium, 30
Egmont Fonden, Denmark, 83
Egmont Foundation, Denmark, 83
EGMONT—Institut Royal des Relations Internationales, Belgium, 29
Einaudi (Luigi), Fondazione, Italy, 178
The Elders Foundation, UK, 352
ELIAMEP—Hellenic Foundation for European and Foreign Policy, Greece, 146
Ellerman (John) Foundation, UK, 361
The ELMA Group of Foundations, USA, 423
Elrha, UK, 352
Elumelu (Tony) Foundation, Nigeria, 238
Emirates Foundation, United Arab Emirates, 334
Empresas Polar Foundation, Venezuela, 487
endPoverty.org, USA, 424
Energies for the World Foundation, France, 105
Enrico Mattei Eni Foundation, Italy, 174
Ente Cassa di Risparmio di Firenze, Italy, 173
Entraide Protestante Suisse, Switzerland, 311
Entraide Universitaire Mondiale du Canada, Canada, 63
Environment and Natural Resources Foundation, Argentina, 7
Environmental Foundation of Jamaica, Jamaica, 184
Equality Fund/Fonds Égalité, Canada, 54
Equity Group Foundation—EGF, Kenya, 198
ERSTE Foundation, Austria, 21
ERSTE Stiftung—Die ERSTE Österreichische Spar-Casse Privatstiftung, Austria, 21
Eskom Development Foundation, South Africa, 279
ETC Group—Action Group on Erosion, Technology and Concentration, Canada, 54
Eugenio Mendoza Foundation, Venezuela, 487
Eurasia Foundation—EF, USA, 424
Eurasia Partnership Foundation-Armenia—EPF-Armenia, Armenia, 9
Eureka Foundation, Bulgaria, 43
EURODAD—European Network on Debt and Development, Belgium, 29
Europe Foundation—EPF, Georgia, 118
European Anti-Poverty Network—EAPN, Belgium, 29
European Center for Constitutional and Human Rights—ECCHR, Germany, 128
European Center for Peace and Development—ECPD, Serbia, 271

INDEX OF MAIN ACTIVITIES

Economic affairs

European Centre for Social Welfare Policy and Research, Austria, 21
European Foundation for the Improvement of Living and Working Conditions—Eurofound, Ireland, 166
European Foundation for Management Development—EFMD, Belgium, 30
European Foundation for Quality Management—EFQM, Belgium, 30
European Foundation for the Sustainable Development of the Regions, Switzerland, 308
European Mediterranean Institute, Spain, 296
European Network on Debt and Development—EURODAD, Belgium, 29
European NGO Confederation for Relief and Development—CONCORD, Belgium, 26
Evrika Foundation, Bulgaria, 43
Evropis Pondis, Georgia, 118
Ewing Marion Kauffman Foundation, USA, 425
ExxonMobil Foundation, USA, 425
F20, Germany, 119
FAFIDESS—Fundación de Asesoría Financiera a Instituciones de Desarrollo y Servicio Social, Guatemala, 148
Fairtrade Nederland, Netherlands, 230
Farm Africa, UK, 354
FARN—Fundación Ambiente y Recursos Naturales, Argentina, 7
FATE Foundation, Nigeria, 237
Fatoumatta Bah-Barrow Foundation—FaBB, Gambia, 117
FDC—Fundação para o Desenvolvimento da Comunidade, Mozambique, 221
Federation of Non-Governmental Organizations for Development in Romania, Romania, 263
Fedesarrollo—Fundación para la Educación Superior y el Desarrollo, Colombia, 71
FEDRE—European Foundation for the Sustainable Development of the Regions, Switzerland, 308
Feed the Children, USA, 425
Feed the Minds, UK, 354
FEEM—Fondazione ENI Enrico Mattei, Italy, 174
Feltrinelli (Giangiacomo), Fondazione, Italy, Italy, 177
FHI 360, USA, 425
FINCA International, USA, 425
Finnish Development Organizations, Finland, 95
First Nations Development Institute, USA, 426
Florence Savings Bank Foundation, Italy, 173
Follereau Foundation Luxembourg, Luxembourg, 209
FOND—Federatia Organizatiilor Neguvernamentale pentru Dezvoltare din Romania, Romania, 263
Fondacioni Shqiptar për të Drejtat e Personave me Aftësi të Kufizuar—FSHDPAK, Albania, 4
FONDAD—Forum on Debt and Development, Netherlands, 225
Fondation Abbé Pierre, France, 108
Fondation Africaine pour les Technologies Agricoles, Kenya, 198
Fondation Agir Contre l'Exclusion—FACE, France, 103
Fondation pour l'Agriculture et la Ruralité dans le Monde—Fondation FARM, France, 106
Fondation Bernheim, Belgium, 31
Fondation BIAT pour la Jeunesse, Tunisia, 326
Fondation BMCE Bank, Morocco, 219
Fondation Charles Léopold Mayer pour le Progrès de l'Homme—FPH, Switzerland, 308
Fondation Digicel Haïti, Haiti, 149
Fondation pour l'Economie et le Développement Durable des Régions d'Europe—FEDRE, Switzerland, 308
Fondation Energies pour le Monde—Fondem, France, 105
Fondation d'Entreprise Crédit Agricole Réunion Mayotte, Réunion, 262
Fondation d'Entreprise VINCI pour la Cité, France, 106
Fondation Espace Afrique, Switzerland, 308
Fondation FARM—Fondation pour l'Agriculture et la Ruralité dans le Monde, France, 106
Fondation Follereau Luxembourg—FFL, Luxembourg, 209
Fondation de France, France, 99
Fondation France Chine—FFC, France, 106
Fondation France-Israël, France, 106
Fondation Grand Cœur—FGC, Chad, 64
Fondation Groupe EDF, France, 107
Fondation Hans Wilsdorf, Switzerland, 309
Fondation Hassan II pour les Marocains Résidant à l'Etranger, Morocco, 220
Fondation Internationale Tierno et Mariam—FITIMA, Burkina Faso, 44
Fondation Jasmin pour la Recherche et la Communication, Tunisia, 326

Fondation Jean Monnet pour l'Europe, Switzerland, 309
Fondation Jean-Paul II pour le Sahel, Burkina Faso, 44
Fondation Joseph Ichame Kamach, Central African Republic, 63
Fondation pour le Logement des Défavorisés, France, 108
Fondation MACIF, France, 108
Fondation MAIF pour la Recherche, France, 108
Fondation Maison des Sciences de l'Homme—FMSH, France, 108
Fondation Marcel Bleustein-Blanchet de la Vocation, France, 109
Fondation Mesmin Kabath—FOMEKA, Congo (Republic), 73
Fondation Mohammed V pour la Solidarité, Morocco, 220
Fondation MTN Côte d'Ivoire, Côte d'Ivoire, 76
Fondation Mutuelles Congolaises d'Epargne et de Crédit—MUCODEC, Congo (Republic), 73
Fondation Nationale pour l'Enseignement de la Gestion des Entreprises, France, 109
Fondation Nationale des Sciences Politiques—SciencesPo, France, 110
Fondation Nicolas Hulot pour la Nature et l'Homme—FNH, France, 110
Fondation Noura, Mauritania, 214
Fondation Orange Mali, Mali, 213
Fondation Orient-Occident—FOO, Morocco, 220
Fondation Perspectives d'Avenir, Congo (Republic), 73
Fondation Rambourg, Tunisia, 326
Fondation pour la Recherche Stratégique, France, 111
Fondation pour le Renforcement des Capacités en Afrique, Zimbabwe, 490
Fondation Rinaldi, Haiti, 149
Fondation Rio Tinto, Guinea, 149
Fondation Robert Schuman, France, 111
Fondation TotalEnergies, France, 112
Fondation Tunisie pour le Développement, Tunisia, 326
Fondazione AVSI, Italy, 175
Fondazione Centesimus Annus—Pro Pontifice, Vatican City, 486
Fondazione Centro Studi Investimenti Sociali—CENSIS, Italy, 172
Fondazione Edoardo Garrone, Italy, 177
Fondazione Giangiacomo Feltrinelli, Italy, 177
Fondazione Giovanni Lorenzini, Italy, 177
Fondazione Giulio Pastore—FGP, Italy, 178
Fondazione Luigi Einaudi, Italy, 178
Fondazione Populorum Progressio, Vatican City, 486
Fondazione Rodolfo Debenedetti—FRDB, Italy, 179
Fondazione Social Venture-Giordano Dell'Amore, Italy, 180
Fondazione Terzo Pilastro – Internazionale, Italy, 180
Fondazione Unipolis, Italy, 181
Fondo Ecuatoriano de Cooperación para el Desarrollo—FECD, Ecuador, 88
Fonds atvērtai sabiedrībai DOTS, Latvia, 204
Fonds Égalité, Canada, 54
Ford Foundation, USA, 427
Foreign Policy and United Nations Association of Austria—UNA-AUSTRIA, Austria, 22
The Forest Trust, Switzerland, 307
Forum on Debt and Development—FONDAD, Netherlands, 225
Forum LSM Internasional untuk Pembangunan Indonesia, Indonesia, 161
Foundation for Analysis and Social Studies, Spain, 288
Foundation of Banks and Savings Banks of CECA, Spain, 289
Foundation for Caribbean Research and Management of Biodiversity, Curaçao, 77
Foundation Centre for the Study of Social Investment, Italy, 172
Foundation for Defense of Democracies—FDD, USA, 427
Foundation for the Financial Assessment of Social Service and Development Institutions, Guatemala, 148
Foundation for Higher Education and Development, Colombia, 71
Foundation for Housing the Disadvantaged, France, 108
Foundation for International Community Assistance, USA, 425
Foundation for Investment and Development of Exports—FIDE, Honduras, 150
Foundation for Latin American Economic Research, Argentina, 7

Foundation for an Open Society DOTS, Latvia, 204
Foundation for the Qualification and Consultancy in Microfinance, El Salvador, 92
Foundation for the Rights of Future Generations, Germany, 141
Foundation Rodolfo Debenedetti, Italy, 179
Foundation for Rural & Regional Renewal—FRRR, Australia, 14
Foundation for Security and Development in Africa—FOSDA, Ghana, 143
Foundation for Social Housing, Venezuela, 488
Foundation of Spanish Commercial Agents, Spain, 287
Foundation for Strategic Research, France, 111
Foundation for the Support of Women's Work, Türkiye, 329
Foundation for the Sustainable Development of Small and Medium-sized Enterprises—FUNDES International, Costa Rica, 74
Foundation for Women, Thailand, 324
Foundation for World Agriculture and Rural Life, France, 106
The Foundation for Young Australians—FYA, Australia, 14
Foundations Platform—F20, Germany, 119
Foundations' Post-Doc Pool, Finland, 95
France China Foundation, France, 106
France-Israel Foundation, France, 106
France-Libertés Fondation Danielle Mitterrand, France, 112
France Nature Environnement, France, 112
Franciscans International, Switzerland, 310
Frank Knox Memorial Fellowships, USA, 428
Fraser Institute, Canada, 55
Fraunhofer-Gesellschaft, Germany, 129
Fraunhofer Society, Germany, 129
FREE Network—Forum for Research on Eastern Europe and Emerging Economies, Sweden, 299
Free Russia Foundation, USA, 428
Freedom Together Foundation, USA, 428
French-American Foundation, USA, 429
French Institute of International Relations, France, 113
French National Foundation for Management Education, France, 109
Frères des Hommes—FDH, France, 113
Friedrich-Ebert-Stiftung eV, Germany, 129
Friedrich Naumann Foundation for Freedom, Germany, 130
Friedrich-Naumann-Stiftung für die Freiheit, Germany, 130
Friends of the Earth International—FOEI, Netherlands, 225
Friends-International, Cambodia, 46
Fund and Endowment Management Foundation, Norway, 240
Fundação Assistência Médica International—AMI, Portugal, 258
Fundação Banco do Brasil, Brazil, 39
Fundação EDP, Portugal, 260
Fundação Getulio Vargas—FGV, Brazil, 40
Fundação José Maria Neves para a Governança, Cabo Verde, 46
Fundació CIDOB, Spain, 287
Fundación de los Agentes Comerciales de España, Spain, 287
Fundación Ambiente y Recursos Naturales—FARN, Argentina, 7
Fundación para el Análisis y los Estudios Sociales—FAES, Spain, 288
Fundación Astur, Uruguay, 485
Fundación AVINA, Panama, 247
Fundación Banco Bilbao Vizcaya Argentaria—Fundación BBVA, Spain, 289
Fundación BANHCAFE—FUNBANHCAFE, Honduras, 150
Fundación Barceló, Spain, 289
Fundación Bariloche, Argentina, 7
Fundación BBVA, Spain, 289
Fundación de las Cajas de Ahorros—FUNCAS, Spain, 289
Fundación Capital, Colombia, 70
Fundación Carlos Slim, Mexico, 215
Fundación Chile—FCH, Chile, 65
Fundación Circulo de Montevideo, Uruguay, 485
Fundación CODESPA, Spain, 290
Fundación Comunitaria de Puerto Rico—FCPR, Puerto Rico, 261
Fundación Corona, Colombia, 71
Fundación Democracia y Desarrollo, Chile, 65
Fundación Dominicana de Desarrollo—FDD, Dominican Republic, 87
Fundación Dr Guillermo Manuel Ungo—FUNDAUNGO, El Salvador, 91
Fundación para la Educación Superior y el Desarrollo—Fedesarrollo, Colombia, 71

Economic affairs

Fundación Empresa-Universidad de Zaragoza, Spain, 290
Fundación Empresas Polar, Venezuela, 487
Fundación Espacio Cívico, Panama, 247
Fundación Eugenio Mendoza—FEM, Venezuela, 487
Fundación Felipe González, Spain, 290
Fundación Futuro Latinoamericano, Ecuador, 88
Fundación Génesis Empresarial, Guatemala, 148
Fundación Global Democracia y Desarrollo—FUNGLODE, Dominican Republic, 87
Fundación para la Inversión y Desarrollo de Exportaciones—FIDE, Honduras, 150
Fundación de Investigaciones Económicas Latinoamericanas—FIEL, Argentina, 7
Fundación Jubileo, Bolivia, 36
Fundación Mediterránea—IERAL, Argentina, 7
Fundación Miguel Alemán AC, Mexico, 215
Fundación Moisés Bertoni—FMB, Paraguay, 248
Fundación Montemadrid, Spain, 292
Fundación Mujer, Costa Rica, 74
Fundación Mujeres en Igualdad—MEI, Argentina, 8
Fundación Nacional para el Desarrollo, El Salvador, 91
Fundación Nacional para el Desarrollo de Honduras—FUNADEH, Honduras, 150
Fundación Nobis, Ecuador, 88
Fundación Oxfam Intermón, Spain, 293
Fundación Paideia Galiza, Spain, 293
Fundación Paraguaya de Cooperación y Desarrollo, Paraguay, 248
Fundación para la Paz y la Democracia—FUNPADEM, Costa Rica, 74
Fundación Princesa de Asturias, Spain, 294
Fundación Rafael del Pino, Spain, 294
Fundación Real Instituto Elcano, Spain, 294
Fundación Repsol, Spain, 295
Fundación Semah-Valencia, Panama, 247
Fundación SES—Sustentabilidad, Educación, Solidaridad, Argentina, 8
Fundación Solidaridad, Dominican Republic, 87
Fundación Telmex Telcel, Mexico, 216
Fundación Tigo, Guatemala, 148
Fundación UNIR Bolivia, Bolivia, 36
Fundación Universidad-Empresa—UE, Spain, 295
Fundación UPM, Uruguay, 485
Fundación de la Vivienda Popular, Venezuela, 488
Fundacja Gospodarcza, Poland, 255
Fundacja Pomocy Wzajemnej Barka, Poland, 256
Fundacja Wspomagania Wsi, Poland, 257
FUNDAMICRO—Fundación de Capacitación y Asesoría en Microfinanzas, El Salvador, 92
FUNDAP—Fundación para el Desarrollo, Guatemala, 148
Fundația Civitas pentru Societatea Civilă, Romania, 263
Fundația Universitară a Mării Negre—FUMN, Romania, 263
FUNDAUNGO—Fundación Dr Guillermo Manuel Ungo, El Salvador, 91
FUNDES—Fundación para el Desarrollo Sostenible de la Pequeña y Mediana Empresa, Costa Rica, 74
Future Foundation, Liechtenstein, 208
FXB International—Association François-Xavier Bagnoud, Switzerland, 310
G. Unger Vetlesen Foundation, USA, 429
The Gaia Foundation, UK, 355
Gapminder, Sweden, 300
Garfield Weston Foundation, UK, 355
Garrone (Edoardo), Fondazione, Italy, 177
Gates (Bill & Melinda) Foundation, USA, 429
Gates Foundation, USA, 429
The Gatsby Charitable Foundation, UK, 355
Gebert Rüf Stiftung, Switzerland, 311
General Service Foundation—GSF, USA, 430
Génesis Empresarial Foundation, Guatemala, 148
Georgian Foundation for Strategic and International Studies (Rondeli Foundation)—GFSIS, Georgia, 118
German Catholic Bishops' Organization for Development Co-operation, Germany, 137
German Council on Foreign Relations, Germany, 124
German Federal Foundation for the Environment, Germany, 124
German Foundation for World Population, Germany, 126
German Institute of Development and Sustainability—IDOS, Germany, 130
German Institute for Global and Area Studies—GIGA, Germany, 130
German Marshall Fund of the United States—GMF, USA, 430
German Savings Banks Foundation for International Co-operation, Germany, 125

Getulio Vargas Foundation, Brazil, 40
Ghazanfar Foundation, Afghanistan, 4
Giangiacomo Feltrinelli Foundation, Italy, 177
Gift of the Givers Foundation, South Africa, 280
Giordano Dell'Amore Social Venture Foundation, Italy, 180
Giovanni Lorenzini Foundation, Italy, 177
Giulio Pastore Foundation, Italy, 178
To Give, Israel, 170
Give2Asia, USA, 394
GiveWell—The Clear Fund, USA, 430
Global Communities, USA, 431
Global Democracy and Development Foundation, Dominican Republic, 87
Global Fund for Women—GFW, USA, 431
Global Greengrants Fund, USA, 431
Global Impact, USA, 395
Global Innovation Fund, UK, 356
Gobabeb Namib Research Institute, Namibia, 222
Goldman Sachs Foundation, USA, 432
Good Neighbors International, Korea (Republic), 201
Good Things Foundation, UK, 356
Google.org—Google Foundation, USA, 432
Gorbachev Foundation, Russian Federation, 266
Gordon (Walter and Duncan) Charitable Foundation, Canada, 62
Graça Machel Trust, South Africa, 280
Graduate Institute of International Studies and Development Studies, Switzerland, 311
Grameen Foundation—GF, USA, 433
Grant (William T.) Foundation, USA, 481
Great Britain Sasakawa Foundation, UK, 356
Greater Kansas City Community Foundation, USA, 433
Grupo Social Fondo Ecuatoriano Populorum Progressio, Ecuador, 89
Guggenheim (Harry Frank) Foundation, USA, 434
Guggenheim (John Simon) Memorial Foundation, USA, 444
Habitat for Humanity International, USA, 433
Hagar NZ, New Zealand, 233
Hammarskjölds (Dag) Minnesfond, Stiftelsen, Sweden, 303
Hanaholmen—Swedish-Finnish Cultural Centre, Finland, 95
HAND—Hungarian Association of NGOs for Development and Humanitarian Aid, Hungary, 152
Haniel Foundation, Germany, 131
Haniel-Stiftung, Germany, 131
Hans Wilsdorf Foundation, Switzerland, 309
Hariri Foundation for Sustainable Human Development, Lebanon, 205
Harp Helú Foundations, Mexico, 216
The Harry Frank Guggenheim Foundation—HFG, USA, 434
Harry and Jeanette Weinberg Foundation, Inc, USA, 434
Hassan II Foundation for Moroccans Living Abroad, Morocco, 220
Havelaar (Max) Foundation, Netherlands, 230
Hawaii Resilience Fund, USA, 458
Health Action International—HAI, Netherlands, 225
Hecht (Lotte and John) Memorial Foundation, Canada, 58
Heifer Foundation, USA, 435
Heinrich Böll Foundation, Germany, 131
Heinrich-Böll-Stiftung, Germany, 131
HEKS—Hilfswerk der Evangelischen Kirchen Schweiz, Switzerland, 311
Hellenic Foundation for European and Foreign Policy—ELIAMEP, Greece, 146
Helmholtz Association, Germany, 132
Helmholtz-Gemeinschaft, Germany, 132
Helmich (Janson Johan og Marcia) Legat, Norway, 242
Helmsley (Leona M. and Harry B.) Charitable Trust, USA, 447
Helvetas Swiss Intercooperation, Switzerland, 311
HER Fund, Hong Kong, 151
Heren Philanthropic Foundation, China (People's Republic), 68
The Heritage Foundation, USA, 436
Heungkong Charitable Foundation, China (People's Republic), 68
Hewlett (William and Flora) Foundation, USA, 481
HIAS—Hebrew Immigrant Aid Society, USA, 436
Higherlife Foundation, Zimbabwe, 491
Hilti Foundation, Liechtenstein, 208
Himalaya Research and Development Foundation—Himalaya Foundation, Taiwan, 321
Hinduja Foundation, India, 157

INDEX OF MAIN ACTIVITIES

History Foundation of Turkey, Türkiye, 329
HOPE International Development Agency, Canada, 56
Horizons of Friendship, Canada, 56
Horn Economic and Social Policy Institute—HESPI, Ethiopia, 94
House of the Human Sciences Foundation, France, 108
Howard Karagheusian Commemorative Corporation—HKCC, USA, 437
Hudson Institute, USA, 437
Hulot (Nicolas), Fondation, France, 110
Human Rights Watch—HRW, USA, 437
Humanity & Inclusion, France, 113
The Hunter Foundation—THF, UK, 359
IAI—Istituto Affari Internazionali, Italy, 182
IBM International Foundation, USA, 438
IBON Foundation, Philippines, 252
Ichikowitz Family Foundation—IFF, South Africa, 280
ICRC—International Red Cross and Red Crescent Movement, Switzerland, 312
The Ideas Institute, Kenya, 199
IDLO—International Development Law Organization, Italy, 181
IDRF—International Development and Relief Foundation, Canada, 56
IIED—International Institute for Environment and Development, UK, 360
IISD—International Institute for Sustainable Development, Canada, 57
IKEA Foundation, Netherlands, 229
İktisadi Kalkınma Vakfı, Türkiye, 328
Îles de Paix, Belgium, 32
IMADR—The International Movement against All Forms of Discrimination and Racism, Japan, 188
Imbuto Foundation, Rwanda, 268
IMPACT Transformer la Gestion des Ressources Naturelles, Canada, 56
IMPACT Transforming Natural Resource Management, Canada, 56
Improving Economies for Stronger Communities—IESC, USA, 438
India Partners, USA, 438
Indian Council of Social Science Research—ICSSR, India, 157
Indonesia Biodiversity Foundation, Indonesia, 162
Innovators and Entrepreneurs Foundation/Fondation d'Innovateurs et d'Entrepreneurs—IEF/FIE, Canada, 57
Institut Europeu de la Mediterrània—IEMed, Spain, 296
Institut FMES—Institut Méditerranéen d'Etudes Stratégiques, France, 113
Institut Français des Relations Internationales—IFRI, France, 113
Institut de Hautes Études Internationales et du Développement—IHEID, Switzerland, 311
Institut for Menneskerettigheder, Denmark, 84
Institut de Recherche Empirique en Économie Politique—IREEP, Benin, 35
Institut Royal des Relations Internationales—EGMONT, Belgium, 33
Institut für Weltwirtschaft—IfW Kiel, Germany, 132
Institute of Baltic Studies, Estonia, 92
Institute of Developing Economies-Japan External Trade Organization—IDE-JETRO, Japan, 188
Institute for the Development of Social Investment, Brazil, 38
Institute of Economic Affairs—IEA, UK, 359
Institute for Empirical Research in Political Economy—IERPE, Benin, 35
The Institute of Energy Economics, Japan—IEEJ, Japan, 188
Institute for European Environmental Policy—IEEP, Belgium, 33
Institute of International Affairs, Italy, 182
Institute of International Law, Argentina, 6
Institute for International Security and Strategic Affairs—ISIAE, Argentina, 6
Institute for Iran-Eurasia Studies—IRAS, Iran, 163
Institute for Latin American and Caribbean Integration, Argentina, 8
Institute for Palestine Studies—IPS, Lebanon, 206
Institute for Private Enterprise and Democracy—IPED, Poland, 257
Institute for Security Studies—ISS, South Africa, 280
Institute of Social Studies—ISS, Netherlands, 226
Institute for Sustainable Communities—ISC, USA, 439

INDEX OF MAIN ACTIVITIES

Instituti Kosovar për Kërkime dhe Zhvillim të Politikave, Kosovo, 203
Instituto Ayrton Senna, Brazil, 41
Instituto para o Desenvolvimento do Investimento Social—IDIS, Brazil, 38
Instituto para la Integración de América Latina y el Caribe—BID-INTAL, Argentina, 8
Instytut Badań nad Demokracją i Przedsiębiorstwem Prywatnym, Poland, 257
Inter-American Foundation—IAF, USA, 439
Inter Pares, Canada, 57
InterAction, USA, 395
Interchurch Aid—HIA Hungary, Hungary, 153
Internationaal Instituut voor Sociale Geschiedenis—IISG, Netherlands, 226
International Alert—Alert, UK, 360
International Center for Research on Women—ICRW, USA, 439
International Civil Society Centre, Germany, 119
International Confederation Catholic Organizations Charitable Social Action, Vatican City, 486
International Co-operation, Italy, 173
International Development Center of Japan, Japan, 189
International Development Law Organization—IDLO, Italy, 181
International Development and Relief Foundation—IDRF, Canada, 56
International Education Research Foundation, Inc—IERF, USA, 440
International Forum Bosnia, Bosnia and Herzegovina, 37
International Foundation for Socio-economic and Political Studies, Russian Federation, 266
International Institute for Environment and Development—IIED, UK, 360
International Institute of Rural Reconstruction—IIRR, Philippines, 252
International Institute of Social History—IISH, Netherlands, 226
International Institute of Social Studies, Netherlands, 226
The International Institute for Strategic Studies—IISS, UK, 360
International Institute for Sustainable Development—IISD, Canada, 57
International Institute of Tropical Agriculture—IITA, Nigeria, 237
International Medical Assistance Foundation, Portugal, 258
International NGO Forum on Indonesian Development—INFID, Indonesia, 161
International Orthodox Christian Charities—IOCC, USA, 441
International Red Cross and Red Crescent Movement—ICRC, Switzerland, 267
International Rescue Committee—IRC, USA, 441
International Research Foundation, Oman, 244
International Solidarity Foundation, Finland, 96
International Water Management Institute—IWMI, Sri Lanka, 297
International Youth Foundation—IYF, USA, 442
Internationalt Uddannelsescenter, Denmark, 84
IOCC—International Orthodox Christian Charities, USA, 441
iPartner India, India, 155
Iraqi Institute for Economic Reform, Iraq, 164
IRC—International Rescue Committee, USA, 441
Irvine (James) Foundation, USA, 443
Isabel Allende Foundation, USA, 442
Islamic Relief Worldwide, UK, 360
Islands of Peace, Belgium, 32
ISPI—Istituto per gli Studi di Politica Internazionale, Italy, 183
IsraAID, Israel, 169
The Israel Democracy Institute—IDI, Israel, 170
Istituto Affari Internazionali—IAI, Italy, 182
Istituto per gli Studi di Politica Internazionale—ISPI, Italy, 183
Italian Institute for International Political Studies, Italy, 183
IUC International Education Center—IUC-Europe, Denmark, 84
Ivey Foundation, Canada, 57
Ivorian Economic and Social Research Centre, Côte d'Ivoire, 75
J. R. McKenzie Trust, New Zealand, 233
The J.W. McConnell Family Foundation, Canada, 57
Jack Ma Foundation—JMF, China (People's Republic), 68
Jahnsson (Yrjö) Foundation, Finland, 98
J'ai Rêvé Foundation, Central African Republic, 63
The James Irvine Foundation, USA, 443
James Michel Foundation, Seychelles, 272
James S. McDonnell Foundation, USA, 443

Janson Johan Helmich and Marcia Jansons Endowment, Norway, 242
Janson Johan Helmich og Marcia Jansons Legat, Norway, 242
Japan Economic Research Institute Inc—JERI, Japan, 189
Japan Foundation Center for Economic Research—JCER, Japan, 189
Japanese-German Centre Berlin, Germany, 133
Japanisch-Deutsches Zentrum Berlin, Germany, 133
Jasmine Foundation for Research and Communication, Tunisia, 326
JCA Charitable Foundation, UK, 361
Jean Monnet Foundation for Europe, Switzerland, 309
Jenny and Antti Wihuri Foundation, Finland, 96
Jenny ja Antti Wihurin Rahasto, Finland, 96
JERI—Japan Economic Research Institute Inc, Japan, 189
JN Foundation, Jamaica, 184
JNF UK—JNF Charitable Trust, UK, 361
John Ellerman Foundation, UK, 361
John Paul II Foundation for the Sahel, Burkina Faso, 44
John Simon Guggenheim Memorial Foundation, USA, 444
John Templeton Foundation, USA, 444
The Johnson Foundation at Wingspread, USA, 444
JOHUD—Jordanian Hashemite Fund for Human Development, Jordan, 196
Jordan River Foundation, Jordan, 196
José Maria Neves Foundation for Governance, Cabo Verde, 46
Joseph Levy Foundation, UK, 362
Joyce Banda Foundation International, Malawi, 210
Joyce Foundation, USA, 445
JPB Foundation, USA, 428
JPMorgan Chase Foundation, USA, 445
Jubilee Foundation, Bolivia, 36
Jubilee USA Network, USA, 445
Kadın Emeğini Değerlendirme Vakfı—KEDV, Türkiye, 329
Kafaa Development Foundation, Libya, 207
Kansainvälinen solidaarisuussäätiö, Finland, 96
Karagheusian (Howard) Commemorative Corporation, USA, 437
Kárpátok Alapítvány, Hungary, 153
KAUTE Foundation, Finland, 96
KAUTE-säätiö, Finland, 96
KDDI Foundation, Japan, 191
KEHATI—Yayasan Keanekaragaman Hayati Indonesia, Indonesia, 162
Kellogg (W. K.) Foundation, USA, 478
Khemka (Nand & Jeet) Foundation, India, 159
KIEDF—Koret Israel Economic Development Funds, Israel, 170
Kiel Institute for the World Economy, Germany, 132
Kind Heart Foundation, Viet Nam, 488
King Khalid Foundation, Saudi Arabia, 269
King Philanthropies, USA, 445
The King's Trust, UK, 363
KK-stiftelsen, Sweden, 301
Knowledge Foundation, Sweden, 301
Knox (Frank) Memorial Fellowships, USA, 428
Koch (Charles) Foundation, USA, 413
Konrad Adenauer Foundation, Germany, 134
Konrad-Adenauer-Stiftung eV—KAS, Germany, 134
Koret Foundation, USA, 446
Koret Israel Economic Development Funds—KIEDF, Israel, 170
Kosovar Institute for Policy Research and Development—KIPRED, Kosovo, 203
Kresge Foundation, USA, 446
Kulika Charitable Trust Uganda, Uganda, 331
Kuok Foundation Berhad, Malaysia, 211
Kusuma Trust UK, UK, 363
Lady Davis Fellowship Trust, Israel, 170
Lafede.cat—Federació d'Organitzacions per a la Justícia Global, Spain, 286
Lafede.cat—Federation of Organizations for Global Justice, Spain, 286
Landesa—Rural Development Institute, USA, 447
LAPAS—Latvijas platforma attīstības sadarbībai, Latvia, 204
Latet Israeli Humanitarian Aid, Israel, 170
Latimpacto—Red Latinoamericana de Inversión Social y Filantropía Estratégica, Colombia, 71
Latin American Association of Development Financing Institutions, Peru, 248
Latin American and Caribbean Committee for the Defence of Women's Rights, Peru, 249
Latin American Future Foundation, Ecuador, 88

Economic affairs

Latin American Network for Economic and Social Justice, Peru, 248
Latin American Venture Philanthropy Network, Colombia, 71
Latindadd—Red Latinoamericana por Justicia Económica y Social, Peru, 248
Latvian Platform for Development Cooperation, Latvia, 204
Laudes Foundation, Switzerland, 313
Laureus Sport for Good, UK, 364
League of Corporate Foundations—LCF, Philippines, 250
Legatum Foundation, United Arab Emirates, 334
Leibniz Association, Germany, 135
Leibniz Gemeinschaft, Germany, 135
Leibniz-Institut für Agrarentwicklung in Transformationsökonomien—IAMO, Germany, 135
Leibniz-Institut für Globale und Regionale Studien, Germany, 130
Leibniz Institute of Agricultural Development in Transition Economies, Germany, 135
The Leona M. and Harry B. Helmsley Charitable Trust, USA, 447
Leonard Cheshire Disability, UK, 364
The Leprosy Mission International, UK, 364
Lesotho Council of Non-Governmental Organisations, Lesotho, 207
Leventis (A. G.) Foundation Nigeria, Nigeria, 237
Leverhulme Trust, UK, 365
Levi Strauss Foundation, USA, 448
Levy (Joseph) Foundation, UK, 362
Liberty Fund, Inc, USA, 448
Light Up the World—LUTW, Canada, 58
Light of the Village Foundation, Indonesia, 162
Litdea Association, Lithuania, 208
Living Culture Foundation Namibia—LCFN, Namibia, 222
Liz Claiborne & Art Ortenberg Foundation, USA, 448
Lloyds Bank Foundation for England and Wales, UK, 365
Lorenzini (Giovanni), Fondazione, Italy, 177
The Lotte and John Hecht Memorial Foundation, Canada, 58
Lowy Institute for International Policy, Australia, 15
Luigi Einaudi Foundation, Italy, 178
Luxembourg Development NGO Co-operation Circle, Luxembourg, 209
Luxemburg (Rosa) Stiftung, Germany, 139
M. S. Swaminathan Research Foundation—MSSRF, India, 158
McCaw (Craig and Susan) Foundation, USA, 418
McConnell (J.W.) Family Foundation, Canada, 57
McDonnell (James S.) Foundation, USA, 443
Macedonian Centre for International Co-operation—MCIC, North Macedonia, 239
Machel (Graça) Trust, South Africa, 280
MACIF Foundation, France, 108
McKenzie (J. R.) Trust, New Zealand, 233
McKnight Foundation, USA, 449
Macquarie Group Foundation, Australia, 15
MADRE, USA, 450
Maecenata Foundation, Germany, 119
Maecenata Stiftung, Germany, 119
MAIF Foundation for Research, France, 108
Maison Franco-Japonaise, Japan, 191
Makyedonski Tzyentar za Myeroonarodna Sorabotka, North Macedonia, 239
Mandela Institute for Development Studies—MINDS, South Africa, 281
Mandela (Nelson) Children's Fund, South Africa, 281
Mani Tese, Italy, 183
Mansour Foundation for Development—MFD, Egypt, 90
Mara Foundation, Uganda, 332
Marcel Bleustein-Blanchet Vocational Foundation, France, 109
Markle Foundation, USA, 451
The MasterCard Foundation, Canada, 59
Mattei (Enrico), Fondazione ENI, Italy, 174
Mawazo Institute, Kenya, 199
Max Bell Foundation, Canada, 59
Max Havelaar Foundation—Fairtrade Netherlands, Netherlands, 230
Max Schmidheiny Foundation at the University of St Gallen, Switzerland, 314
Max Schmidheiny-Stiftung an der Universität St Gallen, Switzerland, 314
Mayer (Charles Léopold Mayer), Fondation, Switzerland, 308
The Maytree Foundation, Canada, 59
Mbeki (Thabo) Foundation, South Africa, 284
Medunarodnog foruma Bosna, Bosnia and Herzegovina, 37
Mediterranean Foundation, Argentina, 7

Economic affairs

Mediterranean Foundation for Strategic Studies Institute, France, 113
Mellon (Richard King) Foundation, USA, 467
Mencap—Royal Mencap Society, UK, 367
Mendoza (Eugenio), Fundación, Venezuela, 487
Mercatus Center, USA, 451
Merchant Navy Fund, UK, 382
Mercy, Ireland, 168
Mercy Corps, USA, 452
M'essh al Sudan, Sudan, 297
Michael & Susan Dell Foundation, USA, 453
Michel (James) Foundation, Seychelles, 272
Microfinance Centre—MFC, Poland, 257
Miguel Alemán Foundation, Mexico, 215
Milieukontakt Macedonia—MKM, North Macedonia, 240
Minderoo Foundation, Australia, 15
Minhaj Welfare Foundation, UK, 368
Minority Rights Group International—MRG, UK, 368
MISEREOR—Bischöfliches Hilfswerk Misereor eV, Germany, 137
Mith Samlanh, Cambodia, 46
Mitterrand (Danielle), Fondation, France, 112
Mo Dewji Foundation, Tanzania, 323
Moawad (René) Foundation, Lebanon, 206
Mohammed bin Rashid Al Maktoum Global Initiatives—MBRGI, United Arab Emirates, 335
Mohammed bin Salman Foundation—Misk Foundation, Saudi Arabia, 269
Moisés Bertoni Foundation, Paraguay, 248
Monnet (Jean), Fondation pour l'Europe, Switzerland, 309
Mønsteds (Otto) Fond, Denmark, 86
Montemadrid Foundation, Spain, 292
Montevideo Circle Foundation, Uruguay, 485
Motsepe Foundation, South Africa, 281
Mouvement International ATD Quart-Monde, France, 115
Mouvement Social, Lebanon, 206
Ms. Foundation for Women, USA, 454
MTN Côte d'Ivoire Foundation, Côte d'Ivoire, 76
MTN Nigeria Foundation, Nigeria, 237
MTN SA Foundation, South Africa, 281
Muriel McBrien Kauffman Foundation, USA, 425
Muslim Aid, UK, 369
Mutual Aid and Liaison Service, France, 116
NAACP Legal Defense and Educational Fund, Inc—LDF, USA, 454
Nadace Vodafone Česká Republika, Czech Republic, 80
Nadácia Pontis, Slovakia, 274
Nand & Jeet Khemka Foundation, India, 159
National Council of Social Development—NCSD, Philippines, 250
National Empowerment Foundation—NEF, Mauritius, 214
National Endowment for Science, Technology and the Arts—Nesta, UK, 370
National Federation of NGOs, Poland, 254
National Foundation for Development, El Salvador, 91
National Foundation for the Development of Honduras, Honduras, 150
National Foundation for Educational Research—NFER, UK, 369
National Foundation for Political Sciences, France, 110
The National Lottery Community Fund, UK, 370
National Organization for Women Foundation, USA, 458
National Science Foundation—NSF, USA, 455
Naumann (Friedrich) Stiftung, Germany, 130
Near East Foundation—NEF, USA, 456
NEF—National Empowerment Foundation, Mauritius, 214
NEF—Near East Foundation, USA, 456
Nelson Mandela Children's Fund, South Africa, 281
Nesta—National Endowment for Science, Technology and the Arts, UK, 370
Network of European Foundations—NEF, Belgium, 27
Network of Foundations and Research Institutions for the Promotion of a Culture of Peace in Africa, Côte d'Ivoire, 75
Network of Foundations Working for Development—netFWD, France, 99
Network for Human Development, Brazil, 41
Network of Information and Support for Non-governmental Organizations, Poland, 254
Network for Social Change Charitable Trust—NSCCT, UK, 370
Neves (José Maria), Fundação para a Governança, Cabo Verde, 46
New Economics Foundation—NEF, UK, 371
New World Foundation—NWF, USA, 456

New Zealand Institute of International Affairs—NZIIA, New Zealand, 234
NFER—National Foundation for Educational Research, UK, 369
NFI—National Foundation for India, India, 159
NGO Center—NGOC, Armenia, 9
Nicolas Hulot Foundation for Nature and Humankind, France, 110
Nigerian Conservation Foundation—NCF, Nigeria, 238
Nigerian Institute of International Affairs—NIIA, Nigeria, 238
Ningxia Yanbao Charity Foundation, China (People's Republic), 69
Nitidæ, France, 115
Nobel Foundation, Sweden, 301
Nobelstiftelsen, Sweden, 301
Nobis Foundation, Ecuador, 88
Non-Governmental Ecological Vernadsky Foundation, Russian Federation, 266
Nonprofit Enterprise and Self-sustainability Team—NESsT, USA, 457
Nordic Africa Institute Scholarships, Sweden, 302
Nordic International Support Foundation—NIS, Norway, 242
Nordiska Afrikainstitutets Stipendier, Sweden, 302
Norsk Utenrikspolitisk Institutt—NUPI, Norway, 242
Norwegian Institute of International Affairs, Norway, 242
NoVo Foundation, USA, 458
NOW Foundation, USA, 458
Nuffield Foundation, UK, 371
NZIIA—New Zealand Institute of International Affairs, New Zealand, 234
Observer Research Foundation—ORF, India, 159
The Ocean Cleanup Foundation, Netherlands, 230
ODI, UK, 371
The Officers' Association, UK, 372
Offor (Sir Emeka) Foundation, Nigeria, 238
Ogólnopolska Federacja Organizacji Pozarządowych—OFOP, Poland, 254
Oil Search Foundation, Papua New Guinea, 247
OISCA International—Organization for Industrial, Spiritual and Cultural Advancement-International, Japan, 192
Ökumenikus Segélyszervezet, Hungary, 153
Oman LNG Development Foundation—ODF, Oman, 244
Omidyar Group, USA, 458
Omidyar Network Fund, USA, 458
One Economy Foundation, Namibia, 222
Open Society Foundation for Albania, Albania, 5
Open Society Foundation South Africa—OSF-SA, South Africa, 282
Open Society Foundation—Western Balkans, Albania, 5
Open Society Foundations, USA, 459
Open Society Initiative for Southern Africa—OSISA, South Africa, 282
Operation USA, USA, 459
Oppenheimer Generations Foundation, South Africa, 282
Opportunity International UK, UK, 372
Orange Botswana Foundation, Botswana, 37
Orange Solidarité Madagascar, Madagascar, 210
Organisation Internationale de Droit du Développement—OIDD, Italy, 181
Organization for Social Science Research in Eastern and Southern Africa—OSSREA, Ethiopia, 94
Orient-Occident Foundation, Morocco, 220
Orji Uzor Kalu Foundation, Nigeria, 238
Österreichische Gesellschaft für Aussenpolitik und Internationale Beziehungen—ÖGAVN, Austria, 22
Östersjöfonden, Finland, 97
Otto Benecke Foundation, Germany, 138
Otto-Benecke-Stiftung eV, Germany, 138
Otto Mønsteds Fond, Denmark, 86
Otto Mønsteds Foundation, Denmark, 86
Our Foundation, Indonesia, 162
Our Future—Foundation for Regional Social Programmes, Russian Federation, 266
Outreach International, USA, 459
Outstretched Hands, Italy, 183
Oxfam America, USA, 460
Oxfam Canada, Canada, 60
Oxfam Denmark, Denmark, 86
Oxfam France, France, 115
Oxfam Hong Kong, Hong Kong, 151
Oxfam India, India, 159
Oxfam Mexico, Mexico, 216
Oxfam South Africa, South Africa, 282

INDEX OF MAIN ACTIVITIES

Pacific Development and Conservation Trust, New Zealand, 234
Pacific Peoples' Partnership, Canada, 61
Pact, USA, 460
PADF—Pan American Development Foundation, USA, 460
PAI—Population Action International, USA, 460
Paideia Galiza Foundation, Spain, 293
Pakistan Institute of International Affairs—PIIA, Pakistan, 245
Pan American Development Foundation—PADF, USA, 460
Paraguayan Foundation for Cooperation and Development, Paraguay, 248
Partners for Equity, Australia, 16
Pastore (Giulio), Fondazione, Italy, 178
Paulo Foundation, Finland, 97
Paulon Säätiö, Finland, 97
PCI Media Impact, USA, 467
PCI—Project Concern International, USA, 431
Peace Direct, UK, 373
Peace Parks Foundation, South Africa, 282
PepsiCo Foundation, Inc, USA, 462
Peres Center for Peace and Innovation, Israel, 171
Peruvian Foundation for Nature Conservation, Peru, 249
The Pew Charitable Trusts, USA, 462
PH International, USA, 463
Philanthropikó Ídryma Stélios Chatzeioánnou stēn Kýpro, Cyprus, 78
Philippine Business for Social Progress—PBSP, Philippines, 250
Plan International Ireland, Ireland, 167
PLAN International—PI, UK, 374
Plataforma Portuguesa das Organizações Não-Governamentais para o Desenvolvimento—ONGD, Portugal, 258
Platforma Mimovládnych Rozvojových Organizácií, Slovakia, 273
Plunkett Foundation, UK, 374
Pontis Foundation, Slovakia, 274
Population Action International—PAI, USA, 460
Populorum Progressio Foundation, Vatican City, 486
Portuguese Platform of Non-Governmental Organizations for Development, Portugal, 258
Practical Action, UK, 374
Praxis Centre for Policy Studies Foundation, Estonia, 93
Première Urgence Internationale, France, 116
Premji (Azim) Foundation, India, 156
Presbyterian World Service & Development—PWS&D, Canada, 61
Primate's World Relief and Development Fund/Le Fonds du Primat Pour le Secours et le Développement Mondial—PWRDF, Canada, 49
Prince's Trust, UK, 363
Princess of Asturias Foundation, Spain, 294
Pro Mujer International, USA, 464
Pro Women International, USA, 464
PRODESSA—Proyecto de Desarrollo Santiago, Guatemala, 148
Project Harmony, USA, 463
ProLiteracy, USA, 464
Pronaturaleza—Fundación Peruana para la Conservación de la Naturaleza, Peru, 249
Prudence Foundation, Hong Kong, 151
Public Studies Centre, Chile, 64
Puerto Rico Community Foundation, Puerto Rico, 261
PwC Charitable Foundation, USA, 465
Quỹ Thiện Tâm, Viet Nam, 488
Quandt (Herbert) Stiftung, Germany, 122
Rabo Foundation, Netherlands, 228
Rafael del Pino Foundation, Spain, 294
The Rainforest Foundation UK—RFUK, UK, 375
Rambourg Foundation, Tunisia, 326
RAND Corporation, USA, 465
Rare, USA, 466
Ravand Institute for Economic and International Studies, Iran, 163
Razumkov Centre, Ukraine, 333
RBC Foundation, Canada, 61
Rebecca Akufo-Addo Foundation—Rebecca Foundation, Ghana, 144
Red Feather, Japan, 185
Red de Mujeres para el Desarrollo, Costa Rica, 75
RED—Ruralité-Environnement-Développement, Belgium, 34
REDEH—Rede de Desenvolvimento Humano, Brazil, 41
Refugee Empowerment International—REI, Japan, 193
Refugee Foundation, Netherlands, 231
Refugees International—RI, USA, 466
Rehabilitation International—RI, USA, 466

INDEX OF MAIN ACTIVITIES

Economic affairs

REI—Refugee Empowerment International, Japan, 193
Reliance Foundation, India, 160
Relief International, USA, 466
René Moawad Foundation—RMF, Lebanon, 206
Repsol Foundation, Spain, 295
Réseau Européen des Associations de Lutte contre la Pauvreté et l'Exclusion Sociale, Belgium, 29
Réseau des Fondations et Institutions de Recherche pour la Promotion d'un Culture de la Paix en Afrique—REFICA, Côte d'Ivoire, 75
Resolution Foundation, UK, 376
The Resource Foundation—TRF, USA, 467
RIA—Royal Irish Academy, Ireland, 167
Richard King Mellon Foundation, USA, 467
Right Livelihood Award Foundation, Sweden, 302
Rising Impact, USA, 467
Robert Schuman Foundation, France, 111
Robert Wood Johnson Foundation—RWJF, USA, 467
The Robertson Trust, UK, 376
Rockefeller Foundation, USA, 468
Rockwool Fonden, Denmark, 86
Rockwool Foundation, Denmark, 86
Rosa Luxemburg Foundation, Germany, 139
Rosa-Luxemburg-Stiftung, Germany, 139
Rössing Foundation, Namibia, 222
The Rotary Foundation, USA, 468
Royal British Legion, UK, 377
Royal Elcano Institute Foundation, Spain, 294
Royal Institute of International Affairs—RIIA—Chatham House, UK, 378
Royal Institute of International Relations—Egmont Institute, Belgium, 29
RSA—Royal Society for the Encouragement of Arts, Manufactures and Commerce, UK, 379
Rüf (Gebert) Stiftung, Switzerland, 311
Rural Development Foundation, Poland, 257
Rural Development Institute—Landesa, USA, 447
Ruralité-Environnement-Développement—RED, Belgium, 34
Rurality Environment Development, Belgium, 34
Russell Sage Foundation—RSF, USA, 469
Russian International Affairs Council—RIAC, Russian Federation, 266
Rytų Europos Studijų Centras—RESC, Lithuania, 209
Säätiöiden post doc-poolin, Finland, 95
Safaricom Foundation, Kenya, 200
Sainsbury Family Charitable Trusts, UK, 380
Sakartvelos Strategiisa da Saertashoriso Urtiertobebis Kvlevis Pondi—Rondelis Pondi, Georgia, 118
El Salvadoran Association for Economic and Social Development FUSADES, El Salvador, 91
Salzburg Global Seminar, Austria, 22
Samsung Foundation, Korea (Republic), 202
San Francisco Foundation—SFF, USA, 470
Sandals Foundation, Jamaica, 184
Santiago Development Project, Guatemala, 148
Santos Foundation, Papua New Guinea, 247
Sarah Scaife Foundation, Inc, USA, 470
The Sasakawa Peace Foundation—SPF, Japan, 194
Save the Children (UK), UK, 381
Sawiris Foundation for Social Development—SFSD, Egypt, 90
SBS Cultural Foundation, Korea (Republic), 202
Scaife (Sarah) Foundation, Inc, USA, 470
Schmidheiny (Max) Stiftung, Switzerland, 314
Schöck (Eberhard) Stiftung, Germany, 127
Schuman (Robert), Fondation, France, 111
Schusterman (Charles and Lynn) Family Foundation, USA, 413
Schwab Foundation for Social Entrepreneurship, Switzerland, 316
Schwarzkopf-Stiftung Junges Europa, Germany, 139
Schwarzkopf Young Europe Foundation, Germany, 139
Schweisfurth Foundation, Germany, 139
Schweisfurth-Stiftung, Germany, 139
Science and Politics Foundation—German Institute for International and Security Affairs, Germany, 141
Scottish Catholic International Aid Fund—SCIAF, UK, 382
The Seafarers' Charity, UK, 382
Seafarers International Relief Fund, UK, 382
SeedChange, Canada, 61
Seeds of Peace, USA, 470
SEEMO—South East Europe Media Organisation, Austria, 23
SEL—Service d'Entraide et de Liaison, France, 116

Self Help Africa—SHA, Ireland, 167
Self Help Development Foundation—SHDF, Zimbabwe, 491
Self-Sufficient People Foundation, Indonesia, 163
Sembrar Sartawi, Bolivia, 36
SEND-West Africa, Ghana, 144
Senna (Ayrton), Instituto, Brazil, 41
Seoam Yoon Se Young Foundation, Korea (Republic), 202
Serrv International, Inc, USA, 471
SES Foundation—Sustainability, Education, Solidarity, Argentina, 8
Seub Nakhasathien Foundation, Thailand, 324
Shanghai Soong Ching Ling Foundation, China (People's Republic), 69
Shaping Our Future Foundation—SOFF, Malawi, 210
Shell Foundation—SF, UK, 382
Siam Society, Thailand, 324
Siamese Heritage Trust, Thailand, 324
Sieć Wspierania Organizacji Pozarządowych—SPLOT, Poland, 254
Sihtasutus Poliitikauuringute Keskus Praxis, Estonia, 93
Silicon Valley Community Foundation—SVCF, USA, 471
Singapore International Foundation—SIF, Singapore, 273
Sir Ahmadu Bello Memorial Foundation, Nigeria, 238
Sir Emeka Offor Foundation, Nigeria, 238
Skoll Foundation, USA, 472
Slim (Carlos), Fundación, Mexico, 215
Sloan (Alfred P.) Foundation, USA, 398
Smallwood Trust, UK, 384
Smith Richardson Foundation, Inc, USA, 472
Social Movement, Lebanon, 206
Software AG Foundation, Germany, 139
Software AG Stiftung, Germany, 139
Solidaarisuus, Finland, 96
Solidarity Foundation, Dominican Republic, 87
Soros Foundation—Kazakhstan, Kazakhstan, 197
Souter Charitable Trust, UK, 384
South African Institute of Race Relations—IRR, South Africa, 283
South East Europe Media Organisation—SEEMO, Austria, 23
South Sudan Center for Strategic and Policy Studies—CSPS, South Sudan, 285
South West International Development Network—SWIDN, UK, 337
Southern Africa Trust, South Africa, 283
Sparkassenstiftung für internationale Kooperation, Germany, 125
The Starr Foundation, USA, 473
Steelworkers Humanity Fund/Le Fonds Humanitaire des Métallos, Canada, 62
Stelios Philanthropic Foundation, Cyprus, 78
Stewardship Foundation, USA, 473
Stichting Dioraphte, Netherlands, 229
Stichting Fonds 1818, Netherlands, 229
Stichting IKEA Foundation, Netherlands, 229
Stichting Max Havelaar—Fairtrade Nederland, Netherlands, 230
Stichting The Ocean Cleanup, Netherlands, 230
Stichting van Schulden naar Kansen, Netherlands, 231
Stichting Triodos Foundation, Netherlands, 231
Stichting Vluchteling, Netherlands, 231
Stiftelsen Dag Hammarskjölds Minnesfond, Sweden, 303
Stiftelsen Gapminder, Sweden, 300
Stiftelsen Riksbankens Jubileumsfond, Sweden, 303
Stiftung für die Rechte zukünftiger Generationen—SRzG, Germany, 141
Stiftung Wissenschaft und Politik—Deutsches Institut für internationale Politik und Sicherheit—SWP, Germany, 141
Stiftung Zukunft.li, Liechtenstein, 208
Stockholm Environment Institute, Sweden, 303
Straits Exchange Foundation—SEF, Taiwan, 321
Streisand (Barbra) Foundation, USA, 408
Strømme Foundation, Norway, 243
Strømmestiftelsen, Norway, 243
Sudan Foundation, Sudan, 297
Sudd Institute, South Sudan, 285
Südosteuropäische Medienorganisation, Austria, 23
SUN Civil Society Network, UK, 381
Suomalaiset kehitysjärjestöt—Fingo, Finland, 95
Surdna Foundation, Inc, USA, 474
Swaminathan (M. S.) Research Foundation, India, 158
Swaziland Charitable Trust, Eswatini, 93
Sweden-Japan Foundation—SJF, Sweden, 304
Swiss Church Aid, Switzerland, 311

SWISSAID Foundation, Switzerland, 318
Synergos—The Synergos Institute, USA, 396
Taiwan NPO Information Platform, Taiwan, 321
Tanager, USA, 397
TANZ—Trade Aid NZ Inc, New Zealand, 235
Tarih Vakfı, Türkiye, 329
Tata Trusts, India, 160
Tearfund, UK, 385
Tearfund Australia, Australia, 18
TechnoServe, USA, 474
Telmex Telcel Foundation, Mexico, 216
Temasek Foundation, Singapore, 273
Templeton (John) Foundation, USA, 444
Templeton Philanthropies, USA, 444
Tencent Foundation, China (People's Republic), 70
Terre Sans Frontières—TSF, Canada, 62
TESEV—Türkiye Ekonomik ve Sosyal Etüdler Vakfı, Türkiye, 329
Tewa, Nepal, 223
Thabo Mbeki Foundation, South Africa, 284
Third Sector Foundation of Turkey, Türkiye, 327
Third World Network—TWN, Malaysia, 211
Thomas B. Thrige Foundation, Denmark, 86
Thomas B. Thriges Fond, Denmark, 86
Thomson Reuters Foundation, UK, 385
Thriges (Thomas B.) Fond, Denmark, 86
Thurgood Marshall Institute, USA, 454
TI—Transparency International, Germany, 142
Tibet Fund, USA, 475
Tides Organizations, USA, 475
Tifa Foundation—Indonesia, Indonesia, 163
Tindall Foundation, New Zealand, 235
Tinh Thuong One Member Limited Liability Microfinance Institution, Viet Nam, 488
Tinker Foundation, Inc, USA, 475
The Todd Foundation, New Zealand, 235
Together for Global Justice—CIDSE, Belgium, 29
Tony Blair Institute for Global Change—TBI, UK, 386
Tony Elumelu Foundation—TEF, Nigeria, 238
TotalEnergies Foundation, France, 112
Trade Aid NZ Inc—TANZ, New Zealand, 235
Transnet Foundation, South Africa, 284
Transparency International—TI, Germany, 142
Triodos Foundation, Netherlands, 231
Trócaire—Catholic Agency for World Development, Ireland, 168
The Trussell Trust, UK, 386
Trust for London, UK, 386
Trust for Social Achievement, Bulgaria, 44
Tujenge Africa Foundation, Burundi, 45
Tulsa Community Foundation—TCF, USA, 476
Tunisia Development Foundation, Tunisia, 326
Turing (Alan) Institute, UK, 339
Turkish Economic and Social Studies Foundation, Türkiye, 329
Turkish Family Health and Planning Foundation, Türkiye, 330
Turkish Foundation for Combating Soil Erosion, for Reforestation and the Protection of Natural Habitats, Türkiye, 330
Türkiye Aile Sağlığı ve Planlaması Vakfı—TAPV, Türkiye, 330
Türkiye Erozyonla Mücadele Ağaçlandırma ve Doğal Varlıkları Koruma Vakfı—TEMA, Türkiye, 330
Türkiye Kalkinma Vakfı, Türkiye, 330
Türkiye Vodafone Vakfı, Türkiye, 331
Turner Foundation, Inc, USA, 476
TÜSEV—Türkiye Üçüncü Sektör Vakfı, Türkiye, 327
Tusk, UK, 387
TY Danjuma Foundation, Nigeria, 239
TYM Fund, Viet Nam, 488
U4 Anti-Corruption Resource Centre, Norway, 241
Ucom Foundation, Armenia, 9
Ufadhili Trust, Kenya, 197
UJIA—United Jewish Israel Appeal, UK, 387
UK Research and Innovation—UKRI, UK, 387
Ukrainian Women's Fund, Ukraine, 333
Uluchay Social-Economic Innovation Center, Azerbaijan, 23
Uluntu Community Foundation—UCF, Zimbabwe, 491
UniCredit Foundation, Italy, 183
UNIFOR—Forvaltningstiftelse for fond og legater, Norway, 240
Unipolis Foundation, Italy, 181
UNIR Bolivia Foundation, Bolivia, 36
Unitarian Universalist Service Committee—UUSC, USA, 476
United Jewish Israel Appeal—UJIA, UK, 387
United Nations Foundation, USA, 476
United Purpose, UK, 387
United States African Development Foundation—USADF, USA, 477
United Way Worldwide, USA, 477

Education

Unity Foundation, Luxembourg, 210
University-Industry Foundation, Spain, 295
University of Zaragoza Business Foundation, Spain, 290
UPM Foundation, Uruguay, 485
UPS Foundation, USA, 477
US Civilian Research & Development Foundation, USA, 419
USPG—United Society Partners in the Gospel, UK, 387
UUSC—Unitarian Universalist Service Committee, USA, 476
Van Leer Foundation, Netherlands, 231
Van Leer Jerusalem Institute, Israel, 171
Vargas (Getulio), Fundação, Brazil, 40
VENRO—Verband Entwicklungspolitik und Humanitäre Hilfe deutscher Nichtregierungsorganizationen, Germany, 120
Vestnordenfonden, Denmark, 86
Vetlesen (G. Unger) Foundation, USA, 429
VIDC—Vienna Institute for International Dialogue and Co-operation, Austria, 23
Vienna Institute for International Dialogue and Co-operation—VIDC, Austria, 23
Village Community Development Foundation, Indonesia, 163
Villar Foundation, Inc, Philippines, 253
Vincent Fairfax Family Foundation—VFFF, Australia, 19
VINCI Corporate Foundation for the City, France, 106
VinFuture Foundation, Viet Nam, 489
Vita, Ireland, 168
Vital Voices Global Partnership, USA, 478
Vivekananda International Foundation—VIF, India, 161
Vodacom Lesotho Foundation, Lesotho, 207
Vodacom Tanzania Foundation—VTF, Tanzania, 323
Vodacom ATH Fiji Foundation, Fiji, 94
Vodafone Czech Republic Foundation, Czech Republic, 80
Vodafone Foundation India, India, 161
Vodafone Foundation New Zealand, New Zealand, 235
Vodafone Idea Foundation, India, 161
Vodafone Türkiye Foundation, Türkiye, 331
Volkart Foundation, Switzerland, 319
Volkart-Stiftung, Switzerland, 319
Voluntary Service Overseas, UK, 388
Volunteer Service Abroad/Te Tūao Tāwāhi—VSA, New Zealand, 236
VSO—Voluntary Service Overseas, UK, 388
W. K. Kellogg Foundation—WKKF, USA, 478
Walk Free, Australia, 15
Walmart Foundation, USA, 478
Walter and Duncan Gordon Charitable Foundation, Canada, 62
Walton Family Foundation, USA, 479
WAMA Foundation, Tanzania, 323
War on Want, UK, 388
Water.org, Inc, USA, 479
WaterAid, UK, 389
The Waterloo Foundation—TWF, UK, 389
Weinberg (Harry and Jeanette) Foundation, USA, 434
West-Nordic Foundation, Denmark, 86
Weston (Garfield) Foundation, UK, 355
Wihuri Foundation for International Prizes, Finland, 98
Wihuri (Jenny and Antti) Foundation, Finland, 96
Wihurin kansainvälisten palkintojen rahasto, Finland, 98
The WILD Foundation—International Wilderness Leadership Foundation, USA, 481
Wilderness Foundation Global—WFG, South Africa, 284
William Buckland Foundation, Australia, 19
The William and Flora Hewlett Foundation, USA, 481
The William H. Donner Foundation, Inc, USA, 481
William T. Grant Foundation, USA, 481
Wilsdorf (Hans), Fondation, Switzerland, 309
Wilson (Woodrow) International Center for Scholars, USA, 482
Winrock International, USA, 481
Winston Churchill Memorial Trust of New Zealand, New Zealand, 236
The Womanity Foundation, Switzerland, 319
Women in Development Foundation, Tanzania, 323
Women in Equality Foundation, Argentina, 8
Women Thrive Fund, UK, 384
WomenLead Institute, USA, 418
Women's Development Network, Costa Rica, 75

Women's Environment & Development Organization—WEDO, USA, 482
Women's Foundation, Costa Rica, 74
The Wood Foundation—TWF, UK, 391
Woodrow Wilson International Center for Scholars, USA, 482
World Alliance of YMCAs—Young Men's Christian Associations, Switzerland, 319
World Economic Forum, Switzerland, 320
World Jewish Relief, UK, 391
World Neighbors, USA, 483
World Resources Institute—WRI, USA, 483
World University Service of Canada/Entraide Universitaire Mondiale du Canada—WUSC/EUMC, Canada, 63
World Vision International, UK, 391
WorldFish, Malaysia, 212
Wujoh Foundation for Media and Development, Yemen, 489
WWF International, Switzerland, 320
The Wyss Foundtion, USA, 484
Xiangjiang Social Relief Fund, China (People's Republic), 68
YADESA—Yayasan Pembinaan Masyarakat Desa, Indonesia, 163
Yanbao Charity Foundation, China (People's Republic), 69
Yayasan Azman Hashim, Malaysia, 212
Yayasan Dian Desa—YDD, Indonesia, 162
Yayasan Geutanyoë, Indonesia, 162
Yayasan Insan Sembada, Indonesia, 163
Yayasan Pembinaan Masyarakat Desa—YADESA, Indonesia, 163
Yayasan Tifa, Indonesia, 163
YMCA—Young Men's Christian Association, UK, 392
Youth Leadership Development Foundation—YLDF, Yemen, 489
Yrjö Jahnsson Foundation, Finland, 98
Yrjö Jahnssonin säätiö, Finland, 98
Zakat House, Kuwait, 203
Zeiss (Carl) Stiftung, Germany, 123
ZOA, Netherlands, 231
Zorig Foundation, Mongolia, 219

EDUCATION

1563 Foundation for the Arts and Culture, Italy, 174
1818 Fund Foundation, Netherlands, 229
The A. G. Leventis Foundation, Cyprus, 77
A. G. Leventis Foundation Nigeria, Nigeria, 237
A. M. M. Sahabdeen Trust Foundation, Sri Lanka, 297
The A. P. Møller and Chastine Mc-Kinney Møller Foundation, Denmark, 82
A. P. Møller og Hustru Chastine Mc-Kinney Møllers Fond til almene Formaal, Denmark, 82
A. S. Hornby Educational Trust, UK, 338
AAUW Educational Foundation, USA, 399
Abdul Hameed Shoman Foundation—AHSF, Jordan, 195
Abdulla Al Ghurair Foundation for Education, United Arab Emirates, 334
Abrinq Foundation for the Rights of Children and Adolescents, Brazil, 39
Academy for the Development of Philanthropy in Poland, Poland, 253
Academy of European Law, Germany, 127
Accademia Musicale Chigiana, Italy, 172
Acíndar Foundation, Argentina, 6
ACLS—American Council of Learned Societies, USA, 399
Acting for Life, France, 100
Action for Children, UK, 338
Action Children's Aid, Denmark, 82
Action Education, France, 100
Active for People in Need Austria, Austria, 20
Acumen, USA, 397
Addoha Foundation, Morocco, 219
Adenauer (Konrad) Stiftung eV, Germany, 134
ADRA—Adventist Development and Relief Agency International, USA, 397
Adriano Olivetti Foundation, Italy, 174
Advance, USA, 397
Adventist Development and Relief Agency International—ADRA, USA, 397
Adyan Foundation, Lebanon, 205
Afghanistan Institute for Civil Society—AICS, Afghanistan, 3
Afghanistan Research and Evaluation Unit, Afghanistan, 3
Africa-America Institute—AAI, USA, 398
Africa Foundation, South Africa, 278
Africa Space Foundation, Switzerland, 308

INDEX OF MAIN ACTIVITIES

African Capacity Building Foundation—ACBF, Zimbabwe, 490
African Wildlife Foundation—AWF, Kenya, 198
African Youth Initiative Network—AYINET, Uganda, 331
Aga Khan Development Network—AKDN, Switzerland, 306
Aga Khan Foundation, Switzerland, 306
Aga Khan Foundation Canada, Canada, 49
Aga Khan Foundation UK, UK, 338
AGIR Association for the Environment and Quality of Life, Mali, 213
Agnelli (Giovanni), Fondazione, Italy, 177
Agora Foundation, Poland, 255
AHA—American Historical Association, USA, 401
AID Foundation, Bangladesh, 24
AINA—Arctic Institute of North America, Canada, 49
Air France Foundation, France, 103
Aisha Buhari Global Foundation, Nigeria, 237
AIT—Asian Institute of Technology, Thailand, 323
Akademia Rozwoju Filantropii w Polsce—ARFP, Poland, 253
Akai Hane—Central Community Chest of Japan, Japan, 185
AKO Foundation, UK, 339
Aktion Børnehjælp, Denmark, 82
Al Jalila Foundation, United Arab Emirates, 334
Al Jisr Foundation, Oman, 244
The Al-Khoei Benevolent Foundation, UK, 339
Al-Mortaqa Foundation for Human Development, Iraq, 164
Al-Zubair Charity Foundation, Sudan, 297
The Alan Turing Institute, UK, 339
Alavi Foundation, USA, 398
Albéniz Foundation, Spain, 288
Alcoa Foundation, USA, 398
Alden (George I.) Trust, USA, 430
Alemán (Miguel), Fundación, Mexico, 215
Alet'Eleym Fewq Alejmey'e, Qatar, 262
Alexander S. Onassis Public Benefit Foundation, Liechtenstein, 207
Alfred P. Sloan Foundation, USA, 398
Alfred Toepfer Foundation FVS, Germany, 121
Alfred Toepfer Stiftung FVS, Germany, 121
Alfried Krupp von Bohlen und Halbach Foundation, Germany, 121
Alfried Krupp von Bohlen und Halbach-Stiftung, Germany, 121
Ali Fulhu Thuthu Foundation, Maldives, 212
Alight, USA, 399
Aliko Dangote Foundation—ADF, Nigeria, 237
Alkhidmat Foundation Pakistan—AKFP, Pakistan, 244
All Good Foundation Charitable Trust, New Zealand, 232
Alliance for International Exchange, USA, 399
Alliance Israélite Universelle, France, 101
Alliance for Securing Democracy, USA, 430
Allianz Foundation, Germany, 121
Almeida (Eng. António de), Fundação, Portugal, 260
Alola Foundation, Timor-Leste, 325
Alvares Penteado (Armando), Fundação, Brazil, 39
Alwaleed Philanthropies, Saudi Arabia, 269
AMADE Mondiale—Association Mondiale des Amis de l'Enfance, Monaco, 217
Aman Foundation, Pakistan, 244
Amancio Ortega Foundation, Spain, 288
Amberes (Carlos de), Fundación, Spain, 289
Ambrela Platform of Development Organizations, Slovakia, 273
Ambrela—Platforma rozvojových organizácií, Slovakia, 273
The Ambrose Monell Foundation, USA, 399
Ambuja Cement Foundation—ACF, India, 156
America for Bulgaria Foundation, Bulgaria, 43
America—Mideast Educational and Training Services Inc, USA, 404
American Association of University Women—AAUW Educational Foundation, USA, 399
American Council of Learned Societies—ACLS, USA, 399
American Councils for International Education, USA, 399
American Enterprise Institute—AEI, USA, 400
American Express Foundation, USA, 400
American Foundation for the Blind—AFB, USA, 400
American Friends Service Committee—AFSC, USA, 401
American Historical Association—AHA, USA, 401
American Institute of Pakistan Studies, USA, 401

INDEX OF MAIN ACTIVITIES   *Education*

American Jewish Joint Distribution Committee—JDC, USA, 402
American Near East Refugee Aid—Anera, USA, 402
American Philosophical Society—APS, USA, 402
American-Scandinavian Foundation—ASF, USA, 403
American Schools of Oriental Research—ASOR, USA, 403
Amerind Foundation, Inc, USA, 403
amfAR—The Foundation for AIDS Research, USA, 403
AMIDEAST—America-Mideast Educational and Training Services, Inc, USA, 404
AMINA—aktiv für Menschen in Not Austria, Austria, 20
Amity Foundation, China (People's Republic), 66
Amnesty International, UK, 340
AMP Foundation, Australia, 10
Amref Health Africa, Kenya, 198
Anders Jahre's Foundation for Humanitarian Purposes, Norway, 240
Anders Jahres Humanitære Stiftelse, Norway, 240
Andrew W. Mellon Foundation, USA, 404
Anera—American Near East Refugee Aid, USA, 402
Anesvad, Spain, 286
Angel of Hope Foundation, Zimbabwe, 490
Angelo Della Riccia Foundation, Italy, 175
Anglo American Foundation, UK, 340
Anguilla Community Fund, Anguilla, 5
Anna Lindh Euro-Mediterranean Foundation for Dialogue between Cultures, Egypt, 90
Anne Çocuk Eğitim Vakfı—AÇEV, Türkiye, 327
Anne Frank-Fonds, Switzerland, 306
Anne Frank Foundation, Netherlands, 224
Anne Frank Fund, Switzerland, 306
Anne Frank Stichting, Netherlands, 224
Anne Ray Foundation, USA, 450
The Annenberg Foundation, USA, 404
The Annie E. Casey Foundation, USA, 404
Anti-Defamation League—ADL, USA, 405
António de Almeida Foundation, Portugal, 260
Apex Foundation, Australia, 10
APHEDA—Union Aid Abroad, Australia, 19
Apprentis d'Auteuil Océan Indien, Réunion, 262
Arab American Institute Foundation—AAIF, USA, 405
Arab Network for Civic Education, Jordan, 195
Arab Thought Foundation—ATF, Lebanon, 205
Arainneachd Eachdraidheil Alba, UK, 358
ArcelorMittal Brazil Foundation, Brazil, 39
Archewell Foundation, USA, 405
Archie Sherman Charitable Trust, UK, 340
Arctic Institute of North America—AINA, Canada, 49
Arcus Foundation, USA, 405
Arengukoostöö Ümarlaud—AKÜ, Estonia, 92
Areumdaun Jaedan, Korea (Republic), 200
Ark, UK, 341
Armando Alvares Penteado Foundation, Brazil, 39
Armanshahr Foundation—OPEN ASIA, Afghanistan, 3
Arthritis Foundation, USA, 406
Arthur Rubinstein International Music Society, Israel, 168
Asahi Group Foundation, Japan, 186
ASEAN Foundation, Indonesia, 161
ASEAN Institutes of Strategic and International Studies—ASEAN ISIS, Indonesia, 162
Asia Africa International Voluntary Foundation—AIV, Japan, 186
Asia New Zealand Foundation/Te Whītau Tūhono, New Zealand, 232
Asia/Pacific Cultural Centre for UNESCO—ACCU, Japan, 186
Asia Philanthropy Circle—APC, Singapore, 272
Asia Society, USA, 406
Asian Community Trust—ACT, Japan, 186
Asian Cultural Council—ACC, USA, 406
Asian Development Research Institute—ADRI, India, 156
Asian Health Institute—AHI, Japan, 187
Asian Institute of Technology—AIT, Thailand, 323
ASKO Europa-Stiftung, Germany, 121
ASKO Europe Foundation, Germany, 121
Asociacija Litdea—Lithuanian Development Education and Awareness Raising Association, Lithuania, 208
Asociación Salvadoreña para el Desarrollo Económico y Social FUSADES, El Salvador, 91
Asotzijazijata za Dyemokratska Initzijativa, North Macedonia, 239
Aspen Institute, USA, 407

Association AGIR pour l'Environnement et la Qualité de la Vie, Mali, 213
Association for Democratic Initiatives—ADI, North Macedonia, 239
Association for Development Policy and Humanitarian Aid, Germany, 120
Association of Non-Governmental Organizations in The Gambia—TANGO, Gambia, 117
Association for Public Benefit Foundations, Austria, 20
Astur Foundation, Uruguay, 485
AT&T Foundation, USA, 407
ATD Fourth World International, France, 115
Atlas Charity Foundation, Poland, 255
Auchan Foundation, France, 103
Aurat Publication & Information Service Foundation—AF, Pakistan, 245
Auschwitz Foundation—Remembrance of Auschwitz, Belgium, 30
Australian Academy of the Humanities, Australia, 11
Australian Academy of Science, Australia, 11
Australian-American Fulbright Commission, Australia, 11
Australian Communities Foundation, Australia, 12
Australian Multicultural Foundation—AMF, Australia, 12
Australian Volunteers International—AVI, Australia, 13
Austrian Foundation for Development Research, Austria, 22
Autonómia Alapítvány, Hungary, 152
Autonómia Foundation, Hungary, 152
Avatud Eesti Fond, Estonia, 92
AVI—Australian Volunteers International, Australia, 13
AVSI Foundation, Italy, 175
Axel Springer Foundation, Germany, 122
Axel-Springer-Stiftung, Germany, 122
Ayala Foundation, Inc—AFI, Philippines, 251
Aydın Doğan Foundation, Türkiye, 328
Aydın Doğan Vakfı, Türkiye, 328
Ayrton Senna Institute, Brazil, 41
Azim Premji Foundation, India, 156
Azman Hashim Foundation, Malaysia, 212
Bagnoud (François-Xavier) Association, Switzerland, 310
Baha'i International Development Organization—BIDO, Israel, 169
Baillet Latour Fund, Belgium, 32
Balti Uuringute Instituut, Estonia, 92
Banco do Brasil Foundation, Brazil, 39
Banda (Joyce) Foundation International, Malawi, 210
Bangladesh Freedom Foundation—BFF, Bangladesh, 24
BANHCAFE Foundation, Honduras, 150
Bank of America Charitable Foundation, USA, 407
The Barack Obama Foundation, USA, 407
Barbados Entrepreneurship Foundation Inc, Barbados, 25
Barça Foundation, Spain, 287
Barceló Foundation, Spain, 289
Barnardo's, UK, 342
Barrié de la Maza (Pedro, Conde de Fenosa), Fundación, Spain, 293
Barzani Charity Foundation—BCF, Iraq, 164
Baxter & Alma Ricard Foundation, Canada, 55
BBC Media Action, UK, 342
BCause Foundation, Bulgaria, 42
The Beautiful Foundation, Korea (Republic), 200
Beisheim Foundation, Germany, 122
Beisheim Stiftung, Germany, 122
Beit Trust, UK, 342
Bell (Max) Foundation, Canada, 59
Bellingcat Foundation, Netherlands, 228
Bello (Sir Ahmadu) Memorial Foundation, Nigeria, 238
Benecke (Otto) Stiftung eV, Germany, 138
Benesco, UK, 347
Berghof Foundation gGmbH, Germany, 122
Berghof Stiftung für Konfliktforschung gGmbH, Germany, 122
Bernadottes (Folke) Minnesfond, Sweden, 299
Bernheim Foundation, Belgium, 31
Bertelsmann Foundation, Germany, 122
Bertelsmann Stiftung, Germany, 122
Bertoni (Moisés) Foundation, Paraguay, 248
Beyaz Nokta Gelişim Vakfı, Türkiye, 328
Bharti Foundation, India, 156
BIAT Youth Foundation, Tunisia, 326
Big Heart Foundation, Chad, 64
Biocon Foundation, India, 157
Bischöfliches Hilfswerk Misereor eV, Germany, 137

Black Sea NGO Network—BSNN, Bulgaria, 42
Black Sea Trust for Regional Cooperation, USA, 430
Black Sea University Foundation—BSUF, Romania, 263
Blanceflor Boncompagni Ludovisi, née Bildt Foundation, Sweden, 303
Blavatnik Family Foundation, USA, 409
Bleustein-Blanchet (Marcel), Fondation de la Vocation, France, 109
Bloomberg Philanthropies, USA, 409
BMCE Bank Foundation, Morocco, 219
Bodossaki Foundation, Greece, 145
Bofill (Jaume), Fundació, Spain, 287
Boghossian Foundation, Belgium, 31
Böll (Heinrich) Stiftung, Germany, 131
Bond, UK, 335
Book Aid International—BAI, UK, 343
Borderland Foundation, Poland, 256
Born Free Foundation, UK, 343
Bosch (Robert) Stiftung GmbH, Germany, 138
Botín Foundation, Spain, 292
Botín (Marcelino), Fundación, Spain, 292
Botswana Institute for Development Policy Analysis—BIDPA, Botswana, 37
BP Foundation, Inc, USA, 409
Braća Karić Foundation, Serbia, 271
BRAC, Bangladesh, 25
Bradley (Lynde and Harry) Foundation, Inc, USA, 449
Brandt (Bundeskanzler Willy) Stiftung, Germany, 123
BrazilFoundation, Brazil, 39
Brenthurst Foundation, South Africa, 282
Bridge House Estates, UK, 348
Brighter Future Myanmar Foundation—BFM, Myanmar, 221
British & Foreign School Society—BFSS, UK, 351
British Academy, UK, 344
The British Council, UK, 344
British Institute of International and Comparative Law—BIICL, UK, 345
British Overseas NGOs for Development, UK, 335
British Red Cross Society, UK, 345
British Schools and Universities Foundation, Inc—BSUF, USA, 410
The Broad Foundation, USA, 410
Brookings Institution, USA, 410
Brother's Brother Foundation, USA, 410
Buchanan Charitable Foundation, New Zealand, 232
Buck (Pearl S.) International, USA, 462
Buckland (William) Foundation, Australia, 19
Buddharaksa Foundation, Thailand, 323
Buffett (Susan Thompson) Foundation, USA, 474
Bulgarian Fund for Women, Bulgaria, 43
Bundeskanzler-Willy-Brandt-Stiftung, Germany, 123
Bunge y Born Foundation, Argentina, 7
Burroughs Wellcome Fund—BWF, USA, 411
C. G. Jung-Institut Zürich, Switzerland, 307
CABI, UK, 345
Cadbury (Edward) Charitable Trust, UK, 351
Cadbury (William Adlington) Charitable Trust, UK, 390
CAF America, USA, 393
CAFOD—Catholic Agency for Overseas Development, UK, 345
Calgary Foundation, Canada, 49
California Community Foundation, USA, 411
Calouste Gulbenkian Foundation, Portugal, 259
Cambodia Development Resource Institute—CDRI, Cambodia, 46
Cambodian Salesian Delegation, Cambodia, 46
Cambridge Commonwealth, European and International Trust, UK, 346
CAMFED International, UK, 346
The Camille and Henry Dreyfus Foundation, Inc, USA, 411
Canada Foundation for Innovation, Canada, 50
Canadian Feed The Children—CFTC, Canada, 50
Canadian International Council/Conseil International du Canada—CIC, Canada, 51
Canadian Organization for Development through Education—CODE, Canada, 52
Canadian Urban Institute/Institut Urbain du Canada—CUI/IUC, Canada, 51
Cancer Research UK, UK, 346
Canon Foundation in Europe, Netherlands, 224
Cape Verdean Student Welfare Foundation, Cabo Verde, 45
CARE International—CI, Switzerland, 307
Cargill (Margaret A.) Philanthropies, USA, 450
Cariplo Foundation, Italy, 175
Caritas de France—Secours Catholique, France, 116

Education

Carlo Cattaneo Institute, Italy, 182
Carlo Pesenti Foundation, Italy, 176
Carlos de Amberes Foundation, Spain, 289
Carlos Slim Foundation, Mexico, 215
CARMABI Foundation, Curaçao, 77
Carnegie Corporation of New York, USA, 411
Carnegie Hero Fund Commission, USA, 412
Carnegie Trust for the Universities of Scotland, UK, 346
Carnegie UK Trust, UK, 346
Carpathian Foundation, Hungary, 153
Casa de Mateus Foundation, Portugal, 259
Casey (Annie E.) Foundation, USA, 404
Cassa di Risparmio di Padova e Rovigo Foundation, Italy, 175
Caterpillar Foundation, USA, 412
Catholic Agency for Overseas Development—CAFOD, UK, 345
Catholic Agency for World Development—Trócaire, Ireland, 168
Catholic Help—Caritas France, France, 116
Cattaneo (Carlo), Istituto, Italy, 182
Caucasus Institute for Peace, Democracy and Development—CIPDD, Georgia, 117
Caucasus Research Resource Center Armenia Foundation—CRRC, Armenia, 9
CBM-International, Germany, 123
CCKF—Chiang Ching-kuo Foundation for International Scholarly Exchange, Taiwan, 321
CEDIAS-Musée Social—Centre d'Etudes, de Documentation, d'Information et d'Action Sociales, France, 101
CEDRO—Centro de Información y Educación para la Prevención del Abuso de Drogas, Peru, 248
CENOZO—Cellule Norbert Zongo pour le Journalisme d'Investigation en Afrique de l'Ouest, Burkina Faso, 44
CENSIS—Fondazione Centro Studi Investimenti Sociali, Italy, 172
Center for China & Globalization—CCG, China (People's Republic), 67
Center for Inquiry—CFI, USA, 412
Center for Training and Consultancy, Georgia, 117
Centras—Assistance Centre for NGOs, Romania, 263
Centras—Centrul de Asistenta pentru Organizatii Neguvernamentale, Romania, 263
Centre for Civil Society—CCS, India, 157
Centre for Development of Non-profit Organizations, Croatia, 76
Centre Européen de la Culture—CEC, Switzerland, 307
Centre for the Information Service, Co-operation and Development of NGOs, Slovenia, 277
Centre for International Studies, Italy, 172
Centre Ivoirien de Recherches Économiques et Sociales—CIRES, Côte d'Ivoire, 75
Centre for Philanthropy, Slovakia, 274
Centre for Social Studies, Documentation, Information and Action, France, 101
Centro de Estudios Públicos—CEP, Chile, 64
Centro de Información y Educación para la Prevención del Abuso de Drogas—CEDRO, Peru, 248
Centro Studi Internazionali—CSI, Italy, 172
Centro Studi e Ricerca Sociale Fondazione Emanuela Zancan, Italy, 172
Centrul de Resurse pentru Drepturile Omului—CReDO, Moldova, 217
Centrum pre Filantropiu, Slovakia, 274
The Century Foundation—TCF, USA, 413
Cera, Belgium, 28
CERANEO—Centar za razvoj neprofitnih organizacija, Croatia, 76
Cercle de Coopération des ONGD du Luxembourg, Luxembourg, 209
Česká spořitelna Foundation, Czech Republic, 79
Česko-německý fond budoucnosti, Czech Republic, 79
Cetana Educational Foundation, USA, 413
Chaabi (Miloud), Fondation, Morocco, 220
Chagnon (Lucie et André), Fondation, Canada, 55
Chandaria Foundation, Kenya, 198
Chang Yung-fa Foundation, Taiwan, 321
Charities Aid Foundation of America—CAF America, USA, 393
Charities Institute Ireland—Cii, Ireland, 165
Charity Islamic Trust Elrahma, UK, 352
Charles Koch Foundation, USA, 413
Charles and Lynn Schusterman Family Philanthropies, USA, 413
Charles Stewart Mott Foundation—CSMF, USA, 414
The Charles Wallace India Trusts, UK, 347
Charles Wolfson Charitable Trust, UK, 347

The Charta 77 Foundation, Czech Republic, 80
The Chatlos Foundation, Inc, USA, 414
Cheshire (Leonard) Foundation, UK, 364
Chia Hsin Foundation, Taiwan, 321
Chiang Ching-kuo Foundation for International Scholarly Exchange—CCKF, Taiwan, 321
The Chicago Community Trust, USA, 414
Chigiana Musical Academy, Italy, 172
ChildFund, New Zealand, 233
ChildFund International, USA, 414
Childhope Philippines, Philippines, 251
Children in Africa Foundation, Germany, 140
Children International—CI, USA, 414
Children of the Mekong, France, 102
Children of Slovakia Foundation, Slovakia, 275
The Children's Investment Fund Foundation, UK, 347
Childwick Trust, UK, 347
Chile Foundation, Chile, 65
China Charities Aid Foundation for Children, China (People's Republic), 67
China Children and Teenagers' Foundation, China (People's Republic), 67
China Foundation for Poverty Alleviation—CFPA, China (People's Republic), 67
China Medical Board—CMB, USA, 415
China Siyuan Foundation for Poverty Alleviation, China (People's Republic), 67
China Youth Development Foundation, China (People's Republic), 68
Christian Aid, UK, 348
The Churchill Fellowship, UK, 348
Churchill (Winston) Foundation of the United States, USA, 482
Churchill (Winston) Memorial Trust, Australia, 19
Churchill (Winston) Memorial Trust of New Zealand, New Zealand, 236
CIEE—Council on International Educational Exchange, USA, 415
Cini (Giorgio), Fondazione, Italy, 177
Citi Foundation, USA, 415
Citizenship Foundation, UK, 392
The City Bridge Trust, UK, 348
City of Lisbon Foundation, Portugal, 259
Civic Democratic Initiative Support Foundation—CDF, Yemen, 489
Civic Initiatives, Serbia, 271
Civil Peace Service—CPS, Germany, 120
Civil Society Development Center—CSDC, Georgia, 117
Civil Society Foundation, Georgia, 118
CLADEM—Comité de América Latina y el Caribe para la Defensa de los Derechos de la Mujer, Peru, 249
Clara Lionel Foundation—CLF, USA, 415
Claudine Talon Foundation, Benin, 35
CLEAR Global, USA, 416
Cleveland Foundation, USA, 416
Cleveland H. Dodge Foundation, Inc, USA, 416
Clinton Foundation, USA, 416
Clore Israel Foundation, Israel, 169
Člověk v tísni, Czech Republic, 79
CNIB Foundation/Fondation INCA, Canada, 52
CNVOS—Zavod Center za Informiranje, Sodelovanje in Razvoj Nevladnih Organizacije, Slovenia, 277
Coady Institute, Canada, 52
Coastline Foundation, Maldives, 212
The Coca-Cola Foundation, Inc, USA, 417
Çocuk (Anne) Eğitim Vakfı, Türkiye, 327
CODE—Canadian Organization for Development through Education, Canada, 52
CODESPA Foundation, Spain, 290
Collier Charitable Fund, Australia, 13
Collodi (Carlo), Fondazione Nazionale, Italy, 179
Comité de América Latina y el Caribe para la Defensa de los Derechos de la Mujer—CLADEM, Peru, 249
Committee of Good Will—Olga Havel Foundation, Czech Republic, 81
Commonwealth Foundation, UK, 348
The Commonwealth Fund, USA, 417
Communication Foundation for Asia, Philippines, 251
Community Chest of Korea—Fruit of Love, Korea (Republic), 200
Community Development Foundation, Mozambique, 221
Community Foundation for Northern Ireland, UK, 349
Community Foundation for the Western Region of Zimbabwe—CFWRZ, Zimbabwe, 490
Concern India Foundation, India, 157
Concern Worldwide, Ireland, 166
CONCORD—European NGO Confederation for Relief and Development, Belgium, 26
Conrad N. Hilton Foundation, USA, 417

Consejo Latinoamericano de Ciencias Sociales—CLACSO, Argentina, 6
Consuelo Zobel Alger Foundation, USA, 417
Cooperazione Internazionale—COOPI, Italy, 173
Coordinadora de ONGD España, Spain, 285
Copperbelt Development Foundation, Zambia, 490
Coram, UK, 349
Corona Foundation, Colombia, 71
Corus International, USA, 418
Costopoulos (J. F.) Foundation, Greece, 146
Coubertin Foundation, France, 105
Council for International Exchange of Scholars—CIES, USA, 418
Covenant Foundation, USA, 418
The Crafoord Foundation, Sweden, 298
Crafoordska stiftelsen, Sweden, 298
The Craig and Susan McCaw Foundation, USA, 418
The CRB Foundation/La Fondation CRB, Canada, 52
CReDO—Centrul de Resurse pentru Drepturile Omului, Moldova, 217
Crown Family Philanthropies, USA, 419
Cruz (Oswaldo), Fundação, Brazil, 40
Culture, Health, Arts, Sports and Education Fund—CHASE, Jamaica, 184
Cundill (Peter) Foundation, Bermuda, 35
Cuso International, Canada, 53
Cyril Ramaphosa Foundation, South Africa, 279
Cystic Fibrosis Trust, UK, 350
Czech-German Fund for the Future, Czech Republic, 79
DAAD—Deutscher Akademischer Austauschdienst, Germany, 125
Dag Hammarskjöld Foundation, Sweden, 303
Daiwa Anglo-Japanese Foundation, UK, 350
Dalia Association, Palestinian Territories, 246
Dalio Foundation, USA, 419
Daniele Agostino Derossi Foundation, USA, 420
Danielle Mitterrand Foundation, France, 112
Danish Cultural Institute—DCI, Denmark, 82
Danish Institute for Human Rights, Denmark, 84
Danish Outdoor Council, Denmark, 83
Danmark-Amerika Fondet, Denmark, 82
Danske Kulturinstitut—DKI, Denmark, 82
David and Lucile Packard Foundation, USA, 420
David Nott Foundation, UK, 350
Davis (Lady) Fellowship Trust, Israel, 170
Daw Khin Kyi Foundation, Myanmar, 221
Debts to Opportunities Foundation, Netherlands, 231
Dell (Michael & Susan) Foundation, USA, 453
del Pino (Rafael), Fundación, Spain, 294
Democracy Fund, USA, 458
Denmark-America Foundation, Denmark, 82
Deripaska (Oleg) Foundation, Russian Federation, 267
Derossi (Daniele Agostino) Foundation, USA, 420
Desmond & Leah Tutu Legacy Foundation, South Africa, 279
Deutsch-Russischer Austausch eV—DRA, Germany, 124
Deutsche Bank Americas Foundation, USA, 420
Deutsche Bank Endowment Fund at the Donors' Association for the Promotion of German Science, Germany, 142
Deutsche Bank Foundation, Germany, 124
Deutsche Bank Stiftung, Germany, 124
Deutsche Bundesstiftung Umwelt—DBU, Germany, 124
Deutsche Krebshilfe eV, Germany, 124
Deutsche Sparkassenstiftung für Internationale Zusammenarbeit, Germany, 125
Deutsche Telekom Foundation, Germany, 125
Deutsche Telekom Stiftung, Germany, 125
Deutscher Akademischer Austauschdienst—DAAD, Germany, 125
Development Cooperation Roundtable, Estonia, 92
Development Foundation, Guatemala, 148
Development Gateway—DG, USA, 420
Development NGO Coordinator Spain, Spain, 285
Dewji (Mo) Foundation, Tanzania, 323
DHL UK Foundation, UK, 350
Dietmar Hopp Foundation, Germany, 126
Dietmar-Hopp-Stiftung, Germany, 126
Digicel Foundation Haiti, Haiti, 149
Digicel Foundation Jamaica, Jamaica, 184
Digicel PNG Foundation, Papua New Guinea, 247
Digicel Trinidad and Tobago Foundation, Trinidad and Tobago, 326
Dioraphte Foundation, Netherlands, 229
DIPF—Leibniz-Institut für Bildungsforschung und Bildungsinformation, Germany, 126
DiploFoundation, Malta, 213
Ditchley Foundation, UK, 351

INDEX OF MAIN ACTIVITIES

Education

Dmitry Likhachev Foundation, Russian Federation, 265
The Do-Nation Foundation, Inc, Saint Lucia, 268
Dóchas—Irish Association of Non-Governmental Development Organisations, Ireland, 165
Dodge (Cleveland H.) Foundation, Inc, USA, 416
Doğan (Aydın) Vakfı, Türkiye, 328
Dollywood Foundation, USA, 420
Dom Manuel II Foundation, Portugal, 260
Dominican Development Foundation, Dominican Republic, 87
Don Bosco Foundation of Cambodia—DBFC, Cambodia, 46
Donner (William H.) Foundation, Inc, USA, 481
Donors' Association for the Promotion of Sciences and Humanities, Germany, 119
Doris Duke Charitable Foundation—DDCF, USA, 421
The Dr Denis Mukwege Foundation, Netherlands, 224
Dr Guillermo Manuel Ungo Foundation, El Salvador, 91
Dr Marcus Wallenberg Foundation for Further Education in International Industry, Sweden, 299
Dr Marcus Wallenbergs Stiftelse för Utbildning i Internationellt Industriellt Företagande, Sweden, 299
Dr Rainer Wild Foundation for Healthy Nutrition, Germany, 126
Dr Rainer Wild-Stiftung—Stiftung für Gesunde Ernährung, Germany, 126
Dr Scholl Foundation, USA, 421
Dreyfus (Camille and Henry) Foundation, USA, 411
Dreyfus Health Foundation, USA, 468
Drug Policy Alliance—DPA, USA, 421
DSW—Deutsche Stiftung Weltbevölkerung, Germany, 126
DTGO Group of Foundations, Thailand, 323
Duke Endowment, USA, 421
Dulverton Trust, UK, 351
Dumbarton Oaks, USA, 421
Dunhe Foundation, China (People's Republic), 68
Dutch-Bangla Bank Foundation, Bangladesh, 25
E. O. Wilson Biodiversity Foundation, USA, 421
Earth Island Institute—EII, USA, 422
Earthworm Foundation, Switzerland, 307
East Asia Institute—EAI, Korea (Republic), 201
East-West Center—EWC, USA, 422
East-West Encounters Charitable Foundation, Germany, 141
Ebelin and Gerd Bucerius ZEIT Foundation, Germany, 143
Eberhard Schöck Foundation, Germany, 127
Eberhard-Schöck-Stiftung, Germany, 127
Ebert (Friedrich) Stiftung, Germany, 129
EcoCiencia—Fundación Ecuatoriana de Estudios Ecologicos, Ecuador, 88
Economic Development Foundation, Türkiye, 328
Economic Foundation, Poland, 255
Ecuadorean Foundation of Ecological Studies, Ecuador, 88
EDF Group Foundation, France, 107
Edmond de Rothschild Foundations, Switzerland, 308
The Edna McConnell Clark Foundation, USA, 422
Ednannia—Initiative Centre to Support Social Action, Ukraine, 332
Edoardo Garrone Foundation, Italy, 177
EDP Foundation, Portugal, 260
Education Above All Foundation—EAA, Qatar, 262
The Education for Development Foundation—EDF, Thailand, 324
Education and Training Foundation—ETF, UK, 351
Educational Opportunity Foundation, UK, 351
Educo, Spain, 286
Edward Cadbury Charitable Trust, UK, 351
Eesti Mittetulundusühingute ja Sihtasutuste Liit, Estonia, 92
Eestimaa Looduse Fond—ELF, Estonia, 92
EFQM—European Foundation for Quality Management, Belgium, 30
Egmont Fonden, Denmark, 83
Egmont Foundation, Denmark, 83
EGMONT—Institut Royal des Relations Internationales, Belgium, 29
Ekofond SPP, Slovakia, 275
Elena & Gennady Timchenko Foundation, Russian Federation, 265
ELEPAP—Rehabilitation for the Disabled, Greece, 145
ELIAMEP—Hellenic Foundation for European and Foreign Policy, Greece, 146
The ELMA Group of Foundations, USA, 423

Elrahma Charity Trust, UK, 352
Emanuela Zancan Foundation Centre for Social Studies and Research, Italy, 172
Embrace the Middle East, UK, 352
Emirates Foundation, United Arab Emirates, 334
Empresas Polar Foundation, Venezuela, 487
Emunah, UK, 353
Enda Third World—Environment and Development Action in the Third World, Senegal, 270
Enda Tiers Monde—Environnement et Développement du Tiers-Monde, Senegal, 270
Energies for the World Foundation, France, 105
Enfants du Mékong, France, 102
The English-Speaking Union—ESU, UK, 353
Ente Cassa di Risparmio di Firenze, Italy, 173
Entraide Protestante Suisse, Switzerland, 311
Entraide Universitaire Mondiale du Canada, Canada, 63
Environmental Foundation of Jamaica, Jamaica, 184
Environmental Partnership Foundation, Poland, 256
Epilepsy Foundation, USA, 424
Equal Justice Initiative—EJI, USA, 424
Equality Fund/Fonds Égalité, Canada, 54
Equity Group Foundation—EGF, Kenya, 198
ERA—Europäische Rechtsakademie, Germany, 127
Ernst Schering Foundation, Germany, 127
Ernst-Schering-Stiftung, Germany, 127
Esquel Group Foundation—Ecuador, Ecuador, 88
Estonian Fund for Nature, Estonia, 92
Estonian National Culture Foundation, Estonia, 93
Ettersberg Foundation, Germany, 140
Eugenio Mendoza Foundation, Venezuela, 487
Eureka Foundation, Bulgaria, 43
Euris Foundation, France, 106
Euro-Mediterranean Centre on Climate Change Foundation, Italy, 176
Europäische Rechtsakademie—ERA, Germany, 127
European Anti-Poverty Network—EAPN, Belgium, 29
European Association for Cancer Research—EACR, UK, 353
European Center for Peace and Development—ECPD, Serbia, 271
European Cultural Centre, Switzerland, 307
European Cultural Foundation—ECF, Netherlands, 225
European Foundation for Management Development—EFMD, Belgium, 30
European Foundation for Quality Management—EFQM, Belgium, 30
European Institute of Health and Social Welfare, Spain, 296
European Mediterranean Institute, Spain, 296
European NGO Confederation for Relief and Development—CONCORD, Belgium, 26
European Roma Rights Centre—ERRC, Belgium, 30
European Training Foundation—ETF, Italy, 173
European Youth Foundation—EYF, France, 112
Europese Culterele Stichting, Netherlands, 225
Evangelisches Studienwerk eV, Germany, 128
Evens Foundation, Belgium, 31
Evrika Foundation, Bulgaria, 43
Ewing Marion Kauffman Foundation, USA, 425
ExxonMobil Foundation, USA, 425
FAI—Fondo per l'Ambiente Italiano, Italy, 174
Faith, UK, 353
The Family Federation of Finland, Finland, 98
Fatoumatta Bah-Barrow Foundation—FaBB, Gambia, 117
FDC—Fundação para o Desenvolvimento da Comunidade, Mozambique, 221
Federacja Funduszy Lokalnych w Polsce, Poland, 254
Federal Chancellor Willy Brandt Foundation, Germany, 123
Federation of Community Foundations in Poland, Poland, 254
Feed the Children, USA, 425
Feed the Minds, UK, 354
FEIM—Fundación para Estudio e Investigación de la Mujer, Argentina, 7
Félix Houphouët-Boigny Foundation for Peace Research, Côte d'Ivoire, 75
Fernand Lazard Foundation, Belgium, 31
Fernando Rielo Foundation, Spain, 290
Ferrero (Piera, Pietro e Giovanni), Fondazione, Italy, 179
FHI 360, USA, 425
FIJI Water Foundation, Fiji, 94
filia.die Frauenstiftung, Germany, 128
filia—the Women's Foundation, Germany, 128

The Film Foundation, USA, 425
FINCA International, USA, 425
Finnish Cultural Foundation, Finland, 97
Finnish Development Organizations, Finland, 95
Finnish Foundation for Technology Promotion, Finland, 98
Finnish Institute in the UK and Ireland Trust, UK, 354
Firelight Foundation, USA, 426
First Nations Development Institute, USA, 426
FirstRand Foundation, South Africa, 280
Flatiron Institute, USA, 472
Florence Gould Foundation, USA, 427
Florence Nightingale International Foundation, Switzerland, 309
Florence Savings Bank Foundation, Italy, 173
FOKAL—Open Society Foundation Haiti, Haiti, 149
Folke Bernadotte Memorial Foundation, Sweden, 299
Folke Bernadottes Minnesfond, Sweden, 299
Follereau Foundation Luxembourg, Luxembourg, 209
Folmer Wisti Fonden for International Forståelse, Denmark, 83
Folmer Wisti Foundation for International Understanding, Denmark, 83
Fondacija Braća Karić, Serbia, 271
Fondacija Cennosti, Bulgaria, 43
Fondacioni i Kosovës për Shoqëri të Hapur, Kosovo, 203
Fondation Addoha, Morocco, 219
Fondation Air France, France, 103
Fondation Auchan, France, 103
Fondation Auschwitz—Mémoire d'Auschwitz, Belgium, 30
Fondation Baxter & Alma Ricard, Canada, 55
Fondation Bernheim, Belgium, 31
Fondation BIAT pour la Jeunesse, Tunisia, 326
Fondation BMCE Bank, Morocco, 219
Fondation Boghossian, Belgium, 31
Fondation Canadienne pour l'Innovation, Canada, 50
Fondation Charles Veillon, Switzerland, 308
Fondation de la Cité Internationale Universitaire de Paris, France, 104
Fondation Claudine Talon, Benin, 35
Fondation du Collège de France, France, 105
Fondation Congo Assistance, Congo (Republic), 73
Fondation de Coubertin, France, 105
Fondation Digicel Haïti, Haiti, 149
Fondation Energies pour le Monde—Fondem, France, 105
Fondation d'Entreprise Crédit Agricole Réunion Mayotte, Réunion, 262
Fondation d'Entreprise Renault, France, 106
Fondation d'Entreprise VINCI pour la Cité, France, 106
Fondation Espace Afrique, Switzerland, 308
Fondation Euris, France, 106
Fondation Européenne de la Culture/Europese Culturele Stichting, Netherlands, 225
Fondation Evens Stichting, Belgium, 31
Fondation Félix Houphouët-Boigny pour la Recherche de la Paix, Côte d'Ivoire, 75
Fondation Fernand Lazard Stichting, Belgium, 31
Fondation Follereau Luxembourg—FFL, Luxembourg, 209
Fondation de France, France, 99
Fondation France Chine—FFC, France, 106
Fondation France-Israël, France, 106
Fondation Franco-Japonaise Sasakawa, France, 106
Fondation Francqui, Belgium, 31
Fondation Grand Cœur—FGC, Chad, 64
Fondation Groupe EDF, France, 107
Fondation Guri Vie Meilleure, Niger, 236
Fondation Hans Wilsdorf, Switzerland, 309
Fondation Hassan II pour les Marocains Résidant à l'Étranger, Morocco, 220
Fondation Internationale Florence Nightingale, Switzerland, 309
Fondation Internationale Tierno et Mariam—FITIMA, Burkina Faso, 44
Fondation ISREC, Switzerland, 309
Fondation J-Louis Lévesque, Canada, 55
Fondation Jean Monnet pour l'Europe, Switzerland, 309
Fondation Jean-Paul II pour le Sahel, Burkina Faso, 44
Fondation Joseph Ichame Kamach, Central African Republic, 63
Fondation Léopold Sédar Senghor, Senegal, 270
Fondation Lucie et André Chagnon, Canada, 55
Fondation Maison des Sciences de l'Homme—FMSH, France, 108

Education

Fondation Mapon, Congo (Democratic Republic), 72
Fondation Marcel Bleustein-Blanchet de la Vocation, France, 109
Fondation Mesmin Kabath—FOMEKA, Congo (Republic), 73
Fondation Miloud Chaâbi, Morocco, 220
Fondation Mohammed V pour la Solidarité, Morocco, 220
Fondation MTN Bénin, Benin, 35
Fondation MTN Cameroun, Cameroon, 47
Fondation MTN Congo, Congo (Republic), 73
Fondation MTN Côte d'Ivoire, Côte d'Ivoire, 76
Fondation Mutuelles Congolaises d'Epargne et de Crédit—MUCODEC, Congo (Republic), 73
Fondation Nationale pour l'Enseignement de la Gestion des Entreprises, France, 109
Fondation Nationale des Sciences Politiques—SciencesPo, France, 110
Fondation Noura, Mauritania, 214
Fondation Orange, France, 110
Fondation Orange Burkina Faso, Burkina Faso, 45
Fondation Orange Cameroun, Cameroon, 47
Fondation Orange-Côte d'Ivoire Télécom—OCIT, Côte d'Ivoire, 76
Fondation Orange Guinée, Guinea, 149
Fondation Orange Mali, Mali, 213
Fondation Orange Tunisie, Tunisia, 326
Fondation Orient-Occident—FOO, Morocco, 220
Fondation Perspectives d'Avenir, Congo (Republic), 73
Fondation Pierre Elliott Trudeau/Pierre Elliott Trudeau Foundation, Canada, 55
Fondation Princesse Charlène de Monaco, Monaco, 218
Fondation Rambourg, Tunisia, 326
Fondation Rawji, Congo (Democratic Republic), 72
Fondation pour le Renforcement des Capacités en Afrique, Zimbabwe, 490
Fondation Rinaldi, Haiti, 149
Fondation Roi Baudouin, Belgium, 33
Fondation Schneider Electric, France, 111
Fondation du Scoutisme Mondial, Switzerland, 320
Fondation Simón I. Patiño, Switzerland, 310
Fondation Sommet Mondial des Femmes, Switzerland, 320
Fondation Sonatel, Senegal, 270
Fondation Stamm, Burundi, 45
Fondation TotalEnergies, France, 112
Fondation Tunisie pour le Développement, Tunisia, 326
Fondation Vodacom RDC, Congo (Democratic Republic), 72
Fondatzija Otvoryeno Opshtyestvo Makyedonija, North Macedonia, 239
Fondazione 1563 per l'Arte e la Cultura, Italy, 174
Fondazione Adriano Olivetti, Italy, 174
Fondazione Angelo Della Riccia, Italy, 175
Fondazione AVSI, Italy, 175
Fondazione Cariplo, Italy, 175
Fondazione Cassa di Risparmio di Padova e Rovigo, Italy, 175
Fondazione Cassa di Risparmio di Torino, Italy, 176
Fondazione Cassa di Risparmio di Verona Vicenza Belluno e Ancona—Fondazione Cariverona, Italy, 176
Fondazione Cavaliere del Lavoro Carlo Pesenti, Italy, 176
Fondazione Centro Euro-Mediterraneo sui Cambiamenti Climatici—CMCC, Italy, 176
Fondazione Centro Studi Investimenti Sociali—CENSIS, Italy, 172
Fondazione Compagnia di San Paolo, Italy, 176
Fondazione Edoardo Garrone, Italy, 177
Fondazione Fratelli Tutti, Vatican City, 486
Fondazione Giorgio Cini, Italy, 177
Fondazione Giovanni Agnelli, Italy, 177
Fondazione Giovanni Lorenzini, Italy, 177
Fondazione Giulio Pastore—FGP, Italy, 178
Fondazione ISMU—Iniziative e Studi sulla Multietnicità, Italy, 178
Fondazione per l'Istituto Svizzero di Roma, Italy, 178
Fondazione Nazionale Carlo Collodi, Italy, 179
Fondazione Piera, Pietro e Giovanni Ferrero, Italy, 179
Fondazione Populorum Progressio, Vatican City, 486
Fondazione Roma, Italy, 179
Fondazione RUI, Italy, 180
Fondazione Terzo Pilastro – Internazionale, Italy, 180
Fondazione Vaticana Giovanni Paolo I, Vatican City, 486

Fondazione di Venezia, Italy, 181
Fondazione Vodafone Italia, Italy, 181
Fondazzjoni Patrimonju Malti, Malta, 213
Fondo para el Desarrollo de los Pueblos Indígenas de América Latina y El Caribe—FILAC, Bolivia, 36
Fonds atvērtai sabiedrībai DOTS, Latvia, 204
Fonds Baillet Latour, Belgium, 32
Fonds Égalité, Canada, 54
Fonds Européen pour la Jeunesse—FEJ, France, 112
Fonds National Suisse de la Recherche Scientifique, Switzerland, 316
Food for the Poor, Inc, USA, 426
For a Healthy Generation, Uzbekistan, 485
Ford Foundation, USA, 427
Foreign Policy Association, USA, 427
The Forest Trust, Switzerland, 307
Forum International de l'Innovation Sociale—FIIS, France, 112
Foundation for AIDS Research—amfAR, USA, 403
Foundation for Assistance, Training and Integration of Disadvantaged People, Spain, 287
Foundation Bofill, Spain, 287
Foundation for Caribbean Research and Management of Biodiversity, Curaçao, 77
Foundation Centre for the Study of Social Investment, Italy, 172
Foundation for the Defence of Nature, Venezuela, 487
Foundation for Environmental Education—FEE, Denmark, 83
Foundation for German-Polish Co-operation, Poland, 257
Foundation of the Hellenic World, Greece, 145
Foundation for International Community Assistance, USA, 425
Foundation for Latin American Economic Research, Argentina, 7
Foundation for National Parks & Wildlife, Australia, 14
Foundation for an Open Society DOTS, Latvia, 204
Foundation Open Society Institute Pakistan, Pakistan, 245
Foundation Open Society Macedonia—FOSIM, North Macedonia, 239
Foundation Orange, Slovakia, 275
Foundation for the Promotion of the German Rectors' Conference, Germany, 140
Foundation 'Remembrance, Responsibility and Future', Germany, 139
Foundation for the Rights of Future Generations, Germany, 141
Foundation for Rural & Regional Renewal—FRRR, Australia, 14
Foundation of Spanish Commercial Agents, Spain, 287
Foundation in Support of Local Democracy, Poland, 256
Foundation for the Support of Women's Work, Türkiye, 329
Foundation for the Swiss Institute of Rome, Italy, 178
Foundation of Weimar Classics, Germany, 134
Foundation for Women, Spain, 293
Foundation for Women's Research and Studies, Argentina, 7
The Foundation for Young Australians—FYA, Australia, 14
Foundation of Youth and Lifelong Learning—INEDIVIM, Greece, 145
Foundation for Youth Research, Germany, 140
Foundations' Post-Doc Pool, Finland, 95
France China Foundation, France, 106
France-Israel Foundation, France, 106
France-Libertés Fondation Danielle Mitterrand, France, 112
Franco-American Fulbright Commission, France, 113
Franco-Japanese Sasakawa Foundation, France, 106
Francqui Foundation, Belgium, 31
Frank (Anne)-Fonds, Switzerland, 306
Frank (Anne) Stichting, Netherlands, 224
Frank Knox Memorial Fellowships, UK, 363
Frankfurt Foundation for German-Italian Studies, Germany, 129
Frankfurter Stiftung für Deutsch-Italienische Studien, Germany, 129
Fraser Institute, Canada, 55
Fratelli Tutti Foundation, Vatican City, 486
Free Russia Foundation, USA, 428
The Freeman Foundation, USA, 428
French-American Foundation, USA, 429

INDEX OF MAIN ACTIVITIES

French National Foundation for Management Education, France, 109
Freudenberg Foundation, Germany, 129
Freudenberg Stiftung, Germany, 129
Friede Springer Foundation, Germany, 129
Friede Springer Stiftung, Germany, 129
Friedensdorf International, Germany, 129
Friedrich-Ebert-Stiftung eV, Germany, 129
Friedrich Naumann Foundation for Freedom, Germany, 130
Friedrich-Naumann-Stiftung für die Freiheit, Germany, 130
Friends-International, Cambodia, 46
Friluftsrådet, Denmark, 83
Fritz Thyssen Foundation, Germany, 130
Fritz Thyssen Stiftung, Germany, 130
FRS-FNRS—Fonds de la Recherche Scientifique, Belgium, 32
FUHEM—Fundación Benéfico-Social Hogar del Empleado, Spain, 286
Fulbright Commission Philippines, Philippines, 253
Fulbright France—Commission Fulbright Franco-Américaine, France, 113
Fulbright Israel, Israel, 169
Fulbright Norway—US-Norway Fulbright Foundation for Educational Exchange, Norway, 241
Fulbright Scholar Program, USA, 418
Fund for the Development of Indigenous Peoples of Latin America and the Caribbean, Bolivia, 36
Fund and Endowment Management Foundation, Norway, 240
Fund for Scientific Research, Belgium, 32
Fundação Abrinq pelos Direitos da Criança e do Adolescente, Brazil, 39
Fundação ArcelorMittal Brasil, Brazil, 39
Fundação Armando Alvares Penteado, Brazil, 39
Fundação Banco do Brasil, Brazil, 39
Fundação Caboverdiana de Acção Social Escolar—FICASE, Cabo Verde, 45
Fundação Calouste Gulbenkian, Portugal, 259
Fundação da Casa de Mateus, Portugal, 259
Fundação Cidade de Lisboa, Portugal, 259
Fundação Dom Manuel II, Portugal, 260
Fundação EDP, Portugal, 260
Fundação Eng. António de Almeida, Portugal, 260
Fundação Getulio Vargas—FGV, Brazil, 40
Fundação Iochpe, Brazil, 40
Fundação Luso-Americana para o Desenvolvimento—FLAD, Portugal, 260
Fundação Maria Cecilia Souto Vidigal, Brazil, 40
Fundação Mário Soares e Maria Barroso, Portugal, 260
Fundação Oriente, Portugal, 260
Fundação Oswaldo Cruz—FIOCRUZ, Brazil, 40
Fundação Ricardo do Espírito Santo Silva, Portugal, 261
Fundação Roberto Marinho, Brazil, 41
Fundação de Serralves, Portugal, 261
Fundação Telefônica Vivo, Brazil, 41
Fundação Vodafone Portugal, Portugal, 261
Fundació Futbol Club Barcelona, Spain, 287
Fundació Gala–Salvador Dalí, Spain, 287
Fundació Jaume Bofill, Spain, 287
Fundación Acindar, Argentina, 6
Fundación AFIM—Ayuda, Formación e Integración del Discapacitado, Spain, 287
Fundación de los Agentes Comerciales de España, Spain, 287
Fundación Albéniz, Spain, 288
Fundación Amancio Ortega, Spain, 288
Fundación Amanecer, Colombia, 70
Fundación Astur, Uruguay, 485
Fundación Bancaria 'la Caixa', Spain, 288
Fundación BANHCAFE—FUNBANHCAFE, Honduras, 150
Fundación Barceló, Spain, 289
Fundación Bigott, Venezuela, 487
Fundación Bunge y Born, Argentina, 7
Fundación Capital, Colombia, 70
Fundación Carlos de Amberes, Spain, 289
Fundación Carlos Slim, Mexico, 215
Fundación Carolina, Spain, 290
Fundación Chile—FCH, Chile, 65
Fundación Científica de la Asociación Española Contra el Cáncer—AECC, Spain, 290
Fundación CODESPA, Spain, 290
Fundación Comunitaria de Puerto Rico—FCPR, Puerto Rico, 261
Fundación Corona, Colombia, 71
Fundación para la Defensa de la Naturaleza—FUDENA, Venezuela, 487
Fundación Dominicana de Desarrollo—FDD, Dominican Republic, 87

INDEX OF MAIN ACTIVITIES

Education

Fundación Dr Guillermo Manuel Ungo—FUNDAUNGO, El Salvador, 91
Fundación Empresa-Universidad de Zaragoza, Spain, 290
Fundación Empresas Polar, Venezuela, 487
Fundación Escuela Nueva, Colombia, 71
Fundación Espacio Cívico, Panama, 247
Fundación para Estudio e Investigación de la Mujer—FEIM, Argentina, 7
Fundación Eugenio Mendoza—FEM, Venezuela, 487
Fundación Felipe González, Spain, 290
Fundación Fernando Rielo, Spain, 290
Fundación Global Democracia y Desarrollo—FUNGLODE, Dominican Republic, 87
Fundación Grupo Esquel—Ecuador, Ecuador, 88
Fundación IE, Spain, 291
Fundación de Investigaciones Económicas Latinoamericanas—FIEL, Argentina, 7
Fundación José Ortega y Gasset—Gregorio Marañón, Spain, 291
Fundación Leo Messi, Spain, 292
Fundación Loewe, Spain, 292
Fundación MAPFRE, Spain, 292
Fundación Marcelino Botín, Spain, 292
Fundación María Francisca de Roviralta, Spain, 292
Fundación Mediterránea—IERAL, Argentina, 7
Fundación Miguel Alemán AC, Mexico, 215
Fundación Moisés Bertoni—FMB, Paraguay, 248
Fundación Montemadrid, Spain, 292
Fundación Mujer, Costa Rica, 74
Fundación Mujeres, Spain, 293
Fundación Mujeres en Igualdad—MEI, Argentina, 8
Fundación Nacional para el Desarrollo de Honduras—FUNADEH, Honduras, 150
Fundación Nobis, Ecuador, 88
Fundación Orange, Spain, 293
Fundación Oxfam Intermón, Spain, 293
Fundación Pablo Neruda, Chile, 65
Fundación Paideia Galiza, Spain, 293
Fundación Paraguaya de Cooperación y Desarrollo, Paraguay, 248
Fundación Pedro Barrié de la Maza, Spain, 293
Fundación Pies Descalzos, Colombia, 71
Fundación Princesa de Asturias, Spain, 294
Fundación Rafa Nadal, Spain, 294
Fundación Rafael del Pino, Spain, 294
Fundación Real Madrid, Spain, 295
Fundación Repsol, Spain, 295
Fundación La Salle de Ciencias Naturales—FLASA, Venezuela, 487
Fundación Semah-Valencia, Panama, 247
Fundación SES—Sustentabilidad, Educación, Solidaridad, Argentina, 8
Fundación SM, Spain, 295
Fundación Tecnologías Sociales—TECSOS, Spain, 296
Fundación Telefónica, Spain, 295
Fundación Telefónica Movistar Argentina, Argentina, 8
Fundación Telefónica Movistar Chile, Chile, 65
Fundación Telefónica Movistar Colombia, Colombia, 71
Fundación Telefónica Movistar Ecuador, Ecuador, 89
Fundación Telefónica Movistar México, Mexico, 216
Fundación Telefónica Movistar Perú, Peru, 249
Fundación Telefónica Movistar Uruguay, Uruguay, 485
Fundación Telmex Telcel, Mexico, 216
Fundación Tigo, Guatemala, 148
Fundación Universidad-Empresa—UE, Spain, 295
Fundación UPM, Uruguay, 485
Fundación Vodafone España, Spain, 296
Fundacja Agory, Poland, 255
Fundacja Dobroczynności Atlas, Poland, 255
Fundacja Gospodarcza, Poland, 255
Fundacja im. Stefana Batorego, Poland, 256
Fundacja Orange, Poland, 255
Fundacja Partnerstwo dla Srodowiska, Poland, 256
Fundacja Pogranicze, Poland, 256
Fundacja POLSAT, Poland, 256
Fundacja Rozwoju Demokracji Loaklnej, Poland, 256
Fundacja Współpracy Polsko-Niemieckiej/Stiftung für Deutsch-Polnische Zusammenarbeit, Poland, 257
Fundacja Wspomagania Wsi, Poland, 257
FUNDAP—Fundación para el Desarrollo, Guatemala, 148
Fundasaun Alola, Timor-Leste, 325
Fundația Orange, Romania, 263
Fundația Orange Moldova, Moldova, 217
Fundația Universitară a Mării Negre—FUMN, Romania, 263
Fundația Vodafone România, Romania, 264
FUNDAUNGO—Fundación Dr Guillermo Manuel Ungo, El Salvador, 91
Future in Our Hands Youth NGO—FIOH, Armenia, 9
FWO—Fonds Wetenschappelijk Onderzoek, Belgium, 32
FXB International—Association François-Xavier Bagnoud, Switzerland, 310
The Gaia Foundation, UK, 355
Gapminder, Sweden, 300
Garden Organic, UK, 355
Garfield Weston Foundation, UK, 355
Garrone (Edoardo), Fondazione, Italy, 177
Gates (Bill & Melinda) Foundation, USA, 429
Gates Foundation, USA, 429
The Gatsby Charitable Foundation, UK, 355
GE Aerospace Foundation, USA, 429
Gebert Rüf Stiftung, Switzerland, 311
The George A. and Eliza Gardner Howard Foundation, USA, 430
The George I. Alden Trust, USA, 430
George and Thelma Paraskevaides Foundation, Cyprus, 78
Georges Lurcy Charitable and Educational Trust, USA, 430
Georgian Foundation for Strategic and International Studies (Rondeli Foundation)—GFSIS, Georgia, 118
Gerda Henkel Foundation, Germany, 130
Gerda Henkel Stiftung, Germany, 130
German Academic Exchange Service, Germany, 125
German Cancer Aid, Germany, 124
German Catholic Bishops' Organization for Development Co-operation, Germany, 137
German Federal Foundation for the Environment, Germany, 124
German Foundation for World Population, Germany, 126
German Institute of Development and Sustainability—IDOS, Germany, 130
German Institute for Global and Area Studies—GIGA, Germany, 130
German Marshall Fund of the United States—GMF, USA, 430
German-Russian Exchange, Germany, 124
German Savings Banks Foundation for International Co-operation, Germany, 125
Getulio Vargas Foundation, Brazil, 40
Ghazanfar Foundation, Afghanistan, 4
Gift of the Givers Foundation, South Africa, 280
Giorgio Cini Foundation, Italy, 177
Giovanni Agnelli Foundation, Italy, 177
Giovanni Lorenzini Foundation, Italy, 177
Giovanni Paolo I, Fondazione Vaticana, Vatican City, 486
Giulio Pastore Foundation, Italy, 178
Give2Asia, USA, 394
Giving USA Foundation, USA, 394
Global Communities, USA, 431
Global Democracy and Development Foundation, Dominican Republic, 87
Global Ethic Foundation, Germany, 141
Global Forest Fund, Denmark, 83
Global Fund for Children, USA, 431
Global Fund for Women—GFW, USA, 431
Global Health Partnerships, UK, 355
Global Impact, USA, 395
Global Innovation Fund, UK, 356
Global Schools Forum, UK, 341
Globetree Association, Sweden, 300
GLOBSEC, Slovakia, 275
Gobabeb Namib Research Institute, Namibia, 222
Goethe-Institut, Germany, 131
Goldman Sachs Foundation, USA, 432
Goldsmith (Horace W.) Foundation, USA, 436
Good Neighbors International, Korea (Republic), 201
Good Things Foundation, UK, 356
Good360, USA, 432
Goodenough College, UK, 356
Goodwill Industries International, Inc—GII, USA, 432
Google.org—Google Foundation, USA, 432
Gorbachev Foundation, Russian Federation, 266
Gordon and Betty Moore Foundation, USA, 432
Gordon (Walter and Duncan) Charitable Foundation, Canada, 62
Gould (Florence) Foundation, USA, 427
Graça Machel Trust, South Africa, 280
Gradjanske inicijative—GI, Serbia, 271
Graduate Institute of International Studies and Development Studies, Switzerland, 311
Graham Foundation for Advanced Studies in the Fine Arts—GF, USA, 432
Grameen Foundation—GF, USA, 433
Grant (William T.) Foundation, USA, 481
The Grass Foundation, USA, 433
Great Britain Sasakawa Foundation, UK, 356
Greater Kansas City Community Foundation, USA, 433
Green Umbrella Children's Foundation—ChildFund Korea, Korea (Republic), 201
Grinspoon (Harold) Foundation, USA, 434
Group of Foundations and Businesses, Argentina, 6
Grupo de Fundaciones y Empresas, Argentina, 6
The Guardian Foundation, UK, 356
Guggenheim (John Simon) Memorial Foundation, USA, 444
Guggenheim (Solomon R.) Foundation, USA, 473
Gulbenkian (Calouste), Fundação, Portugal, 259
Gulf Research Center—GRC, Saudi Arabia, 269
H&M Foundation, Sweden, 300
Haiti Development Institute—HDI, Haiti, 149
Hamdard Foundation Pakistan, Pakistan, 245
Hamlyn (Paul) Foundation, UK, 373
Hammarskjölds (Dag) Minnesfond, Stiftelsen, Sweden, 303
Hanaholmen—Swedish-Finnish Cultural Centre, Finland, 95
HAND—Hungarian Association of NGOs for Development and Humanitarian Aid, Hungary, 152
Haniel Foundation, Germany, 131
Haniel-Stiftung, Germany, 131
Hanns Seidel Foundation, Germany, 131
Hanns-Seidel-Stiftung eV, Germany, 131
Hans Wilsdorf Foundation, Switzerland, 309
Hariri Foundation for Sustainable Human Development, Lebanon, 205
Harold Grinspoon Foundation, USA, 434
Harp Helú Foundations, Mexico, 216
Harry and Jeanette Weinberg Foundation, Inc, USA, 434
Hasbro Childrens Trust, USA, 434
Hasbro Foundation, USA, 434
Hassan II Foundation for Moroccans Living Abroad, Morocco, 220
Hawaii Resilience Fund, USA, 458
He Xiangjian Foundation, China (People's Republic), 68
Headley Trust, UK, 357
Health Volunteers Overseas—HVO, USA, 434
Hearst Foundations, USA, 435
Heart & Stroke, Canada, 56
Heart to Heart International—HHI, USA, 435
Hedwig and Robert Samuel Foundation, Germany, 131
Hedwig und Robert Samuel-Stiftung, Germany, 131
Heinrich Böll Foundation, Germany, 131
Heinrich-Böll-Stiftung, Germany, 131
HEKS—Hilfswerk der Evangelischen Kirchen Schweiz, Switzerland, 311
Hellenic Foundation for Culture, Greece, 145
Hellenic Foundation for European and Foreign Policy—ELIAMEP, Greece, 146
Helmholtz Association, Germany, 132
Helmholtz-Gemeinschaft, Germany, 132
Helmich (Janson Johan og Marcia) Legat, Norway, 242
Helmsley (Leona M. and Harry B.) Charitable Trust, USA, 447
Helsińska Fundacja Praw Człowieka, Poland, 257
Helsinki Foundation for Human Rights, Poland, 257
Hempel Fonden, Denmark, 84
Hempel Foundation, Denmark, 84
Henkel (Gerda) Stiftung, Germany, 130
Henrietta Szold Institute—National Institute for Research in the Behavioural Sciences, Israel, 169
Henry Doubleday Research Association, UK, 355
Henry Luce Foundation, Inc, USA, 435
The Henry Moore Foundation, UK, 358
HER Fund, Hong Kong, 151
Heren Philanthropic Foundation, China (People's Republic), 68
The Heritage Foundation, USA, 436
Heritage Institute for Policy Studies—HIPS, Somalia, 277
HESTIA, Czech Republic, 78
Heungkong Charitable Foundation, China (People's Republic), 68
Hewlett (William and Flora) Foundation, USA, 481
Heydar Aliyev Fondu, Azerbaijan, 23
Heydar Aliyev Foundation, Azerbaijan, 23
Higherlife Foundation, Zimbabwe, 491
Hilti Foundation, Liechtenstein, 208
Hilton (Conrad N.) Foundation, USA, 417

Education

Himalaya Research and Development Foundation—Himalaya Foundation, Taiwan, 321
Hinduja Foundation, India, 157
HIPS—Heritage Institute for Policy Studies, Somalia, 277
Hirschfeld-Eddy Foundation, Germany, 132
Hirschfeld-Eddy-Stiftung, Germany, 132
Hisar Education Foundation—HEV, Türkiye, 328
Historic Environment Scotland, UK, 358
Hitachi Foundation, Japan, 187
Hivos—Humanistisch Instituut voor Ontwikkelings Samenwerking, Netherlands, 226
HJ Foundation, Congo (Democratic Republic), 72
Hodge Foundation, UK, 358
Holt International, USA, 436
Hong Kong Society for the Blind, Hong Kong, 151
Hope, Ireland, 165
Hope Foundation, Türkiye, 331
HOPE International Development Agency, Canada, 56
Hope not Hate Charitable Trust—HNHCT, UK, 358
Hopp (Dietmar) Stiftung, Germany, 126
Horace W. Goldsmith Foundation, USA, 436
Hormuud Salaam Foundation, Somalia, 277
Hornby (A. S.) Educational Trust, UK, 338
Houphouët-Boigny (Félix), Fondation, Côte d'Ivoire, 75
House of the Human Sciences Foundation, France, 108
Howard (George A. and Eliza Gardner) Foundation, USA, 430
Howard Hughes Medical Institute—HHMI, USA, 437
Howard Karagheusian Commemorative Corporation—HKCC, USA, 437
Human Resource Development Foundation, Türkiye, 329
Human Rights Watch—HRW, USA, 437
Humanistic Institute for Co-operation with Developing Countries, Netherlands, 226
Humanitarian Academy for Development—HAD, UK, 359
Humanity & Inclusion, France, 113
Humboldt Forum, Germany, 132
The Hunter Foundation—THF, UK, 359
IACD—Institute of Asian Culture and Development, Korea (Republic), 201
IAESTE—International Association for the Exchange of Students for Technical Experience, Luxembourg, 210
Ian Potter Foundation, Australia, 14
IBM International Foundation, USA, 438
IBON Foundation, Philippines, 252
Ibrahim (Mo) Foundation, UK, 368
Icelandic Human Rights Centre, Iceland, 154
Ichikowitz Family Foundation—IFF, South Africa, 280
The Ideas Institute, Kenya, 199
IDRF—International Development and Relief Foundation, Canada, 56
Idrima Kratikon Ipotrofion, Greece, 147
IE Foundation, Spain, 291
IFES—International Foundation for Electoral Systems, USA, 440
IFRISSE Burkina, Burkina Faso, 45
IHH Humanitarian Relief Foundation, Türkiye, 328
IKGV—İnsan Kaynağını Geliştirme Vakfı, Türkiye, 329
İktisadi Kalkınma Vakfı, Türkiye, 328
IKY—State Scholarships Foundation, Greece, 147
Îles de Paix, Belgium, 32
Imbuto Foundation, Rwanda, 268
Inclusion International, UK, 359
India Partners, USA, 438
Indian Council for Cultural Relations, India, 157
Indian Council of Social Science Research—ICSSR, India, 157
Indian National Trust for Art and Cultural Heritage—INTACH, India, 158
Indonesia Biodiversity Foundation, Indonesia, 162
INEDIVIM—Foundation of Youth and Lifelong Learning, Greece, 145
Information and Education Centre for the Prevention of Drug Abuse, Peru, 248
INHURED International—International Institute for Human Rights, Environment and Development, Nepal, 223
Inlaks Shivdasani Foundation, India, 158
Innovators and Entrepreneurs Foundation/Fondation d'Innovateurs et d'Entrepreneurs—IEF/FIE, Canada, 57

İnsan Hak ve Hürriyetleri İnsani Yardım Vakfı—IHH, Türkiye, 328
İnsan Kaynağını Geliştirme Vakfı—IKGV, Türkiye, 329
Institut Arctique de l'Amérique du Nord—IAAN, Canada, 49
Institut Europeu de la Mediterrània—IEMed, Spain, 296
Institut FMES—Institut Méditerranéen d'Etudes Stratégiques, France, 113
Institut de Hautes Etudes Internationales et du Développement—IHEID, Switzerland, 311
Institut International des Droits de l'Enfant, Switzerland, 312
Institut for Menneskerettigheder, Denmark, 84
Institut Mittag-Leffler, Sweden, 300
Institut Pasteur, France, 114
Institut de Recherche Empirique en Économie Politique—IREEP, Benin, 35
Institut Royal des Relations Internationales—EGMONT, Belgium, 29
Institut für Weltwirtschaft—IfW Kiel, Germany, 132
Institute of Asian Culture and Development—IACD, Korea (Republic), 201
Institute of Baltic Studies, Estonia, 92
Institute of British Geographers, UK, 378
Institute for Citizens & Scholars, USA, 439
Institute of Economic Affairs—IEA, UK, 359
Institute for Empirical Research in Political Economy—IERPE, Benin, 35
Institute of International Education—IIE, USA, 439
Institute of Social Studies—ISS, Netherlands, 226
Instituto Ayrton Senna, Brazil, 41
Instituto Europeo de Salud y Bienestar Social, Spain, 296
Instituto Interamericano de Derechos Humanos—IIDH, Costa Rica, 74
Instituto de Montaña, Peru, 249
Institutul Cultural Român—ICR, Romania, 264
INTACH—Indian National Trust for Art and Cultural Heritage, India, 158
INTEGRATA Foundation, Germany, 132
INTEGRATA—Stiftung für Humane Nutzung der Informationstechnologie, Germany, 132
Inter-American Institute of Human Rights, Costa Rica, 74
Interchurch Aid—HIA Hungary, Hungary, 153
International Baccalaureate—IB, Switzerland, 312
International Blue Crescent Relief and Development Foundation—IBC, Türkiye, 329
International Charitable Fund 'Concord 3000', Ukraine, 333
International Co-operation, Italy, 173
International Development and Relief Foundation—IDRF, Canada, 56
International Education Research Foundation, Inc—IERF, USA, 440
International Forum Bosnia, Bosnia and Herzegovina, 37
International Forum for Social Innovation—IFSI, France, 112
The International Foundation, USA, 440
International Foundation for Electoral Systems—IFES, USA, 440
International Foundation for Science—IFS, Sweden, 300
International Foundation for Socio-economic and Political Studies, Russian Federation, 266
International Historical, Educational, Charitable and Human Rights Society—International Memorial, Russian Federation, 266
International Institute for Applied Systems Analysis—IIASA, Austria, 21
International Institute for Human Rights, Environment and Development, Nepal, 223
International Institute for the Rights of the Child, Switzerland, 312
International Institute of Rural Reconstruction—IIRR, Philippines, 252
International Institute of Social Studies, Netherlands, 226
International Memorial, Russian Federation, 266
International Organization for Relief, Welfare & Development—IORWD, Saudi Arabia, 269
International Orthodox Christian Charities—IOCC, USA, 441
International Renaissance Foundation—IRF, Ukraine, 333
International Rescue Committee—IRC, USA, 441
International Research & Exchanges Board—IREX, USA, 442
International Union for Conservation of Nature and Natural Resources, Switzerland, 313

INDEX OF MAIN ACTIVITIES

International University Centre of Paris Foundation, France, 104
International Visegrad Fund—IVF, Slovakia, 275
International Youth Foundation—IYF, USA, 442
International Youth Library Foundation, Germany, 133
Internationale Jugendbibliothek, Germany, 133
Internationalt Uddannelsescenter, Denmark, 84
INTERSOS, Italy, 182
IOCC—International Orthodox Christian Charities, USA, 441
Iochpe Foundation, Brazil, 40
iPartner India, India, 155
IRC—International Rescue Committee, USA, 441
The Ireland Funds America, USA, 442
IREX—International Research & Exchanges Board, USA, 442
Irvine (James) Foundation, USA, 443
Islands of Peace, Belgium, 32
ISMU Foundation—Initiatives and Studies on Multi-ethnicity, Italy, 178
ISPI—Istituto per gli Studi di Politica Internazionale, Italy, 183
IsraAID, Israel, 169
The Israel Democracy Institute—IDI, Israel, 170
ISREC Foundation, Switzerland, 309
Istituto Carlo Cattaneo, Italy, 182
Istituto Luigi Sturzo, Italy, 182
Istituto di Ricerche Farmacologiche Mario Negri, Italy, 182
Istituto per gli Studi di Politica Internazionale—ISPI, Italy, 183
Istituto Svedese di Studi Classici a Roma, Italy, 183
Italian Institute for International Political Studies, Italy, 183
IUC International Education Center—IUC-Europe, Denmark, 84
IUCN/UICN, Switzerland, 313
Ivorian Economic and Social Research Centre, Côte d'Ivoire, 75
The J. F. Costopoulos Foundation, Greece, 146
J. F. Kapnek Zimbabwe, Zimbabwe, 491
J-Louis Lévesque Foundation, Canada, 55
Jack Ma Foundation—JMF, China (People's Republic), 68
Jacobs Foundation, Switzerland, 313
Jahnsson (Yrjö) Foundation, Finland, 98
Jahres (Anders) Humanitære Stiftelse, Norway, 240
The James Irvine Foundation, USA, 443
James Michel Foundation, Seychelles, 272
James S. McDonnell Foundation, USA, 443
Jan Hus Educational Foundation, Czech Republic, 81
Janson Johan Helmich and Marcia Jansons Endowment, Norway, 242
Janson Johan Helmich og Marcia Jansons Legat, Norway, 242
The Japan Foundation, Japan, 189
Japan Foundation Endowment Committee—JFEC, UK, 361
Japan International Volunteer Center—JVC, Japan, 190
Japan Society for the Promotion of Science—JSPS, Japan, 190
Japanese-German Centre Berlin, Germany, 133
Japanisch-Deutsches Zentrum Berlin, Germany, 133
JCA Charitable Foundation, UK, 361
Jean Monnet Foundation for Europe, Switzerland, 309
JEN, Japan, 190
Jenny and Antti Wihuri Foundation, Finland, 96
Jenny ja Antti Wihurin Rahasto, Finland, 96
Jerusalem Foundation, Israel, 170
The Jerusalem Trust, UK, 361
JFEC—Japan Foundation Endowment Committee, UK, 361
JN Foundation, Jamaica, 184
JNF UK—JNF Charitable Trust, UK, 361
Johanna Quandt Foundation, Germany, 133
Johanna-Quandt-Stiftung, Germany, 133
The John D. and Catherine T. MacArthur Foundation, USA, 443
John Innes Foundation—JIF, UK, 362
John Moores Foundation, UK, 362
John Paul I Vatican Foundation, Vatican City, 486
John Paul II Foundation for the Sahel, Burkina Faso, 44
John S. and James L. Knight Foundation, USA, 444
John Simon Guggenheim Memorial Foundation, USA, 444
Johnson & Johnson Foundation US—JJF, USA, 444
Johnson (Lyndon Baines) Foundation, USA, 449

INDEX OF MAIN ACTIVITIES

Education

Johnson (Stanley Thomas) Foundation, Switzerland, 317
JOHUD—Jordanian Hashemite Fund for Human Development, Jordan, 196
Jordan River Foundation, Jordan, 196
José Ortega y Gasset—Gregorio Marañón Foundation, Spain, 291
Joseph Levy Foundation, UK, 362
Joseph Patrick Trust, UK, 369
Joseph Tanenbaum Charitable Foundation, Canada, 58
Josiah Macy Jr Foundation, USA, 445
Joyce Banda Foundation International, Malawi, 210
Joyce Foundation, USA, 445
JPMorgan Chase Foundation, USA, 445
Jung (C. G.) Institut Zürich, Switzerland, 307
Kade (Max) Foundation, Inc, USA, 451
Kadın Emeğini Değerlendirme Vakfı—KEDV, Türkiye, 329
KAF—Kataliko Actions for Africa, Congo (Democratic Republic), 72
Kafaa Development Foundation, Libya, 207
Kapnek (J. F.) Charitable Trust Zimbabwe, Zimbabwe, 491
Karagheusian (Howard) Commemorative Corporation, USA, 437
Kárpátok Alapítvány, Hungary, 153
Karuna Trust, UK, 363
Kayany Foundation, Lebanon, 206
KCDF—Kenya Community Development Foundation, Kenya, 199
KDDI Foundation, Japan, 191
KEHATI—Yayasan Keanekaragaman Hayati Indonesia, Indonesia, 162
Kellogg (W. K.) Foundation, USA, 478
Kennedy Memorial Trust, UK, 363
Kettering (Charles F.) Foundation, USA, 445
Kettering Foundation—KF, USA, 445
Khalifa Bin Zayed Al Nahyan Foundation, United Arab Emirates, 334
Khemka (Nand & Jeet) Foundation, India, 159
Kiel Institute for the World Economy, Germany, 132
Kind Heart Foundation, Viet Nam, 488
King Baudouin Foundation, Belgium, 33
King Faisal Foundation, Saudi Arabia, 269
King Gustaf V's 90th Birthday Foundation, Sweden, 301
King Hussein Foundation—KHF, Jordan, 196
King Khalid Foundation, Saudi Arabia, 269
King Philanthropies, USA, 445
King Sejong Institute Foundation—KSIF, Korea (Republic), 201
The King's Foundation, UK, 363
The King's Fund, UK, 363
The King's Trust, UK, 363
Kiwanis Children's Fund, USA, 446
KK-stiftelsen, Sweden, 301
Klassik Stiftung Weimar, Germany, 134
Klaus Tschira Foundation, Germany, 134
Klaus Tschira Stiftung GmbH, Germany, 134
Knight (John S. and James L.) Foundation, USA, 444
Knowledge Foundation, Sweden, 301
Knox (Frank) Memorial Fellowships, USA, 428
Knut and Alice Wallenberg Foundation, Sweden, 301
Knut och Alice Wallenbergs Stiftelse, Sweden, 301
Koç (Vehbi), Vakfı, Türkiye, 331
Koch (Charles) Foundation, USA, 413
Kokkalis Foundation, Greece, 146
Koning Boudewijnstichting/Fondation Roi Baudouin, Belgium, 33
Konrad Adenauer Foundation, Germany, 134
Konrad-Adenauer-Stiftung eV—KAS, Germany, 134
Konsultatsiis da Treningis Tsentri, Georgia, 117
Konung Gustaf V's 90-Årsfond, Sweden, 301
Körber Foundation, Germany, 134
Körber-Stiftung, Germany, 134
The Korea Foundation, Korea (Republic), 202
Koret Foundation, USA, 446
The Kosciuszko Foundation, Inc, USA, 446
Kosovo Foundation for Open Society—KFOS, Kosovo, 203
Kresge Foundation, USA, 446
Krupp von Bohlen und Halbach (Alfried) Stiftung, Germany, 121
Kulika Charitable Trust Uganda, Uganda, 331
Kuok Foundation Berhad, Malaysia, 211
Kusuma Trust UK, UK, 363
Kuwait Foundation for the Advancement of Sciences—KFAS, Kuwait, 203
'La Caixa' Banking Foundation, Spain, 288
La Salle Foundation for Natural Sciences, Venezuela, 487

Lady Davis Fellowship Trust, Israel, 170
Lady Khama Charitable Trust, Botswana, 37
Lafede.cat—Federació d'Organitzacions per a la Justícia Global, Spain, 286
Lafede.cat—Federation of Organizations for Global Justice, Spain, 286
Laidlaw Foundation, UK, 364
Laing Family Trusts, UK, 364
Lambrakis Foundation, Greece, 146
Lannan Foundation, USA, 447
LAPAS—Latvijas platforma attīstības sadarbībai, Latvia, 204
Latin American and Caribbean Committee for the Defence of Women's Rights, Peru, 249
Latin American Council of Social Sciences, Argentina, 6
Latter-day Saint Charities—LDSC, USA, 447
Latvia Children's Fund, Latvia, 204
Latvian Platform for Development Cooperation, Latvia, 204
Latvijas Bērnu fonds, Latvia, 204
Lauder (Ronald S.) Foundation, Germany, 138
Laureus Sport for Good, UK, 364
The Lawson Foundation, Canada, 58
Lazard (Fernand), Fondation, Belgium, 31
LBJ Foundation, USA, 449
League of Corporate Foundations—LCF, Philippines, 250
The Leakey Foundation, USA, 447
Learning for Well-being Foundation—L4WB, Netherlands, 227
Legatum Foundation, United Arab Emirates, 334
LEGO Fonden, Denmark, 84
The LEGO Foundation, Denmark, 84
Leibniz Association, Germany, 135
Leibniz Gemeinschaft, Germany, 135
Leibniz-Institut für Globale und Regionale Studien, Germany, 130
Leibniz-Institut für Ost- und Südosteuropaforschung, Germany, 135
Leibniz Institute for East and South-East European Studies, Germany, 135
Leibniz Institute for Research and Information in Education, Germany, 126
Leo Messi Foundation, Spain, 292
The Leona M. and Harry B. Helmsley Charitable Trust, USA, 447
Leonard Cheshire Disability, UK, 364
Léopold Sédar Senghor Foundation, Senegal, 270
The Leprosy Mission International, UK, 364
Leventis (A. G.) Foundation, Cyprus, 77
Leventis (A. G.) Foundation Nigeria, Nigeria, 237
Leverhulme Trust, UK, 365
Levesque (Jean-Louis), Fondation, Canada, 55
Levy (Joseph) Foundation, UK, 362
Li Ka Shing Foundation, Hong Kong, 151
Liberty Fund, Inc, USA, 448
Lien Foundation, Singapore, 273
Lietuvos vaikų fondas, Lithuania, 209
Lifeline Energy, South Africa, 280
Lifewater International, USA, 479
Light Up the World—LUTW, Canada, 58
Light of the Village Foundation, Indonesia, 162
Likhachev (Dmitry) Foundation, Russian Federation, 265
Lilly Endowment, Inc, USA, 448
Limmat Foundation, Switzerland, 314
Limmat Stiftung, Switzerland, 314
Linbury Trust, UK, 365
Lindh (Anna) Euro-Mediterranean Foundation for Dialogue between Cultures, Egypt, 90
Litdea Association, Lithuania, 208
Lithuanian Children's Fund, Lithuania, 209
Littauer (Lucius N.) Foundation, Inc, USA, 449
Living Culture Foundation Namibia—LCFN, Namibia, 222
Lloyd's Register Foundation, UK, 365
Loewe Foundation, Spain, 292
The Long Now Foundation, USA, 449
Lorenzini (Giovanni), Fondazione, Italy, 177
Luce (Henry) Foundation, Inc, USA, 435
Lucie et André Chagnon Foundation, Canada, 55
Lucius N. Littauer Foundation, Inc, USA, 449
Luigi Sturzo Institute, Italy, 182
Lumos Foundation, UK, 366
Lundbeck Foundation, Denmark, 85
Lundbeckfonden, Denmark, 85
Lurcy (Georges) Charitable and Educational Trust, USA, 430
Luso-American Development Foundation, Portugal, 260
The Lutheran World Federation, Switzerland, 314
Lutherischer Weltbund/Fédération Luthérienne Mondiale/Federación Luterana Mundial, Switzerland, 314
Luxembourg Development NGO Co-operation Circle, Luxembourg, 209
Lyford Cay Foundations, Bahamas, 24

Lynde and Harry Bradley Foundation, Inc, USA, 449
Lyndon Baines Johnson Foundation, USA, 449
M. S. Swaminathan Research Foundation—MSSRF, India, 158
M. Venkatarangaiya Foundation—MVF, India, 158
MacArthur (John D. and Catherine T.) Foundation, USA, 444
McCaw (Craig and Susan) Foundation, USA, 418
McConnell Clark (Edna) Foundation, USA, 422
Macdonald Stewart Foundation, Canada, 59
McDonnell (James S.) Foundation, USA, 443
Macedonian Centre for International Co-operation—MCIC, North Macedonia, 239
Machel (Graça) Trust, South Africa, 280
The Mackintosh Foundation, UK, 366
The McLean Foundation, Canada, 59
Macmillan Cancer Support, UK, 366
Macy (Josiah), Jr Foundation, USA, 445
MADRE, USA, 450
MAG—Mines Advisory Group, UK, 366
Maison Franco-Japonaise, Japan, 191
Maj ja Tor Nessling Säätiö, Finland, 96
Maj and Tor Nessling Foundation, Finland, 96
Makyedonski Tzyentar za Myeroonarodna Sorabotka, North Macedonia, 239
Maltese Heritage Foundation, Malta, 213
Mama Cash Foundation, Netherlands, 230
Mandela (Nelson) Foundation, South Africa, 282
The Mandela Rhodes Foundation, South Africa, 281
Mani Tese, Italy, 183
Mannréttindaskrifstofa Íslands, Iceland, 154
Mansour Foundation for Development—MFD, Egypt, 90
MAPFRE Foundation, Spain, 292
Marangopoulos Foundation for Human Rights, Greece, 146
Marcel Bleustein-Blanchet Vocational Foundation, France, 109
Margaret A. Cargill Philanthropies—MACP, USA, 450
Maria Cecilia Souto Vidigal Foundation, Brazil, 40
María Francisca de Roviralta Foundation, Spain, 292
Marinho (Roberto), Fundação, Brazil, 41
Mario Negri Pharmacological Research Institute, Italy, 182
Mário Soares and Maria Barroso Foundation, Portugal, 260
Masason Foundation, Japan, 191
The MasterCard Foundation, Canada, 59
The Matsumae International Foundation, Japan, 191
Mauritius Telecom Foundation—MTF, Mauritius, 214
Mawazo Institute, Kenya, 199
Max Bell Foundation, Canada, 59
Max Kade Foundation, Inc, USA, 451
Max-Planck-Institut für Neurobiologie des Verhaltens—caesar, Germany, 136
Max Planck Institute for Neurobiology of Behavior—caesar, Germany, 136
Max Weber Foundation, Germany, 136
Max Weber Stiftung—MWS, Germany, 136
The Maytree Foundation, Canada, 59
Mbeki (Thabo) Foundation, South Africa, 284
Medunarodnog foruma Bosna, Bosnia and Herzegovina, 37
Media Development Foundation—MDF, Georgia, 118
Mediis Ganvitarebis Pondi, Georgia, 118
Mediterranean Foundation, Argentina, 7
Mediterranean Foundation for Strategic Studies Institute, France, 113
Mellon (Richard King) Foundation, USA, 467
Mencap—Royal Mencap Society, UK, 367
Mendoza (Eugenio), Fundación, Venezuela, 487
Menomadin Foundation, Israel, 170
Menzies Foundation, Australia, 15
Menzies (Sir Robert) Foundation, Australia, 15
The Mercers' Charitable Foundation, UK, 367
Mercy, Ireland, 168
Mercy Corps, USA, 452
Mercy-USA for Aid and Development, USA, 452
Meridian Foundation, Germany, 140
M'essh al Sudan, Sudan, 297
Messi (Leo), Fundación, Spain, 292
Mezhdunarodnyj Memorial, Russian Federation, 266
MFJC—Memorial Foundation for Jewish Culture, USA, 452
Michael & Susan Dell Foundation, USA, 453
Michel (James) Foundation, Seychelles, 272
Miguel Alemán Foundation, Mexico, 215

Milieukontakt Macedonia—MKM, North Macedonia, 240
Miloud Chaâbi Foundation, Morocco, 220
Mines Advisory Group—MAG, UK, 366
Minhaj Welfare Foundation, UK, 368
Minority Rights Group International—MRG, UK, 368
Mirovni Inštitut—Inštitut za sodobne družbene in politične študije, Slovenia, 277
MISEREOR—Bischöfliches Hilfswerk Misereor eV, Germany, 137
Mith Samlanh, Cambodia, 46
Mittag-Leffler Foundation of the Royal Swedish Academy of Sciences, Sweden, 300
Mitterrand (Danielle), Fondation, France, 112
MIUSA—Mobility International USA, USA, 453
Mo Dewji Foundation, Tanzania, 323
Mo Ibrahim Foundation, UK, 368
Moawad (René) Foundation, Lebanon, 206
Mobility International USA—MIUSA, USA, 453
Mohamed Shafik Gabr Foundation for Social Development, Egypt, 90
Mohammed bin Rashid Al Maktoum Global Initiatives—MBRGI, United Arab Emirates, 335
Mohammed bin Salman Foundation—Misk Foundation, Saudi Arabia, 269
Moisés Bertoni Foundation, Paraguay, 248
Møller (A.P.) and Chastine Mc-Kinney Møller Foundation, Denmark, 82
Molson Foundation, Canada, 59
Monell (Ambrose) Foundation, USA, 399
Mongolian Women's Fund—MONES, Mongolia, 218
Monnet (Jean), Fondation pour l'Europe, Switzerland, 309
Mønsteds (Otto) Fond, Denmark, 86
Montemadrid Foundation, Spain, 292
Moore (Gordon and Betty) Foundation, USA, 432
Moore (Henry) Foundation, UK, 358
Moores (John) Foundation, UK, 362
Morehead-Cain Foundation, USA, 453
Morgan Stanley Foundation, USA, 453
Moriya Scholarship Foundation, Japan, 191
Morningside Foundation, USA, 454
Mother Child Education Foundation, Türkiye, 327
Motorola Solutions Foundation, USA, 454
Motsepe Foundation, South Africa, 281
Mountain Institute, Peru, 249
Mouvement International ATD Quart-Monde, France, 115
Mouvement Social, Lebanon, 206
M-PESA Foundation, Kenya, 199
Mshvidobis, Demokratiisa, da Ganvit'arebis Kavkasiuri Instituti, Georgia, 117
MTN Afghanistan Foundation, Afghanistan, 4
MTN Cameroon Foundation, Cameroon, 47
MTN Congo Foundation, Congo (Republic), 73
MTN Côte d'Ivoire Foundation, Côte d'Ivoire, 76
MTN Foundation Benin, Benin, 35
MTN Nigeria Foundation, Nigeria, 237
MTN SA Foundation, South Africa, 281
MTN Uganda Foundation, Uganda, 332
Mukwege (Dr Denis) Foundation, Netherlands, 224
Munich Re Foundation/Münchener Rück Stiftung, Germany, 137
Muriel McBrien Kauffman Foundation, USA, 425
Muscular Dystrophy UK, UK, 369
Music in Africa Foundation—MIAF, South Africa, 281
Musk Foundation, USA, 454
Muslim Aid, UK, 369
The Muttart Foundation, Canada, 59
Myanmar Book Aid and Preservation Foundation—MBAPF, Myanmar, 221
Myanmar/Burma Schools Project Foundation, Canada, 60
Myer Foundation, Australia, 18
Myer (Sidney) Fund, Australia, 18
NAACP Legal Defense and Educational Fund, Inc—LDF, USA, 454
Naandi Foundation—A New Beginning, India, 158
Nadace České spořitelny—Nadace ČS, Czech Republic, 79
Nadace Charty 77, Czech Republic, 80
Nadace Open Society Fund Praha, Czech Republic, 80
Nadace Preciosa, Czech Republic, 80
Nadácia Orange, Slovakia, 275
Nadácia Pontis, Slovakia, 274
Nadácia pre Deti Slovenska, Slovakia, 275
Nadácia SPP, Slovakia, 275
Nadácia Tatra Banky, Slovakia, 276
Nand & Jeet Khemka Foundation, India, 159
National Carlo Collodi Foundation, Italy, 179

National Community Foundation, Saint Lucia, 268
National Empowerment Foundation—NEF, Mauritius, 214
National Endowment for Science, Technology and the Arts—Nesta, UK, 370
National Foundation for the Development of Honduras, Honduras, 150
National Foundation for Educational Research—NFER, UK, 369
National Foundation for Political Sciences, France, 110
National Geographic Society, USA, 455
National Humanities Center—NHC, USA, 455
National Institute for Research in the Behavioural Sciences—Szold (Henrietta) Institute, Israel, 169
National Kidney Foundation—NKF, USA, 455
The National Lottery Community Fund, UK, 370
National Science Foundation—NSF, USA, 455
National Society for the Prevention of Cruelty to Children—NSPCC, UK, 371
National Trust, UK, 370
National Trust of Fiji—NTF, Fiji, 94
The National Trust for Italy, Italy, 174
Naumann (Friedrich) Stiftung, Germany, 130
Near East Foundation—NEF, USA, 456
Nederlandse Organisatie voor Internationale Ontwikkelingssamenwerking—Stichting NOVIB, Netherlands, 228
NEF—National Empowerment Foundation, Mauritius, 214
NEF—Near East Foundation, USA, 456
Negri (Mario), Istituto di Ricerche Farmacologiche, Italy, 182
Nelson Mandela Foundation, South Africa, 282
Neruda (Pablo), Fundación, Chile, 65
Nessling (Maj and Tor) Foundation, Finland, 96
Nesta—National Endowment for Science, Technology and the Arts, UK, 370
Network of Estonian Non-profit Organizations, Estonia, 92
Network of Foundations Working for Development—netFWD, France, 99
Network for Human Development, Brazil, 41
Network for Social Change Charitable Trust—NSCCT, UK, 370
New Carlsberg Foundation, Denmark, 85
New Economics Foundation—NEF, UK, 371
New Myanmar Foundation, Myanmar, 221
New School Foundation, Colombia, 71
New World Foundation—NWF, USA, 456
The New York Community Trust—NYCT, USA, 457
Newberry Library, USA, 457
NFER—National Foundation for Educational Research, UK, 369
NFI—National Foundation for India, India, 159
NGO Center—NGOC, Armenia, 9
Niarchos (Stavros) Foundation, Greece, 147
Nightingale (Florence), Fondation Internationale, Switzerland, 309
Ningxia Yanbao Charity Foundation, China (People's Republic), 69
The Nippon Foundation, Japan, 192
Niwano Peace Foundation, Japan, 192
Nobis Foundation, Ecuador, 88
Non-Governmental Ecological Vernadsky Foundation, Russian Federation, 266
Norbert Zongo Cell for Investigative Journalism in West Africa, Burkina Faso, 44
Nordic Africa Institute Scholarships, Sweden, 302
Nordiska Afrikainstitutets Stipendier, Sweden, 302
Norsk Utenrikspolitisk Institutt—NUPI, Norway, 242
North-South-Bridge Foundation, Germany, 141
Norwegian Institute of International Affairs, Norway, 242
Norwegian Refugee Council—NRC, Norway, 242
Nott (David) Foundation, UK, 350
The Nourafchan Foundation—TNF, Kenya, 199
Novartis US Foundation, USA, 457
NOVIB (Oxfam Netherlands), Netherlands, 228
Novo Nordisk Fonden, Denmark, 85
Novo Nordisk Foundation, Denmark, 85
NRF—National Research Foundation, South Africa, 282
NSPCC—National Society for the Prevention of Cruelty to Children, UK, 371
Nuffic, Netherlands, 227
Nuffield Foundation, UK, 371
Nursultan Nazarbayev Educational Foundation, Kazakhstan, 197
Ny Carlsbergfondet, Denmark, 85
NYCT—The New York Community Trust, USA, 457

Oak Foundation, Switzerland, 315
Obama (Barack) Foundation, USA, 407
OeAD, Austria, 22
Offor (Sir Emeka) Foundation, Nigeria, 238
Oil Search Foundation, Papua New Guinea, 247
OISCA International—Organization for Industrial, Spiritual and Cultural Advancement-International, Japan, 192
Ökumenikus Segélyszervezet, Hungary, 153
Olav Thon Foundation, Norway, 242
Olav Thon Stiftelsen, Norway, 242
Olivetti (Adriano), Fondazione, Italy, 174
Oman LNG Development Foundation—ODF, Oman, 244
Omidyar Group, USA, 458
Omidyar Network Fund, USA, 458
Onassis (Alexander S.) Public Benefit Foundation, Liechtenstein, 207
One Economy Foundation, Namibia, 222
One Foundation, China (People's Republic), 69
OPEN ASIA—Armanshahr Foundation, Afghanistan, 3
Open Estonia Foundation, Estonia, 92
Open Society Africa, Senegal, 270
Open Society Forum (Mongolia), Mongolia, 218
Open Society Foundation Haiti, Haiti, 149
Open Society Foundation—London, UK, 372
Open Society Foundations, USA, 459
Open Society Foundations—Armenia, Armenia, 9
Open Society Foundations in Pakistan, Pakistan, 245
Open Society Fund—Bosnia-Herzegovina, Bosnia and Herzegovina, 37
Open Society Fund Prague—OSF Prague, Czech Republic, 80
Open Society Initiative for Southern Africa—OSISA, South Africa, 282
Open Society Institute—Sofia, Bulgaria, 43
Operation USA, USA, 459
Oppenheimer Generations Foundation, South Africa, 282
Opportunity International UK, UK, 372
Oprah Winfrey Leadership Academy Foundation—OWLAF, USA, 459
Orange Botswana Foundation, Botswana, 37
Orange Foundation, Romania, 263
Orange Foundation Cameroon, Cameroon, 47
Orange Foundation Guinea, Guinea, 149
Orange Foundation Tunisia, Tunisia, 326
Orange Moldova Foundation, Moldova, 217
Orange Solidarité Madagascar, Madagascar, 210
Organization for Social Science Research in Eastern and Southern Africa—OSSREA, Ethiopia, 94
Orient Foundation, Portugal, 260
Orient-Occident Foundation, Morocco, 220
Orji Uzor Kalu Foundation, Nigeria, 238
Ortega (Amancio), Fundación, Spain, 288
Ortega y Gasset (José), Fundación, Spain, 291
Österreichische Forschungsstiftung für Internationale Entwicklung—ÖFSE, Austria, 22
Oswaldo Cruz Foundation, Brazil, 40
Otto Benecke Foundation, Germany, 138
Otto-Benecke-Stiftung eV, Germany, 138
Otto Mønsteds Fond, Denmark, 86
Otto Mønsteds Foundation, Denmark, 86
Our Foundation, Indonesia, 162
Outreach International, USA, 459
OutRight Action International, USA, 460
Outstretched Hands, Italy, 183
Oxfam Denmark, Denmark, 86
Oxfam Deutschland eV, Germany, 138
Oxfam France, France, 115
Oxfam GB, UK, 372
Oxfam Hong Kong, Hong Kong, 151
Oxfam India, India, 159
Oxfam International, Kenya, 200
Oxfam Italia, Italy, 183
Oxfam Mexico, Mexico, 216
Oxfam NOVIB—Nederlandse Organisatie voor Internationale Ontwikkelingssamenwerking, Netherlands, 228
Oxfam NOVIB—Netherlands Organization for International Development Co-operation, Netherlands, 228
Oxfam-Solidariteit/Solidarité, Belgium, 33
OzChild—Children Australia Inc, Australia, 16
Pablo Neruda Foundation, Chile, 65
Pacific Development and Conservation Trust, New Zealand, 234
Pacific Peoples' Partnership, Canada, 61
Packard (David and Lucile) Foundation, USA, 420
PADF—Pan American Development Foundation, USA, 460
Paideia Galiza Foundation, Spain, 293

INDEX OF MAIN ACTIVITIES

Education

Pan American Development Foundation—PADF, USA, 460
The Papal Foundation, USA, 461
Paraguayan Foundation for Cooperation and Development, Paraguay, 248
Paraskevaides (George and Thelma) Foundation, Cyprus, 78
Parasol Foundation Trust, Gibraltar, 144
Partage, France, 116
Partners for Equity, Australia, 16
Partos, Netherlands, 223
Pasteur Institute, France, 114
Pastore (Giulio), Fondazione, Italy, 178
Patiño (Simón I.), Fondation, Switzerland, 310
Paul Hamlyn Foundation—PHF, UK, 373
The Paul Ramsay Foundation, Australia, 16
PCI—Project Concern International, USA, 431
Peace and Disarmament Education Trust—PADET, New Zealand, 234
Peace Institute—Institute for Contemporary Social and Political Studies, Slovenia, 277
Peace Parks Foundation, South Africa, 282
Peace Research Institute Oslo—PRIO, Norway, 242
Peace Village International, Germany, 129
Pearl S. Buck International, USA, 462
Pedro Barrié de la Maza Foundation, Spain, 293
People in Need, Czech Republic, 79
Peres Center for Peace and Innovation, Israel, 171
Perpetual Foundation, Australia, 16
Pestalozzi Children's Foundation, Switzerland, 317
The Peter Cundill Foundation, Bermuda, 35
The Pew Charitable Trusts, USA, 462
PH International, USA, 463
Philanthropikó Idryma Stélios Chatzeioánnou stēn Kýpro, Cyprus, 78
Philanthropy New Zealand/Topūtanga Tuku Aroha o Aotearoa, New Zealand, 232
Philippine-American Educational Foundation—PAEF, Philippines, 253
Philippine Business for Social Progress—PBSP, Philippines, 250
Piera, Pietro and Giovanni Ferrero Foundation, Italy, 179
Pinchuk (Victor) Foundation, Ukraine, 333
Ping Foundation, USA, 415
Plan International Ireland, Ireland, 167
PLAN International—PI, UK, 374
Plataforma Portuguesa das Organizações Não-Governamentais para o Desenvolvimento—ONGD, Portugal, 258
Platforma Mimovládnych Rozvojových Organizácií, Slovakia, 273
Plunkett Foundation, UK, 374
Polish-American Freedom Foundation, Poland, 257
POLSAT Foundation, Poland, 256
Polsko-Amerykańska Fundacja Wolności, Poland, 257
Pontis Foundation, Slovakia, 274
Population Council, USA, 463
Populorum Progressio Foundation, Vatican City, 486
Portuguese Platform of Non-Governmental Organizations for Development, Portugal, 258
Potanin (Vladimir) Foundation, Russian Federation, 267
Potter (Ian) Foundation, Australia, 14
Practical Action, UK, 374
Praemium Erasmianum Foundation, Netherlands, 230
Pratham Education Foundation, India, 159
Pratt Foundation, Australia, 17
Praxis Centre for Policy Studies Foundation, Estonia, 93
Preciosa Foundation, Czech Republic, 80
Premji (Azim) Foundation, India, 156
Presbyterian World Service & Development—PWS&D, Canada, 61
Prince's Trust, UK, 363
Princess of Asturias Foundation, Spain, 294
Princess Charlene of Monaco Foundation, Monaco, 218
PRIO—Peace Research Institute Oslo, Norway, 242
Prix Jeunesse Foundation, Germany, 138
Pro Juventute, Switzerland, 315
Pro Mujer International, USA, 464
Pro Women International, USA, 464
PRODESSA—Proyecto de Desarrollo Santiago, Guatemala, 148
Project Harmony, USA, 463
Project HOPE, USA, 464
Project Trust, UK, 374
ProLiteracy, USA, 464
Protestant Study Foundation, Germany, 128
Prudence Foundation, Hong Kong, 151

Public Health Foundation of India—PHFI, India, 159
Public Studies Centre, Chile, 64
Puerto Rico Community Foundation, Puerto Rico, 261
Pulitzer Center on Crisis Reporting, USA, 464
PwC Charitable Foundation, USA, 465
Qatar Foundation, Qatar, 262
Qattan (A. M.) Foundation, UK, 338
Quandt (Johanna) Stiftung, Germany, 133
Queen Rania Foundation—QRF, Jordan, 196
Quỹ Thiện Tâm, Viet Nam, 488
R. Howard Webster Foundation/Fondation R. Howard Webster, Canada, 61
Rafa Nadal Foundation, Spain, 294
Rafael del Pino Foundation, Spain, 294
Rafto Foundation for Human Rights, Norway, 243
Raftostiftelsen for menneskerettigheter, Norway, 243
Rainforest Action Network—RAN, USA, 465
Rainforest Foundation Norway, Norway, 243
Rainforest Journalism Fund, USA, 464
Rajiv Gandhi Foundation, India, 160
Ramaciotti Foundations, Australia, 17
Rambourg Foundation, Tunisia, 326
Ramsay (Paul) Foundation, Australia, 16
RAN—Rainforest Action Network, USA, 465
RAND Corporation, USA, 465
The Rank Foundation, UK, 375
Rare, USA, 466
RBC Foundation, Canada, 61
Reading Foundation, Germany, 140
Real Madrid Foundation, Spain, 295
Rebecca Akufo-Addo Foundation—Rebecca Foundation, Ghana, 144
Red Feather, Japan, 185
Red Sea Cultural Foundation, Somalia, 278
REDEH—Rede de Desenvolvimento Humano, Brazil, 41
RedR UK, UK, 375
Reeva Rebecca Steenkamp Foundation, South Africa, 283
Refugee Empowerment International—REI, Japan, 193
Regnskogfondet, Norway, 243
Rehabilitation for the Disabled—ELEPAP, Greece, 145
Rehabilitation International—RI, USA, 466
REI—Refugee Empowerment International, Japan, 193
Reliance Foundation, India, 160
Relief International, USA, 466
Renault Foundation, France, 106
René Moawad Foundation—RMF, Lebanon, 206
Repsol Foundation, Spain, 295
Research Corporation for Science Advancement—RCSA, USA, 467
Réseau Européen des Associations de Lutte contre la Pauvreté et l'Exclusion Sociale, Belgium, 29
Resource Centre for the Human Rights Nongovernmental Organizations of Moldova—CReDO, Moldova, 217
The Resource Foundation—TRF, USA, 467
Rhodes Trust, UK, 376
RIA—Royal Irish Academy, Ireland, 167
Ricard (Baxter & Alma), Fondation, Canada, 55
Ricardo do Espírito Santo Silva Foundation, Portugal, 261
Richard Dawkins Foundation for Reason and Science, USA, 412
Richard King Mellon Foundation, USA, 467
Rielo (Fernando), Fundación, Spain, 290
Right Livelihood Award Foundation, Sweden, 302
RNIB Charity, UK, 378
Robert Bosch Foundation, Germany, 138
Robert-Bosch-Stiftung GmbH, Germany, 138
Robert Marinho Foundation, Brazil, 41
Robertson Foundation for Government—RFG, USA, 468
The Robertson Trust, UK, 376
Rockefeller Brothers Fund—RBF, USA, 468
Roger Federer Foundation, Switzerland, 315
Rogosin Institute, USA, 468
Rohini Nilekani Philanthropies, India, 160
Romanian Cultural Institute, Romania, 264
Rome Foundation, Italy, 179
The Ronald S. Lauder Foundation, Germany, 138
Rosetta Foundation, USA, 416
Ross (R. E.) Trust, Australia, 17
The Ross Trust, Australia, 17
Rössing Foundation, Namibia, 222
The Rotary Foundation, USA, 468
Rotary Yoneyama Memorial Foundation, Inc, Japan, 193
Rothschild (Edmond de) Foundations, Switzerland, 308

Roviralta (María Francisca de), Fundación, Spain, 292
Royal Aeronautical Society—RAeS, UK, 376
Royal Air Force Benevolent Fund, UK, 377
Royal Anthropological Institute of Great Britain and Ireland—RAI, UK, 377
Royal Commission for the Exhibition of 1851, UK, 377
The Royal Commonwealth Society—RCS, UK, 377
The Royal Foundation of the Prince and Princess of Wales, UK, 378
Royal Geographical Society (with the Institute of British Geographers)—RGS-IBG, UK, 378
Royal Institute of International Relations—Egmont Institute, Belgium, 29
Royal Literary Fund—RLF, UK, 378
Royal National Institute of Blind People—RNIB, UK, 378
The Royal Society, UK, 379
The Royal Society of Medicine—RSM, UK, 379
Royal Society for the Prevention of Cruelty to Animals—RSPCA, UK, 380
Royal Society for the Protection of Birds—RSPB, UK, 379
Rroma Foundation, Switzerland, 315
Rromani Fundacija, Switzerland, 315
RSA—Royal Society for the Encouragement of Arts, Manufactures and Commerce, UK, 379
RSPB—Royal Society for the Protection of Birds, UK, 379
RSPCA—Royal Society for the Prevention of Cruelty to Animals, UK, 380
Rubinstein (Arthur) International Music Society, Israel, 168
Rüf (Gebert) Stiftung, Switzerland, 311
RUI Foundation, Italy, 180
Ruparelia Foundation, Uganda, 332
Rupert Family Foundations, South Africa, 283
Rural Development Foundation, Poland, 257
Russell Sage Foundation—RSF, USA, 469
Russian International Affairs Council—RIAC, Russian Federation, 266
Rutgers, Netherlands, 228
Saadi Foundation, Iran, 164
SAASTA—South African Agency for Science and Technology Advancement, South Africa, 283
Sääthiöiden post doc-poolin, Finland, 95
Sabancı Vakfı—Hacı Ömer Sabancı Foundation, Türkiye, 329
Safaricom Foundation, Kenya, 200
Sahabdeen (A. M. M.) Trust Foundation, Sri Lanka, 297
SAIA—Slovak Academic Information Agency, Slovakia, 274
Saïd Foundation, UK, 380
Sainsbury Family Charitable Trusts, UK, 380
Saint Cyril and Saint Methodius International Foundation, Bulgaria, 44
Sakartvelos Strategiisa da Saertashoriso Urtiertobebis Kvlevis Pondi—Rondelis Pondi, Georgia, 118
Sakena Fund, USA, 469
Salvador Dalí Foundation, Spain, 287
El Salvadoran Association for Economic and Social Development FUSADES, El Salvador, 91
The Salvation Army International Trust, UK, 381
Salzburg Global Seminar, Austria, 22
Samsung Foundation, Korea (Republic), 202
Samuel (Hedwig und Robert) Stiftung, Germany, 131
The San Diego Foundation, USA, 470
San Francisco Foundation—SFF, USA, 470
Sanaburi Foundation, Japan, 193
Sandals Foundation, Jamaica, 184
Santiago Development Project, Guatemala, 148
Santos Foundation, Papua New Guinea, 247
Sarah Scaife Foundation, Inc, USA, 470
Sasakawa, Fondation Franco-Japonaise, France, 106
The Sasakawa Peace Foundation—SPF, Japan, 194
Save the Children International, UK, 381
Save the Children (UK), UK, 381
Save Our Future Environmental Foundation, Germany, 139
Save Our Future Umweltstiftung—SOF, Germany, 139
Sawiris Foundation for Social Development—SFSD, Egypt, 90
SBS Cultural Foundation, Korea (Republic), 202
Scaife (Sarah) Foundation, Inc, USA, 470
Schering (Ernst) Stiftung, Germany, 127
Schlumberger Foundation, USA, 470
Schneider Electric Foundation, France, 111
Schöck (Eberhard) Stiftung, Germany, 127

Education

Schusterman (Charles and Lynn) Family Foundation, USA, 413
Schwab Foundation for Social Entrepreneurship, Switzerland, 316
Schwarzkopf-Stiftung Junges Europa, Germany, 139
Schwarzkopf Young Europe Foundation, Germany, 139
Schweisfurth Foundation, Germany, 139
Schweisfurth-Stiftung, Germany, 139
Schweizerischer Nationalfonds zur Förderung der Wissenschaftlichen Forschung/Fonds National Suisse de la Recherche Scientifique—SNF, Switzerland, 316
Scientific Foundation of Hisham Adeeb Hijjawi, Jordan, 196
Scientific Foundation of the Spanish Cancer Association, Spain, 290
Scientific Research Foundation, Belgium, 32
Scott Trust Foundation, UK, 356
Scottish Catholic International Aid Fund—SCIAF, UK, 382
Secours Catholique—Caritas de France, France, 116
Seeds of Peace, USA, 470
SEEMO—South East Europe Media Organisation, Austria, 23
Seidel (Hanns) Stiftung, Germany, 131
Self-Sufficient People Foundation, Indonesia, 163
SEND-West Africa, Ghana, 144
Senna (Ayrton), Instituto, Brazil, 41
Sentebale, UK, 382
Seoam Yoon Se Young Foundation, Korea (Republic), 202
Serralves Foundation, Portugal, 261
Serrv International, Inc, USA, 471
Service Civil International—SCI, Belgium, 34
SES Foundation—Sustainability, Education, Solidarity, Argentina, 8
Sesame Workshop, USA, 471
Seub Nakhasathien Foundation, Thailand, 324
Sexual Wellbeing Aotearoa, New Zealand, 235
Seychelles Islands Foundation—SIF, Seychelles, 272
Shafik Gabr (Mohamed) Foundation, Egypt, 90
Shahid Afridi Foundation—SAF, Pakistan, 246
Shanghai Soong Ching Ling Foundation, China (People's Republic), 69
Shaping Our Future Foundation—SOFF, Malawi, 210
Sherman (Archie) Charitable Trust, UK, 340
Shiv Nadar Foundation Group, India, 160
Shoman (Abdul Hameed) Foundation, Jordan, 195
Siam Society, Thailand, 324
Siamese Heritage Trust, Thailand, 324
Sidney Myer Fund & The Myer Foundation, Australia, 18
Sightsavers International, UK, 382
Sihtasutus Eesti Rahvuskultuuri Fond, Estonia, 93
Sihtasutus Poliitikauuringute Keskus Praxis, Estonia, 93
Silicon Valley Community Foundation—SVCF, USA, 471
Silva (Ricardo do Espírito Santo), Fundação, Portugal, 261
Simón I. Patiño Foundation, Switzerland, 310
Simons Foundation, USA, 472
Sinergia—Red Venezolana de OSC, Venezuela, 487
Singapore International Foundation—SIF, Singapore, 273
Sino-British Fellowship Trust—SBFT, UK, 383
Sir Ahmadu Bello Memorial Foundation, Nigeria, 238
Sir Emeka Offor Foundation, Nigeria, 238
Sir Halley Stewart Trust, UK, 383
Sistema Charitable Foundation, Russian Federation, 267
Skinners' Charity Foundation, UK, 383
Skolkovo Foundation—Foundation for Development of the Center for the Development and Commercialization of New Technologies, Russian Federation, 267
Skoll Foundation, USA, 472
Slim (Carlos), Fundación, Mexico, 215
Sloan (Alfred P.) Foundation, USA, 398
Slovak Academic Information Agency—SAIA, Slovakia, 276
Slovak-Czech Women's Fund, Slovakia, 276
Slovak Humanitarian Council, Slovakia, 274
Slovak Security Policy Institute, Slovakia, 276
Slovenian Science Foundation, Slovenia, 277
Slovenská Humanitná Rada, Slovakia, 274
Slovenska znanstvena fundacija—SZF, Slovenia, 277
Slovensko-český enský fond, Slovakia, 276
Slovenský inštitút pre bezpečnostnú politiku, Slovakia, 276

SM Foundation, Spain, 295
Smithsonian Institution, USA, 472
Soares (Mário), Fundação, Portugal, 260
The Sobell Foundation, UK, 384
Social Movement, Lebanon, 206
Society for Education and Training, UK, 351
Software AG Foundation, Germany, 139
Software AG Stiftung, Germany, 139
Sog'lom Avlod Uchun, Uzbekistan, 485
SOHO China Foundation, China (People's Republic), 69
Solidar, Belgium, 34
Solomon R. Guggenheim Foundation, USA, 473
Somalia NGO Consortium, Somalia, 277
Sorenson Legacy Foundation, USA, 473
South African Agency for Science and Technology Advancement—SAASTA, South Africa, 283
South African Institute of Race Relations—IRR, South Africa, 283
South East Europe Media Organisation—SEEMO, Austria, 23
South West International Development Network—SWIDN, UK, 337
Souto Vidigal (Maria Cecilia), Fundação, Brazil, 40
Sparkassenstiftung für internationale Kooperation, Germany, 125
Spencer Foundation, USA, 473
SPP Foundation, Slovakia, 275
Springer (Axel) Stiftung, Germany, 122
Springer (Friede) Stiftung, Germany, 129
St John Ambulance, UK, 380
Stanley Center for Peace and Security, USA, 473
Stanley Thomas Johnson Foundation, Switzerland, 317
The Starr Foundation, USA, 473
State Grid Foundation for Public Welfare, China (People's Republic), 69
State Scholarships Foundation—IKY, Greece, 147
Stavros Niarchos Foundation—SNF, Greece, 147
Steelworkers Humanity Fund/Le Fonds Humanitaire des Metallos, Canada, 62
Steenkamp (Reeva Rebecca) Foundation, South Africa, 283
Stefan Batory Foundation, Poland, 256
Stelios Philanthropic Foundation, Cyprus, 78
Stewart (Sir Halley) Trust, UK, 383
Stichting Bellingcat, Netherlands, 228
Stichting Dioraphte, Netherlands, 229
Stichting Fonds 1818, Netherlands, 229
Stichting Mama Cash, Netherlands, 230
Stichting Praemium Erasmianum, Netherlands, 230
Stichting van Schulden naar Kansen, Netherlands, 231
Stichting Triodos Foundation, Netherlands, 231
Stichting Vodafone Netherlands, Netherlands, 231
Stiftelsen Blanceflor Boncompagni Ludovisi, född Bildt, Sweden, 303
Stiftelsen Dag Hammarskjölds Minnesfond, Sweden, 303
Stiftelsen Gapminder, Sweden, 300
Stiftelsen Tekniken Främjande—Tekniikan Edistämissäätiö, Finland, 98
Stifterverband für die Deutsche Wissenschaft eV, Germany, 119
Stiftung 'Erinnerung, Verantwortung und Zukunft'—EVZ, Germany, 139
Stiftung Ettersberg, Germany, 140
Stiftung zur Förderung der Hochschulrektorenkonferenz, Germany, 140
Stiftung Jugend forscht eV, Germany, 140
Stiftung Kinder in Afrika, Germany, 140
Stiftung Kinderdorf Pestalozzi, Switzerland, 317
Stiftung Lesen, Germany, 140
Stiftung Mercator, Germany, 140
Stiftung Meridian, Germany, 140
Stiftung Nord-Süd-Brücken, Germany, 141
Stiftung Prix Jeunesse, Germany, 138
Stiftung für die Rechte zukünftiger Generationen—SRzG, Germany, 141
Stiftung Vivamos Mejor, Switzerland, 317
Stiftung Weltethos, Germany, 141
Stiftung West-Östliche Begegnungen, Germany, 141
Stiftungsfonds Deutsche Bank im Stifterverband für die Deutsche Wissenschaft, Germany, 142
Street Child, UK, 384
Strickland Foundation, Malta, 214
Strømme Foundation, Norway, 243
Strømmestiftelsen, Norway, 243
Sturzo (Luigi), Istituto, Italy, 182
Sudan Foundation, Sudan, 297
Sudd Institute, South Sudan, 285
Südosteuropäische Medienorganisation, Austria, 23

INDEX OF MAIN ACTIVITIES

Sulaiman Bin Abdul Aziz Bin Saleh Al Rajhi Foundation, Saudi Arabia, 269
Sultan bin Abdulaziz Al Sa'ud Foundation, Saudi Arabia, 270
SUN Civil Society Network, UK, 381
Suomalaiset kehitysjärjestöt—Fingo, Finland, 95
Suomen Kulttuurirahasto, Finland, 97
The Susan Thompson Buffett Foundation—STBF, USA, 474
Sutherland Self Help Trust, New Zealand, 235
Svenska Institutet i Rom/Istituto Svedese di Studi Classici a Roma, Italy, 183
Svenska kulturfonden, Finland, 98
Sverige-Amerika Stiftelsen, Sweden, 304
Swaminathan (M. S.) Research Foundation, India, 158
Swaziland Charitable Trust, Eswatini, 93
Sweden-America Foundation, Sweden, 304
Sweden-Japan Foundation—SJF, Sweden, 304
The Swedish Cultural Foundation in Finland, Finland, 98
Swedish Institute at Athens, Greece, 147
Swedish Institute in Rome, Italy, 183
Swiss Church Aid, Switzerland, 311
Swiss Foundation for Technical Co-operation, Switzerland, 318
Swiss National Science Foundation—SNSF, Switzerland, 316
SWISSAID Foundation, Switzerland, 318
Swisscontact—Swiss Foundation for Technical Co-operation, Switzerland, 318
Syin-Lu Social Welfare Foundation, Taiwan, 321
Syria Al-Gad Relief Foundation, Egypt, 91
Taawon, Palestinian Territories, 246
Tahir Foundation, Indonesia, 162
Taiwan NPO Information Platform, Taiwan, 321
Talon (Claudine), Fondation, Benin, 35
Tanenbaum (Joseph) Charitable Foundation, Canada, 58
Tata Trusts, India, 160
Tatra Bank Foundation, Slovakia, 276
Tearfund Australia, Australia, 18
Tekniikan Edistämissäätiö—Stiftelsen för teknikens främjande—TES, Finland, 98
Telefónica Foundation, Spain, 295
Telefónica Movistar Argentina Foundation, Argentina, 8
Telefónica Movistar Chile Foundation, Chile, 65
Telefónica Movistar Colombia Foundation, Colombia, 71
Telefónica Movistar Ecuador Foundation, Ecuador, 89
Telefónica Movistar México Foundation, Mexico, 216
Telefónica Movistar Perú Foundation, Peru, 249
Telefónica Movistar Uruguay Foundation, Uruguay, 485
Telefónica Vivo Foundation, Brazil, 41
Telmex Telcel Foundation, Mexico, 216
Temasek Foundation, Singapore, 273
Tencent Foundation, China (People's Republic), 70
Terre des Hommes International Federation—TDHIF, Switzerland, 318
Terre Sans Frontières—TSF, Canada, 62
Tewa, Nepal, 223
Thabo Mbeki Foundation, South Africa, 284
Thai Rath Foundation, Thailand, 324
THET, UK, 355
Thomas B. Thrige Foundation, Denmark, 86
Thomas B. Thriges Fond, Denmark, 86
Thomson Foundation, UK, 385
Thomson Reuters Foundation, UK, 385
Thriges (Thomas B.) Fond, Denmark, 86
Thurgood Marshall Institute, USA, 454
Thyssen (Fritz) Stiftung, Germany, 130
TI—Transparency International, Germany, 142
Tibet Fund, USA, 475
Tibet-Institut Rikon, Switzerland, 318
Tides Organizations, USA, 475
Timchenko (Elena & Gennady) Foundation, Russian Federation, 265
Tinker Foundation, Inc, USA, 475
TISCO Foundation, Thailand, 325
TK Foundation, Bahamas, 24
The Todd Foundation, New Zealand, 235
Toepfer (Alfred) Stiftung, Germany, 121
Tokyu Foundation, Japan, 194
Toputānga Tuku Aroha o Aotearoa, New Zealand, 232
TOSA Foundation, USA, 475
Toshiba International Foundation—TIFO, Japan, 194
TotalEnergies Foundation, France, 112
The Toyota Foundation, Japan, 195
Toyota Vietnam Foundation—TVF, Viet Nam, 488
Translators without Borders, USA, 416
Transnet Foundation, South Africa, 284
Transparency International—TI, Germany, 142

INDEX OF MAIN ACTIVITIES

The Trawalla Foundation, Australia, 19
Triodos Foundation, Netherlands, 231
Trócaire—Catholic Agency for World Development, Ireland, 168
Trudeau (Pierre Elliott) Foundation, Canada, 55
Trust for London, UK, 386
Trust for Social Achievement, Bulgaria, 44
Trustees for Harvard University, USA, 421
Trusthouse Charitable Foundation, UK, 386
Tschira (Klaus) Stiftung, Germany, 134
TTF—Toyota Thailand Foundation, Thailand, 325
Tujenge Africa Foundation, Burundi, 45
Tulsa Community Foundation—TCF, USA, 476
Tunisia Development Foundation, Tunisia, 326
Turin Savings Bank Foundation, Italy, 176
Turing (Alan) Institute, UK, 339
Turkish Family Health and Planning Foundation, Türkiye, 330
Turkish Foundation for Combating Soil Erosion, for Reforestation and the Protection of Natural Habitats, Türkiye, 330
Türkiye Aile Sağlığı ve Planlaması Vakfı—TAPV, Türkiye, 330
Türkiye Erozyonla Mücadele Ağaçlandırma ve Doğal Varlıkları Koruma Vakfı—TEMA, Türkiye, 330
Türkiye Vodafone Vakfı, Türkiye, 331
Turquoise Mountain Foundation, UK, 386
Tusk, UK, 387
Tutu (Desmond & Leah) Legacy Foundation, South Africa, 279
TY Danjuma Foundation, Nigeria, 239
UAI—Union des Associations Internationales, Belgium, 27
Ucom Foundation, Armenia, 9
UEFA Foundation for Children, Switzerland, 318
UJIA—United Jewish Israel Appeal, UK, 387
UK Research and Innovation—UKRI, UK, 387
Ukrainian Women's Fund, Ukraine, 333
Uluntu Community Foundation—UCF, Zimbabwe, 491
Umut Vakfı, Türkiye, 331
UNESCO Centre du Patrimoine Mondial, France, 116
UNESCO World Heritage Centre, France, 116
UniCredit Foundation, Italy, 183
UNIFOR—Forvaltningstiftelse for fond og legater, Norway, 240
Union Aid Abroad—APHEDA, Australia, 19
Union des Associations Internationales—UAI, Belgium, 27
Union of International Associations—UIA/Unie van de Internationale Verenigingen—UIV, Belgium, 27
Union for International Cancer Control—UICC, Switzerland, 318
Union Internationale Contre le Cancer, Switzerland, 318
United Jewish Israel Appeal—UJIA, UK, 387
United Nations Foundation, USA, 476
United Purpose, UK, 387
United States African Development Foundation—USADF, USA, 477
United States-Japan Foundation, USA, 477
United Way Worldwide, USA, 477
Unity Foundation, Luxembourg, 210
Universal Foundation, Maldives, 212
Universal Jewish Alliance, France, 101
Universitaire Stichting, Belgium, 34
University Foundation, Belgium, 34
University-Industry Foundation, Spain, 295
University of Zaragoza Business Foundation, Spain, 290
UPM Foundation, Uruguay, 485
UPS Foundation, USA, 477
Usain Bolt Foundation, Jamaica, 185
USC Shoah Foundation—The Institute for Visual History and Education, USA, 477
USPG—United Society Partners in the Gospel, UK, 387
Väestöliitto, Finland, 98
Values Foundation, Bulgaria, 43
Vancouver Foundation, Canada, 62
Van Leer Foundation, Netherlands, 231
Van Leer Jerusalem Institute, Israel, 171
Vargas (Getulio), Fundação, Brazil, 40
Varkey Foundation, UK, 388
Vehbi Koç Foundation, Türkiye, 331
Vehbi Koç Vakfı, Türkiye, 331
Veillon (Charles), Fondation, Switzerland, 308
Venezuelan Network of Civil Society Organizations, Venezuela, 487
Venice Foundation, Italy, 181
Venkatarangaiya (M.) Foundation, India, 158
VENRO—Verband Entwicklungspolitik und Humanitäre Hilfe deutscher Nichtregierungsorganizationen, Germany, 120

Verband für Gemeinnütziges Stiften, Austria, 20
Versus Arthritis, UK, 388
Victor Pinchuk Foundation, Ukraine, 333
Village Community Development Foundation, Indonesia, 163
Villar Foundation, Inc, Philippines, 253
Vincent Fairfax Family Foundation—VFFF, Australia, 19
VINCI Corporate Foundation for the City, France, 106
Vital Strategies, USA, 478
Vivamos Mejor Foundation, Switzerland, 317
Vladimir Potanin Foundation, Russian Federation, 267
Vodacom Foundation, South Africa, 284
Vodacom Foundation DRC, Congo (Democratic Republic), 72
Vodacom Foundation South Africa, South Africa, 284
Vodacom Lesotho Foundation, Lesotho, 207
Vodacom Tanzania Foundation—VTF, Tanzania, 323
Vodafone Albania Foundation, Albania, 5
Vodafone Americas Foundation, USA, 478
Vodafone ATH Fiji Foundation, Fiji, 94
Vodafone Egypt Foundation, Egypt, 91
Vodafone Foundation, UK, 388
Vodafone Foundation Germany, Germany, 142
Vodafone Foundation India, India, 161
Vodafone Foundation New Zealand, New Zealand, 235
Vodafone Ghana Foundation, Ghana, 144
Vodafone Hungary Foundation, Hungary, 153
Vodafone Idea Foundation, India, 161
Vodafone Ireland Foundation, Ireland, 168
Vodafone Italy Foundation, Italy, 181
Vodafone Magyarország Alapítvány, Hungary, 153
Vodafone Netherlands Foundation, Netherlands, 231
Vodafone Portugal Foundation, Portugal, 261
Vodafone Romania Foundation, Romania, 264
Vodafone Spain Foundation, Spain, 296
Vodafone Stiftung Deutschland, Germany, 142
Vodafone Türkiye Foundation, Türkiye, 331
Volkswagen Foundation, Germany, 142
VolkswagenStiftung, Germany, 142
Volnoe Delo—Oleg Deripaska Foundation, Russian Federation, 267
Voluntary Service Overseas, UK, 388
Volunteer Service Abroad/Te Tūao Tāwāhi—VSA, New Zealand, 236
VSO—Voluntary Service Overseas, UK, 388
Výbor dobré vůle—Nadace Olgy Havlové, Czech Republic, 81
Vzdělávací Nadace Jana Husa, Czech Republic, 81
W. K. Kellogg Foundation—WKKF, USA, 478
Wallace (Charles) Trusts, UK, 347
The Wallace Foundation, USA, 478
Wallenberg (Knut och Alice) Stiftelse, Sweden, 301
Walmart Foundation, USA, 478
Walter and Duncan Gordon Charitable Foundation, Canada, 62
Walton Family Foundation, USA, 479
WAMA Foundation, Tanzania, 323
War Child, UK, 388
Water for Good, USA, 479
WaterAid, UK, 389
The Waterloo Foundation—TWF, UK, 389
Weber (Max) Stiftung, Germany, 136
Webster (R. Howard) Foundation, Canada, 61
Weinberg (Harry and Jeanette) Foundation, USA, 434
The Welch Foundation, USA, 479
Welfare Association, Palestinian Territories, 246
Wellcome Trust, UK, 389
Wenner-Gren Foundation for Anthropological Research, Inc, USA, 480
Weston (Garfield) Foundation, UK, 355
Weyerhaeuser Family Foundation, Inc, USA, 480
Whirlpool Foundation, USA, 480
White Point Development Foundation, Türkiye, 328
Wihuri (Jenny and Antti) Foundation, Finland, 96
Wikimedia Foundation, USA, 480
Wild (Dr Rainer) Stiftung, Germany, 126
Wilderness Foundation Global—WFG, South Africa, 284
The Wildlife Trusts, UK, 390
William Adlington Cadbury Charitable Trust, UK, 390
William Buckland Foundation, Australia, 19
The William and Flora Hewlett Foundation, USA, 481
The William H. Donner Foundation, Inc, USA, 481
William Randolph Hearst Foundation, USA, 435

International affairs

William T. Grant Foundation, USA, 481
Wilsdorf (Hans), Fondation, Switzerland, 309
Wilson (E. O.) Biodiversity Foundation, USA, 421
Windle Trust International, UK, 390
Winfrey (Oprah) Leadership Academy Foundation, USA, 459
Winrock International, USA, 481
Winston Churchill Foundation of the United States, USA, 482
Winston Churchill Memorial Trust, Australia, 19
Winston Churchill Memorial Trust of New Zealand, New Zealand, 236
Wisti (Folmer) Foundation for International Understanding, Denmark, 83
The Wolfson Foundation, UK, 390
The Womanity Foundation, Switzerland, 319
Women in Development Foundation, Tanzania, 323
Women in Equality Foundation, Argentina, 8
Women's Foundation, Costa Rica, 74
Women's World Summit Foundation—WWSF, Switzerland, 320
The Wood Foundation—TWF, UK, 391
World Alliance of YMCAs—Young Men's Christian Associations, Switzerland, 319
World Association of Children's Friends, Monaco, 217
World Economic Forum, Switzerland, 320
World Emergency Relief—WER, USA, 483
World Holocaust Forum Foundation—WHF, Israel, 171
World Land Trust—WLT, UK, 391
World Learning, USA, 483
World Neighbors, USA, 483
The World of NGOs, Austria, 20
World Peace Foundation—WPF, USA, 483
World Scout Foundation—Fondation du Scoutisme Mondial—WSF/FSM, Switzerland, 320
World University Service of Canada/Entraide Universitaire Mondiale du Canada—WUSC/EUMC, Canada, 63
World Vision International, UK, 391
WWSF—Women's World Summit Foundation, Switzerland, 320
The Wyss Foundtion, USA, 484
Xiangjiang Social Relief Fund, China (People's Republic), 68
YADESA—Yayasan Pembinaan Masyarakat Desa, Indonesia, 163
Yanai Tadashi Foundation, Japan, 195
Yanbao Charity Foundation, China (People's Republic), 69
Yayasan Azman Hashim, Malaysia, 212
Yayasan Dian Desa—YDD, Indonesia, 162
Yayasan Geutanyoë, Indonesia, 162
Yayasan Insan Sembada, Indonesia, 163
Yayasan Pembinaan Masyarakat Desa—YADESA, Indonesia, 163
Year Out Group, UK, 374
Yellow Feather Fund, USA, 471
Yidan Prize Foundation, Hong Kong, 152
YMCA—Young Men's Christian Association, UK, 392
YongLin Charity Foundation, Taiwan, 322
YORGHAS Foundation, Poland, 258
Young Citizens—Citizenship Foundation, UK, 392
Youth Leadership Development Foundation—YLDF, Yemen, 489
Yrjö Jahnsson Foundation, Finland, 98
Yrjö Jahnssonin säätiö, Finland, 98
Yuan Lin Charity Fund, China (People's Republic), 70
Zakat House, Kuwait, 203
Zancan (Emanuela), Fondazione Centro Studi e Ricerca Sociale, Italy, 172
Zarina & Naushad Merali Foundation, Kenya, 200
Zavod Center za Informiranje, Sodelovanje in Razvoj Nevladnih Organizacije—CNVOS, Slovenia, 277
ZEIT-Stiftung Ebelin und Gerd Bucerius, Germany, 143
Ziviler Friedensdienst—ZFD, Germany, 120
ZOA, Netherlands, 231
Zochonis Charitable Trust, UK, 392
Zonta Foundation for Women, USA, 484
Zorig Foundation, Mongolia, 219
Zuleikhabai Valy Mohamed Gany Rangoonwala Trust—ZVMG Rangoonwala Trust, Pakistan, 246
ZVMG Rangoonwala Trust, Pakistan, 246

INTERNATIONAL AFFAIRS

Academy of European Law, Germany, 127

International affairs

ActionAid International, South Africa, 278
Adenauer (Konrad) Stiftung eV, Germany, 134
Afghanistan Research and Evaluation Unit, Afghanistan, 3
Africa-America Institute—AAI, USA, 398
Africa Institute of South Africa—AISA, South Africa, 279
African Forum and Network on Debt and Development—AFRODAD, Zimbabwe, 490
AFRODAD—African Forum and Network on Debt and Development, Zimbabwe, 490
AIIA—Australian Institute of International Affairs, Australia, 12
AINA—Arctic Institute of North America, Canada, 49
AISA—Africa Institute of South Africa, South Africa, 279
Albanian Institute for International Studies—AIIS, Albania, 4
Alert—International Alert, UK, 360
Alfred Toepfer Foundation FVS, Germany, 121
Alfred Toepfer Stiftung FVS, Germany, 121
Alliance for International Exchange, USA, 399
Alliance for Securing Democracy, USA, 430
Allianz Foundation, Germany, 121
Amberes (Carlos de), Fundación, Spain, 289
America-Mideast Educational and Training Services Inc, USA, 404
American Enterprise Institute—AEI, USA, 400
American Friends Service Committee—AFSC, USA, 401
American Institute of Pakistan Studies, USA, 401
American Jewish World Service—AJWS, USA, 402
American Schools of Oriental Research—ASOR, USA, 403
AMIDEAST—America-Mideast Educational and Training Services, Inc, USA, 404
Amnesty International, UK, 340
Andrews Charitable Trust—ACT, UK, 340
ANGOC—Asian NGO Coalition for Agrarian Reform and Rural Development, Philippines, 251
Ankara İngiliz Arkeoloji Enstitüsü, UK, 345
Anna Lindh Euro-Mediterranean Foundation for Dialogue between Cultures, Egypt, 90
Anti-Defamation League—ADL, USA, 405
Antigua Forum, Guatemala, 147
APHEDA—Union Aid Abroad, Australia, 19
Arab American Institute Foundation—AAIF, USA, 405
Arca Foundation, USA, 405
Arctic Institute of North America—AINA, Canada, 49
Arcus Foundation, USA, 405
Arengukoostöö Ümarlaud—AKÜ, Estonia, 92
Argentine Council for International Relations, Argentina, 6
ASEAN Institutes of Strategic and International Studies—ASEAN ISIS, Indonesia, 162
Asia Foundation, USA, 406
Asia New Zealand Foundation/Te Whītau Tūhono, New Zealand, 232
Asia/Pacific Cultural Centre for UNESCO—ACCU, Japan, 186
Asia Pacific Foundation of Canada—APFCanada, Canada, 49
Asia Philanthropy Circle—APC, Singapore, 272
Asia Society, USA, 406
ASKO Europa-Stiftung, Germany, 121
ASKO Europe Foundation, Germany, 121
Asociación Salvadoreña para el Desarrollo Económico y Social FUSADES, El Salvador, 91
Asotzijatzijata za Dyemokratska Initzijativa, North Macedonia, 239
Aspen Institute, USA, 407
Association for Democratic Initiatives—ADI, North Macedonia, 239
Association for Development Policy and Humanitarian Aid, Germany, 120
Astur Foundation, Uruguay, 485
ATD Fourth World International, France, 115
Atlas Network, USA, 407
Australian-American Fulbright Commission, Australia, 11
Australian Institute of International Affairs—AIIA, Australia, 12
Axel Springer Foundation, Germany, 122
Axel-Springer-Stiftung, Germany, 122
Balti Uuringute Instituut, Estonia, 92
Baltic Sea Foundation, Finland, 97
Ban Ki-Moon Foundation for a Better Future, Korea (Republic), 200
Barcelona Centre for International Affairs, Spain, 287
BBVA Foundation, Spain, 289
Bellingcat Foundation, Netherlands, 228

Berghof Foundation gGmbH, Germany, 122
Berghof Stiftung für Konfliktforschung gGmbH, Germany, 122
Bertelsmann Foundation, Germany, 122
Bertelsmann Stiftung, Germany, 122
Better World Campaign—BWC, USA, 408
Black Sea Trust for Regional Cooperation, USA, 430
Black Sea University Foundation—BSUF, Romania, 263
Blair (Tony) Institute for Global Change, UK, 386
Blavatnik Family Foundation, USA, 409
Bleustein-Blanchet (Marcel), Fondation de la Vocation, France, 109
BMW Foundation Herbert Quandt, Germany, 122
Böll (Heinrich) Stiftung, Germany, 131
Bond, UK, 335
Bosch (Robert) Stiftung GmbH, Germany, 138
Braća Karić Foundation, Serbia, 271
Bradley (Lynde and Harry) Foundation, Inc, USA, 449
Brandt (Bundeskanzler Willy) Stiftung, Germany, 123
Brazilian Center for International Relations, Brazil, 39
Brenthurst Foundation, South Africa, 282
British Academy, UK, 344
British Institute at Ankara, UK, 345
British Institute of International and Comparative Law—BIICL, UK, 345
British Overseas NGOs for Development, UK, 335
Brookings Institution, USA, 410
Bruegel—Brussels European and Global Economic Laboratory, Belgium, 28
Bruno Kreisky Forum for International Dialogue, Austria, 20
Bruno Kreisky Forum für internationalen Dialog, Austria, 20
Buck (Pearl S.) International, USA, 462
Bulgarian Donors' Forum, Bulgaria, 42
Bundeskanzler-Willy-Brandt-Stiftung, Germany, 123
CAF America, USA, 393
The Canada Council for the Arts/Conseil des Arts du Canada, Canada, 50
Canadian Feed The Children—CFTC, Canada, 50
Canadian International Council/Conseil International du Canada—CIC, Canada, 51
Canon Foundation in Europe, Netherlands, 224
Canon Institute for Global Studies—CIGS, Japan, 187
Carlos de Amberes Foundation, Spain, 289
CARMABI Foundation, Curaçao, 77
Carnegie Corporation of New York, USA, 411
Carnegie Endowment for International Peace, USA, 411
Carnegie Foundation, Wateler Fund, Netherlands, 224
Carnegie-Stichting, Watelerfonds, Netherlands, 224
Catholic Agency for World Development—Trócaire, Ireland, 168
Caucasus Institute for Peace, Democracy and Development—CIPDD, Georgia, 117
Caucasus Research Resource Center Armenia Foundation—CRRC, Armenia, 9
CCKF—Chiang Ching-kuo Foundation for International Scholarly Exchange, Taiwan, 321
CENSIS—Fondazione Centro Studi Investimenti Sociali, Italy, 172
Center for China & Globalization—CCG, China (People's Republic), 67
Centras—Assistance Centre for NGOs, Romania, 263
Centras—Centrul de Asistenta pentru Organizatii Neguvernamentale, Romania, 263
Centre for Democracy and Human Rights—CEDEM, Montenegro, 219
Centre for Development of Non-profit Organizations, Croatia, 76
Centre pour le Dialogue Humanitaire, Switzerland, 307
Centre for Dialogue, Research and Cooperation—CDRC, Ethiopia, 94
Centre for Euro-Atlantic Integration and Democracy—CEID, Hungary, 153
Centre Européen de la Culture—CEC, Switzerland, 307
Centre for Humanitarian Dialogue—HD, Switzerland, 307
Centre for International Governance Innovation—CIGI/Centre pour l'Innovation dans la Gouvernance Internationale, Canada, 51
Centre for International Studies, Italy, 172

INDEX OF MAIN ACTIVITIES

Centre for Strategic and International Studies—CSIS, Indonesia, 162
Centro Brasileiro de Relações Internacionais—CEBRI, Brazil, 39
Centro Studi Internazionali—CSI, Italy, 172
The Century Foundation—TCF, USA, 413
CERANEO—Centar za razvoj neprofitnih organizacija, Croatia, 76
Cercle de Coopération des ONGD du Luxembourg, Luxembourg, 209
Charities Aid Foundation of America—CAF America, USA, 393
Charles Koch Foundation, USA, 413
Charles Léopold Mayer Foundation for the Progress of Humankind, Switzerland, 308
Chatham House, UK, 378
Chiang Ching-kuo Foundation for International Scholarly Exchange—CCKF, Taiwan, 321
Chirac (Jacques), Fondation, France, 107
Chr. Michelsen Institute for Science and Intellectual Freedom—CMI, Norway, 241
Churches' Commission for Migrants in Europe, Belgium, 28
Churchill (Winston) Memorial Trust of New Zealand, New Zealand, 236
CIDOB Foundation—Barcelona Centre for International Affairs, Spain, 287
CIDSE—Together for Global Justice, Belgium, 29
Civic Democratic Initiative Support Foundation—CDF, Yemen, 489
Civic Initiatives, Serbia, 271
CMI—Chr. Michelsen Institute for Science and Intellectual Freedom, Norway, 241
Colombian Habitat Foundation, Colombia, 71
Commission des Eglises auprès des Migrants en Europe/Kommission der Kirchen für Migranten in Europa, Belgium, 28
Commonwealth Foundation, UK, 348
Conseil des Arts du Canada, Canada, 50
Consejo Argentino para las Relaciones Internacionales—CARI, Argentina, 6
Consejo Latinoamericano de Ciencias Sociales—CLACSO, Argentina, 6
Conservation International Foundation, USA, 417
Co-operative Development Foundation of Canada—CDF, Canada, 52
Coordinadora de ONGD España, Spain, 285
CRDF Global, USA, 419
Croatian Platform for International Citizen Solidarity, Croatia, 76
CROSOL—Platforma za međunarodnu građansku solidarnost Hrvatske, Croatia, 76
Dag Hammarskjöld Foundation, Sweden, 303
Daiwa Anglo-Japanese Foundation, UK, 350
Danish Institute for Human Rights, Denmark, 84
Danube Institute, Hungary, 153
del Pino (Rafael), Fundación, Spain, 294
Desmond & Leah Tutu Legacy Foundation, South Africa, 279
Deutsch-Russischer Austausch eV—DRA, Germany, 124
Deutsche Gesellschaft für Auswärtige Politik—DGAP, Germany, 124
Deutsche Nationalstiftung, Germany, 125
Deutsche Orient-Stiftung, Germany, 125
Deutsches Institut für internationale Politik und Sicherheit, Germany, 141
Development Cooperation Roundtable, Estonia, 92
Development NGO Coordinator Spain, Spain, 285
Diakonia, Sweden, 298
DiploFoundation, Malta, 213
Ditchley Foundation, UK, 351
Dóchas—Irish Association of Non-Governmental Development Organisations, Ireland, 165
DOEN Foundation, Netherlands, 229
Donner (William H.) Foundation, Inc, USA, 481
Dräger Foundation, Germany, 126
Dräger-Stiftung, Germany, 126
East Asia Institute—EAI, Korea (Republic), 201
East-West Center—EWC, USA, 422
East-West Encounters Charitable Foundation, Germany, 141
Eastern Europe Studies Centre—EESC, Lithuania, 209
Ebert (Friedrich) Stiftung, Germany, 129
Economic Development Foundation, Türkiye, 328
EEB—European Environmental Bureau, Belgium, 30
EGMONT—Institut Royal des Relations Internationales, Belgium, 29
The Elders Foundation, UK, 352
ELIAMEP—Hellenic Foundation for European and Foreign Policy, Greece, 146
ERA—Europäische Rechtsakademie, Germany, 127
Estonian Foreign Policy Institute, Estonia, 93
Eugenio Mendoza Foundation, Venezuela, 487

INDEX OF MAIN ACTIVITIES

Eurasia Foundation—EF, USA, 424
Eurasia Partnership Foundation-Armenia—EPF-Armenia, Armenia, 9
EURODAD—European Network on Debt and Development, Belgium, 29
Europäische Rechtsakademie—ERA, Germany, 127
European Center for Peace and Development—ECPD, Serbia, 271
European Cultural Centre, Switzerland, 307
European Cultural Foundation—ECF, Netherlands, 225
European Environmental Bureau—EEB, Belgium, 30
European Mediterranean Institute, Spain, 296
European Network on Debt and Development—EURODAD, Belgium, 29
European Think Tanks Group—ETTG, Belgium, 26
European Training Foundation—ETF, Italy, 173
European Youth Foundation—EYF, France, 112
Europese Culterele Stichting, Netherlands, 225
Fairtrade Nederland, Netherlands, 230
Federal Chancellor Willy Brandt Foundation, Germany, 123
Fedesarrollo—Fundación para la Educación Superior y el Desarrollo, Colombia, 71
Félix Houphouët-Boigny Foundation for Peace Research, Côte d'Ivoire, 75
Feltrinelli (Giangiacomo), Fondazione, Italy, Italy, 177
Finnish Development Organizations, Finland, 95
Florence Gould Foundation, USA, 427
Folmer Wisti Fonden for International Forståelse, Denmark, 83
Folmer Wisti Foundation for International Understanding, Denmark, 83
Fondacija Braća Karić, Serbia, 271
Fondacija Cennosti, Bulgaria, 43
Fondacioni i Kosovës për Shoqëri të Hapur, Kosovo, 203
FONDAD—Forum on Debt and Development, Netherlands, 225
Fondation Charles Léopold Mayer pour le Progrès de l'Homme—FPH, Switzerland, 308
Fondation Charles Veillon, Switzerland, 308
Fondation Européenne de la Culture/Europese Culterele Stichting, Netherlands, 225
Fondation Félix Houphouët-Boigny pour la Recherche de la Paix, Côte d'Ivoire, 75
Fondation France Chine—FFC, France, 106
Fondation Franco-Japonaise Sasakawa, France, 106
Fondation Jacques Chirac, France, 107
Fondation Jean Monnet pour l'Europe, Switzerland, 309
Fondation Léopold Sédar Senghor, Senegal, 270
Fondation Marcel Bleustein-Blanchet de la Vocation, France, 109
Fondation Nationale des Sciences Politiques—SciencesPo, France, 110
Fondation pour la Recherche Stratégique, France, 111
Fondation Robert Schuman, France, 111
Fondation Sommet Mondial des Femmes, Switzerland, 320
Fondazione Centro Studi Investimenti Sociali—CENSIS, Italy, 172
Fondazione Giangiacomo Feltrinelli, Italy, 177
Fondazione ISMU—Iniziative e Studi sulla Multietnicità, Italy, 178
Fondazione RUI, Italy, 180
Fonds Européen pour la Jeunesse—FEJ, France, 112
Fonds National Suisse de la Recherche Scientifique, Switzerland, 316
Foreign Policy Association, USA, 427
Foreign Policy and United Nations Association of Austria—UNA-AUSTRIA, Austria, 22
Forum on Debt and Development—FONDAD, Netherlands, 225
Forum LSM Internasional untuk Pembangunan Indonesia, Indonesia, 161
Foundation of Banks and Savings Banks of CECA, Spain, 289
Foundation for Caribbean Research and Management of Biodiversity, Curaçao, 77
Foundation Centre for the Study of Social Investment, Italy, 172
Foundation for Defense of Democracies—FDD, USA, 427
Foundation for German-Polish Co-operation, Poland, 257
Foundation for Higher Education and Development, Colombia, 71
Foundation for Latin American Economic Research, Argentina, 7
Foundation for Middle East Peace—FMEP, USA, 428
Foundation for Security and Development in Africa—FOSDA, Ghana, 143
Foundation of Spanish Commercial Agents, Spain, 287
Foundation for Strategic Research, France, 111
Foundation for Women, Spain, 293
Foundation of Youth and Lifelong Learning—INEDIVIM, Greece, 145
France China Foundation, France, 106
Franciscans International, Switzerland, 310
Franco-Japanese Sasakawa Foundation, France, 106
Frank Knox Memorial Fellowships, USA, 428
Fraser Institute, Canada, 55
Free Russia Foundation, USA, 428
Freedom House, Inc, USA, 428
The Freeman Foundation, USA, 428
French-American Foundation, USA, 429
French Institute of International Relations, France, 113
Fridtjof Nansen Institute, Norway, 241
Fridtjof Nansen Institutt—FNI, Norway, 241
Friede Springer Foundation, Germany, 129
Friede Springer Stiftung, Germany, 129
Friedrich-Ebert-Stiftung eV, Germany, 129
Friedrich Naumann Foundation for Freedom, Germany, 130
Friedrich-Naumann-Stiftung für die Freiheit, Germany, 130
Fritz Thyssen Foundation, Germany, 130
Fritz Thyssen Stiftung, Germany, 130
Fulbright Commission Philippines, Philippines, 253
Fundação Getulio Vargas—FGV, Brazil, 40
Fundação Luso-Americana para o Desenvolvimento—FLAD, Portugal, 260
Fundação Mário Soares e Maria Barroso, Portugal, 260
Fundació CIDOB, Spain, 287
Fundación de los Agentes Comerciales de España, Spain, 287
Fundación Astur, Uruguay, 485
Fundación Banco Bilbao Vizcaya Argentaria—Fundación BBVA, Spain, 289
Fundación BBVA, Spain, 289
Fundación de las Cajas de Ahorros—FUNCAS, Spain, 289
Fundación Carlos de Amberes, Spain, 289
Fundación Circulo de Montevideo, Uruguay, 485
Fundación para la Educación Superior y el Desarrollo—Fedesarrollo, Colombia, 71
Fundación Eugenio Mendoza—FEM, Venezuela, 487
Fundación Felipe González, Spain, 290
Fundación Global Democracia y Desarrollo—FUNGLODE, Dominican Republic, 87
Fundación Hábitat Colombia—FHC, Colombia, 71
Fundación de Investigaciones Económicas Latinoamericanas—FIEL, Argentina, 7
Fundación Juan March, Spain, 291
Fundación Mujeres, Spain, 293
Fundación Mujeres en Igualdad—MEI, Argentina, 8
Fundación para la Paz y la Democracia—FUNPADEM, Costa Rica, 74
Fundación Princesa de Asturias, Spain, 294
Fundación Rafael del Pino, Spain, 294
Fundación Real Instituto Elcano, Spain, 294
Fundacja im. Stefana Batorego, Poland, 256
Fundacja Współpracy Polsko-Niemieckiej/Stiftung für Deutsch-Polnische Zusammenarbeit, Poland, 257
Fundația Universitară a Mării Negre—FUMN, Romania, 263
Georgian Foundation for Strategic and International Studies (Rondeli Foundation)—GFSIS, Georgia, 118
German Council on Foreign Relations, Germany, 124
German Foundation for International Legal Co-operation, Germany, 133
German Institute of Development and Sustainability—IDOS, Germany, 130
German Institute for Global and Area Studies—GIGA, Germany, 130
German Marshall Fund of the United States—GMF, USA, 430
German National Trust, Germany, 125
German Orient Foundation, Germany, 125
German-Russian Exchange, Germany, 124
Getulio Vargas Foundation, Brazil, 40
Giangiacomo Feltrinelli Foundation, Italy, 177
Global Democracy and Development Foundation, Dominican Republic, 87
Global Ethic Foundation, Germany, 141
GLOBSEC, Slovakia, 275

International affairs

Goethe-Institut, Germany, 131
Goodenough College, UK, 356
Gorbachev Foundation, Russian Federation, 266
Gould (Florence) Foundation, USA, 427
Gradjanske inicijative—GI, Serbia, 271
Graduate Institute of International Studies and Development Studies, Switzerland, 311
Great Britain Sasakawa Foundation, UK, 356
Guggenheim (Harry Frank) Foundation, USA, 434
Guggenheim (John Simon) Memorial Foundation, USA, 444
Gulf Research Center—GRC, Saudi Arabia, 269
Hammarskjölds (Dag) Minnesfond, Stiftelsen, Sweden, 303
Hanaholmen—Swedish-Finnish Cultural Centre, Finland, 95
HAND—Hungarian Association of NGOs for Development and Humanitarian Aid, Hungary, 152
Hanns Seidel Foundation, Germany, 131
Hanns-Seidel-Stiftung eV, Germany, 131
The Harry Frank Guggenheim Foundation—HFG, USA, 434
Havelaar (Max) Foundation, Netherlands, 230
Heinrich Böll Foundation, Germany, 131
Heinrich-Böll-Stiftung, Germany, 131
Hellenic Foundation for European and Foreign Policy—ELIAMEP, Greece, 146
Helmich (Janson Johan og Marcia) Legat, Norway, 242
Henry Luce Foundation, Inc, USA, 435
The Heritage Foundation, USA, 436
Heritage Institute for Policy Studies—HIPS, Somalia, 277
HIPS—Heritage Institute for Policy Studies, Somalia, 277
Holt International, USA, 436
Hope, Ireland, 165
Hope Foundation, Türkiye, 331
Horn Economic and Social Policy Institute—HESPI, Ethiopia, 94
Houphouët-Boigny (Félix), Fondation, Côte d'Ivoire, 75
Hudson Institute, USA, 437
Human Rights Information and Training Center—HRITC, Yemen, 489
Human Rights Watch—HRW, USA, 437
Humanity United, USA, 438
IAI—Istituto Affari Internazionali, Italy, 182
IBON Foundation, Philippines, 252
Ibrahim (Mo) Foundation, UK, 357
ICVA—International Council of Voluntary Agencies, Switzerland, 305
The Ideas Institute, Kenya, 199
IFES—International Foundation for Electoral Systems, USA, 440
IHH Humanitarian Relief Foundation, Türkiye, 328
IIED—International Institute for Environment and Development, UK, 360
IJ4EU—Investigative Journalism for Europe, Austria, 21
İktisadi Kalkınma Vakfı, Türkiye, 328
Improving Economies for Stronger Communities—IESC, USA, 438
Indian Council of Social Science Research—ICSSR, India, 157
INEDIVIM—Foundation of Youth and Lifelong Learning, Greece, 145
INHURED International—International Institute for Human Rights, Environment and Development, Nepal, 223
İnsan Hak ve Hürriyetleri İnsani Yardım Vakfı—IHH, Türkiye, 328
Institut Arctique de l'Amérique du Nord—IAAN, Canada, 49
Institut Europeu de la Mediterrània—IEMed, Spain, 296
Institut FMES—Institut Méditerranéen d'Etudes Stratégiques, France, 113
Institut Français des Relations Internationales—IFRI, France, 113
Institut de Hautes Études Internationales et du Développement—IHEID, Switzerland, 311
Institut for Menneskerettigheder, Denmark, 84
Institut Royal des Relations Internationales—EGMONT, Belgium, 29
Institut für Weltwirtschaft—IfW Kiel, Germany, 132
Institute of Baltic Studies, Estonia, 92
Institute of Developing Economies-Japan External Trade Organization—IDE-JETRO, Japan, 188
Institute of International Affairs, Italy, 182
Institute of International Education—IIE, USA, 439
Institute of International Law, Argentina, 6

International affairs

Institute for International Security and Strategic Affairs—ISIAE, Argentina, 6
Institute for Iran-Eurasia Studies—IRAS, Iran, 163
Institute for Latin American and Caribbean Integration, Argentina, 8
Institute for Palestine Studies—IPS, Lebanon, 206
Institute for Security Studies—ISS, South Africa, 280
Institute of Social Studies—ISS, Netherlands, 226
Instituti Kosovar për Kërkime dhe Zhvillim të Politikave, Kosovo, 203
Instituto para la Integración de América Latina y el Caribe—BID-INTAL, Argentina, 8
Internationaal Instituut voor Sociale Geschiedenis—IISG, Netherlands, 226
International Alert—Alert, UK, 360
International Center for Transitional Justice—ICTJ, USA, 440
International Centre for Defence and Security—ICDS, Estonia, 93
International Council of Voluntary Agencies—ICVA, Switzerland, 305
International Development Center of Japan, Japan, 189
International Forum Bosnia, Bosnia and Herzegovina, 37
International Foundation for Electoral Systems—IFES, USA, 440
International Foundation for Socio-economic and Political Studies, Russian Federation, 266
International Institute for Applied Systems Analysis—IIASA, Austria, 21
International Institute for Environment and Development—IIED, UK, 360
International Institute for Human Rights, Environment and Development, Nepal, 223
International Institute of Social History—IISH, Netherlands, 226
International Institute of Social Studies, Netherlands, 226
The International Institute for Strategic Studies—IISS, UK, 360
International NGO Forum on Indonesian Development—INFID, Indonesia, 161
International Press Institute—IPI, Austria, 21
International Renaissance Foundation—IRF, Ukraine, 333
International Research & Exchanges Board—IREX, USA, 442
International Society for Human Rights—ISHR, Germany, 133
International Union for Conservation of Nature and Natural Resources, Switzerland, 313
International Youth Foundation—IYF, USA, 442
International Youth Library Foundation, Germany, 133
Internationale Jugendbibliothek, Germany, 133
IREX—International Research & Exchanges Board, USA, 442
IRZ (Deutsche Stiftung für Internationale Rechtliche Zusammenarbeit) eV, Germany, 133
ISMU Foundation—Initiatives and Studies on Multi-ethnicity, Italy, 178
ISPI—Istituto per gli Studi di Politica Internazionale, Italy, 183
IsraAID, Israel, 169
The Israel Democracy Institute—IDI, Israel, 170
Istituto Affari Internazionali—IAI, Italy, 182
Istituto per gli Studi di Politica Internazionale—ISPI, Italy, 183
Italian Institute for International Political Studies, Italy, 183
IUCN/UICN, Switzerland, 313
Jacques Chirac Foundation, France, 107
JANIC—Japanese NGO Center for International Co-operation, Japan, 185
Janson Johan Helmich and Marcia Jansons Endowment, Norway, 242
Janson Johan Helmich og Marcia Jansons Legat, Norway, 242
The Japan Foundation, Japan, 189
Japanese-German Centre Berlin, Germany, 133
Japanisch-Deutsches Zentrum Berlin, Germany, 133
Jean Monnet Foundation for Europe, Switzerland, 309
Jenny and Antti Wihuri Foundation, Finland, 96
Jenny ja Antti Wihurin Rahasto, Finland, 96
JIIA—Japan Institute of International Affairs, Japan, 190
The John D. and Catherine T. MacArthur Foundation, USA, 444
John Simon Guggenheim Memorial Foundation, USA, 444

Joseph Rowntree Charitable Trust—JRCT, UK, 362
Juan March Foundation, Spain, 291
KDDI Foundation, Japan, 191
Kettering (Charles F.) Foundation, USA, 445
Kettering Foundation—KF, USA, 445
Kiel Institute for the World Economy, Germany, 132
Knox (Frank) Memorial Fellowships, USA, 428
Koch (Charles) Foundation, USA, 413
Kofi Annan Foundation, Switzerland, 313
Konrad Adenauer Foundation, Germany, 134
Konrad-Adenauer-Stiftung eV—KAS, Germany, 134
Körber Foundation, Germany, 134
Körber-Stiftung, Germany, 134
The Korea Foundation, Korea (Republic), 202
Kosovar Institute for Policy Research and Development—KIPRED, Kosovo, 203
Kosovo Foundation for Open Society—KFOS, Kosovo, 203
Kulturfonden för Sverige och Finland, Sweden, 301
Lambrakis Foundation, Greece, 146
LAPAS—Latvijas platforma attīstības sadarbībai, Latvia, 204
Latin American Council of Social Sciences, Argentina, 6
Latvian Institute of International Affairs—LIIA, Latvia, 204
Latvian Platform for Development Cooperation, Latvia, 204
Latvijas Ārpolitikas Institūts—LAI, Latvia, 204
Leibniz-Institut für Globale und Regionale Studien, Germany, 135
Leibniz-Institut für Ost- und Südosteuropaforschung, Germany, 135
Leibniz Institute for East and South-East European Studies, Germany, 135
Léopold Sédar Senghor Foundation, Senegal, 270
Leverhulme Trust, UK, 365
Lifeline Consortium, USA, 428
Lindh (Anna) Euro-Mediterranean Foundation for Dialogue between Cultures, Egypt, 90
Lowy Institute for International Policy, Australia, 15
Luce (Henry) Foundation, Inc, USA, 435
Luso-American Development Foundation, Portugal, 260
The Lutheran World Federation, Switzerland, 314
Lutherischer Weltbund/Fédération Luthérienne Mondiale/Federación Luterana Mundial, Switzerland, 314
Luxembourg Development NGO Co-operation Circle, Luxembourg, 209
Luxemburg (Rosa) Stiftung, Germany, 139
Lynde and Harry Bradley Foundation, Inc, USA, 449
MacArthur (John D. and Catherine T.) Foundation, USA, 444
Macedonian Centre for International Co-operation—MCIC, North Macedonia, 239
MADRE, USA, 450
Maecenata Foundation, Germany, 119
Maecenata Stiftung, Germany, 119
MAG—Mines Advisory Group, UK, 366
Maison Franco-Japonaise, Japan, 191
Makyedonski Tzyentar za Myeroonarodna Sorabotka, North Macedonia, 239
Marangopoulos Foundation for Human Rights, Greece, 146
March (Juan), Fundación, Spain, 291
Marcel Bleustein-Blanchet Vocational Foundation, France, 109
Mário Soares and Maria Barroso Foundation, Portugal, 260
Markle Foundation, USA, 451
Mawazo Institute, Kenya, 199
Max Havelaar Foundation—Fairtrade Netherlands, Netherlands, 230
Mayer (Charles Léopold Mayer), Fondation, Switzerland, 308
Mbeki (Thabo) Foundation, South Africa, 284
Medunarodnog foruma Bosna, Bosnia and Herzegovina, 37
Medical Aid for Palestinians—MAP, UK, 367
Mediterranean Foundation for Strategic Studies Institute, France, 113
Mendoza (Eugenio), Fundación, Venezuela, 487
Menzies Foundation, Australia, 15
Menzies (Sir Robert) Foundation, Australia, 15
Mercy, Ireland, 168
Meridian Foundation, Germany, 140
Mines Advisory Group—MAG, UK, 366
Mirovni Inštitut—Inštitut za sodobne družbene in politične študije, Slovenia, 277
The Mission to Seafarers, UK, 368
MIUSA—Mobility International USA, USA, 453

INDEX OF MAIN ACTIVITIES

Mo Ibrahim Foundation, UK, 368
Mobility International USA—MIUSA, USA, 453
Mohammed bin Rashid Al Maktoum Global Initiatives—MBRGI, United Arab Emirates, 335
Monnet (Jean), Fondation pour l'Europe, Switzerland, 309
Montevideo Circle Foundation, Uruguay, 485
Mouvement International ATD Quart-Monde, France, 115
Mshvidobis, Demokratiisa, da Ganvit'arebis Kavkasiuri Instituti, Georgia, 117
Nansen (Fridtjof) Institute, Norway, 241
National Federation of NGOs, Poland, 254
National Foundation for Political Sciences, France, 110
Naumann (Friedrich) Stiftung, Germany, 130
NDI—National Democratic Institute for International Affairs, USA, 456
Network of Foundations and Research Institutions for the Promotion of a Culture of Peace in Africa, Côte d'Ivoire, 75
New World Foundation—NWF, USA, 456
New Zealand Institute of International Affairs—NZIIA, New Zealand, 234
Nigerian Institute of International Affairs—NIIA, Nigeria, 238
Nihon Kokusai Mondai Kenkyusho, Japan, 190
The Nippon Foundation, Japan, 192
Niwano Peace Foundation, Japan, 192
Nobel Foundation, Sweden, 301
Nobelstiftelsen, Sweden, 301
Nordic Africa Institute Scholarships, Sweden, 302
Nordiska Afrikainstitutets Stipendier, Sweden, 302
Norsk Utenrikspolitisk Institutt—NUPI, Norway, 242
Norwegian Institute of International Affairs, Norway, 242
NZIIA—New Zealand Institute of International Affairs, New Zealand, 234
Observer Research Foundation—ORF, India, 159
ODI, UK, 371
Ogólnopolska Federacja Organizacji Pozarządowych—OFOP, Poland, 254
Olof Palme Memorial Fund for International Understanding and Common Security, Sweden, 302
Olof Palmes Minnesfond för internationell förståelse och gemensam säkerhet, Sweden, 302
Open Society Action Fund, USA, 458
Open Society European Policy Institute—OSEPI, Belgium, 29
Open Society Foundation for Albania, Albania, 5
Open Society Foundation—London, UK, 372
Open Society Foundation—Western Balkans, Albania, 5
Open Society Foundations, USA, 459
Open Society Policy Center, USA, 458
Oppenheimer Generations Foundation, South Africa, 282
Organization for Social Science Research in Eastern and Southern Africa—OSSREA, Ethiopia, 94
Orji Uzor Kalu Foundation, Nigeria, 238
Österreichische Gesellschaft für Aussenpolitik und Internationale Beziehungen—ÖGAVN, Austria, 22
Östersjöfonden, Finland, 97
Our Foundation, Indonesia, 162
Oxfam France, France, 115
Oxfam International, Kenya, 200
Pacific Peoples' Partnership, Canada, 61
Pakistan Institute of International Affairs—PIIA, Pakistan, 245
Palestinian NGO Network, Palestinian Territories, 246
Palme (Olof) Minnesfond fr Internationell Frstelse och Gemensam Skerhet, Sweden, 302
Partos, Netherlands, 223
Pathfinder International, USA, 461
Paz y Cooperación, Spain, 296
Peace and Co-operation, Spain, 296
Peace Direct, UK, 373
Peace and Disarmament Education Trust—PADET, New Zealand, 234
Peace Institute—Institute for Contemporary Social and Political Studies, Slovenia, 277
Peace Research Institute Oslo—PRIO, Norway, 242
Peace and Security Funders Group—PSFG, USA, 396
Pearl S. Buck International, USA, 462
Perdana Global Peace Foundation—PGPF, Malaysia, 211
Peres Center for Peace and Innovation, Israel, 171

INDEX OF MAIN ACTIVITIES

The Pew Charitable Trusts, USA, 462
PH International, USA, 463
Philippine-American Educational Foundation—PAEF, Philippines, 253
Ploughshares Fund, USA, 463
Praemium Erasmianum Foundation, Netherlands, 230
Princess of Asturias Foundation, Spain, 294
PRIO—Peace Research Institute Oslo, Norway, 242
Project Harmony, USA, 463
Quandt (Herbert) Stiftung, Germany, 122
Quincy Institute for Responsible Statecraft—QI, USA, 465
Radiation Effects Research Foundation—RERF, Japan, 193
Rafael del Pino Foundation, Spain, 294
Rahvusvaheline Kaitseuuringute Keskus—RKK, Estonia, 93
Rainforest Foundation US—RFUS, USA, 465
Rajiv Gandhi Foundation, India, 160
Ramon Magsaysay Award Foundation, Philippines, 253
RAND Corporation, USA, 465
Rausing (Ruben and Elisabeth) Trust, UK, 383
Ravand Institute for Economic and International Studies, Iran, 163
Razumkov Centre, Ukraine, 333
RED—Ruralité-Environnement-Développement, Belgium, 34
RedR UK, UK, 375
Regional Centre for Strategic Studies—RCSS, Sri Lanka, 297
Regional Environmental Center, Hungary, 153
Rehabilitation International—RI, USA, 466
Réseau des Fondations et Institutions de Recherche pour la Promotion d'un Culture de la Paix en Afrique—REFICA, Côte d'Ivoire, 75
RIA—Royal Irish Academy, Ireland, 167
Robert Bosch Foundation, Germany, 138
Robert-Bosch-Stiftung GmbH, Germany, 138
Robert Schuman Foundation, France, 111
Robertson Foundation for Government—RFG, USA, 468
Rockefeller Brothers Fund—RBF, USA, 468
Rosa Luxemburg Foundation, Germany, 139
Rosa-Luxemburg-Stiftung, Germany, 139
Rowntree (Joseph) Charitable Trust, UK, 362
The Royal Commonwealth Society—RCS, UK, 377
Royal Elcano Institute Foundation, Spain, 294
Royal Institute of International Affairs—RIIA—Chatham House, UK, 378
Royal Institute of International Relations—Egmont Institute, Belgium, 29
The Royal Society, UK, 379
RSA—Royal Society for the Encouragement of Arts, Manufactures and Commerce, UK, 379
RUI Foundation, Italy, 180
Ruralité-Environnement-Développement—RED, Belgium, 34
Rurality Environment Development, Belgium, 34
Russian International Affairs Council—RIAC, Russian Federation, 266
Rytų Europos Studijų Centras—RESC, Lithuania, 209
Sakartvelos Strategiisa da Saertashoriso Urtiertobebis Kvlevis Pondi—Rondelis Pondi, Georgia, 118
El Salvadoran Association for Economic and Social Development FUSADES, El Salvador, 91
Salzburg Global Seminar, Austria, 22
Sarah Scaife Foundation, Inc, USA, 470
Sasakawa, Fondation Franco-Japonaise, France, 106
The Sasakawa Peace Foundation—SPF, Japan, 194
Scaife (Sarah) Foundation, Inc, USA, 470
Schuman (Robert), Fondation, France, 111
Schwarzkopf-Stiftung Junges Europa, Germany, 139
Schwarzkopf Young Europe Foundation, Germany, 139
Schweizerischer Nationalfonds zur Förderung der Wissenschaftlichen Forschung/Fonds National Suisse de la Recherche Scientifique—SNF, Switzerland, 316
Science and Politics Foundation—German Institute for International and Security Affairs, Germany, 141
Seeds of Peace, USA, 470
SEEMO—South East Europe Media Organisation, Austria, 23
Seidel (Hanns) Stiftung, Germany, 131
Service Civil International—SCI, Belgium, 34
Siam Society, Thailand, 324
Siamese Heritage Trust, Thailand, 324

SID—Society for International Development, Italy, 183
Sigrid Rausing Trust—SRT, UK, 383
Singapore International Foundation—SIF, Singapore, 273
SIPRI—Stockholm International Peace Research Institute, Sweden, 304
Skoll Foundation, USA, 472
Slovak Security Policy Institute, Slovakia, 276
Slovenský inštitút pre bezpečnostnú politiku, Slovakia, 276
Smith Richardson Foundation, Inc, USA, 472
Soares (Mário), Fundação, Portugal, 260
Society for International Development—SID, Italy, 183
Solidar, Belgium, 34
South African Institute of International Affairs, South Africa, 283
South African Institute of Race Relations—IRR, South Africa, 283
South East Europe Media Organisation—SEEMO, Austria, 23
South Sudan Center for Strategic and Policy Studies—CSPS, South Sudan, 285
Springer (Axel) Stiftung, Germany, 122
Springer (Friede) Stiftung, Germany, 129
Stanley Center for Peace and Security, USA, 473
The Starr Foundation, USA, 473
Stefan Batory Foundation, Poland, 256
Stichting Bellingcat, Netherlands, 228
Stichting DOEN, Netherlands, 229
Stichting Max Havelaar—Fairtrade Nederland, Netherlands, 230
Stichting Praemium Erasmianum, Netherlands, 230
Stiftelsen Dag Hammarskjölds Minnesfond, Sweden, 303
Stiftelsen Riksbankens Jubileumsfond, Sweden, 303
Stiftung Mercator, Germany, 140
Stiftung Meridian, Germany, 140
Stiftung Weltethos, Germany, 141
Stiftung West-Östliche Begegnungen, Germany, 141
Stiftung Wissenschaft und Politik—Deutsches Institut für internationale Politik und Sicherheit—SWP, Germany, 141
Stockholm Environment Institute, Sweden, 303
Stockholm International Peace Research Institute—SIPRI, Sweden, 304
Straits Exchange Foundation—SEF, Taiwan, 321
Sudd Institute, South Sudan, 285
Südosteuropäische Medienorganisation, Austria, 23
Suomalaiset kehitysjärjestöt—Fingo, Finland, 95
Survival International, UK, 385
Swedish-Finnish Cultural Foundation, Sweden, 301
Swedish Institute at Athens, Greece, 147
Swiss National Science Foundation—SNSF, Switzerland, 316
TESEV—Türkiye Ekonomik ve Sosyal Etüdler Vakfı, Türkiye, 329
TFF–Transnational Foundation for Peace and Future Research, Sweden, 304
TFF–Transnationella Stiftelsen för Freds- och Framtidsforskning, Sweden, 304
Thabo Mbeki Foundation, South Africa, 284
Third Sector Foundation of Turkey, Türkiye, 327
Third World Network—TWN, Malaysia, 211
Thomson Reuters Foundation, UK, 385
Thyssen (Fritz) Stiftung, Germany, 130
TI—Transparency International, Germany, 142
Tinker Foundation, Inc, USA, 475
Toepfer (Alfred) Stiftung, Germany, 121
Together for Global Justice—CIDSE, Belgium, 29
Tony Blair Institute for Global Change—TBI, UK, 386
Toshiba International Foundation—TIFO, Japan, 194
Transparency International—TI, Germany, 142
Trócaire—Catholic Agency for World Development, Ireland, 168
Turkish Economic and Social Studies Foundation, Türkiye, 329
TÜSEV—Türkiye Üçüncü Sektör Vakfı, Türkiye, 327
Tutu (Desmond & Leah) Legacy Foundation, South Africa, 279
U4 Anti-Corruption Resource Centre, Norway, 241
UAI—Union des Associations Internationales, Belgium, 27
Umut Vakfı, Türkiye, 331
UNESCO Centre du Patrimoine Mondial, France, 116
UNESCO World Heritage Centre, France, 116
Union Aid Abroad—APHEDA, Australia, 19

Law, civil society and human rights

Union des Associations Internationales—UAI, Belgium, 27
Union of International Associations—UIA/Unie van de Internationale Verenigingen—UIV, Belgium, 27
United Nations Foundation, USA, 476
United States-Japan Foundation, USA, 477
US Civilian Research & Development Foundation, USA, 419
USC Shoah Foundation—The Institute for Visual History and Education, USA, 477
Values Foundation, Bulgaria, 40
VANI—Voluntary Action Network India, India, 155
Vargas (Getulio), Fundação, Brazil, 40
Veillon (Charles), Fondation, Switzerland, 308
VENRO—Verband Entwicklungspolitik und Humanitäre Hilfe deutscher Nichtregierungsorganizationen, Germany, 120
VIDC—Vienna Institute for International Dialogue and Co-operation, Austria, 23
Vienna Institute for International Dialogue and Co-operation—VIDC, Austria, 23
Vivekananda International Foundation—VIF, India, 161
Voluntary Action Network India—VANI, India, 155
War on Want, UK, 388
Wihuri Foundation for International Prizes, Finland, 98
Wihuri (Jenny and Antti) Foundation, Finland, 96
Wihurin kansainvälisten palkintojen rahasto, Finland, 98
The William H. Donner Foundation, Inc, USA, 481
WILPF—Women's International League for Peace and Freedom, Switzerland, 319
Wilson (Woodrow) International Center for Scholars, USA, 482
Winston Churchill Memorial Trust of New Zealand, New Zealand, 236
Wisti (Folmer) Foundation for International Understanding, Denmark, 83
Women in Equality Foundation, Argentina, 8
Women's Environment & Development Organization—WEDO, USA, 482
Women's International League for Peace and Freedom, Switzerland, 319
Women's World Summit Foundation—WWSF, Switzerland, 320
Woodrow Wilson International Center for Scholars, USA, 482
World Economic Forum, Switzerland, 320
World Holocaust Forum Foundation—WHF, Israel, 171
World Learning, USA, 483
World Peace Foundation—WPF, USA, 483
WWSF—Women's World Summit Foundation, Switzerland, 320
Yayasan Geutanyoë, Indonesia, 162
Yemen Policy Center, Yemen, 489
Yemen Polling Center—YPC, Yemen, 489
Zonta Foundation for Women, USA, 484

LAW, CIVIL SOCIETY AND HUMAN RIGHTS

AAUW Educational Foundation, USA, 399
Abdorrahman Boroumand Center for Human Rights in Iran—ABC, USA, 396
Abdul Hameed Shoman Foundation—AHSF, Jordan, 195
Abilis Foundation, Finland, 95
Abilis-säätiö, Finland, 95
Abrinq Foundation for the Rights of Children and Adolescents, Brazil, 39
Academy for the Development of Philanthropy in Poland, Poland, 253
Academy of European Law, Germany, 127
Access Foundation, Costa Rica, 73
Acción Contra el Hambre–ACH, Spain, 286
Accountable Now, USA, 393
ACDI/VOCA, USA, 397
ACFID—Australian Council for International Development, Australia, 12
ACROTEC Technology Foundation, Italy, 176
ACT Alliance, Switzerland, 306
Action Against Hunger, Spain, 286
Action for Children, UK, 338
Action Children's Aid, Denmark, 82
Action contre la Faim—ACF France, France, 100
Action Group on Erosion, Technology and Concentration, Canada, 54
Action on Poverty, Australia, 10

Law, civil society and human rights

Action Solidarité Tiers Monde—ASTM, Luxembourg, 209
ActionAid International, South Africa, 278
Acumen, USA, 397
Adenauer (Konrad) Stiftung eV, Germany, 134
Adessium Foundation, Netherlands, 223
Adyan Foundation, Lebanon, 205
Afghan Women's Network, Afghanistan, 3
Afghanistan Institute for Civil Society—AICS, Afghanistan, 3
Afghanistan Research and Evaluation Unit, Afghanistan, 3
Africa-America Institute—AAI, USA, 398
Africa Humanitarian Action—AHA, Ethiopia, 93
African Forum and Network on Debt and Development—AFRODAD, Zimbabwe, 490
African Refugees Foundation—AREF, Nigeria, 237
African Women's Development Fund—AWDF, Ghana, 143
African Youth Initiative Network—AYINET, Uganda, 331
Afrobarometer, Ghana, 143
AFRODAD—African Forum and Network on Debt and Development, Zimbabwe, 490
Aga Khan Development Network—AKDN, Switzerland, 306
Aga Khan Foundation, Switzerland, 306
Aga Khan Foundation Canada, Canada, 49
Aga Khan Foundation UK, UK, 338
Age International, UK, 339
AGIR Association for the Environment and Quality of Life, Mali, 213
Agora Foundation, Poland, 255
Agronomes et Vétérinaires sans Frontières—AVSF, France, 100
Agronomists and Veterinarians Without Borders, France, 100
AIC—Association Internationale des Charités, Belgium, 28
Aid to the Church in Need—ACN International, Germany, 120
AID Foundation, Bangladesh, 24
AIIA—Australian Institute of International Affairs, Australia, 12
AINA—Arctic Institute of North America, Canada, 49
Air France Foundation, France, 103
Aisha Buhari Global Foundation, Nigeria, 237
Akademia Rozwoju Filantropii w Polsce—ARFP, Poland, 253
Akai Hane—Central Community Chest of Japan, Japan, 185
Aktion Børnehjælp, Denmark, 82
The Al-Khoei Benevolent Foundation, UK, 339
Al-Mortaqa Foundation for Human Development, Iraq, 164
The Alan Turing Institute, UK, 339
Albanian Disability Rights Foundation, Albania, 4
Albanian Institute for International Studies—AIIS, Albania, 4
Alert—International Alert, UK, 360
Alicia Patterson Foundation—APF, USA, 398
Alight, USA, 399
Alkhidmat Foundation Pakistan—AKFP, Pakistan, 244
All India Disaster Mitigation Institute, India, 155
Allen Lane Foundation, UK, 339
Allen (Paul G.) Family Foundation, USA, 462
Allende (Isabel) Foundation, USA, 442
Alliance for International Exchange, USA, 399
Alliance Israélite Universelle, France, 101
Alliance for Securing Democracy, USA, 430
Allianz Foundation, Germany, 121
Alola Foundation, Timor-Leste, 325
Alongside Hope/Auprès de l'espoir, Canada, 49
Alwaleed Philanthropies, Saudi Arabia, 269
AMADE Mondiale—Association Mondiale des Amis de l'Enfance, Monaco, 217
Amberes (Carlos de), Fundación, Spain, 289
Ambrela Platform of Development Organizations, Slovakia, 273
Ambrela—Platforma rozvojových organizácií, Slovakia, 273
The Ambrose Monell Foundation, USA, 399
Ambuja Cement Foundation—ACF, India, 156
America for Bulgaria Foundation, Bulgaria, 43
America–Mideast Educational and Training Services Inc, USA, 404
American Association of University Women—AAUW Educational Foundation, USA, 399
American Enterprise Institute—AEI, USA, 400
American Express Foundation, USA, 400
American Foundation for the Blind—AFB, USA, 400
American Friends Service Committee—AFSC, USA, 401

American Jewish World Service—AJWS, USA, 402
amfAR—The Foundation for AIDS Research, USA, 403
AMIDEAST—America-Mideast Educational and Training Services, Inc, USA, 404
Amigos de la Tierra, Netherlands, 225
Les Amis de la Terre, Netherlands, 225
Amity Foundation, China (People's Republic), 66
Amnesty International, UK, 340
Analitika—Center for Social Research, Bosnia and Herzegovina, 37
Anders Jahre's Foundation for Humanitarian Purposes, Norway, 240
Anders Jahres Humanitære Stiftelse, Norway, 240
Andrew W. Mellon Foundation, USA, 404
Andrews Charitable Trust—ACT, UK, 340
The Andy Warhol Foundation for the Visual Arts, Inc, USA, 404
Anesvad, Spain, 286
Angel of Hope Foundation, Zimbabwe, 490
ANGOC—Asian NGO Coalition for Agrarian Reform and Rural Development, Philippines, 251
Ankara Ingiliz Arkeoloji Enstitüsü, UK, 345
Anna Lindh Euro-Mediterranean Foundation for Dialogue between Cultures, Egypt, 90
Anne Frank-Fonds, Switzerland, 306
Anne Frank Foundation, Netherlands, 224
Anne Frank Fund, Switzerland, 306
Anne Frank Stichting, Netherlands, 224
The Annenberg Foundation, USA, 404
The Annie E. Casey Foundation, USA, 404
Ansar Burney Trust International, Pakistan, 245
Anti-Corruption Foundation, Russian Federation, 265
Anti-Defamation League—ADL, USA, 405
Anti-Slavery International, UK, 340
Antigua Forum, Guatemala, 147
APHEDA—Union Aid Abroad, Australia, 19
Arab American Institute Foundation—AAIF, USA, 405
Arab Network for Civic Education, Jordan, 195
Arab Organization for Human Rights, Egypt, 90
Arainneachd Eachdraidheil Alba, UK, 358
Arca Foundation, USA, 405
Archewell Foundation, USA, 405
Arctic Institute of North America—AINA, Canada, 49
Arcus Foundation, USA, 405
Arengukoostöö Ümarlaud—AKÜ, Estonia, 92
Areumdaun Jaedan, Korea (Republic), 200
Argentine Council for International Relations, Argentina, 6
Ariadne—European Funders for Social Change and Human Rights, UK, 336
Arias Foundation for Peace and Human Progress, Costa Rica, 74
Armanshahr Foundation—OPEN ASIA, Afghanistan, 3
ASEAN Foundation, Indonesia, 161
ASEAN Institutes of Strategic and International Studies—ASEAN ISIS, Indonesia, 162
Asia Crime Prevention Foundation—ACPF, Japan, 186
Asia Foundation, USA, 406
Asia Philanthropy Circle—APC, Singapore, 272
ASKO Europa-Stiftung, Germany, 121
ASKO Europe Foundation, Germany, 121
Asociacija Litdea—Lithuanian Development Education and Awareness Raising Association, Lithuania, 208
Asociación de Fundaciones Familiares y Empresariales—AFE, Colombia, 70
Asociación Salvadoreña para el Desarrollo Económico y Social FUSADES, El Salvador, 91
Asotzijatzijata za Dyemokratska Initzijativa, North Macedonia, 239
Aspen Institute, USA, 407
Association AGIR pour l'Environnement et la Qualité de la Vie, Mali, 213
Association of Civil Society Development Center, Türkiye, 327
Association for Democratic Initiatives—ADI, North Macedonia, 239
Association for Development Policy and Humanitarian Aid, Germany, 120
Association of Family and Corporate Foundations, Colombia, 70
Association of Foundations, Philippines, 250
Association of Foundations in the Netherlands, Netherlands, 223
Association Internationale des Charités—AIC, Belgium, 28
Association of Italian Foundations and Savings Banks, Italy, 171

INDEX OF MAIN ACTIVITIES

Association of Non-Governmental Organizations in The Gambia—TANGO, Gambia, 117
Associazione di Fondazioni e di Casse di Risparmio SpA—ACRI, Italy, 171
ASTM—Action Solidarité Tiers Monde, Luxembourg, 209
Astur Foundation, Uruguay, 485
ATD Fourth World International, France, 115
Atlas Network, USA, 407
Aurat Publication & Information Service Foundation—AF, Pakistan, 245
Auschwitz-Birkenau Foundation, Poland, 255
Auschwitz Foundation—Remembrance of Auschwitz, Belgium, 30
Australian-American Fulbright Commission, Australia, 11
Australian Communities Foundation, Australia, 12
Australian Conservation Foundation—ACF, Australia, 12
Australian Council for International Development—ACFID, Australia, 12
Australian Foundation for the Peoples of Asia and the Pacific—AFAP, Australia, 10
Australian Institute of International Affairs—AIIA, Australia, 12
Australian Multicultural Foundation—AMF, Australia, 12
Australian Volunteers International—AVI, Australia, 13
Austrian Science Fund, Austria, 21
Autonómia Alapítvány, Hungary, 152
Autonómia Foundation, Hungary, 152
Avatud Eesti Fond, Estonia, 92
AVI—Australian Volunteers International, Australia, 13
AVINA Foundation, Panama, 247
AVSI Foundation, Italy, 175
Azim Premji Foundation, India, 156
BaBe—Budi aktivna, Budi emancipiran, Croatia, 77
Bagnoud (François-Xavier) Association, Switzerland, 310
Baha'i International Development Organization—BIDO, Israel, 169
Balkan Civil Society Development Network—BCSDN, North Macedonia, 239
Balkan Security Platform—BSP, Serbia, 271
Balti Uuringute Instituut, Estonia, 92
Balzan Fonds, Internationale Stiftung, Italy, 181
Ban Ki-Moon Foundation for a Better Future, Korea (Republic), 200
Banda (Joyce) Foundation International, Malawi, 210
BANHCAFE Foundation, Honduras, 150
Bank of America Charitable Foundation, USA, 407
The Barack Obama Foundation, USA, 407
Barbra Streisand Foundation, USA, 408
Barça Foundation, Spain, 287
Barcelona Centre for International Affairs, Spain, 287
Baring Foundation, UK, 341
Barka Foundation for Mutual Assistance, Poland, 256
Barzani Charity Foundation—BCF, Iraq, 164
Basso Issoco (Leilio e Lisli), Fondazione, Italy, 178
Bat Conservation Trust, UK, 342
BBC Media Action, UK, 342
BCause Foundation, Bulgaria, 42
Be Active, Be Emancipated, Croatia, 77
The Beautiful Foundation, Korea (Republic), 200
Bellingcat Foundation, Netherlands, 228
Bello (Sir Ahmadu) Memorial Foundation, Nigeria, 238
Bellona Foundation, Norway, 240
Benaad Enetkhabat Shafaf Afghanistan, Afghanistan, 4
Benecke (Otto) Stiftung eV, Germany, 138
Berghof Foundation gGmbH, Germany, 122
Berghof Stiftung für Konfliktforschung gGmbH, Germany, 122
Bernheim Foundation, Belgium, 31
Bertelsmann Foundation, Germany, 122
Bertelsmann Stiftung, Germany, 122
Bezos Earth Fund, USA, 408
Big Heart Foundation, Chad, 64
Bischöfliches Hilfswerk Misereor eV, Germany, 137
Black Lives Matter Global Network Foundation—BLM Global Network Foundation, USA, 408
Black Sea NGO Network—BSNN, Bulgaria, 42
Black Sea Trust for Regional Cooperation, USA, 430
Black Sea University Foundation—BSUF, Romania, 263
Blair (Tony) Institute for Global Change, UK, 386

INDEX OF MAIN ACTIVITIES

Bleustein-Blanchet (Marcel), Fondation de la Vocation, France, 109
BLM Global Network Foundation, USA, 408
Bloomberg Philanthropies, USA, 409
Blue Marine Foundation—BLUE, UK, 343
BMW Foundation Herbert Quandt, Germany, 122
Bodossaki Foundation, Greece, 145
Böll (Heinrich) Stiftung, Germany, 131
Bond, UK, 335
Borderland Foundation, Poland, 256
Born This Way Foundation, USA, 409
Bosch (Robert) Stiftung GmbH, Germany, 138
Botswana Institute for Development Policy Analysis—BIDPA, Botswana, 37
Braća Karić Foundation, Serbia, 271
BRAC, Bangladesh, 25
Bradley (Lynde and Harry) Foundation, Inc, USA, 449
BrazilFoundation, Brazil, 39
Bread for the World—Protestant Work for Social Welfare and Development, Germany, 123
Bridge House Estates, UK, 348
Brighter Future Myanmar Foundation—BFM, Myanmar, 221
Bristol-Myers Squibb Foundation, USA, 410
British Institute at Ankara, UK, 345
British Institute of International and Comparative Law—BIICL, UK, 345
British Overseas NGOs for Development, UK, 335
British Red Cross Society, UK, 345
Brookings Institution, USA, 410
Brot für die Welt—Evangelisches Werk für Diakonie und Entwicklung, Germany, 123
Brother's Brother Foundation, USA, 410
Brothers of Men, France, 113
Bruno Kreisky Forum for International Dialogue, Austria, 20
Bruno Kreisky Forum für internationalen Dialog, Austria, 20
Buck (Pearl S.) International, USA, 462
Buffett (Susan Thompson) Foundation, USA, 474
Bulgarian Fund for Women, Bulgaria, 43
Bulgarian Platform for International Development—BPID, Bulgaria, 42
Cadbury (Edward) Charitable Trust, UK, 351
Cadbury (William Adlington) Charitable Trust, UK, 390
CAF America, USA, 393
CAF—Charities Aid Foundation, UK, 336
CAF Russia—Charities Aid Foundation Russia, Russian Federation, 264
CAFOD—Catholic Agency for Overseas Development, UK, 345
California Community Foundation, USA, 411
Calouste Gulbenkian Foundation, Portugal, 259
Canadian Centre for International Studies and Co-operation, Canada, 51
Canadian Council for International Co-operation—CCIC/Conseil Canadien pour la Coopération Internationale—CCCI, Canada, 48
Canadian Feed The Children—CFTC, Canada, 50
Canadian Physicians for Aid and Relief—CPAR, Canada, 52
Canon Foundation in Europe, Netherlands, 224
CARE International—CI, Switzerland, 307
Caribbean Policy Development Centre—CPDC, Barbados, 25
Cariplo Foundation, Italy, 175
Caritas Canada, Canada, 53
Caritas de France—Secours Catholique, France, 116
Caritas Internationalis—CI, Vatican City, 486
Carlo Cattaneo Institute, Italy, 182
Carlos de Amberes Foundation, Spain, 289
Carlos Slim Foundation, Mexico, 215
Carlsberg Foundation, Denmark, 82
Carlsbergfondet, Denmark, 82
CARMABI Foundation, Curaçao, 77
Carnegie Corporation of New York, USA, 411
Carnegie Endowment for International Peace, USA, 411
Carnegie Hero Fund Commission, USA, 412
Carnegie Trust for the Universities of Scotland, UK, 346
Carnegie UK Trust, UK, 346
Carpathian Foundation, Hungary, 153
Carrefour International, Canada, 53
The Carter Center, USA, 412
CASE—Centrum Analiz Społeczno-Ekonomicznych, Poland, 255
Casey (Annie E.) Foundation, USA, 404
Catholic Agency for Overseas Development—CAFOD, UK, 345
Catholic Agency for World Development—Trócaire, Ireland, 168
Catholic Help—Caritas France, France, 116

Cattaneo (Carlo), Istituto, Italy, 182
Caucasus Institute for Peace, Democracy and Development—CIPDD, Georgia, 117
Caucasus Research Resource Center Armenia Foundation—CRRC, Armenia, 9
Caucus of Development NGO Networks—CODE-NGO, Philippines, 250
CCKF—Chiang Ching-kuo Foundation for International Scholarly Exchange, Taiwan, 321
CECI—Canadian Centre for International Studies and Co-operation/Centre d'Etudes et de Coopération Internationale, Canada, 51
CEDIAS-Musée Social—Centre d'Etudes, de Documentation, d'Information et d'Action Sociales, France, 101
CEDRO—Centro de Información y Educación para la Prevención del Abuso de Drogas, Peru, 248
CENOZO—Cellule Norbert Zongo pour le Journalisme d'Investigation en Afrique de l'Ouest, Burkina Faso, 44
CENSIS—Fondazione Centro Studi Investimenti Sociali, Italy, 172
Center for China & Globalization—CCG, China (People's Republic), 67
Center for Economic & Social Development—CESD, Azerbaijan, 23
Center for Inquiry—CFI, USA, 412
Center for Social and Economic Research, Poland, 255
Center for Training and Consultancy, Georgia, 117
Center for Victims of Torture—CVT, USA, 413
Centras—Assistance Centre for NGOs, Romania, 263
Centras—Centrul de Asistenta pentru Organizatii Neguvernamentale, Romania, 263
Centre for Civil Society—CCS, India, 157
Centre for Democracy and Human Rights—CEDEM, Montenegro, 219
Centre for the Development of Non-governmental Organizations, Montenegro, 219
Centre for Development of Non-profit Organizations, Croatia, 76
Centre pour le Dialogue Humanitaire, Switzerland, 307
Centre for Dialogue, Research and Cooperation—CDRC, Ethiopia, 94
Centre for Euro-Atlantic Integration and Democracy—CEID, Hungary, 153
Centre Européen de la Culture—CEC, Switzerland, 307
Centre for Humanitarian Action—CHA, Germany, 123
Centre for Humanitarian Dialogue—HD, Switzerland, 307
Centre for the Information Service, Co-operation and Development of NGOs, Slovenia, 277
Centre for International Governance Innovation—CIGI/Centre pour l'Innovation dans la Gouvernance Internationale, Canada, 51
Centre for International Studies, Italy, 172
Centre Ivoirien de Recherches Economiques et Sociales—CIRES, Côte d'Ivoire, 75
Centre for Philanthropy, Slovakia, 274
Centre for Social Impact and Philanthropy—CSIP, India, 154
Centre for Social Studies, Documentation, Information and Action, France, 101
Centre for Strategic and International Studies—CSIS, Indonesia, 162
Centro de Estudios Públicos—CEP, Chile, 64
Centro de Información y Educación para la Prevención del Abuso de Drogas—CEDRO, Peru, 248
Centro Mexicano para la Filantropía—CEMEFI, Mexico, 214
Centro Studi Internazionali—CSI, Italy, 172
Centrul de Resurse pentru Drepturile Omului—CReDO, Moldova, 217
Centrum pre Filantropiu, Slovakia, 274
The Century Foundation—TCF, USA, 413
CERANEO—Centar za razvoj neprofitnih organizacija, Croatia, 76
Cercle de Coopération des ONGD du Luxembourg, Luxembourg, 209
Česká rada sociálních služeb—CRSS, Czech Republic, 78
Česko-německý fond budoucnosti, Czech Republic, 79
Charities Advisory Trust, UK, 336
Charities Aid Foundation of America—CAF America, USA, 393
Charities Aid Foundation—CAF, UK, 336
Charities Aid Foundation Russia—CAF Russia, Russian Federation, 264

Law, civil society and human rights

Charity Islamic Trust Elrahma, UK, 352
Charity Projects, UK, 348
Charles Koch Foundation, USA, 413
Charles Léopold Mayer Foundation for the Progress of Humankind, Switzerland, 308
Charles and Lynn Schusterman Family Philanthropies, USA, 413
Charles Stewart Mott Foundation—CSMF, USA, 414
The Charta 77 Foundation, Czech Republic, 80
Chatham House, UK, 378
The Chatlos Foundation, Inc, USA, 414
Cheshire (Leonard) Foundation, UK, 364
Chia Hsin Foundation, Taiwan, 321
Chiang Ching-kuo Foundation for International Scholarly Exchange—CCKF, Taiwan, 321
The Chicago Community Trust, USA, 414
Child Migrants Trust, UK, 347
ChildFund International, USA, 414
Childhope Philippines, Philippines, 251
Children & War Foundation—CAW, Norway, 240
Children International—CI, USA, 414
Children of the Mekong, France, 102
Children and Sharing, France, 102
The Children's Investment Fund Foundation, UK, 347
Chirac (Jacques), Fondation, France, 107
Chr. Michelsen Institute for Science and Intellectual Freedom—CMI, Norway, 241
Christian Aid, UK, 348
Churches' Commission for Migrants in Europe, Belgium, 28
The Churchill Fellowship, UK, 348
Churchill (Winston) Memorial Trust of New Zealand, New Zealand, 236
CIDOB Foundation—Barcelona Centre for International Affairs, Spain, 287
CIDSE—Together for Global Justice, Belgium, 29
CIMA Research Foundation—Centre for Environmental Monitoring, Italy, 176
Cimade—Ecumenical Care Service, France, 102
La Cimade—Service Oecuménique d'Entraide, France, 102
Citi Foundation, USA, 415
Citizens Foundation, Iceland, 154
Citizenship Foundation, UK, 392
The City Bridge Trust, UK, 348
City of Lisbon Foundation, Portugal, 259
Civic Democratic Initiative Support Foundation—CDF, Yemen, 489
Civic Initiatives, Serbia, 271
CIVICUS—World Alliance for Citizen Participation, South Africa, 278
CiviKos Platform, Kosovo, 202
Civil Peace Service—CPS, Germany, 120
Civil Society Development Center—CSDC, Georgia, 117
Civil Society Foundation, Georgia, 118
Civil Society and Human Rights Network, Afghanistan, 3
Civil Society and Human Rights Organization—CSHRO, Afghanistan, 3
Civitas Foundation for Civil Society, Romania, 263
Civitates, Belgium, 27
CLADEM—Comité de América Latina y el Caribe para la Defensa de los Derechos de la Mujer, Peru, 249
Clara Lionel Foundation—CLF, USA, 415
Claudine Talon Foundation, Benin, 35
CLEAR Global, USA, 416
Cleveland Foundation, USA, 416
Clinton Foundation, USA, 416
Clooney Foundation for Justice—CFJ, USA, 416
Clore Israel Foundation, Israel, 169
Člověk v tísni, Czech Republic, 79
CMDID Foundation—Malian Centre for Inter-Party Dialogue and Democracy, Mali, 213
CMI—Chr. Michelsen Institute for Science and Intellectual Freedom, Norway, 241
CNVOS—Zavod Center za Informiranje, Sodelovanje in Razvoj Nevladnih Organizacije, Slovenia, 277
Coady Institute, Canada, 52
Collier Charitable Fund, Australia, 13
Comic Relief, UK, 348
Comité de América Latina y el Caribe para la Defensa de los Derechos de la Mujer—CLADEM, Peru, 249
Comité de Coordination des ONGI en RCA, Central African Republic, 63
Commission des Eglises auprès des Migrants en Europe/Kommission der Kirchen für Migranten in Europa, Belgium, 28
Committee of Good Will—Olga Havel Foundation, Czech Republic, 81
Common Network, Brazil, 38
Commonwealth Foundation, UK, 348

563

Law, civil society and human rights

Communication Foundation for Asia, Philippines, 251
Community Chest, Singapore, 273
Community Chest of Hong Kong, Hong Kong, 150
Community Chest of Korea—Fruit of Love, Korea (Republic), 200
Community Development Foundation, Mozambique, 221
Community Foundation Partnership, Russian Federation, 264
Community Foundation for the Western Region of Zimbabwe—CFWRZ, Zimbabwe, 490
Concern India Foundation, India, 157
Concern Worldwide, Ireland, 166
CONCORD—European NGO Confederation for Relief and Development, Belgium, 26
The Confederation of Service Charities—Cobseo, UK, 349
Consejo Argentino para las Relaciones Internacionales—CARI, Argentina, 6
Consejo Latinoamericano de Ciencias Sociales—CLACSO, Argentina, 6
Conservation International Foundation, USA, 417
Consuelo Zobel Alger Foundation, USA, 417
Cooperation Canada/Coopération Canada, Canada, 48
Cooperazione Internazionale—COOPI, Italy, 173
Coordinadora de ONGD España, Spain, 285
Coordination SUD, France, 99
Coram, UK, 349
Corona Foundation, Colombia, 71
Corra Foundation, UK, 349
Corus International, USA, 418
Counterpart International, USA, 418
Covenant Foundation, USA, 418
CPAR—Canadian Physicians for Aid and Relief, Canada, 52
CRDF Global, USA, 419
CReDO—Centrul de Resurse pentru Drepturile Omului, Moldova, 217
Croatian Platform for International Citizen Solidarity, Croatia, 76
CROSOL—Platforma za medunarodnu gradansku solidarnost Hrvatske, Croatia, 76
Crossroads International/Carrefour International, Canada, 53
Crown Family Philanthropies, USA, 419
Cuso International, Canada, 53
CVT—Center for Victims of Torture, USA, 413
Czech Council of Social Services, Czech Republic, 78
Czech-German Fund for the Future, Czech Republic, 79
Dag Hammarskjöld Foundation, Sweden, 303
Dalia Association, Palestinian Territories, 246
Daniele Agostino Derossi Foundation, USA, 420
Danielle Mitterrand Foundation, France, 112
Danish Institute for Human Rights, Denmark, 84
Danube Institute, Hungary, 153
David Suzuki Foundation, Canada, 53
Davis (Lady) Fellowship Trust, Israel, 170
Defence for Children International—DCI, Switzerland, 307
DemNet—Demokratikus Jogok Fejlesztéséért Alapítvány, Hungary, 153
DemNet—Foundation for the Development of Democratic Rights, Hungary, 153
Democracy and Development Foundation, Chile, 65
Democracy Fund, USA, 458
Democracy and Human Rights Development Centre, Iraq, 164
Derossi (Daniele Agostino) Foundation, USA, 420
Desmond & Leah Tutu Legacy Foundation, South Africa, 279
Deutsch-Russischer Austausch eV—DRA, Germany, 124
Deutsche Bank Americas Foundation, USA, 420
Deutsche Gesellschaft für Auswärtige Politik—DGAP, Germany, 124
Development Cooperation Roundtable, Estonia, 92
Development Foundation of Turkey, Türkiye, 330
Development Gateway—DG, USA, 420
Development NGO Coordinator Spain, Spain, 285
Development and Peace—Caritas Canada, Canada, 53
Développement et Paix—Caritas Canada, Canada, 53
Diakonia, Sweden, 298
Digicel Foundation Haiti, Haiti, 149
Digicel Foundation Jamaica, Jamaica, 184
Digicel PNG Foundation, Papua New Guinea, 247
Digicel Trinidad and Tobago Foundation, Trinidad and Tobago, 326
Disability Rights Fund, USA, 395
Disabled Peoples' International—DPI, Canada, 54

Dmitry Likhachev Foundation, Russian Federation, 265
Dóchas—Irish Association of Non-Governmental Development Organisations, Ireland, 165
Doctors of the World International, France, 114
DOEN Foundation, Netherlands, 229
Donner (William H.) Foundation, Inc, USA, 481
The Dr Denis Mukwege Foundation, Netherlands, 224
Dr Guillermo Manuel Ungo Foundation, El Salvador, 91
Dr Scholl Foundation, USA, 421
Dräger Foundation, Germany, 126
Dräger-Stiftung, Germany, 126
Drug Policy Alliance—DPA, USA, 421
DSW—Deutsche Stiftung Weltbevölkerung, Germany, 126
Dulverton Trust, UK, 351
Earth Island Institute—EII, USA, 422
Earthrights International—ERI, USA, 422
Earthworm Foundation, Switzerland, 307
East Asia Institute—EAI, Korea (Republic), 201
East-West Encounters Charitable Foundation, Germany, 141
Eastern Europe Studies Centre—EESC, Lithuania, 209
eBay Foundation, USA, 422
Ebelin and Gerd Bucerius ZEIT Foundation, Germany, 143
Ebert (Friedrich) Stiftung, Germany, 129
EcoCiencia—Fundación Ecuatoriana de Estudios Ecologicos, Ecuador, 88
Economic and Social Research Foundation—ESRF, Tanzania, 322
ECPAT International, Thailand, 324
Ecuadorean Foundation of Ecological Studies, Ecuador, 88
Ecuadorean Social Group Fund Populorum Progressio, Ecuador, 89
EDGE Funders Alliance, USA, 394
Edmond de Rothschild Foundations, Switzerland, 308
Ednannia—Initiative Centre to Support Social Action, Ukraine, 332
EDP Foundation, Portugal, 260
Educo, Spain, 286
Edward Cadbury Charitable Trust, UK, 351
EEB—European Environmental Bureau, Belgium, 30
Eesti Mittetulundusühingute ja Sihtasutuste Liit, Estonia, 92
EGMONT—Institut Royal des Relations Internationales, Belgium, 29
Ekopolis Foundation, Slovakia, 275
The Elders Foundation, UK, 352
Electronic Frontier Foundation—EFF, USA, 423
ELIAMEP—Hellenic Foundation for European and Foreign Policy, Greece, 146
Ellerman (John) Foundation, UK, 361
The ELMA Group of Foundations, USA, 423
Elrahma Charity Trust, UK, 352
Elrha, UK, 352
Elton John AIDS Foundation, UK, 352
Embrace the Middle East, UK, 352
EMERGENCY, Italy, 173
Emmaüs International, France, 102
Enda Third World—Environment and Development Action in the Third World, Senegal, 270
Enda Tiers Monde—Environnement et Développement du Tiers-Monde, Senegal, 270
Enfance et Partage, France, 102
Enfants du Mékong, France, 102
EngenderHealth, USA, 424
Enough Project, USA, 416
Entraide Protestante Suisse, Switzerland, 311
Entraide Universitaire Mondiale du Canada, Canada, 63
Environment and Natural Resources Foundation, Argentina, 7
Environmental Justice Foundation—EJF, UK, 353
Equal Justice Initiative—EJI, USA, 424
Equality Fund/Fonds Égalité, Canada, 54
ERA—Europäische Rechtsakademie, Germany, 127
ERSTE Foundation, Austria, 21
ERSTE Stiftung—Die ERSTE Österreichische Spar-Casse Privatstiftung, Austria, 21
Esmée Fairbairn Foundation, UK, 353
Esquel Group Foundation—Ecuador, Ecuador, 88
ETC Group—Action Group on Erosion, Technology and Concentration, Canada, 54
Ettersberg Foundation, Germany, 140
Eurasia Foundation—EF, USA, 424
Eurasia Partnership Foundation-Armenia—EPF-Armenia, Armenia, 9

INDEX OF MAIN ACTIVITIES

Europäische Rechtsakademie—ERA, Germany, 127
Europe Foundation—EPF, Georgia, 118
European Center for Constitutional and Human Rights—ECCHR, Germany, 128
European Center for Peace and Development—ECPD, Serbia, 271
European Centre for Social Welfare Policy and Research, Austria, 21
European Cultural Centre, Switzerland, 307
European Cultural Foundation—ECF, Netherlands, 225
European Environmental Bureau—EEB, Belgium, 30
European Federation of National Organisations Working with the Homeless, Belgium, 26
European Foundation for the Improvement of Living and Working Conditions—Eurofound, Ireland, 166
European NGO Confederation for Relief and Development—CONCORD, Belgium, 26
European Roma Rights Centre—ERRC, Belgium, 30
European Youth For Action—EYFA, Germany, 128
European Youth Foundation—EYF, France, 112
Europese Culterele Stichting, Netherlands, 225
Evens Foundation, Belgium, 31
Evropis Pondis, Georgia, 118
Ewing Marion Kauffman Foundation, USA, 425
ExxonMobil Foundation, USA, 425
EYFA—European Youth For Action, Germany, 128
F. C. Flick Foundation against Xenophobia, Racism and Intolerance, Germany, 128
F. C. Flick-Stiftung gegen Fremdenfeindlichkeit, Rassismus und Intoleranz, Germany, 128
F20, Germany, 119
Fairbairn (Esmée) Foundation, UK, 353
Fairtrade Nederland, Netherlands, 230
Family Restoration Fund, UK, 347
FARN—Fundación Ambiente y Recursos Naturales, Argentina, 7
Fatoumatta Bah-Barrow Foundation—FaBB, Gambia, 117
FDC—Fundação para o Desenvolvimento da Comunidade, Mozambique, 221
FEANTSA—Fédération Européenne des Associations Nationales Travaillant avec les Sans-Abri, Belgium, 26
Federacja Funduszy Lokalnych w Polsce, Poland, 254
Federation of Community Foundations in Poland, Poland, 254
Fédération Européenne des Associations Nationales Travaillant avec les Sans-Abri—FEANTSA, Belgium, 26
Fédération Internationale des Ligues des Droits de L'Homme—FIDH, France, 99
Federation of Non-Governmental Organizations for Development in Romania, Romania, 263
Feed the Children, USA, 425
Feed the Minds, UK, 354
Félix Houphouët-Boigny Foundation for Peace Research, Côte d'Ivoire, 75
Feltrinelli (Giangiacomo), Fondazione, Italy, Italy, 177
Fernand Lazard Foundation, Belgium, 31
FHI 360, USA, 425
filia.die Frauenstiftung, Germany, 128
filia—the Women's Foundation, Germany, 128
FIN—Branchevereniging van Fondsen en Foundations, Netherlands, 223
FINCA International, USA, 425
Finnish Development Organizations, Finland, 95
Finnish Institute in the UK and Ireland Trust, UK, 354
FIPP—Fondation Internationale Pénale et Pénitentiaire, Netherlands, 223
First Nations Development Institute, USA, 426
FirstRand Foundation, South Africa, 280
Flick (F. C.) Stiftung gegen Fremdenfeindlichkeit, Rassismus und Intoleranz, Germany, 128
FOKAL—Open Society Foundation Haiti, Haiti, 149
Follereau Foundation Luxembourg, Luxembourg, 209
FOND—Federatia Organizatiilor Neguvernamentale pentru Dezvoltare din Romania, Romania, 263
Fondacija Balkanska Mreza za Razvoj na Gragjanskoto Opshtestvo, North Macedonia, 239
Fondacija Braća Karić, Serbia, 271
Fondacija Cennosti, Bulgaria, 43
Fondacioni Kosovar per Shoqeri Civile, Kosovo, 202

INDEX OF MAIN ACTIVITIES

Fondacioni i Kosovës për Shoqëri të Hapur, Kosovo, 203
Fondacioni Shqiptar për të Drejtat e Personave me Aftësi të Kufizuar—FSHDPAK, Albania, 4
Fondation Abbé Pierre, France, 108
Fondation Air France, France, 103
Fondation Auschwitz—Mémoire d'Auschwitz, Belgium, 30
Fondation Bernheim, Belgium, 31
Fondation Charles Léopold Mayer pour le Progrès de l'Homme—FPH, Switzerland, 308
Fondation Charles Veillon, Switzerland, 308
Fondation Claudine Talon, Benin, 35
Fondation CMDID—Centre Malien pour le Dialogue Interpartis et la Démocratie, Mali, 213
Fondation Digicel Haïti, Haiti, 149
Fondation d'Entreprise Renault, France, 106
Fondation Européenne de la Culture/Europese Culturele Stichting, Netherlands, 225
Fondation Evens Stichting, Belgium, 31
Fondation Félix Houphouët-Boigny pour la Recherche de la Paix, Côte d'Ivoire, 75
Fondation Fernand Lazard Stichting, Belgium, 31
Fondation Follereau Luxembourg—FFL, Luxembourg, 209
Fondation de France, France, 99
Fondation Franco-Japonaise Sasakawa, France, 106
Fondation Grand Cœur—FGC, Chad, 64
Fondation Guri Vie Meilleure, Niger, 236
Fondation Hassan II pour les Marocains Résidant à l'Étranger, Morocco, 220
Fondation Hirondelle: Media for Peace and Human Dignity, Switzerland, 309
Fondation Internationale Pénale et Pénitentiaire—FIPP, Netherlands, 226
Fondation Internationale Tierno et Mariam—FITIMA, Burkina Faso, 44
Fondation Jacques Chirac, France, 107
Fondation Jasmin pour la Recherche et la Communication, Tunisia, 326
Fondation Jean Jaurès, France, 107
Fondation Jean-Paul II pour le Sahel, Burkina Faso, 44
Fondation Léopold Sédar Senghor, Senegal, 270
Fondation pour le Logement des Défavorisés, France, 108
Fondation MAIF pour la Recherche, France, 108
Fondation Maison des Sciences de l'Homme—FMSH, France, 108
Fondation Marcel Bleustein-Blanchet de la Vocation, France, 109
Fondation pour les Médias en Afrique de l'Ouest, Ghana, 144
Fondation MTN Bénin, Benin, 35
Fondation Nicolas Hulot pour la Nature et l'Homme—FNH, France, 110
Fondation Noura, Mauritania, 214
Fondation Orient-Occident—FOO, Morocco, 220
Fondation P&V, Belgium, 32
Fondation Pierre Elliott Trudeau/Pierre Elliott Trudeau Foundation, Canada, 55
Fondation Rambourg, Tunisia, 326
Fondation pour la Recherche Médicale, France, 110
Fondation pour la Recherche Stratégique, France, 111
Fondation Robert Schuman, France, 111
Fondation Roi Baudouin, Belgium, 31
Fondation Rurale pour l'Afrique de l'Ouest—FRAO, Senegal, 270
Fondation Sommet Mondial des Femmes, Switzerland, 320
Fondation Stamm, Burundi, 45
Fondation TotalEnergies, France, 112
Fondatzija Otvoryeno Opshtyestvo Makyedonija, North Macedonia, 239
Fondazione AVSI, Italy, 175
Fondazione Cariplo, Italy, 175
Fondazione Cassa di Risparmio di Torino, Italy, 176
Fondazione Centesimus Annus—Pro Pontifice, Vatican City, 486
Fondazione Centro Studi Investimenti Sociali—CENSIS, Italy, 172
Fondazione CIMA—Centro Internazionale in Monitoraggio Ambientale, Italy, 176
Fondazione Giangiacomo Feltrinelli, Italy, 177
Fondazione Internazionale Premio Balzan, Italy, 181
Fondazione ISMU—Iniziative e Studi sulla Multietnicità, Italy, 178
Fondazione Lelio e Lisli Basso Issoco—Sezione Internazionale, Italy, 178
Fondazione Populorum Progressio, Vatican City, 486
Fondazione Social Venture-Giordano Dell'Amore, Italy, 180
Fondazione Vodafone Italia, Italy, 181
Fondo para el Desarrollo de los Pueblos Indígenas de América Latina y El Caribe—FILAC, Bolivia, 36
Fonds atvērtai sabiedrībai DOTS, Latvia, 204
Fonds Égalité, Canada, 54
Fonds Européen pour la Jeunesse—FEJ, France, 112
Fonds National Suisse de la Recherche Scientifique, Switzerland, 316
Ford Foundation, USA, 427
The Forest Trust, Switzerland, 307
Forum Darczyńców, Poland, 254
Fórum donorov, Slovakia, 274
Forum International de l'Innovation Sociale—FIIS, France, 112
Forum LSM Internasional untuk Pembangunan Indonesia, Indonesia, 161
FORWARD—Foundation for Women's Health Research and Development, UK, 354
Fös Feminista, USA, 427
Foundation for AIDS Research—amfAR, USA, 403
Foundation for Analysis and Social Studies, Spain, 288
Foundation for Caribbean Research and Management of Biodiversity, Curaçao, 77
Foundation Centre for the Study of Social Investment, Italy, 172
Foundation for Civil Society—FCS, Tanzania, 322
Foundation for Culture and Civil Society—FCCS, Afghanistan, 3
Foundation for the Defence of Nature, Venezuela, 487
Foundation for Defense of Democracies—FDD, USA, 427
Foundation for Democracy and Media, Netherlands, 229
Foundation for Housing the Disadvantaged, France, 108
Foundation for International Community Assistance, USA, 425
Foundation for Latin American Economic Research, Argentina, 7
Foundation for Medical Research, France, 110
Foundation for Middle East Peace—FMEP, USA, 428
Foundation for an Open Society DOTS, Latvia, 204
Foundation Open Society Institute Pakistan, Pakistan, 245
Foundation Open Society Macedonia—FOSIM, North Macedonia, 239
Foundation 'Remembrance, Responsibility and Future', Germany, 139
Foundation for the Rights of Future Generations, Germany, 141
Foundation for Rural & Regional Renewal—FRRR, Australia, 14
Foundation for Security and Development in Africa—FOSDA, Ghana, 143
Foundation for Social Housing, Venezuela, 488
Foundation for Strategic Research, France, 111
Foundation in Support of Local Democracy, Poland, 256
Foundation for the Support of Women's Work, Türkiye, 326
Foundation for the Victims of Terrorism, Spain, 296
Foundation for the Welfare of Holocaust Victims, Israel, 169
Foundation for Women, Spain, 293
Foundation for Women's Health, Research and Development—FORWARD, UK, 354
The Foundation for Young Australians—FYA, Australia, 14
Foundations Platform—F20, Germany, 119
France Amérique Latine—FAL, France, 112
France-Libertés Fondation Danielle Mitterrand, France, 112
France Nature Environnement, France, 112
Franciscans International, Switzerland, 310
Franco-Japanese Sasakawa Foundation, France, 106
Frank (Anne)-Fonds, Switzerland, 306
Frank (Anne) Stichting, Netherlands, 224
Frank Knox Memorial Fellowships, USA, 428
Fraser Institute, Canada, 55
FREE Network—Forum for Research on Eastern Europe and Emerging Economies, Sweden, 299
Free Russia Foundation, USA, 428
Freedom from Torture (Medical Foundation for the Care of Victims of Torture), UK, 354
Freedom House, Inc, USA, 428
Freedom Speech Foundation, Norway, 241

Law, civil society and human rights

Freedom Together Foundation, USA, 428
French-American Foundation, USA, 429
French Institute of International Relations, France, 113
Frères des Hommes—FDH, France, 113
Freudenberg Foundation, Germany, 129
Freudenberg Stiftung, Germany, 129
Fridtjof Nansen Institute, Norway, 241
Fridtjof Nansens Institutt—FNI, Norway, 241
Friede Springer Foundation, Germany, 129
Friede Springer Stiftung, Germany, 129
Friedensdorf International, Germany, 129
Friedrich-Ebert-Stiftung eV, Germany, 129
Friedrich Naumann Foundation for Freedom, Germany, 130
Friedrich-Naumann-Stiftung für die Freiheit, Germany, 130
Friends of the Earth International—FOEI, Netherlands, 225
Friends-International, Cambodia, 46
Front Line Defenders—FLD, Ireland, 166
FUHEM—Fundación Benéfico-Social Hogar del Empleado, Spain, 286
Fulbright Norway—US-Norway Fulbright Foundation for Educational Exchange, Norway, 241
Fund for the Development of Indigenous Peoples of Latin America and the Caribbean, Bolivia, 36
Fund and Endowment Management Foundation, Norway, 240
Fund for Global Human Rights, USA, 395
Fundação Abrinq pelos Direitos da Criança e do Adolescente, Brazil, 39
Fundação Assistência Médica Internacional—AMI, Portugal, 258
Fundação Calouste Gulbenkian, Portugal, 259
Fundação Cidade de Lisboa, Portugal, 259
Fundação EDP, Portugal, 260
Fundação Getulio Vargas—FGV, Brazil, 40
Fundação José Maria Neves para a Governança, Cabo Verde, 46
Fundação Luso-Americana para o Desenvolvimento—FLAD, Portugal, 260
Fundação Mário Soares e Maria Barroso, Portugal, 260
Fundação Vodafone Portugal, Portugal, 261
Fundació CIDOB, Spain, 287
Fundació Futbol Club Barcelona, Spain, 287
Fundación Acceso, Costa Rica, 73
Fundación Ambiente y Recursos Naturales—FARN, Argentina, 7
Fundación para el Análisis y los Estudios Sociales—FAES, Spain, 288
Fundación Arias para la Paz y el Progreso Humano, Costa Rica, 74
Fundación Astur, Uruguay, 485
Fundación AVINA, Panama, 247
Fundación BANHCAFE—FUNBANHCAFE, Honduras, 150
Fundación Carlos de Amberes, Spain, 289
Fundación Carlos Slim, Mexico, 215
Fundación Circulo de Montevideo, Uruguay, 485
Fundación Comunitaria de Puerto Rico—FCPR, Puerto Rico, 261
Fundación Corona, Colombia, 71
Fundación para la Defensa de la Naturaleza—FUDENA, Venezuela, 487
Fundación Democracia y Desarrollo, Chile, 65
Fundación Dr Guillermo Manuel Ungo—FUNDAUNGO, El Salvador, 91
Fundación Espacio Cívico, Panama, 247
Fundación Felipe González, Spain, 290
Fundación Futuro Latinoamericano, Ecuador, 88
Fundación Global Democracia y Desarrollo—FUNGLODE, Dominican Republic, 87
Fundación Grupo Esquel—Ecuador, Ecuador, 88
Fundación de Investigaciones Económicas Latinoamericanas—FIEL, Argentina, 7
Fundación Jubileo, Bolivia, 36
Fundación MAPFRE, Spain, 292
Fundación Montemadrid, Spain, 292
Fundación Mujeres, Spain, 293
Fundación Mujeres en Igualdad—MEI, Argentina, 8
Fundación Nacional para el Desarrollo, El Salvador, 91
Fundación Nacional para el Desarrollo de Honduras—FUNADEH, Honduras, 150
Fundación Nobis, Ecuador, 88
Fundación Orange, Spain, 293
Fundación Oxfam Intermón, Spain, 293
Fundación para la Paz y la Democracia—FUNPADEM, Costa Rica, 74
Fundación Princesa de Asturias, Spain, 294
Fundación Rigoberta Menchú Tum, Guatemala, 148
Fundación Semah-Valencia, Panama, 247

Fundación SES—Sustentabilidad, Educación, Solidaridad, Argentina, 8
Fundación Solidaridad, Dominican Republic, 87
Fundación Tecnologías Sociales—TECSOS, Spain, 296
Fundación Teletón México, Mexico, 216
Fundación Telmex Telcel, Mexico, 216
Fundación Tigo, Guatemala, 148
Fundación UNIR Bolivia, Bolivia, 36
Fundación Víctimas del Terrorismo, Spain, 296
Fundación de la Vivienda Popular, Venezuela, 488
Fundación Vodafone España, Spain, 296
Fundacja Agory, Poland, 255
Fundacja Auschwitz-Birkenau, Poland, 255
Fundacja im. Stefana Batorego, Poland, 256
Fundacja Pogranicze, Poland, 256
Fundacja Pomocy Wzajemnej Barka, Poland, 256
Fundacja Rozwoju Demokracji Loaklnej, Poland, 256
FundAction, USA, 394
Fundasaun Alola, Timor-Leste, 325
Fundasaun Mahein, Timor-Leste, 325
Fundaţia Civitas pentru Societatea Civilă, Romania, 263
Fundaţia Soros—Moldova, Moldova, 217
Fundaţia Universitară a Mării Negre—FUMN, Romania, 263
Fundaţia Vodafone România, Romania, 264
FUNDAUNGO—Fundación Dr Guillermo Manuel Ungo, El Salvador, 91
Future Foundation, Liechtenstein, 208
Future in Our Hands Youth NGO—FIOH, Armenia, 9
FWF—Österreichischer Wissenschaftsfonds, Austria, 21
FXB International—Association François-Xavier Bagnoud, Switzerland, 310
The Gaia Foundation, UK, 355
Gapminder, Sweden, 300
Gates (Bill & Melinda) Foundation, USA, 429
Gates Foundation, USA, 429
Gemeinnützige Hertie-Stiftung, Germany, 130
General Service Foundation—GSF, USA, 430
Georgian Foundation for Strategic and International Studies (Rondeli Foundation)—GFSIS, Georgia, 118
German Academic Scholarship Foundation, Germany, 142
German Catholic Bishops' Organization for Development Co-operation, Germany, 137
German Council on Foreign Relations, Germany, 124
German Foundation for International Legal Co-operation, Germany, 133
German Foundation for World Population, Germany, 126
German Institute of Development and Sustainability—IDOS, Germany, 130
German Institute for Global and Area Studies—GIGA, Germany, 130
German Marshall Fund of the United States—GMF, USA, 430
German-Russian Exchange, Germany, 124
Getty (J. Paul) Trust, USA, 442
Getulio Vargas Foundation, Brazil, 40
Giangiacomo Feltrinelli Foundation, Italy, 177
Gift of the Givers Foundation, South Africa, 280
Giordano Dell'Amore Social Venture Foundation, Italy, 180
To Give, Israel, 170
Give2Asia, USA, 394
GiveWell—The Clear Fund, USA, 430
Glasnost Defence Foundation, Russian Federation, 265
Global Communities, USA, 431
Global Democracy and Development Foundation, Dominican Republic, 87
Global Dialogue, UK, 336
Global Ethic Foundation, Germany, 141
Global Fund for Women—GFW, USA, 431
Global Greengrants Fund, USA, 431
Global Impact, USA, 395
GOAL, Ireland, 166
Goldman Sachs Foundation, USA, 432
Good Neighbors International, Korea (Republic), 201
Good360, USA, 432
Goodenough College, UK, 356
Google.org—Google Foundation, USA, 432
Gordon (Walter and Duncan) Charitable Foundation, Canada, 62
Graça Machel Trust, South Africa, 280
Gradjanske inicijative—GI, Serbia, 271
Graduate Institute of International Studies and Development Studies, Switzerland, 311
Grant (William T.) Foundation, USA, 481
Grassroots International—GRI, USA, 433

Greater Kansas City Community Foundation, USA, 433
Grinspoon (Harold) Foundation, USA, 434
Group of Foundations and Businesses, Argentina, 6
Grupo de Fundaciones y Empresas, Argentina, 6
Grupo Social Fondo Ecuatoriano Populorum Progressio, Ecuador, 89
Guardian Foundation, Timor-Leste, 325
Guggenheim (Harry Frank) Foundation, USA, 434
GuideStar India, India, 155
Gulbenkian (Calouste), Fundação, Portugal, 259
GURT Resource Centre for NGO Development, Ukraine, 332
H&M Foundation, Sweden, 300
Hagar NZ, New Zealand, 233
Hamlyn (Paul) Foundation, UK, 373
Hammarskjölds (Dag) Minnesfond, Stiftelsen, Sweden, 303
Hanaholmen—Swedish-Finnish Cultural Centre, Finland, 95
HAND—Hungarian Association of NGOs for Development and Humanitarian Aid, Hungary, 152
Haniel Foundation, Germany, 131
Haniel-Stiftung, Germany, 131
Harold Grinspoon Foundation, USA, 434
The Harry Frank Guggenheim Foundation—HFG, USA, 434
Harry and Jeanette Weinberg Foundation, Inc, USA, 434
Hassan II Foundation for Moroccans Living Abroad, Morocco, 220
Havelaar (Max) Foundation, Netherlands, 230
Hawaii Resilience Fund, USA, 458
Health Action International—HAI, Netherlands, 225
Heinrich Böll Foundation, Germany, 131
Heinrich-Böll-Stiftung, Germany, 131
HEKS—Hilfswerk der Evangelischen Kirchen Schweiz, Switzerland, 311
Helen Keller International—HKI, USA, 435
Hellenic Foundation for European and Foreign Policy—ELIAMEP, Greece, 146
Helmich (Janson Johan og Marcia) Legat, Norway, 242
HelpAge International, UK, 357
Helsińska Fundacja Praw Człowieka, Poland, 257
Helsingin Sanomain Säätiö, Finland, 96
Helsingin Sanomat Foundation, Finland, 96
Helsinki Foundation for Human Rights, Poland, 257
Helvetas Swiss Intercooperation, Switzerland, 311
Henry Luce Foundation, Inc, USA, 435
The Henry Smith Charity, UK, 358
HER Fund, Hong Kong, 151
The Heritage Foundation, USA, 436
Heritage Institute for Policy Studies—HIPS, Somalia, 277
Hertie Foundation, Germany, 130
HESTIA, Czech Republic, 78
Hewlett (William and Flora) Foundation, USA, 481
HIAS—Hebrew Immigrant Aid Society, USA, 436
Higherlife Foundation, Zimbabwe, 491
Himalaya Research and Development Foundation—Himalaya Foundation, Taiwan, 321
HIPS—Heritage Institute for Policy Studies, Somalia, 277
Hirschfeld-Eddy Foundation, Germany, 132
Hirschfeld-Eddy-Stiftung, Germany, 132
Historic Environment Scotland, UK, 358
History Foundation of Turkey, Türkiye, 329
Hivos—Humanistisch Instituut voor Ontwikkelings Samenwerking, Netherlands, 226
Holt International, USA, 436
Hong Kong Council of Social Service—HKCSS, Hong Kong, 150
Hope, Ireland, 165
Hope Foundation, Türkiye, 331
Hope not Hate Charitable Trust—HNHCT, UK, 358
Horizons of Friendship, Canada, 56
Horn Economic and Social Policy Institute—HESPI, Ethiopia, 94
Houphouët-Boigny (Félix), Fondation, Côte d'Ivoire, 75
House of the Human Sciences Foundation, France, 108
Howard (Katharine) Foundation, Ireland, 167
Hudson Institute, USA, 437
Hulot (Nicolas), Fondation, France, 110
Human Dignity Trust, UK, 359

Human Resource Development Foundation, Türkiye, 329
Human Rights Foundation of Turkey, Türkiye, 330
Human Rights Funders Network—HRFN, USA, 395
Human Rights House Foundation—HRHF, Norway, 241
Human Rights Information and Training Center—HRITC, Yemen, 489
Human Rights Watch—HRW, USA, 437
Humanistic Institute for Co-operation with Developing Countries, Netherlands, 226
Humanitarian Academy for Development—HAD, UK, 359
Humanitarian Coalition, Canada, 48
Humanity & Inclusion, France, 113
Humanity United, USA, 395
IACD—Institute of Asian Culture and Development, Korea (Republic), 201
IAI—Istituto Affari Internazionali, Italy, 182
IBM International Foundation, USA, 438
IBON Foundation, Philippines, 252
Ibrahim (Mo) Foundation, UK, 368
Icelandic Human Rights Centre, Iceland, 154
Ichikowitz Family Foundation—IFF, South Africa, 280
ICRC—International Red Cross and Red Crescent Movement, Switzerland, 312
ICVA—International Council of Voluntary Agencies, Switzerland, 305
The Ideas Institute, Kenya, 199
IDLO—International Development Law Organization, Italy, 181
IFAW—International Fund for Animal Welfare, USA, 438
IFES—International Foundation for Electoral Systems, USA, 440
IHH Humanitarian Relief Foundation, Türkiye, 328
IIED—International Institute for Environment and Development, UK, 360
IISD—International Institute for Sustainable Development, Canada, 57
IJ4EU—Investigative Journalism for Europe, Austria, 21
IKEA Foundation, Netherlands, 229
IKGV—İnsan Kaynağını Geliştirme Vakfı, Türkiye, 329
Îles de Paix, Belgium, 32
IMADR—The International Movement against All Forms of Discrimination and Racism, Japan, 188
Imbuto Foundation, Rwanda, 268
IMPACT Transformer la Gestion des Ressources Naturelles, Canada, 56
IMPACT Transforming Natural Resource Management, Canada, 56
Inamori Foundation, Japan, 188
Inclusion International, UK, 359
Independent Sector, USA, 395
India Partners, USA, 438
Indian Council of Social Science Research—ICSSR, India, 157
Indonesian Forum for the Environment—Friends of the Earth Indonesia, Indonesia, 162
Information and Education Centre for the Prevention of Drug Abuse, Peru, 248
INHURED International—International Institute for Human Rights, Environment and Development, Nepal, 223
İnsan Hak ve Hürriyetleri İnsani Yardım Vakfı—IHH, Türkiye, 328
İnsan Kaynağını Geliştirme Vakfı—IKGV, Türkiye, 329
Institusjonen Fritt Ord, Norway, 241
Institut Arctique de l'Amérique du Nord—IAAN, Canada, 49
Institut Français des Relations Internationales—IFRI, France, 113
Institut de Hautes Études Internationales et du Développement—IHEID, Switzerland, 311
Institut International des Droits de l'Enfant, Switzerland, 312
Institut for Menneskerettigheder, Denmark, 84
Institut de Recherche Empirique en Économie Politique—IREEP, Benin, 35
Institut Royal des Relations Internationales—EGMONT, Belgium, 29
Institut für Weltwirtschaft—IfW Kiel, Germany, 132
Institute of Asian Culture and Development—IACD, Korea (Republic), 201
Institute of Baltic Studies, Estonia, 92
Institute for Citizens & Scholars, USA, 439
Institute of Developing Economies-Japan External Trade Organization—IDE-JETRO, Japan, 188
Institute of Economic Affairs—IEA, UK, 359

INDEX OF MAIN ACTIVITIES

Law, civil society and human rights

Institute for Empirical Research in Political Economy—IERPE, Benin, 35
Institute of International Affairs, Italy, 182
Institute of International Law, Argentina, 6
Institute for International Security and Strategic Affairs—ISIAE, Argentina, 6
Institute for Iran-Eurasia Studies—IRAS, Iran, 163
Institute for Latin American and Caribbean Integration, Argentina, 8
Institute for Palestine Studies—IPS, Lebanon, 206
Institute for Policy and Legal Studies—IPLS, Albania, 4
Institute for Security Studies—ISS, South Africa, 280
Institute of Social Studies—ISS, Netherlands, 226
Institute for Sustainable Communities—ISC, USA, 439
Instituti Kosovar për Kërkime dhe Zhvillim të Politikave, Kosovo, 203
Instituto para la Integración de América Latina y el Caribe—BID-INTAL, Argentina, 8
Instituto Interamericano de Derechos Humanos—IIDH, Costa Rica, 74
Instituto de Montaña, Peru, 249
Inter-American Foundation—IAF, USA, 439
Inter-American Institute of Human Rights, Costa Rica, 74
Inter Pares, Canada, 57
InterAction, USA, 395
Interchurch Aid—HIA Hungary, Hungary, 153
Internationaal Instituut voor Sociale Geschiedenis—IISG, Netherlands, 226
International Alert—Alert, UK, 360
International Association of Charities, Belgium, 28
International Balzan Prize Foundation, Italy, 181
International Blue Crescent Relief and Development Foundation—IBC, Türkiye, 329
International Center for Not-for-Profit Law—ICNL, USA, 396
International Center for Research on Women—ICRW, USA, 439
International Center for Transitional Justice—ICTJ, USA, 440
International Civil Society Centre, Germany, 119
International Confederation Catholic Organizations Charitable Social Action, Vatican City, 486
International Co-operation, Italy, 173
International Council of Voluntary Agencies—ICVA, Switzerland, 305
International Development Center of Japan, Japan, 189
International Development Law Organization—IDLO, Italy, 181
International Federation of Human Rights, France, 99
International Forum Bosnia, Bosnia and Herzegovina, 37
International Forum for Social Innovation—IFSI, France, 112
International Foundation for Electoral Systems—IFES, USA, 440
International Foundation for the Protection of Human Rights Defenders, Ireland, 166
International Fund for Animal Welfare—IFAW, USA, 438
International Historical, Educational, Charitable and Human Rights Society—International Memorial, Russian Federation, 266
International Institute for Environment and Development—IIED, UK, 360
International Institute for Human Rights, Environment and Development, Nepal, 223
International Institute for the Rights of the Child, Switzerland, 312
International Institute of Social History—IISH, Netherlands, 226
International Institute of Social Studies, Netherlands, 226
The International Institute for Strategic Studies—IISS, UK, 360
International Institute for Sustainable Development—IISD, Canada, 57
International Medical Assistance Foundation, Portugal, 258
International Memorial, Russian Federation, 266
International NGO Charter of Accountability, USA, 393
International NGO Coordination Committee in CAR, Central African Republic, 63
International NGO Forum on Indonesian Development—INFID, Indonesia, 161
International Penal and Penitentiary Foundation—IPPF, Netherlands, 226
International Planned Parenthood Federation—IPPF, UK, 360
International Press Institute—IPI, Austria, 21
International Red Cross and Red Crescent Movement—ICRC, Switzerland, 312
International Renaissance Foundation—IRF, Ukraine, 333
International Rescue Committee—IRC, USA, 441
International Research & Exchanges Board—IREX, USA, 442
International Rivers, USA, 441
International Service for Human Rights—ISHR, Switzerland, 312
International Society for Human Rights—ISHR, Germany, 133
International Solidarity Foundation, Finland, 96
International Water Management Institute—IWMI, Sri Lanka, 297
International Women's Health Coalition, USA, 427
International Work Group for Indigenous Affairs—IWGIA, Denmark, 84
International Youth Foundation—IYF, USA, 442
Internationale Stiftung Preis E. Balzan-Fonds, Italy, 181
Internationalt Uddannelsescenter, Denmark, 84
INTERSOS, Italy, 182
INTRAC, UK, 337
iPartner India, India, 155
IPPF—International Planned Parenthood Federation, UK, 360
IRC—International Rescue Committee, USA, 441
The Ireland Funds America, USA, 442
IREX—International Research & Exchanges Board, USA, 442
Irvine (James) Foundation, USA, 443
IRZ (Deutsche Stiftung für Internationale Rechtliche Zusammenarbeit) eV, Germany, 133
Isabel Allende Foundation, USA, 442
Islamic Relief Worldwide, UK, 360
Islands of Peace, Belgium, 32
ISMU Foundation—Initiatives and Studies on Multi-ethnicity, Italy, 178
ISPI—Istituto per gli Studi di Politica Internazionale, Italy, 183
IsraAID, Israel, 169
The Israel Democracy Institute—IDI, Israel, 170
Istituto Affari Internazionali—IAI, Italy, 182
Istituto Carlo Cattaneo, Italy, 182
Istituto per gli Studi di Politica Internazionale—ISPI, Italy, 183
Italian Institute for International Political Studies, Italy, 183
IUC International Education Center—IUC-Europe, Denmark, 84
Ivorian Economic and Social Research Centre, Côte d'Ivoire, 75
J. F. Kapnek Zimbabwe, Zimbabwe, 491
J. Paul Getty Trust, USA, 442
J. R. McKenzie Trust, New Zealand, 233
The J. W. McConnell Family Foundation, Canada, 57
Jacques Chirac Foundation, France, 107
Jahres (Anders) Humanitære Stiftelse, Norway, 240
J'ai Rêvé Foundation, Central African Republic, 63
The James Irvine Foundation, USA, 443
James Michel Foundation, Seychelles, 272
JANIC—Japanese NGO Center for International Co-operation, Japan, 185
Janson Johan Helmich and Marcia Jansons Endowment, Norway, 242
Janson Johan Helmich og Marcia Jansons Legat, Norway, 242
Japan Association of Charitable Organizations—JACO, Japan, 185
Japanese-German Centre Berlin, Germany, 133
Japanisch-Deutsches Zentrum Berlin, Germany, 133
Jasmine Foundation for Research and Communication, Tunisia, 326
Jaurès (Jean), Fondation, France, 107
Jean Jaurès Foundation, France, 107
Jenny and Antti Wihuri Foundation, Finland, 96
Jenny ja Antti Wihurin Rahasto, Finland, 96
JN Foundation, Jamaica, 184
The John D. and Catherine T. MacArthur Foundation, USA, 444
John Ellerman Foundation, UK, 361
John Moores Foundation, UK, 362
John Paul II Foundation for the Sahel, Burkina Faso, 44
John S. and James L. Knight Foundation, USA, 444
The Johnson Foundation at Wingspread, USA, 444
Johnson (Lyndon Baines) Foundation, USA, 449
JOHUD—Jordanian Hashemite Fund for Human Development, Jordan, 196
Jordan River Foundation, Jordan, 196
José Maria Neves Foundation for Governance, Cabo Verde, 46
Joseph Levy Foundation, UK, 362
Joseph Rowntree Charitable Trust—JRCT, UK, 362
Joseph Rowntree Reform Trust Ltd (including the JRSST Charitable Trust), UK, 362
Joyce Banda Foundation International, Malawi, 210
Joyce Foundation, USA, 445
JPB Foundation, USA, 428
JRSST Charitable Trust, UK, 362
Jubilee Foundation, Bolivia, 36
Jubilee USA Network, USA, 445
Kadın Emeğini Değerlendirme Vakfı—KEDV, Türkiye, 329
KAF—Kataliko Actions for Africa, Congo (Democratic Republic), 72
Kafaa Development Foundation, Libya, 207
Kansainvälinen solidaarisuussäätiö, Finland, 96
Kapnek (J. F.) Charitable Trust Zimbabwe, Zimbabwe, 491
Kárpátok Alapítvány, Hungary, 153
Karuna Trust, UK, 363
Katharine Howard Foundation—KHF, Ireland, 167
KCDF—Kenya Community Development Foundation, Kenya, 199
KDDI Foundation, Japan, 191
Keller (Helen) International, USA, 435
Kellogg (W. K.) Foundation, USA, 478
Kiel Institute for the World Economy, Germany, 132
Kind Heart Foundation, Viet Nam, 488
King Baudouin Foundation, Belgium, 33
King Gustaf V's 90th Birthday Foundation, Sweden, 301
King Hussein Foundation—KHF, Jordan, 196
King Philanthropies, USA, 445
The King's Trust, UK, 363
KIOS Foundation, Finland, 96
Knight (John S. and James L.) Foundation, USA, 444
Knox (Frank) Memorial Fellowships, USA, 428
Koç (Vehbi), Vakfı, Türkiye, 331
Koch (Charles) Foundation, USA, 413
Koch Foundation, Inc, USA, 446
Kofi Annan Foundation, Switzerland, 313
Kokkalis Foundation, Greece, 146
Koning Boudewijnstichting/Fondation Roi Baudouin, Belgium, 33
Konrad Adenauer Foundation, Germany, 134
Konrad-Adenauer-Stiftung eV—KAS, Germany, 134
Konsultatsiis da Treningis Tsentri, Georgia, 117
Konung Gustaf V's 90-Årsfond, Sweden, 301
Konzorcijum nezavisnih istraživačkih centara Zapadnog Balkana, Serbia, 271
Körber Foundation, Germany, 134
Körber-Stiftung, Germany, 134
Koret Foundation, USA, 446
Kosovar Civil Society Foundation—KCSF, Kosovo, 202
Kosovar Institute for Policy Research and Development—KIPRED, Kosovo, 203
Kosovo Foundation for Open Society—KFOS, Kosovo, 203
Kresge Foundation, USA, 446
Kuwait Awqaf Public Foundation, Kuwait, 203
Kvinna till Kvinna, Sweden, 301
Lady Davis Fellowship Trust, Israel, 170
Lafede.cat—Federació d'Organitzacions per a la Justícia Global, Spain, 286
Lafede.cat—Federation of Organizations for Global Justice, Spain, 286
Laidlaw Foundation, Canada, 58
Land Network, Timor-Leste, 325
Landesa—Rural Development Institute, USA, 447
LAPAS—Latvijas platforma attīstības sadarbībai, Latvia, 204
Latet Israeli Humanitarian Aid, Israel, 170
Latin America France, France, 112
Latin American and Caribbean Committee for the Defence of Women's Rights, Peru, 249
Latin American and Caribbean Women's Health Network—LACWHN, Ecuador, 89
Latin American Council of Social Sciences, Argentina, 6
Latin American Future Foundation, Ecuador, 88
Latin American Network for Economic and Social Justice, Peru, 248

INDEX OF MAIN ACTIVITIES

Latindadd—Red Latinoamericana por Justicia Económica y Social, Peru, 248
Latter-day Saint Charities—LDSC, USA, 447
Latvia Children's Fund, Latvia, 204
Latvian Platform for Development Cooperation, Latvia, 204
Latvijas Bērnu fonds, Latvia, 204
Laudes Foundation, Switzerland, 313
Laureus Sport for Good, UK, 364
Lazard (Fernand), Fondation, Belgium, 31
LBJ Foundation, USA, 449
League of Corporate Foundations—LCF, Philippines, 250
Legatum Foundation, United Arab Emirates, 334
Leibniz Association, Germany, 135
Leibniz Gemeinschaft, Germany, 135
Leibniz-Institut für Globale und Regionale Studien, Germany, 130
Lelio and Lisli Basso Foundation Onlus, Italy, 178
Leonard Cheshire Disability, UK, 364
Léopold Sédar Senghor Foundation, Senegal, 270
The Leprosy Mission International, UK, 364
Lesotho Council of Non-Governmental Organisations, Lesotho, 207
Leverhulme Trust, UK, 365
Levi Strauss Foundation, USA, 448
Levy (Joseph) Foundation, UK, 362
Liberty Fund, Inc, USA, 448
Lietuvos vaikų fondas, Lithuania, 209
Lifeline Consortium, USA, 428
Likhachev (Dmitry) Foundation, Russian Federation, 265
Liliane Foundation, Netherlands, 229
Lilly Endowment, Inc, USA, 448
Lindh (Anna) Euro-Mediterranean Foundation for Dialogue between Cultures, Egypt, 90
Litdea Association, Lithuania, 208
Lithuanian Children's Fund, Lithuania, 209
Living Culture Foundation Namibia—LCFN, Namibia, 222
Lloyds Bank Foundation for England and Wales, UK, 365
The Long Now Foundation, USA, 449
Luce (Henry) Foundation, Inc, USA, 435
Luso-American Development Foundation, Portugal, 260
The Lutheran World Federation, Switzerland, 314
Lutherischer Weltbund/Fédération Luthérienne Mondiale/Federación Luterana Mundial, Switzerland, 314
Luxembourg Development NGO Co-operation Circle, Luxembourg, 209
Luxemburg (Rosa) Stiftung, Germany, 139
Lynde and Harry Bradley Foundation, Inc, USA, 449
Lyndon Baines Johnson Foundation, USA, 449
MacArthur (John D. and Catherine T.) Foundation, USA, 444
McConnell (J. W.) Family Foundation, Canada, 57
Macedonian Centre for International Co-operation—MCIC, North Macedonia, 239
Machel (Graça) Trust, South Africa, 280
McKenzie (J. R.) Trust, New Zealand, 233
McKnight Foundation, USA, 449
MADRE, USA, 450
Maecenata Foundation, Germany, 119
Maecenata Stiftung, Germany, 119
MAG—Mines Advisory Group, UK, 366
MAIF Foundation for Research, France, 108
Maison Franco-Japonaise, Japan, 191
Makyedonski Tzyentar za Myeroonarodna Sorabotka, North Macedonia, 239
Mama Cash Foundation, Netherlands, 230
Mandela Institute for Development Studies—MINDS, South Africa, 281
Mani Tese, Italy, 183
Mannréttindaskrifstofa Íslands, Iceland, 154
MAPFRE Foundation, Spain, 292
Marangopoulos Foundation for Human Rights, Greece, 146
Marcel Bleustein-Blanchet Vocational Foundation, France, 109
Mário Soares and Maria Barroso Foundation, Portugal, 260
Markle Foundation, USA, 451
Mary Fonden, Denmark, 85
Mary Foundation, Denmark, 85
Masason Foundation, Japan, 191
Mawazo Institute, Kenya, 199
Max Havelaar Foundation—Fairtrade Netherlands, Netherlands, 230
Max Schmidheiny Foundation at the University of St Gallen, Switzerland, 314
Max Schmidheiny-Stiftung an der Universität St Gallen, Switzerland, 314
Mayer (Charles Léopold Mayer), Fondation, Switzerland, 308
The Maytree Foundation, Canada, 59

Mbeki (Thabo) Foundation, South Africa, 284
Medunarodnog foruma Bosna, Bosnia and Herzegovina, 37
Médecins du Monde International, France, 114
Media Development Foundation—MDF, Georgia, 118
Media Foundation for West Africa, Ghana, 144
medica mondiale eV, Germany, 136
Medical Aid for Palestinians—MAP, UK, 367
Medico International, Germany, 136
Mediis Ganvitarebis Pondi, Georgia, 118
Mellon (Richard King) Foundation, USA, 467
Mencap—Royal Mencap Society, UK, 367
Mental Health Foundation, UK, 367
Menzies Foundation, Australia, 15
Menzies (Sir Robert) Foundation, Australia, 15
Mercatus Center, USA, 451
The Mercers' Charitable Foundation, UK, 367
Merchant Navy Fund, UK, 382
Mercy, Ireland, 168
Mercy For Animals—MFA, USA, 452
Mercy Corps, USA, 452
Mertz Gilmore Foundation, USA, 452
M'essh al Sudan, Sudan, 297
Mexican Centre for Philanthropy, Mexico, 214
Mezhdunarodnyj Memorial, Russian Federation, 266
Michel (James) Foundation, Seychelles, 272
Milbank Memorial Fund, USA, 453
Milieukontakt Macedonia—MKM, North Macedonia, 240
Minderoo Foundation, Australia, 15
Mines Advisory Group—MAG, UK, 366
Minhaj Welfare Foundation, UK, 368
Minority Rights Group International—MRG, UK, 368
Mirovni Inštitut—Inštitut za sodobne družbene in politične študije, Slovenia, 277
MISEREOR—Bischöfliches Hilfswerk Misereor eV, Germany, 137
The Mission to Seafarers, UK, 368
Mith Samlanh, Cambodia, 46
Mitterrand (Danielle), Fondation, France, 112
MIUSA—Mobility International USA, USA, 453
Mo Ibrahim Foundation, UK, 368
Moawad (René) Foundation, Lebanon, 206
Mobility International USA—MIUSA, USA, 453
Mohammed bin Rashid Al Maktoum Global Initiatives—MBRGI, United Arab Emirates, 335
Monell (Ambrose) Foundation, USA, 399
Mongolian Women's Fund—MONES, Mongolia, 218
Montemadrid Foundation, Spain, 292
Montevideo Circle Foundation, Uruguay, 485
Moores (John) Foundation, UK, 362
Motorola Solutions Foundation, USA, 454
Mountain Institute, Peru, 249
Mouvement International ATD Quart-Monde, France, 115
Ms. Foundation for Women, USA, 454
Mshvidobis, Demokratiisa, da Ganvit'arebis Kavkasiuri Instituti, Georgia, 117
MTN Afghanistan Foundation, Afghanistan, 4
MTN Foundation Benin, Benin, 35
Mukwege (Dr Denis) Foundation, Netherlands, 224
Muriel McBrien Kauffman Foundation, USA, 425
Muslim Aid, UK, 369
NAACP Legal Defense and Educational Fund, Inc—LDF, USA, 454
Nadace Charty 77, Czech Republic, 80
Nadace Neziskovky.cz, Czech Republic, 79
Nadace Open Society Fund Praha, Czech Republic, 80
Nadace Vodafone Česká Republika, Czech Republic, 80
Nadácia Ekopolis, Slovakia, 275
Nadácia Otvorenej Spoločnosti, Slovakia, 276
Nadácia Pontis, Slovakia, 274
Nansen (Fridtjof) Institute, Norway, 241
National Council of Social Development—NCSD, Philippines, 250
National Council for Voluntary Organisations, UK, 337
National Emergencies Trust, UK, 369
National Endowment for Science, Technology and the Arts—Nesta, UK, 370
National Federation of NGOs, Poland, 254
National Foundation for Development, El Salvador, 91
National Foundation for the Development of Honduras, Honduras, 150
National Foundation for Educational Research—NFER, UK, 369
National Humanities Center—NHC, USA, 455
The National Lottery Community Fund, UK, 370

National Organization for Women Foundation, USA, 458
National Society for the Prevention of Cruelty to Children—NSPCC, UK, 371
National Trust of Fiji—NTF, Fiji, 94
Naumann (Friedrich) Stiftung, Germany, 130
NCVO—National Council for Voluntary Organisations, UK, 337
NDI—National Democratic Institute for International Affairs, USA, 456
Nederlandse Organisatie voor Internationale Ontwikkelingssamenwerking—Stichting NOVIB, Netherlands, 228
Nesta—National Endowment for Science, Technology and the Arts, UK, 370
Network of Estonian Non-profit Organizations, Estonia, 92
Network of European Foundations—NEF, Belgium, 27
Network of Foundations and Research Institutions for the Promotion of a Culture of Peace in Africa, Côte d'Ivoire, 75
Network of Foundations Working for Development—netFWD, France, 99
Network for Human Development, Brazil, 41
Network of Information and Support for Non-governmental Organizations, Poland, 254
Network for Social Change Charitable Trust—NSCCT, UK, 370
Neves (José Maria), Fundação para a Governança, Cabo Verde, 46
New Economics Foundation—NEF, UK, 371
New Myanmar Foundation, Myanmar, 221
New World Foundation—NWF, USA, 456
The New York Community Trust—NYCT, USA, 457
Newberry Library, USA, 457
NFER—National Foundation for Educational Research, UK, 369
NFI—National Foundation for India, India, 159
NGO Center—NGOC, Armenia, 9
NGO Development Centre, Russian Federation, 265
Nicolas Hulot Foundation for Nature and Humankind, France, 110
Nigerian Conservation Foundation—NCF, Nigeria, 238
Nigerian Institute of International Affairs—NIIA, Nigeria, 238
The Nippon Foundation, Japan, 192
Niwano Peace Foundation, Japan, 192
Nobis Foundation, Ecuador, 88
Norbert Zongo Cell for Investigative Journalism in West Africa, Burkina Faso, 44
Nordic Africa Institute Scholarships, Sweden, 302
Nordic International Support Foundation—NIS, Norway, 242
Nordiska Afrikainstitutets Stipendier, Sweden, 302
Norsk Utenrikspolitisk Institutt—NUPI, Norway, 242
Norwegian Institute of International Affairs, Norway, 242
Norwegian Refugee Council—NRC, Norway, 242
Novartis Foundation, Switzerland, 314
NOVIB (Oxfam Netherlands), Netherlands, 228
NoVo Foundation, USA, 458
NOW Foundation, USA, 458
NSPCC—National Society for the Prevention of Cruelty to Children, UK, 371
Nuffield Foundation, UK, 371
NYCT—The New York Community Trust, USA, 457
Oak Foundation, Switzerland, 315
Obama (Barack) Foundation, USA, 407
Observer Research Foundation—ORF, India, 159
ODI, UK, 371
The Officers' Association, UK, 372
Ogólnopolska Federacja Organizacji Pozarządowych—OFOP, Poland, 254
Oil Search Foundation, Papua New Guinea, 247
Ökumenikus Segélyszervezet, Hungary, 153
Olav Thon Foundation, Norway, 242
Olav Thon Stiftelsen, Norway, 242
Omidyar Group, USA, 458
Omidyar Network Fund, USA, 458
One Economy Foundation, Namibia, 222
OPEN ASIA—Armanshahr Foundation, Afghanistan, 3
Open Estonia Foundation, Estonia, 92
Open Society Action Fund, USA, 458
Open Society Africa, Senegal, 270
Open Society European Policy Institute—OSEPI, Belgium, 33
Open Society Forum (Mongolia), Mongolia, 218
Open Society Foundation—Bratislava, Slovakia, 276

INDEX OF MAIN ACTIVITIES

Law, civil society and human rights

Open Society Foundation Haiti, Haiti, 149
Open Society Foundation—London, UK, 372
Open Society Foundation South Africa—OSF-SA, South Africa, 282
Open Society Foundations, USA, 459
Open Society Foundations—Armenia, Armenia, 9
Open Society Foundations in Pakistan, Pakistan, 245
Open Society Fund—Bosnia-Herzegovina, Bosnia and Herzegovina, 37
Open Society Fund Prague—OSF Prague, Czech Republic, 80
Open Society Initiative for Eastern Africa—OSIEA, Kenya, 199
Open Society Initiative for Southern Africa—OSISA, South Africa, 282
Open Society Institute—Sofia, Bulgaria, 43
Open Society Policy Center, USA, 458
Orange Foundation, Spain, 293
Organisation Internationale de Droit du Développement—OIDD, Italy, 181
Organization for Social Science Research in Eastern and Southern Africa—OSSREA, Ethiopia, 94
Orient-Occident Foundation, Morocco, 220
Österreichischer Wissenschaftsfonds—FWF, Austria, 21
Otto Benecke Foundation, Germany, 138
Otto-Benecke-Stiftung eV, Germany, 138
Our Foundation, Indonesia, 162
Our Future—Foundation for Regional Social Programmes, Russian Federation, 266
Outreach International, USA, 459
OutRight Action International, USA, 460
Outstretched Hands, Italy, 183
Oxfam America, USA, 460
Oxfam Aotearoa, New Zealand, 234
Oxfam Australia, Australia, 16
Oxfam Brasil, Brazil, 41
Oxfam Canada, Canada, 60
Oxfam Denmark, Denmark, 86
Oxfam Deutschland eV, Germany, 138
Oxfam France, France, 115
Oxfam GB, UK, 372
Oxfam Hong Kong, Hong Kong, 151
Oxfam India, India, 159
Oxfam International, Kenya, 200
Oxfam Ireland, Ireland, 167
Oxfam Italia, Italy, 183
Oxfam Mexico, Mexico, 216
Oxfam NOVIB—Nederlandse Organisatie voor Internationale Ontwikkelingssamenwerking, Netherlands, 228
Oxfam NOVIB—Netherlands Organization for International Development Co-operation, Netherlands, 228
Oxfam-Québec, Canada, 60
Oxfam-Solidariteit/Solidarité, Belgium, 33
Oxfam South Africa, South Africa, 282
OzChild—Children Australia Inc, Australia, 16
P&V Foundation, Belgium, 32
Pacific Development and Conservation Trust, New Zealand, 234
Pacific Peoples' Partnership, Canada, 61
Pact, USA, 460
PADF—Pan American Development Foundation, USA, 460
PAI—Population Action International, USA, 460
Pakistan Institute of International Affairs—PIIA, Pakistan, 245
Palestinian NGO Network, Palestinian Territories, 246
Pan American Development Foundation—PADF, USA, 460
PANAP—Pesticide Action Network Asia and the Pacific, Malaysia, 211
PANZI Foundation, USA, 461
Partage, France, 116
Partners for Equity, Australia, 16
Partners in Health, USA, 461
Partos, Netherlands, 223
Patterson (Alicia) Foundation, USA, 398
The Paul G. Allen Family Foundation, USA, 462
Paul Hamlyn Foundation—PHF, UK, 373
The Paul Ramsay Foundation, Australia, 16
Paz y Cooperación, Spain, 296
PCI Media Impact, USA, 467
PCI—Project Concern International, USA, 431
Peace Brigades International—PBI, Belgium, 33
Peace and Co-operation, Spain, 296
Peace Direct, UK, 373
Peace and Disarmament Education Trust—PADET, New Zealand, 234
Peace Institute—Institute for Contemporary Social and Political Studies, Slovenia, 277
Peace Research Institute Oslo—PRIO, Norway, 242

Peace and Security Funders Group—PSFG, USA, 396
Peace Village International, Germany, 129
Peace Winds Japan—PWJ, Japan, 192
Pearl S. Buck International, USA, 462
Penal Reform International—PRI, UK, 373
People in Need, Czech Republic, 79
Perdana Global Peace Foundation—PGPF, Malaysia, 211
Peres Center for Peace and Innovation, Israel, 171
Pertubuhan Pertolongan Wanita, Malaysia, 212
Peruvian Foundation for Nature Conservation, Peru, 249
Pestalozzi Children's Foundation, Switzerland, 317
Pesticide Action Network Asia and the Pacific—PANAP, Malaysia, 211
Pesticide Action Network Latin America and the Caribbean, Chile, 65
The Pew Charitable Trusts, USA, 462
PH International, USA, 463
Philanthropikó Ídryma Stélios Chatzeioánnou stēn Kýpro, Cyprus, 78
Philanthropy New Zealand/Tōpūtanga Tuku Aroha o Aotearoa, New Zealand, 232
Philanthropy for Social Justice and Peace, UK, 336
Philippine Council for NGO Certification, Philippines, 250
PHR—Physicians for Human Rights, USA, 463
Physicians for Human Rights—PHR, USA, 463
Pinchuk (Victor) Foundation, Ukraine, 333
Plan International Ireland, Ireland, 167
PLAN International—PI, UK, 374
Plataform CiviKos, Kosovo, 202
Plataforma Portuguesa das Organizações Não-Governamentais para o Desenvolvimento—ONGD, Portugal, 258
Platforma Mimovládnych Rozvojových Organizácií, Slovakia, 273
Ploughshares Fund, USA, 463
Plunkett Foundation, UK, 374
Polish-American Freedom Foundation, Poland, 257
Polish Donors Forum, Poland, 254
Polsko-Amerykańska Fundacja Wolności, Poland, 257
Pontis Foundation, Slovakia, 274
Population Action International—PAI, USA, 460
Populorum Progressio Foundation, Vatican City, 486
Portuguese Platform of Non-Governmental Organizations for Development, Portugal, 258
Potanin (Vladimir) Foundation, Russian Federation, 267
Praemium Erasmianum Foundation, Netherlands, 230
Praxis Centre for Policy Studies Foundation, Estonia, 93
Première Urgence Internationale, France, 116
Premji (Azim) Foundation, India, 156
Presbyterian World Service & Development—PWS&D, Canada, 61
Primate's World Relief and Development Fund/Le Fonds du Primat Pour le Secours et le Développement Mondial—PWRDF, Canada, 49
Prince Claus Fund for Culture and Development, Netherlands, 228
Prince's Trust, UK, 363
Princess of Asturias Foundation, Spain, 294
Prins Claus Fonds Voor Cultuur en Ontwikkeling, Netherlands, 228
PRIO—Peace Research Institute Oslo, Norway, 242
Pro Juventute, Switzerland, 315
Pro Mujer International, USA, 464
Pro Victimis, Switzerland, 315
Pro Women International, USA, 464
Project Harmony, USA, 463
Project HOPE, USA, 464
Project Trust, UK, 374
ProLiteracy, USA, 464
Pronaturaleza—Fundación Peruana para la Conservación de la Naturaleza, Peru, 249
Prospera—International Network of Women's Funds, Canada, 61
Public Studies Centre, Chile, 64
Puerto Rico Community Foundation, Puerto Rico, 261
Pulitzer Center on Crisis Reporting, USA, 464
Quỹ Thiên Tâm, Viet Nam, 488
Quandt (Herbert) Stiftung, Germany, 122
Quincy Institute for Responsible Statecraft—QI, USA, 465
Rafto Foundation for Human Rights, Norway, 243
Raftostiftelsen for menneskerettigheter, Norway, 243

Rainforest Action Network—RAN, USA, 465
Rainforest Foundation Norway, Norway, 243
The Rainforest Foundation UK—RFUK, UK, 375
Rainforest Foundation US—RFUS, USA, 465
Rainforest Journalism Fund, USA, 464
Rajiv Gandhi Foundation, India, 160
Rambourg Foundation, Tunisia, 326
Ramsay (Paul) Foundation, Australia, 16
RAN—Rainforest Action Network, USA, 465
RAND Corporation, USA, 465
Rausing (Ruben and Elisabeth) Trust, UK, 383
Razumkov Centre, Ukraine, 333
RBC Foundation, Canada, 61
Re:wild, USA, 466
Reall—Real Equity for All, UK, 375
Red de Acción en Plaguicidas y sus Alternativas de América Latina—RAP-AL, Chile, 65
Red Feather, Japan, 185
Red de Mujeres para el Desarrollo, Costa Rica, 75
RED—Ruralité-Environnement-Développement, Belgium, Belgium, 34
Red de Salud de las Mujeres Latinoamericanas y del Caribe—RSMLAC, Ecuador, 89
Rede ba Rai, Timor-Leste, 325
Rede Comuá, Brazil, 38
REDEH—Rede de Desenvolvimento Humano, Brazil, 41
Reeva Rebecca Steenkamp Foundation, South Africa, 283
Refugee Empowerment International—REI, Japan, 193
Refugee Foundation, Netherlands, 231
Refugees International—RI, USA, 466
Regional Environmental Center, Hungary, 153
Regnskogfondet, Norway, 243
Rehabilitation International—RI, USA, 466
REI—Refugee Empowerment International, Japan, 193
Relief International, USA, 466
Renault Foundation, France, 106
René Moawad Foundation—RMF, Lebanon, 206
Réseau des Fondations et Institutions de Recherche pour la Promotion d'un Culture de la Paix en Afrique—REFICA, Côte d'Ivoire, 75
Resolution Foundation, UK, 376
Resource Centre for the Human Rights Nongovernmental Organizations of Moldova—CReDO, Moldova, 217
The Resource Foundation—TRF, USA, 467
Rhodes Trust, UK, 376
Richard Dawkins Foundation for Reason and Science, USA, 412
Richard King Mellon Foundation, USA, 467
Right Livelihood Award Foundation, Sweden, 302
Righteous Persons Foundation, USA, 467
Rising Impact, USA, 467
Robert Bosch Foundation, Germany, 138
Robert-Bosch-Stiftung GmbH, Germany, 138
Robert Schuman Foundation, France, 111
Robertson Foundation for Government—RFG, USA, 468
The Robertson Trust, UK, 376
Rockefeller Brothers Fund—RBF, USA, 468
Rockefeller Foundation, USA, 468
Rohini Nilekani Philanthropies, India, 160
Rosa Luxemburg Foundation, Germany, 139
Rosa-Luxemburg-Stiftung, Germany, 139
Rosetta Foundation, USA, 416
The Rotary Foundation, USA, 468
Rothschild (Edmond de) Foundations, Switzerland, 308
Rowntree (Joseph) Charitable Trust, UK, 362
Rowntree (Joseph) Reform Trust, UK, 362
Royal Anthropological Institute of Great Britain and Ireland—RAI, UK, 377
Royal British Legion, UK, 377
The Royal Commonwealth Society—RCS, UK, 377
The Royal Foundation of the Prince and Princess of Wales, UK, 378
Royal Institute of International Affairs—RIIA—Chatham House, UK, 378
Royal Institute of International Relations—Egmont Institute, Belgium, 29
The Royal Society, UK, 379
Royal Society for the Prevention of Cruelty to Animals—RSPCA, UK, 380
Rroma Foundation, Switzerland, 315
Rromani Fundacija, Switzerland, 315
RSA—Royal Society for the Encouragement of Arts, Manufactures and Commerce, UK, 379
RSPCA—Royal Society for the Prevention of Cruelty to Animals, UK, 380
Rural Development Institute—Landesa, USA, 447
Ruralité-Environnement-Développement—RED, Belgium, 34

Rurality Environment Development, Belgium, 34
Russian Donors Forum, Russian Federation, 265
Russian International Affairs Council—RIAC, Russian Federation, 266
Russian LGBT Network, Russian Federation, 267
Rutgers, Netherlands, 228
Rutherford Institute, USA, 469
Ruya Foundation for Contemporary Culture in Iraq, Iraq, 164
Rytų Europos Studijų Centras—RESC, Lithuania, 209
Sabanci Vakfı—Haci Omer Sabanci Foundation, Türkiye, 329
Sainsbury Family Charitable Trusts, UK, 380
Sakartvelos Strategiisa da Saertashoriso Urtiertobebis Kvlevis Pondi—Rondelis Pondi, Georgia, 118
El Salvadoran Association for Economic and Social Development FUSADES, El Salvador, 91
The Salvation Army International Trust, UK, 381
Salzburg Global Seminar, Austria, 22
Samir Kassir Foundation, Lebanon, 206
Samsung Foundation, Korea (Republic), 202
The San Diego Foundation, USA, 470
San Francisco Foundation—SFF, USA, 470
Sanaburi Foundation, Japan, 193
Sandals Foundation, Jamaica, 184
Santos Foundation, Papua New Guinea, 247
Sarah Scaife Foundation, Inc, USA, 470
Sasakawa, Fondation Franco-Japonaise, France, 106
The Sasakawa Peace Foundation—SPF, Japan, 194
Save the Children International, UK, 381
Save the Children (UK), UK, 381
Sawiris Foundation for Social Development—SFSD, Egypt, 90
SBS Cultural Foundation, Korea (Republic), 202
Scaife (Sarah) Foundation, Inc, USA, 470
Schmidheiny (Max) Stiftung, Switzerland, 314
Schuman (Robert), Fondation, France, 111
Schusterman (Charles and Lynn) Family Foundation, USA, 413
Schwab Foundation for Social Entrepreneurship, Switzerland, 316
Schwarzkopf-Stiftung Junges Europa, Germany, 139
Schwarzkopf Young Europe Foundation, Germany, 139
Schweizerischer Nationalfonds zur Förderung der Wissenschaftlichen Forschung/Fonds National Suisse de la Recherche Scientifique—SNF, Switzerland, 316
Scope, UK, 381
Scott Trust Foundation, UK, 356
Scottish Catholic International Aid Fund—SCIAF, UK, 382
The Seafarers' Charity, UK, 382
Seafarers International Relief Fund, UK, 382
Secours Catholique—Caritas de France, France, 116
SeedChange, Canada, 61
Seeds of Affinity, Australia, 17
Seeds of Peace, USA, 470
SEEMO—South East Europe Media Organisation, Austria, 23
Self Help Africa—SHA, Ireland, 167
Self Help Development Foundation—SHDF, Zimbabwe, 491
Self-Sufficient People Foundation, Indonesia, 163
SEND-West Africa, Ghana, 144
Seoam Yoon Se Young Foundation, Korea (Republic), 202
Service Civil International—SCI, Belgium, 34
SES Foundation—Sustainability, Education, Solidarity, Argentina, 8
Sesame Workshop, USA, 471
Shahid Afridi Foundation—SAF, Pakistan, 246
Shelter—National Campaign for Homeless People, UK, 382
Shoman (Abdul Hameed) Foundation, Jordan, 195
SID—Society for International Development, Italy, 183
Sieć Wspierania Organizacji Pozarządowych—SPLOT, Poland, 254
The Sierra Club Foundation, USA, 471
Sightsavers International, UK, 382
Sigrid Rausing Trust—SRT, UK, 383
Sihtasutus Poliitikauuringute Keskus Praxis, Estonia, 93
Silicon Valley Community Foundation—SVCF, USA, 471
Sinergia—Red Venezolana de OSC, Venezuela, 487
Singapore International Foundation—SIF, Singapore, 273
SIPRI—Stockholm International Peace Research Institute, Sweden, 304

Sir Ahmadu Bello Memorial Foundation, Nigeria, 238
Sir Halley Stewart Trust, UK, 383
Sivil Toplum Geliştirme Merkezi—STGM, Türkiye, 327
Skoll Foundation, USA, 472
Slim (Carlos), Fundación, Mexico, 215
Slovak-Czech Women's Fund, Slovakia, 276
Slovak Donors Forum, Slovakia, 274
Slovak Humanitarian Council, Slovakia, 274
Slovak Security Policy Institute, Slovakia, 276
Slovenská Humanitná Rada, Slovakia, 274
Slovensko-český enský fond, Slovakia, 276
Slovenský inštitút pre bezpečnostnú politiku, Slovakia, 276
Smallwood Trust, UK, 384
Smith (Henry) Charity, UK, 358
Smith Richardson Foundation, Inc, USA, 472
Soares (Mário), Fundação, Portugal, 260
The Sobell Foundation, UK, 384
Society for International Development—SID, Italy, 183
Solidaarisuus, Finland, 96
Solidar, Belgium, 34
Solidarity Foundation, Dominican Republic, 87
Somalia NGO Consortium, Somalia, 277
Sorenson Legacy Foundation, USA, 473
Soros Foundation—Kazakhstan, Kazakhstan, 197
Soros Foundation—Moldova, Moldova, 217
Souter Charitable Trust, UK, 384
South African Institute of Race Relations—IRR, South Africa, 283
South East Europe Media Organisation—SEEMO, Austria, 23
South Sudan Center for Strategic and Policy Studies—CSPS, South Sudan, 285
South West International Development Network—SWIDN, UK, 337
Southern Africa Trust, South Africa, 283
Springer (Friede) Stiftung, Germany, 129
St John Ambulance, UK, 380
Stanley Center for Peace and Security, USA, 473
Start Network, UK, 337
Steelworkers Humanity Fund/Le Fonds Humanitaire des Metallos, Canada, 62
Steenkamp (Reeva Rebecca) Foundation, South Africa, 283
Stefan Batory Foundation, Poland, 256
Stelios Philanthropic Foundation, Cyprus, 78
Stewardship Foundation, USA, 473
Stewart (Sir Halley) Trust, UK, 383
Stichting Bellingcat, Netherlands, 228
Stichting Democratie en Media, Netherlands, 229
Stichting DOEN, Netherlands, 229
Stichting IKEA Foundation, Netherlands, 229
Stichting Liliane Fonds, Netherlands, 229
Stichting Mama Cash, Netherlands, 230
Stichting Max Havelaar—Fairtrade Nederland, Netherlands, 230
Stichting Praemium Erasmianum, Netherlands, 230
Stichting Triodos Foundation, Netherlands, 231
Stichting Vluchteling, Netherlands, 231
Stichting Vodafone Netherlands, Netherlands, 231
Stiftelsen Dag Hammarskjölds Minnesfond, Sweden, 303
Stiftelsen Gapminder, Sweden, 300
Stiftelsen Riksbankens Jubileumsfond, Sweden, 303
Stiftung 'Erinnerung, Verantwortung und Zukunft'—EVZ, Germany, 139
Stiftung Ettersberg, Germany, 140
Stiftung Kinderdorf Pestalozzi, Switzerland, 317
Stiftung für die Rechte zukünftiger Generationen—SRzG, Germany, 141
Stiftung Weltethos, Germany, 141
Stiftung West-Östliche Begegnungen, Germany, 141
Stiftung Zukunft.li, Liechtenstein, 208
Stockholm International Peace Research Institute—SIPRI, Sweden, 304
Straits Exchange Foundation—SEF, Taiwan, 321
Street Child, UK, 384
Streisand (Barbra) Foundation, USA, 408
Strømme Foundation, Norway, 243
Strømmestiftelsen, Norway, 243
Studienstiftung des deutschen Volkes, Germany, 142
Sudan Foundation, Sudan, 297
Sudd Institute, South Sudan, 285
Südosteuropäische Medienorganisation, Austria, 23
SUN Civil Society Network, UK, 381
Suomalaiset kehitysjärjestöt—Fingo, Finland, 95
Surdna Foundation, Inc, USA, 474
Survival International, UK, 385

The Susan Thompson Buffett Foundation—STBF, USA, 474
Sutherland Self Help Trust, New Zealand, 235
Suzuki Foundation (David), Canada, 53
Svenska kulturfonden, Finland, 98
Sweden-Japan Foundation—SJF, Sweden, 304
The Swedish Cultural Foundation in Finland, Finland, 98
Swiss Church Aid, Switzerland, 311
Swiss National Science Foundation—SNSF, Switzerland, 316
SWISSAID Foundation, Switzerland, 318
Syin-Lu Social Welfare Foundation, Taiwan, 321
Synergos—The Synergos Institute, USA, 396
Syria Al-Gad Relief Foundation, Egypt, 91
Taawon, Palestinian Territories, 246
Tahir Foundation, Indonesia, 162
Taiwan NPO Information Platform, Taiwan, 321
Talon (Claudine), Fondation, Benin, 35
Tanager, USA, 397
Tang Prize Foundation, Taiwan, 322
TANZ—Trade Aid NZ Inc, New Zealand, 235
Tarih Vakfı, Türkiye, 329
Tata Trusts, India, 160
Tearfund, UK, 385
Tearfund Australia, Australia, 18
Tebtebba Foundation, Philippines, 253
TechnoServe, USA, 474
Teletón México Foundation, Mexico, 216
Telmex Telcel Foundation, Mexico, 216
Templeton Religion Trust, Bahamas, 24
Terre des Hommes International Federation—TDHIF, Switzerland, 318
Terre Sans Frontières—TSF, Canada, 62
TESEV—Türkiye Ekonomik ve Sosyal Etüdler Vakfı, Türkiye, 329
Tewa, Nepal, 223
TFF–Transnational Foundation for Peace and Future Research, Sweden, 304
TFF–Transnationella Stiftelsen för Freds- och Framtidsforskning, Sweden, 304
Thabo Mbeki Foundation, South Africa, 284
Thiel Foundation, USA, 474
Third Sector Foundation of Turkey, Türkiye, 327
Third World Network—TWN, Malaysia, 211
Third World Solidarity Action, Luxembourg, 209
Thomson Foundation, UK, 385
Thomson Reuters Foundation, UK, 385
Thurgood Marshall Institute, USA, 454
TI—Transparency International, Germany, 142
Tibet Fund, USA, 475
Tides Organizations, USA, 475
Tifa Foundation—Indonesia, Indonesia, 163
Tindall Foundation, New Zealand, 235
Tinh Thuong One Member Limited Liability Microfinance Institution, Viet Nam, 488
Tinker Foundation, Inc, USA, 475
The Todd Foundation, New Zealand, 235
Together for Global Justice—CIDSE, Belgium, 29
Tony Blair Institute for Global Change—TBI, UK, 386
Topūtanga Tuku Aroha o Aotearoa, New Zealand, 232
TotalEnergies Foundation, France, 112
The Toyota Foundation, Japan, 195
Trade Aid NZ Inc—TANZ, New Zealand, 235
Translators without Borders, USA, 416
Transparency International—TI, Germany, 142
Transparent Election Foundation of Afghanistan—TEFA, Afghanistan, 4
Triodos Foundation, Netherlands, 231
Trócaire—Catholic Agency for World Development, Ireland, 168
Trudeau (Pierre Elliott) Foundation, Canada, 55
Trust for London, UK, 386
Trust for Mutual Understanding—TMU, USA, 476
Trust for Social Achievement, Bulgaria, 44
TTF—Toyota Thailand Foundation, Thailand, 325
Tujenge Africa Foundation, Burundi, 45
Tulsa Community Foundation—TCF, USA, 476
Turin Savings Bank Foundation, Italy, 176
Turing (Alan) Institute, UK, 339
Turkish Economic and Social Studies Foundation, Türkiye, 329
Turkish Family Health and Planning Foundation, Türkiye, 330
Türkiye Aile Sağlığı ve Planlaması Vakfı—TAPV, Türkiye, 330
Türkiye İnsan Hakları Vakfı—TİHV, Türkiye, 330
Türkiye Kalkınma Vakfı, Türkiye, 330
Türkiye Vodafone Vakfı, Türkiye, 331
Turquoise Mountain Foundation, UK, 386
TÜSEV—Türkiye Üçüncü Sektör Vakfı, Türkiye, 327
Tutu (Desmond & Leah) Legacy Foundation, South Africa, 279
TYM Fund, Viet Nam, 488

INDEX OF MAIN ACTIVITIES

U4 Anti-Corruption Resource Centre, Norway, 241
UAI—Union des Associations Internationales, Belgium, 27
UEFA Foundation for Children, Switzerland, 318
Ufadhili Trust, Kenya, 197
UJIA—United Jewish Israel Appeal, UK, 387
Ukrainian Women's Fund, Ukraine, 333
Uluchay Social-Economic Innovation Center, Azerbaijan, 23
Umut Vakfi, Türkiye, 331
Unbound Philanthropy, USA, 476
UNIFOR—Forvaltningstiftelse for fond og legater, Norway, 240
Union Aid Abroad—APHEDA, Australia, 19
Union des Associations Internationales—UAI, Belgium, 27
Union of International Associations—UIA/Unie van de Internationale Vereinigingen—UIV, Belgium, 27
UNIR Bolivia Foundation, Bolivia, 36
Unitarian Universalist Service Committee—UUSC, USA, 476
United Jewish Israel Appeal—UJIA, UK, 387
United Nations Foundation, USA, 476
United States African Development Foundation—USADF, USA, 477
United States-Japan Foundation, USA, 477
Unity Foundation, Luxembourg, 210
Universal Foundation, Maldives, 212
Universal Jewish Alliance, France, 101
UPS Foundation, USA, 477
US Civilian Research & Development Foundation, USA, 419
USC Shoah Foundation—The Institute for Visual History and Education, USA, 477
USPG—United Society Partners in the Gospel, UK, 387
UUSC—Unitarian Universalist Service Committee, USA, 476
Values Foundation, Bulgaria, 43
Vancouver Foundation, Canada, 62
VANI—Voluntary Action Network India, India, 155
Van Leer Jerusalem Institute, Israel, 171
Vargas (Getulio), Fundação, Brazil, 40
Vehbi Koç Foundation, Türkiye, 331
Vehbi Koç Vakfı, Türkiye, 331
Veillon (Charles), Fondation, Switzerland, 308
Venezuelan Network of Civil Society Organizations, Venezuela, 487
VENRO—Verband Entwicklungspolitik und Humanitäre Hilfe deutscher Nichtregierungsorganizationen, Germany, 120
VIA Foundation, Czech Republic, 81
Victor Pinchuk Foundation, Ukraine, 333
Victoria Children Foundation, Russian Federation, 267
VIDC—Vienna Institute for International Dialogue and Co-operation, Austria, 23
Vienna Institute for International Dialogue and Co-operation—VIDC, Austria, 23
Village Community Development Foundation, Indonesia, 163
VinFuture Foundation, Viet Nam, 489
Vita, Ireland, 168
Vital Strategies, USA, 478
Vital Voices Global Partnership, USA, 478
Vladimir Potanin Foundation, Russian Federation, 267
Vodacom Foundation, South Africa, 284
Vodacom Foundation South Africa, South Africa, 284
Vodacom Lesotho Foundation, Lesotho, 207
Vodafone Americas Foundation, USA, 478
Vodafone ATH Fiji Foundation, Fiji, 94
Vodafone Czech Republic Foundation, Czech Republic, 80
Vodafone Foundation, UK, 388
Vodafone Foundation Germany, Germany, 142
Vodafone Foundation India, India, 161
Vodafone Foundation Luxembourg, Luxembourg, 210
Vodafone Foundation New Zealand, New Zealand, 235
Vodafone Ghana Foundation, Ghana, 144
Vodafone Hungary Foundation, Hungary, 153
Vodafone Idea Foundation, India, 161
Vodafone Ireland Foundation, Ireland, 168
Vodafone Italy Foundation, Italy, 181
Vodafone Magyarország Alapítvány, Hungary, 153
Vodafone Netherlands Foundation, Netherlands, 231
Vodafone Portugal Foundation, Portugal, 261
Vodafone Romania Foundation, Romania, 264
Vodafone Spain Foundation, Spain, 296
Vodafone Stiftung Deutschland, Germany, 142
Vodafone Türkiye Foundation, Türkiye, 331
Volkart Foundation, Switzerland, 319
Volkart-Stiftung, Switzerland, 319
Voluntary Action Network India—VANI, India, 155
Volunteer Service Abroad/Te Tūao Tāwāhi—VSA, New Zealand, 236
Výbor dobré vůle—Nadace Olgy Havlové, Czech Republic, 81
W. K. Kellogg Foundation—WKKF, USA, 478
Wahana Lingkungan Hidup Indonesia—WALHI, Indonesia, 162
WALHI—Wahana Lingkungan Hidup Indonesia, Indonesia, 162
Walk Free, Australia, 15
Walmart Foundation, USA, 478
Walter and Duncan Gordon Charitable Foundation, Canada, 62
War Child, UK, 388
War on Want, UK, 388
WaterAid, UK, 389
Weinberg (Harry and Jeanette) Foundation, USA, 434
Welfare Association, Palestinian Territories, 246
West African Rural Foundation—WARF, Senegal, 270
Westminster Foundation for Democracy—WFD, UK, 389
Wihuri Foundation for International Prizes, Finland, 98
Wihuri (Jenny and Antti) Foundation, Finland, 96
Wihurin kansainvälisten palkintojen rahasto, Finland, 98
Wilderness Foundation Global—WFG, South Africa, 284
William Adlington Cadbury Charitable Trust, UK, 390
The William and Flora Hewlett Foundation, USA, 481
The William H. Donner Foundation, Inc, USA, 481
William T. Grant Foundation, USA, 481
WILPF—Women's International League for Peace and Freedom, Switzerland, 319
Wilson (Woodrow) International Center for Scholars, USA, 482
Windle Trust International, UK, 390
Winston Churchill Memorial Trust of New Zealand, New Zealand, 236
Woman to Woman Foundation, Sweden, 301
The Womanity Foundation, Switzerland, 319
Women in Equality Foundation, Argentina, 8
Women Thrive Fund, UK, 384
WomenLead Institute, USA, 418
Women's Aid, Ireland, 168
Women's Aid Organisation—WAO, Malaysia, 212
Women's Development Network, Costa Rica, 75
Women's Environment & Development Organization—WEDO, USA, 482
Women's Fund Asia, Sri Lanka, 297
Women's International League for Peace and Freedom, Switzerland, 319
Women's World Summit Foundation—WWSF, Switzerland, 320
The Wood Foundation—TWF, UK, 391
Woodrow Wilson International Center for Scholars, USA, 482
World Alliance for Citizen Participation—CIVICUS, South Africa, 278
World Alliance of YMCAs—Young Men's Christian Associations, Switzerland, 319
World Association of Children's Friends, Monaco, 217
World Economic Forum, Switzerland, 320
World Emergency Relief—WER, USA, 483
World Holocaust Forum Foundation—WHF, Israel, 171
World Jewish Relief, UK, 391
World Learning, USA, 483
World Neighbors, USA, 483
The World of NGOs, Austria, 20
World Peace Foundation—WPF, USA, 483
World University Service of Canada/Entraide Universitaire Mondiale du Canada—WUSC/EUMC, Canada, 63
World Vision International, UK, 391
WorldFish, Malaysia, 212
Wujoh Foundation for Media and Development, Yemen, 489
WWF International, Switzerland, 320
WWSF—Women's World Summit Foundation, Switzerland, 320
The Wyss Foundtion, USA, 484
YADESA—Yayasan Pembinaan Masyarakat Desa, Indonesia, 163
Yayasan Geutanyoë, Indonesia, 162
Yayasan Insan Sembada, Indonesia, 163
Yayasan Pembinaan Masyarakat Desa—YADESA, Indonesia, 163
Yayasan Tifa, Indonesia, 163
Year Out Group, UK, 374
Yellow Feather Fund, USA, 471
Yemen Policy Center, Yemen, 489
Yemen Polling Center—YPC, Yemen, 489
YMCA—Young Men's Christian Association, UK, 392
Young Citizens—Citizenship Foundation, UK, 392
Youth Leadership Development Foundation—YLDF, Yemen, 489
Zavod Center za Informiranje, Sodelovanje in Razvoj Nevladnih Organizacije—CNVOS, Slovenia, 277
ZEIT-Stiftung Ebelin und Gerd Bucerius, Germany, 143
Ziviler Friedensdienst—ZFD, Germany, 120
ZOA, Netherlands, 231
Zonta Foundation for Women, USA, 484
Zorig Foundation, Mongolia, 219

MEDICINE AND HEALTH

1818 Fund Foundation, Netherlands, 229
A. G. Leventis Foundation, Greece, 144
A. G. Leventis Foundation Nigeria, Nigeria, 237
A. M. M. Sahabdeen Trust Foundation, Sri Lanka, 297
The A. P. Møller and Chastine Mc-Kinney Møller Foundation, Denmark, 82
A. P. Møller og Hustru Chastine Mc-Kinney Møllers Fond til almene Formaal, Denmark, 82
Abdul Hameed Shoman Foundation—AHSF, Jordan, 195
Abilis Foundation, Finland, 95
Abilis-säätiö, Finland, 95
Acción Contra el Hambre–ACH, Spain, 286
ACRF—Australian Cancer Research Foundation, Australia, 11
ACROTEC Technology Foundation, Italy, 176
Action Against Hunger, Spain, 286
Action for Children, UK, 338
Action Children's Aid, Denmark, 82
Action contre la Faim—ACF France, France, 100
Action Damien/Damiaanactie, Belgium, 28
Action on Poverty, Australia, 10
Action Solidarité Tiers Monde—ASTM, Luxembourg, 209
Active for People in Need Austria, Austria, 20
ADRA—Adventist Development and Relief Agency International, USA, 397
Advance, USA, 397
Adventist Development and Relief Agency International—ADRA, USA, 397
Afghanistan Institute for Civil Society—AICS, Afghanistan, 3
AFPE—American Foundation for Pharmaceutical Education, USA, 401
Africa Foundation, South Africa, 278
Africa Humanitarian Action—AHA, Ethiopia, 93
Africa Space Foundation, Switzerland, 308
The African Agricultural Technology Foundation—AATF, Kenya, 198
African Refugees Foundation—AREF, Nigeria, 237
African Women's Development Fund—AWDF, Ghana, 143
African Youth Initiative Network—AYINET, Uganda, 331
Aga Khan Development Network—AKDN, Switzerland, 306
Aga Khan Foundation, Switzerland, 306
Aga Khan Foundation Canada, Canada, 49
Aga Khan Foundation UK, UK, 338
Age International, UK, 339
AGIR Association for the Environment and Quality of Life, Mali, 213
Agrupació AMCI Foundation, Spain, 286
Ai You Foundation, China (People's Republic), 66
Aisha Buhari Global Foundation, Nigeria, 237
Akai Hane—Central Community Chest of Japan, Japan, 185
Aktion Børnehjælp, Denmark, 82
Al Basar International Foundation, Saudi Arabia, 268
Al Jalila Foundation, United Arab Emirates, 334
Al Jisr Foundation, Oman, 244
Al-Zubair Charity Foundation, Sudan, 297
The Alan Turing Institute, UK, 339
Alavi Foundation, USA, 398
Alemán (Miguel), Fundación, Mexico, 215
Alessio Pezcoller Foundation, Italy, 174
Alexander S. Onassis Public Benefit Foundation, Liechtenstein, 207

Medicine and health

Medicine and health

Alfred Benzon Foundation, Denmark, 82
Alfred Benzons Fond, Denmark, 82
Alfred P. Sloan Foundation, USA, 398
Alfried Krupp von Bohlen und Halbach Foundation, Germany, 121
Alfried Krupp von Bohlen und Halbach-Stiftung, Germany, 121
Ali Fulhu Thuthu Foundation, Maldives, 212
Alicia Patterson Foundation—APF, USA, 398
Alight, USA, 399
Aliko Dangote Foundation—ADF, Nigeria, 237
Alkhidmat Foundation Pakistan—AKFP, Pakistan, 244
All Good Foundation Charitable Trust, New Zealand, 232
Allen (Paul G.) Family Foundation, USA, 462
Allende (Isabel) Foundation, USA, 442
Alola Foundation, Timor-Leste, 325
The Alva Foundation, Canada, 49
Alzheimer Spain Foundation, Spain, 288
Alzheimer's Society, UK, 339
AMADE Mondiale—Association Mondiale des Amis de l'Enfance, Monaco, 217
Aman Foundation, Pakistan, 244
The Ambrose Monell Foundation, USA, 399
Ambuja Cement Foundation—ACF, India, 156
American Enterprise Institute—AEI, USA, 400
American Foundation for the Blind—AFB, USA, 400
American Foundation for Pharmaceutical Education—AFPE, USA, 401
American Heart Association—AHA, USA, 401
American Jewish Joint Distribution Committee—JDC, USA, 402
American Jewish World Service—AJWS, USA, 402
American Near East Refugee Aid—Anera, USA, 402
American Philosophical Society—APS, USA, 402
AmeriCares Foundation, Inc, USA, 403
amfAR—The Foundation for AIDS Research, USA, 403
AMINA—aktiv für Menschen in Not Austria, Austria, 20
Amity Foundation, China (People's Republic), 66
Amref Health Africa, Kenya, 198
Anders Jahre's Foundation for Humanitarian Purposes, Norway, 240
Anders Jahres Humanitære Stiftelse, Norway, 240
Anera—American Near East Refugee Aid, USA, 402
Anesvad, Spain, 286
Angel of Hope Foundation, Zimbabwe, 490
Anglo American Foundation, UK, 340
Anguilla Community Fund, Anguilla, 5
Anne Ray Foundation, USA, 450
The Annenberg Foundation, USA, 404
Apex Foundation, Australia, 10
APHEDA—Union Aid Abroad, Australia, 19
ArcelorMittal Brazil Foundation, Brazil, 39
Archewell Foundation, USA, 405
Archie Sherman Charitable Trust, UK, 340
Areumdaun Jaedan, Korea (Republic), 200
Arthritis Australia, Australia, 10
Arthritis Foundation, USA, 406
Asia Africa International Voluntary Foundation—AIV, Japan, 186
Asia Philanthropy Circle—APC, Singapore, 272
Asian Community Trust—ACT, Japan, 186
Asian Health Institute—AHI, Japan, 187
Asian Venture Philanthropy Network—AVPN, Singapore, 272
Aspen Institute, USA, 407
Association AGIR pour l'Environnement et la Qualité de la Vie, Mali, 213
Association for Development Policy and Humanitarian Aid, Germany, 120
Association of Medical Research Charities—AMRC, UK, 335
Association of Non-Governmental Organizations in The Gambia—TANGO, Gambia, 117
Asthma + Lung UK, UK, 341
ASTM—Action Solidarité Tiers Monde, Luxembourg, 209
Astur Foundation, Uruguay, 485
ATD Fourth World International, France, 115
Auchan Foundation, France, 103
Australian Academy of Technological Sciences and Engineering, Australia, 11
Australian-American Fulbright Commission, Australia, 11
Australian Cancer Research Foundation—ACRF, Australia, 11
Australian Communities Foundation, Australia, 12
Australian Foundation for the Peoples of Asia and the Pacific—AFAP, Australia, 10

Australian Volunteers International—AVI, Australia, 13
Austrian Science Fund, Austria, 21
Autonómia Alapítvány, Hungary, 152
Autonómia Foundation, Hungary, 152
AVI—Australian Volunteers International, Australia, 13
Aviation Sans Frontières—ASF, France, 101
Aviation Without Borders, France, 101
AVSI Foundation, Italy, 175
Aydın Doğan Foundation, Türkiye, 328
Aydın Doğan Vakfı, Türkiye, 328
Azim Premji Foundation, India, 156
Azman Hashim Foundation, Malaysia, 212
Bagnoud (François-Xavier) Association, Switzerland, 310
Baha'i International Development Organization—BIDO, Israel, 169
Baillet Latour Fund, Belgium, 32
Baker Heart & Diabetes Institute, Australia, 13
Balzan Fonds, Internationale Stiftung, Italy, 181
Banda (Joyce) Foundation International, Malawi, 210
Bank of America Charitable Foundation, USA, 407
Barbra Streisand Foundation, USA, 408
Barceló Foundation, Spain, 289
Bariloche Foundation, Argentina, 7
Barnardo's, UK, 342
Barretstown, Ireland, 165
Barrié de la Maza (Pedro, Conde de Fenosa), Fundación, Spain, 293
Barzani Charity Foundation—BCF, Iraq, 164
BBC Media Action, UK, 342
BBVA Foundation, Spain, 289
BCause Foundation, Bulgaria, 42
The Beautiful Foundation, Korea (Republic), 200
Beisheim Foundation, Germany, 122
Beisheim Stiftung, Germany, 122
Beit Trust, UK, 342
Bell (Max) Foundation, Canada, 59
Bello (Sir Ahmadu) Memorial Foundation, Nigeria, 238
Benesco, UK, 347
Benzon (Alfred) Foundation, Denmark, 82
Bertelsmann Foundation, Germany, 122
Bertelsmann Stiftung, Germany, 122
Bettencourt Schueller Foundation, France, 103
Bharti Foundation, India, 156
Big Heart Foundation, Chad, 64
Biocon Foundation, India, 157
Bischöfliches Hilfswerk Misereor eV, Germany, 137
Blair (Tony) Institute for Global Change, UK, 386
Blavatnik Family Foundation, USA, 409
Bleustein-Blanchet (Marcel), Fondation de la Vocation, France, 109
Blood Cancer UK—Bloodwise, UK, 343
Bloomberg Philanthropies, USA, 409
BNP Paribas Foundation, France, 103
Bodossaki Foundation, Greece, 145
Boehringer Ingelheim Fonds—Stiftung für medizinische Grundlagenforschung, Germany, 122
Boghossian Foundation, Belgium, 31
Boltzmann (Ludwig) Gesellschaft, Austria, 21
Bond, UK, 335
Born This Way Foundation, USA, 409
Bosch (Robert) Stiftung GmbH, Germany, 138
BP Foundation, Inc, USA, 409
BRAC, Bangladesh, 25
BrazilFoundation, Brazil, 39
Bread for the World—Protestant Work for Social Welfare and Development, Germany, 123
Breakthrough T1D, USA, 409
Brenthurst Foundation, South Africa, 282
Brighter Future Myanmar Foundation—BFM, Myanmar, 221
BrightFocus Foundation, USA, 409
Bristol-Myers Squibb Foundation, USA, 410
British Heart Foundation—BHF, UK, 344
British Overseas NGOs for Development, UK, 335
British Red Cross Society, UK, 345
The Broad Foundation, USA, 410
Brot für die Welt—Evangelisches Werk für Diakonie und Entwicklung, Germany, 123
Brother's Brother Foundation, USA, 410
Buck (Pearl S.) International, USA, 462
Buckland (William) Foundation, Australia, 19
Buddharaksa Foundation, Thailand, 323
Buffett (Howard G.) Foundation, USA, 437
Buffett (Susan Thompson) Foundation, USA, 474
Bunge y Born Foundation, Argentina, 7
Burroughs Wellcome Fund—BWF, USA, 411
C. G. Jung-Institut Zürich, Switzerland, 307
Cadbury (Edward) Charitable Trust, UK, 351

INDEX OF MAIN ACTIVITIES

Cadbury (William Adlington) Charitable Trust, UK, 390
CAF America, USA, 393
CAFOD—Catholic Agency for Overseas Development, UK, 345
Calgary Foundation, Canada, 49
California Community Foundation, USA, 411
Calouste Gulbenkian Foundation, Portugal, 259
Cambodia Development Resource Institute—CDRI, Cambodia, 46
Canadian Cancer Society, Canada, 50
Canadian Liver Foundation/Fondation Canadienne du Foie, Canada, 58
Canadian Physicians for Aid and Relief—CPAR, Canada, 52
Cancer Council Australia, Australia, 13
Cancer Research UK, UK, 346
Cancer Society of New Zealand/Te Kāhui Matepukupuku o Aotearoa, New Zealand, 233
Cancerfonden, Sweden, 298
Canon Foundation in Europe, Netherlands, 224
Canon Institute for Global Studies—CIGS, Japan, 187
CARE International—CI, Switzerland, 307
Cargill (Margaret A.) Philanthropies, USA, 450
Cariplo Foundation, Italy, 175
Caritas de France—Secours Catholique, France, 116
Carlo Pesenti Foundation, Italy, 176
Carlos Slim Foundation, Mexico, 215
CARMABI Foundation, Curaçao, 77
Carnegie Corporation of New York, USA, 411
The Carter Center, USA, 412
Cassa di Risparmio di Padova e Rovigo Foundation, Italy, 175
Catholic Agency for Overseas Development—CAFOD, UK, 345
Catholic Agency for World Development—Trócaire, Ireland, 168
Catholic Help—Caritas France, France, 116
Caucasus Research Resource Center Armenia Foundation—CRRC, Armenia, 9
CBM-International, Germany, 123
CCKF—Chiang Ching-kuo Foundation for International Scholarly Exchange, Taiwan, 321
CDC Foundation, USA, 412
CEDRO—Centro de Información y Educación para la Prevención del Abuso de Drogas, Peru, 248
CENSIS—Fondazione Centro Studi Investimenti Sociali, Italy, 172
Center for Victims of Torture—CVT, USA, 413
Centre d'Etude du Polymorphisme Humain, France, 107
Centre International de Recherche sur le Cancer—CIRC, France, 101
Centro de Estudios Públicos—CEP, Chile, 64
Centro de Información y Educación para la Prevención del Abuso de Drogas—CEDRO, Peru, 248
The Century Foundation—TCF, USA, 413
Chaabi (Miloud), Fondation, Morocco, 220
Chagnon (Lucie et André), Fondation, Canada, 55
Champalimaud Foundation, Portugal, 259
Chandaria Foundation, Kenya, 198
Chang Yung-fa Foundation, Taiwan, 321
Chantal Biya Foundation, Cameroon, 47
Charities Advisory Trust, UK, 336
Charities Aid Foundation of America—CAF America, USA, 393
Charity Projects, UK, 348
Charles and Lynn Schusterman Family Philanthropies, USA, 413
Charles Wolfson Charitable Trust, UK, 347
The Charta 77 Foundation, Czech Republic, 80
The Chatlos Foundation, Inc, USA, 414
Cheshire (Leonard) Foundation, UK, 364
Chia Hsin Foundation, Taiwan, 321
Chiang Ching-kuo Foundation for International Scholarly Exchange—CCKF, Taiwan, 321
The Chicago Community Trust, USA, 414
ChildFund, New Zealand, 233
ChildFund International, USA, 414
Children & War Foundation—CAW, Norway, 240
Children in Africa Foundation, Germany, 140
Children International—CI, USA, 414
Children of the Mekong, France, 102
Children and Sharing, France, 102
The Children's Investment Fund Foundation, UK, 347
Children's Medical Research Institute—CMRI, Australia, 13
Childs (Jane Coffin) Memorial Fund for Medical Research, USA, 443
Childwick Trust, UK, 347
China Charities Aid Foundation for Children, China (People's Republic), 67

572

INDEX OF MAIN ACTIVITIES

Medicine and health

China Foundation for Poverty Alleviation—CFPA, China (People's Republic), 67
China Medical Board—CMB, USA, 415
China Siyuan Foundation for Poverty Alleviation, China (People's Republic), 67
Chirac (Jacques), Fondation, France, 107
Christian Aid, UK, 348
Christopher & Dana Reeve Foundation, USA, 415
The Churchill Fellowship, UK, 348
Churchill (Winston) Memorial Trust of New Zealand, New Zealand, 236
CIMA Research Foundation—Centre for Environmental Monitoring, Italy, 176
Citi Handlowy Leopold Kronenberg Foundation, Poland, 255
Civic Democratic Initiative Support Foundation—CDF, Yemen, 489
Civil Society Foundation, Georgia, 118
Clara Lionel Foundation—CLF, USA, 415
Claude Pompidou Foundation, France, 104
Claudine Talon Foundation, Benin, 35
CLEAR Global, USA, 416
Cleveland Foundation, USA, 416
Clinton Foundation, USA, 416
CNIB Foundation/Fondation INCA, Canada, 52
Coastline Foundation, Maldives, 212
The Coca-Cola Foundation, Inc, USA, 417
Collier Charitable Fund, Australia, 13
Comic Relief, UK, 348
Committee of Good Will—Olga Havel Foundation, Czech Republic, 81
The Commonwealth Fund, USA, 417
Community Chest, Singapore, 273
Community Chest of Hong Kong, Hong Kong, 150
Community Chest of Korea—Fruit of Love, Korea (Republic), 200
Community Development Foundation, Mozambique, 221
Community Foundation for Northern Ireland, UK, 349
Community Foundation for the Western Region of Zimbabwe—CFWRZ, Zimbabwe, 490
Concern India Foundation, India, 157
Concern Worldwide, Ireland, 166
CONCORD—European NGO Confederation for Relief and Development, Belgium, 26
The Confederation of Service Charities—Cobseo, UK, 349
Conrad N. Hilton Foundation, USA, 417
Consuelo Zobel Alger Foundation, USA, 417
Cooperazione Internazionale—COOPI, Italy, 173
Copperbelt Development Foundation, Zambia, 490
Corona Foundation, Colombia, 71
Corus International, USA, 418
Counterpart International, USA, 418
CPAR—Canadian Physicians for Aid and Relief, Canada, 52
The Crafoord Foundation, Sweden, 298
Crafoordska stiftelsen, Sweden, 298
CRDF Global, USA, 419
Croucher Foundation, Hong Kong, 151
Crown Family Philanthropies, USA, 419
Cruz (Oswaldo), Fundação, Brazil, 40
Culture, Health, Arts, Sports and Education Fund—CHASE, Jamaica, 184
CURE International, USA, 419
The Cure Parkinson's Trust, UK, 349
Cuso International, Canada, 53
CVT—Center for Victims of Torture, USA, 413
Cyril Ramaphosa Foundation, South Africa, 279
Cystic Fibrosis Canada, Canada, 53
Cystic Fibrosis Foundation, USA, 419
Cystic Fibrosis Trust, UK, 350
Dalio Foundation, USA, 419
Dam Foundation, Norway, 243
Damon Runyon Cancer Research Foundation, USA, 419
Daniele Agostino Derossi Foundation, USA, 420
Danish Institute for Human Rights, Denmark, 84
David and Lucile Packard Foundation, USA, 420
David Nott Foundation, UK, 350
Davis (Lady) Fellowship Trust, Israel, 170
Daw Khin Kyi Foundation, Myanmar, 221
Dell (Michael & Susan) Foundation, USA, 453
del Pino (Rafael), Fundación, Spain, 294
Democracy Fund, USA, 458
Dental Aid International, Switzerland, 317
Deripaska (Oleg) Foundation, Russian Federation, 267
Derossi (Daniele Agostino) Foundation, USA, 420
Deutsche AIDS-Stiftung, Germany, 124
Deutsche Krebshilfe eV, Germany, 124
Deutsches Rheuma-Forschungszentrum Berlin, Germany, 126
Development Foundation, Guatemala, 148
Dewji (Mo) Foundation, Tanzania, 323
Diabetes UK, UK, 350

Dietmar Hopp Foundation, Germany, 126
Dietmar-Hopp-Stiftung, Germany, 126
Digicel Foundation Jamaica, Jamaica, 184
Digicel PNG Foundation, Papua New Guinea, 247
Diorapthe Foundation, Netherlands, 229
Direct Relief, USA, 420
Dóchas—Irish Association of Non-Governmental Development Organisations, Ireland, 165
Doctors Without Borders International, Switzerland, 314
Doctors of the World International, France, 114
Doğan (Aydın) Vakfı, Türkiye, 328
Doris Duke Charitable Foundation—DDCF, USA, 421
Dr Rainer Wild Foundation for Healthy Nutrition, Germany, 126
Dr Rainer Wild-Stiftung—Stiftung für Gesunde Ernährung, Germany, 126
Dr Scholl Foundation, USA, 421
Dräger Foundation, Germany, 126
Dräger-Stiftung, Germany, 126
Dreyfus Health Foundation, USA, 468
Drug Policy Alliance—DPA, USA, 421
DSW—Deutsche Stiftung Weltbevölkerung, Germany, 126
DTGO Group of Foundations, Thailand, 323
del Duca (Simone et Cino), Fondation, France, 111
Duke Endowment, USA, 421
Dutch-Bangla Bank Foundation, Bangladesh, 25
Echo Foundation/Fondation Écho, Canada, 54
EcoHealth Alliance, USA, 422
Ecuadorean Social Group Fund Populorum Progressio, Ecuador, 89
Edhi Foundation, Pakistan, 245
Edmond de Rothschild Foundations, Switzerland, 308
The Edna McConnell Clark Foundation, USA, 422
Educo, Spain, 286
Edward Cadbury Charitable Trust, UK, 351
Ekhaga Foundation, Sweden, 299
Ekhagastiftelsen, Sweden, 299
The Elders Foundation, UK, 352
ELEPAP—Rehabilitation for the Disabled, Greece, 145
Elizabeth Glaser Pediatric AIDS Foundation—EGPAF, USA, 423
The ELMA Group of Foundations, USA, 423
Elrha, UK, 352
Else Kröner-Fresenius Foundation, Germany, 127
Else Kröner-Fresenius-Stiftung, Germany, 127
Elton John AIDS Foundation, UK, 352
Embrace the Middle East, UK, 352
EMERGENCY, Italy, 173
Empresas Polar Foundation, Venezuela, 487
Emunah, UK, 353
Enchanted Peach Children's Foundation—EPCF, USA, 423
Enda Third World—Environment and Development Action in the Third World, Senegal, 270
Enda Tiers Monde—Environnement et Développement du Tiers-Monde, Senegal, 270
endPoverty.org, USA, 424
Enfance et Partage, France, 102
Enfants du Mékong, France, 102
EngenderHealth, USA, 424
Eni Foundation, Italy, 173
Ente Cassa di Risparmio di Firenze, Italy, 173
Entraide Protestante Suisse, Switzerland, 311
Epilepsy Foundation, USA, 424
Equality Fund/Fonds Égalité, Canada, 54
Equity Group Foundation—EGF, Kenya, 198
Ernst Schering Foundation, Germany, 127
Ernst-Schering-Stiftung, Germany, 127
Eskom Development Foundation, South Africa, 279
Estonian National Culture Foundation, Estonia, 93
Eureka Foundation, Bulgaria, 43
European Association for Cancer Research—EACR, UK, 353
European Center for Peace and Development—ECPD, Serbia, 271
European Centre for Social Welfare Policy and Research, Austria, 21
European Federation of National Organisations Working with the Homeless, Belgium, 26
European Institute of Health and Social Welfare, Spain, 296
European NGO Confederation for Relief and Development—CONCORD, Belgium, 26
Eurotransplant International Foundation, Netherlands, 225
Evrika Foundation, Bulgaria, 43
ExxonMobil Foundation, USA, 425
Faith, UK, 353
The Family Federation of Finland, Finland, 98

Fatoumatta Bah-Barrow Foundation—FaBB, Gambia, 117
FDC—Fundação para o Desenvolvimento da Comunidade, Mozambique, 221
FEANTSA—Fédération Européenne des Associations Nationales Travaillant avec les Sans-Abri, Belgium, 26
Fédération Européenne des Associations Nationales Travaillant avec les Sans-Abri—FEANTSA, Belgium, 26
Feed the Children, USA, 425
Feed the Minds, UK, 354
FEMSA Foundation, Mexico, 215
Fernando Rielo Foundation, Spain, 290
Ferrero (Piera, Pietro e Giovanni), Fondazione, Italy, 179
FHI 360, USA, 425
Fibrose Kystique Canada, Canada, 53
FIJI Water Foundation, Fiji, 94
FINCA International, USA, 425
Firelight Foundation, USA, 426
First Nations Development Institute, USA, 426
FirstRand Foundation, South Africa, 280
Flatiron Institute, USA, 472
Florence Gould Foundation, USA, 427
Florence Nightingale International Foundation, Switzerland, 309
Florence Savings Bank Foundation, Italy, 173
Follereau Foundation Luxembourg, Luxembourg, 209
Fondation Africaine pour les Technologies Agricoles, Kenya, 198
Fondation pour l'Agriculture et la Ruralité dans le Monde—Fondation FARM, France, 106
Fondation Auchan, France, 103
Fondation de l'Avenir pour la Recherche Médicale Appliquée, France, 103
Fondation Bettencourt Schueller, France, 103
Fondation BNP Paribas, France, 103
Fondation Boghossian, Belgium, 31
Fondation Casip-Cojasor, France, 104
Fondation Chantal Biya—FCB, Cameroon, 47
Fondation Claude Pompidou, France, 104
Fondation Claudine Talon, Benin, 35
Fondation Congo Assistance, Congo (Republic), 73
Fondation Espace Afrique, Switzerland, 308
Fondation FARM—Fondation pour l'Agriculture et la Ruralité dans le Monde, France, 106
Fondation Follereau Luxembourg—FFL, Luxembourg, 209
Fondation de France, France, 99
Fondation Grand Cœur—FGC, Chad, 64
Fondation Guri Vie Meilleure, Niger, 236
Fondation Internationale Florence Nightingale, Switzerland, 309
Fondation Internationale Tierno et Mariam—FITIMA, Burkina Faso, 44
Fondation ISREC, Switzerland, 309
Fondation J-Louis Lévesque, Canada, 55
Fondation Jacques Chirac, France, 107
Fondation Jean Dausset—Centre d'Etude du Polymorphisme Humain—CEPH, France, 107
Fondation Jean-Paul II pour le Sahel, Burkina Faso, 44
Fondation Joseph Ichame Kamach, Central African Republic, 63
Fondation Louis-Jeantet de Médecine, Switzerland, 107
Fondation Lucie et André Chagnon, Canada, 55
Fondation MACIF, France, 108
Fondation MAIF pour la Recherche, France, 108
Fondation Mapon, Congo (Democratic Republic), 72
Fondation Marcel Bleustein-Blanchet de la Vocation, France, 109
Fondation Mérieux, France, 109
Fondation Mesmin Kabath—FOMEKA, Congo (Republic), 73
Fondation Miloud Chaâbi, Morocco, 220
Fondation Mohammed V pour la Solidarité, Morocco, 220
Fondation MTN Bénin, Benin, 35
Fondation MTN Cameroun, Cameroon, 47
Fondation MTN Côte d'Ivoire, Côte d'Ivoire, 76
Fondation Mutuelles Congolaises d'Epargne et de Crédit—MUCODEC, Congo (Republic), 73
Fondation Nestlé pour l'Etude des Problèmes de l'Alimentation dans le Monde, Switzerland, 310
Fondation Noura, Mauritania, 214
Fondation Orange, France, 110
Fondation Orange Burkina Faso, Burkina Faso, 45
Fondation Orange Cameroun, Cameroon, 47
Fondation Orange-Côte d'Ivoire Télécom—OCIT, Côte d'Ivoire, 76
Fondation Orange Guinée, Guinea, 149

Medicine and health

Fondation Orange Mali, Mali, 213
Fondation Orange Tunisie, Tunisia, 326
Fondation Partage et Vie, France, 110
Fondation Perspectives d'Avenir, Congo (Republic), 73
Fondation Princesse Charlène de Monaco, Monaco, 218
Fondation Princesse Grace, Monaco, 218
Fondation Rawji, Congo (Democratic Republic), 72
Fondation pour la Recherche Médicale, France, 110
Fondation pour la Recherche Stratégique, France, 111
Fondation Roi Baudouin, Belgium, 33
Fondation S, France, 111
Fondation Schneider Electric, France, 111
Fondation Simone et Cino del Duca, France, 111
Fondation Sonatel, Senegal, 270
Fondation Stamm, Burundi, 45
Fondation Suisse pour Recherches Alpines—FSRA, Switzerland, 316
Fondation Tunisie pour le Développement, Tunisia, 326
Fondation Vodacom RDC, Congo (Democratic Republic), 72
Fondatzija Otvoryeno Opshtyestvo Makyedonija, North Macedonia, 239
Fondazione Alessio Pezcoller, Italy, 174
Fondazione AVSI, Italy, 175
Fondazione Cariplo, Italy, 175
Fondazione Cassa di Risparmio di Padova e Rovigo, Italy, 175
Fondazione Cassa di Risparmio di Torino, Italy, 176
Fondazione Cassa di Risparmio di Verona Vicenza Belluno e Ancona—Fondazione Cariverona, Italy, 176
Fondazione Cavaliere del Lavoro Carlo Pesenti, Italy, 176
Fondazione Centro Studi Investimenti Sociali—CENSIS, Italy, 172
Fondazione CIMA—Centro Internazionale in Monitoraggio Ambientale, Italy, 176
Fondazione Compagnia di San Paolo, Italy, 176
Fondazione Giovanni Lorenzini, Italy, 177
Fondazione Internazionale Menarini, Italy, 178
Fondazione Internazionale Premio Balzan, Italy, 181
Fondazione Piera, Pietro e Giovanni Ferrero, Italy, 179
Fondazione Populorum Progressio, Vatican City, 486
Fondazione Roma, Italy, 179
Fondazione Salvatore Maugeri—Clinica del Lavoro e della Riabilitazione, Italy, 180
Fondazione Terzo Pilastro – Internazionale, Italy, 180
Fondazione Vodafone Italia, Italy, 181
Fonds Baillet Latour, Belgium, 32
Fonds Égalité, Canada, 54
Fonds National Suisse de la Recherche Scientifique, Switzerland, 316
Food for the Hungry—FH, USA, 426
Food for the Poor, Inc, USA, 426
For a Healthy Generation, Uzbekistan, 485
Forum LSM Internasional untuk Pembangunan Indonesia, Indonesia, 161
FORWARD—Foundation for Women's Health Research and Development, UK, 354
Fòs Feminista, USA, 427
Foundation for AIDS Research—amfAR, USA, 403
Foundation for Basic Research in Biomedicine, Germany, 122
Foundation for Caribbean Research and Management of Biodiversity, Curaçao, 77
Foundation Centre for the Study of Social Investment, Italy, 172
Foundation of the Future for Applied Medical Research, France, 103
Foundation for International Community Assistance, USA, 425
Foundation for Latin American Economic Research, Argentina, 7
Foundation for Medical Research, France, 110
Foundation Open Society Institute Pakistan, Pakistan, 245
Foundation Open Society Macedonia—FOSIM, North Macedonia, 239
Foundation for Rural & Regional Renewal—FRRR, Australia, 14
Foundation for Strategic Research, France, 111
Foundation for the Welfare of Holocaust Victims, Israel, 169
Foundation for Women's Health, Research and Development—FORWARD, UK, 354

Foundation for World Agriculture and Rural Life, France, 106
The Foundation for Young Australians—FYA, Australia, 14
Foundations' Post-Doc Pool, Finland, 95
Fox (Michael J.) Foundation for Parkinson's Research, USA, 453
Frank Knox Memorial Fellowships, USA, 428
Fraser Institute, Canada, 55
Fraunhofer-Gesellschaft, Germany, 129
Fraunhofer Society, Germany, 129
The Fred Hollows Foundation, Australia, 14
Freedom from Torture (Medical Foundation for the Care of Victims of Torture), UK, 354
Freedom Together Foundation, USA, 428
French Institute of International Relations, France, 113
Friedensdorf International, Germany, 129
Friends-International, Cambodia, 46
Fritz Thyssen Foundation, Germany, 130
Fritz Thyssen Stiftung, Germany, 130
Fulbright Commission Philippines, Philippines, 253
Fund and Endowment Management Foundation, Norway, 240
Fundação ArcelorMittal Brasil, Brazil, 39
Fundação Assistência Médica International—AMI, Portugal, 258
Fundação Calouste Gulbenkian, Portugal, 259
Fundação Champalimaud, Portugal, 259
Fundação Getulio Vargas—FGV, Brazil, 40
Fundação Luso-Americana para o Desenvolvimento—FLAD, Portugal, 260
Fundação Maria Cecilia Souto Vidigal, Brazil, 40
Fundação Oswaldo Cruz—FIOCRUZ, Brazil, 40
Fundació Agrupació AMCI, Spain, 286
Fundación Alzheimer España—FAE, Spain, 288
Fundación Astur, Uruguay, 485
Fundación Bancaria 'la Caixa', Spain, 288
Fundación Banco Bilbao Vizcaya Argentaria—Fundación BBVA, Spain, 289
Fundación Barceló, Spain, 289
Fundación Bariloche, Argentina, 7
Fundación BBVA, Spain, 289
Fundación Bunge y Born, Argentina, 7
Fundación Carlos Slim, Mexico, 215
Fundación Científica de la Asociación Española Contra el Cáncer—AECC, Spain, 290
Fundación Comunitaria de Puerto Rico—FCPR, Puerto Rico, 261
Fundación Corona, Colombia, 71
Fundación Empresas Polar, Venezuela, 487
Fundación Espacio Cívico, Panama, 247
Fundación Felipe González, Spain, 290
Fundación FEMSA, Mexico, 215
Fundación Fernando Rielo, Spain, 290
Fundación Global Democracia y Desarrollo—FUNGLODE, Dominican Republic, 87
Fundación de Investigaciones Económicas Latinoamericanas—FIEL, Argentina, 7
Fundación José Ortega y Gasset—Gregorio Marañón, Spain, 291
Fundación Leo Messi, Spain, 292
Fundación MAPFRE, Spain, 292
Fundación María Francisca de Roviralta, Spain, 292
Fundación Miguel Alemán AC, Mexico, 215
Fundación ONCE, Spain, 293
Fundación Oxfam Intermón, Spain, 293
Fundación Pedro Barrié de la Maza, Spain, 293
Fundación Princesa de Asturias, Spain, 294
Fundación Rafael del Pino, Spain, 294
Fundación Semah-Valencia, Panama, 247
Fundación Teletón México, Mexico, 216
Fundación Telmex Telcel, Mexico, 216
Fundación Tigo, Guatemala, 148
Fundacja Citi Handlowy im. Leopolda Kronenberga, Poland, 255
Fundacja POLSAT, Poland, 256
FUNDAP—Fundación para el Desarrollo, Guatemala, 148
Fundasaun Alola, Timor-Leste, 325
Fundația Orange, Romania, 263
Fundația Orange Moldova, Moldova, 217
Fundația Soros-Moldova, Moldova, 217
Fundația Vodafone România, Romania, 264
FWF—Österreichischer Wissenschaftsfonds, Austria, 21
FWO—Fonds Wetenschappelijk Onderzoek, Belgium, 32
FXB International—Association François-Xavier Bagnoud, Switzerland, 310
Gairdner Foundation, Canada, 55
Gapminder, Sweden, 300
Garfield Weston Foundation, UK, 355
Gates (Bill & Melinda) Foundation, USA, 429
Gates Foundation, USA, 429
The Gatsby Charitable Foundation, UK, 355

INDEX OF MAIN ACTIVITIES

GE Aerospace Foundation, USA, 429
Gemeinnützige Hertie-Stiftung, Germany, 130
George and Thelma Paraskevaides Foundation, Cyprus, 78
German Academic Scholarship Foundation, Germany, 142
German AIDS Foundation, Germany, 124
German Cancer Aid, Germany, 124
German Catholic Bishops' Organization for Development Co-operation, Germany, 137
German Foundation for World Population, Germany, 126
German Institute of Development and Sustainability—IDOS, Germany, 130
German Rheumatism Research Centre Berlin, Germany, 126
Getulio Vargas Foundation, Brazil, 40
Ghazanfar Foundation, Afghanistan, 4
Gift of the Givers Foundation, South Africa, 280
Giovanni Lorenzini Foundation, Italy, 177
Give2Asia, USA, 394
GiveWell—The Clear Fund, USA, 430
Glaser (Elizabeth) Pediatric AIDS Foundation, USA, 423
Global Communities, USA, 431
Global Democracy and Development Foundation, Dominican Republic, 87
Global Fund for Women—GFW, USA, 431
Global Health Council, USA, 395
Global Health Partnerships, UK, 355
Global Impact, USA, 395
Global Innovation Fund, UK, 356
Globetree Association, Sweden, 300
GOAL, Ireland, 166
Goethe-Institut, Germany, 131
Goldsmith (Horace W.) Foundation, USA, 436
Good Neighbors International, Korea (Republic), 201
Good Things Foundation, UK, 356
Good360, USA, 432
Google.org—Google Foundation, USA, 432
Gorbachev Foundation, Russian Federation, 266
Gordon and Betty Moore Foundation, USA, 432
Gould (Florence) Foundation, USA, 427
Graça Machel Trust, South Africa, 280
Graduate Institute of International Studies and Development Studies, Switzerland, 311
Grameen Foundation—GF, USA, 433
Grant (William T.) Foundation, USA, 481
The Grass Foundation, USA, 433
Great Britain Sasakawa Foundation, UK, 356
Great Ormond Street Hospital Children's Charity, UK, 356
Greater Kansas City Community Foundation, USA, 433
Green Umbrella Children's Foundation—ChildFund Korea, Korea (Republic), 201
The Greta Thunberg Foundation, Sweden, 300
Group of Foundations and Businesses, Argentina, 6
Grupo de Fundaciones y Empresas, Argentina, 6
Grupo Social Fondo Ecuatoriano Populorum Progressio, Ecuador, 89
Guggenheim (John Simon) Memorial Foundation, USA, 444
Gulbenkian (Calouste), Fundação, Portugal, 259
Hagar NZ, New Zealand, 233
Haiti Development Institute—HDI, Haiti, 149
HALO Trust, UK, 357
Hamdard Foundation Pakistan, Pakistan, 245
Harp Helú Foundations, Mexico, 216
Harry and Jeanette Weinberg Foundation, Inc, USA, 434
Hartford (John A.) Foundation, Inc, USA, 443
Hasbro Childrens Trust, USA, 434
Hasbro Foundation, USA, 434
Hawaii Resilience Fund, USA, 458
Headley Trust, UK, 357
Health Action International—HAI, Netherlands, 225
The Health Foundation, UK, 357
Health Volunteers Overseas—HVO, USA, 434
Hearst Foundations, USA, 435
Heart & Stroke, Canada, 56
Heart to Heart International—HHI, USA, 435
Hecht (Lotte and John) Memorial Foundation, Canada, 58
Heineken Prizes for Arts and Sciences, Netherlands, 225
Heinekenprijzen voor kunst en wetenschap, Netherlands, 225
HEKS—Hilfswerk der Evangelischen Kirchen Schweiz, Switzerland, 311
Helen Keller International—HKI, USA, 435
Helmholtz Association, Germany, 132
Helmholtz-Gemeinschaft, Germany, 132
Helmsley (Leona M. and Harry B.) Charitable Trust, USA, 447

INDEX OF MAIN ACTIVITIES

Medicine and health

Helmut Horten Foundation, Switzerland, 311
Helmut-Horten-Stiftung, Switzerland, 311
HelpAge International, UK, 357
Henry J. Kaiser Family Foundation—KFF, USA, 435
The Henry Smith Charity, UK, 358
Heren Philanthropic Foundation, China (People's Republic), 68
The Heritage Foundation, USA, 436
Hertie Foundation, Germany, 130
Heungkong Charitable Foundation, China (People's Republic), 68
Hewlett (William and Flora) Foundation, USA, 481
Heydar Aliyev Fondu, Azerbaijan, 23
Heydar Aliyev Foundation, Azerbaijan, 23
HIAS—Hebrew Immigrant Aid Society, USA, 436
Higgins (Terrence) Trust, UK, 385
Higherlife Foundation, Zimbabwe, 491
Hilton (Conrad N.) Foundation, USA, 417
Hinduja Foundation, India, 157
Hitachi Foundation, Japan, 187
HJ Foundation, Congo (Democratic Republic), 72
Hjärt-Lungfonden, Sweden, 300
Hodge Foundation, UK, 358
Hollows (Fred) Foundation, Australia, 14
Holt International, USA, 436
Hong Kong Society for the Blind, Hong Kong, 151
Hope, Ireland, 165
HOPE International Development Agency, Canada, 56
Hopp (Dietmar) Stiftung, Germany, 126
Horace W. Goldsmith Foundation, USA, 436
Horizons of Friendship, Canada, 56
Hormuud Salaam Foundation, Somalia, 277
Horten (Helmut) Stiftung, Switzerland, 311
The Howard G. Buffett Foundation, USA, 437
Howard Hughes Medical Institute—HHMI, USA, 437
Howard Karagheusian Commemorative Corporation—HKCC, USA, 437
Howard (Katharine) Foundation, Ireland, 167
Hudson Institute, USA, 437
Human Resource Development Foundation, Türkiye, 329
Human Rights Foundation of Turkey, Türkiye, 330
Human Rights Watch—HRW, USA, 437
Humanitarian Coalition, Canada, 48
Humanity & Inclusion, France, 113
IACD—Institute of Asian Culture and Development, Korea (Republic), 201
Ian Potter Foundation, Australia, 14
IARC—International Agency for Research on Cancer, France, 101
IBM International Foundation, USA, 438
ICRC—International Red Cross and Red Crescent Movement, Switzerland, 312
The Ideas Institute, Kenya, 199
IDLO—International Development Law Organization, Italy, 181
IDRF—International Development and Relief Foundation, Canada, 56
IFRISSE Burkina, Burkina Faso, 45
IHH Humanitarian Relief Foundation, Türkiye, 328
İKGV—İnsan Kaynağını Geliştirme Vakfı, Türkiye, 329
Îles de Paix, Belgium, 32
Imbuto Foundation, Rwanda, 268
India Partners, USA, 438
Indian Council of Social Science Research—ICSSR, India, 157
Information and Education Centre for the Prevention of Drug Abuse, Peru, 248
İnsan Hak ve Hürriyetleri İnsani Yardım Vakfı—IHH, Türkiye, 328
İnsan Kaynağını Geliştirme Vakfı—İKGV, Türkiye, 329
Institut Français des Relations Internationales—IFRI, France, 113
Institut de Hautes Études Internationales et du Développement—IHEID, Switzerland, 311
Institut de Médecine et d'Épidémiologie Appliquée—Fondation Internationale Léon Mba, France, 114
Institut for Menneskerettigheder, Denmark, 84
Institut Pasteur, France, 114
Institut Pasteur de Lille, France, 114
Institut für Weltwirtschaft—IfW Kiel, Germany, 132
Institute of Applied Medicine and Epidemiology—International Foundation Léon Mba, France, 114
Institute of Asian Culture and Development—IACD, Korea (Republic), 201
Institute of Economic Affairs—IEA, UK, 359
Institute for Precision Cardiovascular Medicine, USA, 401

Institute for Scientific Interchange Foundation—ISI, Italy, 181
Institute for Sustainable Communities—ISC, USA, 439
Instituto Europeo de Salud y Bienestar Social, Spain, 296
INTEGRATA Foundation, Germany, 132
INTEGRATA—Stiftung für Humane Nutzung der Informationstechnologie, Germany, 132
Inter Pares, Canada, 57
InterAction, USA, 395
Interchurch Aid—HIA Hungary, Hungary, 153
International Agency for Research on Cancer—IARC, France, 101
International Balzan Prize Foundation, Italy, 181
International Blue Crescent Relief and Development Foundation—IBC, Türkiye, 329
International Charitable Fund 'Concord 3000', Ukraine, 333
International College of Surgeons—ICS, USA, 440
International Co-operation, Italy, 173
International Development Law Organization—IDLO, Italy, 181
International Development and Relief Foundation—IDRF, Canada, 56
International Education Research Foundation, Inc—IERF, USA, 440
International Eye Foundation—IEF, USA, 440
The International Foundation, USA, 440
International Foundation for Socio-economic and Political Studies, Russian Federation, 266
International Medical Assistance Foundation, Portugal, 258
International NGO Forum on Indonesian Development—INFID, Indonesia, 161
International Organization for Relief, Welfare & Development—IORWD, Saudi Arabia, 269
International Orthodox Christian Charities—IOCC, USA, 441
International Planned Parenthood Federation—IPPF, UK, 360
International Red Cross and Red Crescent Movement—ICRC, Switzerland, 312
International Relief Teams—IRT, USA, 441
International Renaissance Foundation—IRF, Ukraine, 333
International Rescue Committee—IRC, USA, 441
International Women's Health Coalition, USA, 427
Internationale Stiftung Preis E. Balzan-Fonds, Italy, 181
INTERSOS, Italy, 182
IOCC—International Orthodox Christian Charities, USA, 441
iPartner India, India, 155
IPPF—International Planned Parenthood Federation, UK, 360
IRC—International Rescue Committee, USA, 441
Isabel Allende Foundation, USA, 442
Islamic Relief Worldwide, UK, 360
Islands of Peace, Belgium, 32
IsraAID, Israel, 169
The Israel Democracy Institute—IDI, Israel, 170
ISREC Foundation, Switzerland, 309
Istituto di Ricerche Farmacologiche Mario Negri, Italy, 182
Izumi Foundation, USA, 442
J. F. Kapnek Zimbabwe, Zimbabwe, 491
J-Louis Lévesque Foundation, Canada, 55
J. R. McKenzie Trust, New Zealand, 233
Jacques Chirac Foundation, France, 107
J'ai Rêvé Foundation, Central African Republic, 63
James S. McDonnell Foundation, USA, 443
Jane Coffin Childs Memorial Fund for Medical Research—JCC Fund, USA, 443
Japan Heart Foundation, Japan, 190
Japanese-German Centre Berlin, Germany, 133
Japanisch-Deutsches Zentrum Berlin, Germany, 133
Jean Dausset Foundation—Centre for the Study of Human Polymorphism, France, 107
Jeans for Genes, Australia, 13
JEN, Japan, 190
Jenny and Antti Wihuri Foundation, Finland, 96
Jenny ja Antti Wihurin Rahasto, Finland, 96
JN Foundation, Jamaica, 184
JNF UK—JNF Charitable Trust, UK, 361
The John A. Hartford Foundation—JAHF, USA, 443
John Moores Foundation, UK, 362
John Paul II Foundation for the Sahel, Burkina Faso, 44

John Simon Guggenheim Memorial Foundation, USA, 444
Johnson & Johnson Foundation US—JJF, USA, 444
Johnson (Stanley Thomas) Foundation, Switzerland, 317
JOHUD—Jordanian Hashemite Fund for Human Development, Jordan, 196
José Ortega y Gasset – Gregorio Marañón Foundation, Spain, 291
Joseph Levy Foundation, UK, 362
Joseph Patrick Trust, UK, 369
Joseph Tanenbaum Charitable Foundation, Canada, 58
Josiah Macy Jr Foundation, USA, 445
Joyce Banda Foundation International, Malawi, 210
JPB Foundation, USA, 428
Jung (C. G.) Institut Zürich, Switzerland, 307
Jusélius (Sigrid) Stiftelse, Finland, 97
Juvenile Diabetes Research Foundation International, USA, 409
Kade (Max) Foundation, Inc, USA, 451
KAF—Kataliko Actions for Africa, Congo (Democratic Republic), 72
Kafaa Development Foundation, Libya, 207
Kaiser (Henry J.) Family Foundation, USA, 435
Kapnek (J. F.) Charitable Trust Zimbabwe, Zimbabwe, 491
Karagheusian (Howard) Commemorative Corporation, USA, 437
Karuna Trust, UK, 363
Katharine Howard Foundation—KHF, Ireland, 167
KDDI Foundation, Japan, 191
Keller (Helen) International, USA, 435
Kellogg (W. K.) Foundation, USA, 478
Khalifa Bin Zayed Al Nahyan Foundation, United Arab Emirates, 334
Kiel Institute for the World Economy, Germany, 132
Kind Heart Foundation, Viet Nam, 488
King Baudouin Foundation, Belgium, 33
King Faisal Foundation, Saudi Arabia, 269
King Hussein Foundation—KHF, Jordan, 196
King Philanthropies, USA, 445
The King's Fund, UK, 363
Kiwanis Children's Fund, USA, 446
Knox (Frank) Memorial Fellowships, USA, 428
Knut and Alice Wallenberg Foundation, Sweden, 301
Knut och Alice Wallenbergs Stiftelse, Sweden, 301
Koç (Vehbi) Vakfı, Türkiye, 331
Kokkalis Foundation, Greece, 146
Komen (Susan G.) Breast Cancer Foundation, USA, 474
Koning Boudewijnstichting/Fondation Roi Baudouin, Belgium, 33
Kresge Foundation, USA, 446
Kronenberg (Leopold) Foundation, Poland, 255
Kröner-Fresenius (Else) Stiftung, Germany, 127
Krupp von Bohlen und Halbach (Alfried) Stiftung, Germany, 121
Kuok Foundation Berhad, Malaysia, 211
Kusuma Trust UK, UK, 363
Kuwait Awqaf Public Foundation, Kuwait, 203
Kuwait Foundation for the Advancement of Sciences—KFAS, Kuwait, 203
Kuwait Institute for Scientific Research—KISR, Kuwait, 203
Kvinna till Kvinna, Sweden, 301
KWF Dutch Cancer Society, Netherlands, 227
KWF Kankerbestrijding, Netherlands, 227
'La Caixa' Banking Foundation, Spain, 288
Lady Davis Fellowship Trust, Israel, 170
Laing Family Trusts, UK, 364
LAPAS—Latvijas platforma attīstības sadarbībai, Latvia, 204
Latin American and Caribbean Women's Health Network—LACWHN, Ecuador, 89
Latter-day Saint Charities—LDSC, USA, 447
Latvia Children's Fund, Latvia, 204
Latvian Platform for Development Cooperation, Latvia, 204
Latvijas Bērnu fonds, Latvia, 204
Laureus Sport for Good, UK, 364
The Lawson Foundation, Canada, 58
League of Corporate Foundations—LCF, Philippines, 250
Legatum Foundation, United Arab Emirates, 334
Leibniz Association, Germany, 135
Leibniz Gemeinschaft, Germany, 135
Leo Messi Foundation, Spain, 292
The Leona M. and Harry B. Helmsley Charitable Trust, USA, 447
Leonard Cheshire Disability, UK, 364
The Leprosy Mission International, UK, 364

Medicine and health

Lesotho Council of Non-Governmental Organisations, Lesotho, 207
Leventis (A. G.) Foundation, Greece, 144
Leventis (A. G.) Foundation Nigeria, Nigeria, 237
Levesque (Jean-Louis), Fondation, Canada, 55
Levi Strauss Foundation, USA, 448
Levy (Joseph) Foundation, UK, 362
Li Ka Shing Foundation, Hong Kong, 151
Lien Foundation, Singapore, 273
Lietuvos vaikų fondas, Lithuania, 209
LifeArc—MRC Technology, UK, 365
Lifewater International, USA, 479
Liliane Foundation, Netherlands, 229
Limmat Foundation, Switzerland, 314
Limmat Stiftung, Switzerland, 314
Linbury Trust, UK, 365
Lithuanian Children's Fund, Lithuania, 209
Liver Canada, Canada, 58
Livestrong Foundation, USA, 448
Lorenzini (Giovanni), Fondazione, Italy, 177
The Lotte and John Hecht Memorial Foundation, Canada, 58
Louis-Jeantet Foundation for Medicine, Switzerland, 310
Lucie et André Chagnon Foundation, Canada, 55
Ludwig Boltzmann Gesellschaft, Austria, 21
Ludwig Cancer Research, USA, 449
Lullaby Trust, UK, 366
Lumos Foundation, UK, 366
Lundbeck Foundation, Denmark, 85
Lundbeckfonden, Denmark, 85
Luso-American Development Foundation, Portugal, 260
McConnell Clark (Edna) Foundation, USA, 422
Macdonald Stewart Foundation, Canada, 59
McDonnell (James S.) Foundation, USA, 443
Machel (Graça) Trust, South Africa, 280
MACIF Foundation, France, 108
McKenzie (J. R.) Trust, New Zealand, 233
The Mackintosh Foundation, UK, 366
McKnight Foundation, USA, 449
The McLean Foundation, Canada, 59
Macmillan Cancer Support, UK, 366
Macy (Josiah), Jr Foundation, USA, 445
MADRE, USA, 450
MAIF Foundation for Research, France, 108
Mandela (Nelson) Children's Fund, South Africa, 281
Mansour Foundation for Development—MFD, Egypt, 90
MAP International—Medical Assistance Programs, USA, 450
MAPFRE Foundation, Spain, 292
Marcel Bleustein-Blanchet Vocational Foundation, France, 109
March of Dimes Foundation, USA, 450
Margaret A. Cargill Philanthropies—MACP, USA, 450
Maria Cecilia Souto Vidigal Foundation, Brazil, 40
María Francisca de Roviralta Foundation, Spain, 292
Marie Curie, UK, 366
Mario Negri Pharmacological Research Institute, Italy, 182
Markle Foundation, USA, 451
Masason Foundation, Japan, 191
Maugeri (Salvatore), Fondazione, Italy, 180
Mauritius Telecom Foundation—MTF, Mauritius, 214
Mawazo Institute, Kenya, 199
Max Bell Foundation, Canada, 59
The Max Foundation, USA, 451
Max Kade Foundation, Inc, USA, 451
Max-Planck-Gesellschaft zur Förderung der Wissenschaften eV, Germany, 135
Max Planck Society for the Advancement of Science, Germany, 135
MDA—Muscular Dystrophy Association, USA, 451
Médecins du Monde International, France, 114
Médecins Sans Frontières International—MSF International, Switzerland, 314
medica mondiale eV, Germany, 136
Medical Aid for Palestinians—MAP, UK, 367
Medico International, Germany, 136
Mellon (Richard King) Foundation, USA, 467
Menarini International Foundation, Italy, 178
Mental Health Foundation, UK, 367
Mercatus Center, USA, 451
Merchant Navy Fund, UK, 382
Mercury Phoenix Trust, UK, 367
Mercy, Ireland, 168
Mercy Corps, USA, 452
Mercy-USA for Aid and Development, USA, 452
Mérieux Foundation, France, 109
M'essh al Sudan, Sudan, 297
Messi (Leo), Fundación, Spain, 292

Michael & Susan Dell Foundation, USA, 453
Michael J. Fox Foundation for Parkinson's Research—MJFF, USA, 453
Miguel Alemán Foundation, Mexico, 215
Milbank Memorial Fund, USA, 453
Miloud Chaâbi Foundation, Morocco, 220
Minhaj Welfare Foundation, UK, 368
Minority Rights Group International—MRG, UK, 368
MISEREOR—Bischöfliches Hilfswerk Misereor eV, Germany, 137
Mith Samlanh, Cambodia, 46
Mo Dewji Foundation, Tanzania, 323
Moawad (René) Foundation, Lebanon, 206
Mohamed Shafik Gabr Foundation for Social Development, Egypt, 90
Mohammed bin Rashid Al Maktoum Global Initiatives—MBRGI, United Arab Emirates, 335
Møller (A.P.) and Chastine Mc-Kinney Møller Foundation, Denmark, 82
Molson Foundation, Canada, 59
Monell (Ambrose) Foundation, USA, 399
Moore (Gordon and Betty) Foundation, USA, 432
Moores (John) Foundation, UK, 362
Morgan Stanley Foundation, USA, 453
Morningside Foundation, USA, 454
Motsepe Foundation, South Africa, 281
Mouvement International ATD Quart-Monde, France, 115
M-PESA Foundation, Kenya, 199
Ms. Foundation for Women, USA, 454
MS Society—Multiple Sclerosis Society of Great Britain and Northern Ireland, UK, 368
MSF International—Médecins Sans Frontières International, Switzerland, 314
MSI Reproductive Choices, UK, 369
MTN Afghanistan Foundation, Afghanistan, 4
MTN Cameroon Foundation, Cameroon, 47
MTN Côte d'Ivoire Foundation, Côte d'Ivoire, 76
MTN Foundation Benin, Benin, 35
MTN Nigeria Foundation, Nigeria, 237
MTN SA Foundation, South Africa, 281
MTN Uganda Foundation, Uganda, 332
Multiple Sclerosis Society of Great Britain and Northern Ireland, UK, 368
Munich Re Foundation/Münchener Rück Stiftung, Germany, 137
Murdoch Children's Research Institute—MCRI, Australia, 15
Muscular Dystrophy UK, UK, 369
Musk Foundation, USA, 454
Muslim Aid, UK, 369
Mutual Aid and Liaison Service, France, 116
Myanmar/Burma Schools Project Foundation, Canada, 60
Nadace Charty 77, Czech Republic, 80
Nadace Preciosa, Czech Republic, 80
Nadácia SPP, Slovakia, 275
Naito Foundation, Japan, 191
Naspa Foundation, Germany, 137
Naspa Stiftung, Germany, 137
National Community Foundation, Saint Lucia, 268
National Emergencies Trust, UK, 369
National Endowment for Science, Technology and the Arts—Nesta, UK, 370
National Heart Foundation of Australia, Australia, 15
National Heart Foundation of New Zealand, New Zealand, 233
National Kidney Foundation—NKF, USA, 455
The National Lottery Community Fund, UK, 370
Nederlandse Organisatie voor Internationale Ontwikkelingssamenwerking—Stichting NOVIB, Netherlands, 228
Negri (Mario), Istituto di Ricerche Farmacologiche, Italy, 182
Nelson Mandela Children's Fund, South Africa, 281
Nesta—National Endowment for Science, Technology and the Arts, UK, 370
Nestlé Foundation for the Study of the Problems of Nutrition in the World, Switzerland, 310
Network of Foundations Working for Development—netFWD, France, 99
Network for Human Development, Brazil, 41
Network for Social Change Charitable Trust—NSCCT, UK, 370
New Economics Foundation—NEF, UK, 371
New World Foundation—NWF, USA, 456
The New York Community Trust—NYCT, USA, 457
NFCR—National Foundation for Cancer Research, USA, 457
NFI—National Foundation for India, India, 159
NHS Charities Together, UK, 371
Niarchos (Stavros) Foundation, Greece, 147

Nightingale (Florence), Fondation Internationale, Switzerland, 309
Ningxia Yanbao Charity Foundation, China (People's Republic), 69
The Nippon Foundation, Japan, 192
Nobel Foundation, Sweden, 301
Nobelstiftelsen, Sweden, 301
Norwegian Refugee Council—NRC, Norway, 242
Nott (David) Foundation, UK, 350
Novartis Foundation, Switzerland, 314
Novartis Foundation for Therapeutic Research, Germany, 137
Novartis-Stiftung für therapeutische Forschung, Germany, 137
Novartis US Foundation, USA, 457
NOVIB (Oxfam Netherlands), Netherlands, 228
Novo Nordisk Fonden, Denmark, 85
Novo Nordisk Foundation, Denmark, 85
NYCT—The New York Community Trust, USA, 457
Oak Foundation, Switzerland, 315
The Ocean Cleanup Foundation, Netherlands, 230
Offor (Sir Emeka) Foundation, Nigeria, 238
Oil Search Foundation, Papua New Guinea, 247
Ökumenikus Segélyszervezet, Hungary, 153
Olav Thon Foundation, Norway, 242
Olav Thon Stiftelsen, Norway, 242
Oman LNG Development Foundation—ODF, Oman, 244
Omidyar Group, USA, 458
Onassis (Alexander S.) Public Benefit Foundation, Liechtenstein, 207
ONCE—Spanish National Organization for the Blind—Foundation, Spain, 293
One Economy Foundation, Namibia, 222
One Foundation, China (People's Republic), 69
OPALS—Organisation Panafricaine de Lutte pour la Santé, France, 115
Open Society Action Fund, USA, 458
Open Society Foundation—London, UK, 372
Open Society Foundation South Africa—OSF-SA, South Africa, 282
Open Society Foundations, USA, 459
Open Society Foundations—Armenia, Armenia, 9
Open Society Foundations in Pakistan, Pakistan, 245
Open Society Initiative for Southern Africa—OSISA, South Africa, 282
Open Society Policy Center, USA, 458
Operation Eyesight Universal/Action Universelle de la Vue, Canada, 60
Operation USA, USA, 459
Oppenheimer Generations Foundation, South Africa, 282
Orange Foundation, Romania, 263
Orange Foundation Cameroon, Cameroon, 47
Orange Foundation Guinea, Guinea, 149
Orange Foundation Tunisia, Tunisia, 326
Orange Moldova Foundation, Moldova, 217
Orange Solidarité Madagascar, Madagascar, 210
Orbis Charitable Trust, UK, 372
Orentreich Foundation for the Advancement of Science, Inc—OFAS, USA, 459
Organisation Internationale de Droit du Développement—OIDD, Italy, 181
Organisation Panafricaine de Lutte pour la Santé—OPALS, France, 115
Organization for Social Science Research in Eastern and Southern Africa—OSSREA, Ethiopia, 94
Orji Uzor Kalu Foundation, Nigeria, 238
Ortega y Gasset (José), Fundación, Spain, 291
Osaka Community Foundation, Japan, 192
Österreichischer Wissenschaftsfonds—FWF, Austria, 21
Oswaldo Cruz Foundation, Brazil, 40
Outreach International, USA, 459
Oxfam America, USA, 460
Oxfam Australia, Australia, 16
Oxfam Canada, Canada, 60
Oxfam Deutschland eV, Germany, 138
Oxfam France, France, 115
Oxfam GB, UK, 372
Oxfam India, India, 159
Oxfam International, Kenya, 200
Oxfam Ireland, Ireland, 167
Oxfam Mexico, Mexico, 216
Oxfam NOVIB—Nederlandse Organisatie voor Internationale Ontwikkelingssamenwerking, Netherlands, 228
Oxfam NOVIB—Netherlands Organization for International Development Co-operation, Netherlands, 228
Oxfam-Québec, Canada, 60
Oxfam-Solidariteit/Solidarité, Belgium, 33
Paavo Nurmen Säätiö, Finland, 97

INDEX OF MAIN ACTIVITIES

Medicine and health

Paavo Nurmi Foundation, Finland, 97
Pacific Leprosy Foundation, New Zealand, 234
Pacific Peoples' Partnership, Canada, 61
Packard (David and Lucile) Foundation, USA, 420
Pact, USA, 460
PAI—Population Action International, USA, 460
Pan-African Organization for Health, France, 115
PAN Europe—Pesticide Action Network Europe, Belgium, 34
PAN UK—Pesticide Action Network UK, UK, 373
Pancare Foundation, Australia, 16
PANNA—Pesticide Action Network North America, USA, 462
PANZI Foundation, USA, 461
Paraskevaides (George and Thelma) Foundation, Cyprus, 78
Parasol Foundation Trust, Gibraltar, 144
Parkinson's Foundation, USA, 461
Partage, France, 116
Partners for Equity, Australia, 16
Partners in Health, USA, 461
Pasteur Institute, France, 114
Pasteur Institute of Lille, France, 114
PATH, USA, 461
Pathfinder International, USA, 461
Patterson (Alicia) Foundation, USA, 398
The Paul G. Allen Family Foundation, USA, 462
The Paul Ramsay Foundation, Australia, 16
Paulo Foundation, Finland, 97
Paulon Säätiö, Finland, 97
PCI Media Impact, USA, 467
PCI—Project Concern International, USA, 431
Peace, Health and Human Development Foundation—PHD Foundation, Japan, 193
Peace Village International, Germany, 129
Peace Winds Japan—PWJ, Japan, 192
Pearl S. Buck International, USA, 462
Pedro Barrié de la Maza Foundation, Spain, 293
PepsiCo Foundation, Inc, USA, 462
Perdana Global Peace Foundation—PGPF, Malaysia, 211
Peres Center for Peace and Innovation, Israel, 171
Perpetual Foundation, Australia, 16
Pesticide Action Network Europe—PAN Europe, Belgium, 34
Pesticide Action Network Latin America and the Caribbean, Chile, 65
Pesticide Action Network North America—PANNA, USA, 462
Pesticide Action Network UK—PAN UK, UK, 373
The Pew Charitable Trusts, USA, 462
Pezcoller (Alessio), Fondazione, Italy, 174
Pfizer Foundation, USA, 462
The PHD Foundation—Peace, Health and Human Development Foundation, Japan, 193
Philanthropikó Ídryma Stélios Chatzeioánnou stēn Kýpro, Cyprus, 78
Philippine-American Educational Foundation—PAEF, Philippines, 253
Philippine Business for Social Progress—PBSP, Philippines, 250
PHR—Physicians for Human Rights, USA, 463
Physicians for Human Rights—PHR, USA, 463
Piera, Pietro and Giovanni Ferrero Foundation, Italy, 179
Pinchuk (Victor) Foundation, Ukraine, 333
Plan International Ireland, Ireland, 167
PLAN International—PI, UK, 374
Planck (Max) Gesellschaft zur Förderung der Wissenschaften eV, Germany, 135
Platform for Development Cooperation and Humanitarian Aid, Slovenia, 276
POLSAT Foundation, Poland, 256
Pompidou (Claude), Fondation, France, 104
Population Action International—PAI, USA, 460
Population Council, USA, 463
Populorum Progressio Foundation, Vatican City, 486
Potter (Ian) Foundation, Australia, 14
Pratt Foundation, Australia, 17
Preciosa Foundation, Czech Republic, 80
Première Urgence Internationale, France, 116
Premji (Azim) Foundation, India, 156
Presbyterian World Service & Development—PWS&D, Canada, 61
Princess of Asturias Foundation, Spain, 294
Princess Charlene of Monaco Foundation, Monaco, 218
Pro Juventute, Switzerland, 315
Pro Mujer International, USA, 464
Pro Women International, USA, 464
Project HOPE, USA, 464
Prudence Foundation, Hong Kong, 151
Public Health Foundation of India—PHFI, India, 159
Public Studies Centre, Chile, 64

Puerto Rico Community Foundation, Puerto Rico, 261
PwC Charitable Foundation, USA, 465
Qatar Foundation, Qatar, 262
Quỹ Thiện Tâm, Viet Nam, 488
Queen Rania Foundation—QRF, Jordan, 196
R. Howard Webster Foundation/Fondation R. Howard Webster, Canada, 61
Radiation Effects Research Foundation—RERF, Japan, 193
Rafael del Pino Foundation, Spain, 294
Rafto Foundation for Human Rights, Norway, 243
Raftostiftelsen for menneskerettigheter, Norway, 243
Rajiv Gandhi Foundation, India, 160
Ramaciotti Foundations, Australia, 17
Ramsay (Paul) Foundation, Australia, 16
RAND Corporation, USA, 465
Rebecca Akufo-Addo Foundation—Rebecca Foundation, Ghana, 144
Red de Acción en Plaguicidas y sus Alternativas de América Latina—RAP-AL, Chile, 65
Red Feather, Japan, 185
Red de Salud de las Mujeres Latinoamericanas y del Caribe—RSMLAC, Ecuador, 89
REDEH—Rede de Desenvolvimento Humano, Brazil, 41
Reeve (Christopher and Dana) Foundation, USA, 415
Refugee Foundation, Netherlands, 231
Refugees International—RI, USA, 466
Rehabilitation for the Disabled—ELEPAP, Greece, 145
Rehabilitation International—RI, USA, 466
Reliance Foundation, India, 160
Relief International, USA, 466
René Moawad Foundation—RMF, Lebanon, 206
The Resource Foundation—TRF, USA, 467
Reumatikerförbundet, Sweden, 302
Rhodes Trust, UK, 376
RIA—Royal Irish Academy, Ireland, 167
Richard King Mellon Foundation, USA, 467
Rielo (Fernando), Fundación, Spain, 290
Right Livelihood Award Foundation, Sweden, 302
Rising Impact, USA, 467
RNIB Charity, UK, 378
Robert Bosch Foundation, Germany, 138
Robert-Bosch-Stiftung GmbH, Germany, 138
Robert Wood Johnson Foundation—RWJF, USA, 467
The Robertson Trust, UK, 376
Rockefeller Foundation, USA, 468
Rogosin Institute, USA, 468
Rome Foundation, Italy, 179
Rosetta Foundation, USA, 416
The Rotary Foundation, USA, 468
Rothschild (Edmond de) Foundations, Switzerland, 308
Roviralta (María Francisca de), Fundación, Spain, 292
Royal Air Force Benevolent Fund, UK, 377
Royal Anthropological Institute of Great Britain and Ireland—RAI, UK, 377
The Royal Australasian College of Physicians—RACP, Australia, 17
Royal British Legion, UK, 377
Royal Flying Doctor Service of Australia—RFDS, Australia, 17
The Royal Foundation of the Prince and Princess of Wales, UK, 378
Royal National Institute of Blind People—RNIB, UK, 378
The Royal Society, UK, 379
The Royal Society of Medicine—RSM, UK, 379
RSA—Royal Society for the Encouragement of Arts, Manufactures and Commerce, UK, 379
Runyon (Damon) Cancer Research Foundation, USA, 419
Ruparelia Foundation, Uganda, 332
Rutgers, Netherlands, 228
Säätiöiden post doc-poolin, Finland, 95
Sabanci Vakfi—Haci Omer Sabanci Foundation, Türkiye, 329
Safaricom Foundation, Kenya, 200
Sahabdeen (A. M. M.) Trust Foundation, Sri Lanka, 297
Saïd Foundation, UK, 380
Sainsbury Family Charitable Trusts, UK, 380
Sakena Fund, USA, 469
The Salvation Army International Trust, UK, 381
Salvatore Maugeri Foundation—Occupational Health and Rehabilitation Clinic, Italy, 180
Salzburg Global Seminar, Austria, 22
Samaritan's Purse, USA, 469
Samsung Foundation, Korea (Republic), 202
The San Diego Foundation, USA, 470
Sandals Foundation, Jamaica, 184
Sander (Wilhelm) Stiftung, Germany, 143

Santé Sud, France, 116
Santos Foundation, Papua New Guinea, 247
Sasakawa Health Foundation—SHF, Japan, 194
Save the Children International, UK, 381
Save the Children (UK), UK, 381
Sawiris Foundation for Social Development—SFSD, Egypt, 90
Schering (Ernst) Stiftung, Germany, 127
Schneider Electric Foundation, France, 111
Schusterman (Charles and Lynn) Family Foundation, USA, 413
Schwab Foundation for Social Entrepreneurship, Switzerland, 316
Schweizerische Akademie der Medizinischen Wissenschaften, Switzerland, 316
Schweizerische Herzstiftung, Switzerland, 316
Schweizerische Stiftung für Alpine Forschungen—SSAF, Switzerland, 316
Schweizerischer Nationalfonds zur Förderung der Wissenschaftlichen Forschung/Fonds National Suisse de la Recherche Scientifique—SNF, Switzerland, 316
Scientific Foundation of the Spanish Cancer Association, Spain, 290
Scientific Research Foundation, Belgium, 32
Scope, UK, 381
The Seafarers' Charity, UK, 382
Seafarers International Relief Fund, UK, 382
Secours Catholique—Caritas de France, France, 116
Secours Dentaire International, Switzerland, 317
SEL—Service d'Entraide et de Liaison, France, 116
Self-Sufficient People Foundation, Indonesia, 163
SEND-West Africa, Ghana, 144
Sentebale, UK, 382
Sesame Workshop, USA, 471
Seva Foundation, USA, 471
Sexual Wellbeing Aotearoa, New Zealand, 235
Shafik Gabr (Mohamed) Foundation, Egypt, 90
Shahid Afridi Foundation—SAF, Pakistan, 246
Shanghai Soong Ching Ling Foundation, China (People's Republic), 69
Sharing and Life Foundation, France, 110
Sherman (Archie) Charitable Trust, UK, 340
Shoman (Abdul Hameed) Foundation, Jordan, 195
SickKids Foundation, Canada, 62
SID—Society for International Development, Italy, 183
Sightsavers International, UK, 382
Signe and Ane Gyllenberg Foundation, Finland, 97
Signe och Ane Gyllenbergs stiftelse, Finland, 97
Sigrid Juséliuksen Säätiö, Finland, 97
Sigrid Jusélius Foundation, Finland, 97
Sihtasutus Eesti Rahvuskultuuri Fond, Estonia, 93
Silicon Valley Community Foundation—SVCF, USA, 471
Simone and Cino del Duca Foundation, France, 111
Simons Foundation, USA, 472
Singapore International Foundation—SIF, Singapore, 273
SIPRI—Stockholm International Peace Research Institute, Sweden, 304
Sir Ahmadu Bello Memorial Foundation, Nigeria, 238
Sir Emeka Offor Foundation, Nigeria, 238
Sir Halley Stewart Trust, UK, 383
The Sir Jules Thorn Charitable Trust, UK, 383
Skoll Foundation, USA, 472
Slim (Carlos), Fundación, Mexico, 215
Sloan (Alfred P.) Foundation, USA, 398
SLOGA—Platforma za Razvojno Sodelovanje in Humanitarno Pomoč, Slovenia, 276
Slovak Humanitarian Council, Slovakia, 274
Slovenská Humanitná Rada, Slovakia, 274
Smallwood Trust, UK, 384
Smith (Henry) Charity, UK, 358
Smithsonian Institution, USA, 472
The Sobell Foundation, UK, 384
Society for International Development—SID, Italy, 183
Software AG Foundation, Germany, 139
Software AG Stiftung, Germany, 139
Sog'lom Avlod Uchun, Uzbekistan, 485
Somalia NGO Consortium, Somalia, 277
Sorenson Legacy Foundation, USA, 473
Soros Foundation—Kazakhstan, Kazakhstan, 197
Soros Foundation—Moldova, Moldova, 217
Souter Charitable Trust, UK, 384
South African Institute of Race Relations—IRR, South Africa, 283
South West International Development Network—SWIDN, UK, 337
Southern Health, France, 116

Science and technology

Souto Vidigal (Maria Cecilia), Fundação, Brazil, 40
Sphere, Switzerland, 305
Spinal Research, UK, 384
SpinalCure Australia, Australia, 18
SPP Foundation, Slovakia, 275
St John Ambulance, UK, 380
Stanley Thomas Johnson Foundation, Switzerland, 317
The Starr Foundation, USA, 473
Start Network, UK, 337
Stavros Niarchos Foundation—SNF, Greece, 147
Stelios Philanthropic Foundation, Cyprus, 78
Stewardship Foundation, USA, 473
Stewart (Sir Halley) Trust, UK, 383
Stichting Diorapthe, Netherlands, 229
Stichting Fonds 1818, Netherlands, 229
Stichting Liliane Fonds, Netherlands, 229
Stichting The Ocean Cleanup, Netherlands, 230
Stichting Triodos Foundation, Netherlands, 231
Stichting Vluchteling, Netherlands, 231
Stiftelsen Dam, Norway, 243
Stiftelsen Gapminder, Sweden, 300
Stiftung Kinder in Afrika, Germany, 140
Stiftung Vivamos Mejor, Switzerland, 317
Stockholm International Peace Research Institute—SIPRI, Sweden, 304
Streisand (Barbra) Foundation, USA, 408
Stroke Association, UK, 384
Studienstiftung des deutschen Volkes, Germany, 142
Sudan Foundation, Sudan, 297
Sudd Institute, South Sudan, 285
Sulaiman Bin Abdul Aziz Bin Saleh Al Rajhi Foundation, Saudi Arabia, 269
Sultan bin Abdulaziz Al Sa'ud Foundation, Saudi Arabia, 270
SUN Civil Society Network, UK, 381
Susan G. Komen Breast Cancer Foundation, USA, 474
The Susan Thompson Buffett Foundation—STBF, USA, 474
Sutherland Self Help Trust, New Zealand, 235
Sweden-Japan Foundation—SJF, Sweden, 304
Swedish Cancer Society, Sweden, 298
The Swedish Heart-Lung Foundation, Sweden, 300
Swedish Rheumatism Association, Sweden, 302
Swiss Academy of Medical Sciences, Switzerland, 316
Swiss Church Aid, Switzerland, 311
Swiss Foundation for Alpine Research—SFAR, Switzerland, 316
Swiss Heart Foundation, Switzerland, 316
Swiss National Science Foundation—SNSF, Switzerland, 316
Sylvia and Charles Viertel Charitable Foundation, Australia, 18
Synergos—The Synergos Institute, USA, 396
Syria Al-Gad Relief Foundation, Egypt, 91
Tahir Foundation, Indonesia, 162
Talon (Claudine), Fondation, Benin, 35
Tanenbaum (Joseph) Charitable Foundation, Canada, 58
Tang Prize Foundation, Taiwan, 322
Tata Trusts, India, 160
Tearfund, UK, 385
Tearfund Australia, Australia, 18
Teletón México Foundation, Mexico, 216
Telmex Telcel Foundation, Mexico, 216
Temasek Foundation, Singapore, 273
Terre des Hommes International Federation—TDHIF, Switzerland, 318
Terre Sans Frontières—TSF, Canada, 62
Terrence Higgins Trust—THT, UK, 385
THET, UK, 355
Third World Network—TWN, Malaysia, 211
Third World Solidarity Action, Luxembourg, 209
Thomson Reuters Foundation, UK, 385
Thorn (The Sir Jules) Charitable Trust, UK, 383
Thrasher Research Fund, USA, 474
Thunberg (Greta) Foundation, Sweden, 300
Thyssen (Fritz) Stiftung, Germany, 130
Tibet Fund, USA, 475
TISCO Foundation, Thailand, 325
Tony Blair Institute for Global Change—TBI, UK, 386
TOSA Foundation, USA, 475
TPG Telecom Foundation, Australia, 19
Translators without Borders, USA, 416
Transnet Foundation, South Africa, 284
Triodos Foundation, Netherlands, 231
Trócaire—Catholic Agency for World Development, Ireland, 168
TTF—Toyota Thailand Foundation, Thailand, 325
Tulsa Community Foundation—TCF, USA, 476
Tunisia Development Foundation, Tunisia, 326
Turin Savings Bank Foundation, Italy, 176

Turing (Alan) Institute, UK, 339
Turkish Family Health and Planning Foundation, Türkiye, 330
Türkiye Aile Sağlığı ve Planlaması Vakfı—TAPV, Türkiye, 330
Türkiye İnsan Hakları Vakfı—TİHV, Türkiye, 330
Turner Foundation, Inc, USA, 476
Turquoise Mountain Foundation, UK, 386
TY Danjuma Foundation, Nigeria, 239
Ucom Foundation, Armenia, 9
UK Research and Innovation—UKRI, UK, 387
UniCredit Foundation, Italy, 183
UNIFOR—Forvaltningstiftelse for fond og legater, Norway, 240
Union Aid Abroad—APHEDA, Australia, 19
Union for International Cancer Control—UICC, Switzerland, 318
Union Internationale Contre le Cancer, Switzerland, 318
United Nations Foundation, USA, 476
United Way Worldwide, USA, 477
Universal Foundation, Maldives, 212
US Civilian Research & Development Foundation, USA, 419
Usain Bolt Foundation, Jamaica, 185
USPG—United Society Partners in the Gospel, UK, 387
Väestöliitto, Finland, 98
Vancouver Foundation, Canada, 62
Van Leer Jerusalem Institute, Israel, 171
Vargas (Getulio), Fundação, Brazil, 40
Vehbi Koç Foundation, Türkiye, 331
Vehbi Koç Vakfı, Türkiye, 331
VENRO—Verband Entwicklungspolitik und Humanitäre Hilfe deutscher Nichtregierungsorganizationen, Germany, 120
Versus Arthritis, UK, 388
Victor Pinchuk Foundation, Ukraine, 333
Victoria Children Foundation, Russian Federation, 267
Viertel (Sylvia and Charles) Charitable Foundation, Australia, 18
Villar Foundation, Inc, Philippines, 253
Vincent Fairfax Family Foundation—VFFF, Australia, 19
VinFuture Foundation, Viet Nam, 489
Vital Strategies, USA, 478
Vivamos Mejor Foundation, Switzerland, 317
Vodacom Foundation, South Africa, 284
Vodacom Foundation DRC, Congo (Democratic Republic), 72
Vodacom Foundation South Africa, South Africa, 284
Vodacom Lesotho Foundation, Lesotho, 207
Vodacom Tanzania Foundation—VTF, Tanzania, 323
Vodafone Albania Foundation, Albania, 5
Vodafone ATH Fiji Foundation, Fiji, 94
Vodafone Egypt Foundation, Egypt, 91
Vodafone Foundation, UK, 388
Vodafone Foundation India, India, 161
Vodafone Ghana Foundation, Ghana, 144
Vodafone Idea Foundation, India, 161
Vodafone Italy Foundation, Italy, 181
Vodafone Romania Foundation, Romania, 264
Volkswagen Foundation, Germany, 142
VolkswagenStiftung, Germany, 142
Volnoe Delo—Oleg Deripaska Foundation, Russian Federation, 267
Voluntary Service Overseas, UK, 388
Volunteer Service Abroad/Te Tūao Tāwāhi—VSA, New Zealand, 236
VSO—Voluntary Service Overseas, UK, 388
Výbor dobré vůle—Nadace Olgy Havlové, Czech Republic, 81
W. K. Kellogg Foundation—WKKF, USA, 478
Wallenberg (Knut och Alice) Stiftelse, Sweden, 301
Walmart Foundation, USA, 478
WAMA Foundation, Tanzania, 323
Water for Good, USA, 479
Water for People, USA, 479
WaterAid, UK, 389
The Waterloo Foundation—TWF, UK, 389
Webster (R. Howard) Foundation, Canada, 61
Weinberg (Harry and Jeanette) Foundation, USA, 434
Wellbeing of Women, UK, 389
Wellcome Trust, UK, 389
Weston (Garfield) Foundation, UK, 355
Weyerhaeuser Family Foundation, Inc, USA, 480
WHO Foundation, Switzerland, 319
Wihuri Foundation for International Prizes, Finland, 98
Wihuri (Jenny and Antti) Foundation, Finland, 96

INDEX OF MAIN ACTIVITIES

Wihurin kansainvälisten palkintojen rahasto, Finland, 98
Wild (Dr Rainer) Stiftung, Germany, 126
Wilhelm Sander Foundation, Germany, 143
Wilhelm-Sander-Stiftung, Germany, 143
William Adlington Cadbury Charitable Trust, UK, 390
William Buckland Foundation, Australia, 19
The William and Flora Hewlett Foundation, USA, 481
William Randolph Hearst Foundation, USA, 435
William T. Grant Foundation, USA, 481
Wilson (Woodrow) International Center for Scholars, USA, 482
Winston Churchill Memorial Trust of New Zealand, New Zealand, 236
The Wolfson Foundation, UK, 390
Woman to Woman Foundation, Sweden, 301
Women in Development Foundation, Tanzania, 323
Women Thrive Fund, UK, 384
WomenLead Institute, USA, 418
Woodrow Wilson International Center for Scholars, USA, 482
World Alliance of YMCAs—Young Men's Christian Associations, Switzerland, 319
World Association of Children's Friends, Monaco, 217
World Economic Forum, Switzerland, 320
World Emergency Relief—WER, USA, 483
World Jewish Relief, UK, 391
World Learning, USA, 483
World Neighbors, USA, 483
World Telehealth Initiative, USA, 484
World Vision International, UK, 391
WorldFish, Malaysia, 212
Worldwide Cancer Research, UK, 392
The Wyss Foundtion, USA, 484
Xiangjiang Social Relief Fund, China (People's Republic), 68
XPRIZE Foundation, USA, 484
Yanbao Charity Foundation, China (People's Republic), 69
Yayasan Azman Hashim, Malaysia, 212
Yayasan Insan Sembada, Indonesia, 163
Yellow Feather Fund, USA, 471
YMCA—Young Men's Christian Association, UK, 392
YongLin Charity Foundation, Taiwan, 322
YORGHAS Foundation, Poland, 258
Yrjö Jahnsson Foundation, Finland, 98
Yrjö Jahnssonin säätiö, Finland, 98
Yuan Lin Charity Fund, China (People's Republic), 70
Zarina & Naushad Merali Foundation, Kenya, 200
ZOA, Netherlands, 231
Zuleikhabai Valy Mohamed Gany Rangoonwala Trust—ZVMG Rangoonwala Trust, Pakistan, 246
Zurich Community Trust—ZCT, UK, 392
ZVMG Rangoonwala Trust, Pakistan, 246

SCIENCE AND TECHNOLOGY

The A. G. Leventis Foundation, Cyprus, 77
A. M. Qattan Foundation, UK, 338
The A. P. Møller and Chastine Mc-Kinney Møller Foundation, Denmark, 82
A. P. Møller og Hustru Chastine Mc-Kinney Møllers Fond til almene Formaal, Denmark, 82
Abdul Hameed Shoman Foundation—AHSF, Jordan, 195
Abdulla Al Ghurair Foundation for Education, United Arab Emirates, 334
Abegg Foundation, Switzerland, 306
Abegg-Stiftung, Switzerland, 306
Access Foundation, Costa Rica, 73
Accion, USA, 397
Acíndar Foundation, Argentina, 6
ACROTEC Technology Foundation, Italy, 176
Action Damien/Damiaanactie, Belgium, 28
Action Group on Erosion, Technology and Concentration, Canada, 54
AFPE—American Foundation for Pharmaceutical Education, USA, 401
The African Agricultural Technology Foundation—AATF, Kenya, 198
Agronomes et Vétérinaires sans Frontières—AVSF, France, 100
Agronomists and Veterinarians Without Borders, France, 100
AINA—Arctic Institute of North America, Canada, 49
AIT—Asian Institute of Technology, Thailand, 323

INDEX OF MAIN ACTIVITIES

Science and technology

The Alan Turing Institute, UK, 339
Albert Schweitzer Ecological Centre, Switzerland, 307
Alcoa Foundation, USA, 398
Alemán (Miguel), Fundación, Mexico, 215
Alessio Pezcoller Foundation, Italy, 174
Alexander von Humboldt Foundation, Germany, 120
Alexander von Humboldt Stiftung, Germany, 120
Alexander S. Onassis Public Benefit Foundation, Liechtenstein, 207
Alfred Benzon Foundation, Denmark, 82
Alfred Benzons Fond, Denmark, 82
Alfred P. Sloan Foundation, USA, 398
Alfred Toepfer Foundation FVS, Germany, 121
Alfred Toepfer Stiftung FVS, Germany, 121
Alfried Krupp von Bohlen und Halbach Foundation, Germany, 121
Alfried Krupp von Bohlen und Halbach-Stiftung, Germany, 121
Alicia Patterson Foundation—APF, USA, 398
Alight, USA, 399
Allen (Paul G.) Family Foundation, USA, 462
Alliance of Bioversity International and the International Center for Tropical Agriculture—CIAT, Italy, 172
Alliance for Securing Democracy, USA, 430
Allianz Foundation, Germany, 121
Alvares Penteado (Armando), Fundação, Brazil, 39
AMADE Mondiale—Association Mondiale des Amis de l'Enfance, Monaco, 217
The Ambrose Monell Foundation, USA, 399
America for Bulgaria Foundation, Bulgaria, 43
American Enterprise Institute—AEI, USA, 400
American Foundation for Pharmaceutical Education—AFPE, USA, 401
American Heart Association—AHA, USA, 401
American Jewish Joint Distribution Committee—JDC, USA, 402
American Near East Refugee Aid—Anera, USA, 402
American Philosophical Society—APS, USA, 402
Amerind Foundation, Inc, USA, 403
Anders Jahre's Foundation for Humanitarian Purposes, Norway, 240
Anders Jahres Humanitære Stiftelse, Norway, 240
Andrew W. Mellon Foundation, USA, 404
Anera—American Near East Refugee Aid, USA, 402
Angelo Della Riccia Foundation, Italy, 175
Anguilla Community Fund, Anguilla, 5
The Annenberg Foundation, USA, 404
Archewell Foundation, USA, 405
Arctic Institute of North America—AINA, Canada, 49
Arcus Foundation, USA, 405
Areces (Ramón), Fundación, Spain, 294
Argentine Council for International Relations, Argentina, 6
Armando Alvares Penteado Foundation, Brazil, 39
Arthritis Foundation, USA, 406
Asahi Glass Foundation, Japan, 186
ASEAN Foundation, Indonesia, 161
Asia Pacific Foundation of Canada—APFCanada, Canada, 49
Asia Philanthropy Circle—APC, Singapore, 272
Asian Institute of Technology—AIT, Thailand, 323
ASKO Europa-Stiftung, Germany, 121
ASKO Europe Foundation, Germany, 121
Aspen Institute, USA, 407
Association of Medical Research Charities—AMRC, UK, 335
Association for Public Benefit Foundations, Austria, 20
Asthma + Lung UK, UK, 341
AT&T Foundation, USA, 407
Aurora Trust, UK, 341
Australian Academy of Science, Australia, 11
Australian Academy of Technological Sciences and Engineering, Australia, 11
Australian-American Fulbright Commission, Australia, 11
Australian Communities Foundation, Australia, 12
Australian Conservation Foundation—ACF, Australia, 12
Australian Volunteers International—AVI, Australia, 13
Austrian Science Fund, Austria, 21
Aventis Foundation, Germany, 121
AVI—Australian Volunteers International, Australia, 13
AVINA Foundation, Panama, 247
AVSI Foundation, Italy, 175

Axel Springer Foundation, Germany, 122
Axel-Springer-Stiftung, Germany, 122
Ayala Foundation, Inc—AFI, Philippines, 251
Azim Premji Foundation, India, 156
Baillet Latour Fund, Belgium, 32
Baker Heart & Diabetes Institute, Australia, 13
Balti Uuringute Instituut, Estonia, 92
Baltic Sea Foundation, Finland, 97
Balzan Fonds, Internationale Stiftung, Italy, 181
Banco do Brasil Foundation, Brazil, 39
Bangladesh Freedom Foundation—BFF, Bangladesh, 24
Barandiarán (José Miguel de), Fundación, Spain, 291
Barbra Streisand Foundation, USA, 408
Bariloche Foundation, Argentina, 7
Barrié de la Maza (Pedro, Conde de Fenosa), Fundación, Spain, 293
Basso Issoco (Leilio e Lisli), Fondazione, Italy, 178
Bat Conservation Trust, UK, 342
BBVA Foundation, Spain, 289
Beisheim Foundation, Germany, 122
Beisheim Stiftung, Germany, 122
Beit Trust, UK, 342
Bell (Max) Foundation, Canada, 59
Bellingcat Foundation, Netherlands, 228
Bellona Foundation, Norway, 240
Benzon (Alfred) Foundation, Denmark, 82
Bertoni (Moisés) Foundation, Paraguay, 248
Bettencourt Schueller Foundation, France, 103
Beyaz Nokta Gelişim Vakfı, Türkiye, 328
Bezos Earth Fund, USA, 408
Biocon Foundation, India, 157
BirdLife International, UK, 343
Black Sea NGO Network—BSNN, Bulgaria, 42
Black Sea Trust for Regional Cooperation, USA, 430
Black Sea University Foundation—BSUF, Romania, 263
Blair (Tony) Institute for Global Change, UK, 386
Blanceflor Boncompagni Ludovisi, née Bildt Foundation, Sweden, 303
Blavatnik Family Foundation, USA, 409
Blood Cancer UK—Bloodwise, UK, 343
Blue Marine Foundation—BLUE, UK, 343
BNP Paribas Foundation, France, 103
Bodossaki Foundation, Greece, 145
Boehringer Ingelheim Fonds—Stiftung für medizinische Grundlagenforschung, Germany, 122
Bofill (Jaume), Fundació, Spain, 287
Boltzmann (Ludwig) Gesellschaft, Austria, 21
Bordoni (Ugo), Fondazione, Italy, 180
Boticário Group Foundation, Brazil, 40
Botín Foundation, Spain, 292
Botín (Marcelino), Fundación, Spain, 292
Brazilian Center for International Relations, Brazil, 39
Breakthrough T1D, USA, 409
Brenthurst Foundation, South Africa, 282
BrightFocus Foundation, USA, 409
Bristol-Myers Squibb Foundation, USA, 410
British Heart Foundation—BHF, UK, 344
The Broad Foundation, USA, 410
Brookings Institution, USA, 410
Bunge y Born Foundation, Argentina, 7
Burroughs Wellcome Fund—BWF, USA, 411
CABI, UK, 345
CAF America, USA, 393
Calouste Gulbenkian Foundation, Portugal, 259
Cambodian Salesian Delegation, Cambodia, 46
The Camille and Henry Dreyfus Foundation, Inc, USA, 411
Canada Foundation for Innovation, Canada, 50
Canadian Cancer Society, Canada, 50
Canadian Liver Foundation/Fondation Canadienne du Foie, Canada, 58
Cancer Research UK, UK, 346
Canon Foundation in Europe, Netherlands, 224
Canon Institute for Global Studies—CIGS, Japan, 187
Cariplo Foundation, Italy, 175
Carl Zeiss Foundation, Germany, 123
Carl-Zeiss-Stiftung, Germany, 123
Carlsberg Foundation, Denmark, 82
Carlsbergfondet, Denmark, 82
CARMABI Foundation, Curaçao, 77
Carnegie Corporation of New York, USA, 411
Carnegie Endowment for International Peace, USA, 411
Carnegie Trust for the Universities of Scotland, UK, 346
Carnegie UK Trust, UK, 346
Casa de Mateus Foundation, Portugal, 259
CASE—Centrum Analiz Społeczno-Ekonomicznych, Poland, 255

Cassa di Risparmio di Padova e Rovigo Foundation, Italy, 175
Caterpillar Foundation, USA, 412
CDC Foundation, USA, 412
CEAS—Centre Ecologique Albert Schweitzer, Switzerland, 307
Center for China & Globalization—CCG, China (People's Republic), 67
Center for Inquiry—CFI, USA, 412
Center for Social and Economic Research, Poland, 255
Centre for Development of Non-profit Organizations, Croatia, 76
Centre Ecologique Albert Schweitzer—CEAS, Switzerland, 307
Centre d'Etude du Polymorphisme Humain, France, 107
Centre for International Governance Innovation—CIGI/Centre pour l'Innovation dans la Gouvernance Internationale, Canada, 51
Centre International de Recherche sur le Cancer—CIRC, France, 101
Centre for International Studies, Italy, 172
Centro Brasileiro de Relações Internacionais—CEBRI, Brazil, 39
Centro Internacional de Mejoramiento de Maíz y Trigo—CIMMYT, Mexico, 215
Centro Studi Internazionali—CSI, Italy, 172
CERANEO—Centar za razvoj neprofitnih organizacija, Croatia, 76
Champalimaud Foundation, Portugal, 259
Charities Aid Foundation of America—CAF America, USA, 393
Charles Darwin Foundation for the Galapagos Islands—CDF, Ecuador, 88
Charles Koch Foundation, USA, 413
The Charta 77 Foundation, Czech Republic, 80
Chatham House, UK, 378
Chemistry Centre Foundation, France, 108
Chia Hsin Foundation, Taiwan, 321
Children's Medical Research Institute—CMRI, Australia, 13
Childs (Jane Coffin) Memorial Fund for Medical Research, USA, 443
Chile Foundation, Chile, 65
Chr. Michelsen Institute for Science and Intellectual Freedom—CMI, Norway, 241
Christopher & Dana Reeve Foundation, USA, 415
The Churchill Fellowship, UK, 348
Churchill (Winston) Foundation of the United States, USA, 482
Churchill (Winston) Memorial Trust of New Zealand, New Zealand, 236
CIAT—Centro Internacional de Agricultura Tropical, Italy, 172
CIDSE—Together for Global Justice, Belgium, 29
CIMA Research Foundation—Centre for Environmental Monitoring, Italy, 176
Citi Handlowy Leopold Kronenberg Foundation, Poland, 255
Citizens Foundation, Iceland, 154
Civic Democratic Initiative Support Foundation—CDF, Yemen, 489
Civil Society Development Center—CSDC, Georgia, 117
Clinton Foundation, USA, 416
Clore Israel Foundation, Israel, 169
CMI—Chr. Michelsen Institute for Science and Intellectual Freedom, Norway, 241
The Commonwealth Fund, USA, 417
Community Foundation Partnership, Russian Federation, 264
Concawe—Oil Companies' European Association for Environment, Health and Safety in Refining and Distribution, Belgium, 29
Consejo Argentino para las Relaciones Internacionales—CARI, Argentina, 6
Conservation International Foundation, USA, 417
Co-op Foundation, UK, 349
Co-operative Community Investment Foundation, UK, 349
Coram, UK, 349
Corus International, USA, 418
The Crafoord Foundation, Sweden, 298
Crafoordska stiftelsen, Sweden, 298
CRDF Global, USA, 419
Croucher Foundation, Hong Kong, 151
Cruz (Oswaldo), Fundação, Brazil, 40
CURE International, USA, 419
Cystic Fibrosis Canada, Canada, 53
Cystic Fibrosis Foundation, USA, 419
Czech Literary Fund Foundation, Czech Republic, 80
Daimler and Benz Foundation, Germany, 123
Daimler und Benz Stiftung, Germany, 123
Dalio Foundation, USA, 419
Dam Foundation, Norway, 243

Science and technology

Damon Runyon Cancer Research Foundation, USA, 419
Darwin (Charles) Foundation for the Galapagos Islands, Ecuador, 88
David and Lucile Packard Foundation, USA, 420
David Suzuki Foundation, Canada, 53
Davis (Lady) Fellowship Trust, Israel, 170
Democracy and Development Foundation, Chile, 65
Democracy Fund, USA, 458
Deripaska (Oleg) Foundation, Russian Federation, 267
Deutsche Bank Endowment Fund at the Donors' Association for the Promotion of German Science, Germany, 142
Deutsche Bundesstiftung Umwelt—DBU, Germany, 124
Deutsche Gesellschaft für Auswärtige Politik—DGAP, Germany, 124
Deutsche Krebshilfe eV, Germany, 124
Deutsche Orient-Stiftung, Germany, 125
Deutsche Telekom Foundation, Germany, 125
Deutsche Telekom Stiftung, Germany, 125
Deutsches Institut für internationale Politik und Sicherheit, Germany, 141
Deutsches Rheuma-Forschungszentrum Berlin, Germany, 126
Development Gateway—DG, USA, 420
Diabetes UK, UK, 350
Dietmar Hopp Foundation, Germany, 126
Dietmar-Hopp-Stiftung, Germany, 126
Digicel Trinidad and Tobago Foundation, Trinidad and Tobago, 326
Dioraphte Foundation, Netherlands, 229
DiploFoundation, Malta, 213
Dom Manuel II Foundation, Portugal, 260
Don Bosco Foundation of Cambodia—DBFC, Cambodia, 46
Donner (William H.) Foundation, Inc, USA, 481
Donors' Association for the Promotion of Sciences and Humanities, Germany, 119
Dr Rainer Wild Foundation for Healthy Nutrition, Germany, 126
Dr Rainer Wild-Stiftung—Stiftung für Gesunde Ernährung, Germany, 126
Dräger Foundation, Germany, 126
Dräger-Stiftung, Germany, 126
Dreyfus (Camille and Henry) Foundation, USA, 411
Dreyfus Health Foundation, USA, 468
DRFN—Desert Research Foundation of Namibia, Namibia, 222
Drug Policy Alliance—DPA, USA, 421
del Duca (Simone et Cino), Fondation, France, 111
E. O. Wilson Biodiversity Foundation, USA, 421
Earth Island Institute—EII, USA, 422
East Asia Institute—EAI, Korea (Republic), 201
eBay Foundation, USA, 422
Ebelin and Gerd Bucerius ZEIT Foundation, Germany, 143
Eberhard Schöck Foundation, Germany, 127
Eberhard-Schöck-Stiftung, Germany, 127
Ebert (Friedrich) Stiftung, Germany, 129
Echo Foundation/Fondation Écho, Canada, 54
EcoHealth Alliance, USA, 422
EDF Group Foundation, France, 107
Edmond de Rothschild Foundations, Switzerland, 308
EDP Foundation, Portugal, 260
Education and Training Foundation—ETF, UK, 351
EFQM—European Foundation for Quality Management, Belgium, 30
Ekhaga Foundation, Sweden, 299
Ekhagastiftelsen, Sweden, 299
Ekofond SPP, Slovakia, 275
Electronic Frontier Foundation—EFF, USA, 423
Elizabeth Glaser Pediatric AIDS Foundation—EGPAF, USA, 423
Else Kröner-Fresenius Foundation, Germany, 127
Else Kröner-Fresenius-Stiftung, Germany, 127
Emirates Foundation, United Arab Emirates, 334
Empresas Polar Foundation, Venezuela, 487
Enda Third World—Environment and Development Action in the Third World, Senegal, 270
Enda Tiers Monde—Environnement et Développement du Tiers-Monde, Senegal, 270
Energies for the World Foundation, France, 105
ENGIE Corporate Foundation, France, 105
Enrico Mattei Eni Foundation, Italy, 174
Ente Cassa di Risparmio di Firenze, Italy, 173
Environment and Natural Resources Foundation, Argentina, 7
Environmental Foundation of Jamaica, Jamaica, 184
Epilepsy Foundation, USA, 424
Equality Fund/Fonds Égalité, Canada, 54
Erik Philip-Sörensen Foundation, Sweden, 299
Erik Philip-Sörensens Stiftelse, Sweden, 299
Ernst Schering Foundation, Germany, 127
Ernst-Schering-Stiftung, Germany, 127
Esquel Group Foundation—Ecuador, Ecuador, 88
Estonian Foreign Policy Institute, Estonia, 93
Estonian National Culture Foundation, Estonia, 93
ETC Group—Action Group on Erosion, Technology and Concentration, Canada, 54
Eurasia Foundation—EF, USA, 424
Eureka Foundation, Bulgaria, 43
Euro-Mediterranean Centre on Climate Change Foundation, Italy, 176
EuroNatur, Germany, 127
European Association for Cancer Research—EACR, UK, 353
European Center for Peace and Development—ECPD, Serbia, 271
European Climate Foundation, Netherlands, 224
European Foundation for Quality Management—EFQM, Belgium, 30
European Foundation for the Sustainable Development of the Regions, Switzerland, 308
Evens Foundation, Belgium, 31
Evrika Foundation, Bulgaria, 43
Farm Africa, UK, 354
FARN—Fundación Ambiente y Recursos Naturales, Argentina, 7
FEDRE—European Foundation for the Sustainable Development of the Regions, Switzerland, 308
FEEM—Fondazione ENI Enrico Mattei, Italy, 174
Félix Houphouët-Boigny Foundation for Peace Research, Côte d'Ivoire, 75
FEMSA Foundation, Mexico, 215
Fernand Lazard Foundation, Belgium, 31
Ferrero (Piera, Pietro e Giovanni), Fondazione, Italy, 179
Fibrose Kystique Canada, Canada, 53
FINCA International, USA, 425
Finnish Cultural Foundation, Finland, 97
Finnish Foundation for Technology Promotion, Finland, 98
Flatiron Institute, USA, 472
Flight Safety Foundation, USA, 426
Florence Savings Bank Foundation, Italy, 173
FOKAL—Open Society Foundation Haiti, Haiti, 149
Fondation Africaine pour les Technologies Agricoles, Kenya, 198
Fondation Bettencourt Schueller, France, 103
Fondation BNP Paribas, France, 103
Fondation Canadienne pour l'Innovation, Canada, 50
Fondation Casip-Cojasor, France, 104
Fondation du Collège de France, France, 105
Fondation pour l'Economie et le Développement Durable des Régions d'Europe—FEDRE, Switzerland, 308
Fondation Energies pour le Monde—Fondem, France, 105
Fondation Ensemble, France, 105
Fondation d'Entreprise Crédit Agricole Réunion Mayotte, Réunion, 262
Fondation d'Entreprise ENGIE, France, 105
Fondation d'Entreprise VINCI pour la Cité, France, 106
Fondation Evens Stichting, Belgium, 31
Fondation Félix Houphouët-Boigny pour la Recherche de la Paix, Côte d'Ivoire, 75
Fondation Fernand Lazard Stichting, Belgium, 31
Fondation de France, France, 99
Fondation France-Israël, France, 106
Fondation Franco-Japonaise Sasakawa, France, 106
Fondation Fyssen, France, 107
Fondation Groupe EDF, France, 107
Fondation Hassan II pour les Marocains Résidant à l'Étranger, Morocco, 220
Fondation Hirondelle: Media for Peace and Human Dignity, Switzerland, 309
Fondation Jean Dausset—Centre d'Etude du Polymorphisme Humain—CEPH, France, 107
Fondation Latsis Internationale, Switzerland, 309
Fondation Léopold Sédar Senghor, Senegal, 270
Fondation Louis-Jeantet de Médecine, Switzerland, 310
Fondation MAIF pour la Recherche, France, 108
Fondation de la Maison de la Chimie, France, 108
Fondation Maison des Sciences de l'Homme—FMSH, France, 108
Fondation Marcel Bleustein-Blanchet de la Vocation, France, 109
Fondation Mérieux, France, 109
Fondation MTN Bénin, Benin, 35
Fondation MTN Cameroun, Cameroon, 47

INDEX OF MAIN ACTIVITIES

Fondation MTN Congo, Congo (Republic), 73
Fondation MTN Côte d'Ivoire, Côte d'Ivoire, 76
Fondation Nestlé pour l'Etude des Problèmes de l'Alimentation dans le Monde, Switzerland, 310
Fondation Nicolas Hulot pour la Nature et l'Homme—FNH, France, 110
Fondation Orange Burkina Faso, Burkina Faso, 45
Fondation Orange-Côte d'Ivoire Télécom—OCIT, Côte d'Ivoire, 76
Fondation Orange Mali, Mali, 213
Fondation Orange Tunisie, Tunisia, 326
Fondation Perspectives d'Avenir, Congo (Republic), 73
Fondation Prince Albert II de Monaco, Monaco, 217
Fondation Prince Pierre de Monaco, Monaco, 218
Fondation pour la Recherche Stratégique, France, 111
Fondation du Roi Abdul-Aziz al-Saoud pour les Études Islamiques et les Sciences Humaines, Morocco, 220
Fondation Schneider Electric, France, 111
Fondation Simone et Cino del Duca, France, 111
Fondation Singer-Polignac, France, 111
Fondation Suisse pour Recherches Alpines—FSRA, Switzerland, 316
Fondation Tunisie pour le Développement, Tunisia, 326
Fondation Vodacom RDC, Congo (Democratic Republic), 72
Fondazione Alessio Pezcoller, Italy, 174
Fondazione Angelo Della Riccia, Italy, 175
Fondazione AVSI, Italy, 175
Fondazione Cariplo, Italy, 175
Fondazione Cassa di Risparmio di Padova e Rovigo, Italy, 175
Fondazione Cassa di Risparmio di Verona Vicenza Belluno e Ancona—Fondazione Cariverona, Italy, 176
Fondazione Centro Euro-Mediterraneo sui Cambiamenti Climatici—CMCC, Italy, 176
Fondazione CIMA—Centro Internazionale in Monitoraggio Ambientale, Italy, 176
Fondazione Giovanni Lorenzini, Italy, 177
Fondazione Internazionale Premio Balzan, Italy, 181
Fondazione per l'Istituto Svizzero di Roma, Italy, 178
Fondazione Lelio e Lisli Basso Issoco—Sezione Internazionale, Italy, 178
Fondazione Piera, Pietro e Giovanni Ferrero, Italy, 179
Fondazione Roma, Italy, 179
Fondazione Ugo Bordoni, Italy, 180
Fondazione di Venezia, Italy, 181
Fondazione Vodafone Italia, Italy, 181
Fonden Realdania, Denmark, 83
Fonds Baillet Latour, Belgium, 32
Fonds Égalité, Canada, 54
Fonds National Suisse de la Recherche Scientifique, Switzerland, 316
Ford Foundation, USA, 427
Foundation for Basic Research in Biomedicine, Germany, 122
Foundation Bofill, Spain, 287
Foundation for Caribbean Research and Management of Biodiversity, Curaçao, 77
Foundation for the Defence of Nature, Venezuela, 487
Foundation for Defense of Democracies—FDD, USA, 427
Foundation for German-Polish Co-operation, Poland, 257
Foundation of the Hellenic World, Greece, 145
Foundation for International Community Assistance, USA, 425
Foundation Open Society Institute Pakistan, Pakistan, 245
Foundation for the Rights of Future Generations, Germany, 141
Foundation for Strategic Research, France, 111
Foundation for the Swiss Institute of Rome, Italy, 178
Foundation for the Welfare of Holocaust Victims, Israel, 169
Foundation of Youth and Lifelong Learning—INEDIVIM, Greece, 145
Foundation for Youth Research, Germany, 140
Foundations' Post-Doc Pool, Finland, 95
Fox (Michael J.) Foundation for Parkinson's Research, USA, 453
France-Israel Foundation, France, 106
France Nature Environnement, France, 112
Franco-Japanese Sasakawa Foundation, France, 106
Frank Knox Memorial Fellowships, USA, 428

INDEX OF MAIN ACTIVITIES

Frankfurt Foundation for German-Italian Studies, Germany, 129
Frankfurter Stiftung für Deutsch-Italienische Studien, Germany, 129
Fraunhofer-Gesellschaft, Germany, 129
Fraunhofer Society, Germany, 129
Free Russia Foundation, USA, 428
Freedom Together Foundation, USA, 428
French-American Foundation, USA, 429
French Institute of International Relations, France, 113
Friede Springer Foundation, Germany, 129
Friede Springer Stiftung, Germany, 129
Friedrich-Ebert-Stiftung eV, Germany, 129
Front Line Defenders—FLD, Ireland, 166
FRS-FNRS—Fonds de la Recherche Scientifique, Belgium, 32
Fulbright Norway—US-Norway Fulbright Foundation for Educational Exchange, Norway, 241
Fund and Endowment Management Foundation, Norway, 240
Fund for Scientific Research, Belgium, 32
Fundação Armando Alvares Penteado, Brazil, 39
Fundação Banco do Brasil, Brazil, 39
Fundação Calouste Gulbenkian, Portugal, 259
Fundação da Casa de Mateus, Portugal, 259
Fundação Champalimaud, Portugal, 259
Fundação Dom Manuel II, Portugal, 260
Fundação EDP, Portugal, 260
Fundação Grupo Boticário de Proteção à Natureza, Brazil, 40
Fundação José Maria Neves para a Governança, Cabo Verde, 46
Fundação Luso-Americana para o Desenvolvimento—FLAD, Portugal, 260
Fundação Mário Soares e Maria Barroso, Portugal, 260
Fundação Oriente, Portugal, 260
Fundação Oswaldo Cruz—FIOCRUZ, Brazil, 40
Fundação Telefônica Vivo, Brazil, 41
Fundação Vodafone Portugal, Portugal, 261
Fundació Jaume Bofill, Spain, 287
Fundación Acceso, Costa Rica, 73
Fundación Acindar, Argentina, 6
Fundación Ambiente y Recursos Naturales—FARN, Argentina, 7
Fundación AVINA, Panama, 247
Fundación Bancaria 'la Caixa', Spain, 288
Fundación Banco Bilbao Vizcaya Argentaria—Fundación BBVA, Spain, 289
Fundación Bariloche, Argentina, 7
Fundación BBVA, Spain, 289
Fundación Bunge y Born, Argentina, 7
Fundación Capital, Colombia, 70
Fundación Carolina, Spain, 290
Fundación Charles Darwin para las Islas Galápagos—FCD, Ecuador, 88
Fundación Chile—FCH, Chile, 65
Fundación Comunitaria de Puerto Rico—FCPR, Puerto Rico, 261
Fundación para la Defensa de la Naturaleza—FUDENA, Venezuela, 487
Fundación Democracia y Desarrollo, Chile, 65
Fundación Empresa-Universidad de Zaragoza, Spain, 290
Fundación Empresas Polar, Venezuela, 487
Fundación Espacio Cívico, Panama, 247
Fundación FEMSA, Mexico, 215
Fundación Global Democracia y Desarrollo—FUNGLODE, Dominican Republic, 87
Fundación Grupo Esquel—Ecuador, Ecuador, 88
Fundación IE, Spain, 291
Fundación José Miguel de Barandiarán, Spain, 291
Fundación Juan March, Spain, 291
Fundación Juanelo Turriano, Spain, 291
Fundación MAPFRE, Spain, 292
Fundación Marcelino Botín, Spain, 292
Fundación María Francisca de Roviralta, Spain, 292
Fundación Miguel Alemán AC, Mexico, 215
Fundación Moisés Bertoni—FMB, Paraguay, 248
Fundación Orange, Spain, 293
Fundación Paideia Galiza, Spain, 293
Fundación Pedro Barrié de la Maza, Spain, 293
Fundación Pies Descalzos, Colombia, 71
Fundación Princesa de Asturias, Spain, 294
Fundación Ramón Areces, Spain, 294
Fundación Real Instituto Elcano, Spain, 294
Fundación Repsol, Spain, 295
Fundación La Salle de Ciencias Naturales—FLASA, Venezuela, 487
Fundación Semah-Valencia, Panama, 247
Fundación SM, Spain, 295
Fundación Tecnologías Sociales—TECSOS, Spain, 296
Fundación Telefónica, Spain, 295
Fundación Telefónica Movistar Argentina, Argentina, 8
Fundación Telefónica Movistar Chile, Chile, 65
Fundación Telefónica Movistar Colombia, Colombia, 71
Fundación Telefónica Movistar Ecuador, Ecuador, 89
Fundación Telefónica Movistar México, Mexico, 216
Fundación Telefónica Movistar Perú, Peru, 249
Fundación Telefónica Movistar Uruguay, Uruguay, 485
Fundación Tigo, Guatemala, 148
Fundación Torcuato Di Tella—FTDT, Argentina, 8
Fundación Universidad-Empresa—UE, Spain, 295
Fundación Vodafone España, Spain, 296
Fundacja Citi Handlowy im. Leopolda Kronenberga, Poland, 255
Fundacja Orange, Poland, 255
Fundacja Współpracy Polsko-Niemieckiej/Stiftung für Deutsch-Polnische Zusammenarbeit, Poland, 257
Fundația Universitară a Mării Negre—FUMN, Romania, 263
Fundația Vodafone România, Romania, 264
Future Foundation, Liechtenstein, 208
FWF—Österreichischer Wissenschaftsfonds, Austria, 21
FWO—Fonds Wetenschappelijk Onderzoek, Belgium, 32
Fyssen Foundation, France, 107
G. Unger Vetlesen Foundation, USA, 429
GAIA—Groupe d'Action dans l'Intérêt des Animaux, Belgium, 32
Gapminder, Sweden, 300
Garden Organic, UK, 355
Garfield Weston Foundation, UK, 355
Gates (Bill & Melinda) Foundation, USA, 429
Gates Foundation, USA, 429
The Gatsby Charitable Foundation, UK, 355
Gebert Rüf Stiftung, Switzerland, 311
Gemeinnützige Hertie-Stiftung, Germany, 130
The General Kashif Al-Getaa Foundation, Iraq, 164
German Academic Scholarship Foundation, Germany, 142
German Cancer Aid, Germany, 124
German Council on Foreign Relations, Germany, 124
German Federal Foundation for the Environment, Germany, 124
German Institute for Global and Area Studies—GIGA, Germany, 130
German Marshall Fund of the United States—GMF, USA, 430
German Orient Foundation, Germany, 125
German Rheumatism Research Centre Berlin, Germany, 126
Giovanni Lorenzini Foundation, Italy, 177
GiveWell—The Clear Fund, USA, 430
Glaser (Elizabeth) Pediatric AIDS Foundation, USA, 423
Global Action in the Interest of Animals, Belgium, 32
Global Democracy and Development Foundation, Dominican Republic, 87
Global Health Council, USA, 395
Global Innovation Fund, UK, 356
GLOBSEC, Slovakia, 275
Gobabeb Namib Research Institute, Namibia, 222
Goethe-Institut, Germany, 131
Good Things Foundation, UK, 356
Goodwill Industries International, Inc—GII, USA, 432
Google.org—Google Foundation, USA, 432
Gordon and Betty Moore Foundation, USA, 432
Gordon (Walter and Duncan) Charitable Foundation, Canada, 62
Graham Foundation for Advanced Studies in the Fine Arts—GF, USA, 432
Grameen Foundation—GF, USA, 433
The Grass Foundation, USA, 433
Great Britain Sasakawa Foundation, UK, 356
Groupe d'Action dans l'Intérêt des Animaux—GAIA, Belgium, 32
Guggenheim (Harry Frank) Foundation, USA, 434
Guggenheim (John Simon) Memorial Foundation, USA, 434
Gulbenkian (Calouste), Fundação, Portugal, 259
HALO Trust, UK, 357
Hamdard Foundation Pakistan, Pakistan, 245
The Harry Frank Guggenheim Foundation—HFG, USA, 434
Hassan II Foundation for Moroccans Living Abroad, Morocco, 220

Science and technology

Hawaii Resilience Fund, USA, 458
Health Action International—HAI, Netherlands, 225
The Health Foundation, UK, 357
Heart & Stroke, Canada, 56
Heineken Prizes for Arts and Sciences, Netherlands, 225
Heinekenprijzen voor kunst en wetenschap, Netherlands, 225
Heineman (Minna-James) Stiftung, Germany, 136
Helmholtz Association, Germany, 132
Helmholtz-Gemeinschaft, Germany, 132
Helmich (Janson Johan og Marcia) Legat, Norway, 242
Helmsley (Leona M. and Harry B.) Charitable Trust, USA, 447
Helmut Horten Foundation, Switzerland, 311
Helmut-Horten-Stiftung, Switzerland, 311
Helvetas Swiss Intercooperation, Switzerland, 311
Hempel Fonden, Denmark, 84
Hempel Foundation, Denmark, 84
Henrietta Szold Institute—National Institute for Research in the Behavioural Sciences, Israel, 169
Henry Doubleday Research Association, UK, 355
The Heritage Foundation, USA, 436
Hertie Foundation, Germany, 130
Hewlett (William and Flora) Foundation, USA, 481
Higherlife Foundation, Zimbabwe, 491
Hirschfeld-Eddy Foundation, Germany, 132
Hirschfeld-Eddy-Stiftung, Germany, 132
Hitachi Foundation, Japan, 187
Hodge Foundation, UK, 358
Honda Foundation, Japan, 187
Hong Kong Society for the Blind, Hong Kong, 151
Hopp (Dietmar) Stiftung, Germany, 126
Hormuud Salaam Foundation, Somalia, 277
Horten (Helmut) Stiftung, Switzerland, 311
Hoso Bunka Foundation, Inc—HBF, Japan, 188
Houphouët-Boigny (Félix), Fondation, Côte d'Ivoire, 75
House of the Human Sciences Foundation, France, 108
Howard Hughes Medical Institute—HHMI, USA, 437
Hudson Institute, USA, 437
Hulot (Nicolas), Fondation, France, 110
von Humboldt (Alexander) Stiftung, Germany, 120
Humboldt Forum, Germany, 132
IACD—Institute of Asian Culture and Development, Korea (Republic), 201
IAESTE—International Association for the Exchange of Students for Technical Experience, Luxembourg, 210
IAI—Istituto Affari Internazionali, Italy, 182
Ian Potter Foundation, Australia, 14
IARC—International Agency for Research on Cancer, France, 101
IBM International Foundation, USA, 438
Ichikowitz Family Foundation—IFF, South Africa, 280
The Ideas Institute, Kenya, 199
IE Foundation, Spain, 291
IFAD—International Fund for Agricultural Development, Italy, 182
IFRISSE Burkina, Burkina Faso, 45
IKEA Foundation, Netherlands, 229
Imbuto Foundation, Rwanda, 268
Inamori Foundation, Japan, 188
Independent Sector, USA, 395
Indian National Trust for Art and Cultural Heritage—INTACH, India, 158
INEDIVIM—Foundation of Youth and Lifelong Learning, Greece, 145
Inlaks Shivdasani Foundation, India, 158
Innovators and Entrepreneurs Foundation/Fondation d'Innovateurs et d'Entrepreneurs—IEF/FIE, Canada, 57
Institut Arctique de l'Amérique du Nord—IAAN, Canada, 49
Institut FMES—Institut Méditerranéen d'Etudes Stratégiques, France, 113
Institut Français des Relations Internationales—IFRI, France, 113
Institut de Médecine et d'Epidémiologie Appliquée—Fondation Internationale Léon Mba, France, 114
Institut Mittag-Leffler, Sweden, 300
Institut Océanographique—Fondation Albert 1er, Prince de Monaco, France, 114
Institut Pasteur, France, 114
Institut Pasteur de Lille, France, 114
Institute of Applied Medicine and Epidemiology—International Foundation Léon Mba, France, 114

Science and technology

Institute of Asian Culture and Development—IACD, Korea (Republic), 201
Institute of Baltic Studies, Estonia, 92
Institute of British Geographers, UK, 378
Institute of Economic Affairs—IEA, UK, 359
The Institute of Energy Economics, Japan—IEEJ, Japan, 188
Institute for European Environmental Policy—IEEP, Belgium, 33
Institute of International Affairs, Italy, 182
Institute of International Law, Argentina, 6
Institute for International Security and Strategic Affairs—ISIAE, Argentina, 6
Institute for Latin American and Caribbean Integration, Argentina, 8
Institute for Precision Cardiovascular Medicine, USA, 401
Institute for Scientific Interchange Foundation—ISI, Italy, 181
Institute for Security Studies—ISS, South Africa, 280
Institute of Social Studies—ISS, Netherlands, 226
Institute for Sustainable Communities—ISC, USA, 439
Instituto para la Integración de América Latina y el Caribe—BID-INTAL, Argentina, 8
Instituto de Montaña, Peru, 249
Institutul Cultural Român—ICR, Romania, 264
INTACH—Indian National Trust for Art and Cultural Heritage, India, 158
INTEGRATA Foundation, Germany, 132
INTEGRATA—Stiftung für Humane Nutzung der Informationstechnologie, Germany, 132
International Agency for Research on Cancer—IARC, France, 101
International Arctic Science Committee—IASC, Iceland, 154
International Balzan Prize Foundation, Italy, 181
International Centre for Defence and Security—ICDS, Estonia, 93
International Development Center of Japan, Japan, 189
International Eye Foundation—IEF, USA, 440
International Forum Bosnia, Bosnia and Herzegovina, 37
The International Foundation, USA, 440
International Foundation of the High-Altitude Research Stations Jungfraujoch and Gornergrat, Switzerland, 313
International Foundation for the Protection of Human Rights Defenders, Ireland, 166
International Foundation for Science—IFS, Sweden, 300
International Fund for Agricultural Development—IFAD, Italy, 182
International Institute for Applied Systems Analysis—IIASA, Austria, 21
International Institute of Social Studies, Netherlands, 226
The International Institute for Strategic Studies—IISS, UK, 360
International Institute of Tropical Agriculture—IITA, Nigeria, 237
International Latsis Foundation, Switzerland, 309
International Maize and Wheat Improvement Center, Mexico, 215
International Research & Exchanges Board—IREX, USA, 442
International Visegrad Fund—IVF, Slovakia, 275
International Water Management Institute—IWMI, Sri Lanka, 297
Internationale Stiftung Hochalpine Forschungsstationen Jungfraujoch und Gornergrat, Switzerland, 313
Internationale Stiftung Preis E. Balzan-Fonds, Italy, 181
IREX—International Research & Exchanges Board, USA, 442
ISPI—Istituto per gli Studi di Politica Internazionale, Italy, 183
The Israel Democracy Institute—IDI, Israel, 170
Istituto Affari Internazionali—IAI, Italy, 182
Istituto di Ricerche Farmacologiche Mario Negri, Italy, 182
Istituto per gli Studi di Politica Internazionale—ISPI, Italy, 183
Istituto Svedese di Studi Classici a Roma, Italy, 183
Italian Institute for International Political Studies, Italy, 183
Ivey Foundation, Canada, 57
Iwatani Naoji Foundation, Japan, 189
J. F. Kapnek Zimbabwe, Zimbabwe, 491
Jack Ma Foundation—JMF, China (People's Republic), 68
Jahres (Anders) Humanitære Stiftelse, Norway, 240
James Michel Foundation, Seychelles, 272
James S. McDonnell Foundation, USA, 443
Jane Coffin Childs Memorial Fund for Medical Research—JCC Fund, USA, 443
Janson Johan Helmich and Marcia Jansons Endowment, Norway, 242
Janson Johan Helmich og Marcia Jansons Legat, Norway, 242
The Japan Foundation, Japan, 189
Japan Society for the Promotion of Science—JSPS, Japan, 190
Japanese-German Centre Berlin, Germany, 133
Japanisch-Deutsches Zentrum Berlin, Germany, 133
Jean Dausset Foundation—Centre for the Study of Human Polymorphism, France, 107
Jeans for Genes, Australia, 13
Jenny and Antti Wihuri Foundation, Finland, 96
Jenny ja Antti Wihurin Rahasto, Finland, 96
JNF UK—JNF Charitable Trust, UK, 361
The John D. and Catherine T. MacArthur Foundation, USA, 444
John Innes Foundation—JIF, UK, 362
John Simon Guggenheim Memorial Foundation, USA, 444
John Templeton Foundation, USA, 444
Johnson & Johnson Foundation US—JJF, USA, 444
JOHUD—Jordanian Hashemite Fund for Human Development, Jordan, 196
José Maria Neves Foundation for Governance, Cabo Verde, 46
José Miguel de Barandiarán Foundation, Spain, 291
Joseph Patrick Trust, UK, 369
Josiah Macy Jr Foundation, USA, 445
JPB Foundation, USA, 428
Juan March Foundation, Spain, 291
Juanelo Turriano Foundation, Spain, 291
Juvenile Diabetes Research Foundation International, USA, 409
Kade (Max) Foundation, Inc, USA, 451
Kajima Foundation, Japan, 191
Kapnek (J. F.) Charitable Trust Zimbabwe, Zimbabwe, 491
KAUTE Foundation, Finland, 96
KAUTE-säätiö, Finland, 96
KDDI Foundation, Japan, 191
Kettering (Charles F.) Foundation, USA, 445
Kettering Foundation—KF, USA, 445
King Abdul-Aziz al-Saoud Foundation for Islamic Study and the Humanities, Morocco, 220
King Faisal Foundation, Saudi Arabia, 269
Klaus Tschira Foundation, Germany, 134
Klaus Tschira Stiftung GmbH, Germany, 134
Knox (Frank) Memorial Fellowships, USA, 428
Knut and Alice Wallenberg Foundation, Sweden, 301
Knut och Alice Wallenbergs Stiftelse, Sweden, 301
Koch (Charles) Foundation, USA, 413
Kokkalis Foundation, Greece, 146
Komen (Susan G.) Breast Cancer Foundation, USA, 474
Koninklijke Hollandsche Maatschappij der Wetenschappen, Netherlands, 226
Körber Foundation, Germany, 134
Körber-Stiftung, Germany, 134
The Kosciuszko Foundation, Inc, USA, 446
Kronenberg (Leopold) Foundation, Poland, 255
Kröner-Fresenius (Else) Stiftung, Germany, 127
Krupp von Bohlen und Halbach (Alfried) Stiftung, Germany, 121
Kuok Foundation Berhad, Malaysia, 211
Kusuma Trust UK, UK, 363
Kuwait Awqaf Public Foundation, Kuwait, 203
Kuwait Foundation for the Advancement of Sciences—KFAS, Kuwait, 203
Kuwait Institute for Scientific Research—KISR, Kuwait, 203
KWF Dutch Cancer Society, Netherlands, 227
KWF Kankerbestrijding, Netherlands, 227
'La Caixa' Banking Foundation, Spain, 288
La Salle Foundation for Natural Sciences, Venezuela, 487
Lady Davis Fellowship Trust, Israel, 170
Laing Family Trusts, UK, 364
Lambrakis Foundation, Greece, 146
LAPAS—Latvijas platforma attīstības sadarbībai, Latvia, 204
Latvian Platform for Development Cooperation, Latvia, 204
Lazard (Fernand), Fondation, Belgium, 31
League of Corporate Foundations—LCF, Philippines, 250
The Leakey Foundation, USA, 447

INDEX OF MAIN ACTIVITIES

Leibniz Association, Germany, 135
Leibniz Gemeinschaft, Germany, 135
Leibniz-Institut für Agrarentwicklung in Transformationsökonomien—IAMO, Germany, 135
Leibniz-Institut für Globale und Regionale Studien, Germany, 130
Leibniz Institute of Agricultural Development in Transition Economies, Germany, 135
Lelio and Lisli Basso Foundation Onlus, Italy, 178
The Leona M. and Harry B. Helmsley Charitable Trust, USA, 447
Léopold Sédar Senghor Foundation, Senegal, 270
Lesotho Council of Non-Governmental Organisations, Lesotho, 207
Leventis (A. G.) Foundation, Cyprus, 77
Leverhulme Trust, UK, 365
Life Sciences Research Foundation—LSRF, USA, 448
LifeArc—MRC Technology, UK, 365
Lifeline Energy, South Africa, 280
Lifewater International, USA, 479
Light Up the World—LUTW, Canada, 58
Limmat Foundation, Switzerland, 314
Limmat Stiftung, Switzerland, 314
Linbury Trust, UK, 365
Liver Canada, Canada, 58
Lloyd's Register Foundation, UK, 365
The Long Now Foundation, USA, 449
Lorenzini (Giovanni), Fondazione, Italy, 177
Louis-Jeantet Foundation for Medicine, Switzerland, 310
Ludwig Boltzmann Gesellschaft, Austria, 21
Ludwig Cancer Research, USA, 449
Lukuru Wildlife Research Foundation, Congo (Democratic Republic), 72
Lullaby Trust, UK, 366
Lundbeck Foundation, Denmark, 85
Lundbeckfonden, Denmark, 85
Luso-American Development Foundation, Portugal, 260
M. S. Swaminathan Research Foundation—MSSRF, India, 158
MacArthur (John D. and Catherine T.) Foundation, USA, 444
McDonnell (James S.) Foundation, USA, 443
McKnight Foundation, USA, 449
Macmillan Cancer Support, UK, 366
Macy (Josiah), Jr Foundation, USA, 445
MAG—Mines Advisory Group, UK, 366
MAIF Foundation for Research, France, 108
Maj ja Tor Nessling Säätiö, Finland, 96
Maj and Tor Nessling Foundation, Finland, 96
MAPFRE Foundation, Spain, 292
Marcel Bleustein-Blanchet Vocational Foundation, France, 109
March (Juan), Fundación, Spain, 291
María Francisca de Roviralta Foundation, Spain, 292
Marie Curie, UK, 366
Mario Negri Pharmacological Research Institute, Italy, 182
Mário Soares and Maria Barroso Foundation, Portugal, 260
Markle Foundation, USA, 451
Masason Foundation, Japan, 191
The Matsumae International Foundation, Japan, 191
Mattei (Enrico), Fondazione ENI, Italy, 174
Mauritius Telecom Foundation—MTF, Mauritius, 214
Mawazo Institute, Kenya, 199
Max Bell Foundation, Canada, 59
The Max Foundation, USA, 451
Max Kade Foundation, Inc, USA, 451
Max-Planck-Gesellschaft zur Förderung der Wissenschaften eV, Germany, 135
Max-Planck-Institut für Neurobiologie des Verhaltens—caesar, Germany, 136
Max Planck Institute for Neurobiology of Behavior—caesar, Germany, 136
Max Planck Society for the Advancement of Science, Germany, 135
MDA—Muscular Dystrophy Association, USA, 451
Medunarodnog foruma Bosna, Bosnia and Herzegovina, 37
Mediterranean Foundation for Strategic Studies Institute, France, 113
Mellon (Richard King) Foundation, USA, 467
Menzies Foundation, Australia, 15
Menzies (Sir Robert) Foundation, Australia, 15
Mercatus Center, USA, 451
Mercy For Animals—MFA, USA, 452
Mercy Corps, USA, 452
Meridian Foundation, Germany, 140
Mérieux Foundation, France, 109
M'essh al Sudan, Sudan, 297

INDEX OF MAIN ACTIVITIES

Science and technology

Michael J. Fox Foundation for Parkinson's Research—MJFF, USA, 453
Michel (James) Foundation, Seychelles, 272
Miguel Alemán Foundation, Mexico, 215
Minderoo Foundation, Australia, 15
Mines Advisory Group—MAG, UK, 366
Minna James Heineman Foundation, Germany, 136
Minna-James-Heineman-Stiftung, Germany, 136
Mittag-Leffler Foundation of the Royal Swedish Academy of Sciences, Sweden, 300
Mohammed bin Rashid Al Maktoum Global Initiatives—MBRGI, United Arab Emirates, 335
Mohammed bin Salman Foundation—Misk Foundation, Saudi Arabia, 269
Moisés Bertoni Foundation, Paraguay, 248
Møller (A.P.) and Chastine Mc-Kinney Møller Foundation, Denmark, 82
Monell (Ambrose) Foundation, USA, 399
Moore (Gordon and Betty) Foundation, USA, 432
Motorola Solutions Foundation, USA, 454
Mountain Institute, Peru, 249
M-PESA Foundation, Kenya, 199
MTN Cameroon Foundation, Cameroon, 47
MTN Congo Foundation, Congo (Republic), 73
MTN Côte d'Ivoire Foundation, Côte d'Ivoire, 76
MTN Foundation Benin, Benin, 35
MTN Nigeria Foundation, Nigeria, 237
MTN SA Foundation, South Africa, 281
MTN Uganda Foundation, Uganda, 332
Munich Re Foundation/Münchener Rück Stiftung, Germany, 137
Murdoch Children's Research Institute—MCRI, Australia, 15
Muscular Dystrophy UK, UK, 369
Musk Foundation, USA, 454
Myanmar Book Aid and Preservation Foundation—MBAPF, Myanmar, 221
Nadace Český literární fond—nclf, Czech Republic, 80
Nadace Charty 77, Czech Republic, 80
Nadace Preciosa, Czech Republic, 80
Nadace Vodafone Česká Republika, Czech Republic, 80
Nadácia Tatra Banky, Slovakia, 276
Naito Foundation, Japan, 191
National Endowment for Science, Technology and the Arts—Nesta, UK, 370
National Geographic Society, USA, 455
National Heart Foundation of Australia, Australia, 15
National Heart Foundation of New Zealand, New Zealand, 233
National Humanities Center—NHC, USA, 455
National Institute for Research in the Behavioural Sciences—Szold (Henrietta) Institute, Israel, 169
National Kidney Foundation—NKF, USA, 455
National Science Foundation—NSF, USA, 455
National Trust, UK, 370
National Trust of Fiji—NTF, Fiji, 94
The Nature Conservancy—TNC, USA, 456
NDI—National Democratic Institute for International Affairs, USA, 456
Negri (Mario), Istituto di Ricerche Farmacologiche, Italy, 182
Nessling (Maj and Tor) Foundation, Finland, 96
Nesta—National Endowment for Science, Technology and the Arts, UK, 370
Nestlé Foundation for the Study of the Problems of Nutrition in the World, Switzerland, 310
Network for Human Development, Brazil, 41
Neves (José Maria), Fundação para a Governança, Cabo Verde, 46
New Economics Foundation—NEF, UK, 371
The New York Community Trust—NYCT, USA, 457
Newberry Library, USA, 457
NFCR—National Foundation for Cancer Research, USA, 457
Nicolas Hulot Foundation for Nature and Humankind, France, 110
The Nippon Foundation, Japan, 192
Nitidæ, France, 115
Nobel Foundation, Sweden, 301
Nobelstiftelsen, Sweden, 301
Nordic Institute for Theoretical Physics, Sweden, 302
NORDITA—Nordiska Institutet för Teoretisk Fysik, Sweden, 302
Novartis US Foundation, USA, 457
Novo Nordisk Fonden, Denmark, 85
Novo Nordisk Foundation, Denmark, 85
NRF—National Research Foundation, South Africa, 282
Nuffield Foundation, UK, 371

NWO Domain Applied and Engineering Sciences, Netherlands, 227
NYCT—The New York Community Trust, USA, 457
Observer Research Foundation—ORF, India, 159
The Ocean Cleanup Foundation, Netherlands, 230
The Ocean Foundation, USA, 458
Oceanographic Institute—Albert I, Prince of Monaco Foundation, France, 114
ODI, UK, 371
OeAD, Austria, 22
Olav Thon Foundation, Norway, 242
Olav Thon Stiftelsen, Norway, 242
Omidyar Group, USA, 458
Omidyar Network Fund, USA, 458
Onassis (Alexander S.) Public Benefit Foundation, Liechtenstein, 207
One Economy Foundation, Namibia, 222
Open Society Foundation for Albania, Albania, 5
Open Society Foundation Haiti, Haiti, 149
Open Society Foundation—London, UK, 372
Open Society Foundation—Western Balkans, Albania, 5
Open Society Foundations, USA, 459
Open Society Foundations in Pakistan, Pakistan, 245
Open Society Initiative for Southern Africa—OSISA, South Africa, 282
Oppenheimer Generations Foundation, South Africa, 282
Orange Botswana Foundation, Botswana, 37
Orange Foundation, Spain, 293
Orange Foundation Tunisia, Tunisia, 326
Orange Solidarité Madagascar, Madagascar, 210
Orbis Charitable Trust, UK, 372
Orentreich Foundation for the Advancement of Science, Inc—OFAS, USA, 459
Orient Foundation, Portugal, 260
Österreichischer Wissenschaftsfonds—FWF, Austria, 21
Östersjöfonden, Finland, 97
Oswaldo Cruz Foundation, Brazil, 40
Pacific Leprosy Foundation, New Zealand, 234
Packard (David and Lucile) Foundation, USA, 420
Paideia Galiza Foundation, Spain, 293
PAN Africa—Pesticide Action Network Africa, Senegal, 271
PAN Europe—Pesticide Action Network Europe, Belgium, 34
PAN UK—Pesticide Action Network UK, UK, 373
PANAP—Pesticide Action Network Asia and the Pacific, Malaysia, 211
PANNA—Pesticide Action Network North America, USA, 462
Parasol Foundation Trust, Gibraltar, 144
Parkinson's Foundation, USA, 461
Partners in Health, USA, 461
Pasteur Institute, France, 114
Pasteur Institute of Lille, France, 114
PATH, USA, 461
Patterson (Alicia) Foundation, USA, 398
The Paul G. Allen Family Foundation, USA, 462
Paulo Foundation, Finland, 97
Paulon Säätiö, Finland, 97
Pedro Barrié de la Maza Foundation, Spain, 293
Peres Center for Peace and Innovation, Israel, 171
Pesticide Action Network Africa—PAN Africa, Senegal, 271
Pesticide Action Network Asia and the Pacific—PANAP, Malaysia, 211
Pesticide Action Network Europe—PAN Europe, Belgium, 34
Pesticide Action Network North America—PANNA, USA, 462
Pesticide Action Network UK—PAN UK, UK, 373
The Pew Charitable Trusts, USA, 462
Pezcoller (Alessio), Fondazione, Italy, 174
Pfizer Foundation, USA, 462
PH International, USA, 463
Philip-Sörensens (Erik) Stiftelse, Sweden, 299
PHR—Physicians for Human Rights, USA, 463
Physicians for Human Rights—PHR, USA, 463
Piera, Pietro and Giovanni Ferrero Foundation, Italy, 179
Planck (Max) Gesellschaft zur Förderung der Wissenschaften eV, Germany, 135
Population Council, USA, 463
Potter (Ian) Foundation, Australia, 14
Practical Action, UK, 374
Pratham Education Foundation, India, 159
Preciosa Foundation, Czech Republic, 80
Premji (Azim) Foundation, India, 156
Prince Bernhard Cultural Foundation, Netherlands, 230
Princess of Asturias Foundation, Spain, 294

Prins Bernhard Culturfonds, Stichting, Netherlands, 230
Project Harmony, USA, 463
Project HOPE, USA, 464
Public Health Foundation of India—PHFI, India, 159
Puerto Rico Community Foundation, Puerto Rico, 261
Qatar Foundation, Qatar, 262
Qattan (A. M.) Foundation, UK, 338
Radiation Effects Research Foundation—RERF, Japan, 193
Rahvusvaheline Kaitseuuringute Keskus—RKK, Estonia, 93
Rainforest Foundation US—RFUS, USA, 465
Ramaciotti Foundations, Australia, 17
Ramón Areces Foundation, Spain, 294
RAND Corporation, USA, 465
Rare, USA, 466
RBC Foundation, Canada, 61
Re:wild, USA, 466
Realdania Foundation, Denmark, 83
RED—Ruralité-Environnement-Développement, Belgium, 34
REDEH—Rede de Desenvolvimento Humano, Brazil, 41
Reeve (Christopher and Dana) Foundation, USA, 415
Rehabilitation International—RI, USA, 466
Reliance Foundation, India, 160
Repsol Foundation, Spain, 295
Research Corporation for Science Advancement—RCSA, USA, 467
Rhodes Trust, UK, 376
RIA—Royal Irish Academy, Ireland, 167
Richard Dawkins Foundation for Reason and Science, USA, 412
Richard King Mellon Foundation, USA, 467
Right Livelihood Award Foundation, Sweden, 302
Rockefeller Foundation, USA, 468
Rogosin Institute, USA, 468
Rohini Nilekani Philanthropies, India, 160
Romanian Cultural Institute, Romania, 264
Rome Foundation, Italy, 179
Rössing Foundation, Namibia, 222
Rotary Yoneyama Memorial Foundation, Inc, Japan, 193
Rothschild (Edmond de) Foundations, Switzerland, 308
Roviralta (María Francisca de), Fundación, Spain, 292
Royal Aeronautical Society—RAeS, UK, 376
Royal Anthropological Institute of Great Britain and Ireland—RAI, UK, 377
Royal Commission for the Exhibition of 1851, UK, 377
Royal Elcano Institute Foundation, Spain, 294
The Royal Foundation of the Prince and Princess of Wales, UK, 378
Royal Geographical Society (with the Institute of British Geographers)—RGS-IBG, UK, 378
Royal Holland Society of Sciences and Humanities, Netherlands, 226
Royal Institute of International Affairs—RIIA—Chatham House, UK, 378
The Royal Society, UK, 379
The Royal Society of Medicine—RSM, UK, 379
Royal Society for the Prevention of Cruelty to Animals—RSPCA, UK, 380
Royal Society for the Protection of Birds—RSPB, UK, 379
RSA—Royal Society for the Encouragement of Arts, Manufactures and Commerce, UK, 379
RSPB—Royal Society for the Protection of Birds, UK, 379
RSPCA—Royal Society for the Prevention of Cruelty to Animals, UK, 380
Rüf (Gebert) Stiftung, Switzerland, 311
Runyon (Damon) Cancer Research Foundation, USA, 419
Ruralité-Environnement-Développement—RED, Belgium, 34
Rurality Environment Development, Belgium, 34
Russian International Affairs Council—RIAC, Russian Federation, 266
SAASTA—South African Agency for Science and Technology Advancement, South Africa, 283
Säätiöiden post doc-poolin, Finland, 95
Sainsbury Family Charitable Trusts, UK, 380
Salzburg Global Seminar, Austria, 22
Samsung Foundation, Korea (Republic), 202
Sander (Wilhelm) Stiftung, Germany, 143
Sasakawa, Fondation Franco-Japonaise, France, 106
Sasakawa Health Foundation—SHF, Japan, 194
The Sasakawa Peace Foundation—SPF, Japan, 194
SBS Cultural Foundation, Korea (Republic), 202

Science and technology

Schering (Ernst) Stiftung, Germany, 127
Schlumberger Foundation, USA, 470
Schneider Electric Foundation, France, 111
Schöck (Eberhard) Stiftung, Germany, 127
Schweisfurth Foundation, Germany, 139
Schweisfurth-Stiftung, Germany, 139
Schweizerische Akademie der Medizinischen Wissenschaften, Switzerland, 316
Schweizerische Stiftung für Alpine Forschungen—SSAF, Switzerland, 316
Schweizerischer Nationalfonds zur Förderung der Wissenschaftlichen Forschung/Fonds National Suisse de la Recherche Scientifique—SNF, Switzerland, 316
Science and Politics Foundation—German Institute for International and Security Affairs, Germany, 141
Scientific Foundation of Hisham Adeeb Hijjawi, Jordan, 196
Scientific Research Foundation, Belgium, 32
SEEMO—South East Europe Media Organisation, Austria, 23
Seoam Yoon Se Young Foundation, Korea (Republic), 202
Sesame Workshop, USA, 471
Seva Foundation, USA, 471
Seychelles Islands Foundation—SIF, Seychelles, 272
Shell Foundation—SF, UK, 382
Shiv Nadar Foundation Group, India, 160
Shoman (Abdul Hameed) Foundation, Jordan, 195
SickKids Foundation, Canada, 62
The Sierra Club Foundation, USA, 471
Sightsavers International, UK, 382
Signe and Ane Gyllenberg Foundation, Finland, 97
Signe och Ane Gyllenbergs stiftelse, Finland, 97
Sihtasutus Eesti Rahvuskultuuri Fond, Estonia, 93
Silicon Valley Community Foundation—SVCF, USA, 471
Simone and Cino del Duca Foundation, France, 111
Simons Foundation, USA, 472
Singapore International Foundation—SIF, Singapore, 273
Singer-Polignac Foundation, France, 111
Sistema Charitable Foundation, Russian Federation, 267
Skolkovo Foundation—Foundation for Development of the Center for the Development and Commercialization of New Technologies, Russian Federation, 267
Skoll Foundation, USA, 472
Sloan (Alfred P.) Foundation, USA, 398
Slovak Security Policy Institute, Slovakia, 276
Slovenian Science Foundation, Slovenia, 277
Slovenska znanstvena fundacija—SZF, Slovenia, 277
Slovenský inštitút pre bezpečnostnú politiku, Slovakia, 276
SM Foundation, Spain, 295
Smithsonian Institution, USA, 472
Snow Leopard Trust, USA, 472
Soares (Mário), Fundação, Portugal, 260
Society for Education and Training, UK, 351
Software AG Foundation, Germany, 139
Software AG Stiftung, Germany, 139
Sorenson Legacy Foundation, USA, 473
Souter Charitable Trust, UK, 384
South African Agency for Science and Technology Advancement—SAASTA, South Africa, 283
South East Europe Media Organisation—SEEMO, Austria, 23
South Sudan Center for Strategic and Policy Studies—CSPS, South Sudan, 285
Spencer Foundation, USA, 473
Spinal Research, UK, 384
SpinalCure Australia, Australia, 18
Springer (Axel) Stiftung, Germany, 122
Springer (Friede) Stiftung, Germany, 129
Stanley Center for Peace and Security, USA, 473
State Grid Foundation for Public Welfare, China (People's Republic), 69
Stichting Bellingcat, Netherlands, 228
Stichting Dioraphte, Netherlands, 229
Stichting IKEA Foundation, Netherlands, 229
Stichting The Ocean Cleanup, Netherlands, 230
Stichting Prins Bernhard Cultuurfonds, Netherlands, 230
Stichting Triodos Foundation, Netherlands, 231
Stichting Vodafone Netherlands, Netherlands, 231
Stiftelsen Blanceflor Boncompagni Ludovisi, född Bildt, Sweden, 303
Stiftelsen Dam, Norway, 243
Stiftelsen Gapminder, Sweden, 300
Stiftelsen Teknikens Främjande—Tekniikan Edistämissäätiö, Finland, 98
Stifterverband für die Deutsche Wissenschaft eV, Germany, 119
Stiftung Jugend forscht eV, Germany, 140
Stiftung Mercator, Germany, 140
Stiftung Meridian, Germany, 140
Stiftung für die Rechte zukünftiger Generationen—SRzG, Germany, 141
Stiftung Wissenschaft und Politik—Deutsches Institut für internationale Politik und Sicherheit—SWP, Germany, 141
Stiftung Zukunft.li, Liechtenstein, 208
Stiftungsfonds Deutsche Bank im Stifterverband für die Deutsche Wissenschaft, Germany, 142
Stockholm Environment Institute, Sweden, 303
Streisand (Barbra) Foundation, USA, 408
Studienstiftung des deutschen Volkes, Germany, 142
Sudan Foundation, Sudan, 297
Südosteuropäische Medienorganisation, Austria, 23
Sulaiman Bin Abdul Aziz Bin Saleh Al Rajhi Foundation, Saudi Arabia, 269
Sultan bin Abdulaziz Al Sa'ud Foundation, Saudi Arabia, 270
Suomen Kulttuurirahasto, Finland, 97
Susan G. Komen Breast Cancer Foundation, USA, 474
Sutherland Self Help Trust, New Zealand, 235
Suzuki Foundation (David), Canada, 53
Svenska Institutet i Rom/Istituto Svedese di Studi Classici a Roma, Italy, 183
Svenska kulturfonden, Finland, 98
Swaminathan (M. S.) Research Foundation, India, 158
Sweden-Japan Foundation—SJF, Sweden, 304
The Swedish Cultural Foundation in Finland, Finland, 98
Swedish Institute in Rome, Italy, 183
Swiss Academy of Medical Sciences, Switzerland, 316
Swiss Foundation for Alpine Research—SFAR, Switzerland, 316
Swiss Foundation for Technical Co-operation, Switzerland, 318
Swiss National Science Foundation—SNSF, Switzerland, 316
Swisscontact—Swiss Foundation for Technical Co-operation, Switzerland, 318
Tang Prize Foundation, Taiwan, 322
Tata Trusts, India, 160
Tatra Bank Foundation, Slovakia, 276
Tea Research Foundation of Central Africa—TRFCA, Malawi, 211
TechnoServe, USA, 474
Tekniikan Edistämissäätiö—Stiftelsen för teknikens främjande—TES, Finland, 98
Telefónica Foundation, Spain, 295
Telefónica Movistar Argentina Foundation, Argentina, 8
Telefónica Movistar Chile Foundation, Chile, 65
Telefónica Movistar Colombia Foundation, Colombia, 71
Telefónica Movistar Ecuador Foundation, Ecuador, 89
Telefónica Movistar México Foundation, Mexico, 216
Telefónica Movistar Perú Foundation, Peru, 249
Telefónica Movistar Uruguay Foundation, Uruguay, 485
Telefônica Vivo Foundation, Brazil, 41
Templeton (John) Foundation, USA, 444
Templeton Philanthropies, USA, 444
Templeton Religion Trust, Bahamas, 24
Tencent Foundation, China (People's Republic), 70
TESEV—Türkiye Ekonomik ve Sosyal Etüdler Vakfı, Türkiye, 329
Thiel Foundation, USA, 474
Thomas B. Thrige Foundation, Denmark, 86
Thomas B. Thriges Fond, Denmark, 86
Thomson Reuters Foundation, UK, 385
Thriges (Thomas B.) Fond, Denmark, 86
Tifa Foundation—Indonesia, Indonesia, 163
TK Foundation, Bahamas, 24
The Todd Foundation, New Zealand, 235
Toegepaste en Technische Wetenschappen, Netherlands, 227
Toepfer (Alfred) Stiftung, Germany, 121
Together for Global Justice—CIDSE, Belgium, 29
Tokyu Foundation, Japan, 194
Tony Blair Institute for Global Change—TBI, UK, 386
Torcuato Di Tella Foundation, Argentina, 8
TOSA Foundation, USA, 475
Toyota Vietnam Foundation—TVF, Viet Nam, 488
Triodos Foundation, Netherlands, 231
Tschira (Klaus) Stiftung, Germany, 134

INDEX OF MAIN ACTIVITIES

Tunisia Development Foundation, Tunisia, 326
Turing (Alan) Institute, UK, 339
Turkish Economic and Social Studies Foundation, Türkiye, 329
Turkish Foundation for Combating Soil Erosion, for Reforestation and the Protection of Natural Habitats, Türkiye, 330
Türkiye Erozyonla Mücadele Ağaçlandırma ve Doğal Varlıkları Koruma Vakfı—TEMA, Türkiye, 330
Türkiye Vodafone Vakfı, Türkiye, 331
Turner Foundation, Inc, USA, 476
Turriano (Juanelo) Fundación, Spain, 291
U4 Anti-Corruption Resource Centre, Norway, 241
Ugo Bordoni Foundation, Italy, 180
UK Research and Innovation—UKRI, UK, 387
UNIFOR—Forvaltningstiftelse for fond og legater, Norway, 240
Union for International Cancer Control—UICC, Switzerland, 318
Union Internationale Contre le Cancer, Switzerland, 318
United Nations Foundation, USA, 476
United States African Development Foundation—USADF, USA, 477
Unity Foundation, Luxembourg, 210
Universitaire Stichting, Belgium, 34
University Foundation, Belgium, 34
University-Industry Foundation, Spain, 295
University of Zaragoza Business Foundation, Spain, 290
UPS Foundation, USA, 477
US Civilian Research & Development Foundation, USA, 419
Van Leer Foundation, Netherlands, 231
Van Leer Jerusalem Institute, Israel, 171
Venice Foundation, Italy, 181
Verband für Gemeinnütziges Stiften, Austria, 20
Versus Arthritis, UK, 388
Vestnordenfonden, Denmark, 86
Vetlesen (G. Unger) Foundation, USA, 429
VINCI Corporate Foundation for the City, France, 106
VinFuture Foundation, Viet Nam, 489
Vital Strategies, USA, 478
Vodacom Foundation, South Africa, 284
Vodacom Foundation DRC, Congo (Democratic Republic), 72
Vodacom Foundation South Africa, South Africa, 284
Vodacom Lesotho Foundation, Lesotho, 207
Vodacom Tanzania Foundation—VTF, Tanzania, 323
Vodafone Albania Foundation, Albania, 5
Vodafone Americas Foundation—USA, 478
Vodafone ATH Fiji Foundation, Fiji, 94
Vodafone Czech Republic Foundation, Czech Republic, 80
Vodafone Egypt Foundation, Egypt, 91
Vodafone Foundation, UK, 388
Vodafone Foundation Germany, Germany, 142
Vodafone Foundation India, India, 161
Vodafone Foundation Luxembourg, Luxembourg, 210
Vodafone Foundation New Zealand, New Zealand, 235
Vodafone Ghana Foundation, Ghana, 144
Vodafone Hungary Foundation, Hungary, 153
Vodafone Idea Foundation, India, 161
Vodafone Ireland Foundation, Ireland, 168
Vodafone Italy Foundation, Italy, 181
Vodafone Magyarország Alapítvány, Hungary, 153
Vodafone Netherlands Foundation, Netherlands, 231
Vodafone Portugal Foundation, Portugal, 261
Vodafone Romania Foundation, Romania, 264
Vodafone Spain Foundation, Spain, 296
Vodafone Stiftung Deutschland, Germany, 142
Vodafone Türkiye Foundation, Türkiye, 331
Volkswagen Foundation, Germany, 142
VolkswagenStiftung, Germany, 142
Volnoe Delo—Oleg Deripaska Foundation, Russian Federation, 267
Walk Free, Australia, 15
Wallenberg (Knut och Alice) Stiftelse, Sweden, 301
Walter and Duncan Gordon Charitable Foundation, Canada, 62
Water for Good, USA, 479
The Welch Foundation, USA, 479
Wellbeing of Women, UK, 389
Wellcome Trust, UK, 389
Wenner-Gren Foundation for Anthropological Research, Inc, USA, 480
Wenner-Gren Foundations, Sweden, 304
West-Nordic Foundation, Denmark, 86
Weston (Garfield) Foundation, UK, 355

INDEX OF MAIN ACTIVITIES

White Point Development Foundation, Türkiye, 328
Whitehall Foundation, Inc, USA, 480
WHO Foundation, Switzerland, 319
Wihuri Foundation for International Prizes, Finland, 98
Wihuri (Jenny and Antti) Foundation, Finland, 96
Wihurin kansainvälisten palkintojen rahasto, Finland, 98
Wikimedia Foundation, USA, 480
Wild (Dr Rainer) Stiftung, Germany, 126
The WILD Foundation—International Wilderness Leadership Foundation, USA, 481
Wilhelm Sander Foundation, Germany, 143
Wilhelm-Sander-Stiftung, Germany, 143
The William and Flora Hewlett Foundation, USA, 481
The William H. Donner Foundation, Inc, USA, 481
Wilson (E. O.) Biodiversity Foundation, USA, 421
Wilson (Woodrow) International Center for Scholars, USA, 482
Winrock International, USA, 481
Winston Churchill Foundation of the United States, USA, 482
Winston Churchill Memorial Trust of New Zealand, New Zealand, 236
The Wolfson Foundation, UK, 390
The Wood Foundation—TWF, UK, 391
Woodrow Wilson International Center for Scholars, USA, 482
World Association of Children's Friends, Monaco, 217
World Economic Forum, Switzerland, 320
World Learning, USA, 483
World Resources Institute—WRI, USA, 483
World Telehealth Initiative, USA, 484
World Vegetable Center, Taiwan, 322
WorldFish, Malaysia, 212
Worldwide Cancer Research, UK, 392
Wujoh Foundation for Media and Development, Yemen, 489
XPRIZE Foundation, USA, 484
Yayasan Tifa, Indonesia, 163
Yellow Feather Fund, USA, 471
YongLin Charity Foundation, Taiwan, 322
Yuan Lin Charity Fund, China (People's Republic), 70
Zeiss (Carl) Stiftung, Germany, 123
ZEIT-Stiftung Ebelin und Gerd Bucerius, Germany, 143
Zonta Foundation for Women, USA, 484

SOCIAL WELFARE

1818 Fund Foundation, Netherlands, 229
The A. G. Leventis Foundation, Cyprus, 77
A. M. M. Sahabdeen Trust Foundation, Sri Lanka, 297
The A. P. Møller and Chastine Mc-Kinney Møller Foundation, Denmark, 82
A. P. Møller og Hustru Chastine Mc-Kinney Møllers Fond til almene Formaal, Denmark, 82
Abilis Foundation, Finland, 95
Abilis-säätiö, Finland, 95
Abrinq Foundation for the Rights of Children and Adolescents, Brazil, 39
Academy for the Development of Philanthropy in Poland, Poland, 253
Acción Contra el Hambre—ACH, Spain, 286
Accountable Now, USA, 393
ACDI/VOCA, USA, 397
ACFID—Australian Council for International Development, Australia, 12
Acíndar Foundation, Argentina, 6
ACT Alliance, Switzerland, 306
Acting for Life, France, 100
Action Against Hunger, Spain, 286
Action for Children, UK, 338
Action Children's Aid, Denmark, 82
Action contre la Faim—ACF France, France, 100
Action Damien/Damiaanactie, Belgium, 28
Action Group on Erosion, Technology and Concentration, Canada, 54
Action on Poverty, Australia, 10
Action Solidarité Tiers Monde—ASTM, Luxembourg, 209
ActionAid International, South Africa, 278
Adenauer (Konrad) Stiftung eV, Germany, 134
Adessium Foundation, Netherlands, 223
ADRA—Adventist Development and Relief Agency International, USA, 397
Advance, USA, 397
Adventist Development and Relief Agency International—ADRA, USA, 397

Afghanistan Institute for Civil Society—AICS, Afghanistan, 3
Afghanistan Research and Evaluation Unit, Afghanistan, 3
Africa-America Institute—AAI, USA, 398
Africa Foundation, South Africa, 278
Africa Humanitarian Action—AHA, Ethiopia, 93
Africa Institute of South Africa—AISA, South Africa, 279
Africa Space Foundation, Switzerland, 308
The African Agricultural Technology Foundation—AATF, Kenya, 198
African Forum and Network on Debt and Development—AFRODAD, Zimbabwe, 490
African Refugees Foundation—AREF, Nigeria, 237
African Venture Philanthropy Alliance—AVPA, Kenya, 197
African Women's Development Fund—AWDF, Ghana, 143
AFRODAD—African Forum and Network on Debt and Development, Zimbabwe, 490
Aga Khan Development Network—AKDN, Switzerland, 306
Aga Khan Foundation, Switzerland, 306
Aga Khan Foundation Canada, Canada, 49
Aga Khan Foundation UK, UK, 338
Age International, UK, 339
AGIR Association for the Environment and Quality of Life, Mali, 213
Agora Foundation, Poland, 255
Agronomes et Vétérinaires sans Frontières—AVSF, France, 100
Agronomists and Veterinarians Without Borders, France, 100
Agrupació AMCI Foundation, Spain, 286
Ai You Foundation, China (People's Republic), 66
AIC—Association Internationale des Charités, Belgium, 28
Aid to the Church in Need—ACN International, Germany, 120
Aid for Development Club, Austria, 20
AID Foundation, Bangladesh, 24
Air France Foundation, France, 103
AISA—Africa Institute of South Africa, South Africa, 279
Aisha Buhari Global Foundation, Nigeria, 237
Akademia Rozwoju Filantropii w Polsce—ARFP, Poland, 253
Akai Hane—Central Community Chest of Japan, Japan, 185
Aktion Børnehjælp, Denmark, 82
Al Jisr Foundation, Oman, 244
The Al-Khoei Benevolent Foundation, UK, 339
Al-Zubair Charity Foundation, Sudan, 297
Alavi Foundation, USA, 398
Albanian Disability Rights Foundation, Albania, 4
Alemán (Miguel), Fundación, Mexico, 215
Ali Fulhu Thuthu Foundation, Maldives, 212
Alicia Patterson Foundation—APF, USA, 398
Alight, USA, 399
Aliko Dangote Foundation—ADF, Nigeria, 237
Alkhidmat Foundation Pakistan—AKFP, Pakistan, 244
All Good Foundation Charitable Trust, New Zealand, 232
All India Disaster Mitigation Institute, India, 155
Allen Lane Foundation, UK, 339
Allen (Paul G.) Family Foundation, USA, 462
Allende (Isabel) Foundation, USA, 442
Allianz Umana Mente Foundation, Italy, 174
Alola Foundation, Timor-Leste, 325
Alongside Hope/Auprès de l'espoir, Canada, 49
The Alva Foundation, Canada, 49
Alwaleed Philanthropies, Saudi Arabia, 269
Alzheimer Spain Foundation, Spain, 288
AMADE Mondiale—Association Mondiale des Amis de l'Enfance, Monaco, 217
Aman Foundation, Pakistan, 244
Amancio Ortega Foundation, Spain, 288
Ambrela Platform of Development Organizations, Slovakia, 273
Ambrela—Platforma rozvojových organizácií, Slovakia, 273
The Ambrose Monell Foundation, USA, 399
Ambuja Cement Foundation—ACF, India, 156
America for Bulgaria Foundation, Bulgaria, 43
American Enterprise Institute—AEI, USA, 400
American Express Foundation, USA, 400
American Foundation for the Blind—AFB, USA, 400
American Friends Service Committee—AFSC, USA, 401
American Jewish Joint Distribution Committee—JDC, USA, 402
American Jewish World Service—AJWS, USA, 402

Social welfare

American Near East Refugee Aid—Anera, USA, 402
AmeriCares Foundation, Inc, USA, 403
amfAR—The Foundation for AIDS Research, USA, 403
Amigos de la Tierra, Netherlands, 225
Les Amis de la Terre, Netherlands, 225
Amity Foundation, China (People's Republic), 66
AMP Foundation, Australia, 10
Anders Jahre's Foundation for Humanitarian Purposes, Norway, 240
Anders Jahres Humanitære Stiftelse, Norway, 240
Andrews Charitable Trust—ACT, UK, 340
The Andy Warhol Foundation for the Visual Arts, Inc, USA, 404
Anera—American Near East Refugee Aid, USA, 402
Angel of Hope Foundation, Zimbabwe, 490
Anglo American Foundation, UK, 340
Anguilla Community Fund, Anguilla, 5
Anna Lindh Euro-Mediterranean Foundation for Dialogue between Cultures, Egypt, 90
Anne Frank-Fonds, Switzerland, 306
Anne Frank Fund, Switzerland, 306
Anne Ray Foundation, USA, 450
The Annenberg Foundation, USA, 404
The Annie E. Casey Foundation, USA, 404
Ansar Burney Trust International, Pakistan, 245
Anti-Slavery International, UK, 340
Apex Foundation, Australia, 10
Apprentis d'Auteuil Océan Indien, Réunion, 262
Arbeiterwohlfahrt Bundesverband eV—AWO, Germany, 121
ArcelorMittal Brazil Foundation, Brazil, 39
Archewell Foundation, USA, 405
Archie Sherman Charitable Trust, UK, 340
Arcus Foundation, USA, 405
Areumdaun Jaedan, Korea (Republic), 200
Ariadne—European Funders for Social Change and Human Rights, UK, 339
Arias Foundation for Peace and Human Progress, Costa Rica, 74
ASEAN Foundation, Indonesia, 161
Asia Foundation, USA, 406
Asia/Pacific Cultural Centre for UNESCO—ACCU, Japan, 186
Asia Philanthropy Circle—APC, Singapore, 272
AsiaDHRRA—Asian Partnership for the Development of Human Resources in Rural Asia, Philippines, 251
Asian Community Trust—ACT, Japan, 186
Asian Development Research Institute—ADRI, India, 156
Asian Partnership for the Development of Human Resources in Rural Asia, Philippines, 251
Asian Venture Philanthropy Network—AVPN, Singapore, 272
Asociacija Litdea—Lithuanian Development Education and Awareness Raising Association, Lithuania, 208
Asociación de Fundaciones Familiares y Empresariales—AFE, Colombia, 70
Aspen Institute, USA, 407
Association AGIR pour l'Environnement et la Qualité de la Vie, Mali, 213
Association for Development Policy and Humanitarian Aid, Germany, 120
Association of Family and Corporate Foundations, Colombia, 70
Association Internationale des Charités—AIC, Belgium, 28
Association of Italian Foundations and Savings Banks, Italy, 171
Association of Non-Governmental Organizations in The Gambia—TANGO, Gambia, 117
Association for Public Benefit Foundations, Austria, 20
Associazione di Fondazioni e di Casse di Risparmio SpA—ACRI, Italy, 171
ASTM—Action Solidarité Tiers Monde, Luxembourg, 209
Astur Foundation, Uruguay, 485
ATD Fourth World International, France, 115
Atlas Charity Foundation, Poland, 255
Auchan Foundation, France, 103
Aurat Publication & Information Service Foundation—AF, Pakistan, 245
Aurora Trust, UK, 341
Australian Communities Foundation, Australia, 12
Australian Council for International Development—ACFID, Australia, 12
Australian Foundation for the Peoples of Asia and the Pacific—AFAP, Australia, 10
Australian Multicultural Foundation—AMF, Australia, 12

Social welfare

Australian Volunteers International—AVI, Australia, 13
Austrian Science Fund, Austria, 21
Autonómia Alapítvány, Hungary, 152
Autonómia Foundation, Hungary, 152
AVI—Australian Volunteers International, Australia, 13
AVINA Foundation, Panama, 247
AVSI Foundation, Italy, 175
Axel Springer Foundation, Germany, 122
Axel-Springer-Stiftung, Germany, 122
Ayala Foundation, Inc—AFI, Philippines, 251
Ayrton Senna Institute, Brazil, 41
Azim Premji Foundation, India, 156
Azman Hashim Foundation, Malaysia, 212
BaBe—Budi aktivna, Budi emancipiran, Croatia, 77
Bagnoud (François-Xavier) Association, Switzerland, 310
Baha'i International Development Organization—BIDO, Israel, 169
Ban Ki-Moon Foundation for a Better Future, Korea (Republic), 200
Banco do Brasil Foundation, Brazil, 39
Banda (Joyce) Foundation International, Malawi, 210
Bangladesh Freedom Foundation—BFF, Bangladesh, 24
BANHCAFE Foundation, Honduras, 150
Bank of America Charitable Foundation, USA, 407
The Barack Obama Foundation, USA, 407
Barbra Streisand Foundation, USA, 408
Barça Foundation, Spain, 287
Barceló Foundation, Spain, 289
Bariloche Foundation, Argentina, 7
Baring Foundation, UK, 341
Barka Foundation for Mutual Assistance, Poland, 256
Barnardo's, UK, 342
Barretstown, Ireland, 165
Barrié de la Maza (Pedro, Conde de Fenosa), Fundación, Spain, 293
Barzani Charity Foundation—BCF, Iraq, 164
BBC Children in Need, UK, 342
BBC Media Action, UK, 342
BBVA Foundation, Spain, 289
BCause Foundation, Bulgaria, 42
Be Active, Be Emancipated, Croatia, 77
The Beautiful Foundation, Korea (Republic), 200
Beit Trust, UK, 342
Bell (Max) Foundation, Canada, 59
Bello (Sir Ahmadu) Memorial Foundation, Nigeria, 238
Benecke (Otto) Stiftung eV, Germany, 138
Benesco, UK, 347
Berghof Foundation gGmbH, Germany, 122
Berghof Stiftung für Konfliktforschung gGmbH, Germany, 122
Bermuda Foundation, Bermuda, 35
Bernheim Foundation, Belgium, 31
Bertelsmann Foundation, Germany, 122
Bertelsmann Stiftung, Germany, 122
Bettencourt Schueller Foundation, France, 103
BIAT Youth Foundation, Tunisia, 326
Big Heart Foundation, Chad, 64
Biocon Foundation, India, 157
Bischöfliches Hilfswerk Misereor eV, Germany, 137
Blair (Tony) Institute for Global Change, UK, 386
Bleustein-Blanchet (Marcel), Fondation de la Vocation, France, 109
BMCE Bank Foundation, Morocco, 219
BNP Paribas Foundation, France, 103
Bodossaki Foundation, Greece, 145
Bofill (Jaume), Fundació, Spain, 287
Boghossian Foundation, Belgium, 31
Böll (Heinrich) Stiftung, Germany, 131
Bond, UK, 335
Born This Way Foundation, USA, 409
Bosch (Robert) Stiftung GmbH, Germany, 138
Bóthar, Ireland, 166
Botín Foundation, Spain, 292
Botín (Marcelino), Fundación, Spain, 292
Botswana Institute for Development Policy Analysis—BIDPA, Botswana, 37
BP Foundation, Inc, USA, 409
Braća Karić Foundation, Serbia, 271
BRAC, Bangladesh, 25
Bradley (Lynde and Harry) Foundation, Inc, USA, 449
BrazilFoundation, Brazil, 39
Bread for the World—Protestant Work for Social Welfare and Development, Germany, 123
Brenthurst Foundation, South Africa, 282
Bridge Asia Japan—BAJ, Japan, 187
Bridge House Estates, UK, 348

Brighter Future Myanmar Foundation—BFM, Myanmar, 221
Bristol-Myers Squibb Foundation, USA, 410
British Gas Energy Trust, UK, 344
British Overseas NGOs for Development, UK, 335
British Red Cross Society, UK, 345
Brot für die Welt—Evangelisches Werk für Diakonie und Entwicklung, Germany, 123
Brother's Brother Foundation, USA, 410
Brothers of Men, France, 113
Bruno Kreisky Forum for International Dialogue, Austria, 20
Bruno Kreisky Forum für internationalen Dialog, Austria, 20
Buck (Pearl S.) International, USA, 462
Buckland (William) Foundation, Australia, 19
Buddharaksa Foundation, Thailand, 323
Buffett (Howard G.) Foundation, USA, 437
Bunge y Born Foundation, Argentina, 7
CABI, UK, 345
Cadbury (Edward) Charitable Trust, UK, 351
Cadbury (William Adlington) Charitable Trust, UK, 390
CAF America, USA, 393
CAF India, India, 155
CAFOD—Catholic Agency for Overseas Development, UK, 345
Calgary Foundation, Canada, 49
California Community Foundation, USA, 411
Calouste Gulbenkian Foundation, Portugal, 259
Cambodia Development Resource Institute—CDRI, Cambodia, 46
Cambodian Salesian Delegation, Cambodia, 46
Campaign Against Exclusion Foundation, France, 103
Canadian Centre for International Studies and Co-operation, Canada, 51
Canadian Council for International Co-operation—CCIC/Conseil Canadien pour la Coopération Internationale—CCCI, Canada, 48
Canadian Feed The Children—CFTC, Canada, 50
Canadian Physicians for Aid and Relief—CPAR, Canada, 52
Cancer Council Australia, Australia, 13
Canon Foundation in Europe, Netherlands, 224
Canon Institute for Global Studies—CIGS, Japan, 187
Cape Verdean Student Welfare Foundation, Cabo Verde, 45
CARE International—CI, Switzerland, 307
Cargill (Margaret A.) Philanthropies, USA, 450
Cariplo Foundation, Italy, 175
Caritas Canada, Canada, 53
Caritas de France—Secours Catholique, France, 116
Caritas Internationalis—CI, Vatican City, 486
Carlo Cattaneo Institute, Italy, 182
Carlo Pesenti Foundation, Italy, 176
Carlos Slim Foundation, Mexico, 215
CARMABI Foundation, Curaçao, 77
Carnegie Corporation of New York, USA, 411
Carnegie Hero Fund Commission, USA, 412
Carnegie UK Trust, UK, 346
Carpathian Foundation, Hungary, 153
Carrefour International, Canada, 53
CASE—Centrum Analiz Społeczno-Ekonomicznych, Poland, 255
Casey (Annie E.) Foundation, USA, 404
Cassa di Risparmio di Padova e Rovigo Foundation, Italy, 175
Caterpillar Foundation, USA, 412
Catholic Agency for Overseas Development—CAFOD, UK, 345
Catholic Agency for World Development—Trócaire, Ireland, 168
Catholic Help—Caritas France, France, 116
Cattaneo (Carlo), Istituto, Italy, 182
Caucus of Development NGO Networks—CODE-NGO, Philippines, 250
CBM-International, Germany, 123
CCKF—Chiang Ching-kuo Foundation for International Scholarly Exchange, Taiwan, 321
CECI—Canadian Centre for International Studies and Co-operation/Centre d'Etudes et de Coopération Internationale, Canada, 51
CEDIAS-Musée Social—Centre d'Etudes, de Documentation, d'Information et d'Action Sociales, France, 101
CEDRO—Centro de Información y Educación para la Prevención del Abuso de Drogas, Peru, 248
CENSIS—Fondazione Centro Studi Investimenti Sociali, Italy, 172
Center for Economic & Social Development—CESD, Azerbaijan, 23

INDEX OF MAIN ACTIVITIES

Center for Social and Economic Research, Poland, 255
Center for Victims of Torture—CVT, USA, 413
Centras—Assistance Centre for NGOs, Romania, 263
Centras—Centrul de Asistenta pentru Organizatii Neguvernamentale, Romania, 263
Centre for Democracy and Human Rights—CEDEM, Montenegro, 219
Centre for Development of Non-profit Organizations, Croatia, 76
Centre d'Études Pour l'Action Sociale—CEPAS, Congo (Democratic Republic), 72
Centre for Humanitarian Action—CHA, Germany, 123
Centre Ivoirien de Recherches Économiques et Sociales—CIRES, Côte d'Ivoire, 75
Centre for Philanthropy, Slovakia, 274
Centre for Social Studies, Documentation, Information and Action, France, 101
Centro de Estudios Públicos—CEP, Chile, 64
Centro de Información y Educación para la Prevención del Abuso de Drogas—CEDRO, Peru, 248
Centro Studi e Ricerca Sociale Fondazione Emanuela Zancan, Italy, 172
Centrum pre Filantropiu, Slovakia, 274
The Century Foundation—TCF, USA, 413
Cera, Belgium, 28
CERANEO—Centar za razvoj neprofitnih organizacija, Croatia, 76
Cercle de Coopération des ONGD du Luxembourg, Luxembourg, 209
Česká rada sociálních služeb—CRSS, Czech Republic, 78
Česko-německý fond budoucnosti, Czech Republic, 79
Chaabi (Miloud), Fondation, Morocco, 220
Chagnon (Lucie et André), Fondation, Canada, 55
Chang Yung-fa Foundation, Taiwan, 321
Chantal Biya Foundation, Cameroon, 47
Charities Advisory Trust, UK, 336
Charities Aid Foundation of America—CAF America, USA, 393
Charity Islamic Trust Elrahma, UK, 352
Charity Projects, UK, 348
Charles and Lynn Schusterman Family Philanthropies, USA, 413
Charles Stewart Mott Foundation—CSMF, USA, 414
Charles Wolfson Charitable Trust, UK, 347
The Charta 77 Foundation, Czech Republic, 80
The Chatlos Foundation, Inc, USA, 414
Cheshire (Leonard) Foundation, UK, 364
Chia Hsin Foundation, Taiwan, 321
Chiang Ching-kuo Foundation for International Scholarly Exchange—CCKF, Taiwan, 321
The Chicago Community Trust, USA, 414
Child Migrants Trust, UK, 347
ChildFund, New Zealand, 233
ChildFund International, USA, 414
Childhope Philippines, Philippines, 251
Children & War Foundation—CAW, Norway, 240
Children in Africa Foundation, Germany, 140
Children International—CI, USA, 414
Children of the Mekong, France, 102
Children and Sharing, France, 102
Children of Slovakia Foundation, Slovakia, 275
The Children's Investment Fund Foundation, UK, 347
Childwick Trust, UK, 347
China Charities Aid Foundation for Children, China (People's Republic), 67
China Children and Teenagers' Foundation, China (People's Republic), 67
China Foundation for Poverty Alleviation—CFPA, China (People's Republic), 67
China Siyuan Foundation for Poverty Alleviation, China (People's Republic), 67
China Youth Development Foundation, China (People's Republic), 68
Chirac (Jacques), Fondation, France, 107
Chr. Michelsen Institute for Science and Intellectual Freedom—CMI, Norway, 241
Christian Aid, UK, 348
Christopher & Dana Reeve Foundation, USA, 415
Churches' Commission for Migrants in Europe, Belgium, 28
The Churchill Fellowship, UK, 348
Churchill (Winston) Memorial Trust of New Zealand, New Zealand, 236
CIDSE—Together for Global Justice, Belgium, 29
Cimade—Ecumenical Care Service, France, 102
La Cimade—Service Oecuménique d'Entraide, France, 102
Citi Foundation, USA, 415
Citi Handlowy Leopold Kronenberg Foundation, Poland, 255

INDEX OF MAIN ACTIVITIES

Social welfare

The City Bridge Trust, UK, 348
Civic Democratic Initiative Support Foundation—CDF, Yemen, 489
Civic Initiatives, Serbia, 271
Civil Society Development Center—CSDC, Georgia, 117
Civitates, Belgium, 27
Claiborne (Liz) & Art Ortenberg Foundation, USA, 448
Clara Lionel Foundation—CLF, USA, 415
Claude Pompidou Foundation, France, 104
Claudine Talon Foundation, Benin, 35
Cleveland Foundation, USA, 416
Cleveland H. Dodge Foundation, Inc, USA, 416
CLIC Sargent, UK, 392
Clinton Foundation, USA, 416
Clore Israel Foundation, Israel, 169
Člověk v tísni, Czech Republic, 79
CMI—Chr. Michelsen Institute for Science and Intellectual Freedom, Norway, 241
CNIB Foundation/Fondation INCA, Canada, 52
Coady Institute, Canada, 52
Coastline Foundation, Maldives, 212
The Coca-Cola Foundation, Inc, USA, 417
CODESPA Foundation, Spain, 290
Collier Charitable Fund, Australia, 13
Colombian Habitat Foundation, Colombia, 71
Comic Relief, UK, 348
Comité de Coordination des ONGI en RCA, Central African Republic, 63
Commission des Eglises auprès des Migrants en Europe/Kommission der Kirchen für Migranten in Europa, Belgium, 28
Committee of Good Will—Olga Havel Foundation, Czech Republic, 81
Common Network, Brazil, 38
Commonwealth Foundation, UK, 348
The Commonwealth Fund, USA, 417
Communication Foundation for Asia, Philippines, 251
Community Chest, Singapore, 273
Community Chest of Hong Kong, Hong Kong, 150
Community Chest of Korea—Fruit of Love, Korea (Republic), 200
Community Development Foundation, Mozambique, 221
Community Foundation for Northern Ireland, UK, 349
Community Foundation for the Western Region of Zimbabwe—CFWRZ, Zimbabwe, 490
Concern India Foundation, India, 157
Concern Worldwide, Ireland, 166
CONCORD—European NGO Confederation for Relief and Development, Belgium, 26
The Confederation of Service Charities—Cobseo, UK, 349
Conrad N. Hilton Foundation, USA, 417
Consejo Latinoamericano de Ciencias Sociales—CLACSO, Argentina, 6
Conservation International Foundation, USA, 417
Consuelo Zobel Alger Foundation, USA, 417
Co-op Foundation, UK, 349
Cooperation Canada/Coopération Canada, Canada, 48
Co-operative Community Investment Foundation, UK, 349
Cooperazione Internazionale—COOPI, Italy, 173
Coordinadora de ONGD España, Spain, 285
Coordination SUD, France, 99
Copperbelt Development Foundation, Zambia, 490
Coram, UK, 349
Corona Foundation, Colombia, 71
Corra Foundation, UK, 349
Corus International, USA, 418
Costopoulos (J. F.) Foundation, Greece, 146
Council of American Development Foundations, Dominican Republic, 87
Counterpart International, USA, 418
Coutu (Marcelle et Jean), Fondation, Canada, 55
CPAR—Canadian Physicians for Aid and Relief, Canada, 52
Croatian Platform for International Citizen Solidarity, Croatia, 76
CROSOL—Platforma za međunarodnu građansku solidarnost Hrvatske, Croatia, 76
Crossroads International/Carrefour International, Canada, 53
Crown Family Philanthropies, USA, 419
Cruz (Oswaldo), Fundação, Brazil, 40
Culture, Health, Arts, Sports and Education Fund—CHASE, Jamaica, 184
Cundill (Peter) Foundation, Bermuda, 35
Cuso International, Canada, 53
CVT—Center for Victims of Torture, USA, 413
Cyril Ramaphosa Foundation, South Africa, 279
Cystic Fibrosis Canada, Canada, 53
Cystic Fibrosis Trust, UK, 350

Czech Council of Social Services, Czech Republic, 78
Czech-German Fund for the Future, Czech Republic, 79
Dalia Association, Palestinian Territories, 246
Dalio Foundation, USA, 419
Dam Foundation, Norway, 243
Daniele Agostino Derossi Foundation, USA, 420
Danielle Mitterrand Foundation, France, 112
Danish Cultural Institute—DCI, Denmark, 82
Danish Institute for Human Rights, Denmark, 84
Danske Kulturinstitut—DKI, Denmark, 82
David and Lucile Packard Foundation, USA, 420
Davis (Lady) Fellowship Trust, Israel, 170
Daw Khin Kyi Foundation, Myanmar, 221
Debts to Opportunities Foundation, Netherlands, 231
DEC—Disasters Emergency Committee, UK, 336
Defence for Children International—DCI, Switzerland, 307
Dell (Michael & Susan) Foundation, USA, 453
del Pino (Rafael), Fundación, Spain, 294
DemNet—Demokratikus Jogok Fejlesztéséért Alapítvány, Hungary, 153
DemNet—Foundation for the Development of Democratic Rights, Hungary, 153
Democracy and Development Foundation, Chile, 65
Democracy Fund, USA, 458
Deripaska (Oleg) Foundation, Russian Federation, 267
Derossi (Daniele Agostino) Foundation, USA, 420
Deutsche AIDS-Stiftung, Germany, 124
Deutsche Bank Americas Foundation, USA, 420
Deutsche Bank Foundation, Germany, 124
Deutsche Bank Stiftung, Germany, 124
Deutsche Bundesstiftung Umwelt—DBU, Germany, 124
Development Foundation, Guatemala, 148
Development Foundation of Turkey, Türkiye, 330
Development Gateway—DG, USA, 420
Development NGO Coordinator Spain, Spain, 285
Development and Peace—Caritas Canada, Canada, 53
Développement et Paix—Caritas Canada, Canada, 53
Dewji (Mo) Foundation, Tanzania, 323
DHL UK Foundation, UK, 350
Digicel Foundation Haiti, Haiti, 149
Digicel Foundation Jamaica, Jamaica, 184
Digicel PNG Foundation, Papua New Guinea, 247
Digicel Trinidad and Tobago Foundation, Trinidad and Tobago, 326
Dioraphte Foundation, Netherlands, 229
Direct Relief, USA, 420
Disabled Peoples' International—DPI, Canada, 54
Disasters Emergency Committee—DEC, UK, 336
The Do-Nation Foundation, Inc, Saint Lucia, 268
Doctors of the World International, France, 114
Dodge (Cleveland H.) Foundation, Inc, USA, 416
DOEN Foundation, Netherlands, 229
Dom Manuel II Foundation, Portugal, 260
Dominican Development Foundation, Dominican Republic, 87
Don Bosco Foundation of Cambodia—DBFC, Cambodia, 46
Donner (William H.) Foundation, Inc, USA, 481
Doris Duke Charitable Foundation—DDCF, USA, 421
The Dr Denis Mukwege Foundation, Netherlands, 224
Dr Guillermo Manuel Ungo Foundation, El Salvador, 91
Dr Scholl Foundation, USA, 421
Dreyfus Health Foundation, USA, 468
Drug Policy Alliance—DPA, USA, 421
DSW—Deutsche Stiftung Weltbevölkerung, Germany, 126
DTGO Group of Foundations, Thailand, 323
Duke Endowment, USA, 421
Dulverton Trust, UK, 351
Dutch-Bangla Bank Foundation, Bangladesh, 25
Earth Island Institute—EII, USA, 422
Earthworm Foundation, Switzerland, 307
East-West Center—EWC, USA, 422
East-West Encounters Charitable Foundation, Germany, 141
eBay Foundation, USA, 422
Ebert (Friedrich) Stiftung, Germany, 129
EcoCiencia—Fundación Ecuatoriana de Estudios Ecologicos, Ecuador, 88
Economic Development Foundation, Türkiye, 328
Economic and Social Research Foundation—ESRF, Tanzania, 322
ECPAT International, Thailand, 324
Ecuadorean Cooperation for Development Fund, Ecuador, 88

Ecuadorean Foundation of Ecological Studies, Ecuador, 88
Ecuadorean Social Group Fund Populorum Progressio, Ecuador, 89
EDF Group Foundation, France, 107
Edhi Foundation, Pakistan, 245
The Edna McConnell Clark Foundation, USA, 422
Ednannia—Initiative Centre to Support Social Action, Ukraine, 332
Edoardo Garrone Foundation, Italy, 177
EDP Foundation, Portugal, 260
The Education for Development Foundation—EDF, Thailand, 324
Educo, Spain, 286
Edward Cadbury Charitable Trust, UK, 351
Egmont Fonden, Denmark, 83
Egmont Foundation, Denmark, 83
Einaudi (Luigi), Fondazione, Italy, 178
Ekopolis Foundation, Slovakia, 275
The Elders Foundation, UK, 352
Elena & Gennady Timchenko Foundation, Russian Federation, 265
ELEPAP—Rehabilitation for the Disabled, Greece, 145
Elizabeth Glaser Pediatric AIDS Foundation—EGPAF, USA, 423
Ellerman (John) Foundation, UK, 361
The ELMA Group of Foundations, USA, 423
Elrahma Charity Trust, UK, 352
Elrha, UK, 352
Elton John AIDS Foundation, UK, 352
Emanuela Zancan Foundation Centre for Social Studies and Research, Italy, 172
Embrace the Middle East, UK, 352
EMERGENCY, Italy, 173
Emirates Foundation, United Arab Emirates, 334
Emmaüs International, France, 102
Emunah, UK, 353
Enchanted Peach Children's Foundation—EPCF, USA, 423
Enda Third World—Environment and Development Action in the Third World, Senegal, 270
Enda Tiers Monde—Environnement et Développement du Tiers-Monde, Senegal, 270
endPoverty.org, USA, 424
Energies for the World Foundation, France, 105
Enfance et Partage, France, 102
Enfants du Mékong, France, 102
ENGIE Corporate Foundation, France, 105
Ente Cassa di Risparmio di Firenze, Italy, 173
Entraide Protestante Suisse, Switzerland, 311
Entraide Universitaire Mondiale du Canada, Canada, 63
Entwicklungshilfe-Klub, Austria, 20
Environmental Foundation of Jamaica, Jamaica, 184
Environmental Justice Foundation—EJF, UK, 353
Equal Justice Initiative—EJI, USA, 424
Equality Fund/Fonds Égalité, Canada, 54
Equity Group Foundation—EGF, Kenya, 198
Ernest Kleinwort Charitable Trust, UK, 353
ERSTE Foundation, Austria, 21
ERSTE Stiftung—Die ERSTE Österreichische Spar-Casse Privatstiftung, Austria, 21
Eskom Development Foundation, South Africa, 279
Esmée Fairbairn Foundation, UK, 353
Esquel Group Foundation—Ecuador, Ecuador, 88
ETC Group—Action Group on Erosion, Technology and Concentration, Canada, 54
Eugenio Mendoza Foundation, Venezuela, 487
Eurasia Foundation—EF, USA, 424
EURODAD—European Network on Debt and Development, Belgium, 29
Europe Foundation—EPF, Georgia, 118
European Anti-Poverty Network—EAPN, Belgium, 29
European Center for Peace and Development—ECPD, Serbia, 271
European Centre for Social Welfare Policy and Research, Austria, 21
European Federation of National Organisations Working with the Homeless, Belgium, 26
European Food Banks Federation—EFBF, Belgium, 26
European Foundation for the Improvement of Living and Working Conditions—Eurofound, Ireland, 166
European Institute of Health and Social Welfare, Spain, 296
European Network on Debt and Development—EURODAD, Belgium, 29
European NGO Confederation for Relief and Development—CONCORD, Belgium, 26
European Youth Foundation—EYF, France, 112

Social welfare

Evropis Pondis, Georgia, 118
Ewing Marion Kauffman Foundation, USA, 425
ExxonMobil Foundation, USA, 425
FAFIDESS—Fundación de Asesoría Financiera a Instituciones de Desarrollo y Servicio Social, Guatemala, 148
Fairbairn (Esmée) Foundation, UK, 353
Fairtrade Nederland, Netherlands, 230
Faith, UK, 353
The Family Federation of Finland, Finland, 98
Family Restoration Fund, UK, 347
Farm Africa, UK, 354
FATE Foundation, Nigeria, 237
Fatoumatta Bah-Barrow Foundation—FaBB, Gambia, 117
FDC—Fundação para o Desenvolvimento da Comunidade, Mozambique, 221
FEANTSA—Fédération Européenne des Associations Nationales Travaillant avec les Sans-Abri, Belgium, 26
Federal Association of Social Welfare Organizations, Germany, 121
Fédération Européenne des Associations Nationales Travaillant avec les Sans-Abri—FEANTSA, Belgium, 26
Fédération Européenne des Banques Alimentaires—FEBA, Belgium, 26
Federation of Non-Governmental Organizations for Development in Romania, Romania, 263
Fedesarrollo—Fundación para la Educación Superior y el Desarrollo, Colombia, 71
Feed the Children, USA, 425
Feed the Minds, UK, 354
FEIM—Fundación para Estudio e Investigación de la Mujer, Argentina, 7
Feltrinelli (Giangiacomo), Fondazione, Italy, 177
FEMSA Foundation, Mexico, 215
Ferrero (Piera, Pietro e Giovanni), Fondazione, Italy, 179
FHI 360, USA, 425
Fibrose Kystique Canada, Canada, 53
FIJI Water Foundation, Fiji, 94
filia.die Frauenstiftung, Germany, 128
filia—the Women's Foundation, Germany, 128
FINCA International, USA, 425
Finnish Development Organizations, Finland, 95
Finnish Institute in the UK and Ireland Trust, UK, 354
Firelight Foundation, USA, 426
First Nations Development Institute, USA, 426
FirstRand Foundation, South Africa, 280
Florence Savings Bank Foundation, Italy, 173
Focus Humanitarian Assistance—FOCUS, Canada, 54
FOKAL—Open Society Foundation Haiti, Haiti, 149
Follereau Foundation Luxembourg, Luxembourg, 209
FOND—Federatia Organizatiilor Neguvernamentale pentru Dezvoltare din Romania, Romania, 263
Fondacija Braća Karić, Serbia, 271
Fondacija Cennosti, Bulgaria, 43
Fondacioni i Kosovës për Shoqëri të Hapur, Kosovo, 203
Fondacioni Shqiptar për të Drejtat e Personave me Aftësi të Kufizuar—FSHDPAK, Albania, 4
Fondation Abbé Pierre, France, 108
Fondation Africaine pour les Technologies Agricoles, Kenya, 198
Fondation Agir Contre l'Exclusion—FACE, France, 103
Fondation Air France, France, 103
Fondation Auchan, France, 103
Fondation de l'Avenir pour la Recherche Médicale Appliquée, France, 103
Fondation Bernheim, Belgium, 31
Fondation Bettencourt Schueller, France, 103
Fondation BIAT pour la Jeunesse, Tunisia, 326
Fondation BMCE Bank, Morocco, 219
Fondation BNP Paribas, France, 103
Fondation Boghossian, Belgium, 31
Fondation Casip-Cojasor, France, 104
Fondation Chantal Biya—FCB, Cameroon, 47
Fondation Claude Pompidou, France, 104
Fondation Claudine Talon, Benin, 35
Fondation Congo Assistance, Congo (Republic), 73
Fondation Digicel Haïti, Haiti, 149
Fondation Energies pour le Monde—Fondem, France, 105
Fondation d'Entreprise Crédit Agricole Réunion Mayotte, Réunion, 262
Fondation d'Entreprise ENGIE, France, 105
Fondation d'Entreprise Renault, France, 106
Fondation d'Entreprise VINCI pour la Cité, France, 106
Fondation Espace Afrique, Switzerland, 308
Fondation Follereau Luxembourg—FFL, Luxembourg, 209
Fondation de France, France, 99
Fondation Grand Cœur—FGC, Chad, 64
Fondation Groupe EDF, France, 107
Fondation Guri Vie Meilleure, Niger, 236
Fondation Hans Wilsdorf, Switzerland, 309
Fondation Hassan II pour les Marocains Résidant à l'Étranger, Morocco, 220
Fondation Hirondelle: Media for Peace and Human Dignity, Switzerland, 309
Fondation Internationale Tierno et Mariam—FITIMA, Burkina Faso, 44
Fondation Jacques Chirac, France, 107
Fondation Jasmin pour la Recherche et la Communication, Tunisia, 326
Fondation Jean-Paul II pour le Sahel, Burkina Faso, 44
Fondation Joseph Ichame Kamach, Central African Republic, 63
Fondation pour le Logement des Défavorisés, France, 108
Fondation Lucie et André Chagnon, Canada, 55
Fondation J-Louis Lévesque, Canada, 55
Fondation MACIF, France, 108
Fondation MAIF pour la Recherche, France, 108
Fondation Maison des Sciences de l'Homme—FMSH, France, 108
Fondation Mapon, Congo (Democratic Republic), 72
Fondation Marcel Bleustein-Blanchet de la Vocation, France, 109
Fondation Marcelle et Jean Coutu, Canada, 55
Fondation Mérieux, France, 109
Fondation Mesmin Kabath—FOMEKA, Congo (Republic), 73
Fondation Miloud Chaâbi, Morocco, 220
Fondation Mohammed V pour la Solidarité, Morocco, 220
Fondation MTN Bénin, Benin, 35
Fondation MTN Cameroun, Cameroon, 47
Fondation MTN Côte d'Ivoire, Côte d'Ivoire, 76
Fondation Mutuelles Congolaises d'Epargne et de Crédit—MUCODEC, Congo (Republic), 73
Fondation Noura, Mauritania, 214
Fondation Orange, France, 110
Fondation Orange Burkina Faso, Burkina Faso, 45
Fondation Orange Cameroun, Cameroon, 47
Fondation Orange Guinée, Guinea, 149
Fondation Orange Mali, Mali, 213
Fondation Orient-Occident—FOO, Morocco, 220
Fondation P&V, Belgium, 32
Fondation Partage et Vie, France, 110
Fondation Perspectives d'Avenir, Congo (Republic), 73
Fondation Princesse Charlène de Monaco, Monaco, 218
Fondation Rambourg, Tunisia, 326
Fondation Rawji, Congo (Democratic Republic), 72
Fondation Rinaldi, Haiti, 149
Fondation Rio Tinto, Guinea, 149
Fondation Roi Baudouin, Belgium, 33
Fondation Schneider Electric, France, 111
Fondation du Scoutisme Mondial, Switzerland, 309
Fondation Sommet Mondial des Femmes, Switzerland, 320
Fondation Stamm, Burundi, 45
Fondation TotalEnergies, France, 112
Fondation Tunisie pour le Développement, Tunisia, 326
Fondation Vodacom RDC, Congo (Democratic Republic), 72
Fondatzija Otvoryeno Opshtyestvo Makyedonija, North Macedonia, 239
Fondazione Allianz Umana Mente, Italy, 174
Fondazione AVSI, Italy, 175
Fondazione Cariplo, Italy, 175
Fondazione Cassa di Risparmio di Padova e Rovigo, Italy, 175
Fondazione Cassa di Risparmio di Torino, Italy, 176
Fondazione Cassa di Risparmio di Verona Vicenza Belluno e Ancona—Fondazione Cariverona, Italy, 176
Fondazione Cavaliere del Lavoro Carlo Pesenti, Italy, 176
Fondazione Centesimus Annus—Pro Pontifice, Vatican City, 486
Fondazione Centro Studi Investimenti Sociali—CENSIS, Italy, 176
Fondazione Compagnia di San Paolo, Italy, 176
Fondazione Edoardo Garrone, Italy, 177
Fondazione Giangiacomo Feltrinelli, Italy, 177
Fondazione Giovanni Lorenzini, Italy, 177

INDEX OF MAIN ACTIVITIES

Fondazione Giulio Pastore—FGP, Italy, 178
Fondazione ISMU—Iniziative e Studi sulla Multietnicità, Italy, 178
Fondazione Luigi Einaudi, Italy, 178
Fondazione Piera, Pietro e Giovanni Ferrero, Italy, 179
Fondazione Populorum Progressio, Vatican City, 486
Fondazione Roma, Italy, 179
Fondazione RUI, Italy, 180
Fondazione Social Venture-Giordano Dell'Amore, Italy, 180
Fondazione Terzo Pilastro – Internazionale, Italy, 180
Fondazione Unipolis, Italy, 181
Fondazione Vodafone Italia, Italy, 181
Fonden Realdania, Denmark, 83
Fondo Ecuatoriano de Cooperación para el Desarrollo—FECD, Ecuador, 88
Fonds Égalité, Canada, 54
Fonds Européen pour la Jeunesse—FEJ, France, 112
Food for the Hungry—FH, USA, 426
Food for the Poor, Inc, USA, 426
For a Healthy Generation, Uzbekistan, 485
Ford Foundation, USA, 427
The Forest Trust, Switzerland, 307
Forum LSM Internasional untuk Pembangunan Indonesia, Indonesia, 161
FORWARD—Foundation for Women's Health Research and Development, UK, 354
Fòs Feminista, USA, 427
Foundation for AIDS Research—amfAR, USA, 403
Foundation for Analysis and Social Studies, Spain, 288
Foundation for Assistance, Training and Integration of Disadvantaged People, Spain, 287
Foundation of Banks and Savings Banks of CECA, Spain, 289
Foundation Bofill, Spain, 287
Foundation for Caribbean Research and Management of Biodiversity, Curaçao, 77
Foundation Centre for the Study of Social Investment, Italy, 176
Foundation for the Financial Assessment of Social Service and Development Institutions, Guatemala, 148
Foundation of the Future for Applied Medical Research, France, 103
Foundation for Higher Education and Development, Colombia, 71
Foundation for Housing the Disadvantaged, France, 108
Foundation for International Community Assistance, USA, 425
Foundation for Latin American Economic Research, Argentina, 7
Foundation Open Society Institute Pakistan, Pakistan, 245
Foundation Open Society Macedonia—FOSIM, North Macedonia, 239
Foundation Orange, Slovakia, 275
Foundation 'Remembrance, Responsibility and Future', Germany, 139
Foundation for the Rights of Future Generations, Germany, 141
Foundation for Rural & Regional Renewal—FRRR, Australia, 14
Foundation for Social Housing, Venezuela, 488
Foundation of Spanish Commercial Agents, Spain, 287
Foundation for the Support of Women's Work, Türkiye, 329
Foundation for the Victims of Terrorism, Spain, 296
Foundation for the Welfare of Holocaust Victims, Israel, 169
Foundation for Women, Spain, 293
Foundation for Women's Health, Research and Development—FORWARD, UK, 354
Foundation for Women's Research and Studies, Argentina, 7
The Foundation for Young Australians—FYA, Australia, 14
Foundation of Youth and Lifelong Learning—INEDIVIM, Greece, 145
Fox (Michael J.) Foundation for Parkinson's Research, USA, 453
France Amérique Latine—FAL, France, 112
France-Libertés Fondation Danielle Mitterrand, France, 112
Franciscans International, Switzerland, 310
Frank (Anne)-Fonds, Switzerland, 306
Fraser Institute, Canada, 55
Freedom from Torture (Medical Foundation for the Care of Victims of Torture), UK, 354

INDEX OF MAIN ACTIVITIES

Social welfare

Freedom Together Foundation, USA, 428
Frères des Hommes—FDH, France, 113
Freudenberg Foundation, Germany, 129
Freudenberg Stiftung, Germany, 129
Friedensdorf International, Germany, 129
Friedrich-Ebert-Stiftung eV, Germany, 129
Friends of the Earth International—FOEI, Netherlands, 225
Friends-International, Cambodia, 46
Fund and Endowment Management Foundation, Norway, 240
Fundação Abrinq pelos Direitos da Criança e do Adolescente, Brazil, 39
Fundação ArcelorMittal Brasil, Brazil, 39
Fundação Assistência Médica International—AMI, Portugal, 258
Fundação Banco do Brasil, Brazil, 39
Fundação Caboverdiana de Acção Social Escolar—FICASE, Cabo Verde, 45
Fundação Calouste Gulbenkian, Portugal, 259
Fundação Dom Manuel II, Portugal, 260
Fundação EDP, Portugal, 260
Fundação Getulio Vargas—FGV, Brazil, 40
Fundação Maria Cecilia Souto Vidigal, Brazil, 40
Fundação Oriente, Portugal, 260
Fundação Oswaldo Cruz—FIOCRUZ, Brazil, 40
Fundació Agrupació AMCI, Spain, 286
Fundació Futbol Club Barcelona, Spain, 287
Fundació Jaume Bofill, Spain, 287
Fundación Acindar, Argentina, 6
Fundación AFIM—Ayuda, Formación e Integración del Discapacitado, Spain, 287
Fundación de los Agentes Comerciales de España, Spain, 287
Fundación Alzheimer España—FAE, Spain, 288
Fundación Amancio Ortega, Spain, 288
Fundación para el Análisis y los Estudios Sociales—FAES, Spain, 288
Fundación Arias para la Paz y el Progreso Humano, Costa Rica, 74
Fundación Astur, Uruguay, 485
Fundación AVINA, Panama, 247
Fundación Bancaria 'la Caixa', Spain, 288
Fundación Banco Bilbao Vizcaya Argentaria—Fundación BBVA, Spain, 289
Fundación BANHCAFE—FUNBANHCAFE, Honduras, 150
Fundación Barceló, Spain, 289
Fundación Bariloche, Argentina, 7
Fundación BBVA, Spain, 289
Fundación Bunge y Born, Argentina, 7
Fundación de las Cajas de Ahorros—FUNCAS, Spain, 289
Fundación Capital, Colombia, 70
Fundación Carlos Slim, Mexico, 215
Fundación Circulo de Montevideo, Uruguay, 485
Fundación CODESPA, Spain, 289
Fundación Comunitaria de Puerto Rico—FCPR, Puerto Rico, 261
Fundación Corona, Colombia, 71
Fundación Democracia y Desarrollo, Chile, 65
Fundación Dominicana de Desarrollo—FDD, Dominican Republic, 87
Fundación Dr Guillermo Manuel Ungo—FUNDAUNGO, El Salvador, 91
Fundación para la Educación Superior y el Desarrollo—Fedesarrollo, Colombia, 71
Fundación Espacio Cívico, Panama, 247
Fundación para Estudio e Investigación de la Mujer—FEIM, Argentina, 7
Fundación Eugenio Mendoza—FEM, Venezuela, 487
Fundación Felipe González, Spain, 290
Fundación FEMSA, Mexico, 215
Fundación Futuro Latinoamericano, Ecuador, 88
Fundación Génesis Empresarial, Guatemala, 148
Fundación Grupo Esquel—Ecuador, Ecuador, 88
Fundación Hábitat Colombia—FHC, Colombia, 71
Fundación IE, Spain, 291
Fundación de Investigaciones Económicas Latinoamericanas—FIEL, Argentina, 7
Fundación Invica, Chile, 65
Fundación Juan March, Spain, 291
Fundación MAPFRE, Spain, 292
Fundación Marcelino Botín, Spain, 292
Fundación María Francisca de Roviralta, Spain, 292
Fundación Miguel Alemán AC, Mexico, 215
Fundación Montemadrid, Spain, 292
Fundación Mujer, Costa Rica, 74
Fundación Mujeres, Spain, 293
Fundación Nacional para el Desarrollo, El Salvador, 91
Fundación Nacional para el Desarrollo de Honduras—FUNADEH, Honduras, 150
Fundación Nobis, Ecuador, 88
Fundación ONCE, Spain, 293
Fundación Orange, Spain, 293

Fundación Oxfam Intermón, Spain, 293
Fundación Paideia Galiza, Spain, 293
Fundación Paraguaya de Cooperación y Desarrollo, Paraguay, 248
Fundación Pedro Barrié de la Maza, Spain, 293
Fundación Princesa de Asturias, Spain, 294
Fundación Promi, Spain, 294
Fundación Rafa Nadal, Spain, 294
Fundación Rafael del Pino, Spain, 294
Fundación Real Madrid, Spain, 295
Fundación Repsol, Spain, 295
Fundación La Salle de Ciencias Naturales—FLASA, Venezuela, 487
Fundación Semah-Valencia, Panama, 247
Fundación SES—Sustentabilidad, Educación, Solidaridad, Argentina, 8
Fundación SM, Spain, 295
Fundación Solidaridad, Dominican Republic, 87
Fundación Tecnologías Sociales—TECSOS, Spain, 296
Fundación Telefónica, Spain, 295
Fundación Telefónica Movistar Colombia, Colombia, 71
Fundación Teletón México, Mexico, 216
Fundación Telmex Telcel, Mexico, 216
Fundación Tigo, Guatemala, 148
Fundación UNIR Bolivia, Bolivia, 36
Fundación UPM, Uruguay, 485
Fundación Víctimas del Terrorismo, Spain, 296
Fundación de la Vivienda Popular, Venezuela, 488
Fundación Vodafone España, Spain, 296
Fundacja Agory, Poland, 255
Fundacja Citi Handlowy im. Leopolda Kronenberga, Poland, 255
Fundacja Dobroczynności Atlas, Poland, 255
Fundacja im. Stefana Batorego, Poland, 256
Fundacja POLSAT, Poland, 256
Fundacja Pomocy Wzajemnej Barka, Poland, 256
FUNDAP—Fundación para el Desarrollo, Guatemala, 148
Fundasaun Alola, Timor-Leste, 325
Fundația Orange, Romania, 263
Fundația Orange Moldova, Moldova, 217
Fundația Vodafone România, Romania, 264
FUNDAUNGO—Fundación Dr Guillermo Manuel Ungo, El Salvador, 91
Future in Our Hands Youth NGO—FIOH, Armenia, 9
FWF—Österreichischer Wissenschaftsfonds, Austria, 21
FWO—Fonds Wetenschappelijk Onderzoek, Belgium, 32
FXB International—Association François-Xavier Bagnoud, Switzerland, 310
The Gaia Foundation, UK, 355
Gapminder, Sweden, 300
Garfield Weston Foundation, UK, 355
Garrone (Edoardo), Fondazione, Italy, 177
Gates (Bill & Melinda) Foundation, USA, 429
Gates Foundation, USA, 429
The Gatsby Charitable Foundation, UK, 355
The General Kashif Al-Getaa Foundation, Iraq, 164
General Service Foundation—GSF, USA, 430
Génesis Empresarial Foundation, Guatemala, 148
German AIDS Foundation, Germany, 124
German Catholic Bishops' Organization for Development Co-operation, Germany, 137
German Federal Foundation for the Environment, Germany, 124
German Foundation for World Population, Germany, 126
German Institute of Development and Sustainability—IDOS, Germany, 130
Getulio Vargas Foundation, Brazil, 40
Ghazanfar Foundation, Afghanistan, 4
Giangiacomo Feltrinelli Foundation, Italy, 177
Gift of the Givers Foundation, South Africa, 280
Giordano Dell'Amore Social Venture Foundation, Italy, 180
Giovanni Lorenzini Foundation, Italy, 177
Giulio Pastore Foundation, Italy, 178
To Give, Israel, 170
Give2Asia, USA, 394
GiveWell—The Clear Fund, USA, 430
Giving USA Foundation, USA, 394
Glaser (Elizabeth) Pediatric AIDS Foundation, USA, 423
Global Communities, USA, 431
Global Dialogue, UK, 336
The Global Foodbanking Network—GFN, USA, 431
Global Fund for Children, USA, 431
Global Fund for Women—GFW, USA, 431
Global Greengrants Fund, USA, 431
Global Impact, USA, 395
Global Innovation Fund, UK, 356
GOAL, Ireland, 166

Goldman Sachs Foundation, USA, 432
Goldsmith (Horace W.) Foundation, USA, 436
Good Neighbors International, Korea (Republic), 201
Good Things Foundation, UK, 356
Good360, USA, 432
Goodenough College, UK, 356
Goodwill Industries International, Inc—GII, USA, 432
Google.org—Google Foundation, USA, 432
Gorbachev Foundation, Russian Federation, 266
Gordon (Walter and Duncan) Charitable Foundation, Canada, 62
Graça Machel Trust, South Africa, 280
Gradjanske inicijative—GI, Serbia, 271
Grameen Foundation—GF, USA, 433
Grant (William T.) Foundation, USA, 481
Grassroots International—GRI, USA, 433
Great Britain Sasakawa Foundation, UK, 356
Greater Kansas City Community Foundation, USA, 433
Green Umbrella Children's Foundation—ChildFund Korea, Korea (Republic), 201
The Greta Thunberg Foundation, Sweden, 300
Grupo Social Fondo Ecuatoriano Populorum Progressio, Ecuador, 89
Gruss (Joseph S. and Caroline) Memorial Fund, Israel, 170
Guggenheim (Harry Frank) Foundation, USA, 434
Guggenheim (John Simon) Memorial Foundation, USA, 444
The Guide Dogs for the Blind Association, UK, 357
GuideStar India, India, 155
Gulbenkian (Calouste), Fundação, Portugal, 259
H&M Foundation, Sweden, 300
Habitat for Humanity International, USA, 433
Hagar NZ, New Zealand, 233
Haiti Development Institute—HDI, Haiti, 149
Hamdard Foundation Pakistan, Pakistan, 245
Hamlyn (Paul) Foundation, UK, 373
Hanaholmen—Swedish-Finnish Cultural Centre, Finland, 95
HAND—Hungarian Association of NGOs for Development and Humanitarian Aid, Hungary, 152
Haniel Foundation, Germany, 131
Haniel-Stiftung, Germany, 131
Hanns Seidel Foundation, Germany, 131
Hanns-Seidel-Stiftung eV, Germany, 131
Hans Wilsdorf Foundation, Switzerland, 309
Hariri Foundation for Sustainable Human Development, Lebanon, 205
Harp Helú Foundations, Mexico, 216
The Harry Frank Guggenheim Foundation—HFG, USA, 434
Harry and Jeanette Weinberg Foundation, Inc, USA, 434
Hasbro Childrens Trust, USA, 434
Hasbro Foundation, USA, 434
Hassan II Foundation for Moroccans Living Abroad, Morocco, 220
Havelaar (Max) Foundation, Netherlands, 230
Hawaii Resilience Fund, USA, 458
He Xiangjian Foundation, China (People's Republic), 68
Headley Trust, UK, 357
The Health Foundation, UK, 357
Hearst Foundations, USA, 435
Heart to Heart International—HHI, USA, 435
Hedwig and Robert Samuel Foundation, Germany, 131
Hedwig und Robert Samuel-Stiftung, Germany, 131
Heifer Foundation, USA, 435
Heinrich Böll Foundation, Germany, 131
Heinrich-Böll-Stiftung, Germany, 131
HEKS—Hilfswerk der Evangelischen Kirchen Schweiz, Switzerland, 311
Helen Keller International—HKI, USA, 435
Helmsley (Leona M. and Harry B.) Charitable Trust, USA, 447
HelpAge International, UK, 357
Helvetas Swiss Intercooperation, Switzerland, 311
Henry J. Kaiser Family Foundation—KFF, USA, 435
The Henry Smith Charity, UK, 358
HER Fund, Hong Kong, 151
Heren Philanthropic Foundation, China (People's Republic), 68
The Heritage Foundation, USA, 436
HESTIA, Czech Republic, 78
Heungkong Charitable Foundation, China (People's Republic), 68
Hewlett (William and Flora) Foundation, USA, 481

Social welfare

HIAS—Hebrew Immigrant Aid Society, USA, 436
Higgins (Terrence) Trust, UK, 385
Higherlife Foundation, Zimbabwe, 491
Hilti Foundation, Liechtenstein, 208
Hilton (Conrad N.) Foundation, USA, 417
Hinduja Foundation, India, 157
History Foundation of Turkey, Türkiye, 329
Hivos—Humanistisch Instituut voor Ontwikkelings Samenwerking, Netherlands, 226
HJ Foundation, Congo (Democratic Republic), 72
Hodge Foundation, UK, 358
Holt International, USA, 436
The Home Depot Foundation, USA, 436
Homeless World Cup Foundation—HWCF, UK, 358
Hong Kong Council of Social Service—HKCSS, Hong Kong, 150
Hong Kong Society for the Blind, Hong Kong, 151
HOPE International Development Agency, Canada, 56
Horace W. Goldsmith Foundation, USA, 436
Horizons of Friendship, Canada, 56
Horn Economic and Social Policy Institute—HESPI, Ethiopia, 94
House of the Human Sciences Foundation, France, 108
The Howard G. Buffett Foundation, USA, 437
Howard Karagheusian Commemorative Corporation—HKCC, USA, 437
Howard (Katharine) Foundation, Ireland, 167
Hudson Institute, USA, 437
Human Resource Development Foundation, Türkiye, 329
Human Rights Foundation of Turkey, Türkiye, 330
Human Rights Information and Training Center—HRITC, Yemen, 489
Humanistic Institute for Co-operation with Developing Countries, Netherlands, 226
Humanitarian Coalition, Canada, 48
Humanity & Inclusion, France, 113
The Hunger Project, USA, 438
The Hunter Foundation—THF, UK, 359
IACD—Institute of Asian Culture and Development, Korea (Republic), 201
Ian Potter Foundation, Australia, 14
IBM International Foundation, USA, 438
IBON Foundation, Philippines, 252
ICRC—International Red Cross and Red Crescent Movement, Switzerland, 312
ICVA—International Council of Voluntary Agencies, Switzerland, 305
The Ideas Institute, Kenya, 199
IDLO—International Development Law Organization, Italy, 181
IDRF—International Development and Relief Foundation, Canada, 56
IE Foundation, Spain, 291
IFAD—International Fund for Agricultural Development, Italy, 182
IHH Humanitarian Relief Foundation, Türkiye, 328
IIED—International Institute for Environment and Development, UK, 360
IKEA Foundation, Netherlands, 229
IKGV—İnsan Kaynağını Geliştirme Vakfı, Türkiye, 329
İktisadi Kalkınma Vakfı, Türkiye, 328
Îles de Paix, Belgium, 32
IMADR—The International Movement against All Forms of Discrimination and Racism, Japan, 188
Imbuto Foundation, Rwanda, 268
Inclusion International, UK, 359
India Partners, USA, 438
Indian Council of Social Science Research—ICSSR, India, 157
Indonesian Forum for the Environment—Friends of the Earth Indonesia, Indonesia, 162
INEDIVIM—Foundation of Youth and Lifelong Learning, Greece, 145
Information and Education Centre for the Prevention of Drug Abuse, Peru, 248
INHURED International—International Institute for Human Rights, Environment and Development, Nepal, 223
Innovators and Entrepreneurs Foundation/Fondation d'Innovateurs et d'Entrepreneurs—IEF/FIE, Canada, 57
İnsan Hak ve Hürriyetleri İnsani Yardım Vakfı—IHH, Türkiye, 328
İnsan Kaynağını Geliştirme Vakfı—IKGV, Türkiye, 329
Institut for Menneskerettigheder, Denmark, 84
Institut de Recherche Empirique en Économie Politique—IREEP, Benin, 35
Institute of Asian Culture and Development—IACD, Korea (Republic), 201

Institute for the Development of Social Investment, Brazil, 38
Institute of Economic Affairs—IEA, UK, 359
Institute for Empirical Research in Political Economy—IERPE, Benin, 35
Institute for Private Enterprise and Democracy—IPED, Poland, 257
Institute of Social Studies—ISS, Netherlands, 226
Institute for Sustainable Communities—ISC, USA, 439
Instituto Ayrton Senna, Brazil, 41
Instituto para o Desenvolvimento do Investimento Social—IDIS, Brazil, 38
Instituto Europeo de Salud y Bienestar Social, Spain, 296
Instytut Badań nad Demokracją i Przedsiębiorstwem Prywatnym, Poland, 257
INTEGRATA Foundation, Germany, 132
INTEGRATA—Stiftung für Humane Nutzung der Informationstechnologie, Germany, 132
Integrated Rural Development Foundation—IRDF, Philippines, 252
Inter-American Foundation—IAF, USA, 439
Inter Pares, Canada, 57
InterAction, USA, 395
Interchurch Aid—HIA Hungary, Hungary, 153
Internationaal Instituut voor Sociale Geschiedenis—IISG, Netherlands, 226
International Association of Charities, Belgium, 28
International Blue Crescent Relief and Development Foundation—IBC, Türkiye, 329
International Center for Research on Women—ICRW, USA, 439
International Charitable Fund 'Concord 3000', Ukraine, 333
International Civil Society Centre, Germany, 119
International Confederation Catholic Organizations Charitable Social Action, Vatican City, 486
International Co-operation, Italy, 173
International Council of Voluntary Agencies—ICVA, Switzerland, 305
International Development Center of Japan, Japan, 189
International Development Law Organization—IDLO, Italy, 181
International Development and Relief Foundation—IDRF, Canada, 56
International Forum Bosnia, Bosnia and Herzegovina, 37
The International Foundation, USA, 440
International Foundation for Socio-economic and Political Studies, Russian Federation, 266
International Fund for Agricultural Development—IFAD, Italy, 182
International Institute for Environment and Development—IIED, UK, 360
International Institute for Human Rights, Environment and Development, Nepal, 223
International Institute of Social History—IISH, Netherlands, 226
International Institute of Social Studies, Netherlands, 226
International Institute of Tropical Agriculture—IITA, Nigeria, 237
International Medical Assistance Foundation, Portugal, 258
International NGO Charter of Accountability, USA, 393
International NGO Coordination Committee in CAR, Central African Republic, 63
International NGO Forum on Indonesian Development—INFID, Indonesia, 161
International Organization for Relief, Welfare & Development—IORWD, Saudi Arabia, 269
International Orthodox Christian Charities—IOCC, USA, 441
International Planned Parenthood Federation—IPPF, UK, 360
International Red Cross and Red Crescent Movement—ICRC, Switzerland, 312
International Renaissance Foundation—IRF, Ukraine, 333
International Rescue Committee—IRC, USA, 441
International Solidarity Foundation, Finland, 96
International Women's Health Coalition, USA, 427
International Youth Foundation—IYF, USA, 442
INTERSOS, Italy, 182
Invica Foundation, Chile, 65
IOCC—International Orthodox Christian Charities, USA, 441
iPartner India, India, 155
IPPF—International Planned Parenthood Federation, UK, 360
IRC—International Rescue Committee, USA, 441

INDEX OF MAIN ACTIVITIES

The Ireland Funds America, USA, 442
Irish Youth Foundation, Ireland, 167
Irvine (James) Foundation, USA, 443
Isabel Allende Foundation, USA, 442
Islamic Relief Worldwide, UK, 360
Islands of Peace, Belgium, 32
ISMU Foundation—Initiatives and Studies on Multi-ethnicity, Italy, 178
IsraAID, Israel, 169
Istituto Carlo Cattaneo, Italy, 182
Ivey Foundation, Canada, 57
Ivorian Economic and Social Research Centre, Côte d'Ivoire, 75
The J. F. Costopoulos Foundation, Greece, 146
J. F. Kapnek Zimbabwe, Zimbabwe, 491
J-Louis Lévesque Foundation, Canada, 55
J. R. McKenzie Trust, New Zealand, 233
The J. W. McConnell Family Foundation, Canada, 57
Jack Ma Foundation—JMF, China (People's Republic), 68
Jacobs Foundation, Switzerland, 313
Jacques Chirac Foundation, France, 107
Jahres (Anders) Humanitære Stiftelse, Norway, 240
J'ai Rêvé Foundation, Central African Republic, 63
The James Irvine Foundation, USA, 443
The Japan Foundation, Japan, 189
Japan International Volunteer Center—JVC, Japan, 190
Japanese-German Centre Berlin, Germany, 133
Japanisch-Deutsches Zentrum Berlin, Germany, 133
Jasmine Foundation for Research and Communication, Tunisia, 326
Jazz Foundation of America—JFA, USA, 443
JCA Charitable Trust, UK, 361
JEN, Japan, 190
The Jerusalem Trust, UK, 361
JN Foundation, Jamaica, 184
JNF UK—JNF Charitable Trust, UK, 361
The John D. and Catherine T. MacArthur Foundation, USA, 444
John Ellerman Foundation, UK, 361
John Moores Foundation, UK, 362
John Paul II Foundation for the Sahel, Burkina Faso, 44
John Simon Guggenheim Memorial Foundation, USA, 444
The Johnson Foundation at Wingspread, USA, 444
Johnson (Stanley Thomas) Foundation, Switzerland, 317
JOHUD—Jordanian Hashemite Fund for Human Development, Jordan, 196
Jordan River Foundation, Jordan, 196
Joseph Levy Foundation, UK, 362
Joseph Patrick Trust, UK, 369
Joseph Rowntree Foundation—JRF, UK, 362
Joseph S. and Caroline Gruss Memorial Fund for the Advancement of Veterans, Israel, 170
Joseph Tanenbaum Charitable Foundation, Canada, 58
Joyce Banda Foundation International, Malawi, 210
Joyce Foundation, USA, 445
JPB Foundation, USA, 428
JPMorgan Chase Foundation, USA, 445
Juan March Foundation, Spain, 291
Jubilee USA Network, USA, 445
Kadın Emeğini Değerlendirme Vakfı—KEDV, Türkiye, 329
Kafaa Development Foundation, Libya, 207
Kaiser (Henry J.) Family Foundation, USA, 435
Kansainvälinen solidaarisuussäätiö, Finland, 96
Kapnek (J. F.) Charitable Trust Zimbabwe, Zimbabwe, 491
Karagheusian (Howard) Commemorative Corporation, USA, 437
Kárpátok Alapítvány, Hungary, 153
Karuna Trust, UK, 363
Katharine Howard Foundation—KHF, Ireland, 167
Kayany Foundation, Lebanon, 206
KCDF—Kenya Community Development Foundation, Kenya, 199
KDDI Foundation, Japan, 191
Keller (Helen) International, USA, 435
Kellogg (W. K.) Foundation, USA, 478
Khalifa Bin Zayed Al Nahyan Foundation, United Arab Emirates, 334
Khemka (Nand & Jeet) Foundation, India, 159
Kind Heart Foundation, Viet Nam, 488
King Baudouin Foundation, Belgium, 33
King Hussein Foundation—KHF, Jordan, 196
King Khalid Foundation, Saudi Arabia, 269
King Philanthropies, USA, 445

INDEX OF MAIN ACTIVITIES

Social welfare

The King's Trust, UK, 363
Kleinwort (Ernest) Charitable Trust, UK, 353
Koç (Vehbi), Vakfı, Türkiye, 331
Koch Foundation, Inc, USA, 446
Kofi Annan Foundation, Switzerland, 313
Kokkalis Foundation, Greece, 146
Koning Boudewijnstichting/Fondation Roi Baudouin, Belgium, 33
Konrad Adenauer Foundation, Germany, 134
Konrad-Adenauer-Stiftung eV—KAS, Germany, 134
Körber Foundation, Germany, 134
Körber-Stiftung, Germany, 134
Koret Foundation, USA, 446
Kosovo Foundation for Open Society—KFOS, Kosovo, 203
Kresge Foundation, USA, 446
Kronenberg (Leopold) Foundation, Poland, 255
Kulika Charitable Trust Uganda, Uganda, 331
Kuok Foundation Berhad, Malaysia, 211
Kusuma Trust UK, UK, 363
Kuwait Awqaf Public Foundation, Kuwait, 203
'La Caixa' Banking Foundation, Spain, 288
La Salle Foundation for Natural Sciences, Venezuela, 487
Lady Davis Fellowship Trust, Israel, 170
Lady Khama Charitable Trust, Botswana, 37
Lafede.cat—Federació d'Organitzacions per a la Justícia Global, Spain, 286
Lafede.cat—Federation of Organizations for Global Justice, Spain, 286
Laidlaw Foundation, Canada, 58
Laing Family Trusts, UK, 364
Laing (J. W.) Trust, UK, 384
Land Network, Timor-Leste, 325
Landesa—Rural Development Institute, USA, 447
LAPAS—Latvijas platforma attīstības sadarbībai, Latvia, 204
Latet Israeli Humanitarian Aid, Israel, 170
Latimpacto—Red Latinoamericana de Inversión Social y Filantropía Estratégica, Colombia, 71
Latin America France, France, 112
Latin American, African and Asian Social Housing Service, Chile, 66
Latin American Council of Social Sciences, Argentina, 6
Latin American Future Foundation, Ecuador, 88
Latin American Network for Economic and Social Justice, Peru, 248
Latin American Venture Philanthropy Network, Colombia, 71
Latindadd—Red Latinoamericana por Justicia Económica y Social, Peru, 248
Latter-day Saint Charities—LDSC, USA, 447
Latvia Children's Fund, Latvia, 204
Latvian Platform for Development Cooperation, Latvia, 204
Latvijas Bērnu fonds, Latvia, 204
Lauder (Ronald S.) Foundation, Germany, 138
Laudes Foundation, Switzerland, 313
Laureus Sport for Good, UK, 364
The Lawson Foundation, Canada, 58
League of Corporate Foundations—LCF, Philippines, 250
Learning for Well-being Foundation—L4WB, Netherlands, 227
The Leona M. and Harry B. Helmsley Charitable Trust, USA, 447
Leonard Cheshire Disability, UK, 364
The Leprosy Mission International, UK, 364
Lesotho Council of Non-Governmental Organisations, Lesotho, 207
Leventis (A. G.) Foundation, Cyprus, 77
Levesque (Jean-Louis), Fondation, Canada, 55
Levi Strauss Foundation, USA, 448
Levy (Joseph) Foundation, UK, 362
Li Ka Shing Foundation, Hong Kong, 151
Liberty Fund, Inc, USA, 448
Lien Foundation, Singapore, 273
Lietuvos vaikų fondas, Lithuania, 209
Lifewater International, USA, 479
Light of the Village Foundation, Indonesia, 162
Liliane Foundation, Netherlands, 229
Lilly Endowment, Inc, USA, 448
Limmat Foundation, Switzerland, 314
Limmat Stiftung, Switzerland, 314
Linbury Trust, UK, 365
Lindh (Anna) Euro-Mediterranean Foundation for Dialogue between Cultures, Egypt, 90
Litdea Association, Lithuania, 208
Lithuanian Children's Fund, Lithuania, 209
Littauer (Lucius N.) Foundation, Inc, USA, 449
Living Culture Foundation Namibia—LCFN, Namibia, 222
Liz Claiborne & Art Ortenberg Foundation, USA, 448

Lloyds Bank Foundation for England and Wales, UK, 365
Lord Mayor's Charitable Foundation, Australia, 14
Lorenzini (Giovanni), Fondazione, Italy, 177
Lucie et André Chagnon Foundation, Canada, 55
Lucius N. Littauer Foundation, Inc, USA, 449
Luigi Einaudi Foundation, Italy, 178
Lullaby Trust, UK, 366
Lumos Foundation, UK, 366
The Lutheran World Federation, Switzerland, 314
Lutherischer Weltbund/Fédération Luthérienne Mondiale/Federación Luterana Mundial, Switzerland, 314
Luxembourg Development NGO Co-operation Circle, Luxembourg, 209
Lynde and Harry Bradley Foundation, Inc, USA, 449
M. S. Swaminathan Research Foundation—MSSRF, India, 158
M. Venkatarangaiya Foundation—MVF, India, 158
MacArthur (John D. and Catherine T.) Foundation, USA, 444
McConnell Clark (Edna) Foundation, USA, 422
McConnell (J. W.) Family Foundation, Canada, 57
Macedonian Centre for International Co-operation—MCIC, North Macedonia, 239
Machel (Graça) Trust, South Africa, 280
MACIF Foundation, France, 108
McKenzie (J. R.) Trust, New Zealand, 233
The Mackintosh Foundation, UK, 366
McKnight Foundation, USA, 449
The McLean Foundation, Canada, 59
Maclellan Foundation, Inc, USA, 450
Macmillan Cancer Support, UK, 366
Macquarie Group Foundation, Australia, 15
MAG—Mines Advisory Group, UK, 366
MAIF Foundation for Research, France, 108
Maison Franco-Japonaise, Japan, 191
Makyedonski Tzyentar za Myeroonarodna Sorabotka, North Macedonia, 239
Mama Cash Foundation, Netherlands, 230
Mandela Institute for Development Studies—MINDS, South Africa, 281
Mandela (Nelson) Children's Fund, South Africa, 281
Mani Tese, Italy, 183
Mansour Foundation for Development—MFD, Egypt, 90
MAPFRE Foundation, Spain, 292
Marangopoulos Foundation for Human Rights, Greece, 146
Marcel Bleustein-Blanchet Vocational Foundation, France, 109
Marcelle et Jean Coutu Foundation, Canada, 55
March of Dimes Foundation, USA, 450
March (Juan), Fundación, Spain, 291
Margaret A. Cargill Philanthropies—MACP, USA, 450
Maria Cecilia Souto Vidigal Foundation, Brazil, 40
María Francisca de Roviralta Foundation, Spain, 292
Marie Curie, UK, 366
Marisla Foundation, USA, 451
Mary Fonden, Denmark, 85
Mary Foundation, Denmark, 85
The MasterCard Foundation, Canada, 59
Mauritius Telecom Foundation—MTF, Mauritius, 214
Mawazo Institute, Kenya, 199
Max Bell Foundation, Canada, 59
Max Havelaar Foundation—Fairtrade Netherlands, Netherlands, 230
Max Schmidheiny Foundation at the University of St Gallen, Switzerland, 314
Max Schmidheiny-Stiftung an der Universität St Gallen, Switzerland, 314
The Maytree Foundation, Canada, 59
Mbeki (Thabo) Foundation, South Africa, 284
MDA—Muscular Dystrophy Association, USA, 451
Medunarodnog foruma Bosna, Bosnia and Herzegovina, 37
Médecins du Monde International, France, 114
medica mondiale eV, Germany, 136
Medical Aid for Palestinians—MAP, UK, 367
Mellon (Richard King) Foundation, USA, 467
Mencap—Royal Mencap Society, UK, 367
Mendoza (Eugenio), Fundación, Venezuela, 487
Menomadin Foundation, Israel, 170
Mental Health Foundation, UK, 367
Menzies Foundation, Australia, 15
Menzies (Sir Robert) Foundation, Australia, 15
Mercatus Center, USA, 451
The Mercers' Charitable Foundation, UK, 367
Merchant Navy Fund, UK, 382

Mercury Phoenix Trust, UK, 367
Mercy, Ireland, 168
Mercy Corps, USA, 452
Mercy-USA for Aid and Development, USA, 452
Mérieux Foundation, France, 109
Mertz Gilmore Foundation, USA, 452
M'essh al Sudan, Sudan, 297
Michael & Susan Dell Foundation, USA, 453
Michael J. Fox Foundation for Parkinson's Research—MJFF, USA, 453
Miguel Alemán Foundation, Mexico, 215
Miloud Chaâbi Foundation, Morocco, 220
Mind, UK, 367
Minderoo Foundation, Australia, 15
Mines Advisory Group—MAG, UK, 366
Minhaj Welfare Foundation, UK, 368
Minority Rights Group International—MRG, UK, 368
Mirovni Inštitut—Inštitut za sodobne družbene in politične študije, Slovenia, 277
MISEREOR—Bischöfliches Hilfswerk Misereor eV, Germany, 137
The Mission to Seafarers, UK, 368
Mith Samlanh, Cambodia, 46
Mitterrand (Danielle), Fondation, France, 112
MIUSA—Mobility International USA, USA, 453
Mo Dewji Foundation, Tanzania, 323
Moawad (René) Foundation, Lebanon, 206
Mobility International USA—MIUSA, USA, 453
Mohamed Shafik Gabr Foundation for Social Development, Egypt, 90
Mohammed bin Rashid Al Maktoum Global Initiatives—MBRGI, United Arab Emirates, 335
Møller (A.P.) and Chastine Mc-Kinney Møller Foundation, Denmark, 82
Molson Foundation, Canada, 59
Monell (Ambrose) Foundation, USA, 399
Mongolian Women's Fund—MONES, Mongolia, 218
Montemadrid Foundation, Spain, 292
Montevideo Circle Foundation, Uruguay, 485
Moores (John) Foundation, UK, 362
Morgan Stanley Foundation, USA, 453
Motorola Solutions Foundation, USA, 454
Motsepe Foundation, South Africa, 281
Mouvement International ATD Quart-Monde, France, 115
Mouvement Social, Lebanon, 206
Ms. Foundation for Women, USA, 454
MTN Afghanistan Foundation, Afghanistan, 4
MTN Cameroon Foundation, Cameroon, 47
MTN Côte d'Ivoire Foundation, Côte d'Ivoire, 76
MTN Foundation Benin, Benin, 35
MTN Uganda Foundation, Uganda, 332
Mukwege (Dr Denis) Foundation, Netherlands, 224
Muriel McBrien Kauffman Foundation, USA, 425
Muscular Dystrophy UK, UK, 369
Muslim Aid, UK, 369
The Muttart Foundation, Canada, 59
Mutual Aid and Liaison Service, France, 116
Myer Foundation, Australia, 18
Myer (Sidney) Fund, Australia, 18
NAACP Legal Defense and Educational Fund, Inc—LDF, USA, 454
Nadace Charty 77, Czech Republic, 80
Nadace Preciosa, Czech Republic, 80
Nadace Vodafone Česká Republika, Czech Republic, 80
Nadácia Ekopolis, Slovakia, 275
Nadácia Orange, Slovakia, 275
Nadácia Otvorenej Spoločnosti, Slovakia, 276
Nadácia Pontis, Slovakia, 274
Nadácia pre Deti Slovenska, Slovakia, 275
Nadácia SPP, Slovakia, 275
Nand & Jeet Khemka Foundation, India, 159
Naspa Foundation, Germany, 137
Naspa Stiftung, Germany, 137
National Community Foundation, Saint Lucia, 268
National Council of Social Development—NCSD, Philippines, 250
National Emergencies Trust, UK, 369
National Empowerment Foundation—NEF, Mauritius, 214
National Endowment for Science, Technology and the Arts—Nesta, UK, 370
National Federation of NGOs, Poland, 254
National Foundation for Development, El Salvador, 91
National Foundation for the Development of Honduras, Honduras, 150
National Foundation for Educational Research—NFER, UK, 369
National Heart Foundation of New Zealand, New Zealand, 233
National Kidney Foundation—NKF, USA, 455

Social welfare

The National Lottery Community Fund, UK, 370
National Organization for Women Foundation, USA, 458
National Society for the Prevention of Cruelty to Children—NSPCC, UK, 371
Near East Foundation—NEF, USA, 456
Nederlandse Organisatie voor Internationale Ontwikkelingssamenwerking—Stichting NOVIB, Netherlands, 228
NEF—National Empowerment Foundation, Mauritius, 214
NEF—Near East Foundation, USA, 456
Neighbour in Need, Austria, 22
Nelson Mandela Children's Fund, South Africa, 281
Nesta—National Endowment for Science, Technology and the Arts, UK, 370
Network of European Foundations—NEF, Belgium, 27
Network of Foundations Working for Development—netFWD, France, 99
Network for Human Development, Brazil, 41
Network of Information and Support for Non-governmental Organizations, Poland, 254
Network for Social Change Charitable Trust—NSCCT, UK, 370
New Economics Foundation—NEF, UK, 371
New World Foundation—NWF, USA, 456
The New York Community Trust—NYCT, USA, 457
NFER—National Foundation for Educational Research, UK, 369
NFI—National Foundation for India, India, 159
NHS Charities Together, UK, 371
Niarchos (Stavros) Foundation, Greece, 147
Nigerian Conservation Foundation—NCF, Nigeria, 238
Ningxia Yanbao Charity Foundation, China (People's Republic), 69
The Nippon Foundation, Japan, 192
Nitidæ, France, 115
Niwano Peace Foundation, Japan, 192
Nobis Foundation, Ecuador, 91
Nonprofit Enterprise and Self-sustainability Team—NESsT, USA, 457
Nordic Africa Institute Scholarships, Sweden, 302
Nordic International Support Foundation—NIS, Norway, 242
Nordiska Afrikainstitutets Stipendier, Sweden, 302
Norwegian Refugee Council—NRC, Norway, 242
The Nourafchan Foundation—TNF, Kenya, 199
Novartis Foundation, Switzerland, 314
Novartis US Foundation, USA, 457
NOVIB (Oxfam Netherlands), Netherlands, 228
NoVo Foundation, USA, 458
Novo Nordisk Fonden, Denmark, 85
Novo Nordisk Foundation, Denmark, 85
NOW Foundation, USA, 458
NSPCC—National Society for the Prevention of Cruelty to Children, UK, 371
Nuffield Foundation, UK, 371
NYCT—The New York Community Trust, USA, 457
Oak Foundation, Switzerland, 315
Obama (Barack) Foundation, USA, 407
ODI, UK, 371
The Officers' Association, UK, 372
Offor (Sir Emeka) Foundation, Nigeria, 238
Ogólnopolska Federacja Organizacji Pozarządowych—OFOP, Poland, 254
Oil Search Foundation, Papua New Guinea, 247
OISCA International—Organization for Industrial, Spiritual and Cultural Advancement-International, Japan, 192
Ökumenikus Segélyszervezet, Hungary, 153
Olof Palme Memorial Fund for International Understanding and Common Security, Sweden, 302
Olof Palmes Minnesfond för internationell förståelse och gemensam säkerhet, Sweden, 302
Oman LNG Development Foundation—ODF, Oman, 244
Omidyar Group, USA, 458
Omidyar Network Fund, USA, 458
ONCE—Spanish National Organization for the Blind—Foundation, Spain, 293
One Economy Foundation, Namibia, 222
One Foundation, China (People's Republic), 69
OneStage, India, 155
OPALS—Organisation Panafricaine de Lutte pour la Santé, France, 115
Open Society Action Fund, USA, 458
Open Society Foundation—Bratislava, Slovakia, 276
Open Society Foundation Haiti, Haiti, 149

Open Society Foundation South Africa—OSF-SA, South Africa, 282
Open Society Foundations—Armenia, Armenia, 9
Open Society Foundations in Pakistan, Pakistan, 245
Open Society Fund—Bosnia-Herzegovina, Bosnia and Herzegovina, 37
Open Society Initiative for Eastern Africa—OSIEA, Kenya, 199
Open Society Initiative for Southern Africa—OSISA, South Africa, 282
Open Society Institute—Sofia, Bulgaria, 43
Open Society Policy Center, USA, 458
Operation USA, USA, 459
Oppenheimer Generations Foundation, South Africa, 282
Oprah Winfrey Leadership Academy Foundation—OWLAF, USA, 459
Orange Foundation, Romania, 263
Orange Foundation Cameroon, Cameroon, 47
Orange Foundation Guinea, Guinea, 149
Orange Moldova Foundation, Moldova, 217
Orange Solidarité Madagascar, Madagascar, 210
Oranje Fonds, Netherlands, 227
ORF Nachbar in Not, Austria, 22
Organisation Internationale de Droit du Développement—OIDD, Italy, 181
Organisation Panafricaine de Lutte pour la Santé—OPALS, France, 115
Organization for Social Science Research in Eastern and Southern Africa—OSSREA, Ethiopia, 94
Orient Foundation, Portugal, 260
Orient-Occident Foundation, Morocco, 220
Orji Uzor Kalu Foundation, Nigeria, 238
Ortega (Amancio), Fundación, Spain, 288
Osaka Community Foundation, Japan, 192
Österreichischer Wissenschaftsfonds—FWF, Austria, 21
Oswaldo Cruz Foundation, Brazil, 40
Otto Benecke Foundation, Germany, 138
Otto-Benecke-Stiftung eV, Germany, 138
Our Foundation, Indonesia, 162
Our Future—Foundation for Regional Social Programmes, Russian Federation, 266
Outreach International, USA, 459
OutRight Action International, USA, 460
Outstretched Hands, Italy, 183
Oxfam America, USA, 460
Oxfam Aotearoa, New Zealand, 234
Oxfam Australia, Australia, 16
Oxfam Brasil, Brazil, 41
Oxfam Canada, Canada, 60
Oxfam Denmark, Denmark, 86
Oxfam Deutschland eV, Germany, 138
Oxfam France, France, 115
Oxfam GB, UK, 372
Oxfam Hong Kong, Hong Kong, 151
Oxfam India, India, 159
Oxfam International, Kenya, 200
Oxfam Ireland, Ireland, 167
Oxfam Italia, Italy, 183
Oxfam Mexico, Mexico, 216
Oxfam NOVIB—Nederlandse Organisatie voor Internationale Ontwikkelingssamenwerking, Netherlands, 228
Oxfam NOVIB—Netherlands Organization for International Development Co-operation, Netherlands, 228
Oxfam-Québec, Canada, 60
Oxfam-Solidariteit/Solidarité, Belgium, 33
Oxfam South Africa, South Africa, 282
OzChild—Children Australia Inc, Australia, 16
P&V Foundation, Belgium, 32
Pacific Development and Conservation Trust, New Zealand, 234
Pacific Leprosy Foundation, New Zealand, 234
Pacific Peoples' Partnership, Canada, 61
Packard (David and Lucile) Foundation, USA, 420
Pact, USA, 460
PADF—Pan American Development Foundation, USA, 460
PAI—Population Action International, USA, 460
Paideia Galiza Foundation, Spain, 293
Palestinian NGO Network, Palestinian Territories, 246
Palme (Olof) Minnesfond fr Internationell Frstelse och Gemensam Skerhet, Sweden, 302
Pan-African Organization for Health, France, 115
Pan American Development Foundation—PADF, USA, 460
PANAP—Pesticide Action Network Asia and the Pacific, Malaysia, 211
PANZI Foundation, USA, 461
The Papal Foundation, USA, 461
Paraguayan Foundation for Cooperation and Development, Paraguay, 248

INDEX OF MAIN ACTIVITIES

Partage, France, 116
Partners for Equity, Australia, 16
Partos, Netherlands, 223
Pastore (Giulio), Fondazione, Italy, 178
PATH, USA, 461
Patterson (Alicia) Foundation, USA, 398
The Paul G. Allen Family Foundation, USA, 462
Paul Hamlyn Foundation—PHF, UK, 373
The Paul Ramsay Foundation, Australia, 16
PCI Media Impact, USA, 467
PCI—Project Concern International, USA, 431
Peace Direct, UK, 373
Peace and Disarmament Education Trust—PADET, New Zealand, 234
Peace, Health and Human Development Foundation—PHD Foundation, Japan, 193
Peace Institute—Institute for Contemporary Social and Political Studies, Slovenia, 277
Peace Parks Foundation, South Africa, 282
Peace Village International, Germany, 129
Peace Winds Japan—PWJ, Japan, 192
Pearl S. Buck International, USA, 462
Pedro Barrié de la Maza Foundation, Spain, 293
Penal Reform International—PRI, UK, 373
People in Need, Czech Republic, 79
PepsiCo Foundation, Inc, USA, 462
Perdana Global Peace Foundation—PGPF, Malaysia, 211
Perpetual Foundation, Australia, 16
Pertubuhan Pertolongan Wanita, Malaysia, 212
Pestalozzi Children's Foundation, Switzerland, 317
Pesticide Action Network Asia and the Pacific—PANAP, Malaysia, 211
The Peter Cundill Foundation, Bermuda, 35
The Pew Charitable Trusts, USA, 462
Pfizer Foundation, USA, 462
PH International, USA, 463
The PHD Foundation—Peace, Health and Human Development Foundation, Japan, 193
Philanthropikó Ídryma Stélios Chatzeioánnou stēn Kýpro, Cyprus, 78
Philanthropy New Zealand/Tōpūtanga Tuku Aroha o Aotearoa, New Zealand, 232
Philanthropy for Social Justice and Peace, UK, 336
Philippine Business for Social Progress—PBSP, Philippines, 250
Piera, Pietro and Giovanni Ferrero Foundation, Italy, 179
Pilgrim Trust, UK, 373
Pinchuk (Victor) Foundation, Ukraine, 333
Plan International Ireland, Ireland, 167
PLAN International—PI, UK, 374
Plataforma Portuguesa das Organizações Não-Governamentais para o Desenvolvimento—ONGD, Portugal, 258
Platform for Development Cooperation and Humanitarian Aid, Slovenia, 276
Platforma Mimovládnych Rozvojových Organizácií, Slovakia, 273
Plunkett Foundation, UK, 374
POLSAT Foundation, Poland, 256
Pompidou (Claude), Fondation, France, 104
Pontis Foundation, Slovakia, 274
Population Action International—PAI, USA, 460
Population Council, USA, 463
Populorum Progressio Foundation, Vatican City, 486
Portuguese Platform of Non-Governmental Organizations for Development, Portugal, 258
Potter (Ian) Foundation, Australia, 14
Praemium Erasmianum Foundation, Netherlands, 230
Pratham Education Foundation, India, 159
Pratt Foundation, Australia, 17
Praxis Centre for Policy Studies Foundation, Estonia, 93
Preciosa Foundation, Czech Republic, 80
Première Urgence Internationale, France, 116
Premji (Azim) Foundation, India, 156
Presbyterian World Service & Development—PWS&D, Canada, 61
Primate's World Relief and Development Fund/Le Fonds du Primat Pour le Secours et le Développement Mondial—PWRDF, Canada, 49
Prince's Trust, UK, 363
Princess of Asturias Foundation, Spain, 294
Princess Charlene of Monaco Foundation, Monaco, 218
Pro Juventute, Switzerland, 315
Pro Mujer International, USA, 464
Pro Victimis, Switzerland, 315
Pro Women International, USA, 464
PRODESSA—Proyecto de Desarrollo Santiago, Guatemala, 148
Project Harmony, USA, 463

INDEX OF MAIN ACTIVITIES
Social welfare

Project HOPE, USA, 464
Project Trust, UK, 374
ProLiteracy, USA, 464
Promi Foundation, Spain, 294
PROVICOOP, Chile, 65
Prudence Foundation, Hong Kong, 151
Public Studies Centre, Chile, 64
Puerto Rico Community Foundation, Puerto Rico, 261
PwC Charitable Foundation, USA, 465
Qatar Foundation, Qatar, 262
Quỹ Thiên Tâm, Viet Nam, 488
Queen Rania Foundation—QRF, Jordan, 196
R. Howard Webster Foundation/Fondation R. Howard Webster, Canada, 61
Rafa Nadal Foundation, Spain, 294
Rafael del Pino Foundation, Spain, 294
The Rainforest Foundation UK—RFUK, UK, 375
Rajiv Gandhi Foundation, India, 160
Rambourg Foundation, Tunisia, 326
Ramsay (Paul) Foundation, Australia, 16
RAND Corporation, USA, 465
The Rank Foundation, UK, 375
Razumkov Centre, Ukraine, 333
Reading Foundation, Germany, 140
Real Madrid Foundation, Spain, 295
Realdania Foundation, Denmark, 83
Reall—Real Equity for All, UK, 375
Rebecca Akufo-Addo Foundation—Rebecca Foundation, Ghana, 144
Red Feather, Japan, 185
Red de Mujeres para el Desarrollo, Costa Rica, 75
Rede ba Rai, Timor-Leste, 325
Rede Comuá, Brazil, 38
REDEH—Rede de Desenvolvimento Humano, Brazil, 41
RedR UK, UK, 375
Reeva Rebecca Steenkamp Foundation, South Africa, 283
Reeve (Christopher and Dana) Foundation, USA, 415
Refugee Empowerment International—REI, Japan, 193
Refugee Foundation, Netherlands, 231
Refugees International—RI, USA, 466
Rehabilitation for the Disabled—ELEPAP, Greece, 145
Rehabilitation International—RI, USA, 466
REI—Refugee Empowerment International, Japan, 193
Reliance Foundation, India, 160
Relief International, USA, 466
Renault Foundation, France, 106
René Moawad Foundation—RMF, Lebanon, 206
Repsol Foundation, Spain, 295
Research Centre for Social Action, Congo (Democratic Republic), 72
Réseau Européen des Associations de Lutte contre la Pauvreté et l'Exclusion Sociale, Belgium, 29
Resolution Foundation, UK, 376
The Resource Foundation—TRF, USA, 467
Reumatikerförbundet, Sweden, 302
Rhodes Trust, UK, 376
RIA—Royal Irish Academy, Ireland, 167
Richard King Mellon Foundation, USA, 467
Right Livelihood Award Foundation, Sweden, 302
Righteous Persons Foundation, USA, 467
Rising Impact, USA, 467
RNIB Charity, UK, 378
Robert Bosch Foundation, Germany, 138
Robert-Bosch-Stiftung GmbH, Germany, 138
Robert Wood Johnson Foundation—RWJF, USA, 467
The Robertson Trust, UK, 376
Rockefeller Brothers Fund—RBF, USA, 468
Rockefeller Foundation, USA, 468
Rockwool Fonden, Denmark, 86
Rockwool Foundation, Denmark, 86
Roger Federer Foundation, Switzerland, 315
Rogosin Institute, USA, 468
Rohini Nilekani Philanthropies, India, 160
Rome Foundation, Italy, 179
The Ronald S. Lauder Foundation, Germany, 138
Rössing Foundation, Namibia, 222
The Rotary Foundation, USA, 468
Roviralta (María Francisca de), Fundación, Spain, 292
Rowntree (Joseph) Foundation, UK, 362
Royal Air Force Benevolent Fund, UK, 377
Royal British Legion, UK, 377
The Royal Commonwealth Society—RCS, UK, 377
Royal Flying Doctor Service of Australia—RFDS, Australia, 17
The Royal Foundation of the Prince and Princess of Wales, UK, 378
Royal Literary Fund—RLF, UK, 378

Royal National Institute of Blind People—RNIB, UK, 378
RSA—Royal Society for the Encouragement of Arts, Manufactures and Commerce, UK, 379
RUI Foundation, Italy, 180
Ruparelia Foundation, Uganda, 332
Rupert Family Foundations, South Africa, 283
Rural Development Institute—Landesa, USA, 447
Russell Sage Foundation—RSF, USA, 469
Russian LGBT Network, Russian Federation, 267
Rutgers, Netherlands, 228
Sabanci Vakfi—Haci Omer Sabanci Foundation, Türkiye, 329
Safaricom Foundation, Kenya, 200
Sahabdeen (A. M. M.) Trust Foundation, Sri Lanka, 297
Saïd Foundation, UK, 380
Sainsbury Family Charitable Trusts, UK, 380
The Salvation Army International Trust, UK, 381
Salzburg Global Seminar, Austria, 22
Samaritans, UK, 381
Samaritan's Purse, USA, 469
Samsung Foundation, Korea (Republic), 202
Samuel (Hedwig und Robert) Stiftung, Germany, 131
The San Diego Foundation, USA, 470
San Francisco Foundation—SFF, USA, 470
Sanaburi Foundation, Japan, 193
Sandals Foundation, Jamaica, 184
Santiago Development Project, Guatemala, 148
Santos Foundation, Papua New Guinea, 247
Sasakawa Health Foundation—SHF, Japan, 194
Save the Children International, UK, 381
Save the Children (UK), UK, 381
Sawiris Foundation for Social Development—SFSD, Egypt, 90
SBS Cultural Foundation, Korea (Republic), 202
Schmidheiny (Max) Stiftung, Switzerland, 314
Schneider Electric Foundation, France, 111
Schusterman (Charles and Lynn) Family Foundation, USA, 413
Schwab Foundation for Social Entrepreneurship, Switzerland, 316
Scientific Foundation of Hisham Adeeb Hijjawi, Jordan, 196
Scientific Research Foundation, Belgium, 32
Scope, UK, 381
Scottish Catholic International Aid Fund—SCIAF, UK, 382
The Seafarers' Charity, UK, 382
Seafarers International Relief Fund, UK, 382
Secours Catholique—Caritas de France, France, 116
SeedChange, Canada, 61
Seeds of Affinity, Australia, 17
Seidel (Hanns) Stiftung, Germany, 131
SEL—Service d'Entraide et de Liaison, France, 116
SELAVIP—Services Latino-Américains, Africains et Asiatiques de Promotion de l'Habitation Populaire, Chile, 66
Self Help Africa—SHA, Ireland, 167
Self Help Development Foundation—SHDF, Zimbabwe, 491
Self-Sufficient People Foundation, Indonesia, 163
SEND-West Africa, Ghana, 144
Senna (Ayrton), Instituto, Brazil, 41
Sentebale, UK, 382
Seoam Yoon Se Young Foundation, Korea (Republic), 202
Serbian Philanthropy Forum, Serbia, 271
Serrv International, Inc, USA, 471
SES Foundation—Sustainability, Education, Solidarity, Argentina, 8
Sesame Workshop, USA, 471
Seva Foundation, USA, 471
Shafik Gabr (Mohamed) Foundation, Egypt, 90
Shahid Afridi Foundation—SAF, Pakistan, 246
Shanghai Soong Ching Ling Foundation, China (People's Republic), 69
Shaping Our Future Foundation—SOFF, Malawi, 210
Sharing and Life Foundation, France, 110
Shell Foundation—SF, UK, 382
Shelter—National Campaign for Homeless People, UK, 382
Sherman (Archie) Charitable Trust, UK, 340
SID—Society for International Development, Italy, 183
Sidney Myer Fund & The Myer Foundation, Australia, 18
Sieć Wspierania Organizacji Pozarządowych—SPLOT, Poland, 254
The Sierra Club Foundation, USA, 471
Sightsavers International, UK, 382
Sihtasutus Poliitikauuringute Keskus Praxis, Estonia, 93

Silicon Valley Community Foundation—SVCF, USA, 471
Singapore International Foundation—SIF, Singapore, 273
Sir Ahmadu Bello Memorial Foundation, Nigeria, 238
Sir Emeka Offor Foundation, Nigeria, 238
Sir Halley Stewart Trust, UK, 383
The Sir Jules Thorn Charitable Trust, UK, 383
Sistema Charitable Foundation, Russian Federation, 267
Skinners' Charity Foundation, UK, 383
Skoll Foundation, USA, 472
Slim (Carlos), Fundación, Mexico, 215
SLOGA—Platforma za Razvojno Sodelovanje in Humanitarno Pomoč, Slovenia, 276
Slovak-Czech Women's Fund, Slovakia, 276
Slovak Humanitarian Council, Slovakia, 274
Slovenská Humanitná Rada, Slovakia, 274
Slovensko-český enský fond, Slovakia, 276
SM Foundation, Spain, 295
Smallwood Trust, UK, 384
Smith (Henry) Charity, UK, 358
Smith Richardson Foundation, Inc, USA, 472
The Snow Foundation, Australia, 18
The Sobell Foundation, UK, 384
Social Movement, Lebanon, 206
Society for International Development—SID, Italy, 183
Software AG Foundation, Germany, 139
Software AG Stiftung, Germany, 139
Sog'lom Avlod Uchun, Uzbekistan, 485
SOHO China Foundation, China (People's Republic), 69
Solidaarisuus, Finland, 96
Solidar, Belgium, 34
Solidarios—Consejo de Fundaciones Americanas de Desarrollo, Dominican Republic, 87
Solidarity Foundation, Dominican Republic, 87
Solidarity Overseas Service Malta—SOS Malta, Malta, 213
Somalia NGO Consortium, Somalia, 277
Sorenson Legacy Foundation, USA, 473
SOS Malta—Solidarity Overseas Service, Malta, 213
Souter Charitable Trust, UK, 384
South Africa Philanthropy Foundation, South Africa, 278
South African Institute of Race Relations—IRR, South Africa, 283
South Sudan Center for Strategic and Policy Studies—CSPS, South Sudan, 285
South West International Development Network—SWIDN, UK, 337
Southern Africa Trust, South Africa, 283
Souto Vidigal (Maria Cecilia), Fundação, Brazil, 40
Sphere, Switzerland, 305
SPP Foundation, Slovakia, 275
Springer (Axel) Stiftung, Germany, 122
Srpski Filantropski Forum, Serbia, 271
St John Ambulance, UK, 380
Stanley Thomas Johnson Foundation, Switzerland, 317
The Starr Foundation, USA, 473
Start Network, UK, 337
State Grid Foundation for Public Welfare, China (People's Republic), 69
Stavros Niarchos Foundation—SNF, Greece, 147
Steelworkers Humanity Fund/Le Fonds Humanitaire des Metallos, Canada, 62
Steenkamp (Reeva Rebecca) Foundation, South Africa, 283
Stefan Batory Foundation, Poland, 256
Stelios Philanthropic Foundation, Cyprus, 78
Stewards Company Limited, UK, 384
Stewardship Foundation, USA, 473
Stewart (Sir Halley) Trust, UK, 383
Stichting Dioraphte, Netherlands, 229
Stichting DOEN, Netherlands, 229
Stichting Fonds 1818, Netherlands, 229
Stichting IKEA Foundation, Netherlands, 229
Stichting Liliane Fonds, Netherlands, 229
Stichting Mama Cash, Netherlands, 230
Stichting Max Havelaar—Fairtrade Nederland, Netherlands, 230
Stichting Praemium Erasmianum, Netherlands, 230
Stichting van Schulden naar Kansen, Netherlands, 231
Stichting Triodos Foundation, Netherlands, 231
Stichting Vluchteling, Netherlands, 231
Stichting Vodafone Netherlands, Netherlands, 231
Stiftelsen Dam, Norway, 243
Stiftelsen Gapminder, Sweden, 300
Stiftung 'Erinnerung, Verantwortung und Zukunft'—EVZ, Germany, 139

Social welfare

Stiftung Kinder in Afrika, Germany, 140
Stiftung Kinderdorf Pestalozzi, Switzerland, 317
Stiftung Lesen, Germany, 140
Stiftung für die Rechte zukünftiger Generationen—SRzG, Germany, 141
Stiftung Vivamos Mejor, Switzerland, 317
Stiftung West-Östliche Begegnungen, Germany, 141
Streisand (Barbra) Foundation, USA, 408
Strickland Foundation, Malta, 214
Stroke Association, UK, 384
Strømme Foundation, Norway, 243
Strømmestiftelsen, Norway, 243
Sudan Foundation, Sudan, 297
Sudd Institute, South Sudan, 285
Sulaiman Bin Abdul Aziz Bin Saleh Al Rajhi Foundation, Saudi Arabia, 269
Sultan bin Abdulaziz Al Sa'ud Foundation, Saudi Arabia, 270
SUN Civil Society Network, UK, 381
Suomalaiset kehitysjärjestöt—Fingo, Finland, 95
Surdna Foundation, Inc, USA, 474
Survival International, UK, 385
Sutherland Self Help Trust, New Zealand, 235
Swaminathan (M. S.) Research Foundation, India, 158
Swaziland Charitable Trust, Eswatini, 93
Swedish Rheumatism Association, Sweden, 302
Swiss Church Aid, Switzerland, 311
SWISSAID Foundation, Switzerland, 318
Syin-Lu Social Welfare Foundation, Taiwan, 321
Synergos—The Synergos Institute, USA, 396
Syria Al-Gad Relief Foundation, Egypt, 91
Taawon, Palestinian Territories, 246
Tahir Foundation, Indonesia, 162
Talk Out Loud, Australia, 18
Talon (Claudine), Fondation, Benin, 35
Tanager, USA, 397
Tanenbaum (Joseph) Charitable Foundation, Canada, 58
Tarih Vakfı, Türkiye, 329
Tata Trusts, India, 160
Tearfund, UK, 385
Tearfund Australia, Australia, 18
TechnoServe, USA, 474
Telefónica Foundation, Spain, 295
Telefónica Movistar Colombia Foundation, Colombia, 71
Teletón México Foundation, Mexico, 216
Telmex Telcel Foundation, Mexico, 216
Tencent Foundation, China (People's Republic), 70
Terre des Hommes International Federation—TDHIF, Switzerland, 318
Terre Sans Frontières—TSF, Canada, 62
Terrence Higgins Trust—THT, UK, 385
TESEV—Türkiye Ekonomik ve Sosyal Etüdler Vakfı, Türkiye, 329
Tewa, Nepal, 223
Thabo Mbeki Foundation, South Africa, 284
Third Sector Foundation of Turkey, Türkiye, 327
Third World Solidarity Action, Luxembourg, 209
Thomson Reuters Foundation, UK, 385
Thorn (The Sir Jules) Charitable Trust, UK, 383
Thunberg (Greta) Foundation, Sweden, 300
Thurgood Marshall Institute, USA, 454
TI—Transparency International, Germany, 142
Tibet Fund, USA, 475
Tibet-Institut Rikon, Switzerland, 318
Tides Organizations, USA, 475
Tifa Foundation—Indonesia, Indonesia, 163
Timchenko (Elena & Gennady) Foundation, Russian Federation, 265
Tindall Foundation, New Zealand, 235
Tinh Thuong One Member Limited Liability Microfinance Institution, Viet Nam, 488
TISCO Foundation, Thailand, 325
TK Foundation, Bahamas, 24
The Todd Foundation, New Zealand, 235
Together for Global Justice—CIDSE, Belgium, 29
Tony Blair Institute for Global Change—TBI, UK, 386
Topūtanga Tuku Aroha o Aotearoa, New Zealand, 232
TOSA Foundation, USA, 475
TotalEnergies Foundation, France, 112
Totto Foundation, Japan, 194
The Toyota Foundation, Japan, 195
TPG Telecom Foundation, Australia, 19
Transnet Foundation, South Africa, 284
Transparency International—TI, Germany, 142
The Trawalla Foundation, Australia, 19
Triodos Foundation, Netherlands, 231
Trócaire—Catholic Agency for World Development, Ireland, 168
The Trussell Trust, UK, 386
Trust for London, UK, 386
Trust for Social Achievement, Bulgaria, 44
Trusthouse Charitable Foundation, UK, 386

TTF—Toyota Thailand Foundation, Thailand, 325
Tulsa Community Foundation—TCF, USA, 476
Tunisia Development Foundation, Tunisia, 326
Turin Savings Bank Foundation, Italy, 176
Turkish Economic and Social Studies Foundation, Türkiye, 329
Turkish Family Health and Planning Foundation, Türkiye, 330
Türkiye Aile Sağlığı ve Planlaması Vakfı—TAPV, Türkiye, 330
Türkiye İnsan Hakları Vakfı—TİHV, Türkiye, 330
Türkiye Kalkınma Vakfı, Türkiye, 330
Türkiye Vodafone Vakfı, Türkiye, 331
Turquoise Mountain Foundation, UK, 386
TÜSEV—Türkiye Üçüncü Sektör Vakfı, Türkiye, 327
TY Danjuma Foundation, Nigeria, 239
TYM Fund, Viet Nam, 488
U4 Anti-Corruption Resource Centre, Norway, 241
Ucom Foundation, Armenia, 9
Ufadhili Trust, Kenya, 197
UJIA—United Jewish Israel Appeal, UK, 387
UK Research and Innovation—UKRI, UK, 387
Ukrainian Women's Fund, Ukraine, 333
Uluchay Social-Economic Innovation Center, Azerbaijan, 23
Uluntu Community Foundation—UCF, Zimbabwe, 491
Unbound Philanthropy, USA, 476
UniCredit Foundation, Italy, 183
UNIFOR—Forvaltningstiftelse for fond og legater, Norway, 240
Unipolis Foundation, Italy, 181
UNIR Bolivia Foundation, Bolivia, 36
Unitarian Universalist Service Committee—UUSC, USA, 476
United Jewish Israel Appeal—UJIA, UK, 387
United Nations Foundation, USA, 476
United Purpose, UK, 387
United States African Development Foundation—USADF, USA, 477
United Way Worldwide, USA, 477
Universal Foundation, Maldives, 212
UPM Foundation, Uruguay, 485
UPS Foundation, USA, 477
Usain Bolt Foundation, Jamaica, 185
USPG—United Society Partners in the Gospel, UK, 387
UUSC—Unitarian Universalist Service Committee, USA, 476
Väestöliitto, Finland, 98
Values Foundation, Bulgaria, 43
Vancouver Foundation, Canada, 62
Van Leer Foundation, Netherlands, 231
Van Leer Jerusalem Institute, Israel, 171
Vargas (Getulio), Fundação, Brazil, 40
Vehbi Koç Foundation, Türkiye, 331
Vehbi Koç Vakfı, Türkiye, 331
Venkatarangaiya (M.) Foundation, India, 158
VENRO—Verband Entwicklungspolitik und Humanitäre Hilfe deutscher Nichtregierungsorganizationen, Germany, 120
Verband für Gemeinnütziges Stiften, Austria, 20
Vestnordenfonden, Denmark, 86
VIA Foundation, Czech Republic, 81
Victor Pinchuk Foundation, Ukraine, 333
Victoria Children Foundation, Russian Federation, 267
Village Community Development Foundation, Indonesia, 163
Villar Foundation, Inc, Philippines, 253
Vincent Fairfax Family Foundation—VFFF, Australia, 19
VINCI Corporate Foundation for the City, France, 106
VinFuture Foundation, Viet Nam, 489
Vita, Ireland, 168
Vital Voices Global Partnership, USA, 478
Vivamos Mejor Foundation, Switzerland, 317
Vodacom Foundation, South Africa, 284
Vodacom Foundation DRC, Congo (Democratic Republic), 72
Vodacom Foundation South Africa, South Africa, 284
Vodacom Lesotho Foundation, Lesotho, 207
Vodacom Tanzania Foundation—VTF, Tanzania, 323
Vodafone Albania Foundation, Albania, 5
Vodafone Americas Foundation, USA, 478
Vodafone ATH Fiji Foundation, Fiji, 94
Vodafone Czech Republic Foundation, Czech Republic, 80
Vodafone Egypt Foundation, Egypt, 91
Vodafone Foundation, UK, 388
Vodafone Foundation India, India, 161

INDEX OF MAIN ACTIVITIES

Vodafone Foundation Luxembourg, Luxembourg, 210
Vodafone Foundation New Zealand, New Zealand, 235
Vodafone Ghana Foundation, Ghana, 144
Vodafone Idea Foundation, India, 161
Vodafone Ireland Foundation, Ireland, 168
Vodafone Italy Foundation, Italy, 181
Vodafone Netherlands Foundation, Netherlands, 231
Vodafone Romania Foundation, Romania, 264
Vodafone Spain Foundation, Spain, 296
Vodafone Türkiye Foundation, Türkiye, 331
Volkart Foundation, Switzerland, 319
Volkart-Stiftung, Switzerland, 319
Volnoe Delo—Oleg Deripaska Foundation, Russian Federation, 267
Voluntary Service Overseas, UK, 388
Volunteer Service Abroad/Te Tūao Tāwāhi—VSA, New Zealand, 236
VSO—Voluntary Service Overseas, UK, 388
Výbor dobré vůle—Nadace Olgy Havlové, Czech Republic, 81
W. K. Kellogg Foundation—WKKF, USA, 478
Wahana Lingkungan Hidup Indonesia—WALHI, Indonesia, 162
WALHI—Wahana Lingkungan Hidup Indonesia, Indonesia, 162
Walk Free, Australia, 15
Walmart Foundation, USA, 478
Walter and Duncan Gordon Charitable Foundation, Canada, 62
WAMA Foundation, Tanzania, 323
War Child, UK, 388
War on Want, UK, 388
WasserStiftung, Germany, 142
Water for Good, USA, 479
Water for People, USA, 479
WaterAid, UK, 389
WaterFoundation, Germany, 142
The Waterloo Foundation—TWF, UK, 389
Webster (R. Howard) Foundation, Canada, 61
Weinberg (Harry and Jeanette) Foundation, USA, 434
Welfare Association, Palestinian Territories, 246
West-Nordic Foundation, Denmark, 86
Weston (Garfield) Foundation, UK, 355
Weyerhaeuser Family Foundation, Inc, USA, 480
Whirlpool Foundation, USA, 480
William Adlington Cadbury Charitable Trust, UK, 390
William Buckland Foundation, Australia, 19
The William and Flora Hewlett Foundation, USA, 481
The William H. Donner Foundation, Inc, USA, 481
William Randolph Hearst Foundation, USA, 435
William T. Grant Foundation, USA, 481
WILPF—Women's International League for Peace and Freedom, Switzerland, 319
Wilsdorf (Hans), Fondation, Switzerland, 309
Winfrey (Oprah) Leadership Academy Foundation, USA, 459
Winrock International, USA, 481
Winston Churchill Memorial Trust of New Zealand, New Zealand, 236
The Womanity Foundation, Switzerland, 319
Women in Development Foundation, Tanzania, 323
Women Thrive Fund, UK, 384
WomenLead Institute, USA, 418
Women's Aid, Ireland, 168
Women's Aid Organisation—WAO, Malaysia, 212
Women's Development Network, Costa Rica, 75
Women's Environment & Development Organization—WEDO, USA, 482
Women's Foundation, Costa Rica, 74
Women's International League for Peace and Freedom, Switzerland, 319
Women's World Summit Foundation—WWSF, Switzerland, 320
The Wood Foundation—TWF, UK, 391
World Alliance of YMCAs—Young Men's Christian Associations, Switzerland, 319
World Association of Children's Friends, Monaco, 217
World Concern, USA, 482
World Economic Forum, Switzerland, 320
World Emergency Relief—WER, USA, 483
World Jewish Relief, UK, 391
World Neighbors, USA, 483
The World of NGOs, Austria, 20
World Scout Foundation—Fondation du Scoutisme Mondial—WSF/FSM, Switzerland, 320
World University Service of Canada/Entraide Universitaire Mondiale du Canada—WUSC/EUMC, Canada, 63

INDEX OF MAIN ACTIVITIES

Social welfare

World Vegetable Center, Taiwan, 322
World Vision International, UK, 391
WorldFish, Malaysia, 212
Wujoh Foundation for Media and Development, Yemen, 489
WWSF—Women's World Summit Foundation, Switzerland, 320
Xiangjiang Social Relief Fund, China (People's Republic), 68
YADESA—Yayasan Pembinaan Masyarakat Desa, Indonesia, 163
Yanbao Charity Foundation, China (People's Republic), 69
Yayasan Azman Hashim, Malaysia, 212
Yayasan Dian Desa—YDD, Indonesia, 162

Yayasan Geutanyoë, Indonesia, 162
Yayasan Insan Sembada, Indonesia, 163
Yayasan Pembinaan Masyarakat Desa—YADESA, Indonesia, 163
Yayasan Tifa, Indonesia, 163
Year Out Group, UK, 374
Yellow Feather Fund, USA, 471
YMCA—Young Men's Christian Association, UK, 392
YongLin Charity Foundation, Taiwan, 322
Young Lives vs Cancer, UK, 392
Youth Leadership Development Foundation—YLDF, Yemen, 489
Yuan Lin Charity Fund, China (People's Republic), 70

Zakat House, Kuwait, 203
Zancan (Emanuela), Fondazione Centro Studi e Ricerca Sociale, Italy, 172
Zarina & Naushad Merali Foundation, Kenya, 200
ZOA, Netherlands, 231
Zochonis Charitable Trust, UK, 392
Zonta Foundation for Women, USA, 484
Zorig Foundation, Mongolia, 219
Zuleikhabai Valy Mohamed Gany Rangoonwala Trust—ZVMG Rangoonwala Trust, Pakistan, 246
Zurich Community Trust—ZCT, UK, 392
ZVMG Rangoonwala Trust, Pakistan, 246

Index by Area of Activity

Note: organizations will appear either in the All Regions index or in one or more of the regions listed below. All Regions means an organization is active in every region of the world. If an organization is listed under All Regions, it will not appear under any other region heading.

All Regions	596
Africa South of the Sahara	601
Australasia	605
Central and South-Eastern Europe	606
East and South-East Asia	609
Eastern Europe and the Republics of Central Asia	612
Middle East and North Africa	615
South America, Central America and the Caribbean	617
South Asia	621
USA and Canada	623
Western Europe	626

ALL REGIONS

30 Million Friends Foundation, France, 102
A. S. Hornby Educational Trust, UK, 338
AAUW Educational Foundation, USA, 399
Abdulla Al Ghurair Foundation for Education, United Arab Emirates, 334
Accademia Musicale Chigiana, Italy, 172
Acción Contra el Hambre–ACH, Spain, 286
Accountable Now, USA, 393
ACDI/VOCA, USA, 397
ACFID—Australian Council for International Development, Australia, 12
ACLS—American Council of Learned Societies, USA, 399
ACROTEC Technology Foundation, Italy, 176
ACT Alliance, Switzerland, 306
Action Against Hunger, Spain, 286
Action Group on Erosion, Technology and Concentration, Canada, 54
ActionAid International, South Africa, 278
Adenauer (Konrad) Stiftung eV, Germany, 134
Adessium Foundation, Netherlands, 223
The Adolph and Esther Gottlieb Foundation, Inc, USA, 397
ADRA—Adventist Development and Relief Agency International, USA, 397
Adventist Development and Relief Agency International—ADRA, USA, 397
Aga Khan Development Network—AKDN, Switzerland, 306
Aga Khan Foundation, Switzerland, 306
Aga Khan Foundation UK, UK, 338
AIC—Association Internationale des Charités, Belgium, 28
Aid to the Church in Need—ACN International, Germany, 120
Air Pollution and Climate Secretariat—AirClim, Sweden, 298
AirClim—Air Pollution and Climate Secretariat, Sweden, 298
Al Jalila Foundation, United Arab Emirates, 334
Al Jisr Foundation, Oman, 244
Alessio Pezcoller Foundation, Italy, 174
Alexander von Humboldt Foundation, Germany, 120
Alexander von Humboldt Stiftung, Germany, 120
Alexander S. Onassis Public Benefit Foundation, Liechtenstein, 207
Alfried Krupp von Bohlen und Halbach Foundation, Germany, 121
Alfried Krupp von Bohlen und Halbach-Stiftung, Germany, 121
Ali Fulhu Thuthu Foundation, Maldives, 212
Alicia Patterson Foundation—APF, USA, 398
Alight, USA, 399
All Good Foundation Charitable Trust, New Zealand, 232
Allen (Paul G.) Family Foundation, USA, 462
Alliance Israélite Universelle, France, 101
Alliance Sud—Swiss Alliance of Development Organizations, Switzerland, 305

Alongside Hope/Auprès de l'espoir, Canada, 49
Alwaleed Philanthropies, Saudi Arabia, 269
American Association of University Women—AAUW Educational Foundation, USA, 399
American Council of Learned Societies—ACLS, USA, 399
American Express Foundation, USA, 400
American Heart Association—AHA, USA, 401
American Jewish Joint Distribution Committee—JDC, USA, 402
amfAR—The Foundation for AIDS Research, USA, 403
Amigos de la Tierra, Netherlands, 225
Les Amis de la Terre, Netherlands, 225
Amnesty International, UK, 340
Andrew W. Mellon Foundation, USA, 404
Andrews Charitable Trust—ACT, UK, 340
Anglo American Foundation, UK, 340
Anne Frank Foundation, Netherlands, 224
Anne Frank Stichting, Netherlands, 224
Anne Ray Foundation, USA, 450
The Annenberg Foundation, USA, 404
Ansar Burney Trust International, Pakistan, 245
Anti-Defamation League—ADL, USA, 405
Anti-Slavery International, UK, 340
Arab Fund for Arts and Culture—AFAC, Lebanon, 205
Argentine Council for International Relations, Argentina, 6
Ariadne—European Funders for Social Change and Human Rights, UK, 336
Asahi Glass Foundation, Japan, 186
ASEAN Institutes of Strategic and International Studies—ASEAN ISIS, Indonesia, 162
Asia Crime Prevention Foundation—ACPF, Japan, 186
Asociacija Litdea—Lithuanian Development Education and Awareness Raising Association, Lithuania, 208
Association Internationale des Charités—AIC, Belgium, 28
AT&T Foundation, USA, 407
ATD Fourth World International, France, 115
Atlas Network, USA, 407
Australian Academy of Technological Sciences and Engineering, Australia, 11
Australian Council for International Development—ACFID, Australia, 12
Austrian Foundation for Development Research, Austria, 22
Aviation Sans Frontières—ASF, France, 101
Aviation Without Borders, France, 101
Baha'i International Development Organization—BIDO, Israel, 169
Baker Heart & Diabetes Institute, Australia, 13
Balzan Fonds, Internationale Stiftung, Italy, 181
Ban Ki-Moon Foundation for a Better Future, Korea (Republic), 200
The Barack Obama Foundation, USA, 407
Barça Foundation, Spain, 287
Bardot (Brigitte), Fondation, France, 104

Barjeel Art Foundation, United Arab Emirates, 334
Basso Issoco (Leilio e Lisli), Fondazione, Italy, 178
Bat Conservation Trust, UK, 342
Bellingcat Foundation, Netherlands, 228
Bellona Foundation, Norway, 240
Bergman (Ingmar), Stiftelsen, Sweden, 303
Bernadottes (Folke) Minnesfond, Sweden, 299
Better World Campaign—BWC, USA, 408
Bezos Earth Fund, USA, 408
BirdLife International, UK, 343
Bischöfliches Hilfswerk Misereor eV, Germany, 137
Blavatnik Family Foundation, USA, 409
Bleustein-Blanchet (Marcel), Fondation de la Vocation, France, 109
Bloomberg Philanthropies, USA, 409
BMW Foundation Herbert Quandt, Germany, 122
Boehringer Ingelheim Fonds—Stiftung für medizinische Grundlagenforschung, Germany, 122
Bond, UK, 335
BP Foundation, Inc, USA, 409
Brandt (Bundeskanzler Willy) Stiftung, Germany, 123
Brazilian Center for International Relations, Brazil, 39
Breakthrough T1D, USA, 409
BrightFocus Foundation, USA, 409
Brigitte Bardot Foundation, France, 104
Bristol-Myers Squibb Foundation, USA, 410
British & Foreign School Society—BFSS, UK, 351
British Academy, UK, 344
The British Council, UK, 344
British Institute of International and Comparative Law—BIICL, UK, 345
British Overseas NGOs for Development, UK, 335
British Red Cross Society, UK, 345
Brookings Institution, USA, 410
Bruegel—Brussels European and Global Economic Laboratory, Belgium, 28
Buffett (Susan Thompson) Foundation, USA, 474
Bundeskanzler-Willy-Brandt-Stiftung, Germany, 123
CABI, UK, 345
CAF America, USA, 393
CAFOD—Catholic Agency for Overseas Development, UK, 345
Calouste Gulbenkian Foundation, Portugal, 259
Cambridge Commonwealth, European and International Trust, UK, 346
The Canada Council for the Arts/Conseil des Arts du Canada, Canada, 50
Canon Institute for Global Studies—CIGS, Japan, 187
Cargill (Margaret A.) Philanthropies, USA, 450
Caritas de France—Secours Catholique, France, 116
Caritas Internationalis—CI, Vatican City, 486
Carlo Pesenti Foundation, Italy, 176

INDEX BY AREA OF ACTIVITY

All Regions

Carnegie Corporation of New York, USA, 411
Carnegie Foundation, Wateler Fund, Netherlands, 224
Carnegie-Stichting, Waterlerfonds, Netherlands, 224
Caterpillar Foundation, USA, 412
Catholic Agency for Overseas Development—CAFOD, UK, 345
Catholic Help—Caritas France, France, 116
CCKF—Chiang Ching-kuo Foundation for International Scholarly Exchange, Taiwan, 321
CDC Foundation, USA, 412
Center for China & Globalization—CCG, China (People's Republic), 67
Center for Inquiry—CFI, USA, 412
Center for Victims of Torture—CVT, USA, 413
Centre d'Etude du Polymorphisme Humain, France, 107
Centre for Humanitarian Action—CHA, Germany, 123
Centre for International Governance Innovation—CIGI/Centre pour l'Innovation dans la Gouvernance Internationale, Canada, 51
Centre International de Recherche sur le Cancer—CIRC, France, 101
Centre for International Studies, Italy, 172
Centro Brasileiro de Relações Internacionais—CEBRI, Brazil, 39
Centro Internacional de Mejoramiento de Maíz y Trigo—CIMMYT, Mexico, 215
Centro Studi Internazionali—CSI, Italy, 172
Centro Studi e Ricerca Sociale Fondazione Emanuela Zancan, Italy, 172
The Century Foundation—TCF, USA, 413
Cera, Belgium, 28
Champalimaud Foundation, Portugal, 259
Charities Aid Foundation of America—CAF America, USA, 393
Charles Koch Foundation, USA, 413
Charles Léopold Mayer Foundation for the Progress of Humankind, Switzerland, 308
Chatham House, UK, 378
The Chatlos Foundation, Inc, USA, 414
Chiang Ching-kuo Foundation for International Scholarly Exchange—CCKF, Taiwan, 321
Chigiana Musical Academy, Italy, 172
Children & War Foundation—CAW, Norway, 240
Childs (Jane Coffin) Memorial Fund for Medical Research, USA, 443
Chirac (Jacques), Fondation, France, 107
Christian Aid, UK, 348
Christopher & Dana Reeve Foundation, USA, 415
The Churchill Fellowship, UK, 348
Churchill (Winston) Memorial Trust, Australia, 19
Churchill (Winston) Memorial Trust of New Zealand, New Zealand, 236
CIDSE—Together for Global Justice, Belgium, 29
CIEE—Council on International Educational Exchange, USA, 415
CIMA Research Foundation—Centre for Environmental Monitoring, Italy, 176
Citi Foundation, USA, 415
Citizens Foundation, Iceland, 154
City of Lisbon Foundation, Portugal, 259
CIVICUS—World Alliance for Citizen Participation, South Africa, 278
Civil Peace Service—CPS, Germany, 120
CLEAR Global, USA, 416
Clinton Foundation, USA, 416
Clooney Foundation for Justice—CFJ, USA, 416
Coady Institute, Canada, 52
The Coca-Cola Foundation, Inc, USA, 417
Collodi (Carlo), Fondazione Nazionale, Italy, 179
The Commonwealth Fund, USA, 417
The Confederation of Service Charities—Cobseo, UK, 349
Conrad N. Hilton Foundation, USA, 417
Conseil des Arts du Canada, Canada, 50
Consejo Argentino para las Relaciones Internacionales—CARI, Argentina, 6
Consejo Latinoamericano de Ciencias Sociales—CLACSO, Argentina, 6
Conservation International Foundation, USA, 417
Coordination SUD, France, 99
Corra Foundation, UK, 349
Corus International, USA, 418
Council for International Exchange of Scholars—CIES, USA, 418
Counterpart International, USA, 418
The Crafoord Foundation, Sweden, 298
Crafoordska stiftelsen, Sweden, 298
Croatian Platform for International Citizen Solidarity, Croatia, 76
CROSOL—Platforma za medunarodnu gradansku solidarnost Hrvatske, Croatia, 76

Croucher Foundation, Hong Kong, 151
Cruz (Oswaldo), Fundação, Brazil, 40
CURE International, USA, 419
The Cure Parkinson's Trust, UK, 349
CVT—Center for Victims of Torture, USA, 413
DAAD—Deutscher Akademischer Austauschdienst, Germany, 125
Dag Hammarskjöld Foundation, Sweden, 303
Daimler and Benz Foundation, Germany, 123
Daimler und Benz Stiftung, Germany, 123
Dalio Foundation, USA, 419
Danielle Mitterrand Foundation, France, 112
Danube Institute, Hungary, 153
David and Lucile Packard Foundation, USA, 420
DEC—Disasters Emergency Committee, UK, 336
Defence for Children International—DCI, Switzerland, 307
Democracy Fund, USA, 458
Deutsche Bundesstiftung Umwelt—DBU, Germany, 124
Deutscher Akademischer Austauschdienst—DAAD, Germany, 125
Deutsches Institut für internationale Politik und Sicherheit, Germany, 141
Development Gateway—DG, USA, 420
DiploFoundation, Malta, 213
Direct Relief, USA, 420
Disability Rights Fund, USA, 395
Disabled Peoples' International—DPI, Canada, 54
Disasters Emergency Committee—DEC, UK, 336
Dmitry Likhachev Foundation, Russian Federation, 265
Doctors Without Borders International, Switzerland, 314
Doctors of the World International, France, 114
Dokolo (Sindika), Fundação, Angola, 5
E. O. Wilson Biodiversity Foundation, USA, 421
Earth Island Institute—EII, USA, 422
eBay Foundation, USA, 422
Ebert (Friedrich) Stiftung, Germany, 129
EcoHealth Alliance, USA, 422
ECPAT International, Thailand, 324
EDF Group Foundation, France, 107
EDGE Funders Alliance, USA, 394
Educational Opportunity Foundation, UK, 351
EFQM—European Foundation for Quality Management, Belgium, 30
EGMONT—Institut Royal des Relations Internationales, Belgium, 29
Ekhaga Foundation, Sweden, 299
Ekhagastiftelsen, Sweden, 299
The Elders Foundation, UK, 352
Electronic Frontier Foundation—EFF, USA, 423
The ELMA Group of Foundations, USA, 423
Elrha, UK, 352
Else Kröner-Fresenius Foundation, Germany, 127
Else Kröner-Fresenius-Stiftung, Germany, 127
Emanuela Zancan Foundation Centre for Social Studies and Research, Italy, 172
Emmaüs International, France, 102
Enchanted Peach Children's Foundation—EPCF, USA, 423
ENGIE Corporate Foundation, France, 105
The English-Speaking Union—ESU, UK, 353
Enough Project, USA, 416
Ernest Kleinwort Charitable Trust, UK, 353
Ernst Schering Foundation, Germany, 127
Ernst-Schering-Stiftung, Germany, 127
ETC Group—Action Group on Erosion, Technology and Concentration, Canada, 54
Eureka Foundation, Bulgaria, 43
EURODAD—European Network on Debt and Development, Belgium, 29
European Association for Cancer Research—EACR, UK, 353
European Center for Constitutional and Human Rights—ECCHR, Germany, 128
European Climate Foundation, Netherlands, 224
European Food Banks Federation—EFBF, Belgium, 26
European Foundation for Management Development—EFMD, Belgium, 30
European Foundation for Quality Management—EFQM, Belgium, 30
European Network on Debt and Development—EURODAD, Belgium, 29
European Think Tanks Group—ETTG, Belgium, 26
European Training Foundation—ETF, Italy, 173
Evrika Foundation, Bulgaria, 43
ExxonMobil Foundation, USA, 425
F20, Germany, 119
Federal Chancellor Willy Brandt Foundation, Germany, 123
Fédération Européenne des Banques Alimentaires—FEBA, Belgium, 26

Fédération Internationale des Ligues des Droits de L'Homme—FIDH, France, 99
Félix Houphouët-Boigny Foundation for Peace Research, Côte d'Ivoire, 75
Fernand Lazard Foundation, Belgium, 31
Fernando Rielo Foundation, Spain, 290
FHI 360, USA, 425
The Film Foundation, USA, 425
Finnish Development Organizations, Finland, 95
FIPP—Fondation Internationale Pénale et Pénitentiaire, Netherlands, 226
Flight Safety Foundation, USA, 426
Florence Nightingale International Foundation, Switzerland, 309
Folke Bernadotte Memorial Foundation, Sweden, 299
Folke Bernadottes Minnesfond, Sweden, 299
FONDAD—Forum on Debt and Development, Netherlands, 225
Fondation 30 Millions d'Amis, France, 102
Fondation Brigitte Bardot, France, 104
Fondation Charles Léopold Mayer pour le Progrès de l'Homme—FPH, Switzerland, 308
Fondation de la Cité internationale des arts, France, 104
Fondation d'Entreprise ENGIE, France, 105
Fondation Félix Houphouët-Boigny pour la Recherche de la Paix, Côte d'Ivoire, 75
Fondation Fernand Lazard Stichting, Belgium, 31
Fondation Franz Weber—FFW, Switzerland, 308
Fondation Fyssen, France, 107
Fondation Gan pour le Cinéma, France, 107
Fondation Groupe EDF, France, 107
Fondation Hassan II pour les Marocains Résidant à l'Étranger, Morocco, 220
Fondation Internationale Florence Nightingale, Switzerland, 309
Fondation Internationale Pénale et Pénitentiaire—FIPP, Netherlands, 226
Fondation Jacques Chirac, France, 107
Fondation Jean Dausset—Centre d'Etude du Polymorphisme Humain—CEPH, France, 107
Fondation MAIF pour la Recherche, France, 108
Fondation Maison des Sciences de l'Homme—FMSH, France, 108
Fondation Marcel Bleustein-Blanchet de la Vocation, France, 109
Fondation Marguerite et Aimé Maeght, France, 109
Fondation Nestlé pour l'Etude des Problèmes de l'Alimentation dans le Monde, Switzerland, 310
Fondation Prince Albert II de Monaco, Monaco, 217
Fondation Princesse Charlène de Monaco, Monaco, 218
Fondation pour la Recherche Médicale, France, 110
Fondation pour la Recherche Stratégique, France, 111
Fondation du Scoutisme Mondial, Switzerland, 320
Fondation Simone et Cino del Duca, France, 111
Fondation Sommet Mondial des Femmes, Switzerland, 320
Fondation Suisse pour Recherches Alpines—FSRA, Switzerland, 316
Fondation TotalEnergies, France, 112
Fondazione Alessio Pezcoller, Italy, 174
Fondazione Cavaliere del Lavoro Carlo Pesenti, Italy, 176
Fondazione CIMA—Centro Internazionale in Monitoraggio Ambientale, Italy, 176
Fondazione Giovanni Lorenzini, Italy, 177
Fondazione Giulio Pastore—FGP, Italy, 178
Fondazione Internazionale Premio Balzan, Italy, 181
Fondazione ITS, Italy, 178
Fondazione Lelio e Lisli Basso Issoco—Sezione Internazionale, Italy, 178
Fondazione Nazionale Carlo Collodi, Italy, 179
Fondazione Social Venture-Giordano Dell'Amore, Italy, 180
Fondazione Vaticana Giovanni Paolo I, Vatican City, 486
Foreign Policy Association, USA, 427
Forum on Debt and Development—FONDAD, Netherlands, 225
Forum International de l'Innovation Sociale—FIIS, France, 112
Foundation for AIDS Research—amfAR, USA, 403
Foundation for Assistance, Training and Integration of Disadvantaged People, Spain, 287
Foundation for Basic Research in Biomedicine, Germany, 122

All Regions

Foundation for Defense of Democracies—FDD, USA, 427
Foundation for Environmental Education—FEE, Denmark, 83
Foundation for Investment and Development of Exports—FIDE, Honduras, 150
Foundation for Medical Research, France, 110
Foundation for the Promotion of the German Rectors' Conference, Germany, 140
Foundation for the Rights of Future Generations, Germany, 141
Foundation for Strategic Research, France, 111
Foundations Platform—F20, Germany, 119
France-Libertés Fondation Danielle Mitterrand, France, 112
Frank (Anne) Stichting, Netherlands, 224
Freedom House, Inc, USA, 428
Friedrich-Ebert-Stiftung eV, Germany, 129
Friedrich Naumann Foundation for Freedom, Germany, 130
Friedrich-Naumann-Stiftung für die Freiheit, Germany, 130
Friends of the Earth International—FOEI, Netherlands, 225
Fritz Thyssen Foundation, Germany, 130
Fritz Thyssen Stiftung, Germany, 130
Front Line Defenders—FLD, Ireland, 166
Fulbright Scholar Program, USA, 418
Fund for Global Human Rights, USA, 395
Fundação Assistência Médica Internacional—AMI, Portugal, 258
Fundação Calouste Gulbenkian, Portugal, 259
Fundação Champalimaud, Portugal, 259
Fundação Cidade de Lisboa, Portugal, 259
Fundação Getulio Vargas—FGV, Brazil, 40
Fundação Oswaldo Cruz—FIOCRUZ, Brazil, 40
Fundação Sindika Dokolo, Angola, 5
Fundació Futbol Club Barcelona, Spain, 287
Fundación AFIM—Ayuda, Formación e Integración del Discapacitado, Spain, 287
Fundación Fernando Rielo, Spain, 290
Fundación para la Inversión y Desarrollo de Exportaciones—FIDE, Honduras, 150
Fundación Juanelo Turriano, Spain, 291
Fundación María Francisca de Roviralta, Spain, 292
Fundación Oxfam Intermón, Spain, 293
Fundación Paraguaya de Cooperación y Desarrollo, Paraguay, 248
Fundación Princesa de Asturias, Spain, 294
Fundación Rafa Nadal, Spain, 294
Fundación Real Instituto Elcano, Spain, 294
Fundación Real Madrid, Spain, 295
Fundación Telefónica, Spain, 295
Fundación Torcuato Di Tella—FTDT, Argentina, 8
Fundación Universidad-Empresa—UE, Spain, 295
FundAction, USA, 394
Fyssen Foundation, France, 107
G. Unger Vetlesen Foundation, USA, 429
The Gaia Foundation, UK, 355
Gairdner Foundation, Canada, 55
Gan Foundation for the Cinema, France, 107
Gapminder, Sweden, 300
Garden Organic, UK, 355
Gates (Bill & Melinda) Foundation, USA, 429
Gates Foundation, USA, 429
GE Aerospace Foundation, USA, 429
Gerda Henkel Foundation, Germany, 130
Gerda Henkel Stiftung, Germany, 130
German Academic Exchange Service, Germany, 125
German Catholic Bishops' Organization for Development Co-operation, Germany, 137
German Federal Foundation for the Environment, Germany, 124
German Institute of Development and Sustainability—IDOS, Germany, 130
Getty (J. Paul) Trust, USA, 442
Getulio Vargas Foundation, Brazil, 40
Giordano Dell'Amore Social Venture Foundation, Italy, 180
Giovanni Lorenzini Foundation, Italy, 177
Giovanni Paolo I, Fondazione Vaticana, Vatican City, 486
Giulio Pastore Foundation, Italy, 178
To Give, Israel, 170
Global Dialogue, UK, 336
Global Environmental Action—GEA, Japan, 187
Global Ethic Foundation, Germany, 141
The Global Foodbanking Network—GFN, USA, 431
Global Forest Fund, Denmark, 83
Global Fund for Community Foundations—GFCF, South Africa, 278
Global Fund for Women—GFW, USA, 431
Global Greengrants Fund, USA, 431

Global Health Council, USA, 395
Global Impact, USA, 395
Global Philanthropy Forum, USA, 395
GLOBSEC, Slovakia, 275
Goethe-Institut, Germany, 131
Good360, USA, 432
Goodwill Industries International, Inc—GII, USA, 432
Google.org—Google Foundation, USA, 432
Gorbachev Foundation, Russian Federation, 266
Gordon and Betty Moore Foundation, USA, 432
Gottlieb (Adolph and Esther) Foundation, Inc, USA, 397
Graduate Institute of International Studies and Development Studies, Switzerland, 311
Graham Foundation for Advanced Studies in the Fine Arts—GF, USA, 432
The Greta Thunberg Foundation, Sweden, 300
Grinspoon (Harold) Foundation, USA, 434
The Guardian Foundation, UK, 356
Guggenheim (Harry Frank) Foundation, USA, 434
Guggenheim (Solomon R.) Foundation, USA, 473
Gulbenkian (Calouste), Fundação, Portugal, 259
Gulf Research Center—GRC, Saudi Arabia, 269
H&M Foundation, Sweden, 300
Habitat for Humanity International, USA, 433
Hammarskjölds (Dag) Minnesfond, Stiftelsen, Sweden, 300
Hanns Seidel Foundation, Germany, 131
Hanns-Seidel-Stiftung eV, Germany, 131
Harold Grinspoon Foundation, USA, 434
The Harry Frank Guggenheim Foundation—HFG, USA, 434
Hasbro Childrens Trust, USA, 434
Hasbro Foundation, USA, 434
Hassan II Foundation for Moroccans Living Abroad, Morocco, 220
Hawaii Resilience Fund, USA, 458
Health Action International—HAI, Netherlands, 225
Heart to Heart International—HHI, USA, 435
Heifer Foundation, USA, 435
Heineken Prizes for Arts and Sciences, Netherlands, 225
Heinekenprijzen voor kunst en wetenschap, Netherlands, 225
Helmholtz Association, Germany, 132
Helmholtz-Gemeinschaft, Germany, 132
Helmich (Janson Johan og Marcia) Legat, Norway, 242
HelpAge International, UK, 357
Helsińska Fundacja Praw Człowieka, Poland, 257
Helsinki Foundation for Human Rights, Poland, 257
Hempel Fonden, Denmark, 84
Hempel Foundation, Denmark, 84
Henkel (Gerda) Stiftung, Germany, 130
Henry Doubleday Research Association, UK, 355
The Henry Moore Foundation, UK, 358
The Heritage Foundation, USA, 436
Hewlett (William and Flora) Foundation, USA, 481
HIAS—Hebrew Immigrant Aid Society, USA, 436
Hilti Foundation, Liechtenstein, 208
Hilton (Conrad N.) Foundation, USA, 417
Hirschfeld-Eddy Foundation, Germany, 132
Hirschfeld-Eddy-Stiftung, Germany, 132
Hodge Foundation, UK, 358
Homeless World Cup Foundation—HWCF, UK, 358
Honda Foundation, Japan, 187
Hornby (A. S.) Educational Trust, UK, 338
Hoso Bunka Foundation, Inc—HBF, Japan, 188
Houphouët-Boigny (Félix), Fondation, Côte d'Ivoire, 75
House of the Human Sciences Foundation, France, 108
Howard Hughes Medical Institute—HHMI, USA, 437
Human Dignity Trust, UK, 359
Human Rights Funders Network—HRFN, USA, 395
Human Rights House Foundation—HRHF, Norway, 241
Human Rights Watch—HRW, USA, 437
Humanity & Inclusion, France, 113
von Humboldt (Alexander) Stiftung, Germany, 120
IAESTE—International Association for the Exchange of Students for Technical Experience, Luxembourg, 210
IAI—Istituto Affari Internazionali, Italy, 182
IARC—International Agency for Research on Cancer, France, 101
IBM International Foundation, USA, 438
ICRC—International Red Cross and Red Crescent Movement, Switzerland, 312

INDEX BY AREA OF ACTIVITY

ICVA—International Council of Voluntary Agencies, Switzerland, 305
IDLO—International Development Law Organization, Italy, 181
Idrima Kratikon Ipotrofion, Greece, 147
IFAW—International Fund for Animal Welfare, USA, 438
IFES—International Foundation for Electoral Systems, USA, 440
IISD—International Institute for Sustainable Development, Canada, 57
IJ4EU—Investigative Journalism for Europe, Austria, 21
IKY—State Scholarships Foundation, Greece, 147
IMADR—The International Movement against All Forms of Discrimination and Racism, Japan, 188
Improving Economies for Stronger Communities—IESC, USA, 438
Inamori Foundation, Japan, 188
Inclusion International, UK, 359
Indian Council for Cultural Relations, India, 157
Ingmar Bergman Foundation, Sweden, 303
Inlaks Shivdasani Foundation, India, 158
Institut de Hautes Études Internationales et du Développement—IHEID, Switzerland, 311
Institut Mittag-Leffler, Sweden, 300
Institut Pasteur, France, 114
Institut Pasteur de Lille, France, 114
Institut Royal des Relations Internationales—EGMONT, Belgium, 29
Institut für Weltwirtschaft—IfW Kiel, Germany, 132
Institute of British Geographers, UK, 378
Institute of Economic Affairs—IEA, UK, 359
The Institute of Energy Economics, Japan—IEEJ, Japan, 188
Institute of International Affairs, Italy, 182
Institute of International Education—IIE, USA, 439
Institute of International Law, Argentina, 6
Institute for International Security and Strategic Affairs—ISIAE, Argentina, 6
Institute for Precision Cardiovascular Medicine, USA, 401
Institute for Scientific Interchange Foundation—ISI, Italy, 181
Institute of Social Studies—ISS, Netherlands, 226
INTEGRATA Foundation, Germany, 132
INTEGRATA—Stiftung für Humane Nutzung der Informationstechnologie, Germany, 132
Internationaal Instituut voor Sociale Geschiedenis—IISG, Netherlands, 226
International Agency for Research on Cancer—IARC, France, 101
International Arctic Science Committee—IASC, Iceland, 154
International Association of Charities, Belgium, 28
International Baccalaureate—IB, Switzerland, 312
International Balzan Prize Foundation, Italy, 181
International Center for Not-for-Profit Law—ICNL, USA, 396
International Center for Research on Women—ICRW, USA, 439
International Center for Transitional Justice—ICTJ, USA, 440
International Civil Society Centre, Germany, 119
International College of Surgeons—ICS, USA, 440
International Confederation Catholic Organizations Charitable Social Action, Vatican City, 486
International Council of Voluntary Agencies—ICVA, Switzerland, 305
International Development Center of Japan, Japan, 189
International Development Law Organization—IDLO, Italy, 181
International Education Research Foundation, Inc—IERF, USA, 440
International Eye Foundation—IEF, USA, 440
International Federation of Human Rights, France, 99
International Forum for Social Innovation—IFSI, France, 112
International Foundation for Electoral Systems—IFES, USA, 440
International Foundation for the Protection of Human Rights Defenders, Ireland, 166
International Foundation for Science—IFS, Sweden, 300
International Foundation for Socio-economic and Political Studies, Russian Federation, 266

INDEX BY AREA OF ACTIVITY

All Regions

International Fund for Animal Welfare—IFAW, USA, 438
International Institute for Applied Systems Analysis—IIASA, Austria, 21
International Institute of Social History—IISH, Netherlands, 226
International Institute of Social Studies, Netherlands, 226
The International Institute for Strategic Studies—IISS, UK, 360
International Institute for Sustainable Development—IISD, Canada, 57
International Lake Environment Committee Foundation, Japan, 189
International Maize and Wheat Improvement Center, Mexico, 215
International Medical Assistance Foundation, Portugal, 258
International Music and Art Foundation, Liechtenstein, 208
International NGO Charter of Accountability, USA, 393
International Office for Water, France, 115
International Organization for Relief, Welfare & Development—IORWD, Saudi Arabia, 269
International Penal and Penitentiary Foundation—IPPF, Netherlands, 226
International Planned Parenthood Federation—IPPF, UK, 360
International Press Institute—IPI, Austria, 21
International Red Cross and Red Crescent Movement—ICRC, Switzerland, 314
International Relief Teams—IRT, USA, 441
International Service for Human Rights—ISHR, Switzerland, 312
International Society for Human Rights—ISHR, Germany, 133
International Union for Conservation of Nature and Natural Resources, Switzerland, 313
International Work Group for Indigenous Affairs—IWGIA, Denmark, 84
International Youth Foundation—IYF, USA, 442
International Youth Library Foundation, Germany, 133
Internationale Jugendbibliothek, Germany, 133
Internationale Stiftung Preis E. Balzan-Fonds, Italy, 181
INTRAC, UK, 337
IPPF—International Planned Parenthood Federation, UK, 360
Islamic Relief Worldwide, UK, 360
ISPI—Istituto per gli Studi di Politica Internazionale, Italy, 183
IsraAID, Israel, 169
Istituto Affari Internazionali—IAI, Italy, 182
Istituto di Ricerche Farmacologiche Mario Negri, Italy, 182
Istituto per gli Studi di Politica Internazionale—ISPI, Italy, 183
Italian Institute for International Political Studies, Italy, 183
ITS Foundation, Italy, 178
IUCN/UICN, Switzerland, 313
J. Paul Getty Trust, USA, 442
Jacques Chirac Foundation, France, 107
James S. McDonnell Foundation, USA, 443
Jane Coffin Childs Memorial Fund for Medical Research—JCC Fund, USA, 443
Janson Johan Helmich and Marcia Jansons Endowment, Norway, 242
Janson Johan Helmich og Marcia Jansons Legat, Norway, 242
Japan Economic Research Institute Inc—JERI, Japan, 189
The Japan Foundation, Japan, 189
Japan Foundation Center for Economic Research—JCER, Japan, 189
Japan Society for the Promotion of Science—JSPS, Japan, 190
Jean Dausset Foundation—Centre for the Study of Human Polymorphism, France, 107
JERI—Japan Economic Research Institute Inc, Japan, 189
Jerusalem Foundation, Israel, 170
John Paul I Vatican Foundation, Vatican City, 486
John Templeton Foundation, USA, 444
Johnson & Johnson Foundation US—JJF, USA, 444
Johnson (Stanley Thomas) Foundation, Switzerland, 317
JPMorgan Chase Foundation, USA, 445
Juanelo Turriano Foundation, Spain, 291
Jubilee USA Network, USA, 445
Juvenile Diabetes Research Foundation International, USA, 409
KDDI Foundation, Japan, 191
Khalifa Bin Zayed Al Nahyan Foundation, United Arab Emirates, 334

Kiel Institute for the World Economy, Germany, 132
King Faisal Foundation, Saudi Arabia, 269
King Sejong Institute Foundation—KSIF, Korea (Republic), 201
Kiwanis Children's Fund, USA, 446
Klaus Tschira Foundation, Germany, 134
Klaus Tschira Stiftung GmbH, Germany, 134
Kleinwort (Ernest) Charitable Trust, UK, 353
Koch (Charles) Foundation, USA, 413
Koch Foundation, Inc, USA, 446
Kofi Annan Foundation, Switzerland, 313
Komen (Susan G.) Breast Cancer Foundation, USA, 474
Konrad Adenauer Foundation, Germany, 134
Konrad-Adenauer-Stiftung eV—KAS, Germany, 134
The Korea Foundation, Korea (Republic), 202
Kröner-Fresenius (Else) Stiftung, Germany, 127
Krupp von Bohlen und Halbach (Alfried) Stiftung, Germany, 121
Laidlaw Foundation, UK, 364
Laing Family Trusts, UK, 364
Laing (J. W.) Trust, UK, 384
Latet Israeli Humanitarian Aid, Israel, 170
Latin American Council of Social Sciences, Argentina, 6
Latter-day Saint Charities—LDSC, USA, 447
Laudes Foundation, Switzerland, 313
Laureus Sport for Good, UK, 364
Lazard (Fernand), Fondation, Belgium, 31
The Leakey Foundation, USA, 447
Legatum Foundation, United Arab Emirates, 334
LEGO Fonden, Denmark, 84
The LEGO Foundation, Denmark, 84
Leibniz Association, Germany, 135
Leibniz Gemeinschaft, Germany, 135
Leibniz-Institut für Agrarentwicklung in Transformationsökonomien—IAMO, Germany, 135
Leibniz Institute of Agricultural Development in Transition Economies, Germany, 135
Lelio and Lisli Basso Foundation Onlus, Italy, 178
Levi Strauss Foundation, USA, 448
Liberty Fund, Inc, USA, 448
Lifeline Consortium, USA, 428
Likhachev (Dmitry) Foundation, Russian Federation, 265
Limmat Foundation, Switzerland, 314
Limmat Stiftung, Switzerland, 314
Linbury Trust, UK, 365
Litdea Association, Lithuania, 208
Lloyd's Register Foundation, UK, 365
Lorenzini (Giovanni), Fondazione, Italy, 177
Lowy Institute for International Policy, Australia, 15
The Lutheran World Federation, Switzerland, 314
Lutherischer Weltbund/Fédération Luthérienne Mondiale/Federación Luterana Mundial, Switzerland, 314
Lyford Cay Foundations, Bahamas, 24
McDonnell (James S.) Foundation, USA, 443
Maclellan Foundation, Inc, USA, 450
Macquarie Group Foundation, Australia, 15
Maecenata Foundation, Germany, 119
Maecenata Stiftung, Germany, 119
Maeght (Marguerite et Aimé), Fondation, France, 109
MAIF Foundation for Research, France, 108
MAP International—Medical Assistance Programs, USA, 450
Marcel Bleustein-Blanchet Vocational Foundation, France, 109
Margaret A. Cargill Philanthropies—MACP, USA, 450
María Francisca de Roviralta Foundation, Spain, 292
Mario Negri Pharmacological Research Institute, Italy, 182
Masason Foundation, Japan, 191
The Matsumae International Foundation, Japan, 191
Max-Planck-Gesellschaft zur Förderung der Wissenschaften eV, Germany, 135
Max Planck Society for the Advancement of Science, Germany, 135
Max Weber Foundation, Germany, 136
Max Weber Stiftung—MWS, Germany, 136
Mayer (Charles Léopold Mayer), Fondation, Switzerland, 308
Mbeki (Thabo) Foundation, South Africa, 284
MDA—Muscular Dystrophy Association, USA, 451
Médecins du Monde International, France, 114
Médecins Sans Frontières International—MSF International, Switzerland, 314
Menzies Foundation, Australia, 15
Menzies (Sir Robert) Foundation, Australia, 15

Mercatus Center, USA, 451
Meridian Foundation, Germany, 140
MFJC—Memorial Foundation for Jewish Culture, USA, 452
Minor Foundation for Major Challenges, Norway, 242
Minority Rights Group International—MRG, UK, 368
Mirovni Inštitut—Inštitut za sodobne družbene in politične študije, Slovenia, 277
MISEREOR—Bischöfliches Hilfswerk Misereor eV, Germany, 137
The Mission to Seafarers, UK, 368
Mittag-Leffler Foundation of the Royal Swedish Academy of Sciences, Sweden, 300
Mitterrand (Danielle), Fondation, France, 112
MIUSA—Mobility International USA, USA, 453
Mobility International USA—MIUSA, USA, 453
Mohammed bin Salman Foundation—Misk Foundation, Saudi Arabia, 269
Moore (Gordon and Betty) Foundation, USA, 432
Moore (Henry) Foundation, UK, 358
Morehead-Cain Foundation, USA, 453
Morgan Stanley Foundation, USA, 453
Mouvement International ATD Quart-Monde, France, 115
MSF International—Médecins Sans Frontières International, Switzerland, 314
MSI Reproductive Choices, UK, 369
Munich Re Foundation/Münchener Rück Stiftung, Germany, 137
Murdoch Children's Research Institute—MCRI, Australia, 15
Music in Africa Foundation—MIAF, South Africa, 281
Musk Foundation, USA, 454
National Carlo Collodi Foundation, Italy, 179
National Endowment for Science, Technology and the Arts—Nesta, UK, 370
National Foundation for Educational Research—NFER, UK, 369
National Geographic Society, USA, 455
National Organization for Women Foundation, USA, 458
National Science Foundation—NSF, USA, 455
Naumann (Friedrich) Stiftung, Germany, 130
Negri (Mario), Istituto di Ricerche Farmacologiche, Italy, 182
Nesta—National Endowment for Science, Technology and the Arts, UK, 370
Nestlé Foundation for the Study of the Problems of Nutrition in the World, Switzerland, 310
Network for Social Change Charitable Trust—NSCCT, UK, 370
New World Foundation—NWF, USA, 456
New Zealand Institute of International Affairs—NZIIA, New Zealand, 234
NFER—National Foundation for Educational Research, UK, 369
Niarchos (Stavros) Foundation, Greece, 147
Nigerian Institute of International Affairs—NIIA, Nigeria, 238
Nightingale (Florence), Fondation Internationale, Switzerland, 309
The Nippon Foundation, Japan, 192
Niwano Peace Foundation, Japan, 192
Nobel Foundation, Sweden, 301
Nobelstiftelsen, Sweden, 301
Nordic Culture Fund, Denmark, 85
Nordisk Kulturfond, Denmark, 85
Norsk Utenrikspolitisk Institutt—NUPI, Norway, 242
Norwegian Institute of International Affairs, Norway, 242
Norwegian Refugee Council—NRC, Norway, 242
Novo Nordisk Fonden, Denmark, 85
Novo Nordisk Foundation, Denmark, 85
NOW Foundation, USA, 458
Nuffic, Netherlands, 227
NZIIA—New Zealand Institute of International Affairs, New Zealand, 234
Oak Foundation, Switzerland, 315
Obama (Barack) Foundation, USA, 407
Observer Research Foundation—ORF, India, 159
The Ocean Cleanup Foundation, Netherlands, 230
The Ocean Foundation, USA, 458
ODI, UK, 371
Office International de l'Eau—OiEau, France, 115
Olav Thon Foundation, Norway, 242
Olav Thon Stiftelsen, Norway, 242
Olof Palme Memorial Fund for International Understanding and Common Security, Sweden, 302
Olof Palmes Minnesfond för internationell förståelse och gemensam säkerhet, Sweden, 302
Omidyar Group, USA, 458

All Regions

Omidyar Network Fund, USA, 458
Onassis (Alexander S.) Public Benefit Foundation, Liechtenstein, 207
Open Society Action Fund, USA, 458
Open Society Foundation—London, UK, 372
Open Society Foundations, USA, 459
Open Society Policy Center, USA, 458
Organisation Internationale de Droit du Développement—OIDD, Italy, 181
Österreichische Forschungsstiftung für Internationale Entwicklung—ÖFSE, Austria, 22
Oswaldo Cruz Foundation, Brazil, 40
OutRight Action International, USA, 460
Oxfam America, USA, 460
Oxfam France, France, 115
Oxfam GB, UK, 372
Oxfam International, Kenya, 200
Oxfam-Solidariteit/Solidarité, Belgium, 33
Packard (David and Lucile) Foundation, USA, 420
PAI—Population Action International, USA, 460
Palme (Olof) Minnesfond fr Internationell Frstelse och Gemensam Skerhet, Sweden, 302
PAN UK—Pesticide Action Network UK, UK, 373
The Papal Foundation, USA, 461
Paraguayan Foundation for Cooperation and Development, Paraguay, 248
Pasteur Institute, France, 114
Pasteur Institute of Lille, France, 114
Pastore (Giulio), Fondazione, Italy, 178
Patterson (Alicia) Foundation, USA, 398
The Paul G. Allen Family Foundation, USA, 462
Paz y Cooperación, Spain, 296
PCI Media Impact, USA, 467
Peace and Co-operation, Spain, 296
Peace Institute—Institute for Contemporary Social and Political Studies, Slovenia, 277
Peace Research Institute Oslo—PRIO, Norway, 242
Peace and Security Funders Group—PSFG, USA, 396
Penal Reform International—PRI, UK, 373
PepsiCo Foundation, Inc, USA, 462
Perdana Global Peace Foundation—PGPF, Malaysia, 211
Pesticide Action Network UK—PAN UK, UK, 373
The Pew Charitable Trusts, USA, 462
Pezcoller (Alessio), Fondazione, Italy, 174
Pfizer Foundation, USA, 462
Philanthropy for Social Justice and Peace, UK, 336
PHR—Physicians for Human Rights, USA, 463
Physicians for Human Rights—PHR, USA, 463
Pinchuk (Victor) Foundation, Ukraine, 333
Ping Foundation, USA, 415
PLAN International—PI, UK, 374
Planck (Max) Gesellschaft zur Förderung der Wissenschaften eV, Germany, 135
Plataforma Portuguesa das Organizações Não-Governamentais para o Desenvolvimento—ONGD, Portugal, 258
Pollock-Krasner Foundation, Inc, USA, 463
Population Action International—PAI, USA, 460
Portuguese Platform of Non-Governmental Organizations for Development, Portugal, 258
Praemium Erasmianum Foundation, Netherlands, 230
Primate's World Relief and Development Fund/Le Fonds du Primat Pour le Secours et le Développement Mondial—PWRDF, Canada, 49
Princess of Asturias Foundation, Spain, 294
Princess Charlene of Monaco Foundation, Monaco, 218
PRIO—Peace Research Institute Oslo, Norway, 242
Prix Jeunesse Foundation, Germany, 138
Pro Helvetia, Switzerland, 315
ProLiteracy, USA, 464
Prospera—International Network of Women's Funds, Canada, 61
Pulitzer Center on Crisis Reporting, USA, 464
PwC Charitable Foundation, USA, 465
Quandt (Herbert) Stiftung, Germany, 122
Quincy Institute for Responsible Statecraft–QI, USA, 465
Rabo Foundation, Netherlands, 228
Rafa Nadal Foundation, Spain, 294
Rafto Foundation for Human Rights, Norway, 243
Raftostiftelsen for menneskerettigheter, Norway, 243
Rainforest Action Network—RAN, USA, 465
Rainforest Journalism Fund, USA, 464
RAN—Rainforest Action Network, USA, 465
RAND Corporation, USA, 465
Rare, USA, 466

Ravand Institute for Economic and International Studies, Iran, 163
RC Forward, Canada, 48
RE:ACT, UK, 375
Re:wild, USA, 466
Real Madrid Foundation, Spain, 295
Reall—Real Equity for All, UK, 375
Reeva Rebecca Steenkamp Foundation, South Africa, 283
Reeve (Christopher and Dana) Foundation, USA, 415
Refugee Foundation, Netherlands, 231
Refugees International—RI, USA, 466
Rehabilitation International—RI, USA, 466
Rethink Charity, Canada, 48
Rhodes Trust, UK, 376
Richard Dawkins Foundation for Reason and Science, USA, 412
Rielo (Fernando), Fundación, Spain, 290
Right Livelihood Award Foundation, Sweden, 302
Rising Impact, USA, 467
Rockefeller Foundation, USA, 468
Rosetta Foundation, USA, 416
The Rotary Foundation, USA, 468
Rotary Yoneyama Memorial Foundation, Inc, Japan, 193
Roviralta (María Francisca de), Fundación, Spain, 292
Royal Aeronautical Society—RAeS, UK, 376
Royal Air Force Benevolent Fund, UK, 377
Royal Anthropological Institute of Great Britain and Ireland—RAI, UK, 377
Royal British Legion, UK, 377
The Royal Commonwealth Society—RCS, UK, 377
Royal Elcano Institute Foundation, Spain, 294
The Royal Foundation of the Prince and Princess of Wales, UK, 378
Royal Geographical Society (with the Institute of British Geographers)—RGS-IBG, UK, 378
Royal Institute of International Affairs—RIIA—Chatham House, UK, 378
Royal Institute of International Relations—Egmont Institute, Belgium, 29
The Royal Society, UK, 379
The Royal Society of Medicine—RSM, UK, 379
RSA—Royal Society for the Encouragement of Arts, Manufactures and Commerce, UK, 379
Russian International Affairs Council—RIAC, Russian Federation, 266
Rutherford Institute, USA, 469
Sabanci Vakfi—Haci Omer Sabanci Foundation, Türkiye, 329
Saint Cyril and Saint Methodius International Foundation, Bulgaria, 44
The Saison Foundation, Japan, 193
The Salvation Army International Trust, UK, 381
Samaritan's Purse, USA, 469
The Sasakawa Peace Foundation—SPF, Japan, 194
Save the Children International, UK, 381
Save the Children (UK), UK, 381
Schering (Ernst) Stiftung, Germany, 127
Schlumberger Foundation, USA, 470
Schwab Foundation for Social Entrepreneurship, Switzerland, 316
Schweizerische Stiftung für Alpine Forschungen—SSAF, Switzerland, 316
Science and Politics Foundation—German Institute for International and Security Affairs, Germany, 141
Scotland's International Development Alliance, UK, 337
Scott Trust Foundation, UK, 356
Secours Catholique—Caritas de France, France, 116
Seidel (Hanns) Stiftung, Germany, 131
Service Civil International—SCI, Belgium, 34
Sesame Workshop, USA, 471
Shell Foundation—SF, UK, 382
SID—Society for International Development, Italy, 183
The Sierra Club Foundation, USA, 471
Signe and Ane Gyllenberg Foundation, Finland, 97
Signe och Ane Gyllenbergs stiftelse, Finland, 97
Silicon Valley Community Foundation—SVCF, USA, 471
Simone and Cino del Duca Foundation, France, 111
Sindika Dokolo Foundation, Angola, 5
SIPRI—Stockholm International Peace Research Institute, Sweden, 304
Skoll Foundation, USA, 472
Smithsonian Institution, USA, 472
Society for International Development—SID, Italy, 183
Solidar, Belgium, 34

INDEX BY AREA OF ACTIVITY

Solidarity Overseas Service Malta—SOS Malta, Malta, 213
Solomon R. Guggenheim Foundation, USA, 473
SOS Malta—Solidarity Overseas Service, Malta, 213
Souter Charitable Trust, UK, 384
Sphere, Switzerland, 305
Spinal Research, UK, 384
Stanley Center for Peace and Security, USA, 473
Stanley Thomas Johnson Foundation, Switzerland, 317
The Starr Foundation, USA, 473
Start Network, UK, 337
State Scholarships Foundation—IKY, Greece, 147
Stavros Niarchos Foundation—SNF, Greece, 147
Steenkamp (Reeva Rebecca) Foundation, South Africa, 283
Stewards Company Limited, UK, 384
Stewardship Foundation, USA, 473
Stichting Bellingcat, Netherlands, 228
Stichting The Ocean Cleanup, Netherlands, 230
Stichting Praemium Erasmianum, Netherlands, 230
Stichting Vluchteling, Netherlands, 231
Stichting Vodafone Netherlands, Netherlands, 231
Stiftelsen Dag Hammarskjölds Minnesfond, Sweden, 303
Stiftelsen Gapminder, Sweden, 300
Stiftelsen Ingmar Bergman, Sweden, 303
Stiftelsen Riksbankens Jubileumsfond, Sweden, 303
Stiftung zur Förderung der Hochschulrektorenkonferenz, Germany, 140
Stiftung Mercator, Germany, 140
Stiftung Meridian, Germany, 140
Stiftung Prix Jeunesse, Germany, 138
Stiftung für die Rechte zukünftiger Generationen—SRzG, Germany, 141
Stiftung Weltethos, Germany, 141
Stiftung Wissenschaft und Politik—Deutsches Institut für internationale Politik und Sicherheit—SWP, Germany, 141
Stockholm Environment Institute, Sweden, 303
Stockholm International Peace Research Institute—SIPRI, Sweden, 304
Stroke Association, UK, 384
SUN Civil Society Network, UK, 381
Suomalaiset kehitysjärjestöt—Fingo, Finland, 95
Susan G. Komen Breast Cancer Foundation, USA, 474
The Susan Thompson Buffett Foundation—STBF, USA, 474
Swiss Alliance of Development Organisations, Switzerland, 305
Swiss Arts Council, Switzerland, 315
Swiss Foundation for Alpine Research—SFAR, Switzerland, 316
Swiss Philanthropy Foundation, Switzerland, 305
Tanager, USA, 397
Tata Trusts, India, 160
Tebtebba Foundation, Philippines, 253
TechnoServe, USA, 474
Telefónica Foundation, Spain, 295
Templeton (John) Foundation, USA, 444
Templeton Philanthropies, USA, 444
Templeton Religion Trust, Bahamas, 24
Thabo Mbeki Foundation, South Africa, 284
Thomson Reuters Foundation, UK, 385
Thrasher Research Fund, USA, 474
Thunberg (Greta) Foundation, Sweden, 300
Thyssen (Fritz) Stiftung, Germany, 130
TI—Transparency International, Germany, 142
Tiffany & Co Foundation, USA, 475
Together for Global Justice—CIDSE, Belgium, 29
Torcuato Di Tella Foundation, Argentina, 8
Toshiba International Foundation—TIFO, Japan, 194
TotalEnergies Foundation, France, 112
Translators without Borders, USA, 416
Transparency International—TI, Germany, 142
Tschira (Klaus) Stiftung, Germany, 134
Turriano (Juanelo) Fundación, Spain, 291
UAI—Union des Associations Internationales, Belgium, 27
UEFA Foundation for Children, Switzerland, 318
UNESCO Centre du Patrimoine Mondial, France, 116
UNESCO World Heritage Centre, France, 116
Union des Associations Internationales—UAI, Belgium, 27
Union of International Associations—UIA/Unie van de Internationale Vereinigingen—UIV, Belgium, 27
Union for International Cancer Control—UICC, Switzerland, 318
Union Internationale Contre le Cancer, Switzerland, 318

INDEX BY AREA OF ACTIVITY

Unitarian Universalist Service Committee—UUSC, USA, 476
United Nations Foundation, USA, 476
United Way Worldwide, USA, 477
Universal Jewish Alliance, France, 101
University-Industry Foundation, Spain, 295
UPS Foundation, USA, 477
USC Shoah Foundation—The Institute for Visual History and Education, USA, 477
UUSC—Unitarian Universalist Service Committee, USA, 476
Van Leer Foundation, Netherlands, 231
Vargas (Getulio), Fundação, Brazil, 40
Varkey Foundation, UK, 388
Vetlesen (G. Unger) Foundation, USA, 429
Victor Pinchuk Foundation, Ukraine, 333
VinFuture Foundation, Viet Nam, 489
Vital Strategies, USA, 478
Vital Voices Global Partnership, USA, 478
Vodafone Americas Foundation, USA, 478
Vodafone Foundation, UK, 388
Vodafone Netherlands Foundation, Netherlands, 231
Volkswagen Foundation, Germany, 142
VolkswagenStiftung, Germany, 142
Walmart Foundation, USA, 478
The Waterloo Foundation—TWF, UK, 389
Weber (Franz), Fondation, Switzerland, 308
Weber (Max) Stiftung, Germany, 136
Wellcome Trust, UK, 389
Wenner-Gren Foundation for Anthropological Research, Inc, USA, 480
Weyerhaeuser Family Foundation, Inc, USA, 480
Whirlpool Foundation, USA, 480
WHO Foundation, Switzerland, 319
Wihuri Foundation for International Prizes, Finland, 98
Wihurin kansainvälisten palkintojen rahasto, Finland, 98
Wikimedia Foundation, USA, 480
The WILD Foundation—International Wilderness Leadership Foundation, USA, 481
Wilderness Foundation Global—WFG, South Africa, 284
The William and Flora Hewlett Foundation, USA, 481
WILPF—Women's International League for Peace and Freedom, Switzerland, 319
Wilson (E. O.) Biodiversity Foundation, USA, 421
Wilson (Woodrow) International Center for Scholars, USA, 482
WINGS—Worldwide Initiatives for Grantmaker Support, Brazil, 38
Winston Churchill Memorial Trust, Australia, 19
Winston Churchill Memorial Trust of New Zealand, New Zealand, 236
The Womanity Foundation, Switzerland, 319
WomenLead Institute, USA, 418
Women's Environment & Development Organization—WEDO, USA, 482
Women's International League for Peace and Freedom, Switzerland, 319
Women's World Summit Foundation—WWSF, Switzerland, 320
Woodrow Wilson International Center for Scholars, USA, 482
World Alliance for Citizen Participation—CIVICUS, South Africa, 278
World Alliance of YMCAs—Young Men's Christian Associations, Switzerland, 319
World Central Kitchen—WCK, USA, 482
World Concern, USA, 482
World Economic Forum, Switzerland, 320
World Emergency Relief—WER, USA, 483
World Holocaust Forum Foundation—WHF, Israel, 171
World Land Trust—WLT, UK, 391
World Learning, USA, 483
World Monuments Fund—WMF, USA, 483
World Peace Foundation—WPF, USA, 483
World Resources Institute—WRI, USA, 483
World Scout Foundation—Fondation du Scoutisme Mondial—WSF/FSM, Switzerland, 320
World Telehealth Initiative, USA, 484
Worldwide Cancer Research, UK, 392
Worldwide Initiatives for Grantmaker Support—WINGS, Brazil, 38
WWF International, Switzerland, 320
WWSF—Women's World Summit Foundation, Switzerland, 320
XPRIZE Foundation, USA, 484
Yellow Feather Fund, USA, 471
Yidan Prize Foundation, Hong Kong, 152
Zancan (Emanuela), Fondazione Centro Studi e Ricerca Sociale, Italy, 172
Ziviler Friedensdienst—ZFD, Germany, 120
Zonta Foundation for Women, USA, 484

Zuleikhabai Valy Mohamed Gany Rangoonwala Trust—ZVMG Rangoonwala Trust, Pakistan, 246
ZVMG Rangoonwala Trust, Pakistan, 246

AFRICA SOUTH OF THE SAHARA

A. G. Leventis Foundation, Greece, 144
A. G. Leventis Foundation Nigeria, Nigeria, 237
AARDO—African-Asian Rural Development Organization, India, 155
Abilis Foundation, Finland, 95
Abilis-säätiö, Finland, 95
Accion, USA, 397
Acting for Life, France, 100
Action Against Hunger, France, 100
Action contre la Faim—ACF France, France, 100
Action Damien/Damiaanactie, Belgium, 28
Action Education, France, 100
Action on Poverty, Australia, 10
Action Solidarité Tiers Monde—ASTM, Luxembourg, 209
Active for People in Need Austria, Austria, 20
Acumen, USA, 397
Advance, USA, 397
Afdi—Agriculteurs Français et Développement International, France, 100
Africa-America Institute—AAI, USA, 398
Africa Foundation, South Africa, 278
Africa Grantmakers' Affinity Group—AGAG, USA, 393
Africa Humanitarian Action—AHA, Ethiopia, 93
Africa Institute of South Africa—AISA, South Africa, 279
Africa Space Foundation, Switzerland, 308
The African Agricultural Technology Foundation—AATF, Kenya, 198
African-Asian Rural Development Organization—AARDO, India, 155
African Capacity Building Foundation—ACBF, Zimbabwe, 490
African Forum and Network on Debt and Development—AFRODAD, Zimbabwe, 490
African Philanthropy Forum, Nigeria, 236
African Refugees Foundation—AREF, Nigeria, 237
African Venture Philanthropy Alliance—AVPA, Kenya, 197
African Wildlife Foundation—AWF, Kenya, 198
African Women's Development Fund—AWDF, Ghana, 143
African Youth Initiative Network—AYINET, Uganda, 331
Afrobarometer, Ghana, 143
AFRODAD—African Forum and Network on Debt and Development, Zimbabwe, 490
Aga Khan Foundation Canada, Canada, 49
AGAG—Africa Grantmakers' Affinity Group, USA, 393
Age International, UK, 339
AGIR Association for the Environment and Quality of Life, Mali, 213
Agriculteurs Français et Développement International, France, 100
Agronomes et Vétérinaires sans Frontières—AVSF, France, 100
Agronomists and Veterinarians Without Borders, France, 100
Air France Foundation, France, 103
AISA—Africa Institute of South Africa, South Africa, 279
Aisha Buhari Global Foundation, Nigeria, 237
AKO Foundation, UK, 339
Al Basar International Foundation, Saudi Arabia, 268
Al-Zubair Charity Foundation, Sudan, 297
Albert Schweitzer Ecological Centre, Switzerland, 307
Alert—International Alert, UK, 360
Alet'Eleym Fewq Alejmey'e, Qatar, 262
Aliko Dangote Foundation—ADF, Nigeria, 237
Alliance of Bioversity International and the International Center for Tropical Agriculture—CIAT, Italy, 172
AMADE Mondiale—Association Mondiale des Amis de l'Enfance, Monaco, 217
American Councils for International Education, USA, 400
American Friends Service Committee—AFSC, USA, 401
American Jewish World Service—AJWS, USA, 402
AmeriCares Foundation, Inc, USA, 403
AMINA—aktiv für Menschen in Not Austria, Austria, 20
Amity Foundation, China (People's Republic), 66
Amref Health Africa, Kenya, 198

Africa South of the Sahara

Anesvad, Spain, 286
Angel of Hope Foundation, Zimbabwe, 490
ANND—Arab NGO Network for Development, Lebanon, 205
APHEDA—Union Aid Abroad, Australia, 19
Apprentis d'Auteuil Océan Indien, Réunion, 262
Arab Image Foundation—AIF, Lebanon, 205
Arcus Foundation, USA, 405
Ark, UK, 341
Asia Africa International Voluntary Foundation—AIV, Japan, 186
Association AGIR pour l'Environnement et la Qualité de la Vie, Mali, 213
Association of Non-Governmental Organizations in The Gambia—TANGO, Gambia, 117
ASTM—Action Solidarité Tiers Monde, Luxembourg, 209
Auchan Foundation, France, 103
Aurora Trust, UK, 341
Australian Foundation for the Peoples of Asia and the Pacific—AFAP, Australia, 10
Australian Volunteers International—AVI, Australia, 13
AVI—Australian Volunteers International, Australia, 13
AVINA Foundation, Panama, 247
AVSI Foundation, Italy, 175
Bagnoud (François-Xavier) Association, Switzerland, 310
Banda (Joyce) Foundation International, Malawi, 210
Bank of America Charitable Foundation, USA, 407
Barceló Foundation, Spain, 289
Barcelona Centre for International Affairs, Spain, 287
Baring Foundation, UK, 341
BBC Media Action, UK, 342
Beit Trust, UK, 342
Bello (Sir Ahmadu) Memorial Foundation, Nigeria, 238
Berghof Foundation gGmbH, Germany, 122
Berghof Stiftung für Konfliktforschung gGmbH, Germany, 122
Big Heart Foundation, Chad, 64
Blair (Tony) Institute for Global Change, UK, 386
Blue Marine Foundation—BLUE, UK, 343
BMCE Bank Foundation, Morocco, 219
BNP Paribas Foundation, France, 103
Böll (Heinrich) Stiftung, Germany, 131
Book Aid International—BAI, UK, 343
Born Free Foundation, UK, 343
Bosch (Robert) Stiftung GmbH, Germany, 138
Bóthar, Ireland, 166
Botswana Institute for Development Policy Analysis—BIDPA, Botswana, 37
BRAC, Bangladesh, 25
Bread for the World—Protestant Work for Social Welfare and Development, Germany, 123
Brenthurst Foundation, South Africa, 282
Brot für die Welt—Evangelisches Werk für Diakonie und Entwicklung, Germany, 123
Brother's Brother Foundation, USA, 410
Brothers of Men, France, 113
Buchanan Charitable Foundation, New Zealand, 232
Buck (Pearl S.) International, USA, 462
Buffett (Howard G.) Foundation, USA, 437
Cadbury (William Adlington) Charitable Trust, UK, 390
CAF—Charities Aid Foundation, UK, 336
CAMFED International, UK, 346
Canadian Centre for International Studies and Co-operation, Canada, 51
Canadian Feed The Children—CFTC, Canada, 50
Canadian Foodgrains Bank, Canada, 50
Canadian Organization for Development through Education—CODE, Canada, 52
Canadian Physicians for Aid and Relief—CPAR, Canada, 52
Cape Verdean Student Welfare Foundation, Cabo Verde, 45
CARE International—CI, Switzerland, 307
Cariplo Foundation, Italy, 175
Caritas Canada, Canada, 53
Carrefour International, Canada, 53
The Carter Center, USA, 412
Catalyste+, Canada, 51
Catholic Agency for World Development—Trócaire, Ireland, 168
CBM-International, Germany, 123
CEAS—Centre Ecologique Albert Schweitzer, Switzerland, 307
CECI—Canadian Centre for International Studies and Co-operation/Centre d'Etudes et de Coopération Internationale, Canada, 51

Africa South of the Sahara

CENOZO—Cellule Norbert Zongo pour le Journalisme d'Investigation en Afrique de l'Ouest, Burkina Faso, 44
Centre pour le Dialogue Humanitaire, Switzerland, 307
Centre for Dialogue, Research and Cooperation—CDRC, Ethiopia, 94
Centre Ecologique Albert Schweitzer—CEAS, Switzerland, 307
Centre d'Etudes Pour l'Action Sociale—CEPAS, Congo (Democratic Republic), 72
Centre for Humanitarian Dialogue—HD, Switzerland, 307
Centre Ivoirien de Recherches Économiques et Sociales—CIRES, Côte d'Ivoire, 75
CESO/SACO—Canadian Executive Service Organization/Service d'Assistance Canadienne aux Organismes, Canada, 51
Chandaria Foundation, Kenya, 198
Chantal Biya Foundation, Cameroon, 47
Charities Aid Foundation—CAF, UK, 336
Charity Projects, UK, 348
Charles Stewart Mott Foundation—CSMF, USA, 414
Cheshire (Leonard) Foundation, UK, 364
Child Migrants Trust, UK, 347
ChildFund, New Zealand, 233
ChildFund International, USA, 414
Children in Africa Foundation, Germany, 140
Children International—CI, USA, 414
Children and Sharing, France, 102
The Children's Investment Fund Foundation, UK, 347
Childwick Trust, UK, 347
China Foundation for Poverty Alleviation—CFPA, China (People's Republic), 67
China Youth Development Foundation, China (People's Republic), 68
Chr. Michelsen Institute for Science and Intellectual Freedom—CMI, Norway, 241
CIAT—Centro Internacional de Agricultura Tropical, Italy, 172
CIDOB Foundation—Barcelona Centre for International Affairs, Spain, 287
Cimade—Ecumenical Care Service, France, 102
La Cimade—Service Oecuménique d'Entraide, France, 102
Claiborne (Liz) & Art Ortenberg Foundation, USA, 448
Clara Lionel Foundation—CLF, USA, 415
Claudine Talon Foundation, Benin, 35
Člověk v tísni, Czech Republic, 79
CMDID Foundation—Malian Centre for Inter-Party Dialogue and Democracy, Mali, 213
CMI—Chr. Michelsen Institute for Science and Intellectual Freedom, Norway, 241
CODE—Canadian Organization for Development through Education, Canada, 52
CODESPA Foundation, Spain, 290
Comic Relief, UK, 348
Comité de Coordination des ONGI en RCA, Central African Republic, 63
Commonwealth Foundation, UK, 348
Community Development Foundation, Mozambique, 221
Community Foundation for the Western Region of Zimbabwe—CFWRZ, Zimbabwe, 490
Concern Worldwide, Ireland, 166
Co-operative Development Foundation of Canada—CDF, Canada, 52
Cooperazione Internazionale—COOPI, Italy, 173
Copperbelt Development Foundation, Zambia, 490
CPAR—Canadian Physicians for Aid and Relief, Canada, 52
The Craig and Susan McCaw Foundation, USA, 418
Crossroads International/Carrefour International, Canada, 53
Crown Family Philanthropies, USA, 419
Cundill (Peter) Foundation, Bermuda, 35
Cuso International, Canada, 53
Cyril Ramaphosa Foundation, South Africa, 279
Danish Institute for Human Rights, Denmark, 84
David Nott Foundation, UK, 350
Dell (Michael & Susan) Foundation, USA, 453
Dental Aid International, Switzerland, 317
Desmond & Leah Tutu Legacy Foundation, South Africa, 279
Deutsche AIDS-Stiftung, Germany, 124
Deutsche Sparkassenstiftung für Internationale Zusammenarbeit, Germany, 125
Development and Peace—Caritas Canada, Canada, 53
Développement et Paix—Caritas Canada, Canada, 53
Dewji (Mo) Foundation, Tanzania, 323
Diakonia, Sweden, 298

Dioraphte Foundation, Netherlands, 229
DOEN Foundation, Netherlands, 229
Dom Manuel II Foundation, Portugal, 260
Doris Duke Charitable Foundation—DDCF, USA, 421
The Dr Denis Mukwege Foundation, Netherlands, 224
DRFN—Desert Research Foundation of Namibia, Namibia, 222
DSW—Deutsche Stiftung Weltbevölkerung, Germany, 126
Dulverton Trust, UK, 351
Earthworm Foundation, Switzerland, 307
East Africa Philanthropy Network—EAPN, Kenya, 197
Economic and Social Research Foundation—ESRF, Tanzania, 322
Education Above All Foundation—EAA, Qatar, 262
Educo, Spain, 286
Elizabeth Glaser Pediatric AIDS Foundation—EGPAF, USA, 423
Elumelu (Tony) Foundation, Nigeria, 238
EMERGENCY, Italy, 173
Enda Third World—Environment and Development Action in the Third World, Senegal, 270
Enda Tiers Monde—Environnement et Développement du Tiers-Monde, Senegal, 270
endPoverty.org, USA, 424
Energies for the World Foundation, France, 105
Enfance et Partage, France, 102
EngenderHealth, USA, 424
Eni Foundation, Italy, 173
Entraide Protestante Suisse, Switzerland, 311
Entraide Universitaire Mondiale du Canada, Canada, 63
Environmental Justice Foundation—EJF, UK, 353
Equality Fund/Fonds Égalité, Canada, 54
Equity Group Foundation—EGF, Kenya, 198
Eskom Development Foundation, South Africa, 279
EWT—Endangered Wildlife Trust, South Africa, 279
Fairtrade Nederland, Netherlands, 230
The Family Federation of Finland, Finland, 98
Family Restoration Fund, UK, 347
Farm Africa, UK, 354
FATE Foundation, Nigeria, 237
Fatoumatta Bah-Barrow Foundation—FaBB, Gambia, 117
FDC—Fundação para o Desenvolvimento da Comunidade, Mozambique, 221
Feed the Children, USA, 425
Feed the Minds, UK, 354
filia.die Frauenstiftung, Germany, 128
filia—the Women's Foundation, Germany, 128
FINCA International, USA, 425
Firelight Foundation, USA, 425
FirstRand Foundation, South Africa, 280
Follereau Foundation Luxembourg, Luxembourg, 209
Fondation Abbé Pierre, France, 108
Fondation Africaine pour les Technologies Agricoles, Kenya, 198
Fondation pour l'Agriculture et la Ruralité dans le Monde—Fondation FARM, France, 106
Fondation Air France, France, 103
Fondation Arabe pour l'Image, Lebanon, 205
Fondation Auchan, France, 103
Fondation BMCE Bank, Morocco, 219
Fondation BNP Paribas, France, 103
Fondation Chantal Biya—FCB, Cameroon, 47
Fondation Claudine Talon, Benin, 35
Fondation CMDID—Centre Malien pour le Dialogue Interpartis et la Démocratie, Mali, 213
Fondation Congo Assistance, Congo (Republic), 73
Fondation Energies pour le Monde—Fondem, France, 105
Fondation Ensemble, France, 105
Fondation d'Entreprise Crédit Agricole Réunion Mayotte, Réunion, 262
Fondation Espace Afrique, Switzerland, 308
Fondation FARM—Fondation pour l'Agriculture et la Ruralité dans le Monde, France, 106
Fondation Follereau Luxembourg—FFL, Luxembourg, 209
Fondation Grand Cœur—FGC, Chad, 64
Fondation Guri Vie Meilleure, Niger, 236
Fondation Hirondelle: Media for Peace and Human Dignity, Switzerland, 309
Fondation Internationale Tierno et Mariam—FITIMA, Burkina Faso, 44
Fondation Jean-Paul II pour le Sahel, Burkina Faso, 44

INDEX BY AREA OF ACTIVITY

Fondation Joseph Ichame Kamach, Central African Republic, 63
Fondation Léopold Sédar Senghor, Senegal, 270
Fondation pour le Logement des Défavorisés, France, 108
Fondation Mapon, Congo (Democratic Republic), 72
Fondation Marcel Hicter, Belgium, 32
Fondation pour les Médias en Afrique de l'Ouest, Ghana, 144
Fondation Mérieux, France, 109
Fondation Mesmin Kabath—FOMEKA, Congo (Republic), 73
Fondation MTN Bénin, Benin, 35
Fondation MTN Cameroun, Cameroon, 47
Fondation MTN Congo, Congo (Republic), 73
Fondation MTN Côte d'Ivoire, Côte d'Ivoire, 76
Fondation Mutuelles Congolaises d'Epargne et de Crédit—MUCODEC, Congo (Republic), 73
Fondation Nicolas Hulot pour la Nature et l'Homme—FNH, France, 110
Fondation Orange, France, 110
Fondation Orange Burkina Faso, Burkina Faso, 45
Fondation Orange Cameroun, Cameroon, 47
Fondation Orange-Côte d'Ivoire Télécom—OCIT, Côte d'Ivoire, 76
Fondation Orange Guinée, Guinea, 149
Fondation Orange Mali, Mali, 213
Fondation Perspectives d'Avenir, Congo (Republic), 73
Fondation Rawji, Congo (Democratic Republic), 72
Fondation pour le Renforcement des Capacités en Afrique, Zimbabwe, 490
Fondation Rio Tinto, Guinea, 149
Fondation Roi Baudouin, Belgium, 33
Fondation Rurale pour l'Afrique de l'Ouest—FRAO, Senegal, 270
Fondation S, France, 111
Fondation Schneider Electric, France, 111
Fondation Sonatel, Senegal, 270
Fondation Stamm, Burundi, 45
Fondation Suisse-Liechtenstein pour les Recherches Archéologiques à l'Etranger, Switzerland, 316
Fondation Vodacom RDC, Congo (Democratic Republic), 72
Fondazione AVSI, Italy, 175
Fondazione Cariplo, Italy, 175
Fonds Égalité, Canada, 54
Food for the Hungry—FH, USA, 426
Ford Foundation, USA, 427
The Forest Trust, Switzerland, 307
FORWARD—Foundation for Women's Health Research and Development, UK, 354
Fòs Feminista, USA, 427
Foundation for Civil Society—FCS, Tanzania, 322
Foundation for Housing the Disadvantaged, France, 108
Foundation for International Community Assistance, USA, 425
Foundation for Security and Development in Africa—FOSDA, Ghana, 143
Foundation for Women, Spain, 293
Foundation for Women's Health, Research and Development—FORWARD, UK, 354
Foundation for World Agriculture and Rural Life, France, 106
Franciscans International, Switzerland, 310
Fraunhofer-Gesellschaft, Germany, 129
Fraunhofer Society, Germany, 129
The Fred Hollows Foundation, Australia, 14
French Agriculturalists and International Development, France, 100
French Institute of International Relations, France, 113
Frères des Hommes—FDH, France, 113
Friedensdorf International, Germany, 129
Fundação Caboverdiana de Acção Social Escolar—FICASE, Cabo Verde, 45
Fundação Dom Manuel II, Portugal, 260
Fundação José Maria Neves para a Governança, Cabo Verde, 46
Fundação Mário Soares e Maria Barroso, Portugal, 260
Fundació CIDOB, Spain, 287
Fundación AVINA, Panama, 247
Fundación Barceló, Spain, 289
Fundación Capital, Colombia, 70
Fundación CODESPA, Spain, 290
Fundación Escuela Nueva, Colombia, 71
Fundación Leo Messi, Spain, 292
Fundación Mujeres, Spain, 293
Fundación Repsol, Spain, 294
FXB International—Association François-Xavier Bagnoud, Switzerland, 310
The Gatsby Charitable Foundation, UK, 355

INDEX BY AREA OF ACTIVITY

Africa South of the Sahara

German AIDS Foundation, Germany, 124
German Foundation for World Population, Germany, 126
German Institute for Global and Area Studies—GIGA, Germany, 130
German Savings Banks Foundation for International Co-operation, Germany, 125
Gift of the Givers Foundation, South Africa, 280
Glaser (Elizabeth) Pediatric AIDS Foundation, USA, 423
Global Communities, USA, 431
Global Fund for Children, USA, 431
Global Health Partnerships, UK, 355
Global Innovation Fund, UK, 356
Global Schools Forum, UK, 341
Globetree Association, Sweden, 300
GOAL, Ireland, 166
Gobabeb Namib Research Institute, Namibia, 222
Good Neighbors International, Korea (Republic), 201
Graça Machel Trust, South Africa, 280
Grameen Foundation—GF, USA, 433
Grassroots International—GRI, USA, 433
Green Umbrella Children's Foundation—ChildFund Korea, Korea (Republic), 201
HALO Trust, UK, 357
Havelaar (Max) Foundation, Netherlands, 230
Headley Trust, UK, 357
Health Volunteers Overseas—HVO, USA, 434
Heinrich Böll Foundation, Germany, 131
Heinrich-Böll-Stiftung, Germany, 131
HEKS—Hilfswerk der Evangelischen Kirchen Schweiz, Switzerland, 311
Helen Keller International—HKI, USA, 435
Helmsley (Leona M. and Harry B.) Charitable Trust, USA, 447
Helvetas Swiss Intercooperation, Switzerland, 311
Heritage Institute for Policy Studies—HIPS, Somalia, 277
Hicter (Marcel), Fondation, Belgium, 32
Higherlife Foundation, Zimbabwe, 491
HIPS—Heritage Institute for Policy Studies, Somalia, 277
Hivos—Humanistisch Instituut voor Ontwikkelings Samenwerking, Netherlands, 226
HJ Foundation, Congo (Democratic Republic), 72
Hollows (Fred) Foundation, Australia, 14
Holt International, USA, 436
HOPE International Development Agency, Canada, 56
Hormuud Salaam Foundation, Somalia, 277
Horn Economic and Social Policy Institute—HESPI, Ethiopia, 94
The Howard G. Buffett Foundation, USA, 437
Hulot (Nicolas), Fondation, France, 110
Humanistic Institute for Co-operation with Developing Countries, Netherlands, 226
Humanitarian Academy for Development—HAD, UK, 359
Humanitarian Coalition, Canada, 48
Humanity United, USA, 438
The Hunger Project, USA, 438
The Hunter Foundation—THF, UK, 359
Ibrahim (Mo) Foundation, UK, 369
Ichikowitz Family Foundation—IFF, South Africa, 280
The Ideas Institute, Kenya, 199
IDRF—International Development and Relief Foundation, Canada, 56
IFAD—International Fund for Agricultural Development, Italy, 182
IFRISSE Burkina, Burkina Faso, 45
IHH Humanitarian Relief Foundation, Türkiye, 328
IIED—International Institute for Environment and Development, UK, 360
IKEA Foundation, Netherlands, 229
Îles de Paix, Belgium, 32
Imbuto Foundation, Rwanda, 268
IMPACT Transformer la Gestion des Ressources Naturelles, Canada, 56
IMPACT Transforming Natural Resource Management, Canada, 56
İnsan Hak ve Hürriyetleri İnsani Yardım Vakfı—IHH, Türkiye, 328
Institut Français des Relations Internationales—IFRI, France, 113
Institut de Médecine et d'Epidémiologie Appliquée—Fondation Internationale Léon Mba, France, 114
Institut for Menneskerettigheder, Denmark, 84
Institut de Recherche Empirique en Économie Politique—IREEP, Benin, 35
Institute of Applied Medicine and Epidemiology—International Foundation Léon Mba, France, 114

Institute of Developing Economies-Japan External Trade Organization—IDE-JETRO, Japan, 188
Institute for Empirical Research in Political Economy—IERPE, Benin, 35
Institute for Security Studies—ISS, South Africa, 280
Inter Pares, Canada, 57
Interchurch Aid—HIA Hungary, Hungary, 153
International Alert—Alert, UK, 360
International Blue Crescent Relief and Development Foundation—IBC, Türkiye, 329
International Co-operation, Italy, 173
International Development and Relief Foundation—IDRF, Canada, 56
The International Foundation, USA, 440
International Fund for Agricultural Development—IFAD, Italy, 182
International Institute for Environment and Development—IIED, UK, 360
International Institute of Rural Reconstruction—IIRR, Philippines, 252
International Institute of Tropical Agriculture—IITA, Nigeria, 237
International NGO Coordination Committee in CAR, Central African Republic, 63
International Orthodox Christian Charities—IOCC, USA, 441
International Rescue Committee—IRC, USA, 441
International Research & Exchanges Board—IREX, USA, 442
International Rhino Foundation—IRF, USA, 441
International Rivers, USA, 441
International Solidarity Foundation, Finland, 96
International Water Management Institute—IWMI, Sri Lanka, 297
International Women's Health Coalition, USA, 427
INTERSOS, Italy, 182
IOCC—International Orthodox Christian Charities, USA, 441
IRC—International Rescue Committee, USA, 441
IREX—International Research & Exchanges Board, USA, 442
Islands of Peace, Belgium, 32
Ivorian Economic and Social Research Centre, Côte d'Ivoire, 75
Izumi Foundation, USA, 442
J. F. Kapnek Zimbabwe, Zimbabwe, 491
Jacobs Foundation, Switzerland, 313
J'ai Rêvé Foundation, Central African Republic, 63
James Michel Foundation, Seychelles, 272
Japan International Volunteer Center—JVC, Japan, 190
The Jerusalem Trust, UK, 361
The John D. and Catherine T. MacArthur Foundation, USA, 444
John Paul II Foundation for the Sahel, Burkina Faso, 44
José Maria Neves Foundation for Governance, Cabo Verde, 46
Joyce Banda Foundation International, Malawi, 210
KAF—Kataliko Actions for Africa, Congo (Democratic Republic), 72
Kansainvälinen solidaarisuussäätiö, Finland, 96
Kapnek (J. F.) Charitable Trust Zimbabwe, Zimbabwe, 491
KCDF—Kenya Community Development Foundation, Kenya, 199
Keller (Helen) International, USA, 435
King Baudouin Foundation, Belgium, 33
King Philanthropies, USA, 445
KIOS Foundation, Finland, 96
Koning Boudewijnstichting/Fondation Roi Baudouin, Belgium, 33
Kulika Charitable Trust Uganda, Uganda, 331
Kvinna till Kvinna, Sweden, 301
Lady Khama Charitable Trust, Botswana, 37
Landesa—Rural Development Institute, USA, 447
Latin American, African and Asian Social Housing Service, Chile, 66
Leibniz-Institut für Globale und Regionale Studien, Germany, 130
Leo Messi Foundation, Spain, 292
The Leona M. and Harry B. Helmsley Charitable Trust, USA, 447
Leonard Cheshire Disability, UK, 364
Léopold Sédar Senghor Foundation, Senegal, 270
The Leprosy Mission International, UK, 364
Lesotho Council of Non-Governmental Organisations, Lesotho, 207
Leventis (A. G.) Foundation, Greece, 144
Leventis (A. G.) Foundation Nigeria, Nigeria, 237
Leverhulme Trust, UK, 365
Lifeline Energy, South Africa, 280

Lifewater International, USA, 479
Liliane Foundation, Netherlands, 229
Living Culture Foundation Namibia—LCFN, Namibia, 222
Liz Claiborne & Art Ortenberg Foundation, USA, 448
Lukuru Wildlife Research Foundation, Congo (Democratic Republic), 72
Lumos Foundation, UK, 366
Luxemburg (Rosa) Stiftung, Germany, 139
MacArthur (John D. and Catherine T.) Foundation, USA, 444
McCaw (Craig and Susan) Foundation, USA, 418
Machel (Graça) Trust, South Africa, 280
McKnight Foundation, USA, 449
MADRE, USA, 450
MAG—Mines Advisory Group, UK, 366
Mama Cash Foundation, Netherlands, 230
Mandela Institute for Development Studies—MINDS, South Africa, 281
Mandela (Nelson) Children's Fund, South Africa, 281
Mandela (Nelson) Foundation, South Africa, 282
The Mandela Rhodes Foundation, South Africa, 281
Mani Tese, Italy, 183
Mara Foundation, Uganda, 332
Marcel Hicter Foundation, Belgium, 32
March of Dimes Foundation, USA, 450
Mário Soares and Maria Barroso Foundation, Portugal, 260
The MasterCard Foundation, Canada, 59
Mawazo Institute, Kenya, 199
The Max Foundation, USA, 451
Max Havelaar Foundation—Fairtrade Netherlands, Netherlands, 230
Media Foundation for West Africa, Ghana, 144
medica mondiale eV, Germany, 136
Medico International, Germany, 136
Menomadin Foundation, Israel, 170
Merchant Navy Fund, UK, 382
Mercury Phoenix Trust, UK, 367
Mercy, Ireland, 168
Mercy Corps, USA, 452
Mercy-USA for Aid and Development, USA, 452
Mérieux Foundation, France, 109
M'essh al Sudan, Sudan, 297
Messi (Leo), Fundación, Spain, 292
Michael & Susan Dell Foundation, USA, 453
Michel (James) Foundation, Seychelles, 272
Mines Advisory Group—MAG, UK, 366
Minhaj Welfare Foundation, UK, 368
Mo Dewji Foundation, Tanzania, 323
Mo Ibrahim Foundation, UK, 369
Mohammed bin Rashid Al Maktoum Global Initiatives—MBRGI, United Arab Emirates, 335
Motsepe Foundation, South Africa, 281
M-PESA Foundation, Kenya, 199
MTN Cameroon Foundation, Cameroon, 47
MTN Congo Foundation, Congo (Republic), 73
MTN Côte d'Ivoire Foundation, Côte d'Ivoire, 76
MTN Foundation Benin, Benin, 35
MTN Nigeria Foundation, Nigeria, 237
MTN SA Foundation, South Africa, 281
MTN Uganda Foundation, Uganda, 332
Mukwege (Dr Denis) Foundation, Netherlands, 224
Muslim Aid, UK, 369
Mutual Aid and Liaison Service, France, 116
The Nature Conservancy—TNC, USA, 456
NDI—National Democratic Institute for International Affairs, USA, 456
Near East Foundation—NEF, USA, 456
Nederlandse Organisatie voor Internationale Ontwikkelingssamenwerking—Stichting NOVIB, Netherlands, 228
NEF—Near East Foundation, USA, 456
Neighbour in Need, Austria, 22
Nelson Mandela Children's Fund, South Africa, 281
Nelson Mandela Foundation, South Africa, 282
Nesr Art Foundation, Angola, 5
Network of Foundations and Research Institutions for the Promotion of a Culture of Peace in Africa, Côte d'Ivoire, 75
Network of Foundations Working for Development—netFWD, France, 99
Neves (José Maria), Fundação para a Governança, Cabo Verde, 46
New School Foundation, Colombia, 71
Nicolas Hulot Foundation for Nature and Humankind, France, 110
Nigerian Conservation Foundation—NCF, Nigeria, 238
Nitidæ, France, 115
Norbert Zongo Cell for Investigative Journalism in West Africa, Burkina Faso, 44

Africa South of the Sahara

Nordic Africa Institute Scholarships, Sweden, 302
Nordic International Support Foundation—NIS, Norway, 242
Nordiska Afrikainstitutets Stipendier, Sweden, 302
North-South-Bridge Foundation, Germany, 141
Nott (David) Foundation, UK, 350
The Nourafchan Foundation—TNF, Kenya, 199
Novartis Foundation, Switzerland, 314
NOVIB (Oxfam Netherlands), Netherlands, 228
NRF—National Research Foundation, South Africa, 282
Offor (Sir Emeka) Foundation, Nigeria, 238
Ökumenikus Segélyszervezet, Hungary, 153
One Economy Foundation, Namibia, 222
OPALS—Organisation Panafricaine de Lutte pour la Santé, France, 115
Open Society Africa, Senegal, 270
Open Society European Policy Institute—OSEPI, Belgium, 33
Open Society Foundation South Africa—OSF-SA, South Africa, 282
Open Society Initiative for Eastern Africa—OSIEA, Kenya, 199
Open Society Initiative for Southern Africa—OSISA, South Africa, 282
Operation Eyesight Universal/Action Universelle de la Vue, Canada, 60
Operation USA, USA, 459
Oppenheimer Generations Foundation, South Africa, 282
Opportunity International UK, UK, 372
Oprah Winfrey Leadership Academy Foundation—OWLAF, USA, 459
Orange Botswana Foundation, Botswana, 37
Orange Foundation, France, 110
Orange Foundation Cameroon, Cameroon, 47
Orange Foundation Guinea, Guinea, 149
Orange Solidarité Madagascar, Madagascar, 210
Orbis Charitable Trust, UK, 372
ORF Nachbar in Not, Austria, 22
Organisation Panafricaine de Lutte pour la Santé—OPALS, France, 115
Organization for Social Science Research in Eastern and Southern Africa—OSSREA, Ethiopia, 94
Orji Uzor Kalu Foundation, Nigeria, 238
Outreach International, USA, 459
Outstretched Hands, Italy, 183
Oxfam Australia, Australia, 16
Oxfam Canada, Canada, 60
Oxfam Denmark, Denmark, 86
Oxfam Deutschland eV, Germany, 138
Oxfam Hong Kong, Hong Kong, 151
Oxfam Ireland, Ireland, 167
Oxfam Italia, Italy, 183
Oxfam Mexico, Mexico, 216
Oxfam NOVIB—Nederlandse Organisatie voor Internationale Ontwikkelingssamenwerking, Netherlands, 228
Oxfam NOVIB—Netherlands Organization for International Development Co-operation, Netherlands, 228
Oxfam-Québec, Canada, 60
Oxfam South Africa, South Africa, 282
Pact, USA, 460
PAN Africa—Pesticide Action Network Africa, Senegal, 271
Pan-African Organization for Health, France, 115
PANZI Foundation, USA, 461
Partage, France, 116
Partners for Equity, Australia, 16
Partners in Health, USA, 461
PATH, USA, 461
Pathfinder International, USA, 461
PCI—Project Concern International, USA, 431
Peace Brigades International—PBI, Belgium, 33
Peace Direct, UK, 373
Peace Parks Foundation, South Africa, 282
Peace Village International, Germany, 129
Peace Winds Japan—PWJ, Japan, 192
Pearl S. Buck International, USA, 462
People in Need, Czech Republic, 79
Pestalozzi Children's Foundation, Switzerland, 317
Pesticide Action Network Africa—PAN Africa, Senegal, 271
The Peter Cundill Foundation, Bermuda, 35
Plan International Ireland, Ireland, 167
Population Council, USA, 463
Practical Action, UK, 374
Pratham Education Foundation, India, 159
Première Urgence Internationale, France, 116
Presbyterian World Service & Development—PWS&D, Canada, 61
Prince Claus Fund for Culture and Development, Netherlands, 228

Prins Claus Fonds Voor Cultuur en Ontwikkeling, Netherlands, 228
Pro Victimis, Switzerland, 315
Project HOPE, USA, 464
Project Trust, UK, 374
Rainforest Foundation Norway, Norway, 243
The Rainforest Foundation UK—RFUK, UK, 375
Rausing (Ruben and Elisabeth) Trust, UK, 383
Rebecca Akufo-Addo Foundation—Rebecca Foundation, Ghana, 144
Red Sea Cultural Foundation, Somalia, 278
RedR UK, UK, 375
Refugee Empowerment International—REI, Japan, 193
Regnskogfondet, Norway, 243
REI—Refugee Empowerment International, Japan, 193
Relief International, USA, 466
Repsol Foundation, Spain, 295
Research Centre for Social Action, Congo (Democratic Republic), 72
Réseau des Fondations et Institutions de Recherche pour la Promotion d'un Culture de la Paix en Afrique—REFICA, Côte d'Ivoire, 75
Robert Bosch Foundation, Germany, 138
Robert-Bosch-Stiftung GmbH, Germany, 138
Roger Federer Foundation, Switzerland, 315
Rosa Luxemburg Foundation, Germany, 139
Rosa-Luxemburg-Stiftung, Germany, 139
Rössing Foundation, Namibia, 222
Royal Society for the Protection of Birds—RSPB, UK, 379
RSPB—Royal Society for the Protection of Birds, UK, 379
The Rufford Foundation, UK, 380
Ruparelia Foundation, Uganda, 332
Rupert Family Foundations, South Africa, 283
Rural Development Institute—Landesa, USA, 447
Rutgers, Netherlands, 228
SAASTA—South African Agency for Science and Technology Advancement, South Africa, 283
Saadi Foundation, Iran, 164
Safaricom Foundation, Kenya, 200
Sainsbury Family Charitable Trusts, UK, 380
Santé Sud, France, 116
Schneider Electric Foundation, France, 111
Schweizerisch-Liechtensteinische Stiftung für Archäologische Forschungen im Ausland—SLSA, Switzerland, 316
Scottish Catholic International Aid Fund—SCIAF, UK, 382
The Seafarers' Charity, UK, 382
Seafarers International Relief Fund, UK, 382
Secours Dentaire International, Switzerland, 317
SeedChange, Canada, 61
SEL—Service d'Entraide et de Liaison, France, 116
SELAVIP—Services Latino-Américains, Africains et Asiatiques de Promotion de l'Habitation Populaire, Chile, 66
Self Help Africa—SHA, Ireland, 167
Self Help Development Foundation—SHDF, Zimbabwe, 491
SEND-West Africa, Ghana, 144
Sentebale, UK, 382
Serrv International, Inc, USA, 471
Seva Foundation, USA, 471
Seychelles Islands Foundation—SIF, Seychelles, 272
Shahid Afridi Foundation—SAF, Pakistan, 246
Shaping Our Future Foundation—SOFF, Malawi, 210
Sightsavers International, UK, 382
Sigrid Rausing Trust—SRT, UK, 383
Sir Ahmadu Bello Memorial Foundation, Nigeria, 238
Sir Emeka Offor Foundation, Nigeria, 238
SNV, Netherlands, 228
Soares (Mário), Fundação, Portugal, 260
Solidaarisuus, Finland, 96
Somalia NGO Consortium, Somalia, 277
South Africa Philanthropy Foundation, South Africa, 278
South African Agency for Science and Technology Advancement—SAASTA, South Africa, 283
South African Institute of International Affairs, South Africa, 283
South African Institute of Race Relations—IRR, South Africa, 283
South Sudan Center for Strategic and Policy Studies—CSPS, South Sudan, 285
Southern Africa Trust, South Africa, 283
Southern Health, France, 116
Sparkassenstiftung für internationale Kooperation, Germany, 125

INDEX BY AREA OF ACTIVITY

Steelworkers Humanity Fund/Le Fonds Humanitaire des Metallos, Canada, 62
Stichting Dioraphte, Netherlands, 229
Stichting DOEN, Netherlands, 229
Stichting IKEA Foundation, Netherlands, 229
Stichting Liliane Fonds, Netherlands, 229
Stichting Mama Cash, Netherlands, 230
Stichting Max Havelaar—Fairtrade Nederland, Netherlands, 230
Stichting Triodos Foundation, Netherlands, 231
Stiftung Kinder in Afrika, Germany, 140
Stiftung Kinderdorf Pestalozzi, Switzerland, 317
Stiftung Nord-Süd-Brücken, Germany, 141
Street Child, UK, 384
Strømme Foundation, Norway, 243
Strømmestiftelsen, Norway, 243
Sudan Foundation, Sudan, 297
Sudd Institute, South Sudan, 285
Survival International, UK, 385
Swaziland Charitable Trust, Eswatini, 93
Swiss Church Aid, Switzerland, 311
Swiss Foundation for Technical Co-operation, Switzerland, 318
Swiss-Liechtenstein Foundation for Archaeological Research Abroad—SLFA, Switzerland, 316
SWISSAID Foundation, Switzerland, 318
Swisscontact—Swiss Foundation for Technical Co-operation, Switzerland, 318
Synergos—The Synergos Institute, USA, 396
Talon (Claudine), Fondation, Benin, 35
TANZ—Trade Aid NZ Inc, New Zealand, 235
Tea Research Foundation of Central Africa—TRFCA, Malawi, 211
Tearfund, UK, 385
Tearfund Australia, Australia, 18
Terre des Hommes International Federation—TDHIF, Switzerland, 318
Terre Sans Frontières—TSF, Canada, 62
THET, UK, 355
Third World Network—TWN, Malaysia, 211
Third World Solidarity Action, Luxembourg, 209
Thomson Foundation, UK, 385
TK Foundation, Bahamas, 24
Tony Blair Institute for Global Change—TBI, UK, 386
Tony Elumelu Foundation—TEF, Nigeria, 238
Trade Aid NZ Inc—TANZ, New Zealand, 235
Transnet Foundation, South Africa, 284
Triodos Foundation, Netherlands, 231
Trócaire—Catholic Agency for World Development, Ireland, 168
Tujenge Africa Foundation, Burundi, 45
Tusk, UK, 387
Tutu (Desmond & Leah) Legacy Foundation, South Africa, 279
TY Danjuma Foundation, Nigeria, 239
U4 Anti-Corruption Resource Centre, Norway, 241
Ufadhili Trust, Kenya, 197
Uluntu Community Foundation—UCF, Zimbabwe, 491
Union Aid Abroad—APHEDA, Australia, 19
United Purpose, UK, 387
United States African Development Foundation—USADF, USA, 477
Unity Foundation, Luxembourg, 210
USPG—United Society Partners in the Gospel, UK, 387
Väestöliitto, Finland, 98
VIDC—Vienna Institute for International Dialogue and Co-operation, Austria, 23
Vienna Institute for International Dialogue and Co-operation—VIDC, Austria, 23
Vita, Ireland, 168
Vodacom Foundation, South Africa, 284
Vodacom Foundation DRC, Congo (Democratic Republic), 72
Vodacom Foundation South Africa, South Africa, 284
Vodacom Lesotho Foundation, Lesotho, 207
Vodacom Tanzania Foundation—VTF, Tanzania, 323
Vodafone Ghana Foundation, Ghana, 144
Vodafone Ireland Foundation, Ireland, 168
Volkart Foundation, Switzerland, 319
Volkart-Stiftung, Switzerland, 319
Voluntary Service Overseas, UK, 388
VSO—Voluntary Service Overseas, UK, 388
WAMA Foundation, Tanzania, 323
War Child, UK, 388
War on Want, UK, 388
WasserStiftung, Germany, 142
Water for Good, USA, 479
Water.org, Inc, USA, 479
Water for People, USA, 479
WaterAid, UK, 389
WaterFoundation, Germany, 142

INDEX BY AREA OF ACTIVITY

West African Rural Foundation—WARF, Senegal, 270
Westminster Foundation for Democracy—WFD, UK, 389
The Whitley Fund for Nature—WFN, UK, 390
William Adlington Cadbury Charitable Trust, UK, 390
Windle Trust International, UK, 390
Winfrey (Oprah) Leadership Academy Foundation, USA, 459
Winrock International, USA, 481
The Wolfson Foundation, UK, 390
Woman to Woman Foundation, Sweden, 301
Women in Development Foundation, Tanzania, 323
The Wood Foundation—TWF, UK, 391
World Animal Protection, UK, 391
World Association of Children's Friends, Monaco, 217
World Jewish Relief, UK, 391
World Neighbors, USA, 483
World University Service of Canada/Entraide Universitaire Mondiale du Canada—WUSC/EUMC, Canada, 63
World Vegetable Center, Taiwan, 322
World Vision International, UK, 391
WorldFish, Malaysia, 212
Year Out Group, UK, 374
YORGHAS Foundation, Poland, 258
Zakat House, Kuwait, 203
Zarina & Naushad Merali Foundation, Kenya, 200
ZOA, Netherlands, 231

AUSTRALASIA

A. M. M. Sahabdeen Trust Foundation, Sri Lanka, 297
ACRF—Australian Cancer Research Foundation, Australia, 11
Action on Poverty, Australia, 10
Action Solidarité Tiers Monde—ASTM, Luxembourg, 209
AIIA—Australian Institute of International Affairs, Australia, 12
Alcoa Foundation, USA, 398
AMP Foundation, Australia, 10
Antarctic Heritage Trust (NZ), New Zealand, 232
Apex Foundation, Australia, 10
Arthritis Australia, Australia, 10
Asia Foundation, USA, 406
Asia New Zealand Foundation/Te Whītau Tūhono, New Zealand, 232
Asia/Pacific Cultural Centre for UNESCO—ACCU, Japan, 186
Asia Pacific Foundation of Canada—APFCanada, Canada, 49
Asia Society, USA, 406
Asian Venture Philanthropy Network—AVPN, Singapore, 272
ASTM—Action Solidarité Tiers Monde, Luxembourg, 209
Australian Academy of the Humanities, Australia, 11
Australian Academy of Science, Australia, 11
Australian-American Fulbright Commission, Australia, 11
Australian Cancer Research Foundation—ACRF, Australia, 11
Australian Communities Foundation, Australia, 11
Australian Conservation Foundation—ACF, Australia, 11
Australian Foundation for the Peoples of Asia and the Pacific—AFAP, Australia, 10
Australian Institute of International Affairs—AIIA, Australia, 12
Australian Multicultural Foundation—AMF, Australia, 12
Australian Volunteers International—AVI, Australia, 13
AVI—Australian Volunteers International, Australia, 13
Bank of America Charitable Foundation, USA, 407
Barzani Charity Foundation—BCF, Iraq, 164
BNP Paribas Foundation, France, 103
British Schools and Universities Foundation, Inc—BSUF, USA, 410
Brothers of Men, France, 113
Buchanan Charitable Foundation, New Zealand, 232
Buckland (William) Foundation, Australia, 19
CAF—Charities Aid Foundation, UK, 336
Cancer Council Australia, Australia, 13
Cancer Society of New Zealand/Te Kāhui Matepukupuku o Aotearoa, New Zealand, 233

Carnegie Endowment for International Peace, USA, 411
CBM-International, Germany, 123
Centre for Strategic and International Studies—CSIS, Indonesia, 162
Charities Aid Foundation—CAF, UK, 336
Charity Projects, UK, 348
Child Migrants Trust, UK, 347
ChildFund, New Zealand, 233
Children's Medical Research Institute—CMRI, Australia, 13
Clean Up Australia, Australia, 13
Climate Cent Foundation, Switzerland, 317
Collier Charitable Fund, Australia, 13
Comic Relief, UK, 348
Commonwealth Foundation, UK, 348
Community Chest of Korea—Fruit of Love, Korea (Republic), 200
Community Foundations of New Zealand, New Zealand, 232
Consuelo Zobel Alger Foundation, USA, 417
Digicel Foundation Jamaica, Jamaica, 184
Digicel PNG Foundation, Papua New Guinea, 247
DOEN Foundation, Netherlands, 229
East-West Center—EWC, USA, 422
Ellerman (John) Foundation, UK, 361
Fairtrade Nederland, Netherlands, 230
Family Restoration Fund, UK, 347
Feed the Minds, UK, 354
Fondation BNP Paribas, France, 103
Fondation d'Entreprise Renault, France, 106
Fondation Roi Baudouin, Belgium, 33
Food for the Hungry—FH, USA, 426
Forest & Bird Te Reo o te Taio, New Zealand, 233
Forum LSM Internasional untuk Pembangunan Indonesia, Indonesia, 161
Foundation for National Parks & Wildlife, Australia, 14
Foundation for Rural & Regional Renewal—FRRR, Australia, 14
The Foundation for Young Australians—FYA, Australia, 14
Franciscans International, Switzerland, 310
Frank Knox Memorial Fellowships, USA, 428
The Fred Hollows Foundation, Australia, 14
Frères des Hommes—FDH, France, 113
Fundación MAPFRE, Spain, 292
German Institute for Global and Area Studies—GIGA, Germany, 130
Give2Asia, USA, 394
Good Neighbors International, Korea (Republic), 200
Good Things Foundation, UK, 356
Good2Give, Australia, 10
Hagar NZ, New Zealand, 233
Haribon Foundation for the Conservation of Natural Resources, Inc, Philippines, 252
Havelaar (Max) Foundation, Netherlands, 230
Health Volunteers Overseas—HVO, USA, 434
Hollows (Fred) Foundation, Australia, 14
Humanitarian Academy for Development—HAD, UK, 359
Humanitarian Coalition, Canada, 48
The Hunger Project, USA, 438
Ian Potter Foundation, Australia, 14
IFAD—International Fund for Agricultural Development, Italy, 182
IHH Humanitarian Relief Foundation, Türkiye, 328
INHURED International—International Institute for Human Rights, Environment and Development, Nepal, 223
İnsan Hak ve Hürriyetleri İnsani Yardım Vakfı—IHH, Türkiye, 328
The International Foundation, USA, 440
International Fund for Agricultural Development—IFAD, Italy, 182
International Institute for Human Rights, Environment and Development, Nepal, 223
International NGO Forum on Indonesian Development—INFID, Indonesia, 161
International Water Management Institute—IWMI, Sri Lanka, 297
The Ireland Funds America, USA, 442
J. R. McKenzie Trust, New Zealand, 233
Jack Ma Foundation—JMF, China (People's Republic), 68
Jeans for Genes, Australia, 13
John Ellerman Foundation, UK, 361
King Baudouin Foundation, Belgium, 33
Knox (Frank) Memorial Fellowships, USA, 428
Koning Boudewijnstichting/Fondation Roi Baudouin, Belgium, 33
Leibniz-Institut für Globale und Regionale Studien, Germany, 130
The Leprosy Mission International, UK, 364
Li Ka Shing Foundation, Hong Kong, 151
Lifeline Energy, South Africa, 280

Australasia

Liliane Foundation, Netherlands, 229
The Long Now Foundation, USA, 449
Lord Mayor's Charitable Foundation, Australia, 14
McKenzie (J. R.) Trust, New Zealand, 233
MAPFRE Foundation, Spain, 292
March of Dimes Foundation, USA, 450
Max Havelaar Foundation—Fairtrade Netherlands, Netherlands, 230
Merchant Navy Fund, UK, 382
Mercy-USA for Aid and Development, USA, 452
Minderoo Foundation, Australia, 15
Moriya Scholarship Foundation, Japan, 191
Morningside Foundation, USA, 454
Myer Foundation, Australia, 18
Myer (Sidney) Fund, Australia, 18
National Heart Foundation of Australia, Australia, 15
National Heart Foundation of New Zealand, New Zealand, 233
The Nature Conservancy—TNC, USA, 456
NDI—National Democratic Institute for International Affairs, USA, 456
NFCR—National Foundation for Cancer Research, USA, 457
Oil Search Foundation, Papua New Guinea, 247
OISCA International—Organization for Industrial, Spiritual and Cultural Advancement-International, Japan, 192
Operation USA, USA, 459
Opportunity International UK, UK, 372
Oxfam Aotearoa, New Zealand, 234
Oxfam Australia, Australia, 16
OzChild—Children Australia Inc, Australia, 16
Pacific Development and Conservation Trust, New Zealand, 234
Pacific Leprosy Foundation, New Zealand, 234
Pacific Peoples' Partnership, Canada, 61
PANAP—Pesticide Action Network Asia and the Pacific, Malaysia, 211
Pancare Foundation, Australia, 16
Partners for Equity, Australia, 16
The Paul Ramsay Foundation, Australia, 16
Peace Brigades International—PBI, Belgium, 33
Peace and Disarmament Education Trust—PADET, New Zealand, 234
Peace, Health and Human Development Foundation—PHD Foundation, Japan, 193
Peace Winds Japan—PWJ, Japan, 192
Perpetual Foundation, Australia, 16
Pesticide Action Network Asia and the Pacific—PANAP, Malaysia, 211
The PHD Foundation—Peace, Health and Human Development Foundation, Japan, 193
Philanthropy Australia, Australia, 10
Philanthropy New Zealand/Tōpūtanga Tuku Aroha o Aotearoa, New Zealand, 232
Potter (Ian) Foundation, Australia, 14
Pratt Foundation, Australia, 17
Project Trust, UK, 374
Queen Elizabeth II National Trust, New Zealand, 234
Rainforest Foundation Norway, Norway, 243
Ramaciotti Foundations, Australia, 17
Ramsay (Paul) Foundation, Australia, 16
Regnskogfondet, Norway, 243
Renault Foundation, France, 106
Ross (R. E.) Trust, Australia, 17
The Ross Trust, Australia, 17
The Royal Australasian College of Physicians—RACP, Australia, 17
Royal Flying Doctor Service of Australia—RFDS, Australia, 17
Royal Society for the Protection of Birds—RSPB, UK, 379
RSPB—Royal Society for the Protection of Birds, UK, 379
Rutgers, Netherlands, 228
Saadi Foundation, Iran, 164
Sahabdeen (A. M. M.) Trust Foundation, Sri Lanka, 297
Santos Foundation, Papua New Guinea, 247
The Seafarers' Charity, UK, 382
Seafarers International Relief Fund, UK, 382
Seeds of Affinity, Australia, 17
Sexual Wellbeing Aotearoa, New Zealand, 235
Shahid Afridi Foundation—SAF, Pakistan, 246
Sidney Myer Fund & The Myer Foundation, Australia, 18
Singapore International Foundation—SIF, Singapore, 273
The Snow Foundation, Australia, 18
SpinalCure Australia, Australia, 18
Stichting DOEN, Netherlands, 229
Stichting Liliane Fonds, Netherlands, 229
Stichting Max Havelaar—Fairtrade Nederland, Netherlands, 230
Stiftung Klimarappen, Switzerland, 317

Central and South-Eastern Europe

Sutherland Self Help Trust, New Zealand, 235
Sylvia and Charles Viertel Charitable Foundation, Australia, 18
Talk Out Loud, Australia, 18
TANZ—Trade Aid NZ Inc, New Zealand, 235
Tearfund Australia, Australia, 18
Third World Solidarity Action, Luxembourg, 209
Tindall Foundation, New Zealand, 235
The Todd Foundation, New Zealand, 235
Tokyu Foundation, Japan, 194
Topūtanga Tuku Aroha o Aotearoa, New Zealand, 232
The Toyota Foundation, Japan, 195
TPG Telecom Foundation, Australia, 19
Trade Aid NZ Inc—TANZ, New Zealand, 235
The Trawalla Foundation, Australia, 19
United Purpose, UK, 387
USPG—United Society Partners in the Gospel, UK, 387
Viertel (Sylvia and Charles) Charitable Foundation, Australia, 18
Vincent Fairfax Family Foundation—VFFF, Australia, 19
Vodafone Foundation New Zealand, New Zealand, 235
Volunteer Service Abroad/Te Tūao Tāwāhi—VSA, New Zealand, 236
Walk Free, Australia, 15
WaterAid, UK, 389
The Whitley Fund for Nature—WFN, UK, 390
William Buckland Foundation, Australia, 19
The Wolfson Foundation, UK, 390
World Animal Protection, UK, 391
World Vision International, UK, 391
WorldFish, Malaysia, 212
Year Out Group, UK, 374
Zorig Foundation, Mongolia, 219

CENTRAL AND SOUTH-EASTERN EUROPE

The A. G. Leventis Foundation, Cyprus, 77
Academy for the Development of Philanthropy in Poland, Poland, 253
Academy of European Law, Germany, 127
Adriano Olivetti Foundation, Italy, 174
Africa Grantmakers' Affinity Group—AGAG, USA, 393
AGAG—Africa Grantmakers' Affinity Group, USA, 393
Age International, UK, 339
Agora Foundation, Poland, 255
Agronomes et Vétérinaires sans Frontières—AVSF, France, 100
Agronomists and Veterinarians Without Borders, France, 100
Air France Foundation, France, 103
AIT—Asian Institute of Technology, Thailand, 323
Akademia Rozwoju Filantropii w Polsce—ARFP, Poland, 253
Albanian Disability Rights Foundation, Albania, 4
Albanian Institute for International Studies—AIIS, Albania, 4
Alcoa Foundation, USA, 398
Alfred Toepfer Foundation FVS, Germany, 121
Alfred Toepfer Stiftung FVS, Germany, 121
Alliance for Securing Democracy, USA, 430
Allianz Foundation, Germany, 121
Ambrela Platform of Development Organizations, Slovakia, 273
Ambrela—Platforma rozvojových organizácií, Slovakia, 273
America for Bulgaria Foundation, Bulgaria, 43
American Councils for International Education, USA, 400
AmeriCares Foundation, Inc, USA, 403
Analitika—Center for Social Research, Bosnia and Herzegovina, 37
Anna Lindh Euro-Mediterranean Foundation for Dialogue between Cultures, Egypt, 90
Anne Çocuk Eğitim Vakfı—AÇEV, Türkiye, 327
Arengukoostöö Ümarlaud—AKÜ, Estonia, 92
Arthur Rubinstein International Music Society, Israel, 168
Asian Institute of Technology—AIT, Thailand, 323
Asociace komunitních nadací v České republice—Spolek AKN, Czech Republic, 78
Asociácia komunitných nadácií Slovenska, Slovakia, 274
Asotsijatzijata za Dyemokratska Initzijativa, North Macedonia, 239
Aspen Institute, USA, 407
Association of Civil Society Development Center, Türkiye, 327
Association for Democratic Initiatives—ADI, North Macedonia, 239
Association of Slovakian Community Foundations, Slovakia, 274
Atlas Charity Foundation, Poland, 255
Auchan Foundation, France, 103
Auschwitz-Birkenau Foundation, Poland, 255
Auschwitz Foundation—Remembrance of Auschwitz, Belgium, 30
Autonómia Alapítvány, Hungary, 152
Autonómia Foundation, Hungary, 152
Avatud Eesti Fond, Estonia, 92
AVSI Foundation, Italy, 175
Axel Springer Foundation, Germany, 122
Axel-Springer-Stiftung, Germany, 122
BaBe—Budi aktivna, Budi emancipiran, Croatia, 77
Balkan Civil Society Development Network—BCSDN, North Macedonia, 239
Balkan Security Platform—BSP, Serbia, 271
Balti Uuringute Instituut, Estonia, 92
Baltic Sea Foundation, Finland, 97
Bank of America Charitable Foundation, USA, 407
Barcelona Centre for International Affairs, Spain, 287
Barka Foundation for Mutual Assistance, Poland, 256
Barzani Charity Foundation—BCF, Iraq, 164
BCause Foundation, Bulgaria, 42
Be Active, Be Emancipated, Croatia, 77
Berghof Foundation gGmbH, Germany, 122
Berghof Stiftung für Konfliktforschung gGmbH, Germany, 122
Bertelsmann Foundation, Germany, 122
Bertelsmann Stiftung, Germany, 122
Black Sea NGO Network—BSNN, Bulgaria, 42
Black Sea Trust for Regional Cooperation, USA, 430
Black Sea University Foundation—BSUF, Romania, 263
BNP Paribas Foundation, France, 103
Bodossaki Foundation, Greece, 145
Boghossian Foundation, Belgium, 31
Böll (Heinrich) Stiftung, Germany, 131
Boltzmann (Ludwig) Gesellschaft, Austria, 21
Book Aid International—BAI, UK, 343
Borderland Foundation, Poland, 256
Bosch (Robert) Stiftung GmbH, Germany, 138
Bóthar, Ireland, 166
Braća Karić Foundation, Serbia, 271
Bread for the World—Protestant Work for Social Welfare and Development, Germany, 123
Brot für die Welt—Evangelisches Werk für Diakonie und Entwicklung, Germany, 123
Brother's Brother Foundation, USA, 410
Bruno Kreisky Forum for International Dialogue, Austria, 20
Bruno Kreisky Forum für internationalen Dialog, Austria, 20
Bulgarian Donors' Forum, Bulgaria, 42
Bulgarian Fund for Women, Bulgaria, 43
Bulgarian Platform for International Development—BPID, Bulgaria, 42
Canon Foundation in Europe, Netherlands, 224
Carlo Cattaneo Institute, Italy, 182
Carpathian Foundation, Hungary, 153
Cartier Foundation for Contemporary Art, France, 104
CASE—Centrum Analiz Społeczno-Ekonomicznych, Poland, 255
Catalyste+, Canada, 51
Cattaneo (Carlo), Istituto, Italy, 182
Center for Social and Economic Research, Poland, 255
Centras—Assistance Centre for NGOs, Romania, 263
Centras—Centrul de Asistenta pentru Organizatii Neguvernamentale, Romania, 263
Centre for Democracy and Human Rights—CEDEM, Montenegro, 219
Centre for the Development of Non-governmental Organizations, Montenegro, 219
Centre for Development of Non-profit Organizations, Croatia, 76
Centre pour le Dialogue Humanitaire, Switzerland, 307
Centre for Euro-Atlantic Integration and Democracy—CEID, Hungary, 153
Centre Européen de la Culture—CEC, Switzerland, 307
Centre for Humanitarian Dialogue—HD, Switzerland, 307
Centre for the Information Service, Co-operation and Development of NGOs, Slovenia, 277
Centre for Philanthropy, Slovakia, 274
Centre for Promotion and Development of Civil Initiatives—OPUS, Poland, 254
Centrum pre Filantropiu, Slovakia, 274
CERANEO—Centar za razvoj neprofitnih organizacija, Croatia, 76
Česká rada sociálních služeb—CRSS, Czech Republic, 78
Česká spořitelna Foundation, Czech Republic, 79
Česko-německý fond budoucnosti, Czech Republic, 79
CESO/SACO—Canadian Executive Service Organization/Service d'Assistance Canadienne aux Organismes, Canada, 51
Charles Stewart Mott Foundation—CSMF, USA, 414
The Charta 77 Foundation, Czech Republic, 80
Children of Slovakia Foundation, Slovakia, 275
Churches' Commission for Migrants in Europe, Belgium, 28
CIDOB Foundation—Barcelona Centre for International Affairs, Spain, 287
Cimade—Ecumenical Care Service, France, 102
La Cimade—Service Oecuménique d'Entraide, France, 102
Citi Handlowy Leopold Kronenberg Foundation, Poland, 255
Civic Forum Foundation, Czech Republic, 80
Civic Initiatives, Serbia, 271
CiviKos Platform, Kosovo, 202
Civil Society Development Foundation, Romania, 263
Civitas Foundation for Civil Society, Romania, 263
Člověk v tísni, Czech Republic, 79
CNVOS—Zavod Center za Informiranje, Sodelovanje in Razvoj Nevladnih Organizacije, Slovenia, 277
Çocuk (Anne) Eğitim Vakfı, Türkiye, 327
Commission des Eglises auprès des Migrants en Europe/Kommission der Kirchen für Migranten in Europa, Belgium, 28
Committee of Good Will—Olga Havel Foundation, Czech Republic, 81
Concawe—Oil Companies' European Association for Environment, Health and Safety in Refining and Distribution, Belgium, 29
CONCORD—European NGO Confederation for Relief and Development, Belgium, 26
Costopoulos (J. F.) Foundation, Greece, 146
CRDF Global, USA, 419
Cultural Foundation of the German Länder, Germany, 134
Czech Association of Community Foundations—AKN Association, Czech Republic, 78
Czech Council of Social Services, Czech Republic, 78
Czech Donors Forum, Czech Republic, 78
Czech-German Fund for the Future, Czech Republic, 79
Czech Literary Fund Foundation, Czech Republic, 80
Czech Music Fund Foundation, Czech Republic, 79
Danish Cultural Institute—DCI, Denmark, 82
Danske Kulturinstitut—DKI, Denmark, 82
DemNet—Demokratikus Jogok Fejlesztéséért Alapítvány, Hungary, 153
DemNet—Foundation for the Development of Democratic Rights, Hungary, 153
Deripaska (Oleg) Foundation, Russian Federation, 267
Deutsche Gesellschaft für Auswärtige Politik—DGAP, Germany, 124
Deutsche Sparkassenstiftung für Internationale Zusammenarbeit, Germany, 125
Development Cooperation Roundtable, Estonia, 92
DSW—Deutsche Stiftung Weltbevölkerung, Germany, 126
Eastern Europe Studies Centre—EESC, Lithuania, 209
Ebelin and Gerd Bucerius ZEIT Foundation, Germany, 143
Eberhard Schöck Foundation, Germany, 127
Eberhard-Schöck-Stiftung, Germany, 127
Economic Development Foundation, Türkiye, 328
Economic Foundation, Poland, 255
EEB—European Environmental Bureau, Belgium, 30
Eesti Mittetulundusühingute ja Sihtasutuste Liit, Estonia, 92
Einaudi (Luigi), Fondazione, Italy, 178
Ekofond SPP, Slovakia, 275
Ekopolis Foundation, Slovakia, 275
ELEPAP—Rehabilitation for the Disabled, Greece, 145
ELIAMEP—Hellenic Foundation for European and Foreign Policy, Greece, 146
Entraide Protestante Suisse, Switzerland, 311
Environment Foundation of Turkey, Türkiye, 330

INDEX BY AREA OF ACTIVITY

Environmental Partnership Foundation, Poland, 256
ERA—Europäische Rechtsakademie, Germany, 127
ERSTE Foundation, Austria, 21
ERSTE Stiftung—Die ERSTE Österreichische Spar-Casse Privatstiftung, Austria, 21
Estonian Foreign Policy Institute, Estonia, 93
Estonian National Culture Foundation, Estonia, 93
Euro-Mediterranean Centre on Climate Change Foundation, Italy, 176
EuroNatur, Germany, 127
Europa Nostra, Netherlands, 224
Europäische Rechtsakademie—ERA, Germany, 127
European Anti-Poverty Network—EAPN, Belgium, 26
European Center for Peace and Development—ECPD, Serbia, 271
European Centre for Social Welfare Policy and Research, Austria, 21
European Community Foundation Initiative—ECFI, Germany, 119
European Cultural Centre, Switzerland, 307
European Cultural Foundation—ECF, Netherlands, 225
European Environmental Bureau—EEB, Belgium, 30
European Federation of National Organisations Working with the Homeless, Belgium, 26
European Foundation for the Improvement of Living and Working Conditions—Eurofound, Ireland, 166
European Foundation for Philanthropy and Society Development, Croatia, 76
European Foundation for the Sustainable Development of the Regions, Switzerland, 308
European Mediterranean Institute, Spain, 296
European NGO Confederation for Relief and Development—CONCORD, Belgium, 26
European Roma Rights Centre—ERRC, Belgium, 30
European Youth For Action—EYFA, Germany, 128
European Youth Foundation—EYF, France, 112
Europese Culterele Stichting, Netherlands, 225
Europska Zaklada za Filantropiju i Društveni Dazvoj, Croatia, 76
Eurotransplant International Foundation, Netherlands, 225
Evangelisches Studienwerk eV, Germany, 128
Evens Foundation, Belgium, 31
EVPA—European Venture Philanthropy Association, Belgium, 27
EYFA—European Youth For Action, Germany, 128
FEANTSA—Fédération Européenne des Associations Nationales Travaillant avec les Sans-Abri, Belgium, 26
Federacja Funduszy Lokalnych w Polsce, Poland, 254
Federation of Community Foundations in Poland, Poland, 254
Fédération Européenne des Associations Nationales Travaillant avec les Sans-Abri—FEANTSA, Belgium, 26
Federation of Non-Governmental Organizations for Development in Romania, Romania, 263
FEDRE—European Foundation for the Sustainable Development of the Regions, Switzerland, 308
filia.die Frauenstiftung, Germany, 128
filia—the Women's Foundation, Germany, 128
FINCA International, USA, 425
Folmer Wisti Fonden for International Forståelse, Denmark, 83
Folmer Wisti Foundation for International Understanding, Denmark, 83
FOND—Federatia Organizatiilor Neguvernamentale pentru Dezvoltare din Romania, Romania, 263
Fondacija Balkanska Mreza za Razvoj na Gragjanskoto Opshtestvo, North Macedonia, 239
Fondacija Braća Karić, Serbia, 271
Fondacija Cennosti, Bulgaria, 43
Fondacioni Kosovar per Shoqeri Civile, Kosovo, 202
Fondacioni i Kosovës për Shoqëri të Hapur, Kosovo, 203
Fondacioni Shqiptar për të Drejtat e Personave me Aftësi të Kufizuar—FSHDPAK, Albania, 4
Fondation Abbé Pierre, France, 108
Fondation Air France, France, 103
Fondation Auchan, France, 103
Fondation Auschwitz—Mémoire d'Auschwitz, Belgium, 30

Fondation BNP Paribas, France, 103
Fondation Boghossian, Belgium, 31
Fondation Cartier pour l'Art Contemporain, France, 104
Fondation Charles Veillon, Switzerland, 308
Fondation pour l'Economie et le Développement Durable des Régions d'Europe—FEDRE, Switzerland, 308
Fondation d'Entreprise VINCI pour la Cité, France, 106
Fondation Européenne de la Culture/Europese Culturele Stichting, Netherlands, 225
Fondation Evens Stichting, Belgium, 31
Fondation Hirondelle: Media for Peace and Human Dignity, Switzerland, 309
Fondation Jean Monnet pour l'Europe, Switzerland, 309
Fondation pour le Logement des Défavorisés, France, 108
Fondation Marc de Montalembert, France, 109
Fondation Marcel Hicter, Belgium, 32
Fondation Nicolas Hulot pour la Nature et l'Homme—FNH, France, 110
Fondation Orange, France, 110
Fondation Robert Schuman, France, 111
Fondation Schneider Electric, France, 111
Fondatzija Otvoryeno Opshtyestvo Makyedonija, North Macedonia, 239
Fondazione Adriano Olivetti, Italy, 174
Fondazione AVSI, Italy, 175
Fondazione Centesimus Annus—Pro Pontifice, Vatican City, 486
Fondazione Centro Euro-Mediterraneo sui Cambiamenti Climatici—CMCC, Italy, 176
Fondazione Internazionale Menarini, Italy, 178
Fondazione ISMU—Iniziative e Studi sulla Multietnicità, Italy, 178
Fondazione Luigi Einaudi, Italy, 178
Fondazione Querini Stampalia—FQS, Italy, 179
Fondazione Terzo Pilastro – Internazionale, Italy, 180
Fonds Européen pour la Jeunesse—FEJ, France, 112
Fórum Dárců, Czech Republic, 78
Fórum donorov, Slovakia, 274
Forum ZaDobro.BIT!, Croatia, 76
Foundation for Analysis and Social Studies, Spain, 288
Foundation for German-Polish Co-operation, Poland, 257
Foundation of the Hellenic World, Greece, 145
Foundation for Housing the Disadvantaged, France, 108
Foundation for International Community Assistance, USA, 425
Foundation Open Society Macedonia—FOSIM, North Macedonia, 239
Foundation Orange, Slovakia, 275
Foundation 'Remembrance, Responsibility and Future', Germany, 139
Foundation in Support of Local Democracy, Poland, 256
Foundation for Women, Spain, 293
Franciscans International, Switzerland, 310
Fraunhofer-Gesellschaft, Germany, 129
Fraunhofer Society, Germany, 129
FREE Network—Forum for Research on Eastern Europe and Emerging Economies, Sweden, 299
Free Russia Foundation, USA, 428
Freedom Speech Foundation, Norway, 241
French Institute of International Relations, France, 113
Fundació CIDOB, Spain, 287
Fundación para el Análisis y los Estudios Sociales—FAES, Spain, 288
Fundación IE, Spain, 291
Fundación MAPFRE, Spain, 292
Fundación Mujeres, Spain, 293
Fundacja Agory, Poland, 255
Fundacja Auschwitz-Birkenau, Poland, 255
Fundacja Citi Handlowy im. Leopolda Kronenberga, Poland, 255
Fundacja Dobroczynności Atlas, Poland, 255
Fundacja Gospodarcza, Poland, 255
Fundacja im. Stefana Batorego, Poland, 256
Fundacja Partnerstwo dla Środowiska, Poland, 256
Fundacja Pogranicze, Poland, 256
Fundacja POLSAT, Poland, 256
Fundacja Pomocy Wzajemnej Barka, Poland, 256
Fundacja Rozwoju Demokracji Loaklnej, Poland, 256
Fundacja Współpracy Polsko-Niemieckiej/ Stiftung für Deutsch-Polnische Zusammenarbeit, Poland, 257
Fundacja Wspomagania Wsi, Poland, 257

Central and South-Eastern Europe

Fundaţia Civitas pentru Societatea Civilă, Romania, 263
Fundaţia pentru Dezvoltarea Societăţii Civile—FDSC, Romania, 263
Fundaţia Orange, Romania, 263
Fundaţia Soros—Moldova, Moldova, 217
Fundaţia Universitară a Mării Negre—FUMN, Romania, 263
Fundaţia Vodafone România, Romania, 264
Future in Our Hands Youth NGO—FIOH, Armenia, 9
Gemeinnützige Hertie-Stiftung, Germany, 130
German Council on Foreign Relations, Germany, 124
German Foundation for International Legal Co-operation, Germany, 133
German Foundation for World Population, Germany, 126
German Marshall Fund of the United States—GMF, USA, 430
German Savings Banks Foundation for International Co-operation, Germany, 125
Gift of the Givers Foundation, South Africa, 280
Global Communities, USA, 431
Global Fund for Children, USA, 431
Goldman Sachs Foundation, USA, 432
Gradjanske inicijative—GI, Serbia, 271
Grupa Zagranica, Poland, 254
HALO Trust, UK, 357
HAND—Hungarian Association of NGOs for Development and Humanitarian Aid, Hungary, 152
Headley Trust, UK, 357
Heinrich Böll Foundation, Germany, 131
Heinrich-Böll-Stiftung, Germany, 131
HEKS—Hilfswerk der Evangelischen Kirchen Schweiz, Switzerland, 311
Hellenic Foundation for Culture, Greece, 145
Hellenic Foundation for European and Foreign Policy—ELIAMEP, Greece, 146
The Henry Smith Charity, UK, 358
Hertie Foundation, Germany, 130
HESTIA, Czech Republic, 78
Hicter (Marcel), Fondation, Belgium, 32
Hivos—Humanistisch Instituut voor Ontwikkelings Samenwerking, Netherlands, 226
Holt International, USA, 436
Hope Foundation, Türkiye, 331
Hulot (Nicolas), Fondation, France, 110
Humanistic Institute for Co-operation with Developing Countries, Netherlands, 226
Humanitarian Academy for Development—HAD, UK, 359
IDRF—International Development and Relief Foundation, Canada, 56
IE Foundation, Spain, 291
IFAD—International Fund for Agricultural Development, Italy, 182
IHH Humanitarian Relief Foundation, Türkiye, 328
IKEA Foundation, Netherlands, 229
İktisadi Kalkınma Vakfı, Türkiye, 328
Impact Europe, Belgium, 27
İnsan Hak ve Hürriyetleri İnsani Yardım Vakfı—IHH, Türkiye, 328
Institusjonen Fritt Ord, Norway, 241
Institut Europeu de la Mediterrània—IEMed, Spain, 296
Institut FMES—Institut Méditerranéen d'Etudes Stratégiques, France, 113
Institut Français des Relations Internationales—IFRI, France, 113
Institute of Baltic Studies, Estonia, 92
Institute for European Environmental Policy—IEEP, Belgium, 33
Institute for Policy and Legal Studies—IPLS, Albania, 4
Institute for Private Enterprise and Democracy—IPED, Poland, 257
Institutul Cultural Român—ICR, Romania, 264
Instytut Badań nad Demokracją i Przedsiębiorstwem Prywatnym, Poland, 257
Interchurch Aid—HIA Hungary, Hungary, 153
International Blue Crescent Relief and Development Foundation—IBC, Türkiye, 329
International Centre for Defence and Security—ICDS, Estonia, 93
International Development and Relief Foundation—IDRF, Canada, 56
International Forum Bosnia, Bosnia and Herzegovina, 37
International Fund for Agricultural Development—IFAD, Italy, 182
International Historical, Educational, Charitable and Human Rights Society—International Memorial, Russian Federation, 266

Central and South-Eastern Europe

International Memorial, Russian Federation, 266
International Orthodox Christian Charities—IOCC, USA, 441
International Rescue Committee—IRC, USA, 441
International Visegrad Fund—IVF, Slovakia, 275
Internationalt Uddannelsescenter, Denmark, 84
INTERSOS, Italy, 182
IOCC—International Orthodox Christian Charities, USA, 441
IRC—International Rescue Committee, USA, 441
IRZ (Deutsche Stiftung für Internationale Rechtliche Zusammenarbeit) eV, Germany, 133
ISMU Foundation—Initiatives and Studies on Multi-ethnicity, Italy, 178
Istituto Carlo Cattaneo, Italy, 182
Istituto Luigi Sturzo, Italy, 182
IUC International Education Center—IUC-Europe, Denmark, 84
The J. F. Costopoulos Foundation, Greece, 146
Jacobs Foundation, Switzerland, 313
Jan Hus Educational Foundation, Czech Republic, 81
Jean Monnet Foundation for Europe, Switzerland, 309
Kade (Max) Foundation, Inc, USA, 451
Kárpátok Alapítvány, Hungary, 153
King Gustaf V's 90th Birthday Foundation, Sweden, 301
Klon/Jawor Association, Poland, 254
Koç (Vehbi), Vakfı, Türkiye, 331
Kokkalis Foundation, Greece, 146
Konung Gustaf V's 90-Årsfond, Sweden, 301
Konzorcijum nezavisnih istraživačkih centara Zapadnog Balkana, Serbia, 271
Körber Foundation, Germany, 134
Körber-Stiftung, Germany, 134
Koret Foundation, USA, 446
The Kosciuszko Foundation, Inc, USA, 446
Kosovar Civil Society Foundation—KCSF, Kosovo, 202
Kosovo Foundation for Open Society—KFOS, Kosovo, 203
Kronenberg (Leopold) Foundation, Poland, 255
Kulturstiftung der Länder—KSL, Germany, 134
Kvinna till Kvinna, Sweden, 301
Lambrakis Foundation, Greece, 146
Landis & Gyr Foundation, Switzerland, 313
Landis & Gyr Stiftung, Switzerland, 313
LAPAS—Latvijas platforma attīstības sadarbībai, Latvia, 204
Latvian Institute of International Affairs—LIIA, Latvia, 204
Latvian Platform for Development Cooperation, Latvia, 204
Latvijas Ārpolitikas Institūts—LAI, Latvia, 204
Lauder (Ronald S.) Foundation, Germany, 138
Leibniz-Institut für Ost- und Südosteuropaforschung, Germany, 135
Leibniz Institute for East and South-East European Studies, Germany, 135
The Leprosy Mission International, UK, 364
Leventis (A. G.) Foundation, Cyprus, 77
Leverhulme Trust, UK, 365
Lietuvos vaikų fondas, Lithuania, 209
Lindh (Anna) Euro-Mediterranean Foundation for Dialogue between Cultures, Egypt, 90
Lithuanian Children's Fund, Lithuania, 209
Ludwig Boltzmann Gesellschaft, Austria, 21
Luigi Einaudi Foundation, Italy, 178
Luigi Sturzo Institute, Italy, 182
Lumos Foundation, UK, 366
Luxemburg (Rosa) Stiftung, Germany, 139
Macedonian Centre for International Co-operation—MCIC, North Macedonia, 239
MAG—Mines Advisory Group, UK, 366
Makyedonski Tzyentar za Myeroonarodna Sorabotka, North Macedonia, 239
Mama Cash Foundation, Netherlands, 230
MAPFRE Foundation, Spain, 292
Marangopoulos Foundation for Human Rights, Greece, 146
Marc de Montalembert Foundation, France, 109
Marcel Hicter Foundation, Belgium, 32
March of Dimes Foundation, USA, 450
The Max Foundation, USA, 451
Max Kade Foundation, Inc, USA, 451
Medunarodnog foruma Bosna, Bosnia and Herzegovina, 37
medica mondiale eV, Germany, 136
Mediterranean Foundation for Strategic Studies Institute, France, 113
Menarini International Foundation, Italy, 178
Mercy-USA for Aid and Development, USA, 452
Mezhdunarodnyj Memorial, Russian Federation, 266
Microfinance Centre—MFC, Poland, 257
Milieukontakt Macedonia—MKM, North Macedonia, 240

Mines Advisory Group—MAG, UK, 366
Minhaj Welfare Foundation, UK, 368
Mohammed bin Rashid Al Maktoum Global Initiatives—MBRGI, United Arab Emirates, 335
Monnet (Jean), Fondation pour l'Europe, Switzerland, 309
de Montalembert (Marc), Fondation, France, 109
Mother Child Education Foundation, Türkiye, 327
Muslim Aid, UK, 369
Nacionalne Zaklade za Razvoj Civilnoga Društva, Croatia, 76
Nadace České spořitelny—Nadace ČS, Czech Republic, 79
Nadace Český Hudebni Fond—NČHF, Czech Republic, 79
Nadace Český literární fond—nčlf, Czech Republic, 80
Nadace Charty 77, Czech Republic, 80
Nadace Neziskovky.cz, Czech Republic, 79
Nadace Občanského fóra—Nadace OF, Czech Republic, 80
Nadace Open Society Fund Praha, Czech Republic, 80
Nadace Preciosa, Czech Republic, 80
Nadace Vodafone Česká Republika, Czech Republic, 80
Nadácia Ekopolis, Slovakia, 275
Nadácia Orange, Slovakia, 275
Nadácia Otvorenej Spoločnosti, Slovakia, 276
Nadácia Pontis, Slovakia, 274
Nadácia pre Deti Slovenska, Slovakia, 275
Nadácia SPP, Slovakia, 275
Nadácia Tatra Banky, Slovakia, 276
National Federation of NGOs, Poland, 254
National Foundation for Civil Society Development, Croatia, 76
National Trust EcoFund, Bulgaria, 43
NDI—National Democratic Institute for International Affairs, USA, 456
Nederlandse Organisatie voor Internationale Ontwikkelingssamenwerking—Stichting NOVIB, Netherlands, 228
Neighbour in Need, Austria, 22
Network of Estonian Non-profit Organizations, Estonia, 92
Network of Information and Support for Non-governmental Organizations, Poland, 254
Nevyriausybinių organizacijų informacijos ir paramos centras, Lithuania, 208
NGO Information and Support Centre—NISC, Lithuania, 208
Nicolas Hulot Foundation for Nature and Humankind, France, 110
NIOK Alapítvány—Nonprofit Információs és Oktató Központ Alapítvány—NIOK, Hungary, 152
NIOK Foundation—Non-Profit Information and Training Centre, Hungary, 152
Nonprofit Enterprise and Self-sustainability Team—NESsT, USA, 457
NOVIB (Oxfam Netherlands), Netherlands, 228
OeAD, Austria, 22
Ogólnopolska Federacja Organizacji Pozarządowych—OFOP, Poland, 254
Ökumenikus Segélyszervezet, Hungary, 153
Olivetti (Adriano), Fondazione, Italy, 174
Open Estonia Foundation, Estonia, 92
Open Society European Policy Institute—OSEPI, Belgium, 33
Open Society Foundation for Albania, Albania, 5
Open Society Foundation—Bratislava, Slovakia, 276
Open Society Foundation—Western Balkans, Albania, 5
Open Society Fund—Bosnia-Herzegovina, Bosnia and Herzegovina, 37
Open Society Fund Prague—OSF Prague, Czech Republic, 80
Open Society Institute—Sofia, Bulgaria, 43
OPUS—Centre for Promotion and Development of Civil Initiatives, Poland, 254
Orange Foundation, Romania, 263
ORF Nachbar in Not, Austria, 22
Östersjöfonden, Finland, 97
Oxfam Deutschland eV, Germany, 138
Oxfam Italia, Italy, 183
Oxfam NOVIB—Nederlandse Organisatie voor Internationale Ontwikkelingssamenwerking, Netherlands, 228
Oxfam NOVIB—Netherlands Organization for International Development Co-operation, Netherlands, 228
PAN Europe—Pesticide Action Network Europe, Belgium, 34
Pan-European Federation for Cultural Heritage, Netherlands, 224

INDEX BY AREA OF ACTIVITY

Partage, France, 116
PCI—Project Concern International, USA, 431
People in Need, Czech Republic, 79
Pestalozzi Children's Foundation, Switzerland, 317
Pesticide Action Network Europe—PAN Europe, Belgium, 34
PH International, USA, 463
Philanthropy Europe Association—Philea, Belgium, 27
Philea—Philanthropy Europe Association, Belgium, 27
Plataform CiviKos, Kosovo, 202
Platform for Development Cooperation and Humanitarian Aid, Slovenia, 276
Platforma Mimovládnych Rozvojových Organizácií, Slovakia, 273
Ploughshares Fund, USA, 463
Polish-American Freedom Foundation, Poland, 257
POLSAT Foundation, Poland, 256
Polsko-Amerykańska Fundacja Wolności, Poland, 257
Pontis Foundation, Slovakia, 274
Praxis Centre for Policy Studies Foundation, Estonia, 93
Preciosa Foundation, Czech Republic, 80
Project Harmony, USA, 463
Project HOPE, USA, 464
Protestant Study Foundation, Germany, 128
Querini Stampalia Foundation, Italy, 179
Rahvusvaheline Kaitseuuringute Keskus—RKK, Estonia, 93
Rausing (Ruben and Elisabeth) Trust, UK, 383
Razumkov Centre, Ukraine, 333
RED—Ruralité-Environnement-Développement, Belgium, Belgium, 34
Regional Environmental Center, Hungary, 153
Rehabilitation for the Disabled—ELEPAP, Greece, 145
Réseau Européen des Associations de Lutte contre la Pauvreté et l'Exclusion Sociale, Belgium, 29
Robert Bosch Foundation, Germany, 138
Robert-Bosch-Stiftung GmbH, Germany, 138
Robert Schuman Foundation, France, 111
Rockefeller Brothers Fund—RBF, USA, 468
Romanian Cultural Institute, Romania, 264
The Ronald S. Lauder Foundation, Germany, 138
Rosa Luxemburg Foundation, Germany, 139
Rosa-Luxemburg-Stiftung, Germany, 139
Rroma Foundation, Switzerland, 315
Rromani Fundacija, Switzerland, 315
Rubinstein (Arthur) International Music Society, Israel, 168
The Rufford Foundation, UK, 380
Rural Development Foundation, Poland, 257
Ruralité-Environnement-Développement—RED, Belgium, 34
Rurality Environment Development, Belgium, 34
Rytų Europos Studijų Centras—RESC, Lithuania, 209
Saadi Foundation, Iran, 164
SAIA—Slovak Academic Information Agency, Slovakia, 274
Sainsbury Family Charitable Trusts, UK, 380
Sasakawa Health Foundation—SHF, Japan, 194
Schneider Electric Foundation, France, 111
Schöck (Eberhard) Stiftung, Germany, 127
Schuman (Robert), Fondation, France, 111
Schwarzkopf-Stiftung Junges Europa, Germany, 139
Schwarzkopf Young Europe Foundation, Germany, 139
Schweisfurth Foundation, Germany, 139
Schweisfurth-Stiftung, Germany, 139
SEEMO—South East Europe Media Organisation, Austria, 23
Serbian Philanthropy Forum, Serbia, 271
Sieć Wspierania Organizacji Pozarządowych—SPLOT, Poland, 254
Sigrid Rausing Trust—SRT, UK, 383
Sihtasutus Eesti Rahvuskultuuri Fond, Estonia, 93
Sihtasutus Poliitikauuringute Keskus Praxis, Estonia, 93
Singapore International Foundation—SIF, Singapore, 273
Sivil Toplum Geliştirme Merkezi—STGM, Türkiye, 327
SLOGA—Platforma za Razvojno Sodelovanje in Humanitarno Pomoč, Slovenia, 276
Slovak Academic Information Agency—SAIA, Slovakia, 274
Slovak-Czech Women's Fund, Slovakia, 276
Slovak Donors Forum, Slovakia, 274
Slovak Humanitarian Council, Slovakia, 274
Slovak Security Policy Institute, Slovakia, 276

INDEX BY AREA OF ACTIVITY

Slovenian Science Foundation, Slovenia, 277
Slovenská Humanitná Rada, Slovakia, 274
Slovenska znanstvena fundacija—SZF, Slovenia, 277
Slovensko-český enský fond, Slovakia, 276
Slovenský inštitút pre bezpečnostnú politiku, Slovakia, 276
Smith (Henry) Charity, UK, 358
Software AG Foundation, Germany, 139
Software AG Stiftung, Germany, 139
Soros Foundation—Moldova, Moldova, 217
South East Europe Media Organisation—SEEMO, Austria, 23
Sparkassenstiftung für internationale Kooperation, Germany, 125
SPP Foundation, Slovakia, 275
Springer (Axel) Stiftung, Germany, 122
Srpski Filantropski Forum, Serbia, 271
Stefan Batory Foundation, Poland, 256
Stichting IKEA Foundation, Netherlands, 229
Stichting Mama Cash, Netherlands, 230
Stichting Triodos Foundation, Netherlands, 231
Stiftung 'Erinnerung, Verantwortung und Zukunft'—EVZ, Germany, 139
Stiftung Kinderdorf Pestalozzi, Switzerland, 317
Stowarzyszenie Klon/Jawor, Poland, 254
Sturzo (Luigi), Istituto, Italy, 182
Südosteuropäische Medienorganisation, Austria, 23
Swiss Church Aid, Switzerland, 311
Swiss Foundation for Technical Co-operation, Switzerland, 318
Swisscontact—Swiss Foundation for Technical Co-operation, Switzerland, 318
Tatra Bank Foundation, Slovakia, 276
Terre des Hommes International Federation—TDHIF, Switzerland, 318
TFF—Transnational Foundation for Peace and Future Research, Sweden, 304
TFF—Transnationella Stiftelsen för Freds- och Framtidsforskning, Sweden, 304
Thomson Foundation, UK, 385
TK Foundation, Bahamas, 24
Toepfer (Alfred) Stiftung, Germany, 121
Transnational Giving Europe—TGE, Belgium, 27
Triodos Foundation, Netherlands, 231
Trust for Mutual Understanding—TMU, USA, 476
Türkiye Çevre Vakfi, Türkiye, 330
Umut Vakfi, Türkiye, 331
UniCredit Foundation, Italy, 183
US Civilian Research & Development Foundation, USA, 419
USPG—United Society Partners in the Gospel, UK, 387
Values Foundation, Bulgaria, 43
Vehbi Koç Foundation, Türkiye, 331
Vehbi Koç Vakfı, Türkiye, 331
Veillon (Charles), Fondation, Switzerland, 308
VIA Foundation, Czech Republic, 81
VIDC—Vienna Institute for International Dialogue and Co-operation, Austria, 23
Vienna Institute for International Dialogue and Co-operation—VIDC, Austria, 23
VINCI Corporate Foundation for the City, France, 106
Vodafone Albania Foundation, Albania, 5
Vodafone Czech Republic Foundation, Czech Republic, 80
Vodafone Hungary Foundation, Hungary, 153
Vodafone Magyarország Alapítvány, Hungary, 153
Vodafone Romania Foundation, Romania, 264
Volnoe Delo—Oleg Deripaska Foundation, Russian Federation, 267
Výbor dobré vůle—Nadace Olgy Havlové, Czech Republic, 81
Vzdělávací Nadace Jana Husa, Czech Republic, 81
Westminster Foundation for Democracy—WFD, UK, 389
The Whitley Fund for Nature—WFN, UK, 390
Winrock International, USA, 481
Wisti (Folmer) Foundation for International Understanding, Denmark, 83
Woman to Woman Foundation, Sweden, 301
World Vision International, UK, 391
The Wyss Foundtion, USA, 484
Zagranica Group, Poland, 254
Zavod Center za Informiranje, Sodelovanje in Razvoj Nevladnih Organizacije—CNVOS, Slovenia, 277
ZEIT-Stiftung Ebelin und Gerd Bucerius, Germany, 143

EAST AND SOUTH-EAST ASIA

A. M. M. Sahabdeen Trust Foundation, Sri Lanka, 297
AARDO—African-Asian Rural Development Organization, India, 155
Abilis Foundation, Finland, 95
Abilis-säätiö, Finland, 95
Accion, USA, 397
Action Against Hunger, France, 100
Action contre la Faim—ACF France, France, 100
Action Damien/Damiaanactie, Belgium, 28
Action Education, France, 100
Action on Poverty, Australia, 10
Action Solidarité Tiers Monde—ASTM, Luxembourg, 209
Acumen, USA, 397
Afdi—Agriculteurs Français et Développement International, France, 100
Afghanistan Institute for Civil Society—AICS, Afghanistan, 3
African-Asian Rural Development Organization—AARDO, India, 155
Age International, UK, 339
Agriculteurs Français et Développement International, France, 100
Agronomes et Vétérinaires sans Frontières—AVSF, France, 100
Agronomists and Veterinarians Without Borders, France, 100
Ai You Foundation, China (People's Republic), 66
Air France Foundation, France, 103
AIT—Asian Institute of Technology, Thailand, 323
Akai Hane—Central Community Chest of Japan, Japan, 185
Alert—International Alert, UK, 360
Alet'Eleym Fewq Alejmey'e, Qatar, 262
Alkhidmat Foundation Pakistan—AKFP, Pakistan, 244
Alliance of Bioversity International and the International Center for Tropical Agriculture—CIAT, Italy, 172
Alola Foundation, Timor-Leste, 325
AMADE Mondiale—Association Mondiale des Amis de l'Enfance, Monaco, 217
American Councils for International Education, USA, 400
American Friends Service Committee—AFSC, USA, 401
American Jewish World Service—AJWS, USA, 402
AmeriCares Foundation, Inc, USA, 403
Amity Foundation, China (People's Republic), 66
ANGOC—Asian NGO Coalition for Agrarian Reform and Rural Development, Philippines, 251
Anne Çocuk Eğitim Vakfı—AÇEV, Türkiye, 327
APHEDA—Union Aid Abroad, Australia, 19
Arbeiterwohlfahrt Bundesverband eV—AWO, Germany, 121
Arcus Foundation, USA, 405
Areumdaun Jaedan, Korea (Republic), 200
Arts Council Korea, Korea (Republic), 200
Asahi Group Foundation, Japan, 186
ASEAN Foundation, Indonesia, 161
Asia Africa International Voluntary Foundation—AIV, Japan, 186
Asia Foundation, USA, 406
Asia New Zealand Foundation/Te Whītau Tūhono, New Zealand, 232
Asia/Pacific Cultural Centre for UNESCO—ACCU, Japan, 186
Asia Pacific Foundation of Canada—APFCanada, Canada, 49
Asia Philanthropy Circle—APC, Singapore, 272
Asia Society, USA, 406
AsiaDHRRA—Asian Partnership for the Development of Human Resources in Rural Asia, Philippines, 251
Asian Community Trust—ACT, Japan, 186
Asian Cultural Council—ACC, USA, 406
Asian Health Institute—AHI, Japan, 187
Asian Institute of Technology—AIT, Thailand, 323
Asian Partnership for the Development of Human Resources in Rural Asia, Philippines, 251
Asian Venture Philanthropy Network—AVPN, Singapore, 272
Aspen Institute, USA, 407
Association of Foundations, Philippines, 250
ASTM—Action Solidarité Tiers Monde, Luxembourg, 209
Auchan Foundation, France, 103
Aurora Trust, UK, 341
Australian Foundation for the Peoples of Asia and the Pacific—AFAP, Australia, 10
Australian Volunteers International—AVI, Australia, 13
AVI—Australian Volunteers International, Australia, 13
AVSI Foundation, Italy, 175

East and South-East Asia

Ayala Foundation, Inc—AFI, Philippines, 251
Azman Hashim Foundation, Malaysia, 212
Bagnoud (François-Xavier) Association, Switzerland, 310
Bank of America Charitable Foundation, USA, 407
Barcelona Centre for International Affairs, Spain, 287
BBC Media Action, UK, 342
The Beautiful Foundation, Korea (Republic), 200
Berghof Foundation gGmbH, Germany, 122
Berghof Stiftung für Konfliktforschung gGmbH, Germany, 122
Bettencourt Schueller Foundation, France, 103
Blakemore Foundation, USA, 408
BNP Paribas Foundation, France, 103
Böll (Heinrich) Stiftung, Germany, 131
Born Free Foundation, UK, 343
Bosch (Robert) Stiftung GmbH, Germany, 138
Bóthar, Ireland, 166
BRAC, Bangladesh, 25
Bread for the World—Protestant Work for Social Welfare and Development, Germany, 123
Bridge Asia Japan—BAJ, Japan, 187
Brighter Future Myanmar Foundation—BFM, Myanmar, 221
British Schools and Universities Foundation, Inc—BSUF, USA, 410
Brot für die Welt—Evangelisches Werk für Diakonie und Entwicklung, Germany, 123
Brother's Brother Foundation, USA, 410
Brothers of Men, France, 113
Buck (Pearl S.) International, USA, 462
Buddharaksa Foundation, Thailand, 323
Cadbury (William Adlington) Charitable Trust, UK, 390
Cambodia Development Resource Institute—CDRI, Cambodia, 46
Cambodian Salesian Delegation, Cambodia, 46
Canadian Centre for International Studies and Co-operation, Canada, 51
Canadian Foodgrains Bank, Canada, 50
Canon Foundation in Europe, Netherlands, 224
CARE International—CI, Switzerland, 307
Caritas Canada, Canada, 53
Carnegie Endowment for International Peace, USA, 411
The Carter Center, USA, 412
Cartier Foundation for Contemporary Art, France, 104
Catalyste+, Canada, 51
Catholic Agency for World Development—Trócaire, Ireland, 168
Caucus of Development NGO Networks—CODE-NGO, Philippines, 250
CBM-International, Germany, 123
CECI—Canadian Centre for International Studies and Co-operation/Centre d'Etudes et de Coopération Internationale, Canada, 51
Centre pour le Dialogue Humanitaire, Switzerland, 307
Centre for Humanitarian Dialogue—HD, Switzerland, 307
Centre for Strategic and International Studies—CSIS, Indonesia, 162
CESO/SACO—Canadian Executive Service Organization/Service d'Assistance Canadienne aux Organismes, Canada, 51
Cetana Educational Foundation, USA, 413
Chang Yung-fa Foundation, Taiwan, 321
Charity Islamic Trust Elrahma, UK, 352
Charity Projects, UK, 348
The Charles Wallace India Trusts, UK, 347
Cheshire (Leonard) Foundation, UK, 364
Chia Hsin Foundation, Taiwan, 321
ChildFund, New Zealand, 233
ChildFund International, USA, 414
Childhope Philippines, Philippines, 251
Children of the Mekong, France, 102
Children and Sharing, France, 102
The Children's Investment Fund Foundation, UK, 347
China Charities Aid Foundation for Children, China (People's Republic), 67
China Charities Alliance, China (People's Republic), 66
China Children and Teenagers' Foundation, China (People's Republic), 67
China Environmental Protection Foundation, China (People's Republic), 67
China Foundation Center—CFC, China (People's Republic), 66
China Foundation for Poverty Alleviation—CFPA, China (People's Republic), 67
China Medical Board—CMB, USA, 415
China Siyuan Foundation for Poverty Alleviation, China (People's Republic), 67

East and South-East Asia

China Youth Development Foundation, China (People's Republic), 68
Chr. Michelsen Institute for Science and Intellectual Freedom—CMI, Norway, 241
CIAT—Centro Internacional de Agricultura Tropical, Italy, 172
CIDOB Foundation—Barcelona Centre for International Affairs, Spain, 287
Civil Society and Human Rights Network, Afghanistan, 3
Civil Society and Human Rights Organization—CSHRO, Afghanistan, 3
Claiborne (Liz) & Art Ortenberg Foundation, USA, 448
Climate Cent Foundation, Switzerland, 317
Člověk v tísni, Czech Republic, 79
CMI—Chr. Michelsen Institute for Science and Intellectual Freedom, Norway, 241
Çocuk (Anne) Eğitim Vakfı, Türkiye, 327
CODESPA Foundation, Spain, 290
Comic Relief, UK, 348
Comité de Coopération Pour le Cambodge, Cambodia, 46
Commonwealth Foundation, UK, 348
Communication Foundation for Asia, Philippines, 251
Community Chest, Singapore, 273
Community Chest of Hong Kong, Hong Kong, 150
Community Chest of Korea—Fruit of Love, Korea (Republic), 200
Community Foundation of Singapore, Singapore, 272
Concern Worldwide, Ireland, 166
Consuelo Zobel Alger Foundation, USA, 417
Cooperation Committee for Cambodia—CCC, Cambodia, 46
Co-operative Development Foundation of Canada—CDF, Canada, 52
The Craig and Susan McCaw Foundation, USA, 418
CRDF Global, USA, 419
Cultural Center of the Philippines—CCP, Philippines, 252
Daiwa Anglo-Japanese Foundation, UK, 350
Danish Cultural Institute—DCI, Denmark, 82
Danish Institute for Human Rights, Denmark, 84
Danske Kulturinstitut—DKI, Denmark, 82
David Nott Foundation, UK, 350
Daw Khin Kyi Foundation, Myanmar, 221
Defense of Green Earth Foundation—DGEF, Japan, 187
Deutsche Gesellschaft für Auswärtige Politik—DGAP, Germany, 124
Deutsche Sparkassenstiftung für Internationale Zusammenarbeit, Germany, 125
Development and Peace—Caritas Canada, Canada, 53
Développement et Paix—Caritas Canada, Canada, 53
Diakonia, Sweden, 298
DOEN Foundation, Netherlands, 229
Dom Manuel II Foundation, Portugal, 260
Don Bosco Foundation of Cambodia—DBFC, Cambodia, 46
DTGO Group of Foundations, Thailand, 323
Dunhe Foundation, China (People's Republic), 68
Earthrights International—ERI, USA, 422
Earthworm Foundation, Switzerland, 307
East Asia Institute—EAI, Korea (Republic), 201
East-West Center—EWC, USA, 422
Education Above All Foundation—EAA, Qatar, 262
The Education for Development Foundation—EDF, Thailand, 324
Educo, Spain, 286
Elena & Gennady Timchenko Foundation, Russian Federation, 265
Elrahma Charity Trust, UK, 352
Elton John AIDS Foundation, UK, 352
Enda Third World—Environment and Development Action in the Third World, Senegal, 270
Enda Tiers Monde—Environnement et Développement du Tiers-Monde, Senegal, 270
endPoverty.org, USA, 424
Enfance et Partage, France, 102
Enfants du Mékong, France, 102
EngenderHealth, USA, 424
Eni Foundation, Italy, 173
Entraide Protestante Suisse, Switzerland, 311
Entraide Universitaire Mondiale du Canada, Canada, 63
Environmental Justice Foundation—EJF, UK, 353
Equality Fund/Fonds Égalité, Canada, 54
Eurasia Foundation—EF, USA, 424
Fairtrade Nederland, Netherlands, 230

Federal Association of Social Welfare Organizations, Germany, 121
Feed the Children, USA, 425
FEMSA Foundation, Mexico, 215
FIJI Water Foundation, Fiji, 94
filia.die Frauenstiftung, Germany, 128
filia—the Women's Foundation, Germany, 128
Fondation Abbé Pierre, France, 108
Fondation pour l'Agriculture et la Ruralité dans le Monde—Fondation FARM, France, 106
Fondation Air France, France, 103
Fondation Auchan, France, 103
Fondation Bettencourt Schueller, France, 103
Fondation BNP Paribas, France, 103
Fondation Cartier pour l'Art Contemporain, France, 104
Fondation Ensemble, France, 105
Fondation d'Entreprise Renault, France, 106
Fondation FARM—Fondation pour l'Agriculture et la Ruralité dans le Monde, France, 106
Fondation France Chine—FFC, France, 106
Fondation Franco-Japonaise Sasakawa, France, 106
Fondation Hirondelle: Media for Peace and Human Dignity, Switzerland, 309
Fondation pour le Logement des Défavorisés, France, 108
Fondation Mérieux, France, 109
Fondation Roi Baudouin, Belgium, 33
Fondation S, France, 111
Fondation Schneider Electric, France, 111
Fondazione AVSI, Italy, 175
Fonds Égalité, Canada, 54
Food for the Hungry—FH, USA, 426
Ford Foundation, USA, 427
The Forest Trust, Switzerland, 307
Forum LSM Internasional untuk Pembangunan Indonesia, Indonesia, 161
Fòs Feminista, USA, 427
Foundation for Housing the Disadvantaged, France, 108
Foundation for Women, Thailand, 324
Foundation for World Agriculture and Rural Life, France, 106
France China Foundation, France, 106
Franciscans International, Switzerland, 310
Franco-Japanese Sasakawa Foundation, France, 106
Fraunhofer-Gesellschaft, Germany, 129
Fraunhofer Society, Germany, 129
The Fred Hollows Foundation, Australia, 14
The Freeman Foundation, USA, 428
French Agriculturalists and International Development, France, 100
French Institute of International Relations, France, 113
Frères des Hommes—FDH, France, 113
Friedensdorf International, Germany, 129
Friends-International, Cambodia, 46
Fulbright Commission Philippines, Philippines, 253
Fundação Dom Manuel II, Portugal, 260
Fundação Oriente, Portugal, 260
Fundació CIDOB, Spain, 287
Fundación Capital, Colombia, 70
Fundación CODESPA, Spain, 290
Fundación FEMSA, Mexico, 215
Fundación IE, Spain, 291
Fundación Leo Messi, Spain, 292
Fundación MAPFRE, Spain, 292
Fundasaun Alola, Timor-Leste, 325
Fundasaun Haburas, Timor-Leste, 325
Fundasaun Mahein, Timor-Leste, 325
Future in Our Hands Youth NGO—FIOH, Armenia, 9
FXB International—Association François-Xavier Bagnoud, Switzerland, 310
German Council on Foreign Relations, Germany, 124
German Foundation for International Legal Co-operation, Germany, 133
German Institute for Global and Area Studies—GIGA, Germany, 130
German Savings Banks Foundation for International Co-operation, Germany, 125
Gift of the Givers Foundation, South Africa, 280
Give2Asia, USA, 394
Global Health Partnerships, UK, 355
Global Innovation Fund, UK, 356
Goldman Sachs Foundation, USA, 432
Good Neighbors International, Korea (Republic), 201
Grameen Foundation—GF, USA, 433
Grassroots International—GRI, USA, 433
Great Britain Sasakawa Foundation, UK, 356
Green Umbrella Children's Foundation—ChildFund Korea, Korea (Republic), 201
Guardian Foundation, Timor-Leste, 325

INDEX BY AREA OF ACTIVITY

Haburas Foundation, Timor-Leste, 325
Hagar NZ, New Zealand, 233
HALO Trust, UK, 357
Haribon Foundation for the Conservation of Natural Resources, Inc, Philippines, 252
Havelaar (Max) Foundation, Netherlands, 230
He Xiangjian Foundation, China (People's Republic), 68
Health Volunteers Overseas—HVO, USA, 434
Hedwig and Robert Samuel Foundation, Germany, 131
Hedwig und Robert Samuel-Stiftung, Germany, 131
Heinrich Böll Foundation, Germany, 131
Heinrich-Böll-Stiftung, Germany, 131
HEKS—Hilfswerk der Evangelischen Kirchen Schweiz, Switzerland, 311
Helen Keller International—HKI, USA, 435
Helvetas Swiss Intercooperation, Switzerland, 311
Henry Luce Foundation, Inc, USA, 435
HER Fund, Hong Kong, 151
Heren Philanthropic Foundation, China (People's Republic), 68
Heungkong Charitable Foundation, China (People's Republic), 68
Himalaya Research and Development Foundation—Himalaya Foundation, Taiwan, 321
Hitachi Foundation, Japan, 187
Hivos—Humanistisch Instituut voor Ontwikkelings Samenwerking, Netherlands, 226
Hollows (Fred) Foundation, Australia, 14
Holt International, USA, 436
Hong Kong Council of Social Service—HKCSS, Hong Kong, 150
Hong Kong Society for the Blind, Hong Kong, 151
HOPE International Development Agency, Canada, 56
Humanistic Institute for Co-operation with Developing Countries, Netherlands, 226
Humanitarian Academy for Development—HAD, UK, 359
Humanitarian Coalition, Canada, 48
Humanity United, USA, 438
IACD—Institute of Asian Culture and Development, Korea (Republic), 201
IBON Foundation, Philippines, 252
IDRF—International Development and Relief Foundation, Canada, 56
IE Foundation, Spain, 291
IFAD—International Fund for Agricultural Development, Italy, 182
IHH Humanitarian Relief Foundation, Türkiye, 328
IIED—International Institute for Environment and Development, UK, 360
IKEA Foundation, Netherlands, 229
IMPACT Transformer la Gestion des Ressources Naturelles, Canada, 56
IMPACT Transforming Natural Resource Management, Canada, 56
Indonesia Biodiversity Foundation, Indonesia, 162
Indonesian Forum for the Environment—Friends of the Earth Indonesia, Indonesia, 162
INHURED International—International Institute for Human Rights, Environment and Development, Nepal, 223
İnsan Hak ve Hürriyetleri İnsani Yardım Vakfı—IHH, Türkiye, 328
Institut Français des Relations Internationales—IFRI, France, 113
Institut de Médecine et d'Epidémiologie Appliquée—Fondation Internationale Léon Mba, France, 114
Institut for Menneskerettigheder, Denmark, 84
Institute of Applied Medicine and Epidemiology—International Foundation Léon Mba, France, 114
Institute of Asian Culture and Development—IACD, Korea (Republic), 201
Institute of Developing Economies-Japan External Trade Organization—IDE-JETRO, Japan, 188
Institute for Iran-Eurasia Studies—IRAS, Iran, 163
Institute for Sustainable Communities—ISC, USA, 439
Institutul Cultural Român—ICR, Romania, 264
Integrated Rural Development Foundation—IRDF, Philippines, 252
Inter Pares, Canada, 57
Interchurch Aid—HIA Hungary, Hungary, 153
International Alert—Alert, UK, 360
International Blue Crescent Relief and Development Foundation—IBC, Türkiye, 329

INDEX BY AREA OF ACTIVITY

East and South-East Asia

International Development and Relief Foundation—IDRF, Canada, 56
The International Foundation, USA, 440
International Fund for Agricultural Development—IFAD, Italy, 182
International Institute for Environment and Development—IIED, UK, 360
International Institute for Human Rights, Environment and Development, Nepal, 223
International Institute of Rural Reconstruction—IIRR, Philippines, 252
International NGO Forum on Indonesian Development—INFID, Indonesia, 161
International Rescue Committee—IRC, USA, 441
International Research & Exchanges Board—IREX, USA, 442
International Rhino Foundation—IRF, USA, 441
International Rivers, USA, 441
International Water Management Institute—IWMI, Sri Lanka, 297
International Women's Health Coalition, USA, 427
IRC—International Rescue Committee, USA, 441
The Ireland Funds America, USA, 442
IREX—International Research & Exchanges Board, USA, 442
IRZ (Deutsche Stiftung für Internationale Rechtliche Zusammenarbeit) eV, Germany, 133
Iwatani Naoji Foundation, Japan, 189
Jack Ma Foundation—JMF, China (People's Republic), 68
JANIC—Japanese NGO Center for International Co-operation, Japan, 185
Japan Association of Charitable Organizations—JACO, Japan, 185
Japan Foundation Center, Japan, 185
Japan Heart Foundation, Japan, 190
Japan International Volunteer Center—JVC, Japan, 190
Japanese-German Centre Berlin, Germany, 133
Japanisch-Deutsches Zentrum Berlin, Germany, 133
JEN, Japan, 190
JIIA—Japan Institute of International Affairs, Japan, 190
Kajima Foundation, Japan, 191
KEHATI—Yayasan Keanekaragaman Hayati Indonesia, Indonesia, 162
Keller (Helen) International, USA, 435
Kind Heart Foundation, Viet Nam, 488
King Baudouin Foundation, Belgium, 33
King Philanthropies, USA, 445
Koning Boudewijnstichting/Fondation Roi Baudouin, Belgium, 33
Körber Foundation, Germany, 134
Körber-Stiftung, Germany, 134
Kuok Foundation Berhad, Malaysia, 211
Land Network, Timor-Leste, 325
Landesa—Rural Development Institute, USA, 447
Latin American, African and Asian Social Housing Service, Chile, 66
League of Corporate Foundations—LCF, Philippines, 250
Leibniz-Institut für Globale und Regionale Studien, Germany, 130
Leo Messi Foundation, Spain, 292
Leonard Cheshire Disability, UK, 364
The Leprosy Mission International, UK, 364
Lien Foundation, Singapore, 273
Lifeline Energy, South Africa, 280
Lifewater International, USA, 479
Light of the Village Foundation, Indonesia, 162
Liliane Foundation, Netherlands, 229
Liz Claiborne & Art Ortenberg Foundation, USA, 448
The Long Now Foundation, USA, 449
Luce (Henry) Foundation, Inc, USA, 435
Luxemburg (Rosa) Stiftung, Germany, 139
McCaw (Craig and Susan) Foundation, USA, 418
MAG—Mines Advisory Group, UK, 366
Maison Franco-Japonaise, Japan, 191
Mama Cash Foundation, Netherlands, 230
MAPFRE Foundation, Spain, 292
March of Dimes Foundation, USA, 450
The Max Foundation, USA, 451
Max Havelaar Foundation—Fairtrade Netherlands, Netherlands, 230
Medico International, Germany, 136
Merchant Navy Fund, UK, 382
Mercury Phoenix Trust, UK, 367
Mercy, Ireland, 168
Mercy For Animals—MFA, USA, 452
Mercy Corps, USA, 452
Mercy-USA for Aid and Development, USA, 452
Mérieux Foundation, France, 109
Messi (Leo), Fundación, Spain, 292
Mines Advisory Group—MAG, UK, 366

Minhaj Welfare Foundation, UK, 368
Mith Samlanh, Cambodia, 46
Mohammed bin Rashid Al Maktoum Global Initiatives—MBRGI, United Arab Emirates, 335
Mongolian Women's Fund—MONES, Mongolia, 218
Moriya Scholarship Foundation, Japan, 191
Morningside Foundation, USA, 454
Mother Child Education Foundation, Türkiye, 327
Muslim Aid, UK, 369
Mutual Aid and Liaison Service, France, 116
Myanmar Book Aid and Preservation Foundation—MBAPF, Myanmar, 221
Myanmar/Burma Schools Project Foundation, Canada, 60
Myer Foundation, Australia, 18
Myer (Sidney) Fund, Australia, 18
Naito Foundation, Japan, 191
National Council of Social Development—NCSD, Philippines, 250
National Trust of Fiji—NTF, Fiji, 94
The Nature Conservancy—TNC, USA, 456
NDI—National Democratic Institute for International Affairs, USA, 456
Nederlandse Organisatie voor Internationale Ontwikkelingssamenwerking—Stichting NOVIB, Netherlands, 228
Neighbour in Need, Austria, 22
Network of Foundations Working for Development—netFWD, France, 99
New Myanmar Foundation, Myanmar, 221
NFCR—National Foundation for Cancer Research, USA, 457
Nihon Kokusai Mondai Kenkyusho, Japan, 190
Ningxia Yanbao Charity Foundation, China (People's Republic), 69
Nordic International Support Foundation—NIS, Norway, 242
North-South-Bridge Foundation, Germany, 141
Nott (David) Foundation, UK, 350
Novartis Foundation, Switzerland, 314
NOVIB (Oxfam Netherlands), Netherlands, 228
NPI Foundation, China (People's Republic), 66
OeAD, Austria, 22
OISCA International—Organization for Industrial, Spiritual and Cultural Advancement-International, Japan, 192
Ökumenikus Segélyszervezet, Hungary, 153
One Foundation, China (People's Republic), 69
Open Society European Policy Institute—OSEPI, Belgium, 33
Open Society Forum (Mongolia), Mongolia, 218
Operation USA, USA, 459
Opportunity International UK, UK, 372
Orangutan Foundation, UK, 372
Orbis Charitable Trust, UK, 372
Orient Foundation, Portugal, 260
Osaka Community Foundation, Japan, 192
Our Foundation, Indonesia, 162
Outreach International, USA, 459
Oxfam Aotearoa, New Zealand, 234
Oxfam Australia, Australia, 16
Oxfam Canada, Canada, 60
Oxfam Deutschland eV, Germany, 138
Oxfam Hong Kong, Hong Kong, 151
Oxfam Italia, Italy, 183
Oxfam NOVIB—Nederlandse Organisatie voor Internationale Ontwikkelingssamenwerking, Netherlands, 228
Oxfam NOVIB—Netherlands Organization for International Development Co-operation, Netherlands, 228
Pact, USA, 460
PANAP—Pesticide Action Network Asia and the Pacific, Malaysia, 211
Partage, France, 116
Partners for Equity, Australia, 16
PATH, USA, 461
Pathfinder International, USA, 461
Paulo Foundation, Finland, 97
Paulon Säätiö, Finland, 97
Peace Direct, UK, 373
Peace, Health and Human Development Foundation—PHD Foundation, Japan, 193
Peace Village International, Germany, 129
Peace Winds Japan—PWJ, Japan, 192
Pearl S. Buck International, USA, 462
People in Need, Czech Republic, 79
Pertubuhan Pertolongan Wanita, Malaysia, 212
Pestalozzi Children's Foundation, Switzerland, 317
Pesticide Action Network Asia and the Pacific—PANAP, Malaysia, 211
PH International, USA, 463

The PHD Foundation—Peace, Health and Human Development Foundation, Japan, 193
Philippine-American Educational Foundation—PAEF, Philippines, 253
Philippine Business for Social Progress—PBSP, Philippines, 250
Philippine Council for NGO Certification, Philippines, 250
Plan International Ireland, Ireland, 167
Platform for Development Cooperation and Humanitarian Aid, Slovenia, 276
Ploughshares Fund, USA, 463
Population Council, USA, 463
Première Urgence Internationale, France, 116
Prince Claus Fund for Culture and Development, Netherlands, 228
Prins Claus Fonds Voor Cultuur en Ontwikkeling, Netherlands, 228
Pro Victimis, Switzerland, 315
Project Harmony, USA, 463
Project HOPE, USA, 464
Project Trust, UK, 374
Prudence Foundation, Hong Kong, 151
Quỹ Thiện Tâm, Viet Nam, 488
Radiation Effects Research Foundation—RERF, Japan, 193
Rainforest Foundation Norway, Norway, 243
Ramon Magsaysay Award Foundation, Philippines, 253
Razumkov Centre, Ukraine, 333
Red Feather, Japan, 185
Rede ba Rai, Timor-Leste, 325
RedR UK, UK, 375
Refugee Empowerment International—REI, Japan, 193
Regnskogfondet, Norway, 243
REI—Refugee Empowerment International, Japan, 193
Relief International, USA, 466
Renault Foundation, France, 106
Robert Bosch Foundation, Germany, 138
Robert-Bosch-Stiftung GmbH, Germany, 138
Rockefeller Brothers Fund—RBF, USA, 468
Rohm Music Foundation, Japan, 193
Romanian Cultural Institute, Romania, 264
Rosa Luxemburg Foundation, Germany, 139
Rosa-Luxemburg-Stiftung, Germany, 139
Royal Society for the Protection of Birds—RSPB, UK, 379
RSPB—Royal Society for the Protection of Birds, UK, 379
The Rufford Foundation, UK, 380
Rural Development Institute—Landesa, USA, 447
Rutgers, Netherlands, 228
Sahabdeen (A. M. M.) Trust Foundation, Sri Lanka, 297
Samsung Foundation, Korea (Republic), 202
Samuel (Hedwig und Robert) Stiftung, Germany, 131
Sanaburi Foundation, Japan, 193
Sasakawa, Fondation Franco-Japonaise, France, 106
Sasakawa Health Foundation—SHF, Japan, 194
SBS Cultural Foundation, Korea (Republic), 202
Schneider Electric Foundation, France, 111
Scottish Catholic International Aid Fund—SCIAF, UK, 382
The Seafarers' Charity, UK, 382
Seafarers International Relief Fund, UK, 382
SeedChange, Canada, 61
SEL—Service d'Entraide et de Liaison, France, 116
SELAVIP—Services Latino-Américains, Africains et Asiatiques de Promotion de l'Habitation Populaire, Chile, 66
Self-Sufficient People Foundation, Indonesia, 163
Sentrong Pangkultura ng Pilipinas, Philippines, 252
Seoam Yoon Se Young Foundation, Korea (Republic), 202
Serrv International, Inc, USA, 471
Seub Nakhasathien Foundation, Thailand, 324
Seva Foundation, USA, 471
Sexual Wellbeing Aotearoa, New Zealand, 235
Shahid Afridi Foundation—SAF, Pakistan, 246
Shanghai Soong Ching Ling Foundation, China (People's Republic), 69
Siam Society, Thailand, 324
Siamese Heritage Trust, Thailand, 324
Sidney Myer Fund & The Myer Foundation, Australia, 18
Singapore International Foundation—SIF, Singapore, 273
Sino-British Fellowship Trust—SBFT, UK, 383
SLOGA—Platforma za Razvojno Sodelovanje in Humanitarno Pomoč, Slovenia, 276
Snow Leopard Trust, USA, 472

Eastern Europe and the Republics of Central Asia

SNV, Netherlands, 228
SOHO China Foundation, China (People's Republic), 69
Sparkassenstiftung für internationale Kooperation, Germany, 125
State Grid Foundation for Public Welfare, China (People's Republic), 69
Steelworkers Humanity Fund/Le Fonds Humanitaire des Metallos, Canada, 62
Stichting DOEN, Netherlands, 229
Stichting IKEA Foundation, Netherlands, 229
Stichting Liliane Fonds, Netherlands, 229
Stichting Mama Cash, Netherlands, 230
Stichting Max Havelaar—Fairtrade Nederland, Netherlands, 230
Stiftung Kinderdorf Pestalozzi, Switzerland, 317
Stiftung Klimarappen, Switzerland, 317
Stiftung Nord-Süd-Brücken, Germany, 141
Straits Exchange Foundation—SEF, Taiwan, 321
Strømme Foundation, Norway, 243
Strømmestiftelsen, Norway, 243
Sweden-Japan Foundation—SJF, Sweden, 304
Swiss Church Aid, Switzerland, 311
Swiss Foundation for Technical Co-operation, Switzerland, 318
SWISSAID Foundation, Switzerland, 318
Swisscontact—Swiss Foundation for Technical Co-operation, Switzerland, 318
Syin-Lu Social Welfare Foundation, Taiwan, 321
Synergos—The Synergos Institute, USA, 396
Tahir Foundation, Indonesia, 162
Taiwan NPO Information Platform, Taiwan, 321
Tang Prize Foundation, Taiwan, 322
TANZ—Trade Aid NZ Inc, New Zealand, 235
Tearfund, UK, 385
Tearfund Australia, Australia, 18
Temasek Foundation, Singapore, 273
Tencent Foundation, China (People's Republic), 70
Terre des Hommes International Federation—TDHIF, Switzerland, 318
TFF—Transnational Foundation for Peace and Future Research, Sweden, 304
TFF—Transnationella Stiftelsen för Freds- och Framtidsforskning, Sweden, 304
Thai Rath Foundation, Thailand, 324
THET, UK, 355
Third World Network—TWN, Malaysia, 211
Third World Solidarity Action, Luxembourg, 209
Thomson Foundation, UK, 385
Tibet Fund, USA, 475
Tifa Foundation—Indonesia, Indonesia, 163
Timchenko (Elena & Gennady) Foundation, Russian Federation, 265
Tinh Thuong One Member Limited Liability Microfinance Institution, Viet Nam, 488
TISCO Foundation, Thailand, 325
Tokyu Foundation, Japan, 194
Totto Foundation, Japan, 194
The Toyota Foundation, Japan, 195
Toyota Vietnam Foundation—TVF, Viet Nam, 488
Trade Aid NZ Inc—TANZ, New Zealand, 235
Trócaire—Catholic Agency for World Development, Ireland, 168
TTF—Toyota Thailand Foundation, Thailand, 325
Turquoise Mountain Foundation, UK, 386
TYM Fund, Viet Nam, 488
U4 Anti-Corruption Resource Centre, Norway, 241
Union Aid Abroad—APHEDA, Australia, 19
United Purpose, UK, 387
United States-Japan Foundation, USA, 477
Unity Foundation, Luxembourg, 210
US Civilian Research & Development Foundation, USA, 419
USPG—United Society Partners in the Gospel, UK, 387
VIDC—Vienna Institute for International Dialogue and Co-operation, Austria, 23
Vienna Institute for International Dialogue and Co-operation—VIDC, Austria, 23
Village Community Development Foundation, Indonesia, 163
Villar Foundation, Inc, Philippines, 253
Vivekananda International Foundation—VIF, India, 161
Vodafone ATH Fiji Foundation, Fiji, 94
Voluntary Service Overseas, UK, 388
VSO—Voluntary Service Overseas, UK, 388
Wahana Lingkungan Hidup Indonesia—WALHI, Indonesia, 162
WALHI—Wahana Lingkungan Hidup Indonesia, Indonesia, 162
Wallace (Charles) Trusts, UK, 347
Walton Family Foundation, USA, 479
War on Want, UK, 388
Water for Good, USA, 479
Water.org, Inc, USA, 479
WaterAid, UK, 389
Westminster Foundation for Democracy—WFD, UK, 389
The Whitley Fund for Nature—WFN, UK, 390
William Adlington Cadbury Charitable Trust, UK, 390
Winrock International, USA, 481
The Wolfson Foundation, UK, 390
Women's Aid Organisation—WAO, Malaysia, 212
Women's Fund Asia, Sri Lanka, 297
World Animal Protection, UK, 391
World Association of Children's Friends, Monaco, 217
World Neighbors, USA, 483
World University Service of Canada/Entraide Universitaire Mondiale du Canada—WUSC/EUMC, Canada, 63
World Vegetable Center, Taiwan, 322
World Vision International, UK, 391
WorldFish, Malaysia, 212
Xiangjiang Social Relief Fund, China (People's Republic), 68
YADESA—Yayasan Pembinaan Masyarakat Desa, Indonesia, 163
Yanai Tadashi Foundation, Japan, 195
Yanbao Charity Foundation, China (People's Republic), 69
Yayasan Azman Hashim, Malaysia, 212
Yayasan Dian Desa—YDD, Indonesia, 162
Yayasan Geutanyoë, Indonesia, 162
Yayasan Insan Sembada, Indonesia, 163
Yayasan Pembinaan Masyarakat Desa—YADESA, Indonesia, 163
Yayasan Tifa, Indonesia, 163
Year Out Group, UK, 374
YongLin Charity Foundation, Taiwan, 322
Yuan Lin Charity Fund, China (People's Republic), 70
Zakat House, Kuwait, 203
ZOA, Netherlands, 231
Zorig Foundation, Mongolia, 219

EASTERN EUROPE AND THE REPUBLICS OF CENTRAL ASIA

The A. G. Leventis Foundation, Cyprus, 77
Abilis Foundation, Finland, 95
Abilis-säätiö, Finland, 95
Abjadnany Sliach, Belarus, 25
Academy of European Law, Germany, 127
Action Against Hunger, France, 100
Action contre la Faim—ACF France, France, 100
Active for People in Need Austria, Austria, 20
Adriano Olivetti Foundation, Italy, 174
Afghanistan Research and Evaluation Unit, Afghanistan, 3
Africa Grantmakers' Affinity Group—AGAG, USA, 393
AGAG—Africa Grantmakers' Affinity Group, USA, 393
Age International, UK, 339
Agronomes et Vétérinaires sans Frontières—AVSF, France, 100
Agronomists and Veterinarians Without Borders, France, 100
Air France Foundation, France, 103
Alert—International Alert, UK, 360
Alliance for Securing Democracy, USA, 430
Allianz Foundation, Germany, 121
American Councils for International Education, USA, 400
AmeriCares Foundation, Inc, USA, 403
AMINA—aktiv für Menschen in Not Austria, Austria, 20
Anti-Corruption Foundation, Russian Federation, 265
Arbeiterwohlfahrt Bundesverband eV—AWO, Germany, 121
Arengukoostöö Ümarlaud—AKÜ, Estonia, 92
Armanshahr Foundation—OPEN ASIA, Afghanistan, 3
Arthur Rubinstein International Music Society, Israel, 168
Aspen Institute, USA, 407
Association of Civil Society Development Center, Türkiye, 327
Atlas Charity Foundation, Poland, 255
Auchan Foundation, France, 103
Auschwitz Foundation—Remembrance of Auschwitz, Belgium, 30
Avatud Eesti Fond, Estonia, 92
AVSI Foundation, Italy, 175
Bagnoud (François-Xavier) Association, Switzerland, 307
Balti Uuringute Instituut, Estonia, 92
Baltic Sea Foundation, Finland, 97
Barcelona Centre for International Affairs, Spain, 287

INDEX BY AREA OF ACTIVITY

BBC Media Action, UK, 342
Berghof Foundation gGmbH, Germany, 122
Berghof Stiftung für Konfliktforschung gGmbH, Germany, 122
Bertelsmann Foundation, Germany, 122
Bertelsmann Stiftung, Germany, 122
Black Sea NGO Network—BSNN, Bulgaria, 42
Black Sea Trust for Regional Cooperation, USA, 430
Black Sea University Foundation—BSUF, Romania, 263
Blue Marine Foundation—BLUE, UK, 343
BNP Paribas Foundation, France, 103
Böll (Heinrich) Stiftung, Germany, 131
Borderland Foundation, Poland, 256
Bosch (Robert) Stiftung GmbH, Germany, 138
Bread for the World—Protestant Work for Social Welfare and Development, Germany, 123
Brot für die Welt—Evangelisches Werk für Diakonie und Entwicklung, Germany, 123
Cadbury (William Adlington) Charitable Trust, UK, 390
CAF—Charities Aid Foundation, UK, 336
CAF Russia—Charities Aid Foundation Russia, Russian Federation, 264
Canadian Foodgrains Bank, Canada, 50
Candid, USA, 393
Canon Foundation in Europe, Netherlands, 224
CARE International—CI, Switzerland, 307
Carnegie Endowment for International Peace, USA, 411
Carpathian Foundation, Hungary, 153
CASE—Centrum Analiz Społeczno-Ekonomicznych, Poland, 255
Catalyste+, Canada, 51
Catholic Agency for World Development—Trócaire, Ireland, 168
Caucasus Institute for Peace, Democracy and Development—CIPDD, Georgia, 117
Caucasus Research Resource Center Armenia Foundation—CRRC, Armenia, 9
Center for Economic & Social Development—CESD, Azerbaijan, 23
Center for Social and Economic Research, Poland, 255
Center for Training and Consultancy, Georgia, 117
Centre pour le Dialogue Humanitaire, Switzerland, 307
Centre for Euro-Atlantic Integration and Democracy—CEID, Hungary, 153
Centre for Humanitarian Dialogue—HD, Switzerland, 307
Centrul Naţional de Asistenţă şi Informare a Organizaţiilor Neguvernamentale din Moldova—Centrul CONTACT, Moldova, 216
Centrul de Resurse pentru Drepturile Omului—CReDO, Moldova, 217
CESO/SACO—Canadian Executive Service Organization/Service d'Assistance Canadienne aux Organismes, Canada, 51
Charities Aid Foundation—CAF, UK, 336
Charities Aid Foundation Russia—CAF Russia, Russian Federation, 264
Charity Projects, UK, 348
Charles and Lynn Schusterman Family Philanthropies, USA, 413
Charles Stewart Mott Foundation—CSMF, USA, 414
ChildFund International, USA, 414
Churches' Commission for Migrants in Europe, Belgium, 28
CIDOB Foundation—Barcelona Centre for International Affairs, Spain, 287
Civil Society Development Center—CSDC, Georgia, 117
Civil Society Foundation, Georgia, 118
Claiborne (Liz) & Art Ortenberg Foundation, USA, 448
Člověk v tísni, Czech Republic, 79
Comic Relief, UK, 348
Commission des Eglises auprès des Migrants en Europe/Kommission der Kirchen für Migranten in Europa, Belgium, 28
Community Foundation Partnership, Russian Federation, 264
CONCORD—European NGO Confederation for Relief and Development, Belgium, 26
Co-operative Development Foundation of Canada—CDF, Canada, 52
Costopoulos (J. F.) Foundation, Greece, 146
CRDF Global, USA, 419
CReDO—Centrul de Resurse pentru Drepturile Omului, Moldova, 217
Czech Donors Forum, Czech Republic, 78
Danish Cultural Institute—DCI, Denmark, 82
Danish Institute for Human Rights, Denmark, 84
Danske Kulturinstitut—DKI, Denmark, 82

INDEX BY AREA OF ACTIVITY

Eastern Europe and the Republics of Central Asia

DemNet—Demokratikus Jogok Fejlesztéséért Alapítvány, Hungary, 153
DemNet—Foundation for the Development of Democratic Rights, Hungary, 153
Deripaska (Oleg) Foundation, Russian Federation, 267
Deutsch-Russischer Austausch eV—DRA, Germany, 124
Deutsche AIDS-Stiftung, Germany, 124
Deutsche Gesellschaft für Auswärtige Politik—DGAP, Germany, 124
Deutsche Sparkassenstiftung für Internationale Zusammenarbeit, Germany, 125
Development Cooperation Roundtable, Estonia, 92
The Dr Denis Mukwege Foundation, Netherlands, 224
Dräger Foundation, Germany, 126
Dräger-Stiftung, Germany, 126
East-West Center—EWC, USA, 422
East-West Encounters Charitable Foundation, Germany, 141
Eastern Europe Studies Centre—EESC, Lithuania, 209
Ebelin and Gerd Bucerius ZEIT Foundation, Germany, 143
Eberhard Schöck Foundation, Germany, 127
Eberhard-Schöck-Stiftung, Germany, 127
Economic Development Foundation, Türkiye, 328
Ednannia—Initiative Centre to Support Social Action, Ukraine, 332
EEB—European Environmental Bureau, Belgium, 30
Eesti Mittetulundusühingute ja Sihtasutuste Liit, Estonia, 92
Eestimaa Looduse Fond—ELF, Estonia, 92
Effekteam Association, Hungary, 152
Elena & Gennady Timchenko Foundation, Russian Federation, 265
ELIAMEP—Hellenic Foundation for European and Foreign Policy, Greece, 146
Elizabeth Glaser Pediatric AIDS Foundation—EGPAF, USA, 423
Elizabeth Kostova Foundation for Creative Writing, Bulgaria, 43
Elton John AIDS Foundation, UK, 352
Environment Foundation of Turkey, Türkiye, 330
ERA—Europäische Rechtsakademie, Germany, 127
Estonian Foreign Policy Institute, Estonia, 93
Estonian Fund for Nature, Estonia, 92
Estonian National Culture Foundation, Estonia, 93
Eurasia Foundation—EF, USA, 424
Eurasia Partnership Foundation-Armenia—EPF-Armenia, Armenia, 9
Europa Nostra, Netherlands, 224
Europäische Rechtsakademie—ERA, Germany, 127
Europe Foundation—EPF, Georgia, 118
European Anti-Poverty Network—EAPN, Belgium, 29
European Center for Peace and Development—ECPD, Serbia, 271
European Centre for Social Welfare Policy and Research, Austria, 14
European Community Foundation Initiative—ECFI, Germany, 119
European Cultural Foundation—ECF, Netherlands, 225
European Environmental Bureau—EEB, Belgium, 30
European Federation of National Organisations Working with the Homeless, Belgium, 26
European Foundation for Philanthropy and Society Development, Croatia, 76
European Foundation for the Sustainable Development of the Regions, Switzerland, 308
European NGO Confederation for Relief and Development—CONCORD, Belgium, 26
European Roma Rights Centre—ERRC, Belgium, 30
European Youth For Action—EYFA, Germany, 128
European Youth Foundation—EYF, France, 112
Europese Culturele Stichting, Netherlands, 225
Europska Zaklada za Filantropiju i Društveni Dazvoj, Croatia, 76
Evangelisches Studienwerk eV, Germany, 128
EVPA—European Venture Philanthropy Association, Belgium, 27
Evropis Pondis, Georgia, 118
EYFA—European Youth For Action, Germany, 128
F. C. Flick Foundation against Xenophobia, Racism and Intolerance, Germany, 128
F. C. Flick-Stiftung gegen Fremdenfeindlichkeit, Rassismus und Intoleranz, Germany, 128

Fairtrade Nederland, Netherlands, 230
The Family Federation of Finland, Finland, 98
FEANTSA—Fédération Européenne des Associations Nationales Travaillant avec les Sans-Abri, Belgium, 26
Federal Association of Social Welfare Organizations, Germany, 121
Fédération Européenne des Associations Nationales Travaillant avec les Sans-Abri—FEANTSA, Belgium, 26
FEDRE—European Foundation for the Sustainable Development of the Regions, Switzerland, 308
filia.die Frauenstiftung, Germany, 128
filia—the Women's Foundation, Germany, 128
FINCA International, USA, 425
Flick (F. C.) Stiftung gegen Fremdenfeindlichkeit, Rassismus und Intoleranz, Germany, 128
Focus Humanitarian Assistance—FOCUS, Canada, 54
Folmer Wisti Fonden for International Forståelse, Denmark, 83
Folmer Wisti Foundation for International Understanding, Denmark, 83
Fondacija Cennosti, Bulgaria, 43
Fondation pour l'Agriculture et la Ruralité dans le Monde—Fondation FARM, France, 106
Fondation Air France, France, 103
Fondation Auchan, France, 103
Fondation Auschwitz—Mémoire d'Auschwitz, Belgium, 30
Fondation BNP Paribas, France, 103
Fondation pour l'Economie et le Développement Durable des Régions d'Europe—FEDRE, Switzerland, 308
Fondation Ensemble, France, 105
Fondation d'Entreprise Renault, France, 106
Fondation Européenne de la Culture/Europese Culturele Stichting, Netherlands, 225
Fondation FARM—Fondation pour l'Agriculture et la Ruralité dans le Monde, France, 106
Fondation Hirondelle: Media for Peace and Human Dignity, Switzerland, 309
Fondation Marcel Hicter, Belgium, 32
Fondation Orange, France, 110
Fondation Robert Schuman, France, 111
Fondation Schneider Electric, France, 111
Fondation Suisse-Liechtenstein pour les Recherches Archéologiques à l'Etranger, Switzerland, 316
Fondazione Adriano Olivetti, Italy, 174
Fondazione AVSI, Italy, 175
Fondazione Prada, Italy, 179
Fonds atvērtai sabiedrībai DOTS, Latvia, 204
Fonds Européen pour la Jeunesse—FEJ, France, 112
For a Healthy Generation, Uzbekistan, 485
Fórum Dárců, Czech Republic, 78
Forum Darczyńców, Poland, 254
Forum ZaDobro.BIT!, Croatia, 76
Fös Feminista, USA, 427
Foundation for Analysis and Social Studies, Spain, 288
Foundation Center, USA, 393
Foundation for International Community Assistance, USA, 425
Foundation for an Open Society DOTS, Latvia, 204
Foundation 'Remembrance, Responsibility and Future', Germany, 139
Foundation in Support of Local Democracy, Poland, 256
Foundation for World Agriculture and Rural Life, France, 106
Foundation of Youth and Lifelong Learning—INEDIVIM, Greece, 145
Fraunhofer-Gesellschaft, Germany, 129
Fraunhofer Society, Germany, 129
FREE Network—Forum for Research on Eastern Europe and Emerging Economies, Sweden, 299
Free Russia Foundation, USA, 428
Freedom Speech Foundation, Norway, 241
French Institute of International Relations, France, 113
Friedensdorf International, Germany, 129
Fundació CIDOB, Spain, 287
Fundación para el Análisis y los Estudios Sociales—FAES, Spain, 288
Fundación IE, Spain, 291
Fundación Paideia Galiza, Spain, 293
Fundacja Dobroczynności Atlas, Poland, 255
Fundacja im. Stefana Batorego, Poland, 256
Fundacja Orange, Poland, 255
Fundacja Pogranicze, Poland, 256
Fundacja Rozwoju Demokracji Loaklnej, Poland, 256
Fundația Orange Moldova, Moldova, 217

Fundația Universitară a Mării Negre—FUMN, Romania, 263
Future in Our Hands Youth NGO—FIOH, Armenia, 9
FXB International—Association François-Xavier Bagnoud, Switzerland, 310
Gebert Rüf Stiftung, Switzerland, 311
Georgian Foundation for Strategic and International Studies (Rondeli Foundation)—GFSIS, Georgia, 118
German AIDS Foundation, Germany, 124
German Council on Foreign Relations, Germany, 124
German Foundation for International Legal Co-operation, Germany, 133
German Marshall Fund of the United States—GMF, USA, 430
German-Russian Exchange, Germany, 124
German Savings Banks Foundation for International Co-operation, Germany, 125
Glaser (Elizabeth) Pediatric AIDS Foundation, USA, 423
Glasnost Defence Foundation, Russian Federation, 265
Global Communities, USA, 431
Goldman Sachs Foundation, USA, 432
GuideStar, USA, 393
GURT Resource Centre for NGO Development, Ukraine, 332
Hagar NZ, New Zealand, 233
HALO Trust, UK, 357
HAND—Hungarian Association of NGOs for Development and Humanitarian Aid, Hungary, 152
Havelaar (Max) Foundation, Netherlands, 230
Headley Trust, UK, 357
Heinrich Böll Foundation, Germany, 131
Heinrich-Böll-Stiftung, Germany, 131
Hellenic Foundation for Culture, Greece, 145
Hellenic Foundation for European and Foreign Policy—ELIAMEP, Greece, 146
Helvetas Swiss Intercooperation, Switzerland, 311
Heydar Aliyev Fondu, Azerbaijan, 23
Heydar Aliyev Foundation, Azerbaijan, 23
Hicter (Marcel), Fondation, Belgium, 32
Howard Karagheusian Commemorative Corporation—HKCC, USA, 437
Humanitarian Academy for Development—HAD, UK, 359
Hungarian Donors Forum, Hungary, 152
IACD—Institute of Asian Culture and Development, Korea (Republic), 201
IDRF—International Development and Relief Foundation, Canada, 56
IE Foundation, Spain, 291
IFAD—International Fund for Agricultural Development, Italy, 182
IHH Humanitarian Relief Foundation, Türkiye, 328
IIED—International Institute for Environment and Development, UK, 360
İktisadi Kalkınma Vakfı, Türkiye, 328
Impact Europe, Belgium, 27
INEDIVIM—Foundation of Youth and Lifelong Learning, Greece, 145
İnsan Hak ve Hürriyetleri İnsani Yardım Vakfı—IHH, Türkiye, 328
Institusjonen Fritt Ord, Norway, 241
Institut Français des Relations Internationales—IFRI, France, 113
Institut for Menneskerettigheder, Denmark, 84
Institute of Asian Culture and Development—IACD, Korea (Republic), 201
Institute of Baltic Studies, Estonia, 92
Institute of Developing Economies-Japan External Trade Organization—IDE-JETRO, Japan, 188
Institute for European Environmental Policy—IEEP, Belgium, 33
Institute for Iran-Eurasia Studies—IRAS, Iran, 163
Institute for Sustainable Communities—ISC, USA, 439
Instituti Kosovar për Kërkime dhe Zhvillim të Politikave, Kosovo, 203
Institutul Cultural Român—ICR, Romania, 264
Interchurch Aid—HIA Hungary, Hungary, 153
International Alert—Alert, UK, 360
International Centre for Defence and Security—ICDS, Estonia, 93
International Charitable Fund 'Concord 3000', Ukraine, 333
International Development and Relief Foundation—IDRF, Canada, 56
International Fund for Agricultural Development—IFAD, Italy, 182

Eastern Europe and the Republics of Central Asia

International Historical, Educational, Charitable and Human Rights Society—International Memorial, Russian Federation, 266
International Institute for Environment and Development—IIED, UK, 360
International Memorial, Russian Federation, 266
International Orthodox Christian Charities—IOCC, USA, 441
International Renaissance Foundation—IRF, Ukraine, 333
International Research & Exchanges Board—IREX, USA, 442
International Visegrad Fund—IVF, Slovakia, 275
International Water Management Institute—IWMI, Sri Lanka, 297
International Women's Health Coalition, USA, 427
Internationalt Uddannelsescenter, Denmark, 84
IOCC—International Orthodox Christian Charities, USA, 441
IREX—International Research & Exchanges Board, USA, 442
IRZ (Deutsche Stiftung für Internationale Rechtliche Zusammenarbeit) eV, Germany, 133
IUC International Education Center—IUC-Europe, Denmark, 84
The J. F. Costopoulos Foundation, Greece, 146
Jacobs Foundation, Switzerland, 313
Japanese-German Centre Berlin, Germany, 133
Japanisch-Deutsches Zentrum Berlin, Germany, 133
Karagheusian (Howard) Commemorative Corporation, USA, 437
Kárpátok Alapítvány, Hungary, 153
King Gustaf V's 90th Birthday Foundation, Sweden, 301
Konsultatsiis da Treningis Tsentri, Georgia, 117
Konung Gustaf V's 90-Årsfond, Sweden, 301
Körber Foundation, Germany, 134
Körber-Stiftung, Germany, 134
Kosovar Institute for Policy Research and Development—KIPRED, Kosovo, 203
Kostova (Elizabeth) Foundation for Creative Writing, Bulgaria, 43
Kvinna till Kvinna, Sweden, 301
Lambrakis Foundation, Greece, 146
Latvia Children's Fund, Latvia, 204
Latvian Institute of International Affairs—LIIA, Latvia, 204
Latvijas Ārpolitikas Institūts—LAI, Latvia, 204
Latvijas Bērnu fonds, Latvia, 204
Lauder (Ronald S.) Foundation, Germany, 138
Leventis (A. G.) Foundation, Cyprus, 77
Liz Claiborne & Art Ortenberg Foundation, USA, 448
Lumos Foundation, UK, 366
Luxemburg (Rosa) Stiftung, Germany, 139
Maj ja Tor Nessling Säätiö, Finland, 96
Maj and Tor Nessling Foundation, Finland, 96
Mama Cash Foundation, Netherlands, 230
Marangopoulos Foundation for Human Rights, Greece, 146
Marcel Hicter Foundation, Belgium, 32
The Max Foundation, USA, 451
Max Havelaar Foundation—Fairtrade Netherlands, Netherlands, 230
Media Development Foundation—MDF, Georgia, 118
Mediis Ganvitarebis Pondi, Georgia, 118
Mercy, Ireland, 168
Mercy Corps, USA, 452
Mezhdunarodnyj Memorial, Russian Federation, 266
Michael Otto Foundation for Environmental Protection, Germany, 136
Michael-Otto-Stiftung für Umweltschutz, Germany, 136
Microfinance Centre—MFC, Poland, 257
Mohammed bin Rashid Al Maktoum Global Initiatives—MBRGI, United Arab Emirates, 335
Mshvidobis, Demokratiisa, da Ganvit'arebis Kavkasiuri Instituti, Georgia, 117
Mukwege (Dr Denis) Foundation, Netherlands, 224
Nadácia Otvorenej Spoločnosti, Slovakia, 276
National Assistance and Information Centre for NGOs in Moldova—CONTACT Centre, Moldova, 216
NDI—National Democratic Institute for International Affairs, USA, 456
Near East Foundation—NEF, USA, 456
Nederlandse Organisatie voor Internationale Ontwikkelingssamenwerking—Stichting NOVIB, Netherlands, 228
NEF—Near East Foundation, USA, 456
Neighbour in Need, Austria, 22

Nessling (Maj and Tor) Foundation, Finland, 96
Network of Estonian Non-profit Organizations, Estonia, 92
Network of Foundations Working for Development—netFWD, France, 99
NGO Center—NGOC, Armenia, 9
NGO Development Centre, Russian Federation, 265
Non-Governmental Ecological Vernadsky Foundation, Russian Federation, 266
NOVIB (Oxfam Netherlands), Netherlands, 228
Nursultan Nazarbayev Educational Foundation, Kazakhstan, 197
OeAD, Austria, 22
OISCA International—Organization for Industrial, Spiritual and Cultural Advancement-International, Japan, 192
Ökumenikus Segélyszervezet, Hungary, 153
Olivetti (Adriano), Fondazione, Italy, 174
OPEN ASIA—Armanshahr Foundation, Afghanistan, 3
Open Estonia Foundation, Estonia, 92
Open Society European Policy Institute—OSEPI, Belgium, 33
Open Society Foundation—Bratislava, Slovakia, 276
Open Society Foundations—Armenia, Armenia, 9
Operation USA, USA, 459
Opportunity International UK, UK, 372
Orange Foundation, Poland, 255
Orange Moldova Foundation, Moldova, 217
ORF Nachbar in Not, Austria, 22
Östersjöfonden, Finland, 97
Otto (Michael) Stiftung, Germany, 136
Our Future—Foundation for Regional Social Programmes, Russian Federation, 266
Oxfam Deutschland eV, Germany, 138
Oxfam NOVIB—Nederlandse Organisatie voor Internationale Ontwikkelingssamenwerking, Netherlands, 228
Oxfam NOVIB—Netherlands Organization for International Development Co-operation, Netherlands, 228
Paavo Nurmen Säätiö, Finland, 97
Paavo Nurmi Foundation, Finland, 97
Pact, USA, 460
Paideia Galiza Foundation, Spain, 293
PAN Europe—Pesticide Action Network Europe, Belgium, 34
Pan-European Federation for Cultural Heritage, Netherlands, 224
Partners in Health, USA, 461
PCI—Project Concern International, USA, 431
Peace Direct, UK, 373
Peace Village International, Germany, 129
People in Need, Czech Republic, 79
Pesticide Action Network Europe—PAN Europe, Belgium, 34
PH International, USA, 463
Philanthropy Europe Association—Philea, Belgium, 27
Philea—Philanthropy Europe Association, Belgium, 27
Ploughshares Fund, USA, 463
Polish-American Freedom Foundation, Poland, 257
Polish Donors Forum, Poland, 254
Polsko-Amerykańska Fundacja Wolności, Poland, 257
Potanin (Vladimir) Foundation, Russian Federation, 267
Prada Foundation, Italy, 179
Praxis Centre for Policy Studies Foundation, Estonia, 93
Première Urgence Internationale, France, 116
Prince Claus Fund for Culture and Development, Netherlands, 228
Prins Claus Fonds Voor Cultuur en Ontwikkeling, Netherlands, 228
Project Harmony, USA, 463
Project HOPE, USA, 464
Protestant Study Foundation, Germany, 128
Rahvusvaheline Kaitseuuringute Keskus—RKK, Estonia, 93
Rausing (Ruben and Elisabeth) Trust, UK, 383
Razumkov Centre, Ukraine, 333
RED—Ruralité-Environnement-Développement, Belgium, Belgium, 34
Regional Environmental Center, Hungary, 153
Relief International, USA, 466
Renault Foundation, France, 106
Réseau Européen des Associations de Lutte contre la Pauvreté et l'Exclusion Sociale, Belgium, 27
Resource Centre for the Human Rights Nongovernmental Organizations of Moldova—CReDO, Moldova, 217

INDEX BY AREA OF ACTIVITY

Robert Bosch Foundation, Germany, 138
Robert-Bosch-Stiftung GmbH, Germany, 138
Robert Schuman Foundation, France, 111
Romanian Cultural Institute, Romania, 264
The Ronald S. Lauder Foundation, Germany, 138
Rosa Luxemburg Foundation, Germany, 139
Rosa-Luxemburg-Stiftung, Germany, 139
Rroma Foundation, Switzerland, 315
Romani Fundacija, Switzerland, 315
Rubinstein (Arthur) International Music Society, Israel, 168
Rüf (Gebert) Stiftung, Switzerland, 311
The Rufford Foundation, UK, 380
Ruralité-Environnement-Développement—RED, Belgium, 34
Rurality Environment Development, Belgium, 34
Russian Donors Forum, Russian Federation, 265
Russian LGBT Network, Russian Federation, 267
Rytų Europos Studijų Centras—RESC, Lithuania, 209
Saadi Foundation, Iran, 164
Sakartvelos Strategiisa da Saertashoriso Urtiertobebis Kvlevis Pondi—Rondelis Pondi, Georgia, 118
Santé Sud, France, 116
Schneider Electric Foundation, France, 111
Schöck (Eberhard) Stiftung, Germany, 127
Schuman (Robert), Fondation, France, 111
Schusterman (Charles and Lynn) Family Foundation, USA, 413
Schwarzkopf-Stiftung Junges Europa, Germany, 139
Schwarzkopf Young Europe Foundation, Germany, 139
Schweisfurth Foundation, Germany, 139
Schweisfurth-Stiftung, Germany, 139
Schweizerisch-Liechtensteinische Stiftung für Archäologische Forschungen im Ausland—SLSA, Switzerland, 316
SEEMO—South East Europe Media Organisation, Austria, 23
Seva Foundation, USA, 471
Sigrid Rausing Trust—SRT, UK, 383
Sihtasutus Eesti Rahvuskultuuri Fond, Estonia, 93
Sihtasutus Poliitikauuringute Keskus Praxis, Estonia, 93
Sistema Charitable Foundation, Russian Federation, 267
Sivil Toplum Gelistirme Merkezi—STGM, Türkiye, 327
Skolkovo Foundation—Foundation for Development of the Center for the Development and Commercialization of New Technologies, Russian Federation, 267
Slovak Security Policy Institute, Slovakia, 276
Slovenský inštitút pre bezpečnostnú politiku, Slovakia, 276
Snow Leopard Trust, USA, 472
The Sobell Foundation, UK, 384
Software AG Foundation, Germany, 139
Software AG Stiftung, Germany, 139
Sog'lom Avlod Uchun, Uzbekistan, 485
Soros Foundation—Kazakhstan, Kazakhstan, 197
South East Europe Media Organisation—SEEMO, Austria, 23
Southern Health, France, 116
Sparkassenstiftung für internationale Kooperation, Germany, 125
Stefan Batory Foundation, Poland, 256
Stichting Mama Cash, Netherlands, 230
Stichting Max Havelaar—Fairtrade Nederland, Netherlands, 230
Stiftung 'Erinnerung, Verantwortung und Zukunft'—EVZ, Germany, 139
Stiftung West-Östliche Begegnungen, Germany, 141
Südosteuropäische Medienorganisation, Austria, 23
Swedish Institute at Athens, Greece, 147
Swiss Foundation for Technical Co-operation, Switzerland, 318
Swiss-Liechtenstein Foundation for Archaeological Research Abroad—SLFA, Switzerland, 316
Swisscontact—Swiss Foundation for Technical Co-operation, Switzerland, 318
Tearfund, UK, 385
Terre des Hommes International Federation—TDHIF, Switzerland, 318
TFF–Transnational Foundation for Peace and Future Research, Sweden, 304
TFF–Transnationella Stiftelsen för Freds- och Framtidsforskning, Sweden, 304
Timchenko (Elena & Gennady) Foundation, Russian Federation, 265
TK Foundation, Bahamas, 24

INDEX BY AREA OF ACTIVITY

Trócaire—Catholic Agency for World Development, Ireland, 168
Trust for Mutual Understanding—TMU, USA, 476
Trust for Social Achievement, Bulgaria, 44
Türkiye Çevre Vakfı, Türkiye, 330
Ucom Foundation, Armenia, 9
Ukrainian Philanthropists Forum, Ukraine, 332
Ukrainian Women's Fund, Ukraine, 333
Uluchay Social-Economic Innovation Center, Azerbaijan, 23
UniCredit Foundation, Italy, 183
United Way—Belarus/NGO Development Centre, Belarus, 25
US Civilian Research & Development Foundation, USA, 419
Väestöliitto, Finland, 98
Values Foundation, Bulgaria, 43
Victoria Children Foundation, Russian Federation, 267
VIDC—Vienna Institute for International Dialogue and Co-operation, Austria, 23
Vienna Institute for International Dialogue and Co-operation—VIDC, Austria, 23
Vladimir Potanin Foundation, Russian Federation, 267
Volnoe Delo—Oleg Deripaska Foundation, Russian Federation, 267
Westminster Foundation for Democracy—WFD, UK, 389
The Whitley Fund for Nature—WFN, UK, 390
William Adlington Cadbury Charitable Trust, UK, 390
Winrock International, USA, 481
Wisti (Folmer) Foundation for International Understanding, Denmark, 83
Woman to Woman Foundation, Sweden, 301
World Jewish Relief, UK, 391
World Vegetable Center, Taiwan, 322
ZEIT-Stiftung Ebelin und Gerd Bucerius, Germany, 143

MIDDLE EAST AND NORTH AFRICA

The A. G. Leventis Foundation, Cyprus, 77
A. M. Qattan Foundation, UK, 338
AARDO—African-Asian Rural Development Organization, India, 155
Abdorrahman Boroumand Center for Human Rights in Iran—ABC, USA, 396
Abdul Hameed Shoman Foundation—AHSF, Jordan, 195
Accion, USA, 397
Action Against Hunger, France, 100
Action contre la Faim—ACF France, France, 100
Action Solidarité Tiers Monde—ASTM, Luxembourg, 209
Addoha Foundation, Morocco, 219
Adyan Foundation, Lebanon, 205
Africa Grantmakers' Affinity Group—AGAG, USA, 393
Africa Humanitarian Action—AHA, Ethiopia, 93
Africa Institute of South Africa—AISA, South Africa, 279
African-Asian Rural Development Organization—AARDO, India, 155
African Forum and Network on Debt and Development—AFRODAD, Zimbabwe, 490
African Philanthropy Forum, Nigeria, 236
African Refugees Foundation—AREF, Nigeria, 237
African Venture Philanthropy Alliance—AVPA, Kenya, 197
Afrobarometer, Ghana, 143
AFRODAD—African Forum and Network on Debt and Development, Zimbabwe, 490
Aga Khan Foundation Canada, Canada, 49
AGAG—Africa Grantmakers' Affinity Group, USA, 393
Age International, UK, 339
Aid for Development Club, Austria, 20
Air France Foundation, France, 103
AISA—Africa Institute of South Africa, South Africa, 279
Al Basar International Foundation, Saudi Arabia, 268
The Al-Khoei Benevolent Foundation, UK, 339
Al-Mortaqa Foundation for Human Development, Iraq, 164
Alert—International Alert, UK, 360
Alet'Eleym Fewq Alejmey'e, Qatar, 262
Alkhidmat Foundation Pakistan—AKFP, Pakistan, 244
Alliance for Securing Democracy, USA, 430
Allianz Foundation, Germany, 121
America—Mideast Educational and Training Services Inc, USA, 404
American Councils for International Education, USA, 400
American Friends Service Committee—AFSC, USA, 401
American Near East Refugee Aid—Anera, USA, 402
American Schools of Oriental Research—ASOR, USA, 403
AmeriCares Foundation, Inc, USA, 403
AMIDEAST—America-Mideast Educational and Training Services, Inc, USA, 404
Anera—American Near East Refugee Aid, USA, 402
Ankara İngiliz Arkeoloji Enstitüsü, UK, 345
Anna Lindh Euro-Mediterranean Foundation for Dialogue between Cultures, Egypt, 90
ANND—Arab NGO Network for Development, Lebanon, 205
Anne Çocuk Eğitim Vakfı—AÇEV, Türkiye, 327
Anne Frank-Fonds, Switzerland, 306
Anne Frank Fund, Switzerland, 306
APHEDA—Union Aid Abroad, Australia, 19
Arab American Institute Foundation—AAIF, USA, 405
Arab Foundations Forum, Jordan, 195
Arab Image Foundation—AIF, Lebanon, 205
Arab Network for Civic Education, Jordan, 195
Arab Network for Environment and Development—RAED, Egypt, 89
Arab Office for Youth and Environment, Egypt, 89
Arab Organization for Human Rights, Egypt, 90
Arab Thought Foundation—ATF, Lebanon, 205
Archie Sherman Charitable Trust, UK, 340
Arengukoostöö Ümarlaud—AKÜ, Estonia, 92
Association of Civil Society Development Center, Türkiye, 327
ASTM—Action Solidarité Tiers Monde, Luxembourg, 209
AVSI Foundation, Italy, 175
Axel Springer Foundation, Germany, 122
Axel-Springer-Stiftung, Germany, 122
Aydın Doğan Foundation, Türkiye, 328
Aydın Doğan Vakfı, Türkiye, 328
Bank of America Charitable Foundation, USA, 407
Bank of Cyprus Cultural Foundation, Cyprus, 77
Barcelona Centre for International Affairs, Spain, 287
Barenboim-Said Foundation, Spain, 289
Barzani Charity Foundation—BCF, Iraq, 164
BBC Media Action, UK, 342
Benecke (Otto) Stiftung eV, Germany, 138
Benesco, UK, 347
Berghof Foundation gGmbH, Germany, 122
Berghof Stiftung für Konfliktforschung gGmbH, Germany, 122
Bertelsmann Foundation, Germany, 122
Bertelsmann Stiftung, Germany, 122
Beyaz Nokta Gelişim Vakfı, Türkiye, 328
BIAT Youth Foundation, Tunisia, 326
Black Sea Trust for Regional Cooperation, USA, 430
Blair (Tony) Institute for Global Change, UK, 386
BMCE Bank Foundation, Morocco, 219
BNP Paribas Foundation, France, 103
Boghossian Foundation, Belgium, 31
Böll (Heinrich) Stiftung, Germany, 131
Book Aid International—BAI, UK, 343
Bosch (Robert) Stiftung GmbH, Germany, 138
Bóthar, Ireland, 166
Bread for the World—Protestant Work for Social Welfare and Development, Germany, 123
British Institute at Ankara, UK, 345
British Schools and Universities Foundation, Inc—BSUF, USA, 410
Brot für die Welt—Evangelisches Werk für Diakonie und Entwicklung, Germany, 123
Brother's Brother Foundation, USA, 410
Campaign Against Exclusion Foundation, France, 103
Canadian Foodgrains Bank, Canada, 50
CARE International—CI, Switzerland, 307
Cariplo Foundation, Italy, 175
Caritas Canada, Canada, 53
Carnegie Endowment for International Peace, USA, 411
The Carter Center, USA, 412
CASE—Centrum Analiz Społeczno-Ekonomicznych, Poland, 255
Catholic Agency for World Development—Trócaire, Ireland, 168
CBM-International, Germany, 123
Center for Economic & Social Development—CESD, Azerbaijan, 23
Center for Social and Economic Research, Poland, 255
Centre pour le Dialogue Humanitaire, Switzerland, 307

Middle East and North Africa

Centre for Humanitarian Dialogue—HD, Switzerland, 307
Çevre Koruma ve Ambalaj Atıkları Değerlendirme Vakfı—ÇEVKO, Türkiye, 328
Chaabi (Miloud), Fondation, Morocco, 220
Charity Islamic Trust Elrahma, UK, 352
Charity Projects, UK, 348
Charles and Lynn Schusterman Family Philanthropies, USA, 413
Charles Wolfson Charitable Trust, UK, 347
Chr. Michelsen Institute for Science and Intellectual Freedom—CMI, Norway, 241
CIDOB Foundation—Barcelona Centre for International Affairs, Spain, 287
Cimade—Ecumenical Care Service, France, 102
La Cimade—Service Oecuménique d'Entraide, France, 102
Civic Democratic Initiative Support Foundation—CDF, Yemen, 489
Cleveland H. Dodge Foundation, Inc, USA, 416
Climate Cent Foundation, Switzerland, 317
Clore Israel Foundation, Israel, 169
Člověk v tísni, Czech Republic, 79
CMI—Chr. Michelsen Institute for Science and Intellectual Freedom, Norway, 241
Çocuk (Anne) Eğitim Vakfı, Türkiye, 327
CODESPA Foundation, Spain, 290
Comic Relief, UK, 348
Commonwealth Foundation, UK, 348
Concern Worldwide, Ireland, 166
Cooperazione Internazionale—COOPI, Italy, 173
Costopoulos (J. F.) Foundation, Greece, 146
The CRB Foundation/La Fondation CRB, Canada, 52
CRDF Global, USA, 419
Crown Family Philanthropies, USA, 419
Dalia Association, Palestinian Territories, 246
Danish Institute for Human Rights, Denmark, 84
David Nott Foundation, UK, 350
Davis (Lady) Fellowship Trust, Israel, 170
Democracy and Human Rights Development Centre, Iraq, 164
Deutsche Orient-Stiftung, Germany, 125
Deutsche Sparkassenstiftung für Internationale Zusammenarbeit, Germany, 125
Development Cooperation Roundtable, Estonia, 92
Development Foundation of Turkey, Türkiye, 330
Development and Peace—Caritas Canada, Canada, 53
Développement et Paix—Caritas Canada, Canada, 53
Diakonia, Sweden, 298
Dodge (Cleveland H.) Foundation, Inc, USA, 416
Doğan (Aydın) Vakfı, Türkiye, 328
Ebelin und Gerd Bucerius ZEIT Foundation, Germany, 143
Economic Development Foundation, Türkiye, 328
Edmond de Rothschild Foundations, Switzerland, 308
Education Above All Foundation—EAA, Qatar, 262
Elena & Gennady Timchenko Foundation, Russian Federation, 265
ELIAMEP—Hellenic Foundation for European and Foreign Policy, Greece, 146
Elrahma Charity Trust, UK, 352
Elumelu (Tony) Foundation, Nigeria, 238
Embrace the Middle East, UK, 352
EMERGENCY, Italy, 173
Emirates Foundation, United Arab Emirates, 334
Emunah, UK, 353
Enda Third World—Environment and Development Action in the Third World, Senegal, 270
Enda Tiers Monde—Environnement et Développement du Tiers-Monde, Senegal, 270
Eni Foundation, Italy, 173
Entraide Protestante Suisse, Switzerland, 311
Entraide Universitaire Mondiale du Canada, Canada, 63
Entwicklungshilfe-Klub, Austria, 20
Environment Foundation of Turkey, Türkiye, 330
Environmental Protection and Packaging Waste Recovery and Recycling Foundation, Türkiye, 328
Eurasia Foundation—EF, USA, 424
Euro-Mediterranean Centre on Climate Change Foundation, Italy, 176
European Cultural Foundation—ECF, Netherlands, 225
European Mediterranean Institute, Spain, 296
European Roma Rights Centre—ERRC, Belgium, 30
Europese Culterele Stichting, Netherlands, 225
EVPA—European Venture Philanthropy Association, Belgium, 27

Middle East and North Africa

F. C. Flick Foundation against Xenophobia, Racism and Intolerance, Germany, 128
F. C. Flick-Stiftung gegen Fremdenfeindlichkeit, Rassismus und Intoleranz, Germany, 128
Faith, UK, 353
FINCA International, USA, 425
Flick (F. C.) Stiftung gegen Fremdenfeindlichkeit, Rassismus und Intoleranz, Germany, 128
Focus Humanitarian Assistance—FOCUS, Canada, 54
Fondation Addoha, Morocco, 219
Fondation Agir Contre l'Exclusion—FACE, France, 103
Fondation Air France, France, 103
Fondation Arabe pour l'Image, Lebanon, 205
Fondation BIAT pour la Jeunesse, Tunisia, 326
Fondation BMCE Bank, Morocco, 219
Fondation BNP Paribas, France, 103
Fondation Boghossian, Belgium, 31
Fondation Européenne de la Culture/Europese Culturele Stichting, Netherlands, 225
Fondation France-Israël, France, 106
Fondation Hirondelle: Media for Peace and Human Dignity, Switzerland, 309
Fondation Jasmin pour la Recherche et la Communication, Tunisia, 326
Fondation Marc de Montalembert, France, 109
Fondation Mérieux, France, 109
Fondation Miloud Chaâbi, Morocco, 220
Fondation Nicolas Hulot pour la Nature et l'Homme—FNH, France, 110
Fondation Noura, Mauritania, 214
Fondation Orange, France, 110
Fondation Orange Tunisie, Tunisia, 326
Fondation Orient-Occident—FOO, Morocco, 220
Fondation Rambourg, Tunisia, 326
Fondation du Roi Abdul-Aziz al-Saoud pour les Études Islamiques et les Sciences Humaines, Morocco, 220
Fondation S, France, 111
Fondation Schneider Electric, France, 111
Fondation Suisse-Liechtenstein pour les Recherches Archéologiques à l'Etranger, Switzerland, 316
Fondation Tunisie pour le Développement, Tunisia, 326
Fondazione AVSI, Italy, 175
Fondazione Cariplo, Italy, 175
Fondazione Centro Euro-Mediterraneo sui Cambiamenti Climatici—CMCC, Italy, 176
Fondazione Terzo Pilastro – Internazionale, Italy, 180
Food for the Hungry—FH, USA, 426
Ford Foundation, USA, 427
Fòs Feminista, USA, 427
Foundation for International Community Assistance, USA, 425
Foundation for Middle East Peace—FMEP, USA, 428
Foundation 'Remembrance, Responsibility and Future', Germany, 139
Foundation in Support of Local Democracy, Poland, 256
Foundation for the Support of Women's Work, Türkiye, 329
Foundation for the Welfare of Holocaust Victims, Israel, 169
France-Israel Foundation, France, 106
Frank (Anne)-Fonds, Switzerland, 306
Fraunhofer-Gesellschaft, Germany, 129
Fraunhofer Society, Germany, 129
The Fred Hollows Foundation, Australia, 14
French Institute of International Relations, France, 113
Friedensdorf International, Germany, 129
FUHEM—Fundación Benéfico-Social Hogar del Empleado, Spain, 286
Fulbright Israel, Israel, 169
Fundació CIDOB, Spain, 287
Fundación Barenboim-Said, Spain, 289
Fundación CODESPA, Spain, 290
Fundación IE, Spain, 291
Fundación Leo Messi, Spain, 292
Fundación MAPFRE, Spain, 292
Fundación Repsol, Spain, 295
Fundacja Rozwoju Demokracji Loaklnej, Poland, 256
Future in Our Hands Youth NGO—FIOH, Armenia, 9
The General Kashif Al-Getaa Foundation, Iraq, 164
George and Thelma Paraskevaides Foundation, Cyprus, 78
German Foundation for International Legal Co-operation, Germany, 133
German Institute for Global and Area Studies—GIGA, Germany, 130
German Marshall Fund of the United States—GMF, USA, 430
German Orient Foundation, Germany, 125
German Savings Banks Foundation for International Co-operation, Germany, 125
Gift of the Givers Foundation, South Africa, 280
Global Communities, USA, 431
Global Fund for Children, USA, 431
Global Innovation Fund, UK, 356
GOAL, Ireland, 166
Goldman Sachs Foundation, USA, 432
Goldsmith (Horace W.) Foundation, USA, 436
Good Neighbors International, Korea (Republic), 201
Graça Machel Trust, South Africa, 280
Grassroots International—GRI, USA, 433
Gruss (Joseph S. and Caroline) Memorial Fund, Israel, 169
Hariri Foundation for Sustainable Human Development, Lebanon, 205
Harry and Jeanette Weinberg Foundation, Inc, USA, 434
Heineman (Minna-James) Stiftung, Germany, 136
Heinrich Böll Foundation, Germany, 131
Heinrich-Böll-Stiftung, Germany, 131
HEKS—Hilfswerk der Evangelischen Kirchen Schweiz, Switzerland, 311
Hellenic Foundation for Culture, Greece, 145
Hellenic Foundation for European and Foreign Policy—ELIAMEP, Greece, 146
Helmsley (Leona M. and Harry B.) Charitable Trust, USA, 447
Henrietta Szold Institute—National Institute for Research in the Behavioural Sciences, Israel, 169
Hisar Education Foundation—HEV, Türkiye, 328
History Foundation of Turkey, Türkiye, 329
Hivos—Humanistisch Instituut voor Ontwikkelings Samenwerking, Netherlands, 226
Hollows (Fred) Foundation, Australia, 14
Hope Foundation, Türkiye, 331
Horace W. Goldsmith Foundation, USA, 436
Howard Karagheusian Commemorative Corporation—HKCC, USA, 437
Hulot (Nicolas), Fondation, France, 110
Human Resource Development Foundation, Türkiye, 329
Human Rights Foundation of Turkey, Türkiye, 330
Human Rights Information and Training Center—HRITC, Yemen, 489
Humanistic Institute for Co-operation with Developing Countries, Netherlands, 226
Humanitarian Academy for Development—HAD, UK, 359
Humanitarian Coalition, Canada, 48
Humanity United, USA, 438
IACD—Institute of Asian Culture and Development, Korea (Republic), 201
Ibrahim (Mo) Foundation, UK, 368
Ichikowitz Family Foundation—IFF, South Africa, 280
The Ideas Institute, Kenya, 199
IDRF—International Development and Relief Foundation, Canada, 56
IE Foundation, Spain, 291
IFAD—International Fund for Agricultural Development, Italy, 182
IHH Humanitarian Relief Foundation, Türkiye, 328
IIED—International Institute for Environment and Development, UK, 360
IKEA Foundation, Netherlands, 229
IKGV—İnsan Kaynağını Geliştirme Vakfı, Türkiye, 329
İktisadi Kalkınma Vakfı, Türkiye, 328
Impact Europe, Belgium, 27
İnsan Hak ve Hürriyetleri İnsani Yardım Vakfı—IHH, Türkiye, 328
İnsan Kaynağını Geliştirme Vakfı—IKGV, Türkiye, 329
Institut Europeu de la Mediterrània—IEMed, Spain, 296
Institut FMES—Institut Méditerranéen d'Etudes Stratégiques, France, 113
Institut Français des Relations Internationales—IFRI, France, 113
Institut International des Droits de l'Enfant, Switzerland, 312
Institut for Menneskerettigheder, Denmark, 84
Institute of Asian Culture and Development—IACD, Korea (Republic), 201
Institute of Developing Economies-Japan External Trade Organization—IDE-JETRO, Japan, 188
Institute for Iran-Eurasia Studies—IRAS, Iran, 163

INDEX BY AREA OF ACTIVITY

Institute for Palestine Studies—IPS, Lebanon, 206
Institute for Security Studies—ISS, South Africa, 280
Institutul Cultural Român—ICR, Romania, 264
Interchurch Aid—HIA Hungary, Hungary, 153
International Alert—Alert, UK, 360
International Blue Crescent Relief and Development Foundation—IBC, Türkiye, 329
International Co-operation, Italy, 173
International Development and Relief Foundation—IDRF, Canada, 56
The International Foundation, USA, 440
International Fund for Agricultural Development—IFAD, Italy, 182
International Institute for Environment and Development—IIED, UK, 360
International Institute for the Rights of the Child, Switzerland, 312
International Orthodox Christian Charities—IOCC, USA, 441
International Research & Exchanges Board—IREX, USA, 442
International Research Foundation, Oman, 244
International Water Management Institute—IWMI, Sri Lanka, 297
International Women's Health Coalition, USA, 427
INTERSOS, Italy, 182
IOCC—International Orthodox Christian Charities, USA, 441
Iraqi Institute for Economic Reform, Iraq, 164
IREX—International Research & Exchanges Board, USA, 442
IRZ (Deutsche Stiftung für Internationale Rechtliche Zusammenarbeit) eV, Germany, 133
The Israel Democracy Institute—IDI, Israel, 170
The J. F. Costopoulos Foundation, Greece, 146
Jack Ma Foundation—JMF, China (People's Republic), 68
Japan International Volunteer Center—JVC, Japan, 190
Jasmine Foundation for Research and Communication, Tunisia, 326
JCA Charitable Foundation, UK, 361
The Jerusalem Trust, UK, 361
JNF UK—JNF Charitable Trust, UK, 361
JOHUD—Jordanian Hashemite Fund for Human Development, Jordan, 196
Jordan River Foundation, Jordan, 196
Joseph S. and Caroline Gruss Memorial Fund for the Advancement of Veterans, Israel, 170
Kadın Emeğini Değerlendirme Vakfı—KEDV, Türkiye, 329
Kafaa Development Foundation, Libya, 207
Kamel Lazaar Foundation—KLF, Tunisia, 327
Karagheusian (Howard) Commemorative Corporation, USA, 437
Kayany Foundation, Lebanon, 206
KIEDF—Koret Israel Economic Development Funds, Israel, 170
King Abdul-Aziz al-Saoud Foundation for Islamic Study and the Humanities, Morocco, 220
King Hussein Foundation—KHF, Jordan, 196
King Khalid Foundation, Saudi Arabia, 269
King Philanthropies, USA, 445
Koç (Vehbi), Vakfı, Türkiye, 331
Körber Foundation, Germany, 134
Körber-Stiftung, Germany, 134
Koret Foundation, USA, 446
Koret Israel Economic Development Funds—KIEDF, Israel, 170
Kuwait Awqaf Public Foundation, Kuwait, 203
Kuwait Foundation for the Advancement of Sciences—KFAS, Kuwait, 203
Kuwait Institute for Scientific Research—KISR, Kuwait, 203
Kvinna till Kvinna, Sweden, 301
Lady Davis Fellowship Trust, Israel, 170
Learning for Well-being Foundation—L4WB, Netherlands, 227
Leibniz-Institut für Globale und Regionale Studien, Germany, 130
Leo Messi Foundation, Spain, 292
The Leona M. and Harry B. Helmsley Charitable Trust, USA, 447
The Leprosy Mission International, UK, 364
Leventis (A. G.) Foundation, Cyprus, 77
Li Ka Shing Foundation, Hong Kong, 151
Liliane Foundation, Netherlands, 229
Lindh (Anna) Euro-Mediterranean Foundation for Dialogue between Cultures, Egypt, 90
Littauer (Lucius N.) Foundation, Inc, USA, 449
Lucius N. Littauer Foundation, Inc, USA, 449
Machel (Graça) Trust, South Africa, 280
MADRE, USA, 450
MAG—Mines Advisory Group, UK, 366
Mama Cash Foundation, Netherlands, 230

INDEX BY AREA OF ACTIVITY

Mandela Institute for Development Studies—MINDS, South Africa, 281
The Mandela Rhodes Foundation, South Africa, 281
Mansour Foundation for Development—MFD, Egypt, 90
MAPFRE Foundation, Spain, 292
Marc de Montalembert Foundation, France, 109
March of Dimes Foundation, USA, 450
Mawazo Institute, Kenya, 199
The Max Foundation, USA, 451
medica mondiale eV, Germany, 136
Medical Aid for Palestinians—MAP, UK, 367
Medico International, Germany, 136
Mediterranean Foundation for Strategic Studies Institute, France, 113
Menomadin Foundation, Israel, 170
Mercury Phoenix Trust, UK, 367
Mercy, Ireland, 168
Mercy Corps, USA, 452
Mercy-USA for Aid and Development, USA, 452
Mérieux Foundation, France, 109
Messi (Leo), Fundación, Spain, 292
Miloud Chaâbi Foundation, Morocco, 220
Mines Advisory Group—MAG, UK, 366
Minhaj Welfare Foundation, UK, 368
Minna James Heineman Foundation, Germany, 136
Minna-James-Heineman-Stiftung, Germany, 136
Mo Ibrahim Foundation, UK, 368
Moawad (René) Foundation, Lebanon, 206
Mohamed Shafik Gabr Foundation for Social Development, Egypt, 90
Mohammed bin Rashid Al Maktoum Global Initiatives—MBRGI, United Arab Emirates, 335
de Montalembert (Marc), Fondation, France, 109
Mother Child Education Foundation, Türkiye, 327
Muslim Aid, UK, 369
National Institute for Research in the Behavioural Sciences—Szold (Henrietta) Institute, Israel, 169
NDI—National Democratic Institute for International Affairs, USA, 456
Near East Foundation—NEF, USA, 456
Nederlandse Organisatie voor Internationale Ontwikkelingssamenwerking—Stichting NOVIB, Netherlands, 228
NEF—Near East Foundation, USA, 456
Network of Foundations Working for Development—netFWD, France, 99
Nicolas Hulot Foundation for Nature and Humankind, France, 110
North-South-Bridge Foundation, Germany, 141
Nott (David) Foundation, UK, 350
Novartis Foundation, Switzerland, 314
NOVIB (Oxfam Netherlands), Netherlands, 228
Ökumenikus Segélyszervezet, Hungary, 153
Oman LNG Development Foundation—ODF, Oman, 244
Open Society European Policy Institute—OSEPI, Belgium, 33
Orange Foundation, France, 110
Orange Foundation Tunisia, Tunisia, 326
Orient-Occident Foundation, Morocco, 220
Otto Benecke Foundation, Germany, 138
Otto-Benecke-Stiftung eV, Germany, 138
Oxfam Australia, Australia, 16
Oxfam Canada, Canada, 60
Oxfam Deutschland eV, Germany, 138
Oxfam Ireland, Ireland, 167
Oxfam Italia, Italy, 183
Oxfam NOVIB—Nederlandse Organisatie voor Internationale Ontwikkelingssamenwerking, Netherlands, 228
Oxfam NOVIB—Netherlands Organization for International Development Co-operation, Netherlands, 228
Oxfam-Québec, Canada, 60
Paraskevaides (George and Thelma) Foundation, Cyprus, 78
Parasol Foundation Trust, Gibraltar, 144
Partage, France, 116
Pathfinder International, USA, 461
PCI—Project Concern International, USA, 431
Peace Direct, UK, 373
Peace Village International, Germany, 129
Peace Winds Japan—PWJ, Japan, 192
People in Need, Czech Republic, 79
Peres Center for Peace and Innovation, Israel, 171
Ploughshares Fund, USA, 463
Population Council, USA, 463
Pratt Foundation, Australia, 17
Première Urgence Internationale, France, 116
Presbyterian World Service & Development—PWS&D, Canada, 61

Prince Claus Fund for Culture and Development, Netherlands, 228
Prins Claus Fonds Voor Cultuur en Ontwikkeling, Netherlands, 228
Pro Victimis, Switzerland, 315
Project HOPE, USA, 464
Project Trust, UK, 374
Qatar Foundation, Qatar, 262
Qattan (A. M.) Foundation, UK, 338
Queen Rania Foundation—QRF, Jordan, 196
Rambourg Foundation, Tunisia, 326
Rausing (Ruben and Elisabeth) Trust, UK, 383
RedR UK, UK, 375
Refugee Empowerment International—REI, Japan, 193
Regional Environmental Center, Hungary, 153
REI—Refugee Empowerment International, Japan, 193
Relief International, USA, 466
René Moawad Foundation—RMF, Lebanon, 206
Repsol Foundation, Spain, 295
Robert Bosch Foundation, Germany, 138
Robert-Bosch-Stiftung GmbH, Germany, 138
Rockefeller Brothers Fund—RBF, USA, 468
Romanian Cultural Institute, Romania, 264
Rothschild (Edmond de) Foundations, Switzerland, 308
Royal Society for the Protection of Birds—RSPB, UK, 379
RSPB—Royal Society for the Protection of Birds, UK, 379
The Rufford Foundation, UK, 380
Rutgers, Netherlands, 228
Ruya Foundation for Contemporary Culture in Iraq, Iraq, 164
Saadi Foundation, Iran, 164
Saïd Foundation, UK, 380
Sainsbury Family Charitable Trusts, UK, 380
Samir Kassir Foundation, Lebanon, 206
Santé Sud, France, 116
Sawiris Foundation for Social Development—SFSD, Egypt, 90
Schneider Electric Foundation, France, 111
Schusterman (Charles and Lynn) Family Foundation, USA, 413
Schweizerisch-Liechtensteinische Stiftung für Archäologische Forschungen im Ausland—SLSA, Switzerland, 316
Scientific Foundation of Hisham Adeeb Hijjawi, Jordan, 196
Scottish Catholic International Aid Fund—SCIAF, UK, 382
Seeds of Peace, USA, 470
SEEMO—South East Europe Media Organisation, Austria, 23
Serrv International, Inc, USA, 471
Seva Foundation, USA, 471
Shafik Gabr (Mohamed) Foundation, Egypt, 90
Shahid Afridi Foundation—SAF, Pakistan, 246
Sherman (Archie) Charitable Trust, UK, 340
Shoman (Abdul Hameed) Foundation, Jordan, 195
Sigrid Rausing Trust—SRT, UK, 383
Sivil Toplum Geliştirme Merkezi—STGM, Türkiye, 327
The Sobell Foundation, UK, 384
South East Europe Media Organisation—SEEMO, Austria, 23
Southern Health, France, 116
Sparkassenstiftung für internationale Kooperation, Germany, 125
Springer (Axel) Stiftung, Germany, 122
Stichting IKEA Foundation, Netherlands, 229
Stichting Liliane Fonds, Netherlands, 229
Stichting Mama Cash, Netherlands, 230
Stichting Triodos Foundation, Netherlands, 231
Stiftung 'Erinnerung, Verantwortung und Zukunft'—EVZ, Germany, 139
Stiftung Klimarappen, Switzerland, 317
Stiftung Nord-Süd-Brücken, Germany, 141
Südosteuropäische Medienorganisation, Austria, 23
Sulaiman Bin Abdul Aziz Bin Saleh Al Rajhi Foundation, Saudi Arabia, 269
Sultan bin Abdulaziz Al Sa'ud Foundation, Saudi Arabia, 270
Swiss Church Aid, Switzerland, 311
Swiss-Liechtenstein Foundation for Archaeological Research Abroad—SLFA, Switzerland, 316
Synergos—The Synergos Institute, USA, 396
Syria Al-Gad Relief Foundation, Egypt, 91
Taawon, Palestinian Territories, 246
Tarih Vakfı, Türkiye, 329
Tearfund, UK, 385
Terre des Hommes International Federation—TDHIF, Switzerland, 318
TESEV—Türkiye Ekonomik ve Sosyal Etüdler Vakfı, Türkiye, 329

South America, Central America and the Caribbean

TFF—Transnational Foundation for Peace and Future Research, Sweden, 304
TFF—Transnationella Stiftelsen för Freds- och Framtidsforskning, Sweden, 304
Third Sector Foundation of Turkey, Türkiye, 327
Third World Solidarity Action, Luxembourg, 209
Thomson Foundation, UK, 385
Timchenko (Elena & Gennady) Foundation, Russian Federation, 265
Tony Blair Institute for Global Change—TBI, UK, 386
Tony Elumelu Foundation—TEF, Nigeria, 238
Triodos Foundation, Netherlands, 231
Trócaire—Catholic Agency for World Development, Ireland, 168
Tunisia Development Foundation, Tunisia, 326
Turkish Economic and Social Studies Foundation, Türkiye, 329
Turkish Family Health and Planning Foundation, Türkiye, 330
Turkish Foundation for Combating Soil Erosion, for Reforestation and the Protection of Natural Habitats, Türkiye, 330
Türkiye Aile Sağlığı ve Planlaması Vakfı—TAPV, Türkiye, 330
Türkiye Çevre Vakfı, Türkiye, 330
Türkiye Erozyonla Mücadele Ağaçlandırma ve Doğal Varlıkları Koruma Vakfı—TEMA, Türkiye, 330
Türkiye İnsan Hakları Vakfı—TİHV, Türkiye, 330
Türkiye Kalkınma Vakfı, Türkiye, 330
Türkiye Vodafone Vakfı, Türkiye, 331
TÜSEV—Türkiye Üçüncü Sektör Vakfı, Türkiye, 327
U4 Anti-Corruption Resource Centre, Norway, 241
UJIA—United Jewish Israel Appeal, UK, 387
Umut Vakfı, Türkiye, 331
Union Aid Abroad—APHEDA, Australia, 19
United Jewish Israel Appeal—UJIA, UK, 387
US Civilian Research & Development Foundation, USA, 419
USPG—United Society Partners in the Gospel, UK, 387
Van Leer Jerusalem Institute, Israel, 171
Vehbi Koç Foundation, Türkiye, 331
Vehbi Koç Vakfı, Türkiye, 331
VIDC—Vienna Institute for International Dialogue and Co-operation, Austria, 23
Vienna Institute for International Dialogue and Co-operation—VIDC, Austria, 23
Vodafone Egypt Foundation, Egypt, 91
Vodafone Türkiye Foundation, Türkiye, 331
War Child, UK, 388
War on Want, UK, 388
WasserStiftung, Germany, 142
WaterFoundation, Germany, 142
Weinberg (Harry and Jeanette) Foundation, USA, 434
Welfare Association, Palestinian Territories, 246
Westminster Foundation for Democracy—WFD, UK, 389
White Point Development Foundation, Türkiye, 328
The Whitley Fund for Nature—WFN, UK, 390
The Wolfson Foundation, UK, 390
Woman to Woman Foundation, Sweden, 301
World University Service of Canada/Entraide Universitaire Mondiale du Canada—WUSC/EUMC, Canada, 63
World Vegetable Center, Taiwan, 322
World Vision International, UK, 391
WorldFish, Malaysia, 212
Wujoh Foundation for Media and Development, Yemen, 489
Year Out Group, UK, 374
Yemen Policy Center, Yemen, 489
Yemen Polling Center—YPC, Yemen, 489
Youth Leadership Development Foundation—YLDF, Yemen, 489
Zakat House, Kuwait, 203
ZEIT-Stiftung Ebelin und Gerd Bucerius, Germany, 143
ZOA, Netherlands, 231

SOUTH AMERICA, CENTRAL AMERICA AND THE CARIBBEAN

Abrinq Foundation for the Rights of Children and Adolescents, Brazil, 39
Access Foundation, Costa Rica, 73
Accion, USA, 397
Acíndar Foundation, Argentina, 6
Acting for Life, France, 100
Action Against Hunger, France, 100
Action contre la Faim—ACF France, France, 100
Action Damien/Damiaanactie, Belgium, 28

South America, Central America and the Caribbean

Action Education, France, 100
Action Solidarité Tiers Monde—ASTM, Luxembourg, 209
Acumen, USA, 397
Advance, USA, 397
Afdi—Agriculteurs Français et Développement International, France, 100
Agriculteurs Français et Développement International, France, 100
Agronomes et Vétérinaires sans Frontières—AVSF, France, 100
Agronomists and Veterinarians Without Borders, France, 100
Aid for Development Club, Austria, 20
Air France Foundation, France, 103
Alcoa Foundation, USA, 398
Alemán (Miguel), Fundación, Mexico, 215
Alet'Eleym Fewq Alejmey'e, Qatar, 262
ALIDE—Asociación Latinoamericana de Instituciones Financieras para el Desarrollo, Peru, 248
Allende (Isabel) Foundation, USA, 442
Alliance of Bioversity International and the International Center for Tropical Agriculture—CIAT, Italy, 172
Alvares Penteado (Armando), Fundação, Brazil, 39
American Friends Service Committee—AFSC, USA, 401
American Jewish World Service—AJWS, USA, 402
AmeriCares Foundation, Inc, USA, 403
Amerind Foundation, Inc, USA, 403
Anguilla Community Fund, Anguilla, 5
Anguilla National Trust—ANT, Anguilla, 6
Anne Çocuk Eğitim Vakfı—AÇEV, Türkiye, 327
The Annie E. Casey Foundation, USA, 404
Antigua Forum, Guatemala, 147
APHEDA—Union Aid Abroad, Australia, 19
Arab Image Foundation—AIF, Lebanon, 205
Arbeiterwohlfahrt Bundesverband eV—AWO, Germany, 121
Arca Foundation, USA, 405
ArcelorMittal Brazil Foundation, Brazil, 39
Archewell Foundation, USA, 405
Arcus Foundation, USA, 405
Arias Foundation for Peace and Human Progress, Costa Rica, 74
Armando Alvares Penteado Foundation, Brazil, 39
Arpad Szenes–Vieira da Silva Foundation, Portugal, 258
Asociación de Fundaciones Familiares y Empresariales—AFE, Colombia, 70
Asociación Latinoamericana de Instituciones Financieras para el Desarrollo—ALIDE, Peru, 248
Asociación Salvadoreña para el Desarrollo Económico y Social FUSADES, El Salvador, 91
Aspen Institute, USA, 407
Association of Family and Corporate Foundations, Colombia, 70
ASTM—Action Solidarité Tiers Monde, Luxembourg, 209
Astur Foundation, Uruguay, 485
AVINA Foundation, Panama, 247
AVSI Foundation, Italy, 175
Ayrton Senna Institute, Brazil, 41
Bagnoud (François-Xavier) Association, Switzerland, 310
Banco do Brasil Foundation, Brazil, 39
BANHCAFE Foundation, Honduras, 150
Bank of America Charitable Foundation, USA, 407
Barbados Entrepreneurship Foundation Inc, Barbados, 25
Barceló Foundation, Spain, 289
Barcelona Centre for International Affairs, Spain, 287
Bariloche Foundation, Argentina, 7
BBC Media Action, UK, 342
BBVA Foundation, Spain, 289
Berghof Foundation gGmbH, Germany, 122
Berghof Stiftung für Konfliktforschung gGmbH, Germany, 122
Bermuda Foundation, Bermuda, 35
Bertoni (Moisés) Foundation, Paraguay, 248
Blue Marine Foundation—BLUE, UK, 343
BNP Paribas Foundation, France, 103
Böll (Heinrich) Stiftung, Germany, 131
Book Aid International—BAI, UK, 343
Bóthar, Ireland, 166
Boticário Group Foundation, Brazil, 40
Botín Foundation, Spain, 292
Botín (Marcelino), Fundación, Spain, 292
BrazilFoundation, Brazil, 39

Bread for the World—Protestant Work for Social Welfare and Development, Germany, 123
Brot für die Welt—Evangelisches Werk für Diakonie und Entwicklung, Germany, 123
Brother's Brother Foundation, USA, 410
Brothers of Men, France, 113
Buffett (Howard G.) Foundation, USA, 437
Bunge y Born Foundation, Argentina, 7
Cadbury (William Adlington) Charitable Trust, UK, 390
CAF—Charities Aid Foundation, UK, 336
Canadian Centre for International Studies and Co-operation, Canada, 51
Canadian Feed The Children—CFTC, Canada, 50
Canadian Foodgrains Bank, Canada, 50
CARE International—CI, Switzerland, 307
Caribbean Policy Development Centre—CPDC, Barbados, 25
Caritas Canada, Canada, 53
Carlos Slim Foundation, Mexico, 215
CARMABI Foundation, Curaçao, 77
The Carter Center, USA, 412
Casey (Annie E.) Foundation, USA, 404
Catalyste+, Canada, 51
Catholic Agency for World Development—Trócaire, Ireland, 168
CBM-International, Germany, 123
CECI—Canadian Centre for International Studies and Co-operation/Centre d'Etudes et de Coopération Internationale, Canada, 51
CEDRO—Centro de Información y Educación para la Prevención del Abuso de Drogas, Peru, 248
Centro de Estudios Públicos—CEP, Chile, 64
Centro de Información y Educación para la Prevención del Abuso de Drogas—CEDRO, Peru, 248
Centro Mexicano para la Filantropía—CEMEFI, Mexico, 214
CERES—Consorcio Ecuatoriano Para La Responsabilidad Social, Ecuador, 87
CESO/SACO—Canadian Executive Service Organization/Service d'Assistance Canadienne aux Organismes, Canada, 51
Charities Aid Foundation—CAF, UK, 336
Charity Projects, UK, 348
Charles Darwin Foundation for the Galapagos Islands—CDF, Ecuador, 88
ChildFund International, USA, 414
Children International—CI, USA, 414
Children and Sharing, France, 102
The Children's Investment Fund Foundation, UK, 347
Chile Foundation, Chile, 65
Chr. Michelsen Institute for Science and Intellectual Freedom—CMI, Norway, 241
CIAT—Centro Internacional de Agricultura Tropical, Italy, 172
CIDOB Foundation—Barcelona Centre for International Affairs, Spain, 287
Cimade—Ecumenical Care Service, France, 102
La Cimade—Service Oecuménique d'Entraide, France, 102
CLADEM—Comité de América Latina y el Caribe para la Defensa de los Derechos de la Mujer, Peru, 249
Claiborne (Liz) & Art Ortenberg Foundation, USA, 448
Clara Lionel Foundation—CLF, USA, 415
Climate Cent Foundation, Switzerland, 317
CMI—Chr. Michelsen Institute for Science and Intellectual Freedom, Norway, 241
Çocuk (Anne) Eğitim Vakfı, Türkiye, 327
CODESPA Foundation, Spain, 290
Colombian Habitat Foundation, Colombia, 71
Comic Relief, UK, 348
Comité de América Latina y el Caribe para la Defensa de los Derechos de la Mujer—CLADEM, Peru, 249
Common Network, Brazil, 38
Commonwealth Foundation, UK, 348
Community of Solidarity Organizations, Chile, 64
Comunalia—Alianza de Fundaciones Comunitarias de México, Mexico, 215
Comunidad de Organizaciones Solidarios, Chile, 64
Concern Worldwide, Ireland, 166
Co-operative Development Foundation of Canada—CDF, Canada, 52
Cooperazione Internazionale—COOPI, Italy, 173
Corona Foundation, Colombia, 71
Council of American Development Foundations, Dominican Republic, 87
Culture, Health, Arts, Sports and Education Fund—CHASE, Jamaica, 184
Cuso International, Canada, 53
Daniele Agostino Derossi Foundation, USA, 420
Danish Cultural Institute—DCI, Denmark, 82

INDEX BY AREA OF ACTIVITY

Danish Institute for Human Rights, Denmark, 84
Danske Kulturinstitut—DKI, Denmark, 82
Darwin (Charles) Foundation for the Galapagos Islands, Ecuador, 88
David Nott Foundation, UK, 350
Democracy and Development Foundation, Chile, 65
Dental Aid International, Switzerland, 317
Derossi (Daniele Agostino) Foundation, USA, 420
Deutsche Bank Americas Foundation, USA, 420
Deutsche Sparkassenstiftung für Internationale Zusammenarbeit, Germany, 125
Development Foundation, Guatemala, 148
Development and Peace—Caritas Canada, Canada, 53
Développement et Paix—Caritas Canada, Canada, 53
Diakonia, Sweden, 298
Digicel Foundation Haiti, Haiti, 149
Digicel Foundation Jamaica, Jamaica, 184
Digicel Trinidad and Tobago Foundation, Trinidad and Tobago, 326
The Do-Nation Foundation, Inc, Saint Lucia, 268
DOEN Foundation, Netherlands, 229
Dom Manuel II Foundation, Portugal, 260
Dominican Development Foundation, Dominican Republic, 87
Dr Guillermo Manuel Ungo Foundation, El Salvador, 91
Earthrights International—ERI, USA, 422
Earthworm Foundation, Switzerland, 307
EcoCiencia—Fundación Ecuatoriana de Estudios Ecologicos, Ecuador, 88
Ecuadorean Consortium for Social Responsibility, Ecuador, 87
Ecuadorean Cooperation for Development Fund, Ecuador, 88
Ecuadorean Foundation of Ecological Studies, Ecuador, 88
Ecuadorean Social Group Fund Populorum Progressio, Ecuador, 89
EDP Foundation, Portugal, 260
Education Above All Foundation—EAA, Qatar, 262
Educo, Spain, 286
Ellerman (John) Foundation, UK, 361
Empresas Polar Foundation, Venezuela, 487
Enda Third World—Environment and Development Action in the Third World, Senegal, 270
Enda Tiers Monde—Environnement et Développement du Tiers-Monde, Senegal, 270
endPoverty.org, USA, 424
Enfance et Partage, France, 102
Entraide Protestante Suisse, Switzerland, 311
Entraide Universitaire Mondiale du Canada, Canada, 63
Entwicklungshilfe-Klub, Austria, 20
Environment and Natural Resources Foundation, Argentina, 7
Environmental Foundation of Jamaica, Jamaica, 184
Environmental Justice Foundation—EJF, UK, 353
Equality Fund/Fonds Égalité, Canada, 54
Esquel Group Foundation—Ecuador, Ecuador, 88
Eugenio Mendoza Foundation, Venezuela, 487
FAFIDESS—Fundación de Asesoría Financiera a Instituciones de Desarrollo y Servicio Social, Guatemala, 148
Fairtrade Nederland, Netherlands, 230
FARN—Fundación Ambiente y Recursos Naturales, Argentina, 7
Federal Association of Social Welfare Organizations, Germany, 121
Fedesarrollo—Fundación para la Educación Superior y el Desarrollo, Colombia, 71
Feed the Children, USA, 425
FEIM—Fundación para Estudio e Investigación de la Mujer, Argentina, 7
FEMSA Foundation, Mexico, 215
Filantrópico, Colombia, 70
FINCA International, USA, 425
FOKAL—Open Society Foundation Haiti, Haiti, 149
Fondation Abbé Pierre, France, 108
Fondation Air France, France, 103
Fondation Arabe pour l'Image, Lebanon, 205
Fondation BNP Paribas, France, 103
Fondation Digicel Haïti, Haiti, 149
Fondation Ensemble, France, 105
Fondation d'Entreprise Renault, France, 106
Fondation FARM—Fondation pour l'Agriculture et la Ruralité dans le Monde, France, 106
Fondation pour le Logement des Défavorisés, France, 108

INDEX BY AREA OF ACTIVITY

South America, Central America and the Caribbean

Fondation Mérieux, France, 109
Fondation Mohammed V pour la Solidarité, Morocco, 220
Fondation Rinaldi, Haiti, 149
Fondation Roi Baudouin, Belgium, 33
Fondation S, France, 111
Fondation Schneider Electric, France, 111
Fondation Simón I. Patiño, Switzerland, 310
Fondation Suisse-Liechtenstein pour les Recherches Archéologiques à l'Etranger, Switzerland, 316
Fondazione AVSI, Italy, 175
Fondazione Populorum Progressio, Vatican City, 486
Fondo para el Desarrollo de los Pueblos Indígenas de América Latina y El Caribe—FILAC, Bolivia, 36
Fondo Ecuatoriano de Cooperación para el Desarrollo—FECD, Ecuador, 88
Fonds Égalité, Canada, 54
Food for the Hungry—FH, USA, 426
Food for the Poor, Inc, USA, 426
Ford Foundation, USA, 427
The Forest Trust, Switzerland, 307
Fòs Feminista, USA, 427
Foundation for Analysis and Social Studies, Spain, 288
Foundation for Caribbean Research and Management of Biodiversity, Curaçao, 77
Foundation for the Conservation of the Atlantic Forest, Brazil, 41
Foundation for the Defence of Nature, Venezuela, 487
Foundation for the Financial Assessment of Social Service and Development Institutions, Guatemala, 148
Foundation for Higher Education and Development, Colombia, 71
Foundation for Housing the Disadvantaged, France, 108
Foundation for International Community Assistance, USA, 425
Foundation for Latin American Economic Research, Argentina, 7
Foundation for Local Development and the Municipal and Institutional Support of Central America and the Caribbean, Costa Rica, 74
Foundation for the Qualification and Consultancy in Microfinance, El Salvador, 92
Foundation for Social Housing, Venezuela, 488
Foundation for the Sustainable Development of Small and Medium-sized Enterprises—FUNDES International, Costa Rica, 74
Foundation for Women, Spain, 293
Foundation for Women's Research and Studies, Argentina, 7
Foundation for World Agriculture and Rural Life, France, 106
France Amérique Latine—FAL, France, 112
Franciscans International, Switzerland, 310
Fraunhofer-Gesellschaft, Germany, 129
Fraunhofer Society, Germany, 129
French Agriculturalists and International Development, France, 100
Frères des Hommes—FDH, France, 113
Friends of Nature Foundation, Bolivia, 36
FUHEM—Fundación Benéfico-Social Hogar del Empleado, Spain, 286
Fund for the Development of Indigenous Peoples of Latin America and the Caribbean, Bolivia, 36
Fundação Abrinq pelos Direitos da Criança e do Adolescente, Brazil, 39
Fundação ArcelorMittal Brasil, Brazil, 39
Fundação Armando Alvares Penteado, Brazil, 39
Fundação Arpad Szenes–Vieira da Silva, Portugal, 258
Fundação Banco do Brasil, Brazil, 39
Fundação Dom Manuel II, Portugal, 260
Fundação EDP, Portugal, 260
Fundação Grupo Boticário de Proteção à Natureza, Brazil, 40
Fundação Iochpe, Brazil, 40
Fundação Maria Cecilia Souto Vidigal, Brazil, 40
Fundação Roberto Marinho, Brazil, 41
Fundação SOS Mata Atlântica, Brazil, 41
Fundação Telefônica Vivo, Brazil, 41
Fundació CIDOB, Spain, 287
Fundación Acceso, Costa Rica, 73
Fundación Acindar, Argentina, 6
Fundación Amanecer, Colombia, 70
Fundación Ambiente y Recursos Naturales—FARN, Argentina, 7
Fundación Amigos de la Naturaleza, Bolivia, 36
Fundación para el Análisis y los Estudios Sociales—FAES, Spain, 288

Fundación Arias para la Paz y el Progreso Humano, Costa Rica, 74
Fundación Astur, Uruguay, 485
Fundación AVINA, Panama, 247
Fundación Banco Bilbao Vizcaya Argentaria—Fundación BBVA, Spain, 289
Fundación BANHCAFE—FUNBANHCAFE, Honduras, 150
Fundación Barceló, Spain, 289
Fundación Bariloche, Argentina, 7
Fundación BBVA, Spain, 289
Fundación Bigott, Venezuela, 487
Fundación Bunge y Born, Argentina, 7
Fundación Capital, Colombia, 70
Fundación Carlos Slim, Mexico, 215
Fundación Carolina, Spain, 290
Fundación Charles Darwin para las Islas Galápagos—FCD, Ecuador, 88
Fundación Chile—FCH, Chile, 65
Fundación Circulo de Montevideo, Uruguay, 485
Fundación CODESPA, Spain, 290
Fundación Comunitaria de Puerto Rico—FCPR, Puerto Rico, 261
Fundación Corona, Colombia, 71
Fundación para la Defensa de la Naturaleza—FUDENA, Venezuela, 487
Fundación Democracia y Desarrollo, Chile, 65
Fundación DEMUCA—Fundación para el Desarrollo Local y el Fortalecimiento Municipal e Institucional de Centroamérica y el Caribe, Costa Rica, 74
Fundación para el Desarrollo Local y el Fortalecimiento Municipal e Institucional de Centroamérica y el Caribe, Costa Rica, 74
Fundación Dominicana de Desarrollo—FDD, Dominican Republic, 87
Fundación Dr Guillermo Manuel Ungo—FUNDAUNGO, El Salvador, 91
Fundación para la Educación Superior y el Desarrollo—Fedesarrollo, Colombia, 71
Fundación Empresas Polar, Venezuela, 487
Fundación Escuela Nueva, Colombia, 71
Fundación Espacio Cívico, Panama, 247
Fundación para Estudio e Investigación de la Mujer—FEIM, Argentina, 7
Fundación Eugenio Mendoza—FEM, Venezuela, 487
Fundación Felipe González, Spain, 290
Fundación FEMSA, Mexico, 215
Fundación Futuro Latinoamericano, Ecuador, 88
Fundación Génesis Empresarial, Guatemala, 148
Fundación Global Democracia y Desarrollo—FUNGLODE, Dominican Republic, 87
Fundación Grupo Esquel—Ecuador, Ecuador, 88
Fundación Hábitat Colombia—FHC, Colombia, 71
Fundación IE, Spain, 291
Fundación de Investigaciones Económicas Latinoamericanas—FIEL, Argentina, 7
Fundación Invica, Chile, 65
Fundación José Ortega y Gasset—Gregorio Marañón, Spain, 291
Fundación Jubileo, Bolivia, 36
Fundación Lealtad, Spain, 285
Fundación Leo Messi, Spain, 292
Fundación MAPFRE, Spain, 292
Fundación Marcelino Botín, Spain, 292
Fundación Mediterránea—IERAL, Argentina, 7
Fundación Miguel Alemán AC, Mexico, 215
Fundación Moisés Bertoni—FMB, Paraguay, 248
Fundación Mujer, Costa Rica, 74
Fundación Mujeres, Spain, 293
Fundación Mujeres en Igualdad—MEI, Argentina, 8
Fundación Nacional para el Desarrollo, El Salvador, 91
Fundación Nacional para el Desarrollo de Honduras—FUNADEH, Honduras, 150
Fundación Nobis, Ecuador, 88
Fundación Pablo Neruda, Chile, 65
Fundación para la Paz y la Democracia—FUNPADEM, Costa Rica, 74
Fundación Pies Descalzos, Colombia, 71
Fundación Repsol, Spain, 295
Fundación Rigoberta Menchú Tum, Guatemala, 148
Fundación La Salle de Ciencias Naturales—FLASA, Venezuela, 487
Fundación Semah-Valencia, Panama, 247
Fundación SES—Sustentabilidad, Educación, Solidaridad, Argentina, 8
Fundación SM, Spain, 295
Fundación Solidaridad, Dominican Republic, 87
Fundación Telefónica Movistar Argentina, Argentina, 8
Fundación Telefónica Movistar Chile, Chile, 65
Fundación Telefónica Movistar Colombia, Colombia, 71

Fundación Telefónica Movistar Ecuador, Ecuador, 89
Fundación Telefónica Movistar México, Mexico, 216
Fundación Telefónica Movistar Perú, Peru, 249
Fundación Telefónica Movistar Uruguay, Uruguay, 485
Fundación Teletón México, Mexico, 216
Fundación Telmex Telcel, Mexico, 216
Fundación Tigo, Guatemala, 148
Fundación UNIR Bolivia, Bolivia, 36
Fundación UPM, Uruguay, 485
Fundación de la Vivienda Popular, Venezuela, 488
FUNDAMICRO—Fundación de Capacitación y Asesoría en Microfinanzas, El Salvador, 92
FUNDAP—Fundación para el Desarrollo, Guatemala, 148
FUNDAUNGO—Fundación Dr Guillermo Manuel Ungo, El Salvador, 91
FUNDES—Fundación para el Desarrollo Sostenible de la Pequeña y Mediana Empresa, Costa Rica, 74
FXB International—Association François-Xavier Bagnoud, Switzerland, 310
General Service Foundation—GSF, USA, 430
Génesis Empresarial Foundation, Guatemala, 148
German Institute for Global and Area Studies—GIGA, Germany, 130
German Savings Banks Foundation for International Co-operation, Germany, 125
GIFE—Grupo de Institutos, Fundações e Empresas, Brazil, 38
Gift of the Givers Foundation, South Africa, 280
Global Communities, USA, 431
Global Democracy and Development Foundation, Dominican Republic, 87
Global Innovation Fund, UK, 356
GOAL, Ireland, 166
Goldman Sachs Foundation, USA, 432
Good Neighbors International, Korea (Republic), 201
Grameen Foundation—GF, USA, 433
Grassroots International—GRI, USA, 433
Green Umbrella Children's Foundation—ChildFund Korea, Korea (Republic), 201
Group of Foundations and Businesses, Argentina, 6
Group of Institutes, Foundations and Enterprises, Brazil, 38
Grupo de Fundaciones y Empresas, Argentina, 6
Grupo Social Fondo Ecuatoriano Populorum Progressio, Ecuador, 89
Guggenheim (John Simon) Memorial Foundation, USA, 444
Haiti Development Institute—HDI, Haiti, 149
Harp Helú Foundations, Mexico, 216
Havelaar (Max) Foundation, Netherlands, 230
Health Volunteers Overseas—HVO, USA, 434
Hearst Foundations, USA, 435
Hedwig and Robert Samuel Foundation, Germany, 131
Hedwig und Robert Samuel-Stiftung, Germany, 131
Heinrich Böll Foundation, Germany, 131
Heinrich-Böll-Stiftung, Germany, 131
HEKS—Hilfswerk der Evangelischen Kirchen Schweiz, Switzerland, 311
Helvetas Swiss Intercooperation, Switzerland, 311
Hivos—Humanistisch Instituut voor Ontwikkelings Samenwerking, Netherlands, 226
Holt International, USA, 436
The Home Depot Foundation, USA, 436
HOPE International Development Agency, Canada, 56
Horizons of Friendship, Canada, 56
The Howard G. Buffett Foundation, USA, 437
Humanistic Institute for Co-operation with Developing Countries, Netherlands, 226
Humanitarian Coalition, Canada, 48
The Hunger Project, USA, 438
Ibero-American Network of Community Foundations, Brazil, 38
IE Foundation, Spain, 291
IFAD—International Fund for Agricultural Development, Italy, 182
IHH Humanitarian Relief Foundation, Türkiye, 328
IIAP—Instituto de Investigaciones de la Amazonía Peruana, Peru, 249
IIED—International Institute for Environment and Development, UK, 360
IKEA Foundation, Netherlands, 229
Iles de Paix, Belgium, 32
IMPACT Transformer la Gestion des Ressources Naturelles, Canada, 56

South America, Central America and the Caribbean

IMPACT Transforming Natural Resource Management, Canada, 56
Independent Sector, USA, 395
Information and Education Centre for the Prevention of Drug Abuse, Peru, 248
İnsan Hak ve Hürriyetleri İnsani Yardım Vakfı—IHH, Türkiye, 328
Institut International des Droits de l'Enfant, Switzerland, 312
Institut de Médecine et d'Epidémiologie Appliquée—Fondation Internationale Léon Mba, France, 114
Institut for Menneskerettigheder, Denmark, 84
Institute of Applied Medicine and Epidemiology—International Foundation Léon Mba, France, 114
Institute of Developing Economies-Japan External Trade Organization—IDE-JETRO, Japan, 188
Institute for the Development of Social Investment, Brazil, 38
Institute for Latin American and Caribbean Integration, Argentina, 8
Institute for Research on the Peruvian Amazon, Peru, 249
Instituto Ayrton Senna, Brazil, 41
Instituto para o Desenvolvimento do Investimento Social—IDIS, Brazil, 38
Instituto para la Integración de América Latina y el Caribe—BID-INTAL, Argentina, 8
Instituto Interamericano de Derechos Humanos—IIDH, Costa Rica, 74
Instituto de Montaña, Peru, 249
Inter-American Foundation—IAF, USA, 439
Inter-American Institute of Human Rights, Costa Rica, 74
Inter Pares, Canada, 57
Interchurch Aid—HIA Hungary, Hungary, 153
International Co-operation, Italy, 173
The International Foundation, USA, 440
International Fund for Agricultural Development—IFAD, Italy, 182
International Institute for Environment and Development—IIED, UK, 360
International Institute for the Rights of the Child, Switzerland, 312
International Orthodox Christian Charities—IOCC, USA, 441
International Research & Exchanges Board—IREX, USA, 442
International Rivers, USA, 441
International Women's Health Coalition, USA, 427
Invica Foundation, Chile, 65
IOCC—International Orthodox Christian Charities, USA, 441
Iochpe Foundation, Brazil, 40
IREX—International Research & Exchanges Board, USA, 442
Isabel Allende Foundation, USA, 442
Islands of Peace, Belgium, 32
Izumi Foundation, USA, 442
Jazz Foundation of America—JFA, USA, 443
JN Foundation, Jamaica, 184
The John D. and Catherine T. MacArthur Foundation, USA, 444
John Ellerman Foundation, UK, 361
John Simon Guggenheim Memorial Foundation, USA, 444
José Ortega y Gasset—Gregorio Marañón Foundation, Spain, 291
Jubilee Foundation, Bolivia, 36
Kellogg (W. K.) Foundation, USA, 478
King Baudouin Foundation, Belgium, 33
King Philanthropies, USA, 445
Koning Boudewijnstichting/Fondation Roi Baudouin, Belgium, 33
KWF Dutch Cancer Society, Netherlands, 227
KWF Kankerbestrijding, Netherlands, 227
La Salle Foundation for Natural Sciences, Venezuela, 487
Latimpacto—Red Latinoamericana de Inversión Social y Filantropía Estratégica, Colombia, 71
Latin America France, France, 112
Latin American, African and Asian Social Housing Service, Chile, 66
Latin American Association of Development Financing Institutions, Peru, 248
Latin American and Caribbean Committee for the Defence of Women's Rights, Peru, 244
Latin American and Caribbean Women's Health Network—LACWHN, Ecuador, 89
Latin American Future Foundation, Ecuador, 88
Latin American Network for Economic and Social Justice, Peru, 248
Latin American Venture Philanthropy Network, Colombia, 71
Latindadd—Red Latinoamericana por Justicia Económica y Social, Peru, 248
Leibniz-Institut für Globale und Regionale Studien, Germany, 130
Leo Messi Foundation, Spain, 292
Leverhulme Trust, UK, 365
Light Up the World—LUTW, Canada, 58
Liliane Foundation, Netherlands, 229
Lilly Endowment, Inc, USA, 448
Liz Claiborne & Art Ortenberg Foundation, USA, 448
Loyalty Foundation, Spain, 285
Lumos Foundation, UK, 366
Luxemburg (Rosa) Stiftung, Germany, 139
MacArthur (John D. and Catherine T.) Foundation, USA, 444
McKnight Foundation, USA, 449
MADRE, USA, 450
MAG—Mines Advisory Group, UK, 366
Mama Cash Foundation, Netherlands, 230
MAPFRE Foundation, Spain, 292
March of Dimes Foundation, USA, 450
Maria Cecilia Souto Vidigal Foundation, Brazil, 40
Marinho (Roberto), Fundação, Brazil, 41
Marisla Foundation, USA, 451
The Max Foundation, USA, 451
Max Havelaar Foundation—Fairtrade Netherlands, Netherlands, 230
Medico International, Germany, 136
Mediterranean Foundation, Argentina, 7
Mendoza (Eugenio), Fundación, Venezuela, 487
Merchant Navy Fund, UK, 382
Mercy, Ireland, 168
Mercy For Animals—MFA, USA, 452
Mercy Corps, USA, 452
Mérieux Foundation, France, 109
Messi (Leo), Fundación, Spain, 292
Mexican Centre for Philanthropy, Mexico, 214
Miguel Alemán Foundation, Mexico, 215
Mines Advisory Group—MAG, UK, 366
Mohammed bin Rashid Al Maktoum Global Initiatives—MBRGI, United Arab Emirates, 335
Moisés Bertoni Foundation, Paraguay, 248
Montevideo Circle Foundation, Uruguay, 485
Mother Child Education Foundation, Türkiye, 327
Mountain Institute, Peru, 249
Mutual Aid and Liaison Service, France, 116
National Community Foundation, Saint Lucia, 268
National Foundation for Development, El Salvador, 91
National Foundation for the Development of Honduras, Honduras, 150
The Nature Conservancy—TNC, USA, 456
NDI—National Democratic Institute for International Affairs, USA, 456
Nederlandse Organisatie voor Internationale Ontwikkelingssamenwerking—Stichting NOVIB, Netherlands, 228
Network of Foundations Working for Development—netFWD, France, 99
Network for Human Development, Brazil, 41
Network of Mexican Community Foundations, Mexico, 215
New School Foundation, Colombia, 71
Nobis Foundation, Ecuador, 88
Nonprofit Enterprise and Self-sustainability Team—NESsT, USA, 457
Nott (David) Foundation, UK, 350
Novartis Foundation, Switzerland, 314
NOVIB (Oxfam Netherlands), Netherlands, 228
OISCA International—Organization for Industrial, Spiritual and Cultural Advancement-International, Japan, 192
Ökumenikus Segélyszervezet, Hungary, 153
Open Society Foundation Haiti, Haiti, 149
Operation USA, USA, 459
Opportunity International UK, UK, 372
Oranje Fonds, Netherlands, 227
Orbis Charitable Trust, UK, 372
Ortega y Gasset (José), Fundación, Spain, 291
Outreach International, USA, 459
Oxfam Brasil, Brazil, 41
Oxfam Canada, Canada, 60
Oxfam Denmark, Denmark, 86
Oxfam Deutschland eV, Germany, 138
Oxfam Italia, Italy, 183
Oxfam Mexico, Mexico, 216
Oxfam NOVIB—Nederlandse Organisatie voor Internationale Ontwikkelingssamenwerking, Netherlands, 228
Oxfam NOVIB—Netherlands Organization for International Development Co-operation, Netherlands, 228
Oxfam-Québec, Canada, 60
Pablo Neruda Foundation, Chile, 65
Pact, USA, 460
PADF—Pan American Development Foundation, USA, 460
Pan American Development Foundation—PADF, USA, 460
PANNA—Pesticide Action Network North America, USA, 462
Partage, France, 116
Partners in Health, USA, 461
PATH, USA, 461
Patiño (Simón I.), Fondation, Switzerland, 310
PCI—Project Concern International, USA, 431
Peace Brigades International—PBI, Belgium, 33
Peace Direct, UK, 373
Peruvian Foundation for Nature Conservation, Peru, 249
Pestalozzi Children's Foundation, Switzerland, 317
Pesticide Action Network Latin America and the Caribbean, Chile, 65
Pesticide Action Network North America—PANNA, USA, 462
Philanthropic, Colombia, 70
Plan International Ireland, Ireland, 167
Population Council, USA, 463
Populorum Progressio Foundation, Vatican City, 486
Practical Action, UK, 374
Presbyterian World Service & Development—PWS&D, Canada, 61
Prince Bernhard Cultural Foundation, Netherlands, 230
Prince Claus Fund for Culture and Development, Netherlands, 228
Prins Bernhard Culturfonds, Stichting, Netherlands, 230
Prins Claus Fonds Voor Cultuur en Ontwikkeling, Netherlands, 228
Pro Mujer International, USA, 464
Pro Victimis, Switzerland, 315
Pro Women International, USA, 464
PRODESSA—Proyecto de Desarrollo Santiago, Guatemala, 148
Project HOPE, USA, 464
Project Trust, UK, 374
Pronaturaleza—Fundación Peruana para la Conservación de la Naturaleza, Peru, 249
PROVICOOP, Chile, 65
Public Studies Centre, Chile, 64
Puerto Rico Community Foundation, Puerto Rico, 261
Rainforest Foundation Norway, Norway, 243
The Rainforest Foundation UK—RFUK, UK, 375
Rainforest Foundation US—RFUS, USA, 465
Red de Acción en Plaguicidas y sus Alternativas de América Latina—RAP-AL, Chile, 65
Red de Mujeres para el Desarrollo, Costa Rica, 75
Red de Salud de las Mujeres Latinoamericanas y del Caribe—RSMLAC, Ecuador, 89
Rede Comuá, Brazil, 38
Rede Iberoamericana de Fundações Civicas ou Comunitárias—RIFC, Brazil, 38
REDEH—Rede de Desenvolvimento Humano, Brazil, 41
Regnskogfondet, Norway, 243
Relief International, USA, 466
Renault Foundation, France, 106
Repsol Foundation, Spain, 295
The Resource Foundation—TRF, USA, 467
Robert Marinho Foundation, Brazil, 41
Rosa Luxemburg Foundation, Germany, 139
Rosa-Luxemburg-Stiftung, Germany, 139
The Rufford Foundation, UK, 380
Rutgers, Netherlands, 228
El Salvadoran Association for Economic and Social Development FUSADES, El Salvador, 91
Samuel (Hedwig und Robert) Stiftung, Germany, 131
Sandals Foundation, Jamaica, 184
Santiago Development Project, Guatemala, 148
Schneider Electric Foundation, France, 111
Schweizerisch-Liechtensteinische Stiftung für Archäologische Forschungen im Ausland—SLSA, Switzerland, 316
Scottish Catholic International Aid Fund—SCIAF, UK, 382
The Seafarers' Charity, UK, 382
Seafarers International Relief Fund, UK, 382
Secours Dentaire International, Switzerland, 317
SeedChange, Canada, 61
SEL—Service d'Entraide et de Liaison, France, 116
SELAVIP—Services Latino-Américains, Africains et Asiatiques de Promotion de l'Habitation Populaire, Chile, 66

INDEX BY AREA OF ACTIVITY

Sembrar Sartawi, Bolivia, 36
Senna (Ayrton), Instituto, Brazil, 41
Serrv International, Inc, USA, 471
SES Foundation—Sustainability, Education, Solidarity, Argentina, 8
Seva Foundation, USA, 471
Sightsavers International, UK, 382
Simón I. Patiño Foundation, Switzerland, 310
Sinergia—Red Venezolana de OSC, Venezuela, 487
Slim (Carlos), Fundación, Mexico, 215
SM Foundation, Spain, 295
Software AG Foundation, Germany, 139
Software AG Stiftung, Germany, 139
Solidarios—Consejo de Fundaciones Americanas de Desarrollo, Dominican Republic, 87
Solidarity Foundation, Dominican Republic, 87
SOS Atlantic Forest Foundation, Brazil, 41
Souto Vidigal (Maria Cecilia), Fundação, Brazil, 40
Sparkassenstiftung für internationale Kooperation, Germany, 125
Steelworkers Humanity Fund/Le Fonds Humanitaire des Metallos, Canada, 62
Stichting DOEN, Netherlands, 229
Stichting IKEA Foundation, Netherlands, 229
Stichting Liliane Fonds, Netherlands, 229
Stichting Mama Cash, Netherlands, 230
Stichting Max Havelaar—Fairtrade Nederland, Netherlands, 230
Stichting Prins Bernhard Cultuurfonds, Netherlands, 230
Stichting Triodos Foundation, Netherlands, 231
Stiftung Kinderdorf Pestalozzi, Switzerland, 317
Stiftung Klimarappen, Switzerland, 317
Stiftung Vivamos Mejor, Switzerland, 317
Survival International, UK, 385
Swiss Church Aid, Switzerland, 311
Swiss Foundation for Technical Co-operation, Switzerland, 318
Swiss-Liechtenstein Foundation for Archaeological Research Abroad—SLFA, Switzerland, 316
SWISSAID Foundation, Switzerland, 318
Swisscontact—Swiss Foundation for Technical Co-operation, Switzerland, 318
Synergos—The Synergos Institute, USA, 396
Szenes (Arpad)-Vieira da Silva, Fundação, Portugal, 258
TANZ—Trade Aid NZ Inc, New Zealand, 235
Tearfund, UK, 385
Telefónica Movistar Argentina Foundation, Argentina, 8
Telefónica Movistar Chile Foundation, Chile, 65
Telefónica Movistar Colombia Foundation, Colombia, 71
Telefónica Movistar Ecuador Foundation, Ecuador, 89
Telefónica Movistar México Foundation, Mexico, 216
Telefónica Movistar Perú Foundation, Peru, 249
Telefónica Movistar Uruguay Foundation, Uruguay, 485
Telefónica Vivo Foundation, Brazil, 41
Teletón México Foundation, Mexico, 216
Telmex Telcel Foundation, Mexico, 216
Terre des Hommes International Federation—TDHIF, Switzerland, 318
Terre Sans Frontières—TSF, Canada, 62
Third World Network—TWN, Malaysia, 211
Third World Solidarity Action, Luxembourg, 209
Tinker Foundation, Inc, USA, 475
TK Foundation, Bahamas, 24
Trade Aid NZ Inc—TANZ, New Zealand, 235
Triodos Foundation, Netherlands, 231
Trócaire—Catholic Agency for World Development, Ireland, 168
U4 Anti-Corruption Resource Centre, Norway, 241
Union Aid Abroad—APHEDA, Australia, 19
UNIR Bolivia Foundation, Bolivia, 36
United Purpose, UK, 387
Unity Foundation, Luxembourg, 210
UPM Foundation, Uruguay, 485
Usain Bolt Foundation, Jamaica, 185
USPG—United Society Partners in the Gospel, UK, 387
Venezuelan Network of Civil Society Organizations, Venezuela, 487
VIDC—Vienna Institute for International Dialogue and Co-operation, Austria, 23
Vienna Institute for International Dialogue and Co-operation—VIDC, Austria, 23
Vivamos Mejor Foundation, Switzerland, 317
Volkart Foundation, Switzerland, 319
Volkart-Stiftung, Switzerland, 319
W. K. Kellogg Foundation—WKKF, USA, 478
Walton Family Foundation, USA, 479
War on Want, UK, 388
WasserStiftung, Germany, 142
Water.org, Inc, USA, 479
Water for People, USA, 479
WaterAid, UK, 389
WaterFoundation, Germany, 142
Weeden Foundation, USA, 479
Westminster Foundation for Democracy—WFD, UK, 389
The Whitley Fund for Nature—WFN, UK, 390
William Adlington Cadbury Charitable Trust, UK, 390
William Randolph Hearst Foundation, USA, 435
Winrock International, USA, 481
The Wolfson Foundation, UK, 390
Women in Equality Foundation, Argentina, 8
Women's Development Network, Costa Rica, 75
Women's Foundation, Costa Rica, 74
World Animal Protection, UK, 391
World Neighbors, USA, 483
World University Service of Canada/Entraide Universitaire Mondiale du Canada—WUSC/EUMC, Canada, 63
World Vision International, UK, 391
Year Out Group, UK, 374
ZOA, Netherlands, 231

SOUTH ASIA

A. M. M. Sahabdeen Trust Foundation, Sri Lanka, 297
AARDO—African-Asian Rural Development Organization, India, 155
Abilis Foundation, Finland, 95
Abilis-säätiö, Finland, 95
Accion, USA, 397
Action Against Hunger, France, 100
Action Children's Aid, Denmark, 82
Action contre la Faim—ACF France, France, 100
Action Damien/Damiaanactie, Belgium, 28
Action Education, France, 100
Action on Poverty, Australia, 10
Action Solidarité Tiers Monde—ASTM, Luxembourg, 209
Acumen, USA, 397
Afdi—Agriculteurs Français et Développement International, France, 100
Afghan Women's Network, Afghanistan, 3
Afghanistan Institute for Civil Society—AICS, Afghanistan, 3
Afghanistan Research and Evaluation Unit, Afghanistan, 3
African-Asian Rural Development Organization—AARDO, India, 155
Aga Khan Foundation Canada, Canada, 49
Age International, UK, 339
Agriculteurs Français et Développement International, France, 100
Agronomes et Vétérinaires sans Frontières—AVSF, France, 100
Agronomists and Veterinarians Without Borders, France, 100
AID Foundation, Bangladesh, 24
Air France Foundation, France, 103
AIT—Asian Institute of Technology, Thailand, 323
AKO Foundation, UK, 339
Aktion Børnehjælp, Denmark, 82
Al Basar International Foundation, Saudi Arabia, 268
Alert—International Alert, UK, 360
Alet'Eleym Fewq Alejmey'e, Qatar, 262
Alkhidmat Foundation Pakistan—AKFP, Pakistan, 244
All India Disaster Mitigation Institute, India, 155
Alliance of Bioversity International and the International Center for Tropical Agriculture—CIAT, Italy, 172
Aman Foundation, Pakistan, 244
Ambuja Cement Foundation—ACF, India, 156
American Councils for International Education, USA, 400
American Institute of Pakistan Studies, USA, 401
American Jewish World Service—AJWS, USA, 402
AmeriCares Foundation, Inc, USA, 403
ANGOC—Asian NGO Coalition for Agrarian Reform and Rural Development, Philippines, 251
Arbeiterwohlfahrt Bundesverband eV—AWO, Germany, 121
Arghyam, India, 156
Ark, UK, 341
Armanshahr Foundation—OPEN ASIA, Afghanistan, 3
Asia Africa International Voluntary Foundation—AIV, Japan, 186
Asia Foundation, USA, 406

South Asia

Asia New Zealand Foundation/Te Whītau Tūhono, New Zealand, 232
Asia/Pacific Cultural Centre for UNESCO—ACCU, Japan, 186
Asia Pacific Foundation of Canada—APFCanada, Canada, 49
Asia Philanthropy Circle—APC, Singapore, 272
Asia Society, USA, 406
AsiaDHRRA—Asian Partnership for the Development of Human Resources in Rural Asia, Philippines, 251
Asian Community Trust—ACT, Japan, 186
Asian Development Research Institute—ADRI, India, 156
Asian Health Institute—AHI, Japan, 187
Asian Institute of Technology—AIT, Thailand, 323
Asian Partnership for the Development of Human Resources in Rural Asia, Philippines, 251
Asian Venture Philanthropy Network—AVPN, Singapore, 272
Aspen Institute, USA, 407
ASTM—Action Solidarité Tiers Monde, Luxembourg, 209
Auchan Foundation, France, 103
Aurat Publication & Information Service Foundation—AF, Pakistan, 245
Aurora Trust, UK, 341
Australian Foundation for the Peoples of Asia and the Pacific—AFAP, Australia, 10
Australian Volunteers International—AVI, Australia, 13
AVI—Australian Volunteers International, Australia, 13
Azim Premji Foundation, India, 156
Bagnoud (François-Xavier) Association, Switzerland, 310
Bangladesh Freedom Foundation—BFF, Bangladesh, 24
Bank of America Charitable Foundation, USA, 407
Barcelona Centre for International Affairs, Spain, 287
Barzani Charity Foundation—BCF, Iraq, 164
BBC Media Action, UK, 342
Benaad Enetkhabat Shafaf Afghanistan, Afghanistan, 4
Berghof Foundation gGmbH, Germany, 122
Berghof Stiftung für Konfliktforschung gGmbH, Germany, 122
Bettencourt Schueller Foundation, France, 103
Bharti Foundation, India, 156
Biocon Foundation, India, 157
Blue Marine Foundation—BLUE, UK, 343
Böll (Heinrich) Stiftung, Germany, 131
Book Aid International—BAI, UK, 343
Born Free Foundation, UK, 343
Bosch (Robert) Stiftung GmbH, Germany, 138
Bóthar, Ireland, 166
BRAC, Bangladesh, 25
Bread for the World—Protestant Work for Social Welfare and Development, Germany, 123
British Schools and Universities Foundation, Inc—BSUF, USA, 410
Brot für die Welt—Evangelisches Werk für Diakonie und Entwicklung, Germany, 123
Brother's Brother Foundation, USA, 410
Brothers of Men, France, 113
CAF—Charities Aid Foundation, UK, 336
CAF India, India, 155
Canadian Centre for International Studies and Co-operation, Canada, 51
Canadian Foodgrains Bank, Canada, 50
CARE International—CI, Switzerland, 307
Caritas Canada, Canada, 53
Carnegie Endowment for International Peace, USA, 411
The Carter Center, USA, 412
Cartier Foundation for Contemporary Art, France, 104
CBM-International, Germany, 123
CECI—Canadian Centre for International Studies and Co-operation/Centre d'Etudes et de Coopération Internationale, Canada, 51
Centre for Civil Society—CCS, India, 157
Centre pour le Dialogue Humanitaire, Switzerland, 307
Centre for Humanitarian Dialogue—HD, Switzerland, 307
Centre for Social Impact and Philanthropy—CSIP, India, 154
Centre for Strategic and International Studies—CSIS, Indonesia, 162
Charitable Impact Foundation, Canada, 47
Charities Advisory Trust, UK, 336
Charities Aid Foundation—CAF, UK, 336
Charity Projects, UK, 348
The Charles Wallace India Trusts, UK, 347

South Asia

Cheshire (Leonard) Foundation, UK, 364
ChildFund International, USA, 414
Children International—CI, USA, 414
Children of the Mekong, France, 102
The Children's Investment Fund Foundation, UK, 347
China Foundation for Poverty Alleviation—CFPA, China (People's Republic), 67
Chr. Michelsen Institute for Science and Intellectual Freedom—CMI, Norway, 241
CIAT—Centro Internacional de Agricultura Tropical, Italy, 172
CIDOB Foundation—Barcelona Centre for International Affairs, Spain, 287
Civil Society and Human Rights Network, Afghanistan, 3
Civil Society and Human Rights Organization—CSHRO, Afghanistan, 3
Claiborne (Liz) & Art Ortenberg Foundation, USA, 448
Climate Cent Foundation, Switzerland, 317
Člověk v tísni, Czech Republic, 79
CMI—Chr. Michelsen Institute for Science and Intellectual Freedom, Norway, 241
Coastline Foundation, Maldives, 212
Comic Relief, UK, 348
Commonwealth Foundation, UK, 348
Community Chest of Korea—Fruit of Love, Korea (Republic), 200
Concern India Foundation, India, 157
Concern Worldwide, Ireland, 166
CRDF Global, USA, 419
Dasra, India, 154
David Nott Foundation, UK, 350
Dell (Michael & Susan) Foundation, USA, 453
Deutsche Gesellschaft für Auswärtige Politik—DGAP, Germany, 124
Deutsche Sparkassenstiftung für Internationale Zusammenarbeit, Germany, 125
Development and Peace—Caritas Canada, Canada, 53
Développement et Paix—Caritas Canada, Canada, 53
Diakonia, Sweden, 298
DOEN Foundation, Netherlands, 229
Dom Manuel II Foundation, Portugal, 260
Dutch-Bangla Bank Foundation, Bangladesh, 25
Earthworm Foundation, Switzerland, 307
East-West Center—EWC, USA, 422
Edhi Foundation, Pakistan, 245
Education Above All Foundation—EAA, Qatar, 262
Educo, Spain, 286
Elizabeth Glaser Pediatric AIDS Foundation—EGPAF, USA, 423
Ellerman (John) Foundation, UK, 361
Elton John AIDS Foundation, UK, 352
EMERGENCY, Italy, 173
Enda Third World—Environment and Development Action in the Third World, Senegal, 270
Enda Tiers Monde—Environnement et Développement du Tiers-Monde, Senegal, 270
endPoverty.org, USA, 424
Enfants du Mékong, France, 102
EngenderHealth, USA, 424
Entraide Protestante Suisse, Switzerland, 311
Entraide Universitaire Mondiale du Canada, Canada, 63
Environmental Justice Foundation—EJF, UK, 353
Equality Fund/Fonds Égalité, Canada, 54
Fairtrade Nederland, Netherlands, 230
The Family Federation of Finland, Finland, 98
Federal Association of Social Welfare Organizations, Germany, 121
Feed the Minds, UK, 354
filia.die Frauenstiftung, Germany, 128
filia—the Women's Foundation, Germany, 128
FINCA International, USA, 425
Focus Humanitarian Assistance—FOCUS, Canada, 54
Fondation Abbé Pierre, France, 108
Fondation pour l'Agriculture et la Ruralité dans le Monde—Fondation FARM, France, 106
Fondation Air France, France, 103
Fondation Auchan, France, 103
Fondation Bettencourt Schueller, France, 103
Fondation Cartier pour l'Art Contemporain, France, 104
Fondation d'Entreprise Renault, France, 106
Fondation FARM—Fondation pour l'Agriculture et la Ruralité dans le Monde, France, 106
Fondation Hirondelle: Media for Peace and Human Dignity, Switzerland, 309
Fondation pour le Logement des Défavorisés, France, 108
Fondation Mérieux, France, 109

Fondation S, France, 111
Fondation Schneider Electric, France, 111
Fondation Suisse-Liechtenstein pour les Recherches Archéologiques à l'Etranger, Switzerland, 316
Fonds Égalité, Canada, 54
Food for the Hungry—FH, USA, 426
Ford Foundation, USA, 427
The Forest Trust, Switzerland, 307
Fòs Feminista, USA, 427
Foundation for Culture and Civil Society—FCCS, Afghanistan, 3
Foundation for Housing the Disadvantaged, France, 108
Foundation for International Community Assistance, USA, 425
Foundation Open Society Institute Pakistan, Pakistan, 245
Foundation for World Agriculture and Rural Life, France, 106
Franciscans International, Switzerland, 310
Fraunhofer-Gesellschaft, Germany, 129
Fraunhofer Society, Germany, 129
The Fred Hollows Foundation, Australia, 14
The Freeman Foundation, USA, 428
French Agriculturalists and International Development, France, 100
French Institute of International Relations, France, 113
Frères des Hommes—FDH, France, 113
Friedensdorf International, Germany, 129
Fundação Dom Manuel II, Portugal, 260
Fundació CIDOB, Spain, 287
Fundación Capital, Colombia, 70
FXB International—Association François-Xavier Bagnoud, Switzerland, 310
German Council on Foreign Relations, Germany, 124
German Foundation for International Legal Co-operation, Germany, 133
German Institute for Global and Area Studies—GIGA, Germany, 130
German Savings Banks Foundation for International Co-operation, Germany, 125
Ghazanfar Foundation, Afghanistan, 4
Gift of the Givers Foundation, South Africa, 280
Give Foundation, India, 155
Give2Asia, USA, 394
GiveIndia, India, 155
Glaser (Elizabeth) Pediatric AIDS Foundation, USA, 423
Global Communities, USA, 431
Global Fund for Children, USA, 431
Global Innovation Fund, UK, 356
Global Schools Forum, UK, 341
Good Neighbors International, Korea (Republic), 201
Grameen Foundation—GF, USA, 433
Grassroots International—GRI, USA, 433
Green Umbrella Children's Foundation—ChildFund Korea, Korea (Republic), 201
GuideStar India, India, 155
Hagar NZ, New Zealand, 233
HALO Trust, UK, 357
Hamdard Foundation Pakistan, Pakistan, 245
Hamlyn (Paul) Foundation, UK, 373
Havelaar (Max) Foundation, Netherlands, 230
Health Volunteers Overseas—HVO, USA, 434
Hedwig and Robert Samuel Foundation, Germany, 131
Hedwig und Robert Samuel-Stiftung, Germany, 131
Heinrich Böll Foundation, Germany, 131
Heinrich-Böll-Stiftung, Germany, 131
HEKS—Hilfswerk der Evangelischen Kirchen Schweiz, Switzerland, 311
Helen Keller International—HKI, USA, 435
Helvetas Swiss Intercooperation, Switzerland, 311
Hinduja Foundation, India, 157
Hivos—Humanistisch Instituut voor Ontwikkelings Samenwerking, Netherlands, 226
Hollows (Fred) Foundation, Australia, 14
Holt International, USA, 436
HOPE International Development Agency, Canada, 56
Humanistic Institute for Co-operation with Developing Countries, Netherlands, 226
Humanitarian Academy for Development—HAD, UK, 359
Humanitarian Coalition, Canada, 48
The Hunger Project, USA, 438
IACD—Institute of Asian Culture and Development, Korea (Republic), 201
IDRF—International Development and Relief Foundation, Canada, 56

INDEX BY AREA OF ACTIVITY

IFAD—International Fund for Agricultural Development, Italy, 182
IHH Humanitarian Relief Foundation, Türkiye, 328
IIED—International Institute for Environment and Development, UK, 360
IKEA Foundation, Netherlands, 229
India Partners, USA, 438
Indian Council of Social Science Research—ICSSR, India, 157
Indian National Trust for Art and Cultural Heritage—INTACH, India, 158
INHURED International—International Institute for Human Rights, Environment and Development, Nepal, 223
İnsan Hak ve Hürriyetleri İnsani Yardım Vakfı—IHH, Türkiye, 328
Institut Français des Relations Internationales—IFRI, France, 113
Institut de Médecine et d'Epidémiologie Appliquée—Fondation Internationale Léon Mba, France, 114
Institute of Applied Medicine and Epidemiology—International Foundation Léon Mba, France, 114
Institute of Asian Culture and Development—IACD, Korea (Republic), 201
Institute of Developing Economies-Japan External Trade Organization—IDE-JETRO, Japan, 188
Institute for Sustainable Communities—ISC, USA, 439
INTACH—Indian National Trust for Art and Cultural Heritage, India, 158
Inter Pares, Canada, 57
Interchurch Aid—HIA Hungary, Hungary, 153
International Alert—Alert, UK, 360
International Blue Crescent Relief and Development Foundation—IBC, Türkiye, 329
International Development and Relief Foundation—IDRF, Canada, 56
The International Foundation, USA, 440
International Fund for Agricultural Development—IFAD, Italy, 182
International Institute for Environment and Development—IIED, UK, 360
International Institute for Human Rights, Environment and Development, Nepal, 223
International Rescue Committee—IRC, USA, 441
International Research & Exchanges Board—IREX, USA, 442
International Rhino Foundation—IRF, USA, 441
International Rivers, USA, 441
International Water Management Institute—IWMI, Sri Lanka, 297
International Women's Health Coalition, USA, 427
iPartner India, India, 155
IRC—International Rescue Committee, USA, 441
IREX—International Research & Exchanges Board, USA, 442
IRZ (Deutsche Stiftung für Internationale Rechtliche Zusammenarbeit) eV, Germany, 133
Japan International Volunteer Center—JVC, Japan, 190
JEN, Japan, 190
The John D. and Catherine T. MacArthur Foundation, USA, 444
John Ellerman Foundation, UK, 361
Karuna Trust, UK, 363
Keller (Helen) International, USA, 435
Khemka (Nand & Jeet) Foundation, India, 159
King Philanthropies, USA, 445
KIOS Foundation, Finland, 96
Kusuma Trust UK, UK, 363
Landesa—Rural Development Institute, USA, 447
Latin American, African and Asian Social Housing Service, Chile, 66
Latin American and Caribbean Women's Health Network—LACWHN, Ecuador, 89
Leibniz-Institut für Globale und Regionale Studien, Germany, 130
Leonard Cheshire Disability, UK, 364
The Leprosy Mission International, UK, 364
Li Ka Shing Foundation, Hong Kong, 151
Lifeline Energy, South Africa, 280
Liliane Foundation, Netherlands, 229
Liz Claiborne & Art Ortenberg Foundation, USA, 448
The Long Now Foundation, USA, 449
Luxemburg (Rosa) Stiftung, Germany, 139
M. S. Swaminathan Research Foundation—MSSRF, India, 158
M. Venkatarangaiya Foundation—MVF, India, 158
MacArthur (John D. and Catherine T.) Foundation, USA, 444

INDEX BY AREA OF ACTIVITY

MAG—Mines Advisory Group, UK, 366
Mama Cash Foundation, Netherlands, 230
March of Dimes Foundation, USA, 450
Mauritius Telecom Foundation—MTF, Mauritius, 214
The Max Foundation, USA, 451
Max Havelaar Foundation—Fairtrade Netherlands, Netherlands, 230
medica mondiale eV, Germany, 136
Medico International, Germany, 136
Merchant Navy Fund, UK, 382
Mercury Phoenix Trust, UK, 367
Mercy For Animals—MFA, USA, 452
Mercy Corps, USA, 452
Mercy-USA for Aid and Development, USA, 452
Mérieux Foundation, France, 109
Michael & Susan Dell Foundation, USA, 453
Mines Advisory Group—MAG, UK, 366
Minhaj Welfare Foundation, UK, 368
Mohammed bin Rashid Al Maktoum Global Initiatives—MBRGI, United Arab Emirates, 335
Moriya Scholarship Foundation, Japan, 191
MTN Afghanistan Foundation, Afghanistan, 4
Muslim Aid, UK, 369
Mutual Aid and Liaison Service, France, 116
Naandi Foundation—A New Beginning, India, 158
Nand & Jeet Khemka Foundation, India, 159
National Empowerment Foundation—NEF, Mauritius, 214
The Nature Conservancy—TNC, USA, 456
NDI—National Democratic Institute for International Affairs, USA, 456
Nederlandse Organisatie voor Internationale Ontwikkelingssamenwerking—Stichting NOVIB, Netherlands, 228
NEF—National Empowerment Foundation, Mauritius, 214
Neighbour in Need, Austria, 22
Network of Foundations Working for Development—netFWD, France, 99
New Myanmar Foundation, Myanmar, 221
NFI—National Foundation for India, India, 159
North-South-Bridge Foundation, Germany, 141
Nott (David) Foundation, UK, 350
Novartis Foundation, Switzerland, 314
NOVIB (Oxfam Netherlands), Netherlands, 228
OISCA International—Organization for Industrial, Spiritual and Cultural Advancement-International, Japan, 192
Ökumenikus Segélyszervezet, Hungary, 153
OneStage, India, 155
OPEN ASIA—Armanshahr Foundation, Afghanistan, 3
Open Society Foundations in Pakistan, Pakistan, 245
Operation Eyesight Universal/Action Universelle de la Vue, Canada, 60
Operation USA, USA, 459
Orbis Charitable Trust, UK, 372
ORF Nachbar in Not, Austria, 22
Outreach International, USA, 459
Oxfam Australia, Australia, 16
Oxfam Canada, Canada, 60
Oxfam Deutschland eV, Germany, 138
Oxfam Hong Kong, Hong Kong, 151
Oxfam India, India, 159
Oxfam Ireland, Ireland, 167
Oxfam Italia, Italy, 183
Oxfam NOVIB—Nederlandse Organisatie voor Internationale Ontwikkelingssamenwerking, Netherlands, 228
Oxfam NOVIB—Netherlands Organization for International Development Co-operation, Netherlands, 228
Pacific Peoples' Partnership, Canada, 61
Pact, USA, 460
Pakistan Centre for Philanthropy—PCP, Pakistan, 244
Pakistan Institute of International Affairs—PIIA, Pakistan, 245
PANAP—Pesticide Action Network Asia and the Pacific, Malaysia, 211
Parasol Foundation Trust, Gibraltar, 144
Partage, France, 116
Partners for Equity, Australia, 16
PATH, USA, 461
Paul Hamlyn Foundation—PHF, UK, 373
PCI—Project Concern International, USA, 431
Peace Brigades International—PBI, Belgium, 33
Peace Direct, UK, 373
Peace, Health and Human Development Foundation—PHD Foundation, Japan, 193
Peace Village International, Germany, 129
Peace Winds Japan—PWJ, Japan, 192
People in Need, Czech Republic, 79

Pestalozzi Children's Foundation, Switzerland, 317
Pesticide Action Network Asia and the Pacific—PANAP, Malaysia, 211
The PHD Foundation—Peace, Health and Human Development Foundation, Japan, 193
Plan International Ireland, Ireland, 167
Ploughshares Fund, USA, 463
Population Council, USA, 463
Practical Action, UK, 374
Pratham Education Foundation, India, 159
Première Urgence Internationale, France, 116
Premji (Azim) Foundation, India, 156
Presbyterian World Service & Development—PWS&D, Canada, 61
Prince Claus Fund for Culture and Development, Netherlands, 228
Prins Claus Fonds Voor Cultuur en Ontwikkeling, Netherlands, 228
Pro Victimis, Switzerland, 315
Project HOPE, USA, 464
Project Trust, UK, 374
Public Health Foundation of India—PHFI, India, 159
Rajiv Gandhi Foundation, India, 160
Ramon Magsaysay Award Foundation, Philippines, 253
Red de Salud de las Mujeres Latinoamericanas y del Caribe—RSMLAC, Ecuador, 89
RedR UK, UK, 375
Regional Centre for Strategic Studies—RCSS, Sri Lanka, 297
Reliance Foundation, India, 160
Relief International, USA, 466
Renault Foundation, France, 106
Robert Bosch Foundation, Germany, 138
Robert-Bosch-Stiftung GmbH, Germany, 138
Rohini Nilekani Philanthropies, India, 160
Rosa Luxemburg Foundation, Germany, 139
Rosa-Luxemburg-Stiftung, Germany, 139
Royal Society for the Protection of Birds—RSPB, UK, 379
RSPB—Royal Society for the Protection of Birds, UK, 379
The Rufford Foundation, UK, 380
Rural Development Institute—Landesa, USA, 447
Rutgers, Netherlands, 228
Sahabdeen (A. M. M.) Trust Foundation, Sri Lanka, 297
Sakena Fund, USA, 469
Samuel (Hedwig und Robert) Stiftung, Germany, 131
Santé Sud, France, 116
Sasakawa Health Foundation—SHF, Japan, 194
Schneider Electric Foundation, France, 111
Schweizerisch-Liechtensteinische Stiftung für Archäologische Forschungen im Ausland—SLSA, Switzerland, 316
Scottish Catholic International Aid Fund—SCIAF, UK, 382
The Seafarers' Charity, UK, 382
Seafarers International Relief Fund, UK, 382
SeedChange, Canada, 61
Seeds of Peace, USA, 470
SEL—Service d'Entraide et de Liaison, France, 116
SELAVIP—Services Latino-Américains, Africains et Asiatiques de Promotion de l'Habitation Populaire, Chile, 66
Serrv International, Inc, USA, 471
Seva Foundation, USA, 471
Shahid Afridi Foundation—SAF, Pakistan, 246
Shiv Nadar Foundation, India, 160
Sightsavers International, UK, 382
Singapore International Foundation—SIF, Singapore, 273
Snow Leopard Trust, USA, 472
SNV, Netherlands, 228
Southern Health, France, 116
Sparkassenstiftung für internationale Kooperation, Germany, 125
Stichting DOEN, Netherlands, 229
Stichting IKEA Foundation, Netherlands, 229
Stichting Liliane Fonds, Netherlands, 229
Stichting Mama Cash, Netherlands, 230
Stichting Max Havelaar—Fairtrade Nederland, Netherlands, 230
Stichting Triodos Foundation, Netherlands, 231
Stiftung Kinderdorf Pestalozzi, Switzerland, 317
Stiftung Klimarappen, Switzerland, 317
Stiftung Nord-Süd-Brücken, Germany, 141
Strømme Foundation, Norway, 243
Strømmestiftelsen, Norway, 243
Survival International, UK, 385
Swaminathan (M. S.) Research Foundation, India, 158
Swiss Church Aid, Switzerland, 311

USA and Canada

Swiss Foundation for Technical Co-operation, Switzerland, 318
Swiss-Liechtenstein Foundation for Archaeological Research Abroad—SLFA, Switzerland, 316
SWISSAID Foundation, Switzerland, 318
Swisscontact—Swiss Foundation for Technical Co-operation, Switzerland, 318
Synergos—The Synergos Institute, USA, 396
TANZ—Trade Aid NZ Inc, New Zealand, 235
Tearfund, UK, 385
Tearfund Australia, Australia, 18
Temasek Foundation, Singapore, 273
Terre des Hommes International Federation—TDHIF, Switzerland, 318
Tewa, Nepal, 223
TFF–Transnational Foundation for Peace and Future Research, Sweden, 304
TFF–Transnationella Stiftelsen för Freds- och Framtidsforskning, Sweden, 304
Third World Network—TWN, Malaysia, 211
Third World Solidarity Action, Luxembourg, 209
Tibet Fund, USA, 475
Tibet-Institut Rikon, Switzerland, 318
Tokyu Foundation, Japan, 194
The Toyota Foundation, Japan, 195
Trade Aid NZ Inc—TANZ, New Zealand, 235
Transparent Election Foundation of Afghanistan—TEFA, Afghanistan, 4
Triodos Foundation, Netherlands, 231
Turquoise Mountain Foundation, UK, 386
U4 Anti-Corruption Resource Centre, Norway, 241
United Purpose, UK, 387
Unity Foundation, Luxembourg, 210
Universal Foundation, Maldives, 212
US Civilian Research & Development Foundation, USA, 419
USPG—United Society Partners in the Gospel, UK, 387
Väestöliitto, Finland, 98
VANI—Voluntary Action Network India, India, 155
Venkatarangaiya (M.) Foundation, India, 158
VIDC—Vienna Institute for International Dialogue and Co-operation, Austria, 23
Vienna Institute for International Dialogue and Co-operation—VIDC, Austria, 23
Vivekananda International Foundation—VIF, India, 161
Vodafone Foundation India, India, 161
Vodafone Idea Foundation, India, 161
Voluntary Action Network India—VANI, India, 155
Voluntary Service Overseas, UK, 388
VSO—Voluntary Service Overseas, UK, 388
Wallace (Charles) Trusts, UK, 347
War Child, UK, 388
War on Want, UK, 388
Water.org, Inc, USA, 479
Water for People, USA, 479
WaterAid, UK, 389
Westminster Foundation for Democracy—WFD, UK, 389
The Whitley Fund for Nature—WFN, UK, 390
Winrock International, USA, 481
The Wolfson Foundation, UK, 390
Women's Fund Asia, Sri Lanka, 297
World Neighbors, USA, 483
World University Service of Canada/Entraide Universitaire Mondiale du Canada—WUSC/EUMC, Canada, 63
World Vegetable Center, Taiwan, 322
World Vision International, UK, 391
WorldFish, Malaysia, 212
Year Out Group, UK, 374
Zakat House, Kuwait, 203
ZOA, Netherlands, 231

USA AND CANADA

Abdorrahman Boroumand Center for Human Rights in Iran—ABC, USA, 396
Accion, USA, 397
Acumen, USA, 397
Adriano Olivetti Foundation, Italy, 174
Advance, USA, 397
AFPE—American Foundation for Pharmaceutical Education, USA, 401
Africa-America Institute—AAI, USA, 398
Africa Foundation, South Africa, 278
Africa Grantmakers' Affinity Group—AGAG, USA, 393
Africa Humanitarian Action—AHA, Ethiopia, 93
African Refugees Foundation—AREF, Nigeria, 237
African Wildlife Foundation—AWF, Kenya, 198

INDEX BY AREA OF ACTIVITY

USA and Canada

Aga Khan Foundation Canada, Canada, 49
AGAG—Africa Grantmakers' Affinity Group, USA, 393
AHA—American Historical Association, USA, 401
AINA—Arctic Institute of North America, Canada, 49
AIT—Asian Institute of Technology, Thailand, 323
Alavi Foundation, USA, 398
Alcoa Foundation, USA, 398
Alden (George I.) Trust, USA, 430
Alfred P. Sloan Foundation, USA, 398
Allende (Isabel) Foundation, USA, 442
Alliance for International Exchange, USA, 399
Alliance for Securing Democracy, USA, 430
The Alva Foundation, Canada, 49
Amancio Ortega Foundation, Spain, 288
The Ambrose Monell Foundation, USA, 399
America for Bulgaria Foundation, Bulgaria, 43
America–Mideast Educational and Training Services Inc, USA, 404
American Councils for International Education, USA, 400
American Enterprise Institute—AEI, USA, 400
American Foundation for the Blind—AFB, USA, 400
American Foundation for Pharmaceutical Education—AFPE, USA, 401
American Friends Service Committee—AFSC, USA, 401
American Historical Association—AHA, USA, 401
American Institute of Pakistan Studies, USA, 401
American Jewish World Service—AJWS, USA, 402
American Near East Refugee Aid—Anera, USA, 402
American Philosophical Society—APS, USA, 402
American-Scandinavian Foundation—ASF, USA, 403
American Schools of Oriental Research—ASOR, USA, 403
AmeriCares Foundation, Inc, USA, 403
Amerind Foundation, Inc, USA, 403
AMIDEAST—America-Mideast Educational and Training Services, Inc, USA, 404
Amref Health Africa, Kenya, 198
The Andy Warhol Foundation for the Visual Arts, Inc, USA, 404
Anera—American Near East Refugee Aid, USA, 402
The Annie E. Casey Foundation, USA, 404
Arab American Institute Foundation—AAIF, USA, 405
Arca Foundation, USA, 405
Archewell Foundation, USA, 405
Arctic Institute of North America—AINA, Canada, 49
Arcus Foundation, USA, 405
Ark, UK, 341
Arthritis Australia, Australia, 10
Arthritis Foundation, USA, 406
Arthur Rubinstein International Music Society, Israel, 168
Asia Foundation, USA, 406
Asia Pacific Foundation of Canada—APFCanada, Canada, 49
Asia Society, USA, 406
Asian Cultural Council—ACC, USA, 406
Asian Institute of Technology—AIT, Thailand, 323
Aspen Institute, USA, 407
Australian-American Fulbright Commission, Australia, 11
AVINA Foundation, Panama, 247
AVSI Foundation, Italy, 175
Banda (Joyce) Foundation International, Malawi, 210
Bank of America Charitable Foundation, USA, 407
Barbra Streisand Foundation, USA, 408
Barka Foundation for Mutual Assistance, Poland, 256
Barzani Charity Foundation—BCF, Iraq, 164
Baxter & Alma Ricard Foundation, Canada, 55
BBVA Foundation, Spain, 289
Bell (Max) Foundation, Canada, 59
Bertelsmann Foundation, Germany, 122
Bertelsmann Stiftung, Germany, 122
Black Lives Matter Global Network Foundation—BLM Global Network Foundation, USA, 408
Black Sea Trust for Regional Cooperation, USA, 430
Blakemore Foundation, USA, 408
BLM Global Network Foundation, USA, 408
BNP Paribas Foundation, France, 103

Böll (Heinrich) Stiftung, Germany, 131
Born Free Foundation, UK, 343
Born This Way Foundation, USA, 409
Bosch (Robert) Stiftung GmbH, Germany, 138
Braća Karić Foundation, Serbia, 271
BRAC, Bangladesh, 25
Bradley (Lynde and Harry) Foundation, Inc, USA, 449
BrazilFoundation, Brazil, 39
British Schools and Universities Foundation, Inc—BSUF, USA, 410
The Broad Foundation, USA, 410
Brother's Brother Foundation, USA, 410
Buck (Pearl S.) International, USA, 462
Buffett (Howard G.) Foundation, USA, 437
Bunge y Born Foundation, Argentina, 7
Burroughs Wellcome Fund—BWF, USA, 411
CAF—Charities Aid Foundation, UK, 336
California Community Foundation, USA, 411
The Camille and Henry Dreyfus Foundation, Inc, USA, 411
Canada Foundation for Innovation, Canada, 50
CanadaHelps, Canada, 47
Canadian Cancer Society, Canada, 50
Canadian Centre for International Studies and Co-operation, Canada, 51
Canadian Council for International Co-operation—CCIC/Conseil Canadien pour la Coopération Internationale—CCCI, Canada, 48
Canadian Feed The Children—CFTC, Canada, 50
Canadian Foodgrains Bank, Canada, 50
Canadian International Council/Conseil International du Canada—CIC, Canada, 51
Canadian Liver Foundation/Fondation Canadienne du Foie, Canada, 58
Canadian Organization for Development through Education—CODE, Canada, 52
Canadian Urban Institute/Institut Urbain du Canada—CUI/IUC, Canada, 51
Candid, USA, 393
Caritas Canada, Canada, 53
Carnegie Endowment for International Peace, USA, 411
Carnegie Hero Fund Commission, USA, 412
Carrefour International, Canada, 53
The Carter Center, USA, 412
Cartier Foundation for Contemporary Art, France, 104
Casey (Annie E.) Foundation, USA, 404
Catalyste+, Canada, 51
CBM-International, Germany, 123
CECI—Canadian Centre for International Studies and Co-operation/Centre d'Etudes et de Coopération Internationale, Canada, 51
CESO/SACO—Canadian Executive Service Organization/Service d'Assistance Canadienne aux Organismes, Canada, 51
Cetana Educational Foundation, USA, 413
Chagnon (Lucie et André), Fondation, Canada, 55
Charitable Impact Foundation, Canada, 47
Charities Aid Foundation—CAF, UK, 336
Charity Islamic Trust Elrahma, UK, 352
Charles and Lynn Schusterman Family Philanthropies, USA, 413
Charles Stewart Mott Foundation—CSMF, USA, 414
The Chicago Community Trust, USA, 414
Child Migrants Trust, UK, 347
ChildFund International, USA, 414
Children International—CI, USA, 414
Children of the Mekong, France, 102
Churchill (Winston) Foundation of the United States, USA, 482
Claiborne (Liz) & Art Ortenberg Foundation, USA, 448
Clara Lionel Foundation—CLF, USA, 415
Cleveland Foundation, USA, 416
Cleveland H. Dodge Foundation, Inc, USA, 416
CNIB Foundation/Fondation INCA, Canada, 52
CODE—Canadian Organization for Development through Education, Canada, 52
Commonwealth Foundation, UK, 348
Community Foundations of Canada, Canada, 47
Cooperation Canada/Coopération Canada, Canada, 48
Co-operative Development Foundation of Canada—CDF, Canada, 52
Costopoulos (J. F.) Foundation, Greece, 146
Council on Foundations—COF, USA, 394
Council of Michigan Foundations—CMF, USA, 394
Coutu (Marcelle et Jean), Fondation, Canada, 55
Covenant Foundation, USA, 418
The Craig and Susan McCaw Foundation, USA, 418
The CRB Foundation/La Fondation CRB, Canada, 52

Crossroads International/Carrefour International, Canada, 53
Crown Family Philanthropies, USA, 419
Cundill (Peter) Foundation, Bermuda, 35
Cuso International, Canada, 53
Cystic Fibrosis Canada, Canada, 53
Cystic Fibrosis Foundation, USA, 419
Damon Runyon Cancer Research Foundation, USA, 419
Danmark-Amerika Fondet, Denmark, 82
Dasra, India, 154
David Suzuki Foundation, Canada, 53
Dell (Michael & Susan) Foundation, USA, 453
Denmark-America Foundation, Denmark, 82
Deutsche Bank Americas Foundation, USA, 420
Deutsche Gesellschaft für Auswärtige Politik—DGAP, Germany, 124
Development and Peace—Caritas Canada, Canada, 53
Développement et Paix—Caritas Canada, Canada, 53
Ditchley Foundation, UK, 351
Dodge (Cleveland H.) Foundation, Inc, USA, 416
Dollywood Foundation, USA, 420
Dom Manuel II Foundation, Portugal, 260
Donner (William H.) Foundation, Inc, USA, 481
Doris Duke Charitable Foundation—DDCF, USA, 421
Dr Scholl Foundation, USA, 421
Dräger Foundation, Germany, 126
Dräger-Stiftung, Germany, 126
Dreyfus (Camille and Henry) Foundation, USA, 411
Dreyfus Health Foundation, USA, 468
Drug Policy Alliance—DPA, USA, 421
Duke Endowment, USA, 421
Dumbarton Oaks, USA, 421
Earthrights International—ERI, USA, 422
Earthworm Foundation, Switzerland, 307
East-West Center—EWC, USA, 422
Echo Foundation/Fondation Écho, Canada, 54
Edmond de Rothschild Foundations, Switzerland, 308
The Edna McConnell Clark Foundation, USA, 422
Elena & Gennady Timchenko Foundation, Russian Federation, 265
ELEPAP—Rehabilitation for the Disabled, Greece, 145
ELIAMEP—Hellenic Foundation for European and Foreign Policy, Greece, 146
Elizabeth Glaser Pediatric AIDS Foundation—EGPAF, USA, 423
Elizabeth Kostova Foundation for Creative Writing, Bulgaria, 43
Elrahma Charity Trust, UK, 352
Elton John AIDS Foundation, UK, 352
endPoverty.org, USA, 424
Enfants du Mékong, France, 102
EngenderHealth, USA, 424
Entraide Universitaire Mondiale du Canada, Canada, 63
Epilepsy Foundation, USA, 424
Equal Justice Initiative—EJI, USA, 424
Equality Fund/Fonds Égalité, Canada, 54
European Center for Peace and Development—ECPD, Serbia, 271
EVPA—European Venture Philanthropy Association, Belgium, 27
Ewing Marion Kauffman Foundation, USA, 425
FAI—Fondo per l'Ambiente Italiano, Italy, 174
Family Restoration Fund, UK, 347
Feed the Children, USA, 425
Fibrose Kystique Canada, Canada, 53
FINCA International, USA, 425
First Nations Development Institute, USA, 426
Flatiron Institute, USA, 472
Florence Gould Foundation, USA, 427
Florida Philanthropic Network—FPN, USA, 394
Focus Humanitarian Assistance—FOCUS, Canada, 54
FOKAL—Open Society Foundation Haiti, Haiti, 149
Fondacija Braća Karić, Serbia, 271
Fondation Baxter & Alma Ricard, Canada, 55
Fondation BNP Paribas, France, 103
Fondation Canadienne pour l'Innovation, Canada, 50
Fondation Cartier pour l'Art Contemporain, France, 104
Fondation Francqui, Belgium, 31
Fondation J-Louis Lévesque, Canada, 55
Fondation Jean Monnet pour l'Europe, Switzerland, 309
Fondation Lucie et André Chagnon, Canada, 55
Fondation Marcelle et Jean Coutu, Canada, 55
Fondation Pierre Elliott Trudeau/Pierre Elliott Trudeau Foundation, Canada, 55

INDEX BY AREA OF ACTIVITY

Fondation Roi Baudouin, Belgium, 33
Fondation Schneider Electric, France, 111
Fondations Philanthropiques Canada—FPC, Canada, 48
Fondazione Adriano Olivetti, Italy, 174
Fondazione AVSI, Italy, 175
Fondazione Centesimus Annus—Pro Pontifice, Vatican City, 486
Fonds Égalité, Canada, 54
Food for the Hungry—FH, USA, 426
Ford Foundation, USA, 427
The Forest Trust, Switzerland, 307
Fòs Feminista, USA, 427
Foundation for Analysis and Social Studies, Spain, 288
Foundation Center, USA, 393
Foundation for International Community Assistance, USA, 425
Foundation for Middle East Peace—FMEP, USA, 428
Foundation 'Remembrance, Responsibility and Future', Germany, 139
Foundation for the Welfare of Holocaust Victims, Israel, 169
Fox (Michael J.) Foundation for Parkinson's Research, USA, 453
Franciscans International, Switzerland, 310
Franco-American Fulbright Commission, France, 113
Francqui Foundation, Belgium, 31
Frank Knox Memorial Fellowships, UK, 363
Fraser Institute, Canada, 55
Fraunhofer-Gesellschaft, Germany, 129
Fraunhofer Society, Germany, 129
Free Russia Foundation, USA, 428
Freedom Together Foundation, USA, 428
The Freeman Foundation, USA, 428
French-American Foundation, USA, 429
French Institute of International Relations, France, 113
Friends-International, Cambodia, 46
Fulbright Commission Philippines, Philippines, 253
Fulbright France—Commission Fulbright Franco-Américaine, France, 113
Fulbright Israel, Israel, 169
Fulbright Norway—US-Norway Fulbright Foundation for Educational Exchange, Norway, 241
Fundação Dom Manuel II, Portugal, 260
Fundação Luso-Americana para o Desenvolvimento—FLAD, Portugal, 260
Fundación Amancio Ortega, Spain, 288
Fundación para el Análisis y los Estudios Sociales—FAES, Spain, 288
Fundación AVINA, Panama, 247
Fundación Banco Bilbao Vizcaya Argentaria—Fundación BBVA, Spain, 289
Fundación BBVA, Spain, 289
Fundación Bunge y Born, Argentina, 7
Fundación Comunitaria de Puerto Rico—FCPR, Puerto Rico, 261
Fundación Global Democracia y Desarrollo—FUNGLODE, Dominican Republic, 87
Fundación IE, Spain, 291
Fundación José Ortega y Gasset—Gregorio Marañón, Spain, 291
Fundación Leo Messi, Spain, 292
Fundación MAPFRE, Spain, 292
Fundacja Pomocy Wzajemnej Barka, Poland, 256
General Service Foundation—GSF, USA, 430
The George A. and Eliza Gardner Howard Foundation, USA, 430
The George I. Alden Trust, USA, 430
George and Thelma Paraskevaides Foundation, Cyprus, 78
Georges Lurcy Charitable and Educational Trust, USA, 430
German Council on Foreign Relations, Germany, 124
German Institute for Global and Area Studies—GIGA, Germany, 130
German Marshall Fund of the United States—GMF, USA, 430
Give Foundation, India, 155
Give2Asia, USA, 394
GiveIndia, India, 155
GiveWell—The Clear Fund, USA, 430
Giving USA Foundation, USA, 394
Glaser (Elizabeth) Pediatric AIDS Foundation, USA, 423
Global Communities, USA, 431
Global Democracy and Development Foundation, Dominican Republic, 87
Global Fund for Children, USA, 431
Global Innovation Fund, UK, 356
Global Schools Forum, UK, 341
Goldman Sachs Foundation, USA, 432

Goldsmith (Horace W.) Foundation, USA, 436
Good Neighbors International, Korea (Republic), 201
Gordon (Walter and Duncan) Charitable Foundation, Canada, 62
Gould (Florence) Foundation, USA, 427
Grameen Foundation—GF, USA, 433
Grant (William T.) Foundation, USA, 481
The Grass Foundation, USA, 433
Grassroots International—GRI, USA, 433
Greater Kansas City Community Foundation, USA, 433
Guggenheim (John Simon) Memorial Foundation, USA, 444
GuideStar, USA, 393
Haiti Development Institute—HDI, Haiti, 149
Harry and Jeanette Weinberg Foundation, Inc, USA, 434
Hartford (John A.) Foundation, Inc, USA, 443
Hearst Foundations, USA, 435
Heart & Stroke, Canada, 56
Hecht (Lotte and John) Memorial Foundation, Canada, 58
Heineman (Minna-James) Stiftung, Germany, 136
Heinrich Böll Foundation, Germany, 131
Heinrich-Böll-Stiftung, Germany, 131
Helen Keller International—HKI, USA, 435
Hellenic Foundation for Culture, Greece, 145
Hellenic Foundation for European and Foreign Policy—ELIAMEP, Greece, 146
Helmsley (Leona M. and Harry B.) Charitable Trust, USA, 447
Henry J. Kaiser Family Foundation—KFF, USA, 435
Henry Luce Foundation, Inc, USA, 435
Hinduja Foundation, India, 157
Holt International, USA, 436
The Home Depot Foundation, USA, 436
Horace W. Goldsmith Foundation, USA, 436
Horizons of Friendship, Canada, 56
The Howard G. Buffett Foundation, USA, 437
Howard (George A. and Eliza Gardner) Foundation, USA, 430
Hudson Institute, USA, 437
Humanitarian Academy for Development—HAD, UK, 359
Humanitarian Coalition, Canada, 48
The Hunger Project, USA, 438
IDRF—International Development and Relief Foundation, Canada, 56
IE Foundation, Spain, 291
Imagine Canada, Canada, 48
Impact Europe, Belgium, 27
IMPACT Transformer la Gestion des Ressources Naturelles, Canada, 56
IMPACT Transforming Natural Resource Management, Canada, 56
Independent Sector, USA, 395
Indian National Trust for Art and Cultural Heritage—INTACH, India, 158
Innovators and Entrepreneurs Foundation/ Fondation d'Innovateurs et d'Entrepreneurs—IEF/FIE, Canada, 57
Institut Arctique de l'Amérique du Nord—IAAN, Canada, 49
Institut Français des Relations Internationales—IFRI, France, 113
Institute for Citizens & Scholars, USA, 439
Institute for Palestine Studies—IPS, Lebanon, 206
Institute for Sustainable Communities—ISC, USA, 439
Institutul Cultural Român—ICR, Romania, 264
INTACH—Indian National Trust for Art and Cultural Heritage, India, 158
Inter-American Foundation—IAF, USA, 439
Inter Pares, Canada, 57
InterAction, USA, 395
International Development and Relief Foundation—IDRF, Canada, 56
International Institute of Rural Reconstruction—IIRR, Philippines, 252
International Institute of Tropical Agriculture—IITA, Nigeria, 237
International Orthodox Christian Charities—IOCC, USA, 441
International Rescue Committee—IRC, USA, 441
International Research & Exchanges Board—IREX, USA, 442
International Women's Health Coalition, USA, 427
Internationalt Uddannelsescenter, Denmark, 84
IOCC—International Orthodox Christian Charities, USA, 441
IRC—International Rescue Committee, USA, 441
The Ireland Funds America, USA, 442
IREX—International Research & Exchanges Board, USA, 442

USA and Canada

Irvine (James) Foundation, USA, 443
Isabel Allende Foundation, USA, 442
IUC International Education Center—IUC-Europe, Denmark, 84
Ivey Foundation, Canada, 57
The J. F. Costopoulos Foundation, Greece, 146
J-Louis Lévesque Foundation, Canada, 55
The J. W. McConnell Family Foundation, Canada, 57
The James Irvine Foundation, USA, 443
Japanese-German Centre Berlin, Germany, 133
Japanisch-Deutsches Zentrum Berlin, Germany, 133
Jazz Foundation of America—JFA, USA, 443
Jean Monnet Foundation for Europe, Switzerland, 309
The John A. Hartford Foundation—JAHF, USA, 443
The John D. and Catherine T. MacArthur Foundation, USA, 444
John S. and James L. Knight Foundation, USA, 444
John Simon Guggenheim Memorial Foundation, USA, 444
The Johnson Foundation at Wingspread, USA, 444
Johnson (Lyndon Baines) Foundation, USA, 449
Jordan River Foundation, Jordan, 196
José Ortega y Gasset—Gregorio Marañón Foundation, Spain, 291
Joseph Tanenbaum Charitable Foundation, Canada, 58
Josiah Macy Jr Foundation, USA, 445
Joyce Banda Foundation International, Malawi, 210
Joyce Foundation, USA, 445
JPB Foundation, USA, 428
Kade (Max) Foundation, Inc, USA, 451
Kaiser (Henry J.) Family Foundation, USA, 435
Keller (Helen) International, USA, 435
Kellogg (W. K.) Foundation, USA, 478
Kennedy Memorial Trust, UK, 363
Kettering (Charles F.) Foundation, USA, 445
Kettering Foundation—KF, USA, 445
King Baudouin Foundation, Belgium, 33
King Hussein Foundation—KHF, Jordan, 196
King Philanthropies, USA, 445
Knight (John S. and James L.) Foundation, USA, 444
Knox (Frank) Memorial Fellowships, USA, 428
Koç (Vehbi), Vakfı, Türkiye, 331
Kokkalis Foundation, Greece, 146
Koning Boudewijnstichting/Fondation Roi Baudouin, Belgium, 33
Koret Foundation, USA, 446
The Kosciuszko Foundation, Inc, USA, 446
Kostova (Elizabeth) Foundation for Creative Writing, Bulgaria, 43
Kresge Foundation, USA, 446
Kress (Samuel H.) Foundation, USA, 469
Laidlaw Foundation, Canada, 58
Lannan Foundation, USA, 447
Lauder (Ronald S.) Foundation, Germany, 138
The Lawson Foundation, Canada, 58
LBJ Foundation, USA, 449
League of California Community Foundations, USA, 396
Learning for Well-being Foundation—L4WB, Netherlands, 227
Leibniz-Institut für Globale und Regionale Studien, Germany, 130
Leo Messi Foundation, Spain, 292
The Leona M. and Harry B. Helmsley Charitable Trust, USA, 447
Levesque (Jean-Louis), Fondation, Canada, 55
Li Ka Shing Foundation, Hong Kong, 151
Life Sciences Research Foundation—LSRF, USA, 448
Lilly Endowment, Inc, USA, 448
Littauer (Lucius N.) Foundation, Inc, USA, 449
Liver Canada, Canada, 58
Livestrong Foundation, USA, 448
Liz Claiborne & Art Ortenberg Foundation, USA, 448
The Long Now Foundation, USA, 449
The Lotte and John Hecht Memorial Foundation, Canada, 58
Luce (Henry) Foundation, Inc, USA, 435
Lucie et André Chagnon Foundation, Canada, 55
Lucius N. Littauer Foundation, Inc, USA, 449
Ludwig Cancer Research, USA, 449
Lukuru Wildlife Research Foundation, Congo (Democratic Republic), 72
Lumos Foundation, UK, 366
Lurcy (Georges) Charitable and Educational Trust, USA, 430
Luso-American Development Foundation, Portugal, 260

Western Europe

Lynde and Harry Bradley Foundation, Inc, USA, 449
Lyndon Baines Johnson Foundation, USA, 449
MacArthur (John D. and Catherine T.) Foundation, USA, 444
McCaw (Craig and Susan) Foundation, USA, 418
McConnell Clark (Edna) Foundation, USA, 422
McConnell (J. W.) Family Foundation, Canada, 57
Macdonald Stewart Foundation, Canada, 59
The Mackintosh Foundation, UK, 366
McKnight Foundation, USA, 449
The McLean Foundation, Canada, 59
Macy (Josiah), Jr Foundation, USA, 445
MADRE, USA, 450
MAPFRE Foundation, Spain, 292
Marangopoulos Foundation for Human Rights, Greece, 146
Marcelle et Jean Coutu Foundation, Canada, 55
March of Dimes Foundation, USA, 450
Marisla Foundation, USA, 451
Markle Foundation, USA, 451
The MasterCard Foundation, Canada, 59
Max Bell Foundation, Canada, 59
The Max Foundation, USA, 451
Max Kade Foundation, Inc, USA, 451
The Maytree Foundation, Canada, 59
Mellon (Richard King) Foundation, USA, 467
Merchant Navy Fund, UK, 382
Mercy For Animals—MFA, USA, 452
Mercy Corps, USA, 452
Mercy-USA for Aid and Development, USA, 452
Mertz Gilmore Foundation, USA, 452
Messi (Leo), Fundación, Spain, 292
Michael & Susan Dell Foundation, USA, 453
Michael J. Fox Foundation for Parkinson's Research—MJFF, USA, 453
Milbank Memorial Fund, USA, 453
Minhaj Welfare Foundation, UK, 368
Minna James Heineman Foundation, Germany, 136
Minna-James-Heineman-Stiftung, Germany, 136
Mith Samlanh, Cambodia, 46
Mohamed Shafik Gabr Foundation for Social Development, Egypt, 90
Molson Foundation, Canada, 59
Monell (Ambrose) Foundation, USA, 399
Monnet (Jean), Fondation pour l'Europe, Switzerland, 309
Morningside Foundation, USA, 454
Ms. Foundation for Women, USA, 454
Muriel McBrien Kauffman Foundation, USA, 425
The Muttart Foundation, Canada, 59
NAACP Legal Defense and Educational Fund, Inc—LDF, USA, 454
National Fish and Wildlife Foundation—NFWF, USA, 455
National Humanities Center—NHC, USA, 455
National Kidney Foundation—NKF, USA, 455
National Park Foundation, USA, 455
The National Trust for Italy, Italy, 174
National Wildlife Federation—NWF, USA, 456
The Nature Conservancy—TNC, USA, 456
NDI—National Democratic Institute for International Affairs, USA, 456
The Neptis Foundation, Canada, 60
The New York Community Trust—NYCT, USA, 457
Newberry Library, USA, 457
NFCR—National Foundation for Cancer Research, USA, 457
Nonprofit Enterprise and Self-sustainability Team—NESsT, USA, 457
Novartis US Foundation, USA, 457
NoVo Foundation, USA, 458
NYCT—The New York Community Trust, USA, 457
Olivetti (Adriano), Fondazione, Italy, 174
Open Society Foundation Haiti, Haiti, 149
Operation Eyesight Universal/Action Universelle de la Vue, Canada, 60
Operation USA, USA, 459
Opportunity International UK, UK, 372
Orbis Charitable Trust, UK, 372
Orentreich Foundation for the Advancement of Science, Inc—OFAS, USA, 459
Ortega (Amancio), Fundación, Spain, 288
Ortega y Gasset (José), Fundación, Spain, 291
Outreach International, USA, 459
Oxfam Canada, Canada, 60
Oxfam-Québec, Canada, 60
Pacific Peoples' Partnership, Canada, 61
PADF—Pan American Development Foundation, USA, 460
Pan American Development Foundation—PADF, USA, 460
PANNA—Pesticide Action Network North America, USA, 462

Paraskevaides (George and Thelma) Foundation, Cyprus, 78
Parasol Foundation Trust, Gibraltar, 144
Parkinson's Foundation, USA, 461
Partners in Health, USA, 461
PATH, USA, 461
PCI—Project Concern International, USA, 431
Peace Brigades International—PBI, Belgium, 33
Peace Direct, UK, 373
Pearl S. Buck International, USA, 462
Pesticide Action Network North America—PANNA, USA, 462
The Peter Cundill Foundation, Bermuda, 35
PH International, USA, 463
Philanthropic Foundations Canada—PFC, Canada, 48
Philippine-American Educational Foundation—PAEF, Philippines, 253
Ploughshares Fund, USA, 463
Population Council, USA, 463
Pratt Foundation, Australia, 17
Presbyterian World Service & Development—PWS&D, Canada, 61
Pro Mujer International, USA, 464
Pro Women International, USA, 464
Project Harmony, USA, 463
Project HOPE, USA, 464
Puerto Rico Community Foundation, Puerto Rico, 261
Queen Rania Foundation—QRF, Jordan, 196
R. Howard Webster Foundation/Fondation R. Howard Webster, Canada, 61
Radiation Effects Research Foundation—RERF, Japan, 193
Razumkov Centre, Ukraine, 333
RBC Foundation, Canada, 61
Red de Mujeres para el Desarrollo, Costa Rica, 75
Rehabilitation for the Disabled—ELEPAP, Greece, 145
Relief International, USA, 466
Research Corporation for Science Advancement—RCSA, USA, 467
The Resource Foundation—TRF, USA, 467
Ricard (Baxter & Alma), Fondation, Canada, 55
Richard King Mellon Foundation, USA, 467
Righteous Persons Foundation, USA, 467
Robert Bosch Foundation, Germany, 138
Robert-Bosch-Stiftung GmbH, Germany, 138
Robert Wood Johnson Foundation—RWJF, USA, 467
Robertson Foundation for Government—RFG, USA, 468
Rockefeller Brothers Fund—RBF, USA, 468
Rogosin Institute, USA, 468
Romanian Cultural Institute, Romania, 264
The Ronald S. Lauder Foundation, Germany, 138
Rothschild (Edmond de) Foundations, Switzerland, 308
Rubinstein (Arthur) International Music Society, Israel, 190
Runyon (Damon) Cancer Research Foundation, USA, 419
Russell Sage Foundation—RSF, USA, 469
Samsung Foundation, Korea (Republic), 202
Samuel H. Kress Foundation, USA, 469
The San Diego Foundation, USA, 470
San Francisco Foundation—SFF, USA, 470
Sandals Foundation, Jamaica, 184
Sarah Scaife Foundation, Inc, USA, 470
Scaife (Sarah) Foundation, Inc, USA, 470
Schneider Electric Foundation, France, 111
Schusterman (Charles and Lynn) Family Foundation, USA, 413
The Seafarers' Charity, UK, 382
Seafarers International Relief Fund, UK, 382
SeedChange, Canada, 61
Seeds of Peace, USA, 470
Sentebale, UK, 382
Serrv International, Inc, USA, 471
Seva Foundation, USA, 471
Shafik Gabr (Mohamed) Foundation, Egypt, 90
Shahid Afridi Foundation—SAF, Pakistan, 246
SickKids Foundation, Canada, 62
Sightsavers International, UK, 382
Simons Foundation, USA, 472
Sloan (Alfred P.) Foundation, USA, 398
Slovak Security Policy Institute, Slovakia, 276
Slovenský inštitút pre bezpečnostnú politiku, Slovakia, 276
Smith Richardson Foundation, Inc, USA, 472
Snow Leopard Trust, USA, 472
Sorenson Legacy Foundation, USA, 473
Spencer Foundation, USA, 473
Steelworkers Humanity Fund/Le Fonds Humanitaire des Metallos, Canada, 62
Stichting Triodos Foundation, Netherlands, 231
Stiftung 'Erinnerung, Verantwortung und Zukunft'—EVZ, Germany, 139

INDEX BY AREA OF ACTIVITY

Streisand (Barbra) Foundation, USA, 408
Surdna Foundation, Inc, USA, 474
Suzuki Foundation (David), Canada, 53
Sverige-Amerika Stiftelsen, Sweden, 304
Sweden-America Foundation, Sweden, 304
Synergos—The Synergos Institute, USA, 396
Taawon, Palestinian Territories, 246
Tanenbaum (Joseph) Charitable Foundation, Canada, 58
Tencent Foundation, China (People's Republic), 70
Terre Sans Frontières—TSF, Canada, 62
Thiel Foundation, USA, 474
Third World Network—TWN, Malaysia, 211
Thurgood Marshall Institute, USA, 454
Tibet Fund, USA, 475
Tides Organizations, USA, 475
Timchenko (Elena & Gennady) Foundation, Russian Federation, 265
TK Foundation, Bahamas, 24
TOSA Foundation, USA, 475
Triodos Foundation, Netherlands, 231
Trudeau (Pierre Elliott) Foundation, Canada, 55
Trust for Mutual Understanding—TMU, USA, 476
Trustees for Harvard University, USA, 421
Tujenge Africa Foundation, Burundi, 45
Tulsa Community Foundation—TCF, USA, 476
Turner Foundation, Inc, USA, 476
Unbound Philanthropy, USA, 476
United States African Development Foundation—USADF, USA, 477
United States-Japan Foundation, USA, 477
Vancouver Foundation, Canada, 62
Vehbi Koç Foundation, Türkiye, 331
Vehbi Koç Vakfı, Türkiye, 331
W. K. Kellogg Foundation—WKKF, USA, 478
The Wallace Foundation, USA, 478
Walter and Duncan Gordon Charitable Foundation, Canada, 62
Walton Family Foundation, USA, 479
WaterAid, UK, 389
Webster (R. Howard) Foundation, Canada, 61
Weeden Foundation, USA, 479
Weinberg (Harry and Jeanette) Foundation, USA, 434
The Welch Foundation, USA, 479
Welfare Association, Palestinian Territories, 246
Whitehall Foundation, Inc, USA, 480
The William H. Donner Foundation, Inc, USA, 481
William Randolph Hearst Foundation, USA, 435
William T. Grant Foundation, USA, 481
Winrock International, USA, 481
Winston Churchill Foundation of the United States, USA, 482
The Wolfson Foundation, UK, 390
Women's Development Network, Costa Rica, 75
World Animal Protection, UK, 391
World Neighbors, USA, 483
World University Service of Canada/Entraide Universitaire Mondiale du Canada—WUSC/EUMC, Canada, 63
World Vision International, UK, 391
The Wyss Foundtion, USA, 484
Yanai Tadashi Foundation, Japan, 195
Zorig Foundation, Mongolia, 219

WESTERN EUROPE

1563 Foundation for the Arts and Culture, Italy, 174
1818 Fund Foundation, Netherlands, 229
The A. G. Leventis Foundation, Cyprus, 77
A. M. Qattan Foundation, UK, 338
The A. P. Møller and Chastine Mc-Kinney Møller Foundation, Denmark, 82
A. P. Møller og Hustru Chastine Mc-Kinney Møllers Fond til almene Formaal, Denmark, 82
Abegg Foundation, Switzerland, 306
Abegg-Stiftung, Switzerland, 306
Académie Goncourt—Société Littéraire des Goncourt, France, 100
Academy of European Law, Germany, 127
ACF—Association of Charitable Foundations, UK, 335
Action for Children, UK, 338
Action Damien/Damiaanactie, Belgium, 28
Acumen, USA, 397
Adriano Olivetti Foundation, Italy, 174
Adyan Foundation, Lebanon, 205
Africa Foundation, South Africa, 278
Africa Grantmakers' Affinity Group—AGAG, USA, 393
Africa Humanitarian Action—AHA, Ethiopia, 93
Africa Space Foundation, Switzerland, 308

INDEX BY AREA OF ACTIVITY

African Refugees Foundation—AREF, Nigeria, 237
African Wildlife Foundation—AWF, Kenya, 198
AGAG—Africa Grantmakers' Affinity Group, USA, 393
Agnelli (Giovanni), Fondazione, Italy, 177
Agrupació AMCI Foundation, Spain, 286
Aid for Development Club, Austria, 20
Air France Foundation, France, 103
AKO Foundation, UK, 339
The Al-Khoei Benevolent Foundation, UK, 339
The Alan Turing Institute, UK, 339
Albéniz Foundation, Spain, 288
Alcoa Foundation, USA, 398
Alfred Benzon Foundation, Denmark, 82
Alfred Benzons Fond, Denmark, 82
Alfred Toepfer Foundation FVS, Germany, 121
Alfred Toepfer Stiftung FVS, Germany, 121
Allen Lane Foundation, UK, 339
Alliance of Community Foundations Germany, Germany, 119
Alliance for Securing Democracy, USA, 430
Allianz Foundation, Germany, 121
Allianz Umana Mente Foundation, Italy, 174
Almeida (Eng. António de), Fundação, Portugal, 260
Almine y Bernard Ruiz-Picasso Foundation, Spain, 288
Alzheimer Spain Foundation, Spain, 288
Alzheimer's Society, UK, 339
AMADE Mondiale—Association Mondiale des Amis de l'Enfance, Monaco, 217
Amancio Ortega Foundation, Spain, 288
Amberes (Carlos de), Fundación, Spain, 289
Ambrosiana Paolo VI Foundation, Italy, 175
American-Scandinavian Foundation—ASF, USA, 403
Amity Foundation, China (People's Republic), 66
Amref Health Africa, Kenya, 198
Anders Jahre's Foundation for Humanitarian Purposes, Norway, 240
Anders Jahres Humanitære Stiftelse, Norway, 240
Angelo Della Riccia Foundation, Italy, 175
Ankara İngiliz Arkeoloji Enstitüsü, UK, 345
Anna Lindh Euro-Mediterranean Foundation for Dialogue between Cultures, Egypt, 90
Anne Çocuk Eğitim Vakfı—AÇEV, Türkiye, 327
Anne Frank-Fonds, Switzerland, 306
Anne Frank Fund, Switzerland, 306
António de Almeida Foundation, Portugal, 260
Arab Organization for Human Rights, Egypt, 90
Arainneachd Eachdraidheil Alba, UK, 358
Arbeiterwohlfahrt Bundesverband eV—AWO, Germany, 121
Archie Sherman Charitable Trust, UK, 340
Arcus Foundation, USA, 405
Areces (Ramón), Fundación, Spain, 294
Ark, UK, 341
Armanshahr Foundation—OPEN ASIA, Afghanistan, 3
Arpad Szenes-Vieira da Silva Foundation, Portugal, 258
Art Fund—National Art Collections Fund, UK, 341
Arthritis Australia, Australia, 10
Arthur Rubinstein International Music Society, Israel, 168
Arts Council England, UK, 341
Asia Society, USA, 406
ASKO Europa-Stiftung, Germany, 121
ASKO Europe Foundation, Germany, 121
Asociación Española de Fundaciones, Spain, 285
Aspen Institute, USA, 407
Association of Charitable Foundations—ACF, UK, 335
Association for Development Policy and Humanitarian Aid, Germany, 120
Association des Fondations Donatrices Suisses, Switzerland, 306
Association of Foundations in the Netherlands, Netherlands, 223
Association of the Friends of the Swedish Institute at Athens, Sweden, 299
Association of German Foundations, Germany, 118
Association of Grantmaking Foundations in Switzerland, Switzerland, 306
Association of Guernsey Charities—AGC, Channel Islands, 64
Association of Italian Foundations and Savings Banks, Italy, 171
Association of Jersey Charities—AJC, Channel Islands, 64
Association of Liechtenstein Charitable Foundations, Liechtenstein, 207
Association of Medical Research Charities—AMRC, UK, 335

Association for Public Benefit Foundations, Austria, 20
Association of Swedish Foundations, Sweden, 298
Associazione di Fondazioni e di Casse di Risparmio SpA—ACRI, Italy, 171
Asthma + Lung UK, UK, 341
Auchan Foundation, France, 103
Aurora Trust, UK, 341
Auschwitz Foundation—Remembrance of Auschwitz, Belgium, 30
Austrian Science Fund, Austria, 21
Avatud Eesti Fond, Estonia, 92
Aventis Foundation, Germany, 121
AVSI Foundation, Italy, 175
Axel Springer Foundation, Germany, 122
Axel-Springer-Stiftung, Germany, 122
Ayrton Senna Institute, Brazil, 41
Bagnoud (François-Xavier) Association, Switzerland, 310
Baillet Latour Fund, Belgium, 32
Baltic Sea Foundation, Finland, 97
Bank of America Charitable Foundation, USA, 407
Barandiarán (José Miguel de), Fundación, Spain, 291
Barceló Foundation, Spain, 289
Barcelona Centre for International Affairs, Spain, 287
Barenboim-Said Foundation, Spain, 289
Baring Foundation, UK, 341
Barka Foundation for Mutual Assistance, Poland, 256
Barnardo's, UK, 342
Barretstown, Ireland, 165
Barrié de la Maza (Pedro, Conde de Fenosa), Fundación, Spain, 293
BBC Children in Need, UK, 342
BBC Media Action, UK, 342
BBVA Foundation, Spain, 289
Beisheim Foundation, Germany, 122
Beisheim Stiftung, Germany, 122
Belém Cultural Centre Foundation, Portugal, 259
Belgian Federation of Philanthropic Foundations, Belgium, 26
Belgische Federatie van Filantropische Stichtingen, Belgium, 26
Benecke (Otto) Stiftung eV, Germany, 138
Benesco, UK, 347
Benetton Foundation for Study and Research, Italy, 175
Benzon (Alfred) Foundation, Denmark, 82
Berghof Foundation gGmbH, Germany, 122
Berghof Stiftung für Konfliktforschung gGmbH, Germany, 122
Bernheim Foundation, Belgium, 31
Bertelsmann Foundation, Germany, 122
Bertelsmann Stiftung, Germany, 122
Bettencourt Schueller Foundation, France, 103
Biblioteca dell'Accademia Nazionale dei Lincei e Corsiniana, Italy, 172
Black Lives Matter Global Network Foundation—BLM Global Network Foundation, USA, 408
Black Sea Trust for Regional Cooperation, USA, 430
Blair (Tony) Institute for Global Change, UK, 386
Blancaflor Boncompagni Ludovisi, née Bildt Foundation, Sweden, 303
BLM Global Network Foundation, USA, 408
Blood Cancer UK—Bloodwise, UK, 343
Blue Marine Foundation—BLUE, UK, 343
BNP Paribas Foundation, France, 103
Bofill (Jaume), Fundació, Spain, 287
Boghossian Foundation, Belgium, 31
Böll (Heinrich) Stiftung, Germany, 131
Boltzmann (Ludwig) Gesellschaft, Austria, 21
Bordoni (Ugo), Fondazione, Italy, 180
Born Free Foundation, UK, 343
Bosch (Robert) Stiftung GmbH, Germany, 138
Bóthar, Ireland, 166
Botín Foundation, Spain, 292
Botín (Marcelino), Fundación, Spain, 292
Braća Karić Foundation, Serbia, 271
BRAC, Bangladesh, 25
Bridge House Estates, UK, 348
British Gas Energy Trust, UK, 344
British Heart Foundation—BHF, UK, 344
British Institute at Ankara, UK, 345
British Schools and Universities Foundation, Inc—BSUF, USA, 410
Brother's Brother Foundation, USA, 410
Brothers of Men, France, 113
Bundesverband Deutscher Stiftungen eV, Germany, 118
Bunge y Born Foundation, Argentina, 7
C. G. Jung-Institut Zürich, Switzerland, 307
Cadbury (Edward) Charitable Trust, UK, 351

Western Europe

Cadbury (William Adlington) Charitable Trust, UK, 390
CAF—Charities Aid Foundation, UK, 336
The Camargo Foundation, France, 101
Campaign Against Exclusion Foundation, France, 103
Cancer Research UK, UK, 346
Cancerfonden, Sweden, 298
Canon Foundation in Europe, Netherlands, 224
Cariplo Foundation, Italy, 175
Carl Zeiss Foundation, Germany, 123
Carl-Zeiss-Stiftung, Germany, 123
Carlo Cattaneo Institute, Italy, 182
Carlos de Amberes Foundation, Spain, 289
Carlsberg Foundation, Denmark, 82
Carlsbergfondet, Denmark, 82
Carnegie Endowment for International Peace, USA, 411
Carnegie Trust for the Universities of Scotland, UK, 346
Carnegie UK Trust, UK, 346
Cartier-Bresson (Henri), Fondation, France, 107
Cartier Foundation for Contemporary Art, France, 104
Casa de Mateus Foundation, Portugal, 259
CASE—Centrum Analiz Społeczno-Ekonomicznych, Poland, 255
Cassa di Risparmio di Padova e Rovigo Foundation, Italy, 175
Catholic Agency for World Development—Trócaire, Ireland, 168
Cattaneo (Carlo), Istituto, Italy, 182
CBM-International, Germany, 123
CEDIAS-Musée Social—Centre d'Etudes, de Documentation, d'Information et d'Action Sociales, France, 101
CENSIS—Fondazione Centro Studi Investimenti Sociali, Italy, 172
Center for Social and Economic Research, Poland, 255
Centre pour le Dialogue Humanitaire, Switzerland, 307
Centre Européen de la Culture—CEC, Switzerland, 307
Centre Français des Fonds et Fondations—CFF, France, 99
Centre for Humanitarian Dialogue—HD, Switzerland, 307
Centre for Social Studies, Documentation, Information and Action, France, 101
Centro Português de Fundações—CPF, Portugal, 258
Cercle de Coopération des ONGD du Luxembourg, Luxembourg, 209
Charities Advisory Trust, UK, 336
Charities Aid Foundation—CAF, UK, 336
Charities Institute Ireland—Cii, Ireland, 165
Charity Islamic Trust Elrahma, UK, 352
Charles Stewart Mott Foundation—CSMF, USA, 414
The Charles Wallace India Trusts, UK, 347
Charles Wolfson Charitable Trust, UK, 347
Chemistry Centre Foundation, France, 108
Cheshire (Leonard) Foundation, UK, 364
Child Migrants Trust, UK, 347
Children of the Mekong, France, 102
Children and Sharing, France, 102
The Children's Investment Fund Foundation, UK, 347
Childwick Trust, UK, 347
Christoph Merian Foundation, Switzerland, 305
Christoph-Merian-Stiftung, Switzerland, 305
Churches' Commission for Migrants in Europe, Belgium, 28
Churchill (Winston) Foundation of the United States, USA, 482
CIDOB Foundation—Barcelona Centre for International Affairs, Spain, 287
Cimade—Ecumenical Care Service, France, 102
La Cimade—Service Oecuménique d'Entraide, France, 102
Cini (Giorgio), Fondazione, Italy, 177
Citizenship Foundation, UK, 392
The City Bridge Trust, UK, 348
Civitates, Belgium, 27
Claude Pompidou Foundation, France, 104
CLIC Sargent, UK, 392
Climate Cent Foundation, Switzerland, 317
Çocuk (Anne) Eğitim Vakfı, Türkiye, 327
Commission des Eglises auprès des Migrants en Europe/Kommission der Kirchen für Migranten in Europa, Belgium, 28
Commonwealth Foundation, UK, 348
Community Foundation for Northern Ireland, UK, 349
Concawe—Oil Companies' European Association for Environment, Health and Safety in Refining and Distribution, Belgium, 29

Western Europe

CONCORD—European NGO Confederation for Relief and Development, Belgium, 26
Co-op Foundation, UK, 349
Co-operative Community Investment Foundation, UK, 349
Coordinadora de ONGD España, Spain, 285
Coram, UK, 349
Le Corbusier Foundation, France, 108
Costopoulos (J. F.) Foundation, Greece, 146
Coubertin Foundation, France, 105
Cultural Foundation of the German Länder, Germany, 134
Cystic Fibrosis Trust, UK, 350
Czech Donors Forum, Czech Republic, 78
Daiwa Anglo-Japanese Foundation, UK, 350
Dam Foundation, Norway, 243
Daniele Agostino Derossi Foundation, USA, 420
Danish Cultural Institute—DCI, Denmark, 82
Danish Institute for Human Rights, Denmark, 84
Danish Outdoor Council, Denmark, 83
Danmark-Amerika Fondet, Denmark, 82
Danske Kulturinstitut—DKI, Denmark, 82
David Nott Foundation, UK, 350
Debenedetti (Rodolfo), Fondazione, Italy, 179
Debts to Opportunities Foundation, Netherlands, 231
del Pino (Rafael), Fundación, Spain, 294
DemNet—Demokratikus Jogok Fejlesztéséért Alapítvány, Hungary, 153
DemNet—Foundation for the Development of Democratic Rights, Hungary, 153
Denmark-America Foundation, Denmark, 82
Derossi (Daniele Agostino) Foundation, USA, 420
Deutsch-Russischer Austausch eV—DRA, Germany, 124
Deutsche AIDS-Stiftung, Germany, 124
Deutsche Bank Endowment Fund at the Donors' Association for the Promotion of German Science, Germany, 142
Deutsche Gesellschaft für Auswärtige Politik—DGAP, Germany, 124
Deutsche Krebshilfe eV, Germany, 124
Deutsche Nationalstiftung, Germany, 125
Deutsche Orient-Stiftung, Germany, 125
Deutsche Sparkassenstiftung für Internationale Zusammenarbeit, Germany, 125
Deutsche Telekom Foundation, Germany, 125
Deutsche Telekom Stiftung, Germany, 125
Deutsches Rheuma-Forschungszentrum Berlin, Germany, 126
Development NGO Coordinator Spain, Spain, 285
DHL UK Foundation, UK, 350
Diabetes UK, UK, 350
Dietmar Hopp Foundation, Germany, 126
Dietmar-Hopp-Stiftung, Germany, 126
Dioraphte Foundation, Netherlands, 229
DIPF—Leibniz-Institut für Bildungsforschung und Bildungsinformation, Germany, 126
Directory of Social Change, UK, 336
Ditchley Foundation, UK, 351
DNB Savings Bank Foundation, Norway, 243
Dóchas—Irish Association of Non-Governmental Development Organisations, Ireland, 165
DOEN Foundation, Netherlands, 229
Dollywood Foundation, USA, 420
Dom Manuel II Foundation, Portugal, 260
Donors' Association for the Promotion of Sciences and Humanities, Germany, 119
Dr Marcus Wallenberg Foundation for Further Education in International Industry, Sweden, 299
Dr Marcus Wallenbergs Stiftelse för Utbildning i Internationellt Industriellt Företagande, Sweden, 299
Dr Rainer Wild Foundation for Healthy Nutrition, Germany, 126
Dr Rainer Wild-Stiftung—Stiftung für Gesunde Ernährung, Germany, 126
Dräger Foundation, Germany, 126
Dräger-Stiftung, Germany, 126
DSW—Deutsche Stiftung Weltbevölkerung, Germany, 126
Dulverton Trust, UK, 351
Earthworm Foundation, Switzerland, 307
East-West Encounters Charitable Foundation, Germany, 141
Eastern Europe Studies Centre—EESC, Lithuania, 209
Ebelin and Gerd Bucerius ZEIT Foundation, Germany, 143
Economic Development Foundation, Türkiye, 328
Edmond de Rothschild Foundations, Switzerland, 308
Edoardo Garrone Foundation, Italy, 177
EDP Foundation, Portugal, 260
Education and Training Foundation—ETF, UK, 351
Educo, Spain, 286
Edward Cadbury Charitable Trust, UK, 351
EEB—European Environmental Bureau, Belgium, 30
Eesti Mittetulundusühingute ja Sihtasutuste Liit, Estonia, 92
Egmont Fonden, Denmark, 83
Egmont Foundation, Denmark, 83
Einaudi (Luigi), Fondazione, Italy, 178
Elena & Gennady Timchenko Foundation, Russian Federation, 265
ELEPAP—Rehabilitation for the Disabled, Greece, 145
ELIAMEP—Hellenic Foundation for European and Foreign Policy, Greece, 146
Elizabeth Kostova Foundation for Creative Writing, Bulgaria, 43
Ellerman (John) Foundation, UK, 361
Elrahma Charity Trust, UK, 352
Elton John AIDS Foundation, UK, 352
EMERGENCY, Italy, 173
Emunah, UK, 353
Enfance et Partage, France, 102
Enfants du Mékong, France, 102
Eni Foundation, Italy, 173
Enrico Mattei Eni Foundation, Italy, 174
Ente Cassa di Risparmio di Firenze, Italy, 173
Entraide Protestante Suisse, Switzerland, 311
Entwicklungshilfe-Klub, Austria, 20
Environmental Justice Foundation—EJF, UK, 353
ERA—Europäische Rechtsakademie, Germany, 127
Erik Philip-Sörensen Foundation, Sweden, 299
Erik Philip-Sörensens Stiftelse, Sweden, 299
Esmée Fairbairn Foundation, UK, 353
Estonian Foreign Policy Institute, Estonia, 93
Ettersberg Foundation, Germany, 140
Euris Foundation, France, 106
Euro-Mediterranean Centre on Climate Change Foundation, Italy, 176
EuroNatur, Germany, 127
Europa Nostra, Netherlands, 224
Europäische Rechtsakademie—ERA, Germany, 127
European Anti-Poverty Network—EAPN, Belgium, 29
European Center for Peace and Development—ECPD, Serbia, 271
European Centre for Social Welfare Policy and Research, Austria, 21
European Community Foundation Initiative—ECFI, Germany, 119
European Cultural Centre, Switzerland, 307
European Cultural Foundation—ECF, Netherlands, 225
European Environmental Bureau—EEB, Belgium, 30
European Federation of National Organisations Working with the Homeless, Belgium, 26
European Foundation for the Improvement of Living and Working Conditions—Eurofound, Ireland, 166
European Foundation for Philanthropy and Society Development, Croatia, 76
European Foundation for the Sustainable Development of the Regions, Switzerland, 308
European Institute of Health and Social Welfare, Spain, 296
European Mediterranean Institute, Spain, 296
European NGO Confederation for Relief and Development—CONCORD, Belgium, 26
European Roma Rights Centre—ERRC, Belgium, 30
European Youth For Action—EYFA, Germany, 128
European Youth Foundation—EYF, France, 112
Europese Culterele Stichting, Netherlands, 225
Europska Zaklada za Filantropiju i Društveni Dazvoj, Croatia, 76
Eurotransplant International Foundation, Netherlands, 225
Evangelisches Studienwerk eV, Germany, 128
Evens Foundation, Belgium, 31
EVPA—European Venture Philanthropy Association, Belgium, 27
EYFA—European Youth For Action, Germany, 128
F. C. Flick Foundation against Xenophobia, Racism and Intolerance, Germany, 128
F. C. Flick-Stiftung gegen Fremdenfeindlichkeit, Rassismus und Intoleranz, Germany, 128
FAI—Fondo per l'Ambiente Italiano, Italy, 174
Fairbairn (Esmée) Foundation, UK, 353
Faith, UK, 353
Family Restoration Fund, UK, 347
FEANTSA—Fédération Européenne des Associations Nationales Travaillant avec les Sans-Abri, Belgium, 26

INDEX BY AREA OF ACTIVITY

Federal Association of Social Welfare Organizations, Germany, 121
Fédération Belge des Fondations Philanthropiques, Belgium, 26
Fédération Européenne des Associations Nationales Travaillant avec les Sans-Abri—FEANTSA, Belgium, 26
FEDRE—European Foundation for the Sustainable Development of the Regions, Switzerland, 308
Feed the Minds, UK, 354
FEEM—Fondazione ENI Enrico Mattei, Italy, 174
Feltrinelli (Giangiacomo), Fondazione, Italy, 177
Ferrero (Piera, Pietro e Giovanni), Fondazione, Italy, 179
FIN—Branchevereniging van Fondsen en Foundations, Netherlands, 223
Finnish Cultural Foundation, Finland, 97
Finnish Foundation for Technology Promotion, Finland, 98
Finnish Institute in the UK and Ireland Trust, UK, 354
Flick (F. C.) Stiftung gegen Fremdenfeindlichkeit, Rassismus und Intoleranz, Germany, 128
Florence Gould Foundation, USA, 427
Florence Savings Bank Foundation, Italy, 173
Follereau Foundation Luxembourg, Luxembourg, 209
Folmer Wisti Fonden for International Forståelse, Denmark, 83
Folmer Wisti Foundation for International Understanding, Denmark, 83
Fondacija Braća Karić, Serbia, 271
Fondacija Cennosti, Bulgaria, 43
Fondacioni Kosovar per Shoqeri Civile, Kosovo, 202
Fondation Abbé Pierre, France, 108
Fondation Agir Contre l'Exclusion—FACE, France, 103
Fondation Air France, France, 103
Fondation Auchan, France, 103
Fondation Auschwitz—Mémoire d'Auschwitz, Belgium, 30
Fondation de l'Avenir pour la Recherche Médicale Appliquée, France, 103
Fondation Bernheim, Belgium, 31
Fondation Bettencourt Schueller, France, 103
Fondation BNP Paribas, France, 103
Fondation Boghossian, Belgium, 31
Fondation Cartier pour l'Art Contemporain, France, 104
Fondation Casip-Cojasor, France, 104
Fondation Charles Veillon, Switzerland, 308
Fondation de la Cité Internationale Universitaire de Paris, France, 104
Fondation Claude Pompidou, France, 104
Fondation du Collège de France, France, 105
Fondation Le Corbusier—FLC, France, 108
Fondation de Coubertin, France, 105
Fondation pour l'Économie et le Développement Durable des Régions d'Europe—FEDRE, Switzerland, 308
Fondation Ensemble, France, 105
Fondation d'Entreprise La Poste, France, 105
Fondation d'Entreprise VINCI pour la Cité, France, 106
Fondation Espace Afrique, Switzerland, 308
Fondation Euris, France, 106
Fondation Européenne de la Culture/Europese Culturele Stichting, Netherlands, 225
Fondation Evens Stichting, Belgium, 31
Fondation Follereau Luxembourg—FFL, Luxembourg, 209
Fondation de France, France, 99
Fondation France Chine—FFC, France, 106
Fondation France-Israël, France, 106
Fondation Franco-Japonaise Sasakawa, France, 106
Fondation Francqui, Belgium, 31
Fondation Hans Wilsdorf, Switzerland, 309
Fondation Henri Cartier-Bresson, France, 107
Fondation Hirondelle: Media for Peace and Human Dignity, Switzerland, 309
Fondation ISREC, Switzerland, 309
Fondation Jean Jaurès, France, 107
Fondation Jean Monnet pour l'Europe, Switzerland, 309
Fondation Latsis Internationale, Switzerland, 309
Fondation pour le Logement des Défavorisés, France, 108
Fondation Louis-Jeantet de Médecine, Switzerland, 310
Fondation MACIF, France, 108
Fondation de la Maison de la Chimie, France, 108
Fondation Marc de Montalembert, France, 109
Fondation Marcel Hicter, Belgium, 32

INDEX BY AREA OF ACTIVITY

Western Europe

Fondation Mohammed V pour la Solidarité, Morocco, 220
Fondation Nationale pour l'Enseignement de la Gestion des Entreprises, France, 109
Fondation Nationale des Sciences Politiques—SciencesPo, France, 110
Fondation Nicolas Hulot pour la Nature et l'Homme—FNH, France, 110
Fondation Orange, France, 110
Fondation Orient-Occident—FOO, Morocco, 220
Fondation P&V, Belgium, 32
Fondation Partage et Vie, France, 110
Fondation du Patrimoine, France, 110
Fondation Prince Pierre de Monaco, Monaco, 218
Fondation Princesse Grace, Monaco, 218
Fondation Rambourg, Tunisia, 326
Fondation Robert Schuman, France, 111
Fondation Roi Baudouin, Belgium, 33
Fondation S, France, 111
Fondation Schneider Electric, France, 111
Fondation Simón I. Patiño, Switzerland, 310
Fondation Singer-Polignac, France, 111
Fondazione 1563 per l'Arte e la Cultura, Italy, 174
Fondazione Adriano Olivetti, Italy, 174
Fondazione Allianz Umana Mente, Italy, 174
Fondazione Ambrosiana Paolo VI, Italy, 175
Fondazione Angelo Della Riccia, Italy, 175
Fondazione AVSI, Italy, 175
Fondazione Benetton Studi Ricerche, Italy, 175
Fondazione Cariplo, Italy, 175
Fondazione Cassa di Risparmio di Padova e Rovigo, Italy, 175
Fondazione Cassa di Risparmio di Torino, Italy, 176
Fondazione Cassa di Risparmio di Verona Vicenza Belluno e Ancona—Fondazione Cariverona, Italy, 176
Fondazione Centesimus Annus—Pro Pontifice, Vatican City, 486
Fondazione Centro Euro-Mediterraneo sui Cambiamenti Climatici—CMCC, Italy, 176
Fondazione Centro Studi Investimenti Sociali—CENSIS, Italy, 172
Fondazione Compagnia di San Paolo, Italy, 176
Fondazione Edoardo Garrone, Italy, 177
Fondazione Fratelli Tutti, Vatican City, 486
Fondazione Giangiacomo Feltrinelli, Italy, 177
Fondazione Giorgio Cini, Italy, 177
Fondazione Giovanni Agnelli, Italy, 177
Fondazione Internazionale Menarini, Italy, 178
Fondazione ISMU—Iniziative e Studi sulla Multietnicità, Italy, 178
Fondazione per l'Istituto Svizzero di Roma, Italy, 178
Fondazione Luigi Einaudi, Italy, 178
Fondazione Piera, Pietro e Giovanni Ferrero, Italy, 179
Fondazione Prada, Italy, 179
Fondazione Querini Stampalia—FQS, Italy, 179
Fondazione Rodolfo Debenedetti—FRDB, Italy, 179
Fondazione Roma, Italy, 179
Fondazione Romaeuropa, Italy, 180
Fondazione RUI, Italy, 180
Fondazione Salvatore Maugeri—Clinica del Lavoro e della Riabilitazione, Italy, 180
Fondazione Terzo Pilastro – Internazionale, Italy, 180
Fondazione Ugo Bordoni, Italy, 180
Fondazione Unipolis, Italy, 181
Fondazione di Venezia, Italy, 181
Fondazione Vodafone Italia, Italy, 181
Fondazzjoni Patrimonju Malti, Malta, 213
Fonden Realdania, Denmark, 83
Fondo para el Desarrollo de los Pueblos Indígenas de América Latina y El Caribe—FILAC, Bolivia, 36
Fonds Baillet Latour, Belgium, 32
Fonds Européen pour la Jeunesse—FEJ, France, 112
Fonds National Suisse de la Recherche Scientifique, Switzerland, 316
Foreign Policy and United Nations Association of Austria—UNA-AUSTRIA, Austria, 22
Föreningen Svenska Atheninstitutets Vänner, Sweden, 299
The Forest Trust, Switzerland, 307
Fórum Dárců, Czech Republic, 78
Forum ZaDobro.BIT!, Croatia, 76
FORWARD—Foundation for Women's Health Research and Development, UK, 354
Foundation for Analysis and Social Studies, Spain, 288
Foundation of Banks and Savings Banks of CECA, Spain, 289
Foundation Bofill, Spain, 287
Foundation Centre for the Study of Social Investment, Italy, 172
Foundation for Democracy and Media, Netherlands, 229
Foundation of the Future for Applied Medical Research, France, 103
Foundation for German-Polish Co-operation, Poland, 257
Foundation of the Hellenic World, Greece, 145
Foundation for Housing the Disadvantaged, France, 108
Foundation 'Remembrance, Responsibility and Future', Germany, 139
Foundation Rodolfo Debenedetti, Italy, 179
Foundation of Spanish Commercial Agents, Spain, 287
Foundation for the Swiss Institute of Rome, Italy, 178
Foundation for the Victims of Terrorism, Spain, 296
Foundation of Weimar Classics, Germany, 134
Foundation for Women, Spain, 293
Foundation for Women's Health, Research and Development—FORWARD, UK, 354
Foundation for Youth Research, Germany, 140
Foundations and Funds Association, Finland, 95
France Amérique Latine—FAL, France, 112
France China Foundation, France, 106
France-Israel Foundation, France, 106
France Nature Environnement, France, 112
Franciscans International, Switzerland, 310
Franco-American Fulbright Commission, France, 113
Franco-Japanese Sasakawa Foundation, France, 106
Francqui Foundation, Belgium, 31
Frank (Anne)-Fonds, Switzerland, 306
Frank Knox Memorial Fellowships, UK, 363
Frankfurt Foundation for German-Italian Studies, Germany, 129
Frankfurter Stiftung für Deutsch-Italienische Studien, Germany, 129
Fratelli Tutti Foundation, Vatican City, 486
Fraunhofer-Gesellschaft, Germany, 129
Fraunhofer Society, Germany, 129
FREE Network—Forum for Research on Eastern Europe and Emerging Economies, Sweden, 299
Free Russia Foundation, USA, 428
Freedom from Torture (Medical Foundation for the Care of Victims of Torture), UK, 354
Freedom Speech Foundation, Norway, 241
French-American Foundation, USA, 429
French Foundation Centre, France, 99
French Institute of International Relations, France, 113
French National Foundation for Management Education, France, 109
Frères des Hommes—FDH, France, 113
Freudenberg Foundation, Germany, 129
Freudenberg Stiftung, Germany, 129
Friede Springer Foundation, Germany, 129
Friede Springer Stiftung, Germany, 129
Friends-International, Cambodia, 46
Friluftsrådet, Denmark, 83
Fridtjof Nansen Institute, Norway, 241
Fridtjof Nansens Institutt—FNI, Norway, 241
FRS-FNRS—Fonds de la Recherche Scientifique, Belgium, 32
FUHEM—Fundación Benéfico-Social Hogar del Empleado, Spain, 286
Fulbright France—Commission Fulbright Franco-Américaine, France, 113
Fulbright Norway—US-Norway Fulbright Foundation for Educational Exchange, Norway, 241
Fund for the Development of Indigenous Peoples of Latin America and the Caribbean, Bolivia, 36
Fund and Endowment Management Foundation, Norway, 240
Fund for Scientific Research, Belgium, 32
Fundação Arpad Szenes–Vieira da Silva, Portugal, 258
Fundação da Casa de Mateus, Portugal, 259
Fundação Centro Cultural de Belém, Portugal, 259
Fundação Dom Manuel II, Portugal, 260
Fundação EDP, Portugal, 260
Fundação Eng. António de Almeida, Portugal, 260
Fundação Luso-Americana para o Desenvolvimento—FLAD, Portugal, 260
Fundação Mário Soares e Maria Barroso, Portugal, 260
Fundação Oriente, Portugal, 260
Fundação Ricardo do Espírito Santo Silva, Portugal, 261
Fundação de Serralves, Portugal, 261
Fundação Vodafone Portugal, Portugal, 261
Fundació Agrupació AMCI, Spain, 286
Fundació CIDOB, Spain, 287
Fundació Gala–Salvador Dalí, Spain, 287
Fundació Jaume Bofill, Spain, 287
Fundación de los Agentes Comerciales de España, Spain, 287
Fundación Albéniz, Spain, 288
Fundación Almine y Bernard Ruiz-Picasso, Spain, 288
Fundación Alzheimer España—FAE, Spain, 288
Fundación Amancio Ortega, Spain, 288
Fundación para el Análisis y los Estudios Sociales—FAES, Spain, 288
Fundación Bancaria 'la Caixa', Spain, 288
Fundación Banco Bilbao Vizcaya Argentaria—Fundación BBVA, Spain, 289
Fundación Barceló, Spain, 289
Fundación Barenboim-Said, Spain, 289
Fundación BBVA, Spain, 289
Fundación Bunge y Born, Argentina, 7
Fundación de las Cajas de Ahorros—FUNCAS, Spain, 289
Fundación Carlos de Amberes, Spain, 289
Fundación Carolina, Spain, 290
Fundación Científica de la Asociación Española Contra el Cáncer—AECC, Spain, 290
Fundación Círculo de Montevideo, Uruguay, 485
Fundación Empresa-Universidad de Zaragoza, Spain, 290
Fundación Felipe González, Spain, 290
Fundación Global Democracia y Desarrollo—FUNGLODE, Dominican Republic, 87
Fundación IE, Spain, 291
Fundación José Miguel de Barandiarán, Spain, 291
Fundación José Ortega y Gasset—Gregorio Marañón, Spain, 291
Fundación Juan March, Spain, 291
Fundación Lealtad, Spain, 285
Fundación Leo Messi, Spain, 292
Fundación Loewe, Spain, 292
Fundación MAPFRE, Spain, 292
Fundación Marcelino Botín, Spain, 292
Fundación Montemadrid, Spain, 292
Fundación Mujeres, Spain, 293
Fundación ONCE, Spain, 293
Fundación Orange, Spain, 293
Fundación Paideia Galiza, Spain, 293
Fundación Pedro Barrié de la Maza, Spain, 293
Fundación Promi, Spain, 294
Fundación Rafael del Pino, Spain, 294
Fundación Ramón Areces, Spain, 294
Fundación Repsol, Spain, 295
Fundación SES—Sustentabilidad, Educación, Solidaridad, Argentina, 8
Fundación SM, Spain, 295
Fundación Tecnologías Sociales—TECSOS, Spain, 296
Fundación Víctimas del Terrorismo, Spain, 296
Fundación Vodafone España, Spain, 296
Fundacja Pomocy Wzajemnej Barka, Poland, 256
Fundacja Współpracy Polsko-Niemieckiej/Stiftung für Deutsch-Polnische Zusammenarbeit, Poland, 257
Fundacja Wspomagania Wsi, Poland, 257
Future Foundation, Liechtenstein, 208
Future in Our Hands Youth NGO—FIOH, Armenia, 9
FWF—Österreichischer Wissenschaftsfonds, Austria, 21
FWO—Fonds Wetenschappelijk Onderzoek, Belgium, 32
FXB International—Association François-Xavier Bagnoud, Switzerland, 310
GAIA—Groupe d'Action dans l'Intérêt des Animaux, Belgium, 32
Garfield Weston Foundation, UK, 355
Garrone (Edoardo), Fondazione, Italy, 177
The Gatsby Charitable Foundation, UK, 355
Gebert Rüf Stiftung, Switzerland, 311
Gemeinnützige Hertie-Stiftung, Germany, 130
Georges Lurcy Charitable and Educational Trust, USA, 430
German Academic Scholarship Foundation, Germany, 142
German AIDS Foundation, Germany, 124
German Cancer Aid, Germany, 124
German Council on Foreign Relations, Germany, 124
German Foundation for World Population, Germany, 126
German Institute for Global and Area Studies—GIGA, Germany, 130
German Marshall Fund of the United States—GMF, USA, 430
German National Trust, Germany, 125
German Orient Foundation, Germany, 125

Western Europe

German Rheumatism Research Centre Berlin, Germany, 126
German-Russian Exchange, Germany, 124
German Savings Banks Foundation for International Co-operation, Germany, 125
Giangiacomo Feltrinelli Foundation, Italy, 177
Gift of the Givers Foundation, South Africa, 280
Giorgio Cini Foundation, Italy, 177
Giovanni Agnelli Foundation, Italy, 177
Give Foundation, India, 155
GiveIndia, India, 155
Global Action in the Interest of Animals, Belgium, 32
Global Democracy and Development Foundation, Dominican Republic, 87
Global Fund for Children, USA, 431
Global Health Partnerships, UK, 355
Global Innovation Fund, UK, 356
Global Schools Forum, UK, 341
Globetree Association, Sweden, 300
GOAL, Ireland, 166
Goldman Sachs Foundation, USA, 432
Goncourt Academy—Goncourt Literary Society, France, 100
Good Neighbors International, Korea (Republic), 201
Good Things Foundation, UK, 356
Goodenough College, UK, 356
Gould (Florence) Foundation, USA, 427
Great Britain Sasakawa Foundation, UK, 356
Great Ormond Street Hospital Children's Charity, UK, 356
Groupe d'Action dans l'Intérêt des Animaux—GAIA, Belgium, 32
The Guide Dogs for the Blind Association, UK, 357
Hamlyn (Paul) Foundation, UK, 373
Hanaholmen—Swedish-Finnish Cultural Centre, Finland, 95
HAND—Hungarian Association of NGOs for Development and Humanitarian Aid, Hungary, 152
Haniel Foundation, Germany, 131
Haniel-Stiftung, Germany, 131
Hans Wilsdorf Foundation, Switzerland, 309
The Health Foundation, UK, 357
Hedwig and Robert Samuel Foundation, Germany, 131
Hedwig und Robert Samuel-Stiftung, Germany, 131
Heineman (Minna-James) Stiftung, Germany, 136
Heinrich Böll Foundation, Germany, 131
Heinrich-Böll-Stiftung, Germany, 131
HEKS—Hilfswerk der Evangelischen Kirchen Schweiz, Switzerland, 311
Hellenic Foundation for Culture, Greece, 145
Hellenic Foundation for European and Foreign Policy—ELIAMEP, Greece, 146
Helmut Horten Foundation, Switzerland, 311
Helmut-Horten-Stiftung, Switzerland, 311
Helsingin Sanomain Säätiö, Finland, 96
Helsingin Sanomat Foundation, Finland, 96
Henie Onstad Art Centre, Norway, 241
Henie Onstad Kunstsenter, Norway, 241
Henri Cartier-Bresson Foundation, France, 107
Heritage Foundation, France, 110
Hertie Foundation, Germany, 139
Hicter (Marcel), Fondation, Belgium, 32
Higgins (Terrence) Trust, UK, 385
Hinduja Foundation, India, 157
Historic Environment Scotland, UK, 358
Hivos—Humanistisch Instituut voor Ontwikkelings Samenwerking, Netherlands, 226
Hjärt-Lungfonden, Sweden, 300
Hope, Ireland, 165
Hope Foundation, Türkiye, 331
Hope not Hate Charitable Trust—HNHCT, UK, 358
Hopp (Dietmar) Stiftung, Germany, 126
Horten (Helmut) Stiftung, Switzerland, 311
Howard (Katharine) Foundation, Ireland, 167
Hulot (Nicolas), Fondation, France, 110
Humanistic Institute for Co-operation with Developing Countries, Netherlands, 226
Humanitarian Academy for Development—HAD, UK, 359
Humboldt Forum, Germany, 132
The Hunger Project, USA, 438
The Hunter Foundation—THF, UK, 359
Ibero-American Network of Community Foundations, Brazil, 38
Ibrahim (Mo) Foundation, UK, 368
Icelandic Human Rights Centre, Iceland, 154
IE Foundation, Spain, 291
İktisadi Kalkınma Vakfı, Türkiye, 328
Îles de Paix, Belgium, 32

Impact Europe, Belgium, 27
Indian National Trust for Art and Cultural Heritage—INTACH, India, 158
Initiative Bürgerstiftungen, Germany, 119
Institusjonen Fritt Ord, Norway, 241
Institut Europeu de la Mediterrània—IEMed, Spain, 296
Institut FMES—Institut Méditerranéen d'Études Stratégiques, France, 113
Institut Français des Relations Internationales—IFRI, France, 113
Institut International des Droits de l'Enfant, Switzerland, 312
Institut de Médecine et d'Epidémiologie Appliquée—Fondation Internationale Léon Mba, France, 114
Institut for Menneskerettigheder, Denmark, 84
Institut Océanographique—Fondation Albert 1er, Prince de Monaco, France, 114
Institute of Applied Medicine and Epidemiology—International Foundation Léon Mba, France, 114
Institute for European Environmental Policy—IEEP, Belgium, 33
Instituto Ayrton Senna, Brazil, 41
Instituto Europeo de Salud y Bienestar Social, Spain, 296
Institutul Cultural Român—ICR, Romania, 264
INTACH—Indian National Trust for Art and Cultural Heritage, India, 158
International Centre for Defence and Security—ICDS, Estonia, 93
International Foundation of the High-Altitude Research Stations Jungfraujoch and Gornergrat, Switzerland, 313
International Historical, Educational, Charitable and Human Rights Society—International Memorial, Russian Federation, 266
International Institute for the Rights of the Child, Switzerland, 312
International Latsis Foundation, Switzerland, 309
International Memorial, Russian Federation, 266
International Orthodox Christian Charities—IOCC, USA, 441
International Rescue Committee—IRC, USA, 441
International Solidarity Foundation, Finland, 96
International University Centre of Paris Foundation, France, 104
Internationale Stiftung Hochalpine Forschungsstationen Jungfraujoch und Gornergrat, Switzerland, 313
Internationalt Uddannelsescenter, Denmark, 84
INTERSOS, Italy, 182
IOCC—International Orthodox Christian Charities, USA, 441
iPartner India, India, 155
IRC—International Rescue Committee, USA, 441
The Ireland Funds America, USA, 442
Irish Youth Foundation, Ireland, 167
Islands of Peace, Belgium, 32
ISMU Foundation—Initiatives and Studies on Multi-ethnicity, Italy, 178
ISREC Foundation, Switzerland, 309
Istituto Carlo Cattaneo, Italy, 182
Istituto Luigi Sturzo, Italy, 182
Istituto Svedese di Studi Classici a Roma, Italy, 183
IUC International Education Center—IUC-Europe, Denmark, 84
The J. F. Costopoulos Foundation, Greece, 146
Jacobs Foundation, Switzerland, 313
Jahnsson (Yrjö) Foundation, Finland, 98
Jahres (Anders) Humanitære Stiftelse, Norway, 240
Japan Foundation Endowment Committee—JFEC, UK, 361
Japanese-German Centre Berlin, Germany, 133
Japanisch-Deutsches Zentrum Berlin, Germany, 133
Jaurès (Jean), Fondation, France, 107
JCA Charitable Foundation, UK, 361
Jean Jaurès Foundation, France, 107
Jean Monnet Foundation for Europe, Switzerland, 309
Jenny and Antti Wihuri Foundation, Finland, 96
Jenny ja Antti Wihurin Rahasto, Finland, 96
JFEC—Japan Foundation Endowment Committee, UK, 361
JNF UK—JNF Charitable Trust, UK, 361
Johanna Quandt Foundation, Germany, 133
Johanna-Quandt-Stiftung, Germany, 133
John Ellerman Foundation, UK, 361
John Innes Foundation—JIF, UK, 362
John Moores Foundation, UK, 362
Jordan River Foundation, Jordan, 196

INDEX BY AREA OF ACTIVITY

José Miguel de Barandiarán Foundation, Spain, 291
José Ortega y Gasset—Gregorio Marañón Foundation, Spain, 291
Joseph Levy Foundation, UK, 362
Joseph Patrick Trust, UK, 369
Joseph Rowntree Charitable Trust—JRCT, UK, 362
Joseph Rowntree Foundation—JRF, UK, 362
Joseph Rowntree Reform Trust Ltd (including the JRSST Charitable Trust), UK, 362
JRSST Charitable Trust, UK, 362
Juan March Foundation, Spain, 291
Jung (C. G.) Institut Zürich, Switzerland, 307
Juselius (Sigrid) Stiftelse, Finland, 97
Kade (Max) Foundation, Inc, USA, 451
KAF—Katalike Actions for Africa, Congo (Democratic Republic), 72
Kamel Lazaar Foundation—KLF, Tunisia, 327
Kansainvälinen solidaarisuussäätiö, Finland, 96
Karuna Trust, UK, 363
Katharine Howard Foundation—KHF, Ireland, 167
KAUTE Foundation, Finland, 96
KAUTE-säätiö, Finland, 96
Kennedy Memorial Trust, UK, 363
King Baudouin Foundation, Belgium, 33
King Gustaf V's 90th Birthday Foundation, Sweden, 301
The King's Foundation, UK, 363
The King's Fund, UK, 363
The King's Trust, UK, 363
KK-stiftelsen, Sweden, 301
Klassik Stiftung Weimar, Germany, 134
Knowledge Foundation, Sweden, 301
Knox (Frank) Memorial Fellowships, USA, 428
Knut and Alice Wallenberg Foundation, Sweden, 301
Knut och Alice Wallenbergs Stiftelse, Sweden, 301
Koç (Vehbi), Vakfı, Türkiye, 331
Kokkalis Foundation, Greece, 146
Koning Boudewijnstichting/Fondation Roi Baudouin, Belgium, 33
Koninklijke Hollandsche Maatschappij der Wetenschappen, Netherlands, 226
Konung Gustaf V's 90-Årsfond, Sweden, 301
Körber Foundation, Germany, 134
Körber-Stiftung, Germany, 134
Kosovar Civil Society Foundation—KCSF, Kosovo, 202
Kostova (Elizabeth) Foundation for Creative Writing, Bulgaria, 43
Kress (Samuel H.) Foundation, USA, 469
Kulturfonden for Sverige och Finland, Sweden, 301
Kulturstiftung der Länder—KSL, Germany, 134
Kulturstiftung Liechtenstein, Liechtenstein, 208
Kusuma Trust UK, UK, 363
Kvinna till Kvinna, Sweden, 301
KWF Dutch Cancer Society, Netherlands, 227
KWF Kankerbestrijding, Netherlands, 227
'La Caixa' Banking Foundation, Spain, 288
Lafede.cat—Federació d'Organitzacions per a la Justícia Global, Spain, 286
Lafede.cat—Federation of Organizations for Global Justice, Spain, 286
Lambrakis Foundation, Greece, 146
Landis & Gyr Foundation, Switzerland, 313
Landis & Gyr Stiftung, Switzerland, 313
Latin America France, France, 112
Latin American and Caribbean Women's Health Network—LACWHN, Ecuador, 89
Latvian Institute of International Affairs—LIIA, Latvia, 204
Latvijas Ārpolitikas Institūts—LAI, Latvia, 204
Lauder (Ronald S.) Foundation, Germany, 138
Learning for Well-being Foundation—L4WB, Netherlands, 227
Leibniz-Institut für Globale und Regionale Studien, Germany, 130
Leibniz-Institut für Ost- und Südosteuropaforschung, Germany, 135
Leibniz Institute for East and South-East European Studies, Germany, 135
Leibniz Institute for Research and Information in Education, Germany, 126
Leo Messi Foundation, Spain, 292
Leonard Cheshire Disability, UK, 364
Léonie Sonning Music Foundation, Denmark, 84
Léonie Sonnings Musikfond, Denmark, 84
The Leprosy Mission International, UK, 364
Leventis (A. G.) Foundation, Cyprus, 77
Leverhulme Trust, UK, 365
Levy (Joseph) Foundation, UK, 362
Li Ka Shing Foundation, Hong Kong, 151
Library of the National Academy of Lincei and Corsiniana, Italy, 172

INDEX BY AREA OF ACTIVITY

Liechtenstein Foundation for Culture, Liechtenstein, 208
LifeArc—MRC Technology, UK, 365
Lindh (Anna) Euro-Mediterranean Foundation for Dialogue between Cultures, Egypt, 90
Living Culture Foundation Namibia—LCFN, Namibia, 222
Lloyds Bank Foundation for England and Wales, UK, 365
Loewe Foundation, Spain, 292
The Long Now Foundation, USA, 449
Louis-Jeantet Foundation for Medicine, Switzerland, 310
Lower Saxony Savings Bank Foundation, Germany, 137
Loyalty Foundation, Spain, 285
Ludwig Boltzmann Gesellschaft, Austria, 21
Ludwig Cancer Research, USA, 449
Luigi Einaudi Foundation, Italy, 178
Luigi Sturzo Institute, Italy, 182
Lullaby Trust, UK, 366
Lumos Foundation, UK, 366
Lundbeck Foundation, Denmark, 85
Lundbeckfonden, Denmark, 85
Lurcy (Georges) Charitable and Educational Trust, USA, 430
Luso-American Development Foundation, Portugal, 260
Luxembourg Development NGO Co-operation Circle, Luxembourg, 209
Luxemburg (Rosa) Stiftung, Germany, 139
MACIF Foundation, France, 108
The Mackintosh Foundation, UK, 366
Macmillan Cancer Support, UK, 366
Maison Franco-Japonaise, Japan, 191
Maj ja Tor Nessling Säätiö, Finland, 96
Maj and Tor Nessling Foundation, Finland, 96
Maltese Heritage Foundation, Malta, 213
Mama Cash Foundation, Netherlands, 230
Mani Tese, Italy, 183
Mannréttindaskrifstofa Íslands, Iceland, 154
MAPFRE Foundation, Spain, 292
Marangopoulos Foundation for Human Rights, Greece, 146
Marc de Montalembert Foundation, France, 109
Marcel Hicter Foundation, Belgium, 32
March (Juan), Fundación, Spain, 291
Marie Curie, UK, 366
Mário Soares and Maria Barroso Foundation, Portugal, 260
Mary Fonden, Denmark, 85
Mary Foundation, Denmark, 85
Mattei (Enrico), Fondazione ENI, Italy, 174
Maugeri (Salvatore), Fondazione, Italy, 180
Max Kade Foundation, Inc, USA, 451
Max-Planck-Institut für Neurobiologie des Verhaltens—caesar, Germany, 136
Max Planck Institute for Neurobiology of Behavior—caesar, Germany, 136
Max Schmidheiny Foundation at the University of St Gallen, Switzerland, 314
Max Schmidheiny-Stiftung an der Universität St Gallen, Switzerland, 314
medica mondiale eV, Germany, 136
Mediterranean Foundation for Strategic Studies Institute, France, 113
Menarini International Foundation, Italy, 178
Mencap—Royal Mencap Society, UK, 367
Mental Health Foundation, UK, 367
The Mercers' Charitable Foundation, UK, 367
Merchant Navy Fund, UK, 382
Mercy, Ireland, 168
Mercy Corps, USA, 452
Merian (Christoph) Stiftung, Switzerland, 305
Messi (Leo), Fundación, Spain, 292
Mezhdunarodnyj Memorial, Russian Federation, 266
Michael Otto Foundation for Environmental Protection, Germany, 136
Michael-Otto-Stiftung für Umweltschutz, Germany, 136
Microfinance Centre—MFC, Poland, 257
Mind, UK, 367
Minhaj Welfare Foundation, UK, 368
Minna James Heineman Foundation, Germany, 136
Minna-James-Heineman-Stiftung, Germany, 136
Mistra—Foundation for Strategic Environmental Research, Sweden, 303
Mith Samlanh, Cambodia, 46
Mo Ibrahim Foundation, UK, 368
Mohamed Shafik Gabr Foundation for Social Development, Egypt, 90
Mohammed bin Rashid Al Maktoum Global Initiatives—MBRGI, United Arab Emirates, 335
Møller (A.P.) and Chastine Mc-Kinney Møller Foundation, Denmark, 82

Monnet (Jean), Fondation pour l'Europe, Switzerland, 309
Mønsteds (Otto) Fond, Denmark, 86
de Montalembert (Marc), Fondation, France, 109
Montemadrid Foundation, Spain, 292
Montevideo Circle Foundation, Uruguay, 485
Moores (John) Foundation, UK, 362
Morningside Foundation, USA, 454
Mother Child Education Foundation, Türkiye, 327
MS Society—Multiple Sclerosis Society of Great Britain and Northern Ireland, UK, 368
Multiple Sclerosis Society of Great Britain and Northern Ireland, UK, 368
Muscular Dystrophy UK, UK, 369
Muslim Aid, UK, 369
Nansen (Fridtjof) Institute, Norway, 241
Naspa Foundation, Germany, 137
Naspa Stiftung, Germany, 137
National Bank of Greece Cultural Foundation, Greece, 147
National Council for Voluntary Organisations, UK, 337
National Emergencies Trust, UK, 369
National Foundation for Political Sciences, France, 110
National Heritage Memorial Fund, UK, 370
The National Lottery Community Fund, UK, 370
The National Lottery Heritage Fund, UK, 370
National Society for the Prevention of Cruelty to Children—NSPCC, UK, 371
National Trust, UK, 370
The National Trust for Italy, Italy, 174
NCVO—National Council for Voluntary Organisations, UK, 337
Nederlandse Organisatie voor Internationale Ontwikkelingssamenwerking—Stichting NOVIB, Netherlands, 228
Nessling (Maj and Tor) Foundation, Finland, 96
Network of Estonian Non-profit Organizations, Estonia, 92
Network of European Foundations—NEF, Belgium, 27
Network of Foundations Working for Development—netFWD, France, 99
New Carlsberg Foundation, Denmark, 85
New Economics Foundation—NEF, UK, 371
NFCR—National Foundation for Cancer Research, USA, 457
NHS Charities Together, UK, 371
Nicolas Hulot Foundation for Nature and Humankind, France, 110
Niedersächsische Sparkassenstiftung, Germany, 137
Nitidæ, France, 115
Non-Governmental Ecological Vernadsky Foundation, Russian Federation, 266
Nonprofit Enterprise and Self-sustainability Team—NESsT, USA, 457
Nordic Africa Institute Scholarships, Sweden, 302
Nordic Institute for Theoretical Physics, Sweden, 302
Nordiska Afrikainstitutets Stipendier, Sweden, 302
NORDITA—Nordiska Institutet för Teoretisk Fysik, Sweden, 302
Norwegian Donors Forum, Norway, 240
Nott (David) Foundation, UK, 350
Novartis Foundation for Therapeutic Research, Germany, 137
Novartis-Stiftung für therapeutische Forschung, Germany, 137
NOVIB (Oxfam Netherlands), Netherlands, 228
NSPCC—National Society for the Prevention of Cruelty to Children, UK, 371
Nuffield Foundation, UK, 371
NWO Domain Applied and Engineering Sciences, Netherlands, 227
Ny Carlsbergfondet, Denmark, 85
Oceanographic Institute—Albert I, Prince of Monaco Foundation, France, 114
OeAD, Austria, 22
The Officers' Association, UK, 372
Olivetti (Adriano), Fondazione, Italy, 174
ONCE—Spanish National Organization for the Blind—Foundation, Spain, 293
Onstad (Henie) Kunstsenter, Norway, 241
OPALS—Organisation Panafricaine de Lutte pour la Santé, France, 115
OPEN ASIA—Armanshahr Foundation, Afghanistan, 3
Open Estonia Foundation, Estonia, 92
Open Society European Policy Institute—OSEPI, Belgium, 33
Operation Eyesight Universal/Action Universelle de la Vue, Canada, 60
Opportunity International UK, UK, 372

Western Europe

Orange Foundation, Spain, 293
Orangutan Foundation, UK, 372
Oranje Fonds, Netherlands, 227
Orbis Charitable Trust, UK, 372
Organisation Panafricaine de Lutte pour la Santé—OPALS, France, 115
Orient Foundation, Portugal, 260
Orient-Occident Foundation, Morocco, 220
Ortega (Amancio), Fundación, Spain, 288
Ortega y Gasset (José), Fundación, Spain, 291
Österreichische Gesellschaft für Aussenpolitik und Internationale Beziehungen—ÖGAVN, Austria, 22
Österreichischer Wissenschaftsfonds—FWF, Austria, 21
Östersjöfonden, Finland, 97
Otto Benecke Foundation, Germany, 138
Otto-Benecke-Stiftung eV, Germany, 138
Otto (Michael) Stiftung, Germany, 136
Otto Mønsteds Fond, Denmark, 86
Otto Mønsteds Foundation, Denmark, 86
Outstretched Hands, Italy, 183
Oxfam Deutschland eV, Germany, 138
Oxfam Ireland, Ireland, 167
Oxfam Italia, Italy, 183
Oxfam NOVIB—Nederlandse Organisatie voor Internationale Ontwikkelingssamenwerking, Netherlands, 228
Oxfam NOVIB—Netherlands Organization for International Development Co-operation, Netherlands, 228
P&V Foundation, Belgium, 32
Paideia Galiza Foundation, Spain, 293
Pan-African Organization for Health, France, 115
PAN Europe—Pesticide Action Network Europe, Belgium, 34
Pan-European Federation for Cultural Heritage, Netherlands, 224
Parasol Foundation Trust, Gibraltar, 144
Partage, France, 116
PATH, USA, 461
Patiño (Simón I.), Fondation, Switzerland, 310
Paul Hamlyn Foundation—PHF, UK, 373
Paulo Foundation, Finland, 97
Paulon Säätiö, Finland, 97
Peace Brigades International—PBI, Belgium, 33
Peace Direct, UK, 373
Pedro Barrié de la Maza Foundation, Spain, 293
Pestalozzi Children's Foundation, Switzerland, 317
Pesticide Action Network Europe—PAN Europe, Belgium, 34
Philanthropikó Ídryma Stélios Chatzeioánnou stēn Kýpro, Cyprus, 78
Philanthropy Europe Association—Philea, Belgium, 27
Philanthropy Ireland, Ireland, 165
Philea—Philanthropy Europe Association, Belgium, 27
Philip-Sörensens (Erik) Stiftelse, Sweden, 299
Piera, Pietro and Giovanni Ferrero Foundation, Italy, 179
Pilgrim Trust, UK, 373
Plan International Ireland, Ireland, 167
Platform for Development Cooperation and Humanitarian Aid, Slovenia, 276
Ploughshares Fund, USA, 463
Plunkett Foundation, UK, 374
Pompidou (Claude), Fondation, France, 104
Portuguese Foundation Centre, Portugal, 258
Post Office Foundation, France, 105
Practical Action, UK, 374
Prada Foundation, Italy, 179
Première Urgence Internationale, France, 116
Prince Bernhard Cultural Foundation, Netherlands, 230
Prince's Trust, UK, 363
Prins Bernhard Culturfonds, Stichting, Netherlands, 230
Pro Juventute, Switzerland, 315
Pro Mujer International, USA, 464
Pro Women International, USA, 464
proFonds, Switzerland, 305
Project Trust, UK, 374
Promi Foundation, Spain, 294
Protestant Study Foundation, Germany, 128
PRS for Music Foundation, UK, 374
Qatar Foundation, Qatar, 262
Qattan (A. M.) Foundation, UK, 338
Quandt (Johanna) Stiftung, Germany, 133
Queen Rania Foundation—QRF, Jordan, 196
Querini Stampalia Foundation, Italy, 179
Rafael del Pino Foundation, Spain, 294
Rahvusvaheline Kaitseuuringute Keskus—RKK, Estonia, 93
The Rainforest Foundation UK—RFUK, UK, 375
Rambourg Foundation, Tunisia, 326
Ramón Areces Foundation, Spain, 294

Western Europe

The Rank Foundation, UK, 375
Razumkov Centre, Ukraine, 333
Reading Foundation, Germany, 140
Realdania Foundation, Denmark, 83
RED—Ruralité-Environnement-Développement, Belgium, Belgium, 34
Red de Salud de las Mujeres Latinoamericanas y del Caribe—RSMLAC, Ecuador, 89
Red Sea Cultural Foundation, Somalia, 278
Rede Iberoamericana de Fundações Cívicas ou Comunitárias—RIFC, Brazil, 38
RedR UK, UK, 375
Rehabilitation for the Disabled—ELEPAP, Greece, 145
Relief International, USA, 466
Repsol Foundation, Spain, 295
Réseau Européen des Associations de Lutte contre la Pauvreté et l'Exclusion Sociale, Belgium, 29
Resolution Foundation, UK, 376
Reumatikerförbundet, Sweden, 302
RIA—Royal Irish Academy, Ireland, 167
Ricardo do Espírito Santo Silva Foundation, Portugal, 261
Rivers Trust, UK, 376
RNIB Charity, UK, 378
Robert Bosch Foundation, Germany, 138
Robert-Bosch-Stiftung GmbH, Germany, 138
Robert Schuman Foundation, France, 111
The Robertson Trust, UK, 376
Rockwool Fonden, Denmark, 86
Rockwool Foundation, Denmark, 86
Roger Federer Foundation, Switzerland, 315
Romaeuropa Foundation, Italy, 180
Romanian Cultural Institute, Romania, 264
Rome Foundation, Italy, 179
The Ronald S. Lauder Foundation, Germany, 138
Rosa Luxemburg Foundation, Germany, 139
Rosa-Luxemburg-Stiftung, Germany, 139
Rotha, Ireland, 165
Rothschild (Edmond de) Foundations, Switzerland, 308
Rowntree (Joseph) Charitable Trust, UK, 362
Rowntree (Joseph) Foundation, UK, 362
Rowntree (Joseph) Reform Trust, UK, 362
Royal Commission for the Exhibition of 1851, UK, 377
Royal Holland Society of Sciences and Humanities, Netherlands, 226
Royal Literary Fund—RLF, UK, 378
Royal National Institute of Blind People—RNIB, UK, 378
Royal Society for the Prevention of Cruelty to Animals—RSPCA, UK, 380
Royal Society for the Protection of Birds—RSPB, UK, 379
Rroma Foundation, Switzerland, 315
Rromani Fundacija, Switzerland, 315
RSPB—Royal Society for the Protection of Birds, UK, 379
RSPCA—Royal Society for the Prevention of Cruelty to Animals, UK, 380
Rubinstein (Arthur) International Music Society, Israel, 168
Rüf (Gebert) Stiftung, Switzerland, 311
RUI Foundation, Italy, 180
Ruiz-Picasso (Almine y Bernard), Fundación, Spain, 288
Rural Development Foundation, Poland, 257
Ruralité-Environnement-Développement—RED, Belgium, 34
Rurality Environment Development, Belgium, 34
Rutgers, Netherlands, 228
Rytų Europos Studijų Centras—RESC, Lithuania, 209
Säätiöt ja rahastot, Finland, 95
Saïd Foundation, UK, 380
Sainsbury Family Charitable Trusts, UK, 380
Salvador Dalí Foundation, Spain, 287
Salvatore Maugeri Foundation—Occupational Health and Rehabilitation Clinic, Italy, 180
Samaritans, UK, 381
Samsung Foundation, Korea (Republic), 202
Samuel H. Kress Foundation, USA, 469
Samuel (Hedwig und Robert) Stiftung, Germany, 131
Sandals Foundation, Jamaica, 184
Sander (Wilhelm) Stiftung, Germany, 143
Santé Sud, France, 116
Sasakawa, Fondation Franco-Japonaise, France, 106
Sasakawa Health Foundation—SHF, Japan, 194
Save Our Future Environmental Foundation, Germany, 139
Save Our Future Umweltstiftung—SOF, Germany, 139
Schmidheiny (Max) Stiftung, Switzerland, 314
Schneider Electric Foundation, France, 111

Schuman (Robert), Fondation, France, 111
Schwarzkopf-Stiftung Junges Europa, Germany, 139
Schwarzkopf Young Europe Foundation, Germany, 139
Schweisfurth Foundation, Germany, 139
Schweisfurth-Stiftung, Germany, 139
Schweizerische Akademie der Medizinischen Wissenschaften, Switzerland, 316
Schweizerische Herzstiftung, Switzerland, 316
Schweizerischer Nationalfonds zur Förderung der Wissenschaftlichen Forschung/Fonds National Suisse de la Recherche Scientifique—SNF, Switzerland, 316
Scientific Foundation of the Spanish Cancer Association, Spain, 290
Scientific Research Foundation, Belgium, 32
Scope, UK, 381
Scottish Council for Voluntary Organisations—SCVO, UK, 337
SCVO—Scottish Council for Voluntary Organisations, UK, 337
The Seafarers' Charity, UK, 382
Seafarers International Relief Fund, UK, 382
Seeds of Peace, USA, 470
SEEMO—South East Europe Media Organisation, Austria, 23
Senna (Ayrton), Instituto, Brazil, 41
Sentebale, UK, 382
Serralves Foundation, Portugal, 261
SES Foundation—Sustainability, Education, Solidarity, Argentina, 8
Shafik Gabr (Mohamed) Foundation, Egypt, 90
Shahid Afridi Foundation—SAF, Pakistan, 246
Sharing and Life Foundation, France, 110
Shelter—National Campaign for Homeless People, UK, 382
Sherman (Archie) Charitable Trust, UK, 340
Sightsavers International, UK, 382
Sigrid Juséliuksen Säätiö, Finland, 97
Sigrid Jusélius Foundation, Finland, 97
Silva (Ricardo do Espírito Santo), Fundação, Portugal, 261
Simón I. Patiño Foundation, Switzerland, 310
Singapore International Foundation—SIF, Singapore, 273
Singer-Polignac Foundation, France, 111
Sino-British Fellowship Trust—SBFT, UK, 383
Sir Halley Stewart Trust, UK, 383
The Sir Jules Thorn Charitable Trust, UK, 383
Skinners' Charity Foundation, UK, 383
SLOGA—Platforma za Razvojno Sodelovanje in Humanitarno Pomoč, Slovenia, 276
Slovak Security Policy Institute, Slovakia, 276
Slovenský inštitút pre bezpečnostnú politiku, Slovakia, 276
SM Foundation, Spain, 295
Smallwood Trust, UK, 384
Smith (Henry) Charity, UK, 358
Soares (Mário), Fundação, Portugal, 260
The Sobell Foundation, UK, 384
Society for Education and Training, UK, 351
Software AG Foundation, Germany, 139
Software AG Stiftung, Germany, 139
Solidaarisuus, Finland, 96
Sonning-Fonden, Denmark, 86
Sonning Foundation, Denmark, 86
Sonning (Léonie) Musikfond, Denmark, 84
South East Europe Media Organisation—SEEMO, Austria, 23
South West International Development Network—SWIDN, UK, 337
Southern Health, France, 116
Spanish Association of Foundations, Spain, 285
Sparebankstiftelsen DNB, Norway, 243
Sparkassenstiftung für internationale Kooperation, Germany, 125
Springer (Axel) Stiftung, Germany, 122
Springer (Friede) Stiftung, Germany, 129
St John Ambulance, UK, 380
Stelios Philanthropic Foundation, Cyprus, 78
Stewart (Sir Halley) Trust, UK, 383
Stichting Democratie en Media, Netherlands, 229
Stichting Dioraphte, Netherlands, 229
Stichting DOEN, Netherlands, 229
Stichting Fonds 1818, Netherlands, 229
Stichting Mama Cash, Netherlands, 230
Stichting Prins Bernhard Cultuurfonds, Netherlands, 230
Stichting van Schulden naar Kansen, Netherlands, 231
Stichting Triodos Foundation, Netherlands, 231
Stiftelsen Blanceflor Boncompagni Ludovisi, född Bildt, Sweden, 303
Stiftelsen Dam, Norway, 243
Stiftelsen för Miljöstrategisk Forskning—Mistra, Sweden, 303

INDEX BY AREA OF ACTIVITY

Stiftelsen Teknikens Främjande—Tekniikan Edistämissäätiö, Finland, 98
Stiftelser i Samverkan, Sweden, 298
Stiftelsesforeningen, Norway, 240
Stifterverband für die Deutsche Wissenschaft eV, Germany, 119
Stiftung 'Erinnerung, Verantwortung und Zukunft'—EVZ, Germany, 139
Stiftung Ettersberg, Germany, 140
Stiftung Jugend forscht eV, Germany, 140
Stiftung Kinderdorf Pestalozzi, Switzerland, 317
Stiftung Klimarappen, Switzerland, 317
Stiftung Lesen, Germany, 140
Stiftung Vivamos Mejor, Switzerland, 317
Stiftung West-Östliche Begegnungen, Germany, 141
Stiftung Zukunft.li, Liechtenstein, 208
Stiftungsfonds Deutsche Bank im Stifterverband für die Deutsche Wissenschaft, Germany, 142
Street Child, UK, 384
Strickland Foundation, Malta, 214
Strømme Foundation, Norway, 243
Strømmestiftelsen, Norway, 243
Studienstiftung des deutschen Volkes, Germany, 142
Sturzo (Luigi), Istituto, Italy, 182
Südosteuropäische Medienorganisation, Austria, 23
Suomen Kulttuurirahasto, Finland, 97
Survival International, UK, 385
Svenska Institutet i Rom/Istituto Svedese di Studi Classici a Roma, Italy, 183
Svenska kulturfonden, Finland, 98
Swaziland Charitable Trust, Eswatini, 93
Sweden-Japan Foundation—SJF, Sweden, 304
Swedish Cancer Society, Sweden, 298
The Swedish Cultural Foundation in Finland, Finland, 98
Swedish-Finnish Cultural Foundation, Sweden, 301
The Swedish Heart-Lung Foundation, Sweden, 300
Swedish Institute in Rome, Italy, 183
Swedish Rheumatism Association, Sweden, 302
Swiss Academy of Medical Sciences, Switzerland, 316
Swiss Church Aid, Switzerland, 311
Swiss Heart Foundation, Switzerland, 316
Swiss National Science Foundation—SNSF, Switzerland, 316
SWISSAID Foundation, Switzerland, 318
SwissFoundations—Verband der Schweizer Förderstiftungen/Association des Fondations Donatrices Suisses, Switzerland, 306
Szenes (Arpad)-Vieira da Silva, Fundação, Portugal, 258
Taawon, Palestinian Territories, 246
Tearfund, UK, 385
Tekniikan Edistämissäätiö-Stiftelsen för teknikens främjande—TES, Finland, 98
Terrence Higgins Trust—THT, UK, 385
TFF—Transnational Foundation for Peace and Future Research, Sweden, 304
TFF—Transnationella Stiftelsen för Freds- och Framtidsforskning, Sweden, 304
THET, UK, 355
Third World Network—TWN, Malaysia, 211
Thomas B. Thrige Foundation, Denmark, 86
Thomas B. Thriges Fond, Denmark, 86
Thomson Foundation, UK, 385
Thorn (The Sir Jules) Charitable Trust, UK, 383
Thriges (Thomas B.) Fond, Denmark, 86
Tibet-Institut Rikon, Switzerland, 318
Timchenko (Elena & Gennady) Foundation, Russian Federation, 265
TK Foundation, Bahamas, 24
Toegepaste en Technische Wetenschappen, Netherlands, 227
Toepfer (Alfred) Stiftung, Germany, 121
Tony Blair Institute for Global Change—TBI, UK, 386
Transnational Giving Europe—TGE, Belgium, 27
Triodos Foundation, Netherlands, 231
Trócaire—Catholic Agency for World Development, Ireland, 168
The Trussell Trust, UK, 386
Trust for London, UK, 386
Trusthouse Charitable Foundation, UK, 386
Turin Savings Bank Foundation, Italy, 176
Turing (Alan) Institute, UK, 339
Turquoise Mountain Foundation, UK, 386
Tusk, UK, 387
Ugo Bordoni Foundation, Italy, 180
UK Community Foundations—UKCF, UK, 338
Umut Vakfı, Türkiye, 331
Unbound Philanthropy, USA, 476
UniCredit Foundation, Italy, 183

INDEX BY AREA OF ACTIVITY

UNIFOR—Forvaltningstiftelse for fond og legater, Norway, 240
Unipolis Foundation, Italy, 181
United Purpose, UK, 387
Universitaire Stichting, Belgium, 34
University Foundation, Belgium, 34
University of Zaragoza Business Foundation, Spain, 290
USPG—United Society Partners in the Gospel, UK, 387
Values Foundation, Bulgaria, 43
Vehbi Koç Foundation, Türkiye, 331
Vehbi Koç Vakfı, Türkiye, 331
Veillon (Charles), Fondation, Switzerland, 308
Venice Foundation, Italy, 181
VENRO—Verband Entwicklungspolitik und Humanitäre Hilfe deutscher Nichtregierungsorganizationen, Germany, 120
Verband für Gemeinnütziges Stiften, Austria, 20
Vereinigung Liechtensteinischer gemeinnütziger Stiftungen eV, Liechtenstein, 207
Versus Arthritis, UK, 388
Vestnordenfonden, Denmark, 86
VIDC—Vienna Institute for International Dialogue and Co-operation, Austria, 23
Vienna Institute for International Dialogue and Co-operation—VIDC, Austria, 23
VINCI Corporate Foundation for the City, France, 106
Vivamos Mejor Foundation, Switzerland, 317
Vodafone Foundation Germany, Germany, 142
Vodafone Foundation Luxembourg, Luxembourg, 210
Vodafone Ireland Foundation, Ireland, 168
Vodafone Italy Foundation, Italy, 181
Vodafone Portugal Foundation, Portugal, 261
Vodafone Spain Foundation, Spain, 296
Vodafone Stiftung Deutschland, Germany, 142
Volkart Foundation, Switzerland, 319
Volkart-Stiftung, Switzerland, 319
Voluntary Service Overseas, UK, 388
VSO—Voluntary Service Overseas, UK, 388
Wallace (Charles) Trusts, UK, 347
Wallenberg (Knut och Alice) Stiftelse, Sweden, 301
Walton Family Foundation, USA, 479
War Child, UK, 388
War on Want, UK, 388
WaterAid, UK, 389
Welfare Association, Palestinian Territories, 246
Wellbeing of Women, UK, 389
Wenner-Gren Foundations, Sweden, 304
West-Nordic Foundation, Denmark, 86
Weston (Garfield) Foundation, UK, 355
The Wheel, Ireland, 165
Wihuri (Jenny and Antti) Foundation, Finland, 96
Wild (Dr Rainer) Stiftung, Germany, 126
The Wildlife Trusts, UK, 390
Wilhelm Sander Foundation, Germany, 143
Wilhelm-Sander-Stiftung, Germany, 143
William Adlington Cadbury Charitable Trust, UK, 390
Wilsdorf (Hans), Fondation, Switzerland, 309
Windle Trust International, UK, 390
Winrock International, USA, 481
Winston Churchill Foundation of the United States, USA, 482
Wisti (Folmer) Foundation for International Understanding, Denmark, 83
The Wolfson Foundation, UK, 390
Woman to Woman Foundation, Sweden, 301
Women Thrive Fund, UK, 384
Women's Aid, Ireland, 168
The Wood Foundation—TWF, UK, 391
World Animal Protection, UK, 391
World Association of Children's Friends, Monaco, 217
World Jewish Relief, UK, 391
The World of NGOs, Austria, 20
World Vision International, UK, 391
The Wyss Foundtion, USA, 484
Yanai Tadashi Foundation, Japan, 195
Year Out Group, UK, 374
Yemen Policy Center, Yemen, 489
Yemen Polling Center—YPC, Yemen, 489
YMCA—Young Men's Christian Association, UK, 392
Young Citizens—Citizenship Foundation, UK, 392
Young Lives vs Cancer, UK, 392
Yrjö Jahnsson Foundation, Finland, 98
Yrjö Jahnssonin säätiö, Finland, 98
Zeiss (Carl) Stiftung, Germany, 123
ZEIT-Stiftung Ebelin und Gerd Bucerius, Germany, 143
ZOA, Netherlands, 231
Zochonis Charitable Trust, UK, 392
Zurich Community Trust—ZCT, UK, 392

9781041053057